YEARBOOK
OF THE
UNITED
NATIONS
2004

Volume 58

Department of Public Information
United Nations, New York

COPYRIGHT © 2006 UNITED NATIONS
Yearbook of the United Nations, 2004
Vol. 58
ISBN: 92-1-100966-9
ISSN: 0082-8521

UNITED NATIONS PUBLICATIONS

SALES NO. E.06.I.1

Printed in Canada

FOREWORD

Addressing UN Member States in late 2003, at the end of a difficult and divisive period for the international community, I expressed my belief that the world had come to a fork in the road. In one direction lay an outdated international security system, ill-equipped to handle the challenges of the twenty-first century; in the other, a renewed commitment to international cooperation, and reformed mechanisms able to address problems without passports.

In 2004, the report of the High-level Panel on Threats, Challenges and Change proposed a new conceptualization of collective security for the 21st century. Addressing a broad range of issues from the use of force to global public health, it recommended fundamental changes in our approach and in the UN itself, and generated lively global debate.

But even as a reform blueprint took shape, the world faced extraordinary challenges. International terrorism wreaked havoc, with attacks in Madrid and Beslan proving the most prominent. Renewed volatility in the Middle East, and an armed conflict in the Darfur region of western Sudan, caused immense suffering. Three new peacekeeping missions were established in quick succession—in Burundi, Côte d'Ivoire and Haiti. And at the end of 2004, a tsunami devastated coastal communities in Indonesia, Sri Lanka, India and Thailand, triggering an unprecedented humanitarian operation.

Throughout an eventful year, the United Nations also continued its long-standing mission to help people achieve the Millennium Development Goals and build better lives for themselves and their children. This work encompassed efforts to combat extreme poverty, end hunger, fight human rights abuse, slow the spread of HIV/AIDS, and ease the plight of refugees and displaced persons. Aided by the report of the Panel of Eminent Persons on United Nations-Civil Society Relations, we sought greater engagement with civil society actors in achieving shared goals.

This edition of the *Yearbook of the United Nations* provides a comprehensive account of the activities undertaken by the United Nations in 2004. It is my hope that it will serve as an important reference tool for all those seeking to learn about our efforts to revitalize our Organization and to create a more peaceful and prosperous world.

KOFI A. ANNAN

Secretary-General of the United Nations
New York, May 2006

Contents

Part One: *Political and security questions*

Part Two: *Human rights*

Part Three: *Economic and social questions*

Part Four: *Legal questions*

Part Five: *Institutional, administrative and budgetary questions*

Part Six: *Intergovernmental organizations related to the United Nations*

Appendices

Indexes

About the 2004 edition of the *Yearbook*

This volume of the *YEARBOOK OF THE UNITED NATIONS* continues the tradition of providing the most comprehensive coverage of the activities of the United Nations. It is an indispensable reference tool for the research community, diplomats, government officials and the general public seeking readily available information on the UN system and its related organizations.

Efforts by the Department of Public Information to achieve a more timely publication have resulted in having to rely on provisional documentation and other materials to prepare the relevant articles. Largely, Economic and Social Council resolutions and some other texts in the present volume are provisional.

Structure and scope of articles

The *Yearbook* is subject-oriented and divided into six parts covering political and security questions; human rights issues; economic and social questions; legal questions; institutional, administrative and budgetary questions; and intergovernmental organizations related to the United Nations. Chapters and topical headings present summaries of pertinent UN activities, including those of intergovernmental and expert bodies, major reports, Secretariat activities and, in selected cases, the views of States in written communications.

Activities of United Nations bodies. All resolutions, decisions and other major activities of the principal organs and, on a selective basis, those of subsidiary bodies are either reproduced or summarized in the appropriate chapter. The texts of all resolutions and decisions of substantive nature adopted in 2004 by the General Assembly, the Security Council and the Economic and Social Council are reproduced or summarized under the relevant topic. These texts are preceded by procedural details giving date of adoption, meeting number and vote totals (in favour–against–abstaining) if any; and an indication of their approval by a sessional or subsidiary body prior to final adoption. The texts are followed by details of any recorded or roll-call vote on the resolution/decision as a whole.

Major reports. Most reports of the Secretary-General, in 2004, along with selected reports from other UN sources, such as seminars and working groups, are summarized briefly.

Secretariat activities. The operational activities of the United Nations for development and humanitarian assistance are described under the relevant topics. For major activities financed outside the UN regular budget, selected information is given on contributions and expenditures.

Views of States. Written communications sent to the United Nations by Member States and circulated as documents of the principal organs have been summarized in selected cases, under the relevant topics. Substantive actions by the Security Council have been analysed and brief reviews of the Council's deliberations given, particularly in cases where an issue was taken up but no resolution was adopted.

Related organizations. The *Yearbook* also briefly describes the 2004 activities of the specialized agencies and other related organizations of the UN system.

Multilateral treaties. Information on signatories and parties to multilateral treaties and conventions is taken from *Multilateral Treaties Deposited with the Secretary-General: Status as at 31 December 2004* (ST/LEG/ SER.E/24 (vols. I & II)), Sales No. E.05.V.3.

Terminology

Formal titles of bodies, organizational units, conventions, declarations and officials are given in full on first mention in an article or sequence of articles. They are also used in resolution/decision texts, and in the SUBJECT INDEX under the key word of the title. Short titles may be used in subsequent references.

How to find information in the *Yearbook*

The user may locate information on the United Nations activities contained in this volume by the use of the Table of Contents, the Subject Index, the Index of Resolutions and Decisions and the Index of Security Council presidential statements. The volume also has five appendices: Appendix I comprises a roster of Member States; Appendix II reproduces the Charter of the United Nations, including the Statute of the International Court of Justice; Appendix III gives the structure of the principal organs of the United Nations; Appendix IV provides the agenda for each session of the principal organs in 2004; and Appendix V gives the addresses of the United Nations information centres and services worldwide.

For more information on the United Nations and its activities, visit our Internet site at:

www.un.org

ABBREVIATIONS COMMONLY USED IN THE *YEARBOOK*

ACABQ	Advisory Committee on Administrative and Budgetary Questions
AU	African Union
CEB	United Nations System Chief Executives Board for Coordination
CIS	Commonwealth of Independent States
CPC	Committee for Programme and Coordination
DPKO	Department of Peacekeeping Operations
DPRK	Democratic People's Republic of Korea
DRC	Democratic Republic of the Congo
ECA	Economic Commission for Africa
ECE	Economic Commission for Europe
ECLAC	Economic Commission for Latin America and the Caribbean
ECOWAS	Economic Community of West African States
ESCAP	Economic and Social Commission for Asia and the Pacific
ESCWA	Economic and Social Commission for Western Asia
EU	European Union
FAO	Food and Agriculture Organization of the United Nations
FYROM	The former Yugoslav Republic of Macedonia
GDP	gross domestic product
GNP	gross national product
HIV/AIDS	human immunodeficiency virus/acquired immunodeficiency syndrome
IAEA	International Atomic Energy Agency
ICAO	International Civil Aviation Organization
ICC	International Criminal Court
ICJ	International Court of Justice
ICRC	International Committee of the Red Cross
ICT	information and communication technology
ICTR	International Criminal Tribunal for Rwanda
ICTY	International Tribunal for the Former Yugoslavia
IDA	International Development Association
IFAD	International Fund for Agricultural Development
IFC	International Finance Corporation
ILO	International Labour Organization
IMF	International Monetary Fund
IMO	International Maritime Organization
ITU	International Telecommunication Union
JIU	Joint Inspection Unit
LDC	least developed country
MDGs	Millennium Development Goals
MINUGUA	United Nations Verification Mission in Guatemala
MINURSO	United Nations Mission for the Referendum in Western Sahara
MINUSTAH	United Nations Stabilization Force in Haiti
MONUC	United Nations Organization Mission in the Democratic Republic of the Congo
MRU	Mano River Union
NATO	North Atlantic Treaty Organization
NGO	non-governmental organization
NSGT	Non-Self-Governing Territory
OAS	Organization of American States
OCHA	Office for the Coordination of Humanitarian Affairs
ODA	official development assistance
OECD	Organisation for Economic Co-operation and Development
OHCHR	Office of the United Nations High Commissioner for Human Rights
OIOS	Office of Internal Oversight Services
ONUB	United Nations Operation in Burundi
OSCE	Organization for Security and Cooperation in Europe
PA	Palestinian Authority
UNAIDS	Joint United Nations Programme on HIV/AIDS
UNAMA	United Nations Assistance Mission in Afghanistan
UNAMI	United Nations Assistance Mission for Iraq
UNAMSIL	United Nations Mission in Sierra Leone
UNCTAD	United Nations Conference on Trade and Development
UNDOF	United Nations Disengagement Observer Force (Golan Heights)
UNDP	United Nations Development Programme
UNEP	United Nations Environment Programme
UNESCO	United Nations Educational, Scientific and Cultural Organization
UNFICYP	United Nations Peacekeeping Force in Cyprus
UNFPA	United Nations Population Fund
UN-Habitat	United Nations Human Settlements Programme
UNHCR	Office of the United Nations High Commissioner for Refugees
UNIC	United Nations Information Centre
UNICEF	United Nations Children's Fund
UNIDO	United Nations Industrial Development Organization
UNIFIL	United Nations Interim Force in Lebanon
UNMEE	United Nations Mission in Ethiopia and Eritrea
UNMIK	United Nations Interim Administration Mission in Kosovo
UNMIL	United Nations Mission in Liberia
UNMOGIP	United Nations Military Observer Group in India and Pakistan
UNMOVIC	United Nations Monitoring, Verification and Inspection Commission
UNOCI	United Nations Operation in Côte d'Ivoire
UNODC	United Nations Office on Drugs and Crime
UNOMIG	United Nations Observer Mission in Georgia
UNOPS	United Nations Office for Project Services
UNRWA	United Nations Relief and Works Agency for Palestine Refugees in the Near East
UNTSO	United Nations Truce Supervision Organization
WFP	World Food Programme
WHO	World Health Organization
WIPO	World Intellectual Property Organization
WMDs	weapons of mass destruction
WMO	World Meteorological Organization
WTO	World Trade Organization
YUN	*Yearbook of the United Nations*

EXPLANATORY NOTE ON DOCUMENTS

References in square brackets in each chapter of Parts One to Five of this volume give the symbols of the main documents issued in 2004 on the topic. The following is a guide to the principal document symbols:

A/- refers to documents of the General Assembly, numbered in separate series by session. Thus, A/59/- refers to documents issued for consideration at the fifty-ninth session, beginning with A/59/1. Documents of special and emergency special sessions are identified as A/S- and A/ES-, followed by the session number.

A/C.- refers to documents of the Assembly's Main Committees, e.g. A/C.1/- is a document of the First Committee, A/C.6/-, a document of the Sixth Committee. A/BUR/- refers to documents of the General Committee. A/AC.- documents are those of the Assembly's ad hoc bodies and A/CN.-, of its commissions; e.g. A/AC.105/- identifies documents of the Assembly's Committee on the Peaceful Uses of Outer Space, A/CN.4/-, of its International Law Commission. Assembly resolutions and decisions since the thirty-first (1976) session have been identified by two arabic numerals; the first indicates the session of adoption; the second, the sequential number in the series. Resolutions are numbered consecutively from 1 at each session. Decisions since the fifty-seventh session are numbered consecutively, from 401 for those concerned with elections and appointments, and from 501 for all other decisions. Decisions of special and emergency special sessions are numbered consecutively, from 11 for those concerned with elections and appointments, and from 21 for all other decisions.

E/- refers to documents of the Economic and Social Council, numbered in separate series by year. Thus, E/2004/- refers to documents issued for consideration by the Council at its 2004 sessions, beginning with E/2004/1. E/AC.-, E/C.- and E/CN.-, followed by identifying numbers, refer to documents of the Council's subsidiary ad hoc bodies, committees and commissions. For example, E/CN.5/- refers to documents of the Council's Commission for Social Development, E/C.2/-, to documents of its Committee on Non-Governmental Organizations. E/ICEF/- documents are those of the United Nations Children's Fund (UNICEF). Symbols for the Council's resolutions and decisions, since 1978, consist of two arabic numerals: the first indicates the year of adoption and the second, the sequential number in the series. There are two series: one for resolutions, beginning with 1 (resolution 2004/1); and one for decisions, beginning with 201 (decision 2004/201).

S/- refers to documents of the Security Council. Its resolutions are identified by consecutive numbers followed by the year of adoption in parentheses, beginning with resolution 1(1946).

ST/-, followed by symbols representing the issuing department or office, refers to documents of the United Nations Secretariat.

Documents of certain bodies bear special symbols, including the following:

CD/-	Conference on Disarmament
CERD/-	Committee on the Elimination of Racial Discrimination
DC/-	Disarmament Commission
DP/-	United Nations Development Programme
HS/-	Commission on Human Settlements
ITC/-	International Trade Centre
TD/-	United Nations Conference on Trade and Development
UNEP/-	United Nations Environment Programme

Many documents of the regional commissions bear special symbols, which are sometimes preceded by the following:

E/ECA/-	Economic Commission for Africa
E/ECE/-	Economic Commission for Europe
E/ECLAC/-	Economic Commission for Latin America and the Caribbean
E/ESCAP/-	Economic and Social Commission for Asia and the Pacific
E/ESCWA/-	Economic and Social Commission for Western Asia

"L" in a symbol refers to documents of limited distribution, such as draft resolutions; "CONF." to documents of a conference; "INF." to those of general information. Summary records are designated by "SR.", verbatim records by "PV.", each followed by the meeting number.

United Nations sales publications each carry a sales number with the following components separated by periods: a capital letter indicating the language(s) of the publication; two arabic numerals indicating the year; a Roman numeral indicating the subject category; a capital letter indicating a subdivision of the category, if any; and an arabic numeral indicating the number of the publication within the category. Examples: E.04.II.A.2; E/F.R.04.II.E.7; E.04.X.1.

Documents cited in the text in square brackets may be obtained through the UN Official Document System by logging on to: http://documents.un.org.

Report of the Secretary-General

Report of the Secretary-General on the work of the Organization

*Following is the Secretary-General's report on the work of the Organization [A/59/1], dated 20 August 2004, submitted to the fifty-ninth session of the General Assembly. The Assembly took note of it on 8 October (**decision 59/504**). On 23 December, the Assembly decided that the agenda item would remain for consideration during the resumed fifty-ninth (2005) session (**decision 59/552**).*

Chapter I

Introduction

1. The United Nations has been through an extraordinarily challenging year. The Security Council had to deal with the controversies surrounding the Iraq crisis and the role to be played by the Organization in the aftermath of the war. There was a surge in demand for peacekeeping operations in a number of countries emerging from violent conflicts. International terrorism and the threat of the use of weapons of mass destruction cast a shadow over all the peoples of the world. Simultaneously, the United Nations also faced a surge in infectious disease as well as the ongoing challenges of extreme poverty and hunger, environmental degradation, human rights violations and humanitarian emergencies. It was against this background that I appointed, last November, a High-level Panel on Threats, Challenges and Change to examine the threats we faced, evaluate our existing policies, processes and institutions and make bold and practicable recommendations.

2. It is worth recalling that the Charter requires the United Nations to promote conditions of economic and social progress and development, as well as solutions to international economic, health and related problems. For the majority of the world's people, the most immediate threats are those of poverty, hunger, unsafe drinking water, environmental degradation and endemic or infectious diseases. The Organization's important work in those areas focuses on the Millennium Development Goals. The eight Goals include halving poverty and hunger, ensuring universal primary education and reversing the spread of HIV/AIDS and other major diseases, all by 2015.

3. While there have been some successes, progress towards achieving the Millennium Development Goals has been mixed. The Goals can be met only through sound economic and social policies, good governance, mobilization of resources and a true partnership between developed and developing nations.

4. An important new programme in the fight against HIV/AIDS is the "three-by-five initiative" of the World Health Organization and the Joint United Nations Programme on HIV/AIDS, which aims to provide antiretroviral treatment to 3 million people by the end of 2005. The need is urgent because 6 million people infected with HIV/AIDS in the developing world need access to antiretroviral therapy to survive. The fight against HIV/AIDS requires strong global leadership, effective global partnership and sustained global action.

5. The gap between increasing demand and limited resources becomes even more evident and urgent when it comes to addressing natural disasters, refugee situations and other humanitarian emergencies. The appeals issued by the United Nations are consistently under-funded, with resulting limits on the services provided. Adequate funding of development and humanitarian causes would be a sound investment. It would also be cost-effective, considering the likely returns in terms of peace and security.

6. The critical situation in Africa and the plight of its peoples is a high-priority concern. The armed conflict in Darfur in western Sudan is a grim reminder of the persistence of deadly conflict on the continent. Half of Africa's people live in poverty, and it is the only region where child malnutrition is getting worse, not better. The HIV/AIDS pandemic has claimed the lives of some 15 million Africans, and continues to cause social and economic devastation in the affected

societies. Yet I have been encouraged by positive trends and the efforts of African States and institutions in dealing with the challenges of peace and security, economic and social development and human rights. African States played an important role in stabilizing Burundi and Liberia. The newly established Peace and Security Council of the African Union has great potential as an instrument for the prevention, management and resolution of violent conflict. Through the New Partnership for Africa's Development and its Peer Review Mechanism, Africa is showing a renewed commitment to poverty reduction, human rights and good governance.

7. The constructive contributions made by non-State actors in achieving progress on issues such as gender, climate change, debt, landmines and HIV/AIDS should not be underestimated. The challenge today is to enrich the unique intergovernmental character of the United Nations through increased openness to establishing partnerships with global civil society.

8. The demand for United Nations peacekeeping operations increased dramatically during the past year, and new operations were launched in Burundi, Haiti, Liberia and the Sudan. At present, more than 56,000 uniformed personnel and some 11,000 civilian staff from 97 countries are serving in 16 missions around the world. Many of those operations are multidimensional, dealing not only with security issues, but also with political problems, the rule of law, human rights, humanitarian concerns and economic reconstruction. The growth in the number of missions reflects the increased demand as well as the continuing importance of peacekeeping in helping to end hostilities and consolidate peace in many countries. At the same time, it places enormous strain on the Organization's resources and its capacity to plan, deploy and manage those operations. Today's operations will not succeed without the sustained political support and commitment of the Member States— and the right resources.

9. The United Nations must of necessity be engaged in the struggle against international terrorism, since effective measures to counter it require broad international cooperation. The Counter-Terrorism Committee of the Security Council, which is central to the Organization's effort, is now to be strengthened by the creation of a Counter-Terrorism Executive Directorate. As we join forces against terrorism, it is imperative that freedom, human rights and the rule of law be upheld and protected.

10. I hope that the momentum gradually building up for the event on the five-year review of the Millennium Declaration in 2005 and the sixtieth anniversary of the United Nations will be sustained and strengthened and will lead to the positive results that our Organization and the world need.

Chapter II

Achieving peace and security

11. Violent internal conflicts continue to engulf millions of civilians around the world, drawing in neighbouring countries and thus posing an even wider threat to international peace and security. Often spurred by the failure of political leaders to provide participatory and accountable governance, such wars can exploit ethnic and religious differences and thrive on economic interests. Participants in such wars often fail to distinguish between combatants, civilians and humanitarian workers. Indeed, civilians have been deliberately attacked, children have been forced to become fighters and aid workers have become strategic targets. The proliferation of weapons of mass destruction and terrorism remain issues of great concern.

12. The United Nations continues to employ a variety of means, including preventive diplomacy, peacemaking, peacekeeping and peacebuilding, to assist Member States in tackling internal as well as more traditional inter-State conflicts. In the course of the past 12 months all of those means were put to use, from good offices in a number of sensitive disputes to a combination of peacekeeping and peacemaking in the cases of Cyprus and Western Sahara to post-conflict peace-building in Sierra Leone. In addition, the United Nations development agencies continued their efforts to assist Member States in addressing the root causes of conflict and in building their long-term capacity for the peaceful settlement of disputes.

13. The past year again saw an increase in the number of United Nations peace-building and peacekeeping missions, demonstrating the central role of our Organization in the pursuit of international peace and security, but also increasing the strains on our human and material resources.

Conflict prevention and peacemaking

14. Because of the serious deterioration of the security environment in Iraq, I decided to temporarily relocate the international staff of the United Nations Assistance Mission for Iraq, as well as of United Nations agencies, programmes and funds, outside the country. However, the United Nations system continued to manage a broad range of essential assistance activities in all

parts of the country, from both within and outside Iraq.

15. In its resolution 1483(2003), the Security Council requested me to terminate the oil-for-food programme in Iraq by 21 November 2003, transferring responsibility for any remaining activity under the programme to the Coalition Provisional Authority. On 21 November 2003, the United Nations handed over all operational responsibilities to the Authority. By 30 June 2004, $8.6 billion of the remaining funds had been transferred to the Development Fund for Iraq. The Office of the Iraq Programme closed down on 31 May.

16. In its resolution 1511(2003), the Security Council invited the Governing Council of Iraq to provide, by 15 December 2003, a timetable and a programme for the drafting of a new constitution for Iraq and for the holding of democratic elections. It also resolved that the United Nations should strengthen and pursue its vital role in Iraq as circumstances permitted and authorized a multinational force to take all necessary measures to contribute to the maintenance of security and stability in Iraq. On 15 November 2003, the Coalition Provisional Authority and the Governing Council signed an agreement setting out a political process for the restoration of sovereignty by 30 June 2004, as well as for the drafting of a new constitution and the holding of elections under that constitution.

17. On 19 January 2004, I convened a meeting in New York with a delegation of the Governing Council and the Coalition Provisional Authority, after which the United Nations was asked to help facilitate a process of dialogue and consensus-building among Iraqis to ensure a peaceful and successful political transition. To that end, my Special Adviser conducted three missions to Iraq. During his first mission, from 6 to 13 February 2004, my Special Adviser, in conjunction with a team from the Electoral Assistance Division of the Department of Political Affairs, concluded that credible elections could not take place by 30 June 2004 and that an interim Government would have to be formed through other means. During his second visit, from 26 March to 16 April, my Special Adviser was able, on the basis of extensive consultations with a broad spectrum of Iraqi society, the Governing Council and the Coalition Provisional Authority, to develop provisional ideas for a successful transition. On 27 April 2004, he presented those ideas to the Security Council. During his third mission, from 1 May to 2 June, my Special Adviser facilitated the formation, on 1 June, of the interim Iraqi Government. Concurrently, an electoral mission was deployed, from 3 May to 6 June, to facilitate

the negotiation of the electoral modalities and establish an electoral institution. On 31 May, the Independent Electoral Commission of Iraq was formed following a country-wide nomination and selection exercise overseen by the United Nations. After consultations with a wide range of Iraqis throughout the country and discussions with the Governing Council and the Coalition Provisional Authority, the legal framework for the electoral system and political parties and entities was promulgated on 7 June.

18. On 8 June 2004, the Security Council adopted resolution 1546(2004), in which it endorsed the proposed timetable for Iraq's political transition and decided that the United Nations should play a leading role, as circumstances permitted, in assisting in convening a national conference, in providing advice on the process for holding elections and in promoting national dialogue and consensus-building on the drafting of a national constitution. The Council also gave UNAMI a mandate in other areas, such as development and humanitarian assistance, human rights and national reconciliation.

19. Under its strengthened mandate provided in resolution 1546(2004), the United Nations will do everything possible to assist the Iraqi people in the transition process. To that end, my new Special Representative will work closely with the interim Government and establish a dialogue with countries in the region and beyond. An expanded role of the United Nations in institution-building, reconstruction, human rights and other areas, however, will depend on whether the overall security environment will allow for a larger presence in Iraq. In the meantime, my Special Representative will focus on the essential priority tasks set out in resolution 1546(2004) from both outside and inside Iraq, as circumstances permit. To succeed, he will need the full support of the international community.

20. Turning to the Israeli-Palestinian conflict, despite the strenuous efforts of the international community through the Quartet (consisting of the United Nations, the European Union, the Russian Federation and the United States of America) and the stated commitment of the parties to the road map initiative, the peace process remained stalled and violence persisted. The humanitarian situation in the occupied Palestinian territory continued to deteriorate, with a subsistence standard of living for many Palestinians being maintained only through assistance from the international donor community, including the United Nations Relief and Works Agency for Palestine Refugees in the Near East and other United Nations agencies and programmes.

21. Over the past 12 months, the Security Council adopted two resolutions on the Middle East. On 19 November 2003, resolution 1515 (2003) endorsed the road map and called upon the parties to fulfil their corresponding obligations. On 19 May 2004, the Council adopted resolution 1544(2004), calling upon Israel to respect its obligations under international humanitarian law, including its obligation not to destroy Palestinian homes in a manner contrary to the law. The General Assembly, at its resumed tenth emergency special session, adopted resolution ES-10/13 on 21 October 2003 demanding that Israel stop and reverse the construction of the wall in the occupied Palestinian territory, including in and around East Jerusalem. On 8 December, the Assembly, again at its resumed tenth emergency special session, adopted resolution ES-10/14 requesting the International Court of Justice to urgently render an advisory opinion on the legal consequences arising from the construction of the wall. The Court rendered its advisory opinion on 9 July 2004, finding that the route of the wall in the occupied Palestinian territory was contrary to international law and that Israel was under an obligation to terminate the building of the wall, to dismantle parts already built and to make reparations for all damage caused to Palestinian property. It also found that States were under an obligation not to recognize the illegal situation and to ensure Israel's compliance with international law under the Fourth Geneva Convention. The Court said that the General Assembly and the Security Council should consider further action. The Assembly reconvened its tenth emergency special session to consider the issue and, on 20 July 2004, adopted resolution ES-10/15, in which it acknowledged the advisory opinion, demanded that Israel comply with its legal obligations as mentioned in the opinion, called upon Member States to comply likewise with their legal obligations and requested me to establish a register of damage caused as a result of the construction of the wall.

22. I have exercised good offices through my direct contacts and those of my Special Coordinator, as well as through the Quartet mechanism. At the meeting of Quartet members, held in New York on 4 May 2004, we reiterated that all final status issues, such as borders and refugees, should be negotiated by the parties and that such negotiations must be based on the internationally accepted framework for the peace process. We also set out principles for the success of a possible Israeli withdrawal from the Gaza Strip and stated that the withdrawal should be complete, that it must lead to an end of the occupation of Gaza and that it must be accompanied by similar steps in the West Bank. Discussion of an action plan has been initiated and designed to move the parties ahead and to help them to meet their obligations.

23. On Cyprus, after two months of intense negotiations by my Special Adviser and with my personal involvement, the Foundation Agreement proposed in the settlement plan was finalized on 31 March 2004 and was submitted to separate simultaneous referendums in the two communities on 24 April. Although it was approved by the Turkish Cypriots by a margin of two to one, the plan was rejected by the Greek Cypriot electorate by a margin of three to one and therefore did not enter into force. At present, I do not see a basis for resuming my good offices in Cyprus. Instead, a broad reassessment of the full range of United Nations peace activities is called for. In this regard, I have called for a review of the United Nations Peacekeeping Force in Cyprus. While the decision of the Greek Cypriots must be respected, I hope they will reflect on their position so that future efforts can have a chance to succeed. I have appealed to the Turkish Cypriots and to Turkey to stand by the community's wish for reunification, and have called upon the Security Council to encourage States to lift unnecessary barriers that isolate the Turkish Cypriots and impede their development.

24. In Burundi, considerable progress was made in the peace process with the signing of the protocols of 8 October and 2 November 2003 and the conclusion on 16 November of the Global Ceasefire Agreement between the Transitional Government of Burundi and the Forces for the Defense of Democracy. By its presidential statement of 22 December 2003, the Security Council recognized the progress made and took note of requests made by the President of Burundi and the Deputy President of South Africa, on behalf of the States of the Regional Initiative, that the United Nations consider taking over from the African Mission in Burundi. The Council also welcomed my decision to examine the situation in further detail. To that end, I fielded an assessment mission to Burundi from 16 to 27 February 2004, following which I recommended the establishment of a multidisciplinary peacekeeping operation in that country. By its resolution 1545(2004) of 21 May, the Council established the United Nations Operation in Burundi, for an initial period of six months as from 1 June 2004, with an authorized troop strength of 5,650 military personnel and up to 120 civilian police personnel. Meanwhile, efforts continued towards a comprehensive and all-inclusive ceasefire, despite serious ongoing challenges.

25. Talks on the Sudan led by the Intergovernmental Authority on Development have made significant progress during the past year, leaving only details of a ceasefire and international guarantees to be negotiated before a comprehensive peace agreement is complete. My Special Adviser provided continuous support to the parties and to the mediation process. I hope that the Sudanese parties will be able to finalize a peace agreement expeditiously. At the request of the Security Council, the United Nations began preparatory work on how best it could fully support the parties during the implementation of a comprehensive peace agreement.

26. During 2004, the launching of an armed rebellion in Darfur in western Sudan and the Government's response led to significant loss of life and massive displacement of civilians in the region, many of whom were forced to seek refuge in neighbouring countries, mainly Chad. As violence targeting the civilian population continued, the humanitarian and human rights situations in the area deteriorated into a full-scale emergency by spring 2004, as detailed in the following chapter. More than 1 million people are internally displaced and over 170,000 refugees are currently in Chad. At the invitation of the Sudanese Government, I dispatched two missions to the area to assess the humanitarian and human rights situations. Persistent reports of massive human rights violations and the humanitarian emergency unfolding in Darfur continued to be a cause of grave concern. I visited the Sudan and Chad in early July 2004 to see what could be done to resolve the root causes and mitigate the consequences of the conflict in Darfur. In a joint communiqué signed at the end of my visit, the Government of the Sudan and the United Nations committed themselves to a wide range of obligations that needed to be met without delay to address the crisis. A joint implementation mechanism, co-chaired by the Sudanese Foreign Minister and my Special Representative for the Sudan, was established to monitor the implementation of the joint communiqué. I also asked my Special Adviser in the region to provide assistance to the African Union in its mediation of the political negotiation on Darfur. On 30 July, the Security Council adopted resolution 1556(2004), in which it demanded that the Government of the Sudan fulfil its commitments to disarm the Janjaweed militias and apprehend and bring to justice Janjaweed leaders and their associates who had incited and carried out human rights and international humanitarian law violations and other atrocities. The Council further requested that I report to it in 30 days, and monthly thereafter, on the progress or lack thereof made by the Government of the Sudan on this matter and expressed its intention to consider further actions in the event of non-compliance.

27. In January 2004, in its resolution 1523(2004), the Security Council extended the mandate of the United Nations Mission for the Referendum in Western Sahara for three months until 30 April to allow my Personal Envoy to consult further with the Government of Morocco on its final response to the Peace Plan for Self-Determination of the People of Western Sahara, which he had submitted to the parties in January 2003. The Frente POLISARIO had informed my Personal Envoy of its acceptance of the Peace Plan in early July 2003. In April 2004, Morocco delivered its final response, in which it expressed a willingness to continue to work to achieve a political solution within the framework of Moroccan sovereignty, thereby rejecting essential elements of the Peace Plan. On 29 April, the Council adopted resolution 1541(2004) extending the mandate of MINURSO until 31 October. The Council also reaffirmed its support for the Peace Plan and my efforts to achieve a mutually acceptable political solution to the dispute over Western Sahara. On 1 June, my Personal Envoy tendered his resignation, citing his belief that he had done all that he could to assist the parties in finding a solution to the conflict. He also stated that, while there had been progress in a number of areas during his seven years of involvement in the issue, the United Nations had not been able to resolve the underlying dispute. Following my Personal Envoy's resignation, I have decided that my current Special Representative for Western Sahara will continue to work with the parties and neighbouring countries in pursuit of a political solution. In the meantime, MINURSO continued to monitor the ceasefire between the parties, which had been in effect since September 1991, and to provide assistance to the implementation of confidence-building measures led by the United Nations High Commissioner for Refugees, including the exchange of family visits between Western Sahara and the Tindouf refugee camps in Algeria, which began in March 2004.

28. Progress made in mid-2004 at the Somalia National Reconciliation Conference in Kenya, held under the auspices of the Intergovernmental Authority on Development, gave cause for cautious optimism. Concerted efforts by the foreign ministers of the Intergovernmental Authority on Development made it possible for the Conference to begin its third and final phase. Somali traditional leaders began negotiating the distribution of parliamentary seats within each of the major clans. Each clan is to submit a list of members of parliament to form the 275-seat transi-

tional federal parliament, which would in turn elect a president. I commend the Governments of the Intergovernmental Authority on Development for demonstrating a renewed cohesiveness on the issue of national reconciliation in Somalia. I personally addressed the Somali delegates at the Conference on 8 July and encouraged them to establish an inclusive governance structure as soon as possible.

29. With regard to United Nations support for the peaceful resolution of potentially violent conflicts, I was pleased with the significant progress achieved by Cameroon and Nigeria, with the assistance of the United Nations, in the implementation of the October 2002 ruling of the International Court of Justice on the land and maritime boundary between the two countries. This progress was achieved within the framework of the Cameroon-Nigeria Mixed Commission, which I established at the request of the heads of State of the two countries and which is chaired by my Special Representative for West Africa. The process initiated by the Commission for the withdrawal of the civilian administration, military and police forces by each of the two States from areas falling within the sovereignty of the other and the corresponding transfer of authority, as called for by the Court, will enhance cooperation between Cameroon and Nigeria. The official visit of Nigerian President Olusegun Obasanjo to Cameroon on 28 and 29 July 2004 demonstrated the two countries' determination to continue to strengthen their bilateral relations through peaceful cooperation and dialogue. In the same vein, the long-standing border dispute between Equatorial Guinea and Gabon seems to be heading towards a mutually acceptable solution following a series of mediation sessions led by my Special Adviser and mediator on this issue. I am pleased to report that on 6 July, the leaders of the two countries signed a memorandum of understanding on the joint development of petroleum and other natural resources in the exclusive economic zones of Equatorial Guinea and Gabon.

30. In the Americas, the United Nations Verification Mission in Guatemala, now in its final year, has been working with domestic institutions and with the newly elected Government to ensure continuity in the implementation of the peace accords and the consolidation of democracy. With organized criminal groups posing a serious threat to the consolidation of the rule of law, the United Nations concluded an agreement with the previous Government, endorsed by the new Government, on the establishment of a Commission for the Investigation of Illegal Groups and Clandestine Security Apparatuses.

The United Nations Office on Drugs and Crime is also helping to strengthen the legal and institutional frameworks to confront organized crime groups, which constitute a serious force destructive to civil society and good governance.

31. Despite multiple peacemaking efforts undertaken by my Special Adviser on Colombia, the Government and the guerrilla groups have not renewed peace talks. Since the end of 2002, the Government has been waging an intensive military campaign against the two major guerrilla groups—the Revolutionary Armed Forces of Colombia and the National Liberation Army. At the same time, it is pursuing talks with some paramilitary groups aimed at their disarmament, demobilization and reintegration. As requested by the Government, the Office of the United Nations High Commissioner for Human Rights examined a draft law on justice and reparations, concluding that it needed to address impunity and past human rights violations. Meanwhile, violence continues and is directly affecting both the humanitarian and human rights situations adversely.

32. In view of the present situation, the second humanitarian action plan, to be launched by the United Nations system in Colombia will provide a comprehensive assistance programme that will require a firm commitment on the part of the Government and other parties. I also urge the Government to implement the recommendations of the Commission on Human Rights. Finally, my good offices remain available in the search for a peaceful solution to the conflict in Colombia. My Special Adviser will continue, through contacts with the Government, guerrilla groups, civil society and the international community, to assist peacemaking efforts.

33. In South Asia, India and Pakistan have made important strides in their efforts to improve their relations and resolve outstanding issues. Following an agreement in January 2004 in Islamabad to resume bilateral dialogue on an agreed range of issues, including Jammu and Kashmir, the two sides have been conducting talks in a purposeful and serious manner. This has brought hope that the two countries will be able to bring an end to the dispute that has troubled their relations since their independence. I have expressed to the leaders of the two countries, both in public and in private, my admiration for their concerted efforts to bring peace to the region and have encouraged them to continue this endeavour. The United Nations will remain at their disposal to assist the process in any way they may deem necessary.

34. In Nepal, the insurgency led by the Communist Party of Nepal (Maoist) has escalated

since the breakdown of peace talks and the cease-fire in August 2003, causing considerable suffering in much of the country. I have intensified my engagement with all concerned with a view to contributing to a political resolution to the conflict. The United Nations Development Programme and the Office of the United Nations High Commissioner for Human Rights are strengthening their support for national efforts to curb conflict-related human rights abuses, and United Nations system agencies are adapting their programmes to ensure that they will be able to deliver protection and assistance to affected communities.

35.   The peace process in Sri Lanka has continued to encounter difficulties and delays. However, the ceasefire has held, demonstrating a desire by all sides for durable peace based on a negotiated agreement. It is my hope that the ongoing efforts to revive negotiations, facilitated by the Government of Norway, will bear fruit and pave the way for the long-awaited reconstruction and rehabilitation of the country, in which the United Nations system stands ready to play a full part.

36.   I am pleased to report that the peace process in Bougainville, Papua New Guinea, has been slowly but steadily moving forward. The downsized successor to the United Nations Political Office in Bougainville, the United Nations Observer Mission in Bougainville has overseen the destruction by the Bougainville parties of over 80 per cent of weapons. Simultaneously, the Bougainville parties, together with the Government of Papua New Guinea, are finalizing the Bougainville constitution. Its adoption will pave the way for the election of an autonomous Bougainville government, hopefully before the end of this year. With the establishment of the autonomous Government, the Mission will have completed its mandate.

37.   I continued to provide good offices aimed at facilitating national reconciliation and democratization in Myanmar. My Special Envoy visited Yangon in September 2003 and March 2004 and engaged relevant actors. On 17 May, the Government reconvened the National Convention to draft a new constitution, regrettably without the participation of the National League for Democracy and some ethnic nationality parties. I have stated that for the Government's political road map to be considered as a credible and all-inclusive vehicle for a democratic transition, the remaining restrictions on Daw Aung San Suu Kyi and her deputy, U Tin Oo, should be lifted and the National League for Democracy's offices permitted to reopen.

38.   Cooperation between the United Nations and the Government of Indonesia, in support of the latter's pursuit of political, economic and social reforms, continues in a constructive manner. Notably, the United Nations provided technical assistance to Indonesia's parliamentary and presidential elections held in recent months. Indonesia's national unity and territorial integrity can best be ensured through respect for democratic norms and the promotion of human rights. In this connection, it should be noted that the Government on 19 May changed the military emergency status in Aceh to a civil emergency. I hope that such a change in status will result in unimpeded access to the population in Aceh so that the Organization can resume all of its humanitarian and developmental activities there. I also remain concerned about the situation in Ambon, Maluku, where sectarian violence flared up again in April. I continue to believe that the perpetrators of serious human rights violations committed in 1999 in Timor-Leste (then East Timor) must be brought to justice.

39.   On the Korean Peninsula, my Personal Envoy continued his efforts to mobilize international humanitarian assistance for the Democratic People's Republic of Korea through the United Nations system, with some progress. I am increasingly concerned about the health situation in the country, of which children are the main victims. Politically, I have focused my efforts on supporting the six-party talks as the most promising way to achieve a nuclear-weapon-free peninsula and a comprehensive settlement of related issues. I remain convinced that durable solutions to these issues will have to take into account the long-term economic needs of the Democratic People's Republic of Korea. In close consultation with that country's Government and other Governments concerned, my Personal Envoy has established expert groups to explore steps and measures by which the international community can best assist the Democratic People's Republic of Korea in meeting its energy needs and modernizing its economy.

40.   The United Nations continues to work on enhancing its institutional capacity for conflict prevention and peacemaking. In response to General Assembly resolution 57/337 of 3 July 2003 on the prevention of armed conflict, the United Nations system has increased its assistance to Member States in building national capacity for the prevention of conflict. Country teams have started to better integrate such assistance into their programmes. United Nations agencies and departments, acting under the auspices of the Inter-agency/Interdepartmental Framework for Coordination, have also assisted a

growing number of Member States, at their request, in building the capacity and skills of institutions, government and civil society for ensuring the peaceful settlement of disputes and enhancing sustainable development and social cohesion, including the consolidation of democratic governance.

Peacekeeping and peace-building

41. The reporting period witnessed a surge in demand for United Nations peacekeeping activities, with the establishment of new and complex operations in Liberia, Côte d'Ivoire, Burundi and Haiti—the last three in quick succession. As at July 2004, the United Nations had more than 56,000 peacekeepers, including troops, military observers and civilian police, serving in 16 operations around the world. The increase in the number of peacekeeping missions poses a serious challenge to the Organization's capacity for effective planning, timely deployment and the provision of sustained support for such operations. The new operations will not succeed without the continued political, financial and human resources of the Member States.

42. Peacekeeping mandates authorized by the Security Council have increasingly sought to create the conditions necessary for preventing a relapse into conflict by helping parties to accelerate national recovery and assume primary responsibility, with support from the international community, for the peace-building process. The effectiveness and success of United Nations peacekeeping and peace-building interventions remain contingent upon the promotion and implementation of regional integrated approaches to challenges when they are transnational in origin and effect. The Office of the Special Representative for West Africa, established in 2002 as the United Nations Office for West Africa, has provided the Security Council with recommendations on practical ways to combat such cross-cutting and subregional problems in West Africa. Under the leadership of my Special Representative, the Office has continued to hold periodic consultations with all heads of United Nations missions in the subregion aimed at promoting inter-mission cooperation.

43. Although some progress has been made in the transitional process in the Democratic Republic of the Congo, the process was impeded by lingering mistrust among various components of the Government of National Unity and Transition. Relations between the Democratic Republic of the Congo and Rwanda and Uganda improved somewhat following the adoption of the Principles on Good Neighbourly Relations and Co-operation between the Democratic Republic of the Congo and Burundi, Rwanda and Uganda in New York in September 2003. Yet the pace of normalization of bilateral relations has slowed down since the beginning of 2004. Meanwhile, the Ituri Brigade of the United Nations Organization Mission in the Democratic Republic of the Congo consolidated its military positions in Ituri and deployed to several locations in the interior of the region, thereby restoring some peace and stability. The leaders of most armed groups in Ituri signed a declaration on 14 May 2004 committing themselves to fully supporting disarmament efforts and the national transitional process. The mine action coordination centre coordinated a survey of mined land and roads in the Ituri District, thus contributing to safe mission deployment. In the Kivus, MONUC also deployed a brigade-sized force. On 26 May 2004, however, fighting broke out in Bukavu, South Kivu, between troops loyal to the Government of National Unity and Transition and those loyal to dissident factions of the former Congolese Rally for Democracy—Goma. While the crisis reached the national level, the situation was brought under control with the withdrawal of troops loyal to the dissident elements from the town. Following the deterioration of bilateral relations between the Democratic Republic of the Congo and Rwanda as a result of the Bukavu crisis, a mini-summit on the Democratic Republic of the Congo was held in the margins of the African Union summit held in Addis Ababa on 6 July, during which it was agreed to establish a Democratic Republic of the Congo/Rwanda joint verification mechanism.

44. The Economic Community of West African States force, which has been deployed in Côte d'Ivoire since January 2003, sharing responsibility for peacekeeping duties with the French force (Licorne), continued to face serious logistical and financial shortfalls. ECOWAS and the Ivorian parties proposed that the United Nations take over peacekeeping functions in Côte d'Ivoire with the establishment of a multidimensional operation. By its resolution 1528(2004) of 27 February 2004, the Security Council established the United Nations Operation in Côte d'Ivoire as from 4 April. Its mandate included monitoring the ceasefire; supporting the implementation of the disarmament, demobilization and reintegration programme; protecting United Nations personnel and civilians under imminent threat of violence; supporting the provision of security for the ministers of the Government of National Reconciliation; facilitating the delivery of humanitarian assistance; providing oversight, guidance and technical assistance for the 2005 elections; and protecting human rights and assisting the Government in reviving and restoring the

rule of law. The Operation had reached its authorized strength of 6,240 troops by mid-August 2004.

45. Serious obstacles to the Ivorian peace process emerged, however, in 2004 in terms of the deepening rift between the President, the Prime Minister and the opposition parties. This eventually led to the opposition's suspension of participation in the Government as from 7 March. On 25 March, opposition demonstrations in Abidjan resulted in violent clashes between the Ivorian security forces and demonstrators and the arrest of opposition members. In response to requests from the President and Prime Minister, an International Commission of Inquiry visited Côte d'Ivoire from 15 to 28 April. The Commission concluded that the demonstrations of 25 March had been used for a carefully planned and executed operation by the Ivorian security forces, as well as special units and parallel forces, targeting opposition parties and community groups. Given the dangerous stalemate in the peace process, I convened a mini-summit on Côte d'Ivoire on 6 July in the margins of the African Union Summit in Addis Ababa. Participants, who included President Laurent Gbagbo, agreed to convene a larger summit in Accra. At the Accra meeting, held from 29 to 31 July, the Ivorian parties agreed on key issues, including resuming the functioning of the Government of National Reconciliation; delegating authority from the President to the Prime Minister and starting the disarmament, demobilization and reintegration programme. I expect all parties to abide fully by their commitments.

46. The United Nations Mission in Sierra Leone continued to successfully implement its mandate to assist the Government of Sierra Leone in consolidating peace. With the support of UNAMSIL and other bilateral and multilateral partners, the Government of Sierra Leone has made significant progress in key areas, such as the reintegration of ex-combatants, the return of refugees, the consolidation of State authority, the restoration of government control of diamond-mining activities and economic recovery.

47. In early February 2004, an interdisciplinary assessment mission travelled to Sierra Leone to take stock of the key security benchmarks and to determine whether a residual UNAMSIL presence would be required beyond December 2004. Following that visit, I submitted my recommendations to the Security Council. Subsequently, in its resolution 1537(2004) of 30 March 2004, the Council authorized a reduced UNAMSIL presence in Sierra Leone for an initial period of six months from 1 January 2005, with a new ceiling of 3,250 troops, 141 military observers and 80 United Nations civilian police personnel. The residual presence of UNAMSIL provides the Government of Sierra Leone with a unique opportunity to further consolidate the peace process and to continue enhancing its security sector.

48. The United Nations peace-building support offices in the Central African Republic and Guinea-Bissau continued to assist the host countries in promoting good governance and mobilizing international support for reconstruction. Despite various destabilizing pressures, including the coups in the Central African Republic in March 2003 and in Guinea-Bissau in September 2003, the United Nations Peace-building Support Office in the Central African Republic and the United Nations Peace-building Support Office in Guinea-Bissau concentrated on the restoration and consolidation of constitutional normality in their respective countries through peaceful political transitions. UNOGBIS contributed to the successful holding of legislative elections in March 2004 and BONUCA facilitated the establishment of a consultative mechanism composed of representatives from the transitional Government, political leaders and civil society.

49. Significant progress was made towards restoring peace in Liberia during the reporting period. By its resolution 1509(2003) of 19 September 2003, the Security Council established the United Nations Mission in Liberia, with a mandate that included implementing the 17 June 2003 ceasefire agreement, supporting security sector reform, contributing to efforts to protect and promote human rights and supporting the implementation of the Comprehensive Peace Agreement signed by the Liberian parties on 18 August 2003 in Accra. UNMIL, with an authorized troop strength of 15,000, took over peace-keeping responsibilities from an ECOWAS force on 1 October 2003.

50. The National Transitional Government of Liberia provided for in the Comprehensive Peace Agreement was inaugurated on 14 October 2003. With the deployment of UNMIL across the country, the security situation improved nationwide. The ceasefire has generally held, although intra-faction disputes at times have resulted in violence. Some 63,000 ex-combatants have been disarmed and demobilized, and programmes to reintegrate them into the community continue. United Nations civilian police, comprising 1,060 personnel, have been working closely with the National Transitional Government of Liberia in restructuring the national police. UNMIL continues to play a central role in supporting the organization of national elections, which are scheduled to be held in October 2005. Humanitarian access

has improved, paving the way for the eventual return of internally displaced persons and refugees. In early February, an international reconstruction conference for Liberia was held at which $520 million was pledged for the reconstruction and humanitarian needs of the country. UNMIL and the United Nations country team are working closely with the National Transitional Government of Liberia and its development partners to ensure that national recovery projects presented at the conference are funded and implemented.

51. Despite the impasse in the peace process between Eritrea and Ethiopia, the situation in the border area remained relatively calm from a military point of view. At the same time, tensions persisted at the political level, exacerbated by spates of inflammatory rhetoric emanating from the two capitals. In order to break the stalemate caused by the lack of progress in the demarcation of the border, I appointed a Special Envoy for Ethiopia and Eritrea to start a dialogue between the two sides. The United Nations Mission in Ethiopia and Eritrea continued to support the peace process by monitoring the temporary security zone between the two countries, chairing the Military Coordination Commission and coordinating humanitarian, human rights and demining activities in the temporary security zone and its adjacent areas. In view of the prevailing circumstances, the effectiveness of UNMEE is currently being reviewed with a view to adjusting and streamlining its operations as necessary. However, no adjustments should be made without careful consideration of the possible implications for the peace process and the results achieved so far.

52. The United Nations Interim Force in Lebanon continued to monitor the Blue Line between Israel and Lebanon and to liaise with the parties to avert, minimize and contain tensions. Unfortunately, the past year saw an increased number of incidents along the Blue Line, with Israeli violations of Lebanese airspace and Hezbollah retaliatory anti-aircraft fire. Israel conducted air raids on suspected Hezbollah positions and there was an exchange of missile, mortar and small arms fire predominantly in the Shab'a farms area. Hezbollah also placed booby traps on the Lebanese side of the Blue Line in close proximity to the Israel Defense Forces patrol routes. I have continued to remind the parties to respect the Blue Line and to abide fully by their obligations. The Lebanese armed forces continue to be active in the south, but the Government of Lebanon has not yet taken all of the steps required to assert and maintain its full authority in the region. The mine action coordination centre continues to assist in clearing land in southern Lebanon of anti-personnel mines; an area of five square kilometres has been cleared since May 2002.

53. During the reporting period, Timor-Leste continued to establish and strengthen its national institutions with assistance from the United Nations Mission of Support in East Timor and United Nations agencies. The security situation remained stable. To safeguard the gains made to date and to help Timor-Leste achieve full self-sufficiency, the Security Council, in its resolution 1543(2004), decided to extend the mandate of UNMISET for a period of six months beyond 20 May 2004, with a view to subsequently extending it for a further and final period of six months. The size of the operation was reduced and its tasks revised to take account of changed circumstances on the ground. The Government of Timor-Leste has assumed full responsibility for maintaining security and stability within the country, although UNMISET remains ready to assist in exceptional circumstances if required. The Mission continues to provide capacity-building assistance to public administration, law enforcement and the judiciary.

54. In Afghanistan, implementation of the Bonn Agreement continued during the review period. The new Afghan constitution was adopted in January 2004 by a Loya Jirga, a disarmament, demobilization and reintegration programme was introduced for ex-combatants and a voter registration drive was initiated on 1 December 2003 in preparation for elections. In March 2004, the Government made public its intention to hold presidential and lower-house parliamentary elections simultaneously in September 2004. Citing legal and technical grounds, the Joint Electoral Management Body announced on 9 July that the presidential elections would be held on 9 October and parliamentary elections in April 2005. Afghanistan remains an insecure environment, with factional fighting in the north and terrorist elements operating in the south. Significant progress on disarmament, demobilization and reintegration is critical to ensure sustainable peace and the holding of elections. The lack of security inside Afghanistan is one of the key factors preventing the return of some 3 million Afghan refugees in the Islamic Republic of Iran and Pakistan, as well as of thousands of internally displaced persons. It is also undermining the political process. Extremists, for example, have deliberately targeted the voter registration drive. A major obstacle to the success of the Bonn process is the increased cultivation of narcotics, which fuels both factional fighting and terrorism. The engagement of the international

community remains a critical factor in keeping the peace and promoting the Bonn process. A conference held in Berlin in March and April 2004 gathered high-level representatives from 56 countries. At the conference, donors pledged $8.2 billion over the next three years to an Afghan-led reconstruction programme. The mine action centre in Afghanistan has been coordinating all mine-related activities, including the clearance of 780 square kilometres of mined land to date.

55. The United Nations Observer Mission in Georgia continued to monitor the implementation of the 1994 Moscow ceasefire agreement by the Georgian and Abkhaz sides and to pursue efforts to achieve a comprehensive settlement of the conflict based on the principle of the territorial integrity of Georgia. Its efforts have focused on maintaining stability on the ground and engaging the two parties on security and political issues, refugee returns and economic cooperation. The Group of Friends continued to support those efforts. Meanwhile, the political change in Georgia brought about by the election of a new President and parliamentary elections in early 2004 has created a new momentum in Georgia's efforts to resolve its internal conflicts, including in Abkhazia. The Abkhaz side, however, has continued to refuse to discuss the status of Abkhazia within the Georgian State, which is a key obstacle in efforts to achieve a negotiated settlement.

56. The United Nations Interim Administration Mission in Kosovo, in furtherance of the establishment of democratic provisional institutions of self-government, devolved powers to the provisional institutions of self-government in accordance with the Constitutional Framework. UNMIK continues to exercise overall authority and to implement the reserved responsibilities listed in chapter 8 of the Constitutional Framework. In March 2004, violence erupted throughout Kosovo, targeting primarily Kosovo Serb community members and institutions, including Serbian Orthodox religious sites. The violence demonstrated that Kosovo still has some way to go in meeting the standards endorsed by the Security Council in its presidential statement of 12 December 2003. As a result, the implementation plan will give additional emphasis to security and the rule of law, minority rights and protection, the return of displaced persons, economic development and decentralization. UNMIK also continued to encourage a direct dialogue on practical matters between Belgrade and Pristina.

57. With the situation in Haiti deteriorating, the Security Council adopted resolution 1529 (2004) on 29 February 2004 authorizing the deployment of a multinational interim force to Haiti and declaring its readiness to establish a follow-on stabilization force to support a peaceful, constitutional political process following the resignation and departure of President Jean-Bertrand Aristide. The Council also approved the establishment of the United Nations Stabilization Mission in Haiti, starting on 1 June 2004 following a multidisciplinary needs assessment mission. The Mission is multidimensional in scope to help Haitians address the complex range of issues they face. Close cooperation with the Organization of American States and the Caribbean Community will be key in ensuring the successful implementation of the Mission's mandate. In July 2004, the transitional Haitian Government presented an Interim Cooperation Framework, prepared with the assistance of the World Bank, UNDP and MINUSTAH, to the donor community in Washington, D.C., and received pledges of $1.3 billion to assist with a wide range of political, social and economic needs.

58. I am thus far encouraged by the dedication and political will demonstrated by the interim Government to put Haiti on a path to democracy and sustainable development. The international community must do its part and remain engaged for the long term, both politically and financially. It must seek creative ways to assist, building on previous experiences, while leaving the ownership of the process firmly in the hands of the Haitian people.

United Nations and regional organizations

59. The United Nations continued to intensify its partnership with regional organizations in pursuit of the shared goals of peace, stability and development in a framework of democratic governance and respect for human rights and the rule of law.

60. In Africa, the United Nations further enhanced its cooperation with the African Union and subregional organizations. We assisted the African Union in developing its policy framework for the establishment of African peace and security structures and continue to cooperate closely with it in that regard, including in the establishment of an African standby force and Military Staff Committee. In an effort to consolidate linkages with ECOWAS in the promotion of peace and stability in the subregion, as called for by the Security Council on a number of occasions, my Special Representative for West Africa held extensive consultations with ECOWAS officials in Nigeria on 31 May and in Senegal on 22 and 23 July 2004 regarding practical modalities for improving working relations. As a result of those consultations, ECOWAS and the Office of the Special Representative of the Secretary-General for West Africa have developed a memorandum of under-

standing and a programme of work for 2004-2005 involving joint activities in the areas of governance and security sector reform, electoral assistance, youth unemployment, free movement of persons and goods, small arms and light weapons and transborder security.

61. The United Nations and the European Union achieved significant progress in cooperation on conflict prevention and post-conflict reconstruction, as well as in crisis management activities. The first desk-to-desk dialogues on conflict prevention, held in Brussels and New York in October 2003 and June 2004, launched a new phase of United Nations–European Union cooperation at both the headquarters and country levels. There was general consensus that the goals of the dialogues had been met in terms of sharing assessments of situations on the ground, deepening interaction between the two organizations, suggesting follow-up actions and identifying specific areas for cooperation on conflict prevention in five targeted countries or subregions. The Joint Declaration on United Nations–European Union Cooperation in Crisis Management, signed in September 2003, committed the two organizations to work together in addressing crisis situations and called for the establishment of a joint consultative mechanism at the working level to examine ways and means to enhance coordination and compatibility. In mid-February 2004, the first meeting of the joint consultative mechanism, the United Nations–European Union steering committee on crisis management, was held at United Nations Headquarters and discussed a range of issues concerning cooperation in planning, training, communications, best practices and supporting African capacity-building initiatives in the area of peacekeeping. Working-level contacts and meetings have continued, and the next steering committee meeting is scheduled for October in Brussels.

62. The United Nations has increased its contacts with member States and the secretariat of the Association of Southeast Asian Nations on matters relating to regional peace and security, in accordance with General Assembly resolution 57/35 of 21 November 2002. In February 2004, at the fourth United Nations–ASEAN regional workshop on conflict prevention, conflict resolution and peace-building in South-East Asia, held in Jakarta (Indonesia being the current Chair of ASEAN), new means to enhance cooperation between the two organizations, specifically in the area of peacekeeping, were recommended, as well as the exchange of lessons learned in the fields of humanitarian assistance, preventive measures and early warning.

63. I welcome the comprehensive review by the Pacific leaders of the functioning of the Pacific Islands Forum and its secretariat, which aims at developing a plan to realize the vision of the Pacific as a region of peace, harmony, security and economic prosperity, and look forward to enhancing our cooperation towards our common objectives.

Electoral assistance

64. Elections can have a polarizing effect and heighten political tensions. Credibly conducted elections encourage those who lose at the ballot box to accept the results, while technically flawed elections provide opportunities for resort to civil disquiet or violence. Requests that the United Nations provide technical assistance to improve the quality of elections and reduce the potential for electoral conflict have increased over the past decade. During the reporting period, 18 new requests were received and 39 countries are currently being assisted. A strong priority of United Nations electoral assistance is enhancing the participation of women in electoral processes through a variety of measures, including public education campaigns and, where relevant, quotas.

65. Of particular importance and prominence has been the involvement of the United Nations with electoral matters in Iraq. Following the determination by a United Nations expert team that credible elections could not be held in the country by 30 June 2004, and as agreed on 15 November 2003 by the Coalition Provisional Authority and the Governing Council of Iraq, a transitional law was adopted that provided for a series of elections beginning in January 2005. United Nations electoral experts subsequently assisted in the establishment of an independent Iraqi electoral commission and are currently contributing technical expertise for the preparation of those elections (see also para. 17 above).

66. In preparation for the elections in Afghanistan (see para. 54), Afghan authorities carried out a countrywide electoral registration drive, with the assistance of the United Nations, between 1 December 2003 and 15 August 2004. This is the first time that Afghan voters have ever been registered. Despite threats and attacks against the process, nearly 9 million Afghans—or more than 90 per cent of the estimated eligible voters—have registered to vote.

67. The peace processes in Burundi, Côte d'Ivoire, the Democratic Republic of the Congo, Liberia and Sierra Leone also include elections as a crucial mechanism for peace-building. In Sierra Leone, following national elections in 2002, the local elections held in May 2004—for which the United Nations provided decisive technical

and logistical support—constituted a further step towards the consolidation of political stability.

Disarmament

68. This year, the Conference on Disarmament benefited from focused high-level discussions during which foreign ministers voiced strong political support for the Conference. Further progress is needed to ensure that the Conference will be able to resume its role of negotiating new arms control and disarmament agreements, with an emphasis on the elimination of weapons of mass destruction. The demonstrated ability of the Conference to devise disarmament treaties should be used to the fullest extent.

69. Several issues relating to weapons of mass destruction remained of great concern to the international community. These included the slow pace of disarmament, violations of non-proliferation commitments, evidence of a clandestine nuclear network and the threat of terrorism. Such developments jeopardize international peace and security and may increase the risk of new instances of unilateral or pre-emptive use of force.

70. I welcome the decision by the Libyan Arab Jamahiriya to renounce its weapons of mass destruction programmes. The States parties' reaffirmation of their commitment to the Chemical Weapons Convention is also encouraging. I urge all States parties to the Treaty on the Non-Proliferation of Nuclear Weapons to confront persisting concerns about compliance and to consider new initiatives to strengthen the treaty while striving for its universality. I also urge further efforts to bring the Comprehensive Nuclear-Test-Ban Treaty into force without delay.

71. Adopted in response to the threat of proliferation of weapons of mass destruction by non-State actors, Security Council resolution 1540 (2004) contains concrete preventive measures to be taken by all States. Its effective implementation would complement ongoing efforts to strengthen existing multilateral disarmament and non-proliferation regimes.

72. The United Nations continued to support efforts by a wide variety of actors to implement the 2001 Programme of Action to Prevent, Combat and Eradicate the Illicit Trade in Small Arms and Light Weapons in All Its Aspects. In particular, it provided assistance to Member States in the establishment of national coordinating bodies, the development of national capacity, the management or destruction of stockpiles, reporting on the implementation of the Programme of Action and the enactment or revision of national legislation on the sale and use of small arms.

73. Multilateral negotiations began in June 2004 on an international instrument to enable States to identify and trace illicit small arms and light weapons. Agreed standards and procedures, as well as increased cooperation, can assist States in gaining greater control over the flow of illicit weapons into and out of their territories. In a further initiative this year, the United Nations conducted broad-based consultations with States, regional and subregional organizations, international agencies and experts in the field on further steps to enhance international cooperation to prevent, combat and eradicate illicit brokering in small arms and light weapons. I encourage Member States to ratify the Protocol against the Illicit Manufacturing of and Trafficking in Firearms, Their Parts and Components and Ammunition, which supplements the United Nations Convention against Transnational Organized Crime, thus enabling its entry into force.

74. With an estimated 15,000 new victims of anti-personnel mines each year and 50 States not yet party to the Mine-Ban Convention, the first review conference of the Convention, the Nairobi Summit for a Mine-Free World, to be held from 29 November to 3 December 2004, will be an opportune moment to redouble efforts to rid the world of these inhumane weapons. I invite those States that have not ratified the Convention to do so promptly and urge all States to participate in the Nairobi Summit at the highest possible level.

Terrorism

75. Events over the past year have underlined the continued threat that terrorism poses to international peace and security and the need for broad-based international cooperation to counter it. During this period, the Security Council Committee established pursuant to resolution 1373 (2001), known as the Counter-Terrorism Committee, continued its efforts to suppress and prevent terrorism and initiated a process of revitalization, which culminated in March 2004 with the adoption of Security Council resolution 1535(2004), aimed at strengthening the reach and effectiveness of the Committee. In accordance with the resolution, on 14 May I appointed an Executive Director of the Counter-Terrorism Executive Directorate, which will be set up later this year.

76. During 2003, working in close coordination with the Counter-Terrorism Committee, the Terrorism Prevention Branch of the United Nations Office on Drugs and Crime provided legislative assistance to more than 70 countries in connection with the ratification and implementation of the 12 universal anti-terrorism conventions and the implementation of Security Coun-

cil resolution 1373(2001). Following the decision of the General Assembly in 2002 to reinforce the work of the Branch, it has provided technical assistance to States, at their own request or that of the Counter-Terrorism Committee. The connection between terrorism and organized crime, as recognized in Security Council resolutions 1373 (2001) and 1456(2003), was discussed at the spring 2004 session of the United Nations System Chief Executives Board for Coordination, along with the need for a global response.

77. I reiterate my conviction that the struggle against terrorism must not take place at the expense of the fundamental freedoms and the basic dignity of individuals. Success in defeating terrorism can come only if we remain true to those values which terrorists eschew. In September 2003, the Office of the United Nations High Commissioner for Human Rights published, in cooperation with the Department of Public Information, the "Digest of Jurisprudence of the United Nations and Regional Organizations on the Protection of Human Rights while Countering Terrorism". The Office of the High Commissioner has supported the work of the Special Rapporteur on human rights and terrorism of the Subcommission on the Promotion and Protection of Human Rights and will be supporting the recently appointed independent expert of the Commission on Human Rights on the protection of human rights and fundamental freedoms while countering terrorism. The Department of Public Information has undertaken a number of activities to enhance outreach to civil society and to inform the public about United Nations activities in the area of counter-terrorism.

Sanctions

78. The Security Council has continued to refine the sanctions instrument so that it can be more effectively applied to new or evolving threats to international peace and security. Following the conclusion of comprehensive peace agreements in the Democratic Republic of the Congo and Liberia, Security Council sanctions were applied with a view to ensuring that continued flows of arms did not undermine the fragile peace processes. The fact that peacekeeping operations were already under way in those countries when the Council adopted the sanctions measures has allowed United Nations military observers and other personnel to play a greater role in sanctions monitoring and enforcement. Aware of the potential unintended effects of such coercive measures on the civilian population in a targeted country, the Council again requested reports assessing the possible humanitarian consequences of United Nations sanctions on Liberia.

79. In its resolution 1493(2003), which imposed the arms embargo on the Democratic Republic of the Congo, the Security Council instructed me to deploy MONUC military observers in North and South Kivu and in Ituri and to report to the Council regularly on information concerning the supply of arms, especially by monitoring the use of airstrips in that region. In the case of Liberia, the Council reviewed its existing measures and made the necessary modifications in response to the changed political situation in that country. In its resolution 1521(2003), the Security Council welcomed the readiness of UNMIL to assist the Committee and the Panel of Experts established by the resolution in monitoring the Council's relevant sanctions measures and also requested the United Nations Mission in Sierra Leone and the United Nations Operation in Côte d'Ivoire to pass to the Committee and the Panel information relevant to the implementation of the sanctions.

80. During the period under review, the Security Council continued to receive detailed information regarding its sanctions regimes from expert groups responsible for monitoring compliance and investigating alleged violations of sanctions. These included the Panel of Experts and Monitoring Group on Somalia, the Panel of Experts on Liberia and the Group of Experts on the Democratic Republic of the Congo. An Analytical Support and Sanctions Monitoring Team was established pursuant to Council resolution 1526(2004) of January 2004 to replace the Monitoring Group on Al-Qaida and the Taliban. In the same resolution, the Council strengthened the mandate of the Al-Qaida and Taliban Sanctions Committee and also encouraged States to inform listed individuals of the measures imposed on them.

81. Regarding Iraq, the Security Council, in its resolution 1518(2003) of 24 November 2003, established a new Committee to continue identifying individuals and entities affiliated with the former Iraqi regime for the purpose of freezing their funds, financial assets and economic resources, which Member States are obligated to transfer to the Development Fund for Iraq.

Chapter III

Meeting humanitarian commitments

82. Since my previous report, the consolidation of peace in several areas of the world has opened windows of opportunity for alleviating suffering and rebuilding the lives of millions of

affected people. At the same time, however, both new and protracted conflicts, as well as natural disasters, continue to take a toll on the world's poor, often undermining whatever progress had been achieved or creating new emergencies.

83. Humanitarian assistance continues to be unevenly allocated and its levels are insufficient to meet needs. I urge the donor community to ensure that funding for humanitarian operations is increased and is provided more consistently across humanitarian emergencies and that it better covers the needs of all sectors.

Protecting and assisting refugees and displaced populations

84. During the past year, the refugee population has decreased significantly. For the second consecutive year the figure has decreased by nearly 1 million persons, falling overall 20 per cent, from 12.1 million at the beginning of 2002 to 9.7 million at present. The total population receiving protection and/or assistance from the Office of the United Nations High Commissioner for Refugees currently stands at some 17 million persons. That figure includes 9.7 million refugees and 4.2 million internally displaced persons. However, the apparent progress in the decline of refugees must be seen against the backdrop of the worldwide total of uprooted persons (including those within and outside the mandate of UNHCR), which is currently estimated at nearly 50 million, or one in every 126 persons on earth. This worldwide figure also includes more than 1.6 million refugees from the occupied Palestinian territory who continue to receive life-saving assistance from UNRWA.

85. I am pleased to report that never before have there been so many opportunities for durable solutions in so many parts of Africa with regard to the situation of refugees and internally displaced persons. In Angola, more than 3.7 million refugees and displaced persons have returned since the conflict ended in April 2002 and plans are in place to return a further 145,000 refugees this year. In Burundi, progress on the political front has enabled more than 130,000 refugees to return since the beginning of 2003. In West Africa, stabilization has led to the return of more than 240,000 refugees to Sierra Leone, including some 25,000 during 2004 alone, and the repatriation programme is expected to draw to a close at the end of this year. In Liberia, repatriation plans are being put in place for more than 320,000 refugees who fled the country, as well as for hundreds of thousands of internally displaced persons, to return once the situation stabilizes further. In the Sudan, positive developments on the political front have opened up

possibilities for the eventual return of millions of refugees and internally displaced persons to the southern part of the country.

86. Despite the progress that has been made, new and lingering conflicts around the world continue to present many challenges for the humanitarian community. For example, the positive steps in the Sudan have been overshadowed by the situation in the western part of the country. More than 1 million persons have become internally displaced in the region of Darfur as a result of direct attacks on their villages and gross human rights violations, while some 170,000 persons have fled to Chad. This has given rise to regional security concerns due to cross-border incursions and the presence of armed groups in the border areas. Despite massive logistical constraints in eastern Chad, UNHCR had managed to move more than 123,000 refugees to nine new refugee camps in safer areas further inland by the end of July 2004. Outbreaks of violence in the eastern part of the Democratic Republic of the Congo in June 2004 resulted in thousands becoming internally displaced while more than 35,000 people fled to Burundi and, in smaller numbers, to Rwanda. The conflict in northern Uganda between government and rebel forces continues to take civilian lives and cause further displacement and increasing vulnerability. More than 1.6 million displaced persons are being sheltered in overcrowded and poorly protected camps where they remain susceptible to attack and abduction by rebel fighters, as well as abuses committed by the local security forces.

87. Outside Africa, tensions in the Middle East, South America and parts of the Balkans are also cause for concern. In Afghanistan, while more than 3.5 million refugees and internally displaced persons have returned to their homes since the end of 2001, it is estimated that there are still around 180,000 internally displaced persons and 2 million refugees remaining in both the Islamic Republic of Iran and Pakistan. Their return is hindered by the continued lack of security inside Afghanistan. In Iraq there were no massive refugee movements in 2003, but the vast insecurity that has prevailed has prevented the return of those who fled the country in previous years. The internal displacement situation in Colombia remains one of the most serious in the world today. An estimated 3 million people have been internally displaced during the country's 40-year conflict, and up to 40,000 have fled to neighbouring countries. Although the war in Kosovo ended more than five years ago, the situation remains perilous for the minority Serb and Roma populations. Clashes between Albanians and Serbs in March 2004 left more than 20

people dead and undermined expectations for more progress on minority returns.

88. Last year UNHCR launched "Convention Plus", an important initiative aimed at strengthening the Convention relating to the Status of Refugees through the use of special multilateral agreements. The objective is to ensure that refugees receive a higher standard of protection as close to home as possible and to increase the level of State involvement as an effective system of international burden-sharing. The agreements will focus on three priority areas: resettlement as a tool of protection, a durable solution and a tangible form of burden-sharing; more effective targeting of development assistance to support durable solutions for refugees; and clarification of the responsibilities of States in the event of secondary movements of refugees and asylum-seekers from an initial country of refuge to another country.

89. Also on the protection front, violence perpetrated against refugee and internally displaced women and children continues to be a major concern. An increase in the use of sexual and gender-based violence as a tool of war has been manifested in Burundi, Chad, Côte d'Ivoire, the Democratic Republic of the Congo and Darfur in western Sudan. In order to better address this growing trend, UNHCR has revised its "Sexual and Gender-based Violence against Refugees, Returnees and Internally Displaced Persons: Guidelines for Prevention and Response". The Guidelines will ensure that better prevention and response mechanisms are put in place. They have already been distributed to a wide range of actors involved in humanitarian work for implementation in the field, and training of staff is also ongoing. Efforts to reinforce cooperation among United Nations agencies in support of children also led to the launch of "Inter-agency Guiding Principles on Unaccompanied and Separated Children" in February 2004. The Guiding Principles will, among other things, strengthen inter-agency collaboration aimed at responding to the problem of forced recruitment of refugee children and addressing family reunification of demobilized children.

90. Coping with the issue of security in the field, for both refugees and humanitarian personnel, has remained a constant challenge. Over the past year there have been a number of direct attacks against humanitarian personnel. Such incidents are often intrinsically linked to the security environment for refugees themselves. In February 2004, more than 200 people were killed in an attack on a camp for displaced persons in northern Uganda. More recently there have been incursions from the Sudan into refugee-populated areas in eastern Chad, where various armed groups are also present. The presence of armed elements in refugee camps and settlements creates a dangerous environment for humanitarian personnel and also has grave consequences for the security and welfare of refugees, including violence and forced recruitment. In June 2004, UNHCR hosted a meeting of experts in Geneva on the issue of maintaining the civilian and humanitarian character of asylum. The meeting brought together the various parts of the United Nations system, including the Department of Peacekeeping Operations, a number of international non-governmental organizations and interested Governments. Participants took stock of lessons learned from the successful process of separating Liberian combatants from refugees in Sierra Leone in 2003, which may be applicable to future cases. A set of operational guidelines, including standards and procedures for the separation of armed elements from refugee populations, will follow later this year.

91. The Office for the Coordination of Humanitarian Affairs, through its Internally Displaced Person Unit, has continued its efforts to improve support for the implementation of a collaborative response to internal displacement. In March 2004, the Inter-Agency Standing Committee endorsed the Unit's development of revised and updated policy guidance on a collaborative response, including the enhancement of protection capacity. To facilitate a more robust assessment and strategic support role for the Unit, the Emergency Relief Coordinator has renamed it the Inter-Agency Internal Displacement Division and appointed a new director, who will also act as his special adviser on internal displacement.

Coordinating and delivering humanitarian assistance

92. Coherent, effective and principled humanitarian response remains a priority for the United Nations. In keeping with its mandate to coordinate humanitarian response to crises, the Office for the Coordination of Humanitarian Affairs has continued to work closely with partner agencies and non-governmental organizations to strengthen key coordination tools and mechanisms for all phases of a crisis. This has included more consistent action to allow improved humanitarian access, information management and financial tracking of aid flows, and improved support for the coordination of protection activities. The Office has also focused increased attention on forgotten emergencies, enhanced its early warning mechanisms, contingency planning capacity and emergency preparedness, and has further

strengthened the strategic planning component of the consolidated appeals process. During the reporting period, such efforts were applied to good effect in response to crises in the Islamic Republic of Iran, Iraq, West and Central Africa and the Sudan.

93. In Darfur, Sudan, massive human rights violations, including forced displacement, extra-judicial killings and gender-based sexual violence, combined with a lack of access to food and water, have left the majority of the population struggling to survive. The World Food Programme has been providing food assistance, while the United Nations Children's Fund has begun constructing and rehabilitating water systems. The World Health Organization has established a system for early warning to respond to outbreaks of disease and, together with UNICEF, is supporting health facilities and other field activities. In addition, my Emergency Relief Coordinator and the investigative missions of the Office of the United Nations High Commissioner for Human Rights have raised the profile of this humanitarian emergency and human rights crisis by briefing the Security Council and holding several high-level meetings with donors and agencies.

94. In northern Uganda, the displaced are dispersed in well over 100 camps, to which access for humanitarian operations is severely constrained. Children suffer disproportionately in this crisis, increasingly as targets of abduction and also through the loss of security. The unique phenomenon of "night commuters", in which more than 50,000 children travel from their homes every night to seek safety in district towns, underlines the tragic humanitarian consequences of this crisis. In this highly insecure environment, WFP has, through the use of armed escorts, managed to sustain the delivery of food supplies to the vulnerable population.

95. Continued insecurity and the cumulative effects of displacement, the depletion of food stocks, the collapse of social services and stagnant economies have kept many countries around the world in need of life-sustaining assistance and have offset prospects for peace. Ongoing fighting, food shortages and weak governance continue to undermine efforts to stabilize the Central African Republic. The eastern regions of the Democratic Republic of the Congo have seen only incremental change since the war ostensibly ended, primarily because of continued efforts by Congolese actors and neighbouring countries to prevent any institution representing the general interest of the country from undermining their established interests. The area continues to be overrun by rebel groups and militias, and mil-

lions struggle to meet their most basic needs. The United Nations is working to meet those needs through efforts such as the rehabilitation of the country's water sources by UNICEF—as more than 54 per cent of the population lack access to potable water—and the support provided by WHO to local and national health authorities.

96. Drought and chronic food supply problems continued to blight Eritrea and Ethiopia. The last six months saw little change in rainfall, crop production or nutritional recovery. The need for measures to improve food security remains acute. WFP has been covering up to 50 per cent of the overall relief food requirements, reaching as many as 3.44 million beneficiaries a month. A joint UNICEF-WFP extended outreach strategy/child survival programme in Ethiopia is aimed at addressing the effect of chronic food insecurity on some 6 million to 8 million children living in the most food-insecure and drought-affected areas. WHO is working closely with the other United Nations agencies and non-governmental organizations for the surveillance and control of health-related problems.

97. In Southern Africa, life expectancy in Lesotho, Malawi, Mozambique, Swaziland, Zambia and Zimbabwe has declined, from an average of 46 years in 1970 to 35 in 2004. At least one child in five in those countries is expected to be an orphan by 2010—and the ratio is even higher in some countries. A deadly combination of HIV/AIDS, food insecurity, weak governance and chronic poverty has led to a crisis of survival and the premature death of millions of people. The concerted efforts of United Nations agencies and non-governmental organizations, through consolidated appeals from mid-2002 to mid-2004, have raised over $800 million, thus enabling the provision of, among other things, food assistance to more than 10 million people, nutritional support to 2 million children, measles immunization to 7 million children and agricultural support to 5.5 million farmers.

98. The integrated, multidimensional character of United Nations missions recently deployed in Burundi, Côte d'Ivoire, Haiti and Liberia creates opportunities for more coherent and effective action in post-conflict situations. Such an integrated approach seeks to advance both humanitarian relief, respect for human rights and the achievement of sustainable peace. In particular, it is essential that the impartiality and neutrality of humanitarian response is maintained in all integrated missions and that the United Nations humanitarian arm is able to fully collaborate with its non-governmental organization partners.

99. United Nations agencies have also been working to facilitate the transition from relief to development in countries emerging from conflict. A recent evaluation of United Nations transition activities in eight countries concluded that a single coherent strategy for the United Nations system was necessary to strengthen transition activities and proposed a standing mechanism to support United Nations country teams engaged in transition planning. The humanitarian and development pillars are already working together more closely to include refugees and displaced persons in transition planning and to promote durable solutions for those populations. The "4 Rs" approach (repatriation, reintegration, rehabilitation and reconstruction) launched jointly two years ago by UNHCR, UNDP and others, is now being tried in pilot projects in Afghanistan, Liberia, Sierra Leone, and Sri Lanka, and there are plans to apply it in Burundi and eventually the Sudan.

100. With the intifada in the occupied Palestinian territory continuing for a fourth year, the socio-economic hardship of the Palestinian population has been worsening as a result of Israeli actions such as closures, curfews and military operations. The emergency interventions of UNRWA continued to be an important source of assistance and stability, although the Agency remained concerned about restrictions on humanitarian access. The construction of a physical barrier in the West Bank has added another obstacle to humanitarian access and has severely affected the livelihoods of the Palestinians affected and their access to essential services. UNRWA also maintained its regular programme of education, health, relief, social and microfinance services to over 4 million Palestine refugees in Jordan, Lebanon and the Syrian Arab Republic, as well as in the West Bank and Gaza Strip.

Funding humanitarian emergencies

101. The message of the consolidated appeals process 2003 midyear review bears repeating: while the general underfunding of consolidated appeals may not be measurable in greater loss of life as is sometimes supposed, greater suffering and recovery denied are persistent themes in all consolidated appeals. The underfunding of humanitarian action persists in 2004, in both absolute and proportional terms. Overall funding requirements for humanitarian assistance in 2004, as registered in the consolidated appeals, totalled $2.9 billion. As at 21 July 2004, contributions totalled $928 million, which (with carry-overs) fulfils only 32 per cent of requirements halfway through the appeal period. This is lower than the response for the same period in 2003, when ap-

proximately 45 per cent of total requirements were funded. In addition, the pattern of funding humanitarian activities remains uneven, leaving some countries substantially under-financed. The response to individual consolidated appeals as at 21 July 2004 ranged from a high of 50 per cent for the northern Caucasus (Russian Federation) and Chad to lows of 16 per cent for Côte d'Ivoire and 15 per cent for Zimbabwe.

102. Overall emergency funding for UNICEF and WHO has provided them with only the minimum capacity to respond to life-sustaining needs. For example, the low level of resources has limited interventions to combat infectious diseases in some West African countries, has restricted education, protection and health-care programmes in Côte d'Ivoire and has impeded support in HIV/AIDS and education activities in Burundi, increasing children's vulnerability and risk for human rights violations.

103. UNHCR, challenged by the system of voluntary contributions, is facing a recurring shortfall in the funding of its life-saving protection and assistance programmes. As in recent years, the impact of the shortfall is being felt mainly in Africa, where the needs are the greatest. Major repatriation operations under way for Liberia and the Sudan may be hindered by a lack of adequate funding. As at the end of July 2004, UNHCR had received only $16.6 million in confirmed contributions out of $39.2 million needed for the repatriation of more than 300,000 Liberians. For the Sudan, UNHCR had received less than half of the $8.8 million needed to begin the expected repatriation and reintegration of up to 600,000 refugees currently in neighbouring countries. The slow pace of funding has also hampered the ability of UNHCR to respond to the crisis of refugees from Darfur in eastern Chad. By the end of July, UNHCR had received $27.8 million out of the $55.8 million needed to respond to the emergency in Chad.

104. The WFP Iraq operation in 2003 was the largest single humanitarian aid operation in history, requiring the Programme and its donors to marshal extraordinary food, cash and human resources. Elsewhere in the world, however, WFP had to face unprecedented needs with insufficient resources. In Africa alone, some 40 million people remained in need of food aid, with roughly $1.8 billion required. WFP struggled to meet the needs of 6.4 million people in the Democratic People's Republic of Korea, covering less than 60 per cent of the operation's requirements. WFP was also forced to cut rations in half for hundreds of thousands of displaced Angolans and thousands of refugees from Ethiopia, Somalia and the Sudan.

105. The Food and Agriculture Organization of the United Nations delivered assistance in the agricultural sector valued at $190 million (of which $111 million was for Iraq). Yet in the consolidated appeals for 2003 it received less than 45 per cent of its requirements. By June 2004, less than 25 per cent of the requirements against the 2004 appeals had been received. FAO provided agricultural inputs, such as seeds and fertilizer, fishing equipment, animal feed and drugs and essential farming tools to restart agricultural production in disaster-affected areas. Where conditions allowed, input distributions were complemented by more sustainable assistance, such as local production of seeds and other planting material, restocking of farm animals, prevention and control of plant and animal diseases, quick-impact rehabilitation of infrastructure such as irrigation schemes and training in improved farming techniques.

106. The $135.8 million shortfall in contributions to the UNRWA emergency appeals for the occupied Palestinian territory was one of the Agency's prime concerns during the year, as needs in the refugee community continued to increase without sufficient resources to address them. In Gaza, UNRWA has been able to rehouse fewer than 10 per cent of the 21,000 Palestinians that have been uprooted by Israeli military operations since October 2000. Funding shortfalls have also made it difficult to maintain emergency food assistance for more than 1 million refugees and to implement the Agency's emergency job creation programme.

107. The United Nations mine action programmes received more than $50 million through the United Nations Voluntary Trust Fund for Assistance in Mine Action during the period covered by the present report. The Trust Fund is managed by the Department of Peacekeeping Operations. Additional funds were received through UNDP and UNICEF thematic trust funds. Shortfalls across the United Nations system compromised assistance efforts in such places as Afghanistan, Angola, Burundi, Colombia, the Democratic Republic of the Congo, the occupied Palestinian territory and the Sudan. As at July 2004, there were funding shortfalls of over $60 million in Afghanistan and the Sudan alone. Contributions to the Trust Fund must be more than doubled if these shortfalls are to be met.

108. During the current reporting period humanitarian workers and operations faced continued risks, particularly in Afghanistan, the Democratic Republic of the Congo and Iraq, where relief workers have been directly targeted. Security is an essential precondition for the delivery of humanitarian assistance in many areas of conflict, and thus forms an integral component of the consolidated appeals. Despite the increased security threats, donor contributions to security sector projects set out in the 2004 consolidated appeals totalled only slightly over $4 million, representing 27 per cent of the overall requirement, as at 27 July 2004. In addition, donors contributed over $6 million for special security requirements for United Nations operations in Iraq outside the consolidated appeals process. While the security sector for Iraq was fully funded, many less prominent emergencies experienced a lack of security personnel, resources and assets.

Natural disaster management

109. In 2003 some 700 disasters resulted in 75,000 deaths and economic losses of more than $65 billion. The death toll was many times higher than that for the previous year, largely because of the earthquake in Bam, Islamic Republic of Iran. In 2004 floods and cyclones in Bangladesh, China, the Dominican Republic, Haiti, India, Madagascar and Sri Lanka affected millions. It is notable that, because of their increased capacity, many of the affected countries did not require external assistance to respond to the floods in 2004. Drought and chronic food supply problems continued to blight the Horn of Africa, where crop production, nutritional recovery and the need for measures to improve food security remained acute. Between September 2003 and June 2004, the Office for the Coordination of Humanitarian Affairs worked with other agencies to coordinate the response to 38 major disasters due to natural or environmental hazards in vulnerable disaster-prone countries. This includes the coordination of the response to major earthquakes in the Islamic Republic of Iran (December 2003) and Morocco (February 2004), cyclone Gafilo in Madagascar (March 2004) and floods in the Dominican Republic and Haiti (May 2004).

110. I am concerned that the consequences of natural hazards pose a great challenge to achieving the Millennium Development Goals and I welcome efforts by humanitarian and development organizations to support the implementation of disaster-reduction activities at the national and local levels. Increased joint planning and collaboration has developed among UNDP, the Office for the Coordination of Humanitarian Affairs, the United Nations Human Settlements Programme and the secretariat of the International Strategy for Disaster Reduction, a primary international mechanism for reducing disaster risk. This cooperation has led to specific collaborative programmes in the Democratic Republic

of the Congo, Ecuador and Peru, as well as regional programming covering eight Central American States. In addition, the Inter-Agency Task Force for Disaster Reduction has re-focused its work to assess the effects of climate change on disaster risk reduction. It has been addressing the increasing vulnerability of urban environments, how to better support disaster response and mitigation in Africa and the continued development of risk and vulnerability information and indicators. In early 2004, UNDP launched a report entitled "Reducing disaster risk: a challenge for development". The report introduced a global Disaster Risk Index, which measures the relative vulnerability of countries to three key natural hazards—earthquakes, tropical cyclones and floods—and identifies development factors that contribute to increased risk levels. In this connection, I am pleased to note that the United Nations University has launched a programme to reduce the risk of catastrophic floods in the Asia and Pacific region by means of a comprehensive approach to reduce hazards and vulnerability.

Protection of civilians in armed conflict

111. The Organization has continued to strengthen and enhance the policy framework for the protection of civilians in armed conflict over the past year. In December 2003, the Under-Secretary-General for Humanitarian Affairs presented to the Security Council a ten-point platform on the protection of civilians in armed conflict, which formed the basis for my fourth report to the Council on the protection of civilians in armed conflict, submitted in May 2004.

112. There has been notable progress in the five years since the agenda on the protection of civilians in armed conflict was launched. Concerns for the protection of civilians are now more effectively integrated into the mandates of peacekeeping operations, as has been the case for the United Nations missions in Burundi, Côte d'Ivoire, the Democratic Republic of the Congo, Liberia and Sierra Leone.

113. During the reporting period, the Office for the Coordination of Humanitarian Affairs completed a series of high-level regional workshops with senior government officials. Those workshops were used to reflect specific regional issues in developing the agenda on the protection of civilians in armed conflict and improving Member States' understanding of their own roles and responsibilities. I am pleased to see regional organizations taking up the agenda, as manifested, for example, by the decision of the African Union to appoint a special representative for the protection of civilians in armed conflict and by the decision of ECOWAS to establish a humani-

tarian division to address issues related to the protection of civilians.

114. The above-mentioned initiatives have been supported by collective mechanisms within the Organization, such as the Executive Committee on Humanitarian Affairs Implementation Group on the Protection of Civilians in Armed Conflict, which has provided a basis for strengthened coordination in this area. Closer coordination has led to the joint development of various tools for the protection of civilians, including an updated aide-memoire reflecting the latest concerns, trends and measures to address them (adopted by the Security Council in December 2003 as an annex to presidential statement S/PRST/2003/27).

115. The serious issue of the sexual exploitation and abuse of women and children in armed conflict by personnel employed by or affiliated with the United Nations—both civilian staff and uniformed peacekeepers—has been the focus of considerable attention since my previous report. In October 2003, I issued a bulletin entitled "Special measures for protection from sexual exploitation and sexual abuse" (ST/SGB/2003/13). The bulletin sets out minimum standards of behaviour expected of all United Nations personnel and measures necessary to maintain an environment that prevents sexual exploitation and abuse. Subsequently, implementation guidelines and tools were issued, and all parts of the United Nations system with field presences have begun working to ensure the coherent implementation of the bulletin at the field level.

Chapter IV

Cooperating for development

Achieving the Millennium Development Goals

116. During the past year, the eight Millennium Development Goals continued to provide a unifying framework for the activities of the United Nations in the area of cooperation for development. The United Nations core strategy—research, campaigning, monitoring and reporting, and country-level operations—guided the Organization's work to achieve the Goals.

117. Although the prospects for meeting the Millennium Development Goals remain uneven, the time-bound and measurable goals are still achievable by the deadline of 2015. However, this will be possible only if developed and developing countries institute the right combination of national and international policies and implement their shared commitments, as set out in the

United Nations Millennium Declaration and the Monterrey Consensus.

118. In assisting Member States to achieve the Millennium Development Goals, the United Nations has adopted a holistic approach. Over the past year, the United Nations has sought to help increase the productive capacity of developing countries and countries with economies in transition through trade, investment, mobilization of resources and technology development. The Organization has also assisted vulnerable groups, such as those living in absolute poverty, women, children, youth, indigenous peoples, refugees, people living with HIV/AIDS and migrants.

119. The United Nations Development Group, comprising the operational agencies working on development, has been developing new policies and guidelines to improve the quality, effectiveness and coordination of programmes at the country level. The common country assessment and the United Nations Development Assistance Framework permit a strategic, coherent and integrated United Nations system response to national priorities and needs within the framework of the Millennium Development Goals. In 2003, 18 United Nations country teams embarked on developing common country assessment and United Nations Development Assistance Frameworks, with 18 more following in 2004.

120. Achieving the Millennium Development Goals continues to require considerable outreach and advocacy. The Millennium Campaign is raising broad-based popular support for the Goals, by working with constituencies in the industrialized countries to gather political momentum behind the eighth Goal, which calls for increased aid, meaningful debt relief and expanded access to trade and technology. In 2003, the Campaign began supporting national campaigns in developing countries, in collaboration with civil society networks.

121. The Millennium Project brings together more than 150 policy experts, development practitioners and top scholars from around the world to research alternative approaches for achieving the Goals. Looking ahead to the 2005 review of the Millennium Declaration, the Project is now working with Governments, international financial institutions and other partners to conduct a series of country-level pilot projects that will look at what each country needs in terms of policies, resources and economic growth to achieve the Goals.

122. As the General Assembly has recognized, effective monitoring of progress towards the achievement of the Goals requires operational and sustainable statistical systems. Sound, reliable and comparable statistical data are indispensable for the formulation and implementation of policies to achieve the Goals. Numerous entities of the system, notably the Statistics Division of the Department of Economic and Social Affairs, under the guidance of the Inter-Agency and Expert Group on the Millennium Development Goal Indicators, have contributed to improving data quality. The Department organized workshops for national statistical capacity-building in 2003. To strengthen tracking of the Goals at the country level, the United Nations Development Group is piloting the roll-out of the DevInfo software, which was in use by 42 national statistical offices in 2003 and is being introduced in another 120 countries in 2004.

123. Science and technology are critical elements in promoting economic and social development to meet the Millennium Development Goals. Many developing countries are unlikely to meet the Goals without a clear political commitment to make science and technology a top priority. Emerging issues include access and connectivity to information and communication technologies and biotechnology, as well as technology transfer and capacity-building. Most entities of the Organization have undertaken work on information and communication technologies and have contributed to the preparatory process of the first phase of the World Summit on the Information Society and to the Summit itself. The Information and Communication Technologies Task Force and the Commission on Science and Technology for Development have played a significant role in disseminating knowledge and sharing information in the field of information and communication technologies for development.

124. Over the past year, the Organization has continued to address the challenge of building national administrative capacity in pursuit of the Millennium Development Goals. The Committee of Experts on Public Administration identified new trends in and opportunities for revitalizing public administration and governance systems to meet the Goals. The *World Public Sector Report 2003: E-Government at the Crossroads* highlighted the power of information and communication technologies and their use in complex environments. Analytical tools and training materials were developed in the field of capacity-building for conflict management.

125. With regard to the goal of eradicating extreme poverty and hunger, the International Fund for Agricultural Development focused on three key measures to reduce poverty in rural areas: strengthening the capacity of the rural poor and their organizations, improving equitable access to productive natural resources and

technology and increasing access to financial services and markets. In 2003, IFAD approved 25 new rural development projects, for a total commitment of $403.6 million towards the achievement of those objectives. In addition, the IFAD grant programme comprised 70 grants amounting to $20.3 million.

126. Through its poverty reduction practice area, UNDP helped countries to develop poverty reduction strategies based on participatory processes, to connect the Millennium Development Goals to national budgets and to improve monitoring of the Goals. It also helped countries to explore feasible policy options and alternative views on human development and poverty reduction through broad national stakeholder consultations and to translate them into the formulation and implementation of poverty reduction strategy papers.

127. Achieving the Millennium Development Goals will reduce the incentive for people to resort to human traffickers to escape poverty. It will also contribute to durable solutions for refugees, internally displaced persons and returnees, who are among the most vulnerable people in the world. People fleeing conflict, human rights violations and persecution should be able to find protection and start their lives anew in a safe and welcoming environment. Jointly, the International Labour Organization, the United Nations Conference on Trade and Development, the Office of the United Nations High Commissioner for Human Rights, the United Nations Office on Drugs and Crime, the International Organization for Migration and UNHCR are strengthening the exchange of information on migration and promoting greater policy coherence. The Department of Economic and Social Affairs contributes to the understanding of the impact of international migration by monitoring levels and trends of such migration and the policies adopted by Governments to shape those trends.

128. Activities carried out at the regional level to combat poverty included pilot projects of the Economic and Social Commission for Western Asia to mobilize local capacity and resources and to strengthen cooperation and collective self-reliance of selected communities in Egypt, Lebanon and the Syrian Arab Republic, leading to the creation of some 1,500 new jobs. The Economic Commission for Latin America and the Caribbean, in its publication *Social Panorama of Latin America 2002-2003*, assessed the chances of halving extreme poverty in the region and documented the scale of undernourishment and child malnutrition as well as trends towards achieving the Millennium Development Goals in those areas.

129. Investing in agriculture and rural areas, particularly in water control technology and rural infrastructure, in food-insecure countries should be the main priority in the fight against hunger. In spite of this, FAO reported that official bilateral development assistance to agriculture from donor countries of the Organization for Economic Cooperation and Development fell from $4.1 billion in 2001 to $3.8 billion in 2002. In commemorating World Food Day 2003, IFAD, FAO and WFP, together with representatives of international and national non-governmental organizations, formally declared their support for the International Alliance Against Hunger, a voluntary association of civil society organizations, social and religious movements and private sector and international organizations committed to the rapid eradication of hunger in the world. More than 50 countries—both developed and developing—have expressed their intent to form or reinforce national alliances against hunger linked to the International Alliance. Through its special programme for food security, which has now been taken up in almost 100 countries, FAO has continued to help low-income food-deficit countries to improve food security at both the national and household levels. This is being achieved through rapid increases in food production and productivity on an economically and environmentally sustainable basis and by improving people's access to food.

130. Increasingly, people living in poverty are located in urban areas. In order to "urbanize" the Millennium Development Goals, UN-Habitat has implemented partial urban inequity surveys in Bangladesh, Bolivia, Egypt, Ghana, the Philippines and Turkey. The UN-Habitat publication, *The Challenge of Slums: Global Report on Human Settlements 2003*, presented the first-ever global estimates of slum populations.

131. Building up the indigenous private sector is essential to achieving growth and development and alleviating poverty. The Commission on the Private Sector and Development's March 2004 report, entitled *Unleashing Entrepreneurship: Making Business Work for the Poor*, details a range of actions that Governments, public development institutions, the private sector and civil society organizations can undertake to spur the growth of small- and medium-sized enterprises. The United Nations Conference on Trade and Development provided services to enhance the competitiveness of small and medium-sized enterprises in developing countries through its Empretec programme. The programme has already been established in over 30 countries, most recently in Angola and Guyana.

132. In 2003, the United Nations Industrial Development Organization assisted some 51 countries through integrated programmes and country service frameworks for industrial development. The aim was to improve industrial governance and institutional infrastructure, strengthen small and medium-sized enterprises, upgrade technological capacity, enhance skills and access to modern technology, build trade and export capability and adopt energy-efficient and cleaner production measures.

133. With regard to achieving universal primary education, UNICEF estimates that 121 million children are still out of school—65 million of them girls. In 2004, the United Nations Educational, Scientific and Cultural Organization initiated a strategic review of its lead coordination role in the Education for All programme, an inter-agency initiative to help countries to achieve and sustain universal primary education of good quality by 2015, relying on the most in-depth statistical evaluation of education ever undertaken on a global scale and covering 180 countries. Among other things, UNESCO is examining ways to advance the monitoring of progress towards the Education for All goals and ways to ensure better coordination among instruments of development cooperation for the programme at the global and country levels. The Education for All Observatory at the UNESCO Institute for Statistics in Montreal continued to provide quality educational data and statistics to help guide decision makers and monitor global progress in achieving Education for All.

134. Efforts to promote gender equality and empower women continued to be an important aspect of the work of the Organization over the past year. The Regional Symposium on Mainstreaming Gender into Economic Policies (Geneva, January 2004), organized jointly by the Economic Commission for Europe and the Office of the Special Adviser on Gender Issues and Advancement of Women, provided an opportunity for exchanging experiences and good practices in selected areas of economic policy. Concrete achievements at the country level, with assistance from United Nations entities, include a growing number of government development professionals trained in gender issues and analysis, more statistical registers with gender-disaggregated data and the progressive inclusion of gender considerations in national poverty reduction strategies and budgets.

135. Progress was achieved in support of major legal instruments, for which Member States received technical cooperation from the Department of Economic and Social Affairs and other entities. The number of States ratifying the Convention on the Elimination of All Forms of Discrimination against Women increased by 3 to reach 177 States parties, and ratifications of the Optional Protocol to the Convention increased by 9 to reach 60 States parties.

136. On reducing child mortality the traditional focus of UNICEF on child survival was strengthened, especially in areas with high mortality rates. Important advances were achieved in the global partnerships against polio and measles, in the development of policies for orphaned children and AIDS prevention and in increasing national focus on child protection issues. UNICEF and its partners are working to ensure the best possible start in life for children and to reduce infant mortality, but this and the other Millennium Development Goals can be achieved only when the needs of children and women are given universal priority.

137. Throughout 2003, in programme design and implementation and in policy dialogue, including dialogue on poverty-reduction strategies, the United Nations Population Fund focused attention on concrete programmes and interventions that linked population dynamics and reproductive health issues, particularly maternal health, to the achievement of the Millennium Development Goals. WHO assisted countries with especially high rates of maternal death to strengthen their health systems to build a "continuum" of care so that all women and their babies can go through pregnancy, childbirth and the post-natal period safely, irrespective of their ability to pay for health services. Such a continuum includes the development of human resources for health; the availability, access, use and quality of services; building the capacity of women, families and the community; and creating collaborative links with other key primary health-care programmes.

138. On establishing global partnerships for development, implementing the Monterrey Consensus adopted at the 2002 International Conference on Financing for Development remains critical for achieving the Millennium Development Goals. As envisaged in the Consensus, on 26 April 2004 the Economic and Social Council held its second high-level meeting with the Bretton Woods institutions and the World Trade Organization. The summary by the President of the Council (A/59/92-E/2004/73) included a number of recommendations to advance the implementation of the policy commitments set out in the Monterrey Consensus.

139. In my view, increased and more equitable world trade holds forth the prospect of helping nations to achieve the Millennium Development Goals. The United Nations regional

commissions provide research and technical assistance programmes focused on enhancing the capacity of their member States to integrate more effectively into the regional and world economy through sustained trade and investment.

140. The conclusion of the Fifth Ministerial Conference of WTO (Cancún, Mexico, September 2003) without substantive results was a major setback, affecting the prospects for concluding the Doha Round of trade negotiations on time. Since then, a framework agreement reached on 31 July 2004 has put the Doha Round back on track. Developing countries continue to receive support from UNCTAD and the regional commissions in those negotiations. Key challenges relate to addressing the core market access agenda of agriculture, non-agricultural products and services and fully integrating the needs and interests of developing countries concerning implementation issues and special and differential treatment.

141. The UNCTAD *Trade and Development Report 2003* examined the developmental implications of new trends in the international pattern of production and investment and made a number of proposals to enhance development strategies and macroeconomic policies in developing countries. The UNCTAD *World Investment Report 2003* focused particularly on the role of national policies and international investment agreements in attracting and benefiting from foreign direct investment. The investment policy reviews and related advisory services provided by UNCTAD helped countries to improve policies and institutions dealing with foreign direct investment and to increase their capacity to attract and benefit from it. During 2003 and the first part of 2004, UNCTAD completed investment policy reviews for Botswana, Ghana, Lesotho, Nepal and Sri Lanka. In collaboration with WTO, UNCTAD assisted developing countries in their negotiations on international investment arrangements, including bilateral investment treaties and double taxation treaties.

Fighting HIV/AIDS

142. The scale and destructive impact of HIV/AIDS places this pandemic at the top of the international agenda as a serious health and development issue. With dedicated efforts by social, political and religious leaders, countries such as Brazil, Cambodia, Senegal, Thailand and Uganda have seen or are beginning to see a decline in infection rates. I wish, however, to reiterate my concern, expressed in my report on progress achieved towards implementation of the Declaration of Commitment on HIV/AIDS, that few countries will meet the goals set in 2001 at the special session of the General Assembly on

HIV/AIDS unless resources and efforts at all levels are increased dramatically.

143. I am happy to report that overall, agencies of the United Nations have increasingly recognized the need to strengthen and better coordinate their efforts at the country level. In 2003, WFP became the ninth co-sponsoring organization of the Joint United Nations Programme on HIV/AIDS, joining ILO, UNICEF, UNDP, UNESCO, the United Nations Office on Drugs and Crime, UNFPA, WHO and the World Bank. The United Nations Development Group has issued new policy guidelines for resident coordinators and United Nations country teams on strengthening the response to HIV/AIDS at the country level and ensuring a unified United Nations policy and programme support. The executive heads of the co-sponsoring agencies of UNAIDS met in March 2004 in Zambia, where they underlined their commitment to coordinated action and enhanced response at the country level and endorsed a new global initiative on preventive education.

144. Globally, the number of women living with HIV now equals the number of men. In sub-Saharan Africa, women now represent 58 per cent of all HIV-infected people. This feminization of the HIV/AIDS epidemic demands an urgent response. In this respect, I welcome the launching in February 2004 by UNAIDS of the Global Coalition on Women and AIDS, which brings together a wide range of individuals and organizations under a steering committee of some 25 high-level leaders representing Governments, activist groups, United Nations agencies and academic institutions and chaired by the Executive Director of UNFPA.

145. UNESCO and UNAIDS are undertaking a participatory joint initiative to empower young people and youth organizations to take action against HIV/AIDS and related discrimination and intolerance in their communities. In 2003, a series of training workshops were held for young people in Africa and the Arab region, and small grants were provided for national and local-level youth initiatives in Bangladesh, Malawi, Mozambique, Sri Lanka and Zambia.

146. As part of a comprehensive HIV/AIDS strategy linking prevention, treatment, care and support for people living with the virus, WHO declared a global treatment emergency in 2003 and launched an initiative to treat 3 million people in developing countries with antiretroviral drugs by the end of 2005.

147. The Department of Economic and Social Affairs convened a training workshop on HIV/AIDS and adult mortality in developing countries for African specialists in September 2003, which provided a solid understanding of the broad de-

mographic aspects of the HIV/AIDS epidemic. The Department also issued a report entitled "*The impact of AIDS*", which documented the massive impact of HIV/AIDS on all sectors of society.

148. The United Nations Development Programme helped countries to mainstream the HIV/AIDS issue and implement responses to the epidemic. UNDP launched the Southern Africa capacity initiative to strengthen the capacity for health care, education and agriculture in the subregion most affected by HIV/AIDS.

149. The programme expenditures of UNICEF on HIV/AIDS have risen rapidly, from $67 million in 2001 to $111 million in 2003. All UNICEF country offices remained involved in the fight against HIV/AIDS, regardless of the current level of incidence of the disease. The UNICEF supply operation helped more than 40 Governments procure antiretroviral drugs and diagnostic equipment.

150. In more than 140 countries, UNFPA contributed to the prevention of HIV/AIDS as part of promoting reproductive health and rights and gender equality through a strategy focused on preventing HIV infection among young people and pregnant women as well as on comprehensive condom-related programming addressing demand, a supportive environment and supply.

151. In 2003, WFP undertook HIV/AIDS interventions in 41 out of the 82 countries in which it operates, including 22 of the 25 countries in the world with the highest prevalence of HIV. Its evolving programming and analytical tools for vulnerability mapping are helping stakeholders to understand and address the links between HIV/AIDS and food insecurity.

152. Refugees with HIV/AIDS face particularly difficult circumstances in locations without sufficient access to adequate health care and social services. In December 2003, the Inter-Agency Standing Committee issued *Guidelines for HIV/AIDS Interventions in Emergency Settings* to address this challenge. The Guidelines serve to help concerned Governments and the international community deliver a comprehensive response to refugees with HIV/AIDS. The Guidelines recognize that during conflict situations, the combined effects of instability, poverty and social dislocation increase the vulnerability of displaced persons to HIV/AIDS. In such circumstances, women and children are particularly at risk, as they can be forced into having sexual relations in order to gain access to basic needs such as food, water or even security.

153. In 2003, UN-Habitat designed an HIV/AIDS orphan shelter programme and completed baseline surveys of the severe orphan situation in the urban slums of Kenya, Swaziland, Uganda, and the United Republic of Tanzania.

154. The United Nations Office on Drugs and Crime continued to assist Governments in the implementation of HIV/AIDS prevention and care programmes for injecting drug users through technical assistance projects, capacity-building, guidance on policy and programme development and monitoring and evaluation, particularly in Eastern Europe and Central, South and South-East Asia.

155. Over the past year, ILO continued to focus on strengthening the capacity of its constituents to contribute to national efforts against HIV/AIDS. ILO sought to ensure that national AIDS plans included the world of work and that labour policy and legislation addressed the implications of HIV/AIDS.

156. The media remains an underutilized sector and resource in the fight against HIV/AIDS. To date, the media have been seen largely as a means of distribution, but have rarely been engaged as a true partner. Therefore, in January of this year, I convened a historic meeting of the leaders of the world's major media companies to focus on what they can contribute to the fight against HIV/AIDS. UNAIDS, the Kaiser Family Foundation and the Department of Public Information are carrying this initiative forward.

Sustainable development

157. Since the World Summit on Sustainable Development (Johannesburg, South Africa, August and September 2002), Member States have emphasized the need to achieve progress in implementing time-bound goals, targets and commitments in sustainable development. This focus on implementation has propelled the Organization's work in support of sustainable development, including through support for capacity-building at the country level.

158. In April 2004, the United Nations Commission on Sustainable Development held its first substantive review of progress on the targets set at the World Summit. The thematic focus of the session was water, sanitation and human settlements, reflecting the priority Member States attached to those issues. The Department of Economic and Social Affairs provided full support to the Commission, assisting it in introducing innovations into the intergovernmental deliberative process to carry out an in-depth review of the three themes, in conjunction with cross-cutting issues. The Partnerships Fair organized during the session showcased some 80 partnership initiatives, providing a timely opportunity for reviewing progress, sharing experiences and networking among partners. At its twelfth session, attended by more than 100 ministers holding a broad range of portfolios, the Commission iden-

tified continuing technical and policy challenges in the area of access to safe drinking water, including effective water sector management, infrastructure investment, regulatory frameworks and local governance; in the area of sanitation, including the need to raise its political profile and funding for it; and in the area of human settlements, including the need for secure property tenure for the poor and legal recognition of women's right to property and inheritance.

159. The General Assembly, in its resolution 58/217 of 23 December 2003, proclaimed the period from 2005 to 2015 the International Decade for Action, "Water for Life", to commence on World Water Day, 22 March 2005. I consider water and its linkages to health, poverty reduction, gender equality, education, environmental protection and peace crucial to sustainable development. Water and its related issues need greater prominence, both globally and locally. Accordingly, I established an Advisory Board on Water and Sanitation, chaired by former Prime Minister Ryutaro Hashimoto of Japan and including other eminent personalities with expertise in the field, in order to raise awareness and help mobilize resources for water and sanitation programmes.

160. Through its energy and environment practice area, UNDP promoted the integration of environmental resource management with poverty reduction efforts. UNDP helped countries to strengthen their capacity to address those challenges at the global, national and community levels, seeking out and sharing best practices, providing innovative policy advice and linking partners through pilot projects that help poor people to build sustainable livelihoods.

161. The Governing Council and the Global Ministerial Environment Forum of the United Nations Environment Programme identified in March 2004 workable approaches for expediting the Millennium Development Goals and the commitments made at the World Summit on Sustainable Development. They addressed goals related to the environmental aspects of water, sanitation, human settlements and the centrality of ecosystem approaches in water management, as well as environmental threats to small island developing States.

162. Over the past year, several environmental instruments have entered into force: the Stockholm Convention on Persistent Organic Pollutants, the Rotterdam Convention on the Prior Informed Consent Procedure for Certain Hazardous Chemicals and Pesticides in International Trade and the Cartagena Protocol on Biosafety to the Convention on Biological Diversity. Although there has been real progress in implementing the Convention on Biological Diversity,

biodiversity itself continues to be lost at an alarming rate. In February 2004, Governments agreed on a more quantitative approach to significantly reducing the current rate of biodiversity loss by 2010.

163. UNEP also continued to foster partnerships for sustainable development, such as the Supporting Entrepreneurs for Environment and Development initiative, launched early in 2004. The initiative, a joint undertaking of UNDP, UNEP, the Stakeholder Forum and the World Conservation Union and supported by the Global Compact, advances new local partnerships in support of the Millennium Development Goals by building the capacity of nascent entrepreneurial partnerships, creating a conduit for investment in partnerships, disseminating good practices and lessons learned and generating evidence-based research to assist policy makers.

164. The first Economic Commission for Europe Regional Implementation Forum on Sustainable Development, held in January 2004, assessed the water, sanitation, and human settlements situation in the ECE region. ECE also initiated a second round of environmental performance reviews for countries with economies in transition, focusing on sustainable development. Two protocols to the ECE Convention on Long-range Transboundary Air Pollution entered into force in 2003: the 1998 Protocol on Heavy Metals and the 1998 Protocol on Persistent Organic Pollutants. The UNDP environmental governance programme initiated regional and cross-border initiatives in Eastern and Central Europe to improve economic opportunities in specific regions while supporting conservation and sustainable management of the region's natural resources.

165. The region served by the Economic and Social Commission for Western Asia suffers from the inefficient use and resulting scarcity of water resources. ESCWA established the Arab Integrated Water Resources Management Network to support research and training institutes for knowledge-sharing and initiated regional cooperation in the management of shared groundwater resources among the member countries. In the energy sector, ESCWA also initiated regional cooperation to promote cross-border energy trade. With the assistance of ESCWA, Egypt, Jordan, Qatar, the Syrian Arab Republic and Yemen adopted new policies on energy pricing and efficiency, codes and standards and promoted the use of efficient appliances in the electric power sector and renewable electricity systems.

166. The environmental management programmes of UNIDO helped countries to address problems of industrial growth, including global warming, water and air pollution, releases of per-

sistent organic pollutants and other toxic substances, land degradation and coastal erosion. UNIDO sought to mitigate those threats by promoting both pre-emptive measures, including the use of cleaner production technologies, and ex post measures, including end-of-pipe treatment of pollutants and other environmental clean-up measures.

167. As the lead agency for the promotion of the United Nations Decade of Education for Sustainable Development, UNESCO prepared a draft international implementation scheme in close consultation with partners from the United Nations, Governments, non-governmental organizations, civil society and individuals. The question is now before the General Assembly at its fifty-ninth session under the agenda item entitled "United Nations Decade of Education for Sustainable Development".

168. The United Nations Forum on Forests continued its work on promoting and facilitating the management, conservation and sustainable development of all types of forests and providing a global framework for policy implementation, coordination and development. In 2004, the Forum considered traditional and scientific forest-related knowledge, social and cultural aspects of forests and means of implementing agreements. The Forum will review the effectiveness of the international arrangement on forests and make recommendations in 2005 to the Economic and Social Council and the General Assembly on the parameters of a mandate for developing a legal framework on all types of forests.

169. FAO helped Member States to build up their capacity to implement Agenda 21, the multisectoral action plan that emerged from the United Nations Conference on Environment and Development (Rio de Janeiro, Brazil, 1992), and provided a neutral forum for international discussions on emerging issues and policy options in food and agriculture. FAO provided support to Member States focusing on strengthening regulatory frameworks for sustainable development; promoting participatory systems-oriented approaches in the management of fisheries, forestry, mountain regions and other natural resources; sharing good practices and policies; promoting an integrated approach to agriculture, forestry and fisheries; and supporting the use of information and communication technologies for development planning at all levels and for specific user groups and localities.

170. To promote sustainable urbanization, UN-Habitat launched the Managing Water for African Cities initiative at the Pan African Implementation and Partnership Conference on Water (Addis Ababa, December 2003) and also established a water and sanitation trust fund. Through the Water for Asian Cities programme, which draws upon the experience of the Managing Water for African Cities programme, UN-Habitat has established a new model for cooperation, closely linking political mobilization and capacity-building to follow-up investment in the sector by the Asian Development Bank.

171. In the field of corporate environmental accounting, UNCTAD in 2004 published *A Manual for the Preparers and Users of Eco-efficiency Indicators*, which standardizes for the first time the presentation and disclosure of a company's environmental performance.

172. A United Nations University study alerted the world to the growing negative environmental impacts of computers. The average 24-kilogram desktop computer with a monitor requires at least 10 times its weight in fossil fuels and chemicals to manufacture, making it five times more materials-intensive than an automobile or refrigerator. The material- and energy-intensive production process, greater adoption of personal computers worldwide and the rapid rate at which they are discarded for newer machines add to resource depletion and environmental pollution. Government incentives are needed worldwide to extend the life of personal computers and to slow the growth of high-tech pollution.

173. To build national capacity for sustainable development, the ILO International Training Centre, based in Turin, Italy, conducted some 700 training activities for 16,000 participants from 177 countries. Some 45 per cent of those activities took place in Turin, 50 per cent in the field and 5 per cent online.

Africa

174. In response to the high priority I have assigned in United Nations reform efforts to addressing the special needs of Africa, all parts of the Organization provided support for African development over the past year. The Office of the Special Adviser on Africa has been established and provides support for the implementation of the New Partnership for Africa's Development through its reporting, advocacy and analytical work. The Office continues to monitor the implementation of the recommendations of my 1998 report on the causes of conflict and the promotion of durable peace and sustainable development in Africa (S/1998/318). In my progress report submitted to the General Assembly at its fifty-eighth session (A/58/352), I noted that while further progress had been made in the implementation of the recommendations in the past year, such progress had been slow and uneven. It concluded that African countries and the

international community needed to accelerate their efforts to implement my recommendations.

175.   To promote technical cooperation for the implementation of NEPAD, the Office of the Special Adviser on Africa in 2004 published *South-South Cooperation in Support of the New Partnership for Africa's Development: Experiences of Africa-Latin America and the Caribbean*, which examines the depth and diversity of South-South cooperation between the two regions and assesses the congruence between NEPAD priorities and existing areas of cooperation.

176.   I have also appointed an independent panel of eminent persons to review and assess the scope and adequacy of international support for NEPAD, to conduct a dialogue with Africa's development partners with a view to promoting support for NEPAD and to make recommendations to me on action the international community could take to enhance support for the implementation of NEPAD and for the development of Africa. The panel is to begin its work in September 2004. The NEPAD secretariat has received institutional, technical and financial support from UNDP.

177.   The prospects for peace in Africa may help to facilitate the return of millions of displaced persons. As part of integrated United Nations efforts in support of the NEPAD peace and security programme, UNHCR focuses on holistic post-conflict and recovery programmes in transition countries.

178.   In November 2003 WFP signed a memorandum of understanding with NEPAD, the focus areas of which included food security, livelihood protection, nutrition, HIV/AIDS, emergency needs assessment, preparedness and response and regional capacity-building. Nearly half, or 46 per cent, of the Programme's development resources were invested in sub-Saharan Africa.

179.   UNEP assisted African Governments in developing the Action Plan for the Environment Initiative of the New Partnership for Africa's Development. The African Union held a donor partners' conference (Algiers, December 2003), at which the Algiers Declaration for a Global Partnership on the Environment Initiative of NEPAD was adopted, recognizing the importance for the initiative of international assistance and national capacity-building and committing all partners and stakeholders to support the implementation phase of the Action Plan.

180.   FAO has provided support to Member States in Africa in capacity-building, technical assistance and the formulation, implementation, monitoring and evaluation of policies and strategies (e.g., in Eritrea, Mozambique, Nigeria, Swaziland, South Africa and the United Republic of Tanzania), as well as in the formulation of regional programmes for food security and support for regional economic organizations. FAO has also assisted in the review and updating of national strategies for food security and agricultural development for the implementation of the NEPAD Comprehensive Africa Agriculture Development Programme. For least developed countries in Africa, UNIDO has launched the African Productive Capacity Initiative, to be implemented in the framework of NEPAD, with the objectives of increasing the share of manufactured products and services in national income, creating environmentally friendly productive entities and generating sustainable jobs.

181.   Jointly with the Government of Japan, the United Nations organized in September 2003 the Tokyo International Conference on African Development. As a follow-up, the Office of the Special Adviser on Africa is assisting United Nations country teams in the preparation of projects for funding from the Japanese Trust Fund for Human Security.

182.   I welcome the Economic and Social Council's initiative to assert its role in African countries emerging from conflict through the work of its ad hoc advisory groups on Burundi and Guinea-Bissau. They presented their recommendations to the Council in February 2004. The groups have called for partnerships between the authorities of the two countries and the international community and have contributed to mobilizing donor support in the critical phase of the transition from relief to development. In this context, working relationships between the Security Council and the Economic and Social Council have been enhanced, as exemplified by joint missions to Guinea-Bissau, thus contributing to promoting a comprehensive approach to peace and development, as called for in the Millennium Declaration.

183.   In 2003, the strategy of UNDP for contributing to the achievement of the Millennium Development Goals in Africa sought to strengthen awareness of the Goals, to strengthen the capacity of African countries for monitoring progress towards the Goals; and to put the Goals into effect at the country level. UNDP organized two subregional Millennium Development Goals forums, for West Africa and Southern Africa, which reinforced the country-level campaigns and rekindled commitment to the Goals. Various governance programmes helped to create an enabling environment for the Goals and to strengthen political commitment to their achievement. UNDP also supported the efforts of many countries in Africa to incorporate the Goals in their medium-

to long-term national poverty reduction strategies, including poverty reduction strategy papers.

184. The Global Partnership for Clean Fuels and Vehicles has also made substantial progress. The Partnership, focusing on sub-Saharan Africa and coordinated by UNEP, was set up to support the global phase-out of leaded gasoline as part of a commitment made at the World Summit on Sustainable Development. At a conference held at UNEP headquarters in May 2004, it was reported that over half of all petrol sold in sub-Saharan Africa was now unleaded, a dramatic increase since 2001, when virtually all petrol sold was leaded.

185. The interventions of UNFPA in Africa focused on evidence-based policy dialogue, national capacity-building for the management of population and reproductive health programmes and data for development.

186. In 2004, 63 UN-Habitat-supported projects and programmes for urban development and management were under execution in 30 countries in Africa, addressing the formulation of national housing policies and programmes, promoting appropriate building materials and technologies, improving access by the poor to basic services and promoting sustainable livelihoods.

187. The United Nations Office on Drugs and Crime continued to provide capacity-building support to the Eastern and Southern Africa Anti-Money Laundering Group and its 14 member States. The Office also completed operational research in Kenya, Malawi and Mauritius jointly with UNAIDS on drug abuse and HIV/AIDS linkages and appropriate prevention responses. The Office also provided African Governments with technical and advisory services to develop drug demand-reduction programmes in national policies.

188. ILO supported the African Union in preparing for the Extraordinary Summit on Employment and Poverty Reduction in Africa, to be held in September 2004. As a result of ILO advice, a number of poverty reduction strategy papers in Africa have incorporated issues of employment, social protection, social dialogue and principles, and rights at work.

Addressing the needs of the least developed countries, landlocked developing countries and small island developing States

189. Developments during the past year show that the most vulnerable groups of countries remain marginalized in the global economy. The targets set by the international community to assist them, in particular with regard to halving extreme poverty and hunger by 2015, seem, on the basis of current trends, unlikely to be achieved in most cases. The Office of the High Representative for the Least Developed Countries, Landlocked Developing Countries and Small Island Developing States increased its efforts to address the special needs of these three groups of countries and assisted me in ensuring coordinated follow-up of the implementation of the respective programmes of action referred to below.

190. At its high-level segment in June 2004, the Economic and Social Council adopted a ministerial declaration on resource mobilization and creation of an enabling environment for poverty eradication in the context of the implementation of the Programme of Action for the Least Developed Countries for the Decade 2001-2010, adopted in Brussels in 2001, which renewed the call for the effective implementation of the Programme of Action and again urged donor countries to provide more than 0.2 per cent of their gross national product as official development assistance to those countries.

191. The Brussels Programme of Action remains the most comprehensive programme addressing all the special needs of the least developed countries. The establishment of national mechanisms, including national focal points, is crucial for its implementation at the national level. As at May 2004, 47 countries had identified a national focal point and 18 national forums had been established, as compared with 11 focal points and 9 national forums a year ago. Within the United Nations and other multilateral organizations, 19 entities have now mainstreamed the Brussels Programme of Action into their activities and programmes of work. Moreover, partnerships with civil society, the private sector and intergovernmental organizations have been either initiated or strengthened.

192. The landlocked developing countries received a special boost in their efforts from the International Ministerial Conference on Transit Transport Cooperation (Almaty, Khazakstan, August 2003), which was the first United Nations conference ever to address this group's special needs. Its outcome, the Almaty Programme of Action, was the result of a participatory preparatory process involving all stakeholders, and is balanced, focused and implementable. A road map for the implementation of the Almaty Programme of Action has been prepared and validated through a meeting of United Nations entities and agencies, including the World Bank Group. I have invited Member States to take advantage of the United Nations annual treaty event to become party to the conventions on transit transport.

193. Regarding the needs of the third vulnerable group, the small island developing States,

the Organization continued to assist Member States in implementing, through analytical and operational activities, the Barbados Programme of Action adopted at the Global Conference on the Sustainable Development of Small Island Developing States (Bridgetown, April and May 1994). In April 2004, the Commission on Sustainable Development convened a three-day preparatory meeting on the International Meeting to Review the Implementation of the Programme of Action for the Sustainable Development of Small Island Developing States, to be held in Mauritius in January 2005.

194. The least developed countries, landlocked developing countries and small island developing States have received broad-based support from the United Nations. One of the numerous activities of UNCTAD, both analytical and operational, with regard to those countries was the publication of *The Least Developed Countries Report 2004*. The report assesses the relationship between international trade and poverty and identifies national and international policies that would make trade a more effective mechanism for poverty reduction in the least developed countries. The Integrated Framework for Trade-Related Technical Assistance to Least Developed Countries, consisting of six agencies—the International Monetary Fund, the International Trade Centre UNCTAD/WTO, UNCTAD, UNDP, the World Bank and the World Trade Organization—continued to support the least developed countries in their capacity development for trade. In January 2004, FAO issued a paper on FAO and the small island developing States: challenges and emerging issues in agriculture, forestry and fisheries.

195. WFP dedicated 71 per cent of its development resources to the least developed countries and 99 per cent to low-income food-deficit countries. Similarly, UNFPA devoted most of its resources and programme efforts to least developed countries and small island developing States, in particular those whose population and social development indicators fell considerably short of internationally agreed standards. UN-Habitat continued to carry out capacity-building programmes in the least developed countries, landlocked developing countries and small island developing States through its various programmes and its regional offices. The United Nations Office on Drugs and Crime, jointly with the Commonwealth Secretariat, continued to provide technical assistance to several Pacific island States identified as international financial centres at high risk for money-laundering.

196. At the regional level, the Economic and Social Commission for Asia and the Pacific, in its panel discussion on achieving the Millennium Development Goals in the least developed countries through regional development cooperation, held at its sixtieth session (Shanghai, China, April 2004), highlighted the modalities of regional development cooperation required to ensure socio-economic progress in the least developed countries. A Pacific regional workshop on urban management (Nadi, Fiji, December 2003), organized jointly by ESCAP, UN-Habitat, UNDP and the Pacific Islands Forum Secretariat, resulted in a draft Pacific Urban Agenda, which was adopted by ESCAP. ESCAP also convened the eighth session of the Special Body on Pacific Island Developing Countries in April 2004, which arrived at a set of recommendations in regard to experiences and challenges in urban management issues in Pacific island countries. As a follow-up to the Almaty conference, the Economic Commission for Europe initiated the promotion of accession to the ECE legal instruments on transport by least developed countries, and together with ESCAP convened the first Expert Group Meeting on Developing Euro-Asian Transport Linkages in March 2004, covering landlocked and transit developing countries as well as transition countries in the Euro-Asian region.

Chapter V

International legal order and human rights

Human rights development

197. As I stated in my report of September 2002 entitled "strengthening of the United Nations: an agenda for further change", building strong human rights institutions at the country level is what, in the long run, will ensure that human rights are protected and advanced in a sustained manner. In follow-up, the Office of the United Nations High Commissioner for Human Rights, the United Nations Development Group and the Executive Committee on Humanitarian Affairs have developed and adopted a joint plan of action for the period 2004-2006 designed to strengthen human rights-related United Nations action at the country level. The focus of the plan is to improve the capacity of United Nations country teams to assist Member States, at their request, in their efforts to establish and operate national human rights promotion and protection systems. Measures are being developed in the areas of needs assessment and planning, training and facilitating closer linkages between national systems and the international human rights mechanisms. The plan also includes the development of appropriate methodological tools and

resource materials for use by country teams, national authorities and civil society. Specific projects are aimed at enhancing the role of national courts in human rights protection.

198. Human rights advisers have been assigned to a number of country teams. This relatively new concept has proven to be an effective way to develop human rights capacity and to support the human rights elements of peace processes as well as in conflict or post-conflict situations. OHCHR currently maintains field presences in more than 40 countries and manages some 40 technical cooperation projects and programmes in all parts of the world. Moreover, to alleviate the causes of violence and related human rights violations, as well as to combat impunity, which, if left unaddressed, can reverse or halt progress, OHCHR has been called upon to coordinate or carry out investigations into major human rights violations.

199. Progress in the protection of human rights depends on the strength of the international legal framework. It is heartening to note that the number of ratifications of international human rights treaties has continued to increase, moving us closer to achieving one of the goals of the United Nations Millennium Declaration. I would like to make a special reference to the International Convention on the Protection of the Rights of All Migrant Workers and Members of their Families, the States parties to which met for the first time on 11 December 2003 to elect the 10 members of the Committee monitoring the implementation of the Convention. The Committee held its first session from 1 to 5 March 2004 at the United Nations Office at Geneva. I am convinced that the Committee has an essential role to play in a neglected area and hope that States Members of the United Nations will make every possible effort to accede to or ratify this important instrument, as well as all other fundamental international human rights treaties.

200. The work of the expert bodies established under the human rights treaties continues to be of critical importance. From the date of my last report until 1 June 2004, the Human Rights Committee, the Committee on Economic, Social and Cultural Rights, the Committee on the Elimination of Racial Discrimination, the Committee on the Rights of the Child, the Committee on the Elimination of Discrimination against Women and the Committee against Torture have considered the reports of 87 States parties and adopted four general comments that clarify the meaning of the treaties and offer practical advice on their implementation. The treaty bodies have continued to harmonize their working methods and to consider means to assist States parties to fulfil

their substantive commitments and meet their reporting obligations. OHCHR has developed guidelines for an expanded core document designed to streamline the reporting process for the consideration of treaty bodies.

201. The petitions procedures operating under a number of international human rights treaties offer valuable opportunities for individuals directly to seek redress for alleged violations of their rights. Over the past year, expert bodies have adopted well over 100 decisions and views on individual cases.

202. The special rapporteurs and experts (mandate holders) appointed by the Commission on Human Rights have continued to make valuable contributions to the protection of fundamental rights. Over the past year, some 90 reports submitted to the Commission by the mandate holders—as well as more than 20 reports submitted to the General Assembly—have touched upon numerous human rights themes, reminding the international community of the need to uphold domestic and international human rights standards. The mandate holders have visited more than 40 countries in the framework of their fact-finding activities. Through their numerous confidential urgent appeals and other communications to some 164 countries, the mandate holders have contributed to keeping the concerned Governments aware of the need to conform in practice with international human rights norms and standards. Those communications sought the protection of individuals whose rights had allegedly been violated with no due process of law or, more generally, drew attention to global phenomena and developments threatening the full enjoyment of human rights.

203. In addition, the Commission established new thematic mechanisms on trafficking in persons, especially women and children, and on impunity. On the latter issue, the Commission asked me to appoint an independent expert to update the 1997 Set of Principles for the protection and promotion of human rights through action to combat impunity. The newly established Special Rapporteur on trafficking is to focus on the human rights aspects of the victims of trafficking in persons, especially women and children. New special procedures mechanisms were also established by the Commission for Belarus, Chad, the Democratic People's Republic of Korea, the Democratic Republic of the Congo, the Sudan and Uzbekistan.

204. At its sixtieth session, the Commission on Human Rights commemorated the International Day of Reflection on the 1994 Genocide in Rwanda. I attended this important meeting, at which I announced my Plan of Action to Prevent

Genocide, in particular my intention to appoint a Senior Adviser on the Prevention of Genocide to work closely with the High Commissioner for Human Rights and the United Nations system to ensure that we are better equipped to anticipate and prevent such horrors in the future. On 12 July, I informed the Security Council of my intention to appoint Juan Méndez to this position.

205. This year the Commission on Human Rights attracted almost 5,000 participants, including representatives of Member States, nongovernmental organizations, independent experts, United Nations agencies and national human rights institutions. A total of 82 senior government officials, primarily foreign and justice ministers, attended the high-level segment opening the Commission, a significant increase over the previous year. Despite broad participation, however, there continues to be disquiet over the fact that a number of Governments accused of gross violations of human rights are elected to membership in the Commission, about the high level of politicization of the Commission's debates and about the lack of consideration of certain situations involving grave human rights violations.

206. On 1 July 2004, Louise Arbour took up her responsibilities as High Commissioner following the General Assembly's endorsement of my decision to appoint her to that post. For the past year, the Office of the High Commissioner has been ably led by Bertrand Ramcharan, following the tragic death on 19 August 2003 of Sergio Vieira de Mello, the High Commissioner for Human Rights and my Special Representative in Iraq, who was killed, along with 21 colleagues, in a terrorist attack on the United Nations headquarters in Baghdad. I take this opportunity to put on record the remarkable contribution that Mr. Vieira de Mello made to the principles and purposes of the United Nations throughout his long career as an outstanding international civil servant.

International Criminal Court

207. The International Criminal Court is now operational in The Hague. The United Nations is proud to have played an important role in its establishment and in making arrangements for the commencement of its operations. As at 31 December 2003, the United Nations Secretariat ceased to act as the secretariat of the Assembly of States Parties.

208. The second session of the Assembly of States Parties was held in September 2003. The Assembly elected the Deputy Prosecutor, the Board of Directors of the Victims Trust Fund and the remaining members of the Committee on Budget and Finance. It adopted the staff regulations of the Court as well as the 2004 budget,

which signals that the Court may soon begin to carry out its judicial functions. The Assembly also established its own secretariat and a trust fund for the participation of least developed countries in its activities.

209. Pursuant to General Assembly resolution 58/79 of 9 December 2003, the United Nations Secretariat has assisted in the orderly and smooth transition of work to the secretariat of the Assembly of States Parties. In accordance with the same resolution, I have also taken steps to conclude a relationship agreement to guide future cooperation between the United Nations and the Court and to facilitate the discharge of responsibilities of the two institutions under their constituent instruments. On 7 June 2004, the Acting Legal Counsel on my behalf and the Chef de Cabinet of the President of the International Criminal Court initialled the negotiated draft relationship agreement, thereby completing the negotiations at the working level. The General Assembly and the Assembly of States Parties to the Rome Statute of the International Criminal Court now must approve the agreement before it can be signed and enter into force.

210. As at 23 July 2004, 94 States were parties to the Rome Statute of the International Criminal Court. Although the pace of accession and ratification has slowed down, I remain confident that we can assume that the 100 mark will be reached soon. Universal participation in the Rome Statute would be an indelible contribution to the cause of justice in a world where many still commit, without punishment, egregious crimes that numb the human conscience. It should remain the ultimate goal. Once again, I appeal to those countries which have not yet done so to consider acceding to or ratifying the Rome Statute. I was pleased that, in June 2004, the Security Council did not renew the request that it had made in previous years that in the next 12 months the International Criminal Court not commence or proceed with the investigation or prosecution of any case involving officials or personnel from a contributing State not a party to the Rome Statute in respect of acts or omissions relating to an operation authorized or established by the United Nations. This development represents a significant contribution to the efforts of the Organization to promote justice and the rule of law in international affairs.

International Tribunals

International Tribunal for the Former Yugoslavia

211. The International Tribunal for the Former Yugoslavia has continued to implement the

completion strategy endorsed by the Security Council in its resolutions 1503(2003) and 1534 (2004). The three trial chambers operate at full capacity, hearing six cases simultaneously and preparing to begin new cases as soon as ongoing cases are completed. On 6 April 2004, the judges amended rule 28 (A) of the Tribunal's Rules of Procedure and Evidence to comply with the Security Council's directive in its resolution 1534 (2004) that indictments concentrate on the most senior leaders suspected of being most responsible for crimes within the Tribunal's jurisdiction.

212. The Tribunal has taken an active role in preparing domestic judicial institutions in the States of the former Yugoslavia for the referral of cases from the Tribunal. The Tribunal hosted a donors' conference on 30 October 2003 that raised 15.7 million euros for the planned war crimes chamber within the State Court of Bosnia and Herzegovina, a project endorsed by the Security Council in its resolutions 1503(2003) and 1534(2004). The Chamber, which is being established by the Office of the High Representative for Bosnia and Herzegovina, is expected to be operational by January 2005 and, provided adequate detention facilities are available, should be able to receive cases referred by the Tribunal shortly thereafter. The Tribunal is also engaged in a number of initiatives designed to share expertise and information with the national authorities of Croatia and Serbia and Montenegro in order to facilitate the possible referral of cases to domestic jurisdictions in those States.

213. Six trials, involving a total of eight accused, are under way in the Tribunal's trial chambers. An additional 20 cases, involving 34 accused, are in the pre-trial phase. The total number of guilty pleas has risen to 18. Some of the accused pleading guilty have provided important evidence about the crimes they committed and events they witnessed. The trial chambers have rendered 14 judgements during the past year, and the Appeals Chamber has rendered 3. Four hundred and ten witnesses have testified. As at 20 July 2004, 59 persons were being detained at the Tribunal's detention facility. The Tribunal has transferred two convicted persons to Member States to serve their sentences: one to Austria and one to Norway.

214. Nearly 20 indictees, including some former high-ranking military and political officials, notably Radovan Karadzic, Ratko Mladic and Ante Gotovina, remain at large. The full cooperation of the international community, especially the States of the former Yugoslavia, remains essential in order to accomplish the Tribunal's mandate, complete its operations on time and have a lasting impact on the rule of law

in the former Yugoslavia. On 4 May 2004, the President of the Tribunal reported to the Security Council the consistent failure of Serbia and Montenegro to comply with its obligations under article 29 of the Tribunal's Statute and rule 39 of its Rules of Procedure and Evidence. That report stated that the level of Serbia and Montenegro's cooperation with the Tribunal had started to fall off after the December 2003 elections in that country and had now reached the point where it was almost non-existent.

International Criminal Tribunal for Rwanda

215. The International Criminal Tribunal for Rwanda has worked to achieve the goals set out in Security Council resolution 1503(2003), in which the Council urges it to complete investigations by 2004, trials by 2008 and appeals by 2010. The Tribunal has now rendered 17 judgements involving 23 accused. The trials of 19 accused are under way at different stages. The judicial capacity of the trial chambers was increased following the Security Council's grant of ad litem judges, nine of whom can now operate at any given time. Additional measures have been taken to streamline the judicial process. So, for example, a Trial Committee, composed of representatives of the Chambers, the Prosecution and the Registry, is now in place and is responsible for planning and streamlining pre-trial proceedings so as to ensure that cases are ready for trial on schedule.

216. Following the adoption of Security Council resolution 1503(2003), a separate position of Prosecutor was established for the Tribunal. The Prosecutor has reviewed the cases and determined which should be pursued before the Tribunal and which could be transferred to national jurisdictions for prosecution. Concrete steps are now being taken to assess the suitability of some national systems, including that of Rwanda, to adjudicate cases in compliance with international standards.

217. The Registry continues to provide support to the other organs to facilitate their work. Reform of the legal aid system is under way in order to control unnecessary or excessive defence fees. The Registrar has signed agreements on the enforcement of sentences with France, Italy and Sweden, and is working towards the early conclusion of similar agreements with other countries, including Rwanda.

Special Court for Sierra Leone

218. In the past year the Special Court for Sierra Leone has continued to lay the groundwork for the start of trials of those alleged to bear the greatest responsibility for the atrocities com-

mitted during the conflict in that country. On 16 September 2003, the Special Court issued its latest indictment and arrest warrant against Santigie Borbor Kanu, who was arrested while in the custody of the authorities of Sierra Leone awaiting trial for treason and transferred to the detention facility of the Special Court. To date, the Special Court has approved 13 indictments. On 5 December 2003, the Prosecutor withdrew the indictments against Foday Sankoh and Sam Bockarie in view of their deaths. Two indictees, Johnny Paul Koroma and Charles Taylor, remain at large, and nine are detained in the custody of the Special Court, all of whom have pleaded not guilty.

219. On 28 January 2004, the trial chamber issued decisions as a result of which three trials, instead of nine separate ones, will be held involving the nine accused who are currently in the custody of the Court. The trials in the cases of the Civil Defence Forces and the Revolutionary United Front started on 3 June and 5 July 2004 respectively. The trial in the case of the Armed Forces Revolutionary Council is expected to start in the autumn of 2004, when a second trial chamber will be appointed.

220. The Special Court's progress has been achieved against constant funding insecurity and fiscal constraints. The funding requirement of $19 million for the first year of operation (July 2002–June 2003) were met entirely through voluntary contributions. However, during the past year it has become apparent that pledges and contributions from a group of interested States would not be sufficient to fund operations for the minimum three-year timeline, which I had previously indicated as being necessary for the investigation, prosecution and trial of a very limited number of accused. As a result of the continuing funding uncertainty, in March 2004 I sought a subvention from the General Assembly of $40 million for completion of the Court's work—$16.7 million for the period from 1 July to 31 December 2004 and the remaining $23.3 million for 2005. By its resolution 58/284 of 8 April 2004, the General Assembly authorized a subvention of up to $16.7 million from the regular budget appropriations for the period from 1 July to 31 December 2004. I will report to the Assembly at its fifty-ninth session on the status of this subvention and seek approval for release of the balance.

221. After only two years of operation, the Special Court is already preparing for the post-trial phase by working on its completion and exit strategies. These will include winding down its core activities, devising mechanisms to continue necessary residual activities and leaving behind a legacy of accountability for violations of international humanitarian law. In addition, it is hoped that there will be a contribution to legal reform efforts in Sierra Leone through the dissemination of information regarding the Special Court's work and the transfer of expertise, equipment and facilities to the local legal community.

Enhancing the rule of law

222. On 24 September 2003, the Security Council held its first general consideration of the topic of justice and the rule of law. In a statement to the Council, I shared a number of lessons that the Secretariat has learned from its experience over the years in dealing with post-conflict situations and trying to help rebuild shattered societies. Foremost among those was that we must make the rule of law and justice central objectives of our peace operations, for when people do not feel safe from crime or confident that past injustices are being redressed, they will lose faith in a peace process and that process will ultimately fail. As far as re-establishing the rule of law is concerned, I noted that we cannot focus, as we sometimes have in the past, solely on rebuilding law enforcement institutions. Instead, we must take a comprehensive approach that encompasses the entire criminal justice process—police, prosecutors, defence lawyers, judges, court administrators and prison officers. A second major lesson I recalled was the need to avoid a "one-size-fits-all" approach. Rather, we must tailor solutions to local circumstances and traditions. We must also resist the temptation to think that we know best, but must involve local actors from the start and try to help them to find their own solutions. As for the pursuit of justice, I identified two major challenges. First, there is a need to look beyond questions of individual responsibility for serious crimes and to give greater consideration to meeting the needs both of victims and of the wider societies from which they come. This may mean that we will need, on occasion, to supplement criminal trials with other mechanisms, such as truth commissions, commissions of inquiry and reparation programmes. The second major challenge is how to resolve the demands of justice and of reconciliation when they compete. As I noted, the relentless pursuit of justice may at times be an obstacle to peace, making it difficult to reach an agreement that will stop the bloodshed or placing a delicate and hard-won peace agreement in peril. That might mean that we sometimes must accept less than perfect justice or will need to devise alternatives to prosecutions, such as truth and reconciliation processes, or will have to put off the day when we bring the guilty to trial. At other times we might need simply to accept the risk to peace in the hope that, in the

long term, a peace that is founded in justice will be more secure and likely to endure.

223. In August 2004, I submitted a report to the Security Council identifying a number of further practical lessons that we in the Secretariat have learned in this field which the Council might apply and build upon in its future work. Central among those were a number of precepts or ground rules that I suggested the Organization should adhere to when negotiating peace agreements and adopting mandates for its operations. Among them were the need to reject any amnesty for genocide, war crimes or crimes against humanity and ensure that any amnesty already granted for those crimes is not a bar to prosecution before any court created or assisted by the United Nations; to avoid establishing or participating directly in any tribunal that can impose capital punishment; to ensure that all courts created or assisted by the United Nations are structured and organized in a way that will ensure that the process of prosecution and trial is credible, that it complies with established international standards regarding the independence and impartiality of the judiciary, the effectiveness, impartiality and fairness of prosecutors and the integrity of the judicial process; to consider, where mixed tribunals are envisaged and there are no clear guarantees regarding the real and perceived objectivity, impartiality and fairness of the national judiciary, insisting on a majority of international judges and an international prosecutor; to recognize and respect the rights of victims and ensure that relevant processes include specific measures for their participation and protection; to recognize and respond to the differential impact of conflicts and international crimes on women; and to ensure that initiatives for the restoration of the rule of law and transitional justice mechanisms are adequately resourced through viable and sustainable funding mechanisms, including, where United Nations–sponsored tribunals are involved, at least partial funding through assessed contributions. I also announced my intention to instruct my Executive Committee on Peace and Security to propose concrete action on the matters discussed in my report, with a view to strengthening United Nations support for transitional justice and the rule of law in conflict and post-conflict countries.

224. In September 2003, I appointed a full-time coordinator to secure and organize the assistance that the United Nations is to provide to the Government of Cambodia under our June 2003 agreement on the establishment of extraordinary chambers within the existing courts of Cambodia for the prosecution of serious violations of Cambodian law and international law committed during the period of Democratic Kampuchea. To form a better picture of the probable requirements of the extraordinary chambers, I sent a planning mission to Phnom Penh in December 2003 and another in March 2004. As a result, agreement was reached with Cambodia on a range of key planning parameters. Suitable premises for a courtroom and accommodation for the related institutions and support services have also been identified and detailed budget estimates prepared. I shall soon be launching an appeal to States and will be reporting in depth to the General Assembly at its fifty-ninth session on progress achieved. Meanwhile, with a new Government in place, the Cambodian authorities have assured me that ratification of the agreement will be a priority on the agenda of the National Assembly.

225. During the past year, five new multilateral treaties were deposited with me, bringing the total number of active treaties deposited to 510. Ten treaties, related to human rights, health, transnational organized crime and the environment, entered into force. The annual treaty event that I initiated in 2000 will this year be entitled "Focus 2004: treaties on the protection of civilians". In March, I invited Governments to participate in the event, to be held during the fifty-ninth session of the General Assembly. I have pledged to provide requesting States with the legal technical assistance necessary to participate in the multilateral treaty framework. The Office of Legal Affairs jointly with the United Nations Institute for Training and Research offers biannual training on treaty law and practice at Headquarters. In 2003, this training was expanded to the regional level. To enhance knowledge of the technical aspects of treaties deposited with me, a new *Handbook of Final Clauses* has been published to complement the existing *Treaty Handbook*. Contributing to the wide dissemination of treaty-related information, the United Nations Treaty Collection on the Internet provides on a daily basis the updated status of all treaties deposited with me. This site now receives over 1.7 million hits per month.

Legal affairs

226. The International Law Commission completed its first reading of draft articles on diplomatic protection and advanced its work on reservations to treaties. It also made progress on the other topics on its agenda, including international liability in case of loss from transboundary harm arising out of hazardous activities; responsibility of international organizations; shared natural resources; unilateral acts of States; and fragmentation of international law. The Ad Hoc

Committee established pursuant to General Assembly resolution 51/210 of 17 December 1996 was reconvened and continued its efforts to elaborate a draft comprehensive convention on international terrorism and a draft convention for the suppression of acts of nuclear terrorism. Meanwhile, by its resolution 58/74 of 9 December 2003, the General Assembly decided to reconvene the Ad Hoc Committee on Jurisdictional Immunities of States and Their Property with a mandate to formulate a preamble and final clauses with a view to completing a convention on jurisdictional immunities of States and their property. In March 2004, the Ad Hoc Committee adopted the text of a draft convention, which it recommended for adoption by the Assembly.

227. At its session in 2004, the United Nations Commission on International Trade Law adopted a legislative guide on insolvency law. The objective of the guide is to assist national authorities in preparing new laws and in reviewing existing laws to establish an effective legal framework to address the financial difficulties of debtors, thereby providing market certainty and promoting economic growth and stability. The Commission is also preparing international standards in the fields of secured credit, arbitration, electronic contracting, transport and Government procurement law. In the past year, the International Trade Law Branch of the Office of Legal Affairs, which received additional resources to address an increased workload, particularly in the area of training and legal assistance, continued to assist the Commission, whose membership was increased from 36 to 60 States.

228. With respect to the law of the sea, the fifth meeting of the Open-ended Informal Consultative Process on Oceans and the Law of the Sea discussed how States could better address the increasing threats to biodiversity in areas beyond national jurisdiction. In relation to the request by the General Assembly to establish a regular process for global reporting and assessment of the state of the marine environment, including socio-economic aspects, an international workshop was held in conjunction with the fifth meeting of the Consultative Process. This represented the first opportunity for States to discuss the practical implications of the establishment of a global marine assessment process. Inter-agency cooperation and coordination to address all these issues has been enhanced by the establishment of the Oceans and Coastal Areas Network (UN-Oceans), the general mechanism for inter-agency cooperation in ocean affairs. The date 16 November 2004 marks the tenth anniversary of the entry into force of the United Nations Convention on the Law of the Sea. One hundred and forty-five

States are now parties to the Convention, demonstrating the considerable progress that has been made towards universal participation.

229. During the past year, the Office of Legal Affairs provided advice on legal issues arising from the situation in Iraq, including on relevant Security Council resolutions and the question of Iraq's representation in the United Nations, as well as on the activities of the United Nations Assistance Mission for Iraq, the winding-up of the oil-for-food programme and the transfer of responsibility for the programme to the Coalition Provisional Authority.

230. The Office provided procedural advice to the tenth emergency special session of the General Assembly, which ultimately requested the International Court of Justice to give an advisory opinion on the legal consequences of the construction by the occupying Power of a wall in the occupied Palestinian territory. The Office prepared a dossier of relevant documents and assisted in the preparation of my written statement to the Court.

231. With respect to the International Tribunals, the Office provided advice in relation to requests for access to documentary evidence and witnesses. It also assisted the Management Committee of the Special Court for Sierra Leone on legal and operational aspects of the Court. The Office provided support to peacekeeping missions and assistance with respect to the establishment of a number of new and expanded operations, including the United Nations Mission in Liberia, the United Nations Operation in Côte d'Ivoire, the United Nations Stabilization Mission in Haiti and the United Nations Operation in Burundi.

232. The Office also provided advice on a wide range of other matters of concern to the Organization, including personnel reform, procurement practices and guidelines on cooperation with the private sector. It continued to draft and negotiate a series of complex contracts for the capital master plan and a related security-strengthening initiative for the Headquarters complex in New York.

Chapter VI

Management

Administration and management

233. The Organization continued its efforts to improve client servicing and place a stronger emphasis on delivering results. An Organization-wide client survey of services provided by the Department of Management was carried out to es-

tablish benchmarks against which future performance can be measured. The survey revealed that while respondents viewed recent efforts to upgrade the management of services as being headed in the right direction, there was much room for improvement, particularly with respect to client focus and meeting client needs, enhanced consultation with clients in the policy-making process and flexibility in the application of policies and rules. An important development was a retreat in May 2004 that brought together all the chief administrative officers from offices away from Headquarters and senior Headquarters administrative staff. This has led to mechanisms being put in place for increased dialogue and closer collaboration in the area of administration and management.

234. Practical steps have been taken to improve high-priority administrative services. In view of increased security threats, the Organization's ability to respond quickly and effectively to crises has been enhanced by building up its capacity to deal with the needs of staff, their families and others who may be affected. The administration of justice has become more efficient through the assignment of additional resources and streamlining procedures, which has led to significant reductions in case backlogs.

Information and communication technology services

235. The information and communication technology strategy (A/57/620) to ensure efficiency, automation and coordination in the Organization's internal decision-making is being implemented, and a Project Review Committee has been established to enforce standards on all initiatives in the area of information and communication technology and to ensure that all related investments are justified. The United Nations is upgrading its global information and communication technology network to make it more robust and sufficiently powerful to support multimedia applications such as desktop video-conferencing. Network security risk assessments have been undertaken to mitigate security risks at four duty stations.

Security and safety services

236. In view of significantly increased threats to the United Nations and its staff, the Organization undertook a number of initiatives to enhance security at Headquarters and field offices. Measures in New York include the replacement of the perimeter fence and the development of an electronic access control system. The development of a system-wide standardized access control system is under way. To ensure a safe and secure working environment, risk assessment, mitigation measures and strategies in the form of Headquarters minimum operating security standards were developed and established in January 2004. All United Nations system offices at Headquarters have agreed to adhere to the standards.

237. In the wake of the attack on the United Nations office in Baghdad on 19 August 2003, the Department of Management worked very closely with the United Nations Security Coordinator, the Department of Peacekeeping Operations, the Office for the Coordination of Humanitarian Affairs and the Department of Political Affairs to compile an implementation plan to improve crisis response on the basis of lessons learned. Recommendations cover the areas of disaster preparedness and planning, formulation of clear definitions of roles and responsibilities, development of emergency procedures, creation of a full inventory of operational response capabilities, proper selection and training of crisis response personnel and dedicated follow-up on administrative matters.

238. Training programmes on security have been instituted, including one on basic security in the field, which is mandatory for all staff. Increased security awareness of staff before and during a crisis has been promoted through a hotline, a web site and an emergency preparedness booklet, and post-crisis support programmes for staff are provided by the Staff Counsellor's Office.

Common support services

239. The United Nations Global Marketplace, a common Internet-based supplier registration and database facility that is expected to become a "one-stop shop" for all United Nations-related procurement information for both procurement professionals in the Organization and the public, was launched in February 2004. The consolidation of requirements and direct negotiations with manufacturers and developers rather than the retailer have led to global arrangements, that benefit all United Nations system organizations, thus avoiding duplication of effort and providing improved volume discounts, increased control over the procurement process, elimination of non-value-added tasks and reduction of long purchase cycles. Particularly beneficial are travel-related contracts and contracts for information technology and telecommunications (software and hardware), office supplies, vehicles and security-related equipment. New office facilities are being built in Addis Ababa, Nairobi and Santiago to ensure that disparate offices are situated in one location in line with the "United

Nations House" concept. In terms of security, they will conform to the new electronic access control system and the Headquarters minimum operating security standards.

Human resources management

240. Implementation of the integrated human resources management reform programme continued with human resource practices and procedures being further refined in order to meet the needs of programme managers and staff at large. Particular emphasis was given to supporting the new staff selection system, which incorporates recruitment, placement, promotion and managed mobility. Information technology tools have been leveraged with the Organization-wide roll-out of a fully electronic Performance Appraisal System (e-PAS), the further development of the electronic Human Resources Handbook and enhancements to the Galaxy tool, which supports the staff selection system. The Office of Human Resources Management continues to work in partnership with department heads in developing and monitoring human resources action plans, which set departmental goals related to, among other things, geographical distribution, gender, staff development and PAS compliance.

241. The core values and competencies have now been incorporated into all aspects of human resources management, including recruitment, performance management, career development and learning. Major emphasis has been placed on developing a culture of continuous learning, building leadership and management capacity, providing guidance for staff and managers on emergency preparedness and supporting career development and mobility for staff at all levels. Increased attention has been paid to the work-life agenda, including the design and implementation of worksite wellness programmes, further implementation of the United Nations policy on HIV/AIDS, the introduction of flexible working arrangements and the provision of expanded staff counselling and advisory services.

Capital master plan

242. The United Nations has entered into contracts for the design development phase of the refurbishment of the Headquarters complex. They cover various design services related to infrastructure, architecture and engineering, as well as measures to strengthen security. In February 2004 the United States of America, as the host country, extended a provisional offer, subject to approval by the United States Congress, of an interest-bearing loan of $1.2 billion to finance the capital master plan. Subsequently the host country proposed alternative repayment scenarios for consideration by the General Assembly. Preparatory work is moving ahead, and an architect has been selected for the design and construction of the new building south of Headquarters that would serve as alternate accommodation during the renovation phase.

Financial management

243. The results-based-budgeting framework has continued to be further refined to improve managerial accountability, including the introduction of the new two-year strategic framework to replace the medium-term plan and a redesigned programme performance report.

244. A worrisome development during the past year has been the deterioration in the financial situation of the International Tribunals for the Former Yugoslavia and Rwanda, with an increasing number of Member States failing to pay their assessed contributions. Unless Member States respond positively and promptly by paying their dues, the future of the Tribunals may be jeopardized.

245. The payment of regular budget contributions has also fallen behind in comparison with the previous year, with the amount unpaid at the end of 2003 totalling $441.7 million, versus $304.7 million at the end of 2002. Only 127 Member States had paid their assessed contributions in full by the end of 2003. Those developments, together with recent decisions of the General Assembly that surplus balances from closed peacekeeping missions should be returned to Member States, have severely curtailed the level of available cash. Under these circumstances, full and timely payments by Member States become even more necessary in order to not affect the mandated operations of the United Nations.

Accountability and oversight

246. This year marks the tenth anniversary of the establishment of the Office of Internal Oversight Services, which was created by the General Assembly in July 1994 to enhance oversight functions within the Organization. The Assembly will conduct its second five-year evaluation and review of the functions and reporting procedures of the Office at its fifty-ninth session. To assist the Assembly, the Office undertook a comprehensive internal assessment of its activities, concluding that while the quality of its activities had improved over the past five years, there was a need to strengthen coordination of oversight reports in the Secretariat to enhance the impact of recommendations and overall accountability.

Monitoring, evaluation and consulting

247.   Intensive training of managers and staff carried out by the Office of Internal Oversight Services contributed to the strengthening of results-based management. The format and content of my report on the programme performance of the United Nations for the biennium 2002-2003 (A/59/69) were substantially improved to showcase the key results achieved under each programme and subprogramme of the Organization's programme budget.

248.   In its evaluation of the recent restructuring of the Department of Peacekeeping Operations (A/58/746), the Office of Internal Oversight Services concluded that the reform was on the right track but that more time was needed for its impact to be realized fully. Among other things, the Office recommended improving personnel management, institutionalizing best practices and implementing information management and technology objectives.

249.   The Office of Internal Oversight Services continued to provide consulting services to Secretariat departments to assist them in changing their work processes and structures, including by completing a report on the integration of global management in conference services (A/59/133) and assessments of the children and armed conflict programme and the human resources reform programme.

Internal audit

250.   The Office of Internal Oversight Services conducted approximately 100 audits and issued five reports to the General Assembly covering a wide range of issues, including peacekeeping operations, the activities of the Office of the United Nations High Commissioner for Refugees, procurement and programme management. As a result of its audit of the Headquarters Committee on Contracts, the Office of Internal Oversight Services made recommendations for improving the efficiency of the review process (A/58/294). In its report on the audit of the Office of the Prosecutor of the International Tribunals for Rwanda and the Former Yugoslavia (A/58/677), which was still a joint office at the time, it recommended strengthening planning and monitoring activities and expediting the recruitment of senior officials. Two audit reports submitted to the General Assembly dealt with the administration of peacekeeping trust funds (A/58/613) and the policies and procedures for recruiting Department of Peacekeeping Operations staff (A/58/704).

Investigations

251.   In September 2003, the Investigations Division of the Office of Internal Oversight Services opened a new office at the United Nations Office at Vienna. Approximately 90 per cent of cases investigated by the Division are located away from Headquarters. With the move of most of the Headquarters-based investigators to the new location, the Division has been able to realize substantial cost savings and be in closer contact with many of the offices for which it conducts investigations.

252.   At my request, an investigation was conducted into allegations that the United Nations had possession of a cockpit voice recorder ("black box") from the Falcon 50 aircraft that was carrying the Presidents of Rwanda and Burundi when it crashed on 6 April 1994, precipitating the Rwandan genocide. A cockpit voice recorder had indeed been stored at the United Nations since 1994, but the investigation revealed that it was not from the presidential aircraft and did not contain any relevant information about the crash of that aircraft.

253.   The Investigations Division is leading the Investigation Task Force in Kosovo, which was established as a result of last year's investigation into the fraudulent diversion of $4.3 million by a senior staff member of the reconstruction pillar of the United Nations Interim Administration Mission in Kosovo (see A/58/592 and Corr.1). As a joint investigative body, the Task Force is mandated to initiate, conduct and coordinate investigations to identify fraud and corruption involving funds from the Kosovo consolidated budget. The Anti-Fraud Office of the European Union and the Financial Investigation Unit of UNMIK, composed of police from the Guardia di Finanza of Italy, are the other members of the Task Force. This initiative is being run in close collaboration with the senior management of UNMIK so that corrective action can be taken promptly.

254.   On 21 April 2004, I appointed a high-level Independent Inquiry Committee to investigate allegations of impropriety in the administration and management of the oil-for-food programme in Iraq. To ensure a thorough and meticulous inquiry, the members of the Committee have access to all relevant United Nations records and information and the authority to interview all relevant officials and personnel. The Committee is authorized to obtain records and interviews from persons unaffiliated with the United Nations who may have knowledge relevant to the inquiry and to seek cooperation from Member States in the conduct of its inquiry. I was encouraged by the unanimous welcoming of the

Committee's appointment by the Security Council through its resolution 1538(2004) and its calling upon the Coalition Provisional Authority, Iraq and all other Member States, including their national regulatory authorities, to cooperate fully with the inquiry.

Strengthening the Organization

255. The implementation of my agenda for further change, submitted to the General Assembly two years ago, is now largely complete. Last autumn, I submitted a progress report to the Assembly at its fifty-eighth session (A/58/351), along with a number of subsidiary reports on specific reform proposals. The programme budget proposal for the biennium 2004-2005 debated by the Assembly last autumn reflected an alignment of activities of the Organization with the priorities agreed upon at the Millennium Summit and the global conferences of the 1990s. It also reflected a major reorganization of two large departments—the Department for General Assembly and Conference Management and the Department of Public Information—and the discontinuation of a large number of reports, meetings and activities of marginal utility. In terms of resources, more than $100 million was reallocated within or between programmes and significant increases in the funds dedicated to information and communication technology and staff training were approved.

256. Reporting is one area in which measurable improvements have been made. Efforts to consolidate reports for the fifty-eighth session of the General Assembly resulted in a 13 per cent reduction in the number of reports. An additional reduction of 16 per cent is proposed for the fifty-ninth session. In the area of public information, the structural changes made to the Department of Public Information are beginning to show results—with more focused attention being given to priority activities and better leveraging of technology. A single regional information hub was established in Brussels in January 2004, replacing nine under-resourced and disparate centres located throughout Western Europe. Further efforts to consolidate the network of information centres in other regions will proceed in the coming year.

257. With regard to the planning and budgeting system, a two-year strategic framework replaced the four-year medium-term plan. The first proposed strategic framework, for the period 2006-2007, will be submitted to the General Assembly at its fifty-ninth session. In addition, processes for programme planning and resource allocation are now better aligned and the intergovernmental review process has been streamlined. The budget document for 2004-2005 was considerably shorter than in previous bienniums and was better presented. In late 2004, Member States were also expected to consider specific measures to improve the system of monitoring and evaluation, another important element in the planning and budgeting cycle.

258. The reforms introduced in the Office of the United Nations High Commissioner for Human Rights are described in some detail in chapter V, including proposed measures to strengthen national protection systems, improve treaty implementation and enhance the management of the Office. The question of strengthening support for rapporteurs and the special procedures system remains a priority policy issue. The new High Commissioner will address this and other concerns, in particular as regards the staffing of her Office, in the coming year.

259. Two major reports arising out of the 2002 reform package were completed in the past year: one that clarifies the Organization's roles and responsibilities in technical cooperation on a number of selected issues and the other reflecting the work of the Panel of Eminent Persons on United Nations–Civil Society Relations. Considerable follow-up work will be needed, particularly on the latter report, since the Panel's recommendations have important institutional and systemic implications for the United Nations. Chapter VII contains additional details on the Panel's findings and proposed next steps.

260. The funds and programmes have made further progress in strengthening their presence at the country level. Measures include the development of guidelines for joint programming and identification of lessons learned in countries emerging from conflict. Modalities for the joint management of resources, knowledge-sharing systems and strengthening of the resident coordinators are being developed.

261. A comprehensive report on the progress made to implement the 10 building blocks of the Organization's human resources strategy will be considered by the General Assembly in late 2004. Concerning specific proposals contained in the 2002 package, implementation is in progress. For example, measures to harmonize contracts and benefits for staff in the field have been developed; however, the financial impact of those proposals is still under review. Practical measures to improve opportunities for General Service staff are being developed, within the restrictions imposed by recent resolutions of the General Assembly. A review of delegated authority has pointed to the need for more explicit guidance from the Department of Management on management and administrative functions. Better

systems of monitoring are also anticipated—including the reconfiguration of the Organization's Accountability Panel—and more attention will be given to managerial training.

262. I would also like to draw attention to a recent review conducted by the General Accounting Office of the United States Government on the progress of United Nations reform. It is encouraging to note that, at the time of its review, the Office estimated that 85 per cent of the reforms proposed in the 1997 and 2002 reform packages had been either fully or partly implemented.

Chapter VII

Partnerships

Communication

263. As detailed in my previous report on the work of the Organization, the Department of Public Information has undergone a major reorganization of its priorities, structures and processes. Its new operating model is based on the premise that its role is to manage and coordinate the content of United Nations communications and to strategically convey this content to achieve the greatest public impact. Through the reorganization process, the Department has acquired the tools it needed to deliver on the challenges I set for it in my 2002 report entitled "Strengthening of the United Nations: an agenda for further change (A/57/387 and Corr.1)". After a period of transition, initial problems with the new structures and processes have been overcome. The reformed and restructured Department now understands what is expected of it, is mastering the means to deliver on those expectations and has gained practical experience in their execution. It is ready to apply the lessons learned, as well as its new-found confidence, to further improve the products and services it offers.

264. In December 2003, through its resolution 58/101 B, the General Assembly endorsed my proposals regarding the rationalization of the network of United Nations information centres around the world and laid out a clear sequence of steps to be undertaken by the Department of Public Information to implement those proposals. The first such step was the creation of a regional United Nations information centre for Western Europe, established on 1 January 2004 in Brussels immediately following the closure of nine Western European information centres on 31 December 2003. With the establishment of this modern and adequately resourced centre, the Organization will, for the first time, be able to properly implement a robust, coherent and coordinated public information outreach programme throughout Western Europe.

265. I have asked the Department of Public Information to review the Western European experience to derive lessons that may be valuable as we continue the process of regionalization of the United Nations information centres. It is clear that the regional model that will ultimately be applied in the developing world will differ from that used in Western Europe, as the needs of each region are different. At this stage, I envisage the establishment, in consultation with Member States, of a significant number of smaller hubs in key media centres throughout the developing world, with sites chosen and resources allocated in such a way as to ensure that distance and linguistic diversity do not hamper their operations.

266. A feature of United Nations information activities over the past 12 months was the establishment of small expert groups to deal with the public information consequences of emerging crises. These groups, generally with participants from the Department of Public Information and the relevant substantive offices of the Secretariat, are guided by senior management and provide strategic advice and guidance on how we might publicly address the crises in question. Another group, composed of United Nations system information officers from the Middle East and the Arab world, held two meetings and developed a strategic plan to bolster the flagging image of the Organization in that region.

267. The importance of effective public information for the success of peacekeeping operations was underlined as the Secretariat sought to ensure that the United Nations was equipped to meet the recent dramatic surge in demand for such operations. The Department of Public Information, in fulfilling its responsibilities with regard to the public information aspects of peacekeeping, has set in place new strategies aimed at generating support for new and expanding operations among Member States, the general public and the local populations in the areas where such operations are deployed.

268. To implement the aforementioned strategies, there is an increasing need to rapidly deploy expert public information personnel to new field missions. Preliminary training of United Nations staff who could be deployed rapidly to peacekeeping missions was conducted at the United Nations Logistics Base at Brindisi in June, under the auspices of the Department of Public Information and with funding from the United Kingdom of Great Britain and Northern Ireland. I hope to continue this training to ensure that we have a full cadre of qualified staff avail-

able when needed. Training has also been provided to information staff currently serving with United Nations peacekeeping missions on ways to support specific mission priorities, such as disarmament, demobilization and reintegration. Experts from the Department of Public Information now take part, as a matter of course, in multidisciplinary assessment missions that precede the deployment of peacekeeping or political missions. In the past 12 months, assessment missions to Burundi, Côte d'Ivoire, Haiti, Liberia and the Sudan have benefited from input by public information officers, and a preliminary media needs-assessment mission was undertaken to Iraq.

269. A number of new techniques and activities have been employed to increase the scope of United Nations outreach. The use of external public venues for United Nations observances and commemorations has proved to be a most successful innovation, quadrupling attendance at the annual New York observance of World AIDS Day (1 December), for example.

270. Similarly, the use of multi-site videoconferences and Internet exchanges, linking students and civil society partners around the world, has boosted our capacity to encourage public dialogue on many important issues. Special web events held in the lead-up to and during the first phase of the World Summit for the Information Society (Geneva, December 2003), attracted large and enthusiastic participation from students in many countries. The annual Department of Public Information Non-Governmental Organizations Conference, which brought a record 2,000 representatives from civil society organizations from 86 countries to New York, was followed by many more interested organizations and individuals via a live webcast.

271. Another innovative means used to promote public understanding of the work of the Organization was allowing the filming on location at United Nations Headquarters of *The Interpreter*, a feature film. This decision was taken after considerable thought and discussion, and ultimately rested on the assessment that the net result would be increased awareness of the United Nations among a broad audience.

272. In an effort to focus attention on important issues that often go underreported, the Department of Public Information launched a list of "10 stories the world should hear more about". Featured on the list was the plight of child soldiers in Uganda, the crisis in the Central African Republic, developments that may lead to a new treaty on the rights of the disabled and the threat posed by overfishing to the livelihoods of 200 million people worldwide. The initiative received a positive response from United Nations offices and agencies that contributed ideas to the project and succeeded in drawing the attention of numerous news organizations both to the specific stories themselves and to the broader question of what role the media plays in raising public awareness.

273. The Dag Hammarskjöld Library employed technology to upgrade its products, with its UNBISnet catalogue now linked to the full text of all documents on the Official Document System, in all six official languages. Additional links have been provided in the index to speeches to the full text of speeches and in the voting records to the full texts of resolutions. A thorough revision of the voting records database, currently under way, is expected to be completed by the end of 2004.

274. The continuous development and improvement of the United Nations web site allows us to harness the power of the Internet towards familiarizing more people around the world with the work of our Organization and issues of common concern. In 2003 the site recorded over 2,100 million hits, compared to 1,695 million hits in 2002. On an average day, over 940,000 pages are viewed by users. Substantial increases in visits to the various language sites were also recorded in the course of 2003: 126 per cent for Arabic, 792 per cent for Chinese, 77 per cent for English, 108 per cent for French, 173 per cent for Russian and 115 per cent for Spanish. The size of these increases reflects the phenomenal growth in overall Internet use in such countries as China, as well as the significant measures taken by the Secretariat to promote multilingualism by making more pages available in all the official languages. The introduction of a new search engine that can be employed for searching in all official languages is also making it much easier to locate relevant materials.

275. To facilitate movement towards parity among the official languages, the Department of Public Information has been establishing partnerships with academic institutions that provide pro bono translations. Agreements have already been signed with Minsk State Linguistic University (Belarus), Shaoxing University (China) and the University of Salamanca (Spain). Discussions with possible partners on arrangements that would enhance the Arabic language site are well under way.

276. Special measures are being implemented to improve access to content on the web site for users with disabilities. Technical guidelines have been drafted by a working group of the Publications Board, and all content-providing

offices are being encouraged to conform with them to the maximum extent possible.

277. The United Nations News Centre online portal, which is now available in all official languages, continues to draw a steadily growing number of visitors. The stories posted there by News Services Section staff appear with ever greater frequency on the web sites of various United Nations offices and agencies, as well as major media outlets, non-governmental organizations and other external entities. The portal's e-mail news service in English and French now has over 25,000 subscribers in more than 100 countries. This service should be available in all official languages before the end of 2004.

278. Turning to our more traditional outreach activities, it is encouraging to note that after a dip in the number of visitors to United Nations Headquarters in the wake of the events of 11 September 2001, the number of people taking guided tours rose again in the period covered by the present report.

279. United Nations Radio continues to provide daily and weekly news reports and features in the six official languages, as well as Portuguese and Kiswahili, to hundreds of radio stations around the globe. Weekly programmes in seven other non-official languages are also distributed. The audience for this programming is conservatively estimated at 200 million people. The radio service is expanding the material on offer with a new programme on Africa and the development of a dramatic programme for children.

280. United Nations Television estimates that an audience of 2 billion people sees its programming, including hundreds of hours of coverage supplied to the world's broadcasters through daily feeds covering meetings of the General Assembly, the Security Council and other events and conferences. Through an expanding network of partnerships with major broadcasters, United Nations Television's productions of "World Chronicle" (a weekly talk show), "UN in Action" (a series of features on the work of the United Nations system) and the annual "Year in Review" have enjoyed larger audiences than ever before, as have its latest productions: "The United Nations: Working for Us All" and "The Security Council: Keeping the Peace".

281. Over the past year, the Department of Public Information has also co-produced a series of public service announcements in connection with the observance of 13 international days. These announcements, produced in association with an outside partner, were distributed to 200 television broadcasters in 70 countries and received positive feedback.

United Nations Fund for International Partnerships

282. The successful partnership between the United Nations Fund for International Partnerships and the United Nations Foundation entered into its seventh year in March 2004. Since the inception of this partnership in 1998 and until the end of 2003, a total of $563 million had been allocated to fund 292 projects with activities in 121 countries and involving 35 United Nations entities. The cumulative amount of co-financing from other funding partners, such as multilateral and bilateral donors, was $187.4 million. Projects have been funded worldwide in four programme areas: children's health; population and women; environment; and peace, security and human rights.

283. Over time, the focus of the UNF-UNFIP partnership has developed from the exclusive programming and funding of individual projects to also "telling the story" of such projects and of the work of the United Nations in general. The Foundation plays a unique advocacy role by virtue of its ability to increase understanding of the United Nations on the part of potential partners and the public. At the same time, the Foundation's extrabudgetary contributions are able to be used in ways that core funds cannot, opening up possibilities for innovation and creativity that the Organization alone would not be able to provide. Through UNF matching grants, new partners have come forward to collaborate on United Nations causes in a range of areas, such as protecting biodiversity, preserving World Heritage sites and combating disease.

284. Building on a series of innovative initiatives, UNF, the Coalition for Environmentally Responsible Economies, UNEP and UNFIP hosted the Institutional Investor Summit on Climate Risk in November 2003. The Summit brought together 200 pension fund managers, United States state treasurers, government officials, business executives, representatives of non-governmental organizations and senior United Nations staff to explore the connection between climate risk and fiduciary responsibility. It culminated in the signing of a 10-point call to action by key participants with responsibility for over $1 trillion in assets.

285. As a result of the success of the UNF-UNFIP partnership, UNFIP now functions as a clearing house for partnership information and a facilitator of funding opportunities for the United Nations. Increasingly, UNFIP provides a full range of services to build key networks, alliances and partnerships. A recent example of this is the Citigroup Private Bank partnership with UNDP. This collaboration brought a dozen of the

Bank's clients to Mozambique and South Africa in April 2004 to explore opportunities to support the United Nations projects they visited.

286. UNFIP often provides advice to the private sector and foundations on United Nations policies and procedures, as well as suggestions on strategic ways for external entities to support the achievement of the Millennium Development Goals. In 2003, UNFIP was instrumental in getting the European Foundation Centre (an umbrella organization of over 500 foundations) to adopt the Goals as their framework for action, with an emphasis on supporting the fight against HIV/AIDS. New partnerships were established with a number of institutions, foundations and corporations, including the Citigroup Private Bank and Citigroup Foundation, the Committee to Encourage Corporate Philanthropy, the Council on Foundations, the Education Development Centre, Europe in the World, Hewlett-Packard, the Hilton Foundation, Microsoft, the Network of European Foundations for Innovative Cooperation, Pricewaterhouse-Coopers, the United States Chamber of Commerce and Vodafone.

287. In 2004, UNFIP assumed responsibility for providing support to my Special Adviser on Sport for Development and Peace, particularly with regard to his activities aimed at promoting field-level projects using sport as a tool for development.

Project services

288. In a multi-year effort initiated in 2003, the United Nations Office for Project Services set out to strengthen its financial condition, improve its competitive edge and streamline people, processes and technologies to acquire new business and meet client and market needs cost-effectively and efficiently. To position UNOPS for long-term viability, its management must make a series of strategic investments in 2004 and 2005. The goal is to recast UNOPS as a client-centred organization that contributes effectively to the realization of the Millennium Development Goals and the broader peace and development agenda of the United Nations.

289. In terms of 2003 performance, UNOPS continued to adhere to its self-financing principle. Total project delivery for 2003 amounted to $490.6 million, with revenue totalling $66.2 million and expenditures $47.8 million. UNDP remained the primary client of UNOPS, which continued to be a valued partner also of the International Fund for Agricultural Development and other lending institutions because of its acknowledged expertise in loan supervision and disbursements.

Civil society and business partnerships

290. After a year of extensive consultations at the country, regional and global levels, my Panel of Eminent Persons on United Nations–Civil Society Relations submitted its report entitled "We the peoples: civil society, the United Nations and global governance" (A/58/817). The Panel based its proposals on four main principles, namely, that the United Nations needed: to become a more outward-looking organization in response to the changing nature of multilateralism; to embrace a plurality of constituencies and establish new partnerships to tackle global challenges; to connect the global goals with local reality; and to accept a more explicit role in strengthening global governance, emphasizing participatory democracy and deeper accountability of institutions to the global public. Building on those principles, the Panel made a total of 30 proposals in the following areas: the convening role of the United Nations—fostering multi-constituency processes; investing more in partnerships; focusing on the country level; strengthening Security Council dialogue with civil society; engaging with elected representatives and parliamentarians; streamlining and depoliticizing civil society accreditation and access to the United Nations; providing the necessary additional resources; and providing global leadership in enhancing engagement with civil society.

291. The Panel's report is a valuable contribution to the reform process of the United Nations. I am particularly pleased that the Panel has proposed a number of concrete ways of increasing the participation of civil society representatives from developing countries, strengthening partnerships with civil society in the humanitarian and development areas and encouraging greater involvement of parliamentarians in the work of the United Nations. As the Panel suggests, the effectiveness and the relevance of the Organization would increase if we found ways to strengthen the involvement and participation of civil society. I intend to submit to the General Assembly, at its fifty-ninth session, further comments and suggestions regarding practical steps that might be taken in response to the Panel's recommendations.

292. The past year witnessed rapid growth in the Global Compact, the corporate citizenship initiative I launched in July 2000 to advance universal principles in the areas of human rights, labour conditions and the environment. An impact assessment undertaken by the international consultancy McKinsey & Company observed that the Global Compact, with more than 1,500 companies from 70 countries, was the largest corporate citizenship initiative in the world. Moreover,

the assessment concluded that the Global Compact had, overall, had a positive impact by encouraging companies to adopt or enhance policies related to social and environmental issues while galvanizing partnerships between businesses, labour groups, civil society organizations and other stakeholders.

293. A major milestone was the Global Compact Leaders Summit, which I convened on 24 June at United Nations Headquarters. With nearly 500 leaders in attendance, it was the largest gathering ever of chief executive officers, government officials and heads of labour and civil society organizations on the topic of global corporate citizenship. One of the most noteworthy Summit outcomes was the adoption of the tenth Global Compact principle, dealing with anti-corruption. The Compact thus entered the worldwide fight against corruption, a scourge whose main victims are the world's poor. There was a range of other important outcomes, chief among them: (a) a pledge by 20 major financial companies to begin integrating social, environmental and governance issues into investment analysis and decision-making; (b) an announcement by a number of stock exchanges that they would explore collaboration with the Global Compact, with many agreeing to actively share information on the Compact and on corporate responsibility with their listed companies; and (c) an announcement by the Department of Management of the Secretariat that the Global Compact's principles would be adopted in key areas of the Organization's administration, such as procurement, investment management, facilities management and human resources.

294. The Summit also featured calls to improve the accountability and integrity of the initiative. Leaders from several civil society organizations expressed keen concern about the Global Compact's credibility, urging that the initiative further explore ways to ensure that the commitments by companies to the Global Compact's principles are translated into concrete and transparent action. Indeed, it is crucial that the reputation of the United Nations not be threatened or harmed by a failure to focus on quality assurance. Therefore, I announced at the Summit that the Global Compact Office would begin a process to improve the overall governance of the initiative in order to provide such safeguards. It is also clear the Global Compact's more than 40 country networks hold great promise. Moving forward, the Global Compact Office will focus on helping to make such local networks truly dynamic and sustainable. They will be key assets as we strive to realize the vision of the Global Compact: a more sustainable and inclusive global economy.

Chapter VIII

Conclusion

295. As the present report demonstrates, the United Nations has continued to carry out a wide range of activities in difficult times, consistent with the principles and purposes of its Charter. These activities reflect all the major international problems and concerns, and are a part of the struggle for a world of greater justice. Despite formidable challenges and obstacles, the Organization's efforts are helping us to build a better future.

296. The architects of the Charter were guided by a central idea—that durable international peace could be built only on foundations of interdependence. Underpinning this idea was the rule of law and multilateralism as the only rational basis for civilized discourse among nations. Shared responsibility was at the heart of the United Nations Millennium Declaration adopted in September 2000. Much has changed since the Millennium Summit, and even more since the Charter was adopted. Yet the values of interdependence and shared responsibility remain fundamental.

297. Next year we will celebrate the sixtieth anniversary of the United Nations. It will provide an opportunity for fresh thinking about the problems of our world and how the Organization can address them. It is my hope that in the coming months, Member States, the Secretariat and other entities of the United Nations system, civil society and business organizations, as well as individuals around the world will work together to ensure that the anniversary will be worthy of the United Nations and everything for which it stands.

PART ONE

Political and security questions

Chapter I

International peace and security

In 2004, the resolve of the international community to promote and maintain international peace and security continued to be tested by new acts of international terrorism, the unstable security situation in Iraq, a deteriorating Israeli-Palestinian conflict, a surge in violent internal conflicts in Africa and Haiti, and questions about the effectiveness of the Organization's response to those and other situations. In August, the General Assembly reaffirmed the central role of the United Nations in the maintenance of international peace and security and the promotion of international cooperation, and, in December, the Secretary-General submitted to the Assembly a report entitled "A more secure world: our shared responsibility" by the High-level Panel on Threats, Challenges and Change, which he had appointed in 2003 to evaluate UN performance in addressing threats and challenges to international security and to make recommendations for strengthening the Organization. The Panel offered a vision of a United Nations for the twenty-first century and made recommendations for change in each of its principal organs, including the Security Council, and proposed the establishment of a new intergovernmental body, the Peace-building Commission. Also, the Assembly, recalling that 2005 would mark the sixtieth anniversary of the end of the Second World War, declared 8 and 9 May as a time of remembrance and reconciliation to be observed annually and decided to hold a solemn meeting in May 2005 in commemoration of all victims of the war.

The devastating consequences of international terrorism continued to be felt in 2004, with particularly vicious incidents in Spain and the Russian Federation. The Security Council condemned those atrocities and urged that those responsible be brought to justice. To counter the continuing threat posed by international terrorism, the Council established a working group to make recommendations on measures it could impose on individuals, groups and entities involved or associated with terrorist activities, including more effective procedures for prosecuting them and seizing their assets. It called for the establishment of an international fund to compensate victims of terrorist acts and their families. The Council also adopted measures to revitalize and strengthen the Counter-Terrorism Committee,

including the creation of the Counter-Terrorism Committee Executive Directorate and the appointment of an Executive Director.

The Council considered ways to improve the quality of the UN response in complex crises. It also examined the Organization's conflict prevention activities, including the role of diamonds in fuelling conflict and the progress made in implementing the Kimberley Process for the certification of rough diamonds, and the role of businesses in conflict prevention, peacekeeping and post-conflict peace-building. In the area of post-conflict peace-building, the Council met at ministerial level to examine the civilian aspects of conflict management and peace-building. It also considered the role of civil society in post-conflict peace-building, the UN role in post-conflict national reconciliation, the rule of law and transitional justice in conflict and post-conflict situations, and UN cooperation with regional organizations to maximize efficiency in stabilization processes.

The Organization maintained 14 political and peace-building missions during 2004. The surge in demand for UN peacekeeping forces in 2004, with the establishment of new and complex operations in Burundi, Côte d'Ivoire and Haiti, in quick succession, posed a serious challenge to the Organization's capacity for effective planning, timely deployment, management and the provision of sustained support for such operations. In May, the Council studied those challenges during its consideration of strategic directions and future trends of peacekeeping operations. The Council also considered the recommendations of the Special Committee on Peacekeeping Operations, which met in March/April to discuss comprehensive strategies for complex peacekeeping operations, enhancing UN peacekeeping capacity and that of African peacekeeping, consultations with troop-contributing countries, safety and security issues in the light of the 2003 bombing of the UN headquarters in Iraq, the contribution of regional arrangements to the management of UN peacemaking missions, and gender mainstreaming in peacekeeping operations. At the end of 2004, 64,701 military and civilian police were serving under UN command in 16 peacekeeping missions, compared to 45,815 at the end of 2003.

The financial position of UN peacekeeping operations was significantly affected by the rapid expansion of peacekeeping activities. During the reporting period, expenditures increased to $2,933.8 million, compared to a final figure of $2,499.8 million for the previous year. Unpaid assessed contributions increased to $1.5 billion, compared to $1.1 billion the previous year. The Assembly considered several aspects of peacekeeping financing, including the peacekeeping support account, the disposition of the assets of closed missions, the peacekeeping Reserve Fund, experience with the creation of regional hubs of auditors and investigators for financial oversight of peacekeeping operations, and reimbursement issues. It also considered the management of peacekeeping assets, including the financing of the United Nations Logistics Base and the strategic deployment stocks, an analysis of the establishment of a global procurement hub for all peacekeeping missions, the question of air safety in the procurement of aircraft, and policies and procedures for the recruitment of peacekeeping staff.

Promotion of international peace and security

UN role in the maintenance of international peace and security

On 5 August [meeting 93], the General Assembly met to consider, under the agenda item "Strengthening of the United Nations system", a draft resolution [A/58/L.67/Rev.1] on reaffirming the central role of the United Nations in the maintenance of international peace and security and the promotion of international cooperation.

Malaysia, in introducing the draft on behalf of the Non-Aligned Movement, said that developments in global affairs in recent years raised serious concerns about the primacy of the United Nations, its relevance in multilateral decision-making, and the gradual erosion of its role as the primary interlocutor in addressing global challenges and in fulfilling its responsibilities as envisaged in the Charter. That view had been emphasized by world leaders before the Assembly in September 2003 and was echoed by the general public, civil society and mass media worldwide. The draft resolution was a broad-based initiative for Member States to reaffirm their support for and political commitment and adherence to the central role of the United Nations in fulfilling its role and responsibilities; it provided a strong pol-itical platform that would enhance the Organization's role in the maintenance of peace and security and the promotion of economic and social development.

Canada said that the draft resolution, despite its stated intent, would not strengthen the role and capacity of the United Nations. It went beyond just renewing commitment to the ideals and purposes of the United Nations; it was interpretative of those ideals and purposes and disregarded elements that would impart sufficient balance to attract consensus. Its selectivity risked undermining, or at least complicating, the Assembly's work on key issues linked to the new realities of the international environment and could contribute to the United Nations seeing the world through outdated and blurred lenses.

GENERAL ASSEMBLY ACTION

On 5 August [meeting 93], the Assembly adopted **resolution 58/317** [draft: A/58/L.67/Rev.1] by recorded vote (93-2-47) [agenda item 59].

Reaffirming the central role of the United Nations in the maintenance of international peace and security and the promotion of international cooperation

The General Assembly,

Bearing in mind the Charter of the United Nations, including the purposes and principles contained therein, and especially the determination to save succeeding generations from the scourge of war, and emphasizing its paramount importance for the maintenance of international peace and security and the development of friendly relations and cooperation among States,

Considering that the promotion of respect for the obligations arising from the Charter and other instruments and rules of international law is among the basic purposes and principles of the United Nations, and in this context recalling the Declaration on Principles of International Law concerning Friendly Relations and Cooperation among States in accordance with the Charter of the United Nations, annexed to its resolution 2625(XXV) of 24 October 1970,

Recalling the United Nations Millennium Declaration, adopted by heads of State and Government at the Millennium Summit of the United Nations on 8 September 2000,

Reaffirming its determination to establish and maintain a just and lasting international peace and security in accordance with the Charter and relevant resolutions of the United Nations, upholding the need to abide strictly by the relevant provisions of the Charter on the sovereign equality of all Member States, respect for their territorial integrity and political independence and non-interference in their internal affairs, the non-use of force or threat of force, resolution of disputes by peaceful means in conformity with the principles of justice and international law, the right to self-determination of peoples remaining under colonial or other forms of alien domination or foreign occupation, respect for human rights and fundamental freedoms, respect for the equal rights of all without distinction as to race, sex, language or religion, and international cooperation in solving international problems of an economic, social, cultural or humanitarian character, and convinced that development can be achieved only in a climate of peace, security and mutual confidence both within and among Member States,

Reiterating that the responsibility for managing and achieving worldwide economic and social development, as well as responding to threats to international peace and security, must be shared among all nations of the world and exercised multilaterally and that, in this context, as the most universal and most representative intergovernmental organization, the United Nations must play the central role,

1. *Reiterates* the need for full observance of the Charter of the United Nations and the unrestricted application of all the principles and the achievement of the purposes that it enshrines, including, inter alia, the principles regarding the sovereign equality of Member States and the necessity of respecting the political independence of nations, and reaffirms the central role of the United Nations in the maintenance of international peace and security and the strengthening of international cooperation in conformity with the Charter;

2. *Reaffirms* the irreplaceable role of the United Nations and the necessity of ensuring the equal participation of all Member States, in a transparent manner, in a multilateral system, guided by the Charter and founded on universally recognized values and norms;

3. *Also reaffirms* its commitment to multilateralism, which entails, inter alia, respect for the Charter and the principles and norms of international law and the adoption of measures to prevent the use or the threat of use of force and the exercise of pressure and coercion as a means for obtaining certain political objectives, and in this context underlines the fact that Member States have committed themselves to refraining in their international relations from the threat or use of force against the territorial integrity or political independence of any State, or in any other manner inconsistent with the purposes of the United Nations, and to upholding the principle of settlement of international disputes by peaceful means in such a manner as not to endanger international peace and security and justice, bearing in mind the need to allay the legitimate concern of Member States with regard to ensuring lasting safety and security for their peoples;

4. *Re-emphasizes* the respective prerogatives and functions of the General Assembly, the Security Council and the Economic and Social Council as defined in the Charter, and the need to enhance the coordination among these organs, which constitute the framework for the achievement of the purposes of the United Nations, and underlines its conviction regarding the need to sustain as a priority in the process of reform of the United Nations, the revitalization and strengthening of the Assembly and the reforms of the Security Council and the Economic and Social Council, with a view to strengthening further the capacity of the United Nations so as to enable it to improve its performance in undertaking its functions and responsibilities, mindful, in this context, of the need to involve all Member States in these processes in order to ensure that their perspectives, concerns and interests will be taken fully into account;

5. *Welcomes* the establishment by the Secretary-General of the High-level Panel on Threats, Challenges and Change, and takes note of its terms of reference;

6. *Calls upon* all States to cooperate fully through constructive dialogue in order to ensure the full enjoyment, promotion and protection of all human rights and fundamental freedoms for all, as well as in the promotion of the peaceful resolution of international problems, including those of a humanitarian character, the prevention and end of genocide, crimes against humanity and war crimes and the prosecution of those responsible for such crimes, and, in their actions towards that purpose, calls upon them to comply strictly with the principles and norms of international law, inter alia, by fully respecting their obligations under international human rights instruments and humanitarian law;

7. *Reaffirms* the right to self-determination of peoples that remain under colonial or other forms of alien domination or foreign occupation, in conformity with the Charter and the relevant resolutions of the United Nations;

8. *Expresses its deep concern* over any act or threat of foreign intervention or occupation of any State or territory in contravention of the Charter;

9. *Underlines* the need to strengthen the capacity of the United Nations in the areas of prevention and resolution of armed conflict, including relevant peace-building and development activities, as well as in the areas of peacemaking and peacekeeping, in accordance with the Charter, and calls for the building up of consensus among Member States in defining the scope, orientation and needs of such capacity in the light of current and evolving challenges and threats to international peace and security, taking into consideration, in this context, the need for partnership between the United Nations and relevant regional and subregional intergovernmental organizations in accordance with Chapter VIII of the Charter;

10. *Reaffirms* the important role of women in the prevention and resolution of conflicts and in peace-building, and stresses the importance of their full and equal participation in all efforts to maintain and promote peace and security and the need to increase their role in decision-making with regard to conflict prevention and resolution and the rebuilding of post-conflict societies;

11. *Condemns* acts of terrorism in all its forms and manifestations, wherever and by whomsoever committed, reiterates its call upon all States to adopt and implement further measures to prevent terrorism and to strengthen international cooperation in combating terrorism, and reaffirms that measures taken by States must be in accordance with the Charter and must comply with their obligations under international law and the relevant resolutions of the United Nations;

12. *Reaffirms* the importance of achieving the total elimination of all weapons of mass destruction globally, in particular nuclear weapons, which pose the greatest danger to mankind and the survival of civilization, reiterates in this context its deep concern over the slow pace of progress towards nuclear disarmament, emphasizes that the achievement of genuine peace and security demands that the policies of States be directed towards the elimination of the threat of war, in particular nuclear war, bearing also in mind all the resulting predictable consequences of the resurgence of a new

arms race among States, also reaffirms the need for all
Member States to fulfil their obligations in relation to
arms control and disarmament and to prevent the proliferation in all its aspects of weapons of mass destruction, and further reaffirms that the ultimate objective
of the efforts of States in the disarmament process is
general and complete disarmament;

13. *Reiterates its call upon* all States urging them, as
well as the relevant United Nations bodies, to take appropriate measures to fully implement the Programme of
Action to Prevent, Combat and Eradicate the Illicit Trade
in Small Arms and Light Weapons in All Its Aspects;

14. *Emphasizes* that the United Nations has a central
role in promoting and coordinating international cooperation for development, as well as in the follow-up
to international economic affairs and the outcome of
the major United Nations conferences and summits in
the economic and social fields and in promoting policy
coherence on global economic, social and development issues, in consonance with the relevant provisions
of the Charter, and expresses its commitment to work
for the strengthening of its role as coordinator of the
efforts carried out by the international community in
this regard, with a view to ensuring the achievement of
a fair, democratic, transparent and equitable international economic environment, in which the opportunities offered by globalization are to the advantage of all
countries, in particular the developing countries.

RECORDED VOTE ON RESOLUTION 58/317:

In favour: Algeria, Angola, Antigua and Barbuda, Argentina, Armenia,
Azerbaijan, Bahrain, Barbados, Belarus, Bhutan, Bolivia, Brazil, Brunei
Darussalam, Burundi, Cambodia, Cameroon, Cape Verde, Chile, China,
Colombia, Costa Rica, Côte d'Ivoire, Cuba, Democratic People's Republic
of Korea, Djibouti, Dominica, Dominican Republic, Ecuador, Egypt, El Sal-
vador, Gambia, Ghana, Grenada, Guatemala, Guyana, Haiti, Honduras,
India, Indonesia, Iran, Jamaica, Jordan, Kenya, Kuwait, Kyrgyzstan, Lao
People's Democratic Republic, Lebanon, Lesotho, Madagascar, Malay-
sia, Maldives, Mali, Mauritania, Mauritius, Mexico, Micronesia, Mongo-
lia, Morocco, Mozambique, Myanmar, Namibia, Nepal, Nicaragua, Nige-
ria, Oman, Pakistan, Panama, Paraguay, Peru, Philippines, Qatar, Russian
Federation, Saint Lucia, Saudi Arabia, Senegal, Singapore, South Africa,
Sri Lanka, Sudan, Suriname, Syrian Arab Republic, Thailand, Timor-
Leste, Togo, Trinidad and Tobago, Tunisia, United Arab Emirates, United
Republic of Tanzania, Venezuela, Viet Nam, Yemen, Zambia, Zimbabwe.

Against: Israel, United States.

Abstaining: Albania, Andorra, Australia, Austria, Belgium, Bosnia and
Herzegovina, Bulgaria, Canada, Croatia, Cyprus, Czech Republic, Den-
mark, Finland, France, Germany, Greece, Hungary, Iceland, Ireland, Italy,
Japan, Latvia, Liechtenstein, Lithuania, Luxembourg, Malta, Marshall Is-
lands, Monaco, Netherlands, New Zealand, Norway, Poland, Portugal,
Republic of Korea, Romania, San Marino, Serbia and Montenegro,
Slovakia, Slovenia, Spain, Sweden, Switzerland, The former Yugoslav
Republic of Macedonia, Tonga, Turkey, Ukraine, United Kingdom.

The United States, speaking after the vote, declared that the resolution was premature since it
attempted to address a matter that was currently
being reviewed by the High-level Panel on
Threats, Challenges and Change (see below).
Furthermore, it reaffirmed some principles of
international law and not others, thus rendering
the text incomplete.

High-level Panel on Threats,
Challenges and Change

In a December note [A/59/565 & Corr.1], the
Secretary-General transmitted to the General Assembly the report of the High-level Panel on
Threats, Challenges and Change entitled "A
more secure world: our shared responsibility".
He appointed the Panel in 2003 [YUN 2003, p. 49] to
evaluate how existing UN policies and institutions had performed in addressing threats and
challenges to international security and to make
recommendations for strengthening the Organization in providing collective security in the
twenty-first century.

The Panel, chaired by Anand Panyarachun
(Thailand), put forward a new vision of collective
security, one that addressed all of the major
threats to international peace and security. It examined the case for a new security consensus, including elements of a credible collective security
system; collective security and the challenge of
prevention; collective security and the use of
force, including questions of legitimacy, peace
enforcement, peacekeeping capability and post-
conflict peace-building; and a more effective
United Nations for the twenty-first century. The
report addressed specific threats and identified
new ways of understanding the connections between them and the implications for the policies
and institutions that had to be put in place.

The Panel concluded that 60 years after the
creation of the United Nations, the biggest
security threats went far beyond States waging
aggressive war, extending to poverty, infectious
disease and environmental degradation; war and
violence within States; the spread and possible
use of nuclear, radiological, chemical and biological weapons; terrorism; and transnational organized crime. Those threats came from both States
and non-State actors. The system of collective
security created by the UN founders was, in a traditional military sense, a pledge for collective
action against aggression. The central challenge
for the twenty-first century was to fashion a new
and broader understanding, bringing together
all the strands of collective security, in order to
form a collective security system that would be
effective, efficient and equitable.

The case for collective security currently
rested on three basic pillars: that threats recognized no national boundaries, were connected,
and had to be addressed at the global, regional
and national levels; no State alone could make itself invulnerable to those threats; and it could not
be assumed that every State would always be able,
or willing, to meet its responsibility to protect its
own peoples and not to harm its neighbours.
Without mutual recognition of threats, there
could be no collective security. What was needed
was a new consensus between frayed alliances, between wealthy and poor nations, and among peoples mired in mistrust across a widening cultural
abyss.

The Panel identified six clusters of threats with which the world should be concerned: economic and social threats, including poverty, infectious diseases and environmental degradation; inter-State conflict; internal conflict, including civil war, genocide and other large-scale atrocities; nuclear, radiological, chemical and biological weapons; terrorism; and transnational organized crime. The primary challenge was to ensure that distant threats did not become imminent and those that were imminent did not become destructive. That required a framework for preventive action, especially leadership at the domestic and international levels to act early, decisively and collectively. Meeting the challenge of prevention had to begin with development because it was the foundation for a collective security system and was vital in helping States prevent or reverse the erosion of State capacity, and was part of a long-term strategy for preventing civil war and for addressing the environments in which both terrorism and organized crime flourished.

The Panel addressed the circumstances in which effective collective security might require the backing of military force. It identified "five criteria of legitimacy" that the Security Council should always consider when deciding to authorize or apply military force. Those guidelines (seriousness of threat, proper purpose, last resort, proportional means and balance of consequences) should significantly improve the chances of reaching international consensus on deeply divisive issues.

In addressing the issue of reforming the United Nations, the Panel found that it was currently just as important as it had been in 1945: to combine power with principle. Recommendations that ignored underlying power realities would be doomed to failure or irrelevance, just as recommendations that simply reflected raw distributions of power and made no effort to bolster international principles were unlikely to gain the widespread adherence required to shift international behaviour. Proposed changes should be driven by real-world need. The Panel identified the institutional weaknesses in current responses to threats as those urgently in need of remedy. The General Assembly had lost vitality and often failed to focus on the most compelling issues of the day. The Security Council needed to be more proactive, with those who contributed most to the Organization financially, militarily and diplomatically participating more in Council decision-making, and those who participated in Council decision-making contributing more to the Organization. The Council needed greater credibility, legitimacy and representation to do all that

was demanded of it. It also needed to avail itself more of the potential advantages of working with regional and subregional organizations. There was a major institutional gap in addressing countries under stress and countries emerging from conflict. There should be new institutional arrangements to address the economic and social threats to international security. The Commission on Human Rights suffered from a legitimacy deficit that cast doubts on the overall reputation of the United Nations. A more professional and better organized Secretariat that was much more capable of concerted action was needed.

The Panel made a number of recommendations for addressing the issues raised in its report. In the area of collective security and the challenge of prevention, it recommended that all States recommit themselves to the goals of eradicating poverty, achieving sustained economic growth and promoting sustainable development. The donor countries not reaching the goal of 0.7 per cent of gross national product for official development assistance should establish a timetable for doing so. World Trade Organization members should strive to conclude the Doha development round of multilateral trade negotiations [YUN 2001, p. 1432] at the latest in 2006. Lender Governments and international financial institutions should provide highly indebted poor countries with greater debt relief, longer debt payment schedules and improved access to global markets. More than $10 billion annually was needed to stem the HIV/AIDS pandemic. Leaders of countries affected by HIV/AIDS needed to mobilize resources, commit funds and engage civil society and the private sector in disease-control efforts. The Security Council, with the Joint United Nations Programme on HIV/AIDS, should host a second special session on HIV/AIDS as a threat to international peace and security, to explore the future effects of HIV/AIDS on States and societies, generate research and identify a long-term strategy for diminishing the threat. International donors, working with national authorities and local civil society organizations, should undertake a new global initiative to rebuild local and national public health systems throughout the developing world. Greater resources should be provided to the World Health Organization Global Outbreak Alert and Response Network to increase its capacity to cope with potential disease outbreaks. States should provide incentives for development of renewable energy sources and begin to phase out environmentally harmful subsidies, especially for fossil fuel. Member States were urged to reflect on the gap between the promise of the Kyoto Protocol [YUN 1997, p. 1048] to the United Nations Framework Convention on Climate Change [YUN 1992, p. 681] and its performance, re-engage on the problem of global warming and begin new negotiations to produce a new long-term strategy for reducing global warming beyond the period covered by the Protocol (up to 2012).

To deal with conflicts between States, the Security Council should use its authority under the Rome Statute of the International Criminal Court [YUN 1998, p. 1209] to refer cases of suspected war crimes and crimes against humanity to the Court. The United Nations should work with national authorities, international financial institutions, civil society organizations and the private sector to develop norms governing the management of natural resources for countries emerging from or at risk of conflict. It should build on the experience of regional organizations in developing frameworks for minority rights and for protecting democratically elected Governments from unconstitutional overthrow. Member States should negotiate legally binding agreements on the marking, tracing, brokering and transfer of small arms and light weapons, and report on all elements of the United Nations Register of Conventional Arms, with the Secretary-General providing an annual account to the General Assembly and the Security Council on reporting inadequacies. A training and briefing facility should be established for special representatives of the Secretary-General and other UN mediators, and the Department of Political Affairs should be given additional resources and be restructured to provide more consistent and professional mediation support, taking into account the need for the United Nations to have a field-oriented mediation support capacity; competence on recurrent thematic issues in peace negotiations; greater interaction with national mediators, regional organizations and non-governmental organizations (NGOs) involved in conflict resolution; and greater involvement of important voices from civil society, especially those of women in peace processes. National leaders and parties to conflict should use the option of preventive deployment of peacekeepers.

Regarding collective security and the use of force, the Panel agreed that Article 51 of the Charter should be neither rewritten nor reinterpreted, to extend its scope to allow preventive measures to non-imminent threats or to restrict its application to actual attacks. The Security Council was fully empowered under Chapter VII of the Charter to address the full range of security threats with which States were concerned. The task was not to find alternatives to the Council as a source of authority but to make the Council work better. The Panel en-

dorsed the emerging norm that there was a collective international responsibility to protect, exercisable by the Council authorizing military intervention as a last resort, in the event of genocide and other large-scale killing, ethnic cleansing or serious violations of humanitarian law which sovereign Governments had proved powerless or unwilling to prevent. In considering whether to authorize or endorse military force, the Council should always address the five basic criteria of legitimacy (see p. 55). Those guidelines for authorizing the use of force should be embodied in declaratory resolutions of the Council and the Assembly.

Regarding peace enforcement and peacekeeping capability, the Panel said that developed States should do more to transform their existing force capacities into suitable contingents for peace operations; Member States should support the Department of Peacekeeping Operations to meet deadlines for deployment; States with advanced military capacities should establish high readiness, self-sufficient battalions to reinforce UN missions and place them at the disposal of the United Nations; troop strength for peacekeeping missions should be sufficient to deter and repel hostile factions; and the United Nations should have a small corps of between 50 and 100 senior police officers and managers to undertake mission assessments and organize the start-up of police components of peace operations.

Other recommendations were made in respect of nuclear, radiological, chemical and biological weapons (see p. 554); terrorism (see p. 576); transnational organized crime (see p. 1117); the role of sanctions (see p. 331); peace enforcement and peacekeeping capability (see p. 81); post-conflict peace-building (see p. 63); protecting civilians (see p. 60); and for a more effective United Nations in the twenty-first century (see p. 1360).

The Secretary-General wholly endorsed the core arguments for a broader, more comprehensive concept of collective security. The recommendations required a wide-ranging response and he would move quickly to consider and implement, as appropriate, those under his purview, while those pertaining to the Secretariat would need the approval and support of the relevant legislative bodies. Other recommendations were directed at UN intergovernmental organs and the highest levels of government. He said that action on the recommendations need not await consideration by the Assembly at its sixtieth (2005) session but could commence whenever possible.

Complex crises and UN response

The Security Council met on 28 May [meeting 4980] to consider complex crises and the United

Nations response, having before it suggestions for discussion submitted by Pakistan [S/2004/423]. According to Pakistan, the Council and the UN system had been increasingly called upon since 1990 to intervene in complex crises—conflicts that had military and security dimensions, as well as political, economic, social and humanitarian facets. An effective collective response required action on several interrelated tracks, including containment and resolution of conflict, establishing security, protection of civilians, security sector reforms, humanitarian relief strategies, establishing justice and the rule of law, promoting good governance, and development of democratic institutions. To be effective, certain elements were necessary: timely analysis and assessment of potential and actual conflicts and crises; strategic coherence in policy response; enhanced UN system coordination; and closer cooperation with regional and subregional organizations, regional countries and humanitarian and development partners.

On 8 September [S/2004/723], the Council President issued a summary of the important ideas and suggestions presented during the debate. According to the summary, most of the issues currently under consideration by the Council were complex crises, requiring solutions to meet both security and development needs. The link between peace and development had to remain at the core of the UN response to complex crises, with major investment by the international community, the General Assembly, the Security Council, the Economic and Social Council and the Secretariat. In tackling complex crises, prevention should be the first priority. The United Nations should therefore move from a culture of response to a culture of prevention. Preventive action should address the deep-rooted socioeconomic, cultural, environmental, institutional and other structural causes often underlying immediate political symptoms of conflicts. The resource gap in the comprehensive, integrated response sought by the international community for conflict prevention and ensuring human security should be overcome by a bolder, more precise approach to detecting and preventing conflicts and by making development a dimension of complex UN operations. At the policy level, priority should be given to preventive diplomacy. The UN system needed to be strengthened to deal with short- and long-range early warning factors, with better use of existing and non-UN capacities to analyse and anticipate crises and help defuse them in the early stages.

Concerning conflict management and resolution, the Assembly should play a larger role in considering general principles of cooperation in the maintenance of international peace and security and in drawing the attention of the Council to situations likely to endanger peace and security. The Council should pay greater attention to resolving conflicts using measures mentioned in Chapter VI of the Charter.

Peacekeeping could be enhanced by incorporating more elements of peace-building and post-conflict reconstruction. A great deal remained to be done to improve the UN peacekeeping potential, especially in the areas of rapid response, the effective use of material resources, financing, transport and training. The Secretariat and the international community should significantly restructure their work in peacekeeping.

At the root of most conflicts were issues of poverty, corruption, deliberate manipulation of minority groups, and social inequality and exclusion, which had to be addressed by the Council. The United Nations should devote greater attention to development, strive to help developing countries eradicate poverty and increase its involvement in post-conflict reconstruction. It was important to develop a framework and an enabling environment for peace-building activities, including a speedy operational response, the optimum mobilization of resources and preventing the outbreak or recurrence of conflicts.

Recognizing that one of the greatest weaknesses of the international system was follow-up, Council members suggested that the United Nations consider political and administrative mechanisms to follow up on progress, warn of obstacles and propose remedies. Those mechanisms should involve the Council, the countries concerned, major donors, regional and subregional organizations and international financial agencies and institutions.

Conflict prevention

In 2004, the General Assembly and the Security Council considered various measures for the prevention of armed conflict, including the economic measures of the Kimberley Process for the certification of rough diamonds and the role that business could play in conflict prevention.

On 23 December, the Assembly decided that the item on the prevention of armed conflict would remain for consideration at its resumed fifty-ninth (2005) session (**decision 59/552**).

Conflict diamonds

Kimberley Process. Two plenary meetings of the Kimberley Process were held in 2003 (Johannesburg, 28-30 April, and Sun City, South Africa,

29-31 October) to review implementation of the Kimberley Process Certification Scheme (KPCS), established in 2003 [YUN 2003, p. 55] to stop the use of conflict diamonds in fuelling armed conflict, protect the legitimate diamond industry and ensure implementation of resolutions on trade in conflict diamonds [A/58/623]. The Johannesburg meeting, in recognition of the challenges faced by certain participants, extended the tolerance period for implementing KPCS until 31 May 2003. The Sun City meeting welcomed the addition of Brazil, Romania and Togo to the list of KPCS participants, bringing the total number, as at October 2003, to 45 States and the European Union (EU). Canada and the Russian Federation were elected KPCS Chair and Vice-Chair, respectively, for 2004, and the Russian Federation as Chair for 2005. The meeting agreed to establish a peer review mechanism to guarantee that KPCS was upheld.

GENERAL ASSEMBLY ACTION

On 14 April [meeting 85], the General Assembly adopted **resolution 58/290** [draft: A/58/L.59 & Add.1] without vote [agenda item 21].

The role of diamonds in fuelling conflict: breaking the link between the illicit transaction of rough diamonds and armed conflict as a contribution to prevention and settlement of conflicts

The General Assembly,

Recognizing that the trade in conflict diamonds is a matter of serious international concern, which can be directly linked to the fuelling of armed conflict, the activities of rebel movements aimed at undermining or overthrowing legitimate Governments and the illicit traffic in and proliferation of armaments, especially small arms and light weapons,

Recognizing also the devastating impact of conflicts fuelled by the trade in conflict diamonds on the peace, safety and security of people in affected countries, and the systematic and gross human rights violations that have been perpetrated in such conflicts,

Noting the negative impact of such conflicts on regional stability and the obligations placed upon States by the Charter of the United Nations regarding the maintenance of international peace and security,

Recognizing, therefore, that continued action to curb the trade in conflict diamonds is imperative,

Recognizing also the positive benefits of the legitimate diamond trade to producing countries, and underlining the need for continued international action to prevent the problem of conflict diamonds from negatively affecting the trade in legitimate diamonds, which makes a critical contribution to the economies of many of the producing, exporting and importing States, especially developing States,

Noting that the vast majority of rough diamonds produced in the world are from legitimate sources,

Recalling the Charter and all the relevant resolutions of the Security Council related to conflict diamonds, and determined to contribute to and support the im-

plementation of the measures provided for in those resolutions,

Recalling also Security Council resolution 1459(2003) of 28 January 2003, in which the Council strongly supported the Kimberley Process Certification Scheme as a valuable contribution against trafficking in conflict diamonds,

Welcoming the important contribution of the Kimberley Process, which was initiated by African diamond-producing countries,

Believing that the implementation of the Kimberley Process Certification Scheme should substantially reduce the opportunity for conflict diamonds to play a role in fuelling armed conflict and should help to protect legitimate trade and ensure the effective implementation of the relevant resolutions on trade in conflict diamonds,

Recalling its resolutions 55/56 of 1 December 2000, 56/263 of 13 March 2002 and 57/302 of 15 April 2003, in which it called for the development and implementation of proposals for a simple, effective and pragmatic international certification scheme for rough diamonds,

Welcoming, in this regard, the implementation of the Kimberley Process Certification Scheme in such a way that it does not impede the legitimate trade in diamonds or impose an undue burden on Governments or industry, particularly smaller producers, and does not hinder the development of the diamond industry,

Welcoming also the decision of countries and one regional economic integration organization to address the problem of conflict diamonds by participating in the Kimberley Process and to implement the Kimberley Process Certification Scheme,

Welcoming further the important contribution made by the diamond industry, in particular the World Diamond Council, as well as civil society, to assist international efforts to stop the trade in conflict diamonds,

Welcoming the voluntary self-regulation initiatives for the diamond industry announced by the World Diamond Council, and recognizing that a system of such voluntary self-regulation will contribute, as described in the Interlaken Declaration of 5 November 2002 on the Kimberley Process Certification Scheme for Rough Diamonds, to ensuring the effectiveness of national systems of internal control for rough diamonds,

Noting with appreciation that the Kimberley Process has pursued its deliberations on an inclusive basis, involving concerned stakeholders, including producing, exporting and importing States, the diamond industry and civil society,

Recognizing that State sovereignty should be fully respected and that the principles of equality, mutual benefits and consensus should be adhered to,

Recognizing also that the Kimberley Process Certification Scheme, which came into effect on 1 January 2003, will be credible only if all participants have established internal systems of control designed to eliminate the presence of conflict diamonds in the chain of producing, exporting and importing rough diamonds within their own territories, while taking into account that differences in production methods and trading practices, as well as differences in institutional controls thereof, may require different approaches to meet minimum standards,

1. *Reaffirms its strong support* for the Kimberley Process Certification Scheme;

2. *Recognizes* that the Kimberley Process Certification Scheme can help to ensure the effective implementation of relevant resolutions of the Security Council containing sanctions on the trade in conflict diamonds, and calls for the full implementation of existing Council measures targeting the illicit trade in rough diamonds that play a role in fuelling conflict;

3. *Stresses* that the widest possible participation in the Kimberley Process Certification Scheme is essential and should be encouraged, urges all Member States to participate actively in the Certification Scheme by complying with its undertakings, and welcomes the establishment at the plenary meeting of the Kimberley Process, held in Johannesburg, South Africa, from 28 to 30 April 2003, of a Participation Committee to ensure that participants and applicants willing to join the Certification Scheme meet the minimum standards;

4. *Notes with appreciation* the report of the Chair of the Kimberley Process submitted pursuant to resolution 57/302, and congratulates the Governments, regional economic integration organization representatives, the organized diamond industry and civil society participating in the Kimberley Process for contributing to the development and implementation of the Kimberley Process Certification Scheme;

5. *Takes note* of the decision of the General Council of the World Trade Organization of 15 May 2003 granting a waiver with respect to the measures taken to implement the Kimberley Process Certification Scheme;

6. *Welcomes* the progress achieved at the plenary meeting of the Kimberley Process held in Sun City, South Africa, from 29 to 31 October 2003 by the adoption of a decision on a peer review system for the effective implementation of the Kimberley Process Certification Scheme;

7. *Encourages* participants in the Kimberley Process to allow voluntary review visits in accordance with the decision mentioned in paragraph 6 above, and welcomes the readiness of some participants to host such visits;

8. *Also encourages* participants in the Kimberley Process Certification Scheme to submit annual reports on the implementation of the Certification Scheme to the Chair of the Kimberley Process;

9. *Further encourages* all participants in the Kimberley Process Certification Scheme to collate and submit relevant statistical data on the production of and international trade in rough diamonds as a tool for effective implementation and as envisaged by the Certification Scheme;

10. *Acknowledges with great appreciation* the important contribution that the Government of South Africa has made to the efforts to curb the trade in conflict diamonds in its capacity as the Chair of the Kimberley Process from May 2000 to December 2003, and welcomes the selection of Canada as the Chair and the Russian Federation as the Vice-Chair of the Process for 2004;

11. *Requests* the Chair of the Kimberley Process to submit a report on the implementation of the Process to the General Assembly at its fifty-ninth session;

12. *Decides* to include in the provisional agenda of its fifty-ninth session the item entitled "The role of diamonds in fuelling conflict".

At the 2004 Kimberley Process meeting (Gatineau, Quebec, 27-29 October) [A/59/590], the Chair (Canada) reported that 42 Governments and the EU (following its enlargement, all EU countries participated as a single participant) were implementing KPCS, encompassing the majority of the production and trade in rough diamonds. The Scheme accounted for more than 99.8 per cent of global production, valued at $8.5 billion. Under KPCS, 47,598 certificates were issued for more than $20 billion in trade. Under the peer review system adopted in October 2003, eight participants had already received review visits and another seven were scheduled to do so before the end of 2004. The meeting endorsed the report of the Working Group on Monitoring, including a provisional schedule of review visits in 2005 and 2006. To improve the comparability of statistics submitted by participants, the meeting established a maximum period for the validity of KPCS certificates at 60 calendar days from the date of issuance and asked the Working Group on Statistics to study aspects of national methodologies that constrained statistical reporting. Participants established a framework for the three-year review of KPCS and created an ad hoc working group to carry out the review and report before 31 July 2006.

The Assembly took further action on conflict diamonds in December (see p. 506).

Role of business in conflict prevention, peacekeeping and post-conflict peace-building

On 15 April [meeting 4943], the Security Council considered the role of business in conflict prevention, peacekeeping and post-conflict peace-building. The Council President, in opening the debate, said that political and economic stability in conflict prevention, as well as in post-conflict recovery, were closely interrelated and had to be reflected inside and outside the broader UN system, including the international financial institutions such as the World Bank. The role of the private sector deserved particular attention in that context, especially its huge potential in development or reconstruction strategy at national and regional levels.

The Secretary-General told the Council that the economic dimensions of armed conflict, though often overlooked, should never be underestimated. Private companies operated in many conflict zones and conflict-prone countries and their decisions on investment and employment, on relations with local communities, on protection for the local environment, and on their own security arrangements could either help a country turn its back on conflict or exacerbate the tensions that fuelled conflict in the first place. Private companies also manufactured and sold the hardware of conflict and were involved in the exploitation of, and trade in, lucrative local natural resources. The challenges were complex, touching on fundamental questions of sovereignty, democratic governance, corporate accountability and individual integrity. Business itself had an enormous stake in the search for solutions, since companies required a stable environment to conduct their operations; their bottom lines could not be separated from some of the key UN goals of peace, development and equity.

The Security Council, for its part, had already addressed many of those issues, but the time had come to translate its ad hoc efforts into a more systematic approach, so as to promote greater cooperation between the security and development arms of the United Nations, give it the tools to influence more actively the economic incentives and disincentives that drove the dynamics of armed conflict, and ensure that those factors were reflected in efforts to prevent conflict, in peace agreements and in the mandates given to peace operations.

In that context, the Secretary-General indicated that he had established an inter-agency group, chaired by the Department of Political Affairs, to look at the political economy of armed conflict and make recommendations for improving the response of the UN system and of Member States. He urged the Council and Member States to focus greater attention on the issue and to engage more dynamically with the private sector.

President's summary. The Security Council President summarized the discussion in a document circulated on 25 May [S/2004/441]. Among the observations, speakers said that business had a crucial role to play in situations of armed conflict. Private companies' decisions on investment and employment, on relations with local communities and on protection for local environments could ease or exacerbate tensions. Giving people work and opportunity was a key factor in preventing and in emerging from conflict. Domestic small and medium-size enterprises played an especially important role in that context, creating most of the jobs, especially employment opportunities for demobilized fighters.

Business itself had an enormous stake in the search for solutions. Requiring a stable environment to carry out their operations and minimize their risks, companies looked for a reasonable level of security, adequate infrastructure, financ-

ing for reconstruction programmes and a perspective afforded by visible progress. In long-term conflict prevention, key elements were education, sustainable economic growth and the private sector's contribution to it. The resolution of violent conflicts required a concerted effort by all major stakeholders. The United Nations, the international financial institutions and Member States were called on to cooperate closely with the private sector to set the necessary political, security, legal, economic and financial framework.

A number of participants expressed their hope for a follow-up to the Council's meeting, with some suggesting that the Secretary-General report on further developments. The President concluded that the meeting was a clear signal for a more coherent approach by all respective institutions within and outside the UN system to use the potential of entrepreneurial initiative in conflict situations more effectively.

Peacemaking and peace-building

The High-level Panel on Threats, Challenges and Change, in its December report [A/59/565], made recommendations on post-conflict peace-building. It said that special representatives of the Secretary-General should have the authority and guidance to work with relevant parties to establish robust donor-coordinating mechanisms and have the required resources. Funding should be provided for disarmament and demobilization programmes from assessed budgets and a standing fund established for peace-building at the minimum level of $250 million to finance the recurrent expenditures of a nascent Government and critical agency rehabilitation and reintegration programmes.

The Panel proposed the establishment of a peace-building commission to identify countries that were under stress and risked sliding towards collapse; organize proactive assistance in preventing that process from developing further; assist in planning for transitions between conflict and post-conflict peace-building; and marshall and sustain the international community's efforts in post-conflict peace-building for as long as necessary. A peace-building support office should also be established in the Secretariat to support the commission and ensure that the Secretary-General was able to integrate system-wide peace-building strategies, develop best practices and provide cohesive support for field operations.

Civilian aspects of conflict management and peace-building

Security Council consideration. On 22 September [meeting 5041], the Security Council met at the ministerial level to consider the civilian aspects of conflict management and peace-building. The President (Spain), in an 8 September letter [S/2004/722], remarked on the importance of the civilian aspects of crisis management in complex crisis situations, as the ability of international military operations was limited in terms of socio-economic rehabilitation and political reconciliation. The importance of civil-military cooperation had to be acknowledged. In a civil-military operation, civilian aspects could not be achieved without security, and civilian success was the key for the exit strategy of the military. Unlike the military, civilian crisis management did not have a body of agreed doctrine and relied on individual entrepreneurship in the field. Demanding Council mandates on the Secretariat and other bodies made the setting up of civilian teams and means for a successful operation difficult. Therefore, the Council should address such issues as the nature of the growing responsibilities of civilian elements in civil-military operations; ways for organizations involved in deploying such operations to enhance their cooperation in order to increase the availability of resources and their interoperability; options for cooperation in crisis management between the United Nations and Member States and other international organizations; institutional issues regarding the deployment of coordinated civilian-military components for a particular operation; and improvements to civilian crisis management by focusing on building a more cohesive international approach.

The Secretary-General told the Council that peace-building was complex and drew in many actors, including the Council, UN agencies, funds and programmes, regional organizations and NGOs. The United Nations needed to be realistic about what was achievable and to have a clear political strategy for success, with benchmarks for progress towards the goal of building legitimate and effective States, including clear priorities, particularly in the areas of security, the rule of law and immediate economic opportunities. The Organization needed to sustain its focus on those long-term commitments and ensure adequate resources. It had to make sure that its efforts were well integrated, working with other organizations, bilateral donors and NGOs on the basis of shared goals and priorities, and to maintain an international cadre of highly skilled civilian staff for peace-building. Peace-building required a clear strategy, developed and executed by highly skilled professionals, grounded in local conditions and reflected in realistic mandates, supported by all parts of the UN system and

backed by the Council and the membership of the Organization as a whole.

The African Union (AU) Commissioner for Peace and Security, the High Representative for the EU's Common Foreign and Security Policy, and the Secretary-General of the League of Arab States also addressed the Council.

SECURITY COUNCIL ACTION

On 22 September [meeting 5041], following consultations among Security Council members, the President made statement **S/PRST/2004/33** on behalf of the Council:

The Security Council met at the ministerial level on 22 September 2004 to consider "Civilian aspects of conflict management and peace-building". Ministers recognized the increasing importance of civilian aspects of conflict management in addressing complex crisis situations and in preventing the recurrence of conflict. They affirmed the importance of conflict resolution in accordance with the relevant provisions of the Charter of the United Nations.

Ministers also acknowledged the importance of civilian-military cooperation in crisis management. Military and police components are essential to address and stabilize certain serious crisis situations and to guarantee security. Moreover, the participation of a strong civilian component is key to the provision of humanitarian assistance, the re-establishment of public order, functioning public institutions, reconstruction, rehabilitation and peace-building for longer-term sustainable development. A substantial civilian participation in crisis management is also essential for a strategy of military disengagement and plays a crucial role in the phase of post-conflict peace-building. In this context, it is important that there is coordination between the civilian and military components in crisis management from the first phase of integrated mission planning. In addition, there should be significant coordination with actors involved in longer-term reconstruction and development, including in particular the other organs of the United Nations system in accordance with their respective mandates and the international financial institutions, as well as cooperation with the business sector.

Ministers recognized the increasing role of some regional and subregional and other international organizations in crisis management. They also recalled that Articles 52 and 53 of the Charter set forth the contribution of regional organizations to conflict management, as well as the relationship between the United Nations and regional organizations. They encouraged these organizations, whenever possible, to continue to develop their crisis management capabilities, including in the civilian field, in close coordination with the United Nations and in accordance with the provisions of Article 54 of the Charter. When applicable, clear schemes for joint operations should be developed. Also, greater coordination and interoperability among those organizations, as well as developing and sharing common strategies, operational policies and best practices in civilian crisis management, would enhance efficiency and coherence in crisis management. Continued internal coordination in this field among all relevant United Nations organs and agencies should also be strengthened.

Ministers supported the efforts by Member States to continue to develop, as appropriate, their own civilian crisis management capabilities, including, inter alia, rapid civilian response teams, and they also supported their initiatives to make these capabilities available to the United Nations and other relevant regional or subregional organizations, as a contribution to their efforts in the maintenance of international peace and security. Adequate capabilities should be developed in key areas of civilian crisis management, such as police, justice and the rule of law, preparation of electoral processes and electoral observation, civil protection and public administration. The Council should consider the nature and availability of these capabilities when approving the necessary mandates for United Nations operations.

Adequate and flexible means for transitional peace support and crisis management activities, such as protection of civilians, including United Nations and humanitarian personnel, disarmament, demobilization and reintegration of former combatants, the end of impunity, public institution-building and transitional justice, as well as the promotion and protection of human rights and the integration of a gender perspective, are essential to ensure lasting peace after a conflict. Also, the involvement of local actors in the policy-making process and a fruitful relationship with civil society should be among the priorities of any post-conflict strategy.

The Security Council commends the efforts of the Secretary-General in addressing all relevant issues relating to the civilian aspects of crisis management, and invites him, other institutions and agencies of the United Nations system, regional and subregional organizations and Member States to continue to give serious consideration to this matter, with a view to making further progress in this field.

Role of civil society in post-conflict peace-building

On 22 June [meeting 4993], the Security Council met to consider the role of civil society in post-conflict peace-building. It had before it a non-paper submitted by the President (Philippines) [S/2004/442] on the questions to be discussed, which drew attention to the crucial role played by civil society organizations in the comprehensive and multidimensional approach to conflict prevention and post-conflict peace-building. In addition to their contributions to peacekeeping, relief and humanitarian efforts, those organizations were a source of information on the ground. They had become a force to reckon with in post-conflict areas, with their public advocacy role and media campaigns often helping to shape public understanding of the crises and bringing pressure to bear on Governments to act, and an actor in the policy process, whose support was at times essential to the success of government policies and Council initiatives. However, more needed to be done to harness civil society in the structural

and operational dimensions of post-conflict peace-building.

The Secretary-General told the Council that the partnership between the United Nations and civil society had grown considerably, reflecting the increasing role of civil society in helping to shape and scrutinize government policies, in holding Governments accountable and in contributing to international decision-making. If peace-building missions were to be effective, they should, as part of a clear political strategy, work with and strengthen those civil society forces that were helping people to voice their concerns and to act on them in peaceful ways. The aim should be to create a synergy with those civil society groups that were bridge-builders, truth-finders, watchdogs, human rights defenders and agents of social protection and economic revitalization. Civil society groups also had a role to play in UN deliberative processes. The Secretary-General called on the Council to deepen its dialogue with civil society groups and thus benefit from their expertise, focus and insight. He asked the Council to pay attention to the report of the Panel of Eminent Persons on United Nations–Civil Society Relations (see p. 63), especially the measures proposed for increasing the participation of civil society representatives from developing countries, for strengthening the partnership with civil society in UN humanitarian and development work, and on how the Council might engage more effectively with civil society. The Secretary-General said that he had high hopes for the 2005 international conference on conflict prevention which civil society groups were organizing in response to the recommendation in his 2001 report on conflict prevention [YUN 2001, p. 48].

The President of the Economic and Social Council told the Security Council that civil society organizations were significant actors in crisis and post-crisis situations. Their number, diverse mandates and varying operational capacities made coordination essential to ensure the coherence and impact of their efforts. Many donors, including the United Nations, relied on NGOs as implementing partners of channels for assistance, and, in violent conflicts, they were the principal delivery vehicles. NGOS faced particular challenges, and international organizations and Governments should support them in their efforts. The Economic and Social Council was uniquely placed to interact and consult with civil society, and its various subsidiary bodies had established close contacts with NGOs and other private entities to hear their views on the topics that the intergovernmental bodies were addressing.

On 3 August [S/2004/624], the Security Council President, in a summary of the debate, said that Member States recognized the need to establish a mechanism or a strategy to foster the partnership between the United Nations and civil society organizations. They lauded the organizations' efforts in providing grass-roots information and early warning for conflict prevention, as well as in national reconstruction and rehabilitation. Most members supported the practice of holding "Arria-plus formula" meetings (the "Arria formula" enabled Council members to discuss matters with invited personalities in an informal and closed setting), but others cautioned against formalizing such meetings or other interaction between the Council and those organizations. Member States recognized the need to enhance coordination and cooperation among the Security Council, the General Assembly, the Economic and Social Council and other UN bodies and institutions involved in conflict prevention and post-conflict peace-building.

Specific recommendations were made for the establishment of a strategy/framework/mechanism for post-conflict peace-building; maintaining governmental/intergovernmental and civil society communication and coordination; incorporating economic and social development in post-conflict peace-building; enhancing and developing creative and cooperative relationships among civil society, the Security Council and the UN system as a whole; following up on the recommendations of the Panel on UN relationships with civil society (see below); making use of the Arria-formula type of meetings; correcting the representational imbalance of civil society organizations; and convening independent commissions of inquiry following UN operations.

Report of Panel on UN-Civil Society Relations. The Panel of Eminent Persons on United Nations–Civil Society Relations, in its June report "We the peoples: civil society, the United Nations and global governance" [A/58/817] (see p. 1360), noted that the Security Council had greatly enhanced its relations with civil society in recent years, largely in response to its changing roles in the post–cold war era and the changing nature of conflicts. That expanded engagement was largely with NGOs in the areas of international humanitarian assistance and human rights and, to a lesser extent, with religious leaders. It had taken the form of more frequent Arria formula meetings, regular meetings with the NGO Working Group on the Security Council, expanded contacts with international NGOs and more frequent field visits of Council members to meet with civil society. While some civil society actors regarded those informal consultations as

sufficient, others believed that they were not inclusive enough and mechanisms for exchanges with civil society should be enhanced through a more formal UN instrument.

The Panel proposed that Council members should further strengthen their dialogue with civil society by improving the planning and effectiveness of the Arria formula meetings; ensuring that the Council's field missions met regularly with appropriate local civil society leaders, international humanitarian NGOs and others; holding a series of Council seminars to discuss issues of emerging importance, which would include presentations by civil society and other constituencies; and convening independent commissions of inquiry after Council-mandated operations.

UN role in post-conflict national reconciliation

On 26 January [meeting 4903], the Security Council considered the agenda item "Post-conflict national reconciliation: role of the United Nations".

The Council President, in opening the debate, said that post-conflict national reconciliation presented challenges for the work of the United Nations, raising questions as to what role the Organization should have in national reconciliation processes; whether it should incorporate the need for reconciliation into exit strategies for post-conflict situations or design specific strategies for reconciliation; and what role other principal UN organs should play. Other questions concerned the principles and mechanisms of reconciliation, and the instruments for seeking truth, such as truth and reconciliation commissions, consensus-building among political actors, reparations for victims and the role of justice.

The Assistant Secretary-General for Political Affairs, Tuliameni Kalomoh, in his briefing, contended that post-conflict reconciliation was closely related to the broader discussion of the rule of law and to addressing the root causes of the conflict. The Council, in its 2003 debate on the issue [YUN 2003, p. 59], had identified the need to incorporate rule of law concerns into UN activities (see p. 65). The international community had employed a number of instruments to address the issue of reconciliation, such as tribunals, truth and reconciliation commissions, amnesties (except for genocide, war crimes and crimes against humanity), reparations and targeted assistance programmes. Although it was difficult to apply standard prescriptions for reconciliation to every situation, some general observations could be informative. First, peace without reconciliation was hardly ever durable. Secondly, it was difficult to achieve reconciliation without a significant measure of justice. Thirdly, there were some crimes that were so heinous that they required that justice be done. Fourthly, the pursuit of justice should not become an obstacle to establishing or maintaining peace. Reconciliation was a complex, often difficult process in which contradictions might be inevitable. It involved accounting for the past and meeting demands for justice and the degree of forgiveness that would allow for the reconstruction of the social fabric, and striking a balance between the aggrieved and the aggressors, the pursuit of justice and stability. It was a long-term process and the right combination of measures would depend on the specific conditions in each post-conflict situation.

The Administrator of the United Nations Development Programme (UNDP), Mark Malloch Brown, speaking about UNDP's role in reconciliation, said that, since the submission of the report of the Panel on United Nations Peace Operations (Brahimi report) [YUN 2000, p. 83], there had been a clear understanding of the different roles played by the various parts of the United Nations, under the leadership of the Department for Political Affairs, in post-conflict reconstruction in general and in reconciliation in particular. For UNDP, that presented some critical issues. First, there was a significant funding gap in every post-conflict situation during the process from relief to reconciliation. Secondly, although UNDP was much less well resourced in areas such as disarmament, demobilization and reintegration, the rule of law and justice and early support for building electoral systems, it worked in all of those areas. However, despite its strengthened capacity in those areas, it was difficult to provide adequate support to half a dozen of those activities around the world at the same time. UNDP had therefore begun to discuss with key supporters how to strengthen its own capabilities and how the international community could make funds available more quickly for the early steps of reconciliation.

Carolyn McAskie, Deputy Emergency Relief Coordinator, said that a principled and strategic approach to humanitarian assistance was required so as to ensure that it did not perpetuate grievance or hamper longer-term development, and adequate funding was necessary not only for life-sustaining assistance but also for programmes that had a significant impact on national reconciliation. There was considerable scope to look further into ways to channel reconciliation efforts into the programmatic work of UN agencies, bearing in mind the fact that humanitarians played an important bridging role. The United Nations Children's Fund, the Office of the United Nations High Commissioner for Refugees, the World Food Programme and other humanitarian agencies already played that role in their everyday work. Humanitarian aid had to be consistently and equitably provided. Legal and judicial mechanisms, international humanitarian law, property restitution, reintegration and reparations had to be consistently applied if reconciliation was to have a solid base. However, humanitarian assistance alone would not provide a solution to crises. Without reconciliation, rehabilitation, reconstruction and development, countries would slip back into the horrors of war, and the efforts of the humanitarian community would be lost. Sixty-five per cent of the countries emerging from conflict in Africa were slipping back into violence, and the international community could not afford to be complacent on that front. It was therefore vital to have an international support strategy to ensure that humanitarian activities were reinforced with reconciliation, rehabilitation and reconstruction efforts.

SECURITY COUNCIL ACTION

On 26 January [meeting 4903], following consultations among Security Council members, the President made statement **S/PRST/2004/2** on behalf of the Council:

The Security Council met on 26 January 2004 to consider the item entitled "Post-conflict national reconciliation: role of the United Nations". Members expressed their respective views and understandings on, and reaffirmed the vital importance of, this matter, stressing the necessary close cooperation needed in the United Nations system, including the Council, on this issue.

The statements underscored the important tasks that must be addressed in post-conflict situations in order to reach the goal of national reconciliation, as well as the relevant experience and expertise that exist within the United Nations system and in Member States.

Members considered that it would be appropriate to examine further how to harness and direct this expertise and experience drawn up from several key areas, so that it would be more readily accessible to the Council, to the wider United Nations system and membership, and to the international community as a whole, so that the lessons and experience of the past could be, as appropriate, learned and built on.

The Council invites the Secretary-General to give consideration to the relevant views expressed in this debate in preparation of his report on the role of the United Nations in justice and the rule of law.

The Council invites all Members of the United Nations, and other parts of the United Nations system with relevant experience and expertise, to contribute to this process.

The rule of law and transitional justice in conflict and post-conflict situations

Consideration by Commission on Crime Prevention and Criminal Justice. The Commission on Crime Prevention and Criminal Justice, at its thirteenth session (11-20 May) [E/2004/30], recommended to the Economic and Social Council for adoption a draft resolution entitled "The rule of law and development: strengthening the rule of law and the reform of criminal justice institutions, with emphasis on technical assistance, including in post-conflict reconstruction". That resolution was adopted by the Council as **resolution 2004/25** (see p. 1111).

Report of Secretary-General. In August [S/2004/616], the Secretary-General submitted a report on the rule of law and transitional justice in conflict and post-conflict societies, highlighting the key issues and lessons learned from UN experience in promoting justice and the rule of law in those societies. The report took into account the views expressed during the Security Council's 26 January debate on the UN role in post-conflict national reconciliation, as requested by the Council in presidential statement **S/PRST/2004/2** (see p. 64). Among the key issues discussed were: strengthening the rule of law and transitional justice in the wake of conflict; articulating a common language of justice for the United Nations; assistance based on international norms and standards; identifying the UN role in peace operations; assessing national needs and capacities; supporting domestic reform; filling a rule of law vacuum; developing national justice systems; learning lessons from ad hoc tribunals; facilitating truth telling; delivering reparations; and coordinating UN efforts.

The Secretary-General said that in recent years, the United Nations had increasingly focused on questions of transitional justice and the rule of law in conflict and post-conflict societies, gaining important lessons for future activities. Success would depend on critical factors such as the need to ensure a common basis in international norms and standards and to mobilize the necessary resources for a sustainable investment in justice. The United Nations should support domestic reform constituencies, help build the capacity of national justice sector institutions, facilitate national consultations on justice reform and transitional justice and help fill the rule of law vacuum evident in so many post-conflict societies. In some cases, international or mixed tribunals had been established to address past crimes in war-torn societies. While they had helped to bring justice and hope to victims, combat impunity and enrich the jurisprudence of international criminal law, they were expensive and contributed little to sustainable national capacities for justice administration. The International Criminal Court offered hope for a permanent reduction in the phenomenon of impunity, and the further ratification of its statute was to be encouraged. Truth commissions, also valuable in the quest for justice and reconciliation, had proved to be a vital element of transitional justice and were key to restoring public trust in national institutions of governance. Strengthening UN support in those areas would require efforts to enhance coordination among all actors, develop rosters of experts and technical tools, and more systematically record, analyse and apply those lessons in Council mandates, peace processes and the operations of UN peace missions.

The Secretary-General recommended that peace agreements and Council resolutions and mandates: give priority to the restoration of and respect for the rule of law; respect, incorporate and apply international standards for fairness, due process and human rights in the administration of justice; reject any amnesty for genocide, war crimes or crimes against humanity, including ethnic, gender and sexually based international crimes; ensure that the United Nations did not establish or participate in any tribunal that included capital punishment among possible sanctions; require that all judicial processes be credible, fair, independent and impartial; recognize and respect the rights of victims and accused persons, particularly the most affected groups; recognize the differential impact of conflict and rule of law deficits on women and children and the need to ensure gender sensitivity in the restoration of rule of law and transitional justice; fund national needs assessment and consultation processes; where mixed tribunals were envisaged for divided societies, consider mandating a majority of international judges to enhance the credibility and perceived fairness of such tribunals; insist on full governmental cooperation with international and mixed tribunals, including in the surrender of accused persons; adopt an integrated and comprehensive approach to the rule of law and transitional justice; ensure the provision of adequate resources, including a sustainable funding mechanism; and consider the establishment of national human rights commissions during transitional arrangements.

The Secretary-General announced his intention to instruct the Executive Committee on Peace and Security to propose action on the matters discussed in the report, with the aim of strengthening UN support for transitional justice and the rule of law in conflict and post-conflict countries and ensured their integration into planning of UN peace operations. The Committee should, among other actions, propose new or enhanced UN system mechanisms for collecting and developing best practices, documentation, guidelines and other tools for transitional justice and for justice sector development; develop workable national-level rule of law coordination mechanisms; and ensure that all programmes and policies supporting constitutional, judicial and legislative reform promoted gender equality.

Statement by Secretary-General. The Secretary-General, introducing his 2004 report on the work of the Organization [A/59/1] (see p. 3) before the General Assembly on 21 September [meeting 3], said that the rule of law was at risk around the world. Laws were shamelessly disregarded as civilians were massacred in cold blood, while relief workers, journalists and other noncombatants were taken hostage or put to death in the most barbarous fashion, prisoners were abused and whole populations displaced and their homes destroyed, while rape was used as a deliberate strategy. No cause, no grievance, however legitimate, could justify such acts, the prevalence of which reflected the collective failure to uphold the rule of law and instil respect for human life. The current international framework of fair rules, norms and laws was riddled with gaps and weaknesses, applied selectively, enforced arbitrarily, and lacked the teeth to make it into an effective legal system. Where enforcement capacity existed, as in the Security Council, many felt it was not always used fairly or effectively and where the rule of law was most earnestly invoked, as in the Commission on Human Rights, those invoking it did not always practise what they preached. By reintroducing the rule of law and confidence in its impartial application, societies shattered by conflict could be resuscitated.

The Secretary-General recalled his promise to the Security Council to make strengthening the rule of law and transitional justice in conflict and post-conflict societies a priority for the remainder of his tenure. He urged the Assembly to do more to foster the rule of law, to sign and implement treaties on the protection of civilians, and to support the measures he would propose on improving the security of UN staff (see p. 1475).

The United States President, George W. Bush, proposed the establishment of a UN democracy fund to help countries lay the foundation of democracy by instituting the rule of law, independent courts, a free press, political parties and trade unions, and to help set up and support election monitors. The United States would make an initial contribution to the fund and he urged other nations to do likewise.

SECURITY COUNCIL ACTION

On 6 October [meeting 5052], following consultations among Security Council members, the President made statement **S/PRST/2004/34** on behalf of the Council:

The Security Council thanks the Secretary-General for his report of 3 August 2004, which was reissued on 23 August 2004, and reaffirms the vital importance that the Council attaches to promoting justice and the rule of law, and post-conflict national reconciliation. The Council will consider, as appropriate in its deliberations, the recommendations set out in paragraph 64 of the report.

The Council urges the Secretariat to make proposals for implementation of the recommendations set out in paragraph 65 of the report, and draws attention in particular to the importance of the practical measures set out in that paragraph that can be implemented rapidly, including coordinating existing expertise and resources, setting up databases and web-based resources, developing rosters of experts and organizing workshops and training programmes. The Council urges Member States that are interested in doing so to contribute national expertise and materials to these developments, within their means, and to improve their capacities in these areas.

The Council recalls the important statement made by the Secretary-General to the fifty-ninth session of the General Assembly on 21 September 2004, and endorses his view that "it is by reintroducing the rule of law, and confidence in its impartial application, that we can hope to resuscitate societies shattered by conflict". The Council stresses the importance and urgency of the restoration of justice and the rule of law in post-conflict societies, not only in order to come to terms with past abuses, but also to promote national reconciliation and to help prevent a return to conflict in the future. The Council emphasizes that such processes must be inclusive, gender-sensitive and open to the full participation of women.

The Council underlines the importance of assessing the particular justice and rule of law needs in each host country, taking into consideration the nature of the country's legal system, traditions and institutions, and of avoiding a "one size fits all" approach. The Council recognizes that building national capacities and independent national institutions is essential, that local ownership and leadership in that process should be encouraged and respected, and that international structures can play a complementary and supportive role.

The Council emphasizes that ending the climate of impunity is essential to the efforts of a conflict and post-conflict society to come to terms with past abuses and in preventing future abuses. The Council draws attention to the full range of mechanisms of transitional justice that should be considered, including national, international and "mixed" criminal tribunals and truth and reconciliation commissions, and underlines the fact that those mechanisms should concentrate not only on individual responsibility for serious crimes, but also on the need to seek peace, truth and national reconciliation. The Council welcomes the report's balanced appraisal of the lessons to be learned from the experience of the ad hoc international criminal tribunals and "mixed" tribunals.

The Council recalls that justice and the rule of law at the international level are of key importance for promoting and maintaining peace, stability and development in the world. The Council underlines also the importance of helping to prevent future conflicts through addressing their root causes in a legitimate and fair manner.

The Council warmly welcomes the Secretary-General's decision to make the United Nations work to strengthen the rule of law and transitional justice in conflict and post-conflict societies a priority for the remainder of his tenure. The Council invites the Secretary-General to keep it informed of the Secretariat's progress in taking forward the recommendations set out in paragraph 65 of the report, and expresses the intention to consider this matter again within six months.

Cooperation with regional organizations

Security Council consideration (May). On 7 May [meeting 4964], the Chairman-in-Office of the Organization for Security and Cooperation in Europe (OSCE) briefed the Security Council on its cooperation with the United Nations, the EU, the North Atlantic Treaty Organization (NATO) and other regional organizations. He said that OSCE had helped to end the civil war in Tajikistan, constrained conflict in Georgia, the Republic of Moldova and the former Yugoslav Republic of Macedonia and, with the United Nations, continued to play a major role in building civil society in post-conflict Bosnia and Herzegovina and the Serbia and Montenegro province of Kosovo. Currently, OSCE had 18 field missions, mostly in the Caucasus and in Central Asian countries, which helped it deal with new threats to security. In its efforts to combat terrorism, OSCE worked closely with the Council's Counter-Terrorism Committee. It also worked in controlling the spread of small arms. In March, with the UN Office on Drugs and Crime, it hosted the third special meeting of the Counter-Terrorism Committee with international, regional and subregional organizations [S/2004/276]. In cooperation with the United Nations Educational, Scientific and Cultural Organization, it was paying attention to the role of education in building tolerance and inter-cultural understanding. The United Nations and OSCE worked well together in the field, especially in Kosovo, where it was an integral part of the United Nations Interim Administration Mission in Kosovo. In Georgia, OSCE supported the efforts

of the United Nations Observer Mission in Georgia to bring about a comprehensive settlement of the conflict in Abkhazia.

In its wide range of activities, OSCE had good working relations with the United Nations, which could be further strengthened. It would continue to cooperate with the United Nations, the EU and NATO to improve their ability to respond quickly in addressing major contemporary challenges.

Security Council consideration (July). On 20 July [meeting 5007], the Security Council met to discuss cooperation between the United Nations and regional organizations in stabilization processes. Attending the meeting were representatives of the AU, the Association of Southeast Asian Nations, the Commonwealth of Independent States (CIS), the Economic Community of West African States, the EU, the League of Arab States, NATO, the Organization of the Islamic Conference and OSCE.

The Council President (Romania), in a background document on the subject [S/2004/546], stated that the purpose of the meeting was to identify new methods of cooperation and interaction between the United Nations and regional organizations and innovative approaches in conflict stabilization processes. It would also review progress made since its 2003 meeting on the theme "The Security Council and regional organizations: facing the new challenges to international peace and security" [YUN 2003, p. 58].

Addressing the Council, the Secretary-General said that the United Nations was currently cooperating with regional organizations in stabilization processes in many countries, particularly with the AU and the EU in Africa, the EU and NATO in Europe, the Organization of American States and the Caribbean Community in Haiti, and with coalition forces in Afghanistan. That cooperation had shown that, in many instances, regional organizations could be on the ground much faster than the United Nations. Indeed, the AU, the EU and NATO had either established or were developing rapid response capabilities for peacekeeping operations. Not all regional organizations, however, could sustain deployments over a long period, and the legitimacy that flowed from UN operations was often needed for longer-term sustainability.

The cooperative efforts of the United Nations with regional organizations had not been without problems. Full integration was not always easy, due to different mandates, organizational cultures and leadership roles. In trying to enhance cooperation, the United Nations had to consider the comparative strengths of different organizations and work to create strategic partnerships that met challenges. Moreover, UN co-operation with regional organizations, though established across a wide range of activities, was often ad hoc. More institutionalized channels of cooperation would help ensure greater efficiency and effectiveness and economies of scale. To that end, the Secretary-General exchanged views regularly with heads of regional organizations on issues of common concern. He would discuss with them cooperation mechanisms for monitoring the protection of civilians in armed conflict, measures for building tolerance and promoting a dialogue among civilizations and lessons learned from field experiences, such as military-civilian cooperation, policing, institution-building and confidence-building measures. The 2005 high-level meeting between the United Nations and regional organizations would review progress in implementing decisions on those issues.

Report of Secretary-General. The Secretary-General, in his report on the work of the Organization [A/59/1] (see p. 3), gave examples of UN co-operation with regional organizations in pursuit of the shared goals of peace, stability and development in a framework of democratic governance and respect for human rights and the rule of law.

SECURITY COUNCIL ACTION

On 20 July [meeting 5007], following consultations among Security Council members, the President made statement **S/PRST/2004/27** on behalf of the Council:

> The Security Council met on 20 July 2004 to consider the item entitled "Cooperation between the United Nations and regional organizations in stabilization processes". Members recalled that Articles 52 and 53 of the Charter of the United Nations set forth the contribution of regional organizations to the settlement of disputes, as well as the relationship between the United Nations and regional organizations.
>
> The Council recalls its invitation of January 1993 to regional organizations to improve coordination with the United Nations, the Declaration of the General Assembly of December 1994 on the enhancement of cooperation between the United Nations and regional arrangements or agencies, and its meeting on "The Security Council and regional organizations: facing the new challenges to international peace and security", held on 11 April 2003 under the Mexican presidency of the Council.
>
> On 20 July 2004, members expressed their views on the cooperation between the United Nations and regional organizations and acknowledged the important role that can be played by the latter in the prevention, resolution and management of conflicts, including by addressing their root causes.
>
> The statements emphasized that the Council has primary responsibility for the maintenance of international peace and security and that effectively addressing the numerous conflict situations confronting the international community would require an increased level of cooperation with regional organizations, where appropriate.
>
> Member States and heads of regional organizations participating in the meeting stressed their interest in enhancing cooperation between the United Nations and regional organizations in the maintenance of international peace and security. They also considered that regular dialogue on specific issues between the Council and regional organizations would bring significant added value in this respect.
>
> It was stressed that common and coordinated efforts undertaken by the United Nations and regional organizations in stabilization processes should be based on complementarity and their comparative advantages, making full use of their experience, in accordance with the Charter and the relevant statutes of the regional organizations.
>
> The statements reiterated the importance of a coherent approach to stabilization processes through improved cooperation and collaboration, including increased and timely exchange of information between United Nations and regional organizations, in accordance with the provisions of Article 54 of the Charter.
>
> The Council welcomes the ongoing practice of high-level meetings of the Secretary-General with regional organizations and the consensus reached over modalities of cooperation in conflict prevention and principles of cooperation in peace-building. It invites the Secretary-General to give consideration to the relevant views expressed in this debate in preparation of the next high-level meeting and to keep the Council informed as appropriate.
>
> The Council invites regional organizations to take necessary steps to increase collaboration with the United Nations in order to maximize efficiency in stabilization processes and also encourages enhanced cooperation and coordination among regional and subregional organizations themselves, in particular through the exchange of information and by sharing experience and best practices.
>
> The Council invites all Members of the United Nations to contribute to the strengthening of the capacity of regional and subregional organizations in all parts of the world, including through the provision of human, technical and financial assistance.
>
> The Council invites all Members of the United Nations, and other parts of the United Nations system with relevant experience and expertise, to contribute to this process.

The Council, in statement **S/PRST/2004/44** of 19 November (see p. 282), recognized the importance of cooperation between the United Nations and the AU to build capacity to deal with collective security challenges.

Political and peace-building missions in 2004

During 2004, 15 UN political offices and peace-building missions were in operation: 8 in

Africa, 1 in the Americas, 5 in Asia and the Pacific and 1 in the Middle East.

Among those missions in Africa, the United Nations Office in Burundi was absorbed into the United Nations Operation in Burundi in May (see p. 141). The Secretary-General extended the mandate of the United Nations Peace-building Office in the Central African Republic until 31 December 2005. The Security Council extended the mandate of the United Nations Peace-building Support Office in Guinea-Bissau until 22 December 2005, which it also revised. The United Nations Mission in Côte d'Ivoire was extended twice, to 27 February and 4 April, and was absorbed as of that date into the United Nations Operation in Côte d'Ivoire (see p. 170). The United Nations Advance Mission in the Sudan was established on 11 June. The United Nations Political Office for Somalia continued to monitor the situation in that country. The mandate of the Office of the Special Representative of the Secretary-General for the Great Lakes Region was extended until 31 December 2005, and that of the United Nations Office for West Africa was extended for three years, from 1 January 2005 to 31 December 2007.

In the Americas, the United Nations Verification Mission in Guatemala concluded its mandate on 31 December 2004.

In Asia and the Pacific, the mandate of the United Nations Tajikistan Office of Peace-building was extended until 1 June 2005. The mandate of the United Nations Observer Mission in Bougainville, established from 1 January 2004 to replace the United Nations Political Office in Bouganville, was extended to the end of the year. The United Nations Assistance Mission in Afghanistan was extended to 26 March 2005, and the mandate of the United Nations Assistance Mission for Iraq was extended until 12 August 2005. In the Democratic People's Republic of Korea, the United Nations Command continued to maintain implementation of the 1953 Armistice Agreement [YUN 1953, p. 136].

In the Middle East, the Office of the United Nations Special Coordinator for the Middle East contributed to the implementation of peace agreements. The Council, in other action, decided to send visiting missions to Haiti (13-16 April) (see p. 288), West Africa (20-29 June) (see p. 164) and Central Africa (20-25 November) (see p. 160).

(For the financing of UN political and peace-building missions, see PART FIVE, Chapter II.)

Roster of 2004 political and peace-building offices

The figures for mission strength listed for the following missions and offices are as at 1 December 2004.

UNOB

United Nations Office in Burundi
Established: 25 October 1993.
Ended: 21 May 2004.
Mandate: To assist the parties to the peace process with regard to the building of an internal political partnership within the context of the Arusha peace process; extended in 2001 to help in the consolidation of peace and security.
Head of Mission: Berhanu Dinka (Ethiopia).

MINUGUA

United Nations Verification Mission in Guatemala
Established: 19 September 1994.
Ended: 31 December 2004.
Mandate: To verify implementation of the Comprehensive Agreement on Human Rights.
Representative of the Secretary-General and Chief of Mission: Tom Koenigs (Germany).
Strength: 26 international civilian staff, 1 civilian police adviser, 45 local civilian staff.

UNPOS

United Nations Political Office for Somalia
Established: 15 April 1995.
Mandate: To monitor the situation in Somalia and keep the Security Council informed, particularly about developments affecting the humanitarian and security situation, repatriation of refugees and impact on neighbouring countries.
Representative of the Secretary-General and Head of Office: Winston A. Tubman (Liberia).
Strength: 5 international civilian staff, 3 local civilian staff.

Great Lakes region

Office of the Special Representative of the Secretary-General for the Great Lakes Region
Established: 19 December 1997.
Mandate: To monitor developments in the region and their implications for peace and security and contribute to regional efforts in the prevention or peaceful settlement of conflicts.
Special Representative of the Secretary-General: Ibrahima Fall (Senegal).
Strength: 8 international civilian staff, 8 local civilian staff.

UNOGBIS

United Nations Peace-building Support Office in Guinea-Bissau

Established: 3 March 1999.

Mandate: To assist in the transition from conflict management to post-conflict peace-building and reconstruction; revised in 2004 to include the promotion of national reconciliation, and assistance in holding elections and in reform of security and justice sectors.

Representative of the Secretary-General and Head of Office: João Bernardo Honwana (Mozambique).

Strength: 11 international civilian staff, 2 military advisers, 1 civilian police adviser, 13 local civilian staff.

UNSCO

Office of the United Nations Special Coordinator for the Middle East

Established: 1 October 1999.

Mandate: To act as the focal point for the United Nations contribution to the implementation of the peace agreements and to enhance UN assistance.

Special Coordinator for the Middle East Peace Process and Personal Representative of the Secretary-General: Terje Roed-Larsen (Norway).

Strength: 21 international civilian staff, 21 local civilian staff.

BONUCA

United Nations Peace-building Office in the Central African Republic

Established: 15 February 2000.

Mandate: To support efforts to consolidate peace and promote national reconstruction and economic recovery.

Representative of the Secretary-General and Head of Office: General Lamine Cissé (Senegal).

Strength: 22 international civilian staff, 5 military advisers, 6 civilian police, 30 local civilian staff.

UNTOP

United Nations Tajikistan Office of Peace-building

Established: 1 June 2000.

Mandate: To provide a political framework and leadership for post-conflict peace-building.

Representative of the Secretary-General: Vladimir Sotirov (Bulgaria) (from 1 October).

Strength: 10 international civilian staff, 1 civilian police adviser, 17 local civilian staff.

UNOWA

United Nations Office for West Africa

Established: 1 January 2002.

Mandate: To ensure the strengthening of harmonization and coordination of UN system activities in an integrated regional perspective and development of a partnership with the Economic Community of West African States, other sub-regional organizations and international and national actors, including civil society.

Special Representative of the Secretary-General: Ahmedou Ould-Abdallah (Mauritania).

Strength: 7 international civilian staff, 7 local civilian staff.

UNAMA

United Nations Assistance Mission in Afghanistan

Established: 28 March 2002.

Mandate: To fulfil the tasks and responsibilities entrusted to the United Nations in the Bonn Agreement; promote national reconciliation and rapprochement; manage all UN humanitarian relief, recovery and reconstruction activities; and assist in the promotion of the political process.

Special Representative of the Secretary-General: Jean Arnault (France).

Strength: 186 international civilian staff, 734 local civilian staff, 10 military observers, 8 civilian police.

MINUCI

United Nations Mission in Côte d'Ivoire

Established: 13 May 2003.

Ended: 4 April 2004, with its merger into the United Nations Operation in Côte d'Ivoire.

UNAMI

United Nations Assistance Mission for Iraq

Established: 14 August 2003.

Mandate: To support the Secretary-General in the fulfilment of his mandate under Security Council resolution 1483(2003).

Special Representative of the Secretary-General: Ashraf Jehangir Qazi (Pakistan).

Strength: 132 international civilian staff, 187 local civilian staff, 3 military advisers.

UNOMB

United Nations Observer Mission in Bougainville (Papua New Guinea)

Established: 1 January 2004.

Mandate: To assist in the promotion of the political process under the Lincoln Agreement.

Head of Office: Tor Stenbock (Norway).

Strength: 2 international civilian staff.

UNAMIS

United Nations Advance Mission in the Sudan

Established: 11 June 2004.

Mandate: To prepare for the international monitoring foreseen in the 2003 Naivasha Agreement on Security Arrangements, to facilitate contacts with the parties concerned and to prepare for the introduction of a peace support operation following the signing of a comprehensive peace agreement.

Special Representative of the Secretary-General: Jan Pronk (Netherlands).

Strength: 154 international civilian staff, 141 local civilian staff, 25 military personnel.

Commemoration of the sixtieth anniversary of the end of the Second World War

On 22 November [meeting 59], the General Assembly adopted **resolution 59/26** [draft: A/59/L.28/Rev.2, as orally revised] without vote [agenda item 158].

Commemoration of the sixtieth anniversary of the end of the Second World War

The General Assembly,

Recalling that 2005 marks the sixtieth anniversary of the end of the Second World War, the war which brought untold sorrow to mankind,

Stressing that this historic event established the conditions for the creation of the United Nations, designed to save succeeding generations from the scourge of war,

Calling upon the States Members of the United Nations to unite their efforts in dealing with new challenges and threats, with the United Nations playing a central role, and to make every effort to settle all disputes by peaceful means in conformity with the Charter of the United Nations and in such a manner that international peace and security are not endangered,

Underlining the progress made since the end of the Second World War in overcoming its legacy and towards establishing reconciliation, international and regional cooperation and the promotion of democratic values, human rights and fundamental freedoms, in particular through the United Nations, and the establishment of regional organizations and other appropriate frameworks,

1. *Declares* 8-9 May as a time of remembrance and reconciliation and, while recognizing that Member States may have individual days of victory, liberation and commemoration, invites all Member States, organizations of the United Nations system, non-governmental organizations and individuals to observe annually either one or both of these days in an appropriate manner to pay tribute to all victims of the Second World War;

2. *Requests* the President of the General Assembly to hold a special solemn meeting of the General Assembly in the second week of May 2005 in commemoration of all victims of the war;

3. *Requests* the Secretary-General to bring the present resolution to the attention of all Member States and organizations of the United Nations system and to take measures necessary for its implementation.

The Assembly, by **decision 59/552** of 23 December, decided that the item entitled "Declaration by the United Nations of 8 and 9 May as days of remembrance and reconciliation" would remain for consideration during its resumed fifty-ninth (2005) session.

Threats to international peace and security

International terrorism

High-level Panel on Threats, Challenges and Change

The High-level Panel on Threats, Challenges and Change, in its report transmitted to the General Assembly in December [A/59/565 & Corr.1], described the effects of terrorism and made recommendations for its prevention. The Panel said that terrorism attacked the values that lay at the heart of the United Nations Charter—respect for human rights, the rule of law, rules of war to protect civilians, tolerance among people and nations, and the peaceful resolution of conflict. Two new dynamics gave the terrorist threat greater urgency—the instance (not likely to be the last) of an armed non-State network (Al-Qaida) with global reach and sophisticated capacity; and the threat that terrorists, for whatever motivation, would seek to cause mass casualties.

The Panel recommended that the United Nations, with the Secretary-General taking a leading role, promote a comprehensive strategy against terrorism. That strategy would include dissuasion, working to reverse the causes or facilitators of terrorism through promoting social and political rights and the rule of law, and to end occupations, address major political grievances, combat organized crime, reduce poverty and unemployment, and stop State collapse. It should also encompass efforts to counter extremism and intolerance, including through education and fostering public debate; development of better instruments for global counter-terrorism cooperation, within a legal framework that was respectful of civil liberties and human rights; building State capacity to prevent terrorist recruitment and operations; and control of dangerous materials and public health defence.

Member States that had not done so were urged to sign and ratify all 12 international conventions against terrorism [YUN 2001, p. 69], and adopt the eight Special Recommendations on Terrorist Financing issued by the Organisation for Economic Co-operation and Development–supported Financial Action Task Force on

Money-Laundering [ibid., p. 68] and the measures recommended in its various best practices papers. The General Assembly should rapidly complete negotiations on a comprehensive convention on terrorism, incorporating a definition of terrorism. The Security Council should extend the authority of the Counter-Terrorism Executive Directorate (see p. 79) to act as a clearing house for State-to-State provision of military, police and border control assistance for developing domestic counter-terrorism capacities. The Council should devise a schedule of predetermined sanctions for State non-compliance with the Council's counter-terrorism resolutions. To help Member States comply with their counter-terrorism obligations, the United Nations should establish a capacity-building trust fund.

2004 terrorist incidents

Spain

On 11 March, a terrorist attack on commuter trains in Madrid, Spain, claimed the lives of 200 people and caused over 1,400 other casualties, some 190 of whom were in serious or critical condition. Among the dead and wounded were nationals not only of Spain, but of over 20 other countries.

SECURITY COUNCIL ACTION

On the same day [meeting 4923], the Security Council unanimously adopted **resolution 1530 (2004)**. The draft [S/2004/186] was prepared in consultations among Council members.

The Security Council,

Reaffirming the purposes and principles of the Charter of the United Nations and its relevant resolutions, in particular its resolution 1373(2001) of 28 September 2001,

Reaffirming also the need to combat by all means, in accordance with the Charter, threats to international peace and security caused by terrorist acts,

1. *Condemns in the strongest terms* the bomb attacks in Madrid perpetrated by the terrorist group Euskadi ta Askatasuna (ETA) on 11 March 2004, in which many lives were lost and people injured, and regards such acts, like any act of terrorism, as a threat to peace and security;

2. *Expresses its deepest sympathy and condolences* to the people and Government of Spain and to the victims of the terrorist attacks and their families;

3. *Urges* all States, in accordance with their obligations under resolution 1373(2001), to cooperate actively in efforts to find and bring to justice the perpetrators, organizers and sponsors of these terrorist attacks;

4. *Expresses its reinforced determination* to combat all forms of terrorism, in accordance with its responsibilities under the Charter of the United Nations.

Communications. On 12 March [S/2004/196], Romania, in a letter addressed to the Council President, noted that among those killed were two Romanian citizens and 75 others were injured. Romania emphasized the importance of elaborating and enforcing comprehensive counter-terrorism legislation and urged the Council to continue to discharge its responsibility for international peace and security, including through its Counter-Terrorism Committee. The adoption of resolution 1530(2004) should be followed by concrete and firm measures to bring to justice the perpetrators and sponsors of such heinous acts.

On 15 March [S/2004/204], Spain conveyed its appreciation for the expressions of sympathy and cooperation demonstrated by the Council in resolution 1530(2004), adopted only a few hours after the attacks. It said that when the Council adopted that text, the Spanish Government was firmly convinced that the terrorist group ETA was behind the 11 March events. Since then, new evidence pointed to the involvement of citizens of other countries and investigations were continuing. In a further communication of 31 March [S/2004/269], Spain expressed its regret at its earlier conclusion and reported that the attacks were committed by radical Islamist elements, many of whom were Moroccans. With the collaboration of the Moroccan police, an investigation was being conducted into the terrorist organization Moroccan Islamic Combat Group. It had been determined that individuals, whose whereabouts were unknown and who apparently took part in preparing and carrying out the attacks, were involved in drug trafficking. The investigation was ongoing and the Spanish police were processing the relevant international arrest warrants.

Russian Federation

Grozny incident

On 10 May [meeting 4966], following consultations among Security Council members, the President made statement **S/PRST/2004/14** on behalf of the Council:

The Security Council unequivocally condemns the terrorist bomb attack that took place on 9 May 2004 in Grozny, Russian Federation, as a result of which many people were injured and killed, including the President of the Chechen Republic of the Russian Federation, Mr. Ahmad Kadyrov.

The Council condemns in the strongest terms the perpetrators of this heinous act committed against innocent people at the stadium when celebrating Victory Day—the most solemn national holiday in the Russian Federation.

The Council expresses its deepest sympathy and condolences to the people and to the Government of the Russian Federation and to the victims and their families.

The Council urges all States, in accordance with their obligation under resolution 1373(2001) of 28 September 2001, to cooperate with the Russian authorities in their efforts to bring to justice the perpetrators, organizers and sponsors of this attack.

The Council reaffirms that terrorism in all its forms and manifestations constitutes one of the most serious threats to international peace and security and that any acts of terrorism are criminal and unjustifiable, regardless of their motivation, whenever and by whomsoever committed.

The Council expresses its determination to combat all forms of terrorism, in accordance with its responsibilities under the Charter of the United Nations.

Beslan incident

On 1 September, more than 30 armed men seized a school in the town of Beslan in the North Ossetia region of the Russian Federation during a ceremony to mark the first day of the school term, taking more than 1,000 people hostage. The siege, which ended two days later, resulted in the death of 360 persons, of whom 172 were children and 30 members of the gang that seized the school.

SECURITY COUNCIL ACTION

On the same day [meeting 5026], following consultations among Security Council members, the President made statement **S/PRST/2004/31** on behalf of the Council:

The Security Council condemns in the strongest terms the heinous terrorist act involving the taking of hostages at a secondary school in the town of Beslan, Russian Federation, on 1 September 2004, as well as other terrorist attacks committed recently against innocent civilians in Moscow and on two Russian airliners, in which many lives were claimed and people injured.

The Council demands the immediate and unconditional release of all hostages in the terrorist attack.

The Council expresses its deepest sympathy and condolences to the people and the Government of the Russian Federation and to the victims of the terrorist acts and their families.

The Council urges all States, in accordance with their obligations under resolution 1373(2001), to cooperate actively with the Russian authorities in their efforts to find and bring to justice the perpetrators, organizers and sponsors of these terrorist acts.

The Council reaffirms that terrorism in all its forms and manifestations constitutes one of the most serious threats to international peace and security and that any acts of terrorism are criminal and unjustifiable, regardless of their motivation, whenever and by whomsoever committed.

The Council expresses its determination to combat all forms of terrorism, in accordance with its responsibilities under the Charter of the United Nations.

Communications. The Russian Federation President, Vladimir Putin, in a 4 September statement [A/59/337-S/2004/721], said that the Beslan incident was an inhuman crime by terrorists and a direct intervention on the part of international terrorists against Russia, which had to create a more effective security system and demand that its law enforcement agencies took actions commensurate with the level and scale of the new threats.

The heads of the member States of CIS, in a 16 September statement [A/59/537-S/2004/868], expressed their solidarity with the Russian Federation in its fight against terrorism and their conviction that only concerted efforts in combating international terrorism would prevent its spread. The heads of State instructed the relevant national structures to prepare a concept of cooperation between CIS member States in combating terrorism and other violent manifestations of extremism, and pledged to contribute to the struggle waged by the international community against the threat of terrorism.

The State Duma of the Federal Assembly of the Russian Federation, in a 22 September statement [A/59/538], expressed gratitude to all national parliaments, international organizations, State and public figures and peoples of foreign States for their expression of sympathy and called for international solidarity in combating terrorism, given the expanding geographical scope of terrorist acts, their brutality and the transformation of civilians, and even children, into the main target of terror.

Other incidents

On 8 October, the Security Council President made a press statement [SC/8215], affirming that Council members strongly condemned recent terrorist attacks in which many lives were claimed and people injured, including the horrific attacks in Pakistan, the 7 October heinous attack in Taba, Egypt, and the murder of a British civilian in Baghdad. By adopting resolution 1566(2004) by consensus, the Council had reaffirmed the central role of the United Nations in the fight against terrorism and the Council's determination to stand together in confronting terrorism. The Council urged all States, in accordance with their obligations under resolution 1373(2001) [YUN 2001, p. 61] and other relevant Council resolutions, to cooperate actively in their efforts to find and bring to justice the perpetrators, organizers and sponsors of terrorist acts. They reaffirmed their view that terrorism in all its forms and manifestations constituted one of the most serious threats to international peace and security, and that any acts of terrorism were criminal and unjustifiable.

Anniversary of bombing of UN Baghdad office

On 19 August, the Security Council President issued a press statement on the first anniversary of the bombing of the UN headquarters in Baghdad [SC/8170-IK/455], stating that Council members together with the entire system commemorated that day as one of the most tragic days in the history of the Organization. A year earlier, the UN family lost Sergio Vieira de Mello and 21 other UN staff members in the bombing. Their deaths came as a result of the terrorist attack aimed at breaking the will of the international community, which came to Iraq with no other mission than to help its people regain control of their own destiny and build a better future of peace, justice, sovereignty and full independence. Those who killed the UN staff members had committed a crime, not only against the United Nations, but also against Iraq itself, the statement said. Paying tribute to those who lost their lives in that attack, members of the Council noted the continuing terrorist attacks on the representatives of the international community working in Iraq and strongly condemned them.

Measures to eliminate terrorism

During 2004, the United Nations pursued action on several fronts to combat and eliminate international terrorism. The General Assembly, on 2 December, adopted **resolution 59/46** (see p. 1311) on measures to eliminate international terrorism.

The Security Council, by **resolution 1526 (2004)** of 30 January (see p. 332), decided to improve implementation of the measures imposed by its previous resolutions against Al-Qaida, the Taliban and their associates. On 28 April, by **resolution 1540(2004)** (see p. 544), the Council, concerned by the threat of illicit trafficking in nuclear, chemical and biological weapons and their means of delivery, decided that all States should establish domestic controls to prevent the proliferation of those weapons and their means of delivery. In October, during consideration of the agenda item "Threats to international peace and security caused by terrorist acts", the Council adopted additional measures to be taken to combat terrorism (see below).

SECURITY COUNCIL ACTION

On 8 October [meeting 5053], the Security Council unanimously adopted **resolution 1566(2004)**.

The draft [S/2004/792] was prepared in consultations among Council members.

The Security Council,

Reaffirming its resolutions 1267(1999) of 15 October 1999 and 1373(2001) of 28 September 2001, as well as its other resolutions concerning threats to international peace and security caused by terrorism,

Recalling, in this regard, its resolution 1540(2004) of 28 April 2004,

Reaffirming the imperative to combat terrorism in all its forms and manifestations by all means, in accordance with the Charter of the United Nations and international law,

Deeply concerned by the increasing number of victims, including children, of acts of terrorism motivated by intolerance or extremism in various regions of the world,

Calling upon States to cooperate fully with the Security Council Committee established pursuant to resolution 1373(2001) concerning counter-terrorism (the Counter-Terrorism Committee), including the recently established Counter-Terrorism Committee Executive Directorate, the Security Council Committee established pursuant to resolution 1267(1999) concerning Al-Qaida and the Taliban and associated individuals and entities and its Analytical Support and Sanctions Monitoring Team, and the Security Council Committee established pursuant to resolution 1540 (2004), and further calling upon such bodies to enhance cooperation with each other,

Reminding States that they must ensure that any measures taken to combat terrorism comply with all their obligations under international law, and should adopt such measures in accordance with international law, in particular international human rights, refugee and humanitarian law,

Reaffirming that terrorism in all its forms and manifestations constitutes one of the most serious threats to peace and security,

Considering that acts of terrorism seriously impair the enjoyment of human rights and threaten the social and economic development of all States and undermine global stability and prosperity,

Emphasizing that enhancing dialogue and broadening understanding among civilizations, in an effort to prevent the indiscriminate targeting of different religions and cultures, and addressing unresolved regional conflicts and the full range of global issues, including development issues, will contribute to international cooperation, which by itself is necessary to sustain the broadest possible fight against terrorism,

Reaffirming its profound solidarity with victims of terrorism and their families,

Acting under Chapter VII of the Charter,

1. *Condemns in the strongest terms* all acts of terrorism irrespective of their motivation, whenever and by whomsoever committed, as one of the most serious threats to peace and security;

2. *Calls upon* States to cooperate fully in the fight against terrorism, especially with those States where or against whose citizens terrorist acts are committed, in accordance with their obligations under international law, in order to find, deny safe haven and bring to justice, on the basis of the principle of extradite or prosecute, any person who supports, facilitates, participates or attempts to participate in the financing, planning,

preparation or commission of terrorist acts or provides safe havens;

3. *Recalls* that criminal acts, including against civilians, committed with the intent to cause death or serious bodily injury, or taking of hostages, with the purpose of provoking a state of terror in the general public or in a group of persons or particular persons, intimidating a population or compelling a government or an international organization to do or to abstain from doing any act, which constitute offences within the scope of and as defined in the international conventions and protocols relating to terrorism, are under no circumstances justifiable by considerations of a political, philosophical, ideological, racial, ethnic, religious or other similar nature, and calls upon all States to prevent such acts and, to ensure that such acts if not prevented, are punished by penalties consistent with their grave nature;

4. *Calls upon* all States to become party, as a matter of urgency, to the relevant international conventions and protocols whether or not they are party to regional conventions on the matter;

5. *Calls upon* Member States to cooperate fully on an expedited basis in resolving all outstanding issues with a view to adopting by consensus the draft comprehensive convention on international terrorism and the draft international convention for the suppression of acts of nuclear terrorism;

6. *Calls upon* relevant international, regional and subregional organizations to strengthen international cooperation in the fight against terrorism and to intensify their interaction with the United Nations and, in particular, the Security Council Committee established pursuant to resolution 1373(2001) concerning counter-terrorism (the Counter-Terrorism Committee), with a view to facilitating full and timely implementation of resolution 1373(2001);

7. *Requests* the Counter-Terrorism Committee, in consultation with relevant international, regional and subregional organizations and the United Nations bodies to develop a set of best practices to assist States in implementing the provisions of resolution 1373(2001) related to the financing of terrorism;

8. *Directs* the Counter-Terrorism Committee, as a matter of priority and, when appropriate, in close cooperation with relevant international, regional and subregional organizations, to start visits to States, with the consent of the States concerned, in order to enhance the monitoring of the implementation of resolution 1373(2001) and facilitate the provision of technical and other assistance for such implementation;

9. *Decides* to establish a working group consisting of all members of the Security Council to consider and submit recommendations to the Council on practical measures to be imposed upon individuals, groups or entities involved in or associated with terrorist activities, other than those designated by the Security Council Committee established pursuant to resolution 1267 (1999) concerning Al-Qaida and the Taliban and associated individuals and entities, including more effective procedures considered to be appropriate for bringing them to justice through prosecution or extradition, freezing their financial assets, preventing their movement through the territories of Member States, and preventing supply to them of all types of arms and related material, and on the procedures for implementing these measures;

10. *Requests* the working group established pursuant to paragraph 9 above to consider the possibility of establishing an international fund to compensate victims of terrorist acts and their families, which might be financed through voluntary contributions, which could consist in part of assets seized from terrorist organizations, their members and their sponsors, and submit its recommendations to the Council;

11. *Requests* the Secretary-General to take, as a matter of urgency, appropriate steps to make the Counter-Terrorism Committee Executive Directorate fully operational and to inform the Council by 15 November 2004;

12. *Decides* to remain actively seized of the matter.

The Russian Federation, in a statement after the vote, said that the unprecedented escalation of international terrorism (see p. 72) pointed to the need for the Council to further develop a global anti-terrorist strategy, as defined in resolution 1373(2001) [YUN 2001, p. 61]. Resolution 1566 (2004) set out concrete steps to strengthen security mechanisms and to improve legal instruments for enhancing coordination of international counter-terrorism actions. However, identifying additional anti-terrorist measures posed a problem, and the Council's working group entrusted with that task should, as a priority, search for ways to identify terrorists, possibly drafting a relevant list of those who might subsequently be brought to justice.

Communications. On 12 May [A/59/83-S/2004/387], the Sudan transmitted to the Secretary-General the Khartoum Declaration on Combating Terrorism and Transnational Organized Crime, issued by the Intergovernmental Authority on Development (Khartoum, 17-19 January).

On 23 March [A/58/745-S/2004/235], Cuba protested the inclusion in the United States delegation to the sixtieth session of the Commission on Human Rights of the "notorious terrorist" of Cuban origin, Luis Zúñiga Rey. It said that his inclusion was a sign of disrespect for the United Nations and it jeopardized the security of the Organization.

By letters dated 2 and 21 September [A/58/884-S/2004/718, A/59/371], Cuba informed the Secretary-General that, as a result of Panama's President, Mireya Moscoso, having pardoned four Cuban-born terrorists (Luis Faustino Clemente Posada Carriles, Gaspar Eugenio Jiménez Escobedo, Guillermo Novo Sampoll and Pedro Remón Rodríguez), who were sentenced in Panama for the attempted assassination of Cuban President Fidel Castro in November 2000, it was severing indefinitely diplomatic relations with Panama. Also on 21 September [S/2004/753], Cuba provided further information on the four suspects and requested the Counter-Terrorism

Committee to evaluate the situation in the hope of bringing an end to impunity for those terrorists and to inform Cuba of its conclusions, in the light of resolution 1373(2001).

On 22 September [A/59/383-S/2004/758], Costa Rica conveyed to the Secretary-General the proposal of its President, Abel Pacheco de la Espriella, for establishing a United Nations High Commissioner on Terrorism. The office of such a High Commissioner would be an independent body for coordinating international counter-terrorism activities. The President recommended that the General Assembly request the Secretary-General to report in 2005 on the possible methods, mandate and structure of such an office, which could be operational by December 2007, and to establish a working group for that purpose.

Counter-Terrorism Committee

In 2004, the Counter-Terrorism Committee (CTC), established by Security Council resolution 1373(2001) [YUN 2001, p. 61], updated the consolidated directory of contact points in each State, in a number of international/regional organizations and agencies, and in the UN Secretariat, that would provide information or assistance in connection with matters arising under resolution 1373(2001). The revisions were transmitted by the Committee Chairman to the Council President on 28 April [S/2004/346] and 24 September [S/2004/659].

The Chairman also submitted CTC's work programmes for the 90-day periods 1 January to 31 March [S/2004/32], 1 April to 30 June [S/2004/284], 1 July to 30 September [S/2004/541] and 1 October to 31 December [S/2004/820]. The Council considered those reports at meetings held on 19 July and 19 October under the agenda item "Threats to international peace and security caused by terrorist acts".

In a 28 May note [S/2004/436], the Council President reported that Council members had agreed to elect Alexander V. Konuzin (Russian Federation) as CTC Chairman and Abdallah Baali (Algeria), Ismael Abraão Gaspar Martins (Angola) and Ronaldo Mota Sardenberg (Brazil) as Vice-Chairmen until 31 December 2004.

Security Council consideration (March). The CTC Chairman, reporting on 4 March [meeting 4921] to the Security Council on the Committee's work, said that the Committee had approved 44 reports from States on their implementation of resolution 1373(2001) under its October to December 2003 programme of work [YUN 2003, p. 66] and its subcommittees had reviewed another 37. As part of that work programme, the report on the problems encountered by States and CTC in

implementing resolution 1373(2001) (see p. 78) was submitted to the Council on 14 November 2003. CTC would report on measures to be taken to solve those problems (see p. 77). CTC expanded contacts and cooperation with international, regional and subregional organizations, including participating in their meetings.

Communications. On 1 April [S/2004/276], the CTC Chairman transmitted to the Council President the declaration adopted by the follow-up meeting to the CTC special meeting of 6 March 2003, hosted by OSCE in cooperation with the United Nations Office on Drugs and Crime (Vienna, 11-12 March 2004), in which international, regional and subregional organizations agreed, among other actions, to enhance the effectiveness of their efforts against terrorism and to coordinate and exchange information with CTC, one another and other relevant international actors to meet the capacity-building needs of their members so as to assist them to implement fully their obligations under resolution 1373(2001).

On 7 May [S/2004/361], the CTC Chairman, in accordance with resolution 1456(2003) [YUN 2003, p. 63], reported on States' reporting to CTC and indicated that, as at 7 May, 71 States had failed to meet the reporting deadlines for the submission of second, third and fourth reports. Of those States, 11 had requested an extension.

Security Council consideration (July). Reporting to the Council on 19 July [meeting 5006], the CTC Chairman, referring to the Committee's report for April to June [S/2004/284], said that during the transition period following the adoption of resolution 1535(2004) (see p. 79) on the revitalization of CTC, the review of reports submitted by States had slowed down. Only 25 of the 65 planned reviews were actually completed, but CTC had taken measures to accelerate the process. The Committee began integrating the analysis of country assessments of assistance needs into the review process, thereby ensuring that global technical assistance efforts were better adjusted to needs. CTC intended to assume a more active role in coordinating technical assistance, particularly through direct dialogue with Member States and through information exchange with the donor community. With regard to transparency, CTC resumed the practice of regular briefings by its Chairman with interested delegations. Given the lack of public awareness about its activities and the resulting misconceptions about its work, it would continue to improve its communication methods. Through CTC efforts, the number of States becoming parties to the 12 terrorism-related international conventions [YUN 2001, p. 69] had increased.

Referring to the Committee's report for July to September [S/2004/541], the CTC Chairman said that, as at 30 June, CTC had received 515 reports from Member States and others, including 162 second, 116 third and 40 fourth reports. However, 71 States had not met the deadline for submission of their reports. CTC's main task was implementing resolution 1535(2004), and in that regard it expected to consider in July the draft organizational plan for the CTC Executive Directorate (see p. 79). It had agreed on formal cooperation with the Security Council Committee established pursuant to resolution 1267(1999) [YUN 1999, p. 265] concerning Al-Qaida and the Taliban and would seek appropriate working relations with the Security Council Committee established pursuant to resolution 1540(2004) (see p. 544) concerning non-proliferation problems in the context of the terrorist threat. The Committee would begin preparations for its first visit to a Member State to ensure monitoring of resolution 1373(2001). It would also develop direct dialogue with Member States seeking assistance in strengthening their capacities to combat terrorism.

SECURITY COUNCIL ACTION (July)

On 19 July [meeting 5006], following consultations among Security Council members, the President made statement **S/PRST/2004/26** on behalf of the Council:

The Security Council welcomes the briefing by the Chairman of the Security Council Committee established pursuant to resolution 1373(2001) concerning counter-terrorism (the Counter-Terrorism Committee) on the work of the Committee.

The Council reaffirms that terrorism in all its forms and manifestations constitutes one of the most serious threats to peace and security and that any acts of terrorism are criminal and unjustifiable, regardless of their motivation, whenever and by whomsoever committed.

The Council recalls the statement by its President on 16 October 2003 (S/PRST/2003/17) and its resolution 1535(2004) of 26 March 2004, which indicated the intention of the Council to review the structure and activities of the Counter-Terrorism Committee.

The Council expresses its appreciation for the work of Mr. Inocencio Arias, of Spain, as Chairman of the Counter-Terrorism Committee and also expresses its confidence that the new Chairman, supported by the new Bureau of the Committee, will continue the effective coordination of the Committee in the global fight against terrorism under the aegis of the United Nations by monitoring the implementation of resolution 1373(2001) of 28 September 2001.

The Council invites the Counter-Terrorism Committee to pursue its agenda as set out in the work programme for the Committee for the twelfth 90-day period, focusing on practical measures to implement resolution 1535(2004) on the revitalization of the Committee, including by considering the organizational plan for the newly established Counter-Terrorism Committee Executive Directorate.

The Council notes the importance of continuing the efforts of the Counter-Terrorism Committee aimed at increasing the capabilities of Member States to combat terrorism, to identify and address the problems faced by States in implementing resolution 1373(2001), to facilitate the provision of technical assistance adjusted to the countries' needs, to encourage the largest possible number of States to become parties to the international conventions and protocols related to counter-terrorism, and to strengthen its dialogue and cooperation with international, regional and subregional organizations acting in the areas outlined by resolution 1373(2001).

The Council invites the Counter-Terrorism Committee to accelerate its work on country assessments of assistance needs that can be shared with interested donor States and organizations and welcomes the initiation of preparations for the first visit by the Committee to a Member State with its consent in order to enhance the monitoring of the implementation of resolution 1373(2001), focusing in particular on the assistance that might be available to address States' needs.

The Council notes that, as of 30 June 2004, 71 States had not met the deadline for submission of their respective reports to the Counter-Terrorism Committee as set out in resolution 1373(2001). It calls upon them urgently to do so, in order to maintain the universality of response which resolution 1373 (2001) requires.

The Council invites the Counter-Terrorism Committee to continue reporting on its activities at regular intervals and expresses its intention to review the structure and activities of the Committee in October 2004.

Security Council consideration (October). The CTC Chairman, reporting to the Council on 19 October [meeting 5059] on CTC's work programme for July to September [S/2004/541], said that, as at 30 September, CTC had received 526 reports from Member States and others, including 197 first reports, 162 second reports and 118 third reports. However, 78 Member States had not submitted their reports on time.

During the reporting period, CTC approved a guidance document for making assessments of each country's assistance needs and intended to rely on the assessment process to enhance the dialogue with Member States and the donor community with a view to making technical assistance more effective and relevant. In July, the Chairman requested Member States to update on a regular basis the Directory of Counter-Terrorism Information and Sources of Assistance and the Assistance Matrix. The Committee also adopted general guidelines for conducting visits to Member States and procedures for the preparation, conduct and evaluation of CTC visits. The CTC web page was substantially improved and updated. The Chairman submitted the 90-day work programme for October to December [S/2004/820].

SECURITY COUNCIL ACTION (October)

On 19 October [meeting 5059], following consultations among Security Council members, the President made statement **S/PRST/2004/37** on behalf of the Council:

The Security Council welcomes the briefing by the Chairman of the Security Council Committee established pursuant to resolution 1373(2001) concerning counter-terrorism (the Counter-Terrorism Committee) on the work of the Committee.

The Council reaffirms that terrorism in all its forms and manifestations constitutes one of the most serious threats to peace and security and that any acts of terrorism are criminal and unjustifiable, regardless of their motivation, whenever and by whomsoever committed.

The Council recalls the statement by its President of 19 July 2004, resolution 1535(2004), which indicated the intention of the Council to review the structure and activities of the Counter-Terrorism Committee, and resolution 1566(2004) emphasizing additional measures aimed at strengthening international cooperation in combating terrorism.

The Council invites the Counter-Terrorism Committee to pursue its agenda as set out in the work programme for the Committee for the thirteenth 90-day period, focusing on practical measures to implement resolution 1535(2004) on the revitalization of the Committee, including implementation of the organizational plan for the Counter-Terrorism Committee Executive Directorate, and resolution 1566(2004). These measures will embrace further work to increase the capacity of the Committee, including through enhanced cooperation with the Security Council Committee established pursuant to resolution 1267(1999) concerning Al-Qaida and the Taliban and associated individuals and entities and the Security Council Committee established pursuant to resolution 1540 (2004).

The Council notes the importance of continuing the efforts of the Counter-Terrorism Committee to enhance the capabilities of Member States to combat terrorism, to identify and address the problems faced by States in implementing resolution 1373 (2001), to facilitate the provision of technical assistance adjusted to the countries' needs, to encourage the largest possible number of States to become parties to the international conventions and protocols related to counter-terrorism, and to strengthen its dialogue and cooperation with international, regional and subregional organizations acting in the areas outlined in resolution 1373(2001).

The Council invites the Counter-Terrorism Committee to continue preparing and begin sending to Member States assessments of their assistance needs for eventual sharing with interested donor States and organizations, and to accelerate the preparations for the first visits to Member States with their consent in order to enhance the monitoring of the implementation of resolution 1373(2001) and facilitate the provision of technical and other assistance for such implementation.

The Council, recalling paragraph 7 of resolution 1566(2004), invites the Counter-Terrorism Committee to start, in consultation with relevant international, regional and subregional organizations and United Nations bodies, to develop a set of best practices to assist States in implementing the provisions of resolution 1373(2001) related to the financing of terrorism.

The Council notes that, as of 30 September 2004, 78 States had not submitted their respective reports to the Counter-Terrorism Committee on time as set out in resolution 1373(2001). It calls upon them urgently to do so, in order to maintain the universality of response which resolution 1373(2001) requires.

The Council invites the Counter-Terrorism Committee to continue reporting on its activities at regular intervals and expresses its intention to review the structure and activities of the Committee in January 2005.

Report of CTC Chairman. On 16 December [S/2004/982], the CTC Chairman, in accordance with the Committee's eleventh 90-day work programme [S/2004/284], presented to the Security Council a list of 75 States that had failed to meet the reporting deadlines for the submission of second, third and fourth reports, of which 7 had requested an extension.

Arrangements for the CTC Bureau

On 30 March [meeting 4939], following consultations among Security Council members, the President made statement **S/PRST/2004/8** on behalf of the Council:

The Security Council recalls the statement by its President of 16 October 2003 (S/PRST/2003/17), which confirmed the continuation of the current arrangements for the Bureau of the Security Council Committee established pursuant to resolution 1373 (2001) concerning counter-terrorism for another six months, until 4 April 2004.

The said six months having elapsed, the Council confirms the continuation of the current arrangements for the Bureau of the Committee for another six months, until 4 October 2004.

Implementation of resolution 1373(2001)

By a January note [S/2004/70], the Security Council President transmitted to the Council the report of the Chair of CTC on the problems encountered in the implementation of resolution 1373(2001) [YUN 2001, p. 61].

The report concluded that implementation of resolution 1373(2001) was encountering serious problems, at the level of both States and CTC. Implementation of the obligations for suppressing the financing of terrorism was placing new burdens on banking institutions and financial professions, legislation on money-laundering was not specific enough, international financial transactions lacked transparency, and national legislation was weak and often did not include provisions for freezing funds. It was also difficult, for both technical and political reasons, to monitor certain non-profit organizations used by terrorists to disseminate propaganda or collect funds on their behalf. Some States were reluctant to create a legislative mechanism for prosecuting those responsible for acts of terrorism wherever committed. Although many States had ratified the main international anti-terrorist conventions, a number of those had not adopted internal enforcement measures.

Because of the relationship between organized crime and terrorism, CTC needed to give greater attention in its dialogue with States to publicizing the means of combating organized crime. It should also play a more proactive role in promoting implementation of anti-terrorist action plans related to weapons of mass destruction, legal obligations in the fields of disarmament, arms limitation and non-proliferation, and instruments aimed at combating the manufacturing and trafficking of small arms and weapons.

Technical assistance was a major component of CTC work. As CTC was assuming a more proactive role in that area, its structure and working methods needed to be revisited in order to increase efficiency. It needed to evaluate the specific needs of States in that area, enhance relations with assistance providers, serve as a focal point for counter-terrorism action plans and monitor the assistance provided to States. In terms of CTC's structure and procedures, the CTC monitoring mechanism, based on the stages States had reached in adopting anti-terrorism legislation, had become artificial. Moreover, Member States perceived the stages system as an evaluation by CTC of their performance in fighting terrorism and believed that the system did not provide a clear picture of the States' real situation or efforts in implementing resolution 1373(2001). Other deficiencies were related to the need for consistency in reporting, the decision-making process, inadequacy of follow-up to CTC decisions, lack of adequate accountability, the responsibilities of the Chair, the functioning of the Bureau, recruitment of personnel of the CTC secretariat and the need to find a better contractual arrangement for CTC experts. In an effort to find solutions to the problems raised, the CTC Chair would submit a further report, including specific measures for complying with resolution 1373(2001).

Revitalization of Counter-Terrorism Committee

On 19 February [S/2004/124], the CTC Chairman submitted his proposals for the revitalization of the Committee, aimed at consolidating achievements made in the fight against terrorism, intensifying CTC's and the Security Council's work in that field, and giving CTC further means for monitoring implementation of resolution 1373 (2001). The revitalized CTC would consist of the Plenary, composed of Security Council member States, which would focus on strategic and policy decisions; the Bureau, composed of the Chair and Vice-Chairs; and the Executive Directorate (CTED), made up of experts and Secretariat staff and comprising the Assessment and Technical Assistance Office and the Information and Administrative Office. CTED would be headed by an Executive Director, to be appointed by the Secretary-General. A draft resolution reflecting the main ideas of the report was to be presented to the Council.

Security Council consideration (4 March). The CTC Chairman, Inocencio Arias (Spain), told the Security Council on 4 March [meeting 4921] that CTC revitalization was urgent and necessary and would provide the means for making it more operational, proactive and visible. The goals of revitalization were to promote and monitor implementation of resolution 1373(2001) through dialogue; strengthen the provision of technical assistance to States and cooperation within the United Nations and among international and regional organizations; improve CTC's capacity to collect information and to make concrete recommendations to the Council on all aspects of resolution 1373(2001); and expedite CTC's work and simplify its procedures, including adoption of a proactive communication strategy. The Chairman stressed that the Executive Directorate would not be a permanent structure, but would have a sunset clause of 31 December 2007 and would not set a precedent for other Council bodies.

SECURITY COUNCIL ACTION

On 26 March [meeting 4936], the Security Council unanimously adopted **resolution 1535(2004)**. The draft [S/2004/238] was prepared in consultations among Council members.

The Security Council,

Reaffirming its resolution 1373(2001) of 28 September 2001, adopted under Chapter VII of the Charter of the United Nations, and the ministerial declarations annexed to its resolutions 1377(2001) of 12 November 2001 and 1456(2003) of 20 January 2003, as well as its other resolutions concerning threats to international peace and security caused by terrorist acts,

Reaffirming also that terrorism in all its forms and manifestations constitutes one of the most serious threats to peace and security,

Reaffirming its reinforced determination to combat all forms of terrorism, in accordance with its responsibilities under the Charter,

Reminding States that they must ensure that any measures taken to combat terrorism comply with all their obligations under international law, and should adopt such measures in accordance with international law, in particular international human rights, refugee and humanitarian law,

Reaffirming its call upon States to become party, as a matter of urgency, to all relevant international conventions and protocols relating to terrorism and to support all international initiatives taken with that aim, and to make full use of the sources of assistance and guidance which are now available,

Commending Member States for their cooperation with the Counter-Terrorism Committee, and calling upon all of them to continue to cooperate fully with the Committee,

Commending the progress made so far by the Counter-Terrorism Committee, established by the Security Council under paragraph 6 of resolution 1373(2001), acting under Chapter VII of the Charter, in discharging its important responsibility to monitor the implementation of that resolution,

Stressing the important role that international, regional and subregional organizations play in the fight against terrorism, urging them to intensify their assistance to Member States with respect to the implementation of resolution 1373(2001), and commending the coordination by the Committee of counter-terrorism efforts with such organizations,

Recognizing that many States continue to require assistance in implementing resolution 1373(2001), and urging States and organizations to inform the Committee of areas in which they are able to offer assistance,

Recognizing also the need for the Committee, where appropriate, to visit States, with the consent of the State concerned, and to engage in a detailed discussion to monitor the implementation of resolution 1373 (2001),

Recognizing further that such visits should be conducted, when appropriate, in close cooperation with relevant international, regional and subregional organizations and other United Nations bodies, including the United Nations Office on Drugs and Crime, in particular with its Terrorism Prevention Branch, taking special care of the assistance that might be available to address the needs of States,

Stressing the importance of enhancing the monitoring of the implementation of resolution 1373(2001),

Having considered the report of the Chairman of the Committee on the problems encountered both by Member States and by the Committee itself in the implementation of resolution 1373(2001),

Stressing the importance of addressing these difficulties so as to enable the Committee to monitor effectively the implementation of resolution 1373(2001) and to enhance the capacity-building work in which it is engaged,

Bearing in mind the special nature of resolution 1373(2001), the continuing threats to peace and security caused by terrorism, the important role the United Nations and the Security Council must continue to play in the global fight against terrorism, and the need to reinforce the Committee as the subsidiary body of the Council with responsibility in this area, without setting a precedent for other bodies of the Council,

1. *Endorses* the report of the Security Council Committee established pursuant to resolution 1373(2001) concerning counter-terrorism on its revitalization;

2. *Decides* that the revitalized Committee shall consist of the Plenary, composed of the member States of the Security Council, and the Bureau, composed of the Chair and the Vice-Chairs, assisted by the Counter-Terrorism Committee Executive Directorate (hereinafter "CTED") to be established as a special political mission, under the policy guidance of the Plenary, for an initial period ending 31 December 2007 and subject to a comprehensive review by the Council by 31 December 2005, so as to enhance the ability of the Committee to monitor the implementation of resolution 1373 (2001) and effectively continue the capacity-building work in which it is engaged;

3. *Decides also* that CTED, headed by an Executive Director, shall be responsible for the tasks set out in the report of the Committee, and requests the Secretary-General, within forty-five days of the adoption of the present resolution, to appoint, after consultation with and subject to the approval of the Council, an Executive Director of CTED who will take up office as soon as possible;

4. *Requests* the Executive Director of CTED, within thirty days of taking office, in consultation with and through the Secretary-General, to submit to the Plenary, for its endorsement, an organizational plan for CTED, consistent with the report of the Committee and United Nations rules and regulations, including its structure, staffing requirements, budget needs, management guidelines, recruitment procedures, recognizing in particular the need for an effective, cooperative management structure for the new body, and staffing with suitably qualified and experienced personnel, who would be international civil servants subject to Article 100 of the Charter of the United Nations, securing the highest standards of efficiency, competence and integrity and paying due regard to the importance of recruiting the staff on as wide a geographical basis as possible;

5. *Requests* the Chairman of the Committee to present the organizational plan to the Council for its endorsement, and further requests the Secretary-General to take the appropriate steps to implement it on an expedited basis, including, at the appropriate time, seeking the approval of the General Assembly;

6. *Decides* that the Committee shall continue to report to the Council on a regular basis;

7. *Stresses* the importance of ensuring that the Committee continues to operate effectively during the consolidation of the support structure of the Committee into CTED, and, in this regard, decides that the Committee shall continue to operate with its present support structure until the Committee determines, in consultation with the Secretary-General, that CTED is operational;

8. *Decides* to remain actively seized of the matter.

The Secretary-General, following consultations with Security Council members, appointed on 12 May [S/2004/388, S/2004/389] Javier Rupérez (Spain) as CTED Executive Director, which the

Council approved two days later [S/2004/390]. On 11 August [S/2004/642], the Council endorsed CTED's organizational plan.

Report of Secretary-General. As requested by resolution 1566(2004) (see p. 74), the Secretary-General submitted to the Council on 15 November [S/2004/914] a report on steps to make CTED, currently functioning within the budget of the Department of Political Affairs (DPA) with support from the DPA Executive Office, fully operational. He said that, in addition to the appointment of an Executive Director and endorsement by CTC of the CTED organizational plan (see above), administrative arrangements were put in place to facilitate recruitment of support personnel. Vacancy announcements for specialists in areas such as legislative drafting, financial law enforcement, extradition law, customs and border control, technical assistance and administrative support would be circulated. Budget requirements for 2004 (July to December) amounting to $617,700 were being met through redeployment of resources appropriated under section 3, Political affairs, of the 2004-2005 programme budget. The requirement for 2005 would be submitted to the General Assembly during its fifty-ninth (2004) session.

The Secretary-General, in his November report [A/59/534/Add.1] on estimates in respect of special political missions, good offices and other political initiatives authorized by the Assembly and/or the Council, presented overall resource requirements for CTED in 2005 at $6,085,000 net ($7,071,800 gross). That amount was approved by the Assembly, on the recommendation of the Advisory Committee on Administrative and Budgetary Questions (ACABQ) [A/59/569/Add.1], in section VII of **resolution 59/276**.

Reports of States. Between January and December, the CTC Chairman transmitted to the Council President reports submitted by Member States on action they had taken or planned to take to implement resolution 1373(2001) and letters from the Committee requesting follow-up information: [S/2004/19, S/2004/21-23, S/2004/36-38, S/2004/57-60, S/2004/65, S/2004/86, S/2004/89-96, S/2004/118-119, S/2004/124, S/2004/127-130, S/2004/131 & Corr.1, S/2004/132-133, S/2004/136, S/2004/149-159, S/2004/170-171, S/2004/179, S/2004/181, S/2004/214 & Corr.1, S/2004/215, S/2004/226-227, S/2004/252-255, S/2004/286, S/2004/295-296, S/2004/323-324, S/2004/340, S/2004/342-344, S/2004/358-360, S/2004/362-372, S/2004/374-377, S/2004/403-405, S/2004/429, S/2004/450-451, S/2004/475-477, S/2004/479-483, S/2004/502, S/2004/523 & Add.1, S/2004/552-559, S/2004/578-580, S/2004/589, S/2004/658-659, S/2004/660 & Add.1, S/2004/661-664, S/2004/670, S/2004/683-691, S/2004/745-746, S/2004/778, S/2004/791, S/2004/834-855, S/2004/863, S/2004/872, S/2004/876, S/2004/884-885, S/2004/899-900, S/2004/918-919, S/2004/945, S/2004/964, S/2004/983, S/2004/991-993, S/2004/1000-1001, S/2004/1003-1006, S/2004/1023-1024].

Action by Commission on Crime Prevention and Criminal Justice

The Commission on Crime Prevention and Criminal Justice, at its thirteenth session (11-20 May) [E/2004/30], recommended to the Economic and Social Council for approval a draft resolution for adoption by the General Assembly entitled "Strengthening international cooperation and technical assistance in promoting the implementation of the universal conventions and protocols related to terrorism within the framework of the activities of the United Nations Office on Drugs and Crime". That resolution was approved by the Council as **resolution 2004/19** and adopted by the Assembly as **resolution 59/153** (see p. 1125).

IAEA action

The General Conference of the International Atomic Energy Agency (IAEA), at its forty-eighth session (Vienna, 20-24 September) (see p. 548), adopted resolution GC(48)/RES/11 relating to progress on measures to protect against nuclear and radiological terrorism. It called on member States to continue to provide political, financial and technical support to improve nuclear and radiological security, prevent nuclear and radiological terrorism, and support the Nuclear Security Fund.

Peacekeeping operations

In 2004, the General Assembly and the Security Council continued to oversee the management and operations of UN peacekeeping missions. The Council addressed a number of key issues aimed at strengthening and streamlining the overall conduct of those operations. It renewed the mandates of several ongoing operations and created new ones in the face of deteriorating security conditions. The Assembly took action on a number of financial and administrative matters. The Department of Peacekeeping Operations (DPKO) continued to implement the recommendations contained in the 2000 report of the Panel on United Nations Peace Operations (the Brahimi report) [YUN 2000, p. 83] and those of the Special Committee on Peacekeeping Operations, whose mandate was to review the whole question of peacekeeping operations in all their aspects. The Special Committee held a general debate on 29 and 30 March, during which it approved a number of recommendations for submission to the Assembly. It also considered other general issues related to peacekeeping operations and made recommendations for improving their effectiveness.

General aspects of UN peacekeeping

Security Council Working Group on Peacekeeping Operations

The Security Council Working Group on Peacekeeping Operations held four meetings in 2004 (2 April, 11 June, 2 July and 27 August). The Chairman of the Working Group, in his personal report on the Group's activities, transmitted in December to the Council [S/2004/1040], said that the Group, in addition to dealing with various issues concerning the relationship between troop contributors and peacekeeping operations, focused on the relationship between the Council and DPKO and how to deal with the demands of peacekeeping from the perspective of new and increasingly complex operations and the management of ongoing operations.

The Chairman proposed that the Working Group become a full-fledged subsidiary organ of the Council so that it could have a more effective role in terms of peacekeeping mandates.

On 30 December [S/2004/1032], the Council President stated that Council members had agreed that the Working Group would continue its work until 31 December 2005.

Decision-making in peacekeeping operations

By a 5 February letter [S/2004/99], Brazil, Canada, Egypt, Germany, Ghana, India, Japan, Mexico, Pakistan and South Africa drew the attention of the Security Council to their concern regarding decision-making in peacekeeping operations. According to them, decision-making in peacekeeping operations was confined to Council members, the Secretariat and troop-contributing countries. While there were mechanisms provided for in resolution 1353(2001) [YUN 2001, p. 80] for the inclusion of other interested Member States on a case-by-case basis, those mechanisms had not been successful in allowing for substantial input by major stakeholders in peacekeeping operations. Meetings with troop-contributing countries were largely informative and technical, with little or no relevance for Council decisions. The potential for a broad-based approach remained mostly untapped. New ways to organize a more comprehensive and rational decision-making process, involving all stakeholders, was needed. Apart from improving the basis for decision-making in the Council, the inclusion of major stakeholders would also create a considerable incentive for the general membership to support peacekeeping operations. The solution would be to schedule regular meetings of the Security Council Working Group on Peacekeeping Operations as the forum for open debate, allowing all interested parties to make their views known on issues concerning peacekeeping operations. The Chairman of the Working Group would then report back to the Council. As for the question of determining which States had a legitimate interest in participating, the Council's precedent of allowing non-members with a stake in the agenda item to speak in the Council's public meetings, upon request, should be followed.

Strategic direction and future trends of UN peacekeeping operations

During its presidency of the Security Council, Pakistan informed the members that it was holding a debate on 17 May on UN peacekeeping operations [S/2004/378]. In its working paper on the subject, Pakistan said that, with the recent upsurge in demand for peacekeeping operations and the four years that had elapsed since the release of the Brahimi report, it was timely to evaluate the strategic direction of peacekeeping operations and analyse trends. That would involve reviewing the efficacy and effectiveness of the principles, policies, structures and mechanisms governing the planning, establishment, deployment and conduct of peacekeeping operations, what had and had not worked since the Brahimi reforms, as well as the level of logistic, financial and political support for those operations and future requirements.

Opening the debate on 17 May [meeting 4970], Pakistan, as Council President, said that it was appropriate to highlight the challenges in peacekeeping and to help generate sufficient levels of political, financial, human and logistical support required in establishing new missions. It hoped that the exchange of views would promote better preparation for the challenges and for utilizing more effectively the instrument of UN peacekeeping in the furtherance of international peace and security.

The Secretary-General told the Council that the United Nations was facing a surging demand for peacekeeping. As at April, more than 53,000 troops, military observers and civilian police were serving in 15 UN missions around the world, the highest number since October 1995. Many of those missions were large and complex and went beyond the limited military functions of traditional peacekeeping missions. The Council had recently authorized a new mission in Haiti and expanded the one in Côte d'Ivoire, while other missions were being planned for Burundi and the Sudan. To absorb the new costs, an extra $1 billion above the current $2.82 billion would be needed by the end of the year for the peacekeeping budget. The United Nations had a duty to meet that demand and to seize the opportunities to bring long-standing conflicts to an end, as UN peacekeeping missions offered the best and sometimes only hope of emerging from conflict towards a safe and stable future.

Peacekeeping had become increasingly multidimensional and, as the complexity of mandates had increased, so too had public expectations about what those missions could achieve. Peacekeeping operations had to be part of a longer-term strategy to solidify the foundation of peace, lest, as in Haiti and Liberia, the United Nations had to return again. To that end, the international community should better integrate the security, political, economic and social levers at its disposal to keep and build peace in the immediate post-conflict period and beyond. As the United Nations moved into non-traditional aspects of peacekeeping, it also needed to have a clear picture of the environments in which it was operating, with the required information, the capacity to analyse that information and the means to conduct its mission.

To deal with those challenges, the United Nations had to show commitment and be prepared to stay the course with political will and resources to ensure that peace processes did not falter into renewed conflict. To succeed, Council mandates had to be clear, implementable and achievable and missions needed to receive the requisite troops and resources. Council support was especially important when a mission faced challenges to the legitimacy of its mandate.

Although many of the recommendations in the Brahimi report had been implemented, the scale of the current surge in peacekeeping operations might well outstrip the Organization's capacities to backstop those operations, and it would have to augment those capacities. UN missions remained hampered by a lack of specialized military capacities, generally available from developed countries, which made only limited contributions of troops to peacekeeping operations. At the same time, many willing troop-contributor States had difficulty in deploying staff within the necessary time frames.

The Secretary-General urged Member States to help fill those gaps so that UN peacekeeping operations could draw on specialized capacities and deploy rapidly. The United Nations was also working with regional, subregional and international arrangements to ensure complementary capacities, such as early temporary force deployments that could bridge the gap until the UN peacekeepers could deploy. Another critical gap was the need for French-speaking personnel, especially police, to tackle assignments in Francophone countries. As missions in Haiti, Côte d'Ivoire and possibly Burundi were expanded, that pressure would intensify.

UN peacekeeping missions had a long history and the lessons of the past had to be recalled to ensure that everything would be done to ensure success. New missions should be guaranteed the necessary resources and commitment to handle the complex and challenging tasks to which they were called.

SECURITY COUNCIL ACTION

On 17 May [meeting 4970], following consultations among Security Council members, the President made statement **S/PRST/2004/16** on behalf of the Council:

The Security Council recalls its primary responsibility for the maintenance of international peace and security and reaffirms its commitment to the purposes and principles enshrined in the Charter of the United Nations, in particular, of the political independence, sovereignty and territorial integrity of all States in conducting all peacekeeping and peacebuilding activities and the need for States to comply with their obligations under international law.

The Council recognizes that, as experience confirms, United Nations peacekeeping operations play a critical role in the maintenance of international peace and security, preventing and containing conflicts, promoting compliance with international norms and Council decisions, and building peace in post-conflict situations.

It further notes that United Nations peacekeeping missions are charged with increasingly difficult and complex mandates assigned to them by the Council and recognizes in this regard the need for a continued review of United Nations peacekeeping.

The Council notes that, in addition to the existing fourteen United Nations peacekeeping operations, there has been a recent surge in demand for new peacekeeping operations. It is cognizant of the challenges this represents for the United Nations system in terms of generating the necessary resources, personnel and other capabilities to meet the increased demand.

The Council calls upon Member States to ensure that the United Nations is provided with full political and financial support to meet these challenges effectively, keeping in view the specific requirements of each mission and bearing in mind the human and financial resource implications for the United Nations. The Council also stresses that it is also important to ensure that, while meeting the demand for new peacekeeping operations, the resources available for and the effective management of the existing operations are not adversely affected. At the same time it underscores the need for efficient and effective management of resources.

The Council calls upon Member States to contribute sufficient levels of trained troops, police and civilian personnel, including those with specialized capabilities and skills, bearing in mind the need for an increased percentage of female personnel at all decision-making levels, as well as the mobilization of logistic and administrative support, to allow the multiple operations to start optimally and fulfil their respective mandates in an effective manner. Enhancing the Secretariat's capacities and using them in a rational and efficient manner will constitute a crucial element of this response.

The Council also stresses the need for improved integrated mission planning, as well as enhanced capacity for rapid deployment of personnel and materiel to ensure efficient start-up of peacekeeping operations. The timely and adequate replenishment of strategic deployment stocks is essential to meet current and future demands.

The Council recognizes the need to work, as appropriate, with regional and subregional organizations and multinational arrangements in peacekeeping operations in accordance with Chapter VIII of the Charter of the United Nations to ensure complementary capacities and approaches before and during the deployment and after the withdrawal of United Nations peacekeeping missions.

The Council recognizes its responsibility to provide clear, realistic and achievable mandates for peacekeeping missions. The Council values, in this regard, the assessments and recommendations provided by the Secretariat for informed decisions on the scope and composition of new peacekeeping operations as well as their mandates, concept of operations and force levels and structures.

The Council believes that there is need to strengthen the relationship between those who plan, mandate and manage peacekeeping operations, and those who implement the mandates for these operations. Troop-contributing countries, through their experience and expertise, can greatly contribute to the planning process and can assist the Council in taking appropriate, effective and timely decisions on peacekeeping operations. The Council recognizes, in this regard, that the meetings and mechanisms established by its resolution 1353(2001) of 13 June 2001 serve to facilitate the consultations process.

The Council recognizes that in peacekeeping operations there are contributors, other than troop-contributing countries, whose views should also be taken into account as appropriate.

The Council stresses that, in challenging environments, United Nations peacekeepers may need to be provided with sufficiently robust rules of engagement and the necessary military resources to enable them to fulfil their mandate and, if necessary, to defend themselves. In all cases, the Council considers the safety and security of all United Nations personnel to be a priority. It stresses, in this context, the importance of enhanced capacity to gather and manage information in the field.

The Council takes notes of recent efforts to increase coordination between missions in adjacent countries and encourages Special Representatives of the Secretary-General to explore synergies to ensure effective management of peacekeeping missions in the same regions or subregions.

The Council stresses the need to regularly assess the size, mandate and structure of peacekeeping operations with a view to making the necessary adjustments, including downsizing, where appropriate, according to progress achieved. It also encourages the continued commitment of the international community to consolidate and sustain the peace on the ground during and beyond the life of the mission.

The Council further recognizes the importance of a gender perspective, including gender training for peacekeepers, in peacekeeping operations, in accordance with Council resolution 1325(2000) of 31 October 2000 and the importance of protection of children in armed conflict in accordance with Council resolution 1379(2001) of 20 November 2001.

The Council recognizes the increased risk of the spread of communicable diseases and certain criminal activities in post-conflict areas. The Council welcomes efforts by the Secretariat to sensitize peacekeeping personnel in the prevention of HIV/AIDS and other communicable diseases in compliance with Council resolution 1308(2000) of 17 July 2000, and encourages the Secretariat to continue implementing its guidelines on prostitution and trafficking.

The Council recognizes that effective peacekeeping operations should be part of an overall strategy to consolidate and sustain peace. In this regard, it stresses the need to ensure from the outset the coordination, coherence and continuity between the different parts of this overall strategy, in particular between peacekeeping on the one hand and peacebuilding on the other. To this end, the Council encourages closer cooperation between all relevant United Nations agencies, funds and programmes and international financial institutions, regional and subregional organizations and the private sector. Ensuring lasting peace in the aftermath of conflict may require sustained support from the United Nations and its humanitarian and development partners.

The Council notes that training is increasingly becoming a critical element in peacekeeping operations and recognizes the need to utilize the expertise of experienced troop-contributing countries. It encourages international cooperation and support for the establishment of peacekeeping training centres, which could provide a wide range of training opportunities to new and emerging troop contributors.

The Council recognizes that meeting the demands of an increasing number of United Nations peacekeeping missions will require the concerted efforts of the Security Council, the General Assembly, the States Members of the United Nations and the Secretary-General so as to ensure that the necessary resources and operational support are provided. The Council encourages follow-up consultations on the surge in demand, and invites the Secretary-General to provide regularly, in a timely manner, to Member States assessments of evolving needs and shortfalls in United Nations peacekeeping, in order to identify critical gaps and unmet requirements as well as steps required to meet these.

The Council underscores the useful role of its Working Group on Peacekeeping Operations in the consultation process at different stages of peacekeeping operations. It encourages the Working Group to pay special attention to matters relating to the surge in demand in United Nations peacekeeping over the coming year and, as necessary, to report to the Council.

The Council pays high tribute to all the men and women who have served and continue to serve in United Nations peacekeeping operations for their high level of professionalism, dedication and courage. It honours the memory of those who lost their lives in the service of the United Nations and the noble cause of peace.

The Secretary-General, in an August report [A/59/282] to the General Assembly on the implementation of the United Nations Millennium Declaration [YUN 2000, p. 49], discussed the Organization's achievements in peace and security, particularly in peacekeeping in the light of the jump in demand for UN peacekeeping operations (see p. 51).

Strategies for complex peacekeeping operations

The Special Committee on Peacekeeping Operations, at its 2004 substantive session (New York, 29 March–16 April) [A/58/19], recognized the need for DPKO to plan for peacekeeping missions in such a manner as to facilitate postconflict peace-building and long-term prevention of recurrence of armed conflict. In that context, it encouraged the Secretariat to develop comprehensive strategies and integrated mission planning in disarmament, demobilization and reintegration, strengthening the rule of law, security sector reform, quick-impact projects and mine action, with a view to restoring security and stability in post-conflict societies. The Committee called for the inclusion of peace-building elements in mandates to generate conditions for preventing the recurrence of armed conflict. It stressed the need for cooperation and coordination among UN specialized agencies, funds and programmes, as well as with the Bretton Woods institutions (the World Bank Group and the International Monetary Fund), international donors, humanitarian organizations, NGOs and civil society for ensuring operational clarity and coherence on the ground during implementation of those comprehensive strategies in the postconflict peace-building phases, so as to ensure a smooth transition to long-term development activities. It looked forward to the detailed review of UN capacity in that regard, to be included in the Secretary-General's report on the implementation of resolution 57/337 [YUN 2003, p. 50] to the General Assembly at its fifty-ninth (2004) session.

Regarding disarmament, demobilization and reintegration, the Special Committee stressed the importance of planning and preparations at UN Headquarters of comprehensive strategies from the outset, and underscored the valuable role that the Peacekeeping Best Practices Unit could play in that regard. Efforts should be undertaken to identify with the donor community ways to secure financing for all components of the disarmament, demobilization and reintegration programmes. All disarmament, demobilization and reintegration processes should take into account the special needs of child and women soldiers and children and women dependants of ex-combatants. Peacekeeping missions should be committed to implementing those strategies in cooperation with local authorities and relevant partners. At the earliest stage of the peace negotiation process preceding the establishment of a mission, there should be identification, preparation and coordination of all relevant actors in order to develop, well in advance, a successful disarmament, demobilization and reintegration strategy. The Special Committee underlined the importance of effective disarmament measures, including the collection, safe storage, disposal or destruction of arms from ex-combatants.

The Special Committee recognized that establishment of local rule-of-law capacities was an essential element in creating and sustaining stability in a post-conflict environment. A peacekeeping mission might provide technical advice to reform the local justice system. The Special Committee noted the report of the Executive Committee on Peace and Security regarding the need for enhanced UN system-wide coordination to strengthen its rule-of-law capacities and mobilize identified resources. The Special Committee believed that the report identified available expertise within and outside the UN system and suggested possible arrangements through which UN departments and agencies and external entities could provide expertise. It asked the Secretariat to assess the work undertaken thus far in that area, particularly in justice and corrections. The Committee noted the Secretary-General's request, in his report on the implementation of its recommendations [A/58/694] (see p. 81), for additional resources for DPKO's support for justice and corrections issues and sought clarification on the resources requested.

Concerning quick-impact projects, the Special Committee suggested that they be not only an integral part of mission planning and development, but also part of the implementation of comprehensive strategies to meet the challenges facing complex peacekeeping operations. Selection procedures for those projects should be more flexible and be addressed at the field level. The necessary resources should be made available through the second year of a peacekeeping operation, provided they directly supported the mission's mandate and either responded to needs not covered by existing assistance or served as a catalyst to broaden those efforts.

In the area of mine action, the Special Committee encouraged stakeholders to use standardized information management systems, such as the Information Management System for Mine Action, for the collection, analysis and dissemination of mine-related information. The Committee further encouraged the development and application of standardized mine-action training modules, mine-risk education materials and operating procedures for use by troop-contributing countries.

Enhancing UN peacekeeping capacity

The Special Committee on Peacekeeping Operations [A/58/19], in emphasizing the need to further improve the Organization's rapid deployment capabilities, suggested that the Secretariat use the United Nations Standby Arrangements System database as a starting point for the force-generation process and improve the efficacy of all aspects of pre-mandate operational preparedness, especially the timely dissemination of information on upcoming missions to troop-contributing countries to meet required deployment deadlines. More efficient management of the financial and logistical aspects would also contribute to rapid deployments. Further study and proposals on the requirements for rapidly deployable reserve forces were welcomed.

The Special Committee encouraged DPKO to assess the effectiveness of the Standby Arrangements System and optimize the strategic deployment stocks system in the light of lessons learned. It supported using the rapid deployment level early in the force-generation process to link troops from one Member State with equipment and training from other sources. The Special Committee stressed the need for militarily coherent and well-trained headquarters to achieve the degree of command and control necessary for effective implementation of complex mandates, and urged wider use of rapidly deployable headquarters in the initial phase of a peacekeeping operation. The earliest possible selection of the force commander, police commissioner and headquarters staff was recommended, to allow for their training and engagement in the pre-mission planning process.

The Special Committee reiterated its request for the creation of a working group to consider the funding difficulties of troop-contributing countries in complying with rapid deployment requirements, especially ways of assuring rapid reimbursement in the rapid deployment phase, and asked the Secretariat to produce a study on possible options. It welcomed the initiatives for improving the capacity for rapid deployment of civil personnel. Given the likely surge in peacekeeping activities in 2004, it requested DPKO to explore alternative means of placing staff on standby, in addition to expanding the rapid deployment team concept.

Noting the ongoing review of strategic deployment stocks, the Special Committee called on the Secretariat to ensure that all aspects of pre-mandate operational readiness were covered so as to reduce preparation time. To overcome the equipment shortfall faced by troop-contributing countries, it recommended that the United Nations continue to facilitate various enabling arrangements, including through other Member States and bilateral arrangements.

Concerning the challenges faced in meeting the demands of surges in operational activity, the Special Committee recommended that the United Nations implement an integrated mission-planning process across all departments and stakeholders, producing a mission concept of operations and component plans that were fully understood, integrated, rehearsed and owned. It should also seek additional surge-planning capacity from external sources, such as regional headquarters, national staff or teams of international experts on a time-, objective- or mission-oriented basis.

The Special Committee noted the focus of the Peacekeeping Best Practices Unit on policy development, lessons learned and knowledge management and expected the Unit to play a part in developing generic peacekeeping policies, and in integrating lessons learned and best practices in the planning and conduct of missions. It welcomed the launch of the Unit's website and the publication of the handbook on multidimensional peacekeeping.

Consultations with troop contributors

The Special Committee on Peacekeeping Operations [A/58/19] reiterated the need for substantive consultations between the Security Council, the Secretariat and troop-contributing countries in planning and managing peacekeeping operations. It recognized that the meetings and mechanisms established by the Council in resolution 1353(2001) [YUN 2001, p. 80] had facilitated the consultation process. It looked forward to the implementation of the Council's recommendations [YUN 2002, p. 65] regarding the establishment of a mechanism for strengthening the Council's cooperation with troop-contributing countries and encouraged increased consultations between the Security Council Working Group on Peacekeeping Operations and troop contributors on specific peacekeeping issues and individual peacekeeping operations. The Special Committee recommended that the Secretariat continue to look at ways to improve modalities for information-sharing with troop-contributing countries, particularly with respect to the Situation Centre's briefings and reports. It encouraged DPKO to make more use of issue-specific workshops and briefings to enhance cooperation on peacekeeping.

The Peacekeeping Best Practices Unit should consult with troop-contributing countries, and the Secretariat should convene periodic meetings, with the participation of former force commanders and national contingent commanders, to develop validation mechanisms for lessons learned and best practices. The Secretariat should consult with the troop-contributing countries in a timely manner when planning any change in the tasks, mission-specific rules of engagement, operational concepts or command and control structure which had an impact on the personnel, equipment, training and logistics requirements, and when planning a drawdown of troops in any peacekeeping operation.

The Special Committee requested that a list of the existing and anticipated peacekeeping-related policy papers, guidelines, manuals, standard operating procedures and training materials issued by DPKO be provided to Member States at regular intervals and be made available on the Department's web site.

Safety and security

The Special Committee on Peacekeeping Operations [A/58/19] expressed concern over the precarious security environment in many field missions and called on the Secretariat to give the utmost priority to enhancing the safety and security of UN and associated personnel in the field. It supported the ongoing overall review of the UN security management system, and was of the view that the Secretary-General's request for a full-time safety and security focal point and a mission security management unit within DPKO should be considered within the context of that review. In the meantime, DPKO and related Secretariat bodies should address security concerns in missions in coordination with the field.

The Committee believed that joint mission analysis cells, established to improve enhancing information-gathering capacity in the field and to assess operating environments, should be properly equipped, adequately staffed and have access to all available information. The Secretariat should report on that capacity to the Committee in 2005. Recognizing the need to improve information collection, analysis and dissemination at Headquarters as well as in the field, and pending the security management review, the Committee requested the Secretariat to inform Member States as quickly as possible, particularly in crisis situations, of changes in the security situation in the field or when casualties had occurred. It recommended that DPKO institute contingency arrangements for each mission to facilitate the evacuation of personnel.

The Committee welcomed the development and use of minimum operating security standards for peacekeeping missions and urged that they be reviewed and updated as circumstances changed. It reiterated its requests for information on the status of the Secretariat's work to formalize a policy on protection from nuclear, biological and chemical threats in the field.

Cooperation with regional arrangements

The Special Committee on Peacekeeping Operations [A/58/19], while emphasizing the central role of the United Nations in peacekeeping operations, welcomed the new partnerships with relevant regional organizations that had enabled the Organization in recent years to make use of regional capacities. Assisting regional and subregional organizations in strengthening their capacities for peacekeeping would prove beneficial to those organizations, to confidence-building in the regions concerned and to peace and stability of the international community as a whole. At the same time, more deliberation should be encouraged on the optimal relationship between the United Nations and regional and subregional entities with regard to peacekeeping.

The Committee recognized that regional organizations had capacities for supporting UN peacekeeping operations in rapid-reaction capabilities, over-the-horizon capabilities, coordinated civilian and civilian police capabilities, specialized capabilities, provision of coherent headquarters, regional expertise, and sharing of best practices and training. They could also identify contributions offered by their own member States, or act as a one-stop shop. However, development of regional capacities should be in addition to bilateral contributions from Member States.

The Committee recommended that DPKO expand its contacts with regional organizations and their subregional partners, especially at the working level, in order to implement practical means for partnership. In addition, the Peacekeeping Best Practices Unit should continue to develop lessons learned in consultation with regional organizations, building on its studies of the Interim Emergency Multinational Force in the Democratic Republic of the Congo, authorized by Security Council resolution 1484(2003) [YUN 2003, p. 126], and the multinational force of the Economic Community of West African States Mission in Liberia [ibid., p. 190], and those lessons should be incorporated in future partnerships with regional organizations.

Women and peacekeeping

The Special Committee on Peacekeeping Operations [A/58/19], taking note of the Secretary-General's 2003 report on gender mainstreaming in peacekeeping activities [YUN 2003, p. 74], stressed the need for ongoing reporting on the implementation of gender mainstreaming in the field and at Headquarters. It shared the Secretary-General's concern over the low representation of women in peacekeeping operations and expressed its wish to see more female candidates for senior civilian appointments and for military and civilian police positions at all levels. The Committee encouraged the Secretariat to pursue its policy of mainstreaming a gender perspective into DPKO activities and to implement the recommendations made by the Secretary-General in his report on women, peace and security relating to peacekeeping [YUN 2002, p. 67].

Recognizing the need for a gender mainstreaming strategy for UN peacekeeping operations, the Committee recommended that gender experts be included in pre-mandate assessments and planning to ensure that the gender dimension was fully addressed in mission mandates. It welcomed DPKO's decision to focus in the coming year on establishing procedures for gender mainstreaming, including developing an organizational action plan for implementing the elements in Security Council resolution 1325(2000) [YUN 2000, p. 1113] relating to peacekeeping. The Committee encouraged the Secretariat to take into account the recommendations on peacekeeping operations contained in the relevant resolution of the Commission on the Status of Women [E/2004/27 (res. 48/4)] (see p. 1170), as well as the guidelines provided in the Commission's agreed conclusions on women's equal participation in conflict prevention, management and conflict resolution and in post-conflict peace-building, adopted by the Economic and Social Council in **resolution 2004/12** (see p. 1154).

Report of Secretary-General. Responding to Security Council presidential statement S/PRST/2002/32 [YUN 2002, p. 1143], the Secretary-General, in October [S/2004/814], reported on the implementation of Council resolution 1325(2000) [YUN 2000, p. 1113] on women and peace and security. He stated that the most significant progress in its implementation was made in peacekeeping. In 2000, there was only minimal mention of gender issues in peacekeeping mandates and two gender advisers were assigned to peacekeeping operations. Currently, gender concerns were raised in all new peacekeeping mandates and there were 10 full-time gender adviser positions in 17 peacekeeping operations. The gender adviser within DPKO would support the mainstreaming of gender perspectives in all DPKO offices, provide policy and operational guidance to gender advisers in the field, and disseminate lessons learned and best practices on gender and peacekeeping.

Gender units and advisers in peacekeeping operations provided technical guidance to ensure gender perspectives were incorporated in all functional areas of peacekeeping and to increase women's participation in implementing the mission's mandate. Gender advisers participated in inter-agency assessment missions conducted prior to the establishment of the mandates of operations in Burundi, Côte d'Ivoire, Haiti and Liberia.

Military, civilian police and civilian peacekeeping personnel were trained on the protection, rights and particular needs of women, as well as the importance of involving women in all peacekeeping functions. Canada and the United Kingdom developed a gender training initiative for military and civilian personnel involved in peace support operations. Within the UN system, the Department of Management supported a variety of capacity-building initiatives on mainstreaming gender perspectives in peacekeeping, while DPKO focused on improving the gender-mainstreaming training materials and tools. In addition, the United Nations Institute for Training and Research conducted training on women and children for civilian personnel in several peacekeeping operations.

To deal with the emerging problem of human trafficking in some peacekeeping operations, DPKO developed a policy on human trafficking and was producing, with United States support, a package of guidance for peacekeeping operations, which would include model legislation and awareness-raising materials. A number of peacekeeping operations had also established specific units in police stations to assist victims of sexual violence. Gender-sensitive HIV/AIDS awareness training was included in induction training for peacekeepers.

According to the Secretary-General, a more coherent strategy for gender mainstreaming in peacekeeping was needed to increase the understanding of the relevance of gender issues to peacekeeping and to detail how to integrate gender concerns into the various pillars of an operation, including greater attention to data collection and reporting. He intended to develop a comprehensive strategy and action plan for mainstreaming gender perspectives into peacekeeping activities, with specific monitoring and reporting mechanisms, and urged the Security Council to monitor the implementation of the strategy and action plan.

As to enhancing the gender balance in recruitment, DPKO had introduced specific language into vacancy announcements, targeting professional women's organizations in order to encourage female candidates to apply. It had also made efforts to increase the representation of women among uniformed personnel.

The Secretary-General called on Member States, UN entities and civil society organizations to further analyse the obstacles to increasing women's representation in peace operations and humanitarian response and develop and implement appropriate recruitment strategies, including in military and police services, and create a pool of precertified female candidates for senior-level positions to ensure rapid deployment.

The Security Council, in presidential statement **S/PRST/2004/40** (see p. 1152) of 28 October, welcomed the Secretary-General's recommendations for developing a strategy and action plan for mainstreaming a gender perspective into peacekeeping activities and operations and for recruiting more female candidates in peace operations, particularly for senior-level positions, including in the military and civilian police services.

In related action, the Council, in **resolution 1539(2004)** (see p. 787) of 22 April, noted with concern all the cases of sexual exploitation and abuse of women and children, especially girls, in humanitarian crises, including those involving humanitarian workers and peacekeepers, and requested contributing countries to incorporate the six core principles of the Inter-Agency Standing Committee on emergencies into pertinent codes of conduct for peacekeeping personnel and to develop appropriate disciplinary and accountability mechanisms.

Peacekeeping and the international legal system

During informal consultations of the Security Council on 19 May, the United States introduced a draft resolution which sought to renew the request contained in Council resolution 1487(2003) [YUN 2003, p. 77] that the International Criminal Court not commence or proceed, for a period of 12 months starting on 1 July 2003, with investiga-

tion or prosecution of any case involving current or former officials or personnel from a contributing State not a party to the Rome Statute establishing the Court [YUN 1998, p. 1209] over acts or omission relating to a UN established or authorized operation, unless the Council otherwise decided.

On 20 May [S/2004/412], Ireland, Jordan, Liechtenstein and Switzerland requested that the Council convene a public meeting and invite interested States to discuss the proposed renewal of resolution 1487(2003) since it had implications of direct import to Member States, including those that were parties to the Rome Statute, relating to international peacekeeping, fundamental questions of international law and the Council's role in promoting law and accountability. They suggested that the issue would benefit from discussion in the wider UN membership. The Council President, Pakistan, in the assessment of its presidency for May [S/2004/614], reported that, during informal discussions on 21 May, the public meeting and the vote were deferred. Subsequently, the sponsor informed the Council that the request had been withdrawn for the time being. No further action was taken in 2004 on the draft resolution.

Comprehensive review of peacekeeping

Special Committee on Peacekeeping Operations

As requested by the General Assembly in resolution 57/336 [YUN 2003, p. 79], the Special Committee on Peacekeeping Operations and its Working Group continued their comprehensive review of the whole question of peacekeeping operations in all their aspects [A/58/19]. In response to the Committee's request, the Secretary-General submitted a January report on the implementation of the Committee's recommendations [A/58/694].

The Committee, during its general debate on 29 and 30 March, considered guiding principles, definitions and implementation of peacekeeping mandates; safety and security of UN and associated personnel; cooperation with troop-contributing countries; cooperation with regional arrangements; enhancing African peacekeeping; comprehensive strategies for complex peacekeeping operations; enhancing UN capacity for peacekeeping; civilian police; gender and peacekeeping; children and peacekeeping; public information; and financial issues (for details, see subjects above).

On 1 July [meeting 92], the General Assembly, on the recommendation of the Fourth (Special Political and Decolonization) Committee [A/58/474/Add.1], adopted **resolution 58/315** without vote [agenda item 85].

Comprehensive review of the whole question of peacekeeping operations in all their aspects

The General Assembly,

Recalling its resolution 2006(XIX) of 18 February 1965 and all other relevant resolutions,

Recalling also, in particular, its resolutions 57/336 of 18 June 2003 and 57/129 of 11 December 2002,

Affirming that the efforts of the United Nations in the peaceful settlement of disputes, including through its peacekeeping operations, are indispensable,

Convinced of the need for the United Nations to continue to improve its capabilities in the field of peacekeeping and to enhance the effective and efficient deployment of its peacekeeping operations,

Considering the contribution that all States Members of the United Nations make to peacekeeping,

Noting the widespread interest in contributing to the work of the Special Committee on Peacekeeping Operations expressed by Member States, in particular troop-contributing countries,

Bearing in mind the continuous necessity of preserving the efficiency and strengthening the effectiveness of the work of the Special Committee,

1. *Welcomes* the report of the Special Committee on Peacekeeping Operations;

2. *Endorses* the proposals, recommendations and conclusions of the Special Committee, contained in paragraphs 29 to 177 of its report;

3. *Urges* Member States, the Secretariat and relevant organs of the United Nations to take all necessary steps to implement the proposals, recommendations and conclusions of the Special Committee;

4. *Reiterates* that those Member States that become personnel contributors to the United Nations peacekeeping operations in years to come or participate in the future in the Special Committee for three consecutive years as observers shall, upon request in writing to the Chairman of the Special Committee, become members at the following session of the Special Committee;

5. *Decides* that the Special Committee, in accordance with its mandate, shall continue its efforts for a comprehensive review of the whole question of peacekeeping operations in all their aspects and shall review the implementation of its previous proposals and consider any new proposals so as to enhance the capacity of the United Nations to fulfil its responsibilities in this field;

6. *Requests* the Special Committee to submit a report on its work to the General Assembly at its fifty-ninth session;

7. *Decides* to include in the provisional agenda of its fifty-ninth session the item entitled "Comprehensive review of the whole question of peacekeeping operations in all their aspects".

By **decision 59/517** of 10 December, the Assembly took note of the report [A/59/472] of the Fourth Committee on its consideration of the agenda item "Comprehensive review of the whole question of peacekeeping operations in all their aspects". On 23 December, the Assembly decided that the agenda item would remain for consideration at its resumed fifty-ninth (2005) session (**decision 59/552**).

Operations in 2004

On 1 January 2004, 13 peacekeeping operations were in place—5 in Africa, 3 in Asia, 2 in Europe and 3 in the Middle East. During the year, three new missions were launched (in Burundi, Côte d'Ivoire and Haiti), bringing the total number of missions in place at the end of the year to 16.

Africa

In Africa, the mandate of the United Nations Mission in Sierra Leone (UNAMSIL) was extended by the Security Council to 30 June 2005. The Council also extended the mandate of the United Nations Organization Mission in the Democratic Republic of the Congo (MONUC) until 31 March 2005, authorized an increase in its strength by 5,900 personnel and expanded its mandate. The mandate of the United Nations Mission for the Referendum in Western Sahara (MINURSO) was extended until 30 April 2005 and that of the United Nations Mission in Ethiopia and Eritrea (UNMEE) until 15 March 2005. The Council extended the mandate of the United Nations Mission in Liberia (UNMIL) to 19 September 2005. The Council established, in February, the United Nations Operation in Côte d'Ivoire (UNOCI) until 4 April 2005 to, among other tasks, monitor the ceasefire and movement of armed groups, and to assist in disarmament, demobilization, reintegration and resettlement. In May, it authorized the deployment of the United Nations Operation in Burundi (ONUB) until 1 June 2005, with a mandate to ensure respect of the ceasefire agreements, promote the re-establishment of confidence between forces, carry out disarmament and create security conditions for humanitarian assistance, among other responsibilities.

Americas

In the Americas, the Security Council established as of 1 June the United Nations Stabilization Mission in Haiti (MINUSTAH) to, among other tasks, secure a stable environment, support the constitutional and political process and the conduct of free and fair elections, and extend State authority throughout the country. The

Council extended the MINUSTAH mandate until 1 June 2005.

Asia

In Asia, the United Nations Military Observer Group in India and Pakistan (UNMOGIP), established in 1949, remained in place to monitor the ceasefire in Jammu and Kashmir. The Council extended the mandate of the United Nations Mission of Support in East Timor (UNMISET) until 20 May 2005.

In related action, the Council extended in September the authorization of the International Security Assistance Force in Afghanistan for a further period of 12 months beyond 13 October 2004 (**resolution 1563(2004)**).

Europe

In Europe, the Security Council extended the mandate of the United Nations Observer Mission in Georgia (UNOMIG) until 31 January 2005. The Council extended the mandate of the United Nations Peacekeeping Force in Cyprus (UNFICYP) until 15 June 2005 and endorsed the Secretary-General's recommendations for amending the concept of operations and troop levels. The United Nations Interim Administration Mission in Kosovo (UNMIK), Serbia and Montenegro, remained in place. The Council also authorized Member States, acting through or in cooperation with the European Union, to establish for an initial period of 12 months a multinational stabilization force (EUFOR), to replace the NATO-led stabilization force in Bosnia and Herzegovina (**resolution 1575(2004)**).

Middle East

Three long-standing operations continued in the Middle East: the United Nations Truce Supervision Organization (UNTSO), which continued to observe the truce in Palestine; the United Nations Interim Force in Lebanon (UNIFIL), whose mandate was extended until 31 January 2005; and the United Nations Disengagement Observer Force (UNDOF), whose mandate was renewed until 30 June 2005.

Roster of 2004 operations

UNTSO

United Nations Truce Supervision Organization
Established: June 1948.
Mandate: To assist in supervising the observance of the truce in Palestine.

Strength as at December 2004: 153 military observers.

UNMOGIP

United Nations Military Observer Group in India and Pakistan
Established: January 1949.
Mandate: To supervise the ceasefire between India and Pakistan in Jammu and Kashmir.
Strength as at December 2004: 44 military observers.

UNFICYP

United Nations Peacekeeping Force in Cyprus
Established: March 1964.
Mandate: To prevent the recurrence of fighting between the two Cypriot communities.
Strength as at December 2004: 1,226 troops, 45 civilian police.

UNDOF

United Nations Disengagement Observer Force
Established: June 1974.
Mandate: To supervise the ceasefire between Israel and the Syrian Arab Republic and the disengagement of Israeli and Syrian forces in the Golan Heights.
Strength as at December 2004: 1,041 troops.

UNIFIL

United Nations Interim Force in Lebanon
Established: March 1978.
Mandate: To restore peace and security and assist the Lebanese Government in ensuring the return of its effective authority in the area.
Strength as at December 2004: 2,001 troops.

MINURSO

United Nations Mission for the Referendum in Western Sahara
Established: April 1991.
Mandate: To monitor and verify the implementation of a settlement plan for Western Sahara and assist in the holding of a referendum in the Territory.
Strength as at December 2004: 222 military observers; 2 civilian police.

UNOMIG

United Nations Observer Mission in Georgia
Established: August 1993.
Mandate: To verify compliance with a ceasefire agreement between the parties to the conflict in Georgia and investigate ceasefire violations; expanded in 1994 to include monitoring the imple-

mentation of an agreement on a ceasefire and separation of forces and observing the operation of a multinational peacekeeping force.

Strength as at December 2004: 122 military observers, 11 civilian police.

UNMIK

United Nations Interim Administration Mission in Kosovo

Established: June 1999.

Mandate: To promote, among other things, the establishment of substantial autonomy and self-government in Kosovo, perform basic civilian administrative functions, organize and oversee the development of provisional institutions, facilitate a political process to determine Kosovo's future status, support reconstruction of key infrastructure, maintain civil law and order, protect human rights and assure the return of refugees and displaced persons.

Strength as at December 2004: 3,616 civilian police, 37 military observers.

UNAMSIL

United Nations Mission in Sierra Leone

Established: October 1999.

Mandate: To cooperate with the Government of Sierra Leone and other parties in the implementation of the Peace Agreement signed in Lomé, Togo, on 7 July 1999, including, among other things, to assist in the implementation of the disarmament, demobilization and reintegration plan, monitor adherence to the ceasefire agreement of 18 May 1999 and facilitate the delivery of humanitarian assistance.

Strength as at December 2004: 5,409 troops, 118 civilian police.

MONUC

United Nations Organization Mission in the Democratic Republic of the Congo

Established: November 1999.

Mandate: To establish contacts with the signatories to the Ceasefire Agreement, provide technical assistance in implementation of the Agreement, provide information on security conditions, plan for the observation of the ceasefire, facilitate the delivery of humanitarian assistance and assist in the protection of human rights.

Strength as at December 2004: 11,415 troops, 155 civilian police.

UNMEE

United Nations Mission in Ethiopia and Eritrea

Established: July 2000.

Mandate: To establish and put into operation the mechanism for verifying the cessation of hostilities and to assist the Military Coordination Commission in tasks related to demining and in administrative support to its field offices.

Strength as at December 2004: 4,071 troops.

UNMISET

United Nations Mission of Support in East Timor

Established: May 2002.

Mandate: To provide assistance to the core administrative structures and interim law enforcement and public security of East Timor (renamed Timor-Leste), including assisting in the development of the East Timor Police Service, and contribute to the maintenance of East Timor's external and internal security.

Strength as at December 2004: 466 troops, 149 civilian police.

UNMIL

United Nations Mission in Liberia

Established: September 2003.

Mandate: To support the implementation of the ceasefire agreement and the peace process; protect UN staff and facilities and civilians; support humanitarian and human rights activities; and assist in national security reform, including national police training and formation of a new, restructured military.

Strength as at December 2004: 14,684 troops, 1,097 civilian police.

UNOCI

United Nations Operation in Côte d'Ivoire

Established: 4 April 2004.

Mandate: To monitor the implementation of the 3 May 2003 comprehensive ceasefire agreement and the movement of armed groups; assist in disarmament, demobilization, reintegration, repatriation and resettlement; protect UN personnel, institutions and civilians; support humanitarian assistance; support implementation of the peace process; and assist in human rights, public information and law and order.

Strength as at December 2004: 5,995 troops, 213 civilian police.

MINUSTAH

United Nations Stabilization Mission in Haiti

Established: 1 June 2004.

Mandate: To ensure a secure and stable environment in support of the Transitional Government; to support the constitutional and political process; to assist the Transitional Government in bringing about national dialogue, conducting free and fair elections and extending State authority throughout the country; to promote and protect human rights; and to cooperate with the Transitional Government in providing humanitarian assistance.

Strength as at December 2004: 4,790 troops, 1,270 civilian police.

ONUB

United Nations Operation in Burundi
Established: 1 June 2004.

Mandate: To monitor implementation of ceasefire agreements; to assist in disarmament and demobilization activities; to create security conditions for the provision of humanitarian assistance and the voluntary return of refugees; to assist in the electoral process; and to protect civilians under threat and UN personnel and facilities.

Strength as at December 2004: 5,475 troops, 82 civilian police.

Financial and administrative aspects of peacekeeping operations

Financing

Expenditures for United Nations peacekeeping operations for the period 1 July 2003 to 30 June 2004 totalled $2,933.8 million, compared to a final figure of $2,499.8 million for the previous 12-month period. The 17 per cent increase in expenditure was attributable to the operations of four new peacekeeping missions (UNMIL, UNOCI, MINUSTAH, ONUB) and MONUC, offset by a decrease in expenditure levels at UNIFIL, UNAMSIL, UNMIK, UNMISET and UNMEE.

In terms of the overall financial situation, assessments, unpaid assessments and expenditures of active missions all increased on account of the establishment of four new peacekeeping operations, with a corresponding decrease in liquidity. Unpaid assessments for active peacekeeping missions rose by $501.7 million or 109 per cent, with the four new missions accounting for 88 per cent of that increase. Unpaid assessments for closed missions did not change significantly. As at 30 June 2004, total unpaid assessments amounted to $1.5 billion, compared to $1.1 billion in the previous financial period.

The liquidity of active missions was negatively affected by the start-up of the four new missions, which were financed initially by loans from the Peacekeeping Reserve Fund. The liquidity position of closed missions with cash surpluses deteriorated as they continued to be the only source of lending to active peacekeeping missions, the Tribunals and the regular budget. Available cash for active missions totalled $1,052.3 million, while liabilities reached $1,599.6 million. Available cash for closed missions totalled $307.7 million, while liabilities came to $345.6 million.

Notes of Secretary-General. In accordance with General Assembly resolution 49/233 A [YUN 1994, p. 1338], the Secretary-General submitted to the General Assembly's Fifth (Administrative and Budgetary) Committee a February note [A/C.5/58/35] updating information provided in March 2003 [YUN 2003, p. 82] on proposed budgetary requirements for current peacekeeping operations, the United Nations Logistics Base (UNLB) and the support account for the period 1 July 2003 to 30 June 2004 amounting to $2,689,945,400. That figure took into account 2003 Assembly decisions in respect of UNMISET, MONUC and UNMIL.

In May [A/C.5/58/36], the Secretary-General submitted information on proposed budgetary requirements for 1 July 2004 to 30 June 2005 in the amount of $2,504,803,100.

Financial performance and proposed budgets

In April [A/58/759], ACABQ considered the financial performance report for 1 July 2002 to 30 June 2003 and the proposed budget for 1 July 2004 to 30 June 2005 for the support account for peacekeeping operations [A/58/760]; the Secretary-General's overview of the financing of the UN peacekeeping operations: budget performance for 1 July 2002 to 30 June 2003 and budget for the period from 1 July 2004 to 30 June 2005 [A/58/705]; the performance report on the budget for the support account for peacekeeping operations for 1 July 2002 to 30 June 2003 [A/58/703 & Add.1]; and the proposed budget for the support account for peacekeeping operations for 1 July 2004 to 30 June 2005 [A/58/715].

Expenditure for peacekeeping missions, including UNLB and the support account for peacekeeping operations, for the year ending 30 June 2003 amounted to $2,392.4 million, against appropriations of $2,606.5 million, leaving an unencumbered balance of $214.1 million.

ACABQ, while welcoming improvements made in the budget presentation using results-based budgeting, noted that little progress had been made in enhancing the capability of existing financial systems to support results-based budgeting, and was concerned that, as at the end of March, operational resources and costs could not be attributed, monitored and recorded automatically for the results-based budgeting framework of each mission and that additional systems would need to be installed. The Committee pointed to the need for missions to state more clearly mission-specific objectives in budget documents. It also stressed the importance of clearly drafting expected accomplishments, indicators of achievement and planned outputs under each component, identifying time frames to facilitate monitoring and reporting, and allowing objective measurement of progress in implementing expected accomplishments and the mission's objective.

ACABQ emphasized that the timely recruitment of staff for DPKO was critical and all efforts should be made to reach recruitment goals. The Committee joined the Board of Auditors in recommending that the administration evaluate the level of incumbents appointed to budgeted posts at missions to ensure that staff occupied posts at the appropriate level and that the level of posts be re-evaluated and inconsistencies rectified. It regretted that DPKO managerial, staffing and operational reviews of mission activities were not reflected in budget proposals and recommended that the Board of Auditors follow up on the issue of periodic and timely management reviews. It believed there was a need to establish a common approach for restructuring the supervision of the technical support areas of peacekeeping missions.

ACABQ considered the proposed conversion of staff in peacekeeping missions from the 300 series of the staff rules to the 100 series, and noted that during the 2004/05 period some 1,600 Professional and 5,000 national staff members would be so converted. It requested further information in the next submission on the matter. Noting that 300-series appointment was limited to four years, ACABQ pointed out that those appointments were never intended to create long-term career opportunities. Such a wholesale conversion raised a number of policy issues, including the net impact on the equitable geographical distribution of staff, the potential impact on the long-term contractual obligations of the Organization, and the cost implications. The proposed action represented a change in the scope of application of the 300 series and should be reported to the Fifth Committee for possible comment or further direction. ACABQ therefore recommended that the Secretary-General present a comprehensive proposal on the matter in the context of his report on human resources management to be submitted to the General Assembly at its fifty-ninth (2004) session and, pending the Assembly's consideration, defer any action on the proposed conversion.

ACABQ considered the issue of hiring individuals on procurement contracts without benefits for functions necessary for the day-to-day running of long-term peacekeeping operations. It was of the opinion that, in a number of instances, those services could be outsourced instead of employing individuals as staff members or issuing them special service contracts. It underlined the necessity for the Secretariat to develop a coherent, comprehensive and cost-effective policy on outsourcing for peacekeeping missions in implementation of resolution 55/232 [YUN 2000, p. 1401]. In the meantime, it would make recommendations on a case-by-case basis.

GENERAL ASSEMBLY ACTION

On 18 June [meeting 91], the General Assembly, on the recommendation of the Fifth Committee [A/58/821], adopted **resolution 58/296** without vote [agenda items 127 & 134].

Administrative and budgetary aspects of the financing of the United Nations peacekeeping operations

The General Assembly,

Having considered the report of the Secretary-General entitled "Overview of the financing of the United Nations peacekeeping operations: budget performance for the period from 1 July 2002 to 30 June 2003 and budget for the period from 1 July 2004 to 30 June 2005" and the report of the Advisory Committee on Administrative and Budgetary Questions,

1. *Requests* the Secretary-General to submit to the General Assembly at the main part of its fifty-ninth session a comprehensive report on the use, including the conversion, of 300 series contracts, addressing in particular the strategy of the Organization for meeting current and future human resources requirements for peacekeeping missions, taking into account the observations and recommendations of the Advisory Committee on Administrative and Budgetary Questions;

2. *Endorses* the observations and recommendations of the Advisory Committee contained in paragraphs 35 to 39 of its report, concerning the wholesale conversion, bearing in mind the fact that the General Assembly has taken no decision to support the replacement of the 300 series contracts as a mechanism for the employment of staff in peacekeeping missions;

3. *Decides* to suspend the application of the four-year maximum limit for appointments of limited duration under the 300 series of the staff rules in peacekeeping operations, until 31 December 2004, pending a decision by the General Assembly on this matter at its fifty-ninth session.

On 29 October, the Assembly requested the Secretary-General to submit at the second part of its resumed fifty-ninth (2005) session a report on the review of the management structure of all peacekeeping operations, including through administrative comparisons, taking into account the complexities, mandates and specificities of each operation and the necessity of carrying out effectively and efficiently each operation (**decision 59/507**).

On 23 December, the Assembly decided that the item on the administrative and budgetary aspects of the financing of the United Nations peacekeeping operations would remain for consideration during its resumed fifty-ninth session (**decision 59/552**).

Funds from closed missions

In March [A/58/723], the Secretary-General, in response to the General Assembly's request contained in resolution 57/323 [YUN 2003, p. 85] that he postpone the return of 50 per cent ($84,446,000) of the net cash available for credit to Member States as a result of a number of peacekeeping missions having been closed, reported that the amount available as at 29 February 2004 was $57,399,000.

In the light of the establishment of missions in Côte d'Ivoire and Haiti, the extension of UNMISET until May 2005, and potential missions in Burundi and the Sudan, which would give rise to increased requirements before the Assembly was in a position to review and approve the related budgets, the Secretary-General proposed that, out of prudence, the return of the amount of $84,446,000, representing 50 per cent of the cash available to Member States as at 30 June 2002, be postponed. He also proposed that the Assembly revisit the issue at the main part of its fifty-ninth (2004) session.

ACABQ, in a March report [A/58/732], expressed the view that the postponement of the return of "available cash" to Member States was a policy decision to be determined by the Assembly, while pointing out that cash from closed missions appeared to be the only source for temporary cross-borrowing, as well as for funding new missions, in addition to the Peacekeeping Reserve Fund.

GENERAL ASSEMBLY ACTION

On 8 April [meeting 83], the General Assembly, on the recommendation of the Fifth Committee [A/58/582/Add.1], adopted **resolution 58/288** without vote [agenda item 134].

Implementation of paragraph 3 of General Assembly resolution 57/323

The General Assembly,

Recalling its resolution 57/323 of 18 June 2003,

Having considered the note by the Secretary-General on the implementation of paragraph 3 of General Assembly resolution 57/323 and the related report of the Advisory Committee on Administrative and Budgetary Questions,

1. *Takes note* of the proposal by the Secretary-General and the related report of the Advisory Committee on Administrative and Budgetary Questions;

2. *Decides* to postpone to 30 June 2004 the return of the remaining 50 per cent of the net cash available for credit to Member States as at 30 June 2002, in the amount of 84,446,000 United States dollars, in respect of the fund balances of the United Nations Mission in Haiti; the United Nations Observer Group in Central

America and the United Nations Observer Mission in El Salvador; the United Nations Preventive Deployment Force; the United Nations Protection Force, the United Nations Confidence Restoration Operation in Croatia, the United Nations Preventive Deployment Force and the United Nations Peace Forces headquarters; the United Nations Transitional Administration for Eastern Slavonia, Baranja and Western Sirmium and the Civilian Police Support Group; the United Nations Angola Verification Mission and the United Nations Observer Mission in Angola; the United Nations Observer Mission Uganda-Rwanda and the United Nations Assistance Mission for Rwanda; the United Nations Mission of Observers in Tajikistan; the United Nations Transition Assistance Group; and the United Nations Observer Mission in Liberia;

3. *Also decides* that credits or disbursements to Member States may be made at the discretion of the Member State concerned as from 1 July 2004;

4. *Encourages* Member States that are owed credits for the closed peacekeeping mission accounts to apply those credits to any accounts where the Member State concerned has outstanding assessed contributions.

In April [A/58/778], the Secretary-General updated the information, as at 30 June 2003, on the financial position of 18 closed peacekeeping missions for which financial performance reports had already been submitted: the Military Observer Group of the United Nations Verification Mission in Guatemala (MINUGUA); the United Nations Mission in Haiti (UNMIH); the United Nations Observer Group in Central America (ONUCA) and the United Nations Observer Mission in El Salvador (ONUSAL); the United Nations Operation in Mozambique (ONUMOZ); the United Nations Operation in Somalia (UNOSOM); the United Nations Preventive Deployment Force (UNPREDEP); the United Nations Protection Force, the United Nations Confidence Restoration Operation in Croatia, UNPREDEP and the United Nations Peace Forces headquarters (UNPF); the United Nations Support Mission in Haiti (UNSMIH) and the United Nations Civilian Police Mission in Haiti (MIPONUH); the United Nations Transitional Administration for Eastern Slavonia, Baranja and Western Sirmium (UNTAES) and the Civilian Police Support Group; the United Nations Transitional Authority in Cambodia (UNTAC); the United Nations Mission of Observers in Tajikistan (UNMOT); the United Nations Angola Verification Mission (UNAVEM) and the United Nations Observer Mission in Angola (MONUA); the United Nations Observer Mission in Liberia (UNOMIL); the United Nations Observer Mission Uganda-Rwanda (UNOMUR) and the United Nations Assistance Mission for Rwanda (UNAMIR); the United Nations Military Liaison Team in Cambodia (UNMLT); the United Nations Iran-Iraq Military Observer Group (UNIIMOG); the United Nations Mission in the

Central African Republic (MINURCA); and the United Nations Transition Assistance Group (UNTAG).

The Secretary-General reported that, as at 30 June 2003, the net cash available for credit to Member States amounted to $178,684,000, inclusive of the $84,446,000 to be credited to Member States, in accordance with resolution 58/288 (see above). He proposed that the balance of $94,238,000 be retained until 31 October 2004 to supplement the Peacekeeping Reserve Fund in order to finance the initial requirement for the new peacekeeping operations. The available cash in the Fund ($150.3 million) was insufficient to meet the foreseeable cash requirements in the first quarter of the forthcoming financial year.

ACABQ, in a May report [A/58/799], reiterated that the postponement of the return of available cash was a policy decision to be determined by the Assembly.

On 18 June, by **decision 58/564 C**, the Assembly deferred until its fifty-ninth session the Secretary-General's report on the updated financial position of closed peacekeeping missions as at 30 June 2003 and the related ACABQ report.

Peacekeeping support account

The Secretary-General, in February [A/58/703 & Add.1], submitted the performance report on the budget of the support account for peacekeeping operations for 1 July 2002 to 30 June 2003. Expenditures for the period totalled $97,145,400 against an apportionment of $100,896,200, resulting in an unencumbered balance of $3,750,800, attributable mainly to the vacancy rate and underexpenditures for consultants, official travel and information technology. The Secretary-General recommended that the unencumbered balance and other income and adjustments of $4,600,000 be applied to the 2004/2005 budget (see below).

Also in February [A/58/715], the Secretary-General submitted the budget for the support account for peacekeeping operations for 1 July 2004 to 30 June 2005 in the amount of $122,093,400, which provided for 762 posts. In April [A/58/760], ACABQ recommended reductions to that budget totalling $814,500 and that the Assembly approve total staffing and non-staffing requirements of $121,278,900 gross ($104,870,200 net). It proposed that miscellaneous income of $4,600,000, the amount of $127,800 that was not applied to offset the amounts prorated among individual peacekeeping budgets for 1 July 2002 to 30 June 2003, and the amount of $741,000 relating to additional staff assessment income be applied to the resources required for 1 July 2004 to 30 June 2005

and that the balance be prorated among individual peacekeeping operation budgets for that period.

GENERAL ASSEMBLY ACTION

On 18 June [meeting 91], the General Assembly, on the recommendation of the Fifth Committee [A/58/582/Add.2], adopted **resolution 58/298** without vote [agenda item 134].

Support account for peacekeeping operations
The General Assembly,

Recalling its resolutions 45/258 of 3 May 1991, 47/218 A of 23 December 1992, 48/226 A of 23 December 1993, 56/241 of 24 December 2001, 56/293 of 27 June 2002 and 57/318 of 18 June 2003, its decisions 48/489 of 8 July 1994, 49/469 of 23 December 1994 and 50/473 of 23 December 1995 and other relevant resolutions of the General Assembly,

Having considered the reports of the Secretary-General on the financing of the support account for peacekeeping operations and the related reports of the Advisory Committee on Administrative and Budgetary Questions,

Recognizing the importance of the United Nations being able to respond and deploy rapidly to a peacekeeping operation upon adoption of a relevant resolution of the Security Council, within thirty days for traditional peacekeeping operations and ninety days for complex peacekeeping operations,

Recognizing also the need for adequate support during all phases of peacekeeping operations, including the liquidation and termination phases,

Mindful that the level of the support account should broadly correspond to the mandate, number, size and complexity of peacekeeping missions,

1. *Takes note* of the reports of the Secretary-General on the financing of the support account for peacekeeping operations;

2. *Reaffirms* the need for effective and efficient administration and financial management of peacekeeping operations, and urges the Secretary-General to continue to identify measures to increase the productivity and efficiency of the support account;

3. *Also reaffirms* the need for adequate funding for the backstopping of peacekeeping operations, as well as the need for full justification for that funding in support account budget submissions;

4. *Endorses* the conclusions and recommendations contained in the relevant report of the Advisory Committee on Administrative and Budgetary Questions;

5. *Decides* to maintain, for the period from 1 July 2004 to 30 June 2005, the funding mechanism for the support account used in the current period, from 1 July 2003 to 30 June 2004, as approved in paragraph 3 of its resolution 50/221 B of 7 June 1996;

6. *Reaffirms* the need for the Secretary-General to ensure that delegation of authority to the Department of Peacekeeping Operations of the Secretariat and field missions is in strict compliance with relevant resolutions and decisions and the relevant rules and procedures of the General Assembly on this matter;

7. *Also reaffirms* paragraph 15 of its resolution 56/293, regrets that the report requested in paragraph 10 of its resolution 57/318 was not submitted at its fifty-

eighth session, and decides to consider it at its fifty-ninth session;

8. *Decides* to continue its consideration of the implementation of the restructuring of the Department of Peacekeeping Operations, in the context of the review requested in paragraph 14 of resolution 57/318, at the second part of its resumed fifty-ninth session;

9. *Requests* the Secretary-General to report to the General Assembly at its fifty-ninth session on the status of the civilian rapid deployment roster, including measures to improve its utility, taking into account recent experiences with its use;

10. *Also requests* the Secretary-General to review the level of the support account, including the need for existing posts, in future budget submissions, taking into consideration the number, size and complexity of peacekeeping operations;

11. *Notes with concern*, as observed by the Advisory Committee in paragraph 21 of its report, that the implementation of paragraph 18 of resolution 57/318 is not consistent with the requirement of the resolution;

12. *Reiterates* paragraph 18 of resolution 57/318, and requests the Secretary-General to submit, during future considerations of the support account budget, information as outlined in paragraph 22 of the report of the Advisory Committee with respect to posts that will have been vacant for at least 12 months by 30 June of a given year on the understanding that, in the interim, until such consideration by the General Assembly, the recruitment process will not be affected;

**Financial performance report for
the period from 1 July 2002 to 30 June 2003**

13. *Takes note* of the report of the Secretary-General on the financial performance of the support account for peacekeeping operations for the period from 1 July 2002 to 30 June 2003;

**Budget estimates for the
period from 1 July 2004 to 30 June 2005**

14. *Approves* the support account requirements in the amount of 121,610,300 United States dollars for the period from 1 July 2004 to 30 June 2005, including 743 continuing and 18 new temporary posts and their related post and non-post requirements;

Financing of the budget estimates

15. *Decides* that the requirements for the support account for peacekeeping operations for the period from 1 July 2004 to 30 June 2005 shall be financed as follows:

(*a*) The unencumbered balance and other income in the total amount of 8,478,600 dollars, comprising 8,350,800 dollars in respect of the period ended 30 June 2003 and the adjustment of 127,800 dollars related to the period ended 30 June 2001, to be applied to the resources required for the period from 1 July 2004 to 30 June 2005;

(*b*) The increase of 59,000 dollars in the estimated staff assessment income, representing the difference between 682,000 dollars in respect of the financial period ended 30 June 2003 and the adjustment of 741,000 dollars related to the period ended 30 June 2001, to be applied to the amount referred to in subparagraph (*a*) above;

(*c*) The balance of 113,131,700 dollars to be prorated among the budgets of the active peacekeeping operations for the period from 1 July 2004 to 30 June 2005;

(*d*) The estimated staff assessment income of 16,509,400 dollars for the period from 1 July 2004 to 30 June 2005 to be set off against the balance referred to in subparagraph (*c*) above, to be prorated among the budgets of the individual active peacekeeping operations.

Peacekeeping Reserve Fund

The Secretary-General, in response to General Assembly resolution 57/317 [YUN 2003, p. 88], reported in March [A/58/724] that the level of the Peacekeeping Reserve Fund, established in 1992 [YUN 1992, p. 1022] to ensure the rapid deployment of peacekeeping operations, stood at $194.3 million as at 30 June 2003. As at 29 February 2004, the balance was $163 million, with $74 million available in cash. The Secretary-General recommended that the Fund be maintained at the level of $150 million and that the balance in excess of that amount ($11 million) be applied to the support account for peacekeeping operations for 1 July 2004 to 30 June 2005.

In March [A/58/732], ACABQ expressed the view that an increase in the Fund's level would have little or no impact on the short-term cash-flow problem, which could be solved only by payment of assessed contributions. It recommended that the Assembly accept the Secretary-General's recommendations on the Fund's level and the treatment of the balance in excess of that level. By **decision 58/564 C** of 18 June, the Assembly deferred consideration of the Secretary-General's report on the Peacekeeping Reserve Fund and the related ACABQ report until its fifty-ninth (2004) session.

Accounts and auditing

At its resumed fifty-eighth session, the General Assembly considered the financial report and audited financial statements for UN peacekeeping operations for 1 July 2002 to 30 June 2003 [A/58/5, vol. II], the Secretary-General's report on the implementation of the recommendations of the Board of Auditors [A/58/737] and the related ACABQ report [A/58/759].

GENERAL ASSEMBLY ACTION

On 18 June [meeting 91], the General Assembly, on the recommendation of the Fifth Committee [A/58/570/Add.1], adopted **resolution 58/249 B** without vote [agenda item 118].

Financial reports and audited financial statements, and reports of the Board of Auditors

The General Assembly,

Having considered the financial report and audited financial statements for the twelve-month period from

1 July 2002 to 30 June 2003 and the report of the Board of Auditors on United Nations peacekeeping operations, the related section of the report of the Advisory Committee on Administrative and Budgetary Questions and the report of the Secretary-General on the implementation of the recommendations of the Board of Auditors concerning United Nations peacekeeping operations in respect of that period,

1. *Accepts* the audited financial statements on the United Nations peacekeeping operations for the period from 1 July 2002 to 30 June 2003;

2. *Takes note* of the observations and endorses the recommendations contained in the report of the Board of Auditors;

3. *Also takes note* of the observations and endorses the recommendations contained in the report of the Advisory Committee on Administrative and Budgetary Questions related to the report of the Board of Auditors;

4. *Commends* the Board of Auditors for the quality of its report and the streamlined format thereof;

5. *Takes note* of the report of the Secretary-General on the implementation of the recommendations of the Board of Auditors concerning United Nations peacekeeping operations in respect of the financial period ended 30 June 2003;

6. *Requests* the Secretary-General to continue to ensure that internal control in peacekeeping missions is improved with respect to the optimum use of audit resources;

7. *Also requests* the Secretary-General to ensure the full implementation of the recommendations of the Board of Auditors and the related recommendations of the Advisory Committee in a prompt and timely manner.

Regional auditors and investigators

In November [A/59/546], the Secretary-General transmitted the report of the Office of Internal Oversight Services (OIOS) on the first year of experience of regional investigators in two hubs, Vienna and Nairobi, in response to General Assembly resolution 57/318 [YUN 2003, p. 86]. The report assessed the OIOS Investigations Division's regional investigator programme, under which regional investigators, operating from Nairobi and Vienna, conducted inquiries at peacekeeping missions. It also provided an overview of the caseload of the two regional hubs, highlighted some of the significant matters investigated and assessed the impact of the new concept.

OIOS concluded that, given the limited resources, the regional investigators working on cases at peacekeeping operations had performed well. Significant matters had been investigated, particularly corruption and sexual exploitation and abuse, and recommendations issued, accepted and implemented. The OIOS work was generally well received by DPKO and mission management. The first year of operation revealed the merits of the regional hubs, especially in terms of costs and reduced travel times com-

pared to those for investigations handled by staff based at UN Headquarters. Relying only on regional investigators, however, meant that OIOS investigators, unlike resident investigators, could not develop detailed knowledge of the individual missions, nor readily respond to requests from missions, given the travel and time requirements. The larger and more complex missions, however, needed the presence of resident investigators.

OIOS believed that the most effective approach was a combination of regional and resident investigators, with resident investigators based at and providing services to the larger missions, and an additional six regional investigator posts to provide services to both the larger missions in regard to complex cases and the smaller missions. It would submit, for the Assembly's consideration, a proposal for additional posts in its budget submission for the support account for peacekeeping operations for 1 July 2005 to 30 June 2006.

Reimbursement issues

Equipment

The Secretary-General, in response to General Assembly resolution 55/274 [YUN 2001, p. 100], submitted in August [A/59/292] a report on reformed procedures for determining reimbursement to Member States for contingent-owned equipment, which summarized the findings and recommendations of the 2004 Working Group on Contingent-Owned Equipment (23 February–5 March) [A/C.5/58/37 & Corr.1]. The Working Group conducted a triennial review of reimbursement rates and updated the standards of major equipment and self-sustainment categories. It agreed on criteria for reimbursement of commercial pattern support vehicles as military pattern vehicles; standard reimbursement rates for certain special cases and new categories of major equipment; a threshold value of $500 for special cases major equipment; and the frequency of verification reports by field missions (quarterly). Consensus was not reached on the triennial review of reimbursement rates for major equipment and self-sustainment; a refinement of the methodology for triennial rate review of contingent-owned equipment; a mechanism to provide guidance and decision-making on contingent-owned equipment; a modular medical concept; and a methodology to review reimbursement rates for troop costs.

The Secretary-General recommended that the Assembly approve the criteria for reimbursement of commercial pattern support vehicles as military vehicles, the reimbursement rates for new items of major equipment and the quarterly cycle of verification reports; and agree to distribution of the updated Contingent-Owned Equipment Manual as an official UN document. He also suggested that the Assembly convene the next Working Group in 2008 instead of 2007 to review the contingent-owned equipment system; establish a methodology for reviewing reimbursement rates; set up consultations between the Secretariat and Member States on the system; make recommendations on the costing and medical staffing level of the modular medical concept; adopt the proposed format for collecting national cost data on medical equipment for the Working Group to review; and discuss the maintenance of current reimbursement rates for troop costs and the determination by the Assembly of when an adjustment was warranted.

Management of peacekeeping assets

UN Logistics Base

The General Assembly, at its resumed fifty-eighth session, considered the financial performance report of the United Nations Logistics Base (UNLB) in Brindisi, Italy, for 1 July 2002 to 30 June 2003 [A/58/702]. Expenditures for the period totalled $14,447,500 gross ($13,360,600 net), against total appropriations of $14,293,200, resulting in a deficit of $154,300. The Assembly was asked to approve the additional requirement of $154,300, to apply other income/adjustments for that period amounting to $3,328,000 to offset the additional requirements and to decide on the treatment of the balance of $3,173,700.

The Assembly also had before it the proposed budget for 1 July 2004 to 30 June 2005 [A/58/706] amounting to $28,799,700 gross ($27,104,600 net), which represented an increase of $6,591,600 in total resources over the previous 12-month period. The proposed increase reflected a 17.7 per cent increase in operational costs, a 55.2 per cent increase in personnel costs, and a 34.7 per cent increase in staff assessment. The budget provided for the deployment of 37 international and 114 national staff.

ACABQ, in April [A/58/759/Add.9], noted that the report on UNLB's financial performance did not contain information on measures taken in response to its requests and asked that the next report contain such information. It requested that a methodology be developed to identify and estimate reimbursable costs and utilized for the next budget estimate. Regarding the 2004/05 budget, ACABQ's recommendations would result in a reduction of $377,700. It also made recommenda-

tions on the administration and management of UNLB and opportunities for further savings.

In May [A/C.5/58/36], the Secretary-General submitted to the Fifth Committee a note on amounts to be apportioned in respect of each peacekeeping mission, including the prorated share of UNLB for 1 July 2004 to 30 June 2005.

The Assembly also considered reports on the status of implementation of strategic deployment stocks [A/58/707], progress in implementing the field assets control system [YUN 2003, p. 94], an analysis of establishing a global procurement hub for all peacekeeping missions in Brindisi [A/58/762] and the related ACABQ reports [A/58/759/Add.9 & A/58/796] (these reports are dealt with in the respective sections).

GENERAL ASSEMBLY ACTION

On 18 June [meeting 91], the General Assembly, on the recommendation of the Fifth Committee [A/58/582/Add.2], adopted **resolution 58/297** without vote [agenda item 134].

Financing of the United Nations Logistics Base at Brindisi, Italy

The General Assembly,

Recalling section XIV of its resolution 49/233 A of 23 December 1994,

Recalling also its decision 50/500 of 17 September 1996 on the financing of the United Nations Logistics Base at Brindisi, Italy, and its subsequent resolutions and decisions thereon, the latest of which was decision 58/557 of 23 December 2003,

Recalling further its resolution 56/292 of 27 June 2002 concerning the establishment of the strategic deployment stocks and its subsequent resolution 57/315 of 18 June 2003 on the status of the implementation of the strategic deployment stocks,

Having considered the reports of the Secretary-General on the financing of the United Nations Logistics Base, the status of the implementation of strategic deployment stocks, progress in the implementation of the field assets control system and the analysis of establishing a global procurement hub for all peacekeeping missions in Brindisi and the related reports of the Advisory Committee on Administrative and Budgetary Questions,

Reiterating the importance of establishing an accurate inventory of assets,

1. *Notes with appreciation* the facilities provided by the Government of Italy to the United Nations Logistics Base at Brindisi;

2. *Endorses* the observations and recommendations contained in the reports of the Advisory Committee on Administrative and Budgetary Questions, and requests the Secretary-General to ensure their full implementation;

3. *Reiterates* the need to implement, as a matter of priority, an effective inventory management standard, especially in respect of peacekeeping operations involving high inventory value;

4. *Also reiterates* paragraph 2 of its resolution 56/292, and requests the Secretary-General to report thereon expeditiously;

Field assets control system

5. *Takes note* of the report of the Secretary-General on progress in the implementation of the field assets control system;

Strategic deployment stocks

6. *Also takes note* of the report of the Secretary-General on the status of the implementation of the strategic deployment stocks;

7. *Requests* the Secretary-General to report to the General Assembly at its fifty-ninth session on the functioning of existing mechanisms of the strategic deployment stocks, in the light of lessons learned from experiences with mission start-ups;

Global procurement hub

8. *Takes note* of the report of the Secretary-General on the analysis of establishing a global procurement hub for all peacekeeping missions in Brindisi;

9. *Endorses* the observations and recommendations contained in the report of the Advisory Committee on Administrative and Budgetary Questions, and requests the Secretary-General to ensure their full implementation;

Financial performance report for the period from 1 July 2002 to 30 June 2003

10. *Takes note* of the report of the Secretary-General on the financial performance of the United Nations Logistics Base at Brindisi for the period from 1 July 2002 to 30 June 2003;

Budget estimates for the period from 1 July 2004 to 30 June 2005

11. *Approves* the cost estimates for the United Nations Logistics Base at Brindisi amounting to 28,422,000 United States dollars for the period from 1 July 2004 to 30 June 2005;

Financing of the budget estimates

12. *Decides* to apply the balance of other income and adjustments in the total amount of 3,173,700 dollars in respect of the financial period ended 30 June 2003 to the resources required for the period from 1 July 2004 to 30 June 2005;

13. *Also decides* that the increase of 9,900 dollars in the estimated staff assessment income in respect of the financial period ended 30 June 2003 shall be added to the credits from the amount referred to in paragraph 12 above;

14. *Further decides* to prorate the balance of 25,248,300 dollars among the individual active peacekeeping operation budgets to meet the financing requirements of the United Nations Logistics Base at Brindisi for the period from 1 July 2004 to 30 June 2005;

15. *Decides* to set off against the balance referred to in paragraph 14 above the estimated staff assessment income of 1,412,500 dollars for the period from 1 July 2004 to 30 June 2005, representing the difference between the estimated staff assessment income of 1,560,600 dollars for the period from 1 July 2004 to 30 June 2005 and the adjustment in the staff assessment income of 148,100 dollars related to the period ended

30 June 2001, to be prorated among the individual active peacekeeping operation budgets;

16. *Also decides* to consider at its fifty-ninth session the question of the financing of the United Nations Logistics Base at Brindisi.

Strategic deployment stocks

In response to General Assembly resolution 57/315 [YUN 2003, p. 73], the Secretary-General submitted a February report on the status of implementation of the strategic deployment stocks [A/58/707]. He stated that DPKO had positioned sufficient stocks at UNLB and had significantly advanced towards having the capability to deploy rapidly the immediate operational capability for a traditional peacekeeping mission. As at 31 December 2003, strategic deployment stocks facilitated the rapid deployment and operational readiness of UNMIL, UNOCI, the United Nations Monitoring, Verification and Inspection Commission and the Office of the Special Representative of the Secretary-General in Iraq.

As at 30 June 2003, strategic deployment stock holdings were valued at $23 million, and equipment transferred from DPKO's reserve and surplus stocks from peacekeeping missions was valued at $21 million. Out of the total budget of $141,546,000, expenditures amounted to $88,902,181. As the Assembly in resolution 57/315 had extended the validity of the approved resources to 30 June 2004, the balance of $52,643,816 had been carried forward to the 2003/04 financial period. The Secretary-General also reported that the Galileo Inventory Management System had been implemented at UNLB and at Headquarters to manage the strategic deployment stocks.

ACABQ, in its April report on UNLB [A/58/759/Add.9], expressed regret that the Secretary-General's report did not provide sufficient information on the administration of the strategic deployment stocks, including problems incurred. ACABQ suggested that the next budget submission should include information on lessons learned and deficiencies to be corrected, and reiterated its previous recommendation that the report on strategic deployment stocks should be consolidated with that on UNLB. It urged the Secretariat to address the factors hampering the acquisition and replenishment of the strategic stocks, such as contractual problems and the selection of vendors; to consider improving replenishment policies and procedures, while maintaining those stocks in good condition; and to include that information in the Secretary-General's annual report on strategic deployment stocks. ACABQ was of the view that the role of the Steering Group on Strategic Deployment Stocks and its Finance Working Group should be enhanced to make them an effective tool in a coordinated approach to strategic deployment stocks.

Procurement

Reports of Secretary-General. In April [A/58/762], the Secretary-General, responding to General Assembly resolution 57/320 [YUN 2003, p. 96], submitted an analysis of the merits of establishing a global procurement hub for all peacekeeping missions in Brindisi. The Secretary-General, reviewing the possibility of transferring the logistics support function to UNLB, focused on the advantages and disadvantages of creating such a hub and its operational impact on the functioning of DPKO's Logistics Support Division and the Office of Central Support Services of the Department of Management.

The review concluded that, while there were some advantages to creating such a hub, such as operating in a closer time zone to the majority of peacekeeping missions, enhanced ability to perform on-site contract management for strategic deployment stocks and reduced operating costs, they were far outweighed by the disadvantages. Those disadvantages related to the difficulty of attracting and maintaining qualified international staff, coordination challenges of operating in a time zone different from Headquarters, the loss of surge capacity (specifically, the inability to utilize Headquarters staff during peak demands), relocation costs and duplication of support and liaison infrastructures.

In May [A/58/796], ACABQ, noting that the Secretary-General's report dealt only with a few of the operational and administrative challenges of establishing a hub, called for a more thorough review, providing a technical, managerial and financial analysis, and recommended that the Assembly defer action until a comprehensive report was submitted.

Also in April [A/58/761], the Secretary-General reported on procurement and contract management for peacekeeping operations, in response to Assembly resolution 57/290 B [YUN 2003, p. 83], the recommendation of the Board of Auditors on UN peacekeeping operations for the year ended 30 June 2002 [ibid., p. 91] and the comments of ACABQ [ibid., p. 95]. The Secretary-General stated that new initiatives, including ethics training and the drafting of ethical guidelines, had been put in place to ensure that all staff working in procurement understood their responsibilities. The newly revised Procurement Manual contained a chapter entitled "Ethics and Professional Responsibility". The Procurement Division issued an instruction reminding all procurement staff

of their responsibilities relating to the signature of a declaration of independence and, in particular, of the need to ensure confidentiality of information associated with their functions. To improve procurement and contract management in peacekeeping missions, plans were reviewed by the Logistics Support Division at Headquarters to determine how best to fulfil requirements, taking into account surplus assets at other missions and strategic stock at UNLB. Although the quality and timeliness of the procurement submissions from the missions had improved, further improvement needed to be made in that area. Over the previous 12 months, the Procurement Division undertook management missions to a number of peacekeeping operations, during which specific issues were addressed. It released staff to participate in fact-finding and start-up phases of new missions to develop procurement capacity on the ground at the outset of those missions. Field procurement training took place in the first quarter of 2004 in six locations and the Procurement Division worked with UN organizations to develop a system-wide common procurement and certification programme under the auspices of the Inter-Agency Procurement Working Group to meet longer-term training needs.

To improve procurement lead time, the Procurement Division, with the Logistics Support Division, established a "24/7" hotline and a designated focal point for direct communications between procurement officers in the field and the Procurement Division. Recommendations of local committees on contracts were forwarded directly to the Procurement Division for presentation to the Headquarters Committee on Contracts. The two Divisions were developing a common procurement management system to facilitate the exchange of procurement-related data between Headquarters and peacekeeping missions.

OIOS report. In September [A/59/347], the Secretary-General transmitted the OIOS report on the audit of safeguarding air safety standards while procuring air services for UN peacekeeping missions, prepared pursuant to General Assembly resolution 57/279 [YUN 2002, p. 1358]. As of 31 January 2004, DPKO, through 12 long-term and four short-term commercial contracts with a total value of $132.5 million, deployed 136 aircraft to peacekeeping missions, and projected deployment of over 200 in 2004, owing to the increase in peacekeeping operations.

Among efforts to improve air safety, DPKO and the World Food Programme developed the Aviation Standards for Peacekeeping and Humanitarian Air Transport Operations. Efforts were still needed in air safety policy setting, procurement, and organization and staffing of DPKO and peacekeeping mission units responsible for air safety. The audit also found that, although DPKO had an accident prevention programme, no trend analyses or lessons learned had been issued. For missions in Sierra Leone, Liberia and Côte d'Ivoire, where a total of 40 aircraft were deployed, a regional aviation safety office would be more cost-effective than deploying aviation safety officers at each mission, and would help to improve consistency in the application of DPKO's accident prevention programme. Within DPKO, the prolonged periods during which the positions of Chief, Air Transport Section, and Chief, Aviation Safety Unit, remained vacant, and the limited progress in implementing the International Civil Aviation Organization's recommendations for strengthening DPKO's civil aviation capacity, made it difficult for the Department to develop and sustain a sound air safety strategy.

Regarding procurement, OIOS noted that, due to budgetary constraints, visits by DPKO staff to vendor sites to evaluate vendor capability in providing technically acceptable and safe air services were infrequent. The Procurement Division and the Department needed to agree on a vendor prequalification process to allow wider participation of vendors in UN bids, while allowing sufficient scrutiny of prospective vendors' documentation. There were divergent opinions within DPKO concerning the use of cargo aircraft for transporting cargo and passengers. After two accidents involving non-UN cargo aircraft carrying passengers resulted in mass fatalities in 2002-2003, the Department stopped transporting passengers on cargo aircraft as of April 2004.

OIOS issued 20 recommendations to enhance policy and procedures on safeguarding air safety standards while procuring air services for UN peacekeeping missions. DPKO's management agreed with all the recommendations and had started to implement them.

Restructuring issues

OIOS report. In March [A/58/746], the Secretary-General transmitted the OIOS report on the evaluation of the impact of the recent restructuring of DPKO, prepared in response to General Assembly resolution 56/241 [YUN 2001, p. 74]. The evaluation focused on the impact of the restructuring on DPKO's performance in the backstopping of peacekeeping operations.

OIOS was of the view that, while the reform would require more time to produce its full impact, the process was on the right track. It had enhanced DPKO's capacity to strategize, analyse and tackle complex, multidimensional problems and to improve its rapid deployment capacity and backstopping of field operations. However, DPKO faced four main challenges: to develop a comprehensive, clearly structured and evolving doctrine comprising the totality of its policies and guidelines; to operationalize the process of learning lessons and translating them into policies and practice; to establish a sound and transparent procedure for adjusting its staffing from peak to routine levels and managing the resultant staff mobility; and to exploit fully information management to strengthen its capacity.

Among its recommendations, OIOS proposed that DPKO redesign the integrated mission task forces concept, including DPKO's role in making it operational, and that a reliable mechanism be established for apprising those involved in mission planning of lessons learned and best practices. DPKO and the Department of Political Affairs should develop a mechanism for subregional political cooperation between missions. In addition, DPKO should advance inter-mission flexibilities and establish mechanisms for better integration between missions. DPKO should review annually the capacity, structure, preparedness and effectiveness of each peacekeeping force, identify the problems in implementing the Standards, Verification and Control of Contingent-Owned Equipment for Major Equipment and Self-Sustainment (COE Manual), issue standard operating procedures to guide the missions and revise the Guidelines to Troop-Contributing Countries for Military Units (TCC Guidelines). Other recommendations called on DPKO to define the functions of the Situation Centre and determine whether additional functions could be supported by reassigning or delaying resources, pending the provision of additional resources; finalize the organizational streamlining of the Civilian Police Division; ensure that its work plans were sound, realistic and flexible and periodically evaluated; and develop the law and order segment of a departmental "generic" exit strategy with a view to preventing a law-and-order vacuum when the United Nations departed.

The Department was called on to recommend to the Controller expanding the authority of missions funded from the regular budget in line with the policy promulgated in July 2002, while the Personnel Management and Support Service was urged to reassess its projects in succession planning and developing recruitment policies and procedures for the field to ensure further delegation of authority. The restructuring review of the Field Service category should resume, and the roster of available staff members should be updated. A mechanism for institutionalizing best practices as policies and operational modalities should be established. DPKO's training strategy should promote an integrated approach to the training of civilian, police and military components and address capacity development in political affairs and other areas where the Department did not have primary responsibility or dedicated units.

OIOS recommended that the Communications and Information Technology Service adopt an action plan for developing an information and communications technology strategy and a strategic plan for the Department and field missions. DPKO was urged to set up a committee for the information management strategy and policy and prepare a work plan for its implementation.

The Director of Change Management should lead the review of the Department's organizational structure with a view to formalizing it in a revised Secretary-General's bulletin. The review should define limited and continuous functions and refine the delineation of responsibilities between DPKO and peacekeeping operations and between DPKO and the Department of Management. DPKO should make its future business plans more sound and realistic, reflecting staff strength and skills mix, prioritizing tasks, having flexibility for exigencies and realistic deadlines. Implementation of the plans should be monitored and efficiency of implementation periodically evaluated.

The General Assembly, in **resolution 58/299** of 18 June, took note of the OIOS report. It noted that the Board of Auditors would act on Assembly resolution 57/318 [YUN 2003, p. 86] once it had considered the OIOS report and assessed what additional evaluation it might provide. The Assembly might revert at that time to the OIOS report.

Personnel matters

Recruitment policies and procedures

OIOS report. In February [A/58/704], the Secretary-General transmitted an OIOS report on the audit of the policies and procedures for recruiting DPKO staff, prepared pursuant to General Assembly resolution 57/287 A [YUN 2002, p. 1360]. The audit found that the average recruiting time for DPKO staff in the Professional category and above was 347 days, significantly higher than the goal of 120 days envisaged in the Secretary-General's report on human resources management reform [YUN 2000, p. 1337]. OIOS considered that DPKO should be able to significantly reduce the recruitment time frame in future years, particularly because the surge in vacancies experienced during 2001 and 2002 appeared unlikely to recur in the near future.

The criteria for determining staff members' eligibility to apply for vacancies had undergone significant changes with the issuance of an administrative instruction [ST/AI/2002/4] promulgating the new staff selection system from 1 May 2002. Section 5.6 of the instruction appeared to indicate that a staff member who had served the minimum occupancy period in a post was eligible to be considered for any post, even if it was two or more grades higher than the staff member's current level. OIOS was concerned that that provision was not articulated in the Secretary-General's report on human resources management reform or explicitly enunciated in the administrative instruction. The audit also identified instances in which ineligible staff members were shortlisted and evaluated for an advertised post. In several cases, errors were made in determining the eligibility of candidates at the 15-day and 30-day marks because of the lack of clear eligibility requirements. OIOS recommended that the Office of Human Resources Management (OHRM) clarify the eligibility requirements to ensure transparency and equity in recruitment and promotion.

The biggest challenge facing managers in DPKO and OHRM was reviewing the large number of applications received in response to vacancy announcements issued during 2002, as the Galaxy system did not possess a filtering mechanism to assist them in excluding unqualified candidates. OIOS recommended that OHRM work closely with managers to develop appropriate filtering techniques for screening applications. OIOS also found that numeric scoring methods were not used by DPKO managers for evaluating candidates, evidently because OHRM had said it was optional. OIOS recommended that OHRM ensure that managers used numeric ratings based on predetermined evaluation criteria.

The General Assembly, in **resolution 58/299**, decided to revert to consideration of the OIOS report during its fifty-ninth (2004) session, in the context of its consideration of the items on human resources management and the administrative and budgetary aspects of the financing of peacekeeping operations.

Report of Secretary-General. In April [A/58/767], the Secretary-General reported on the criteria used for recruitment to support account posts, in particular those in DPKO, in response to Assembly resolutions 56/293 [YUN 2002, p. 77] and 57/318 [YUN 2003, p. 86]. The report presented details on the selection criteria for such posts, outlined the criteria used for the selection of staff for posts subject to geographical distribution and analysed possible future criteria for consideration in recruitment against peacekeeping support account posts.

The report noted that the posts financed under the peacekeeping support account were not governed by the system of desirable ranges for the geographic distribution of staff in the Professional category and above, as set out by the Assembly most recently in resolution 53/221 [YUN 1999, p. 1324]. Consequently, numerical targets did not exist for those posts. However, in recruitment against support account posts, due regard was given to equitable geographical representation and gender balance, as well as to candidates with the requisite qualifications already in the service of the United Nations. A troop contribution factor was added by the Assembly in resolution 55/238 [YUN 2000, p. 1300]. Therefore, in filling those posts, primary consideration was given to identifying the most qualified candidates, while taking the other criteria into account. Senior managers also reviewed both individual cases and the overall pattern of recommendations in the context of legislative mandates with regard to gender parity, geographical diversity and proper representation of troop- and police-contributing countries.

The Secretary-General proposed using the system of desirable ranges as a workable hypothesis to be applied to various options for filling posts under the support account budget and presented options for determining desirable ranges for nationals in those posts. To illustrate the ramifications of varying the relative weights of the factors of population, size, the total number of UN members, and contribution amount and introducing the new troop contribution factor, the report offered six options with resultant desirable ranges, allowing for shifts in the relative weight of the factors.

The Secretary-General concluded that the differences between the options were small. Variations up to 15 per cent in the weight of the contribution factor in favour of the new troop contribution factor had only a marginal impact on Member States' representation status. The number of overrepresented Member States remained unchanged. Five Member States that stood to benefit (China, France, Germany, Italy, United States) were among major troop-contributing countries, and would move from their current status of underrepresentation to within range. The proposed options would not change the status of two underrepresented Member States (Japan, Spain).

Staffing of field missions

Report of Secretary-General (April). In April [A/58/765], the Secretary-General reported on the greater use of national staff (national professional officers (NPOs) and national general service staff) in field missions, as requested by the General Assembly in resolution 57/290 B [YUN 2003, p. 83]. He recalled the policy governing the use of NPOs adopted by the Assembly in resolution 49/223 [YUN 1994, p. 1374], which restricted their service to the country of their nationality. Their use was also limited to functions with a national content, requiring national experience and knowledge of local culture, language traditions and institutions. In December 2003, authority was delegated to DPKO to recruit NPOs in governance-oriented missions, both necessary and desirable in view of the expanded field of activities requiring national experience and local knowledge. The increased utilization of national staff also strengthened national capacity and development, providing national staff with the opportunity to contribute directly to reconciliation, recovery and reconstruction efforts. As at January 2004, a total of 9,231 national posts had been approved and established, of which 306 were NPO posts in eight peacekeeping and special political missions and 8,925 were national general service posts.

The Secretary-General concluded that overall, the experience of using national staff in the various missions had been positive. NPOs had generally produced high-quality work in their area of competence and their knowledge of local institutions, culture and language had proved especially helpful. All missions that currently had NPOs had indicated their interest in maintaining and expanding that particular expertise. Some missions, however, had encountered difficulties in identifying suitable national staff as a result of UN language requirements. The greater use of NPOs in peacekeeping operations was also limited by the conditions governing their employment. However, within that framework, it had been possible to increase significantly their use in such missions as UNMIK and UNAMA. In staffing missions in the future, DPKO would use the experience gained at those two missions to expand the use of NPOs where feasible and cost-effective.

OHRM and DPKO were monitoring the use of NPOs within the framework of the delegation of authority granted in December 2003. The currently applied criteria for their recruitment might be further reviewed to allow the Secretariat, and DPKO in particular, to be in a better position to develop flexible staffing strategies for expanding their use in field missions.

OIOS report. In July [A/59/152], the Secretary-General transmitted an OIOS report on the follow-up audit of DPKO policies and procedures for recruiting international civilian staff for field missions, prepared in response to General Assembly resolution 57/322 [YUN 2003, p. 98]. The report discussed OHRM's monitoring role, the global strategy for civilian staffing and management of the recruitment function.

OIOS found that, despite the additional resources provided, OHRM's monitoring of DPKO's delegated recruitment authority was weak. Contrary to expectations, the Galaxy system for filling vacancies did not result in continuous monitoring of recruitment actions by DPKO because the system had not been used for processing the recruitment of international civilian staff for field missions. OIOS also found instances where Field Service staff had been converted to the Professional category contrary to staff rules, and OHRM gave no clear policy guidance regarding DPKO's practice of "promoting" certain staff members by treating successive mission appointments as independent of each other, while reassigning others from one mission to another without a review of their salary level/grade. In the opinion of OIOS, the monitoring of delegated recruitment authority needed to be strengthened through more intensive reviews and provision of policy guidance to DPKO. OHRM should ensure enforcement of the policy guidance on the conversion of Field Service appointments to the Professional category and provide policy guidance to ensure that DPKO's recruitment practices were consistent with those of the Organization. DPKO, in consultation with OHRM, should resolve the problems concerning the Galaxy system, develop policy guidelines on geographical distribution and gender balance, and finalize arrangements with Member States for deploying civilian specialists in field missions through institutional relationships.

Work needed to be done in human resources planning, streamlining the recruitment process, screening applications for inclusion in the roster of available staff, expanding the sources of recruitment, and delegating authority to field missions. OIOS also found that an Intranet/Internet-based roster of candidates from which field missions could select suitable candidates had not been established; some 120,000 applications received in response to the generic vacancy announcements issued through the Galaxy system had not been screened; recruitment procedures were still in draft form; and DPKO was yet to expand the delegation of recruitment authority beyond the two missions to which that authority had been delegated in 2000. In the opinion of OIOS, DPKO needed to formulate a realistic timetable for completing the tasks assigned to its Personnel Management and Support Service, and to hold its managers accountable. The efficiency gains resulting from implementing new information technology systems and delegating recruitment authority to the field should lead to resizing of the Service's staffing levels based on an assessment of its workload.

The Secretary-General, in his transmittal note, said that he concurred with the OIOS recommendations, many of which were accepted by OHRM and action initiated.

Report of Secretary-General (August). The Secretary-General submitted in August [A/59/291] a comprehensive report on the staffing of field missions, including the use of 300 and 100 series appointments, as requested by the General Assembly in resolution 58/296 (see p. 94). The report addressed the current international context in which peacekeeping operations were deployed and the Organization's strategy for meeting current and future resource requirements for peacekeeping missions, the use of 300 series contracts and the financial implications.

In view of the larger and more complex mandates of peacekeeping missions, the Secretary-General said that supporting those multidimensional operations in increasingly dangerous circumstances required that the Secretariat have at its disposal a cadre of experienced, trained and multi-skilled civilian peacekeepers. Developing such a capacity required strengthened human resources structures and policies, including equitable contracts and updated conditions of service that facilitated the interest, recruitment and retention of qualified staff. In response to the increase in peacekeeping missions and the resulting high mobility in the field, DPKO, with legislative bodies and OHRM, designed its human resources strategy with the objective of developing such a cadre in a variety of occupational fields. The elements of that strategy included the establishment of mission templates to ensure consistent and rational organizational structures within which jobs would be defined and linked to generic job profiles; introduction of the performance appraisal system in peacekeeping missions; development of a strategic framework for training; appropriate contractual arrangements to retain staff in whom significant investment had been made; and fair and equitable conditions of service.

Various contractual mechanisms were needed to facilitate the employment of staff on short-, medium- and long-term bases. For the past 10 years, the practice had been to recruit all staff for special missions on appointments of limited duration under the 300 series of the staff rules (with fewer benefits), initially for six months with six-month extensions, subject to the mission's mandate. The 300 series of the staff rules were intended to meet the special needs of short-term appointments, especially in field operations, and were to be applied to assignments not expected to exceed three years, with a possibility of extension for a fourth and final year. Over time, the appointment was used for the initial recruitment of all staff for service in a special mission, becoming, in essence, a probationary trial period, after which it was the normal practice to consider staff for reappointment under a 100 series fixed-term appointment limited to service with a specific mission.

As at 30 June 2004, DPKO employed 3,921 international staff from 157 countries in peacekeeping operations, of whom 1,535 were engaged under appointments of limited duration, 1,500 were on 100 series fixed-term appointments limited to service with a specific mission, 336 were Field Service Officers, and the remaining 550 on assignment from Headquarters and other offices. In accordance with **resolution 58/296** (see p. 94), by which the Assembly suspended the application of the four-year maximum limit for appointments of limited duration under the 300 series in peacekeeping operations until 31 December 2004, the Secretariat ceased the practice of reviewing 300 series staff for reappointment under the 100 series fixed-term appointments after reaching their fourth year under an appointment of limited duration.

Peremptorily separating staff on appointments of limited duration after reaching their maximum of four years without due consideration for the needs of the Organization for skilled, experienced field staff did not, in DPKO's view, represent sound managerial practice. The practice would only add to the high vacancy rate and the pressures placed on the Organization to deliver high-quality mission operations in the field, and would have serious consequences for the operation of missions. In 2003, 417 staff members reached their fourth year on appointments of limited duration. If the Department were obliged to separate them, much institutional knowledge, talent and skill would be lost, and another 417 vacancies would be added to the already high number due to the current surge in new and expanding missions.

The Secretary-General concluded that, to respond effectively to the growing and changing demands for more complex peacekeeping activities, the Secretariat had to ensure that it had the resources and capacity to rapidly deploy the required experienced and multi-skilled civilian staff to field missions. The development of such staff involved investing in people and often retaining their services for more than four years. Appropriate contractual arrangements were crit-

ical for enabling the Secretariat to attract, recruit and retain staff in field operations. He was therefore seeking the Assembly's endorsement to use the 100 series of the staff rules for the appointment of staff in field missions for periods of six months or longer, for functions for which there was a continuing requirement. Appointments of limited duration would be used only for time-limited activities such as technical assessments, short-term assistance or special projects.

ACABQ response. ACABQ, in its October report on human resources management [A/59/446], said that the solution proposed by the Secretary-General raised a number of questions. To provide assistance for an informed discussion, it submitted two options. In the first, the Assembly could endorse the Secretary-General's proposal for using the 100 series of the staff rules, but adjustments and refinements would have to be made during its implementation since the wholesale incorporation into the 100 series would lead to complications, such as the lack of transparency, the disparities in conditions of service between UN field staff and those of funds and programmes, the career aspirations of national staff and problems that might arise when some 100 series staff were required to reapply at the end of each mission, while others, outposted from Headquarters, were guaranteed reabsorption upon completion of their field assignment.

In the second option, the Assembly would recognize that a piecemeal, ad hoc approach was not appropriate in dealing with such a significant number of staff performing a major activity (a total of 6,082 were currently holding appointments of limited duration), and that a "one size fits all" approach was not transparent and might only lead to difficulties in implementation. It would call for an innovative and comprehensive system incorporating features of both the 100 and 300 series, as well as the work to be done by the Secretariat on improving equity in the conditions of service among field staff and what might emerge from the involvement of the International Civil Service Commission (ICSC). The financial implications should also be clearly spelled out. That system would thus be uniquely suited to the needs of the field staff supporting peacekeeping operations and the current and long-term requirements of the Organization. As an interim measure, the arrangements contemplated by the Secretary-General could be applied.

Conduct and discipline

The Special Committee on Peacekeeping Operations, in its April report [A/58/19], noted that the meeting it had requested the Secretariat to convene in 2003 with Member States to discuss ways of meeting the challenges of developing standard procedures for dealing with alleged violations of the code of conduct for peacekeepers and for minimizing misconduct [YUN 2003, p. 99] had not been held and requested that it be convened before its 2005 session. It emphasized that cases of alleged misconduct should be handled through cooperation between the troop-contributing countries concerned and the mission leadership. The Committee, while urging the Secretariat to involve the contributing country concerned from the outset in an investigation into any case of alleged misconduct, regretted that the Secretariat withheld, at its own discretion, certain elements of the investigation outcome of cases of misconduct from the troop- or police-contributing country whose national was the subject of investigation. The Committee stressed that the investigation outcome, including all related evidence, should be made available to that country to enable its national authorities to take legal steps.

To help improve discipline, the Special Committee encouraged Member States contributing formed units to UN peacekeeping missions to deploy trained counsellors with those units. It recognized the need to strengthen DPKO systems for monitoring and reporting all cases of misconduct in peacekeeping operations and for greater accountability and transparency in dealing with such cases. In that regard, it welcomed the Secretary-General's bulletin [ST/SGB/2003/13] on special measures for protection from sexual exploitation and sexual abuse, and steps taken by the Department to ensure that each mission had an active strategy to prevent and respond to the problems of sexual exploitation and abuse as they related to peacekeeping operations. The Committee noted the development of DPKO's web-based training module on the ICSC standards of conduct and the prevention of sexual exploitation, abuse and harassment. It requested that Member States be briefed on the progress of the DPKO review on how to improve notification and monitoring of conduct in field missions.

UN Volunteers

The General Assembly, by **decision 58/567** of 8 April, deferred consideration of the Secretary-General's report on the participation of United Nations Volunteers in peacekeeping operations [YUN 2001, p. 814] and the related ACABQ report [ibid., p. 94] until its fifty-ninth (2004) session.

Chapter II

Africa

In 2004, Africa remained a priority concern for the United Nations, whose efforts to restore the conflict zones, especially the Great Lakes region and West Africa, to peace and stability were marked by progress and setbacks. While countries such as Sierra Leone and Liberia, with UN encouragement and assistance, were well on their way to overcoming obstacles that had blocked progress in the search for peace, others, including Côte d'Ivoire, Ethiopia and Eritrea, and Western Sahara, remained mired in conflict with little immediate prospects of finding mutually agreed solutions. The region suffered a further setback with the rapid escalation of the conflict situation in the Darfur region of western Sudan, which risked further destabilizing the continent. Concerned about Africa's future stability, the Security Council sent missions to both the Great Lakes region and West Africa during the year to urge leaders and parties to the conflicts to make decisions that would lead to negotiated settlements. The Council held one of its sessions in Nairobi, Kenya, to demonstrate its deep concern for the problems facing the continent. Many of those problems were addressed by the Council, including the causes of conflict and the promotion of durable peace and sustainable development in Africa, and enhancing Africa's peacekeeping capacity.

As the countries of the Great Lakes region continued to experience conflict, especially the Democratic Republic of the Congo (DRC) and Burundi, the First International Conference on the Great Lakes Region was held in November under the auspices of the United Nations and the African Union (AU). The Conference called for measures to address the priority issues of peace and security, governance and democracy, economic development, and social and humanitarian issues. Also in November, the Council sent a mission to the region, which reported that both the DRC and Burundi were at critical turning points in their peace processes as they were faced with implementing the remaining aspects of their agreed transition process, before proceeding with elections that could lead to durable peace and stability.

The military situation in the eastern part of the DRC deteriorated in mid-year, following months of slow progress in advancing the func-

tioning of the Transitional Government established under the terms of a 2002 peace agreement. Subsequently, an integrated army command was instituted by the Transitional Government and the principal political institutions began to function. Despite that progress, the remaining problems, including the slow pace in adopting legislation, the need for State administration throughout the country, further integration of former opposing forces and preparation for elections, appeared intractable. Violence erupted in the east of the country, with charges by the DRC of Rwandan involvement. The United Nations Organization Mission in the DRC (MONUC) worked to halt the fighting and arranged for the disarmament, demobilization and reintegration of armed forces. In October, the Council increased the Mission's size and expanded its mandate, giving it the authority to use all necessary means to carry out its responsibilities, including the protection of civilians and officials.

In Burundi, the transitional process was well under way, as positive steps were taken to implement the 2000 Arusha Agreement on Peace and Reconciliation, despite the refusal of one main armed movement to join the process. In May, the Council established the United Nations Operation in Burundi (ONUB), which took over from the AU peacekeeping mission. Its main tasks were to monitor ceasefire agreements, promote confidence between the forces, assist in the delivery of humanitarian assistance, contribute to the electoral process and protect civilians.

In the Central African Republic, the United Nations Peace-building Support Office in the Central African Republic (BONUCA) supported the Government's efforts to achieve reconciliation and reconstruction, following years of unrest. The Government made progress in preparing for elections, scheduled for 2005, by adopting an electoral schedule and drafting a constitution and electoral laws. The constitution was adopted by the people in a December referendum.

The region of West Africa was marked by mixed progress in addressing conflicts. The Secretary-General, through the United Nations Office for West Africa (UNOWA), sought solutions to combat the regional cross-border problems. In that regard, he requested his Special Representative for West Africa to coordinate activities with the UN missions in the region and regional organizations, in particular the Economic Community of West African States (ECOWAS) and the Mano River Union (MRU). The Council called for a comprehensive and composite approach for solutions to the conflicts in West Africa and made recommendations to address the root causes of conflict and promote sustainable peace, security and good governance.

In Côte d'Ivoire, disagreements between political parties over the delegation of powers in the Government of National Reconciliation and the refusal of armed factions to lay down arms blocked further implementation of the 2003 Linas-Marcoussis Agreement. Three main rebel groups continued to hold the northern half of the country. In February, the Council established the United Nations Operation in Côte d'Ivoire (UNOCI), which created a zone of confidence between the south and the rebel-controlled north. After months of political stalemate and violent clashes between security forces and demonstrators, the parties signed the Accra III Agreement on reactivating the peace process. Little progress followed, however, and further hostilities erupted in November when Government forces attacked rebels' positions in the north. Mediation efforts, led by President Thabo Mbeki of South Africa, were undertaken to assist the parties to reach an agreement.

In Liberia, the National Transitional Government succeeded in restoring State authority over the entire country, with the assistance of the United Nations Mission in Liberia (UNMIL). The disarmament process was completed in October and armed groups were disbanded. However, the peace process remained fragile, as demonstrated by the outbreak of violence in late October.

Sierra Leone also made strides in consolidating stability, having fulfilled nearly all provisions of the 2000 Agreement on the Ceasefire and Cessation of Hostilities. That progress led to the drawdown of the United Nations Mission in Sierra Leone (UNAMSIL) from 11,500 troops to 5,000 by the end of the year. The disarmament, demobilization and reintegration programme for ex-combatants was closed on 31 March after four years. The Truth and Reconciliation Commission completed its trials of those accused of serious human rights abuses and crimes against humanity during the 10 years of civil war, and released its final report to the public.

Progress was also recorded in the Guinea-Bissau situation, as it complied with the terms of the 2003 Political Transitional Charter by holding legislative elections leading to the formation of a new Government in May. Preparations were under way for holding presidential elections. That progress was temporarily halted in October by a military mutiny, but calm was restored when the Government paid salary arrears of the armed forces and civil services. The United Nations Peace-building Support Office in Guinea-Bissau (UNOGBIS) continued to support the peace process.

Cameroon and Nigeria, acting through the Cameroon-Nigeria Mixed Commission, took steps to resolve their border issues, following the 2002 ruling of the International Court of Justice on the land and maritime boundary. Work began on the delimitation of the border.

The situation in the Sudan drew international attention when what appeared to be ethnic-based violence erupted in the Darfur region of western Sudan, complicating an already protracted civil war and creating a serious humanitarian situation. A peace process led by the Intergovernmental Authority on Development (IGAD) and assisted by the AU was directed at helping the parties implement the 2002 Machakos Protocol dealing with the issues of the right to self-determination for the people of southern Sudan, and the status of State and religion, and the 2003 Framework Agreement on Security Arrangements signed by the Government, the main rebel group, and the Sudan People's Liberation Movement/Army (SPLM/A). On 26 May 2004, the parties agreed on a power-sharing mechanism under a Government of National Unity and on the administration of certain conflict areas. Meanwhile in the south, rebel militias, known as the Janjaweed, carried out attacks on civilians in villages and settlements in the Darfur region. By mid-2004, over a million people were in need of urgent humanitarian assistance and about 200,000 refugees had fled to Chad. The UN Secretary-General responded to the situation by proposing that an advance team be sent there to prepare for international monitoring of the 2003 security agreement. The United Nations and the Sudan signed on 5 August a Plan of Action on Darfur, by which the Sudan pledged to restore security to Darfur, enable delivery of aid and assist in the voluntary return of displaced persons. However, on 18 September, the Security Council said that the Government had not met its commitments to improve the security of the civilian population of Darfur. The Council supported the AU plans to augment its monitoring mission in Darfur, and urged the Government and the rebel groups to reach a political solution. Towards the end of the year, the parties completed the process for the full implementation of the peace framework, with the Government and SPLM/A agreeing on a series of documents to be incorporated into a comprehensive peace agreement and signed in 2005. However, the situation in Darfur remained a matter of concern. The Secretary-General, as requested by the Council, established the International Commission of Inquiry for Darfur to investigate reports of serious violations of international humanitarian law and human rights law.

Slow but steady progress was made in the national reconciliation process in Somalia, which began in 2002 at the Eldoret (Kenya) Conference under the auspices of IGAD. In January 2004, Somali leaders signed a declaration on agreement of issues related to a transitional federal government. At the Somali National Reconciliation Conference, held in Kenya intermittently over a period of two years and attended by numerous representatives of Somali factions and clans, with the notable exception of Somaliland, the participants agreed to form the Transitional Federal Parliament. In late 2004, that body elected its Speaker and the Transitional President, thereby establishing the first national governmental institutions since the country's central Government disintegrated under the pressures of civil war 14 years earlier. IGAD, as organizer of the Conference, convened ministerial committee meetings which reached agreement on various aspects of the planned transitional federal Government, and the AU dispatched a reconnaissance mission to prepare for deploying military monitors to Somalia. The United Nations Political Office for Somalia (UNPOS) remained involved in the peace process and humanitarian efforts and continued to operate from Nairobi. The monitoring group established by the Secretary-General to investigate violations of the arms embargo against Somalia reported in August that weapons continued to flow into, through and out of Somalia, in contravention of the embargo.

Little headway was made in the border dispute between Eritrea and Ethiopia. The United Nations Mission in Ethiopia and Eritrea (UNMEE), which maintained its presence along the border zone, continued to monitor the implementation of the 2000 Algiers Peace Agreements between the two countries. Although a decision on delimitation of the border had been made in 2002 by the Boundary Commission and the Secretary-General's Special Envoy continued to negotiate with both sides, the physical demarcation process remained stalled throughout 2004. In November, Ethiopia proposed a plan for resolving the dispute through peaceful means, including the suggestion that both sides implement the Boundary Commission's decision. Eritrea was dismissive of the plan.

The question of the future of Western Sahara also remained unresolved due to a lack of compromise by the two parties to the dispute, Morocco and the Frente Popular para la Liberación de Saguía el-Hamra y de Río de Oro (POLISARIO), despite their 1990 agreement to hold a referendum for the people to decide between independence or integration of the Territory with Morocco. The latest peace plan, drawn up in 2003 by the Secretary-General's Personal Envoy, would divide governmental and administrative responsibilities between the parties before the results of the referendum were finalized. POLISARIO eventually accepted that plan, but Morocco continued to reject it. By the end of the year, the Secretary-General said that an agreement appeared more distant than a year earlier, as there was no consensus on how to proceed to overcome the deadlock. The United Nations Mission for the Referendum in Western Sahara (MINURSO) continued to monitor the ceasefire.

In December 2003, the Libyan Arab Jamahiriya announced its decision to abandon programmes for developing weapons of mass destruction and their means of delivery. The International Atomic Energy Agency (IAEA), on 10 March, welcomed the voluntary decision and Libya's request that IAEA ensure verification that all its nuclear activities would be under safeguards and exclusively for peaceful purposes. In April, the Security Council also welcomed the decision and encouraged Libya to ensure the verified elimination of all of its weapons of mass destruction programmes.

Promotion of peace in Africa

The United Nations remained engaged in 2004 in the search to resolve the root causes of conflict and to encourage peace and sustainable development in Africa.

In August, the Secretary-General reported on implementation of his 1998 recommendations on overcoming the root causes of conflict and promoting durable peace, focusing on progress and hindrances encountered over the previous two years. He found that, while progress had been made in tackling conflict situations, some worrisome trends had emerged. The General Assembly welcomed the progress as reported by the Secretary-General and his recommendation that Member States strengthen cooperation between the UN system and the AU and other African organizations in the maintenance of peace and security. The Secretary-General was requested to explore suitable arrangements through which Member States could support Africa's efforts to address the multiple causes of conflict.

The Secretary-General, reporting in November on the peacekeeping capacity in Africa, discussed the efforts of the AU and other African regional and subregional organizations in strengthening their continental security architecture, including the establishment of an African Standby Force, and proposed measures the United Nations could adopt in support of that initiative.

Working Group. In an 8 January note [S/2004/5], the Security Council President said that, after consultations among the members, it had been agreed that Ismael Abraão Gaspar Martins (Angola) would serve as Chairman of the Ad Hoc Working Group on Conflict Prevention and Resolution in Africa until the end of 2004. In a 30 December note [S/2004/1031], the President stated that the Council members had agreed that the Ad Hoc Working Group would continue its work until 31 December 2005.

That Working Group, established in 2002 [YUN 2002, p. 93], reported in December 2004 [S/2004/989] on its 2003-2004 activities. It provided assistance to a number of meetings and panels related to conflict prevention and resolution, contributed to Council missions to Africa, and enhanced its working relationship with Economic and Social Council advisory groups dealing with African countries emerging from conflict. It also examined regional and cross-conflict issues that affected the Security Council's work, and developed partnerships with other institutions, such as the International Peace Academy.

Security Council consideration. The Security Council, on 22 December [meeting 5106], heard a statement by the Chairman of the Ad Hoc Working Group on the Group's 2003 report [YUN 2003, p. 105]. He recalled the Group's round-table discussion with the International Peace Academy, which included the Secretary-General's suggestion to consider how to deal with Governments that had been democratically elected but defied constitutional order and flouted basic governance. Referring to the Council's invitation, in presidential statement S/PRST/2004/44 (see p. 282), to the Secretary-General to explore new means of cooperation between the United Nations and the AU, he said that the Working Group could play a pivotal role in enhancing cooperation between the Council and the AU's newly established Peace and Security Council. He suggested that the Working Group reflect on how it could better implement its mandate, including through the continued development of partnerships with other institutions, and on its

future status within the Council in order to respond to new trends in the search for solutions to African conflicts.

Economic and Social Council action. The Economic and Social Council considered the work of its ad hoc advisory groups on African countries emerging from conflict and, in July, it adopted **resolution 2004/59** on its assessment of those advisory groups (see pp. 156 and 932).

Implementation of Secretary-General's 1998 recommendations on promotion of peace

Report of Secretary-General (August). The Secretary-General, in response to General Assembly resolution 58/235 [YUN 2003, p. 106], submitted on 20 August [A/59/285] a report on implementation of the recommendations contained in his 1998 report on the causes of conflict and promotion of durable peace and sustainable development in Africa [YUN 1998, p. 66]. The report, which updated information since his 2003 review [YUN 2003, p. 106], highlighted progress in the implementation of those recommendations, identified challenges and constraints and made specific proposals on measures to accelerate the implementation of those recommendations. He reported that, while steady progress was made in peacemaking and peacekeeping, progress was slow in other areas, such as the strengthening of democratic governance, enhancing administrative capacity, ensuring the independence of the judiciary and promoting transparency and accountability.

The number of countries in the region experiencing armed conflict had dropped from 14 in 1998, to six in 2004 and very few others were facing deep political crises. Most African countries were relatively stable politically and were governed by democratically elected regimes. Their efforts were directed at economic reconstruction and at combating poverty and underdevelopment. Peace agreements were negotiated in Burundi, Côte d'Ivoire, the Democratic Republic of the Congo (DRC), Eritrea, Ethiopia, Liberia and the Sudan. Under the auspices of the AU, African countries had established a legal framework and structures to deal with conflicts, such as the Peace and Security Council and the protocol relating to its establishment, and the Committee of the Wise which supported the Council. They also deployed peacekeeping forces and military observers in a number of African countries and were establishing an African standby force to enable them to participate more effectively in peace operations. The number of military coups had diminished and those countries that had experienced attempted or successful coups (Central African Republic, Comoros, Guinea-Bissau, Sao

Tome and Principe and Sierra Leone) had restored or were attempting to return to law and order. Efforts were also under way in the areas of governance and human rights. Some 23 countries had acceded to the African Peer Review Mechanism of the New Partnership for Africa's Development (NEPAD) [YUN 2001, p. 899], set up by the AU to promote political, economic and corporate governance and human rights observance. The long-standing issue of Angola had been resolved, and the Security Council had approved new peacekeeping missions in Burundi, Côte d'Ivoire, the DRC and Liberia, and an advance team for the Sudan. In general, there were increased prospects for peace restoration in all countries experiencing armed conflict, although instability continued in the Great Lakes region, the member countries of the Mano River Union and in parts of Central Africa.

The report provided details of action taken to implement the recommendations as well as constraints in the following areas of peacemaking: the appointment of special mediators and special commissions; mobilizing international support for peace efforts; improving the effectiveness of sanctions; stopping the proliferation of arms; establishing multidisciplinary peacekeeping missions that bridged the gap to integrated reconstruction and development; supporting efforts by African regional organizations in peacekeeping; providing UN and other support for regional and subregional initiatives; protecting civilians in situations of conflict; addressing refugee security issues; coordinating humanitarian assistance; ensuring post-conflict peace-building; financing recovery, especially by the International Monetary Fund and the World Bank; working towards a coordinated international response; securing respect for human rights and the rule of law; promoting transparency and accountability in public administration; managing natural resources; and eliminating discrimination against women.

The Secretary-General noted that slow progress was shown in poverty reduction, despite African countries' efforts to implement NEPAD and create an enabling environment for economic growth and sustainable development. Efforts were under way to reduce trade in small arms and to prevent the harbouring of opponents with military capabilities in neighbouring countries and uncontrolled military groups.

However, certain trends threatened to affect peace in Africa adversely, including the worsening conditions for young people, in particular high unemployment rates, the spread of the HIV/AIDS pandemic, and the illicit exploitation of and trade in natural resources. Demographic pressures and issues of migration were becoming an increasing source of tension in West, Central and East Africa, as a result of high fertility rates and a shortage of arable land. Those pressures threatened to undermine UN and African Governments' efforts in peace-building, the promotion of good governance and democratization. The Secretary-General urged the international community to take steps to reverse those trends, including tightening the rules and controls to regulate the trade in diamonds (see p. 57) and engaging more seriously in the fight against poverty, and to support efforts to strengthen cooperation among the UN system, the AU and other African regional organizations. In that regard, he instructed relevant UN agencies, departments and offices to look into new ways of collaboration.

GENERAL ASSEMBLY ACTION

On 23 December [meeting 76], the General Assembly adopted **resolution 59/255** [draft: A/59/L.50/Rev.1 & Add.1] without vote [agenda item 38 (b)].

Implementation of the recommendations contained in the report of the Secretary-General on the causes of conflict and the promotion of durable peace and sustainable development in Africa

The General Assembly,

Recalling the report of the Open-ended Ad Hoc Working Group on the Causes of Conflict and the Promotion of Durable Peace and Sustainable Development in Africa, and its resolutions 53/92 of 7 December 1998, 54/234 of 22 December 1999, 55/217 of 21 December 2000, 56/37 of 4 December 2001, 57/296 of 20 December 2002, 57/337 of 3 July 2003 and 58/235 of 23 December 2003, as well as resolution 59/213 of 20 December 2004 on cooperation between the United Nations and the African Union,

Recalling also, in this context, Security Council resolutions 1325(2000) of 31 October 2000 on women and peace and security, and 1366(2001) of 30 August 2001 on the role of the Council in the prevention of armed conflicts,

Recalling further the creation by the Economic and Social Council, by its resolution 2002/1 of 15 July 2002, of ad hoc advisory groups on African countries emerging from conflict,

Reaffirming that the implementation of the recommendations contained in the report of the Secretary-General on the causes of conflict and the promotion of durable peace and sustainable development in Africa must remain a priority on the agenda of the United Nations system and for Member States,

Noting with concern the slow progress in the implementation of many of the recommendations contained in the report of the Secretary-General, as well as the emergence of trends that could potentially affect the peace and stability of Africa,

Stressing that the responsibility for peace and security in Africa, including the capacity to address the root causes of conflict and to resolve conflicts in a peaceful manner, lies primarily with African countries, while recognizing the need for support from the international community,

Reaffirming the need to strengthen the synergies between Africa's economic and social development programmes and its peace and security agenda,

1. *Takes note* of the progress report of the Secretary-General on the implementation of the recommendations contained in his report on the causes of conflict and promotion of durable peace and sustainable development in Africa, including an overview of trends and challenges as well as further advances in a wide range of areas made since the last progress report;

2. *Welcomes* the progress that has been made in the prevention and settlement of disputes and the sustained efforts by African regional and subregional initiatives to mediate and resolve conflicts, and the support given by the international community and the United Nations to those efforts;

3. *Notes with appreciation* the efforts to enhance coordination to ensure that African regional and subregional initiatives continue to be taken in close consultation and coordination with the United Nations in order to ensure that the United Nations can play a clear role, as appropriate, in the subsequent implementation of mediated settlements;

4. *Welcomes* the successful establishment of the Peace and Security Council of the African Union, and looks forward to the establishment of other supporting elements such as a Panel of the Wise, a continental early warning system, an African standby force and a special fund;

5. *Encourages*, in this context, the international community to continue to support the ongoing efforts of African countries to develop their capacity to undertake peace support operations at regional and subregional levels, including their effort to establish a continental early warning system;

6. *Welcomes* the establishment and coming into force of the African Peace Facility of the European Union to support the implementation of peace initiatives undertaken by the African Union and African subregional organizations;

7. *Also welcomes* the recommendation of the Secretary-General to Member States to strengthen cooperation between the United Nations system, the African Union and other African organizations in the maintenance of international peace and security;

8. *Further welcomes* the decision of the Secretary-General to instruct relevant agencies, departments and offices of the United Nations to look into new ways of collaborating with the African Union in order to boost its efforts in undertaking peace operations;

9. *Recognizes* the contribution made by the ad hoc advisory groups on African countries emerging from conflict of the Economic and Social Council, as well as by the Ad Hoc Working Group on Conflict Prevention and Resolution in Africa of the Security Council, in promoting peace and sustainable development, and emphasizes the need for continued collaboration between the Economic and Social Council and the Security Council in generating a coherent approach to the challenges of conflict prevention, conflict resolution and post-conflict reconstruction in Africa;

10. *Notes* the support offered by the United Nations system in the context of conflict prevention and peace consolidation, and in this regard calls upon Member States, in particular donor countries, as well as other development partners and relevant regional and subregional organizations as appropriate, to continue to provide financial and technical assistance, in a coordinated and sustained manner, to support activities in Africa, inter alia, to eradicate poverty, promote respect for human rights and strengthen the rule of law and transparent and accountable public administration;

11. *Requests* the Secretary-General to explore and recommend suitable arrangements and mechanisms through which Member States could more effectively support Africa's efforts to address the multiple causes of conflict in Africa, including their regional dimensions, and to strengthen, in a coordinated and sustained manner, preventive action as well as post-conflict peacebuilding;

12. *Decides* to continue to monitor the implementation of the recommendations contained in the report of the Secretary-General on the causes of conflict and the promotion of durable peace and sustainable development in Africa;

13. *Requests* the Secretary-General to submit to the General Assembly at its sixtieth session a progress report on the implementation of the present resolution.

African peacekeeping capacity

Consideration by Special Committee on Peacekeeping Operations. The Special Committee on Peacekeeping Operations, at its 2004 session (New York, 29 March–16 April), discussed enhancing African peacekeeping. It recognized the effort to establish the African Standby Force (see below) through regional partnership arrangements and the need to further expand the pool of African military, civilian police and civilian specialists available for peacekeeping operations. It requested that efforts to train African peacekeeping military personnel be enhanced and conducted according to UN standards and that regional and subregional organizations and Member States expand training for civilian police and specialists. The Special Committee welcomed the new partnerships for building Africa's capacity for conflict prevention, peacekeeping and peace-building between the United Nations, the AU and other regional organizations and bodies, and individual Member States, and looked forward to the Secretary-General's comprehensive report on the enhancement of Africa's peacekeeping capacity.

Report of Secretary-General. In accordance with General Assembly resolution 57/48 [YUN 2002, p. 235], the Secretary-General reported on 30 November [A/59/591] on the enhancement of African peacekeeping capacity. The report examined the role of African regional and subregional organizations in peacekeeping and that of the African Standby Force in a response system, and the way forward. The report noted that, since 1999, the United Nations had faced a surge in demand for peacekeeping and, of the more than 53,000 troops, military observers and civilian police currently serving in 17 UN missions, more than half of them were in Africa. In the previous year, the Security Council had authorized new missions in Burundi and Liberia, expanded those in Côte d'Ivoire and the DRC, and was planning another for the Sudan (see p. 247).

In the past five years, the AU and subregional organizations, such as the Economic Community of West African States (ECOWAS), had played an increasingly prominent role in the maintenance of peace and security in African regions. Cooperation with ECOWAS included support to its missions in Côte d'Ivoire, Liberia and Sierra Leone in the form of the provision of logistical and financial advice, planning and deployment and sustainment. The Secretary-General's Special Representative for West Africa worked with States and organizations on issues of cross-border security problems, such as illicit trafficking of weapons and combatants, and conflict prevention in the Mano River region. In East Africa, the United Nations supported the Intergovernmental Authority on Development (IGAD).

A new AU security structure was expected to have profound implications for peacekeeping on the continent, particularly the Policy Framework Document approved by the AU Summit (Addis Ababa, Ethiopia, 6-8 July), establishing the Standby Force and the Military Staff Committee. A standby brigade from each of the five subregions, established by 2010, would be composed of nationally based units available for rapid deployment under the auspices of such organizations as the AU, ECOWAS or the Southern African Development Community (SADC) or a coalition of the willing. The Standby Force, which would participate in various peacekeeping scenarios, from ceasefire monitoring to multidimensional peacekeeping and peace enforcement, would allow African Member States to contribute more effectively to both African and UN-led peacekeeping operation in Africa and elsewhere and would be a welcome addition to tools available to the international community for managing crises in Africa and other parts of the world.

In addressing the way forward, the Secretary-General welcomed the commitment made by the Group of 8 at their annual summit (Sea Islands, United States, June), in response to the AU's appeal for assistance in setting up the Standby Force, to train and help equip 75,000 peacekeepers by 2010 as part of a plan to expand global capability for peace support operations. He also welcomed the commitment of the European Union (EU) to strengthening the AU's ability to conduct peace support operations, including

through the establishment of the African Peace Facility [S/2004/444] at a cost of 250 million euros, which became operational on 25 May. It also provided funds for the AU to expand its peace and security staff capacity; in a 6 July declaration, it reiterated its intention to support the strengthening of peace and security mechanisms in Africa.

For its part, the United Nations focused on building the capacity of individual African troop contributors to participate in UN peacekeeping operations. It could do more to assist the AU, but it had to have a clear mandate and the required resources. The Organization, with its partners, also needed to coordinate efforts within the framework of a joint action plan that reflected comparative advantage in delivering peace and security and the needs and wishes of the providers and beneficiaries of peacekeeping operations. Such a plan should address issues such as a common doctrine and training standards; equipment and adequate logistical support, including sea and airlift capabilities; funding; and planning and management capacity for peacekeeping operations. The Secretary-General suggested concrete initiatives the United Nations could undertake in collaboration with key African partners in those areas, including: the establishment of a revolving fund to allow African Member States to obtain equipment from liquidating peacekeeping missions in Africa or to purchase from the United Nations strategic deployment stocks; promoting the use of a common set of equipment; making available to the AU, to strengthen its strategic headquarters capacity, the significant UN capacity to plan, launch, manage and conduct peacekeeping operations; and promoting longer-term programmes for the exchange of staff.

Those measures should be seen as part of an "open door" policy to give African regional and subregional organizations full access to updated information on conflicts and potential conflicts, best practices and lessons learned, mission planning templates and other relevant documents.

Central Africa and Great Lakes region

The volatile situation in Central Africa and the Great Lakes region remained a major concern to the international community in 2004, in particular the conflicts in the Democratic Republic of the Congo (DRC), Burundi and Rwanda. During the year, the United Nations continued its search for political solutions to the widespread unrest in the Great Lakes region. In support of that effort, it organized in November, in collaboration with the AU, the First International Conference on the Great Lakes Region, which outlined a number of measures to address the priority issues of peace and security, governance and democracy, economic development, and social and humanitarian issues. In addition, the United Nations Standing Advisory Committee on Security Questions in Central Africa met at the ministerial level in June to discuss the geopolitical and security situation in the region.

Meanwhile, the Security Council, as it had done in the previous four years, sent a mission to the region in late November to assess the situation. The mission reported that both the DRC and Burundi were at a crucial turning point in their peace processes and faced the similar challenge of implementing the outstanding aspects of their respective transition process, such as conducting credible elections that would lead to durable peace and stability. Both also had transitional Governments in place and, with assistance from UN peacekeeping forces, were attempting to solve the issue of armed groups by bringing them into the peace process and arranging disarmament and reintegration programmes.

In the DRC, following months of slow progress to advance the establishment and functioning of the transitional Government, as outlined in the 2002 Global and All-Inclusive Agreement [YUN 2002, p. 125] signed by a number of armed factions, the transitional Government in Kisangani took steps to establish an integrated army command and to operationalize the principal political institutions. However, a number of challenges remained, including the slow pace in adopting needed legislation, the extension of State administration throughout the country, military integration and reintegration of former forces, and preparation for elections. The situation was further complicated by the outbreak of violence in eastern DRC, causing the military and security situation to deteriorate. The Governments of the DRC and Rwanda accused each other of involvement in the violence by supporting antigovernment armed groups. The United Nations Mission in the Democratic Republic of the Congo (MONUC) took action to halt the fighting and coordinated with the Government and opposing parties to arrange the disarmament, demobilization, resettlement and reintegration of armed forces. The Security Council expressed concern about the continuation of hostilities in eastern DRC and warned neighbouring States of the consequences of supporting armed rebel groups.

Acting on the recommendation of the Secretary-General, the Security Council, in October, authorized the increase of MONUC military personnel to 16,700 and expanded its mandate, giving it the authority to use all necessary means to carry out its tasks. Those tasks included deployment to volatile areas, ensuring the protection of civilians, seizing illegal arms, protection of officials and contributing to the electoral process.

Relations with Rwanda remained tense as the two countries continued to make charges and counter-charges of invasion and threats of invasion and of assisting opposing armed factions. Nevertheless, the two countries were among the regional States which signed the Tripartite Agreement and the Dar es Salaam Declaration on Peace, Security, Democracy and Development in the Great Lakes Region. They also established the Joint Verification Mission to monitor the border between their countries.

As requested by the Council, the Secretary-General established a Group of Experts to report on the flows of arms in the region. The Group found that Rwanda supported dissident military leaders in eastern DRC and violated the arms embargo. In July, the Council extended the arms embargo for another year, until 31 July 2005, and requested the Secretary-General to re-establish the Group of Experts.

The transitional process in Burundi also made some progress towards implementation of the peace agreement between rebel forces. The 2000 Arusha Agreement on Peace and Reconciliation [YUN 2000, p. 146] provided for political reform during a three-year transition period. By 2004, only one main armed movement had not joined the political process and hostilities continued throughout the year in one area of Burundi where that group continued to operate. In May, the Security Council established the United Nations Operation in Burundi with a maximum force of 5,650 military personnel to monitor ceasefire agreements, promote confidence between Burundi forces, monitor the illegal flow of arms and the quartering of Burundi armed forces, assist in providing safe conditions for delivery of humanitarian assistance, contribute to the electoral process and protect civilians. The UN mission took over from the African Mission in Burundi set up by the AU in 2003, and it incorporated the existing United Nations Office in Burundi.

In August, some 150 refugees from the DRC were massacred in Gatumba, Burundi, in what appeared to be an ethnically motivated crime. Investigations were unable to determine who had organized and carried it out. In December, the Security Council called on the DRC and Rwanda to cooperate with Burundi in the investigation of the massacre, and it requested the UN missions in those countries to assist the investigation and strengthen the security of vulnerable populations. The Council stated its intention to consider measures against those who threatened the national reconciliation process in Burundi.

Towards the end of the year, progress was made, especially with regard to the peaceful extension of the Burundi transitional Government for at least six months after its original deadline of 31 October 2004, the establishment of an electoral calendar, and the adoption of a post-transition constitution to be put to a popular referendum. Legislation remained to be adopted on electoral procedure and reform of the armed forces and police.

The Central African Republic was also run by a transitional Government in 2004, following a coup d'état in March 2003. In similar steps as in other regional countries, the Government, which included all political factions, made progress towards elections, scheduled for 2005, having adopted an electoral schedule and having drafted a constitution, electoral code and laws on political parties. The constitution was approved by the people of the Central African Republic in a December referendum. The United Nations Peace-building Support Office in the Central African Republic remained in the country to support the Government's efforts to achieve reconciliation and reconstruction following years of unrest and continued serious crime. The crises of the region and, in particular, the burgeoning problems in the Sudanese region of Darfur, were also areas of concern for the Central African Republic.

The year 2004 marked the tenth anniversary of the 1994 genocide in Rwanda, for which the General Assembly held a solemn commemoration.

On 11 November [S/2004/904], the Secretary-General stated that the mandate of his Special Representative for the Great Lakes Region would expire on 31 December. In view of the first and second conferences on the Great Lakes, he affirmed his intention to extend the mandate until 31 December 2005. The Council took note of the intention on 16 November [S/2004/905].

International Conference on Great Lakes

The First International Conference on Peace, Security, Democracy and Development in the Great Lakes Region was held on 19 and 20 November in Dar es Salaam, United Republic of Tanzania. Organized under the auspices of the United Nations and the AU, the summit meeting was preceded by the Pre-Summit Meeting of the Ministers for Foreign Affairs (Dar es Salaam, 16-17 November), the First Great Lakes Regional Women's Meeting (Kigali, Rwanda, 7-9 October) and the Meeting of Regional Non-Governmental

Organizations from the Great Lakes Region (Arusha, United Republic of Tanzania, 20-24 September). The Conference concluded with the adoption and signing of the Dar es Salaam Declaration on Peace, Security, Democracy and Development in the Great Lakes Region by the heads of State and Government of Angola, Burundi, the Central African Republic, the Congo, the DRC, Kenya, Rwanda, the Sudan, Uganda, the United Republic of Tanzania and Zambia.

The Declaration, which provided a vision and follow-up mechanism, addressed the four themes of the Conference: peace and security, democracy and governance, economic development and regional integration, and humanitarian and social issues. The leaders expressed their commitment to: support the national peace processes in the region and refrain from negatively impacting them; establish a regional security framework for the prevention, management and settlement of conflicts; strengthen cooperation in defence and security; ensure security at borders; prevent assistance to armed groups; support national disarmament and demobilization programmes; fight trans-border crime and terrorism; protect vulnerable groups; promote democracy and good governance; promote multiculturalism, tolerance and human rights; cooperate in enhancing economic growth through economic integration; establish or strengthen regional legal, administrative and institutional frameworks for regional integration; adopt regional policies to promote the private sector; promote cooperation in trade, monetary policies, energy, transport, tourism, culture, environment and information technologies; pursue a collective strategy on enhanced access to international markets; find solutions to the problems of displaced and refugee populations; guarantee the safety of humanitarian personnel; establish an early warning and rapid response mechanism for natural and man-made disasters; prohibit the recruitment of children into armed forces; and promote strategies to curb the spread of endemic diseases such as HIV/AIDS, tuberculosis and malaria.

The participants decided to set up a Regional Inter-Ministerial Committee, assisted by the Regional Preparatory Committee, to prepare draft protocols and programmes of action to be submitted to the second summit which would form the Declaration part of a pact on security, stability and development in the Great Lakes region.

Conference preparations

The Secretary-General, in a 12 March letter to the Security Council [S/2004/528], noted the progress in the preparations for the international conference on the Great Lakes region and stated that, in order to assist in follow-up to the conference's preparatory meetings and in the establishment of the national preparatory committees, the Office of his Special Representative would need nine international civil servants, in addition to its current seven administrators. On 30 June [S/2004/529], the Council President responded that members had requested more detailed information on the need for nine additional staff.

The EU, in a 19 October statement of its Presidency, on the occasion of the meeting of the Preparatory Committee for the International Conference on the Great Lakes Region (Kinshasa, DRC) [S/2004/864], pledged the financial, technical and diplomatic support of the Group of Friends of the Great Lakes Region, of which the EU was a member, to help make the conference a success.

Security Council consideration. On 27 October [meeting 5065], the Security Council was briefed by Ibrahima Fall, the Special Representative of the Secretary-General for the Great Lakes Region, on the status of preparations for the First International Conference to be followed by a second and final summit in 2005. He said that the entire process had given rise to ideas and suggestions for the regional preparatory meetings, on the basis of which the Dar es Salaam declaration would be finalized. The inclusive preparatory meetings allowed for a geographical broadening among countries participating, which increased from seven to eleven, with the addition of Angola, the Central African Republic, the Congo and the Sudan. Four priority areas had been identified for the conference: peace and security; governance and democracy; economic development and regional integration; and social and humanitarian issues.

Members of the Council continued informal consultations on the subject.

Security Council missions to Central Africa

Follow-up to 2003 mission. The Secretary-General, in response to Security Council presidential statement S/PRST/2003/12 [YUN 2003, p. 109], submitted a 20 January progress report [S/2004/52] on advances made in the implementation of the recommendations of the Council's 2003 mission to Central Africa [YUN 2003, p. 109] regarding the situations in the DRC and Burundi (see pp. 120 and 142), and detailed preparations for the convening of an international conference on the Great Lakes region (see p. 116).

The Council, on 17 February [meeting 4911], considered the Secretary-General's progress report. The Assistant Secretary-General for Political Affairs, Tuliameni Kalomoh, told the Council that substantial progress had been made in the peace

processes in both countries since the Council's mission in 2003. However, much remained to be done to consolidate the historic advances and to build sustainable peace in the region. The international community's commitment to continue supporting peace efforts in the subregion was therefore as critical as ever. The mission provided an added impetus, encouraging the parties to fulfil their commitments to the peace process in both Burundi and the DRC.

2004 mission. On 8 November [S/2004/891], the Council President informed the Secretary-General that the Council had decided to send another mission to Central Africa from 20 to 25 November, headed by Jean-Marc de La Sablière (France). The mission would visit Burundi, the DRC, Rwanda and Uganda. In its general mandate, the mission would, among other tasks, stress the need to continue the peace and transitional processes in the DRC and Burundi (see pp. 119 and 152) and to bring them to a successful conclusion in 2005. It would call on Governments of the region to cooperate in areas of security, including joint monitoring of borders and combating the illegal traffic in arms, and economic development. The mandate also addressed the specific situations and actions to be accomplished in each of the countries to be visited.

On 30 November [S/2004/934], the mission reported on its visit, the fifth in as many years. The mission observed that, while the Council had recognized the linkages between the peace processes of the DRC and Burundi, the regional dimension of the conflict had become more prominent over the previous 18 months, as was demonstrated by the massacre on 13 August in a refugee transit centre in Gatumba, Burundi (see p. 150). The resulting refugee flows affected all countries in the subregion. The mission was also concerned by unconfirmed reports of cross-border cooperation between different armed groups. Despite the reinforcement of MONUC and the establishment of ONUB, the task remained vast. With no fewer than 325 identified airstrips, illicit arms continued to flow through the porous borders into the DRC. The mission condemned the prevalence of sexual violence in both the DRC and Burundi, perpetrated by almost all armed groups, including army units of the two countries. However, it was convinced that the provisions of the Dar es Salaam Declaration (see p. 116) provided a solid basis for consolidating peace and promoting cooperation between the countries of the Great Lakes region. The successful conclusion of the First International Conference on the Great Lakes Region gave hope for regional cooperation. Rwanda's threatened preparedness to cross the border to "neutralize" the former Armed

Forces of Rwanda (ex-FAR/Interahamwe) reinforced the need for stronger regional cooperation.

The mission exchanged views with President Museveni of Uganda on the status of the peace processes and on the humanitarian situation in Uganda. In regard to northern Uganda, Mr. Museveni expressed the view that the conflict there would soon cease, given the recent developments in the Sudanese peace process (see p. 236) as a result of the curbing of cross-border operations of the Lord's Resistance Army, whose combatants had become "fugitives".

The mission concluded that, in spite of the remaining challenges, there had been a steady positive trend in the promotion of regional security. Since the adoption of the Principles on Good-Neighbourly Relations and Cooperation between the DRC and its eastern neighbours in September 2003 [YUN 2003, p. 133], much progress had been made, leading up to the adoption of the Dar es Salaam Declaration. The mission recommended that the Council encourage the participants in the International Conference on the Great Lakes Region to focus on the development of priorities and speedy implementation.

Security Council consideration. The Council, on 30 November [meeting 5091], heard a briefing by the head of the mission, Mr. de La Sablière, who said that the mission came back encouraged, even though much remained to be done, by the widely shared determination by Congolese and Burundian officials to move to elections and, by the extent of the progress achieved since the Council's 2003 mission. The international community should exert effective influence in its engagement in the two countries. To that end, better use should be made of the coordination mechanisms in the DRC. It was equally essential that the elections scheduled for 2005 should not be jeopardized by new outbreaks of violence, particularly in the eastern part of the DRC. The regional dimension of certain problems made it clear that the success of the Great Lakes Conference had to be followed up by the swift implementation of the Dar es Salaam Declaration by establishing priorities. Thinking about the post-electoral period should also begin.

Standing Advisory Committee on Security Questions

The United Nations Standing Advisory Committee on Security Questions in Central Africa, at its twenty-first ministerial meeting (Malabo, Equatorial Guinea, 21-25 June) [A/59/154-S/2004/576], discussed the geopolitical and security situation in Burundi, the Central African Republic, Chad, the DRC, Equatorial Guinea, and Sao Tome and Principe; cooperation between the United Nations and the Economic Community of Central African States (ECCAS); and the Committee's future.

Concerning Burundi, the Committee welcomed the 2003 signing of the Global Ceasefire Agreement [YUN 2003, p. 152] but remained concerned about the lack of resources for initiating the disarmament, demobilization and reintegration (DDR) process. It recommended the establishment of an electoral and political system which encouraged compromise, the search for consensus to facilitate national reconciliation, and the observance of the electoral timetable stipulated in the 2000 Arusha Agreement [YUN 2000, p. 146]. The Committee called on ECCAS to become more involved in the search for a lasting solution to the crisis in Burundi.

The Committee welcomed the efforts of the transitional Government in the Central African Republic to implement the recommendations of the 2003 national dialogue [YUN 2003, p. 158], including the electoral timetable. It appealed to bilateral and multilateral donors to support the economic and financial needs of the country.

Noting the situation in the DRC, the Committee appealed to all political actors to abide by the provisions of the Global and All-Inclusive Agreement on the Transition of the DRC Government [YUN 2002, p. 125]. The international community was urged to support reconstruction, national reconciliation and election preparations.

The Committee noted with satisfaction the climate in which the legislative and municipal elections had been held in April in Equatorial Guinea (see p. 234) and condemned the attempts to overturn the democratically elected institutions by force. In view of the magnitude of the problems relating to mercenary activities, the Committee decided to include the issue in the agenda of its next meeting. It encouraged Equatorial Guinea and Cameroon to implement the decisions taken in the framework of the ad hoc joint commission on security questions between the two countries, which met in Malabo in June (see p. 234).

The Committee welcomed the efforts of all political actors in Sao Tome and Principe to find a consensus-based solution to the political crisis in the country, and encouraged the Government to continue efforts aimed at restructuring and training the country's security forces. It welcomed the mission sent by ECCAS in March to that country.

Condemning the attempted coup in Chad on 16 May, the Committee expressed concern about the general situation on the border between Chad and the Sudan (see p. 239) and welcomed the mediation efforts led by President Idriss Déby of Chad to find a solution to the problems in the Darfur region.

The Committee called for further cooperation between ECCAS and the United Nations. In regard to its own future, the Committee decided on action for its revitalization and to enhance the effectiveness of its functioning, including the establishment by member States of follow-up and evaluation mechanisms and holding thematic meetings on major issues.

The Committee assisted ECCAS in establishing a mechanism for conflict prevention and management (the Council for Peace and Security in Central Africa (COPAX)), and appealed to the ECCAS secretariat to operationalize COPAX as soon as possible.

Democratic Republic of the Congo

In 2004, the Security Council worked towards building on the recent progress achieved in the peace process in the DRC as a result of the conclusion of the Global and All-Inclusive Agreement signed by the parties to the conflict in late 2002 [YUN 2002, p. 125] and the establishment in 2003 of the Government of National Unity and Transition [YUN 2003, p. 129], which provided for a two-year transitional Government to be followed by national elections. Those efforts were supported by the International Committee in Support of the Transition, comprising the five permanent Security Council members (China, France, Russian Federation, United Kingdom, United States), plus Belgium and Canada, four African countries (Angola, Gabon, South Africa, Zambia), the EU and the AU, which provided advice and guidance for the Congolese transition, and by the United Nations Organization Mission in the Democratic Republic of the Congo (MONUC), headed by William Lacy Swing (United States), the Special Representative of the Secretary-General. MONUC's mission, as set out in Council resolution 1493(2003) [ibid., p. 130], was to, among other things, provide assistance for the reform of the security forces, the re-establishment of a State based on the rule of law and the preparation and holding of elections throughout the country. In October, the Council, in resolution 1565 (2004), extended MONUC's mandate until 31 March 2005 and restructured it to deploy and maintain a presence in the key areas of potential volatility to promote the re-establishment of confidence, discourage violence and allow UN personnel to operate freely, particularly in the eastern part of the country; ensure the protection of civilians, including humanitarian personnel; seize or collect the arms that were in violation of the arms embargo; assist the Congolese authori-

ties in maintaining order; support the disarmament of foreign combatants; and assist in the promotion of human rights. The Council also increased its strength by 5,900 personnel, including up to 341 civilian police.

The Secretary-General, on 18 November [SG/A/896-AFR/1067-BIO/3624], announced the appointment of Ross Mountain (New Zealand) as his Deputy Special Representative for the DRC, and Resident Coordinator and Humanitarian Coordinator for the DRC.

Political and military developments

Formation of national army

The Secretary-General, in his fifteenth report on MONUC [S/2004/251] (see p. 121), reported that initial steps had been taken towards restructuring the national army, to be known as the Forces armées de la République démocratique du Congo (FARDC). A draft law on defence and the armed forces, which was approved by the Council of Ministers in January, was being considered by the National Assembly. The transitional Government issued decrees establishing a Commission de contrôle des effectifs de l'armée, charged with overseeing the identification of elements belonging to hitherto different military organizations, and the État-Major technique d'intégration, which was to plan and undertake the operational aspects of integration. On 12 January, President Kabila swore in one military region commander and two deputies, replacing previous nominees who had not reported for duty. Through Belgian bilateral assistance, senior officers from all armed components participated in a seminar in Kinshasa in January to plan military integration.

The Security Council considered the situation in the DRC on 15 January and welcomed efforts currently under way to set up the first integrated and unified brigade in Kisangani, as a step towards the formation of a Congolese national army. By resolution 1522(2004) (below), it adjusted one of its prior demands so that the integrated brigade could operate in that city.

SECURITY COUNCIL ACTION (January)

On 15 January [meeting 4894], the Security Council unanimously adopted **resolution 1522(2004)**. The draft [S/2004/25] was prepared in consultations among Council members.

The Security Council,

Recalling its resolutions and the statements by its President on the situation concerning the Democratic Republic of the Congo,

Encouraged by the progress achieved in the peace process in the Democratic Republic of the Congo since the conclusion of the Global and All-Inclusive Agreement on the Transition in the Democratic Republic of the Congo, signed at Pretoria on 17 December 2002, and the subsequent establishment of the Government of National Unity and Transition,

Considering that the reform of the security sector, including the disarmament, demobilization and reintegration of former combatants, the effective restructuring and integration of the armed forces of the former Congolese belligerents and the establishment of an integrated national police, are key elements for the success of the transition process in the Democratic Republic of the Congo,

Reaffirming, in this regard, that overall responsibility lies with the Government of National Unity and Transition, welcoming the establishment of an integrated High Command, and calling for effective cooperation at all levels of the Congolese armed forces,

1. *Welcomes* the efforts currently being undertaken to set up the first integrated and unified brigade in Kisangani as a step towards the elaboration and implementation of a comprehensive programme for the formation of a Congolese integrated national army;

2. *Decides* that, since the Government of National Unity and Transition has been established and is in place, its demand for the demilitarization of Kisangani and its surroundings laid down in paragraph 3 of resolution 1304(2000) of 16 June 2000 shall not apply to the restructured and integrated forces of the Democratic Republic of the Congo and to the armed forces included in the comprehensive programme for the formation of an integrated and restructured national army;

3. *Urges* the Government of National Unity and Transition to take the appropriate measures for the restructuring and integration of the armed forces of the Democratic Republic of the Congo in accordance with the Global and All-Inclusive Agreement on the Transition in the Democratic Republic of the Congo, including setting up a Supreme Defence Council and the elaboration of a national plan for disarmament, demobilization and reintegration, as well as the necessary legislative framework;

4. *Calls upon* the international community to provide further assistance for the integration and restructuring of the armed forces of the Democratic Republic of the Congo, in accordance with Security Council resolution 1493(2003) of 28 July 2003;

5. *Decides* to remain actively seized of the matter.

Meeting on security sector reform

On 9 February, the United Nations convened a meeting in New York between the DRC transitional Government and Member States concerned to review the status of security sector reform and to reach an understanding on the key issues to be addressed to meet the timetable for the transition, the Secretary-General reported [S/2004/251]. The meeting agreed that the Government should develop a national security policy, finance the establishment and maintenance of security entities, and ensure that DDR bodies coordinated their work under a common vision and strategy. A number of military reform issues were also agreed upon, including the review and adop-

tion of the law on the general organization of defence and the armed forces; establishment of the conseil supérieur de la défense; adoption and implementation of a coherent military integration plan, complemented by a national DDR programme and production of plans for the deployment of integrated FARDC units. Agreement was also reached on the need to elaborate the future role of the police service by holding a national seminar on police issues, to adopt decrees appointing the national police high command, to establish the protection corps and to designate the command structure of the Integrated Police Unit.

The meeting also agreed to set up an advisory group on security sector reform.

Communication (March). Belgium, on 12 March [S/2004/201], in response to resolution 1522 (2004) (above) and the 9 February meeting on the DRC's security sector reform (above), informed the Council President of its support to the DRC by providing training for an initial integrated brigade in peacekeeping operations. France was also participating in the training programme.

Follow-up to 2003 mission

The Secretary-General, in a 20 January report [S/2004/52], described progress on the implementation of recommendations made by the Security Council's 2003 mission to Central Africa [YUN 2003, p. 127] (see also pp. 117 and 142). In regard to the DRC, those recommendations concerned the installation of the transitional Government and the creation of a unified national army, the situation in Bunia and in North Kivu, the need for regional countries to exert a positive influence on the situation, and efforts to end impunity and establish the rule of law. The Secretary-General updated the Council on action taken in 2003 to implement those recommendations. Regarding the establishment of the transitional institutions, he also reported that, on 7 January 2004, the transitional Parliament met in extraordinary session to tackle the backlog in the examination and adoption of key legislation.

Security Council consideration. On 11 February [S/2004/224], the Council was briefed by the Secretary-General's Special Representative, William Lacy Swing. In a press statement of the same date [SC/8000-AFR/833], the Council President said that Council members were encouraged by the positive developments in the peace and national reconciliation process. They shared the concern of the International Committee in Support of the Transition with regard to the work still to be done leading up to national elections in 2005 and stressed the need for the disarmament, demobilization and reintegration of Congolese combatants to be implemented and for a national coordinator to ensure a unified approach. Council members called on the international community to assist the Government, and took note of the progress made and the actions agreed upon at the 9 February meeting on security sector reform (see p. 120) as a basis for integrating and restructuring the military and police.

On 17 February [meeting 4911], during the Council's consideration of the Secretary-General's 20 January report, the Assistant Secretary-General for Political Affairs, Mr. Kalomoh, said that the transitional Government's comprehensive programme of work, having been approved by the new Parliament, was well under way. Progress was made in normalizing relations between the DRC and its neighbours, but much more could be done in that area. The pace of DDR and resettlement and/or repatriation of Rwandans, Ugandan and Burundian armed elements had accelerated beyond expectations. The International Committee in Support of the Transition had been meeting in Kinshasa on a regular basis, under the chairmanship of the Special Representative, and had been instrumental in resolving several deadlocks between and among the parties.

In Bunia, MONUC had been enforcing a weapons-free policy, and the first phase of the Mission's military expansion outside Bunia was under way.

Political developments and MONUC activities

Report of Secretary-General (March). On 25 March [S/2004/251], the Secretary-General, in response to Security Council resolution 1493(2003) [YUN 2003, p. 130], issued his fifteenth report on MONUC, covering developments since November 2003. He reported that eight months after the establishment of the transitional Government, despite initial progress in national reunification, the peace process was facing daunting challenges. The most crucial issue concerned the ability of the transitional leaders to act as a truly unified government and to overcome the atmosphere of distrust.

During the reporting period, the principal political institutions of the transitional Government continued to function and several steps were taken to implement the Global and All-Inclusive Agreement on the Transition. The ordinary session of Parliament concluded on 3 January, with many items remaining on its agenda. An extraordinary session opened on 7 Janaury to address the legislative backlog, but only the laws establishing the Independent Electoral Commission, the High Media Authority, the Ethics and Anti-corruption Commission and the National Human Rights Observatory, and the law on political parties, had been adopted by the National Assembly. Although initial steps were taken towards restructuring and integrating the national army (see p. 128), lack of equipment and sustainment raised serious concerns regarding its future operational capacity.

Pending the development of a national DDR programme, MONUC was expected to assume functions, such as monitoring of disarmament and demobilization, including the registration and storage of arms; carrying out voluntary disarmament of individuals and small groups outside government centres; providing assistance in the destruction of arms; and monitoring human rights. As numerous Mayi-Mayi had requested to be disarmed and reintegrated into the national army, MONUC would assist the Government in emergency disarmament needs by undertaking voluntary disarmament as a security measure. It was also planning with the United Nations Development Programme (UNDP) ways to better utilize the rapid-response mechanism, a financial and operational tool for responding to contingencies in connection with DDR. Progress in the reform and restructuring of the Congolese national police was stymied by delays in the appointment of a unified police command. Training for the establishment of the Integrated Police Unit, with EU support, was expected to start in mid-June.

Considerable preparatory work was needed for the holding of elections by 30 June 2005, such as adopting laws to establish a viable Independent Electoral Commission, and laws on nationality, decentralization, amnesty and political parties, as well as the drafting of a new constitution that would be submitted to a referendum. Decisions were also needed on voter registration, demarcation of constituencies and the electoral system. The pace of normalization of relations with neighbouring countries slowed down, as the transitional Government had not followed up on the agreed-upon confidence-building measures with its neighbours, such as setting up a joint bilateral commission with Rwanda. Meetings of the joint security commission of the DRC and Uganda were postponed several times.

MONUC continued the eastward deployment of its military contingents. The MONUC brigade in Ituri consolidated its positions in Bunia and deployed to seven locations in the interior of the region. It was scheduled to deploy to two other areas by the end of March. Nevertheless, volatility in Ituri had increased, mainly as a result of restricted operating space for armed groups due to the extension of Ituri brigade operations, slow progress in the integration of the district into national structures, possible involvement of external actors and delays in launching a local disarmament and reintegration initiative. Those factors contributed to shifting alliances among the armed groups in the region, no longer necessarily along ethnic lines. Reflecting a new trend among militia hardliners to target MONUC, attacks on the Mission occurred on 16, 19 and 20 January. A MONUC military observer was killed on 12 February in an ambush of a convoy en route to Bunia. As a result, the Ituri brigade took additional preventive measures through patrols, augmented checkpoint control and cordon and search operations.

During the reporting period, there was limited progress in solidifying the political process in Ituri. On 20 January, the Ituri operational plan, prepared by the Government, UNDP, the United Nations Children's Fund and MONUC, was formally adopted. It was to be implemented pending the adoption of the national DDR programme. However, the Ituri Interim Administration had not extended its reach much beyond Bunia, where armed groups were jockeying for power and remained a source of instability. The Secretary-General's Special Representative urged President Kabila, at a 24 February meeting, to extend State authority to Ituri and proposed measures the transitional Government could take towards that end, including the appointment of a governor for Orientale province and a district commissioner for Ituri.

In late January, MONUC received reports of a massacre in the village of Gobu on Lake Albert. MONUC determined that most of the population had fled as a result of the massacre, which was led by an alliance of a Lendu militia and the branch of the Union des patriotes congolais (UPC) led by Thomas Lubanga (UPC-L).

In Bunia, as part of efforts to end impunity and restore the justice capacity, MONUC and its partners refurbished the Bunia prison, courthouse, police headquarters and accommodations for judges. MONUC trained 81 police officers on urban law enforcement and provided advisers to support local police in investigations, patrol duties and other functions.

In the Kivus, intermittent skirmishes were attributable to the accelerated pace of disarmament, demobilization, repatriation, resettlement or reintegration of Rwandan elements previously incorporated into Mayi-Mayi groups and the repatriation of some prominent Rwandan rebel leaders, which altered the balance of power among various local groups. MONUC reacted quickly to restore security, as well as to assist in DDR activities and humanitarian efforts. It was also developing a strategy for extending State authority to the Kivus, including the implementation of integrated security activities, community relations and economic recovery. It intended to form a 3,500-member brigade for deployment in the Kivus, with headquarters in Bukavu. In February, tensions mounted in Bukavu as a result of deep divisions within the transitional Government (see p. 124).

The pace of repatriation of Rwandan armed groups accelerated, rising from 2,900 people in November 2003 to 9,658 by 10 March 2004. MONUC began, for the first time, repatriations to Burundi and Uganda, with a total of 3,085 and 501 persons, respectively, as at 10 March.

Human rights abuses involved violations of the right to security and private property committed by armed elements, militia members, foreign armed groups and State law enforcement agencies, who were also responsible for killings, torture and inhuman and degrading treatment. Throughout the country, looting, armed robberies, extortions, illegal taxation, arbitrary arrest and illegal detention were the key means of subsistence for unpaid soldiers. MONUC investigated reports of serious human rights abuses against children, including killings and sexual abuse. It was also undertaking a study of the issue and was setting up mixed commissions in three locations to assist victims. MONUC also provided military protection for large-scale humanitarian deliveries in South Kivu and logistical assistance to humanitarian agencies and to Congolese authorities, and assisted humanitarian actors in addressing the problem of the return of some of the 3.4 million internally displaced persons in the DRC to their places of origin.

The Secretary-General, noting the delays in the transition process, identified a number of priorities that needed to be addressed to adhere to the time lines for the transition. Those included enacting the legislative framework for security sector reform, DDR, extension of State administration and elections and addressing problems such as Mayi-Mayi integration into the armed forces. MONUC was following up on the understandings reached at the 9 February meeting on security sector reform (see p. 120), and the Secretary-General indicated that he would propose additional recommendations on the support MONUC could provide for the integration and development of the national police. The Secretary-General called on the DRC to improve its relations with its neighbours in the search for sustainable peace in Central Africa, and urged Rwanda and Uganda to play a constructive role in that regard (see p. 126).

March incidents in Kinshasa. The EU, in a 30 March statement [S/2004/307], expressed concern at incidents that occurred during the night of 28

March in Kinshasa. The EU encouraged the Congolese leaders, the institutions of the transition and the Congolese people to remain calm and committed to the transition process.

The Security Council President, in a press statement of 31 March [SC/8047-AFR/878], following a briefing by the Under-Secretary-General for Peacekeeping Operations, said that Council members expressed concern over the serious incidents in Kinshasa on 28 March and called on all parties to ensure the transition was not jeopardized. They called on the Congolese leaders to make every effort to proceed with the full implementation of the Global and All-Inclusive Agreement on Transition and to take steps for the DDR of combatants, reform of the security sector, the full re-establishment of State authority and the successful organization of elections.

Communications (April). By a letter of 16 April [S/2004/312], Uganda announced that, as part of its efforts to promote good-neighbourly relations in the Great Lakes region, it had reopened its embassy in Kinshasa, which had been closed since 1998.

The DRC, on 21 April [S/2004/318], transmitted the schedule of its election procedure, in accordance with the Global and All-Inclusive Agreement.

Events in eastern DRC

Cross-border tensions (April)

On 26 April [S/2004/327], the DRC expressed its gratitude to MONUC for having confirmed that soldiers of the regular Rwandan army were still present in the DRC in North and South Kivu, in violation of the agreements signed between the two countries [YUN 2003, p. 133]. The DRC protested the presence of those soldiers, who it said were helping to exacerbate tension at the border and might undermine the tenuous progress towards peace in the Great Lakes region. The DRC requested the Secretary-General to send a fact-finding commission to study the latest developments in the region, and reiterated its request for an urgent meeting of the Council on the situation in the DRC.

Rwanda, in a 29 April response [S/2004/335], rejected those allegations and called on MONUC to investigate the matter more thoroughly. Rwanda stated that there were no Rwandan troops in the Bunangana area in the DRC and urged MONUC to exercise more caution before labelling Kinyarwanda-speaking Congolese as nationals of Rwanda. At the same time, Rwanda expressed concern at the failure of the international community to address the presence of the Interahamwe, the militia responsible for the 1994 genocide [YUN 1994,

p. 283], who were based in the DRC and were terrorizing people in western Rwanda and eastern DRC. In Rwanda's view, the Interahamwe militia was the principal source of insecurity and violence in the Great Lakes region. Rwanda also appealed to the Council to investigate the source of arms supplied to that militia.

On 10 May [S/2004/385], the EU expressed concern at reports of an attack led by the Democratic Liberation Forces of Rwanda (FDLR) on Rwandan territory and of an incident involving Rwandan troops inside DRC territory. The EU believed that MONUC should intervene to counter any attempt by FDLR to infiltrate Rwandan territory, with a view to establishing real stability in the DRC. It called on the DRC and Rwanda to hold direct consultations to improve relations and indicated its support for the establishment of a bilateral mechanism for monitoring the border area, backed by MONUC.

SECURITY COUNCIL ACTION (May)

On 14 May [meeting 4969], following consultations among Security Council members, the President made statement **S/PRST/2004/15** on behalf of the Council:

> The Security Council expresses its serious concern regarding recent reports of an incursion into the Democratic Republic of the Congo by elements of the Rwandan army.
>
> The Council further expresses its concern at the reports of increased military activities of the Forces démocratiques de libération du Rwanda in the eastern part of the Democratic Republic of the Congo and of incursions made by them on the territory of Rwanda.
>
> The Council condemns in this context any impediments to the freedom of movement of the United Nations Organization Mission in the Democratic Republic of the Congo and reaffirms its full support for the efforts of the Mission to stabilize the situation in the eastern part of the Democratic Republic of the Congo, and encourages the Mission to continue to report to it on the military situation in the eastern part of the Democratic Republic of the Congo, in accordance with its mandate.
>
> The Council attaches great importance to respect for the national sovereignty and territorial integrity of the Democratic Republic of the Congo, of which it condemns any violation, as well as any violation of its relevant resolutions.
>
> The Council also attaches great importance to respect for the national sovereignty and territorial integrity of Rwanda, and condemns any incursions of armed groups into that country.
>
> The Council demands that the Government of Rwanda take measures to prevent the presence of any of its troops on the territory of the Democratic Republic of the Congo.
>
> The Council calls upon the Governments of the Democratic Republic of the Congo and Rwanda to investigate jointly, with the assistance of the Mission,

the substance of recent reports on armed incursions across their mutual border.

The Council further calls upon both Governments to establish border security mechanisms to prevent the recurrence of such incidents.

The Council reaffirms its support for the commitments made by the Governments of the Democratic Republic of the Congo and Rwanda in Pretoria on 27 November 2003, and urges both Governments to implement expeditiously the provisions contained in the communiqué issued on that date.

The Council further underlines the fact that the disarmament and the demobilization of all armed groups, including in particular the ex-Forces armées rwandaises and Interahamwe combatants, are essential to the settlement of the conflict in the Democratic Republic of the Congo, and calls upon the Governments of Rwanda and the Democratic Republic of the Congo to take all necessary measures to facilitate the swift and voluntary repatriation of Rwandan combatants from the Democratic Republic of the Congo.

The Council encourages the Governments of the Democratic Republic of the Congo and Rwanda to continue to take steps to normalize their relations. It commends, in this context, the Government of the Democratic Republic of the Congo for the efforts that led to the arrest of Mr. Yusufu Munyakazi, indicted, inter alia, on charges of genocide, and his subsequent transfer to the International Tribunal for Rwanda, and it calls upon all Member States to intensify efforts to arrest and transfer suspects sought by the Tribunal.

The Council urges all Governments in the region to encourage the re-establishment of confidence between neighbouring countries, in accordance with the declaration of Principles on Good-neighbourly Relations and Cooperation between the Democratic Republic of the Congo and Burundi, Rwanda and Uganda, adopted in New York by leaders of the region on 25 September 2003, with a view to achieving the normalization of their relations.

The Bukavu crisis

The Secretary-General reported in March [S/2004/251] that, despite the improvement of the overall situation in the Kivus, the mounting tension in Bukavu in February underscored the deep divisions within the transitional Government, particularly within the presidency, the integrated military high command and local political and military arrangements in Bukavu. Following the discovery of an arms cache at a residence of an associate of the former Rassemblement congolais pour la démocratie–Goma (RCD-G) South Kivu Governor Chiribanya, a confrontation on 3 February between elements loyal to the commander of the tenth military region, Brigadier General Prosper Nabyolwa, and those loyal to the Governor's allies resulted in at least two persons being killed. The situation was defused by MONUC and some weapons were handed over to the Mission. On 7 February, the

Council of Ministers suspended Governor Chiribanya and decided not to arrest him for the possession of arms. On 22 February, under General Nabyolwa's order, the homes of two former RCD-G officers associated with the suspended Governor were raided, resulting in the arrest of an RCD-G military officer, Major Kasongo, who was subsequently transferred to Kinshasa. Major Kasongo had been convicted by the military court in absentia for his alleged role in the assassination of President Laurent-Désiré Kabila and sentenced to death. His transfer to Kinshasa heightened tensions within the leadership of the tenth military region. In reaction, RCD-G threatened to withdraw from the transitional institutions if Major Kasongo was not sent back to Bukavu. That, in turn, triggered statements from ministers close to the President and the Mayi-Mayi component of the transitional Government criticizing RCD-G and accusing it of "preparing a third rebellion" in the Kivus. Following an agreement between President Kabila and Vice-President Azarias Ruberwa, MONUC transported Major Kasongo back to Bukavu on 25 February, thus helping to stabilize the town. Meanwhile, hard-line elements fomented a campaign against MONUC, claiming that it had not acted impartially. The spread of hate propaganda against the Banyamulenge ethnic group was also observed. On 8 March, at the request of President Kabila, MONUC transported General Nabyolwa to Kinshasa for consultations.

Communications. On 1 June [S/2004/454], the DRC reported to the Council President that, since 26 May, soldiers under the command of Colonel Jules Mutebusi, deputy commander of the military region around Bukavu, had committed acts of insubordination and had crossed the border into Rwanda. Colonel Mutebutsi had dispatched reinforcements to forcibly release one of his loyal soldiers arrested at the border. On 28 May, General Laurent Mihigo Nkunda dispatched five battalions from Goma to Bukavu to reinforce Colonel Mutebutsi's troops, while troops stationed in the Ruzizi plain also began to move towards Bukavu. On 31 May, the mutinous troops were in the vicinity of the airport at Kavumu and on the outskirts of Bukavu. The DRC Foreign Minister led a high-level delegation to Rwanda to convince Rwandan President Paul Kagame not to become involved in a problem that was internal to the Congolese armed forces. Some 50 people, mostly civilians, had been killed and property looted and plundered. On 2 June, Bukavu had fallen to the mutineers, who were supported by a third column from the east of the DRC. The transitional Government said that the mutiny would not affect the continuation of the process towards democratic elections and that the law would be applied against the perpetrators. It called for an urgent meeting of the Council to, among other things, impose sanctions if it turned out that the mutineers had benefited from outside assistance.

On 3 June [S/2004/452], Rwanda, expressing concern that the situation did not spill over into that country, and about statements by DRC President Joseph Kabila implicating Rwanda in the fighting in Bukavu, reiterated that there were no Rwandan troops in the DRC. It was of the view that the problem in Bukavu was an internal Congolese matter. It requested the Congolese forces involved in the events in Bukavu to support the DRC transition process, and called on the international community and the regional leaders to revive the verification mechanisms provided for under the 1999 Lusaka Ceasefire Agreement [YUN 1999, p. 87]. On the same date [S/2004/455], the DRC transmitted a communiqué issued at the extraordinary session of the Council of Ministers, held on 2 June, in which it condemned the violation of DRC's territorial integrity and sovereignty by Rwanda and requested that the Council strongly condemn Rwanda for its aggression and take measures under the Charter to put it to an end. The DRC reiterated its request that the Council impose sanctions on Rwanda, which, it said, remained the sole obstacle to the overall peace process taking place in the Great Lakes region.

Rwanda, on 7 June [S/2004/459], said that it was concerned that the DRC Government intended to wage war on Rwanda. It reiterated that its forces were not involved in the fall of Bukavu and announced the closure of the border with the DRC on 6 June to allow those concerned to verify and arrest, or otherwise deal with members of Rwanda's armed forces allegedly present on DRC territory until the United Nations and/or the AU clarified the events in Bukavu, and the eastern DRC in general. Rwanda also requested that the two bodies set up a verification mechanism to investigate and report on the allegations against Rwanda.

The AU Peace and Security Council (Addis Ababa, 4 June) [S/2004/458] released a statement condemning the 2 June occupation of Bukavu by dissident soldiers of the new Congolese national army. It took note of the mutineers' announcement that they would withdraw from Bukavu and demanded that they transfer the administration of the province to the authorities designated by the Government. It urged the UN Security Council to increase MONUC's size and resources to effectively support the DRC peace process, and requested AU members to provide troops for that force. The AU welcomed the decision of the Chairperson of its Commission to dispatch an Envoy to the DRC and Rwanda.

The EU also issued a statement on 4 June [S/2004/467] condemning the clashes in Bukavu and calling for an immediate end to hostilities and for the rebel forces to lay down their arms and leave Bukavu. It called on the DRC, Rwanda and Uganda to cooperate to reduce the tension in eastern DRC.

SECURITY COUNCIL ACTION (7 June)

On 7 June [meeting 4985], following consultations among Security Council members, the President made statement **S/PRST/2004/19** on behalf of the Council:

> The Security Council condemns with the utmost firmness the seizure of the town of Bukavu, on 2 June 2004, by dissident forces led by former Rassemblement congolais pour la démocratie-Goma commanders Major General Laurent Nkunda, Colonel Jules Mutebutsi and others. It also condemns atrocities and human rights violations which have occurred in this context. It declares its profound concern regarding reports of military actions that these forces have undertaken in other parts of the Democratic Republic of the Congo. It considers that all such actions constitute a serious threat to the peace process and to the transition and demands that they cease immediately.

> The Council reaffirms its commitment to and respect for the national sovereignty, political independence, territorial integrity and unity of the Democratic Republic of the Congo. It expresses its solidarity with the Congolese people and its full support to the Government of National Unity and Transition. It calls for the prompt and peaceful extension of State authority throughout the Congolese territory, in particular in Bukavu.

> The Council urges all parties represented in the Government of National Unity and Transition to remain fully committed to the peace process and to abstain from any action that could endanger the unity of the transitional Government.

> The Council warns solemnly the States neighbouring the Democratic Republic of the Congo of the consequences of support to the armed rebel groups. It urges the Government of Rwanda, taking into account its previous relationship with the Rassemblement congolais pour la démocratie-Goma, and all other neighbouring States, to do all in their power to support the peace process and help to secure a peaceful resolution to this crisis, while at the same time refraining from any action or declaration that might impact negatively on the situation in the Democratic Republic of the Congo. It recalls the terms of its resolutions 1493(2003) of 28 July 2003 and 1533(2004) of 12 March 2004, especially those elements relating to regional security across the Great Lakes, and calls upon all Member States, in particular those in the region, to fulfil their responsibilities accordingly.

> The Council welcomes the initiative of the Chairperson of the Commission of the African Union

aimed at overcoming the current crisis, including in its human dimension, and at facilitating the successful conclusion of the peace process in the Democratic Republic of the Congo.

The Council reiterates its full support to the United Nations Organization Mission in the Democratic Republic of the Congo. It condemns the recent killing of three of the Mission's personnel. It calls upon all Congolese parties to support the work of the Mission and demands that they refrain from any hostile action against the personnel or facilities of the United Nations.

Communications (mid-June). Reacting to the Council statement (see above), Rwanda, on 10 June [S/2004/474], said that it was disturbed that the Council's reaction was based on orchestrated disinformation. Rwanda intended to continue playing a positive role in the search for regional peace and stability and urged the Council to demand that the DRC Government desist from its bellicose statements and hatred against Rwanda. It noted that the DRC was opposed to the proposed verification mechanisms under the Lusaka Ceasefire Agreement. On 22 June [S/2004/509], Rwanda said that, based on the information received from the Secretary-General's Special Representative that the DRC was finally ready to establish the verification mechanism, it had, on 18 June, submitted to MONUC a draft agreement for the establishment of a permanent joint commission between the two countries to finalize the work of the Third Party Verification Mechanism, which was an indication of its efforts to ensure transparency. Rwanda also brought to the Council's attention the fact that Colonel Mutebutsi, a DRC national, along with about 300 men, had fled to Rwanda where he was allowed to enter on humanitarian grounds but would not be permitted to engage in activities to undermine the DRC's transitional Government and that country's security.

On 10 June [S/2004/489], the DRC confirmed that its forces had peacefully regained control of Bukavu. In response to Rwanda's communications (above), it repeated its accusation of renewed aggression by Rwanda in violation of the Charter and Council resolutions, and reaffirmed that it had no hidden agenda in Rwanda. The DRC requested that the Council ensure that Rwanda lifted the border closure to facilitate the return of Congolese nationals who had fled the Bukavu fighting, of former Colonel Mutebutsi and his men who found refuge in Rwanda and armed Rwandan elements remaining in the DRC.

SECURITY COUNCIL ACTION (22 June)

On 22 June [meeting 4994], following consultations among Security Council members, the President made statement **S/PRST/2004/21** on behalf of the Council:

The Security Council reiterates its grave concern at the continued violence and instability in the eastern part of the Democratic Republic of the Congo and at reports of threats to the peace and transition process. It condemns in the strongest terms any involvement by outside forces in the Democratic Republic of the Congo.

The Council urges all Congolese parties to remain fully committed to the peace process of the Global and All-Inclusive Agreement on the Transition in the Democratic Republic of the Congo and to respect the Government of National Unity and Transition as the sole legitimate governing authority in the Democratic Republic of the Congo. It warns all parties against any attempt to seize power by force. It urges all parties to refrain from statements or actions which might inflame the situation, including by supporting armed elements.

The Council warns all parties against any attempt at engaging in belligerent actions or violations of the embargo imposed by resolution 1493(2003) of 28 July 2003, in the eastern part of the Democratic Republic of the Congo. It invites the Secretary-General to determine further the need for a possible rapid reaction capability for the United Nations Organization Mission in the Democratic Republic of the Congo.

The Council calls upon the Government of National Unity and Transition to begin work immediately with the International Committee in Support of the Transition and with the Mission to establish mechanisms for closer coordination, in order to expedite security sector reform, the adoption of essential legislation and electoral preparations.

The Council urges the Governments of the Democratic Republic of the Congo and Rwanda to respond without further delay to the efforts undertaken by the Mission under its current mandate to establish, as soon as possible, a joint verification mechanism for their common security, including verification of cross-border movements.

The Council strongly encourages the heads of State of the Democratic Republic of the Congo, Rwanda, Uganda and Burundi to work together to reduce tensions and restore confidence in the region, in accordance with the commitments made in the declaration on good-neighbourly relations of 25 September 2003 including by holding meetings at the earliest possible opportunity.

The Council urges Rwanda not to provide any practical or political support to armed groups in the Democratic Republic of the Congo, in particular those led by Mr. Laurent Nkunda or Mr. Jules Mutebutsi. It further urges Rwanda to use its influence positively to de-escalate the current crisis and support the restoration of stability.

The Council reminds Uganda not to interfere in the Democratic Republic of the Congo, including through military support for armed groups.

The Council calls upon Burundi to prevent any support from its territory to armed groups in the Democratic Republic of the Congo. It encourages the Transitional Government to facilitate humanitarian assistance for Congolese refugees now in Burundi, and the international community to provide its full assistance.

The Council underlines that any attempt to disrupt the peace and transition process in the Democratic Republic of the Congo, including through support for armed groups, will not be tolerated.

The Council condemns the deaths of innocent civilians and human rights abuses in the eastern part of the Democratic Republic of the Congo and calls for such incidents to be fully investigated. Those responsible for atrocities and human rights abuses should be held to account, and the Government of National Unity and Transition should take immediate steps, with support from the international community, to reverse the current climate of impunity.

Uganda, on 23 June [S/2004/511], said that the part of the Council statement reminding Uganda not to interfere in the DRC suggested that Uganda was or might be contemplating interfering in DRC internal affairs, which was uncalled for. Uganda urged the Council President to correct the false impression. In a further communication of 28 June [S/2004/517], Uganda affirmed that it had no intention of getting involved in Congolese affairs. It rejected any attempt to reintroduce a military solution to the DRC crisis and declared that it would not provide sanctuary to Mr. Nkunda. Uganda called on the United Nations to support the democratization process that would lead to elections in the DRC.

Rwanda, in a response of the same date [S/2004/518], expressed its concerns arising from the Council statement (above). It felt that the Council was falling prey to the deliberate misrepresentation as a result of a disinformation campaign and, in turn, presented its own information to correct that situation. Rwanda reiterated its readiness to proceed with the proposed verification mechanism and urged MONUC to facilitate a meeting with DRC officials.

On 2 July [S/2004/534], Rwanda confirmed that its President, Paul Kagame, had met with DRC President Joseph Kabila on 24 June in Abuja, Nigeria, to recommit themselves to implementation of the 2002 Pretoria Agreement [YUN 2002, p. 115] on the withdrawal of Rwandan troops from DRC territory through the reactivation of the joint verification mechanism and by addressing other outstanding issues, especially the disarmament, demobilization, repatriation and rehabilitation of the ex-FAR/Interahamwe by the DRC. It also announced the reopening of the border, effective 3 July.

SECURITY COUNCIL ACTION (July)

On 29 July [meeting 5014], the Security Council unanimously adopted **resolution 1555(2004)**. The draft [S/2004/605] was prepared in consultations among Council members.

The Security Council,

Recalling its relevant resolutions and the statements by its President on the situation concerning the Democratic Republic of the Congo, in particular resolutions 1493(2003) of 28 July 2003 and 1533(2004) of 12 March 2004,

Reaffirming its commitment to respect for the sovereignty, territorial integrity and political independence of the Democratic Republic of the Congo and all the States in the region,

Reiterating its full support to the Government of National Unity and Transition of the Democratic Republic of the Congo,

Deeply concerned by the ongoing tensions and by the continuation of hostilities in the eastern part of the Democratic Republic of the Congo, particularly in the provinces of North and South Kivu, as well as in the Ituri district,

Reaffirming its readiness to support the peace and national reconciliation process, in particular through the United Nations Organization Mission in the Democratic Republic of the Congo,

Welcoming the readiness of the Mission to take an active part in the joint verification mechanism whose creation was announced by the Presidents of the Democratic Republic of the Congo and of the Republic of Rwanda in Abuja on 25 June 2004,

Noting that the situation in the Democratic Republic of the Congo continues to constitute a threat to international peace and security in the region,

1. *Decides* to extend the mandate of the United Nations Organization Mission in the Democratic Republic of the Congo, as contained in resolutions 1493(2003) and 1533(2004), both adopted under Chapter VII of the Charter of the United Nations, until 1 October 2004;

2. *Requests* the Secretary-General to submit a report to the Council, before 16 August 2004, on the execution by the Mission of its mandate;

3. *Decides* to remain actively seized of the matter.

Further political developments

Report of Secretary-General (August). On 16 August [S/2004/650], the Secretary-General, in response to Security Council resolution 1555(2004) (above), submitted his third special report on MONUC, which covered political and military developments since his previous report in March (see p. 121). The preparations for elections, which would include a referendum on a new constitution and legislative elections, culminating in presidential elections in July 2005, posed a number of challenges, given the size of the DRC, its population of over 50 million and the absence of basic infrastructure. On 5 June, President Kabila promulgated the organic law on the establishment of the Independent Electoral Commission, which had since adopted a provisional timetable for electoral operations and had begun preparations for the registration of an estimated 28 million voters. While the law on the registration of voters was being prepared, work on the electoral law could not begin until there was agreement on the type of political system and constitutional principles to be adopted. In June, the Senate drafted the general provisions of the new constitution and started consultations on such issues as the form of the State and its name, the political regime and territorial delimitation.

State administration remained weak or absent in many parts of the country, where parallel administrations run by armed groups maintained control. However, some progress was made in extending State authority, with the installation of governors and vice-governors in the 11 provinces.

The lack of progress on military integration was a significant destabilizing factor. With the exception of one integrated brigade that was trained by a Belgian team, military regional commanders had little control over the armed elements under their command. FARDC's poor command and control structure and the lack of support and payment of salaries contributed to indiscipline among the ranks, which depended on the local population for their sustenance. In view of the continuing delays in security sector reform, a meeting was convened on 29 June, as a follow-up to the 9 February meeting (see p. 120), to review progress and identify and coordinate bilateral efforts. The meeting agreed that MONUC would revive efforts to establish a consortium of Member States to assist the Congolese in the development of an overall plan for military reform. MONUC established a steering committee of potential donors, the first meeting of which was held on 13 July. The World Bank, in May, approved a $100 million grant to support the national DDR programme, the operational plans of which were being finalized. Pending its implementation, MONUC and UNDP assisted the Government in disarming some 535 Mayi-Mayi soldiers in eastern DRC.

Some progress was made in integrating the Congolese police forces, comprising some 70,000 personnel. The police high command was appointed, followed by the appointment in July of provincial police inspectors. MONUC and the Government drew up plans to train and deploy 6,000 police officers during 2004-2005. France trained and equipped a 500-member rapid intervention police unit.

The situation in Ituri remained tense, as rifts between moderates and hardliners emerged within the armed groups. In an effort to extend State authority, President Kabila consulted the leaders of armed groups from 10 to 14 May. The participants signed an *acte d'engagement*, committing themselves to the transition process and participation in the pilot disarmament and reinser-

tion programme. The new District Commissioner was appointed in June. The judicial tribunal in Bunia began to hear criminal cases and the local police began assuming their law enforcement responsibility. The MONUC Ituri brigade had so far deployed to eight locations.

Serious allegations of sexual exploitation and misconduct by MONUC civilian and military personnel in Bunia were uncovered by the Mission during May, including sexual exploitation of girls and women at the camp for internally displaced persons and other locations. Those allegations were under investigation by the UN Office of Internal Oversight Services (OIOS).

In addition to the crisis in Bukavu (see p. 124), on 11 June, about 40 presidential guards attempted a coup d'état, without success. On 14 July, eight RCD-Goma members of the National Assembly suspended their membership of the Assembly, but were condemned by the RCD-Goma leadership. FARDC increased its presence in eastern DRC by deploying some 15,000 troops. General Nkunda's fate remained unresolved as he and his troops remained located between Goma and Bukavu on Lake Kivu, creating a tense situation.

Bilateral relations suffered setbacks during the reporting period. In April, Rwanda claimed that elements of the ex-FAR/Interahamwe, also referred to as FDLR, attacked its territory from the DRC, while the latter claimed that Rwandans had invaded its territory (see p. 124). Steps were taken to strengthen bilateral contacts with Uganda, despite the continued presence of Ugandan armed groups in north-eastern DRC. The establishment in December 2003 of the DRC/Uganda Joint Bilateral Security Intelligence Commission with MONUC assistance had contributed to the strengthening of bilateral relations. Following a meeting in May, a joint MONUC/DRC/Uganda border verification mechanism was established.

The Secretary-General noted that, overall, the prevailing mistrust and lack of political determination continued to impede the transitional Government from moving forward on its agreed agenda. Some influential elements among the ex-belligerents were working against the transition, and the security situation remained unstable, as evidenced by the May/June activity in Bukavu and Kinshasa. A clear political strategy was therefore necessary, requiring a step-by-step approach. He urged the Government to engage in such a process, following the steps outlined in the report, and called on the DRC, Rwanda and Uganda to normalize their bilateral relations as a matter of priority.

The Secretary-General said that MONUC was authorized to use all necessary means to fulfil its mandate in the Ituri district and in North and South Kivu. There was a wide gap between the expectations that the Mission would enforce peace and the Mission's capacity to fulfil them. In the Secretary-General's view, MONUC's key role was to use its good offices to build confidence among the leaders of the transition and to strengthen the Government. Given the size of the DRC, MONUC could not be deployed everywhere, nor in sufficient strength. Hence strategic areas of operation had to be identified. If the Council were to mandate MONUC to assist in the creation of stability in areas other than Ituri, the conditions under which the Mission would use force to deter dissident elements from using violence to derail the political process should be clearly defined.

The Secretary-General recommended that the transitional Government should ensure that support to ex-FAR/Interahamwe was terminated; MONUC should be augmented and fully deployed in the Kivus, participate in DDR and support FARDC; MONUC should prevent reprisal attacks by foreign elements against Congolese civilians; and support should be provided to the Joint Verification Mechanism. He cautioned, however, that MONUC could not assume responsibility for the maintenance of law and order in the DRC. Its primary role in deterring armed challenges was to use its political good offices to mediate disputes.

The military concept of MONUC's operations would allow it to act as a deterrent in unstable areas, on the one hand, and as a rapid reaction force, on the other. It would have to maintain a credible and secure presence in key areas of potential volatility to undertake surge operations in crisis areas, in addition to its regular tasks, which would require flexible and mobile reserve capability of an additional 13,100 military personnel.

The Secretary-General called on the Security Council to endorse his transitional agenda to strengthen the political process and on the transitional Government to implement it. The Governments of the DRC, Rwanda and Uganda needed to ensure that the flow of arms across their borders ended; to settle the question of the foreign armed groups, in particular the ex-FAR/Interahamwe; and to legitimize the exploitation of natural resources. Those goals could be achieved through the Joint Verification Mechanism or by establishing normal bilateral relations, with the exchange of ambassadors. He recommended that the Council increase MONUC's military strength from 10,800 all ranks to 23,900 and extend the mandate of its civilian police component and increase its strength from the current 140 to 507 personnel. The implementation of the Mission's revised military tasks would require the addition of formed and enabling units, as well as improving its information-gathering and analysis capacity.

Letter and statement of Secretary-General. On 3 September [S/2004/715], the Secretary-General, in a letter to the Council President, noted that Council members had recognized the need to enhance the UN involvement in the DRC's peace process. However, the possibility of a further deterioration in the situation could not be ruled out, given the speed with which events were unfolding. Pending the Council's decision on the recommendations contained in his report, he proposed that the Council deploy emergency reinforcements to MONUC, consisting of two additional infantry battalions and four attack helicopters, to address immediate security concerns, without prejudice to the long-term requirement of reinforcing MONUC.

The Secretary-General, in a statement to the press issued on 19 November [SG/SM/9605-AFR/1069-PKO/115], expressed outrage at the findings of a UN investigation into allegations of sexual exploitation and abuse in MONUC, which showed clear evidence that acts of gross misconduct had taken place. The investigation should be accelerated and those involved held accountable. Prince Zeid Ra'ad Al-Hussein (Jordan) had agreed to be his adviser on the issue. The Secretary-General declared that he was considering additional measures and had instructed the Department of Peacekeeping Operations (DPKO) urgently to send a special investigation team to the DRC to examine the outstanding cases.

SECURITY COUNCIL ACTION (October)

On 1 October [meeting 5048], the Security Council unanimously adopted **resolution 1565(2004)**. The draft [S/2004/774] was prepared in consultations among Council members.

The Security Council,

Recalling its previous resolutions and the statements by its President concerning the Democratic Republic of the Congo,

Reaffirming its commitment to respect the sovereignty, territorial integrity and political independence of the Democratic Republic of the Congo and all the States of the region,

Reaffirming its support for the process of the Global and All-Inclusive Agreement on the Transition in the Democratic Republic of the Congo, signed in Pretoria on 17 December 2002, welcoming the efforts made to date for its implementation by the Government of National Unity and Transition, and calling upon all the Congolese parties to honour their commitments in this regard, in particular so that free, fair and peaceful elections can take place within the agreed time frame,

Deeply concerned by the continuation of hostilities in the eastern part of the Democratic Republic of the Congo, particularly in the provinces of North and South Kivu and in the Ituri district, and by the grave violations of human rights and of international humanitarian law that accompany them,

Recalling that all the parties bear responsibility for ensuring security with respect to the civilian populations, and recalling in particular, in this regard, its resolutions 1325(2000) of 31 October 2000 on women and peace and security, 1379(2001) of 20 November 2001, 1460(2003) of 30 January 2003 and 1539(2004) of 22 April 2004 on children in armed conflict, and 1265 (1999) of 17 September 1999 and 1296(2000) of 19 April 2000 on the protection of civilians in armed conflict,

Taking note of the third special report of the Secretary-General of 16 August 2004 on the United Nations Organization Mission in the Democratic Republic of the Congo, and of the recommendations contained therein,

Taking note also of the letter dated 3 September 2004 from the Secretary-General to the President of the Security Council,

Noting that the situation in the Democratic Republic of the Congo continues to constitute a threat to international peace and security in the region,

Acting under Chapter VII of the Charter of the United Nations,

1. *Decides* to extend the deployment of the United Nations Organization Mission in the Democratic Republic of the Congo until 31 March 2005;

2. *Requests* the Secretary-General to arrange the rapid deployment of additional military capabilities for the Mission in accordance with the recommendation contained in his letter dated 3 September 2004, and, beyond, to deploy as soon as possible in the provinces of North and South Kivu all the brigades and appropriate force enablers;

3. *Authorizes* the increase in the Mission's strength by 5,900 personnel, including up to 341 civilian police personnel, as well as the deployment of appropriate civilian personnel, appropriate and proportionate air mobility assets and other force enablers, and expresses its determination to keep the Mission's strength and structure under regular review, taking into account the evolution of the situation on the ground;

4. *Decides* that the Mission will have the following mandate:

(*a*) To deploy and maintain a presence in the key areas of potential volatility in order to promote the reestablishment of confidence, to discourage violence, in particular by deterring the use of force to threaten the political process, and to allow United Nations personnel to operate freely, particularly in the eastern part of the Democratic Republic of the Congo;

(*b*) To ensure the protection of civilians, including humanitarian personnel, under imminent threat of physical violence;

(*c*) To ensure the protection of United Nations personnel, facilities, installations and equipment;

(*d*) To ensure the security and freedom of movement of its personnel;

(*e*) To establish the necessary operational links with the United Nations Operation in Burundi, and with the Governments of the Democratic Republic of the Congo and Burundi, in order to coordinate efforts towards monitoring and discouraging cross-border movements of combatants between the two countries;

(*f*) To monitor the implementation of the measures imposed by paragraph 20 of resolution 1493(2003) of 28 July 2003, including on the lakes, in cooperation with the Operation and, as appropriate, with the Governments concerned and with the Group of Experts referred to in paragraph 10 of resolution 1533(2004) of 12 March 2004, including by inspecting, as it deems it necessary and without notice, the cargo of aircraft and of any transport vehicle using the ports, airports, airfields, military bases and border crossings in North and South Kivu and in Ituri;

(*g*) To seize or collect, as appropriate, arms and any related materiel whose presence in the territory of the Democratic Republic of the Congo violates the measures imposed by paragraph 20 of resolution 1493 (2003), and to dispose of such arms and related materiel as appropriate;

(*h*) To observe and report, in a timely manner, on the position of armed movements and groups and the presence of foreign military forces in the key areas of volatility, especially by monitoring the use of landing strips and the borders, in particular on the lakes;

5. *Decides* that the Mission will also have the following mandate, in support of the Government of National Unity and Transition:

(*a*) To contribute to arrangements made for the security of the institutions and the protection of officials of the transition in Kinshasa until the integrated police unit in Kinshasa is ready to take on this responsibility, and to assist the Congolese authorities in the maintenance of order in other strategic areas, as recommended in paragraph 103 (*c*) of the third special report of the Secretary-General;

(*b*) To contribute to the improvement of the security conditions in which humanitarian assistance is provided, and to assist in the voluntary return of refugees and internally displaced persons;

(*c*) To support operations to disarm foreign combatants led by the armed forces of the Democratic Republic of the Congo, including by undertaking the steps listed in paragraphs 75 (*b*) to (*e*) of the third special report of the Secretary-General;

(*d*) To facilitate the demobilization and voluntary repatriation of disarmed foreign combatants and their dependants;

(*e*) To contribute to the disarmament portion of the national programme of disarmament, demobilization and reintegration of Congolese combatants and their dependants, in monitoring the process and providing, as appropriate, security in some sensitive locations;

(*f*) To contribute to the successful completion of the electoral process stipulated in the Global and All-Inclusive Agreement on the Transition in the Democratic Republic of the Congo, by assisting in the establishment of a secure environment for free, transparent and peaceful elections to take place;

(*g*) To assist in the promotion and protection of human rights, with particular attention to women, children and vulnerable persons, to investigate human rights violations to put an end to impunity, and to continue to cooperate with efforts to ensure that those responsible for serious violations of human rights and international humanitarian law are brought to justice, while working closely with the relevant United Nations agencies;

6. *Authorizes* the Mission to use all necessary means, within its capacity and in the areas where its armed units are deployed, to carry out the tasks listed in paragraphs 4 *(a)* to *(g)* above, and in paragraphs 5 *(a)* to *(c)*, *(e)* and *(f)* above;

7. *Decides* that the Mission will also have the mandate, within its capacity and without prejudice to carrying out tasks stipulated in paragraphs 4 and 5 above, to provide advice and assistance to the Transitional Government and authorities, in accordance with the commitments of the Global and All-Inclusive Agreement, including by supporting the three joint commissions outlined in paragraph 62 of the third special report of the Secretary-General, in order to contribute to their efforts, with a view to take forward:

(a) Essential legislation, including the future constitution;

(b) Security sector reform, including the integration of national defence and internal security forces together with disarmament, demobilization and reintegration and, in particular, the training and monitoring of the police, while ensuring that they are democratic and fully respect human rights and fundamental freedoms;

(c) The electoral process;

8. *Requests* the Secretary-General to report to the Council, within one month of the adoption of the present resolution, on reforms necessary to improve the structures of command and control and the management of military information within the Mission, and to rationalize the civilian and police components of the Mission;

9. *Also requests* the Secretary-General, through his Special Representative for the Democratic Republic of the Congo, to coordinate all the activities of the United Nations system in the Democratic Republic of the Congo;

10. *Further requests* the Secretary-General to ensure that his Special Representatives for the Democratic Republic of the Congo and for Burundi coordinate the activities of the Mission and the Operation, in particular:

(a) By sharing military information at their disposal, especially concerning cross-border movements of armed elements and arms trafficking;

(b) By pooling their logistic and administrative resources, to an extent that does not prejudice the ability of the missions to carry out their respective mandates, in order to ensure their maximum efficiency and cost-effectiveness;

(c) By coordinating, as appropriate, the implementation of the national programmes for disarmament and demobilization and repatriation, reintegration and resettlement;

11. *Stresses* the need for the Government of National Unity and Transition to carry out the process provided for by the Global and All-Inclusive Agreement, and in particular to implement the recommendations listed in paragraph 54 of the third special report of the Secretary-General, including by producing, with the support of the Mission, precise plans and time lines in each of the fields identified;

12. *Calls upon* the Government of National Unity and Transition to cooperate closely with the Mission in establishing three joint commissions on essential legislation, security sector reform and elections, and in implementing security sector reform, in accordance with paragraph 7 above;

13. *Urges* the Government of National Unity and Transition to continue, with determination and rapidity, the integration of the security forces, in particular the integration of the armed forces, and underlines the importance of regular meetings of the Supreme Defence Council and of its cooperation with the international partners of the Democratic Republic of the Congo, especially with the Mission, as positive signals of the commitment of the Government of National Unity and Transition in this regard;

14. *Also urges* the Government of National Unity and Transition to develop without further delay a plan for the disarmament of foreign combatants, and to entrust its implementation to the armed forces of the Democratic Republic of the Congo, with the support of the Mission;

15. *Urges* the Governments of the Democratic Republic of the Congo, Burundi, Rwanda and Uganda to each ensure that its territory is not used to infringe the sovereignty of the others, to realize without further delay the complete normalization of their bilateral relations, and to cooperate actively in assuring security along their common borders, in particular by implementing agreements they have signed for the establishment of joint verification mechanisms with the active participation of the Mission, and exhorts them to comply in this regard with the recommendations listed in paragraph 55 of the third special report of the Secretary-General;

16. *Urges*, in particular, the Governments of the Democratic Republic of the Congo and Rwanda to work together and with the Mission and the African Union, with a view to removing the threat posed by foreign armed groups, as they have agreed to in the Peace Agreement signed in Pretoria on 30 July 2002 and the Declaration signed in Pretoria on 27 November 2003, and in accordance with the terms of reference for the Joint Verification Mechanism signed in New York on 22 September 2004;

17. *Calls upon* the Government of National Unity and Transition and Congolese officials at all levels to take all necessary steps, while respecting freedom of expression and of the press, to prevent the use of the media to incite hatred or tensions among communities;

18. *Calls upon* Member States, the international organizations concerned and the community of donors to provide their full support to the transitional process, the extension of State authority throughout the territory and long-term social and economic development in the Democratic Republic of the Congo, and encourages them in this regard to respond positively to the recommendations listed in paragraph 57 of the third special report of the Secretary-General;

19. *Strongly condemns* violence and other violations of international humanitarian law and human rights, in particular those perpetrated against civilians, in the Democratic Republic of the Congo, and demands that all parties and Governments concerned in the region, including the Government of National Unity and Transition, take without delay all necessary steps to bring to justice those responsible for these violations and to ensure respect for human rights and international humanitarian law, as appropriate with relevant

international assistance, as well as to guarantee the security and well-being of the civilian population;

20. *Demands* that all parties cooperate fully with the operations of the Mission and that they ensure the safety of as well as unhindered and immediate access for United Nations and associated personnel in carrying out their mandate, throughout the territory of the Democratic Republic of the Congo, demands in particular that all parties provide full access to Mission military observers, including in all ports, airports, airfields, military bases and border crossings, and requests the Secretary-General to report without delay any failure to comply with these demands;

21. *Recalls* its resolution 1502(2003) of 26 August 2003, reaffirms the obligation of all parties to comply fully with the rules and principles of international humanitarian law applicable to them related to the protection of humanitarian and United Nations personnel, and urges all those concerned to allow immediate, full and unimpeded access by humanitarian personnel to all people in need of assistance, as set forth in applicable international humanitarian law;

22. *Also recalls* the link between the illicit exploitation and trade of natural resources in certain regions and the fuelling of armed conflicts, and, in line with its resolutions 1493(2003), 1533(2004) and 1552(2004) of 27 July 2004, condemns categorically the illegal exploitation of the natural resources and other sources of wealth of the Democratic Republic of the Congo, urges all States, especially those in the region including the Democratic Republic of the Congo itself, to take appropriate steps in order to end these illegal activities, including if necessary through judicial means, and to report to the Council as appropriate, and exhorts the international financial institutions to assist the Government of National Unity and Transition in establishing efficient and transparent control of the exploitation of natural resources;

23. *Welcomes* the convening of the International Conference on Peace, Security, Democracy and Development in the Great Lakes Region, with inclusive participation by all the Governments concerned, under the aegis of the African Union and the United Nations, with a view to strengthening stability in the region and working out conditions that will enable each State to enjoy the right to live in peace;

24. *Encourages* all Member States to increase international political engagement in the peace process in the region, as requested in paragraph 57 of the third special report of the Secretary-General;

25. *Expresses grave concern* at the allegations of sexual exploitation and misconduct by civilian and military personnel of the Mission, requests the Secretary-General to continue to fully investigate these allegations, to take the appropriate action in accordance with the Secretary-General's bulletin on special measures for protection from sexual exploitation and sexual abuse and to keep the Council informed, further encourages the Mission to conduct training for personnel targeted to ensure full compliance with its code of conduct regarding sexual misconduct, and urges troop-contributing countries to take appropriate disciplinary and other action to ensure full accountability in cases of such misconduct involving their personnel;

26. *Requests* the Secretary-General to keep it informed regularly of developments in the situation in the Democratic Republic of the Congo, and to submit to the Council before 28 February 2005 a report on the execution of the Mission's mandate, including an evaluation of the structure and strength of its military, civilian and police components, with a view to their adjustment according to the progress made on the ground and the tasks remaining to be accomplished;

27. *Reiterates its strong support* for the Special Representative of the Secretary-General and the Mission, and for the efforts they continue to make to assist the parties in the Democratic Republic of the Congo and in the region to advance the peace process;

28. *Decides* to remain actively seized of the matter.

Following the adoption of resolution 1565 (2004) (above), the Secretary-General said that the Council's action, while improving the Mission's operational capacities, fell well below the requested additional forces. Therefore, he had instructed DPKO to review the tasks that could be performed by MONUC, with a view to revising the scope of its military and civilian police concepts of operation. He hoped that the Council would favourably revisit MONUC's requirements in the future.

Rwanda, in a 4 October letter [S/2004/788], expressed disappointment that the Council had not mandated MONUC to forcefully disarm the ex-FAR/Interahamwe.

Security Council mission. The Security Council mission to Central Africa (21-25 November) (see p. 117) had as its key objective, during its visit to the DRC, to observe the achievements made in the peace and transition process since its last visit to the country in June 2003 [YUN 2003, p. 127]. It discussed the political transition process, the continuing insecurity and the need for good-neighbourly relations in eastern DRC, the situation in Bukavu and the roles of MONUC and the international community.

In its report [S/2004/934], the mission noted that the main transitional institutions had been established and were operational; an integrated high command had been set up for the armed forces and police service; the Governors and Vice-Governors of the provinces had been appointed; and some key laws, such as the nationality law, had been adopted. The mission had a strong impression of the Congolese people's desire to hold elections and concluded that the parties should reach an understanding on the post-transitional period to ensure long-term stability. The mission, stressing the need to respect the deadline for completing the electoral process by the target date of June 2005, said that much work remained to be done in that regard, in particular the integration of the armed forces, the adoption of the constitution and election laws. President Kabila had reaffirmed his determination to hold elections within the agreed time frame.

The mission noted the restructuring challenges that MONUC was facing and underlined the importance of early, detailed planning for its role in supporting the election process.

The Security Council discussed the report on 8 December [meeting 5096].

Further cross-border tension (November)

The DRC, on 30 November [S/2004/935], informed the Council President that Rwandan regular troops had crossed the Congolese border to attack the town of Mutongo in North Kivu province and requested that the Council meet to condemn the aggression. In a 1 December statement [S/2004/949] of its Foreign Minister, the DRC accused Rwanda of using the fight against the ex-FAR/Interahamwe as an excuse to return to the DRC. The DRC was aware that it had to resolve the Interahamwe issue and was committed to doing so, but questioned Rwanda's real objective in trying to disarm the ex-FAR/Interahamwe. It rejected Rwandan President Kagame's proposals for neutralizing the ex-FAR/Interahamwe but was willing to accept assistance from African States and their partners, including MONUC, to settle, by force if necessary, the Interahamwe and ex-FAR issue.

On 2 December [SG/SM/9631-AFR/1076], the Secretary-General, in a statement attributable to his Spokesman, said that he was disturbed by the increasing tension between the DRC and Rwanda, particularly by indications from Rwanda of military operations on DRC territory against ex-FAR/Interahamwe elements, which Rwanda maintained was a threat to its security. He called on Rwanda to refrain from military action in the DRC, which would disrupt the transition process, and on the DRC to intensify efforts to disarm and repatriate elements still in the DRC. He added that MONUC was prepared to activate the Joint Verification Mechanism for disarming and repatriating those groups.

Rwanda, in a 6 December communiqué [S/2004/951], expressed surprise that the DRC President had called on the Congolese people to mobilize to fight a Rwandan invasion on DRC territory, and reiterated that there were no Rwandan troops currently on DRC territory. Rwanda added that ex-FAR/Interahamwe elements were present and active in massive numbers there, and intended to launch an attack against Rwanda. Rwanda had fulfilled its obligations under all agreements it had signed with the DRC, while the DRC had not done so; specifically, it had not disarmed and demobilized those elements on its territory.

The AU Peace and Security Council, in a 7 December decision [S/2004/966], expressed concern about the continued presence of ex-FAR/Interahamwe in the DRC and its effect on the stability of the region. It called for a DRC-Rwanda summit, with the AU, the United Nations and other stakeholders, to defuse the tension and consider ways to address the disarmament and demobilization of the ex-FAR/Interahamwe. The AU Council appealed to the United Nations to strengthen MONUC so that it could participate in the disarmament and demobilization and called for the speedy establishment of the Joint Verification Mechanism.

SECURITY COUNCIL ACTION (December)

On 7 December [meeting 5095], following consultations among Security Council members, the President made statement **S/PRST/2004/45** on behalf of the Council:

The Security Council expresses its very deep concern at multiple reports of military operations by the Rwandan army in the eastern part of the Democratic Republic of the Congo and at threats by the Government of Rwanda in this regard. It recalls its adherence to the respect for the sovereignty of all States, and underlines the fact that the threat or use of force against the territorial integrity of any State is contrary to the purposes and principles stated in the Charter of the United Nations.

The Council strongly condemns any and all such military action, recalling that they are contrary to its resolutions, and in particular to resolution 1565 (2004), by which it urged the Governments of the Democratic Republic of the Congo, Burundi, Rwanda and Uganda to each ensure that the territory of its country was not used to infringe the sovereignty of the others.

The Council demands that the Government of Rwanda withdraw without delay any forces it may have in the territory of the Democratic Republic of the Congo, and calls upon all States in the region to refrain from any action or statement that contravenes international law, undermines the already fragile stability in the region or the transitional process supported by the international community.

The Council notes that these reported events and threats are contrary to all peace agreements, declarations and protocols signed by regional States since the 1998 commencement of hostilities in the Democratic Republic of the Congo. It underlines the fact that these events and threats, arising after the International Conference on the Great Lakes Region, are contrary to the commitments taken by the regional Heads of State, in the Declaration adopted in Dar es Salaam on 20 November 2004, to settle their disputes in a peaceful manner, and are all the more unacceptable.

The Council calls upon all Governments in the region, to commit themselves to and make full use of multilateral mechanisms they have agreed to establish, including the Joint Verification Mechanism and the Tripartite Commission, for the peaceful resolution of their disputes. It further calls upon the Government of Rwanda, as well as all Governments in the region, to devote their resources to the promotion of peace, stability, democracy and development.

The Council urges all Member States fully to comply with their obligations under resolution 1493 (2003), which imposed an arms embargo in the district of Ituri and the provinces of North and South Kivu.

The Council recognizes that continued tension in the eastern part of the Democratic Republic of the Congo undermines peace and security in the region, and in particular that the presence of ex-Forces armées rwandaises and Interahamwe elements in the eastern Democratic Republic of the Congo is a source of instability, a threat to civilian populations and an impediment to good neighbourly relations between the Democratic Republic of the Congo and Rwanda. It considers the armed presence and activities of ex-Forces armées rwandaises and Interahamwe elements in the eastern part of the Democratic Republic of the Congo to be unacceptable and demands that they disarm and disband without delay, with a view to their repatriation or resettlement.

In this regard, the Council welcomes steps taken to set up the plan established by the Congolese authorities, with the support of the United Nations Organization Mission in the Democratic Republic of the Congo, aimed at accelerating the disarmament and demobilization of foreign armed groups. It calls upon the Governments of Rwanda and the Democratic Republic of the Congo to explore ways to facilitate the voluntary repatriation of these combatants, based on the existing mechanisms. It urges the Congolese authorities to do everything possible to effectively disarm these armed groups as a matter of urgency, in the interest of stability in the Democratic Republic of the Congo, the security of Rwanda and Burundi, and the establishment of peace and stability in the region.

The Council further calls upon, in this regard, the Congolese authorities to accelerate the integration of the armed forces of the Democratic Republic of the Congo, and encourages the donor community to provide coordinated financial and technical assistance to this important task.

The Council condemns any attempt aimed at undermining the unity and territorial integrity of the Democratic Republic of the Congo.

The Council expresses its intention to consider further actions, including measures that may be taken against those individuals who, by their actions or statements, compromise the peace and transition process in the Democratic Republic of the Congo.

The DRC, on 20 December [S/2004/984], said that, in the light of Rwanda's refusal to withdraw its troops in compliance with statement S/PRST/2004/45 (above), it was calling on the Council to take steps against Rwanda, including the imposition of a total embargo on arms sales to Rwanda (see p. 160), the suspension of bilateral and multilateral aid, the freezing of the assets and prohibition of the movement of Rwandan authorities.

Situation at end of year

Progress continued to be made in the transition to a new Government, but the security situation in eastern DRC remained volatile, the Secretary-General reported in December [S/2004/1034]. The May/June Bukavu crisis (see p. 124) and the Gatumba massacre in Burundi in August (see p. 150) had polarized the government components, leading RCD-G to temporarily suspend its participation in the transitional Government on 23 August. Subsequently, the Government prepared a new road map to ensure implementation of the Global and All-Inclusive Agreement; the road map was adopted by the Council of Ministers and was being reviewed monthly. However, progress remained slow. The Senate prepared a first draft of the constitution, which provided for a unitary State with considerable powers devolved to the provinces, although key issues, such as the electoral system and the balance of power between the President and the Prime Minister, remained to be clarified. The laws on nationality and the armed forces were promulgated on 12 November, while the amnesty, decentralization and electoral laws were under discussion in the Parliament. The voter registration law was adopted but had not been promulgated.

Among developments in regional relations, the DRC and Rwanda signed, on 22 September, the terms of reference for the Joint Verification Mechanism to address cross-border issues, including the remaining ex-FAR/Interahamwe in the DRC. The Mechanism was composed of the Joint Verification Commission, a policy-making and review body, and Joint Verification Teams comprising technical experts and representatives of MONUC and the AU. The first meeting of the Commission was held in Kigali, Rwanda, on 5 October. On 29 November, the parties endorsed the concept of operations for the Teams. Separately, on 26 October, the DRC, Rwanda and Uganda signed an agreement on regional security, with a view to strengthening trilateral relations and preventing the use of their territories by foreign combatants. The agreement also committed the parties to ensuring the DDR of foreign armed groups within 12 months and established a Tripartite Joint Commission. On 19 and 20 November, the leaders of 11 African States participated in the International Conference on Peace, Security, Democracy and Development in the Great Lakes Region, which agreed on guiding principles in the areas of peace and security and good governance, among others (see p. 116).

In accordance with resolution 1565(2004), by which the Security Council mandated the establishment of joint commissions with a view to assisting the transitional Government in security sector reform, essential legislation and elections, the National Assembly and Senate agreed on the establishment of the Joint Commission on Essential Legislation, to be chaired by MONUC, which convened on 7 November a meeting of donors to discuss its terms of reference. The Commission would advise on the elaboration and implementation of key legislation, including the constitution and laws on nationality, voter registration, referendums, decentralization and elections. The Joint Commission on Security Sector Reform would coordinate and supplement assistance in support of integration and reform of the armed forces, provide technical advice and coordinate donor assistance for security sector reform.

The security situation in Ituri, which had improved earlier in the year, deteriorated sharply. In Katanga and Kasai, armed men from the Revolutionary Movement for the Liberation of Katanga captured the town of Kilwa on 13 and 14 October, resulting in the displacement of its population. FARDC regained control of the town on 15 October. In the Kivus, tensions increased between political and military factions, while security along the border with Rwanda deteriorated, with accusations and counter-accusations of border violations. On 29 November, the transitional Government officially complained to the Joint Verification Mechanism about the presence of thousands of Rwandan troops in the Kivus since January. However, security concerns forced the Verification Team to cancel its investigation. On 19 December, Rwanda's Foreign Minister stated that his Government was withdrawing its "threat" to send troops into the DRC, noting that it would trust the international community to address the matter of the remaining ex-FAR/Interahamwe on Congolese territory.

In Ituri, the Government, with MONUC and UNDP assistance, began a disarmament and reintegration programme for an estimated 15,000 militia members. However, by mid-December, only 1,506 former combatants had registered for the programme. Overall, by the end of the year, more than 11,300 foreign combatants and their dependants had been repatriated from the DRC to Burundi, Rwanda and Uganda. Three FARDC brigades were deployed to South Kivu to conduct operations to disarm and repatriate FDLR.

MONUC and the UN Secretariat continued to follow up on allegations of sexual exploitation and abuse by MONUC personnel. Between June and September, an OIOS investigation into sexual misconduct in Bunia revealed that 8 of 72 allegations could be corroborated. All of the cases were being followed up to ensure that appropriate disciplinary action was taken, and a number of staff were suspended, pending completion of the in-

vestigations. The Secretary-General emphasized zero tolerance towards sexual exploitation and abuse and said that he would develop a comprehensive strategy to prevent and respond to such activities in all peacekeeping operations.

The Secretary-General concluded that the transitional process was steadily, albeit slowly, progressing towards elections, despite remaining challenges. He urged the parties to turn their attention to real power-sharing and overcoming the mistrust that continued to impede the establishment of a unified country. The Congolese parties needed to assure the population that elections would be conducted fairly and free from political violence. Although there had been some visible progress with regard to the extension of State authority, transparent and legitimate local governance had yet to take root in many areas because of the lack of infrastructure, the irregular payment of salaries of civil servants and the illegal exploitation of natural resources. The difficulties encountered in the reform of the security sector remained daunting, while relations with neighbouring States remained tense. The Secretary-General urged the DRC and Rwanda to cooperate to restore peace in eastern DRC, and called on Uganda to assist the DRC in extending its authority throughout Ituri.

MONUC financing

The General Assembly considered several reports by the Secretary-General concerning the financing of MONUC.

A performance report on the MONUC budget, covering 1 July 2002 to 30 June 2003 [A/58/684], stated that total expenditure amounted to $481.7 million, out of a total apportionment of $584.7 million. The difference of $102.9 million, a variance of 17.6 per cent, was primarily attributable to the delayed deployment of military and civilian personnel. The Secretary-General recommended that the Assembly decide on the treatment of the unencumbered balance and on the treatment of other income, amounting to $31,456,000, mostly derived from savings on or cancellation of prior-period obligations ($22,581,000) and from interest income ($6,547,000).

The MONUC budget for 1 July 2004 to 30 June 2005 [A/58/701] totalled $721.4 million, inclusive of voluntary contributions in kind valued at $3.1 million. It provided for the deployment of 10,040 military contingent personnel, 760 military observers, 182 civilian police, 972 international staff, 1,354 national staff and 490 United Nations Volunteers.

The Advisory Committee on Administrative and Budgetary Questions (ACABQ), in its April report [A/58/759/Add.10], recommended that the unencumbered balance for the earlier period, as well as other adjustments, be credited to Member States. In regard to the proposed 2004/05 budget, it recommended that the total requirement be reduced by $9.2 million and that the Assembly appropriate $709.1 million gross ($691.6 million net) for the maintenance of MONUC for the 12 months.

The Secretary-General, in an April note [A/58/772], reported that the appropriation for 1 July 2003 to 30 June 2004 for MONUC was projected to be fully utilized, primarily due to the full deployment of military contingents and resulting requirement for the reimbursement of troop-contributing Governments. The difference between the projected expenditures and the amount appropriated by the Assembly was $59 million gross ($57.1 million net). Therefore, he requested that the Assembly assess and apportion that amount among Member States. ACABQ, in a May report [A/58/794], endorsed that request.

GENERAL ASSEMBLY ACTION

On 18 June [meeting 91], the General Assembly, on the recommendation of the Fifth (Administrative and Budgetary) Committee [A/58/583/Add.1], adopted **resolution 58/259 B** without vote [agenda item 138].

Financing of the United Nations Organization Mission in the Democratic Republic of the Congo

The General Assembly,

Having considered the reports of the Secretary-General and his note on the financing of the United Nations Organization Mission in the Democratic Republic of the Congo and the related reports of the Advisory Committee on Administrative and Budgetary Questions,

Recalling Security Council resolutions 1258(1999) of 6 August 1999 and 1279(1999) of 30 November 1999 regarding, respectively, the deployment to the Congo region of military liaison personnel, and the establishment of the United Nations Organization Mission in the Democratic Republic of the Congo, and the subsequent resolutions by which the Council extended the mandate of the Mission, the latest of which was resolution 1493(2003) of 28 July 2003, by which the Council also authorized increasing the military strength of the Mission,

Recalling also its resolution 54/260 A of 7 April 2000 on the financing of the Mission, and its subsequent resolutions thereon, the latest of which was resolution 58/259 A of 23 December 2003,

Reaffirming the general principles underlying the financing of United Nations peacekeeping operations, as stated in General Assembly resolutions 1874(S-IV) of 27 June 1963, 3101(XXVIII) of 11 December 1973 and 55/235 of 23 December 2000,

Noting with appreciation that voluntary contributions have been made to the Mission,

Mindful of the fact that it is essential to provide the Mission with the necessary financial resources to en-

able it to fulfil its responsibilities under the relevant resolutions of the Security Council,

1. *Takes note* of the status of contributions to the United Nations Organization Mission in the Democratic Republic of the Congo as at 15 April 2004, including the contributions outstanding in the amount of 111.1 million United States dollars, representing some 6 per cent of the total assessed contributions, notes with concern that only thirty-six Member States have paid their assessed contributions in full, and urges all other Member States, in particular those in arrears, to ensure payment of their outstanding assessed contributions;

2. *Expresses its appreciation* to those Member States which have paid their assessed contributions in full, and urges all other Member States to make every possible effort to ensure payment of their assessed contributions to the Mission in full;

3. *Expresses concern* at the financial situation with regard to peacekeeping activities, in particular as regards the reimbursements to troop contributors that bear additional burdens owing to overdue payments by Member States of their assessments;

4. *Also expresses concern* at the delay experienced by the Secretary-General in deploying and providing adequate resources to some recent peacekeeping missions, in particular those in Africa;

5. *Emphasizes* that all future and existing peacekeeping missions shall be given equal and non-discriminatory treatment in respect of financial and administrative arrangements;

6. *Also emphasizes* that all peacekeeping missions shall be provided with adequate resources for the effective and efficient discharge of their respective mandates;

7. *Reiterates its request* to the Secretary-General to make the fullest possible use of facilities and equipment at the United Nations Logistics Base at Brindisi, Italy, in order to minimize the costs of procurement for the Mission;

8. *Endorses* the conclusions and recommendations contained in the reports of the Advisory Committee on Administrative and Budgetary Questions, subject to the provisions of the present resolution, and requests the Secretary-General to ensure their full implementation;

9. *Requests* the Secretary-General to take all necessary measures in order to improve the distribution of food rations in the Mission;

10. *Also requests* the Secretary-General, in the context of the comprehensive review of the organizational structure of the Mission, to consider the posts required for the election process;

11. *Authorizes* the Secretary-General to employ, if necessary, 17 additional staff, up to a total of 34, in the Office of Public Information for the purposes of the election process, within the approved budget level for 2004-2005, and to report thereon in the context of the next performance report of the Mission;

12. *Requests* the Secretary-General to present in his next budget proposal workload indicators for the international staff in the Office of Public Information;

13. *Also requests* the Secretary-General to take all necessary action to ensure that the Mission is administered with a maximum of efficiency and economy, particularly with regard to air transport;

14. *Further requests* the Secretary-General, in order to reduce the cost of employing General Service staff, to continue efforts to recruit local staff for the Mission

against General Service posts, commensurate with the requirements of the Mission;

Financial performance report for the period from 1 July 2002 to 30 June 2003

15. *Takes note* of the report of the Secretary-General on the financial performance of the Mission for the period from 1 July 2002 to 30 June 2003;

Budget estimates for the period from 1 July 2004 to 30 June 2005

16. *Decides* to appropriate to the Special Account for the United Nations Organization Mission in the Democratic Republic of the Congo the amount of 746,072,500 dollars for the period from 1 July 2004 to 30 June 2005, inclusive of 709,123,200 dollars for the maintenance of the Mission, 30,207,700 dollars for the support account for peacekeeping operations and 6,741,600 dollars for the United Nations Logistics Base;

Financing of the appropriation

17. *Decides also* to apportion among Member States the amount of 746,072,500 dollars at a monthly rate of 62,172,708 dollars, in accordance with the levels set out in General Assembly resolution 55/235, as adjusted by the Assembly in its resolution 55/236 of 23 December 2000 and updated in its resolution 58/256 of 23 December 2003, and taking into account the scale of assessments for 2004 and 2005, as set out in its resolution 58/1 B of 23 December 2003, subject to a decision of the Security Council to extend the mandate of the Mission;

18. *Decides further* that, in accordance with the provisions of its resolution 973(X) of 15 December 1955, there shall be set off against the apportionment among Member States, as provided for in paragraph 17 above, their respective share in the Tax Equalization Fund of 22,311,400 dollars, comprising the estimated staff assessment income of 17,523,300 dollars approved for the Mission, the prorated share of 4,408,300 dollars of the estimated staff assessment income approved for the support account and the prorated share of 379,800 dollars of the estimated staff assessment income approved for the United Nations Logistics Base;

19. *Decides* that for Member States that have fulfilled their financial obligations to the Mission, there shall be set off against their apportionment, as provided for in paragraph 17 above, their respective share of the unencumbered balance and other income in the total amount of 133,437,500 dollars in respect of the financial period ended 30 June 2003, in accordance with the levels set out in General Assembly resolution 55/235, as adjusted by the Assembly in its resolution 55/236 and its resolution 57/290 A of 20 December 2002, taking into account the scale of assessments for 2003 as set out in its resolutions 55/5 B of 23 December 2000 and 57/4 B of 20 December 2002;

20. *Decides also* that for Member States that have not fulfilled their financial obligations to the Mission, there shall be set off against their outstanding obligations their respective share of the unencumbered balance and other income in the total amount of 133,437,500 dollars in respect of the financial period ended 30 June 2003, in accordance with the scheme set out in paragraph 19 above;

21. *Decides further* that the increase in the estimated staff assessment income of 393,400 dollars in respect of the financial period ended 30 June 2003 shall be added to the credits from the amount referred to in paragraphs 19 and 20 above and that the respective shares of Member States therein shall be applied in accordance with the provisions of those paragraphs, as appropriate;

Financing of the appropriation for the period from 1 July 2003 to 30 June 2004

22. *Takes note* of the note by the Secretary-General on the financing arrangements for the Mission for the period from 1 July 2003 to 30 June 2004;

23. *Decides* to apportion among Member States the amount of 59,038,300 dollars already appropriated for the maintenance of the Mission for the period from 1 July 2003 to 30 June 2004 under the terms of General Assembly resolution 58/259 A, in accordance with the levels set out in Assembly resolution 55/235, as adjusted by the Assembly in its resolutions 55/236 and 57/290 A and updated in its resolution 58/256, taking into account the scale of assessments for 2003, as set out in its resolutions 55/5 B and 57/4 B, and the scale of assessments for 2004, as set out in its resolution 58/1 B;

24. *Decides also* that, in accordance with the provisions of its resolution 973(X), there shall be set off against the apportionment among Member States, as provided for in paragraph 23 above, their respective share in the Tax Equalization Fund of the estimated additional staff assessment income of 1,936,764 dollars approved for the Mission;

25. *Emphasizes* that no peacekeeping mission shall be financed by borrowing funds from other active peacekeeping missions;

26. *Encourages* the Secretary-General to continue to take additional measures to ensure the safety and security of all personnel under the auspices of the United Nations participating in the Mission;

27. *Invites* voluntary contributions to the Mission in cash and in the form of services and supplies acceptable to the Secretary-General, to be administered, as appropriate, in accordance with the procedure and practices established by the General Assembly;

28. *Decides* to include in the provisional agenda of its fifty-ninth session the item entitled "Financing of the United Nations Organization Mission in the Democratic Republic of the Congo".

On 23 December, the Assembly decided that the agenda item on the financing of MONUC would remain for consideration during its resumed fifty-ninth (2005) session (**decision 59/552**).

Arms embargo

In March, the Security Council, having considered the fourteenth report of the Secretary-General on MONUC [YUN 2003, p. 134], established a committee to review and monitor the arms embargo imposed by resolution 1493(2003) [ibid., p. 130] against armed groups operating in the DRC (see below).

SECURITY COUNCIL ACTION (March)

On 12 March [meeting 4926], the Security Council unanimously adopted **resolution 1533(2004)**.

The draft [S/2004/192] was prepared in consultations among Council members.

The Security Council,

Recalling its resolutions and the statements by its President concerning the Democratic Republic of the Congo,

Reiterating its concern regarding the presence of armed groups and militias in the eastern part of the Democratic Republic of the Congo, particularly in North and South Kivu and in Ituri, which perpetuates a climate of insecurity in the whole region,

Condemning the continuing illicit flow of weapons into the Democratic Republic of the Congo, and declaring its determination to monitor closely compliance with the arms embargo imposed by its resolution 1493(2003) of 28 July 2003,

Underscoring the right of the Congolese people to control their own natural resources, recalling in this regard the statement made by its President on 19 November 2003, which emphasizes the connection, in the context of the continuing conflict, between the illegal exploitation of natural resources and trafficking in raw materials and arms, as highlighted in the final report of the Panel of Experts on the Illegal Exploitation of Natural Resources and Other Forms of Wealth of the Democratic Republic of the Congo, and stressing for this purpose the need for all Member States to work to achieve an end to the illegal exploitation of natural resources,

Encouraging all States signatories to the Nairobi Declaration on the Problem of the Proliferation of Illicit Small Arms and Light Weapons in the Great Lakes Region and the Horn of Africa of 15 March 2000 to implement quickly the measures required by the Coordinated Agenda for Action, as an important means of support of the measures imposed by paragraph 20 of resolution 1493(2003),

Taking note of the fourteenth report of the Secretary-General on the United Nations Organization Mission in the Democratic Republic of the Congo, of 17 November 2003, and of the recommendations contained therein,

Noting that the situation in the Democratic Republic of the Congo continues to constitute a threat to international peace and security in the region,

Acting under Chapter VII of the Charter of the United Nations,

1. *Reaffirms* the demand, laid down in paragraph 20 of resolution 1493(2003), that all States take the necessary measures to prevent the supply of arms and any related materiel or assistance to armed groups operating in North and South Kivu and in Ituri, and to groups not party to the Global and All-Inclusive Agreement on the Transition in the Democratic Republic of the Congo, signed at Pretoria on 17 December 2002;

2. *Welcomes* the recommendations contained in paragraph 72 of the fourteenth report of the Secretary-General on the United Nations Organization Mission in the Democratic Republic of the Congo;

3. *Requests* the Mission to continue to use all means, within its capabilities, to carry out the tasks outlined in paragraph 19 of resolution 1493(2003), and in particular to inspect, without notice as it deems it necessary, the cargo of aircraft and of any transport vehicle using the ports, airports, airfields, military bases and border crossings in North and South Kivu and in Ituri;

4. *Authorizes* the Mission to seize or collect, as appropriate, the arms and any related materiel whose presence in the territory of the Democratic Republic of the Congo violates the measures imposed by paragraph 20 of resolution 1493(2003), and to dispose of such arms and related materiel as appropriate;

5. *Reiterates its demand* that all parties provide immediate, unconditional and unhindered access to Mission personnel, in accordance with paragraphs 15 and 19 of resolution 1493(2003), to enable them to carry out the tasks outlined in paragraphs 3 and 4 above;

6. *Reiterates its condemnation* of the continuing illegal exploitation of natural resources in the Democratic Republic of the Congo, especially in the eastern part of the country, which contributes to the perpetuation of the conflict, and reaffirms the importance of bringing to an end these illegal activities, including by applying the necessary pressure on the armed groups, traffickers and all other actors involved;

7. *Urges* all States, and especially those in the region, to take the appropriate steps to end these illegal activities, including through judicial means where possible, and, if necessary, to report to the Council;

8. *Decides* to establish, in accordance with rule 28 of its provisional rules of procedure, a Committee of the Security Council consisting of all members of the Council ("the Committee"), to undertake the following tasks:

(*a*) To seek from all States, and particularly those in the region, information regarding the actions taken by them to implement effectively the measures imposed by paragraph 20 of resolution 1493(2003) and to comply with paragraphs 18 and 24 of the same resolution, and thereafter to request from them whatever further information it may consider useful, including by providing States with an opportunity, at the request of the Committee, to send representatives to meet with the Committee for more in-depth discussion of relevant issues;

(*b*) To examine, and to take appropriate action on, information concerning alleged violations of the measures imposed by paragraph 20 of resolution 1493(2003) and information on alleged arms flows highlighted in the reports of the Panel of Experts on the Illegal Exploitation of Natural Resources and Other Forms of Wealth of the Democratic Republic of the Congo, identifying, where possible, individuals and legal entities reported to be engaged in such violations, as well as aircraft or other vehicles used;

(*c*) To present regular reports to the Council on its work, with its observations and recommendations, in particular on the ways to strengthen the effectiveness of the measures imposed by paragraph 20 of resolution 1493(2003);

(*d*) To consider the lists referred to in paragraph 10 (*g*) below with a view to submitting recommendations to the Council for possible future measures to be taken in this regard;

(*e*) To receive notifications in advance from States made under paragraph 21 of resolution 1493(2003) and to decide, if need be, upon any action to be taken;

9. *Requests* all States, in particular those in the region, to report to the Committee, within sixty days of the date of adoption of the present resolution, on the actions that they have taken to implement the measures

imposed by paragraph 20 of resolution 1493(2003), and authorizes the Committee thereafter to request from Member States whatever further information it may consider necessary;

10. *Requests* the Secretary-General, in consultation with the Committee, to establish, within thirty days of the date of adoption of the present resolution, and for a period expiring on 28 July 2004, a group of experts consisting of no more than four members ("the Group of Experts"), having the necessary skills to perform the following mandate:

(*a*) To examine and analyse information gathered by the Mission in the context of its monitoring mandate;

(*b*) To gather and analyse all relevant information in the Democratic Republic of the Congo, countries of the region and, as necessary, in other countries, in co-operation with the Governments of those countries, on flows of arms and related materiel, as well as networks operating in violation of the measures imposed by paragraph 20 of resolution 1493(2003);

(*c*) To consider and recommend, where appropriate, ways of improving the capabilities of interested States, in particular those of the region, to ensure that the measures imposed by paragraph 20 of resolution 1493(2003) are effectively implemented;

(*d*) To report to the Council in writing before 15 July 2004, through the Committee, on the implementation of the measures imposed by paragraph 20 of resolution 1493(2003), with recommendations in this regard;

(*e*) To keep the Committee frequently updated on its activities;

(*f*) To exchange with the Mission, as appropriate, information that might be of use in the fulfilment of its monitoring mandate as described in paragraphs 3 and 4 above;

(*g*) To provide the Committee, in its reports, with a list, with supporting evidence, of those found to have violated the measures imposed by paragraph 20 of resolution 1493(2003), and those found to have supported them in such activities, for possible future measures by the Council;

11. *Requests* the Special Representative of the Secretary-General for the Democratic Republic of the Congo to communicate, as appropriate, to the Security Council, through the Committee, information gathered by the Mission and, when possible, reviewed by the Group of Experts concerning supply of arms and related materiel to armed groups and militias and any possible presence of foreign military in the Democratic Republic of the Congo;

12. *Urges* all States, relevant United Nations bodies and, as appropriate, other organizations and interested parties, to cooperate fully with the Committee and with the Group of Experts and the Mission, in particular by supplying any information at their disposal on possible violations of the measures imposed by paragraph 20 of resolution 1493(2003);

13. *Calls upon* the international community, in particular the specialized international organizations concerned, to provide financial and technical assistance to the Government of the Democratic Republic of the Congo with a view to helping it to exercise effective control over its borders and its airspace;

14. *Decides* to remain actively seized of the matter.

Council members elected the Chairman and vice-chairmen of the Security Council Committee established pursuant to resolution 1533 (2004), as announced by the Council President on 8 April [S/2004/280].

In May and June, Honduras [S/AC.43/2004/17], Jordan [S/AC.43/2004/25], Kuwait [S/AC.43/2004/24], Norway [S/AC.43/2004/18], South Africa [S/AC.43/2004/9], Sweden [S/AC.43/2004/7] and the Syrian Arab Republic [S/AC.43/2004/19] informed the Committee of measures they had taken to comply with the requirements contained in paragraphs 18 and 24 of resolution 1533(2004).

Appointment of Group of Experts. The Secretary-General, on 21 April [S/2004/317] and 24 August [S/2004/677], informed the Council of the names of the four experts he had appointed to serve on the Group of Experts, in accordance with paragraph 10 of resolution 1533(2004) (above). On 21 September [S/2004/750], he informed the Council of the replacement of one of those members who was unable to assume his functions.

Report of Group of Experts. The Group of Experts on the DRC released its report on 15 July [S/2004/551]. The report described the political and military situation leading to the imposition and monitoring of the arms embargo established by resolution 1493(2003) [YUN 2003, p. 130], examined the elements that contributed to border porosity and arms trafficking, issues related to air transport and trafficking, aiding and abetting, the involvement of foreign forces and military alliances with uncontrolled armed groups.

The group noted that the transitional Government exerted little or no authority over extended parts of DRC's eastern border, whose porosity, permeability and permissibility constituted the most critical factor undermining its ability and that of the international community to monitor the flow of weapons and other illicit commodities into the country. Moreover, local, regional and international capacities, controls and surveillance were weak or totally inadequate. There was therefore ample opportunity to traffic weapons into the DRC overland, facilitated by the informal trading across the border, as well as by way of inter-State lakes and by aircraft using the more than 450 known airports and airfields, many of them in remote areas but long enough to accommodate medium-weight aircraft.

The Group examined the case of Rwandan support for the mutinous forces of Jules Mutebutsi and Laurent Nkunda. It concluded that Rwanda's violations involved direct and indirect support, in both the DRC and Rwanda, to those mutinous troops during their armed military operations against FARDC, allowing them to flee back into Rwanda where they regrouped and remained a latent threat to the DRC. Both Mr. Mutebutsi's and Mr. Nkunda's forces had looted areas of Bukavu, gaining $1 million to $3 million in cash for recruitment and for the payment and supply of troops. Prior to the outbreak of the Bukavu conflict, Rwandan officials also lent their support to General Nkunda on recruitment drives inside Rwanda. The Group of Experts confirmed reports that, from mid-May to June 2004, Rwandan troops had ordered the deforestation of the southern sector of the DRC's Virunga National Park. Rwanda's deployment to that area was in violation of the embargo. It also confirmed that Rwandan forces maintained positions in the Congolese border town of Bunagana and surroundings.

The Group noted that political and military alliances of convenience could be construed as violations of the arms embargo in giving direct or indirect support to groups not party to the Global and All-Inclusive Agreement or to an uncontrolled armed group operating out of Ituri and the Kivus, adding that the ambiguity of interpretation of the embargo needed to be clarified.

Among its recommendations, the Group called for Governments party to the Northern Corridor Transit Agreement to amend the Agreement to permit physical inspection of transit trade goods en route to areas under the exclusive domain of uncontrolled armed groups and other embargoed parties. To prevent all forms of assistance reaching the Ituri armed groups, it urged control of all inter-State trade with such groups, as well as commercial flights, until MONUC was able to deploy to those territories or the State extended its authority there.

Aware of Uganda's security concerns, the Group suggested that Uganda provide adequate protection so that it could deploy immigration and customs agents to its border areas with the DRC and strengthen its capacity to patrol Lake Albert and Lake Edward. Procedures at border crossings with areas controlled by Ituri armed groups should be enhanced by the presence of more accredited agents, tighter procedures on the declaration of goods to and from the DRC, improved inspection of goods entering areas controlled by Ituri armed groups and systematic registration of individuals exiting and entering Uganda.

In regard to Rwanda, the Group recommended the restoration of civilian oversight and monitoring of activities along its borders with the DRC, and the restriction of immigration, safe residence and freedom of movement of dissident or mutinous forces and other individuals allied with such forces except for international peace negotiations. The Group urged the Joint Verification Mechanism, as agreed by the 24 June summit in Abuja between Rwanda and the DRC (see p. 127), to begin its work. The Group said that the extension of the transitional authority throughout the DRC remained a prerequisite, which should be followed by unified governmental control of the borders in order to stem the flow of arms and other illicit commodities into the country. The control of movements in the air and on the ground should be improved by establishing an independent air-traffic services unit.

Pointing to the need to respect the civilian nature of refugee camps, in particular by abstaining from voluntary and forced recruitment within them, the Group called on Rwanda to prohibit recruitment drives and to expel Congolese who had conducted them. The disarmament, demobilization, repatriation, reintegration and resettlement mechanism would benefit from a donor-funded external verification mission to follow up on the status of demobilized soldiers after their return to Rwanda. Such a mission could ensure that demobilized soldiers were not being recruited to fight in the DRC. The Group also recommended that Mutebutsi's troops fleeing across the border be disarmed and cantoned and that the DRC and Rwanda reach an agreement on the fate of Mutebutsi and his troops.

Improvement of MONUC's monitoring and interdiction capacity could be achieved with appropriate lake patrol and air-surveillance capabilities, and more troops to monitor airports, areas under the control of the Ituri armed groups, Idjwi Island and other flashpoints along the DRC-Rwanda border.

The Group of Experts recommended the renewal of the arms embargo in the DRC for the period covering MONUC's next mandate. It added that monitoring of the embargo was essential to enhance its effectiveness.

Communications. The DRC, in a 21 July letter [S/2004/586], welcomed the Group's report which, it said, confirmed the DRC's views on the continued presence of the Rwandan Defence Forces on its territory, with the concealed motive of exploiting the natural resources in the DRC. It supported the recommendations and called on the Council to impose further sanctions targeted at the Rwandan leaders, including a travel ban, the freezing of their bank assets and an arms embargo.

In its reaction to the report, also of 21 July [S/2004/587], Rwanda refuted many of the statements contained therein. It said that the most serious threat to the region was the presence of the ex-FAR/Interahamwe, whereas the report focused on Mutebutsi and his men. The United Nations, Rwanda said, should work with regional States to strengthen their capacity in border control and customs procedures and operations. The Experts should have focused on those needs. On 26 July [S/2004/593], Rwanda expanded on its comments, stating that the Group of Experts had completely ignored or trivialized the information that Rwanda had provided, including responses to specific questions. Rwanda stated that the report therefore lacked credibility.

On 23 July [S/2004/591] and 27 July [S/2004/607], Uganda submitted its comments and observations on the report, particularly references to Uganda, which it denied, and factual errors, which, it said, were intended to portray Uganda in a bad light. Solutions to Congolese problems required strengthening regional cooperation and governmental structures, rather than inquiries by expert groups, it added.

SECURITY COUNCIL ACTION (July)

On 27 July [meeting 5011], the Security Council unanimously adopted **resolution 1552(2004)**. The draft [S/2004/594] was prepared in consultations among Council members.

The Security Council,

Recalling its resolutions and the statements by its President concerning the Democratic Republic of the Congo, in particular resolutions 1493(2003) of 28 July 2003 and 1533(2004) of 12 March 2004,

Reiterating its concern regarding the presence of armed groups and militias in the eastern part of the Democratic Republic of the Congo, particularly in the provinces of North and South Kivu and in the Ituri district, which perpetuates a climate of insecurity in the whole region,

Condemning the continuing illicit flow of weapons within and into the Democratic Republic of the Congo, and declaring its determination to monitor closely compliance with the arms embargo imposed by its resolution 1493(2003),

Taking note of the report and the recommendations, of 9 July 2004, of the Group of Experts referred to in paragraph 10 of resolution 1533(2004), transmitted by the Security Council Committee established in accordance with paragraph 8 of the same resolution (hereinafter "the Committee"),

Noting that the situation in the Democratic Republic of the Congo continues to constitute a threat to international peace and security in the region,

Acting under Chapter VII of the Charter of the United Nations,

1. *Reaffirms* the demands set out in paragraphs 15, 18 and 19 of resolution 1493(2003);

2. *Decides,* in the light of the failure of the parties to comply with those demands, to renew, until 31 July 2005, the provisions of paragraphs 20 to 22 of resolution 1493(2003) and all the provisions of resolution 1533(2004);

3. *Expresses its intention* to modify or to remove those provisions if it determines that the demands noted above have been satisfied;

4. *Decides* that it will review those measures by 1 October 2004, and periodically thereafter;

5. *Requests,* to this end, the Secretary-General, in consultation with the Committee, to re-establish, within thirty days of the date of adoption of the present resolution, and for a period expiring on 31 January 2005, the Group of Experts referred to in paragraph 10 of resolution 1533(2004);

6. *Requests* the Group of Experts to report to the Council in writing before 15 December 2004, through the Committee, on the implementation of the measures imposed by paragraph 20 of resolution 1493(2003), with recommendations in this regard, in particular regarding the lists provided for by paragraph 10 (*g*) of resolution 1533(2004);

7. *Decides* to remain actively seized of the matter.

Burundi

In 2004, the United Nations, through the United Nations Office in Burundi (UNOB), headed by the Special Representative of the Secretary-General for Burundi, continued to assist the parties (Jean Bosco Ndayikengurukiye's faction of the Conseil national pour la défense dela démocratie–Forces pour la défense de la démocratie (CNDD-FDD), Alain Mugabarabona's faction of the Parti pour la libération du peuple hutu–Forces nationales de libération (PALIPEHUTU-FNL), Pierre Nkurunziza's faction of the CNDD-FDD and Agathon Rwasa's Forces nationales de libération (FNL (Rwasa), also known as Palipehutu-FNL) in the implementation of the 2000 Arusha Agreement on Peace and Reconciliation [YUN 2000, p. 146], particularly its transition to full democratic governance. The Implementation Monitoring Committee, charged with supervising the implementation of the Agreement, met under the chairmanship of the United Nations. The Committee's subsidiary organ, the Joint Ceasefire Commission, established in 2003, coordinated and resolved military issues related to the implementation of the ceasefire agreements between and among the parties. The United Nations worked closely with the Great Lakes Regional Peace Initiative under the chairmanship of Uganda; the Facilitation, a regional peace initiative under the direction of South Africa's Deputy President, Jacob Zuma, and the Transitional Government, established in 2001 for a three-year period.

The security aspects were covered by the AU African Mission in Burundi (AMIB), established in 2003 to provide security for the cantonment of combatants and assist in the demobilization, disarmament and reintegration of armed groups. In May 2004, the Security Council established the

United Nations Operation in Burundi (ONUB), incorporating UNOB and AMIB, with a mandate to monitor ceasefire agreements, promote confidence between the Burundian forces through disarmament and demobilization measures, monitor the illegal flow of arms and the quartering of Burundi armed forces, assist the transitional Government in establishing safe conditions for providing humanitarian assistance, contribute to the electoral process, and protect civilians under threat and UN personnel and property. The Council extended ONUB's mandate until 1 June 2005.

Political and military developments

Follow-up to recommendations of 2003 mission

Forum of Burundi's Development Partners. Burundi forwarded to the Security Council President the final communiqué of the Forum of Burundi's Development Partners (Brussels, Belgium, 13-14 January) [S/2004/49].

Burundi's international partners pledged a total of 810 million euros ($1,032 million) to cover the priority programmes for the second phase of its transition, covering economic recovery, capacity-building for good governance, repatriation of refugees and rehabilitation of survivors, and the establishment of a new defence and security force. In its transmittal letter, Burundi requested the Council to ensure that the amounts pledged were disbursed and expressed its hope that the Council would strengthen the peace process by taking over the responsibilities of AMIB through a UN peacekeeping operation and provide assistance in combating impunity.

Netherlands ceasefire talks. Burundi also transmitted to the Council President the communiqué issued at the end of talks (Oisterwijk, Netherlands, 18-21 January) [S/2004/62] between President Domitien Ndayizeye and Ibrahim Ntakirutimana and his PALIPEHUTU-FNL delegation. The parties agreed on the establishment of an international commission of inquiry into the death of the Apostolic Nuncio, Archbishop Michael Courtney [S/2004/46]; ending the violence to create a climate of trust and an end to the clashes between PALIPEHUTU-FNL and CNDD-FDD; and to meet without delay to discuss matters related to the Burundi peace process. The Netherlands declared its readiness to assist the parties in pursuing the discussions and following up on the agreements reached.

Statement by Council President. In a 23 January statement [SC/7988-AFR/817], the Council President said that the Council welcomed the discussions and the role played by the Dutch Gov-

ernment. It noted the final communiqué signed by the parties and encouraged them to continue their discussions, with a view to a complete cessation of hostilities and PALIPEHUTU-FNL entering the transitional institutions.

EU statement. The EU, in a 27 January statement [S/2004/109], called on the Government of Burundi and FNL to hold a follow-up meeting at the earliest opportunity, to cease all hostilities and to conclude a ceasefire agreement.

Establishment of commission of inquiry. As recommended by the mission [YUN 2003, p. 149], the Security Council President, on 26 January [S/2004/72], responding to Burundi's 2002 request that the Council establish an international judicial commission of inquiry as provided for in the Arusha Agreement, affirmed the Council's agreement to request the Secretary-General to send an assessment mission to Burundi to consider the advisability and feasibility of establishing such a commission. The terms of reference of the mission, approved by the Council on 23 January, were annexed to the President's letter.

Report of Secretary-General. Reporting on those and other developments relating to the implementation of the recommendations pertaining to Burundi of the Council's 2003 mission to the Great Lakes region, the Secretary-General, in a 20 January report [S/2004/52], said that, in connection with the international community's assistance to AMIB, UN agencies and AMIB maintained regular consultations, and UN agencies in Bujumbura, with political guidance from UNOB, provided assistance in disarmament, demobilization and reintegration activities and security sector reform, in cooperation with AMIB and the Joint Ceasefire Commission (JCC). A new impetus was given to JCC activities with the arrival in Bujumbura of the representatives of CNDD-FDD (Nkurunziza) in December 2003. At the time of the report, all the parties except FNL (Rwasa) were represented in JCC. They visited the three proposed demobilization sites in December and January. JCC took formal decisions on those matters on 5 January.

The Secretary-General drew attention to the Forum of Burundi's Development Partners (see above), organized with UNDP assistance, and other UN initiatives to provide assistance to restore Burundi's economy. On the humanitarian side, the United Nations and its partners, in November 2003, launched the 2004 consolidated appeal for some $71 million for humanitarian needs.

Efforts continued to end impunity for human rights violations. However, the establishment of the Truth and Reconciliation Commission, which was expected to play a major role in the reconciliation process, was stalled in Parliament due to disagreement between the two major political groupings comprising the transitional institutions. The Field Office of the High Commissioner for Human Rights continued to monitor the human rights situation and to strengthen the judiciary.

UNOB provided support, both diplomatic and financial, to facilitate the regional peace initiative. Its efforts contributed to the comprehensive ceasefire agreement of 16 November 2003, signed by the Transitional Government and CNDD-FDD (Nkurunziza) [YUN 2003, p. 152]. That permitted CNDD-FDD (Nkurunziza) representatives to return to Bujumbura and participate in the transitional institutions. In his new year address, President Ndayizeye called on stakeholders to accelerate implementation, and CNDD-FDD (Nkurunziza) responded by announcing that it would have its combatants gathered in the assembly areas by 10 January 2004. On 6 January, the President signed a decree appointing 33 members of the joint military high command, 20 from the army and 13 from FDD (Nkurunziza).

Security Council consideration. At the Security Council's 17 February meeting [meeting 4911] to discuss the Secretary-General's report, the Assistant Secretary-General for Political Affairs, Tuliameni Kalomoh, said that significant progress had been achieved towards implementation of the Council mission's recommendations. The January meeting between President Ndayizeye and a high-level FNL (Rwasa) delegation in Oisterwijk (see p. 142) provided further grounds for optimism.

Many challenges lay ahead, as the transitional period was expected to end in November with elections. In that regard, a UN multidisciplinary reconnaissance mission was due to arrive in Bujumbura on 17 February to examine the situation on the ground and assess support for the Transitional Government.

Burundi told the Council that all that remained was to canton the CNDD-FDD combatants and to begin disarmament, demobilization and reintegration operations. The other movements were in the process of gathering their combatants, most of whom were returning to the DRC with MONUC's help. Only PALIPEHUTU-FNL remained outside the peace process, but it had met with the Transitional Government. Burundi urged the Council to send a peacekeeping mission to the country, a step it described as vital to the success of the Burundi peace process and which could help stabilize the Great Lakes region. Burundi welcomed the Council's request that the Secretary-General send a fact-finding mission to the country with a view to establishing an international judicial commission of inquiry.

It was also pleased with the role played by the Economic and Social Council's Ad Hoc Advisory Group on Burundi (see p. 912).

Multidisciplinary assessment mission

Report of Secretary-General (March). The Secretary-General, in response to presidential statement S/PRST/2003/30 [YUN 2003, p. 153], submitted on 16 March [S/2004/210] a report which contained the findings of his multidisciplinary assessment mission to Burundi (16-27 February) to examine UN support to the implementation of the Arusha Agreement. The mission observed the political, military, security, humanitarian and economic situations, as well as human rights and the status of implementation of the Agreement.

Reporting on the political situation, the mission observed that significant progress had been made towards ending hostilities. Most of the armed political parties and movements had joined the peace process, with the exception of FNL (Rwasa), which continued to reject the Arusha Agreement on the grounds that it was a power-sharing deal between political elites and did not address the plight of the disenfranchised, nor brought them into the process. Although it held meetings in January in the Netherlands with the Transitional Government (see p. 142), the group cancelled further meetings, citing ongoing hostilities. In the meantime, the deadline for joining the process imposed on FNL (Rwasa) by the Regional Peace Initiative in November 2003 [YUN 2003, p. 151] expired on 16 February. Fighting between FNL (Rwasa) and joint Burundian Armed Forces (FAB)/CNDD-FDD (Nkurunziza) elements continued, resulting in the Government refusing to end military action until FNL (Rwasa) agreed to negotiate with it, and the latter refusing to do so as long as the Government was waging military action against it. Meanwhile, members of the international community were attempting to bring FNL (Rwasa) into the process. Despite those difficulties, the mission found that progress had been made in achieving an all-inclusive peace process since the inauguration of the transitional Government in 2001 and that both sides seemed ready to open discussions if the right framework could be found.

The ceasefire was generally holding and major military operations had ceased throughout most of the country despite continuing operations against FNL (Rwasa), which harassed the capital from neighbouring Bujumbura Rurale. The security situation had also improved and calm had been restored to most provinces. However, ongoing hostilities between FAB/CNDD-FDD (Nkurunziza) in Bujumbura Rurale continued to seriously affect security in those areas, forcing the capital to remain under curfew. Criminality had increased, aided by the large number of weapons in circulation and the Government's inability to control the situation.

The civil conflict in Burundi had led to massive refugee flows, much internal displacement and the disruption of daily life over the decade of conflict. Currently, there were 320,000 Burundians living in camps in the United Republic of Tanzania, and an estimated 281,000 internally displaced persons at 230 sites. Reports indicated that large numbers of internally displaced persons had begun returning to their original locations in recent months, but their return, as well as that of refugees, constituted a major humanitarian challenge in the coming months. The re-establishment of sustainable livelihoods would, however, require a shift in emphasis by the international community from humanitarian assistance and emergency interventions to recovery programming.

The human rights situation in Burundi had not improved much in recent months. Summary executions of civilians had decreased, but torture and illegal and arbitrary detention persisted. The civilian population, especially the elderly, women and children, were the primary victims of the acts of violence, which were committed with impunity. Incidents of rape were on the rise and individuals accused of witchcraft were killed by mobs. The incapacity of the judicial system to act in a timely and impartial manner remained a matter of grave concern. The Office of the United Nations High Commissioner for Human Rights (OHCHR) maintained its office in Burundi for monitoring, investigating and promoting human rights, with a reduced staff of three, down from 23 in 1999.

Implementation of the Arusha Agreement had accelerated since the integration of the armed groups into the Transitional Government, and the working relationship between the parties had been more cooperative in recent months. Further progress was needed in security sector reform, judicial reform, adoption of legal instruments and the organization of elections, in view of the end of the transitional period set for 31 October. While the United Nations was following up on Burundi's request for an assessment mission (see p. 142) to advise on the establishment of an international judicial commission of inquiry, with the exception of the law on genocide, very few of the other measures called for in the Arusha Agreement had been implemented.

To facilitate the integration process, the Government had established a National Commission for Demobilization, Reinsertion and Reintegration and an Executive Secretariat. In February, the Commission completed the preparation of a national demobilization, reinsertion and reintegration programme costing $84.4 million, to be financed through the World Bank.

With less than eight months left in the transitional period, the organization of credible elections represented one of the greatest political and practical challenges ahead. The Transitional Government anticipated holding *colline* elections in July, commune elections in August and parliamentary and presidential elections in October. However, the legal framework for elections had not yet been adopted. Proposals had been drawn up for the post-transition constitution, the electoral code, the law on political parties and the law on the reorganization of communal administration. Legislation on elections was needed to continue the planning, and a civic education campaign and registration of voters would be required. Another obstacle was the cantonment of armed forces, which had stalled, thereby preventing those groups from registering as political parties.

UNOB, headed by the Special Representative of the Secretary-General, Berhanu Dinka, continued to work with the Regional Initiative on Burundi, under the chairmanship of Uganda, in moving the peace process forward, and with the Facilitation, under the leadership of the Deputy President of South Africa, Jacob Zuma, in its work to bring about a comprehensive ceasefire. The Implementation Monitoring Committee, mandated by the Arusha Agreement to monitor, supervise and ensure implementation of the Agreement, under the chairmanship of the United Nations, held its seventeenth session from 10 to 13 February, at which it continued to press for a post-transition constitution and the electoral law. JCC, a subsidiary body of the Committee, worked on military issues relating to the ceasefire agreements. In January, the Commission approved the site for the two demobilization centres and 11 pre-disarmament assembly areas. AMIB, the AU peacekeeping mission, with a strength of 2,523 troops and 43 military observers as at February, served to stabilize the situation in Burundi and gave confidence to the armed groups to begin the assembly and cantonment process; however, it suffered from a lack of funds and logistic support, preventing it from fully implementing its mandate.

The Secretary-General also made recommendations for reinforcing the UN role in Burundi (see p. 145).

Establishment of ONUB

Report of Secretary-General. The Secretary-General, in his March report on Burundi

[S/2004/210], said that, in view of the expressed readiness of the parties to cooperate in a spirit of national reconciliation and the significant progress made to date, the assessment mission to Burundi concluded that the UN role there could be expanded to provide the support required to consolidate the peace process. The election of a new Government was scheduled for 31 October, at which time the transition process would end. Because of the serious financial and logistical difficulties facing AMIB, the AU, on 17 March [S/2004/270], had requested UN assistance in taking over and expanding its presence in Burundi. That request was strongly supported by the Government of Burundi [S/2004/208]. The Secretary-General therefore recommended that the Council authorize the deployment of a multidimensional UN peacekeeping operation (the United Nations Mission in Burundi (ONUB) to support the peace process.

The operation would be headed by a Special Representative of the Secretary-General, who would chair the Implementation Monitoring Committee. JCC would report directly to the Force Commander. The Deputy Special Representative would serve concurrently as United Nations Resident Coordinator and Humanitarian Coordinator. The Mission would comprise a military component based on the reassignment of AMIB, with a total troop strength of 5,650 all ranks, including 200 military observers and 125 headquarters staff, as well as a civilian component, which would build on current UNOB capabilities, to monitor and provide security at predisarmament assembly sites, collect and secure weapons, monitor the cantonment of FAB elements and weapons, and participate in joint liaison teams of JCC to monitor the disarmament and disbanding of militia groups by the Transitional Government. It would also be responsible for protecting UN personnel, equipment and facilities. The Secretary-General suggested that the force be deployed under robust rules of engagement and that an "over-the-horizon" force be established.

The civilian police component would support the preparation of a comprehensive plan for the integration and development of the Burundi National Police. There would also be a security sector reform and disarmament, demobilization, reinsertion and reintegration component, a rule of law and civil affairs component, an electoral component, a human rights component, and a public information component. The Mission would cooperate closely with MONUC in the DRC, particularly on gathering information on cross-border movements of armed elements and arms trafficking.

The Secretary-General said that a Council decision was needed soon, in view of the expiration of the AMIB mandate on 2 April and the planned elections. The force should remain in place after the elections and its mandate should be reviewed within the following six months. As a first priority, the Secretary-General called on the Government and FNL (Rwasa) to immediately cease hostilities and enter into dialogue with a view to becoming part of the peace process.

The Secretary-General informed the Council that the financial implications of deploying ONUB would amount to some $418 million for a 12-month period [S/2004/210/Add.1], and of his intention to immediately begin planning and preparations for the Mission [S/2004/274]. On 1 April [S/2004/275], the Council, without prejudice to any decision it might take on establishing such an operation, approved his proposal.

The AU Peace and Security Council, at its second session (Addis Ababa, 25 March) [S/2004/261], adopted a communiqué on Burundi in which it urged the UN Security Council to authorize the early deployment of a UN peacekeeping mission as the Secretary-General had recommended. In the meantime, it decided to renew the AMIB mandate for one month, until 2 May, on the understanding that the Council would deploy a peacekeeping mission in Burundi before the end of the new mandate. The AU appealed to PALIPEHUTU-FNL (Rwasa) to work towards a ceasefire agreement with the Transitional Government and to join the peace process.

Burundi, on 21 April [S/2004/316], expressed concerns about the preparations for the deployment of the peacekeeping mission in Burundi and hoped that they would be reflected in the draft resolution that was being prepared, especially regarding the task of the mission to create favourable conditions for the investigative work of the International Judicial Commission of Inquiry and the National Truth and Reconciliation Commission, which were important for the peace process. Noting that armed groups had crossed into Burundi from both the DRC and the United Republic of Tanzania, Burundi stated that the future peacekeeping mission should not include any nationals from its immediate neighbours. Burundi expected the Council to accept the Secretary-General's proposals concerning ONUB.

SECURITY COUNCIL ACTION (May)

On 21 May [meeting 4975], the Security Council unanimously adopted **resolution 1545(2004)**. The draft [S/2004/410] was prepared in consultations among Council members.

The Security Council,

Recalling its resolutions as well as the statements by its President on Burundi, in particular its resolution 1375(2001) of 29 October 2001 and the statements by its President of 18 December 2002 and 22 December 2003,

Reaffirming its strong commitment to the respect of the sovereignty, independence, territorial integrity and unity of Burundi, and recalling the importance of the principles of good-neighbourliness and non-interference, and of regional cooperation,

Reaffirming its full support for the process of the Arusha Peace and Reconciliation Agreement for Burundi, signed at Arusha, United Republic of Tanzania, on 28 August 2000 (hereinafter "the Arusha Agreement"), calling upon all the Burundian parties to honour fully their commitments, and assuring them of its determination to support their efforts to that end,

Encouraging in particular the transitional institutions of Burundi to enact without delay the laws and regulations required for the organization of the electoral process under the Arusha Agreement, so that this process can take place before the expiration of the transitional period on 31 October 2004,

Taking note with satisfaction of the ceasefire agreement signed on 7 October 2002 by the Transitional Government of Burundi with the Forces pour la défense de la démocratie of Mr. Jean Bosco Ndayikengurukiye and the Parti pour la libération du peuple hutu-Forces nationales de libération of Mr. Alain Mugabarabona, as well as the Global Ceasefire Agreement signed on 16 November 2003 at Dar-es-Salaam, United Republic of Tanzania, between the Transitional Government and the Conseil national pour la défense de la démocratie-Forces pour la défense de la démocratie of Mr. Pierre Nkurunziza,

Reiterating its concern at the continuing hostilities in certain parts of the country, underlining that there cannot be a military solution to Burundi's problems, urging all the parties to observe an immediate ceasefire, and stressing the importance attached to the Parti pour la libération du peuple hutu-Forces nationales de libération of Mr. Agathon Rwasa, the last armed movement that has still not done so, participating in the peace process of the Arusha Agreement,

Taking note in this regard of the talks which were started between the President of the Republic of Burundi, Mr. Domitien Ndayizeye, and this armed movement at the meeting held at Oisterwijk, the Netherlands, from 18 to 21 January 2004, as well as the congress held at Kigoma, United Republic of Tanzania, from 18 to 21 April 2004 by the Parti pour la libération du peuple hutu-Forces nationales de libération of Mr. Agathon Rwasa, and urging the latter to conclude an agreement with the Transitional Government without delay with a view to a complete cessation of hostilities and its participation in the transitional institutions,

Condemning all acts of violence, as well as human rights and international humanitarian law violations, and particularly concerned by the increasing incidents of rape, including mass rapes,

Reaffirming its determination to support the efforts of Burundians to bring the perpetrators of such acts and violations to justice on the basis of the rule of law in order to put an end to situations of impunity, and call-ing upon the parties and transitional authorities to take without delay all necessary measures to that end,

Expressing its concern at the tragic humanitarian situation of a large majority of the Burundian population, recalling that all the parties are responsible for the security of the civilian populations, and recalling in particular, in this regard, its resolution 1325(2000) of 31 October 2000 on women and peace and security, its resolutions 1379(2001) of 20 November 2001, 1460(2003) of 30 January 2003 and 1539(2004) of 22 April 2004 on children and armed conflict, and its resolutions 1265(1999) of 17 September 1999 and 1296(2000) of 19 April 2000 on the protection of civilians in armed conflict,

Taking note of the progress achieved in preparing the disarmament, demobilization and reintegration programme for the combatants, calling upon the parties to commit themselves firmly to that programme without delay, and encouraging the international financial institutions and donors to support the programme,

Expressing its concern at the deteriorating economic situation in Burundi in the context of the conflict, and recognizing that any improvement in security should be matched by tangible economic and social benefits for the population,

Considering that the voluntary and sustainable return of refugees and internally displaced persons will be a critical factor for the consolidation of the peace process, and will require a just solution of the issue of land ownership,

Welcoming the conclusions of the Forum of Burundi's Development Partners, which was held at Brussels on 13 and 14 January 2004, and calling upon donors to honour their pledges,

Paying tribute to the efforts made by the African Union as well as by the States which are members of the Regional Initiative, especially Uganda and the United Republic of Tanzania, and the Facilitation, in particular South Africa, to bring peace to Burundi, and encouraging the African Union to maintain a strong presence in Burundi to accompany the efforts of the Burundian parties, as specified in the Arusha Agreement and subsequent agreements,

Welcoming the efforts of the African Mission in Burundi and the contingents from South Africa, Ethiopia and Mozambique which make it up, as well as the Member States which have assisted the Mission in its deployment,

Encouraging the efforts being undertaken to train a joint Burundian protection unit to ensure continuing security of the leaders of the transitional institutions, and underlining the need for that unit to be operational as soon as possible,

Taking note of the statements made before the Council by the President of Burundi on 22 September 2003 and by the Deputy President of the Republic of South Africa, Mr. Jacob Zuma, on 4 December 2003, in favour of transforming the African Mission in Burundi into a United Nations peacekeeping operation, and taking note also, in that regard, of the letter dated 15 March 2004 from Mr. Thérence Sinunguruza, Minister for Foreign Affairs and Cooperation of Burundi, addressed to the President of the Security Council, as well as the letter dated 17 March 2004 from Mr. Alpha Oumar Konaré, Chairperson of the Commission of the African Union, addressed to the Secretary-General,

Aware of the difficulty of sustaining stability in Burundi unless peace is restored beyond its borders, in particular in the Democratic Republic of the Congo, and underlining how important it is for all the States concerned, especially those of the region, to cooperate towards that end, and for the United Nations to coordinate its efforts in the two countries,

Having considered the report of the Secretary-General on Burundi,

Welcoming with satisfaction and encouraging the efforts of the United Nations to enhance the awareness of peacekeeping personnel of the need to prevent and combat HIV/AIDS and other communicable diseases,

Noting that obstacles remain to Burundi's stability, and determining that the situation in that country continues to constitute a threat to international peace and security in the region,

Acting under Chapter VII of the Charter of the United Nations,

1. *Welcomes* the recommendations contained in the report of the Secretary-General on Burundi;

2. *Decides* to authorize, for an initial period of six months as from 1 June 2004, with the intention to renew it for further periods, the deployment of a peacekeeping operation called the United Nations Operation in Burundi (the acronym ONUB to be used in all languages), pursuant to the mandate specified in paragraphs 5 to 7 below, in order to support and help to implement the efforts undertaken by Burundians to restore lasting peace and bring about national reconciliation, as provided under the Arusha Agreement;

3. *Decides also* that ONUB shall be headed by the Special Representative of the Secretary-General for Burundi, who chairs the Implementation Monitoring Committee of the Arusha Agreement, and shall initially be composed of existing forces of the African Mission in Burundi, and therefore requests the Secretary-General, acting in liaison with the African Union, to ensure the transfer of authority over the Mission, within the framework of ONUB, to his Special Representative;

4. *Decides further* that ONUB shall consist of a maximum of 5,650 military personnel, including 200 observers and 125 staff officers, and up to 120 civilian police personnel, as well as the appropriate civilian personnel;

5. *Authorizes* ONUB to use all necessary means to carry out the following mandate, within its capacity and in the areas where its armed units are deployed, and in coordination with humanitarian and development communities:

(*a*) To ensure the respect of the ceasefire agreements, by monitoring implementation and investigating violations of those agreements;

(*b*) To promote the re-establishment of confidence between the Burundian forces present, monitor and provide security at their pre-disarmament assembly sites, collect and secure weapons and materiel to dispose of it as appropriate, and contribute to the dismantling of militias as called for in the ceasefire agreements;

(*c*) To carry out the disarmament and demobilization portions of the national programme of disarmament, demobilization and reintegration of combatants;

(*d*) To monitor the quartering of the Armed Forces of Burundi and their heavy weapons, as well as the disarmament and demobilization of the elements that need to be disarmed and demobilized;

(*e*) To monitor, to the extent possible, the illegal flow of arms across the national borders, including Lake Tanganyika, in cooperation with the United Nations Organization Mission in the Democratic Republic of the Congo and, as appropriate, with the group of experts referred to in paragraph 10 of resolution 1533(2004) of 12 March 2004;

(*f*) To contribute to the creation of the necessary security conditions for the provision of humanitarian assistance and facilitate the voluntary return of refugees and internally displaced persons;

(*g*) To contribute to the successful completion of the electoral process stipulated in the Arusha Agreement by ensuring a secure environment for free, transparent and peaceful elections to take place;

(*h*) Without prejudice to the responsibility of the Transitional Government of Burundi, to protect civilians under imminent threat of physical violence;

(*i*) To ensure the protection of United Nations personnel, facilities, installations and equipment, as well as the security and freedom of movement of ONUB personnel, and to coordinate and conduct, as appropriate, mine action activities in support of its mandate;

6. *Decides* that ONUB shall provide advice and assistance, within its capacity and subject to carrying out tasks stipulated in paragraph 5 above, to the Transitional Government and authorities to contribute to their efforts:

(*a*) To monitor Burundi's borders, with special attention to refugees, as well as to movements of combatants, especially in the Cibitoké province;

(*b*) To carry out institutional reforms as well as the constitution of the integrated national defence and internal security forces and, in particular, the training and monitoring of the police, while ensuring that they are democratic and fully respect human rights and fundamental freedoms;

(*c*) To proceed with electoral activities;

(*d*) To complete implementation of the reform of the judiciary and correction system, in accordance with the Arusha Agreement;

(*e*) To ensure, in close liaison with the Office of the United Nations High Commissioner for Human Rights, the promotion and protection of human rights, with particular attention to women, children and vulnerable persons, and investigate human rights violations to put an end to impunity;

7. *Decides also* that ONUB shall cooperate with the Government and authorities of Burundi, as well as their international partners, to ensure the coherence of their work, in assisting the Government and authorities of Burundi in:

(*a*) Extending State authority and utilities throughout the territory, including civilian police and judicial institutions;

(*b*) Carrying out the national programme of disarmament, demobilization and reintegration of combatants and members of their families, including those coming from the territory of the Democratic Republic of the Congo, in liaison with the Government of that country and the United Nations Organization Mission in the Democratic Republic of the Congo, and with particular attention to the specific needs of women and children;

8. *Requests* the Secretary-General, through his Special Representative for Burundi, to conduct all the activities of the United Nations system in Burundi and to facilitate the coordination with other national, regional and international actors, in particular the African Union, of activities in support of the transition process, while ensuring that ONUB personnel give special attention to issues related to gender equality, as well as to the specific needs of children;

9. *Also requests* the Secretary-General to conclude agreements with States neighbouring Burundi to enable ONUB forces to cross their respective borders in pursuit of armed combatants, as may be necessary while carrying out their mandate;

10. *Requests* the Transitional Government of Burundi to conclude a status-of-forces agreement for ONUB with the Secretary-General within thirty days of the adoption of the present resolution, taking into consideration General Assembly resolution 58/82 of 9 December 2003 on the scope of legal protection under the Convention on the Safety of United Nations and Associated Personnel, and notes that, pending the conclusion of such an agreement, the model status-of-forces agreement for peacekeeping operations of 9 October 1990 shall apply provisionally;

11. *Requests* all parties to cooperate fully with the deployment and operations of ONUB, in particular by ensuring the safety and freedom of movement of United Nations and associated personnel, as well as the personnel of humanitarian, development and aid organizations, throughout the territory of Burundi;

12. *Recalls* its resolution 1502(2003) of 26 August 2003, reaffirms the obligation of all parties to comply fully with the rules and principles of international humanitarian law applicable to them related to the protection of humanitarian and United Nations personnel, and urges all those concerned to allow full, unimpeded access by humanitarian personnel to all people in need of assistance as set forth in applicable international humanitarian law;

13. *Requests* all parties and concerned States to facilitate the voluntary, safe and sustainable return of refugees and internally displaced persons, and to cooperate fully to this end with ONUB and the relevant international organizations;

14. *Underlines* the need for ONUB to have at its disposal an effective public information capacity, including through local and national radio, television and newspaper channels, to promote understanding of the peace process and the role of ONUB among local communities and the parties;

15. *Stresses* the importance of the full and unconditional implementation of the Arusha Agreement, and demands that all parties fulfil their obligations under that agreement in order to allow the electoral process, in particular the legislative elections, to take place before 31 October 2004;

16. *Reaffirms* the need for all parties to complete in a timely manner the execution of the programme for the regrouping and cantonment of combatants and to begin implementing as soon as possible the programme to dismantle all armed groups, including the militias, and the disarmament, demobilization and reintegration programme, giving particular attention to the specific needs of women and children, and to pro-

ceed as well, in parallel, with the restructuring of the armed forces and the internal security forces;

17. *Reaffirms also* the continued need to promote peace and national reconciliation and to foster accountability and respect for human rights in Burundi, and urges the Government of Burundi, specialized agencies, other multilateral organizations, civil society and Member States to accelerate their efforts to establish the Truth and Reconciliation Commission, as provided for in the Arusha Agreement;

18. *Expresses its deep concern* over the illicit flow of arms to armed groups and movements, in particular those which are not parties to the peace process under the Arusha Agreement, calls upon all States to halt that flow without prejudice to the Burundian national army and police forces whose integration is in progress, and expresses its intention to consider this issue further as soon as possible after the deployment of ONUB;

19. *Urges* the international financial institutions and the donor community to continue to contribute to the economic development of Burundi, in particular for the long term, including through the realization of pledges already made, to enable that country to achieve sustainable stability, and in order also to contribute to the wider stability of the region;

20. *Requests* the Secretary-General to ensure that his Special Representatives for Burundi and for the Democratic Republic of the Congo coordinate the activities of ONUB and the United Nations Organization Mission in the Democratic Republic of the Congo, share military information at their disposal, in particular concerning cross-border movements of armed elements and arms trafficking, and pool their logistic and administrative resources, to an extent that does not affect the ability to carry out their respective mandates, in order to maximize efficiency and cost-effectiveness;

21. *Decides* that ONUB shall carry out its mandate in close cooperation with the Mission, in particular concerning monitoring and prevention of movements of combatants across the border between Burundi and the Democratic Republic of the Congo, as well as the implementation of the disarmament and demobilization programmes;

22. *Requests* the Secretary-General to keep the Council informed on a regular basis of developments in the situation in Burundi, the implementation of the Arusha Agreement and the execution of the mandate of ONUB and to submit a report on those developments every three months, including an evaluation of the strength of the military component, with a view to its adjusted reduction, taking account of the progress made on the ground and the tasks remaining to be accomplished;

23. *Decides* to remain actively seized of the matter.

Appointments. The Secretary-General, on 24 May [S/2004/433], informed the Security Council of his intention to appoint Carolyn McAskie (Canada) as his Special Representative for Burundi and Head of ONUB, replacing Berhanu Dinka (Ethiopia). The Council took note of the appointment on 28 May [S/2004/434]. Similarly, on 16 July [S/2004/583], the Secretary-General informed the Council of his nomination of Major

General Derrick Mbuyiselo Mgwebi (South Africa), formerly AMIB Force Commander, as ONUB Force Commander. The Council took note of that information on 21 July [S/2004/584].

Communications (May and July). In a statement forwarded to the Security Council on 28 May [S/2004/448], the EU welcomed the establishment of ONUB and called on PALIPEHUTU-FNL to seize the opportunity for peace. It encouraged the Regional Peace Initiative on Burundi (see below), in particular Uganda, the United Republic of Tanzania and South Africa, to continue the efforts to support the transition in Burundi. In another statement of 19 July [S/2004/608], the EU reiterated its support, particularly regarding financial support, for the disarmament, demobilization and reintegration process and the reform of the defence and security forces of Burundi. It called for the electoral process to be set in motion and considered that the urgent establishment of the Independent National Electoral Commission, the adoption of the electoral code and communal law, and the adoption of the post-transition constitution would start the process rapidly and definitively.

Regional Peace Initiative

The Great Lakes Regional Peace Initiative on Burundi, at its twenty-first summit (Dar es Salaam, 5 June), discussed the elections scheduled for October and the non-participation of PALIPEHUTU-FNL in the peace process. In a communiqué transmitted on 8 June [S/2004/471], the summit directed that the electoral process start without further delay with a view to holding elections by 31 October, as stipulated in the Arusha Agreement, and mandated the Facilitator, Deputy President Zuma, to help the Government and the Burundi parties to reach a compromise on outstanding issues relating to power-sharing. Noting that the continued intransigence of PALIPEHUTU-FNL posed an obstacle to the peace process, the summit urged the AU Peace and Security Council to recommend appropriate political and legal action within three months and called on PALIPEHUTU-FNL to take advantage of that time period and join the peace process. It decided to impose restrictions on the movement of that group's leaders and invited the international community to do likewise. The summit mandated the Chairperson of the Regional Initiative, Ugandan President Yoweri Museveni, to approach the United Nations for assistance in providing protection services for Burundi leaders who requested it.

The AU Peace and Security Council, at its twelfth meeting (Addis Ababa, 4 July) [S/2004/561], endorsed the decision of the Regional Initiative summit to extend the deadline for PALIPEHUTU-FNL to join the peace process by three months and to impose restrictions on the movements of its members.

At its twenty-second summit meeting (Dar es Salaam, 18 August) [S/2004/665], the Regional Peace Initiative took note of the consultations on power-sharing held in Pretoria and Bujumbura between the Burundi parties, and endorsed the power-sharing agreement concluded in Pretoria on 6 August as the appropriate mechanism for ensuring ethnic balance. It endorsed their acknowledgement that the provisions of the Arusha Agreement be incorporated in the Burundi constitution and in all other relevant legislation. It invited the Transitional Government to ensure that the Independent Electoral Commission was in place by 29 August and that the National Assembly decide on the draft constitution three weeks later, failing which it should be submitted to a referendum or to the Implementation Monitoring Committee.

The summit condemned the terrorist attack against the UN refugee camp in Gatumba, Burundi, on 13 August (see below). In the light of recent incidents and of the refusal of PALIPEHUTU-FNL to renounce violence and participate in the peace process, the summit declared PALIPEHUTU-FNL a terrorist organization.

Gatumba massacre

On 14 August [S/2004/652], Rwanda issued a communiqué expressing its shock and horror at the massacre of more than 150 Congolese Banyamulenge refugees at the UNHCR transit camp at Gatumba on the night of 13 August. Information available indicated that the attack was perpetrated by a combined force of ex-FAR/Interahamwe and Mayi-Mayi from the DRC, in cooperation with PALIPEHUTU-FNL elements.

Rwanda added that, during and following the May/June events in Bukavu (see p. 124), Banyamulenge refugees in Rwanda and Burundi affirmed that they had fled targeted massacres against them by DRC armed forces under the command of Mbuza Mabe, acting in concert with ex-FAR/Interahamwe. Rwanda expressed concern that for 10 years the international community refused to disarm the ex-FAR/Interahamwe, the force that committed the genocide in Rwanda, or to take any decisive action against them. Rwanda again called on the international community to take action against the incipient ethnic cleansing in the region, especially in eastern DRC. It called for the forcible disarmament, demobilization and repatriation of the ex-FAR/Interahamwe currently deployed along Rwanda's border and in many cases co-located with DRC armed forces.

As the Secretary-General reported in his 25 August report [S/2004/682] (see p. 151), the massacre occurred after a period of escalating tension in Bujumbura Rurale, while other areas of the country were relatively stable. The instability in the area ignited with the Gatumba massacre. An investigation of the event by the United Nations yielded inconclusive results (see below).

SECURITY COUNCIL ACTION (August)

On 15 August [meeting 5021], following consultations among Security Council members, the President made statement **S/PRST/2004/30** on behalf of the Council:

The Security Council condemns with the utmost firmness the massacre of refugees from the Democratic Republic of the Congo which occurred on the territory of Burundi, in Gatumba, on 13 August 2004.

The Council requests the Special Representative of the Secretary-General for Burundi, in close contact with the Special Representative of the Secretary-General for the Democratic Republic of the Congo, to establish the facts and report on them to the Council as quickly as possible.

The Council calls upon the authorities of Burundi and of the Democratic Republic of the Congo to cooperate actively so that the perpetrators and those responsible for those crimes can be brought to justice without delay.

The Council calls upon all States in the region to ensure that the territorial integrity of their neighbours is respected. It recalls in this respect the declaration of principles on good-neighbourly relations and cooperation adopted in New York on 25 September 2003. It encourages them to redouble their efforts in order to provide security for the civilian populations on their territory, including for the foreigners to whom they grant refuge.

The Council requests the United Nations Operation in Burundi and the United Nations Organization Mission in the Democratic Republic of the Congo to offer their assistance to the Burundian and Congolese authorities with a view to facilitating the investigation and to strengthening the security of vulnerable populations.

Communications. The AU Peace and Security Council, at its fifteenth meeting (Addis Ababa, 17 August) [S/2004/656], condemned the massacre and stressed the need to establish the Joint DRC/ Rwanda Verification Mechanism. The Council recalled its decision of 4 July calling for an examination of PALIPEHUTU/FNL activities and reiterated its appeal to AU member States to impose, with immediate effect, restrictions on the movement of their leaders and members, as recommended by the twenty-first summit of the Regional Peace Initiative (see p. 149).

The Fourteenth Ministerial Conference of the Non-Aligned Movement (Durban, South Africa, 19 August) [S/2004/694] supported the Regional Peace Initiative's decision (see p. 149) to declare PALIPEHUTU-FNL, which had claimed responsibility for the massacre, a terrorist organization, and urged the United Nations and the AU to reinforce that position. It also supported the proposal to conduct an international investigation into the massacre.

Reports on investigation into massacre. On 3 September [S/2005/6], the Security Council received a preliminary oral report on the ongoing investigation, conducted by MONUC, ONUB and OHCHR, of the massacre committed in the refugee camp at Gatumba. Council members, reaffirming their condemnation of the attack on defenceless refugees, expressed their expectation that they would soon receive a final report on the investigation.

On 15 October [S/2004/821], the Secretary-General transmitted to the Council the joint report on the Gatumba massacre (see above), as it had requested in presidential statement S/PRST/ 2004/30 (see above). According to the report, despite an extensive investigation, the UN team was unable to conclusively identify who authorized, financed or carried out the killings. Nevertheless, sufficient information was collected to warrant further investigation. Evidence pointed to PALIPEHUTU-FNL, the only group claiming responsibility, as probably having participated in the massacre but unlikely to have done so on its own. Evidence of other groups' participation was credible but could not be confirmed. The attack, apparently ethnically and politically motivated, targeted Banyamulenge refugees from the DRC who had fled fighting there in June. The Banyamulenge were viewed as pro-Rwanda by many, even though they participated on both sides of the fighting in June. The Governments of Burundi and Rwanda, as well as the Munyamulenge Vice-President of the DRC, charged that the refugees were killed by an alliance of anti-Tutsi groups based in eastern DRC, which might have included elements of FARDC, members of a Rwandan Hutu rebel group partly composed of ex-FAR/ Interahamwe and Mayi-Mayi. The UN team investigated all leads but was unable to find conclusive evidence.

The massacre was committed at a critical moment in the peace processes in both the DRC and Burundi and threatened to scuttle both. Information suggesting the potential involvement of one or more actors in the DRC warranted a continuation of the investigation. The team collected sufficient information about the crime to recommend a thorough judicial inquiry at both the national level, led by Burundi, and the international level, led by the International Criminal Court (ICC).

The team recommended that the Council encourage the immediate initiation of national and international judicial proceedings to ensure that the authors and perpetrators of the killings were identified, prosecuted and brought to justice, and that Burundi should seek international technical assistance for the investigation and should be able to rely on the full cooperation of the DRC and Rwanda. Burundi should also immediately invoke the jurisdiction of ICC. In view of the political instability in the region, Governments and others in the region should be called on to exercise restraint in their declarations concerning the massacre. Burundi should also be requested to immediately take all measures necessary to protect refugee and internally displaced populations.

Burundi, reacting to the report on 29 October [S/2004/867], said that it was conducting an investigation and intended to release its own report shortly. It pointed out and gave examples of omissions, confused interpretations of facts and assertions that were contrary to stated facts in the UN report. It declared its intention to pursue a thorough judicial investigation at the national and subregional levels with the cooperation of the DRC and Rwanda to bring the culprits to justice and would refer the matter to ICC.

Further political developments

Report of Secretary-General (August). On 25 August [S/2004/682], the Secretary-General issued his first report on ONUB, covering developments since his 16 March report (see p. 143).

During the reporting period, the Burundian parties engaged in intense negotiations on the electoral process and post-transitional power-sharing arrangements. On 26 March, President Ndayizeye invited 27 armed political parties and movements to an all-party forum to discuss the election and legal instruments to govern Burundi in the post-transition period, but no consensus was reached. Thereafter, the Facilitation (South Africa) met with those organizations five times from April to July in Bujumbura and Pretoria. The Secretary-General's Special Representative also worked closely with the Facilitation and the parties to move the process forward. The Tutsi parties called for revisions to the Arusha Agreement and subsequent agreements, particularly to provide for an alternating presidency between Hutu and Tutsi parties; one (Tutsi) Vice-President with veto power, instead of two from different ethnic groups, as called for in the Arusha Agreement; and a 10-year interim period between the transition and full democracy, instead of five. By law, political parties were required to be ethnically mixed, with every party having a 30 per cent minimum representation of each ethnic group. The Tutsi parties argued that, to be fairly represented in legislative bodies, at least 70 per cent of the 40 per cent of the seats reserved for them had to be occupied by Tutsis representing Tutsi-led parties and the remaining 30 per cent by Tutsis representing parties with a Hutu majority. The Hutu-dominated parties opposed those amendments. At an 18-21 July meeting, the Facilitation stressed that the agreements should be adhered to, a position accepted by the Hutu parties but rejected by the Tutsis. In July, Vice-President Alphonse Kadege of the Tutsi-dominated UPRONA party denounced the discussions as favouring the Hutu parties.

To break the deadlock, the Facilitation, in co-ordination with ONUB, invited all armed political parties and movements to Pretoria for consultations on 4 and 5 August. CNDD-FDD (Nkurunziza) declined to participate. The talks ended with 20 predominantly Hutu parties agreeing to the power-sharing formula suggested by the Facilitation and 11 predominantly Tutsi parties rejecting it. However, the Hutu parties made the concession to increase by 21 the number of seats for minority groups in the National Assembly. Meanwhile, efforts continued to convince CNDD-FDD representatives to occupy the seats reserved for them in the National Assembly, the Senate and the Cabinet, which they refused to do in protest against the presence of former army officers in the National Assembly. On 27 July, after a meeting with the President, CNDD-FDD (Nkurunziza) agreed to resume its activities in the National Assembly and the Cabinet, but no agreement was reached on its participation in the Senate.

On 28 May, the Cabinet agreed to postpone the elections by one year on technical grounds, which was rejected by CNDD-FDD (Nkurunziza) and the Front for Democracy in Burundi (FRODEBU), but welcomed by the Union for National Progress, Burundi (UPRONA). ONUB encouraged the parties to separate the technical aspects of the electoral process from the political negotiations in order to move the process along. The Independent Electoral Commission was established on 5 August, but the five commissioners had not been nominated or approved.

The Special Representative worked with the Facilitation and others concerned to build confidence between the Transitional Government and FNL. The latter offered to cease fire if certain conditions were met, including the return of CNDD-FDD to its cantonment areas and the confinement of the Burundian Armed Forces to barracks. The Transitional Government rejected the offer but did indicate its willingness to engage in formal ceasefire negotiations at a later date. In the meantime, tensions in Bujumbura Rurale escalated, culminating in the massacre at the Gatumba refugee camp on 13 August (see p. 149). President Ndayizeye, at a meeting with the Special Representative on 15 August, expressed concern about a possible alliance of FNL, Congolese Mayi-Mayi and ex-FAR/Interahamwe forces.

In other developments, the Implementation Monitoring Committee, meeting in April (20-23) and again in July (12-14) under the Chairmanship of the Special Representative, urged the adoption of the necessary legislation for the electoral process and the fulfilment of the disarmament, demobilization and reintegration process. It urged the parties to set up the Electoral Commission and decided that, if the parties failed to agree on a post-transition constitution by 31 July, it would, in accordance with the Arusha Agreement, hire experts to draft the document.

With regard to military integration, the Joint Ceasefire Commission endorsed, on 17 June, an operations plan for the pre-disarmament, disarmament and demobilization of combatants, which was approved by the Cabinet, but the Government still had to prepare an operational plan for the integration, demobilization and reform of the military and a budget to support that process. Belgium, France, the Netherlands and the United Kingdom contributed to the integrated training of combatants from the various armed political parties and movements. As to the implementation of the disarmament, demobilization and reintegration programme, technical preparations were moving forward and a demobilization centre was set up. Members of various groups were assembled in 12 pre-disarmament assembly areas throughout the country, but the Burundian Armed Forces had not begun cantoning its troops, on the grounds that their deployment was required because of ongoing hostilities with FNL (Rwasa). Although funding was available for demobilization and reintegration, primarily through the World Bank, the lack of an operational plan remained a concern. Efforts were also under way to enhance the functioning of the local police.

ONUB's police component had begun assessing the current police structure, analysing the training required and assisting in the formulation of a comprehensive plan for security arrangements during the elections.

The deployment of ONUB, which totalled 3,312 troops as at 23 August, was behind schedule due primarily to lack of donor response, particularly for the maritime unit and the "over-the-horizon" force proposed by the Secretary-General (see p. 145). The mission sent a battalion each to Gitega and Bubanza, and a company remained in

Bujumbura, which would be built up to battalion strength. Daily patrols began in Bujumbura Rurale and some 100 military observers were deployed to field sites, mostly in Bujumbura Rurale, where they encountered some difficulties with freedom of movement. A maritime unit patrolled Lake Tanganyika.

In his observations, the Secretary-General called on Burundi, the DRC and the international community to ensure that those responsible for the Gatumba massacre were held responsible. He expressed concern about the possibility of heightened ethnic tensions in Burundi following the massacre, and urged those Governments and Rwanda to work together to end ethnic-based hostilities that had afflicted the subregion for so long.

Noting that the negotiations on post-transition power-sharing had shown signs that the parties were willing to find common ground to implement the Arusha timetable and preserve peace, he called on them to continue in that direction. He also noted that the parties had yet to demonstrate the good faith and political will necessary to fulfil their commitments to each other and to the Security Council.

Communication (September). The EU, in a statement issued on 6 September [S/2004/737], welcomed Burundi's establishment of an Independent Electoral Commission which would play the leading role in the organization of local, regional, parliamentary and presidential elections. Its creation made it possible to proceed with the adoption of a new constitution and electoral laws. The EU also welcomed the law creating the Truth and Reconciliation Commission and expressed its willingness to assist Burundi in the organization of elections.

Security Council communiqué. At a closed meeting held on 23 September [meeting 5042], the Security Council heard a briefing by Burundian President Ndayizeye, who, according to the Council President, in his summary of the Council's activities in September [S/2005/6], informed the Council of the latest developments in Burundi, including the adoption of a draft constitution and the decision of the Transitional Government to hold a referendum on the draft constitution. Council members encouraged the President to continue to work for a successful conclusion of the transition.

Extension of transitional period

The twenty-third summit of the Great Lakes Regional Peace Initiative on Burundi (Nairobi, 15 October) [S/2004/894] welcomed the progress made by the Transitional Government, specifically the establishment of the Independent Electoral Commission, the adoption of the draft post-transitional constitution, and President Ndayizeye's announcement of 20 October as the date of the referendum on the post-transitional constitution. Based on the reality on the ground, the summit accepted that elections could not take place before 1 November, and it endorsed the Independent Electoral Commission's electoral calendar, which rescheduled the constitutional referendum for 26 November, local elections (COLLINE) on 9 February 2005, commune council elections on 23 February 2005, National Assembly elections on 9 March 2005, Senate elections on 23 March 2005 and the presidential election on 22 April 2005. As a consequence, the summit noted that the life of the transition institutions and administration had to be extended. It noted that that issue was addressed in the draft constitution passed by the National Assembly and the Senate. The summit decided that the draft constitution should be endorsed before 25 October 2004, as an interim constitution until the referendum, to facilitate the election process in line with the calendar of the Independent Electoral Commission. The summit also decided that the region should assist Burundi to secure the financial resources required for elections by ensuring that the donors who had pledged funds met their obligations.

Burundi, in its 8 November letter transmitting the summit's communiqué, reported that the Congress had approved the interim constitution, which came into force on 1 November. In addition, the President had appointed the provincial electoral committees, which worked under the authority of the Independent Electoral Commission. According to the Chairman of that Commission, the electoral timetable was provisional and adherence to those dates would depend on the security situation in the country. Moreover, the holding of the constitutional referendum would also depend on such factors as availability of resources for a census and the manufacture of identification cards and voting cards.

Situation at end of year

The Secretary-General, in his 15 November report on ONUB [S/2004/902], which covered events since 25 August, said that the reporting period was marked by major developments in the last few months of the original 36-month transitional period, which ended on 31 October. Among the remaining challenges were the adoption of key legislation, including the communal law, repeal of the law banning assembly, and laws governing the establishment of the new military and security forces, and the adoption of a new electoral code before elections could be held. Dis-

armament needed to proceed without delay, so that armed groups could become eligible to register as political parties before the elections. Demobilization and integration should proceed for the creation of integrated security services, and the issue of the proliferation of arms should be addressed to ensure security for elections. The question of FNL (Rwasa), which remained outside the peace process, would have to be resolved.

On 20 October, the President, after consultations, signed a law declaring the draft constitution, adopted on 17 September, to be the interim constitution until the referendum was held. After some initial refusals, 9 of the 10 Tutsi-dominated G-10 parties accepted the interim constitution. However, some prominent Tutsi leaders, including the Vice-President, Alphonse Kadege, continued to call for a debate on the proposed constitution. Mr. Kadege was later dismissed by the President. The tenth party, PARENA, did not participate in the political process and refused to pronounce itself on the matter.

UNDP and ONUB estimated that $23 million was required to fund the electoral process, including the constitutional referendum, of which $19.5 million had been pledged but only $1.87 million had been received.

The military situation remained generally stable, with the exception of three western provinces, Bujumbura Rurale, Cibitoké and Bubanza, where frequent clashes occurred between FAB/CNDD-FDD and RNL (Rwasa). The hostilities caused temporary displacements of the local population. Crime, which was on the rise, was characterized by indiscriminate and opportunistic incidents, including organized crime. On 26 September, a United Nations Volunteer was murdered in Bujumbura, the first civilian casualty in the mission. The instability in eastern DRC continued to contribute to increased tensions in Burundi. In mid-October, roughly 3,000 Burundians, mostly Tutsis, citing fear of election-related violence, crossed into Rwanda, which prompted UPRONA to accuse CNDD-FDD (Nkurunziza) of conducting a "terror campaign". More than half had returned a month later.

In order to speed up disarmament, training of combatants to form joint security brigades began. On 23 September, 1,000 FAB and 800 CNDD-FDD (Nkurunziza) elements completed a month-long training programme and were deployed to replace the Burundian Armed Forces units in Bujumbura Rurale. The five smaller armed parties and political movements had not yet begun participating, pending an agreement with the Transitional Government on selection criteria and disarmament procedures.

An estimated 12,000 combatants were expected to be demobilized before elections in April 2005, but disagreements on procedure for integration and reform prevented disarmament and demobilization from starting. However, there was agreement on the demobilization of child soldiers by the end of 2004. Despite the political problems, most of the technical preparations for disarmament, demobilization and reintegration were completed, including the establishment of three demobilization centres and arrangements to supply them. The Transitional Government and ONUB had prepared a disarmament, demobilization and reintegration plan. As at 18 October, 20,979 members of the armed political parties and movements had been assembled in 12 pre-disarmament assembly areas monitored by ONUB. All the parties provided the Joint Ceasefire Commission with lists of their combatants, which were being verified by the joint liaison teams. The Council of Ministers adopted a decree on the formation, organization and mandate of the National Burundian Police.

The Secretary-General reported that overall, steady progress had been observed in the peace process, especially with regard to the extension of the transition and the establishment of a clear electoral calendar, thereby averting a constitutional crisis. Major political and social tensions in the country remained, however, fuelled by mistrust between the parties. Having made major political achievements in the last six months, Burundi found itself at the beginning of a dynamic but potentially volatile electoral process. In the light of the progress, and in view of the remaining priorities of the transition, he recommended that ONUB's mandate be extended for an additional six months, until 31 May 2005.

Report of Security Council 2004 mission. The Security Council mission to the Great Lakes region (21-25 November) (see p. 115), in its report to the Council [S/2004/934], said that it was greatly impressed by the progress made in the peace process in Burundi and expressed its support for the transitional process based on the principles of dialogue, power-sharing and reconciliation. Welcoming the decision on extension of the transitional process, the mission expressed concern over delays encountered in the critical areas of the adoption of the electoral code and the commune act, essential prerequisites for the elections, and in progress in disarmament, demobilization and reintegration in order to create conditions for holding elections.

In discussions with Burundian leaders, the mission emphasized the need to ensure stability in the post-transition period. It noted the call by many of its interlocutors that an international judicial commission of inquiry be established to support the fight against impunity, and that the draft legislation on the national Truth and Reconciliation Commission had been adopted by the Parliament. The mission also heard that the security situation had improved. With the exception of Bujumbura Rurale, most of the country was considered stable. As in previous Council visits to the country, the interlocutors appealed for help in overcoming the dire poverty facing the country, which was a root cause of the conflict.

The mission recommended that the Council consider the issue of FNL, with a view to ascertaining what additional measures could be taken against those in the movement who compromised the peace process; consider the feasibility of establishing an international judicial commission of inquiry; and urge donor countries to disburse financial aid and extend technical assistance to Burundi. It also recommended the extension of ONUB's mandate.

Security Council consideration. The Council considered the mission's report on 30 November [meeting 5091] and 8 December [meeting 5096], and heard presentations by the head of the mission, who noted that the framework for the end of the transition and the post-transition period had largely been agreed and a referendum on the constitution was set for 22 December. As in the DRC, the mission was encouraged by what it had seen, despite remaining difficulties, which should not be underestimated. In Burundi, the process was more on track; it was currently a question of will and determination. Burundi faced the problem of FNL receiving support in the DRC from the ex-FAR/Interahamwe.

SECURITY COUNCIL ACTION (December)

On 1 December [meeting 5093], the Security Council unanimously adopted **resolution 1577 (2004)**. The draft [S/2004/930] was prepared in consultations among Council members.

The Security Council,

Recalling its resolution 1545(2004) of 21 May 2004 and the statement by its President of 15 August 2004,

Reaffirming its strong commitment to the respect of the sovereignty, independence, territorial integrity and unity of Burundi, and recalling the importance of the principles of good-neighbourliness and non-interference, and of regional cooperation,

Reaffirming its full support for the process of the Arusha Peace and Reconciliation Agreement for Burundi signed at Arusha, United Republic of Tanzania, on 28 August 2000 (hereinafter "the Arusha Agreement"), calling upon all the Burundian parties to honour fully their commitments, and assuring them of its determination to support Burundi's efforts to bring the transition to an end successfully through the holding of free and fair elections,

Welcoming the positive achievements that have been made so far by the Burundian sides, including since the deployment of the United Nations Operation in Burundi on 1 June 2004,

Welcoming in particular the agreement signed by the Burundian parties at Pretoria on 6 August 2004, and the subsequent adoption by the Parliament of an interim Constitution, on 20 October 2004, which provides guarantees for all communities to be represented in the post-transition institutions,

Encouraging all Burundian parties to continue their dialogue in a spirit of compromise, in particular during the campaign to explain the interim Constitution and the drawing-up of the electoral code, with a view to a lasting political solution,

Recalling that there is no alternative to the holding of elections as provided for by the Arusha Agreement, and calling upon the transitional authorities to carry through the electoral process scheduled to take place until 22 April 2005,

Paying tribute to the efforts made by the States of the Regional Peace Initiative on Burundi, especially Uganda and the United Republic of Tanzania, and the Facilitation, in particular South Africa, to support the peace process in Burundi, and encouraging them to continue to accompany the efforts of the Burundian parties,

Encouraging the international donor community to respond to requests from the Government of Burundi to strengthen its national judicial institutions and rule-of-law capacity,

Condemning all acts of violence as well as violations of human rights and international humanitarian law,

Reiterating its strong condemnation of the Gatumba massacre, and reaffirming that perpetrators of such crimes must be brought to justice,

Taking note of the joint report of the United Nations Operation in Burundi, the United Nations Organization Mission in the Democratic Republic of the Congo and the Office of the United Nations High Commissioner for Human Rights regarding the Gatumba massacre on 13 August 2004, and taking note also of the statement by the Government of Burundi of 29 October 2004 and of its commitment to bring its investigation into the Gatumba massacre to a prompt conclusion, with international support as appropriate,

Taking note also of the report of the Secretary-General of 15 November 2004,

Noting that obstacles remain to Burundi's stability, and determining that the situation in that country continues to constitute a threat to international peace and security in the region,

Acting under Chapter VII of the Charter of the United Nations,

1. *Decides* that the mandate of the United Nations Operation in Burundi, as defined in resolution 1545(2004), shall be extended until 1 June 2005;

2. *Urges* all the Governments and parties concerned in the region to denounce the use of and incitement to violence, to condemn unequivocally violations of human rights and of international humanitarian law, and actively to cooperate with the United Nations Operation in Burundi and the United Nations Organization Mission in the Democratic Republic of the Congo and with efforts of States aimed at ending impunity;

3. *Calls upon* the Governments of the Democratic Republic of the Congo and of Rwanda to cooperate unreservedly with the Government of Burundi to ensure that the investigation into the Gatumba massacre is completed and that those responsible are brought to justice;

4. *Requests* the United Nations Operation in Burundi and the United Nations Organization Mission in the Democratic Republic of the Congo to continue to provide their assistance, within their mandates, to the Burundian and Congolese authorities, with a view to facilitating the completion of the investigation into the Gatumba massacre and strengthening the security of vulnerable populations;

5. *Deeply troubled* by the fact that the Parti pour la libération du peuple hutu-Forces nationales de libération of Mr. Agathon Rwasa has claimed responsibility for the Gatumba massacre, expresses its intention to consider appropriate measures that might be taken against those individuals who threaten the peace and national reconciliation process in Burundi;

6. *Requests* the Secretary-General to keep it informed on a regular basis of developments in the situation in Burundi, the implementation of the Arusha Agreement, the execution of the mandate of the United Nations Operation in Burundi and the action taken by the Burundian authorities following the recommendations of the Council in the fight against impunity, and to submit a report on those developments every three months;

7. *Decides* to remain actively seized of the matter.

Further developments. Despite slippages in the electoral calendar, there was some progress at the end of the year in the preparation for the referendum on the constitution and elections [S/2005/149]. Voter registration commenced on 20 November and lasted until the end of the month, with extensive logistical support mobilized by ONUB, including transport of registration and electoral materials to all 17 provinces. In total, 3,134,116 Burundians registered to vote, estimated to represent, by province, from 60 to 90 per cent of those eligible.

The Implementation Monitoring Committee, at its twenty-fourth session (17 December), called on the Government to finalize an electoral code and communal law and to collaborate on issues of military rank harmonization within the context of the overall security sector reform/demobilization, disarmament and reintegration programme. On 2 December, President Ndayizeye launched the disarmament and demobilization process in Muramvya, and on 31 December, signed a decree consolidating the combatants of the six armed political parties and movements located in the 12 pre-disarmament assembly areas into five cantonment sites, which paved the way for the transformation and subsequent registration of the armed political parties and movements.

Ad Hoc Advisory Group. The Economic and Social Council's Ad Hoc Advisory Group on Burundi, established in 2003 to examine the humanitarian and economic needs of the country, issued a report in February [S/2004/11] and made recommendations in April [S/2004/266] on action to be taken by both the Economic and Social Council and the Security Council. After considering the reports, the Economic and Social Council took action on those aspects of the situation in Burundi in **resolution 2004/2** of 3 May (see p. 933) and **resolution 2004/60** of 23 July (see p. 934).

ONUB financing

The Secretary-General, pending the submission of a full budget for the maintenance of ONUB, submitted on 24 May [A/58/802] an interim budget for the period from 21 April to 30 June and from 1 July to 31 December, which reflected the preliminary financial requirements of $58,421,400 and $145,267,500, respectively.

ACABQ, on 24 May [A/58/811], recommended that the Assembly approve a total commitment authority of $156,043,900 to be assessed for ONUB, which included commitment authority in the amount of $49,709,300, inclusive of an amount of $49,491,200 it had already authorized, for the period 21 April to 30 June, and the amount of $106,334,600 for the period from July to October.

GENERAL ASSEMBLY ACTION (June)

On 18 June [meeting 91], the General Assembly, on the recommendation of the Fifth Committee [A/58/833], adopted **resolution 58/312** without vote [agenda item 170].

Financing of the United Nations Operation in Burundi

The General Assembly,

Having considered the report of the Secretary-General on the financing of the United Nations Operation in Burundi and the related report of the Advisory Committee on Administrative and Budgetary Questions,

Recalling Security Council resolution 1545(2004) of 21 May 2004, by which the Council authorized, for an initial period of six months as from 1 June 2004, with the intention to renew it for further periods, the deployment of a peacekeeping operation called the United Nations Operation in Burundi,

Recognizing that the costs of the Operation are expenses of the Organization to be borne by Member States in accordance with Article 17, paragraph 2, of the Charter of the United Nations,

Reaffirming the general principles underlying the financing of United Nations peacekeeping operations, as stated in its resolutions 1874(S-IV) of 27 June 1963, 3101(XXVIII) of 11 December 1973 and 55/235 of 23 December 2000,

Mindful of the fact that it is essential to provide the Operation with the necessary financial resources to enable it to fulfil its responsibilities under the relevant resolution of the Security Council,

1. *Expresses concern* at the financial situation with regard to peacekeeping activities, in particular as regards the reimbursements to troop contributors that bear additional burdens owing to overdue payments by Member States of their assessments;

2. *Also expresses concern* at the delay experienced by the Secretary-General in deploying and providing adequate resources to some recent peacekeeping missions, in particular those in Africa;

3. *Emphasizes* that all future and existing peacekeeping missions shall be given equal and non-discriminatory treatment in respect of financial and administrative arrangements;

4. *Also emphasizes* that all peacekeeping missions shall be provided with adequate resources for the effective and efficient discharge of their respective mandates;

5. *Reiterates its request* to the Secretary-General to make the fullest possible use of facilities and equipment at the United Nations Logistics Base at Brindisi, Italy, in order to minimize the costs of procurement for the Operation;

6. *Endorses* the conclusions and recommendations contained in the report of the Advisory Committee on Administrative and Budgetary Questions, and requests the Secretary-General to ensure their full implementation;

7. *Requests* the Secretary-General to take all necessary action to ensure that the Operation is administered with a maximum of efficiency and economy;

8. *Also requests* the Secretary-General, in order to reduce the cost of employing General Service staff, to continue efforts to recruit local staff for the Operation against General Service posts, commensurate with the requirements of the Operation;

Budget estimates for the period from 21 April to 31 October 2004

9. *Authorizes* the Secretary-General to establish a special account for the United Nations Operation in Burundi for the purpose of accounting for the income received and expenditure incurred in respect of the Operation;

10. *Also authorizes* the Secretary-General to enter into commitments for the Operation for the period from 21 April to 31 October 2004 in a total amount not exceeding 156,043,900 United States dollars, comprising the amount of 49,709,300 dollars for the period from 21 April to 30 June 2004 for the establishment of the Operation, inclusive of the amount of 49,491,200 dollars previously authorized by the Advisory Committee for the period from 21 April to 30 June 2004 under the terms of section IV of General Assembly resolution 49/233 A of 23 December 1994, and the amount of 106,334,600 dollars for the period from 1 July to 31 October 2004 for the maintenance of the Operation;

Financing of the commitment authority

11. *Decides* to apportion among Member States the total amount of 156,043,900 dollars, comprising the amount of 49,709,300 dollars for the period from 21 April to 30 June 2004 and the amount of 106,334,600 dollars for the period from 1 July to 31 Oc-

tober 2004, in accordance with the levels set out in General Assembly resolution 55/235, as adjusted by the Assembly in its resolution 55/236 of 23 December 2000 and updated in its resolution 58/256 of 23 December 2003, taking into account the scale of assessments for 2004, as set out in its resolution 58/1 B of 23 December 2003;

12. *Decides also* that, in accordance with the provisions of its resolution 973(X) of 15 December 1955, there shall be set off against the apportionment among Member States, as provided for in paragraph 11 above, their respective share in the Tax Equalization Fund of 149,400 dollars, representing the estimated staff assessment income approved for the Operation for the period from 21 April to 30 June 2004, and 1,187,900 dollars, representing the estimated staff assessment income approved for the Operation for the period from 1 July to 31 October 2004;

13. *Emphasizes* that no peacekeeping mission shall be financed by borrowing funds from other active peacekeeping missions;

14. *Encourages* the Secretary-General to continue to take additional measures to ensure the safety and security of all personnel under the auspices of the United Nations participating in the Operation;

15. *Invites* voluntary contributions to the Operation in cash and in the form of services and supplies acceptable to the Secretary-General, to be administered, as appropriate, in accordance with the procedure and practices established by the General Assembly;

16. *Decides* to include in the provisional agenda of its fifty-ninth session the item entitled "Financing of the United Nations Operation in Burundi".

On 26 August [A/59/300] the Secretary-General issued the budget for ONUB for the period from 1 July 2004 to 30 June 2005, in the amount of $333,174,000. It incorporated and superseded the budgetary proposal for ONUB for 1 July to 31 December 2004 (see above).

ACABQ, on 5 October [A/59/412], recommended that the total estimated budget requirements for that period be reduced to $329,714,400.

GENERAL ASSEMBLY ACTION (October)

On 29 October [meeting 46], the General Assembly, on the recommendation of the Fifth Committee [A/59/528], adopted **resolution 59/15** without vote [agenda item 153].

Financing of the United Nations Operation in Burundi

The General Assembly,

Having considered the report of the Secretary-General on the financing of the United Nations Operation in Burundi and the related report of the Advisory Committee on Administrative and Budgetary Questions,

Recalling Security Council resolution 1545(2004) of 21 May 2004, by which the Council authorized, for an initial period of six months as from 1 June 2004, with the intention to renew it for further periods, the deployment of a peacekeeping operation in Burundi entitled the United Nations Operation in Burundi,

Recalling also its resolution 58/312 of 18 June 2004 on the financing of the Operation,

Reaffirming the general principles underlying the financing of United Nations peacekeeping operations, as stated in General Assembly resolutions 1874(S-IV) of 27 June 1963, 3101(XXVIII) of 11 December 1973 and 55/235 of 23 December 2000,

Mindful of the fact that it is essential to provide the Operation with the necessary financial resources to enable it to fulfil its responsibilities under the relevant resolution of the Security Council,

1. *Takes note* of the status of contributions to the United Nations Operation in Burundi as at 30 September 2004, including the contributions outstanding in the amount of 100.3 million United States dollars, representing some 65 per cent of the total assessed contributions, notes with concern that only twenty-seven Member States have paid their assessed contributions in full, and urges all other Member States, in particular those in arrears, to ensure payment of their outstanding assessed contributions;

2. *Expresses its appreciation* to those Member States which have paid their assessed contributions in full, and urges all other Member States to make every possible effort to ensure payment of their assessed contributions to the Operation in full;

3. *Expresses concern* at the financial situation with regard to peacekeeping activities, in particular as regards the reimbursements to troop contributors that bear additional burdens owing to overdue payments by Member States of their assessments;

4. *Also expresses concern* at the delay experienced by the Secretary-General in deploying and providing adequate resources to some recent peacekeeping missions, in particular those in Africa;

5. *Emphasizes* that all future and existing peacekeeping missions shall be given equal and non-discriminatory treatment in respect of financial and administrative arrangements;

6. *Also emphasizes* that all peacekeeping missions shall be provided with adequate resources for the effective and efficient discharge of their respective mandates;

7. *Reiterates its request* to the Secretary-General to make the fullest possible use of facilities and equipment at the United Nations Logistics Base at Brindisi, Italy, in order to minimize the costs of procurement for the Operation;

8. *Endorses* the conclusions and recommendations contained in the report of the Advisory Committee on Administrative and Budgetary Questions, subject to the provisions of the present resolution;

9. *Authorizes* the Secretary-General to fill the following posts at appropriate grades until 30 June 2005:

Director in the Office of the Special Representative of the Secretary-General;

Political Affairs Officer in the Office of the Special Representative of the Secretary-General;

Protocol Officer in the Office of the Special Representative of the Secretary-General;

Political Affairs Officer in the Office of the Principal Deputy Special Representative of the Secretary-General;

Administrative Assistant in the Office of the Principal Deputy Special Representative of the Secretary-General;

Deputy Special Representative of the Secretary-General (Humanitarian and Development Coordination);

Special Assistant to the Deputy Special Representative of the Secretary-General;

Principal Legal Adviser;

Chief of the Communications and Public Information Office;

Spokesperson;

and requests the Secretary-General to re-justify these posts in his next budget with additional information on appropriate grades;

10. *Requests* the Secretary-General to take all necessary action to ensure that the mission is administered with a maximum of efficiency and economy;

11. *Also requests* the Secretary-General, in order to reduce the cost of employing General Service staff, to continue efforts to recruit local staff for the Operation against General Service posts, commensurate with the requirements of the Operation;

**Budget estimates for the period
from 1 July 2004 to 30 June 2005**

12. *Decides* to appropriate to the Special Account for the United Nations Operation in Burundi the amount of 329,714,400 dollars for the maintenance of the Operation for the period from 1 July 2004 to 30 June 2005, inclusive of the amount of 106,334,600 dollars previously authorized by the General Assembly under the terms of its resolution 58/312 for the period from 1 July to 31 October 2004;

Financing of the appropriation

13. *Decides*, taking into account the amount of 106,334,600 dollars already apportioned by the General Assembly for the period from 1 July to 31 October 2004 under the terms of its resolution 58/312, to apportion among Member States the additional amount of 31,046,400 dollars for the period from 1 July to 30 November 2004, in accordance with the levels set out in General Assembly resolution 55/235, as adjusted by the Assembly in its resolution 55/236 of 23 December 2000 and updated in its resolution 58/256 of 23 December 2003, taking into account the scale of assessments for 2004, as set out in its resolution 58/1 B of 23 December 2003;

14. *Decides also* that, in accordance with the provisions of its resolution 973(X) of 15 December 1955, there shall be set off against the apportionment among Member States, as provided for in paragraph 13 above, their respective share in the Tax Equalization Fund of 1,076,225 dollars, representing the estimated additional staff assessment income approved for the Operation for the period from 1 July to 30 November 2004;

15. *Decides further* to apportion among Member States the amount of 192,333,400 dollars at a monthly rate of 27,476,200 dollars for the maintenance of the Operation for the period from 1 December 2004 to 30 June 2005, in accordance with the scheme set out in paragraph 13 above and taking into account the scale of assessments for 2004 and 2005, as set out in its resolution 58/1 B, subject to a decision of the Security Council to extend the mandate of the Operation;

16. *Decides* that, in accordance with the provisions of its resolution 973(X), there shall be set off against the apportionment among Member States, as provided for in paragraph 15 above, their respective share in the Tax Equalization Fund of 3,169,775 dollars, representing the staff assessment income approved for the Operation for the period from 1 December 2004 to 30 June 2005;

17. *Emphasizes* that no peacekeeping mission shall be financed by borrowing funds from other active peacekeeping missions;

18. *Encourages* the Secretary-General to continue to take additional measures to ensure the safety and security of all personnel under the auspices of the United Nations participating in the Operation;

19. *Invites* voluntary contributions to the Operation in cash and in the form of services and supplies acceptable to the Secretary-General, to be administered, as appropriate, in accordance with the procedure and practices established by the General Assembly;

20. *Decides* to keep under review during its fifty-ninth session the item entitled "Financing of the United Nations Operation in Burundi".

On 23 December, the Assembly decided that the agenda item on financing ONUB would remain for consideration during its resumed fifty-ninth (2005) session (**decision 59/552**).

Rwanda

Throughout the year, Rwanda and the DRC exchanged charges of interference in each other's internal affairs. The DRC complained on numerous occasions that Rwanda was supporting military operations in DRC territory, while Rwanda alleged that groups opposing its Government were operating from the DRC. (For further information on the charges concerning DRC territory, see section on DRC, above). Rwanda claimed that lack of action by the international community, and particularly on the part of MONUC peacekeepers in the DRC, had emboldened its opponents.

The year 2004 marked the tenth anniversary of the 1994 genocide in Rwanda, for which the General Assembly held a solemn commemoration.

Military situation

Rwanda, on 30 November [S/2004/933], informed the Security Council of the continued violation of its sovereignty and territorial integrity by forces operating from the DRC with relative impunity. Despite Council action, the ex-FAR/Interahamwe forces continued to operate from, and receive supplies in, the territory of another State and to recruit and train troops. Eastern DRC had become a recruiting ground and crucible for the ideology of hate, destruction and extermination in the region. Over the previous three months, those forces had carried out a series of attacks on Rwandan territory, killing people and destroying property. Intending to complete the genocide of 1994 [YUN 1994, p. 282], the forces had also targeted infrastructure vital for Rwanda's economy. Recalling recent incidents, including the attack at Gatumba (see p. 149), Rwanda deplored the international community's lack of reaction, which it claimed had encouraged those groups. Rwanda believed that MONUC should focus on disarming them, as failure to do so would increase tension in the region and undermine the transitional processes in the DRC and Burundi. Rwanda stated that the problem of the genocidal forces was a matter for the Council to resolve. Since all options for resolving the situation had been rejected by the DRC, Rwanda could not stand by and see its people attacked, its infrastructure destroyed and destabilization continue. Having lost one million of its citizens in 1994, Rwanda had a responsibility to protect and defend its people.

The Secretary-General, in a 2 December statement released by his Spokesman [SG/SM/9631-AFR/1076], said that he was disturbed by the increasing tension between the DRC and Rwanda, particularly by indications of military operations on DRC territory against ex-FAR/Interahamwe elements, which Rwanda maintained was a threat to its security. He called on Rwanda to refrain from any military action on DRC territory, which would disrupt the transitional process in that country, and to work within the established process for disarming and repatriating the remaining ex-FAR/Interahamwe elements still in DRC territory. The Secretary-General called on the DRC to intensify its efforts to disarm and repatriate such elements, and indicated that MONUC was prepared to activate the Joint Verification Mechanism for disarming and repatriating those groups.

The Council, in presidential statement **S/PRST/2004/45** (see p. 133), expressed concern at reports of military operations by the Rwandan army in eastern DRC and demanded that Rwanda withdraw without delay any forces it might have in the DRC. The Council noted that the presence of ex-FAR and Interahamwe elements in eastern DRC was a source of instability.

Tenth anniversary of 1994 genocide

In 2004, several events were organized at the United Nations to mark the tenth anniversary of the 1994 genocide in Rwanda [YUN 1994, p. 282]. Canada and Rwanda organized the Memorial Conference on the Rwanda Genocide (New York, 26 March). The Secretary-General, in his address, said that the international community had failed Rwanda. However, the United Nations was currently helping the people to recover and reconcile. It was clearing mines, repatriating refugees, rehabilitating clinics and schools, and building up the judicial system, among other things, while the United Nations International Criminal Tribunal for Rwanda continued to pursue the perpetrators of the genocide (see p. 1286). The genocide in Rwanda had raised questions that affected all mankind, and the question remained as to whether, confronted by a new Rwanda situation, the response would be effective and timely.

General Assembly commemorative meeting. The General Assembly, having designated 7 April as the International Day of Reflection on the 1994 Genocide in Rwanda in resolution 58/234 [YUN 2003, p. 154], held a commemorative meeting [meeting 82] that day in New York to mark the tenth anniversary of that tragedy. The meeting was addressed by the Presidents of the General Assembly and the Security Council, the Vice-President of the Economic and Social Council, Rwandan President Paul Kagame, the Deputy-Secretary-General and Jacqueline Murekatete, a survivor of the genocide.

The Assembly President, in his statement, said that the Assembly shared the hopes and aspirations of the Government and people of Rwanda in seeking to heal and rebuild a democratic nation, with an overarching vision of economic and social progress for all. The tragedy afforded the United Nations the opportunity to confront the issues that could lead to such situations, determine its own shortcomings in Rwanda and consider what remained to be done to prevent genocide in future years. For his part, the Secretary-General suggested areas for future activities to prevent genocide.

On 8 April [S/2004/310], the EU said that the anniversary was an occasion for reflection by the international community. It was heartened by UN efforts to forewarn the world against future genocide and supported the Secretary-General's proposals to prevent genocide, in particular his decision to appoint a Special Adviser on the Prevention of Genocide (see p. 730). The EU pledged to support Rwanda's recovery.

GENERAL ASSEMBLY ACTION

On 10 December [meeting 71], the General Assembly adopted **resolution 59/137** [draft: A/59/L.45 & Add.1] without vote [agenda item 39 (a)].

Assistance to survivors of the 1994 genocide in Rwanda, particularly orphans, widows and victims of sexual violence

The General Assembly,

Guided by the Charter of the United Nations and the Universal Declaration of Human Rights,

Recalling the findings and recommendations of the independent inquiry commissioned by the Secretary-General, with the approval of the Security Council, into the actions of the United Nations during the 1994 genocide in Rwanda,

Recalling also the report containing the findings and recommendations of the International Panel of Eminent Personalities commissioned by the Organization of African Unity to investigate the genocide in Rwanda and the surrounding events, entitled "Rwanda: The Preventable Genocide",

Recalling further its resolution 58/234 of 23 December 2003, by which it declared 7 April 2004 the International Day of Reflection on the Genocide in Rwanda,

Noting decision EX.CL/Dec.154(V) on the report of the Chairperson of the African Union on the commemoration of the tenth anniversary of the Rwandan genocide, adopted by the Executive Council of the African Union at its fifth ordinary session, held in Addis Ababa from 30 June to 3 July 2004,

Recognizing the numerous difficulties faced by survivors of the 1994 genocide in Rwanda, particularly the orphans, widows and victims of sexual violence, who are poorer and more vulnerable as a result of the genocide, especially the many victims of sexual violence who have contracted HIV and have since either died or become seriously ill with AIDS,

Firmly convinced of the necessity to restore the dignity of the survivors of the 1994 genocide in Rwanda, which would help to promote reconciliation and healing in Rwanda,

Commending the tremendous efforts of the Government and people of Rwanda and civil society organizations, as well as international efforts, to provide support for restoring the dignity of the survivors, including the allocation by the Government of Rwanda of 5 per cent of its national budget every year to support genocide survivors,

1. *Requests* the Secretary-General to encourage the relevant agencies, funds and programmes of the United Nations system to continue to work with the Government of Rwanda in developing and implementing programmes aimed at supporting vulnerable groups that continue to suffer from the effects of the 1994 genocide, in alleviating poverty, disease and suffering and in promoting development in Rwanda;

2. *Invites* the relevant agencies, funds and programmes of the United Nations system to continue to develop and implement those programmes, utilizing existing resources and encouraging the mobilization of additional voluntary contributions;

3. *Invites* agencies, funds and programmes of the United Nations system to ensure that assistance is provided in the specific areas identified as priorities by the Government of Rwanda, notably education for orphans, medical care and treatment for victims of sexual violence, including HIV-positive victims, trauma and psychological counselling for genocide survivors and skills training and microcredit programmes aimed at promoting self-sufficiency and alleviating poverty;

4. *Encourages* all Member States to seriously consider promoting the implementation of the recommendations contained in the report of the independent inquiry into the actions of the United Nations during the 1994 genocide in Rwanda, and also encourages all Member States to provide assistance to genocide survivors and other vulnerable groups in Rwanda in support of the present resolution;

5. *Expresses its appreciation* for development assistance and support for the reconstruction and rehabilitation of Rwanda after the 1994 genocide, and calls upon Member States to continue to support the development of Rwanda, inter alia, through programmes under the poverty reduction strategy;

6. *Requests* the Secretary-General, in view of the critical situation of the survivors of the 1994 genocide in Rwanda, particularly orphans, widows and victims of sexual violence, to take all necessary and practicable measures for the implementation of the present resolution, and to report thereon to the General Assembly at its sixtieth session.

Arms embargo

On 19 February [S/2004/134], the Security Council Committee established pursuant to resolution 918(1994) [YUN 1994, p. 285] concerning the arms embargo against Rwanda issued a report covering its activities from 1 January to 31 December 2003. In the absence of a specific monitoring mechanism to ensure implementation of the arms embargo, the Committee repeated its previous observation [YUN 2002, p. 142] that it relied solely on the cooperation of States and organizations in a position to provide information on violations of the arms embargo. During the reporting period, no violations were brought to the Committee's attention.

Central African Republic

The United Nations Peace-building Support Office in the Central African Republic (BONUCA), established by Security Council presidential statement S/PRST/2000/5 [YUN 2000, p. 162], continued in 2004 to support the Government's efforts to return to stability and achieve reconciliation and reconstruction, following the 2003 coup d'état [YUN 2003, p. 156]. The political situation in the country was marked by progress towards elections, scheduled for early 2005, which were designed to restore constitutional order. The transitional Government, established in 2003 [YUN 2003, p. 156], adopted a schedule for elections and considered a draft constitution, electoral code and laws on political parties. The draft constitution was approved by the people of the Central African Republic in a referendum on 5 December and work continued on the draft legislation.

However, the security situation remained precarious, with acts of violence, including summary executions, armed robbery and roadblocks continuing to occur, despite the deployment of defence and security detachments backed by the Central African Economic and Monetary Community (CEMAC) multinational force. There was concern over the possible consequences to the Central African Republic of the crises in the subregion, in particular the Sudanese region of Darfur.

The Secretary-General extended BONUCA's mandate for an additional year, until 31 December 2005.

Political and security developments

Press statement (23 January). The Security Council President, in a 23 January press statement [SC/7989-AFR/818], following a briefing by the Secretary-General's Representative on the situation in the Central African Republic and BONUCA activities, said that Council members noted with satisfaction that the authorities of the Central African Republic had maintained efforts towards reconciliation and reconstruction, and underlined that the continuation of the national dialogue and the restructuring of the national security forces were positive elements. They called for the strengthening of the CEMAC international force and invited the Central African authorities to ensure that human rights violations did not remain unpunished. The members called on the authorities to allow the electoral operations to take place according to schedule and invited the Secretary-General to examine ways in which BONUCA could assist in that regard.

Communication. On 10 February [S/2004/125], the Central African Republic transmitted to the Council President the calendar for the referendum and elections, adopted by consensus on 23 January by the Office of the President of the Republic, the Government and the Bureau of the National Transition Council (NTC), in the presence of the bureau of the committee to oversee the implementation of the outcome of the national dialogue. The calendar envisaged the holding of the referendum on the constitution in October/November 2004 and presidential and legislative elections in January 2005.

Report of Secretary-General (June). The Secretary-General, in response to presidential statement S/PRST/2001/25 [YUN 2001, p. 156], submitted a 16 June report on the situation in the Central African Republic and BONUCA activities [S/2004/496], covering the first half of 2004.

The political situation during the period was marked by the launching of the electoral process with a view to restoring constitutional legality and the rule of law in 2005. The transitional Government adopted a schedule for the elections and a timeline, which it forwarded to the Security Council on 10 February (see above). The transitional Government transmitted to NTC for its views the draft constitution, the electoral code and ordinances on political parties and the status of the opposition, and on the constitutional court and decentralization. The draft constitution was based on the 1995 Constitution, suspended since the coup d'état of March 2003, and on the recommendations of the national dialogue. The document would be submitted to the people for approval by a referendum in November 2004, followed by legislative and presidential elections in early 2005.

On 30 April, the head of State established the Mixed and Independent Electoral Commission (CEMI) to make preparations for and conduct the elections and ensure implementation of the Electoral Code. Political parties expressed concern over CEMI's independence and integrity. BONUCA established a framework for political consultations with foreign partners who supported the electoral process and the UN system, and UNDP established a technical advisory committee under its project of support to the electoral process. BONUCA also worked to defuse tensions through mediation and good offices with political parties, civil society, trade unions and public authorities, and with the transitional authorities in drafting legal texts.

The Central African authorities remained concerned about the security situation. The lack of security was most evident in the rural areas, where the civilian population was vulnerable to attacks, especially by "former liberators" who assisted General François Bozizé during the 2003 coup d'état. They severely tested the Government, demanding "bonuses promised" in return for their support of the rebellion and holding demonstrations that led to confrontations with the regular forces. Negotiations with the parties, including the Secretary-General's Representative, led to a solution to the problem of the former liberators, but it was uncertain whether the settlement was definitive.

The process of restructuring the defence and security forces was continuing, as was military training and equipping. In the area of subregional security cooperation, NTC authorized the ratification of the Protocol to the Treaty establishing the Economic Community of Central African States (ECCAS) on the Council for Peace and Security in Central Africa, adopted in Malabo, Equatorial Guinea, in February 2000. The Government was also pursuing disarmament, particularly in Bangui, and had approved a project for the reintegration of former combatants and support to communities. BONUCA and UNDP were assisting the Government in implementing the project.

The economic situation was characterized by a continued decline in production in most sectors, in particular in timber and diamonds due to the Government's temporary suspension of concessions and operating permits, pending their overhaul. Consequently, tax revenue declined by 30 per cent. The poverty and vulnerability of the population remained a major concern. Despite the prevailing insecurity, operational agencies of the UN system, in particular UNICEF, WHO, UNDP, WFP, UNHCR and FAO, concentrated on humanitarian activities and on active participation in the implementation of emergency programmes. The agencies adopted a development assistance framework for the Central African Republic, highlighting good governance, socio-economic recovery and prevention of HIV/AIDS, which depended on support from the donor community and the availability of additional resources. Despite the difficulties, the overall economic situation was improving, mainly as a result of the gradual resumption of mining and forestry production.

The human rights situation was also improving slowly. General Bozizé appointed a special adviser responsible for human rights and good governance, and the Government established a national committee to draft reports on the human rights situation and formulate a national plan of action for promoting and protecting human rights. BONUCA continued its observation and investigation of human rights violations, meeting victims and visiting detention centres, organizing training of law enforcement officers and providing media coverage of human rights activities.

According to the Secretary-General, the fact that the parties were opting for management by consensus of the transition with a view to a return to constitutional order through legislative and presidential elections in 2005 offered hope for a return to stability. Assistance was urgently needed to consolidate the achievements made and to build confidence. He noted the geostrategic position of the Central African Republic and the possible humanitarian and security impact of the conflict in the Sudanese region of Darfur. If that crisis persisted, he warned, Sudanese refugees living in camps near the Chad-Central African Republic border would be pushed towards the Central African Republic. He welcomed the recent decision of the International Monetary Fund (IMF), the World Bank and the African Development Bank to support the efforts of the Central African authorities.

UN Standing Advisory Committee consideration. The United Nations Standing Advisory Committee on Security Questions in Central Africa, at its twenty-first meeting (21-25 June), welcomed the efforts of the transitional Government to implement the recommendations of the 2003 national dialogue and the current political consensus in the country. It expressed concern about the precarious economic and security situation, improvement of which would make it easier to meet the various electoral deadlines and consolidate the positive political developments. The Committee appealed to donors and international financial institutions to provide the Central African Republic with the necessary support; to CEMAC to strengthen efforts to ensure security in the country, particularly in disarmament and the restructuring of the defence and security forces; and to the ECCAS General Secretariat to become actively involved with the electoral process.

Press statement (7 July). Security Council members, in a 7 July press statement by its President [SC/8142-AFR/992], noted the positive evolution of the political situation and progress in the economic and financial fields in the Central African Republic. They welcomed the establishment of CEMI as an important step towards the restoration of constitutional legality and encouraged the Central African authorities to maintain efforts to organize free, transparent and democratic elections in 2005. Members expressed concern regarding the possible consequences to the Central African Republic of the crisis in the subregion, in particular the crisis in Darfur (see p. 235).

Extension of BONUCA's mandate. The Secretary-General, on 18 October [S/2004/874], informed the Security Council of his intention to extend BONUCA's mandate for an additional year, until 31 December 2005. The extension would enable the Office to support efforts to restore constitutional legality and help to create a propitious political environment for holding elections. In addition, he had asked BONUCA to assess developments in neighbouring countries on the situation in the Central African Republic and vice versa. On 28 October [S/2004/875], the Council took note of the proposal.

SECURITY COUNCIL ACTION

On 28 October [meeting 5067], following consultations among Security Council members, the President made statement **S/PRST/2004/39** on behalf of the Council:

The Security Council commends the Central African authorities, the political parties and civil society of the Central African Republic for the efforts they have made for the ongoing success of the transition process. The Council welcomes in particular the spirit of consensus which the Central African parties have shown and which attests to their determination to continue the transition process to the end.

The Council encourages the Central Africans to continue their efforts to ensure the success of the constitutional referendum in November and the satisfactory organization of free, transparent and democratic presidential and legislative elections in January 2005.

The Council also pays tribute to the United Nations system in the Central African Republic and in particular to the Representative of the Secretary-General, General Lamine Cissé, for his work at the head of the United Nations Peacebuilding Support Office in the Central African Republic, and reaffirms to him its full support. The Council is pleased that the Secretary-General intends to renew the mandate of the Office until 31 December 2005.

The Council welcomes the assistance provided by the international community to the stabilization and recovery of the Central African Republic as well as the considerable efforts made by the member States of the Central African Economic and Monetary Community in the political, economic and security fields.

The Council calls upon international donors and the international financial institutions to continue to provide resolute support to the Central African Republic, including on the preparation of the upcoming legislative and presidential elections. It also emphasizes that their support will be essential for the country's economic and social recovery, and encourages them to formulate, in close consultation with relevant development agencies and with the Government of the Central African Republic, a concerted development strategy for the country.

However, the Council expresses its concern at the deterioration of the State's finances and of the public sector, and calls upon the Central African authorities to act with determination in order to address this situation.

The Council reiterates its full support for the Central African Economic and Monetary Community multinational force, and calls for the continuation of the restructuring of the Central African Republic's defence and security forces.

The Council also encourages the Central African authorities to continue to combat, with determination, human rights violations.

The Council again expresses its concern at the possible consequences to the Central African Republic of the crises in the subregion. Accordingly, it welcomes with satisfaction the Secretary-General's initiative in asking the United Nations Peacebuilding Support Office in the Central African Republic to assess the implications of developments in neighbouring countries on the situation in Central African Republic and vice versa.

Report of Secretary-General (December). On 23 December [S/2004/1012], the Secretary-General, reporting on the situation in the Central African Republic and BONUCA activities, said that the electoral process for the holding of general elections continued, supported by the Committee of Foreign Partners to Follow Up on the Electoral Process (China, France, Germany, the EU, UN system agencies, and the CEMAC Executive Secretariat and Force Commander). NTC, at its second session, which closed on 15 July, amended the draft constitution and the draft electoral code,

and transmitted them to the Government for adoption. The amendments concerned, among other things, the type of regime to be adopted, the powers of the Prime Minister, the length of the presidential term of office, the conditions for eligibility to the legislature and the presidency, and the conditions for establishing the criminal liability of the head of State. The head of State initialled and distributed the draft constitution and signed and enacted the ordinance on the electoral code.

NTC, at its third session (16 August–1 October), adopted the draft ordinance on political parties and the status of the opposition. National Councillors separately considered the draft constitution, and, with BONUCA's assistance, resolved discrepancies with respect to amendments made in accordance with the recommendations of the 2003 national dialogue. The Government amended the ordinance on the electoral code, modified the draft constitution and enacted it by decree. The draft constitution was approved by the people of the Central African Republic in a referendum on 5 December.

At its fourth session (8-26 November), NTC adopted draft ordinances on the establishment, organization and functioning of the transitional constitutional court, on the establishment of a commission to oversee freedom of the press (Haut Conseil de la communication) and on freedom of the press, all of which were submitted to the Government for adoption.

On 23 August, CEMI set up, in partnership with BONUCA and NTC, a committee of experts to develop an interpretation of the electoral code and measures for applying it to the election dates. An electoral census was carried out from 16 to 24 October. A total of 4,020 voting stations were set up within the country and abroad for 1,400,882 registered voters.

The overall security situation remained precarious. Acts of violence and summary executions attributable to law enforcement forces and robbery and roadblocks by armed groups continued to occur. On 14 September, a National Commission for Disarmament, Demobilization and Reintegration was established.

The economic and social situation continued to be affected by the poor economic performances of 2002 and 2003, despite the commitments and adjustments made by the Government in agreement with the Bretton Woods institutions (the World Bank Group and IMF) to gradually restore security throughout the country, reduce State spending and combat bad governance and impunity. Personal income and State revenue declined, while earnings growth remained weak. The agricultural sector continued to be affected by the fall in world coffee and cotton prices. Public expenditure fell as a result of the authorities' commitments to cut State spending. Civil servants and State officials reported that they would be owed salary arrears for five months by the end of 2004.

The humanitarian situation remained precarious, and the poor condition of roads and the prevailing insecurity made it difficult for humanitarian organizations to reach vulnerable population groups. There were around 200,000 displaced persons in the Central African Republic at the end of 2004 and almost 30,000 Central African refugees in Goré, Chad, following the events of 15 March 2003 [YUN 2003, p. 156]. The Central African Republic was hosting almost 46,000 people of Sudanese, Chadian, DRC, Rwandan and Burundian origin. A repatriation operation for DRC refugees living in the Central African Republic began in October.

The Secretary-General determined that the situation in the Central African Republic was gradually improving in spite of shortcomings in governance and human rights. The programmes adopted in August by IMF and the World Bank sent a signal to the authorities to continue their efforts to raise tax revenues. Meanwhile, election preparations were proceeding on schedule, and on 11 December General Bozizé announced his candidacy for president. The compromise achieved with regard to the draft constitution and the draft electoral code significantly improved relations between the Government and NTC, giving rise to new hope for a favourable outcome to the transition, as demonstrated by the smooth holding of the constitutional referendum on 5 December. The Secretary-General encouraged the donor community and friends of the Central African Republic to provide material, financial and technical resources to ensure a lasting consolidation of its institutions.

Other matters. The Central African Republic, by a 4 March letter [S/2004/195], informed the Secretary-General that General Bozizé had agreed to receive and welcome the Haitian President, Jean-Bertrand Aristide, as a purely humanitarian act. (See PART ONE, Chapter II, for more information.)

West Africa

In 2004, the countries in conflict in West Africa recorded modest progress in their search for peace and a return to stability, with the exception of Côte d'Ivoire, where tension remained high.

In March, the Security Council expressed concern about the continuing instability in the region, called for a comprehensive and composite approach to durable solutions to the crises and conflicts that would address the root causes, and considered means to promote peace and security. In that regard, the Council sent a fact-finding mission to the region in June to, among other tasks, identify a coherent UN intervention strategy. The mission made a number of recommendations for addressing the complex problems facing the region and the countries individually, stressing the need for a collective approach and support of the efforts of the Economic Community of West African States (ECOWAS).

In further efforts to promote a regional approach to addressing the serious challenges to peace and security facing West Africa, the Security Council met in March to consider the Secretary-General's report and recommendations for combating subregional and cross-border problems. The Council adopted many of the Secretary-General's recommendations, particularly those relating to the plight of child soldiers and the use and proliferation of mercenaries and small arms, within the context of a regional approach. Other recommendations dealt with disarmament and reintegration of ex-combatants, security sector reform, good governance, halting human rights and humanitarian abuses, and an international presence in post-conflict countries. The Secretary-General also submitted to the Council an assessment of the role and performance of the United Nations Office for West Africa (UNOWA) in promoting regional solutions to cross-border and regional problems and conflict prevention.

In Côte d'Ivoire, progress in implementing the 2003 Linas-Marcoussis Agreement was stymied by the disagreements among the political parties over the delegation of powers in the Government of National Reconciliation and their refusal to lay down their arms. In February, the Security Council established the United Nations Operation in Côte d'Ivoire (UNOCI), thereby expanding the UN presence in the country. A demonstration in March led to violent clashes in Abidjan between the Ivorian security forces and demonstrators and led to the withdrawal of opposition forces from the Government. After months of political stalemate, the parties signed the Accra III Agreement on reactivating the peace process and on means for implementing the Linas-Marcoussis Agreement. However, little progress followed, and hostilities erupted again in November when government forces attacked rebels' strongholds in the north, crossing the Zone of Confidence, a belt across the middle of the country controlled by UNOCI. The Council imposed an arms embargo and adopted other sanctions on Côte d'Ivoire. To get the peace process back on track, mediation efforts were led by President Thabo Mbeki of South Africa, which resulted in the parties' agreement in December on a plan of action for advancing the peace process. By the end of the year, tensions in the capital, Abidjan, and the rest of the country had decreased and significant progress was made in fulfilling all outstanding requirements under the Linas-Marcoussis Agreement.

Both Liberia and Sierra Leone experienced positive movement in efforts to stabilize their respective political situations. In Liberia, concerted efforts were made to implement the 2003 Comprehensive Peace Agreement, the framework for the establishment of the National Transitional Government and the end of civil strife. The United Nations Mission in Liberia (UNMIL), established in 2003, monitored the ceasefire, assisted in disarming combatants and facilitated the delivery of humanitarian aid. The deployment of the Mission's troops throughout the country in 2004 brought relative calm and security that permitted progress towards the restoration of State authority. The disarmament and demobilization of the armed forces were completed in October and resettlement of displaced persons commenced. The Government continued to encounter difficulties in delivering basic services, extending civil administration throughout the country and establishing electoral procedures. The outbreak of violence in Monrovia in late October was a reminder of the fragility of the peace process.

Sierra Leone was able to consolidate its stability in 2004, implementing most of the provisions of the 2000 Agreement on the Ceasefire and Cessation of Hostilities (Abuja Agreement). That progress and fulfilment of the benchmarks for the drawdown of the United Nations Mission in Sierra Leone (UNAMSIL) created the conditions for the reduction of the Mission from 11,500 troops at the beginning of the year to 5,000. Meanwhile, Sierra Leone continued efforts to enhance the capacity of its armed forces and police to enable them to ensure security and stability. The disarmament, demobilization and reintegration programme was formally closed on 31 March, with more than 54,000 ex-combatants having received benefits. Local elections were held in May for the first time in 32 years. The Truth and Reconciliation Commission released its final report to the public, and the Special Court for Sierra Leone continued to try those accused of serious human rights abuses and crimes against humanity during the 10 years of civil war.

In view of the progress achieved, the Security Council, in September, redefined the UNAMSIL mandate. As the country remained generally calm, UNAMSIL proceeded with its drawdown and transferred responsibility for national security to the Government of Sierra Leone.

Guinea-Bissau was also successful in implementing the terms of its peace framework, the 2003 Political Transition Charter. The main achievements in 2004 were the holding of legislative elections in March and the formation of a new Government in May, the resumption by some governmental institutions of their functions and the start of preparations for presidential elections in April 2005. The United Nations Peace-building Support Office in Guinea-Bissau (UNOGBIS) continued to support the Government in the peace process and to promote social and economic development, which remained in a critical socio-economic situation. Progress in implementing the Political Transition Charter was halted temporarily by a military mutiny in October; however, the situation was ameliorated when the Government, having received international assistance and adopted fiscal reforms, was able to satisfy one of the grievances that led to the march, paying the salary arrears of the armed forces and civil services. Presidential elections were scheduled for 2005 and efforts were made to restructure the security sector. To assist the Government in those efforts, the Security Council in December extended the UNOGBIS mandate and expanded its responsibilities.

Cameroon and Nigeria took steps in 2004 to resolve their border issues, with UN assistance, mainly through the Cameroon-Nigeria Mixed Commission. The Commission, established by the Secretary-General following the 2002 ruling of the International Court of Justice on the land and maritime boundary between the two countries, began work on the delimitation of the land and maritime borders.

Regional issues

Threats to peace and security

Report of Secretary-General. The Secretary-General, on 12 March [S/2004/200], reported on ways to combat subregional and cross-border problems in West Africa, as requested by the Security Council in presidential statement S/PRST/2003/11 [YUN 2003, p. 176]. The Secretary-General noted that, while the three cross-border problems of child soldiers, mercenaries and small arms were important contributory causes of conflict in West Africa, their relationship with the instability was primarily symptomatic, not causal.

Based on extensive consultations by his Special Representative for West Africa within the UN system and in the subregion, he made recommendations to address the cross-border problems, in the areas of improving UN harmonization, ratification and observance of existing conventions, collaboration in the Mano River Union (MRU) area, strengthening the ECOWAS secretariat and implementating the 1998 ECOWAS moratorium on the importation, exportation and manufacture of small arms and light weapons in West Africa, supporting national commissions, disarmament, demobilization and reintegration programmes, security sector reform, reducing extortion at roadblocks within and between countries, strengthening civil society participation and awareness-raising, and "naming and shaming" small arms exporters and private security companies.

To improve harmonization among the UN actors active in West Africa, the Secretary-General suggested that his Special Representative for West Africa organize meetings among the senior staff of the UN political and peacekeeping missions in the region, and the regional heads of UN agencies and programmes, with the participation of senior ECOWAS officials and civil society representatives. He called on regional Governments to ratify and observe existing conventions on small arms, child soldiers and mercenaries and to adopt policies against the recruitment of child soldiers and mercenaries. ECOWAS and the United Nations, with the MRU countries (Guinea, Liberia, Sierra Leone), should explore ways of enhancing international attention to the priority cross-border problems, including the convening of an international conference on assistance to that region. MRU States and Côte d'Ivoire, with UN and other assistance, should initiate joint security patrols and common border management. ECOWAS should reinforce its four observation and monitoring zones to gather more information on cross-border problems, authorize information-sharing and set up a database of individuals and groups suspected of trafficking in small arms, mercenaries and child soldiers. It should also adopt a legally binding instrument to complement the work done so far under its 1998 moratorium, due to expire in 2004, including a ban on mercenaries; harmonize national legislation and common penalties; and begin work on a regional arms register. ECOWAS should also support the strengthening of national arms control commissions. A register of arms held by the military and security agencies should be maintained.

In the area of disarmament, demobilization and reintegration, the lessons learned in Mali and Sierra Leone should be applied in other areas in West Africa, and UNOWA and UN missions in Côte d'Ivoire, Liberia and Sierra Leone should collaborate regarding a true disarmament, demobilization and reintegration process. Development projects should be made contingent on the collection of arms, and disarmament, demobilization and reintegration programmes should contain specific elements for child and women combatants. Security sector reform could be improved, including in human rights and humanitarian law, and by convening a meeting of defence and interior ministers. The capacity of frontier services should also be strengthened. To reduce extortion at roadblocks, ECOWAS members should abide by their commitments to free passage for people and goods and reduce illegitimate checkpoints.

To halt human rights and humanitarian abuses, the Secretary-General called for further concerted pressure, including international sanctions, against the recruiters of children and mercenaries, as well as commercial companies and individuals involved in such recruitment and which exported small arms to the subregion. Among other measures to control small arms, he proposed that exporting countries should force manufacturers to inscribe indelible serial numbers on weapons and importing countries should strengthen licensing procedures.

The Secretary-General said that addressing the cross-border regional issues identified by the Council in a comprehensive manner required a fundamental change in the political approach. The regional and international communities should help Governments by providing targeted assistance and ensuring that international standards were respected, and by responding at an earlier stage to governance and humanitarian crises. The international community should also maintain a robust presence in post-conflict countries to prevent regression into conflict and to promote good governance and peace-building. The Secretary-General hoped that Council members would explore ways to enhance the ECOWAS capacity to address cross-border regional issues, support the activities of civil society organizations, including women's associations, and identify specific recommendations from among those in his report for further action.

Security Council consideration. At the Security Council's 25 March meeting [meeting 4933] to consider cross-border issues in West Africa, the Secretary-General said that ECOWAS had taken important initiatives to tackle the serious challenges to peace and security in West Africa, demonstrating the resolve of Africans to settle African problems in cooperation with the international community. The recommendations in his report could not be implemented solely on a country-by-country basis but required a multifaceted regional approach. Special attention should be paid to the proliferation of small arms, the illegal exploitation of natural resources and the use of child soldiers and mercenaries, as well as roadblocks. To build on his report on the subject (see p. 165), he had asked his Special Representative for West Africa to convene a meeting to explore how ECOWAS and the relevant UN entities could best move ahead.

The ECOWAS Chairman (Ghana) said that, though the Secretary-General's recommendations for joint security patrols and common border management were laudable, ECOWAS felt that the best solution was finding a way to restore peace to the entire region. He stated that, with the drawdown of UNAMSIL (see p. 212), there was a need to ensure that the withdrawal took account of the Government's ability to assume responsibility for overall security, enhance control of natural resources and consolidate civil administration throughout the country. It was also vital that UNAMSIL continue to monitor the movement of armed elements along Liberia's borders to prevent incursions. UNOWA should be tasked with getting the leaders of Côte d'Ivoire, Sierra Leone and Guinea to stay engaged in the disarmament process and to help UNMIL to monitor the concealment of arms in Liberia's neighbouring States.

SECURITY COUNCIL ACTION (March)

On 25 March [meeting 4933], following consultations among Security Council members, the President made statement **S/PRST/2004/7** on behalf of the Council:

> The Security Council, recalling its relevant resolutions and the statements by its President, emphasizes the importance of addressing the continuing factors of instability in West Africa within a regional framework. It recognizes the need for a comprehensive and composite approach for durable solutions to the complex crises and conflicts in West Africa. Such an approach should address the root causes of conflict and consider means to promote sustainable peace and security, including development and economic revival, good governance and political reform.
>
> The Council takes note in this regard of the report of the Secretary-General of 12 March 2004 and its recommendations to address cross-border issues, in particular the plight of child soldiers and the use and proliferation of mercenaries and small arms, within the context of a regional approach. The Council believes action on the report should be taken as part of a wider strategy of conflict prevention, crisis management and post-conflict stabilization in the subregion.
>
> The Council welcomes the principles set out by the African Union and the New Partnership for Africa's Development which provide an important framework for such action. It encourages the States members of the Economic Community of West African States to ensure that these are fully imple-

mented. It consequently urges the Economic Community of West African States to work closely with the United Nations system, the international financial institutions and other international and regional organizations concerned, including the newly established African Union Peace and Security Council, as well as with interested States, in drafting a regional conflict prevention policy taking fully into account the recommendations of the recent joint United Nations and European Union mission to the region.

> The Council stresses the importance of the role of the Special Representative of the Secretary-General for West Africa in facilitating the coordination of a coherent United Nations approach to cross-border and transnational problems in the subregion.
>
> The Council encourages the Special Representative of the Secretary-General for West Africa to continue to hold regular meetings on coordination among the United Nations missions in the region in the interest of improved cohesion and maximum efficiency of United Nations activities in West Africa. It also encourages the greatest possible harmonization among United Nations agencies within countries of the subregion.
>
> The Council requests the Secretary-General to encourage the United Nations missions in West Africa to share information and their logistic and administrative resources as far as possible, without impeding the satisfactory execution of their respective mandates, in order to increase their effectiveness and reduce costs.
>
> The Council expresses its intention to consider the recommendations of the Secretary-General to facilitate cross-border operations and to strengthen cooperation among the United Nations missions in the region, including the possibility of 'hot pursuit' operations, joint air patrolling, shared border responsibility, the possible reinforcement of airspace monitoring and joint planning for the repatriation of foreign combatants. It looks forward to receiving, as soon as possible, the recommendations of the Secretary-General, after due consultation with the Governments concerned. It also encourages the States in the subregion to organize common patrols along their respective borders, jointly if need be, with the respective United Nations peacekeeping operations.
>
> The Council invites the Secretary-General and the Economic Community of West African States to take the requisite practical decisions to improve the coordination of the activities of the United Nations and the Economic Community of West African States in West Africa.
>
> The Council stresses the importance of a regional approach in the preparation and implementation of demobilization, disarmament and reintegration programmes. To this end it invites the United Nations missions in West Africa, the Governments concerned, the appropriate financial institutions, international development agencies and donor countries to work together to harmonize individual country demobilization, disarmament and reintegration programmes within an overarching regional strategy to design community development programmes to be implemented alongside demobilization, disarmament and reintegration programmes, and to pay special attention to the specific needs of children in armed conflict.

The Council reiterates the importance of finding durable solutions to the problem of refugees and displaced persons in the subregion, and urges the States in the region to promote necessary conditions for their voluntary and safe return with the support of relevant international organizations and donor countries.

The Council considers that illegal trafficking in arms poses a threat to international peace and security in the region. It, therefore, urges the States members of the Economic Community of West African States to fully implement their moratorium on the import, export and manufacture of light weapons, signed in Abuja on 31 October 1998. It also invites them to study the possibility of strengthening its provisions.

The Council invites the States members of the Economic Community of West African States to take all necessary steps to better combat illegal trafficking in small arms and light weapons in the region, such as the establishment of a regional register of small arms and light weapons. The Council calls on donor countries to help the member States implement these steps.

The Council urges all States, in particular those in the region and those with a capacity to export arms, to ensure that arms embargoes are fully implemented in the subregion. It expresses its intention to pay close attention and remain in consultation with the Economic Community of West African States and Member States on steps to stop the illicit flows of arms to conflict zones in the region.

The Council recognizes the need to address both the supply and demand side with regard to private companies selling illegally small arms or security services, and invites the Governments concerned to take appropriate steps to prevent such illegal sales.

The Council recalls the measures it has implemented on the illegal exploitation and trade of diamonds and timber in the subregion, and encourages the Economic Community of West African States and its member States to promote transparent and sustainable exploitation of those resources.

The Council encourages the Economic Community of West African States to publicly identify parties and actors who are shown to engage in illicit trafficking of small arms in the subregion and use mercenaries, and expresses its intention to consider adopting this practice in relation to the conflicts in West Africa.

The Council recalls that the existence of the many illegitimate checkpoints and the practice of extortion at those checkpoints in the region harms the security of civilians and is a major stumbling block to the economic development of all West Africa. It therefore invites the Governments concerned to take the necessary steps to effectively address this impediment to regional economic integration with the support of the international community.

The Council calls upon the States members of the Economic Community of West African States to work together to agree to a coherent approach to the problem of foreign combatants.

The Council calls upon the Mano River Union States to resume dialogue and to consider holding a summit of heads of State and meetings of ministers to develop a common approach to their shared security issues and confidence-building measures.

The Council considers that civil society actors, including the media, have an important role to play in crisis management and conflict prevention in the region and that their efforts in this regard deserve to be actively supported by the regional States, the Economic Community of West African States, the international community and the United Nations system. Increased support should be provided for the media to raise awareness about the plight of child soldiers, the use and proliferation of small arms and the recruitment of mercenaries.

The Council welcomes the consideration being given in the International Contact Group on Liberia to broadening its mandate to the cross-border issues concerning Liberia and its neighbouring countries.

The Council considers reform of the security sector an essential element for peace and stability in West Africa, and urgently calls upon donor countries and the international financial community to coordinate their efforts to support the Economic Community of West African States, in particular its Executive Secretariat, and to assist the States in the subregion in their efforts to reform the security sector.

The Council, in the context of its emphasis on the regional dimension of the problems in West Africa, expresses its intention to keep under review the implementation of the above-mentioned recommendations, and requests the Secretary-General to report on them at the occasion of his regular reports on the United Nations missions in the subregion.

MRU summit. The Mano River Union countries, at their summit on 20 May in Conakry, Guinea [S/2004/468], expressed satisfaction at the implementation of the disarmament, demobilization, reintegration and rehabilitation programme, which made possible the voluntary repatriation of Sierra Leonean refugees. The summit considered that all armed individuals conducting destabilizing activities against a legally established Government were to be considered as rebels or mercenaries, and that MRU member States should take legal and security measures to render them harmless. They called on the regional States to establish cooperation and monitoring mechanisms to combat that problem.

Security Council missions to West Africa

Report on 2003 mission

Security Council consideration. On 23 January [meeting 4899], the Security Council considered the progress report of the Secretary-General on its 2003 mission to West Africa [YUN 2003, p. 164]. The Assistant Secretary-General for Political Affairs briefed the Council on developments in the countries visited since the publication of the report. He concluded that, by and large, progress continued to be made in implementing the mission's recommendations. Having invested so much already in the subregion in terms of capital and resources, it was important that the Council remain engaged to build upon the progress being made in Guinea-Bissau, Côte d'Ivoire, Liberia and Sierra Leone and address the cross-cutting regional issues relating to peace and security and governance.

2004 mission

On 15 June [S/2004/491], the Security Council President informed the Secretary-General that the Council was sending a mission to West Africa (Ghana, Côte d'Ivoire, Liberia, Sierra Leone, Nigeria, Guinea-Bissau and Guinea), headed by Emyr Jones Parry (United Kingdom), from 20 to 29 June to, among other tasks, identify a coherent strategy for UN intervention in conflict prevention and peace-building, encourage ECOWAS to implement a subregional conflict prevention strategy, and strengthen UN-ECOWAS-MRU cooperation. Specific tasks were identified for the mission in each of the countries concerned.

In its 2 July report to the Council [S/2004/525], the mission stated that it had focused on the link between security and development, the need to build good governance and respect for human rights as the necessary foundation for lasting peace and prosperity. The region's borders were so porous and the problems, including the prevalence of small arms, fighters, child soldiers and HIV/AIDS, moved so easily across them that a collective approach was necessary to effect real and lasting change. A collective and integrated UN strategy should encompass the transition from peacekeeping to peace-building and development, including the role of UN peacekeeping operations in helping to create the right socio-economic conditions for lasting stability. ECOWAS was taking an increasingly active role by mobilizing regional countries to undertake peacekeeping missions; leading conflict resolution initiatives, as in Côte d'Ivoire, Guinea-Bissau and Liberia; and working with UNOWA on a regional conflict prevention strategy. Those efforts were gradually helping to build security and stability in the subregion, which, in turn, would lay the basis for greater economic integration and growth. The mission noted the progress in peace-building in the region in general, but was concerned by the breakdown in the peace process in Côte d'Ivoire.

The mission was gratified to learn about the enlarged programme of collaboration between ECOWAS and UNOWA to address cross-border problems in the subregion. The mission supported the efforts by the EU, UNDP and UNOWA to establish a strategic and operational planning capacity in the office of the ECOWAS Executive

Secretary. It also welcomed the ECOWAS and UNOWA initiative to identify ways of preventing military coups and other unconstitutional means of seizing or holding power, as well as mitigating the abuses of power that were usually the root causes of such actions.

The mission called on all parties to cease the use of child soldiers, emphasized the need to reintegrate former child combatants, and welcomed the efforts of the United Nations Children's Fund (UNICEF) and others to strengthen the ECOWAS Child Protection Unit. It recommended that additional resources be provided rapidly for UNOWA. It underlined the need to include in the regional approach to disarmament, demobilization and reintegration programmes not only those countries emerging from conflict but also those seriously affected by conflicts in neighbouring countries, such as Guinea, Mali and Burkina Faso.

With regard to small arms, the mission called on exporting countries to take action against those transgressing national laws or UN sanctions. The mission called on donors and institutions to provide assistance, particularly transport capacity and logistical assistance to increase the subregion's peacekeeping capacity. It encouraged ECOWAS, working with UNOWA, to develop a conflict prevention strategy, and recommended that the UN system develop strategies to deal with problems afflicting border regions in order to prevent conflicts from spreading further. Countries should also ensure that border controls curbed unauthorized cross-border movements, and UN peacekeeping operations should pay special attention to the monitoring of border areas.

The mission appealed to donors to increase contributions to humanitarian appeals, and encouraged greater support to West African civil society organizations. To promote job creation and economic opportunity, it recommended that Governments in the region work towards greater accountability and transparency, through such measures as anti-corruption campaigns and policies. Noting the principle of no impunity for serious human rights abuses, the mission urged the Council to take measures at the appropriate time, including the imposition of targeted sanctions against the individuals concerned.

The Council heard an oral briefing by the head of the mission on its visit to West Africa on 30 June [meeting 5000] and considered the mission's written report on 16 July [meeting 5005].

UNOWA activities

On 4 October [S/2004/797], the Secretary-General transmitted to the Security Council a review of the activities of the United Nations Office for West Africa. The Office, established in 2001 [YUN 2001, p. 162], became operational only in January 2003 in Dakar, Senegal. The review stated that, despite initial administrative and logistical constraints and unforeseen developments in the region, the Office had made considerable progress. It had proved useful in raising public awareness about cross-border and subregional problems, bringing a regional perspective to issues and promoting conflict prevention. It also developed mechanisms and promoted plans of action for enhancing linkages with other UN entities and national and international partners, supported peacemaking efforts, especially in Côte d'Ivoire and Liberia, undertook studies on subregional issues and conducted field missions to assess developments in tension-prone areas. The Secretary-General had also entrusted UNOWA with following up on the implementation of the 2002 decision [YUN 2002, p. 1265] of the International Court of Justice on land and maritime boundaries between Cameroon and Nigeria (see p. 230).

Promoting an integrated regional approach to the complex challenges facing West Africa remained a long-term process requiring sustained interaction between UNOWA and its partners. To that end, the Secretary-General recommended that UNOWA's mandate be extended for another period of three years, from 1 January 2005 to 31 December 2007, subject to a midterm review in July 2006. He intended to strengthen UNOWA, as called for by the Council's mission to West Africa (see p. 169).

Côte d'Ivoire

Concerted efforts by the United Nations, ECOWAS and the international community continued in 2004 to help facilitate a return to peace and stability in Côte d'Ivoire through implementation of the 2003 Linas-Marcoussis Agreement [YUN 2003, p. 166], including providing assistance to the Government of National Reconciliation of Côte d'Ivoire, established under that Agreement. The main responsibility for peacekeeping rested with the Licorne (French forces) and the ECOWAS Mission in Côte d'Ivoire (ECOMICI), whose deployment was endorsed by the Security Council in resolution 1464(2003) [ibid., p. 168]. Forces from both entities were deployed along the Zone of Confidence separating the Government-controlled south of the country from the north, controlled by the rebel movement, Forces nouvelles. Those efforts were supported by the United Nations Mission in Côte d'Ivoire (MINUCI), established in May 2003 [YUN 2003, p. 172] to facilitate implementation of the Linas-Marcoussis Agreement, monitor the security situation and complement the ECOWAS and French peacekeeping forces. The mission was headed by the Special Representative of the Secretary-General.

During the year, the Government of National Reconciliation attempted to fulfil its tasks as outlined by the Agreement and to work towards national elections in 2005. However, implementation was hampered by continued disagreements over the delegation of powers. Based on reports of an investigative mission sent to evaluate MINUCI's progress, the Secretary-General recommended that the United Nations expand its peacekeeping mission. The Security Council established the United Nations Operation in Côte d'Ivoire (UNOCI) in February, with a maximum strength of 6,240 UN military personnel, and requested the Secretary-General to transfer authority from MINUCI and ECOWAS forces to UNOCI. At the same time, the Council authorized the French forces to use all necessary means to support UNOCI. The UN mission's wide-ranging mandate included responsibilities for monitoring the ceasefire and movements of armed groups; assisting in disarmament, demobilization, reintegration, repatriation and resettlement programmes; protecting UN personnel, institutions and civilians; facilitating humanitarian assistance; supporting implementation of the peace process; contributing to the protection of human rights; promoting the peace process through public information; and assisting the Government in restoring law and order.

The peace process stalled in March, due to rising political tension and lack of progress in implementing the terms of the Linas-Marcoussis Agreement. Some parties refused to lay down their arms, and others either suspended participation in the Government of National Reconciliation or announced their intention to do so. As frustration mounted, demonstrations were held, despite a government ban, resulting in violent clashes in the capital, Abidjan, between the Ivorian security forces and demonstrators. Investigation into the events determined that the excessive use of force was not proportional to the situation.

A series of diplomatic efforts by a number of heads of regional States and others to steer the peace process back on track, including a visit by the Security Council mission to the subregion, resulted in the signing on 30 July of the Accra III Agreement, which committed the parties to a framework for reactivating the peace process and fully implementing the terms of the Linas-Marcoussis Agreement, including resolving the issue of eligibility for the presidency, adoption of all legal reforms envisaged under the Linas-Marcoussis Agreement, and agreeing on a clear delegation of powers from the President to the Prime Minister. The Council welcomed the Agreement and urged all parties to implement it in good faith.

However, the parties failed to make much progress in fulfilling the terms of the Agreement in the following months. Hostilities broke out again in early November when government forces launched attacks against positions held by the Forces nouvelles in the north. Fighting and violent demonstrations quickly spread to other parts of the country, and nine French peacekeepers were killed by government forces. On 6 November, the Secretary-General asked the Security Council to confirm that UNOCI could use all necessary means to prevent any hostile action in the Zone of Confidence, which it did on the same day. Nine days later the Council took punitive action against those involved in the fighting by imposing an arms embargo against Côte d'Ivoire and a travel ban and a freeze of funds against those blocking the peace process. The Council established a committee to designate those individuals and entities subject to the sanctions.

The events in November were a serious setback to the prospects for peace. For the remainder of the year, there was some progress in returning to negotiations, principally through the mediation efforts of President Thabo Mbeki of South Africa, who led an AU diplomatic initiative in cooperation with the United Nations and ECOWAS. By late December, most of the major legislative reforms envisaged in the peace agreements had been drafted, including an amendment to article 35 of the Constitution on eligibility for the presidency.

Political and security developments

The Secretary-General reported [S/2004/443] a number of encouraging developments in the peace process at the beginning of the year. On 6 January, the Forces nouvelles returned to the Government of National Reconciliation and participated in subsequent meetings of the Council of Ministers, where major legal reforms envisaged in the Linas-Marcoussis Agreement were considered. On 14 January, the Secretary-General of the Forces nouvelles reaffirmed his movement's commitment to remain in the Government. The first extraordinary session of the National Assembly was convened to consider some of the draft laws envisaged under the Agreement, including those related to the identification of the population and the residence status of foreigners, the reconstitution of the In-

dependent Electoral Commission, the establishment of the National Commission on Human Rights, and land reform. On 12 January, President Laurent Gbagbo met with Guillaume Soro, leader of the Forces nouvelles, for the first time since that party had suspended participation in the Government. On 28 January, President Gbagbo agreed to restructure the management of the Ivorian Radio and Television, which had been a source of major political friction. In addition, the Government took steps towards deploying State administration and providing basic services to Forces nouvelles–controlled areas.

In the area of military cooperation, on 9 January, the quadripartite commission (Forces armées nationales de Côte d'Ivoire (FANCI), the armed wing of Forces nouvelles, ECOMICI and Licorne) signed the Yamoussoukro Agreement on the joint operational plan and guidelines for the disarmament, demobilization and reintegration programme. Both FANCI and the Forces nouvelles committed themselves to implementing the programme. On 14 February, the commission met to consider further plans and agreed on an exchange of prisoners to be carried out on 4 March. The Prime Minister, Seydou Diarra, announced that the programme would start on 8 March. However, the political climate began to worsen. On 26 February, Mr. Soro declared that, unless all key issues of the Linas-Marcoussis Agreement were addressed, his movement would not lay down arms before the October 2005 elections.

Communications (January/February). President Gbagbo, in a speech delivered on 20 January [S/2004/67], reported on the Government's efforts towards achieving a peaceful solution to the crisis, and indicated that, within the powers granted to him by the Constitution, he intended to submit a number of issues to referendum.

The AU Central Organ of the Mechanism for Conflict Prevention, Management and Resolution, at a meeting on 30 January [S/2004/88], expressed satisfaction at the progress made in the Ivorian peace process, particularly the return of the Forces nouvelles to the Government. It encouraged the Ivorian political forces to continue to honour their commitments, in conformity with the Linas-Marcoussis Agreement, and supported the requests by Côte d'Ivoire and ECOWAS for the speedy deployment of a peacekeeping force in that country and the Secretary-General's proposal for such a mission [YUN 2003, p. 171].

Report of assessment mission. On 6 January [S/2004/3], the Secretary-General reported on MINUCI's efforts to facilitate peace and security in the country, including the report of an assessment mission sent to Côte d'Ivoire from 3 to 11

December 2003 [YUN 2003, p. 183] and his recommendation for expanding MINUCI's mandate in the light of the realities on the ground. In the meantime, the President of the General Assembly, in an 8 January letter [S/2004/100] to the Security Council President, drew attention to resolution 58/275 [YUN 2003, p. 175] concerning consideration of the financing of MINUCI at the Assembly's resumed fifty-eighth (2004) session, scheduled for 8 March to 2 April.

SECURITY COUNCIL ACTION (4 February)

On 4 February [meeting 4909], the Council unanimously adopted **resolution 1527(2004)**. The draft [S/2004/82] was prepared in consultations among Council members.

The Security Council,

Reaffirming its previous resolutions concerning Côte d'Ivoire, in particular its resolutions 1514(2003) of 13 November 2003, 1498(2003) of 4 August 2003 and 1464(2003) of 4 February 2003,

Reaffirming its strong commitment to the sovereignty, independence, territorial integrity and unity of Côte d'Ivoire, and recalling the importance of the principles of good-neighbourliness, non-interference and cooperation in relations between the States of the region,

Reaffirming its endorsement of the agreement signed by the Ivorian political forces at Linas-Marcoussis, France, on 23 January 2003 ("the Linas-Marcoussis Agreement") and approved by the Conference of Heads of State on Côte d'Ivoire held in Paris on 25 and 26 January 2003,

Stressing the importance of the complete and unconditional implementation of the measures provided for under the Linas-Marcoussis Agreement, and taking note with satisfaction of the progress made recently in this regard,

Recalling its full support for the efforts of the Economic Community of West African States and France to promote a peaceful settlement of the conflict, and welcoming in particular the effective action taken by the Economic Community of West African States Mission in Côte d'Ivoire in order to stabilize the country, as well as the commitment of the African Union in supporting the process of national reconciliation in Côte d'Ivoire,

Taking note of the message addressed to the Security Council on 10 November 2003 by the President of the Republic of Côte d'Ivoire, in which he requested the transformation of the United Nations Mission in Côte d'Ivoire into a peacekeeping operation,

Noting the need for the Mission to continue carrying out its mandate as outlined in its resolution 1479(2003) of 13 May 2003,

Affirming its readiness to consider the recommendations contained in the report of the Secretary-General of 6 January 2004 as well as the need for coordination of the United Nations efforts in West Africa,

Noting with concern the continued existence of challenges to the stability of Côte d'Ivoire, and determining that the situation in Côte d'Ivoire continues to constitute a threat to international peace and security in the region,

Acting under Chapter VII of the Charter of the United Nations,

1. *Decides* that the mandate of the United Nations Mission in Côte d'Ivoire shall be extended until 27 February 2004;

2. *Decides also* to renew until 27 February 2004 the authorization given to Member States participating in forces of the Economic Community of West African States, together with French Forces supporting them;

3. *Takes note with appreciation* of the report of the Secretary-General of 6 January 2004 on the United Nations Mission in Côte d'Ivoire;

4. *Calls upon* the signatories to the Linas-Marcoussis Agreement to carry out expeditiously their responsibilities under the Linas-Marcoussis Agreement;

5. *Also calls upon* the signatories to the Linas-Marcoussis Agreement to take the steps called for by the Secretary-General in paragraph 86 of his report, and expresses its readiness to help them to achieve lasting peace and stability;

6. *Requests* the Secretary-General, pending a decision by the Security Council on the reinforcement of the United Nations presence in Côte d'Ivoire as recommended in paragraph 61 of the report of the Secretary-General, to prepare the possible deployment of a peacekeeping operation within five weeks after such decision by the Council;

7. *Decides* to remain actively seized of the matter.

Establishment of UNOCI

To help him finalize his proposals for expanding the UN peacekeeping mission in Côte d'Ivoire, the Secretary-General sent a technical team to that country from 16 to 27 January to evaluate the situation. In his 9 February report [S/2004/3/Add.1], he pointed out that under the Linas-Marcoussis Agreement, the international community was requested to support the Government of National Reconciliation in restructuring the security forces. However, the conduct of the National Police and the Gendarmerie, including human rights violations, corruption and extortion at checkpoints along major arteries, contributed to a widespread culture of impunity. The security forces had ceased to function in the northern part of the country, where law enforcement and policing activities were carried out by "interim structures". A plan was being prepared for the return and reintegration of the National Police and the Gendarmerie to the north, which appeared to have the agreement of the Forces nouvelles, but the latter insisted on a neutral UN presence during the transition period. Another important concern to be urgently addressed was the restoration of law enforcement institutions and personnel in the zone of confidence. The judicial system had also ceased functioning in the north and in the zone of confidence. The prison system was underfunded and prisoners were held without access to proper judicial procedures.

The Secretary-General proposed that in the southern part of the country where national police operations had not been disrupted, the main role of the UN civilian police would be to advise the Government on restructuring the Gendarmerie and the National Police. It would also advise law enforcement authorities and observe their operation, with a view to deterring excesses and abuses. In the north and in the zone of confidence, the UN civilian police would advise the Government on the restoration of a police presence and instil confidence in the population so as to facilitate the restoration of that presence there. The UN civilian police, comprising 350 UN officers, would provide advice and support aimed at enhancing the operational capabilities and professionalism of the police and gendarmerie, and the restoration of law enforcement institutions and personnel in the zone of confidence and in the north. The deployment of all UN civilian police would begin in Abidjan in the south and Bouaké in the north, and gradually expand throughout the country.

The Secretary-General also recommended the establishment of a small judicial unit to help address key outstanding issues identified in the Linas-Marcoussis Agreement relating to strengthening the independence of the judiciary, national identification and citizenship, human rights, land tenure, and the criteria for eligibility for the presidency and other elections-related issues. The unit, comprising up to five international staff, would support and advise judicial authorities and the Government on the re-establishment of an impartial judicial system in areas where the administration of justice had broken down, and encourage the transparency of the justice system. It would follow legislative, judicial and administrative developments on matters central to implementation of the Linas-Marcoussis Agreement. In view of the need to re-establish a prison system in the north and to strengthen the system in the south, it was recommended that the civilian police and judicial component of the proposed peacekeeping operation also include a corrections unit to advise national authorities.

In a later addendum [S/2004/3/Add.2], the Secretary-General informed the Security Council that the financial implications for the deployment of a UN peacekeeping operation in Côte d'Ivoire were projected at $303 million for a six-month period, including $149 million in recurrent and $154 million in non-recurrent costs. The projections, which took into account MINUCI's personnel and assets, provided for the deployment of 6,240 military personnel and 435 international and 529 national staff, as well as 119 United Nations Volunteers.

SECURITY COUNCIL ACTION (27 February)

On 27 February [meeting 4918], the Security Council unanimously adopted **resolution 1528 (2004)**. The draft [S/2004/146] was prepared in consultations among Council members.

The Security Council,

Recalling its resolutions 1464(2003) of 4 February 2003, 1479(2003) of 13 May 2003, 1498(2003) of 4 August 2003, 1514(2003) of 13 November 2003 and 1527 (2004) of 4 February 2004, and the statements by its President on Côte d'Ivoire,

Reaffirming its strong commitment to the sovereignty, independence, territorial integrity and unity of Côte d'Ivoire, and recalling the importance of the principles of good-neighbourliness, non-interference and regional cooperation,

Recalling that it endorsed the agreement signed by the Ivorian political forces at Linas-Marcoussis, France, on 23 January 2003 ("the Linas-Marcoussis Agreement") and approved by the Conference of Heads of State on Côte d'Ivoire, held in Paris on 25 and 26 January 2003,

Taking note with satisfaction of the recent progress, in particular the return of the Forces nouvelles to the Government, the agreement reached on the implementation of the programme of disarmament, demobilization and reintegration, and the talks between the President of the Republic of Côte d'Ivoire and the Forces nouvelles,

Considering that the Ivorian parties have made the progress called for by the Secretary-General towards the steps mentioned in paragraph 86 of his report of 6 January 2004 on the United Nations Mission in Côte d'Ivoire, as confirmed to the Council on 4 February 2004, and encouraging the Ivorian parties to continue their efforts in that direction,

Calling upon the parties and the Government of National Reconciliation to take all necessary steps to prevent further violations of human rights and international humanitarian law and to put an end to impunity,

Reaffirming its resolution 1325(2000) of 31 October 2000 on women and peace and security, its resolutions 1379(2001) of 20 November 2001 and 1460(2003) of 30 January 2003 on children and armed conflict, and its resolutions 1265(1999) of 17 September 1999 and 1296(2000) of 19 April 2000 on the protection of civilians in armed conflict,

Welcoming and encouraging efforts by the United Nations to sensitize peacekeeping personnel in the prevention and control of HIV/AIDS and other communicable diseases in all its peacekeeping operations,

Deeply concerned by the deteriorating economic situation in Côte d'Ivoire and its serious impact on the subregion as a whole,

Welcoming the commitment of the African Union in supporting the process of national reconciliation in Côte d'Ivoire,

Recalling its full support for the efforts of the Economic Community of West African States and France to promote a peaceful settlement of the conflict, and welcoming in particular the effective action taken by the forces of the Economic Community of West African States in order to stabilize the country,

Taking note of the message addressed to the Security Council on 10 November 2003 by the President of the

Republic of Côte d'Ivoire, in which he requested the transformation of the United Nations Mission in Côte d'Ivoire into a peacekeeping operation,

Taking note also of the request made by the Economic Community of West African States to the Security Council on 24 November 2003 to establish a peacekeeping operation in Côte d'Ivoire,

Noting that lasting stability in Côte d'Ivoire will depend on peace in the subregion, especially in Liberia, and emphasizing the importance of cooperation among the countries of the subregion to this end, as well as the need for coordination of the efforts of the United Nations missions in the subregion to contribute to the consolidation of peace and security,

Having considered the report of the Secretary-General on the United Nations Mission in Côte d'Ivoire,

Taking note of the letter dated 8 January 2004 from the President of the General Assembly addressed to the President of the Security Council,

Aware of the persistent challenges to the stability of Côte d'Ivoire, and determining that the situation in Côte d'Ivoire continues to pose a threat to international peace and security in the region,

Acting under Chapter VII of the Charter of the United Nations,

1. *Decides* to establish the United Nations Operation in Côte d'Ivoire for an initial period of twelve months as from 4 April 2004, and requests the Secretary-General to transfer authority from the United Nations Mission in Côte d'Ivoire and the forces of the Economic Community of West African States to the United Nations Operation in Côte d'Ivoire on that date, and decides, therefore, to renew the mandate of the United Nations Mission in Côte d'Ivoire until 4 April 2004;

2. *Decides also* that the United Nations Operation in Côte d'Ivoire shall comprise, in addition to the appropriate civilian, judiciary and corrections component, a military strength of a maximum of 6,240 United Nations personnel, including 200 military observers and 120 staff officers, and up to 350 civilian police officers, as required to perform the mandated tasks described in paragraph 6 below;

3. *Requests* the Secretary-General to encourage the United Nations missions in West Africa to share logistic and administrative support, to the extent possible, without prejudicing their operational capabilities with respect to their mandates, in order to maximize effectiveness and minimize the cost of the missions;

4. *Requests* the United Nations Operation in Côte d'Ivoire to carry out its mandate in close liaison with the United Nations missions in Sierra Leone and in Liberia, including, especially, in the prevention of movements of arms and combatants across shared borders and the implementation of disarmament and demobilization programmes;

5. *Reaffirms its strong support* for the Special Representative of the Secretary-General for Côte d'Ivoire, and approves his full authority for the coordination and conduct of all the activities of the United Nations system in Côte d'Ivoire;

6. *Decides* that the mandate of the United Nations Operation in Côte d'Ivoire, in coordination with the French forces authorized in paragraph 16 below, shall be the following:

Monitoring of the ceasefire and movements of armed groups

(a) To observe and monitor the implementation of the comprehensive ceasefire agreement of 3 May 2003, and to investigate violations of the ceasefire;

(b) To liaise with the National Armed Forces of Côte d'Ivoire and the military elements of the Forces nouvelles in order to promote, in coordination with the French forces, the re-establishment of trust between all the Ivorian forces involved, as stated in its resolution 1479(2003);

(c) To assist the Government of National Reconciliation in monitoring the borders, with particular attention to the situation of Liberian refugees and to the movement of combatants;

Disarmament, demobilization, reintegration, repatriation and resettlement

(d) To assist the Government of National Reconciliation in undertaking the regrouping of all the Ivorian forces involved and to ensure the security of their cantonment sites;

(e) To help the Government of National Reconciliation to implement the national programme for the disarmament, demobilization and reintegration of the combatants, with special attention to the specific needs of women and children;

(f) To coordinate closely with the United Nations missions in Sierra Leone and in Liberia in the implementation of a voluntary repatriation and resettlement programme for foreign ex-combatants, with special attention to the specific needs of women and children, in support of the efforts of the Government of National Reconciliation and in cooperation with the Governments concerned, relevant international financial institutions, international development organizations and donor nations;

(g) To ensure that the programmes mentioned in subparagraphs (e) and (f) above take into account the need for a regional approach;

(h) To guard weapons, ammunition and other materiel handed over by the former combatants and to secure, neutralize or destroy such materiel;

Protection of United Nations personnel, institutions and civilians

(i) To protect United Nations personnel, installations and equipment, provide the security and freedom of movement of United Nations personnel and, without prejudice to the responsibility of the Government of National Reconciliation, to protect civilians under imminent threat of physical violence, within its capabilities and its areas of deployment;

(j) To support, in coordination with the Ivorian authorities, the provision of security for the ministers of the Government of National Reconciliation;

Support for humanitarian assistance

(k) To facilitate the free flow of people, goods and humanitarian assistance, inter alia, by helping to establish the necessary security conditions;

Support for the implementation of the peace process

(l) To facilitate, in cooperation with the Economic Community of West African States and other international partners, the re-establishment by the Government of National Reconciliation of the authority of the State throughout Côte d'Ivoire;

(*m*) To provide oversight, guidance and technical assistance to the Government of National Reconciliation, with the assistance of the Economic Community of West African States and other international partners, to prepare for and assist in the conduct of free, fair and transparent electoral processes linked to the implementation of the Linas-Marcoussis Agreement, in particular the presidential election;

Assistance in the field of human rights

(*n*) To contribute to the promotion and protection of human rights in Côte d'Ivoire, with special attention to violence committed against women and girls, and to help to investigate human rights violations with a view to helping to end impunity;

Public information

(*o*) To promote understanding of the peace process and the role of the United Nations Operation in Côte d'Ivoire among local communities and the parties through an effective public information capacity, including the establishment, as necessary, of a United Nations radio broadcasting capability;

Law and order

(*p*) To assist the Government of National Reconciliation, in conjunction with the Economic Community of West African States and other international organizations, in restoring a civilian policing presence throughout Côte d'Ivoire, and to advise the Government of National Reconciliation on the restructuring of the internal security services;

(*q*) To assist the Government of National Reconciliation, in conjunction with the Economic Community of West African States and other international organizations, in re-establishing the authority of the judiciary and the rule of law throughout Côte d'Ivoire;

7. *Requests* the Secretary-General to give special attention to the gender and child-protection components within the staff of the United Nations Operation in Côte d'Ivoire;

8. *Authorizes* the United Nations Operation in Côte d'Ivoire to use all necessary means to carry out its mandate, within its capabilities and its areas of deployment;

9. *Requests* the Secretary-General and the Government of National Reconciliation to conclude a status-of-forces agreement within thirty days of the adoption of the present resolution, taking into consideration General Assembly resolution 58/82 of 9 December 2003 on the scope of legal protection under the Convention on the Safety of United Nations and Associated Personnel, and notes that, pending the conclusion of such an agreement, the model status-of-forces agreement dated 9 October 1990 shall apply provisionally;

10. *Stresses* the importance of the complete and unconditional implementation of the measures provided for under the Linas-Marcoussis Agreement, and demands that the parties fulfil their obligations under the Linas-Marcoussis Agreement so that, in particular, the forthcoming presidential election can be held in 2005 in accordance with the constitutional deadlines;

11. *Calls upon* all parties to cooperate fully in the deployment and operations of the United Nations Operation in Côte d'Ivoire, in particular by guaranteeing the safety, security and freedom of movement of United Nations personnel as well as associated personnel throughout the territory of Côte d'Ivoire;

12. *Reaffirms,* in particular, the need for the Government of National Reconciliation to undertake the complete and immediate implementation of the disarmament, demobilization and reintegration programme, including the disbanding of all armed groups, in particular the militias, the curbing of all kinds of disruptive street protests, especially of the various youth groups, and the restructuring of the armed forces and the internal security services;

13. *Urges* the international community to continue considering how it might help further economic development in Côte d'Ivoire, with a view to achieving long-term stability in Côte d'Ivoire and the whole sub-region;

14. *Requests* the Secretary-General to keep the Council regularly informed of the situation in Côte d'Ivoire, the implementation of the Linas-Marcoussis Agreement and the implementation of the mandate of the United Nations Operation in Côte d'Ivoire, and to report to it in this regard every three months, including a review of the troop level, with a view to a phasing-down in the light of the progress achieved on the ground and the tasks remaining to be fulfilled;

15. *Decides* to renew until 4 April 2004 the authorization given to the French forces and the forces of the Economic Community of West African States through its resolution 1527(2004);

16. *Authorizes,* for a period of twelve months from 4 April 2004, the French forces to use all necessary means in order to support the United Nations Operation in Côte d'Ivoire, in accordance with the agreement to be reached between the United Nations Operation in Côte d'Ivoire and the French authorities, and in particular:

(*a*) To contribute to the general security of the area of activity of the international forces;

(*b*) To intervene at the request of the United Nations Operation in Côte d'Ivoire in support of its elements whose security may be threatened;

(*c*) To intervene against belligerent actions, if the security conditions so require, outside the areas directly controlled by the United Nations Operation in Côte d'Ivoire;

(*d*) To help to protect civilians in the deployment areas of their units;

17. *Requests* France to continue to report to it periodically on all aspects of its mandate in Côte d'Ivoire;

18. *Decides* to remain actively seized of the matter.

The Secretary-General, speaking after the vote, said that Côte d'Ivoire had come a long way from the crisis that erupted in 2002. He noted that the parties had recently agreed on arrangements to implement the disarmament, demobilization, reintegration and repatriation programme, which was to start on 8 March. Other positive developments were the return of the Forces nouvelles to the Government of National Reconstruction on 6 January and consideration by the Council of Ministers of draft legislation and other reforms envisaged in the Linas-Marcoussis Agreement. A strengthened UN presence would make implementation of the disarmament, demobilization and reintegration programme easier, facilitate the provision of humanitarian assistance and the restoration of State authority throughout the country, contribute to the promotion of human rights and the re-establishment of the rule of law, and help the country prepare for elections in 2005.

Appointment. On 25 March [S/2004/267], the Secretary-General informed the Security Council of his intention to appoint Major General Abdoulaye Fall (Senegal) as Force Commander of UNOCI. The Council, on 31 March [S/2004/268], took note of his intention.

Events of late March

Following those positive developments in the peace process, the political climate in Côte d'Ivoire began to worsen, the Secretary-General stated in his first report on UNOCI [S/2004/443]. Following Mr. Soro's 26 February declaration on conditions for laying down arms (see p. 171), a number of political parties announced their intention to suspend participation in the Government due to concerns over the pace of implementation of the reforms envisaged under the Linas-Marcoussis Agreement, in particular those relating to the devolution of power from the President to the Government and the discretionary authority of ministers to make certain senior appointments within departments under their purview. Forces from the parties were deployed along the zone of confidence separating the Government-controlled south of the country from the rebel-controlled north. As a result of the political stalemate, the disarmament, demobilization and reintegration programme did not start as planned on 8 March. Two days later, supporters of the President stormed the Ministry of Justice to protest appointments made by the Justice Minister, Alassane Ouattara, who was also President of the opposition party, Rally of the Republicans. ECOWAS and French forces prevented them from attacking the residence of the Forces nouvelles ministers in Abidjan. Following those developments, the Council of Ministers, on 11 March, banned all demonstrations. In defiance, the "Coalition des Marcoussistes" (a coalition of opposition parties, including Forces nouvelles) announced that it would organize a demonstration on 25 March to protest the stalemate in the peace process and to show support for implementation of the Linas-Marcoussis Agreement. Despite a decree signed by President Gbagbo on 23 March limiting public demonstrations to enclosed spaces, the opposition parties maintained their determination to proceed with the rally. In a broadcast to the nation on the same day [S/2004/241], the President announced that a meeting had been scheduled for 29 March to examine all the issues outlined in a "Memorandum of Political Signatories of the Linas-Marcoussis and Accra II Agreements" presented to him by a delegation of "Marcoussistes".

On 24 March, the Secretary-General urged all Ivorian parties to exercise restraint and avoid exacerbating the situation. He appealed to the leaders of all Ivorian political parties to engage in consultations in order to move forward with implementation of the Agreement, as did a number of African leaders. Meanwhile, the Ivorian armed forces and gendarmerie moved into the centre of Abidjan. Public institutions and schools were closed until 29 March.

On 25 March, demonstrations took place in several parts of Abidjan, resulting in violent clashes between the Ivorian security forces and demonstrators. Violence and sporadic shooting occurred for two days in and around the capital. At least 120 people were killed, 274 wounded and 20 disappeared. Demonstrations also took place in Yamoussoukro and in Bouaké. The Secretary-General issued another statement, again urging all parties to put the national interest foremost, stop confrontations and resume implementation of the Agreement.

The events of 25 and 26 March dealt a serious blow to the peace process. Following those events, Mr. Soro stated that his movement ruled out any possibility of disarmament or a return to the Government as long as President Gbagbo remained in power. However, on 31 March, the "Marcoussistes" presented a number of conditions for the resumption of dialogue with President Gbagbo, including recognition of their constitutional right to demonstrate; enhanced security for signatories of the Agreement to be provided by Ivorian, French and UN forces; balanced coverage for all political parties in State-owned media; permission to organize funerals and commemorative ceremonies for those who died on 25 March; and the establishment of an international commission of inquiry to investigate all human rights violations committed in connection with the 25-26 March events. President Gbago [S/2004/257] and Prime Minister Diarra [S/2004/258] also requested the establishment of an international commission of inquiry and called on all the parties that had signed the Agreement but had suspended their participation in governmental bodies to return to their places and to implement it fully.

The Secretary-General supported the requests for an International Commission of Inquiry and instructed the Office of the United Nations High Commissioner for Human Rights (OHCHR) to proceed with its establishment (see p. 177).

Security Council President press statement. The Security Council President, in a 26 March press statement [SC/8043-AFR/869], said that Council members expressed grave concern at the events and stressed the importance of implementing all the commitments in the Linas-Marcoussis Agreement, in particular disarmament, to ensure the redeployment of the administration throughout the territory.

Communications (April). The EU, in a statement issued on 8 April [S/2004/309], deplored the events of 25 March. It emphasized the importance of prompt deployment of UN peacekeeping forces in Côte d'Ivoire to support implementation of the Agreement and urged the parties to resume political dialogue and participate again in the Government of National Reconciliation.

On 22 April [S/2004/321], Côte d'Ivoire transmitted to the Council the common platform on conditions for the resumption of the political dialogue, submitted by the Directorate for the Coordination of Political Forces for National Reconciliation, signatories of the Linas-Marcoussis Agreement, concluded during a meeting held on 13, 15 and 17 April to consider the social and economic situation following the events of 25-26 March. Those conditions, as agreed to by the Government of National Reconciliation, concerned security guarantees for civilians and political leaders; the right to demonstrate; the holding of a public commemoration for victims; the establishment of an international commission of inquiry to investigate the events of 25-26 March; and the impartial treatment of information by the State-run media. The letter also contained a schedule of specific actions in regard to each of the conditions, and a list of legislation relating to the Agreement that had been submitted to and/or adopted by Parliament.

SECURITY COUNCIL ACTION (April)

On 30 April [meeting 4959], following consultations among Security Council members, the President made statement **S/PRST/2004/12** on behalf of the Council:

The Security Council expresses its grave concern at the events which occurred in Côte d'Ivoire at the end of March 2004 and at the current impasse in the peace process defined in the Linas-Marcoussis Agreement.

The Council underscores the importance of investigating all alleged violations of human rights committed in Côte d'Ivoire so that those responsible do not remain unpunished.

The Council reaffirms its strong commitment to the territorial integrity and unity of Côte d'Ivoire.

The Council recalls that it endorsed the Linas-Marcoussis Agreement, which remains the only possible solution to the crisis in Côte d'Ivoire.

The Council further recalls that all Ivorian political forces have committed themselves to implement fully and with no conditions the Linas-Marcoussis Agreement. The Council decided, on the basis of this commitment, to deploy the United Nations Operation in Côte d'Ivoire to support the process of peaceful settlement of the crisis, which is to culminate in 2005 with the organization of free, fair and transparent elections.

The Council emphasizes the individual responsibility of each of the Ivorian actors in the settlement of the crisis.

The Council expresses its readiness to consider further steps to encourage full implementation of the Linas-Marcoussis Agreement and to promote the process of national reconciliation in Côte d'Ivoire, including actions that might be taken, if necessary, against individuals whose activities are an obstacle to the full implementation of the Linas-Marcoussis Agreement.

Commission of inquiry

OHCHR, as requested by the Secretary-General, led the investigation into alleged human rights violations committed in connection with the demonstrations of 25 March. The commission of inquiry visited Abidjan from 15 to 28 April. In its report [S/2004/384], the commission concluded that the 25 March demonstration was used for what turned out to be a carefully planned operation by the Ivorian security forces, as well as special units and the so-called parallel forces, targeting opposition parties and community groups not only in Côte d'Ivoire, but also in Burkina Faso, Mali and the Niger. In spite of public statements to the contrary, all evidence suggested that there was no significant threat to the security forces by the demonstrators and that the repression and killings on 25 March and the following days represented a level of violence and excessive use of force that were not proportional to the situation, resulting in indiscriminate killing of innocent civilians and massive human rights violations. The events had to be seen in the broader context of a fragile political system and a struggle for power, which was often violent. The political responsibility of those who planned the march, in spite of the ban, the tense climate created by the drawing of a "red zone" (forbidden area for unauthorized persons) and the mobilization and use of the army were major factors in the escalation of tension. Many of the killings took place in the houses of would-be demonstrators or even innocent civilians targeted by the security forces. Most of the human rights violations could be characterized as a massacre in which summary executions, torture, disappearances and arbitrary detentions were repeatedly committed by units of the security forces, acting in coordination or in collusion with the parallel forces.

In addition, the commission believed that other massive human rights violations committed since 19 September 2002 also needed to be investigated, and proposed the establishment of an international commission of inquiry for that purpose. It also stated that other relevant issues needed to be resolved, such as reducing the uneven distribution of wealth, the systematic exclusion of community groups and the low level of literacy, compounded by unemployment.

Among its proposals, the commission recommended: the conduct of criminal investigations for those responsible for the massacres; the expansion of the UNOCI mandate to ensure the protection of witnesses to the indiscriminate killings of 25 March and of relatives of massacre victims; the establishment of a mixed human rights court, with the participation of international judges, mandated to prosecute all past serious human rights violations, including those committed prior to 25 March 2004; the dismantlement and disarmament of all armed groups, including the so-called parallel forces, with the possible integration of those forces into regular security structures of the State; ensuring more effective protection of the basic human rights and fundamental freedoms of all individuals in Abidjan, to create an environment conducive to holding fair elections in 2005; reform and training of the police and security forces; reform and strengthening of the judiciary; restructuring of the armed forces with the participation of all ethnic groups; establishment of a UN radio station to encourage mutual respect and tolerance; and the establishment of an independent human rights mechanism of the Commission on Human Rights, such as a country-based special rapporteur or an independent expert.

Security Council consideration. The Security Council, in a 14 May press statement of the President [SC/8094-AFR/929-HR/4756], following a briefing by the Acting High Commissioner for Human Rights, welcomed OHCHR's intention to establish a commission to look into events dating back to September 2002. They expressed their determination to consider rapidly steps to ensure that those responsible for the violations of human rights in Cote d'Ivoire since September 2002 were held accountable for their actions. Council members urged the immediate establishment of the National Human Rights Commission called for in the Linas-Marcoussis Agreement.

Communications. President Gbagbo, on 18 [S/2004/411] and 20 [S/2004/414] May, welcomed the decision to send a new commission of inquiry to conduct a comprehensive review of the violations from September 2002. He also indicated that two national commissions of inquiry had been established to investigate the events of 25-26 March and that action would be taken to follow up on the conclusions of the Council's inquiries.

SECURITY COUNCIL ACTION (May)

On 25 May [meeting 4977], following consultations among Security Council members, the President made statement **S/PRST/2004/17** on behalf of the Council:

> The Security Council reiterates its grave concern at the events which occurred in Côte d'Ivoire at the end of March 2004 and at the current impasse in the peace process defined in the Linas-Marcoussis Agreement.
>
> The Council recalls that it endorsed the Linas-Marcoussis Agreement, which is the only solution to the crisis in Côte d'Ivoire.
>
> The Council reaffirms the individual responsibility of each of the Ivorian actors to ensure the full implementation of the Linas-Marcoussis Agreement. It reiterates its complete readiness to take any necessary further steps against individuals who block the full implementation of the Linas-Marcoussis Agreement.
>
> The Council takes note with deep concern of the report of the commission of inquiry of the Office of the United Nations High Commissioner for Human Rights on the events that occurred in Abidjan on 25 and 26 March 2004. It expresses its appreciation for the work of the Office of the High Commissioner.
>
> The Council strongly condemns the violations of human rights and international humanitarian law committed in Côte d'Ivoire, including those that occurred in Abidjan on 25 and 26 March 2004, and expresses its determination to ensure that those responsible for all these violations are identified and that the Government of Côte d'Ivoire brings them to justice. The Council expects President Laurent Gbagbo to comply fully with the commitment he has made in this regard, through the letter dated 20 May 2004 from the Permanent Representative of Côte d'Ivoire to the United Nations addressed to the President of the Security Council.
>
> The Council therefore requests the Secretary-General to establish as soon as possible the international commission of inquiry, as recommended by the commission of inquiry of the Office of the United Nations High Commissioner for Human Rights and requested by the Government of Côte d'Ivoire, in order to investigate all human rights violations committed in Côte d'Ivoire since 19 September 2002 and determine responsibility. The Council calls upon all the Ivorian parties to cooperate fully with this international commission of inquiry.
>
> The Council reiterates its demand for the Government of Côte d'Ivoire to bring to justice those responsible for these violations of human rights. In this regard, it expresses its complete readiness to encourage possible international assistance to the Ivorian judicial authorities to this end and requests

the Secretary-General to submit recommendations on the various possible options for such assistance.

The Council is deeply concerned by slogans and declarations of hate, in particular those directed against the personnel of the United Nations Operation in Côte d'Ivoire, and urges all the Ivorian actors to refrain from any action or statement, especially in the media, which put at risk the security of United Nations personnel and, more globally, the process of national reconciliation. The Council recalls the obligation of all Ivorian actors, in particular the Government of Côte d'Ivoire, to cooperate fully in the deployment and operations of the United Nations Operation in Côte d'Ivoire, which is there at the request of the Government, in particular by guaranteeing the safety, security and freedom of movement of all United Nations personnel.

The Council requests the United Nations Operation in Côte d'Ivoire to establish without delay its broadcasting capacity, as mandated in its resolution 1528 (2004) of 27 February 2004.

The Council recalls that it decided, on the basis of the commitment of all Ivorian political forces to implement fully and without conditions the Linas-Marcoussis Agreement, to deploy the United Nations Operation in Côte d'Ivoire to support the process of peaceful settlement of the crisis, which is to lead to the organization in 2005 of open, free and transparent elections.

The Council underlines the fact that no concrete progress can be made in the implementation of the Linas-Marcoussis Agreement until the Government of National Reconciliation composed on 13 March 2003 and completed on 12 September 2003 meets again under the authority of the Prime Minister.

The Council is therefore deeply concerned by the recent announcement by President Laurent Gbagbo that he would dismiss opposition ministers. The Council also reiterates its concerns at the continuing non-participation of the opposition parties in the Government of National Reconciliation. The Council considers that such decisions undermine the normal functioning of Ivorian institutions and the resumption of dialogue between Ivorian parties which is the basis of the Linas-Marcoussis Agreement.

The Council underscores the importance of having all relevant Ivorian parties participate fully in the Government of National Reconciliation. In this regard, the Council calls upon all Ivorian parties to apply faithfully all the provisions of the Linas-Marcoussis Agreement, including those regarding the composition and the functioning of the Government of National Reconciliation, and to resume immediately political dialogue with a view to ensuring the effective functioning of the Government of National Reconciliation.

The Council reiterates its full support to Prime Minister Seydou Diarra, head of the Government of National Reconciliation, and encourages him to carry on his task until the completion of the peace process, as foreseen in the Linas-Marcoussis Agreement.

The Council recalls the importance it attaches to the early and full adoption of the constitutional and legislative reforms provided for in the Linas-Marcoussis Agreement.

The Council takes note in this regard of the renewed commitment of President Laurent Gbagbo, in his message to the nation on 18 May 2004, to apply fully the Linas-Marcoussis Agreement, and his request addressed to the Parliament to accelerate the achievement of the legislative reforms. It now expects these commitments to be fulfilled in order that concrete steps can be undertaken to restore confidence.

The Council also reaffirms the urgency of disbanding militias and armed groups and proceeding with operations to regroup the opposing forces in order to permit the start of disarmament and demobilization, which must precede their reintegration into the regular army or civilian life.

The Council firmly rejects the assertion that disarmament can be delayed until after the 2005 elections and calls upon all parties to move immediately to begin this process.

The Council underlines the responsibilities of the Monitoring Committee as the guarantor of the implementation of the Linas-Marcoussis Agreement and expresses its appreciation for further efforts it may undertake in order to overcome the current impasse in the peace process as well as in supporting the United Nations Operation in Côte d'Ivoire in carrying out its mandate.

The Council calls upon all parties to take immediate action to implement the steps above and emphasizes that these measures are essential to enable Côte d'Ivoire and Ivorians to return to the path to peace, stability and economic development."

Further developments in peace process

Report of Secretary-General (June). The Secretary-General, in his first report on UNOCI, issued on 2 June [S/2004/443] in response to resolution 1528(2004) (see p. 173), said that, in an effort to give new impetus to the peace process, a high-level delegation, led by the Under-Secretary-General for Peacekeeping Operations, Jean-Marie Guéhenno, visited Côte d'Ivoire from 15 to 20 April. The delegation conveyed the international community's preparedness to help Côte d'Ivoire restore peace and normalcy, including through the deployment of UNOCI, but the Ivorian parties had the responsibility to proceed without further delay and in good faith with implementation of the Linas-Marcoussis Agreement. It encouraged the President to use his authority to establish all necessary conditions to enable the Government to function effectively, including full support for his Prime Minister, greater freedom for the ministers to appoint their aides and the immediate dismantling of any parallel government structures. The delegation called on the Forces nouvelles to proceed with disarmament without delay.

On 24 April, the "Coalition des Marcoussistes" held a memorial service to honour the victims of the 25 and 26 March events, which took place without any serious incidents. The following day, supporters of President Gbagbo held a rally in Abidjan, demanding that UNOCI immediately disarm Forces nouvelles and the right to hold a rally in the Forces nouvelles stronghold of Bouaké. In the meantime, the political stalemate continued and the parties hardened their positions. On 26 April, the Forces nouvelles leader said that his movement would not disarm or return to the Government as long as President Gbagbo remained in power and would re-establish social services and a police force in the areas under its control. Two days later, a delegation of the "Coalition des Marcoussistes", escorted by UNOCI troops, travelled to northern Côte d'Ivoire for meetings aimed at promoting reconciliation. On 5 May, Prime Minister Diarra gave the Coalition assurances of impartial treatment in access to the State media and enhanced security, thereby satisfying the two remaining preconditions for the return of their ministers to the Government. In addition, the National Assembly decided to resume the debate on the law on identification and to consider other draft laws envisaged under the Linas-Marcoussis Agreement.

On 18 May, however, President Gbagbo announced the suspension of support to the opposition ministers who had boycotted Cabinet meetings since early March, and signed a decree announcing the dismissal of three of them, including Mr. Soro. Forces nouvelles responded by withdrawing all its remaining representatives from the capital to Bouaké. The tension continued to mount the next few days in Abidjan and several businesses and schools were closed. Threats to UNOCI from pro-Gbagbo supporters escalated, and the Secretary-General called on all parties concerned to desist from action that might lead to further violence and to cooperate with the Linas-Marcoussis Monitoring Committee and his Special Representative in resolving outstanding issues. The Monitoring Committee formulated a programme of work to help the parties overcome the political stalemate and proceed with implementation of the Agreement. The programme included a timetable for disarmament, demobilization and reintegration operations; legislation relating to the identification process; the reunification of the country, including by redeploying the State administration and the provision of basic services throughout Côte d'Ivoire; the reconstitution of the Independent Electoral Commission; equal access by all political groups to public media; security arrangements for leaders of political parties and candidates for presidential elections; and measures aimed at economic recovery.

The security situation, which deteriorated following the events of 25-26 March, remained fragile throughout the country. Serious tensions resulted in shootings and violent attacks against villagers. There was also an increase in militia activities in the western region. Ethnic and party clashes were also reported. In the north, in February and March, inter-factional fighting escalated between the military wings of Forces nouvelles. The continued de facto partitioning of the country contributed to the climate of uncertainty, and reinforced fears of a resumption of civil conflict. Forces nouvelles was reported to be strengthening its administrative activities in the areas under its control, including the payment of salaries to elements of the army and police and the establishment of custom services. Forces nouvelles suspended its participation in meetings of the quadripartite military commission, while FANCI no longer participated in joint patrols with Forces nouvelles. In Abidjan, the security situation deteriorated, with various demonstrations, mainly organized by pro–Ivorian Patriotic Front supporters to protest the findings of the international commission of inquiry (see p. 177) and delays in implementing the disarmament, demobilization and reintegration programme. UNOCI and French troops also came under attacks by groups of violent protesters.

The human rights situation throughout Côte d'Ivoire also deteriorated, with violations including arbitrary detention, extrajudicial killings and discrimination and violence on the basis of nationality, ethnic origin, gender and political opinion. In the northern area, there were acts of extortion, arbitrary tax collection, forceful abduction and summary execution. The collapse of the judicial system led to a dramatic increase in child prostitution and sexual violence perpetrated by various uniformed elements.

The current political crisis had a negative effect on election preparations. The National Assembly adopted a law on the identification and residence of aliens and the Government promulgated decrees on the establishment of a National Identification Supervisory Commission, changes to the National Identification Office, procedures for the issuance and format of the national identity card, and appointments to the National Identification Supervisory Commission. However, several draft laws were still awaiting legislative assent. An electoral needs assessment mission, sent to Côte d'Ivoire from 26 January to 6 February by the Secretary-General, recommended the establishment of an electoral component within UNOCI to provide technical assistance to national electoral authorities and monitor electoral preparations throughout the country.

The crisis also affected significantly the overall humanitarian and economic situation in the country and the West African subregion. Surveys indicated that malnutrition rates were on the rise in the western part of the country owing to the loss of harvests, continued displacements, poor roads and limited access to health facilities. In the north, the lack of deployment of local administration in the territory under the control of Forces nouvelles impacted negatively on the provision of health services and education in those areas. The health situation remained precarious, owing to the closure of most health-care centres following the departure of up to 85 per cent of the medical staff and lack of medical supplies.

The Secretary-General concluded that Côte d'Ivoire had reached a crossroads. He appealed to the Security Council, the AU, ECOWAS and other international stakeholders to continue to play an active role in encouraging all Ivorian parties to resume political dialogue, and to all opposition parties to return to the Government of National Reconciliation without delay. He said that the Security Council's upcoming mission to West Africa (see below) would provide an opportunity to remind all Ivorian parties of their respective responsibilities. He urged President Gbagbo to ensure that the ban on disruptive activities was enforced without discrimination, that all Ivorians were free to move safely throughout the country and that the Government was allowed to initiate the process of legislative reform unhindered.

Report of Security Council mission. The Security Council mission to West Africa (20-29 June) (see p. 169) visited Côte d'Ivoire on 22 and 23 June. In its report, submitted on 2 July [S/2004/525], the mission said that it had emphasized to leaders of Côte d'Ivoire its concern over the breakdown in the peace process, the impasse in the implementation of the Linas-Marcoussis Agreement and the non-functioning of the Government. It identified three concrete measures as vital for restarting the peace process: the reconstitution of the Government, the resumption of its work and the establishment of a schedule for implementing the Linas-Marcoussis Agreement; the early adoption by the National Assembly of political reforms envisaged in the Agreement; and the parties acting in unity to forge a better future for the country. The mission stressed that attacks against UN personnel and property had to cease.

The mission agreed that failure to resolve the political impasse would not only provoke a major socio-economic and humanitarian disaster and compound the existing North-South divide in the country, but would seriously upset the stability of the whole subregion. It noted the concern expressed by the UNOCI Force Commander that, unlike the French Licorne force, the mission's rules of engagement did not permit it to use force in monitoring the ceasefire and protecting civilians in the Zone of Confidence, making it difficult for the two forces to cooperate effectively.

The mission recommended that the President and the Prime Minister should consult with all the signatories to the Agreement on reconstituting and reactivating the Government, including an implementation schedule and ensuring that draft laws on political reform were adopted by the National Assembly by 28 July; the parties should commit to regular high-level dialogue without preconditions; the Government should halt hostile actions against UNOCI and UN and other foreign representatives in the country; and UNOCI should be brought up to full strength. In that regard, the Council would welcome advice on redefining the UNOCI mandate to allow for readjustment of its rules of engagement. The mission also recommended that the Government honour its commitment to authorize the operation of UNOCI's radio by early July; the Monitoring Committee should work with the Government and ECOWAS in monitoring the schedule of compliance with the Agreement; UN representatives should work with civil society organizations to advance the peace process; the Government should ensure that those responsible for human rights violations were brought to justice; the parties should commit themselves to cooperating with the international commission of inquiry (see p. 177) into human rights violations since September 2002; UNOCI should assist in preparations for general elections; ECOWAS should remain engaged in efforts to resume the national dialogue and help expedite legislative reforms provided for in the Agreement; and the Security Council should monitor fulfilment of the pledges made by President Gbagbo and other Ivorian parties, particularly the adoption of laws and the resolution of the issues of the status-of-forces agreement and the operation of UNOCI radio by early July. The Council should consider targeted measures against individuals who obstructed implementation of those pledges.

Côte d'Ivoire, in its observations on the report of the Security Council mission [S/2004/610], transmitted on 27 July, affirmed that President Gbagbo would ensure that the bills provided for in the Agreement were adopted in compliance with the national Constitution.

Accra III Agreement

As the Ivorian peace process continued to face serious difficulties, numerous initiatives were taken in mid-2004 by international stakeholders to defuse the tensions, the Secretary-General reported [S/2004/697]. His Special Representative, Albert Tévoédjrè, consulted with the President, other government leaders and those of Ivorian political parties on ways to overcome the impasse in the peace process, while the Prime Minister consulted with the "Coalition des Marcoussistes". On 20 June, the Presidents of Ghana, Nigeria and Togo and the ECOWAS Executive Secretary met with President Gbagbo in Abuja, Nigeria, at an ECOWAS mini-summit at which strategies for putting the Ivorian peace process back on track were discussed. Following the summit, President Gbagbo, in a 21 June speech, announced his determination to remove all obstacles to the peace process and condemned attacks against French citizens and UN personnel. He encouraged the Government to submit all remaining draft laws under the Linas-Marcoussis Agreement to the National Assembly for adoption.

Following further diplomatic initiatives by the President of Gabon, President Gbagbo met with the major Ivorian political forces, including the "Coalition des Marcoussistes", and separately with them on 29 and 30 June, in an attempt to restart the political dialogue. That meeting discussed the return of the three dismissed ministers to the Government of National Reconciliation and the delegation of powers from the President to the Prime Minister. Forces nouvelles did not participate in the meeting, but indicated that it would abide by any agreement reached by the other members of the Coalition. The AU Peace and Security Council (Addis Ababa, Ethiopia, 4 July) [S/2004/561] welcomed the ECOWAS mediation efforts to relaunch the peace and reconciliation process as well as the resumption of dialogue between the President and the political opposition, and urged the Forces nouvelles to rejoin the negotiation process.

On 6 July, the Secretary-General convened a mini-summit on Côte d'Ivoire, on the sidelines of the third AU summit in Addis Ababa. Attended by the Presidents of Benin, Burkina Faso, Côte d'Ivoire, Gabon, Ghana, Mali and Nigeria, the Prime Minister of Togo and the ECOWAS Executive Secretary, the summit called on the Ivorian parties to increase efforts to overcome the political impasse; restore the integrity of, and confidence in, the Government of National Reconciliation; and dismantle all paramilitary and militia groups. The President and Prime Minister were called upon to resume the effective functioning of the Government, which should address all remaining legal reforms. The Ivorian parties were urged to establish security conditions necessary for State administration and economic activities nationwide, and for the preparation of elections, and participate in the disarmament, demobilization and reintegration programme. It was also decided that a meeting of all the Ivorian political forces would be convened in Accra, Ghana, on 29 July to give impetus to the peace process. Prior to that meeting, a number of confidence-building measures were to be taken: President Gbagbo would meet with the leaders of all Ivorian political forces; the National Assembly would adopt all legal reforms envisaged under the Agreement before the end of July; the Joint Côte d'Ivoire–Burkina Faso and Côte d'Ivoire–Mali Commissions would be reactivated; and the heads of State of Burkina Faso, Côte d'Ivoire and Mali would hold a tripartite meeting to prepare for the Accra summit.

The high-level meeting on Côte d'Ivoire was held in Accra on 29 and 30 July, bringing together 13 African heads of State, President Gbagbo and Prime Minister Diarra, and most of the leaders of the 10 Ivorian political forces signatory to the Linas-Marcoussis Agreement. The parties reached a consensus on addressing the key outstanding issues facing the peace process, and signed the Accra III Agreement on 30 July. The text of the Agreement was forwarded to the Security Council on 2 August [S/2004/629] by Ghana.

The Accra III Agreement provided a framework and a timetable for the reactivation of the peace process, with a view to ensuring the full implementation of the Linas-Marcoussis Agreement. With regard to the revision of article 35 of the Constitution concerning eligibility to the presidency, the parties agreed that President Gbagbo should use his constitutional powers to implement that provision by the end of September. They also agreed that the National Assembly should adopt, by the end of August, all legal reforms envisaged under the Agreement. They committed themselves to the commencement of the disarmament, demobilization and reintegration process by 15 October, which should include all paramilitary and militia groups. The parties agreed on the need for a clear delegation of powers from the President to the Prime Minister, to urgently resume the work of the Government of National Reconciliation and to convene a meeting of the Council of Ministers.

The parties also committed themselves to cooperating fully with the international commission of inquiry to investigate the human rights violations perpetrated in Côte d'Ivoire since

September 2002 (see p. 177) and on the urgent need to establish the National Human Rights Commission. They agreed to establish a tripartite monitoring group, comprising representatives of ECOWAS, the AU and UNOCI, which would submit fortnightly reports on progress in implementing the Accra III Agreement to the ECOWAS and AU Chairpersons and to the UN Secretary-General.

In a statement issued on 5 August [S/2004/641], the EU welcomed the Accra III Agreement and urged all the parties concerned to commit themselves to the full application of its provisions.

SECURITY COUNCIL ACTION (August)

On 5 August [meeting 5018], following consultations among Security Council members, the President made statement **S/PRST/2004/29** on behalf of the Council:

The Security Council welcomes the signing, on 30 July 2004 at Accra, by the President of the Republic of Côte d'Ivoire, Mr. Laurent Gbagbo, the Prime Minister of the Government of National Reconciliation, Mr. Seydou Elimane Diarra, and all the political forces of Côte d'Ivoire, of an agreement ("the Accra III Agreement") that consolidates the implementation of the Linas-Marcoussis process. The Council recalls that it endorsed the Linas-Marcoussis Agreement. It welcomes the resolute commitment of the African Heads of State and Government, in particular of the Chairman of the Economic Community of West African States, Mr. John Agyekum Kufuor, President of the Republic of Ghana, and the Chairperson of the African Union, Mr. Olusegun Obasanjo, President of the Federal Republic of Nigeria, as well as of the Secretary-General of the United Nations and the other participants in the summit held in Accra on 29 and 30 July 2004, thanks to which the conclusion of the Accra III Agreement was made possible.

The Council welcomes the spirit of dialogue and responsibility shown by President Gbagbo and each of the Ivorian parties, who have clearly demonstrated their willingness to lead the political process in Côte d'Ivoire to its completion. It welcomes the concrete measures agreed upon by the signatories to the Accra III Agreement with a view to facilitating the full and comprehensive implementation of the Linas-Marcoussis Agreement and because of the serious threats, caused by the continuing crisis, which persist against the territorial integrity of Côte d'Ivoire. It urges the parties to adhere strictly to the deadlines that have been fixed, in particular to settle the issue of eligibility for the Presidency of the Republic and to begin disarmament, in accordance with the Linas-Marcoussis Agreement, for all paramilitary groups and militias and disband disruptive youth groups.

The Council urges all parties to implement in good faith, without delays or preconditions, the obligations they have undertaken in signing the Accra III Agreement. It calls upon them, in particular, to remain committed so that open, free and transparent elections can be held, as agreed, before the end of 2005. It reaffirms its complete readiness to take any appropriate measure against individuals who impede the full implementation of the Linas-Marcoussis Agreement.

The Council takes note with profound concern of the preliminary results of the investigation led by the United Nations Operation in Côte d'Ivoire of the massacres that occurred in Korhogo. It reiterates its firm condemnation of all atrocities and violations of human rights and international humanitarian law committed in Côte d'Ivoire and in particular those that occurred in Abidjan on 25 and 26 March 2004. It reiterates its full support to the international commission of inquiry put in place by the United Nations High Commissioner for Human Rights in order to establish the facts and circumstances of the perpetration of violations of human rights and international humanitarian law which have occurred in Côte d'Ivoire since 19 September 2002, and, as far as possible, to identify their authors. It recalls that all persons responsible for such violations will be brought to justice. It encourages the Ivorian parties to establish without further delay, in accordance with the commitment they have undertaken, the National Human Rights Commission provided for in the Linas-Marcoussis Agreement.

The Council expresses its intention to continue to follow closely developments in the situation in Côte d'Ivoire and the implementation of the Linas-Marcoussis Agreement. It emphasizes in this regard the importance of the follow-up mechanism and looks forward to the regular reports provided for in the Accra III Agreement of 30 July 2004. In this regard, the Council requests the Secretary-General to keep it regularly informed of the implementation of commitments under the Accra III Agreement.

President Gbagbo, in an address to his country on 6 August [S/2004/632], expressed his Government's intention to implement the Accra Agreement.

Tripartite Monitoring Group

The tripartite Monitoring Group, set up in accordance with the Accra III Agreement to review progress in its implementation, issued seven reports in 2004 covering the periods 1 to 31 August [S/2004/667, S/2004/716], 1 to 15 September [S/2004/748], 15 to 30 September [S/2004/800], 1 to 15 October [S/2004/878], 15 to 30 October [S/2004/944] and 16 to 30 November [S/2004/976]. Developments from 1 to 17 December and from 18 December to the end of the year were detailed in a later report [S/2005/82]. (For details of the last three reports, see p. 191.)

The Group reported, among the major developments, that the Council of Ministers met on 9 August and issued decrees reinstating the three dismissed ministers to their previous posts in the Government; appointing a new government spokesperson; and delegating power to the Prime

Minister. The Group followed the status of implementation of the pertinent texts of legislation and decrees envisaged under the Linas-Marcoussis and Accra III Agreements, and, in its second report, included a timetable for the disarmament, demobilization and reintegration programme and a table setting out progress in respect of the legislative texts. The Group noted sharp divisions between the parties over appointments to the Independent Electoral Commission. In addition, the gridlock in the National Assembly did not augur well for the remaining legislation to be considered and adopted by the Assembly, as scheduled. The Group warned that the political atmosphere could lead to a revival of animosities, which could erode commitment to the Accra III Agreement.

By mid-September, the Group reported that, while the legislative process was slow, some progress was achieved in the disarmament, demobilization and reintegration programme. However, the critical problem of identification had to be solved before that exercise could begin. It also noted some encouraging developments in human rights, specifically, that checkpoints and the number of arrests, detentions and disappearances had decreased. In the light of the stalemate within the National Assembly and the trend of political debate over issues relating to implementation of the Agreements, the tripartite Monitoring Group recommended that consultations be held with President Gbagbo and other political stakeholders to ascertain the difficulties facing them in regard to the passage of the relevant legal reforms, and with the four major Ivorian political leaders (President Gbagbo, Mr. Soro, Mr. Konan Bedie, Mr. Alassane Ouattara) to find a solution to the controversy surrounding article 35 of the Constitution. However, the situation remained deadlocked over the issues of constitutional reform and disarmament.

UNOCI activities

Report of Secretary-General (August). On 27 August [S/2004/697], the Secretary-General, in response to Security Council resolution 1528(2004) (see p. 173), issued his second report on UNOCI, covering developments since his 2 June report, including events leading to the 30 July signing of the Accra III Agreement (see p. 183).

With a troop strength of 5,877 as at 20 August, UNOCI's activities focused on patrolling, including border patrolling and guard duties, and liaising with FANCI, the military elements of Forces nouvelles and the Licorne force. It coordinated with humanitarian and development agencies to facilitate the delivery of assistance. The civilian police force, which had 160 officers, out of an authorized strength of 350, assisted the mixed national force of gendarmes, comprising Ivorian internal security forces and Forces nouvelles elements, in training and facilitated cooperation between the two sides. The UNOCI deployment had a generally positive impact on the security situation in the country, which had become more stable. However, violent incidents, mostly involving rival factions of Forces nouvelles in the north, various youth groups in Abidjan and militias in other parts of the country, led to an increased level of tension. The presence of mercenaries was also reported in both northern and southern areas. In the north, "unidentified" heavily armed elements, allegedly supporters of Staff Sergeant Ibrahim Coulibaly, launched an attack against the military elements of Forces nouvelles stationed in the Korhogo area on 20 June, resulting in 11 civilian deaths. The same elements then attacked the convoy of the Secretary-General of Forces nouvelles, Mr. Soro, but no injuries were reported. Forces nouvelles issued a communiqué accusing the attackers of receiving support from President Gbagbo and Guinean President Lansana Conté. On 21 June, clashes between the rival factions of Mr. Soro and Mr. Coulibaly in Bouaké resulted in a series of summary executions. On 25 and 26 June, sporadic shooting between rival factions of Forces nouvelles was again reported in Korhogo. Mass graves discovered in Korhogo were investigated by UNOCI, which confirmed the existence of three such graves containing at least 99 bodies. The situation in Abidjan was calm, with a strong presence of FANCI and Ivorian security forces. FANCI reinforced its positions along the southern edge of the Zone of Confidence to track possible infiltration by armed elements from the north. Western areas of the country remained volatile, mainly owing to a large presence of Liberian and Burkinabé refugees. Tensions were also rising between local military forces in both the north and south and the impartial forces, particularly the French Licorne force. A positive development was the resumption on 16 August of the Quadripartite Commission meetings of FANCI, Forces nouvelles, ONUCI and the Licorne force.

The human rights situation in Côte d'Ivoire continued to be of serious concern. Grave violations occurred in the north, following interfactional fighting within Forces nouvelles. In the Government-controlled area, the situation was marked by reports of ethnic tensions, including harassment and intimidation of foreigners and civilians from the north by paramilitary and militia groups and other disruptive youth groups. In western areas, the situation was dominated by intercommunal conflict, with land ownership at the core of tensions. That dispute led to the exclusion of foreign migrants, mainly from Mali, Guinea and Burkina Faso, and northern ethnic groups. On 22 June, OHCHR established the International Commission of Inquiry to investigate human rights violations since September 2002, which arrived in the country on 15 July to begin its work. Progress was made in the public information area with the mission's radio station, covering the greater Abidjan area, beginning regular broadcasts on 13 August.

The humanitarian situation was complicated by the internal displacement of an estimated 800,000 persons, of whom 500,000 had yet to be resettled. Humanitarian agencies reported a near total collapse of the provision of basic services in health, water and sanitation, education and protection in the north. Some 70,000 Liberian refugees continued to live in Côte d'Ivoire, where they encountered hostility from local extremist groups and some political leaders.

The Secretary-General observed that the Accra III Agreement, containing a framework for implementation of the main provisions of the Linas-Marcoussis Agreement, provided a clear road map for progress in the peace process. Some progress had been made, although much remained to be done to meet the established deadlines. Reminding the Ivorian parties of their personal responsibility for ensuring that the commitments made in Accra were carried out, he also drew their attention to the Council's stated intention to consider appropriate, targeted measures against individuals who obstructed the implementation of the Linas-Marcoussis Agreement. While the international community remained ready to assist the Ivorian parties to bring the crisis to an end, it looked to President Gbagbo and the Ivorian leadership to ensure that progress was made in the peace process.

Security Council consideration. The Security Council was briefed on 27 September on the situation in Côte d'Ivoire by the Secretary-General's Special Representative, Albert Tévoédjrè. In a 27 September press statement of its President [SC/8197-AFR/1036], Council members noted the resumption of the activities of the Government of National Reconciliation, in accordance with the commitments made at the Accra III summit (see p. 182), but expressed concern over the lack of progress in other key sectors. They underlined that the situation was not only holding back the peace process in Côte d'Ivoire, but was also detrimental to further progress in the subregion. The members exhorted President Gbagbo to do everything in his power to ensure the revision of article 35 of the Constitution, and exhorted Forces nouvelles to start as soon as possible, without pre-

conditions, the disarmament, demobilization and reintegration process to which they both had committed themselves. They also called on military groups to disarm and on members of Parliament to accelerate consideration of legislative reforms.

Communication. Mr. Gbagbo, in an address to Ivorians on 12 October [S/2004/817], said that he would submit to Parliament the draft amendment to article 35 of the Constitution on eligibility, as soon as disarmament began. He reported that the armed forces on both sides had declared themselves ready to begin disarmament on 15 October and he appealed to the political leaders to play their part.

Renewed hostilities

Despite the general improvement in security between September and mid-October, the situation remained tense in Man and around Guiglo where militias operated freely, the Secretary-General reported [S/2004/962]. The level of co-operation between FANCI and the military elements of Forces nouvelles also improved, culminating in the adoption on 11 October of the Yamoussoukro Joint Declaration, in which the parties reaffirmed an earlier decision not to resume armed hostilities and their commitment to commencing the disarmament process. However, the lack of progress in the peace process impacted on the military and security situation in Côte d'Ivoire, with both FANCI and Forces nouvelles increasing their states of alert. Tensions mounted as the deadline for the disarmament process approached, and demonstrations were held in three northern towns in early October, targeting both UNOCI and Licorne troops. On 26 October, Forces nouvelles claimed to have discovered a large quantity of weapons and ammunition in a truck entering Bouaké. That led to the suspension two days later of their participation in the Government of National Reconciliation. Forces nouvelles declared a "state of emergency", imposed a curfew in areas under its control, withdrew from the disarmament, demobilization and reintegration process and announced that all vehicles entering areas under its control, including UN and humanitarian vehicles, would be searched.

On 4 November, FANCI launched a military operation against Forces nouvelles positions in Bouaké and Korhogo. In Abidjan, the so-called "young patriots", supporters of President Gbagbo, forcibly tried to seize the residence of Forces nouvelles ministers. Meanwhile, the office of the Prime Minister was seized by FANCI and the staff expelled. The "young patriots" also ransacked the offices of the National Commission for Disarmament, Demobilization and Reintegration and those of the opposition parties, and burned and looted the offices of three major newspapers. Following the attacks, the Secretary-General of Forces nouvelles declared the Accra III and the Linas-Marcoussis Agreements "null and void".

On 5 November, FANCI forces carried out additional attacks against Forces nouvelles, resulting in further deaths of civilians and soldiers. Despite UNOCI efforts to prevent infiltration through the zone of confidence, on 6 November large numbers of FANCI troops moved across the zone and clashed with Forces nouvelles in Sakassou, south of Bouaké, and in Bouaké itself. Meanwhile, President Gbagbo informed the UN Secretary-General that the military operations under way were "limited and targeted at the recapture of specific towns". On the same day, a base of the French Licorne force was bombed, resulting in the deaths of nine French soldiers and one American citizen, and the wounding of 38 French soldiers. The French forces responded by destroying the planes used by FANCI during the raids, and military helicopters on the ground in Yamoussoukro. The Ivorian authorities accused the Licorne force of a disproportionate use of force in response to a "mistake" by the Ivorian security and defence forces, as the Government explained in a letter of 16 November [S/2004/910]. The Ivorian authorities asked for an international inquiry into the French action. That action had also heightened tensions in Abidjan and other major towns, fuelled by messages broadcast on State-run radio and television inciting hatred and violence against French forces and citizens, leading to violent demonstrations. Calm was restored on 7 November, as FANCI troops were ordered to withdraw to their positions south of the Zone of Confidence and President Gbagbo appealed for calm and for demonstrators to return to their homes.

The Secretary-General, on 6 November [S/2004/886], sought the Security Council's confirmation that, in accordance with resolution 1528 (2004) (see p. 173), UNOCI was authorized to use all necessary means within its capabilities and areas of deployment to prevent any hostile action within the zone of confidence, where the UNOCI and the French forces were deployed.

SECURITY COUNCIL ACTION (6 November)

On 6 November [meeting 5072], following consultations among Security Council members, the President made statement **S/PRST/2004/42** on behalf of the Council:

The Security Council condemns the attack against French forces in Bouaké on 6 November 2004 that resulted in fatalities and other casualties, as well as the fatal air strikes in the north by the national armed forces of Côte d'Ivoire, as violations of the ceasefire agreement of 3 May 2003.

The Council further condemns any effort by any party to send forces through the Zone of Confidence.

The Council demands the immediate cessation of all military operations by all Ivorian parties and full compliance with the ceasefire agreement of 3 May 2003.

The Council expresses its full support for the action undertaken by French forces and the United Nations Operation in Côte d'Ivoire.

The Council confirms that French forces and the United Nations Operation in Côte d'Ivoire are authorized to use all necessary means to carry out fully their mandate in accordance with its resolution 1528(2004) of 27 February 2004. It confirms also that the United Nations Operation in Côte d'Ivoire, within its capabilities and areas of deployment, is authorized to prevent any hostile action, in particular within the Zone of Confidence.

The Council strongly recalls the obligations of all Ivorian parties, the Government of Côte d'Ivoire as well as the Forces nouvelles, to refrain from any violence against civilians and to cooperate fully with the activities of the United Nations Operation in Côte d'Ivoire. The Council firmly reminds all parties of the need to guarantee the security and freedom of movement of all United Nations personnel.

The Council intends to examine rapidly further actions, including individual measures to be taken.

The AU Peace and Security Council, in a communiqué on Côte d'Ivoire adopted on 8 November [S/2004/896], urged the Government and the parties to exercise maximum restraint, desist from pronouncements that might incite hatred and violence, and recommit themselves to dialogue and negotiations. It supported the decision of the AU Chairperson to mandate President Thabo Mbeki of South Africa to undertake a mission to the country to promote a political solution.

On 29 November [S/2004/931], Côte d'Ivoire provided its version of the events that took place from 4 to 10 November and called for the forces in the zone of confidence to be unified under the United Nations.

Arms embargo

On 10 November [S/2004/895], the Gambia, on behalf of the African Group of States, expressed deep regrets over the events that had occurred in Bouaké since 4 November. The Group expressed reservations about the proposed Security Council resolution recommending the imposition of punitive measures against Côte d'Ivoire as they were incompatible with the AU's strategy of engagement with all the parties concerned, and appealed to the Council that the AU be allowed more time for its diplomatic efforts to come to fruition.

SECURITY COUNCIL ACTION (15 November)

On 15 November [meeting 5078], the Security Council unanimously adopted **resolution 1572 (2004)**. The draft [S/2004/892] was submitted by Chile, France, Germany, Romania, Spain, the United Kingdom and the United States.

The Security Council,

Recalling its resolution 1528(2004) of 27 February 2004, as well as the relevant statements by its President, in particular those of 5 August and 6 November 2004,

Reaffirming its strong commitment to the sovereignty, independence, territorial integrity and unity of Côte d'Ivoire, and recalling the importance of the principles of good-neighbourliness, non-interference and regional cooperation,

Recalling that it endorsed the agreement signed by the Ivorian political forces at Linas-Marcoussis, France, on 23 January 2003 (the Linas-Marcoussis Agreement) and approved by the Conference of Heads of State on Côte d'Ivoire, held in Paris on 25 and 26 January 2003, and the agreement signed at Accra on 30 July 2004 (the Accra III Agreement),

Deploring the resumption of hostilities in Côte d'Ivoire and the repeated violations of the ceasefire agreement of 3 May 2003,

Deeply concerned by the humanitarian situation in Côte d'Ivoire, in particular in the northern part of the country, and by the use of the media, in particular radio and television broadcasts, to incite hatred and violence against foreigners in Côte d'Ivoire,

Strongly recalling the obligations of all Ivorian parties, the Government of Côte d'Ivoire as well as the Forces nouvelles, to refrain from any violence against civilians, including against foreign citizens, and to cooperate fully with the activities of the United Nations Operation in Côte d'Ivoire,

Welcoming the ongoing efforts of the Secretary-General, the African Union and the Economic Community of West African States towards re-establishing peace and stability in Côte d'Ivoire,

Determining that the situation in Côte d'Ivoire continues to pose a threat to international peace and security in the region,

Acting under Chapter VII of the Charter of the United Nations,

1. *Condemns* the air strikes committed by the national armed forces of Côte d'Ivoire, which constitute flagrant violations of the ceasefire agreement of 3 May 2003, and demands that all Ivorian parties to the conflict, the Government of Côte d'Ivoire as well as the Forces nouvelles, fully comply with the ceasefire;

2. *Reiterates its full support* for the action undertaken by the United Nations Operation in Côte d'Ivoire and French forces in accordance with their mandate under its resolution 1528(2004) and with the statement by its President of 6 November 2004;

3. *Emphasizes again* that there can be no military solution to the crisis and that the full implementation of the Linas-Marcoussis Agreement and the Accra III Agreement remains the only way to resolve the crisis persisting in the country;

4. *Urges*, as a consequence, the President of the Republic of Côte d'Ivoire, the heads of all the Ivorian political parties and the leaders of the Forces nouvelles immediately to begin resolutely implementing all the commitments they have made under those agreements;

5. *Expresses its full support* for the efforts of the Secretary-General, the African Union and the Economic Community of West African States, and encourages them to continue these efforts in order to relaunch the peace process in Côte d'Ivoire;

6. *Demands* that the Ivorian authorities stop all radio and television broadcasting inciting hatred, intolerance and violence, requests the United Nations Operation in Côte d'Ivoire to strengthen its monitoring role in this regard, and urges the Government of Côte d'Ivoire and the Forces nouvelles to take all necessary measures to ensure the security and safety of civilian persons, including foreign nationals and their property;

7. *Decides* that all States shall, for a period of thirteen months from the date of adoption of the present resolution, take the necessary measures to prevent the direct or indirect supply, sale or transfer to Côte d'Ivoire from their territories or by their nationals, or using their flag vessels or aircraft, of arms or any related materiel, in particular military aircraft and equipment, whether or not these originated in their territories, as well as the provision of any assistance, advice or training related to military activities;

8. *Decides also* that the measures imposed by paragraph 7 above shall not apply to:

(a) Supplies and technical assistance intended solely for the support of or use by the United Nations Operation in Côte d'Ivoire and the French forces supporting them;

(b) Supplies of non-lethal military equipment intended solely for humanitarian or protective use, and related technical assistance and training, as approved in advance by the Committee established pursuant to paragraph 14 below;

(c) Supplies of protective clothing, including flak jackets and military helmets, temporarily exported to Côte d'Ivoire by United Nations personnel, representatives of the media and humanitarian and development workers and associated personnel for their personal use only;

(d) Supplies temporarily exported to Côte d'Ivoire to the forces of a State which is taking action, in accordance with international law, solely and directly to facilitate the evacuation of its nationals and those for whom it has consular responsibility in Côte d'Ivoire, as notified in advance to the Committee established pursuant to paragraph 14 below;

(e) Supplies of arms and related materiel and technical training and assistance intended solely for the support of or use in the process of restructuring defence and security forces pursuant to paragraph 3 (f) of the Linas-Marcoussis Agreement, as approved in advance by the Committee established pursuant to paragraph 14 below;

9. *Decides further* that all States shall take the necessary measures, for a period of twelve months, to prevent the entry into or transit through their territories of all persons designated by the Committee established pursuant to paragraph 14 below who constitute

a threat to the peace and national reconciliation process in Côte d'Ivoire, in particular those who block the implementation of the Linas-Marcoussis and Accra III Agreements, any other person determined to be responsible for serious violations of human rights and international humanitarian law in Côte d'Ivoire on the basis of relevant information, any other person who publicly incites hatred and violence, and any other person determined by the Committee to be in violation of the measures imposed by paragraph 7 above, provided that nothing in the present paragraph shall oblige a State to refuse entry into its territory to its own nationals;

10. *Decides* that the measures imposed by paragraph 9 above shall not apply where the Committee established pursuant to paragraph 14 below determines that such travel is justified on the grounds of humanitarian need, including religious obligation, or where the Committee concludes that an exemption would further the objectives of the resolutions of the Council, for peace and national reconciliation in Côte d'Ivoire and stability in the region;

11. *Decides also* that all States shall, for the same period of twelve months, freeze immediately the funds, other financial assets and economic resources that are in their territories on the date of adoption of the present resolution or at any time thereafter, that are owned or controlled directly or indirectly by the persons designated pursuant to paragraph 9 above by the Committee established pursuant to paragraph 14 below, or that are held by entities owned or controlled directly or indirectly by any persons acting on their behalf or at their direction, as designated by the Committee, and decides further that all States shall ensure that any funds, financial assets or economic resources are prevented from being made available by their nationals or by any persons within their territories to or for the benefit of such persons or entities;

12. *Decides further* that the provisions of paragraph 11 above do not apply to funds, other financial assets and economic resources:

(a) That have been determined by relevant States to be necessary for basic expenses, including payment for foodstuffs, rent or mortgage, medicines and medical treatment, taxes, insurance premiums and public utility charges, or exclusively for payment of reasonable professional fees and reimbursement of incurred expenses associated with the provision of legal services, or fees or service charges, in accordance with national laws, for routine holding or maintenance of frozen funds, other financial assets and economic resources, after notification by the relevant States to the Committee established pursuant to paragraph 14 below of the intention to authorize, where appropriate, access to such funds, other financial assets and economic resources and in the absence of a negative decision by the Committee within two working days of such notification;

(b) That have been determined by relevant States to be necessary for extraordinary expenses, provided that such determination has been notified by the relevant States to the Committee and has been approved by the Committee; or

(c) That have been determined by relevant States to be the subject of a judicial, administrative or arbitral lien or judgement, in which case the funds, other financial assets and economic resources may be used to satisfy that lien or judgement, provided that the lien or judgement was entered prior to the date of the present resolution, is not for the benefit of a person referred to in paragraph 11 above or an individual or entity identified by the Committee, and has been notified by the relevant States to the Committee;

13. *Decides* that, at the end of a period of thirteen months from the date of adoption of the present resolution, the Security Council shall review the measures imposed by paragraphs 7, 9 and 11 above, in the light of progress accomplished in the peace and national reconciliation process in Côte d'Ivoire as defined by the Linas-Marcoussis and Accra III Agreements, and expresses its readiness to consider the modification or termination of those measures before the aforesaid period of thirteen months only if the Linas-Marcoussis and Accra III Agreements have been fully implemented;

14. *Decides also* to establish, in accordance with rule 28 of its provisional rules of procedure, a Committee of the Security Council consisting of all the members of the Council (the Committee), to undertake the following tasks:

(a) To designate the individuals and entities subject to the measures imposed by paragraphs 9 and 11 above, and to update that list regularly;

(b) To seek from all States concerned, and particularly those in the region, information regarding the actions taken by them to implement the measures imposed by paragraphs 7, 9 and 11 above, and whatever further information it may consider useful, including by providing them with an opportunity to send representatives to meet with the Committee to discuss in more detail any relevant issues;

(c) To consider and decide upon requests for the exemptions set out in paragraphs 8, 10 and 12 above;

(d) To make relevant information publicly available through appropriate media, including the list of persons referred to in subparagraph (a) above;

(e) To promulgate guidelines as may be necessary to facilitate the implementation of the measures imposed by paragraphs 11 and 12 above;

(f) To present regular reports to the Council on its work, with its observations and recommendations, in particular on ways to strengthen the effectiveness of the measures imposed by paragraphs 7, 9 and 11 above;

15. *Requests* all States concerned, in particular those in the region, to report to the Committee, within ninety days of the date of adoption of the present resolution, on the actions they have taken to implement the measures imposed by paragraphs 7, 9 and 11 above, and authorizes the Committee to request whatever further information it may consider necessary;

16. *Urges* all States, relevant United Nations bodies and, as appropriate, other organizations and interested parties, to cooperate fully with the Committee, in particular by supplying any information at their disposal on possible violations of the measures imposed by paragraphs 7, 9 and 11 above;

17. *Expresses its determination* to consider without delay further steps to ensure the effective monitoring and implementation of the measures imposed by paragraphs 7, 9 and 11 above, in particular the establishment of a panel of experts;

18. *Requests* the Secretary-General to submit a report to the Council by 15 March 2005, drawing on information from all relevant sources, including the Government of National Reconciliation in Côte d'Ivoire, the United Nations Operation in Côte d'Ivoire, the Economic Community of West African States and the African Union, on progress made towards the goals described in paragraph 13 above;

19. *Decides* that the measures imposed by paragraphs 9 and 11 above shall enter into force on 15 December 2004, unless the Council shall determine before then that the signatories to the Linas-Marcoussis and Accra III Agreements have implemented all their commitments under the Accra III Agreement and are embarked towards full implementation of the Linas-Marcoussis Agreement;

20. *Decides also* to remain actively seized of the matter.

The Council, by a 6 December note of its President [S/2004/950], agreed that Gunter Pleuger (Germany) would serve, from 6 to 31 December 2004, as Chairman of the Security Council Committee established pursuant to resolution 1572 (2004) (above) concerning Côte d'Ivoire. The Committee held its first meeting on 6 December [SC/8261-AFR/1077].

End-of-year developments

Report of Secretary-General (December). The Secretary-General, on 9 December, issued his third progress report on UNOCI [S/2004/962 & Add.1], covering developments since his 27 August report (see p. 184). He continued to report a lack of progress in the implementation of the peace agreements, which was further complicated by the launching of a military operation by FANCI in early November (see p. 185). Following the outbreak of hostilities, actions by the AU, ECOWAS and the United Nations focused on the restoration of calm and security and on facilitating a resumption of dialogue among the Ivorian parties.

On 7 November, President Gbagbo appealed for calm and for demonstrators to return to their homes, and the next day, UNOCI and FANCI resumed joint patrols, both of which contributed to a reduction of tensions. The Ivorian authorities reported that 57 people were killed during the November disturbances. Some 9,000 expatriates left the country, and a number of UN staff were relocated to Accra, Ghana. Throughout the crisis, UNOCI troops maintained contacts with both FANCI and Forces nouvelles.

On 9 November, President Mbeki of South Africa led an AU mission to Abidjan aimed at bringing about a resumption of the peace process. The mission held discussions with President Gbagbo and other leaders. On 11 November, President Mbeki held further consultations in Pretoria, South Africa, with several opposition leaders, and with Burkina Faso's President on 13 November. Following further meetings in Pretoria on 20 and 21 November with the Secretary-General of Forces nouvelles, President Mbeki returned to Côte d'Ivoire on 2 December for a four-day visit to meet with the Ivorian parties and examine proposals for the resumption of the peace process. During that visit, the parties agreed on a plan of action for resuming the peace process.

In other developments, on 14 November, President Obasanjo of Nigeria, in his capacity as AU Chairperson, convened a summit in Abuja, attended by six regional heads of State, which urged all Ivorian parties to observe the ceasefire and called on the international community to stop the flow of arms to the country.

On 18 November, for the first time since the outbreak of hostilities, the Council of Ministers met under the chairmanship of President Gbagbo. None of the Forces nouvelles ministers attended. The meeting examined draft legislation to enact the reforms envisaged under the Linas-Marcoussis Agreement. The second ordinary session of the National Assembly resumed on 29 November.

The National Commission for Disarmament, Demobilization and Reintegration indicated that some 30,000 ex-combatants would participate in the programme, including 26,000 from Forces nouvelles, of which 3,000 were children. However, the programme did not commence as scheduled in October because Forces nouvelles was not prepared to disarm in the absence of progress in the adoption of key constitutional and legal reforms. The rehabilitation of the disarmament, demobilization and reintegration sites in the south were completed, while those in the north were not, due to continued protests and lack of authorization for access. The programme continued to face severe financial difficulties. However, France had provided 1 million euros, which enabled the programme to begin in the eastern region.

On 15 October, the International Commission of Inquiry, established under the Linas-Marcoussis Agreement to investigate all serious violations of human rights and humanitarian law perpetrated in Côte d'Ivoire since 19 September 2002, submitted its report to the United Nations High Commissioner for Human Rights. It was subsequently circulated to the Ivorian parties signatory to that Agreement for their comments and was finalized and submitted to the Secretary-General on 19 November for transmission to the Security Council (see p. 177). During the crisis, the UNOCI public information unit increased its monitoring and analysis of daily media and launched a public information strategy focusing on countering disinformation, propaganda and media broadcasts inciting hatred, intolerance and violence.

The Secretary-General observed that the November crisis had strained UNOCI's capacity to implement its mandate. As an emergency measure, he recommended that the mission be reinforced by an additional infantry battalion of 850 military personnel to act as a reserve force to be stationed in Abidjan. It would be reinforced by an additional aviation unit of both attack and light helicopters and 270 support personnel, as well as a small-boat unit of 30 personnel. He also proposed the deployment of an additional 76 personnel to provide protection to ministers of the Government, bringing the level of the gendarme unit to 282. Those adjustments would increase the total UNOCI force to 7,466 military personnel. A formed police unit of 125 personnel was also recommended to assist in protecting of UNOCI headquarters and a level 1+ military medical facility for emergency requirements.

In an addendum to the report [S/2004/962/Add.1], the Secretary-General informed the Council that the financial implications arising from the reinforcement of UNOCI was estimated, on a full-cost basis, at some $27.3 million for the period ending 30 June 2005.

Communication. Côte d'Ivoire, on 21 December [S/2004/988], commented on and raised objections to some of the statements in the Secretary-General's report, which, it said, failed to take into account several relevant concerns on the ground and to address those expressed by the Ivorian President and Government well before its preparation. Côte d'Ivoire had called for a Security Council meeting on France's "reprisals" and for an international inquiry to be conducted into the events of 4 to 10 November (see p. 185). It also urged that the French Licorne force be placed under UNOCI command.

SECURITY COUNCIL ACTION (December)

On 16 December [meeting 5103], following consultations among Security Council members, the President made statement **S/PRST/2004/48** on behalf of the Council:

The Security Council commends the efforts made by the African Union and, in particular, the personal involvement of Mr. Thabo Mbeki, President of the Republic of South Africa, to promote dialogue and relaunch the peace and national reconciliation process in Côte d'Ivoire. It expresses its full support for the facilitation mission undertaken by President Mbeki on behalf of the African Union.

The Council welcomes the encouraging prospects resulting from these efforts and the commitments made by all Ivorian parties, demands that all Ivorian parties fully comply with their commitments, and

underlines that it will monitor with vigilance their full implementation.

The Council reaffirms its conviction that the full implementation of resolution 1572(2004) is a key element in ensuring that all Ivorian parties commit themselves fully to the implementation of the peace and national reconciliation process in Côte d'Ivoire, and deplores the fact that the signatories to the Linas-Marcoussis Agreement and the Accra III Agreement have not implemented by 15 December 2004 all their commitments under the Accra III Agreement.

The Council underlines that any failure by any Ivorian party to respect its commitments made to President Mbeki would constitute a threat to the implementation of the peace and national reconciliation process as defined in the Linas-Marcoussis and Accra III Agreements, and recalls in this regard the measures referred to in paragraphs 9 and 11 of resolution 1572(2004).

The Council requests the Committee established pursuant to resolution 1572(2004) to continue its work, taking fully into account the developments in the peace process in Côte d'Ivoire arising from the facilitation efforts undertaken by the African Union.

In addition, the Council demands that all Ivorian parties stop all incitement to violence and hatred in broadcast, written and other media, and calls upon the Committee to monitor this closely without delay.

The Council also demands that all Ivorian parties ensure freedom of the press and unlimited access to information throughout Côte d'Ivoire.

The Council expresses its intention to consider without delay further steps to ensure the effective monitoring and implementation of the arms embargo imposed by resolution 1572(2004).

The Council expresses its appreciation to the Special Representative of the Secretary-General for Côte d'Ivoire, Mr. Albert Tévoédjrè, for his unsparing efforts to support the restoration of a durable peace in Côte d'Ivoire under challenging circumstances.

Later developments. In a later report [S/2005/186], the Secretary-General said that President Gbagbo's decision in late December to ban street marches and demonstrations in Abidjan for three months helped calm the situation in the city, but the security situation in the country as a whole remained very tense.

Before the completion of its extraordinary session in late December, the National Assembly adopted most of the major legislative reforms (the amendment to the Citizenship Code, the Special Law on Naturalization and the law consenting to a proposed amendment to articles 35 and 55 of the Constitution) envisaged in the Linas-Marcoussis Agreement, which were subsequently promulgated. In that context, the Assembly's adoption of the amendment to article 35 of the Constitution relating to eligibility of candidates for the presidency was a significant step forward. However, Mr. Gbagbo had repeatedly stated his intention to submit the proposed amendment to a national referendum. That position was challenged by the opposition parties. The G-7, a group of opposition political parties, further claimed that some of the legislation was not in conformity with the Linas-Marcoussis Agreement and called for the revision of those laws. The Assembly also adopted a new law on the press and one on audio-visual communication. A presidential decree was issued on 24 December changing the status of the Ivorian Radio and Television into a State-owned company.

Communication. On 20 December [S/2004/987], Côte d'Ivoire informed the Security Council that the basic laws called for under the Linas-Marcoussis and Accra III Agreements were approved by the National Assembly on 17 December, and that other related bills would be concluded on 31 December. Côte d'Ivoire reiterated President Gbagbo's position that the amendment to article 35 required approval in a national referendum. Drawing attention to article 127 of the Constitution which stated that no amendment procedure might be initiated so long as the integrity of the national territory was threatened, it said that, while President Gbagbo wished to finish amending article 35, adherence to the rule of law and the Constitution required that the country be reunified so that the amendment could be put to a referendum.

Monitoring Group (December). On 2 December [S/2004/944], the Secretary-General forwarded to the Security Council the sixth and seventh reports of the tripartite Monitoring Group established under the Accra III Agreement, covering the periods from 15 to 30 October and from 1 to 15 November. The Group noted that the deadline of 15 October passed without the commencement of the disarmament, demobilization and reintegration programme, underscoring the failure of the parties to implement the time frame set under that Agreement. Furthermore, the conditions for the organization of the elections had not been met. The FANCI military operations in early November, followed by retaliatory action by the Licorne force, which destroyed much Ivorian military equipment, led to rising tensions. The resumption of armed hostilities had complicated, if not scuttled, the initiatives that were ongoing in search of a way out of the Ivorian crisis. By mid-November, the atmosphere for negotiations was confused even as reports of consultations and good offices might have otherwise given hope for some compromise.

The situation had not changed much by the end of the month, as the Monitoring Group observed in its eighth report [S/2004/976], covering the period from 16 to 30 November. While the overall military situation had calmed down,

the confusion and uncertainties in the general political and social situation had scuttled any local initiatives for restoring dialogue among the Ivorian political actors. The ongoing consultations by President Mbeki (see p. 189) were the only glimmer of hope in the prevailing circumstances, and it was in the interest of the international community to support that AU initiative.

In the report covering activities from 1 to 17 December [S/2005/82], the Group provided information on the broad outlines agreed upon by the Ivorian parties under the five clusters proposed by the AU facilitation mission (2-6 December): the legislative programme; disarmament, demobilization and reintegration; functioning of the Government of National Reconciliation; creating a climate conducive to free political activity and the functioning of State institutions; and restoration of social services and redeployment of administration throughout the country. Under the programme of action, the parties agreed that the Government would forward to the National Assembly all outstanding legislative texts envisaged under the Linas-Marcoussis Agreement. All parties agreed that the disarmament, demobilization and reintegration programme would start immediately and would be carried out in the context of the Agreement reached earlier at Yamoussoukro among the military Quadripartite Commission. Implementation would be the responsibility of the National Commission for Disarmament, Demobilization and Reintegration, although Forces nouvelles insisted that only UNOCI should carry out the exercise in zones under its control. It was agreed that all ministers of the Government should return to their posts and work as a team. However, security had to be improved for their safety. To enhance general security, the parties agreed on joint patrols by FANCI and UNOCI; the "young patriots" should be encouraged to get off the streets; restoration of the regular management of the national television company; and an end to the hate campaign in the media. It was also agreed that measures would be taken progressively to urgently restore social services and public utilities.

UNOCI financing

The Secretary-General submitted the UNOCI budget for the period from 4 April to 30 June 2004 and from 1 July 2004 to 30 June 2005, which amounted to a total of $502,354,400 ($101,061,200 and $401,293,200, respectively) [A/58/788].

ACABQ, in its report [A/58/806] on the proposed budget, recommended that the total be reduced by $205,339,700, bringing the total figure to $297,014,700, due to delayed deployment rates for military and other personnel and the vacancy rates in authorized posts.

GENERAL ASSEMBLY ACTION (June)

On 18 June [meeting 91], the General Assembly, on the recommendation of the Fifth Committee [A/58/831], adopted **resolution 58/310** without vote [agenda item 167].

Financing of the United Nations Operation in Côte d'Ivoire

The General Assembly,

Having considered the report of the Secretary-General on the financing of the United Nations Operation in Côte d'Ivoire and the related report of the Advisory Committee on Administrative and Budgetary Questions,

Recalling Security Council resolution 1528(2004) of 27 February 2004, by which the Council established the United Nations Operation in Côte d'Ivoire for an initial period of twelve months as from 4 April 2004,

Recognizing that the costs of the Operation are expenses of the Organization to be borne by Member States in accordance with Article 17, paragraph 2, of the Charter of the United Nations,

Reaffirming the general principles underlying the financing of United Nations peacekeeping operations, as stated in General Assembly resolutions 1874(S-IV) of 27 June 1963, 3101(XXVIII) of 11 December 1973 and 55/235 of 23 December 2000,

Mindful of the fact that it is essential to provide the Operation with the necessary financial resources to enable it to fulfil its responsibilities under the relevant resolution of the Security Council,

1. *Expresses concern* at the financial situation with regard to peacekeeping activities, in particular as regards the reimbursements to troop contributors that bear additional burdens owing to overdue payments by Member States of their assessments;

2. *Also expresses concern* at the delay experienced by the Secretary-General in deploying and providing adequate resources to some recent peacekeeping missions, in particular those in Africa;

3. *Emphasizes* that all future and existing peacekeeping missions shall be given equal and non-discriminatory treatment in respect of financial and administrative arrangements;

4. *Also emphasizes* that all peacekeeping missions shall be provided with adequate resources for the effective and efficient discharge of their respective mandates;

5. *Reiterates its request* to the Secretary-General to make the fullest possible use of facilities and equipment at the United Nations Logistics Base at Brindisi, Italy, in order to minimize the costs of procurement for the Operation;

6. *Endorses* the conclusions and recommendations contained in the report of the Advisory Committee on Administrative and Budgetary Questions, and requests the Secretary-General to ensure their full implementation, subject to the provisions of the present resolution;

7. *Requests* the Secretary-General to review the organizational and management structures of the Operation and, in this regard, to pay particular attention to the level and functions of the Deputy Special Representative of the Secretary-General posts and provide detailed information thereon in the next budget submission;

8. *Takes note* of paragraphs 26 to 28 of the report of the Advisory Committee, and requests the Secretary-General to ensure that the functions assigned to the Deputy Special Representatives of the Secretary-General are performed consistent with the mandate of the Operation, until such time as the General Assembly is able to take a decision on the revised organizational structure;

9. *Requests* the Secretary-General to take all necessary action to ensure that the Operation is administered with a maximum of efficiency and economy;

10. *Also requests* the Secretary-General, in order to reduce the cost of employing General Service staff, to continue efforts to recruit local staff for the Operation against General Service posts, commensurate with the requirements of the Operation;

Budget estimates for the period from 4 April to 31 December 2004

11. *Authorizes* the Secretary-General to establish a special account for the United Nations Operation in Côte d'Ivoire for the purpose of accounting for the income received and expenditure incurred in respect of the Operation;

12. *Decides* to appropriate to the Special Account for the United Nations Operation in Côte d'Ivoire the amount of 96,368,100 United States dollars for the period from 4 April to 30 June 2004 for the establishment of the Operation, inclusive of the amount of 49,943,300 dollars previously authorized by the Advisory Committee under the terms of section IV of General Assembly resolution 49/233 A of 23 December 1994;

13. *Decides also* to appropriate to the Special Account for the Operation the amount of 211,101,400 dollars, inclusive of 200,646,600 dollars for the maintenance of the Operation for the period from 1 July to 31 December 2004, 8,547,300 dollars for the support account for peacekeeping operations and 1,907,500 dollars for the United Nations Logistics Base for the period from 1 July 2004 to 30 June 2005;

Financing of the appropriation

14. *Decides further* to apportion among Member States the amount of 96,368,100 dollars for the Operation for the period from 4 April to 30 June 2004, in accordance with the levels set out in General Assembly resolution 55/235, as adjusted by the Assembly in its resolution 55/236 of 23 December 2000 and updated in its resolution 58/256 of 23 December 2003, taking into account the scale of assessments for 2004, as set out in its resolution 58/1 B of 23 December 2003;

15. *Decides* that, in accordance with the provisions of its resolution 973(X) of 15 December 1955, there shall be set off against the apportionment among Member States, as provided for in paragraph 14 above, their respective share in the Tax Equalization Fund of 766,900 dollars, representing the estimated staff assessment income approved for the Operation for the period from 4 April to 30 June 2004;

16. *Decides also* to apportion among Member States the amount of 200,646,600 dollars for the Operation for the period from 1 July to 31 December 2004, in ac-

cordance with the scheme set out in paragraph 14 above;

17. *Decides further* that, in accordance with the provisions of its resolution 973(X), there shall be set off against the apportionment among Member States, as provided for in paragraph 16 above, their respective share in the Tax Equalization Fund of 3,588,000 dollars, representing the estimated staff assessment income approved for the Operation for the period from 1 July to 31 December 2004;

18. *Decides* to apportion among Member States the amount of 8,547,300 dollars for the support account and the amount of 1,907,500 dollars for the United Nations Logistics Base for the period from 1 July 2004 to 30 June 2005, in accordance with the scheme set out in paragraph 14 above and taking into account the scale of assessments for 2004 and 2005, as set out in its resolution 58/1 B;

19. *Decides also* that, in accordance with the provisions of its resolution 973(X), there shall be set off against the apportionment among Member States, as provided for in paragraph 18 above, their respective share in the Tax Equalization Fund of 1,354,700 dollars for the period from 1 July 2004 to 30 June 2005, comprising the prorated share of 1,247,300 dollars of the estimated staff assessment income approved for the support account and the prorated share of 107,400 dollars of the estimated staff assessment income approved for the United Nations Logistics Base;

20. *Emphasizes* that no peacekeeping mission shall be financed by borrowing funds from other active peacekeeping missions;

21. *Encourages* the Secretary-General to continue to take additional measures to ensure the safety and security of all personnel under the auspices of the United Nations participating in the Operation;

22. *Invites* voluntary contributions to the Operation in cash and in the form of services and supplies acceptable to the Secretary-General, to be administered, as appropriate, in accordance with the procedure and practices established by the General Assembly;

23. *Decides* to include in the provisional agenda of its fifty-ninth session the item entitled "Financing of the United Nations Operation in Côte d'Ivoire".

On 23 August [A/59/289], the Secretary-General submitted the UNOCI budget for the period from 1 July 2004 to 30 June 2005, which amounted to $384,350,400 and superseded the budgetary proposals for the same period set out earlier (see p. 191).

ACABQ, in its report [A/59/419 & Corr.1], recommended a reduction of $5,877,600 from the proposed budget, for a total amount of $378,472,800 gross ($372,129,600 net), inclusive of the $200,646,600 already appropriated under Assembly resolution 58/310 (above).

GENERAL ASSEMBLY ACTION (October)

On 29 October [meeting 46], the General Assembly, on the recommendation of the Fifth Committee [A/59/529], adopted **resolution 59/16** without vote [agenda item 154].

Financing of the United Nations Operation in Côte d'Ivoire

The General Assembly,

Having considered the report of the Secretary-General on the financing of the United Nations Operation in Côte d'Ivoire and the related report of the Advisory Committee on Administrative and Budgetary Questions,

Recalling Security Council resolution 1528(2004) of 27 February 2004, by which the Council established the United Nations Operation in Côte d'Ivoire for an initial period of twelve months as from 4 April 2004,

Recalling also its resolution 58/310 of 18 June 2004 on the financing of the Operation,

Reaffirming the general principles underlying the financing of United Nations peacekeeping operations, as stated in General Assembly resolutions 1874(S-IV) of 27 June 1963, 3101(XXVIII) of 11 December 1973 and 55/235 of 23 December 2000,

Mindful that it is essential to provide the Operation with the necessary financial resources to enable it to fulfil its responsibilities under the relevant resolution of the Security Council,

1. *Takes note* of the status of contributions to the United Nations Operation in Côte d'Ivoire as at 30 September 2004, including the contributions outstanding in the amount of 201.2 million United States dollars, representing some 66 per cent of the total assessed contributions, notes with concern that only thirty-one Member States have paid their assessed contributions in full, and urges all other Member States, in particular those in arrears, to ensure payment of their outstanding assessed contributions;

2. *Expresses its appreciation* to those Member States which have paid their assessed contributions in full, and urges all other Member States to make every possible effort to ensure payment of their assessed contributions to the Operation in full;

3. *Expresses concern* at the financial situation with regard to peacekeeping activities, in particular as regards the reimbursements to troop contributors that bear additional burdens owing to overdue payments by Member States of their assessments;

4. *Also expresses concern* at the delay experienced by the Secretary-General in deploying and providing adequate resources to some recent peacekeeping missions, in particular those in Africa;

5. *Emphasizes* that all future and existing peacekeeping missions shall be given equal and non-discriminatory treatment in respect of financial and administrative arrangements;

6. *Also emphasizes* that all peacekeeping missions shall be provided with adequate resources for the effective and efficient discharge of their respective mandates;

7. *Reiterates its request* to the Secretary-General to make the fullest possible use of facilities and equipment at the United Nations Logistics Base at Brindisi, Italy, in order to minimize the costs of procurement for the Operation;

8. *Endorses* the conclusions and recommendations contained in the report of the Advisory Committee on Administrative and Budgetary Questions, subject to the provisions of the present resolution;

9. *Authorizes* the Secretary-General to fill the following posts at appropriate grades until 30 June 2005:

Director in the Office of the Special Representative of the Secretary-General;

Special Assistant to the Special Representative;

Two Protocol Officers (one Professional and one National Officer);

Deputy Special Representative for Humanitarian Coordination, Recovery and Reconstruction;

Principal Legal Adviser;

Chief of the Communications and Public Information Office;

Spokesperson;

and requests the Secretary-General to re-justify these posts in his next budget with additional information on appropriate grades;

10. *Requests* the Secretary-General to take all necessary action to ensure that the Operation is administered with a maximum of efficiency and economy;

11. *Also requests* the Secretary-General, in order to reduce the cost of employing General Service staff, to continue efforts to recruit local staff for the Operation against General Service posts, commensurate with the requirements of the Operation;

Budget estimates for the period from 1 July 2004 to 30 June 2005

12. *Decides* to appropriate to the Special Account for the United Nations Operation in Côte d'Ivoire the amount of 177,826,200 dollars for the maintenance of the Operation for the period from 1 July 2004 to 30 June 2005, in addition to the amount of 200,646,600 dollars already appropriated for the maintenance of the Operation for the period from 1 July to 31 December 2004 under the terms of General Assembly resolution 58/310;

Financing of the appropriation

13. *Decides also* to apportion among Member States the amount of 92,864,793 dollars for the Operation for the period from 1 January to 4 April 2005, in addition to the amount of 200,646,600 dollars already apportioned for the period from 1 July to 31 December 2004 under the terms of its resolution 58/310, in accordance with the levels set out in General Assembly resolution 55/235, as adjusted by the Assembly in its resolution 55/236 of 23 December 2000, and updated in its resolution 58/256 of 23 December 2003, taking into account the scale of assessments for 2005, as set out in its resolution 58/1 B of 23 December 2003;

14. *Decides further* that, in accordance with the provisions of its resolution 973(X) of 15 December 1955, there shall be set off against the apportionment among Member States, as provided for in paragraph 13 above, their respective share in the Tax Equalization Fund of 1,438,826 dollars, representing the estimated additional staff assessment income approved for the Operation for the period from 1 January to 4 April 2005;

15. *Decides* to apportion among Member States the amount of 84,961,407 dollars at a monthly rate of 29,637,700 dollars for the period from 5 April to 30 June 2005, in accordance with the scheme set out in paragraph 13 above, and taking into account the scale of assessments for 2005, as set out in its resolution 58/1 B, subject to a decision of the Security Council to extend the mandate of the Operation;

16. *Decides also* that, in accordance with the provisions of its resolution 973(X), there shall be set off against the apportionment among Member States, as provided for in paragraph 15 above, their respective share in the Tax Equalization Fund of 1,316,374 dollars, representing the estimated staff assessment income approved for the Operation for the period from 5 April to 30 June 2005;

17. *Emphasizes* that no peacekeeping mission shall be financed by borrowing funds from other active peacekeeping missions;

18. *Encourages* the Secretary-General to continue to take additional measures to ensure the safety and security of all personnel under the auspices of the United Nations participating in the Operation;

19. *Invites* voluntary contributions to the Operation in cash and in the form of services and supplies acceptable to the Secretary-General, to be administered, as appropriate, in accordance with the procedure and practices established by the General Assembly;

20. *Decides* to keep under review during its fifty-ninth session the item entitled "Financing of the United Nations Operation in Côte d'Ivoire".

On 23 December, the Assembly, by **decision 59/552**, decided that the agenda item on UNOCI financing would remain for consideration during its resumed fifty-ninth (2005) session.

Liberia

Liberia's political transition showed measured progress in 2004, as efforts intensified to implement the 2003 Comprehensive Peace Agreement [YUN 2003, p. 192] concluded by Liberia's Government, the two main rebel groups (the Liberians United for Reconciliation and Democracy (LURD) and the Movement for Democracy in Liberia (MODEL)), 18 political parties and civil society leaders. That Agreement, which ended the war and provided for the establishment of a National Transitional Government, was monitored by three mechanisms: the Joint Monitoring Committee, chaired by the Force Commander of the United Nations Mission in Liberia (UNMIL), which assessed the compliance by armed groups with the ceasefire; the Implementation Monitoring Committee, chaired by ECOWAS and charged with monitoring and ensuring implementation of the Agreement; and the International Contact Group on Liberia. UNMIL, established in 2003 with an authorized strength of 15,000, continued to observe and monitor the implementation of the agreed ceasefire, assist in developing cantonment sites and disarming combatants, monitor disengagement and cantonment, and facilitate delivery of humanitarian aid. As at 1 December 2004, the Mission's strength stood at 14,541 troops and 1,104 civilian police.

Throughout 2004, UNMIL made progress in stabilizing Liberia and providing assistance to create the security conditions for the full implementation of the Agreement. The deployment of its troops in all areas brought relative calm and security that facilitated the delivery of humanitarian assistance and progress towards the restoration of State authority. On 31 October, the disarmament and demobilization of armed forces was completed, and the armed factions were formally disbanded. By the end of the year, further progress was made, including the commencement of the repatriation of refugees and the resettlement of internally displaced persons. State authority was extended to most counties and the new Liberian National Police Service was strengthened through recruitment and training, with UN assistance. Despite those achievements, many challenges remained, in particular the limitations on the capacity of the National Transitional Government to deliver basic services and to extend civil administration throughout the entire country. The electoral reform bill was held up due to disagreement on the allocation of seats in the future legislative assembly, and disagreements within the LURD leadership complicated negotiations among the parties on power sharing.

However, the peace process encountered serious setbacks, especially the outbreak of violence in Monrovia from 28 to 31 October, apparently fueled by ethnic divisions and exploited by former combatants. The security situation remained relatively calm, although it was marred by an increasing number of incidents of mob violence and armed robberies.

The Security Council considered the reports of its two subsidiary bodies established to assess the effectiveness of its arms embargo, diamond and timber sanctions against Liberia, and a ban on travel of individuals deemed to be harmful to the peace process, and those of the Panel of Experts appointed to advise on compliance with those sanctions. While noting that the Transitional Government had made progress in meeting the conditions for lifting the measures, in particular diamond and timber sanctions, the Council determined that much remained to be done to fulfil the conditions for lifting the sanctions and therefore decided to renew the measures. It also imposed further measures against former President Charles Taylor and his immediate family.

Peace-building efforts

Report of Secretary-General (March). In response to Security Council resolution 1509(2003) [YUN 2003, p. 194], the Secretary-General, on 22 March [S/2004/229], issued his second progress report on UNMIL, covering the period since his previous report of 15 December 2003 [YUN 2003, p. 197]. The Mission, whose task was to stabilize the country and create conditions for the implemen-

tation of the other aspects of its mandate, was deployed throughout the country, with the exception of the area along the border with Côte d'Ivoire in Grand Gedeh and Maryland counties. During the reporting period, there was general compliance with the ceasefire in most of the country, except for reports of minor violations by all three armed groups (LURD, MODEL and former Government of Liberia forces) outside the capital, including illegal checkpoints and sporadic shooting, as well as the harassment of civilians, extortion and looting. Security in areas where UNMIL had deployed improved and armed groups in those areas generally respected the ban on the public display of arms.

The Joint Monitoring Committee continued to monitor the ceasefire, maintain dialogue among the armed groups and facilitate contacts between UNMIL and ground commanders of the three factions. It held six meetings during the reporting period to discuss ceasefire violations, preparations for disarmament, demobilization, reintegration and repatriation, and efforts to retrieve looted vehicles from the armed factions. UNMIL pressed the factions to submit lists of their combatants, indicating their locations and military equipment. MODEL and forces of the former Government of Liberia forces indicated that they were finalizing nominal lists, while LURD had yet to provide a response.

The Implementation Monitoring Committee met on 4 March to review preparations for relaunching the disarmament, demobilization, reintegration and repatriation process. UNMIL, ECOWAS and the International Contact Group on Liberia were also working to advance the peace process, calling on all parties to refrain from action that could jeopardize the work of the National Transitional Government, and to turn to the politics of dialogue and accommodation.

The National Transitional Legislative Assembly completed the nomination of 19 of the 23 ministerial positions as allocated by the Agreement. However, the issue of appointments to 84 assistant ministerial positions not provided for under the Agreement continued to be a source of tension between some leaders of the armed factions and Chairman Charles Gyude Bryant of the National Transitional Government. By early March, the Transitional Government submitted 66 nominations to the Transitional Legislative Assembly for those posts, but none had been formally confirmed. The approval process was also complicated by a leadership struggle within LURD.

The situation in Liberia further heightened tension in the region, and Chairman Bryant paid visits to Guinea and Sierra Leone to help revive cooperation among the Mano River Union (MRU) countries. A meeting of the Force Commanders of UNMIL, UNAMSIL and MINUCI was held in Abidjan on 13 February to discuss regional aspects of conflicts, including military coordination in addressing cross-border activities. The Secretary-General's Special Representatives for Liberia, Côte d'Ivoire, Sierra Leone, Guinea-Bissau and West Africa met in Dakar from 18 to 21 February to review and address cross-border issues, such as the movement of combatants, the use of mercenaries, the circulation of small arms and the repatriation of foreign combatants. The International Contact Group on Liberia, in a statement issued following its 5 February meeting, urged all States in the subregion to prevent their territories from being used by armed elements to destabilize their neighbours and to strengthen subregional cooperation. It urged UNMIL, the Transitional Government and the leadership of the warring parties to contain all Liberian fighters within the territory of Liberia to enable the peace process in neighbouring countries to succeed.

The disarmament, demobilization and reintegration process, which was suspended in December 2003 [YUN 2003, p. 199], was revived at a meeting held on 15 January 2004 among UNMIL, the faction commanders, the Transitional Government, UN agencies and other stakeholders. The meeting agreed that the programme would be contingent on the implementation of a sensitization campaign for combatants; provision by the three armed factions of lists of their combatants, locations and weapons; the establishment of cantonment sites; and adequate deployment of UNMIL troops to provide security. The Technical Coordination Committee completed the operational plans for the disarmament and demobilization process and identified disarmament and cantonment sites, in conjunction with UNMIL. The Government arranged for the distribution of rice to combatants, for which UNMIL provided logistical assistance. As at 5 March, $11.3 million in pledges had been made to the UNDP Trust Fund for disarmament demobilization, reintegration and repatriation, of which $8 million had been received, but additional funds were urgently needed.

The UNMIL civilian police worked to re-establish police services where the police had been forced to withdraw for security reasons. It also conducted joint force patrols to locations throughout the country. On 12 January, UNMIL launched a training programme for a Liberian interim police force of 400 officers. The civilian police consulted with justice officials to improve conditions in the correctional system, which faced such problems as insufficient prison facilities, untimely processing of cases and a lack of security.

UNMIL assisted the Transitional Government to prepare for the re-establishment of State authority throughout the country. Progress was made in meeting civil servants' salary arrears, but most ministries still lacked operational facilities, having been looted during the fighting in Monrovia in 2003. UNMIL assisted ministries and other governmental institutions to develop plans for restructuring and enhancing their operational capacities and for restoring civil administration in the interior of the country. Its civil affairs officers helped to resolve disputes over illegally occupied dwellings and land restitution. The human rights and protection component worked with the gender unit in building the capacity of the Ministry of Gender and Development. It also assisted the Transitional Government in preparing draft legislation for the establishment of the Truth and Reconciliation Commission and other human rights legislation. The Mission's public information component promoted the peace process through UNMIL Radio, working with national and international media.

With the deployment of UNMIL outside Monrovia, humanitarian access to vulnerable populations in the interior of the country improved. About 12,000 refugees from neighbouring countries returned home spontaneously, raising protection concerns in those parts of the country where UNMIL had not been deployed. The Office of the United Nations High Commissioner for Refugees (UNHCR) led the overall programme for the eventual return and resettlement of refugees and other displaced persons. However, the humanitarian situation in the camps for internally displaced persons around Monrovia, hosting some 250,000 people, was dire. Between November 2003 and January 2004, UN agencies and NGOs relocated about 25,000 internally displaced persons from shelters in Monrovia back to their homes or to recognized camps. An estimated 10,000 internally displaced persons had spontaneously returned from camps to areas that were relatively accessible, such as Bomi, Bong, Margibi and Grand Cape Mount counties. However, they all faced problems of lack of housing, food, tools for farming and poor infrastructure. A number of UN aid agencies were working to meet those challenges.

By early March, UNMIL had undertaken over 50 quick-impact projects in Monrovia utilizing local contractors, and another 45 projects were under review, mainly in the education, health, water and sanitation areas. Support was made available by UNDP, the World Bank and UNICEF, among others. A results-focused transition framework addressing Liberia's short- to medium-term reconstruction and development needs was presented at the International Reconstruction Conference for Liberia (New York, 5-6 February), where $522 million was pledged for relief and reconstruction.

The Secretary-General concluded that notwithstanding the difficulties encountered in launching the disarmament, demobilization, reintegration and repatriation programme, significant progress was made in improving security, facilitating the delivery of humanitarian assistance and implementing the peace process. He emphasized the need for the parties to work together constructively and refrain from jeopardizing the functioning of the National Transitional Government. He added that there were still many difficult challenges requiring careful management, and the Implementation Monitoring Committee would have to play a more central role in the coming months to facilitate dialogue among the parties and in helping to overcome any obstacles to the peace process.

Security Council consideration. On 29 March [S/2004/328], the Under-Secretary-General for Peacekeeping Operations briefed the Security Council during consideration of the Secretary-General's report. Council members welcomed the significant progress made towards improving security in Liberia, while recognizing that much more remained to be done, especially disarmament, demobilization, reintegration and repatriation, one of the biggest challenges ahead. They noted that the increased stability in the country should encourage the Government to extend State authority throughout Liberia.

Report of Secretary-General (May). In May [S/2004/430 & Corr.1], the Secretary-General, updating the information on Liberia since his March report (see p. 196), indicated that UNMIL was able to move into areas previously controlled by LURD elements along the Guinea-Liberia border and along Liberia's borders with Sierra Leone and Côte d'Ivoire. The ceasefire continued to hold, although the security situation remained fragile, mainly because the disarmament process was yet to be completed. Intra-faction disputes, particularly within LURD, created tension and resulted in some shooting incidents. The Joint Monitoring Committee held five meetings during the reporting period and noted that, while fighting among the armed groups had almost completely ended, intra-faction disputes and criminal activities remained a serious threat to security.

The International Contact Group on Liberia met in London on 11 May to assess progress made in the Liberian peace process. It recognized the need for a subregional approach to resolving many of the issues at hand and, to that end, proposed that the Group's mandate be expanded to cover not only Liberia but also the wider subregional issues.

Both the National Transitional Government and the National Transitional Legislative Assembly were making sincere efforts to carry out their responsibilities. The major issue of appointments to the Transitional Government, which had strained relations between Chairman Bryant and the armed factions and made it difficult for the Transitional Government to function, was largely resolved. The process of confirming nominees to the 81 assistant ministerial and other executive positions began, and the 21-member Cabinet was formally sworn in on 23 March. However, two seats in the Legislative Assembly remained vacant because of ongoing disagreements among the stakeholders in Grand Kru county and the All Liberian Coalition Party.

On 15 April, UNMIL re-launched the disarmament, demobilization, rehabilitation and reintegration programme at a cantonment site in Gbarnga for LURD combatants. Additional cantonment sites were opened in Buchanan (for MODEL), in Tubmanburg (for LURD) and near Monrovia (for former government forces). Disarmament commenced on 6 May for ex-Government of Liberia militias at Kakata and the next day in the Buchanan cantonment site initially used for MODEL combatants, without major problems. However, on 17 May, riots erupted in Monrovia when a group of armed ex-Government of Liberia combatants, demanding to be transported to a cantonment site to be disarmed, were informed that they were scheduled to undergo the process at a later stage. UNMIL troops and civilian police had to intervene to prevent the situation from escalating. As at 18 May, 17,485 combatants had been disarmed since 15 April, bringing the overall total to nearly 31,000 since December 2003, out of an anticipated caseload of 53,000. Some 14,368 weapons were also surrendered, but there were signs that some of the heavy weapons were not being turned in, while others were being smuggled across Liberia's borders. Modalities were being finalized for the voluntary reintegration and repatriation of foreign combatants to their countries of origin, with particular attention to the special needs of women and children associated with the fighting forces. With disarmament and demobilization components of the programme on track, UNMIL and others concerned turned their focus to the reintegration aspects of the programme, in collaboration with a number of agencies, including UN agencies, the United States Agency for International Development, the EU and NGOs.

In the security sector, the registration of Liberian law enforcement personnel was proceeding on schedule. The process, due to be completed by September, had enabled, as at 1 May, 3,492 members of the Liberian National Police to be registered. UNMIL provided training for 530 officers. A Rule of Law Implementation Committee was established to coordinate the reform of the police, the judiciary and correctional institutions. It was formulating a strategy for the reform and restructuring of the police force, renamed the Liberian Police Service. UNMIL also worked on problems facing the legal and judicial system, including rehabilitation work on the infrastructure of the Temple of Justice in Monrovia and coordinating plans for opening circuit and magistrates courts.

UNMIL continued to work with the Liberian authorities to formulate and execute a comprehensive strategy for the return of government officials to their areas of authority. A task force for the restoration of civil authority was established to formulate a gradual deployment of government officials to all counties.

As preparations for elections continued, an assessment mission was sent to Liberia in April to develop proposals on the UN role in supporting that process. The assessment team drew up proposals for the reform of the electoral system and a possible time line of activities. It recommended that a meeting be held as soon as possible with all signatories to the Agreement to clarify issues such as voter education and registration, constituency delimitation and polling.

Security Council consideration. The Security Council, at a 3 June meeting [meeting 4981] to consider the Secretary-General's third progress report on UNMIL (see p. 197), was briefed by the Special Representative of the Secretary-General for Liberia, Jacques Paul Klein. He reported that progress had been made in deploying troops throughout Liberia, disarming armed groups and restructuring the law and order institutions, which had exceeded the Mission's expectations. UNMIL's deployment throughout Liberia had greatly improved security along its porous borders. The United Nations was pleased that the United States had offered to take the lead in assisting and advising the National Transitional Government on the restructuring of the army. Meanwhile, UNMIL was preparing a draft restructuring scheme, and a draft defence policy was being reviewed. Developments in the surrounding countries were of concern as they negatively impacted on the Liberian peace process.

The improved security situation and the resumption of the disarmament process had enabled humanitarian agencies and human rights groups to extend their activities to formerly inaccessible areas, and displaced people and refugees were returning to their former homes. UNMIL also assisted in the restoration of the judicial system and prisons, with 17 courts being reconstituted in the Monrovia area.

The Special Representative observed that there were numerous challenges ahead, as progress was still fragile. Ensuring weapons handover remained a priority. Until the disarmament, demobilization, reintegration and repatriation programme and the troop deployment process were completed, inter- and intra-factional conflicts might persist in remote parts of the country. The capacity of the Transitional Government to deliver services and extend its authority throughout the country also remained very limited. However, he anticipated no major setback in efforts to bring peace and stability to Liberia.

Security Council mission. The Security Council mission to West Africa (see p. 169), which visited Liberia on 24 June, reported on 2 July [S/2004/525] that it was impressed by the progress made there since the National Transitional Government took office and UNMIL deployment in October 2003. It recognized, however, that the challenges of reconstruction and peace-building were so great that the international community would have to remain engaged for some time to come. The mission identified several immediate priorities for Liberia, the most urgent of which was establishing security, particularly in view of reports of cross-border movements. The mission recommended that UNMIL pay particular attention to monitoring Liberia's external borders. To help establish government authority throughout the country, it recommended that the remaining UNMIL civilian personnel, including human rights officers, be deployed as soon as possible. It welcomed the United States assistance in military training. The mission encouraged donors to provide financial and technical support for election preparations and underlined the importance of helping women to participate in those elections. It also urged donors to disburse quickly the pledges made at the international donors' conference on Liberia in February (see p. 915).

In regard to sanctions imposed against Liberia (see p. 204) by Security Council resolution 1521 (2003) [YUN 2003, p. 208], the mission reiterated the Council's wish to see sanctions ended as soon as the conditions outlined in that resolution were met. It clarified that the diamond ban could be lifted once Liberia had a transparent and internationally verifiable diamond certification scheme, thus paving the way for the country to join the Kimberley Process for diamond certification (see p. 57). The mission recommended that the Government continue efforts to achieve the goals in its action plan on timber, including the transparent management of government revenues. It also recommended that the Council consider the Special Representative's proposal that UNMIL play a more active role in monitoring sanctions.

The mission encouraged the Government to combat corruption and to explore ways of attracting private investment, in conjunction with donors and development partners. The mission recommended that UNMIL continue to coordinate with other UN missions in the subregion to develop a more effective response to cross-border problems, such as the movements of arms and mercenaries and human trafficking.

The Council considered the mission's visit and report at meetings held on 30 June and 16 July [meetings 5000 & 5005].

Report of Secretary-General (September). The Secretary-General, in his 10 September report on UNMIL [S/2004/725], covering developments in Liberia since his 26 May report (see p. 197), said that the overall security situation remained calm, although there were a few minor skirmishes and incidents, primarily related to the intra-faction dispute within LURD. Disarmament was nearing completion and UNMIL continued searches to curb the illegal movement of weapons across the country. In July, a large quantity of arms and ammunition was confiscated during checkpoint and search-and-seizure operations in central Liberia. The Mission also continued to conduct land and air patrols to monitor the situation along the borders. At the same time, there was an increase in minor crimes and civil unrest, particularly in Monrovia, where many disarmed ex-combatants had moved. However, the security situation around the city had improved overall, primarily owing to the presence of UNMIL troops and joint patrols by UNMIL civilian police and the Liberian National Police throughout the capital. The patrols quelled demonstrations by ex-combatants and others, which at times turned violent. Criminal activity and violent incidents also increased in some areas in the interior, partially linked to growing frustration among combatants still awaiting the commencement of the disarmament and demobilization programme in outlying counties and those awaiting the start of the rehabilitation and reintegration programme in their chosen communities.

The third phase of the disarmament and demobilization programme commenced, with disarmament carried out in several remote border areas, and new cantonment sites opened in Zwedru (for MODEL) and Ganta (for the former Government of Liberia forces). Operations at the cantonment sites in Gbarnga (for LURD) and Buchanan (for MODEL) concluded in July. As at 30 August, a total of 71,000 combatants had been disarmed since December 2003. UNMIL had registered 530 foreign combatants, most of whom were from Guinea, Sierra Leone and Côte d'Ivoire. UNMIL worked with UN and other agencies to strengthen linkages between the reintegration of ex-combatants and internally displaced persons and refugees who returned to their communities.

UNMIL also worked with the Liberian National Police Service in recruiting and training police officers. Through quick-impact projects, it helped to facilitate the rehabilitation and reopening of the law school, and provided legal support to committees and organizations to build capacity for good governance, transparency and the supremacy of the rule of law. It also worked with the juvenile justice system by collaborating with national counterparts, through education and legal reform initiatives. UNMIL developed, in collaboration with others, training programmes for justices of the peace, magistrates and circuit and specialized court judges, and strengthened the correctional system.

Some progress was made towards the restoration of State authority throughout the country. UNMIL assisted the national Task Force for the Restoration of State Authority in the Ministry of Internal Affairs in developing and implementing a nationwide programme for that purpose, and helped in the deployment of immigration and customs officials to border crossing points. UNMIL civil affairs officers were deployed to all 15 counties, where they supported the restoration of State authority and the revival of government institutions, including negotiating with members of the armed factions to ensure that they vacated State-owned buildings.

ECOWAS, UNMIL and the National Elections Commission, at a meeting on 31 May, agreed that the Commission would be responsible for conducting elections and that the United Nations would take the lead in coordinating all electoral assistance for the Commission. At subsequent meetings, the Commission determined that there was general consensus that the local elections would take place after the presidential and legislative elections in October 2005 and after the elected government had taken office. On 30 August, the Commission submitted the draft electoral reform legislation to the National Transitional Legislative Assembly. Voter registration was expected to begin in April 2005.

The Secretary-General, while noting the progress made in stabilizing Liberia and in creating the security conditions for implementation of the Comprehensive Peace Agreement, said that he remained concerned about the capacity of the National Transitional Government to deliver basic services and extend civil administration throughout the country. Protracted disputes, including over claims by some ministers that individuals from their respective factions should be nominated to key government and parastatal positions, had hindered the functioning of the Transitional Government, as had the continuing divisions within LURD. Liberia was entering the rehabilitation and reintegration phase of the disarmament, demobilization, reintegration and repatriation programme, a vital element in the process of ensuring durable peace and in enhancing subregional security. There were some 70,000 ex-combatants seeking to benefit from the reintegration programme, which was experiencing a funding shortfall. In the light of the new phase of UNMIL operations, focusing on rehabilitation and reintegration, the restoration of State administration nationwide, the strengthening of the rule-of-law institutions, promotion of recovery and reconstruction, and the organization of elections, the Secretary-General recommended that the UNMIL mandate be extended for 12 months, until 19 September 2005.

SECURITY COUNCIL ACTION (September)

On 17 September [meeting 5036], the Security Council unanimously adopted **resolution 1561 (2004)**. The draft [S/2004/740] was prepared in consultations among Council members.

The Security Council,

Recalling its previous resolutions and statements by its President on Liberia, including its resolutions 1497(2003) of 1 August 2003 and 1509(2003) of 19 September 2003 and the statement by its President of 27 August 2003, and other relevant resolutions and statements,

Welcoming the report of the Secretary-General of 10 September 2004 and its recommendations,

Recognizing the critical role the Economic Community of West African States continues to play in the Liberian peace process, and welcoming the support and continued engagement of the African Union and its close coordination with the Economic Community of West African States and the United Nations,

Noting the substantial progress made to date in the disarmament phase of the programme of disarmament, demobilization, rehabilitation and reintegration of ex-combatants,

Recalling that its resolutions 1521(2003) of 22 December 2003 and 1532(2004) of 12 March 2004 provide

for measures against any individuals engaged in activities aimed at undermining peace and stability in Liberia and the subregion,

1. _Decides_ to extend the mandate of the United Nations Mission in Liberia until 19 September 2005;

2. _Calls upon_ all Liberian parties to demonstrate their full commitment to the peace process and to work together to ensure that free, fair and transparent elections take place as planned no later than October 2005;

3. _Calls upon_ the international community to respond to the continuing need for funds for the critically important rehabilitation and reintegration phase and to fulfil pledges made at the International Reconstruction Conference on Liberia, held in New York on 5 and 6 February 2004;

4. _Requests_ the Secretary-General through his Special Representative to continue to report periodically to the Council on the progress made by the Mission in the implementation of its mandate;

5. _Decides_ to remain actively seized of the matter.

The United States, speaking in explanation of its vote, said that its policy was to ensure that its armed services participating in UN peace operations were protected from criminal prosecution or other assertion of jurisdiction by the International Criminal Court. Normally, it would seek express provisions providing such protection for personnel from States not party to the Rome Statute establishing the Court [YUN 1998, p. 1209]. However, the United States maintained sufficient bilateral protections with Liberia to facilitate its continued participation in UNMIL, absent such express provisions (see p. 198).

Report of Secretary-General (December). The Secretary-General, on 17 December [S/2004/972], issued his fifth progress report on UNMIL, covering developments in Liberia since his 10 September report (see p. 199). During that period, progress was made in implementing the Comprehensive Peace Agreement, including the completion of disarmament and demobilization on 31 October, the formal disbandment of the armed factions on 3 November, the commencement of the repatriation of refugees on 1 October and the resettlement of internally displaced persons on 8 November. State authority was extended to several additional counties and the training of recruits for the new Liberian National Police Service continued.

At the same time, the peace process encountered several major challenges, in particular an outbreak of violence in Monrovia from 28 to 31 October, resulting in destruction of property and loss of life, continued disputes among the LURD leadership, violent demonstrations by various disaffected groups and slow progress in the reintegration of ex-combatants. Progress was also hampered by the limited capacity of the National Transitional Government to provide social services and consolidate State authority, disputes among the former armed factions regarding the distribution of government posts, and delays in the passage of the electoral reform bill.

Early reports of the October disturbances indicated that a land dispute might have triggered the rioting, which rapidly assumed ethnic and religious dimensions involving members of the predominantly Mandingo ethnic group. The situation was exploited by disgruntled combatants awaiting reintegration, loyalists of former President Charles Taylor and some elements of the opposing factions within LURD. A number of religious, commercial and residential properties were destroyed during the uprising and 19 people killed. UNMIL initially responded to the riots by deploying its civilian police and Liberian police units, but as the situation escalated, its troops had to undertake robust action to bring it under control. The continuing disagreement among splinter groups within LURD posed serious problems for the peace process, and there were reports that some members were attempting to unseat Chairman Bryant and unravel the peace process. To guard against the derailment of the peace process, UNMIL, in a meeting with other international partners on 13 and 15 October, agreed that the National Transitional Government should be encouraged to address the grievances of the population, specifically: paying civil servants' salary arrears; instituting measures to address corruption; ensuring transparency in the management of public funds; and improving communication with the public. It urged the National Transitional Government to consult civil society groups, and Chairman Bryant to convene regular Cabinet meetings so as to ensure transparency and inclusiveness in decision-making.

On 18 October, the Implementation Monitoring Committee issued a press statement warning the Liberian factions that the international community would not allow any disruption of the functioning of the National Transitional Government, including the unseating of Chairman Bryant, and drawing attention to the measures provided for in Security Council resolutions 1521(2003) [YUN 2003, p. 208] and 1532(2004) (see p. 204) that would be taken against any individual undermining peace and stability in Liberia and the subregion. On 19 October, the Minister of Justice announced that the National Transitional Government had commenced legal action to freeze the economic assets of the former Commissioner of the Maritime Bureau, Benoni Urey, and the former Finance Minister, Emmanuel Shaw. However, following a legal petition by the two men, the Liberian Supreme Court ordered a suspension of the freeze until a hearing on 2 November. As at 1 December, the Supreme Court had yet to rule on the matter. (See section on sanctions.)

Divisions within LURD deepened on 27 October, when one faction unilaterally elected new executive members for LURD. At the intervention of the Special Representative and regional leaders, the leadership of the two opposing LURD factions were brought together at a 30 October meeting, at which a memorandum of understanding was signed for transforming LURD into a political movement; however, feuding flared up again shortly thereafter.

Meanwhile, there were growing signs of public dissatisfaction with the limited progress of the Government in improving basic living conditions. Several protests occurred linked to low or delayed payment of salaries, labour disputes, poor teaching conditions and high registration fees for high school students.

Following the completion of the disarmament and demobilization exercise, which officially ended on 31 October, 48 commanders from the three armed factions handed in their weapons and demobilized on 2 November. The next day, the three armed factions signed a joint declaration attesting to the completion of disarmament and demobilization and acknowledging the cessation of their military existence with the disbandment of their forces and command structures. As at 1 December, a total of 101,449 combatants had been disarmed and demobilized, including over 22,000 women and nearly 11,000 children, and 27,892 weapons and 33,000 pieces of heavy munitions and unexploded ordnance had been collected. UNMIL continued to make payments to the demobilized combatants, but implementation of an effective rehabilitation and reintegration programme for those ex-combatants remained a major challenge. UNMIL also initiated discussions with neighbouring countries on the repatriation of disarmed combatants who had identified themselves as nationals of those States.

Some progress was made in the restoration of State authority. During the reporting period, Chairman Bryant submitted for confirmation the names of eight nominees for county superintendent posts. UNMIL, in collaboration with UNDP, facilitated the establishment of District Development Councils to enhance community participation in local projects and governance. Meanwhile, the United Nations Office for Project Services assisted in the development of a national plan for reconstruction, including rehabilitation of the free port area in Monrovia. UNMIL also assisted the Government with the deployment of officials, particularly at the border entry points. However, the deployed officials' ability to function was hampered by a lack of adequate facilities and equipment. UNMIL civil affairs county coordinators continued to support the restoration of State authority and the revival of government institutions.

The National Transitional Legislative Assembly reached its full strength of 76 members, with the 12 October election of the representative for Grand Kru county, thereby fulfilling another provision of the Comprehensive Peace Agreement. The electoral reform bill had not been adopted due to disagreement on the basis to be used for allocating seats (either on the number of registered voters or on actual population figures). The delay hindered preparations for the October 2005 elections.

On 1 October, UNHCR, in collaboration with the Government, began to facilitate the voluntary repatriation of Liberian refugees from neighbouring countries, estimated to total nearly 100,000 by the end of the year. That action followed the signing of agreements between UNHCR and Liberia, Sierra Leone, Côte d'Ivoire, Ghana and Guinea, providing the legal framework for repatriation. In addition, it was estimated that there were more than 260,000 internally displaced persons in Liberia. UN organizations, such as WFP, FAO, UNICEF, WHO and the United Nations Human Settlements Programme (UN-Habitat) increased their deployment throughout the country to bring humanitarian aid to those outside the capital.

The Secretary-General said that the peace process was at a critical juncture, with the focus of attention shifting to the preparations for the October 2005 elections, the need to resettle internally displaced persons and refugees and provide reintegration opportunities for ex-combatants, and further the extension of State authority nationwide. Many serious issues remained to be effectively addressed, so that the gains made so far were not undermined. In addition to paying civil servants' salaries, the Government needed to address corruption and ensure transparency in order to attract donor funding for reconstruction. Consideration should also be given to increasing independent oversight of the Government's public revenue management. The Government should also actively engage and consult with civil society, as part of an overall strategy to enhance public understanding of and promote support for the transition process, expand its authority nationwide and promote reconciliation and religious tolerance among the diverse groups in the country. The reintegration of ex-combatants, largely unemployed and restive, was

essential to counter the threat they posed to security and stability.

UNMIL financing

2003/04 financial arrangements and performance

In a 12 May note [A/58/792] on financing arrangements for UNMIL for the period from 1 August 2003 to 30 June 2004, the Secretary-General reported that, as at 30 March 2004, expenditures incurred by UNMIL amounted to $237,837,300 gross ($237,260,700 net), or 42 per cent of the $564,494,300 gross ($560,733,400 net) appropriated by the General Assembly for that period to the Special Account for UNMIL in resolution 58/261 A [YUN 2003, p. 200]. It was anticipated that the remainder would be fully utilized and that an additional $114,494,300 would be needed for the budget, as States had been apportioned for only $450,000,000. The Assembly was also requested to approve the reduction in the estimated staff assessment income from $5,210,000 as apportioned to $3,760,900.

On 20 December [A/59/624], the Secretary-General issued a performance report on the UNMIL budget for the period from 1 August 2003 to 30 June 2004. Actual expenditure amounted to $548,178,700, a variance of 2.9 per cent, leaving an unencumbered balance of $16,315,600.

2004/05 budget estimates

On 22 March [A/58/744], the Secretary-General submitted the budget for UNMIL for the period from 1 July 2004 to 30 June 2005, which amounted to $839,711,300, inclusive of budgeted voluntary contributions in kind valued at $120,000.

ACABQ, in its 14 May report [A/58/798], having considered the financial arrangements for the period from 1 August 2003 to 30 June 2004 and the 2004/05 budget, proposed a number of revisions to the budget, particularly for streamlining UNMIL's structure and downgrading five posts. It recommended that the estimated budget requirement be reduced to $821,986,000.

GENERAL ASSEMBLY ACTION

On 18 June [meeting 91], the General Assembly, on the recommendation of the Fifth Committee [A/58/589/Add.1], adopted **resolution 58/261 B** without vote [agenda item 165].

Financing of the United Nations Mission in Liberia
The General Assembly,
Having considered the reports of the Secretary-General and his note on the financing of the United Nations Mission in Liberia and the related reports of the Advisory Committee on Administrative and Budgetary Questions,

Recalling Security Council resolution 1497(2003) of 1 August 2003, by which the Council declared its readiness to establish a United Nations stabilization force to support the transitional government and to assist in the implementation of a comprehensive peace agreement in Liberia,

Recalling also Security Council resolution 1509(2003) of 19 September 2003, by which the Council decided to establish the United Nations Mission in Liberia for a period of twelve months,

Recalling further its resolution 58/261 A of 23 December 2003 on the financing of the Mission,

Reaffirming the general principles underlying the financing of United Nations peacekeeping operations, as stated in General Assembly resolutions 1874 (S-IV) of 27 June 1963, 3101(XXVIII) of 11 December 1973 and 55/235 of 23 December 2000,

Noting with appreciation that voluntary contributions have been made to the Mission,

Mindful of the fact that it is essential to provide the Mission with the necessary financial resources to enable it to fulfil its responsibilities under the relevant resolution of the Security Council,

1. *Takes note* of the status of contributions to the United Nations Mission in Liberia as at 15 April 2004, including the contributions outstanding in the amount of 139.3 million United States dollars, representing some 31 per cent of the total assessed contributions, notes with concern that only thirty-eight Member States have paid their assessed contributions in full, and urges all other Member States, in particular those in arrears, to ensure payment of their outstanding assessed contributions;

2. *Expresses its appreciation* to those Member States which have paid their assessed contributions in full, and urges all other Member States to make every possible effort to ensure payment of their assessed contributions to the Mission in full;

3. *Expresses concern* at the financial situation with regard to peacekeeping activities, in particular as regards the reimbursements to troop contributors that bear additional burdens owing to overdue payments by Member States of their assessments;

4. *Also expresses concern* at the delay experienced by the Secretary-General in deploying and providing adequate resources to some recent peacekeeping missions, in particular those in Africa;

5. *Emphasizes* that all future and existing peacekeeping missions shall be given equal and non-discriminatory treatment in respect of financial and administrative arrangements;

6. *Also emphasizes* that all peacekeeping missions shall be provided with adequate resources for the effective and efficient discharge of their respective mandates;

7. *Reiterates its request* to the Secretary-General to make the fullest possible use of facilities and equipment at the United Nations Logistics Base at Brindisi, Italy, in order to minimize the costs of procurement for the Mission;

8. *Endorses* the conclusions and recommendations contained in the report of the Advisory Committee on Administrative and Budgetary Questions, subject to the provisions of the present resolution, and requests the Secretary-General to ensure their full implementation;

9. *Requests* the Secretary-General to review the projects that may require the services of consultants, in order to ensure the implementation of those projects that are required for the successful implementation of the mandate, and to report thereon in the performance report;

10. *Also requests* the Secretary-General to take all necessary action to ensure that the Mission is administered with a maximum of efficiency and economy;

11. *Further requests* the Secretary-General, in order to reduce the cost of employing General Service staff, to continue efforts to recruit local staff for the Mission against General Service posts, commensurate with the requirements of the Mission;

Budget estimates for the period from 1 July 2004 to 30 June 2005

12. *Decides* to appropriate to the Special Account for the United Nations Mission in Liberia the amount of 864,815,900 dollars for the period from 1 July 2004 to 30 June 2005, inclusive of 821,986,000 dollars for the maintenance of the Mission, 35,015,300 dollars for the support account for peacekeeping operations and 7,814,600 dollars for the United Nations Logistics Base;

Financing of the appropriation

13. *Decides also* to apportion among Member States the amount of 864,815,900 dollars at a monthly rate of 72,067,991 dollars, in accordance with the levels set out in General Assembly resolution 55/235, as adjusted by the Assembly in its resolution 55/236 of 23 December 2000 and updated in its resolution 58/256 of 23 December 2003, taking into account the scale of assessments for 2004 and 2005 as set out in its resolution 58/1 B of 23 December 2003, subject to a decision of the Security Council to extend the mandate of the Mission;

14. *Decides further* that, in accordance with the provisions of its resolution 973(X) of 15 December 1955, there shall be set off against the apportionment among Member States, as provided for in paragraph 13 above, their respective share in the Tax Equalization Fund of 15,634,600 dollars, comprising the estimated staff assessment income of 10,084,900 dollars approved for the Mission, the prorated share of 5,109,600 dollars of the estimated staff assessment income approved for the support account and the prorated share of 440,100 dollars of the estimated staff assessment income approved for the United Nations Logistics Base;

Financing of the appropriation for the period from 1 August 2003 to 30 June 2004

15. *Takes note* of the note by the Secretary-General on the financing arrangements of the Mission for the period from 1 August 2003 to 30 June 2004;

16. *Decides* to apportion among Member States the additional amount of 114,494,300 dollars already appropriated for the maintenance of the Mission for the period from 1 August 2003 to 30 June 2004 under the terms of General Assembly resolution 58/261 A, at a monthly rate of 10,408,600 dollars, in accordance with the levels set out in Assembly resolution 55/235, as adjusted by the Assembly in its resolution 55/236 and its resolution 57/290 A of 20 December 2002 and updated in its resolution 58/256, and taking into account the scale of assessments for 2003, as set out in its resolutions 55/5 B of 23 December 2000 and 57/4 B of 20 December 2002 and the scale of assessments for 2004 as set out in its resolution 58/1 B;

17. *Approves* the reduction in the estimated staff assessment income approved for the Mission in the amount of 1,449,100 dollars, from 5,210,000 dollars to 3,760,900 dollars;

18. *Emphasizes* that no peacekeeping mission shall be financed by borrowing funds from other active peacekeeping missions;

19. *Encourages* the Secretary-General to continue to take additional measures to ensure the safety and security of all personnel under the auspices of the United Nations participating in the Mission;

20. *Invites* voluntary contributions to the Mission in cash and in the form of services and supplies acceptable to the Secretary-General, to be administered, as appropriate, in accordance with the procedure and practices established by the General Assembly;

21. *Decides* to include in the provisional agenda of its fifty-ninth session the item entitled "Financing of the United Nations Mission in Liberia".

2005/06 budget estimates

On 20 December [A/59/630], the Secretary-General submitted proposed budget estimates for the maintenance of UNMIL for the period from 1 July 2005 to 30 June 2006, which amounted to $722,753,600 inclusive of budgeted voluntary contributions in kind in the amount of $120,000.

On 23 December, the General Assembly decided that the agenda item on UNMIL financing would remain for consideration at its resumed fifty-ninth (2005) session (**decision 59/552**). The Assembly also called on the international community to provide assistance for the rehabilitation and reconstruction of Liberia in **resolution 59/219** (see p. 929).

Sanctions

The Security Council received several reports on the implementation of sanctions imposed on Liberia pursuant to Council resolutions 1343 (2001) [YUN 2001, p. 181], 1478(2003) [YUN 2003, p. 203] and 1521(2003) [ibid., p. 208]. Those sanctions banned arms and related materiel, military training, the export of Liberian timber products and rough diamonds and international travel of those individuals so designated, who constituted a threat to the peace process in Liberia and the subregion. On 12 March 2004, the Council imposed further financial sanctions on Charles Taylor and his immediate family (see below).

On 16 January [S/2004/40], the Secretary-General informed the Council, as requested by resolution 1521(2003), of his appointment of five members of the Panel of Experts established pursuant to resolution 1478(2003). The Panel was mandated to conduct a follow-up assessment mission to Liberia and neighbouring States, to investigate and report on the implementation of resolution 1521(2003) and violations of the sanctions, including any violations involving rebel movements and neighbouring countries, and any information relevant to the designation by the Committee established pursuant to resolution 1521(2003) of the individuals described in the resolution, and the various sources of financing, such as from natural resources, for the illicit trade of arms.

SECURITY COUNCIL ACTION (March)

On 12 March [meeting 4925], the Security Council unanimously adopted **resolution 1532(2004)**. The draft [S/2004/189] was prepared in consultations among Council members.

The Security Council,

Recalling its resolution 1521(2003) of 22 December 2003 and its other resolutions and the statements by its President on the situation in Liberia and West Africa,

Noting with concern that the actions and policies of former President of Liberia Charles Taylor and other persons, in particular their depletion of Liberian resources and their removal from Liberia and secreting of Liberian funds and property, have undermined Liberia's transition to democracy and the orderly development of its political, administrative and economic institutions and resources,

Recognizing the negative impact on Liberia of the transfer abroad of misappropriated funds and assets and the need for the international community to ensure as soon as possible, in accordance with paragraph 6 below, the return of such funds and assets to Liberia,

Expressing concern that former President Taylor, in collaboration with others still closely associated with him, continues to exercise control over and to have access to such misappropriated funds and property, with which he and his associates are able to engage in activities that undermine peace and stability in Liberia and the region,

Determining that this situation constitutes a threat to international peace and security in West Africa, in particular to the peace process in Liberia,

Acting under Chapter VII of the Charter of the United Nations,

1. *Decides* that, to prevent former President of Liberia Charles Taylor, his immediate family members, in particular Jewel Howard Taylor and Charles Taylor, Jr., senior officials of the former Taylor regime, or other close allies or associates as designated by the Committee established pursuant to paragraph 21 of resolution 1521(2003) (hereinafter "the Committee") from using misappropriated funds and property to interfere in the restoration of peace and stability in Liberia and the subregion, all States in which there are, at the date of adoption of the present resolution or at any time thereafter, funds, other financial assets and economic resources owned or controlled directly or indirectly by Charles Taylor, Jewel Howard Taylor and Charles Taylor, Jr. and/or those other individuals designated by the Committee, including funds, other financial assets and economic resources held by entities owned or controlled, directly or indirectly, by any of them or by any persons acting on their behalf or at

their direction, as designated by the Committee, shall freeze without delay all such funds, other financial assets and economic resources and shall ensure that neither these nor any other funds, other financial assets or economic resources are made available, by their nationals or by any persons within their territory, directly or indirectly, to or for the benefit of such persons;

2. *Decides also* that the provisions of paragraph 1 above do not apply to funds, other financial assets and economic resources:

(*a*) That have been determined by relevant State(s) to be necessary for basic expenses, including payment for foodstuffs, rent or mortgage, medicines and medical treatment, taxes, insurance premiums and public utility charges, or exclusively for payment of reasonable professional fees and reimbursement of incurred expenses associated with the provision of legal services, or fees or service charges for routine holding or maintenance of frozen funds, other financial assets and economic resources, after notification by the relevant State(s) to the Committee of the intention to authorize, where appropriate, access to such funds, other financial assets and economic resources and in the absence of a negative decision by the Committee within two working days of such notification;

(*b*) That have been determined by relevant State(s) to be necessary for extraordinary expenses, provided that such determination has been notified by the relevant State(s) to the Committee and has been approved by the Committee; or

(*c*) That have been determined by relevant State(s) to be the subject of a judicial, administrative or arbitral lien or judgement, in which case the funds, other financial assets and economic resources may be used to satisfy that lien or judgement, provided that the lien or judgement was entered prior to the date of the present resolution, is not for the benefit of a person referred to in paragraph 1 above or an individual or entity identified by the Committee, and has been notified by the relevant State(s) to the Committee;

3. *Decides further* that all States may allow for the addition to accounts subject to the provisions of paragraph 1 above of:

(*a*) Interest or other earnings due on those accounts; and

(*b*) Payments due under contracts, agreements or obligations that arose prior to the date on which those accounts became subject to the provisions of paragraph 1 above;

provided that any such interest, other earnings and payments continue to be subject to those provisions;

4. *Decides* that the Committee shall:

(*a*) Identify individuals and entities of the types described in paragraph 1 above and promptly circulate to all States a list of said individuals and entities, including by posting such a list on the web site of the Committee;

(*b*) Maintain and regularly update and review every six months the list of those individuals and entities identified by the Committee as being subject to the measures set forth in paragraph 1 above;

(*c*) Assist States, where necessary, in tracing and freezing the funds, other financial assets and economic resources of such individuals and entities;

(*d*) Seek from all States information regarding the actions taken by them to trace and freeze such funds, other financial assets and economic resources;

5. *Decides also* to review the measures imposed by paragraph 1 above at least once a year, the first review taking place by 22 December 2004 in conjunction with its review of the measures imposed by paragraphs 2, 4, 6 and 10 of resolution 1521(2003), and to determine at that time what further action is appropriate;

6. *Expresses its intention* to consider whether and how to make available the funds, other financial assets and economic resources frozen pursuant to paragraph 1 above to the Government of Liberia, once that Government has established transparent accounting and auditing mechanisms to ensure the responsible use of government revenue to benefit directly the people of Liberia;

7. *Decides* to remain actively seized of the matter.

Implementation of sanctions regime

Report of Committee established pursuant to resolution 1343(2001). On 23 February [S/2004/139 & Corr.1], the Security Council Committee established pursuant to resolution 1343(2001) concerning Liberia reported to the Council. It was tasked with reporting on any Liberian military or financial support to the Revolutionary United Front (RUF) of Sierra Leone and other rebel movements, including transfer of arms, military training and provision of communications and logistical assistance, as well as on the bans on the travel of key individuals providing support to rebels and the import of Sierra Leone rough diamonds not controlled through the certificate-of-origin regime. The report covered the period from 21 December 2002 to 22 December 2003, when the Council decided, in resolution 1521 (2003), to dissolve the Committee and to revise the legal basis of the sanctions to reflect the changed circumstances in Liberia, in particular the departure of former President Charles Taylor, the formation of the National Transitional Government and progress with the peace process in Sierra Leone. During the reporting period, the Committee received 11 notifications of travel of individuals on the travel ban list and granted 22 of the 29 requests for waivers of the ban. It conducted reviews of the travel ban list on three occasions, and removed the names of two RUF members from the list of persons to be expelled from Liberia. In response to the Council's request, the Committee received a total of 116 replies from States on measures they had taken to implement the travel ban. The Committee sought information from States on alleged violations reported by the Panel of Experts of the Liberia sanctions regime. At its request, the Committee received a report from the Panel of Experts on violations of the embargo on the importation of all round logs and timber products originating in Liberia.

Report of Secretary-General (April). In response to Security Council resolution 1478(2003) [YUN 2003, p. 203], the Secretary-General, on 1 April [S/2004/272], reported on Liberia's compliance with that resolution. Since his 22 April 2003 report [YUN 2003, p. 202], there had been significant developments in Liberia, in particular the resignation of President Charles Taylor on 11 August 2003 and his departure from the country, the signing of the Comprehensive Peace Agreement [ibid., p. 192] and the establishment of UNMIL [ibid., p. 194]. The report also described the dissolution of RUF in Sierra Leone over the previous two years, and its transformation into a political party, the Revolutionary United Front Party. Subsequently, there were reports of former RUF members being recruited to fight in Liberia on behalf of the forces of the Government of Liberia or LURD. However, with the deaths of some RUF fighters, including its leader, Sam Bockarie, the force was substantially weakened. Noting the changed circumstances, the Council had accordingly revised the legal basis of its sanctions and agreed not to renew the prohibition against the import of rough diamonds from Sierra Leone not controlled by the certificate-of-origin regime, thus making the demand contained in paragraph 2 (c) of resolution 1343(2001) obsolete. Therefore, the Secretary-General intended to make the report currently before the Council his last, pursuant to paragraph 20 of resolution 1478(2003). He would report to the Council by 30 May on progress made towards the revised benchmarks for lifting sanctions, in accordance with paragraph 26 of resolution 1521(2003).

Report of Secretary-General (May). On 26 May [S/2004/428], the Secretary-General submitted a report pursuant to Security Council resolution 1521(2003) regarding Liberia, covering progress made towards the goals described in paragraphs 5, 7 and 11 of that resolution, which dealt with the imposition of arms, diamond and timber sanctions. The report described progress in a number of areas: disarmament, demobilization, reintegration and repatriation; restructuring the security sector; implementing the Comprehensive Peace Agreement; maintaining stability in Liberia and the subregion; establishing a certificate-of-origin regime for trade in Liberian rough diamonds; and control over the timber-producing areas and use of revenues from the timber industry.

Since its establishment on 14 October 2003, the National Transitional Government had made some encouraging progress towards meeting the objectives contained in paragraphs 5, 7 and 11,

the Secretary-General said, notwithstanding a number of serious resource and operational constraints. Much remained to be done to apply and implement the recommendations for reform of the timber sector made by the Timber Sanctions Review Committee. The reform programme needed to be developed into a comprehensive package, with fully defined recommendations, an implementation strategy and timelines. Although some steps had been taken, such as a review of logging concessions, there were still concerns about the current pace of the review process and the way concessions could be awarded by the Government. The Forestry Development Authority would need to ensure transparency in revising all forestry concession agreements to reflect international standards and sustainable forest management practices.

The Government did not have full authority and control over the timber-producing areas. However, with the steady deployment and patrolling of UNMIL forces throughout the country, in particular to logging areas such as Buchanan, Greenville and Zwedru, the Government's capacity was increasing, although it would take some time to establish local administration in forest areas. The most pressing concerns continued to be the lack of structure, oversight and accountability in the financial management systems of the timber sector.

In the diamond sector, the Government was making gradual progress in preparing its application to join the Kimberley Process for the certification of rough diamonds (see p. 198). In doing so, the Government would need to ensure transparency in its procedures and methods for instituting controls over the export, import and transit of rough diamonds.

Report of Panel of Experts (June). The Panel of Experts established pursuant to paragraph 22 of Security Council resolution 1521(2003) concerning sanctions against Liberia transmitted a report to the Council on 1 June [S/2004/396 & Corr.1,2]. The Panel, having visited the country, said that it found no evidence of weapons trafficking into Liberia since August 2003; however, organized, international smuggling networks remained in place. Disarmament was progressing, but there was a strong possibility that factions might have cached weapons either within Liberia or in neighbouring countries, making regional stability a continuing concern. Therefore, it affirmed that the arms sanctions should remain in place, the ECOWAS moratorium on small arms should be implemented (see p. 166), and the origin of weapons surrendered in the disarmament process should be established. Regarding civil aviation, the Panel said that the Government was currently applying international civil aviation regulations and flights were operating more safely than in the past when arms were entering the country. It recommended that the Liberian civil aviation authority continue to implement the international standards.

In the context of the poor internal security situation, diamond mining in Liberia had virtually ceased, and consequently the current level of diamond smuggling was negligible. The Government had taken steps towards establishing an effective certificate-of-origin scheme for trade in rough diamonds that was transparent and internationally verifiable, with a view to joining the Kimberley Process. The Panel recommended that those positive steps be accelerated by providing financial and technical support.

Sanctions on timber products appeared to be effective, as there was no evidence of widespread exports. However, UNMIL had not deployed to the heavily forested south-east of Liberia, and the Forestry Development Authority did not function outside Monrovia. Given the evidence of the Authority's past complicity with human rights abuses and widespread corruption, an independent review of the industry was required. The lack of trained personnel suggested that a management company should be appointed to run the Authority. Until the Authority was operational and security achieved, the conditions necessary to lift sanctions would not be met, as the revenue from forestry and the security forces used by logging companies could be a source of regional instability.

In terms of the humanitarian impact, the Panel determined that the sanctions against Liberia had contributed significantly to ending the country's 14-year cycle of armed conflicts and laying the foundations for lasting peace and good governance. The erosion of former President Taylor's power base was a direct result of the sanctions, as had been the inability of former warring factions and their expatriate counterparts to use diamonds and timber to prolong the conflict. At the same time, the sanctions on diamonds and timber had had some adverse effects, such as the absence of employment for thousands of Liberians, the loss of tax revenues to the Government and road maintenance opportunities previously provided by logging companies. Nevertheless, Liberians seemed to understand the rationale for their imposition and viewed the international community's efforts to facilitate reforms in Liberia as positive.

On several occasions throughout the year [SC/8027, SC/8033, SC/8062, SC/8123, SC/8133, SC/8145, SC/8147, SC/8176/Rev.1, SC/8211], the Security Council Committee established pursuant to resolution 1521(2003) approved additions to the list of individuals subject to the travel restrictions imposed by paragraph 4 *(a)* of that resolution.

Security Council consideration. The Security Council, which considered the 26 May report of the Secretary-General on 3 June [meeting 4981], heard a statement by the Special Representative for Liberia, who affirmed that, as part of its mandate, UNMIL monitored progress made by the Government to put in place mechanisms to ensure the proper management of the natural resource industries under sanctions, namely diamonds and timber. He pointed out that the Government badly needed reliable sources of revenue in order to function effectively. Liberia's long-term security and stability would come only with a robust economy that could offer steady employment for young adult males, supported by a responsible credible, democratic and accountable Government. It was therefore necessary for the international community to provide all necessary support to enable the Government to meet the requirements of resolution 1521(2003).

The Chairman of the National Transitional Government of Liberia, Charles Gyude Bryant, in his address to the Council, made the case for lifting the sanctions, especially those on diamonds and timber. He said that the forestry sector held the greatest short-term promise for job creation and fostering economic recovery, and diamond production was an economic mainstay for a substantial number of people and a foreign exchange earner. He enumerated the steps Liberia had taken to meet the demands of the Council for lifting the sanctions in both industries and drew attention to the fact that the United States had unilaterally lifted sanctions on the importation of diamonds from Liberia.

On 10 June, the Council conducted a mid-term review of the sanctions imposed on Liberia. In a statement of the same day issued by its President [SC/8119-AFR/966], Council members acknowledged progress made by the Liberian Government in meeting the conditions for lifting the measures, in particular the diamonds and timber sanctions. While noting that no major violations of the arms embargo and the diamond and timber sanctions had been reported since August 2003, the members felt that the conditions for lifting the sanctions were yet to be fully met. They also noted the views expressed by the Special Representative and the Chairman of the National Transitional Government, and said that the measures were not meant to be punitive but to ensure that the peace process was irreversible. They expressed their readiness to keep the measures on diamonds and timber under regular review with a view to their possible termination, based on further evaluation of progress made on the benchmarks established for lifting them.

SECURITY COUNCIL ACTION (June)

On 17 June [meeting 4991], the Security Council unanimously adopted **resolution 1549(2004)**. The draft [S/2004/495] was prepared in consultations among Council members.

The Security Council,

Recalling its resolutions, in particular resolutions 1521(2003) of 22 December 2003 and 1532(2004) of 12 March 2004, on the situation in Liberia and West Africa,

Taking note of the report of the Secretary-General on Liberia of 26 May 2004 and the report of the Panel of Experts on Liberia of 17 May 2004, both submitted pursuant to resolution 1521(2003),

Taking note also of the views expressed by the Chairman of the National Transitional Government of Liberia in the Security Council on 3 June 2004 appealing for the lifting of current sanctions on Liberia's timber and diamonds, and the request that Council experts visit Liberia within the next ninety days to assess the performance of the Transitional Government in fulfilling the conditions for the lifting of sanctions,

1. *Decides* to re-establish the Panel of Experts appointed pursuant to paragraph 22 of resolution 1521 (2003) for a further period commencing no later than 30 June and ending on 21 December 2004 to undertake the following tasks:

(a) To conduct a follow-up assessment mission to Liberia and neighbouring States in order to investigate and compile a report on the implementation, and any violations, particularly ongoing violations, of the measures referred to in paragraphs 2, 4, 6 and 10 of resolution 1521(2003), including any violations involving rebel movements and neighbouring countries, and including any information relevant to designation by the Security Council Committee established pursuant to resolution 1521(2003) (hereinafter "the Committee") of the individuals described in paragraph 4 (a) of resolution 1521(2003), and also including the various sources of financing, such as from natural resources, for the illicit trade in arms;

(b) To assess the progress made towards the goals described in paragraphs 5, 7 and 11 of resolution 1521 (2003);

(c) To monitor the implementation and enforcement of the measures imposed by paragraph 1 of resolution 1532(2004), particularly in Liberia and in neighbouring States, as well as in other regions, and to provide the Committee with any information that the Panel acquires which will facilitate the identification of individuals and entities of the types described in paragraph 1 of resolution 1532(2004), and with recommendations on technical assistance that Liberia and other States might require to implement the measures;

(d) To assess the socio-economic and humanitarian impact of the measures imposed by resolutions 1521 (2003) and 1532(2004);

2. *Requests* the Panel to provide a mid-term report to the Council for its review, through the Committee, no later than 30 September 2004, with its observations and recommendations, taking into consideration pro-

gress made towards the goals identified in resolution 1521(2003), in particular in paragraphs 7 and 11 of that resolution, and also requests that the Panel present a final report to the Council, through the Committee, no later than 10 December 2004, covering all the tasks assigned to it in paragraph 1 above;

3. *Requests* the Secretary-General, upon adoption of the present resolution and acting in consultation with the Committee, to appoint by 30 June 2004 no more than five experts, with the range of expertise necessary to fulfil the mandate of the Panel referred to above, drawing as much as possible and as appropriate on the expertise of the members of the Panel of Experts appointed pursuant to paragraph 22 of resolution 1521(2003), and further requests the Secretary-General to make the necessary financial arrangements to support the work of the Panel;

4. *Encourages* the National Transitional Government of Liberia to take urgent steps to establish an effective certificate-of-origin regime for trade in Liberian rough diamonds that is transparent and internationally verifiable, and urges the Transitional Government to establish its full authority and control over the timber-producing areas and to take all necessary steps to ensure that government revenues from the Liberian timber industry are not used to fuel conflict or otherwise in violation of the resolutions of the Council but are used for legitimate purposes for the benefit of the Liberian people, including development;

5. *Reiterates its call upon* States, relevant international organizations and others in a position to do so to offer assistance to the National Transitional Government of Liberia in achieving the objectives set forth in paragraphs 5, 7 and 11 of resolution 1521(2003);

6. *Reiterates its previous appeals* to the international community to provide timely and adequate assistance for the reconstruction and economic recovery of Liberia and, in particular, to redeem the pledges made at the International Reconstruction Conference on Liberia, held in New York on 5 and 6 February 2004;

7. *Urges* all States, relevant United Nations bodies and, as appropriate, other organizations and interested parties to cooperate fully with the Committee and the Panel of Experts, including by supplying information on possible violations of the measures imposed by paragraphs 2, 4, 6 and 10 of resolution 1521(2003) and paragraph 1 of resolution 1532(2004);

8. *Decides* to remain actively seized of the matter.

The Secretary-General, on 2 July [S/2004/531], informed the Security Council of the names of the five experts he had appointed to the Panel of Experts pursuant to resolution 1549(2004) (above).

Report of Expert Panel (September). The Panel of Experts submitted, on 23 September [S/2004/752], its midterm report, prepared in accordance with resolution 1549(2004) (above). The Panel, which visited Liberia in August, reported, with regard to the timber industry, that sanctions remained effective and appeared to have halted exports of timber. There was no evidence of widespread logging and the Panel could not confirm allegations of exports to Côte d'Ivoire and Guinea. However, a pre-audit of the Forestry Development Authority, the Government's regulatory agency, revealed a complete lack of financial management systems. An independent firm was appointed to provide financial management. The Government, which had, in December 2003, produced a road map of reforms necessary for sanctions to be lifted, reported on progress in meeting those reforms. The Panel pointed out that, without sufficient security, conflict could resume; without financial oversight, misappropriation would facilitate corruption; and without enforcement, timber companies might violate regulations with impunity; therefore reform was required. Because reforms had not been instituted, nor had the conditions set out in Security Council resolution 1521(2003) been met, the Panel recommended that the timber sanctions remain in place.

The Panel reported that illegal Liberian exports of rough diamonds continued to be negligible. That situation was a result of poor weather conditions, concerns regarding overall security in mining areas, particularly as disarmament remained to be completed in those areas, and acute shortages of mining equipment. In August, the National Transitional Legislative Assembly adopted an Act amending the Minerals and Mining Law, providing for controls on the export, import and transit of rough diamonds. In addition, some institutional and technical structures were set up for implementing the Kimberley Process Certification Scheme. In that regard, the Ministry of Lands, Mines and Energy would monitor buying and selling transactions to ensure greater transparency in the flow of diamonds from the mine to the granting of a Kimberley Process certificate and export. A plan was drawn up for establishing mining cooperatives and for training mines inspectors. Overall, the Panel determined that the Government was proceeding well towards meeting the Council's requirements for lifting sanctions on the export of Liberian rough diamonds. However, its biggest obstacle remained funding for the materials and mechanisms necessary for implementing the Kimberley Process Certification Scheme; without funding, it was unlikely that the Government would be able to meeting those requirements by the end of 2004.

Security Council consideration. Following a review of the sanctions on Liberia by the Security Council, the President, in a 7 October press statement [SC/8212-AFR/1045], said that Council members, noting that no violations of the diamond and timber sanctions were reported in recent months, appreciated the Government's efforts to meet the goals identified in resolution 1521(2003) for lifting sanctions. They encouraged the Liberian authorities to take the necessary measures to establish full authority and control over the timber-producing areas and to ensure proper utilization of the revenues of the timber industry. While recognizing the need to lift the diamonds and timber sanctions as soon as possible, and acknowledging the progress made so far, Council members concluded that the conditions for lifting them were not fully met and called on the Government to take the necessary steps for meeting those benchmarks.

Report of Expert Panel (December). The Panel of Experts transmitted a report to the Security Council on 6 December [S/2004/955], covering the socio-economic and humanitarian situation in the country, the impact of sanctions on that situation, weapons trafficking, the travel ban against certain individuals, diamond mining and trading, and the timber industry. It reported that small quantities of arms imported to Liberia were smuggled in from neighbouring countries, such as Guinea and Sierra Leone, for the purpose of being surrendered in the disarmament, demobilization, reintegration and repatriation process in Liberia. More than 27,000 weapons were recovered, indicating a benchmark return rate of more than 60 per cent.

The Government remained committed to meeting the requirements for lifting the embargo on rough diamonds, but it was hampered by a lack of funding and institutional capacity. With the onset of the dry season and better security, mining activity had increased, much of which was, however, illegal. Reports indicated that the production from those mines was being smuggled through neighbouring countries to reach the international market. There was widespread compliance with timber sanctions. However, the Forestry Development Authority had not completed the reforms required by the Council, such as financial oversight and expansion of its operations to the field. The Panel recommended that the current embargoes on Liberian diamond and timber exports remain in effect.

The Panel criticized the Government's handling of the national budget, which reflected misplaced priorities. In addition, the Government had not prepared accounts for the previous two budgets, and, from February to June, had allowed excess expenditure of $8.6 million without any allotments from the Bureau of the Budget, nor any supplementary budget approved by the National Assembly. There were also large variations between amounts budgeted and amounts spent and a lack of audits. Among its recommendations, the Panel proposed that UNMIL be empowered to take a proactive stance in identifying and publicizing high-level corruption and other violations of public trust, so as to emphasize the importance of and urgent need for accountability and transparency.

The Government had delayed action to freeze the assets of the persons designated by the Security Council, and finally took action against 2 of the 26 persons on the list, and without proper preparation. The Panel, having contacted a number of countries to obtain information about the assets frozen by them, in pursuance of Council resolution 1532(2004), learned that Germany, the United Kingdom and the United States had identified and frozen the assets of three listed individuals.

The Panel was concerned about aircraft registered in Liberia, as it believed that Liberian registered aircraft were still flying elsewhere in the world for illicit activities. The Panel approved the permanent presence of UNMIL police officers at Robertsfield International Airport to enhance security procedures and allow for overall supervision of airport civilian security personnel.

SECURITY COUNCIL ACTION (December)

On 21 December [meeting 5105], the Security Council unanimously adopted **resolution 1579 (2004)**. The draft [S/2004/981] was prepared in consultations among Council members.

The Security Council,

Recalling its previous resolutions and the statements by its President on the situation in Liberia and West Africa,

Taking note of the reports of the Panel of Experts on Liberia of 24 September and 6 December 2004 submitted pursuant to resolution 1549(2004) of 17 June 2004,

Taking note also of the letter dated 13 December 2004 from the Special Representative of the Secretary-General in Liberia to the Chairman of the Security Council Committee established pursuant to paragraph 21 of resolution 1521(2003) of 22 December 2003,

Recognizing the linkage between the illegal exploitation of natural resources such as diamonds and timber, the illicit trade in such resources and the proliferation and trafficking of arms as one of the sources of fuelling and exacerbating conflicts in West Africa, particularly in Liberia,

Recalling that the measures imposed under resolution 1521(2003) were designed to prevent such illegal exploitation from fuelling a resumption of the conflict in Liberia, as well as to support the implementation of the Comprehensive Peace Agreement signed at Accra on 18 August 2003, and the extension of the authority, throughout Liberia, of the National Transitional Government of Liberia,

Expressing its satisfaction that the full deployment of the United Nations Mission in Liberia has contributed to the improvement of security throughout Liberia, while recognizing that the National Transitional Government of Liberia has not yet established its authority throughout Liberia,

Expressing concern that former President of Liberia Charles Taylor and others still closely associated with him continue to engage in activities that undermine peace and stability in Liberia and the region,

Having reviewed the measures imposed by paragraphs 2, 4, 6 and 10 of resolution 1521(2003) and paragraph 1 of resolution 1532(2004) of 12 March 2004 and the progress made towards achieving the objectives set forth in paragraphs 5, 7 and 11 of resolution 1521 (2003),

Welcoming the steps taken by the National Transitional Government of Liberia towards meeting the conditions established by the Security Council for lifting the measures imposed by resolution 1521(2003),

Noting the completion of demobilization and disarmament, respect for the ceasefire, and implementation of the Comprehensive Peace Agreement, but emphasizing that significant challenges remain in completing the reintegration, repatriation and restructuring of the security sector, as well as establishing and maintaining stability in Liberia and the subregion,

Noting with concern that, despite having initiated important reforms, the National Transitional Government of Liberia has made only limited progress towards establishing its full authority and control over the timber-producing areas and towards ensuring that government revenues from the Liberian timber industry are not used to fuel conflict or otherwise in violation of the resolutions of the Council but are used for legitimate purposes for the benefit of the Liberian people, including development,

Welcoming the start of preparations by the National Transitional Government of Liberia to establish an effective certificate-of-origin regime for trade in rough diamonds that is transparent and internationally verifiable, looking forward to the visit by representatives of the Kimberley Process to Liberia in early 2005, encouraging the Government to continue its preparations in that regard, and urging States to increase their support for its efforts,

Determining that the situation in Liberia continues to constitute a threat to international peace and security in the region,

Acting under Chapter VII of the Charter of the United Nations,

1. *Decides,* on the basis of its assessments above of progress made by the National Transitional Government of Liberia towards meeting the conditions for lifting the measures imposed by resolution 1521(2003):

(*a*) To renew the measures on arms and travel imposed by paragraphs 2 and 4 of resolution 1521(2003) for a further period of twelve months from the date of adoption of the present resolution, and to review them after six months;

(*b*) To renew the measures on timber imposed by paragraph 10 of resolution 1521(2003) for a further period of twelve months from the date of adoption of the present resolution, and to review them after six months;

(*c*) To renew the measures on diamonds imposed by paragraph 6 of resolution 1521(2003) for a further period of six months from the date of adoption of the present resolution, but to review them after three months in the light of the visit by representatives of the Kimberley Process and the preliminary report of the

Panel of Experts on Liberia, requested in paragraph 8 (*f*) below, with a view to lifting the measures as soon as possible, when the Council concludes that the National Transitional Government has established an effective certificate-of-origin regime for trade in rough diamonds that is transparent and internationally verifiable;

2. *Reiterates* the Council's readiness to terminate these measures once the conditions referred to in paragraph 1 above have been met;

3. *Encourages* the National Transitional Government of Liberia to intensify its efforts to meet these conditions, in particular by implementing the Liberia Forest Initiative and the necessary reforms in the Forestry Development Authority, and urges all members of the National Transitional Government to commit themselves to this end for the benefit of the Liberian people;

4. *Notes* that the measures imposed by paragraph 1 of resolution 1532(2004) remain in force to prevent former President Charles Taylor, his immediate family members, senior officials of the former Taylor regime, or other close allies or associates from using misappropriated funds and property to interfere in the restoration of peace and stability in Liberia and the subregion, and reconfirms its intention to review these measures at least once a year;

5. *Reiterates its call upon* the international donor community to continue to provide assistance to the peace process, including for reintegration and reconstruction, to contribute generously to consolidated humanitarian appeals, to disburse as soon as possible the pledges made at the International Reconstruction Conference on Liberia, held in New York on 5 and 6 February 2004, and to respond to the immediate financial, administrative and technical needs of the National Transitional Government of Liberia, in particular to assist the Government to meet the conditions referred to in paragraph 1 above, so that the measures can be lifted as soon as possible;

6. *Restates its demand* that all States refrain from any action that might contribute to further destabilization of the situation in the subregion, and further demands that all West African States take action to prevent armed individuals and groups from using their territory to prepare and commit attacks on neighbouring countries;

7. *Reminds* all States of their obligation to implement all the measures under resolutions 1521(2003) and 1532(2004), and particularly urges the National Transitional Government of Liberia to implement without delay its obligations under paragraph 1 of resolution 1532(2004) to freeze the assets of all persons designated by the Security Council Committee established pursuant to paragraph 21 of resolution 1521 (2003) (hereinafter "the Committee");

8. *Decides* to re-establish the Panel of Experts appointed pursuant to resolution 1549(2004) for a further period until 21 June 2005 to undertake the following tasks:

(*a*) To conduct a follow-up assessment mission to Liberia and neighbouring States in order to investigate and compile a report on the implementation, and any violations, of the measures referred to in paragraph 1 above, including any information relevant to the designation by the Committee of the individuals described

in paragraph 4 (*a*) of resolution 1521(2003) and paragraph 1 of resolution 1532(2004), and including the various sources of financing, such as from natural resources, for the illicit trade of arms;

(*b*) To assess the impact and effectiveness of the measures imposed by paragraph 1 of resolution 1532 (2004);

(*c*) To assess the progress made towards meeting the conditions referred to in paragraph 1 above;

(*d*) To assess the humanitarian and socio-economic impact of the measures imposed by paragraphs 2, 4, 6 and 10 of resolution 1521(2003);

(*e*) To report to the Council, through the Committee, by 7 June 2005 on all the issues listed in the present paragraph;

(*f*) To provide a preliminary report to the Council, through the Committee, by 21 March 2005 on progress made towards meeting the conditions for lifting the measures on diamonds imposed by paragraph 6 of resolution 1521(2003);

9. *Requests* the Secretary-General, acting in consultation with the Committee, to appoint as soon as possible no more than five experts, with the appropriate range of expertise, in particular on arms, timber, diamonds, finance, humanitarian and socio-economic and any other relevant issues, drawing as much as possible on the expertise of the members of the Panel of Experts established pursuant to resolution 1549(2004), and further requests the Secretary-General to make the necessary financial and security arrangements to support the work of the Panel;

10. *Calls upon* the United Nations Mission in Liberia, the United Nations Mission in Sierra Leone and the United Nations Mission in Côte d'Ivoire to continue assisting the Committee and the Panel of Experts in accordance with paragraph 23 of resolution 1521(2003);

11. *Calls upon* all States and the National Transitional Government of Liberia to cooperate fully with the Panel of Experts;

12. *Requests* the Secretary-General to submit a report to the Council by 7 June 2005, drawing on information from all relevant sources, including the National Transitional Government of Liberia, the United Nations Mission in Liberia and the Economic Community of West African States, on progress made towards meeting the conditions mentioned in paragraph 1 above;

13. *Decides* to remain seized of the matter.

Security Council Committee. On 31 December 2004 [S/2004/1025], the Security Council Committee established pursuant to resolution 1521 (2003) concerning Liberia submitted a report on its activities since its establishment on 22 December 2003.

Since the adoption of that resolution, the Committee received and approved one request to permit UNMIL to import into Liberia weapons and ammunition to be used in the training of Liberian police. The Committee considered 10 requests for travel-ban waivers, of which 7 were granted. It held quarterly reviews of the travel-ban list established on 16 March 2004, retaining the names of 19 persons and adding five more to that list. The Committee conducted its first formal review of the assets-freeze list on 17 and 20 December, placing three persons on the list during the reporting period.

The Committee adopted procedures for updating and maintaining its travel-ban list, handling requests for exemptions and conducting reviews of its travel-ban and assets-freeze lists. Fifteen States responded to the Committee's request for information regarding their actions to enforce the sanctions.

No major violations of the arms embargo were reported, and the diamond and timber sanctions were being largely implemented. No responses had been received to its request to 13 States for information on alleged violations.

Sierra Leone

In 2004, Sierra Leone, building on the progress achieved in 2003 in implementing the provisions of the 2000 Agreement on the Ceasefire and Cessation of Hostilities (Abuja Agreement) [YUN 2000, p. 210], made significant strides in the peace consolidation process in the country, with the completion of the disarmament, demobilization and reintegration process, the holding of local elections, the successful ending of the work of the Truth and Reconciliation Commission, the gradual handover of responsibility for security to the Government and the progressive consolidation of State authority.

The United Nations Mission in Sierra Leone (UNAMSIL) continued in 2004 to assist the Government in re-establishing a functioning State and in meeting the benchmarks for the Mission's drawdown and eventual withdrawal by the end of 2004. The Security Council, while noting the progress made by Sierra Leone, extended the Mission's mandate until 30 September. However, recognizing that some major gaps still existed, in particular with regard to the capacity of the Sierra Leone police and armed forces to maintain security and stability, the Council acted on the Secretary-General's recommendation that the timetable for the drawdown be extended to ensure a more gradual reduction in military strength, thus allowing for a smooth transition to a follow-on mission and eventual assumption by the Government of primary responsibility for national security. The Council decided that a residual UNAMSIL presence would remain in Sierra Leone, for an initial period of six months from 1 January 2005, to be reduced from 5,000 troops at the end of 2004 to 3,250 troops by 28 February 2005.

Throughout 2004, Sierra Leone, with international assistance, worked to increase the size of its police force and to enhance its capabilities so that officers could be deployed to all provinces, including the diamond-mining and border areas. At the same time, the Government took steps to strengthen the operational capacity of its armed forces, to enable it to assume responsibility for external security and to backstop the police in maintaining public order, which allowed it to extend State authority to all 12 administrative districts of the country. However, the judicial system was unable to function effectively due to lack of trained magistrates and other personnel, logistics and infrastructure.

As the security situation remained stable, UNAMSIL was able to hand over to the Government the primary responsibility for security in the north and south of the country first and later in the eastern and western areas, but continued to cooperate with Sierra Leone forces in patrolling and monitoring border areas. The disarmament, demobilization and reintegration programme closed on 31 March after four years, with a total of 54,000 ex-combatants having received benefits.

Other significant achievements recorded by Sierra Leone included the successful holding of local elections on 22 May for the first time in 32 years, the completion by the Special Court for Sierra Leone of two full years of operation in trying those accused of serious human rights abuses and crimes against humanity during the decade-long civil war, the completion in July of the repatriation by UNHCR of Sierra Leonean refugees, mainly from Guinea and Liberia, and the release, in October, of the final report of the Truth and Reconciliation Commission, which provided an analysis of the causes, nature and circumstances that fuelled the war.

Having received reports of gradual and steady progress in the Government's achievement of the benchmarks, the Council, in September, extended UNAMSIL's mandate for nine months. It also defined the military, civilian police and civilian tasks of UNAMSIL's residual presence, which would remain in Sierra Leone for an initial period of six months from 1 January 2005. The Council agreed to review the presence of the residual force in 2005.

UNAMSIL activities

Report of Secretary-General (March). On 19 March [S/2004/228], the Secretary-General issued his twenty-first report on UNAMSIL, in which he outlined his proposals for a residual UN peacekeeping presence in Sierra Leone after the termination of UNAMSIL's mandate, based on the findings of a UN interdepartmental assessment mission, which visited Sierra Leone (9-19 February) to evaluate progress and collect information.

The mission reported that the drawdown of UNAMSIL, which was scheduled to take place in December, was proceeding according to the plan outlined in resolution 1492(2003) [YUN 2003, p. 217]. While significant progress had been made in meeting the benchmarks [YUN 2002, p. 155] required for that process to continue, some major gaps remained, particularly with regard to the security sector, in consolidating State administration throughout the country and restoring government control over diamond-mining activities. The Sierra Leone police force, with assistance in training and recruiting provided by an international police team, made progress in building its capacity to assume full responsibility for internal security. As of February, some 980 recruits were trained, bringing its strength to 7,115 officers, with the eventual aim of reaching its pre-war level of 9,500 officers. The newly trained police were being deployed to the provinces, especially in areas vacated by UNAMSIL and to the diamond-mining and border areas in the east. The Government re-established a police presence in all provincial and district headquarters and major towns, and intended to deploy police in each chiefdom. UNAMSIL also provided advice on cross-border policing, airport security, criminal intelligence, policy and planning, and juvenile justice. Despite those gains, the national police force was not yet capable of handling widespread public disturbances, particularly in Freetown and the diamond-mining areas. In addition, the force lacked the necessary accommodation and police stations.

With regard to the armed forces, the Government, with international assistance, launched a programme for building their operational capacity to assume responsibility for external security and to backstop the police in maintaining public order. Those measures included the deployment of three brigades to the provinces and border areas; the restructuring of the armed forces to reduce troop strength from 14,000 to 10,500; and forging a cooperative relationship between the armed forces, the National Security Council and the National Security Council Coordinating Group.

UNAMSIL continued to conduct joint patrols and exercises with the Sierra Leone forces and police, but leaders stated that the armed forces were not fully prepared or equipped to take over security responsibilities from UNAMSIL by the end of the year, an assessment shared by all stakeholders and the UN assessment team.

The Government closed the initial programme for the reintegration of ex-combatants on 31 December 2003, with a total of 51,000 individuals having received medium-term reintegration assistance. The majority of the 6,845 child combatants who were demobilized were reunited with their families.

State authority was consolidated, with government officials deployed in all 12 administrative districts of the country and the return of paramount chiefs to their chiefdoms. Magistrate courts were rehabilitated in all districts, but the recruitment of judges and magistrates was hampered by the poor conditions of service. Only five magistrates were assigned to service the 12 districts. As a temporary measure, justices of the peace, trained with UNDP support, were deployed to 18 locations to perform judicial functions under the supervision of the magistrates. Progress was also made in re-establishing government administrative, security and judicial structures throughout the country, but their capacity to function remained severely limited by the lack of logistics, infrastructure and qualified personnel.

The Government reasserted its control over diamond mining through vigorous law-enforcement measures, including the deployment of mine monitors and wardens in mining areas, and incentives to encourage legal mining. UNAMSIL cooperated with the Government in conducting aerial surveys and ground patrols of mining areas. Among challenges faced by the industry were the fact that more than 50 per cent of diamond-mining activities in the country remained unlicensed and disputes continued among chiefdoms over diamond-mining rights and boundaries.

The assessment mission made suggestions for remedial action that the Government and its partners could take to accelerate progress on the benchmarks, minimize threats to stability and enable national institutions to take primary responsibility for security and national recovery. The Government needed to sensitize the general populace and explain the measures it was taking to address the economic and social challenges, and encourage potential investors, in particular in the agriculture and mining sectors, to create employment opportunities for youth. Preparations for the elections needed to be transparent and the necessary security arrangements put in place. In that respect, UNAMSIL conducted a threat assessment and a security plan was drawn up, in coordination with the Sierra Leone police.

At the subregional level, the MRU countries (Guinea, Liberia and Sierra Leone) should resume dialogue aimed at building subregional security structures and revitalizing the MRU secretariat. The three UN peacekeeping missions in the area (UNAMSIL, UNMIL and MINUCI) should continued cooperating on cross-border issues and in joint planning and sharing of information.

Under consideration were the possibility of "hot pursuit" operations, joint air patrolling, shared border responsibility, the establishment of a subregional reserve force and joint planning for the repatriation of foreign combatants.

In view of its assessment that key security benchmarks would most likely not be met by December, the mission reported that all national and international stakeholders had emphasized the need to maintain a post-UNAMSIL peacekeeping presence to, among other tasks, assist the country in assuming its full responsibilities in the security sector.

The Secretary-General recommended that the UNAMSIL drawdown plan be adjusted to avoid a steep drop in the Mission's military strength in the remaining phases of the withdrawal process, reducing the military strength gradually from the current level of 11,500 to 5,000 between June and 31 December 2004. A new follow-on mission would be established, whose primary purpose would be to provide back-up security and accompany the transition to national primacy until the Government's security sector was adequately developed. The post-UNAMSIL peacekeeping mission would focus on three geographical areas: the west, including Freetown; the centre of the country, which was the stronghold of the former Civil Defence Force (CDF); and the east, specifically the border and diamond-mining areas. In the centre, the new mission would act as a deterrent against possible destabilization of the work of the Special Court for Sierra Leone or the Government, backstop the police in maintaining security, provide security for UN personnel and reinforce the western and eastern areas. In the east, it would compensate for the lack of capacity by the Sierra Leone police and army to fully monitor the border and maintain security in other parts of the country. The mission would consist of three battalions, with 3,250 troops, 141 military observers and 80 civilian police personnel. Certain tasks currently performed by UNAMSIL would be assumed by other UN agencies by the end of 2004, while some of its offices, such as the electoral unit, would be phased out. The new mission would have a public information unit and a political policy and planning unit. It would be headed by the Special Representative of the Secretary-General and supported by a Deputy Special Representative, who would also serve as the UN Resident Coordinator and Humanitarian Coordinator. Wherever UN military observers, civil affairs, political and human rights officers and civilian police personnel were co-deployed, they would function as integrated units, in close collaboration with the UN country team and its transitional support teams. The proposed mission would remain in Sierra Leone until the end of 2005, with a midyear review.

The Secretary-General invited the Security Council to authorize the establishment of a residual UN peacekeeping operation in Sierra Leone, as well as an appropriate adjustment in the current drawdown plan of UNAMSIL, which would include the retention of 1,500 troops from relevant UNAMSIL support units, for two months, to facilitate a seamless transition to the follow-on mission.

SECURITY COUNCIL ACTION (March)

On 30 March [meeting 4938], the Security Council unanimously adopted **resolution 1537(2004)**. The draft [S/2004/256] was prepared in consultations among Council members.

The Security Council,

Recalling its resolutions and the statements by its President concerning the situation in Sierra Leone,

Affirming the commitment of all States to respect the sovereignty, political independence and territorial integrity of Sierra Leone,

Commending the efforts of the Economic Community of West African States towards building peace in the subregion, and encouraging the Presidents of the member States of the Mano River Union to resume dialogue and to renew their commitment to building regional peace and security,

Expressing its appreciation to those Member States providing troops, civilian police personnel and support elements to the United Nations Mission in Sierra Leone,

Having considered the report of the Secretary-General of 19 March 2004,

Welcoming the significant progress made towards the benchmarks for the drawdown of the Mission, in accordance with Security Council resolutions 1436(2002) of 24 September 2002 and 1492(2003) of 18 July 2003, and commending the Mission for the progress made to date in the adjustments to its size, composition and deployment,

Noting, however, that progress towards the benchmarks remains fragile and some major gaps still remain, in particular with regard to the capacity of the Sierra Leone police and armed forces to maintain security and stability effectively,

Reiterating the importance of the effective consolidation of stability and State authority throughout Sierra Leone, particularly in the sensitive diamond-producing areas and in the border areas, and stressing continued United Nations support to the Government of Sierra Leone in fulfilling these objectives,

Emphasizing the importance of free, fair and transparent local elections in May 2004, and encouraging the Government of Sierra Leone to make the necessary preparations, assisted by the Mission, within its mandate,

Encouraging the Truth and Reconciliation Commission to produce its report as soon as possible, and welcoming the intention of the Government of Sierra Leone to establish a Human Rights Commission thereafter,

Noting the Secretary-General's analysis of the need for a significantly reduced United Nations peace-keeping presence to remain in Sierra Leone into 2005,

Emphasizing the importance of the Government of Sierra Leone assuming full responsibility for national security as soon as possible,

1. *Decides* that the mandate of the United Nations Mission in Sierra Leone shall be extended for a period of six months until 30 September 2004;

2. *Welcomes* the intention of the Secretary-General to adjust the timetable for the drawdown of the Mission during 2004, in order to ensure a more gradual reduction in its military strength, as outlined in paragraph 72 of his report;

3. *Urges* the Government of Sierra Leone to intensify its efforts to develop an effective and sustainable police force, army, penal system and independent judiciary, so that the Government can rapidly take over from the Mission full responsibility for maintaining law and order throughout Sierra Leone, and encourages donors and the Mission, in accordance with its mandate, to continue to assist the Government in this regard;

4. *Also urges* the Government of Sierra Leone to continue to strengthen its control over and regulation of diamond mining, including through the High-level Steering Committee;

5. *Decides* that a residual Mission presence will remain in Sierra Leone, for an initial period of six months from 1 January 2005, reduced from the December 2004 level of 5,000 troops to a new ceiling of 3,250 troops, 141 military observers and 80 United Nations civilian police personnel by 28 February 2005, and requests the Secretary-General to proceed with planning on the basis of the recommendations contained in his report, in order to ensure a seamless transition from the current configuration of the Mission to the residual presence;

6. *Affirms its intention* to confirm the precise tasks of the residual Mission presence, and the benchmarks for its duration, no later than 30 September 2004;

7. *Requests* the Secretary-General to provide by 15 September 2004 a progress report, including progress made in the work of the Special Court for Sierra Leone, progress in resolving the conflict in Liberia, further increases in the capability of the Sierra Leone police and armed forces and strengthened cooperation among United Nations missions in the subregion, with recommendations for any modifications that such progress might allow to the size, composition, duration and benchmarks of the residual Mission presence;

8. *Welcomes* the intention of the Secretary-General to keep the security, political, humanitarian and human rights situation in Sierra Leone under close review and to report to the Council, after due consultations with troop-contributing countries and the Government of Sierra Leone, including by quarterly assessments of progress against the benchmarks for the drawdown of the Mission, including the capacity of the Sierra Leone security sector;

9. *Expresses its appreciation* for the essential work being carried out by the Special Court for Sierra Leone, notes with serious concern the precarious financial situation of the Court for its third year of operation, urges all countries to submit their outstanding pledged funds immediately, supports the request by the Secretary-General to the General Assembly to consider a contribution to the financing of the Court from the regular budget, as contained in the report of the Secretary-General to the General Assembly of 15 March 2004, and urges all States to cooperate fully with the Court;

10. *Commends* the efforts of the Secretary-General to establish cooperation between the United Nations missions in the subregion, and welcomes his intention, set out in paragraph 65 of his report, to submit recommendations to the Council by the end of 2004 on how such cooperation might be strengthened;

11. *Requests* the Mission to share its experience with the United Nations Mission in Liberia and the United Nations Operation in Côte d'Ivoire and to carry out its mandate in close liaison with them, especially in the prevention of movements of arms and combatants across borders and in the implementation of disarmament, demobilization and reintegration programmes;

12. *Decides* to remain actively seized of the matter.

Security Council mission. The Security Council mission to West Africa (see p. 169), which visited Sierra Leone on 25 June, reported on 2 July [S/2004/525] that it was pleased to see that significant progress had been achieved in the peace consolidation process in the country. However, the gains remained fragile and considerable challenges still faced the Government, such as widespread unemployment; trials under way at the Special Court for Sierra Leone; control over the diamond-mining areas; and potential external threats from spillover from other conflicts in the region. Noting President Alhaji Ahmad Tejan Kabbah's hope that the maintenance of UNAMSIL's presence in the country from January 2005 would allow the Sierra Leone army and police force to strengthen their capacity and resources to assume responsibility for national security, the mission underlined the importance of that goal and encouraged donors to contribute to the restructuring and strengthening of the security sector. It also encouraged donors to contribute to the Court for Sierra Leone, given its importance for long-term reconciliation. The mission stressed the need to address the root causes of the conflict, including through a poverty reduction strategy, the continuing consolidation of State authority throughout the country and anti-corruption measures.

Report of Secretary-General (July). On 6 July [S/2004/536], the Secretary-General, in his twenty-second report on UNAMSIL, noted that the overall political and security situation in Sierra Leone remained stable, allowing the Mission to continue with its drawdown and withdrawal plan to handover to the Government the primary responsibility for security in the Northern and Southern Provinces and to support the national police in those areas. The handover of responsibility for security to the Government in the Eastern Province and the Western Area (Freetown and outlying parts) was scheduled to take place in August and September, respectively. UNAMSIL and the Government jointly evaluated the security situation at the National Security Council Coordinating Group's weekly meetings. The Mission worked with the provincial and district security committees and conducted joint exercises with the Sierra Leone police and Republic of Sierra Leone Armed Forces (RSLAF). The security environment in the border areas needed robust patrolling and monitoring, particularly along the border with Guinea, where some Guinean troops had crossed over to engage in farming and hunting inside Sierra Leone.

Local elections were held on 22 May, the first in 32 years, and were contested by 1,115 candidates, the majority of whom belonged to the two main parties, the Sierra Leone People's Party and the All People's Congress (APC), as well as 347 independent candidates. The Revolutionary United Front Party did not take part in the elections, reportedly owing to financial constraints. A total of 2,271,435 voters were registered. The elections resulted in 475 posts of councillor being filled in 394 wards nationwide. UNAMSIL provided logistical support for the elections, including land and air transport to most chiefdoms, communications support, technical assistance to the National Electoral Commission (NEC) and election policing, while UNDP funded civic education activities. With a view to preparing for national elections in 2007, NEC requested further technical assistance from the United Nations; an electoral needs assessment mission was dispatched to Sierra Leone in June.

In terms of meeting the benchmarks for the drawdown of UNAMSIL, the Sierra Leone police made progress towards assuming responsibility for the maintenance of law and order. The pace of training and recruitment had accelerated, bringing the total force to 7,903. UNAMSIL continued to assist in raising the professional standards of the police by conducting in-service courses. With other UN agencies, it was also running human rights workshops. RSLAF made progress in restructuring, and the envisaged downsizing from 14,000 to 10,500 by 2007 was on track. UNAMSIL provided training in military policing, vehicle maintenance, information technology and communications.

The disarmament, demobilization and reintegration programme was officially closed on 31 March, with a total of 54,000 ex-combatants having received reintegration benefits over the previous four years. As agreed by Sierra Leone and Liberia, the estimated 500 to 2,000 Sierra Leonean ex-combatants in Liberia would undergo disarmament and demobilization in Liberia, and would have the option of staying or returning to Sierra Leone. A similar choice would be given to the 500 to 800 Sierra Leonean ex-combatants in Côte d'Ivoire.

The Special Court for Sierra Leone commenced joint trials of indictees on 3 June, with the trial of members of the former CDF, including the former Minister of the Interior, Sam Hinga Norman. The trial of members of the former RUF was scheduled to begin in July, while that of the former Armed Forces Revolutionary Council members depended on the appointment of a second trial chamber and the readiness of the defence team. In planning its exit strategy, the Court was negotiating bilateral agreements with several countries for the enforcement of sentences and the relocation of witnesses. Some Governments had already responded positively.

Overall, the Secretary-General found that the Government had made significant progress in consolidating peace and in promoting national reconciliation and economic recovery. He urged the newly elected local councils to become instruments for improving the life of communities. He expressed regret at incidents between the armed forces and the Sierra Leone police as the Government took over responsibility for security from UNAMSIL throughout the country. It was essential for the Government to implement expeditiously its plan for addressing major security sector gaps.

Security Council consideration. At consultations held on 15 July [S/2004/623] on the Secretary-General's report (above), Security Council members took note of the significant progress in consolidating peace in Sierra Leone, facilitated by the implementation of the UNAMSIL drawdown plan. However, they noted the fragility of the gains made so far and underlined the need for accelerated progress on the key benchmarks.

Report of Secretary-General (September). The Secretary-General, on 9 September [S/2004/724], issued his twenty-third report on UNAMSIL. He stated that the improved security situation enabled the Mission to hand over primary responsibility for security in the Eastern Province to the Government on 4 August. The relationship between RSLAF and the Sierra Leone police improved and measures were taken to improve collaboration between them. The security situation in the border areas remained volatile, with reports of arms smuggling into Liberia from Sierra Leone. The security environment along the border with Guinea was also of concern in the light of reports that some Guinean armed forces were harassing Sierra Leonean civilians. In that regard, the 5 August meeting in Conakry between the two Governments on resolving the boundary dispute in the area of Yenga was a welcome development. In a meeting on the Yenga issue between President Kabbah and Guinean President Lansana Conté in Conakry on 2 September, the two leaders agreed that the village of Yenga belonged to Sierra Leone, in accordance with the 1912 treaty signed between France and the United Kingdom. On 6 September, the two countries agreed to establish joint investigation and technical committees to prepare reports on the Yenga issue.

In reviewing the transition to a residual UN presence in Sierra Leone and the required benchmarks, the Secretary-General stated that, despite the efforts of the Government and a military training team from the United Kingdom, several factors hampered the operational effectiveness of both the Sierra Leone police and RSLAF. Unless the issues of logistics, communications, accommodation and transport shortfalls were addressed, the security sector would not be able to assume full security responsibilities in the future. RSLAF's capacity to assume effective responsibility for security against external threats would remain a key benchmark in reviewing the tasks of the residual UNAMSIL presence after 2004. Before UNAMSIL completed its drawdown by the end of 2005, RSLAF should have a fully operational company, with a full complement of vehicles, radios and accommodation, the ability to deploy within 48 hours into border areas to prevent armed incursions, and a fully operational infantry battalion to deploy anywhere in the country in support of the national police within 24 hours. The army would also need to establish a reliable military communications system. By the end of 2005, the police force should have completed all planned deployments to the provinces, attained the planned level of 9,500 personnel and ensured that its units were adequately equipped before UNAMSIL's withdrawal. Another benchmark for drawdown was the full deployment of the United Nations Mission in Liberia, especially in areas close to Liberia's border with Sierra Leone. The Secretary-General suggested that the benchmarks be reviewed by mid-2005, with a view to determining further adjustments in UNAMSIL components.

On 29 June, a UNAMSIL civil contractor helicopter carrying 24 UN and non-UN personnel crashed, and all aboard were killed. The cause of the crash was under investigation at the time of the report.

The human rights situation had gradually improved as a result of UNAMSIL's training and sensitization efforts, in partnership with the Government and local human rights organizations. On 30 July, the Sierra Leone Parliament passed an act establishing the National Human Rights Commission. A Law Reform Commission was also established to review existing laws and to make recommendations for the repeal, amendment or enactment of new laws. The entire justice system needed urgent reform to address the problems of inadequate personnel, lack of access to current legislation and jurisprudence in codified form, respect for human rights in the administration of justice and the lack of resources. On 21 July, 64 former RUF members and 33 of the so-called West Side Boys, detained in Pademba prison for over three years, rioted to protest another postponement of their court appearances. The police brought the situation under control, and a month later, the Government released 16 of them on the advice of the international community.

The Truth and Reconciliation Commission completed its operational mandate, having collected over 8,000 statements on the issues, events and violations of human rights that occurred during the decade-long civil war. The Special Court for Sierra Leone, which had completed two years of operation, began the trial of three members of the former CDF on 3 July and continued with the trial of three former RUF members.

The repatriation by UNHCR of Sierra Leonean refugees, mainly from Guinea and Liberia, was completed on 21 July. Since the repatriation began in 2001, UNHCR had repatriated 179,000 refugees, with 25,913 Sierra Leoneans repatriated in 2004. Another 92,000 refugees returned unassisted and an estimated 15,000 opted to stay in other countries. Sierra Leone continued to host some 66,000 Liberian refugees.

The Secretary-General concluded that the overall gradual progress and stable political environment in Sierra Leone continued to facilitate the consolidation of peace. The Government had made significant progress towards accomplishing a number of benchmarks for the withdrawal of UNAMSIL. That situation had permitted a slow increase in economic and commercial activity throughout the country. Further progress would depend on continued support from international donors. In order to continue with the gradual drawdown of UNAMSIL and to ensure a smooth transition from the current configuration of the Mission to its residual presence in Sierra Leone, he recommended that its mandate be extended for nine months, until 30 June 2005.

SECURITY COUNCIL ACTION (September)

On 17 September [meeting 5037], the Security Council unanimously adopted **resolution 1562 (2004)**. The draft [S/2004/741] was prepared in consultations among Council members.

The Security Council,

Recalling its previous resolutions and the statements by its President concerning the situation in Sierra Leone,

Affirming the commitment of all States to respect the sovereignty, political independence and territorial integrity of Sierra Leone,

Commending the efforts of the Economic Community of West African States towards building peace in the subregion, and encouraging the Mano River Union member States to continue their dialogue aimed at building regional peace and security,

Encouraging the United Nations missions in the region to continue their efforts towards developing inter-mission cooperation, especially in the prevention of movements of arms and combatants across borders and in the implementation of disarmament, demobilization and reintegration programmes,

Having considered the report of the Secretary-General of 9 September 2004,

Welcoming the further progress made towards the benchmarks for drawdown of the United Nations Mission in Sierra Leone, and commending the Mission for the progress made to date in the adjustments to its size, composition and deployment,

Underlining the importance of additional efforts to strengthen the capacity of the Sierra Leone police and armed forces to maintain security and stability effectively,

Underlining also the importance of increasingly close collaboration between the Mission and the United Nations country team in Sierra Leone, to ensure a smooth transition after the final departure of the Mission,

Expressing its appreciation for the essential work of the Special Court for Sierra Leone, noting its vital contribution to the establishment of the rule of law in Sierra Leone, and encouraging all States to cooperate fully with the Court,

Determining that the situation in Sierra Leone continues to constitute a threat to international peace and security in the region,

Acting under Chapter VII of the Charter of the United Nations,

1. *Decides* that the mandate of the United Nations Mission in Sierra Leone shall be extended until 30 June 2005;

2. *Decides also* that the tasks of the residual Mission presence, which shall remain in Sierra Leone for an initial period of six months from 1 January 2005, as set out in paragraph 5 of resolution 1537(2004) of 30 March 2004, shall be the following:

Military and civilian police tasks

— To monitor, in conjunction with district and provincial security committees, the overall security situation, to support the Sierra Leone armed forces and police in patrolling the border and diamond-mining areas, including through joint planning and joint operations where appropriate, and to monitor the growing capacity of the Sierra Leone security sector;

— To support the Sierra Leone police in maintaining internal security, including security for the Special Court for Sierra Leone while the Mission remains deployed in Sierra Leone;

— To assist the Sierra Leone police with its programme of recruitment, training and mentoring designed to strengthen further the capacity and resources of the police;

— To protect United Nations personnel, installations and equipment and ensure the security and freedom of movement of United Nations personnel, within its capabilities and its areas of deployment;

Civilian tasks

— To monitor the repatriation, reception, resettlement and reintegration of Sierra Leonean ex-combatants from abroad;

— To monitor, investigate, report and promote the observance of human rights;

— To disseminate information on the mandate and purpose of the mission and publicize the Government's primary responsibility for national security, including through United Nations radio;

— To monitor progress towards consolidation of State authority throughout the country;

3. *Authorizes* the residual Mission presence to use all necessary means to carry out its mandate, within its capabilities and its areas of deployment;

4. *Expresses its intention* to review regularly the residual Mission presence against the following benchmarks:

— Strengthening the capacity of the Sierra Leone armed forces and police to maintain security and stability effectively throughout the country;

— Consolidating State authority throughout the country;

— Consolidating the deployment of the United Nations Mission in Liberia throughout Liberia;

5. *Welcomes* the Secretary-General's assurance, as set out in paragraph 91 of his report of 19 March 2004, that where military observers, civil affairs officers, political affairs officers, human rights officers and civilian police personnel are co-deployed, they will function as integrated units and work in close collaboration with the United Nations country team;

6. *Urges* the Government of Sierra Leone to intensify its efforts to develop an effective and sustainable police force, armed forces, penal system and independent judiciary, so that the Government can take over from the United Nations Mission in Sierra Leone as soon as possible full responsibility for maintaining law and order throughout Sierra Leone, including in the sensitive diamond-producing areas, and encourages donors and the Mission, in accordance with its mandate, to continue to assist the Government in this regard, as well as to assist the Government in restoring public services throughout the country;

7. *Welcomes* the Secretary-General's intention to keep the security, political, humanitarian and human rights situation in Sierra Leone under close review and to report regularly to the Council, after due consultations with troop-contributing countries and the Government of Sierra Leone;

8. *Decides* to remain actively seized of the matter.

Report of Secretary-General (December). In his twenty-fourth report on UNAMSIL issued on 10 December [S/2004/965], the Secretary-General said that, on 23 September, UNAMSIL transferred to the Government primary responsibility for security in the western area, thereby completing the overall transfer. Consequently, the Mission's role was readjusted to that of providing support to the national security services. The relationship between the Sierra Leone armed forces and police continued to improve, as the leadership of the two agencies committed themselves, in a 9 August joint communiqué, to enhancing cooperation. However, the issue of the border village of Yenga remained a cause for concern. Despite the 2 September agreement (see p. 216) affirming Sierra Leone's sovereignty over the village, Guinean armed forces maintained a small presence in the area, and there were reports of Sierra Leonean civilians being harassed by them. The issue continued to generate tensions and had the potential of negatively affecting relations between the two countries.

The drawdown of UNAMSIL remained on track. A national security exercise was held in November to test planning procedures following UNAMSIL's disengagement, including the operational preparedness of the Sierra Leone police and armed forces joint force command. Meanwhile, to ensure a seamless transition from peacekeeping to peace-building in Sierra Leone, UNAMSIL and the UN country team jointly developed a transition plan, identifying priority tasks to be implemented in 2005, with a focus on national capacity-building, strengthening national ownership and ensuring the Government's lead in the formulation and implementation of policies and programmes in key areas, and ensuring that it addressed the root causes of the conflict.

The final report of the Truth and Reconciliation Commission was presented to President Kabbah on 5 October and subsequently released to the public [ECOSOC/6140-GA/10287-SC/8227]. The report covered the 10-year conflict, its causes, nature, human rights violations, the role of external actors and circumstances that fuelled the war, such as mineral resources. On 15 October, the Special Court signed its first agreement on the enforcement of sentences, which would allow some of those convicted to serve their sentences outside Sierra Leone. It also concluded a limited number of witness relocation agreements and finalized its work completion strategy. In the justice sector, appointment by the Government of a number of High Court judges would help to expedite adjudication of the large backlog of cases pending before the courts.

The Secretary-General observed that, as Sierra Leone moved from recovery and reconstruction to the development phase, concerted and highly focused actions by the Government and its international partners should address poverty alleviation to ensure that the improvements in the macroeconomic situation had a positive impact on the living standards of the population. The poverty reduction strategy paper, which was being finalized, would provide the framework for such action, while post-conflict aid would need to be followed by adequate longer-term donor assistance and development.

UNAMSIL financing

The Secretary-General submitted to the General Assembly at its resumed fifty-eighth (2004) session the performance report on the UNAMSIL budget for 1 July 2002 to 30 June 2003 [A/58/660], which showed that, of a total appropriation of $669,476,400, actual expenditure amounted to $603,085,500, a variance of 9.9 per cent. He also submitted the proposed budget for the maintenance of the Mission for the period from 1 July 2004 to 30 June 2005 [A/58/661], totalling $199,799,800 gross.

ACABQ, having reviewed the reports, recommended on 8 April [A/58/759/Add.3] that the approved appropriation for 2002/03 be reduced to $633,447,400 and that the total apportionment granted by the Assembly for the maintenance of the Mission during the same period be increased from $622,469,200 to $633,447,400. The Assembly should decide on the treatment of other income and adjustments for 2002/03 in the amount of $27,223,300. ACABQ made suggestions for reducing costs and recommended that the estimated budget for the 2004/05 period be reduced from $199,799,800 to $196,982,200.

GENERAL ASSEMBLY ACTION (June)

On 18 June [meeting 91], the General Assembly, on the recommendation of the Fifth Committee [A/58/829], adopted **resolution 58/308** without vote [agenda item 146].

Financing of the United Nations Mission in Sierra Leone

The General Assembly,

Having considered the reports of the Secretary-General on the financing of the United Nations Mission in Sierra Leone and the related reports of the Advisory Committee on Administrative and Budgetary Questions,

Bearing in mind Security Council resolution 1270 (1999) of 22 October 1999, by which the Council established the United Nations Mission in Sierra Leone, and the subsequent resolutions by which the Council revised and extended the mandate of the Mission, the latest of which was resolution 1537(2004) of 30 March 2004,

Recalling its resolution 53/29 of 20 November 1998 on the financing of the United Nations Observer Mission in Sierra Leone and subsequent resolutions on the financing of the United Nations Mission in Sierra Leone, the latest of which was resolution 57/291 B of 18 June 2003,

Reaffirming the general principles underlying the financing of United Nations peacekeeping operations, as stated in General Assembly resolutions 1874(S-IV) of 27 June 1963, 3101(XXVIII) of 11 December 1973 and 55/235 of 23 December 2000,

Noting with appreciation that voluntary contributions have been made to the Mission,

Mindful of the fact that it is essential to provide the Mission with the necessary financial resources to enable it to fulfil its responsibilities under the relevant resolutions of the Security Council,

1. *Takes note* of the status of contributions to the United Nations Observer Mission in Sierra Leone and the United Nations Mission in Sierra Leone as at 15 April 2004, including the contributions outstanding in the amount of 85.5 million United States dollars, representing some 6.5 per cent of the total assessed contributions, notes with concern that only thirty Member States have paid their assessed contributions in full, and urges all other Member States, in particular those in arrears, to ensure payment of their outstanding assessed contributions;

2. *Expresses its appreciation* to those Member States which have paid their assessed contributions in full, and urges all other Member States to make every possible effort to ensure payment of their assessed contributions to the Mission in full;

3. *Expresses concern* at the financial situation with regard to peacekeeping activities, in particular as regards the reimbursements to troop contributors that bear additional burdens owing to overdue payments by Member States of their assessments;

4. *Also expresses concern* at the delay experienced by the Secretary-General in deploying and providing adequate resources to some recent peacekeeping missions, in particular those in Africa;

5. *Emphasizes* that all future and existing peacekeeping missions shall be given equal and non-discriminatory treatment in respect of financial and administrative arrangements;

6. *Also emphasizes* that all peacekeeping missions shall be provided with adequate resources for the effective and efficient discharge of their respective mandates;

7. *Reiterates its request* to the Secretary-General to make the fullest possible use of facilities and equipment at the United Nations Logistics Base at Brindisi, Italy, in order to minimize the costs of procurement for the Mission;

8. *Endorses* the conclusions and recommendations contained in the report of the Advisory Committee on Administrative and Budgetary Questions, and requests the Secretary-General to ensure their full implementation, bearing in mind that the budget may be revised in light of Security Council resolution 1537(2004);

9. *Requests* the Secretary-General to take all necessary action to ensure that the Mission is administered with a maximum of efficiency and economy;

10. *Also requests* the Secretary-General, in order to reduce the cost of employing General Service staff, to continue efforts to recruit local staff for the Mission against General Service posts, commensurate with the requirements of the Mission;

Financial performance report for the period from 1 July 2002 to 30 June 2003

11. *Takes note* of the report of the Secretary-General on the financial performance of the Mission for the period from 1 July 2002 to 30 June 2003;

12. *Decides* to reduce the appropriation authorized for the Mission for the period from 1 July 2002 to 30 June 2003 under the terms of its resolution 56/251 B of 27 June 2002 from 699,838,300 dollars to 633,447,400 dollars;

13. *Decides also*, taking into account the amount of 622,469,200 dollars already apportioned for the period from 1 July 2002 to 30 June 2003 in accordance with the provisions of its resolution 56/251 B and its resolution 57/291 A of 20 December 2002, to apportion among Member States the additional amount of 10,978,200 dollars for the period from 1 July 2002 to 30 June 2003, in accordance with the levels set out in General Assembly resolution 55/235, as adjusted by the Assembly in its resolutions 55/236 of 23 December 2000 and 57/290 A of 20 December 2002, taking into account the scale of assessments for 2002 and 2003, as set out in its resolutions 55/5 B of 23 December 2000 and 57/4 B of 20 December 2002;

14. *Decides further* that, in accordance with the provisions of its resolution 973(X) of 15 December 1955, there shall be set off against the apportionment among Member States, as provided for in paragraph 13 above, their respective share in the Tax Equalization Fund of the estimated increase in the staff assessment income of 230,000 dollars approved for the Mission for the period from 1 July 2002 to 30 June 2003;

15. *Decides* to approve the decrease in the estimated staff assessment income for the period from 1 July 2002 to 30 June 2003 from 10,678,500 dollars to 9,560,600 dollars;

Budget estimates for the period from 1 July 2004 to 30 June 2005

16. *Decides also* to appropriate to the Special Account for the United Nations Mission in Sierra Leone the amount of 207,246,100 dollars for the period from 1 July 2004 to 30 June 2005, inclusive of 196,982,200 dollars for the maintenance of the Mission, 8,391,200 dollars for the support account for peacekeeping operations and 1,872,700 dollars for the United Nations Logistics Base;

Financing of the appropriation

17. *Decides further* to apportion among Member States the amount of 207,246,100 dollars at a monthly rate of 17,270,508 dollars, in accordance with the levels set out in General Assembly resolution 55/235, as adjusted by the Assembly in its resolution 55/236 and updated in its resolution 58/256 of 23 December 2003, taking into account the scale of assessments for 2004 and 2005, as set out in its resolution 58/1 B of 23 December 2003, subject to a decision of the Security Council to extend the mandate of the Mission;

18. *Decides* that, in accordance with the provisions of its resolution 973(X), there shall be set off against the apportionment among Member States, as provided for in paragraph 17 above, their respective share in the Tax Equalization Fund of 5,610,700 dollars at a monthly rate of 467,558 dollars, comprising the estimated staff assessment income of 4,280,600 dollars approved for the Mission, the prorated share of 1,224,600 dollars of the estimated staff assessment income ap-

proved for the support account and the prorated share of 105,500 dollars of the estimated staff assessment income approved for the United Nations Logistics Base;

19. *Decides also* that, for Member States that have fulfilled their financial obligations to the Mission, there shall be set off against their apportionment, as provided for in paragraph 17 above, their respective share of the other income in the amount of 27,223,000 dollars in respect of the financial period ended 30 June 2003, in accordance with the levels set out in General Assembly resolution 55/235, as adjusted by the Assembly in its resolutions 55/236 and 57/290 A, taking into account the scale of assessments for 2003 as set out in its resolutions 55/5 B and 57/4 B;

20. *Decides further* that, for Member States that have not fulfilled their financial obligations to the Mission, there shall be set off against their outstanding obligations their respective share of the other income in the amount of 27,223,000 dollars in respect of the financial period ended 30 June 2003, in accordance with the scheme set out in paragraph 19 above;

21. *Emphasizes* that no peacekeeping mission shall be financed by borrowing funds from other active peacekeeping missions;

22. *Encourages* the Secretary-General to continue to take additional measures to ensure the safety and security of all personnel under the auspices of the United Nations participating in the Mission;

23. *Invites* voluntary contributions to the Mission in cash and in the form of services and supplies acceptable to the Secretary-General, to be administered, as appropriate, in accordance with the procedure and practices established by the General Assembly;

24. *Decides* to include in the provisional agenda of its fifty-ninth session the item entitled "Financing of the United Nations Mission in Sierra Leone".

The Secretary-General, in August [A/59/286], submitted revised estimates for the UNAMSIL budget for the period from 1 July 2004 to 30 June 2005, consequent upon the Security Council's decision in resolution 1537(2004) (see p. 214) to retain a residual UNAMSIL presence in Sierra Leone from 1 January 2005. The revised budget amounted to $291,603,600, an increase of $94,621,400.

ACABQ, in its October report [A/59/417] on the revised budget, recommended approval of the full amount proposed by the Secretary-General.

GENERAL ASSEMBLY ACTION (October)

On 29 October [meeting 46], the General Assembly, on the recommendation of the Fifth Committee [A/59/527], adopted **resolution 59/14** without vote [agenda item 136].

Financing of the United Nations Mission in Sierra Leone

The General Assembly,

Having considered the report of the Secretary-General on the financing of the United Nations Mission in Sierra Leone and the related report of the Advisory Committee on Administrative and Budgetary Questions,

Bearing in mind Security Council resolution 1270 (1999) of 22 October 1999, by which the Council established the United Nations Mission in Sierra Leone, and the subsequent resolutions by which the Council revised and extended the mandate of the Mission, the latest of which was resolution 1562(2004) of 17 September 2004,

Recalling its resolution 53/29 of 20 November 1998 on the financing of the United Nations Observer Mission in Sierra Leone and subsequent resolutions on the financing of the United Nations Mission in Sierra Leone, the latest of which was resolution 58/308 of 18 June 2004,

Reaffirming the general principles underlying the financing of United Nations peacekeeping operations, as stated in General Assembly resolutions 1874(S-IV) of 27 June 1963, 3101(XXVIII) of 11 December 1973 and 55/235 of 23 December 2000,

Noting with appreciation that voluntary contributions have been made to the Mission,

Mindful of the fact that it is essential to provide the Mission with the necessary financial resources to enable it to fulfil its responsibilities under the relevant resolutions of the Security Council,

1. *Takes note* of the status of contributions to the United Nations Observer Mission in Sierra Leone and the United Nations Mission in Sierra Leone as at 30 September 2004, including the contributions outstanding in the amount of 84.9 million United States dollars, representing some 3 per cent of the total assessed contributions, notes with concern that only thirty-four Member States have paid their assessed contributions in full, and urges all other Member States, in particular those in arrears, to ensure payment of their outstanding assessed contributions;

2. *Expresses its appreciation* to those Member States which have paid their assessed contributions in full, and urges all other Member States to make every possible effort to ensure payment of their assessed contributions to the Mission in full;

3. *Expresses concern* at the financial situation with regard to peacekeeping activities, in particular as regards the reimbursements to troop contributors that bear additional burdens owing to overdue payments by Member States of their assessments;

4. *Also expresses concern* at the delay experienced by the Secretary-General in deploying and providing adequate resources to some recent peacekeeping missions, in particular those in Africa;

5. *Emphasizes* that all future and existing peacekeeping missions shall be given equal and non-discriminatory treatment in respect of financial and administrative arrangements;

6. *Also emphasizes* that all peacekeeping missions shall be provided with adequate resources for the effective and efficient discharge of their respective mandates;

7. *Reiterates its request* to the Secretary-General to make the fullest possible use of facilities and equipment at the United Nations Logistics Base at Brindisi, Italy, in order to minimize the costs of procurement for the Mission;

8. *Endorses* the conclusions and recommendations contained in the report of the Advisory Committee on Administrative and Budgetary Questions, and requests the Secretary-General to ensure their full implementation;

9. *Requests* the Secretary-General to take all necessary action to ensure that the Mission is administered with a maximum of efficiency and economy;

10. *Also requests* the Secretary-General, in order to reduce the cost of employing General Service staff, to continue efforts to recruit local staff for the Mission against General Service posts, commensurate with the requirements of the Mission;

Revised budget estimates for the period from 1 July 2004 to 30 June 2005

11. *Decides* to appropriate to the Special Account for the United Nations Mission in Sierra Leone the amount of 94,621,400 dollars for the maintenance of the Mission for the period from 1 July 2004 to 30 June 2005, in addition to the amount of 207,246,100 dollars already appropriated for the same period under the terms of its resolution 58/308;

Financing of the appropriation

12. *Decides also*, taking into account the amount of 207,246,100 dollars previously apportioned under the terms of its resolution 58/308, to apportion among Member States the additional amount of 94,621,400 dollars at a monthly rate of 7,885,117 dollars, in accordance with the levels set out in General Assembly resolution 55/235, as adjusted by the Assembly in its resolution 55/236 of 23 December 2000 and updated in its resolution 58/256 of 23 December 2003, taking into account the scale of assessments for 2004 and 2005, as set out in its resolution 58/1 B of 23 December 2003;

13. *Decides further* that, in accordance with the provisions of its resolution 973(X) of 15 December 1955, there shall be set off against the apportionment among Member States, as provided for in paragraph 12 above, their respective share in the Tax Equalization Fund of the amount of 2,096,500 dollars, at a monthly rate of 174,708 dollars, representing the additional estimated staff assessment income approved for the Mission;

14. *Emphasizes* that no peacekeeping mission shall be financed by borrowing funds from other active peacekeeping missions;

15. *Encourages* the Secretary-General to continue to take additional measures to ensure the safety and security of all personnel under the auspices of the United Nations participating in the Mission;

16. *Invites* voluntary contributions to the Mission in cash and in the form of services and supplies acceptable to the Secretary-General, to be administered, as appropriate, in accordance with the procedure and practices established by the General Assembly;

17. *Decides* to keep under review during its fifty-ninth session the item entitled "Financing of the United Nations Mission in Sierra Leone".

The Assembly, on 23 December, decided that the agenda item on UNAMSIL financing would remain for consideration at its resumed fifty-ninth (2005) session (**decision 59/552**).

Financing of Special Court

The Secretary-General, on 26 February [S/2004/182], informed the Security Council of the shortfall in the budget for the third year of operation of the Special Court for Sierra Leone, estab-

lished in 2002 [YUN 2002, p. 164] as requested by the Council in resolution 1315(2000) [YUN 2000, p. 205]. Since voluntary contributions for the operation of the Court, to date, were estimated at only $8 milion, the anticipated shortfall was projected between $20 million and $22 million. To address the situation, the Secretary-General proposed that the shortfall for all or part of the third-year costs of the Court be provided by assessment and invited the Council to bring the matter to the attention of the General Assembly.

On 10 March [S/2004/183], the Security Council President informed the Secretary-General that it had no objection to his proposal for supplementing the voluntary contributions for financing the Court.

The Secretary-General, on 15 March [A/58/733], submitted to the Assembly for approval a request for a subvention to the Special Court for Sierra Leone for the period from 1 July 2004 to 31 December 2005 of up to $40 million, of which $16.7 million related to the period from 1 July to 31 December 2004 and the remaining $23.3 million to 2005. The amount requested would supplement voluntary contributions, including those pledged but not yet paid. Any voluntary contributions received would reduce the amount to be assessed.

On 17 March [A/58/7/Add.30], ACABQ, having reviewed the request, recommended that commitment authority be granted in the amount of $16.7 million. ACABQ intended to revert to the matter when it had received a detailed submission, and would provide a detailed recommendation to the Assembly on the required level of financial assistance and the source of financing.

GENERAL ASSEMBLY ACTION (April)

On 8 April [meeting 83], the General Assembly, on the recommendation of the Fifth Committee [A/58/573/Add.1], adopted **resolution 58/284** without vote [agenda item 121].

Special Court for Sierra Leone

The General Assembly,

Having considered the report of the Secretary-General on the request for a subvention to the Special Court for Sierra Leone submitted in response to the exchange of letters between the Secretary-General and the President of the Security Council and the related report of the Advisory Committee on Administrative and Budgetary Questions,

1. *Endorses* the conclusions and recommendations of the Advisory Committee on Administrative and Budgetary Questions contained in its report, subject to the provisions of the present resolution, and in this regard requests the Secretary-General to provide the necessary report to the General Assembly at its fifty-ninth session;

2. *Authorizes* the Secretary-General, as an exceptional measure, to enter into commitments in an amount not to exceed 16.7 million United States dollars to supplement the financial resources of the Special Court for Sierra Leone for the period from 1 July to 31 December 2004, on the understanding that any regular budget funds appropriated for the Court would be refunded to the United Nations at the time of liquidation of the Court should sufficient voluntary contributions be received;

3. *Requests* the Secretary-General, in concert with the Management Committee, to redouble efforts to raise voluntary contributions to support the work of the Court, and to report to the General Assembly at its fifty-ninth session on progress made;

4. *Appeals* to Member States, as a matter of urgency, to contribute voluntary funds in support of the Court and to honour existing pledges;

5. *Notes* that the Court is expected to complete its work by 31 December 2005;

6. *Requests* the Secretary-General to invite the Court to adopt a completion strategy, and also requests the Secretary-General to inform the Security Council and the General Assembly at its fifty-ninth session about this matter;

7. *Invites* the Management Committee to review the structure of the Court with a view to minimizing the cost of completing the Court's work, without adversely affecting the implementation of the legal agreement between the United Nations and the Government of Sierra Leone.

The Secretary-General, as requested in resolution 58/284 (above), reported on 7 December [A/59/534/Add.2] on the request for a subvention to the Special Court. He said that, owing to the continuing availability of voluntary contributions, the Special Court would not require the $16.7 million authorized by the General Assembly for the period ending 31 December 2004. It was anticipated, however, that the Special Court would exhaust its available voluntary contributions and a subvention from the United Nations would be required from early 2005. The Assembly was being requested to appropriate the amount of $20 million for that purpose.

ACABQ, on 10 December [A/59/569/Add.2], reviewed the Secretary-General's report and recommended that commitment authority be granted in an amount not to exceed $20 million, so that the Court could continue operations until 30 June 2005. The Committee would revert to the matter on the basis of the detailed report to be submitted to the Assembly at its resumed fifty-ninth (2005) session.

The Assembly, in section VII of **resolution 59/276** of 23 December (see p. 1383), authorized the Secretary-General to enter into commitments not to exceed $20 million to supplement the financial resources of the Court, with effect from 1 January to 30 June 2005, under special political missions of section 3, Political affairs, of the 2004-2005 programme budget. He should continue to raise voluntary contributions for the Court and submit a progress report at the Assembly's resumed fifty-ninth session. Member States were asked to continue to provide funds in support of the Court.

Sanctions

The Chairman of the Security Council Committee established pursuant to resolution 1132 (1997) [YUN 1997, p. 135] on Sierra Leone, reported on 27 February [S/2004/166] on its activities in 2003. The Committee sought the views of the Sierra Leone Government and the Special Representative of the Secretary-General on the criteria for reviewing and revising the travel-ban list and on redefining the legal basis of the travel ban. The Committee removed the names of eight persons confirmed deceased from the list and approved one request for an exemption of the travel restrictions. The Committee also considered allegations of violations of the diamond sanctions. In the absence of a specific monitoring mechanism, the Committee urged States and organizations to provide it with pertinent information.

In a later report [S/2005/44], the Committee described its 2004 activities. On 25 February, the Committee issued a revised travel-ban list [SC/8008]. On Sierra Leone's recommendation, the Committee removed the names of 16 individuals from the list and issued a new one on 20 September [SC/8192]. The Committee reviewed a request from the Special Court for Sierra Leone that five individuals in the Court's custody be allowed to be granted a waiver so that they could travel abroad for medical treatment, and the Acting Chairman indicated that the Committee would look constructively upon such requests. It considered a notification from the United States [S/2004/395] of the export of non-lethal spare parts for RSLAF helicopters, and information from Argentina on steps it had taken to implement the arms sanctions. On 5 November, the Committee adopted revised guidelines for the conduct of its work.

Guinea-Bissau

In 2004, progress was made towards restoring constitutional rule in Guinea-Bissau through implementation of the terms of the Political Transitional Charter, signed in September 2003 [YUN 2003, p. 227]. The Charter, signed by the Military Committee, 23 of the 24 registered political parties and civil society organizations, set up a Transitional Government and the National Transitional Council, following the coup d'état staged by the military. As called for in the Charter, legislative elections were held in March 2004, and a new Government was formed in May. The Interim President, Henrique Pereira Rosa, and the new Government undertook to restore law and order and institutional stability. Some governmental institutions resumed their functions and preparations began for presidential elections, scheduled for April 2005.

The United Nations Peace-building Support Office in Guinea-Bissau (UNOGBIS), headed by the Secretary-General's Representative for Guinea-Bissau, continued to support the Government's efforts to monitor internal developments, to promote peace and security, and to coordinate efforts aimed at social and economic development in the country. It reported that the socio-economic situation in Guinea-Bissau remained critical, and the Government lacked the resources to meet expenditure and pay salary arrears of the civil services and armed forces.

Progress in implementing the Transitional Charter was stalled by a military mutiny on 6 October, resulting in the assassination of the Chief of General Staff and the Chief of Human Resources. Condemning the use of force to settle differences, the Security Council urged the political parties to continue working with national authorities to complete the implementation of the Charter before the holding of presidential elections. The Council welcomed the financial support provided by ECOWAS for the payment of some of the salary arrears of military personnel.

By the end of the year, the transitional process was back on track, and the new Government formed after the legislative elections of March made further efforts towards restoring constitutional rule and institutional stability. The executive, legislative and judiciary branches began to function, and progress was made in organizing presidential elections. The Government's fiscal reforms made it possible for civil servants and the security forces to be paid after a long hiatus. According to the Secretary-General, Guinea-Bissau's new Government needed assistance in organizing presidential elections, restructuring the security sector and building the capacity of the executive and judiciary branches. To help the Government meet those challenges, he proposed that the UNOGBIS presence in Guinea-Bissau be extended and its mandate expanded. Acting on that recommendation, the Security Council, on 22 December, extended the mandate for one year and revised it. Among its tasks, UNOGBIS would support national reconciliation; promote respect for the rule of law and human rights; support the restoration of constitutional normalcy; assist in elections; strengthen national mechanisms for conflict prevention; support security sector reform; and mobilize international financial assistance.

Elections and new Government

Following the 26 January elections for the President and the Vice-President of the Supreme Court of Justice, legislative elections were held in Guinea-Bissau on 28 and 30 March, a significant step in the implementation of the transitional process due to end with the holding of presidential elections in March 2004. The National Electoral Commission announced on 4 April that the African Party for the Independence of Guinea-Bissau and Cape Verde (PAIGC) obtained 45 seats in the 102-member National Popular Assembly, the party of former President Koumba Yala, the Party of Social Renewal (PRS), 35 seats, the United Social Democratic Party, led by Francisco Fadul, 17 seats, the Electoral Union two seats and the United Popular Alliance (APU) one seat. Thus, none of the parties received an absolute majority. After the ruling by the Supreme Court rejecting claims of fraud by PRS and APU, all parties accepted the results. With the transfer, on 7 May, by the National Transition Council of its power to the newly elected National Popular Assembly and the Assembly's inauguration, the Council ceased to exist as provided for in the Transition Charter.

Following the inauguration of the Assembly, the President appointed Carlos Gomes Junior, head of PAIGC, as Prime Minister. Mr. Gomes Junior announced a 24-member Government, representing all ethnic groups and including five women.

The EU, in a 2 April statement of its Presidency [S/2004/283], welcomed the calmness and public-spiritedness which characterized the electoral process. It found the elections to be fair, free and transparent. The EU reaffirmed its willingness to help Guinea-Bissau in normalizing its economic and social situations.

Developments and UNOGBIS activities

Report of Secretary-General (June). The Secretary-General, in response to Security Council resolution 1233(1999) [YUN 1999, p. 140], reported on 4 June [S/2004/456] on developments in Guinea-Bissau and UNOGBIS. He said that important progress continued to be made towards restoring constitutional order, in accordance with the Transitional Charter provisions. Following the formation of the new Government, the new authorities set priority objectives, among which were the creation of institutional capacity for assuming national responsibility for good governance, accountable and transparent financial management and the improvement of socio-economic conditions.

The overall situation in the country remained peaceful; however, the ethnic imbalance within the military, unpaid salary arrears for the security forces and the poor condition of barracks and infrastructure were potentially destabilizing factors. The authorities recognized that the reorganization of the armed forces was one of the country's top priorities. In that regard, UNOGBIS, in collaboration with ECOWAS and bilateral partners, initiated planning for the reform of the armed forces. The reintegration component of the disarmament, reinsertion and reintegration programme was proceeding well and the Government received additional resources from the World Bank to increase the number of beneficiaries to 7,376 from 4,372.

Among efforts to reinforce national capacity for the protection and respect of human rights, UNOGBIS helped to develop a National Human Rights Action Plan to be submitted to the National Popular Assembly. UNOGBIS followed closely the cases of 20 persons accused of attempted coups d'état and arbitrarily detained since December 2002, given that many of them had not been formally charged. UNOGBIS received assurances that the trial of the detainees would proceed in criminal courts to avoid further delays, as the military tribunal lacked logistical and financial means.

The economic situation in Guinea-Bissau remained difficult, with two out of three people living in poverty. To respond to the country's economic and budgetary crisis, the Transitional Government, supported by IMF, the World Bank, the African Development Bank and UNDP, formulated an emergency budget for 2004 and an emergency economic management plan. To support the country in the implementation of that plan, a multi-donor Emergency Economic Management Fund for Guinea-Bissau, initiated by the Ad Hoc Advisory Group on Guinea-Bissau of the Economic and Social Council, was set up to enable the Government to resume social services and key public administration activities. The Fund, administered by UNDP and expected to be operational until the end of 2004, had so far received just over $4 million of the $18.3 million required.

The Secretary-General observed that the democratization process in Guinea-Bissau remained fragile. It lacked the resources to strengthen the capacity of State institutions to address the country's deep-rooted structural problems. The country needed the support of the international community to complete the transition to constitutional order.

Ad Hoc Advisory Group. The Ad Hoc Advisory Group on Guinea-Bissau issued two reports [E/2004/10, E/2004/92], highlighting its efforts to assist the country with its development priorities. The Economic and Social Council in **resolution 2004/1** of 3 May (see p. 935), and **resolution 2004/61** of 23 July (see p. 936), called on donors to support Guinea-Bissau's development efforts, including through the Emergency Economic Management Fund. The Economic and Social Council drew the Security Council's attention to the Group's work in a 2 November letter [S/2004/898].

Security Council consideration. On 6 April, the Security Council was briefed, during informal consultations, on the situation in Guinea-Bissau by David Stephen, the Representative of the Secretary-General and Head of UNOGBIS. In a press statement issued that day [SC/8054-AFR/887] by the President, Council members took note of the announcement by the PAIGC leader of the party's intention to form a broad-based government and urged all the Guinean actors to work together for a smooth completion of the transitional period. Members commended ECOWAS for its mediation and facilitation role, as well as for the timely and constructive contribution brought to the political environment immediately after the elections. They also expressed concern at the persistence of serious economic difficulties in Guinea-Bissau and appealed to the international community to consider the situation in the country as a matter of urgency, requiring strengthened support of its economic reconstruction and rehabilitation efforts.

SECURITY COUNCIL ACTION (June)

On 18 June [meeting 4992], following consultations among Security Council members, the President made statement **S/PRST/2004/20** on behalf of the Council:

The Security Council, recalling its previous statements on Guinea-Bissau, in particular the statement by its President of 19 June 2003, welcomes the report of the Secretary-General of 4 June 2004 on developments in Guinea-Bissau and on activities of the United Nations Peace-building Support Office in that country.

In this regard, the Council expresses its satisfaction regarding progress made by national authorities towards restoring constitutional order, in accordance with the Transition Charter provisions and calendar, in particular the installation of a new National Popular Assembly and a new Government, thus completing the first phase of the transitional process due to end with the holding of presidential elections by March 2005, and generating the environment for growing international confidence and support.

The Council acknowledges, with appreciation, the manner in which the country's principal actors and the political forces managed to reach consensus on critical political challenges they faced during and after the elections, and encourages them to stay the course.

The Council also encourages all parties, and the new Government established on 12 May 2004, to faithfully adhere to the provisions of the Transition Charter in order to achieve and consolidate national reconciliation and to ensure the full restoration of constitutional order. It further encourages the authorities to continue to strengthen the rule of law and respect for human rights and to resolve outstanding human rights issues.

The Council commends the national authorities and the people of Guinea-Bissau for their continued commitment and dedication to democracy.

The Council expresses, nonetheless, its concern with the fragility of the democratization process in Guinea-Bissau, due mainly to the country's deep-rooted structural problems, including the weakness of State institutions and structures, as well as the persistent economic and social crisis.

The Council further expresses its concern about the need to improve the situation of the military, in particular the payment of salary arrears, which continues to be seen as a potentially destabilizing factor. It welcomes the Government's commitment to make all efforts aimed at addressing the issue of salary arrears and the reorganization of the national armed forces and invites the international community to fully support such efforts.

The Council welcomes the improved dialogue between the Government of Guinea-Bissau and the Bretton Woods institutions, and urges the Government to continue to implement its commitments in the areas of fiscal responsibility and good governance. It highlights the importance that those efforts be matched by the resumption of adequate levels of international assistance.

The Council acknowledges and also welcomes the assistance provided to Guinea-Bissau by bilateral and multilateral partners, in particular the United Nations Development Programme and the World Bank, and encourages their enhanced constructive involvement in the country.

The Council underlines the importance it attaches to the organization of a round-table conference to take place in the last quarter of 2004, which it considers of utmost relevance to addressing some of the most urgent needs of Guinea-Bissau. In the interim, the Council reiterates its appeals to the international community to contribute financially to the Emergency Economic Management Fund for Guinea-Bissau, managed by the United Nations Development Programme.

The Council recognizes and commends the work of the United Nations Peace-building Support Office in Guinea-Bissau and the entire United Nations country team for their outstanding support and contribution to the process of normalization of the political situation and stability in Guinea-Bissau.

The Council reaffirms the importance of the regional dimension in the solution of the problems faced by Guinea-Bissau, and, in this regard, welcomes the role being played by the African Union, the West African Economic and Monetary Union, the Economic Community of West African States and the Community of Portuguese-speaking Countries in the peace-building process in Guinea-Bissau.

The Council also commends the efforts by the Ad Hoc Working Group on Conflict Prevention and Resolution in Africa of the Council, the Ad Hoc Advisory Group on Guinea-Bissau of the Economic and Social Council and the Group of Friends of Guinea-Bissau aimed at assisting the country to address both its short-term post-conflict crisis and longer-term development goals.

The Council looks forward to conclusions and recommendations of its mission to West Africa, which includes Guinea-Bissau.

Security Council mission. The Security Council mission to West Africa (see p. 169) visited Guinea-Bissau on 27 and 28 June, jointly with the Economic and Social Council's Ad Hoc Advisory Group on Guinea-Bissau and the Group of Friends of Guinea-Bissau. In its 2 July report [S/2004/525], the mission welcomed the progress in the political transition and commended the Government's efforts to meet its short-term priorities, including paying current salaries to civil servants and the armed forces and ensuring accountability and transparency in the management of public funds.

The mission, noting that the overall situation in the country remained fragile, despite the progress made in the transition, highlighted the remaining major challenges as restructuring the armed forces into a professional force; strengthening national public institutions; redressing social and economic inequities; promoting inclusive internal political dialogue; and mobilizing resources from bilateral and multilateral sources, to promote social and economic development and to ensure regular payment of salaries to civil servants and the military.

The mission recommended that development partners and donors, including the Bretton Woods institutions (the World Bank Group and IMF) and the EU, should help Guinea-Bissau to meet its most immediate needs; the Government and IMF should discuss resuming an IMF programme; UNDP should assist in preparing for the round-table conference to take place late in 2004; the Government should strengthen a culture of good governance, democracy and respect for the rule of law and human rights; and bilateral and/or multilateral partners should support the restructuring of the armed forces. The mission also recommended that the Ad Hoc Advisory Group on Guinea-Bissau and the Security Council continue to monitor and support political, economic and social developments in Guinea-Bissau. ECOWAS was called on to include Guinea-

Bissau in regional policies for containing the proliferation of small arms and other security threats in the region.

The Security Council considered the mission's report on 16 July [meeting 5005].

Appointment. On 1 September [S/2004/713], the Secretary-General informed the Security Council of his intention to designate Jono Bernardo Honwana (Mozambique) as his Representative in Guinea-Bissau and Head of UNOGBIS as from 15 September, to succeed David Stephen, who retired in April. The Council, on 3 September [S/2004/714], took note of the Secretary-General's intention.

Military revolt

On 6 October, a group of military officers led a revolt, which resulted in the assassination of the Chief of General Staff, General Verissimo Correia Seabra, and the spokesman for the armed forces, Colonel Domingos de Barros.

The officers involved stated afterwards that their actions had been motivated mainly by grievances over salaries, poor living conditions and corruption in the military hierarchy. They insisted that the mutiny had not been a coup d'état or aimed at changing the political status quo. Subsequently, they sought, and obtained from the authorities, the appointment of Major General Tagme Na Waie as new Chief of General Staff. General Tagme and new chiefs of the navy, air force and army were sworn in on 11 November, ending the month-long vacuum of military leadership. The appointments, however, were viewed as caving in on the part of the civilian authorities to pressures from the military and as a sign of further erosion of the authority of the constitutional Government and its institutions. In addition, misgivings were expressed about impunity following the Government's commitment in a memorandum of understanding, signed with the military, to a possible amnesty for all involved in military interventions since 1980.

Following the installation of the new officers, the interim President underlined the importance of proceeding with the long-planned reform of the armed forces, a goal endorsed by the new Chief of General Staff, who announced the military leadership's readiness to work towards reform. ECOWAS and the Community of Portuguese-speaking Countries provided material and technical assistance to the Government of Guinea-Bissau after the mutiny, including a cash donation of $500,000 towards paying some of the salary arrears owed to the military. The Community dispatched a good offices mission to Bissau on 15 November to assist the civilian and military authorities to find peace.

Security Council consideration. The Security Council was briefed by the Assistant Secretary-General for Political Affairs on the developments that took place on 6 October. In a 7 October statement of the President [SC/8213-AFR/1047], Council members expressed concern over the tragic events at a time when Guinea-Bissau was making steady progress towards the full restoration of constitutional order. They condemned the use of force to settle long-standing problems in the military sector and the subsequent loss of life. They called on all concerned to come to a speedy agreement consistent with respect for constitutional authority and the rule of law.

SECURITY COUNCIL ACTION (October)

On 2 November [meeting 5069], following consultations among Security Council members, the President made statement **S/PRST/2004/41** on behalf of the Council:

The Security Council expresses its deep concern at developments in Guinea-Bissau that led to the killings, on 6 October 2004, of the Chief of General Staff of the Armed Forces, General Veríssimo Correia Seabra, and of the Chief of Human Resources, Colonel Domingos de Barros. The Council condemns in the strongest terms such use of force to settle differences or address grievances and, bearing in mind the position of the African Union on unconstitutional changes of government, as stated in the 1999 Algiers Declaration and the 2000 Lomé Declaration, calls upon the Guinea-Bissau parties to refrain from attempting to seize power in Guinea-Bissau by force.

The Council takes note of the signature of a memorandum of understanding, in Bissau, on 10 October 2004, and of the establishment of a commission to monitor its implementation, and underlines that the Government of Guinea-Bissau and national authorities must remain committed to the promotion of the rule of law and to the fight against impunity, including when considering ways of implementing the above-mentioned agreement.

The Council urges all political parties to continue working, in good faith, with national authorities to complete the implementation of the Political Transition Charter before the holding of presidential elections by April 2005.

The Council reaffirms that peace and stability in Guinea-Bissau are critical for peace and security in the West African subregion. As the Government of Guinea-Bissau tackles the military, political, institutional and economic problems that are responsible for recurrent political turmoil and instability in Guinea-Bissau, the Council underlines the importance of addressing their root causes as well as finding immediate solutions to improve the situation in the short term.

The Council stresses the need for urgent measures by the international community to assist the Government of Guinea-Bissau to overcome the present crisis, in particular to reinforce the capacity of legitimate authorities to maintain political stability and to determine sound solutions to the country's most urgent and fundamental challenges, particularly the restructuring of the Armed Forces, the strengthening of the State and its institutions and the promotion of social and economic development.

The Council welcomes the timely financial support already provided by the Economic Community of West African States and its members to the Government of Guinea-Bissau towards the payment of salary arrears due to military personnel. The Council calls upon international donors to contribute urgently to the Government of Guinea-Bissau's budget for civil service and military salaries and also encourages them to contribute to the Emergency Economic Management Fund, managed by the United Nations Development Programme.

The Council also takes note, with appreciation, of the recent visit of a fact-finding mission from the Community of Portuguese-speaking Countries to Guinea-Bissau.

The Council reiterates its call upon the international community to maintain its confidence in the process of democratic consolidation in Guinea-Bissau and to uphold its commitments to development in that country, particularly through its active preparation for and participation in the round-table conference scheduled to take place next December, in Brussels.

The Council reaffirms its full support for the Representative of the Secretary-General in Guinea-Bissau and indicates its intention to consider suitable ways of improving the role of the United Nations Peacebuilding Support Office in Guinea-Bissau in the promotion of peace and security, as well as in the coordination of efforts aiming at social and economic development in the country.

The Council requests the Secretary-General to submit to the United Nations, in his next report on the Support Office and the situation in Guinea-Bissau, suggestions on what contribution the United Nations could make towards an active and coordinated international effort to assist Guinea-Bissau.

Report of Secretary-General (December). The Secretary-General, in his 15 December report on developments in Guinea-Bissau and UNOGBIS activities [S/2004/969], said that prior to the mutiny of 6 October (see p. 227), the political situation in that country showed signs of progress and promise towards restoring constitutional rule and institutional stability. The executive, legislative and judiciary branches began to function within the parameters of the powers envisaged in the Constitution. The National Electoral Commission was established to organize polls and presidential elections in 2005, which would complete the political transition and mark the full restoration of constitutional normalcy. The military mutiny jeopardized those and other gains and demonstrated the fragility of the continuing transitional process and of the society as a whole. It also increased the danger of polarizing of the society along ethnic lines, especially given the widespread perception that the revolt was inspired by Balanta elements in the armed forces.

The Government's fiscal and governance reforms resulted in improved revenue collection, making it possible for it to meet its commitments to pay current salaries to civil servants and the security forces. However, the Government did not have the resources to meet recurrent expenditures and pay the huge backlog of salary arrears inherited from the previous Government. Moreover, the Emergency Economic Management Fund had been depleted and would cease to be operational at the end of the year. However, the Government anticipated accessing a second tranche of an EU budget support package, contingent upon an agreed macroeconomic framework with IMF, which had scheduled a mission to Guinea-Bissau from 4 to 18 December to assist the authorities with preparing the 2005 budget. The Government also worked with the Bretton Woods institutions to begin finalization of the poverty reduction strategy paper for submission to the round table initially scheduled for December 2004, but postponed after the 6 October mutiny.

The health and education sectors suffered from inadequate infrastructure, financial resources and qualified human resources. With teaching materials financed through the Emergency Economic Management Fund, State schools were able to commence the 2004/05 school year on time in October for the first time in three years. The national polio vaccination campaign covered 97 per cent of children and the United Nations provided substantial support for the campaign against malaria. The first national forum on HIV/AIDS was held in September.

The re-evaluation of the preparatory process for planning the reform of the armed forces and reconciliation among the military factions prior to the military mutiny, interrupted by the events of 6 October, would resume as new military leadership had been appointed. The police force, which also needed reform, faced a shortage of equipment, funds and capacity to enable it to fulfil its public security role. With UNDP support, the national mine action coordination authority supervised the removal by NGOs of 2,599 mines and 34,900 pieces of unexploded ordnance, while the International Organization for Migration provided administrative and financial management support to the demobilization, reinsertion and reintegration programme.

The human rights situation was a cause of concern, and the events of 6 October intensified the climate of uncertainty and insecurity, especially since no official investigation was launched. By November, all 20 prisoners accused of attempted coups d'état and arbitrarily detained since December 2002 were provisionally released.

The Secretary-General observed that the challenges confronting Guinea-Bissau were complex and multisectoral, and complicated as a result of the 6 October mutiny. With a view to building sustainable peace and progress, he proposed that the Security Council extend the UNOGBIS presence and revise its mandate to take into account the diverse tasks at hand and the importance of strengthening the capacity of national stakeholders to confront those challenges. That new mandate would allow the Office, working with the UN country team, to integrate development and peace and security activities into a cohesive peace-building strategy for the immediate, medium and longer terms; help Guinea-Bissau overcome its difficulties, including the organization of presidential elections, and with the country team contribute to institutional capacity-building to enable the legislative, the executive and the judiciary branches to function more effectively; and support efforts to implement military reform. Training and advocacy in the advancement of respect for human rights and the rule of law would be intensified. The Office would also promote the development of national mechanisms of conflict prevention and management.

Concerning international assistance to Guinea-Bissau, the Secretary-General recommended that the Emergency Economic Management Fund be extended beyond the end of 2004 to 30 June 2005 to enable the Government to meet its urgent budgetary priorities. Once the Government and the military authorities had defined the nature and scope of such reform, the international community should provide support, through a special fund, so that the process could proceed expeditiously. UNOGBIS and the country team would work with national authorities to define programmes in support of that process and to mobilize resources. The United Nations would also assist the authorities to implement the Programme of Action to Prevent, Combat and Eradicate the Illicit Trade in Small Arms and Light Weapons in All Its Aspects [YUN 2001, p. 499]. The Government, in cooperation with ECOWAS and others, should address the regional proliferation of small arms and other cross-border issues. In terms of medium- and longer-term priorities, the United Nations and other donors should develop programmes to strengthen national institutions in the political, judiciary, social and economic realms; develop and empower civil society bodies; address the plight of youth; and rebuild social and public infrastructure. ECOWAS, the Community of Portuguese-speaking Countries and

the United Nations should ensure complementarity and avoid duplication of efforts. At the same time, UNOGBIS and the UN country team would strengthen the judiciary system through capacity-building and resource allocation.

The Secretary-General said it was regrettable that, since the beginning of the transition, qualified optimism was replaced by growing scepticism and a perception that the military posed the greatest obstacle to the consolidation of democracy, peace and economic opportunities. He encouraged the authorities to complete the political transition peacefully, including by holding presidential elections as envisaged in the Political Transition Charter. He urged the international community and all donors to be generous in their assistance, including providing contributions to the Emergency Economic Management Fund and financial and technical support for holding presidential elections in 2005.

SECURITY COUNCIL ACTION (December)

On 22 December [meeting 5107], the Security Council unanimously adopted **resolution 1580 (2004)**. The draft [S/2004/986] was prepared in consultations among Council members.

The Security Council,

Reaffirming its previous resolutions 1216(1998) of 21 December 1998 and 1233(1999) of 6 April 1999, and the statement by its President of 2 November 2004,

Expressing its deep concern at recent developments in Guinea-Bissau, particularly the military mutiny of 6 October 2004 that resulted in the assassinations of the Chief of General Staff of the Armed Forces, General Veríssimo Correia Seabra, and the Armed Forces spokesman, Colonel Domingos de Barros, and which has jeopardized gains made since the installation of the new Government after the legislative elections of March 2004,

Stressing the fact that such developments demonstrate the fragility of the ongoing transitional process and of national political institutions, and recognizing the risks they present to the conclusion of the transitional process,

Noting with concern that repeated acts of instability and unrest threaten efforts towards sustainable social and economic development, and may erode the confidence of bilateral partners and the international community,

Underlining the fact that the Government of Guinea-Bissau and national authorities must remain committed to the promotion of the rule of law and fight against impunity,

Welcoming the report of the Secretary-General on developments in Guinea-Bissau and on the activities of the United Nations Peacebuilding Support Office in that country of 15 December 2004, and his recommendations contained therein,

Reaffirming its full commitment to the promotion of peace and stability in Guinea-Bissau,

1. *Decides* to extend the mandate of the United Nations Peacebuilding Support Office in Guinea-

Bissau, as a special political mission, for one year from the date of adoption of the present resolution;

2. *Decides also* to revise the mandate of the Support Office as follows:

(a) To support all efforts to enhance political dialogue, to promote national reconciliation and respect for the rule of law and human rights;

(b) To support the efforts of all national stakeholders to ensure the full restoration of constitutional normalcy in accordance with the provisions of the Political Transition Charter of 28 September 2003, including through the holding of free and transparent presidential elections;

(c) To assist with these elections in close cooperation with the United Nations country team and other international partners;

(d) To assist in strengthening the national mechanisms for conflict prevention during the remainder of the transitional period and beyond;

(e) To encourage and support national efforts to reform the security sector, including the development of stable civil-military relations, and to attract international support for these efforts;

(f) To encourage the Government to fully implement the Programme of Action to Prevent, Combat and Eradicate the Illicit Trade in Small Arms and Light Weapons in All Its Aspects;

(g) To work closely with the Resident Coordinator and the United Nations country team to mobilize international financial assistance to enable the Government to meet its immediate financial and logistical needs and implement its national reconstruction and social and economic development strategy;

(h) Within the framework of a comprehensive peacebuilding strategy, to actively support efforts of the United Nations system and Guinea-Bissau's other partners, towards strengthening State institutions and structures to enable them to uphold the rule of law, respect for human rights and the unimpeded and independent functioning of the executive, legislative and judicial branches of government;

3. *Encourages* the authorities of Guinea-Bissau to enhance political dialogue and pursue constructive civil-military relations, as a way forward, towards the peaceful completion of the political transition, including the holding of presidential elections as envisaged in the Political Transition Charter;

4. *Calls upon* the National Assembly of Guinea-Bissau, while addressing the issue of granting an amnesty for all those involved in military interventions since 1980, to take account of the principles of justice and fight against impunity;

5. *Strongly urges* the Government, together with military authorities and other concerned parties, to agree, as soon as possible, on a national plan for the reform of the security sector, in particular military reform;

6. *Invites* the Secretary-General to establish an emergency fund, to be administered by the United Nations Development Programme, to support efforts related to the planning and implementation of military reform;

7. *Appeals* to the international community to continue to provide assistance to help Guinea-Bissau to meet its immediate needs as well as its structural challenges, particularly by providing additional contribu-

tions to the Emergency Economic Management Fund as well as to the new fund mentioned above;

8. *Encourages* the establishment of a joint coordinating mechanism among the United Nations, the Economic Community of West African States and the Community of Portuguese-speaking Countries to ensure synergy and complementarity;

9. *Commends* the Bretton Woods institutions for their continued engagement in Guinea-Bissau and encourages them to continue their assistance;

10. *Requests* the Secretary-General to conduct a review of the Support Office with a view to adjusting its capacities to meet the requirements of its revised mandate;

11. *Also requests* the Secretary-General to keep the Security Council closely and regularly informed of developments on the ground and of the implementation of the present resolution, in particular of paragraphs 2 and 5 above, and in that regard requests the Secretary-General to submit a report every three months from the date of adoption of the present resolution;

12. *Decides* to remain actively seized of the matter.

Cameroon-Nigeria

Cameroon and Nigeria cooperated to resolve border issues, with UN assistance, through the Cameroon-Nigeria Mixed Commission. The Commission was established by the Secretary-General following the ruling of the International Court of Justice (ICJ) of 10 October 2002 on the land and maritime boundary between those two countries [YUN 2002, p. 1265].

Cameroon-Nigeria Mixed Commission

On 17 March [S/2004/298], the Secretary-General informed the Security Council of the activities undertaken by Cameroon and Nigeria, through his good offices and with the assistance of the Secretariat, to implement the ICJ ruling. Prior to that ruling, Cameroon's President, Paul Biya, and Nigeria's President, Olusegun Obasanjo, had agreed to respect the Court's ruling, establish an implementation mechanism with UN support and adopt confidence-building measures. Following the ICJ ruling in October 2002, they asked the Secretary-General to establish a Mixed Commission, to be chaired by his Special Representative, Ahmedou Ould-Abdallah, to consider the implications of the ICJ decision, including: the demarcation of the land boundary; recommendations on confidence-building measures, such as projects to promote joint economic ventures and cross-border cooperation; troop withdrawal from boundary areas; demilitarization of the Bakassi peninsula, with the possibility of deploying international personnel to observe the withdrawal; and reactivation of the Lake Chad Basin Commission

(Cameroon, Central African Republic, Chad, Niger, Nigeria). The Mixed Commission, which met bimonthly, alternately in Yaoundé, Cameroon, and Abuja, Nigeria, established, at its first meeting (Yaoundé, December 2002), a subcommission, consisting of legal experts and cartographers from both countries and the United Nations, with responsibility for demarcating the land boundary between the two countries. The subcommission, at its first meeting (Geneva, January 2003), prepared a small-scale map indicating the boundary and a work programme for the demarcation exercise, which was approved by the Mixed Commission in February 2003. The demarcation exercise was expected to last 96 weeks.

The Mixed Commission also established a subcommission on affected populations. Acting on the decision of the Mixed Commission, the two subcommissions carried out a field visit in February 2004 to the southern part of the land boundary between Cameroon and Nigeria and the Bakassi peninsula. The Mixed Commission also decided that it would carry out field visits to the land boundary area and the Bakassi peninsula itself in March.

The Mixed Commission also established a working group, composed of five experts each from Nigeria and Cameroon, and UN experts, to make a preliminary study and recommendations for delineating the maritime boundary in conformity with the ICJ decision and to produce a map on that basis. To promote confidence-building, the Mixed Commission identified possible projects to promote cross-border cooperation and joint economic ventures, including the reactivation of the Lake Chad Basin Commission.

One of the most important tasks carried out by the Mixed Commission was the withdrawal of and transfer of authority from the civil administration and military and police forces in the Lake Chad area. In December 2003, Nigeria handed over 28 villages to Cameroon, while Cameroon transferred one village to Nigeria. To consolidate the withdrawal and transfer of authority, the Mixed Commission established an observer personnel group for a year, composed of five members each from Nigeria and Cameroon and five UN representatives.

At their third summit (Geneva, 31 January 2004), Presidents Biya and Obasanjo reaffirmed their commitment to implementing the Mixed Commission's agreed work plan and to strengthen confidence-building measures through the exchange of ambassadors, the opening of consulates along the common border and the introduction of joint security patrols. The two leaders also considered concluding a bilateral treaty of friendship and non-aggression. They decided that the Joint Commission would meet annually at a higher level.

The cost of the demarcation exercise and for UN support to the Mixed Commission through 2005 was estimated at $25 million. The Secretary-General intended to seek regular budget support to continue the work of the Commission.

On 15 April [S/2004/299], the Council President informed the Secretary-General that the Council had noted his intention to continue the activities of the UN support team to the Cameroon-Nigeria Mixed Commission with funding from the regular budget and urged the parties of the Mixed Commission to seek further contributions.

On 29 July [S/2004/612], Cameroon informed the Council that Presidents Obasanjo and Biya discussed on 28 and 29 July, among other things, the work of the Mixed Commission and issues relating to peace and security, economic development and regional and international integration. They agreed to open discussions with a view to signing a non-aggression pact.

Financing of Mixed Commission

The Secretary-General, in his report on estimates in respect of special political missions, good offices and other political initiatives authorized by the General Assembly and/or the Security Council [A/C.5/58/20/Add.1], proposed requirements in the amount of $6,902,900 to support the Cameroon-Nigeria Mixed Commission for the period from 1 June to 31 December 2004, to be charged against the unallocated balance in the provision for special political missions for the 2004-2005 biennium.

The Chairman of ACABQ, in an oral report to the Fifth Committee on 26 May [A/C.5/58/SR.49], said that, pending consideration of a new submission, ACABQ recommended that the Secretary-General be granted commitment authority of up to $6,902,900.

GENERAL ASSEMBLY ACTION

On 18 June [meeting 91], the General Assembly, on the recommendation of the Fifth Committee [A/58/573/Add.2], adopted **resolution 58/294** without vote [agenda item 121].

Estimates in respect of special political missions, good offices and other political initiatives authorized by the General Assembly and/or the Security Council

The General Assembly,

Having considered the report of the Secretary-General on the estimates in respect of special political missions, good offices and other political initiatives authorized by the General Assembly and/or the Security Council and the oral statement made by the

Chairman of the Advisory Committee on Administrative and Budgetary Questions,

1. *Emphasizes* the importance of the work of the good offices of the Secretary-General in support of the work of Cameroon-Nigeria Mixed Commission;

2. *Takes note* of the report of the Secretary-General on estimates in respect of special political missions, good offices and other political initiatives authorized by the General Assembly and/or the Security Council;

3. *Notes with concern* the late submission of the report of the Secretary-General;

4. *Endorses* the observations and recommendations as orally presented by the Chairman of the Advisory Committee on Administrative and Budgetary Questions, subject to the provisions of the present resolution;

5. *Requests* the Secretary-General to submit to the General Assembly, by the end of its fifty-eighth session, a comprehensive financial report on the requirements for United Nations support to the Cameroon-Nigeria Mixed Commission, including clearly defined requirements to be provided from the regular budget and elements being financed from other sources, for its consideration at the early part of its fifty-ninth session;

6. *Authorizes* the Secretary-General to enter into commitments in the amount of 6 million United States dollars for United Nations support to the Cameroon-Nigeria Mixed Commission until 30 November 2004, on the understanding that any decision on further financing must be taken by 31 October 2004;

7. *Urges* the Secretary-General to seek further voluntary contributions for United Nations support to the Cameroon-Nigeria Mixed Commission.

In response to that request, the Secretary-General, on 9 September [A/58/886], proposed revised requirements from the regular budget in the amount of $5,419,300 for the seven month period from 1 June to 31 December, and voluntary contributions estimated at $8.3 million.

On 5 October [A/59/411], ACABQ recommended that the Assembly approve the revised requirements for that period and that further voluntary contributions be sought to support the Commission.

GENERAL ASSEMBLY ACTION

On 29 October [meeting 46], the General Assembly, on the recommendation of the Fifth Committee [A/59/448], adopted **resolution 59/12** without vote [agenda item 108].

Estimates in respect of special political missions, good offices and other political initiatives authorized by the General Assembly and/or the Security Council: United Nations support to the Cameroon-Nigeria Mixed Commission

The General Assembly,

Recalling its resolution 58/294 of 18 June 2004, in which it authorized a commitment authority in the amount of 6 million United States dollars for the United Nations support to the Cameroon-Nigeria Mixed Commission,

Having considered the report of the Secretary-General on the estimates in respect of special political missions, good offices and other political initiatives authorized by the General Assembly and/or the Security Council and the related report of the Advisory Committee on Administrative and Budgetary Questions,

1. *Takes note* of the revised requirements for the United Nations support to the Cameroon-Nigeria Mixed Commission for the period from 1 June to 31 December 2004, which amount to 5,419,300 dollars;

2. *Endorses* the observations and recommendations of the Advisory Committee on Administrative and Budgetary Questions, and approves the charging of 5,419,300 dollars against the unallocated balance of funds appropriated under section 3, Political affairs, of the programme budget for the biennium 2004-2005, for special political missions;

3. *Requests* the Secretary-General to ensure that budget presentations for special political missions, to the extent possible, utilize the format of peacekeeping operations and contain information and justification for proposals for post and non-post requirements, subject to the considerations of timeliness and the need for expeditious financing action.

Equatorial Guinea

The EU Presidency, in a 17 June statement on Equatorial Guinea [S/2004/515], welcomed the forthcoming opening of the country's new Parliament after the parliamentary and municipal elections held on 25 April. Although it considered that the electoral campaign was peaceful, the EU noted that Spanish parliamentary observers had detected irregularities that distorted the electoral process, in violation of the agreements between the Government and the opposition reached in Mbini in August 2003. It believed that the elections failed to constitute a Parliament reflecting the political diversity of the society of the country, given that the opposition was not adequately represented in the elections. It called on the authorities to allow the opposition to participate freely in parliamentary sessions.

The United Nations Standing Advisory Committee on Security Questions in Central Africa, at its twenty-first ministerial meeting (Malabo, Equatorial Guinea, 21-25 June) [A/59/154-S/2004/576], noted the climate in which the legislative and municipal elections had been held in April and welcomed the desire for liberalization, characterized by the formation of a new Government with the participation of political parties other than the Democratic Party of Equatorial Guinea. The Committee condemned the attempt to overturn the democratically elected institutions by force and welcomed the support given by States in the subregion to the Government of Equatorial Guinea during those events. The Committee encouraged Equatorial Guinea and

Cameroon to implement the decisions taken in the framework of the ad hoc joint commission on security questions between the two countries, which met in Malabo in June.

Horn of Africa

In 2004, the countries in the Horn of Africa continued to be torn by civil strife, especially in the Sudan, where a protracted civil war increased in intensity, as fighting flared up in the Darfur area of western Sudan and armed militias attacked civilian settlements. That created one of the worst humanitarian crises ever, coupled with serious violations of human rights. The fighting complicated efforts to reach a comprehensive settlement to end the civil war between the north and south of the country, which had been raging for over 21 years. As the situation in Darfur deteriorated, the African Union (AU), took the lead in trying to bring the parties together both to resolve the Darfur crisis and to end the civil war by sending a mission of observers to the region. The Security Council established a special political mission in the Sudan, with a view to preparing for a UN peace support operation to help implement any final agreement reached by the parties. It also requested the Secretary-General to establish a Commission of Inquiry to investigate reports of the serious violations of international humanitarian law and human rights. Although the security and humanitarian situation remained precarious throughout the year, the Sudanese parties succeeded in concluding a comprehensive peace agreement in December, which was expected to be signed in early 2005.

In Somalia, some progress was made towards national reconciliation, with the signing by Somali leaders of a declaration on agreement of issues related to the transitional federal government. Somaliland, however, continued to remain outside the political process. The Somali National Reconciliation Conference continued to meet, and agreement was reached on the formation of a transitional Federal Parliament and a power-sharing arrangement for a transitional period of five years. Established in September, the new Parliament in October elected Colonel Abdullahi Yusuf Ahmed as President of Somalia. However, the security situation remained volatile, and the UN arms embargo continued to be violated by all parties.

The border dispute between Eritrea and Ethiopia remained contentious, with no progress made in implementing the 2000 Algiers ceasefire and peace agreement between the two countries and the 2002 decision of the Ethiopia and Eritrea Boundary Commission, established under that agreement, on the delimitation of the border. The Secretary-General appointed a Special Envoy to discuss with both countries ways of ending the stalemate so that demarcation of the border could continue. However, Eritrea refused to receive him. In November, Ethiopia put forward a five-point peace proposal for resolving the dispute, which was rejected by Eritrea. By the end of the year, reports were received of a steady increase in the build-up of the armed forces of both countries near the Temporary Security Zone.

Appointment. The Secretary-General, on 22 December [S/2004/1019], informed the Security Council that his Special Adviser, Mohamed Sahnoun, had been following developments in the Horn of Africa region, especially in Somalia and the Sudan, and had been providing advice on what role the United Nations could play to promote negotiated settlements of conflicts in the region. During the first months of 2004, Mr. Sahnoun led the UN observer delegation at the Sudan peace talks in Kenya; he followed the talks on the Darfur region of the Sudan as well as the peace process in Somalia. To allow Mr. Sahnoun to continue his efforts, the Secretary-General extended his appointment until 31 December 2005, which the Council noted [S/2004/1020].

Sudan

In 2004, violence broke out in the Darfur region of western Sudan among the two armed groups, the Sudan People's Liberation Movement/Army (SPLM/A) and the Justice and Equality Movement (JEM), the Government of Sudan forces and a supposedly Government-backed militia composed of a loose collection of fighters, mainly of Arab background, known as the Janjaweed. The fighting there created one of the worst humanitarian crises ever, with serious violations of human rights and international humanitarian law, and complicated an already protracted and devastating civil war in the Sudan between government troops based in the north and rebel forces (SPLM/A) based in the south. Attempts to end the civil war, which erupted in 1983, following the breakdown of the 1972 Addis Ababa agreement, were initiated in 1993 by the heads of State of the then Intergovernmental Authority on Drought and Development, renamed the Intergovernmental Authority on Development (IGAD). That process was relaunched in 2002 [YUN 2002, p. 217] with the signing of the Machakos (Kenya) Protocol, which resolved two main issues: the right to self-determination for the people of southern Sudan and the status of State and religion. By that document, the parties agreed to establish a democratic system of governance in which power and wealth would be equitably shared and human rights guaranteed, and to set up a six-year interim period of governance, followed by a referendum to confirm the unity of the Sudan or to move towards secession.

The Machakos Protocol was followed by the signing in September 2003, in Naivasha, Kenya, of the Framework Agreement on Security Arrangements during the Interim Period [YUN 2003, p. 257]. Under its terms, the Sudan would have two armies under separate command during the six-year interim period: the government troops in the north and SPLM/A in the south; both would downsize their forces and contribute forces to joint/integrated units; and a ceasefire would be observed by international monitors, once a comprehensive peace agreement was signed.

As the fighting intensified in 2004, several efforts were made by international and regional actors, primarily the AU, to bring the parties to the negotiating table to conclude a comprehensive peace agreement and to settle the Darfur conflict. On 8 April 2004, the Government, SPLM/A and JEM signed a Humanitarian Ceasefire Agreement in N'Djamena, Chad, to allow international access to the population in need in Darfur. The agreement also included the establishment of a ceasefire commission to monitor its observance and provided for AU monitors on the ground in Darfur. Parallel to those efforts, negotiations on a comprehensive peace agreement, led by IGAD, intensified. Having completed the last three of the six protocols provided for under the Machakos Protocol, including one on power-sharing, the parties, on 5 June, signed the Nairobi Declaration confirming the agreement on the six protocols and committing themselves to completing the final stages of the peace process.

Meanwhile, the Secretary-General, in anticipation of the conclusion of a comprehensive peace agreement, began preparations for UN support to the implementation of such an agreement. He proposed that an advance team be established as a special political mission to the Sudan, which the Security Council endorsed in June as the United Nations Advance Mission in the Sudan (UNAMIS). The Council also declared its readiness to consider establishing a UN peace support operation and asked the Secretary-General to make recommendations on such an operation.

While progress was made on the peace process, the security situation deteriorated dramatically and remained serious throughout the year, with reports of extreme violence and violations of human rights and international humanitarian law

against civilians in the Darfur region by all parties to the crisis, in particular by the Janjaweed. By mid-2004, over 1 million people were in need of urgent humanitarian assistance and about 200,000 refugees had fled to Chad. Following a visit by the Secretary-General to the Sudan, the United Nations and the Government signed, on 3 July, a joint communiqué, by which the Sudan committed itself to disarming the Janjaweed and other armed outlaw groups, to end impunity, to lift all restrictions on humanitarian relief deliveries, and to resume political talks with opposing parties. For its part, the United Nations agreed to assist the deployment of AU ceasefire monitors and to mediate in the dispute.

The Security Council, on 30 July, called on the Sudan to fulfil its commitments stated in the joint communiqué, and endorsed the deployment of international monitors, including the protection force envisioned by the AU, to the Darfur region under AU leadership. In addition, the Council decided to impose an arms embargo against non-governmental entities and individuals operating in Darfur and extended the special political mission it set up in June for an additional 90 days, until 10 December. The United Nations and the Sudan signed on 5 August a Plan of Action to facilitate implementation of Security Council demands and of the 3 July agreement between the Government and the United Nations, by which the Sudan would take specific actions within 30 days to create the conditions for restoration of peace and security.

Following the failure of the Government to fully comply with the Council's demands and its own commitments, the Council, on 18 September, supported the AU's intention to enhance and augment its monitoring mission in the Darfur region and requested the Secretary-General to establish an international commission of inquiry to investigate reports of violations of international humanitarian law and human rights in Darfur. In the event that the Sudan failed to comply with the terms of the resolution, the Council would consider sanctions against the Government.

Despite the worsening security and humanitarian situation, particularly the growing insecurity and violence in Darfur, repeated ceasefire breaches and the appearance of new rebel groups, progress continued to be made in the peace talks. On 19 November, the Government and SPLM/A signed the "Declaration on the conclusion of IGAD negotiations on peace in the Sudan" during the Security Council's Meeting in Nairobi, Kenya. The Declaration and the six protocols referred to in the Nairobi Declaration of 5 June constituted the core Peace Agreement and marked an important step towards the finalization of a comprehensive peace agreement, which the parties agreed to complete by the end of the year. The Council welcomed the signing of the Declaration and pledged to assist the people of the Sudan, upon the signing of a comprehensive agreement, to establish a united and prosperous nation. It also mentioned its readiness to establish a UN peace support operation to support implementation of the agreement.

On 31 December, the Government of the Sudan and SPLA initialled the last two agreements, which set the stage for the official signing, scheduled for early 2005, of the Comprehensive Peace Agreement, the culmination of negotiations over two and a half years of work since the signing of the Machakos Protocol.

Outbreak of crisis in Darfur

The EU, in statements forwarded to the Security Council on 12 January [S/2004/44] and 26 February [S/2004/177], expressed concern about the situation in Darfur, and called on the Government and SPLM/A to respect the September 2003 ceasefire agreement. It remarked that the scale of the humanitarian crisis was escalating, with more than 700,000 internally displaced persons needing urgent assistance. The EU called on the Government to grant the United Nations and other relief organizations full access to all areas of Darfur, to put an end to the Janjaweed atrocities and to ensure that the perpetrators were brought to justice. It called on rebel groups operating in the Darfur region to commit themselves to providing safe passage for relief agencies. It also urged the parties to the conflict to agree to an immediate ceasefire and hold peace talks.

The United Nations Emergency Relief Coordinator, Jan Egeland, reported that, since the fighting started between rebel groups, militias and the Government months earlier, the United Nations had received reports of systematic raids against civilian populations, including burning and looting of villages, large-scale killings and abductions. Humanitarian agencies had also been targeted, with their staff being abducted and relief trucks looted. He announced on 10 February [AFR/830-IHA/861] that Sudan's President, Omer Hassan Ahmed Al Bashir, had promised to allow aid workers access to the nearly 3 million suffering civilians in Darfur, who were still without essential aid. UN agencies estimated that they had been able to reach only 15 per cent of those in need. Some 110,000 had also fled to Chad in the past three months, in addition to the 700,000 displaced.

N'Djamena Humanitarian Ceasefire Agreement and follow-up

On 31 March, during ceasefire talks on Darfur held in N'Djamena, Chad, the Secretary-General issued a statement [SG/SM/9238-AFR/877] expressing dismay over the casualties and serious human rights violations in Darfur. He welcomed the efforts of President Idriss Derby of Chad, the Government of the Sudan, the parties to the conflict and the international community to achieve a cessation of hostilities and ultimately a long-term solution to the conflict. He said that the fighting had to stop and encouraged the parties to work towards an effective humanitarian ceasefire, which would provide unimpeded access to all those in need.

The Security Council President, in a 2 April press statement [SC/8050-AFR/883], said that Council members welcomed the ongoing negotiations in N'Djamena, with the support of the United Nations, the EU and the United States, and called on the Government of the Sudan and opposition groups to conclude a humanitarian ceasefire and to reach a political settlement to the dispute.

On 8 April [SG/SM/9250-AFR/898], the Government of the Sudan, SPLM/A and JEM signed the N'Djamena Humanitarian Ceasefire Agreement. Welcoming that development, the Secretary-General expressed the hope that it would result in an immediate cessation of hostilities and an end to attacks against civilians, as well as full humanitarian access to all people in need of assistance and protection.

The EU, in a 15 April statement of its Presidency [S/2004/337] welcoming the agreement, called on all parties to scrupulously observe and respect its rules, and on the Sudanese Government to fulfil its commitment to control the Janjaweed forces.

On 25 May [S/2004/425], the Sudan informed the Security Council President that, as of 24 May, it would grant entry visas to all humanitarian workers within 48 hours, suspend travel permit procedures to Darfur, and facilitate the entry and clearance of equipment to be used for humanitarian purposes. The Government had appealed to the AU for the expeditious deployment of ceasefire observers, and to the population to return to their villages, with a reaffirmation of its commitment to provide them security and protection.

The EU, on 26 May [S/2004/445], welcomed the Sudan's decision to lift restrictions on humanitarian agency workers travelling to Darfur. It called on the Government to condemn the actions of the Janjaweed militias in Darfur and to bring them under control. It welcomed the establishment by the Government of a Commission of Inquiry to investigate human rights violations by armed groups in Darfur and expected swift action to be taken on its findings. The EU supported the work of the AU to establish a ceasefire commission and monitoring mechanism for the Darfur region.

Meanwhile, the Office of the United Nations High Commissioner for Human Rights (OHCHR) sent two missions (5-15 April and 21 April–2 May) to the region in response to reports of alleged human rights violations. In its 7 May report to the Commission on Human Rights [E/CN.4/ 2005/3] (see p. 803), OHCHR recommended, among other things, the establishment of an international commission of inquiry.

SECURITY COUNCIL ACTION (May)

On 25 May [meeting 4978], following consultations among Security Council members, the President made statement **S/PRST/2004/18** on behalf of the Council:

The Security Council expresses its grave concern over the deteriorating humanitarian and human rights situation in the Darfur region of the Sudan. Noting that thousands have been killed and that hundreds of thousands of people are at risk of dying in the coming months, the Council emphasizes the need for immediate humanitarian access to the vulnerable population.

The Council also expresses its deep concern at the continuing reports of large-scale violations of human rights and of international humanitarian law in Darfur, including indiscriminate attacks on civilians, sexual violence, forced displacement and acts of violence, especially those with an ethnic dimension, and demands that those responsible be held accountable. The Council strongly condemns these acts which jeopardize a peaceful solution of the crisis, stresses that all parties to the N'Djamena humanitarian ceasefire agreement have committed themselves to refraining from any act of violence or any other abuse against civilian populations, in particular women and children, and that the Government of the Sudan has also committed itself to neutralizing the armed Janjaweed militias, and urges all parties to take the necessary steps to put an end to violations of human rights and international humanitarian law. In this regard, the Council takes note of the recommendations of the United Nations High Commissioner for Human Rights in his report of 7 May 2004.

The Council reiterates its call upon the parties to ensure the protection of civilians and to facilitate humanitarian access to the affected population. In that regard, the Council emphasizes the need for the Government of the Sudan to facilitate the voluntary and safe return of refugees and displaced persons to their homes, and to provide protection for them, and also calls upon all parties, including opposition groups, to support these objectives. The Council calls upon all parties, in accordance with the provisions of its resolution 1502 (2003) of 26 August 2003, to allow full unimpeded access by humanitarian personnel to all people in need of assistance, and to make available, as far as possible, all necessary facilities for their operations, and to promote the safety, security and freedom of movement of humanitarian personnel and their assets.

The Council, while welcoming the ceasefire agreement signed on 8 April 2004 in N'Djamena emphasizes the urgent need for all parties to observe the ceasefire and to take immediate measures to end the violence, and calls upon the Government of the Sudan to respect its commitments to ensure that the Janjaweed militias are neutralized and disarmed. Stressing that a ceasefire commission with international representation is a central component of the 8 April agreement, the Council expresses its full and active support for the efforts of the African Union to establish the ceasefire commission and protection units, and calls upon the opposition groups and the Government of the Sudan to facilitate the immediate deployment of monitors in Darfur and to ensure their free movement throughout Darfur. The Council also calls upon Member States to provide generous support for the efforts of the African Union.

The Council welcomes the announcement by the Government of the Sudan that it will issue visas to all humanitarian workers within 48 hours of application, eliminate the need for travel permits, and facilitate the entrance and clearance of equipment imported for humanitarian purposes. The Council acknowledges the appointment of a fact-finding commission by presidential decree. The Council, however, is seriously concerned about continued logistical impediments prohibiting a rapid response in the face of a stark and mounting crisis and calls upon the Government to fulfil its announced commitment to cooperate fully and expeditiously with humanitarian efforts to provide assistance to the imperiled populations of Darfur, noting with particular concern that the humanitarian challenge will be aggravated by the imminent onset of the rainy season.

The Council calls upon the international community to respond rapidly and effectively to the consolidated appeal for Darfur.

The Council observes with distress the prolonged absence of an accredited Resident Coordinator/ Humanitarian Coordinator and affirms the need for the immediate appointment and appropriate accreditation of a permanent Resident Coordinator/ Humanitarian Coordinator to ensure daily coordination in order to address impediments to humanitarian access brought to the attention of the United Nations by the international aid community.

The Council encourages the parties to step up their efforts to reach a political settlement to their dispute in the interest of the unity and sovereignty of the Sudan.

The Council requests that the Secretary-General keep it informed of the humanitarian and human rights crisis as it unfolds, and, as necessary, to make recommendations.

Developments in Sudan's peace process

Naivasha protocols

After months of negotiations, the Government of the Sudan and SPLM/A reached agreement on the remaining three protocols on power-sharing;

the areas of the Nuba Mountains (Southern Kordofan) and Blue Nile; and Abyei, the Secretary-General reported [S/2004/453]. They completed a series of six agreements, concluded over two years since the signature of the first protocol in Machakos, Kenya, in July 2002, followed by protocols on security arrangements in September 2003 [YUN 2003, p. 257], and on wealth-sharing in January 2004.

In a 26 May statement [SG/SM/9332-AFR/946], the Secretary-General said that he had been following the peace talks on the Sudan, facilitated by the Inter-Governmental Authority on Development (IGAD), and had been in touch with Sudan's President, Hassan Al-Bashir, and the Chairman of SPLM/A, John Garang. He was heartened to learn that the parties had initialled the three protocols, in Naivasha, Kenya, and urged them to reach agreement on the remaining issues, especially the ceasefire arrangements, the implementation modalities and international guarantees for a future comprehensive peace agreement. He also called on the Government and the armed opposition in Darfur to seize the momentum created in Naivasha to reach a political solution in western Sudan.

The EU, on 2 June [S/2004/466], welcomed the signing of the three protocols as a significant step towards lasting peace in southern Sudan, and urged the parties to sustain the momentum towards peace and to begin a discussion on a comprehensive peace agreement. At the same time, it reiterated its concern at the humanitarian crisis unfolding in Darfur and called on the Government and all parties to show a similar commitment to bring peace and stability to that region.

Nairobi Declaration. On 5 June [S/2004/490], the Government and SPLM/A signed in Nairobi, Kenya, a Declaration confirming their agreement on the six peace protocols. By that Declaration, the Government and SPLM/A recommitted themselves to their obligations contained in the six protocols agreed to since the relaunching of the IGAD peace process in Machakos in July 2002 [YUN 2002, p. 217], the Secretary-General said in a later report on the Sudan [S/2004/763]. They also committed themselves to completing the final stages of peace negotiations and appealed to the international community to support them during the implementation period.

UN peace support

Report of Secretary-General (June). On 3 June [S/2004/453], the Secretary-General reported on the situation in the Sudan, in response to Security Council presidential statement S/PRST/2003/16 [YUN 2003, p. 257], which had requested him to initiate preparatory work on the nature of UN support for the implementation of a comprehensive peace agreement between the Government and SPLM/A.

The Secretary-General declared that, by completing a series of framework protocols, the Government of the Sudan and SPLM/A were poised to put an end to the long war that had defied attempts by various external actors, including neighbouring States, donors and other States, and by the parties themselves to bring it to an end. It was up to the parties to conclude negotiations and sign a comprehensive peace agreement. Certain that the international community and the UN operation would face difficult times in assisting and working with the parties through the interim periods of peace implementation, the Secretary-General had established an Interdepartmental Task Force (ITF) on the Sudan to develop a common UN strategy to support implementation of the final agreement and had sent an assessment mission to the Sudan and Kenya from 27 November to 16 December 2003. Since April 2004, a group of UN technical experts had been in the Sudan working with the country team to develop further a common logistics and support strategy for the peace implementation phase. That team would be augmented immediately with additional support staff and subsumed into a UN advance team, which the Secretary-General would propose to the Council for approval. The advance team would ensure cohesive preparations for the Organization's role in post-conflict Sudan and establish contacts and working relationships with the parties on the ground; it would include up to 25 military liaison officers and support elements. The advance team would be subsequently absorbed into a full mission should the Council so decide.

The Secretary-General believed that the Sudan was at a historic juncture that represented the best chance to bring to a close one of Africa's most intractable wars. As the Government and SPLM/A were pledging themselves to peace, however, fighting continued to rage in parts of the country. Noting that the situation in Darfur would make a Sudanese peace agreement much harder to implement, he called on the Government and SPLM/A to use their influence to bring a halt to the fighting, since a meaningful agreement on Darfur was fundamental to the success of a UN role in the Sudan. The Secretary-General urged the parties to that conflict to conclude a political agreement without delay. He recommended that the Council support the creation of an advance team for an initial period of three months.

On 11 June [meeting 4988], the Security Council unanimously adopted **resolution 1547(2004)**. The draft [S/2004/473] was prepared in consultations among Council members.

The Security Council,

Welcoming the signing of the declaration on 5 June 2004 in Nairobi, in which the parties confirmed their agreement to the six protocols signed between the Government of the Sudan and the Sudan People's Liberation Movement/Army and reconfirmed their commitment to completing the remaining stages of negotiations,

Commending the work and continued support of the Intergovernmental Authority on Development, in particular, the Government of Kenya as Chair of the Subcommittee on the Sudan, in facilitating the peace talks, and recognizing the efforts of the Civilian Protection Monitoring Team, the Joint Military Commission in the Nuba Mountains and the Verification and Monitoring Team in support of the peace process, and expressing the hope that the Intergovernmental Authority will continue to play a vital role during the transitional period,

Reaffirming its support for the Machakos Protocol of 20 July 2002 and subsequent agreements based on that Protocol,

Reaffirming its commitment to the sovereignty, independence and unity of the Sudan,

Recalling the statements by its President of 10 October 2003 and 25 May 2004,

Condemning all acts of violence and violations of human rights and international humanitarian law by all parties, and expressing its utmost concern at the consequences of the prolonged conflict for the civilian population of the Sudan, including women, children, refugees and internally displaced persons,

Urging the two parties involved to conclude speedily a comprehensive peace agreement, and believing that the progress now being made in the Naivasha negotiation process will contribute to improved stability and peace in the Sudan,

Welcoming the report of the Secretary-General of 3 June 2004,

1. *Welcomes* the proposal of the Secretary-General to establish, for an initial period of three months and under the authority of a special representative of the Secretary-General, a United Nations advance team in the Sudan as a special political mission dedicated to preparation for the international monitoring foreseen in the Framework Agreement on Security Arrangements during the Interim Period, signed in Naivasha, Kenya, on 25 September 2003, to facilitate contacts with the parties concerned and to prepare for the introduction of a peace support operation following the signing of a comprehensive peace agreement;

2. *Endorses* the proposals of the Secretary-General for the staffing of the advance team, and in this regard requests the Secretary-General to conclude all necessary agreements with the Government of the Sudan as expeditiously as possible;

3. *Declares its readiness* to consider establishing a United Nations peace support operation to support the implementation of a comprehensive peace agreement, and requests the Secretary-General to submit to the Council his recommendations for the size, structure and mandate of this operation as soon as possible after the signing of a comprehensive peace agreement;

4. *Requests* the Secretary-General, pending the signing of a comprehensive peace agreement, to take the necessary preparatory steps, including, in particular, pre-positioning the most critical logistical and personnel requirements to facilitate the rapid deployment of the above-mentioned possible operation, principally to assist the parties in monitoring and verifying compliance with the terms of a comprehensive peace agreement as well as to prepare for the role of the Organization during the transitional period in the Sudan;

5. *Underlines* the need for an effective public information capacity, including through local and national radio, television and newspaper channels, in order to promote an understanding of the peace process and the role a United Nations peace support operation will play among local communities and the parties;

6. *Endorses* the conclusions of the Secretary-General with regard to the situation in the Sudan, in particular in Darfur and the Upper Nile, as set out in paragraph 22 of his report, calls upon the parties to use their influence to bring an immediate halt to the fighting in the Darfur region, in the Upper Nile and elsewhere, urges the parties to the ceasefire agreement signed in N'Djamena on 8 April 2004 to conclude a political agreement without delay, welcomes the efforts of the African Union to that end, and calls upon the international community to be prepared for constant engagement, including extensive funding in support of peace in the Sudan;

7. *Requests* the Secretary-General to keep it informed of developments in the Sudan, particularly on the Naivasha negotiation process, the implementation of the peace process and the execution by the advance team of its mandate, and to submit a report to the Council no later than three months after the adoption of the present resolution;

8. *Decides* to remain seized of the matter.

The Sudan, in an 11 June letter [S/2004/490], transmitted to the Council a statement, which its Permanent Representative to the United Nations was not allowed to deliver during the Council's consideration on that date of the draft resolution on the Sudan. In a 17 June reply [S/2004/498], the Council President recalled his discussions with the Sudan on the issue of its desire to address the Council and proposed convening a meeting to allow the Sudan to fully express its views on matters of common interest between it and the Council.

Appointment. On 17 June [S/2004/503], the Secretary-General informed the Council that he would appoint Jan Pronk (Netherlands) as his Special Representative for the Sudan and head of the peace support operation, which might be authorized by the Council at the conclusion of the Comprehensive Peace Agreement between the Sudan and SPLM/A. The Council, on 18 June [S/2004/504], took note of his intention.

Security Council action. On 30 July, the Council, in resolution 1556(2004) (see p. 240) extended the special political mission set out in the foregoing resolution for an additional 90 days, to 10 December, and requested the Secretary-General to incorporate into the mission contingency planning for Darfur.

Further developments in the Darfur situation

Sudan's emergency measures. The Sudan informed the Security Council of the measures decreed by President Al-Bashir on 18 June [S/2004/513] to alleviate the situation in Darfur. They included the declaration of a general mobilization of the State apparatuses, with a view to consolidating security, pursuing and disarming outlawed groups, including the Janjaweed, Tora Bora and Peshmerga, and bringing them to justice, and stopping groups from crossing the borders and threatening the stability of neighbouring Chad; establishment by the judiciary in Darfur of special courts to prosecute bandits and criminals; the deployment of police forces to protect municipalities so that citizens could return to their villages; and provision of basic services and humanitarian assistance. The Sudan called on all citizens, including those in Darfur, to attend a conference that would promote national dialogue to bring about national reconciliation.

UN/Sudan 3 July agreement. The Secretary-General visited the Sudan and Chad from 29 June to 3 July, meeting with his senior advisers, Sudanese Cabinet ministers, and United States Secretary of State Colin Powell, in Khartoum; he later visited a number of camps for internally displaced persons in Darfur [SG/T/2412]. On 3 July [S/2004/635], at the conclusion of the visit, the Government of the Sudan and the United Nations issued a joint communiqué in which they expressed concern about the grave situation in the Darfur region, and the number and severity of the conditions of the internally displaced in Darfur and refugees in Chad. They were aware of the need to stop the attacks on the targeted civilian population in Darfur, particularly by the Janjaweed and other outlaw armed groups, and to ensure security in the region consistent with the N'Djamena Humanitarian Ceasefire Agreement (see p. 235).

The United Nations pledged to help alleviate the humanitarian needs of the affected population in Darfur and Sudanese refugees in Chad, to assist in the quick deployment of AU ceasefire monitors and to continue preparations for a possible peacekeeping role when agreements were reached.

The Sudan committed itself to taking a number of measures to halt restrictions on humanitarian work in Darfur, to end impunity for human rights abuses, investigate all cases of violations and to bring those accused to justice without delay. It pledged to deploy a strong police force and ensure that no militias were present in all areas surrounding the camps of displaced persons. It would immediately start disarming the Janjaweed and other armed outlaw groups. Finally, it would resume political talks on Darfur to reach a comprehensive solution acceptable to all parties.

The Government and the United Nations agreed to form a high-level Joint Implementation Mechanism, led by the Foreign Minister of the Sudan and the Special Representative of the Secretary-General, to follow and appraise developments and report on the implementation of their agreement.

AU and LAS meetings. The AU Peace and Security Council, in a communiqué issued at its twelfth meeting at ministerial level (Addis Ababa, 4 July) [S/2004/561], noted that, although the crisis in Darfur was grave, the situation could not be defined as genocide but should be addressed with urgency to avoid further escalation. It urged the Sudan to follow through on the commitments made on 3 July (above), and that all parties refrain from any further actions that could constitute violations of all the agreements signed so far. It stressed that the AU should continue to lead efforts to address the crisis in Darfur, supported by the international community. It welcomed the establishment of the Ceasefire Commission (CFC) in Al Fasher on 9 June, and the partial deployment of AU military observers in the Darfur region, and urged CFC to expedite the process, including the deployment of protection elements within the framework of the 28 May Agreement on the Establishment of the CFC and Deployment of Observers. The Council also welcomed the convening of the first meeting (N'Djamena, 2 July) of the Joint Commission provided for in the Humanitarian Ceasefire Agreement, and urged the Sudanese parties to participate in the meeting scheduled for 15 July to discuss political issues, with a view to reaching a comprehensive agreement. It expressed concern over the impact of the Darfur conflict on the stability of Chad and the rest of the region, and encouraged the Sudan and Chad to enhance security along their common border.

The third ordinary session of the AU Assembly of heads of State and Government (Addis Ababa, 6-8 July), in a decision on Darfur, decided to increase the number of AU observers to a minimum of 80 and to deploy the protection force immediately. It agreed that, under AU monitoring, the rebel forces should be cantoned at mutually agreed sites and the militias disarmed by the Sudanese Government. It further agreed that the political dialogue should resume as scheduled on 15 July, with a view to reaching a political agreement that would create conditions for convening an all-party conference as provided for in the N'Djamena Humanitarian Ceasefire Agreement, with the participation of the rebel movements. The Assembly acknowledged the agreement signed between the Sudan and the United Nations, which it described as consistent with the AU peace efforts.

At its thirteenth meeting (Addis Ababa, 27 July) [S/2004/603], the AU Peace and Security Council underlined the need to implement the AU Assembly decision on Darfur (see p. 239), which provided a framework for addressing the crisis. The Council welcomed the meeting of the parties (Addis Ababa, 15 July) but regretted the failure of SPLM/A and JEM leadership to attend. It called on the parties to be represented at the highest level at the next round of political talks aimed at finding a lasting solution to the Darfur conflict. The Council took note of the progress in deploying military observers and the protection force, and requested the CFC chairperson to prepare a comprehensive plan for enhancing the effectiveness of the AU Mission, including the possibility of transforming it into a full-fledged peacekeeping mission with the requisite mandate and size to ensure implementation of the Humanitarian Ceasefire Agreement, with emphasis on the disarmament of the Janjaweed, the protection of the civilian population and the facilitation of delivery of humanitarian aid.

On 8 August [S/2004/674], the Ministerial Council of the League of Arab States, at its extraordinary session, called on the Security Council to allow the Sudanese Government sufficient time to implement the undertakings and commitments contained in the joint communique signed with the United Nations and the 5 August Darfur Plan of Action (see p. 242) issued by its Foreign Minister and the Secretary-General's Special Representative. It rejected any suggestion of coercive military intervention in the region or the imposition of sanction on the Sudan and offered support for the return of emigrants and refugees and full Arab support to the AU in its efforts to resolve the crisis in Darfur.

SECURITY COUNCIL ACTION (July)

On 30 July [meeting 5015], the Security Council adopted **resolution 1556(2004)** by vote (13-0-2). The draft [S/2004/611] was submitted by Chile, France, Germany, Romania, Spain, the United Kingdom and the United States.

The Security Council,

Recalling the statement by its President of 25 May 2004, its resolution 1547(2004) of 11 June 2004 and its resolution 1502(2003) of 26 August 2003 on the access of humanitarian workers to populations in need,

Welcoming the leadership role and the engagement of the African Union regarding the situation in Darfur, and expressing its readiness to support fully those efforts,

Welcoming also the communiqué dated 27 July 2004, issued by the Peace and Security Council of the African Union,

Reaffirming its commitment to the sovereignty, unity, territorial integrity and independence of the Sudan as consistent with the Machakos Protocol of 20 July 2002 and subsequent agreements based thereon, as agreed to by the Government of the Sudan,

Welcoming the joint communiqué dated 3 July 2004, issued by the Government of the Sudan and the Secretary-General, including the creation of the Joint Implementation Mechanism, and acknowledging steps taken towards improved humanitarian access,

Taking note of the report of the Secretary-General of 3 June 2004 on the Sudan, and welcoming the appointment by the Secretary-General of a Special Representative for the Sudan and his efforts to date,

Reiterating its grave concern at the ongoing humanitarian crisis and widespread human rights violations, including continued attacks on civilians, that are placing the lives of hundreds of thousands at risk,

Condemning all acts of violence and violations of human rights and international humanitarian law by all parties to the crisis, in particular by the Janjaweed militias, including indiscriminate attacks on civilians, rapes, forced displacements and acts of violence, especially those with an ethnic dimension, and expressing its utmost concern at the consequences of the conflict in Darfur on the civilian population, including women, children, internally displaced persons, and refugees,

Recalling, in this regard, that the Government of the Sudan bears the primary responsibility to respect human rights while maintaining law and order and protecting its population within its territory and that all parties are obliged to respect international humanitarian law,

Urging all parties to take the necessary steps to prevent and to put an end to violations of human rights and international humanitarian law, and underlining the fact that there will be no impunity for violators,

Welcoming the commitment of the Government of the Sudan to investigate the atrocities and prosecute those responsible,

Emphasizing the commitment of the Government of the Sudan to mobilize the armed forces of the Sudan immediately to disarm the Janjaweed militias,

Recalling in this regard its resolutions 1325(2000) of 31 October 2000 on women and peace and security, 1379(2001) of 20 November 2001, 1460(2003) of 30 January 2003 and 1539(2004) of 22 April 2004 on children and armed conflict, and 1265(1999) of 17 September 1999 and 1296(2000) of 19 April 2000 on the protection of civilians in armed conflict,

Expressing concern at reports of violations of the ceasefire agreement signed in N'Djamena on 8 April

2004, and reiterating that all parties to the ceasefire must comply with all of the terms contained therein,

Welcoming the donor consultation held in Geneva in June 2004 as well as subsequent briefings highlighting urgent humanitarian needs in the Sudan and Chad, and reminding donors of the need to fulfil commitments that have been made,

Recalling that over one million people are in need of urgent humanitarian assistance, that with the onset of the rainy season the provision of assistance has become increasingly difficult, and that without urgent action to address the security, access, logistics, capacity and funding requirements the lives of hundreds of thousands of people will be at risk,

Expressing its determination to do everything possible to halt a humanitarian catastrophe, including by taking further action if required,

Welcoming the ongoing international diplomatic efforts to address the situation in Darfur,

Stressing that any return of refugees and displaced persons to their homes must take place voluntarily, with adequate assistance and with sufficient security,

Noting with grave concern that up to 200,000 refugees have fled to the neighbouring State of Chad, which constitutes a serious burden upon that country, expressing grave concern at reported cross-border incursions by Janjaweed militias of the Darfur region of the Sudan into Chad, and also taking note of the agreement between the Governments of the Sudan and Chad to establish a joint mechanism to secure the borders,

Determining that the situation in the Sudan constitutes a threat to international peace and security and to stability in the region,

Acting under Chapter VII of the Charter of the United Nations,

1. *Calls upon* the Government of the Sudan to fulfil immediately all of the commitments it made in the joint communiqué of 3 July 2004, including particularly by facilitating international relief for the humanitarian disaster by means of a moratorium on all restrictions that might hinder the provision of humanitarian assistance and access to the affected populations, by advancing independent investigation in cooperation with the United Nations of violations of human rights and international humanitarian law, by the establishment of credible security conditions for the protection of the civilian population and humanitarian actors, and by the resumption of political talks with dissident groups from the Darfur region, specifically the Justice and Equality Movement and the Sudan Liberation Movement and Sudan Liberation Army on Darfur;

2. *Endorses* the deployment of international monitors, including the protection force envisioned by the African Union, to the Darfur region of the Sudan, under the leadership of the African Union, urges the international community to continue to support those efforts, welcomes the progress made in deploying monitors, including the offers to provide forces by members of the African Union, and stresses the need for the Government of the Sudan and all involved parties to facilitate the work of the monitors in accordance with the N'Djamena ceasefire agreement of 8 April 2004 and with the Addis Ababa agreement of 28 May 2004 on the modalities of establishing an observer mission to monitor the ceasefire;

3. *Urges* Member States to reinforce the international monitoring team, led by the African Union, including the protection force, by providing personnel and other assistance including financing, supplies, transport, vehicles, command support, communications and headquarters support as needed for the monitoring operation, and welcomes the contributions already made by the European Union and the United States to support the African Union-led operation;

4. *Welcomes* the work done by the United Nations High Commissioner for Human Rights to send human rights observers to the Sudan, and calls upon the Government of the Sudan to cooperate with the High Commissioner in the deployment of those observers;

5. *Urges* the parties to the N'Djamena ceasefire agreement to conclude a political agreement without delay, notes with regret that the failure of senior rebel leaders to participate in the talks held on 15 July 2004 in Addis Ababa, was unhelpful to the process, and calls for renewed talks under the sponsorship of the African Union, and its chief mediator, Mr. Hamid Algabid, to reach a political solution to the tensions in Darfur, and strongly urges rebel groups to respect the ceasefire, end the violence immediately, engage in peace talks without preconditions, and act in a positive and constructive manner to resolve the conflict;

6. *Demands* that the Government of the Sudan fulfil its commitments to disarm the Janjaweed militias and apprehend and bring to justice Janjaweed leaders and their associates who have incited and carried out human rights and international humanitarian law violations and other atrocities, requests the Secretary-General to report in thirty days, and monthly thereafter, to the Council on the progress, or lack thereof, by the Government of the Sudan on this matter, and expresses its intention to consider further actions, including measures as provided for in Article 41 of the Charter of the United Nations, on the Government of the Sudan, in the event of non-compliance;

7. *Decides* that all States shall take the necessary measures to prevent the sale or supply to all non-governmental entities and individuals, including the Janjaweed militias, operating in the states of North Darfur, South Darfur and West Darfur, by their nationals or from their territories or using their flag vessels or aircraft, of arms and related materiel of all types, including weapons and ammunition, military vehicles and equipment, paramilitary equipment, and spare parts for the aforementioned, whether or not originating in their territories;

8. *Decides also* that all States shall take the necessary measures to prevent any provision to the non-governmental entities and individuals identified in paragraph 7 above operating in the states of North Darfur, South Darfur and West Darfur, by their nationals or from their territories, of technical training or assistance related to the provision, manufacture, maintenance or use of the items listed in paragraph 7 above;

9. *Decides further* that the measures imposed by paragraphs 7 and 8 above shall not apply to:

(a) Supplies and related technical training and assistance to monitoring, verification or peace support operations, including such operations led by regional organizations, that are authorized by the United

Nations or are operating with the consent of the relevant parties;

(b) Supplies of non-lethal military equipment intended solely for humanitarian, human rights monitoring or protective use, and related technical training and assistance;

(c) Supplies of protective clothing, including flak jackets and military helmets, for the personal use of United Nations personnel, human rights monitors, representatives of the media and humanitarian and development workers and associated personnel;

10. *Expresses its intention* to consider the modification or termination of the measures imposed under paragraphs 7 and 8 above when it determines that the Government of the Sudan has fulfilled its commitments described in paragraph 6 above;

11. *Reiterates its support* for the Framework Agreement on Security Arrangements during the Interim Period, signed in Naivasha, Kenya on 25 September 2003 by the Government of the Sudan and the Sudan People's Liberation Movement/Army, and looks forward to effective implementation of the Agreement and a peaceful, unified Sudan working in harmony with all other States for the development of the Sudan, and calls upon the international community to be prepared for constant engagement, including necessary funding, in support of peace and economic development in the Sudan;

12. *Urges* the international community to make available much needed assistance to mitigate the humanitarian catastrophe now unfolding in the Darfur region, calls upon Member States to honour pledges that have been made against needs in Darfur and Chad, and underscores the need to contribute generously towards fulfilling the unmet portion of the United Nations consolidated appeals;

13. *Requests* the Secretary-General to activate interagency humanitarian mechanisms to consider what additional measures may be needed to avoid a humanitarian catastrophe and to report regularly to the Council on progress made;

14. *Encourages* the Special Representative of the Secretary-General for the Sudan and the independent expert of the Commission on Human Rights to work closely with the Government of the Sudan in supporting independent investigations of violations of human rights and international humanitarian law in the Darfur region;

15. *Extends* the special political mission set out in resolution 1547(2004) for an additional ninety days, to 10 December 2004, and requests the Secretary-General to incorporate into the mission contingency planning for the Darfur region;

16. *Expresses its full support* for the African Union-led ceasefire commission and monitoring mission in Darfur, requests the Secretary-General to assist the African Union with planning and assessments for its mission in Darfur and, in accordance with the joint communiqué, to prepare to support the implementation of a future agreement in Darfur in close cooperation with the African Union, and also requests the Secretary-General to report to the Security Council on the progress made;

17. *Decides* to remain seized of the matter.

RECORDED VOTE ON RESOLUTION 1556(2004):

In favour: Algeria, Angola, Benin, Brazil, Chile, France, Germany, Philippines, Romania, Russian Federation, Spain, United Kingdom, United States.
Against: None.
Abstaining: China, Pakistan.

China, speaking before the vote, said that the Government of the Sudan bore primary responsibility for resolving the Darfur situation and should be assisted by the international community in that effort. The Council should listen to the AU, and its actions should be conducive to securing the cooperation of the Sudanese Government. The draft resolution included mandatory measures against the Government, which could not be helpful in resolving the situation and might even complicate it.

After the vote, the United States said that responsibility for the disaster lay squarely with the Government of the Sudan. The resolution, in stern and unambiguous terms, put the Government on notice that it had to fulfil its commitments in the 3 July UN/Sudan communiqué (see p. 239). It should know that serious measures (international sanctions) were looming if it refused to do so. The purpose of the resolution was to relieve the suffering in Darfur, not to punish the Sudan. The choice was up to the Government.

Pakistan did not believe that the threat or imposition of sanctions was advisable and trusted that the Council would not take such further measures. Pakistan looked forward to the Secretary-General's report to be issued in 30 days, which it hoped would confirm that the Sudanese Government and the rebel groups were complying with their commitments and obligations.

On the same day [S/2004/639], the EU, expressing support for resolution 1556(2004), supported the call on the Sudan to fulfil all the commitments it made on 3 July and reiterated its determination to continue to play an active role in the situation by sending an assessment team to the region to recommend how best to further support the AU Observer Mission, including the protection force.

Implementation of resolution 1556(2004)

Darfur Plan of Action. The Foreign Minister of the Sudan, Mustafa Osman Ismail, acting on behalf of his Government, and Jan Pronk, Special Representative of the Secretary-General, signed on 5 August the Darfur Plan of Action [S/2004/636]. Drawn up following discussions at the second meeting of the Joint Implementation Mechanism (2 August), the Plan's objective was to create conditions for the restoration of peace, security and development in Darfur. To that end, the Sudan committed itself to indicating its progress in complying with Security Council resolution 1556(2004) (see p. 240) by the original deadline of 30 August, and with its 3 July commitments.

According to the Plan, the Sudan would identify parts of Darfur that could be made secure and safe within 30 days and its police forces would provide secure routes to and between those areas. All offensive military operations by the Government's armed forces in those areas would cease immediately, including any offensive actions against rebel groups. The armed forces would be redeployed so that they were not in contact with the camps and civilians. In accordance with the ceasefire agreement, the Government would ask the rebel groups participating in the Darfur peace talks immediately to cease offensive military operations in the proposed safe areas and to lay down their weapons as part of a disarmament, demobilization and reintegration programme. The Government would identify and declare those militias over whom it had influence and instruct them to cease their activities and lay down their weapons. Observance of those commitments would be monitored by the Ceasefire Commission. The Government would make a declaration of commitment to start the Darfur peace talks as soon as possible in a venue proposed by the AU, and it expected the Council and the AU to pressure the rebels to do likewise. It would seek financial and logistic support from the AU, the League of Arab States and other partners. The Government would sign an agreement with the International Organization for Migration to oversee and assist in the voluntary return of internally displaced persons to their homes, and confirmed its policy of no involuntary return. It would hold a conference of local leaders to seek their help in building confidence and contributing to security, administration and in resolving disputes, and start talks with community leaders and others to establish a commission for rehabilitation, recovery, development and reconciliation in Darfur. With the support of the international community, the Government would improve the humanitarian situation in Darfur, including by extending the fast-track procedure for access until July 2005.

Communications. The Sudan, responding on 17 August [S/2004/671] to resolution 1556(2004), said that it was proceeding with the implementation of the resolution's provisions on humanitarian assistance, disarmament, security and protection of human rights, and a political settlement. Specifically, it had taken measures to disarm the militias, but warned of the enormity of the task, saying that the entire process depended on a comprehensive settlement. It had also mobilized all its resources to provide security for the voluntary return of emigrants to their villages and to provide for their humanitarian needs in those villages. It had responded to the AU's call for negotiations with the rebels in Abuja, Nigeria, on 23 August. Commenting on resolution 1556(2004), the Sudan drew attention to: the challenge of the severe shortage of humanitarian assistance supplies; its position that the rebel movements bore responsibility for the deteriorating situation in Darfur and its hope that the Council would exert pressure on them to put a stop to their activities in the emigrant and refugee camps; the need for the Council to affirm unconditionally its respect for the Sudan's sovereignty, unity, territorial integrity and independence; the targeting of the Sudan's police and civilian security agencies and the urgency for the international community to pressure the rebels to respect the ceasefire; and Eritrea's role in undermining stability in the region. The Sudan affirmed its willingness to cooperate with the United Nations and the international community in addressing the humanitarian situation and its desire to achieve a political settlement of the Darfur conflict.

On 31 August [S/2004/701], the Sudan forwarded to the Council a list of measures it had taken to comply with the Darfur Plan of Action and with resolution 1556(2004) in the areas of relief assistance, health services, human rights, security, reining in the militias, the voluntary repatriation of internally displaced persons, political negotiations and participation in them of tribal leaders from Darfur, and the presence of AU monitors in the Sudan.

Report of Secretary-General (August). In response to resolution 1556(2004), the Secretary-General, on 30 August [S/2004/703], reported on the Sudan's progress in fulfilling its terms. He stated that the Joint Implementation Mechanism, which had held meetings on 15 July and 2, 12 and 19 August, sent a joint verification mission to Darfur from 26 to 28 July, which concluded that no forced returns had been observed in those areas it visited, and security in camps for internally displaced persons had improved. However, there was a clear need to accelerate implementation of the Government's commitments in other areas. The Government had not taken any measures to disarm the Janjaweed and other armed outlaw groups. It agreed that the Government should lay out a road map indicating actions to be taken within 30 days, covering certain regions and selected militias over which it had influence, on the understanding that those actions should start the disarmament process. The Government could prove its commitment to the international community by achieving substantial and verifiable progress on the ground within the first 30-day reporting period.

With respect to the Darfur Plan of Action (see p. 242), the Secretary-General reported that, on 15 August, the Government announced the selection of the areas that it would make safe and secure by the end of August, including areas in each of the three States of Darfur, with an estimated 375,000 internally displaced persons, or 30 per cent of the total number (about 1,227,000) in Darfur as at 1 August. On 19 August, it presented to the Joint Implementation Mechanism a list of immediate measures it was taking, including the deployment, from 10 to 20 August, of 2,000 additional police and 100 armed vehicles, and protection for villages within a 20-kilometre radius around the major towns identified. The military would be redeployed to administrative headquarters and garrisons to avoid direct contact with civilians. Internal security of the identified areas would be the responsibility of the police.

As required by the Plan, a conference of local leaders was held (Khartoum, 11-12 August) to review draft legislation on the native administration of the three Darfur States. It also discussed social reconciliation and the role of the traditional administration in the disarmament process. All major tribes and interests of both pastoralists and nomads were represented. The Native Administration Law for the Darfur States was adopted on 19 August by presidential order, with provisions on administrative, security, judicial, executive and other issues.

The most critical commitment still to be implemented related to the armed militias who continued to pose a serious threat to the civilian population. Despite various commitments to disarm them, the Government had stated repeatedly that it had no control over the militias accused of attacking civilians and committing other atrocities in Darfur. However, during discussions in the Joint Implementation Mechanism, the Government did accept the UN position that some militias were under its influence and should be identified and instructed to lay down their weapons, and that they were not limited to those previously incorporated into the Popular Defence Forces, but included outside militias that were later linked with those forces.

While the disarming of members of the Popular Defence Forces had begun in several locations, militia activities were reported in all three States of Darfur, with villages wantonly attacked, looted and destroyed and over 50 people killed. The Government provided no evidence that it had identified any militias outside the Popular Defence Forces or had issued instructions to the leaders of militias under its influence to disarm. A comprehensive demobilization, disarmament and reintegration programme was urgently needed, for which the Government should accept international assistance if it was unable to stop the attacks and protect civilians.

The capacity of humanitarian agencies on the ground continued to increase. The United Nations and the Red Cross and Red Crescent missions were already operating in Darfur, and 10 other organizations were about to start operations. The number of displaced persons increased by about 200,000 to more than 1.2 million, and that of host communities and others requiring relief by more than 60,000. Total UN funding requirements in response to the Darfur crisis was estimated at $531 million.

The United Nations collaborated with the AU to produce a comprehensive plan for an expanded AU mission in Darfur (AUMIS), to include logistical support and budgetary requirements and support to the AU in managing and directing a complicated field operation. A UN assessment team also found a need for a substantial civilian police component to assist with monitoring and capacity-building of the national police.

The Secretary-General concluded that, after 18 months of conflict and 30 days after the adoption of resolution 1556(2004), the Government had been unable to resolve the crisis in Darfur and had not met some of its core commitments. However, the search for a political solution was under way in Abuja, through a UN-supported AU mediation effort. The Secretary-General believed that a substantially increased international presence in Darfur was required as quickly as possible to monitor the implementation of the parties' commitments more effectively. The crisis in Darfur could not be seen in isolation from the search for a comprehensive peace in the Sudan. While efforts were being made to find a solution to the Darfur crisis, simultaneous efforts were required promptly to restart and conclude the IGAD-led peace talks (see p. 234). However, any effort to make the conclusion of the IGAD process conditional on an end to the crisis in Darfur would be counter-productive, with consequences that could further destabilize the country and the region.

Security Council consideration. At the Security Council's consideration of the Secretary-General's report, on 2 September [meeting 5027], the Special Representative affirmed that the United Nations had maintained pressure on the Sudanese Government to show progress in improving security, through the framework of the

Joint Implementation Mechanism. The Government had made some progress in that regard in the 30-day initial period but had not met its commitments in two key areas: stopping attacks against civilians by militias and disarming them; and no concrete steps had been taken to bring to justice any of the militia leaders or the perpetrators of the attacks or even to identify them. There was thus distrust among the displaced due to their perception that the Government was behind the terror and trauma they had experienced. The Special Representative, noting that negotiations towards a political solution were under way in Abuja, urged the parties to redouble their efforts and seek assistance from the AU and UN facilitators and mediators. He further urged that the IGAD peace talks be resumed concurrently with those negotiations.

Communication. Australia, Canada and New Zealand, in a joint letter of 10 September [S/2004/739], agreed with the Special Representative that pressure be maintained on the Government of the Sudan to carry out its commitments. They urged the Council to support the AU, including the deployment of a significantly expanded AU mission and to establish clear benchmarks and time lines for actions expected of the Government with regard to disarming the Janjaweed; identifying those groups over which the Government had influence; apprehending and prosecuting those suspected of inciting and carrying out war crimes and crimes against humanity; and continuing to remove barriers to access by humanitarian and human rights monitors. They called on the Secretary-General to establish an impartial commission of experts to investigate allegations of war crimes and crimes against humanity, especially of sexual violence.

SECURITY COUNCIL ACTION (September)

On 18 September [meeting 5040], the Security Council adopted **resolution 1564(2004)** by vote (11-0-4). The draft [S/2004/744] was submitted by Germany, Romania, Spain, the United Kingdom and the United States.

The Security Council,

Recalling its resolution 1556(2004) of 30 July 2004, the statement by its President of 25 May 2004, its resolution 1547(2004) of 11 June 2004 and resolution 1502 (2003) of 26 August 2003, and taking into account the Plan of Action agreed by the Special Representative of the Secretary-General for the Sudan and the Government of the Sudan,

Welcoming the report of the Secretary-General of 30 August 2004 and the progress achieved on humanitarian access, and expressing concern that paragraphs 59 to 67 indicate that the Government of the Sudan has not fulfilled the entirety of its commitments under resolution 1556(2004) and taking into account the need to foster and restore the confidence of vulnerable populations and to improve radically the overall security environment in Darfur; and welcoming the recommendations contained in the report, particularly those concerning the desirability of a substantially increased presence of the African Union mission in the Darfur region of the Sudan,

Welcoming also the leadership role and the engagement of the African Union in addressing the situation in Darfur,

Welcoming further the letter dated 6 September 2004 to the President of the Security Council from the Chairman of the African Union, the President of the Federal Republic of Nigeria, Mr. Olusegun Obasanjo, including his appeal for international support for the extension of the African Union mission in Darfur,

Reaffirming its commitment to the sovereignty, unity, territorial integrity and independence of the Sudan, as consistent with the Machakos Protocol of 20 July 2002 and subsequent agreements based thereon, as agreed to by the Government of the Sudan,

Recalling the joint communiqué of 3 July 2004 issued by the Government of the Sudan and the Secretary-General, and recognizing the efforts undertaken by the Joint Implementation Mechanism and the Special Representative of the Secretary-General to advance the aims of the communiqué and the requirements of resolution 1556(2004),

Welcoming the fact that the Government of the Sudan has taken a number of steps to lift administrative obstructions to the delivery of humanitarian relief, which has resulted in access for an increased number of humanitarian personnel in Darfur, as well as international human rights non-governmental institutions, and recognizing that the Government of the Sudan has broadened its cooperation with United Nations humanitarian agencies and their partners,

Urging the Government of the Sudan and the rebel groups to facilitate this humanitarian relief by allowing unfettered access for humanitarian supplies and workers, including across the borders of the Sudan with Chad and Libya by land and by air as may be required,

Expressing grave concern at the lack of progress with regard to security and the protection of civilians, disarmament of the Janjaweed militias and the identification and bringing to justice of the Janjaweed leaders responsible for violations of human rights and international humanitarian law in Darfur,

Recalling that the Government of the Sudan bears the primary responsibility to protect its population within its territory, to respect human rights and to maintain law and order, and that all parties are obliged to respect international humanitarian law,

Stressing that the Sudanese rebel groups, particularly the Justice and Equality Movement and the Sudan Liberation Movement/Army, must also take all necessary steps to respect international humanitarian and human rights law,

Emphasizing that the ultimate resolution of the crisis in Darfur must include the safe and voluntary return of internally displaced persons and refugees to their original homes, and noting in that regard the memorandum of understanding of 21 August 2004 between the Government of the Sudan and the International Organization for Migration,

Expressing its determination to do everything possible to end the suffering of the people of Darfur,

Determining that the situation in the Sudan constitutes a threat to international peace and security and to stability in the region,

Acting under Chapter VII of the Charter of the United Nations,

1. *Declares its grave concern* that the Government of the Sudan has not fully met its obligations noted in resolution 1556(2004) and the joint communiqué of 3 July 2004 with the Secretary-General to improve, as expected by the Security Council, the security of the civilian population of Darfur in the face of continued depredations, and deplores the recent ceasefire violations by all parties, in particular the reports by the Ceasefire Commission of the Government of the Sudan's helicopter assaults and Janjaweed attacks on Yassin, Hashaba and Gallab villages on 26 August 2004;

2. *Welcomes and supports* the intention of the African Union to enhance and augment its monitoring mission in the Darfur region of the Sudan, and encourages the undertaking of proactive monitoring;

3. *Urges* Member States to support the African Union in these efforts, including by providing all equipment, logistical, financial, material and other resources necessary to support the rapid expansion of the African Union mission and by supporting the efforts of the African Union aimed at a peaceful conclusion of the crisis and the protection of the welfare of the people of Darfur, welcomes the Government of the Sudan's request to the African Union to increase its monitoring presence in Darfur in its letter dated 9 September 2004 to the Council, and urges the Government of the Sudan to take all steps necessary to follow through with this commitment and to cooperate fully with the African Union to ensure a secure and stable environment;

4. *Calls upon* the Government of the Sudan and the rebel groups, particularly the Justice and Equality Movement and the Sudan Liberation Movement/Army, to work together under the auspices of the African Union to reach a political solution in the negotiations currently being held in Abuja under the leadership of President Obasanjo, notes the progress made to date, urges the parties to the negotiations to sign and implement the humanitarian agreement immediately and to conclude a protocol on security issues as soon as possible, and underscores and supports the role of the African Union in monitoring the implementation of all such agreements reached;

5. *Urges* the Government of the Sudan and the Sudan People's Liberation Movement to conclude a comprehensive peace accord expeditiously as a critical step towards the development of a peaceful and prosperous Sudan;

6. *Affirms* that internally displaced persons, refugees and other vulnerable peoples should be allowed to return to their homes voluntarily, in safety and with dignity, and only when adequate assistance and security are in place;

7. *Reiterates its call for* the Government of the Sudan to end the climate of impunity in Darfur by identifying and bringing to justice all those responsible, including members of popular defence forces and Janjaweed militias, for the widespread human rights abuses and violations of international humanitarian law, and insists that the Government of the Sudan take all appropriate steps to stop all violence and atrocities;

8. *Calls upon* all Sudanese parties to take the necessary steps to ensure that violations reported by the Ceasefire Commission are addressed immediately and that those responsible for such violations are held accountable;

9. *Demands* that the Government of the Sudan submit to the African Union mission for verification, documentation, particularly the names of Janjaweed militiamen disarmed and names of those arrested for human rights abuses and violations of international humanitarian law, with regard to its performance relative to resolution 1556(2004) and the N'Djamena ceasefire agreement of 8 April 2004;

10. *Also demands* that all armed groups, including rebel forces, cease all violence, cooperate with international humanitarian relief and monitoring efforts and ensure that their members comply with international humanitarian law, and facilitate the safety and security of humanitarian staff;

11. *Reiterates its full support* for the N'Djamena ceasefire agreement, and in this regard urges the Government of the Sudan to refrain from conducting military flights in and over the Darfur region in accordance with its commitments;

12. *Requests* that the Secretary-General rapidly establish an international commission of inquiry in order immediately to investigate reports of violations of international humanitarian and human rights law in Darfur by all parties, to determine also whether or not acts of genocide have occurred, and to identify the perpetrators of such violations with a view to ensuring that those responsible are held accountable, calls upon all parties to cooperate fully with such a commission, and also requests the Secretary-General, in conjunction with the Office of the United Nations High Commissioner for Human Rights, to take appropriate steps to increase the number of human rights monitors deployed to Darfur;

13. *Calls upon* Member States to provide in an urgent manner generous and sustained contributions to the humanitarian efforts under way in Darfur and Chad to address the shortfall in response to continued United Nations appeals, emphasizes the need for Member States to fulfil their pledges forthwith, and welcomes the substantial contributions made to date;

14. *Declares* that, in the event that the Government of the Sudan fails to comply fully with resolution 1556(2004) or the present resolution, including, as determined by the Council after consultations with the African Union, failure to cooperate fully with the expansion and extension of the African Union monitoring mission in Darfur, the Council shall consider taking additional measures as contemplated in Article 41 of the Charter of the United Nations, such as actions to affect the Sudan's petroleum sector and the Government of the Sudan or individual members of the Government, in order to take effective action to obtain such full compliance or full cooperation;

15. *Requests* that, in the monthly reports pursuant to resolution 1556(2004), the Secretary-General report to the Council on the Government of the Sudan's progress or lack thereof in complying with the Council's demands in the present resolution and the effort by

the Government of the Sudan and the Sudan People's Liberation Movement to conclude a comprehensive peace accord on an urgent basis;

16. *Decides* to remain seized of the matter.

RECORDED VOTE ON RESOLUTION 1564(2004):

In favour: Angola, Benin, Brazil, Chile, France, Germany, Philippines, Romania, Spain, United Kingdom, United States.
Against: None.
Abstaining: Algeria, China, Pakistan, Russian Federation.

The countries which abstained in the vote had expressed opposition beforehand to the Council's use of the threat of sanctions as a means of achieving its objectives. After the vote, the Sudan said that it had honoured its commitments and that the Council knew better than anyone that the problem had its roots in the country's economic and social backwardness; it wondered whether sanctions would help resolve the problem. The adoption of the resolution, it said, had torpedoed all negotiations and undermined the AU's efforts.

Further communications. On 22 September [S/2004/751], the Sudan expressed its belief that resolution 1564(2004) had encouraged the rebels to adopt a position that led to the deadlock in the Abuja negotiations and to violations of the ceasefire agreement, as demonstrated by their attacks on villages on 16 and 18 September.

The EU, on 23 September [S/2004/803], welcomed resolution 1564(2004), including its stated preparedness to consider measures, such as sanctions, should the Sudan fail to comply with previous Council demands.

The AU Peace and Security Council, in a communiqué on the situation in Darfur issued at its sixteenth meeting (Addis Ababa, 17 September) [S/2004/755], welcomed the convening in Abuja, since 23 August, of the inter-Sudanese peace talks, and urged the parties (the Government of the Sudan, JEM, SPLM/A) to comply with the 8 April N'Djamena Humanitarian Ceasefire Agreement, cooperate with the AU, remain committed to the negotiation process and work towards a political settlement.

The EU External Relations Council, on 13 September [S/2004/766], issued conclusions on Darfur indicating the EU's intention to take appropriate measures, including sanctions, against the Government of the Sudan if no tangible progress was made in meeting the Security Council demands in resolution 1556(2004), and to increase its humanitarian support as well as support to the AU mission in the Sudan.

On 27 September, the Sudan informed the Security Council President that Darfur rebels raided the village of Ghibaish, in Western State, on 22 September, thus extending their operations to areas outside Darfur and showing a lack of interest in a political settlement [S/2004/762]; that rebel elements attacked the camp for inter-

nally displaced persons at Kalma, in Southern Darfur State [S/2004/767]; and that rebels continued to refuse to specify their positions as required under the N'Djamena ceasefire agreement [S/2004/769]. It also informed the Council that a conference on the native administrative system and its role in restoring tranquility, security and peace in Darfur (Al Fasher, North Darfur, 18-19 September), attended by community leaders, tribal chieftains, heads of political parties, civil leaders and representatives of Darfur in the National Assembly, issued a final communiqué and an agreement on resolving the Darfur crisis through dialogue among the people of Darfur within the context of one homeland [S/2004/768]. On 28 September [S/2004/772], the Sudan drew attention to four recent ceasefire violations.

UN Advance Mission in Sudan

The United Nations, as requested by the Security Council in resolution 1547(2004), established, in June, a special political mission, the United Nations Advance Mission in the Sudan (UNAMIS), headed by Jan Pronk (Netherlands) Special Representative for the Sudan. He was supported by two Deputy Special Representatives, who were appointed by the Secretary-General, one of whom would function as Resident Coordinator/Humanitarian Coordinator. Also appointed were the mission's Chief Military Adviser and a chief civilian police adviser. The mission was headquartered in Khartoum, with a liaison office in Nairobi. The international staff would include military liaison and political and civil affairs staff, public information officers and experts in logistics and administration. On 5 August, the Government signed an agreement with the United Nations on the status of the mission and its personnel.

UNAMIS financing

The Secretary-General, on 27 October [A/59/534], submitted proposed resource requirements for UNAMIS from 11 September to 10 December 2004, estimated at $21,008,100 net ($21,789,400 gross). That amount included $998,600 remaining unencumbered from the $16,636,600 approved for the initial phase (11 June–10 September) of the mission.

ACABQ, having reviewed the estimates, recommended in its 11 November report [A/59/569] approval of the full amount.

GENERAL ASSEMBLY ACTION

On 3 December [meeting 66], the General Assembly, on the recommendation of the Fifth Committee [A/59/448/Add.1], adopted **resolution 59/58** without vote [agenda item 108].

Estimates in respect of special political missions, good offices and other political initiatives authorized by the General Assembly and/or the Security Council: United Nations advance team in the Sudan

The General Assembly,

Having considered the report of the Secretary-General on the estimates in respect of special political missions, good offices and other political initiatives authorized by the General Assembly and/or the Security Council and the related report of the Advisory Committee on Administrative and Budgetary Questions,

1. *Endorses* the observations and recommendations of the Advisory Committee on Administrative and Budgetary Questions;

2. *Decides* to approve the budget for the United Nations advance team in the Sudan for the period from 11 September to 10 December 2004 in the amount of 21,789,400 United States dollars gross (21,008,100 dollars net);

3. *Notes* that part of the requirements would be met from the unspent balance of 998,600 dollars of the amount already provided for the mission;

4. *Decides* to approve a charge, against the provision for special political missions appropriated under section 3, Political affairs, of the programme budget for the biennium 2004–2005, in the amount of 3,002,600 dollars, corresponding to the unassigned balance in that provision;

5. *Also decides* to appropriate, under the procedure provided for in paragraph 11 of annex I to General Assembly resolution 41/213 of 19 December 1986, the amount of 17,006,900 dollars under section 3, Political affairs, and 781,300 dollars under section 34, Staff assessment, of the programme budget for the biennium 2004–2005, the amount of 781,300 dollars to be offset by a corresponding amount in the income estimates under income section 1, Income from staff assessment, of the programme budget.

Developments in the peace processes and security situation

Report of Secretary-General (September). The Secretary-General reported on 28 September [S/2004/763] that the IGAD-led peace process was scheduled to resume in early October and UNAMIS would have to be ready to assist and be in a position to deploy an operation in a timely manner following a final breakthrough and the signing of a comprehensive peace agreement. In that regard, several additional tasks were identified for the mission, including helping the AU to deploy and support an expanded mission in Darfur, establishing four field offices in Darfur and Kassala and enhancing the ability of the advance mission's headquarters to support the new tasks and offices in Darfur. The Secretary-General said that the expanded tasks would re-

quire an additional six military officers and six police officers.

Meanwhile, the humanitarian challenge in the Sudan remained enormous as the crisis continued in Darfur, and other parts of the country remained beset by ethnic tensions. The number of vulnerable people in the south requiring immediate assistance in food, health, water and sanitation under Operation Lifeline Sudan was around 3 million. While humanitarian access had improved, government restrictions in southern Blue Nile limited the capacity for humanitarian action. Hostilities linked to oilfield development and militia realignment in and around western Upper Nile, hostile actions by the Ugandan Lord's Resistance Army and intra-ethnic conflict in some areas of Equatoria and in the Shilluk Kingdom earlier in the year led to new displacement and suffering, and access restrictions. Internally displaced persons returning to their home areas were also putting a strain on the humanitarian situation.

The Secretary-General observed that the decision of the Government and SPLM/A to resume negotiations on 7 October in the context of the IGAD-led peace process restored optimism that progress was possible, and he was heartened by the parties' recent positive attitude towards concluding the negotiations as soon as possible. That peace process was central to comprehensive peace in the Sudan, as it addressed the fundamental roots of the conflict in southern Sudan. While the process did not offer a comprehensive solution to the country's problems, the breadth of the agreements reached in the Naivasha protocols (see p. 236) offered a basis for answers to the wider issues of insecurity and conflict. In his view, the current crisis in Darfur was emblematic of that problem. The rebel groups in Darfur were only two of an array of peoples and groups that had complained of systematic marginalization over the course of recent Sudanese history. An agreement between the Government and SPLM/A, he said, would be a catalyst to addressing the Darfur crisis and the wider problems of economic and political marginalization.

Security Council consideration. The Security Council, during its consideration of the Secretary-General's report on 5 October [meeting 5050], was told by the Special Representative that, despite the Government's pledges to take action, there was no systematic improvement in people's security in the Sudan and no progress on ending impunity. Ceasefire breaches also continued. Pressure had to be put on the current political leaders to change their policies. Such pressure should be constructive, with no mixed signals or messages and should be combined with adequate monitoring and a fair degree of trust and acknowledgment of good performance. There should be no room for options other than complying with the demands of the international community. The conflicts in the Sudan had to be prevented from turning into general antagonism between people of different religions or different ethnic backgrounds.

Report of Secretary-General (October). The Secretary-General, in response to resolution 1564(2004), reported on 4 October [S/2004/787] on the situation in the Sudan, in particular on the security and humanitarian situations. With regard to the security situation, the Secretary-General said that the Joint Implementation Mechanism, at its 17 September meeting, concluded that progress towards full security implied that achievements would be maintained and improved upon and that there could be no trade off between security in the initial areas and security elsewhere in Darfur. In the coming months, that meant that the Government had to take action to stop attacks on the civilian population by its forces and by others such as the Janjaweed militia. It should request international assistance to fulfil its responsibility in that regard. During the meeting, the Government promised to commit no further breaches of the ceasefire and to accept international assistance, including more AU forces to carry out tasks beyond the ceasefire monitoring. The Government proposed three new areas it would make safe and secure around the camps for internally displaced persons at Kass, Kutum and Zallingi, in Southern, Northern and Western Darfur, respectively. At its 24 September meeting, the Monitoring Committee agreed on a procedure designed to avoid situations that might lead to a breach of the N'Djamena ceasefire agreement. On 26 September, however, the Government informed the United Nations that it could not agree to the procedure owing to failure on the part of SPLM/A and JEM to meet their obligations under the N'Djamena agreement.

The Secretary-General said it was clear that the ceasefire was not holding in many parts of Darfur. Violence was reported throughout September, with clashes at Sayyah, north of Al Fasher, and attacks by Government-aligned militia against SLA at Abu Dalek. Attacks against civilians continued, including attacks by uniformed men and abduction of young women. Other incidents included assault, killings, collection of unlawful taxes by the militias, general banditry and inter-tribal fighting. Ever increasing numbers of the population of Darfur were exposed, without any protection from the Government, to hunger, fear and violence, and the suffering was being prolonged by inaction. The Government had not fulfilled its commitments and obligations on disarming the militia and had not presented the details of a plan to establish a commission to collect weapons, as promised at the 17 September Joint Implementation Mechanism meeting.

Impunity among members of the armed forces remained a concern. The Government had taken only minimal steps towards military or criminal prosecution of those already identified as responsible for ceasefire violations and offences under international humanitarian law.

The humanitarian situation had deteriorated since the objectives of the 90-day UN humanitarian plan for Darfur were set. There were more displaced people than previously thought, with new arrivals to some camps numbering in the tens of thousands. The number of conflict-affected people could rise above 2 million if continuation of the civil war caused further displacements. In general, the Government continued to fulfil its commitments regarding humanitarian access. Assistance was beginning to flow into SPLM/A controlled-areas, although complete freedom of access was not possible.

As to the Darfur peace process, political talks between the Government and the rebel movements began on 23 August at Abuja, under the auspices of Nigerian President Olusegun Obasanjo, with the United Nations supporting the mediation effort. The parties agreed on a text for a protocol on humanitarian access, by which they would take measures to prevent violence against civilians, reaffirm the need to protect the rights of internally displaced persons and refugees, and form an implementation mechanism, namely, the Joint Humanitarian Facilitation and Monitoring Unit. While the parties declined to sign that protocol, the Government, on 17 September, agreed to act as if it had been signed. Negotiations were ongoing on a security protocol, but a wide gap between the parties prevented them from reaching agreement.

The Secretary-General observed that the most important step to be taken in the coming weeks was the deployment of the expanded AU force. That force needed to be sizeable and speedily deployed. It also needed a broad mandate that went beyond overseeing the ceasefire and that should include: ensuring protection of the rights of internally displaced persons and refugees in their areas of origin; providing safety of displaced persons in the camps and safe and voluntary return of refugees and displaced persons to their areas of origin; monitoring the behaviour of the police; and disarming fighters. The second issue to be addressed was the resumption of the political talks between the Government and SPLM/A. The outcome of those talks, intended to bring peace, a new constitution, a federal structure for the State, national differentiation and a broad-based Government, could serve as a model for Darfur.

International Commission of Inquiry. The Secretary-General, as requested by the Security Council in resolution 1564(2004), established the International Commission of Inquiry for Darfur to investigate reports of serious violations of international humanitarian law and human rights law in that region by all parties in the current conflict; qualify crimes and determine whether acts of genocide had occurred or were occurring; and identify the perpetrators of such violations and recommend accountability mechanisms before which they would be brought to account. On 4 October [S/2004/812], he informed the Council of his appointment of a five-member Commission, to be chaired by Antonio Cassese (Italy).

In conducting its inquiry, the Commission would enjoy the full cooperation of the Government of the Sudan, and would be provided with the necessary facilities to enable it to operate, and, in particular, be guaranteed freedom of movement throughout the territory, and freedom of access to all sources of information and documentary material. Appropriate security arrangements for the Commission's personnel and documents would be provided, and protection of victims and witnesses would be guaranteed. The Commission was requested to report to the Secretary-General within 90 days from the start of its activities.

SECURITY COUNCIL ACTION (October)

On 26 October [meeting 5063], the Security Council unanimously adopted **resolution 1569(2004)**. The draft [S/2004/857] was prepared in consultations among Council members.

The Security Council,

Acting in accordance with Article 28, paragraph 3, of the Charter of the United Nations,

1. *Decides* to hold meetings in Nairobi starting on 18 November 2004 and ending on 19 November 2004, and that the agenda for these meetings will be "The reports of the Secretary-General on the Sudan";

2. *Decides also* to discuss the Sudan with representatives of the African Union and the Intergovernmental Authority on Development at the above-mentioned meetings, and to take the opportunity of the presence of the Security Council in Nairobi to discuss other peace efforts in the region with both the African Union and the Intergovernmental Authority on Development;

3. *Decides further*, with respect to the meetings referred to in paragraph 1 above, to waive the requirement set out in rule 49 of its provisional rules of procedure that the verbatim record of each meeting of the Council shall be made available on the first working day following the meeting, and decides that the verbatim record shall be issued subsequently in New York.

Report of Secretary-General (November). Reporting on developments in the Sudan since his September report (see p. 248), the Secretary-General, on 2 November [S/2004/881], said that the month of October saw a deterioration in security conditions in Darfur, as reported by observers and humanitarian agencies. Ceasefire violations increased on both sides. SPLM/A and the Government were seeking to claim a bigger area of Darfur. The Government responded to attacks by launching operations using army, police and militia, including the Janjaweed. In an apparent drift towards lawlessness, cases of banditry and abduction dramatically increased, affecting civilian traffic, including pilgrims travelling through the Sudan for the hajj, and hampering delivery of humanitarian aid. Various sources reported the emergence of a new rebel movement in Darfur, known as the National Movement for Reformation and Development (NMRD), which claimed responsibility for attacks against Government troops and also threatened the AU Ceasefire Commission. There were also clashes between JEM and NMRD. In addition, a new anti-Government armed group called Al-Shahamah (nobility) emerged in Western Kordofan, calling for a fair distribution of wealth and power, better education and employment opportunities, a review of the power- and wealth-sharing protocols, and revision of the protocol on the Nuba Mountains and the southern Blue Nile regions signed by the Government and SPLM/A. The spread of fighting between rebel movements and activities in areas outside Darfur increased insecurity.

On 20 October, the AU Peace and Security Council announced it would increase its mission in Darfur to 3,320 persons, including 2,341 military personnel and up to 815 civilian police. It expanded its mandate to include the monitoring and verification of the security provided for returning internally displaced persons, of the Government's efforts to disarm Government-controlled militias, and of the protection of civilians under imminent threat and in the immediate vicinity of AU troops and monitors. On 26 October, the Sudanese Parliament endorsed the deployment of the additional AU forces, and the Government accepted verification by the AU Mission on whether Janjaweed had been recruited into the police. A UN assistance cell in Addis Ababa was integrated into and co-located with elements of the AU office dealing with management of the AU Mission in Darfur.

Peace negotiations. The Secretary-General also reported that the IGAD-led peace process had recently shown signs of progress, as the political process addressing the north-south conflict had resumed. From 7 to 16 October, the First Vice-President of the Sudan, Ali Osman Taha, and SPLM/A Chairman John Garang met in Nairobi to resolve outstanding security issues and to plan for the completion of the peace negotiations. They resolved most of the issues for a permanent ceasefire arrangement, including the deployment of joint integrated units in eastern Sudan and the collaborative approach in handling other armed groups during the transition period, but not for the funding of the armed forces of southern Sudan and the timing of the incorporation and integration of other armed groups into the respective structures of the Sudan armed forces and SPLA.

From 17 to 30 October, the parties held technical-level negotiations on implementation modalities, focusing on the Machakos protocol, the power-sharing and wealth-sharing protocols and the protocol on the conflict areas. They consulted the United Nations on aspects of the ceasefire, envisaging a UN monitoring and verification role during the implementation phase. At the conclusion of the talks, the parties announced that they had been able to resolve certain concerns raised by the United Nations regarding specific elements of its role.

Political talks between the Government and the rebel movements in the Darfur peace process resumed on 21 October in Abuja, during which the Government, SPLM/A and JEM reaffirmed their commitment to the ceasefire and to the need to reach a political solution to the Darfur conflict. While the parties continued to discuss their security concerns in the framework of the Security Committee, they commenced negotiations on political issues on 29 October, having expressed their readiness to negotiate a declaration of principles. The Special Representative urged them to sign the protocol on improving the humanitarian situation (see p. 249) and stressed the need for the establishment of mechanisms to facilitate implementation.

The Secretary-General commented that the ongoing talks in Nairobi were proceeding well and that the AU force was expanding rapidly. In spite of that progress, ceasefire breaches had increased as had violence, affecting civilians indirectly and directly, especially in Darfur, where attacks and killings continued at an unacceptable scale. The increase in the number of internally displaced persons reflected the severity of the protection and security situation in Darfur, which the conflicting parties should take as a clear message to pursue urgently a peace agreement. The Secretary-General was of the view that

the north-south round of talks had a good chance of being completed by the year's end, and the international community should ensure that the momentum was maintained. Meanwhile, violence in Darfur was on the rise and new movements were threatening the peace in Kordofan, in the east and in Khartoum. The Secretary-General proposed that the Security Council consider what action it could take to ensure effective implementation of the demands set out in its resolutions on the Sudan at its meetings to be held in Nairobi (see below).

Security Council consideration (4 November). The Security Council reviewed the Secretary-General's report on 4 November [meeting 5071]. Addressing the meeting, the Special Representative said that progress on the political front was slow, and regression on the ground was alarming, as instability had increased in October. Political agreements might come too late to stop the rising violence. Both sides were trying to widen the area of their control. Fighting was occurring in more places, militias were ganging up, and the Government did not fully control its own forces. Within the rebel movements, there was a leadership crisis. The situation could only be reversed by a three-pronged approach: a third party (the AU) should be deployed to deter violations; all negotiation processes should be speeded up; and political leaders, official and self-elected, should be held accountable for violations of agreements and further human misery.

In a statement released the same day [SC/8283], the Council President said that Council members expressed concern about the Government's forced relocations of internally displaced persons in Otash, Old Sharief and New Sharief. They also condemned ongoing violations of international human rights and humanitarian law, such as attacks on civilians, sexual violence and hostage-taking that were being perpetrated in Darfur by all parties including the Government, rebel groups, and the Janjaweed militias.

Communications. Australia, on 8 November [S/2004/887], said it supported the Special Representative's suggestion that the Council use its forthcoming Nairobi meetings to maintain strong pressure on the Sudanese parties to meet their obligations to protect civilians and work towards a peaceful settlement of the country's conflicts.

The EU, on 11 November [S/2004/912], welcomed the progress in the Abuja peace talks and the signing of the Humanitarian and Security Protocols on 9 November. It confirmed its commitment to contribute to the peace and reconciliation processes in the Sudan, which did not exclude the use of sanctions against all parties to the conflict.

Security Council consideration (18-19 November). The Council met in Nairobi on 18 and 19 November [meetings 5080-5082], in accordance with resolution 1569(2004) (see p. 250). In attendance at the first and third meetings were the Sudan's First Vice-President, Ali Othman Taha, and the Chairman of SPLM/A, John Grang. At the first meeting, the Secretary-General said that, while the Council should place its primary focus on the conclusion of the north-south talks, also demanding its attention was the conflict in Darfur, where the security situation continued to deteriorate, despite the ceasefire agreements signed earlier in N'Djamena and Abuja. It was time to conclude the Naivasha process, he said, and involve all Sudanese stakeholders in a national conference to discuss the future governance of the country.

Vice-President Taha reiterated his Government's firm commitment to concluding negotiations as soon as possible and announced that it had reached an understanding with SPLM/A and the IGAD secretariat, as reflected in the common memorandum of understanding committed to by the parties for the conclusion of the negotiations within the agreed framework contained therein and to be signed in the presence of Council members. The Government's vision of a peaceful political resolution in Darfur was based on the Naivasha agreements (see p. 236) and on the establishment of a foundation for decentralized government within a federal network, which would include an agreement on the sharing of national resources and wealth in a manner that provided every governorate, State and region in the Sudan with a proportional share. The Government had also prepared a three-year medium-term development plan to be implemented after the signing of a peace agreement on Darfur that would address urgent assistance to facilitate the return of displaced persons and refugees, develop agricultural and other income-generating sectors, and focus on providing clean water for industry and people.

Chairman Garang, in stating the SPLM/A position, said that, with the six protocols already in place, it considered negotiations on the comprehensive peace agreement on the Sudan complete. Outstanding were two issues in each of its two annexes: those in the comprehensive ceasefire annex concerned the funding of the armed forces and the time frame for incorporating other armed groups into the Sudan Armed Forces or SPLM/A structures; those in the annex on implementation modalities concerned the system of funds transfer in local currency of the Government's share of southern Sudan's oil revenues and the sharing of information on existing oil

contracts. He assured the Council that SPLM/A was willing to work with the other parties in resolving those issues and with the National Congress Party in establishing a new Government of national unity.

SECURITY COUNCIL ACTION (November)

On 19 November [meeting 5082], the Security Council unanimously adopted **resolution 1574 (2004)**. The draft [S/2004/903] was prepared in consultation among Council members.

The Security Council,

Recalling its resolutions 1547(2004) of 11 June 2004, 1556(2004) of 30 July 2004 and 1564(2004) of 18 September 2004 and the statements by its President concerning the Sudan,

Reaffirming its commitment to the sovereignty, unity, independence and territorial integrity of the Sudan, and recalling the importance of the principles of good-neighbourliness, non-interference and regional cooperation,

Reaffirming its support for the Machakos Protocol of 20 July 2002 and subsequent agreements based on that Protocol,

Expressing its determination to help the people of the Sudan to promote national reconciliation, lasting peace and stability, and to build a prosperous and united Sudan in which human rights are respected and the protection of all citizens is assured,

Recalling that it welcomed the signature of the declaration on 5 June 2004 in Nairobi, in which the parties confirmed their agreement to the six protocols signed between the Government of the Sudan and the Sudan People's Liberation Movement/Army and reconfirmed their commitment to completing the remaining stages of negotiations,

Commending again the work and continued support of the Intergovernmental Authority on Development, in particular, the Government of Kenya as Chair of the Subcommittee on the Sudan, in facilitating the peace talks in Nairobi, recognizing the efforts of the Civilian Protection Monitoring Team, the Joint Military Commission in the Nuba Mountains and the Verification and Monitoring Team in support of the peace process, and expressing its hope that the Intergovernmental Authority will continue to play a vital role during the transitional period,

Encouraging the parties to conclude speedily a comprehensive peace agreement, and stressing the need for the international community, once such an agreement has been signed and implementation begins, to provide assistance towards its implementation,

Emphasizing that progress towards resolution of the conflict in Darfur would create conditions conducive for delivery of such assistance,

Expressing its serious concern at the growing insecurity and violence in Darfur, the dire humanitarian situation, continued violations of human rights and repeated breaches of the ceasefire, and reiterating in this regard the obligation of all parties to implement the commitments, referred to in its previous resolutions on the Sudan,

Condemning all acts of violence and violations of human rights and international humanitarian law by all parties, and emphasizing the need for perpetrators of all such crimes to be brought to justice without delay,

Recalling, in this regard, that all parties, including the Sudanese rebel groups such as the Justice and Equality Movement and the Sudan Liberation Army, must respect human rights and international humanitarian law, and also recalling the primary responsibility of the Government of the Sudan to protect its population within its territory and to maintain law and order, while respecting human rights,

Stressing the importance of further progress towards resolving the crisis in Darfur, welcoming the vital and wide-ranging role being played by the African Union towards that end, and welcoming the decision of the Government of the Sudan in favour of the expansion of the African Union mission,

Taking note of the reports of the Secretary-General of 28 September 2004 and 2 November 2004,

Deeply concerned by the situation in the Sudan and its implications for international peace and security and stability in the region,

1. *Declares its strong support* for the efforts of the Government of the Sudan and the Sudan People's Liberation Movement/Army to reach a comprehensive peace agreement, encourages the parties to redouble their efforts, welcomes the signing of the memorandum of understanding in Nairobi on 19 November 2004 entitled "Declaration on the conclusion of negotiations of the Intergovernmental Authority on Development on peace in the Sudan", annexed to the present resolution, and the agreement that the six protocols referred to in the Nairobi Declaration of 5 June 2004 constitute and form the core peace agreement, and strongly endorses the parties' commitment to reach a final comprehensive agreement by 31 December 2004, and expects that it will be fully and transparently implemented, with the appropriate international monitoring;

2. *Declares its commitment*, upon conclusion of a comprehensive peace agreement, to assist the people of the Sudan in their efforts to establish a peaceful, united and prosperous nation, on the understanding that the parties are fulfilling all their commitments, including those agreed in Abuja and N'Djamena;

3. *Urges* the joint assessment mission of the United Nations, the World Bank and the parties, in association with other bilateral and multilateral donors, to continue their efforts to prepare for the rapid delivery of an assistance package for the reconstruction and economic development of the Sudan, including official development assistance, possible debt relief and trade access, to be implemented once a comprehensive peace agreement has been signed and its implementation begins;

4. *Welcomes* the initiative of the Government of Norway to convene an international donors conference for the reconstruction and economic development of the Sudan upon the signing of a comprehensive peace agreement;

5. *Also welcomes* the continued operations of the Joint Military Commission, the Civilian Protection Monitoring Team, and the Verification and Monitoring Team, in anticipation of the implementation of a comprehensive peace agreement and the establishment of a United Nations peace support operation;

6. *Reiterates its readiness*, upon the signature of a comprehensive peace agreement, to consider establishing a United Nations peace support operation to support the implementation of that agreement, and reiterates its request to the Secretary-General to submit to the Security Council, as soon as possible after the signing of a comprehensive peace agreement, recommendations for the size, structure and mandate of such an operation, including also a timetable for its deployment;

7. *Welcomes* the preparatory work already carried out by the United Nations Advance Mission in the Sudan, established by its resolution 1547(2004), endorses the proposals in the reports of the Secretary-General of 28 September 2004 and 2 November 2004 to increase its staffing, extends the mandate of the Advance Mission by a further three months until 10 March 2005, and calls upon the Sudan People's Liberation Movement/Army to commit to full cooperation with the Advance Mission,

8. *Calls upon* all countries in the region to do their utmost to support actively the full and timely implementation of a comprehensive peace agreement;

9. *Emphasizes* that a comprehensive peace agreement will contribute towards sustainable peace and stability throughout the Sudan and to the efforts to address the crisis in Darfur, and underlines the need for a national and inclusive approach, including the role of women, towards reconciliation and peacebuilding;

10. *Underlines* the importance of progress in peace talks in Abuja between the Government of the Sudan and the Sudan Liberation Army and the Justice and Equality Movement towards resolving the crisis in Darfur, insists that all parties to the Abuja peace talks negotiate in good faith to reach agreement speedily, welcomes the signature in Abuja of the Humanitarian and Security Protocols on 9 November 2004, urges the parties to implement them rapidly, and looks forward to the early signature of a declaration of principles with a view to a political settlement;

11. *Demands* that Government and rebel forces and all other armed groups immediately cease all violence and attacks, including abduction, refrain from forcible relocation of civilians, cooperate with international humanitarian relief and monitoring efforts, ensure that their members comply with international humanitarian law, facilitate the safety and security of humanitarian staff, and reinforce throughout their ranks their agreements to allow unhindered access and passage by humanitarian agencies and those in their employ, in accordance with resolution 1502(2003) of 26 August 2003 on the access of humanitarian workers to populations in need and with the Abuja Protocols of 9 November 2004;

12. *Decides*, in accordance with its previous resolutions on the Sudan, to monitor compliance by the parties with their obligations in that regard and, subject to a further decision of the Council, to take appropriate action against any party failing to fulfil its commitments;

13. *Strongly supports* the decisions of the African Union to increase its mission in Darfur to 3,320 personnel and to enhance its mandate to include the tasks listed in paragraph 6 of the communiqué of 20 October 2004 of the Peace and Security Council of the African Union, urges Member States to provide the required equipment, logistical, financial, material and other necessary resources, and urges the Government of the Sudan and all rebel groups in Darfur to cooperate fully with the African Union;

14. *Reiterates its call upon* Member States to provide urgent and generous contributions to the humanitarian efforts under way in the Sudan and Chad;

15. *Calls upon* all parties to cooperate fully with the International Commission of Inquiry established by the Secretary-General, as described in his letter dated 4 October 2004 to the President of the Security Council, the outcome of which will be communicated to the Council;

16. *Reiterates* the importance of deploying more human rights monitors to Darfur;

17. *Requests* the Secretary-General to keep it regularly informed of developments in the Sudan, and to make any recommendations for action to ensure implementation of the present resolution and its previous resolutions on the Sudan;

18. *Decides* to remain seized of the matter.

Annex

Declaration on the conclusion of negotiations of the Intergovernmental Authority on Development on peace in the Sudan

Gigiri, Nairobi: Friday, 19 November 2004

WHEREAS the Government of the Republic of the Sudan and the Sudan People's Liberation Movement/Army (the Parties) reconfirmed in the Nairobi Declaration of 5 June 2004, on the final phase of the negotiations on peace in the Sudan led by the Intergovernmental Authority on Development, their agreement on the six texts, including the Machakos Protocol as well as the texts relating to power sharing, wealth sharing, security arrangements, and resolution of the conflict in southern Kordofan/Nuba Mountains, Blue Nile, and Abyei area;

WHEREAS the Parties in a joint press statement on 16 October 2004, "recommitted themselves to finalize and conclude the comprehensive peace agreement in recognition that prompt completion of the peace process is essential for all the people of the Sudan as it will help in resolving all challenges facing the country";

ACKNOWLEDGING the progress made to date on the security arrangements and ceasefire details including the extensive work that has been accomplished in the implementation modalities annexes; and

DECLARING that the conclusion of the initiative led by the Intergovernmental Authority on Development is central to a comprehensive peace agreement in the Sudan including the resolution of the conflict in Darfur;

NOW HEREBY THE PARTIES AFFIRM that the six protocols referred to in the Nairobi Declaration of 5 June 2004 constitute and form the core peace agreement and therefore invite the United Nations Security Council in this, its Nairobi sitting, to pass a resolution endorsing the six protocols.

FURTHER the Parties declare their commitment to expeditiously complete negotiations on the two annexes on ceasefire agreement and implementation modalities so as to conclude and sign the comprehensive peace agreement no later than 31 December 2004.

For the Government of the Republic of the Sudan
(*Signed*) Mr. Yahya Hussein **Babikar**
For the Sudan People's Liberation Movement/Army
(*Signed*) Cdr. Nhial **Deng Nhial**

Witnessed by:
On behalf of the envoys of the Intergovernmental Authority on Development:
(*Signed*) Lt. Gen. Lazaro K. **Sumbeiywo** (Rtd.)
Special Representative of the Secretary-General of the United Nations
(*Signed*) Mr. Jan **Pronk**
In the presence of the United Nations Security Council:
Permanent Representative of Algeria to the United Nations
(*Signed*) Ambassador Abdallah **Baali**
Permanent Representative of Angola to the United Nations
(*Signed*) Ambassador Ismael Gaspar **Martins**
Permanent Representative of Benin to the United Nations
(*Signed*) Ambassador Joël **Adechi**
Permanent Representative of Brazil to the United Nations
(*Signed*) Ambassador Ronaldo **Sardenberg**
Permanent Representative of Chile to the United Nations
(*Signed*) Ambassador Heraldo **Muñoz**
Permanent Representative of China to the United Nations
(*Signed*) Ambassador **Wang** Guangya
Permanent Representative of France to the United Nations
(*Signed*) Ambassador Jean-Marc **de La Sablière**
Permanent Representative of Germany to the United Nations
(*Signed*) Ambassador Gunter **Pleuger**
Permanent Representative of Pakistan to the United Nations
(*Signed*) Ambassador Munir **Akram**
Permanent Representative of the Philippines to the United Nations
(*Signed*) Ambassador Lauro **Baja**, Jr.
Permanent Representative of Romania to the United Nations
(*Signed*) Ambassador Mihnea **Motoc**
Permanent Representative of the Russian Federation to the United Nations
(*Signed*) Ambassador Andrey **Denisov**
Permanent Representative of Spain to the United Nations
(*Signed*) Ambassador Juan Antonio **Yáñez-Barnuevo**
Permanent Representative of the United Kingdom of Great Britain and Northern Ireland to the United Nations
(*Signed*) Ambassador Emyr **Jones Parry**
Permanent Representative of the United States of America to the United Nations
(*Signed*) Ambassador John **Danforth**

Report of Secretary-General (December). On 3 December [S/2004/947], the Secretary-General, reporting on developments in the Sudan, stated that, following the signing on 9 November of the Humanitarian and Security Protocols in Abuja (see p. 251), the situation in Darfur was calm for about one week and deteriorated towards the end of November, with increased clashes between Government forces and SPLM/A resulting in many police and civilian deaths. The violence reached a high point on 22 November, when SPLA attacked Tawilla in northern Darfur and took control of all police posts. The Sudanese army launched heavy retaliatory attacks, reportedly using bomber planes, forcing SPLA to withdraw. Fighting continued until 24 November, causing extensive casualties. Both sides proclaimed they were no longer bound by the ceasefire and a state of emergency was declared in Northern Darfur. In addition, on 13 and 22 November, SPLA attacked a police station near Kalma camp for internally displaced persons in Southern Darfur, killing several people. The AU was investigating reports of both incidents. The Special Representative advised the Government to exercise maximum restraint when responding to attacks, refrain from conducting hostile military flights, avoid targeting civilians in any military action and ensure that militias under their influence did likewise.

The Joint Ceasefire Commission was convened in N'Djamena to discuss the violence. Both parties blamed each other for initiating the violence, but reconfirmed their commitment to the ceasefire agreement. The AU criticized the parties for their repeated failure to live up to their commitments; requested the Government to submit plans and time lines to neutralize the armed militias, including the Janjaweed; and demanded that SPLA and JEM submit information on the locations of their forces. The AU also recommended the establishment of an agreed framework to deal with ceasefire violations and the accelerated deployment of AU troops in Darfur.

Despite the renewed violence, the Abuja peace talks on Darfur were proceeding. The parties made substantive progress towards finalizing the declaration of principles and had agreed to reconvene in Abuja for the next round of talks scheduled for 10 December. A draft prepared by the AU mediation team was based on the demands put forward by the parties, including recognition of the ethnic, cultural, religious and social diversity in the Sudan, a commitment to the unity and sovereignty of the Sudan, the need for an equitable distribution of power and national wealth, and the reaffirmation of the principles of equality, citizenship, the rule of law and the protection of human rights.

The IGAD-led north-south peace process on the Sudan continued in Naivasha to work towards a comprehensive peace agreement. Talks resumed on 26 November at the technical level to find an acceptable compromise to the outstanding issues, including funding for the army of the south during the pre-interim and interim periods. A UN team of experts was dispatched to assist the parties.

The Secretary-General remarked that the optimism generated on the political front was overshadowed by regression in the security situation. In Darfur, chaos loomed as order was collapsing. He called on the parties to abide by their commitments by providing the AU with information on the location of their troops and exercising full control over them. The conclusion of a comprehensive peace agreement would have far-reaching implications for the Sudan and raise challenges for UNAMIS. While calling on the international community to sustain interest in the Sudan, the Secretary-General announced that the United Nations was planning for the implementation phase of a comprehensive peace agreement and would make recommendations to the Security Council on the size, structure and mandate of a full UN mission to succeed UNAMIS.

Security Council consideration. The Security Council considered the Secretary-General's report on 7 December [meeting 5094]. Addressing the Council, Under-Secretary-General for Political Affairs, Kieran Prendergast, remarking on the worsening security situation, drew attention to other incidents of violence in Darfur throughout November, including attacks by the new rebel movement, the National Movement for Reform and Development (NMRD), in the Kulbus area, and cross-border operations by elements of the Chadian army in support of NMRD. The Jebel Moon area in North Darfur was also tense, with the reported presence of three rebel groups, government forces and armed tribesmen. Increased activity by the Janjaweed and other pro-government militias were also reported, all of which threatened to plunge Darfur into chaos. The international community, he said, should send an unequivocal message to all Sudanese parties that violence and hostile military actions were not an acceptable means to achieve political gains.

Press statements (December). In a statement to the press on 21 December [SC/8274-AFR/1083], the Security Council President said Council members, following consultations held that day, expressed concern at the serious degradation of the security and humanitarian situation in Darfur and at the repeated violations of the ceasefire. They condemned the violations and the shooting at an AU helicopter. Reiterating their support for the AU efforts and its mission in Darfur, they called for the expeditious and full deployment of the African force. The Council called on both parties, when they resumed their talks in January 2005 in Abuja to achieve a political agreement without delay. The Council expressed readiness to consider a full range of options to exercise pressure on the parties to ensure full compliance with its resolutions.

Further political progress

The Secretary-General, in a 31 December press statement [SG/SM/9661-AFR/1086], welcomed the initialling that day by the Government of the Sudan and SPLA of the last two agreements of the north-south peace process: the Agreement on the Implementation Modalities of the Protocols and Agreements, and the Agreement on the Permanent Ceasefire and Security Agreements Implementation Modalities, which constituted integral parts of a comprehensive peace agreement and marked the parties' commitment to end more than two decades of civil war. The Secretary-General looked forward to the official signing of the Comprehensive Peace Agreement in January 2005, ushering in a new era of peace in the Sudan, in which the United Nations was prepared to play a significant role.

Eritrea-Sudan

On 4 and 22 January, the Sudan accused Eritrea of inciting, supporting and training groups of outlaws in the Darfur region of the country as part of its attempts to destabilize the Sudan and the ongoing peace process [A/58/669-S/2004/14]. It also said that, according to news reports, an outlaw group in eastern Sudan, the Beja Congress, had forged an alliance with the outlaw groups in the Darfur region, with support from Eritrea [A/58/693-S/2004/66]. Eritrea, on 22 January [S/2004/63], rejected those claims as attempts to isolate Eritrea and to divert Sudanese public attention from the country's domestic problems. On 10 August [S/2004/638], the Sudan again informed the Security Council of what it called Eritrea's continuing hostility towards the Sudan and its involvement in the conflict in Darfur.

Somalia

In 2004, progress was made in the national reconciliation process of Somalia, which was based on the outcome of the 2002 Eldoret (Kenya) Conference, held under the auspices of IGAD, and which led to the signing of the Declaration on Cessation of Hostilities and the Structures and Principles of the Somalia National Reconciliation Process (the Eldoret Declaration) [YUN 2002, p. 202]. That Declaration was signed in December 2002 by five Mogadishu faction leaders and the Transitional National Government (TNG), established by the Arta (Djibouti) Conference in 2000 [YUN 2000, p. 215]. It set up a national reconciliation process, aimed at bringing the factions into agreement on a national government. Some pro-

gress was made in 2003 in five of the six reconciliation committees of the process, and agreement was reached by participating Somali leaders at a conference in September 2003 on a transitional federal government [YUN 2003, p. 248]. However, the TNG President and some faction leaders rejected the document and opposed the proposed federal system. During the negotiations on reconciliation, Somaliland, in the northwest, remained outside the process.

The first sign of progress in 2004 was the signing by Somali leaders, on 29 January, of a declaration on agreement of issues related to the transitional federal government. That meeting was part of the ongoing IGAD-sponsored Somali National Reconciliation Conference in Kenya, which aimed to establish a viable transitional government. In mid-2004, IGAD held a series of Ministerial Facilitation Committee meetings on the Conference and launched its third and final phase, which led to the establishment of the Transitional Federal Government of Somalia. The Security Council, in July, welcomed the AU's decision to dispatch a reconnaissance mission to prepare for deploying military monitors to Somalia.

The Conference, meeting in Kenya and attended by representatives of the numerous factions and clans of Somalia, with the notable exception of Somaliland, agreed to form the Transitional Federal Parliament, with members selected by the factions at the Conference. That body elected the Speaker of Parliament and the Transitional President, important steps towards the re-establishment of stability. The peace process produced a power-sharing arrangement for a transitional period of five years. The inclusive peace process involved all clans and most major faction leaders. At the same time, fighting inside Somalia continued.

The United Nations Political Office for Somalia (UNPOS), led by the Secretary-General's Special Representative, Winston A. Tubman (Liberia), remained involved in the peace process and humanitarian efforts, and continued to operate from Nairobi.

The Secretary-General, in response to a 2003 Council request, established a Monitoring Group of four experts to investigate violations of the arms embargo against Somalia, and to provide a draft list of the individuals continuing to violate it. The Group reported to the Council in August that weapons and ammunition continued to flow into, through and out of Somalia, in contravention of the embargo; and that to fully investigate violations, it required more time than specified in its mandate. Therefore, the Council called for the re-establishment of the Group, for a period of six months, to continue its functions and to update the draft list.

The economic and social situation in Somalia continued to suffer as a result of the chronic warfare and drought. At times, UN activities had to be curtailed due to insecurity in various parts of the country. The General Assembly, in **resolution 59/218** (see p. 913), noted the urgent need for humanitarian and reconstruction assistance and urged the international community to respond accordingly. In related action, the Executive Board of UNDP and the United Nations Population Fund, in decision 2004/35 (see p. 879), endorsed UNDP's approach in promoting security by reducing poverty and encouraging good governance. The Board authorized the UNDP Administrator to approve projects consistent with the strategic approach of promoting peace and security on a case-by-case basis.

National reconciliation process and security situation

Report of Secretary-General (February). The Secretary-General, in a 12 February report on the situation in Somalia [S/2004/115 & Corr.1], submitted in response to the Security Council's request in the President's statement S/PRST/2001/30 [YUN 2001, p. 210], described developments since his previous report in October 2002 [YUN 2003, p. 248].

He reported that, on 29 January, at the Somali Leaders' Consultation Meeting (Nairobi), organized by IGAD under the chairmanship of the President of Uganda, Yoweri Museveni, and the President of Kenya, Mwai Kibaki, participating Somali leaders signed a document entitled "Declaration on the Harmonization of Various Issues Proposed by the Somali Delegates at the Somali Consultative Meetings from 9 to 29 January 2004". The Declaration consisted of proposed amendments to the transitional federal charter adopted on 15 September 2003 [YUN 2003, p. 248]. The leaders decided that the charter would be called the transitional federal charter of the Somali republic, and the government, the transitional federal government, whose term would last for five years. The transitional federal parliament would consist of 275 members, 12 per cent of whom would be women. A national census would be undertaken during the drafting of a new constitution, which would be approved by an internationally supervised national referendum. A controversy subsequently arose, however, over the method for selecting members of parliament.

The security situation at the beginning of 2004 remained serious in many Somali regions and affected humanitarian aid delivery. In the north, Somaliland and Puntland gave assurances of safe access to the contested areas of the Sool and Sanaag regions. Intense inter-clan fighting occurred in the central region, forcing 9,000 people to flee to surrounding towns and preventing adequate intervention. In southern and central Somalia, violence and armed conflict continued to hamper access and humanitarian programming.

The Secretary-General commented that the agreement at the leaders' consultation marked a breakthrough that could lead to further progress at the Somali National Reconciliation Conference, which had been stalled for some time. The next and final phase of the reconciliation process would involve the selection of members of the transitional national parliament, who would elect a president to lead the country during the transitional period. The Secretary-General stressed that progress in the political arena should be accompanied by efforts by the Somali leaders to improve the security situation on the ground so as to make it conducive to the implementation of a political agreement, thereby according credibility to the agreement.

Communications. On 30 January, the AU [S/2004/88] and the EU [S/2004/112] welcomed the signing of the Declaration. The AU Central Organ of the Mechanism for Conflict Prevention, Management and Resolution called on the Somali factions and leaders to continue to uphold the spirit of the 2002 Eldoret Declaration and to refrain from action that would jeopardize the Somali reconciliation process at Mbagathi, Kenya, which was approaching conclusion. It called on the authorities of Puntland and Somaliland to desist from resorting to military means to resolve their territorial dispute in the provinces of Sool and Sanaag. The statement released by the EU Presidency reiterated EU support to the IGAD-sponsored national reconciliation process, to which there was no alternative for the restoration of effective government, peace and stability in Somalia.

SECURITY COUNCIL ACTION (February)

On 25 February [meeting 4915], following consultations among Security Council members, the President made statement **S/PRST/2004/3** on behalf of the Council:

The Security Council, recalling its previous decisions concerning the situation in Somalia, in particular the statement by its President of 11 November 2003 and welcoming the report of the Secretary-General of 12 February 2004, reaffirms its commitment to a comprehensive and lasting settlement of the situation in Somalia and its respect for the sovereignty, territorial integrity, political independence and unity of the country, consistent with the purposes and principles of the Charter of the United Nations.

The Council reiterates its firm support for the Somali National Reconciliation Process and the ongoing Somali National Reconciliation Conference in Kenya, launched under the auspices of the Intergovernmental Authority on Development.

The Council commends President Mwai Kibaki of Kenya, President Yoweri Museveni of Uganda, other leaders of the Intergovernmental Authority, and international supporters of the Somali National Reconciliation Conference for their perseverance to help Somalis achieve national reconciliation.

The Council welcomes the signing in Nairobi, on 29 January 2004, of the Declaration on the Harmonization of Various Issues Proposed by the Somali Delegates at the Somali Consultative Meetings, held from 9 to 29 January 2004, as an important step towards lasting peace and reconciliation in Somalia, and urges all signatories to the agreement to fully abide by their commitment to move the peace process forward.

The Council calls upon the Somali parties to build on the progress achieved and swiftly conclude the Somali National Reconciliation Conference with a durable and inclusive solution to the conflict in Somalia by establishing a viable transitional government.

The Council reiterates that the Somali parties should abide by and implement expeditiously the Eldoret Declaration of 27 October 2002 on the cessation of hostilities, and calls upon the Somali parties to continue working towards a comprehensive security arrangement for Somalia.

The Council stresses the urgent need for a comprehensive ceasefire throughout Somalia, and stresses also that the Somali parties themselves bear the responsibility for achieving it. The Council calls upon the Somali parties to implement the ceasefire fully, to ensure security, and to resolve their differences by peaceful means.

The Council condemns those who obstruct the peace process, and stresses that those who persist on the path of confrontation and conflict will be held accountable. The Council will continue to monitor the situation closely.

The Council calls upon all neighbouring States to continue their endeavour to participate fully and constructively for the success of the Somali National Reconciliation Process and the attainment of peace in the region.

The Council welcomes the commitment and preparation by the African Union to deploy a military observer mission to Somalia and calls upon the international community to support the African Union's efforts to improve the security situation in Somalia.

The Council calls upon the international community to continue its efforts to support the Intergovernmental Authority in its facilitation of the Somali National Reconciliation Conference, and calls upon the donor countries to contribute to the Conference, the Trust Fund for Peace-building in Somalia and the United Nations Consolidated Inter-Agency Appeal for Somalia.

The Council expresses serious concern regarding the humanitarian situation in Somalia, and calls upon the leaders of Somalia to facilitate the delivery of much-needed humanitarian assistance and to as-sure the safety of all international and national aid workers.

The Council reiterates its concern over the continued flow of weapons and ammunition supplies to Somalia, welcomes the establishment of the Monitoring Group pursuant to resolution 1519(2003) of 16 December 2003, and calls upon relevant States and entities to comply scrupulously with the arms embargo and to cooperate with the Monitoring Group.

The Council welcomes the readiness of the Secretary-General to enhance the attention of the United Nations to developments in Somalia within existing resources. The Council reiterates that a comprehensive peace-building programme with special emphasis on disarmament, demobilization, rehabilitation and reintegration will be important to post-conflict Somalia as stipulated in the statement by its President of 28 March 2002.

The Council requests the Secretary-General to consider and to suggest in his next report ways to develop the role of the United Nations in support of the Intergovernmental Authority-facilitated Somali reconciliation process.

The Council reiterates its readiness to assist the Somali parties and support the Intergovernmental Authority in the implementation of the agreements reached in the Somali National Reconciliation Conference.

Report of Secretary-General (June). On 9 June [S/2004/469], the Secretary-General, reporting further on the situation in Somalia, said that the controversy that arose immediately after the signing of the 29 January Declaration on outstanding issues (see p. 257) stalled the national reconciliation process for four months. On 4 February, some members of the Somalia Restoration and Reconciliation Council issued a press statement contesting the Declaration's validity. On 8 February, the Transitional National Assembly endorsed the Declaration. Following approval of the draft transitional charter by the plenary of the Somalia National Reconciliation Conference, the IGAD Facilitation Committee began preparations for phase III of the Conference. A delegation composed of the AU Special Envoy for Somalia, an IGAD official, and officials from Kenya, Sweden and the United Kingdom met with the newly created National Organizing Council for Somalia members in Jowhar on 17 March, to persuade them to return to the Conference. The Organizing Council demanded that no further amendments be made to the charter, that the political leaders to select members of parliament be limited to the 24 signatories of the Eldoret Declaration and President Hassan, and that the latter no longer act as President. Should IGAD fail to meet those demands, the Organizing Council would press to convene phase III of the Conference within Somalia. Other Somali Restoration and Reconciliation Council leaders met in Nairobi on 25 March and decided to remain engaged in the Conference, while others left for various reasons.

On 22 April, the Kenyan Foreign Minister announced a road map with fixed dates for the completion of the Conference, and requiring all political leaders absent from Nairobi to return and the traditional leaders to arrive at the Conference venue within a stated time frame. The process would culminate in the swearing in of a president for the transitional federal government of Somalia on 1 July. The fifth IGAD Ministerial Facilitation Committee meeting was fixed for 6 May, when the Ministers were expected to launch phase III of the Conference.

The Facilitation Committee met as scheduled in Nairobi, with all IGAD Foreign Ministers in attendance. In a joint communiqué, the Ministers appealed to Somali leaders to return to the Conference by 20 May and for the Conference to conclude successfully by the end of July. They agreed to hold their next meeting in Nairobi on 20 May; the Jowhar group indicated its intention to rejoin the Conference by that date.

Following the sixth IGAD Ministerial Facilitation Committee meeting (Nairobi, 21-22 May), the Ministers stated that they had consulted all Somali clans for the completion of the third and final phase of the Conference. They called for the early arrival of traditional leaders at the Conference site and for the cooperation of Somali political leaders in selecting the members of the transitional federal parliament. They warned that absent leaders would not be allowed to hold the process hostage, and that punitive measures would be taken against those obstructing the completion of the reconciliation process.

The security situation on the ground remained of concern, with an increase in threats and attacks on international and national aid workers. The security situation was particularly serious in Mogadishu, western Somaliland, Kismaayo town, and parts of the western border area with Kenya. In Somaliland, the United Nations was forced to reduce its international staff and non-governmental organizations (NGOs) had curtailed activities there since mid-March. As a result of an April UN/NGO security mission to the area, additional international support was provided to the Special Protection Unit dedicated to protecting aid workers. Strengthened security measures were also being put in place throughout Somalia.

The humanitarian situation was also grave, following four consecutive years of drought in northern Somalia, causing massive livestock deaths and further impoverishing pastoralist families. UN agencies and NGOs responded with short-term interventions, including water trucking, food aid and supplementary feeding, mobile health clinics, veterinary services and cash grants. During the reporting period, UNHCR repatriated 2,918 Somali refugees from camps in Djibouti to Somaliland and implemented reintegration projects in Somalia to generate employment, provide education and assist the special needs of girls.

In his observations, the Secretary-General expressed hope that the two recent IGAD Ministerial Facilitation Committee meetings would help the Somali National Reconciliation Conference to conclude with an accepted outcome. The end-of-July time frame given by IGAD, by which to conclude the Conference, placed enormous pressure on the Somali parties and the region. It was incumbent on them to demonstrate the necessary political will to reach agreement on the remaining contentious issues. While the responsibility for peace in Somalia rested with all Somalis, it was at the same time incumbent on the international community to find a way to engage the country. He urged IGAD, the AU, the League of Arab States (LAS), the EU and the Security Council to consider additional measures in support of peace and national reconciliation in Somalia, and suggested that the Arms Embargo Monitoring Group could provide an impetus in that regard (see p. 263).

Communication. The EU, in a 28 May statement issued by its Presidency [S/2004/446], welcomed the outcome of the sixth IGAD ministerial meeting, which officially launched phase III of the Somali National Reconciliation Conference, and the commitment of IGAD member States to adopt a common approach based on political consensus. It appealed to all parties to continue their engagement with the reaffirmation of the importance of Somali ownership and consensus by all Somali clans on the principles and guidelines for the third and final phase; and agreement on a timetable for the remainder of the Conference and on a list of parliament members by the next IGAD meeting on 21 June.

SECURITY COUNCIL ACTION (July)

On 14 July [meeting 5003], following consultations among Security Council members, the President made statement **S/PRST/2004/24** on behalf of the members:

The Security Council, recalling its previous decisions concerning the situation in Somalia, in particular the statement by its President of 25 February 2004, and welcoming the report of the Secretary-General of 9 June 2004, reaffirms its commitment to a comprehensive and lasting settlement of the situation in Somalia and its respect for the sovereignty, territorial integrity, political independence and unity of the country, consistent with the purposes and principles of the Charter of the United Nations.

The Council reiterates its firm support for the Somali National Reconciliation Process and the ongoing Somali National Reconciliation Conference in Kenya, launched under the auspices of the Intergovernmental Authority on Development, and commends the Intergovernmental Authority leaders, in particular the Government of Kenya, for their efforts in the search for peace in Somalia. The Council also commends the international observers for their active engagement in the process.

The Council welcomes the outcome of the fifth, sixth, and seventh Intergovernmental Authority on Development Ministerial Facilitation Committee meetings on the Somali National Reconciliation Conference, which demonstrated the coherent regional approach and commitment of States members of the Intergovernmental Authority to national reconciliation in Somalia.

The Council welcomes the launching of phase III of the Somali National Reconciliation Conference, and encourages all parties to continue in their ongoing efforts to move the process forward and agree on a durable and inclusive solution to the conflict in Somalia and the establishment of a transitional federal Government for Somalia.

The Council recognizes that, while the establishment of a transitional federal Government will be an important step towards establishing sustainable peace and stability in Somalia, much effort will lie ahead if this objective is to be achieved. The Council emphasizes the need for the new Government, once formed, to engage with the international community and to use the transition period constructively for the purposes of reconciliation, stability and reconstruction.

The Council reiterates that the Somali parties should abide by and implement expeditiously the Eldoret Declaration of 27 October 2002 on the cessation of hostilities, and calls upon the Somali parties to continue working towards a comprehensive security arrangement for Somalia.

The Council reiterates that the Somali parties themselves bear the main responsibility for achieving a comprehensive ceasefire throughout Somalia. The Council calls upon the Somali parties to implement the ceasefire fully, to ensure security, and to resolve their differences by peaceful means.

The Council condemns those who obstruct the peace process, fully supports, in this regard, the warning of the Intergovernmental Authority ministers, and reiterates that those who persist upon the path of confrontation and conflict will be held accountable. The Council will continue to monitor the situation closely.

The Council welcomes the decision by the African Union to dispatch a reconnaissance mission to prepare the ground for the deployment of military monitors to Somalia, and calls upon Somali leaders to cooperate with this initiative.

The Council calls upon the international community to continue to support the Intergovernmental Authority in its facilitation of the Somali National Reconciliation Conference, and calls upon donor countries and organizations to contribute to the Conference, the Trust Fund for Peace-building in Somalia and the United Nations Consolidated Inter-Agency Appeal for Somalia.

The Council reiterates serious concern regarding the humanitarian situation in Somalia, and calls upon Somali leaders to facilitate the delivery of much-needed humanitarian assistance and to assure the safety of all international and national aid workers.

The Council reiterates its concern over the continued flow of weapons and ammunition supplies to Somalia, commends the work of the Monitoring Group established pursuant to resolution 1519(2003) of 16 December 2003, and urges relevant States and entities to comply scrupulously with the arms embargo and to cooperate with the Monitoring Group.

The Council commends the work of Mr. Winston A. Tubman, the Representative of the Secretary-General, welcomes his visit to the region in support of the Intergovernmental Authority on Development-sponsored Somali peace process, and encourages him to continue his facilitation efforts.

The Council welcomes the Secretary-General's meeting with the Somali parties on 8 July 2004 in Mbagathi, Kenya, and requests the Secretary-General to keep the Council regularly informed of developments at the Somali National Reconciliation Conference and to make timely recommendations on what additional measures could be taken by the Council in support of the Conference and its outcome.

Establishment of Transitional Federal Parliament

At the end of June, the controversies regarding the method of selecting members of the transitional federal parliament led Somali leaders to absent themselves from the Somali National Reconciliation Conference (Mbagathi), the Secretary-General stated in his 8 October report on Somalia [S/2004/804]. However, concerted efforts by IGAD member States led to their gradual return in July. Each Somali clan (Hawiye, Darod, Digil and Mirifle, Dir and the "Allied" clans) was requested to propose names for members of the Somali National Arbitration Committee and the collective leadership of the Conference (the Presidium), and a list of 61 members of parliament by 5 July, with the exception of the "Allied" clans, which were asked to submit a list of 31 members. On 8 July, the Secretary-General, addressing the Somali delegates at the Conference, reiterated the UN commitment to support the Conference's outcome.

Negotiations on the number of seats to be allotted to each of the sub-clans proved challenging, but the problem was resolved during six IGAD ministerial meetings held in Nairobi over five months and the willingness of Somali leaders to compromise. At the tenth IGAD Ministerial Facilitation Committee meeting (Nairobi, 21-22 August), the Ministers focused on facilitating the selection of Somali members of parliament.

On 22 August, 194 members of the Transitional Federal Parliament of Somalia were sworn into office. Differences within the Harti sub-clan (Darod) over their choice were resolved after the intervention of the Kenyan President, Mwai Kibaki, and international observers. On 29 August, an additional 66 members were sworn in in the presence of the Kenyan Vice-President, who declared the Parliament formally inaugurated. By mid-September, 268 of a total membership of 275 had been sworn in.

The Transitional Federal Parliament held its first meeting in Nairobi on 2 September, at which five of its remaining seven members were sworn in. On 15 September, Sharif Hassan Sheikh Aden was elected Speaker of Parliament. Despite the efforts of international observers, only 23 women members were sworn in, well short of the agreed 33, or 12 per cent of the total membership, as stipulated by the transitional federal charter. To raise the level of inclusiveness at the Conference, and to gain support for its outcome, a dialogue with the Somali business community was held (Djibouti, 21-22 July) with the participation of regional ministers and UN senior staff.

The absence of General Mohamed Hersi "Morgan" from the Conference and reports that he was planning a military attack on Kismaayo caused concern among the civilian population of the region. He had been reported to be gathering his militia with the intention of attacking the Juba Valley Alliance (JVA), which had ousted him from Kismaayo in 1999. The JVA leader, Colonel Barre Hirale, a member of the transitional federal parliament, left the Conference and returned to Kismaayo. On 27 July, the Conference Chairman, Bethuel Kiplagat (Kenya), issued a press release on behalf of the IGAD Facilitation Committee, calling on regional countries to apply sanctions against General "Morgan" by, among other things, denying him entry to IGAD member States. General "Morgan" announced his intention to return to the Conference, on the condition, he said on 14 September, that JVA not attack his militia.

The question of Somaliland remained to be resolved. "President" Dahir Riyale Kahin of the "Republic of Somaliland" issued a press release on 7 July, warning that any attempt to resurrect the former Somali Union would trigger a new cycle of civil war that would engulf the entire Horn of Africa. He expressed satisfaction with international community pronouncements that the current Conference would be followed by the formation of a government for Somalia that would then enter into dialogue with the "government of Somaliland".

The Secretary-General, in his observations, welcomed the planning under way in Nairobi, involving the United Nations Political Office for Somalia (UNPOS), the UN country team, the Somalia Aid Coordination Body, the European Commission, LAS and others, to arrive at a peace-building framework leading to the formulation of a rapid assistance package for the Somali transitional federal government.

He pointed to the likelihood, at the current stage of the Somali peace process, of a call for an expanded UN peace-building role. He proposed that any enhanced UN role in Somalia be incremental and based on discussions with the new government. In the meantime, he also proposed that resources for UNPOS for 2004-2005 be maintained at the current level. He appealed to the Somali leaders to improve security on the ground, and to the international community to support the peace process.

Communications. The AU and the EU issued statements welcoming the establishment of the Transitional Federal Parliament. In a 17 September communiqué [S/2004/755], the AU Peace and Security Council (Addis Ababa) commended the efforts of the IGAD Facilitation Committee. It encouraged the members of Parliament to work for the early election of a president and formation of a transitional federal government. In a 4 August statement of its Presidency [S/2004/640], the EU appealed to all parties to continue their engagement with the aim of establishing an inclusive government committed to an effective ceasefire, to the creation of a stable national environment, to working for humanitarian access across Somalia, to a federal Somalia and to cooperating with the international community.

Election of President

The members of the Transitional Federal Parliament elected on 10 October Colonel Abdullahi Yusuf Ahmed as President of Somalia, after three rounds of voting [S/2005/89]. In the final round, Colonel Yusuf obtained 189 votes and the runner-up, Abdullahi Ahmed Addow, obtained 79 votes. Mr. Addow pledged to cooperate with the President. Prior to the vote, all 26 presidential candidates signed a declaration to support the elected President and to demobilize their militias.

In a 14 October statement issued by its Presidency [S/2004/865], the EU welcomed the election, which it believed would pave the way for the establishment of a transitional federal government, and pledged to support the transition to a federal State.

On 26 October [meeting 5064], following consultations among Security Council members, the President made statement **S/PRST/2004/38** on behalf of the Council:

The Security Council reaffirms its previous resolutions and the statements by its President concerning the situation in Somalia, in particular resolution 1558(2004) of 17 August 2004 and the statement by its President of 14 July 2004.

The Council reiterates its commitment to a comprehensive and lasting settlement of the situation in Somalia and its respect for the sovereignty, territorial integrity, political independence and unity of Somalia, consistent with the purposes and principles of the Charter of the United Nations.

The Council commends the recent progress made at the Somali National Reconciliation Conference in Nairobi, including the establishment of the Transitional Federal Parliament of Somalia and the subsequent election of the Speaker of Parliament and the transitional President, which are important steps towards the re-establishment of peace and stability in Somalia.

The Council, underscoring the importance of consolidating the gains made so far, looks forward to the formation, in the near future, of a Transitional Federal Government inside Somalia, capable of beginning reconciliation and reconstruction in a spirit of consensus and dialogue with all the Somali parties.

The Council, in this regard, encourages the Transitional Federal Parliament and the President to take further steps to select a Prime Minister and an efficient and effective Cabinet, and to develop a preliminary programme of action and timetable for the transitional period. The Council urges the transitional federal institutions to involve women fully in post conflict reconciliation and reconstruction. The Council also notes the ongoing discussion to outline possible coordination mechanisms between the Transitional Federal Government and the international community.

The Council commends member States of the Intergovernmental Authority on Development, in particular the Government of Kenya, as well as other countries and organizations for constructively supporting the Somali National Reconciliation Process for the past two years, and encourages them to continue their efforts in support of the cause of peace in Somalia.

The Council welcomes and expresses its support for the commitment of the African Union to assist the transitional process in Somalia, in particular through planning for a peace support mission to Somalia, including options for disarmament, demobilization and reintegration, and encourages the international donor community to contribute to these efforts.

The Council further welcomes the efforts of the United Nations Political Office for Somalia, the United Nations country team, the Somalia Aid Coordination Body, the European Union, the Intergovernmental Authority on Development Partners Forum, the League of Arab States and others engaged in developing a peacebuilding framework leading to the formation of a rapid assistance package and calls upon the international community to support this package as well as emergency rehabilitation and economic development programmes as security returns to Somalia.

The Council shares the Secretary-General's assessment that "at this stage of progress in the Somali peace process, there will likely be a call for an expanded peacebuilding role and presence for the United Nations, in order that it may assist the Somali parties in implementing their agreement. At the same time, it is clear that any enhanced role for the Organization in Somalia must be incremental, and should be based on the outcome of discussions with the new government." The Council looks forward to the recommendations of the Secretary-General in this regard.

The Council urges the Somali leaders to create a favourable environment for the future Transitional Federal Government by making determined efforts to bring about improvements in the security situation on the ground and reiterates that those who persist on the path of confrontation and conflict will be held accountable. The Council will continue to monitor the situation closely.

Formation of Transitional Federal Government

As later reported by the Secretary-General [S/2005/89], the Transitional Federal Government of Somalia had been formed by the end of the year, with the completion of: the appointment by the President, on 3 November, of Ali Mohammed Gedi, a member of the Hawiye clan predominant in Mogadishu, as Prime Minister, which was endorsed by Parliament on 23 December; and the appointment by the Prime Minister, early in December, of 73 Ministers, Assistant Ministers and Ministers of State, which some in Parliament criticized as not in line with the "4.5 formula" for clan representation followed during the National Reconciliation Conference.

Earlier, a donors meeting (Stockholm, Sweden, 29 October) discussed options for a coordination structure to oversee and guide assistance to Somalia and requested the United Nations to take the lead role at the political and planning levels. They formed a Coordination and Monitoring Committee co-chaired by the United Nations and the Transitional Federal Government, which held its first meeting on 11 November. A UN inter-agency fact-finding mission visited Ethiopia and Kenya from 13 to 17 December to assess the progress made in the Somali peace process. The mission, which held talks with the President, the Speaker of Parliament, representatives of IGAD countries and donors, among others, stressed the need to provide support for the outcome of the peace process.

On 25 October, President Yusuf urged the AU Peace and Security Council to support his Government through the provision of 15,000 to 20,000 peacekeeping troops in order to restore security in Somalia. He based those figures on the existence of an estimated 55,000 armed militiamen, 500 "technicals" and 2 million small arms in the country. In response, the AU organized a planning seminar (Addis Ababa, 4-5 November) for the stabilization of Somalia through the transitional period.

An IGAD special summit on Somalia (Nairobi, 14 October) recognized the Government of President Yusuf and agreed to hold talks with the AU, the United Nations, LAS, EU and the United States to make a case for a peace enforcement force in Somalia. On 17 November, the IGAD Council of Ministers agreed to establish an IGAD monitoring and follow-up team to continue to support the Somali peace process to succeed its Facilitation Committee.

Meanwhile in Somalia, the Somaliland Cabinet issued a statement on 11 October reiterating the "sovereignty and territorial integrity" of "Somaliland" as non-negotiable and requesting the international community's help to prevent conflict between Somalia and "Somaliland". Intermittent fighting continued throughout Somalia, and the prevailing insecurity and violence prevented the United Nations from implementing programmes in large areas of the country. Reports indicated large-scale violations of the arms embargo. Above-normal rainfall in most of Somalia during late 2004 brought a four-year drought to an end, providing relief to the country's largely pastoral economy. However, the humanitarian emergency continued in drought-affected regions in the north and in other parts.

Security Council consideration. President Ahmed, addressing the Security Council on 19 November [meeting 5083] during its session in Nairobi, said that the Government was working on the two main objectives of consolidating reconciliation talks with the armed groups and realizing a tangible peace-building plan. He requested the Council to phase in a peace-building mission, including the deployment of a stabilization force in Somalia. Noting that the Government would not generate revenue for some time, he drew attention to the urgent need for financial resources for it to function and requested the Council to take measures to provide financial and diplomatic support.

SECURITY COUNCIL ACTION (November)

On 19 November [meeting 5083], following consultations among Security Council members, the President made statement **S/PRST/2004/43** on behalf of the Council:

The Security Council reaffirms all its previous resolutions and the statements by its President concerning the situation in Somalia, in particular the statement by its President of 26 October 2004.

The Council reiterates its commitment to a comprehensive and lasting settlement of the situation in Somalia and its respect for the sovereignty, territorial integrity, political independence and unity of Somalia, consistent with the purposes and principles of the Charter of the United Nations.

The Council welcomes the progress made in the Somali National Reconciliation Process, in particular the establishment of the Transitional Federal Parliament, the election of the Speaker of Parliament and the President and the appointment of the Prime Minister, which provides a sound and solid framework to achieve a comprehensive and lasting solution to the Somalia situation. The Council reiterates its expectation of the establishment of a broad-based, all-inclusive and effective government inside Somalia that will continue the reconciliation efforts with all Somali parties.

The Council stresses that it is the responsibility of all Somali parties to work together to consolidate the gains made so far and to achieve further progress. The Council calls upon them to seize this historic opportunity for peace in Somalia by developing a programme of action and timetable for the transitional period, creating a favourable environment for long-term stability and making determined efforts to rebuild the country.

The Council commends member States of the Intergovernmental Authority on Development, in particular the Government of Kenya, as well as other countries and organizations for all their constructive efforts to facilitate the Somali National Reconciliation Process.

The Council reaffirms its support for the commitment of the African Union to assist the transitional process in Somalia, in particular the planning for a mission in Somalia, including options for disarmament, demobilization and reintegration.

The Council encourages and urges donor countries and regional and subregional organizations to provide support to the efforts of the future Somali government and institutions to ensure their ability to function inside Somalia, and to assist in the reconstruction of Somalia. The Council encourages a dialogue between the international donor community and the future Transitional Federal Government on the principles and modalities of international coordination under discussion, including at the meeting held in Stockholm on 29 October 2004, and welcomes the United Nations lead facilitating role in that dialogue and in the subsequent coordination arrangements.

The Council reaffirms its full support for the peace process in Somalia and the commitment of the United Nations to assist the regional and subregional efforts in this regard.

The Council expresses its determination to continue to monitor the situation closely.

Arms embargo

Monitoring Group. In response to Security Council resolution 1519(2003) [YUN 2003, p. 254], the Secretary-General established a Monitoring Group charged with, among other tasks, investigating violations of the arms embargo covering access to Somalia by land, air and sea. On 22 January [S/2004/73], the Secretary-General informed the Council of his appointment of four experts to the Group.

The Monitoring Group's report was transmitted on 11 August [S/2004/604] by the Security Council Committee established pursuant to resolution 751(1992) [YUN 1992, p. 202] concerning Somalia. The investigations revealed that arms continued to flow into, within and out of Somalia and were circulating inside the country. The pattern of the arms traffic and the resulting violations seemed to have changed, as arms traders and other businessmen were replacing warlords as the main importers of arms. Arms continued to be sold openly in local arms markets, in particular at the Bakaaraha arms markets in Mogadishu, the main source for arms in Somalia. The level of arms shipments to specific warlords from external sources had not changed, particularly arms obtained by special order, such as heavy weapons and ammunition. Arms flow out of Somalia was light but occurred daily, in particular to Kenya. Somali warlords, some of whom were involved in drug trafficking, were all violating the arms embargo.

The transportation of arms by air had decreased, the preferred means of transport being by land and sea. There was evidence that arms smuggled from one neighbouring Gulf State were transported to a port in another neighbouring State and thence to Somalia by road or by sea. The arms were delivered from external sources to the north and south of Somalia to several places along the Somali coastline, often by dhows and in some cases large vessels, and distributed by road. Sources indicated that some Somali warlords were not keen on seeing a government in place because it would undermine their business operations. Money obtained from arms and drug trafficking and other illegal activities was used to buy goods that were then smuggled into neighbouring countries. The Customs and border control of the neighbouring States were ineffective in enforcing the arms embargo due to a lack of capability and corruption.

The Monitoring Group considered premature the preparation of a draft list of those who continued to violate the arms embargo inside and outside Somalia, together with their supports for possible Council action, as requested in resolution 1519(2003). It recommended that the draft list be called a watch list, remain confidential and include individuals to be investigated further to establish whether they continued to violate the arms embargo. Continued monitoring of the arms embargo was necessary to ensure its effectiveness, but the limited duration of the Group's mandate did not offer enough opportunity to investigate fully some of the alleged violations, thus making it difficult to come up with clear-cut and definitive cases of violation. Continuity of the Group was imperative at the current critical stage of the Somali National Reconciliation Conference (see p. 260), to enable it to act as a deterrent to potential violators and to ensure that opposition groups did not destabilize any new transitional government that might emerge from the Conference.

SECURITY COUNCIL ACTION (August)

On 17 August [meeting 5022], the Security Council unanimously adopted **resolution 1558(2004)**. The draft [S/2004/648] was prepared in consultations among Council members.

The Security Council,

Reaffirming its previous resolutions and the statements by its President concerning the situation in Somalia, in particular resolution 733(1992) of 23 January 1992, which established an embargo on all deliveries of weapons and military equipment to Somalia (hereinafter referred to as "the arms embargo"), and resolution 1519(2003) of 16 December 2003,

Reiterating its firm support for the Somali National Reconciliation Process and the ongoing Somali National Reconciliation Conference under the sponsorship of the Intergovernmental Authority on Development, and reaffirming the importance of the sovereignty, territorial integrity, political independence and unity of Somalia,

Condemning the continued flow of weapons and ammunition supplies to and through Somalia, in contravention of the arms embargo, and expressing its determination that violators should be held accountable,

Reiterating the importance of enhancing the monitoring of the arms embargo in Somalia through persistent and vigilant investigation into the violations, bearing in mind that the Somali National Reconciliation Process and the implementation of the arms embargo serve as mutually reinforcing processes,

Determining that the situation in Somalia constitutes a threat to international peace and security in the region,

Acting under Chapter VII of the Charter of the United Nations,

1. *Stresses* the obligation of all States to comply fully with the measures imposed by resolution 733(1992);

2. *Takes note* of the report of the Monitoring Group of 11 August 2004 submitted pursuant to paragraph 6 of resolution 1519(2003), and the observations and recommendations contained therein, and expresses its intention to give them due consideration in order to improve compliance with the measures imposed by resolution 733(1992);

3. *Requests* the Secretary-General, in consultation with the Security Council Committee established pursuant to resolution 751(1992) concerning Somalia (hereinafter referred to as "the Committee"), to re-establish, within thirty days of the date of adoption of the present resolution, and for a period of six months,

the Monitoring Group as referred to in paragraph 2 of resolution 1519(2003), with the following mandate:

(a) To continue the tasks outlined in paragraphs 2 *(a)* to *(d)* of resolution 1519(2003);

(b) To continue refining and updating information on the draft list of those who continue to violate the arms embargo inside and outside Somalia, and their active supporters, for possible future measures by the Council, and to present such information to the Committee as and when the Committee deems appropriate;

(c) To continue making recommendations based on its investigations, on the previous reports of the Panel of Experts appointed pursuant to resolutions 1425 (2002) of 22 July 2002 and 1474(2003) of 8 April 2003, and on the first report of the Monitoring Group;

(d) To work closely with the Committee on specific recommendations for additional measures to improve overall compliance with the arms embargo;

(e) To provide to the Council, through the Committee, a midterm report and a final report covering all the tasks set out above;

4. *Also requests* the Secretary-General to make the necessary financial arrangements to support the work of the Monitoring Group;

5. *Reaffirms* the need for implementation of the actions set out in paragraphs 4, 5, 7, 8 and 10 of resolution 1519(2003);

6. *Expects* the Committee, in accordance with its mandate, to recommend to the Council appropriate measures in response to violations of the arms embargo, by considering and developing, in close consultation with the Monitoring Group, specific proposals to improve compliance with the arms embargo;

7. *Decides* to remain actively seized of the matter.

In response to resolution 1558(2004) (above) recommending the re-establishment of the Monitoring Group, the Secretary-General, on 23 August [S/2004/676], appointed four experts as members of the Group.

Security Council Committee. On 29 December, the Chairman of the Security Council Committee established pursuant to resolution 751(1992) [YUN 1992, p. 202] concerning the arms embargo on Somalia submitted a report covering its activities in 2004 [S/2004/1017]. The Committee held 3 formal and 10 informal meetings during the year. It discussed the work of the Monitoring Group and the replies received from 19 Member States to its request for information on violations of the arms embargo. As in the past, the Committee relied on the cooperation of States and organizations in a position to provide such information.

Eritrea-Ethiopia

The United Nations maintained its presence in Eritrea and Ethiopia, as it continued to monitor implementation of the 2000 Algiers ceasefire and peace agreements between the two countries [YUN 2000, p. 180] (known collectively as the Algiers Agreements), which regulated their border dispute that had led to armed conflict in 1998 and intermittent fighting since then. The United Nations Mission in Ethiopia and Eritrea (UNMEE), established in 2000, continued to monitor the border region inside and near the Temporary Security Zone and to support the work of the Boundary Commission, set up by the Agreements to determine the border. In 2002, the Commission completed the delimitation of the border and began the demarcation process, which was stalled by the end of 2003 when Ethiopia rejected significant parts of the Commission's decision, which it had previously accepted as final and binding. At the beginning of 2004, both sides continued to restrict the freedom of movement of UNMEE in areas inside and adjacent to the Temporary Security Zone and both banned direct flights by UN aircraft between the Ethiopian capital of Addis Ababa and the Eritrean capital of Asmara.

Although no major incidents between the two countries occurred in early 2004, the lack of progress in the political situation, in particular the demarcation of the border, threatened the stability of the subregion. The Secretary-General, seeking to rekindle the political process, appointed a Special Envoy to explore with both Governments ways of overcoming the impasse. Eritrea, however, refused to receive him on the grounds that it would not entertain any new process before the implementation of the Commission's decision.

The Security Council, in September, extended the UNMEE mandate and approved reductions in its size and operations, as proposed by the Secretary-General, and took note of some positive developments in relations between UNMEE and both countries.

Ethiopia, on 25 November, proposed a five-point peace plan for resolving the bilateral dispute through peaceful means, which included working towards normalization of relations and opening dialogue on implementing the Boundary Commission's decision on delimitation. Eritrea was dismissive of the proposal, stating that Ethiopia needed to express unconditional support of the Commission and its decision, withdraw from Eritrean territory and cooperate on demarcation of the border. In December, there was a steady increase of Ethiopian armed forces near the security zone.

Implementation of Algiers Agreements

Security Council consideration. On 7 January, at an informal meeting of the Security Council to consider the Secretary-General's December 2003 report on the situation in Ethiopia and Eritrea

[YUN 2003, p. 238], Assistant Secretary-General in the Department of Peacekeeping Operations, Hédi Annabi, briefed the Council on recent developments.

In a press statement issued on that date [SC/7972-AFR/807], the Council President said that the Council members expressed concern about the lack of progress in the demarcation process. They reaffirmed the final and binding nature of the Eritrea-Ethiopia Boundary Commission's decision and underlined the importance of its expeditious implementation within the framework of the Agreements. They also expressed disappointment about Ethiopia's rejection of parts of the decision and its refusal to fully cooperate with the Commission. The Council members, while acknowledging the cooperative attitude of the Eritrean Government, appealed to both parties to initiate demarcation expeditiously. They supported the additional measures being considered by the Secretary-General to move demarcation and the peace process forward and urged both countries to respond positively to his proposals.

The Council members also expressed concern at the recent sharp increase in the restriction of UNMEE's movement by Eritrea and the persisting administrative difficulties imposed by both parties. They urged both to provide full support to UNMEE, facilitate unrestricted movement of its personnel and establish a route for UNMEE flights between the two capitals. Noting recent inflammatory rhetoric by both sides, Council members called on them to engage in a broad political dialogue with a view to improving their relations and defusing tensions.

Appointment. The Secretary-General, on 29 January [S/2004/102], appointed Lloyd Axworthy (Canada) as his Special Envoy for Ethiopia and Eritrea to explore with them ways to overcome the current impasse in the implementation of the Algiers Agreements. He underscored that the offer of good offices did not represent a new initiative or alternative mechanism but would focus on the implementation of the Agreements, the Boundary Commission's decision and relevant Security Council resolutions and decisions. On 9 February [S/2004/103], the Council welcomed the appointment and expressed support for the Secretary-General's mission of good offices.

Communications. On 13 February [S/2004/116], Eritrea forwarded to the Council three letters from its President, Isaias Afwerki, to the Secretary-General concerning the peace process. The communications expressed Eritrea's position on the matter of the Secretary-General's Special Envoy, stating that Eritrea sensed an imposition on it to accept the new mission of the Special

Envoy. Eritrea had decided not to entertain any new process, political or otherwise, before the full and expeditious implementation of the 2002 decision of the Boundary Commission [YUN 2002, p. 187] demarcating the border. In the letters, the President reiterated Eritrea's position that the introduction of another process would serve no useful purpose. Eritrea blamed Ethiopia for the stalemate in the implementation process caused by its rejection of the Commission's decision.

Report of Secretary-General (March). In his 5 March [S/2004/180] progress report on Ethiopia and Eritrea, the Secretary-General updated developments and described UNMEE activities since his December 2003 report [YUN 2003, p. 238]. Annexed to the report was the twelfth report of the Eritrea-Ethiopia Boundary Commission, covering the period from 1 December 2003 to 26 February 2004, which had been unable to advance its demarcation activities.

The Secretary-General's Special Envoy visited the region in late February, consulting with the Ethiopian leadership and AU officials in Addis Ababa; he did not visit Asmara because of Eritrea's opposition to his mission.

The general situation in the Temporary Security Zone and the adjacent areas remained relatively stable but fragile during the reporting period. In the absence of progress in the demarcation of the border, UNMEE continued to patrol the Zone, monitor the redeployed positions of the parties' armed forces in the adjacent areas, and observe the activities of the Eritrean militia and police in and around the Zone. UNMEE observed an increase in training activities, in particular by the Ethiopian Armed Forces, which conducted such exercise near the southern boundary of the Zone. Incursions by Ethiopian herdsmen and their livestock into the Zone decreased marginally, and incidents of Ethiopian militia accompanying them had all but ceased. Meanwhile, allegations by both parties of cattle rustling and attacks on UNMEE property and/or personnel increased. On 2 February, Ethiopia severely restricted UNMEE's freedom of movement by closing almost all roads leading into the country for 48 hours. On the Eritrean side, UNMEE movements were also restricted in areas adjacent to, and sometimes within, the Zone. UNMEE staff continued to experience difficulties at the airports in Addis Ababa and Asmara, and direct flights between the two capitals were still not permitted by both countries. The Military Coordination Commission, chaired by UNMEE, met on 2 February and endorsed a framework for the conduct of sector-level military coordination commissions, the first of which was convened on the Mereb River Bridge on 3 March. The

Secretary-General appealed to Eritrea to sign the status-of-forces agreement with the United Nations without delay.

UN agencies continued to assist in addressing medium- to long-term food insecurity in an attempt to break the cycle of persistent emergency and need for humanitarian response in both countries. The full caseload of those requiring aid was estimated to be some 7.2 million people. UNMEE completed 88 quick-impact projects in the Temporary Security Zone and adjacent areas. However, the Trust Fund to Support the Peace Process in Ethiopia and Eritrea was almost depleted.

The Secretary-General said that the appointment of his Special Envoy was intended to provide an opportunity for both parties to present their positions and ideas on how to move the process forward. He reiterated his appeal to them, especially to Eritrea, to give his Special Envoy the opportunity to meet and discuss with their leadership how best his mission of good offices could help them overcome the impasse.

The continuing stalemate raised questions about the future of UNMEE, which was not meant to support a status quo indefinitely. Possible benchmarks for its reduction would include an improvement in the security environment, well-functioning sector military coordination commissions and meaningful progress in demarcation. UNMEE's effectiveness would be kept under review and its operations adjusted and streamlined as needed. Meanwhile, the Secretary-General recommended that the Mission's mandate be extended for six months, until 15 September.

SECURITY COUNCIL ACTION (March)

On 12 March [meeting 4924], the Security Council unanimously adopted **resolution 1531(2004)**. The draft [S/2004/188] was prepared in consultations among Council members.

The Security Council,

Reaffirming all its previous resolutions and the statements by its President pertaining to the situation between Ethiopia and Eritrea, and the requirements contained therein, including in particular resolution 1507(2003) of 12 September 2003,

Reiterating its support for the peace process and its unwavering commitment, including through the role played by the United Nations Mission in Ethiopia and Eritrea, to the full and expeditious implementation of the comprehensive Peace Agreement signed at Algiers by the Governments of Ethiopia and Eritrea (hereinafter referred to as "the parties") on 12 December 2000 and the preceding Agreement on Cessation of Hostilities signed on 18 June 2000 ("the Algiers Agreements"), and the delimitation decision of the Boundary Commission of 13 April 2002, embraced by the parties as final and binding in accordance with the Algiers Agreements,

Noting with concern the continuing impasse in the peace process, due mainly to the lack of progress in the demarcation of the border,

Taking note with concern of the twelfth report on the work of the Eritrea-Ethiopia Boundary Commission, of 27 February 2004, in particular its conclusion that under the present circumstances the Commission is unable to progress with demarcation activities,

Expressing its concern about Ethiopia's rejection of significant parts of the decision of the Boundary Commission and its current lack of cooperation with the Commission,

Expressing disappointment about Eritrea's refusal at present to engage with the Special Envoy of the Secretary-General for Ethiopia and Eritrea,

Emphasizing that cooperation with the Special Envoy offers both parties a concrete opportunity to move the peace process forward,

Recognizing the increasing demand for United Nations peacekeeping and resources from the international community for peacekeeping and peace-building purposes, and recalling the additional operational costs due to the delays in the demarcation process,

Expressing its support for the Special Representative of the Secretary-General for Ethiopia and Eritrea and for the Mission,

Having considered the report of the Secretary-General of 5 March 2004, and fully supporting the observations made therein,

1. *Decides* to extend the mandate of the United Nations Mission in Ethiopia and Eritrea until 15 September 2004 at the troop and military observer levels authorized by its resolution 1320(2000) of 15 September 2000;

2. *Strongly urges* the parties once again to cooperate fully and expeditiously with the Mission in the implementation of its mandate and to step up their efforts to ensure the security of all Mission staff, and reiterates in the strongest terms its demand that the parties allow the Mission full freedom of movement and remove with immediate effect and without preconditions any and all restrictions on, and impediments to the work of, the Mission and its staff in the discharge of their mandate;

3. *Stresses* that the primary responsibility for the implementation of the Algiers Agreements and the decision of the Eritrea-Ethiopia Boundary Commission lies with both parties;

4. *Calls upon* the parties to cooperate fully and promptly with the Boundary Commission and to create the necessary conditions for demarcation to proceed expeditiously, including through the unequivocal restating of Ethiopia's acceptance of the decision of the Commission, the appointment by Ethiopia of field liaison officers and the payment of its dues to the Commission;

5. *Reaffirms* the crucial importance of a political dialogue between the two countries for the completion of the peace process and the consolidation of progress achieved so far, and urges both parties to normalize their relations, including through confidence-building measures, and to refrain from any threat or use of force against each other;

6. *Reiterates its support* for the initiative of the Secretary-General to exercise his good offices by appointing a Special Envoy in order to facilitate the implementation of the Algiers Agreements, the decision of the Boundary Commission and the relevant resolutions and decisions of the Security Council and to encourage the normalization of diplomatic relations between the two countries, and emphasizes that this appointment does not constitute an alternative mechanism;

7. *Expresses its full support* for the Special Envoy of the Secretary-General for Ethiopia and Eritrea, Mr. Lloyd Axworthy, stresses that the Special Envoy enjoys the unanimous support of the witnesses to the Algiers Agreements, namely the United Nations, the United States of America, Algeria, the African Union and the European Union, and urges both parties, in particular the Government of Eritrea, to engage constructively and without further delay with the Special Envoy;

8. *Urges* both parties once again to establish expeditiously a direct high-altitude flight route between Asmara and Addis Ababa to relieve the unnecessary additional cost to the Mission and Member States;

9. *Decides* to monitor closely the steps taken by the parties in the implementation of their commitments under the Algiers Agreements, including through the Boundary Commission, and to review any implications for the Mission;

10. *Requests* the Secretary-General to monitor the situation closely and to keep under review the effectiveness of the mission, and to adjust and streamline its operations as needed, taking into account also the mandate of the Mission as outlined in paragraph 2 of resolution 1320(2000);

11. *Decides* to remain actively seized of the matter.

Council President's press statement. Following informal consultations in the Security Council and a Secretariat briefing on 4 May, the Council President released a press statement [SC/8085-AFR/918] expressing members' concern at the deterioration in Eritrea's cooperation with UNMEE and continuing restrictions on its freedom of movement, especially in areas adjacent to the Temporary Security Zone; the increase in detention of UNMEE local staff; the closure of the main supply route to UNMEE troops in Sector West by Eritrean authorities; and recent public allegations by a senior Eritrean government official that might negatively affect the security of UNMEE staff. Members were disappointed with Ethiopia's continued rejection of significant parts of the Boundary Commission decision, which heightened regional tension and blocked completion of UNMEE's mandate. Eritrea's and Ethiopia's actions raised questions about UNMEE's long-term viability. Members were also concerned about the lack of progress in the implementation of the Boundary Commission's demarcation decision and reiterated their support for the Special Envoy's efforts to engage the two parties in

order to overcome the current stalemate in the peace process.

Report of Secretary-General (July). On 7 July [S/2004/543], the Secretary-General, in his progress report on Ethiopia and Eritrea, said that, during the reporting period, relations between the Eritrean authorities and UNMEE had deteriorated, as a result of the government measures noted by the Council in its presidential statement (above). The Eritrean authorities had closed the main road from Asmara to Barentu, UNMEE's main supply route to troops in Sector West. The Special Representative had written to President Isaias Afwerki asking for his personal intervention to reverse the trend, as had the Secretary-General. The Foreign Minister had assured a visiting UN team that Eritrea was prepared to resolve any problems amicably.

Cooperation with Ethiopia remained at a workable level. Training activities by the Ethiopian Armed Forces continued, including the firing of heavy-calibre weapons close to the southern boundary of the Zone. Following discussions with the sector-level of the Military Coordination Commission, the Forces agreed to move live firing exercises at least five kilometres away from the Zone.

Reports of violations of the Zone, mostly cattle rustling, increased. In April, Eritrea reported three violations, which allegedly resulted in exchanges of fire between Eritrean militia and Ethiopians entering the Zone. Eritrean militia arrested two individuals of the Kunama ethnic group. On 25 May, a large explosion occurred in Barentu, in Sector West, killing an unconfirmed number of people and injuring dozens. As UNMEE continued to encounter restrictions of movement in areas adjacent to the Zone within Eritrea, its ability to monitor the redeployed positions of the Eritrean Defence Forces remained constrained.

The Military Coordination Commission met (Nairobi, 15 March and 10 May) to discuss the military situation in the Mission area, focusing on security aspects impacting on UNMEE operations. Sector-level coordination meetings were initiated in Sectors West and Centre, with meetings held in March, April and May.

The Boundary Commission, in its thirteenth report annexed to the Secretary-General's report, reiterated that the stalemate persisted; consequently, it was maintaining its presence in the area, at a reduced level, so that it could resume operations if required. It also noted that Ethiopia had not paid its portion of the Commission's expenses.

An escalation of public rhetoric on both sides was noted, and reports indicated that each continued to upgrade and strengthen its armed forces. The Secretary-General expressed concern about public statements by Eritrean authorities attacking the peacekeeping operation and its staff. He noted the 7 April statement by the Ethiopian Foreign Ministry reiterating that the current demarcation line would disrupt the lives of border communities and lead to future conflict, and describing the demarcation process as flawed. He reminded the parties, in particular Ethiopia, that they themselves had entrusted the Boundary Commission with the entire demarcation process, had drawn up its mandate and had selected its Commissioners. Aware of the questions being raised about the long-term effectiveness of UNMEE, the Secretary-General initiated a review aimed at adjusting and streamlining UNMEE's operations as needed, keeping in mind its mandate and the need to uphold the integrity of the ceasefire arrangements.

Communication. Eritrea, on 14 July [S/2004/571], characterized the Secretary-General's report as replete with factual inaccuracies, biased against Eritrea, and portraying a distorted picture of the reality on the ground. It failed to recognize Ethiopia's violation of international law and glossed over its provocative act of building new settlements in Badme, the seriousness of which the United Nations could not downplay. It was also silent on Ethiopia's responsibility for the current state of affairs.

Eritrea stated that it fully respected UNMEE's unhindered freedom of movement in the Zone. However, it could not accept a unilateral extension of the Zone by another stretch of territory termed "adjacent area", nor did it subscribe to UNMEE's interpretation of the 2000 Algiers Peace Agreements [YUN 2000, p. 180] as implying freedom of random inspection without prior notice and government approval. Eritrea cited examples of what it called UNMEE's intrusive and unwarranted activities outside the Zone and emphasized the need for UNMEE to be neutral.

Appointment. On 6 July [S/2004/548], the Secretary-General informed the Security Council of the appointment of Major-General Rajender Singh (India) as UNMEE Force Commander, to replace Major-General Robert Gordon (United Kingdom) whose tour of duty was ending. The Council took note of the information [S/2004/549].

Press statement (July). The Security Council President, in a 15 July press statement [SC/8150-AFR/995], said that Council members were satisfied that some restrictions on UNMEE's freedom of movement had decreased, but stressed that several other open questions, such as direct flights between Addis Ababa and Asmara, re-

mained unresolved. They called on both parties to continue to cooperate constructively with the Mission to maintain stability and prevent incidents in the border area. They also welcomed UNMEE's ongoing efforts to streamline its operations.

Members welcomed the recent visit (3-7 July) of the Secretary-General to both capitals and expressed the hope that his meetings with Eritrea's President Isaias Afwerki and Ethiopia's Prime Minister Meles Zenawi would provide new momentum for the involvement of both parties with the Special Envoy.

Report of Secretary-General (September). In his 2 September progress report on Ethiopia and Eritrea [S/2004/708], the Secretary-General said that the general situation in the Temporary Security Zone and adjacent areas remained stable. Improvement in the cooperation of both parties with UNMEE had had a positive effect on the overall security environment. Restrictions imposed by Eritrea on UNMEE patrols inside and near the Zone had decreased. The main supply route to UNMEE troops in Sector West was reopened on 9 August but closed again from 1 September. Detentions by Eritrea of locally recruited UN staff had also decreased. Cooperation between UNMEE and the military authorities on the Ethiopian side remained satisfactory. Except for a few incidents, the Ethiopian Armed Forces had imposed no restrictions on UNMEE patrols in the adjacent areas south of the Zone.

On 18 August, Prime Minister Meles Zenawi informed the Secretary-General of Ethiopia's decision to allow UN aircraft to fly directly between Asmara and Addis Ababa without deviation, and on 31 August, an UNMEE team met with Ethiopian authorities to work out the technical details.

Under the chairmanship of the UNMEE Force Commander, the twenty-fifth meeting of the Military Coordination Commission was held (Nairobi, 5 July). A total of six sector-level meetings had been held to review the military situation.

As requested by the Security Council in resolution 1531(2004) (see p. 267), the Secretary-General conducted a review of UNMEE's effectiveness. He determined that the Mission's military component was a vital factor of stability and cautioned the United Nations to be careful not to leave a security vacuum. At the same time, there was a realization that, after four years, the time had come to adjust its configuration, particularly since some areas of the Zone had been militarily stable since UNMEE's establishment. Any change in the force structure should be gradual, taking into consideration the security dynamics so as not to undermine UNMEE's core monitoring function or the Boundary Commission's prospect of resuming its work. Should the current stalemate in the peace process be broken, leading to the demarcation of the border, the Secretary-General said that he would recommend the temporary strengthening of UNMEE in a number of areas, including humanitarian, human rights and legal affairs. In the current circumstances, however, he recommended adjustments in two phases. Phase I, already in progress, included replacing the military demining contingent, which had left in June, with a modest commercial capacity, resulting in annual savings of $6 million and reducing force headquarters staff by up to 30 per cent. Phase II would entail repatriating the infantry battalion and support elements from Sector East and consolidating the existing three sectors into two. The remaining two infantry battalions would adjust their areas of responsibility to support and secure the military observers remaining in Sector East. The troop drawdown would be offset by an increase in air patrols. At the completion of Phase II, the military structure would comprise a force headquarters, two infantry battalions, two demining units, other support elements and up to 220 military observers. The force reserve would come from the remaining force structure. The number of civilian staff would be reduced commensurately. Further reductions might be justified following completion of Phase II and would depend on the situation on the ground.

The persistent humanitarian needs in Ethiopia and Eritrea remained of concern to UN agencies and implementing partners. Given that situation, the Secretary-General extended the mandate of his Special Envoy for the Humanitarian Crisis in the Horn of Africa, Martti Ahtisaari, for another six months to enable him to work with the two Governments, the donor community, the UN country teams and other stakeholders in identifying longer-term solutions to the humanitarian challenges.

Having met with the leaders of both countries during his visit in early July, the Secretary-General remained concerned about the absence of prospects for breaking the stalemate on the demarcation of the border. Neither side had offered any new ideas on how the peace process could be advanced. It should be clear to both parties that progress would not be made by merely restating and maintaining positions. It was time that the more cooperative spirit they had recently demonstrated towards UNMEE be applied to the broader political process in order to move it forward. While awaiting their further moves, the Secretary-General recommended that the UNMEE mandate be extended for a further six months, until 15 March 2005, and that the Security Council authorize the proposed adjustments indicated.

SECURITY COUNCIL ACTION (September)

On 14 September [meeting 5032], the Security Council unanimously adopted **resolution 1560 (2004)**. The draft [S/2004/728] was prepared in consultations among Council members.

The Security Council,

Reaffirming all its previous resolutions and statements pertaining to the situation between Ethiopia and Eritrea, and the requirements contained therein, including in particular resolution 1531(2004) of 12 March 2004,

Stressing its unwavering commitment to the peace process, including through the role played by the United Nations Mission in Ethiopia and Eritrea, and to the full and expeditious implementation of the comprehensive Peace Agreement signed on 12 December 2000 at Algiers by the Governments of Ethiopia and Eritrea (hereinafter referred to as "the parties") and the preceding Agreement on Cessation of Hostilities signed on 18 June 2000 ("the Algiers Agreements"), and the delimitation decision of the Eritrea-Ethiopia Boundary Commission of 13 April 2002, embraced by the parties as final and binding in accordance with the Algiers Agreements,

Recalling that lasting peace between Ethiopia and Eritrea, as well as in the region, cannot be achieved without the full demarcation of the border between the parties,

Noting with concern, in this regard, the lack of progress made in the demarcation of the border, as reflected in the fourteenth report on the work of the Boundary Commission, of 20 August 2004, which concludes that under the present circumstances the Commission is unable to progress with demarcation activities,

Expressing its concern about Ethiopia's ongoing rejection of significant parts of the decision of the Boundary Commission and its current lack of cooperation with the Commission,

Expressing disappointment about the continuing refusal of Eritrea to engage with the Special Envoy of the Secretary-General for Ethiopia and Eritrea, whose good offices represent a concrete opportunity for the parties to move the peace process forward,

Recalling the recent increase in United Nations peacekeeping activities and the need to allocate peacekeeping resources in the most effective manner, and recalling in this regard the additional burden caused by the delays in the demarcation process,

Having considered the report of the Secretary-General of 2 September 2004, and fully supporting the observations made therein,

1. *Decides* to extend the mandate of the United Nations Mission in Ethiopia and Eritrea until 15 March 2005;

2. *Approves* the adjustments to the Mission, including its presence and operations, as recommended by the Secretary-General in paragraphs 13 to 18 of his report;

3. *Calls upon* the parties to cooperate fully and expeditiously with the Mission in the implementation of

its mandate, to ensure the security of all staff of the Mission, and to remove immediately and unconditionally all restrictions on and impediments to the work and to the full and free movement of the Mission and its staff;

4. *Takes note* of positive developments in some areas of relations between the Mission and the parties, in this regard welcomes particularly the recent decision by Ethiopia to allow a direct high-altitude flight route between Asmara and Addis Ababa without any deviation, urges Ethiopia and Eritrea to take immediate steps, in consultation with the Mission, towards implementing the direct flights between the two capitals, and also in this regard calls upon Eritrea to reopen the Asmara to Barentu road;

5. *Stresses* that Ethiopia and Eritrea have the primary responsibility for the implementation of the Algiers Agreements and the decision of the Eritrea-Ethiopia Boundary Commission, and calls upon the parties to show political leadership to achieve a full normalization of their relationship, including through the adoption of further confidence-building measures;

6. *Calls upon* the parties to cooperate fully and promptly with the Boundary Commission and to create the necessary conditions for demarcation to proceed expeditiously, including through the payment of Ethiopia's dues to the Commission and the appointment of field liaison officers;

7. *Urges* Ethiopia to show the political will to reaffirm unequivocally its acceptance of the decision of the Boundary Commission, and to take the necessary steps to enable the Commission to demarcate the border without further delay;

8. *Reiterates its full support* for the Special Envoy of the Secretary-General for Ethiopia and Eritrea, Mr. Lloyd Axworthy, in his efforts to facilitate the implementation of the Algiers Agreements, the decision of the Boundary Commission and the normalization of diplomatic relations between the two countries through his good offices, and emphasizes that this appointment does not constitute an alternative mechanism;

9. *Calls upon* Eritrea to enter into dialogue and cooperation with the Special Envoy;

10. *Decides* to continue monitoring closely the steps taken by the parties in the implementation of their commitments under the relevant resolutions of the Security Council and under the Algiers Agreements, including through the Boundary Commission, and to review any implications for the Mission;

11. *Requests* the Secretary-General to continue to monitor the situation closely, to review the mission's mandate in the light of progress made in the peace process and changes made to the Mission;

12. *Decides* to remain actively seized of the matter.

Communication. The EU, in a 17 September statement by its Presidency [S/2004/802], welcomed resolution 1560(2004) and supported the Mission's rationalization. It expressed concern about the continuing stalemate and urged the two countries to use the next six months to implement measures that might help to break the current deadlock and allow demarcation to proceed.

Five-point peace proposal. On 25 November [S/2004/943], the House of Peoples' Representa-

tives of Ethiopia, reiterating Ethiopia's firm position that the decision of the Boundary Commission was flawed but realizing that lasting peace between Ethiopia and Eritrea was more important, adopted a five-point proposal on peace between them, submitted by Prime Minister Meles Zenawi. By the proposal, Ethiopia would resolve their dispute only through peaceful means and the root causes of their conflict through dialogue; it would accept in principle the Commission's decision, agree to pay its Commission dues and appoint field liaison officers; and it would immediately start dialogue with a view to implementing the decision in question in a manner consistent with the promotion of sustainable peace. Ethiopia's communication to the Secretary-General included the Prime Minister's statement to the House announcing the proposal.

The EU, on 29 November [S/2004/938], welcomed Ethiopia's announcement of the five-point peace plan and said that its agreement to accept the Boundary Commission's decision was an indication of its commitment. The EU remained ready to play a supportive role in the peace process and emphasized that the normalization of relations would be an essential element for regional peace and security.

Eritrea, responding in a 12 December press release [S/2004/968], said that the way forward lay with Ethiopia's full and unconditional respect of the Algiers Agreements; strict compliance with the Boundary Commission's decision; withdrawal of its forces from Eritrean territories; and cooperation with the Commission to ensure expeditious demarcation of the boundary. Eritrea called on the international community to help secure peace and stability by putting pressure on Ethiopia to ensure demarcation.

On 15 December [S/2004/970], Ethiopia, in an aide-memoire said that it found Eritrea's rejection of its five-point peace proposal puzzling as it addressed all of Eritrea's concerns. Ethiopia said that its acceptance of the Boundary Commission's decision was unequivocal and unconditional, but it had used the wording "accepts in principle" in recognition of the technical requirement for adjustments which required dialogue and the Commission's identification of the "anomalies" and "impracticalities" of its decision, which could only be overcome by dialogue.

The Security Council President, in a 21 December press statement [SC/8276-AFR/1084], said that Council members welcomed the Ethiopian announcement of the five-point peace plan and Eritrea's continued acceptance of the Commission's decision. They were encouraged by the movement towards a peaceful solution of the border dispute and looked forward to the beginning of the border demarcation process. They encouraged both countries to work towards a full normalization of their relations, to reiterate their commitment to solving their differences peacefully and to refrain from any destabilizing action in the border area.

Report of Secretary-General (December). The Secretary-General, in his 16 December progress report on Ethiopia and Eritrea [S/2004/973 & Corr.1 & Add.1], referred to Ethiopia's five-point plan and Eritrea's 10 December letter to the Boundary Commission. He stated that it was incumbent upon Ethiopia to express immediately unconditional respect for the Commission's work, including full acceptance of its 13 April 2002 decision, and that Ethiopia had to withdraw its troops from Eritrean territory and cooperate fully with the expeditious demarcation of the border. He stated further that Ethiopia had not complied with the Commission's order to remove illegal settlements from Eritrean territory.

As for the status of the Temporary Security Zone and adjacent areas, the general situation remained calm and the level of cooperation of the military authorities of both countries with UNMEE was satisfactory. During the reporting period, UNMEE observed incursions by both Ethiopian and Eritrean troops into the Zone. Freedom of movement for UNMEE personnel in Eritrea improved; however, the road from Asmara to Keren via Barentu remained closed to UNMEE, and immigration procedures imposed on its staff at Ethiopia and Eritrea airports remained in place. While Ethiopia had approved direct flights between the two capitals, efforts to secure Eritrea's approval were unsuccessful. The Secretary-General appealed to Eritrea to avoid further delay in finalizing the necessary direct flights arrangements with UNMEE.

At meetings of the Military Coordination Commission, UNMEE put forward proposals for improving communications and the security situation, including the establishment of a communications hotline, the inclusion of local police and civil administrators as observers in future meetings and military and police withdrawal from within 250 metres of both sides of the Zone.

In general, the Secretary-General was encouraged by the parties' continued commitment to the ceasefire, as manifested in the relative military stability in the border area and regular meetings of the Military Coordination Commission, and in their cooperation with UNMEE. However, serious improvement was still required as the protracted stalemate in the peace process continued. Noting Ethiopia's intention to resolve the dispute through peaceful means, he welcomed any step

that might contribute to the implementation of the Algiers Agreements and the Boundary Commission's decision, the initiation of dialogue between Eritrea and Ethiopia and the willingness to address the root causes of the conflict and to normalize bilateral relations. He encouraged Ethiopia to formally initiate implementation of its proposal through the Boundary Commission and called on both parties to refrain from any action in the border area that could be viewed as destabilizing.

Annexed to the Secretary-General's report was the fifteenth report [S/2004/973/Corr.1] of the Boundary Commission covering the period 20 August to 14 December, which indicated no further progress in its demarcation activities. Noting Ethiopia's five-point peace proposal, it said that Ethiopia had yet to pay its outstanding dues. An addendum to the Commission's report was issued on 27 December [S/2004/973/Add.1].

UNMEE financing

On 21 January [A/58/633], the Secretary-General submitted the performance report on UNMEE's budget for the period 1 July 2002 to 30 June 2003. Total expenditure for that period amounted to $209,619,100 out of an apportionment of $220,830,200, a variance of $11,211,100, or 5.1 per cent.

ACABQ reviewed the financial performance report on 12 April [A/58/759/Add.8] and recommended that the unencumbered balance of $11,211,100 and other income and adjustments totalling $13,294,000, be credited to Member States in a manner to be determined by the General Assembly. It recommended that the estimated budget requirement as requested be reduced by $3,129,200, to $198,331,600 gross ($193,774,200 net).

GENERAL ASSEMBLY ACTION

On 18 June [meeting 91], the General Assembly, on the recommendation of the Fifth Committee [A/58/824], adopted **resolution 58/302** without vote [agenda item 141].

Financing of the United Nations Mission in Ethiopia and Eritrea

The General Assembly,

Having considered the reports of the Secretary-General on the financing of the United Nations Mission in Ethiopia and Eritrea and the related reports of the Advisory Committee on Administrative and Budgetary Questions,

Bearing in mind Security Council resolution 1312 (2000) of 31 July 2000, by which the Council established the United Nations Mission in Ethiopia and Eritrea, and the subsequent resolutions by which the Council extended the mandate of the Mission, the latest of which was resolution 1531(2004) of 12 March 2004,

Recalling its resolution 55/237 of 23 December 2000 on the financing of the Mission and its subsequent resolutions thereon, the latest of which was resolution 57/328 of 18 June 2003,

Reaffirming the general principles underlying the financing of United Nations peacekeeping operations, as stated in General Assembly resolutions 1874 (S-IV) of 27 June 1963, 3101(XXVIII) of 11 December 1973 and 55/235 of 23 December 2000,

Noting with appreciation that voluntary contributions have been made to the Mission,

Mindful of the fact that it is essential to provide the Mission with the necessary financial resources to enable it to fulfil its responsibilities under the relevant resolutions of the Security Council,

1. *Takes note* of the status of contributions to the United Nations Mission in Ethiopia and Eritrea as at 15 April 2004, including the contributions outstanding in the amount of 24.8 million United States dollars, representing some 4 per cent of the total assessed contributions, notes with concern that only thirty-six Member States have paid their assessed contributions in full, and urges all other Member States, in particular those in arrears, to ensure payment of their outstanding assessed contributions;

2. *Expresses its appreciation* to those Member States which have paid their assessed contributions in full, and urges all other Member States to make every possible effort to ensure payment of their assessed contributions to the Mission in full;

3. *Expresses concern* at the financial situation with regard to peacekeeping activities, in particular as regards the reimbursements to troop contributors that bear additional burdens owing to overdue payments by Member States of their assessments;

4. *Also expresses concern* at the delay experienced by the Secretary-General in deploying and providing adequate resources to some recent peacekeeping missions, in particular those in Africa;

5. *Emphasizes* that all future and existing peacekeeping missions shall be given equal and non-discriminatory treatment in respect of financial and administrative arrangements;

6. *Also emphasizes* that all peacekeeping missions shall be provided with adequate resources for the effective and efficient discharge of their respective mandates;

7. *Reiterates its request* to the Secretary-General to make the fullest possible use of facilities and equipment at the United Nations Logistics Base at Brindisi, Italy, in order to minimize the costs of procurement for the Mission;

8. *Endorses* the conclusions and recommendations contained in the report of the Advisory Committee on Administrative and Budgetary Questions, and requests the Secretary-General to ensure their full implementation;

9. *Requests* the Secretary-General to take all action necessary to ensure that the Mission is administered with a maximum of efficiency and economy;

10. *Also requests* the Secretary-General, in order to reduce the cost of employing General Service staff, to continue efforts to recruit local staff for the Mission against General Service posts, commensurate with the requirements of the Mission;

Financial performance report for the period from 1 July 2002 to 30 June 2003

11. *Takes note* of the report of the Secretary-General on the financial performance of the Mission for the period from 1 July 2002 to 30 June 2003;

Budget estimates for the period from 1 July 2004 to 30 June 2005

12. *Decides* to appropriate to the Special Account for the United Nations Mission in Ethiopia and Eritrea the amount of 216,030,500 dollars for the period from 1 July 2004 to 30 June 2005, inclusive of 198,331,600 dollars for the maintenance of the Mission, 7 million dollars for the strengthening of the safety and security of the staff and premises of the Mission, 8,746,800 dollars for the support account for peacekeeping operations and 1,952,100 dollars for the United Nations Logistics Base;

Financing of the appropriation

13. *Decides also* to apportion among Member States the amount of 216,030,500 dollars at a monthly rate of 18,002,541 dollars, in accordance with the levels set out in General Assembly resolution 55/235, as adjusted by the Assembly in its resolution 55/236 of 23 December 2000 and updated in its resolution 58/256 of 23 December 2003, taking into account the scale of assessments for 2004 and 2005, as set out in its resolution 58/1 B of 23 December 2003, subject to a decision of the Security Council to extend the mandate of the Mission;

14. *Decides further* that, in accordance with the provisions of its resolution 973(X) of 15 December 1955, there shall be set off against the apportionment among Member States, as provided for in paragraph 13 above, their respective share in the Tax Equalization Fund of 5,943,800 dollars at a monthly rate of 495,316 dollars, comprising the estimated staff assessment income of 4,557,400 dollars approved for the Mission, the prorated share of 1,276,400 dollars of the estimated staff assessment income approved for the support account and the prorated share of 110,000 dollars of the estimated staff assessment income approved for the United Nations Logistics Base;

15. *Decides* that, for Member States that have fulfilled their financial obligations to the Mission, there shall be set off against their apportionment, as provided for in paragraph 13 above, their respective share of the unencumbered balance and other income in the total amount of 24,505,100 dollars in respect of the financial period ended 30 June 2003, in accordance with the levels set out in General Assembly resolution 55/235, as adjusted by the Assembly in its resolution 55/236 and its resolution 57/290 A of 20 December 2002, taking into account the scale of assessments for 2003 as set out in its resolutions 55/5 B of 23 December 2000 and 57/4 B of 20 December 2002;

16. *Decides also* that, for Member States that have not fulfilled their financial obligations to the Mission, there shall be set off against their outstanding obligations their respective share of the unencumbered balance and other income in the total amount of 24,505,100 dollars in respect of the financial period ended 30 June 2003, in accordance with the scheme set out in paragraph 15 above;

17. *Decides further* that the decrease of 5,100 dollars in the estimated staff assessment income in respect of the financial period ended 30 June 2003 shall be set off against the credits from the amount referred to in paragraphs 15 and 16 above;

18. *Emphasizes* that no peacekeeping operation shall be financed by borrowing funds from other active peacekeeping operations;

19. *Encourages* the Secretary-General to continue to take additional measures to ensure the safety and security of all personnel under the auspices of the United Nations participating in peacekeeping operations;

20. *Invites* voluntary contributions to the Mission in cash and in the form of services and supplies acceptable to the Secretary-General, to be administered, as appropriate, in accordance with the procedure and practices established by the General Assembly;

21. *Decides* to include in the provisional agenda of its fifty-ninth session the item entitled "Financing of the United Nations Mission in Ethiopia and Eritrea".

On 16 December [A/59/616], the Secretary-General submitted the performance report on UNMEE's budget for the period 1 July 2003 to 30 June 2004 showing a total expenditure of $183,600,200 out of an apportionment of $188,400,000, a variance of $4,799,800 or 2.5 per cent. On 21 December [A/59/636], the Secretary-General submitted UNMEE's budget for the period 1 July 2005 to 30 June 2006, amounting to $176,716,200.

The Assembly, on 23 December, decided that the agenda item on UNMEE financing would remain for consideration during its resumed fifty-ninth (2005) session (**decision 59/552**).

North Africa

Western Sahara

The United Nations continued its search in 2004 for an end to the dispute over the question of governance of Western Sahara, despite a lack of movement in narrowing the negotiating positions of the two parties to the dispute, Morocco and the Frente Popular para la Liberación de Saguía el-Hamra y de Río de Oro (POLISARIO). Since the parties' agreement in 1990 to hold a referendum for the people to decide between independence or integration of the Territory with Morocco, progress had been made in establishing voter rolls, but plans to organize elections had met with objections from both sides. In 2003, the Personal Envoy of the Secretary-General proposed a Peace Plan for Self-Determination of the People of Western Sahara, dividing responsibilities of governance between the parties before

holding a referendum, but not requiring the approval of both sides for every step of implementation. POLISARIO eventually accepted the plan, but Morocco rejected it and continued to do so in 2004. In the Secretary-General's view, an agreement appeared more distant by the end of 2004 than it had a year earlier, given the lack of consensus on measures to overcome the existing deadlock.

In June, the Secretary-General's Personal Envoy, James A. Baker III, resigned, having concluded that he had done all he could on the issue. The Secretary-General requested his Special Representative for Western Sahara, Alvaro de Soto, to continue to work with the parties and the neighbouring States towards a mutually acceptable political solution.

The United Nations Mission for the Referendum in Western Sahara (MINURSO), established by Security Council resolution 690(1991) [YUN 1991, p. 794] to implement the UN settlement plan proposed by the Secretary-General, continued to monitor the ceasefire between the two parties and to report on developments, as it had for 13 years. On three occasions in 2004, the Council renewed its mandate, maintaining its authorized strength at 230 military personnel.

There was some progress in the implementation of confidence-building measures. The parties resumed family visits between Western Saharan refugees living in camps in Algeria and their relatives in the Territory, and telephone service was expanded in the camps. In February and June, POLISARIO released a total of 200 Moroccan prisoners of war, leaving another 412 such prisoners still in detention by late 2004, some of them for more than 20 years.

Peace-making efforts

Report of Secretary-General (January). The Secretary-General, in response to Security Council resolution 1513(2003) [YUN 2003, p. 264], reported on 19 January [S/2004/39] on developments in Western Sahara since his previous report [YUN 2003, p. 262]. During that period, his recently appointed Special Representative for Western Sahara, Alvaro de Soto (Peru), held talks with officials from Morocco, POLISARIO, Algeria and Mauritania. The area of responsibility of MINURSO remained calm, with no indication that either side intended to resume hostilities. Under the command of Major General Gyorgy Száraz (Hungary), it continued to monitor the ceasefire, conduct ground and air patrols, and inspect units larger than company size of the Royal Moroccan Army (RMA) and POLISARIO military forces. Both sides carried out routine maintenance and training activities. Some limitations on MINURSO's freedom of movement were imposed by POLISARIO in areas east of the berm. MINURSO continued to cooperate with the parties on the marking and disposal of mines and unexploded ordnance. That situation remained the pattern throughout 2004.

The Secretary-General reported that, since the release of 643 Moroccan prisoners of war in 2003 [YUN 2003, p. 258], 613 such prisoners remained held by POLISARIO, most of them for over 20 years. He reiterated his call for the release of all remaining prisoners of war and for both sides to account for those still missing in relation to the conflict. The situation of Western Saharan refugees deteriorated in early 2004, due to shortages of relief aid that resulted in acute and chronic malnutrition of those in the Tindouf area in Algeria. The World Food Programme (WFP) and UNHCR were planning a joint mission to the refugee camps. The UNHCR-operated telephone connection between the refugee camps in Algeria and the Territory was re-established on 12 January, and telephone service between one camp in the Tindouf area and the Territory was to be extended to other locations.

The Secretary-General's Personal Envoy, James A. Baker III (United States), having held discussions with Moroccan officials in December 2003, was of the view that the MINURSO mandate should be extended until 30 April 2004 to allow him time to consult further with Morocco on its final response to the Peace Plan for Self-Determination of the People of Western Sahara, which he proposed to the parties in January 2003 [YUN 2003, p. 259]. The Secretary-General concurred with his view and recommended that the Council extend the mandate for three months.

SECURITY COUNCIL ACTION (January)

On 30 January [meeting 4905], the Security Council unanimously adopted **resolution 1523 (2004)**. The draft [S/2004/76] was prepared in consultations among Council members.

The Security Council,

Recalling all its resolutions on Western Sahara, and reaffirming in particular resolution 1495(2003) of 31 July 2003,

1. *Decides* to extend the mandate of the United Nations Mission for the Referendum in Western Sahara until 30 April 2004;

2. *Requests* that the Secretary-General provide a report on the situation before the end of the present mandate;

3. *Decides* to remain seized of the matter.

Report of Secretary-General (April). As requested by the foregoing resolution, the Secretary-General, in a 23 April report [S/2004/325 & Add.1], described developments relating to Western Sahara since his January report.

His Personal Envoy held meetings with Moroccan officials on 2 and 15 April to discuss issues pertaining to Morocco's final response to resolution 1495(2003) [YUN 2003, p. 262], calling on the parties to work with the United Nations and with each other towards accepting and implementing its terms. He also met with POLISARIO in March. During a meeting with the Personal Envoy on 15 April, Morocco delivered its final response to the plan, which was annexed to the report, raising issues that it considered unacceptable. It believed that the autonomy-based political solution offered to the people as a transitional step could only be final; it could therefore not agree to a transition period marked by uncertainty as to the final status of the Territory. On the other hand, the autonomy solution, as agreed to by the parties, by definition ruled out the possibility for the independence option to be submitted to the population. It was, therefore, out of the question for Morocco to engage in negotiations with anyone over its sovereignty and territorial integrity. With those aspects ruled out from the plan, Morocco was prepared to negotiate a final settlement through a viable autonomy status for the Sahara region.

During the reporting period, MINURSO conducted ground and air patrols to inspect Moroccan and POLISARIO forces. The limitations on the Mission's freedom of movement in areas of the Territory east of the berm did not significantly affect its ability to monitor the situation in those areas. In February, MINURSO's Force Commander became Officer-in-Charge also of the Mission during the absence of the Special Representative for Western Sahara, who had been asked by the Secretary-General to head his mission of good offices mission in Cyprus.

On 13 February, POLISARIO announced the release of a further 100 Moroccan prisoners of war, who were subsequently repatriated under the auspices of the International Committee of the Red Cross (ICRC), reducing the number of remaining prisoners to 514.

WFP and UNHCR undertook a joint assessment mission to the Tindouf refugee camps in January, where, despite improvements in donor support, the food situation remained unstable. The Special Representative and UNHCR promoted confidence-building measures aimed at facilitating person-to-person contacts between refugees in the camps in Algeria and their communities of origin in Western Sahara. The parties and Algeria, as the country of asylum, approved the revised UNHCR plan of action for family visits for refugees in the camps, which had been submitted to them in December 2003 [YUN

2003, p. 264]. The first exchange of family visits between Western Saharan refugees living in the Tindouf camps and their relatives in the town of Laayoune in the Territory began on 5 March, followed by four more exchanges of visits, all involving a total of 240 people from both sides. As at 31 March, over 8,500 people had sought to be included in the exchange programme. MINURSO civilian police escorted flights carrying visitors to and from the Territory and the Tindouf refugee camps.

The Secretary-General stated that opposition to a non-consensual solution to the conflict over Western Sahara was clear. He believed that Morocco's final response to the Peace Plan would require the parties to agree to negotiate a solution based on "autonomy within the framework of Moroccan sovereignty". Sovereignty, he noted, was the fundamental issue dividing the parties. Given their positions, the Council could either terminate MINURSO and return the issue of Western Sahara to the General Assembly, or try again to get them to work towards acceptance and implementation of the Peace Plan, which still constituted the best political solution to the conflict. The Secretary-General therefore hoped that the Council would reaffirm its recent unanimous support for the Plan and call upon the parties to work towards its implementation. To allow them sufficient time to work towards that goal, he recommended that MINURSO's mandate be extended for 10 months, until 28 February 2005.

SECURITY COUNCIL ACTION (April)

On 29 April [meeting 4957], the Security Council unanimously adopted **resolution 1541(2004)**. The draft [S/2004/330] was prepared in consultations among Council members.

The Security Council,

Recalling all its resolutions on Western Sahara, and reaffirming, in particular resolution 1495 (2003) of 31 July 2003,

Reaffirming its commitment to assist the parties to achieve a just, lasting and mutually acceptable political solution which will provide for the self-determination of the people of Western Sahara in the context of arrangements consistent with the purposes and principles of the Charter of the United Nations, and noting the role and responsibilities of the parties in this respect,

Having considered the report of the Secretary-General,

1. *Reaffirms its support* for the Peace Plan for Self-Determination of the People of Western Sahara as an optimum political solution on the basis of agreement between the two parties;

2. *Reaffirms its strong support* for the efforts of the Secretary-General and his Personal Envoy to achieve a mutually acceptable political solution to the dispute over Western Sahara;

3. *Calls upon* all the parties and the States of the region to cooperate fully with the Secretary-General and his Personal Envoy;

4. *Decides* to extend the mandate of the United Nations Mission for the Referendum in Western Sahara until 31 October 2004;

5. *Requests* that the Secretary-General provide a report on the situation before the end of the present mandate, and also requests the Secretary-General to include in this report an evaluation of the mission size necessary for the Mission to carry out its mandated tasks, with a view towards its possible reduction;

6. *Decides* to remain seized of the matter.

Resignation of Personal Envoy. On 11 June [S/2004/492], the Secretary-General informed the Security Council that his Personal Envoy for Western Sahara, who had served in that capacity for seven years, had offered his resignation, which the Secretary-General had accepted with deep regret. The Secretary-General thanked the Envoy for the considerable effort and time he had devoted to helping the parties, and indicated that his Special Representative for Western Sahara, Mr. de Soto, would continue to work with the parties and neighbouring countries in pursuit of a just and lasting peace that would provide for the self-determination of the people of Western Sahara.

Statements of position (August/September). Algeria, POLISARIO and Morocco put forward their positions on Western Sahara in letters to the Security Council dated 17 August [A/58/873-S/2004/657], 30 August [A/59/314-S/2004/704] and 24 September [S/2004/760], respectively.

Algeria regarded the question of Western Sahara as one of decolonization, to be resolved through the exercise by the Saharans of their right to self-determination. Since the conflict involved Western Sahara and Morocco, the occupying Power, any settlement had to be reached only by those two parties. To place the problem in an Algerian-Moroccan context was a delaying tactic because Algeria, which had no direct part in the conflict, could not and would not replace Western Sahara in determining its future.

POLISARIO, in its letter, transmitted by Namibia, reviewed the history of the conflict and peace-making attempts. It agreed with the Secretary-General's conclusion that Morocco had reneged on its commitments under the 1991 UN settlement plan [YUN 1991, p. 793], which it had accepted. Illegally occupying a neighbouring country for 30 years, Morocco had plundered its natural resources, caused wars in the region and frustrated the international community's peace-making efforts. Western Sahara would continue to resist that foreign occupation until the attainment of its right to self-determination and independence.

Morocco annexed to its letter a memorandum of clarification in response to what it called the other parties' diplomatic campaign to delay a definitive, consensual political solution. It asserted that its status with respect to Sahara was not that of a foreign State or of an occupying Power as Algeria had suggested, since "Sahara had been an integral part of the Kingdom of Morocco since time immemorial", notwithstanding a colonial hiatus. Morocco had participated in good faith in the implementation of the UN settlement plan but had been thwarted by POLISARIO's constant efforts to distort the voter identification process for the referendum envisaged in that plan. For both legal and political reasons, it had rejected the Personal Envoy's Peace Plan. Morocco believed that the search for a mutually acceptable political solution remained the best path to a definitive settlement of the regional dispute.

Report of Secretary-General (October). The Secretary-General, in response to resolution 1541 (2004) (see p. 276), submitted a 20 October report [S/2004/827] covering developments in Western Sahara since his April report. He indicated that his Special Representative, having completed his temporary assignment in Cyprus, resumed his responsibilities in respect of Western Sahara in July and, in September, conducted a round of consultations with the King of Morocco, the President of Mauritania, the Foreign Minister of Algeria and POLISARIO leaders on the Peace Plan. He ascertained that Morocco continued to reject elements of the Plan but was prepared to negotiate a mutually acceptable autonomy status, while POLISARIO maintained its support for it. Both POLISARIO and Algeria were opposed to discussing any aspect of the Plan unless Morocco agreed to support it. Mauritania maintained its willingness to support any solution that was mutually agreeable to the parties.

In June, POLISARIO announced the release of a further 100 Moroccan prisoners of war, who were repatriated to Morocco under ICRC auspices, leaving 412 prisoners in detention. UNHCR and the Special Representative urged the parties, during a series of consultations, to implement confidence-building measures. Exchange of visits between Western Saharan refugees in the Tindouf refugee camps in Algeria and their family members in the Territory took place on 31 August, with MINURSO support. The number of persons involved in the six months of the operation of the programme totalled 19,009, including 11,884 from the Tindouf area camps and 7,125 from the Territory. After a review of the first implementation phase of the confidence-building measures with the parties, they expressed their commitment to the continuation of those meas-

ures. They also agreed to continue the family visits and maintain the telephone service until the end of 2004 in order to give all concerned sufficient time to further review the draft plan of action for the second phase.

An assessment team from the Department of Peacekeeping Operations visited the area and identified two options regarding the strength of MINURSO's military component. The first option would maintain the current level of 203 military observers working out of nine team sites on both sides of the buffer strip, with two sector headquarters and one force headquarters. The second would involve closing the two sector headquarters; increasing headquarters staff for personnel matters, logistics, operations and planning; and closing one of the team sites, thus reducing MINURSO's total military strength to 193.

The Secretary-General observed that agreement on the Peace Plan appeared more distant than six months earlier, with no agreement on how to overcome the deadlock. However, he would continue to look for opportunities to advance the goal of enabling the people of Western Sahara to exercise their right to self-determination. Expressing concern about the recent escalation in public rhetoric emanating from the parties and the region, he viewed the renewal of the family visits as a welcome sign. He appealed to POLISARIO to release all remaining Moroccan prisoners of war, and to both Morocco and POLISARIO to cooperate with ICRC in accounting for all missing persons. The Secretary-General also noted the appearance in the heavily mined buffer strip of clandestine migrants, groups of whom occasionally remained stranded there without means of sustainment. That was part of a broader phenomenon of trafficking in human beings through the region, including through the MINURSO area of operations, which had no mandate or resources to deal with it.

In general, the effective monitoring of the ceasefire between the two countries by MINURSO over the previous 13 years had been a major stabilizing and confidence-building achievement. Both sides, having held consultations with the MINURSO Force Commander, preferred that the Mission's size not be reduced. The Secretary-General, expressing his preference for maintaining the Mission's military component as currently structured and staffed, recommended that the Security Council extend MINURSO's mandate for six months, until 30 April 2005.

SECURITY COUNCIL ACTION (October)

On 28 October [meeting 5068], the Security Council unanimously adopted **resolution 1570(2004)**. The draft [S/2004/869] was submitted by France, the Russian Federation, Spain, the United Kingdom and the United States.

The Security Council,

Recalling all its previous resolutions on Western Sahara, including resolutions 1495(2003) of 31 July 2003 and 1541(2004) of 29 April 2004,

Reaffirming its commitment to assist the parties to achieve a just, lasting and mutually acceptable political solution which will provide for the self-determination of the people of Western Sahara in the context of arrangements consistent with the principles and purposes of the Charter of the United Nations, and noting the role and responsibilities of the parties in this respect,

Reiterating its call upon the parties and States of the region to continue to cooperate fully with the United Nations to end the current impasse and to achieve progress towards a political solution,

Having considered the report of the Secretary-General of 20 October 2004,

1. Decides to extend the mandate of the United Nations Mission for the Referendum in Western Sahara until 30 April 2005;

2. Requests that the Secretary-General provide a report on the situation before the end of the mandate period and an interim report, within three months from adoption of the resolution, on the evolution of the situation and on the Mission's size and concept of operation, with further detail on the options discussed in the report of the Secretary-General of 20 October 2004 on the possible reduction of the Mission staff, including civilian and administrative personnel;

3. Calls upon Member States to consider voluntary contributions to fund confidence-building measures that allow for increased person-to-person contact, in particular the exchange of family visits;

4. Decides to remain seized of the matter.

GENERAL ASSEMBLY ACTION

The General Assembly had before it the Secretary-General's July report [A/59/134] summarizing reports on Western Sahara that had been submitted to the Security Council from 1 July 2003 to 30 June 2004.

On 10 December [meeting 71], the Assembly, on the recommendation of the Fourth (Special Political and Decolonization) Committee [A/59/478], adopted **resolution 59/131** by recorded vote (50-0-100) [agenda item 20].

Question of Western Sahara

The General Assembly,

Having considered in depth the question of Western Sahara,

Reaffirming the inalienable right of all peoples to self-determination and independence, in accordance with the principles set forth in the Charter of the United Nations and General Assembly resolution 1514(XV) of 14 December 1960 containing the Declaration on the Granting of Independence to Colonial Countries and Peoples,

Recalling its resolution 58/109 of 9 December 2003,

Recalling also all resolutions of the General Assembly and the Security Council on the question of Western Sahara,

Recalling further Security Council resolutions 658(1990) of 27 June 1990 and 690(1991) of 29 April 1991, by which the Security Council approved the settlement plan for Western Sahara,

Recalling Security Council resolutions 1359(2001) of 29 June 2001 and 1429(2002) of 30 July 2002, as well as resolution 1495(2003) of 31 July 2003, in which the Council expressed its support of the peace plan for self-determination of the people of Western Sahara as an optimum political solution on the basis of agreement between the two parties, and resolution 1541 (2004) of 29 April 2004,

Taking note of the responses of the parties and neighbouring States to the Personal Envoy of the Secretary-General, concerning the peace plan, contained in the report of the Secretary-General of 23 May 2003,

Reaffirming the responsibility of the United Nations towards the people of Western Sahara,

Noting with satisfaction the entry into force of the ceasefire in accordance with the proposal made by the Secretary-General, and stressing the importance it attaches to the maintenance of the ceasefire as an integral part of the settlement plan,

Underlining, in this regard, the validity of the settlement plan, while noting the fundamental differences between the parties in its implementation,

Stressing that the lack of progress in the settlement of the dispute on Western Sahara continues to cause suffering to the people of Western Sahara, remains a source of potential instability in the region and obstructs the economic development of the Maghreb region and that, in view of this, the search for a political solution is critically needed,

Welcoming the efforts of the Secretary-General in search of a mutually acceptable political solution, which will provide for self-determination of the people of Western Sahara,

Having examined the relevant chapter of the report of the Special Committee on the Situation with regard to the Implementation of the Declaration on the Granting of Independence to Colonial Countries and Peoples,

Having also examined the report of the Secretary-General,

1. Takes note of the report of the Secretary-General;

2. Underlines Security Council resolution 1495 (2003), in which the Council expressed its support of the peace plan for self-determination of the people of Western Sahara as an optimum political solution on the basis of agreement between the two parties;

3. Continues to support strongly the efforts of the Secretary-General in order to achieve a mutually acceptable political solution to the dispute over Western Sahara;

4. Commends the Secretary-General for his outstanding efforts and the two parties for the spirit of cooperation they have shown in the support they provide for those efforts;

5. Calls upon all the parties and the States of the region to cooperate fully with the Secretary-General;

6. Reaffirms the responsibility of the United Nations towards the people of Western Sahara;

7. Calls upon the parties to cooperate with the International Committee of the Red Cross in its efforts to solve the problem of the fate of the people unaccounted for, and calls upon the parties to abide by their

obligations under international humanitarian law to release without further delay all those held since the start of the conflict;

8. *Requests* the Special Committee on the Situation with regard to the Implementation of the Declaration on the Granting of Independence to Colonial Countries and Peoples to continue to consider the situation in Western Sahara and to report thereon to the General Assembly at its sixtieth session;

9. *Invites* the Secretary-General to submit to the General Assembly at its sixtieth session a report on the implementation of the present resolution.

RECORDED VOTE ON RESOLUTION 59/131:

In favour: Algeria, Angola, Antigua and Barbuda, Armenia, Bahamas, Barbados, Belarus, Belize, Bolivia, Botswana, Burundi, Cambodia, Colombia, Cuba, Democratic People's Republic of Korea, Dominica, Egypt, Eritrea, Ethiopia, Grenada, Guinea-Bissau, Guyana, Jamaica, Kenya, Lao People's Democratic Republic, Lesotho, Liberia, Mauritius, Mexico, Mozambique, Myanmar, Namibia, Nauru, Panama, Papua New Guinea, Russian Federation, Rwanda, Saint Lucia, Saint Vincent and the Grenadines, Samoa, South Africa, Suriname, Timor-Leste, Trinidad and Tobago, Uganda, United Republic of Tanzania, Venezuela (Bolivarian Republic of), Viet Nam, Zambia, Zimbabwe.

Against: None.

Abstaining: Albania, Andorra, Argentina, Australia, Austria, Azerbaijan, Bahrain, Bangladesh, Belgium, Benin, Bosnia and Herzegovina, Brazil, Brunei Darussalam, Bulgaria, Burkina Faso, Cameroon, Canada, Central African Republic, Chile, Comoros, Costa Rica, Côte d'Ivoire, Croatia, Cyprus, Czech Republic, Democratic Republic of the Congo, Denmark, Dominican Republic, Ecuador, El Salvador, Equatorial Guinea, Estonia, Finland, France, Gabon, Germany, Greece, Guatemala, Guinea, Haiti, Honduras, Hungary, Iceland, India, Indonesia, Ireland, Israel, Japan, Jordan, Kuwait, Kyrgyzstan, Latvia, Liechtenstein, Lithuania, Luxembourg, Malaysia, Maldives, Malta, Marshall Islands, Monaco, Mongolia, Morocco, Nepal, Netherlands, New Zealand, Nicaragua, Norway, Pakistan, Palau, Peru, Philippines, Poland, Portugal, Qatar, Republic of Moldova, Romania, San Marino, Sao Tome and Principe, Saudi Arabia, Senegal, Serbia and Montenegro, Sierra Leone, Singapore, Slovakia, Slovenia, Somalia, Spain, Sri Lanka, Sweden, Switzerland, Thailand, The former Yugoslav Republic of Macedonia, Togo, Turkey, Ukraine, United Arab Emirates, United Kingdom, United States, Uruguay, Yemen

MINURSO

In 2004, the military component of the United Nations Mission for the Referendum in Western Sahara (MINURSO), which was under the command of Major General György Száraz (Hungary), continued to monitor the ceasefire between the Royal Moroccan Army and the POLISARIO forces that had been in effect since 1991 [YUN 1991, p. 796]. Its strength throughout the year remained at approximately 230 troops, its authorized size.

MINURSO financing

The General Assembly, at its resumed fifty-eighth session, had before it the performance report on the MINURSO budget for 1 July 2002 to 30 June 2003 [A/58/642 & Corr.1], showing a total expenditure of $40,976,400 for the reporting period, out of an apportionment of $45,200,300; and the MINURSO budget for 1 July 2004 to 30 June 2005 [A/58/657], amounting to $44,134,700, inclusive of budgeted voluntary contributions in kind totalling $2,144,700.

ACABQ, having reviewed both reports, recommended, on 12 April [A/58/759/Add.2], that the unencumbered balance of $3,120,500 for the period

1 July 2002 to 30 June 2003 and other income and adjustments in the amount of $2,833,000, be credited to Member States in a manner to be determined by the Assembly. It also recommended that the estimated requirements in the proposed budget for 1 July 2004 to 30 June 2005 of $41,990,000 be reduced by $130,000, to $41,860,000, should the Security Council decide to continue the mandate of the Mission beyond 30 April 2004.

GENERAL ASSEMBLY ACTION

On 18 June [meeting 91], the General Assembly, on the recommendation of the Fifth Committee [A/58/830], adopted **resolution 58/309** without vote [agenda item 147].

Financing of the United Nations Mission for the Referendum in Western Sahara

The General Assembly,

Having considered the reports of the Secretary-General on the financing of the United Nations Mission for the Referendum in Western Sahara and the related reports of the Advisory Committee on Administrative and Budgetary Questions,

Recalling Security Council resolution 690(1991) of 29 April 1991, by which the Council established the United Nations Mission for the Referendum in Western Sahara, and the subsequent resolutions by which the Council extended the mandate of the Mission, the latest of which was resolution 1541(2004) of 29 April 2004,

Recalling also its resolution 45/266 of 17 May 1991 on the financing of the Mission and its subsequent resolutions and decisions thereon, the latest of which was resolution 57/331 of 18 June 2003,

Reaffirming the general principles underlying the financing of United Nations peacekeeping operations, as stated in General Assembly resolutions 1874 (S-IV) of 27 June 1963, 3101(XXVIII) of 11 December 1973 and 55/235 of 23 December 2000,

Noting with appreciation that voluntary contributions have been made to the Mission,

Mindful of the fact that it is essential to provide the Mission with the necessary financial resources to enable it to fulfil its responsibilities under the relevant resolutions of the Security Council,

1. *Takes note* of the status of contributions to the United Nations Mission for the Referendum in Western Sahara as at 15 April 2004, including the contributions outstanding in the amount of 44.9 million United States dollars, representing some 8 per cent of the total assessed contributions, notes with concern that only thirty-three Member States have paid their assessed contributions in full, and urges all other Member States, in particular those in arrears, to ensure payment of their outstanding assessed contributions;

2. *Expresses its appreciation* to those Member States which have paid their assessed contributions in full;

3. *Expresses concern* at the financial situation with regard to peacekeeping activities, in particular as regards the reimbursements to troop contributors that bear additional burdens owing to overdue payments by Member States of their assessments;

4. *Urges* all other Member States to make every possible effort to ensure payment of their assessed contributions to the Mission in full;

5. *Expresses concern* at the delay experienced by the Secretary-General in deploying and providing adequate resources to some recent peacekeeping missions, in particular those in Africa;

6. *Emphasizes* that all future and existing peacekeeping missions shall be given equal and non-discriminatory treatment in respect of financial and administrative arrangements;

7. *Also emphasizes* that all peacekeeping missions shall be provided with adequate resources for the effective and efficient discharge of their respective mandates;

8. *Reiterates its request* to the Secretary-General to make the fullest possible use of facilities and equipment at the United Nations Logistics Base at Brindisi, Italy, in order to minimize the costs of procurement for the Mission;

9. *Endorses* the conclusions and recommendations contained in the report of the Advisory Committee on Administrative and Budgetary Questions, and requests the Secretary-General to ensure their full implementation;

10. *Requests* the Secretary-General to take all necessary action to ensure that the Mission is administered with a maximum of efficiency and economy;

11. *Also requests* the Secretary-General, in order to reduce the cost of employing General Service staff, to continue efforts to recruit local staff for the Mission against General Service posts, commensurate with the requirements of the Mission;

Financial performance report for the period from 1 July 2002 to 30 June 2003

12. *Takes note* of the report of the Secretary-General on the financial performance of the Mission for the period from 1 July 2002 to 30 June 2003;

Budget estimates for the period from 1 July 2004 to 30 June 2005

13. *Decides* to appropriate to the Special Account for the United Nations Mission for the Referendum in Western Sahara the amount of 44,041,200 dollars for the period from 1 July 2004 to 30 June 2005, inclusive of 41,860,000 dollars for the maintenance of the Mission, 1,783,200 dollars for the support account for peacekeeping operations and 398,000 dollars for the United Nations Logistics Base;

Financing of the appropriation

14. *Decides also* to apportion among Member States the amount of 44,041,200 dollars at a monthly rate of 3,670,100 dollars, in accordance with the levels set out in General Assembly resolution 55/235, as adjusted by the Assembly in its resolution 55/236 of 23 December 2000 and updated in its resolution 58/256 of 23 December 2003, taking into account the scale of assessments for 2004 and 2005, as set out in its resolution 58/1 B of 23 December 2003, subject to a decision of the Security Council to extend the mandate of the Mission;

15. *Decides further* that, in accordance with the provisions of its resolution 973(X) of 15 December 1955, there shall be set off against the apportionment among Member States, as provided for in paragraph 14 above, their respective share in the Tax Equalization Fund of 3,191,600 dollars, comprising the estimated staff assessment income of 2,908,900 dollars approved for the Mission, the prorated share of 260,200 dollars of the

estimated staff assessment income approved for the support account and the prorated share of 22,500 dollars of the estimated staff assessment income approved for the United Nations Logistics Base;

16. *Decides* that, for Member States that have fulfilled their financial obligations to the Mission, there shall be set off against their apportionment, as provided for in paragraph 14 above, their respective share of the unencumbered balance and other income in the total amount of 5,953,500 dollars in respect of the financial period ended 30 June 2003, in accordance with the levels set out in General Assembly resolution 55/235, as adjusted by the Assembly in its resolution 55/236 and its resolution 57/290 A of 20 December 2002, taking into account the scale of assessments for 2003, as set out in its resolutions 55/5 B of 23 December 2000 and 57/4 B of 20 December 2002;

17. *Decides also* that, for Member States that have not fulfilled their financial obligations to the Mission, there shall be set off against their outstanding obligations their respective share of the unencumbered balance and other income in the total amount of 5,953,500 dollars in respect of the financial period ended 30 June 2003, in accordance with the scheme set out in paragraph 16 above;

18. *Decides further* that the decrease of 444,800 dollars in the estimated staff assessment income in respect of the financial period ended 30 June 2003 shall be set off against the credits from the amount referred to in paragraphs 16 and 17 above;

19. *Emphasizes* that no peacekeeping mission shall be financed by borrowing funds from other active peacekeeping missions;

20. *Encourages* the Secretary-General to continue to take additional measures to ensure the safety and security of all personnel under the auspices of the United Nations participating in the Mission;

21. *Invites* voluntary contributions to the Mission in cash and in the form of services and supplies acceptable to the Secretary-General, to be administered, as appropriate, in accordance with the procedure and practices established by the General Assembly;

22. *Decides* to include in the provisional agenda of its fifty-ninth session the item entitled "Financing of the United Nations Mission for the Referendum in Western Sahara".

On 23 December, the Assembly decided that the agenda item on MINURSO financing would remain for consideration during its resumed fifty-ninth (2005) session (**decision 59/552**).

Libyan Arab Jamahiriya

Implementation of NPT Safeguards Agreement

The Board of Governors of the International Atomic Energy Agency (IAEA), in its resolution 2004/18 of 10 March [GOV/2004/18] (see p. 549), welcomed the 19 December 2003 decision of the Libyan Arab Jamahiriya [YUN 2003, p. 269] to abandon its programmes for developing weapons of mass destruction and their means of delivery, and its request to IAEA to ensure verification that all its nuclear activities would be under safeguards and exclusively for peaceful purposes [YUN 2003, p. 550]. IAEA appreciated Libya's active cooperation and openness since that date to facilitate the Agency's verification work and the elimination of those programmes.

SECURITY COUNCIL ACTION

On 22 April [meeting 4949], following consultations among Security Council members, the President made statement **S/PRST/2004/10** on behalf of the Council:

The Security Council takes note of resolution 2004/18 of 10 March 2004 of the Board of Governors of the International Atomic Energy Agency regarding the implementation of the safeguards agreement of the Socialist People's Libyan Arab Jamahiriya, a State party to the Treaty on the Non-proliferation of Nuclear Weapons, by which the Board requested the Director General of the International Atomic Energy Agency to report a case of non-compliance to the Security Council for information purposes only, while commending the Socialist People's Libyan Arab Jamahiriya for the actions it has taken to date and those it has proposed to take to remedy it.

The Council welcomes the decision by the Socialist People's Libyan Arab Jamahiriya to abandon its programmes for developing weapons of mass destruction and their means of delivery and the positive steps taken to fulfil its commitments and obligations, including its active cooperation with the International Atomic Energy Agency and the Organization for the Prohibition of Chemical Weapons.

The Council takes note that in its resolution 2004/18 the Board of Governors of the International Atomic Energy Agency recognized the decision of the Socialist People's Libyan Arab Jamahiriya as a step towards the realization of the goal of an Africa and a Middle East free of weapons of mass destruction and at peace.

The Council reaffirms the need to seek to resolve proliferation problems by peaceful means through political and diplomatic channels.

The Council welcomes existing and future efforts to assist the Socialist People's Libyan Arab Jamahiriya in this task, and expresses the hope that the steps taken by the Socialist People's Libyan Arab Jamahiriya would facilitate and improve international cooperation with and enhance the security of that country.

The Council encourages the Socialist People's Libyan Arab Jamahiriya to ensure the verified elimination of all of its weapons of mass destruction programmes. It welcomes the roles played in that regard by the International Atomic Energy Agency and the Organization for the Prohibition of Chemical Weapons in facilitating the fulfilment of the commitments of the Socialist People's Libyan Arab Jamahiriya, demonstrating the importance and usefulness of existing international treaty regimes.

The Council expresses the hope that resolution 2004/18 will be implemented in the spirit of continued cooperation.

Southern Africa

Angola

The General Assembly, in **resolution 59/216** of 22 December, welcomed the successful implementation of the 2002 Memorandum of Understanding additional to the Lusaka Protocol [YUN 2002, p. 221], which ended hostilities in Angola and created unprecedented conditions for the re-establishment and consolidation of peace in Angola. The Assembly requested Angola and the United Nations, and invited international financial institutions, to prepare and organize an international donors conference for long-term development and reconstruction of the country, including special economic assistance (see p. 927).

Following completion of the mandates and subsequent closure of the United Nations Angola Verification Mission (UNAVEM) (in 1997) and the United Nations Observer Mission in Angola (MONUA) (in 1999), the Assembly decided on 13 September 2004 to defer consideration of the agenda item on the financing of those two missions and to include it in the draft agenda of its fifty-ninth (2004) session (**decision 58/577**). On 23 December, the Assembly decided that the item would remain for consideration during its resumed fifty-ninth (2005) session (**decision 59/552**).

Mozambique

The General Assembly, by **resolution 59/214** of 22 December, commended Mozambique for its efforts in the maintenance of peace, stability, economic growth and development and for the enhancement of democracy and the consolidation of national reconciliation in the country. It requested the Secretary-General to make arrangements to continue to mobilize and coordinate humanitarian and reconstruction assistance to support Mozambique (see p. 930).

Zimbabwe

In statements released on 15 April and 28 May [S/2004/336, S/2004/447] and forwarded to the Security Council, the EU Presidency condemned the violence, intimidation and irregularities before and during parliamentary by-elections in Zimbabwe. In a further statement on 23 June [S/2004/516], the EU condemned the Government's closure of a newspaper prior to elections.

Other issues

Comoros

The AU Central Organ of the Mechanism for Conflict Prevention, Management and Resolution, in a communiqué issued on 30 January and transmitted to the Security Council [S/2004/88], welcomed the signing of the Moroni agreement on 20 December 2003 on the Transitional Arrangements in the Comoros and the outcome of the first meeting of the Follow-up Committee on the agreement (5 - 7 January 2004), as well as the progress made since then in the search for a lasting solution to the Comorian crisis.

The Central Organ authorized the deployment of an AU Observer Mission (MIOC) for a period of four months, as recommended in the report of the Chairperson of the Commission on the Situation in the Comoros. It welcomed the positive outcome of the meeting convened in Paris on 21 January to establish the trust fund to support the ongoing transition in the Comoros.

Cooperation between the AU and the UN system

In 2004, the Security Council, at its 19 November meeting [meeting 5084] in Nairobi, considered its institutional relationship with the AU. The representative of the AU Chairman, in his address to the Council, drew attention to the various areas of cooperation between the United Nations and the AU, particularly in the establishment of the AU Peace and Security Council, the Military Staff Committee, the African Standby Force and the early warning system in Africa (see p. 114). He hoped that the cooperation for capacity-building in Africa would be further enhanced in all those areas. He also praised support for the AU Commission and the New Partnership for Africa's Development.

The EU, in a 25 May statement [S/2004/444], welcomed the launching of the AU Peace and Security Council.

SECURITY COUNCIL ACTION

On 19 November [meeting 5084], following consultations among Security Council members, the President made statement **S/PRST/2004/44** on behalf of the Council:

The Security Council reiterates its primary responsibility for the maintenance of international peace and security, and recalls that cooperation with regional and subregional organizations in matters relating to the maintenance of peace and security is an important pillar of the system of collective security established by the Charter of the United Nations, as provided for in Chapter VIII thereof.

The Council reaffirms the statement by its President of 20 July 2004, which underscores the importance of a stronger relationship between the United Nations and regional organizations consistent with the principles set forth in Articles 52 and 53 of the Charter.

The Council, at its meeting on 19 November 2004 in Nairobi, addressed the institutional relationship between the United Nations and the African Union, including their collective efforts to resolve African conflicts and to promote sustainable peace, development and stability.

The Council, referring to the Constitutive Act of the African Union, welcomes the establishment of the Peace and Security Council of the African Union, and expresses its support for early ratification of the Peace and Security Protocol by all African States and the establishment of an African standby force and an early warning system in Africa. The completion of these efforts will allow for better coordination of regional mechanisms to foster peace and security, sustainable development and the eradication of poverty in Africa, as set forth in the New Partnership for Africa's Development.

The Council recognizes the importance of strengthening cooperation with the African Union in order to help build its capacity to deal with collective security challenges, including through the establishment of rapid and appropriate responses to emerging crisis situations and the development of effective strategies for conflict prevention, peacekeeping and peacebuilding.

The Council welcomes, in this regard, the provision by the United Nations and donors of technical, logistical and military planning support to the African Union in the establishment of African Union peace and security mechanisms and operations.

The Council particularly welcomes the leading role of the African Union in efforts to settle crises on the African continent, and expresses its full support for the peace initiatives conducted by the African Union, and through subregional organizations such as the Economic Community of West African States, the Southern African Development Community, the Central African Economic and Monetary Community, the Intergovernmental Authority on Development and other regional agreements committed to the peaceful settlement of disputes in Africa. The Council underlines the importance of being kept fully informed, consistent with Article 54 of the Charter.

The Council also welcomes the strengthening of practical cooperation between the United Nations and the African Union, as demonstrated in the case of the African Mission in the Sudan and the African Mission in Burundi, to support and enhance the management and operational capacities of the African Union in the field of peacekeeping and peacebuilding.

The Council calls upon the international community to support the efforts of the African Union to strengthen its capacities for peacekeeping, conflict resolution and post-conflict reconstruction, through the provision of information, training, expertise and resources, and to support the activities of the United Nations and its agencies in this regard.

The Council further invites the Secretary-General to explore, in close consultation with the Chairperson of the African Union Commission, new means of cooperation between the United Nations and the African Union, especially taking into consideration the expanded mandate and the new organs of the African Union.

Report of Secretary-General. The Secretary-General, in his 1 September consolidated report on cooperation between the United Nations and regional and other organizations [A/59/303], said that consultations continued to be held on a regular basis and at all levels between the United Nations and the AU. He described specific areas of cooperation between them and efforts to strengthen that cooperation.

GENERAL ASSEMBLY ACTION

On 20 December [meeting 74], the General Assembly adopted **resolution 59/213** [draft A/59/L.54 & Add.1] without vote [agenda item 56 (*a*)].

Cooperation between the United Nations and the African Union

The General Assembly,

Having considered the report of the Secretary-General on cooperation between the United Nations and regional and other organizations,

Recalling the provisions of Chapter VIII of the Charter of the United Nations, as well as its resolutions 55/218 of 21 December 2000, 56/48 of 7 December 2001 and 57/48 of 21 November 2002,

Recalling also the principles enshrined in the Constitutive Act of the African Union adopted at the meeting of the Heads of State and Government of the African Union, held in Lomé from 10 to 12 July 2000,

Recalling further the decisions and declarations adopted by the Assembly of the African Union at its first, second and third ordinary sessions, held in Durban, South Africa, on 9 and 10 July 2002, in Maputo from 10 to 12 July 2003 and in Addis Ababa from 6 to 8 July 2004, respectively,

Welcoming the entry into force of the Protocol relating to the Establishment of the Peace and Security Council of the African Union, on 26 December 2003, and the policy framework document on the establishment of an African standby force and a military staff committee,

Welcoming also the statement by the President of the Security Council at the 5084th meeting of the Security Council, held in Nairobi on 19 November 2004, on the institutional relationship with the African Union,

Welcoming further the Vision and Mission of the African Union and the proposals contained in the Strategic Plan of the Commission of the African Union, as adopted at the meeting of the Heads of State and Government of the African Union, held in Addis Ababa from 6 to 8 July 2004,

Bearing in mind the United Nations Declaration on the New Partnership for Africa's Development, contained in its resolution 57/2 of 16 September 2002, and its resolutions 57/7 of 4 November 2002 and 58/233 of 23 December 2003, and welcoming the renewed commitments by the international community to support the New Partnership and other related initiatives for Africa,

Welcoming decision AU/Dec.38(III) adopted by the third ordinary session of the Assembly of the African Union, on the implementation of the New Partnership,

Bearing in mind the Declaration and the Plan of Action contained in the document entitled "A world fit for children", adopted at the special session of the General Assembly on children, held in New York from 8 to 10 May 2002 and the African Common Position on Children, endorsed by the Assembly of Heads of State and Government of the Organization of African Unity at its thirty-seventh ordinary session, held in Lusaka from 9 to 11 July 2001,

Appreciating the continuous efforts of African countries in mainstreaming gender perspectives and the empowerment of women in decision-making organs, and in this regard welcoming the Solemn Declaration on Gender Equality in Africa, adopted at the third ordinary session of the Assembly of the African Union,

Taking note of the Plan of Action on the Family in Africa launched by the African Union at its extraordinary summit meeting on the family in Africa, held in Cotonou, Benin, from 25 to 27 July 2004, as Africa's contribution to the celebration of the tenth anniversary of the International Year of the Family,

Taking note also of the Declaration on Employment and Poverty Alleviation in Africa adopted at the extraordinary summit meeting of the African Union on employment and poverty alleviation in Africa, held in Ouagadougou from 3 to 9 September 2004,

Noting the efforts to be undertaken by the African Union and its organs and regional economic communities and bodies in the area of economic integration, and the need to accelerate the process of the full establishment and consolidation of the African Union so as to achieve sustainable development,

Stressing the urgent need to address the plight of refugees and internally displaced persons in Africa, and noting in this context decision EX.CL/Dec.127(V) on the situation of refugees, returnees and displaced persons in Africa, adopted by the Executive Council of the African Union at its fifth ordinary session, held in Addis Ababa from 30 June to 3 July 2004, and the conference convened by the African Parliamentary Union and the United Nations High Commissioner for Refugees on "Refugees in Africa: the challenges of protection and solutions", held in Cotonou from 1 to 3 June 2004,

Recognizing the importance of developing and maintaining a culture of peace, tolerance and harmonious relationships based on the promotion of economic development, democratic principles, good governance, the rule of law, human rights, social justice and international cooperation, as reflected in the Constitutive Act of the African Union and the Declaration on Democracy, Political, Economic and Corporate Governance of the New Partnership for Africa's Development,

Stressing the need for extending the scope of cooperation between the United Nations and the African Union in the area of combating illegal exploitation of natural resources,

Emphasizing the importance of the effective, coordinated and integrated implementation of the United Nations Millennium Declaration, the Doha Development Agenda, the Monterrey Consensus of the International Conference on Financing for Development and the Plan of Implementation of the World Summit on Sustainable Development ("Johannesburg Plan of Implementation"),

Welcoming the adoption of the Protocol establishing the African Court on Human and Peoples' Rights to complement the African Commission on Human and Peoples' Rights,

Acknowledging the entry into force of the 1999 Algiers Convention on the Prevention and Combating of Terrorism, and noting the centrality of international partnership and cooperation between the African Union, the relevant United Nations organs and the wider international community in the global fight against terrorism,

Taking note of the Abuja Declaration on HIV/AIDS, Tuberculosis and Other Related Infectious Diseases, and the Framework for Action thereon, and the Maputo Declaration on Malaria, HIV/AIDS, Tuberculosis and Other Related Infectious Diseases,

Acknowledging the contribution of the United Nations Liaison Office in strengthening coordination and cooperation between the African Union and the United Nations, as well as the need to consolidate it so as to enhance its performance,

Convinced that strengthening cooperation between the United Nations and the African Union and its organs will contribute to the advancement of the principles of the Constitutive Act of the African Union and to the development of Africa,

1. *Takes note with appreciation* of the report of the Secretary-General;

2. *Welcomes* the cooperation between the African Union and the United Nations and, in this respect, the continuing participation in and constructive contribution of the African Union and its specialized agencies to the work of the United Nations, and calls upon the two organizations to enhance the involvement of the African Union in all United Nations activities concerning Africa;

3. *Stresses* the need for closer cooperation and coordination between the African Union and the United Nations, and urges the United Nations system to continue to support the African Union on an ongoing basis in accordance with the Cooperation Agreement between the two organizations as well as other memorandums of understanding;

4. *Calls upon* the Secretary-General to involve the African Union and its organs closely in the implementation of the commitments contained in the United Nations Millennium Declaration, especially those that relate to addressing the special needs of Africa;

5. *Invites* the Secretary-General to request all relevant United Nations agencies to intensify their cooperation with the African Union in the establishment of its organs, including through the implementation of the protocols to the Constitutive Act of the African Union and the Treaty establishing the African Economic Community, and to assist in the effective harmonization of the programmes of the African Union with those of the regional economic communities;

6. *Requests* the agencies of the United Nations system working in Africa to include in their programmes at the national, subregional and regional levels, activities to support African countries in their efforts to enhance regional economic cooperation and integration;

7. *Invites* the Secretary-General to request the United Nations system to enhance its support to the African Union in the implementation of its Vision and Mission and the Strategic Plan of the Commission of the African Union, particularly in the following areas:

(a) Setting up of support structures and management;

(b) Adaptation of structure to strategy and strengthening of skills in institutional consolidation;

(c) Modernization of information and communication technology and advancement of indigenous technology;

(d) Building of internal capacity to mainstream gender;

(e) Promotion of free and democratic elections;

(f) Disaster management;

(g) Integrated health system in Africa;

(h) Elaboration of an African social policy model: children first;

(i) Support for the African Committee of Experts on the Rights and Welfare of the Child;

(j) Global advocacy for the African Union vision, to consolidate integration and promote sustainable development in Africa;

8. *Requests* the United Nations system, while acknowledging its primary role in the promotion and maintenance of international peace and security, to intensify its assistance to the African Union, as appropriate, in strengthening the institutional and operational capacity of its Peace and Security Council, in particular in the following areas:

(a) Development of its early warning system, including the Situation Room of the Peace and Security Directorate;

(b) Training of civilian and military personnel, including a staff exchange programme;

(c) Regular and continued exchange and coordination of information, including between the early warning systems of the two organizations;

(d) Peace support missions of the African Union in its various member States, in particular in the area of communication and other related logistical support;

(e) Capacity-building for peacebuilding before and after the termination of hostilities on the continent;

(f) Support for the Peace and Security Council in taking humanitarian action on the continent in accordance with the Protocol relating to the Establishment of the Peace and Security Council;

(g) Establishment of the African standby force and the military staff committee;

9. *Invites* the Secretary-General to explore, in close consultation with the Chairperson of the Commission of the African Union, new means of cooperation between the United Nations and the African Union, especially taking into consideration the expanded mandate and the new organs of the African Union;

10. *Urges* the United Nations to encourage donor countries, in consultation with the African Union, to contribute to adequate funding, training and logistical support for African countries in their efforts to en-

hance their peacekeeping capabilities, with a view to enabling those countries to participate actively in peacekeeping operations within the framework of the Protocol relating to the Establishment of the Peace and Security Council and the framework of the United Nations;

11. *Stresses* the urgent need for the United Nations and the African Union to develop close cooperation and concrete programmes aimed at addressing the problems posed by the proliferation of small arms and light weapons and anti-personnel mines, within the framework of the relevant declarations and resolutions adopted by the two organizations;

12. *Calls upon* the United Nations system and the international community to continue to support the New Partnership for Africa's Development and its Peer Review Mechanism as African-owned and led initiatives and programmes of the African Union;

13. *Calls upon* the United Nations system, the African Union and the international community to intensify their cooperation in the global fight against terrorism through the implementation of the relevant international and regional treaties and protocols and, in particular, the African Plan of Action adopted in Algiers on 14 September 2002, as well as their support for the operation of the African Centre for Studies and Research on Terrorism, inaugurated in Algiers in October 2004;

14. *Calls upon* the United Nations system to intensify its efforts, in collaboration with the African Union, in combating illegal exploitation of natural resources, particularly in conflict areas, in accordance with relevant resolutions and decisions of the United Nations and the African Union;

15. *Encourages* the United Nations system to effectively support the efforts of the African Union in urging the international community to duly implement the Doha Development Agenda, including negotiations aimed at substantial improvements in market access to promote sustainable growth in Africa;

16. *Invites* the United Nations system to enhance its support to African countries in their efforts to implement the Johannesburg Plan of Implementation;

17. *Encourages* the United Nations to take special measures to address the challenges of poverty eradication through debt cancellation, enhanced official development assistance, increases in flows of foreign direct investments, as well as transfers of technology;

18. *Calls upon* the United Nations system to accelerate the implementation of the Plan of Action contained in the document entitled "A world fit for children", adopted at the special session of the General Assembly on children, and to provide assistance, as appropriate, to the African Union and its member States in this regard;

19. *Calls upon* the United Nations system and the African Union to develop a coherent and effective strategy, including through joint programmes and activities, for the promotion and protection of human rights in Africa, within the framework of the implementation of regional and international treaties, resolutions and plans of action adopted by the two organizations;

20. *Urges* the United Nations system to increase its support for Africa in the implementation of the declaration of the extraordinary summit meeting of the Assembly of Heads of State and Government of the Organization of African Unity on HIV/AIDS, tuberculosis and other related infectious diseases, and the Declaration of Commitment on HIV/AIDS, so as to arrest the spread of these diseases, inter alia, through sound capacity-building in human resources;

21. *Invites* the United Nations system and the international community to provide adequate support to the African Commission on Human and Peoples' Rights, aimed at finalizing the process leading to the establishment of the African Court on Human and Peoples' Rights;

22. *Urges* the United Nations system speedily to implement resolution 58/149 of 22 December 2003 on assistance to refugees, returnees and displaced persons in Africa, and effectively to support African countries in their effort to incorporate the problems of refugees into national and regional development plans;

23. *Urges* the Secretary-General to encourage the United Nations system to work towards ensuring the effective and equitable representation of African men and women at senior and policy levels at the respective headquarters of its organizations and in their regional fields of operation;

24. *Requests* the United Nations system to cooperate with the African Union and its member States in the implementation of appropriate policies for the promotion of the culture of democracy, good governance, respect for human rights and the rule of law, and the strengthening of democratic institutions which will enhance the popular participation of the peoples of the continent in these issues, in accordance with the purposes and principles of the Constitutive Act of the African Union and the New Partnership for Africa's Development;

25. *Calls upon* the United Nations system and invites the Bretton Woods institutions to support, within their respective mandates, and where necessary and possible, the establishment of the institutional structures of the African Union, including the Pan-African Parliament, the Court of Justice, the Economic, Social and Cultural Council and the Financial Institutions;

26. *Requests* the Secretary-General to report to the General Assembly at its sixty-first session on the implementation of the present resolution.

Chapter III

Americas

In 2004, the United Nations continued to advance the cause of lasting peace, human rights, sustainable development and the rule of law in the Americas.

In Guatemala, peaceful elections in December 2003 and the orderly handover of power in January 2004 brought a sense of relief and renewed optimism. The United Nations Verification Mission in Guatemala (MINUGUA) continued to fulfil its mandate of verifying compliance with the peace accords signed in 1996 between the Government of Guatemala and the Unidad Revolucionaria Nacional Guatemalteca. MINUGUA, in anticipation of the termination of its mandate at the end of the year, continued its two-year phase-down of operations and carried out a transition strategy designed to build national capacity to promote the goals of the peace accords. The formal public closure of the Mission took place in November.

Despite efforts in January by the Caribbean Community (CARICOM) to end the polarization and build consensus in Haiti, the political and security crisis in that country escalated into violence in February. President Jean-Bertrand Aristide resigned and the constitutional President, Boniface Alexandre, requested UN assistance to restore peace and stability, thereby authorizing international troops to enter Haiti. The Multinational Interim Force (MIF) was immediately deployed and an interim government was selected. May floods and Hurricane Jeanne exacerbated the situation and appeals to donors were made. In view of the unstable and complex security situation, the Security Council established the United Nations Stabilization Mission in Haiti (MINUSTAH), which assumed the operations from MIF in June. In December, in response to a number of kidnappings in the capital and warnings of possible increased violence, MINUSTAH conducted an intensive patrolling operation, which resulted in a peaceful and secure environment through the end of the year.

In other developments in the region, the Andean Zone of Peace was established at the fifteenth meeting of the Andean Presidential Council in Ecuador. Cuba denounced new restrictions placed by the United States on visits to Cuba by relatives, family remittances to Cubans and tourist travel. The General Assembly again called on States to refrain from promulgating laws and measures such as the ongoing embargo against Cuba by the United States. It also adopted resolutions on strengthening United Nations cooperation with the Organization of American States and CARICOM.

The General Assembly requested the Secretary-General to submit a report on the situation in Central America in 2005 and decided to consider the item every two years.

On 23 December, by **decision 59/552**, the General Assembly decided to consider the item "The situation in Central America: progress in fashioning a region of peace, freedom, democracy and development" at its resumed fifty-ninth (2005) session.

Central America

Guatemala

Following the successful conclusion of elections in Guatemala in 2003 [YUN 2003, p. 282] for the third time since the signing of the Guatemala peace agreements in 1996 [YUN 1996, p. 168], the orderly handover of power in January brought a sense of relief and renewed optimism to the population. The country continued to make significant progress in consolidating the peace and laid a firmer foundation on which to construct a better future. Notable progress was made in the areas of human rights, demilitarization and the strengthening of civilian authority, and in decentralization, which allowed the increased participation of citizens in decision-making. However, in the socio-economic sphere, especially agrarian reform, progress remained limited, due mainly to inadequate financing.

The United Nations Verification Mission in Guatemala (MINUGUA) (see below) continued to verify the 1996 Agreement on a Firm and Lasting Peace [YUN 1996, p. 168], signed by the Government of Guatemala and the Unidad Revolucionaria Nacional Guatemalteca (URNG), and to monitor compliance with the 2000-2004 verification timetable [YUN 2000, p. 239]. In anticipation of its departure at the end of 2004, MINUGUA continued its two-year phase-down of operations and carried out a transition strategy designed to build national capacity to promote the goals of the peace accords. The formal public closure of the Mission took place on 15 November. MINUGUA received Guatemala's highest civilian honours, the Order of the Quetzal, in recognition of its work.

MINUGUA

The mandate of MINUGUA, which had been extended to 31 December 2004 by General Assembly resolution 58/238 [YUN 2003, p. 283], focused in 2004 on verification of two areas—human rights, and demilitarization and the strengthening of civilian power—as outlined in the 1996 Agreement on a Firm and Lasting Peace [YUN 1996, p. 168].

Report of Secretary-General. In response to Assembly resolution 58/238, the Secretary-General submitted on 30 August [A/59/307] the ninth and final report on the implementation of the Guatemalan peace agreements, which summarized political developments during the previous year, and the status of the implementation of the peace accords. The Secretary-General said that the political environment had improved considerably since his last report [YUN 2003, p. 280] and that the electoral defeat of General Efraín Ríos Montt [ibid., p. 279], under whose 1982-1983 rule the army committed some of the worst atrocities of the conflict, was a sign that Guatemalans were rejecting the past and looking towards the future.

Regarding the implementation of the peace accords (1996-2004), the Secretary-General said that it had been plagued by obstacles and setbacks, and the resistance of powerful groups that felt threatened by change. On 25 February, President Oscar Berger pledged to reinvigorate implementation of the peace accords with the support of a new National Peace Accords Commission.

In the area of human rights, the Secretary-General said that the overall assessment of progress was positive. Advances included: the creation of a new civilian police force, an independent Public Prosecutor's Office and a Public Defender's Institute; the enactment of a judicial career law which had improved the selection, training and evaluation of judges; improvements in technology and expansions in the physical infrastructure of the courts, as well as better access for indigenous people through the hiring of bilingual staff and interpreters; and the creation of five Justice Administration Centres in the country's predominantly indigenous areas. The main challenge was to consolidate the rule of law amid a surge in crime and manifold evidence that key institutional reform processes launched under the accords had lost momentum or had regressed. The National Human Rights Movement reported 18 incidents of harassment during the

first half of 2004, mainly threats to human rights organizations or others involved in judicial processes. A 2003 initiative, reached in agreement with the United Nations and the former Government to create the Commission for the Investigation of Illegal Groups and Clandestine Security Organizations (CICIACS) to investigate clandestine groups, was withdrawn from Congress in May amid constitutional objections. Although several articles of the agreement were declared unconstitutional by the Constitutional Court, the new Government said it remained committed to creating CICIACS and would propose modifications to the United Nations after consultations with human rights groups and other interested actors. Public security remained a major concern to Guatemalans, who were suffering under a surge of violent crime common to post-conflict societies. Guatemala's location in the drug trafficking corridor made it vulnerable to organized crime groups, and the deplorable condition of the National Civilian Police had allowed crime to proliferate, resulting in increasing and serious abuse by its members, including kidnapping, social cleansing and torture. The naming of a well-regarded human rights activist, Frank Larue, to head the Presidential Commission on Human Rights had instilled new dynamism in that institution. Reparations to human rights abuse victims would be a test of Guatemala's commitment to human rights. The Government provided initial funding for a National Reparations Programme for the victims of human rights violations, and named Rosalina Tuyuc, a respected indigenous leader and victims' representative, to head the commission overseeing the programme. However, the programme still needed to be placed on firmer legal and financial footing. The Office of the Human Rights Ombudsman also needed to be strengthened, and international observation of and assistance for the human rights situation in Guatemala continued. The proposed office of the High Commissioner for Human Rights would make an important contribution in that regard.

In the area of identity and rights of indigenous peoples, reforms had taken place at the legal and institutional levels through the creation of special programmes and agencies, as envisaged in the peace accords. Debate was also taking place on the topics of racism and discrimination. However, the everyday reality for most indigenous people had changed little. Except for access to communications media from which it had been traditionally excluded, the indigenous population remained outside the mainstream of national life and the worst social indicators continued to be registered in predominantly indigenous areas.

The report noted that great changes in the area of demilitarization and the strengthening of civilian authority had occurred during the past year. The army was trimmed from 27,000 to 15,500 troops and officers, a new military budget ceiling was set at 0.33 per cent of gross domestic product, and the Presidential General Staff was eliminated and a professional civilian presidential security force created in its place. Although a new human rights–based military doctrine was presented publicly in July, more still needed to be done to institutionalize civilian control over the armed forces and intelligence structures.

Little actual change was noted in the inter-related areas of socio-economic aspects, the agrarian situation and gender issues. The Secretary-General remarked that only limited results had been achieved in agrarian reform. Despite increases in social spending and the creation of new institutions to address land issues, public services remained inadequate, rural development opportunities scarce and land conflicts persistent. The percentage of the population living in poverty remained at 57 per cent, while the number of those living in extreme poverty had increased. One of the main limitations to improving the situation was the chronic lack of government funds to finance the expansion of State services benefiting the poor, resulting from its failure to increase the tax base. Efforts to improve access to land and resolve land conflicts had also been insufficient. The government agency responsible for providing credit for land purchases remained severely underfunded, as was the one created for mediating land disputes, which also lacked the institutional stability to play that role in a sustained manner. Improvements in Guatemala's health system were modest and the country continued to exhibit some of the worst primary health indicators in Latin America. However, one positive step was the creation of the integrated health-care system for the rural areas. Although significant progress had been made in the area of education reform, much more needed to be done. Increases in education spending were hampered by the inadequacy of the education budget. The Government succeeded in lowering illiteracy rates to 30 per cent and started bilingual education, but that was available to less than 10 per cent of indigenous children. The most important advance in the area of decentralization was the increase in citizen participation in local decision-making. In many parts of the country, civil society groups were beginning to play a more active role in influencing municipal and departmental policy-making, and the new Administration named several governors proposed by the Departmental Development Councils. Significant efforts were made

to reform laws, create institutions and formulate public policies favouring women and gender equality; however, domestic violence, unequal access to education and jobs, and low levels of political participation among women persisted. Funding shortages limited the reach and impact of newly created institutions for dealing with women's issues.

The process of demobilizing and reintegrating the URNG combatants into civilian life was successful. However, the process fell short in providing viable economic opportunities for ex-combatants, due to insufficient government assistance in providing land, housing, credit and other basic services. A similar situation confronted returning former refugees and internally displaced persons.

The Secretary-General observed that Guatemala could not rest on its achievements, as the deeper structural reforms envisaged by the peace accords lagged far behind the political advances. Crime and insecurity were the greatest dangers to Guatemala's democracy and economic future, and halting the deterioration of the National Civilian Police had become a matter of national urgency. Other areas needing attention included unpaid debt to victims; the investigation and punishment of those responsible for acts of genocide and other crimes against humanity; tax reform; a functional State with sufficient resources to make major public investments in health, education, security and justice; and policies to help lift more than half its citizens out of poverty. The Secretary-General stated that the peace process had matured and the democratic framework in Guatemala had been consolidated to the point where it should be possible to address unresolved issues peacefully through national mechanisms and more standard forms of international cooperation. It was essential that UN agencies, funds and programmes remain guided by the accords, directing funding to priority areas. He emphasized the importance of continued support by the donor community, and of further engagement in projects supporting the peace accords and political dialogue with the Government on implementation of the accords.

Haiti

Political and security situation

During 2004, the political and security crisis in Haiti escalated into violence. The situation originated in 2000, when Haitian President Jean-Bertrand Aristide and his Fanmi Lavalas party claimed victory in presidential and parliamentary elections, in which voter turnout hardly rose above 10 per cent of the electorate. The opposition and members of the international community contested the results, accusing the Government of manipulating them. Subsequent dialogue between the Government and the opposition on resolving the situation broke down. The opposition was increasingly repressed by politicized sectors of the Haitian National Police and by irregular armed groups supportive of the Government. By late 2003, a newly united opposition movement, comprising political parties, civil society actors and the private sector, was calling for President Artistide's resignation.

In January 2004, the Caribbean Community (CARICOM), in an initiative to resolve the crisis, sent a fact-finding mission to Haiti to meet with President Aristide and the opposition, and presented proposals for moving the process forward at a meeting with the major political stakeholders (Nassau, Bahamas, 20-21 January) and including observers from the United States, Canada and the Organization of American States (OAS). In a subsequent meeting hosted by the Jamaican Prime Minister, P. J. Patterson, in his capacity as CARICOM Chairman (Kingston, Jamaica, 31 January), and attended by international partners, including the European Union (EU), the CARICOM Prior Action Plan on Haiti was submitted. The Plan involved measures to improve the security climate and to build confidence, and included compliance with previous OAS resolutions, negotiation of rules for demonstrations, the release of detainees, disarmament of strong-arm groups, the strengthening of the police force and the enjoyment of fundamental freedoms. The Plan envisaged the establishment of an electoral commission, the formation of a council of eminent persons and the appointment of a neutral and independent prime minister. It also called for the formation of a new Government through a process of consultations. A plan of action to facilitate implementation of the CARICOM Prior Action Plan was drawn up at a subsequent meeting in Washington, D.C. That plan was accepted by President Aristide but rejected by the opposition.

In early February, armed conflict broke out in the northern city of Gonaives and in the following days fighting spread to other cities. Insurgents took control of the northern part of the country. Despite diplomatic efforts, the armed opposition threatened to march on the capital, Port-au-Prince. The already weakened and outnumbered Haitian National Police were forced to abandon their posts or protectively barricade themselves against mounting attacks of the rebel groups. Some 70 persons were killed in February.

Security Council press statement. The Security Council President, on 18 February [S/2004/224], issued a press statement in which Council members expressed deep concern over the increasing violence and political crisis in Haiti, the deterioration of the humanitarian situation, and the massive violations of human rights. They called on President Aristide's Government and the opposition to restore dialogue to overcome their differences peacefully and democratically. The Council expressed support for the CARICOM and OAS initiative to bring the crisis to an end, and deplored the decision of the opposition to reject the CARICOM-OAS Action Plan (see above). It called on both parties to accept and implement its provisions and pertinent OAS resolutions. The Council called on the international community to respond to the serious humanitarian situation in Haiti.

Communications (23-26 February). On 23 February [S/2004/143], Jamaica, on behalf of the CARICOM members, requested a meeting of the Security Council in the light of the steadily deteriorating situation in Haiti.

France, in a letter of 25 February [S/2004/145], urged the international community to take action to preserve Haiti from disorder and violence. Stressing the need to establish a transitional Government of national unity in Haiti, France expressed its willingness to play a role in the international mobilization effort and proposed an initiative, which broadened the CARICOM Prior Action Plan (see above) to include the establishment of a civilian peacekeeping force, international assistance in preparing for elections, the delivery of humanitarian aid, the dispatch of human rights observers and a long-term commitment to providing aid for Haiti's economic and social reconstruction.

On 26 February [S/2004/148], OAS called on the Security Council to address the crisis in Haiti, and requested that the Secretaries-General of OAS and the United Nations remain in close contact to ensure coordination and complementarity in the roles of the two organizations.

Appointment of Special Adviser. On 26 February [A/58/722-E/2004/13, S/2004/161], the Secretary-General appointed John Reginald Dumas (Trinidad and Tobago) as his Special Adviser on Haiti. Mr. Dumas would examine ways in which the Organization could enhance its contributions to alleviating the political, economic and social crises in the country. On 27 February [S/2004/162], the Security Council noted the Secretary-General's decision.

Security Council consideration. The Security Council met on 26 February [meeting 4917] to discuss the question concerning Haiti, as requested by Jamaica (see p. 289). Speaking before the Council, the Jamaican representative said that the past 20 months had been challenging and without much progress towards ending polarization or building a political consensus in Haiti. He cited recent CARICOM efforts initiated in January, which included fact-finding missions to Haiti, meetings with President Jean-Bertrand Aristide and with the opposition, in addition to a CARICOM initiative presented in January in the Bahamas (ibid.).

Drawing attention to the political upheaval that had escalated in the past weeks, Jamaica concluded that the situation within Haiti could no longer be viewed as an internal matter and posed a serious threat to regional peace and security, given the outflow of refugees, which threatened to overwhelm the resources of neighbouring States. Incursions by rebel forces from the north had resulted in reprisal killings, the destruction of property and general lawlessness, creating a state of anarchy in much of the country. Immediate action was needed to safeguard democracy and to avert bloodshed and a humanitarian disaster.

Jamaica also stated that President Aristide had requested international community assistance, specifically, from CARICOM to strengthen the Haitian National Police. While CARICOM continued to seek a political solution to the Haitian crisis, its member States sought direct and immediate UN intervention, as the situation was one of utmost urgency and the need for decisive action was paramount. The immediate need was for the Security Council to authorize the deployment of a multinational force, in addition to addressing the growing humanitarian crisis and extending assistance to Haiti's long-term economic and social reconstruction. It was also imperative that affected States be assisted to offset the costs for relief and humanitarian assistance to the refugees.

SECURITY COUNCIL ACTION (26 February).

On 26 February [meeting 4917], following consultations among Security Council members, the President made statement [S/PRST/2004/4] on behalf of the Council:

> The Security Council expresses deep concern in regard to the deterioration of the political, security and humanitarian environment in Haiti. It deplores the loss of life that has already occurred and fears that the failure, thus far, to reach a political settlement may result in further bloodshed. Continued violence and the breakdown of law and order in Haiti could have destabilizing effects in the region.
>
> The Council commends the Organization of American States and the Caribbean Community for their lead role in promoting a peaceful solution and

for trying to re-establish confidence among the parties, in particular through their Plan of Action.

> The Council supports the Caribbean Community and the Organization of American States as they continue to work towards a peaceful and constitutional solution to the current impasse. The principles outlined in the Caribbean Community/Organization of American States Plan of Action represent an important basis for a solution to the crisis. The Council calls upon the parties to act responsibly by choosing negotiation instead of confrontation. An accelerated timetable now seems necessary.
>
> The Council is deeply concerned with the prospect of further violence in Haiti and acknowledges the call for international involvement in Haiti. The Council will consider urgently options for international engagement, including that of an international force in support of a political settlement in accordance with the Charter of the United Nations.
>
> The Council calls upon all sides in Haiti's conflict to facilitate the distribution of food and medicine and ensure the protection of civilians. It calls upon all sides to respect international humanitarian personnel and facilities and to ensure that humanitarian assistance reaches those who need it.
>
> The Council calls upon the Government and all other parties to respect human rights and to cease the use of violence to advance political goals. Those responsible for human rights violations will be held accountable.
>
> The Council supports the Secretary-General's decision to name a Special Advisor for Haiti.
>
> The Council will continue to monitor closely the situation in Haiti and remains seized of the matter.

Deployment of Multinational Interim Force

Early on 29 February, Mr. Aristide left the country. His letter of resignation was read out by the Prime Minister, Yvon Neptune. In accordance with the constitutional rules of succession, Boniface Alexandre, the President of the Supreme Court, was sworn in as interim President.

Security Council consideration (29 February). On 29 February [meeting 4919], the Security Council met to discuss the situation in Haiti. The Council had before it an appeal [S/2004/163] by Mr. Alexandre for support to the Haitian constitutional process and authorizing international security forces to enter Haiti to help bring a climate of security and stability to support the political process and facilitate the provision of humanitarian assistance.

SECURITY COUNCIL ACTION (29 February)

On 29 February [meeting 4919], the Security Council unanimously adopted **resolution 1529 (2004)**. The draft [S/2004/164] was prepared in consultations among Council members.

The Security Council,

Recalling its resolutions as well as the statements by its President concerning Haiti, in particular the statement of 26 February 2004 (S/PRST/2004/4),

Deeply concerned by the deterioration of the political, security and humanitarian situation in Haiti and deploring the loss of life that has already occurred,

Expressing its utmost concern at the continuing violence in Haiti, as well as the potential for a rapid deterioration of the humanitarian situation in that country, and its destabilizing effect on the region,

Stressing the need to create a secure environment in Haiti and the region that enables respect for human rights, including the well-being of civilians, and supports the mission of humanitarian workers,

Commending the Organization of American States and the Caribbean Community for their lead efforts to advance a peaceful solution and for attempting to establish confidence among the parties, in particular through their Plan of Action,

Taking note of the resignation of Jean-Bertrand Aristide as President of Haiti and the swearing-in of Boniface Alexandre as the Acting President of Haiti in accordance with the Constitution of Haiti,

Acknowledging the appeal of the new President of Haiti for the urgent support of the international community to assist in restoring peace and security in Haiti and to further the constitutional political process now under way,

Determined to support a peaceful and constitutional solution to the current crisis in Haiti,

Determining that the situation in Haiti constitutes a threat to international peace and security and to stability in the Caribbean, especially through the potential outflow of people to other States in the subregion,

Acting under Chapter VII of the Charter of the United Nations,

1. *Calls upon* Member States to support the constitutional succession and political process now under way in Haiti and the promotion of a peaceful and lasting solution to the current crisis;

2. *Authorizes* the immediate deployment of a Multinational Interim Force in Haiti for a period of not more than three months from adoption of the present resolution:

(a) To contribute to a secure and stable environment in the Haitian capital and elsewhere in the country, as appropriate and as circumstances permit, in order to support Haitian President Alexandre's request for international assistance to support the constitutional political process under way in Haiti;

(b) To facilitate the provision of humanitarian assistance and the access of international humanitarian workers to the Haitian people in need;

(c) To facilitate the provision of international assistance to the Haitian police and the Haitian Coast Guard in order to establish and maintain public safety and law and order and to promote and protect human rights;

(d) To support the establishment of conditions for international and regional organizations, including the United Nations and the Organization of American States, to assist the Haitian people;

(e) To coordinate, as needed, with the Special Mission of the Organization of American States and with the United Nations Special Adviser for Haiti, to prevent further deterioration of the humanitarian situation;

3. *Declares its readiness* to establish a follow-on United Nations stabilization force to support continuation of a peaceful and constitutional political process and the maintenance of a secure and stable environment, and in this regard requests the Secretary-General, in consultation with the Organization of American States, to submit to the Council recommendations, preferably by thirty days from the adoption of the present resolution, for the size, structure and mandate of such a force, including the role of international police and means of coordination with the Special Mission of the Organization of American States, and for subsequent deployment of the United Nations force not later than three months from the adoption of the present resolution;

4. *Welcomes* the appointment by the Secretary-General on 26 February of a Special Adviser for Haiti, and requests the Secretary-General to elaborate a programme of action for the United Nations to assist the constitutional political process and support humanitarian and economic assistance and promote the protection of human rights and the development of the rule of law;

5. *Calls upon* Member States to contribute personnel, equipment and other necessary financial and logistic resources on an urgent basis to the Multinational Interim Force, invites contributing Member States to inform the leadership of the Force and the Secretary-General of their intent to participate in the mission, and stresses the importance of voluntary contributions to help defray the expenses of the Force that participating Member States will bear;

6. *Authorizes* the Member States participating in the Multinational Interim Force to take all necessary measures to fulfil its mandate;

7. *Demands* that all parties to the conflict in Haiti cease using violent means, reiterates that all parties must respect international law, including with respect to human rights, and that there will be individual accountability and no impunity for violators, and also demands that parties respect the constitutional succession and the political process under way to resolve the current crisis and enable legitimate Haitian security forces and other public institutions to perform their duties and provide access to humanitarian agencies to carry out their work;

8. *Further calls upon* all parties in Haiti and on Member States to cooperate fully with the Multinational Interim Force in the execution of its mandate and to respect the security and freedom of movement of the Force, as well as to facilitate the safe and unimpeded access of international humanitarian personnel and aid to populations in need in Haiti;

9. *Requests* the leadership of the Multinational Interim Force to report periodically to the Council, through the Secretary-General, on the implementation of its mandate;

10. *Calls upon* the international community, in particular the United Nations, the Organization of American States and the Caribbean Community, to work with the people of Haiti in a long-term effort to promote the rebuilding of democratic institutions and to assist in the development of a strategy to promote social and economic development and to combat poverty;

11. *Decides* to remain seized of the matter.

Report of Multinational Force. On 23 March [S/2004/239], the United States submitted to the

Secretary-General, in accordance with resolution 1529(2004), an interim report of the Multinational Interim Force in Haiti (MIF), whose strength stood at 3,400 troops as at that date. The Force began operations on 29 February, and within days armed gangs had begun to withdraw from Port-au-Prince, looting was significantly reduced, and by 11 March the main airports and seaports had been secured. The Force undertook stabilization efforts in northern Haiti, deploying troops to the rebel stronghold cities of Gonaïves and Cap-Haïtien, and established roving patrols to provide a visible presence. Similar patrols were also established in Port-au-Prince and in central and southern Haiti. However, the number of troops available was still insufficient to guard the large number of static sites. MIF assisted the local police in "practical disarmament", detaining illegally armed persons and confiscating arms, and worked with humanitarian personnel to improve the coordination of assistance. That allowed staff of international and regional organizations to return to work and assistance projects to resume. The Force also began to work with the Haitian National Police and Coast Guard in support of patrols to maintain law and order. The police requested MIF assistance in vetting existing police units to remove human rights abusers, finding new officers and procuring vehicles and fuel. MIF would work closely with the United Nations and OAS to establish the conditions for the deployment of a follow-on UN force and to facilitate international efforts to assist the Haitian National Police. With the MIF mandate concluding on 1 June, planning had begun for the transition to a UN stabilization force. The MIF troop contributors recommended that a UN transition team be deployed to Haiti by mid-April.

Security Council consideration. On 23 March [S/2004/328], the Assistant Secretary-General for Political Affairs, in a briefing to the Council on the situation in Haiti, stated that MIF, having deployed in the capital and other areas of the country, had made considerable progress in stabilizing a situation characterized by a collapse of public structures, looting and widespread violence. Calm had been restored in Port-au-Prince but there was still an urgent need for increased security in other localities. The Secretariat was continuing close consultations with MIF with the aim of facilitating the transition to a UN operation. A secure corridor from Port-au-Prince to Cap-Haïtien had been opened allowing for the resumption of activities by UN agencies. A multidisciplinary assessment mission under the auspices of the Secretary-General's Special Adviser was being conducted and would soon report to the Council.

The members of the Council took note of the presentation given by the United States delegation in the name of the countries participating in MIF. They welcomed CARICOM's agreement to participate in a forthcoming UN stabilization force and stressed that the international community should be mobilized in order to create the necessary conditions to restore a secure political, social, economic and humanitarian environment in Haiti in the long term.

Departure of Haitian President

On 4 March [S/2004/195], the President of the Central African Republic informed the Secretary-General that his country had agreed to receive and welcome the former President of Haiti, Jean-Bertrand Aristide, as a humanitarian act.

On 11 March [A/58/731-S/2004/191], Jamaica transmitted the text of a statement issued by CARICOM heads of Government at their emergency meeting (Kingston, Jamaica, 2-3 March), which expressed the view that the circumstances under which Mr. Aristide demitted office set a dangerous precedent for democratically elected Governments everywhere and that no action should be taken to legitimize the rebel forces nor should they be included in any interim government. They called for an investigation, under UN auspices, to clarify the circumstances leading to his relinquishing the Presidency.

The Security Council held consultations on 30 March with the Special Adviser to the Secretary-General [S/2004/328], who had visited Haiti and countries of the area and had attended the CARICOM summit in Saint Kitts and Nevis. Council members focused on the disarmament of armed groups, the need for national reconciliation and the timely organization of elections. They agreed that stabilization of the country and creating the necessary conditions for security were the most urgent needs.

Further political developments

The Secretary-General, in his April report on Haiti [S/2004/300], said that on 4 March, a Tripartite Council was named, consisting of one representative each from the Fanmi Lavalas party, the Plateforme démocratique and the international community. The following day, that group selected seven eminent persons to form the Conseil des sages, which would in turn select a Prime Minister. The Council included representatives of key sectors of Haitian society, including human rights groups, churches, academia, the private sector and political groups. On 9 March, the Conseil des sages selected Gérard Latortue as

Prime Minister, who, in consultation with it, formed a 13-member Transitional Government. Some supporters of the Fanmi Lavalas party and others contested the Transitional Government's legitimacy. To build political consensus for the work of the Transitional Government, a political pact, called the Consensus on the Political Transition Pact, was signed on 4 April by the Prime Minister, members of the Conseil des sages, representatives of political groups, except the Fanmi Lavalas party which denounced it, and civil society organizations. The understanding reached provided for the holding of municipal, parliamentary and presidential elections in 2005. Members of the Transitional Government, the electoral council and the Conseil des sages agreed not to contest those elections. Until the next parliament was in place, the Conseil des sages would advise the Transitional Government on important matters such as the budget, agreements and decrees, and draw attention to questions requiring high-level intervention. The Pact also provided for procedures to address vacancies in the executive branch; measures to be undertaken during the transition period in the areas of security, development, the fight against impunity and corruption, decentralization, elections, judicial reform, a national conference and a new social contract; institutional strengthening of political parties and civil society organizations; reintegration of former armed elements; and professionalization of the Haitian National Police. It was agreed to establish commissions to address human rights abuses, financial wrongdoing and matters related to the former military, and to discuss with the United Nations the status of MIF and the follow-on peacekeeping operation.

The Secretary-General said that a major test for the Transitional Government was extending State authority outside Port-au-Prince, as many communities were without legitimate local governments and were controlled by irregular armed groups. Self-appointed or insurgent-designated mayors and leaders had replaced some local bodies. The intended nomination by the Transitional Government of provisional municipal committees would require consensus at the local level.

The Secretary-General reported that he had dispatched on 11 March a multidisciplinary assessment mission to Haiti, comprising representatives of several Secretariat departments, to gather information on the ground, specifically on the political and security situation (see p. 292), the police, judicial and corrections institutions, human rights, the humanitarian situation, development issues, gender issues, the situation of the media, and the activities of regional and sub-regional organizations.

According to the Secretary-General, the security situation remained uncertain and would be influenced by the political process; the pace and efficacy of the restoration of government authority and State institutions, particularly the Haitian National Police, throughout the country; the durability of the measures undertaken by MIF, particularly with regard to disarmament; and the willingness of armed groups to cooperate with disarmament and reintegration plans. To date, weapons handovers had been largely symbolic and pledges by rebels to lay down arms upon the establishment of the Transitional Government had not been followed through. In the circumstances, an international presence would be needed to provide a security umbrella and, in conjunction with the police, to confiscate illicit arms and seize caches. A comprehensive programme for the disarmament, demobilization and reintegration of armed groups would be required. The international community would support the national capacity to develop, coordinate and implement such a strategy. Support could be provided for the development of national legal, law enforcement and administrative capacities for weapons control, collection, management, stockpiling, destruction and disposal and to combat illicit trafficking.

During the period of unrest, the police almost completely collapsed and were reduced to a strength of no more than 2,500. Stations were vandalized, burnt and seriously damaged, while equipment, records and archives were looted or destroyed. Law enforcement officers had begun to return to work and efforts were being made to bring back more officers and recruit new ones. A successful restoration of the rule of law and public security in Haiti would require a comprehensive approach to assist the police with sustainable reform and institutional strengthening, with parallel improvements in other areas of the criminal justice system. The administration of justice was greatly affected by the crisis, and considerable improvements were needed to ensure lasting peace and security.

To ensure an effective and timely response to the emergency humanitarian situation and rehabilitation needs, a quick and generous response from donors was essential. The United Nations issued a flash appeal for Haiti in 2004, requesting $35 million for six months (see p. 938). With regard to medium- and longer-term assistance needs, a Haiti Contact Group meeting (Washington, D.C., 23 March) agreed to prepare an interim framework, focusing on the current economic, social and institutional needs of Haiti.

The Secretary-General said that, on the basis of the findings of the multidisciplinary team, he was recommending the establishment of a multidimensional stabilization operation in Haiti, to be known as the United Nations Stabilization Mission in Haiti (MINUSTAH), for an initial period of 24 months, to help the country address a range of complex issues in a sustainable manner, achieve peace and stability, build and strengthen functioning democratic institutions, support the re-establishment of the rule of law and promote social and economic development and good governance. It would be composed of a strong civilian component, including 1,622 UN civilian police, backed up by a robust UN military force of up to 6,700 troops. It would also include a humanitarian affairs and development pillar and a civilian affairs pillar, under the overall leadership of the Special Representative of the Secretary-General.

SECURITY COUNCIL ACTION (April)

On 30 April [meeting 4961], the Security Council unanimously adopted **resolution 1542(2004)**. The draft [S/2004/334] was prepared in consultations among Council members.

The Security Council,

Recalling its resolution 1529(2004) of 29 February 2004,

Welcoming the report of the Secretary-General of 16 April 2004, and supporting its recommendations,

Affirming its strong commitment to the sovereignty, independence, territorial integrity and unity of Haiti,

Deploring all violations of human rights, particularly against the civilian population, and urging the Transitional Government of Haiti ("Transitional Government") to take all necessary measures to put an end to impunity and to ensure that the continued promotion and protection of human rights and the establishment of a State based on the rule of law and an independent judiciary are among its highest priorities,

Reaffirming its resolution 1325(2000) of 31 October 2000 on women and peace and security and its resolutions 1379(2001) of 20 November 2001, 1460(2003) of 30 January 2003 and 1539(2004) of 22 April 2004 on children in armed conflict, as well as its resolutions 1265(1999) of 17 September 1999 and 1296(2000) of 19 April 2000 on the protection of civilians in armed conflict,

Welcoming and encouraging efforts by the United Nations to sensitize peacekeeping personnel in the prevention and control of HIV/AIDS and other communicable diseases in all its peacekeeping operations,

Commending the rapid and professional deployment of the Multinational Interim Force in Haiti and the stabilization efforts it has undertaken,

Taking note of the political agreement reached by some key parties on 4 April 2004, and urging all parties to work without delay towards a broad political consensus on the nature and duration of the political transition,

Reiterating its call upon the international community to continue to assist and support the economic, social

and institutional development of Haiti over the long term, and welcoming the intention of the Organization of American States, the Caribbean Community, and of the international donor community, as well as international financial institutions, to participate in those efforts,

Noting the existence of challenges to the political, social and economic stability of Haiti, and determining that the situation in Haiti continues to constitute a threat to international peace and security in the region,

1. *Decides* to establish the United Nations Stabilization Mission in Haiti, the stabilization force called for in resolution 1529(2004), for an initial period of six months, with the intention to renew it for further periods, and requests that authority be transferred from the Multinational Interim Force in Haiti to the Mission on 1 June 2004;

2. *Authorizes* remaining elements of the Multinational Interim Force to continue carrying out its mandate under resolution 1529(2004) within the means available for a transition period not exceeding thirty days from 1 June 2004, as required and requested by the Mission;

3. *Requests* the Secretary-General to appoint a Special Representative for Haiti, who will have overall authority on the ground for the coordination and conduct of all the activities of the United Nations agencies, funds and programmes in Haiti;

4. *Decides* that the Mission will consist of a civilian and a military component, in accordance with the report of the Secretary-General on Haiti, the civilian component to include a maximum of 1,622 civilian police, including advisers and formed units, and the military component to include up to 6,700 troops of all ranks, and requests further that the military component report directly to the Special Representative through the Force Commander;

5. *Supports* the establishment of a Core Group chaired by the Special Representative and comprising also his/her Deputies, the Force Commander, representatives of the Organization of American States and the Caribbean Community, other regional and subregional organizations, international financial institutions and other major stakeholders, in order to facilitate the implementation of the Mission's mandate, promote interaction with the Haitian authorities as partners, and enhance the effectiveness of the international community's response in Haiti, as outlined in the report of the Secretary-General;

6. *Requests* that, in carrying out its mandate, the Mission cooperate and coordinate with the Organization of American States and the Caribbean Community;

7. *Acting* under Chapter VII of the Charter of the United Nations with regard to section I below, decides that the Mission shall have the following mandate:

I. *Secure and stable environment:*

(a) To ensure a secure and stable environment, in support of the Transitional Government, within which the constitutional and political process in Haiti can take place;

(b) To assist the Transitional Government in monitoring, restructuring and reforming the Haitian National Police, consistent with democratic policing standards, including through the vetting and certification of its personnel, advising on its reorganization and training, including gender training, as well as monitoring/mentoring members of the Haitian National Police;

(c) To assist the Transitional Government, particularly the Haitian National Police, with comprehensive and sustainable disarmament, demobilization and re-integration programmes for all armed groups, including women and children associated with such groups, as well as weapons control and public security measures;

(d) To assist with the restoration and maintenance of the rule of law, public safety and public order in Haiti through the provision, inter alia, of operational support to the Haitian National Police and the Haitian Coast Guard, as well as with their institutional strengthening, including the re-establishment of the corrections system;

(e) To protect United Nations personnel, facilities, installations and equipment and to ensure the security and freedom of movement of its personnel, taking into account the primary responsibility of the Transitional Government in that regard;

(f) To protect civilians under imminent threat of physical violence, within its capabilities and areas of deployment, without prejudice to the responsibilities of the Transitional Government and of police authorities;

II. *Political process:*

(a) To support the constitutional and political process under way in Haiti, including through good offices, and to foster principles of democratic governance and institutional development;

(b) To assist the Transitional Government in its efforts to bring about a process of national dialogue and reconciliation;

(c) To assist the Transitional Government in its efforts to organize, monitor, and carry out free and fair municipal, parliamentary and presidential elections at the earliest possible date, in particular through the provision of technical, logistical, and administrative assistance and continued security, with appropriate support to an electoral process with voter participation that is representative of the national demographics, including women;

(d) To assist the Transitional Government in extending State authority throughout Haiti and support good governance at local levels;

III. *Human rights:*

(a) To support the Transitional Government as well as Haitian human rights institutions and groups in their efforts to promote and protect human rights, particularly of women and children, in order to ensure individual accountability for human rights abuses and redress for victims;

(b) To monitor and report on the human rights situation, in cooperation with the Office of the United Nations High Commissioner for Human Rights, including on the situation of returned refugees and displaced persons;

8. *Decides* that the Mission, in collaboration with other partners, shall provide advice and assistance within its capacity to the Transitional Government:

(a) In the investigation of human rights violations and violations of international humanitarian law, in collaboration with the Office of the High Commissioner, to put an end to impunity;

(b) In the development of a strategy for reform and institutional strengthening of the judiciary;

9. *Decides also* that the Mission shall coordinate and cooperate with the Transitional Government, as well as with their international partners, in order to facilitate the provision and coordination of humanitarian assistance and access of humanitarian workers to Haitian people in need, with a particular focus on the most vulnerable segments of society, particularly women and children;

10. *Authorizes* the Secretary-General to take all necessary steps to facilitate and support the early deployment of the Mission in advance of the United Nations assumption of responsibilities from the Multinational Interim Force;

11. *Requests* the Haitian authorities to conclude a status-of-forces agreement for peacekeeping operations with the Secretary-General within thirty days of adoption of the present resolution, and notes that, pending the conclusion of such an agreement, the model status-of-forces agreement dated 9 October 1990 shall apply provisionally;

12. *Demands* strict respect for the persons and premises of the United Nations and associated personnel, the Organization of American States, the Caribbean Community and other international and humanitarian organizations, as well as diplomatic missions in Haiti, and that no acts of intimidation or violence be directed against personnel engaged in humanitarian, development or peacekeeping work, and demands further that all parties in Haiti provide safe and unimpeded access to humanitarian agencies to allow them to carry out their work;

13. *Emphasizes* the need for Member States, United Nations organs, bodies and agencies and other international organizations, in particular the Organization of American States and the Caribbean Community, other regional and subregional organizations, international financial institutions and non-governmental organizations to continue to contribute to the promotion of the social and economic development of Haiti, in particular for the long term, in order to achieve and sustain stability and combat poverty;

14. *Urges* all the above-mentioned stakeholders, in particular the United Nations organs, bodies and agencies to assist the Transitional Government of Haiti in the design of a long-term development strategy to this effect;

15. *Calls upon* Member States to provide substantial international aid to meet the humanitarian needs in Haiti and to permit the reconstruction of the country, utilizing relevant coordination mechanisms, and further calls upon States, in particular those in the region, to provide appropriate support for the actions undertaken by the United Nations organs, bodies and agencies;

16. *Requests* the Secretary-General to provide an interim report to the Council on the implementation of the present mandate, and to provide an additional report, prior to the expiration of the mandate, containing recommendations to the Council on whether to extend, restructure or reshape the Mission in order to

ensure that the Mission and its mandate remain relevant to changes in the political, security and economic development situation in Haiti;

17. *Decides* to remain seized of the matter.

MIF-MINUSTAH transition

In May [S/2004/386], the Secretary-General transmitted the 60-day report on MIF activities, which provided an update on the status of the tasks assigned to the Force. It indicated that the constitutional political process had remained consistent, and MIF had provided security to the Presidential Palace and the Primature so they could continue to function. All appropriate humanitarian assistance requests for support through the Civil Military Operations Centre had been fulfilled, and MIF collaborated with humanitarian organizations to distribute assistance in targeted areas. The report also cited the development of long-term training plans for the Haitian Coast Guard; the establishment of a rewards programme for seizure of weapon caches; continued work towards facilitating the transfer of authority to MINUSTAH; and the progress made since the March report in returning portions of the country to an acceptable level of stability.

In a 16 June report [S/2004/497], the Secretary-General stated that an ongoing MIF assessment revealed stable and relatively secure conditions in the southern claw region, which allowed forces to withdraw and focus on Hinche and the Port-au-Prince area. The political process had significantly improved since the establishment of the Transitional Government. MIF and MINUSTAH held a joint planning conference (3-7 May), which resulted in a draft transition document. The report also covered MIF activities to facilitate humanitarian assistance, including relief to the heavily flooded towns of Fond Verrettes and Mapou; to assist the Haitian National Police and the Haitian Coast Guard to support public safety and human rights; to establish conditions so that international and regional organizations could assist the Haitian people; and to coordinate with OAS and the United Nations Special Adviser to prevent further deterioration of the humanitarian situation.

The Assistant Secretary-General for Peacekeeping Operations, on 16 June [S/2004/622], briefed the Security Council on the situation in Haiti. Outlining the efforts to establish MINUSTAH and envisaging the transfer of authority from MIF to MINUSTAH on or before 1 July, he stressed the need for continued support from donor countries, troop-contributing countries and the Council for MINUSTAH to succeed. MINUSTAH assumed operational responsibilities on 25 June.

Appointments. On 27 May [S/2004/439], the Secretary-General informed the Security Council of his intention to appoint Lieutenant General Augusto Heleno Ribeiro Pereira (Brazil) to the post of Force Commander of MINUSTAH, which formally assumed authority from MIF on 1 June. On 12 July [S/2004/565], he indicated his intention to appoint Juan Gabriel Valdés (Chile) as his Special Representative and Head of MINUSTAH. The Council took note of those intentions [S/2004/440, S/2004/566].

MINUSTAH activities

Report of Secretary-General (August). In an August report [S/2004/698], the Secretary-General described progress in the implementation of the MINUSTAH mandate, including the deployment of military troops and civilian police, whose strength was 2,755 and 240, respectively, at the time of the report. Troops were deployed to every area in Haiti except in the north where patrols were conducted in Cap-Haitien and Fort-Liberté. More troops would be required to deal with the challenges in the more remote municipalities and along the border with the Dominican Republic. Civilian police officers were deployed outside the capital from 26 July. Regional operational centres were set up in every region. To support the Haitian National Police in re-establishing their presence and enhance confidence, civilian police advisers would be deployed at every decision-making level of the national police force.

The Transitional Government, having taken office on 17 March, had begun to restore governance and prepare the ground for transition to an elected Government, in accordance with the time line agreed in the Consensus on the Political Transition Pact (see below). In May, with the support of bilateral and multilateral agencies and the United Nations, it prepared the interim cooperation framework, setting out priorities and targets to respond to the country's urgent and medium-term development needs, assessed at $1,370 million, of which $446 million had already been committed by donors. At the International Donors Conference on Haiti (Washington, D.C., 19-20 July), the international community pledged another $1,085 million.

The signatories of the Consensus on the Political Transition Pact agreed on 23 July to the formation of a Follow-up Committee, comprising representatives of the Transitional Government, the Conseil des sages, political parties and civil society groups, to institutionalize the process of overseeing its implementation. However, Fanmi Lavalas remained outside the main political transition process. Tensions continued to characterize the relationship between the Transitional Government and Fanmi Lavalas, which alleged that its members were subject to political persecution and pointed to the 27 June arrest of former Prime Minister Yvon Neptune as evidence. Mr. Neptune had been detained for his alleged involvement in the February massacre in Saint-Marc, but no charges had so far been brought against him. The Government had also placed a number of Fanmi Lavalas supporters on a list of those barred from leaving the country. The Secretary-General's Special Adviser tried to broker an agreement between the Transitional Government and Fanmi Lavalas on the latter's entry into the political process. The Fanmi Lavalas party itself had shown signs of increasing internal divisions, with moderates considering joining the political transition process. A group of former Fanmi Lavalas members formed a new political party on 31 July—the Mouvement démocratique et réformateur haitien, which indicated its intention to compete in the next elections and take part in the political process. In addition, more than 70 new political parties and groups had emerged, making the Haitian political landscape very fragmented.

The Provisional Electoral Council, which was mired in internal disputes, had not drawn up time frames for the elections or taken a decision regarding the sequence and number of votes. On 15 April, the Transitional Government requested UN electoral assistance. A UN mission was sent to Haiti (8-17 June) to assess its electoral needs and determine the modalities for assistance. The assessment mission recommended action to amend the electoral law and related regulations, training and direct assistance to the Provisional Electoral Council, the establishment of a voters list and the development of a civic education campaign. It also recommended that joint municipal and parliamentary elections be held towards the middle of 2005 and presidential polls towards the end of 2005. MINUSTAH would supervise the electoral process and coordinate and monitor international technical assistance.

During the reporting period, the Transitional Government made moderate strides in extending State authority outside Port-au-Prince. By August, it had appointed 103 of the 139 municipal commissions. However, a number of municipalities remained without a mayor and, in those where a local government was in place, infrastructure and basic facilities were lacking. MINUSTAH established contact with the various levels of State administration to identify local needs and develop a municipal database. It assessed needs in public administration, local management skills and good governance and was working with the United Nations Development Programme (UNDP), OAS and the EU on decentralization and the establishment and strengthening of local authority.

While the security situation improved, armed groups continued to control parts of the country, particularly in the north and the east along the border with the Dominican Republic. Isolated instances of violence and gunfire, home invasions, acts of retaliation, kidnappings, gang activity and confrontation between the National Police and former soldiers of the disbanded Haitian armed forces were reported. On 8 July the Transitional Government's Superior Council on the National Police stated that the activities of armed groups presenting themselves as security forces were illegal and action would be taken against them, with MINUSTAH help, if they were still operating after 15 September.

With regard to disarmament, demobilization and reintegration, a mixed inter-ministerial commission, essential for developing a national programme, had not yet been established. The Transitional Government, however, did establish the commission, led by the Minister of the Interior, to examine the situation of the former armed forces, and on 13 August announced the formation of an inter-ministerial commission to study issues related to back pay and retirement funds and to formulate recommendations on the reorganization of the military. A worrisome development was the refusal of the former military to disarm until their demands were met. Meanwhile, the National Police had increased from 2,500 to 3,567 officers, which was still insufficient to provide adequate security.

Insecurity and problems in the functioning of law enforcement structures contributed to the continuing precariousness of the human rights situation. The trial of Louis Jodel Chamblain, accused of participating in the assassination of Antroine Izmery, a businessman and adviser to former President Aristide, in September 1993, opened on 16 August. Mr. Chamblain and his co-defendant were acquitted but remained in prison pending further trials. The international community denounced the trial as not meeting minimum legal standards and expressed concern at the haste with which the Transitional Government had arrested members of Fanmi Lavalas suspected of political violence and corruption, while failing to act against perpetrators of serious human rights violations.

The humanitarian situation remained complex, compounded by chronic poverty and environmental degradation. MINUSTAH initiated preparations to support the response to complex emergencies. UN inter-agency assessment missions were deployed to follow up on the floods in southern Haiti and to identify possible vulnerable areas.

The Secretary-General said that the restoration of the rule of law would be crucial to restoring confidence in the institutions of the State. The Government of Haiti had to do more to establish a well-functioning and impartial justice system. The Secretary-General remained concerned by reports of double standards in the administration of justice. He urged the Government to strengthen the country's legitimate democratic institutions, while overhauling or abolishing those that did not meet democratic standards, and to establish, as a priority, a national commission on disarmament, demobilization and reintegration. The Secretary-General called on all concerned to lay down their arms and to refrain from violence so as to allow the political process, including the electoral process, to unfold free from pressure.

SECURITY COUNCIL ACTION (September)

On 10 September [meeting 5030], following consultations among Security Council members, the President made statement **S/PRST/2004/32** on behalf of the Council:

The Security Council extends its appreciation to participating countries of the United Nations Stabilization Mission in Haiti, and hopes that those countries that have pledged to contribute troops and civilian police will do their utmost to expedite the early deployment of their personnel.

The Council notes that, while the overall situation in Haiti has improved since last February, challenges by illegal armed groups to the authority of the Transitional Government are undermining stability and security in some parts of the country.

The Council condemns attempts by some illegal armed groups to perform unauthorized law enforcement functions in some Haitian cities. The Council underscores the need for the Transitional Government to extend its control and authority throughout the country. It stresses the need for the Mission actively to assist the Transitional Government's security institutions in addressing the activities of all illegal armed groups, in accordance with the mandate provided in resolution 1542(2004).

The Council stresses the urgency of disbanding and disarming all illegal armed groups. It calls upon the Transitional Government to complete without delay the establishment of the required structures and the adoption of the required legal framework for the implementation of a national disarmament, demobilization and reintegration programme. It notes that the Mission will assist the Transitional Government in these efforts.

The Council underlines the fact that stability and security remain key to the political and economic reconstruction efforts of the Transitional Government and the international community. It stresses the importance of building the capacity of an effective and professional national police in Haiti. It reiterates the importance of effective coordination and cooperation between the Mission and the Haitian National Police. It also underlines the urgency of improving the situation of human rights in the country, including women's rights.

The Council underlines the fact that only a comprehensive and inclusive dialogue in Haiti can lay down the foundations of a peaceful and democratic political environment. It calls upon all Haitian political actors to participate in the national dialogue, as well as in the transition and in the electoral process to occur in 2005.

The Council welcomes the fact that the Provisional Electoral Council has marked the start of the electoral process in Haiti by holding a broad dialogue on the preparation of elections. The Council encourages the United Nations and the Organization of American States to finalize a memorandum of understanding outlining the election responsibilities of each organization as soon as possible.

The Council reiterates that an end to impunity is key to national reconciliation in Haiti. The Council stresses that justice should apply equally to all citizens in that country and be carried out by an independent judicial system with the support of a reformed correctional system. The Council expresses its strong concern at reports of double standards in the administration of justice. The Council welcomes the intention expressed by the Transitional Government to cease travel restrictions without judicial justification in place against former civil servants and politicians. It urges the Transitional Government to end such restrictions without delay.

The Council welcomes the results of the donors conference held in Washington, D.C., on 19 and 20 July 2004, and urges a timely disbursement of the funds pledged. The Council looks forward to the follow-up implementation meeting to be held in Port-au-Prince from 22 and 23 September 2004, taking into account the priorities identified by the Haitian Government's Interim Cooperation Framework.

The Council reiterates its support for the establishment of a core group to maintain the mobilization of the international community, to increase the consultation among major stakeholders to enhance the coordination and effectiveness of the assistance for Haiti, and to contribute to the definition of a long-term development strategy aimed at the promotion of lasting peace and stability in that country.

The Council welcomes the appointment of Mr. Juan Gabriel Valdés as Special Representative of the Secretary-General and Head of the United Nations Stabilization Mission in Haiti, and commits its full support to his work.

Report of Secretary-General (November). The Secretary-General, in his November report on MINUSTAH [S/2004/908], stated that the Mission had deployed throughout Haiti and had a permanent presence in all important areas, except in Jérémie and Port-de-Paix. The security situation had deteriorated, particularly in Port-au-Prince, and the political climate remained tense. Armed groups remained the main threat, some of which increasingly defied and confronted the Transitional Government. In late August and early September, former military officers occupied police stations in Petit-Goâve, Thomazeau and Terre-Rouge, and, in November, took possession of an unoccupied station near Saint-Marc. The National Police, with MINUSTAH assistance, expelled them from the Thomazeau police station and prevented them from occupying other public buildings. On 29 September, MINUSTAH forces denied them entry to Gonaives.

On 30 September, violence broke out during demonstrations organized by supporters of former President Aristide to commemorate the thirteenth anniversary of the 1991 military coup [YUN 1991, p. 151]. On 4 October, the Secretary-General's Special Representative expressed regret that a peaceful demonstration had served as an excuse for a series of brutal and violent actions and appealed to all Haitians not to be drawn into a vicious cycle of revenge and violence and to embark on the path of dialogue, reconciliation and peace. During the demonstrations, more than 60 people were killed, including 13 National Police officers, three of whom were beheaded. The unrest disrupted the daily life of city residents and brought port activities in Port-au-Prince to a standstill, preventing the unloading of humanitarian assistance. To counter the spread of violence, the Joint MINUSTAH/Haitian National Police Operations Centre was established on 4 October in Port-au-Prince as a means of enhancing coordination between the Mission and the National Police. Regular joint patrols contributed to the normalization of public markets and the reopening of schools. In addition, MINUSTAH forces and civilian police patrolled outside the capital to provide a visible security presence and protect key installations, and established checkpoints which monitored movement and searched for illegal weapons.

The Transitional Government blamed former President Aristide and his armed supporters for instigating the violence. Several political leaders and civil society representatives urged the Transitional Government to take stronger action against them, including declaring Fanmi Lavalas a "terrorist" organization and outlawing it, and issuing an international warrant for Mr. Aristide's arrest. The Prime Minister called on the non-violent Fanmi Lavalas elements to condemn the violence and join the transition process. Meanwhile, Fanmi Lavalas supporters continued to denounce the political persecution and repression of their movement.

On 26 October, in the Fort-National district of Port-au-Prince, at least seven young people were executed. At the urging of the Special Representa-tive, the Transitional Government ordered an investigation into the reported deaths. Two days later, four other youths were killed in similar circumstances in Carrefour-Péan.

The Transitional Government took steps to address the grievances of the former military by creating three commissions. On the recommendation of one of the commissions, the Transitional Government, on 6 October, set up a Demobilized Soldiers Management Bureau to reintegrate the demobilized soldiers into the country's economic and social life. To enhance their public image, the former military offered assistance in restoring public order and some were cooperating with the National Police. However, the police spokesperson stated that only demobilized soldiers who had been integrated into its structures would be recognized.

On 21 October, Prime Minister Latortue reshuffled his cabinet, the first since the Transitional Government took office on 17 March, and appointed a former military officer as Secretary of State in charge of public security, reporting to the Minister of Justice. The Special Representative met with political leaders and civil society representatives to discuss a national dialogue, its objectives and format. The Transitional Government reiterated its commitment to organize free, fair and credible elections in 2005, and allocated funds to the Provisional Electoral Council to launch its preparatory activities. The Council, on 5 October, decided to set local elections for 6 November 2005, the first round of national (presidential and legislative) for 27 November 2005, and the second round of voting for 18 December 2005. Fifty per cent of the vote would be needed to be elected president, senator or member of parliament. A memorandum of understanding between the United Nations and OAS concerning electoral assistance to Haiti was signed on 2 and 3 November.

On 9 September, the Special Representative formally established the Core Group on Haiti, comprising representatives of the diplomatic corps, international financial institutions and regional and subregional organizations.

In view of the changing situation in Haiti, the Secretary-General proposed a number of modifications to MINUSTAH's structure to increase its capacity to implement its mandate. They included: adding a police unit of 125 officers to be stationed in Port-au-Prince to provide operational support to the National Police and to strengthen security arrangements in the capital; continuation of quick-impact humanitarian projects beyond the first year of the Mission; augmenting MINUSTAH's capacity to implement disarmament, demobilization and reintegration projects; strengthening its capacity to monitor community-based projects and to support the Transitional Government in developing legal and institutional frameworks for disarmament, demobilization and reintegration; the addition of an engineering company; and the strengthening of the humanitarian and development coordination pillar. The Secretary-General recommended that the Security Council extend the MINUSTAH mandate for a further 18 months, until 31 May 2006.

SECURITY COUNCIL ACTION (November)

On 29 November [meeting 5090], the Security Council unanimously adopted **resolution 1576 (2004)**. The draft [S/2004/923] was prepared in consultations among Council members.

The Security Council,

Reaffirming its resolution 1542(2004) of 30 April 2004, and recalling resolution 1529(2004) of 29 February 2004 and relevant statements by its President on the situation in Haiti,

Commending the work of the Special Representative of the Secretary-General in support of the efforts of the Transitional Government of Haiti and all political actors in Haiti towards a comprehensive and inclusive national dialogue and reconciliation process, including the holding of fair and free elections in 2005 and the subsequent transfer of power to elected authorities,

Underlining the fact that political reconciliation and economic reconstruction efforts remain key to the stability and security of Haiti, and in that regard stressing that all Member States, especially those in the region, should continue to support the Transitional Government in those efforts,

Urging the Transitional Government to continue to make progress in the implementation of the Interim Cooperation Framework, including by developing concrete projects for economic development, in close cooperation with, and with the full assistance of, the international community, in particular the United Nations and international financial institutions,

Welcoming the establishment of the Core Group on Haiti and the Ad Hoc Advisory Group on Haiti of the Economic and Social Council,

Condemning all acts of violence and the attempts by some armed groups to perform unauthorized law enforcement functions in the country,

Stressing, in that context, the urgency of conducting disarmament, demobilization and reintegration programmes, and urging the Transitional Government to establish, without delay, the national commission on disarmament, demobilization and reintegration,

Condemning all violations of human rights and urging the Transitional Government to take all necessary measures to put an end to impunity,

Concerned by any arbitrary detention of people solely for their political affiliation, and calling upon the Transitional Government to release those against whom no charges have been brought,

Calling upon the international community to continue to address, in full support of the Transitional Government, the humanitarian needs caused by natural disasters in various parts of the country,

Welcoming the contribution made by Member States to the United Nations Stabilization Mission in Haiti, and urging troop- and police-contributing countries to abide by the deployment schedules agreed, and noting in particular the need for more French-speaking police officers,

Noting the continuing existence of challenges to the political, social and economic stability of Haiti, and determining that the situation in Haiti continues to constitute a threat to international peace and security in the region,

Acting under Chapter VII of the Charter of the United Nations, as described in paragraph 7, section I, of resolution 1542(2004),

1. *Decides* to extend the mandate of the United Nations Stabilization Mission in Haiti as contained in resolution 1542(2004), until 1 June 2005, with the intention to renew for further periods;

2. *Encourages* the Transitional Government to continue to explore actively all possible ways to include in the democratic and electoral process those who currently remain outside the transition process but have rejected violence;

3. *Welcomes* the report of the Secretary-General of 18 November 2004 on the Mission, and endorses the Secretary-General's recommendations as outlined in paragraphs 52 to 57 thereof;

4. *Urges* relevant international financial institutions and donor countries to disburse promptly the funds pledged at the International Donors Conference on Haiti, held in Washington, D.C., on 19 and 20 July 2004;

5. *Requests* the Secretary-General to provide a report to the Council at least every three months on the implementation by the Mission of its mandate;

6. *Decides* to remain seized of the matter.

Further developments. In a later report [S/2005/124], the Secretary-General indicated that on 14 December MINUSTAH troops and civilian police officers, jointly with the National Police, launched an operation to restore law and order in the shantytown of Cité Soleil in Port-au-Prince. Forces met with little resistance and no casualties were reported. On 15 December, a group of former soldiers illegally occupied the abandoned private residence of former President Aristide in the Port-au-Prince suburb of Tabarre. At the request of the Transitional Government, MINUSTAH and the Haitian National Police surrounded the residence. When a delegation from the Government and another one composed of political parties and civil society leaders failed to reach a negotiated solution, MINUSTAH troops took over the residence and disarmed 43 individuals there. In retaliation, former soldiers attacked police officers and police stations. MINUSTAH responded promptly and retook control of the police stations seized in Grand-Goâve, Mirebalais and Petit-Goâve.

As the holiday season approached, there were warnings of a possible increase in violence by armed gangs associated with Mr. Aristide, and a number of kidnappings took place in the capital. MINUSTAH conducted its largest patrolling operation in Port-au-Prince to date, which resulted in a peaceful and secure environment during the holidays. A total of 41 suspects were arrested and six weapons seized, in addition to ammunition being confiscated. It also prevented a widely announced march by former soldiers through Port-au-Prince.

On 20 December, the Transitional Government announced the launching of a compensation programme for members of the former military demobilized in 1995 and made some $2.8 million available for that purpose. Payment of the first of three instalments began on 28 December and was expected to be completed in March 2005. MINUSTAH's improved military and police operations in some of the most volatile areas contributed to an improved environment conducive to implementing disarmament, demobilization and reintegration programmes. Preliminary discussions on those programmes began with gang members and community leaders.

Most political actors appeared to favour a national dialogue and the holding of elections. On 6 December, the Prime Minister invited the leader of the Congrès national des mouvements démocratiques to contact various political, social and religious sectors and interested personalities to formally advance the process of national dialogue. An ad hoc group (Groupe de réflexion et de promotion du dialogue national) was formed, which reported to the Prime Minister on 31 December. The Prime Minister also established the Committee on Assistance for Victims of Violence to provide assistance to those who had been wounded, lost relatives or been displaced because of their political beliefs. The commission, created on 6 October to investigate the financial management of the Lavalas Government between February 2001 and February 2004, continued its activities. Relations between Fanmi Lavalas and the Transitional Government remained tense, despite the release of several party leaders, while differences within Fanmi Lavalas resulted in growing ambiguity regarding its legitimate leaders. On 16 December, Fanmi Lavalas created a 19-member commission, which, according to a press release, would be allowed to engage in political discussions on behalf of the party.

Programme of support for Haiti

Report of Secretary-General. On 16 June, the Secretary-General submitted a report [E/2004/80] on the development of a long-term programme of support for Haiti, which elaborated on the national and economic situation, provided an overview of UN system activities in the country, and re-evaluated the existing long-term programme of support. The report indicated that Haiti remained the poorest nation in the western hemisphere and that the country's critical economic condition was negatively affected by its political situation. On 22 April, major development partners met to elaborate a plan of action. UNDP and the World Bank decided to lead the process for the preparation of the Interim Cooperation Framework for donors, and a round table was scheduled for July.

The report also covered humanitarian assistance and other UN activities, including: ensuring the availability of food; restoring the public health sector; combating HIV/AIDS; ensuring public security and the rule of law; tracking the Millennium Development Goals [YUN 2000, p. 51]; and monitoring human rights violations.

Economic and Social Council action. On 23 July, the Economic and Social Council adopted **resolution 2004/52** on the long-term programme of support for Haiti (see p. 938); on 11 November, it adopted **decision 2004/322** on the Ad Hoc Advisory Group on Haiti (see p. 939); and, on 22 July, it adopted **resolution 2004/46** on support for MINUSTAH (see p. 1025).

Financing of MINUSTAH

On 3 May [A/58/236], the Secretary-General requested the inclusion in the agenda of the resumed fifty-eighth session of the General Assembly the item entitled "Financing of the United Nations Stabilization Mission in Haiti".

Pending submission to the Assembly during its fifty-ninth session of a full budget for MINUSTAH for 1 May 2004 to 30 June 2005, including results-based frameworks, the Secretary-General submitted on 17 May [A/58/800] an interim budget for the Mission for 1 May to 30 June 2004 and from 1 July to 31 December 2004, which reflected preliminary financial requirements for MINUSTAH amounting to $49,259,800 and $215,552,000, respectively.

The Advisory Committee on Administrative and Budgetary Questions (ACABQ), in its May report [A/58/809], noted that it had already concurred on commitment authority of up to $49,259,800 for MINUSTAH for 1 May to 30 June, and recommended that the Assembly approve a total assessment of $221,740,300.

GENERAL ASSEMBLY ACTION (June)

On 18 June [meeting 91], the General Assembly, on the recommendation of the Fifth (Administrative and Budgetary) Committee [A/58/832], adopted **resolution 58/311** without vote [agenda item 168].

Financing of the United Nations Stabilization Mission in Haiti

The General Assembly,

Having considered the report of the Secretary-General on the financing of the United Nations Stabilization Mission in Haiti and the related report of the Advisory Committee on Administrative and Budgetary Questions,

Recalling Security Council resolution 1529(2004) of 29 February 2004, by which the Council declared its readiness to establish a United Nations stabilization force to support continuation of a peaceful and constitutional political process and the maintenance of a secure and stable environment in Haiti,

Recalling also Security Council resolution 1542 (2004) of 30 April 2004, by which the Council decided to establish the United Nations Stabilization Mission in Haiti for an initial period of six months,

Recognizing that the costs of the Mission are expenses of the Organization to be borne by Member States in accordance with Article 17, paragraph 2, of the Charter of the United Nations,

Reaffirming the general principles underlying the financing of United Nations peacekeeping operations, as stated in General Assembly resolutions 1874(S-IV) of 27 June 1963, 3101(XXVIII) of 11 December 1973 and 55/235 of 23 December 2000,

Mindful of the fact that it is essential to provide the Mission with the necessary financial resources to enable it to fulfil its responsibilities under the relevant resolution of the Security Council,

1. *Expresses concern* at the financial situation with regard to peacekeeping activities, in particular as regards the reimbursements to troop contributors that bear additional burdens owing to overdue payments by Member States of their assessments;

2. *Also expresses concern* at the delay experienced by the Secretary-General in deploying and providing adequate resources to some recent peacekeeping missions, in particular those in Africa;

3. *Emphasizes* that all future and existing peacekeeping missions shall be given equal and non-discriminatory treatment in respect of financial and administrative arrangements;

4. *Also emphasizes* that all peacekeeping missions shall be provided with adequate resources for the effective and efficient discharge of their respective mandates;

5. *Requests* the Secretary-General to make the fullest possible use of facilities and equipment at the United Nations Logistics Base at Brindisi, Italy, in order to minimize the costs of procurement for the Mission;

6. *Endorses* the conclusions and recommendations contained in the report of the Advisory Committee on Administrative and Budgetary Questions, and requests the Secretary-General to ensure their full implementation;

7. *Requests* the Secretary-General to take all necessary action to ensure that the Mission is administered with a maximum of efficiency and economy;

8. *Also requests* the Secretary-General, in order to reduce the cost of employing General Service staff, to make efforts to recruit local staff for the Mission against General Service posts, commensurate with the requirements of the Mission;

Budget estimates for the period from 1 May to 31 October 2004

9. *Authorizes* the Secretary-General to establish a special account for the United Nations Stabilization Mission in Haiti for the purpose of accounting for income received and expenditure incurred in respect of the Mission;

10. *Also authorizes* the Secretary-General to enter into commitments in the amount of 172,480,500 United States dollars for the period from 1 July to 31 October 2004 for the maintenance of the Mission, in addition to the amount of 49,259,800 dollars for the period from 1 May to 30 June 2004 authorized by the Advisory Committee for the establishment of the Mission under the terms of section IV of General Assembly resolution 49/233 A of 23 December 1994;

Financing of the commitment authority

11. *Decides* to apportion among Member States the amount of 221,740,300 dollars, comprising the amount of 49,259,800 dollars for the period from 1 May to 30 June 2004 and the amount of 172,480,500 dollars for the period from 1 July to 31 October 2004, in accordance with the levels set out in General Assembly resolution 55/235, as adjusted by the Assembly in its resolution 55/236 of 23 December 2000 and updated in its resolution 58/256 of 23 December 2003, taking into account the scale of assessments for 2004 as set out in its resolution 58/1 B of 23 December 2003;

12. *Decides also* that, in accordance with the provisions of its resolution 973(X) of 15 December 1955, there shall be set off against the apportionment among Member States, as provided for in paragraph 11 above, their respective share in the Tax Equalization Fund of 2,272,000 dollars, comprising the estimated staff assessment income of 387,000 dollars approved for the Mission for the period from 1 May to 30 June 2004 and the estimated staff assessment income of 1,885,000 dollars approved for the Mission for the period from 1 July to 31 October 2004;

13. *Emphasizes* that no peacekeeping mission shall be financed by borrowing funds from other active peacekeeping missions;

14. *Encourages* the Secretary-General to take additional measures to ensure the safety and security of all personnel under the auspices of the United Nations participating in the Mission;

15. *Invites* voluntary contributions to the Mission in cash and in the form of services and supplies acceptable to the Secretary-General, to be administered, as appropriate, in accordance with the procedure and practices established by the General Assembly;

16. *Decides* to include in the provisional agenda of its fifty-ninth session the item entitled "Financing of the United Nations Stabilization Mission in Haiti".

On 20 August [A/59/288], the Secretary-General presented a report containing the budget for MINUSTAH for 1 May 2004 to 30 June 2005, which amounted to $428,306,600 and included the budgetary proposals for 1 May to

31 December 2004, set out in the Secretary-General's 17 May report (see p. 296).

In a 29 September report [A/59/390], ACABQ reviewed budget proposals and identified reductions totalling $9,312,400. However, it recommended approval of the full amount proposed by the Secretary-General due to the effects of Hurricane Jeanne (see p. 942) on the Mission's activities, facilities and infrastructure, and with regard to the additional tasks the Mission was being called upon to perform in relation to humanitarian assistance and food distribution.

GENERAL ASSEMBLY ACTION (October)

On 29 October [meeting 46], the General Assembly, on the recommendation of the Fifth Committee [A/59/530], adopted **resolution 59/17** without vote [agenda item 155].

Financing of the United Nations Stabilization Mission in Haiti

The General Assembly,

Having considered the report of the Secretary-General on the financing of the United Nations Stabilization Mission in Haiti and the related report of the Advisory Committee on Administrative and Budgetary Questions,

Recalling Security Council resolution 1529(2004) of 29 February 2004, by which the Council declared its readiness to establish a United Nations stabilization force to support continuation of a peaceful and constitutional political process and the maintenance of a secure and stable environment in Haiti,

Recalling also Security Council resolution 1542 (2004) of 30 April 2004, by which the Council decided to establish the United Nations Stabilization Mission in Haiti for an initial period of six months,

Recalling further its resolution 58/311 of 18 June 2004 on the financing of the Mission,

Reaffirming the general principles underlying the financing of United Nations peacekeeping operations, as stated in General Assembly resolutions 1874(S-IV) of 27 June 1963, 3101(XXVIII) of 11 December 1973 and 55/235 of 23 December 2000,

Mindful of the fact that it is essential to provide the Mission with the necessary financial resources to enable it to fulfil its responsibilities under the relevant resolution of the Security Council,

Stressing the role of the Fifth Committee in the consideration and approval of the budgetary proposals of the Secretary-General,

1. *Takes note* of the status of contributions to the United Nations Stabilization Mission in Haiti as at 30 September 2004, including the contributions outstanding in the amount of 144.4 million United States dollars, representing some 65 per cent of the total assessed contributions, notes with concern that only thirty-two Member States have paid their assessed contributions in full, and urges all other Member States, in particular those in arrears, to ensure payment of their outstanding assessed contributions;

2. *Expresses its appreciation* to those Member States that have paid their assessed contributions in full, and urges all other Member States to make every possible effort to ensure payment of their assessed contributions to the Mission in full;

3. *Expresses concern* at the financial situation with regard to peacekeeping activities, in particular as regards the reimbursements to troop contributors that bear additional burdens owing to overdue payments by Member States of their assessments;

4. *Also expresses concern* at the delay experienced by the Secretary-General in deploying and providing adequate resources to some recent peacekeeping missions, in particular those in Africa;

5. *Emphasizes* that all future and existing peacekeeping missions shall be given equal and non-discriminatory treatment in respect of financial and administrative arrangements;

6. *Also emphasizes* that all peacekeeping missions shall be provided with adequate resources for the effective and efficient discharge of their respective mandates;

7. *Reiterates its request* to the Secretary-General to make the fullest possible use of facilities and equipment at the United Nations Logistics Base at Brindisi, Italy, in order to minimize the costs of procurement for the Mission;

8. *Requests* the Secretary-General to make all efforts to provide the necessary facilities to expedite the deployment of troops and to take all necessary measures to repair the infrastructures required for the operational needs of the Mission;

9. *Endorses* the conclusions and recommendations contained in the report of the Advisory Committee on Administrative and Budgetary Questions, subject to the provisions of the present resolution;

10. *Authorizes* the Secretary-General to fill the following posts at appropriate grades until 30 June 2005:

Director of the Office of the Special Representative of the Secretary-General;
Special Assistant to the Director;
Special Assistant to the Special Representative;
Protocol Officer;
Political Affairs Officer;
Deputy Special Representative of the Secretary-General for Humanitarian and Development Coordination;
Senior Humanitarian and Development Officer;
Humanitarian and Development Officer;
Principal Legal Adviser;
Chief of Public Information;
Spokesperson;
Head of the Political Affairs and Planning Division;
and requests the Secretary-General to re-justify these posts in his next budget with additional information on the appropriate grades;

11. *Requests* the Secretary-General to take all necessary action to ensure that the Mission is administered with a maximum of efficiency and economy;

12. *Also requests* the Secretary-General, in order to reduce the cost of employing General Service staff, to continue to make efforts to recruit local staff for the Mission against General Service posts, commensurate with the requirements of the Mission;

Budget estimates for the period from 1 May 2004 to 30 June 2005

13. *Takes note* that in paragraph 7.II (c) of its resolution 1542(2004), the Security Council mandates the

Mission to assist in organizing, monitoring and carrying out free and fair municipal, parliamentary and presidential elections;

14. *Requests* the Secretary-General to implement fully the mandate given to him and to measure the Mission's accomplishments, in particular expected accomplishment 2.3, fully in accordance with the Security Council mandate;

15. *Decides* to appropriate to the Special Account for the United Nations Stabilization Mission in Haiti the amount of 49,259,800 dollars for the period from 1 May to 30 June 2004 previously authorized by the Advisory Committee on Administrative and Budgetary Questions for the establishment of the Mission under the terms of section IV of General Assembly resolution 49/233 A of 23 December 1994;

16. *Decides also* to appropriate to the Special Account for the United Nations Stabilization Mission in Haiti the amount of 379,046,800 dollars for the period from 1 July 2004 to 30 June 2005, inclusive of the amount of 172,480,500 dollars previously authorized by the Assembly in its resolution 58/311 for the period from 1 July to 31 October 2004;

Financing of the appropriation

17. *Decides further* to apportion among Member States the amount of 206,566,300 dollars at a monthly rate of 25,820,787 dollars for the maintenance of the Mission for the period from 1 November 2004 to 30 June 2005, taking into account the amount of 172,480,500 dollars already apportioned by the General Assembly for the period from 1 July to 31 October 2004 in its resolution 58/311, in accordance with the levels set out in its resolution 55/235, as adjusted by the Assembly in its resolution 55/236 of 23 December 2000 and updated in its resolution 58/256 of 23 December 2003, taking into account the scale of assessments for 2004 and 2005 as set out in its resolution 58/1 B of 23 December 2003, subject to a decision of the Security Council to extend the mandate of the Mission;

18. *Decides* that, in accordance with the provisions of its resolution 973(X) of 15 December 1955, there shall be set off against the apportionment among Member States, as provided for in paragraph 17 above, their respective share in the Tax Equalization Fund of 4,371,700 dollars approved for the Mission for the period from 1 November 2004 to 30 June 2005;

19. *Emphasizes* that no peacekeeping mission shall be financed by borrowing funds from other active peacekeeping missions;

20. *Encourages* the Secretary-General to continue to take additional measures to ensure the safety and security of all personnel under the auspices of the United Nations participating in the Mission;

21. *Invites* voluntary contributions to the Mission in cash and in the form of services and supplies acceptable to the Secretary-General, to be administered, as appropriate, in accordance with the procedure and practices established by the General Assembly;

22. *Decides* to keep under review during its fifty-ninth session the item entitled "Financing of the United Nations Stabilization Mission in Haiti".

On 23 December, by **decision 59/552**, the Assembly decided that the item on financing of

MINUSTAH would remain for consideration during its resumed fifty-ninth (2005) session.

Other questions

Andean Zone of Peace

By a 12 October letter [A/59/235], Bolivia, Colombia, Ecuador, Peru and Venezuela—the member countries of the Andean Community—transmitted to the Secretary-General the Declaration of San Francisco de Quito on the Establishment and Development of the Andean Zone of Peace, adopted on 12 July by the Presidents of those countries at the fifteenth meeting of the Andean Presidential Council held in Quito, Ecuador.

The General Assembly, in **resolution 59/54** (see p. 592) of 2 December, welcomed the Declaration.

Colombia

In a letter dated 2 July [S/2004/569], the Netherlands, on behalf of the EU, transmitted a statement on the occasion of the formal start of talks between the Government of Colombia and the Autodefensas Unidas de Colombia (AUC) paramilitary groups. The EU confirmed its readiness to assist in reaching a peaceful and durable solution to the conflict, within the framework of a credible and comprehensive peace strategy, and in that regard, underlined the importance of the good offices of the Secretary-General of the United Nations and of regular constructive dialogue between the Government and civil society.

Cuba–United States

In a letter dated 10 May [A/58/789], Cuba denounced the 6 May announcement by the United States Government of new measures against Cuba. The measures, described by Cuba as part of the United States "aggressive and hostile" policy against Cuba, dealt with restricting visitation to Cuba by relatives and United States citizens, limiting family remittances from Cubans residing in the United States, and discouraging tourist travel to Cuba.

On 1 July [A/58/851], Cuba, in a declaration by its National Assembly, objected to the implementation on 30 June of the new measures, which included the cancellation of almost all United States citizens' visitation licences, as well as to threats by the United States of applying more aggressively sections of its Helms-Burton Act [YUN

1996, p. 194] that would penalize businessmen from third countries dealing with Cuba.

On 8 September [A/59/348], Cuba submitted a report on the implementation of General Assembly resolution 58/7 [YUN 2003, p. 286], which described, in addition to the new measures, the extraterritorial nature of the United States embargo policy, the embargo's impact on the Cuban national health system and economy, and damage to exchanges between the Cuban and American peoples.

Reports of Secretary-General. On 27 August [A/59/302, Part I] and on 5 October [A/59/302, Part II], the Secretary-General, in response to General Assembly resolution 58/7, forwarded replies by Governments on their actions to implement that resolution. That text had called on States to refrain from unilateral application of economic and trade measures against other States, and urged them to repeal or invalidate such measures. The two reports included, in addition to the replies from 86 States, statements from the EU, eight UN bodies and ten specialized agencies.

GENERAL ASSEMBLY ACTION

On 28 October [meeting 44], the General Assembly adopted **resolution 59/11** [draft: A/59/L.2] by recorded vote (179-4-1) [agenda item 28].

Necessity of ending the economic, commercial and financial embargo imposed by the United States of America against Cuba

The General Assembly,

Determined to encourage strict compliance with the purposes and principles enshrined in the Charter of the United Nations,

Reaffirming, among other principles, the sovereign equality of States, non-intervention and non-interference in their internal affairs and freedom of international trade and navigation, which are also enshrined in many international legal instruments,

Recalling the statements of the Heads of State or Government at the Ibero-American Summits concerning the need to eliminate the unilateral application of economic and trade measures by one State against another that affect the free flow of international trade,

Concerned at the continued promulgation and application by Member States of laws and regulations, such as that promulgated on 12 March 1996 known as the "Helms-Burton Act", the extraterritorial effects of which affect the sovereignty of other States, the legitimate interests of entities or persons under their jurisdiction and the freedom of trade and navigation,

Taking note of declarations and resolutions of different intergovernmental forums, bodies and Governments that express the rejection by the international community and public opinion of the promulgation and application of regulations of the kind referred to above,

Recalling its resolutions 47/19 of 24 November 1992, 48/16 of 3 November 1993, 49/9 of 26 October 1994, 50/10 of 2 November 1995, 51/17 of 12 November 1996, 52/10 of 5 November 1997, 53/4 of 14 October 1998, 54/21 of 9 November 1999, 55/20 of 9 November 2000, 56/9 of 27 November 2001, 57/11 of 12 November 2002 and 58/7 of 4 November 2003,

Concerned that, since the adoption of its resolutions 47/19, 48/16, 49/9, 50/10, 51/17, 52/10, 53/4, 54/21, 55/20, 56/9, 57/11 and 58/7, further measures of that nature aimed at strengthening and extending the economic, commercial and financial embargo against Cuba continue to be promulgated and applied, and concerned also at the adverse effects of such measures on the Cuban people and on Cuban nationals living in other countries,

1. *Takes note* of the report of the Secretary-General on the implementation of resolution 58/7;

2. *Reiterates its call upon* all States to refrain from promulgating and applying laws and measures of the kind referred to in the preamble to the present resolution in conformity with their obligations under the Charter of the United Nations and international law, which, inter alia, reaffirm the freedom of trade and navigation;

3. *Once again urges* States that have and continue to apply such laws and measures to take the necessary steps to repeal or invalidate them as soon as possible in accordance with their legal regime;

4. *Requests* the Secretary-General, in consultation with the appropriate organs and agencies of the United Nations system, to prepare a report on the implementation of the present resolution in the light of the purposes and principles of the Charter and international law and to submit it to the General Assembly at its sixtieth session;

5. *Decides* to include in the provisional agenda of its sixtieth session the item entitled "Necessity of ending the economic, commercial and financial embargo imposed by the United States of America against Cuba".

RECORDED VOTE ON RESOLUTION 59/11:

In favour: Afghanistan, Albania, Algeria, Andorra, Angola, Antigua and Barbuda, Argentina, Armenia, Australia, Austria, Azerbaijan, Bahamas, Bahrain, Bangladesh, Barbados, Belarus, Belgium, Belize, Benin, Bhutan, Bolivia, Bosnia and Herzegovina, Botswana, Brazil, Brunei Darussalam, Bulgaria, Burkina Faso, Burundi, Cambodia, Cameroon, Canada, Cape Verde, Central African Republic, Chile, China, Colombia, Comoros, Congo, Costa Rica, Côte d'Ivoire, Croatia, Cuba, Cyprus, Czech Republic, Democratic People's Republic of Korea, Democratic Republic of the Congo, Denmark, Djibouti, Dominica, Dominican Republic, Ecuador, Egypt, Equatorial Guinea, Eritrea, Estonia, Ethiopia, Fiji, Finland, France, Gabon, Gambia, Georgia, Germany, Ghana, Greece, Grenada, Guatemala, Guinea, Guinea-Bissau, Guyana, Haiti, Honduras, Hungary, Iceland, India, Indonesia, Iran, Ireland, Italy, Jamaica, Japan, Jordan, Kazakhstan, Kenya, Kiribati, Kuwait, Kyrgyzstan, Lao People's Democratic Republic, Latvia, Lebanon, Lesotho, Liberia, Libyan Arab Jamahiriya, Liechtenstein, Lithuania, Luxembourg, Madagascar, Malawi, Malaysia, Maldives, Mali, Malta, Mauritania, Mauritius, Mexico, Monaco, Mongolia, Mozambique, Myanmar, Namibia, Nauru, Nepal, Netherlands, New Zealand, Niger, Nigeria, Norway, Oman, Pakistan, Panama, Papua New Guinea, Paraguay, Peru, Philippines, Poland, Portugal, Qatar, Republic of Korea, Republic of Moldova, Romania, Russian Federation, Rwanda, Saint Kitts and Nevis, Saint Lucia, Saint Vincent and the Grenadines, Samoa, San Marino, Sao Tome and Principe, Saudi Arabia, Senegal, Serbia and Montenegro, Seychelles, Sierra Leone, Singapore, Slovakia, Slovenia, Solomon Islands, Somalia, South Africa, Spain, Sri Lanka, Sudan, Suriname, Swaziland, Sweden, Switzerland, Syrian Arab Republic, Tajikistan, Thailand, The Former Yugoslav Republic of Macedonia, Timor-Leste, Togo, Tonga, Trinidad and Tobago, Tunisia, Turkey, Turkmenistan, Tuvalu, Uganda, Ukraine, United Arab Emirates, United Kingdom, United Republic of Tanzania, Uruguay, Venezuela, Viet Nam, Yemen, Zambia, Zimbabwe.

Against: Israel, Marshall Islands, Palau, United States.

Abstaining: Micronesia.

El Salvador-Honduras

On 5 January [S/2004/9], Honduras transmitted to the Security Council President an Application for the revision of the Judgment of 11 September 1992 [YUN 1992, p. 983] in the case concerning the *Land, Island and Maritime Frontier Dispute (El Salvador/Honduras: Nicaragua intervening) (El Salvador v. Honduras)* dated 18 December 2003 [YUN 2003, p. 1306].

Cooperation between the United Nations and regional organizations

Caribbean Community

In response to General Assembly resolution 57/41 [YUN 2002, p. 254] on cooperation between the United Nations and the Caribbean Community (CARICOM), the Secretary-General summarized, in his September consolidated report on cooperation between the United Nations and regional and other organizations [A/59/303], UN-CARICOM collaborative activities, including high-level consultations in early 2004 on the unfolding political crisis in Haiti (see p. 288) and subsequent cooperation with MINUSTAH.

The third general meeting between the United Nations and CARICOM was held in New York in April. The meeting, which reviewed follow-up action to the second meeting, considered that substantial progress had been achieved in cooperation between the two organizations, especially in the areas of conflict prevention, governance and security. The meeting also discussed institutional arrangements for cooperation and training and the need for improved coordination of activities. It stressed the need to convene regular review meetings to deal with constraints in the relationship between the two organizations.

GENERAL ASSEMBLY ACTION

On 10 December [meeting 71], the General Assembly adopted **resolution 59/138** [draft: A/59/L.25 & Add.1, as orally revised] without vote [agenda item 56 (*e*)].

Cooperation between the United Nations and the Caribbean Community

The General Assembly,

Recalling its resolutions 46/8 of 16 October 1991, 49/141 of 20 December 1994, 51/16 of 11 November 1996, 53/17 of 29 October 1998, 55/17 of 7 November 2000 and 57/41 of 21 November 2002,

Bearing in mind the provisions of Chapter VIII of the Charter of the United Nations on the existence of regional arrangements or agencies for dealing with such matters relating to the maintenance of international peace and security as are appropriate for regional action and other activities consistent with the purposes and principles of the United Nations,

Bearing in mind also the assistance given by the United Nations towards the maintenance of peace and security in the Caribbean region,

Recalling the signing, on 27 May 1997, by the Secretary-General of the United Nations and the Secretary-General of the Caribbean Community of a cooperation agreement between the secretariats of the two organizations,

Noting with satisfaction that the third general meeting between representatives of the Caribbean Community and its associated institutions and of the United Nations system was held in New York on 12 and 13 April 2004,

Bearing in mind that, in its resolutions 54/225 of 22 December 1999, 55/203 of 20 December 2000 and 57/261 of 20 December 2002, it recognized the importance of adopting an integrated management approach to the Caribbean Sea area in the context of sustainable development,

Bearing in mind also that in the United Nations Millennium Declaration, adopted by resolution 55/2 of 8 September 2000, Heads of State and Government resolved to address the special needs of small island developing States by implementing the Barbados Programme of Action and the outcome of the twenty-second special session of the General Assembly rapidly and in full,

Noting that the World Summit for Sustainable Development, held in Johannesburg, South Africa, from 26 August to 4 September 2002, considered the specific issues and problems facing small island developing States, and noting that a special meeting to review the implementation of the Barbados Programme of Action will be convened in Mauritius in January 2005,

Noting also that the Declaration of Commitment on HIV/AIDS adopted by the General Assembly in resolution S-26/2 of 27 June 2001 recognized the Caribbean region as having the second-highest rate of infection after sub-Saharan Africa and that the region therefore needs special attention and assistance from the international community,

Noting further that the Caribbean region has been hard hit, and in some cases devastated, by hurricanes in 2004, and concerned that their frequency, intensity and destructive power pose a challenge to the development endeavours of the region,

Affirming the need to strengthen the cooperation that already exists between entities of the United Nations system and the Caribbean Community in the areas of economic and social development, as well as the areas of political and humanitarian affairs,

Convinced of the need for the coordinated utilization of available resources to promote the common objectives of the two organizations,

Having considered the report of the Secretary-General on cooperation between the United Nations and regional and other organizations,

1. *Takes note* of the report of the Secretary-General, in particular section IV on the Caribbean Community, as well as efforts to strengthen cooperation;

2. *Calls upon* the Secretary-General of the United Nations, in association with the Secretary-General of the Caribbean Community, as well as the relevant regional organizations, to continue to assist in furthering the development and maintenance of peace and security within the Caribbean region;

3. *Invites* the Secretary-General to continue to promote and expand cooperation and coordination between the United Nations and the Caribbean Community in order to increase the capacity of the two organizations to attain their objectives;

4. *Urges* the specialized agencies and other organizations and programmes of the United Nations system to cooperate with the Secretary-General of the United Nations and the Secretary-General of the Caribbean Community in order to initiate, maintain and increase consultations and programmes with the Caribbean Community and its associated institutions in the attainment of their objectives, with special attention to the areas and issues identified at the third general meeting, as set out in the report of the Secretary-General, as well as in resolutions 54/225, 55/203, 55/2 and S-26/2 and the decision of the World Summit on Sustainable Development on the sustainable development of small island developing States;

5. *Invites* the organizations of the United Nations system as well as Member States to increase financial and other assistance to the countries of the Caribbean Community to help to implement the priorities of the Caribbean Regional Strategic Plan of Action, which sets out realistic targets for reducing the rate of new infections, raising the quality and coverage of care, treatment and support and building institutional capacity, and to cope with the problems and the burden caused by the HIV/AIDS pandemic;

6. *Invites* the Secretary-General to consider utilizing a strategic programming framework modality to strengthen the coordination and cooperation between the two secretariats as well as between the United Nations field offices and the Caribbean Community;

7. *Calls upon* the United Nations, the specialized agencies and other organizations and programmes of the United Nations system to assist the countries of the Caribbean, in particular those in greatest need, such as Grenada and Haiti, in their rebuilding efforts after the hurricane damage of 2004;

8. *Welcomes* the initiatives of Member States in assisting in the cooperation between the United Nations and the Caribbean Community, and encourages their continuing efforts;

9. *Recommends* that the fourth general meeting between representatives of the Caribbean Community and its associated institutions and of the United Nations system be held in the Caribbean in early 2006 in order to review and appraise progress in the implementation of the agreed areas and issues and to hold consultations on such additional measures and procedures as may be required to facilitate and strengthen cooperation between the two organizations;

10. *Requests* the Secretary-General to submit to the General Assembly at its sixty-first session a report on the implementation of the present resolution;

11. *Decides* to include in the provisional agenda of its sixty-first session the sub-item entitled "Cooperation between the United Nations and the Caribbean Community".

Cooperation with OAS

In response to General Assembly resolution 57/157 [YUN 2002, p. 253] on cooperation between the United Nations and the Organization of American States (OAS), the Secretary-General, in his September consolidated report on cooperation between the United Nations and regional and other organizations [A/59/303], reviewed the continued collaborative activities of MINUSTAH and OAS in Haiti; close cooperation between OAS and the Department for Disarmament Affairs through the United Nations Regional Centre for Peace, Disarmament and Development in Latin American and the Caribbean, including work on a jointly designed web-based small arms and light weapons administration system; coordination between the Economic Commission for Latin America and the Caribbean and OAS; and consultations and exchange of information on a regular basis between OAS and the UN Secretariat, funds, programmes and agencies.

GENERAL ASSEMBLY ACTION

On 23 December [meeting 76], the General Assembly adopted **resolution 59/257** [draft: A/59/L.41/Rev.1 & Add.1] without vote [agenda item 56 *(o)*].

Cooperation between the United Nations and the Organization of American States

The General Assembly,

Recalling that the purposes of the United Nations are, inter alia, to achieve international cooperation in solving international problems of an economic, social, cultural or humanitarian character and in promoting and encouraging respect for human rights and fundamental freedoms, and to be a centre for harmonizing the actions of nations in the attainment of these common ends,

Recalling also that the Charter of the Organization of American States reaffirms these purposes and principles and provides that that organization is a regional agency under the terms of the Charter of the United Nations,

Recalling further that both organizations seek, inter alia, to promote social advancement, improve the standards of living of peoples, particularly in developing countries, and promote the protection of all human rights and fundamental freedoms,

Recalling its resolution 57/157 of 16 December 2002 on promoting cooperation between the United Nations and the Organization of American States,

Aware that the United Nations and the Organization of American States signed a memorandum of understanding on 3 November 2004 concerning the provision of assistance for the planning, organization and monitoring of the elections in Haiti,

Recalling that one of the common goals of the two organizations is to combat corruption and impunity, and noting that the Inter-American Convention against Corruption is a pioneering international instrument in that field,

Recalling also the fifth high-level meeting between the Secretary-General and heads of regional organizations, held in New York on 29 and 30 July 2003 to review the new threats to international peace and security, including international terrorism, civil and international conflicts, the proliferation of weapons of mass destruction, poverty, organized crime and violations of human rights, which demonstrated the need for greater synergy in the efforts made by the two organizations,

Noting that during the Special Conference on Security, held in Mexico City on 27 and 28 October 2003, the States members of the Organization of American States defined a new concept of security that is multidimensional in scope and includes traditional and new threats, concerns and challenges to their security,

Mindful of the meeting held in March 2004 between the secretariats of the Organization of American States and the United Nations, which reviewed the progress made in promoting transparency in the area of conventional weapons, and reviewed their cooperation with a view to curbing the illicit traffic in weapons,

Aware of the increased cooperation between bodies of the inter-American system for the protection of human rights and the United Nations Commission on Human Rights,

Noting with grave concern the continuing spread of the HIV/AIDS pandemic in the region, which requires coordinated action at the national, regional and global levels,

1. *Takes note with satisfaction* of the report of the Secretary-General on cooperation between the United Nations and the Organization of American States and his continuing efforts to strengthen that cooperation;

2. *Notes with satisfaction* the cooperation between the Organization of American States and the United Nations Stabilization Mission in Haiti as well as other bodies and programmes of the system providing assistance and support for the recovery and stability of Haiti, and calls upon them to continue to support the planning, organization and monitoring of elections in 2005 in that country;

3. *Calls for* a prompt mobilization of resources to meet the emergency needs of the Caribbean countries, especially Haiti and Grenada, in the wake of the serious floods and hurricanes that affected that region;

4. *Expresses its appreciation* to the Economic Commission for Latin America and the Caribbean for the initiatives to strengthen cooperation with inter-American institutions in various fields, in particular, hemispheric integration, statistics, women and development;

5. *Recognizes* the work of the Organization of American States in promoting democracy, in the field of regional cooperation and in connection with its task of coordination with the United Nations;

6. *Also recognizes* the close cooperation between the United Nations and the Organization of American States in promoting the necessary transparency in all matters concerning the registration of conventional weapons, and calls upon them to continue intra-regional dialogue and coordination with a view to curbing the illicit traffic in weapons;

7. *Calls upon* the Organization of American States to actively participate in the International Meeting to Review the Implementation of the Barbados Programme of Action for the Sustainable Development of Small Island Developing States, to be held in Port Louis from 10 to 14 January 2005;

8. *Invites* the Organization of American States to participate actively in the World Conference on Disaster Reduction, to be held in Kobe, Japan, from 18 to 22 January 2005;

9. *Calls for* an increase in financial resources and the strengthening of national and regional programmes for combating HIV/AIDS, as well as an increase in the supply of safe, effective and essential medicines at a reasonable cost;

10. *Calls upon* the United Nations and the Organization of American States to continue to develop their mutual cooperation in accordance with their respective mandates, jurisdiction and composition and to adapt to each specific situation in accordance with the Charter of the United Nations;

11. *Notes with satisfaction* the holding of periodic meetings between representatives of the United Nations and the Organization of American States, as well as the exchange of information taking place between the two organizations, and recommends that these practices be maintained;

12. *Requests* the Secretary-General to submit to the General Assembly at its sixty-first session a report on the implementation of the present resolution, as appropriate;

13. *Decides* to include in the provisional agenda of its sixty-first session the sub-item entitled "Cooperation between the United Nations and the Organization of American States".

Observer status

On 2 December, the General Assembly, by **resolution 59/52** (see p. 1460), granted observer status to the Organisation of Eastern Caribbean States in the work of the Assembly.

Chapter IV

Asia and the Pacific

In 2004, the security challenges in Asia and the Pacific, especially in Afghanistan and Iraq, continued to test the resolve of the international community in its efforts to restore peace and stability to that region, return it to democratic governance, and promote and strengthen its economic and social development.

In Afghanistan, where institutions of security and justice and the provision of basic services were still weak and dependent on the international community, significant progress was made towards the implementation of the benchmarks contained in the Bonn Agreement [YUN 2001, p. 263] governing Afghanistan's transition to peace and democracy. With United Nations support, provided through the United Nations Assistance Mission in Afghanistan (UNAMA), headed by the Secretary-General's Special Representative, Lakhdar Brahimi, the Constitutional Loya Jirga (grand council) finalized and adopted in January a constitution for Afghanistan, paving the way for the re-establishment of the rule of law and the holding of democratic elections. Those elections, which were held without any major security incidents, allowed President Hamid Karzai and a new cabinet to take office in December and to begin planning for parliamentary and provincial elections in 2005.

The international community's commitment to a stable and peaceful Afghanistan was reaffirmed at a conference held in Berlin, Germany, on 31 March. Delegates, among other things, pledged $8.2 billion towards an Afghan-led reconstruction programme and adopted the Berlin Declaration, which expressed the determination of the Afghan Government and the international community to continue the tasks of rebuilding and reforming the political, social and economic structures of Afghanistan. The conference also adopted the Berlin Declaration on Counter-Narcotics, which called for regional cooperation in the fight against the cultivation and trafficking of illicit drugs.

In March, the Security Council extended the UNAMA mandate to provide support for the implementation of the Bonn Agreement for an additional period of one year.

The International Security Assistance Force (ISAF), a multinational force established by Security Council resolution 1386(2001) [YUN 2001, p. 267], continued to assist the Afghan Government in the maintenance of security in Kabul and its surrounding areas. It expanded its support role through the deployment of provincial reconstruction teams in other parts of the country. The North Atlantic Treaty Organization (NATO) continued to carry out its role as lead command for ISAF throughout 2004.

In January, the Council further refined the sanctions measures against Osama bin Laden, Al-Qaida, the Taliban and their associates. It also strengthened the mandate of the Al-Qaida and Taliban Sanctions Committee and established, for a period of 18 months, an Analytical Support and Sanctions Monitoring Team to report on the implementation of the measures by States and to recommend further action for consideration by the Council. In addition, it improved the Committee's consolidated list, which remained a critical tool for implementing all sanctions measures.

The Economic and Social Council, in July, adopted **resolution 2004/37**, on providing support to the Government of Afghanistan in its efforts to eliminate illicit opium and foster stability and security in the region (see p. 1244). By **resolution 59/161**, the General Assembly, in December, also called on the international community to support the Afghan Government in its efforts to eliminate opium production (see p. 1244). The Economic and Social Council, in July, adopted **resolution 2004/10** on the situation of women and girls in Afghanistan (see p. 1163).

In Iraq, the challenges to peace and security were a major priority for the international community and the United Nations. Despite the enormous security constraints, the United Nations continued to promote an inclusive, participatory and transparent political transition process, provide reconstruction, development and humanitarian assistance, and promote the protection of human rights, national reconciliation and judicial and legal reform.

On 28 June, the Coalition Provisional Authority (CPA), established in 2003 by the occupying forces to provide for the interim administration of Iraq, handed over authority over the entire territory to the Interim Iraqi Government, which was officially established on that same day. Consequently, the Governing Council of Iraq ceased to exist.

The Secretary-General's Special Adviser, Lakhdar Brahimi (Algeria), at the request of the Governing Council of Iraq and CPA, undertook three missions to Iraq between February and June 2004. During those visits, which also included a team from the UN Electoral Assistance Division, he helped the Iraqis to negotiate an appropriate modality and schedule for the holding of elections and facilitated a consultative process, which resulted in an agreement on the structure and composition of a sovereign and independent Interim Government. UN electoral experts assisted in the establishment of an independent Iraqi electoral commission and contributed technical expertise for the preparation of general elections, scheduled to take place in January 2005.

In March, the Iraqi Governing Council approved the Transitional Administrative Law, which served as the legal basis for the Interim Government until the ratification of a permanent constitution.

On 8 June, the Security Council adopted **resolution 1546(2004)**, by which it endorsed the proposed timetable for Iraq's political transition, including the formation of a sovereign Interim Government of Iraq by 30 June 2004 and the convening of a national conference. It endorsed the holding no later than 31 January 2005 of direct democratic elections for a Transitional National Assembly, which would have responsibility, among other things, for forming a Transitional Government and for drafting a permanent constitution leading to a constitutionally elected Government by 31 December 2005. The resolution gave the United Nations a strong and clearly defined mandate and took note of the intention to create a distinct entity under unified command of the multinational force to provide security for the UN presence in Iraq. Moreover, the resolution reaffirmed the authorization for the multinational force under unified command established under resolution 1511(2003), and decided that the force should have the authority to take all necessary measures to contribute to the maintenance of security and stability in Iraq.

In August, the United Nations helped to convene a national conference at which an Interim National Council was elected.

Meanwhile, the security environment continued to deteriorate throughout 2004, with attacks, including acts of terror, against Iraqi civilians, State representatives and members of the multinational force. In November, the Interim Iraqi Government declared a 60-day state of emergency throughout the country, with the exception of the three northern governorates. Due to a lack of security, the United Nations Assistance Mission for Iraq (UNAMI), established in 2003, carried out its activities from outside the country, specifically in Cyprus, Jordan and Kuwait. International and regional efforts were made to foster greater stability in Iraq, including a ministerial meeting in Sharm El Sheik in late November, which the Secretary-General attended.

The United Nations Monitoring, Verification and Inspection Commission (UNMOVIC) and the International Atomic Energy Agency (IAEA) assessed material that was in the public domain on the issues pertaining to Iraq's alleged weapons of mass destruction. They also investigated the discovery of items relevant to their mandates that had been exported from Iraq as scrap metal.

In April, the Secretary-General appointed a high-level Independent Inquiry Committee, chaired by Paul A. Volcker (United States), to investigate allegations of impropriety in the administration and management of the oil-for-food programme. The Committee submitted a status report and a briefing paper.

Progress was made in the identification and return of remains of missing Kuwaiti and third-country nationals from Iraq, and on the return of all Kuwaiti property seized by Iraq during the 1990 invasion and occupation of Kuwait.

In 2004, Timor-Leste continued to establish and strengthen its national institutions with assistance from the United Nations Mission of Support in East Timor (UNMISET) and UN agencies. As the security situation remained stable throughout the year, and to help Timor-Leste achieve full self-sufficiency, the Security Council, in May, extended the UNMISET mandate for a period of six months beyond 20 May 2004, but reduced the size of the operation and revised its tasks to take account of the changed circumstances on the ground. In November, the Council extended the Mission's mandate for a final period until 20 May 2005. The Government of Timor-Leste assumed full responsibility for maintaining security and stability within the country, although UNMISET remained ready to assist in exceptional circumstances. UNMISET continued to provide capacity-building assistance to public administration, law enforcement and the judiciary. In October, a UN technical assessment mission made recommendations pertaining to UNMISET's tasks and composition.

In other developments, local elections, the first ever to be conducted by Timorese authorities, were held in December. Relations between Timor-Leste and Indonesia continued to improve, although the two countries did not reach final agreement on the demarcation of their land border. Marine boundary negotiations between Timor-Leste and Australia continued, though no final agreement was reached on the exploitation of petroleum and natural gas resources in the area.

After a prolonged stalemate, the political and institutional processes in Cambodia resumed in 2004. In November, Cambodia ratified the Agreement between the United Nations and the Cambodian Government concerning the prosecution of crimes committed during the period of Democratic Kampuchea. The Agreement would enter into force once the United Nations was satisfied that sufficient funding was in place to support the operations and staffing of the Extraordinary Chambers for a sustained period of time.

In 2004, the peace process in Bougainville, Papua New Guinea, moved forward slowly but steadily. The United Nations Observer Mission in Boungainville (UNOMB) oversaw the destruction by the Bougainville parties of over 90 per cent of weapons. The Boungainville parties together with the Government of Papua New Guinea finalized a constitution. Its adoption would pave the way for the election, scheduled for early 2005, of an autonomous Bougainville Government. UNOMB's mandate was extended for a final period until 30 June 2005.

Among other concerns in the region that were brought to the attention of the United Nations were relations between India and Pakistan; developments in the Democratic People's Republic of Korea; the situation in Myanmar; the issue of the Greater Tunb, Lesser Tunb and Abu Musa islands in the Arabian Gulf; and cooperation with the Pacific Islands Forum. The activities of the United Nations Tajikistan Office of Peacebuilding were extended for another year, until 1 June 2005, in order to continue to support Tajikistan in its post-conflict peace-building efforts.

Afghanistan

Implementation of Bonn Agreement

In 2004, the United Nations continued to assist the Afghan Transitional Administration (TA) in implementing the 2001 Agreement on Provisional Arrangements in Afghanistan Pending the Re-establishment of Permanent Government Institutions (the Bonn Agreement) [YUN 2001, p. 263], with support provided by the United Nations Assistance Mission in Afghanistan (UNAMA), led by the Special Representative of the Secretary-General and Head of Mission, and by the International Security Assistance Force (ISAF), led by the North Atlantic Treaty Organization (NATO).

The Secretary-General submitted three progress reports to the General Assembly and the Security Council on the implementation of the Bonn Agreement and on the activities of UNAMA [A/58/742-S/2004/230, A/58/868-S/2004/634, A/59/581-S/2004/925]. ISAF activities were reported to the Council by the NATO Secretary-General through the UN Secretary-General [S/2004/222, S/2004/537, S/2004/785]. The Council extended UNAMA's mandate until 26 March 2005 (**resolution 1536 (2004)**) (see p. 313) and ISAF's authorization until 13 October 2005 (**resolution 1563(2004)**) (see p. 331).

On 10 February, the Council took note of the Secretary-General's intention to appoint Jean Arnault (France) as his Special Representative for Afghanistan to replace Lakhdar Brahimi (Algeria), who relinquished his post on 6 January [S/2004/104, S/2004/105].

Finalization of Afghan Constitution

Under the terms of the Bonn Agreement, the Constitutional Loya Jirga, which commenced its consideration in December 2003 [YUN 2003, p. 308] of the draft constitution for Afghanistan, successfully concluded its deliberations on 4 January 2004, with almost unanimous agreement among the 502 delegates on the final draft. The various groups reached compromise on many of the issues before them, including the powers of the President, the nationality of ministers, the creation of a commission to oversee the implementation of the Constitution, the timing of the elections and the national anthem and language. The final text agreed provided for a presidential system, but with great emphasis on parliamentary control of the executive. The Constitution vested most powers in the central Government and did not devolve much authority to the provinces. It also called for an independent judiciary and a legal framework consistent with the "beliefs and prescriptions" of Islam. It explicitly included all minority groups in the definition of the nation and recognized Dari and Pashto as official languages, and other languages as official in the areas where they were spoken by the majority. It also provided equal rights to men and women and guaranteed women at least 25 per cent of the representatives in the lower house of parliament.

Statement of Security Council President. The Security Council President, in a 6 January press statement [SC/7971-AFG/241], said that Council members welcomed the new Constitution agreed by the Loya Jirga on 4 January as a significant step towards a peaceful, prosperous and democratic Afghanistan that respected the rights of all citizens, men and women. Council members paid tribute to the delegates of the Constitutional Loya Jirga for their work in completing that long and complex process. They also recognized the important role played by the Secretary-General's Special Representative, Mr. Brahimi.

EU declaration. The European Union (EU), in a 6 January declaration [S/2004/42] of its Presidency (Ireland), welcomed the approval by the Loya Jirga of a Constitution for Afghanistan and reconfirmed its full commitment to the Afghan peace process.

Security Council consideration (January). At the Security Council's 15 January meeting [meeting 4893] to discuss the situation in Afghanistan, the Secretary-General told the Council that, since his December 2003 report on the situation there [YUN 2003, p. 307], the adoption of the new Constitution was an important and very encouraging development in the implementation of the Bonn peace process. The Constitution, which had entered into force, provided a permanent foundation for re-establishing the rule of law in Afghanistan. It defined a political order through a strong presidential system of government with a bicameral legislature, established a judicial system in compliance with Islam, and included provisions for ensuring full respect for fundamental human rights, including equal rights for women. However, the Constitution by itself could not guarantee peace and stability. Afghans, with the international community's support, had to tackle the troubling security situation, ensure an inclusive and broadly representative Government, and accelerate the pace of reconstruction.

The Secretary-General's Special Representative said that the near unanimous acclamation of the new Constitution was a further step in the Bonn transitional plan. The Constitutional Loya Jirga was to a large degree representative of Afghanistan taken as a whole and included delegates from every province and from a wide sector of society, including women. Much of the Constitutional Loya Jirga provided public debate not seen in the country for many years. The Jirga reached early consensus on some 120 of the 160 articles of the draft constitution, but it saw difficult debate and hard bargaining on a number of issues, such as the form of Government and the role of the courts. Though there were also some signs of polarization along ethnic lines, in the end, delegates reached a compromise and made concessions in order to arrive at a text that all could accept. The fundamental law they had written should, if implemented, provide a solid foundation upon which to continue the task of addressing the real needs facing Afghans daily. The first task in implementing the Constitution was to make it a living reality as expectations had been raised that the Government and its international partners would deliver on their promise of peace and stability.

The adoption of the Constitution was a great accomplishment, but the ultimate test of each element of the Bonn process would be whether or not Afghanistan would move towards "the irreversibility of peace". From that perspective, the new constitutional order would have meaning for the average Afghan only if security improved and the rule of law was strengthened. Thus the major challenges in implementing the Constitution remained the challenges of the peace process as a whole: the disarmament of factional forces, the protection of the basic rights of every Afghan citizen, the demand for increased reconstruction, the reform of national institutions, and reform also across the Government to ensure better representation. Further gains could be made if the effort to reform the national security institutions, the Ministry of Defence, the Ministry of the Interior and the intelligence services were to pick up pace. The disarmament, demobilization and reintegration (DDR) programme had also not progressed far enough. In addition, the threat factional forces posed to the peace process had been increasingly compounded by the terrorist tactics of extremists. The pattern continued of challenging the central Government's authority and disrupting the peace process by attacking targets of opportunity, be they the Government, nongovernmental organizations (NGOs), the United Nations or ordinary citizens. Those attacks coincided with signals that extremist elements were rallying support against the peace process and had the effect of blocking reconstruction and limiting the presence of the Government in the affected areas. While the United States and Pakistan were interdicting extremist elements at the border, some press reports claimed that Taliban leaders were moving more or less freely in and between cities in Pakistan. Afghan and Pakistani authorities were discussing those issues of concern in a constructive manner. At the same time, the Government, along with UNAMA, UN agencies and international security forces, was working out integrated packages to improve district-level governance, strengthen the formal and traditional justice system, increase the presence of police and reach out with focused reconstruction assistance to communities.

Mr. Brahimi said that it was too early to draw lessons from the first two years of the Bonn process, but he believed that one clear lesson related to the difficulty of carrying out post-conflict transitional processes without equivalent and dedicated security assistance. Until Afghan security institutions were further strengthened, there would be a need in other parts of the country for the sort of assistance that ISAF had given in Kabul. The launch of the German provincial reconstruction team (PRT) in Kunduz was the first sign of ISAF's expansion, as called for by Security Council resolution 1510(2003) [YUN 2003, p. 310]. The United States had also indicated its intention to create a broader PRT presence in the south.

Mr. Brahimi expressed concern over the extent to which the Afghan economy was becoming dependent on the drug trade. The Government had shown a commitment to tackling the problem, but its efforts had concentrated on building government institutions and on drafting legislation. While those activities were essential in the long-term fight against drugs, they had not had an immediate effect on the amount of opium cultivated or trafficked. The problem would not be solved over the long term without development and achievements being made in other sectors, including in providing alternative livelihoods, building up the judicial and penal systems and reducing demand for opium derivatives both domestically and abroad.

Mr. Brahimi said that the success of the Constitutional Loya Jirga and of the political debate that had begun offered hope, but it was a success that had to be quickly capitalized on, lest it did no more than raise false expectations.

Report of Secretary-General (March). In his 19 March report on the situation in Afghanistan and its implications for international peace and security [A/58/742-S/2004/230], submitted in response to Security Council resolution 1471(2003) [YUN 2003, p. 295] and General Assembly resolutions 58/27 A [ibid., p. 304] and 58/27 B [ibid., p. 934], the Secretary-General summarized the key developments in Afghanistan since his 30 December 2003 report [ibid., p. 307]. He said that the positive outcome of the Constitutional Loya Jirga had affected the political dynamics of the nation. The unity and purpose demonstrated by delegates from the southern provinces contrasted with the fragmentation observed in the past, and suggested renewed interest and optimism about national politics within that important constituency. The Security Council had been repeatedly informed of the concern that a continued sense of alienation in southern Afghanistan was a factor of instability. The perception that the new Constitution offered a credible framework for power-sharing was therefore welcomed.

Security Council consideration (March). On 24 March [meeting 4931], the Security Council discussed the situation in Afghanistan. Assistant Secretary-General for Peacekeeping Operations Hédi Annabi said that after 26 months of steady progress in the implementation of the Bonn Agreement's political agenda, the process had reached one of its last major benchmarks: the holding of free and fair elections. The Constitution required elections for the presidency and for the upper and lower houses of the national assembly. At the implementation level, notwithstanding the many complexities associated with the carrying out of multi-level and simultaneous elections in Afghanistan, around 40,000 Afghans would be trained to manage 4,700 polling sites on election day. The United Nations would verify the work of the registration and polling teams, which would be composed entirely of Afghans. The Electoral Secretariat would implement the instructions of the Joint Electoral Management Body (JEMB), composed of six Afghan electoral commissioners and five international electoral experts. JEMB would take the lead role in deciding when elections would take place and it would also be responsible for the preparation, conduct and oversight of those elections. In the meantime, the first phase of the registration process had progressed more or less on target, with the registration of 1.56 million voters; of those, around 28 per cent were women. Preparations were being made to launch the second phase of the registration process, when registration teams would deploy to provincial capitals. That phase was scheduled to begin on 1 May and to continue at some 4,200 sites for approximately one month. Success in completing the registration and in holding the elections would depend on support from Afghan and international security forces. President Karzai had requested NATO to provide additional security during the election period. UNAMA was holding discussions with NATO on those security issues. The financial requirements for registration were almost fully pledged. Delays, however, in actually disbursing funds to the United Nations Development Programme (UNDP) trust fund continued to hinder and delay procurement, staffing and planning activities.

SECURITY COUNCIL ACTION (March)

On 26 March [meeting 4937], the Security Council unanimously adopted **resolution 1536(2004).** The draft [S/2004/249] was prepared in consultations among Council members.

The Security Council,

Reaffirming its previous resolutions on Afghanistan, in particular resolution 1471(2003) of 28 March 2003 extending the mandate of the United Nations Assistance Mission in Afghanistan through 27 March 2004,

Reaffirming its strong commitment to the sovereignty, independence, territorial integrity and national unity of Afghanistan,

Welcoming the Constitution adopted by the Loya Jirga on 4 January 2004 which reflects the determination of the Afghan people to ensure the transition of their country towards a stable and democratic State,

Recognizing that the United Nations must continue to play its central and impartial role in the international efforts to assist the Afghan people in consolidating peace in Afghanistan and rebuilding their country,

Reaffirming the Transitional Administration as the sole legitimate government of Afghanistan pending the democratic presidential and parliamentary elections envisioned in the Agreement on Provisional Arrangements in Afghanistan Pending the Re-establishment of Permanent Government Institutions, signed in Bonn, Germany, on 5 December 2001 (the Bonn Agreement) and in the Afghan Constitution,

Reiterating its strong support for the full implementation of the Bonn Agreement, and supporting also the objectives of the international conference scheduled to take place in Berlin on 31 March and 1 April 2004 to allow the Afghan authorities and the international community to reaffirm their long-term commitment to take the transitional process in Afghanistan forward, including by demonstrating support for the Afghan political process and its national security, as well as by confirming and generating international financial and other donations,

Recalling the importance of the coming elections to establish democratic Afghan authorities as a further step towards implementation of the Bonn Agreement, and welcoming in that regard the creation of a Joint Electoral Management Body and the initial progress made in voter registration,

Recalling and emphasizing the importance of the Declaration on Good-neighbourly Relations, signed in Kabul on 22 December 2002, and encouraging all States concerned to continue to follow up on the Kabul Declaration and the Declaration on Encouraging Closer Trade, Transit and Investment Cooperation signed in Dubai, United Arab Emirates, on 22 September 2003,

Stressing also the importance of extending central government authority to all parts of Afghanistan, of comprehensive nationwide disarmament, demobilization and reintegration of all armed factions, and of security sector reform, including reconstitution of the new Afghan National Army and Afghan National Police,

Welcoming the visit of the Security Council mission to Afghanistan from 31 October to 7 November 2003, and taking note of its report and recommendations,

1. *Decides* to extend the mandate of the United Nations Assistance Mission in Afghanistan for an additional period of twelve months from the date of adoption of the present resolution;

2. *Welcomes* the report of the Secretary-General of 19 March 2004 and the recommendations contained therein;

3. *Stresses* the importance of the provision of sufficient security and of significant donor support for the holding of credible national elections in accordance with the Afghan Constitution and the Agreement on Provisional Arrangements in Afghanistan Pending the Re-establishment of Permanent Government Institutions (the Bonn Agreement), and to this end urges Member States and international organizations to coordinate closely with the Mission and the Transitional Administration;

4. *Encourages* Afghan authorities to enable an electoral process that provides for voter participation that is representative of the national demographics, including women and refugees, and calls upon all eligible Afghans to participate fully in the registration and electoral processes;

5. *Encourages* the Mission and the Afghan authorities, in this regard, to accelerate voter registration efforts in preparation for elections, and urges close coordination between Afghan and United Nations authorities;

6. *Welcomes* the progress made since the commencement of the disarmament, demobilization and reintegration process in October 2003 and the contribution of the International Observer Group in this regard; stresses that efforts on the part of the Afghan authorities and all Afghan parties, supported by the international community, to achieve further progress on the disarmament, demobilization and reintegration process are critical, particularly for the creation of an environment more conducive to the conduct of free and fair elections; and in this regard calls upon all Afghan parties to abide by commitments made in the Bonn Agreement, including in annex I thereto;

7. *Welcomes* the efforts to date of the Afghan authorities to implement their National Drug Control Strategy adopted on 22 May 2003, and urges the Afghan authorities to make further efforts in that regard and Member States to support its implementation with the necessary resources;

8. *Stresses* that tackling the drug trade cannot be separated from creating a strong economy and a secure environment in Afghanistan and cannot be achieved without increased cooperation among neighbouring States and countries along trafficking routes to strengthen anti-narcotic controls to curb the drug flow, and notes with concern in this regard the assessment made by the United Nations Office on Drugs and Crime in its last Afghan opium survey;

9. *Welcomes* the appointment of Mr. Jean Arnault as the new Special Representative of the Secretary-General for Afghanistan, reaffirms its continued strong support for the Special Representative and the concept of a fully integrated mission, and endorses his full authority, in accordance with all relevant resolutions, over all United Nations activities in Afghanistan;

10. *Requests* the Mission, with the support of the Office of the United Nations High Commissioner for Human Rights, to continue to assist the Afghan Independent Human Rights Commission in the full implementation of the human rights provisions of the new Afghan Constitution, in particular those regarding the full enjoyment by women of their human rights, and requests also that the Mission support the establishment of a fair and transparent judicial system and work towards the strengthening of the rule of law;

11. *Calls upon* all Afghan parties to cooperate with the Mission in the implementation of its mandate and to ensure the security and freedom of movement of its staff throughout the country;

12. *Welcomes* the progress made by the International Security Assistance Force in expanding its presence outside of Kabul and in implementing its mandate in accordance with resolutions 1444(2002) of 27 November 2002 and 1510(2003) of 13 October 2003, requests that the Force continue working in close consultation with the Secretary-General and his Special Representative, and calls upon troop contributors to provide the necessary resources to ensure the full implementation of the mandate of the Force;

13. *Welcomes also* the development of the new Afghan National Army and Afghan National Police as important steps towards the goal of Afghan security forces providing security and ensuring the rule of law throughout the country, and welcomes further the readiness of the Force to provide security assistance for the organization of the forthcoming elections in support of the Afghan authorities and the Mission, in accordance with resolution 1510(2003);

14. *Requests* the Secretary-General to report to the Council in a timely manner on developments in Afghanistan, including, after elections, on the future role of the Mission;

15. *Decides* to remain actively seized of the matter.

Berlin Conference on Afghanistan

The International Conference on "Afghanistan and the International Community—A Partnership for the Future" (Berlin, Germany, 31 March–1 April), sponsored by the Governments of Afghanistan, Germany and Japan together with the United Nations, brought together high-level representatives from 65 countries to evaluate the progress made in the Bonn process and to determine the path forward.

The Conference adopted the Berlin Declaration, in which it noted the substantial progress achieved under the Bonn Agreement in fostering peace, stability, national unity, democratization and economic development in Afghanistan, and welcomed in particular the announcement to hold direct presidential and parliamentary elections in September. It agreed that ISAF, currently under NATO command, and Operation Enduring Freedom would continue until the new Afghan security and armed forces were sufficiently constituted and operational. The Conference agreed that the international community would assist further in stabilizing the security situation throughout the country; that it was necessary to implement the first phase of the DDR programme to be completed by June and to intensify it ahead of the 2004 elections; to continue the formation of the Afghan national army; and to fully establish the rule of law and a functioning judicial system. It also agreed to do everything, including the development of economic alternatives, to reduce and eliminate the threat posed to the rule of law and development by opium poppy cultivation, drug production and trafficking.

The Conference endorsed the Work Plan entitled "The Way Ahead" put forward by the Government of Afghanistan, annexed it to the Declaration, and welcomed the multiyear commitments made at the Conference for reconstruction and development totalling $8.2 billion for fiscal years March 2004 to March 2007, including a pledge of $4.4 billion for March 2004 to March 2005 to implement the investment programme outlined in the document submitted to the Conference entitled "Securing Afghanistan's Future". The Work Plan outlined measures for holding free and fair elections, institution-building and development.

The Conference also welcomed NATO's commitment to expand ISAF by establishing additional PRTs and the further steps made by Afghanistan and its neighbours to foster regional cooperation.

Also annexed to the Declaration were the Berlin Declaration on Counter-Narcotics within the framework of the Kabul Declaration on Good-neighbourly Relations [YUN 2002, p. 274], and a progress report on the implementation of the Bonn Agreement.

Security Council consideration (April). The Under-Secretary-General for Peacekeeping Operations, Jean-Marie Guéhenno, in his briefing to the Security Council on 6 April [meeting 4941], said that the Conference reasserted the unity of purpose and long-term commitment that had been a hallmark of the international community's engagement in Afghanistan and demonstrated the international community's resolve to assist the Afghan Government. The $4.4 billion committed for fiscal year 2004 was over 100 per cent of the amount that had been sought, and the $8.2 billion committed for three years represented 69 per cent of the funds requested for that period by Afghanistan. In the margins of the intergovernmental Conference, two other meetings were held: a meeting of Afghan civil society members and a donor meeting, at which $68 million was pledged, against needs of some $135 million, for the presidential and parliamentary elections and for the Afghan refugee communities in Pakistan and Iran. The Conference highlighted, among other things, the challenges on the reconstruction and development front, as well as the rising tide of the drug economy.

The holding of national elections posed the greatest short-term challenge in the next stage of the Bonn process. In the Work Plan annexed to the Berlin Declaration, the Afghan Government agreed to help ensure freedom of expression and political organization, a level playing field for political parties and their candidates, a neutral civil service and military, freedom of the press and equal access to it. At the request of the Government, the United Nations was prepared, jointly with the Afghan Human Rights Commission, to monitor the implementation of political rights across the country to achieve those benchmarks. Without substantial improvement in the security situation, the elections would be threatened. The Work Plan provided for the intensification of DDR efforts to encompass 40 per cent of the militia and the cantonment of all heavy weapons by June 2004. Success in DDR programmes would depend to a great degree on the leadership of the Afghan Government.

The Under-Secretary-General underscored the need for adequate international security assistance to support the Afghan Government in the electoral process and to protect it from factional threats and attempts to terminate it. The United Nations joined President Karzai's appeal to NATO and the coalition to increase deployment of international forces to help the Afghan Government fulfil its commitment to hold free and fair elections.

SECURITY COUNCIL ACTION (April)

On 6 April [meeting 4941], following consultations among Security Council members, the President made statement **S/PRST/2004/9** on behalf of the Council:

The Security Council welcomes the results of the Berlin Conference on Afghanistan, held on 31 March and 1 April 2004, co-chaired by the United Nations, Afghanistan, Germany and Japan. The Council thanks Afghanistan and Germany for jointly hosting this event, an important milestone on the way to a secure, stable, free, prosperous and democratic Afghanistan.

The Council expresses its full support for the commitment of Afghanistan and the international community to successfully complete the implementation of the Agreement on Provisional Arrangements in Afghanistan Pending the Re-establishment of Permanent Government Institutions, signed in Bonn, Germany, on 5 December 2001 (the Bonn Agreement) and to continue the transition process in Afghanistan through a lasting partnership, thus reflecting a model for a common endeavour of the international community in its fight against terrorism.

The Council endorses the Berlin Declaration and stresses the relevance of the Work Plan of the Afghan Government, the Progress Report on the Implementation of the Bonn Agreement, and the Berlin Declaration on Counter-Narcotics, annexed to the Berlin Declaration, and welcomes the significant financial multiyear commitments made by the international donor community.

The Council in particular expresses full support for the commitment by the Government of Afghanistan to pursue the necessary reform steps and actions as outlined in the Work Plan.

The Council welcomes the announcement of President Karzai to hold direct presidential and parliamentary elections by September of this year. The Council stresses the importance of a secure environment for free, fair and credible democratic elections, and stresses that to this end further efforts of the Government of Afghanistan and of the international community are needed.

The Council welcomes in this regard the decision taken by the President of Afghanistan to implement vigorously the disarmament, demobilization and reintegration programme, in particular to intensify it ahead of the 2004 elections, and to continue the formation of the Afghan National Army and the Afghan National Police.

The Council also acknowledges the commitment by the North Atlantic Treaty Organization to expand the mission of the International Security Assistance Force by establishing five additional Provincial Reconstruction Teams by summer 2004 and further Provisional Reconstruction Teams thereafter, as well as the readiness of the Force and Operation Enduring Freedom to assist in securing the conduct of elections.

The Council welcomes the commitments totalling $8.2 billion for the fiscal years March 2004–March 2007 made by participants at the Berlin Conference for the reconstruction and development of Afghanistan and stresses the importance, with increasing absorption capacity, for a growing share of this assistance to be channelled through the Afghan budget as direct budget support or as contributions to the Afghanistan Reconstruction Trust Fund and to the Law and Order Trust Fund.

The Council stresses that opium poppy cultivation, drug production and trafficking pose a serious threat to the rule of law and development in Afghanistan as well as to international security, and that therefore Afghanistan and the international community shall endeavour to reduce and eventually eliminate this threat, including through the development of economic alternatives. The Council reiterates the importance of increased cooperation among neighbouring States and countries along trafficking routes to strengthen anti-narcotic controls.

The Council takes note of the appeal of President Karzai at the Berlin Conference for additional international support needed in countering narcotics. The Council refers in this context to the necessary implementation of the Afghan National Drug Control Strategy and the Counter-Narcotics Action Plans in the areas of law enforcement, judicial reform, alternative livelihoods, demand reduction and public awareness. The Council calls upon Member States to support the implementation of these Action Plans. Afghanistan needs both human and financial resources to tackle this problem.

The Council welcomes, in particular, the Berlin Declaration on Counter-Narcotics within the framework of the Declaration on Good-neighbourly Relations, signed in Kabul on 22 December 2002 by Afghanistan and its neighbours, as well as the planned Conference on Regional Police Cooperation to be held in Doha on 18 and 19 May 2004.

The Council invites the Secretary-General to include in his future reports to the Council and the

General Assembly on the situation in Afghanistan, in addition to the information on implementation of the Bonn Agreement, chapters on progress achieved in the implementation of the Berlin Declaration, the Work Plan of the Afghan Government and in the promotion of regional and international cooperation with Afghanistan.

The Council reaffirms its full support for the actions taken by the Special Representative of the Secretary-General and the United Nations Assistance Mission in Afghanistan and reiterates the central and impartial role of the United Nations in the international efforts to assist the Afghan people in consolidating peace in Afghanistan and rebuilding their country.

The Council will remain seized of the matter.

As a follow-up to the Berlin Conference, the Afghanistan Development Forum met at ministerial level (Kabul, 20-22 April) to discuss how the pledges made in Berlin could be translated into specific programmes. The meeting emphasized such cross-cutting themes as gender, human rights and the environment. Investment in security and the rule of law as prerequisites for all other activities were also emphasized.

Communication. By a 1 July letter to the Secretary-General [A/59/124-S/2004/532], Uzbekistan transmitted the text of the Tashkent Declaration by the heads of State of the members of the Shanghai Cooperation Organization (China, Kazakhstan, Kyrgyzstan, Russian Federation, Tajikistan, Uzbekistan), adopted at a summit meeting (Tashkent, Uzbekistan, 17 June). The members welcomed the formation of a widely representative Government in Afghanistan. They also said that they would strive to promote international cooperation in the fight against terrorism, extremism and drug trafficking in order to establish security, peace and tranquillity, as well as to create the essential conditions for the peaceful renewal of Afghanistan.

Security situation

The Secretary-General, in his March report on the situation in Afghanistan and its implications for international peace and security [A/58/742-S/2004/230], said that security in Afghanistan showed no signs of significant improvement. Civilians continued to be killed in inter-factional fighting and attacks by extremist elements on national and international aid agencies and on government officials continued to occur, predominantly in the southern provinces, constraining implementation of activities such as reconstruction, the census and voter registration in rural areas. Attacks against ISAF on 27 and 28 January suggested that the risk of suicide attacks against well-protected, international military targets remained high. At the same time, factional feuds,

rivalries and drug-related incidents continued to affect the lives of the population. However, the weak or corrupt provincial and district administrations, the continued rule of local commanders and the absence of effective national law enforcement were more common sources of insecurity for the population than terrorist violence. Those factors contributed to a deterioration of security in the north-east, traditionally one of the safest regions of the country, where rival commanders had been fighting over land, possibly driven by attempts to expand drug production. Aware that the UN presence contributed to stability, security measures were being taken to enable the United Nations to operate safely in as many areas as possible. As a result of the implementation of additional security measures and guarantees from the national authorities of Afghanistan and Pakistan, the Office of the United Nations High Commissioner for Refugees (UNHCR), on 29 February, resumed the repatriation of Afghan refugees living in Pakistan, which had been suspended after the assassination of a UNHCR staff member in November 2003 [YUN 2003, p. 307]. As part of a longer-term approach to security, a security, stabilization and reconstruction programme combined the deployment of better trained and equipped police forces, reconstruction projects and improvements in the provincial and district administration. A pilot project was launched in Kandahar under the leadership of the provincial governor and with the support of UNAMA and the coalition-led provincial reconstruction team. The national programme was officially launched on 21 January.

By mid-year, the security situation in Afghanistan had become volatile, having seriously deteriorated in certain parts of the country, said the Secretary-General in his August report [A/58/868-S/2004/634]. Attacks on national and international forces and on electoral, government and humanitarian workers and their premises in southern Afghanistan had intensified. Several of the most serious acts of violence took place in the north and west of the country, areas that had so far been considered low-risk. Acts of violence were increasingly being directed at the staff and offices of the electoral secretariat and UN workers. Four Afghan female registration staff were killed in the east in two separate bomb attacks on 26 June and 8 July. In the south, a team leader of the Joint Electoral Management Body (JEMB) in Uruzgan province and a village chief were ambushed and shot dead on 24 July. A protracted attack on an electoral convoy, in clearly marked UN vehicles with a police convoy, took place in broad daylight in the south-east on 6 June and rocket-propelled grenades were fired at a UN Mine Action Centre for Afghanistan demining convoy in the central and south-eastern regions on 12 June and on a UNHCR compound in the southern province of Kandahar on 18 June.

The view of the north as the safest area of the country was seriously undermined by a succession of violent acts. A brutal attack left 10 Chinese construction workers dead in the city of Jilawugir (Baghlan province) on 10 June; five days later, an attack with improvised explosive devices in the town of Kondoz killed four Afghans. On 2 June, gunmen in the west ambushed a Médecins sans frontières vehicle in Badghis province, and shot and killed five of its staff, including three international staff, causing the organization to withdraw completely from the country.

In addition to those attacks, the north and west of the country experienced an unprecedented level of factional fighting. Fighting between the forces loyal to Governor Ismail Khan and General Zahir in the town of Herat on 21 March resulted in some 50 to 100 people killed, including the central Government's Minister of Aviation and a son of the Governor, and forced General Zahir and his forces to take refuge in the neighbouring province of Badghis. In a negotiated agreement between the central Government and Governor Khan, troops were deployed to Herat to help restore order. Herat's intelligence chief was implicated in the incident and dismissed; however, his successor, appointed by the central Government, was denied access to his office by the Governor. On 4 July, commanders loyal to the Governor ransacked the intelligence chief's temporary office and attacked his staff, critically injuring two. In Faryab province, factional tensions culminated on 8 April when the Governor and senior officials of his administration were forced out of office by a violent crowd. The central Government deployed Afghan national army troops to the area to restore order. Nevertheless, factional elements had thwarted the efforts by the central Government to install a new governor. Similarly, in Samangan and Sar-i-Pul, factional elements continued to prevent the governors-designate from taking up their posts.

In the months prior to election day and the deployment of additional security forces, which took place in the final weeks before the elections (see below), there was a build-up of serious security incidents, some of which were directed against the electoral effort, but others were directed more generally against peace and reconstruction activities. On 12 September, following the decision by President Karzai to replace the Governor of Herat, Ismail Khan, several hundred protesters attacked and burned the UNAMA office in Herat and looted the offices of other UN agencies, NGOs and the Afghan Independent Human Rights Commission. The fact that those attacks occurred in areas previously thought not to be at high risk was of serious concern. Similarly, security in the south and south-east deteriorated to the point where large areas were effectively out of bounds to the assistance community, and government officials were frequent targets of attacks. There were real concerns over the impact that that obvious deterioration of the security situation might have on the credibility of the elections. Significant extraordinary measures were therefore taken to safeguard the election.

The generally calm security environment on election day was due in part to the additional ISAF and coalition troops deployed before the election. Security was also greatly enhanced by progress made in the training and deployment of the Afghan army and police forces, which performed extremely well on election day, whether in protecting polling stations, deterring threats or escorting election materials.

In the aftermath of the election, and with a reduction in the coalition and ISAF forces, three broad security threats continued to effect the Bonn process: extremist or terrorist attacks, factional violence among militia forces and violence and other threats to security personnel by criminal elements, in particular those involved in the trafficking of drugs. That reality was tragically borne out by a suicide bombing in the centre of Kabul on 23 October, in which two people lost their lives. A few days later, on 28 October, three international electoral staff were abducted in the Kart-e-Parwan district of Kabul in broad daylight. As a result, additional security measures were taken to enhance the safety of staff, the most stringent measures since 2001. The abducted staff were subsequently released on 22 November.

Elections

Security Council consideration (March). On 24 March [meeting 4931], during the Security Council's consideration of the situation in Afghanistan, the Assistant Secretary-General for Peacekeeping Operations, Mr. Annabi, reported that after 26 months of steady progress in the implementation of the Bonn Agreement's political agenda, the process had reached one of its last major benchmarks: the holding of free and fair elections for the presidency and for the upper and lower houses of the national assembly. At the implementation level, some 40,000 Afghans would be trained to manage 4,700 polling sites on election day. The United Nations would verify the work of the registration and polling teams, which would be composed entirely of Afghans.

The Electoral Secretariat would implement the instructions of JEMB, composed of six Afghan electoral commissioners and five international electoral experts. JEMB would take the lead role in deciding when elections would take place and would also be responsible for their preparation, conduct and oversight. In the meantime, the first phase of the registration process had progressed, with the registration of 1.56 million voters. The second phase, which would involve deploying registration teams to provincial capitals, was scheduled to begin on 1 May at some 4,200 sites. Success in completing the registration and in holding the elections would depend on support from Afghan and international security forces. President Karzai had requested NATO to provide additional security during the election period and UNAMA was holding discussions with NATO on those security issues. The financial requirements for registration were almost fully pledged. Delays, however, in actual disbursing funds to the UNDP trust fund continued to hinder and delay procurement, staffing and planning activities.

Report of Secretary-General. In March, following broad consultations, the Afghan Government announced its intention to hold presidential and lower-house parliamentary elections simultaneously in September 2004, and for the upper house in the spring of 2005, said the Secretary-General [A/58/868-S/2004/634]. The Electoral Law was passed by the Cabinet on 27 May 2004, codifying the electoral rules for the transitional period and providing for a system of single non-transferable votes with multiple-seat constituencies, and ensuring, in accordance with the Constitution, that 68 of the total 249 seats in the lower house would be held by women. On 5 June, the Decree on Provincial Boundaries, delineating administrative divisions for electoral purposes, was signed, creating two new provinces (Panjshir and Daikundi). On 10 July, the Cabinet decided to base the apportionment of seats in the legislature on the provincial population figures of the 1979 census, and requested the United Nations to provide technical assistance to update those figures and to supervise the publication of the final outcome. While the Constitution provided that every effort be made to hold the presidential and parliamentary elections together, JEMB was compelled to take into account a number of legal and technical factors that affected the credibility of the elections and the parliamentary elections in particular. On 9 July, JEMB announced that the elections would be separated: the presidential election would be held on 9 October 2004 and elections for both the lower and upper houses of parliament would be held in April 2005.

Nominations for presidential candidates closed on 26 July, with 23 candidates having submitted applications to contest the ballot and 30 political parties having been formally registered out of the 62 that applied.

As requested by the Government of Afghanistan on 20 June, the Afghan Independent Human Rights Commission and UNAMA began an open-ended process to evaluate the exercise of political rights throughout Afghanistan, with particular focus on the freedoms of expression, assembly, association and movement. The first report on the findings of the verification campaign presented on 16 July contained recommendations to address the problems identified during the investigation.

Security Council consideration (May). On 27 May [meeting 4979], the Security Council discussed the situation in Afghanistan and was briefed on the latest developments by the newly appointed Special Representative of the Secretary-General for Afghanistan and Head of UNAMA, Jean Arnault, who reported that the security situation continued to evolve negatively. An increase in the number of incidents and in the number of resulting casualties was consistent with the spring surge in extremists' attacks. According to coalition forces, various extremist groups were involved, including the Taliban operating in the south, foreign fighters in the south-east and Hezb-i-Islami/Hekmatyar in the east. Drug-related violence was also an important factor of insecurity. In addition, militias involved in combating the Taliban were believed to be responsible for a high percentage of incidents in the areas where they operated. In the north and north-east, tensions between two ethnic factions remained high. However, the deployment in that region and in the city of Herat of the new Afghan army had had a stabilizing impact and had prevented further escalation. Though the voter registration process had been affected by the overall increase in incidents, it was unclear whether attacks against registration teams had been directed against the electoral operation per se or whether they were intended against government targets. The level of violent opposition to the electoral process was therefore still difficult to gauge, but precautions were being taken as registration was pushing into the rural areas. Since the beginning of May, close to a million people had been registered, which brought the total number of registered voters to 2.7 million. Although the registration process was well under way, a number of concerns remained, foremost the problem of security and the possibility that insecurity could lead to under-registration in some provinces. Another challenge related to the determination of population figures themselves. Under the new Electoral Law, the figures that would be used to define the number of representatives per province would be based on a survey done by the Afghan Central Statistical Office. However, due to insecurity, it was likely that a number of provinces would not be surveyed, or only partially. A third challenge was funding. The voter registration process itself was almost fully funded, with a shortfall of just $2.6 million, but the election itself was only partially funded. The registration of political parties had been slow and difficult, due in part to the fact that the Political Party Law sought to limit the right to operate legally to those groups that were not related to military organizations. In order to hold free and fair elections, a new Media Law, among other things, had been passed and electoral authorities were in the process of establishing a media monitoring commission. Security in general, and that of the electoral process in particular, was ultimately an Afghan responsibility, but it was a responsibility that Afghans could not shoulder without international assistance. A widespread, robust international military presence in support of domestic security forces remained critical.

SECURITY COUNCIL ACTION

On 15 July [meeting 5004], following consultations among Security Council members, the President made statement **S/PRST/2004/25** on behalf of the Council:

The Security Council, taking note of the decision announced by the Joint Electoral Management Body established by the Afghan authorities, welcomes and supports the holding of the presidential election in Afghanistan on 9 October 2004. This election is a key requirement under the Agreement on Provisional Arrangements in Afghanistan Pending the Re-establishment of Permanent Government Institutions, signed in Bonn, Germany, on 5 December 2001 (the Bonn Agreement) and represents a new milestone in the process of constructing a democratic, stable and prosperous Afghanistan.

The Council further takes note of the decision of the Body to hold parliamentary elections in April 2005. The Council understands that technical and logistical reasons made it impossible, as reported by the Secretariat, to hold simultaneous presidential and parliamentary elections by September of this year. The Council stresses the importance of using the remaining months to ensure that the necessary preparations are completed and the conditions met for free and fair elections according to the timetables of the Body.

The Council calls upon the Afghan Government and the international community to maintain and intensify, ahead of the presidential and parliamentary elections, their efforts to strengthen the national army and national police, to accelerate the disarmament, demobilization and reintegration process, and

to support the Afghan Government in its strategy to eliminate opium production. The Council stresses the importance of accelerated progress on disarmament, demobilization and reintegration in order to create a safer environment for the election process, including security for electoral staff and Afghan voters, to help ensure a free and credible outcome to the electoral process, and otherwise to help create a secure environment in which the rule of law is respected. The Council reiterates its call upon all eligible Afghans to fully participate in the registration and electoral processes for the presidential and parliamentary elections.

The Council encourages Afghan authorities to enable an electoral process to provide for voter participation that is representative of the national demographics including women and refugees, and in this regard calls for the determination of practical modalities for the registration and participation of the Afghan refugees in Iran and Pakistan in the ongoing Afghan electoral process.

The Council acknowledges the commitment by the North Atlantic Treaty Organization, Operation Enduring Freedom and Member States to assist in establishing a secure environment for the conduct of elections, and calls upon the international community to further increase its security assistance to Afghanistan. The Council also acknowledges the intention of the European Union and bilateral donors to contribute to the conduct of free and fair elections and notes ongoing discussions within the Organization for Security and Cooperation in Europe on a possible contribution in that context.

The Council stresses the importance of providing the necessary funding for the timely implementation of the timetables of the Joint Electoral Management Body. It acknowledges the contribution of the international donor community in support of the elections, calls upon donors to implement their pledges, and encourages the international community to consider further commitments to make the costs for elections as inclusive as possible.

The Council reaffirms its full support for the Special Representative of the Secretary-General and the United Nations Assistance Mission in Afghanistan and reiterates the central and impartial role of the United Nations in the international efforts to assist the Afghan people in consolidating peace in Afghanistan and rebuilding their country.

The Council will remain seized of the matter.

Security Council consideration (August). At the Security Council's 25 August meeting [meeting 5025] to discuss the situation in Afghanistan, the Special Representative of the Secretary-General said that preparations for the presidential elections were under way. JEMB was finalizing regulations applicable to the electoral campaign, scheduled to start on 7 September, which included campaign financing, electoral activities and public order, access to the media and the misuse of government resources for political purposes. The overall security plan for the pre-polling phase, for election day and for post-election processes had also been finalized, with polling-site security being the responsibility primarily of the Ministry of the Interior, which by polling day would have 20,000 police, while the security areas around the polling sites would be protected by military personnel from the Afghan national army, ISAF and the coalition. Factional rivalries had not been able to derail the electoral process or undermine popular participation in registration in the country's east and south-east. However, their impact on the south had been more tangible, depriving part of the population there of the possibility of participating in the election. There were clear indications that the Taliban and similar groups were preparing to escalate their attacks against the last stage of the election. Action was therefore necessary against those who were planning to carry out those attacks. A welcome development, in that regard, was the assurance by Pakistan's President Pervez Musharraf, during an August meeting with President Karzai, that he would not allow Pakistan's territory to be used for actions against Afghanistan's interests. At the same time, preparations for registration and voting of Afghan refugees in neighbouring Iran and Pakistan had made substantial progress. Following the signing of memorandums of understanding between both Governments, and between Afghanistan and UNAMA, the implementing partner, the International Organization for Migration, had begun to operate in both countries.

Security Council consideration (September). On 28 September [meeting 5045], the Security Council discussed the situation in Afghanistan. The Under-Secretary-General for Peacekeeping Operations, Mr. Guéhenno, said that the logistical preparations were on track for the 9 October polling date. Despite episodes of violence in Herat, which delayed the pre-election operations in western Afghanistan, the tensions in that part of the country had subsided, enabling the electoral preparations to resume despite the damage caused to the offices of UNAMA and JEMB during incidents on 12 September. Eighteen presidential and 36 vice-presidential candidates, including three women, had been campaigning in the presidential election since the official start of the campaign on 7 September. The Afghan Independent Human Rights Commission and UNAMA continued to monitor and report on the exercise of political rights throughout the country. JEMB had also accredited 11 national and international monitoring organizations, and 14 more were expected to be accredited before the elections. Despite a slow start, registration and voting preparations for Afghan refugees in Pakistan and Iran were under way. Efforts were being made to de-

fine with tribal and community leaders their role in local security arrangements on election day, particularly in the east, south-east and south, in view of the fact that security forces were thinly spread out throughout the country. The DDR process had gained some momentum due to the renewed commitment by the Ministry of Defence to implement the programme and efforts by the Ministry of Justice to apply the law establishing that political parties could be registered only if they severed links with militia forces.

Presidential elections

The Secretary-General reported in November [A/59/581-S/2004/925] that 10.5 million Afghans had registered to vote, 41 per cent of whom were women, for the presidential election, which was held on schedule on 9 October. Eighteen candidates, including one woman, contested the elections. Some 8,128,940 ballots were cast, representing 70 per cent of the registered voters. Polling also took place in Pakistan and Iran, where over 580,000 and 240,000 Afghan refugees, respectively, voted. The elections were followed by some 5,321 domestic and 121 international observers and monitors, 22,000 party agents and 52,000 agents of candidates, as well as national and international media. President Karzai was declared the winner with 55.4 per cent of the vote. He was followed by Yonous Qanooni, with 16.3 per cent, Haji Mohammad Mohaqeq, with 11.6 per cent, and Abdul Rashid Dostum, with 10 per cent, and the remaining 14 candidates, 6 per cent collectively. The candidates agreed to accept the election results.

Despite fears that the process might be attacked by anti-Government elements, no major security incidents occurred. A number of opposition candidates, however, raised allegations regarding the fairness of the process, including problems with the use of indelible ink to mark voters' thumbs and assertions of undue influence on voters by polling staff and candidates' representatives. Those opposition candidates issued an appeal midway through the polling for voters to boycott the ballot, which was largely ignored by voters. In the days after the ballot, most of the candidates who had called for a boycott continued to allege serious irregularities and called for the reopening of some polling centres and for their complaints to be investigated by an independent panel. JEMB requested UNAMA to nominate an independent panel of international electoral experts to investigate their complaints. The panel's report, made public on 2 November, found that the irregularities observed did not have a material impact on the overall outcome of the election.

Security Council consideration (October). On 12 October [meeting 5055], the Security Council discussed the situation in Afghanistan. The Assistant Secretary-General for Peacekeeping Operations, Mr. Annabi, said that the impressive participation, the enthusiasm and pride of women and men voting for the first time and the peaceful and orderly environment in which the electoral operation unfolded promised well for Afghanistan's journey towards democracy. The fact that the elections were not marred by violence was a tribute not only to the Afghan voters but also to the national army and police, who provided a safe environment with the assistance of the international security forces. The elections, of course, were not perfect, due to trouble experienced with the application of indelible ink, allegations of intimidation and other irregularities. Security conditions on election day exceeded expectations, though some incidents were reported. The presidential elections had helped to add momentum to disarmament efforts, for, by election day, more than 22,500 personnel had been disarmed and 2,780 serviceable heavy weapons had been disabled or cantoned. That corresponded to 33 per cent of estimated actual personnel targets and to 68 per cent of the heavy weapons target.

SECURITY COUNCIL ACTION (October)

On 12 October [meeting 5056], following consultations among Security Council members, the President made statement **S/PRST/2004/35** on behalf of the Council:

The Security Council welcomes the presidential election that took place on 9 October 2004 in Afghanistan, stresses its historic importance as a milestone in the political process, and congratulates the millions of Afghan voters, many of them women and refugees, who showed their commitment to democracy by participating in the first popular election of their Head of State. The Council welcomes further the broad political representation, as manifested by the 18 presidential candidates. The Council commends the Afghan National Police and the Afghan National Army for their role, with the assistance of the international security forces, in bolstering security during the election period.

The Council appreciates the effort of the Joint Electoral Management Body and the United Nations Assistance Mission in Afghanistan for their excellent achievement in the preparations for the presidential election. The Council appreciates the electoral management body's efforts to address any candidate's concerns and to further enhance the transparency of the electoral process, and looks forward to a final statement.

The Council urges the Government of Afghanistan, with the help of the international community, to continue to confront the challenges that remain in Afghanistan, including security, timely preparation of the parliamentary elections in April 2005, the reconstruction of institutions, the fight against narcotics, and the disarmament, demobilization and reintegration of Afghan militias.

The Council calls upon the Afghan authorities to plan and carry out without delay inclusive parliamentary elections, and calls upon the international community to support them in completing the electoral process set out in the Bonn Agreement.

The Council pledges its continued support for the Government and people of a sovereign Afghanistan as they rebuild their country, strengthen the foundations of constitutional democracy, and assume their rightful place in the community of nations, and calls upon the international community, with the United Nations in a central role, to support them in these efforts.

On 3 November, after the certification of the official electoral results by JEMB, Hamid Karzai was declared Afghanistan's first elected President.

Communications. On 1 October [A/59/425-S/2004/808], Turkey transmitted to the Secretary-General the final communiqué of the annual coordination meeting of the Ministers for Foreign Affairs of the States members of the Organization of the Islamic Conference (New York, 28 September), expressing their hope that the holding of the presidential elections on 9 October and parliamentary elections in April 2005 would pave the way towards the restoration of full democracy in Afghanistan. They also called on States to consider making donations to the Afghan People Assistance Fund.

Post-electoral phase

Security Council consideration (November). On 9 November [meeting 5073], the Security Council was briefed by the Under-Secretary-General for Peacekeeping Operations, Mr. Guéhenno, who said that attention had shifted to the post-election political phase, including the task of forming the next Government and the challenges of parliamentary and local elections. President Karzai had already identified security as the most important issue, especially the further disarmament of private military forces. Security, in fact, remained a significant concern. A suicide bombing carried out in Kabul on 23 October, in which two people lost their lives, signalled the end of the period of relative calm that prevailed during the presidential election. Parliamentary elections would be much more complicated and fraught with security concerns. There were five essential issues, in particular, that had to be resolved in order to hold parliamentary elections within the time frame prescribed by the electoral law: districts' boundaries—and in some cases provinces—had to be officially delimited; population figures had to be agreed upon for the assignment of parliamentary seats; the voters' list had to be analysed, refined and in some cases updated, in order to prepare specific voter lists for each polling station; a complaints mechanism and electoral offence prosecution system had to be developed at the local level; and the qualifications of potential candidates had to be vetted prior to their registration.

The parliamentary elections would inevitably be affected by local tensions and would be more susceptible to fraud and intimidation than were the presidential elections. For those reasons, the influence of local commanders, the widespread web of narcotics and arms and the absence of an efficient local civil administration constituted serious obstacles to holding legitimate elections in April 2005. The issue of irregular militias was also an emerging problem that needed to be tackled in advance of the next round of elections. The production and trafficking of illicit drugs also contributed to local insecurity and risked becoming a major impediment to holding credible parliamentary and local elections. The expansion of the formal security apparatus would be key to the success of those elections. In particular, the deployment of Afghan professional police was absolutely necessary for safe district elections. However, while domestic security forces would necessarily be called on to play a major role, international forces remained indispensable both in the direct provision of security and in backing up national efforts.

Report of Secretary-General (November). In his November report [A/59/581-S/2004/952] describing key political and humanitarian developments in Afghanistan, the Secretary-General observed that the major reason for the success of the electoral process was the desire of the Afghan people to ensure that it would succeed. That was a decisive indication that the Bonn process and the institutions that were being formed within it, had the backing of a large majority of the Afghan people. The successful presidential election redeemed the difficult decision by JEMB to separate presidential and parliamentary elections. The complexities avoided by postponing parliamentary elections allowed all actors to focus on carrying out the presidential elections as well as possible. Fulfilling the spirit of the Bonn Agreement required more than fulfilling the letter of its defined political process. In particular, much more needed to be achieved towards the fundamental goal of building the capacity of government at all levels and extending its authority to all parts of the country. That extension of authority was required in order to ensure the rule of law, the functioning of the legal economy, the practice of human and political rights and positive relations with neighbouring countries. The gradual handing over of functions to the Afghan Government was a positive indicator of progress made since 2001. The overall policy direction, and the planning of reconstruction, had been successfully taken over by the Afghan Government. The year ahead would present many challenges to the political and economic recovery of the country. For the first time, however, Afghanistan would face those challenges with a directly elected President endowed with a strong popular mandate. The United Nations remained committed to assisting the new Government as it continued to fulfil the letter and the spirit of the Bonn Agreement.

In a later report [A/59/744-S/2005/183], the Secretary-General said that, on 7 December, President Karzai was inaugurated, and the formation of the new 27-member Cabinet was announced on 23 December. The overall security situation remained relatively calm during the last months of 2004, due mainly to the severe winter season. However, coalition forces, the Afghan national army and government institutions continued to be targeted by extremist elements employing anti-tank mines, small unit ambushes and rocket attacks. A new law on money-laundering was adopted in late 2004.

GENERAL ASSEMBLY ACTION

On 8 December [meeting 69], the General Assembly adopted **resolution 59/112 A** [draft: A/59/L.44 & Add.1] without vote [agenda items 27 and 39 (d)].

The situation in Afghanistan and its implications for international peace and security

The General Assembly,

Recalling its resolution 58/27 A of 5 December 2003 and all its previous relevant resolutions,

Recalling also all relevant Security Council resolutions and statements by the President of the Council on the situation in Afghanistan, in particular the most recent resolutions 1536(2004) of 26 March 2004 and 1563(2004) of 17 September 2004, as well as statements by the President of the Council on 6 April and 15 July 2004 and 12 October 2004,

Reaffirming its strong commitment to the sovereignty, independence, territorial integrity and national unity of Afghanistan, and respecting its multicultural, multi-ethnic and historical heritage,

Applauding the adoption of a pluralistic and democratic constitution on 4 January 2004, the first direct election of a Head of State in the history of Afghanistan, on 9 October 2004, and the substantive progress achieved in the empowerment of women in Afghan politics as historic milestones in the political process, which will help to consolidate durable peace and national stability in Afghanistan,

Emphasizing the desirability of a new government being representative of the ethnic, cultural and geographical diversity of the country,

Recognizing the urgent need to tackle the remaining challenges in Afghanistan, including the lack of security in certain areas, terrorist threats, the comprehensive nationwide disarmament, demobilization and reintegration of Afghan militias, the timely preparation of the parliamentary and local elections scheduled for the spring of 2005, the reconstruction of institutions, the promotion and protection of human rights and the fight against narcotics,

Reaffirming in this context its continued support for the implementation of the provisions of the Bonn Agreement of 5 December 2001, and of the Berlin Declaration, including the annexes thereto, of 1 April 2004, and pledging its continued support thereafter for the Government and people of Afghanistan as they rebuild their country, strengthen the foundations of a constitutional democracy and assume their rightful place in the community of nations,

Expressing its appreciation and strong support for the ongoing efforts of the Secretary-General and his Special Representative for Afghanistan, and stressing the central and impartial role that the United Nations continues to play to promote peace and stability in Afghanistan,

Recognizing the need for a continued strong international commitment to humanitarian assistance and for programmes, under the ownership of the Government of Afghanistan, of rehabilitation and reconstruction, and noting that visible progress in this regard can further enhance the authority of the Government and greatly contribute to the peace process,

Expressing in this context its deep concern over attacks against Afghan civilians, United Nations staff, national and international humanitarian personnel and the International Security Assistance Force,

Noting that, despite improvements in building the security sector, terrorist attacks caused by Al-Qaida operatives, the Taliban and other extremist groups and the lack of security caused by factional violence and criminal activity, including the illicit production of and trafficking in drugs, still remain a serious challenge, threatening the democratic process as well as reconstruction and economic development,

Noting also that the responsibility for providing security and law and order throughout the country resides with the Government of Afghanistan, welcoming its continuing cooperation with the Assistance Force and the Operation Enduring Freedom coalition, and stressing the importance of extending central government authority to all parts of Afghanistan,

Commending the Afghan national army and police, the Assistance Force and the Operation Enduring Freedom coalition for their contributions in improving security conditions, including for the electoral process, in Afghanistan,

Commending also, among others, the countries neighbouring Afghanistan for the commitment they have shown to the Afghan presidential election, including their cooperation and support for the successful staging of out-of-country voting in the Islamic Republic of Iran and in Pakistan,

Welcoming the determination of the Afghan authorities to plan and carry out without delay parliamentary and local elections, scheduled for the spring of 2005,

Deeply concerned about the continued increase in the cultivation, production of and trafficking in narcotic drugs in Afghanistan, which is undermining stability and security as well as the political and economic re-

construction of Afghanistan and which has dangerous repercussions in the region and far beyond, and commending in this context the reaffirmed commitment of the Government of Afghanistan to rid the country of this pernicious production and trade, including by decisive law enforcement measures,

Recognizing that the social and economic development of Afghanistan, specifically the development of gainful and sustainable livelihoods in the formal productive sector, is an important condition for the successful implementation of the comprehensive Afghan national drug control strategy and depends to a large extent on enhanced international cooperation with the Government of Afghanistan,

1. *Welcomes* the report of the Secretary-General and the recommendations contained therein;

2. *Congratulates* the democratically elected Head of State of Afghanistan, the newly appointed Government of Afghanistan and millions of Afghan voters, who have participated in the first popular election of their Head of State;

3. *Stresses* the importance of the provision of sufficient security for the holding of credible parliamentary elections, and to this end calls upon Member States to contribute personnel, equipment and other resources to the International Security Assistance Force, thus assisting in securing the conduct of free and fair elections, including through the progressive establishment of provincial reconstruction teams in other parts of Afghanistan, and to coordinate closely with the United Nations Assistance Mission in Afghanistan and the Government of Afghanistan;

4. *Welcomes* the progress made since the commencement of the disarmament, demobilization and reintegration process in October 2003, including extensive demobilization and heavy weapons cantonment, and stresses the importance of addressing the issues of irregular militias and ammunition stockpiles and the need to substantially complete the process in a comprehensive manner throughout the country in accordance with the Bonn Agreement in order to create an environment more conducive to the conduct of free and fair parliamentary elections;

5. *Also welcomes* the development of the new professional Afghan national army and Afghan national police and the progress made in the creation of a fair and effective justice system as important steps towards the goal of strengthening Afghan government authority, providing security, ensuring the rule of law and eliminating corruption throughout the country, and urges the international community to continue to support the efforts of the Government of Afghanistan in these areas in a coordinated manner;

6. *Calls upon* the Government of Afghanistan, with the assistance of the international community, including through the Operation Enduring Freedom coalition and the Assistance Force, in accordance with their respective designated responsibilities, to continue to address the threat to the security and stability of Afghanistan posed by Al-Qaida operatives, the Taliban and other extremist groups, factional violence among militia forces and criminal violence, in particular violence involving the drug trade;

7. *Reiterates* the importance of the implementation of the timetable of the Joint Electoral Management

Body for parliamentary and local elections scheduled for the spring of 2005;

8. *Calls upon* the Assistance Mission to continue to provide the necessary support to the Government of Afghanistan in order to facilitate timely and inclusive parliamentary and local elections;

9. *Calls upon* the Assistance Mission and the Joint Electoral Management Body to provide sufficient training to the election personnel as well as voter and civic education, with a particular focus on women, before parliamentary and local elections;

10. *Calls upon* the Joint Electoral Management Body, with the assistance of the Assistance Mission, to provide budgetary targets for the elections, and urges the donor community to consider making further commitments to meet those targets in time;

11. *Calls upon* regional organizations and Member States to contribute to the conduct of free and fair parliamentary elections by providing international election monitors;

12. *Reiterates* the important role of the Afghan Independent Human Rights Commission in the promotion and protection of human rights and fundamental freedoms, and stresses the need to expand its range of operations in all parts of Afghanistan in accordance with the Afghan Constitution;

13. *Calls for* full respect for human rights and international humanitarian law throughout Afghanistan and, with the assistance of the Assistance Mission, full implementation of the human rights provisions of the new Afghan Constitution, including those regarding the full enjoyment by women of their human rights, and commends the commitment of the Government of Afghanistan in this respect;

14. *Welcomes* the efforts to date of the Afghan authorities to implement their comprehensive national drug control strategy adopted in May 2003, and urges the Government of Afghanistan to take decisive action, in particular to stop the processing of and trade in drugs, by pursuing the concrete steps set out in the work plan of the Government of Afghanistan, presented at the International Conference on Afghanistan, held in Berlin on 31 March and 1 April 2004;

15. *Calls upon* the international community to assist the Government of Afghanistan in the implementation of its comprehensive national drug control strategy, aimed at eliminating illicit poppy cultivation, including through support for increased law enforcement, interdiction, demand reduction, eradication of illicit crops, crop substitution and other alternative livelihood and development programmes, increasing public awareness and building the capacity of drug control institutions;

16. *Supports* the fight against the illicit trafficking in drugs and precursors within Afghanistan and in neighbouring States and countries along trafficking routes, including increased cooperation among them to strengthen anti-narcotic controls to curb the drug flow, and welcomes in this context the signing on 1 April 2004 of the Berlin Declaration on Counter-Narcotics within the framework of the Kabul Declaration on Good-neighbourly Relations of 22 December 2002;

17. *Commends* the continuing efforts of the signatories of the Kabul Declaration on Good-neighbourly Relations to implement their commitments under the Declaration, including, within this framework, those under the Declaration on Encouraging Closer Trade, Transit and Investment Cooperation, and furthermore calls upon all other States to respect and support the implementation of these provisions and to promote regional stability;

18. *Appreciates* the efforts of the members of the Tripartite Commission, namely, Afghanistan, Pakistan and the United States of America, to continue to address cross-border activities in accordance with its mandate;

19. *Calls for* the provision of continued international assistance to the vast number of Afghan refugees and internally displaced persons to facilitate their safe and orderly return and sustainable reintegration into society so as to contribute to the stability of the entire country;

20. *Requests* the Secretary-General to report to the General Assembly every six months during its fifty-ninth session on developments in Afghanistan, including after parliamentary elections, and on the future role of the Assistance Mission, and to report to the Assembly at its sixtieth session on the progress made in the implementation of the present resolution;

21. *Decides* to include in the provisional agenda of its sixtieth session the item entitled "The situation in Afghanistan and its implications for international peace and security".

On the same day, the Assembly adopted **resolution 59/112 B** on emergency international assistance for peace, normalcy and reconstruction of war-stricken Afghanistan (see p. 917).

On 23 December, the Assembly decided that the item on the situation in Afghanistan and its implications for international peace and security would remain for consideration at its resumed fifty-ninth (2005) session (**decision 59/552**).

Sectoral issues

Judicial system and the rule of law

The Afghan justice system suffered from weak management and communications among justice institutions, the absence of implementing legislation for organizing the system, and a lack of the required number of skilled staff and the need to build the capacities of existing staff. The process of reforming the justice sector, led by Italy, was based on two complementary efforts: strengthening political will and providing financial and technical assistance. The new Constitution had also introduced several changes to the judicial system, with the Supreme Court as the highest judicial organ in Afghanistan and its structure and administration well defined.

The decree on the reformed code of criminal procedure was issued in mid-February, providing a versatile system under which jurisdiction could be shifted to provincial courts from districts courts. On 21 February, a two-week training-of-trainers seminar was initiated with senor judicial and law enforcement personnel on the new criminal procedural code. A year-long training programme organized by the Judicial Reform Commission for young professionals was concluded and the International Development Law Organization continued to run courses for judges, prosecutors, defence lawyers and policemen. Other initiatives included the establishment of a department for the administration of juvenile justice within the Ministry of Justice and the start of a legal aid project. In the area of law reform, a juvenile code and by-laws for the new code of criminal procedure were being developed.

The physical facilities of the permanent justice institutions, including the Supreme Court, the Attorney General's office and the Ministry of Justice, were undergoing rehabilitation with UNDP support. Construction of provincial courts was under way in nine capitals, while the prioritization of district courts would be determined by the Provincial Stabilization Strategy.

Complementary to the justice reform effort was the rehabilitation of the correctional system, supported by the United Nations Office on Drugs and Crime (UNODC). Reform of the correctional system focused on Kabul, where UNODC completed the first round of rehabilitation and reconstruction of the male detention centre in February. Work was progressing on the main prison at Pol-e-Charki and the Kabul female detention centre. The Transitional Administration (TA) had devised a long-term redevelopment plan for reforming the national prison system. However, because of competing fiscal priorities facing the Government and the low level of donor support for the rehabilitation for the correctional system, very limited progress was made in that area. Progress was also hampered by a lack of coordination between the main justice institutions, the inroads by the drug mafia, the slow expansion of effective national security institutions, and interference by civil and military authorities in the administration of justice. A key reform was the transfer of prison administration from the Ministry of the Interior to the Ministry of Justice, which was reviewing a draft penitentiary law finalized by UNODC.

A total of 4,339 police officers, including border police, had been trained through the German Police Programme and United States training programmes. Police instruction was being conducted by Afghans, following the completion of the training-of-trainers programme. However, an insufficient number of trained and well-equipped police in the provinces was one of the major obstacles to the expansion of government authority. To redress the shortfall, seven regional police training centres were being established by the United States and were expected to be operational by the end of March. Support for the payment of police salaries was ongoing through the UNDP-managed Law and Order Trust Fund for Afghanistan. Some 19,500 police had by August received training. The target strength of the force provided for a core of the 47,500 national police, 12,500 border police and 2,500 highway police to be reached by the end of 2005.

International support for Afghanistan's police was reaffirmed and increased through the holding of a conference on police reconstruction in Afghanistan (Doha, Qatar, 18-19 May). The conference confirmed that $350 million in international resources would be earmarked for police programmes over the next few years. An immediate need was the provision of some $148.6 million in donor funding for the Law and Order Trust Fund for Afghanistan to cover salaries, equipment, institutional development and rehabilitation of police stations until 31 March 2005.

Security sector reform

Efforts were being made to accelerate the process of strengthening the newly created Afghan security institutions, which, together with their international counterparts, were developing mechanisms to ensure a holistic approach to security sector reform, in particular DDR; reforming and strengthening the justice sector (see p. 325); and combating illicit narcotics (see p. 327). Although further progress was made in the reforms of principal ministries, it was not enough after two years. The first two phases of the reform of the Ministry of Defence had been completed and the next phase commenced with the identification of candidates for the 700 third-tier positions. However, the prevalence of parallel military structures continued to impede the establishment of the national security forces.

Under the lead of the United States, assisted by France, the Afghan national army had been formed, with a strength of some 15,000 trained personnel in 18 battalions deployed around the country on security and "show of force" tasks. At full strength, it would consist of approximately 70,000 soldiers organized in five corps: the central corps in Kabul and four regional corps in Kandahar, Paktia, Herat and Balkh. The three brigades in the central corps were by November at full strength, with 15 battalions altogether. Plans were under way to develop the more technical elements of the corps, especially artillery, air defence and engineering. The process of establishing the regional corps, expected to take 5 to 7 years, had begun with the appointment on 1 September of four regional corps commanders and some key staff. The officer corps was being trained at the Command and General Staff College, which was formally inaugurated on 14 February. Measures had been implemented to address problems of recruitment and attrition. Attrition had been reduced from 15 per cent in November 2003 to 3 per cent per month, owing in part to improved living conditions, a campaign to attract back deserters and the increasing diversity of the armed forces.

The main accomplishment of the Afghan national army during the year was the provision of security for the presidential elections (see p. 321), which was an integral part of the nationwide security plan. It also provided security, in isolated cases, for the mobile disarmament units conducting the DDR programme, and was instrumental in separating the forces of Ismail Khan and his opponents in western Afghanistan during the conflict in August.

Disarmament, demobilization and reintegration

The voluntary DDR programme, under the leadership of UNDP and Japan, which began in October 2003, had two major components: the demobilization of soldiers from existing military units and the cantonment of heavy weapons. The programme showed some success but fell short of expectations. A review of pilot projects in Kondoz, Gardez, Mazar-e-Sharif and Kabul revealed shortcomings typical of such operations. A worrying pattern was the widespread extortion of demobilized soldiers by local commanders, which led the Afghan New Beginnings Programme to stop severance payments to soldiers as part of the overall reintegration package. The pilot projects also showed the need for more high-level political engagement to pave the way for more significant DDR. As at 6 March, only 5,373 ex-soldiers or officers had been demobilized. The commitment made at the Berlin Conference (see p. 315) was to achieve the DDR of no less than 40 per cent of the stated troop strength of 100,000 Afghan militia forces, as well as the cantonment of all heavy weapons under credible supervision by June, ahead of the 2004 elections. As at 31 July, the number of men who had turned in their weapons and entered the programme stood at some 12,245 or some 12 per cent of the militia forces' troop strength. Of the total number, some 10,380 had started their reintegration. To accelerate demobilization and disarmament, in July the President issued a decree identifying additional units to be demobilized prior to the elections and instructing the Ministries of Defence and of Finance to begin to apply financial sanctions in cases of non-compliance. By the end of September, an additional 5,480 soldiers had entered the programme. Over 20,000 soldiers had begun the process of reintegration.

The issue of irregular militias also needed to be addressed, since they were not in the programme but were increasingly responsible for insecurity in many parts of the country.

A survey of the cantonment process at the end of July showed that a total of 6,099 heavy weapons were recorded, with 1,657 deemed to be operational, 3,071 classified as reparable and 1,371 classified as unusable. Cantonment had started in Gardez, Kabul, Shiberghan and Mazar-e-Sharif. The problem of guarding the cantonment sites was yet to be resolved and that of the existence of large amounts of ammunition in many parts of the country was still to be addressed.

Counter-narcotics activities

The UNODC *Opium Survey 2004* indicated that opium cultivation increased by two thirds in 2004, reaching an unprecedented 131,000 hectares in all provinces. Afghanistan remained the world's largest opium producer, accounting for 75 per cent of global production. In 2003, the value of the crop in Afghanistan was about $2 billion to $3 billion, or 68 per cent of the country's gross domestic product. Economic dependency on poppy cultivation, limited law enforcement resources, corruption and the lack of an effective institutional framework for drug control added to the complexity of the situation. Narcotics were becoming an increasing threat to national security, social stability and governmental effectiveness. The burgeoning illicit drug trade was threatening reconstruction efforts and state-building in the country as well as long-term peace and stability in the region. It was undermining legitimate economic activities and the establishment of the rule of law, and was responsible for supporting factional agendas and anti-government elements, impeding DDR and promoting the development of private militias.

Against that background, efforts to combat illegal drugs continued. The narcotic drugs law, drafted by the Ministry of Justice and UNODC, came into force on 25 January, providing a robust legal framework for prosecuting drug-related offences. The Government, with support from coalition forces, had initiated a strategy to combat narcotics more robustly and conducted several interdiction operations. In addition, a Central Eradication Planning Cell was being established, with international support, to identify target districts for poppy eradication and to assess the effectiveness of the eradication campaign.

The international counter-narcotics conference on Afghanistan (Kabul, 8-9 February) facilitated discussion between key players in the provinces, the central Government and the international community. The conference identified among its priorities the mainstreaming of drug control into all development sectors, improvement of coordination across all principal ministries and donors, extending the counternarcotics police to priority regions and providing effective drug-awareness programmes and specialized skill-based training in drug abuse prevention.

In April, the Central Eradication Planning Cell launched an opium poppy eradication campaign in 16 opium-producing provinces. In addition, the Central Poppy Eradication Force, consisting of police officers from the Ministry of the Interior, began eradication activities in May, covering over 600 hectares of opium poppy in Wardak province. The Special Narcotics Force of the Ministry of the Interior, created in January to conduct interdiction operations, had been active also in the destruction of laboratories. Steps were also taken to improve coordination, with the setting up in May of a Counter-Narcotics Steering Group.

The Counter-Narcotics Directorate, previously under the National Security Adviser's office, was elevated to a full ministry. President Karzai convened a National Counter-Narcotics Jirga (9-10 December), with the participation of governors, security officials, elders, tribal and religious leaders and dignitaries from all Afghan provinces. Participants pledged to use their political, religious and social influence to combat cultivation, production and smuggling of illegal narcotics.

Communication (October). On 27 October [A/59/541-S/2004/873], Kazakhstan transmitted to the Secretary-General the text of the declaration of the Ministers for Foreign Affairs of the States members of the Conference on Interaction and Confidence-Building Measures in Asia, adopted at their ministerial meeting (Almaty, Kazakhstan, 22 October). The Ministers, among other things, called for a comprehensive strategy of international actions to counter the drug threat originating from Afghanistan.

Recovery, rehabilitation and reconstruction

While the Afghan Government had a coherent vision of its post-war reconstruction, its capacity remained weak in terms of public administration, institutions and ability to extend its development plans to provincial governments and to deliver essential public services. Many provincial governments remained semi-autonomous in relation to the central Government, particularly with regard to the remittance of tax revenue and the implementation of national laws at the provincial level. The uncertain security situation and the unchecked development of a parallel and illicit narco-economy exacerbated that weakness and seriously challenged further development.

However, the Government had made significant progress in meeting a number of the commitments contained in the Work Plan endorsed at the Berlin Conference (see p. 315). Benchmarks had been met in the areas of public administration, fiscal management and some aspects of private sector and economic and social development, but progress was slower in the rule of law, land management, disarmament and especially counter-narcotics. President Karzai, at a second meeting of the Afghanistan Development Forum (Kabul, 20-22 April), announced a series of new national priority programmes and made a commitment to overhaul the ministerial structure. The discussions facilitated the finalization of the development budget, approved by the Cabinet on 30 June, with total development expenditures targeted at $4.5 billion, of which $3.7 billion in funding had been identified.

The Priority Reform and Restructuring Decree continued to be the primary vehicle for reforming and modernizing the most critical functions of government. A critical measure of the Decree, which was helping effect reform of the bureaucracy, allowed ministries and other government entities to place key staff on an elevated pay scale for a fixed term. The next step called for extension of the process to provincial governments. The Government had also introduced an integrated framework for short-term capacity-building, which would allow key civil servants to be paid salaries comparable with rates paid to Afghan nationals employed by NGOs, enabling it to compete effectively for the best recruits. The Government also developed a mechanism for recruiting exceptionally qualified Afghans as long-term advisers and, through the Afghanistan Reconstruction Trust Fund, was able to hire international technical assistants for short-term technical, design and feasibility studies.

The Government began to put in place a legal framework to ensure that civil servants were accountable for the execution of their duties. The proposed public finance and expenditure management law imposed specific penalties on any civil servant who used his or her position for material gain or who otherwise abused it. The proposed procurement law was expected to include similar provisions. The draft civil service law would include a code of conduct specifying conflict-of-interest rules and other provisions to increase accountability and transparency. The Government appointed a new Anti-Corruption Commissioner. Reforms to the Auditor-General's office and Attorney-General's office, however, needed greater support if those offices were to be effective.

The National Solidarity Programme, one of several national priority programmes, continued to make progress. Over 4,300 community development councils were elected by secret ballot and $12 million in block grants disbursed to them. A number of the implementing NGOs were experiencing severe security constraints, which had slowed down the implementation of Programme projects.

A high-level conference on regional economic cooperation (Bishkek, Kyrgyzstan, 10-12 May), supported by UNDP, discussed public and private sector assistance initiatives and how the region could contribute to Afghanistan's economic growth, focusing in particular on efforts to reduce trade barriers, improve transport infrastructure and streamline border bottlenecks. The declaration adopted by the conference stressed the importance of regional cooperation for Afghanistan's recovery and the stability of the region. The declaration also urged donor support, especially for private sector development, through the establishment of an export and investment guarantee fund. The Government of Afghanistan hosted the Second Economic Cooperation Organization Regional Trade and Investment Conference in Kabul from 18 to 20 April, with 1,000 participants, including high-level officials and delegates. The Conference noted Afghanistan's potential for sustainable investment and trade.

The underlying strategy of UN relief, recovery and reconstruction efforts since the signing of the Bonn Agreement (see p. 311) was to move from the direct implementation of projects to supporting the Government's own development plans. Between May and October, the UN country team, with the Government, NGOs, donor communities and international institutions, conducted Afghanistan's first common country assessment of the country's development challenges in the areas of institutional development and governance, peace, security and justice, economic development and growth, and social well-being.

Communications. The heads of State of the members of the Central Asian Cooperation Organization (Kazakhstan, Kyrgyzstan, Tajikistan, Uzbekistan) (Astana, Kazakhstan, 28 May) [A/58/838-S/2004/432], noted that the consolidation of peace in Afghanistan and the establishment of good-neighbourly relations with that country were in keeping with the fundamental interests of the Central Asian countries. Joint efforts to restore Afghanistan's economy and infrastructure would contribute to ensuring regional security and stability. The members also reaffirmed their desire to involve Afghanistan in the region's integration process.

On 25 June [A/58/849-S/2004/520], in identical letters to the Secretary-General and the Council President, Turkey transmitted the text of the Istanbul Declaration adopted by the Islamic Conference of Foreign Ministers at its thirty-first session (see below), reaffirming, among other things, the Conference's support for Afghanistan's rebuilding process.

Bishkek Conference

The Islamic Conference of Foreign Ministers, at its thirty-first session (Istanbul, Turkey, 14-16 June) [A/58/856-S/2004/582 & Corr.1], adopted a resolution on the situation in Afghanistan, in which Ministers, among other things, commended the constructive efforts of the United Nations and welcomed the convening of an international conference in Bishkek in May (see above) to discuss regional economic cooperation.

The high-level international conference "Afghanistan and Regional Economic Cooperation: Central Asia, Iran and Pakistan", organized by UNDP (Bishkek, 10-12 May) [A/59/163-S/2004/585], adopted the Bishkek Declaration, by which participants recognized the leading role of the United Nations and the Government of Afghanistan in organizing international assistance to the Afghan people and in the reconstruction of the country. They confirmed their readiness to participate in programmes for the reconstruction of Afghanistan, to provide humanitarian, technical and advisory services and to facilitate private sector initiatives. They urged donors, international financial institutions and humanitarian organizations to increase their participation in the comprehensive revival of the Afghan State.

Social aspects

The human rights situation in Afghanistan was a continuing source of serious concern. In the north, north-east and west, commanders acted with impunity and were seen by many as responsible for a wide range of repressive activities. The role of local authorities in carrying out violations was particularly worrisome. The reappointment of confirmed human rights violators to government posts compounded the problem. In April, the Secretary-General appointed an independent expert on human rights in Afghanistan to develop a programme of advisory services to ensure full respect for and protection of human

rights and to help prevent human rights violations.

There were continuing reports of trafficking,
kidnapping and smuggling of children, and their
subsequent deportation from countries of destination. With support from the United Nations
Children's Fund, the Government had begun to
address the problem and to formulate a national
plan of action on combating child trafficking.

In certain areas of the country, strong social
and cultural norms continued to limit women's
public role, and conservative ideologues denied
them their rights. Health and educational services were unevenly and insufficiently available.
Institutional mechanisms to address those issues,
including the Ministry of Women's Affairs, were
weak.

However, some progress was made to strength-
en the position of women in the country, including through the newly adopted Constitution (see
p. 311), which had a number of provisions securing the political participation of women. At the
Berlin Conference (see p. 315), the Government
stated its commitment to increase the number of
women in the civil service.

As at 20 May, UNHCR had facilitated the return
of 156,426 individual refugees to Afghanistan in
2004. Of those, 116,400 came from Pakistan and
39,897 from Iran. Since the operation began in
March 2002, a total of 2,432,127 individuals had
been repatriated. The Government estimated
that at least 2.5 million to 3 million Afghans were
still outside the country, in addition to approximately 200,000 internally displaced persons
based in the south and west of the country.

UNAMA

The United Nations Assistance Mission in Afghanistan was established by Security Council
resolution 1401(2002) [YUN 2002, p. 264] to promote, among other tasks, national reconciliation
and the responsibilities entrusted to the United
Nations under the Bonn Agreement. It comprised the Office of the Special Representative,
which included four special advisers in the cross-
cutting fields of human rights, demobilization,
gender and the rule of law, as well as three sub-
components: two substantive pillars, one political
(Pillar I) and one relief, recovery and reconstruction (Pillar II), and an administrative component.
UNAMA was headquartered in Kabul, with re-
gional offices in Bamiyan, Gardez, Herat,
Jalalabad, Kandahar, Kunduz and Mazar-e-
Sharif and three sub-offices in Faizabad,
Maimana and Panjao. UNAMA was headed by the
Special Representative of the Secretary-General.
In February, the Secretary-General appointed
Jean Arnault (France) as Special Representative

and Head of UNAMA to replace Lakhdar Brahimi
(Algeria) (see p. 311). By **resolution 1536(2004)**
(see p. 313), the Security Council extended
UNAMA's mandate until 26 March 2005.

International Security Assistance Force

During the year, the Secretary-General submitted to the Security Council, in accordance
with resolutions 1386(2001) [YUN 2001, p. 267] and
1510(2003) [YUN 2003, p. 310], reports on the activities of ISAF, covering the periods November 2003
to February 2004 [S/2004/222], February to May
[S/2004/537] and May to August [S/2004/785]. Activities from August to the end of the year were covered in a later report [S/2005/131].

As at 31 December 2004, the Force, a multinational force operating under NATO leadership,
comprised 9,000 personnel from 26 NATO
nations and 10 non-NATO countries.

ISAF continued to implement its activities mandated by Council resolution 1386(2001) to assist
the Afghan Government in the maintenance of
security in Kabul and its surrounding areas and
by resolution 1510(2003) to provide support for
and to strengthen the ability of the Government
to provide a more secure environment throughout the country. It executed its framework
security tasks in association with the Afghan national army and the Kubul police. As a result of
suicide attacks on 27 and 28 January, two ISAF soldiers were killed and six others severely
wounded. ISAF provided security for the Constitutional Loya Jirga, which concluded on 4 January (see p. 311), and supported the voter registration process in Kabul. The ISAF-assisted DDR
pilot project was completed on 29 January and
discussions were ongoing with the Afghan Ministry of Defence to assess how best to maintain the
momentum created so that a smooth transition
could be achieved to a more substantial DDR. It
initiated a heavy weapons cantonment programme in Kabul and its environs on 15 January.
It also remained active in security sector reform,
continued to support the training of the Afghan
national army and the national police and assisted in the counter-narcotics programme. On
1 June, ISAF assumed responsibility for the operation of the military part of Kabul's international
airport, and in July expanded its mandate to nine
provinces, known as area north, outside Kabul
and its environs. On 23 July, the NATO Council
decided to deploy two battalions to augment ISAF
forces during the presidential elections (see
p. 321). During the election period, ISAF participated in the Afghan electoral management structure and provided limited support to international observers and to the Joint Electoral
Management Body, including the handling of in-

coming election material and providing flights between Kabul and Pakistan and Iran to move the ballot papers of Afghans in refugee camps. From August, ISAF took over new provincial reconstruction teams at Pol-e-Khumri and Feyzabad. It was increasing its training and development activities in support of the Afghan national army and would organize, with UNAMA, legal training sessions for Afghan administrative and judicial personnel. ISAF civil-military cooperation was shifting its focus from quick-reaction projects and short-term assessments to a more long-term vision aimed at meeting requirements of the Afghan national priority programme and harmonizing its activities with those of the international community.

Extension of ISAF mandate

On 17 September [meeting 5038], the Security Council unanimously adopted **resolution 1563 (2004)**. The draft [S/2004/742] was prepared in consultations among Council members.

The Security Council,

Reaffirming its previous resolutions on Afghanistan, in particular resolutions 1386(2001) of 20 December 2001, 1413(2002) of 23 May 2002, 1444(2002) of 27 November 2002 and 1510(2003) of 13 October 2003,

Reaffirming its strong commitment to the sovereignty, independence, territorial integrity and national unity of Afghanistan,

Reaffirming its resolutions 1368(2001) of 12 September 2001 and 1373(2001) of 28 September 2001, and reiterating its support for international efforts to root out terrorism in accordance with the Charter of the United Nations,

Recognizing that the responsibility for providing security and law and order throughout the country resides with the Afghans themselves, and welcoming the continuing cooperation of the Afghan Transitional Administration with the International Security Assistance Force,

Reaffirming the importance of the Bonn Agreement of 5 December 2001 and the Berlin Declaration of 1 April 2004, and recalling in particular annex I to the Bonn Agreement which, inter alia, provides for the progressive expansion of the Force to other urban centres and other areas beyond Kabul,

Stressing the importance of extending central government authority to all parts of Afghanistan, of conducting free and fair elections, of comprehensive disarmament, demobilization and reintegration of all armed factions, of justice sector reform, of security sector reform, including reconstitution of the Afghan National Army and Police, and of combating narcotics trade and production, and recognizing certain progress that has been made in these and other areas with the help of the international community,

Recognizing the constraints upon the full implementation of the Bonn Agreement resulting from concerns about the security situation in parts of Afghanistan, in particular in the light of the upcoming elections,

Welcoming, in this context, the commitment by lead nations of the North Atlantic Treaty Organization to establish further Provincial Reconstruction Teams, as well as the readiness of the Force and the Operation Enduring Freedom Coalition to assist in securing the conduct of national elections,

Expressing its appreciation to Eurocorps for taking over the lead from Canada in commanding the Force, and to Canada for its leadership of the Force during the past year, and recognizing with gratitude the contributions of many nations to the Force,

Determining that the situation in Afghanistan still constitutes a threat to international peace and security,

Determined to ensure the full implementation of the mandate of the Force, in consultation with the Afghan Transitional Administration and its successors,

Acting for these reasons under Chapter VII of the Charter,

1. *Decides* to extend the authorization of the International Security Assistance Force, as defined in resolutions 1386(2001) and 1510(2003), for a period of twelve months beyond 13 October 2004;

2. *Authorizes* the Member States participating in the Force to take all necessary measures to fulfil its mandate;

3. *Recognizes* the need to strengthen the Force, and in this regard calls upon Member States to contribute personnel, equipment and other resources to the Force, and to make contributions to the Trust Fund established pursuant to resolution 1386(2001);

4. *Calls upon* the Force to continue to work in close consultation with the Afghan Transitional Administration and its successors and the Special Representative of the Secretary-General, as well as with the Operation Enduring Freedom Coalition in the implementation of the mandate of the Force;

5. *Requests* the leadership of the Force to provide quarterly reports on the implementation of its mandate to the Security Council through the Secretary-General;

6. *Decides* to remain actively seized of the matter.

Sanctions

In 2004, the Security Council adopted new measures against Osama bin Laden, Al-Qaida, the Taliban, their associates and associated entities. By resolution 1526(2004) (see p. 332), the Council further refined the financial measures, travel ban and arms embargo imposed on those persons identified in the consolidated list created pursuant to resolution 1267(1999) [YUN 1999, p. 265] and also sought to improve the list. In addition to further strengthening the mandate of the Sanctions Committee, the Council established an Analytical Support and Sanctions Monitoring Team (the Monitoring Team) to report on the implementation of the measures by States and to recommend further action for consideration by the Council.

Communication (January). On 9 January [S/2004/10], Switzerland transmitted to the Council President its comments on the December 2003 report of the Monitoring Group on Afghanistan

[YUN 2003, p. 314], whose mandate expired on 17 January 2004.

Security Council consideration. At the Council's 12 January meeting [meeting 4892] to consider the threats to international peace and security caused by terrorist acts, the Chairman of the Security Council Committee established pursuant to resolution 1267(1999) (the Al-Qaida and Taliban Sanctions Committee) provided an oral assessment, pursuant to Council resolution 1455 (2003) [YUN 2003, p. 311], of the implementation by Member States of the measures included in the consolidated list maintained by the Committee, which constituted the fourth 90-day report on the work of the Committee and its Monitoring Group. He also reported on missions conducted in October and December 2003 to 10 countries in the Arabian Gulf, West Asia and South-East Asia.

In reviewing the reports submitted by States, the Chairman said that, although many States had taken positive steps, including the adoption of special legislation, to curb the financing of Al-Qaida's activities, a number of areas needed improvement, such as the freezing of assets other than bank accounts, cash flows to finance terrorist activities, full implementation of the travel ban, and the arms embargo, the most difficult to implement because of national security concerns. He suggested that to improve the implementation of the travel ban the list should be improved and the technical capacity of States increased. As to the arms embargo, he suggested that it needed to be defined in a more specific and targeted way, including the mention of specific goods and materials, and to strengthen cooperation at the regional and international levels to avoid the diversion of weapons and dangerous material to Al-Qaida.

The Chairman reported that to date a total of 93 reports had been submitted under resolution 1455(2003), with 98 States or 51 per cent not having submitted a report. That seriously hampered the Committee in accomplishing its task. The Committee, in analysing the possible reasons why States had not submitted reports, identified a possible lack of political will, reporting fatigue, a lack of resources and technical capacity, and coordination difficulties at the national level. In addition, some States might have considered the submission guidelines to be too detailed, and in some cases inapplicable to their situation.

SECURITY COUNCIL ACTION (January)

On 30 January [meeting 4908], the Security Council unanimously adopted **resolution 1526(2004)**. The draft [S/2004/79] was prepared in consultations among Council members.

The Security Council,

Recalling its resolutions 1267(1999) of 15 October 1999, 1333(2000) of 19 December 2000, 1363(2001) of 30 July 2001, 1373(2001) of 28 September 2001, 1390 (2002) of 16 January 2002, 1452(2002) of 20 December 2002 and 1455(2003) of 17 January 2003,

Underlining the obligation placed upon all Member States to implement, in full, resolution 1373(2001), including with regard to any member of the Taliban and Al-Qaida, and any individuals, groups, undertakings and entities associated with the Taliban and Al-Qaida, who have participated in the financing, planning, facilitating and preparation or perpetration of terrorist acts or in supporting terrorist acts, as well as to facilitate the implementation of counter-terrorism obligations in accordance with relevant Security Council resolutions,

Reaffirming the need to combat by all means, in accordance with the Charter of the United Nations and international law, threats to international peace and security caused by terrorist acts,

Noting that, in giving effect to the measures in paragraph 4 (b) of resolution 1267(1999), paragraph 8 (c) of resolution 1333(2000) and paragraphs 1 and 2 of resolution 1390(2002), full account is to be taken of the provisions of paragraphs 1 and 2 of resolution 1452 (2002),

Reiterating its condemnation of the Al-Qaida network and other associated terrorist groups for ongoing and multiple criminal terrorist acts, aimed at causing the deaths of innocent civilians and other victims and the destruction of property, and greatly undermining stability,

Reiterating its unequivocal condemnation of all forms of terrorism and terrorist acts,

Stressing to all States, international bodies and regional organizations the importance of ensuring that resources are committed, including through international partnership, to meet the ongoing threat that Al-Qaida and members of the Taliban, and any individuals, groups, undertakings and entities associated with them, represent to international peace and security,

Acting under Chapter VII of the Charter,

1. *Decides* to improve, as set out below, the implementation of the measures imposed by paragraph 4 (b) of resolution 1267(1999), paragraph 8 (c) of resolution 1333(2000) and paragraphs 1 and 2 of resolution 1390 (2002) with respect to Osama bin Laden, members of Al-Qaida and the Taliban and other individuals, groups, undertakings and entities associated with them, as referred to in the list created pursuant to resolutions 1267(1999) and 1333(2000) ("the Committee list"), namely:

(a) To freeze without delay the funds and other financial assets or economic resources of those individuals, groups, undertakings and entities, including funds derived from property owned or controlled, directly or indirectly, by them or by persons acting on their behalf or at their direction, and ensure that neither these nor any other funds, financial assets or economic resources are made available, directly or indirectly, for the benefit of such persons by their nationals or by any persons within their territory;

(b) To prevent the entry into or the transit through their territories of those individuals, provided that nothing in the present paragraph shall oblige any State to deny entry into or require the departure from its territories of its own nationals and that the present paragraph shall not apply where entry or transit is necessary for the fulfilment of a judicial process, or the Committee determines on a case-by-case basis only that entry or transit is justified;

(c) To prevent the direct or indirect supply, sale or transfer to those individuals, groups, undertakings and entities from their territories or by their nationals outside their territories, or using their flag vessels or aircraft, of arms and related materiel of all types, including weapons and ammunition, military vehicles and equipment, paramilitary equipment and spare parts for the aforementioned, and technical advice, assistance, or training related to military activities;

and recalls that all States shall implement the measures with respect to listed individuals and entities;

2. *Decides also* to strengthen the mandate of the Security Council Committee established pursuant to resolution 1267(1999) ("the Committee") to include, in addition to the oversight of the implementation by States of the measures referred to in paragraph 1 above, a central role in assessing information for review by the Council regarding effective implementation of the measures, as well as in recommending improvements to the measures;

3. *Decides further* that the measures referred to in paragraph 1 above shall be further improved in eighteen months, or sooner if necessary;

4. *Calls upon* States to move vigorously and decisively to cut the flows of funds and other financial assets and economic resources to individuals and entities associated with Al-Qaida, Osama bin Laden and/or the Taliban, taking into account, as appropriate, international codes and standards for combating the financing of terrorism, including those designed to prevent the abuse of non-profit organizations and informal/alternative remittance systems;

5. *Urges* all States and encourages regional organizations, as appropriate, to establish internal reporting requirements and procedures on the trans-border movement of currency based on applicable thresholds;

6. *Decides*, in order to assist the Committee in the fulfilment of its mandate, to establish for a period of eighteen months a New York–based Analytical Support and Sanctions Monitoring Team ("the Monitoring Team") under the direction of the Committee, with the responsibilities enumerated in the annex to the present resolution;

7. *Requests* the Secretary-General, upon adoption of the present resolution and acting in close consultation with the Committee, to appoint, consistent with United Nations rules and procedures, no more than eight members, including a coordinator, of the Monitoring Team, who demonstrate expertise in one or more of the following areas related to activities of Al-Qaida and/or the Taliban, including counter-terrorism and related legislation; financing of terrorism and international financial transactions, including technical banking expertise; alternative remittance systems, charities and use of couriers; border enforcement, including port security; arms embargoes and export controls; and drug trafficking;

8. *Requests* the Monitoring Team to submit, in writing, three comprehensive, independent reports to the Committee, the first by 31 July 2004, the second by 15 December 2004 and the third by 30 June 2005, on im-

plementation by States of the measures referred to in paragraph 1 above, including concrete recommendations for improved implementation of the measures and possible new measures;

9. *Requests* the Secretary-General to provide cost-effective support, as needed by the Committee, in the light of the increased workload entailed by the present resolution;

10. *Requests* the Committee to consider, where and when appropriate, visits to selected countries by the Chairman and/or Committee members to enhance the full and effective implementation of the measures referred to in paragraph 1 above, with a view to encouraging States to comply fully with the present resolution and resolutions 1267(1999), 1333(2000), 1390 (2002) and 1455(2003);

11. *Also requests* the Committee to follow up via oral and/or written communications with States regarding effective implementation of the sanctions measures and to provide States with an opportunity, at the request of the Committee, to send representatives to meet with the Committee for more in-depth discussion of relevant issues;

12. *Further requests* the Committee, through its Chairman, to report orally to the Council in detail at least every one hundred and twenty days on the overall work of the Committee and the Monitoring Team, including a summary of progress by States in submitting the reports referred to in paragraph 6 of resolution 1455(2003) and any follow-up communications with States regarding additional requests for information and assistance;

13. *Requests* the Committee, based on its ongoing oversight of implementation by States of the measures referred to in paragraph 1 above, to prepare and to circulate to the Council within seventeen months of the adoption of the present resolution a written analytical assessment on implementation of the measures, including States' successes and challenges in implementing them, with a view to recommending further measures for consideration by the Council;

14. *Requests* all States, and encourages regional organizations, relevant United Nations bodies and, as appropriate, other organizations and interested parties to cooperate fully with the Committee and the Monitoring Team, including by supplying such information as may be sought by the Committee pursuant to the present resolution and resolutions 1267(1999), 1333 (2000), 1390(2002), 1452(2002) and 1455(2003), to the extent possible;

15. *Reiterates* the need for close coordination and concrete exchange of information between the Committee and the Security Council Committee established pursuant to resolution 1373(2001) ("the Counter-Terrorism Committee");

16. *Reiterates* to all States the importance of proposing to the Committee the names of members of Al-Qaida and the Taliban or individuals associated with Osama bin Laden and other individuals, groups, undertakings and entities associated with them for inclusion in the Committee list, unless to do so would compromise investigations or enforcement actions;

17. *Calls upon* all States, when submitting new names to the Committee list, to include identifying information and background information, to the greatest extent possible, that demonstrates the association

of the individuals and/or entities with Osama bin Laden or with members of Al-Qaida and/or the Taliban, in line with the guidelines of the Committee;

18. *Strongly encourages* all States to inform, to the extent possible, individuals and entities included in the Committee list of the measures imposed on them, and of the guidelines of the Committee and resolution 1452(2002);

19. *Requests* the Secretariat to communicate to Member States the Committee list at least every three months to facilitate implementation by States of the measures on entry and travel imposed by paragraph 2 (b) of resolution 1390(2002), and further requests that the Committee list, whenever amended, be automatically conveyed by the Secretariat to all States and regional and subregional organizations for the inclusion, to the extent possible, of listed names in their respective electronic databases and relevant border enforcement and entry/exit tracking systems;

20. *Reiterates* the urgency for all States to comply with their existing obligations to implement the measures referred to in paragraph 1 above and to ensure that their domestic legislative enactments or administrative measures, as appropriate, permit the immediate implementation of those measures with respect to their nationals and other individuals or entities located or operating in their territory, and with respect to funds, other financial assets and economic resources over which they have jurisdiction, and to inform the Committee of the adoption of such measures, and invites States to report the results of all related investigations and enforcement actions to the Committee, unless to do so would compromise the investigations or enforcement actions;

21. *Requests* that the Committee seek from States, as appropriate, status reports on the implementation of the measures referred to in paragraph 1 above concerning listed individuals and entities, specifically with respect to the aggregate amounts of the frozen assets of the listed individuals and entities;

22. *Requests* all States that have not yet done so to submit to the Committee by 31 March 2004 the updated reports called for in paragraph 6 of resolution 1455(2003), following as closely as possible the guidance document previously provided by the Committee, and further requests all States that have not submitted those reports to explain in writing to the Committee by 31 March 2004 their reasons for non-reporting;

23. *Requests* the Committee to circulate to the Council a list of those States that have not submitted by 31 March 2004 reports pursuant to paragraph 6 of resolution 1455(2003), including an analytical summary of the reasons put forward by States for non-reporting;

24. *Urges* all States and encourages relevant international, regional and subregional organizations to become more directly involved in capacity-building efforts and to offer technical assistance in areas identified by the Committee, in consultation with the Counter-Terrorism Committee;

25. *Decides* to remain actively seized of the matter.

Annex

In accordance with paragraph 6 of resolution 1526(2004), the Analytical Support and Sanctions Monitoring Team shall operate under the direction of the Security Council Committee established pursuant to resolution 1267(1999) and shall have the following responsibilities:

— To collate, assess, monitor and report on and make recommendations regarding implementation of the measures; to pursue case studies, as appropriate; and to explore in depth any other relevant issues as directed by the Committee;

— To submit a comprehensive programme of work to the Committee for its approval and review, as necessary, in which the Monitoring Team should detail the activities envisaged in order to fulfil its responsibilities, including proposed travel;

— To analyse reports submitted pursuant to paragraph 6 of resolution 1455(2003) and any subsequent written responses provided by States to the Committee;

— To work closely and share information with Counter-Terrorism Committee experts to identify areas of convergence and to help facilitate concrete coordination between the two Committees;

— To consult with States in advance of travel to selected States, based on its programme of work approved by the Committee;

— To consult with States, including through engaging in regular dialogue with representatives in New York and in capitals, taking into account comments from States, especially regarding any issues that might be contained in the reports of the Monitoring Team referred to in paragraph 8 of resolution 1526(2004);

— To report to the Committee, on a regular basis or when the Committee so requests, through oral and/or written briefings on the work of the Monitoring Team, including on its visits to States and its activities;

— To assist the Committee in preparing its oral and written assessments to the Council, in particular the analytical summaries referred to in paragraphs 12 and 13 of resolution 1526(2004);

— Any other responsibility identified by the Committee.

Sanctions Committee activities

The Al-Qaida and Taliban Sanctions Committee submitted a report [S/2004/1039] covering its activities from 1 January to 31 December 2004. During that period, the Committee held three formal meetings and 36 informal consultations at the expert level.

The Security Council, in resolution 1526(2004) (see above), created a new, more demanding conceptual and substantive framework for the Committee's future activities on an 18-month basis, by clearly defining the mandatory sanctions measures, including the freezing of financial assets, the travel ban and the arms embargo, to be applied by States, individuals and entities referred to in the Committee's consolidated list. It also strengthened the Committee's central role in monitoring and assessing information for the Council's review regarding the effectiveness of the measures and in recommending improvements, by establishing, for a period of 18 months, an Analytical Support and Sanctions Monitoring Team under the Committee's direction. The Council also emphasized the need for dialogue between the Committee and Member States.

Those measures, in addition to enhanced cooperation with the Council's Counter-Terrorism Committee, and increased contact with relevant specialized international bodies, such as Interpol, allowed the Committee in 2004 to move to a qualitatively higher level in implementing its mandate, in particular in monitoring the implementation of the sanctions measures by States.

To cover the new conditions introduced by the Council in resolutions 1455(2003) [YUN 2003, p. 311] and 1526(2004), the Committee revised the guidelines adopted in 2002 for the conduct of its work. It continued to update its consolidated list of individuals and entities associated with Al-Qaida and the Taliban, adding 29 individuals and 15 entities, and approved extensive technical corrections to the list on the basis of information provided by Member States. The Committee established a list of focal points similar to the one used by the Counter-Terrorism Committee (see p. 76), with more than 300 contact points. The contact list became operational at the end of 2004. The Committee continued to consider notifications and/or requests for exceptions to the sanctions measures, which increased compared to 2003, although the sums notified were quite low. It also considered the recommendations submitted by the Monitoring Team in its first and second reports (see p. 336) with the aim of agreeing on follow-up action.

Report of Sanctions Committee (April). Pursuant to resolution 1526(2004), the Sanctions Committee Chairman transmitted to the Council President, on 27 April, a list [S/2004/349] of those States that had not submitted by 31 March 2004 reports pursuant to paragraph 6 of resolution 1455(2003), as well as an analytical summary of the reasons put forward by States for non-reporting.

By 31 March, the Committee had received 123 reports from Member States pursuant to resolution 1455(2003) and 15 letters from States pursuant to resolution 1526(2004) explaining their reasons for non-reporting. The number of States which had neither reported nor explained their reasons for non-reporting totalled 53. Most of the written explanations from non-reporting States cited a lack of resources, rendering it difficult to submit the reports in a timely manner. The Committee believed that a proper analysis of the reasons for non-reporting could not be conducted on the basis of only 15 responses. The Monitoring Team was requested to contact a number of rep-

resentatives of non-reporting States to assist them in providing the information needed. The Committee Chairman was also requested to report to the Council in May, at which time he would give a reassessment of the reasons given by States for non-reporting.

Security Council consideration (May). On 25 May [meeting 4976], the Security Council discussed threats to international peace and security caused by terrorist acts. The Chairman of the Al-Qaida and Taliban Sanctions Committee, Heraldo Muñoz, presented his first oral assessment of the overall work of the Committee and the Monitoring Team, summarized States' progress in implementing the sanctions measures and addressed communications with States regarding additional requests for information and assistance.

Mr. Muñoz said that the Committee, at the initiative of some members, had started discussing definitions of terms used in resolution 1526 (2004) and other relevant resolutions, particularly the definition of the freezing of funds or other financial assets or economic resources, with the purpose of providing more clarity and precision to the Committee's monitoring functions and to Member States in their implementation efforts. The Monitoring Team began its work in April and had since submitted to the Committee an initial work plan and was preparing its first report and an analysis of all reports submitted under resolution 1455(2003). The Team was designing a new database that would include information on the implementation of Al-Qaida and Taliban-related sanctions. It was also working to maximize the impact of the consolidated list by correcting entries, seeking improvements to the identifiers, encouraging States to contribute names, analysing why States were reluctant to submit names and looking at specific incidents of cross-border funding of Al-Qaida-associated terrorists.

The Team carried out a preliminary assessment of the sanctions implementation, based on 43 reports submitted by Member States. According to the reports, many States did not incorporate the sanctions measures in their domestic legislation or administrative rules, considering their existing laws sufficient to deal with all forms of terrorism. However, that did not always appear to be supported by the facts, especially with regard to the freezing of financial assets and economic resources. Some States argued that special laws to implement the measures were not needed and only a few stated their intention to amend their laws. For the purpose of assets freezing, the consolidated list continued to have a limited distribution in most States, usually being made available only to banks. Most States reported new regulations governing charities, including requirements for licensing or registration, proper record-keeping of all transactions and audited accounts. In some States, charities were subjected to inspection to ensure compliance with their charters, while in others they were examined for tax liability. The majority of States did not provide any information on efforts to regulate alternative remittance systems. As to the travel ban, most States had integrated the consolidated list into their border-control systems, but only a few were able to do so electronically or in a way that allowed immediate research and regular and timely updates. Concerning the arms embargo, although most States appeared to have adequate regulations to deal with the illegal acquisition or retention of conventional and unconventional arms, many reported not having taken any specific measures to implement the arms embargo or to enact legislation aimed specifically at Al-Qaida and the Taliban.

The Committee Chairman led a mission to Algeria, Senegal, Spain and Tunisia (1-8 May) in order to engage in a dialogue, to learn from the experiences of the countries visited and to understand their preoccupations and concerns. An issue discussed in all countries was the need for cooperation and information-sharing among States. He also discussed new ways in which terrorist organizations raised funds, including the use of legitimate or illegitimate commercial means such as owning import-export companies. Other issues discussed included the tracing of money, control over non-governmental and other civil organizations, the freezing of assets, reporting on the transborder movement of currency, the arms embargo and the consolidated list. Among its recommendations, the mission suggested increased cooperation among Member States and information-sharing, and addressing questions such as poverty reduction, employment and education in the fight against terrorism. There continued to be a need for assistance in a number of countries. Awareness had to be raised on the impact of terrorist financing through kidnappings and commercial enterprises used for raising or transmitting funds.

With regard to the reasons for the non-submission of reports, the Commitee Chairman said that the Monitoring Team had contacted a number of non-reporting States to seek further clarification. The Team found that many States lacked a clear understanding of the differences between the scope of the Committee's work and that of the Counter-Terrorism Committee, considering the reports they had submitted to the latter sufficient for satisfying their reporting obligations to the Committee. The Team also found a lack of supervision and coordination mechanisms at the national level, delays in governmental processes and a lack of information exchange between ministries and departments.

Monitoring Team

The Analytical Support and Sanctions Monitoring Team (the Monitoring Team), established by Security Council resolution 1526(2004) (see p. 332), had the mandate of collating, assessing, monitoring, reporting on and making recommendations regarding the implementation of measures imposed in that resolution.

On 15 March [S/2004/207], the Secretary-General informed the Council President of the appointment of eight members of the Monitoring Team. Richard Barrett (United Kingdom) was appointed Coordinator. On 31 March [S/2004/264] and 24 September [S/2004/759], the Secretary-General informed the Council President of the appointment of two new experts of the Monitoring Team to replace two original experts who were unable to assume their functions.

Report of Monitoring Team (August). Pursuant to Council resolution 1526(2004), the Sanctions Committee Chairman, on 23 August [S/2004/679], transmitted to the Council President the first report of the Monitoring Team. The report noted that Al-Qaida had evolved into a global network of groups without any organizational structure but held together by a set of overlapping goals, whose leaders had tried to distort the basic Muslim duty of Jihad to justify terrorist campaigns. Perceived injustices and images of violent confrontation had ensured a steady flow of new supporters. The sanctions, aimed at curbing the Taliban and Al-Qaida terrorism, had achieved less than was hoped for, partly because they addressed a set of circumstances that no longer applied, and partly because effective sanctions were hard to design, let alone impose, against the new form of Al-Qaida-associated terrorism. While the sanctions against the financing of terrorism had had some effect, and some millions of dollars of assets had been frozen, there was a need to update them, based on the new methods used by Al-Qaida to raise and transfer money. There was a similar need to improve the consolidated list, the travel ban and the arms embargo to reflect Al-Qaida's new methodology.

As at July, 130 Member States had submitted reports on the implementation of resolution 1455(2003). While many reported action taken against Al-Qaida, few offered specific details or referred directly to those named on the consolidated list. Only 19 States had recorded the presence of any individual or entity associated with Al-Qaida inside their borders, although the true number was most certainly higher. Thirty-four States reported freezing assets, though in some cases it had been difficult to discern what that really entailed, what those assets were, their value or ownership. No State had reported stopping anyone on the consolidated list from travelling, or taking action against them in respect of the arms embargo.

The most important reason for the limited impact of the sanctions was that the Council had reacted to events, while Al-Qaida had shown great flexibility and adaptability in staying ahead of them. Moreover, the structure of Al-Qaida had evolved into a loose network of affiliated underground groups with certain common goals, and it would always be difficult to design and enforce sanctions against diverse groups of individuals who were not in one location, could adopt different identities and who needed no special equipment to launch their attacks.

The impact and the credibility of the Council's work against Al-Qaida and the Taliban depended on the content and utility of the consolidated list. Twenty-one States had submitted names for inclusion on the list, which comprised 143 individuals and one entity associated with the Taliban, and 174 individuals and 111 entities associated with Al-Qaida. The number of contributors to the list suggested that many States were reluctant to provide names. The list could only be truly useful if it achieved international acceptance as a register of the key components of the Al-Qaida network. In the absence of an agreed definition of terrorism, the list provided the only consensus on what Al-Qaida comprised. Apart from its relevance, a further key factor governing the utility of the list was its accuracy. Technical and practical problems with the list included the lack of basic identifiers for many entries, such as date of birth, nationality and passport information, making enforcement action virtually impossible, and inconsistencies and inaccuracies in the spelling and transliteration of names. Though the Sanctions Committee had issued a reformatted version of the list in 2003 [YUN 2003, p. 312], the Monitoring Team called for further technical correction to about one third of all entries and recommended that, where names were too vague to allow effective application, they should be removed from the list until sufficient detail was available. The Team had also requested the 80 Member States that had either submitted names or had some connection to individuals on the list to examine the entries for accuracy and completeness. A further issue that needed resolution was the procedure for removing a name from the list. The Team, among other things, recommended that there should be an agreed process for notifying the Sanctions Committee when someone on the list was detained, and for sharing internationally any useful information.

As a result of national and international action, Al-Qaida's funding had decreased significantly, but so too had its need for money. Nevertheless, Al-Qaida still needed to raise and move money; a legal basis for freezing assets related to Al-Qaida, the Taliban and associated groups still existed in all but three Member States. The Team was concerned that many States had merely amended anti-money-laundering legislation to cover terrorist crime as well. As terrorist-related financial transactions generally took place before the crime occurred, States would encounter problems when applying to terrorist financiers measures designed to deal with the proceeds of crime. Successes in countering terrorist financing would also encourage Al-Qaida and its associates to seek alternative means to raise and move their assets in ways that were less open to scrutiny, and adaptable to local circumstances, such as using the trade in counterfeit currency in Somalia, exploiting the potential for credit card fraud in Western Europe and the Asia/Pacific region, and benefiting from the drug trade in Afghanistan and North Africa. There were some 32 international and regional organizations working to establish standards and policies to combat terrorist financing. The most comprehensive regulatory regimes were those in greatest compliance with standards set by the Financial Action Task Force's (FATF's) 40 recommendations on anti-money-laundering and eight special recommendations on counter-terrorist financing [YUN 2001, p. 68]. However, FATF did not attract universal support and could not by itself achieve a properly supervised global regime for the financial sector. Over 90 States had set up financial intelligence units, which analysed suspicious transaction reports submitted by banks and other entities as part of national efforts against money-laundering and counter-terrorist financing. The Team recommended that Member States circulate the consolidated list beyond their banks to non-bank financial institutions and to any non-financial entities where assets might be held.

There was potential also for the abuse of alternative remittance systems, such as hawala, by Al-Qaida-associated terrorists, but few States had reported action to regulate them. As to the Council's urging in resolution 1526(2004) that all States establish internal reporting requirements and procedures on the transborder movement of currency, initial research by the Team showed that although States had regulations governing the transborder movement of currency by individuals, there was no universal standard on the amounts to be declared. The movement of relatively large amounts of cash was not remarkable and attracted little scrutiny. Al-Qaida's exploitation of charities and other non-profit organizations as a way to raise and move money had led some States to introduce licensing and better regulation of those bodies.

Most Member States believed that they had achieved effective implementation of the Al-Qaida/Taliban arms embargo by incorporating its measures into existing legislation. However, most Al-Qaida-related terrorist attacks had involved arms and explosives not covered by those measures. The difficulty of ensuring an effective arms embargo on Al-Qaida was self-evident. However, Member States could restrict the scale of Al-Qaida-associated terrorism by impeding their access to larger weapons systems, and restricting their ability to construct non-conventional bombs designed to cause mass casualties. There was evidence that Al-Qaida remained interested in acquiring the means to construct bombs that could disperse a chemical, biological or radiological pollutant. Al-Qaida-related groups had tried at least twice to buy the basic ingredients for a so-called dirty bomb and a good deal of the necessary technical knowledge was available on the Internet.

In view of the Taliban's and Al-Qaida's proven ability to adapt and to evade the measures imposed by the Council, and considering the porous nature of most borders, it was not surprising that the implementation of the travel ban appeared to have little or no effect on their activities. The ability of the terrorists to acquire identity documents and to avoid border controls exceeded the capability of many Member States to impose effective restrictions. The Team noted the need for better distribution internationally of information on stolen or lost travel documents, and for the introduction of border control systems linked to databases that made use of forged documents more difficult. Ultimately, there should be an extensive international database of forensic information on Al-Qaida-associated terrorists to include DNA and fingerprints to help States uncover the real identity of suspects stopped at borders.

The Monitoring Team, among other things, provided an analysis of why 65 Member States had failed to report by the extended deadline of 31 March 2004, as requested under Council resolutions 1455(2003) [YUN 2003, p. 311] and 1390(2002) [YUN 2002, p. 281]. The Team observed that the lack of a report from a State did not necessarily denote any lack of will to produce one or a lack of commitment to international efforts against Al-Qaida and the Taliban, but some Member States just lacked the capacity to produce a report. There was a particular need for some States to bring their national agencies responsible for counter-terrorism into the reporting process. As at 31 July, of those States listed as non-reporting in May 2004, four had subsequently submitted reports and a further eight had undertaken to do so as soon as possible.

The Monitoring Team aimed to consult a wide range of national authorities directly engaged in the fight against terrorism in order to develop ideas as to what further measures the Council might consider. The Team had already visited a number of Member States, including Afghanistan and Pakistan.

Security Council consideration (September). At the Security Council's 13 September meeting [meeting 5031] to discuss threats to international peace and security caused by terrorist acts, the Chairman of the Sanctions Committee, Mr. Muñoz, briefed the Council on the Monitoring Team's first report (see above). The Committee had discussed an informal document presented by its Chairman on non-mandatory measures contained in resolution 1526(2004). Such measures were recognized as important for the implementation of the sanctions regime, as they provided ideas as to how States might further enhance their counter-terrorism efforts. The Committee, among other things, revised the guidelines for the conduct of its work, added names of new individuals and entities to the consolidated list, and established an active working relationship with the Counter-Terrorism Committee.

The Monitoring Team provided the Committee with support in promoting the effective implementation of relevant resolutions, assessed the impact of the measures detailed in those resolutions and made recommendations as to how those measures might be made more effective. The Committee stressed that there were no quick fixes, short-cuts or easy remedies to the threat posed by international terrorism. Rather, the task required systematic, persistent and exacting work, accompanied by constant analysis of what had been carried out.

Report of Sanctions Committee (December). Pursuant to Council resolution 1455(2003) [YUN 2003, p. 311], the Sanctions Committee Chairman, on 16 December [S/2004/1037], transmitted to the Council President a written assessment of the actions taken by States to implement the measures in paragraph 1 of that resolution (the travel ban, arms embargo and assets freeze targeting individuals and entities belonging to or associated with the Taliban and Al-Qaida). On 15 October, the Monitoring Team, at the Committee's request, provided an analysis of all the States' reports received pursuant to resolution 1455(2003), which was annexed to the written assessment. The analysis pointed out that there were different levels of implementation of measures by States. Some States had technical, financial and human resources potential and had demonstrated their willingness and readiness to prevent and neutralize possible terrorist activities, but remained vulnerable to Al-Qaida's increasingly sophisticated operational activities. Other States had sufficient potential to take all necessary measures to prevent terrorist acts, but had not demonstrated in their reports that they had done so. Some States had provided implementation reports in which they admitted difficulties caused, among other things, by limitations in their implementation capacities. In addition, almost one third of all States had not submitted a report. The Committee presumed that most non-reporting States lacked the capacity to do so, but was unaware of what kind of assistance they required. Those States were urged to submit their reports no later than 31 December 2004.

Most reporting States made appropriate use of the Committee's list and were also advancing in their capacity to implement the assets freeze. However, steps such as regulating the activities of non-banking financial entities, cash couriers and charities had yet to be implemented in a number of countries. The implementation of the travel ban continued to be a concern for the Committee, since, in the five years it had been in place, not a single individual was reported to have been stopped at a border as a consequence of being on the Committee's list. Some States had problems disseminating list updates to all relevant border checkpoints and consular offices. As with the travel ban, no cases of enforcement of the arms embargo had been reported to the Committee. Furthermore, little information on legislation and enforcement measures had been provided by Member States.

The reports submitted by Member States had provided the Committee with valuable information on the level of implementation of sanctions measures, issues of concern, questions relating to the use of the list and, to some extent, needs for assistance. Together with other means of communication, those reports allowed the Committee to improve the sanctions measures on a regular basis and to focus its work on pertinent issues.

Security Council consideration (December). On 17 December [meeting 5104], during the Security Council's discussion of threats to international peace and security caused by terrorist acts, the Chairman of the Sanctions Committee presented his third oral assessment on the Committee's activities covering the period since his last report. The Committee had reviewed the Monitoring Team's first report (see p. 336) and its recommendations. It also received two specialized briefings: one on how Al-Qaida operations had evolved over the past few years, and the other on the workings of Interpol and ways to enhance cooperation between Interpol and the Committee.

The Committee also sought to engage Member States in a more active dialogue. Towards that end, the Committee Chairman continued to conduct trips to a number of countries where he discussed the implementation of the sanctions. Some States raised concerns about the quality of the consolidated list, while others expressed frustration with what they saw as Western double standards in the fight against terrorism, pointing to the protection of perceived terrorists under the guise of refugee law and sometimes even support for organizations that those countries considered to be terrorist groups. Many States underlined the need for regional and subregional cooperation aimed at enhancing capacities in the fight against terrorism. The Committee's priorities remained its list and the identification of possible improvements to the sanctions measures. The Committee had shifted its focus from comprehensive reporting of State implementation to active dialogue with Member States.

Iraq

Situation in Iraq

In 2004, the United Nations, through the Secretary-General's Special Adviser for Iraq, Lakhdar Brahimi, and the United Nations Assistance Mission for Iraq (UNAMI), continued to assist Iraq to achieve a successful transition to democratic governance, the establishment of democratic institutions, and reconstruction and reconciliation in the context of Security Council resolution 1483(2003) [YUN 2003, p. 338].

On 19 January, the Secretary-General convened a meeting in New York with the Governing Council of Iraq and the Coalition Provisional Authority (CPA). On the same day, the Security Council held a private meeting [meeting 4897], during which it had a constructive exchange of views with the Chairman of the Iraqi Governing Council, Adnan Pachachi.

The Security Council President, in his assessment of the Council's work for the month of January [S/2004/524], said that the Iraqi Governing Council Chairman reported on progress achieved in the country and the remaining problems, and requested the Secretary-General to send a mission to Iraq to determine the feasibility of holding direct elections at an early date. The Secretary-General subsequently decided to dispatch a fact-finding mission to Iraq, led by his Special Adviser.

Communications (January/February). By a 26 January letter to the Council President [S/2004/84], the League of Arab States transmitted a summary of the proposals and projects presented by the Arab organizations and funds, as well as the conclusions of the second meeting of the Arab Specialized Organizations and Financial Institutions on Assisting Iraq (Amman, Jordan, 6 January). Representatives of Arab States, organizations, funds and financial institutions participated in the meeting, along with representatives of the United Nations, the World Bank, the International Monetary Fund, the Saudi Fund for Development and the Union of Arab Investors. The meeting produced recommendations affirming the importance of effective participation in the international efforts to assist Iraq and of the establishment of a mechanism for cooperation comprising the Iraqi, Arab and international actors involved in the reconstruction of Iraq.

On 18 February [S/2004/121], Kuwait transmitted to the Secretary-General and the Council President the final communiqué of the Fifth Conference of the Ministers for Foreign Affairs of States Neighbouring Iraq (Bahrain, Egypt, Iran, Iraq, Jordan, Kuwait, Saudi Arabia, Syria and Turkey) (Kuwait City, 14-15 February). The Ministers re-emphasized the principle of non-interference in Iraq's internal affairs and stressed the right of the Iraqi people to freely determine their future. They reaffirmed the importance of enhancing the role of the United Nations so that it could assume its central responsibilities throughout the transitional process in Iraq. They welcomed the Secretary-General's establishment of an advisory group consisting of representatives of States neighbouring Iraq as well as Security Council members. They also welcomed all relevant Council resolutions, especially 1511(2003) [YUN 2003, p. 348], which called for a timetable for the transfer of power to the Iraqi people and also on the United Nations to facilitate the transfer of power by 30 June 2004 as agreed by the Transitional Governing Council of Iraq and CPA. The Ministers condemned terrorist acts against civilians, Iraqi policemen and security forces, humanitarian and religious institutions, and international organizations and diplomatic missions operating in Iraq. The Ministers condemned the killing of Kuwaiti and Iranian prisoners of war and third-country nationals by the previous regime. They also com-

mended the decision of the Iraqi people to bring the leaders of the previous regime, particularly the former President of Iraq, to justice and to try them for their crimes against humanity. Finally, they welcomed the Secretary-General's decision to dispatch an assessment team to Iraq (see below).

Fact-finding mission (February)

The fact-finding mission visited Iraq from 6 to 13 February. Its terms of reference called for an assessment of the feasibility of holding direct elections before 30 June, a determination of the time frame and conditions required for conducting credible elections consistent with UN principles and practices, and whether there were other options for representing the will of the Iraqi people within the time frame of the 15 November 2003 agreement [YUN 2003, p. 350], acceptable to all parties and guaranteeing a transparent and inclusive mechanism.

The report, transmitted by the Secretary-General [S/2004/140], stated that the fact-finding mission held wide-ranging discussions, met with a cross-section of Iraqis, including political, religious and tribal leaders. On the basis of those discussions, the mission was able to develop an understanding of the political environment and recent political developments related to the ongoing debate on the governance transition and to form an opinion on specific issues. There was near unanimous agreement that the United Nations should act as a facilitator of the process, providing technical assistance and helping form a consensus on the various issues.

The mission took place against the background of the political developments arising from the 15 November 2003 agreement on the political process to accelerate the transfer of sovereignty from CPA to an Iraqi administration by the end of June 2004. That agreement set out the conditions for the dissolution of CPA, with a new transitional assembly and provisional government assuming power. However, key Iraqi figures, including the Governing Council itself and a number of political and religious groups, opposed the caucus-style process suggested for choosing the transitional assembly. Many, including Ayatollah Sistani, demanded direct general elections and claimed that it was possible to organize a reasonably credible election before 30 June. There was therefore a deadlock over the issue of direct elections versus the caucus-style process prescribed in the 15 November agreement. At the end of long discussions with the mission at both the political and technical levels, a consensus emerged that it would be extremely difficult and even hazardous to try to organize general elections before 30 June and that the caucus system was not a viable option. However, as indicated in the technical report appended to the main report, elections would need a minimum preparation time of about eight months after the legal framework had been completed. If the required political consensus was reached fairly rapidly, it would be possible to hold elections by the end of 2004. Several other options were explored, including extending the existing Governing Council. Many Iraqis stressed that new initiatives were urgently needed to rebuild trust, promote inclusion and explore new options. Others affirmed that the way out of the impasse was for the United Nations to assist the Iraqis in building consensus on a political framework that would produce a road map for the governance transition and assist in the establishment of a transitional government to bring that to fruition.

The mission concluded that Iraq faced the difficult task of finding institutions capable of channelling political contestation into legitimate directions. Iraqis were eager to move to a new chapter in their history by finding political solutions to their problems through consensus-building. The challenges of working out a legitimate political process leading to a democratically elected government were enormous, as were establishing security throughout the country, building trust with the Iraqi people, drafting a constitution and building consensus among different Iraqi factions. Iraqis believed that the sooner an Iraqi government was in place the better, and that there should be no delay in the restoration of Iraqi sovereignty. There appeared to be an emerging consensus that a provisional government would need to be formed by 30 June through some mechanism other than direct elections.

The mission, in its recommendations, said that a consensus existed in Iraq that elections were a necessary step in the process of building democratic governance and reconstruction, but credible elections could not take place by 30 June. Preparations would need at least eight months after a legal institutional framework had been established. Agreement on the electoral legal framework should be reached as soon as possible so that preparations for establishing the various operational modalities could begin. The mission was told that a political agreement on the legal framework could be reached by May, paving the way for elections by the end of 2004 or shortly thereafter. The United Nations recommended that an autonomous and independent Iraqi Electoral Commission should be established, with financial and human resources being made available so that it could begin planning and preparing the process in a timely manner. Many Iraqis

agreed that a single elected assembly should be chosen through elections held by the end of 2004 or shortly thereafter, with the dual functions of drafting a constitution and acting as the principal law-making body or legislature. There was also consensus that the 30 June deadline for the transfer of sovereignty to a provisional government should be maintained. The United Nations would be willing to assist in building consensus among Iraqis on the specific powers, structure and composition of such a provisional governance body and the process through which it could be established, and provide advisory services and technical assistance towards the establishment of an electoral legal framework. Security remained of paramount importance, both for the success of those processes and for UN participation. Discussions were already under way with the Governing Council and CPA; those discussions needed to be intensified to complete arrangements for expanding UN activities in Iraq.

The Secretary-General, in his transmittal letter, said that the fact-finding mission facilitated the emergence among Iraqis of a wide measure of agreement on the need for direct national elections, to be prepared and held under optimal technical, security and political conditions. There remained, however, a number of outstanding questions, including the choice of a transitional mechanism that would enjoy the broadest support among Iraqi constituencies and how to implement such a mechanism.

Further political developments

Security Council consideration (February). On 24 February [meeting 4914], the Security Council discussed the situation between Iraq and Kuwait.

The United States representative, in updating the Council on developments in Iraq, said that the Transitional Administrative Law to govern Iraq during its transition to full democracy, with the establishment of a duly elected government under a permanent constitution, was nearing completion. Iraqis were working with each other and the international community to map their own political future and the number of Iraqis contributing to the security effort had virtually doubled. Saddam Hussein was in custody and would undergo due process for crimes committed against the Iraqi people and humanity. However, difficult and significant challenges remained. Former regime loyalists, foreign fighters and international terrorists continued to attack police stations, religious gatherings and schools, and had also directed their efforts against CPA partners, NGOs and the United Nations itself. The campaign of terror also targeted critical infrastructure throughout Iraq. Many nations had stepped forward to assist in the rebirth of Iraq. As President George W. Bush had stressed, the United Nations had a vital role to play in Iraq both before and after 1 July. The Iraqi people, the United Nations and CPA supported the transfer of sovereignty by 30 June and direct national elections as soon as practical thereafter.

Since Saddam Hussein's arrest in December 2003, the number of attacks against multinational force troops had decreased, although attacks on both Iraqi security forces and civilians had increased. In spite of that, the determination of the Iraqi people to assume primary responsibility for their own security remained undeterred. The Iraqi Civil Defence Corps had more than doubled in size, to approximately 25,000 personnel, since December 2003. The Corps performed a range of duties, including fixed site security, convoy route security, patrols, cordons and checkpoints establishment. The number of Iraqi armed forces personnel had also more than doubled to approximately 3,500 personnel, 2,000 of whom had been trained while the remaining 1,500 were in training. The Iraqi police force totalled about 75,000 personnel, and the border police and immigration and customs inspectors had grown to approximately 23,000. Troops deployed from 35 countries participating in the multinational force were also supporting the Iraqi people. New and renewed contributions represented the international community's commitment to improving Iraq's future.

On the issue of governance, the United States representative said that the broad framework of the political process would be underpinned by the work under way within the Iraqi Governing Council to draft a Transitional Administrative Law, the basis for the Iraqi transitional government until a permanent constitution was ratified. The United States also welcomed the UN fact-finding mission's report (see above). The mechanism for governing Iraq between the transfer of sovereignty and the national elections remained to be worked out. The Iraqi people, the Governing Council, CPA and the United Nations would work to reach agreement on a transition mechanism that would have the broad-based support of the Iraqi people. With the oil-for-food programme terminated, the World Food Programme was assisting CPA and the Iraqi Ministry of Trade with procurement and logistics assistance necessary to keep the public distribution system supplied with food-basket goods. Shipments of food and other humanitarian supplies were managed by the newly established Coordination Centre, jointly staffed by Iraqi and Coali-

tion officials. The Centre's role was to ensure the steady, secure and managed flow of remaining oil-for-food goods and newly procured goods. The Ministry of Trade would take complete control of procurement on 1 April and would assume full responsibility for all aspects of the programme on 1 July.

On the disarmament of Iraq, the Iraq Survey Group continued its search for weapons of mass destruction (WMDs), prohibited missile-delivery systems and related infrastructure. The Survey Group had discovered clear evidence that Saddam Hussein's regime hid WMD programme activities from the United Nations Monitoring, Verification and Inspection Commission (UNMOVIC), and concluded that Iraq was in violation of previous Security Council resolutions. To meet the tasks ahead, the Survey Group maintained a sizeable number of specialists dedicated to interviewing individuals connected with Iraq's WMD programmes; obtaining and analysing documents, computer hard drives and other materials; and assessing and exploiting potential WMD-related sites. Some Iraqis were cooperating in that effort, thought fear of reprisal was inhibiting cooperation by others. Some officials with close ties to the previous regime seemed determined to avoid cooperating in any way. In addition, document analysis had been obstructed by the destruction of documents and computers in the immediate post-conflict period.

The United Kingdom representative reported that progress was continuing on the provision of basic services, economic and reconstruction issues and human rights and justice. The focus was on rehabilitation of water and sanitation networks, including Baghdad's sewage plants. Power generation had improved to a February average of 4,260 megawatts, and long-term repairs and scheduled maintenance were being undertaken throughout the country to build a sustainable power grid. Key bridges were also being rebuilt. Progress was also being made in health and education. A key focus was the establishment of a sound economic framework and a transparent public expenditure system. The Central Bank law had been enacted, granting it full independence. The balance of the Development Fund for Iraq totalled $8.8 billion as at 12 February. To date, total disbursements from the Fund amounted to $3.2 billion. On 7 February, the International Advisory and Monitoring Board and CPA agreed on the statement of work for the independent public accountant to audit the sale and export of Iraqi oil.

Efforts were also made to create new jobs, as unemployment levels remained very high. The national employment programme and the additional employment programme in the northern governorates had so far created close to 110,000 jobs out of a target of 155,000 new public work jobs.

In coordination with CPA, the Iraqi Ministry of Justice had developed strategies and activities to ensure the establishment or reconstruction of basic Iraqi criminal justice facilities.

France said that the deadline of 30 June should not simply mark, in legal terms, the end of the occupation regime. It had to lead to a genuine restoration of Iraqi sovereignty and therefore to a genuine handover of authority and resources to the Iraqis. The United Nations would most likely be called on to be involved with the Iraqis, who wanted to see a robust involvement by the Organization in all areas. The United Nations would require a clear and specific mandate that would guarantee its independence and take into account its new circumstances. A new Council resolution would be necessary to support the restoration of Iraqi sovereignty and to support or define new arrangements.

Communication of Secretary-General (March). On 18 March [S/2004/225], the Secretary-General reported to the Council President that he had received letters from the Interim President of the Iraqi Governing Council, Mohammed Bahr Al-Uloom, and from the CPA Administrator, L. Paul Bremer, informing him that, on 8 March, the Governing Council had adopted the Transitional Administrative Law, an important step towards the establishment of an independent, democratic State. The Governing Council invited the United Nations to Iraq to assist with both the formation of the Interim Government, to which sovereignty would be transferred on 30 June, and in the preparations for national direct elections, scheduled to be held before the end of January 2005. CPA supported that request and assured the Secretary-General of its cooperation in providing the security required for the United Nations to carry out those missions.

In view of the Governing Council's request, the Secretary-General asked his Special Adviser, Mr. Brahimi, and his team and an electoral assistance team to return to Iraq as soon as possible.

SECURITY COUNCIL ACTION (March)

On 24 March [meeting 4930], following consultations among Security Council members, the President made statement **S/PRST/2004/6** on behalf of the Council:

> The Security Council welcomes the Secretary-General's letter dated 18 March 2004 and the exchange of letters with Dr. Mohammed Bahr Al-Uloom, President of the Governing Council of Iraq for the month of March 2004, and Mr. L. Paul Bre-

mer III, Administrator of the Coalition Provisional Authority.

> The Council also welcomes and strongly supports the decision of the Secretary-General to dispatch to Iraq his Special Adviser Mr. Lakhdar Brahimi and his team, as well as an electoral assistance team, as soon as possible, in order to lend assistance and advice to the Iraqi people in the formation of an interim Iraqi government to which sovereignty will be transferred on 30 June 2004, as well as in the preparations for direct elections to be held before the end of January 2005.

> The Council calls upon all parties in Iraq to cooperate fully with these United Nations teams and welcomes the security and other support provided to them by the Governing Council and the Coalition Provisional Authority.

Security Council consideration (16 April). The Security Council discussed the situation between Iraq and Kuwait on 16 April [meeting 4944], during which it was briefed by the United States representative on the situation in Iraq. He said that threat elements continued to challenge all those who were working for a better Iraq. The violence, which included ambush and mutilation as well as riots and attacks, was perpetrated by three groups: insurgents including former regime loyalists, terrorists who had infiltrated Iraq and militias affiliated with radical elements. The multinational force, which comprised 24,000 personnel from over 30 countries, had conducted the full spectrum of military operations, which ranged from the provision of humanitarian assistance, civil affairs and relief and reconstruction activities to the detention of those who were threats to security. It searched for weapons that threatened Iraq's stability, gathered intelligence and carried out offensive combat operations. The force also performed or assisted in many humanitarian and reconstruction activities and in the area of local governance.

One of the key long-term objectives of the multinational force and a major challenge was to recruit, train and equip Iraqi security forces in preparation for their assumption of the responsibility for maintaining security and enforcing the rule of law. The force had made significant progress in "standing up" Iraqi security forces. Despite the increase in attacks targeting Iraqi forces, Iraqis continued to join and the multinational force was working to build professional entities to provide a stabilizing influence. As at the beginning of April, some 200,000 members of Iraq's security forces were either on duty or in training.

The United States was committed to working with the international community to ensure that the security needs of the United Nations were met, both before and after 30 June. It continued to work with a UN team of security experts in

Iraq to establish a strong relationship with the multinational force to facilitate the return of international UN personnel. With UN support, the United States had begun to solicit force contributions for the protection of a broad-based UN mission, whose role would be further defined by Council action. Operating as part of the multinational force, such forces would be dedicated solely to providing security for UN personnel and facilities.

The end of the occupation and the assumption of governing authority by the Iraqi Interim Government on 30 June would mark the beginning of a new era for the Iraqi people. Mr. Brahimi had consulted with a wide range of Iraqis during April and had made preliminary recommendations for the transition process, which the United States looked forward to hearing about in greater detail (see below). CPA's commitment to Iraq would continue well beyond 30 June, nonetheless. The transfer of sovereignty would not bring total calm to Iraq, and the multinational force would be needed to continue to support Iraq's security forces until they could assume sole responsibility for the security and stability of their country.

UN team visit to Iraq (April)

On 27 April [meeting 4952], the Council was briefed by the Secretary-General's Special Adviser, Mr. Brahimi, who led a team of political advisers in Iraq from 4 to 15 April to assist and advise the Iraqi people in the formation of an Interim Government to which sovereignty would be transferred on 30 June. Concurrently with his visit, a UN electoral mission also visited Iraq to support and advise on the preparations for direct elections to be held before the end of January 2005. Mr. Brahimi said that the security situation remained extremely worrying with an atmosphere of great tension and anxiety in the face of the siege of Fallujah by coalition forces, the Mahdi army's uprising in the south and the general increase in violence throughout the country. Hopes for a peaceful resolution to the stand-off in Fallujah had not yet materialized. On 22 April, staff of UNAMI, based in Amman, received a delegation from Fallujah, which claimed that several hundred of Fallujah's inhabitants had died and that well over 1,000 had been wounded. The United Nations was not in a position to verify those figures or the cause of death and injury, but there was little doubt that many lives had been lost and much suffering endured by civilians. The same was true of the precarious and complicated situation in Najaf and Karbala, two of the holiest cities for Shi'a in Iraq. Despite the prevailing insecurity situation, which affected its visit,

the UN team was able to meet with a large cross-section of Iraqis. A key question was whether a credible political process was even viable under such circumstances. According to Mr. Brahimi, there was, in fact, no alternative but to find a way of making the process viable and credible. There was a dialectical link between security on the one hand, and the end of occupation, the restoration of sovereignty and independence and the advent of a legitimate Iraqi Government and political regime on the other. Security was essential for the process to be completed, and the sooner a credible Iraqi Government was in place the better. Virtually every Iraqi with whom the UN team met urged that there be no delay in bringing an end to the occupation, even though they understood that a democratically elected Government would not be in place by 30 June. The majority of Iraqis also favoured the handover of power by CPA on 30 June to a new caretaker Government composed of technically qualified persons, led by a qualified prime minister. The UN team suggested that a president should serve as head of State, with two vice-presidents. The caretaker Government would tend to the day-to-day administration of the country until such time as a democratically elected Government could be put in place. In doing so, the members of the caretaker Government had to be careful not to use their positions to give advantage to any political party or group. To prevent even the perception that they might do so, it would be best if they did not stand for election. It should refrain from entering into long-term commitments that could and should await decision by an elected Government, and consult with representatives of all parts of Iraqi society. To that end, the UN team suggested the establishment of a consultative assembly or council. Ideally, the Iraqis themselves should select the caretaker Government and the United Nations could help in that process. The UN team believed that it would be possible to identify by the end of May a group of people respected by and acceptable to Iraqis across the country to form the caretaker Government. Many Iraqis had suggested that the United Nations convene a national conference to engage in a genuine national dialogue on the country's challenges. The UN team, while agreeing that such a conference would be worthwhile, was of the view that it should be convened by an Iraqi preparatory committee, which should identify the modalities for the conference.

The conference, which could be convened in July at the earliest, should bring together between 1,000 and 1,500 people representing a wide sample of Iraqi society from every province in the country, all political parties, tribal chiefs and leaders, trade and professional unions, universities, women's groups, youth organizations, writers, artists and religious leaders, among others. It would discuss ways to address the security situation and ideas on how to organize timely and successful elections, and review the contentious aspects of the Transitional Administrative Law (see p. 341). It would also appoint a consultative council to advise the Government. Mr. Brahimi said that the convening of the national conference might ultimately constitute an important step towards, among other things, national reconciliation. It would have to deal with issues such as the manner in which the new army was formed, how the issue of "de-Baathification" was handled and how concerns about due process for current detainees were addressed. In that regard, Mr. Brahimi drew attention to the announcement by the CPA Administrator that, as of 10 May, it would regularly post lists of detainees at police stations and courthouses throughout the country. Grievances about the way in which the "de-Baathification" policy was being implemented, especially with respect to teachers and university professors, among others, would be addressed. CPA was also considering the dissolution of existing militias, including the Mahdi army and other armies. Mr. Brahimi said that the UN team would resume its consultations in Iraq as soon as possible in order to build broad consensus and move forward towards the establishment of an Interim Government by 30 June.

SECURITY COUNCIL ACTION

On 27 April [meeting 4953], following consultations among Security Council members, the President made statement **S/PRST/2004/11** on behalf of the Council:

The Security Council welcomes with appreciation the comprehensive briefing provided by the Special Adviser to the Secretary-General on Iraq, Mr. Lakhdar Brahimi.

Recalling the statement by its President of 24 March 2004 (S/PRST/2004/6), the Council considers the efforts of the Special Adviser and his team as well as those of the United Nations electoral assistance team to be of particular importance and urgency.

The Council strongly supports the efforts and the dedication of the Special Adviser and welcomes the provisional ideas that he has submitted as a basis for the formation of an interim Iraqi government to which sovereignty will be transferred on 30 June 2004.

The Council encourages the Secretary-General and his Special Adviser to continue diligently with the efforts that they are employing and welcomes the intention of the Special Adviser to return to Iraq shortly, and looks forward to a further briefing upon his return.

The Council calls upon all Iraqi parties to co-operate fully with the Special Adviser, and also calls upon Iraq's neighbours and the international community at large to lend all possible support to these efforts.

Communication. On 30 April [A/58/783-S/2004/354], Malaysia transmitted to the Presidents of the Security Council and the General Assembly a declaration on Iraq, adopted at the tenth session of the Islamic Summit Conference (Putrajaya, Malaysia, 22 April). The declaration, among other things, condemned the acts of terrorism carried out in Iraqi places of worship, and urged the Council to adopt a resolution, which would effectively help to restore the sovereignty and full independence of Iraq and empower the United Nations with the necessary mandate and authority to ensure the achievement of that goal.

Final report on implementation of resolution 1483(2003)

Security Council consideration (19 May). On 19 May [meeting 4971], the representatives of the United States and the United Kingdom briefed the Council on their last quarterly report on the implementation of resolution 1483(2003) [YUN 2003, p. 338]. The United States said that on 30 June, CPA and the framework of occupation recognized and established under that resolution would come to an end. The Iraqi Governing Council would cease to exist by that date, and an Interim Government of Iraq would assume the responsibility and authority for governing a sovereign Iraq. Among other tasks, it would prepare for elections for a Transitional National Assembly, to be held no later than 31 January 2005. The security situation since the 16 April report (see p. 343) had been particularly difficult. The multinational force was on the offensive against former regime elements and foreign terrorists in Fallujah and Ramadi. It responded to the string of kidnappings and was working to stop the lawlessness instigated by Muqtada Al-Sadr's Mahdi militia in Baghdad and southern Iraq.

More than 210,000 Iraqi citizens were serving in various components of the Iraqi security forces. The response of the various forces was uneven, and the United States was focusing on improving the quality and leadership of those forces. A Ministry of Defence and a Ministry of the Interior had been established as well as a Ministerial Committee on National Security. Coordination and consultative arrangements would be established between the multinational force and the Interim Government of Iraq. International security forces would be expanded to support the return of UN international personnel to Iraq, and a unit was being established within the multinational force under unified command to provide security for UN personnel and facilities in Iraq. The Transitional Administrative Law, adopted in February by the Governing Council, confirmed Iraq as a single State with federal structures, and affirmed civilian control of Iraq's security services and the independence of the judiciary. The Law also codified that elections for the Transitional National Assembly had to be held before the end of January 2005 and the drafting of a permanent constitution by 15 August 2005, with the transition to a constitutionally elected Government by 31 December 2005. A key milestone in Iraq's political transition would be the establishment of a Government chosen by democratic elections. The UN electoral assistance team was working with the Iraqi people in developing an independent election commission, an agreement on electoral modalities and a political parties law. The preparations for the establishment of an independent election commission were advancing. A nationwide nomination process was under way to select the seven commissioners.

Iraq continued to receive goods purchased under the oil-for-food programme, and the coordination centre established by CPA oversaw the shipment of food and other humanitarian supplies remaining in the oil-for-food pipeline. Capacity-building and technical support programmes had been initiated in relevant Iraqi ministries to improve Iraqi capabilities to procure essential items and monitor incoming oil-for-food shipments. That would help ensure that the Iraqis would be able to manage remaining oil-for-food contracts and projects when the coordination centre and the Office of Project Coordination were phased out. The Iraqi Board of Supreme Audit had collected, centralized and safeguarded oil-for-food documents in preparation for its own investigation of the programme and had signalled its readiness to assist the UN and other investigations into alleged abuses. The United States representative referred to the abuse of Iraqi detainees at Abu Ghraib prison, which, he said, stained the honour and reputation of the United States. To date, seven military personnel had been charged with criminal offences and two officers relieved of their command. A number of investigations were proceeding. Immediate steps had been taken to reinforce existing military policies to ensure that United States forces understood, were fully trained in and adhered to the Geneva Conventions.

Communication (2 June). On 2 June [A/58/818-S/2004/449], Jordan transmitted to the Presidents of the Council and the Assembly the statement made by the speakers of the parliaments of the neighbouring countries of Iraq at the meeting convened by the Inter-Parliamentary Union (Amman, 12-13 May). Calling for, among other things, a broader and more central role for the United Nations in Iraq based on a clearly defined, realistic and achievable mandate from the Council, they welcomed the resumption of UN activities in Iraq and concurred with the recommendations submitted by the Secretary-General's Special Adviser.

Establishment of Interim Government and transfer of sovereignty

Security Council consideration (3 June). On 3 June [meeting 4982], the Council discussed the situation between Iraq and Kuwait. It was briefed by the Minister for Foreign Affairs of Iraq who said that on 1 June the Iraqi people took the first step towards regaining their full sovereignty and independence. The Secretary-General's Special Adviser supervised the introduction of a new Interim Iraqi Government to assume authority on 30 June. It comprised 32 ministers, 6 of whom were women. The formation of the Interim Government, the result of an extensive consultation process promoted by Mr. Brahimi, was based on merit and qualifications with an element of political and social balancing. Iraq urged the international community to endorse the establishment of the sovereign Interim Government through the adoption of a new Council resolution, which should underline the transfer of full sovereignty to the Iraqi people on 30 June. That meant investing full authority in the Interim Government to run Iraq's affairs, including authority over security matters, full control of Iraq's resources and assets and a leading role in mechanisms agreed by the Council to monitor disbursement of its resources. The Transitional Administrative Law would remain the only legal framework until the end of 2005. To make the democratic process more inclusive, there were plans to hold a national conference by July 2004 to allow all those parties and individuals who wished to be represented to have a say. A preparatory committee for the conference had already been identified. An electoral commission had also been established to supervise elections, with the support and help of the United Nations. Part of the mandate of the caretaker Government was to work closely with the United Nations to prepare for general elections in 2005. The Foreign Minister stressed that Iraq had not yet reached a stage to maintain its own security. Political development in Iraq was progressive and inclusive and the country remained committed to the clear steps it had to take towards elections in 2005. Any premature departure of international troops would lead to chaos and the real possibility of a civil war. Iraqi forces would be under Iraqi command, operating in liaison and partnership with the multinational force.

Security Council consideration (7 June). At its 7 June meeting [meeting 4984] to consider the situation between Iraq and Kuwait, the Secretary-General told the Security Council that his Special Adviser, Mr. Brahimi, would give a briefing on the process leading to the announcement of the Iraqi Interim Government on 1 June. In his own introductory comments, the Secretary-General said that since the outbreak of the Iraq crisis, the UN role had been difficult, often dangerous, hedged about with constraints and controversy. To understand the role played by Mr. Brahimi and his team and by the United Nations Electoral Assistance Division, headed by Carina Perelli, it was important to set their efforts in a wider and longer perspective. It was no secret that the events leading up to the war in Iraq, and developments since then, had been among the most divisive that the Council had had to deal with since the end of the cold war. Against that background of strongly held views on both sides of the argument, it was inevitable that agreement on the role to be played by the United Nations in the aftermath of the war, especially in the political process, would also be elusive. Although Member States were able to agree that the United Nations should play a vital or central role, that role was never specifically defined. Moreover, the deadly attack on UN headquarters in Baghdad in August 2003 [YUN 2003, p. 346] greatly reduced the UN capacity to act inside Iraq, for it brought to a virtual halt the on-the-ground involvement of the United Nations in the political process in Iraq. It remained clear since then that any UN role in Iraq, political or otherwise, would face serious security constraints.

The Secretary-General said that there had to be some symmetry between the risks the United Nations was asked to accept and the role it was being called to play. The temporary relocation of UN international staff from the country did not mean that the Organization had disengaged from Iraq's political process. On the contrary, contacts were intensified with Governments around the world from UN Headquarters, and Iraq remained a constant agenda item in virtually all of the Secretary-General's meetings with heads of State or Government and Foreign Ministers. His primary message was the need for the occupation to be brought to an end as soon as possible and for the Iraqis to regain control of their sovereignty, political destiny and natural resources. While most Iraqis welcomed that a date had been set for the formation of a sovereign Iraqi Government,

prominent figures representing key constituencies threatened to reject the outcome of the caucus-style method prescribed in the 15 November 2003 agreement [YUN 2003, p. 354] for selecting that Government. There was a real risk that the political process might collapse. Against that background, the President of the Iraqi Governing Council wrote to the Secretary-General at the end of 2003 [ibid., p. 355], requesting help in answering two specific questions: whether elections were feasible by 30 June 2004, and, if not, by what alternative means an Interim Government could be formed, to which sovereignty would be restored. The Secretary-General responded positively to that request, having been given strong assurance that there was a clear role for the United Nations, and everything possible would be done to provide security for its personnel. The Secretary-General's position was that whatever role the United Nations undertook should be proportionate to the risks that UN staff had to assume. It was within that context that he asked Mr. Brahimi to play a role in the political transition process. On the basis of the report presented to the Council on his fact-finding visit to Iraq (see p. 344), the process began leading to the formation of the Interim Government and the preparation of elections to be held by January 2005. That process was completed on time and in full. The UN role was to facilitate national dialogue and consensus-building among Iraqis, leading to the formation of an Interim Government, including its structure and composition. Mr. Brahimi had also helped forge consensus on a chairman for the committee that would prepare the national conference in early July 2004. The UN electoral experts helped the Iraqis lay the groundwork for elections. The establishment of the Independent Electoral Commission of Iraq was complete. Seven Iraqi commissioners and a National Electoral Director were selected by the United Nations. Agreement was reached on the legislative framework for the elections, including the electoral system, political parties and representation, and criteria for voter registration. The Council was discussing a draft resolution that addressed, among other things, the future role of the United Nations in Iraq. The Secretary-General looked forward to a clear definition of that role and to the creation of the conditions, including the provision of security for UN staff and resources, which would allow the United Nations to implement its mandate satisfactorily.

The Secretary-General's Special Adviser briefed the Council on the consultation process that led to the formation of the Interim Government, and, in particular, the selection of Ayad

Allawi as interim Prime Minister. He said that the Council of Ministers reflected to a large extent the regional, ethnic and religious diversity of Iraq and was composed largely of technocrats.

Communication of Secretary-General. The Secretary-General transmitted to the Council President a copy of that briefing [S/2004/461], which constituted Mr. Brahimi's report on his third and latest mission to Iraq from 1 May to 2 June.

The Secretary-General fully endorsed Mr. Brahimi's observations. He emphasized that the United Nations had consistently held that there was no substitute for the legitimacy derived from free and fair elections. The elections scheduled to take place by early 2005 were therefore the most important milestone in Iraq's transitional political process. The formation of the Interim Government marked a first step in that process, and deserved to be given a fair chance and full support. Iraq's challenges, however, would take years, not months, to overcome. A major task for the Interim Government was dealing with the grave insecurity that affected Iraq. The United Nations stood ready to contribute to the restoration of peace and stability in a democratic Iraq.

SECURITY COUNCIL ACTION (June)

On 8 June [meeting 4987], the Council unanimously adopted **resolution 1546(2004)**. The draft [S/2004/460] was submitted by Romania, the United Kingdom and the United States.

The Security Council,

Welcoming the beginning of a new phase in Iraq's transition to a democratically elected government, and looking forward to the end of the occupation and the assumption of full responsibility and authority by a fully sovereign and independent Interim Government of Iraq by 30 June 2004,

Recalling all of its relevant resolutions on Iraq,

Reaffirming the independence, sovereignty, unity and territorial integrity of Iraq,

Reaffirming also the right of the Iraqi people freely to determine their own political future and control their own natural resources,

Recognizing the importance of international support, particularly that of countries in the region, Iraq's neighbours, and regional organizations, for the people of Iraq in their efforts to achieve security and prosperity, and noting that the successful implementation of the present resolution will contribute to regional stability,

Welcoming the efforts of the Special Adviser to the Secretary-General to assist the people of Iraq in achieving the formation of the Interim Government of Iraq, as set out in the letter dated 7 June 2004 from the Secretary-General addressed to the President of the Security Council,

Taking note of the dissolution of the Governing Council of Iraq, and welcoming the progress made in implementing the arrangements for Iraq's political transition referred to in resolution 1511(2003) of 16 October 2003,

Welcoming the commitment of the Interim Government of Iraq to work towards a federal, democratic, pluralist and unified Iraq, in which there is full respect for political and human rights,

Stressing the need for all parties to respect and protect the archaeological, historical, cultural and religious heritage of Iraq,

Affirming the importance of the rule of law, national reconciliation, respect for human rights, including the rights of women, fundamental freedoms, and democracy, including free and fair elections,

Recalling the establishment of the United Nations Assistance Mission for Iraq on 14 August 2003, and affirming that the United Nations should play a leading role in assisting the Iraqi people and government in the formation of institutions for representative government,

Recognizing that international support for the restoration of stability and security is essential to the well-being of the people of Iraq as well as to the ability of all concerned to carry out their work on behalf of the people of Iraq, and welcoming contributions by Member States in this regard under resolution 1483(2003) of 22 May 2003 and resolution 1511(2003),

Recalling the report provided by the United States of America to the Security Council on 16 April 2004 on the efforts and progress made by the multinational force,

Recognizing the request, conveyed in the letter dated 5 June 2004 from the Prime Minister of the Interim Government of Iraq addressed to the President of the Security Council, which is annexed to the present resolution, to retain the presence of the multinational force,

Recognizing also the importance of the consent of the sovereign Government of Iraq for the presence of the multinational force and of close coordination between the multinational force and that government,

Welcoming the willingness of the multinational force to continue efforts to contribute to the maintenance of security and stability in Iraq in support of the political transition, especially for upcoming elections, and to provide security for the United Nations presence in Iraq, as described in the letter dated 5 June 2004 from the Secretary of State of the United States of America addressed to the President of the Security Council, which is annexed to the present resolution,

Noting the commitment of all forces promoting the maintenance of security and stability in Iraq to act in accordance with international law, including obligations under international humanitarian law, and to cooperate with relevant international organizations,

Affirming the importance of international assistance in the reconstruction and development of the Iraqi economy,

Recognizing the benefits to Iraq of the immunities and privileges enjoyed by Iraqi oil revenues and by the Development Fund for Iraq, and noting the importance of providing for continued disbursements of that fund by the Interim Government of Iraq and its successors upon the dissolution of the Coalition Provisional Authority,

Determining that the situation in Iraq continues to constitute a threat to international peace and security,

Acting under Chapter VII of the Charter of the United Nations,

1. *Endorses* the formation of a sovereign Interim Government of Iraq, as presented on 1 June 2004, which will assume full responsibility and authority by 30 June 2004 for governing Iraq while refraining from taking any actions affecting Iraq's destiny beyond the limited interim period until an elected Transitional Government of Iraq assumes office as envisaged in paragraph 4 below;

2. *Welcomes* the fact that, also by 30 June 2004, the occupation will end and the Coalition Provisional Authority will cease to exist, and that Iraq will reassert its full sovereignty;

3. *Reaffirms* the right of the Iraqi people freely to determine their own political future and to exercise full authority and control over their financial and natural resources;

4. *Endorses* the proposed timetable for Iraq's political transition to democratic government, including:

(a) The formation of the sovereign Interim Government of Iraq that will assume governing responsibility and authority by 30 June 2004;

(b) The convening of a national conference reflecting the diversity of Iraqi society;

(c) The holding of direct democratic elections, by 31 December 2004 if possible, and in no case later than 31 January 2005, to a Transitional National Assembly, which will, inter alia, have responsibility for forming a Transitional Government of Iraq and drafting a permanent constitution for Iraq leading to a constitutionally elected government by 31 December 2005;

5. *Invites* the Government of Iraq to consider how the convening of an international meeting could support the above-mentioned process, and notes that it would welcome such a meeting to support the Iraqi political transition and Iraqi recovery, to the benefit of the Iraqi people and in the interest of stability in the region;

6. *Calls upon* all Iraqis to implement these arrangements peaceably and in full, and calls upon all States and relevant organizations to support such implementation;

7. *Decides* that, in implementing, as circumstances permit, their mandate to assist the Iraqi people and government, the Special Representative of the Secretary-General and the United Nations Assistance Mission for Iraq, as requested by the Government of Iraq, shall:

(a) Play a leading role:

(i) To assist in the convening, during the month of July 2004, of a national conference to select a Consultative Council;

(ii) To advise and support the Independent Electoral Commission of Iraq, as well as the Interim Government of Iraq and the Transitional National Assembly, in the process for holding elections;

(iii) To promote national dialogue and consensus-building on the drafting of a national constitution by the people of Iraq;

(b) And also:

(i) To advise the Government of Iraq in the development of effective civil and social services;

(ii) To contribute to the coordination and delivery of reconstruction, development and humanitarian assistance;

(iii) To promote the protection of human rights, national reconciliation, and judicial and legal reform in order to strengthen the rule of law in Iraq;

(iv) To advise and assist the Government of Iraq on initial planning for the eventual conduct of a comprehensive census;

8. *Welcomes* ongoing efforts by the incoming Interim Government of Iraq to develop Iraqi security forces including the Iraqi armed forces (hereinafter referred to as "Iraqi security forces"), operating under the authority of the Interim Government of Iraq and its successors, which will play a progressively greater role and ultimately assume full responsibility for the maintenance of security and stability in Iraq;

9. *Notes* that the presence of the multinational force in Iraq is at the request of the incoming Interim Government of Iraq, and therefore reaffirms the authorization for the multinational force under unified command established under resolution 1511(2003), having regard to the letters annexed to the present resolution;

10. *Decides* that the multinational force shall have the authority to take all necessary measures to contribute to the maintenance of security and stability in Iraq in accordance with the letters annexed to the present resolution expressing, inter alia, the Iraqi request for the continued presence of the multinational force and setting out its tasks, including by preventing and deterring terrorism, so that, inter alia, the United Nations can fulfil its role in assisting the Iraqi people as outlined in paragraph 7 above and the Iraqi people can implement freely and without intimidation the timetable and programme for the political process and benefit from reconstruction and rehabilitation activities;

11. *Welcomes,* in this regard, the letters annexed to the present resolution stating, inter alia, that arrangements are being put in place to establish a security partnership between the sovereign Government of Iraq and the multinational force and to ensure coordination between the two, and notes also in this regard that Iraqi security forces are responsible to appropriate Iraqi ministers, that the Government of Iraq has the authority to commit Iraqi security forces to the multinational force to engage in operations with it, and that the security structures described in the letters will serve as the forums for the Government of Iraq and the multinational force to reach agreement on the full range of fundamental security and policy issues, including policy on sensitive offensive operations, and will ensure full partnership between Iraqi security forces and the multinational force, through close coordination and consultation;

12. *Decides* that the mandate of the multinational force shall be reviewed at the request of the Government of Iraq or twelve months from the date of adoption of the present resolution, and that this mandate shall expire upon the completion of the political process set out in paragraph 4 above, and declares that it will terminate this mandate earlier if requested by the Government of Iraq;

13. *Notes* the intention, set out in the letter from the Secretary of State of the United States of America annexed to the present resolution, to create a distinct en-

tity under unified command of the multinational force with a dedicated mission to provide security for the United Nations presence in Iraq, recognizes that the implementation of measures to provide security for staff members of the United Nations system working in Iraq would require significant resources, and calls upon Member States and relevant organizations to provide such resources, including contributions to that entity;

14. *Recognizes* that the multinational force will also assist in building the capability of the Iraqi security forces and institutions, through a programme of recruitment, training, equipping, mentoring and monitoring;

15. *Requests* Member States and international and regional organizations to contribute assistance to the multinational force, including military forces, as agreed with the Government of Iraq, to help to meet the needs of the Iraqi people for security and stability, humanitarian and reconstruction assistance, and to support the efforts of the United Nations Assistance Mission for Iraq;

16. *Emphasizes* the importance of developing effective Iraqi police, border enforcement and the Facilities Protection Service, under the control of the Interior Ministry of Iraq, and, in the case of the Facilities Protection Service, other Iraqi ministries, for the maintenance of law, order and security, including combating terrorism, and requests Member States and international organizations to assist the Government of Iraq in building the capability of those Iraqi institutions;

17. *Condemns* all acts of terrorism in Iraq, reaffirms the obligations of Member States under resolutions 1373(2001) of 28 September 2001, 1267(1999) of 15 October 1999, 1333(2000) of 19 December 2000, 1390 (2002) of 16 January 2002, 1455(2003) of 17 January 2003 and 1526(2004) of 30 January 2004 and other relevant international obligations with respect, inter alia, to terrorist activities in and from Iraq or against its citizens, and specifically reiterates its call upon Member States to prevent the transit of terrorists to and from Iraq, arms for terrorists and financing that would support terrorists, and re-emphasizes the importance of strengthening the cooperation of the countries of the region, particularly neighbours of Iraq, in this regard;

18. *Recognizes* that the Interim Government of Iraq will assume the primary role in coordinating international assistance to Iraq;

19. *Welcomes* efforts by Member States and international organizations to respond in support of requests by the Interim Government of Iraq to provide technical and expert assistance while Iraq is rebuilding administrative capacity;

20. *Reiterates its request* that Member States, international financial institutions and other organizations strengthen their efforts to assist the people of Iraq in the reconstruction and development of the Iraqi economy, including by providing international experts and necessary resources through a coordinated programme of donor assistance;

21. *Decides* that the prohibitions related to the sale or supply to Iraq of arms and related materiel under previous resolutions shall not apply to arms or related materiel required by the Government of Iraq or the multinational force to serve the purposes of the pres-

ent resolution, stresses the importance for all States to abide strictly by them, and notes the significance of Iraq's neighbours in this regard, and calls upon the Government of Iraq and the multinational force each to ensure that appropriate implementation procedures are in place;

22. *Notes* that nothing in paragraph 21 above affects the prohibitions on or obligations of States related to items specified in paragraphs 8 and 12 of resolution 687(1991) of 3 April 1991 or activities described in paragraph 3 (*f*) of resolution 707(1991) of 15 August 1991, and reaffirms its intention to revisit the mandates of the United Nations Monitoring, Verification, and Inspection Commission and the International Atomic Energy Agency;

23. *Calls upon* Member States and international organizations to respond to Iraqi requests to assist Iraqi efforts to integrate Iraqi veterans and former militia members into Iraqi society;

24. *Notes* that, upon the dissolution of the Coalition Provisional Authority, the funds in the Development Fund for Iraq shall be disbursed solely at the direction of the Government of Iraq, and decides that the Development Fund for Iraq shall be utilized in a transparent and equitable manner and through the Iraqi budget, including to satisfy outstanding obligations against the Development Fund for Iraq, that the arrangements for the depositing of proceeds from export sales of petroleum, petroleum products and natural gas established in paragraph 20 of resolution 1483(2003) shall continue to apply, that the International Advisory and Monitoring Board shall continue its activities in monitoring the Development Fund for Iraq and shall include as an additional full voting member a duly qualified individual designated by the Government of Iraq, and that appropriate arrangements shall be made for the continuation of deposits of the proceeds referred to in paragraph 21 of resolution 1483(2003);

25. *Decides* that the provisions in paragraph 24 above for the deposit of proceeds into the Development Fund for Iraq and for the role of the International Advisory and Monitoring Board shall be reviewed at the request of the Transitional Government of Iraq or twelve months from the date of adoption of the present resolution, and shall expire upon the completion of the political process set out in paragraph 4 above;

26. *Decides also* that, in connection with the dissolution of the Coalition Provisional Authority, the Interim Government of Iraq and its successors shall assume the rights, responsibilities and obligations relating to the oil-for-food programme that were transferred to the Authority, including all operational responsibility for the programme and any obligations undertaken by the Authority in connection with such responsibility, and responsibility for ensuring independently authenticated confirmation that goods have been delivered, and further decides that, following a transition period of one hundred and twenty days from the date of adoption of the present resolution, the Interim Government of Iraq and its successors shall assume responsibility for certifying delivery of goods under previously prioritized contracts, and that such certification shall be deemed to constitute the independent authentication required for the release of funds associated with such contracts, consulting as appropriate to

ensure the smooth implementation of these arrangements;

27. *Decides further* that the provisions of paragraph 22 of resolution 1483(2003) shall continue to apply, except that the privileges and immunities provided in that paragraph shall not apply with respect to any final judgement arising out of a contractual obligation entered into by Iraq after 30 June 2004;

28. *Welcomes* the commitments of many creditors, including those of the Paris Club, to identify ways to reduce substantially Iraq's sovereign debt, calls upon Member States, as well as international and regional organizations, to support the Iraq reconstruction effort, urges the international financial institutions and bilateral donors to take the immediate steps necessary to provide their full range of loans and other financial assistance and arrangements to Iraq, recognizes that the Interim Government of Iraq will have the authority to conclude and implement such agreements and other arrangements as may be necessary in this regard, and requests creditors, institutions and donors to work as a priority on these matters with the Interim Government of Iraq and its successors;

29. *Recalls* the continuing obligations of Member States to freeze and transfer certain funds, assets and economic resources to the Development Fund for Iraq in accordance with paragraphs 19 and 23 of resolution 1483(2003) and with resolution 1518(2003) of 24 November 2003;

30. *Requests* the Secretary-General to report to the Council within three months from the date of adoption of the present resolution on the operations in Iraq of the United Nations Assistance Mission for Iraq, and on a quarterly basis thereafter on the progress made towards national elections and the fulfilment of all the responsibilities of the Mission;

31. *Requests* that the United States of America, on behalf of the multinational force, report to the Council within three months of the date of the present resolution on the efforts and progress of the force, and on a quarterly basis thereafter;

32. *Decides* to remain actively seized of the matter.

Annex

Text of letters from the Prime Minister of the Interim Government of Iraq, Dr. Ayad Allawi, and the Secretary of State of the United States of America, Mr. Colin L. Powell, addressed to the President of the Security Council

Letter dated 5 June 2004 from the Prime Minister of the Interim Government of Iraq, Dr. Ayad Allawi

On my appointment as Prime Minister of the Interim Government of Iraq, I am writing to express the commitment of the people of Iraq to complete the political transition process to establish a free and democratic Iraq and to be a partner in preventing and combating terrorism. As we enter a critical new stage, regain full sovereignty and move towards elections, we will need the assistance of the international community.

The Interim Government of Iraq will make every effort to ensure that these elections are fully democratic, free and fair. Security and stability continue to be essential to our political transition. There continue, however, to be forces in Iraq, including foreign elements, that are opposed to our transition to peace, democracy and security. The Government is determined to overcome these forces and to develop security forces capable of providing adequate security for the Iraqi people. Until we are able to provide security for ourselves, including the defence of Iraq's land, sea and air space, we ask for the support of the Security Council and the international community in this endeavour. We seek a new resolution on the Multinational Force mandate to contribute to maintaining security in Iraq, including through the tasks and arrangements set out in the letter from Secretary of State Colin Powell to the President of the Security Council. The Government requests that the Security Council review the mandate of the MNF at the request of the Transitional Government of Iraq, or twelve months from the date on which such a resolution is adopted.

In order to discharge the Iraqi Government's responsibility for security, I intend to establish appropriate security structures that will allow my Government and Iraqi security forces to progressively take on that responsibility. One such structure is the Ministerial Committee for National Security, consisting of myself as the Chair, the Deputy Prime Minister and the Ministers for Defence, the Interior, Foreign Affairs, Justice and Finance. The National Security Advisor and Director of the Iraqi National Intelligence Service will serve as permanent advisory members of the Committee. This forum will set the broad framework for Iraqi security policy. I intend to invite, as appropriate, the MNF commander, his deputy or the MNF commander's designated representative, and other appropriate individuals, to attend and participate as well, and will stand ready to discuss mechanisms of coordination and cooperation with the MNF. Iraqi armed forces will be responsible to the Chief of Staff and Minister for Defence. Other security forces (the Iraqi police, border guards and the Facilities Protection Service) will be responsible to the Minister of the Interior or other government ministers.

In addition, the relevant ministers and I will develop further mechanisms for coordination with the MNF. I intend to create with the MNF coordination bodies at the national, regional and local levels that will include Iraqi security forces' commanders and civilian leadership, to ensure that Iraqi security forces will coordinate with the MNF on all security policy and operations issues in order to achieve unity of command of military operations in which Iraqi forces are engaged with the MNF. In addition, the MNF and Iraqi government leaders will keep each other informed of their activities, consult regularly to ensure effective allocation and use of personnel, resources and facilities, will share intelligence and will refer issues up the respective chains of command where necessary. Iraqi security forces will take on progressively greater responsibility as Iraqi capabilities improve.

The structures I have described in this letter will serve as the forums for the MNF and the Iraqi government to reach agreement on the full range of fundamental security and policy issues, including policy on sensitive offensive operations, and will ensure full partnership between Iraqi forces and the MNF, through close coordination and consultation. Since these are sensitive issues for a number of sovereign governments, including Iraq and the United States of

America, they need to be resolved within the framework of a mutual understanding on our strategic partnership. We will be working closely with the MNF leadership in the coming weeks to ensure that we have such an agreed strategic framework.

We are ready to take sovereign responsibility for governing Iraq by 30 June. We are well aware of the difficulties facing us, and of our responsibilities to the Iraqi people. The stakes are great, and we need the support of the international community to succeed. We ask the Security Council to help us by acting now to adopt a Security Council resolution giving us the necessary support.

I understand that the co-sponsors intend to annex this letter to the resolution on Iraq under consideration. In the meantime, I request that you provide copies of this letter to members of the Council as quickly as possible.

Letter dated 5 June 2004 from the Secretary of State of the United States of America, Mr. Colin L. Powell

Recognizing the request of the government of Iraq for the continued presence of the Multinational Force in Iraq, and following consultations with Prime Minister Ayad Allawi of the Iraqi Interim Government, I am writing to confirm that the MNF under unified command is prepared to continue to contribute to the maintenance of security in Iraq, including by preventing and deterring terrorism and protecting the territory of Iraq. The goal of the MNF will be to help the Iraqi people to complete the political transition and will permit the United Nations and the international community to work to facilitate Iraq's reconstruction.

The ability of the Iraqi people to achieve their goals will be heavily influenced by the security situation in Iraq. As recent events have demonstrated, continuing attacks by insurgents, including former regime elements, foreign fighters and illegal militias challenge all those who are working for a better Iraq.

The development of an effective and cooperative security partnership between the MNF and the sovereign Government of Iraq is critical to the stability of Iraq. The commander of the MNF will work in partnership with the sovereign Government of Iraq in helping to provide security while recognizing and respecting its sovereignty. To that end, the MNF stands ready to participate in discussions of the Ministerial Committee for National Security on the broad framework of security policy, as referred to in the letter dated 5 June 2004 from Prime Minister Allawi of the Interim Government of Iraq. On the implementation of this policy, recognizing that Iraqi security forces are responsible to the appropriate Iraqi ministers, the MNF will coordinate with Iraqi security forces at all levels—national, regional and local—in order to achieve unity of command of military operations in which Iraqi forces are engaged with the MNF. In addition, the MNF and the Iraqi government leaders will keep each other informed of their activities, consult regularly to ensure effective allocation and use of personnel, resources and facilities, will share intelligence and will refer issues up the respective chains of command where necessary. We will work in the forums described by Prime Minister Allawi in his letter dated 5 June 2004 to reach agreement on the full range of fundamental security and policy issues, including policy on sensitive offensive operations, and will ensure full partnership between MNF and Iraqi forces, through close coordination and consultation.

Under the agreed arrangement, the MNF stands ready to continue to undertake a broad range of tasks to contribute to the maintenance of security and to ensure force protection. These include activities necessary to counter ongoing security threats posed by forces seeking to influence Iraq's political future through violence. This will include combat operations against members of these groups, internment where this is necessary for imperative reasons of security, and the continued search for and securing of weapons that threaten Iraq's security. A further objective will be to train and equip Iraqi security forces that will increasingly take responsibility for maintaining Iraq's security. The MNF also stands ready as needed to participate in the provision of humanitarian assistance, civil affairs support, and relief and reconstruction assistance requested by the Iraqi Interim Government and in line with previous Security Council resolutions.

In addition, the MNF is prepared to establish or support a force within the MNF to provide for the security of personnel and facilities of the United Nations. We have consulted closely with United Nations officials regarding the United Nations' security requirements and believe that a brigade-size force will be needed to support the United Nations' security effort. This force will be under the command and control of the MNF commander, and its missions will include static and perimeter security at United Nations facilities and convoy escort duties for the United Nations mission's travel requirements.

In order to continue to contribute to security, the MNF must continue to function under a framework that affords the force and its personnel the status that they need to accomplish their mission, and in which the contributing States have responsibility for exercising jurisdiction over their personnel and which will ensure arrangements for, and use of assets by, the MNF. The existing framework governing these matters is sufficient for these purposes. In addition, the forces that make up the MNF are and will remain committed at all times to act consistently with their obligations under the law of armed conflict, including the Geneva Conventions.

The MNF is prepared to continue to pursue its current efforts to assist in providing a secure environment in which the broader international community is able to fulfil its important role in facilitating Iraq's reconstruction. In meeting these responsibilities in the period ahead, we will act in full recognition of and respect for Iraqi sovereignty. We look to other Member States and international and regional organizations to assist the people of Iraq and the sovereign Iraqi government in overcoming the challenges that lie ahead to build a democratic, secure and prosperous country.

The co-sponsors intend to annex this letter to the resolution on Iraq under consideration. In the meantime, I request that you provide copies of this letter to members of the Council as quickly as possible.

Speaking after the vote, the United States said that the resolution defined the key political tasks in which the United Nations would play a leading and vital role to support Iraqi efforts. The annexed letters to the resolution described the security partnership that was being put into place between Iraq and the multinational force.

The United Kingdom said that the resolution made an important contribution to Iraq's development. Besides endorsing the formation of an Interim Government, it set a clear path for the future political process, which would end with elections on the basis of a constitution approved by the Iraqi people. It gave the United Nations a leading role, as circumstances permitted, to assist Iraq in that process. In addition, as requested by the Iraqi Government, the resolution authorized the continued presence of the multinational force. The United Kingdom stood ready to participate fully in those arrangements.

Communications. On 25 June [S/2004/519], Turkey transmitted to the Secretary-General the text of the Chairman's statement on the results of the meeting of the Regional Initiative on Iraq (Istanbul, Turkey, 15 June), with the participation of Egypt, Iran, Iraq, Jordan, Kuwait, Saudi Arabia, the Syrian Arab Republic and Turkey. The Chairman welcomed the adoption of Council resolution 1546(2004) and expressed the hope that the United Nations would be able to perform its functions in Iraq with the full cooperation of all.

On the same day [A/58/849-S/2004/520], Turkey transmitted to the Secretary-General and the Council President the text of the Istanbul Declaration, adopted by the Islamic Conference of Foreign Ministers at its thirty-first session (Istanbul, 14-16 June), supporting the steps taken towards ending the occupation in Iraq and the process by which the Iraqis would assume their sovereignty. They welcomed in that respect the adoption of resolution 1546(2004).

The Sixth Conference of the Ministers for Foreign Affairs of States Neighbouring Iraq (Cairo, Egypt, 21 July), in its final statement transmitted to the Council President [S/2004/590], welcomed the transfer of authority to the sovereign Interim Government of Iraq and the adoption of resolution 1546(2004).

The Ministers for Foreign Affairs of the States members of the Organization of the Islamic Conference, in the final communiqué of their annual coordination meeting (New York, 28 September), noted with satisfaction the role assigned to the United Nations under resolution 1546(2004) and welcomed the transfer of authority to the Interim Government on 28 June and the convening of the Iraqi national conference [A/59/425-S/2004/808].

International Advisory and Monitoring Board

The International Advisory and Monitoring Board for Iraq (IAMB), established by Security Council resolution 1483(2003) [YUN 2003, p. 338] to ensure that the Development Fund for Iraq was used in a transparent manner for the purposes set out in paragraph 14 of that resolution and that the Iraqi export sales of petroleum products and natural gas were consistent with international market best practices, commenced overseeing the audit of the Fund.

In a 30 June letter [S/2004/542] submitted by the Secretary-General to the Council President on 6 July, the Secretary-General's representative on and Chairman of IAMB reported that, on 24 March, the Board approved the appointment of the auditing firm of KPMG to conduct the audit of the Fund. It also completed the review of the statement of work of the auditors and submitted it to the CPA Administrator. The Board identified a number of issues of concern which it conveyed to CPA and the public, such as controls over the extraction of oil, bartering and sole-sourced contracts.

The Board appointed two observers from the Iraqi Governing Council and one from CPA and requested the CPA Administrator to designate an official to act as counterpart to the Board after 30 June. As a result of resolution 1546(2004) (see p. 348), the Board was revising its terms of reference. It established a website to ensure the widest availability of documentation and information related to its operations.

On 28 June, responsibility for decisions regarding the use of the Fund was handed over from CPA to the Iraqi Interim Government.

UN Assistance Mission for Iraq

The United Nations Assistance Mission for Iraq (UNAMI), established by Security Council resolution 1500(2003) [YUN 2003, p. 346] to support the Secretary-General in the fulfilment of his mandate under resolution 1483(2003) [ibid., p. 338], operated from temporary headquarters located in Larnaca, Cyprus, until 22 June, and in Amman and Kuwait. It was also in the process of establishing bases of operation in Baghdad, Basrah and Erbil. UNAMI's mission was expanded by Council resolution 1546(2004) (see p. 348) to include assisting in the convening of a national conference to select a Consultative Council, advising on the holding of elections, promoting national dialogue and consensus-building on the drafting of a new constitution, advising on the development of effective civil and social services and contributing to the coordination and delivery of reconstruction, development and humanitarian assistance.

On 12 July [S/2004/563], the Secretary-General informed the Security Council that he intended to appoint Ashraf Jehangir Qazi (Pakistan) as his Special Representative for Iraq and Head of UNAMI to replace Ross Mountain. The Security Council, on 13 July [S/2004/546], noted the Secretary-General's intention.

During the year, the Secretary-General submitted three reports [S/2004/625, S/2004/710 & Corr.1, S/2004/959] on UNAMI's activities.

Report of Secretary-General (August). In response to resolution 1483(2003) [YUN 2003, p. 338] and resolution 1511(2003) [ibid., p. 348], the Secretary-General submitted an August report [S/2004/625] on UNAMI activities and key developments in Iraq since his December 2003 report [ibid., p. 352].

Staff security remained the overriding constraint for all UN activities in Iraq. The acting UN Security Coordinator assessed the risks to UN personnel in Iraq as being in the high to critical category, and for the foreseeable future the United Nations would remain a high-value, high-impact target for attacks. UNAMI and UN agencies and programmes would therefore continue to limit their activities inside Iraq to the essential. In the absence of a significant improvement in the overall security situation, the United Nations had to continue to incorporate into all plans and activities the special measures outlined in the Secretary-General's December 2003 report. All UN staff were therefore required to undergo security awareness and information training as a precondition for deployment in Iraq, and any long-term deployment would require the prior development of UN living and working facilities to the minimum operating security standards requirements. It would also require security arrangements by the multinational force and the United Nations in line with their respective responsibilities. Accordingly, the Secretary-General welcomed the provision in resolution 1546(2004) for protection by a distinct entity under unified command of the multinational force. Planning was under way with a view to concluding a formal agreement on protection, exchange of information, emergency medical evacuation and other assistance. As the United Nations lacked the resources for its own security responsibilities in Iraq, it would have to rely on the Interim Government and the multinational force to provide security on the initial re-entry of UN international staff. The assistance of Member States was being sought for the establishment by UNAMI of security units. Outside UN premises, the multinational force would initially serve as the guarantor of the overall security.

In July 2004, UNAMI supported the electoral process by providing logistics, communications, information technology and voter education supplies. UNAMI fostered a sustained effort by UN agencies and programmes to support Iraqi ministries and civil society in the delivery of services to the Iraqi people. It also helped in coordinating assistance with donors and NGOs.

In February 2004, the country team, composed of all UN agencies, offices, funds and programmes with activities in Iraq, developed a strategic planning framework for all UN activities in Iraq. Under the framework, there were 11 clusters (education and culture; health; water and sanitation; infrastructure and housing; agriculture, water resources and environment; food security; mine action; internally displaced persons and refugees; governance and civil society; poverty reduction and human development; and support to the electoral process) informed by five cross-cutting themes—security, human rights, gender, environment and employment generation. UNAMI and the UN country team undertook a wide range of capacity-building, reconstruction, development and humanitarian assistance planning activities. UNAMI established an inter-agency, multisectoral Emergency Response Working Group in April to deal with humanitarian monitoring and early warning, contingency planning, coordination, information management and advocacy and was developing a contingency plan for Iraq. It also worked with the United Nations Development Group agencies and the World Bank to establish the mechanisms for the International Reconstruction Fund Facility for Iraq to accept funds and identify, appraise, approve, implement and monitor projects in the difficult security conditions.

Notwithstanding the constraints imposed by the temporary relocation of UN international staff from Iraq, the United Nations remained engaged in Iraq's political transition process. The United Nations intensified high-level contacts with Iraqis and Governments around the world to discuss the situation and the prospects for an orderly political transition, culminating in credible elections.

On 8 June, the Iraqi Prime Minister–designate requested the United Nations to assist in the preparations for the convening of a national conference which would represent all the colours of the Iraqi political spectrum. The Secretary-General therefore dispatched a small team led by Jamal Benomar to Iraq to assist the Preparatory Committee for the National Conference.

The UN electoral assistance team helped the Iraqis to lay the groundwork for holding elections. Under a plan designed and supervised by the UN Electoral Assistance Division, a national nomination and selection process was conducted to identify candidates for posts as Electoral Commissioners and the Chief Electoral Officer, both of which were appointed by the CPA Administrator on 31 May. From 20 June to 9 July, the Division, with the assistance of Mexico, undertook an intensive training programme with the Iraqi Electoral Commissioners and Chief Electoral Officer. On 30 June, the Chairman of the Electoral Commission requested the United Nations to assist in establishing the Commission as an institution and in the planning, preparation and organization of the electoral process.

The Secretary-General observed that resolution 1546(2004) gave the United Nations a strong and clearly defined mandate. At the same time, the situation in Iraq remained a major challenge both for the Iraqi people and for the international community as a whole. The United Nations would concentrate its efforts on the task set forth in its mandate pursuant to resolution 1546(2004), as requested by the Iraqi Government, and with full consideration given to the deadlines set out in the time frame of Iraq's transitional process. The primary task of the Special Representative would be to assist the Iraqis in implementing the proposed transitional timetable leading to the establishment of a constitutionally elected Government by 31 December 2005. Security would remain the primary obstacle and constraint. A qualitative improvement in the overall security environment was an essential prerequisite for the success of UN efforts in Iraq. The security and safety of all UN staff would therefore remain the overarching guiding principle for all UN activities. Until overall security conditions in Iraq improved significantly, UNAMI would have to continue to operate primarily from the region. UNAMI was promoting operational and sustained contacts with Iraqi ministries to assist in enhancing national capacity and was preparing for the resumption of in-country activities when circumstances would permit. In the light of the essential role that it was playing in supporting the transition process in Iraq, the Secretary-General recommended that UNAMI's mandate be extended for a further period of 12 months.

SECURITY COUNCIL ACTION (August)

On 12 August [meeting 5020], the Security Council unanimously adopted **resolution 1557(2004)**. The draft [S/2004/637] was prepared in consultations among Council members.

The Security Council,

Recalling all its previous relevant resolutions on Iraq, in particular resolutions 1500(2003) of 14 August 2003 and 1546(2004) of 8 June 2004,

Reaffirming the independence, sovereignty, unity and territorial integrity of Iraq,

Recalling the establishment of the United Nations Assistance Mission for Iraq on 14 August 2003, and re-

affirming that the United Nations should play a leading role in assisting the Iraqi people and government in the formation of institutions for representative government,

Welcoming the appointment by the Secretary-General of his new Special Representative for Iraq,

Having considered the report of the Secretary-General of 5 August 2004,

1. *Decides* to extend the mandate of the United Nations Assistance Mission for Iraq for a period of twelve months from the date of the present resolution;

2. *Expresses its intention* to review the mandate of the Mission in twelve months or sooner if requested by the Government of Iraq;

3. *Decides* to remain seized of the matter.

Report of Secretary-General (September). In response to resolution 1546(2004), the Secretary-General submitted a 3 September report [S/2004/710 & Corr.1] on UNAMI's operations and on the progress made towards national elections since his August report (see p. 354). Since its formation on 28 June 2004, the Interim Government of Iraq had taken steps to rebuild Iraq, such as fostering development and economic recovery by improving education and training, creating employment opportunities and promoting business and trade. However, the security situation remained volatile and generally unreceptive to significant economic and political initiatives. Governance structures in the provinces and administrative links with Baghdad had yet to be fully established. Economic opportunities were limited across the country and threats to oil facilities further indicated the challenges within which the Interim Government was trying to establish its authority. Military combat, violence, assassinations and abductions continued to be reported across the country, exacting a huge toll on human life. Armed militias connected to key political parties and figures remained active. Insurgents continued to challenge the presence of the multinational force and the new security forces of the Interim Government. Members of the Iraqi security forces appeared to have competing loyalties to various entities, including family, tribe and party, as well as the Iraqi State. Political violence was directed against senior and middle-ranking government officials, as well as senior officials of various political parties. Such tactics were aimed at demoralizing Iraqi public servants and deterring potential candidates from competing for public office, thereby reducing the pool of talent in government and politics. The pervasive sense of insecurity felt by Iraqis as a result of extortion, kidnappings and other criminal activities eroded public confidence in the capacity of political leaders to improve the security situation. The humanitarian situation was characterized by a marked disregard for international humanitarian and human rights law. Attacks on Iraqi civilians, residential areas and the nascent police forces were widespread. Places of sanctity were targeted or used by combatants.

While fighting was ongoing in several localities in Iraq, the crisis in the city of Najaf was particularly serious. Fighting escalated between an armed militia loyal to Moqtada al-Sadr, Iraqi security forces and the multinational force and was concentrated close to the Imam Ali Shrine. On 27 August, a mediation initiative, led by Grand Ayatollah Ali al-Sistani, resulted in a five-point agreement with the militia, which led to the cessation of hostilities and the transfer of control of the shrine to the senior cleric. The plan, among other things, stated that the cities of Najaf and Kufa had to be disarmed and that all armed elements had to withdraw. It also called on all parties and movements to join in a process leading to general elections and full sovereignty. The Secretary-General, in his statements of 7 and 13 August, encouraged the promotion of the rule of law and a peaceful and reconciliatory approach to bring the fighting in Najaf to an end.

The national conference, scheduled to take place in July 2004, was held from 15 to 18 August in Baghdad, after the Iraqi Preparatory Committee for the Conference, on the advice of the UN team, decided to postpone it for two weeks in order to expand participation. The conference was attended by more than 1,100 delegates from all Iraqi governorates, representing a wide spectrum of Iraqi society. The conference decided to establish an Interim National Council, one of whose key functions would be to monitor the work of the Interim Government. The national conference was held against the backdrop of ongoing fighting in Najaf, which prevented the participation of a number of political actors, who argued that there could not be a genuine dialogue under the circumstances. There was also a perception among several participants that the conference was organized by one of the major political parties and was dominated by established political parties. Despite those shortcomings, the conference completed its task and provided the first opportunity for the Interim Government to demonstrate its commitment to a transparent and inclusive political process leading to national elections in 2005.

The security assessment and related measures for UN staff protection in Iraq remained unchanged during the period under review. The small UN staff presence in the international zone was operating at the outer limit of acceptable and prudent risk. The ceiling for the deployment of UN international substantive, support and security staff in Iraq stood at 35. Efforts by the multinational force to establish a distinct entity with a dedicated mission to provide security for the UN presence in Iraq continued. The United Nations, at the request of the multinational force, had encouraged Member States to provide troops or make financial contributions to such an entity, which should consist of military units of about three battalions. Eighteen Member States responded positively. There was also a need for integrated security arrangements for UNAMI (for details, see below). Discussions were held with six Member States with regard to the provision of paramilitary, civilian police and military guard units. However, a specific Security Council mandate to obtain and deploy the guard units was required. In addition, indications from Member States approached thus far were that, without a clear and unambiguous legal basis, many if not all of the potential contributors would possibly decline to contribute units.

The greatest challenge facing the electoral process in Iraq was the insecure environment in which the preparatory work was being done. While the United Nations continued to assist in the electoral process, as circumstances permitted, the responsibility for organizing and conducting the election rested with the Iraqi authorities. UN electoral assistance was concentrated on consolidating the Electoral Commission, in particular its presence throughout the country and the induction and training of staff, and assisting in the preparation, organization and planning of electoral activities in order to meet the 31 January 2005 deadline. UNAMI's electoral component, in cooperation with the Electoral Assistance Division of the Department of Political Affairs, was coordinating the provision of international financial and technical assistance to the Commission.

The Secretary-General's Special Representative and Head of UNAMI, Mr. Qazi, arrived in Baghdad on 13 August with a seven-member core team. His initial engagements included the national conference and contacts aimed at a peaceful settlement of the conflict in Najaf.

The Secretary-General observed that the convening of the national conference, though not as broad-based and as inclusive as most Iraqis would have wanted, made advances on several critical aspects. At the same time, however, the overall security environment had not seen any significant improvement. A crucial challenge for the Interim Government would be to create the necessary conditions to allow Iraq to become a society based on the rule of law. That implied a coordinated effort in the transformation of law and order institutions, encompassing police, judicial and penal reform. All parties had to support the Government's decision to disband militias, whose members had to be reintegrated into civil society. The problem of insecurity could be addressed only through a political process and a shared willingness to engage in sustained and transparent dialogue in a spirit of mutual understanding and compromise.

A conducive security environment was clearly and intimately linked to the performance of UN operations in Iraq. Circumstances did not permit the United Nations to implement its mandate to the fullest extent. Unless and until there was significant improvement in the overall security situation, UNAMI would have to continue working both inside and outside Iraq, as circumstance permitted, with a restricted presence on the ground in Iraq. It was important that the entity of the multinational force mandated to provide security for the UN presence be identified or deployed prior to the deployment of UNAMI guard units. The Secretary-General expected the full support of Member States, particularly in the Security Council, to contribute to that common endeavour.

Security Council consideration (14 September). On 14 September [meeting 5033], the Council was briefed by the Secretary-General's Special Representative for Iraq, Mr. Qazi, and by the United States representative on behalf of the multinational force.

Mr. Qazi reviewed the Secretary-General's first report pursuant to resolution 1546(2004) (see above). He said that the security environment was far from conducive to the deployment of UNAMI's international staff to Iraq, except in minimal numbers. It also confined UNAMI's movements to the international zone, which limited UNAMI's ability to interact with a sufficiently wide range of the Iraqi political spectrum.

The United States said that the security situation was fragile, attacks were persistent and lives continued to be lost. The multinational force had employed new counter-insurgency tactics and continued to train and deploy Iraqi security forces. The key to defeating the insurgents and terrorists was to continue training and deploying Iraqi forces at an accelerated pace. As at 10 September, the Iraqi Ministry of Defence had over 231,000 Iraqi security forces either on duty or in training. The Iraqi police numbered over 86,000, with a goal of hiring 135,000; the Department of Border Enforcement had hired over 14,000 border police, with a goal of hiring 32,000. The multinational force also worked to restore essential services to the Iraqi people, such as repairing bridges, ports, roads and railroads. It constructed hospitals, schools, post offices and other public buildings, while medical units had developed children's vaccination programmes. The United States and the multinational force remained committed to working with the international community to ensure that the security needs of the United Nations were met, but that effort merited international support if it were to be successful.

A longer, written version of the United States report was provided to the Council on that same day [S/2004/730].

Security arrangements for UNAMI

In a 21 September letter to the Security Council President [S/2004/764], the Secretary-General set out UNAMI's security arrangements, subject to the Council's approval. To expand its staffing and activities in Iraq, UNAMI, in addition to the protection provided by the multinational force, would have to establish an integrated UN security structure to carry out access control and patrols within UNAMI facilities; provide personal security details for personnel both within UN premises and on the move; and conduct training and coordinate security arrangements between UNAMI and other UN organizations, and with the multinational force. UNAMI's integrated security structure would consist of international security staff, protection coordination officers, personal security details and guard units. Their deployment would be subject to ongoing assessments of the overall security situation in Iraq and the related deployment of substantive staff, as well as on the completion of logistical arrangements, including secure office and living accommodation. The guard units would form part of that integrated security structure. Three formed units would be needed, each consisting of up to 160 armed civilian police, paramilitary or military personnel, to be provided as contingents from Member States. The guard units would form part of UNAMI, with the specific responsibility of controlling access to and conducting patrols within UNAMI premises.

In a 1 October letter [S/2004/765], the Council President welcomed the Secretary-General's proposed security arrangements for UNAMI and urged Member States to respond positively with contributions. On the same day [S/PV.5047], the Council endorsed its President's reply.

Establishment of UN trust fund

On 26 November [S/2004/927], the Netherlands drew the attention of the Security Council President to an exchange of letters between the Netherlands and the Secretary-General concerning the European Union's offer to contribute $12 million for financing the middle ring of the proposed UN protection force in Iraq, its request for information regarding the administrative details for the transfer of those funds, including the establishment of a UN trust fund for that purpose, and the Secretary-General's indication of his willingness to establish such a fund provided he received a mandate from the Council.

The Council President, in his 30 November reply [S/2004/929], said that the Council endorsed the creation of a trust fund to accept and administer contributions from Member States and requested the Secretary-General to establish the fund no later than 3 December.

On the same day [S/PV.5092], the Council endorsed the President's reply to the Secretary-General.

Sharm El Sheik meeting

The International Ministerial Meeting of the Countries Neighbouring Iraq (Egypt, Iran, Iraq, Jordan, Kuwait, Saudi Arabia, Syrian Arab Republic, Turkey), the Group of Eight (Canada, France, Germany, Italy, Japan, Russian Federation, United Kingdom, United States) and China (Sharm El Sheik, 23 November) was convened by Egypt with the objective of supporting the Iraqi people, the political process set out in Security Council resolution 1546(2004) (see p. 348) and the efforts of the Interim Government in that process. In his address to the meeting, the Secretary-General emphasized the need to promote convergence both inside Iraq and in the international community.

In a final communiqué transmitted by Egypt to the Council President on 26 November [S/2004/928], the ministers affirmed the right of the Iraqi people to a secure and stable life and to determine freely their future through democratic means and to exercise full control over their natural and financial resources. They underlined the importance of the United Nations continuing to play a leading role in that effort, and called on the international community to provide the assistance necessary for protecting the United Nations in Iraq. They encouraged the Interim Government to convene, before the general elections of 2005, representatives of the Iraqi political spectrum and civil society in order to share with them the results of the Sharm El Sheik meeting, so as to advance nation-building and national reconciliation with a view to encouraging broader participation in the general elections. The ministers called on all parties concerned to prevent the transit of terrorists to and from Iraq and financing that supported terrorists. They reiterated that the mandate of the multinational force in Iraq was not open-ended, for it would expire in accordance with resolution 1546(2004) on completion of the political process. They also reiterated the importance of humanitarian assistance and support for the reconstruction of Iraq, and called on Iraq's creditors to reduce substantially Iraq's sovereign debt. The ministers reaffirmed the importance of bringing to justice members of the previous Iraqi regime who had committed war crimes against Iran and Kuwait and crimes against humanity affecting the Iraqi people. Participants were directed to review regularly progress in implementing the conclusions reached at the meeting and to report to ministers on the outcome of their follow-up meetings, the first of which was to be held in February 2005.

Further reports of Secretary-General pursuant to resolution 1546(2004)

Pursuant to resolution 1546(2004), the Secretary-General submitted an 8 December report [S/2004/959] on UNAMI activities in Iraq since his September report (see p. 355). The security situation remained a major challenge. Although certain parts of the country, especially in the south, remained relatively calm, violence continued to adversely affect the centre of Iraq, particularly in and around Baghdad and other key cities, such as Fallujah, Samarra, Ramadi and Mosul. Iraq's security and law enforcement institutions remained fragile. Attacks, including acts of terror against State institutions and government officials, multinational force members, Iraqi security forces and civilians, continued unabated. Abductions and hostage-taking were also reported almost on a daily basis. On 7 November, the Interim Government declared a 60-day state of emergency in all parts of Iraq, except in the three northern governorates. Specific measures were announced for Fallujah and Ramadi, including the imposition of a 24-hour curfew in Fallujah, disbandment of the local police, and the closure of borders with the Syrian Arab Republic and Jordan. On 3 November, the Interim Government authorized Iraqi security forces and the multinational force to regain control of Fallujah through military action. While the Interim Government appeared to have regained control over most of the city, some insurgent groups might have relocated to other localities outside of the city. South of Baghdad also witnessed armed encounters between sectarian groups. In Sadr City, Iraqi security forces and the multinational force were engaged in military combat. An arrangement was reached whereby insurgents were to lay down their arms in a government weapons buy-out programme in exchange for a commitment by the authorities to rehabilitate long-neglected neighbourhoods. A partial amnesty was also announced and, eventually, order was restored in Sadr City. Violence also increased in Kirkuk and Mosul.

The priorities in the transitional process were the preparations for direct and democratic elections. Technical preparations for the elections remained on schedule. On 21 November, the Independent Electoral Commission of Iraq announced that the elections had been scheduled for 30 January 2005. While a number of parties and other entities announced their support for the elections, others indicated that they might boycott them.

In view of the very high and in some cases intensifying levels of violence in certain parts of Iraq, staff security remained the overriding constraint for all UN activities throughout the country. The deployment of UN staff in Iraq, which has been undertaken primarily in support of the electoral process, was confined to the international zone in Baghdad, and movement outside that zone remained extremely hazardous. The multinational force was providing security for UN personnel and controlling access to and protecting the outer perimeter of UN facilities. An agreement was being negotiated with the United States concerning protection by the multinational force of the UN presence in Iraq. The United Nations and the United States exchanged letters recording their mutual understanding of the security framework applicable in respect of UNAMI. The United Nations continued to support efforts by the multinational force to encourage Member States to provide troops or to make financial contributions for the creation of a UN protection force in Iraq (see p. 356). An initial group of protection coordination officers were recruited and deployed to Iraq as part of an integrated UN security structure. They were undergoing final equipping, training and technical certification for duty in Iraq. A UN guard unit of 135 military personnel had been provided by a Member State. That unit would control access to and conduct patrols within UNAMI facilities. The United Nations would continue to rely on the multinational force and Member States for air transport to and from Baghdad, and within Iraq, until it had the capability to resume its own flight operations.

The Special Representative and his political team continued to forge contacts with the Interim Government, political and religious leaders, public figures and representatives of civil society. The Special Representative and UNAMI closely followed developments in and around Fallujah and met with key officials of the Interim Government and representatives of the diplomatic community and of the multinational force to obtain a comprehensive understanding of the situation. The Special Representative engaged as wide a section of the Iraqi political spectrum as possible on how to advance the political process and to establish a conducive environment for the planned elections.

The Independent Electoral Commission had established itself as a credible institution and was carrying out its tasks in an effective manner. UNAMI guidance during the formative phase of institution-building was critical, as was the international expertise provided through Member States and other electoral organizations. An electoral cluster was established under the United Nations Development Group Iraq Trust Fund within the International Reconstruction Fund Facility for Iraq. The cluster encompassed all support activities to the Independent Electoral Commission for the preparation, administration and organization of the elections of January 2005. It also provided indirect electoral activities such as enhancement of women's participation, national observation, media development, political entity development and support to vulnerable groups. To date the cluster had received voluntary contributions of $110 million. Concurrently with the growth of the electoral administration, international technical assistance coordinated by UNAMI was consolidated. Training of election staff was a high priority for UNAMI, which also assisted in the development of the electoral regulations. Voter registration started on 1 November and was to continue until 15 December. The period of certification of political entities and coalitions and the nomination of candidates also began on 1 November. As at 29 November, 240 entity certification applications had been received, 228 of which received certification. Increasing emphasis was being placed on the public information programme to ensure that the public was informed about the electoral process. With the exception of Al Anbar province, all election materials needed for that stage of the election process had reached their destination.

Humanitarian, reconstruction and development activities remained constrained by the security situation and the resulting limitation on the number of staff deployed inside Iraq. Kidnappings and murders of national and international aid personnel prompted more international agencies to cease operation in November. Despite the fragile security environment, the United Nations was able to focus on a broad range of capacity-building activities and to continue reconstruction and rehabilitation efforts throughout Iraq, in partnership with other organizations. The donor committee of the International Reconstruction Fund Facility for Iraq held its third meeting (Tokyo, Japan, 13-14 October), at which donors were updated on World Bank and United Nations Development Group Trust Fund activities. Over $600 million had been pledged so far, of which $447 million had been received. At the meeting, the Interim Government presented the national development strategy for Iraq, which was formulated with UN assistance.

The UNAMI Public Information Unit worked on creating a better public understanding of the UN mandate in support of the transitional political process in Iraq and highlighted UN efforts aimed at support for reconstruction and humanitarian activities. It also addressed misconceptions about the United Nations through a coherent media policy.

The Secretary-General observed that credible and inclusive elections were the keystone for achieving legitimacy and stability in Iraq, and, as such, they would be the foundation for the next chapter in Iraq's history. If elections were to have an optimal impact, there was a need for sustained political efforts aimed at making the transition as inclusive, participatory and transparent as possible. Iraqis had to be reassured that the transition process was on track, enabling them to see light at the end of the tunnel. That required simultaneous progress in three mutually reinforcing areas: the security, political and economic areas, which should be addressed at the same time with equal attention. For its part, the United Nations, despite its limited presence, was determined to do its utmost to implement the mandate entrusted to it under resolution 1546(2004).

In a later report [S/2005/141 & Corr.1], the Secretary-General said that the month of December 2004 was critical for making final preparations for the January 2005 elections. On 15 December, the Fijian guard unit assumed from the multinational force the responsibility for inner ring protection of UN facilities within the Baghdad international zone. On 29 December, a bilateral agreement was concluded with the United States to obtain catering services, facility construction and renovation, vehicle maintenance, fuel supply, medical and military defence materials, training areas and welfare and recreation facilities for UN staff in Baghdad.

Security Council consideration (December). On 13 December [meeting 5099], the Council was briefed on the situation in Iraq by the Secretary-General's Special Representative for Iraq and by the United States representative.

The Special Representative said that the forthcoming elections represented a test of the new political order and of the transition process and, while there was a widespread desire among Iraqis to participate in them, some important segments of the population still felt alienated or excluded from the political transition. The desire to find political solutions to Iraq's political problems was by and large shared by all Iraqis, with the exception of a few irreconcilable extremists. The United Nations had actively continued to engage in dialogue those Iraqis outside the political mainstream to understand their needs and aspirations and encourage them to enter the political process. Equally, the Interim Government had made efforts to reach out to alienated elements and was continuing to do so.

The Special Representative said that he was optimistic that the Interim Government and the people of Iraq were willing and able to successfully negotiate the transition to a united democratic and prosperous Iraq. In support of that effort, the Paris Club (an informal group of official creditors) had decided to significantly reduce the country's external debt burden, and hoped that other creditors nations would do likewise.

The United States representative, updating the Council on the situation in Iraq on behalf of the multinational force, summarized a report provided to the Council on that same day [S/2004/967] and said that the security situation in Iraq remained difficult. The multinational force continued to work alongside their Iraqi counterparts to combat terrorism, destroy weapons that threatened Iraq's stability, gather intelligence and wage combat operations against insurgents and terrorists. It was helping to build that capability through the recruiting, training, equipping and mentoring of the Iraqi security forces. Those forces had almost tripled since the last reporting period and currently numbered some 116,240 people. While those trends were positive, much work remained before Iraq's forces could take full responsibility for the country's security. In the absence of a distinct entity to provide security for UN personnel in Iraq, United States troops had undertaken that task. He urged the United Nations to put additional personnel on the ground, as UN support was essential to the future of Iraq, and especially to the success of the elections.

UN Monitoring, Verification and Inspection Commission and IAEA activities

UNMOVIC

By an 8 January letter [S/2004/28], the Secretary-General proposed to the Security Council that Anatoliy Scherba (Ukraine) be appointed to the UNMOVIC College of Commissioners, replacing Kostyantyn Gryshchenko (Ukraine). On 13 January [S/2004/29], the Council agreed with the Secretary-General's proposal.

Reports of UNMOVIC (February, May, August, November). As called for in Security Council resolution 1284(1999) [YUN 1999, p. 230], UNMOVIC submitted to the Council, through the Secretary-General, four quarterly reports on its activities. Throughout the year, the Executive Chairman continued his practice of providing monthly briefings to the Council President and kept the Secretary-General informed about UNMOVIC's activities. UNMOVIC staff training courses were held throughout the year.

The February report [S/2004/160] said that, during the period from 1 December 2003 to 29 February 2004, no official information was available to UNMOVIC on either the work or the results of the investigations of the United States–led Iraq Survey Group in Iraq, nor had the Survey Group requested any information from UNMOVIC. However, note had been made of the testimony of David Kay, the former head of the Survey Group, before the Armed Services Committee of the United States Senate on 28 January, in which he said, among other things, that it was unlikely that there were large stockpiles of chemical and biological weapons in Iraq. UNMOVIC continued to assess material in the public domain on issues pertaining to Iraq's weapons of mass destruction (WMDs) and to compare it with what was known by UNMOVIC about Iraq's various weapons programmes. A summary of known UNMOVIC findings with respect to Iraq's chemical and biological munitions and a report on UNMOVIC's network of laboratories were appended to the report.

UNMOVIC continued the work on draft modifications to the monitoring and verification plan for Iraq and its annexes, approved by the Council in resolution 715(1991) [YUN 1991, p. 194], including the legal framework, operating procedures and practical arrangements regarding monitoring and verification. The work also aimed to take account of the changed circumstances on the ground in Iraq following the 2003 war. Another major effort was the compilation of a compendium on the nature and extent of Iraq's past proscribed weapons and programmes. The compendium looked at the origins of the programmes, including the political and security environment that led to their establishment. The College of Commissioners recognized that, while an early discussion of the future role of UNMOVIC by the Council would be desirable, the time frame for such a discussion was a matter for the Council.

In the May report [S/2004/435] covering the period from 1 March to 31 May, UNMOVIC indicated that its experts investigated, with the IAEA Iraq Nuclear Verification Office, the discovery of items from Iraq at a scrap yard in the Netherlands. The team of experts confirmed that a missile engine salvaged from the scrap metal process

was one from an SA-2 missile that had been tagged by UN inspectors in the past and had not been declared as having been fired. Despite the cooperation of the Government of the Netherlands and the scrapyard company concerned, it was not possible to determine how many other engines and other material previously subject to monitoring in Iraq might have passed through that scrapyard or others. UNMOVIC was aware from comparative analysis of satellite imagery that a number of sites previously known to have contained equipment and materials subject to monitoring had been either cleaned out or destroyed. It was not known whether such equipment and materials were still at the sites during the time of coalition action in March and April 2003. However, it was possible that some of the materials might have been removed from Iraq by looters of those sites and sold as scrap. In the meantime, UNMOVIC continued to compile its compendium of proscribed weapons and programmes, focusing on the period from 1999 to 2002 when inspectors were absent from the country, and during which time Iraq utilized a sophisticated procurement network for the acquisition of foreign materials, equipment and technology. According to UNMOVIC, from 1999 to 2002 Iraq produced a variety of dual-use biological and chemical items and materials, but there was no evidence that they were used for proscribed chemical or biological weapon purposes. Although some of the goods might have been acquired by Iraq outside the framework of the Security Council mechanisms, most of them were later declared by Iraq to UNMOVIC in its semi-annual monitoring declarations. However, in several instances Iraq provided misleading declarations regarding the suppliers, sources of the items and materials and procurement channels. The College of Commissioners, noting that UNMOVIC's mandate to verify the disarmament of Iraq and to conduct monitoring and verification was still in place, underlined that UNMOVIC's priority was to maintain its readiness to resume operations in Iraq until the Council revisited the mandate, as set out in resolution 1483(2003) [YUN 2003, p. 338].

In the August report [S/2004/693], covering the period from 1 June to 31 August, UNMOVIC said that it continued to investigate the discovery of items exported from Iraq as scrap metal. At the beginning of June, Commission experts visited a number of trading companies in Jordan dealing in the export of scrap metal from Iraq to Jordan. A number of items relevant to the UNMOVIC mandate were observed at the scrap yards, including 20 SA-2 missile engines. The scrap company managers estimated that a total of 130,000 tons of Iraqi scrap metal had passed through Jordan's largest free trade zone, though that amount was only a small part of all scrap materials exported from Iraq to the other neighbouring countries and further to Europe, North Africa and Asia. Other high-quality industrial production equipment from facilities all over Iraq had been purchased by unnamed contractors at low cost, dismantled and moved out of the country. According to some of the merchants, the authorities in Iraq had overall control of the scrap export business. A team of UNMOVIC and IAEA experts also visited a scrap yard in Turkey in July, though no items of relevance were found there. With the agreement of the relevant Member States, UNMOVIC intended to observe the destruction of the SA-2 missile engines located in Jordan and the Netherlands together with other tagged and dual-use equipment that had been under monitoring in Iraq. Using commercially available satellite imagery, UNMOVIC continued to assess the status of sites subjected to monitoring that were damaged during the war and in some cases completely razed. The systematic removal of items subject to monitoring affected UNMOVIC's ability to maintain an accurate and up-to-date assessment of Iraq's capabilities.

Another issue under evaluation was the examination of information available on past storage, handling and deployment of chemical and biological munitions by Iraq, a summary of which was appended to the report. In the publicly released testimony of the head of the United States–led Iraq Survey Group in March, mention was made of the uncovering of a very robust Iraqi programme for delivery systems that had not been reported to the United Nations. While not much specific detail was provided in the statement by the Survey Group, UNMOVIC considered it important to set out what it knew about those programmes and their relationship to the delivery of chemical and/or biological warfare agents. A short summary of UNMOVIC's findings on those issues was also appended to the report.

The November report [S/2004/924], covering the period from 1 September to 30 November, indicated that the comprehensive report of Charles Duelfer, the Special Adviser to the United States Director of Central Intelligence for Iraq's Weapons of Mass Destruction, was made public on 6 October. Mr. Duelfer and a team from the Iraq Survey Group visited UNMOVIC on 8 October to present their findings, the scope of their work and the methodology used, while acknowledgeing that extensive documentation still had to be analysed. UNMOVIC was studying the report and was comparing its own knowledge and findings with those of the Survey Group. Initial comments on specific findings of the report were appended to the report.

During the period under review, UNMOVIC's experts continued to use commercial satellite imagery to assess the status of sites subject to monitoring, particularly the Muthanna State Establishment and Al Qaa Qaa State Establishment, given their involvement in Iraq's past weapons programmes, their size and inventory of WMD-related material. The Muthanna State Establishment was Iraq's prime chemical weapon research, production and storage facility. As of May 2004, no changes at the area of the two sealed bunkers were observed; however, analysis of imagery revealed that some other structures had been demolished and removed, together with other equipment which, although rendered harmless, was not fully destroyed in the 1990s. The report of the Iraq Survey Group stated that all sealed structures at the site had been breached and some equipment and materials removed. Stockpiles of chemical munitions were still stored in the bunkers, which tested positive for chemical weapon agents. In addition, the extent of looting made it impossible to determine whether the Iraqi Government removed equipment after 1998, or after March 2003. However, UNMOVIC responded that, in December 2002, it had inspected the bunker area of the facility and found all sealed structures intact and guarded by Iraqi security. If that structure had actually been breached, as stated by the Iraq Survey Group in its report, there could no longer be any certainty about whether all its contents were intact.

The other site, the Al Qaa Qaa State Establishment, was one of the major weapons-related industrial complexes in Iraq. As of November 2004, the fate of about 800 pieces of declared chemical equipment known to have been at the site was uncertain. Analysis of satellite imagery of November 2003 revealed that all buildings at the chemical raw materials stores at the site had been destroyed, while others appeared to have war damage. With the Jordanian Government's support, a number of SA-2 engines and other missiles and chemical-related dual-use items were destroyed in Jordan in August and October, in the presence of an UNMOVIC inspector. Late in November, Dutch authorities destroyed, also in the presence of an UNMOVIC inspector, the 22 SA-2 missile engines found in a Rotterdam scrap yard.

Also in November, UNMOVIC convened a panel of external technical experts to assist in a technical review of the provisions concerning biological matters and the associated annex (annex III) of the monitoring and verification plan approved by Council resolution 715(1991). The panel made specific recommendations on items covered by the plan, in the light of UN monitoring and verification experience and bio-technical advances. Similar review processes would be conducted for the chemical and missile provisions and related annexes. Once the whole process was completed, the revised annexes would be submitted to the Council for information. UNMOVIC retained a core staff of nine local nationals in Baghdad who maintained the existing offices, laboratories and other equipment. The Cyprus Field Office continued to store and maintain UNMOVIC inspection and monitoring equipment recovered from Iraq.

IAEA

IAEA reports (April and October). In accordance with Security Council resolution 1051 (1996) [YUN 1996, p. 218], IAEA submitted to the Council, through the Secretary-General, two consolidated six-monthly reports, on 11 April [S/2004/285] and 1 October [S/2004/786], on the Agency's verification activities in Iraq.

In April, IAEA said that, since 17 March 2003, it had not been in a position to implement its mandate in Iraq under Council resolution 687(1991) [YUN 1991, p. 172] and related resolutions. It was IAEA's understanding that its obligations pursuant to those resolutions remained valid unless and until the Council decided otherwise. During the period under review, IAEA continued to consolidate and further analyse information collected and activities implemented since 1991, so as to identify lessons learned and decide whether and to what extent its plan for resuming verification activities needed to be adapted in the light of those lessons and the changing situation in Iraq. The information obtained was derived principally from open sources and commercial satellite imagery of locations of interest to IAEA for potential future verification in Iraq. IAEA was concerned about the implications of the results of its review of satellite imagery, especially with respect to sites known to have contained items subject to monitoring under the monitoring and verification plan. The imagery showed that there had been extensive removal of equipment and, in some instances, of entire buildings. In addition, large quantities of scrap, some of it contaminated, had been transferred out of Iraq, from IAEA-monitored sites. It was not clear whether the removal of those items was the result of looting in the aftermath of the 2003 war in Iraq, or part of systematic efforts to rehabilitate some of the locations. In any event, those activities might have a significant impact on IAEA's continuity of knowledge of Iraq's remaining nuclear-related capabilities, and raised concern with regard to the proliferation risk associated with dual-use material and equipment disappearing to unknown destinations. IAEA remained ready, subject to Council guidance, to resume its mandated verification activities in Iraq. In the meantime, Member States were expected to provide any information relevant to prohibited programmes in Iraq or aspects of the IAEA mandate, with a view to enabling IAEA to fulfil its responsibilities.

In October, IAEA reported that, on 6 July, it was informed by the United States of the removal and transfer to the United States, with the consent of the Interim Iraqi Government, of nuclear material (see below). Pursuant to Iraq's safeguards agreement with IAEA, on 3 and 4 August, IAEA carried out its annual physical inventory verification of the remaining 550 tons of nuclear material in Iraq located at the location C nuclear material storage facility and verified the presence of the nuclear material subject to safeguards. Following the transfer of responsibility and authority for governing Iraq to the Interim Government on 30 June 2004, the Iraqi Minister of Science and Technology visited IAEA in July and discussed, among other issues, matters related to the implementation of relevant Council resolutions. In September, Iraq requested IAEA assistance with the sale of the remaining nuclear material at Tuwaitha (with the exception of a small quantity to be retained for research purposes), the dismantling and decontamination of former nuclear facilities, and the resumption of assistance under a number of technical cooperation projects approved by the Sanctions Committee for Iraq, but which were put on hold following the suspension of inspections in December 1998. IAEA was assessing the possibility of providing such assistance.

IAEA communications. On 6 July [S/2004/538], IAEA notified the Security Council President, through the Secretary-General, that it had been advised by the United States, due to security concerns, of the transfer on 23 June to the United States of 1.8 tons of uranium enriched to 2.6 per cent in uranium-235, 3 kilograms of uranium of various low enrichments and some 1,000 highly radioactive sources, most of which had been stored at location C. The nuclear material that remained at location C was mostly natural uranium, some depleted uranium and some low enriched uranium waste.

On 25 October [S/2004/831], IAEA informed the Council, through the Secretary-General, that it had been advised on 10 October by the General Director of the Planning and Following Up Directorate of the Iraqi Ministry of Science and Technology of the loss, after 9 April 2003, through theft and looting, of high explosives subject to IAEA monitoring. On 15 October, IAEA informed the multinational force about the matter.

Iraq-Kuwait

Oil-for-food programme: High-level Independent Inquiry Committee

The oil-for-food programme, established by Security Council resolution 986(1995) [YUN 1995, p. 475] authorizing the sale of Iraqi petroleum and petroleum products as a temporary measure to finance humanitarian assistance, thereby alleviating the adverse consequences of the sanctions regime imposed by the Council, was phased out on 21 November 2003 [YUN 2003, p. 362].

On 19 March 2004, the Secretary-General informed the Council President of his intention to establish an independent, high-level inquiry concerning matters arising from public news reports and commentaries that had called into question the administration and management of the programme, including allegations of fraud and corruption. On 26 March, he communicated to the Council President the terms of reference of the independent inquiry, which were to determine: whether UN procedures for the processing and approving of contracts under the programme, the monitoring of the sale and delivery of petroleum and petroleum products and the purchase of and delivery of humanitarian goods had been violated; whether any UN officials, personnel, agents or contractors had engaged in any illicit or corrupt activities in the carrying out of their respective roles in relation to the programme; and whether the accounts of the programme were in order and were maintained in accordance with UN Financial Regulations and Rules.

The Secretary-General requested the UN Office of Internal Oversight Services (OIOS) to terminate the inquiry it had commenced into those allegations and to hand over the documents and other materials it had collected in connection with its investigation.

The independent inquiry was expected to submit to the Secretary-General within three months a report on the status of its work. The inquiry's final report would be made available to the public. The Secretary-General undertook, based on the findings of the report, to take appropriate action within his authority in regard to individuals or entities found in violation of UN rules of procedure, or having engaged in abusive, illicit or corrupt activities.

On 21 April, the Secretary-General announced the formation of the Independent Inquiry Com-

mittee (IIC) to look into the oil-for-food programme, headed by Paul A. Volcker, former Chairman of the Board of Governors of the United States Federal Reserve System, and comprising Justice Richard Goldstone (South Africa) and Mark Pieth (Switzerland). He also indicated that the panel would have the authority to access all relevant UN records and information and interview relevant UN officials and personnel. He would employ his authority so that the United Nations privileges and immunities would not impede efforts to hold accountable those who had engaged in unacceptable conduct.

SECURITY COUNCIL ACTION

On 21 April [meeting 4946], the Security Council unanimously adopted **resolution 1538(2004)**. The draft [S/2004/311] was submitted by France, Germany, Spain, the United Kingdom and the United States.

The Security Council,

Expressing the desire to see a full and fair investigation of efforts by the former Government of Iraq, including through bribery, kickbacks, surcharges on oil sales and illicit payments in regard to purchases of humanitarian goods, to evade the provisions of resolution 661(1990) of 6 August 1990 and subsequent relevant resolutions,

Concerned by public news reports and commentaries that have called into question the administration and management of the oil-for-food programme (hereinafter "the Programme") established pursuant to resolution 986(1995) of 14 April 1995 and subsequent relevant resolutions, including allegations of fraud and corruption,

Affirming that any illicit activity by United Nations officials, personnel and agents, as well as contractors, including entities that have entered into contracts under the Programme, is unacceptable,

Emphasizing the importance of full cooperation with the independent high-level inquiry by all United Nations officials and personnel, the Coalition Provisional Authority, Iraq and all other Member States,

Affirming the letter of its President of 31 March 2004 welcoming the decision of the Secretary-General to create an independent high-level inquiry to investigate the administration and management of the Programme, and taking note of the details relating to its organization and terms of reference,

1. *Welcomes* the appointment of the independent high-level inquiry;

2. *Calls upon* the Coalition Provisional Authority, Iraq and all other Member States, including their national regulatory authorities, to cooperate fully by all appropriate means with the inquiry;

3. *Looks forward* to receiving the final report of the inquiry;

4. *Decides* to remain actively seized of the matter.

IIC status report and first briefing paper

On 9 August, the Independent Inquiry Committee submitted a status report describing the initiation and progress of its investigation (www.iic-offp.org).

The inquiry was to be conducted from three office locations—New York, Paris and Baghdad, by line staff organized into a number of investigation teams, each of which included legal, investigative, accounting and technology professionals, with a common background in the fraud and corruption investigations involving multiple jurisdictions. IIC conducted investigative missions in Iraq, Europe and the Middle East. Those Member States that had been approached by IIC had offered to cooperate with the inquiry. IIC had identified and started interviewing individuals with responsibility for establishing and operating the various aspects of the programme on behalf of the UN and its related agencies, and contractors involved with the programme. The Committee initiated methodical identification, securing and screening of all UN programme documents and financial records. It also met with representatives from a number of national governmental investigative authorities concerned about conduct that might have occurred within their countries. IIC would cooperate with those additional inquiries to the extent consistent with maintaining the integrity of its own investigation.

In a 21 October briefing paper, reviewing the status of the investigation into the oil-for-food programme, IIC reported that it had made substantial progress towards the goal of assessing the allegations of maladministration and corruption. The Committee and its staff had conducted scores of witness interviews in Europe, the United States, Iraq and elsewhere in the Middle East. They were also reviewing UN records and had obtained additional informaiton in Iraq. The briefing paper also detailed facts about oil sales and the purchase of humanitarian goods and oil spare parts, as well as programme revenue and expenditures.

POWs, Kuwaiti property and missing persons

Reports of Secretary-General (April, August, December). Pursuant to Security Council resolution 1284(1999) [YUN 1999, p. 230], the Secretary-General submitted reports in April [S/2004/301], August [S/2004/645] and December [S/2004/961] on compliance by Iraq with its obligations regarding the repatriation or return of all Kuwaiti and third-country nationals or their remains, and on the return of all Kuwaiti property, including archives, seized by Iraq during its occupation of Kuwait, which began in August 1990 [YUN 1990, p. 189]. The High-level Coordinator for compli-

ance by Iraq with its obligations regarding the return of Kuwaiti nationals and property, Yuri M. Vorontsov (Russian Federation), regularly briefed the Security Council throughout the year.

In April, the Secretary-General observed that progress had been made in closing the files of the Kuwaiti prisoners of war and third-country nationals since his December 2003 report [YUN 2003, p. 357]. That was evidence of a steady movement forward and a result of cooperation among the members of the Tripartite Commission (France, Iraq, Kuwait, Saudi Arabia, United Kingdom, United States), established in 1991 under the auspices of the International Committee of the Red Cross. From the end of 1998 to the end of 2002, Iraq did not participate in the Commission's work. In December 2002, for the first time in four years, Iraq participated on the sidelines of the Commission's meeting. The Secretary-General reiterated his strong condemnation of the execution of Kuwaiti and third-country nationals by the previous Iraqi regime, as detailed in his December 2003 report, and stressed that the perpetrators of those crimes should be brought to justice. The extension by the Council on 18 December 2003 [ibid.] of the Coordinator's mandate should contribute to bringing to a closure the remaining humanitarian issues of concern to the people of Kuwait. Mr. Vorontsov would visit Baghdad to establish contacts with the new Iraqi authorities and would continue to confer with CPA representatives in order to fulfil his mandate.

In August, the Secretary-General said that the number of resolved cases of persons still unaccounted for had increased. Given that some 340 mortal remains had already been brought to Kuwait, their positive identification would mean that in the near future about one half of the Kuwaiti and third-country prisoners would have found their final resting place. As at 12 August, not a single person from the initial list of 605 Kuwaiti and third-country nationals had been found alive. The Secretary-General welcomed the establishment of contact between the High-level Coordinator and the Iraqi Interim Government, and took note of the new Iraqi authorities' determination to assist Mr. Vorontsov in resolving remaining humanitarian issues.

In December, the Secretary-General said that the remains of Kuwaiti and third-country nationals continued to be repatriated to Kuwait and identified. Progress in the discovery and identification of mortal remains was evidence of the enhanced cooperation between the Tripartite Commission and its Technical Subcommittee, established in 1994 to expedite the search for all persons for whom inquiry files had been opened. In November, the Interim Government returned to Kuwait property seized by the previous Iraqi regime. That important step should trigger further efforts on the part of the new Iraqi authorities in finding other stolen items, foremost among them the Kuwaiti national archives.

UN Iraq-Kuwait Observation Mission

The United Nations Iraq-Kuwait Observation Mission (UNIKOM), established by Security Council resolution 687(1991) [YUN 1991, p. 172], discharged its functions until 6 October 2003 [YUN 2003, p. 358] in accordance with its terms of reference, as expanded by resolution 806(1993) [YUN 1993, p. 406].

Financing

On 18 June [meeting 91], the General Assembly considered the Secretary-General's performance reports on UNIKOM's budget for the period from 1 July 2002 to 30 June 2003 [A/58/630], and the overview of the financing of UN peacekeeping operations: budget performance for the period from 1 July 2002 to 30 June 2003 and budget for the period from 1 July 2004 to 30 June 2005 [A/58/705], together with the related reports of the Advisory Committee on Administrative and Budgetary Questions (ACABQ) on the financial performance report of UNIKOM for the period from 1 July 2002 to 30 June 2003 [A/58/759 & Add.12].

On the recommendation of the Fifth (Administrative and Budgetary) Committee [A/58/585/Add.1], the Assembly adopted **resolution 58/304** without vote [agenda item 143 *(a)*].

Financing of the United Nations Iraq-Kuwait Observation Mission

The General Assembly,

Having considered the reports of the Secretary-General on the financing of the United Nations Iraq-Kuwait Observation Mission and the related reports of the Advisory Committee on Administrative and Budgetary Questions,

Recalling Security Council resolutions 687(1991) of 3 April 1991 and 689(1991) of 9 April 1991, by which the Council decided to establish the United Nations Iraq-Kuwait Observation Mission and to review the question of its termination or continuation every six months, and resolution 1490(2003) of 3 July 2003, by which the Council decided to continue the mandate of the Observation Mission for a final period until 6 October 2003,

Recalling also its resolution 45/260 of 3 May 1991 on the financing of the Observation Mission and its subsequent resolutions and decisions thereon, the latest of which was decision 58/559 of 23 December 2003,

Reaffirming the general principles underlying the financing of United Nations peacekeeping operations, as stated in General Assembly resolutions 1874(S-IV)

of 27 June 1963, 3101(XXVIII) of 11 December 1973 and 55/235 of 23 December 2000,

Expressing its appreciation for the substantial voluntary contributions made to the Observation Mission by the Government of Kuwait and the contributions of other Governments,

Mindful of the fact that it is essential to provide the Observation Mission with the necessary resources to enable it to meet its outstanding liabilities,

1. *Takes note* of the status of contributions to the United Nations Iraq-Kuwait Observation Mission as at 15 April 2004, including the contributions outstanding in the amount of 7 million United States dollars, representing some 2 per cent of the total assessed contributions, notes with concern that only eighty-one Member States have paid their assessed contributions in full, and urges all other Member States, in particular those in arrears, to ensure the payment of their outstanding assessed contributions;

2. *Expresses its continued appreciation* of the decision of the Government of Kuwait to defray two thirds of the cost of the Observation Mission, effective 1 November 1993;

3. *Expresses its appreciation* to those Member States which have paid their assessed contributions in full, and urges all other Member States to make every possible effort to ensure payment of their assessed contributions to the Observation Mission in full;

4. *Expresses concern* at the financial situation with regard to peacekeeping activities, in particular as regards the reimbursements to troop contributors that bear additional burdens owing to overdue payments by Member States of their assessments;

5. *Also expresses concern* at the delay experienced by the Secretary-General in deploying and providing adequate resources to some recent peacekeeping missions, in particular those in Africa;

6. *Emphasizes* that all future and existing peacekeeping missions shall be given equal and non-discriminatory treatment in respect of financial and administrative arrangements;

7. *Also emphasizes* that all peacekeeping missions shall be provided with adequate resources for the effective and efficient discharge of their respective mandates;

8. *Endorses* the conclusions and recommendations contained in the report of the Advisory Committee on Administrative and Budgetary Questions, and requests the Secretary-General to ensure their full implementation;

Financial performance report for the period from 1 July 2002 to 30 June 2003

9. *Takes note* of the report of the Secretary-General on the financial performance of the Observation Mission for the period from 1 July 2002 to 30 June 2003;

10. *Decides*, taking into account the unencumbered balance and other income in the total amount of 12,657,400 dollars in respect of the financial period ended 30 June 2003, that Member States that have fulfilled their financial obligations to the Observation Mission shall be credited their respective share of the unencumbered balance and other income in the total amount of 4,295,733 dollars, in accordance with the levels set out in General Assembly resolution 55/235, as adjusted by the Assembly in its resolutions 55/236

of 23 December 2000 and 57/290 A of 20 December 2002, and taking into account the scale of assessments for 2003, as set out in its resolutions 55/5 B of 23 December 2000 and 57/4 B of 20 December 2002;

11. *Decides also* that, for Member States that have not fulfilled their financial obligations to the Observation Mission, their respective share of the unencumbered balance and other income in the total amount of 4,295,733 dollars in respect of the financial period ended 30 June 2003 shall be set off against their outstanding obligations, in accordance with the scheme set out in paragraph 10 above;

12. *Decides further* that the decrease of 114,900 dollars in the estimated staff assessment income in respect of the financial period ended 30 June 2003 shall be set off against the credits from the amount referred to in paragraphs 10 and 11 above, and that the respective shares of Member States therein shall be applied in accordance with the provisions of those paragraphs, as appropriate;

13. *Decides* that, taking into account the voluntary contribution of the Government of Kuwait in respect of the financial period ended 30 June 2003, two thirds of the net unencumbered balance and other income in the total amount of 8,361,667 dollars in respect of the financial period ended 30 June 2003 shall be returned to the Government of Kuwait;

14. *Emphasizes* that no peacekeeping mission shall be financed by borrowing funds from other active peacekeeping missions;

15. *Decides* to include in the provisional agenda of its fifty-ninth session, under the item entitled "Financing of the activities arising from Security Council resolution 687(1991)", the sub-item entitled "United Nations Iraq-Kuwait Observation Mission".

On 23 December, the Assembly decided that the item on the financing of activities arising from resolution 687(1991) remained for consideration at the resumed fifty-ninth (2005) session (**decision 59/552**).

UN Compensation Commission and Fund

The United Nations Compensation Commission (UNCC), established in 1991 [YUN 1991, p. 195] for the resolution and payment of claims against Iraq for losses and damage resulting from its 1990 invasion and occupation of Kuwait [YUN 1990, p. 189], continued in 2004 to expedite the prompt settlement of claims through the United Nations Compensation Fund, which was established at the same time as the Commission.

Governing Council. The Commission's Governing Council held four sessions in Geneva during the year—the fifty-first (9-11 March) [S/2004/213], the fifty-second (29 June-2 July) [S/2004/547], the fifty-third (21-23 September) [S/2004/773] and the fifty-fourth (7-9 December) [S/2004/977]—at which it considered the reports and recommendations of the Panels of Commissioners appointed to review specific instalments of various

categories of claims. The Governing Council also acted on the Executive Secretary's report submitted at each session, which, in addition to providing a summary of the previous period's activities, covered the processing, withdrawal and payment of claims.

Other matters considered by the Council during the year included the processing and payment of claims, requests for late filing of claims, contributions to the Compensation Fund and arrangements for ensuring that payments were made into the Fund.

Oversight activities

On 5 October [S/2004/789], the Secretary-General transmitted to the Security Council the report of the Board of Auditors on the financial statements of UNCC for the biennium ended 31 December 2003. The Board reported that the claim-processing performance of UNCC had been acceptable in regard to international practices. UNCC still had no proper assurance that past payments reached the claimants, but expected the newly requested audit certificates to do so. The Board regretted that more internal audits could not be accomplished due to insufficient staff by the Governing Council. The Board recommended that UNCC conduct a joint risk-assessment with OIOS, request all paying Governments and agents to provide updated information on their compensation payment system, provide OIOS with appropriate internal audit post, and establish an audit committee.

Timor-Leste

UN Mission of Support in East Timor

The United Nations Mission of Support in East Timor (UNMISET), established under Security Council resolution 1410(2002) [YUN 2002, p. 321], continued to carry out its mandate in Timor-Leste, which included providing assistance to the administrative, law enforcement and public security structures critical to the viability and political stability of Timor-Leste, in addition to contributing to the maintenance of its external and internal security. In order to help Timor-Leste achieve full self-sufficiency, the Security Council in May extended UNMISET's mandate for six months beyond 20 May 2004, and, in November, for a final period until 20 May 2005.

On 19 May [S/2004/418], the Secretary-General informed the Council that he intended to appoint Sukehiro Hasegawa (Japan) as his Special

Representative for Timor-Leste and Head of UNMISET, replacing Kamalesh Sharma (India). On 21 May [S/2004/419], the Council took note of that intention.

Communications (February). On 11 February [S/2004/108], Portugal informed the Council President that, in spite of impressive progress achieved in Timor-Leste, the international community's substantial engagement and support would still be needed to ensure stability and security in the new State. As threats to that stability could be expected to continue beyond the conclusion of UNMISET's mandate on 20 May, and given Timor-Leste's assessment of its own limitations in coping with internal and external security problems, Portugal strongly favoured that the post-UNMISET presence in Timor-Leste include a military force to maintain a sufficient deterrent. Portugal would be available to participate in that common effort.

On 12 February [S/2004/114], Timor-Leste informed the Secretary-General that its forces were still not ready to deal independently with internal tensions, nor with the general volatility of a nascent country and with that in the region. Timor-Leste was therefore convinced that it was necessary to extend the presence of a UN battalion of peacekeeping forces, backed by helicopters, in the country beyond May.

Report of Secretary-General (February). Pursuant to Council resolution 1410(2002), the Secretary-General submitted a 13 February special report [S/2004/117] on UNMISET's activities and proposals on how the international community could assist in promoting the security and stability of Timor-Leste after the end of UNMISET's mandate on 20 May.

The Secretary-General said that Timor-Leste's political institutions continued to strengthen and evolve, though the relationships between them were at an early stage of development and in some respects remained fragile. The security situation had largely remained calm, despite occasional demonstrations. While no new violence was carried out by former militia or armed groups, reports of sightings of armed gangs and criminal elements in districts bordering West Timor continued. The border remained porous, and illegal hunting, trade and crossings continued, as did other criminal activity. The Government responded with a number of police investigations and arrests to deter such activity. On 25 January, there was a confrontation between members of the Timorese armed forces (F-FDTL) and the police (Policia Nacional de Timor-Leste (PNTL)) in the town of Los Palos, in which a number of police were briefly detained by F-FDTL officers. In response to that incident, President

Xanana Gusmão called for the creation of an independent commission to assess the problems faced by F-FDTL and to recommend solutions.

In general, relations between Timor-Leste and Indonesia continued to develop, supported by commitment at the highest political levels on both sides. However, the two countries needed to make further progress in addressing the problems posed by the continued presence of 28,000 former refugees from Timor-Leste in West Timor, only 452 of whom returned to Timor-Leste in 2003, notwithstanding ongoing efforts to promote long-term reconciliation. While the introduction by the Office of the United Nations High Commissioner for Refugees (UNHCR) of a resettlement and return plan contributed to a reduction of tension in the remaining camps, the situation remained volatile.

The Secretary-General said that planning for UNMISET was predicated upon the assumption that Timor-Leste would be able to achieve self-sufficiency within two years after independence. However, it was clear that further assistance would be crucial in a number of areas after UNMISET's mandate expired on 20 May. The UN Secretariat had further analysed Timor-Leste's likely requirements after that date. It sent a technical assessment mission, including civilian, military and police expertise, to Timor-Leste early in January to review the situation on the ground.

The report provided an analysis of the status of progress, together with detailed proposals for assistance after 20 May, in each of UNMISET's three programme areas: stability, democracy and justice; internal security and law enforcement; and external security and border-control. The Secretary-General recommended that the Security Council extend UNMISET for a further 12-month "consolidation phase" to provide assistance to the justice system and to core administrative structures critical to the viability and political stability of Timor-Leste, and to contribute to the development of the national police and to the maintenance of security and stability in Timor-Leste. The Mission could continue to support efforts by the Governments of Timor-Leste and Indonesia to resolve pending bilateral issues and their increasing cooperation, in particular border demarcation and the development of appropriate mechanisms for managing the border regions, as well as to ensure that those responsible for serious crimes in 1999 were brought to justice. UNMISET, under the continued leadership of the Secretary-General's Special Representative, would include multidimensional peacekeeping units, advisers on gender and HIV/AIDS, a human rights capacity, and civilian, police and military components, in a reduced and modified form, so as to complete key tasks and enable Timor-Leste to attain self-sufficiency.

The Secretary-General recommended the retention of a component of 58 civilian advisers to provide advice and support to the public administration and justice system; the continuing support to prosecutions and trials related to the serious crimes committed in 1999; the retention of 157 civilian police advisers to assist in the continued development of the police; and the deployment of 42 military liaison officers to monitor security-related developments and support demarcation efforts. The Secretary-General also recommended that a security force, comprising some 310 military personnel, be deployed to provide protection for the military liaison officers, maintain a reassuring presence in the border regions and provide a quick-reaction capability if required. Those recommendations focused on areas that had an impact on the security and stability of Timor-Leste, and where bilateral assistance was unavailable or not well suited to meet requirements. They also included a transition strategy that would allow the peacekeeping assistance to be phased out within a year, mostly on the basis of developing sufficient Timorese capabilities, although it relied in some cases on transition to bilateral assistance. The validity of and the benefits from those proposals depended on a number of key political decisions, including the adoption by Timor-Leste of a Civil Service Act, of the law creating the Office of the Provedor (Prosecutor), and of strong transparency and accountability legislation against corruption; the adoption of legislation defining the respective relationships between PNTL and F-FDTL and between various PNTL units; the establishment of oversight mechanisms for PNTL; and promulgation and strict implementation of a code of conduct.

Security Council consideration (20 February). On 20 February [meeting 4913], the Security Council discussed the situation in Timor-Leste, with particular reference to the Secretary-General's February report. The UN Under-Secretary-General for Peacekeeping Operations, Jean-Marie Guéhenno, brought to the Council's attention two recent developments. First, President Gusmão approved the law on village elections, an important advance in terms of reinforcing the role of electoral processes in Timor-Leste and in fostering local engagement in governance. It was expected that further steps would be taken to clarify the role and responsibility of village chiefs and village councils. Secondly, the 29 January incident during which villagers from West Timor entered Tomor-Leste, burning structures and stealing livestock, suggested the continuing fragility of the situation on the ground. Mr. Guéhenno said that the continued presence of a small peacekeeping operation for an additional one-year consolidation period would make a meaningful difference in enabling the country to reach the threshold of self-sufficiency. However, there were limits to what could be achieved and some further long-term assistance might be required even after that period. For that reason, the responsibilities of civilian advisers would include identification of alternative solutions by which to continue support after that period had ended. The Government had launched intensive discussion on ensuring a smooth transition after that assistance ended. Support of serious crime investigations and proceedings would allow progress in an area where much had already been done, considering that 81 indictments had been issued, with 369 indictees, resulting in 48 convictions. However, a number of trials would remain pending by 20 May and further indictments were in the process of preparation, including those related to the killing of two local UN staff. The great majority of those who had been indicted remained outside the country. Close cooperation among Member States would be essential to ensure that all those responsible were brought to justice.

Notable progress had been achieved in the establishment of an effective and professional police force. In February, the Timorese police force, numbering 3,024, assumed responsibility for all daily patrolling throughout the country, including along the border area, where they were playing a key role under difficult circumstances. The United Nations had retained daily operational responsibilities for crowd control only, so that the Timorese riot unit could undergo additional intensive training before 20 May. The international police contingent included only that 125-officer formed police unit and some 200 officers who were advising and discharging residual headquarters functions. International assistance would remain crucial for a further 12 months after 20 May to ensure the police service's effective functioning and to reinforce professional values and skills. That would be based on the continued deployment of 157 civilian police advisers after May, with staffing requirements to be reviewed by the end of 2004.

Finally, progress in external security and border control had benefited from the statesmanlike commitment shown by the Indonesian and Timorese leadership. However, agreement on the border and practical arrangements for its management had yet to be reached, and the potential for tensions or destabilizing actions remained within communities in the western districts. At the same time, the creation of structures and relationships on the ground required further time. While the Border Patrol Unit had assumed its responsibilities, and while F-FDTL continued to develop, both institutions remained thinly stretched, and further clarification of their responsibilities was essential. In addition, the establishment of the Rapid Deployment Service was considerably behind schedule. In that context, an essential role continued to be played by military observers, who were monitoring developments within a potentially volatile area and they were supporting close relationships between Timorese and Indonesian border personnel. The retention of a small group of 42 military liaison officers along the border to discharge similar functions, as proposed by the Secretary-General (see p. 368) for a further year after 20 May, could be reviewed in December, against progress in border arrangements and the development of necessary Timorese capacity.

Timor-Leste said that, while peace was a reality, it was still very fragile; so were the institutions of law and order and the State public administration. For those reasons, the Government of Timor-Leste, in a 12 February letter to the Secretary-General (see p. 368), had appealed for the continuation of a peacekeeping component in a new UN mission in Timor-Leste, as the best deterrence against any potential violent conflict.

Report of Secretary-General (April). The Secretary-General, in a 29 April report [S/2004/333] describing UNMISET's activities since his February special report (see above), said that several important steps were taken towards preparation for Timor-Leste's first elections since the country's independence in 2002 [YUN 2002, p. 323]. President Gusmão, on 10 February 2004, promulgated a village elections bill providing for the establishment of the National Electoral Commission, which was sworn in on 19 March. He signed on 26 March a bill regulating political parties and, on 1 April, a decree-law defining the roles and functions of the village heads and councils. The elections, scheduled for the last quarter of 2004, posed a significant logistical challenge for the Government, particularly voter registration, due to begin on 31 May, with final voter lists to be published on 20 September. Further progress was also made towards the adoption of legislation for key public institutions. The National Parliament adopted the Civil Service Act on 19 April, as well as the Organic Law on the Office of the Presidency on 20 May, paving the way for the establishment of two other constitutional bodies, the Superior Council of Defence and Security and the Council of State. The Parliament was also considering a bill related to the creation of the

Office of the Provedor for Human Rights and Justice, an independent institution to support good governance and civil rights. However, the law on PNTL had yet to be approved. A defence act and acts related to the establishment of other constitutional bodies with security responsibility, which were in various stages of preparation and consideration, were vital for the long-term viability and sustainability of Timor-Leste's security structure. The Secretary-General emphasized that, for the effective maintenance of law and order, the roles of Timorese police and armed forces should be clarified in advance of 20 May, when Timor-Leste would assume full responsibility for its internal and external security, and UNMISET's role would be reduced to one of support. The need for clarity in the country's security policy and structure was also apparent from the preliminary findings emerging from reviews of the 25 January 2004 incident in Los Palos, where members of F-FDTL became involved in a confrontation with PNTL. Three separate inquiries, established by President Gusmão, pointed out that F-FDTL was confronted with serious institutional problems, including a poorly understood definition of its role, low morale, lack of respect for discipline and authority, insufficient training and unresolved relations with former combatants.

Concerning relations between Timor-Leste and Indonesia, the finalization of an agreement between them on a border line remained elusive. Significant technical work was completed, as reflected in preparation of an interim report of the Joint Border Committee, for which further input was expected from Indonesia. However, political engagement was necessary for the swift conclusion of border management arrangements, including cooperation on security and regulation of economic activity, and the implementation of agreements on the issuance of border passes and the establishment of a transit facility linking Oecussi with the rest of Timor-Leste.

Efforts continued to address the problem of the former refugees remaining in camps in West Timor, on the basis of cooperation between Indonesia and Timor-Leste, supported by UNHCR and the International Organization for Migration. A five-point strategy proposed by UNHCR, and agreed to by both Governments, resulted in the relocation in the second half of 2003 of some 12,000 former refugees from camps to other areas of West Timor, where they could more easily integrate in a sustainable manner, leaving a caseload of 16,000 refugees in West Timor. However, less than 100 former refugees returned to Timor-Leste in the first three months of 2004.

The second round of negotiations on the maritime boundary between Timor-Leste and Australia began on 19 April. Further talks were scheduled for September. Progress in that area was crucial to permit full development of the petroleum and natural gas resources in the region and to ensure appropriate and mutually agreed sharing of the benefits.

The security situation had generally remained calm and peaceful, despite unconfirmed reports of the presence of armed groups in western districts. The Tactical Coordination Line—the informal boundary agreed to by the United Nations Transitional Administration in East Timor and the Indonesian authorities pending formal demarcation of the border—remained porous along a significant part of its length, and disputes between villages situated in its vicinity continued, as did illegal trade, hunting and crossings, and miscellaneous minor criminal activity. Security and stability were promoted by regular patrolling activities throughout Timor-Leste by UNMISET's 1,750-member military component, which would remain at that strength until 20 May. Its military component continued to transfer skills and knowledge to F-FDTL members and to encourage and assist the Border Patrol Unit in the execution of its border security management and patrolling tasks.

The Secretary-General observed that the international community's peacekeeping activities in Timor-Leste had created a window of opportunity for progress. The extraordinary progress that had so far taken place had permitted a swift downsizing in the international presence on the ground, and left no doubt as to the momentum of transfer of responsibility to Timor-Leste. Nonetheless, there was a limit to what could be achieved in so short a time. Since 2002, the leadership of Timor-Leste had demonstrated an ability to work closely together to meet national challenges, and had maintained close cooperation with the Special Representative. Similar coordination and cooperation would be essential to enable the Timorese people to derive full benefit from the additional year of peacekeeping assistance. However, certain immediate steps were crucial, including agreement on arrangements to permit civilian advisers to assume their functions, selection of Timorese counterparts, and clarification of the precise responsibilities of Timorese security agencies on an interim basis. The Timorese leadership could lay the foundations for future progress by fostering a culture of political dialogue and debate, anchored in the values of human rights, tolerance and respect for the law, and by providing a firm legislative basis for the development of the public administration's machinery.

Security Council consideration (May). On 10 May [meeting 4965], the Council discussed the situation in Timor-Leste, including the Secretary-General's April report. The Special Representative of the Secretary-General, Kamalesh Sharma, told the Council that the Timorese national police had assumed responsibility for policing in all 13 districts and for a vast majority of headquarters functions. The United Nations was therefore confident about transferring executive responsibility for policing to Timor-Leste on 19 May. However, the creation of a professional, apolitical, accountable and responsive police service, with well-established traditions of integrity and a mindset of service to the community, would require further efforts and time. UNMISET's military component continued to be downsized according to the revised schedule approved in Council resolution 1473(2003) [YUN 2003, p. 374]. Unconfirmed reports of criminal elements, both inside and outside Timor-Leste, continued to be received. Indonesia's commitment to controlling such elements was encouraging, as were the continuing efforts of Timor-Leste to develop the capabilities of its security agencies to deal with them, including through the establishment of PNTL's Rapid Deployment Service. UNMISET would continue to cooperate with the Government of Timor-Leste in building the capacities of PNTL's specialized units, including the training of the Rapid Deployment Service during the consolidation phase. Through its institution- and capacity-building activities, UNMISET had contributed significantly to the viability and political stability of the State institutions, including through mentoring and coaching Timorese counterparts, assistance in the preparation of legal frameworks, formalizing related rules and regulations and institutionalization of operational procedures.

The innovative and pioneering experiment sanctioned by Council resolution 1410(2002) revealed that the requirements for human and institutional capacity development were far more demanding than originally envisaged, requiring the presence of important adviser positions beyond May. A robust exit strategy to ensure sustainability would be the major challenge during UNMISET's consolidation phase. Likewise, the assistance provided through UNMISET's serious crimes programme offered crucial reinforcement to the Council's commitment that perpetrators of such crimes should be brought to justice. The sustainability of the justice sector could be achieved only through the direct support of bilateral and multilateral development partners.

On 14 May [meeting 4968], the Security Council unanimously adopted **resolution 1543(2004)**. The draft [S/2004/383] was prepared in consultations among Council members.

The Security Council,

Reaffirming its previous resolutions on the situation in Timor-Leste, in particular resolutions 1410(2002) of 17 May 2002, 1473(2003) of 4 April 2003 and 1480 (2003) of 19 May 2003,

Commending the progress achieved by the people and Government of Timor-Leste, with the assistance of the international community, towards developing, in so short a time, the nation's infrastructure, public administration, law enforcement and defence capacities,

Commending also the work of the United Nations Mission of Support in East Timor, under the leadership of the Special Representative of the Secretary-General, and welcoming the progress made towards the accomplishment of key tasks inscribed in its mandate, in accordance with resolutions 1410(2002), 1473(2003) and 1480(2003),

Expressing its appreciation to those Member States providing troops, civilian police personnel and support elements to the Mission,

Having considered the statement of 20 February 2004 by the Minister for Foreign Affairs of Timor-Leste to the Security Council, requesting a one-year extension of the Mission,

Taking note of the special report of the Secretary-General of 13 February 2004 on the United Nations Mission of Support in East Timor as well as his report of 29 April 2004,

Welcoming the recommendation of the Secretary-General to extend the Mission for a further one-year consolidation phase, in order to allow key tasks to be performed and to sustain, strengthen and build upon the gains made to date, thereby permitting Timor-Leste to attain self-sufficiency,

Noting that the emerging institutions in Timor-Leste are still in the process of consolidation and that further assistance is required to ensure the sustained development and strengthening of key sectors, mainly justice, public administration, including the National Police, and the maintenance of security and stability in Timor-Leste,

Encouraging the Government of Timor-Leste to adopt, as soon as possible, legislation and other appropriate measures referred to in paragraph 69 of the report of the Secretary-General of 29 April 2004, and further outlined as Timor-Leste action required in annexes I to III of the same report,

Welcoming the excellent communication and goodwill that have characterized relations between Timor-Leste and Indonesia, and encouraging continued cooperation between the two Governments and cooperation with the Mission towards further progress in resolving pending bilateral issues, including those relating to the demarcation and management of the border and to the provision of justice for those responsible for serious crimes committed in 1999,

Remaining fully committed to the promotion of security and long-lasting stability in Timor-Leste,

1. *Decides* to extend the mandate of the United Nations Mission of Support in East Timor for a period of six months, with a view to subsequently extending the mandate for a further and final period of six months, until 20 May 2005;

2. *Decides also* to reduce the size of the Mission and to revise its tasks, in accordance with the recommendations of the Secretary-General in section III of his report of 29 April 2004;

3. *Decides*, accordingly, that the mandate of the Mission shall consist of the following elements, as outlined in the report of the Secretary-General of 29 April 2004:

(a) Support for the public administration and justice system of Timor-Leste and for justice in the area of serious crimes;

(b) Support to the development of law enforcement in Timor-Leste;

(c) Support for the security and stability of Timor-Leste;

4. *Decides* that the Mission shall include up to 58 civilian advisers, 157 civilian police advisers, 42 military liaison officers, 310 formed troops and a 125-person International Response Unit;

5. *Decides also* that internationally accepted human rights principles shall continue to form an integral part of training and capacity-building carried out by the Mission under paragraph 3 above;

6. *Requests* the Secretary-General to keep the Security Council closely and regularly informed of developments on the ground and of the implementation of the present resolution, in particular with regard to progress towards the achievement of key tasks in the mandate of the Mission, and in that regard requests the Secretary-General to submit a report within three months of the date of adoption of the present resolution and every three months thereafter, with recommendations for any modifications such progress might allow to the size, composition and tasks of the Mission, with a view to completing its mandate by 20 May 2005;

7. *Also requests* the Secretary-General to include in the reports requested under paragraph 6 above recommendations on tasks and configuration of police and military components for Security Council review in November 2004;

8. *Reaffirms* the need to fight against impunity and the importance for the international community to lend its support in this regard, and emphasizes that the Serious Crime Unit should complete all investigations by November 2004 and should conclude trials and other activities as soon as possible and no later than 20 May 2005;

9. *Underlines* the fact that further United Nations assistance to Timor-Leste should be coordinated with the efforts of bilateral and multilateral donors, regional mechanisms, non-governmental organizations, private sector entities and other actors from within the international community;

10. *Urges* the donor community as well as United Nations agencies, funds and programmes and multilateral financial institutions to continue providing essential resources and assistance for the implementation of projects towards sustainable and long-term development in Timor-Leste;

11. *Decides* to remain actively seized of the matter.

Report of Secretary-General (August). Pursuant to Security Council resolution 1543(2004) (see above), the Secretary-General submitted a 13

August progress report [S/2004/669] covering UNMISET activities since his April report (see p. 370).

The Government of Timor-Leste had taken several important steps towards self-sufficiency, such as formally assuming responsibility for internal and external security on 20 May. In addition, several key pieces of legislation establishing legal and institutional frameworks were adopted, and efforts continued for the promotion of a culture of free political dialogue and resolution of bilateral issues. Voter registration for Timor-Leste's first elections since independence commenced in May. One of the opposition political groupings did not recognize the validity of the voter registration cards; it nonetheless decided to allow its members to participate in the elections. The respective roles of the national security institutions were established prior to the transfer of internal and external security responsibilities from UNMISET to Timor-Leste, with the promulgation in May of the organic laws for PNTL and F-FDTL. To supplement the legislation on the national police, a government decree establishing a police oversight committee that included members of civil society was adopted and a PNTL disciplinary regulation was promulgated.

As regards the justice sector, the law establishing the Office of the Provedor for Human Rights and Justice was promulgated in May. Progress was also made in formulating a policy on veterans. On 8 June, President Gusmão formally presented to the National Parliament the report of the Veterans Commission, which contained a number of recommendations to the Government, including forms of recognition and material benefits to the veterans. The Parliament formed an ad hoc committee to study the report and was considering possible legislation on the issue. However, the impatience of veterans for swifter progress was underlined by the decision in June by several veterans groups to form, together with other political groups, an organization to press demands for their quick identification and recognition and for material benefits. The groups also made political demands related to the composition of the national police and the resignation of certain government ministers. Those demands were the subject of a public demonstration on 19 July, which was dispersed the following day by police officers using tear gas. The incident underlined the potential for friction posed by veterans' concerns and the need for swift action by the Government.

While progress was made in laying the legislative framework of the institutions of State, the Government was aware of the need to enhance the effectiveness of those institutions, in order to sustain stability and improve socio-economic conditions. For that purpose, the Government was negotiating with Australia on the maritime boundary between the two countries and on the sharing of regional petroleum and natural gas resources. Representatives of the Governments of Timor-Leste and Indonesia continued to meet on the delineation of the land border between the two countries. During a meeting of the Joint Border Commission in Jakarta on 24 and 25 June, the two sides approved the interim report on the Joint Border Survey conducted earlier, which provided a basis for agreement on approximately 90 per cent of the border.

Since the beginning of its consolidation phase on 20 May, UNMISET had made further progress towards the main objectives of its mandate, while adapting its tasks and reducing its civilian, police and military personnel. Progress in the prosecution of serious crimes continued. The Special Panels for serious crimes completed the trials in five additional cases since May. Since their inception, the Panels had rendered a total of 58 verdicts, with 55 defendants being convicted of at least one charge and three defendants acquitted.

The Secretary-General observed that UNMISET civilian advisers and civilian police advisers were working to enhance the professional skills and performance of their Timorese counterparts, while UNMISET's military component continued to support Timor-Leste's management of its security. Progress in those areas would be kept under close assessment, with a view to determining the feasibility of modifying UNMISET's size, composition and tasks, including the configuration of its police and military components.

Security Council consideration (August). On 24 August [meeting 5024], the Council considered the Secretary-General's August report. The UN Assistant Secretary-General for Peacekeeping Operations, Hédi Annabi, said that progress was being made towards formulating a policy on veterans. The National Parliament was considering the report of the President's commissions on veterans and ex-combatants. Bilateral and multilateral assistance would be required to implement concrete projects to address the most deserving and the most needy cases, including those who participated in the independence struggle from the outset as well as their widows and orphans. Progress had also been made on the finalization of the land border between Timor-Leste and Indonesia. Agreement on 90 per cent of the border had largely been achieved and it was expected that agreement would be reached at the political level on the remaining 10 per cent in the near future.

With regard to the 58 civilian advisers to be provided for the most critical positions in public administration, UNMISET had recruited and deployed 51 of them in the field; an additional four advisers would be deployed in September, and a decision by the Government on the three remaining positions was awaited. It was incumbent on the Government to recruit the counterparts to the advisers as expeditiously as possible so as to be able to benefit from UNMISET's expertise and skills during the remaining months of its mandate. The civilian advisers were informed of the importance of preparing and implementing exit strategies for UNMISET. They would focus on institutional capacity development through well-targeted, formalized training programmes, including fostering a culture of transparency, accountability and respect for human rights.

The justice sector continued to be affected by a shortage of qualified personnel and limited infrastructure, which contributed in turn to a continued backlog of cases, detentions on expired warrants and violations of human rights. The number of detainees held on expired warrants was considerably reduced after a judicial review by the President of the Court of Appeal following a formal request from the Special Representative. The UNMISET police component continued to assist PNTL to develop into a professional and impartial police service through mentoring and monitoring. It developed a skills development plan based on a needs assessment of areas requiring continued assistance. Meanwhile, the response of the anti-riot rapid intervention unit to the 19 and 20 July demonstrations in Dili suggested the importance of further training for that particular unit. The security situation in the border districts, and indeed in all of Timor-Leste, had generally been calm and peaceful. The majority of the personnel of UNMISET's reduced military component were deployed in the western border districts, while one platoon of the international response unit was deployed in Dili. Development of the defence forces, which continued to suffer from a lack of experience and skilled personnel, proper training and equipment and a very limited logistical capability for deployment, would continue to depend on external support through the provision of equipment and training.

Report of Secretary-General (November). The Secretary-General submitted a 9 November progress report on UNMISET, covering the period since his August report (see p. 372). The report also included recommendations based on the findings of an integrated technical assessment mission that visited Timor-Leste in October.

During the reporting period, Timor-Leste remained peaceful and stable after the demonstration dispersed by the police with the use of tear gas on 20 July (see above). The Government addressed pressing issues confronting the country, including the veterans issue and violence between martial arts groups. Following successful voter registration, which ended on 31 July, preparations for local elections were under way. On 16 and 17 August, the National Parliament made determined efforts to select the Provedor for Human Rights and Justice, but so far without success. Timor-Leste's relations with neighbouring countries continued to grow, but that had yet to result in any concrete agreements on border delineation and other pending issues. The National Electoral Commission and the Technical Secretariat for Electoral Administration continued to make preparations for local elections, which were to be conducted in a phased manner throughout the country before July 2005.

Realizing the urgent need for solutions of the veterans issue, the Government held a meeting with the diplomatic corps in Dili on 26 October, soliciting their support for a programme that would recognize and honour the contributions made by veterans and ex-combatants, help their reintegration into civilian life and provide financial assistance to the neediest among them and their families. President Gusmão constituted the Commission for Resistance Cadres Affairs to identify civilian members of the resistance. On 18 August, he provided members of the diplomatic corps and UNMISET with the final report of the Independent Commission of Inquiry into the incident of 24 January at Los Palos, where members of the armed forces were involved in a confrontation with police. The report presented a general overview of the poor conditions of F-FDTL, proposing some solutions to the problems confronting them, but did not address the issue of individual accountability for misconduct in the incident.

Relations between Timor-Leste and Indonesia were strengthened by the visit of the Timorese Prime Minister to Jakarta from 19 to 22 October, on the occasion of the swearing-in of the new President of Indonesia, Susilo Bambang Yudhoyono. However, border demarcation talks did not result in a final agreement. The second round of maritime boundary negotiations with Australia was held in Canberra and Darwin in September and again in Dili in October. It was hoped that a mutually beneficial arrangement that permitted the successful exploitation of petroleum and natural gas resources in the area would be concluded as early as possible.

Following discussions on the Secretary-General's August report in the Security Council on 24 August 2004, the Special Representative constituted eight working groups to assist in the timely identification of activities required for a smooth transition from the peacekeeping and peace-building operation to more traditional institution-building and sustainable developmental assistance. A coordinated and systematic campaign of public information within the country would be critical as UNMISET drew to a close to reassure the local population of the continuation of international assistance from the wider UN system and other bilateral and multilateral development partners. That process was already under way by means of a new programme broadcast weekly on national radio in Tetum, the local language.

In accordance with Security Council resolution 1543(2004), an integrated technical assessment mission from UN Headquarters visited Timor-Leste early in October to review the situation on the ground. During its visit, the mission held extensive discussions with Timorese leaders, NGOs and members of civil society, political parties, representatives of the diplomatic community, UN programmes and agencies, the Bretton Woods institutions and UNMISET. The mission also travelled to the border districts. It found that, since the inception of UNMISET's consolidation phase in May, Timor-Leste had made further progress in developing key State institutions and security agencies, and adopted a number of important pieces of legislation. Nevertheless, major challenges remained and continuing international assistance was essential. There was a consensus that UNMISET should maintain its current tasks, composition and size, including those of the military and police components, until May 2005.

The overall security situation in Timor-Leste remained calm and peaceful during the reporting period. However, smuggling and illegal trading in the border areas continued. The capacity of F-FDTL continued to grow, but it remained hampered by a lack of experienced personnel, appropriate training regimes and equipment, and by limited logistic capacity. Work on the defence plan "Defence 2020" continued with the assistance of a bilaterally supported adviser. The defence force conducted a new recruitment drive; once that process was completed, the training for the 260 new recruits would start in mid-November. UNMISET's military component continued to support the efforts of the Timorese security agencies in maintaining the security and stability of the country. Five training modules, covering military policing, engineering, operational staff work, military information collection and logistic staff work, were initiated in August

and September. The programme was scheduled to continue until the end of UNMISET's mandate in May 2005 and would include further specialized training. At the same time, the military component made efforts to foster close collaboration between the Timorese and Indonesian security agencies. As part of UNMISET's exit strategy, the military component established arrangements for regular meetings between the Timorese and Indonesian sides that would continue after May 2005. UNMISET military liaison officers played a pivotal role in monitoring security-related developments along the border and in facilitating contacts between the Timorese and Indonesian border security agencies.

Progress in border security had been slower than expected and therefore many of the factors that warranted the presence of UNMISET's military component had not changed. Timor-Leste and Indonesia had still not reached final agreement on the demarcation of their land border. The Timorese border security agencies had not gained sufficient capacity to manage the border affairs alone, neither had they reached the point where they could interact with the Indonesian border security agencies on their own without facilitation of UNMISET's military component. As the national police force was gaining skills and experience, its ability to meet security challenges had improved, but not to the level of providing protection and evacuation to UNMISET's military liaison officers. The Secretary-General said that, in view of the above and the fact that the strength of the military component was already at its bare minimum, it would be necessary to retain the 477 authorized military personnel for the next six months. The 125-person International Response Unit would continue to undertake preventive and response operations in exceptional circumstances. While that assistance would be available until May 2005, it was imperative that Timor-Leste and Indonesia intensify their efforts to conclude an agreement on land border demarcation as early as possible. Pending such an agreement, the adoption of an interim arrangement would be necessary to facilitate border management.

The Secretary-General observed that the situation on the ground did not warrant any modification of UNMISET's tasks as mandated by Council resolution 1543(2004), or any change in its size or composition. He therefore recommended retaining UNMISET with its existing configuration, size and tasks until 20 May 2005. That final period would allow UNMISET to complete its key tasks and to consolidate the gains that had been made up to that point. At the same time, UNMISET would need to prepare its exit strategy, making sure that the country could continue to function without suffering from the impact of its withdrawal. That called for UNMISET to redouble its efforts to encourage the involvement and ownership of the Timorese in UNMISET's programme areas and to identify bilateral or multilateral partners. The UN system funds, programmes and specialized agencies and other development partners had complemented UNMISET's role in Timor-Leste's institution-building process. During the next six months, their support would be even more critical in facilitating a smooth transition from a peacekeeping operation to a sustainable, traditional, development assistance framework.

Security Council consideration (November). On 15 November [meeting 5076], the Security Council discussed the Secretary-General's November report (see above) and was briefed by the Secretary-General's Special Representative, Mr. Hasegawa.

Mr. Hasegawa said, among other things, that the civilian advisers were not only actively training and mentoring their East Timorese counterparts, they were also formulating exit strategies with their counterparts so as to ensure a smooth transition at the end of UNMISET's mandate. The prosecutors, defence lawyers and trial judges of the serious crimes process were making strenuous efforts to complete investigations by November 2004, as well as trials by May 2005, as stipulated in Council resolution 1543(2004). The serious crimes process would not be able to respond fully to the desire for justice for all of the victims of the violence in 1999 with the limited time and resources available. There were several ideas and proposals in that regard to address the issue. The Secretary-General would examine those ideas and proposals, with a view to identifying the most appropriate arrangement to resolve the issue. Meanwhile, the Special Representative proposed to deploy additional data experts and specialists who could assist in the processing and archiving of all the evidentiary and testimonial materials obtained during investigations and trials. The eight working groups that the Special Representative had constituted in August (see p. 375) started identifying specific measures required for a smooth transition from peacekeeping operations to development assistance. The final reports from each of the eight groups would be ready by mid-January 2005 and their recommendations would be reflected in the Secretary-General's next report to the Council.

SECURITY COUNCIL ACTION (November)

On 16 November [meeting 5079], the Security Council unanimously adopted **resolution 1573**

(2004). The draft [S/2004/901] was prepared in consultations among Council members.

The Security Council,

Reaffirming its previous resolutions on the situation in Timor-Leste, in particular resolutions 1410(2002) of 17 May 2002, 1473(2003) of 4 April 2003, 1480(2003) of 19 May 2003 and 1543(2004) of 14 May 2004,

Commending the people and the Government of Timor-Leste for the peace and stability they have achieved in the country, as well as for their continuing efforts towards consolidating democracy and building State institutions,

Also commending the United Nations Mission of Support in East Timor, under the leadership of the Special Representative of the Secretary-General, and welcoming the continuing progress made towards the accomplishment of key tasks inscribed in its mandate, particularly during its consolidation phase, in accordance with resolution 1543(2004),

Paying tribute to Timor-Leste's bilateral and multilateral partners for their invaluable assistance, particularly with regard to institutional capacity-building and social and economic development,

Noting that, despite notable advances achieved in the last months, Timor-Leste has not yet reached the critical threshold of self-sufficiency, mainly in key areas such as public administration, law enforcement and security,

Welcoming the strengthening of cooperation and good relations between Timor-Leste and its neighbours, and encouraging further progress towards concrete agreements on border delineation and other pending issues,

Commending the Serious Crimes Unit for the efforts it has undertaken in order to complete its investigations by November 2004, and any further trials and other activities no later than 20 May 2005,

Noting with concern that it may not be possible for the Serious Crimes Unit to fully respond to the desire for justice of those affected by the violence in 1999 bearing in mind the limited time and resources that remain available,

Taking note of the report of the Secretary-General of 29 April 2004 on the Mission as well as his report of 19 November 2004, and welcoming his recommendations contained therein,

Remaining fully committed to the promotion of security and long-lasting stability in Timor-Leste,

1. *Decides* to extend the mandate of the United Nations Mission of Support in East Timor for a final period of six months until 20 May 2005;

2. *Decides also* to maintain the current tasks, configuration and size of the Mission in order to allow it to complete key tasks of its mandate and consolidate gains made thus far;

3. *Requests* the Mission to focus increasingly on implementing its exit strategy, particularly with a view to ensuring increasing involvement and ownership of the Timorese in the three programme areas of the Mission, so that, when it departs Timor-Leste, its responsibilities can be taken over by the Timorese, with the continued assistance of the United Nations system and bilateral and multilateral partners;

4. *Urges* the donor community to continue providing its indispensable assistance to Timor-Leste, in-

cluding through active participation in the donors, conference scheduled to be held in March 2005;

5. *Urges*, in particular, United Nations development and humanitarian agencies and multilateral financial institutions to start immediately planning for a smooth transition, in Timor-Leste, from a peace-keeping operation to a sustainable development assistance framework;

6. *Reaffirms* the need to fight against impunity, and in this regard takes note of the Secretary-General's intention to continue to explore possible ways to address this issue with a view to making proposals as appropriate;

7. *Requests* the Secretary-General to keep the Security Council closely and regularly informed of developments on the ground and of the implementation of the present resolution, in particular of paragraphs 3 and 5 above, and in that regard requests the Secretary-General to submit a report within three months of the date of adoption of the present resolution, followed by a final report in May 2005;

8. *Decides* to remain actively seized of the matter.

Later developments. In a later report [S/2005/99], the Secretary-General said that local elections, the first ever conducted by Timorese national authorities, were successfully held in two districts in two phases, on 18 and 22 December. Voter turnout was very high, exceeding 90 per cent in some areas; people voted in an orderly manner, in an atmosphere free of intimidation or interference. However, the Technical Secretariat for Electoral Administration encountered numerous logistical difficulties, including many errors in the voter roll in the first phase of the elections, which prevented some voters from casting their ballots. Problems arose between the Timorese armed forces and the national police despite efforts to improve their relationship. On 16 December, a group of armed soldiers attacked a police station in Dili, injuring two officers and causing damage to the premises. Relations between Timor-Leste and Indonesia continued to improve. In December, the two countries agreed to form a Truth and Friendship Commission to deal with human rights abuses perpetrated in 1999 and other bilateral issues. However, no further progress was made on the delineation of the land border between the two countries.

Financing of UN operations

During 2004, the General Assembly considered the financing of two UN missions in Timor-Leste—UNMISET and the United Nations Mission in East Timor (UNAMET). UNMISET was established by Council resolution 1410(2002) [YUN 2002, p. 321] to provide assistance to the administrative, law enforcement and public security structures critical to the viability and political stability of Timor-Leste, in addition to contributing to the maintenance of its external and internal security.

UNAMET was established by Council resolution 1246(1999) [YUN 1999, p. 283] to conduct the 1999 popular consultations on East Timor's autonomy [ibid., p. 288]; its mandate ended on 30 November 1999, in accordance with resolution 1262(1999) [ibid., p. 287].

UNMISET

In May [A/58/795], the Secretary-General submitted to the General Assembly an interim budget for UNMISET for the period from 1 July to 31 December 2004, which reflected preliminary financial requirements in the amount of $45,728,400 exclusive of budgeted voluntary contributions in kind. Owing to UNMISET's extension for a period of six months by Security Council resolution 1543(2004) (see p. 372), the report superseded the budgetary proposals of December 2003 on UNMISET's financing [A/58/645], which contained UNMISET's liquidation budget.

In May [A/58/809], ACABQ, in reviewing UNMISET's interim budget for the period from 1 July to 31 December 2004, noted that the requirements presented constituted more of a projection than fully justifiable estimates. It would therefore be unrealistic for either it or the Fifth Committee to attempt a detailed examination of UNMISET's requirements at that stage. ACABQ intended to conduct such an examination on the basis of the fully justified estimates later in 2004. Accordingly, it requested information from the UN Secretariat on the financial requirements for the period between July and October 2004. ACABQ recommended that the Assembly approve commitment authority with assessment for UNMISET in the amount of $30,485,600.

GENERAL ASSEMBLY ACTION (June)

On 18 June [meeting 91], the General Assembly, on the recommendation of the Fifth Committee [A/58/584/Add.1], adopted **resolution 58/260 B** without vote [agenda item 140].

Financing of the United Nations Mission of Support in East Timor

The General Assembly,

Having considered the report of the Secretary-General on the financing of the United Nations Mission of Support in East Timor and the related report of the Advisory Committee on Administrative and Budgetary Questions,

Recalling Security Council resolution 1272(1999) of 25 October 1999 regarding the establishment of the United Nations Transitional Administration in East Timor and the subsequent resolutions by which the Council extended the mandate of the Transitional Administration, the last of which was resolution 1392(2002) of 31 January 2002, by which the mandate was extended until 20 May 2002,

Recalling also Security Council resolution 1410(2002) of 17 May 2002, by which the Council established the United Nations Mission of Support in East Timor as from 20 May 2002 for an initial period of twelve months, and the subsequent resolutions by which the Council extended the mandate of the Mission, the latest of which was resolution 1543(2004) of 14 May 2004, by which the Council extended the Mission for a period of six months, with a view to subsequently extending the mandate for a further and final period of six months, until 20 May 2005,

Recalling further its resolution 54/246 A of 23 December 1999 on the financing of the United Nations Transitional Administration in East Timor and its subsequent resolutions on the financing of the United Nations Mission of Support in East Timor, the latest of which was resolution 58/260 A of 23 December 2003,

Mindful of the fact that it is essential to provide the Mission with the financial resources necessary to enable it to fulfil its responsibilities under the relevant resolutions of the Security Council,

1. *Endorses* the conclusions and recommendations contained in the report of the Advisory Committee on Administrative and Budgetary Questions, and requests the Secretary-General to ensure their full implementation;

2. *Emphasizes* that it will consider the number and level of posts, the administrative structure, lines of accountability and reporting in support of the substantive mandate in the context of the full budget proposal to be submitted to the General Assembly at its fifty-ninth session;

**Budget estimates for the period
from 1 July to 31 October 2004**

3. *Authorizes* the Secretary-General to enter into commitments in the amount of 30,485,600 United States dollars for the maintenance of the Mission for the period from 1 July to 31 October 2004;

Financing of the commitment authority

4. *Decides* to apportion among Member States the amount of 30,485,600 dollars for the Mission for the period from 1 July to 31 October 2004 in accordance with the levels set out in General Assembly resolution 55/235 of 23 December 2000, as adjusted by the Assembly in its resolution 55/236 of 23 December 2000 and updated in its resolution 58/256 of 23 December 2003, taking into account the scale of assessments for 2004 as set out in its resolution 58/1 B of 23 December 2003;

5. *Decides also* that, in accordance with the provisions of its resolution 973(X) of 15 December 1955, there shall be set off against the apportionment among Member States, as provided for in paragraph 4 above, their respective share in the Tax Equalization Fund of 2,086,400 dollars, representing the estimated staff assessment income approved for the Mission for the period from 1 July to 31 October 2004;

6. *Decides further* to include in the provisional agenda of its fifty-ninth session the item entitled "Financing of the United Nations Mission of Support in East Timor".

In December 2003 [A/58/636], the Secretary-General submitted to the Assembly a performance report on the UNMISET budget for the pe-

riod from 1 July 2002 to 30 June 2003. Expenditure for the period totalled $288,001,100, resulting in an unencumbered balance of $4,058,900. The Assembly was requested to decide on the treatment of that unencumbered balance and on the treatment of other income for the period ended 30 June 2003, amounting to $10,525,000.

In August 2004 [A/59/290], the Secretary-General submitted UNMISET's budget for the period from 1 July 2004 to 30 June 2005, in the amount of $85,393,400, comprising $77,304,800 for UNMISET's maintenance for the period from 1 July 2004 to 20 May 2005 and $8,088,600 for the commencement of the liquidation activities for the period from 21 May to 30 June 2005. It was inclusive of budgeted voluntary contributions in kind in the amount of $60,000, consisting of $53,300 and $6,700 for the maintenance and the commencement of liquidation periods, respectively. The report incorporated and superseded the May 2004 budgetary proposals for UNMISET for the period from 1 July to 31 December 2004 (see p. 377).

In September [A/59/384], ACABQ presented its comments and recommendations on the Secretary-General's reports on UNMISET's financial performance for the period from 1 July 2002 to 30 June 2003 and on UNMISET's proposed budget for the period from 1 July 2004 to 30 June 2005 (see above).

GENERAL ASSEMBLY ACTION (October)

On 29 October [meeting 46], the General Assembly, on the recommendation of the Fifth Committee [A/59/531], adopted **resolution 59/13** without vote [agenda item 129].

**Financing of the United Nations Mission of
Support in East Timor**

The General Assembly,

Having considered the reports of the Secretary-General on the financing of the United Nations Mission of Support in East Timor, and the related report of the Advisory Committee on Administrative and Budgetary Questions,

Recalling Security Council resolution 1272(1999) of 25 October 1999 regarding the establishment of the United Nations Transitional Administration in East Timor and the subsequent resolutions by which the Council extended the mandate of the Transitional Administration, the last of which was resolution 1392 (2002) of 31 January 2002, by which the mandate was extended until 20 May 2002,

Recalling also Security Council resolution 1410(2002) of 17 May 2002, by which the Council established the United Nations Mission of Support in East Timor as of 20 May 2002 for an initial period of twelve months, and the subsequent resolutions by which the Council extended the mandate of the Mission, the latest of which was resolution 1543(2004) of 14 May 2004, by which the Council extended the mandate of the Mission for a period of six months, with a view to subsequently extending the mandate for a further and final period of six months, until 20 May 2005,

Recalling further its resolution 54/246 A of 23 December 1999 on the financing of the United Nations Transitional Administration in East Timor and its subsequent resolutions on the financing of the United Nations Mission of Support in East Timor, the latest of which was resolution 58/260 B of 18 June 2004,

Reaffirming the general principles underlying the financing of United Nations peacekeeping operations, as stated in General Assembly resolutions 1874(S-IV) of 27 June 1963, 3101(XXVIII) of 11 December 1973 and 55/235 of 23 December 2000,

Noting with appreciation that voluntary contributions have been made to the Mission and to the Trust Fund for the United Nations Transitional Administration in East Timor,

Mindful of the fact that it is essential to provide the Mission with the necessary financial resources to enable it to fulfil its responsibilities under the relevant resolutions of the Security Council,

Taking note of the views expressed by Member States,

1. *Takes note* of the status of contributions to the United Nations Transitional Administration in East Timor and the United Nations Mission of Support in East Timor as at 30 September 2004, including the contributions outstanding in the amount of 74.8 million United States dollars, representing some 4 per cent of the total assessed contributions, notes with concern that only thirty-three Member States have paid their assessed contributions in full, and urges all other Member States, in particular those in arrears, to ensure payment of their outstanding assessed contributions;

2. *Expresses its appreciation* to those Member States which have paid their assessed contributions in full, and urges all other Member States to make every possible effort to ensure payment of their assessed contributions to the Transitional Administration and the Mission in full;

3. *Expresses concern* at the financial situation with regard to peacekeeping activities, in particular as regards the reimbursements to troop contributors that bear additional burdens owing to overdue payments by Member States of their assessments;

4. *Also expresses concern* at the delay experienced by the Secretary-General in deploying and providing adequate resources to some recent peacekeeping missions, in particular those in Africa;

5. *Emphasizes* that all future and existing peacekeeping missions shall be given equal and non-discriminatory treatment in respect of financial and administrative arrangements;

6. *Also emphasizes* that all peacekeeping missions shall be provided with adequate resources for the effective and efficient discharge of their respective mandates;

7. *Reiterates its request* to the Secretary-General to make the fullest possible use of facilities and equipment at the United Nations Logistics Base at Brindisi, Italy, in order to minimize the costs of procurement for the Mission;

8. *Endorses* the conclusions and recommendations contained in the report of the Advisory Committee on Administrative and Budgetary Questions, subject to the provisions of the present resolution, and requests the Secretary-General to ensure their full implementation, in particular:

(*a*) That the staffing of the Serious Crimes Unit will be further adjusted after the completion of the investigations to be commensurate with such residual tasks as it may have once the investigations have been completed;

(*b*) That the Mission, to the extent possible, recruit National Officers and national General Service staff locally to fill international Professional and General Service posts;

9. *Requests* the Secretary-General to report on the implementation of the above-mentioned paragraphs of the present resolution in the context of his performance report;

10. *Endorses* the view of the Advisory Committee on Administrative and Budgetary Questions in paragraph 31 of its report that the position of Force Commander should be classified at the D-1 level, but authorizes the Secretary-General, as an exceptional measure and without prejudice to other peacekeeping missions, to maintain the incumbent at the D-2 level given the difficulties in recruiting a replacement owing to the short time remaining until the completion of the Mission;

11. *Emphasizes* that the Serious Crimes Unit should complete all investigations by November 2004 and should conclude trials and other activities as soon as possible and no later than 20 May 2005;

12. *Requests* the Secretary-General to measure the accomplishments of the Mission fully in accordance with Security Council resolution 1543(2004);

Financial performance report for the period from 1 July 2002 to 30 June 2003

13. *Takes note* of the report of the Secretary-General on the financial performance of the Mission for the period from 1 July 2002 to 30 June 2003;

Budget estimates for the period from 1 July 2004 to 30 June 2005

14. *Decides* to appropriate to the Special Account for the United Nations Mission of Support in East Timor the amount of 85,153,700 dollars for the period from 1 July 2004 to 30 June 2005, inclusive of the amount of 30,485,600 dollars previously authorized by the General Assembly for the Mission for the period from 1 July to 31 October 2004 under the terms of its resolution 58/260 B, and comprising the amount of 77,071,800 dollars for the period from 1 July 2004 to 20 May 2005 for the maintenance of the Mission and the amount of 8,081,900 dollars for the commencement of the liquidation activities of the Mission for the period from 21 May to 30 June 2005;

Financing of the appropriation

15. *Decides also*, taking into account the amount of 30,485,600 dollars already apportioned under the terms of its resolution 58/260 B, to apportion among Member States the additional amount of 3,530,657 dollars for the Mission for the period from 1 July to 20 November 2004, in accordance with the levels set out in General Assembly resolution 55/235, as adjusted by the Assembly in its resolutions 55/236 of 23 December 2000, and updated in its resolution 58/256 of 23 December 2003, taking into account the scale of assessments for 2004, as set out in its resolution 58/1 B of 23 December 2003;

16. *Decides further* that, in accordance with the provisions of its resolution 973(X) of 15 December 1955, there shall be set off against the apportionment among Member States, as provided for in paragraph 15 above, their respective share in the Tax Equalization Fund of the amount of 287,709 dollars, representing the estimated additional staff assessment income approved for the Mission for the period from 1 July to 20 November 2004;

17. *Decides* to apportion among Member States the amount of 43,055,543 dollars for the period from 21 November 2004 to 20 May 2005, in accordance with the scheme set out in paragraph 15 above and taking into account the scale of assessments for 2004 and 2005, as set out in its resolution 58/1 B, subject to a decision of the Security Council to extend the mandate of the Mission;

18. *Decides also* that, in accordance with the provisions of its resolution 973(X), there shall be set off against the apportionment among Member States, as provided for in paragraph 17 above, their respective share in the Tax Equalization Fund of the amount of 3,004,991 dollars, representing the estimated staff assessment income approved for the Mission for the period from 21 November 2004 to 20 May 2005;

19. *Decides further* to apportion among Member States the amount of 8,081,900 dollars for the Mission for the period from 21 May to 30 June 2005, in accordance with the scheme set out in paragraph 15 above and taking into account the scale of assessments for 2005, as set out in its resolution 58/1 B;

20. *Decides* that, in accordance with the provisions of its resolution 973(X), there shall be set off against the apportionment among Member States, as provided for in paragraph 19 above, their respective share in the Tax Equalization Fund of the amount of 382,900 dollars, representing the estimated staff assessment income approved for the Mission for the period from 21 May to 30 June 2005;

21. *Decides also* that for Member States that have fulfilled their financial obligations to the Mission, there shall be set off against their apportionment, as provided for in paragraph 15 above, their respective share of the unencumbered balance and other income in the total amount of 14,583,900 dollars in respect of the financial period ended 30 June 2003, in accordance with the levels set out in General Assembly resolution 55/235, as adjusted by the Assembly in its resolution 55/236 and its resolution 57/290 A of 20 December 2002, taking into account the scale of assessments for 2003 as set out in its resolutions 55/5 B of 23 December 2000 and 57/4 B of 20 December 2002;

22. *Decides further* that for Member States that have not fulfilled their financial obligations to the Mission, there shall be set off against their outstanding obligations their respective share of the unencumbered balance and other income in the total amount of 14,583,900 dollars in respect of the financial period ended 30 June 2003, in accordance with the scheme set out in paragraph 21 above;

23. *Decides* that the decrease of 181,300 dollars in the estimated staff assessment income in respect of the financial period ended 30 June 2003 shall be set off against the credits from the amount referred to in paragraphs 21 and 22 above;

24. *Emphasizes* that no peacekeeping mission shall be financed by borrowing funds from other active peacekeeping missions;

25. *Encourages* the Secretary-General to continue to take additional measures to ensure the safety and security of all personnel under the auspices of the United Nations participating in the Mission;

26. *Invites* voluntary contributions to the Mission in cash and in the form of services and supplies acceptable to the Secretary-General, to be administered, as appropriate, in accordance with the procedure and practices established by the General Assembly;

27. *Decides* to keep under review during its fifty-ninth session the item entitled "Financing of the United Nations Mission of Support in East Timor".

On 23 December, the Assembly decided that the agenda item on financing of UNMISET would remain for consideration at its resumed fifty-ninth (2005) session (**decision 59/552**).

UNAMET

On 13 September, the General Assembly decided to defer consideration of the item on the financing of UNAMET and to include it in the draft agenda of its fifty-ninth (2004) session (**decision 58/578**).

On 23 December, the Assembly decided that the agenda item on UNAMET's financing would remain for consideration at its resumed fifty-ninth (2005) session (**decision 59/552**).

Other matters

Cambodia

Following the approval by the General Assembly in resolution 57/228 B [YUN 2003, p. 385] of the Agreement between the United Nations and the Royal Government of Cambodia concerning Prosecution under Cambodian Law of Crimes Committed during the Period of Democratic Kampuchea (1975-1979), the Secretary-General, pursuant to that resolution, in his October report on Khmer Rouge trials [A/59/432], described progress achieved and measures to be taken in preparing for the entry into force and implementation of the Agreement, as well as resource requirements and mobilization. According to the Secretary-General, the formation of a new Government on 15 July allowed Cambodia to address the many issues facing the country, particularly the advancement of the rule of law and the process of judiciary reform and national reconciliation. In that context, the National Assembly and the Senate, in October, approved the Agreement, together with amendments to the Cambodian

Law on the Establishment of Extraordinary Chambers in the Courts of Cambodia for the Prosecution of Crimes Committed during the Period of Democratic Kampuchea ("the Law") aimed at bringing that Law into conformity with the Agreement. It was expected that the relevant authorities would proceed with ratification of the Agreement in the near future.

The Secretary-General said that, in the planning and preparation for the Extraordinary Chambers, he had worked closely with the acting governmental authorities, pending the constitution of a new Royal Government of Cambodia and ratification of the Agreement by the legislative organs. That planning had included: designing a concept of operations for the Extraordinary Chambers and their related institutions based on the Agreement; identifying premises, together with related utilities, equipment, facilities and services; developing parameters for budget estimates; apportioning between Cambodia and the United Nations responsibilities for the costs of utilities and services and for safety and security arrangements in accordance with the Agreement; and identifying such other limited assistance as the United Nations might need to provide to ensure the smooth functioning of the investigation, the prosecution and trials. UN support for the establishment and the operation of the Extraordinary Chambers was being organized as a UN technical assistance project. A UN technical team, which visited Phnom Penh from 8 to 20 March, prepared preliminary cost estimates and clarified the division of operational responsibilities between Cambodia and the United Nations pursuant to the Agreement. The choice of premises for the court offices and for the trial venue was finalized.

In describing the concept of operations for the Extraordinary Chambers, the Secretary-General said that the Agreement would not enter into force until both parties had notified each other that all the legal requirements for entry into force had been complied with. Setting up the Extraordinary Chambers could be initiated only when sufficient funds were in place for staffing and sustaining the operations of the Chambers. The Secretary-General would consider that condition to be met when pledges for the full three years of operation of the Chambers and actual contributions for its first year had been received. The three-year overall time frame for the Chambers' operations would begin from the commencement of operations by the Prosecutor's Office to the completion of all trials and appeals. Trial judges, co-investigating judges and co-prosecutors would be appointed two months after the entry into force of the Agreement. It was anticipated

that the investigation phase would last a year and a half to two years. It would be the prerogative of the co-prosecutors and co-investigating judges, within the parameters laid down in the Agreement, to decide who was to be investigated and prosecuted. Trials were expected to start 18 months after the entry into force of the Agreement and last from nine months to a year and a half in each case. Two or more trials could be held simultaneously. Proceedings, which would be conducted in three languages (Khmer, English and French), would require simultaneous interpretation. There would be full audio/video recording, as well as written summary records, of trial proceedings. Considerable public outreach needs and media interest were expected, justifying audio/video broadcast of the trial proceedings, live or time-delayed, as might be decided by the Chambers on a case-by-case basis. Some 200,000 pages of documentary evidence were expected to be examined, the bulk of which was held by the Documentation Centre of Cambodia, an NGO dedicated to research and preservation of documentation on crimes perpetrated during the period of Democratic Kampuchea. Several other sources of documentary evidence, both inside and outside Cambodia, might need to be accessed. The bulk of the documentation was in Khmer and only a small part of it had been translated to date. An intense translation effort was therefore required before actual investigative work could start. Up to 150 witnesses and/or plaintiffs (some 100 from within Cambodia and some 50 from abroad) were expected to be called on by the co-investigating judges, with about one fifth of those also having to appear at the trials proper. Up to 10 international experts, scholars and researchers were to be appointed by the Chambers for brief periods. The international judges, the international co-prosecutor and the international co-investigating judge would be accorded the status of UN officials for the purposes of their terms and conditions of service, which would allow them to maintain the credibility of the Extraordinary Chambers and ensure their impartiality and independence, both actual and perceived.

In a November addendum [A/59/432/Add.1], the Secretary-General said that, on 2 November, Cambodia had provided the Organization with an original copy of the Instrument of Ratification of the Agreement between the United Nations and Cambodia, done on 19 October. In accordance with article 32 of the Agreement, by which it would enter into force once both parties had notified each other in writing that the legal requirements for entry into force had been complied with, Cambodia, on 16 November, provided the United Nations with its notification. The Secretary-General said that the United Nations would provide Cambodia with its notification when pledges for the full three years of the Extraordinary Chambers' operations and actual contributions for its first year of operations had been received.

In December, the Secretary-General sent a third planning mission to Cambodia to complete work on identifying the probable requirements of the Chambers.

On 20 December, the Assembly took note of the Secretary-General's report on Khmer Rouge trials (**decision 59/528**).

India-Pakistan

India and Pakistan made important strides in 2004 to improve their relations and resolve outstanding issues. Following an agreement in January in Islamabad, Pakistan, to resume bilateral dialogue on an agreed range of issues, including Jammu and Kashmir, the two sides continued to conduct talks in a purposeful and serious manner. The Secretary-General expressed to the leaders of the countries, both in public and in private, his admiration for their concerted efforts to bring peace to the region and encouraged them to continue that endeavour.

On 6 January [S/2004/41], the EU welcomed the successful conclusion of the Twelfth Summit meeting of the South Asian Association for Regional Cooperation (Islamabad, 4-6 January), which provided an opportunity for President Pervez Musharraf of Pakistan and Prime Minister Atal Bihari Vajpayee of India to build on positive developments in their bilateral relations. The statement by both countries that they had agreed to commence a process of composite dialogue was particularly welcomed. The EU lauded the commitment of both leaders to the peaceful settlement of all bilateral issues and shared their view that constructive dialogue would promote progress towards their common objective of peace, security and economic development for their people.

The United Nations Military Observer Group in India and Pakistan (UNMOGIP) continued in 2004 to monitor the situation in Jammu and Kashmir. On 24 August [S/2004/695], the Secretary-General informed the Security Council President of his intention to appoint Major General Guido Palmieri (Italy) as Chief Military Observer of UNMOGIP, replacing Major General Pertti Puonti (Finland), who relinquished his post on 28 July. The Council took note of the Secretary-General's intention on 27 August [S/2004/696].

Korea question

On the Korean peninsula, the United Nations focused efforts on supporting the six-party talks (China, the Democratic People's Republic of Korea (DPRK), Japan, the Republic of Korea, the Russian Federation and the United States) aimed at achieving a nuclear-weapon-free peninsula and a comprehensive settlement of related issues. In consultations with the Government of the DPRK, the Secretary-General's Pesonal Envoy had established expert groups to explore steps and measures by which the international community could best assist that country in meeting its energy needs and modernizing its economy.

By a 26 July letter [S/2004/592] to the Secretary-General, the DPRK said that there was an impending danger of war hanging over the Korean peninsula due to the United States forceful attempts to increase its armed forces in the Republic of Korea. The DPRK said that it could not remain indifferent to those moves behind the six-way talks over an alleged settlement of the nuclear issue.

On 25 October [A/59/533-S/2004/860], the DPRK addressed identical letters to the Secretary-General and the Security Council President, drawing attention to the joint naval exercise to be staged by the United States and Japan in the Tokyo Wan from 26 October. The exercise constituted a breach of the UN Charter and international law and order, was a dangerous act that could entail global instability, and would create an obstacle to the peaceful solution of the nuclear issue of the Korean peninsula.

Myanmar

In 2004, the Secretary-General continued to provide his good offices in order to facilitate national reconciliation and democratization in Myanmar. On 17 May, the Government reconvened the National Convention to draft a new constitution, though without the participation of the National League for Democracy and some ethnic nationality parties. The Government's political road map could be considered a credible and all-inclusive vehicle for a democratic transition only if the remaining restrictions on Daw Aung San Suu Kyi and her deputy, U Tin Oo, were lifted and the National League for Democracy's offices permitted to reopen.

On 10 December [S/2004/978], the EU condemned the continued detention of Daw Aung San Suu Kyi and regretted that, although a small number of political prisoners had been released, a large number remained in detention.

Responding on 28 December [S/2004/1018], Myanmar said that the EU's attempt to place the issue of Myanmar on the Security Council's agenda was unacceptable, as the situation in Myanmar was not an issue of international peace and security and was considered annually under an agenda item of the General Assembly's Third (Social, Humanitarian and Cultural) Committee.

On 30 January, the Executive Board of the United Nations Development Programme (UNDP)/ United Nations Population Fund took note of the UNDP Administrator's note on assistance to Myanmar [DP/2004/8] and the report by the independent assessment mission to Myanmar [E/2004/35 (dec. 2004/2)] (see p. 878).

Papua New Guinea

In 2004, the peace process in the Papua New Guinea province of Bougainville moved forward slowly but steadily. The United Nations, through its new mission, the United Nations Observer Mission in Bougainville (UNOMB), continued to assist in the implementation of the 2001 Bougainville Peace Agreement, concluded between the Papua New Guinea Government and the Bougainville parties. The Agreement, which had established the framework for a peace process, including a permanent ceasefire, as provided for in the 1998 Lincoln Agreement [YUN 1998, p. 319] and its annex, the Arawa Agreement [ibid.], covered issues of autonomy, the holding of a referendum and agreements on weapons disposal.

Security Council consideration (May). On 6 May [meeting 4962], the Security Council was briefed by the Assistant Secretary-General for Political Affairs on the situation in Bougainville since his last report on 15 December 2003 [YUN 2003, p. 394].

The agreement on the destruction of all contained weapons between the Bougainville Revolutionary Army (BRA) and the Bougainville Resistance Force (BRF) was transformed into a binding resolution on 17 December 2003 at a meeting of the Peace Process Consultative Committee.

UNOMB, established in December 2003 [YUN 2003, p. 395] and headed since 1 March 2004 by Tor Stenbock (Norway) who replaced Noel Sinclair (Guyana), was working in close cooperation and consultation with the Government of Papua New Guinea and the Bougainville leaders. UNOMB had been given a mandate to monitor, among other things, weapons destruction and the Bougainville constitutional process, and was also expected to verify and to certify that the level of security was conducive to holding elections.

Phase III, the final phase, of the weapons disposal programme had commenced. As at 6 May, 1,588 pieces of contained weapons—81 per cent of the arsenals of BRA and BRF—had been destroyed. UNOMB had certified that 5 of 10 Bougainville districts had completed the weapons disposal programme. The destruction of the weapons had been accompanied by ceremonies, which were used as opportunities to promote awareness of the peace process across the island.

At the Peace Process Consultative Committee meeting held on 25 February, the Papua New Guinea Government provided the Bougainvillean leaders with its comments on the second draft of the Bougainville constitution. The Bougainville Constitutional Commission would incorporate those comments into the third and final draft, which was expected to be produced by the end of May, after which it would be submitted for approval by the Bougainville Constituent Assembly in June, and for endorsement by the national Government by the end of July. Elections would then be planned for the end of November or the beginning of December. The Bougainville Interim Provincial Government had begun preparations for the electoral process and had established a Ministry for Peace and Autonomy to act as a counterpart to the national Government's Bougainville Peace and Restoration Office.

In a move designed to create greater autonomy, the former leader of BRF was appointed as Bougainville's first Minister of Police. In addition to the delegation of police powers, Bougainville's policing and judicial institutions were further strengthened through the law and justice programmes of Australia and New Zealand. It was hoped that those programmes would, over time, help to build capacity for Bougainville's police, justice and correctional institutions.

Progress was made in efforts to involve Francis Ona and his supporters in the peace process. The so-called "A" company, the dominant force in Mr. Ona's Me'ekamui Defence Force, joined the peace process, and in April completed the destruction of its weapons. It was also active in conducting peace awareness meetings in the so-called "no-go zone". However, other elements of the Me'ekamui Defence Force had not contained their weapons. UNOMB was informed that the zone's inhabitants were dissatisfied with restrictions on the freedom of their movement caused by the roadblocks, which inhibited access and the free flow of services and goods to the "no-go zone". Regrettably, Mr. Ona continued to avoid discussing the matter with the Bougainvillean leaders and the national Government. On the whole, UNOMB believed that Mr. Ona's influence continued to be reduced.

UNOMB continued to work with UNDP, the United Nations Children's Fund and other UN organizations on the practical aspects of peace-building in Bougainville. UNDP had nearly completed preparations for the implementation of its second-phase rehabilitation programme for Bougainville, which would include assistance in agriculture, capacity-building and other areas.

The Papua New Guinea representative told the Council that the Bougainville peace process had passed a number of significant milestones on the way to self-sustaining peace. They included the withdrawal of the last in a series of neutral regional supports for the peace process: the Bougainville Transition Team, made up of unarmed civilians from Australia, Fiji, New Zealand and Vanuatu. Also, the Peace Process Consultative Committee met in December 2003 and resolved that the guns contained under the agreed weapons disposal plan would be destroyed. The meeting was held within the time frame set in the plan, which formed part of the Bougainville Peace Agreement. With UNOMB's support, implementation had been truly impressive. Former combatants had displayed real determination in putting away and destroying their guns. That did not mean that Bougainville would be completely free of the presence and the threat of guns. However, the main former combatant groups would have contained and destroyed their guns, and the way would be clear for holding free and democratic elections for the autonomous Bougainville government.

Australia and New Zealand had given valued financial and technical support for strengthening policing in Bougainville, including the training of both additional general duties police and community auxiliary police. The establishment of the Governance and Implementation Fund would allow those two countries and other aid donors to contribute to practical peace-building in Bougainville, providing resources for implementation of a jointly developed work plan which was supported by the national Government and the Bougainville transitional administration. Priorities included promoting awareness and building capacity, both nationally and in Bougainville, to make sure that the arrangements for Bougainville autonomy developed and operated as agreed.

Letter of Secretary-General (June). On 25 June [S/2004/526], the Secretary-General informed the Security Council President that Papua New Guinea, on 14 June, had requested the extension of UNOMB's mandate. Since the Council's meeting on 6 May, UNOMB had reported further progress by the parties in the implementation of the Bougainville Peace Agreement, including, as of 21 June, the destruction of 1,651 or 85 per cent of the contained weapons, and the

completion of the weapons disposal programme in six of Bougainville's ten districts. UNOMB continued to receive requests to supervise weapons containment in the "no-go zone". Given UNOMB's crucial role in building confidence among the parties and the need for it to complete the remaining mandated tasks, the Secretary-General recommended the extension of UNOMB's mandate for a further six-month period, from 1 July to 31 December 2004.

On 30 June [S/2004/527], the Council took note of the Secretary-General's recommendation and expressed its intention to extend UNOMB for a final period of six months. The Council requested the Secretary-General to report within three months on an assessment of the ground situation and on a mission-closure plan.

Report of Secretary-General. On 29 September [S/2004/771], the Secretary-General submitted a report on UNOMB, with particular attention to weapons disposal, the development of a constitution for an autonomous Bougainville government, preparations for elections and the plan for UNOMB's closing. A copy of an aide-memoire, dated 17 September, from the Government of Papua New Guinea on UNOMB's role and its remaining responsibilities was attached to the Secretary-General's report.

As at 29 September, Bougainville ex-combatants had destroyed a total of 1,841 weapons, or 92.6 per cent of the total amount. The weapons disposal plan had been completed in seven of the ten districts of the province. UNOMB was working very closely with the parties on the expeditious completion of the weapons disposal plan in the remaining districts. At the same time, UNOMB was expanding its weapons awareness campaign to the adjacent "no-go zone" not covered by the weapons disposal plan, encouraging former combatants and other individuals in the area to turn in their weapons.

Steady progress in weapons disposal contributed to an improved level of law and order throughout the province. Policing was strengthened with the deployment of 50 Bougainville police who had completed their training, and the recruitment of a further 50 police who were undergoing training. The Australian Federal Police, who had deployed to Bougainville in early September, had started to work side by side with the Bougainville police. In addition, more than 400 community auxiliary police were at work or undergoing retraining in Bougainville. Community policing was being facilitated by New Zealand. Progress was also being made in improving access to courts and upgrading the correctional services.

The Bougainville Constitutional Commission submitted the third draft of the constitution to the Bougainville Constituent Assembly on 1 September. The Constituent Assembly introduced amendments, which resulted in a fourth draft of the constitution. The report of the Constitutional Commission and the third and fourth drafts of the proposed constitution were submitted to the national Government in mid-September. The Government expected that consultations between the bipartisan National Committee and the Constituent Assembly would be undertaken in the near future. To ensure that the Bougainville constitution complied with that of Papua New Guinea, the amendments to the fourth draft would have to be reviewed by the Office of the Attorney-General. The Government had expressed its concern over a number of public policy issues, including the affordability of the proposed system of government. It had nevertheless acknowledged that, while the Bougainville constitution had to be consistent with the constitution of Papua New Guinea, public policy issues were a matter for consultation. If such issues did not violate the constitution of Papua New Guinea, they would be left to the Bougainville leaders to decide. The Papua New Guinea Chief Electoral Commissioner visited Bougainville to assess technical and other electoral needs, and drew up a programme of work in close consultation with officials on the ground.

Together with UN agencies and programmes, the donor community was working closely with the Bougainville provincial administration to lay a solid economic foundation for the future government. A work plan had been prepared jointly by the national Government and the Bougainville Interim Provincial Administration, to be financed through the Governance and Implementation Fund. The medium-term priorities for the Fund would be to transfer essential powers from the national Government to the Bougainville administration, prepare and hold elections for an autonomous government and reform the Bougainville public sector.

In accordance with the Security Council's request, UNOMB drew up a Mission liquidation plan and had made a complete inventory of its assets, including recommendations on how they should be liquidated, which would take an estimated six to eight weeks after the expiration of UNOMB's mandate.

The Secretary-General observed that, in view of the situation in the province, it would not be possible to hold elections by the end of 2004, in spite of continuing solid progress in weapons disposal, constitution drafting and preparations for elections. In the coming months, and until an autonomous government was established in Bougainville, UNOMB would continue to chair the Peace Process Consultative Committee so that the parties could consult on the peace process and on preparations for elections in particular. UNOMB would also continue to monitor and report to that Committee on the verification and certification of compliance by the parties in the handing over of weapons, especially on the surrendered or contained weapons in the "no-go zone" in the period leading up to elections. UNOMB had gained the full trust and confidence of all the parties and of a significant segment of the population in the "no-go zone". There was concern that UNOMB's premature closure could have a negative impact on the peace process during the critical months ahead. The national Government and the Bougainville leaders were aware of the Council's concerns regarding the open-ended nature of UNOMB's mandate. The Mission would continue to support their efforts to move the peace process forward in the remaining period of its current mandate.

Letter of Secretary-General (December). On 21 December [S/2004/1015], the Secretary-General informed the Council President that, by a 14 December letter, Papua New Guinea had requested a further extension of UNOMB's mandate. The Secretary-General commended the Government of Papua New Guinea and the Bougainville parties for overcoming their differences and adopting the Bougainville constitution, thereby opening the way for the holding of elections for an autonomous Bougainville government. Preparations for those elections had already begun, the details of which were contained in Papua New Guinea's 14 December letter, annexed to that of the Secretary-General. A schedule for elections had also been drawn up by the Papua New Guinea Electoral Commission in consultation with the Bougainville Administration.

Efforts continued to encourage former combatants to destroy the remaining 6 per cent of the contained weapons. Meanwhile, the renewed activities of Francis Ona across Bougainville made it imperative that UNOMB continue to facilitate a dialogue between his supporters and the Bougainville leaders until the voting was completed. When established, the autonomous Bougainville government would assume the functions of the Peace Process Consultative Committee, currently chaired by UNOMB, whose responsibilities would have been fully implemented.

The transparent and thorough electoral preparations undertaken by the Government of Papua New Guinea were positive developments and every effort should be made to enable the parties to reach a successful conclusion of the peace process in June 2005. Accordingly, the Secretary-General recommended that the Mission's mandate be extended for a period of six months, until 30 June 2005, so that it could complete the tasks which the Council had endorsed.

On 23 December [S/2004/1016], the Council took note of the Secretary-General's recommendation and requested him to submit a report within three months on an assessment of the ground situation and on a mission-closure plan.

Tajikistan

The Secretary-General, on 23 April [S/2004/331], informed the Security Council of his intention to continue the activities of the United Nations Tajikistan Office of Peace-building (UNTOP) for another year, until 1 June 2005, in view of its role and the country's need for continuing support in its post-conflict peace-building efforts. The Council took note of his intention on 28 April [S/2004/332].

UNTOP, established in 2000 [YUN 2000, p. 315] following the withdrawal of the United Nations Mission of Observers in Tajikistan, focused its activities during 2004 on the consolidation of peace and national reconciliation, the promotion of the rule of law, the strengthening of democratic institutions and support for national capacity-building in human rights. The Secretary-General reported that UNTOP continued to conduct Political Discussion Club meetings on political pluralism, democratization and consolidation of peace in Tajikistan, attended by national and local government officials, leaders of political parties and representatives of civil society. As a result of the Club's catalytic effect, new forms of partnership between the State and civil society had emerged and conditions had improved for the freer functioning of political parties. UNTOP also supported the development of national law enforcement capacities. The viability of the peace process in Tajikistan and the strength of its democratic institutions would be tested by parliamentary elections in early 2005. In April 2004, UNTOP facilitated a needs assessment mission led by the Electoral Assistance Division of the UN Department of Political Affairs. The assistance to be provided to Tajikistan would aim at contributing to the improvement of the transparency and credibility of the 2005 parliamentary elections and at promoting democratization.

On 1 April [A/58/754], Tajikistan informed the Secretary-General that the last of its stocks of anti-personnel mines, numbering 200 items, were destroyed on 31 March at a military testing ground, in accordance with the 1997 Ottawa Convention on the Prohibition of the Use, Stockpiling, Production and Transfer of Anti-personnel Mines and on Their Destruction [YUN 1997, p. 503].

On 19 April [A/58/773], Tajikistan reported that, with the support of UNDP and the Geneva International Centre for Humanitarian Demining, it had convened a conference on the topic "Progress towards the Ottawa Convention's Aims in Central Asia" (Dushanbe, Tajikistan, 15-16 April).

On 8 June [A/58/838-S/2004/432], Kazakhstan, Kyrgyzstan, Tajikistan and Uzbekistan submitted to the Secretary-General the text of a joint statement signed by the Presidents of the four countries at a meeting of the heads of State of the Organization of Central Asian Cooperation (Astana, Kazakhstan, 28 May), in which they confirmed their desire to pursue the steady expansion of the integration process in every area of regional cooperation.

United Arab Emirates–Iran

Greater Tunb, Lesser Tunb and Abu Musa

The United Arab Emirates, in a 1 March letter to the Secretary-General [S/2004/169], requested the Security Council to retain on its agenda for 2004 the item entitled "Letter dated 3 December 1971 from the Permanent Representatives of Algeria, Iraq, the Libyan Arab Jamahiriya and the People's Democratic Republic of Yemen to the United Nations addressed to the President of the Security Council (S/10409)", concerning Iran's occupation of three islands belonging to the United Arab Emirates, namely Greater Tunb, Lesser Tunb and Abu Musa, until a settlement of the dispute was achieved by peaceful means through direct negotiations or through recourse to the International Court of Justice.

On 9 June [S/2004/486], the League of Arab States (LAS) informed the Council President that the LAS Council had adopted a resolution at its sixteenth regular session (Tunis, Tunisia, 22-23 May) on the occupation by Iran of the three Arab islands belonging to the United Arab Emirates. The resolution called on the Secretary-General and the Council President to maintain that issue among the matters of which the Council was seized until Iran ended its occupation of the three islands.

On 29 June [S/2004/530], the United Arab Emirates transmitted to the Secretary-General the text of a press release issued by the Ministerial Council of the Gulf Cooperation Council at its ninety-first session (Jeddah, Saudi Arabia, 30 June), reiterating its support of the sovereignty of the United Arab Emirates over the three islands.

On 30 July [S/2004/617], Iran stated that the islands were integral parts of the Iranian territory and rejected any claim to the contrary. Iran had always offered to negotiate with the United Arab Emirates to remove any misunderstanding between the two countries.

United Nations–Pacific Islands Forum cooperation

On 4 June [A/59/95], New Zealand transmitted to the Secretary-General the decisions and the Auckland Declaration adopted at the Special Leaders' Retreat of the Pacific Islands Forum (Auckland, New Zealand, 6 April). The leaders, among other things, agreed to a Pacific Vision statement that set the region on a new path of enhanced regional cooperation. The Vision statement would be elaborated through the development of a Pacific Plan. That undertaking would identify how better sharing of resources and alignment of policies would improve the well-being of the region.

Cooperation between the United Nations and the Pacific Islands Forum was highlighted by the Secretary-General in a September report [A/59/303] on cooperation between the United Nations and regional and other organizations.

GENERAL ASSEMBLY ACTION

On 8 November [meeting 50], the General Assembly adopted **resolution 59/20** [draft: A/59/L.11 & Add.1] without vote [agenda item 56 (*q*)].

Cooperation between the United Nations and the Pacific Islands Forum

The General Assembly,

Recalling its resolutions 56/41 of 7 December 2001 and 57/37 of 21 November 2002,

Welcoming the ongoing efforts towards closer cooperation between the United Nations and the Pacific Islands Forum and its associated institutions,

Reaffirming that one of the guiding principles for cooperation in peace-building adopted by the fourth high-level meeting between the United Nations and heads of regional organizations is that, as the promotion of self-reliance should be a fundamental goal of all cooperative and peace-building activities, peace-building must be a home-grown process in which the role of the United Nations and regional organizations is to support national endeavours,

Noting the outcomes of the Special Leaders' Retreat of the Pacific Islands Forum, held in New Zealand in April 2004,

Taking note of the communiqué of the thirty-fifth meeting of the Pacific Islands Forum, held in Apia from 5 to 7 August 2004,

Having considered the report of the Secretary-General on cooperation between the United Nations and regional and other organizations,

1. *Takes note* of the report of the Secretary-General, in particular the section on cooperation between the United Nations and the Pacific Islands Forum, and encourages further such cooperation;

2. *Welcomes* the ongoing work of various international organizations, United Nations agencies, funds and programmes in advancing knowledge in the key strategic areas related to governance, security, economic growth, trade and sustainable development, as well as in the implementation of the internationally agreed development goals, including those in the United Nations Millennium Declaration, in the Pacific island countries;

3. *Also welcomes* the decision of the Pacific Islands Forum to develop a "Pacific Plan", which is aimed at enhancing regional integration and cooperation among its members and cooperation with the international community, including the United Nations system;

4. *Further welcomes* the steps taken by the Secretary-General for the sixth high-level meeting between the United Nations and heads of regional organizations, to be convened in mid-2005, and recognizes the tasks before the United Nations departments and organizations in leading the process of implementing the recommendations of the last meeting and in formulating practical follow-up plans for discussion during the next meeting;

5. *Notes with satisfaction* that regular consultations continue at all levels between the United Nations and the Secretariat of the Pacific Islands Forum and that the United Nations also participated in the 2004 session of the Pacific Islands Forum Regional Security Committee and at the Leaders' Forum, held in Apia in August 2004;

6. *Welcomes* the ongoing efforts of the Pacific Islands Forum to promote, primarily through the Regional Security Committee, law enforcement cooperation, the rule of law and regional peace and security, including combating all types of terrorism, in implementing the core United Nations treaties on anti-terrorism, anti-money-laundering, transnational crime and the financing of terrorism;

7. *Requests*, in this regard, that the United Nations continue to assist the Pacific Islands Forum to enable the timely implementation of relevant United Nations mandates, and invites States to contribute to the Biketawa Trust Fund, which is administered by the Pacific Islands Forum for confidence-building measures and conflict prevention;

8. *Welcomes* the significant efforts of the Pacific Islands Forum in enhancing peace and security in the region, including through the Regional Assistance Mission to Solomon Islands;

9. *Also welcomes* the readiness of the United Nations, in cooperation with the Pacific Islands Forum, to field an inter-agency mission to Nauru to identify ways of assisting that country to cope with its current situation;

10. *Notes with appreciation* the role of the United Nations in the Bougainville peace process in Papua New Guinea and the steady progress being made by the parties;

11. *Welcomes* plans for the joint hosting of a regional seminar with the Pacific Islands Forum on "Conflict prevention and peace-building", to be held in early 2005;

12. *Requests* that the Department of Political Affairs of the Secretariat and the United Nations Development Programme, in cooperation with the Pacific Islands Forum, promote joint cooperative needs assessment missions in the region to determine additional support to enhance peace-building and reconciliation processes and to complement the activities of regional missions and mechanisms;

13. *Takes note* of steps taken by the Pacific Islands Forum to solidify its partnership with non-State actors in the region in promoting governance and sustainable development issues;

14. *Invites* the United Nations Institute for Training and Research to develop, in close consultation with the Pacific Islands Forum and other interested agencies, a Pacific-specific regional training programme on "Preventive diplomacy and post-conflict resolution", and to convene this programme in the Pacific in 2005;

15. *Urges* all States to participate, at the highest level possible, in the International Meeting to Review the Implementation of the Programme of Action for the Sustainable Development of Small Island Developing States, to be held in Mauritius;

16. *Recognizes* the burden placed on small States by growing international reporting requirements, and encourages the investigation of innovative reporting modalities, including regional reporting, where appropriate;

17. *Calls upon* the Office of the United Nations High Commissioner for Human Rights to provide technical support to Pacific Islands Forum members to contribute to the regional efforts in promoting awareness and knowledge of all international human rights treaties;

18. *Requests* the Secretary-General to submit to the General Assembly at its sixty-first session a report on the implementation of the present resolution;

19. *Decides* to include in the provisional agenda of its sixty-first session the sub-item entitled "Cooperation between the United Nations and the Pacific Islands Forum".

UN-ASEAN cooperation

The United Nations and the Association of Southeast Asian Nations (ASEAN) increased contacts and cooperation on matters relating to regional peace and security during 2004, as detailed in a September report [A/59/303] by the Secretary-General on cooperation between the United Nations and regional and other organizations. A joint communiqué issued by the 37th Ministerial Meeting of ASEAN (Jakarta, Indonesia, 30 June) stated that ASEAN was considering requesting observer status with the United Nations and that an institutional relationship with the United Nations would support the realization of the goals of the ASEAN community and efforts to strengthen cooperation between the two organizations.

GENERAL ASSEMBLY ACTION

On 22 October [meeting 40], the General Assembly adopted **resolution 59/5** [draft: A/59/L.6 & Add.1] without vote [agenda item 56 (c)].

Cooperation between the United Nations and the Association of Southeast Asian Nations

The General Assembly,

Bearing in mind the aims and purposes of the Association of Southeast Asian Nations, as enshrined in the Bangkok Declaration of 8 August 1967, in particular the maintenance of close and beneficial cooperation with existing international and regional organizations with similar aims and purposes,

Recalling its resolution 57/35 of 21 November 2002 on cooperation between the United Nations and the Association,

Noting with appreciation the report of the Secretary-General on cooperation between the United Nations and the Association,

Noting with satisfaction that the activities of the Association are consistent with the purposes and principles of the United Nations,

Welcoming the ongoing efforts that strengthen the cooperation between the United Nations system and the Association,

Welcoming also the participation of the Association in the high-level meetings between the United Nations and regional organizations, as well as the collaboration between the Association and the Economic and Social Commission for Asia and the Pacific to promote dialogue and cooperation among regional organizations in Asia and the Pacific,

1. *Commends* the President of the General Assembly, the Secretary-General of the United Nations and the Ministers for Foreign Affairs of the States members of the Association of Southeast Asian Nations for their efforts to hold regular meetings, on an annual basis, with the presence of the Secretary-General of the Association, during the regular session of the Assembly, with a view to further strengthening the cooperation between the United Nations and the Association;

2. *Continues to encourage* both the United Nations and the Association to further increase contacts and strengthen areas of cooperation, as appropriate;

3. *Requests* the Secretary-General to submit to the General Assembly at its sixty-first session a report on the implementation of the present resolution;

4. *Decides* to include in the provisional agenda of its sixty-first session the sub-item entitled "Cooperation between the United Nations and the Association of Southeast Asian Nations".

Chapter V

Europe and the Mediterranean

In 2004, progress towards the restoration of peace and stability and the settlement of several long-standing disputes in Europe and the Mediterranean suffered serious setbacks, as renewed violence risked derailing the stabilization and normalization process in the Serbia and Montenegro province of Kosovo, and almost brought the Georgian/Abkhaz peace process to a standstill, while efforts to reunite Cyprus in a bizonal, bicommunal federation ended in a stalemate with no immediate prospects of a way forward. Only in Bosnia and Herzegovina was there any significant progress to report regarding United Nations efforts to restore stability.

Bosnia and Herzegovina made steps towards restoring normality to its institutions and promoting further Euro-Atlantic integration by adopting requisite legislation and establishing new State-level institutions, although the continued lack of cooperation, especially by its constituent Republic, Republika Srpska, with the International Tribunal for the Former Yugoslavia resulted in the country being denied membership in the North Atlantic Treaty Organization (NATO) Partnership for Peace programme. Because of the positive security situation in the country, NATO announced in June that it was ending its multinational Stabilization Force there in December. The European Union (EU) indicated its intention to fill the resulting gap by installing an EU force as the successor to the NATO Force, which the Security Council authorized in December.

In the Serbia and Montenegro province of Kosovo, an eruption of violence in March caused a serious setback to the stabilization and normalization processes aimed at assisting the authorities and people of Kosovo to build a modern, multi-ethnic society. Despite the outbreak, the United Nations Interim Administration Mission in Kosovo and the Special Representative of the Secretary-General launched the Kosovo Standards Implementation Plan, which included priority actions in response to the March violence. Also arising out of the March events, the Secretary-General appointed a team to conduct a comprehensive review of the policies and practices of all actors. The team, among its recommendations, suggested that a comprehensive and integrated strategy be elaborated and that the

"standards before status" policy, which established in 2002 benchmarks for Kosovo to attain before talks on its status could begin, be replaced by a priority-based policy to facilitate future status discussions. General elections, organized for the first time by Kosovo authorities, were held on 23 October leading to the formation of a coalition Government.

The Georgian/Abkhaz peace process came perilously close to a standstill. While the parties came together during the course of the year on some substantive issues, efforts to advance a dialogue on the 2001 Basic Principles for the Distribution of Competences between Tbilisi (Georgia's Government) and Sukhumi (the Abkhaz leadership) encountered serious challenges. The Principles, which were intended to serve as a basis for negotiations on the status of Abkhazia as a sovereign entity within the State of Georgia, encountered serious challenges. Renewed violence in March led to a chain of events that brought all contacts between the sides to a halt. The Georgian side announced a proposal for settling the conflict, which included substantial autonomy for a reintegrated Abkhazia into the State of Georgia and power sharing at the national level, but there was no movement in the position of the Abkhaz side.

No progress was made towards a settlement of the conflict between Armenia and Azerbaijan over the Nagorny Karabakh region in Azerbaijan.

In the Mediterranean, after a 40-year effort by the United Nations, the Cyprus problem remained unresolved at the end of 2004 with no obvious avenue to achieve successful negotiations. The Secretary-General reconvened talks in February in Cyprus, which were resumed in Bürgenstock, Switzerland, on 24 March. As no agreement was achievable during those negotiations between the two sides—the Greek Cypriots and the Turkish Cypriots—the Secretary-General, in accordance with prior agreements, finalized a text on the basis of his proposed settlement plan. The "Comprehensive Settlement of the Cyprus Problem", which comprised, among other documents, a Foundation Agreement and constituent State constitutions, was submitted for approval by each side in simultaneous referenda on 24 April. The Greek Cypriot electorate, by a margin of three to one, rejected the settlement proposal; the Turkish Cypriot side approved it by a margin of two to one. The Foundation Agreement could not therefore enter into force and all the agreements of the Comprehensive Settlement became null and void. The Republic of Cyprus acceded to EU membership on 1 May, putting into question the future status of the northern part of the island. In those circumstances, the Secretary-General reviewed the mandate and concept of operations of the United Nations Peacekeeping Force in Cyprus and recommended a reduction in the mission's military component. He undertook to maintain continuous contact at the highest level with the parties and promised to designate on an ad hoc basis senior Secretariat officials to deal with any particular aspect of his mission of good offices that might require attention.

The former Yugoslavia

UN operations

In 2004, the United Nations maintained only one peacekeeping mission in the territories of the former Yugoslavia. Through the United Nations Interim Administration Mission in Kosovo (UNMIK), it continued efforts to restore peace and stability to the province of Kosovo in Serbia and Montenegro. Peace activities in Bosnia and Herzegovina were conducted by the European Union Police Mission.

Financing and liquidation of closed peacekeeping operations

The Secretary-General's April report on the updated financial position of closed peacekeeping missions as at 30 June 2003 [A/58/778] (see p. 95], included information on the financing of the United Nations Preventive Deployment Force (UNPREDEP), which ended in 1999; the United Nations Protection Force (UNPROFOR), which ended in 1999; the United Nations Confidence Restoration Operation in Croatia (UNCRO), which ended in 1996; and UNPREDEP—known collectively as the United Nations Peace Forces (UNPF)—and the UNPF Headquarters (UNPF-HQ); and the United Nations Transitional Administration for Eastern Slavonia, Baranja and Western Sirmium (UNTAES).

UNMIBH

In January [A/58/632], the Secretary-General submitted the performance report on the budget of the United Nations Mission in Bosnia and Herzegovina (UNMIBH), which ended on 31 December 2002, for the period from 1 July 2002 to 30 June 2003, in which he recommended that the General Assembly decide on the treatment of the unencumbered balance of $8,236,800 and other income/adjustments amounting to $8,603,000. In February [A/58/720], he reported on the final disposition of UNMIBH assets, which had an inventory value of $59,564,700 as at 31 December 2002.

In its April financial performance report on UNMIBH [A/58/759/Add.11], the Advisory Committee on Administrative and Budgetary Questions (ACABQ) recommended that the unencumbered balance and the amount resulting from other income and adjustments for that period be credited to Member States in a manner to be determined by the Assembly.

On 18 June [meeting 91], the General Assembly, on the recommendation of the Fifth (Administrative and Budgetary) Committee [A/58/822], adopted **resolution 58/300** without vote [agenda item 136].

Financing of the United Nations Mission in Bosnia and Herzegovina

The General Assembly,

Having considered the reports of the Secretary-General on the financing of the United Nations Mission in Bosnia and Herzegovina and the related reports of the Advisory Committee on Administrative and Budgetary Questions,

Recalling Security Council resolution 1035(1995) of 21 December 1995 regarding the establishment of the United Nations Mission in Bosnia and Herzegovina and the subsequent resolutions by which the Council extended the mandate of the Mission, the latest of which was resolution 1423(2002) of 12 July 2002, by which the Council extended the mandate of the Mission until 31 December 2002,

Recalling also Security Council resolution 1437(2002) of 11 October 2002, in which the Council authorized the United Nations military observers to continue to monitor the demilitarization of the Prevlaka peninsula until 15 December 2002,

Recalling further its decision 50/481 of 11 April 1996 on the financing of the Mission and its subsequent resolutions and decisions thereon, the latest of which was resolution 57/334 of 18 June 2003,

Reaffirming the general principles underlying the financing of United Nations peacekeeping operations, as stated in General Assembly resolutions 1874(S-IV) of 27 June 1963, 3101(XXVIII) of 11 December 1973 and 55/235 of 23 December 2000,

Noting with appreciation that voluntary contributions have been made to the Mission,

Mindful of the fact that it is essential to provide the Mission with the necessary financial resources to enable it to meet its outstanding liabilities,

1. *Takes note* of the status of contributions to the United Nations Mission in Bosnia and Herzegovina as

at 15 April 2004, including the contributions outstanding in the amount of 38 million United States dollars, representing some 4 per cent of the total assessed contributions, notes with concern that only ninety-seven Member States have paid their assessed contributions in full, and urges all other Member States, in particular those in arrears, to ensure payment of their outstanding assessed contributions;

2. *Expresses its appreciation* to those Member States which have paid their assessed contributions in full, and urges all other Member States to make every possible effort to ensure payment of their assessed contributions to the Mission in full;

3. *Expresses concern* at the delay experienced by the Secretary-General in deploying and providing adequate resources to some recent peacekeeping missions, in particular those in Africa;

4. *Emphasizes* that all future and existing peacekeeping missions shall be given equal and non-discriminatory treatment in respect of financial and administrative arrangements;

5. *Also emphasizes* that all peacekeeping missions shall be provided with adequate resources for the effective and efficient discharge of their respective mandates;

6. *Endorses* the conclusions and recommendations contained in the report of the Advisory Committee on Administrative and Budgetary Questions, and requests the Secretary-General to ensure their full implementation;

Final disposition of assets

7. *Takes note* of the report of the Secretary-General on the final disposition of the assets of the Mission;

Financial performance report for the period from 1 July 2002 to 30 June 2003

8. *Also takes note* of the report of the Secretary-General on the financial performance of the Mission for the period from 1 July 2002 to 30 June 2003;

9. *Decides* that Member States that have fulfilled their financial obligations to the Mission shall be credited their respective share of the unencumbered balance and other income in the total amount of 16,839,800 dollars in respect of the financial period ended 30 June 2003, in accordance with the levels set out in General Assembly resolution 55/235, as adjusted by the Assembly in its resolutions 55/236 of 23 December 2000 and 57/290 A of 20 December 2002, and taking into account the scale of assessments for 2003, as set out in its resolutions 55/5 B of 23 December 2000 and 57/4 B of 20 December 2002;

10. *Decides also* that, for Member States that have not fulfilled their financial obligations to the Mission, their respective share of the unencumbered balance and other income in the total amount of 16,839,800 dollars in respect of the financial period ended 30 June 2003 shall be set off against their outstanding obligations, in accordance with the scheme set out in paragraph 9 above;

11. *Decides further* that the increase of 342,600 dollars in the estimated staff assessment income in respect of the financial period ended 30 June 2003 shall be added to the credits from the amount referred to in paragraphs 9 and 10 above, and that the respective shares of Member States therein shall be applied in ac-

cordance with the provisions of those paragraphs, as appropriate;

12. *Emphasizes* that no peacekeeping mission shall be financed by borrowing funds from other active peacekeeping missions;

13. *Decides* to include in the provisional agenda of its fifty-ninth session the item entitled "Financing of the United Nations Mission in Bosnia and Herzegovina.

On 23 December, the Assembly decided that the item on the financing of UNMIBH would remain for consideration during its resumed fifty-ninth (2005) session (**decision 59/552**).

Bosnia and Herzegovina

In 2004, efforts to assist the two entities comprising the Republic of Bosnia and Herzegovina—the Federation of Bosnia and Herzegovina (where mainly Bosnian Muslims (Bosniacs) and Bosnian Croats resided) and Republika Srpska (where mostly Bosnian Serbs resided)—in implementing the 1995 General Framework Agreement for Peace in Bosnia and Herzegovina and the annexes thereto (the Peace Agreement) [YUN 1995, p. 544] were directed by the European Union (EU). Those efforts were accomplished through the activities of the Office of the High Representative for the Implementation of the Peace Agreement on Bosnia and Herzegovina, responsible for the Agreement's civilian aspects [YUN 1996, p. 293], and the European Union Police Mission in Bosnia and Herzegovina (EUPM). The North Atlantic Treaty Organization (NATO) continued to execute its responsibilities for the Agreement's military aspects, which were transferred to the EU Force (EUFOR) mission in December. NATO maintained a headquarters in Sarajevo, following the transfer of responsibilities. The Peace Implementation Council (PIC) and its Steering Board continued to oversee and facilitate the Agreement's implementation.

The High Representative reported on the progress made in the implementation process and related political developments in the country during the year in the context of his mission implementation plan, which set out a number of core tasks to be accomplished [YUN 2003, p. 401]. Bosnia and Herzegovina undertook a number of reforms, particularly in the areas of the rule of law, refugee return and economic development, in accordance with European standards, as it continued work towards full integration into Europe through the EU Stabilization and Association Pro-

cess and NATO's Partnership for Peace requirements.

Implementation of Peace Agreement

Civilian aspects

The civilian aspects of the 1995 Peace Agreement entailed a wide range of activities, including humanitarian aid, infrastructure rehabilitation, establishment of political and constitutional
institutions, promoting respect for human rights
and the holding of free and fair elections. The
High Representative for the Implementation of
the Peace Agreement, who chaired the PIC Steering Board and other key implementation bodies,
was the final authority with regard to implementing the civilian aspects of the Peace Agreement
[YUN 1995, p. 547]. The reports on the activities of
EUPM were submitted by the EU Secretary-
General and High Representative for the Common Foreign and Security Policy, Javier Solana,
to the Security Council President through the
UN Secretary-General.

Office of High Representative

Reports of High Representative. The High
Representative, Lord Paddy Ashdown (United
Kingdom), reported to the Council through the
Secretary-General on the peace implementation
process for the periods from 1 January to 30 June
[S/2004/807] and from 1 July to 31 December
[S/2005/156], describing progress in the imple-
mentation of the Peace Agreement's civilian as-
pects, which the High Representative had been
mandated to monitor, mobilize and coordinate.
(For details on the reports' specific topics, see
below.)

The Security Council, on 3 March, considered
the High Representative's report covering late
2003 [YUN 2003, p. 402]. On 11 November, it considered the report covering the first half of 2004.

SECURITY COUNCIL ACTION

On 3 March [meeting 4920], the Security Council
considered the High Representative's report for
the period from 1 September to 31 December
2003 [YUN 2003, p. 402]. On 9 July [meeting 5001], it
unanimously adopted **resolution 1551(2004)**.
The draft [S/2004/545] was submitted by France,
Germany, Italy, Romania, the Russian Federation, Spain, the United Kingdom and the United
States.

The Security Council,

Recalling all its relevant resolutions concerning the
conflicts in the former Yugoslavia and the relevant
statements by its President, including resolutions
1031(1995) of 15 December 1995, 1088(1996) of 12 De-

cember 1996, 1423(2002) of 12 July 2002 and 1491
(2003) of 11 July 2003,

Reaffirming its commitment to the political settlement
of the conflicts in the former Yugoslavia, preserving
the sovereignty and territorial integrity of all States
there within their internationally recognized borders,

Emphasizing its full support for the continued role in
Bosnia and Herzegovina of the High Representative
for the Implementation of the Peace Agreement on
Bosnia and Herzegovina,

Underlining its commitment to support the implementation of the General Framework Agreement for Peace
in Bosnia and Herzegovina and the annexes thereto
(collectively the "Peace Agreement"), as well as the relevant decisions of the Peace Implementation Council,

Emphasizing its appreciation to the High Representative, the Commander and personnel of the multinational Stabilization Force, the Organization for
Security and Cooperation in Europe, the European
Union, and the personnel of other international organizations and agencies in Bosnia and Herzegovina
for their contributions to the implementation of the
Peace Agreement,

Emphasizing that a comprehensive and coordinated
return of refugees and displaced persons throughout
the region continues to be crucial to lasting peace,

Recalling the declarations of the ministerial meetings of the Peace Implementation Council,

Taking note of the reports of the High Representative, including his latest report, of 18 February 2004,

Determining that the situation in the region continues
to constitute a threat to international peace and
security,

Determined to promote the peaceful resolution of the
conflicts in accordance with the purposes and principles of the Charter of the United Nations,

Recalling the relevant principles contained in the
Convention on the Safety of United Nations and Associated Personnel of 9 December 1994 and the statement by its President of 9 February 2000,

Welcoming and encouraging efforts by the United
Nations to sensitize peacekeeping personnel in the
prevention and control of HIV/AIDS and other communicable diseases in all its peacekeeping operations,

Taking note of the decisions set out in paragraph 8 of
the communiqué of the summit of the North Atlantic
Treaty Organization held in Istanbul, Turkey, on
28 June 2004, which refers to the intention of that organization to conclude its Stabilization Force operation
in Bosnia and Herzegovina by the end of 2004,

Taking note also of the intention of the European
Union to launch a European Union mission to Bosnia
and Herzegovina, including a military component,
from December 2004, under the terms set out in the
letter dated 29 June 2004 from the Minister for Foreign Affairs of Ireland and President of the Council of
the European Union addressed to the President of the
Security Council,

Acting under Chapter VII of the Charter,

I

1. *Reaffirms once again its support* for the General
Framework Agreement for Peace in Bosnia and Herze-
govina and the annexes thereto (collectively the "Peace
Agreement"), as well as for the Dayton Agreement on
Implementing the Federation of Bosnia and Herze-

govina of 10 November 1995, calls upon the parties to comply strictly with their obligations under those Agreements, and expresses its intention to keep the implementation of the Peace Agreement, and the situation in Bosnia and Herzegovina, under review;

2. *Reiterates* that the primary responsibility for the further successful implementation of the Peace Agreement lies with the authorities in Bosnia and Herzegovina themselves and that the continued willingness of the international community and major donors to assume the political, military and economic burden of implementation and reconstruction efforts will be determined by the compliance and active participation by all the authorities in Bosnia and Herzegovina in implementing the Peace Agreement and rebuilding a civil society, in particular in full cooperation with the International Tribunal for the Prosecution of Persons Responsible for Serious Violations of International Humanitarian Law Committed in the Territory of the Former Yugoslavia since 1991, in strengthening joint institutions, which foster the building of a fully functioning self-sustaining State able to integrate itself into the European structures, and in facilitating returns of refugees and displaced persons;

3. *Reminds* the parties once again that, in accordance with the Peace Agreement, they have committed themselves to cooperate fully with all entities involved in the implementation of this peace settlement, as described in the Peace Agreement, or which are otherwise authorized by the Security Council, including the International Tribunal for the Former Yugoslavia, as it carries out its responsibilities for dispensing justice impartially, and underlines that full cooperation by States and entities with the Tribunal includes, inter alia, the surrender for trial of all persons indicted by the Tribunal and the provision of information to assist in Tribunal investigations;

4. *Emphasizes its full support* for the continued role of the High Representative for the Implementation of the Peace Agreement on Bosnia and Herzegovina in monitoring the implementation of the Peace Agreement and giving guidance to and coordinating the activities of the civilian organizations and agencies involved in assisting the parties to implement the Peace Agreement, and reaffirms that, under annex 10 of the Peace Agreement, the High Representative is the final authority in theatre regarding the interpretation of civilian implementation of the Peace Agreement and that, in case of dispute, he may give his interpretation and make recommendations, and make binding decisions as he judges necessary on issues as elaborated by the Peace Implementation Council in Bonn, Germany, on 9 and 10 December 1997;

5. *Expresses its support* for the declarations of the ministerial meetings of the Peace Implementation Council;

6. *Recognizes* that the parties have authorized the multinational force referred to in paragraph 11 below to take such actions as required, including the use of necessary force, to ensure compliance with annex 1-A of the Peace Agreement;

7. *Reaffirms its intention* to keep the situation in Bosnia and Herzegovina under close review, taking into account the reports submitted pursuant to paragraphs 19 and 23 below, and any recommendations those reports might include, and its readiness to consider the imposition of measures if any party fails significantly to meet its obligations under the Peace Agreement;

II

8. *Pays tribute* to those Member States which participated in the multinational Stabilization Force established in accordance with its resolution 1088(1996), and welcomes their willingness to assist the parties to the Peace Agreement by continuing to deploy a multinational stabilization force;

9. *Notes* the support of the parties to the Peace Agreement for the continuation of the multinational Stabilization Force, set out in the declaration of the ministerial meeting of the Peace Implementation Council in Madrid on 16 December 1998;

10. *Welcomes* the decision of the North Atlantic Treaty Organization to conclude its current Stabilization Force operation in Bosnia and Herzegovina by the end of 2004, and further welcomes the intention of the European Union to launch a European Union mission to Bosnia and Herzegovina, including a military component, from December 2004;

11. *Authorizes* the Member States acting through or in cooperation with the organization referred to in annex 1-A of the Peace Agreement to continue for a further planned period of six months the multinational Stabilization Force as established in accordance with its resolution 1088(1996) under unified command and control in order to fulfil the role specified in annexes 1-A and 2 of the Peace Agreement;

12. *Expresses its intention* to consider the terms of further authorization as necessary, in the light of developments in the implementation of the Peace Agreement and the situation in Bosnia and Herzegovina;

13. *Authorizes* the Member States acting under paragraph 11 above to take all necessary measures to effect the implementation of and to ensure compliance with annex 1-A of the Peace Agreement, stresses that the parties shall continue to be held equally responsible for compliance with that annex and shall be equally subject to such enforcement action by the Force as may be necessary to ensure implementation of that annex and the protection of the Force, and takes note that the parties have consented to the Force taking such measures;

14. *Authorizes* Member States to take all necessary measures, at the request of the Force, either in defence of the Force or to assist the Force in carrying out its mission, and recognizes the right of the Force to take all necessary measures to defend itself from attack or threat of attack;

15. *Authorizes* the Member States acting under paragraph 11 above, in accordance with annex 1-A of the Peace Agreement, to take all necessary measures to ensure compliance with the rules and procedures established by the Commander of the Force, governing command and control of airspace over Bosnia and Herzegovina with respect to all civilian and military air traffic;

16. *Requests* the authorities in Bosnia and Herzegovina to cooperate with the Commander of the Force to ensure the effective management of the airports of Bosnia and Herzegovina, in the light of the responsibilities conferred on the Force by annex 1-A of the Peace Agreement with regard to the airspace of Bosnia and Herzegovina;

17. *Demands* that the parties respect the security and freedom of movement of the Force and other international personnel;

18. *Recalls* all the agreements concerning the status of forces as referred to in appendix B to annex 1-A of the Peace Agreement, and reminds the parties of their obligation to continue to comply therewith;

19. *Requests* the Member States acting through or in cooperation with the organization referred to in annex 1-A of the Peace Agreement to continue to report to the Security Council, through the appropriate channels and at least at monthly intervals;

20. *Decides* that the status-of-forces agreements currently contained in appendix B to annex 1-A of the Peace Agreement shall apply provisionally in respect of the proposed European Union mission and its forces, including from the point of their build-up in Bosnia and Herzegovina, in anticipation of the concurrence of the parties to those agreements to that effect;

21. *Invites* all States, in particular those in the region, to continue to provide appropriate support and facilities, including transit facilities, for the Member States acting under paragraphs 11 and 20 above;

* * *

22. *Welcomes* the deployment by the European Union of its Police Mission to Bosnia and Herzegovina since 1 January 2003;

23. *Requests* the Secretary-General to continue to submit to the Council reports from the High Representative, in accordance with annex 10 of the Peace Agreement and the conclusions of the Peace Implementation Conference held in London on 4 and 5 December 1996, and later Peace Implementation Conferences, on the implementation of the Peace Agreement and in particular on compliance by the parties with their commitments under that Agreement;

24. *Decides* to remain seized of the matter.

Mission implementation plan

The High Representative presented to the PIC Steering Board, in June, an update of the mission implementation plan of his Office, drawn up in 2002 [YUN 2002, p. 359] and introduced in 2003 [YUN 2003, p. 401]. Reporting in October [S/2004/807], he said that there had been notable advances in executing all four core tasks: rule of law; reforming the economy; strengthening the capacity of Bosnia and Herzegovina institutions; and defence reform. Notably, the Independent Judicial Commission completed its operations with the establishment of a single Bosnia and Herzegovina High Judicial and Prosecutorial Council in June. The package of laws for the State Investigation and Protection Agency was enacted, representing a critical step in re-shaping criminal enforcement, and progress was made towards the adoption of several key economic-related laws. In March, the intelligence law was adopted, leading to the establishment of the State Intelligence and Security Agency. The appointment in March of a Minister of Defence was fol-

lowed by other appointments to key State-level military posts and the establishment of the defence institutions. The identity-card management programme gave the State the means to manage and vouch for the integrity of identity documents, despite politically motivated attempts to undermine it.

In a later report [S/2005/156], the High Representative stated that progress in the 2004 mission implementation plan, made up of 26 programmes, included the establishment of the Indirect Tax Authority Governing Board, the State Ministry of Defence and the State Intelligence and Security Agency, the unification of the city of Mostar (see p. 395) and progress in regulating the entities' internal debts. Four of the 26 programmes were completed by the end of the year, including the State Management of Identity Documents, the Parliamentary Oversight over the Armed Forces and the Security Policy. Of the 230 programme items, 116 had been completed by the end of the year.

Civil affairs

The High Representative, in his reports covering 1 January to 30 June [S/2004/807] and 1 July to 31 December [S/2005/156], stated that Bosnia and Herzegovina was concentrating on meeting the conditions contained in the EU Commission's feasibility study for negotiating a stabilization and association agreement and the requirements for meeting NATO's benchmarks for the country's entry into the Partnership for Peace programme [YUN 2003, p. 403]. The Bosnia and Herzegovina authorities succeeded in fulfilling some of the key conditions set by the EU and NATO, notably by adopting most of the requisite legislation and establishing new State-level institutions. A total of 18 laws were enacted, many of them introducing significant structural changes in crime prevention, the judiciary, the development of a single economic space and the functioning of the energy market. An additional 21 laws adopted by the Council of Ministers were awaiting enactment by the Bosnia and Herzegovina Parliamentary Assembly.

However, the continued failure of the Republika Srpska authorities to cooperate fully with the International Tribunal for the Former Yugoslavia (ICTY) caused NATO to deny Bosnia and Herzegovina entry into the Partnership for Peace programme at its June summit (Istanbul, Turkey, 28-29 June), and forced the High Representative to introduce punitive measures against those individuals and organizations identified as supporting suspected war criminals. Fifty-nine individuals were removed from party and other public positions, including the Republika Srpska

Interior Minister and the President of the Serbian Democratic Party (SDS). Despite the adoption by the Republika Srpska government of the final report of the Srebrenica Commission (see below), which it established in 2003 [YUN 2003, p. 404] to investigate missing persons, among other duties, and the arrest by Republika Srpska Special Police of eight Bosnian Serbs on suspicion of war crimes on warrants issued by the Sarajevo Cantonal Court, the North Atlantic Council, at its ministerial meeting (Brussels, Belgium, 9 December), considered that Bosnia and Herzegovina was still not cooperating with ICTY, making it ineligible for the second time in a year for membership in NATO's Partnership for Peace programme. Subsequently, the Office of the High Representative, with EUFOR and the United States, announced further punitive sanctions, including removal of nine officials, the blocking of the bank accounts of others suspected of abetting Tribunal fugitives, requiring the Republika Srpska government to verify if those persons mentioned in the Commission's report were still in government service, and requesting acceleration of defence reforms through the early closure of the entities' ministries of defence. In the wake of those measures, ministers of the Party of Democratic Progress at both the Republika Srpska and State level resigned, prompting President Dragan Cavic to convene talks with the Serb-dominated parties on the way forward. In late December, the six Serb-based parties signed an agreement confirming, among other things, Republika Srpska's commitment to dealing with the ICTY issue.

In the area of defence reform, the State-level Ministry of Defence became functional, with the filling of all top military posts and the approval by the Council of Ministers, on 20 May, of the Book of Rules on Internal Organization for the Ministry of Defence, the Joint Staff and the Operational Command. Both entity armies downsized by at least 25 per cent. The Presidency's decision in March on the size and structure of the Armed Forces of Bosnia and Herzegovina envisaged a much-reduced force of 12,000 full-time military professionals and 60,000 reserves, and the restructuring and downsizing of the Republika Srpska Army General Staff and the Federation Army Joint Command. The intake of conscripts and the duration of military service were also being cut. The Intelligence and Security Agency became operational on 1 June. The High Representative established the post of supervisor for intelligence reform to ensure the Agency's development.

The first municipal elections administrated wholly by local institutions were held in October, but the turnout was very low, particularly among the Bosniak community. The elections were conducted peaceably in Republika Srpska, with further gains for the Independent Social Democratic Party (SNSD) and erosion of SDS's pre-eminence.

Concerning the city of Mostar, the United Nations sought to produce a permanent statute for the city, based on compromises that would eliminate the ethnic and political divisions sustained by the existence of the six so-called "city-municipalities" and "central zone". As agreed in 2003 [YUN 2003, p. 403], the High Representative, in view of the need to provide solutions to the still-contentious issues of the system of elections and the status of the existing municipalities [ibid.], imposed on 28 January a statute for Mostar. Under the statute, the "city-municipalities" were abolished and transformed into "city areas", making them, in effect, branch offices of the unified administration as well as electoral districts. The statute also guaranteed power-sharing through national quotas and safeguards for vital national interests in the composition and rules of the city council, thereby preventing domination by a single nationality, while ensuring broad national balance in the future city government. Along with the statute, a decision was issued on the steps and timetable for the city's unification. A Mostar Implementation Unit to assist in carrying out the reform measures and a Committee on Confidence-Building Measures to win popular support for the unification process were established.

Implementation of the statute proceeded relatively well. A compromise city budget was adopted by the City Council in mid-year and some success was achieved in joining divided institutions. The opening of the rebuilt Old Bridge on 23 July helped to normalize the atmosphere in the city, and post-war internal ethnic boundaries were gradually losing their significance. Since the October elections (see p. 416) produced no clear majority in the Council, a Croat mayor was elected with cross-party and cross-ethnic support after extensive power-sharing negotiations. However, the political situation remained fragile and potentially volatile and much of the technical process of unification was still to be completed.

Srebrenica

The Srebrenica Commission, appointed by Republika Srpska in December 2003 [YUN 2003, p. 404] to investigate and report on persons missing as a result of the 1995 Srebrenica massacre [YUN 1995, p. 529], was established in January 2004. The High Representative, although not having any formal role in the Commission, monitored the Commission's activity.

The Commission's report, issued in June, indicated that Republika Srpska had recognized, for the first time, the origins, nature and extent of the atrocities committed in and around Srebrenica and disclosed the location of previously unknown primary and secondary mass graves, documents and other evidence that might serve as bases for further prosecution of war crimes. The report established that, between 10 and 19 July 1995, some 8,000 Bosniaks were liquidated and that the perpetrators took elaborate measures to conceal those crimes by relocating the bodies. It identified, in particular, 32 locations of mass graves, 11 of them previously unknown, and elaborated on the participation of particular Republika Srpska military and police units in the 1995 events and aftermath. The report cited documents making clear that those events had three planned phases: the attack on Srebrenica, the separation of women and children, and the execution of males. The Commission promised to produce a consolidated list of all the persons still unaccounted for, but wanted better access to relevant documentation of competent Republika Srpska institutions and Federation records. On 11 June, the High Representative forwarded to the EU and NATO copies of the report and his assessment of it.

Judicial reform

The High Representative, reporting in October [S/2004/807] on steps taken to establish the rule of law in Bosnia and Herzegovina, said that the financial help pledged during the 2003 donors' conference [YUN 2003, p. 408] to defray the costs of trying war crime cases transferred by ICTY to local Bosnia and Herzegovina courts enabled the project to proceed. The plan called for the creation of a special chamber within the State Court to try such cases, and for a registrar's office within the court to provide logistical and administrative support (see p. 1293).

The development of an anti-money-laundering programme progressed. As part of the package of laws expanding the role of the State Investigation and Protection Agency, a new law was enacted in June, making the Agency primarily responsible for compiling and analysing information from financial transactions in order to initiate appropriate criminal investigations. A draft law for seizing assets acquired through or used in criminal activities was submitted to the Council of Ministers for consideration and adoption.

Regarding the process of reappointing judges and prosecutors at all levels in Bosnia and Herzegovina, out of some 1,000 vacancies advertised, 877 judges and prosecutors were appointed or re-

appointed. Establishing adequate budgets for courts was hindered by the need to pay compensation paid to judges who were not reappointed, and judicial salaries and fees for attorneys representing criminal defendants. The Disciplinary Prosecutor received cases against 142 judges and prosecutors. Sanctions were imposed in 14 cases of established judicial misconduct.

The Office of the High Representative worked on building the capacities of the State Court. The new, single High Judicial and Prosecutorial Council was established as a State-level institution on 1 May, thus terminating the mandate of the Independent Judicial Commission. The Rule of Law Pillar was dissolved in October and replaced by a substantially reduced Rule of Law Department. The Office of the High Representative would continue to work closely with the Rule of Law and Legal Departments on issues of common interest, and supported the Council in dealing with the unresolved issues of judicial, prosecutorial and defence counsel compensation, court budgets and minor offence courts.

Economic reform and reconstruction

The High Representative reported that, although notable progress was made in economic reform, the economy of Bosnia and Herzegovina had yet to register concrete benefits from the legal, fiscal and structural changes. However, domestic authorities had asserted greater ownership over some important economic issues, particularly in regard to fiscal and customs reforms. The Indirect Taxation Authority, which commenced operation in January, would operate an integrated and indirect tax-collection service and a State-level customs service, implementing a single set of rules, applicable throughout the country, which should make it possible to launch the collection of value added tax by the end of 2005. In December, State-level laws on sales and excise taxation were passed and the double taxation within the territory of Bosnia and Herzegovina was abolished.

The Office of the High Representative was instrumental in efforts to resolve the long-standing problem of the entities' internal indebtedness, a major obstacle to investment and job creation. An enabling law was passed in Republika Srpska, but enactment of similar legislation in the Federation was proving contentious on both political and fiscal grounds.

Advances were made to restructure the public utilities sector. The Law on Civil Aviation was successfully implemented during the year, and the drafting of the railway law was under way. The laws establishing the Electricity Transmission Company and the Independent System Operator were passed, enabling the proper functioning of the electricity transmission system and preparing it for reconnection to the European electricity grid on 10 October.

Given the ongoing need to improve the business environment and standards of corporate governance in Bosnia and Herzegovina, the Office of the High Representative supported the drafting of laws on public enterprises, investment of public funds and public procurement. The Bulldozer Initiative, coordinated by the Office, had some success in cutting bureaucracy and removing regulations inimical to investment. The Framework Law on Business Registration was adopted, and the authorities were creating a single business registration system to reduce registration time and cost. The State-level Law on Public Procurement was enacted, and the new Law on Accounting and Auditing was aimed at putting in place a uniform set of international accounting and auditing standards. The Office of the High Representative continued to centralize the process of privatizing enterprises across Bosnia and Herzegovina. A single information point for privatization opportunities was established in March, with a website offering information for potential investors. The Office was also successful in assisting the State Veterinary Institute in becoming operational.

In the light of mismanagement, incompetence and political manipulation within publicly owned companies in Republika Srpska, the Office amended, in December, relevant legislation, thus requiring special audits of such companies by the Republika Srpska Auditor General. In response, the entity governments committed themselves to implementing reforms to improve management practices and eliminate endemic corruption in the public sector.

Public administration reform

The Office of the High Representative developed a State Government Strengthening Plan, focusing on staffing and premises, to help the Chairman of the Council of Ministers make State ministries and the Council fully operational. It commissioned a review of the application of the State Civil Service Law by the State Civil Service Agency. The Agency's March report recommended a number of managerial and legal changes, which were incorporated in an action plan. The Agency initiated changes in its personnel structure and was drafting by-laws and amendments to the Civil Service Law. The High Representative established the Police Restructuring Commission on 2 July, with a mandate to restructure Bosnia and Herzegovina's police forces and to propose a single police structure.

Reviews of the public sector, funded by the European Commission, were in progress. When completed, a comprehensive strategy for improving Bosnia and Herzegovina's public administration would follow.

Refugees

In 2004, the number of refugees returning to Bosnia and Herzegovina since the signing of the Peace Agreement reached 1 million. The Bosnia and Herzegovina authorities assumed responsibility for implementation of annex VII of the Peace Agreement at the beginning of 2004 and, in November, the Office of the High Representative closed its unit that monitored returns. Implementation of property law, a precondition for returns, increased and the process was expected to end by April 2005. The transfer of responsibilities from the Commission for Real Property Claims to the Bosnia and Herzegovina authorities was completed. A body charged with reviewing Commission decisions was established and commissioners appointed.

The Bosnia and Herzegovina State Commission for Refugees and Displaced Persons continued to act as the coordinating body between the State, the entities and Brcko District. A return fund was established, to which the State, Brcko and Republika Srpska had transferred their financial commitments, but the Federation was tardy in doing so. However, with loans secured for 2005, the State ministry and the State Commission for Refugees and Displaced Persons would have sufficient means to implement their returns policy.

Media development

Reform of the public broadcasting system encountered serious obstacles during 2004. In April, the Council of Ministers endorsed public broadcasting draft legislation, aimed at bringing Bosnia and Herzegovina into compliance with the EU feasibility study requirements—to create a single, self-sustainable public broadcasting system within a common infrastructure. However, the Bosnia and Herzegovina Parliament failed to adopt the legislation, due to the opposition by Republika Srpska delegates to amendments that would have allowed for the creation of a sound common resource corporation. In addition, Croatian Democratic Union members pushed for the establishment of three separate "national" channels, in addition to the two existing entity broadcasters. With the help of the Office of the High Representative and the European Commission, the outstanding issues were renegotiated and resolved, and the draft legislation was awaiting adoption by the Council of Ministers.

The State-wide television service, launched in August, was well accepted in both entities and was addressing the challenges of the broadcasting market.

Relations with other countries

Bosnia and Herzegovina, during its presidency of the South-East European Cooperation Process, including the first meeting of defence ministers from the region, demonstrated its capacity to play a valuable political role at the regional level. The first International Investment Conference organized by the Government of Bosnia and Herzegovina was held in Mostar on 26 and 27 February. Although overshadowed by the tragic deaths of President Boris Trajkovski of The Former Yugoslav Republic of Macedonia and his delegation when their aircraft crashed while approaching Mostar, the Conference facilitated business contacts and investment opportunities. In addition to the 12 concrete investment projects that were presented to potential investors, the Conference sent out positive political and economic signals to the international business community.

The wave of intercommunal violence that roiled the Serbia and Montenegro province of Kosovo in mid-March (see p. 405) did not spill over into Bosnia and Herzegovina. Bosnia and Herzegovina's relations with Serbia and Montenegro improved, assisted by the election of Boris Tadic as President of Serbia. Mr. Tadic paid a visit to Bosnia and Herzegovina, during which he apologized for "those who committed crimes in the name of the Serb people" during the war. Bilateral forums functioned on a regular basis, including efforts to delimit the exact border on the lower Drina River near Zvornik.

Bosnia and Herzegovina and Croatia made progress towards normalizing their relations. Meetings at the presidential level between the two countries were held twice annually. Croatian Prime Minister Ivo Sanader had taken a constructive approach to Bosnia and Herzegovina and the position of Croats in the country. Border issues were almost entirely resolved, with the notable exception of Croatia's failure to ratify the treaty granting Bosnia and Herzegovina free-port rights at Ploce.

European Union Police Mission in Bosnia and Herzegovina

Reports of EU Secretary-General. As invited by the Security Council in presidential statement S/PRST/2002/33 [YUN 2002, p. 363], the EU Secretary-General and High Representative for the Common Foreign and Security Policy re-ported on the activities of the EU Police Mission (EUPM) covering the periods 1 January to 30 June [S/2004/709] and 1 July to 31 December [S/2005/66].

As at 31 December, the Mission numbered 862 personnel, of whom 472 were seconded civilian police officers, 61 international civilians and 329 national staff from Bosnia and Herzegovina. All but 1 of the 25 EU member States participated in the Mission (420 police officers) and 9 non-EU contributing States (52 police officers). The Mission was headed by Kevin Carty (Ireland) from 1 March, following the death of Sven Frederiksen (Denmark) on 26 January.

In the first report, the EU Secretary-General highlighted the achievements made in the programmes administered by EUPM [YUN 2003, p. 409]. Under the crime police programme, EUPM introduced an intelligence-led approach to policing that was helping Bosnia and Herzegovina fight major and organized crime more effectively. Crucial to that, a national intelligence model was introduced countrywide. The criminal justice programme was aimed at establishing the State judicial police and the two court police forces at entity level. A new programme focusing on a police education and training system was launched. Under the internal affairs programme, seven professional standards units and nine public complaints bureaux were established. Guidelines for preventing serious crowd disturbances during major public events were being implemented. The State Border Service (SBS) strengthened its cooperation with the multinational Stabilization Force (SFOR) and other entity-based police forces, including through regular joint border operations. The Council of Ministers, in March, expanded the powers of the State Investigation and Protection Agency (SIPA), enhancing its responsibility in the fight against organized crime. The related laws were before the Parliamentary Assembly of Bosnia and Herzegovina for approval. Technical amendments to the Bosnia and Herzegovina Criminal Procedure Code and Law on Civil Service were also necessary to harmonize those laws with other SIPA laws.

Implementation of EUPM's programmes was hampered by legal challenges to the UNMIBH/International Police Task Force (IPTF) police certification process, by which law enforcement officers were vetted before receiving final certification [YUN 2001, p. 332] (see p. 399).

A review commissioned by the European Commission on police structures concluded that Bosnia and Herzegovina had too many levels of policing and identified options for restructuring. A Police Restructuring Commission was launched in July to make recommendations for a single police structure for the whole country.

In the report covering the second half of 2004 [S/2005/66], the EU Secretary-General said that, in terms of the strategic priorities, the Mission had made solid progress. The Ministry of Security had recruited more staff and established internal departments covering all areas of responsibility, and the Minister of Security had assumed the chairmanship of the Ministerial Consultative Meeting on Police Matters, which coordinated and oversaw the political aspects of all State-level police agencies. New laws were adopted, including a law creating a new Immigration Service, an updated law governing the working of SBS and a law on police officials.

SIPA was established in temporary accommodation in Sarajevo and planning was ongoing to secure permanent facilities. The Agency's legal framework and operating rules were established, and a headquarters and two regional offices were set up; a total of 279 police officers had been recruited by the end of the year. The Criminal Investigation Department had begun conducting investigations, and a cell for criminal intelligence was set up as the focal point for intelligence from international stakeholders.

Interpol established a national office in Sarajevo. Technical agreements between Interpol Sarajevo and the entity and State-level law enforcement agencies were drawn up, giving those police forces direct access to the Interpol database. All aspects of police education were brought together in May, and an agreement was reached on the creation of a national training system. A project was launched to harmonize the curriculum for all three training schools in Bosnia and Herzegovina.

In the fight against organized crime and corruption, a nationwide national intelligence system was introduced. An agreement was reached on expanding the country's forensic capabilities. To help achieve financial viability and sustainability of the local police, EUPM helped to develop local capacity regarding salary scales and budget planning.

In the view of the High Representative, EUPM, as it entered the last year of its mandate, was well placed, in partnership with the local authorities, to complete its prime directive of leaving in place sustainable and effective policing arrangements in Bosnia and Herzegovina, in line with the best European practices and through implementation of the Police Restructuring Commission's recommendations. Consideration would need to be given as to how best to support that work.

Police certification

In a briefing to the Security Council on 3 March [meeting 4920], which was considering a report on EUPM activities during late 2003 [YUN 2003, p. 402], the High Representative, Lord Paddy Ashdown, drew the Council's attention to the problem of the growing number of challenges within the courts of Bosnia and Herzegovina to the UN-led police certification process, instituted in 2001 [YUN 2001, p. 332] by IPTF in Bosnia and Herzegovina, whose mission terminated at the end of 2002. That de-certification process weeded out police officers whose past, particularly during the war, disqualified them from remaining in the police. More than 150 non-certified police officers had asked the courts to assess the legality of their dismissal. In January 2004, the first non-certified police officer dismissed under IPTF was reinstated, following an order from a domestic court. The situation was deteriorating, as the Human Rights Chamber of Bosnia and Herzegovina had decided that it was competent to examine whether such dismissals were carried out in accordance with the provisions of the European Convention on Human Rights.

The High Representative, with the UN Department of Peacekeeping Operations, had been trying to identify a solution to those challenges.

SECURITY COUNCIL ACTION

On 25 June [meeting 4997], following consultations among Security Council members, the President made statement **S/PRST/2004/22** on behalf of the Council:

The Security Council notes the report of the High Representative for the Implementation of the Peace Agreement on Bosnia and Herzegovina to the Secretary-General of 18 February 2004 which refers to the increasing number of challenges to the police certification process conducted by the United Nations Mission in Bosnia and Herzegovina International Police Task Force.

The Council recalls its relevant resolutions and its support for the General Framework Agreement for Peace in Bosnia and Herzegovina and the annexes thereto (collectively the "Peace Agreement"). The parties to the Peace Agreement had the responsibility to cooperate fully with, and to instruct their respective responsible officials and authorities to provide their full support to, the International Police Task Force during its mandate on all relevant matters. The Council affirms that such responsibility included giving full and immediate effect to the decisions issued by the Task Force, including decisions to deny certification. The Council also affirms that Bosnia and Herzegovina has the obligation to respect fully and to promote the fulfilment of its responsibilities under the Peace Agreement.

The Council reaffirms the legal basis in the Charter of the United Nations on which the International Police Task Force was given its mandate. The Council recalls that during its mandate the Task Force was entrusted with the tasks set out in annex 11 of the Peace Agreement, including the tasks referred to in the conclusions of the London, Bonn, Luxembourg, Madrid and Brussels Conferences and agreed by the authorities in Bosnia and Herzegovina.

The Council affirms that the certification process was carried out pursuant to the mandate of the International Police Task Force and fully endorses this process. The comprehensive and rigorous vetting procedure was designed to create a police force comprised entirely of personnel meeting internationally recognized standards of personal integrity and professional performance.

The Council expresses concern at the failure of the competent authorities in Bosnia and Herzegovina to take due steps to implement decisions to deny certification. The Council notes that this failure has already led to several challenges before the courts in Bosnia and Herzegovina brought by persons whose employment in Bosnia and Herzegovina's law enforcement agencies was terminated pursuant to a denial of certification by the International Police Task Force.

The Council further notes that in some cases such persons have been reinstated following decisions of some local courts. The Council calls upon the authorities in Bosnia and Herzegovina to ensure, including through the adoption or amendment of domestic legislation, that all certification decisions of the International Police Task Force are fully and effectively implemented and that the employment of persons who were denied certification by the Task Force is terminated, and that such persons will be precluded from employment, either now or in the future, in any position within any law enforcement agency in Bosnia and Herzegovina.

Military aspects

Stabilization Force

Under the command of NATO, the multinational Stabilization Force (SFOR), also known as Operation Joint Guard, continued in 2004 to oversee implementation of the military aspects of the 1995 Peace Agreement. Its 2004 activities were recorded in 10 reports [S/2004/174, S/2004/263, S/2004/488, S/2004/588, S/2004/654, S/2004/731, S/2004/784, S/2004/889, S/2004/936, S/2005/67], submitted by the NATO Secretary-General to the Security Council, in accordance with Council resolution 1088(1996) [YUN 1996, p. 310]. Another report [S/2005/226] covered December activities of EUFOR (see p. 404).

SFOR's strength decreased from just over 11,400 in December 2003 to 7,526 on 30 November 2004. The Council, by resolution 1551(2004) of 9 July (see p. 392), welcoming NATO's intention to conclude the SFOR operation by the end of 2004, authorized its continuation for a further period of six months.

During the year, SFOR continued to contribute to the maintenance of a safe and secure environment in Bosnia and Herzegovina, monitor terrorist-related threats throughout the country and engage in weapons collection and destruction. Its operations also focused on the detention of persons indicted for war crimes. In January it launched, with the Republika Srpska Ministry of the Interior, a cordon-and-search operation to detain Radovan Karadzic, indicted by ICTY for war crimes. Although he was not detained, substantial evidence was collected. In February, the High Representative and the SFOR Commander announced actions against several individuals for supporting persons indicted for war crimes, including freezing their bank accounts, dismissal from political office and prohibition from standing for office again. On 15 April, the Bosnian-Croat Federation State and the entity authorities signed a declaration on cooperation with ICTY and called on all indicted persons to surrender. On 19 May, the Republika Srpska Parliament issued a declaration calling on all persons indicted for war crimes to surrender and all related authorities to cooperate with ICTY. Fifteen arrest warrants were posted on the Republika Srpska website, as well as a list of persons indicted for war crimes, including for the first time, Radovan Karadzic and Ratko Mladic.

The results of the weapons collection effort, known as Operation Harvest, showed success and the need for further efforts. On 13 May, the Multinational Specialized Unit found a large weapons cache in Ugljevik and, on 20 May, SFOR confirmed that a secret arms depot was found in a wire factory in Cazin. As part of SFOR's strategy to facilitate the transfer of responsibilities to nascent authorities, the local police would be increasingly encouraged to lead Operation Harvest activities.

On 18 May, the Bosnia and Herzegovina Parliament adopted the new Defence Law and the Army Service Law, while the Council of Ministers approved the book of rules on the internal organization of the Ministry of Defence. Work on the implementation of the structure of the armed forces continued with discussion of the internal organization and responsibilities of the State-level Ministry of Defence, Joint Staff and Operational Command. SFOR established a new initiative, the Advice and Assistance Implementation Initiative, to assist in implementing the new structure.

SFOR, on 1 June, forwarded the results of the vetting process for generals' posts in the new combined armed forces of Bosnia and Herzegovina to the President's Office and to the Bosnia and Herzegovina and Federation defence ministries. On 9 June, the candidates for the generals' posts in the joint institutions were announced. Republika Srpska also adopted, in accordance with the defence reforms, a new organizational structure for the military, controlled by a civilian-led Ministry of Defence.

Transition from SFOR to EUFOR

NATO, in a communiqué issued by the heads of State and Government after a 28-29 June meeting in Istanbul, Turkey, announced that, as the security situation in Bosnia and Herzegovina had evolved positively, it had decided to conclude the SFOR operation by the end of the year. As its long-term commitment to Bosnia and Herzegovina remained unchanged, it would maintain a residual military presence in the country. NATO-HQ Sarajevo would advise on defence reform, undertake certain operational supporting tasks, support ICTY with regard to the detention of persons indicted for war crimes and share intelligence with the EU.

Ireland, in its capacity as President of the EU Council, requested on 29 June [S/2004/522] that the Security Council President inform the Security Council of the EU's intention to launch an EU mission, including a military component, following NATO's announced termination of SFOR in December to fulfil the role specified in annexes 1-A and 2 of the Peace Agreement and contribute to the safe and secure environment in Bosnia and Herzegovina. The EU would welcome the Council's determination that the status-of-forces agreements currently contained in appendix B to annex 1-A would apply provisionally in respect of the EU-led military operation (EUFOR), in anticipation of the concurrence of the parties to those agreements to that effect.

On 22 October [S/2004/883], Bosnia and Herzegovina welcomed NATO's continued commitment through its headquarters in Sarajevo. Given all the reforms in defence and security systems that had been carried out, the uniform chain of command established and democratic control secured, conditions had been created in Bosnia and Herzegovina for the transfer from NATO's SFOR to EUFOR. It supported the announced EU mission and the transfer of responsibilities and announced its intention to cooperate on a partnership basis.

Roles of EU and NATO. By an exchange of letters dated 19 November [S/2004/916, S/2004/915], forwarded by the Netherlands and Germany, respectively, to the Council President, the EU High Representative and the NATO Secretary-General outlined the respective roles of their organizations in Bosnia and Herzegovina after the transition from SFOR to EUFOR's Operation Althea.

The two organizations would have access to the full authorities under annexes 1-A and 2 of the Peace Agreement. EUFOR would have the main peace stabilization role under the Peace Agreement through a robust military presence in order to: deter the former Entity Armed Forces and other armed groups; monitor and ensure compliance with the military aspects of the Peace Agreement; and prevent a resumption of violence. It would have full authority to fulfil the role specified in annexes 1-A and 2 of the Peace Agreement, monitor implementation of its military aspects, and assess and address non-compliance by the parties.

EUFOR would also support, with the EU and international community actors, the core tasks of the mission implementation plan of the Office of the High Representative and other civil implementation organizations regarding counter-terrorism, the fight against organized crime, returns of displaced persons and refugees, the rule of law and implementation of other civilian aspects of the Peace Agreement. It would also provide support to ICTY and relevant authorities, including the detention of persons indicted for war crimes.

NATO's presence would be based on the June 2004 Istanbul summit communiqué (see above) and on other NATO decisions, and would exercise its authority only when necessary to fulfil its tasks, including for Force protection. Both NATO headquarters in Sarajevo and EUFOR would be the legal successors to SFOR for the fulfilment of their missions.

Also on 19 November [S/2004/917], Bosnia and Herzegovina informed the Council President that its Presidency fully accepted EUFOR and NATO as the legal successors to the NATO-SFOR mission and mandate, under the same terms. It offered its unreserved support and cooperation and expected to be consulted and regularly informed on the duration of the EUFOR and NATO missions.

The Council, in resolution 1575(2004) (below) of 22 November, authorized the establishment of EUFOR for an initial period of 12 months.

SECURITY COUNCIL ACTION

On 22 November [meeting 5085], the Security Council unanimously adopted **resolution 1575 (2004)**. The draft [S/2004/920] was prepared in consultations among Council members.

The Security Council,

Recalling all its previous relevant resolutions concerning the conflicts in the former Yugoslavia and relevant statements by its President, including resolutions 1031(1995) of 15 December 1995, 1088(1996) of 12 December 1996, 1423(2002) of 12 July 2002, 1491 (2003) of 11 July 2003 and 1551(2004) of 9 July 2004,

Reaffirming its commitment to the political settlement of the conflicts in the former Yugoslavia, preserving the sovereignty and territorial integrity of all States there within their internationally recognized borders,

Emphasizing its full support for the continued role in Bosnia and Herzegovina of the High Representative for the Implementation of the Peace Agreement on Bosnia and Herzegovina,

Underlining its commitment to support the implementation of the General Framework Agreement for Peace in Bosnia and Herzegovina and the annexes thereto (collectively the "Peace Agreement"), as well as the relevant decisions of the Peace Implementation Council,

Recalling all the agreements concerning the status of forces referred to in appendix B to annex 1-A of the Peace Agreement, and reminding the parties of their obligation to continue to comply therewith,

Recalling also the provisions of its resolution 1551 (2004) concerning the provisional application of the status-of-forces agreements contained in appendix B to annex 1-A of the Peace Agreement,

Emphasizing its appreciation to the High Representative, the Commander and personnel of the multinational Stabilization Force, the Organization for Security and Cooperation in Europe, the European Union and the personnel of other international organizations and agencies in Bosnia and Herzegovina for their contributions to the implementation of the Peace Agreement,

Emphasizing that a comprehensive and coordinated return of refugees and displaced persons throughout the region continues to be crucial to lasting peace,

Recalling the declarations of the ministerial meetings of the Peace Implementation Council,

Taking note of the reports of the High Representative, including his latest report, of 6 October 2004,

Determined to promote the peaceful resolution of the conflicts in accordance with the purposes and principles of the Charter of the United Nations,

Recalling the relevant principles contained in the Convention on the Safety of United Nations and Associated Personnel of 9 December 1994 and the statement by its President of 9 February 2000,

Welcoming and encouraging efforts by the United Nations to sensitize peacekeeping personnel in the prevention and control of HIV/AIDS and other communicable diseases in all its peacekeeping operations,

Recalling the decisions set out in paragraph 8 of the communiqué of the summit of the North Atlantic Treaty Organization held in Istanbul, Turkey, on 28 June 2004, which refers to the intention of the Organization to conclude the Stabilization Force operation in Bosnia and Herzegovina by the end of 2004 and to establish a headquarters of the Organization in Sarajevo that will constitute its residual military presence,

Recalling also that in resolution 1551(2004) the Security Council took note of the intention of the European Union to launch a European Union mission to Bosnia and Herzegovina, including a military component, from December 2004, under the terms set out in the letter dated 29 June 2004 from the Minister for Foreign Affairs of Ireland and President of the Council of the European Union to the President of the Security Council,

Taking note of the letters between the European Union and the North Atlantic Treaty Organization, sent to the Security Council on 19 November 2004, on how those organizations will cooperate together in Bosnia and Herzegovina, in which both organizations recognize that the European Union Force will have the

main peace stabilization role under the military aspects of the Peace Agreement,

Taking note also of the confirmation by the Presidency of Bosnia and Herzegovina, on behalf of Bosnia and Herzegovina, including its constituent entities, of the arrangements for the European Union Force and the North Atlantic Treaty Organization headquarters presence,

Welcoming, in the light of the forthcoming European Union mission, the increasing engagement in Bosnia and Herzegovina of the European Union,

Welcoming also tangible signs of Bosnia and Herzegovina's progress towards European integration,

Determining that the situation in the region continues to constitute a threat to international peace and security,

Acting under Chapter VII of the Charter,

I

1. *Reaffirms once again its support* for the General Framework Agreement for Peace in Bosnia and Herzegovina and the annexes thereto (collectively the "Peace Agreement"), as well as for the Dayton Agreement on Implementing the Federation of Bosnia and Herzegovina of 10 November 1995, and calls upon the parties to comply strictly with their obligations under those Agreements;

2. *Reiterates* that the primary responsibility for the further successful implementation of the Peace Agreement lies with the authorities in Bosnia and Herzegovina themselves and that the continued willingness f the international community and major donors to assume the political, military and economic burden of implementation and reconstruction efforts will be determined by the compliance and active participation by all the authorities in Bosnia and Herzegovina in implementing the Peace Agreement and rebuilding a civil society, in particular in full cooperation with the International Tribunal for the Prosecution of Persons Responsible for Serious Violations of International Humanitarian Law Committed in the Territory of the Former Yugoslavia since 1991, in strengthening joint institutions, which foster the building of a fully functioning self-sustaining State able to integrate itself into the European structures, and in facilitating returns of refugees and displaced persons;

3. *Reminds* the parties once again that, in accordance with the Peace Agreement, they have committed themselves to cooperate fully with all entities involved in the implementation of this peace settlement, as described in the Peace Agreement, or which are otherwise authorized by the Security Council, including the International Tribunal for the Former Yugoslavia, as it carries out its responsibilities for dispensing justice impartially, and underlines that full cooperation by States and entities with the Tribunal includes, inter alia, the surrender for trial of all persons indicted by the Tribunal and the provision of information to assist in Tribunal investigations;

4. *Emphasizes its full support* for the continued role of the High Representative for the Implementation of the Peace Agreement on Bosnia and Herzegovina in monitoring the implementation of the Peace Agreement and giving guidance to and coordinating the activities of the civilian organizations and agencies involved in assisting the parties to implement the Peace Agreement, and reaffirms that, under annex 10 of the Peace

Agreement, the High Representative is the final authority in theatre regarding the interpretation of civilian implementation of the Peace Agreement and that, in case of dispute, he may give his interpretation and make recommendations, and make binding decisions as he judges necessary on issues as elaborated by the Peace Implementation Council in Bonn, Germany, on 9 and 10 December 1997;

5. *Expresses its support* for the declarations of the ministerial meetings of the Peace Implementation Council;

6. *Reaffirms its intention* to keep implementation of the Peace Agreement and the situation in Bosnia and Herzegovina under close review, taking into account the reports submitted pursuant to paragraphs 18 and 21 below, and any recommendations that those reports might include, and its readiness to consider the imposition of measures if any party fails significantly to meet its obligations under the Peace Agreement;

II

7. *Acknowledges* the support of the authorities of Bosnia and Herzegovina for the European Union Force and the continued North Atlantic Treaty Organization presence and their confirmation that both are the legal successors to the Stabilization Force for the fulfilment of their missions for the purposes of the Peace Agreement, its annexes and appendices and relevant Security Council resolutions and can take such actions as are required, including the use of force, to ensure compliance with annexes 1-A and 2 of the Peace Agreement and relevant Council resolutions;

8. *Pays tribute* to those Member States which participated in the multinational Stabilization Force established in accordance with its resolution 1088(1996), and expresses its appreciation of their efforts and achievements in Bosnia and Herzegovina;

9. *Welcomes* the intention of the European Union to launch a European Union military operation to Bosnia and Herzegovina from December 2004;

10. *Authorizes* the Member States acting through or in cooperation with the European Union to establish for an initial planned period of twelve months a multinational stabilization force, the European Union Force, as a legal successor to the Stabilization Force under unified command and control, which will fulfil its missions in relation to the implementation of annexes 1-A and 2 of the Peace Agreement in cooperation with the North Atlantic Treaty Organization headquarters presence in accordance with the arrangements agreed between the Organization and the European Union as communicated to the Security Council in their letters of 19 November 2004, which recognize that the European Union Force will have the main peace stabilization role under the military aspects of the Peace Agreement;

11. *Welcomes* the decision of the North Atlantic Treaty Organization to conclude the Stabilization Force operation in Bosnia and Herzegovina by the end of 2004 and to maintain a presence in Bosnia and Herzegovina through the establishment of a headquarters of the Organization in order to continue to assist in implementing the Peace Agreement in conjunction with the European Union Force, and authorizes the Member States acting through or in cooperation with the Organization to establish a headquarters of the Organ-

ization as a legal successor to the Stabilization Force under unified command and control, which will fulfil its missions in relation to the implementation of annexes 1-A and 2 of the Peace Agreement in cooperation with the European Union Force in accordance with the arrangements agreed between the Organization and the European Union as communicated to the Security Council in their letters of 19 November 2004, which recognize that the European Union Force will have the main peace stabilization role under the military aspects of the Peace Agreement;

12. *Recognizes* that the Peace Agreement and the provisions of its previous relevant resolutions shall apply to and in respect of both the European Union Force and the North Atlantic Treaty Organization presence as they have applied to and in respect of the Stabilization Force and that, therefore, references in the Peace Agreement, in particular in annex 1-A and the appendices thereto, and in relevant resolutions to the Implementation Force and/or the Stabilization Force, the North Atlantic Treaty Organization and the North Atlantic Council shall henceforth be read as applying, as appropriate, to the North Atlantic Treaty Organization presence, the European Union Force, the European Union and the Political and Security Committee and Council of the European Union respectively;

13. *Expresses its intention* to consider the terms of further authorization as necessary in the light of developments in the implementation of the Peace Agreement and the situation in Bosnia and Herzegovina;

14. *Authorizes* the Member States acting under paragraphs 10 and 11 above to take all necessary measures to effect the implementation of and to ensure compliance with annexes 1-A and 2 of the Peace Agreement, stresses that the parties shall continue to be held equally responsible for compliance with those annexes and shall be equally subject to such enforcement action by the European Union Force and the North Atlantic Treaty Organization presence as may be necessary to ensure implementation of those annexes and the protection of the Force and the Organization presence;

15. *Authorizes* Member States to take all necessary measures, at the request of either the European Union Force or the North Atlantic Treaty Organization headquarters, in defence of the Force or the Organization presence respectively, and to assist both organizations in carrying out their missions, and recognizes the right of both the Force and the Organization presence to take all necessary measures to defend themselves from attack or threat of attack;

16. *Authorizes* the Member States acting under paragraphs 10 and 11 above, in accordance with annex 1-A of the Peace Agreement, to take all necessary measures to ensure compliance with the rules and procedures governing command and control of airspace over Bosnia and Herzegovina with respect to all civilian and military air traffic;

17. *Demands* that the parties respect the security and freedom of movement of the European Union Force, the North Atlantic Treaty Organization presence, and other international personnel;

18. *Requests* the Member States acting through or in cooperation with the European Union and the Member States acting through or in cooperation with the North Atlantic Treaty Organization to report to the Security Council on the activity of the European Union Force and

the North Atlantic Treaty Organization headquarters presence respectively, through the appropriate channels and at least at three-monthly intervals;

19. *Invites* all States, in particular those in the region, to continue to provide appropriate support and facilities, including transit facilities, for the Member States acting under paragraphs 10 and 11 above;

20. *Reiterates its appreciation* for the deployment by the European Union of its Police Mission to Bosnia and Herzegovina since 1 January 2003;

21. *Requests* the Secretary-General to continue to submit to the Security Council reports from the High Representative, in accordance with annex 10 of the Peace Agreement and the conclusions of the Peace Implementation Conference held in London on 4 and 5 December 1996, and later Peace Implementation Conferences, on the implementation of the Peace Agreement and in particular on compliance by the parties with their commitments under that Agreement;

22. *Decides* to remain seized of the matter.

EUFOR report. In his first report [S/2005/226] on EUFOR's activities, the EU Secretary-General and High Representative for the Common Foreign and Security Policy said that the EU launched Operation Althea in December in line with its mandate. The new operation reinforced the EU's comprehensive approach towards Bosnia and Herzegovina and supported the country's progress towards EU integration by its own efforts, with the objective of signing a stabilization and association agreement as a medium-term objective. The political scene was dominated by the eight measures announced by the High Representative on 16 December to address the continued failure of Republika Srpska to cooperate fully with ICTY (see p. 1283) and the subsequent resignation of its Prime Minister, Dragan Mikerevic, and the Bosnia and Herzegovina Foreign Minister, Mladen Ivanic. In mid-December, EUFOR inspected the Han Pijesak military installation, 40 kilometres north-east of Sarajevo, an area suspected of having been used by persons indicted for war crimes to escape apprehension. In the view of the EU, that assertive and high-profile operation established EUFOR's visibility and authority and made a positive impact both nationally and internationally.

Serbia and Montenegro

In 2004, the United Nations continued to assist the authorities and people of the Kosovo province of Serbia and Montenegro in their efforts to build a modern, European, multi-ethnic society. The United Nations Interim Administration Mission in Kosovo (UNMIK) cooperated with the Kosovo authorities in strengthening the Pro-

visional Institutions of Self-Government, mainly the Kosovo Assembly and the Kosovo Government, and in transferring authority to those institutions, in accordance with the 2001 Constitutional Framework for Provisional Self-Government [YUN 2001, p. 352]. It also monitored progress towards the fulfilment of the eight standards set out in the 2003 "standards for Kosovo" document [YUN 2003, p. 420], as endorsed by the Security Council in presidential statement S/PRST/2003/26 [ibid.], that Kosovo had to meet in preparation for talks on its future status. However, a resurgence of violence in March stalled progress on the implementation of the standards and was a serious setback to building a democratic, multi-ethnic and stable Kosovo, seriously damaging the process of normalization and reconciliation.

Despite the setback, UNMIK and the Special Representative of the Secretary-General, Harri Holkeri, launched the Kosovo Standards Implementation Plan, which included six priority actions in response to the March violence. Also resulting from the March events, the Secretary-General appointed a team to conduct a comprehensive review of the policies and practices of all actors. The team, among its recommendations, suggested that a comprehensive and integrated strategy be elaborated and that the "standards before status" policy be replaced by a priority-based policy within that strategy to facilitate future status discussions. General elections, organized for the first time by Kosovo authorities, were held on 23 October. Taking place without incident, they were certified as free and fair by the Council of Europe, leading to the formation of a coalition Government.

Situation in Kosovo

The United Nations continued to work towards the full implementation of Security Council resolution 1244(1999) [YUN 1999, p. 353], which set out the modalities for a political solution to the crisis in the Serbia and Montenegro province of Kosovo, and of resolutions 1160(1998) [YUN 1998, p. 369], 1199(1998) [ibid., p. 377], 1203(1998) [ibid., p. 382] and 1239(1999) [YUN 1999, p. 349]. The civilian aspects of resolution 1244(1999) were being implemented by UNMIK and the military aspects by the international security presence (KFOR), led by NATO.

Appointment of Special Representative. UNMIK was headed by the Special Representative of the Secretary-General. In June, the Secretary-General informed the Security Council of his intention to appoint Søren Jessen-Petersen (Denmark) to replace Harri Holkeri (Finland) in that position [S/2004/500]. The Council took note of that intention on 18 June [S/2004/501].

Resurgence of violence

Communication. On 24 February [S/2004/141], Serbia and Montenegro brought to the attention of the Security Council the ambush and killing of two Serb civilians in the Lipljan area, which, it said, brought into question KFOR's decision a few days earlier to withdraw the multinational brigade "Centre" in charge of security in that area. Recalling previous crimes committed against Kosovo Serbs and the failure of condemnations by the Council and others to improve security or apprehend the perpetrators, Serbia and Montenegro said such incidents raised concerns about the authority of KFOR, UNMIK and the Council in implementing resolution 1244(1999), and the impunity enjoyed by the extremists in Kosovo and Metohija. Serbia and Montenegro expected the Council to take action to identify and bring to justice the perpetrators of the current and other crimes.

Report of Secretary-General. The Secretary-General, in his report on UNMIK activities in Kosovo from 1 January to 31 March [S/2004/348], said that the defining event during that period was the widespread violence that occurred in March. The onslaught, led by Kosovo Albanian extremists against the Kosovo Serb, Roma and Ashkali communities, was an organized, widespread and targeted campaign, resulting in the deaths of 19 persons, of whom 11 were Kosovo Albanians and 8 were Kosovo Serbs, and there were 954 persons injured. In addition, 65 international police officers, 58 Kosovo Police Service (KPS) officers and 61 KFOR personnel were injured. Approximately 730 houses belonging to minorities, mostly Kosovo Serbs, were damaged or destroyed, and 36 Orthodox churches, monasteries and other religious and cultural sites were also damaged or destroyed. Sporadic attacks, including attacks against the international security and police presence, continued, the worst occurring on 23 March, when a Ghanaian UNMIK police officer and a Kosovo Albanian KPS officer were killed.

The violence, which began in earnest on 17 March, appeared to have been sparked by the shooting of a Kosovo Serb youth in the village of Caglavica (Pristina region) on 15 March, followed the next day by a blockade by Kosovo Serbs of the main Pristina-Skopje road outside Pristina, demonstrations by some 18,000 Kosovo Albanians to protest the arrest of four members of the Kosovo Liberation Army, and the drowning of three Kosovo Albanian children in the River Ibar near Zubin Potok (Mitrovica region). Those and other incidents, made worse by inflammatory and biased media reporting, resulted in demonstrations, which were quickly taken over by organized elements.

The Special Representative took political and operational measures to stem the spread of the violence. UNMIK and KFOR established a senior crisis team to coordinate policy and security actions and launched efforts to apprehend those involved in violent actions. KFOR temporarily deployed some 2,000 additional troops and reestablished some checkpoints, primarily in Kosovo Serb areas. UNMIK police made 260 arrests in connection with the violence and a further 400 for curfew violations.

Kosovo Albanian leaders were mostly reluctant to condemn the violence in general and against the Kosovo Serb community in particular. During the most violent days, most central-level government officials of the main political parties and in the municipalities renewed demands for the independence of Kosovo and the transfer of competencies from UNMIK. On 17 March, the Kosovo Prime Minister, Bajram Rexhepi, acting with the Special Representative, issued statements calling for an end to the violence. At the same time, other members of the Provisional Institutions appeared to justify or even condone the violence, blaming it on the continuing existence of parallel structures, roadblocks set up by Kosovo Serbs, the death of the Kosovo Albanian children, the division of the city of Mitrovica and UNMIK. While both Kosovo President Ibrahim Rugova and the head of the Kosovo Protection Corps made television addresses calling for calm, those and other initial statements avoided specifically referring to the Kosovo Serb community as the target of most of the violence. The Kosovo Assembly issued a statement which focused on parallel structures rather than on the evolving violence.

International condemnation of the violence caused Kosovo Albanian leaders to change the focus of their statements, although they still largely failed to expressly condemn the attacks on the Kosovo Serb community. The Special Representative, at an 18 March meeting with local political and institutional leaders, emphasized that statements blaming the United Nations, KFOR or parallel structures for the violence had to stop. Following that meeting, the Prime Minister convinced Kosovo Albanian protestors to lift their siege of the Kosovo Serb majority village of Caglavica.

On 2 April, Kosovo Albanian officials within the Provisional Institutions, political leaders and representatives of the Turkish, Bosniac, Egyptian, Ashkali and Roma communities signed an open letter addressed to the population, condemning the violence and promising that politicians and the people of all ethnicities would work together to build a better Kosovo. They also called for a memorandum of understanding on a partnership between Kosovo Albanians and Kosovo Serbs based on mutual respect and the marginalization of extremists on both sides, and a memorandum of understanding between the population and religious leaders, who would preach tolerance and respect. The Government committed itself to establishing a fund to repair damaged buildings and religious sites and identified 11.6 million euros in the 2004 budget for reconstruction. UNMIK provided technical assistance and support for the reconstruction effort and was negotiating with the United Nations Educational, Scientific and Cultural Organization on the establishment of assessment teams to evaluate the damage.

The authorities in Belgrade played a role in collective efforts to stem the violence and prevent extremist reaction. On 26 March, the Serbian Parliament issued a declaration calling for the Serb community in Kosovo to be granted political and territorial autonomy and for a reconsideration and change of policy in Kosovo, and urged the international community to punish the perpetrators and to effect rapid reconstruction of homes and religious sites. A similar declaration was adopted by the State Union of Serbia and Montenegro Assembly on 1 April.

Security Council consideration. At the request of Serbia and Montenegro [S/2004/220], the Security Council met on 18 March [meeting 4928] to consider the latest outbreak of violence in Kosovo and Metohija.

The Secretary-General told the Council that the overall security situation throughout Kosovo was still highly unstable, and that the United Nations could not close its eyes to the fact that it was ethnically motivated. The deliberate targeting of houses and religious sites was inexcusable, as were the subsequent attacks against mosques in other parts of Serbia and Montenegro. The attacks on UNMIK and KFOR staff should also be condemned in the strongest possible terms. The situation in Mitrovica had become sufficiently serious to warrant the relocation of international staff. The events highlighted the fragility of the structures and relationships in Kosovo, and showed that, despite the progress made since 1999, the United Nations had not gone far enough. He reminded the leaders of the Kosovo Albanian community that, as the largest ethnic group, they had the responsibility to protect and promote the rights of all people within Kosovo, particularly its minorities.

SECURITY COUNCIL ACTION (March)

On 18 March [meeting 4928], following consultations among Security Council members, the President made statement **S/PRST/2004/5** on behalf of the Council:

The Security Council strongly condemns the large-scale inter-ethnic violence in Kosovo, Serbia and Montenegro, that began yesterday and in which many people have been killed and hundreds injured. It also strongly condemns the attacks on the troops of the Kosovo Force and the personnel and sites of the United Nations Interim Administration Mission in Kosovo. Such violence is unacceptable and must stop immediately. Those responsible must be brought to justice. The perpetrators must understand that an attack on the international presence is an attack on the international community as a whole and that extremism has no role in Kosovo's future.

The Council calls upon all communities in Kosovo, taking into account their respective responsibilities, to stop all acts of violence, to avoid further escalation and to restore calm. The Council urges the parties to refrain from irresponsible and inflammatory statements and accusations. The Council reiterates that the population in Kosovo must employ peaceful, democratic means and work through the recognized and legitimate channels, including the United Nations and the structures of the Provisional Institutions of Self-Government, to address their grievances. It stresses that legal investigations by the authorities in Kosovo, in particular into the incidents involving the shooting of a Kosovo Serb teenager in Pristina and the deaths of three Kosovo Albanian children in Mitrovica, are under way, and calls for thorough investigations of all other incidents.

The Council deplores the reported deaths and injuries among the population of Kosovo as well as casualties among the Kosovo Police Service, the international civilian police of the United Nations Interim Administration Mission in Kosovo and the troops of the Kosovo Force. The Council extends its condolences to the families of all the victims.

The Council reiterates the urgent need for the authorities in Kosovo to take effective steps to enforce the rule of law, ensure proper security for all ethnic communities and bring to justice all the perpetrators of criminal acts. The establishment of a multi-ethnic, tolerant, democratic society in a stable Kosovo remains the fundamental objective of the international community in implementing Security Council resolution 1244(1999) of 10 June 1999. The Council will closely monitor the implementation by the parties of their obligations according to the "Standards for Kosovo" document.

The Council expresses its full support for the efforts of the Special Representative of the Secretary-General, the United Nations Interim Administration Mission in Kosovo and the Kosovo Force, and welcomes the fact that the international security presence is continuing to undertake additional measures, as deemed necessary, to stabilize the situation throughout Kosovo. It calls on the Provisional Institutions of Self-Government, the authorities in Belgrade and all concerned to cooperate fully. The Council takes note of the joint statement of the Special Representative, the Provisional Institutions of Self-Government, political leaders and others of 17 March 2004.

Communication (March). The Russian Federation Ministry of Foreign Affairs, in a 20 March statement [S/2004/237], expressed concern over developments in Kosovo. Russia said that it had repeatedly drawn attention to the danger of such a development and to the inadequate response from the international presences in the province. A simple numerical increase in NATO troops was not enough. They were duty-bound to take action to suppress violence and protect the civilian population and, with UNMIK, make the Kosovo Albanian leaders fulfil the Council's demands. The Council had to insist on the implementation of its resolutions.

Security Council consideration. The Security Council, on 13 April [meeting 4942], continued consideration of the March events. The Under-Secretary-General for Peacekeeping Operations, briefing the Council, said that UNMIK was investigating and assessing the violence, which had so far resulted in 183 arrests. International prosecutors were currently working on 42 cases and an additional 90 cases were being handled by the local judiciary. However, given the scale of the violence, additional investigative capacity would be needed. To that end, UNMIK had asked for 100 additional police investigators. The Under-Secretary-General stated that the events indicated that Kosovo still had a long way to go on the path to multi-ethnicity. The standards implementation process needed to be put back on track and the Kosovo Standards Implementation Plan (see p. 408) should be launched to move the process forward so as not to lose momentum. Further review and revision of the Plan, with additional emphasis on security and the rule of law, minority rights and protection and returns, and on decentralization, might be necessary in the wake of the violence.

UNMIK had set up a crisis management review body to evaluate its response and was engaged in establishing a basis of confidence for Kosovo Serbs and fostering reconciliation among Kosovo's communities. The events had shown that the international community's determination to ensure coexistence and reconciliation among the communities was, by itself, not sufficient, but needed to be complemented by concrete action by Kosovo's leaders and its people to address the root causes of the ethnically motivated violence.

Follow-up to March events

The Secretary-General, in his July report on UNMIK [S/2004/613], said that considerable progress had been made to bring to justice those responsible for the violence in March. International prosecutors were currently handling 52 cases involving serious crimes, including judicial investigations into the 20 deaths connected with the violence. The local judiciary was handling more than 260 cases. Some 80 individuals had already been convicted of minor offences in municipal courts. Allegations of misconduct made against some 100 KPS officers during the March violence were being examined. Kosovo Serb KPS officers had returned to work, and mixed Kosovo Albanian/Kosovo Serb patrols had resumed. The prompt arrest by Kosovo Albanian KPS officers of two Kosovo Albanians within hours of the murder of a 17-year-old Kosovo Serb on 5 June in Gracanica (Pristina region) was a further encouraging sign.

The Secretary-General indicated that, in the wake of the March violence, he had requested Kai Eide (Norway) to conduct a comprehensive review of the policies and practices of all actors in Kosovo and to provide recommendations for further thinking on the way forward. That review had been completed and recommendations submitted for the Secretary-General's consideration (see p. 431).

The Secretary-General also reported that the reconstruction programme of the Provisional Institutions had moved forward significantly. According to governmental figures, 263 properties had been repaired, reconstruction was ongoing on 161 properties, contracts were about to be awarded for 70 more, and tenders for 180 others were soon to be issued.

While the Provisional Institutions had not yet developed a systematic programme to reach out to minority communities, Kosovo Albanian leaders, especially the Prime Minister, had visited those communities and reconstruction sites as part of his "internal dialogue with communities" initiative. Some municipal authorities also tried to improve community relations.

Meanwhile, Kosovo Serb involvement in the political process remained a cause for concern, particularly in the context of the October elections (see p. 416). Kosovo Serbs had remained outside the Kosovo Assembly since March and did not participate in the work of the Provisional Institutions at both the central and local levels. Nonetheless, there were signs of renewed interest in participation, and political relations at the central level among community leaders improved. A meeting held in Pristina on 23 June between Kosovo Albanian and Serb leaders was well attended and produced statements on the need for renewed inter-ethnic dialogue. The leaders also met outside Kosovo on a number of occasions.

The enhanced international scrutiny of inter-community relations, following the March violence, fostered dialogue between Kosovo Albanians and Kosovo Serbs. The newly constituted "Contact Group Plus", which included representatives of the Contact Group countries (France, Germany, Italy, Russian Federation, United Kingdom, United States), the EU and NATO, supported the work of political and community leaders on the implementation of standards. A "troika" composed of the EU, the United States and NATO focused on standards and security issues. In a significant development, President Rugova, Prime Minister Rexhepi and Kosovo Albanian and Kosovo Serb leaders, at a meeting facilitated by the United States and the EU (Pristina, 14 July), signed a declaration announcing that all houses damaged during the violence would be rebuilt before winter, expressing a commitment to ensure that internally displaced persons could return, and calling for the establishment of a ministry for community matters, human rights and returns. A Kosovo Security Advisory Group, consisting of KFOR, UNMIK and Kosovo Albanian and Kosovo Serb representatives of the Provisional Institutions, was established to enhance the flow of security information and prevent a recurrence of violence. The Group held its first meeting on 14 July.

Security Council consideration. During its consideration of the Secretary-General's reports on UNMIK [S/2004/348, S/2004/613] on 11 May [meeting 4967] and 5 August [meeting 5017], the Security Council was further updated on the implications of the March violence. At the May meeting, the Special Representative noted that the speed with which the violence spread over Kosovo overwhelmed the capacity of KFOR and UNMIK to respond. UNMIK had no means of augmenting its forces and KFOR forces were not reinforced until after the violence ended. He said he would act on the recommendations of the board he had appointed to review operational procedures and coordination in response to crises, and asked the Council to consider the effectiveness of UNMIK's structures and organization in the current circumstances. The security environment in Kosovo was not conducive to the forcible return of minority communities. The Special Representative urged countries granting temporary protection to persons from Kosovo's minority communities to continue to do so until conditions of safety and dignity could be guaranteed.

At the Council's August meeting, the Assistant Secretary-General for Peacekeeping Operations, Hédi Annabi, reported that the overall security situation in Kosovo remained calm and stable, with few significant security incidents that could not be attributable to extremist groups. The programme for reconstruction of damaged or destroyed properties, for which the Provisional Institutions were responsible, was entrusted to an inter-ministerial Reconstruction Commission. As at 30 July, 331 of the 935 damaged or destroyed properties had been rebuilt, 277 were under reconstruction, and contracts for a further 36 properties were soon to be awarded. While those results were noteworthy, much more needed to be done to ensure that all homes were rebuilt before the winter and that schools were reconstructed before the start of the school year. The encouraging steps taken by Kosovo Albanian leaders to mend the damage to inter-ethnic reconciliation should be followed by public commitment and concrete action to rebuild trust between Kosovo's communities.

Kosovo Standards Implementation Plan

The "standards for Kosovo" document [YUN 2003, p. 420], supported by the Security Council in presidential statement S/PRST/2003/26 [ibid.], set out eight standards (in the areas of functioning democratic institutions, rule of law, freedom of movement, returns and reintegration, economy, property rights, dialogue with Belgrade, and the Kosovo Protection Corps) that Kosovo had to meet to comply with resolution 1244(1999) [YUN 1999, p. 353], the Constitutional Framework for Provisional Self-Government [YUN 2001, p. 352], and the original standards/benchmark statement endorsed by the Council in presidential statement S/PRST/2002/11 [YUN 2002, p. 369]. In his April report on UNMIK [S/2004/348], the Secretary-General stated that the Kosovo Standards Implementation Plan, prepared by the five joint UNMIK–Provisional Institutions working groups, was launched on 31 March. Kosovo Serb political leaders had not participated in development of the Plan, and the Government of Serbia joined them in claiming that the Plan was a road map to independence for Kosovo. The Plan set out actions and policies for reaching the standards and identified actions to be undertaken by the Provisional Institutions of Self-Government, UNMIK and other institutions to achieve them and a timeline for doing so.

The Plan set specific goals in such areas as the building of democratic institutions, the enforcement of rights for minorities and the creation of a functioning economy. Its provisions also included the holding of free and fair elections and the establishment of an impartial judicial system. The Plan was revised to take into account the March events and their aftermath (see p. 405), by including, among other things, priority actions to be carried out by the Provisional Institutions: implementation of a reconstruction programme with funding for reconstruction and loss of property; implementation of initiatives to rebuild trust between communities; the sanctioning of civil servants and party leaders who did not respond appropriately during the violence; and public condemnation of hate speech. The sections of the Plan dealing with freedom of movement and sustainable returns and the rights of communities and their members were to be further revised in the light of the March violence.

SECURITY COUNCIL ACTION (April)

On 30 April [meeting 4960], following consultations among Security Council members, the President made statement **S/PRST/2004/13** on behalf of the Council:

The Security Council notes that the presentation of the Kosovo Standards Implementation Plan on 31 March 2004 at Pristina in Kosovo, Serbia and Montenegro, is a step forward in the standards process. The Council reiterates that the Implementation Plan should serve as a basis for the assessment of the progress of the Provisional Institutions of Self-Government in meeting the standards. The Council in this respect urges strongly the Provisional Institutions of Self-Government to demonstrate their full and unconditional commitment to a multi-ethnic Kosovo, in particular with respect to the promotion and protection of the rights of members of the minority communities as well as of human rights, equal security, freedom of movement and sustainable returns for all inhabitants of Kosovo. The Council reiterates further that the progress by the Provisional Institutions of Self-Government in meeting the standards, which should be reflected throughout Kosovo, will be assessed periodically and that the advancement towards a process to determine the future status of Kosovo in accordance with resolution 1244(1999) of 10 June 1999 will depend on the positive outcome of a comprehensive review.

The Council reaffirms its full support for the "standards before status" policy that was devised for Kosovo and endorsed by the Council in application of its resolution 1244(1999). It recalls in this context the "standards for Kosovo" document presented on 10 December 2003 and subsequently supported by the Council in the statement by its President of 12 December 2003, which outlined the standards that are to be achieved in order to reach the goal of establishing in Kosovo a multi-ethnic, stable and democratic society.

The Council stresses that it is essential, as indicated in the Implementation Plan, to review and revise in a timely manner two key sections of the document, namely "sustainable returns and the rights of communities and their members" and "freedom of movement". The Council calls upon the Provisional Institutions of Self-Government to take urgent steps on these two standards in order to rebuild and reach out to the Serb and other communities who suffered most in the large-scale inter-ethnic violence of 17 to 20 March 2004 that resulted in many dead and wounded and the destruction of personal property and Serbian Orthodox churches and monasteries in Kosovo.

The Council, strongly condemning those events, emphasizes that no party can be allowed to profit or to advance a political agenda through violent measures. It calls upon the Provisional Institutions of Self-Government and all political leaders to take responsibility in the current situation and to ensure that such acts and threats of violence are not repeated. The Council underscores that immediate actions should be taken aimed at the establishment of and public respect for the rule of law, including prosecution of perpetrators, effective collection of illegal weapons and combating organized crime. The Council urges the Provisional Institutions of Self-Government to take concrete steps to fulfil their commitment to rebuild multi-ethnicity and reconciliation throughout Kosovo, as promised in the open letter of institutional and political leaders of 2 April 2004. The Council asserts further that, in addition, there must be rapid steps taken by the Provisional Institutions of Self-Government to fulfil their commitment to rebuild or provide appropriate compensation for damaged or destroyed property and to rebuild holy sites and to facilitate the return of those displaced from their homes.

When assessing the progress made by the Provisional Institutions of Self-Government, the Council would pay particular attention to the adoption and the implementation of laws and regulations, policies and attitudes of the Provisional Institutions of Self-Government, among others, in the following areas: the fight against discrimination, corruption and economic crime, the propagation of hate by the media, as well as the support for multi-ethnicity and reconciliation, genuine devolution, orderly and sustainable returns, effective functioning of the Assembly and of the political parties, disciplinary procedures for the civil service, building-up of a professional, politically neutral and multi-ethnic administration, at the central and local levels, with a view to providing public services to every community on an equal footing, an efficient strategy for the return of refugees and internally displaced persons in safe conditions, a constructive engagement with the United Nations Interim Administration Mission in Kosovo, and full participation in the direct dialogue with Belgrade.

The Council underlines the importance that the Special Representative of the Secretary-General, within his authority as set out in resolution 1244 (1999), inter alia, in the context of the review mechanism, continue to consult closely with interested parties, in particular the Contact Group. The Council reaffirms its intention to continue to consider the regular reports of the Secretary-General, including an assessment by the Special Representative, as to the progress of the Provisional Institutions of Self-Government towards meeting the standards. The Council takes note of the fact that the Contact Group intends to make a substantive contribution to the regular reviews and to submit its assessments to the Special Representative.

The Council requests the Secretary-General, in his next report to the Council, to include a comprehensive assessment of the violence of 17 to 20 March 2004.

The Council also requests the Secretary-General to present recommendations on possible new institutional arrangements respectful of the objective of building a democratic and multi-ethnic Kosovo to allow more effective local government through the devolution of central non-reserved responsibilities to local authorities and communities in Kosovo, taking into account relevant studies and recommendations of interested parties and international organizations. How that local government is organized is a matter for further discussion between interested parties in Kosovo.

The Council welcomes the strong measures by the international presence in Kosovo aimed at enhancing the security and protection of all communities, as well as their religious, historical and cultural sites, with the goal of ensuring lasting stability in Kosovo. It calls in this respect for the full cooperation of the Provisional Institutions of Self-Government and all concerned.

The Council will continue to follow the matter closely.

Communication. Serbia and Montenegro transmitted to the Council President the Plan for the Political Solution to the Situation in Kosovo and Metohija [S/2004/352], adopted on 29 April by the National Assembly of the Republic of Serbia, which, it said, represented the framework for possible discussions on territorial autonomy in the province of Kosovo and Metohija with representatives of the international community within and outside the province. The Plan offered an outline of institutional guarantees for the Serb community through territorial autonomy.

Progress on standards implementation

In his July report on UNMIK [S/2004/613], the Secretary-General reported that the Provisional Institutions of Self-Government had moved forward with the implementation of the Kosovo Standards Implementation Plan at both the central and municipal levels, albeit slowly and with difficulty. Transforming the Plan into real change on the ground was challenging, due mainly to the lack of capacity and experience within the Provisional Institutions. The 30 April deadline for the creation of revised plans for the standards relating to freedom of movement and sustainable returns and rights of communities was not met, but Prime Minister Rexhepi committed his office to working directly with UNMIK to ensure their completion. While progress was made on four of the six priority actions to be carried out by the Provisional Institutions (see p. 408), no action was taken with respect to two—the requirement that they investigate and sanc-

tion authorities and political leaders who contributed to the violence through public statements or actions or who failed to exercise their authority properly, and that they publicly condemn print and broadcast media reports that contributed to ethnic violence and support the recommendations of the temporary Media Commissioner in relation to his investigation into those reports. The Prime Minister stated that the Government would be unable to fulfil those actions.

The Office of the Prime Minister took steps to move the standards implementation process forward. A matrix detailing the work required by the ministries of the Provisional Institutions to fulfil the actions listed in the Plan, including detailed assignments and timelines for completion, was prepared, and focal points on standards were appointed in every ministry and municipality. The joint UNMIK–Provisional Institutions working groups, which had prepared the Plan, were relaunched to monitor progress and implementation difficulties, and UNMIK established assessment committees to report on implementation. UNMIK, in cooperation with the Provisional Institutions, organized a public information campaign, which benefited from the support of key political leaders.

In a November report on UNMIK [S/2004/907], the Secretary-General said that a technical assessment by his Special Representative of progress on the standards showed that tangible and encouraging progress had been made in specific areas, but concrete progress was limited and the standards had not yet been met. Encouraging progress had been made in the reconstruction of destroyed houses and schools, investigating and prosecuting those responsible for the violence, reform of local government, and elections on 23 October for Kosovo's Assembly. The lack of progress in key areas, such as return and reconciliation efforts, security conditions and freedom of movement for the Kosovo minorities, in particular Kosovo Serbs, remained cause for concern. Even though Provisional Institutions' authorities, notably Prime Minister Rexhepi, had engaged in outreach activities to ethnic communities, a systematic, properly resourced outreach programme, including reconciliation and interethnic dialogue, was not yet in place. Neither Provisional Institutions nor party leaders had investigated the involvement of public authorities in the March violence or publicly condemned media reports that incited ethnic violence.

The security of the Kosovo minority groups, in particular Kosovo Serbs, remained precarious, with substantial limitations on their freedom of movement. Meanwhile, the rate of returns following the March events was significantly reduced, and the safety and sustainability of those returns remained fragile. Furthermore, participation of minority communities, in particular Kosovo Serbs, in the Provisional Institutions had not improved.

Progress on specific standards

Functioning democratic institutions. The Provisional Institutions suffered from a lack of capacity in implementing key aspects of the Kosovo Standards Implementation Plan. The enhancement of the professional competence of the civil service posed a challenge, as did the need to insulate the civil service from political interference. The task was complicated by the continued existence of Serbian parallel structures which took orders from Belgrade and contributed to the alienation of Kosovo Serbs from mainstream politics and public administration.

Minority employment in the Provisional Institutions continued to be low and confined to areas below the decision-making level, and mostly in the offices catering to minorities themselves. In the central ministries, minorities occupied 9.6 per cent of total posts, against the minimum stipulated level of 16.6 per cent. In the municipalities, the employment of Kosovo Serbs and other minorities was also very limited. Most institutions had not taken the initiatives required to bring minorities into decision-making levels for all communities.

The Kosovo Assembly continued to hold plenary sessions on a monthly rather than a weekly basis, leading to longer sessions, the postponement or delay of agenda items, and rushed debates and voting because of the packed agenda. On 8 July, the Kosovo Assembly proposed 38 amendments to the Constitutional Framework, despite clear warnings by UNMIK that such changes were outside its powers. The amendments were forwarded to UNMIK in September for consideration; UNMIK continued to object to them but agreed to study specific areas. The Assembly held its final session on 27 September. During its three-year mandate, it adopted 83 laws, of which 74 were formally submitted to UNMIK and 51 promulgated. Following the elections on 23 October, the new Assembly held its first session on 3 December.

The Office of the Prime Minister tried to consolidate the professional policy-making capacity and executive bodies of the Provisional Institutions but with few concrete results. The absence of rules of procedure for the working of the Government and the central ministries affected their effectiveness and coordination.

Operational responsibility for running the 2004 Assembly elections (see p. 416) was en- trusted to the multi-ethnic Central Election Commission created for that purpose. Little progress was achieved in the implementation of standards in the media, which, with few exceptions, had not begun to approach the standards of tolerance, civility and fairness set out in the Standards Implementation Plan. The temporary Media Commissioner issued a report criticizing media performance, in particular by Radio Television Kosovo and two private television stations.

A Law on Gender Equality in Kosovo, promulgated by the Special Representative on 7 June, provided for the establishment of an Office for Gender Equality. Municipal gender officer positions were included in the Kosovo consolidated budget, but those officers were unable to introduce gender concerns in the municipal agendas. Gender affairs officers were appointed in 4 of the 10 ministries.

The working group on local government finalized a framework document for local government reform in Kosovo, which addressed calls for greater democracy, increased participation, the provision of services and sustainable security at the local level, and provided for much devolution of power from the central to the local level.

Rule of law. Progress was made in the investigation and prosecution of those responsible for the March violence. At the same time, UNMIK's efforts to create a multi-ethnic justice system accessible to all communities suffered a setback as a result of the March riots. The three UNMIK court liaison offices in the Pristina, Gnjilane and Pec regions were working at limited capacity as a result of staff security issues and most municipal courts in Kosovo remained inaccessible to minority communities. Kosovo Serb prosecutors and judges declined to take up their work following the March violence. Of a total of 310 judges and 85 prosecutors, there were 16 Kosovo Serb judges and 3 prosecutors. Parallel court structures, which had ceased to function before March, resumed in Leposavic (Mitrovica region), Mitrovica and Lipljan (Pristina region). The development of KPS was re-evaluated after the March violence, focusing on the schedule for transition of station command from UNMIK police to KPS, among other things. UNMIK police revised its transition plan to ensure that command of stations that performed well would be changed earlier than problematic ones. By November, 15 stations were under KPS control.

An anti-corruption strategy, which included public awareness-raising measures, strengthening and reform of legislation and the establishment of an independent anti-corruption unit, was launched in March. However, implementation remained weak as abuse of internal controls and procurement mechanisms continued to be widespread in some ministries. Progress was made in both ministries and municipalities in establishing systems of internal audit and financial control, and on 8 September, the Assembly adopted an anti-corruption law. At the central level, the Kosovo Security Advisory Group was established as a forum for the Provisional Institutions and all communities to discuss security concerns with UNMIK and KFOR.

Freedom of movement. The freedom of movement of minority communities in Kosovo, particularly Kosovo Serbs, continued to be limited. In some regions, Kosovo Serbs travelled through Kosovo Albanian majority areas only with escorts, using special transport services, or in vehicles with special license plates. Members of other minority communities, including Kosovo Albanians in predominantly Serb municipalities, enjoyed more freedom of movement, but still faced problems. More than 300 police escorts were required each month in connection with the transport of Kosovo Serb political authorities, visits by internally displaced persons, the holding of cultural or religious events, and travel to work or school. The absence of escorts prevented Kosovo Serb children in the rural areas north of Pristina and in Obilic from attending school for several weeks in September. The Government funded a civil service bus line and a train line for minority members. Special arrangements were generally required for minority public service employees to work in majority areas.

Returns and reintegration. Prior to the events in March, there were limited but encouraging prospects for returns in 2004, with returns projects involving every ethnicity ongoing in each area of Kosovo. That situation was completely reversed after March. In less than 48 hours, 4,100 minority community members had become newly displaced, the majority from the Pristina and southern Mitrovica regions. Of the displaced, 82 per cent were Kosovo Serbs and the remaining 18 per cent were mostly Roma and Ashkali. As at 24 September, 2,288 people who had been displaced in March had not returned to their homes.

By the end of August, the number of minority returns to Kosovo in 2004 stood at 1,300, only 40 per cent of the previous year's total. While the level of municipal engagement in the returns process had increased, most municipalities lacked the capacity and political will to assume responsibility for it. Many municipalities were developing return strategies; however, direct engagement by municipalities in the development or implementation of returns projects was still limited. The Provisional Institutions increased

funding for returns from 7 million euros in 2003 to 10.5 million in 2004. In July, Kosovo political leaders endorsed the creation of a ministry for community matters, human rights and returns.

Economy. The March violence damaged the economy in terms of weakened investor interest and confidence. That, combined with the high level of unemployment, made the short- and medium-term economic outlook a cause for concern in spite of a projected 4 per cent growth in 2004. Focus was directed to the priorities outlined in the "standards for Kosovo" document, including the establishment of a legal framework for a sustainable, competitive market economy, the development of a non-discriminatory economic policy, and the strengthening of local institutions. A regulation on public procurement was promulgated in February and an EU-compliant Customs Code entered into force in March. The Kosovo Assembly adopted a number of relevant laws, including those on obligations, consumer protection, concessions, copyright, patents, profit tax, personal income tax and tax administration.

The privatization process advanced towards meeting the objective of completion by late 2006. The Kosovo Trust Agency (KTA) privatized an average of 25 socially owned enterprises each month. Remaining concerns included the determination of the status of socially owned enterprises, immunity for the KTA Board and management, and the liquidation of the assets and/or land of such enterprises. To improve transparency, KTA planned to introduce to those enterprises new corporate governance that would include boards of directors and supervisory boards.

The collection of revenue for public utility providers continued to be problematic. Within the Post and Telecommunications Company, collections were approaching 100 per cent of billed revenues, except for fixed-line telephony. In contrast, the Kosovo Electricity Company (KEK) was only able to collect on 32 per cent of electricity delivered. The Energy Office was consulting with KEK management on measures to improve billing and collections. Seven regional water and seven regional waste companies were created from the previous 42 municipal operations to improve revenue collection through consolidation. The average revenue collection rate in that sector was 52 per cent.

No formal tax compliance indicators had been developed, but the Tax Administration developed performance indicators that measured the efficiency of the Administration itself. Compliance with taxes was low, with only 20 per cent of total tax revenues derived from internal collection. International cooperation, along with anti-smuggling efforts and cooperation with police and KFOR, improved compliance.

The budget process functioned unsatisfactorily. Medium-term expenditure frameworks, a public investment plan and sector-spending budgets did not exist, and there was ongoing disagreement between the Provisional Institutions and UNMIK regarding the allocation of the budget surplus.

On 1 April, the Pristina Airport was transferred from military (KFOR) to civilian (UNMIK) control. An agreement was finalized between UNMIK and Iceland for the provision by Iceland of certain civil aviation services. Those measures ensured that the airport was operated in conformity with applicable international standards and practices.

Property rights. Little progress was made regarding the illegal occupation of residential, agricultural and commercial land, as implementation and enforcement of legal instruments protecting property rights remained inadequate. Municipalities had not made a concerted effort to prevent illegal occupation through the enforcement of regulations, and there was no coordinated public awareness campaign. However, the Expert Group on Property, in August, finalized its terms of reference and formed a subgroup to compile an inventory of central and municipal property legislation, and to prepare a needs assessment and legislative action plan.

Concerning residential property, the Housing and Property Directorate and the Housing and Property Claims Commission continued to work through their caseload. As at 30 September, Directorate and Commission decisions had been issued for 19,875 of 29,028 claims (68 per cent), although only 8,996 (46 per cent) had been enforced or fully implemented. To continue its work at planned levels, the Directorate asked for an additional 200,000 euros to meet its original requirement of 1.2 million euros. Its projected deficit for 2005 stood at $2.3 million. The establishment of the immovable property rights and cadastral registries was moving forward, although neither was fully functional.

As to informal settlements, a stakeholders group was established and met frequently. No action was taken by the Provisional Institutions to launch an awareness-raising campaign about informal settlements and the property rights of their inhabitants, despite ongoing urban planning activity. Limited progress was noted in the provision of alternative housing for the socially vulnerable. Two pilot social housing projects, initiated centrally and developed and co-financed at the municipal level, were completed in September, and three more were under development.

Dialogue with Belgrade. Despite the promising start in early 2004 of the working groups on direct dialogue between Pristina and Belgrade on energy and on missing persons, the mid-March violence and a variety of other issues impeded resumption, owing to Belgrade's reluctance. Kosovo Prime Minister Rexhepi expressed to the International Committee of the Red Cross his willingness to resume the dialogue on missing persons. A meeting of advisers on the reform of local government (Vienna, 28 September) did, however, indicate that a dialogue was still possible.

Kosovo Protection Corps. The Kosovo Protection Corps (KPC) continued to comply with the rule of law and to exercise its mandate but did not hide its frustration at not being given greater tasks. At the tactical and operational levels, KPC performed well, especially in mine clearance and search and rescue operations; however, more training and equipment were needed for it to achieve European professional standards. The withdrawal of the training provided by the International Organization for Migration would have a significant impact on both general and specialist training. Command, control and coordination measures needed to be developed between KPC and other emergency services. KPC was also constrained by lack of funding, essential equipment, training and supervision. Discipline within KPC was improving. The revision of the disciplinary code had been delayed by political issues but steps were being taken to resolve them. A plan for recruiting minorities, in order to raise their numbers to 10 per cent from the current 4.75 per cent, was drawn up.

Comprehensive review of policies and practices

Following the March events, the Secretary-General appointed a team headed by Kai Eide (Norway) to conduct a comprehensive review of the policies and practices of all actors in Kosovo and to make recommendations on a way forward. The team's report was submitted to the Security Council in August. On 17 November [S/2004/932], the Secretary-General transmitted the report, together with his own recommendations.

The team observed that Kosovo was characterized by growing dissatisfaction and frustration. For the Kosovo Albanian majority, the main issues were a serious lack of economic opportunities and the absence of a clear political perspective, while the Kosovo Serbs saw themselves as victims of a campaign to reduce their presence in Kosovo to a scattered rural population. The March violence had taken the international community by surprise because it had failed to read the mood in the population and to understand the depth of the dissatisfaction of the majority and the vulnerability of the minorities. UNMIK itself had become the main target of criticism from all sides, although it had also been a victim of the lack of a clear political perspective.

However, a new tone had emerged as a result of clearer messages coming from the international community. The Kosovo Albanians seemed to accept that their efforts to stem the violence in March were inadequate, damaging their reputation and support in the international community. The Serbs, for their part, understood that they could not and should not remain outside the political process when their Kosovo Albanian counterparts were seen to accommodate their demands; consequently, the Serbs appeared more willing to participate in common efforts, although a decision to take part in elections (see p. 416) and return to the Provisional Institutions of Self-Government had not been made. The joint declaration on reconstruction of houses, signed on 14 July, reflected those positive trends (see below).

The international community faced several tests, the first of which was to maintain strong pressure to return to the political process. The second was managing the interim period, including the transfer of more authority to Kosovo institutions and having a more dynamic standards policy. The current "standards before status" policy lacked credibility, as implementing those standards was seen as unachievable. Standards implementation should be an integral part of a wider policy to bring Kosovo closer to European standards. The third test related to preparations for future status discussions. In the light of the growing frustration, the faltering economy and the eventual reduction of international forces, raising the future status question soon seemed the better option. The international community needed to intensify its dialogue with Belgrade, which would be one of the parties to the future status negotiations.

UNMIK needed to be restructured to allow it to concentrate on priorities. The United Nations should prepare to gradually reduce its presence in Kosovo, with a parallel increase in that of the EU and a continuation of the presence of the Organization for Security and Cooperation in Europe (OSCE).

Recommendations of review team. The team recommended a comprehensive and integrated strategy, covering the period from the time of the report through 2005, to be elaborated in consultation with relevant partners. The strategy should: meet immediate requirements relating to security and prosecution, reconstruction, return and decentralization; formulate a more dynamic standards policy with achievable priorities; outline further transfer of responsibilities and competencies to Kosovo authorities; demonstrate resolve to sanction Kosovo authorities for misuse of powers; develop a comprehensive capacity-building policy for self-government; reform the structures of the international presence in Kosovo; and prepare for discussions on future status. Discussions should be held with the Security Council, other organizations and key Member States to secure commitment for the resources and support required to implement that strategy. Pressure should be maintained to strengthen positive trends, including progress in security, reconstruction, prosecution of those responsible for the March events and local government reform. The "standards before status" policy should be replaced by a dynamic priority-based standards policy within the framework of the integrated strategy to facilitate orderly future status discussions and regional and European integration efforts. Three intermediary standards reviews should be scheduled before the mid-2005 review. Transferring further competencies should be launched without delay, giving the Provisional Institutions a greater sense of ownership, responsibility and accountability. That should include establishing new ministries of energy, of justice and of community matters, human rights and returns.

A process of gradually handing over operational control of KPS to the Provisional Institutions, with UNMIK maintaining overall executive authority, should be elaborated and implemented. KPS units should be given proper training and equipment and the handover of remaining UN police responsibilities to the EU or OSCE should be explored. The Special Representative of the Secretary-General should make greater use of sanctions and interventions and draw up an inventory of possible measures.

A more coherent and ambitious capacity-building policy should be elaborated and implemented under OSCE leadership. UNMIK should be streamlined to provide new energy and a more concentrated effort on key challenges. A comprehensive restructuring of the international presence as a whole should be undertaken in 2005 with a gradual reduction of UNMIK as it completed its mandate and handed over responsibilities to other authorities and organizations.

The EU should prepare an economic development strategy and consolidate its various presences in Kosovo. NATO should maintain KFOR's presence to ensure a safe and secure environment, with a view to ensuring an adequate force level during the future status process. The broader international community should provide a more concerted and coordinated engagement.

The dialogue with Belgrade should be improved and a high-level international consultative mechanism for Kosovo, involving key capitals and headquarters, should be established. Discussion of the future status question should be undertaken by the United Nations, beginning later in the year.

Recommendations of Secretary-General. The Secretary-General, in his recommendations on the way forward, said that consultations on the review team's recommendations with the Contact Group, other European members of the Security Council, the EU, OSCE and NATO, held on 20 September, resulted in a general understanding of and support for an integrated strategy for the way forward in Kosovo up to mid-2005 and in preparation for the future status process. There was broad agreement on the need to focus on the economy and on security, the need to engage with Belgrade and to bring the Kosovo Serbs into the process, the importance of the standards process, and on support for a subregional approach that would not focus exclusively on Kosovo.

The Secretary-General emphasized that all processes in Kosovo had to remain within the parameters of Security Council resolution 1244 (1999). A comprehensive and integrated strategy, based on a decision by the Council, would be put in place leading to the future status process, the main components of which would be: strengthening current efforts to deal with the causes and consequences of the March violence; improving dialogue at all levels; initiating a more comprehensive dialogue with Belgrade; recalibrating the standards policy; transferring further competencies to the Provisional Institutions and increasing their accountability; increasing oversight and intervention by UNMIK; enhancing capacity-building for the Provisional Institutions; implementing a stronger economic development policy with short- and long-term measures; and realigning and streamlining UNMIK.

Achieving progress on the eight standards remained the basis of UN policy within the overall framework of the integrated strategy. UNMIK would review progress towards implementing the standards by providing quarterly technical assessments, which would provide the basis for the political assessments by the Secretary-General in reports to the Council. On the basis of a comprehensive review, to be conducted in mid-2005, the Council would decide whether to initiate the process leading to a determination of the future status of Kosovo.

UNMIK reviewed the competencies it currently managed and identified those that might be transferred to the Provisional Institutions, as well as areas for enhanced operational involvement of the Provisional Institutions. The transfer policy was linked to greater accountability and responsibility of the Provisional Institutions and a greater degree of oversight. UNMIK was putting in place more effective mechanisms for oversight and remedial interventions to ensure the full implementation of resolution 1244(1999) and compliance with the Constitutional Framework [YUN 2001, p. 352] and applicable legislation.

Recommendations on new institutional arrangements for more effective local government through the devolution of central non-reserved responsibilities to local authorities would be submitted by the Secretary-General. Institutions would have to be created to deal with the consequences and causes of the March events and to ensure the active engagement of the leaders and people of Kosovo for a multi-ethnic society. Current efforts for ensuring the prosecution of those responsible, the improvement of security and the reconstruction of destroyed homes and religious sites should be reinforced, and the conditions necessary for the safe and sustainable return of all displaced persons put in place.

Revitalization of the economy remained an overriding concern. A midterm and long-term economic strategy should be complemented by effective short-term measures. The Secretary-General called on the EU to design and implement an economic development strategy for Kosovo. Dialogue among the communities in Kosovo and between Belgrade and Pristina should be intensified. A more intense and comprehensive dialogue with Belgrade was being initiated, taking into account its legitimate concerns. UNMIK was being streamlined and realigned to focus on the key challenges and priorities, which could involve the EU and OSCE taking on additional competencies, including financial commitments, within UNMIK. NATO was urged to maintain KFOR to implement its responsibilities under resolution 1244(1999), particularly to ensure a safe and secure environment, including the provision of an adequate force level during the future status process and the implementation of an eventual political settlement.

The Secretary-General concluded that the coordinated support of the international community, particularly that of key Member States, was essential for success. The people of Kosovo from all communities, their representatives in the Provisional Institutions and political leaders had to work towards the strategy goals and ensure that there was sufficient progress to move gradually into talks on the future status of Kosovo.

UNMIK priorities

The Secretary-General reported in November [S/2004/907] that, in the light of the situation in Kosovo, his Special Representative outlined UNMIK's priorities for the near future. They included achieving progress on the eight standards as the basic policy framework; prioritizing actions within each standard to ensure the sustained action needed to deal with the consequences of the March events, establish the necessary institutions for that purpose and secure the engagement of the Kosovo leaders and people for creating a multi-ethnic society; and engagement by both the Provisional Institutions and the Kosovo Serb and other minority communities in the Kosovo Security Advisory Group and local crime prevention councils to address the security concerns of minorities. The local crime prevention councils, which brought together police, KFOR, municipal authorities and community representatives, would also help to address local security requirements. The Special Representative also proposed to the Serbian Government that high-level talks be held on Kosovo security issues.

UNMIK undertook initiatives to improve coordination in building additional capacities within the Provisional Institutions to permit the further transfer of competencies. Together with the Provisional Institutions, it would proceed as quickly as possible with decentralization of pilot projects and the drafting of laws on local government and finances. It would cooperate with KFOR to improve security and freedom of movement. An action plan was being prepared to support positive measures by local authorities in the area of returns, particularly at the municipal level, and to deal directly with those obstructing returns. Those efforts needed to be accompanied by a programme of outreach by the Provisional Institutions to Kosovo Serb and other minority communities.

Concerning economic development, quick-impact projects at the municipal level would be implemented with donors and UN agencies in order to lay the groundwork for economic recovery. Kosovo communities should engage in internal dialogue, and dialogue between Pristina and Belgrade should be enhanced. The constructive engagement of Belgrade was needed in a variety of fields beyond decentralization, such as missing persons, returns and the economy. Consideration would be given to resuming meetings of the working groups in the direct dialogue between Pristina and Belgrade, and the involvement of

Kosovo in regional dialogue and initiatives would be enhanced.

Parliamentary elections

The Secretary-General reported in November [S/2004/907] that elections for the Kosovo Assembly were held on 23 October, organized for the first time to a large extent by the people of Kosovo themselves. The multi-ethnic Central Elections Commission and its secretariat certified 33 political entities which contested the elections. The election campaign began on 22 September and was largely conducted in a calm and dignified manner. Although many Kosovo Serb political leaders wished to participate in the elections, parties in Serbia proper largely opposed participation. Serbia and Montenegro Prime Minister Vojislav Kostunica maintained that conditions were not in place for Kosovo Serbs to vote and urged them not to go to the polls. However, on 5 October, Serbian President Boris Tadic publicly supported Kosovo Serb participation, and the Special Representative allowed the late registration of a new Kosovo Serb political entity, the Serbian List for Kosovo and Metohija, which submitted a list of 33 candidates; another Kosovo Serb civic list claiming to represent Kosovo Serb internally displaced persons was also certified. On 8 October, a technical memorandum of understanding was signed with the Serbian Commissariat for Refugees on the opening of polling centres in Serbia proper, leading to 15 polling and registration centres being set up and run by OSCE there. The vote was held in an orderly manner, with no significant security incidents.

Official results showed a turnout of around 54 per cent (in Kosovo), down from 64 per cent in the first Assembly elections in 2001 [YUN 2001, p. 360]. Around 2,000 Kosovo Serbs, or under 1 per cent of the potential Kosovo Serb electorate, voted. The low turnout meant that there would not be any directly elected Kosovo Serb representatives in the Assembly and it remained uncertain if the 10 seats set aside would be filled. Support for the main Kosovo Albanian parties did not vary considerably from that in the 2001 elections: the Democratic League of Kosovo (LDK) obtained 45.4 per cent of the votes, the Democratic Party of Kosovo (PDK) 28.9 per cent, and the Alliance for the Future of Kosovo (AAK) 8.4 per cent. A new Kosovo Albanian political formation, ORA ("Time"), obtained 6.2 per cent. Negotiations among the main Kosovo Albanian parties on the formation of a coalition Government began immediately after the vote.

Security Council consideration. The Special Representative, in his briefing to the Security Council on 29 November [meeting 5089], said that the 23 October elections, monitored by a broad cross-section of some 13,000 local observers, were determined to be free and fair by the Council of Europe. No significant incidents of a political or security nature interrupted polling, which generally took place in a secure environment. While the overall turnout was good, he regretted the low turnout of the Kosovo Serbs. He noted that LDK and AAK had decided to form a coalition and prepare for government. However, the agreement and the possible appointment of Ramush Haradinaj as Prime Minister raised some concerns in view of reports that ICTY was pursuing a case related to him. The Special Representative noted that Kosovo would, for the first time, have a strong parliamentary opposition, which he trusted would play a democratic role and show mature political judgement in the interest of Kosovo's move towards a review of standards and status talks.

Other developments. In late 2004, Mr. Rugova was re-elected President of Kosovo, Nexhat Daci was elected President of the Assembly and Mr. Haradinaj was appointed Prime Minister. New portfolios of Deputy Prime Minister and 15 deputy ministers were agreed upon. The Government allocated 3 of the 13 ministerial positions to representatives of minority communities. Three new ministries were established in the areas of energy, local-government administration, and returns and communities.

Communication. On 4 December [S/2004/960], the Government of the Republic of Serbia adopted a conclusion concerning the appointment of Mr. Haradinaj as Prime Minister of Kosovo and Metohija, in which it noted his "criminal past" during the war, the arrest warrant issued by the War Crimes Panel of the Belgrade District Court for his alleged involvement in war crimes, and the investigation being conducted by ICTY. Serbia denounced his election as Prime Minister and demanded that the Special Representative revoke it.

UN Interim Administration Mission in Kosovo (UNMIK)

The United Nations Interim Administration Mission in Kosovo, established in 1999 [YUN 1999, p. 357] to facilitate a political process to determine Kosovo's political future, comprised five components referred to as pillars: interim administration (led by the United Nations); institution-building (led by OSCE); economic reconstruction (led by the EU); humanitarian affairs (led by the Office of the United Nations High Commissioner for Refugees (UNHCR)); and police and justice (led by the United Nations). UNMIK was headed by the Special Representative of the

Secretary-General. Søren Jessen-Petersen replaced Harri Holkeri as Special Representative on 18 June.

The Secretary-General reported to the Security Council on the activities of UNMIK and developments in Kosovo for the periods 1 January to 31 March [S/2004/348], 1 April to 15 July [S/2004/613] and 16 July to 31 October [S/2004/907]. Activities for the remainder of the year were covered in a later report [S/2005/88].

Financing

On 18 June [meeting 91], the General Assembly, having considered the financial performance report for UNMIK for the period 1 July 2002 to 30 June 2003 [A/58/634], the proposed budget for 1 July 2004 to 30 June 2005 [A/58/638 & Corr.1] and the related comments and recommendations of ACABQ [A/58/759/Add.5], adopted, on the recommendation of the Fifth Committee [A/58/826], **resolution 58/305** without vote [agenda item 144].

Financing of the United Nations Interim Administration Mission in Kosovo

The General Assembly,

Having considered the reports of the Secretary-General on the financing of the United Nations Interim Administration Mission in Kosovo and the related reports of the Advisory Committee on Administrative and Budgetary Questions,

Recalling Security Council resolution 1244(1999) of 10 June 1999 regarding the establishment of the United Nations Interim Administration Mission in Kosovo,

Recalling also its resolution 53/241 of 28 July 1999 on the financing of the Mission and its subsequent resolutions thereon, the latest of which was resolution 57/326 of 18 June 2003,

Acknowledging the complexity of the Mission,

Reaffirming the general principles underlying the financing of United Nations peacekeeping operations, as stated in General Assembly resolutions 1874(S-IV) of 27 June 1963, 3101(XXVIII) of 11 December 1973 and 55/235 of 23 December 2000,

Mindful of the fact that it is essential to provide the Mission with the necessary financial resources to enable it to fulfil its responsibilities under the relevant resolution of the Security Council,

1. *Takes note* of the status of contributions to the United Nations Interim Administration Mission in Kosovo as at 15 April 2004, including the contributions outstanding in the amount of 108.2 million United States dollars, representing some 6 per cent of the total assessed contributions, notes with concern that only thirty-two Member States have paid their assessed contributions in full, and urges all other Member States, in particular those in arrears, to ensure payment of their outstanding assessed contributions;

2. *Expresses its appreciation* to those Member States which have paid their assessed contributions in full, and urges all other Member States to make every possible effort to ensure payment of their assessed contributions to the Mission in full;

3. *Expresses concern* at the financial situation with regard to peacekeeping activities, in particular as regards the reimbursements to troop contributors that bear additional burdens owing to overdue payments by Member States of their assessments;

4. *Also expresses concern* at the delay experienced by the Secretary-General in deploying and providing adequate resources to some recent peacekeeping missions, in particular those in Africa;

5. *Emphasizes* that all future and existing peacekeeping missions shall be given equal and non-discriminatory treatment in respect of financial and administrative arrangements;

6. *Also emphasizes* that all peacekeeping missions shall be provided with adequate resources for the effective and efficient discharge of their respective mandates;

7. *Reiterates its request* to the Secretary-General to make the fullest possible use of facilities and equipment at the United Nations Logistics Base at Brindisi, Italy, in order to minimize the costs of procurement for the Mission;

8. *Endorses* the conclusions and recommendations contained in the report of the Advisory Committee on Administrative and Budgetary Questions, and requests the Secretary-General to ensure their full implementation, bearing in mind the fact that the Special Representative of the Secretary-General has requested additional police and judicial resources in response to recent events in Kosovo (Serbia and Montenegro);

9. *Requests* the Secretary-General to take all necessary action to ensure that the Mission is administered with a maximum of efficiency and economy;

10. *Also requests* the Secretary-General, in order to reduce the cost of employing General Service staff, to continue efforts to recruit local staff for the Mission against General Service posts, commensurate with the requirements of the Mission;

**Financial performance report for
the period from 1 July 2002 to 30 June 2003**

11. *Takes note* of the report of the Secretary-General on the financial performance of the Mission for the period from 1 July 2002 to 30 June 2003;

**Budget estimates for the
period from 1 July 2004 to 30 June 2005**

12. *Decides* to appropriate to the Special Account for the United Nations Interim Administration Mission in Kosovo the amount of 278,413,700 dollars for the period from 1 July 2004 to 30 June 2005, inclusive of 264,625,200 dollars for the maintenance of the Mission, 11,272,700 dollars for the support account for peacekeeping operations and 2,515,800 dollars for the United Nations Logistics Base;

Financing of the appropriation

13. *Decides also* to apportion among Member States the amount of 278,413,700 dollars at a monthly rate of 23,201,142 dollars, in accordance with the levels set out in General Assembly resolution 55/235, as adjusted by the Assembly in its resolution 55/236 of 23 December 2000 and updated in its resolution 58/256 of 23 December 2003, taking into account the scale of assessments for 2004 and 2005, as set out in its resolution 58/1 B of 23 December 2003;

14. *Decides further* that, in accordance with the provisions of its resolution 973(X) of 15 December 1955,

there shall be set off against the apportionment among Member States, as provided for in paragraph 13 above, their respective share in the Tax Equalization Fund of 20,572,400 dollars, comprising the estimated staff assessment income of 18,785,600 dollars approved for the Mission, the prorated share of 1,645,100 dollars of the estimated staff assessment income approved for the support account and the prorated share of 141,700 dollars of the estimated staff assessment income approved for the United Nations Logistics Base;

15. *Decides* that, for Member States that have fulfilled their financial obligations to the Mission, there shall be set off against their apportionment, as provided for in paragraph 13 above, their respective share of the unencumbered balance and other income in the total amount of 10,804,200 dollars in respect of the financial period ended 30 June 2003, in accordance with the levels set out in General Assembly resolution 55/235, as adjusted by the Assembly in its resolution 55/236 and its resolution 57/290 A of 20 December 2002, taking into account the scale of assessments for 2003, as set out in its resolutions 55/5 B of 23 December 2000 and 57/4 B of 20 December 2002;

16. *Decides also* that, for Member States that have not fulfilled their financial obligations to the Mission, there shall be set off against their outstanding obligations their respective share of the unencumbered balance and other income in the total amount of 10,804,200 dollars in respect of the financial period ended 30 June 2003, in accordance with the scheme set out in paragraph 15 above;

17. *Decides further* that the increase of 2,113,600 dollars in the estimated staff assessment income in respect of the financial period ended 30 June 2003 shall be added to the credits from the amount referred to in paragraphs 15 and 16 above;

18. *Emphasizes* that no peacekeeping mission shall be financed by borrowing funds from other active peacekeeping missions;

19. *Encourages* the Secretary-General to continue to take additional measures to ensure the safety and security of all personnel under the auspices of the United Nations participating in the Mission;

20. *Invites* voluntary contributions to the Mission in cash and in the form of services and supplies acceptable to the Secretary-General, to be administered, as appropriate, in accordance with the procedure and practices established by the General Assembly;

21. *Decides* to include in the provisional agenda of its fifty-ninth session the item entitled "Financing of the United Nations Interim Administration Mission in Kosovo".

In December, the Secretary-General submitted the performance report for UNMIK for the period 1 July 2003 to 30 June 2004 [A/59/623] and the proposed budget for 1 July 2005 to 30 June 2006 [A/59/633].

By **decision 59/552** of 23 December, the Assembly decided that the item on UNMIK financing would remain for consideration at its resumed fifty-ninth (2005) session.

International security presence (KFOR)

The Secretary-General transmitted to the Security Council, in accordance with resolution 1244(1999) [YUN 1999, p. 353], reports on the activities of the international security presence in Kosovo (KFOR), also known as Operation Joint Guard, covering the periods 1 January to 29 February [S/2004/175, S/2004/262], and 1 April to 31 December [S/2004/487, S/2004/649, S/2004/655, S/2004/732, S/2004/799, S/2004/859, S/2004/937, S/2005/20, S/2005/332]. As at 31 December, the force, which operated under NATO leadership, comprised 17,170 troops, including 2,788 from non-NATO countries.

KFOR continued operations to secure the theatre, prevent ethnic violence and protect patrimonial sites. KFOR remained vigilant to deter possible threats directed against international organizations and military bases. It continued to improve its crowd and riot control capabilities so as to be better prepared to counter a resurgence of violence.

Regional cooperation

Regional cooperation, in particular between Kosovo and The former Yugoslav Republic of Macedonia (FYROM) and Albania, continued to develop. On 11 June, UNMIK, acting for the Provisional Institutions, signed the Memorandum of Understanding on the Development of the South-East Europe Core Regional Transport Network, aimed at enhancing cooperation on transport issues among the signatories and providing the precondition for the development of road and railway links, waterways, ports and airport networks in the region. On 28 September, UNMIK and Albania signed an agreement to eliminate double taxation for businesses and persons from Albania operating in Kosovo, and vice versa. Slovenia and Romania opened liaison offices in Pristina and FYROM was due to open an office of its Chamber of Commerce. The Provisional Institutions, working in coordination with UNMIK, participated in regular multilateral forums, such as meetings of the Stability Pact and the EU Western Balkans Forum.

The European Commission Stabilization and Association Process Tracking Mechanism continued to guide Kosovo towards EU-compatible reforms. The fifth meeting of the Mechanism (Brussels, 17 September) between the European Commission, the Provisional Institutions and UNMIK discussed the economy and environment issues, and the recently adopted European Partnership with Serbia and Montenegro, including Kosovo, which identified priorities for moving closer to the EU. The recently established Office for European Integration Processes in the Prime Minister's Office would increase the Provisional Institutions' capacities to respond effectively to the European Partnership.

Cooperation with ICTY

On 4 May [S/2004/353] (see p. 1283), the President of the International Tribunal for the Former Yugoslavia brought to the attention of the Security Council the report of the ICTY Prosecutor, indicating that Serbia and Montenegro had failed to comply with its obligations under the Statute of the Tribunal and its Rules of Procedure and Evidence, in particular to execute arrest warrants issued by the Tribunal and to respond to requests by the Registrar to explain those failures. Its cooperation with the Tribunal, which had declined since December 2003, was currently non-existent.

Former Yugoslav Republic of Macedonia

Relations with Greece

On 4 November, the United States announced its official recognition of the "Republic of Macedonia" as the name of the country recognized by the United Nations as "The former Yugoslav Republic of Macedonia" (FYROM). Its decision, according to United States State Department spokesman Richard Boucher, was without prejudice to the ongoing negotiations between the two countries under the auspices of the United Nations over the name of the country. On the same date, the EU reiterated its support for the name as recognized by the United Nations.

In accordance with the 1995 Interim Accord on the normalization of relations between FYROM and Greece [YUN 1995, p. 599], representatives of both countries met on 6 December under the auspices of the Secretary-General. The countries exchanged views in the context of article 5 of the Accord, which provided for the continuation of negotiations with a view to reaching agreement on their differences, as described in Security Council resolutions 817(1993) [YUN 1993, p. 208] and 845(1993) [ibid., p. 209], concerning the name of the State of FYROM. They decided to meet again on 12 January 2005.

Statement by Secretary-General. The Secretary-General, in a 26 February press statement [SG/SM/9172], said that he had learned with sadness of the death of the FYROM President, Boris Trajkovski, and members of his delegation in a plane crash that day.

Georgia

In 2004, the Georgian/Abkhaz peace process came perilously close to a standstill. While the parties came together during the course of the year on some issues, efforts to advance a dialogue based on the 2001 paper known as Basic Principles for the Distribution of Competences between Tbilisi (Georgia's Government) and Sukhumi (the Abkhaz leadership) [YUN 2001, p. 386], which was intended to serve as a framework for substantive negotiations over the status of Abkhazia as a sovereign entity within the State of Georgia, encountered serious challenges.

Renewed violence in the zone of conflict in March led to a chain of events that brought all contacts between the sides to a halt, as the Abkhaz side refused to participate in the weekly quadripartite meetings and the joint fact-finding groups were suspended. The Abkhaz side also maintained its refusal to discuss the Basic Principles and the transmittal letter, despite a more positive attitude expressed by the new Georgian administration. The political uncertainty in Sukhumi due to the unclear results of the de facto presidential elections in October seriously limited the possibility of continued dialogue. However, the high-level meeting of the Group of Friends of the Secretary-General (France, Germany, Russian Federation, United Kingdom, United States), which met on 13 and 14 December in Geneva, presented a timely opportunity to consider the state of the peace process and how to rekindle the search for a lasting and comprehensive solution. The Georgian side put forward a proposal for settling the conflict that included substantial autonomy for a reintegrated Abkhazia into the State of Georgia and power sharing at the national level.

UN Observer Mission in Georgia

The United Nations Observer Mission in Georgia (UNOMIG), established by Security Council resolution 858(1993) [YUN 1993, p. 509], continued to monitor compliance with the 1994 Agreement on a Ceasefire and Separation of Forces (Moscow Agreement) [YUN 1994, p. 583] and to fulfil other tasks as mandated by Council resolution 937(1994) [ibid., p. 584]. The Mission operated in close collaboration with the collective peacekeeping force of the Commonwealth of Independent States (CIS) that had been in the zone of conflict, at the request of the parties, since 1994 [ibid., p. 583]. The Council extended the Mission's mandate twice during the year, the first

time until 31 July 2004 and the second until 31 January 2005.

UNOMIG's main headquarters was located in Sukhumi (Abkhazia, Georgia), with some administrative headquarters in Pitsunda, a liaison office in the Georgian capital of Tbilisi and team bases and a sector headquarters in each of the Gali and Zugdidi sectors. A team base in the Kodori Valley was manned by observers operating from Sukhumi. As at 31 December 2004, UNOMIG had a strength of 117 military observers and 11 civilian police officers.

Heidi Tagliavini (Switzerland) continued as the Secretary-General's Special Representative for Georgia and Head of UNOMIG. She was assisted by Major General Kazi Ashfaq Ahmed (Bangladesh), UNOMIG's Chief Military Observer, who was succeeded on 24 May by Major General Hussein Ghobashi (Egypt).

Political aspects of the conflict

Report of Secretary-General (January). The Secretary-General, in his 14 January report [S/2004/26] on the situation in Abkhazia, Georgia, and UNOMIG operations [YUN 2003, p. 438], welcomed the momentum gained by the peace process in 2003, the increased involvement of the Group of Friends and the renewed willingness of the sides to engage constructively in the key areas of economic cooperation, return of refugees and internally displaced persons, and political and security matters. Progress, however, remained slow. Moreover, the increasingly complex political situation on both sides of the ceasefire line and the events that led to the resignation of President Eduard Shevardnadze [YUN 2003, p. 438] had put the peace process temporarily on hold. The Secretary-General noted that two years after the finalization of the Basic Principles on the Distribution of Competences and the transmittal letter, the negotiations on the future political status of Abkhazia within the State of Georgia had not begun. He appealed to the Abkhaz side to abandon its uncompromising position on the paper and take advantage of the change of leadership in Tbilisi to negotiate a mutually acceptable and lasting settlement.

As UNOMIG's presence remained critical for the maintenance of stability in the conflict zone and for advancing the peace process towards a comprehensive political settlement, the Secretary-General recommended that its mandate be extended until 31 July 2004.

Other developments. Presidential elections were held in Georgia on 4 January, resulting in the election of Mikhail Saakashvili as President. The EU, in a 6 January statement [S/2004/43], welcomed the preliminary findings of the OSCE Office for Democratic Institutions and Human Rights International Election Observation Mission that the recent elections demonstrated notable progress over previous elections and brought Georgia closer to meeting international standards for democratic elections. The high rate of participation of the population and the clear mandate given to Mr. Saakashvili represented a positive signal for Georgia's future and opened new opportunities for the country.

SECURITY COUNCIL ACTION

The Security Council held private meetings on 23 January [meeting 4900] and 27 January [meeting 4904] to discuss UNOMIG and the situation in Georgia. On 30 January [meeting 4906], the Council unanimously adopted **resolution 1524(2004)**. The draft [S/2004/77] was prepared in consultations among Council members.

The Security Council,

Recalling all its relevant resolutions, in particular resolution 1494(2003) of 30 July 2003,

Having considered the report of the Secretary-General of 14 January 2004,

Recalling the conclusions of the summits of the Organization for Security and Cooperation in Europe held in Lisbon in December 1996 and in Istanbul on 18 and 19 November 1999, regarding the situation in Abkhazia, Georgia,

Recalling also the relevant principles contained in the Convention on the Safety of United Nations and Associated Personnel of 9 December 1994,

Deploring the fact that the perpetrators of the shooting down of a helicopter of the United Nations Observer Mission in Georgia on 8 October 2001, which resulted in the death of nine people on board, have still not been identified,

Stressing that the continued lack of progress on key issues of a comprehensive settlement of the conflict in Abkhazia, Georgia, is unacceptable,

Welcoming, however, the positive momentum given to the United Nations–led peace process by regular high-level meetings of the Group of Friends of the Secretary-General in Geneva and the Georgian-Russian summit meeting held in Sochi, Russian Federation, on 6 and 7 March 2003,

Noting the holding of presidential elections in Georgia in January 2004, and encouraging the new Georgian leadership as well as the Abkhaz side to pursue a comprehensive, peaceful political settlement of the conflict in Abkhazia, Georgia,

Welcoming the important contributions made by the Mission and the collective peacekeeping force of the Commonwealth of Independent States in stabilizing the situation in the zone of conflict, and stressing its attachment to the close cooperation existing between them in the performance of their respective mandates,

1. *Welcomes* the report of the Secretary-General of 14 January 2004;

2. *Reaffirms* the commitment of all Member States to the sovereignty, independence and territorial integrity of Georgia within its internationally recognized borders, and the necessity to define the status of Abkhazia within the State of Georgia in strict accordance with these principles;

3. *Commends and strongly supports* the sustained efforts of the Secretary-General and his Special Representative, with the assistance of the Russian Federation in its capacity as facilitator, as well as of the Group of Friends of the Secretary-General, and of the Organization for Security and Cooperation in Europe, to promote the stabilization of the situation and the achievement of a comprehensive political settlement, which must include a settlement of the political status of Abkhazia within the State of Georgia;

4. *Stresses, in particular, its strong support* for the document entitled "Basic Principles for the Distribution of Competences between Tbilisi and Sukhumi" and for its letter of transmittal, finalized by, and with the full support of, all members of the Group of Friends of the Secretary-General;

5. *Deeply regrets* the continued refusal of the Abkhaz side to agree to a discussion on the substance of that document, again strongly urges the Abkhaz side to receive the document and its letter of transmittal, urges both parties thereafter to give them full and open consideration and to engage in constructive negotiations on their substance, and urges those having influence with the parties to promote this outcome;

6. *Regrets* the lack of progress on the initiation of political status negotiations, and recalls once again that the purpose of those documents is to facilitate meaningful negotiations between the parties, under the leadership of the United Nations, on the status of Abkhazia within the State of Georgia, and is not an attempt to impose or dictate any specific solution to the parties;

7. *Underlines further* the fact that the process of negotiation leading to a lasting political settlement acceptable to both sides will require concessions from both sides;

8. *Welcomes* the convening of regular meetings of senior representatives of the Group of Friends of the Secretary-General in Geneva and the intention expressed by the parties to accept the invitation to participate in the forthcoming meeting, and calls upon them to participate again in a positive spirit;

9. *Urges* the parties to participate in a more active, regular and structured manner in the task forces established in the first Geneva meeting (to address issues in the priority areas of economic cooperation, the return of internally displaced persons and refugees, and political and security matters) and complemented by the working groups established in Sochi, Russian Federation, and stresses that results-oriented activities in these three priority areas remain key to building common ground between the Georgian and Abkhaz sides and ultimately for concluding meaningful negotiations on a comprehensive political settlement based on the document entitled "Basic Principles for the Distribution of Competences between Tbilisi and Sukhumi" and its letter of transmittal;

10. *Welcomes* the joint Georgian-Abkhaz high-level visit to Bosnia and Herzegovina and to Kosovo, Serbia and Montenegro, led by the Special Representative of the Secretary-General, as agreed in the second Geneva meeting;

11. *Calls upon* the parties to spare no effort to overcome their ongoing mutual mistrust;

12. *Calls again upon* the parties to ensure the necessary revitalization of the peace process in all its major aspects, including their work in the Coordinating Council and its relevant mechanisms, to build on the results of the third meeting on confidence-building measures between the Georgian and Abkhaz sides, held in Yalta, Ukraine, on 15 and 16 March 2001, to implement the proposals agreed on that occasion in a purposeful and cooperative manner, and to consider holding a fourth meeting on confidence-building measures;

13. *Reminds* all concerned to refrain from any action that might impede the peace process;

14. *Stresses* the urgent need for progress on the question of the refugees and internally displaced persons, calls upon both sides to display a genuine commitment to make returns the focus of special attention and to undertake this task in close coordination with the United Nations Observer Mission in Georgia and in consultation with the Office of the United Nations High Commissioner for Refugees and the Group of Friends of the Secretary-General, and recalls the understanding reached at the Sochi summit that the reopening of the Sochi-Tbilisi railway would be undertaken in parallel with the return of refugees and displaced persons, starting in the Gali district;

15. *Reaffirms* the unacceptability of the demographic changes resulting from the conflict, and reaffirms also the inalienable right of all refugees and internally displaced persons affected by the conflict to return to their homes in secure and dignified conditions, in accordance with international law and as set out in the Quadripartite Agreement on the Voluntary Return of Refugees and Displaced Persons of 4 April 1994 and the Yalta Declaration;

16. *Recalls* that the Abkhaz side bears a particular responsibility to protect the returnees and to facilitate the return of the remaining displaced population;

17. *Welcomes* the mission led by the United Nations Development Programme to the Gali region from 30 November to 17 December 2003 to assess the feasibility of a sustainable recovery process for the local population and potential returnees and to identify further actions to improve the overall security conditions and ensure sustainable return, and looks forward to the publication of the resulting report;

18. *Welcomes also* the positive consideration given by the parties to the recommendations of the joint assessment mission to the Gali district, urges them once again to implement those recommendations, and in particular calls upon the Abkhaz side to agree to the opening as soon as possible of the Gali branch of the human rights office in Sukhumi and to provide security conditions for its unhindered functioning;

19. *Welcomes further* the start of the deployment of a civilian police component as part of the Mission, as endorsed in resolution 1494(2003) and agreed by the parties, looks forward to an early confirmation by the Abkhaz side that the deployment in the Gali district of the remaining police officers can proceed, and calls upon the parties to cooperate and actively support the police component;

20. *Calls in particular upon* the Abkhaz side to improve law enforcement involving the local population and to address the lack of instruction in their mother tongue for the ethnic Georgian population;

21. *Calls upon* both parties further to publicly dissociate themselves from any militant rhetoric and demonstrations of support for military options or for the activities of illegal armed groups, notes the efforts undertaken by the Georgian side to put an end to the activities of illegal armed groups, and encourages the parties, in particular the Georgian side, to maintain their efforts;

22. *Condemns* any violations of the provisions of the Agreement on a Ceasefire and Separation of Forces signed in Moscow on 14 May 1994;

23. *Welcomes* the continuing relative calm in the Kodori Valley and the intention reaffirmed by the parties to resolve the situation peacefully, recalls its strong support for the protocol signed by the two sides on 2 April 2002 regarding the situation in the valley, and calls upon the sides to continue to fully implement the protocol;

24. *Deplores* the deterioration in the security environment in the Gali sector, including repeated killings and abductions;

25. *Welcomes* the holding of a quadripartite meeting with high-level representation by the parties on 19 January 2004 and their signing of a protocol on security issues, and urges the parties to abide by the provisions of that protocol and the protocol signed by them on 8 October 2003 and to cooperate more closely with each other to improve security in the Gali sector;

26. *Calls upon* the Georgian side to continue to improve security for joint patrols of the Mission and the collective peacekeeping force of the Commonwealth of Independent States in the Kodori Valley to enable them to resume independent and regular monitoring of the situation when road conditions permit;

27. *Underlines* the fact that it is the primary responsibility of both sides to provide appropriate security and to ensure the freedom of movement of the Mission, the collective peacekeeping force and other international personnel, strongly condemns the repeated abductions of personnel of those missions, deeply deplores the fact that none of the perpetrators have ever been identified or brought to justice, and reiterates that it is the responsibility of the parties to end this impunity;

28. *Urges* the parties, once again, to take all necessary steps to identify those responsible for the shooting down of a Mission helicopter on 8 October 2001, to bring them to justice, and to inform the Special Representative of the steps taken;

29. *Decides* to extend the mandate of the Mission for a new period terminating on 31 July 2004, subject to a review, as appropriate, of its mandate by the Council in the event of changes in the mandate of the collective peacekeeping force;

30. *Requests* the Secretary-General to continue to keep the Council regularly informed and to report three months from the date of the adoption of the present resolution on the situation in Abkhazia, Georgia;

31. *Decides* to remain actively seized of the matter.

Statement by President of Georgia. The Security Council, at a meeting on 26 February [meeting 4916] on the situation in Georgia, heard a statement by Georgian President Mikhail

Saakashvili. He affirmed, on behalf of the new Government, commitment to the peaceful resolution of the conflict in Abkhazia, Georgia, and added that the Government was encouraged by certain positive developments in the peace process. Referring to the meetings in Geneva of the Group of Friends, the President said that his Government attached great importance to the outcome of the Geneva process. The task forces established in that framework might form a powerful mechanism for the entire peace process. He expected the Geneva process to be results-oriented in all three designated directions (economic cooperation, return of refugees and internally displaced persons, and security matters). Specifically, the deployment of a civilian police unit in the Gali region would be helpful for the return of the internally displaced persons and refugees.

President Saakashvili said that, at his meeting two weeks earlier with Russian President Vladimir Putin, he felt there was a move towards positive relations, as they were able to define a common set of interests. In concrete terms, that would mean Russia ending the policy of granting citizenship to the population of the conflict regions of Abkhazia and the former South Ossetia, and ending the illegal acquisition of property on Abkhazian soil. He appealed to all Council members to work to reverse those policies.

In presenting his vision for the peace process, Mr. Saakashvili maintained that the definition of Abkhazia's political status, as outlined in the Basic Principles for the Distribution of Competences between Tbilisi and Sukhumi [YUN 2001, p. 386], provided the key to resolving the conflict. He called on the Abkhaz people to seize the opportunity presented as a result of the recent changes in Georgia to jointly build a common future. A solution should be based on guarantees of security, human rights and the promise of living in a free and open society. Mr. Saakashvili declared his readiness to guarantee the highest possible degree of autonomy to Abkhazia within the Georgian State and resources for the development of Abkhazia's economy. He was prepared to consider different kinds of relationships, such as broad autonomy in a united Georgian State, and elements of a federal relationship that provided for the territorial integrity of Georgia and human rights guarantees.

The new leadership in Tbilisi was offering a new set of principles. It had demonstrated its political will by cracking down on those forces that believed that solutions to conflict were based on violence or on using illegitimate means against people, and he called on the de facto leadership

in Abkhazia to take similar steps and to recognize that their current path was counter-productive.

He suggested that the process initiated in Sochi by President Putin (when the two sides discussed railroad links, returns and energy projects) [YUN 2003, p. 433], a part of the Geneva process, be advanced. He also called on the Council to establish a firm policy in support of peace and reconciliation, making it clear that those who were not on the side of peace would be held accountable, that there would be sanctions, and that the International Criminal Court (see p. 1295) awaited those who perpetrated criminal acts.

Meeting of Group of Friends (February). The third meeting of senior representatives of the Group of Friends (Geneva, 17-18 February) considered political and security matters, return of refugees and internally displaced persons, and economic cooperation. The Special Representative, the United Nations High Commissioner for Refugees and representatives of the United Nations Development Programme (UNDP) participated in the meeting. Representatives of both sides were also invited to participate. While the Georgian side accepted the invitation, the Abkhaz side declined, reiterating in a letter from the de facto President, Vladislav Ardzinba, its refusal to accept the Basic Principles on the Distribution of Competences between Tbilisi and Sukhumi and the transmittal letter and requesting a resumption of the Coordinating Council meetings, suspended since 2001 [YUN 2001, p. 378].

The Group of Friends welcomed the efforts of the Special Representative to bring the sides together on the issue of security guarantees and supported her proposal to submit to the two sides a letter of intent in support of returns. The Group also reaffirmed the central role of the Geneva process in achieving a political settlement.

Report of Secretary-General (April). In a 20 April report [S/2004/315] on the situation in Abkhazia, Georgia, the Secretary-General stated that his Special Representative maintained an active dialogue with the two sides in the Georgian/Abkhaz conflict and with the Group of Friends, both in Tbilisi and in their respective capitals. In follow-up to the 2003 meeting on security guarantees [YUN 2003, p. 434], the Special Representative convened a second meeting of the sides (Tbilisi, 10 February), with the participation of the Group of Friends. In the light of proposals presented by both Georgian and Abkhaz representatives, she offered to organize informal consultations between them and international experts in April in Geneva in preparation for the third meeting scheduled for Sukhumi in May. She had also organized a meeting on 19 January on implementation of the 2003 Gali protocol [ibid., p. 440].

Concerning the return of refugees, the Special Representative submitted to both sides a draft letter of intent, which would be a political signal of commitment to returns and provide the basis for increased involvement by UN bodies in the process, in particular UNHCR. UNOMIG finalized a draft paper on the return process and forwarded it to the participants in the Sochi working group on the return of internally displaced persons and refugees, created in 2003 [YUN 2003, p. 433].

UNOMIG's efforts to advance the peace process were affected by the complex political situation on both sides of the ceasefire line. In Tbilisi, State structures had begun to stabilize since the election of President Saakashvili on 4 Janaury, the formation of a Government the following month and the election of a new parliament on 28 March. The Secretary-General, in meetings with Mr. Saakashvili (Davos, France, January; New York, 26 February), assured him of the UN commitment to a lasting settlement with respect for Georgia's sovereignty and territorial integrity, and encouraged him to maintain the dialogue with the Abkhaz side. Presidents Putin and Saakashvili, at their first meeting (Moscow, 10-11 February), agreed to revitalize the implementation of the 2003 Sochi agreement. In Sukhumi, political leaders were preparing for elections for the de facto presidency, scheduled for the latter part of the year, creating an atmosphere which made it difficult to advance the peace process. Relations between Tbilisi and Sukhumi were also strained by the seizure by the Georgian side of six foreign fishing vessels operating in waters off the Abkhaz coast. The Abkhaz side threatened to use force to prevent further incursions into its "sovereign territory", while the Georgian side maintained that the foreign vessels were operating illegally in Georgian territorial waters.

Security Council consideration. During the Security Council's 29 April meeting [meeting 4958] to consider the Secretary-General's April report (see above), Zurab Zhvania, Prime Minister of Georgia, reiterated Georgia's commitment to a negotiated, peaceful resolution of the conflict. Georgia regretted that the investigation into the 2001 shooting down of a UNOMIG helicopter [YUN 2001, p. 383] was hampered by the refusal of the Abkhaz leadership to allow the investigation to be carried out in territory under its control. While Georgia supported the introduction of the civilian police component to the Gali region, the Abkhaz authorities obstructed its deployment. Georgia was participating in the Geneva process, while the Abkhaz side refused to participate in the third meeting on refugees and displaced persons. Georgia believed that it was time for the Council to pay more attention to the position of the separatists and to draw the appropriate conclusions.

Report of Secretary-General (July). In his 14 July report on Abkhazia, Georgia [S/2004/570], the Secretary-General reported that the Special Representative maintained dialogue with both sides at the highest level, and with representatives of the Group of Friends. The Secretary-General discussed the situation in Georgia with Prime Minister Zhvania (New York, 29 April), who briefed him on developments in Georgia and the Government's efforts to combat crime, including in the zone of conflict.

At the third meeting on security guarantees between the Georgian and Abkhaz sides (Sukhumi, 20 May), with the participation of representatives of the Group of Friends, OSCE and the CIS collective peacekeeping force, discussions continued on the issue of guarantees, including their international dimension, and on mechanisms for their implementation in the context of the 2001 Yalta Declaration on confidence-building measures [YUN 2001, p. 377], as well as on the proposals submitted at the second meeting in February (see p. 423). Also discussed was the implementation of existing agreements in relation to the Kodori Valley [YUN 2002, pp. 385 & 390], in particular the importance of resuming regular patrolling. The sides welcomed the Special Representative's proposal for a special UN mission to the Kodori Valley to ascertain the facts and undertake an assessment of the situation in the event of a crisis. They agreed to appoint contact persons for consultations and preparatory work before the next meeting, scheduled for 15 September.

The Russian Federation convened a further meeting of the Sochi working group on the return of refugees and internally displaced persons (Moscow, 26-27 April), with the participation of the Abkhaz side for the first time, the Special Representative, UNHCR officials and the CIS peacekeeping force, to discuss the draft UNOMIG/UNHCR letter of intent, endorsed by the Group of Friends in February (see p. 423). The Abkhaz side questioned the references in the letter to relevant Council resolutions and the role of the Group of Friends and presented its own draft. No agreement was reached, but the sides agreed to work on the text at the next meeting in July. Both sides confirmed their support for UNHCR's direct involvement in the return process, with the Abkhaz side emphasizing the UNHCR role in the registration of returnees. UNHCR, while expressing readiness to support the return process, stressed that prerequisites for its engagement were a formal confirmation of the intent of the two sides and an agreement on conditions to allow voluntary returns in safety and dignity.

Meanwhile, the crisis in the adjacent Georgian Republic of Ajaria came to an end with the resignation of the Ajarian leader, facilitated by the engagement of the Russian Federation and new elections. In the separatist region of South Ossetia, high-level tensions continued, following Georgia's establishment, in late May, of anti-smuggling checkpoints and the deployment of special forces to protect them. South Ossetian forces were put on high alert and the movement of troops and arms was reported in the area. The Abkhaz side followed developments in Ajaria and in South Ossetia with concern and focused on statements by some Georgian politicians that Sukhumi would be next in their reintegration effort, which led to an enhanced Abkhaz security presence in the Gali district in the lead-up to Georgia's National Day, 26 May. In the light of the escalating tensions, the Special Representative and UNOMIG took measures to defuse the situation, including additional patrols and encouragement for both sides to refrain from actions and rhetoric that could cause the situation to deteriorate. The Special Representative maintained regular contact with both sides and facilitated direct contacts between them, which were instrumental in assuring the Abkhaz side that it was not Tbilisi's intention to destabilize the situation and in persuading the Georgian side from taking reciprocal additional security measures.

In his address to the nation on 26 May, President Saakashvili reiterated that one of the core aims of his Government was reunification with Abkhazia and South Ossetia. Appealing to Abkhaz and Ossetians to start talks, he stressed that Tbilisi was prepared to consider any State model that took into account the interests of the population in the regions and ensured their future development. He confirmed Georgia's policy of reintegration exclusively through dialogue and peaceful means and offered to the Abkhaz side the highest possible federal status, with international guarantees. The Abkhaz side, however, rejected Mr. Saakashvili's overture, stating that, while it was ready to discuss the non-resumption of hostilities and the restoration of trust and normal relations, its status was not open for discussion. The Secretary-General expressed his hope that with time, the leadership in Sukhumi would reconsider its stance and respond constructively to the offer of the new Georgian leadership for direct dialogue.

Communications. The EU, in a 17 March statement [S/2004/245] concerning the Georgian Autonomous Republic of Ajaria, reaffirmed its attachment to the sovereignty and territorial integrity of Georgia and called on all sides to refrain from any further escalation which could result in violence. It urged the central Government in Tbilisi and the authorities in the Ajaria capital of Batumi to re-establish dialogue at the highest level with a view to finding a peaceful solution acceptable to all and in the interest of Georgia.

Georgia, in a 26 July letter [S/2004/595] to the Security Council, affirmed its commitment to a peaceful solution and its hope that the new leader of the secessionists would take more constructive positions. It recalled the idea considered previously of a Council visit to Abkhazia, stating that the time might be right for such a visit. Georgia mentioned the issues that it found contrary to a peaceful solution: the enforcement of the visa-free regime on the Abkhaz and former South Ossetian segments of the Georgia-Russian border; the granting of Russian citizenship to the population of the separatist regions; the illegal acquisition of land and property in Abkhazia, Georgia; the training of Abkhaz separatists in Russian Federation military schools; the unresolved issue of the military base in Gudauta; and the entering into Georgian territory of hundreds of armed mercenaries from Russia to conduct so-called "joint manoeuvres". The only way out of the situation was through decisive actions of a unified and resolute Security Council.

SECURITY COUNCIL ACTION (July)

On 29 July [meeting 5013], the Security Council unanimously adopted **resolution 1554(2004)**. The draft [S/2004/600] was prepared in consultations among Council members.

The Security Council,

Recalling all its relevant resolutions, in particular resolution 1524(2004) of 30 January 2004,

Welcoming the report of the Secretary-General of 14 July 2004,

Recalling the conclusions of the summits of the Organization for Security and Cooperation in Europe held in Lisbon in December 1996 and in Istanbul on 18 and 19 November 1999, regarding the situation in Abkhazia, Georgia,

Recalling also the relevant principles contained in the Convention on the Safety of United Nations and Associated Personnel of 9 December 1994,

Deploring the fact that the perpetrators of the shooting down of a helicopter of the United Nations Observer Mission in Georgia on 8 October 2001, which resulted in the death of nine people on board, have still not been identified,

Stressing that the continued lack of progress on key issues of a comprehensive settlement of the conflict in Abkhazia, Georgia, is unacceptable,

Welcoming, however, the positive momentum given to the United Nations-led peace process by regular high-level meetings of the Group of Friends of the

Secretary-General in Geneva and the Georgian-Russian summit meetings,

Welcoming the important contributions made by the Mission and the collective peacekeeping force of the Commonwealth of Independent States in stabilizing the situation in the zone of conflict, and stressing its attachment to the close cooperation existing between them in the performance of their respective mandates,

1. *Reaffirms* the commitment of all Member States to the sovereignty, independence and territorial integrity of Georgia within its internationally recognized borders, and the necessity to define the status of Abkhazia within the State of Georgia in strict accordance with these principles;

2. *Commends and strongly supports* the sustained efforts of the Secretary-General and his Special Representative, with the assistance of the Russian Federation in its capacity as facilitator, as well as of the Group of Friends of the Secretary-General, and of the Organization for Security and Cooperation in Europe to promote the stabilization of the situation and the achievement of a comprehensive political settlement, which must include a settlement of the political status of Abkhazia within the State of Georgia;

3. *Reiterates its strong support* for the document entitled "Basic Principles for the Distribution of Competences between Tbilisi and Sukhumi" and for its letter of transmittal, finalized by, and with the full support of, all members of the Group of Friends of the Secretary-General;

4. *Deeply regrets* the continued refusal of the Abkhaz side to agree to a discussion on the substance of that document, again strongly urges the Abkhaz side to receive the document and its letter of transmittal, urges both parties thereafter to give them full and open consideration and to engage in constructive negotiations on their substance, and urges those having influence with the parties to promote this outcome;

5. *Regrets* the lack of progress on the initiation of political status negotiations, and recalls once again that the purpose of those documents is to facilitate meaningful negotiations between the parties, under the leadership of the United Nations, on the status of Abkhazia within the State of Georgia, and is not an attempt to impose or dictate any specific solution to the parties;

6. *Calls upon* the parties to spare no effort to overcome their ongoing mutual mistrust, and underlines the fact that the process of negotiation leading to a lasting political settlement acceptable to both sides will require concessions from both sides;

7. *Welcomes* the commitment by the Georgian side to a peaceful resolution of the conflict, and calls upon both parties further to publicly dissociate themselves from all militant rhetoric and demonstrations of support for military options;

8. *Reminds* all concerned to refrain from any action that might impede the peace process;

9. *Welcomes* the convening of regular meetings of senior representatives of the Group of Friends of the Secretary-General and the United Nations in Geneva, and, while regretting that the Abkhaz side did not participate in the last meeting, looks forward to the constructive participation of the parties in the forthcoming meetings;

10. *Urges* the parties to participate in a more active, regular and structured manner in the task forces established in the first Geneva meeting (to address issues in the priority areas of economic cooperation, the return of internally displaced persons and refugees, and political and security matters) and complemented by the working groups established in Sochi, Russian Federation, in March 2003, and reiterates that results-oriented activities in these three priority areas remain key to building common ground between the Georgian and Abkhaz sides and ultimately for concluding meaningful negotiations on a comprehensive political settlement based on the document entitled "Basic Principles for the Distribution of Competences between Tbilisi and Sukhumi" and its letter of transmittal;

11. *Encourages* the sides in that respect to continue their discussion on security guarantees, and welcomes the meeting held in Sukhumi on 20 May 2004 on this issue;

12. *Calls again upon* the parties to take concrete steps to revitalize the peace process in all its major aspects, including their work in the Coordinating Council and its relevant mechanisms, to build on the results of the third meeting on confidence-building measures between the Georgian and Abkhaz sides, held in Yalta, Ukraine, on 15 and 16 March 2001 and to implement the proposals agreed on that occasion in a purposeful and cooperative manner, with a view to holding a fourth meeting on confidence-building measures;

13. *Stresses* the urgent need for progress on the question of the refugees and internally displaced persons, calls upon both sides to display a genuine commitment to make returns the focus of special attention and to undertake this task in close coordination with the Observer Mission in Georgia and in consultation with the Office of the United Nations High Commissioner for Refugees and the Group of Friends of the Secretary-General;

14. *Calls for* the rapid finalization and signature of the letter of intent on returns proposed by the Special Representative of the Secretary-General, and welcomes the recent meetings, with the participation of the Special Representative and the Office of the High Commissioner, of the Sochi working group on refugees and internally displaced persons;

15. *Reaffirms* the unacceptability of the demographic changes resulting from the conflict, and reaffirms also the inalienable right of all refugees and internally displaced persons affected by the conflict to return to their homes in secure and dignified conditions, in accordance with international law and as set out in the Quadripartite Agreement on the Voluntary Return of Refugees and Displaced Persons of 4 April 1994 and the Yalta Declaration;

16. *Recalls* that the Abkhaz side bears a particular responsibility to protect the returnees and to facilitate the return of the remaining displaced population;

17. *Welcomes* the report of the mission led by the United Nations Development Programme to the Gali region from 30 November to 17 December 2003 to assess the feasibility of a sustainable recovery process for the local population and potential returnees and to identify further actions to improve the overall security conditions and ensure sustainable return, and looks forward to further consultations by the United Nations

Development Programme and the Mission with the parties, aimed at implementing its recommendations;

18. *Urges* the parties once again to implement the recommendations of the joint assessment mission of November 2000 to the Gali sector, regrets that there has been no progress to that effect despite the positive consideration by the parties given to those recommendations in the first Geneva meeting, and calls again upon the Abkhaz side to agree to the opening as soon as possible of the Gali branch of the human rights office in Sukhumi and to provide security conditions for its unhindered functioning;

19. *Expresses concern* that despite the start of the deployment of a civilian police component as part of the Mission, as endorsed in resolution 1494(2003) of 30 July 2003 and agreed upon by the parties, the deployment of the remaining officers in the Gali sector is still outstanding, and calls upon the Abkhaz side to allow for a swift deployment of the police component in that region;

20. *Calls in particular upon* the Abkhaz side to improve law enforcement involving the local population and to address the lack of instruction in their mother tongue for the ethnic Georgian population;

21. *Welcomes* the measures taken by the Georgian side to put an end to the activities of illegal armed groups, and encourages the maintenance of those efforts;

22. *Condemns* any violations of the provisions of the Agreement on a Ceasefire and Separation of Forces signed in Moscow on 14 May 1994;

23. *Welcomes* the continuing relative calm in the Kodori Valley, and condemns the killings and abductions of civilians as well as the attack on a checkpoint of the collective peacekeeping force of the Commonwealth of Independent States in the Gali sector;

24. *Urges* the parties to abide by the provisions of the protocols on security issues in the Gali sector, signed on 8 October 2003 and 19 January 2004, to continue their regular meetings and to cooperate more closely with each other to improve security in the sector;

25. *Calls upon* the Georgian side to provide comprehensive security guarantees to allow for independent and regular monitoring of the situation in the upper Kodori Valley by joint patrols of the Mission and the collective peacekeeping force;

26. *Underlines* the fact that it is the primary responsibility of both sides to provide appropriate security and to ensure the freedom of movement of the Mission, the collective peacekeeping force and other international personnel, strongly condemns in that respect the repeated abductions of personnel of those missions in the past, deeply deplores the fact that none of the perpetrators have ever been identified or brought to justice, and reiterates again that it is the responsibility of the parties to end this impunity;

27. *Urges* the parties, once again, to take all necessary steps to identify those responsible for the shooting down of a Mission helicopter on 8 October 2001, to bring them to justice, and to inform the Special Representative of the steps taken;

28. *Decides* to extend the mandate of the Mission for a new period terminating on 31 January 2005, subject to a review as appropriate of its mandate by the Council in the event of changes in the mandate of the collective peacekeeping force;

29. *Requests* the Secretary-General to continue to keep the Council regularly informed and to report three months from the date of the adoption of the present resolution on the situation in Abkhazia, Georgia;

30. *Decides* to remain actively seized of the matter.

Report of Secretary-General (October). In his 18 October report [S/2004/822] on the situation in Abkhazia, Georgia, the Secretary-General said that, at a meeting of the Georgian-Russian Sochi working group on the return of refugees and internally displaced persons convened by the Russian Federation on 20 July, with the participation of the Special Representative, UNHCR and the Commander of the CIS peacekeeping force, the Georgian and Abkhaz sides again discussed the draft letter of intent prepared by UNOMIG and UNHCR but were still unable to agree on the text and again undertook to work on agreeable formulations before the next meeting in November. The sides also discussed the UNHCR draft concept paper on the registration of returnees in the Gali district and agreed to exchange more substantial comments prior to the next meeting.

The political situation deteriorated on 30 July when a Georgian coast guard vessel fired on a foreign cargo ship in coastal waters near Sukhumi, in what Georgia regarded as a law enforcement action to assert control over its internationally recognized territorial waters in the Black Sea, including international shipping to and from ports in Abkhazia. The following day, the Abkhaz authorities suspended their participation in the negotiation process and called for an investigation into and a legal assessment of the incident by the United Nations, the CIS peacekeeping force and the international community as a precondition for returning to the negotiating table. The Abkhaz side also suspended its participation in the ceasefire monitoring and security-related mechanisms, including the weekly quadripartite meetings and the joint fact-finding group.

To defuse the situation, the Special Representative met with both sides and issued a statement, urging them to resolve such incidents through negotiations and to refrain from action that could negatively affect the peace process. She reiterated her offer to convene a meeting on maritime issues. Her efforts were supported by the Group of Friends, which held high-level meetings with the sides in Tbilisi and Sukhumi, and she urged them to adhere to the 1994 Moscow Agreement [YUN 1994, p. 583], resume unconditionally the negotiations and address maritime issues at the planned meeting on security guarantees. While the Georgian side responded positively, the Abkhaz side maintained its position. Under those circumstances, the meeting on security guarantees planned for 15 September had to be postponed. In a parallel effort, the Russian Federation offered to convene a meeting on maritime issues on 25 September in Sochi, with the participation of the sides and UNOMIG. That meeting was postponed also at the request of the Abkhaz side.

Tensions also emerged in the relations between Georgia and the Russian Federation. Georgia officially protested against tourist visits to Abkhazia, Georgia, and the resumption on 10 September, after a 12-year interruption, of the Sukhumi-Sochi-Moscow passenger rail line as violations of Georgia's sovereignty, international law and bilateral agreements. Georgia also protested against the continued visits to Abkhazia by high-profile Russian politicians. President Putin and President Saakashvili, during the summit of CIS heads of State (Astana, Kazakhstan, 16 September), discussed bilateral relations between their two countries, including conflict resolution issues. In a meeting with President Saakashvili in New York on 21 September to discuss the situation in Georgia, the Secretary-General noted the challenges that Georgia and the region had faced during the preceding months and stressed his commitment to work with the parties to the Georgian-Abkhaz conflict. Mr. Saakashvili, for his part, underlined the importance of the continuing involvement of the United Nations and suggested elements for a solution to Georgia's internal conflicts, such as confidence-building measures, demilitarization of the conflict zone and the widest possible autonomy for Abkhazia with international guarantees. The Secretary-General also reported that Mr. Saakashvili had written to him on 16 August, expressing his concern over the situation in South Ossetia and reiterating Georgia's rejection of the use of force for conflict resolution.

In Sukhumi, de facto presidential elections were held on 3 October. The United Nations maintained the position set out in Security Council resolution 1255(1999) [YUN 1999, p. 380], affirming that the holding of self-styled elections in Abkhazia, Georgia, were unacceptable and illegitimate in the absence of the majority of the population and the determination of the political status of the territory. The Georgian side warned against legitimization of the elections and regretted outside support for one of the candidates.

In other developments, following the acceptance by both sides of the recommendations of the UNDP-led feasibility study for the Gali, Ochamchira and Tqvarcheli districts, as a result

of a 2003 mission to the region [YUN 2003, p. 440], UNDP, in collaboration with UNOMIG, initiated a rehabilitation programme focusing on agriculture, health, water and sanitation, and capacity-building for non-governmental organizations (NGOs). UNOMIG and UNDP were finalizing an agreement with the EU, which would contribute to the UNDP programme and to the UNOMIG trust fund for quick-impact rehabilitation projects in the zone of conflict.

Statement by President of Georgia. Speaking during the general debate of the General Assembly on 21 September [A/59/PV.4], Georgian President Saakashvili proposed a stage-by-stage settlement plan to resolve conflicts in Georgia. The first step was the initiation of confidence-building measures through joint economic projects, restoring the right of internally displaced persons to return home and ensuring human rights. Step two would focus on demilitarization and transforming the current peacekeeping operation into an international operation to protect the people of those regions from militias, irregulars and violent gangs. The third stage envisioned guarantees that would lead to the establishment of the broadest form of autonomy—one that protected culture and language and guaranteed self-governance, fiscal control and meaningful representation and power-sharing at the national government level.

Communication. Georgia, in a 26 October letter to the Security Council [S/2004/861], said that the UN-led peace process in the region had reached a critical juncture. The holding of the illegitimate and self-styled presidential elections by the Abkhaz separatists on 3 October was another attempt to imbue legality to the demographic changes resulting from the conflict, in disregard of the international community's position. The Russian Federation, which praised the elections on 4 October as "calm and democratic", appeared to be the only dissenter to that position. Georgia was committed to resuming negotiations for settling the conflict with any leader who succeeded the de facto Abkhazia president Ardzinba. However, progress would require political will on the Abkhaz side for constructive engagement in the negotiations, in particular on the Basic Principles for the Distribution of Competences between Tbilisi and Sukhumi, allowing the establishment of a branch of the UN Human Rights Office in Gali, addressing the problem of teaching Georgian children in Abkhazia in their native language, and agreeing to the deployment of UNOMIG civilian police in the Gali district. The Security Council needed to take the lead in reinvigorating the peace process, and should consider a field visit to Georgia, particularly to

Sukhumi, to learn first-hand the reality on the ground and to try to resolve the stalemate in the conflict resolution process.

Press statement. The Security Council President issued a press statement on 27 October [SC/8228] confirming that the members, having heard a briefing by the Special Representative, shared the concern of the Secretary-General on the absence of tangible progress in the Georgian/Abkhaz peace process. They underlined the need for renewed efforts to achieve a lasting political solution to the conflict with the support of the United Nations and the assistance of the Russian Federation in its capacity as facilitator, as well as the Group of Friends of the Secretary-General.

Further report of Secretary-General. In a report covering developments in Georgia during late 2004 [S/2005/32], the Secretary-General stated that the Abkhaz side remained preoccupied with internal political developments related to the self-styled presidential elections of 3 October and their outcome. Following contradictory decisions by local authorities, tensions between followers of the two main contenders, Sergey Bagapsh and Raul Khadjimba, led to demonstrations and takeovers of public buildings. The situation was defused on 6 December when the two candidates reached an agreement to run on a single ticket in a new "election" scheduled for 12 January 2005. The agreement was signed by the two candidates, the highest Abkhaz leadership and two visiting Russian officials. The Georgian side protested visits by Russian officials to Sukhumi without prior notification to Tbilisi and Russian involvement in political developments there. The Russian Federation said its involvement was aimed at preventing possible armed conflict and creating conditions for solving the Georgian-Abkhaz dispute.

The Special Representative stayed in close contact with the leadership of both sides, in particular in Sukhumi, emphasizing the need to avoid increasing instability within the conflict zone and to create conditions for resumption of negotiations. She encouraged the Abkhaz side to resume, as a first step, its participation in both the weekly quadripartite meetings and in the joint fact-finding group. While it initially maintained its position not to resume the peace process dialogue or to participate in related meetings until the internal situation in Sukhumi was resolved and the international community had assessed the 30 July maritime incident (see p. 427), the Abkhaz side, on 16 December, in a first encouraging sign, resumed participation in those bodies.

The Special Representative maintained high-level contacts with the Group of Friends in her efforts to re-establish the dialogue. In October she met with the Group of Friends in New York and in Washington, D.C., and later held discussions with representatives of the individual Group members. She also met with the United Nations High Commissioner for Refugees during his visit to the region and the EU Special Representative for the South Caucasus, Heikki Talvitie.

Meeting of Group of Friends (December). High-level representatives of the Group of Friends convened in Geneva on 13 and 14 December under the chairmanship of the Under-Secretary-General for Peacekeeping Operations to review the status of the peace process. The Special Representative and the High Commissioner for Refugees participated in the discussion. The Friends agreed that negotiating efforts should intensify as soon as the new leadership was formed in Sukhumi. They tentatively planned a meeting for early 2005, for which the United Nations would prepare proposals on security guarantees and related confidence-building measures. In that context, they agreed to address maritime security as a priority. The Friends emphasized the importance of the return of refugees and internally displaced persons and acknowledged the key roles of UNOMIG and UNHCR in that regard. They agreed that work in the relevant Sochi working groups on the rehabilitation of the Sochi-Tbilisi railroad and the Inguri power plant should continue. Participants appreciated the humanitarian and rehabilitation work carried out by UNOMIG and UNDP in the Gali district and adjacent areas and welcomed the EU commitment to finance economic projects.

Situation on the ground

Kodori Valley

In the Kodori Valley, the upper part of which was controlled by Georgia and the lower part by the de facto Abkhaz authorities, a number of UNOMIG/CIS patrols were conducted between 12 May and 2 September. Reporting the situation to be calm, they confirmed that the road through the valley damaged by floods in 2003 was again passable up to the broken bridge between the Abkhaz-controlled lower part and the Georgian-controlled upper part. Although the Abkhaz side alleged that the Georgian side had introduced additional forces in the upper Kodori Valley in violation of the 1994 Moscow Agreement [YUN 1994, p. 583], a joint CIS/Georgian patrol on 15 June did not confirm those allegations.

UNOMIG/CIS patrols in the upper valley were suspended later in the year for security reasons and poor road conditions. Discussions were held with the parties on resuming patrolling, including security guarantees. Helicopter patrols remained suspended, while administrative flights continued on authorized flight routes over the Black Sea. The Georgian side reported several overflights by unauthorized aircraft. No patrolling was conducted in the lower valley, owing to the inability of the Abkhaz side to guarantee security.

Gali and Zugdidi sectors

The overall situation in the Gali sector was generally calm. However, tensions developed in the weeks leading up to Georgia's National Day, 26 May. Additional Abkhaz law enforcement personnel were deployed and temporary security posts were established in advance of the holiday. To defuse the situation, UNOMIG increased its patrolling and encouraged both sides to refrain from militant actions and rhetoric. After 26 May, the tension subsided and most of the additional law enforcement personnel were removed. Similar Abkhaz reinforcement took place on 21 and 22 June, when the Georgian authorities distributed fertilizers to residents of some villages in the Gali district.

The number of criminal incidents in the Gali sector decreased in the earlier part of the year, but as the year progressed, criminality and law-lessness increased significantly, particularly in the lower Gali area. The Abkhaz militia carried out several operations in the lower Gali district, detaining a number of people, most of whom were later released. Following one of those operations, the commander of an Abkhaz observation post was abducted on 6 April and released after three weeks. On 3 July, a CIS peacekeeping force checkpoint near the ceasefire line came under fire. In addition to their annual military exercises, the Abkhaz authorities reinforced security, especially along the ceasefire line, in the lead-up to the de facto presidential elections on 3 October.

Throughout the year, the overall situation in the Zugdidi sector was generally calm, with a relatively low level of criminal incidents reported. The Georgian side conducted a large-scale military exercise from 30 April to 3 May in the Kulevi training area, adjacent to the restricted-weapons zone. UNOMIG observed the exercise and reported no violations of the ceasefire agreement. The Georgian authorities continued to conduct anti-crime operations throughout the area. On 14 June, the Georgian police detained two trucks along the Abkhaz side of the ceasefire line during an anti-smuggling operation. On 7 May, CIS reported a Georgian police convoy crossing the ceasefire line on its way back from Svanetia, carrying some 500 small arms confiscated there. CIS reported an attack on 4 July on one of its checkpoints near the ceasefire line; no casualties occurred.

Humanitarian situation and human rights

United Nations agencies, international organizations and NGOs continued to provide food, medical aid and infrastructural assistance to the conflict zone in Abkhazia, Georgia; in addition to strictly humanitarian work, some development-related activity also took place. UNHCR completed the last portion of its school rehabilitation project, from which more than 14,000 children in 80 schools in Abkhazia benefited. The United Nations Children's Fund delivered health and education assistance, including the second consignment of immunization supplies, and worked with local partners in improving vaccine storage, delivery and monitoring. It began a training programme for health-care providers and primary caregivers in the Gali, Ochamchira, Sukhumi and Tqvarcheli districts. The United Nations Development Fund for Women supported women in leadership, people-to-people dialogue and youth and education activities, with a focus on conflict prevention and resolution, gender equality and peace-building. The United Nations Volunteers focused on developing the capacity of local NGOs and the promotion of small-scale income-generation projects. Various NGOs provided health care and medicine, laboratory equipment, food assistance, improvements to housing and education and demining services and mine-awareness training.

UNOMIG continued to implement quick-impact projects, designed to improve living conditions and to repair basic infrastructure in the zone of conflict. Since its inception in 2002, 66 projects had been approved, of which 43 were completed. UNOMIG and the EU were finalizing negotiations to secure some 4 million euros to fund a two-year programme of major rehabilitation in the health, education and electricity sectors.

The precarious human rights situation in Abkhazia showed no signs of improvement. The rule of law, the administration of justice and law enforcement mechanisms remained weak and did not provide adequate protection of the right to life and physical security, nor public order, particularly in the Gali district. Murders, abductions and robberies mostly went unpunished. Cases of prolonged detention, violation of the right to legal protection, extortion and use of violence by uniformed Abkhaz personnel were reported. The United Nations Human Rights Office in Sukhumi provided legal advisory services to the local population, monitored court trials and places of pre-trial detention, and promoted human rights awareness. The Office of the United Nations High Commissioner for Human Rights (OHCHR) developed a human rights training programme for local law enforcement agencies. In partnership with organizations, OHCHR implemented projects for strengthening the non-governmental sector and building local capacity to promote human rights.

The human rights situation was influenced by preparations for the de facto presidential elections in October (see p. 429), as the Abkhaz authorities deferred action on human rights issues until after the "elections". In addition, they remained unable to create an environment conducive to the safe and dignified return of internally displaced persons.

Adoption by the de facto Abkhaz Parliament of the long-overdue "criminal code" and "criminal procedure code" was further delayed. Restrictions were placed on independent media, including the tightening of de facto governmental control of electronic and print media.

Financing

The General Assembly considered the UNOMIG financial performance report for 1 July 2002 to 30 June 2003 [A/58/639], the budget for the maintenance of UNOMIG for 1 July 2004 to 30 June 2005 [A/58/640], and ACABQ's related comments and recommendations [A/58/759/Add.1].

On 18 June [meeting 91], the Assembly adopted, on the recommendation of the Fifth Committee [A/58/825], **resolution 58/303** without vote [agenda item 142].

Financing of the United Nations Observer Mission in Georgia

The General Assembly,

Having considered the reports of the Secretary-General on the financing of the United Nations Observer Mission in Georgia and the related reports of the Advisory Committee on Administrative and Budgetary Questions,

Recalling Security Council resolution 854(1993) of 6 August 1993, by which the Council approved the deployment of an advance team of up to ten United Nations military observers for a period of three months and the incorporation of the advance team into a United Nations observer mission if such a mission was formally established by the Council,

Recalling also Security Council resolution 858(1993) of 24 August 1993, by which the Council established the United Nations Observer Mission in Georgia, and the subsequent resolutions by which the Council extended the mandate of the Observer Mission, the latest of which was resolution 1524(2004) of 30 January 2004,

Recalling further its decision 48/475 A of 23 December 1993 on the financing of the Observer Mission and its subsequent resolutions and decisions thereon, the latest of which was resolution 57/333 of 18 June 2003,

Reaffirming the general principles underlying the financing of United Nations peacekeeping operations, as stated in General Assembly resolutions 1874(S-IV) of 27 June 1963, 3101(XXVIII) of 11 December 1973 and 55/235 of 23 December 2000,

Mindful of the fact that it is essential to provide the Observer Mission with the financial resources necessary to enable it to fulfil its responsibilities under the relevant resolutions of the Security Council,

1. *Takes note* of the status of contributions to the United Nations Observer Mission in Georgia as at 15 April 2004, including the contributions outstanding in the amount of 12.4 million United States dollars, representing some 6 per cent of the total assessed contributions, notes with concern that only thirty Member States have paid their assessed contributions in full, and urges all other Member States, in particular those in arrears, to ensure payment of their outstanding assessed contributions;

2. *Expresses its appreciation* to those Member States which have paid their assessed contributions in full, and urges all other Member States to make every possible effort to ensure payment of their assessed contributions to the Observer Mission in full;

3. *Expresses concern* at the delay experienced by the Secretary-General in deploying and providing adequate resources to some recent peacekeeping missions, in particular those in Africa;

4. *Emphasizes* that all future and existing peacekeeping missions shall be given equal and non-discriminatory treatment in respect of financial and administrative arrangements;

5. *Also emphasizes* that all peacekeeping missions shall be provided with adequate resources for the effective and efficient discharge of their respective mandates;

6. *Reiterates its request* to the Secretary-General to make the fullest possible use of facilities and equipment at the United Nations Logistics Base at Brindisi, Italy, in order to minimize the costs of procurement for the Observer Mission;

7. *Endorses* the conclusions and recommendations contained in the report of the Advisory Committee on Administrative and Budgetary Questions, and requests the Secretary-General to ensure their full implementation;

8. *Requests* the Secretary-General to take all action necessary to ensure that the Observer Mission is administered with a maximum of efficiency and economy;

9. *Also requests* the Secretary-General, in order to reduce the cost of employing General Service staff, to continue efforts to recruit local staff for the Observer Mission against General Service posts, commensurate with the requirements of the Mission;

Financial performance report for the period from 1 July 2002 to 30 June 2003

10. *Takes note* of the report of the Secretary-General on the financial performance of the Observer Mission for the period from 1 July 2002 to 30 June 2003;

**Budget estimates for the period
from 1 July 2004 to 30 June 2005**

11. *Decides* to appropriate to the Special Account for the United Nations Observer Mission in Georgia the amount of 33,589,200 dollars for the period from 1 July 2004 to 30 June 2005, inclusive of 31,925,700 dollars for the maintenance of the Observer Mission, 1,360,000 dollars for the support account for peacekeeping operations and 303,500 dollars for the United Nations Logistics Base;

Financing of the appropriation

12. *Decides also* to apportion among Member States the amount of 33,589,200 dollars at a monthly rate of 2,799,100 dollars, in accordance with the levels set out in General Assembly resolution 55/235, as adjusted by the Assembly in its resolution 55/236 of 23 December 2000 and updated in its resolution 58/256 of 23 December 2003, taking into account the scale of assessments for 2004 and 2005 as set out in its resolution 58/1 B of 23 December 2003, subject to a decision of the Security Council to extend the mandate of the Mission;

13. *Decides further* that, in accordance with the provisions of its resolution 973(X) of 15 December 1955, there shall be set off against the apportionment among Member States, as provided for in paragraph 12 above, their respective share in the Tax Equalization Fund of 2,339,800 dollars, comprising the estimated staff assessment income of 2,124,200 dollars approved for the Observer Mission, the prorated share of 198,500 dollars of the estimated staff assessment income approved for the support account and the prorated share of 17,100 dollars of the estimated staff assessment income approved for the United Nations Logistics Base;

14. *Decides* that, for Member States that have fulfilled their financial obligations to the Observer Mission, there shall be set off against their apportionment, as provided for in paragraph 12 above, their respective share of the unencumbered balance and other income in the amount of 4,096,100 dollars in respect of the financial period ended 30 June 2003, in accordance with the levels set out in General Assembly resolution 55/235, as adjusted by the Assembly in its resolution 55/236 and its resolution 57/290 A of 20 December 2002, taking into account the scale of assessments for 2003 as set out in its resolutions 55/5 B of 23 December 2000 and 57/4 B of 20 December 2002;

15. *Decides also* that, for Member States that have not fulfilled their financial obligations to the Observer Mission, there shall be set off against their outstanding obligations their respective share of the unencumbered balance and other income in the amount of 4,096,100 dollars in respect of the financial period ended 30 June 2003, in accordance with the scheme set out in paragraph 14 above;

16. *Decides further* that the increase of 142,200 dollars in the estimated staff assessment income in respect of the financial period ended 30 June 2003 shall be added to the credits from the amount referred to in paragraphs 14 and 15 above and that the respective shares of Member States therein shall be applied in accordance with the provisions of those paragraphs, as appropriate;

17. *Emphasizes* that no peacekeeping mission shall be financed by borrowing funds from other active peacekeeping missions;

18. *Encourages* the Secretary-General to continue to take additional measures to ensure the safety and security of all personnel participating in the Observer Mission under the auspices of the United Nations;

19. *Invites* voluntary contributions to the Observer Mission in cash and in the form of services and supplies acceptable to the Secretary-General, to be administered, as appropriate, in accordance with the procedure and practices established by the General Assembly;

20. *Decides* to include in the provisional agenda of its fifty-ninth session the item entitled "Financing of the United Nations Observer Mission in Georgia".

On 23 December, the Assembly decided that the item on the financing of UNOMIG would remain for consideration during its resumed fifty-ninth (2005) session (**decision 59/552**).

Armenia and Azerbaijan

In 2004, the Minsk Group of OSCE (France, Russian Federation, United States) continued efforts to mediate the dispute between Armenia and Azerbaijan, which had erupted in armed conflict in 1992 [YUN 1992, p. 388] after four years of sporadic ethnic fighting in the Nagorny Karabakh region in Azerbaijan. However, there was no change in the position of either country with regard to the conflict during the year. Both sides continued to address communications to the Secretary-General, clarifying their positions regarding the conflict or lodging complaints against the actions of the other.

The General Assembly, by **decision 59/552** of 23 December, decided that the item on the situation in the occupied territories of Azerbaijan would remain for consideration during its resumed fifty-ninth (2005) session.

Communications. On 19 February [S/2004/123], Armenia brought to the Secretary-General's attention the murder that day of an Armenian Armed Forces officer, Lieutenant Gurgen Margarian, by an Azerbaijani military officer, while both were attending a language course in Budapest, Hungary, of the NATO Partnership for Peace Programme. According to Armenia, the crime was a consequence of the anti-Armenian hysteria by the Azeri authorities over the years and recent militarist propaganda. On 23 February [S/2004/138], Azerbaijan expressed its regret over the incident and explained the circumstances that might have affected the suspect's emotional condition. Azerbaijan urged Armenia not to allow the incident to damage the already tense relations between the two countries. Armenia, in a 1 March letter [S/2004/168], outlined its concerns arising from what it viewed as the encouragement by Azerbaijani officials of hate propaganda following the incident. The significant increase of propaganda from Azerbaijani officials to distort the roots and causes of the Nagorny Karabakh conflict and their efforts to nullify the international community's 12-year efforts to achieve a resolution to the conflict served to discredit the international mediation process, threatened the ceasefire regime and increased the instability and insecurity in the region. Armenia gave a historical overview of the Nagorny Karabakh problem.

Azerbaijan, responding on 15 March [S/2004/209], presented its own views and historical background to dispel the Armenian "myth" concerning the origins of the Nagorny Karabakh problem, the accusations of massacres of Armenians in Sumgayit, Ganja and Baku, and the argument that Armenian aggression against Azerbaijan was carried out to ensure the right to self-determination by Armenians in Nagorny Karabakh. As to the 19 February incident, Azerbaijan advised against making accusations while the investigation was still under way, and capitalizing on the incident to appease internal consumption and misguide the international community. In response to accusations that its leadership was "fuelling aggressiveness", Azerbaijan said that its society was determined to resolve the conflict by peaceful means and that Armenia was trying to camouflage its annexationist plans.

On 16 March [A/59/66-S/2004/219], Azerbaijan transmitted to the Secretary-General and the Security Council President a memorandum on the legal aspects of the conflict in and around the Nagorny Karabakh region of Azerbaijan. In a communication of 11 May [S/2004/380], its Foreign Minister, on the occasion of the tenth anniversary of the ceasefire, said that despite the numerous mediation efforts of the international community, in particular the OSCE Minsk Group, no real progress had been made to achieve a peaceful settlement of the conflict, and proposed, as an initial step towards such a settlement, the evacuation of Azerbaijan's territories currently under occupation and the restoration of transportation links in the region.

On 12 July [S/2004/562], Azerbaijan said that the Armenian separatist regime established in the occupied territories of Azerbaijan had declared its intention to hold "elections" to the "local self-governance bodies" on 8 August. Such "elections" had no legitimacy as they contravened international law and Azerbaijan's national legisla-

tion and would negatively affect the search for a peaceful settlement of the conflict. Azerbaijan reaffirmed that the formation of legitimate authorities of any kind in the Nagorny Karabakh region of Azerbaijan was possible only when a just settlement of the conflict was achieved on the basis of international law, Security Council resolutions and relevant OSCE decisions.

Armenia confirmed, on 20 July [S/2004/581], that local self-governance elections in Nagorny Karabakh were to be held on 8 August, as the most recent of a series of presidential, parliamentary and local elections held there over the past 10 years. Popularly elected authorities were an important factor in the negotiation and implementation process of any agreement that might be reached, and an expression of the people's right to self-determination. Elections did not adversely affect the negotiations, nor legitimize the current status. Armenia suggested that the international community consider monitoring the elections to ascertain their compliance with international standards.

On 4 August [A/59/212-S/2004/626], Azerbaijan expressed concern over military training exercises conducted in the occupied territories of Azerbaijan by Armenian armed forces, which, it said, were really illegal armed groups of the separatist regime established by Armenia. Together with the intention to hold illegal elections in the occupied territories of Azerbaijan on 8 August, the holding of such exercises was just another provocation by the Armenian side, which exacerbated the atmosphere surrounding the proposed participation of Armenia in the NATO Cooperative Best Effort 2004 exercises in September in Azerbaijan, and complicated preparations for the forthcoming negotiations between the two countries.

Armenia, on 17 August [A/59/273-S/2004/653], described the Azerbaijan complaint as another attempt to divert the international community's attention from its unconstructive stance in the negotiations within the framework of the Minsk Group on the Nagorny Karabakh conflict. Armenia called on the Azerbaijani authorities to engage constructively and pragmatically in the peace process.

Azerbaijan complained on 3 September [A/59/333-S/2004/717] that Armenia was establishing illegal settlements in the occupied Azerbaijani territories by settling the Armenian population in those territories, in an effort to annex that region through a forceful solution.

Armenia transmitted to the Secretary-General on 18 November [A/59/576-S/2004/913] excerpts of speeches by Azerbaijani leaders as examples of their unwillingness to engage in the search for a peaceful resolution of the Nagorny Karabakh conflict.

Azerbaijan, on 26 February [S/2004/165], transmitted a statement by Khojaly refugees addressed to the United Nations, the Council of Europe and OSCE, adopted at a meeting of Khojaly refugees on 12 February, in connection with the twelfth anniversary of the Khojaly genocide committed by Armenian forces in Nagorny Karabakh on 26 February 1992.

EU statement on Azerbaijan. The EU, in a 9 January statement [S/2004/47] on Azerbaijan, welcomed the decree issued by its President on 29 December 2003 pardoning 160 prisoners, more than a third of whom were political prisoners, as a positive step by Azerbaijan in respect of its obligations to the Council of Europe. However, the EU remained concerned about the situation of those arrested following the disturbances of 16 October 2003 and urged the Azeri authorities to ensure that they would soon be brought to a fair and open trial or released.

Cyprus

After more than 40 years of efforts by the United Nations, through the Secretary-General's mission of good offices, the Cyprus problem remained unresolved at the end of 2004, with little immediate prospects of reaching an understanding on how to proceed. Following a breakdown of negotiations in 2003 between the Greek Cypriot and Turkish Cypriot sides, the Secretary-General, after receiving assurances from both sides of their determination to resume those efforts, convened talks on 10 February 2004 in Cyprus, which resulted in the 13 February Agreement on the modalities for negotiating and finalizing the text of a settlement. Talks were reconvened in Cyprus on 19 February and continued in Bürgenstock, Switzerland, on 24 March. As no further agreement was achieved, the Secretary-General, in accordance with the 13 February Agreement, finalized the text on the basis of his own plan. The "Comprehensive Settlement of the Cyprus Problem", which comprised, among other things, a Foundation Agreement, constituent State constitutions, a treaty on matters related to the new state of affairs, and a draft act of adaptation of the terms of accession to the EU, was submitted for approval by each side in simultaneous referenda held on 24 April. The Greek Cypriot electorate, by a margin of three to one, rejected the settlement proposal; on the Turkish Cypriot side, it was approved by a margin of two to one.

Therefore, the Foundation Agreement could not enter into force and all the related agreements of the Comprehensive Settlement became null and void. The Republic of Cyprus acceded to EU membership on 1 May, putting into question the future status of the northern part of the island.

The Secretary-General said that he respected the outcome of the referenda but ended his mission of good offices. In the circumstances, he reviewed the mandate and concept of operations of the United Nations Peacekeeping Force in Cyprus (UNFICYP) and recommended a reduction in the mission's military component and a new concept of operations based on increased mobility. He undertook to maintain continuous contact at the highest level with the parties and promised to designate, on an ad hoc basis, senior Secretariat officials to deal with various aspects of his mission of good offices. The Security Council extended UNFICYP's mandate, as revised, until June 2005.

Incidents and position statements

Communications. Throughout 2004, the Secretary-General received letters from the Government of Cyprus and from the Turkish Cypriot authorities containing charges and countercharges, protests and accusations, and explanations of position regarding the question of Cyprus. The letters from the "Turkish Republic of Northern Cyprus" were transmitted by Turkey.

In communications dated between 16 March and 16 December, Cyprus reported violations of its national airspace and unauthorized intrusions into Nicosia's flight information region by Turkish military aircraft, while those from the "Turkish Republic of Northern Cyprus" claimed the existence of two independent States on the island of Cyprus and that the flights mentioned took place within the sovereign airspace of the "Turkish Republic of Northern Cyprus" [A/58/739-S/2004/218, A/58/797-S/2004/391, A/58/804-S/2004/399, A/58/844-S/2004/507, A/58/858-S/2004/597, A/58/880-S/2004/700, A/58/885-S/2004/720, A/59/564-S/2004/893, A/59/589-S/2004/940, A/59/627-S/2004/980].

In other communications, the "Turkish Republic of Northern Cyprus", on 8 January [A/58/678-S/2004/13], and 24 November [A/59/580-S/2004/926] refuted allegations against Turkey and the "Turkish Republic of Northern Cyprus" contained in statements made by the representatives of the Greek Cypriot administration during meetings of the various committees of the General Assembly at its fifty-eighth session and at a 27 October meeting of the Fourth (Special Political and Decolonization) Committee during the Assembly's fifty-ninth session under the agenda item "Comprehensive review of the whole question of peacekeeping operations in all their aspects".

In a 28 May letter [A/58/815-S/2004/438], Cyprus outlined the social benefits that its Government offered to Turkish Cypriots in the south and efforts to expand intra-island trade, and all measures aimed at promoting reunification of the island and allowing the Turkish Cypriots to enjoy the benefits of the accession of Cyprus to the EU, effective 1 May. On 23 July [A/58/857-S/2004/596], Cyprus described its recent confidence-building measures aimed at promoting cooperation and confidence between the two communities. It proposed the opening of eight additional crossing points along the ceasefire line, demining by both sides, disengagement of military forces from the walled part of the capital, Nicosia, and from the wider Dherinia-Famagusta and Strovilia areas, and restricting military manoeuvres. On 6 August [A/58/865-S/2004/628], Cyprus informed the Secretary-General of further confidence-building measures it had recently announced. They included measures on the circulation of public-service vehicles owned by Turkish Cypriots, and measures to facilitate the movement of goods and the development of contacts and economic relations between Greek Cypriots and Turkish Cypriots. The measures were in line with the EU policy to facilitate reunification of the island by encouraging the economic development of the Turkish Cypriot community, through proposals aimed at the economic integration of the island and contacts between the two communities and with the EU.

The "Turkish Republic of Northern Cyprus", in an 18 August response [A/58/876-S/2004/675], said that the so-called confidence-building measures were beyond comprehension, as they were presented at the time when the Greek Cypriots had rejected, in the April referendum (see p. 440), the Secretary-General's plan for a power-sharing arrangement, thereby ensuring that the proposed measures and their benefits, including unification, did not materialize. The proposals were aimed at preventing the European Council's proposals on special conditions for trade with North Cyprus from materializing. By the same letter, the "Turkish Republic of Northern Cyprus" rejected the claim by Cyprus, conveyed in a 26 July letter to the Secretary-General [A/58/859-S/2004/ 598], that Turkey was trying to legitimize partition through force and wanted to consolidate the status quo.

In a 6 September letter [A/58/887-S/2004/727], the "Turkish Republic of Northern Cyprus" said that further confidence-building proposals of the Greek Cypriot administration showed its intention to extend its illegal authority to the Turk-

ish Cypriot economic side and to hold Turkish Cypriot development hostage to its political considerations.

Good offices mission

Resumption of negotiations

The Secretary-General, following the failure in 2003 of his efforts to resolve the Cyprus problem on the basis of his 2002 settlement plan "Basis for Agreement on a Comprehensive Settlement of the Cyprus Problem" [YUN 2002, p. 400] as revised in 2003 [YUN 2003, p. 448], and in keeping with his decision [ibid., p. 449] not to take a new initiative unless there was reason to believe that the political will existed for a successful outcome, sought an unequivocally stated preparedness on the part of the leaders of both sides to resume negotiations. He described the UN efforts at mediation in reports to the Security Council of 16 April [S/2004/302], 28 May [S/2004/437] and 24 September [S/2004/756].

Turkey's Prime Minister, Recep Tayyip Erdogan, at a meeting with the Secretary-General in Davos, Switzerland, on 24 January, conveyed Turkey's new policy on Cyprus and expressed its support for a resumption of negotiations. He preferred that the main issues be dealt with by 1 May, the date of Cyprus's entry into the EU, and that a political figure be appointed to handle the negotiations. Turkey had no objection to the Secretary-General finalizing the plan should the parties fail to agree on all issues. The Greek Cypriot leader reiterated to the Secretary-General in Brussels, at a meeting on 29 January, his call for the resumption of substantive negotiations on the basis of the Secretary-General's revised settlement plan, stressing categorically that he sought a solution before 1 May. He reassured the Secretary-General that the changes he sought would not be overly numerous, set out his view that negotiations should resume before a decision was taken about holding a referendum, and promised to get back to the Secretary-General on his idea that there should be parameters to guide the Secretary-General should it fall to him to finalize the plan.

The Greek Government and the leader of the opposition supported a renewal of the Secretary-General's efforts. The EU, preferring the accession of a reunited Cyprus on 1 May to EU membership, concurred.

The Secretary-General, in letters of 4 February, invited Tassos Papadopoulos, the President of Cyprus, and Rauf Denktash, the Turkish Cypriot leader, to begin negotiations on 10 February in New York. He also invited the Prime Ministers of the guarantor Powers (Greece, Turkey, United Kingdom), and suggested modalities to ensure that negotiations would be completed and the plan finalized by 31 March, and that referenda would be conducted on a fixed date before 1 May. The proposal was accepted by all parties. Among the procedures outlined by the Secretary-General were the following: the parties would meet to negotiate, on the basis of the plan, changes to the Foundation Agreement; Greece and Turkey would meet on issues of security; and the parties would appoint technical committees to complete the texts on constitutional laws, co-operation agreements and federal laws, as well as a list of treaties binding on the United Cyprus Republic. The parties would also agree on the nominees to the Supreme Court and the transitional Board of the Central Bank; appoint anthem committees to recommend a flag and anthem of the United Cyprus Republic; and provide the Secretary-General with a proposed Constituent State constitution consistent with the Foundation Agreement. If the parties failed to agree, the Secretary-General would, by 31 March, complete the text, on the basis of which the three guarantor Powers would confirm their agreement to put the Foundation Agreement to separate simultaneous referenda and their commitment to sign, together with the United Cyprus Republic, the treaty on matters related to the new state of affairs in Cyprus. The parties would ask the Security Council to take decisions as set out in the appendix to the plan entitled "Matters to Be Submitted to the United Nations Security Council for Decision". Should the Foundation Agreement be approved, it would enter into force the day after confirmation by the Secretary-General; if not, it would be null and void and the commitments undertaken by the parties would have no legal effect.

The 13 February agreement

On 10 February, each leader put forward, at the Secretary-General's request, an overview of the changes sought to the plan. However, neither Mr. Papadopoulos nor Mr. Denktash accepted the proposed procedures either for formalizing the finalization of the plan or the commitment to hold a referendum. In a change of position, Mr. Denktash proposed, on 11 February, a three-stage procedure, which, he said, had the support of Turkey and conformed broadly with the parameters proposed by the Secretary-General. That procedure would enlarge the Secretary-General's role from completing any unfinished parts of the plan to resolving any deadlocks in the negotiations. To facilitate agreement, the Secretary-General proposed a draft press statement, retaining the core el-

ements of Mr. Denktash's proposal while incorporating the clarifications sought by Mr. Papadopoulos and other elements contained in the Secretary-General's 4 February letter (see p. 435).

The Secretary-General's Special Adviser, Alvaro de Soto, negotiated the final terms of that statement (see below) between the leaders, and the representatives of Greece and Turkey. The main issues dividing the parties were whether organizations other than the United Nations should participate in the negotiations, and the way in which the role of Greece and Turkey in the culminating phases of the process would be presented. On 13 February, all parties agreed to the Secretary-General's final proposal to resolve those issues. The 13 February agreement, as it came to be known, committed the parties to a three-phase process leading to referenda on a finalized plan before 1 May 2004.

Press statement by Secretary-General. The Secretary-General, in a 13 February press statement, announced that the parties had committed to negotiating in good faith on the basis of his plan to achieve a comprehensive settlement of the Cyprus problem through separate and simultaneous referenda before 1 May. To that end, they would seek to agree on changes sought and to complete the plan in all aspects by 22 March, within the framework of the Secretary-General's mission of good offices, so as to produce a finalized text. In the absence of such an agreement, the Secretary-General would convene a meeting of the two sides, with the participation of Greece and Turkey, in an effort to agree on a finalized text by 29 March. As a final resort, in the event of continuing deadlock, the parties would invite the Secretary-General to use his discretion to finalize the text to be submitted to referenda on the basis of the plan. The parties also agreed to other suggestions contained in the Secretary-General's 4 February letter. They decided to form a technical committee on economic and financial aspects of implementation, to be chaired by the United Nations. The guarantor Powers had signified their commitment to that process and to meeting their obligations under it.

The talks would reconvene in Cyprus on 19 February, with direct meetings between the two parties in the presence of the Special Adviser, with the technical committees on laws and treaties reconvening on the same day.

Negotiating process

Cyprus phase (phase 1)

The first phase of the resumed negotiations was held in Cyprus between 19 February and 22 March. The Special Adviser asked the parties to explain in specific terms, with proposed textual amendments, the changes they sought to the plan. On 24 February, the Turkish Cypriot side submitted a list of proposed changes, covering all issues, a number of which would have substantially altered key parameters of the plan. Those initial proposals were replaced in mid-March by less far-reaching proposed textual amendments, described as a priority list. Despite its expressed interest in demarcating the boundary between the constituent States, the Turkish Cypriot side failed to produce a territorial proposal, or to propose a way for the issue to be discussed.

The Greek Cypriot side, by contrast, took each issue in turn, producing dense and lengthy papers explaining the changes sought and annexing proposed textual amendments. Declining to provide a comprehensive text of proposed changes or to prioritize its demands, it stated that none of its proposed changes took away any rights from the Turkish Cypriots, and few, if any, required trade-offs on subjects of interest to the Turkish Cypriots. While the Turkish Cypriot side was generally prepared to engage on Greek Cypriot proposals and to discuss matters on a realistic basis and made counter-offers and compromise proposals, the Greek Cypriot side insisted on full satisfaction of its demands, while arguing that the Turkish Cypriot 24 February paper (see above) was outside the parameters of the plan and thus precluded engagement with Turkish Cypriot proposals. It did not alter its attitude to Turkish Cypriot concerns. The Turkish Cypriot side argued that the Greek Cypriot delay in exposing the extent of its demands was preventing the beginning of real negotiation, and amounted to filibustering. The Greek Cypriot side countered that the Turkish Cypriot failure to produce a territorial proposal left a hole at the centre of its demands and the Greek Cypriot side in the dark.

Since progress was proving difficult through either face-to-face meetings or working-level bilateral consultations, the two sides agreed to the Special Adviser's suggestion that the direct meetings be replaced, beginning on 15 March, by proximity talks in an effort to narrow differences and facilitate give and take in the run-up to phase 2 of the process. He also proposed a framework to allow for trade-offs, and encouraged the two sides to identify priorities, reaffirming that changes to the plan would have to be balanced across all issues.

The Greek Cypriot side was critical of the suggested framework, while the Turkish Cypriot side responded more positively. The asymmetry of the response, together with the mini-crisis provoked by Mr. Denktash's decision not to attend phase 2 of the process, prevented the United Nations from proposing trade-offs on the remaining major issues in phase 1. To resolve at least some of the secondary issues before the end of phase 1, a final meeting of the leaders on the island was held on 22 March. During the first phase, representatives of Greece and Turkey met in Athens, Greece, on 17 March, at the invitation of the United Nations, to discuss security.

In contrast to the slow progress at the political level, the seven technical committees produced 131 completed laws and cooperation agreements, a list of 1,134 treaties and instruments binding on the United Cyprus Republic, recommendations on a flag and an anthem, detailed recommendations on the economic and financial aspects of the plan and its implementation, the organizational charts of the federal Government, comprising 6,181 positions, and a list of buildings on each side to house the federal Government during a transitional period.

Bürgenstock phases (phases 2 and 3)

Phase 2 of the talks began in Bürgenstock, Switzerland, on 24 March. It was attended by Mr. Papadopoulos, the Foreign Ministers of Greece and Turkey, later joined on 28 and 29 March by their respective Prime Ministers, the Secretary-General and the European Commissioner for Enlargement. Rauf Denktash did not attend, but authorized Mehmet Ali Talat and Serdar Denktash to negotiate with full powers on behalf of the Turkish Cypriots. Due to differing views as to the appropriate format, it was not possible to have face-to-face meetings. The United Nations therefore consulted with all parties, exploring compromise suggestions and ascertaining their priorities and possible areas of flexibility. Despite those efforts, the opportunity was not taken for open and frank dialogue. The Secretary-General subsequently made bridging proposals in the form of a revised text. The Turkish Cypriot side and Turkey suggested further amendments, while the Greek Cypriot side made public its dissatisfaction with the Secretary-General's proposals. On 30 March, it communicated, for the first time, its views on the UN proposals regarding a framework for signature and expressed interest in additional territory. Greece expressed concern about certain aspects of the security provisions of the settlement.

As no agreement was achievable at that stage, the process moved to phase 3 as envisaged in the 13 February agreement (see p. 436), in which the Secretary-General would use his discretion and finalize the text on the basis of his plan. On 31 March, he presented a finalized plan, which included further changes beyond those already suggested in his bridging proposals and outlined the procedures to be followed during April in the run-up to the referenda. The text of the "Comprehensive Settlement of the Cyprus Problem" (www.annanplan.org) called for action by the Security Council.

Comprehensive Settlement of the Cyprus Problem

The "Comprehensive Settlement of the Cyprus Problem" comprised, as appendices, a Foundation Agreement, constituent State constitutions, the treaty on matters related to the new state of affairs in Cyprus, the draft act of adaptation of the terms of accession of the United Cyprus Republic to the EU, matters to be submitted to the Security Council for decision (see p. 436) and measures to be taken during April 2004.

The Foundation Agreement included the 14 main articles, which summarized the key elements of the plan, and to which were annexed the Constitution of the United Cyprus Republic, its constitutional laws, its Federal Laws, the cooperation agreements between the federal Government and the constituent States, the list of international treaties and instruments that the United Cyprus Republic would accede to, the territorial arrangements, the provisions relating to property affected by events since 1963, the provisions establishing the Reconciliation Commission, and the provisions on the coming into being of the new state of affairs in Cyprus. That was the part of the plan to be put to referenda on 24 April, together with the respective constituent State constitutions.

The treaty on matters related to the new state of affairs in Cyprus provided for a Monitoring Committee and for Additional Protocols to the Treaties of Establishment, Guarantee and Alliance, and transitional security arrangements related to the dissolution of local forces and withdrawal and redeployment of Greek and Turkish forces. Following the completion of all internal ratification procedures by the guarantors after the referenda, the treaty was to be signed into force on 29 April; the Foundation Agreement would only enter into force when the guarantors had signed the treaty, thereby bringing into being the new state of affairs in Cyprus, after which the Co-Presidents of the United Cyprus Republic would sign, bringing the treaty itself into force.

The Security Council would take decisions to enter into force simultaneously with the Foundation Agreement—it would endorse that Agreement, prohibit the supply of arms to Cyprus and authorize a UN operation there (see below).

Measures to be taken during April, contained in a work programme, were to ensure that the federal public service and federal property and buildings would be provided for, that a list of no more than 45,000 persons would be provided for the purposes of the federal citizenship law, and that the members of the transitional Government would be identified should the referenda be successful.

Security Council consideration. The Security Council met on 2 April [meeting 4940] to consider the situation in Cyprus. In his briefing to the Council, the Secretary-General's Special Adviser said that the most important change made to the plan during the March talks related to the reinstatement of property to people who were dispossessed. Under the revised scheme, the amount of land reinstated to dispossessed owners and the number of displaced and dispossessed persons to be reinstated to some of their property would increase. Certain restrictions on the acquisition of property in the Turkish Cypriot State would be permissible during a transitional period.

The revised plan also dealt with the issues of the residency by persons from one constituent State in the other constituent State and the establishment of residency by Greek and Turkish nationals in Cyprus. The transitional limitations were designed to prevent, on either side, unrestricted residence and immigration or unlimited property purchases, and to ensure that the identity of Cyprus and its constituent States was maintained. There were no permanent derogations from the EU acquis communautaire (the body of European treaties, regulations and judgements).

The workings of the federal Government were revised in three respects. First, the transitional periods were shortened, with elections to be held at the federal and constituent State levels, along with European Parliament elections, on 13 June. Secondly, membership of the Presidential Council was increased from six to nine members, with provision for two persons not from the same constituent State to rotate in the offices of President and Vice-President in three 20-month periods over the 60-month term of the Presidential Council. Thirdly, voting for the Senate would be on the basis of mother tongue, rather than internal citizenship status, to ensure that political equality was not undermined over time.

Improvements were made regarding the economic and financial aspects of the plan, largely based on the agreed recommendations of experts from each side in the technical committees.

The map in the plan was not changed, but the plan envisaged that, in the last months of each phased handover of territory, the United Nations would supervise the transfer of areas subject to territorial adjustment. New details of measures to assist in relocation of persons who had to move as a result of territorial adjustment were introduced.

Important refinements were made regarding security. The provisions relating to troop withdrawal were altered, so that the 6,000 Greek and Turkish troops permitted to remain in Cyprus under the previous plan, on the proviso that all would leave should Turkey accede to the EU, would drop to 3,000 in 2011 and to 950 Greek troops and 650 Turkish troops (the same number permitted under the 1960 Treaty of Alliance) in 2018 or upon Turkey's EU accession (whichever was earlier).

Press statement by Security Council President. The Security Council President, in a 16 April press statement [SC/8061], said that Council members welcomed the results of the preparatory International Donors Conference for Cyprus held on 15 April in Brussels to cover costs linked to a possible political settlement to the Cyprus question. They recognized the commitments of the donors as a demonstration of their willingness to provide the necessary financial resources to implement the Secretary-General's "Comprehensive Settlement of the Cyprus Problem" should the Cypriots vote to approve the plan. Council members affirmed that it was for the Cypriots to take a historic decision concerning their future in the 24 April referenda. Should the plan be approved, Council members stood ready to take further actions as provided for in the plan, including the establishment of a new UN operation in support of swift and full implementation by all parties. Council members would be committed to helping ensure that the parties fully met their commitments under the settlement.

*Matters submitted
to Security Council for decision*

As provided for in the "Comprehensive Settlement of the Cyprus Problem", the Secretary-General, in his 16 April report on Cyprus [S/2004/302], mentioned those matters requiring Security Council action, including: endorsement of the Foundation Agreement, in particular taking note that any unilateral change in the state of affairs established by the Agreement was prohibited; prohibition of the supply of arms to Cyprus; and establishing a UN peacekeeping operation in Cyprus with the concurrence of the constituent States to monitor implementation of the Foundation Agreement, promote compliance with it and contribute to the maintenance of a secure environment.

The Secretary-General said that the decisions requested of the Council were a crucial part of the overall framework of the settlement, providing additional assurance that it would be implemented in the framework of UN principles. He

was requesting the Council to consider his submission in advance of the 24 April referenda, in the hope that it would assure Cypriots that the United Nations was prepared to meet its responsibilities foreseen under the plan. In accordance with the plan, the Council decisions would enter into force simultaneously with the Foundation Agreement on 29 April.

Security Council consideration. The Security Council met on 21 April [meeting 4947] to consider the Secretary-General's 16 April report. It had before it a draft resolution [S/2004/313] submitted by the United Kingdom and the United States, by which the Council, following notification by the Secretary-General to the Council President that the Foundation Agreement had entered into force, would have terminated UNFICYP's mandate and established the United Nations Settlement Implementation Mission in Cyprus (UNSIMIC) to monitor implementation of the Foundation Agreement and the security and political situation, promote compliance with the Agreement and contribute to a secure environment. The Council would also have decided that all States should prevent the sale, supply or transfer of arms and related materiel to Cyprus, except for those circumstances specified in the draft resolution, and established a committee to monitor implementation of that decision.

Speaking before the vote, the Russian Federation said that it had consistently supported the Secretary-General's good offices mission and his efforts aimed at a just settlement of the Cyprus problem; however, it believed that the 24 April referenda should take place without external interference or pressure and that the Council should await the results before taking a decision. The draft resolution involved the formulation of a serious decision on the parameters of a new UN operation in Cyprus and the imposition of an arms embargo. Such a technically and legally complex decision called for the most thorough and careful analysis. Opposition to such precipitous action on the eve of the referenda was expressed by the parties directly interested in the settlement and by the majority of Council members. Under those circumstances, the Russian Federation had no other choice but to exercise a veto on technical grounds. It was prepared to take part in formulating a draft resolution on the issue after the referenda.

The draft resolution was not adopted owing to the negative vote of a permanent member (Russian Federation) of the Council (14-1).

Speaking after the vote, the United Kingdom said the fact that the overwhelming majority of the Council had voted in favour of the draft sent a strong message of support for the Secretary-

General's efforts and his plan. The draft resolution remained on the table and the United Kingdom would ask the Council to take speedy action after the referenda. The United States said the vote demonstrated that the opposition to the draft resolution was isolated. If the settlement was approved by Cypriots in the referenda, the Council would act rapidly to establish UNSIMIC and an arms embargo.

The 24 April referenda

After the Bürgenstock meetings, the leaders on each side took positions regarding the 24 April referenda. On the Turkish Cypriot side, one of their negotiators, Mr. Talat, came out strongly in favour of a "Yes" vote, while the Turkish Cypriot leader, Rauf Denktash, opposed it. The other negotiator, Serdar Denktash, took a neutral position. Turkey's Prime Minister Erdogan and Foreign Minister Abdullah Gül spoke out strongly in favour of a "Yes" vote. Messrs. Erdogan, Gül and Talat also sought to convey to the Greek Cypriot public, by statements, interviews and Mr. Talat's visit to the south, the determination of the Turkish Cypriots and Turkey to abide by their commitments under the plan and fully implement a settlement.

On the Greek Cypriot side, the situation was more complex. Mr. Papadopoulos, in a speech on 7 April, called on the people to reject the plan with a "resounding No" and challenged the wisdom of "doing away with our internationally recognized State exactly at the very moment it strengthens its political weight, with its accession to the European Union". The Secretary-General expressed surprise at the statement, in the light of what Mr. Papadopoulos had said to him in Brussels. In addition to the support of the Greek Government, the plan received the unequivocal support of Mr. Papadopoulos's two immediate predecessors, Glafcos Clerides and George Vassiliou, and of the leader of the second largest political party, Nicos Anastasiades. After calling for the postponement of the referenda, Mr. Papadopoulos's coalition partner in government, which was the largest political party in Cyprus, called for a "soft No" to the plan, unless additional guarantees were provided regarding security and implementation.

The United Nations had made the plan and information about it available on its website in Greek and Turkish since early 2003. It also provided information and gave briefings to civil society groups on request. However, its efforts were hampered by the media climate on the island.

The referenda were held on 24 April. The plan was rejected by 75.8 per cent of Greek Cypriot voters and approved by 24.2 per cent. On the Turkish Cypriot side, the plan was approved by 64.9 per cent of voters and rejected by 35.1 per cent.

Statement by Secretary-General. In a statement [S/2004/437, annex III] issued on 24 April, the Secretary-General, while affirming that a unique opportunity to resolve the Cyprus problem had been missed, said that he respected the outcome of the two referenda. He applauded the Turkish Cypriots, who approved the plan notwithstanding the significant sacrifices that it entailed for many of them. He regretted that they would not enjoy the benefits of EU membership as of 1 May, but hoped that ways would be found to ease their plight. The Secretary-General remained convinced that the settlement plan represented a fair, viable and carefully balanced compromise. Noting that a large majority of the Greek Cypriot electorate did not share that view, he hoped that they might arrive at a different view after a profound and sober assessment of the decision. He would report to the Council, which might wish to evaluate the outcome and its implications.

Security Council consideration. The Security Council met on 28 April [meeting 4954] to consider the situation in Cyprus, having before it the Secretary-General's April report [S/2004/302] (see p. 439). In briefing the Council, the Under-Secretary-General for Political Affairs said that the full implications of the outcome of the referenda would take a while to become apparent. While the results were disappointing and the Secretary-General's objective of reuniting Cyprus in time for accession to the EU by 1 May had not been met, the United Nations had nevertheless come closer than ever before to resolving one of the most delicate and complex conflicts on its agenda. That achievement should be preserved, pending a fundamental re-evaluation on the Greek Cypriot side.

The Council continued discussion on the subject in informal consultations.

Implications of the vote

The Secretary-General, in his 28 May report [S/2004/437] on his mission of good offices, described the entire 2004 negotiating process and assessed its outcome. He commented that the fate of his plan was a powerful illustration of the difficulties of finding a solution to that long-standing problem. While a comprehensive settlement had proved elusive, a great deal had been achieved in the course of the past four and a half years. The obstacles that had prevented Cyprus initiatives from getting beyond generalities were overcome, resulting in a comprehensive and carefully balanced settlement proposal, ready to be implemented. Although the plan was legally null and void in the aftermath of the referenda, its acceptance by the Turkish Cypriot electorate meant that the shape of any final settlement to re-unify Cyprus would appear to be set. The plan remained the only foreseeable basis for Cypriots to achieve a settlement.

The rejection of the plan by the Greek Cypriot electorate was a major setback. What was rejected was the solution itself rather than a mere blue-print. Benefits that the Greek Cypriots had sought for decades (including the reunification of Cyprus, the return of a large swathe of terri-tory, the return of most displaced persons to their homes, the withdrawal of all troops not permit-ted by international treaties, the halting of fur-ther Turkish immigration and the return to Tur-key of a number of "settlers") had been foregone. The result was the maintenance of the status quo.

Greek Cypriots rightly expected the interna-tional community to respect their decision, but there was a possibility that, following a period of reflection, a way might emerge to refloat the plan and salvage a settlement. In that context, fears re-garding security and implementation appeared to be prominent among Greek Cypriots. Without reopening the provisions of the plan, the Council should address such fears, provided they could be clearly articulated by the Greek Cypriot side. However, the sheer size of the "No" vote raised even more fundamental questions. That was the first time that the Greek Cypriot public had been asked to vote on a bicommunal, bizonal federal solution of the Cyprus problem. Such a solution meant not just two constituent States, but also political equality and the sharing of power. If the Greek Cypriots were ready to share power and prosperity with the Turkish Cypriots in a federal structure based on political equality, that needed to be demonstrated not just by word but by action.

For their part, the Turkish Cypriots had clearly come out in favour of reunification of Cyprus in a bicommunal, bizonal federation. In opting for a settlement, the Turkish Cypriots had broken with the decades-old policies of seeking recognition of the "State" they purported to have created in 1983 [YUN 1983, p. 253]. While the Turkish Cypriots might feel rebuffed after the 24 April vote, their best course was not to turn their back on reunifi-cation, but to redouble their determination to achieve it. They, and Turkey, should reach out to the Greek Cypriots and promote reconciliation. The situation of the Turkish Cypriots called for the attention of the international community, in-cluding the Security Council. The Turkish Cyp-riot leadership pointed to the disparity between the outcomes of the referenda as evidence that the Greek Cypriot leadership did not speak for the Turkish Cypriots. The vote had undone what-ever rationale might have existed for pressuring and isolating them. The Secretary-General had taken note of the expressed Greek Cypriot inten-tion for the Republic of Cyprus, as an EU mem-ber, to extend to the Turkish Cypriots as many of the benefits of EU membership as were "possible and permissible".

The way ahead

The Secretary-General stated that, as for the future of his mission of good offices, the out-come of the referenda had resulted in a stale-mate. As neither of the parties had made a propo-sal for resolving that impasse, there was no basis for resuming his mission of good offices. In the aftermath of the vote, the Secretary-General be-lieved that a fundamental reassessment of the full range of UN peace activities in Cyprus was timely. He intended to complete a review within three months, of UNFICYP's mandate, force levels and concept of operations, in the light of the de-velopments on the ground, the positions of the parties and any views the Council might have. He urged Council members to encourage the Turk-ish Cypriots and Turkey to remain committed to reunification. For that purpose, he hoped States would cooperate to eliminate unnecessary re-strictions and barriers that had isolated the Turk-ish Cypriots and impeded their development.

The Security Council met on 8 June [meeting 4986] to consider the Secretary-General's May re-port on his mission of good offices (above). The Special Adviser, in briefing the Council, said that while the outcome of the negotiating effort had not been a success, there were achievements that should be built on to keep alive the prospects of reconciliation and reunification in the future. He remarked that what was rejected on 24 April was a comprehensive plan for a settlement, ready for implementation, with nothing further to be ne-gotiated, rather than a mere framework or set of principles for future negotiations. The approval by the Turkish Cypriots of the plan, signalling their commitment to reunification, indicated they had clearly backed away from a search for a separate, sovereign statehood, a fundamental turnabout in their direction for more than two decades. The Secretary-General recommended that the Council encourage the Turkish Cypriots to remain committed to that goal. His call on all States to cooperate to eliminate unnecessary re-strictions and barriers that had the effect of iso-lating the Turkish Cypriots was not meant to give State rights, State functions or State institutions to the so-called "Turkish Republic of Northern Cyprus", nor to afford recognition or assist secession, but rather to promote reunification and reconciliation.

Post referendum positions

President Papadopoulos of Cyprus, in a letter of 7 June [A/58/835-S/2004/464] to the Secretary-General, presented the official Greek Cypriot position on the Secretary-General's May report on his mission of good offices in Cyprus (see p. 440). He said that the concerns of the Greek Cypriot community, which had not been adequately addressed in the final plan of 31 March, were mainly the question of Turkish mainland settlers, the permanent stationing of Turkish military forces in Cyprus, and the expansion of the guarantor Powers' rights emanating from the Treaty of Guarantee, through the inclusion of an additional protocol. He declared that the Cypriot proposal for resolving the disagreement over the interpretation of the rights of the Treaty of Guarantee, between Cyprus and Turkey, was never entertained by the Special Adviser. Under its proposal, a triggering-off mechanism would be set up for the exercise of the right of intervention under the Treaty. Another issue of significance was the lack of time and the tight deadlines, which did not allow for substantial negotiations to take place or for agreed conclusions to be reached.

Mr. Papadopoulos said that there were serious inaccuracies and wrong assumptions in the Secretary-General's report, the most serious being the interpretation of the Greek Cypriot community's choice at the 24 April referendum as a vote against reunification of their country, and that the Greek Cypriots were turning away from a solution based on a bizonal, bicommunal federation. He reiterated his commitment and that of the Greek Cypriot people to such a solution.

Mr. Papadopoulos considered inaccurate the allegation in the Secretary-General's report that the overall amount of property in the Turkish Cypriot State eligible to be reinstated to Greek Cypriots would be roughly doubled as compared with the previous version of the plan, since it included preconditions limiting substantially the right of Greek Cypriots to reinstatement and the percentage of properties to be reinstated. The report also omitted reference to Turkey's benefits under the plan, especially the indefinite stationing of Turkish troops on the island. The plan would have given immediately the Turkish Cypriots considerable benefits governmentally, politically, internationally, economically and security-wise, while the two benefits for Greek Cypriots, namely territorial adjustments and reductions in the size of the Turkish Army in Cyprus, would have taken years to be phased in. Implementation of the plan, especially those provisions of crucial interest to the Greek Cypriots, would have been contingent to Turkey's good will. The new provisions in the plan serving Turkish interests in Cyprus explained why it was overwhelmingly rejected by the Greek Cypriots, approved by the Turkish Cypriot side and so emphatically endorsed by the Turkish Government. The Greek Cypriots also objected to the proposal for the elimination of restrictions and barriers that had the effect of isolating the Turkish Cypriots.

The Secretary-General, in a 15 June response [A/58/843-S/2004/493], said that he stood fully by his report, including the narrative and the analysis, his appeals and recommendations, to which he hoped the Greek Cypriot side would respond positively. The Secretary-General stated that he did not share Mr. Papadopoulos's characterization of the conduct of UN efforts.

Mr. Papadopoulos, in his address during the general debate of the General Assembly on 23 September [A/59/PV.7], outlined the reasons for the failure of the Secretary-General's settlement plan. He stated it was not the product of negotiation, did not constitute an agreed solution between the parties, did not place the necessary emphasis on achieving a central Government able to guarantee the single, sovereign character of Cyprus, and failed to address the Greek Cypriot concerns regarding security and implementation of the plan. In rejecting the plan, the Greek Cypriots did not reject the solution or the reunification of their country; they rejected that particular plan as not achieving that objective. They insisted on certain parameters—the withdrawal of Turkish troops and settlers and respect for the human rights of all Cypriots, the underlying structures for a functioning economy, the functionality and workability of the new state of affairs, the just resolution of land and property issues in accordance with the decisions of the European Court of Human Rights, and respect for refugees' right of return. Cyprus should, in the future, proceed without any grey areas with regard to its sovereignty or its relations with third-party States.

In the EU framework, Cyprus was pursuing policies for the economic development of the Turkish Cypriots, which, while not a substitute for a solution, were the most effective way to foster economic integration of the two communities and increase contact between them so as to ensure the viability of a future solution. The new context defined by the accession of Cyprus to the EU and by the expressed will of Turkey to advance on the European path could have a catalytic effect in reaching a settlement in Cyprus. Cyprus called on Turkey to join it in seeking mutually beneficial solutions to the various aspects of the Cyprus problem.

In a 4 October letter [A/59/434-S/2004/815] transmitted to the Secretary-General by Turkey,

Mr. Talat, Prime Minister of the "Turkish Republic of Northern Cyprus", responding to Mr. Papadopoulous's statement, said that Mr. Papadopoulous himself and his administration were behind the collapse of the Secretary-General's initiative. The Greek Cypriot people were misled by the Greek Cypriot leader in a 7 April address (see p. 440), when he called for his people to reject the plan in order to "achieve their joint strategic goal", which he described as "politically upgrading and shielding their internationally recognized State, the Republic of Cyprus". The Turkish Cypriot leader rejected Mr. Papadopoulos's assertion that the Secretary-General's plan did not adequately address the Greek Cypriot parameters for a solution, and his allegation that the UN plan failed to address Greek Cypriot concerns regarding security and implementation. In Mr. Talat's view, the claim that the plan was not the product of negotiation was inconceivable.

The results of the referenda clearly demonstrated the strong desire of the Turkish Cypriot people for a settlement based on partnership and equality. The Greek Cypriot side, which opted for no settlement, continued to enjoy the benefits of the usurped title of "Republic of Cyprus" and had become an EU member, whereas the Turkish Cypriot side, which voted for a peaceful reunification, not only remained outside the EU but continued to be subjected to political and economic restrictions and isolation. The question was whether the world should continue to close its eyes to that unjust situation and allow the Greek Cypriots to continue pretending that they represented the whole island or honour the Turkish Cypriots with their vested rights to speak and act for themselves. The Turkish Cypriot people expected the international community to address the unjust circumstances and lift the restrictions on economic, social and political development. In that context, the Turkish Cypriot leader welcomed the international community's efforts in response to the Secretary-General's call to eliminate the unnecessary restrictions. However, those efforts aimed at supporting the Turkish Cypriot people's development were being seriously hampered by the Greek Cypriot administration. The Turkish Cypriot side therefore called on the international community to end the isolation of the Turkish Cypriot people and lift the restrictions on their economic and social life in order to facilitate their overall development.

Cyprus, in a letter of 12 August [A/58/869-S/2004/646], drew the Secretary-General's attention to the issue of property rights, specifically the intensification of the illegal exploitation of Greek Cypriot properties in the Turkish occupied areas of Cyprus, through construction on Greek Cypriot-owned land and/or the sale of Greek Cypriot properties to foreigners, and expressed its concern over the repercussions that such actions might have on efforts to find a solution to the Cyprus problem.

The "Turkish Republic of Northern Cyprus", in its response transmitted by Turkey to the Secretary-General on 15 September [A/59/363-S/2004/738], underlined that transactions involving the sale of property in the "Turkish Republic of Northern Cyprus" were a matter concerning only the relevant authorities of the State. The Greek Cypriot claims that the property transactions were illegal and constituted liabilities to the people who purchased them were totally unfounded.

Positions on EU representation

Turkey's Ministry of Foreign Affairs, in a 1 May statement [A/58/781-S/2004/351], affirmed that the Turkish Cypriot people had expressed through a referendum their wish for a political future within the EU as a constituent partner of a united Cyprus. It was incumbent on the EU to acknowledge and act on the free and genuine expression of the will of the Turkish Cypriot people in that regard. It noted that the separate referenda underlined the fact of the existence of two separate peoples on the island, neither of which represented the other. In those circumstances, it was only the Greek Cypriots who would join the EU on 1 May under the terms of the 2003 Treaty of Accession, which was based on a political and legal situation of a divided island and did not allow for accession of a united Cyprus to the EU. The Greek Cypriots, who would join the EU on 1 May, therefore had no legitimate authority to represent the whole of Cyprus or the Turkish Cypriots.

The Cyprus Ministry of Foreign Affairs, in a 17 May response [A/58/803-S/2004/398], stated that the Government of the Republic of Cyprus was the internationally recognized Government in Cyprus, with the competence and authority to represent the State, notwithstanding the de facto division of the island. As from 1 May, the Republic of Cyprus was a full member of the EU. The Treaty of Accession provided for the terms of accession in the event that a comprehensive settlement of the Cyprus problem had not been reached by the date of accession. In that event and even though the entire territory of the Republic of Cyprus became part of the EU, the application of the acquis was suspended in the areas in which the Government did not exercise effective control.

With the aim of facilitating the reunification of Cyprus, the Republic of Cyprus announced to the EU on 26 April its intention to expand the package of measures benefiting the Turkish Cypriots to include trade as well as intra-island trade of manufactured goods produced in the occupied area, and advocated that the 259 million euros earmarked by the EU for 2004-2006 for the Turkish Cypriots in the event of a settlement be made available immediately.

UNFICYP

The United Nations Peacekeeping Force in Cyprus, established in 1964 [YUN 1964, p. 165], continued in 2004 to monitor the ceasefire lines between the Turkish and Turkish Cypriot forces on the northern side and the Cypriot National Guard on the southern side of the island; to maintain the military status quo and prevent a recurrence of fighting; and to undertake humanitarian and economic activities. In the absence of a formal ceasefire agreement, UNFICYP's task was to judge whether changes in military positions constituted violations of the military status quo, as recorded by the Force in 1974. UNFICYP, under the overall authority of the Special Representative and Chief of Mission, Zbigniew Wlosowicz (Poland), continued to keep the area between the ceasefire lines, known as the buffer zone, under constant surveillance through a system of observation posts and through air, vehicle and foot patrols.

During 2004, Alvaro de Soto continued as the Secretary-General's Special Adviser on Cyprus until 24 April. No successor was appointed in 2004.

As at 31 December, UNFICYP, under the command of Major General Herbert Joaquin Figoli Almandos (Uruguay), comprised 1,226 troops and 45 civilian police.

Activities

Report of Secretary-General (May). The Secretary-General, in his 26 May report covering UNFICYP activities and developments from 11 November 2003 to 20 May 2004 [S/2004/427], said that the military situation along the ceasefire line remained generally calm, but the number of air violations increased. The restrictions imposed on UNFICYP's movement in 2000 [YUN 2000, p. 404] by the Turkish Cypriot authorities continued to hinder its operations. The violation of the military status quo in Strovilia persisted. In the latter half of the reporting period, UNFICYP conducted training and planning for a possible transition to a new UN operation in Cyprus, in the event of a settlement. Among its humanitarian tasks,

UNFICYP assisted the orderly movement of civilians and vehicles through the buffer zone at the authorized crossing points at Ledra, Ayios Dometios/Metehan, Pergamos and Strovilia. It monitored and followed up on more than 50 cases of unauthorized crossings, thefts, traffic violations, accidents and unauthorized photography, and also facilitated 32 cases of medical evacuation from the north to medical facilities in the south. UNFICYP also facilitated 138 bicommunal events at the Ledra Palace Hotel, bringing together Greek and Turkish Cypriots. It provided support for civilian activities in the buffer zone, facilitating a project funded by the United Nations Office for Project Services in February to restore the historic Venetian Castle.

The Secretary-General said that, in view of the watershed vote of 24 April (see p. 440), and as part of an overall reappraisal of UN peace activities in Cyprus, he intended to review within three months UNFICYP's mandate, force levels and concept of operations, in the light of developments on the ground, the positions of the parties and any views the Security Council might have. He would submit recommendations on the adjustments or restructuring that might be required. Meanwhile, he recommended that the Council extend UNFICYP's mandate until 15 December 2004.

SECURITY COUNCIL ACTION (June)

On 11 June [meeting 4989], the Security Council unanimously adopted **resolution 1548(2004)**. The draft [S/2004/484] was submitted by the United Kingdom.

The Security Council,

Welcoming the report of the Secretary-General of 26 May 2004 on the United Nations operation in Cyprus, and in particular the call to the parties to assess and address the humanitarian issue of missing persons with due urgency and seriousness,

Noting that the Government of Cyprus has agreed that, in view of the prevailing conditions on the island, it is necessary to keep the United Nations Peacekeeping Force in Cyprus beyond 15 June 2004,

Welcoming the intention of the Secretary-General to conduct a review, to be completed within three months, on the mandate, force levels and concept of operation of the Force, in view of the referenda on 24 April 2004 and taking into account developments on the ground and the views of the parties,

Welcoming and encouraging efforts by the United Nations to sensitize peacekeeping personnel in the prevention and control of HIV/AIDS and other communicable diseases in all its peacekeeping operations,

1. *Reaffirms* all its relevant resolutions on Cyprus, in particular resolution 1251(1999) of 29 June 1999 and subsequent resolutions;

2. *Decides* to extend the mandate of the United Nations Peacekeeping Force in Cyprus for a further period, ending 15 December 2004, and to consider the

recommendations of the Secretary-General in his review of the Force and to act upon them within one month of receiving them;

3. *Urges* the Turkish Cypriot side and the Turkish forces to rescind without delay all remaining restrictions on the Force, and calls upon them to restore in Strovilia the military status quo which existed there prior to 30 June 2000;

4. *Requests* the Secretary-General to submit a report on the implementation of the present resolution concurrent with the report provided for above;

5. *Decides* to remain seized of the matter.

Report of Secretary-General (September). In a 24 September report on UNFICYP [S/2004/756], the Secretary-General stated that official contacts between leaders of the two sides had ceased since the referenda, and signs of mutual distrust had reappeared. Their position on the Secretary-General's mission of good offices had not changed and, accordingly, he saw no basis for resuming his good offices as long as the impasse continued. On 1 May, Cyprus joined the EU, but key decisions on EU relations with Turkey and with the Turkish Cypriots had yet to be taken, which caused considerable uncertainty on both sides of the island. The Greek Cypriot side opposed the EU's recommendations on direct trade and had proposed its own set of economic and confidence-building measures, which were largely dismissed by the Turkish Cypriot side (see p. 442). Despite the absence of direct relations at the official level, contacts between ordinary Cypriots continued to grow. The movement of people was further facilitated by the Greek Cypriot side's willingness to accept entry to the south by EU nationals and Cyprus visa holders entering the island through ports in the north. For their part, the Turkish Cypriot authorities agreed to accept Greek Cypriot identity cards, rather than passports, when crossing the buffer zone to the north.

In terms of confidence-building measures, the Greek Cypriot side proposed in June, through UNFICYP, the withdrawal of military equipment and the unmanning of positions around the old town of Nicosia and in the Dherynia-Famagusta area, and a ban on military exercises and use of heavy equipment for 2 kilometres on both sides of the ceasefire line. Those proposals had yet to be taken up by the other side. The Greek Cypriot side also proposed the opening of eight additional crossing points, which the Turkish Cypriot side welcomed in principle and (see p. 443) UNFICYP supported. UNFICYP also facilitated land passage given to Turkish Cypriots for the annual August visit to Kokkina. The Turkish Cypriots allowed the opening of a secondary school in the Karpas for Greek Cypriot children. The Committee on Missing Persons in Cyprus resumed meetings on 30 August, after a hiatus of more than four years.

In response to resolution 1548(2004) (see p. 444), UNFICYP review teams conducted an in-depth assessment of the developments on the ground and the evolving role of UNFICYP's three components (political/civil affairs, civilian police and military) over the years. Also participating in the review, a Secretariat team visited UNFICYP from 29 August to 5 September and consulted with both sides. The Secretary-General concurred with the findings and recommended a reduction of the strength of the UNFICYP military component from an authorized strength of 1,230 to 860 all ranks, including 40 military observers/liaison officers. The civilian police deployment, currently at 44, should be increased, while remaining within the authorized strength of 69. The new concept of operations, to be known as "concentration with mobility", would shift from static to mobile surveillance, better use of technology, including closed circuit television and improved information technology, and additional helicopter hours. The mission's political and civil affairs component would be strengthened by a small increase in staff. Those measures would allow UNFICYP to carry out its mandated tasks, while taking into account the changed environment and achieving a more efficient use of resources. A further review was to take place before the end of the next mandate period, in mid-2005.

The Secretary-General indicated that he did not intend to appoint a full-time Special Adviser at that time, although political developments might require an appointment at some stage. Therefore, the Chief of Mission would act as the Special Representative to maintain continuous contact at the highest level with the two sides and other key players. In support of the expanded function, UNFICYP's capacity for political analysis and reporting needed to be strengthened. He would consider designating, on an ad hoc basis, senior Secretariat officials to deal with any particular aspects of the Secretary-General's mission of good offices that might require special attention. He recommended that the Council approve UNFICYP's amended concept of operations and force level and extend its mandate until 15 June 2005 to allow for implementation of the restructuring and for experience to be gained before a further review.

SECURITY COUNCIL ACTION (October)

On 22 October [meeting 5061], the Security Council unanimously adopted **resolution 1568**

(2004). The draft [S/2004/829] was submitted by the United Kingdom.

The Security Council,

Welcoming the report of the Secretary-General of 24 September 2004 on the United Nations operation in Cyprus,

Reiterating its call to the parties to assess and address the humanitarian issue of missing persons with due urgency and seriousness, and welcoming in this regard the resumption of the activities of the Committee on Missing Persons since August 2004,

Welcoming the Secretary-General's review of the United Nations Peacekeeping Force in Cyprus, pursuant to resolution 1548(2004) of 11 June 2004,

Noting that the Government of Cyprus has agreed that in view of the prevailing conditions on the island it is necessary to keep the Force beyond 15 December 2004,

Taking note of the assessment of the Secretary-General that the security situation on the island has become increasingly benign over the last few years and that a recurrence of fighting in Cyprus is increasingly unlikely,

Welcoming the Secretary-General's intention to conduct a further review on the mandate, force levels and concept of operation of the Force in advance of the next renewal of its mandate, continuing to take into account developments on the ground and the views of the parties,

Echoing the Secretary-General's gratitude to the Government of Cyprus and the Government of Greece for their voluntary contributions to the funding of the Force, and his request for further voluntary contributions from other countries and organizations,

Welcoming and encouraging efforts by the United Nations to sensitize peacekeeping personnel in the prevention and control of HIV/AIDS and other communicable diseases in all its peacekeeping operations,

1. *Reaffirms* all its relevant resolutions on Cyprus, in particular resolution 1251(1999) of 29 June 1999 and subsequent resolutions;

2. *Endorses* the recommendations of the Secretary-General for the amendment of the concept of operations and force level of the United Nations Peacekeeping Force in Cyprus, as outlined in his report of 24 September 2004;

3. *Decides* to extend the mandate of the Force for a further period ending 15 June 2005;

4. *Urges* the Turkish Cypriot side and Turkish forces to rescind without delay all remaining restrictions on the Force, and calls upon them to restore in Strovilia the military status quo which existed there prior to 30 June 2000;

5. *Requests* the Secretary-General to submit a report on the implementation of the present resolution concurrent with the review provided for above;

6. *Decides* to remain seized of the matter.

In a 24 November letter [A/59/580-S/2004/926] to the Secretary-General, the "Turkish Republic of Northern Cyprus" said that, notwithstanding the 30 per cent reduction in its force level and the amended concept of operations, the Secretary-General's review of UNFICYP fell short of updating the Force's mandate in line with the changed circumstances on the ground. However, that issue could be dealt with in the context of the further review to be conducted prior to June 2006.

Financing

On 18 June [meeting 91], the General Assembly, having considered the Secretary-General's report on UNFICYP's financial performance for 1 July 2002 to 30 June 2003 [A/58/631], the proposed budget for UNFICYP's maintenance for 1 July 2004 to 30 June 2005 [A/58/644 & Corr.1], and ACABQ's related comments and recommendations [A/58/759/Add.4], adopted, on the recommendation of the Fifth Committee [A/58/823], **resolution 58/301** without vote [agenda item 137].

Financing of the United Nations Peacekeeping Force in Cyprus

The General Assembly,

Having considered the reports of the Secretary-General on the financing of the United Nations Peacekeeping Force in Cyprus and the related reports of the Advisory Committee on Administrative and Budgetary Questions,

Recalling Security Council resolution 186(1964) of 4 March 1964, regarding the establishment of the United Nations Peacekeeping Force in Cyprus, and the subsequent resolutions by which the Council extended the mandate of the Force, the latest of which was resolution 1548(2004) of 11 June 2004,

Recalling also its resolution 47/236 of 14 September 1993 on the financing of the Force for the period beginning 16 June 1993 and its subsequent resolutions and decisions thereon, the latest of which was resolution 57/332 of 18 June 2003,

Reaffirming the general principles underlying the financing of United Nations peacekeeping operations as stated in General Assembly resolutions 1874(S-IV) of 27 June 1963, 3101(XXVIII) of 11 December 1973 and 55/235 of 23 December 2000,

Noting with appreciation that voluntary contributions have been made to the Force by certain Governments,

Noting that voluntary contributions were insufficient to cover all the costs of the Force, including those incurred by troop-contributing Governments prior to 16 June 1993, and regretting the absence of an adequate response to appeals for voluntary contributions, including that contained in the letter dated 17 May 1994 from the Secretary-General to all Member States,

Mindful of the fact that it is essential to provide the Force with the necessary financial resources to enable it to fulfil its responsibilities under the relevant resolutions of the Security Council,

1. *Takes note* of the status of contributions to the United Nations Peacekeeping Force in Cyprus as at 15 April 2004, including the contributions outstanding in the amount of 15.7 million United States dollars, representing some 7 per cent of the total assessed contributions, notes with concern that only thirty-eight Member States have paid their assessed contributions in full, and urges all other Member States, in particular those in arrears, to ensure payment of their outstanding assessed contributions;

2. *Expresses its appreciation* to those Member States which have paid their assessed contributions in full, and urges all other Member States to make every possible effort to ensure payment of their assessed contributions to the Force in full;

3. *Expresses concern* at the financial situation with regard to peacekeeping activities, in particular as regards the reimbursements to troop contributors that bear additional burdens owing to overdue payments by Member States of their assessments;

4. *Also expresses concern* at the delay experienced by the Secretary-General in deploying and providing adequate resources to some recent peacekeeping missions, in particular those in Africa;

5. *Emphasizes* that all future and existing peacekeeping missions shall be given equal and non-discriminatory treatment in respect of financial and administrative arrangements;

6. *Also emphasizes* that all peacekeeping missions shall be provided with adequate resources for the effective and efficient discharge of their respective mandates;

7. *Reiterates its request* to the Secretary-General to make the fullest possible use of facilities and equipment at the United Nations Logistics Base at Brindisi, Italy, in order to minimize the costs of procurement for the Force;

8. *Endorses* the conclusions and recommendations contained in the report of the Advisory Committee on Administrative and Budgetary Questions, and requests the Secretary-General to ensure their full implementation;

9. *Requests* the Secretary-General to take all action necessary to ensure that the Force is administered with a maximum of efficiency and economy;

10. *Also requests* the Secretary-General, in order to reduce the cost of employing General Service staff, to continue efforts to recruit local staff for the Force against General Service posts, commensurate with the requirements of the Force;

Financial performance report for the period from 1 July 2002 to 30 June 2003

11. *Takes note* of the report of the Secretary-General on the financial performance of the Force for the period 1 July 2002 to 30 June 2003;

Budget estimates for the period from 1 July 2004 to 30 June 2005

12. *Decides* to appropriate to the Special Account for the United Nations Peacekeeping Force in Cyprus the amount of 51,992,200 dollars for the period from 1 July 2004 to 30 June 2005, inclusive of 47,240,400 dollars for the maintenance of the Force, 2,176,900 dollars for strengthening the security and safety of the staff and premises of the Force, 2,105,100 dollars for the support account for peacekeeping operations and 469,800 dollars for the United Nations Logistics Base;

Financing of the appropriation

13. *Notes with appreciation* that a one-third share of the net appropriation, equivalent to 16,444,900 dollars, will be funded through voluntary contributions from the Government of Cyprus and the amount of 6.5 million dollars from the Government of Greece;

14. *Decides* to apportion among Member States the amount of 29,047,300 dollars at a monthly rate of 2,420,608 dollars, in accordance with the levels set out in General Assembly resolution 55/235, as adjusted by the Assembly in its resolution 55/236 of 23 December 2000 and updated in its resolution 58/256 of 23 December 2003, taking into account the scale of assessments for 2004 and 2005, as set out in its resolution 58/1 B of 23 December 2003, subject to a decision of the Security Council to extend the mandate of the Force;

15. *Decides also* that, in accordance with the provisions of its resolution 973(X) of 15 December 1955, there shall be set off against the apportionment among Member States, as provided for in paragraph 14 above, their respective share in the Tax Equalization Fund of 2,657,500 dollars, comprising the estimated staff assessment income of 2,323,800 dollars approved for the Force, the prorated share of 307,200 dollars of the estimated staff assessment income approved for the support account and the prorated share of 26,500 dollars of the estimated staff assessment income approved for the United Nations Logistics Base;

16. *Decides further* that, for Member States that have fulfilled their financial obligations to the Force, there shall be set off against their apportionment, as provided for in paragraph 14 above, their respective share of the unencumbered balance and other income in the amount of 1,005,879 dollars for the financial period ended 30 June 2003, in accordance with the levels set out in General Assembly resolution 55/235, as adjusted by the Assembly in its resolution 55/236 and its resolution 57/290 A of 20 December 2002, taking into account the scale of assessments for 2003, as set out in its resolutions 55/5 B of 23 December 2000 and 57/4 B of 20 December 2002;

17. *Decides* that, for Member States that have not fulfilled their financial obligations to the Force, there shall be set off against their outstanding obligations their respective share of the unencumbered balance and other income in the amount of 1,005,879 dollars in respect of the financial period ended 30 June 2003, in accordance with the scheme set out in paragraph 16 above;

18. *Decides also* that the increase in the estimated staff assessment income of 85,500 dollars in respect of the financial period ended 30 June 2003 shall be added to the credits from the amount referred to in paragraphs 16 and 17 above, and that the respective shares of Member States therein shall be applied in accordance with the provisions of those paragraphs, as appropriate;

19. *Decides further*, taking into account its voluntary contribution for the financial period ended 30 June 2003, that one third of other income in the amount of 641,666 dollars in respect of the financial period ended 30 June 2003 shall be returned to the Government of Cyprus;

20. *Decides* that, taking into account its voluntary contribution for the financial period ended 30 June 2003, the prorated share of other income in the amount of 286,055 dollars in respect of the financial period ended 30 June 2003 shall be returned to the Government of Greece;

21. *Decides also* to continue to maintain as separate the account established for the Force for the period prior to 16 June 1993, invites Member States to make voluntary contributions to that account, and requests

the Secretary-General to continue his efforts in appealing for voluntary contributions to the account;

22. *Emphasizes* that no peacekeeping mission shall be financed by borrowing funds from other active peacekeeping missions;

23. *Encourages* the Secretary-General to continue to take additional measures to ensure the safety and security of all personnel under the auspices of the United Nations participating in the Force;

24. *Invites* voluntary contributions to the Force in cash and in the form of services and supplies acceptable to the Secretary-General, to be administered, as appropriate, in accordance with the procedure and practices established by the General Assembly;

25. *Decides* to include in the provisional agenda of its fifty-ninth session the item entitled "Financing of the United Nations Peacekeeping Force in Cyprus".

On 23 December, the Assembly decided that the agenda on UNFICYP financing would remain for consideration at its resumed fifty-ninth (2005) session (**decision 59/552**).

Other issues

Strengthening of security and cooperation in the Mediterranean

In response to General Assembly resolution 58/70 [YUN 2003, p. 455], the Secretary-General submitted a July report with a later addendum [A/59/130 & Add.1], containing replies received from Algeria, Jordan, Lebanon, Mexico, Morocco, Panama and Venezuela to his 18 February note verbale requesting the views of States and intergovernmental organizations on ways to strengthen security and cooperation in the Mediterranean region.

GENERAL ASSEMBLY ACTION

On 3 December [meeting 66], the General Assembly, on the recommendation of the First (Disarmament and International Security) Committee [A/59/464], adopted **resolution 59/108** without vote [agenda item 70].

Strengthening of security and cooperation in the Mediterranean region

The General Assembly,

Recalling its previous resolutions on the subject, including resolution 58/70 of 8 December 2003,

Reaffirming the primary role of the Mediterranean countries in strengthening and promoting peace, security and cooperation in the Mediterranean region,

Bearing in mind all the previous declarations and commitments, as well as all the initiatives taken by the riparian countries at the recent summits, ministerial meetings and various forums concerning the question of the Mediterranean region,

Recognizing the indivisible character of security in the Mediterranean and that the enhancement of cooperation among Mediterranean countries with a view to promoting the economic and social development of all peoples of the region will contribute significantly to stability, peace and security in the region,

Recognizing also the efforts made so far and the determination of the Mediterranean countries to intensify the process of dialogue and consultations with a view to resolving the problems existing in the Mediterranean region and to eliminating the causes of tension and the consequent threat to peace and security, and their growing awareness of the need for further joint efforts to strengthen economic, social, cultural and environmental cooperation in the region,

Recognizing further that prospects for closer Euro-Mediterranean cooperation in all spheres can be enhanced by positive developments worldwide, in particular in Europe, in the Maghreb and in the Middle East,

Reaffirming the responsibility of all States to contribute to the stability and prosperity of the Mediterranean region and their commitment to respecting the purposes and principles of the Charter of the United Nations as well as the provisions of the Declaration on Principles of International Law concerning Friendly Relations and Cooperation among States in accordance with the Charter of the United Nations,

Noting the peace negotiations in the Middle East, which should be of a comprehensive nature and represent an appropriate framework for the peaceful settlement of contentious issues in the region,

Expressing its concern at the persistent tension and continuing military activities in parts of the Mediterranean that hinder efforts to strengthen security and cooperation in the region,

Taking note of the report of the Secretary-General,

1. *Reaffirms* that security in the Mediterranean is closely linked to European security as well as to international peace and security;

2. *Expresses its satisfaction* at the continuing efforts by Mediterranean countries to contribute actively to the elimination of all causes of tension in the region and to the promotion of just and lasting solutions to the persistent problems of the region through peaceful means, thus ensuring the withdrawal of foreign forces of occupation and respecting the sovereignty, independence and territorial integrity of all countries of the Mediterranean and the right of peoples to self-determination, and therefore calls for full adherence to the principles of non-interference, non-intervention, non-use of force or threat of use of force and the inadmissibility of the acquisition of territory by force, in accordance with the Charter of the United Nations and the relevant resolutions of the United Nations;

3. *Commends* the Mediterranean countries for their efforts in meeting common challenges through coordinated overall responses, based on a spirit of multilateral partnership, towards the general objective of turning the Mediterranean basin into an area of dialogue, exchanges and cooperation, guaranteeing peace, stability and prosperity, encourages them to strengthen such efforts through, inter alia, a lasting multilateral and action-oriented cooperative dialogue among States of the region, and recognizes the role of the United Nations in promoting regional and international peace and security;

4. *Recognizes* that the elimination of the economic and social disparities in levels of development and other obstacles as well as respect and greater understanding among cultures in the Mediterranean area will contribute to enhancing peace, security and cooperation among Mediterranean countries through the existing forums;

5. *Calls upon* all States of the Mediterranean region that have not yet done so to adhere to all the multilaterally negotiated legal instruments related to the field of disarmament and non-proliferation, thus creating the necessary conditions for strengthening peace and cooperation in the region;

6. *Encourages* all States of the region to favour the necessary conditions for strengthening the confidence-building measures among them by promoting genuine openness and transparency on all military matters, by participating, inter alia, in the United Nations system for the standardized reporting of military expenditures and by providing accurate data and information to the United Nations Register of Conventional Arms;

7. *Encourages* the Mediterranean countries to strengthen further their cooperation in combating terrorism in all its forms and manifestations, taking into account the relevant resolutions of the United Nations, and in combating international crime and illicit arms transfers and illicit drug production, consumption and trafficking, which pose a serious threat to peace, security and stability in the region and therefore to the improvement of the current political, economic and social situation and which jeopardize friendly relations among States, hinder the development of international cooperation and result in the destruction of human rights, fundamental freedoms and the democratic basis of pluralistic society;

8. *Requests* the Secretary-General to submit a report on means to strengthen security and cooperation in the Mediterranean region;

9. *Decides* to include in the provisional agenda of its sixtieth session the item entitled "Strengthening of security and cooperation in the Mediterranean region".

Stability and development in South-Eastern Europe

On 3 December [meeting 66], the General Assembly, on the recommendation of the First Committee [A/59/452], adopted **resolution 59/59** without vote [agenda item 58].

Maintenance of international security— good-neighbourliness, stability and development in South-Eastern Europe

The General Assembly,

Recalling the purposes and principles of the Charter of the United Nations and the Final Act of the Conference on Security and Cooperation in Europe, signed in Helsinki on 1 August 1975,

Recalling also the United Nations Millennium Declaration,

Recalling further its previous resolutions on the subject, including resolution 57/52 of 22 November 2002,

Welcoming with appreciation the increased cooperation among countries in the region of South-Eastern Europe on issues related to security, economy, trade, transport, cross-border cooperation, human rights and justice and home affairs,

Reiterating the importance of the South-East European Cooperation Process for further enhancing regional cooperation and stability, which constitutes one of the main elements of the Stabilization and Association Process, and welcoming the positive results of the South-East European Cooperation Process summit meeting, held in Sarajevo on 21 April 2004,

Welcoming the conclusions reached at the Summit of the European Council, held in Thessaloniki, Greece, on 19 and 20 June 2003, and the decisions of the European Council on the principles, priorities and conditions contained in the European Partnerships with all countries of the Stabilization and Association Process,

Noting the progress made by the countries of the Stabilization and Association Process in fulfilling the criteria for membership in the European Union and, in this context, the first entry into force of a Stabilization and Association Agreement, as well as Croatia's becoming a candidate country for membership in the European Union,

Emphasizing the crucial importance of the full implementation of Security Council resolution 1244 (1999) of 10 June 1999 on Kosovo, Serbia and Montenegro, and stressing, inter alia, the role and responsibility of the United Nations Interim Administration Mission in Kosovo, supported by the Organization for Security and Cooperation in Europe and the European Union, and of the North Atlantic Treaty Organization and its Kosovo Force in that regard,

Reaffirming the validity of the Agreement for the delineation of the borderline between the former Yugoslav Republic of Macedonia and Serbia and Montenegro, signed in Skopje on 23 February 2001, and encouraging the parties to cooperate in its timely implementation,

Noting the importance of the Regional Conference on Border Security and Management, held in Ohrid, the former Yugoslav Republic of Macedonia, on 22 and 23 May 2003,

Emphasizing the crucial importance of strengthening regional efforts in South-Eastern Europe on arms control, demining, disarmament and confidence-building measures and non-proliferation of weapons of mass destruction, and concerned that, in spite of ongoing efforts, the illicit trade in small arms and light weapons in all its aspects persists in some parts of the region,

Affirming its support for all regional initiatives on combating the illicit proliferation of small arms and light weapons, including the activities undertaken at the national level for their collection and destruction,

Mindful of the importance of national, regional and international activities of all relevant organizations aimed at the creation of peace, security, stability, democracy, cooperation and economic development and the observance of human rights and good-neighbourliness in South-Eastern Europe,

Reaffirming its determination that all nations should live together in peace with one another as good neighbours,

1. *Reaffirms* the need for full observance of the Charter of the United Nations;

2. *Calls upon* all States, the relevant international organizations and the appropriate organs of the United Nations to respect the principles of territorial integrity and sovereignty of all States and the inviolability of international borders, to continue to take measures in accordance with the Charter and the commitments of the Organization for Security and Co-operation in Europe and through further development of regional arrangements, as appropriate, to eliminate threats to international peace and security and to help to prevent conflicts in South-Eastern Europe, which can lead to the violent disintegration of States;

3. *Acknowledges* the positive results achieved so far by the countries of the region, urges them to invest further efforts in consolidating South-Eastern Europe as a region of peace, security, stability, democracy, the rule of law, cooperation and economic development and for the promotion of good-neighbourliness and the observance of human rights, thus contributing to the maintenance of international peace and security and enhancing the prospects for sustained development and prosperity for all peoples in the region as an integral part of Europe, and recognizes the role of the United Nations, the Organization for Security and Co-operation in Europe and the European Union in successfully promoting regional disarmament;

4. *Calls upon* all participants in the Stability Pact for South-Eastern Europe, as well as all concerned international organizations, to continue to support the efforts of the States of South-Eastern Europe towards regional stability and cooperation so as to enable them to pursue sustainable development and integration into European structures, taking also into account trans-Atlantic relations;

5. *Calls upon* all States and relevant international organizations to contribute to the full implementation of Security Council resolution 1244(1999), on Kosovo, Serbia and Montenegro, as well as of Council resolutions 1345(2001) of 21 March 2001 and 1371(2001) of 26 September 2001, and emphasizes the importance of the standards review process, of the implementation of the "Standards for Kosovo" document endorsed by the Security Council in its presidential statement of 12 December 2003 and of the Kosovo Standards Implementation Plan of 31 March 2004;

6. *Recognizes* the efforts made and activities undertaken in Kosovo by the United Nations and the Kosovo Force for the establishment of a multi-ethnic and stable Kosovo, thus contributing to a further improvement of the overall security situation in the region;

7. *Rejects* the use of violence in pursuit of political aims, and stresses that only peaceful political solutions can assure a stable and democratic future for South-Eastern Europe;

8. *Stresses* the importance of good-neighbourliness and the development of friendly relations among States, and calls upon all States to resolve their disputes with other States by peaceful means, in accordance with the Charter;

9. *Urges* the strengthening of relations among the States of South-Eastern Europe on the basis of respect for international law and agreements, in accordance with the principles of good-neighbourliness and mutual respect;

10. *Recognizes* the efforts of the international community, and welcomes in particular the assistance already provided by the European Union and the Stability Pact for South-Eastern Europe, as well as other contributors, in promoting the long-term process of democratic and economic development of the region;

11. *Calls upon* all States to intensify cooperation with and render all necessary assistance to the International Tribunal for the Prosecution of Persons Responsible for Serious Violations of International Humanitarian Law Committed in the Territory of the Former Yugoslavia since 1991 to bring all at-large indictees to surrender to the Tribunal in line with Security Council resolutions 1503(2003) of 28 August 2003 and 1534 (2004) of 26 March 2004;

12. *Stresses* the importance of enhanced regional cooperation for the development of the South-Eastern European States in the priority areas of infrastructure, transport, trade, energy and environment, as well as in other areas of common interest;

13. *Also stresses* that the rapprochement of the South-Eastern European States with the European Union will favourably influence the security, political and economic situation in the region, as well as good-neighbourly relations among the States;

14. *Emphasizes* the importance of continuous regional efforts and intensified dialogue in South-Eastern Europe aimed at arms control, disarmament and confidence-building measures, as well as strengthening cooperation and undertaking appropriate measures at the national, subregional and regional levels against the proliferation of weapons of mass destruction and to prevent all acts of terrorism;

15. *Recognizes* the seriousness of the problem of anti-personnel mines and explosive remnants of war in some parts of South-Eastern Europe, welcomes in this context the efforts of the countries in the region and of the international community in support of mine action, and encourages States to join and support these efforts;

16. *Urges* all States to take effective measures against the illicit trade in small arms and light weapons in all its aspects and to help programmes and projects aimed at the collection and safe destruction of surplus stocks of small arms and light weapons, and stresses the importance of closer cooperation among States, inter alia, in crime prevention, combating terrorism, trafficking in human beings, organized crime and corruption, drug trafficking and money-laundering;

17. *Calls upon* all States and the relevant international organizations to communicate to the Secretary-General their views on the subject of the present resolution;

18. *Decides* to include in the provisional agenda of its sixty-first session the item entitled "Maintenance of international security—good-neighbourliness, stability and development in South-Eastern Europe".

Cooperation with the Council of Europe

The Secretary-General, in response to General Assembly **resolution 58/316** (see p. 1374), submitted, in his September consolidated report [A/58/303] on cooperation between the United Nations and regional organizations, a section on cooperation activities with the Council of Europe.

On 10 December [meeting 71], the General Assembly adopted **resolution 59/139** [draft: A/59/L.31 & Add.1] without vote [agenda item 56 (f)].

Cooperation between the United Nations and the Council of Europe

The General Assembly,

Recalling the Agreement between the Council of Europe and the Secretariat of the United Nations signed on 15 December 1951 and the Arrangement on Cooperation and Liaison between the secretariats of the United Nations and the Council of Europe of 19 November 1971,

Welcoming the report of the Secretary-General on cooperation between the United Nations and the Council of Europe,

1. *Reiterates its appreciation* for the ongoing fruitful cooperation between the United Nations and its agencies and the Council of Europe, including its Commissioner for Human Rights and its partial and enlarged agreements, both at the level of headquarters and in the field;

2. *Notes* the constructive interest of the Parliamentary Assembly of the Council of Europe in the reform process of the United Nations, including its willingness to contribute to the discussion on how to give a parliamentary dimension to the world Organization;

3. *Requests* the Secretary-General of the United Nations to continue exploring, with the Secretary-General of the Council of Europe, possibly by arranging a meeting of representatives of the two organizations in the light of the outcome of the Third Summit of the Council of Europe, possibilities for further enhancement of cooperation between the organizations;

4. *Decides* to include in the provisional agenda of its sixty-first session the sub-item entitled "Cooperation between the United Nations and the Council of Europe", and requests the Secretary-General to submit to the General Assembly at its sixty-first session a report on cooperation between the United Nations and the Council of Europe in general and, in particular, the results of the efforts referred to in paragraph 3 above to explore possibilities for further cooperation between the two organizations.

Cooperation with the Organization for Security and Cooperation in Europe

The Secretary-General, in his September consolidated report on cooperation between the United Nations and regional organizations [A/59/303], outlined cooperation activities undertaken by the United Nations and the Organization for Security and Cooperation in Europe (OSCE). Consultations continued to be held at all levels between the secretariats of the two organizations. The annual working-level meetings, which were initiated in 2001 and later held in Vienna (May 2003) and New York (May 2004), enhanced contacts between the secretariats' substantive units. The UN Secretariat also participated in a number of conferences organized by OSCE. Specific cooperation activities continued within the context of the United Nations Interim Administration Mission in Kosovo (see p. 404) and the United Nations Observer Mission in Georgia (see p. 420). The Economic Commission for Europe enjoyed a close working relationship with OSCE in the economic and environmental areas, with the Commission providing OSCE economic analyses and information on various norms, standards and conventions and on its extensive network of experts. The United Nations Children's Fund collaborated with OSCE in the promotion of the rights of women and children, juvenile justice, the development of the Roma strategy, education and the problem of children affected by armed conflict.

In the context of the tripartite process of informal consultations among the United Nations, OSCE and the Council of Europe, the thirteenth high-level meeting (February 2004) examined how to respond to threats to security and stability and reached agreement on improved collaboration, at the field and headquarters levels, in responding to such threats and on the need for a common and effective framework to combat terrorist acts and a comprehensive approach to security.

By **decision 59/552** of 23 December, the General Assembly decided that the item on cooperation between the United Nations and OSCE would remain for consideration during its resumed fifty-ninth (2005) session.

Chapter VI

Middle East

The political and security situation in the Middle East in 2004 was characterized by a stalled peace process and continuing high levels of violence. Throughout the year, both Palestinians and Israelis suffered from violence and ever-mounting death tolls. However, by the end of the year, there were some signs of dialogue and cooperation between Israeli and Palestinian authorities.

The Quartet, a coordinating mechanism for international peace efforts, comprising the Russian Federation, the United States, the European Union and the United Nations, continued its efforts to promote the road map initiative as the best solution to the conflict. The road map, which was endorsed by the Security Council in 2003, aimed to achieve progress through parallel and reciprocal steps by Israel and the Palestinian Authority (PA) in the political, security, economic, humanitarian and institution-building areas, under an international monitoring system. Despite those efforts, little progress was made in the road map's implementation.

In February 2004, Israel's Prime Minister, Ariel Sharon, announced a unilateral initiative to withdraw all Israeli civilian settlements, military forces and installations from the Gaza Strip and from an area in the northern part of the West Bank. The Quartet welcomed the plan, which was officially approved by the Israeli Knesset in October. Meanwhile, the situation on the ground continued to deteriorate, especially in the Gaza Strip. Israeli mounted several military operations, while the PA, for its part, failed to halt attacks against Israelis emanating from territories under its control. In May, the Rafah area in Gaza was subjected to a major Israeli military operation, "Operation Rainbow", aimed at preventing weapons smuggling between Gaza and Egypt. Israeli military bulldozers demolished hundreds of houses in order to widen the border area (known as the Philadelphi route) between Rafah and Egypt. In response to the deteriorating situation, the Security Council, in May, called on Israel to respect its obligations under international humanitarian law and not to undertake demolition of homes contrary to that law. A month-long siege in and around the Gaza town of Beit Hanoun in July left behind broken buildings and flattened crops. On 28 September, a massive military operation was launched in the northern Gaza Strip,

particularly in the densely populated towns of Beit Lahiya and Beit Hanoun and the Jabaliya refugee camp, home to over 100,000 refugees. Over 80 Palestinians were killed and more than 300 were injured within a week. Other Palestinian cities, towns and refugee camps (Bethlehem, Jenin, Khan Yunis, Zeitoun, Balata refugee camp) also suffered incursions and blockades, as the crisis intensified, hindering the work of humanitarian aid workers. Israel carried out extrajudicial killings throughout the year, killing, among others, the spiritual leader of the Palestinian Islamist organization Hamas, Sheikh Ahmed Yassin, in March, and Abdel Aziz Al-Rantisi, a political leader of Hamas, in April.

On 11 November, the President of the PA, Yasser Arafat, died of natural causes in Paris. President Arafat had been confined throughout most of 2004 to his headquarters compound in Ramallah under de facto house arrest. Following Mr. Arafat's death, security cooperation between Israel and the PA resumed and Israel scaled back military activity in areas under the Authority's control. Palestinian presidential elections were scheduled to take place in January 2005.

Concerned about the continued deterioration of the situation in the region, the Security Council convened on a monthly basis during the year, and at times even more frequently, to discuss the situation in the Middle East, including the Palestinian question. On 25 March, a draft resolution, by which the Council would have condemned the killing of Sheikh Yassin, as well as all terrorist attacks against civilians, was not adopted due to the negative vote of a permanent Council member, nor was a 5 October draft resolution which would have demanded the immediate cessation of all military operations in northern Gaza and the withdrawal of Israeli forces from that area.

The International Court of Justice (ICJ), on 9 July, rendered an advisory opinion on the legal consequences arising from the construction of a separation wall by Israel in the Occupied Palestinian Territory, as requested by the General Assembly in December 2003. The Court, among other things, found that the route of the wall was contrary to international law and that Israel was under an obligation to terminate the construction, to dismantle parts already built and to make reparations for all damage caused to Palestinian property. On 30 June, Israel's Supreme Court ruled, among other things, that sections of the wall required re-routing, and the Israeli Government declared that it would abide by the Court's ruling. Meanwhile, construction of the wall continued throughout the year.

The General Assembly convened its resumed tenth emergency special session in July to discuss the item "Illegal Israeli actions in Occupied East Jerusalem and the rest of the Occupied Palestinian Territory". It adopted a resolution which acknowledged the ICJ advisory opinion and demanded that Israel comply with its legal obligations as defined in the opinion.

International attention focused on Lebanon in early September when the Lebanese Parliament amended the constitution to extend President Emile Lahoud's six-year term, which was about to expire, by another three years. The Syrian Arab Republic, which maintained a large military presence in Lebanon, supported the move. The amendment was adopted the day after the Security Council adopted a resolution calling for free and fair presidential elections in Lebanon and for the full withdrawal of foreign forces from the country and the disbanding and disarmament of all militias. Syria redeployed some of its troops, but by the end of the year had not withdrawn all of its troops from Lebanon. In October, Prime Minister Rafik Hariri resigned from his post and was replaced by Omar Karami.

In southern Lebanon, Israeli forces and their main Lebanese opponent, the paramilitary group Hizbullah, continued to face each other across the Blue Line, the provisional border drawn by the United Nations following the withdrawal of Israeli troops from southern Lebanon in 2000. Israeli violations of Lebanese airspace continued, while Hizbullah, on a number of occasions, directed anti-aircraft fire at Israeli villages across the Blue Line. The first municipal elections in southern Lebanon since the Israeli withdrawal of 2000 were held in May, with a high voter turnout.

The mandates of the United Nations Interim Force in Lebanon and of the United Nations Disengagement Observer Force in the Golan Heights were extended twice during the year, and the United Nations Truce Supervision Organization continued to assist both peacekeeping operations in their tasks.

The United Nations Relief and Works Agency for Palestine Refugees in the Near East continued to provide education and health and social services to over 4 million Palestinian refugees living both in and outside camps in the West Bank and the Gaza Strip, as well as in Jordan, Lebanon and Syria. With the Government of Switzerland, the Agency, in June co-hosted its first major international conference since its inception.

During the year, the Special Committee to Investigate Israeli Practices Affecting the Human Rights of the Palestinian People and Other Arabs of the Occupied Territories reported to the Assembly on the situation in the West Bank, including East Jerusalem, the Gaza Strip and the Golan Heights. The Committee on the Exercise of the Inalienable Rights of the Palestinian People continued to mobilize international support for the Palestinians.

Peace process

Overall situation

The Secretary-General, in a November report on the peaceful settlement of the question of Palestine [A/59/574-S/2004/909] (see also p. 486), said that, despite the efforts of the international community through the Quartet and the stated commitment of the parties to the road map initiative as expressed at the summit meeting in Aqaba, Jordan, on 4 June 2003 [YUN 2003, p. 465], the situation in the Middle East was characterized by a stalled peace process and continuing high levels of violence. Throughout 2004, both Palestinians and Israelis suffered from violence and ever-mounting death tolls. The humanitarian situation in the Occupied Palestinian Territory continued to deteriorate sharply, with even a minimum standard of living for many Palestinians being sustained only by assistance from the donor community, particularly by the United Nations Relief and Works Agency for Palestine Refugees in the Near East (UNRWA) and other UN programmes. The rising number of deaths and injuries was evidence of the lack of progress in advancing the peace process in 2004. As at 16 September, 825 Palestinians and 136 Israelis had lost their lives in the conflict in the preceding 12 months. Since the eruption of the violence in September 2000 [YUN 2000, p. 416], 3,633 Palestinians and 966 Israelis had been killed.

Neither side took adequate steps to protect civilians, and both were in breach of their international legal obligations. Israel, as the occupying Power, had clear obligations to protect Palestinian civilians and their property. Nevertheless, Palestinian civilians continued to be killed and injured in Israeli military operations, including incursions and pre-emptive strikes, as well as Israeli extrajudicial killings. The scale of destruction of Palestinian property by the Israeli military raised serious concerns about collective punishment. For its part, the PA had obligations under agreements reached with Israel, international humanitarian law and the road map to protect Israeli civilians from attacks emanating from territories under its control. It failed to live up to those obligations, and Israeli civilians continued to suffer terrorist attacks from Palestinian militant groups, including suicide bombings and Qassam rocket strikes. For each side to cite the actions of the other excused neither from fulfilling its own obligations. More broadly, the parties had not lived up to their road map obligations. The Israeli Government made no progress on its core obligation to dismantle settlement outposts erected since March 2001 and to freeze settlement activities, including natural growth. The PA made no progress on its core obligations to take immediate action to end violence and combat terror. The PA and the Israeli Government needed to take the necessary first steps to restore momentum towards peace, otherwise the stalemate would continue and there would be no lasting ceasefire. Those first steps, as outlined by the Secretary-General, were clear: on the Israeli side, the dismantling of settlement outposts and the implementation of a full freeze of all settlement activities, and on the Palestinian side, the implementation of meaningful security reforms and bringing to an end the use of violence in all its forms.

Israel's settlement expansion and lack of action on removing the outposts erected since 2001 severely undermined Palestinian trust in Israel's intentions and contributed to strengthening extremist opinion among Palestinians. Despite repeated promises by the Israeli Government, settlement construction continued at a considerable pace, in particular in large settlement blocs. In and around East Jerusalem, settlement activity, both governmental and privately sponsored, proceeded at a rate that observers described as unmatched since 1992. In addition, Israel persisted in confining the elected PA President, Yasser Arafat, to his headquarters in the West Bank.

The security measures taken by the PA remained limited and unclear. Reform of the Palestinian security services was needed to restore law and order as well as the PA's diminished credibility, specifically the consolidation of all security services into three main bodies, with a professional leadership, under the authority of an effective interior minister.

Throughout 2004, the situation in the Middle East, including the Palestinian question, remained the subject of extensive consultations and debates in the Security Council. On 19 May, the Council adopted resolution 1544(2004), calling on Israel to respect its obligations under international humanitarian law, including its obligation not to destroy Palestinian homes in an illegal manner.

Israel continued construction of the security barrier in parts of the West Bank. On 9 July, the International Court of Justice (ICJ) rendered an advisory opinion on the legal consequences of the wall (see p. 465), declaring that the construction was contrary to international law. The Assembly, in resolution ES-10/15 of 20 July (see p. 465), demanded that Israel comply with its legal obligations.

In February, Prime Minister Ariel Sharon of Israel announced an initiative to withdraw Israeli armed forces from Gaza and parts of the West Bank and to evacuate all settlements in the Gaza Strip, as well as four settlements in the northern West Bank. The Quartet welcomed that step and stated that for the withdrawal to be a real contribution to the peace process, it should lead to an end of the occupation of Gaza and be accompanied by similar steps in the West Bank.

Occupied Palestinian Territory

Communication (14 January). On 14 January [A/58/682-S/2004/33], Israel informed the Secretary-General and the Security Council President that on that day a female suicide bomber perpetrated an attack in the Gaza Strip, killing four Israeli citizens and wounding 12 others. Hamas and Al-Aqsa Martyrs Brigade jointly claimed responsibility for the bombing.

Security Council consideration (January). The Security Council met on 16 January [meeting 4895] to discuss the situation in the Middle East, including the Palestinian question.

The Under-Secretary-General (USG) for Political Affairs, Kieran Prendergast, said that there had been little progress towards peace since the last Council briefing in December 2003 [YUN 2003, p. 483], and the peace process remained stalemated. That process would resume only when both parties recognized that their mutual concerns could be addressed solely through parallel steps, and not in a sequential manner littered with preconditions. That approach, adopted by the road map, would require both the Palestinians and the Israelis to acknowledge and address each other's core concerns.

Israel's most basic concern remained the security of the State and the Israeli people. In response, as a necessary first step, the PA should take action to halt all acts of violence against Israelis. The Palestinians' most basic concerns were territory and viability—meaning the end of occupation and the establishment of an independent, sovereign and viable State in the West Bank and Gaza Strip. In response, and also as a necessary first step, Israel should halt settlement expansion, the construction of the separation wall and all action that worked against the contiguity of the State. Despite initial contacts between the new Palestinian Government and the Israeli Government, both parties continued to ignore each other's core concerns, thereby falling short of carrying out their preliminary commitments under the Quartet's road map.

The PA had taken no tangible measures to establish control over the various groups that used violence and terror. It also failed to reform its security apparatus or to consolidate it under the authority of an empowered interior minister, as called for in the road map. At the same time, Palestinian militant factions failed to agree on a comprehensive cessation of violence, although they continued their dialogue thanks to the efforts of the Egyptian Government. In addition, there was a deterioration in the PA's capability to maintain domestic law and order. If that trend continued, there could be more unrest on Palestinian streets, with negative repercussions for the PA's governing control.

The Israeli Government repeatedly committed itself to implementation of the road map; however, its statements were not matched by action. Israel did not fulfil its core commitment to remove all settlements erected since March 2001 and to implement a complete settlement freeze. In fact, settlement outposts had increased and the Government was proceeding with the construction of the West Bank barrier. Together with other settlement infrastructure and a tight closure policy, that construction was fragmenting the West Bank into non-contiguous patches of territory and was eroding Palestinians' trust in the peace process.

In the face of the discouraging situation, the international community had to maintain its involvement in the peace process, in the view of the USG. The Security Council, the General Assembly and the Quartet had made efforts to revive the peace process; nevertheless, it was all too apparent that a more vigorous involvement of the key players in the international community was needed.

During the preceding month, both sides continued to experience violence: 58 Palestinians and 11 Israelis were killed, and 440 Palestinians and 65 Israelis were wounded. Israel Defense Forces (IDF) resumed extrajudicial killings and launched at least 15 incursions into Palestinian villages and refugee camps, which often involved the use of disproportionate and deadly force in civilian areas.

The situation on the ground caused great harm to the Palestinian economy. Israel's internal and external closures of the Occupied Palestinian Territory remained the central impediment to economic stabilization and recovery. Slight economic improvement was reported in places, due in part to IDF troops moving out of some Palestinian cities, but closure remained the defining reality for those areas, with roadblocks and, in some places, construction of the barrier almost completely halting movement. The closure system continued to impede the international community's efforts to deliver humanitarian aid.

Communications (30 January, 11 February). On 30 January [A/58/697-S/2004/80], Israel informed the Secretary-General and the Council President that on 29 January a PA policeman perpetrated a suicide attack in central Jerusalem, killing 10 people and wounding over 50.

On 11 February [A/ES-10/256-S/2004/107], the Permanent Observer of Palestine said that on that day Israeli forces, backed by tanks, raided a densely populated neighbourhood in Gaza City, killing at least 12 Palestinians and wounding 50 others.

Israeli withdrawal plan

In early February, Prime Minister Sharon announced that Israel would unilaterally undertake military disengagement leading to eventual total withdrawal of settlements from the Gaza Strip and from an area in the northern Samaria in the West Bank. Israel planned to maintain a military presence along the border between the Gaza Strip and Egypt (Philadelphi route) and to continue construction of the barrier for security purposes. The evacuation process was scheduled to be completed by the end of 2005. Upon completion, there would no longer be any permanent presence of Israeli security forces or Israeli civilians in Gaza and the Samaria area, according to the announcement.

Security Council consideration (18 February). The Security Council, on 18 February [meeting 4912], discussed the situation in the Middle East, including the Palestinian question.

The Special Coordinator for the Middle East Peace Process and Personal Representative of the Secretary-General, Terje Roed-Larsen, noted that key Israeli and Palestinian officials had met recently. He welcomed Mr. Sharon's bold step—the announcement about the planned Israeli withdrawal from the Gaza Strip, where Israelis controlled about 40 per cent of the land. Palestinian Prime Minister Ahmed Qurei had also welcomed the initiative, saying he would accept it as a first step of a broader withdrawal. Similarly, the Secretary-General said that the withdrawal from Gaza had to be seen as a first step, and it had to be made in the context of the road map and as part of a cooperative engagement between Israel, the PA and the international community. The announcement set the stage for three possible scenarios in the coming months. One was the resumption of a vigorous peace process, with re-engagement between Israel and many of its Arab partners. The second was unilateral Israeli disengagement from parts of the Occupied Palestinian Territory, starting in Gaza, but not as part of a process or re-engagement. The third centred on the inability of the parties to enact that withdrawal, thereby maintaining the status quo, with all its attendant violence and misery. The Personal Representative urged the two leaders to work to fulfil their obligations under the road map and urged the Quartet to re-engage with the parties.

Meanwhile, the situation on the ground remained in a stalemate characterized by continued violence and lack of constructive progress on the road map, with Israeli occupation firmly entrenched and little concrete Palestinian movement on reform. The withdrawal announcement occurred in the context of an upsurge in violence that led to more bloodshed, loss of life and misery. Since the last briefing on 16 January (see above), 11 Israelis and 65 Palestinians were killed, and at least 305 Palestinians and 58 Israelis were injured. The humanitarian situation remained dire in the West Bank and Gaza Strip. Continued closures and Israeli military operations hindered Palestinian economic and social activity and caused the Palestinian people to endure daily humiliations. The economic situation was marked by high unemployment and widespread poverty. However, the West Bank economy stabilized in 2003, attributed in part to some easing of the closure measures, and, according to international financial institutions, its economy grew by 4.5 per cent in 2003, with a concurrent gain in employment.

Communications (24 February–17 March). In a series of letters to the Secretary-General and the Council President between 24 February and 17 March [A/58/721-S/2004/142, A/58/726-S/2004/172, A/58/735-S/2004/211, A/58/736-S/2004/212], Israel detailed Palestinian terrorist attacks against Israeli civilians. On 22 February, a Palestinian terrorist killed eight people and wounded 73 others on a commuter bus in Jerusalem. On 14 March, two Palestinians carried out a bombing attack at the port of Ashdod, killing 10 Israelis and wounding 18. Israel also said that a number of terrorist attempts were averted by IDF.

The Permanent Observer of Palestine, in letters during that period [A/ES-10/257-S/2004/167, A/ES-10/258-S/2004/173, A/ES-10/259-S/2004/178, A/ES-10/260-S/2004/187, A/ES-10/261-S/2004/216], informed the Secretary-General and the Council President that Israel continued to kill and wound Palestinian civilians. On 7 March, IDF raided two refugees camps in the Gaza Strip, killing 14 Palestinians and injuring more than 80 other civilians. On 10 March, an Israeli raid in the city of Jenin resulted in the death of seven Palestinians. IDF fired two missiles into the Rafah refugee camp on 17 March, killing four Palestinians and wounding several others.

Security Council consideration (18 March). The Security Council, on 18 March [meeting 4927], discussed the situation in the Middle East, including the Palestinian question.

The Assistant Secretary-General for Political Affairs, Danilo Türk, said that despite the rise in violence since the 18 February briefing (see p. 455), the possibility of peace remained open. Prime Minister Sharon's announcement of a plan for disengaging from the Gaza Strip had attracted substantial attention. To garner the support of the international community and strengthen its chances for success, the withdrawal should have four main features: it should be part of the Quartet's road map; it should occur in partnership with the PA; the withdrawal should be complete; and it should be considered by all as a first step towards the end of Israeli occupation, as set forth in relevant Council resolutions. Quartet envoys met on 10 March in Washington, D.C., to discuss the possible Gaza Strip withdrawal and other relevant issues. They agreed to work towards a Quartet principals' meeting in the next few months, and considered ways to revitalize the road map process. Those efforts were taking place while violence continued unabated. Since the last briefing to the Council, 101 people lost their lives to the conflict—80 Palestinians and 21 Israelis. The toll from Israeli military operations in the Gaza Strip grew, and Israel carried out extrajudicial killings during the reporting period. Israel had a duty to protect its citizens from terrorist attacks, and it had a concomitant responsibility under international law to protect the lives of the civilians in the territory it occupied. Thus, in the aftermath of an operation carried out on 7 March in a densely populated part of the Gaza Strip that resulted in the deaths of 14 Palestinians—including several children—the Secretary-General called on the Israeli Government to abide by its obligations under international humanitarian law to avoid civilian casualties and to desist from the use of disproportionate force in densely populated areas. The reporting period also witnessed terrorist attacks against Israeli civilians. The United Nations was of the view that no cause could justify such acts, and it called on the PA to take up its security responsibilities under the road map. It was imperative that those who planned, carried out and facilitated terrorist acts be brought to justice.

West Bank barrier construction continued at a rapid pace around Jerusalem and Ramallah. However, the Israeli High Court of Justice extended a freeze until 17 March on construction of a section north-west of Jerusalem to examine petitions brought by eight Palestinian villages. The Court ordered the Government to respond to claims that the barrier harmed Palestinian villagers. The Government agreed to modify certain plans and to negotiate with villagers on others.

Assassination of Sheikh Yassin

On 22 March [A/ES-10/262-S/2004/231], the Permanent Observer of Palestine said that Israeli forces carried out on that day an extrajudicial execution by killing Sheikh Ahmed Yassin in Gaza City. On the same day [S/2004/242], the European Union (EU) condemned the extrajudicial killing of Sheikh Yassin by IDF in a missile attack.

Security Council consideration (23 and 25 March). At the request of the Libyan Arab Jamahiriya, on behalf of the Arab Group [S/2004/233], the Security Council, on 23 [meeting 4929] and 25 March [meeting 4934], considered the situation in the Middle East, including the Palestinian question.

At the 23 March meeting, the Permanent Observer of Palestine described the murder of the spiritual leader of the Hamas movement, Sheikh Yassin, in an attack which Israeli Prime Minister Sharon indicated he personally supervised and said that he would continue that policy. The Permanent Observer said that the Palestinians valued the readiness of the vast majority of the Council members to take a clear position vis-à-vis what had happened. As far as Prime Minister Sharon's plan for withdrawal from Gaza was concerned, the Permanent Observer said that a unilateral step could not be part of the road map, for disengagement could not be part of a negotiated withdrawal. He also expressed concern about Israel's construction of a separation wall, even after the matter was submitted to ICJ for an advisory opinion. The wall represented an illegitimate annexation, as a fait accompli, of large areas of Palestinian land, and it rendered impossible any implementation of the two-State solution. The wall was the central issue for the Israeli Government; halting its construction and destroying it was a major issue for the international community.

Israel said that in the three and a half years of Palestinian terrorist attacks that had murdered hundreds of innocent Israeli civilians, the Coun-

cil had not met even once to condemn an attack. The Council, instead, was meeting to come to the defence of one of its prime perpetrators. Although the Council never met to discuss the attacks for which Sheikh Yassin was responsible, the list was gruesome and shocking. Under Sheikh Yassin's direct leadership, Hamas had perpetrated over 425 attacks that killed 377 Israelis and wounded 2,076 in less than three and a half years. He stood at the head of a command and control structure dedicated to the destruction of Israel. Sheikh Yassin personally instigated and authorized homicide attacks, encouraged individuals to become suicide bombers, ordered missile attacks against Israeli communities, coordinated activities with other terrorist organizations and collected funds for terrorist activity, campaigning throughout the Arab world to raise millions of dollars to improve Hamas terrorist capabilities. Through his words he spawned an ideology of hatred, incitement and murder, glorified as martyrdom. By any reasonable standard of international law, Israel had a legitimate right, in fact a duty, to defend itself against illegal combatants and their commanders. The Palestinian leadership had proved beyond any doubt that it had no intention of fighting terrorism, as it was legally and morally obliged to do. Sheikh Yassin lived and operated for years in the safe haven of the PA, in violation of the most basic international norms. The operation against Sheikh Yassin constituted a stride forward in Israel's march against fundamentalist terrorism, as Sheikh Yassin was one of the greatest obstacles to the cessation of hostilities and the renewal of negotiations. The road map explicitly required the elimination of Hamas and all other terrorist organizations and called for an end to funding and support for their efforts.

On 25 March, the Council had before it a draft resolution sponsored by Algeria and the Libyan Arab Jamahiriya [S/2004/240], by which the Council would have condemned the killing of Sheikh Yassin, as well as all terrorist attacks against any civilians.

The United States said that it would vote against the draft resolution because it was silent about the terrorist atrocities committed by Hamas, did not reflect the realities of the Middle East conflict, and would not further the goals of peace and security. The United States was deeply troubled by the killing of Sheikh Yassin, which had led to escalated tensions in Gaza and the region and could set back efforts to resume progress towards peace. However, events needed to be considered in their context, and the Council did nothing to contribute to a settlement when it condemned one party's actions and turned a blind eye to other developments. The draft resolution condemned the killing of the leader of Hamas, a terrorist organization dedicated to the destruction of Israel, but failed to condemn the suicide bombing carried out by Hamas in the Israeli port of Ashdod that had killed 10 Israelis, despite the request of Member States that such references be included. The Council should focus on ways to advance the goal of the two States—Israel and Palestine—living side by side in peace and security. The draft resolution did not advance that goal.

The draft resolution was not adopted owing to the negative vote of a permanent member of the Council (11-1-3).

Speaking after the vote, the Russian Federation expressed regret that the Council was unable to respond to the development of events in the Palestinian territories resulting from the killing of Sheikh Yassin. Russia voted in favour of the draft because it condemned all terrorist attacks against civilians.

Other developments

Communications (7 and 19 April). On 7 April [A/ES-10/263-S/2004/279], the Permanent Observer of Palestine said that following the killing of Sheikh Yassin, Israeli government and military officials made repeated statements hinting that similar action would be taken against Yasser Arafat, the PA President. At the same time, IDF continued to kill and wound Palestinian civilians. In fact, at least 23 Palestinians had been killed since 22 March.

On 19 April [A/ES-10/264-S/2004/304], the Permanent Observer said that, two days earlier, Israeli forces carried out another extrajudicial execution by killing Abdel Aziz Al-Rantisi, a political leader of Hamas.

Security Council consideration (19 April). At the request of Egypt, on behalf of the Arab Group [S/2004/303], the Security Council, on 19 April [meeting 4945], considered the situation in the Middle East, including the Palestinian question.

The Permanent Observer of Palestine said that, on 17 April, less than four weeks after the death of Sheikh Yassin, IDF committed another extrajudicial execution by killing Mr. Al-Rantisi. That crime was carried out following repeated threats by Prime Minister Sharon and other Israeli officials to target Palestinian leaders, in flagrant violation of international law. Unable to uphold its duties for the maintenance of international peace and security when it came to the Occupied Palestinian Territory, the Council had allowed Israel to continue acting beyond the parameters of international law, and failed to take measures to ensure the protection of the Pal-

estinian civilian population in the occupied territories. With regard to Israel's decision to unilaterally withdraw from Gaza, the proposal fell far short of any real withdrawal, as control of international borders, airspace and water remained in the hands of the occupier. Israel continued to use the pretext of fighting terrorists to justify all its actions against the Palestinian people. The Permanent Observer said that terrorism and violence constituted one of the dynamics of the conflict. It was a dynamic that had taken on more prominence in recent years, but it did not constitute the conflict itself. The conflict was about the belligerent military occupation of another people and their land by a foreign Power for nearly four decades. The Council had to take bold actions to ensure compliance with its own resolutions and adherence to international law and to bring an end to the cycle of violence that had prevented the realization of genuine peace.

Israel said that the Council was convened again not to condemn the murder of innocent civilians by organizations such as Hamas, but to denounce the demise of a key architect of those massacres. Just hours before the targeted counter-terrorist operation against Mr. Rantisi, the organization he headed claimed responsibility, together with the Al Aqsa Martyrs Brigade, for yet another suicide attack against Israelis. Mr. Rantisi sought to destroy any peace initiative and called for the destruction of Israel. He developed alliances with terrorist groups operating around the world, supported by regimes in Syria and Iran, and was committed to fostering terrorism in Iraq and throughout the Western world. A paediatrician by training, that doctor led the campaign to mobilize women and children for use in homicide bombings. Had it been possible to arrest Mr. Rantisi, while minimizing harm to civilian life, Israel would have done so, but in the absence of cooperation from the PA, Israel was left with no choice but to target those who planned and executed the murder of innocent Israeli civilians. The targeting of Mr. Rantisi was not merely a necessary defensive act to prevent ongoing and planned attacks against innocent civilians, but it was part of the global struggle against terrorism. As the struggle against terrorism continued, Prime Minister Sharon launched a bold and unprecedented initiative to bring new hope and opportunity to the peace process. The disengagement plan, when approved, would lead to the evacuation of settlements and military installations in the Gaza Strip and parts of the West Bank. Although not required by the road map, it was an opportunity to restart that process, to which Israel remained committed. In the absence of a peace partner, Israel was compelled to propose that unprecedented initiative itself, but it hoped to implement it in a coordinated fashion that would ensure stability and security for Israelis and Palestinians, provide a humanitarian infrastructure and rekindle the peace process.

The United States urged all parties to exercise maximum restraint and stressed that it was committed to ensuring that Mr. Sharon's plan was consistent with the road map and the realization of two States, Israel and Palestine, living side by side in peace and security. An Israeli withdrawal from Gaza would provide a rare opportunity for real progress. It was particularly noteworthy that that step was being proposed by Mr. Sharon, who was an architect of the Israeli settlements policy of the 1970s. The proposal was an important and positive development.

Egypt deplored the extrajudicial assassinations of Palestinians by the Israeli army. It said that any withdrawal from the Palestinian territories had to be coordinated with the Palestinians and followed up by other measures in order to implement the concept of two neighbouring States living side by side in peace and security and within guaranteed borders.

Communication (22 April). On 22 April [A/ES-10/265-S/2004/319], the Permanent Observer of Palestine said that, beginning on 20 April, IDF launched a raid on the town of Beit Lahiya in the northern Gaza Strip. The raid lasted three days and resulted in the death of 13 Palestinians.

Security Council consideration (23 April). The Security Council, on 23 April [meeting 4951], heard a briefing by the Special Coordinator for the Middle East Peace Process and Personal Representative of the Secretary-General, who used his monthly briefing to focus on what he saw as a crucial and potentially seminal juncture for peace efforts in the region.

Mr. Roed-Larsen said that the Gaza withdrawal, if carried out in the right way, could usher in a new era of peacemaking in the Middle East, but if implemented in the wrong way, would lead to more violence. Any Israeli withdrawal from the West Bank and Gaza that restored Palestinian rights was a welcome development. The withdrawal plans would deliver almost the whole remaining 40 per cent of the Gaza Strip to the Palestinians, in addition to the 60 per cent that was handed over to the PA 10 years earlier. They would also include withdrawals in the north of the West Bank. However, for the Gaza withdrawal to mark the beginning of an era of peace and security, it needed to contain two main elements. First, the withdrawal should be full and complete and should be recognized as such by the international community, and second, it should be accompanied by the implementation of other Pal-

estinian and Israeli obligations under the road map. Occupation would end only when Palestinians gained control over their affairs in Gaza, and thus robust and reliable security and administrative arrangements were needed for post-withdrawal Gaza. The withdrawal from Gaza confronted Israel with a security dilemma: if it withdrew completely but in a context of hostility and mistrust, Gaza could become a launching pad for more attacks against its own territory. If, on the other hand, Israel retained control over territory in, or international access to, Gaza, the occupation would continue, and so, most probably, would violent acts against Israel. That, in turn, would defeat the very purpose of the withdrawal plan. One way to resolve that dilemma was through temporary and internationally supervised security arrangements. An international presence, with the consent of the parties, would enable Israel to withdraw completely from Gaza and free itself from the occupation. It would also enable the Palestinians to live normally, free from Israeli controls, while rebuilding their shattered security capabilities and fighting terrorism and violence in cooperation with regional and international players.

Meanwhile, the PA had to reorganize its ailing security system under the authority of an empowered interior minister and had to curb violence and terror, for there was no excuse for the PA to avoid fulfilling that obligation any longer. Fighting terrorism was not a payoff that depended on the reciprocity of Israeli measures. While preparing for the withdrawal, Israel should remove all settlement outposts erected since March 2001 and completely freeze settlement activities in the West Bank. In short, the withdrawal from Gaza had to be part of the implementation of the road map, not a substitute, for it represented the consensus of the international community on how to resolve the Arab-Israeli conflict in a realistic, gradual and comprehensive way, encompassing the Syrian and Lebanese tracks. It tackled both immediate concerns and final status issues. Regarding security and territory, the road map laid out concrete, reciprocal and parallel steps that both parties should take to reverse the situation.

Both parties failed to meet their obligations. Israel did not dismantle the settlement outposts, implement a settlement freeze or abstain from taking measures undermining trust. In fact, by the time the road map implementation collapsed in 2003, settlement outposts had actually increased. Large tracts of Palestinian land were confiscated for the construction of the barrier, directly impacting tens of thousands of people. Also during the attempted implementation of the road map, many Palestinians were killed and extrajudicial assassinations continued. Despite the efforts of Prime Minister Mahmoud Abbas, the PA failed to curb violence or reorganize its security services under the Interior Minister. Terrorist attacks continued, claiming more innocent Israeli lives and raising Israeli scepticism about Palestinian commitment. Unable to exercise his powers, Mr. Abbas resigned, bringing the road map process to a halt. Since then, and despite the goodwill of the new Prime Minister, Ahmed Qurei, the PA's credibility was diminishing. In fact, the PA had reached a state of near paralysis.

Palestinians needed to be reassured that a final status agreement would respect their basic rights regarding the refugees, the settlements, the status of Jerusalem and the borders. Israelis needed to be reassured that the final peace agreement would really be final, ending violence and leading to Israel's acceptance by all its neighbours, and that it would be a negotiated, fair and realistic deal. By articulating such a political horizon to the parties, the road map aimed to embolden them to perform the most difficult immediate tasks, notably on security and territory. However, it was unrealistic to expect that the parties, mired in a violent relationship devoid of trust, would take, on their own, all the decisions necessary to return to the path of peace. Therefore, it was incumbent on the international community, with the Council at the fore, to lead the parties towards a viable solution. By adopting resolution 1397 (2002) [YUN 2002, p. 418], the Council enshrined the end goal of the peace process: two States, Israel and Palestine, living side by side in peace and security. The Council also adopted the way to achieve that goal, the road map, in resolution 1515(2003) [YUN 2003, p. 483].

Communications (30 April and 3 May). On 30 April [A/58/783-S/2004/354], Malaysia, as Chairman of the tenth session of the Islamic Summit Conference, transmitted the Declaration on Palestine, adopted at a special meeting on the Middle East (Putrajaya, Malaysia, 22 April). The Declaration, among other things, rejected the unilateral Israeli plan as it breached resolutions on international legitimacy and contradicted the provisions of the road map. It called on Israel to stop and reverse the construction of the wall in the occupied territories and urged the Security Council to consider the deployment of a UN peacekeeping force or a mechanism to monitor the implementation of the road map.

On 3 May [A/58/780-S/2004/350], Israel said that on the previous day two Palestinian terrorists killed a pregnant Israeli mother and her four young daughters in the Gaza Strip.

Quartet meeting (4 May)

Representatives of the Quartet—the UN Secretary-General, the Russian Foreign Minister, the Irish Foreign Minister, the United States Secretary of State, the High Representative for European Common Foreign and Security Policy and the European Commissioner for External Affairs—met in New York on 4 May to review developments since their last meeting [YUN 2003, p. 473]. The Quartet, in a joint statement [S/2004/421], called on the two sides to implement the road map. It condemned the continuing terror attacks on Israel, and called on the PA to take immediate action against those who planned and executed them. The Quartet members recognized Israel's legitimate right to self-defence in the face of terrorist attacks, within the parameters of international humanitarian law. They called on Israel to ease the humanitarian and economic plight of the Palestinian people, including increasing freedom of movement for people and goods both within and from the West Bank and Gaza, removing checkpoints, and taking other steps to respect the dignity of the Palestinian people and improve their quality of life. As stipulated in the road map, Israel should take no actions undermining trust, including deportations, attacks on civilians, and confiscation and/or demolition of Palestinian homes and property. The Quartet noted the Israeli Government's pledge that the barrier under construction would be a security rather than a political barrier, and would be temporary rather than permanent. It expressed concern that the proposed route of the barrier restricted the movement of people and goods, and undermined Palestinians' trust in the road map process as it appeared to prejudge the final borders of a future Palestinian State.

The Quartet welcomed the announced intention of Israeli Prime Minister Sharon to withdraw from all Gaza settlements and parts of the West Bank, as potentially a rare opportunity in the search for peace in the Middle East. That initiative, which had to bring about a full Israeli withdrawal, could be a step towards achieving the two-State vision. According to the Quartet, any unilateral initiatives by Israel should be undertaken in a manner consistent with the road map and the two-State vision, and no party should take unilateral actions that sought to predetermine issues that could be resolved only through negotiation and agreement between the two parties.

The Quartet and the international community were prepared to intensify their engagement with the Palestinians to restore momentum on the road map, enhance Palestinian humanitarian and economic conditions, build transparent and accountable Palestinian institutions, ensure security and stability in Gaza and the West Bank, prevent all acts of terrorism, and ensure the dismantlement of armed terrorist groups. In furtherance of those goals, the Quartet would take the following steps, with mechanisms to monitor performance by all sides: it would act on an urgent basis, in conjunction with the World Bank, the Office of the United Nations Special Coordinator for the Middle East Peace Process and the Ad Hoc Liaison Committee, on the basis of a World Bank/Office of the Special Coordinator rapid-assessment study, to ensure that Palestinian humanitarian needs were met, Palestinian infrastructure was restored and developed, and economic activity was reinvigorated. The Quartet was prepared to engage with a responsible and accountable Palestinian leadership, committed to reform and security performance. Through an empowered Prime Minister and Cabinet, the Task Force on Palestinian Reform, and in connection with the major donors working through the Ad Hoc Liaison Committee and the Local Aid Coordination Committee, the Quartet would engage the Palestinians to reinvigorate the reform agenda of the road map, paying particular attention to areas from which Israel planned to withdraw. The Quartet would seek to ensure that arrangements were put in place to ensure security for Palestinians and Israelis as well as freedom of movement and greater mobility and access for Palestinians. It underscored the need for agreed, transparent arrangements with all sides on access, mobility and safety for international organizations and bilateral donors and their personnel. As Israel withdrew, custody of Israeli-built infrastructure and land evacuated by Israel should be transferred through an appropriate mechanism to a reorganized PA in coordination with representatives of Palestinian civil society, the Quartet and other representatives of the international community to determine equitable and transparent arrangements for the ultimate disposition of those areas as quickly as possible. In coordination with, and under the auspices of, an oversight committee led by the United States, and in coordination with the empowered PA Prime Minister and Cabinet, Palestinian security services should be restructured and retrained, consistent with the road map, to provide law and order and security to the Palestinians, to end terror attacks against Israel and Israelis and to dismantle terrorist capabilities and infrastructure. The Quartet reminded all parties of the obligation to make rapid progress towards resumption of the political dialogue, and added that a coordinating and oversight mechanism under its auspices would be established.

Israeli military operations in Gaza

Communications (12-19 May). In communications dated between 12 and 19 May [A/ES-10/266-S/2004/382, A/ES-10/267-S/2004/394, A/ES-10/268-S/2004/402, A/ES-10/269-S/2004/409], the Permanent Observer of Palestine said that Israel continued to launch military attacks against the Palestinian population in the occupied territories. During a raid on 11 and 12 May in Gaza City, IDF killed 15 Palestinians, including 7 children. Widespread destruction was caused by repeated raids in the Rafah refugee camp, which killed at least 21 Palestinians. On 19 May, IDF opened fire on a large crowd of demonstrators in the Rafah area, killing at least 10 people and wounding more than 60 others.

Press statement of Secretary-General (19 May). The Secretary-General, on 19 May, condemned the killing and injuring of Palestinian demonstrators in southern Gaza on that day. He called on Israel to halt the military operations immediately. The Secretary-General was distressed by the killing of peaceful demonstrators, many of them women and children. He again warned Israel that it had to abide by its obligations as an occupying Power, which included protecting the civilian population and eschewing the disproportionate or indiscriminate use of force.

SECURITY COUNCIL ACTION (19 May)

On 19 May [meeting 4972], the Security Council adopted **resolution 1544(2004)** by vote (14-0-1). The draft [S/2004/400] was submitted by Algeria and Yemen.

The Security Council,

Reaffirming its resolutions 242(1967) of 22 November 1967, 338(1973) of 22 October 1973, 446(1979) of 22 March 1979, 1322(2000) of 7 October 2000, 1397 (2002) of 12 March 2002, 1402(2002) of 30 March 2002, 1403(2002) of 4 April 2002, 1405(2002) of 19 April 2002, 1435(2002) of 24 September 2002 and 1515(2003) of 19 November 2003,

Reiterating the obligation of Israel, the occupying Power, to abide scrupulously by its legal obligations and responsibilities under the Geneva Convention relative to the Protection of Civilian Persons in Time of War, of 12 August 1949,

Calling upon Israel to address its security needs within the boundaries of international law,

Expressing grave concern at the continued deterioration of the situation on the ground in the territory occupied by Israel since 1967,

Condemning the killing of Palestinian civilians that took place in the Rafah area,

Gravely concerned by the recent demolition of homes committed by Israel, the occupying Power, in the Rafah refugee camp,

Recalling the obligations of the Palestinian Authority and the Government of Israel under the road map,

Condemning all acts of violence, terror and destruction,

Reaffirming its support for the road map, endorsed in its resolution 1515(2003),

1. *Calls upon* Israel to respect its obligations under international humanitarian law, and insists, in particular, on its obligation not to undertake the demolition of homes contrary to that law;

2. *Expresses grave concern* regarding the humanitarian situation of Palestinians made homeless in the Rafah area, and calls for the provision of emergency assistance to them;

3. *Calls for* the cessation of violence and for respect of and adherence to legal obligations, including those under international humanitarian law;

4. *Calls upon* both parties to implement immediately their obligations under the road map;

5. *Decides* to remain seized of the matter.

VOTE ON RESOLUTION 1544(2004):

In favour: Algeria, Angola, Benin, Brazil, Chile, China, France, Germany, Pakistan, Philippines, Romania, Russian Federation, Spain, United Kingdom.

Against: None.

Abstaining: United States.

Speaking after the vote, the United States said that while it believed that Israel had the right to act to defend itself, its operations in Gaza did not serve the purposes of peace and security, but had actually worsened the humanitarian situation and resulted in confrontations between Israeli forces and Palestinians. Noting that the Israeli Government had expressed regret for what it called a tragic event, the United States said those events served as a reminder of the wisdom of Israel disengaging from Gaza and having its security presence replaced by reformed Palestinian security forces. While concerned about Israel's operations in Gaza, the United States could not vote in favour of the resolution because it did not sufficiently address the context of the events in Gaza. It was clear that Palestinian terrorists were smuggling weapons into Gaza through tunnels in Rafah and that the PA failed to address that threat or to end terrorist acts. Because those issues were not addressed, the United States abstained.

The Permanent Observer of Palestine said that the slaughter of innocent Palestinians in the Rafah camp was the most recent illustration of the barbaric action of the occupying Power and an act of State terrorism. During the preceding few days, that practice had escalated in the Rafah area, causing vast destruction. IDF, by using armoured bulldozers, tanks and helicopter gunships, raided the area, destroying more than 100 homes. More than 1,100 Palestinians were made homeless and hundreds of others fled the area. Since September 2000, more than 1,300 homes in Rafah alone had been demolished or made unliveable. Israel's aim was the effective levelling of the Rafah camp and areas in the city of Rafah to allow for the enlargement of its so-called security zone.

Israel said that the Council had convened again at the behest of the Palestinian Observer, under a barrage of misinformation. According to Israel, during a procession of several thousand demonstrators, which was organized by the PA and included many gunmen, seven Palestinians were killed, of whom four or five were armed terrorists. While Israel regretted any loss of civilian life, those numbers put the incident into proportion. The city of Rafah served as the PA's main pipeline for transporting weapons and ammunition in Gaza. Since September 2000, subterranean tunnels constructed underneath the "Philadelphi route" had been used by Iran and Hizbullah, as well as by Palestinian terrorist organizations like Hamas, for turning the Gaza Strip into a base for missile and rocket attacks against Israeli targets. The tunnels were typically dug from inside homes to evade discovery by Israeli security personnel. The purpose of the IDF action in Gaza was to terminate the transfer of all illegal weapons by underground tunnels to Gaza. Since April 2004, IDF had exposed eight such tunnels in the Rafah area, in addition to 101 tunnels found since the beginning of the intifada in September 2000. IDF demolished only those structures involved in terror and violence against Israeli civilians, and under international law those structures were considered legitimate military targets.

Communication (20 May). On 20 May [A/58/810-S/2004/413], the Permanent Observer of Palestine said that in the immediate wake of the adoption of resolution 1544(2004) (above), several Israeli officials publicly declared the intention to continue the military campaign; meanwhile, IDF continued killing Palestinian civilians (more than 100 in the preceding three weeks) and destroying Palestinian homes in the Rafah area. In the light of that situation, it was imperative that concerted efforts be taken by the United Nations to ensure compliance by Israel with that resolution.

Security Council consideration (21 May). The Security Council, on 21 May [meeting 4974], discussed the situation in the Middle East, including the Palestinian question.

The USG for Political Affairs, Mr. Prendergast, said that the situation since the last briefing of 23 April (see p. 459) had been characterized by growing violence, destruction and despair. Since then, 128 Palestinians and 19 Israelis had been killed, and hundreds more injured. IDF demolished hundreds of Palestinian homes and continued its policy of extrajudicial killings, in breach of its obligations under international law. Economic conditions continued to worsen, bringing yet more suffering. At the political level, deadlock prevailed. The Quartet, on 4 May, reiterated its commitment to assisting Israelis and Palestinians out of the morass through implementation of the road map. However, action by the international community or the Quartet was no substitute for steps taken by the parties. In early May, a majority of the Likud party voted against Prime Minister Sharon's initiative to withdraw unilaterally from the Gaza Strip; nevertheless, Mr. Sharon reiterated his intention to pursue the plan. Support for a withdrawal was expressed by the tens of thousands of Israelis who demonstrated in Tel Aviv and by opinion polls that showed strong popular support for a Gaza pull-out. Unfortunately, that debate cast a shadow over more fundamental issues, namely, the nature, scope and terms of a Gaza withdrawal, and its relationship to implementation of the road map. Consequently, a stalemate had developed while awaiting political decisions for transforming the initiative into a specific plan leading to the end of the occupation. Israeli settlement expansion continued unabated in Gaza and the West Bank, prompting Palestinians to wonder if all the talk about evacuation was a cover-up for more expansion. In addition, the construction of the barrier continued to erode Palestinian territory and Palestinian hope. According to estimates, the latest Israeli construction plans would put more than 12 per cent of the West Bank—plus occupied East Jerusalem—on the Israeli side of the barrier. Although Mr. Sharon stated that the barrier was temporary, the Palestinians saw it as the greatest single threat to the viability of a future State.

Communications (9-21 June). In communications dated between 9 and 21 June [A/58/839-S/2004/470, A/ES-10/270-S/2004/485, A/ES-10/271-S/2004/506], the Permanent Observer of Palestine said that Israel continued to carry out illegal policies and practices against the Palestinian people and their leadership in the Occupied Palestinian Territory. In violation of resolution 1544 (2004), Israel continued to kill Palestinian civilians and to destroy homes and property in the Rafah area. Israel also issued land confiscation orders in preparation for further expansion of the separation wall inside Palestinian territory.

Security Council consideration (23 June). The Security Council, on 23 June [meeting 4995], met to discuss the situation in the Middle East, including the Palestinian question.

The USG for Political Affairs said that the situation remained tense; the conflict continued to claim lives, economic conditions worsened, hope for a better future was low, and suffering continued—all of which contributed to a climate of despair and extremism. Since his May briefing, 39 Palestinians and two Israelis were killed and 309 Palestinians and 32 Israelis were wounded. Once the Israeli incursion into Rafah ended on 24 May, a full picture emerged of the impact that Israel's Operation Rainbow had had on the ground. According to UNRWA, 167 buildings, housing 379 families or 2,066 people, were destroyed or damaged beyond repair by Israeli forces in what was one of the most destructive operations in the Gaza Strip since September 2000. Since that date, a total of 3,437 Palestinians and 942 Israelis had been killed, and 1,476 structures were destroyed in Rafah town and refugee camp, affecting almost 15,000 people. In the course of Operation Rainbow, 53 Palestinians were killed. The operation uncovered three tunnels used to smuggle weapons. On 2 and 3 June, Israeli forces, with tanks and bulldozers, again entered Rafah town and camp, demolishing 11 more buildings, 4 of them partially. Closures continued throughout the West Bank. IDF conducted a number of search-and-arrest operations following security warnings, and extrajudicial killings continued. Curfews were imposed repeatedly in most West Bank Palestinian towns and villages. Bethlehem was declared a closed military zone for almost a week. Construction of the Israeli barrier continued at a rapid pace in and around Jerusalem, and more Palestinian land was confiscated for the construction. An increasing number of Palestinians and international peace activists demonstrated against the barrier. Attacks against and harassment of UN staff and property by IDF forces also increased. Palestinian violence continued as well, with mortars fired on Israeli settlements in Gaza and a suicide bomb attack.

The proposed Israeli withdrawal from the Gaza Strip and parts of the West Bank could help to break the political stalemate. On 7 June, the Israeli Government adopted a plan related to that initiative. Under that plan, disengagement would proceed in four stages and would involve the evacuation of all settlements and military installations in the Gaza Strip as well as the dismantling of four settlements in the northern West Bank, by the end of 2005. First, the isolated Gaza settlements of Morag, Netzarim and Kfar Darom would be evacuated, followed by the West Bank settlements of Kadim, Ganim, Sanur and Homesh. Then the remaining Gush Katif settlements would be evacuated, and finally, the northern Gaza settlements of Nissanit, Elei Sinai and Dugit would be dismantled. Another vote by the Israeli cabinet would be necessary before implementation could begin. Palestinian Prime Minister Qurei stated that the PA welcomed the disengagement plan so long as it was implemented as a part of the road map. However, if the withdrawal from Gaza and parts of the West Bank was to mark a new beginning in the peace process, both sides, Israeli and Palestinian, would have to play a part. Although the initiative was unilateral, its successful application required cooperation between all parties. The PA had a major role to play in the success of the withdrawal, and that role was contingent on the Palestinian leadership also fulfilling its obligations under the road map. The PA had to establish security control in the vacated areas. It also had to revitalize, reorganize and reform itself. Among the most urgent tasks were the strengthening of Palestinian institutions and promotion of the rule of law. That included the genuine empowerment of Prime Minister Qurei and his cabinet, and the unification of the Palestinian security forces into three components under the authority of an empowered interior minister.

Communications (25 June–15 July). On 25 June [A/58/849-S/2004/520], Turkey transmitted to the United Nations the text of the declaration adopted by the Islamic Conference of Foreign Ministers at its thirty-first session (Istanbul, Turkey, 14-16 June). The declaration, among other things, urged the Quartet to work to stop the Israeli aggression in all its forms and secure protection for the Palestinian people. In a resolution adopted at the meeting [A/58/856-S/2004/582 & Corr.1], transmitted on 15 July, the Foreign Ministers rejected the Israeli unilateral plan and condemned Israel for the assassination of Sheikh Yassin. It called for the cessation of all political contacts with the Israeli Government as long as the blockade against the Palestinian people continued.

On 28 June [A/58/850-S/2004/521], Israel said that on that day Palestinian terrorists fired four rockets on the southern town of Sderot, killing two Israeli civilians and injuring at least 11 others.

On 7 July [A/ES-10/272-S/2004/544], the Permanent Observer of Palestine said that Israel continued to invade Palestinian towns and used excessive and indiscriminate force against the Palestinian civilian population. Over the previous month, IDF killed at least 55 Palestinians. Israeli forces also continued to attack the Rafah area.

Security Council consideration (13 July). The Security Council, on 13 July [meeting 5002], discussed the situation in the Middle East and heard a briefing by the Special Coordinator for the Middle East Peace Process and Personal Representative of the Secretary-General, Mr. Roed-Larsen, who described the latest round of the conflict. Since the last monthly briefing of 23 June, violence continued, claiming the lives of 61

Palestinians and seven Israelis, and wounding more than 580 Palestinians and 71 Israelis. The PA, despite promises by its leadership, made no progress on its core obligation to end violence, combat terror and reform and reorganize itself. Israel made no progress either on its core obligation to dismantle settlement outposts erected since March 2001 and to move towards a complete freeze of settlement activities. The slow progress on the implementation of Palestinian reform could not be explained except by the lack of political will. The PA decided to begin holding local elections as early as the autumn of 2004. The commitment to holding elections was a step towards creating more democratic local institutions; however, the PA had not responded to calls by the international community to reform its electoral institutional framework to meet minimal international standards. In the areas of finance and public administration, reform had proceeded well.

Regarding security reform, President Arafat had lent only nominal support to an Egyptian plan to reform the Palestinian security services, consistent with the road map, with support of the international community. Those efforts were necessary to end the emerging chaos in Palestinian areas, to restore law and order and, most importantly, to re-establish the PA as a credible partner for the international community. The Quartet as well as the Arab peace partners had been active in trying to bring about the necessary reforms. The Palestinian Prime Minister needed to be empowered to enable him and the cabinet to make the necessary changes, but that had not happened. Mr. Arafat remained confined to his headquarters in Ramallah in difficult conditions, under de facto house arrest. However, that was not an excuse for passivity and inaction. There was currently no sign of constructive movement. Despite a well-intentioned Prime Minister, the paralysis of the PA was evident and the deterioration of law and order in Palestinian areas was worsening. Clashes and showdowns between branches of Palestinian security forces were common in the Gaza Strip, where the PA's legal authority was receding fast in the face of the mounting power of arms, money and intimidation. Lawlessness and gang rule were becoming common in Nablus, while the perceived PA abdication of responsibility had led many Rafah residents to take matters into their own hands, with some of them establishing a private checkpoint, preventing PA officials from crossing to Egypt or from entering Rafah. Jericho was becoming the only Palestinian city with a functioning police. That collapse of authority could not be attributed only to the Israeli incursions and operations inside

Palestinian towns; the PA was in deep distress and in real danger of collapse.

Israel's lack of compliance on the issue of settlements was equally frustrating. Territory lay at the heart of the conflict. The drafters of the road map were careful to require from Israel an immediate dismantling of all outposts erected since March 2001, in order to send a clear and positive message to the Palestinians that a paradigm shift was taking place. A full and comprehensive freeze on settlement activities was to have been achieved as the security situation improved, but that had not been the case.

Emergency special session

In accordance with General Assembly decision ES-10/22 [YUN 2003, p. 481] and at the request of Jordan [A/ES-10/274] in its capacity as Chairman of the Arab Group and on behalf of the League of Arab States (LAS), as well as at the request of Malaysia, on behalf of the Chairman of the Coordinating Bureau of the Non-Aligned Movement [A/ES-10/275], the tenth emergency special session of the Assembly resumed on 16 July to discuss "Illegal Israeli actions in Occupied East Jerusalem and the rest of the Occupied Palestinian Territory". In particular, the Assembly discussed the 9 July ICJ advisory opinion on the legal consequences of the construction of a wall in the Occupied Palestinian Territory, including in and around East Jerusalem (see below). The session was first convened in April 1997 [YUN 1997, p. 394] and resumed in July and November of that year, as well as in March 1998 [YUN 1998, p. 425], February 1999 [YUN 1999, p. 402], October 2000 [YUN 2000, p. 421], December 2001 [YUN 2001, p. 414], May 2002 [YUN 2002, p. 428] and in August of that year [ibid., p. 435], September 2003 [YUN 2003, p. 472] and resumed in October [ibid., p. 476] and December of that year [ibid., p. 479].

ICJ advisory opinion

On 9 July, at the request of the General Assembly in resolution ES-10/14 [YUN 2003, p. 480], ICJ rendered its advisory opinion (see p. 1272) on the legal consequences arising from the construction by Israel of the separation wall in the Occupied Palestinian Territory [A/ES-10/273 & Corr.1]. The Court found that the route of the wall in the occupied territory, including in and around East Jerusalem, was contrary to international law and that Israel was under an obligation to terminate the building of the wall, to dismantle parts already built and to make reparations for all damage caused to Palestinian property. It also found that States were under an obligation not to recognize the illegal situation and to ensure Israel's compli-ance with international law under the Fourth Geneva Convention. The Court affirmed that the Assembly and the Security Council should consider further action.

The Assembly reconvened the emergency special session to consider the issue.

GENERAL ASSEMBLY ACTION

On 20 July [meeting 27], the General Assembly adopted **resolution ES-10/15** [draft: A/ES-10/L.18/Rev.1] by recorded vote (150-6-10) [agenda item 5].

Advisory opinion of the International Court of Justice on the *Legal Consequences of the Construction of a Wall in the Occupied Palestinian Territory, including in and around East Jerusalem*

The General Assembly,

Guided by the principles enshrined in the Charter of the United Nations,

Considering that the promotion of respect for the obligations arising from the Charter and other instruments and rules of international law is among the basic purposes and principles of the United Nations,

Recalling its resolution 2625(XXV) of 24 October 1970, on the Declaration on Principles of International Law concerning Friendly Relations and Cooperation among States in accordance with the Charter of the United Nations,

Reaffirming the illegality of any territorial acquisition resulting from the threat or use of force,

Recalling the Regulations annexed to the Hague Convention Respecting the Laws and Customs of War on Land of 1907,

Recalling also the Geneva Convention relative to the Protection of Civilian Persons in Time of War of 12 August 1949, and relevant provisions of customary law, including those codified in Additional Protocol I to the Geneva Conventions,

Recalling further the International Covenant on Civil and Political Rights, the International Covenant on Economic, Social and Cultural Rights and the Convention on the Rights of the Child,

Reaffirming the permanent responsibility of the United Nations towards the question of Palestine until it is resolved in all aspects in a satisfactory manner on the basis of international legitimacy,

Recalling relevant Security Council resolutions, including resolutions 242(1967) of 22 November 1967, 338(1973) of 22 October 1973, 446(1979) of 22 March 1979, 452(1979) of 20 July 1979, 465(1980) of 1 March 1980, 476(1980) of 30 June 1980, 478(1980) of 20 August 1980, 904(1994) of 18 March 1994, 1073(1996) of 28 September 1996, 1397(2002) of 12 March 2002, 1515 (2003) of 19 November 2003 and 1544(2004) of 19 May 2004,

Recalling also the resolutions of its tenth emergency special session on illegal Israeli actions in Occupied East Jerusalem and the rest of the Occupied Palestinian Territory,

Reaffirming the most recent resolution of the fifty-eighth session of the General Assembly on the status of the Occupied Palestinian Territory, including East Jerusalem, resolution 58/292 of 6 May 2004,

Reaffirming also the right of the Palestinian people to self-determination, including their right to their independent State of Palestine,

Reaffirming further the commitment to the two-State solution of Israel and Palestine, living side by side in peace and security within recognized borders, based on the pre-1967 borders,

Condemning all acts of violence, terrorism and destruction,

Calling upon both parties to fulfil their obligations under relevant provisions of the road map, the Palestinian Authority to undertake visible efforts on the ground to arrest, disrupt and restrain individuals and groups conducting and planning violent attacks, and the Government of Israel to take no actions undermining trust, including deportations and attacks on civilians and extrajudicial killings,

Reaffirming that all States have the right and the duty to take actions in conformity with international law and international humanitarian law to counter deadly acts of violence against their civilian population in order to protect the lives of their citizens,

Recalling its resolution ES-10/13 of 21 October 2003, in which it demanded that Israel stop and reverse the construction of the wall in the Occupied Palestinian Territory, including in and around East Jerusalem,

Recalling also its resolution ES-10/14 of 8 December 2003, in which it requested the International Court of Justice to urgently render an advisory opinion on the following question:

"What are the legal consequences arising from the construction of the wall being built by Israel, the occupying Power, in the Occupied Palestinian Territory, including in and around East Jerusalem, as described in the report of the Secretary-General, considering the rules and principles of international law, including the Fourth Geneva Convention, of 1949, and relevant Security Council and General Assembly resolutions?",

Having received with respect the advisory opinion of the Court on the *Legal Consequences of the Construction of a Wall in the Occupied Palestinian Territory*, rendered on 9 July 2004,

Noting in particular that the Court replied to the question put forth by the General Assembly in resolution ES-10/14 as follows:

"A. The construction of the wall being built by Israel, the occupying Power, in the Occupied Palestinian Territory, including in and around East Jerusalem, and its associated regime, are contrary to international law;

"B. Israel is under an obligation to terminate its breaches of international law; it is under an obligation to cease forthwith the works of construction of the wall being built in the Occupied Palestinian Territory, including in and around East Jerusalem, to dismantle forthwith the structure therein situated, and to repeal or render ineffective forthwith all legislative and regulatory acts relating thereto, in accordance with paragraph 151 of this Opinion;

"C. Israel is under an obligation to make reparation for all damage caused by the construction of the wall in the Occupied Palestinian Territory, including in and around East Jerusalem;

"D. All States are under an obligation not to recognize the illegal situation resulting from the construction of the wall and not to render aid or assistance in maintaining the situation created by such construction; all States Parties to the Fourth Geneva Convention relative to the Protection of Civilian Persons in Time of War of 12 August 1949 have in addition the obligation, while respecting the United Nations Charter and international law, to ensure compliance by Israel with international humanitarian law as embodied in that Convention;

"E. The United Nations, and especially the General Assembly and the Security Council, should consider what further action is required to bring to an end the illegal situation resulting from the construction of the wall and the associated regime, taking due account of the present Advisory Opinion.",

Noting that the Court concluded that "the Israeli settlements in the Occupied Palestinian Territory (including East Jerusalem) have been established in breach of international law",

Noting also the statement made by the Court that "Israel and Palestine are under an obligation scrupulously to observe the rules of international humanitarian law, one of the paramount purposes of which is to protect civilian life", and that "in the Court's view, this tragic situation can be brought to an end only through implementation in good faith of all relevant Security Council resolutions, in particular resolutions 242 (1967) and 338(1973)",

Considering that respect for the Court and its functions is essential to the rule of law and reason in international affairs,

1. *Acknowledges* the advisory opinion of the International Court of Justice of 9 July 2004 on the *Legal Consequences of the Construction of a Wall in the Occupied Palestinian Territory*, including in and around East Jerusalem;

2. *Demands* that Israel, the occupying Power, comply with its legal obligations as mentioned in the advisory opinion;

3. *Calls upon* all States Members of the United Nations to comply with their legal obligations as mentioned in the advisory opinion;

4. *Requests* the Secretary-General to establish a register of damage caused to all natural or legal persons concerned in connection with paragraphs 152 and 153 of the advisory opinion;

5. *Decides* to reconvene to assess the implementation of the present resolution, with the aim of ending the illegal situation resulting from the construction of the wall and its associated regime in the Occupied Palestinian Territory, including East Jerusalem;

6. *Calls upon* both the Government of Israel and the Palestinian Authority to immediately implement their obligations under the road map, in cooperation with the Quartet, as endorsed by Security Council resolution 1515(2003), to achieve the vision of two States living side by side in peace and security, and emphasizes that both Israel and the Palestinian Authority are under an obligation scrupulously to observe the rules of international humanitarian law;

7. *Calls upon* all States parties to the Fourth Geneva Convention to ensure respect by Israel for the Conven-

tion, and invites Switzerland, in its capacity as the depositary of the Geneva Conventions, to conduct consultations and to report to the General Assembly on the matter, including with regard to the possibility of resuming the Conference of High Contracting Parties to the Fourth Geneva Convention;

8. *Decides* to adjourn the tenth emergency special session temporarily and to authorize the President of the General Assembly at its most recent session to resume its meeting upon request from Member States.

RECORDED VOTE ON RESOLUTION ES-10/15:

In favour: Afghanistan, Albania, Algeria, Andorra, Antigua and Barbuda, Argentina, Armenia, Austria, Azerbaijan, Bahamas, Bahrain, Bangladesh, Barbados, Belarus, Belgium, Belize, Bhutan, Bolivia, Bosnia and Herzegovina, Botswana, Brazil, Brunei Darussalam, Bulgaria, Burkina Faso, Burundi, Cambodia, Cape Verde, Chile, China, Colombia, Congo, Costa Rica, Croatia, Cuba, Cyprus, Czech Republic, Democratic People's Republic of Korea, Denmark, Djibouti, Dominica, Dominican Republic, Ecuador, Egypt, Eritrea, Estonia, Fiji, Finland, France, Gabon, Gambia, Germany, Ghana, Greece, Grenada, Guatemala, Guinea, Guyana, Haiti, Honduras, Hungary, Iceland, India, Indonesia, Iran, Ireland, Italy, Jamaica, Japan, Jordan, Kazakhstan, Kenya, Kuwait, Kyrgyzstan, Lao People's Democratic Republic, Latvia, Lebanon, Lesotho, Libyan Arab Jamahiriya, Liechtenstein, Lithuania, Luxembourg, Malaysia, Maldives, Mali, Malta, Mauritania, Mauritius, Mexico, Monaco, Mongolia, Morocco, Mozambique, Myanmar, Namibia, Nepal, Netherlands, New Zealand, Nicaragua, Nigeria, Norway, Oman, Pakistan, Panama, Paraguay, Peru, Philippines, Poland, Portugal, Qatar, Republic of Korea, Romania, Russian Federation, Saint Lucia, Saint Vincent and the Grenadines, San Marino, Saudi Arabia, Senegal, Serbia and Montenegro, Sierra Leone, Singapore, Slovakia, Slovenia, South Africa, Spain, Sri Lanka, Sudan, Suriname, Swaziland, Sweden, Switzerland, Syrian Arab Republic, Thailand, The former Yugoslav Republic of Macedonia, Timor-Leste, Togo, Trinidad and Tobago, Tunisia, Turkey, Turkmenistan, Tuvalu, Ukraine, United Arab Emirates, United Kingdom, United Republic of Tanzania, Uzbekistan, Venezuela, Viet Nam, Yemen, Zambia, Zimbabwe.

Against: Australia, Israel, Marshall Islands, Micronesia, Palau, United States.

Abstaining: Cameroon, Canada, El Salvador, Nauru, Papua New Guinea, Solomon Islands, Tonga, Uganda, Uruguay, Vanuatu.

The Permanent Observer of Palestine, speaking before the vote [meeting 24], said that the ICJ advisory opinion was a pivotal development that brought international law back to the forefront of the dialogue on the question of Palestine and the Israeli-Palestinian conflict. While the outcome might be considered a victory for the Palestinian people, it was also a victory for all the peoples of the region and for the region's future. The Court's position on the issue, on the basis of international law, was conclusive, and there could be no further question as to the illegal status of the wall or the settlements that Israel was building in the Occupied Palestinian Territory. ICJ's conclusions on the wall were definitive and non-negotiable. The aim of the draft resolution before the Assembly was twofold: acceptance of the advisory opinion and a call for compliance by Israel and by Member States with international legal obligations as set out in the advisory opinion. The PA expected States to undertake actions consistent with their legal obligations as determined by ICJ, including action against settlement activities and sanctions against companies involved in the wall construction. Israel had already declared its rejection of the Court's authority

and the advisory opinion as well as its intention to continue constructing the wall.

Israel said that, together with a large number of Member States, it did not support the request for the advisory opinion, which it found inappropriate, a misuse of the advisory opinion procedure and damaging to the road map. Israel was dismayed that the opinion did not seriously address the terrorism facing Israeli civilians or the Palestinian leadership's refusal to bring that terrorism to an end. Those crimes were the very reason that the fence was being erected, and Israel found that omission legally inexplicable and morally inexcusable. Israel recognized that the security fence raised complex legal and humanitarian issues. Accordingly, the fence and its route were subject to a process of constant review and change, including the right of those affected, Palestinian or Israeli, to petition Israel's Supreme Court. On 30 June, in response to such a petition, that Court recognized Israel's authority to erect a fence as a defensive measure against terrorist attacks, though it stressed that the fence had to be balanced against the rights of those affected. The Israeli Court laid out a detailed proportionality test by which such a balance could be reached, and it found that sections of the fence required re-routing. The Court's ruling was petitioned by Palestinians and Israelis who wanted practical solutions on the ground; the Court sought to find a balance between competing rights; it had before it specific evidence on all aspects of routing, the security rationale and associated humanitarian effects; and its ruling was binding upon Israel. ICJ, on the other hand, was asked only about the rights of one side; it was supplied only with partial and often misleading information; it was asked a question as part of a political and manipulative campaign; and its opinion was advisory only. Following the judgement of the Israeli Court, the Government announced that it would not only re-route those parts of the fence that were the subject of the petition, but would re-examine the entire routing so as to ensure that it complied with international law. That re-examination had already led to a decision to re-route large portions of the fence. ICJ's opinion did not rule out the authority to erect a security fence; indeed, it recognized that military exigencies and security imperatives could justify such action, but it failed to properly examine those exigencies.

The United States [meeting 25] said that the draft resolution and ICJ's opinion that the text endorsed pointed away from a political solution to the Israeli-Palestinian crisis that would embody the vision of two States living side by side in peace and security. Moreover, the draft resolution was one-sided, and it adopted a confusing interpretation of Article 51 of the UN Charter on the right to self-defence.

The Assembly continued its discussion on the agenda item on 19 and 20 July [meetings 26 & 27]. Speaking after the vote, the Netherlands, on behalf of the EU and other Member States, said the ICJ advisory opinion largely coincided with the EU's position on the legality of the barrier built by Israel on the Palestinian side of the Green Line (the de facto border between Israel and Palestine). The EU expressed its opposition to the route of the barrier.

Further developments

Communication (6 August). On 6 August [A/ES-10/276-S/2004/630], the Permanent Observer of Palestine said that Israel continued to kill and injure Palestinian civilians and to destroy property in the occupied territories. For more than a month, Israeli forces had laid siege to the area of Beit Hanoun in Gaza, repeatedly carrying out attacks in the area and causing destruction to private and public property. Israel also continued to construct the wall and to build illegal settlements.

Security Council consideration (11 August). The Security Council, at a meeting on 11 August [meeting 5019], heard a statement by the USG for Political Affairs, Mr. Prendergast, who said that there had been no tangible progress towards resuming the peace process since the 13 July briefing (see p. 464), and violence continued to claim innocent lives. Neither side took adequate steps to protect civilians, and both were in breach of their international legal obligations. Palestinian civilians continued to fall victim in Israeli military operations. The scale of destruction of Palestinian property by the Israeli military raised concerns about collective punishment. For its part, the PA had obligations under agreements reached with Israel, under international humanitarian law and in accordance with its commitments under the road map to protect Israeli civilians from attacks emanating from territories in its control. It failed to live up to those obligations, and Israeli civilians continued to suffer attacks from Palestinians, most recently in the form of Qassam rockets. Over the past month, 54 Palestinians had been killed and 400 Palestinians and 23 Israelis injured.

A new pattern had emerged: Palestinian militants launched Qassam rockets into Israel, followed by Israeli helicopter missile strikes into the Gaza Strip and ever-deeper incursions into areas adjacent to Israel. The northern Gaza Strip was the focus of a large-scale Israeli operation—operation Forward Shield—around the city of Beit

Hanoun, begun on 29 June in the wake of a Qassam attack on Sderot and continued in many areas of Beit Hanoun and beyond, towards the Jabalya refugee camp. During the reporting period, more than 60 rockets were launched from Beit Hanoun at Israeli communities near the Gaza Strip, causing injury and property damage. Israel continued to carry out extrajudicial killings, as well as search and arrest campaigns throughout the West Bank and the Gaza Strip.

Progress on the implementation of Palestinian reform continued to be slow and mostly cosmetic. On 17 July, Prime Minister Qurei submitted his resignation, citing the state of unprecedented chaos. President Arafat announced a series of security measures to prevent further deterioration, including the appointment of the chief of military intelligence as head of national security forces and the appointment of a new police chief in Gaza. However, those measures led to further unrest as thousands took to the streets in Gaza City in protest. The next day, demonstrations involved clashes among various factions of Fatah. After that attack, manifestations of unrest, popular discontent and chaos increased. Finally, political mediation, notably by a group of Palestinian Legislative Council members, led to an agreement by which President Arafat agreed to grant Prime Minister Qurei full authority over the security agencies, and to abide by the Basic Law as far as the powers of the Prime Minister were concerned. On 27 July, Mr. Qurei retracted his resignation. However, despite those developments, ultimate authority and control over all PA security agencies remained with the National Security Council, headed by President Arafat.

Israel also failed to implement its core commitments under the road map. Settlement expansion and lack of action on removing the outposts erected since 2001 severely undermined Palestinian trust in Israel's intentions and contributed to strengthening hardliners among Palestinians. Despite repeated promises by the Israeli Government, settlement activities continued. Support for Prime Minister Sharon's initiative to withdraw the Israeli armed forces from Gaza and parts of the West Bank and to evacuate all settlements in the Gaza Strip and four settlements in the northern West Bank was gaining momentum within Israel. Despite vocal opposition from segments of the settler community, polls showed that 60 per cent of Israelis supported the disengagement initiative.

Communications (12 August–14 September). In communications dated 12 and 31 August [A/58/870-S/2004/647, A/58/881-S/2004/702], Israel detailed Palestinian attacks against Israelis. On 11 August, Palestinian terrorists detonated a bomb at a checkpoint in Jerusalem, wounding six Israeli soldiers and 12 Palestinians and killing two Palestinian bystanders. On 31 August, two Palestinian suicide bombers killed 16 Israelis and wounded over 100 more in the city of Be'er Sheva.

In communications dated between 19 August and 14 September [A/ES-10/277-S/2004/668, A/ES-10/278-S/2004/673, A/58/877-S/2004/678, A/ES-10/279-S/2004/719, A/ES-10/281-S/2004/729], the Permanent Observer of Palestine said that Israel continued to carry out illegal policies and practices against the Palestinian people. On 15 August, more than 2,000 Palestinian prisoners and detainees being held in Israeli jails started a series of hunger strikes to protest the violation of their rights and their living conditions. On 7 September, IDF carried out a missile attack in the neighbourhood of Shijaia in Gaza City, killing 15 Palestinians and wounding at least 40 others. Between 7 and 14 September, IDF killed at least 16 Palestinians and wounded dozens of others in the occupied territories.

Security Council consideration (17 September). The Security Council, on 17 September [meeting 5039], heard a briefing by the USG for Political Affairs. He said that it had been a bad month in the Middle East, with a marked increase in casualties on both sides and a resumption of suicide bombings. Nor was there good news to report in terms of implementation of the road map. Prime Minister Sharon had said that Israel was not following the road map and that it might stay in the West Bank long after any withdrawal from Gaza. Meanwhile, new decisions were announced on settlement activity and Palestinian reform remained stalled.

In terms of specific events, the previous month was marked by the first major suicide bombing since March and a number of Israeli military operations, incursions and acts of destruction. On 31 August, 16 Israelis were killed and more than 100 injured in a double suicide bombing on two buses in the Israeli city of Be'er Sheva. Responsibility for that terror attack was claimed by Hamas, which stated that it was an act of revenge for Israel's assassinations of its spiritual leader and his successor in the spring. In all, 80 Palestinians and 17 Israelis were killed in five weeks; 630 Palestinians and 133 Israelis were injured. Violence in and around Gaza continued. On several occasions, Palestinian militants launched Qassam rockets and mortar shells against Israeli settlements in Gaza and against the Israeli town of Sderot, causing damage and injury. On 6 September, Israeli helicopter gunships, tanks and warplanes attacked a Hamas training site in Gaza City, killing 14 Palestinians—mostly militants—and injuring 30 others, leading to further retaliatory action.

The Israeli policy of confiscating and/or levelling Palestinian land in the context of military operations and for the construction of the wall also continued. Israel was revising long sections of the barrier route in accordance with a ruling of the Israeli Supreme Court, which also instructed the Government to respond to the advisory opinion rendered by ICJ on 9 July. Meanwhile, however, Israel continued to construct the barrier east of Jerusalem, and there were reports that construction would be speeded up south of Jerusalem. The UN Secretariat was working on terms of reference for establishing a registry of damages, as requested by the General Assembly. On 31 August, Prime Minister Sharon underlined his commitment to implement the withdrawal of all armed forces from Gaza and parts of the West Bank and to evacuate all settlements in the Gaza Strip, as well as four settlements in the northern West Bank, and outlined a timetable for the legislative process arising from the plan, which had already begun. On 14 September, the Israeli security cabinet approved the legislative package for the implementation of the disengagement plan, including principles for the evacuation of settlements and compensation for settlement residents. The Government also approved advance compensation for those settlers relocating voluntarily.

For its part, the PA failed to make progress on its obligation to end the violence and combat terror and to institute meaningful reform measures, despite President Arafat's statements on commitment to reform. On the positive side, the voter registration process began on 4 September under the auspices of the Central Elections Commission.

Quartet meeting (22 September)

The Quartet, meeting informally in New York on 22 September, issued a statement [SG/2091] in which it reaffirmed its 4 May communiqué (see p. 460). It noted that the situation remained difficult and no significant progress was made on the road map. The Quartet said that genuine action was needed so that an empowered Palestinian Prime Minister and cabinet could fulfil the PA's obligations under the road map, including an end to violence and terrorism and the dismantlement of terrorist capabilities and infrastructure. It also noted the need for the PA to prepare for assumption of control over Gaza, in particular by reforming its security forces and re-establishing the rule of law. Welcoming steps towards Palestinian municipal elections, it urged Israel and the PA to cooperate towards that goal. It also urged

Israel to dismantle settlement outposts erected since March 2001 and to impose a settlement freeze. In addition, Israel should ease the humanitarian and economic plight of the Palestinian people. Taking note of the 9 July ICJ advisory opinion on the Israeli separation barrier, the Quartet urged positive action by Israel with respect to the barrier's route. It encouraged Prime Minister Sharon's intention to withdraw from all Gaza settlements and parts of the West Bank and for the two parties to coordinate implementation of the withdrawal.

Escalation of violence

Communications (23 September–4 October). On 23 September [A/59/380-S/2004/757], Israel said that on the previous day a Palestinian suicide bomber killed two Israeli security officers and wounded 30 civilians in northern Jerusalem. On 23 September, Palestinian gunmen killed three military personnel in Gaza.

In communications dated between 27 September and 4 October [A/ES-10/282-S/2004/761, A/ES-10/283-S/2004/776, A/ES-10/285-S/2004/790, A/ES-10/284-S/2004/782], the Permanent Observer of Palestine said that, on 26 September, Israel killed Izzedine Al-Sheikh Khalil, a leader of Hamas, when a car bomb was detonated in Damascus, Syrian Arab Republic. On 29 and 30 September, IDF killed at least 33 Palestinians and wounded more than 100 others in Gaza. On 1 October, 8 more Palestinian civilians were killed and 17 others wounded by Israeli forces in continued military attacks at the Jabaliya refugee camp.

On 1 October [A/59/425-S/2004/808], Turkey transmitted to the Secretary-General the final communiqué of the annual coordination meeting of Foreign Ministers of the States members of the Organization of the Islamic Conference (New York, 28 September). The meeting took note of Israel's defiant response to the ICJ advisory opinion and called for further measures to be taken by the United Nations, in accordance with paragraph 5 of resolution ES-10/15 (see p. 465). It also called on UN Member States to prevent any products of the Israeli settlements from entering their markets, to decline entry to Israeli settlers and to impose sanctions against companies and entities involved in the construction of the wall in the Occupied Palestinian Territory.

On 4 October [S/2004/795], the Permanent Observer of LAS transmitted to the Security Council President the text of a resolution on the deterioration of the situation in the Palestinian territories, adopted by the extraordinary session of the LAS Council (Cairo, Egypt, 3 October). The resolution, among other things, called on the Quartet to take a decisive stand to stop the Israeli

aggression against the Palestinian people and requested the Secretary-General to report on the crimes and practices of Israel in the occupied territories.

Security Council consideration (4-5 October). At the request of Tunisia on behalf of the Arab Group and LAS [S/2004/779], the Security Council, on 4 and 5 October [meetings 5049 & 5051], considered the situation in the Middle East, including the Palestinian question.

Speaking on 4 October, the Permanent Observer of Palestine said that since 29 September, IDF had killed 83 Palestinians, including 20 children, injured hundreds and caused widespread destruction, including the demolition of homes and the destruction of farmland, economic installations and infrastructure such as roads, water and electricity networks. The bulk of those losses occurred when IDF swept through the northern part of the Gaza Strip, including the Jabaliya refugee camp, rushing more than 2,000 soldiers, 100 tanks and 100 armoured vehicles and bulldozers to the area, in addition to helicopter gunships. Hundreds of Palestinians were without shelter as a result. Tens of thousands were without water or electricity and were suffering from severe shortages of food and medicine. Israel claimed that it swept through the northern part of the Gaza Strip and committed those acts in response to the launching of rockets from that area on an Israeli town that resulted in the killing of two Israeli children. There was absolutely no justification, under any circumstances, for the Israelis to carry out widespread killing and destruction. Perhaps what was taking place in Gaza was related in some way to the so-called unilateral disengagement plan, which was aimed at dismantling the settlements and military installations in the Gaza Strip, as well as four settlement outposts in the northern West Bank, while laying siege to the Gaza Strip and maintaining control over its land, airspace and water. The plan also aimed at continuing the construction of the separation wall and the building of settlements in the West Bank. In brief, it aimed at a long-term movement to surround the Gaza Strip while maintaining the colonization of the West Bank.

Israel said that on 29 September two Israeli children were murdered by Qassam rockets fired at the Israeli town of Sderot. The Palestinian terror organization Hamas claimed responsibility for that attack, which was only the latest of such incidents. Palestinian terror organizations had been producing Qassam rockets in workshops dispersed throughout the Gaza Strip. The ease with which those rockets were hidden, transported and launched made them a weapon of choice. Those rocket attacks from Gaza did not target only Israeli civilians; Palestinian lives were also put at risk by terrorists' use of human shields. Virtually all terrorist fire directed from Gaza against Israeli targets emanated from crowds or residential buildings, and explosive charges and mines were planted within the civilian infrastructure. Israel was compelled to act in accordance with its right and duty of self-defence in an effort to halt the firing of rockets and the murder of its citizens. While the latest operation was broader than its predecessors, it was relatively limited, with the aim of refraining from deeply penetrating densely populated areas.

On 5 October, a vote was taken on a draft resolution [S/2004/783] submitted by Algeria, Pakistan and Tunisia, by which the Security Council would have demanded the immediate cessation of all military operations in northern Gaza and the withdrawal of the Israeli occupying forces from that area. The vote was 11 to 1, with 3 abstentions. The draft resolution was not adopted owing to the negative vote of a permanent member of the Council (United States). Speaking after the vote, the United Kingdom said that the draft resolution wrongly gave the impression that fault lay only with the Israeli side. The responsibility for taking steps to end the violence lay with both sides; for that reason, the United Kingdom abstained. France said it voted in favour of the draft resolution for it called for an immediate cessation of Israeli military operations in the north of Gaza and included a condemnation of acts of terror and the need for the speedy implementation of the road map. Those two factors were essential and ensured that the text was balanced.

Communications (7-18 October). In communications dated between 7 and 18 October [A/ES-10/286-S/2004/801, A/59/427-S/2004/806, A/ES-10/287-S/2004/811, A/ES-10/288-S/2004/816, A/ES-10/289-S/2004/824], the Permanent Observer of Palestine said that in a one-week period IDF killed 26 Palestinian children in northern Gaza. At least 21 Palestinian civilians were killed by IDF between 7 and 11 October. On 14 October, Israeli forces killed five more Palestinians in two air missile strikes against refugee camps in Gaza. In the three-week period since 29 September, IDF killed at least 150 Palestinians and injured at least 500 others.

Security Council consideration (22 October). On 22 October [meeting 5060], the Council heard a briefing by the USG for Political Affairs, Mr. Prendergast, who said a major Israeli military operation in the Gaza Strip resulted in the deaths of large numbers of Palestinians. Since the last monthly briefing (see p. 469), 206 Palestinians and 13 Israelis were killed and 1,033 Palestinians and 62 Israelis were injured. Violence in and around the Gaza Strip sharply escalated during the reporting period and the Occupied Palestinian Territory drifted towards chaos. On 29 September, Qassam rockets fired from Gaza at the Israeli town of Sderot killed two children. The next day, Israel launched a major military operation in northern Gaza. A large contingent of Israeli troops entered Beit Lahiya, Beit Hanoun and the Jabaliya refugee camp. By 15 October, when Israeli troops started redeploying, 135 Palestinians had been killed in Gaza, 114 of them in the northern part of the Strip. UN agencies' operations were severely affected by Israeli restrictions on movement. During the reporting period, UNRWA was forced to suspend many of its normal operations, including the resumption of emergency food aid in the Gaza Strip. With few exceptions, since 21 September, Israeli forces had denied UN personnel unimpeded access into Gaza, hindering the delivery of humanitarian aid. Israel continued its policies of demolishing houses and of confiscating and/or levelling Palestinian land for the construction of the barrier, which continued, especially around Jerusalem. On 11 October, Prime Minister Sharon stated that Israel adhered to its support of the road map, which he said was the only plan to enable progress towards a viable political agreement. His withdrawal initiative was scheduled to enter the legislative process in the Knesset (parliament) on 25 October.

Communications (25 October and 2 November). On 25 October [A/ES-10/290-S/2004/856], the Permanent Observer of Palestine said that from 18 to 25 October, IDF killed 31 Palestinians and wounded dozens of other people. On 25 October, IDF launched a large-scale military attack on the Khan Younis refugee camp in Gaza.

On 2 November [A/59/548-S/2004/880], Israel said that the day before a Palestinian suicide bomber killed three Israeli civilians and wounded 30 others in Tel Aviv.

Further developments in the peace process

Security Council consideration (15 November and 16 December). The Security Council, on 15 November [meeting 5077], heard a briefing by the Special Coordinator for the Middle East Peace Process, Mr. Roed-Larsen. He said that on 11 November, President Arafat died in a hospital in Paris. A funeral ceremony was held for him in Cairo on 12 November, before he was buried in Ramallah. The Palestinian leadership had taken steps towards a smooth transition of power and, by and large, prevented unrest in the areas under PA control.

The Middle East had reached a critical juncture even before the death of President Arafat. In late October, the Israeli Knesset approved Prime Minister Sharon's initiative to withdraw from the Gaza Strip and parts of the West Bank. That historic decision paved the way for the evacuation of Israeli settlements in the Occupied Palestinian Territory for the first time since the occupation began in 1967. The recent violence followed a pattern that had emerged since September 2000 and especially in 2004, with Palestinian extremists and militants organizing and carrying out suicide bombings and other acts of terror against Israeli civilians, as they did once again on 1 November, killing three people in Tel Aviv and wounding many more. Palestinian militants also fired Qassam rockets and mortar shells against cities inside Israel and against Israeli targets in the Occupied Palestinian Territory. Israel maintained the illegal practice of targeted assassinations, including in densely populated areas where there was a high risk of so-called collateral damage. Israel's military operations and incursions in the occupied territories raised the spectre of disproportionate use of force and collective punishment through the destruction of civilian property and infrastructure.

Briefing the Council on 16 December [meeting 5102], the USG for Political Affairs, Mr. Prendergast, said that there had been a marked number of positive developments since the 15 November briefing, which afforded a window of opportunity to revitalize the peace process. Significant strides were made towards ensuring that the Palestinian presidential elections scheduled for 9 January 2005 would be conducted in a free and fair manner, in accordance with international standards, and monitored by more than 400 international electoral observers, with UN technical assistance provided to the Central Elections Commission. Registration for Palestinian voters reopened on 24 November and continued until 1 December. Campaigning would officially begin on 26 December and last through 7 January 2005.

Security reform and the establishment of full control by the PA over the Palestinian areas continued to be a major challenge facing the Palestinian leadership. The Israeli Government contributed to enabling a positive transition period following the death of President Arafat. Security cooperation between the parties resumed. Israel scaled back military activity in areas under PA control, and Prime Minister Sharon announced his willingness to cease all military incursions into Palestinian areas if calm prevailed. In recognition of a long-standing Quartet condition, Mr. Sharon said that Israel would want to coordinate security arrangements with the PA for the planned withdrawal of Israeli troops and settlers from the Gaza Strip and parts of the West Bank

and for the transfer of the evacuated areas to the Palestinians. In addition, Mr. Sharon publicly acknowledged that incitement in the Palestinian media had dropped noticeably, in accordance with Palestinian obligations under the road map. The overall level of violence had dropped during the period under review, but casualty figures were still too high; 52 Palestinians and seven Israelis were killed, and 172 Palestinians and 29 Israelis were injured. While there was a reduction in the number of incidents, Palestinian militants continued to fire mortar shells and Qassam rockets against Israeli settlements and targets inside Israel. Israel continued to demolish houses and restricted movement for the Palestinians, although in an eased form. Israel's construction of the barrier in the West Bank also continued, with worrisome consequences for Palestinians, despite Israel's revision of the barrier's route, closer to the Green Line.

Meanwhile, the Quartet principals, at a meeting on 23 November in Sharm el-Sheikh, Egypt, discussed the transition in the PA and agreed that the immediate priorities were to provide technical support for the elections and to help ensure the fiscal stability of the Palestinian governing body.

In a later briefing to the Council [meeting 5111], Mr. Prendergast said that the first round of elections to Palestinian municipal councils was held in 26 communities on 23 December, with some 150,000 eligible voters choosing from among more than 800 candidates. Those elections—the first at the municipal level since 1967—witnessed a voter turnout of up to 81 per cent. Women won 51 out of the total of 297 seats. The next round of local elections was due to take place in 11 communities in Gaza on 27 January 2005.

Communications (29-30 December). In a 29 December letter [A/ES-10/291-S/2004/1028], the Permanent Observer of Palestine said that, as 2004 came to a close, the situation in the Occupied Palestinian Territory continued to be critical. IDF killed nearly 1,000 Palestinians during the year and injured thousands more, while causing massive destruction of homes, properties, land and infrastructure, particularly in and around the refugee camps of the Gaza Strip. Even after the death of President Arafat, Israel continued to wage its military campaign, inflicting almost daily casualties on the Palestinian civilian population. Since 25 October, at least 113 Palestinians were killed as a result of the ongoing violence and attacks. In addition, Israel continued to construct the wall and to expand its settlements. Despite the assurances given by Israel that it would not hinder the election process, it continued to restrict movement, preventing candidates from campaigning and creating obstacles for voter registration. On 30 December [A/ES-10/292-S/2004/1029], the Permanent Observer made similar claims.

Jerusalem

East Jerusalem, where most of the city's Arab inhabitants lived, remained one of the most sensitive issues in the Middle East peace process and a focal point of concern for the United Nations in 2004.

Committee on Palestinian Rights. In its annual report [A/59/35], the Committee on the Exercise of the Inalienable Rights of the Palestinian People (Committee on Palestinian Rights) said that in and around East Jerusalem settlement activity proceeded at a rate unmatched since 1992. Settlement activity connecting East Jerusalem and the "Ma'ale Adumim" settlement could result in splitting the West Bank into two separate Palestinian cantons, having serious implications for the territorial contiguity of the West Bank. In addition, the construction by Israel of the wall in the Occupied Palestinian Territory, including in and around East Jerusalem, continued to cause great hardship to the Palestinians.

Transfer of diplomatic missions

Report of Secretary-General. On 12 October [A/59/431], the Secretary-General reported that five Member States, including Israel, had replied to his request for information on steps taken or envisaged to implement General Assembly resolution 58/22 [YUN 2003, p. 484], which addressed the transfer by some States of their diplomatic missions to Jerusalem in violation of Security Council resolution 478(1980) [YUN 1980, p. 426]. Israel viewed those resolutions as unbalanced and said that they threatened to prejudice the outcome of the Middle East peace process. The Syrian Arab Republic said Council resolution 478(1980) affirmed that Israel's decision to impose its laws, jurisdiction and administration on Jerusalem was illegal and consequently null and void and lacking in validity. The respondents made no mention of specific steps taken to implement resolution 58/22.

GENERAL ASSEMBLY ACTION

On 1 December [meeting 64], the General Assembly adopted **resolution 59/32** [draft: A/59/L.39] by recorded vote (155-7-15) [agenda item 36].

Jerusalem

The General Assembly,

Recalling its resolution 181(II) of 29 November 1947, in particular its provisions regarding the City of Jerusalem,

Recalling also its resolution 36/120 E of 10 December 1981 and all subsequent resolutions, including resolution 56/31 of 3 December 2001, in which it, inter alia, determined that all legislative and administrative measures and actions taken by Israel, the occupying Power, which have altered or purported to alter the character and status of the Holy City of Jerusalem, in particular the so-called "Basic Law" on Jerusalem and the proclamation of Jerusalem as the capital of Israel, were null and void and must be rescinded forthwith,

Recalling further Security Council resolutions relevant to Jerusalem, including resolution 478(1980) of 20 August 1980, in which the Council, inter alia, decided not to recognize the "Basic Law" and called upon those States which had established diplomatic missions in Jerusalem to withdraw such missions from the Holy City,

Recalling the advisory opinion rendered on 9 July 2004 by the International Court of Justice on the *Legal Consequences of the Construction of a Wall in the Occupied Palestinian Territory*, and recalling resolution ES-10/15 of 20 July 2004,

Expressing its grave concern at any action taken by any body, governmental or non-governmental, in violation of the above-mentioned resolutions,

Reaffirming that the international community, through the United Nations, has a legitimate interest in the question of the City of Jerusalem and the protection of the unique spiritual, religious and cultural dimensions of the city, as foreseen in relevant United Nations resolutions on this matter,

Having considered the report of the Secretary-General,

1. *Reiterates its determination* that any actions taken by Israel to impose its laws, jurisdiction and administration on the Holy City of Jerusalem are illegal and therefore null and void and have no validity whatsoever;

2. *Deplores* the transfer by some States of their diplomatic missions to Jerusalem in violation of Security Council resolution 478(1980), and calls once more upon those States to abide by the provisions of the relevant United Nations resolutions, in conformity with the Charter of the United Nations;

3. *Stresses* that a comprehensive, just and lasting solution to the question of the City of Jerusalem should take into account the legitimate concerns of both the Palestinian and Israeli sides and should include internationally guaranteed provisions to ensure the freedom of religion and of conscience of its inhabitants, as well as permanent, free and unhindered access to the holy places by the people of all religions and nationalities;

4. *Requests* the Secretary-General to report to the General Assembly at its sixtieth session on the implementation of the present resolution.

RECORDED VOTE ON RESOLUTION 59/32:

In favour: Afghanistan, Algeria, Andorra, Argentina, Armenia, Australia, Austria, Azerbaijan, Bahamas, Bahrain, Bangladesh, Barbados, Belarus, Belgium, Belize, Benin, Bhutan, Bolivia, Bosnia and Herzegovina, Botswana, Brazil, Brunei Darussalam, Bulgaria, Burkina Faso, Burundi, Cambodia, Canada, Cape Verde, Central African Republic, Chile, China, Colombia, Congo, Côte d'Ivoire, Croatia, Cuba, Cyprus, Czech Republic, Democratic People's Republic of Korea, Denmark, Djibouti, Dominica, Dominican Republic, Ecuador, Egypt, Eritrea, Estonia, Ethiopia, Finland, France, Gabon, Gambia, Georgia, Germany, Ghana, Greece, Guinea, Guinea-Bissau, Guyana, Hungary, Iceland, India, Indonesia, Iran, Iraq, Ireland, Italy, Jamaica, Japan, Jordan, Kazakhstan, Kuwait, Kyrgyzstan, Lao People's Democratic Republic, Latvia, Lebanon, Lesotho, Liberia, Libyan Arab Jamahiriya, Liechtenstein, Lithuania, Luxembourg, Madagascar, Malaysia, Maldives, Mali, Malta, Mauritania, Mauritius, Mexico, Monaco, Mongolia, Morocco, Mozambique, Myanmar, Namibia, Nepal, Netherlands, New Zealand, Niger, Nigeria, Norway, Oman, Pakistan, Panama, Paraguay, Peru, Philippines, Poland, Portugal, Qatar, Republic of Korea, Republic of Moldova, Romania, Russian Federation, Saint Lucia, Saint Vincent and the Grenadines, San Marino, Saudi Arabia, Senegal, Serbia and Montenegro, Seychelles, Sierra Leone, Singapore, Slovakia, Slovenia, Somalia, South Africa, Spain, Sri Lanka, Sudan, Suriname, Swaziland, Sweden, Switzerland, Syrian Arab Republic, Tajikistan, Thailand, The former Yugoslav Republic of Macedonia, Togo, Trinidad and Tobago, Tunisia, Turkey, Turkmenistan, Uganda, Ukraine, United Arab Emirates, United Kingdom, United Republic of Tanzania, Uruguay, Venezuela, Viet Nam, Yemen, Zambia, Zimbabwe.

Against: Costa Rica, Grenada, Israel, Marshall Islands, Micronesia, Palau, United States.

Abstaining: Albania, Cameroon, El Salvador, Fiji, Guatemala, Haiti, Honduras, Kenya, Nauru, Nicaragua, Papua New Guinea, Samoa, Solomon Islands, Tonga, Vanuatu.

Economic and social situation

A June report on the economic and social repercussions of the Israeli occupation on the living conditions of Palestinians in the occupied territory, including Jerusalem, and of the Arab population in the occupied Syrian Golan [A/59/89-E/2004/21] was prepared by the Economic and Social Commission for Western Asia (ESCWA), in accordance with Economic and Social Council resolution 2003/59 [YUN 2003, p. 486] and General Assembly resolution 58/229 [ibid., p. 487]; it covered developments since the last ESCWA report [ibid., p. 485].

The report noted that the occupation of Palestinian territory by Israel continued to deepen the economic and social hardship for Palestinians. The Israeli army continued to resort to extrajudicial killings, arbitrary detention, household demolition, severe mobility restrictions and closure policies. Economic indicators showed negative trends: unemployment reaching 70 per cent in some areas; greater dependence on food aid; and untold losses from physical destruction of Palestinian homes, public buildings, agricultural assets, infrastructure and private property. Israel's confiscation of Palestinian land and water resources for settlements and the erection of the West Bank wall accelerated, affecting one third of West Bank inhabitants, mostly refugees, women and children. Malnutrition and other health problems afflicted a growing number of Palestinians at a time of curtailed access to needed services. Israeli restrictions regularly impeded humanitarian services to the Occupied Palestinian Territory, while Israeli settlements and the construction of a barrier in the occupied territories continued to fuel the Israeli-Palestinian conflict. At the same time, expansion of Israeli settlements in the occupied Syrian Golan Heights continued unabated. Access to natural resources and social services, in particular schooling, higher education and medical facilities, remained inadequate for the Arab population in the Golan Heights.

ECONOMIC AND SOCIAL COUNCIL ACTION

On 23 July [meeting 50], the Economic and Social Council adopted **resolution 2004/54** [draft: E/2004/L.25, orally amended] by recorded vote (51-1-1) [agenda item 11].

Economic and social repercussions of the Israeli occupation on the living conditions of the Palestinian people in the Occupied Palestinian Territory, including Jerusalem, and the Arab population in the occupied Syrian Golan

The Economic and Social Council,

Recalling General Assembly resolution 58/229 of 23 December 2003,

Also recalling its resolution 2003/59 of 24 July 2003,

Guided by the principles of the Charter of the United Nations affirming the inadmissibility of the acquisition of territory by force, and recalling relevant Security Council resolutions, including resolutions 242(1967) of 22 November 1967, 338(1973) of 22 October 1973, 446(1979) of 22 March 1979, 452(1979) of 20 July 1979, 465(1980) of 1 March 1980, 476(1980) of 30 June 1980, 478(1980) of 20 August 1980, 497(1981) of 17 December 1981, 904(1994) of 18 March 1994, 1073 (1996) of 28 September 1996, 1397(2002) of 12 March 2002, 1515(2003) of 19 November 2003 and 1544(2004) of 19 May 2004,

Recalling the resolutions of the tenth emergency special session of the General Assembly, including resolutions ES-10/13 of 21 October 2003, ES-10/14 of 8 December 2003 and ES-10/15 of 20 July 2004,

Reaffirming the applicability of the Geneva Convention relative to the Protection of Civilian Persons in Time of War, of 12 August 1949, to the Occupied Palestinian Territory, including East Jerusalem, and other Arab territories occupied by Israel since 1967,

Stressing the importance of the revival of the Middle East peace process on the basis of Security Council resolutions 242(1967), 338(1973), 425(1978) of 19 March 1978, 1397(2002), 1515(2003) and 1544 (2004) and the principle of land for peace, as well as compliance with the agreements reached between the Government of Israel and the Palestine Liberation Organization, the representative of the Palestinian people,

Reaffirming the principle of the permanent sovereignty of peoples under foreign occupation over their natural resources,

Convinced that the Israeli occupation has gravely impeded the efforts to achieve sustainable development and a sound economic environment in the Occupied Palestinian Territory, including East Jerusalem, and the occupied Syrian Golan,

Gravely concerned about the deterioration of the economic and living conditions of the Palestinian people in the Occupied Palestinian Territory, including East Jerusalem, and of the Arab population of the occupied Syrian Golan and the exploitation by Israel, the occupying Power, of their natural resources,

Gravely concerned also by the grave impact on the economic and social conditions of the Palestinian people caused by the construction of the wall by Israel inside the Occupied Palestinian Territory and the resulting violation of their economic and social rights, including the rights to work, to health, to education and to an adequate standard of living,

Gravely concerned at the extensive destruction by Israel, the occupying Power, of agricultural land and orchards in the Occupied Palestinian Territory, including East Jerusalem, during the recent period, including, and in particular, as a result of the construction of the wall,

Acknowledging the advisory opinion rendered on 9 July 2004 by the International Court of Justice on the *Legal Consequences of the Construction of a Wall in the Occupied Palestinian Territory*,

Expressing grave concern about the continuation of the recent tragic and violent events since September 2000 that have led to many deaths and injuries,

Aware of the important work being done by the United Nations and the specialized agencies in support of the economic and social development of the Palestinian people, as well as the assistance being provided in the humanitarian field,

Conscious of the urgent need for the reconstruction and development of the economic and social infrastructure of the Occupied Palestinian Territory, including East Jerusalem, as well as the urgent need to address the dire humanitarian crisis facing the Palestinian people,

Calling upon both parties to fulfil their obligations under the road map in cooperation with the Quartet,

1. *Stresses* the need to preserve the national unity and the territorial integrity of the Occupied Palestinian Territory, including East Jerusalem, and to guarantee the freedom of movement of persons and goods in the Territory, including the removal of restrictions on going into and from East Jerusalem, and the freedom of movement to and from the outside world;

2. *Also stresses* the vital importance of the construction and operation of the seaport in Gaza and safe passage for the economic and social development of the Palestinian people;

3. *Demands* the complete cessation of all acts of violence, including all acts of terror, provocation, incitement and destruction;

4. *Calls upon* Israel, the occupying Power, to end its occupation of Palestinian cities, towns and other populated centres, to end the imposition of all forms of closure and curfew and to cease its destruction of homes and properties, economic institutions and agricultural fields;

5. *Reaffirms* the inalienable right of the Palestinian people and the Arab population of the occupied Syrian Golan to all their natural and economic resources, and calls upon Israel, the occupying Power, not to exploit, endanger or cause loss or depletion of these resources;

6. *Also reaffirms* that Israeli settlements in the Occupied Palestinian Territory, including East Jerusalem, and the occupied Syrian Golan are illegal and an obstacle to economic and social development;

7. *Stresses* the importance of the work of the organizations and agencies of the United Nations and of the United Nations Special Coordinator for the Middle East Peace Process and Personal Representative of the Secretary-General to the Palestine Liberation Organization and the Palestinian Authority;

8. *Urges* Member States to encourage private foreign investment in the Occupied Palestinian Territory, including East Jerusalem, in infrastructure, job-creation projects and social development in order to alleviate the hardship of the Palestinian people and improve their living conditions;

9. *Requests* the Secretary-General to submit to the General Assembly at its fifty-ninth session, through the Economic and Social Council, a report on the implementation of the present resolution and to continue to include in the report of the United Nations Special Coordinator an update on the living conditions of the Palestinian people, in collaboration with relevant United Nations agencies;

10. *Decides* to include the item entitled "Economic and social repercussions of the Israeli occupation on the living conditions of the Palestinian people in the Occupied Palestinian Territory, including East Jerusalem, and the Arab population in the occupied Syrian Golan" in the agenda of its substantive session of 2005.

RECORDED VOTE ON RESOLUTION 2004/54:

In favour: Armenia, Azerbaijan, Bangladesh, Belgium, Belize, Benin, Bhutan, Burundi, Canada, Chile, China, Colombia, Congo, Cuba, Ecuador, Finland, France, Germany, Ghana, Greece, Guatemala, Hungary, India, Indonesia, Ireland, Italy, Jamaica, Japan, Kenya, Libyan Arab Jamahiriya, Malaysia, Mauritius, Mozambique, Namibia, Nicaragua, Nigeria, Panama, Poland, Qatar, Republic of Korea, Russian Federation, Saudi Arabia, Senegal, Sweden, Tunisia, Turkey, Ukraine, United Arab Emirates, United Kingdom, United Republic of Tanzania, Zimbabwe.
Against: United States.
Abstaining: Australia.

On the same date (**decision 2004/298**), the Council took note of the note by the Secretary-General transmitting the report prepared by ESCWA (see p. 474).

GENERAL ASSEMBLY ACTION

On 22 December [meeting 75], the General Assembly, on the recommendation of the Second (Economic and Financial) Committee [A/59/489], adopted **resolution 59/251** by recorded vote (156-5-11) [agenda item 91].

Permanent sovereignty of the Palestinian people in the Occupied Palestinian Territory, including East Jerusalem, and of the Arab population in the occupied Syrian Golan over their natural resources

The General Assembly,

Recalling its resolution 58/229 of 23 December 2003, and taking note of Economic and Social Council resolution 2004/54 of 23 July 2004,

Recalling also its resolution 58/292 of 6 May 2004,

Reaffirming the principle of the permanent sovereignty of peoples under foreign occupation over their natural resources,

Guided by the principles of the Charter of the United Nations, affirming the inadmissibility of the acquisition of territory by force, and recalling relevant Security Council resolutions, including resolutions 242(1967) of 22 November 1967, 465(1980) of 1 March 1980 and 497(1981) of 17 December 1981,

Recalling its resolution 2625(XXV) of 24 October 1970,

Reaffirming the applicability of the Geneva Convention relative to the Protection of Civilian Persons in Time of War, of 12 August 1949, to the Occupied Palestinian Territory, including East Jerusalem, and other Arab territories occupied by Israel since 1967,

Recalling the advisory opinion rendered on 9 July 2004 by the International Court of Justice on the *Legal*

Consequences of the Construction of a Wall in the Occupied Palestinian Territory, and recalling also its resolution ES-10/15 of 20 July 2004,

Expressing its concern at the exploitation by Israel, the occupying Power, of the natural resources of the Occupied Palestinian Territory, including East Jerusalem, and other Arab territories occupied by Israel since 1967,

Expressing its concern also at the extensive destruction by Israel, the occupying Power, of agricultural land and orchards in the Occupied Palestinian Territory during the recent period, including the uprooting of a vast number of olive trees,

Aware of the detrimental impact of the Israeli settlements on Palestinian and other Arab natural resources, especially as a result of the confiscation of land and the forced diversion of water resources, and of the dire economic and social consequences in this regard,

Aware also of the detrimental impact on Palestinian natural resources being caused by the unlawful construction of the wall by Israel, the occupying Power, in the Occupied Palestinian Territory, including in and around East Jerusalem, and of its grave effect on the economic and social conditions of the Palestinian people,

Reaffirming the need for the immediate resumption of negotiations within the Middle East peace process, on the basis of Security Council resolutions 242(1967), 338(1973) of 22 October 1973, 425(1978) of 19 March 1978 and 1397(2002) of 12 March 2002, the principle of land for peace and the Quartet performance-based road map to a permanent two-State solution to the Israeli-Palestinian conflict, as endorsed by the Security Council in its resolution 1515(2003) of 19 November 2003, and for the achievement of a final settlement on all tracks,

Recalling the need to end all acts of violence, including acts of terror, provocation, incitement and destruction,

Taking note of the note by the Secretary-General transmitting the report prepared by the Economic and Social Commission for Western Asia on the economic and social repercussions of the Israeli occupation on the living conditions of the Palestinian people in the Occupied Palestinian Territory, including Jerusalem, and of the Arab population in the occupied Syrian Golan,

1. *Reaffirms* the inalienable rights of the Palestinian people and the population of the occupied Syrian Golan over their natural resources, including land and water;

2. *Calls upon* Israel, the occupying Power, not to exploit, damage, cause loss or depletion of or endanger the natural resources in the Occupied Palestinian Territory, including East Jerusalem, and in the occupied Syrian Golan;

3. *Recognizes* the right of the Palestinian people to claim restitution as a result of any exploitation, damage, loss or depletion, or endangerment of their natural resources, and expresses the hope that this issue will be dealt with in the framework of the final status negotiations between the Palestinian and Israeli sides;

4. *Requests* the Secretary-General to report to it at its sixtieth session on the implementation of the present resolution, and decides to include in the provisional agenda of its sixtieth session the item entitled "Permanent sovereignty of the Palestinian people in the Occupied Palestinian Territory, including East Jerusalem, and of the Arab population in the occupied Syrian Golan over their natural resources".

RECORDED VOTE ON RESOLUTION 59/251:

In favour: Afghanistan, Algeria, Andorra, Angola, Antigua and Barbuda, Argentina, Armenia, Austria, Azerbaijan, Bahamas, Bahrain, Bangladesh, Barbados, Belarus, Belgium, Belize, Benin, Bolivia, Bosnia and Herzegovina, Botswana, Brazil, Brunei Darussalam, Bulgaria, Burkina Faso, Burundi, Cambodia, Canada, Cape Verde, Chile, China, Colombia, Comoros, Congo, Costa Rica, Croatia, Cuba, Cyprus, Czech Republic, Democratic People's Republic of Korea, Denmark, Djibouti, Dominica, Ecuador, Egypt, El Salvador, Eritrea, Estonia, Ethiopia, Fiji, Finland, France, Gabon, Georgia, Germany, Ghana, Greece, Grenada, Guatemala, Guyana, Hungary, Iceland, India, Indonesia, Iran, Iraq, Ireland, Italy, Jamaica, Japan, Jordan, Kazakhstan, Kenya, Kuwait, Lao People's Democratic Republic, Latvia, Lebanon, Lesotho, Liberia, Libyan Arab Jamahiriya, Liechtenstein, Lithuania, Luxembourg, Madagascar, Malaysia, Maldives, Mali, Malta, Mauritius, Mexico, Monaco, Mongolia, Morocco, Mozambique, Myanmar, Namibia, Nepal, Netherlands, New Zealand, Nicaragua, Niger, Nigeria, Norway, Oman, Pakistan, Panama, Paraguay, Peru, Philippines, Poland, Portugal, Qatar, Republic of Korea, Republic of Moldova, Romania, Russian Federation, Saint Lucia, Saint Vincent and the Grenadines, San Marino, Sao Tome and Principe, Saudi Arabia, Senegal, Serbia and Montenegro, Seychelles, Sierra Leone, Singapore, Slovakia, Slovenia, Somalia, South Africa, Spain, Sri Lanka, Sudan, Suriname, Sweden, Switzerland, Syrian Arab Republic, Thailand, The former Yugoslav Republic of Macedonia, Timor-Leste, Togo, Trinidad and Tobago, Tunisia, Turkey, Turkmenistan, Uganda, Ukraine, United Arab Emirates, United Kingdom, United Republic of Tanzania, Uruguay, Uzbekistan, Venezuela, Viet Nam, Yemen, Zambia, Zimbabwe.

Against: Israel, Marshall Islands, Micronesia, Palau, United States.

Abstaining: Albania, Australia, Cameroon, Central African Republic, Côte d'Ivoire, Dominican Republic, Haiti, Nauru, Tonga, Tuvalu, Vanuatu.

Other aspects

Special Committee on Israeli Practices. In response to General Assembly resolution 58/96 [YUN 2003, p. 490], the Special Committee to Investigate Israeli Practices Affecting the Human Rights of the Palestinian People and Other Arabs of the Occupied Territories, in September, reported for the thirty-sixth time to the General Assembly on events and the human rights situation in the territories it considered occupied—the Golan Heights, the West Bank, including East Jerusalem, and the Gaza Strip [A/59/381]. The report reflected the substance of information gathered during the Committee's mission to Lebanon, Egypt and the Syrian Arab Republic from 25 May to 8 June. In those three countries, the Committee met with 84 witnesses representing associations of Palestinian refugees in Lebanon, Palestinian non-governmental organizations (NGOs) from the occupied territories and Israeli NGOs, as well as individuals from Syria. The report reviewed the human rights situation in the occupied territories and described developments in relation to the human rights situation in the occupied Syrian Golan.

The Committee urged international and national media to give the matter broader coverage in order to make the appalling human rights situation of Palestinians and other Arabs in the occupied territories better known to the world. National public opinion, concerned civil society groups and diplomatic, academic and other circles should take the lead in assembling and disseminating information about the violations of international law and international humanitarian law perpetrated daily in the Occupied Palestinian Territory that were generating destruction of human life, infrastructure, cultivated land and economic wealth. The construction of the wall was causing major changes to the social fabric of Palestinian communities. The Committee was also alarmed at the regional and international dimensions of the Palestinian issue and was convinced that the international community had to act, especially in view of the advisory opinion rendered by ICJ and the ensuing adoption by the General Assembly of resolution ES-10/15 (see p. 465).

Report of Secretary-General. On 9 September [A/59/345], the Secretary-General informed the General Assembly that Israel had not replied to his August request for information on steps taken or envisaged to implement Assembly resolution 58/99 [YUN 2003, p. 489], demanding that Israel, among other things, cease all practices and actions that violated the human rights of the Palestinian people, and condemning all acts of terror, provocation, incitement and destruction, especially the excessive use of force by Israeli forces against Palestinian civilians.

Commission on Human Rights. In a 27 February addendum [E/CN.4/2004/6/Add.1] to his September 2003 report on the human rights situation in the occupied territories [YUN 2003, p. 488], the Special Rapporteur of the Commission on Human Rights, John Dugard (South Africa), stated that the situation was characterized by serious violations of human rights law, and that terrorism was a constant feature of the conflict in the occupied territories and neighbouring Israel. Both Palestinians and Israelis were responsible for inflicting a reign of terror on civilians.

Focusing on the separation wall being constructed by Israel, the Special Rapporteur said that insofar as it was built on Palestinian territory, it could not be justified as a legitimate or proportionate response to terrorism. The wall, which penetrated deep into Palestinian territory, had resulted in the creation of a zone between the Green Line and the wall inside the Occupied Palestinian Territory. Israel designated that area as "closed" to all Palestinians. Palestinians who lived, farmed, worked or went to school within that closed zone required special permits from the Israeli authorities. Both the construction of the wall and the operation of the permit system for the closed zone had caused great hardships to Palestinians and violated norms of human rights law and international humanitarian law. In addition, the construction of the wall had resulted in large-scale destruction of Palestinian property.

Notice of seizure of land had been served in an arbitrary manner and there were no real means for landowners to contest the seizure. The wall had infrequent gates for the purpose of crossing, thus those farmers granted permits to farm their land had difficulty gaining access. The permit system also interfered with education, health care and family life. There was a real prospect that life would become so intolerable for villagers living in the closed zone that they would abandon their homes and migrate to the West Bank. The main beneficiaries of the wall were settlers: 54 settlements and 142,000 settlers (63 per cent of the West Bank settlement population) would find themselves on the Israeli side of the wall, with access to land separated from its Palestinian owners. The wall might have been justified as a security measure to prevent would-be suicide bombers from entering Israel had it followed the course of the Green Line; however, as it was built largely on Palestinian territory, it could not be justified on those grounds. The route of the wall suggested that its main purpose was the annexation, by de facto means, of additional land for Israel. In addition, the wall violated the prohibition on the acquisition of territory by forcible means, and undermined the right to self-determination of the Palestinian people by reducing the size of a future Palestinian State.

In a 12 August interim report [A/59/256], the Special Rapporteur said that since February, IDF had intensified its military incursions into the Gaza Strip, resulting in deaths and a massive and wanton destruction of property. Despite Israel's announced intention to withdraw from Gaza, in reality it planned to retain ultimate control by controlling its borders, territorial sea and airspace.

The wall that Israel was constructing within the Palestinian territory was held to be contrary to international law by ICJ on 9 July 2004. Israel announced that it would not comply with that advisory opinion, but indicated that it would abide by the ruling of its own High Court in respect of sections of the wall still to be built.

Israel claimed that the purpose of the wall was to secure Israel from terrorist attacks and claimed that such attacks inside Israel had dropped by over 80 per cent as a result of the wall. The Special Rapporteur noted that there was no compelling evidence that suicide bombers could not have been as effectively prevented from entering Israel if the wall had been built along the Green Line or within the Israeli side of that Line. In his view, there were more convincing explanations for the construction of the wall, such as the incorporation of settlers within Israel, the confiscation of Palestinian land and the inducement to

Palestinians to leave their lands by making life intolerable for them. In deciding on the route of the wall, Israel had seized rich agricultural land and water resources along the Green Line. In the Jerusalem area, the wall was being built around an expanded East Jerusalem to incorporate some 247,000 settlers in 12 settlements and some 249,000 Palestinians within the wall. The seizure of land in East Jerusalem would have serious implications for Palestinians, for, among other things, it would prohibit over 100,000 Palestinians in West Bank neighbourhoods who were dependent upon the facilities of East Jerusalem, including hospitals, universities, schools, employment and markets for agricultural goods, from entering East Jerusalem.

Freedom of movement was severely curtailed in the West Bank and Gaza. The inhabitants of Gaza were effectively imprisoned by a combination of wall, fence and sea. Within Gaza freedom of movement was severely restricted by roadblocks which effectively divided the small territory. The inhabitants of the West Bank were subjected to a system of curfews and checkpoints that denied freedom of movement. Palestinians living in the West Bank needed permits to travel from one city to another and permits were arbitrarily withheld and seldom granted for private vehicles.

GENERAL ASSEMBLY ACTION

On 10 December [meeting 71], the General Assembly, on the recommendation of the Fourth (Special Political and Decolonization) Committee [A/59/471], adopted **resolution 59/124** by recorded vote (149-7-22) [agenda item 76].

Israeli practices affecting the human rights of the Palestinian people in the Occupied Palestinian Territory, including East Jerusalem

The General Assembly,

Recalling its relevant resolutions, including resolution 58/292 of 6 May 2004, as well as those adopted at its tenth emergency special session,

Recalling also the relevant resolutions of the Commission on Human Rights,

Bearing in mind the relevant resolutions of the Security Council,

Having considered the report of the Special Committee to Investigate Israeli Practices Affecting the Human Rights of the Palestinian People and Other Arabs of the Occupied Territories and the report of the Secretary-General,

Taking note of the report of the Human Rights Inquiry Commission established by the Commission on Human Rights and the recent reports of the Special Rapporteur of the Commission on Human Rights on the situation of human rights in the Palestinian territories occupied by Israel since 1967,

Recalling the advisory opinion rendered on 9 July 2004 by the International Court of Justice, and recalling also General Assembly resolution ES-10/15 of 20 July 2004,

Noting in particular the Court's reply, including that the construction of the wall by Israel, the occupying Power, in the Occupied Palestinian Territory, including in and around East Jerusalem, and its associated regime are contrary to international law,

Recalling the International Covenant on Civil and Political Rights, the International Covenant on Economic, Social and Cultural Rights and the Convention on the Rights of the Child, and affirming that these human rights instruments must be respected in the Occupied Palestinian Territory, including East Jerusalem,

Aware of the responsibility of the international community to promote human rights and ensure respect for international law, and recalling in this regard its resolution 2625(XXV) of 24 October 1970,

Reaffirming the principle of the inadmissibility of the acquisition of territory by force,

Reaffirming also the applicability of the Geneva Convention relative to the Protection of Civilian Persons in Time of War, of 12 August 1949, to the Occupied Palestinian Territory, including East Jerusalem, and other Arab territories occupied by Israel since 1967,

Reaffirming further the obligation of the States parties to the Fourth Geneva Convention under articles 146, 147 and 148 with regard to penal sanctions, grave breaches and responsibilities of the High Contracting Parties,

Reaffirming that all States have the right and the duty to take actions in conformity with international law and international humanitarian law to counter deadly acts of violence against their civilian population in order to protect the lives of their citizens,

Stressing the need for full compliance with the Israeli-Palestinian agreements reached within the context of the Middle East peace process and the implementation of the Quartet road map to a permanent two-State solution to the Israeli-Palestinian conflict,

Concerned about the continuing systematic violation of the human rights of the Palestinian people by Israel, the occupying Power, including that arising from the excessive use of force, the use of collective punishment, the reoccupation and closure of areas, the confiscation of land, the establishment and expansion of settlements, the construction of the wall inside the Occupied Palestinian Territory in departure from the Armistice Line of 1949, the destruction of property and all other actions by it designed to change the legal status, geographical nature and demographic composition of the Occupied Palestinian Territory, including East Jerusalem,

Gravely concerned about the military actions that have been carried out since 28 September 2000 and that have led to thousands of deaths among Palestinian civilians, including hundreds of children, and tens of thousands of injuries,

Expressing deep concern about the extensive destruction caused by the Israeli occupying forces, including of religious, cultural and historical sites, of vital infrastructure and institutions of the Palestinian Authority, and of agricultural land throughout Palestinian cities, towns, villages and refugee camps,

Expressing deep concern also about the Israeli policy of closure and the severe restrictions, including curfews, that continue to be imposed on the movement of persons and goods, including medical and humanitarian personnel and goods, throughout the Occupied Palestinian Territory, including East Jerusalem, and the consequent negative impact on the socio-economic situation of the Palestinian people, which remains that of a dire humanitarian crisis,

Expressing concern that thousands of Palestinians continue to be held in Israeli prisons or detention centres under harsh conditions that impair their well-being, and also expressing concern about the ill-treatment and harassment of any Palestinian prisoners and all reports of torture,

Convinced of the need for an international presence to monitor the situation, to contribute to ending the violence and protecting the Palestinian civilians and to help the parties to implement agreements reached, and, in this regard, recalling the positive contribution of the Temporary International Presence in Hebron,

Stressing the necessity for the full implementation of all relevant Security Council resolutions,

1. *Reiterates* that all measures and actions taken by Israel, the occupying Power, in the Occupied Palestinian Territory, including East Jerusalem, in violation of the relevant provisions of the Geneva Convention relative to the Protection of Civilian Persons in Time of War, of 12 August 1949, and contrary to the relevant resolutions of the Security Council, are illegal and have no validity;

2. *Demands* that Israel, the occupying Power, comply fully with the provisions of the Fourth Geneva Convention of 1949 and cease immediately all measures and actions taken in violation and in breach of the Convention, including the extrajudicial executions;

3. *Condemns* all acts of violence, including all acts of terror, provocation, incitement and destruction, especially the excessive use of force by the Israeli occupying forces against Palestinian civilians, resulting in extensive loss of life, vast numbers of injuries and massive destruction of homes, properties, agricultural lands and vital infrastructure;

4. *Expresses grave concern* at the use of suicide bombing attacks against Israeli civilians, resulting in extensive loss of life and injury;

5. *Condemns* the events that occurred in the Jenin refugee camp in April 2002, including the loss of life, injury, widespread destruction and displacement inflicted on many of its civilian inhabitants;

6. *Condemns also* the killing of Palestinian civilians and the widespread demolition of homes by Israel, the occupying Power, in the Rafah refugee camp in May 2004 and in the Jabaliya refugee camp in October 2004;

7. *Demands* that Israel, the occupying Power, cease all practices and actions which violate the human rights of the Palestinian people, respect human rights law and comply with its obligations;

8. *Demands also* that Israel, the occupying Power, comply with its legal obligations under international law, as mentioned in the advisory opinion rendered on 9 July 2004 by the International Court of Justice and as demanded in resolution ES-10/15 and resolution ES-10/13 of 21 October 2003, and that it cease the construction of the wall in the Occupied Palestinian Territory, including in and around East Jerusalem, dismantle forthwith the structure situated therein, repeal or render ineffective all legislative and regulatory acts re-

lating thereto, and make reparation for all damage caused by the construction of the wall;

9. *Stresses* the need to preserve the territorial integrity of all the Occupied Palestinian Territory and to guarantee the freedom of movement of persons and goods within the Palestinian territory, including the removal of restrictions on movement into and from East Jerusalem, and the freedom of movement to and from the outside world;

10. *Requests* the Secretary-General to report to the General Assembly at its sixtieth session on the implementation of the present resolution.

RECORDED VOTE ON RESOLUTION 59/124:

In favour: Afghanistan, Algeria, Andorra, Antigua and Barbuda, Argentina, Armenia, Austria, Azerbaijan, Bahamas, Bahrain, Bangladesh, Barbados, Belarus, Belgium, Belize, Benin, Bolivia, Bosnia and Herzegovina, Botswana, Brazil, Brunei Darussalam, Bulgaria, Burkina Faso, Burundi, Cambodia, Cape Verde, Chile, China, Colombia, Comoros, Croatia, Cuba, Cyprus, Czech Republic, Democratic People's Republic of Korea, Denmark, Djibouti, Dominica, Ecuador, Egypt, Eritrea, Estonia, Ethiopia, Fiji, Finland, France, Gabon, Georgia, Germany, Ghana, Greece, Guinea, Guinea-Bissau, Guyana, Hungary, India, Indonesia, Iran, Iraq, Ireland, Italy, Jamaica, Japan, Jordan, Kazakhstan, Kuwait, Kyrgyzstan, Lao People's Democratic Republic, Latvia, Lebanon, Lesotho, Libyan Arab Jamahiriya, Liechtenstein, Lithuania, Luxembourg, Madagascar, Malaysia, Maldives, Mali, Malta, Mauritius, Mexico, Monaco, Mongolia, Morocco, Mozambique, Myanmar, Namibia, Nepal, Netherlands, New Zealand, Nigeria, Norway, Oman, Pakistan, Panama, Paraguay, Peru, Philippines, Poland, Portugal, Qatar, Republic of Korea, Republic of Moldova, Romania, Russian Federation, Saint Lucia, Saint Vincent and the Grenadines, Samoa, San Marino, Sao Tome and Principe, Saudi Arabia, Senegal, Serbia and Montenegro, Seychelles, Sierra Leone, Singapore, Slovakia, Slovenia, Somalia, South Africa, Spain, Sri Lanka, Sudan, Suriname, Swaziland, Sweden, Switzerland, Syrian Arab Republic, Tajikistan, Thailand, The former Yugoslav Republic of Macedonia, Timor-Leste, Togo, Trinidad and Tobago, Tunisia, Turkey, Turkmenistan, Ukraine, United Arab Emirates, United Kingdom, United Republic of Tanzania, Uruguay, Venezuela, Viet Nam, Yemen, Zambia, Zimbabwe.

Against: Australia, Israel, Marshall Islands, Micronesia, Nauru, Palau, United States.

Abstaining: Albania, Cameroon, Canada, Costa Rica, Côte d'Ivoire, Dominican Republic, El Salvador, Equatorial Guinea, Grenada, Guatemala, Haiti, Honduras, Iceland, Kenya, Nicaragua, Papua New Guinea, Solomon Islands, Tonga, Tuvalu, Uganda, Uzbekistan, Vanuatu.

By **resolution 59/179** of 20 December, the Assembly reaffirmed the right of the Palestinian people to self-determination, including the right to their State, and urged all States and UN specialized agencies and organizations to support the Palestinian people in their quest for self-determination (see p. 486).

Work of Special Committee

In a September report [A/59/344], the Secretary-General stated that all necessary facilities were provided to the Special Committee on Israeli Practices, as requested in General Assembly resolution 58/96 [YUN 2003, p. 490]. Arrangements were made for it to meet in March and May in Geneva, and a field mission was carried out to Lebanon, Egypt and the Syrian Arab Republic from 25 May to 8 June. Due to the restrictions imposed on the production of Assembly reports, the Special Committee did not submit periodic reports during the period under review. The UN Department of Public Information continued to provide press coverage of Special Committee meetings and to disseminate information on its activities.

GENERAL ASSEMBLY ACTION

On 10 December [meeting 71], the General Assembly, on the recommendation of the Fourth Committee [A/59/471], adopted **resolution 59/121** by recorded vote (84-9-80) [agenda item 76].

Work of the Special Committee to Investigate Israeli Practices Affecting the Human Rights of the Palestinian People and Other Arabs of the Occupied Territories

The General Assembly,

Guided by the purposes and principles set forth in the Charter of the United Nations,

Guided also by international humanitarian law, in particular the Geneva Convention relative to the Protection of Civilian Persons in Time of War, of 12 August 1949, as well as international standards of human rights, in particular the Universal Declaration of Human Rights and the International Covenants on Human Rights,

Recalling its relevant resolutions, including resolutions 2443(XXIII) of 19 December 1968 and 58/96 of 9 December 2003, and the relevant resolutions of the Commission on Human Rights,

Recalling also the relevant resolutions of the Security Council,

Taking into account the advisory opinion rendered on 9 July 2004 by the International Court of Justice on the *Legal Consequences of the Construction of a Wall in the Occupied Palestinian Territory*, and recalling in this regard General Assembly resolution ES-10/15 of 20 July 2004,

Convinced that occupation itself represents a gross and grave violation of human rights,

Gravely concerned about the continuation of the tragic events that have taken place since 28 September 2000, including the excessive use of force by the Israeli occupying forces against Palestinian civilians, resulting in thousands of deaths and injuries,

Having considered the report of the Special Committee to Investigate Israeli Practices Affecting the Human Rights of the Palestinian People and Other Arabs of the Occupied Territories and the relevant reports of the Secretary-General,

Recalling the Declaration of Principles on Interim Self-Government Arrangements of 13 September 1993 and the subsequent implementation agreements between the Palestinian and Israeli sides,

Expressing the hope that the Israeli occupation will be brought to an early end and that therefore the violation of the human rights of the Palestinian people will cease, and recalling in this regard its resolution 58/292 of 6 May 2004,

1. *Commends* the Special Committee to Investigate Israeli Practices Affecting the Human Rights of the Palestinian People and Other Arabs of the Occupied Territories for its efforts in performing the tasks assigned to it by the General Assembly and for its impartiality;

2. *Reiterates its demand* that Israel, the occupying Power, cooperate with the Special Committee in implementing its mandate;

3. *Deplores* those policies and practices of Israel that violate the human rights of the Palestinian people and other Arabs of the occupied territories, as reflected in the report of the Special Committee covering the reporting period;

4. *Expresses grave concern* about the continuing crisis situation in the Occupied Palestinian Territory, including East Jerusalem, since 28 September 2000, as a result of unlawful Israeli practices and measures, and especially condemns the excessive and indiscriminate use of force against the civilian population, including extrajudicial executions, which has resulted in more than 3,400 Palestinian deaths, including those of more than 750 children, and tens of thousands of injuries;

5. *Requests* the Special Committee, pending complete termination of the Israeli occupation, to continue to investigate Israeli policies and practices in the Occupied Palestinian Territory, including East Jerusalem, and other Arab territories occupied by Israel since 1967, especially Israeli violations of the Geneva Convention relative to the Protection of Civilian Persons in Time of War, of 12 August 1949, and to consult, as appropriate, with the International Committee of the Red Cross according to its regulations in order to ensure that the welfare and human rights of the peoples of the occupied territories are safeguarded and to report to the Secretary-General as soon as possible and whenever the need arises thereafter;

6. *Also requests* the Special Committee to submit regularly to the Secretary-General periodic reports on the current situation in the Occupied Palestinian Territory, including East Jerusalem;

7. *Further requests* the Special Committee to continue to investigate the treatment of prisoners and detainees in the Occupied Palestinian Territory, including East Jerusalem, and other Arab territories occupied by Israel since 1967;

8. *Requests* the Secretary-General:

(a) To provide the Special Committee with all necessary facilities, including those required for its visits to the occupied territories, so that it may investigate Israeli policies and practices referred to in the present resolution;

(b) To continue to make available such staff as may be necessary to assist the Special Committee in the performance of its tasks;

(c) To circulate regularly to Member States the periodic reports mentioned in paragraph 6 above;

(d) To ensure the widest circulation of the reports of the Special Committee and of information regarding its activities and findings, by all means available, through the Department of Public Information of the Secretariat and, where necessary, to reprint those reports of the Special Committee that are no longer available;

(e) To report to the General Assembly at its sixtieth session on the tasks entrusted to him in the present resolution;

9. *Decides* to include in the provisional agenda of its sixtieth session the item entitled "Report of the Special Committee to Investigate Israeli Practices Affecting the Human Rights of the Palestinian People and Other Arabs of the Occupied Territories".

RECORDED VOTE ON RESOLUTION 59/121:

In favour: Afghanistan, Algeria, Armenia, Azerbaijan, Bahrain, Bangladesh, Barbados, Belarus, Belize, Benin, Bolivia, Botswana, Brazil, Brunei Darussalam, Burkina Faso, Cambodia, Cape Verde, Chile, China, Colombia, Comoros, Cuba, Democratic People's Republic of Korea, Djibouti, Dominica, Ecuador, Egypt, Gabon, Ghana, Guinea, Guinea-Bissau, Guyana, India, Indonesia, Iran, Iraq, Jamaica, Jordan, Kuwait, Lao People's Democratic Republic, Lebanon, Lesotho, Libyan Arab Jamahiriya, Madagascar, Malaysia, Maldives, Mali, Mauritania, Mauritius, Morocco, Mozambique, Myanmar, Namibia, Nepal, Nigeria, Oman, Pakistan, Paraguay, Qatar, Saint Lucia, Sao Tome and Principe, Saudi Arabia, Senegal, Sierra Leone, Singapore, Somalia, South Africa, Sri Lanka, Sudan, Suriname, Syrian Arab Republic, Tajikistan, Togo, Trinidad and Tobago, Tunisia, Turkey, Turkmenistan, United Arab Emirates, United Republic of Tanzania, Venezuela, Viet Nam, Yemen, Zambia, Zimbabwe.

Against: Australia, Canada, Grenada, Israel, Marshall Islands, Micronesia, Nauru, Palau, United States.

Abstaining: Albania, Andorra, Antigua and Barbuda, Argentina, Austria, Bahamas, Belgium, Bosnia and Herzegovina, Bulgaria, Burundi, Cameroon, Costa Rica, Côte d'Ivoire, Croatia, Cyprus, Czech Republic, Denmark, Dominican Republic, El Salvador, Equatorial Guinea, Estonia, Ethiopia, Fiji, Finland, France, Georgia, Germany, Greece, Guatemala, Haiti, Honduras, Hungary, Iceland, Ireland, Italy, Japan, Kazakhstan, Kenya, Latvia, Liechtenstein, Lithuania, Luxembourg, Malta, Mexico, Monaco, Mongolia, Netherlands, New Zealand, Nicaragua, Norway, Panama, Papua New Guinea, Peru, Philippines, Poland, Portugal, Republic of Korea, Republic of Moldova, Romania, Russian Federation, Saint Vincent and the Grenadines, Samoa, San Marino, Serbia and Montenegro, Slovakia, Slovenia, Solomon Islands, Spain, Sweden, Switzerland, Thailand, The former Yugoslav Republic of Macedonia, Tonga, Tuvalu, Uganda, Ukraine, United Kingdom, Uruguay, Uzbekistan, Vanuatu.

Fourth Geneva Convention

Report of Secretary-General. In September [A/59/339], the Secretary-General informed the General Assembly that Israel had not replied to his August request for information on steps taken or envisaged to implement Assembly resolution 58/97 [YUN 2003, p. 491] demanding that Israel accept the de jure applicability of the Fourth Geneva Convention in the Occupied Palestinian Territory, including East Jerusalem, and that it comply scrupulously with its provisions. The Secretary-General noted that he had drawn the attention of all States parties to the Convention to paragraph 3 of resolution 58/97 calling on them to exert all efforts to ensure respect by Israel for the Convention's provisions, and to paragraph 6 of resolution 58/100 [ibid., p. 524] calling on States not to recognize any legislative or administrative measures and actions taken by Israel in the occupied Syrian Golan.

The High Contracting Parties to the Fourth Geneva Convention had reaffirmed the applicability of the Convention to the Occupied Palestinian Territory at meetings in 1999 [YUN 1999, p. 415] and in 2001 [YUN 2001, p. 425].

GENERAL ASSEMBLY ACTION

On 10 December [meeting 71], the General Assembly, on the recommendation of the Fourth Committee [A/59/471], adopted **resolution 59/122** by recorded vote (160-7-11) [agenda item 76].

Applicability of the Geneva Convention relative to the Protection of Civilian Persons in Time of War, of 12 August 1949, to the Occupied Palestinian Territory, including East Jerusalem, and the other occupied Arab territories

The General Assembly,

Recalling its relevant resolutions, including its resolution 58/292 of 6 May 2004,

Recalling also its resolution ES-10/15 of 20 July 2004,

Bearing in mind the relevant resolutions of the Security Council,

Recalling the Regulations annexed to the Hague Convention IV of 1907, the Geneva Convention relative to the Protection of Civilian Persons in Time of War, of 12 August 1949, and relevant provisions of customary law, including those codified in Additional Protocol I to the four Geneva Conventions,

Having considered the report of the Special Committee to Investigate Israeli Practices Affecting the Human Rights of the Palestinian People and Other Arabs of the Occupied Territories and the relevant reports of the Secretary-General,

Considering that the promotion of respect for the obligations arising from the Charter of the United Nations and other instruments and rules of international law is among the basic purposes and principles of the United Nations,

Recalling the advisory opinion rendered on 9 July 2004 by the International Court of Justice, and also recalling General Assembly resolution ES-10/15,

Noting in particular the Court's reply, including that the Fourth Geneva Convention is applicable in the Occupied Palestinian Territory, including East Jerusalem, and that Israel is in breach of several of the provisions of the Convention,

Noting the convening for the first time, on 15 July 1999, of a Conference of High Contracting Parties to the Fourth Geneva Convention, as recommended by the General Assembly in its resolution ES-10/6 of 9 February 1999, on measures to enforce the Convention in the Occupied Palestinian Territory, including East Jerusalem, and to ensure respect thereof in accordance with article 1 common to the four Geneva Conventions, and aware of the statement adopted by the Conference,

Welcoming the reconvening of the Conference of High Contracting Parties to the Fourth Geneva Convention on 5 December 2001 in Geneva and stressing the importance of the Declaration adopted by the Conference, and underlining the need for the parties to follow up the implementation of the Declaration,

Welcoming and encouraging the initiatives by States parties to the Convention, both individually and collectively, according to article 1 common to the four Geneva Conventions, aimed at ensuring respect for the Convention,

Stressing that Israel, the occupying Power, should comply strictly with its obligations under international law, including international humanitarian law,

1. *Reaffirms* that the Geneva Convention relative to the Protection of Civilian Persons in Time of War, of 12 August 1949, is applicable to the Occupied Palestinian Territory, including East Jerusalem, and other Arab territories occupied by Israel since 1967;

2. *Demands* that Israel accept the de jure applicability of the Convention in the Occupied Palestinian Territory, including East Jerusalem, and other Arab territories occupied by Israel since 1967, and that it comply scrupulously with the provisions of the Convention;

3. *Calls upon* all High Contracting Parties to the Convention, in accordance with article 1 common to the four Geneva Conventions and as mentioned in the advisory opinion of the International Court of Justice of 9 July 2004, to continue to exert all efforts to ensure respect for its provisions by Israel, the occupying

Power, in the Occupied Palestinian Territory, including East Jerusalem, and other Arab territories occupied by Israel since 1967;

4. *Reiterates* the need for speedy implementation of the relevant recommendations contained in the resolutions of its tenth emergency special session, including resolution ES-10/15, with regard to ensuring respect by Israel, the occupying Power, for the provisions of the Convention;

5. *Requests* the Secretary-General to report to the General Assembly at its sixtieth session on the implementation of the present resolution.

RECORDED VOTE ON RESOLUTION 59/122:

In favour: Afghanistan, Algeria, Andorra, Antigua and Barbuda, Argentina, Armenia, Austria, Azerbaijan, Bahamas, Bahrain, Bangladesh, Barbados, Belarus, Belgium, Belize, Benin, Bolivia, Bosnia and Herzegovina, Botswana, Brazil, Brunei Darussalam, Bulgaria, Burkina Faso, Burundi, Cambodia, Canada, Cape Verde, Chile, China, Colombia, Comoros, Congo, Costa Rica, Croatia, Cuba, Cyprus, Czech Republic, Democratic People's Republic of Korea, Denmark, Djibouti, Dominica, Ecuador, Egypt, El Salvador, Equatorial Guinea, Eritrea, Estonia, Ethiopia, Fiji, Finland, France, Gabon, Georgia, Germany, Ghana, Greece, Guatemala, Guinea, Guinea-Bissau, Guyana, Honduras, Hungary, Iceland, India, Indonesia, Iran, Ireland, Italy, Jamaica, Japan, Jordan, Kazakhstan, Kenya, Kuwait, Kyrgyzstan, Lao People's Democratic Republic, Latvia, Lebanon, Lesotho, Libyan Arab Jamahiriya, Liechtenstein, Lithuania, Luxembourg, Madagascar, Malaysia, Maldives, Mali, Malta, Mauritius, Mexico, Monaco, Mongolia, Morocco, Mozambique, Myanmar, Namibia, Nepal, Netherlands, New Zealand, Nicaragua, Nigeria, Norway, Oman, Pakistan, Panama, Paraguay, Peru, Philippines, Poland, Portugal, Qatar, Republic of Korea, Republic of Moldova, Romania, Russian Federation, Saint Lucia, Saint Vincent and the Grenadines, Samoa, San Marino, Sao Tome and Principe, Saudi Arabia, Senegal, Serbia and Montenegro, Seychelles, Sierra Leone, Singapore, Slovakia, Slovenia, Solomon Islands, Somalia, South Africa, Spain, Sri Lanka, Sudan, Suriname, Swaziland, Sweden, Switzerland, Syrian Arab Republic, Tajikistan, Thailand, The former Yugoslav Republic of Macedonia, Timor-Leste, Togo, Tonga, Trinidad and Tobago, Tunisia, Turkey, Turkmenistan, Ukraine, United Arab Emirates, United Kingdom, United Republic of Tanzania, Uruguay, Uzbekistan, Venezuela, Viet Nam, Yemen, Zambia, Zimbabwe.

Against: Grenada, Israel, Marshall Islands, Mauritania, Micronesia, Palau, United States.

Abstaining: Albania, Australia, Cameroon, Côte d'Ivoire, Dominican Republic, Haiti, Nauru, Papua New Guinea, Tuvalu, Uganda, Vanuatu.

Israeli settlements

Report of Secretary-General. On 9 September [A/59/343], the Secretary-General informed the General Assembly that Israel had not replied to his August request for information on steps taken or envisaged to implement the relevant provisions of resolution 58/98 [YUN 2003, p. 492], demanding that Israel, among other things, cease all construction of the wall and new settlements in the Occupied Palestinian Territory, including East Jerusalem.

GENERAL ASSEMBLY ACTION

On 10 December [meeting 71], the General Assembly, on the recommendation of the Fourth Committee [A/59/471], adopted **resolution 59/123** by recorded vote (155-8-15) [agenda item 76].

Israeli settlements in the Occupied Palestinian Territory, including East Jerusalem, and the occupied Syrian Golan

The General Assembly,

Guided by the principles set forth in the Charter of the United Nations, and affirming the inadmissibility of the acquisition of territory by force,

Recalling its relevant resolutions, including resolution 58/292 of 6 May 2004, as well as those resolutions adopted at its tenth emergency special session,

Recalling also relevant Security Council resolutions, including resolutions 242(1967) of 22 November 1967, 446(1979) of 22 March 1979, 465(1980) of 1 March 1980, 476(1980) of 30 June 1980, 478(1980) of 20 August 1980, 497(1981) of 17 December 1981 and 904 (1994) of 18 March 1994,

Reaffirming the applicability of the Geneva Convention relative to the Protection of Civilian Persons in Time of War, of 12 August 1949, to the Occupied Palestinian Territory, including East Jerusalem, and to the occupied Syrian Golan,

Considering that the transfer by the occupying Power of parts of its own civilian population into the territory it occupies is a breach of the Fourth Geneva Convention and relevant provisions of customary law, including those codified in Additional Protocol I to the Geneva Conventions,

Recalling the advisory opinion rendered on 9 July 2004 by the International Court of Justice on the *Legal Consequences of the Construction of a Wall in the Occupied Palestinian Territory*, and recalling also General Assembly resolution ES-10/15 of 20 July 2004,

Noting that the Court concluded that "the Israeli settlements in the Occupied Palestinian Territory (including East Jerusalem) have been established in breach of international law",

Taking note of the recent report of the Special Rapporteur of the Commission on Human Rights on the situation of human rights in the Palestinian territories occupied by Israel since 1967,

Recalling the Declaration of Principles on Interim Self-Government Arrangements of 13 September 1993 and the subsequent implementation agreements between the Palestinian and Israeli sides,

Recalling also the Quartet road map to a permanent two-State solution to the Israeli-Palestinian conflict, and noting specifically its call for a freeze on all settlement activity,

Aware that Israeli settlement activities have involved, inter alia, the transfer of nationals of the occupying Power into the occupied territories, the confiscation of land, the exploitation of natural resources and other illegal actions against the Palestinian civilian population,

Bearing in mind the detrimental impact of Israeli settlement policies, decisions and activities on efforts to achieve peace in the Middle East,

Expressing grave concern about the continuation by Israel, the occupying Power, of settlement activities, in violation of international humanitarian law, relevant United Nations resolutions and the agreements reached between the parties, including the construction and expansion of the settlements in Jabal Abu-Ghneim and Ras Al-Amud in and around Occupied East Jerusalem,

Expressing grave concern also about the continuing unlawful construction by Israel of the wall inside the Occupied Palestinian Territory, including in and around East Jerusalem, and expressing its concern in particular about the route of the wall in departure from the Armistice Line of 1949, which could prejudice future negotiations and make the two-State solution physically impossible to implement and which is causing the Palestinian people further humanitarian hardship,

Deeply concerned that the wall's route has been traced in such a way as to include the great majority of the Israeli settlements in the Occupied Palestinian Territory, including East Jerusalem,

Reiterating its opposition to settlement activities in the Occupied Palestinian Territory, including East Jerusalem, and to any activities involving the confiscation of land, the disruption of the livelihood of protected persons and the de facto annexation of land,

Recalling the need to end all acts of violence, including acts of terror, provocation, incitement and destruction,

Gravely concerned about the dangerous situation resulting from actions taken by the illegal armed Israeli settlers in the occupied territory,

Taking note of the relevant reports of the Secretary-General,

1. *Reaffirms* that Israeli settlements in the Palestinian territory, including East Jerusalem, and in the occupied Syrian Golan are illegal and an obstacle to peace and economic and social development;

2. *Calls upon* Israel to accept the de jure applicability of the Geneva Convention relative to the Protection of Civilian Persons in Time of War, of 12 August 1949, to the Occupied Palestinian Territory, including East Jerusalem, and to the occupied Syrian Golan and to abide scrupulously by the provisions of the Convention, in particular article 49;

3. *Reiterates its demand* for the complete cessation of all Israeli settlement activities in the Occupied Palestinian Territory, including East Jerusalem, and in the occupied Syrian Golan, and calls for the full implementation of the relevant Security Council resolutions;

4. *Demands* that Israel, the occupying Power, comply with its legal obligations, as mentioned in the advisory opinion rendered on 9 July 2004 by the International Court of Justice;

5. *Stresses* the need for full implementation of Security Council resolution 904(1994), in which, among other things, the Council called upon Israel, the occupying Power, to continue to take and implement measures, including confiscation of arms, with the aim of preventing illegal acts of violence by Israeli settlers, and called for measures to be taken to guarantee the safety and protection of the Palestinian civilians in the occupied territory;

6. *Reiterates its calls* for the prevention of all acts of violence by Israeli settlers, especially against Palestinian civilians and property, particularly in the light of recent developments;

7. *Requests* the Secretary-General to report to the General Assembly at its sixtieth session on the implementation of the present resolution.

RECORDED VOTE ON RESOLUTION 59/123:

In favour: Afghanistan, Algeria, Andorra, Antigua and Barbuda, Argentina, Armenia, Austria, Azerbaijan, Bahamas, Bahrain, Bangladesh, Barbados, Belarus, Belgium, Belize, Benin, Bolivia, Bosnia and Herzegovina, Botswana, Brazil, Brunei Darussalam, Bulgaria, Burkina Faso, Burundi, Cambodia, Canada, Cape Verde, Chile, China, Colombia, Comoros, Congo, Costa Rica, Croatia, Cuba, Cyprus, Czech Republic, Democratic People's Republic of Korea, Denmark, Djibouti, Dominica, Ecuador, Egypt, El Salvador, Eritrea, Estonia, Ethiopia, Fiji, Finland, France, Gabon, Georgia, Germany, Ghana, Greece, Guatemala, Guinea, Guinea-Bissau, Guyana, Honduras, Hungary, Iceland, India, Indonesia, Iran, Iraq, Ireland, Italy, Jamaica, Japan, Jordan, Kazakhstan, Kuwait, Kyrgyzstan, Lao Peo-

ple's Democratic Republic, Latvia, Lebanon, Lesotho, Libyan Arab Jamahiriya, Liechtenstein, Lithuania, Luxembourg, Madagascar, Malaysia, Maldives, Mali, Malta, Mauritania, Mauritius, Mexico, Monaco, Mongolia, Morocco, Mozambique, Myanmar, Namibia, Nepal, Netherlands, New Zealand, Nigeria, Norway, Oman, Pakistan, Panama, Paraguay, Peru, Philippines, Poland, Portugal, Qatar, Republic of Korea, Republic of Moldova, Romania, Russian Federation, Saint Lucia, Saint Vincent and the Grenadines, Samoa, San Marino, Sao Tome and Principe, Saudi Arabia, Senegal, Serbia and Montenegro, Seychelles, Sierra Leone, Singapore, Slovakia, Slovenia, Somalia, South Africa, Spain, Sri Lanka, Sudan, Suriname, Swaziland, Sweden, Switzerland, Syrian Arab Republic, Tajikistan, Thailand, The former Yugoslav Republic of Macedonia, Timor-Leste, Togo, Tunisia, Turkey, Turkmenistan, Ukraine, United Arab Emirates, United Kingdom, United Republic of Tanzania, Uruguay, Venezuela, Viet Nam, Yemen, Zambia, Zimbabwe.

Against: Australia, Grenada, Israel, Marshall Islands, Micronesia, Nauru, Palau, United States.

Abstaining: Albania, Cameroon, Côte d'Ivoire, Dominican Republic, Equatorial Guinea, Haiti, Kenya, Nicaragua, Papua New Guinea, Solomon Islands, Tonga, Tuvalu, Uganda, Uzbekistan, Vanuatu.

Palestinian women

The Secretary-General, in a report [E/CN.6/2004/4] to the Commission on the Status of Women, as requested by the Economic and Social Council in resolution 2003/42 [YUN 2003, p. 494], reviewed the situation of Palestinian women and assistance provided by UN organizations from September 2002 to September 2003. He said that during that period, the occupation of Palestinian territory by Israel continued to have a detrimental effect on all aspects of the living conditions of the Palestinian people. Unemployment increased threefold and poverty rose among more than two thirds of the population. Women and children bore a special and enduring burden resulting from the occupation. Under the new Israeli rule, Palestinian women living in East Jerusalem were regarded as mere residents and were not allowed to give their nationality or residency to their husbands or children. Women's responsibilities within households were expanded due to the death, imprisonment or unemployment of male members. Many women were placed in the position of being a primary household provider, caregiver and the main strategist for coping financially, mentally and physically with the new situation. The closures of roads, local curfews and numerous checkpoints prevented thousands of ordinary Palestinians from going to work, cultivating their fields or sending their children to school. About 140 checkpoints operated in the West Bank, and 25 to 30 others in the Gaza Strip. Hundreds of farmers lost their income since they were unable to cultivate their fields, and women were severely affected by the decline in the agricultural sector, a vital source of income for the household.

Although the situation in the Occupied Palestinian Territory made it difficult for international organizations to provide direct assistance to Palestinian women, the UN system continued to respond to their needs. The United Nations Development Programme (UNDP) provided assistance to Palestinian women through project activities targeting female-headed rural households. UNDP also provided technical and financial support as well as training for community-based women's organizations. The United Nations Conference on Trade and Development collaborated with Palestinian ministries to support Palestinian farmers, including women, by assisting them in marketing their surplus olive oil. The International Labour Organization (ILO) provided assistance to Palestinian women, including through an interregional programme on capacity-building for gender equality, employment promotion and poverty eradication. The World Bank incorporated gender dimensions in its activities and participated in the Gender Task Force in the West Bank and Gaza. In response to emergency needs, the World Bank managed $25 million in bilateral donor funds for job-creation projects. One of the main selection criteria for emergency grants was a project's ability to benefit women. The Bank supported a counselling centre for women in difficult circumstances, aimed at providing support, therapy, advocacy and vocational training services to Palestinian women subjected to domestic violence. The Bank also completed a beneficiary assessment report of the second Community Development Project, which found that nearly 40 per cent of all schools rehabilitated under the project were girls' or co-educational schools. Among other Bank projects were construction of a girls' orphanage, vocational training to women under development grants and an integrated educational programme for women with children.

The Secretary-General observed that the humanitarian and socio-economic crisis in the Occupied Palestinian Territory had reached unprecedented levels. The capacity of Palestinian women to cope with that new situation had been declining, and the number of women dependent on emergency assistance, particularly food assistance, had risen. The status and living conditions of Palestinian women were linked to the achievement of a peaceful resolution of the conflict. There were important differences in how women and men were affected by the socio-economic and political situation, which were apparent in such areas as basic social services, including education and health, economic opportunities and means of livelihood. Those differences needed to be taken into account in research, data collection, policy and strategy development, and implementation and monitoring of projects on the ground. It was also important that efforts be made to increase women's full participation in decision-making processes at all levels. It was essential for UN entities to operate in the Occupied Palestin-

ian Territory and the refugee camps, and to provide Palestinian women with food security, psychosocial/trauma counselling, health services, including reproductive health, education, and human rights and economic empowerment. Further opportunities should be sought to highlight the specific ways in which the crisis impacted on women as compared to men so that targeted actions could be taken to mitigate negative gender-specific impacts. The collection of data disaggregated by sex and studies on the impact of the crisis on women in particular areas should be encouraged, and the linkage between the ongoing crisis and the increase in domestic violence could be further explored. In the Secretary-General's view, efforts should be undertaken to address gender perspectives in international assistance programmes, in addition to implementing projects specifically targeting women.

ECONOMIC AND SOCIAL COUNCIL ACTION

On 23 July [meeting 51], the Economic and Social Council, on the recommendation of the Commission on the Status of Women [E/2004/27], adopted **resolution 2004/56** by recorded vote (49-1-3) [agenda item 14 (*a*)].

Situation of and assistance to Palestinian women

The Economic and Social Council,

Having considered with appreciation the report of the Secretary-General,

Recalling the Nairobi Forward-looking Strategies for the Advancement of Women, in particular paragraph 260 concerning Palestinian women and children, the Beijing Platform for Action adopted at the Fourth World Conference on Women and the outcome of the twenty-third special session of the General Assembly, entitled "Women 2000: gender equality, development and peace for the twenty-first century",

Recalling also its resolution 2003/42 of 22 July 2003 and other relevant United Nations resolutions,

Recalling further the Declaration on the Elimination of Violence against Women as it concerns the protection of civilian populations,

Expressing the urgent need for the resumption of negotiations within the Middle East peace process on its agreed basis and towards the speedy achievement of a final settlement between the Palestinian and Israeli sides,

Concerned about the grave deterioration of the situation of Palestinian women in the Occupied Palestinian Territory, including East Jerusalem, and about the severe consequences of continuous illegal Israeli settlements activities as well as the harsh economic conditions and other severe consequences of the continuing Israeli attacks and sieges on Palestinian cities, towns, villages and refugee camps, which has resulted in the dire humanitarian crisis being faced by Palestinian women and their families,

Concerned also that the route marked out for the wall under construction by Israel, the occupying Power, in the Occupied Palestinian Territory, including in and around East Jerusalem, could prejudice future negotiations and make the two-State solution physically impossible to implement and would cause further humanitarian hardship to the Palestinians, in particular women and children,

Expressing its condemnation of all acts of violence, including all acts of terror, provocation, incitement and destruction, especially the excessive use of force against Palestinian civilians, many of them women and children, resulting in injury and loss of human life,

1. *Calls upon* the concerned parties, as well as the international community, to exert all the efforts necessary to ensure the immediate resumption of the peace process on its agreed basis, taking into account the common ground already gained, and calls for measures for tangible improvement of the difficult situation on the ground and the living conditions faced by Palestinian women and their families;

2. *Reaffirms* that the Israeli occupation remains a major obstacle for Palestinian women with regard to their advancement, self-reliance and integration in the development planning of their society;

3. *Demands* that Israel, the occupying Power, comply fully with the provisions and principles of the Universal Declaration of Human Rights, the Regulations annexed to The Hague Convention IV, of 18 October 1907 and the Geneva Convention relative to the Protection of Civilian Persons in Time of War, of 12 August 1949, in order to protect the rights of Palestinian women and their families;

4. *Calls upon* Israel to facilitate the return of all refugees and displaced Palestinian women and children to their homes and properties, in compliance with the relevant United Nations resolutions;

5. *Calls upon* the international community to continue to provide urgently needed assistance and services in an effort to alleviate the dire humanitarian crisis being faced by Palestinian women and their families and to help in the reconstruction of relevant Palestinian institutions;

6. *Requests* the Commission on the Status of Women to continue to monitor and take action with regard to the implementation of the Nairobi Forward-looking Strategies for the Advancement of Women, in particular paragraph 260 concerning Palestinian women and children, the Beijing Platform for Action and the outcome of the twenty-third special session of the General Assembly, entitled "Women 2000: gender equality, development and peace for the twenty-first century";

7. *Requests* the Secretary-General to continue to review the situation and to assist Palestinian women by all available means, including those set out in his report, and to submit to the Commission on the Status of Women at its forty-ninth session a report, including information provided by the Economic and Social Commission for Western Asia, on the progress made in the implementation of the present resolution.

RECORDED VOTE ON RESOLUTION 2004/56:

In favour: Armenia, Azerbaijan, Bangladesh, Belgium, Belize, Benin, Bhutan, Burundi, Chile, China, Colombia, Congo, Cuba, Ecuador, Finland, France, Germany, Ghana, Greece, Guatemala, Hungary, India, Indonesia, Ireland, Italy, Jamaica, Japan, Kenya, Libyan Arab Jamahiriya, Malaysia, Mauritius, Mozambique, Namibia, Nigeria, Panama, Poland, Qatar, Republic of Korea, Russian Federation, Saudi Arabia, Senegal, Sweden, Tunisia, Turkey, Ukraine, United Arab Emirates, United Kingdom, United Republic of Tanzania, Zimbabwe.

Against: United States.

Abstaining: Australia, Canada, Nicaragua.

Palestinian children

On 20 December [meeting 74], the General Assembly, on the recommendation of the Third (Social, Humanitarian and Cultural) Committee [A/59/499], adopted **resolution 59/173** by recorded vote (117-5-62) [agenda item 101].

The situation of and assistance to Palestinian children

The General Assembly,

Recalling the Convention on the Rights of the Child,

Bearing in mind the conclusion by the International Court of Justice, in its advisory opinion of 9 July 2004, that the Convention on the Rights of the Child is applicable within the Occupied Palestinian Territory,

Recalling the World Declaration on the Survival, Protection and Development of Children and the Plan of Action for Implementing the World Declaration on the Survival, Protection and Development of Children in the 1990s adopted by the World Summit for Children, held in New York on 29 and 30 September 1990,

Recalling also the Declaration and Plan of Action adopted by the General Assembly at its twenty-seventh special session,

Recalling further the relevant provisions of the International Covenant on Economic, Social and Cultural Rights,

Noting with grave concern that the Palestinian children under Israeli occupation remain deprived of many basic rights under the Convention on the Rights of the Child,

Concerned about the continued grave deterioration of the situation of Palestinian children in the Occupied Palestinian Territory, including East Jerusalem, the severely detrimental impact of the continuing Israeli assaults and sieges on Palestinian cities, towns, villages and refugee camps, and the continuing dire humanitarian crisis on the safety and well-being of Palestinian children,

Concerned also about the severely detrimental impact being caused by the unlawful construction of the wall by Israel, the occupying Power, in the Occupied Palestinian Territory, including in and around East Jerusalem, and its associated regime, on the socio-economic conditions of Palestinian children and their families and on the enjoyment by Palestinian children of their right to education, to an adequate standard of living, including adequate food, clothing and housing, to health and to be free from hunger, in accordance with the Convention on the Rights of the Child and the International Covenant on Economic, Social and Cultural Rights,

Emphasizing the importance of the safety and well-being of all children in the whole Middle East region,

Expressing its condemnation of all acts of violence, resulting in extensive loss of human life and injuries, including among Palestinian children,

Deeply concerned about the negative consequences, including psychological consequences, of the Israeli military actions for the present and future well-being of Palestinian children,

1. *Stresses* the urgent need for Palestinian children to live a normal life free from foreign occupation, destruction and fear in their own State;

2. *Demands*, in the meanwhile, that Israel, the occupying Power, respect relevant provisions of the Con-

vention on the Rights of the Child and comply fully with the provisions of the Geneva Convention relative to the Protection of Civilian Persons in Time of War, of 12 August 1949, in order to ensure the well-being and protection of Palestinian children and their families;

3. *Calls upon* the international community to provide urgently needed assistance and services in an effort to alleviate the dire humanitarian crisis being faced by Palestinian children and their families and to help in the reconstruction of relevant Palestinian institutions.

RECORDED VOTE ON RESOLUTION 59/173:

In favour: Afghanistan, Algeria, Angola, Antigua and Barbuda, Argentina, Armenia, Azerbaijan, Bahamas, Bahrain, Bangladesh, Barbados, Belarus, Belize, Bhutan, Bolivia, Botswana, Brazil, Brunei Darussalam, Burkina Faso, Burundi, Cambodia, Cape Verde, Chad, Chile, China, Comoros, Costa Rica, Côte d'Ivoire, Cuba, Democratic People's Republic of Korea, Democratic Republic of the Congo, Djibouti, Dominica, Dominican Republic, Ecuador, Egypt, Equatorial Guinea, Eritrea, Ethiopia, Fiji, Gabon, Gambia, Ghana, Grenada, Guinea, Guinea-Bissau, Guyana, Honduras, India, Indonesia, Iran, Iraq, Jamaica, Jordan, Kazakhstan, Kenya, Kuwait, Kyrgyzstan, Lao People's Democratic Republic, Lebanon, Lesotho, Liberia, Libyan Arab Jamahiriya, Madagascar, Malawi, Malaysia, Maldives, Mali, Mauritania, Mauritius, Mongolia, Morocco, Mozambique, Myanmar, Namibia, Nauru, Nepal, Niger, Nigeria, Oman, Pakistan, Panama, Paraguay, Philippines, Qatar, Russian Federation, Saint Lucia, Saint Vincent and the Grenadines, Sao Tome and Principe, Saudi Arabia, Senegal, Seychelles, Sierra Leone, Singapore, Somalia, South Africa, Sri Lanka, Sudan, Suriname, Swaziland, Syrian Arab Republic, Tajikistan, Thailand, Togo, Trinidad and Tobago, Tunisia, Turkey, Turkmenistan, Uganda, United Arab Emirates, United Republic of Tanzania, Uzbekistan, Venezuela, Viet Nam, Yemen, Zambia, Zimbabwe.

Against: Israel, Marshall Islands, Micronesia, Palau, United States.

Abstaining: Albania, Andorra, Australia, Austria, Belgium, Benin, Bosnia and Herzegovina, Bulgaria, Cameroon, Canada, Colombia, Croatia, Cyprus, Czech Republic, Denmark, El Salvador, Estonia, Finland, France, Georgia, Germany, Greece, Guatemala, Haiti, Hungary, Iceland, Ireland, Italy, Japan, Latvia, Liechtenstein, Lithuania, Luxembourg, Malta, Mexico, Monaco, Netherlands, New Zealand, Norway, Papua New Guinea, Peru, Poland, Portugal, Republic of Korea, Republic of Moldova, Romania, Samoa, San Marino, Serbia and Montenegro, Slovakia, Slovenia, Solomon Islands, Spain, Sweden, Switzerland, The former Yugoslav Republic of Macedonia, Tonga, Tuvalu, Ukraine, United Kingdom, Uruguay, Vanuatu.

Issues related to Palestine

General aspects

The General Assembly again considered the question of Palestine in 2004. Having discussed the annual report of the Committee on the Exercise of the Inalienable Rights of the Palestinian People (Committee on Palestinian Rights) [A/59/35], the Assembly adopted five resolutions, reaffirming, among other things, the necessity of achieving a peaceful settlement of the Palestine question—the core of the Arab-Israeli conflict—and stressing the need for the realization of the inalienable rights of the Palestinians, primarily the right to self-determination, for Israeli withdrawal from the Palestinian territory occupied since 1967 and for resolving the problem of the Palestine refugees. The Assembly also affirmed that the status of the Palestinian territory remained one of military occupation. It called on

the Secretariat to continue its activities to promote and raise awareness of Palestinian rights.

In observance of the International Day of Solidarity with the Palestinian People, celebrated annually on 29 November in accordance with Assembly resolution 32/40 B [YUN 1977, p. 304], the Committee held a solemn meeting. The Permanent Observer Mission of Palestine, under the Committee's auspices, presented an exhibit entitled "Steadfast in Palestine".

Report of Secretary-General. In a November report on the peaceful settlement of the question of Palestine [A/59/574-S/2004/909], submitted in response to Assembly resolution 58/21 [YUN 2003, p. 497], the Secretary-General made observations on the Middle East peace process (see also p. 453). On 12 April, the Secretary-General sought the positions of Egypt, Israel, Jordan, Lebanon, the Syrian Arab Republic and the Permanent Observer of Palestine regarding steps taken to implement the resolution. As at 17 September, Israel, Syria and the Permanent Observer had responded.

Israel said that it viewed the resolution as unbalanced and as an undue interference in matters which the parties had agreed to resolve within the context of direct bilateral negotiations. The violence in the region was a result of a Palestinian decision to abandon peace negotiations and pursue their goals through violence and terrorism. The one-sided approach of the resolution, which sought to dictate the outcome of the negotiating process, effectively rewarded violence at a time when the Palestinian side should discontinue such acts and boldly pursue peaceful dialogue.

Syria affirmed that Israel's determination to continue its expansionist policy inside Palestinian territory, especially while it was building the separation wall, and its non-compliance with Assembly resolutions, were blatant examples of its illegitimate actions and a denial of the principle of equal and inalienable rights and self-determination of peoples.

The Permanent Observer said that Israel's withdrawal from Palestinian territory was a fundamental requisite for solving the question of Palestine and achieving a peaceful settlement of the Israeli-Palestinian conflict, based on the two-State solution. Israel's settler policy and its construction of the wall in the Occupied Palestinian Territory, including East Jerusalem, were the antithesis of withdrawal and actually constituted the main obstacle to the realization of the national rights of the Palestinian people and the achievement of the two-State solution. Without the complete cessation and reversal of all settlement activities and of the construction of the wall, there could be no hope for the road map and for a peaceful settlement. The international community had to face that reality and take the necessary measures to reach that result.

The Secretary-General, summarizing developments during the year, observed that the rising number of deaths and violence in the Middle East were evidence of the lack of progress in advancing the peace process. In general, both parties had not lived up to their road map obligations. On the economic front, the picture remained grim. The Palestinian economy was in tatters and stood little chance of recovery unless immediate action was taken. Forty-seven per cent of the Palestinian population lived in poverty. Unemployment among Palestinians stood at 34.3 per cent, or 28.6 per cent at the ILO-adjusted rate, which excluded discouraged workers. UNRWA and the World Food Programme were providing food to 39 per cent of the Palestinian population in the occupied territory. The economic crisis, according to the World Bank, was contributing to the impoverishment of an entire generation of young Palestinians, as well as to the undermining of the credibility of the PA, and, inevitably, it was increasing the popular appeal of militant factions. The primary cause of that crisis was the closure regime imposed by Israel and, without a significant change in that regime, the Palestinian economy would not be revived. According to the World Bank, Israel's disengagement plan would have limited impact on the Palestinian economy if it were not accompanied by a radical easing of closure that encompassed three elements: the removal of internal obstacles to movement in the West Bank; the opening of Palestinian external borders to commodity trade; and a return to a reasonable flow of Palestinian labour into Israel. If those conditions were met, additional donor money could be raised, but donors needed some assurance that their contributions would have an impact. Aid would be provided in the context of a successful comprehensive Israeli withdrawal from the Gaza Strip and the northern West Bank, as a first step in the implementation of the road map.

The Secretary-General said that it was particularly disquieting that Israel had announced its intention to phase out completely Palestinian employment inside Israel by 2008. The number of Palestinians employed in Israel had decreased significantly since September 2000, and the Palestinian economy was dependent on the Israeli economy, not only for employment but also for raw materials and trade. A revival of the Palestinian economy in the short term depended on a return to reasonable levels of Palestinian employment in Israel. Should Israel insist on ending Palestinian employment and implement the dis-

engagement plan without accompanying measures to ease closure, unemployment and poverty would continue to soar among Palestinians. The Secretary-General called on the international community to provide the resources necessary to support UN programmes in addressing the deteriorating economic and humanitarian situation of the Palestinian people.

GENERAL ASSEMBLY ACTION

On 1 December [meeting 64], the General Assembly adopted **resolution 59/31** [draft: A/59/L.37 & Add.1] by recorded vote (161-7-10) [agenda item 37].

Peaceful settlement of the question of Palestine

The General Assembly,

Recalling its relevant resolutions, including those adopted at the tenth emergency special session,

Recalling also its resolution 58/292 of 6 May 2004,

Recalling further the relevant Security Council resolutions, including resolutions 242(1967) of 22 November 1967, 338(1973) of 22 October 1973, 1397(2002) of 12 March 2002, 1515(2003) of 19 November 2003 and 1544(2004) of 19 May 2004,

Welcoming the affirmation by the Security Council of the vision of a region where two States, Israel and Palestine, live side by side within secure and recognized borders,

Noting with concern that it has been fifty-seven years since the adoption of resolution 181(II) of 29 November 1947 and thirty-seven years since the occupation of Palestinian territory, including East Jerusalem, in 1967,

Having considered the report of the Secretary-General submitted pursuant to the request made in its resolution 58/21 of 3 December 2003,

Reaffirming the permanent responsibility of the United Nations with regard to the question of Palestine until the question is resolved in all its aspects in accordance with international law,

Recalling the advisory opinion rendered on 9 July 2004 by the International Court of Justice on the *Legal Consequences of the Construction of a Wall in the Occupied Palestinian Territory*, and recalling also its resolution ES-10/15 of 20 July 2004,

Convinced that achieving a final and peaceful settlement of the question of Palestine, the core of the Arab-Israeli conflict, is imperative for the attainment of comprehensive and lasting peace and stability in the Middle East,

Aware that the principle of equal rights and self-determination of peoples is among the purposes and principles enshrined in the Charter of the United Nations,

Affirming the principle of the inadmissibility of the acquisition of territory by war,

Recalling its resolution 2625(XXV) of 24 October 1970,

Reaffirming the illegality of the Israeli settlements in the territory occupied since 1967 and of Israeli actions aimed at changing the status of Jerusalem,

Reaffirming also that the construction by Israel, the occupying Power, of a wall in the Occupied Palestinian Territory, including in and around East Jerusalem, and its associated regime, are contrary to international law,

Affirming once again the right of all States in the region to live in peace within secure and internationally recognized borders,

Recalling the mutual recognition between the Government of the State of Israel and the Palestine Liberation Organization, the representative of the Palestinian people, and the agreements concluded between the two sides, and the need for full compliance with those agreements,

Recalling also the endorsement by the Security Council, in resolution 1515(2003), of the Quartet road map to a permanent two-State solution to the Israeli-Palestinian conflict, and stressing the urgent need for its implementation and compliance with its provisions,

Noting the establishment of the Palestinian Authority, and recognizing the urgent need to rebuild, reform and strengthen its damaged institutions,

Welcoming the contribution to the peace process of the United Nations Special Coordinator for the Middle East Peace Process and Personal Representative of the Secretary-General to the Palestine Liberation Organization and the Palestinian Authority, including in the framework of the activities of the Quartet,

Welcoming also the convening of international donor meetings, as well as the establishment of international mechanisms to provide assistance to the Palestinian people,

Expressing its grave concern over the tragic events in the Occupied Palestinian Territory, including East Jerusalem, since 28 September 2000 and the continuing deterioration of the situation, including the rising number of deaths and injuries, mostly among Palestinian civilians, the deepening humanitarian crisis facing the Palestinian people and the widespread destruction of Palestinian property and infrastructure, both private and public, including institutions of the Palestinian Authority,

Expressing its grave concern also over the repeated military actions in the Occupied Palestinian Territory and the reoccupation of Palestinian population centres by the Israeli occupying forces,

Emphasizing the importance of the safety and well-being of all civilians in the whole Middle East region, and condemning all acts of violence and terror against civilians on both sides, including the suicide bombings, the extrajudicial executions and the excessive use of force,

Gravely concerned over the increased suffering and casualties on both the Palestinian and Israeli sides, the loss of confidence on both sides and the dire situation facing the Middle East peace process,

Aware of the urgent need for revitalized and active international involvement to support both parties in overcoming the current dangerous impasse in the peace process,

Affirming the urgent need for the parties to cooperate with all international efforts, including the efforts of the Quartet, to end the current tragic situation and to resume and accelerate negotiations towards a final peace settlement,

Welcoming the initiatives and efforts undertaken by civil society in pursuit of a peaceful settlement of the question of Palestine,

Taking note of the findings by the International Court of Justice, in its advisory opinion, including on the urgent necessity for the United Nations as a whole to redouble its efforts to bring the Israeli-Palestinian conflict, which continues to pose a threat to international peace and security, to a speedy conclusion, thereby establishing a just and lasting peace in the region,

1. *Reaffirms* the necessity of achieving a peaceful settlement of the question of Palestine, the core of the Arab-Israeli conflict, in all its aspects, and of intensifying all efforts towards that end;

2. *Reaffirms its full support* for the Middle East peace process, which began in Madrid, and the existing agreements between the Israeli and Palestinian sides, stresses the necessity for the establishment of a comprehensive, just and lasting peace in the Middle East, and welcomes in this regard the ongoing efforts of the Quartet;

3. *Welcomes* the Arab Peace Initiative adopted by the Council of the League of Arab States at its fourteenth session, held in Beirut on 27 and 28 March 2002;

4. *Calls upon* both parties to fulfil their obligations in implementation of the road map by taking parallel and reciprocal steps in this regard, and stresses the importance and urgency of establishing a credible and effective third-party monitoring mechanism including all members of the Quartet;

5. *Stresses* the need for a speedy end to the reoccupation of Palestinian population centres and for the complete cessation of all acts of violence, including military attacks, destruction and acts of terror;

6. *Calls upon* the parties, with the support of the Quartet and other interested parties, to exert all efforts necessary to halt the deterioration of the situation, to reverse all measures taken on the ground since 28 September 2000 and to facilitate a speedy resumption of the peace process and the conclusion of a final peaceful settlement;

7. *Demands* that Israel, the occupying Power, comply with its legal obligations, as mentioned in the advisory opinion, and calls upon all States Members of the United Nations to comply with their legal obligations as mentioned in the advisory opinion;

8. *Reaffirms its commitment*, in accordance with international law, to the two-State solution of Israel and Palestine, living side by side in peace and security within recognized borders, based on the pre-1967 borders;

9. *Reiterates its demand* for the complete cessation of all Israeli settlement activities in the Occupied Palestinian Territory, including East Jerusalem, and in the occupied Syrian Golan, and calls for the implementation of the relevant Security Council resolutions;

10. *Stresses* the need for:

(a) The withdrawal of Israel from the Palestinian territory occupied since 1967;

(b) The realization of the inalienable rights of the Palestinian people, primarily the right to self-determination and the right to their independent State;

11. *Also stresses* the need for resolving the problem of the Palestine refugees in conformity with its resolution 194(III) of 11 December 1948;

12. *Urges* Member States to expedite the provision of economic, humanitarian and technical assistance to

the Palestinian people and the Palestinian Authority during this critical period to help to alleviate the suffering of the Palestinian people, rebuild the Palestinian economy and infrastructure and support the restructuring and reform of Palestinian institutions;

13. *Requests* the Secretary-General to continue his efforts with the parties concerned, and in consultation with the Security Council, towards the attainment of a peaceful settlement of the question of Palestine and the promotion of peace in the region and to submit to the General Assembly at its sixtieth session a report on these efforts and on developments on this matter.

RECORDED VOTE ON RESOLUTION 59/31:

In favour: Afghanistan, Albania, Algeria, Andorra, Angola, Argentina, Armenia, Austria, Azerbaijan, Bahamas, Bahrain, Bangladesh, Barbados, Belarus, Belgium, Belize, Benin, Bhutan, Bolivia, Bosnia and Herzegovina, Botswana, Brazil, Brunei Darussalam, Bulgaria, Burkina Faso, Burundi, Cambodia, Canada, Cape Verde, Central African Republic, Chile, China, Colombia, Congo, Costa Rica, Côte d'Ivoire, Croatia, Cuba, Cyprus, Czech Republic, Democratic People's Republic of Korea, Denmark, Djibouti, Dominica, Dominican Republic, Ecuador, Egypt, El Salvador, Eritrea, Estonia, Fiji, Finland, France, Gabon, Gambia, Georgia, Germany, Ghana, Greece, Guatemala, Guinea, Guinea-Bissau, Guyana, Hungary, Iceland, India, Indonesia, Iran, Iraq, Ireland, Italy, Jamaica, Japan, Jordan, Kazakhstan, Kenya, Kuwait, Kyrgyzstan, Lao People's Democratic Republic, Latvia, Lebanon, Lesotho, Liberia, Libyan Arab Jamahiriya, Liechtenstein, Lithuania, Luxembourg, Madagascar, Malaysia, Maldives, Mali, Malta, Mauritania, Mauritius, Mexico, Monaco, Mongolia, Morocco, Mozambique, Myanmar, Namibia, Nepal, Netherlands, New Zealand, Nicaragua, Niger, Nigeria, Norway, Oman, Pakistan, Panama, Paraguay, Peru, Philippines, Poland, Portugal, Qatar, Republic of Korea, Republic of Moldova, Romania, Russian Federation, Saint Lucia, Saint Vincent and the Grenadines, San Marino, Saudi Arabia, Senegal, Serbia and Montenegro, Seychelles, Sierra Leone, Singapore, Slovakia, Slovenia, Somalia, South Africa, Spain, Sri Lanka, Sudan, Suriname, Sweden, Switzerland, Syrian Arab Republic, Tajikistan, Thailand, The former Yugoslav Republic of Macedonia, Timor-Leste, Togo, Trinidad and Tobago, Tunisia, Turkey, Turkmenistan, Ukraine, United Arab Emirates, United Kingdom, United Republic of Tanzania, Uruguay, Uzbekistan, Venezuela, Viet Nam, Yemen, Zambia, Zimbabwe.

Against: Australia, Grenada, Israel, Marshall Islands, Micronesia, Palau, United States.

Abstaining: Cameroon, Haiti, Honduras, Nauru, Papua New Guinea, Samoa, Solomon Islands, Tonga, Uganda, Vanuatu.

By **decision 59/552** of 23 December, the Assembly decided that the agenda items entitled "The situation in the Middle East" and "Question of Palestine" would remain for consideration during its resumed fifty-ninth (2005) session.

Status of the Occupied Palestinian Territory

On 6 May [meeting 87], the General Assembly adopted **resolution 58/292** [draft: A/58/L.61/Rev.1] by recorded vote (140-6-11) [agenda item 38].

Status of the Occupied Palestinian Territory, including East Jerusalem

The General Assembly,

Recalling its resolutions 3237(XXIX) of 22 November 1974, 43/177 of 15 December 1988 and 52/250 of 7 July 1998,

Recalling also Security Council resolutions 242(1967) of 22 November 1967, 338(1973) of 22 October 1973, 1397(2002) of 12 March 2002 and 1515(2003) of 19 November 2003,

Recalling further the relevant provisions of international law, as well as relevant United Nations resolutions, with regard to Israeli settlements and to Occupied East Jerusalem,

Reaffirming the principle of the inadmissibility of the acquisition of territory by force,

Noting that Palestine, in its capacity as observer and pending its attainment of full membership in the United Nations, does not present credentials to the General Assembly,

Affirming the need to enable the Palestinian people to exercise sovereignty and to achieve independence in their State, Palestine,

1. *Affirms* that the status of the Palestinian territory occupied since 1967, including East Jerusalem, remains one of military occupation, and affirms, in accordance with the rules and principles of international law and relevant resolutions of the United Nations, including Security Council resolutions, that the Palestinian people have the right to self-determination and to sovereignty over their territory and that Israel, the occupying Power, has only the duties and obligations of an occupying Power under the Geneva Convention relative to the Protection of Civilian Persons in Time of War, of 12 August 1949 and the Regulations annexed to the Hague Convention respecting the Laws and Customs of War on Land of 1907;

2. *Expresses its determination* to contribute to the achievement of the inalienable rights of the Palestinian people and the attainment of a just and comprehensive negotiated peace settlement in the Middle East resulting in two viable, sovereign and independent States, Israel and Palestine, based on the pre-1967 borders and living side by side in peace and security.

RECORDED VOTE ON RESOLUTION 58/292:

In favour: Algeria, Andorra, Antigua and Barbuda, Argentina, Armenia, Austria, Azerbaijan, Bahrain, Bangladesh, Barbados, Belarus, Belgium, Belize, Bolivia, Bosnia and Herzegovina, Botswana, Brazil, Brunei Darussalam, Bulgaria, Burkina Faso, Burundi, Cambodia, Canada, Central African Republic, Chile, China, Colombia, Comoros, Congo, Croatia, Cuba, Cyprus, Czech Republic, Democratic People's Republic of Korea, Denmark, Djibouti, Dominica, Ecuador, Egypt, Eritrea, Estonia, Ethiopia, Finland, France, Gabon, Gambia, Georgia, Germany, Ghana, Greece, Grenada, Guinea, Guinea-Bissau, Guyana, Haiti, Hungary, Iceland, India, Indonesia, Iran, Ireland, Italy, Jamaica, Japan, Jordan, Kazakhstan, Kenya, Kuwait, Lao People's Democratic Republic, Latvia, Lebanon, Lesotho, Libyan Arab Jamahiriya, Liechtenstein, Lithuania, Luxembourg, Malaysia, Maldives, Mali, Malta, Mauritius, Mexico, Monaco, Mongolia, Morocco, Mozambique, Myanmar, Namibia, Nepal, Netherlands, New Zealand, Niger, Nigeria, Norway, Oman, Pakistan, Paraguay, Philippines, Poland, Portugal, Qatar, Republic of Korea, Republic of Moldova, Romania, Russian Federation, Saint Lucia, Saint Vincent and the Grenadines, San Marino, Saudi Arabia, Senegal, Sierra Leone, Singapore, Slovakia, Slovenia, Somalia, South Africa, Spain, Sri Lanka, Sudan, Sweden, Switzerland, Syrian Arab Republic, Tajikistan, Thailand, The former Yugoslav Republic of Macedonia, Timor-Leste, Togo, Trinidad and Tobago, Tunisia, Turkey, Uganda, Ukraine, United Arab Emirates, United Kingdom, United Republic of Tanzania, Uruguay, Venezuela, Viet Nam, Yemen, Zambia.

Against: Israel, Marshall Islands, Micronesia, Nauru, Palau, United States.

Abstaining: Australia, Costa Rica, Dominican Republic, Guatemala, Honduras, Nicaragua, Peru, Serbia and Montenegro, Solomon Islands, Tonga, Tuvalu.

Speaking after the vote, Israel said it objected to the resolution because of what it ignored and what it misrepresented, and because the motive of its primary sponsor in submitting the text was to undermine and prejudge the negotiating process, not to further it. The resolution ignored the Quartet statement made on 4 May (see p. 460) and violated the central tenet of the peace process, reiterated in the Quartet statement, which was to avoid prejudging the outcome of negotiations. The resolution also misrepresented reality, for it was a matter of fact and of law that the 1949 Armistice Lines (the wording in the draft text was changed in operative paragraph 2 to read "pre-1967 borders", replacing "1949 Armistice Lines") had never represented borders, as the resolution could be taken to imply.

The Permanent Observer of Palestine said that the resolution reaffirmed basic issues, including the status of the Palestinian territory occupied since 1967, including East Jerusalem, as territory under military occupation. It also reaffirmed that the Palestinian people had the right to self-determination and to exercise sovereignty over their territory. Moreover, the resolution affirmed that Israel, the occupying Power, needed to comply with its duties and obligations under the Fourth Geneva Convention and the Fourth Hague Convention. Those were all important matters that pertained to the core of the conflict and to the foundation of rights of the Palestinian people.

Committee on Palestinian Rights

As mandated by General Assembly resolution 58/18 [YUN 2003, p. 500], the Committee on the Exercise of the Inalienable Rights of the Palestinian People reviewed the situation relating to the Palestine question, reported on it and made suggestions to the Assembly and the Security Council.

The Committee followed the Palestine-related activities of intergovernmental bodies, such as the African Union, the Non-Aligned Movement and the Organization of the Islamic Conference, and, through its Chairman, participated in meetings of those bodies. In June, the Committee's Bureau held consultations with EU representatives to build a constructive relationship on issues of common concern. Throughout the year, the Committee held a number of international events, including the United Nations International Meeting on the Impact of the Construction of the Wall in the Occupied Palestinian Territory, including in and around East Jerusalem (Geneva, 15-16 April); the United Nations African Meeting in Support of the Inalienable Rights of the Palestinian People (Cape Town, South Africa, 29-30 June); the United Nations Forum of Civil Society in Support of Middle East Peace (Cape Town, 1 July); and the United Nations International Conference of Civil Society in Support of the Palestinian People (New York, 13-14 September).

In its annual report to the Assembly [A/59/35] covering the period from 10 October 2003 to 6 October 2004, the Committee said that the unremitting Israeli military incursions in areas under Palestinian control continued, increasing the numbers of those killed and wounded and resulting in the devastation of Palestinian cities and communities. The Committee was deeply troubled by the disproportionate and indiscriminate use of force by the Israeli army and the practice of collective punishment. The expansion of settlements and outposts and the construction of the wall in the West Bank continued at a brisk pace, along with the demolition of houses, confiscation of Palestinian property and unprecedented restrictions of movement. The number of Palestinians killed, in the four years of the intifada (uprising), reached a total of over 3,700, with some 35,700 injured. The Committee remained concerned over Israeli military operations in densely populated residential areas in the Occupied Palestinian Territory, especially the Gaza Strip. Since the start of the intifada, more than 65,998 Palestinian buildings, including homes, were destroyed or damaged. The Israeli army intensified extrajudicial killings, a policy the Committee had repeatedly condemned as inadmissible under international humanitarian law. At the same time, it strongly condemned all terrorist attacks against civilians in Israel, which also could not be justified. In addition, the Committee condemned Israel's continued siege on PA President Arafat in Ramallah, preventing him for almost three years from properly carrying out his duties. A worsening fiscal crisis likewise affected the PA's effectiveness in delivering core services to the population. Despite a financial gap of $890 million for 2004, it managed to provide for basic needs, including education, health, water, electricity and sewerage, although the standards of those services had declined. Efforts were made by the PA to introduce reforms in the finance and public administration areas. Security services members began receiving their salaries through bank accounts, replacing payment in person. The PA announced in August that simultaneous presidential, parliamentary and municipal elections would be held by spring 2005, though the Palestinian Central Elections Committee expressed concern about the registration of voters, given the curfews and Israeli military incursions.

The Committee noted with growing concern that Israel continued the expansion of settlements, in violation of its obligation under the road map. Based on a June survey, settlement expansion was under way at 73 of 211 settlement locations, including 12 of the 21 settlements in the Gaza Strip. In and around East Jerusalem, settlement activity proceeded at a rate unmatched since 1992. The total area of expansion was close to 500,000 square metres and included land development for settlement, new infrastructure, construction within the settlements, internal road works and the placement of new caravans.

The construction by Israel of the wall in the Occupied Palestinian Territory, including in and around East Jerusalem, caused great hardship to the Palestinians. Some 875,000 Palestinians in the West Bank, 38 per cent of the population, had been affected by the wall. Some 263,200 living in 81 localities had become isolated. The wall created a fait accompli that could become permanent and lead to the de facto annexation of Palestinian land. The Committee welcomed the advisory opinion of ICJ, in which the Court determined, among other things, that Israel was under an obligation to cease the construction and to dismantle portions built on Palestinian land (see p. 465). On 30 June, the Israeli High Court of Justice ordered changes in the trajectory of the wall along a 30-kilometre segment north of Jerusalem, stating that the separation from their agricultural land injured local inhabitants in a severe and acute way. In response to the ruling, the Israeli Defence Ministry presented changes in the route of the wall south of Hebron, which would be closer to the Armistice Line of 1949 (known as the Green Line). However, 15 square kilometres of Palestinian land remained on the Israeli side of the wall. The system of curfews and closures imposed by Israel, which severely restricted the movement of Palestinian people, goods and services, remained the central impediment to economic stabilization and recovery.

The Committee maintained that the continuing Israeli occupation remained at the core of the Israeli-Palestinian conflict and that a negotiated solution that would end the occupation and enable the Palestinian people to exercise its inalienable rights was urgently needed. In its view, the road map remained the best way to achieve a comprehensive, just and lasting solution through the establishment of two States, Israel and Palestine, based on the 1967 borders. Any unilateral moves by either party would not contribute to a durable settlement unless they were based on negotiations between the two sides and were part of the implementation of the road map. The existence of the wall rendered the vision of a two-State solution almost impossible.

GENERAL ASSEMBLY ACTION

On 1 December [meeting 64], the General Assembly adopted **resolution 59/28** [draft: A/59/L.34 & Add.1] by recorded vote (104-7-63) [agenda item 37].

Committee on the Exercise of the Inalienable Rights of the Palestinian People

The General Assembly,

Recalling its resolutions 181(II) of 29 November 1947, 194(III) of 11 December 1948, 3236(XXIX) of 22 November 1974, 3375(XXX) and 3376(XXX) of 10 November 1975, 31/20 of 24 November 1976 and all subsequent relevant resolutions, including those adopted by the General Assembly at its emergency special sessions and resolution 58/18 of 3 December 2003,

Recalling also its resolution 58/292 of 6 May 2004,

Having considered the report of the Committee on the Exercise of the Inalienable Rights of the Palestinian People,

Recalling the mutual recognition between the Government of the State of Israel and the Palestine Liberation Organization, the representative of the Palestinian people, as well as the existing agreements between the two sides and the need for full compliance with those agreements,

Recalling also the Quartet road map to a permanent two-State solution to the Israeli-Palestinian conflict,

Recalling further the advisory opinion rendered on 9 July 2004 by the International Court of Justice on the *Legal Consequences of the Construction of a Wall in the Occupied Palestinian Territory*, and recalling also its resolution ES-10/15 of 20 July 2004,

Reaffirming that the United Nations has a permanent responsibility towards the question of Palestine until the question is resolved in all its aspects in a satisfactory manner in accordance with international legitimacy,

1. *Expresses its appreciation* to the Committee on the Exercise of the Inalienable Rights of the Palestinian People for its efforts in performing the tasks assigned to it by the General Assembly, and takes note of its annual report, including the conclusions and recommendations contained in chapter VII thereof;

2. *Requests* the Committee to continue to exert all efforts to promote the realization of the inalienable rights of the Palestinian people, to support the Middle East peace process and to mobilize international support for and assistance to the Palestinian people, and authorizes the Committee to make such adjustments in its approved programme of work as it may consider appropriate and necessary in the light of developments and to report thereon to the General Assembly at its sixtieth session and thereafter;

3. *Also requests* the Committee to continue to keep under review the situation relating to the question of Palestine and to report and make suggestions to the General Assembly, the Security Council or the Secretary-General, as appropriate;

4. *Further requests* the Committee to continue to extend its cooperation and support to Palestinian and other civil society organizations in order to mobilize international solidarity and support for the achievement by the Palestinian people of its inalienable rights and for a peaceful settlement of the question of Palestine, and to involve additional civil society organizations in its work;

5. *Requests* the United Nations Conciliation Commission for Palestine, established under General Assembly resolution 194(III), and other United Nations bodies associated with the question of Palestine to continue to cooperate fully with the Committee and to make available to it, at its request, the relevant information and documentation which they have at their disposal;

6. *Invites* all Governments and organizations to extend their cooperation to the Committee in the performance of its tasks;

7. *Requests* the Secretary-General to circulate the report of the Committee to all the competent bodies of the United Nations, and urges them to take the necessary action, as appropriate;

8. *Also requests* the Secretary-General to continue to provide the Committee with all the necessary facilities for the performance of its tasks.

RECORDED VOTE ON RESOLUTION 59/28:

In favour: Afghanistan, Algeria, Argentina, Armenia, Azerbaijan, Bahamas, Bahrain, Bangladesh, Belarus, Belize, Benin, Bhutan, Bolivia, Botswana, Brazil, Brunei Darussalam, Burkina Faso, Cambodia, Cape Verde, Central African Republic, Chile, China, Colombia, Congo, Côte d'Ivoire, Cuba, Cyprus, Democratic People's Republic of Korea, Djibouti, Dominica, Ecuador, Egypt, El Salvador, Eritrea, Ethiopia, Fiji, Gabon, Gambia, Ghana, Guinea, Guinea-Bissau, Guyana, India, Indonesia, Iran, Iraq, Jamaica, Jordan, Kazakhstan, Kuwait, Kyrgyzstan, Lao People's Democratic Republic, Lebanon, Lesotho, Liberia, Libyan Arab Jamahiriya, Madagascar, Malaysia, Maldives, Mali, Malta, Mauritania, Mauritius, Mexico, Morocco, Mozambique, Myanmar, Namibia, Nepal, Niger, Nigeria, Oman, Pakistan, Panama, Paraguay, Philippines, Qatar, Saint Lucia, Saint Vincent and the Grenadines, Saudi Arabia, Senegal, Seychelles, Sierra Leone, Singapore, Somalia, South Africa, Sri Lanka, Sudan, Suriname, Syrian Arab Republic, Tajikistan, Togo, Trinidad and Tobago, Tunisia, Turkey, Turkmenistan, United Arab Emirates, United Republic of Tanzania, Uzbekistan, Venezuela, Viet Nam, Yemen, Zambia, Zimbabwe.

Against: Australia, Canada, Israel, Marshall Islands, Micronesia, Palau, United States.

Abstaining: Albania, Andorra, Austria, Belgium, Bosnia and Herzegovina, Bulgaria, Burundi, Cameroon, Costa Rica, Croatia, Czech Republic, Denmark, Dominican Republic, Estonia, Finland, France, Georgia, Germany, Greece, Guatemala, Haiti, Honduras, Hungary, Iceland, Ireland, Italy, Japan, Kenya, Latvia, Liechtenstein, Lithuania, Luxembourg, Monaco, Nauru, Netherlands, New Zealand, Nicaragua, Norway, Papua New Guinea, Peru, Poland, Portugal, Republic of Korea, Republic of Moldova, Romania, Russian Federation, Samoa, San Marino, Serbia and Montenegro, Slovakia, Slovenia, Solomon Islands, Spain, Sweden, Switzerland, Thailand, The former Yugoslav Republic of Macedonia, Tonga, Uganda, Ukraine, United Kingdom, Uruguay, Vanuatu.

Division for Palestinian Rights

Under the guidance of the Committee on Palestinian Rights, the Division for Palestinian Rights of the UN Secretariat continued to research, monitor, prepare studies, and collect and disseminate information on all issues related to the Palestine question. The Division responded to requests for information and issued the following publications: a monthly bulletin covering action by the United Nations and intergovernmental organizations on the issue of Palestine; a monthly chronology of events relating to the question of Palestine, based on media reports and other sources; reports of meetings organized under the auspices of the Committee; a special bulletin on the observance of the International Day of Solidarity with the Palestinian People (29 November); periodic reviews of developments relating to Middle East peace efforts; and an annual compilation of relevant General Assembly and Security Council action.

The Committee, in its annual report [A/59/35], requested the Division to continue its programme of publications and other informational activities, including further expansion of the electronic United Nations Information System on the Question of Palestine and the graphic enhancement of the "Question of Palestine" website. It requested that the annual training programme for PA staff be continued.

GENERAL ASSEMBLY ACTION

On 1 December [meeting 64], the General Assembly adopted **resolution 59/29** [draft: A/59/L.35 & Add.1] by recorded vote (103-8-64) [agenda item 37].

Division for Palestinian Rights of the Secretariat

The General Assembly,

Having considered the report of the Committee on the Exercise of the Inalienable Rights of the Palestinian People,

Taking note in particular of the relevant information contained in chapter V.B of that report,

Recalling its resolution 32/40 B of 2 December 1977 and all subsequent relevant resolutions, including resolution 58/19 of 3 December 2003,

1. *Notes with appreciation* the action taken by the Secretary-General in compliance with its resolution 58/19;

2. *Considers* that the Division for Palestinian Rights of the Secretariat continues to make a useful and constructive contribution;

3. *Requests* the Secretary-General to continue to provide the Division with the necessary resources and to ensure that it continues to carry out its programme of work as detailed in the relevant earlier resolutions, in consultation with the Committee on the Exercise of the Inalienable Rights of the Palestinian People and under its guidance, including, in particular, the organization of meetings in various regions with the participation of all sectors of the international community, the further development and expansion of the documents collection of the United Nations Information System on the Question of Palestine, the preparation and widest possible dissemination of publications and information materials on various aspects of the question of Palestine and the provision of the annual training programme for staff of the Palestinian Authority;

4. *Also requests* the Secretary-General to ensure the continued cooperation of the Department of Public Information and other units of the Secretariat in enabling the Division to perform its tasks and in covering adequately the various aspects of the question of Palestine;

5. *Invites* all Governments and organizations to extend their cooperation to the Division in the performance of its tasks;

6. *Requests* the Committee and the Division, as part of the observance of the International Day of Solidarity with the Palestinian People on 29 November, to continue to organize an annual exhibit on Palestinian rights or a cultural event in cooperation with the Permanent Observer Mission of Palestine to the United Nations, and encourages Member States to continue to give the widest support and publicity to the observance of the Day of Solidarity.

RECORDED VOTE ON RESOLUTION 59/29:

In favour: Afghanistan, Algeria, Argentina, Azerbaijan, Bahamas, Bahrain, Bangladesh, Barbados, Belarus, Belize, Benin, Bhutan, Bolivia, Botswana, Brazil, Brunei Darussalam, Burkina Faso, Cambodia, Cape Verde, Central African Republic, Chile, China, Colombia, Congo, Côte d'Ivoire, Cuba, Cyprus, Democratic People's Republic of Korea, Djibouti, Ecuador,

Egypt, El Salvador, Eritrea, Ethiopia, Gabon, Gambia, Ghana, Guinea, Guinea-Bissau, Guyana, India, Indonesia, Iran, Iraq, Jamaica, Jordan, Kazakhstan, Kuwait, Kyrgyzstan, Lao People's Democratic Republic, Lebanon, Lesotho, Liberia, Libyan Arab Jamahiriya, Madagascar, Malaysia, Maldives, Mali, Malta, Mauritania, Mauritius, Mexico, Morocco, Mozambique, Myanmar, Namibia, Nepal, Niger, Nigeria, Oman, Pakistan, Panama, Paraguay, Philippines, Qatar, Saint Lucia, Saint Vincent and the Grenadines, Saudi Arabia, Senegal, Seychelles, Sierra Leone, Singapore, Somalia, South Africa, Sri Lanka, Sudan, Suriname, Syrian Arab Republic, Tajikistan, Togo, Trinidad and Tobago, Tunisia, Turkey, Turkmenistan, United Arab Emirates, United Republic of Tanzania, Uruguay, Uzbekistan, Venezuela, Viet Nam, Yemen, Zambia, Zimbabwe.

Against: Australia, Grenada, Israel, Marshall Islands, Micronesia, Nauru, Palau, United States.

Abstaining: Albania, Andorra, Armenia, Austria, Belgium, Bosnia and Herzegovina, Bulgaria, Burundi, Cameroon, Canada, Costa Rica, Croatia, Czech Republic, Denmark, Dominican Republic, Estonia, Fiji, Finland, France, Georgia, Germany, Greece, Guatemala, Haiti, Honduras, Hungary, Iceland, Ireland, Italy, Japan, Kenya, Latvia, Liechtenstein, Lithuania, Luxembourg, Monaco, Netherlands, New Zealand, Nicaragua, Norway, Papua New Guinea, Peru, Poland, Portugal, Republic of Korea, Republic of Moldova, Romania, Russian Federation, Samoa, San Marino, Serbia and Montenegro, Slovakia, Slovenia, Solomon Islands, Spain, Sweden, Switzerland, Thailand, The former Yugoslav Republic of Macedonia, Tonga, Uganda, Ukraine, United Kingdom, Vanuatu.

Special information programme

As requested in General Assembly resolution 58/20 [YUN 2003, p. 502], the UN Department of Public Information (DPI) in 2004 continued its special information programme on the question of Palestine, which included the maintenance of the web page on the question of Palestine under "Global Issues" and other pages of the UN website, the issuing of press releases and the organization of its annual training programme for Palestinian broadcasters and journalists. The Radio Section provided coverage of various aspects of the question of Palestine in its broadcasts in all six UN official languages. The quarterly *UN Chronicle* and *UN Chronicle Online* reported on relevant issues and action taken by the Assembly and the Security Council. DPI, in cooperation with the Foreign Ministry of China, organized an international media seminar on peace in the Middle East (Beijing, 16-17 June).

As in previous years, the network of United Nations information centres (UNICs) and other UN offices carried out activities in connection with the International Day of Solidarity with the Palestinian People. Throughout the year, many UNICs dealt with the Palestine question and organized related outreach activities.

GENERAL ASSEMBLY ACTION

On 1 December [meeting 64], the General Assembly adopted **resolution 59/30** [draft: A/59/L.36 & Add.1] by recorded vote (162-7-9) [agenda item 37].

Special information programme on the question of Palestine of the Department of Public Information of the Secretariat

The General Assembly,

Having considered the report of the Committee on the Exercise of the Inalienable Rights of the Palestinian People,

Taking note in particular of the information contained in chapter VI of that report,

Recalling its resolution 58/20 of 3 December 2003,

Convinced that the worldwide dissemination of accurate and comprehensive information and the role of civil society organizations and institutions remain of vital importance in heightening awareness of and support for the inalienable rights of the Palestinian people,

Recalling the mutual recognition between the Government of the State of Israel and the Palestine Liberation Organization, the representative of the Palestinian people, as well as the existing agreements between the two sides and the need for full compliance with those agreements,

Recalling also the Quartet road map to a permanent two-State solution to the Israeli-Palestinian conflict,

Taking note of the advisory opinion rendered on 9 July 2004 by the International Court of Justice on the *Legal Consequences of the Construction of a Wall in the Occupied Palestinian Territory,*

1. *Notes with appreciation* the action taken by the Department of Public Information of the Secretariat in compliance with resolution 58/20;

2. *Considers* that the special information programme on the question of Palestine of the Department is very useful in raising the awareness of the international community concerning the question of Palestine and the situation in the Middle East and that the programme is contributing effectively to an atmosphere conducive to dialogue and supportive of the peace process;

3. *Requests* the Department, in full cooperation and coordination with the Committee on the Exercise of the Inalienable Rights of the Palestinian People, to continue, with the necessary flexibility as may be required by developments affecting the question of Palestine, its special information programme for the biennium 2004-2005, in particular:

(a) To disseminate information on all the activities of the United Nations system relating to the question of Palestine, including reports on the work carried out by the relevant United Nations organizations;

(b) To continue to issue and update publications on the various aspects of the question of Palestine in all fields, including materials concerning the recent developments in that regard, in particular the prospects for peace;

(c) To expand its collection of audio-visual material on the question of Palestine and to continue the production and preservation of such material and the updating of the exhibit in the Secretariat;

(d) To organize and promote fact-finding news missions for journalists to the Occupied Palestinian Territory, including East Jerusalem;

(e) To organize international, regional and national seminars or encounters for journalists, aiming in particular at sensitizing public opinion to the question of Palestine;

(f) To continue to provide assistance to the Palestinian people in the field of media development, in particular to strengthen the training programme for Palestinian broadcasters and journalists initiated in 1995.

RECORDED VOTE ON RESOLUTION 59/30:

In favour: Afghanistan, Albania, Algeria, Andorra, Argentina, Armenia, Austria, Azerbaijan, Bahamas, Bahrain, Bangladesh, Barbados, Belarus,

Belgium, Belize, Benin, Bhutan, Bolivia, Bosnia and Herzegovina, Botswana, Brazil, Brunei Darussalam, Bulgaria, Burkina Faso, Burundi, Cambodia, Canada, Cape Verde, Central African Republic, Chile, China, Colombia, Congo, Costa Rica, Côte d'Ivoire, Croatia, Cuba, Cyprus, Czech Republic, Democratic People's Republic of Korea, Denmark, Djibouti, Dominica, Dominican Republic, Ecuador, Egypt, El Salvador, Eritrea, Estonia, Ethiopia, Fiji, Finland, France, Gabon, Gambia, Georgia, Germany, Ghana, Greece, Guatemala, Guinea, Guinea-Bissau, Guyana, Honduras, Hungary, Iceland, India, Indonesia, Iran, Iraq, Ireland, Italy, Jamaica, Japan, Jordan, Kazakhstan, Kenya, Kuwait, Kyrgyzstan, Lao People's Democratic Republic, Latvia, Lebanon, Lesotho, Liberia, Libyan Arab Jamahiriya, Liechtenstein, Lithuania, Luxembourg, Madagascar, Malaysia, Maldives, Mali, Malta, Mauritania, Mauritius, Mexico, Monaco, Mongolia, Morocco, Mozambique, Myanmar, Namibia, Nepal, Netherlands, New Zealand, Nicaragua, Niger, Nigeria, Norway, Oman, Pakistan, Panama, Paraguay, Peru, Philippines, Poland, Portugal, Qatar, Republic of Korea, Republic of Moldova, Romania, Russian Federation, Saint Lucia, Saint Vincent and the Grenadines, San Marino, Saudi Arabia, Senegal, Serbia and Montenegro, Seychelles, Sierra Leone, Singapore, Slovakia, Slovenia, Somalia, South Africa, Spain, Sri Lanka, Sudan, Suriname, Sweden, Switzerland, Syrian Arab Republic, Tajikistan, Thailand, The former Yugoslav Republic of Macedonia, Timor-Leste, Togo, Trinidad and Tobago, Tunisia, Turkey, Turkmenistan, Ukraine, United Arab Emirates, United Kingdom, United Republic of Tanzania, Uruguay, Uzbekistan, Venezuela, Viet Nam, Yemen, Zambia, Zimbabwe.

Against: Grenada, Israel, Marshall Islands, Micronesia, Nauru, Palau, United States.

Abstaining: Australia, Cameroon, Haiti, Papua New Guinea, Samoa, Solomon Islands, Tonga, Uganda, Vanuatu.

Assistance to Palestinians

UN activities

In response to General Assembly resolution 58/113 [YUN 2003, p. 504], the Secretary-General submitted a June report [A/59/121-E/2004/88] describing UN and other assistance to the Palestinian people from May 2003 to April 2004.

During the reporting period, new hope for a peaceful solution to the Palestinian-Israeli conflict was brought about by the road map proposed by the Quartet [YUN 2003, p. 464], spelling out concrete steps towards the fulfilment of the vision of two States, Israel and Palestine, living side by side in peace and security. However, neither side honoured its commitments, for Israel did not stop settlement activities and continued its military operations in Palestinian areas and the construction of the security wall, while the PA did not bring an end to violence and terrorism. Throughout the reporting period, UN agencies in the Occupied Palestinian Territory had to seek additional resources to meet increasing emergency needs while trying to maintain their development activities, and the focus of those activities shifted even more to humanitarian aid as compared to the previous year. The UN system provided assistance in a number of areas, including institutional capacity-building, human resources and social development, human rights and women, infrastructure and natural resources management, and productive sectors.

The Quartet's Task Force on Palestinian Reform, established in 2002 [YUN 2002, p. 432], continued to monitor and support the implementation of Palestinian civil reforms and guide the international donor community in assisting the Palestinian reform agenda. Significant technical and programmatic donor support in all reform areas continued to be forthcoming. The Task Force worked with Palestinians to update the Palestinian reform action plan, which, on a continuing basis, highlighted Palestinian commitments, reviewed benchmarks, identified obstacles to reform and proposed areas for donor assistance. The Task Force conducted its activities through seven reform support groups in the areas of elections, financial accountability, judicial and rule of law reform, legislative reform, market economics, local government, and public administration and civil service reform. At its meeting in Rome on 11 December 2003, the Task Force noted that Palestinian political instability, continued Israeli restrictions on freedom of movement and the significant deterioration of security contributed to paralysis and delay in the reform process. While expressing concern that that process had been largely stalled over the previous four months, it nonetheless welcomed the progress made in several areas of Palestinian civil reform, in particular the implementation of higher standards of fiscal transparency and accountability, and work towards developing public institutions and laws to promote a market economy. The Palestinian efforts to establish a centrally coordinated and proactive approach to reform through the PA Reform Coordination Support Unit, under the auspices of the Prime Minister, and the establishment of the Palestinian National Reform Committee, composed of representatives from the Government, the legislature, the business community and civil society, were positive steps towards developing a more comprehensive reform agenda. In its progress report of February 2004, the Task Force expressed disappointment at the overall pace of reform. It noted that significant measures had been adopted, such as the passing by the Palestinian Legislative Council of the 2004 budget, the start of voter registration and the decision to pay all security personnel through bank transfers. However, it observed that a real political commitment by both parties was still lacking and was hampering progress in many areas, especially in the judicial and legislative fields.

The Secretary-General observed that a two-track strategy—balancing emergency needs against development goals that supported a viable PA—had been the basis of the UN approach since 2001. Although less than preferable, it had become the modus operandi for relief efforts in the Occupied Palestinian Territory. As a result of their considerable efforts, the UN system and donors had achieved measured success in both emergency and development assistance. The successes had been overshadowed by the escalation of the crisis, which had led not only to loss of life, but also to a reversal in the progress made in the socio-economic sectors. Humanitarian and financial assistance alone would not serve as a solution to the political crisis. A solution regarding the status of the Palestinian people, as well as the economic situation and humanitarian crisis, were linked directly to respect for international law and the achievement of a peaceful resolution of the conflict. Israel had to ease restrictions and work closely with those providing aid and development projects, and the PA needed to take steps to lessen Israel's security concerns.

The Economic and Social Council, on 23 July, took note of the Secretary-General's report (**decision 2004/297**).

UNCTAD assistance to Palestinians

At its fifty-first session (Geneva, 4-15 October) [A/59/15], the Trade and Development Board of the United Nations Conference on Trade and Development (UNCTAD) considered the report on UNCTAD assistance to the Palestinian people [TD/B/51/2]. The report underlined the urgency of bringing relief, rehabilitation and development efforts into a cohesive framework determined by a Palestinian development vision and agenda. The Palestinian economy continued to feature structural imbalances and distortions, owing to occupation, geographic isolation and fragmentation, war and institutional attrition, and the uncertainty of implementation of the proposed two-State solution and the international community's road map. UNCTAD supported Palestinian development efforts and the establishment of new partnerships with the private sector and international development organizations. Increasingly, donors considered UNCTAD to be a transparent development agency capable of delivering cost-effective technical assistance to the Palestinian people. However, funding constraints were becoming increasingly critical, and that had impaired the efficiency and impact of technical assistance. The secretariat's ability to forge ahead with the design and initiation of planned technical assistance activities was undermined by recurrent limitations and the unpredictability and reduction of resources. Regular budgetary resources were sufficient to maintain the secretariat's specialized knowledge and policy analysis capacity in specific areas, and to provide occasional advisory services, but they were not adequate for managing a multisectoral technical assistance programme, or to enable Palestinian representatives to participate fully in UNCTAD expert meetings. In order to remedy that situation, the secretariat was prepared to follow up on the Board deliberations with proactive resource mobilization efforts.

GENERAL ASSEMBLY ACTION

On 2 December [meeting 65], the General Assembly adopted **resolution 59/56** [draft: A/59/L.24 & Add.1, orally revised] without vote [agenda item 39 (c)].

Assistance to the Palestinian people

The General Assembly,

Recalling its resolution 58/113 of 17 December 2003, as well as previous resolutions on the question,

Recalling also the signing of the Declaration of Principles on Interim Self-Government Arrangements in Washington, D.C., on 13 September 1993, by the Government of the State of Israel and the Palestine Liberation Organization, the representative of the Palestinian people, and the subsequent implementation agreements concluded by the two sides,

Gravely concerned at the deterioration in the living conditions of the Palestinian people throughout the occupied territory, which constitutes a mounting humanitarian crisis,

Conscious of the urgent need for improvement in the economic and social infrastructure of the occupied territory,

Aware that development is difficult under occupation and is best promoted in circumstances of peace and stability,

Noting the great economic and social challenges facing the Palestinian people and their leadership,

Conscious of the urgent necessity for international assistance to the Palestinian people, taking into account the Palestinian priorities,

Welcoming the results of the Conference to Support Middle East Peace, convened in Washington, D.C., on 1 October 1993, the establishment of the Ad Hoc Liaison Committee and the work being done by the World Bank as its secretariat and the establishment of the Consultative Group, as well as all follow-up meetings and international mechanisms established to provide assistance to the Palestinian people,

Welcoming also the work of the Joint Liaison Committee, which provides a forum in which economic policy and practical matters related to donor assistance are discussed with the Palestinian Authority,

Stressing the continued importance of the work of the Ad Hoc Liaison Committee in the coordination of assistance to the Palestinian people,

Noting the upcoming meeting of the Ad Hoc Liaison Committee to review the state of the Palestinian economy,

Stressing the need for the full engagement of the United Nations in the process of building Palestinian institutions and in providing broad assistance to the Palestinian people, and welcoming in this regard the support provided to the Palestinian Authority by the Task Force on Palestinian Reform, established by the Quartet in 2002,

Noting, in this regard, the active participation of the United Nations Special Coordinator for the Middle East Peace Process and Personal Representative of the Secretary-General to the Palestine Liberation Organization and the Palestinian Authority in the activities of the Special Envoys of the Quartet,

Welcoming the endorsement by the Security Council, in its resolution 1515(2003) of 19 November 2003, of the performance-based road map to a permanent two-State solution to the Israeli-Palestinian conflict, and stressing the need for its implementation and compliance with its provisions,

Having considered the report of the Secretary-General,

Expressing grave concern at the continuation of the recent tragic and violent events that have led to many deaths and injuries,

1. *Takes note* of the report of the Secretary-General;

2. *Also takes note* of the report of the Personal Humanitarian Envoy of the Secretary-General on the humanitarian conditions and needs of the Palestinian people;

3. *Expresses its appreciation* to the Secretary-General for his rapid response and efforts regarding assistance to the Palestinian people;

4. *Also expresses its appreciation* to the Member States, United Nations bodies and intergovernmental, regional and non-governmental organizations that have provided and continue to provide assistance to the Palestinian people;

5. *Stresses* the importance of the work of the United Nations Special Coordinator for the Middle East Peace Process and Personal Representative of the Secretary-General to the Palestine Liberation Organization and the Palestinian Authority and of the steps taken under the auspices of the Secretary-General to ensure the achievement of a coordinated mechanism for United Nations activities throughout the occupied territories;

6. *Urges* Member States, international financial institutions of the United Nations system, intergovernmental and non-governmental organizations and regional and interregional organizations to extend, as rapidly and as generously as possible, economic and social assistance to the Palestinian people, in close cooperation with the Palestine Liberation Organization and through official Palestinian institutions;

7. *Calls upon* relevant organizations and agencies of the United Nations system to intensify their assistance in response to the urgent needs of the Palestinian people in accordance with Palestinian priorities set forth by the Palestinian Authority;

8. *Urges* Member States to open their markets to exports of Palestinian products on the most favourable terms, consistent with appropriate trading rules, and to implement fully existing trade and cooperation agreements;

9. *Calls upon* the international donor community to expedite the delivery of pledged assistance to the Palestinian people to meet their urgent needs;

10. *Stresses*, in this context, the importance of ensuring the free passage of aid to the Palestinian people and the free movement of persons and goods;

11. *Urges* the international donor community, United Nations agencies and organizations and non-governmental organizations to extend as rapidly as possible emergency economic and humanitarian assistance to the Palestinian people to counter the impact of the current crisis;

12. *Stresses* the need to implement the Paris Protocol on Economic Relations of 29 April 1994, fifth annex to the Israeli-Palestinian Interim Agreement on the West Bank and the Gaza Strip, signed in Washing-ton, D.C., on 28 September 1995, in particular with regard to the full and prompt clearance of Palestinian indirect tax revenues, and welcomes the progress made in this regard;

13. *Suggests* the convening in 2005 of a United Nations–sponsored seminar on assistance to the Palestinian people;

14. *Requests* the Secretary-General to submit a report to the General Assembly at its sixtieth session, through the Economic and Social Council, on the implementation of the present resolution, containing:

(a) An assessment of the assistance actually received by the Palestinian people;

(b) An assessment of the needs still unmet and specific proposals for responding effectively to them;

15. *Decides* to include in the provisional agenda of its sixtieth session the sub-item entitled "Assistance to the Palestinian people".

UNRWA

In 2004, the United Nations Relief and Works Agency for Palestine Refugees in the Near East continued to provide vital education, health and relief and social services to an ever-growing refugee population, despite a severe budget deficit and a cash flow crisis.

As at 30 June, almost 4 million refugees were registered with UNRWA, an increase of 2.56 per cent over the 2003 figure of 4.08 million. Approximately 68 per cent of the registered refugee population was living outside the 59 officially recognized refugee camps. The largest refugee population was registered in Jordan (42 per cent of the Agency-wide total), followed by the Gaza Strip (22.41 per cent), the West Bank (16.13 per cent), the Syrian Arab Republic (9.98 per cent) and Lebanon (9.48 per cent). Of those registered, 43.54 per cent were 19 years of age or under.

In his annual report on the work of the Agency from 1 July 2003 to 30 June 2004 [A/59/13], the UNRWA Commissioner-General said that the reporting period was characterized by the continuation of conditions of strife in the Occupied Palestinian Territory. UNRWA recognized the right and duty of Israel to protect its citizens, but that did not affect Israel's obligations under international humanitarian law, which prohibited, among other things, disproportionate military responses, the killing of innocent civilians and collective punishment. The large-scale military operations undertaken by Israel Defence Forces (IDF) caused heavy loss of life and widespread damage to and destruction of Palestinian property and infrastructure. The number of suicide bombings inside Israel decreased significantly, while rocket and mortar attacks from the Gaza Strip on targets within Israel and against settlements and IDF positions within the Gaza Strip continued. Military incursions into refugee camps were particularly extensive during the reporting period, which was characterized by a dramatic increase in shelter and home demolition.

The severe economic depression that the Palestinian economy had been experiencing since September 2000 continued unabated. According to the World Bank, unemployment remained at over 25 per cent, and real wages declined by 2.6 per cent. The resumption of tax revenue transfers from Israel to the PA provided a one-time boost to the Palestinian economy; nevertheless, Palestinian per capita income remained 35 per cent lower than its pre-intifada level. As a result, over half the Palestinian population continued to live below the poverty line.

During the reporting period, 34 UNRWA staff members were detained by Israeli authorities, and the Agency was refused access to detained staff members. Despite assurances to the contrary, the Israeli Foreign Ministry had yet to follow up on any of UNRWA's requests for official information and documents concerning the charges against those staff members, or the status of legal proceedings, convictions or appeals.

The environment in which UNRWA carried out its operations in the Occupied Palestinian Territory continued to affect negatively its ability to deliver services. Among UNRWA buildings damaged and equipment destroyed by the conflict were schools, training centres and health-care facilities. Closures and checkpoint delays prevented schools from operating normally as large numbers of teachers and students could not reach their schools or return to their homes. Office workers, doctors and nurses could not reach their places of work, trucks carrying humanitarian supplies could not reach their destinations, ambulances were delayed or prevented from moving patients needing urgent treatment, and UNRWA school buildings were taken over by Israeli forces and used as bases and detention centres. There were also a few instances where Palestinian militants entered UNRWA premises. In the West Bank, IDF military operations, including curfews and closed military zones, adversely impacted UNRWA's ability to carry out its humanitarian functions in support of Palestine refugees. In Gaza, the external closures imposed on the area and the internal closures that effectively bisected or trisected the Strip for significant periods of time led to disruption in the delivery of UNRWA humanitarian supplies.

The largest activity of UNRWA's extensive emergency assistance programme for refugees affected by the conflict was the provision of food aid to over 1.3 million refugees. Owing to insufficient funding, UNRWA was forced to curtail provision of remedial education to its pupils and psychological counselling to children and adults. The Agency provided temporary accommodation and emergency assistance to refugees whose shelters were destroyed. In the West Bank, the implementation of the Jenin camp reconstruction project neared completion. Meanwhile, the destruction of shelter in Gaza increased significantly, necessitating the expansion of reconstruction and rehousing programmes there.

During the reporting period, two appeals for assistance from the international community to fund the Agency's emergency programmes were launched for the second half of 2003 ($102.8 million) and for 2004 ($193.6 million). The international community's response to those appeals gradually decreased as the crisis entered its fourth year and other world crises diverted donors' attention. In 2003, contributions covered 47 per cent of the needs documented in UNRWA appeals, while the proportion for 2004 stood at 32 per cent as at 30 June 2004.

Advisory Commission. By a 30 September letter to the Commissioner-General, which was included in his annual report [A/59/13], the Chairperson of the Advisory Commission of UNRWA noted with concern the continuing deterioration in the political, economic and social situation in the Occupied Palestinian Territory, including the escalation of armed attacks during the reporting period. The humanitarian crisis was evidenced primarily by high levels of poverty, deteriorating health conditions, the displacement of an increasing number of Palestinians following the destruction of their homes, and the increasing exhaustion of the capacity of the Palestinian population to sustain itself in the face of the decline in economic and social conditions since September 2000. He noted that the Agency had launched appeals totalling $209.4 million for 2004, though the international community's level of response stagnated, in that as at mid-September only $89.5 million had been pledged and $82.9 million actually received. The Commission underscored the need for a growing level of contributions to the Agency's regular budget.

Report of Conciliation Commission. The United Nations Conciliation Commission for Palestine, in its fifty-eighth report covering the period from 1 September 2003 to 31 August 2004 [A/59/260], submitted in response to General Assembly resolution 58/91 [YUN 2003, p. 509], noted its August 2003 report [ibid., p. 507] and observed that it had nothing new to report since its submission.

Projects

During 2003/04, project funding enabled UNRWA to complete the construction of four schools and one health centre, among other construction projects, and the rehabilitation/construction of 239 shelters. Several environmental health projects were also completed, in particular the construction of facilities to improve the water supply and sewerage systems. Project funding helped to sustain regular Agency programmes through the upgrading of facilities and the introduction of courses at several of UNRWA's vocational training centres, the operations support programme in the West Bank and Gaza and the provision of medical supplies. During the reporting period, UNRWA received new pledges for projects in the amount of $24.6 million. Of the new funding, $9.5 million (39 per cent) was allocated to the relief and social services sector, $3.4 million to the health sector, $3.4 million to the education sector and $3.8 million to other projects, while $4.5 million had not been allocated. Projects in the Occupied Palestinian Territory received $7.2 million, those in Syria $6.3 million, Lebanon $3.2 million and Jordan $0.4 million. Agency-wide activities received $7.5 million. The Peace Implementation Programme, established in 1993 [YUN 1993, p. 569] to fund extrabudgetary activities within the Agency's major service areas and later merged under the projects' budget [YUN 2000, p. 450], enabled UNRWA, among other things, to complete the construction of 20 additional classrooms.

Emergency appeals

UNRWA continued its programme of emergency assistance, focusing on food aid, emergency employment creation, shelter repair and rebuilding, cash assistance, health and education. During the reporting period, UNRWA launched three appeals. A six-month appeal was launched in June 2003 for $102.9 million, covering July-December 2003 ($53.3 million received as at 30 June 2004), followed by a year-long appeal for 2004 for $193.6 million ($55.9 million received). In May 2004, the destruction wrought by the Israeli military operation in the city of Rafah in Gaza led to a supplementary appeal for that area for $15.8 million ($4.4 million received). Owing to a lack of funds, the Agency was forced to set new priorities for its emergency appeal to focus primarily on food aid, emergency employment creation and cash assistance, and to reduce the number of beneficiaries receiving food parcels in the West Bank, as well as the caloric value of rations in the West Bank and Gaza. Furthermore, UNRWA was unable to rebuild approximately 1,500 shelters that had been destroyed by IDF since the intifada began in September 2000. With the available emergency appeal funds, UNRWA rebuilt or repaired a total of 735 shelters

in Gaza and 366 in the West Bank, and it provided 19,550 short-term jobs for Palestine refugees and created 1,595,604 job/days either through direct hire or community-based construction projects. Food distribution continued, targeting 128,000 families in the Gaza Strip and 94,294 in the West Bank.

Geneva conference

UNRWA, together with the Swiss Government, co-hosted its first major international conference (Geneva, 7-8 June) since its inception, entitled "Meeting the Humanitarian Needs of the Palestine Refugees in the Near East: Building Partnerships in Support of UNRWA". The Agency stressed the need for increased mutual engagement between itself and the international community, including greater support for UNRWA to keep up with the increasing needs of a growing refugee population, and to upgrade UNRWA services and rehabilitate infrastructure. The conference identified numerous areas where a stronger and more substantive tripartite partnership among donors, host countries and UNRWA could lead to improvements in the responsiveness, effectiveness and efficiency of the Agency's operations in providing services to the refugees. A structural linkage was set between the conference and UNRWA's future planning process to ensure that the recommendations from the conference would be reflected in the Agency's medium-term plan for 2005-2009 and in its budget preparation processes.

Major service areas

UNRWA continued to implement its regular programme, providing education, health, social services and microcredit assistance to Palestine refugees throughout the occupied territories. It also pursued internal management reform, with a view to enhancing its overall efficiency and effectiveness.

UNRWA's education programme was its largest activity, consisting of 658 schools that provided basic and preparatory education to approximately 490,000 pupils, five secondary schools in Lebanon, eight vocational training centres and three teacher training colleges. The schools followed the national curricula of the host countries in each of UNRWA's five fields of operations. As a result, UNRWA was required to implement improvements to the curriculum introduced by the host country authorities. However, because of its precarious financial situation, UNRWA was struggling to keep pace with such developments, which included the introduction of a tenth year in basic education in the Occupied Palestinian

Territory, English language in elementary schools in Jordan and computer science in Jordanian and Syrian preparatory schools. UNRWA's university scholarship programme was discontinued owing to financial constraints. Despite the financial challenges, UNRWA's Education Department continued to implement reform and improvement of internal processes, as well as specific projects, such as the computer information technology initiative. UNRWA continued to introduce secondary schooling in Lebanon as a result of restrictions in access for Palestine refugees to the Lebanese public education system. In the West Bank and Gaza Strip, operations were severely hampered by the ongoing crisis. Israeli military action left 29 pupils dead and 147 injured in the reporting period.

Technical supervision of UNRWA's health programme was provided by the World Health Organization, which also supplied the services of senior management staff and short-term consultants, as well as technical publications. UNRWA focused on sustaining adequate levels of investment in primary health care, with special emphasis on maternal and child health and disease prevention and control, enhancing the process of institutional capacity-building and developing its human resources. Management reforms led to the introduction of new systems relating to health information, hospital management and drug supply management. The situation in the Occupied Palestinian Territory caused a significant deterioration of the refugees' health. Studies documented the increasing prevalence of acute and chronic malnutrition as well as iron-deficiency anaemia and low birth weight. Studies also warned of breakdowns in preventive services to women and children owing to closures and curfews, resulting in fewer infants completing immunizations on schedule. In Lebanon, UNRWA strengthened its cooperation with the Palestinian Red Crescent Society facilities, providing cost-effective secondary health care to refugees unable to afford the cost of private hospitalization. The Agency also continued its environmental health services in refugee camps throughout its areas of operation, introducing and/or improving sewage disposal, storm water drainage, provision of safe drinking water and refuse collection.

UNRWA's relief and social services programme addressed the needs of the most vulnerable among the refugee population and sought to reduce poverty. It fostered community-based organizations with a special focus on women, children and youth, as well as physically/mentally challenged refugees. UNRWA's special hardship programme was in increasing demand owing to the difficult socio-economic situation in Jordan. Shelter rehabilitation continued insofar as extra-budgetary funding was forthcoming. Funding by Governments and the provision of land by the host authority enabled UNRWA to implement housing projects in Gaza, following large-scale destruction of refugee shelters.

UNRWA continued to promote income-generation activities on two levels—in the overall context of its relief and social services programme, and as a commercial, self-sustaining and market-oriented microfinance and microenterprise programme. The latter programme expanded its operations in Jordan and the Syrian Arab Republic. It provided 15,740 loans worth $12.34 million in the region. That programme came under great strain owing to the severe decline in economic conditions in the Occupied Palestinian Territory since October 2000; nevertheless, it was returned to financial self-sufficiency.

GENERAL ASSEMBLY ACTION

On 10 December [meeting 71], the General Assembly, on the recommendation of the Fourth Committee [A/59/470], adopted **resolution 59/117** by recorded vote (167-1-11) [agenda item 75].

Assistance to Palestine refugees

The General Assembly,

Recalling its resolution 194(III) of 11 December 1948 and all its subsequent resolutions on the question, including resolution 58/91 of 9 December 2003,

Recalling also its resolution 302(IV) of 8 December 1949, by which, inter alia, it established the United Nations Relief and Works Agency for Palestine Refugees in the Near East,

Recalling further relevant Security Council resolutions,

Aware of the fact that, for more than five decades, the Palestine refugees have suffered from the loss of their homes, lands and means of livelihood,

Affirming the imperative of resolving the problem of the Palestine refugees for the achievement of justice and for the achievement of lasting peace in the region,

Acknowledging the essential role that the United Nations Relief and Works Agency for Palestine Refugees in the Near East has played for more than fifty-four years since its establishment in ameliorating the plight of the Palestine refugees in the fields of education, health and relief and social services,

Taking note of the report of the Commissioner-General of the United Nations Relief and Works Agency for Palestine Refugees in the Near East covering the period from 1 July 2003 to 30 June 2004,

Aware of the continuing needs of the Palestine refugees throughout all the fields of operation, namely Jordan, Lebanon, the Syrian Arab Republic and the Occupied Palestinian Territory,

Expressing grave concern at the especially difficult situation of the Palestine refugees under occupation, including with regard to their safety, well-being and living conditions, and the continuous deterioration of those conditions during the recent period,

Noting the signing of the Declaration of Principles on Interim Self-Government Arrangements on 13 September 1993 by the Government of Israel and the Palestine Liberation Organization and the subsequent implementation agreements,

Aware of the important role to be played in the peace process by the Multilateral Working Group on Refugees of the Middle East peace process,

1. *Notes with regret* that repatriation or compensation of the refugees, as provided for in paragraph 11 of General Assembly resolution 194(III), has not yet been effected and that, therefore, the situation of the Palestine refugees continues to be a matter of grave concern;

2. *Also notes with regret* that the United Nations Conciliation Commission for Palestine has been unable to find a means of achieving progress in the implementation of paragraph 11 of General Assembly resolution 194(III), and requests the Conciliation Commission to exert continued efforts towards the implementation of that paragraph and to report to the Assembly as appropriate, but no later than 1 September 2005;

3. *Affirms* the necessity for the continuation of the work of the United Nations Relief and Works Agency for Palestine Refugees in the Near East and the importance of its operation and its services for the well-being of the Palestine refugees and for the stability of the region, pending the resolution of the question of the Palestine refugees;

4. *Calls upon* all donors to continue to make the most generous efforts possible to meet the anticipated needs of the Agency, including those mentioned in recent emergency appeals;

5. *Decides* to extend the mandate of the Agency until 30 June 2008, without prejudice to the provisions of paragraph 11 of General Assembly resolution 194(III).

RECORDED VOTE ON RESOLUTION 59/117:

In favour: Afghanistan, Algeria, Andorra, Angola, Antigua and Barbuda, Argentina, Armenia, Australia, Austria, Azerbaijan, Bahamas, Bahrain, Bangladesh, Barbados, Belarus, Belgium, Belize, Benin, Bolivia, Bosnia and Herzegovina, Botswana, Brazil, Brunei Darussalam, Bulgaria, Burkina Faso, Burundi, Cambodia, Canada, Cape Verde, Central African Republic, Chile, China, Colombia, Comoros, Congo, Costa Rica, Côte d'Ivoire, Croatia, Cuba, Cyprus, Czech Republic, Democratic People's Republic of Korea, Denmark, Djibouti, Dominica, Dominican Republic, Ecuador, Egypt, El Salvador, Equatorial Guinea, Eritrea, Estonia, Ethiopia, Fiji, Finland, France, Gabon, Georgia, Germany, Ghana, Greece, Guatemala, Guinea, Guinea-Bissau, Guyana, Hungary, Iceland, India, Indonesia, Iran, Iraq, Ireland, Italy, Jamaica, Japan, Jordan, Kazakhstan, Kenya, Kuwait, Kyrgyzstan, Lao People's Democratic Republic, Latvia, Lebanon, Lesotho, Libyan Arab Jamahiriya, Liechtenstein, Lithuania, Luxembourg, Madagascar, Malaysia, Maldives, Mali, Malta, Mauritania, Mauritius, Mexico, Monaco, Mongolia, Morocco, Mozambique, Myanmar, Namibia, Nauru, Nepal, Netherlands, New Zealand, Nicaragua, Nigeria, Norway, Oman, Pakistan, Panama, Paraguay, Peru, Philippines, Poland, Portugal, Qatar, Republic of Korea, Republic of Moldova, Romania, Russian Federation, Saint Lucia, Saint Vincent and the Grenadines, Samoa, San Marino, Sao Tome and Principe, Saudi Arabia, Senegal, Serbia and Montenegro, Seychelles, Sierra Leone, Singapore, Slovakia, Slovenia, Solomon Islands, Somalia, South Africa, Spain, Sri Lanka, Sudan, Suriname, Sweden, Switzerland, Syrian Arab Republic, Tajikistan, Thailand, The former Yugoslav Republic of Macedonia, Timor-Leste, Togo, Tonga, Trinidad and Tobago, Tunisia, Turkey, Turkmenistan, Uganda, Ukraine, United Arab Emirates, United Kingdom, United Republic of Tanzania, Uruguay, Uzbekistan, Venezuela, Viet Nam, Yemen, Zambia, Zimbabwe.

Against: Israel.

Abstaining: Cameroon, Grenada, Haiti, Honduras, Marshall Islands, Micronesia, Palau, Papua New Guinea, Tuvalu, United States, Vanuatu.

The Assembly, also on 10 December [meeting 71] and on the Fourth Committee's recommendation

[A/59/470], adopted **resolution 59/119** by recorded vote (163-6-7) [agenda item 75].

Operations of the United Nations Relief and Works Agency for Palestine Refugees in the Near East

The General Assembly,

Recalling its resolutions 194(III) of 11 December 1948, 212(III) of 19 November 1948, 302(IV) of 8 December 1949 and all subsequent related resolutions, including resolution 58/93 of 9 December 2003,

Recalling also the relevant Security Council resolutions,

Having considered the report of the Commissioner-General of the United Nations Relief and Works Agency for Palestine Refugees in the Near East covering the period from 1 July 2003 to 30 June 2004,

Taking note of the letter dated 30 September 2004 from the Chairperson of the Advisory Commission of the United Nations Relief and Works Agency for Palestine Refugees in the Near East addressed to the Commissioner-General,

Deeply concerned about the continuing critical financial situation of the Agency and its effect on the continuing provision of necessary Agency services to the Palestine refugees, including its emergency-related and development programmes,

Recalling Articles 100, 104 and 105 of the Charter of the United Nations and the Convention on the Privileges and Immunities of the United Nations,

Recalling also the Convention on the Safety of United Nations and Associated Personnel,

Affirming the applicability of the Geneva Convention relative to the Protection of Civilian Persons in Time of War, of 12 August 1949, to the Palestinian territory occupied since 1967, including East Jerusalem,

Aware of the continuing needs of the Palestine refugees throughout the Occupied Palestinian Territory and in the other fields of operation, namely, in Jordan, Lebanon and the Syrian Arab Republic,

Gravely concerned about the increased suffering of the Palestine refugees, including that resulting from loss of life, injury and extensive destruction and damage to their shelters and properties, during the ongoing crisis in the Occupied Palestinian Territory, including East Jerusalem,

Expressing grave concern about the grave impact of the events that occurred in the Jenin refugee camp in April 2002, the Rafah refugee camp in May 2004 and the Jabaliya refugee camp in October 2004, including the loss of life, injury, destruction and displacement inflicted on many of the civilian inhabitants,

Aware of the extraordinary efforts being undertaken by the Agency for the repair or rebuilding of thousands of damaged or destroyed refugee shelters,

Aware also of the valuable work done by the refugee affairs officers of the Agency in providing protection to the Palestinian people, in particular Palestine refugees,

Gravely concerned about the endangerment of the safety of the Agency's staff and about the damage caused to facilities of the Agency as a result of Israeli military operations during the reporting period,

Deploring the killing of twelve Agency staff members by the Israeli occupying forces since September 2000,

Deploring also the killing and wounding of children in the Agency's schools by the Israeli occupying forces,

Expressing deep concern about the continuing policies of closure and severe restrictions, including the curfews, that have been imposed on the movement of persons and goods throughout the Occupied Palestinian Territory, including East Jerusalem, and which have had a grave impact on the socio-economic situation of the Palestine refugees and have greatly contributed to the dire humanitarian crisis facing the Palestinian people,

Deeply concerned about the continuing imposition of restrictions on the freedom of movement of the Agency's staff, vehicles and goods, the harassment and intimidation of the Agency's staff and the serious accusations made against the Agency, which proved to be unfounded, all of which undermine and obstruct the Agency's work, including its ability to provide its essential services, notably its education, health and relief and social services,

Recalling the signing, on 13 September 1993, of the Declaration of Principles on Interim Self-Government Arrangements by the Government of Israel and the Palestine Liberation Organization and the subsequent implementation agreements,

Aware of the agreement between the Agency and the Government of Israel,

Taking note of the agreement reached on 24 June 1994, embodied in an exchange of letters between the Agency and the Palestine Liberation Organization,

1. *Expresses its appreciation* to the Commissioner-General of the United Nations Relief and Works Agency for Palestine Refugees in the Near East, as well as to all of the staff of the Agency, for their tireless efforts and valuable work, particularly in the light of the increasingly difficult conditions during the past year;

2. *Also expresses its appreciation* to the Advisory Commission of the United Nations Relief and Works Agency for Palestine Refugees in the Near East, and requests it to continue its efforts and to keep the General Assembly informed of its activities, including the full implementation of Assembly decision 48/417 of 10 December 1993;

3. *Takes note with appreciation* of the report of the Working Group on the Financing of the United Nations Relief and Works Agency for Palestine Refugees in the Near East and the efforts of the Working Group to assist in ensuring the financial security of the Agency, and requests the Secretary-General to provide the necessary services and assistance to the Working Group for the conduct of its work;

4. *Commends* the continuing efforts of the Commissioner-General to increase the budgetary transparency and efficiency of the Agency, as reflected in the Agency's programme budget for the biennium 2004-2005;

5. *Acknowledges* the support provided by the host Governments to the Agency in the discharge of its duties;

6. *Welcomes* the convening, on 7 and 8 June 2004, of the Geneva conference by the United Nations Relief and Works Agency for Palestine Refugees in the Near East and the Swiss Agency for Development and Cooperation to increase support for the United Nations Relief and Works Agency;

7. *Encourages* the Agency's further consideration of the needs and rights of children in its operations in accordance with the Convention on the Rights of the Child;

8. *Expresses concern* about the temporary relocation of the headquarters international staff of the Agency from Gaza City and the disruption of operations at the headquarters;

9. *Calls upon* Israel, the occupying Power, to comply fully with the provisions of the Geneva Convention relative to the Protection of Civilian Persons in Time of War, of 12 August 1949;

10. *Also calls upon* Israel to abide by Articles 100, 104 and 105 of the Charter of the United Nations and the Convention on the Privileges and Immunities of the United Nations in order to ensure the safety of the personnel of the Agency, the protection of its institutions and the safeguarding of the security of its facilities in the Occupied Palestinian Territory, including East Jerusalem;

11. *Urges* the Government of Israel speedily to compensate the Agency for damage to its property and facilities resulting from actions by the Israeli side, particularly during the reporting period;

12. *Calls upon* Israel particularly to cease obstructing the movement of the staff, vehicles and supplies of the Agency and to cease the levying of extra fees and charges, which affect the Agency's operations detrimentally;

13. *Requests* the Commissioner-General to proceed with the issuance of identification cards for Palestine refugees and their descendants in the Occupied Palestinian Territory;

14. *Affirms* that the functioning of the Agency remains essential in all fields of operation;

15. *Notes* the success of the Agency's microfinance and microenterprise programme, and calls upon the Agency, in close cooperation with the relevant agencies, to continue to contribute to the development of the economic and social stability of the Palestine refugees in all fields of operation;

16. *Reiterates its request* to the Commissioner-General to proceed with the modernization of the archives of the Agency through the Palestine Refugee Records Project, and to indicate the progress made in this regard in his report to the General Assembly at its sixtieth session;

17. *Reiterates its previous appeals* to all States, specialized agencies and non-governmental organizations to continue and to augment the special allocations for grants and scholarships for higher education to Palestine refugees in addition to their contributions to the regular budget of the Agency and to contribute to the establishment of vocational training centres for Palestine refugees, and requests the Agency to act as the recipient and trustee for the special allocations for grants and scholarships;

18. *Urges* all States, specialized agencies and non-governmental organizations to continue and to increase their contributions to the Agency so as to ease the ongoing financial constraints, exacerbated by the current humanitarian situation on the ground, and to support the Agency's valuable work in assisting the Palestine refugees.

RECORDED VOTE ON RESOLUTION 59/119:

In favour: Afghanistan, Algeria, Andorra, Angola, Antigua and Barbuda, Argentina, Armenia, Australia, Austria, Azerbaijan, Bahamas, Bahrain, Bangladesh, Barbados, Belarus, Belgium, Belize, Benin, Bolivia,

Bosnia and Herzegovina, Botswana, Brazil, Brunei Darussalam, Bulgaria, Burkina Faso, Cambodia, Canada, Cape Verde, Chile, China, Colombia, Comoros, Congo, Costa Rica, Croatia, Cuba, Cyprus, Czech Republic, Democratic People's Republic of Korea, Denmark, Djibouti, Dominica, Dominican Republic, Ecuador, Egypt, El Salvador, Equatorial Guinea, Eritrea, Estonia, Ethiopia, Fiji, Finland, France, Gabon, Georgia, Germany, Ghana, Greece, Guatemala, Guinea, Guinea-Bissau, Guyana, Hungary, Iceland, India, Indonesia, Iran, Iraq, Ireland, Italy, Jamaica, Japan, Jordan, Kazakhstan, Kenya, Kuwait, Kyrgyzstan, Lao People's Democratic Republic, Latvia, Lebanon, Lesotho, Libyan Arab Jamahiriya, Liechtenstein, Lithuania, Luxembourg, Madagascar, Malaysia, Maldives, Mali, Malta, Mauritania, Mauritius, Mexico, Monaco, Mongolia, Morocco, Mozambique, Myanmar, Namibia, Nauru, Nepal, Netherlands, New Zealand, Nigeria, Norway, Oman, Pakistan, Panama, Paraguay, Peru, Philippines, Poland, Portugal, Qatar, Republic of Korea, Republic of Moldova, Romania, Russian Federation, Saint Lucia, Saint Vincent and the Grenadines, Samoa, San Marino, Sao Tome and Principe, Saudi Arabia, Senegal, Serbia and Montenegro, Seychelles, Sierra Leone, Singapore, Slovakia, Slovenia, Solomon Islands, Somalia, South Africa, Spain, Sri Lanka, Sudan, Suriname, Sweden, Switzerland, Syrian Arab Republic, Tajikistan, Thailand, The former Yugoslav Republic of Macedonia, Timor-Leste, Togo, Tonga, Trinidad and Tobago, Tunisia, Turkey, Turkmenistan, Uganda, Ukraine, United Arab Emirates, United Kingdom, United Republic of Tanzania, Uruguay, Uzbekistan, Venezuela, Viet Nam, Yemen, Zambia, Zimbabwe.

Against: Grenada, Israel, Marshall Islands, Micronesia, Palau, United States.

Abstaining: Burundi, Cameroon, Côte d'Ivoire, Haiti, Honduras, Nicaragua, Papua New Guinea.

On 23 December, the Assembly decided that the agenda item on UNRWA would remain for consideration at its resumed fifty-ninth (2005) session (**decision 59/552**).

UNRWA financing

UNRWA ended 2003 with a positive working capital balance of $32.2 million. It was able to achieve a relatively favourable financial result owing, in part, to the positive impact of United States dollar depreciation against other currencies, with the result that UNRWA made $4 million in exchange rate gains in 2003. Working capital, defined as the difference between assets and liabilities in the regular budget for the calendar year, stood at $36.7 million as at 31 December 2003. However, $4.5 million represented funds earmarked to procure basic commodities, leaving a real positive working capital balance of $32.2 million for the cash budget. The end-of-year excess of income over expenditure of $23.5 million, minus the $10 million reserve for currency fluctuations, was added to the working capital of $18.7 million carried forward from December 2002.

UNRWA's cash position improved during the reporting period, in part because of the reimbursement by the PA of a large amount of value-added tax (VAT) due from prior years. However, there remained outstanding cash pledges under the regular budget amounting to $8.4 million and approximately $13 million in respect of VAT due from the PA.

Working Group. The Working Group on the Financing of UNRWA held two meetings in 2004, on 7 and 15 October. In its report to the General Assembly [A/59/442], the Working Group said

that, by the end of September, UNRWA faced the prospect of a funding gap in its 2004 regular cash budget of $7.3 million. Income for 2004 was expected to be $309.1 million (of which $291.7 million was income from donors, $15.9 million was from UN agencies and $1.5 million was interest income and exchange rate gains), against a net cash expenditure of $316.4 million. Furthermore, of the $291.7 million in income expected from donors for the regular budget in 2004, $270.6 million had been received by the end of September and $21.1 million was outstanding. The Agency continued to try to attract a reliable, sustainable flow of funds so as not to have to depend upon stopgap measures to meet funding needs.

The Working Group remained concerned about the increasing shortfalls in funding for its 2004 appeals. Against a total request of $209.4 million for emergency appeals during 2004, the Agency had received only $89.4 million in pledges. In addition, against a total request for $529.8 million for prior years' emergency appeals, the Agency had received only $323.3 million in pledges. The shortfalls in emergency appeal contributions seriously curtailed the Agency's humanitarian activities, such as food distribution, emergency employment generation programmes, trauma counselling and other emergency health activities. UNRWA's budget requirements for the 2004-2005 biennium were estimated at $805 million, compared with $791.7 million for 2002-2003.

The Working Group said that the problem of the refugees was deeply rooted in a political issue that originated more than half a century earlier, and that it remained essential to settle that problem once and for all in accordance with all relevant UN resolutions. The problems faced by the refugees were, however, humanitarian ones that needed to be addressed as a shared international responsibility. The services provided by UNRWA should be viewed as the minimum required to enable the refugees to lead productive lives. Any further reduction in those services would not only unfairly deprive the refugees of the minimum level of support to which they were entitled, but could also have a destabilizing effect on the entire region.

Displaced persons

In a July report [A/59/151] on compliance with General Assembly resolution 58/92 [YUN 2003, p. 514], which called for accelerated return of all persons displaced as a result of the June 1967 and subsequent hostilities to their homes or former places of residence in the territories occupied by Israel since 1967, the Secretary-General said that, since UNRWA was not involved in arrangements for the return of either refugees or displaced persons not registered with it, the Agency's information was based on requests by returning registered refugees for the transfer of their entitlements to their areas of return. Displaced refugees known by UNRWA to have returned to the West Bank and Gaza Strip since 1967 totalled about 24,600. As far as UNRWA knew, between 1 July 2003 and 30 June 2004, 550 registered refugees had returned to the West Bank and 148 to Gaza from places outside the occupied territory. Some of those refugees might not have been displaced since 1967, but were possibly family members of a displaced registered refugee.

GENERAL ASSEMBLY ACTION

On 10 December [meeting 71], the General Assembly, on the recommendation of the Fourth Committee [A/59/470], adopted **resolution 59/118** by recorded vote (162-6-9) [agenda item 75].

Persons displaced as a result of the June 1967 and subsequent hostilities

The General Assembly,

Recalling its resolutions 2252(ES-V) of 4 July 1967, 2341 B (XXII) of 19 December 1967 and all subsequent related resolutions,

Recalling also Security Council resolutions 237(1967) of 14 June 1967 and 259(1968) of 27 September 1968,

Taking note of the report of the Secretary-General submitted in pursuance of its resolution 58/92 of 9 December 2003,

Taking note also of the report of the Commissioner-General of the United Nations Relief and Works Agency for Palestine Refugees in the Near East covering the period from 1 July 2003 to 30 June 2004,

Concerned about the continuing human suffering resulting from the June 1967 and subsequent hostilities,

Taking note of the relevant provisions of the Declaration of Principles on Interim Self-Government Arrangements of 1993 with regard to the modalities for the admission of persons displaced in 1967, and concerned that the process agreed upon has not yet been effected,

1. *Reaffirms* the right of all persons displaced as a result of the June 1967 and subsequent hostilities to return to their homes or former places of residence in the territories occupied by Israel since 1967;

2. *Expresses deep concern* that the mechanism agreed upon by the parties in article XII of the Declaration of Principles on Interim Self-Government Arrangements of 1993 on the return of displaced persons has not been complied with, and stresses the necessity for an accelerated return of displaced persons;

3. *Endorses*, in the meanwhile, the efforts of the Commissioner-General of the United Nations Relief and Works Agency for Palestine Refugees in the Near East to continue to provide humanitarian assistance, as far as practicable, on an emergency basis, and as a temporary measure, to persons in the area who are currently displaced and in serious need of continued assistance as a result of the June 1967 and subsequent hostilities;

4. *Strongly appeals* to all Governments and to organizations and individuals to contribute generously to the Agency and to the other intergovernmental and non-governmental organizations concerned for the above-mentioned purposes;

5. *Requests* the Secretary-General, after consulting with the Commissioner-General, to report to the General Assembly before its sixtieth session on the progress made with regard to the implementation of the present resolution.

RECORDED VOTE ON RESOLUTION 59/118:

In favour: Afghanistan, Algeria, Andorra, Antigua and Barbuda, Argentina, Armenia, Australia, Austria, Azerbaijan, Bahamas, Bahrain, Bangladesh, Barbados, Belarus, Belgium, Belize, Benin, Bolivia, Bosnia and Herzegovina, Botswana, Brazil, Brunei Darussalam, Bulgaria, Burkina Faso, Burundi, Cambodia, Canada, Cape Verde, Chile, China, Colombia, Comoros, Congo, Costa Rica, Croatia, Cuba, Cyprus, Czech Republic, Democratic People's Republic of Korea, Denmark, Djibouti, Dominica, Dominican Republic, Ecuador, Egypt, El Salvador, Equatorial Guinea, Eritrea, Estonia, Ethiopia, Fiji, Finland, France, Gabon, Georgia, Germany, Ghana, Greece, Guatemala, Guinea, Guinea-Bissau, Guyana, Hungary, Iceland, India, Indonesia, Iran, Iraq, Ireland, Italy, Jamaica, Japan, Jordan, Kazakhstan, Kenya, Kuwait, Kyrgyzstan, Lao People's Democratic Republic, Latvia, Lebanon, Lesotho, Libyan Arab Jamahiriya, Liechtenstein, Lithuania, Luxembourg, Madagascar, Malaysia, Maldives, Mali, Malta, Mauritania, Mauritius, Mexico, Monaco, Mongolia, Morocco, Mozambique, Myanmar, Namibia, Nepal, Netherlands, New Zealand, Nicaragua, Nigeria, Norway, Oman, Pakistan, Panama, Paraguay, Peru, Philippines, Poland, Portugal, Qatar, Republic of Korea, Republic of Moldova, Romania, Russian Federation, Saint Lucia, Saint Vincent and the Grenadines, Samoa, San Marino, Sao Tome and Principe, Saudi Arabia, Senegal, Serbia and Montenegro, Seychelles, Sierra Leone, Singapore, Slovakia, Slovenia, Solomon Islands, Somalia, South Africa, Spain, Sri Lanka, Sudan, Suriname, Sweden, Switzerland, Syrian Arab Republic, Tajikistan, Thailand, The former Yugoslav Republic of Macedonia, Timor-Leste, Togo, Tonga, Trinidad and Tobago, Tunisia, Turkey, Turkmenistan, Uganda, Ukraine, United Arab Emirates, United Kingdom, United Republic of Tanzania, Uruguay, Venezuela, Viet Nam, Yemen, Zambia, Zimbabwe.

Against: Grenada, Israel, Marshall Islands, Micronesia, Palau, United States.

Abstaining: Cameroon, Côte d'Ivoire, Haiti, Honduras, Nauru, Papua New Guinea, Tuvalu, Uzbekistan, Vanuatu.

Property rights

In response to General Assembly resolution 58/94 [YUN 2003, p. 514], the Secretary-General submitted an August report [A/59/279] on steps taken to protect and administer Arab property, assets and property rights in Israel, and establish a fund for income derived therefrom, on behalf of the rightful owners. He indicated that he had transmitted the resolution to Israel and all other Member States, requesting information on any steps taken or envisaged to implement it. The report also detailed replies received from six Member States, including Israel, covering various aspects of Assembly resolutions 58/91 to 58/95 [YUN 2003, pp. 509-514] pertaining to assistance to Palestine refugees. In its reply, Israel said that it supported UNRWA's humanitarian mission and recognized its contribution to the welfare of Palestinian refugees. It was concerned, however, about what it regarded as the politicization of UNRWA operations and the need to take account of the campaign of terror being waged against Israel's citizens. Israel urged UNRWA to draw attention to the misuse of refugee camps by armed elements in violation of international law.

GENERAL ASSEMBLY ACTION

On 10 December [meeting 71], the General Assembly, on the recommendation of the Fourth Committee [A/59/470], adopted **resolution 59/120** by recorded vote (161-6-9) [agenda item 75].

Palestine refugees' properties and their revenues

The General Assembly,

Recalling its resolutions 194(III) of 11 December 1948, 36/146 C of 16 December 1981 and all its subsequent resolutions on the question,

Taking note of the report of the Secretary-General submitted in pursuance of its resolution 58/94 of 9 December 2003,

Taking note also of the report of the United Nations Conciliation Commission for Palestine for the period from 1 September 2003 to 31 August 2004,

Recalling that the Universal Declaration of Human Rights and the principles of international law uphold the principle that no one shall be arbitrarily deprived of his or her property,

Recalling in particular its resolution 394(V) of 14 December 1950, in which it directed the Conciliation Commission, in consultation with the parties concerned, to prescribe measures for the protection of the rights, property and interests of the Palestine refugees,

Noting the completion of the programme of identification and evaluation of Arab property, as announced by the Conciliation Commission in its twenty-second progress report, and the fact that the Land Office had a schedule of Arab owners and file of documents defining the location, area and other particulars of Arab property,

Expressing its appreciation for the work done to preserve and modernize the existing records, including the land records, of the Conciliation Commission and the importance of such records for a just resolution of the plight of the Palestine refugees in conformity with resolution 194(III),

Recalling that, within the framework of the Middle East peace process, the Palestine Liberation Organization and the Government of Israel agreed, in the Declaration of Principles on Interim Self-Government Arrangements of 13 September 1993, to commence negotiations on permanent status issues, including the important issue of the refugees,

1. *Reaffirms* that the Palestine refugees are entitled to their property and to the income derived therefrom, in conformity with the principles of equity and justice;

2. *Requests* the Secretary-General to take all appropriate steps, in consultation with the United Nations Conciliation Commission for Palestine, for the protection of Arab property, assets and property rights in Israel;

3. *Calls once again upon* Israel to render all facilities and assistance to the Secretary-General in the implementation of the present resolution;

4. *Calls upon* all the parties concerned to provide the Secretary-General with any pertinent information in their possession concerning Arab property, assets

and property rights in Israel that would assist him in the implementation of the present resolution;

5. *Urges* the Palestinian and Israeli sides, as agreed between them, to deal with the important issue of Palestine refugees' properties and their revenues within the framework of the final status negotiations of the Middle East peace process;

6. *Requests* the Secretary-General to report to the General Assembly at its sixtieth session on the implementation of the present resolution.

RECORDED VOTE ON RESOLUTION 59/120:

In favour: Afghanistan, Algeria, Andorra, Antigua and Barbuda, Argentina, Armenia, Australia, Austria, Azerbaijan, Bahamas, Bahrain, Bangladesh, Barbados, Belarus, Belgium, Belize, Benin, Bolivia, Bosnia and Herzegovina, Botswana, Brazil, Brunei Darussalam, Bulgaria, Burkina Faso, Burundi, Cambodia, Canada, Cape Verde, Chile, China, Colombia, Comoros, Congo, Costa Rica, Croatia, Cuba, Cyprus, Czech Republic, Democratic People's Republic of Korea, Denmark, Djibouti, Dominica, Dominican Republic, Ecuador, Egypt, El Salvador, Equatorial Guinea, Eritrea, Estonia, Ethiopia, Fiji, Finland, France, Gabon, Georgia, Germany, Ghana, Greece, Guatemala, Guinea, Guinea-Bissau, Guyana, Hungary, Iceland, India, Indonesia, Iran, Iraq, Ireland, Italy, Jamaica, Japan, Jordan, Kazakhstan, Kenya, Kuwait, Kyrgyzstan, Lao People's Democratic Republic, Latvia, Lebanon, Lesotho, Libyan Arab Jamahiriya, Liechtenstein, Lithuania, Luxembourg, Madagascar, Malaysia, Maldives, Mali, Malta, Mauritania, Mauritius, Mexico, Monaco, Mongolia, Morocco, Mozambique, Myanmar, Namibia, Nepal, Netherlands, New Zealand, Nicaragua, Nigeria, Norway, Oman, Pakistan, Panama, Paraguay, Peru, Philippines, Poland, Portugal, Qatar, Republic of Korea, Republic of Moldova, Romania, Russian Federation, Saint Lucia, Saint Vincent and the Grenadines, Samoa, San Marino, Sao Tome and Principe, Saudi Arabia, Senegal, Serbia and Montenegro, Seychelles, Sierra Leone, Singapore, Slovakia, Slovenia, Solomon Islands, Somalia, South Africa, Spain, Sri Lanka, Sudan, Suriname, Sweden, Switzerland, Syrian Arab Republic, Tajikistan, Thailand, The former Yugoslav Republic of Macedonia, Timor-Leste, Togo, Tonga, Trinidad and Tobago, Tunisia, Turkey, Turkmenistan, Ukraine, United Arab Emirates, United Kingdom, United Republic of Tanzania, Uruguay, Venezuela, Viet Nam, Yemen, Zambia, Zimbabwe.

Against: Grenada, Israel, Marshall Islands, Micronesia, Palau, United States.

Abstaining: Cameroon, Côte d'Ivoire, Haiti, Honduras, Nauru, Papua New Guinea, Tuvalu, Uzbekistan, Vanuatu.

Peacekeeping operations

In 2004, the United Nations Truce Supervision Organization (UNTSO), originally set up to monitor the ceasefire called for by the Security Council in resolution S/801 of 29 May 1948 [YUN 1947-48, p. 427] in newly partitioned Palestine, continued its work. UNTSO's unarmed military observers fulfilled evolving mandates—from supervising the original four armistice agreements between Israel and its neighbours (Egypt, Jordan, Lebanon, Syrian Arab Republic) to observing and monitoring other ceasefires, as well as performing a number of additional tasks. During the year, UNTSO personnel worked with the two remaining UN peacekeeping forces in the Middle East—the United Nations Disengagement Observer Force (UNDOF) in the Golan Heights and the United Nations Interim Force in Lebanon (UNIFIL).

On 5 October [S/2004/809], the Secretary-General informed the Council of his intention to appoint Brigadier General Clive Lilley (New Zealand) as the Chief of Staff of UNTSO, replacing Major General Carl Dodd (Ireland). On 8 October [S/2004/810], the Council took note of his intention.

Lebanon

Lebanon became a focus of international attention on 3 September 2004, when Lebanese President Emile Lahoud's six-year term was extended for another three years by a constitutional amendment enacted by the parliament. It was widely contended in Lebanon that the extension of President Lahoud's term in office was the result of pressure by the Government of the Syrian Arab Republic. The day before, the Security Council, in resolution 1559(2004) (see p. 506), had called for free and fair presidential elections in Lebanon, the full withdrawal of foreign forces from the country and the disbanding and disarmament of militias. Lebanese Prime Minister Rafik Hariri resigned on 20 October, and was replaced by Omar Karami, who formed a new Government on 26 October. Mr. Karami's Government was widely perceived as favourably disposed towards a Syrian presence and influence in Lebanon.

The Secretary-General appointed a Special Envoy, Terje Roed-Larsen, to oversee the resolution's implementation. Mr. Roed-Larsen was already serving as the Special Coordinator for the Middle East Peace Process and Personal Representative of the Secretary-General. In monthly briefings to the Security Council on the Palestine question, including East Jerusalem, Mr. Roed-Larsen and the Under-Secretary-General for Political Affairs, Kieran Prendergast, covered developments in southern Lebanon.

The paramilitary group Hizbullah continued to carry out attacks against positions of the Israel Defence Forces (IDF) in farmlands and targets inside Israel, and IDF continued to carry out attacks within Lebanon. The Shab'a farmlands had been an area of contention since the withdrawal of Israeli forces from Lebanon in June 2000 [YUN 2000, p. 465]. According to the Lebanese Government, Israel's withdrawal from southern Lebanon was incomplete, as Israeli forces continued to occupy the Shab'a farms, while Israel held the view that the area was occupied Syrian territory and thus within the purview of Security Council resolution 242(1967) [YUN 1967, p. 257] on the Israeli-Syrian conflict, and not resolution 425 (1978) [YUN 1978, p. 312], which dealt with Israel's withdrawal from Lebanon. However, Lebanon and the Syrian Arab Republic maintained that the Shab'a farmlands were inside Lebanese territory.

The first municipal elections in southern Lebanon since the Israeli withdrawal in 2000 were held in May 2004.

Staffan de Mistura continued to act as the Secretary-General's Personal Representative for Southern Lebanon, responsible for coordinating UN activities in the area.

Communications. In communications received throughout the year [A/58/672-S/2004/6, A/58/679-S/2004/15, A/58/690-S/2004/55, A/58/689-S/2004/54, A/58/691-S/2004/64, A/58/699-S/2004/83, A/58/700-S/2004/85, A/58/738-S/2004/217, A/58/747-S/2004/250, A/58/749-S/2004/260, A/58/757-S/2004/278, A/58/770-S/2004/297, A/58/775-S/2004/320, A/58/784-S/2004/355, A/58/786-S/2004/357, A/58/790-S/2004/373, S/2004/379, A/58/791-S/2004/381, A/58/805-S/2004/401, A/58/813-S/2004/424, A/58/834-S/2004/457, A/58/836-S/2004/463, A/58/842-S/2004/494, A/58/845-S/2004/508, A/58/852-S/2004/574, A/58/853-S/2004/575, A/58/854-S/2004/577, A/58/867-S/2004/633, A/58/872-S/2004/651, A/58/875-S/2004/672, A/58/882-S/2004/705, A/59/362-S/2004/734, A/59/392-S/2004/775, A/59/435-S/2004/818, A/59/535-S/2004/866, A/59/575-S/2004/911, A/59/577-S/2004/922, A/59/594-S/2004/954, A/59/595-S/2004/956, A/59/596-S/2004/957, A/59/611-S/2004/971, A/59/658-S/2004/1021], Lebanon detailed Israel's violations of the Blue Line, the provisional border drawn by the United Nations following the withdrawal of Israeli troops from southern Lebanon in 2000, and consequently of Lebanese sovereignty and territorial integrity.

In letters sent throughout the year [A/58/687-S/2004/61, A/58/837-S/2004/465, A/59/559-S/2004/890, A/59/571-S/2004/906], Israel reported attacks carried out by Hizbullah and other militias against Israeli military and civilian targets across the Blue Line. Israel also alleged that Hizbullah was supported by the Governments of Iran, Lebanon and the Syrian Arab Republic.

On 29 December [A/59/659-S/2004/1027], Iran refuted Israel's allegations and considered them a deliberate attempt to distract the international community's attention from Israel's acts of aggression that aggravated the situation in the Middle East.

Relations with Syrian Arab Republic

On 30 August [A/58/879-S/2004/699], Lebanon informed the Secretary-General and the Security Council President of an initiative to submit to the Council a draft resolution, sponsored by France and the United States, urging the Syrian Arab Republic to withdraw its troops from Lebanon, to refrain from interfering in the Lebanese presidential elections and to cease supporting terrorist groups in Lebanon. That draft resolution, according to Lebanon, would set a dangerous precedent, for it would coincide with the forthcoming presidential elections and, thus, could adversely affect the electoral process. The presence of Syrian troops in Lebanon was linked to the 1989 Taif Agreement and other bilateral agreements between Lebanon and Syria. That presence was under the auspices and supervision of the competent institutions in each country. No external entity was entitled to intervene with regard to its modalities or to impose changes. According to Lebanon, that presence served the common interests of the two countries. In addition, the allegation that Syria was backing terrorist organizations in Lebanon defied the truth. Syria's role in Lebanon had always been to support and strengthen the official security institutions and thereby contribute to the maintenance of security.

On 1 September [A/58/883-S/2004/706], Syria said that it rejected any discussion of the proposed draft resolution because, among other things, Lebanon itself rejected raising the issue. In addition, the issue was a domestic concern and did not constitute a threat to international peace and security; consequently, the overall question did not fall under the Council's jurisdiction.

SECURITY COUNCIL ACTION

On 2 September [meeting 5028], the Security Council adopted **resolution 1559(2004)** by vote (9-0-6). The draft [S/2004/707] was submitted by France, Germany, the United Kingdom and the United States.

The Security Council,

Recalling all its previous resolutions on Lebanon, in particular resolutions 425(1978) and 426(1978) of 19 March 1978, resolution 520(1982) of 17 September 1982 and resolution 1553(2004) of 29 July 2004, as well as the statements by its President on the situation in Lebanon, in particular the statement of 18 June 2000 (S/PRST/2000/21),

Reiterating its strong support for the territorial integrity, sovereignty and political independence of Lebanon within its internationally recognized borders,

Noting the determination of Lebanon to ensure the withdrawal of all non-Lebanese forces from Lebanon,

Gravely concerned at the continued presence of armed militias in Lebanon, which prevents the Government of Lebanon from exercising its full sovereignty over all Lebanese territory,

Reaffirming the importance of the extension of the control of the Government of Lebanon over all Lebanese territory,

Mindful of the upcoming Lebanese presidential elections, and underlining the importance of free and fair elections according to Lebanese constitutional rules devised without foreign interference or influence,

1. *Reaffirms its call for* the strict respect of the sovereignty, territorial integrity, unity and political independence of Lebanon under the sole and exclusive authority of the Government of Lebanon throughout Lebanon;

2. *Calls upon* all remaining foreign forces to withdraw from Lebanon;

3. *Calls for* the disbanding and disarmament of all Lebanese and non-Lebanese militias;

4. *Supports* the extension of the control of the Government of Lebanon over all Lebanese territory;

5. *Declares its support* for a free and fair electoral process in Lebanon's upcoming presidential elections conducted according to Lebanese constitutional rules devised without foreign interference or influence;

6. *Calls upon* all parties concerned to cooperate fully and urgently with the Security Council for the full implementation of the present resolution and all relevant resolutions concerning the restoration of the territorial integrity, full sovereignty and political independence of Lebanon;

7. *Requests* that the Secretary-General report to the Council within thirty days on the implementation by the parties of the present resolution, and decides to remain actively seized of the matter.

VOTE ON RESOLUTION 1559(2004):

In favour: Angola, Benin, Chile, France, Germany, Romania, Spain, United Kingdom, United States.

Against: None.

Abstaining: Algeria, Brazil, China, Pakistan, Philippines, Russian Federation.

Speaking before the vote, Lebanon said that the draft resolution did not take into account the unique relations between Lebanon and Syria, for the Syrian Government had helped Lebanon to maintain security and stability within its borders. In addition, the draft dealt with a purely internal issue, the presidential electoral process under way in Lebanon as the mandate of the current President would end on 23 November. The draft text referred to support for free and fair presidential elections in Lebanon. Lebanon did not believe that an issue such as that, which was an internal matter for a Member State, had ever been discussed in the Council. Lebanon's parliamentarians had the right to take decisions pertaining to elections. Syrian troops came to Lebanon in response to the Government's legitimate request. Those troops had been redeployed many times, and their presence was invisible. They contributed to rebuffing Israel's radical and excessive actions, which continued to include totally unjustifiable and excessive acts of violence.

Speaking after the vote, the United States said that it believed that Lebanon should be allowed to determine its own future and assume control of its own territory, yet the Lebanese people were still unable to exercise their rights as a free people to make those choices as a nation. Syria had imposed its political will on Lebanon and had compelled the cabinet and the parliament to amend its Constitution and abort the electoral process by extending the term of the President by three years. It was clear that Lebanese parliamentarians had been pressured, and even threatened, by Syria and its agents to make them comply. The United States supported the extension of the Lebanese Government's control over all Lebanese territory, including southern Lebanon, as called for by the Council. The continued presence of armed Hizbullah militia elements, as well as the presence of the Syrian military and Iranian forces in Lebanon, hindered that goal. The United States believed that it was wrong for Syria to continue to maintain its forces in Lebanon and to continue to interfere in the Lebanese electoral process.

Report of Secretary-General (October). In response to Council resolution 1559(2004) (see above), the Secretary-General submitted an October report on the implementation by the parties of that resolution [S/2004/777].

The Secretary-General, noting that the resolution called for the withdrawal of all remaining foreign forces from Lebanon, said that apart from UNIFIL, the only significant foreign forces deployed in Lebanon as at 30 September were Syrian. Syria had maintained forces in Lebanon since 1976. The troops were initially deployed at the request of the Lebanese President; that deployment was transformed into an Arab Deterrent Force sanctioned by the League of Arab States, at the request of the Government of Lebanon, and was joined by troops from other Arab countries. The Governments of both Lebanon and Syria had told the Secretary-General that the Syrian forces present in Lebanon—which at one point numbered 40,000, according to Lebanon—were there at the invitation of Lebanon and by mutual agreement. Specifically, they were said to be deployed pursuant to the 1989 Taif Agreement and the 1991 Syria-Lebanon Treaty of Cooperation. As far as the Secretary-General was aware, the two Governments had not, to date, concluded an agreement to determine the strength and duration of the presence of Syrian forces, as provided for in both those instruments.

The Syrian Government had informed the United Nations that, in addition to uniformed armed forces, it also stationed in Lebanon a substantial presence of non-uniformed military intelligence officials that were usual components of military units. Those officials, together with the uniformed forces, constituted the full Syrian troop strength. The Syrian military and intelligence apparatus in Lebanon had not been withdrawn as of 30 September. However, according to the two Governments, Syria had redeployed approximately 3,000 of its forces formerly deployed south of Beirut. It had not been made clear to the United Nations whether those redeployments were confined to regular troops or included non-uniformed military intelligence officers, and whether they had all returned to Syria. The Syrian Government indicated to the Secretary-General that a total of about 14,000 Syrian troops remained in Lebanon, most of whom were based near the Syrian border and not deep inside Lebanon. The Lebanese and Syrian Governments told the Secretary-General that the timing of further withdrawals would be determined by the security situation in Lebanon and the region and through the joint military committee established pursuant to the Taif Agreement. Lebanon also informed him that the fragile security situation in the region and its risks to Lebanon's domestic stability made it difficult to set a timetable for the full withdrawal of Syrian forces. Similarly, Syria informed the Secretary-General that it could not provide him with numbers and timetables for any future withdrawal. The Lebanese Government stated that its ultimate goal was the complete withdrawal of all foreign forces from its territory, and the two Governments were discussing the nature and extent of the current deployment.

Resolution 1559(2004) also called for the disbanding and disarmament of all Lebanese and non-Lebanese militias. As at 30 September, several armed elements remained in the southern part of Lebanon. The most significant remaining armed group was Hizbullah, and UN staff on the ground had not discerned any change in the status of Hizbullah since the adoption of resolution 1559(2004). Regarding Palestinian armed groups, Lebanon assured the Secretary-General that Palestinian militants were not allowed to leave their refugee camps with weapons. UN personnel in the region indicated that Lebanon had positioned its armed forces outside the camps, apparently to enforce that policy.

As at 30 September, the Lebanese Government had not extended its control over all of its territory, as called for in resolution 1559(2004). Although Lebanon held peaceful municipal elections in the south in May (see p. 511), the area around the Blue Line remained tense. Hizbullah operations frequently violated the Blue Line. It was widely asserted that Hizbullah operations were carried out independently of Lebanese government control or sanction. More than four years after the Israeli withdrawal from southern Lebanon, movement in the region remained restricted. Hizbullah had established checkpoints throughout southern Lebanon and movements of Lebanese officials, UNIFIL personnel and diplomats were hindered at times by armed elements.

On 3 September, the day after resolution 1559(2004) was adopted, the Lebanese Chamber of Deputies approved a law that extended President Emile Lahoud's term by three years, ending on 23 November 2007. According to the Lebanese Government, that law was adopted in accordance with Lebanese constitutional rules. However, it was widely contended in Lebanon, and asserted by the sponsors of resolution 1559(2004), that the extension of the President's term was the result of direct intervention by the Syrian Government. It was widely alleged in Lebanon that the Syrian military presence, including a substantial component of non-uniformed intelligence officials, afforded Syria considerable leverage over Lebanese domestic affairs, though the Lebanese and Syrian Governments denied that Syria intervened in Lebanon's internal affairs.

Since October 2000, Israeli aircraft had regularly violated Lebanese sovereignty by flying into Lebanese airspace, at times crossing the Blue Line. They frequently penetrated deep into Lebanese territory and generated sonic booms over populated areas. Israel claimed that those overflights were carried out for security reasons. Hizbullah anti-aircraft rounds had fallen across the Blue Line into Israel, causing Israeli casualties.

The Secretary-General observed that the requirements imposed on the various parties as set out in resolution 1559(2004) had not been met. The Lebanese and Syrian Governments had assured him of their respect for the Council, and that consequently they would not contest it. The parties had provided the Secretary-General with information and had given him certain assurances. The Secretary-General had requested from the parties a timetable for their full implementation. As for the electoral process, it had long been the Secretary-General's belief that Governments and leaders should not hold office beyond prescribed term limits. Lebanese public opinion appeared to be divided over such issues as the Syrian military presence in Lebanon, the constitutional situation as it related to presidential elections, and the continued existence of armed groups not under the direct control of the Government. However, many were of the view that full implementation of resolution 1559 (2004) would be in the interest not just of Lebanon, but of Syria too, and of the region and the wider international community. The Secretary-General said that it was time, 14 years after the end of hostilities and four years after the Israeli withdrawal from Lebanon, for all parties to set aside the remaining vestiges of the past. The withdrawal of foreign forces and the disbandment and disarmament of militias would, with finality, end that sad chapter of Lebanese history.

Communications (October). On 5 October [S/2004/794 & Corr.1], Lebanon said that the Secretary-General's October report (see above) did not take into account the historical responsibility borne by Israel for pursuing a policy of destruction in Palestine, Syria and Lebanon. Lebanon reiterated that the question of the departure of Syrian troops from the country was governed by bilateral relations and agreements between Lebanon and Syria and depended on peace and defence requirements and mutual security interests. Hizbullah was an occupation resistance party to which the Lebanese provided political protection. Its resistance would come to an end with the end of the residual occupation by Israel of Lebanese territory. The extension of the Lebanese President's term took place in accordance with the rules set out in the Lebanese Constitution and it was the rule of the majority that determined the results.

Syria, on 6 October [S/2004/796], said that the Lebanese and Syrian Governments could decide to redeploy Syrian forces within Lebanon in case of need, and, following the decision of the joint Lebanese-Syrian military committee, Syrian troops were redeployed for a fifth time. In Syria's view, the real cause of the troubled situation in the region was the absence of a just and comprehensive peace, owing to Israel's defiance of the UN Charter, refusal to implement relevant Council resolutions and continuing violations of the Geneva Conventions in the Occupied Palestinian Territory.

On 1 October [A/59/425-S/2004/808], Turkey transmitted to the Secretary-General the final communiqué of the annual coordination meeting of the Foreign Ministers of the States members of the Organization of the Islamic Conference (New York, 28 September). The Ministers supported Lebanon in its efforts to complete the liberation of all its remaining territories under Israeli occupation and urged the United Nations to compel Israel to pay reparations for all the losses it had inflicted as a result of its aggression against Lebanon. They reaffirmed the right of Palestine refugees to return to their homes and rejected settling them in Lebanon.

SECURITY COUNCIL ACTION

On 19 October [meeting 5058], following consultations among Security Council members, the President made statement **S/PRST/2004/36** on behalf of the Council:

The Security Council welcomes the report of the Secretary-General of 1 October 2004 on the implementation of resolution 1559(2004) of 2 September 2004.

The Council takes note of the letter dated 5 October 2004 from the Permanent Representative of Lebanon to the United Nations addressed to the Secretary-General and of the note verbale dated 6 October 2004 from the Permanent Mission of the Syrian Arab Republic to the United Nations addressed to the President of the Security Council.

The Council reaffirms its strong support for the territorial integrity, sovereignty and political independence of Lebanon within its internationally recognized borders.

The Council notes with concern that the requirements set out in resolution 1559(2004) have not been met, as reported by the Secretary-General. The Council urges relevant parties to implement fully all provisions of that resolution, and welcomes the Secretary-General's readiness to assist the parties in this regard.

The Council appreciates the intention of the Secretary-General to keep the Council updated. It requests that he continue to report to the Council on the implementation of the resolution every six months.

Appointment. In a 14 December letter to the Council President [S/2004/974], the Secretary-General said he had decided to appoint Terje Roed-Larsen (Norway) as his Special Envoy for the implementation of Council resolution 1559 (2004) at the level of Under-Secretary-General. On 16 December [S/2004/975], the Council took note of the Secretary-General's intention.

UNIFIL

In 2004, the United Nations Interim Force in Lebanon continued to discharge its mandate by observing, monitoring and reporting on developments in its area of operation. The Security Council twice extended UNIFIL's mandate in 2004, in January and in July, each time for a six-month period.

UNIFIL, established by Council resolution 425(1978) following Israel's invasion of Lebanon [YUN 1978, p. 296], was originally entrusted with confirming the withdrawal of Israeli forces, restoring international peace and security, and assisting Lebanon in regaining authority in southern Lebanon. Following a second invasion in 1982 [YUN 1982, p. 428], the Council, in resolution 511(1982) [ibid., p. 450], authorized the Force to carry out the additional task of providing protection and humanitarian assistance to the local population. With the withdrawal of IDF from Lebanon in June 2000 [YUN 2000, p. 465], UNIFIL's operational role changed. A reinforcement was initiated to enable UNIFIL to monitor Israel's withdrawal, which included extending its operations into those territories previously occupied by IDF [ibid.]. In 2001, having fulfilled those responsibilities, UNIFIL began a reconfiguration and redeployment phase [YUN 2001, p. 453], which was completed in December 2002 [YUN 2002, p. 478].

The Force headquarters, based in Naqoura, provided command and control, and liaison with Lebanon and Israel, UNDOF, UNTSO and a number of NGOs.

Composition and deployment

As at 31 December 2004, UNIFIL comprised 2,001 troops from France (204), Ghana (652), India (650), Ireland (5), Italy (54), Poland (238) and Ukraine (198). The Force was assisted in its tasks by 51 UNTSO military observers. It employed 407 civilian staff, of whom 104 were recruited internationally and 303 locally. On 26 January [S/2004/69], the Security Council took note of the Secretary-General's intention [S/2004/68] to appoint Major General Alain Pellegrini (France) as Force Commander to replace Major General Lalit Mohan Tewari (India), who would complete his tour of duty on 17 February.

Since UNIFIL's establishment, 246 members had lost their lives: 79 as a result of firings or bomb explosions, 105 in accidents and 62 from other causes.

Activities

Report of Secretary-General (January). In a report on developments from 24 July 2003 to 19 January 2004 in the UNIFIL area of operations [S/2004/50], the Secretary-General said that the situation on the ground was marked by numerous incidents threatening the stability of southern Lebanon, including renewed exchanges of fire in the Shab'a farms area and attacks across the Blue Line. UNIFIL remained focused on maintaining the ceasefire through mobile and air patrols along the Blue Line, observation from fixed positions and contact with the parties.

The Secretary-General expressed concern at Israel's persistent air violations of sovereign Lebanese territory. Hizbullah's firing of anti-aircraft rounds across the Blue Line was also a violation. Israel's air strikes against Hizbullah positions added a serious new dimension to the cycle. He added that Lebanon had demonstrated its capacity to exercise its authority throughout southern Lebanon, particularly through the activities of the Joint Security Forces and the Lebanese Army during periods of heightened regional and local tension. He urged Lebanon to exert control over the use of force on its entire territory and to prevent all attacks across the Blue Line. The Secretary-General recommended that the Force's mandate be extended for another six months, until 31 July 2004.

By a 14 January letter [S/2004/35], Lebanon requested that UNIFIL's mandate, due to expire at the end of the month, be extended for six months.

On 30 January [meeting 4907], the Security Council unanimously adopted **resolution 1525 (2004)**. The draft [S/2004/78] was prepared in consultations among Council members.

The Security Council,

Recalling all its resolutions on Lebanon, in particular resolutions 425(1978) and 426(1978) of 19 March 1978 and 1496(2003) of 31 July 2003, as well as the statements by its President on the situation in Lebanon, in particular the statement of 18 June 2000 (S/PRST/2000/21),

Recalling also the letter dated 18 May 2001 from the President of the Security Council to the Secretary-General,

Recalling further the conclusion of the Secretary-General that, as of 16 June 2000, Israel had withdrawn its forces from Lebanon in accordance with resolution 425(1978) and met the requirements defined in the report of the Secretary-General of 22 May 2000, as well as the conclusion of the Secretary-General that the United Nations Interim Force in Lebanon had essentially completed two of the three parts of its mandate, focusing now on the remaining task of restoring international peace and security,

Emphasizing the interim nature of the Force,

Recalling its resolution 1308(2000) of 17 July 2000,

Recalling also its resolution 1325(2000) of 31 October 2000,

Recalling further the relevant principles contained in the Convention on the Safety of United Nations and Associated Personnel of 9 December 1994,

Responding to the request of the Government of Lebanon, as stated in the letter dated 14 January 2004 from the Permanent Representative of Lebanon to the United Nations addressed to the Secretary-General,

Expressing its concern over the tensions and potential for escalation as noted in the report of the Secretary-General of 20 January 2004,

1. *Endorses* the report of the Secretary-General of 20 January 2004 on the United Nations Interim Force in Lebanon, and in particular its recommendation to renew the mandate of the Force for a further period of six months;

2. *Decides* to extend the present mandate until 31 July 2004;

3. *Reiterates its strong support* for the territorial integrity, sovereignty and political independence of Lebanon within its internationally recognized boundaries;

4. *Encourages* the Government of Lebanon to continue efforts to ensure the return of its effective authority throughout the south, including the deployment of Lebanese armed forces, stresses the importance of the Government of Lebanon continuing to extend those measures, and calls upon the Government of Lebanon to do its utmost to ensure a calm environment throughout the south, including along the Blue Line;

5. *Calls upon* the parties to ensure that the Force is accorded full freedom of movement in the discharge of its mandate throughout its area of operation as outlined in the report of the Secretary-General;

6. *Reiterates its call upon* the parties to continue to fulfil the commitments they have given to respect fully the withdrawal line identified by the United Nations, as set out in the report of the Secretary-General of 16 June 2000, to exercise the utmost restraint and to cooperate fully with the United Nations and the Force;

7. *Condemns* all acts of violence, expresses great concern about the serious breaches and the sea, land and continuing air violations of the withdrawal line, and urges the parties to put an end to these violations, to refrain from any act or provocation that could further escalate the tension and to abide scrupulously by their obligation to respect the safety of personnel of the Force and other United Nations personnel;

8. *Supports* the continued efforts of the Force to maintain the ceasefire along the withdrawal line through mobile patrols and observation from fixed positions and through close contacts with the parties to correct violations, resolve incidents and prevent the escalation thereof;

9. *Welcomes* the continued contribution of the Force to operational demining, applauds the progress in demining efforts noted by the Secretary-General in his report, encourages further assistance in mine action by the United Nations to the Government of Lebanon in support of both the continued development of its national mine action capacity and emergency demining activities in the south, commends donor countries for supporting these efforts through financial and in-kind contributions and encourages further international contributions, takes note of the communication to the Government of Lebanon and the Force of maps and information on the location of mines, and stresses the necessity to provide the Government of Lebanon and the Force with any additional maps and records on the location of mines;

10. *Requests* the Secretary-General to continue consultations with the Government of Lebanon and other parties directly concerned on the implementation of the present resolution and to report thereon to the Council before the end of the present mandate as well as on the activities of the Force and the tasks presently carried out by the United Nations Truce Supervision Organization;

11. *Looks forward* to the early fulfilment of the mandate of the Force;

12. *Stresses* the importance of, and the need to achieve, a comprehensive, just and lasting peace in the Middle East, based on all its relevant resolutions, including its resolution 242(1967) of 22 November 1967 and 338(1973) of 22 October 1973.

By a 30 January letter [A/58/698-S/2004/81], Lebanon welcomed the renewal of UNIFIL's mandate.

Report of Secretary-General (July). In response to resolution 1525(2004) (above), the Secretary-General submitted a July report on UNIFIL covering 21 January to 21 July [S/2004/572 & Add.1]. He said that the situation on the ground was characterized by numerous armed encounters across the Blue Line, the majority of which were between Hizbullah and IDF and some of which involved unknown or Palestinian actors. He described incidents which tended to set off a chain of escalating exchanges, elevating tensions for periods of several days at a time. Air strikes and shooting incidents resulted in the deaths of one Israeli soldier, one Lebanese civilian and two Palestinians. Israeli violations of Lebanese airspace continued, and on at least two occasions Hizbullah directed anti-aircraft fire towards Israeli villages. While conditions of relative stability were maintained in southern Lebanon, friction between the parties posed a threatening counterpoint. Israeli air incursions into Lebanon were on the whole less frequent than in the previous six months, although they were notable for their intensity and the large number of aircraft involved, and the number of instances of Hizbullah anti-aircraft fire dropped significantly.

The first municipal elections in southern Lebanon since the Israeli withdrawal were held on 23 May. There was high voter turnout throughout the south, and polling was conducted in an orderly manner, with no reports of intimidation or major disturbances. The elections bolstered local governing structures and marked an advance in integration of the formerly occupied zone with the rest of the country. The vast majority of seats were won by Hizbullah and the other dominant political party in the south, Amal.

The Lebanese Joint Security Force and the Lebanese Army continued to operate in the areas vacated by Israel in 2000. The strength and activity of the Joint Security Force generally remained the same, apart from an increase in activities in late March and early June, when tensions heightened, and in May during the elections. The Force also intervened on several occasions to control demonstrations and took other measures to restrict access to the technical fence. Nevertheless, the Lebanese Government maintained the position that, so long as there was no comprehensive peace with Israel, Lebanese armed forces would not be deployed along the Blue Line. Under those circumstances, Hizbullah maintained its visible presence near the Line through its mobile and fixed positions and generally refrained from interfering with UNIFIL. Israel and Hizbullah concluded an agreement, brokered by German mediators, for a prisoner exchange, which took place on 29 and 30 January.

UNIFIL provided assistance to the Lebanese civilian population in the form of medical care, water projects and equipment and services for schools, and supplied social services to the needy. It cooperated on humanitarian matters with the Lebanese authorities, UN agencies and other organizations operating in Lebanon. The presence of a large number of minefields in UNIFIL's area of operation, largely concentrated along the Blue Line owing to comprehensive demining in other sectors, remained a serious concern. UNIFIL continued its demining activities, clearing over 800 mines and pieces of unexploded ordnance, and carried out mine-risk education for schoolchildren. In southern Lebanon, the United Nations collaborated with the Lebanese Government and various donors on landmine clearance.

The Secretary-General observed that the situation in southern Lebanon in early 2004 was replete with contradictions. While both Israel and Lebanon proclaimed their aspirations to avoid destabilization of the area, only one month passed without confrontation. Furthermore, single incidents often sparked a chain reaction of violence to which both sides contributed. Importantly, none of those events spiralled out of control, and for that the parties and UNIFIL, all deserved credit. Nevertheless, the risk remained that hostile acts would escalate and lead to conflict. Further efforts were required to maintain calm in the south and to halt violations of the Blue Line. The Secretary-General recommended that the Force's mandate be extended for another six months, until 31 January 2005.

Communication. On 9 July [S/2004/560], Lebanon requested that UNIFIL's mandate be extended for six months, as a reaffirmation of the international community's commitment to the restoration of Lebanon's sovereignty over its entire territory.

SECURITY COUNCIL ACTION (July)

On 29 July [meeting 5012], the Council unanimously adopted **resolution 1553(2004)**. The draft [S/2004/599] was prepared in consultations among Council members.

The Security Council,
Recalling all its resolutions on Lebanon, in particular resolutions 425(1978) and 426(1978) of 19 March 1978 and 1525(2004) of 30 January 2004 as well as the statements by its President on the situation in Lebanon, in particular the statement of 18 June 2000 (S/PRST/2000/21),
Recalling also the letter dated 18 May 2001 from the President of the Security Council to the Secretary-General,
Recalling further the conclusion of the Secretary-General that, as of 16 June 2000, Israel had withdrawn its forces from Lebanon in accordance with resolution 425(1978) and met the requirements defined in the report of the Secretary-General of 22 May 2000, as well as the conclusion of the Secretary-General that the United Nations Interim Force in Lebanon had essentially completed two of the three parts of its mandate, focusing now on the remaining task of restoring international peace and security,

Emphasizing the interim nature of the Force,

Recalling its resolution 1308(2000) of 17 July 2000,

Recalling also its resolution 1325(2000) of 31 October 2000,

Recalling further the relevant principles contained in the Convention on the Safety of United Nations and Associated Personnel of 9 December 1994,

Responding to the request of the Government of Lebanon to extend the mandate of the Force for a new period of six months presented in the letter dated 9 July 2004 from the Permanent Representative of Lebanon to the United Nations addressed to the Secretary-General,

Expressing its concern over the tensions and potential for escalation as noted in the report of the Secretary-General of 21 July 2004,

1. *Endorses* the report of the Secretary-General of 21 July 2004 on the United Nations Interim Force in Lebanon and in particular its recommendation to renew the mandate of the Force for a further period of six months;

2. *Decides* to extend the present mandate until 31 January 2005;

3. *Reiterates its strong support* for the territorial integrity, sovereignty and political independence of Lebanon within its internationally recognized boundaries;

4. *Encourages* the Government of Lebanon to continue efforts to ensure the return of its effective authority throughout the south, including the deployment of Lebanese armed forces, stresses the importance of the Government of Lebanon to continue to extend these measures, and calls upon the Government of Lebanon to do its utmost to ensure a calm environment throughout the south, including along the Blue Line;

5. *Calls upon* the parties to ensure that the Force is accorded full freedom of movement in the discharge of its mandate throughout its area of operation as outlined in the report of the Secretary-General;

6. *Reiterates its call upon* the parties to continue to fulfil the commitments they have given to respect fully the withdrawal line identified by the United Nations, as set out in the report of the Secretary-General of 16 June 2000, to exercise utmost restraint and to cooperate fully with the United Nations and the Force;

7. *Condemns* all acts of violence, expresses great concern about the serious breaches and the sea, land and continuing air violations of the withdrawal line, and urges the parties to put an end to these violations, to refrain from any act or provocation that could further escalate the tension and to abide scrupulously by the obligation to respect the safety of the personnel of the Force and other United Nations personnel;

8. *Supports* the continued efforts of the Force to maintain the ceasefire along the withdrawal line through mobile patrols and observation from fixed positions and through close contacts with the parties to correct violations, resolve incidents and prevent the escalation thereof;

9. *Welcomes* the continued contribution of the Force to operational demining, applauds the successful completion of Operation Emirates Solidarity noted by the Secretary-General in his report, encourages further assistance in mine action by the United Nations to the Government of Lebanon in support of both the continued development of its national mine action capacity and emergency demining activities in the south, commends donor countries for supporting these efforts through financial and in-kind contributions and encourages further international contributions, takes note of the communication to the Government of Lebanon and the Force of maps and information on the location of mines, and stresses the necessity to provide the Government of Lebanon and the Force with any additional maps and records on the location of mines;

10. *Requests* the Secretary-General to continue consultations with the Government of Lebanon and other parties directly concerned on the implementation of the present resolution and to report thereon to the Council before the end of the present mandate as well as on the activities of the Force and the tasks presently carried out by the United Nations Truce Supervision Organization;

11. *Looks forward* to the early fulfilment of the mandate of the Force;

12. *Stresses* the importance of, and the need to achieve, a comprehensive, just and lasting peace in the Middle East, based on all its relevant resolutions, including resolutions 242(1967) of 22 November 1967 and 338(1973) of 22 October 1973.

Further developments. In a report on developments during the second half of 2004 [S/2005/36], the Secretary-General said that a relatively quiet but tense situation prevailed in UNIFIL's area of operation, with a notable absence of armed exchanges between Hizbullah and IDF. There were two serious violations of the Blue Line involving rocket fire by unidentified, presumably Palestinian, armed elements operating from southern Lebanon, but no casualties resulted. Israeli air incursions into Lebanese airspace continued with little change and, in a new development, on one occasion, Hizbullah launched a remotely piloted aerial vehicle, or drone, that penetrated Israeli airspace. There were, however, no instances of Hizbullah anti-aircraft fire across the Line. UNIFIL continued to provide assistance to the Lebanese civilian population.

Financing

In June 2004, the General Assembly considered the performance report on UNIFIL's budget for 1 July 2002 to 30 June 2003 [A/58/637], submitted by the Secretary-General. Total expenditure for the period amounted to $107,596,800, compared with a total apportionment of $112,376,000, resulting in an unencumbered balance of $4,779,200, or 4.3 per cent.

The Assembly also had before it the proposed UNIFIL budget for 1 July 2004 to 30 June 2005 [A/58/659] in the amount of $94,741,200 and the overview report of the financing of UN peacekeeping operations: budget performance for the period from 1 July 2002 to 30 June 2003 and budget for the period from 1 July 2004 to 30 June 2005 [A/58/705]. Also considered were the comments and recommendations of the Advisory Committee on Administrative and Budgetary Questions (ACABQ) on the budgets [A/58/759/ Add.6].

GENERAL ASSEMBLY ACTION

On 18 June [meeting 91], the General Assembly, on the recommendation of the Fifth (Administrative and Budgetary) Committee [A/58/828], adopted **resolution 58/307** by recorded vote (131-2) [agenda item 145 (b)].

Financing of the United Nations Interim Force in Lebanon

The General Assembly,

Having considered the reports of the Secretary-General on the financing of the United Nations Interim Force in Lebanon, the related reports of the Advisory Committee on Administrative and Budgetary Questions and the report of the Board of Auditors,

Recalling Security Council resolution 425(1978) of 19 March 1978 regarding the establishment of the United Nations Interim Force in Lebanon and the subsequent resolutions by which the Council extended the mandate of the Force, the latest of which was resolution 1525(2004) of 30 January 2004,

Recalling also its resolution S-8/2 of 21 April 1978 on the financing of the Force and its subsequent resolutions thereon, the latest of which was resolution 57/325 of 18 June 2003,

Reaffirming its resolutions 51/233 of 13 June 1997, 52/237 of 26 June 1998, 53/227 of 8 June 1999, 54/267 of 15 June 2000, 55/180 A of 19 December 2000, 55/180 B of 14 June 2001, 56/214 A of 21 December 2001, 56/214 B of 27 June 2002 and 57/325 of 18 June 2003,

Reaffirming also the general principles underlying the financing of United Nations peacekeeping operations, as stated in General Assembly resolutions 1874 (S-IV) of 27 June 1963, 3101(XXVIII) of 11 December 1973 and 55/235 of 23 December 2000,

Noting with appreciation that voluntary contributions have been made to the Force,

Mindful of the fact that it is essential to provide the Force with the necessary financial resources to enable it to fulfil its responsibilities under the relevant resolutions of the Security Council,

1. *Takes note* of the status of contributions to the United Nations Interim Force in Lebanon as at 15 April 2004, including the contributions outstanding in the amount of 77 million United States dollars, representing some 2 per cent of the total assessed contributions, notes with concern that only twenty-eight Member States have paid their assessed contributions in full, and urges all other Member States, in particular those in arrears, to ensure payment of their outstanding assessed contributions;

2. *Expresses its appreciation* to those Member States that have paid their assessed contributions in full, and urges all other Member States to make every possible effort to ensure payment of their assessed contributions to the Force in full;

3. *Expresses deep concern* that Israel did not comply with General Assembly resolutions 51/233, 52/237, 53/227, 54/267, 55/180 A, 55/180 B, 56/214 A, 56/214 B and 57/325;

4. *Stresses once again* that Israel should strictly abide by General Assembly resolutions 51/233, 52/237, 53/227, 54/267, 55/180 A, 55/180 B, 56/214 A, 56/214 B and 57/325;

5. *Expresses concern* at the financial situation with regard to peacekeeping activities, in particular as regards the reimbursements to troop contributors that bear additional burdens owing to overdue payments by Member States of their assessments;

6. *Also expresses concern* at the delay experienced by the Secretary-General in deploying and providing adequate resources to some recent peacekeeping missions, in particular those in Africa;

7. *Emphasizes* that all future and existing peacekeeping missions shall be given equal and non-discriminatory treatment in respect of financial and administrative arrangements;

8. *Also emphasizes* that all peacekeeping missions shall be provided with adequate resources for the effective and efficient discharge of their respective mandates;

9. *Reiterates its request* to the Secretary-General to make the fullest possible use of facilities and equipment at the United Nations Logistics Base at Brindisi, Italy, in order to minimize the costs of procurement for the Force;

10. *Endorses* the conclusions and recommendations contained in the report of the Advisory Committee on Administrative and Budgetary Questions, requests the Secretary-General to ensure their full implementation, and, with regard to the recommendation contained in paragraph 16 concerning the Secretary-General's proposal to convert 45 individual special service agreements into 45 national posts, requests the Secretary-General to provide further information in order to take a decision on this question at its fifty-ninth session;

11. *Requests* the Secretary-General to take all necessary action to ensure that the Force is administered with a maximum of efficiency and economy;

12. *Also requests* the Secretary-General, in order to reduce the cost of employing General Service staff, to continue efforts to recruit local staff for the Force against General Service posts, commensurate with the requirements of the Force;

13. *Reiterates its request* to the Secretary-General to take the measures necessary to ensure the full implementation of paragraph 8 of its resolution 51/233, paragraph 5 of its resolution 52/237, paragraph 11 of its resolution 53/227, paragraph 14 of its resolution 54/267, paragraph 14 of its resolution 55/180 A, paragraph 15 of its resolution 55/180 B, paragraph 13 of its resolution 56/214 A, paragraph 13 of its resolution 56/214 B and paragraph 14 of its resolution 57/325, stresses once again that Israel shall pay the amount of 1,117,005 dollars resulting from the incident at Qana on 18 April 1996, and requests the Secretary-General to report on this matter to the General Assembly at its resumed fifty-ninth session;

Financial performance report for the period from 1 July 2002 to 30 June 2003

14. *Takes note* of the report of the Secretary-General on the financial performance of the Force for the period from 1 July 2002 to 30 June 2003;

Budget estimates for the period from 1 July 2004 to 30 June 2005

15. *Decides* to appropriate to the Special Account for the United Nations Interim Force in Lebanon the amount of 97,804,100 dollars for the period from 1 July 2004 to 30 June 2005, inclusive of 92,960,300 dollars for the maintenance of the Force, 3,960,000 dollars for the support account for peacekeeping operations and 883,800 dollars for the United Nations Logistics Base;

Financing of the appropriation

16. *Also decides* to apportion among Member States the amount of 97,804,100 dollars at a monthly rate of 8,150,341 dollars, in accordance with the levels set out in General Assembly resolution 55/235, as adjusted by the Assembly in its resolution 55/236 of 23 December 2000 and updated in its resolution 58/256 of 23 December 2003, and taking into account the scale of assessments for 2004 and 2005, as set out in its resolution 58/1 B of 23 December 2003, subject to a decision of the Security Council to extend the mandate of the Force;

17. *Further decides* that, in accordance with the provisions of its resolution 973(X) of 15 December 1955, there shall be set off against the apportionment among Member States, as provided for in paragraph 16 above, their respective share in the Tax Equalization Fund of 5,313,100 dollars, comprising the estimated staff assessment income of 4,685,400 dollars approved for the Force, the prorated share of 577,900 dollars of the estimated staff assessment income approved for the support account and the prorated share of 49,800 dollars of the estimated staff assessment income approved for the United Nations Logistics Base;

18. *Decides* that, for Member States that have fulfilled their financial obligations to the Force, there shall be set off against their apportionment, as provided for in paragraph 16 above, their respective share of the unencumbered balance and other income in the total amount of 15,788,700 dollars in respect of the financial period ended 30 June 2003, in accordance with the levels set out in General Assembly resolution 55/235, as adjusted by the Assembly in its resolution 55/236 and its resolution 57/290 A of 20 December 2002, and taking into account the scale of assessments for 2003, as set out in its resolutions 55/5 B of 23 December 2000 and 57/4 B of 20 December 2002;

19. *Also decides* that, for Member States that have not fulfilled their financial obligations to the Force, there shall be set off against their outstanding obligations their respective share of the unencumbered balance and other income in the total amount of 15,788,700 dollars in respect of the financial period ended 30 June 2003, in accordance with the scheme set out in paragraph 18 above;

20. *Further decides* that the increase of 878,900 dollars in the estimated staff assessment income in respect of the financial period ended 30 June 2003 shall be added to the credits from the amount referred to in paragraphs 18 and 19 above, and that the respective shares of Member States therein shall be applied in accordance with the provisions of those paragraphs, as appropriate;

21. *Decides* that, for Member States that have fulfilled their financial obligations to the Force, there shall be set off against their apportionment, as provided for in paragraph 16 above, their respective share of the retained surplus in the total amount of 63,312,709 dollars, representing the net accumulated surplus in the account of the Force from 1978 to 1993, in accordance with the composition of groups set out in paragraphs 3 and 4 of General Assembly resolution 43/232 of 1 March 1989, as adjusted by the Assembly in its resolutions 44/192 B of 21 December 1989, 45/244 of 21 December 1990, 46/194 of 20 December 1991, 47/218 A of 23 December 1992 and 51/218 B and C of 18 December 1996, and taking into account the scale of assessments for 1993 as set out in its resolution 46/221 A of 20 December 1991, as adjusted by the Assembly in its decision 47/456 of 23 December 1992 and its resolution 48/223 A of 23 December 1993;

22. *Also decides* that, for Member States that have not fulfilled their financial obligations to the Force, there shall be set off against their outstanding obligations their respective share of the retained surplus in the total amount of 63,312,709 dollars, in accordance with the scheme set out in paragraph 21 above;

23. *Emphasizes* that no peacekeeping mission shall be financed by borrowing funds from other active peacekeeping missions;

24. *Encourages* the Secretary-General to continue to take additional measures to ensure the safety and security of all personnel under the auspices of the United Nations participating in the Force;

25. *Invites* voluntary contributions to the Force in cash and in the form of services and supplies acceptable to the Secretary-General, to be administered, as appropriate, in accordance with the procedure and practices established by the General Assembly;

26. *Decides* to include in the provisional agenda of its fifty-ninth session, under the item entitled "Financing of the United Nations peacekeeping forces in the Middle East", the sub-item entitled "United Nations Interim Force in Lebanon".

RECORDED VOTE ON RESOLUTION 58/307:

In favour: Afghanistan, Algeria, Andorra, Argentina, Armenia, Australia, Austria, Azerbaijan, Bahamas, Bahrain, Bangladesh, Belarus, Belgium, Belize, Bosnia and Herzegovina, Brazil, Brunei Darussalam, Bulgaria, Burkina Faso, Burundi, Cambodia, Canada, Central African Republic, Chile, China, Colombia, Costa Rica, Côte d'Ivoire, Croatia, Cuba, Cyprus, Czech Republic, Denmark, Djibouti, Dominican Republic, Ecuador, Egypt, El Salvador, Estonia, Ethiopia, Finland, France, Gabon, Gambia, Germany, Ghana, Greece, Guatemala, Guinea, Guyana, Haiti, Honduras, Hungary, Iceland, India, Indonesia, Ireland, Italy, Jamaica, Japan, Jordan, Kazakhstan, Kenya, Kuwait, Latvia, Lebanon, Lesotho, Libyan Arab Jamahiriya, Liechtenstein, Lithuania, Luxembourg, Malaysia, Maldives, Mali, Malta, Mauritius, Mexico, Monaco, Morocco, Mozambique, Myanmar, Namibia, Nepal, Netherlands, New Zealand, Nicaragua, Niger, Nigeria, Norway, Oman, Pakistan, Panama, Peru, Poland, Portugal, Qatar, Republic of Korea, Republic of Moldova, Russian Federation, San Marino, Saudi Arabia, Senegal, Serbia and Montenegro, Sierra Leone, Singapore, Slovakia, Slovenia, South Africa, Spain, Sri Lanka, Sudan, Sweden, Switzerland, Syrian Arab Republic, Thailand, Timor-Leste, Togo, Trinidad and Tobago, Tunisia, Turkey, Uganda, Ukraine, United Arab Emirates, United Kingdom, United Republic of Tanzania, Uruguay, Venezuela, Viet Nam, Yemen, Zambia, Zimbabwe.

Against: Israel, United States.

The Assembly adopted the fourth preambular paragraph and operative paragraphs 3, 4 and 13 by a single recorded vote of 75 to 2, with 48 abstentions. The Committee adopted those paragraphs in the same manner, by 80 to 2, with 51 abstentions.

On 23 December, the Assembly decided that the item on the financing of UN peacekeeping forces in the Middle East would remain for consideration at its resumed fifty-ninth (2005) session (**decision 59/552**).

Syrian Arab Republic

In 2004, the General Assembly again called for Israel's withdrawal from the Golan Heights in the Syrian Arab Republic, which it had occupied since 1967. The area was effectively annexed by Israel when it extended its laws, jurisdiction and administration to the territory towards the end of 1981 [YUN 1981, p. 309].

Alleged Syrian interference in the Lebanese presidential elections in early September led to the adoption of Security Council resolution 1559 (2004) (see p. 506).

Israeli policies and measures affecting the human rights of the population in the Golan Heights and other occupied territories were monitored by the Special Committee to Investigate Israeli Practices Affecting the Human Rights of the Palestinian People and Other Arabs of the Occupied Territories (Committee on Israeli Practices) and were the subject of resolutions adopted by the Commission on Human Rights (see PART TWO, Chapter III) and the Assembly.

Communications. In a 5 January letter [A/58/670-S/2004/1], the Syrian Arab Republic said that the Israeli Government gave its authorization for the construction of nine new settlements in the occupied Syrian Golan and for the expansion of existing Israeli settlements in that area.

Syria, in a letter of 15 March [A/58/734-S/2004/205], stated that on 4 March the Israeli occupation authorities proceeded to confiscate further territory in the occupied Syrian Golan. That confiscation came on the heels of the Israeli Government's approval of nine new settlement units, the construction of 900 new houses and the allocation of funds for implementing the Israeli Government's plan to increase the number of Israeli settlers in the Syrian Golan and expand existing Israeli settlements. The residents of the occupied Golan had declared a peaceful general strike for 14 March as a day for defending the land and defying the occupation authorities.

On 22 June [A/58/846-S/2004/510], Syria, in response to allegations made by Israel that the Syrian Government had trained, sponsored and financed terrorist groups, said that the Israeli claims constituted a distortion of the facts and an attempt to justify its terrorism against the Lebanese people and its occupation of Arab lands.

Bahrain transmitted to the Secretary-General the final communiqué and the Manama Declaration adopted by the Supreme Council of the Gulf Cooperation Council at its twenty-fifth session (Manama, Bahrain, 20-21 December) [A/59/663-S/2005/5]. The Supreme Council demanded that Israel withdraw from all the occupied Arab lands in Palestine and the occupied Golan Heights to the line of 4 June 1967 and from the Shab'a farms in southern Lebanon.

Committee on Israeli Practices. In its annual report [A/59/381], the Committee on Israeli Practices stated that it had visited Damascus, Syria, and Quneitra province, which bordered the occupied area, where it met with Syrian authorities and received information from witnesses with personal knowledge of the human rights situation in the occupied Syrian Golan. Syrian government officials emphasized that the situation continued to deteriorate and that Israel was still pursuing its policy of settlement expansion and land expropriation. The population of 44 Jewish settlements, which had 20,000 inhabitants, was expected to increase by 15,000 settlers over the next three years, following a decision by the Israeli authorities on 1 January. Authorization already had been granted for nine new settlements and for extending the existing ones, which implied further expropriation of Arab land. The laying of anti-personnel landmines continued. The Israeli authorities laid mines in 1,000 dunums of land in the Quneitra area along the Golan border strip and fenced them in with barbed wire, preventing farmers from cultivating their lands, and in the Harmon area, where trees had been uprooted. A matter of even greater concern was the burial of nuclear waste close to the Syrian border. It was feared that the nuclear waste, sealed in glass containers or reinforced cement chambers, would be affected by climatic conditions after 30 to 50 years and would start leaking depleted uranium, with a catastrophic environmental impact. Israel had refused to allow its nuclear reactors to be monitored by the International Atomic Energy Agency, and it refused to comply with relevant international conventions. Syrian Arabs in the occupied Golan had to pay taxes at higher rates than Israeli settlers for all kinds of purposes, including television licence fees, housing, income and property, and health insurance. Markets were closed to Syrian farmers as a result of the Israeli occupation, and there was a decline in agricultural production.

Reports of Secretary-General. On 9 September [A/59/338], the Secretary-General reported that no reply had been received from Israel to his August request for information on steps taken or envisaged to implement General Assembly resolution 58/100 [YUN 2003, p. 524], which called on

Israel to desist from changing the physical character, demographic composition, institutional structure and legal status of the Golan, and from its repressive measures against the population.

By a 12 October report [A/59/431], the Secretary-General transmitted replies received from five Member States, including Israel, in response to his request for information on steps taken or envisaged to implement Assembly resolution 58/23 [YUN 2003, p. 524], which dealt with Israeli policies in the Syrian territory occupied since 1967, and resolution 58/22 [ibid., p. 484] on the transfer by some States of their diplomatic missions to Jerusalem (see p. 473).

GENERAL ASSEMBLY ACTION

On 1 December [meeting 64], the General Assembly adopted **resolution 59/33** [draft: A/59/L.40 & Add.1] by recorded vote (111-6-60) [agenda item 36].

The Syrian Golan

The General Assembly,

Having considered the item entitled "The situation in the Middle East",

Taking note of the report of the Secretary-General,

Recalling Security Council resolution 497(1981) of 17 December 1981,

Reaffirming the fundamental principle of the inadmissibility of the acquisition of territory by force, in accordance with international law and the Charter of the United Nations,

Reaffirming once more the applicability of the Geneva Convention relative to the Protection of Civilian Persons in Time of War, of 12 August 1949, to the occupied Syrian Golan,

Deeply concerned that Israel has not withdrawn from the Syrian Golan, which has been under occupation since 1967, contrary to the relevant Security Council and General Assembly resolutions,

Stressing the illegality of the Israeli settlement construction and other activities in the occupied Syrian Golan since 1967,

Noting with satisfaction the convening in Madrid on 30 October 1991 of the Peace Conference on the Middle East, on the basis of Security Council resolutions 242(1967) of 22 November 1967, 338(1973) of 22 October 1973 and 425(1978) of 19 March 1978 and the formula of land for peace,

Expressing grave concern over the halt in the peace process on the Syrian track, and expressing the hope that peace talks will soon resume from the point they had reached,

1. *Declares* that Israel has failed so far to comply with Security Council resolution 497(1981);

2. *Also declares* that the Israeli decision of 14 December 1981 to impose its laws, jurisdiction and administration on the occupied Syrian Golan is null and void and has no validity whatsoever, as confirmed by the Security Council in its resolution 497(1981), and calls upon Israel to rescind it;

3. *Reaffirms its determination* that all relevant provisions of the Regulations annexed to the Hague Convention of 1907, and the Geneva Convention relative to the Protection of Civilian Persons in Time of War, continue to apply to the Syrian territory occupied by Israel since 1967, and calls upon the parties thereto to respect and ensure respect for their obligations under those instruments in all circumstances;

4. *Determines once more* that the continued occupation of the Syrian Golan and its de facto annexation constitute a stumbling block in the way of achieving a just, comprehensive and lasting peace in the region;

5. *Calls upon* Israel to resume the talks on the Syrian and Lebanese tracks and to respect the commitments and undertakings reached during the previous talks;

6. *Demands once more* that Israel withdraw from all the occupied Syrian Golan to the line of 4 June 1967 in implementation of the relevant Security Council resolutions;

7. *Calls upon* all the parties concerned, the co-sponsors of the peace process and the entire international community to exert all the necessary efforts to ensure the resumption of the peace process and its success by implementing Security Council resolutions 242(1967) and 338(1973);

8. *Requests* the Secretary-General to report to the General Assembly at its sixtieth session on the implementation of the present resolution.

RECORDED VOTE ON RESOLUTION 59/33:

In favour: Afghanistan, Algeria, Argentina, Armenia, Azerbaijan, Bahamas, Bahrain, Bangladesh, Barbados, Belarus, Belize, Benin, Bhutan, Bolivia, Botswana, Brazil, Brunei Darussalam, Burkina Faso, Cambodia, Cape Verde, Central African Republic, Chile, China, Colombia, Côte d'Ivoire, Cuba, Democratic People's Republic of Korea, Djibouti, Dominica, Ecuador, Egypt, El Salvador, Eritrea, Ethiopia, Fiji, Gabon, Gambia, Ghana, Guinea, Guinea-Bissau, Guyana, Honduras, India, Indonesia, Iran, Iraq, Jamaica, Jordan, Kazakhstan, Kuwait, Kyrgyzstan, Lao People's Democratic Republic, Lebanon, Lesotho, Liberia, Libyan Arab Jamahiriya, Madagascar, Malaysia, Maldives, Mali, Mauritania, Mauritius, Mexico, Mongolia, Morocco, Mozambique, Myanmar, Namibia, Nepal, Nicaragua, Niger, Nigeria, Oman, Pakistan, Panama, Papua New Guinea, Paraguay, Philippines, Qatar, Russian Federation, Saint Lucia, Saint Vincent and the Grenadines, Saudi Arabia, Senegal, Seychelles, Sierra Leone, Singapore, Somalia, South Africa, Sri Lanka, Sudan, Suriname, Swaziland, Syrian Arab Republic, Tajikistan, Thailand, Timor-Leste, Togo, Trinidad and Tobago, Tunisia, Turkey, Turkmenistan, Uganda, United Arab Emirates, United Republic of Tanzania, Uzbekistan, Venezuela, Viet Nam, Yemen, Zambia, Zimbabwe.

Against: Grenada, Israel, Marshall Islands, Micronesia, Palau, United States.

Abstaining: Albania, Andorra, Australia, Austria, Belgium, Bosnia and Herzegovina, Bulgaria, Burundi, Cameroon, Canada, Costa Rica, Croatia, Cyprus, Czech Republic, Denmark, Dominican Republic, Estonia, Finland, France, Georgia, Germany, Greece, Guatemala, Haiti, Hungary, Iceland, Ireland, Italy, Japan, Kenya, Latvia, Liechtenstein, Lithuania, Luxembourg, Malta, Monaco, Nauru, Netherlands, New Zealand, Norway, Peru, Poland, Portugal, Republic of Korea, Republic of Moldova, Romania, Samoa, San Marino, Serbia and Montenegro, Slovakia, Slovenia, Spain, Sweden, Switzerland, The former Yugoslav Republic of Macedonia, Tonga, Ukraine, United Kingdom, Uruguay, Vanuatu.

On 10 December [meeting 71], the Assembly, under the agenda item on the report of the Committee on Israeli Practices and on the Fourth Committee's recommendation [A/59/471], adopted **resolution 59/125** by recorded vote (160-2-15) [agenda item 76].

The occupied Syrian Golan

The General Assembly,

Having considered the report of the Special Committee to Investigate Israeli Practices Affecting the Human Rights of the Palestinian People and Other Arabs of the Occupied Territories,

Deeply concerned that the Syrian Golan, occupied since 1967, has been under continued Israeli military occupation,

Recalling Security Council resolution 497(1981) of 17 December 1981,

Recalling also its previous relevant resolutions, the most recent of which was resolution 58/100 of 9 December 2003,

Having considered the report of the Secretary-General submitted in pursuance of resolution 58/100,

Recalling its previous relevant resolutions in which, inter alia, it called upon Israel to put an end to its occupation of the Arab territories,

Reaffirming once more the illegality of the decision of 14 December 1981 taken by Israel to impose its laws, jurisdiction and administration on the occupied Syrian Golan, which has resulted in the effective annexation of that territory,

Reaffirming that the acquisition of territory by force is inadmissible under international law, including the Charter of the United Nations,

Reaffirming also the applicability of the Geneva Convention relative to the Protection of Civilian Persons in Time of War, of 12 August 1949, to the occupied Syrian Golan,

Bearing in mind Security Council resolution 237 (1967) of 14 June 1967,

Welcoming the convening at Madrid of the Peace Conference on the Middle East on the basis of Security Council resolutions 242(1967) of 22 November 1967 and 338(1973) of 22 October 1973 aimed at the realization of a just, comprehensive and lasting peace, and expressing grave concern about the stalling of the peace process on all tracks,

1. *Calls upon* Israel, the occupying Power, to comply with the relevant resolutions on the occupied Syrian Golan, in particular Security Council resolution 497(1981), in which the Council, inter alia, decided that the Israeli decision to impose its laws, jurisdiction and administration on the occupied Syrian Golan was null and void and without international legal effect, and demanded that Israel, the occupying Power, rescind forthwith its decision;

2. *Also calls upon* Israel to desist from changing the physical character, demographic composition, institutional structure and legal status of the occupied Syrian Golan and in particular to desist from the establishment of settlements;

3. *Determines* that all legislative and administrative measures and actions taken or to be taken by Israel, the occupying Power, that purport to alter the character and legal status of the occupied Syrian Golan are null and void, constitute a flagrant violation of international law and of the Geneva Convention relative to the Protection of Civilian Persons in Time of War, of 12 August 1949, and have no legal effect;

4. *Calls upon* Israel to desist from imposing Israeli citizenship and Israeli identity cards on the Syrian citizens in the occupied Syrian Golan, and from its repressive measures against the population of the occupied Syrian Golan;

5. *Deplores* the violations by Israel of the Geneva Convention relative to the Protection of Civilian Persons in Time of War, of 12 August 1949;

6. *Calls once again upon* Member States not to recognize any of the legislative or administrative measures and actions referred to above;

7. *Requests* the Secretary-General to report to the General Assembly at its sixtieth session on the implementation of the present resolution.

RECORDED VOTE ON RESOLUTION 59/125:

In favour: Afghanistan, Algeria, Andorra, Antigua and Barbuda, Argentina, Armenia, Australia, Austria, Azerbaijan, Bahamas, Bahrain, Bangladesh, Barbados, Belarus, Belgium, Belize, Benin, Bolivia, Bosnia and Herzegovina, Botswana, Brazil, Brunei Darussalam, Bulgaria, Burkina Faso, Burundi, Cambodia, Canada, Cape Verde, Chile, China, Colombia, Comoros, Congo, Costa Rica, Croatia, Cuba, Cyprus, Czech Republic, Democratic People's Republic of Korea, Denmark, Djibouti, Dominica, Ecuador, Egypt, El Salvador, Eritrea, Estonia, Ethiopia, Fiji, Finland, France, Gabon, Georgia, Germany, Ghana, Greece, Guatemala, Guinea, Guinea-Bissau, Guyana, Honduras, Hungary, Iceland, India, Indonesia, Iran, Ireland, Italy, Jamaica, Japan, Jordan, Kazakhstan, Kuwait, Kyrgyzstan, Lao People's Democratic Republic, Latvia, Lebanon, Lesotho, Libyan Arab Jamahiriya, Liechtenstein, Lithuania, Luxembourg, Madagascar, Malaysia, Maldives, Mali, Malta, Mauritania, Mauritius, Mexico, Monaco, Mongolia, Morocco, Mozambique, Myanmar, Namibia, Nepal, Netherlands, New Zealand, Nicaragua, Nigeria, Norway, Oman, Pakistan, Panama, Papua New Guinea, Paraguay, Peru, Philippines, Poland, Portugal, Qatar, Republic of Korea, Republic of Moldova, Romania, Russian Federation, Saint Lucia, Saint Vincent and the Grenadines, Samoa, San Marino, Sao Tome and Principe, Saudi Arabia, Senegal, Serbia and Montenegro, Seychelles, Sierra Leone, Singapore, Slovakia, Slovenia, Somalia, South Africa, Spain, Sri Lanka, Sudan, Suriname, Swaziland, Sweden, Switzerland, Syrian Arab Republic, Tajikistan, Thailand, The former Yugoslav Republic of Macedonia, Timor-Leste, Togo, Trinidad and Tobago, Tunisia, Turkey, Turkmenistan, Uganda, Ukraine, United Arab Emirates, United Kingdom, United Republic of Tanzania, Uruguay, Uzbekistan, Venezuela, Viet Nam, Yemen, Zambia, Zimbabwe.

Against: Israel, Palau.

Abstaining: Albania, Cameroon, Côte d'Ivoire, Dominican Republic, Equatorial Guinea, Grenada, Haiti, Kenya, Marshall Islands, Micronesia, Nauru, Tonga, Tuvalu, United States, Vanuatu.

UNDOF

The mandate of the United Nations Disengagement Observer Force, established by Security Council resolution 350(1974) [YUN 1974, p. 205] to supervise the observance of the ceasefire between Israel and the Syrian Arab Republic in the Golan Heights and ensure the separation of their forces, was renewed twice in 2004, in June and December, each time for a six-month period.

UNDOF maintained an area of separation, which was some 80 kilometres long and varied in width between approximately 12.5 kilometres in the centre to less than 400 metres in the extreme south. The area of separation was inhabited and policed by the Syrian authorities, and no military forces other than UNDOF were permitted within it.

As at 26 November, UNDOF comprised 1,039 troops from Austria (375), Canada (192), Japan (30), Poland (349), Nepal (2) and Slovakia (91). It was assisted by 77 UNTSO military observers.

The Secretary-General appointed Major General Bala Nanda Sharma (Nepal) as Force Commander [S/2004/30] to succeed Major General Franciszek Gagor (Poland), who completed his tour of duty on 16 January. The Security Council took note of the Secretary-General's intention on 14 January [S/2004/31].

Reports of Secretary-General. The Secretary-General reported to the Security Council on UNDOF activities between 9 December 2003 and 21 June 2004 [S/2004/499] and between 22 June and 7 December 2004 [S/2004/948]. Both reports noted that the UNDOF area of operation remained calm, except in the Shab'a farms area (see p. 509). UNDOF continued in 2004 to supervise the area of separation between Israeli and Syrian troops in the Golan Heights, to ensure that no military forces of either party were deployed there, by means of fixed positions and patrols. The Force, accompanied by liaison officers from the party concerned, carried out fortnightly inspections of equipment and force levels in the area of limitation. As in the past, both sides denied inspection teams access to some of their positions and imposed restrictions on the Force's freedom of movement. Mines, especially in the area of separation, continued to pose a threat to UNDOF personnel and local inhabitants. The Force assisted the International Committee of the Red Cross with mail facilities and the passage of persons through the area of separation, and supported the United Nations Children's Fund in mine-awareness activities.

The Secretary-General observed that the situation in the Middle East continued to be very tense and was likely to remain so, unless and until a comprehensive settlement covering all aspects of the problem could be reached. He hoped that determined efforts would be made by all concerned to tackle the problem in all its aspects, with a view to arriving at a just and durable peace settlement, as called for by Council resolution 338(1973) [YUN 1973, p. 213]. Stating that he considered the Force's continued presence in the area to be essential, the Secretary-General, with the agreement of both Israel and Syria, recommended in the June report that UNDOF's mandate be extended until 31 December 2004 and in the December report, until 30 June 2005.

SECURITY COUNCIL ACTION

On 29 June [meeting 4998], the Council unanimously adopted **resolution 1550(2004)**. The draft [S/2004/514] was prepared in consultations among Council members.

The Security Council,

Having considered the report of the Secretary-General of 21 June 2004 on the United Nations Disengagement Observer Force, and reaffirming its resolution 1308(2000) of 17 July 2000,

1. *Calls upon* the parties concerned to implement immediately Security Council resolution 338(1973) of 22 October 1973;

2. *Decides* to renew the mandate of the United Nations Disengagement Observer Force for a period of six months, that is, until 31 December 2004;

3. *Requests* the Secretary-General to submit, at the end of this period, a report on developments in the situation and the measures taken to implement resolution 338(1973).

On 15 December [meeting 5101], the Council unanimously adopted **resolution 1578(2004)**. The draft [S/2004/963] was prepared during consultations among Council members.

The Security Council,

Having considered the report of the Secretary-General of 7 December 2004 on the United Nations Disengagement Observer Force, and reaffirming its resolution 1308(2000) of 17 July 2000,

1. *Calls upon* the parties concerned to implement immediately its resolution 338(1973) of 22 October 1973;

2. *Decides* to renew the mandate of the United Nations Disengagement Observer Force for a period of six months, that is, until 30 June 2005;

3. *Requests* the Secretary-General to submit, at the end of this period, a report on developments in the situation and the measures taken to implement resolution 338(1973).

After the adoption of each resolution, the President, following consultations among Council members, made identical statements **S/PRST/2004/23** [meeting 4998] on 29 June and **S/PRST/2004/47** [meeting 5101] on 15 December, on behalf of the Council:

> In connection with the resolution just adopted on the renewal of the mandate of the United Nations Disengagement Observer Force, I have been authorized to make the following complementary statement on behalf of the Security Council:
>
> > As is known, the report of the Secretary-General on the United Nations Disengagement Observer Force states in paragraph 12: "... the situation in the Middle East is very tense and is likely to remain so, unless and until a comprehensive settlement covering all aspects of the Middle East problem can be reached". That statement of the Secretary-General reflects the view of the Security Council.

Financing

Reports of Secretary-General and ACABQ. On 18 December 2003, the Secretary-General presented a performance report on UNDOF's budget for 1 July 2002 to 30 June 2003 [A/58/641]. Expenditures totalled $38,975,700, against an apportionment of $38,991,800, resulting in an unencumbered balance of $16,100. On 22 December, he submitted UNDOF's budget for 1 July 2004 to 30 June 2005 [A/58/662 & Corr.1], totalling $40,902,100. On 9 February 2004, he submitted an overview report on the financing of UN peacekeeping operations: budget performance for the period from 1 July 2002 to 30 June 2003 and the budget for 1 July 2004 to 30 June 2005 [A/58/705].

ACABQ's comments and recommendations on the two December reports were contained in an April 2004 report [A/58/759/Add.7].

GENERAL ASSEMBLY ACTION

On 18 June [meeting 91], the General Assembly, on the recommendation of the Fifth Committee [A/58/827], adopted **resolution 58/306** without vote [agenda item 145 (a)].

Financing of the United Nations Disengagement Observer Force

The General Assembly,

Having considered the reports of the Secretary-General on the financing of the United Nations Disengagement Observer Force and the related reports of the Advisory Committee on Administrative and Budgetary Questions,

Recalling Security Council resolution 350(1974) of 31 May 1974 regarding the establishment of the United Nations Disengagement Observer Force and the subsequent resolutions by which the Council extended the mandate of the Force, the latest of which was resolution 1520(2003) of 22 December 2003,

Recalling also its resolution 3211 B (XXIX) of 29 November 1974 on the financing of the United Nations Emergency Force and of the United Nations Disengagement Observer Force, and its subsequent resolutions thereon, the latest of which was resolution 57/324 of 18 June 2003,

Reaffirming the general principles underlying the financing of United Nations peacekeeping operations, as stated in General Assembly resolutions 1874(S-IV) of 27 June 1963, 3101(XXVIII) of 11 December 1973 and 55/235 of 23 December 2000,

Mindful of the fact that it is essential to provide the Force with the necessary financial resources to enable it to fulfil its responsibilities under the relevant resolutions of the Security Council,

1. *Takes note* of the status of contributions to the United Nations Disengagement Observer Force as at 15 April 2004, including the contributions outstanding in the amount of 17.4 million United States dollars, representing some 1 per cent of the total assessed contributions, notes with concern that only thirty-eight Member States have paid their assessed contributions in full, and urges all other Member States, in particular those in arrears, to ensure the payment of their outstanding assessed contributions;

2. *Expresses its appreciation* to those Member States which have paid their assessed contributions in full;

3. *Expresses concern* at the financial situation with regard to peacekeeping activities, in particular as regards the reimbursements to troop contributors that bear additional burdens owing to overdue payments by Member States of their assessments;

4. *Urges* all Member States to make every possible effort to ensure payment of their assessed contributions to the Force in full;

5. *Expresses concern* at the delay experienced by the Secretary-General in deploying and providing adequate resources to some recent peacekeeping missions, in particular those in Africa;

6. *Emphasizes* that all future and existing peacekeeping missions shall be given equal and non-discriminatory treatment in respect of financial and administrative arrangements;

7. *Also emphasizes* that all peacekeeping missions shall be provided with adequate resources for the effective and efficient discharge of their respective mandates;

8. *Reiterates its request* to the Secretary-General to make the fullest possible use of facilities and equipment at the United Nations Logistics Base at Brindisi, Italy, in order to minimize the costs of procurement for the Force;

9. *Endorses* the conclusions and recommendations contained in the report of the Advisory Committee on Administrative and Budgetary Questions, except those in paragraphs 16 and 20, and requests the Secretary-General to ensure their full implementation;

10. *Authorizes* the Secretary-General to fund the 14 contractual posts mentioned in paragraph 10 of his report on the budget for the Force for the period from 1 July 2004 to 30 June 2005 through general temporary assistance, without prejudice to a future discussion and decision on the proposal, and requests the Secretary-General to resubmit with full justification this request in the context of the budget proposal for the period from 1 July 2005 to 30 June 2006, taking into account the recommendation of the Advisory Committee contained in paragraph 19 of its report;

11. *Requests* the Secretary-General to take all necessary action to ensure that the Force is administered with a maximum of efficiency and economy;

12. *Also requests* the Secretary-General, in order to reduce the cost of employing General Service staff, to continue efforts to recruit local staff for the Force against General Service posts, commensurate with the requirements of the Force;

Financial performance report for the period from 1 July 2002 to 30 June 2003

13. *Takes note* of the report of the Secretary-General on the financial performance of the Force for the period from 1 July 2002 to 30 June 2003;

Budget estimates for the period from 1 July 2004 to 30 June 2005

14. *Decides* to appropriate to the Special Account for the United Nations Disengagement Observer Force the amount of 43,033,400 dollars for the period from 1 July 2004 to 30 June 2005, inclusive of 40,902,100 dollars for the maintenance of the Force, 1,742,400 dollars for the support account for peacekeeping operations and 388,900 dollars for the United Nations Logistics Base;

Financing of the appropriation

15. *Decides also* to apportion among Member States the amount of 43,033,400 dollars at a monthly rate of 3,586,116 dollars, in accordance with the levels set out in General Assembly resolution 55/235, as adjusted by the Assembly in its resolution 55/236 of 23 December 2000 and updated in its resolution 58/256 of 23 December 2003, and taking into account the scale of assessments for 2004 and 2005, as set out in its resolution 58/1 B of 23 December 2003, subject to a decision of the Security Council to extend the mandate of the Force;

16. *Decides further* that, in accordance with the provisions of its resolution 973(X) of 15 December 1955, there shall be set off against the apportionment among

Member States, as provided for in paragraph 15 above, their respective share in the Tax Equalization Fund of 1,451,700 dollars, comprising the estimated staff assessment income of 1,175,400 dollars approved for the Force, the prorated share of 254,300 dollars of the estimated staff assessment income approved for the support account and the prorated share of 22,000 dollars of the estimated staff assessment income approved for the United Nations Logistics Base;

17. *Decides* that, for Member States that have fulfilled their financial obligations to the Force, there shall be set off against their apportionment, as provided for in paragraph 15 above, their respective share of the unencumbered balance and other income in the total amount of 1,891,100 dollars in respect of the financial period ended 30 June 2003, in accordance with the levels set out in General Assembly resolution 55/235, as adjusted by the Assembly in its resolution 55/236 and its resolution 57/290 A of 20 December 2002, and taking into account the scale of assessments for 2003, as set out in its resolutions 55/5 B of 23 December 2000 and 57/4 B of 20 December 2002;

18. *Decides also* that, for Member States that have not fulfilled their financial obligations to the Force, their respective share of the unencumbered balance and other income in the total amount of 1,891,100 dollars in respect of the financial period ended 30 June 2003 shall be set off against their outstanding obliga-tions in accordance with the scheme set out in paragraph 17 above;

19. *Decides further* that the increase of 86,600 dollars in the estimated staff assessment income in respect of the financial period ended 30 June 2003 shall be added to the credits from the amount referred to in paragraphs 17 and 18 above and that the respective shares of Member States therein shall be applied in accordance with the provisions of those paragraphs, as appropriate;

20. *Emphasizes* that no peacekeeping mission shall be financed by borrowing funds from other active peacekeeping missions;

21. *Encourages* the Secretary-General to continue to take additional measures to ensure the safety and security of all personnel under the auspices of the United Nations participating in the Force;

22. *Invites* voluntary contributions to the Force in cash and in the form of services and supplies acceptable to the Secretary-General, to be administered, as appropriate, in accordance with the procedure and practices established by the General Assembly;

23. *Decides* to include in the provisional agenda of its fifty-ninth session, under the item entitled "Financing of the United Nations peacekeeping forces in the Middle East", the sub-item entitled "United Nations Disengagement Observer Force".

Chapter VII

Disarmament

Although Member States continued to differ in 2004 on many disarmament issues, relative progress was made in addressing challenges relating to weapons of mass destruction and conventional weapons, particularly small arms and light weapons, and in promoting transparency in armaments.

The Conference on Disarmament remained unable to reach consensus on a comprehensive programme of work, and consequently did not take action on its agenda items for the sixth consecutive year. However, the Conference was able to adopt a decision on enhancing the engagement of civil society in its work. Similarly, continuing discord among Member States prevented the Disarmament Commission from reaching agreement on its substantive agenda for the 2004 session.

In April, owing to increasing concern over threats to international peace and security associated with the potential proliferation of weapons of mass destruction, the Security Council called on States to ensure compliance with their commitments under multilateral non-proliferation treaties, and established a Committee to monitor their efforts in that regard. The General Assembly reaffirmed the importance of effective verification measures in non-proliferation and other disarmament agreements and asked the Secretary-General to establish a panel of governmental experts to explore the question of verification in all its aspects.

Regarding conventional weapons, Member States maintained progress in efforts to combat the proliferation of small arms and light weapons, particularly regarding the implementation of the Programme of Action adopted by the 2001 UN Conference on the Illicit Trade in Small Arms and Light Weapons in All Its Aspects. National, regional and subregional initiatives undertaken within that framework increased significantly during the year, including the adoption and strengthening of national laws, weapons collection and destruction activities, and the establishment of arrangements for cooperation. Member States of the Economic Community of West African States began efforts to transform into a legally-binding instrument their 1998 Moratorium on the Importation, Exportation and Manufacture of Small Arms and Light Weapons in West Africa. The Protocol on the Control of Firearms, Ammunition and Other Related Materials, adopted in 2001 by member States of the Southern African Development Community, entered into force in November. The open-ended working group established in 2003 to negotiate an international instrument to help identify and trace illicit small arms and light weapons began its work and resolved to produce and circulate the first draft of the proposed instrument in early 2005. The Security Council encouraged international cooperation to prevent the diversion of small arms and light weapons to terrorist groups, particularly Al-Qaida, while the General Assembly asked the Secretary-General to continue consultations with Member States with a view to establishing no later than 2007, a group of governmental experts to consider further steps to enhance such cooperation in combating illicit brokering of those weapons.

Concerning the United Nations Register of Conventional Arms, the Secretary-General reported in July an adjustment to its scope in conformity with the recommendations of the Group of Governmental Experts that reviewed the Register's operation in 2003 and proposed measures to enhance its effectiveness and relevance.

In November, the First Review Conference of the States Parties to the Convention on the Prohibition of the Use, Stockpiling, Production and Transfer of Anti-personnel Mines and on Their Destruction (Mine-Ban Convention) reviewed the Convention's operation and status and adopted an action plan for ending the suffering caused by anti-personnel mines.

The Group of Governmental Experts established to undertake the second review since 1981 of the relationship between disarmament and development reaffirmed the findings of the 1987 Conference on the issue that, although disarmament and development had their logics and existed independently of each other, progress in one could create a conducive environment for the other.

On the bilateral level, the United States and the Russian Federation held meetings during the year to discuss the implementation of their Strategic Offensive Reductions Treaty (Moscow Treaty), which entered into force in 2003.

UN role in disarmament

UN machinery

Disarmament issues before the United Nations were considered mainly through the General Assembly and its First (Disarmament and International Security) Committee, the Disarmament Commission (a deliberative body) and the Conference on Disarmament (a multilateral negotiating forum, which met in Geneva). By **decision 59/544** of 23 December, the General Assembly took note of the First Committee's report [A/59/618].

The Department for Disarmament Affairs of the UN Secretariat continued to support the work of Member States and treaty bodies, to service the Advisory Board on Disarmament Matters and to administer the UN disarmament fellowship programme.

Fourth special session devoted to disarmament

The General Assembly had decided, by resolution 51/45 C [YUN 1996, p. 447], to convene its fourth special session devoted to disarmament in 1999, subject to the emergence of consensus on its agenda and objectives, which had not been achieved.

In 2004, the Assembly established an open-ended working group (see below) to consider, on the basis of consensus, the objectives and agenda of the special session and asked it to report on its work before the end of the Assembly's sixtieth session. A similar working group established previously, which completed its work in 2003 [YUN 2003, p. 530], had not been able to reach consensus on the issue.

GENERAL ASSEMBLY ACTION

On 3 December [meeting 66], the General Assembly, on the recommendation of the First Committee [A/59/459 & Corr.1], adopted **resolution 59/71** without vote [agenda item 65 *(dd)*].

Convening of the fourth special session of the General Assembly devoted to disarmament

The General Assembly,

Recalling its resolutions 49/75 I of 15 December 1994, 50/70 F of 12 December 1995, 51/45 C of 10 December 1996, 52/38 F of 9 December 1997, 53/77 AA of 4 December 1998, 54/54 U of 1 December 1999, 55/33 M of 20 November 2000, 56/24 D of 29 November 2001 and 57/61 of 22 November 2002 and its decision 58/521 of 8 December 2003,

Recalling also that, there being a consensus to do so in each case, three special sessions of the General Assembly devoted to disarmament were held in 1978, 1982 and 1988,

Bearing in mind the Final Document of the Tenth Special Session of the General Assembly, adopted by consensus at the first special session devoted to disarmament,

Bearing in mind also the ultimate objective of general and complete disarmament under effective international control,

Taking note of paragraph 98 of the Final Document of the Thirteenth Conference of Heads of State or Government of Non-Aligned Countries, held at Kuala Lumpur from 20 to 25 February 2003, and paragraph 91 of the Final Document of the Fourteenth Ministerial Conference of the Movement of Non-Aligned Countries, held at Durban, South Africa, from 17 to 19 August 2004, which supported the convening of the fourth special session of the General Assembly devoted to disarmament, which would offer an opportunity to review, from a perspective more in tune with the current international situation, the most critical aspects of the process of disarmament and to mobilize the international community and public opinion in favour of the elimination of nuclear and other weapons of mass destruction and of the control and reduction of conventional weapons,

Recalling the United Nations Millennium Declaration, adopted by the Heads of State and Government during the Millennium Summit of the United Nations, held in New York from 6 to 8 September 2000, in which they resolved "to strive for the elimination of weapons of mass destruction, particularly nuclear weapons, and to keep all options open for achieving this aim, including the possibility of convening an international conference to identify ways of eliminating nuclear dangers",

Reiterating its conviction that a special session of the General Assembly devoted to disarmament can set the future course of action in the fields of disarmament, arms control, non-proliferation and related international security matters,

Emphasizing the importance of multilateralism in the process of disarmament, arms control, non-proliferation and related international security matters,

Taking note of the report of the Open-ended Working Group to consider the objectives and agenda, including the possible establishment of the preparatory committee, for the fourth special session of the General Assembly devoted to disarmament,

1. *Decides* to establish an open-ended working group, working on the basis of consensus, to consider the objectives and agenda, including the possible establishment of the preparatory committee, for the fourth special session of the General Assembly devoted to disarmament, taking note of the paper presented by the Chairman of Working Group II during the 1999 substantive session of the Disarmament Commission and the written proposals and views submitted by Member States as contained in the working papers presented during the three substantive sessions of the Open-ended Working Group in 2003, as well as the reports of the Secretary-General regarding the views of Member States on the objectives, agenda and timing of the fourth special session of the General Assembly devoted to disarmament;

2. *Requests* the Open-ended Working Group to hold an organizational session in order to set the dates for its substantive sessions in 2006, and to submit a report on its work, including possible substantive recommendations, before the end of the sixtieth session of the General Assembly;

3. *Requests* the Secretary-General, within existing resources, to provide the Open-ended Working Group with the necessary assistance and services as may be required to discharge its tasks;

4. *Decides* to include in the provisional agenda of its sixtieth session the item entitled "Convening of the fourth special session of the General Assembly devoted to disarmament".

Disarmament Commission

In 2004, the Disarmament Commission, composed of all UN Member States, held nine formal and five informal meetings (New York, 5-23 April) [A/59/42] and an organizational meeting on 22 December [A/60/42], at which the Commission discussed possible agenda items, including issues relating to nuclear disarmament (see p. 528) and conventional disarmament (see p. 564). Proposals in that regard were submitted by Indonesia, on behalf of the Non-Aligned Movement; Ireland, on behalf of the European Union (EU); and the United States, which also proposed measures for improving the effectiveness of the UN disarmament machinery. Deliberations revealed a wide gap among delegations on agenda items, and, in efforts to narrow the gap, the Chairman presented a new proposal that drew from others, to serve as a basis for discussion; however, the Commission was unable to reach agreement on its substantive agenda. On 23 April, the Commission decided to continue deliberations on agenda items for its 2005 session, and requested its Chairman to continue informal consultations and to present the outcome to the Commission's organizational meeting in December 2004.

GENERAL ASSEMBLY ACTION

On 3 December [meeting 66], the General Assembly, on the recommendation of the First Committee [A/59/461], adopted **resolution 59/105** without vote [agenda item 67 (d)].

Report of the Disarmament Commission

The General Assembly,

Having considered the report of the Disarmament Commission,

Recalling its resolutions 47/54 A of 9 December 1992, 47/54 G of 8 April 1993, 48/77 A of 16 December 1993, 49/77 A of 15 December 1994, 50/72 D of 12 December 1995, 51/47 B of 10 December 1996, 52/40 B of 9 December 1997, 53/79 A of 4 December 1998, 54/56 A of 1 December 1999, 55/35 C of 20 November 2000, 56/26 A of 29 November 2001, 57/95 of 22 November 2002 and 58/67 of 8 December 2003,

Considering the role that the Disarmament Commission has been called upon to play and the contribution that it should make in examining and submitting recommendations on various problems in the field of disarmament and in the promotion of the implementation of the relevant decisions adopted by the General Assembly at its tenth special session,

Bearing in mind its decision 52/492 of 8 September 1998,

1. *Takes note* of the report of the Disarmament Commission;

2. *Reaffirms* the importance of further enhancing the dialogue and cooperation among the First Committee of the General Assembly, the Disarmament Commission and the Conference on Disarmament;

3. *Also reaffirms* the role of the Disarmament Commission as the specialized, deliberative body within the United Nations multilateral disarmament machinery that allows for in-depth deliberations on specific disarmament issues, leading to the submission of concrete recommendations on those issues;

4. *Requests* the Disarmament Commission to continue its work in accordance with its mandate, as set forth in paragraph 118 of the Final Document of the Tenth Special Session of the General Assembly, and with paragraph 3 of Assembly resolution 37/78 H of 9 December 1982, and to that end to make every effort to achieve specific recommendations on the items on its agenda, taking into account the adopted "Ways and means to enhance the functioning of the Disarmament Commission";

5. *Recommends* that the Disarmament Commission consider the following items at its 2005 substantive session:

   (*a*) [To be determined];

   (*b*) [To be determined];

6. *Requests* the Disarmament Commission to meet for a period not exceeding three weeks during 2005, namely, from 18 July to 5 August, and to submit a substantive report to the General Assembly at its sixtieth session;

7. *Requests* the Secretary-General to transmit to the Disarmament Commission the annual report of the Conference on Disarmament, together with all the official records of the fifty-ninth session of the General Assembly relating to disarmament matters, and to render all assistance that the Commission may require for implementing the present resolution;

8. *Also requests* the Secretary-General to ensure full provision to the Disarmament Commission and its subsidiary bodies of interpretation and translation facilities in the official languages and to assign, as a matter of priority, all the necessary resources and services, including verbatim records, to that end;

9. *Decides* to include in the provisional agenda of its sixtieth session the item entitled "Report of the Disarmament Commission".

Conference on Disarmament

The Conference on Disarmament, a multilateral negotiating body, held a three-part session in Geneva in 2004 (19 January–26 March, 10 May–25 June and 26 July–8 September) [A/59/27].

The Conference continued to consider the cessation of the nuclear arms race and nuclear disarmament; prevention of nuclear war; prevention of an arms race in outer space; effective international arrangements to assure non-nuclear-weapon States against the use or threat of use of nuclear weapons; new types of weapons of mass destruction (WMDs) and new systems of such weapons; radiological weapons; a comprehensive programme of disarmament; and transparency in armaments.

Besides the continuing lack of consensus on a programme of work, which had undermined progress in the Conference for many years, another area of disagreement in 2004 was how to approach new issues that could be relevant to the current international environment, particularly terrorism and WMDs and compliance with arms control and disarmament agreements. A number of Member States expressed interest in addressing those issues without including them in the agenda. Subsequently, the Conference considered them in informal plenary meetings as "additional issues". In efforts to resolve the impasse on a programme of work, successive Presidents of the Conference held consultations, at which a number of informal proposals on the work programme were considered. Deliberations were based mainly on the 2003 cross-group proposal put forward by five former Presidents ("A-5 proposal") [YUN 2003, p. 531], which many members regarded as the most promising solution. While a number of delegations advocated a comprehensive approach to the work programme as a guarantee for addressing the security concerns of all States, others criticized such linking of issues. The Conference concluded its 2004 session without resolving the deadlock and, once again, did not set up any mechanism to deal with its agenda items. Nonetheless, members were able to take a decision on enhancing the engagement of civil society in the Conference's work. The Conference decided to hold its 2005 session between January and September and requested its current President and incoming President to hold consultations during the intersessional period and make recommendations, taking into account all proposals.

GENERAL ASSEMBLY ACTION

On 3 December [meeting 66], the General Assembly, on the recommendation of the First Committee [A/59/461], adopted **resolution 59/104** without vote [agenda item 67].

Report of the Conference on Disarmament

The General Assembly,

Having considered the report of the Conference on Disarmament,

Convinced that the Conference on Disarmament, as the single multilateral disarmament negotiating forum of the international community, has the primary role in substantive negotiations on priority questions of disarmament,

Recognizing the need to conduct multilateral negotiations with the aim of reaching agreement on concrete issues,

Recalling, in this respect, that the Conference has a number of urgent and important issues for negotiation,

Taking note of active discussions held on the programme of work during the 2004 session of the Conference, as duly reflected in the report and the records of the plenary meetings,

Taking note also of significant contributions made during the 2004 session to promote substantive discussions on issues on the agenda, as well as of discussions held on other issues that could also be relevant to the current international security environment,

Stressing the urgent need for the Conference to commence its substantive work at the beginning of its 2005 session,

Taking note of the decision reached on 12 February 2004 with regard to enhancement of the engagement of civil society in the work of the Conference and the statement by the President made thereafter,

1. *Reaffirms* the role of the Conference on Disarmament as the single multilateral disarmament negotiating forum of the international community;

2. *Calls upon* the Conference to intensify consultations and explore possibilities with a view to reaching an agreement on a programme of work;

3. *Takes note* of the strong collective interest of the Conference in commencing substantive work as soon as possible during its 2005 session;

4. *Welcomes* the decision of the Conference to request its current President and the incoming President to conduct consultations during the intersessional period and, if possible, to make recommendations, taking into account all relevant proposals, including those submitted as the documents of the Conference, views presented and discussions held, and to endeavour to keep the membership of the Conference informed, as appropriate, of their consultations, as expressed in paragraph 46 of its report;

5. *Requests* all States members of the Conference to cooperate with the current President and successive Presidents in their efforts to guide the Conference to the early commencement of substantive work in its 2005 session;

6. *Requests* the Secretary-General to continue to ensure the provision to the Conference of adequate administrative, substantive and conference support services;

7. *Requests* the Conference to submit a report on its work to the General Assembly at its sixtieth session;

8. *Decides* to include in the provisional agenda of its sixtieth session the item entitled "Report of the Conference on Disarmament".

Multilateral disarmament agreements

As at 31 December 2004, the following numbers of States had become parties to the multilateral agreements listed below (in chronological order, with the years in which they were initially signed or opened for signature).

(Geneva) Protocol for the Prohibition of the Use in War of Asphyxiating, Poisonous or Other Gases, and of Bacteriological Methods of Warfare (1925): 133 parties

The Antarctic Treaty (1959): 45 parties

Treaty Banning Nuclear Weapon Tests in the Atmosphere, in Outer Space and under Water (1963): 124 parties

Treaty on Principles Governing the Activities of States in the Exploration and Use of Outer Space, including the Moon and Other Celestial Bodies (1967) [YUN 1966, p. 41, GA res. 2222(XXI), annex]: 98 parties

Treaty for the Prohibition of Nuclear Weapons in Latin America and the Caribbean (Treaty of Tlatelolco) (1967): 39 parties

Treaty on the Non-Proliferation of Nuclear Weapons (1968) [YUN 1968, p. 17, GA res. 2373(XXII), annex]: 189 parties

Treaty on the Prohibition of the Emplacement of Nuclear Weapons and Other Weapons of Mass Destruction on the Seabed and the Ocean Floor and in the Subsoil Thereof (1971) [YUN 1970, p. 18, GA res. 2660(XXV), annex]: 92 parties

Convention on the Prohibition of the Development, Production and Stockpiling of Bacteriological (Biological) and Toxin Weapons and on Their Destruction (1972) [YUN 1971, p. 19, GA res 2826 (XXVI), annex]: 153 parties

Convention on the Prohibition of Military or Any Other Hostile Use of Environmental Modification Techniques (1977) [YUN 1976, p. 45, GA res. 31/72, annex]: 69 parties

Agreement Governing the Activities of States on the Moon and Other Celestial Bodies (1979) [YUN 1979, p. 111, GA res. 34/68, annex]: 11 parties

Convention on Prohibitions or Restrictions on the Use of Certain Conventional Weapons Which May Be Deemed to Be Excessively Injurious or to Have Indiscriminate Effects (1981): 97 parties

South Pacific Nuclear Free Zone Treaty (Treaty of Rarotonga) (1985): 17 parties

Treaty on Conventional Armed Forces in Europe (CFE Treaty) (1990): 30 parties

Treaty on Open Skies (1992): 31 parties

Convention on the Prohibition of the Development, Production, Stockpiling and Use of Chemical Weapons and on Their Destruction (1993): 166 parties

Treaty on the South-East Asia Nuclear-Weapon-Free Zone (Bangkok Treaty) (1995): 10 parties

African Nuclear-Weapon-Free Zone Treaty (Pelindaba Treaty) (1996): 22 parties

Comprehensive Nuclear-Test-Ban Treaty (1996): 120 parties

Inter-American Convention against the Illicit Manufacturing of and Trafficking in Firearms, Ammunition, Explosives, and Other Related Materials (1997): 26 parties

Convention on the Prohibition of the Use, Stockpiling, Production and Transfer of Anti-personnel Mines and on Their Destruction (Mine-Ban Convention, formerly known as Ottawa Convention) (1997): 144 parties

Inter-American Convention on Transparency in Conventional Weapons Acquisitions (1999): 9 parties

Agreement on Adaptation of the CFE Treaty (1999): 3 parties

[*The United Nations Disarmament Yearbook*, vol. 29: *2004*, Sales No. E.05.IX.1]

Nuclear disarmament

Conference on Disarmament

In 2004, the Conference on Disarmament was not able to establish any subsidiary body to deal with nuclear disarmament owing to the continuing lack of agreement on a programme of work (see p. 524). Consequently, the question of nuclear disarmament was addressed only at plenary meetings, where delegations reaffirmed or further elaborated their respective positions on the item. Concerns were expressed about the proliferation of WMDs, especially nuclear weapons and related technologies; underscored was the importance of Security Council resolutions 1373 (2001) on measures to eliminate international terrorism [YUN 2001, p. 61] and 1540(2004) on the non-proliferation of WMDs (see p. 544).

Fissile material

In 2004, as in previous years, difficulties in reaching agreement on a comprehensive programme of work (see p. 524) that would take into account Member States' negotiating priorities, prevented the Conference on Disarmament from establishing an ad hoc committee to consider the issue of the prohibition of the production of fissile material for nuclear weapons and other nuclear explosive devices. Nonetheless, the issue was addressed during plenary meetings and an informal meeting, at which delegations reaffirmed their views on the subject. While countries of the Non-Aligned Movement emphasized that any treaty on that subject should include existing stockpiles of such material, others, mostly Western States and China, supported the United States new position, which, while reaffirming commitment to negotiations on a legally binding treaty banning the production of fissile material for nuclear weapons and other nuclear explosive devices, raised concerns about effective verification. The President of the Conference drew attention to a proposal for establishing an expert group to address related technical issues [CD/1734].

On 3 December [meeting 66], the General Assembly, on the recommendation of the First Committee [A/59/459 & Corr.1], adopted **resolution 59/81** by recorded vote (179-2-2) [agenda item 65].

The Conference on Disarmament decision (CD/1547) of 11 August 1998 to establish, under item 1 of its agenda entitled "Cessation of the nuclear arms race and nuclear disarmament", an ad hoc committee to negotiate, on the basis of the report of the Special Coordinator (CD/1299) and the mandate contained therein, a non-discriminatory, multilateral and internationally and effectively verifiable treaty banning the production of fissile material for nuclear weapons or other nuclear explosive devices

The General Assembly,

Recalling its resolutions 48/75 L of 16 December 1993, 53/77 I of 4 December 1998, 55/33 Y of 20 November 2000, 56/24 J of 29 November 2001, 57/80 of 22 November 2002 and 58/57 of 8 December 2003,

Convinced that a non-discriminatory, multilateral and internationally and effectively verifiable treaty banning the production of fissile material for nuclear weapons or other nuclear explosive devices would be a significant contribution to nuclear disarmament and nuclear non-proliferation,

Recalling the 1998 report of the Conference on Disarmament, in which, inter alia, the Conference recorded that, in proceeding to take a decision on this matter, that decision was without prejudice to any further decisions on the establishment of further subsidiary bodies under agenda item 1 and that intensive consultations would be pursued to seek the views of the members of the Conference on Disarmament on appropriate methods and approaches for dealing with agenda item 1, taking into consideration all proposals and views in that respect,

1. *Recalls* the decision of the Conference on Disarmament to establish, under item 1 of its agenda entitled "Cessation of the nuclear arms race and nuclear disarmament", an ad hoc committee which shall negotiate, on the basis of the report of the Special Coordinator and the mandate contained therein, a non-discriminatory, multilateral and internationally and effectively verifiable treaty banning the production of fissile material for nuclear weapons or other nuclear explosive devices;

2. *Urges* the Conference on Disarmament to agree on a programme of work that includes the immediate commencement of negotiations on such a treaty.

RECORDED VOTE ON RESOLUTION 59/81:

In favour: Afghanistan, Albania, Algeria, Andorra, Angola, Antigua and Barbuda, Argentina, Armenia, Australia, Austria, Azerbaijan, Bahamas, Bahrain, Bangladesh, Barbados, Belarus, Belgium, Belize, Benin, Bhutan, Bolivia, Bosnia and Herzegovina, Botswana, Brazil, Brunei Darussalam, Bulgaria, Burkina Faso, Burundi, Cambodia, Cameroon, Canada, Cape Verde, Central African Republic, Chile, China, Colombia, Comoros, Congo, Costa Rica, Côte d'Ivoire, Croatia, Cuba, Cyprus, Czech Republic, Denmark, Djibouti, Dominica, Dominican Republic, Ecuador, Egypt, El Salvador, Equatorial Guinea, Eritrea, Estonia, Ethiopia, Fiji, Finland, France, Gabon, Gambia, Georgia, Germany, Ghana, Greece, Grenada, Guatemala, Guinea-Bissau, Guyana, Haiti, Honduras, Hungary,

Iceland, India, Indonesia, Iran, Iraq, Ireland, Italy, Jamaica, Japan, Jordan, Kazakhstan, Kenya, Kuwait, Kyrgyzstan, Lao People's Democratic Republic, Latvia, Lebanon, Lesotho, Liberia, Libyan Arab Jamahiriya, Liechtenstein, Lithuania, Luxembourg, Madagascar, Malawi, Malaysia, Maldives, Mali, Malta, Marshall Islands, Mauritius, Mexico, Micronesia, Monaco, Mongolia, Morocco, Mozambique, Myanmar, Namibia, Nauru, Nepal, Netherlands, New Zealand, Nicaragua, Niger, Nigeria, Norway, Oman, Pakistan, Panama, Papua New Guinea, Paraguay, Peru, Philippines, Poland, Portugal, Qatar, Republic of Korea, Republic of Moldova, Romania, Russian Federation, Rwanda, Saint Lucia, Saint Vincent and the Grenadines, Samoa, San Marino, Sao Tome and Principe, Saudi Arabia, Senegal, Serbia and Montenegro, Seychelles, Sierra Leone, Singapore, Slovakia, Slovenia, Solomon Islands, Somalia, South Africa, Spain, Sri Lanka, Sudan, Suriname, Swaziland, Sweden, Switzerland, Syrian Arab Republic, Tajikistan, Thailand, The former Yugoslav Republic of Macedonia, Timor-Leste, Togo, Tonga, Trinidad and Tobago, Tunisia, Turkey, Tuvalu, Uganda, Ukraine, United Arab Emirates, United Republic of Tanzania, Uruguay, Uzbekistan, Vanuatu, Venezuela, Viet Nam, Yemen, Zambia, Zimbabwe.

Against: Palau, United States.

Abstaining: Israel, United Kingdom.

Security assurances

The Conference on Disarmament addressed the issue of security assurances for non-nuclear-weapon States against the use or threat of use of nuclear weapons. During plenary meetings, delegations reaffirmed or further elaborated their respective positions on the item. Many non-nuclear-weapon States emphasized their interest in a binding instrument to provide them with security assurances, which they noted would strengthen the nuclear non-proliferation regime.

On 3 December [meeting 66], the General Assembly, on the recommendation of the First Committee [A/59/457], adopted **resolution 59/64** by recorded vote (118-0-63) [agenda item 63].

Conclusion of effective international arrangements to assure non-nuclear-weapon States against the use or threat of use of nuclear weapons

The General Assembly,

Bearing in mind the need to allay the legitimate concern of the States of the world with regard to ensuring lasting security for their peoples,

Convinced that nuclear weapons pose the greatest threat to mankind and to the survival of civilization,

Welcoming the progress achieved in recent years in both nuclear and conventional disarmament,

Noting that, despite recent progress in the field of nuclear disarmament, further efforts are necessary towards the achievement of general and complete disarmament under effective international control,

Convinced that nuclear disarmament and the complete elimination of nuclear weapons are essential to remove the danger of nuclear war,

Determined to abide strictly by the relevant provisions of the Charter of the United Nations on the non-use of force or threat of force,

Recognizing that the independence, territorial integrity and sovereignty of non-nuclear-weapon States need to be safeguarded against the use or threat of use of force, including the use or threat of use of nuclear weapons,

Considering that, until nuclear disarmament is achieved on a universal basis, it is imperative for the international community to develop effective measures and arrangements to ensure the security of non-nuclear-weapon States against the use or threat of use of nuclear weapons from any quarter,

Recognizing that effective measures and arrangements to assure non-nuclear-weapon States against the use or threat of use of nuclear weapons can contribute positively to the prevention of the spread of nuclear weapons,

Bearing in mind paragraph 59 of the Final Document of the Tenth Special Session of the General Assembly, the first special session devoted to disarmament, in which it urged the nuclear-weapon States to pursue efforts to conclude, as appropriate, effective arrangements to assure non-nuclear-weapon States against the use or threat of use of nuclear weapons, and desirous of promoting the implementation of the relevant provisions of the Final Document,

Recalling the relevant parts of the special report of the Committee on Disarmament submitted to the General Assembly at its twelfth special session, the second special session devoted to disarmament, and of the special report of the Conference on Disarmament submitted to the Assembly at its fifteenth special session, the third special session devoted to disarmament, as well as the report of the Conference on its 1992 session,

Recalling also paragraph 12 of the Declaration of the 1980s as the Second Disarmament Decade, contained in the annex to its resolution 35/46 of 3 December 1980, which states, inter alia, that all efforts should be exerted by the Committee on Disarmament urgently to negotiate with a view to reaching agreement on effective international arrangements to assure non-nuclear-weapon States against the use or threat of use of nuclear weapons,

Noting the in-depth negotiations undertaken in the Conference on Disarmament and its Ad Hoc Committee on Effective International Arrangements to Assure Non-Nuclear-Weapon States against the Use or Threat of Use of Nuclear Weapons, with a view to reaching agreement on this question,

Taking note of the proposals submitted under the item in the Conference on Disarmament, including the drafts of an international convention,

Taking note also of the relevant decision of the Thirteenth Conference of Heads of State or Government of Non-Aligned Countries, held in Kuala Lumpur from 20 to 25 February 2003, as well as the relevant recommendations of the Organization of the Islamic Conference,

Taking note further of the unilateral declarations made by all the nuclear-weapon States on their policies of non-use or non–threat of use of nuclear weapons against the non-nuclear-weapon States,

Noting the support expressed in the Conference on Disarmament and in the General Assembly for the elaboration of an international convention to assure non-nuclear-weapon States against the use or threat of use of nuclear weapons, as well as the difficulties pointed out in evolving a common approach acceptable to all,

Taking note of Security Council resolution 984(1995) of 11 April 1995 and the views expressed on it,

Recalling its relevant resolutions adopted in previous years, in particular resolutions 45/54 of 4 December 1990, 46/32 of 6 December 1991, 47/50 of 9 December 1992, 48/73 of 16 December 1993, 49/73 of 15 December 1994, 50/68 of 12 December 1995, 51/43 of 10 December 1996, 52/36 of 9 December 1997, 53/75 of 4 December 1998, 54/52 of 1 December 1999, 55/31 of 20 November 2000, 56/22 of 29 November 2001, 57/56 of 22 November 2002 and 58/35 of 8 December 2003,

1. *Reaffirms* the urgent need to reach an early agreement on effective international arrangements to assure non-nuclear-weapon States against the use or threat of use of nuclear weapons;

2. *Notes with satisfaction* that in the Conference on Disarmament there is no objection, in principle, to the idea of an international convention to assure non-nuclear-weapon States against the use or threat of use of nuclear weapons, although the difficulties with regard to evolving a common approach acceptable to all have also been pointed out;

3. *Appeals* to all States, especially the nuclear-weapon States, to work actively towards an early agreement on a common approach and, in particular, on a common formula that could be included in an international instrument of a legally binding character;

4. *Recommends* that further intensive efforts be devoted to the search for such a common approach or common formula and that the various alternative approaches, including, in particular, those considered in the Conference on Disarmament, be explored further in order to overcome the difficulties;

5. *Also recommends* that the Conference on Disarmament actively continue intensive negotiations with a view to reaching early agreement and concluding effective international arrangements to assure the non-nuclear-weapon States against the use or threat of use of nuclear weapons, taking into account the widespread support for the conclusion of an international convention and giving consideration to any other proposals designed to secure the same objective;

6. *Decides* to include in the provisional agenda of its sixtieth session the item entitled "Conclusion of effective international arrangements to assure non-nuclear-weapon States against the use or threat of use of nuclear weapons".

RECORDED VOTE ON RESOLUTION 59/64:

In favour: Afghanistan, Algeria, Angola, Antigua and Barbuda, Azerbaijan, Bahamas, Bahrain, Bangladesh, Barbados, Belize, Benin, Bhutan, Brunei Darussalam, Burkina Faso, Burundi, Cambodia, Cameroon, Cape Verde, Central African Republic, China, Colombia, Comoros, Congo, Costa Rica, Côte d'Ivoire, Cuba, Democratic People's Republic of Korea, Djibouti, Dominica, Dominican Republic, Ecuador, Egypt, El Salvador, Equatorial Guinea, Eritrea, Ethiopia, Gabon, Gambia, Ghana, Grenada, Guatemala, Guinea-Bissau, Guyana, Honduras, India, Indonesia, Iran, Iraq, Jamaica, Japan, Jordan, Kazakhstan, Kenya, Kuwait, Kyrgyzstan, Lao People's Democratic Republic, Lebanon, Lesotho, Liberia, Libyan Arab Jamahiriya, Madagascar, Malawi, Malaysia, Maldives, Mali, Mauritius, Mexico, Mongolia, Morocco, Mozambique, Myanmar, Namibia, Nepal, Nicaragua, Niger, Nigeria, Oman, Pakistan, Panama, Paraguay, Peru, Philippines, Qatar, Rwanda, Saint Kitts and Nevis, Saint Lucia, Saint Vincent and the Grenadines, Samoa, Sao Tome and Principe, Saudi Arabia, Senegal, Sierra Leone, Singapore, Somalia, South Africa, Sri Lanka, Sudan, Suriname, Swaziland, Syrian Arab Republic, Thailand, Timor-Leste, Togo, Tonga, Trinidad and Tobago, Tunisia, Turkmenistan, Uganda, Ukraine, United Arab Emirates, United Republic of Tanzania, Uruguay, Uzbekistan, Venezuela, Viet Nam, Yemen, Zambia, Zimbabwe.

Against: None.

Abstaining: Albania, Andorra, Argentina, Armenia, Australia, Austria, Belarus, Belgium, Bolivia, Bosnia and Herzegovina, Brazil, Bulgaria, Canada, Chile, Croatia, Cyprus, Czech Republic, Denmark, Estonia, Fiji, Finland, France, Germany, Greece, Haiti, Hungary, Iceland, Ireland, Israel, Italy, Liechtenstein, Lithuania, Luxembourg, Malta, Marshall Islands, Micronesia, Monaco, Nauru, Netherlands, New Zealand, Norway, Palau,

Poland, Portugal, Republic of Korea, Republic of Moldova, Romania, Russian Federation, San Marino, Serbia and Montenegro, Slovakia, Slovenia, Solomon Islands, Spain, Sweden, Switzerland, Tajikistan, The former Yugoslav Republic of Macedonia, Turkey, Tuvalu, United Kingdom, United States, Vanuatu.

Disarmament Commission

In April [A/59/42], the Disarmament Commission, while deliberating on possible agenda items on nuclear disarmament, considered conference room papers on related topics and the Chairman's proposal on guidelines for nuclear disarmament and non-proliferation of nuclear weapons in all its aspects, including, in particular, strategies for dealing with illicit activities that undermined nuclear disarmament and non-proliferation objectives. However, the Commission was not able to reach agreement on its substantive agenda for 2004 and decided to continue deliberations in 2005 on its agenda (see p. 523).

START and other bilateral agreements and unilateral measures

In an 11 February statement [CD/1728] to the National Defense University (Washington, D.C.), transmitted to the Conference on Disarmament, United States President George W. Bush announced seven proposals for strengthening global efforts to combat the spread of WMDs, including direct action against proliferation networks and measures to strengthen the regime set up by the Treaty on the Non-Proliferation of Nuclear Weapons (NPT) (see p. 542) and related activities of the International Atomic Energy Agency (IAEA) (see p. 1481). On 13 February [CD/1732], the Foreign Minister of Malaysia expressed disappointment that Mr. Bush, in that statement, appeared to question the commitment of his Government on nuclear non-proliferation.

The Bilateral Implementation Commission, established by the 2002 Strategic Offensive Reductions Treaty (SORT), or the Moscow Treaty [YUN 2002, p. 493] between the United States and the Russian Federation, which entered into force in 2003 [YUN 2003, p. 535], held its first meeting (Geneva, 8-9 April) to discuss both sides' efforts to implement the Treaty. Senior officials from the two countries held additional meetings during the year for that purpose. Both sides announced that they would continue to consider, within the context of their implementation of the 1991 Treaty on the Reduction and Limitation of Strategic Offensive Arms (START I) [YUN 1991, p. 34] and 1993 START II process [YUN 1993, p. 117], the possible extension of SORT beyond its current expiration date of 31 December 2012.

The United States Secretary of Energy, at a meeting with IAEA officials (Vienna, 26 May),

launched the Global Threat Reduction Initiative (GTRI), designed to secure and remove high-risk nuclear and radiological materials that posed a threat to the United States and the international community. Later in the year, the United States and the Russian Federation, with IAEA support, convened a GTRI Partners Conference in Vienna to discuss the collection and security of proliferation-attractive materials and to review GTRI. The Conference recommended that IAEA member States work with the Agency to coordinate a mechanism to address opportunities for implementing related projects.

The heads of State and Government of member countries of the North Atlantic Treaty Organization (NATO), at their summit meeting (Istanbul, Turkey, 28-29 June), welcomed seven new members (Bulgaria, Estonia, Latvia, Lithuania, Romania, Slovakia and Slovenia) and issued the Istanbul Declaration on "our security in a new era", by which they renewed commitment to addressing threats facing NATO, including terrorism (see p. 576) and the proliferation of WMDs (see p. 543). In the Istanbul Summit Communiqué, they reaffirmed that NATO policy of support for arms control, disarmament and non-proliferation would continue to play a major role in the achievement of security objectives.

Report of Secretary-General. In response to General Assembly resolutions 58/46 [YUN 2003, p. 552], 58/47 [ibid., p. 536], 58/51 [ibid., p. 538] and 58/56 [ibid., p. 541], the Secretary-General, in a September report [A/59/136], assessed progress made in addressing nuclear disarmament issues. He observed that nuclear disarmament and non-proliferation remained priority issues for international peace and security and that the international community faced continuing dangers from the acquisition, possession and possible use of WMDs, including nuclear weapons. Reducing such threats required efforts at the unilateral, bilateral and multilateral levels. Unilateral measures to reduce existing nuclear arsenals by nuclear-weapon States were essential, and some progress had been made in that regard. Steady implementation of the Moscow Treaty by the Russian Federation and the United States would help strengthen international peace and security. At the same time, it was important for the international community to strengthen arms control and disarmament agreements by achieving universal adherence to them and implementing them. Reflecting on the status of NPT, which remained the cornerstone of the non-proliferation regime, (see p. 542) and on related challenges, particularly regarding preparations for the upcoming Review Conference of States parties in 2005, the Secretary-General noted that a successful outcome at the Conference would be critical in maintaining the validity of the regime. He advocated measures to achieve the entry into force of the Comprehensive Nuclear-Test-Ban Treaty (see p. 538), revitalize the Conference on Disarmament (see p. 523) and explore ways to implement the recommendations contained in the 2001 report of the Advisory Board on Disarmament Matters [YUN 2001, p. 474] on measures that might reduce the risk of nuclear war. Remarking that the threat of proliferation of WMDs, their means of delivery and related materials had increased the challenges to multilateral disarmament efforts, the Secretary-General declared the Organization's commitment to assist Member States in tackling the problems.

Communications. The Ministers attending the Fourteenth Ministerial Conference of the Non-Aligned Movement (Durban, South Africa, 17-19 August) expressed concern at strategic defence doctrines that set out rationales for the use of nuclear weapons, and at the slow pace of progress with nuclear disarmament, which they described as their highest priority. They underscored the need for nuclear-weapon States to implement the commitments made at the 2000 NPT Review Conference [YUN 2000, p. 487], so as to accomplish the total elimination of nuclear weapons.

The Foreign Ministers of States members of the Organization of the Islamic Conference (New York, 28 September) [A/59/425-S/2004/808] reaffirmed the need to promote multilateral diplomacy in resolving disarmament and non-proliferation concerns and underlined that multilateral institutions established under UN auspices were the sole legitimate bodies to ensure compliance with relevant international agreements.

GENERAL ASSEMBLY ACTION

On 3 December [meeting 66], the General Assembly, on the recommendation of the First Committee [A/59/459 & Corr.1], adopted five resolutions and one decision related to nuclear disarmament. The Assembly adopted **resolution 59/75** by recorded vote (151-6-24) [agenda item 65 (t)].

Accelerating the implementation of nuclear disarmament commitments

The General Assembly,

Recalling its resolution 58/51 of 8 December 2003, and mindful of the upcoming 2005 Review Conference of the Parties to the Treaty on the Non-Proliferation of Nuclear Weapons,

Expressing its grave concern at the danger to humanity posed by the possibility that nuclear weapons could be used and at the lack of implementation of binding obligations and agreed steps towards nuclear disarmament, and reaffirming that nuclear disarmament and nuclear non-proliferation are mutually reinforcing processes requiring urgent irreversible progress on both fronts,

Recalling the unequivocal undertaking by the nuclear-weapon States to accomplish the total elimination of their nuclear arsenals, leading to nuclear disarmament, in accordance with commitments made under article VI of the Treaty on the Non-Proliferation of Nuclear Weapons, and noting that the ultimate objective of the disarmament process is general and complete disarmament under strict and effective international control,

1. *Calls upon* all States to comply fully with commitments made regarding nuclear disarmament and nuclear non-proliferation and not to act in any way that may be detrimental to nuclear disarmament and non-proliferation or that may lead to a new nuclear arms race;

2. *Also calls upon* all States to spare no efforts to achieve universal adherence to the Treaty on the Non-Proliferation of Nuclear Weapons and the early entry into force of the Comprehensive Nuclear-Test-Ban Treaty;

3. *Calls upon* all States parties to the Treaty on the Non-Proliferation of Nuclear Weapons to accelerate the implementation of the practical steps for systematic and progressive efforts to achieve nuclear disarmament that were agreed upon at the 2000 Review Conference of the Parties to the Treaty on the Non-Proliferation of Nuclear Weapons;

4. *Calls upon* the nuclear-weapon States to take further steps to reduce their non-strategic nuclear arsenals and not to develop new types of nuclear weapons, in accordance with their commitment to diminish the role of nuclear weapons in their security policies;

5. *Agrees* urgently to strengthen efforts towards both nuclear disarmament and nuclear non-proliferation through the resumption in the Conference on Disarmament of negotiations on a non-discriminatory, multilateral and internationally and effectively verifiable treaty banning the production of fissile material for nuclear weapons or other nuclear explosive devices, in accordance with the statement of the Special Coordinator in 1995 and the mandate contained therein, taking into account both nuclear disarmament and nuclear non-proliferation objectives, as well as the completion and implementation of arrangements by all nuclear-weapon States to place fissile material no longer required for military purposes under international verification;

6. *Calls for* the establishment of an appropriate subsidiary body in the Conference on Disarmament to deal with nuclear disarmament;

7. *Underlines* the imperative of the principles of irreversibility and transparency for all nuclear disarmament measures and the need to develop further adequate and efficient verification capabilities;

8. *Decides* to include in the provisional agenda of its sixtieth session an item entitled "Towards a nuclear-weapon-free world: accelerating the implementation of nuclear disarmament commitments", and to review the implementation of the present resolution at that session.

RECORDED VOTE ON RESOLUTION 59/75:

In favour: Afghanistan, Algeria, Andorra, Angola, Antigua and Barbuda, Argentina, Armenia, Austria, Azerbaijan, Bahamas, Bahrain, Bangladesh, Barbados, Belgium, Belize, Benin, Bhutan, Bolivia, Botswana, Brazil, Brunei Darussalam, Burkina Faso, Burundi, Cambodia, Cameroon, Canada, Cape Verde, Central African Republic, Chile, China,

Colombia, Comoros, Congo, Costa Rica, Côte d'Ivoire, Croatia, Cuba, Cyprus, Djibouti, Dominica, Dominican Republic, Ecuador, Egypt, El Salvador, Equatorial Guinea, Eritrea, Ethiopia, Fiji, Finland, Gabon, Gambia, Germany, Ghana, Grenada, Guatemala, Guinea-Bissau, Guyana, Haiti, Honduras, Indonesia, Iran, Iraq, Ireland, Jamaica, Japan, Jordan, Kazakhstan, Kenya, Kuwait, Kyrgyzstan, Lao People's Democratic Republic, Lebanon, Lesotho, Liberia, Libyan Arab Jamahiriya, Liechtenstein, Lithuania, Luxembourg, Madagascar, Malawi, Malaysia, Maldives, Mali, Malta, Marshall Islands, Mauritius, Mexico, Micronesia, Mongolia, Morocco, Mozambique, Myanmar, Namibia, Nauru, Nepal, Netherlands, New Zealand, Nicaragua, Niger, Nigeria, Norway, Oman, Pakistan, Panama, Papua New Guinea, Paraguay, Peru, Philippines, Qatar, Republic of Korea, Republic of Moldova, Rwanda, Saint Lucia, Saint Vincent and the Grenadines, Samoa, San Marino, Sao Tome and Principe, Saudi Arabia, Senegal, Seychelles, Sierra Leone, Singapore, Solomon Islands, Somalia, South Africa, Sri Lanka, Sudan, Suriname, Swaziland, Sweden, Switzerland, Syrian Arab Republic, Tajikistan, Thailand, Timor-Leste, Togo, Trinidad and Tobago, Tunisia, Turkey, Tuvalu, Uganda, Ukraine, United Arab Emirates, United Republic of Tanzania, Uruguay, Vanuatu, Venezuela, Viet Nam, Yemen, Zambia, Zimbabwe.

Against: France, Israel, Latvia, Palau, United Kingdom, United States.

Abstaining: Albania, Australia, Belarus, Bosnia and Herzegovina, Bulgaria, Czech Republic, Denmark, Estonia, Georgia, Greece, Hungary, Iceland, India, Italy, Poland, Portugal, Romania, Russian Federation, Serbia and Montenegro, Slovakia, Slovenia, Spain, The former Yugoslav Republic of Macedonia, Uzbekistan.

The First Committee adopted paragraph 2 by a separate recorded vote of 153 to 4, with 5 abstentions. The Assembly retained the paragraph by a recorded vote of 169 to 4, with 4 abstentions.

The Assembly adopted **resolution 59/76** by recorded vote (165-3-16) [agenda item 65].

A path to the total elimination of nuclear weapons

The General Assembly,

Recalling its resolutions 49/75 H of 15 December 1994, 50/70 C of 12 December 1995, 51/45 G of 10 December 1996, 52/38 K of 9 December 1997, 53/77 U of 4 December 1998, 54/54 D of 1 December 1999, 55/33 R of 20 November 2000, 56/24 N of 29 November 2001, 57/78 of 22 November 2002 and 58/59 of 8 December 2003,

Recognizing that the enhancement of international peace and security and the promotion of nuclear disarmament mutually complement and strengthen each other,

Expressing deep concern regarding the growing dangers posed by the proliferation of weapons of mass destruction, including that caused by proliferation networks,

Welcoming the decision of the Libyan Arab Jamahiriya, announced on 19 December 2003, to renounce all its weapons of mass destruction programmes,

Welcoming also the adoption of Security Council resolution 1540(2004) of 28 April 2004 as an important step for global efforts to prevent the proliferation of weapons of mass destruction,

Convinced that every effort should be made to avoid nuclear war and nuclear terrorism,

Reaffirming the crucial importance of the Treaty on the Non-Proliferation of Nuclear Weapons as the cornerstone of the international regime for nuclear non-proliferation and as an essential foundation for the pursuit of nuclear disarmament,

Bearing in mind that challenges to the Treaty and to the nuclear non-proliferation regime have further increased the necessity of full compliance and that the Treaty can fulfil its role only if there is confidence in compliance by all States parties,

Recognizing the progress made by the nuclear-weapon States in the reduction of their nuclear weapons unilaterally or through their negotiations, including the entry into force of the Treaty between the United States of America and the Russian Federation on Strategic Offensive Reductions, which should serve as a step for further nuclear disarmament, and the efforts for nuclear disarmament and non-proliferation by the international community,

Welcoming the ongoing efforts aimed at the reduction of nuclear-weapons-related materials deployed within the framework of international cooperation, such as the Cooperative Threat Reduction programme,

Reaffirming the conviction that further advancement in nuclear disarmament will contribute to consolidating the international regime for nuclear non-proliferation, ensuring international peace and security,

Welcoming the continuation of a moratorium on nuclear-weapon-test explosions or any other nuclear explosions since the last nuclear tests, in 1998,

Welcoming also the successful adoption of the Final Document of the 2000 Review Conference of the Parties to the Treaty on the Non-Proliferation of Nuclear Weapons, and stressing the importance of implementing its conclusions,

Recognizing the active discussions at the third session, held from 26 April to 7 May 2004, of the Preparatory Committee for the 2005 Review Conference of the Parties to the Treaty on the Non-Proliferation of Nuclear Weapons, and emphasizing the importance of a successful Review Conference in 2005, the year of the sixtieth anniversary of the atomic bombings,

Welcoming the steady increase in the number of States that have signed and/or concluded additional protocols to their International Atomic Energy Agency safeguards agreements in recent years, and sharing the hope that the Agency's safeguards system will be further strengthened through the universalization of safeguards agreements and the additional protocols,

Encouraging the Russian Federation and the United States of America to implement fully the Treaty on Strategic Offensive Reductions and to continue their intensive consultations in accordance with the Joint Declaration on the New Strategic Relationship between the two States,

Welcoming the Final Declaration of the third Conference on Facilitating the Entry into Force of the Comprehensive Nuclear-Test-Ban Treaty, convened in Vienna from 3 to 5 September 2003 in accordance with article XIV of the Treaty, and the Joint Ministerial Statement of the second meeting of Friends of the Comprehensive Nuclear-Test-Ban Treaty in September 2004,

Encouraging all States to make maximum efforts to bring about the early entry into force of the Comprehensive Nuclear-Test-Ban Treaty, progress on which would contribute to a positive outcome of the 2005 Review Conference of the Parties to the Treaty on the Non-Proliferation of Nuclear Weapons,

Recognizing the importance of preventing terrorists from acquiring or developing nuclear weapons or related materials, radioactive materials, equipment and technology, and underlining the role of the International Atomic Energy Agency in this regard,

Stressing the importance of education on disarmament and non-proliferation for future generations and of efforts to tackle the current non-proliferation and disarmament problems,

1. *Reaffirms* the importance of achieving the universality of the Treaty on the Non-Proliferation of Nuclear Weapons, and calls upon States not parties to the Treaty to accede to it as non-nuclear-weapon States without delay and without conditions;

2. *Also reaffirms* the importance for all States parties to the Treaty on the Non-Proliferation of Nuclear Weapons to fulfil their obligations under the Treaty;

3. *Stresses* the central importance of the following practical steps for the systematic and progressive efforts to implement article VI of the Treaty on the Non-Proliferation of Nuclear Weapons, and paragraphs 3 and 4 *(c)* of the decision on principles and objectives for nuclear non-proliferation and disarmament of the 1995 Review and Extension Conference of the Parties to the Treaty:

(a) The importance and urgency of signatures and ratifications, without delay and without conditions and in accordance with constitutional processes, to achieve the early entry into force of the Comprehensive Nuclear-Test-Ban Treaty as well as a moratorium on nuclear-weapon-test explosions or any other nuclear explosions pending the entry into force of that Treaty;

(b) The establishment of an ad hoc committee in the Conference on Disarmament as early as possible during its 2005 session to negotiate a non-discriminatory, multilateral and internationally and effectively verifiable treaty banning the production of fissile material for nuclear weapons or other nuclear explosive devices, in accordance with the report of the Special Coordinator of 1995 and the mandate contained therein, taking into consideration both nuclear disarmament and non-proliferation objectives, with a view to its conclusion within five years and, pending its entry into force, a moratorium on the production of fissile material for nuclear weapons;

(c) The establishment of an appropriate subsidiary body with a mandate to deal with nuclear disarmament in the Conference on Disarmament as early as possible during its 2005 session in the context of establishing a programme of work;

(d) The inclusion of the principle of irreversibility to apply to nuclear disarmament, nuclear and other related arms control and reduction measures;

(e) An unequivocal undertaking by the nuclear-weapon States, as agreed at the 2000 Review Conference of the Parties to the Treaty on the Non-Proliferation of Nuclear Weapons, to accomplish the total elimination of their nuclear arsenals, leading to nuclear disarmament, to which all States parties to the Treaty are committed under article VI of the Treaty;

(f) Deep reductions by the Russian Federation and the United States of America in their strategic offensive arsenals, while placing great importance on the existing multilateral treaties, with a view to maintaining and strengthening strategic stability and international security;

(g) Steps by all the nuclear-weapon States leading to nuclear disarmament in a way that promotes international stability, and based on the principle of undiminished security for all:

(i) Further efforts by all the nuclear-weapon States to continue to reduce their nuclear arsenals unilaterally;

(ii) Increased transparency by the nuclear-weapon States with regard to their nuclear weapons capabilities and the implementation of agreements pursuant to article VI of the Treaty and as voluntary confidence-building measures to support further progress on nuclear disarmament;

(iii) The further reduction of non-strategic nuclear weapons, based on unilateral initiatives and as an integral part of the nuclear arms reduction and disarmament process;

(iv) Concrete agreed measures to reduce further the operational status of nuclear weapons systems;

(v) A diminishing role for nuclear weapons in security policies to minimize the risk that these weapons will ever be used and to facilitate the process of their total elimination;

(vi) The engagement, as soon as appropriate, of all the nuclear-weapon States in the process leading to the total elimination of their nuclear weapons;

(h) Reaffirmation that the ultimate objective of the efforts of States in the disarmament process is general and complete disarmament under effective international control;

4. *Recognizes* that the realization of a world free of nuclear weapons will require further steps, including deeper reductions in all types of nuclear weapons by all the nuclear-weapon States in the process of working towards achieving their elimination;

5. *Invites* the nuclear-weapon States to keep the Members of the United Nations duly informed of the progress or efforts made towards nuclear disarmament;

6. *Encourages* all States parties to the Treaty on the Non-Proliferation of Nuclear Weapons to make maximum efforts for a successful Review Conference in 2005;

7. *Welcomes* the ongoing efforts in the dismantlement of nuclear weapons, notes the importance of the safe and effective management of the resultant fissile materials, and calls for arrangements by all the nuclear-weapon States to place, as soon as practicable, fissile material designated by each of them as no longer required for military purposes under International Atomic Energy Agency or other relevant international verification and arrangements for the disposition of such material for peaceful purposes to ensure that such material remains permanently outside of military programmes;

8. *Stresses* the importance of further development of the verification capabilities, including International Atomic Energy Agency safeguards and Comprehensive Nuclear-Test-Ban Treaty verification regimes, that will be required to provide assurance of compliance with nuclear disarmament agreements for the achievement and maintenance of a nuclear-weapon-free world;

9. *Calls upon* all States to redouble their efforts to prevent and curb the proliferation of nuclear and other weapons of mass destruction, confirming and strengthening, if necessary, their policies not to transfer equipment, materials or technology that could contribute to the proliferation of those weapons, while ensuring that such policies are consistent with the

obligations of States under the Treaty on the Non-Proliferation of Nuclear Weapons;

10. *Also calls upon* all States to maintain the highest possible standards of security, safe custody, effective control and physical protection of all materials that could contribute to the proliferation of nuclear and other weapons of mass destruction in order, inter alia, to prevent those materials from falling into the hands of terrorists;

11. *Welcomes* the adoption of resolution GC(48)/RES/14 on 24 September 2004 by the General Conference of the International Atomic Energy Agency, in which it is recommended that States members of the Agency continue to consider implementing the elements of the plan of action outlined in resolution GC(44)/RES/19, adopted on 22 September 2000 by the General Conference of the Agency, and in the Agency's updated plan of action of February 2004, with the aim of facilitating the entry into force of comprehensive safeguards agreements and additional protocols, and calls for the early and full implementation of that resolution;

12. *Encourages* all States to implement, as appropriate, the recommendations in the report of the Secretary-General on the United Nations study on disarmament and non-proliferation education, submitted to the General Assembly at its fifty-seventh session, and voluntarily to share information on efforts they have been undertaking to that end;

13. *Encourages* the constructive role played by civil society in promoting nuclear non-proliferation and nuclear disarmament.

RECORDED VOTE ON RESOLUTION 59/76:

In favour: Afghanistan, Albania, Algeria, Andorra, Angola, Antigua and Barbuda, Argentina, Armenia, Australia, Austria, Azerbaijan, Bahamas, Bahrain, Bangladesh, Barbados, Belarus, Belgium, Belize, Benin, Bolivia, Bosnia and Herzegovina, Botswana, Brunei Darussalam, Bulgaria, Burkina Faso, Burundi, Cambodia, Cameroon, Canada, Cape Verde, Central African Republic, Chile, Colombia, Comoros, Congo, Costa Rica, Côte d'Ivoire, Croatia, Cyprus, Czech Republic, Denmark, Djibouti, Dominica, Dominican Republic, Ecuador, El Salvador, Equatorial Guinea, Eritrea, Estonia, Ethiopia, Fiji, Finland, France, Gabon, Gambia, Georgia, Germany, Ghana, Greece, Grenada, Guatemala, Guinea-Bissau, Guyana, Haiti, Honduras, Hungary, Iceland, Indonesia, Iraq, Italy, Jamaica, Japan, Jordan, Kazakhstan, Kenya, Kuwait, Kyrgyzstan, Lao People's Democratic Republic, Latvia, Lebanon, Lesotho, Liberia, Libyan Arab Jamahiriya, Liechtenstein, Lithuania, Luxembourg, Madagascar, Malawi, Malaysia, Maldives, Mali, Marshall Islands, Mauritius, Micronesia, Monaco, Mongolia, Morocco, Mozambique, Namibia, Nauru, Nepal, Netherlands, Nicaragua, Niger, Nigeria, Norway, Oman, Panama, Papua New Guinea, Paraguay, Peru, Philippines, Poland, Portugal, Qatar, Republic of Korea, Republic of Moldova, Romania, Russian Federation, Rwanda, Saint Lucia, Saint Vincent and the Grenadines, Samoa, San Marino, Sao Tome and Principe, Saudi Arabia, Senegal, Serbia and Montenegro, Seychelles, Sierra Leone, Singapore, Slovakia, Slovenia, Solomon Islands, Somalia, Spain, Sri Lanka, Sudan, Suriname, Swaziland, Switzerland, Syrian Arab Republic, Tajikistan, Thailand, The former Yugoslav Republic of Macedonia, Timor-Leste, Togo, Tonga, Trinidad and Tobago, Tunisia, Turkey, Tuvalu, Uganda, Ukraine, United Arab Emirates, United Kingdom, United Republic of Tanzania, Uruguay, Uzbekistan, Vanuatu, Venezuela, Viet Nam, Yemen, Zambia, Zimbabwe.

Against: India, Palau, United States.

Abstaining: Bhutan, Brazil, China, Cuba, Democratic People's Republic of Korea, Egypt, Iran, Ireland, Israel, Malta, Mexico, Myanmar, New Zealand, Pakistan, South Africa, Sweden.

The Assembly adopted **resolution 59/77** by recorded vote (117-43-21) [agenda item 65].

Nuclear disarmament

The General Assembly,

Recalling its resolution 49/75 E of 15 December 1994 on a step-by-step reduction of the nuclear threat, and

its resolutions 50/70 P of 12 December 1995, 51/45 O of 10 December 1996, 52/38 L of 9 December 1997, 53/77 X of 4 December 1998, 54/54 P of 1 December 1999, 55/33 T of 20 November 2000, 56/24 R of 29 November 2001, 57/79 of 22 November 2002 and 58/56 of 8 December 2003 on nuclear disarmament,

Reaffirming the commitment of the international community to the goal of the total elimination of nuclear weapons and the establishment of a nuclear-weapon-free world,

Bearing in mind that the Convention on the Prohibition of the Development, Production and Stockpiling of Bacteriological (Biological) and Toxin Weapons and on Their Destruction of 1972 and the Convention on the Prohibition of the Development, Production, Stockpiling and Use of Chemical Weapons and on Their Destruction of 1993 have already established legal regimes on the complete prohibition of biological and chemical weapons, respectively, and determined to achieve a nuclear weapons convention on the prohibition of the development, testing, production, stockpiling, loan, transfer, use and threat of use of nuclear weapons and on their destruction, and to conclude such an international convention at an early date,

Recognizing that there now exist conditions for the establishment of a world free of nuclear weapons, and stressing the need to take concrete practical steps towards achieving this goal,

Bearing in mind paragraph 50 of the Final Document of the Tenth Special Session of the General Assembly, the first special session devoted to disarmament, calling for the urgent negotiation of agreements for the cessation of the qualitative improvement and development of nuclear-weapon systems, and for a comprehensive and phased programme with agreed time frames, wherever feasible, for the progressive and balanced reduction of nuclear weapons and their means of delivery, leading to their ultimate and complete elimination at the earliest possible time,

Reaffirming the conviction of the States parties to the Treaty on the Non-Proliferation of Nuclear Weapons that the Treaty is a cornerstone of nuclear non-proliferation and nuclear disarmament and the importance of the decision on strengthening the review process for the Treaty, the decision on principles and objectives for nuclear non-proliferation and disarmament, the decision on the extension of the Treaty and the resolution on the Middle East, adopted by the 1995 Review and Extension Conference of the Parties to the Treaty on the Non-Proliferation of Nuclear Weapons,

Stressing the importance of the thirteen steps for the systematic and progressive efforts to achieve the objective of nuclear disarmament leading to the total elimination of nuclear weapons, as agreed to by the States parties in the Final Document of the 2000 Review Conference of the Parties to the Treaty on the Non-Proliferation of Nuclear Weapons,

Reiterating the highest priority accorded to nuclear disarmament in the Final Document of the Tenth Special Session of the General Assembly and by the international community,

Reiterating its call for an early entry into force of the Comprehensive Nuclear-Test-Ban Treaty,

Stressing the importance of the forthcoming 2005 Review Conference of the Parties to the Treaty on the Non-Proliferation of Nuclear Weapons and the need for a positive and substantive outcome of the Conference in a manner that will preserve the integrity of the three pillars of the Treaty regime, that is, nuclear disarmament, nuclear non-proliferation and peaceful uses of nuclear energy,

Noting with appreciation the entry into force of the Treaty on the Reduction and Limitation of Strategic Offensive Arms (START I), to which Belarus, Kazakhstan, the Russian Federation, Ukraine and the United States of America are States parties,

Noting with appreciation also the entry into force of the Treaty between the United States of America and the Russian Federation on Strategic Offensive Reductions ("the Moscow Treaty") as a significant step towards reducing their deployed strategic nuclear weapons, while calling for further irreversible deep cuts in their nuclear arsenals,

Noting with appreciation further the unilateral measures taken by the nuclear-weapon States for nuclear arms limitation, and encouraging them to take further such measures,

Recognizing the complementarity of bilateral, plurilateral and multilateral negotiations on nuclear disarmament, and that bilateral negotiations can never replace multilateral negotiations in this respect,

Noting the support expressed in the Conference on Disarmament and in the General Assembly for the elaboration of an international convention to assure non-nuclear-weapon States against the use or threat of use of nuclear weapons, and the multilateral efforts in the Conference on Disarmament to reach agreement on such an international convention at an early date,

Recalling the advisory opinion of the International Court of Justice on the *Legality of the Threat or Use of Nuclear Weapons*, issued on 8 July 1996, and welcoming the unanimous reaffirmation by all Judges of the Court that there exists an obligation for all States to pursue in good faith and bring to a conclusion negotiations leading to nuclear disarmament in all its aspects under strict and effective international control,

Mindful of paragraph 74 and other relevant recommendations in the Final Document of the Thirteenth Conference of Heads of State or Government of Non-Aligned Countries, held at Kuala Lumpur from 20 to 25 February 2003, calling upon the Conference on Disarmament to establish, as soon as possible and as the highest priority, an ad hoc committee on nuclear disarmament and to commence negotiations on a phased programme for the complete elimination of nuclear weapons with a specified framework of time,

Recalling paragraph 61 of the Final Document of the Fourteenth Ministerial Conference of the Movement of Non-Aligned Countries, held in Durban, South Africa, from 17 to 19 August 2004,

Reaffirming the specific mandate conferred by the General Assembly in its decision 52/492 of 8 September 1998 upon the Disarmament Commission to discuss the subject of nuclear disarmament as one of its main substantive agenda items,

Recalling the United Nations Millennium Declaration, in which Heads of State and Government resolve to strive for the elimination of weapons of mass destruction, in particular nuclear weapons, and to keep all options open for achieving this aim, including the possibility of convening an international conference to identify ways of eliminating nuclear dangers,

Reaffirming that, in accordance with the Charter of the United Nations, States should refrain from the use or the threat of use of nuclear weapons in settling their disputes in international relations,

Seized of the danger of the use of weapons of mass destruction, particularly nuclear weapons, in terrorist acts and the urgent need for concerted international efforts to control and overcome it,

1. *Recognizes* that, in view of recent political developments, the time is now opportune for all the nuclear-weapon States to take effective disarmament measures with a view to achieving the elimination of these weapons;

2. *Reaffirms* that nuclear disarmament and nuclear non-proliferation are substantively interrelated and mutually reinforcing, that the two processes must go hand in hand and that there is a genuine need for a systematic and progressive process of nuclear disarmament;

3. *Welcomes and encourages* the efforts to establish new nuclear-weapon-free zones in different parts of the world on the basis of agreements or arrangements freely arrived at among the States of the regions concerned, which is an effective measure for limiting the further spread of nuclear weapons geographically and contributes to the cause of nuclear disarmament;

4. *Recognizes* that there is a genuine need to diminish the role of nuclear weapons in strategic doctrines and security policies to minimize the risk that these weapons will ever be used and to facilitate the process of their total elimination;

5. *Urges* the nuclear-weapon States to stop immediately the qualitative improvement, development, production and stockpiling of nuclear warheads and their delivery systems;

6. *Also urges* the nuclear-weapon States, as an interim measure, to de-alert and deactivate immediately their nuclear weapons and to take other concrete measures to reduce further the operational status of their nuclear-weapon systems;

7. *Reiterates its call upon* the nuclear-weapon States to undertake the step-by-step reduction of the nuclear threat and to carry out effective nuclear disarmament measures with a view to achieving the total elimination of these weapons;

8. *Calls upon* the nuclear-weapon States, pending the achievement of the total elimination of nuclear weapons, to agree on an internationally and legally binding instrument on a joint undertaking not to be the first to use nuclear weapons, and calls upon all States to conclude an internationally and legally binding instrument on security assurances of non-use and non-threat of use of nuclear weapons against non-nuclear-weapon States;

9. *Urges* the nuclear-weapon States to commence plurilateral negotiations among themselves at an appropriate stage on further deep reductions of nuclear weapons as an effective measure of nuclear disarmament;

10. *Underlines* the importance of applying the principle of irreversibility to the process of nuclear disarmament, nuclear and other related arms control and reduction measures;

11. *Underscores* the importance of the unequivocal undertaking by the nuclear-weapon States, in the Final Document of the Review Conference of the Parties

to the Treaty on the Non-Proliferation of Nuclear Weapons, held in New York from 24 April to 19 May 2000, to accomplish the total elimination of their nuclear arsenals leading to nuclear disarmament, to which all States parties are committed under article VI of the Treaty, and the reaffirmation by the States parties that the total elimination of nuclear weapons is the only absolute guarantee against the use or threat of use of nuclear weapons;

12. *Calls for* the full and effective implementation of the thirteen steps for nuclear disarmament contained in the Final Document of the 2000 Review Conference of the Parties to the Treaty on the Non-Proliferation of Nuclear Weapons;

13. *Urges* the nuclear-weapon States to carry out further reductions of non-strategic nuclear weapons, based on unilateral initiatives and as an integral part of the nuclear arms reduction and disarmament process;

14. *Calls for* the immediate commencement of negotiations in the Conference on Disarmament on a non-discriminatory, multilateral and internationally and effectively verifiable treaty banning the production of fissile material for nuclear weapons or other nuclear explosive devices on the basis of the report of the Special Coordinator and the mandate contained therein;

15. *Urges* the Conference on Disarmament to agree on a programme of work which includes the immediate commencement of negotiations on such a treaty with a view to their conclusion within five years;

16. *Calls for* the conclusion of an international legal instrument or instruments on adequate security assurances to non-nuclear-weapon States;

17. *Also calls for* the early entry into force and strict observance of the Comprehensive Nuclear-Test-Ban Treaty;

18. *Expresses its regret* that the Conference on Disarmament was unable to establish an ad hoc committee on nuclear disarmament at its 2004 session, as called for in General Assembly resolution 58/56;

19. *Reiterates its call upon* the Conference on Disarmament to establish, on a priority basis, an ad hoc committee to deal with nuclear disarmament early in 2005 and to commence negotiations on a phased programme of nuclear disarmament leading to the eventual total elimination of nuclear weapons;

20. *Calls for* the convening of an international conference on nuclear disarmament in all its aspects at an early date to identify and deal with concrete measures of nuclear disarmament;

21. *Requests* the Secretary-General to submit to the General Assembly at its sixtieth session a report on the implementation of the present resolution;

22. *Decides* to include in the provisional agenda of its sixtieth session the item entitled "Nuclear disarmament".

RECORDED VOTE ON RESOLUTION 59/77:

In favour: Afghanistan, Algeria, Angola, Antigua and Barbuda, Bahamas, Bahrain, Bangladesh, Barbados, Belize, Benin, Bhutan, Bolivia, Botswana, Brazil, Brunei Darussalam, Burkina Faso, Burundi, Cambodia, Cameroon, Cape Verde, Central African Republic, Chile, China, Colombia, Comoros, Congo, Costa Rica, Côte d'Ivoire, Cuba, Democratic People's Republic of Korea, Djibouti, Dominica, Dominican Republic, Ecuador, Egypt, El Salvador, Equatorial Guinea, Eritrea, Ethiopia, Fiji, Gabon, Gambia, Ghana, Grenada, Guatemala, Guinea-Bissau, Guyana, Honduras, Indonesia, Iran, Iraq, Jamaica, Jordan, Kenya, Kuwait, Lao People's Democratic Republic, Lebanon, Lesotho, Liberia, Libyan Arab Jamahiriya, Madagascar, Malawi, Malaysia, Maldives, Mali, Marshall Islands, Mexico, Mongolia, Morocco, Mozambique, Myanmar, Namibia,

Nepal, New Zealand, Nicaragua, Niger, Nigeria, Oman, Panama, Papua New Guinea, Paraguay, Peru, Philippines, Qatar, Rwanda, Saint Lucia, Saint Vincent and the Grenadines, Samoa, Sao Tome and Principe, Saudi Arabia, Senegal, Sierra Leone, Singapore, Solomon Islands, Somalia, South Africa, Sri Lanka, Sudan, Suriname, Swaziland, Syrian Arab Republic, Thailand, Timor-Leste, Togo, Tonga, Trinidad and Tobago, Tunisia, Tuvalu, Uganda, United Arab Emirates, United Republic of Tanzania, Uruguay, Venezuela, Viet Nam, Yemen, Zambia, Zimbabwe.

Against: Albania, Andorra, Australia, Austria, Belgium, Bosnia and Herzegovina, Bulgaria, Canada, Croatia, Cyprus, Czech Republic, Denmark, Estonia, Finland, France, Germany, Greece, Hungary, Iceland, Israel, Italy, Latvia, Liechtenstein, Lithuania, Luxembourg, Micronesia, Monaco, Netherlands, Norway, Palau, Poland, Portugal, Romania, San Marino, Serbia and Montenegro, Slovakia, Slovenia, Spain, Switzerland, The former Yugoslav Republic of Macedonia, Turkey, United Kingdom, United States.

Abstaining: Argentina, Armenia, Azerbaijan, Belarus, Georgia, Haiti, India, Ireland, Japan, Kazakhstan, Kyrgyzstan, Malta, Mauritius, Pakistan, Republic of Korea, Republic of Moldova, Russian Federation, Sweden, Tajikistan, Ukraine, Uzbekistan.

The Assembly adopted **resolution 59/79** by recorded vote (116-46-18) [agenda item 65].

Reducing nuclear danger

The General Assembly,

Bearing in mind that the use of nuclear weapons poses the most serious threat to mankind and to the survival of civilization,

Reaffirming that any use or threat of use of nuclear weapons would constitute a violation of the Charter of the United Nations,

Convinced that the proliferation of nuclear weapons in all its aspects would seriously enhance the danger of nuclear war,

Convinced also that nuclear disarmament and the complete elimination of nuclear weapons are essential to remove the danger of nuclear war,

Considering that, until nuclear weapons cease to exist, it is imperative on the part of the nuclear-weapon States to adopt measures that assure non-nuclear-weapon States against the use or threat of use of nuclear weapons,

Considering also that the hair-trigger alert of nuclear weapons carries unacceptable risks of unintentional or accidental use of nuclear weapons, which would have catastrophic consequences for all mankind,

Emphasizing the imperative need to adopt measures to avoid accidental, unauthorized or unexplained incidents arising from computer anomaly or other technical malfunctions,

Conscious that limited steps relating to detargeting have been taken by the nuclear-weapon States and that further practical, realistic and mutually reinforcing steps are necessary to contribute to the improvement in the international climate for negotiations leading to the elimination of nuclear weapons,

Mindful that reduction of tensions brought about by a change in nuclear doctrines would positively impact on international peace and security and improve the conditions for the further reduction and the elimination of nuclear weapons,

Reiterating the highest priority accorded to nuclear disarmament in the Final Document of the Tenth Special Session of the General Assembly and by the international community,

Recalling that in the advisory opinion of the International Court of Justice on the *Legality of the Threat or Use of Nuclear Weapons* it is stated that there exists an obligation for all States to pursue in good faith and bring to a conclusion negotiations leading to nuclear disarmament in all its aspects under strict and effective international control,

Recalling also the call in the United Nations Millennium Declaration to seek to eliminate the dangers posed by weapons of mass destruction and the resolve to strive for the elimination of weapons of mass destruction, particularly nuclear weapons, including the possibility of convening an international conference to identify ways of eliminating nuclear dangers,

1. *Calls for* a review of nuclear doctrines and, in this context, immediate and urgent steps to reduce the risks of unintentional and accidental use of nuclear weapons;

2. *Requests* the five nuclear-weapon States to take measures towards the implementation of paragraph 1 above;

3. *Calls upon* Member States to take the necessary measures to prevent the proliferation of nuclear weapons in all its aspects and to promote nuclear disarmament, with the objective of eliminating nuclear weapons;

4. *Takes note* of the report of the Secretary-General submitted pursuant to paragraph 5 of General Assembly resolution 58/47 of 8 December 2003;

5. *Requests* the Secretary-General to intensify efforts and support initiatives that would contribute towards the full implementation of the seven recommendations identified in the report of the Advisory Board on Disarmament Matters that would significantly reduce the risk of nuclear war, and also to continue to encourage Member States to endeavour to create conditions that would allow the emergence of an international consensus to hold an international conference as proposed in the United Nations Millennium Declaration, to identify ways of eliminating nuclear dangers, and to report thereon to the General Assembly at its sixtieth session;

6. *Decides* to include in the provisional agenda of its sixtieth session the item entitled "Reducing nuclear danger".

RECORDED VOTE ON RESOLUTION 59/79:

In favour: Afghanistan, Algeria, Angola, Antigua and Barbuda, Bahamas, Bahrain, Bangladesh, Barbados, Belize, Benin, Bhutan, Bolivia, Botswana, Brazil, Brunei Darussalam, Burkina Faso, Burundi, Cambodia, Cameroon, Cape Verde, Central African Republic, Chile, Colombia, Comoros, Congo, Costa Rica, Côte d'Ivoire, Cuba, Democratic People's Republic of Korea, Djibouti, Dominica, Dominican Republic, Egypt, El Salvador, Equatorial Guinea, Eritrea, Ethiopia, Fiji, Gabon, Gambia, Ghana, Grenada, Guatemala, Guinea-Bissau, Guyana, Honduras, India, Indonesia, Iran, Iraq, Jamaica, Jordan, Kenya, Kuwait, Lao People's Democratic Republic, Lebanon, Lesotho, Liberia, Libyan Arab Jamahiriya, Madagascar, Malawi, Malaysia, Maldives, Mali, Marshall Islands, Mauritius, Mexico, Mongolia, Morocco, Mozambique, Myanmar, Namibia, Nauru, Nepal, Nicaragua, Niger, Nigeria, Oman, Pakistan, Panama, Peru, Philippines, Qatar, Rwanda, Saint Lucia, Saint Vincent and the Grenadines, Samoa, Sao Tome and Principe, Saudi Arabia, Senegal, Sierra Leone, Singapore, Somalia, South Africa, Sri Lanka, Sudan, Suriname, Swaziland, Syrian Arab Republic, Thailand, Timor-Leste, Togo, Tonga, Trinidad and Tobago, Tunisia, Tuvalu, Uganda, United Arab Emirates, United Republic of Tanzania, Uruguay, Vanuatu, Venezuela, Viet Nam, Yemen, Zambia, Zimbabwe.

Against: Albania, Andorra, Australia, Austria, Belgium, Bosnia and Herzegovina, Bulgaria, Canada, Croatia, Cyprus, Czech Republic, Denmark, Estonia, Finland, France, Germany, Greece, Hungary, Iceland, Ireland, Italy, Latvia, Liechtenstein, Lithuania, Luxembourg, Malta, Micronesia, Monaco, Netherlands, New Zealand, Norway, Palau, Poland, Portugal, Romania, San Marino, Serbia and Montenegro, Slovakia, Slovenia, Spain, Sweden, Switzerland, The former Yugoslav Republic of Macedonia, Turkey, United Kingdom, United States.

Abstaining: Argentina, Armenia, Azerbaijan, Belarus, China, Ecuador, Georgia, Israel, Japan, Kazakhstan, Kyrgyzstan, Paraguay, Republic of Korea, Republic of Moldova, Russian Federation, Tajikistan, Ukraine, Uzbekistan.

The Assembly adopted **resolution 59/94** without vote [agenda item 65].

Bilateral strategic nuclear arms reductions and the new strategic framework

The General Assembly,

Recalling its resolution 57/68 of 22 November 2002,

Noting with satisfaction the new strategic relationship between the United States of America and the Russian Federation, built on the principles of mutual security, trust, openness, cooperation and predictability, as affirmed in their Joint Declaration of 24 May 2002,

Noting the increasing cooperation between the United States of America and the Russian Federation in addressing significant challenges to international security, as illustrated by their joint efforts regarding Security Council resolution 1540(2004) of 28 April 2004,

Welcoming the determination of the two countries to work together, and with other nations and international organizations, to meet their respective obligations under article VI of the Treaty on the Non-Proliferation of Nuclear Weapons which was opened for signature on 1 July 1968,

Mindful of the obligation of all parties to the Treaty to abide by all of their commitments under the Treaty,

1. *Welcomes* the entry into force of the Treaty on Strategic Offensive Reductions ("the Moscow Treaty") on 1 June 2003, under which the United States of America and the Russian Federation are committed to reducing and limiting their strategic nuclear warheads so that by 31 December 2012, the aggregate number of such warheads does not exceed 1,700 to 2,200 for each party;

2. *Supports* the continued commitment of the United States of America and the Russian Federation to cooperative efforts in strategic offensive reductions, inter alia, through meetings of the Bilateral Implementation Commission for the Moscow Treaty, as well as increased strategic stability through discussions in the working groups established under the Consultative Group for Strategic Security;

3. *Recognizes* that the Moscow Treaty is an important result of the new bilateral strategic relationship, which will help in establishing more favourable conditions for actively promoting security and cooperation, and enhancing international stability;

4. *Acknowledges* the contribution that the United States of America and the Russian Federation have made to nuclear disarmament by reducing their deployed strategic warheads by about half since the end of the cold war;

5. *Recognizes* the importance of the Treaty on the Reduction and Limitation of Strategic Offensive Arms (START), which is still in force, and of its provisions, which will lay the foundation for ensuring confidence, transparency and predictability in further strategic offensive reductions;

6. *Also recognizes* that, since the end of the cold war, the United States of America has reduced the number of its START-accountable deployed strategic warheads from over 10,000 to less than 6,000, and has also eliminated 1,032 launchers for intercontinental ballistic missiles and submarine-launched ballistic missiles, 350 heavy bombers and 28 ballistic missile submarines, and removed 4 additional ballistic missile submarines from strategic service;

7. *Further recognizes* that, in the same time period, the Russian Federation has reduced the number of its START-accountable deployed strategic warheads to less than 5,000, and has also eliminated 1,250 launchers for intercontinental ballistic missiles and submarine-launched ballistic missiles, 43 ballistic missile submarines and 65 heavy bombers;

8. *Recognizes* the importance of the 1991 and 1992 initiatives put forward by the Presidents of the United States of America and the Union of Soviet Socialist Republics/Russian Federation, which represent a major step forward in the meeting by the Russian Federation and the United States of America of their obligations under article VI of the Treaty on the Non-Proliferation of Nuclear Weapons;

9. *Notes with approval* that, since the end of the cold war, the United States of America and the Russian Federation have halted the production of fissile material for nuclear weapons and have committed themselves to eliminating excess fissile material resulting from the dismantlement of weapons no longer needed for national security;

10. *Welcomes*, in this context, the implementation of the 1993 Agreement concerning the Disposition of Highly Enriched Uranium Extracted from Nuclear Weapons, signed by the Governments of the Russian Federation and the United States of America, under which more than 216 metric tons of excess Russian highly enriched uranium have been down-blended for use as power reactor fuel, and the fact that, under the Agreement, 30 metric tons of highly enriched uranium from dismantled nuclear weapons will be down-blended per year until a total of 500 metric tons has been processed;

11. *Also welcomes* the independent action taken by the United States of America to dispose of 174 metric tons of excess highly enriched uranium from its nuclear weapons programme, of which 50 metric tons have already been down-blended for use as reactor fuel;

12. *Supports* continued efforts by the United States of America and the Russian Federation to implement the 1997 Agreement concerning Cooperation regarding Plutonium Production Reactors and the 2000 Agreement concerning the Management and Disposition of Plutonium Designated as No Longer Required for Defence Purposes and Related Cooperation;

13. *Invites* the United States of America and the Russian Federation to keep other States Members of the United Nations duly informed of their nuclear reduction activities;

14. *Decides* to include in the provisional agenda of its sixtieth session the item entitled "Bilateral strategic nuclear arms reductions and the new strategic framework".

The Assembly adopted **decision 59/514** by recorded vote (138-5-38) [agenda item 65 *(aa)*].

United Nations conference to identify ways of eliminating nuclear dangers in the context of nuclear disarmament

At its 66th plenary meeting, on 3 December 2004, the General Assembly, by a recorded vote of 138 to 5, with 38 abstentions, and on the recommendation of the First Committee, decided to include in the provisional agenda of its sixtieth session the item entitled "United Nations conference to identify ways of eliminating nuclear dangers in the context of nuclear disarmament".

RECORDED VOTE ON DECISION 59/514:

In favour: Afghanistan, Algeria, Angola, Antigua and Barbuda, Argentina, Armenia, Bahamas, Bahrain, Bangladesh, Barbados, Belarus, Belize, Benin, Bhutan, Bolivia, Botswana, Brazil, Brunei Darussalam, Burkina Faso, Burundi, Cambodia, Cameroon, Cape Verde, Central African Republic, Chile, China, Colombia, Comoros, Congo, Costa Rica, Côte d'Ivoire, Cuba, Cyprus, Democratic People's Republic of Korea, Djibouti, Dominica, Dominican Republic, Ecuador, Egypt, El Salvador, Equatorial Guinea, Eritrea, Ethiopia, Fiji, Gabon, Gambia, Ghana, Grenada, Guatemala, Guinea-Bissau, Guyana, Haiti, Honduras, India, Indonesia, Iran, Iraq, Ireland, Jamaica, Japan, Jordan, Kazakhstan, Kenya, Kuwait, Kyrgyzstan, Lao People's Democratic Republic, Lebanon, Lesotho, Liberia, Libyan Arab Jamahiriya, Madagascar, Malawi, Malaysia, Maldives, Mali, Malta, Marshall Islands, Mauritius, Mexico, Mongolia, Morocco, Mozambique, Myanmar, Namibia, Nauru, Nepal, Netherlands, New Zealand, Nicaragua, Niger, Nigeria, Oman, Pakistan, Panama, Papua New Guinea, Paraguay, Peru, Philippines, Qatar, Rwanda, Saint Lucia, Saint Vincent and the Grenadines, Samoa, Sao Tome and Principe, Saudi Arabia, Senegal, Seychelles, Sierra Leone, Singapore, Solomon Islands, Somalia, South Africa, Sri Lanka, Sudan, Suriname, Swaziland, Sweden, Syrian Arab Republic, Tajikistan, Thailand, Timor-Leste, Togo, Tonga, Trinidad and Tobago, Tunisia, Tuvalu, Uganda, Ukraine, United Arab Emirates, United Republic of Tanzania, Uruguay, Uzbekistan, Vanuatu, Venezuela, Viet Nam, Yemen, Zambia, Zimbabwe.

Against: France, Palau, Poland, United Kingdom, United States.

Abstaining: Albania, Andorra, Australia, Austria, Azerbaijan, Belgium, Bosnia and Herzegovina, Bulgaria, Canada, Croatia, Denmark, Estonia, Finland, Georgia, Germany, Greece, Hungary, Iceland, Israel, Italy, Latvia, Liechtenstein, Lithuania, Luxembourg, Norway, Portugal, Republic of Korea, Republic of Moldova, Romania, Russian Federation, San Marino, Serbia and Montenegro, Slovakia, Slovenia, Spain, Switzerland, The former Yugoslav Republic of Macedonia, Turkey.

ABM Treaty and other missile issues

In 2004, missile defence issues, particularly the proliferation of long-range ballistic missiles and United States efforts to build a missile defence system [YUN 1999, p. 469], remained an area of international concern. During the year, the United States installed six interceptor missiles at its missile defence complex at Fort Greely, Alaska, designed to destroy an incoming warhead before it reached its target anywhere in the country, thus completing the first phase of its planned missile defence system. Despite the system's failure during a test on 15 December, United States officials reaffirmed the Government's intention to pursue development of the system. By year's end, 18 countries were either actively involved in the project or were exploring missile defence cooperation with the United States. The North Atlantic Treaty Organization (NATO) was also involved in the project.

On 2 December, the Russian Federation decided to expand its role in a joint project with India to build a sophisticated cruise missile, and it assured India of steady supplies of military spare parts.

On 28 December, India and Pakistan issued a joint statement indicating that they were working towards an early finalization of an agreement for mutual pre-launch notification before testing ballistic missiles.

The subscribing States to the non-legally binding international code of conduct against ballistic missile proliferation, also known as the Hague Code of Conduct, adopted in 2002 [YUN 2002, p. 504], held their third regular meeting (New York, 17-18 November), at which they discussed, among other things, further implementation of confidence-building measures, future outreach activities and methods of communication. The meeting agreed that annual declarations were to cover the period from 1 January to 31 December, with 31 March of the following year as the deadline for submission. The fourth regular meeting was scheduled to take place in Vienna in June 2005, when confidence-building measures and universalization of the Code would be discussed. At year's end, subscribing States numbered 117.

Report of Secretary-General. In response to General Assembly resolution 58/37 [YUN 2003, p. 546], the Secretary-General, in a July report with a later addendum [A/59/137 & Add.1], presented the replies of seven Member States to his request for their views on the issue of missiles in all its aspects.

Expert panel. In August [A/59/278 & Corr.1], the Secretary-General reported on the activities of the Panel of Governmental Experts he had established to explore the issue of missiles in all its aspects pursuant to Assembly resolution 58/37. The Panel met (New York, 23-27 February, 17-21 May and 19-23 July) and held an in-depth discussion, taking into account Member States' views (see above) and papers put forward by its members. However, given the complexity of the issues at hand, the Panel was not able to reach consensus on the preparation of a final report. The first panel of governmental experts completed its work in 2002 [YUN 2002, p. 504].

Communications. In April, the Libyan Arab Jamahiriya announced plans to reduce the range of its Scud B missiles below their current range of 185 miles, and to reduce the missiles' maximum payload from 2,200 pounds to less than 1,100 pounds. It agreed to allow monitors from the United States and the United Kingdom to observe the conversions and ensure that they were irreversible.

On 9 August [CD/1742], the Russian Federation pointed out a potential threat to its deterrent forces, following a 6 August agreement between Denmark and the United States on the modernization of the United States radar station in Thule, Greenland. Despite United States assurances that its anti-missile defence would not be directed against Russia, the location of the radar station suggested otherwise and Russia reserved the right to maintain its security at the appropriate level.

Ministers of the Non-Aligned Movement, at their Fourteenth Ministerial Conference (Durban, South Africa, 17-19 August), reaffirmed the need for a multilaterally negotiated, universal, comprehensive, transparent and non-discriminatory approach towards the issue of missiles in all its aspects.

GENERAL ASSEMBLY ACTION

On 3 December [meeting 66], the General Assembly, on the recommendation of the First Committee [A/59/459 & Corr.1], adopted **resolution 59/67** by recorded vote (119-4-60) [agenda item 65 (*g*)].

Missiles

The General Assembly,

Recalling its resolutions 54/54 F of 1 December 1999, 55/33 A of 20 November 2000, 56/24 B of 29 November 2001, 57/71 of 22 November 2002 and 58/37 of 8 December 2003,

Reaffirming the role of the United Nations in the field of arms regulation and disarmament and the commitment of Member States to take concrete steps to strengthen that role,

Realizing the need to promote regional and international peace and security in a world free from the scourge of war and the burden of armaments,

Convinced of the need for a comprehensive approach towards missiles, in a balanced and non-discriminatory manner, as a contribution to international peace and security,

Bearing in mind that the security concerns of Member States at the international and regional levels should be taken into consideration in addressing the issue of missiles,

Underlining the complexities involved in considering the issue of missiles in the conventional context,

Expressing its support for the international efforts against the development and proliferation of all weapons of mass destruction,

Considering that the Secretary-General, in response to resolution 58/37, established in 2004 a Panel of Governmental Experts, which had a comprehensive, in-depth exchange of views on the issue of missiles in all its aspects,

Taking note of the report of the Secretary-General on the issue of missiles in all its aspects, in which he stated that given the complexity of the issues at hand, no consensus had been reached on the preparation of a final report by the Panel,

1. *Takes note* of the report of the Secretary-General containing the replies from Member States on the report on the issue of missiles in all its aspects, submitted pursuant to resolution 58/37;

2. *Requests* the Secretary-General to prepare a report, with the support of qualified consultants and the United Nations Institute for Disarmament Research, as appropriate, taking into account the views expressed by Member States, to contribute to the United Nations endeavour to address the issue of missiles in all its aspects, by identifying areas where consensus can be reached, and to submit it to the General Assembly at its sixty-first session;

3. *Also requests* the Secretary-General, with the assistance of a Panel of Governmental Experts, to be es-

tablished in 2007 on the basis of equitable geographical distribution, to further explore further ways and means to address within the United Nations the issue of missiles in all its aspects, including identifying areas where consensus can be reached, and to submit a report for consideration by the General Assembly at its sixty-third session;

4. *Decides* to include in the provisional agenda of its sixtieth session the item entitled "Missiles".

RECORDED VOTE ON RESOLUTION 59/67:

In favour: Afghanistan, Algeria, Angola, Antigua and Barbuda, Bahamas, Bahrain, Bangladesh, Barbados, Belarus, Belize, Benin, Bhutan, Botswana, Brazil, Brunei Darussalam, Burkina Faso, Burundi, Cambodia, Cameroon, Cape Verde, Central African Republic, Chile, China, Colombia, Comoros, Congo, Costa Rica, Côte d'Ivoire, Cuba, Democratic People's Republic of Korea, Djibouti, Dominica, Dominican Republic, Ecuador, Egypt, El Salvador, Equatorial Guinea, Eritrea, Ethiopia, Gabon, Gambia, Ghana, Grenada, Guatemala, Guinea-Bissau, Guyana, India, Indonesia, Iran, Jamaica, Jordan, Kazakhstan, Kenya, Kuwait, Kyrgyzstan, Lao People's Democratic Republic, Lebanon, Lesotho, Libyan Arab Jamahiriya, Madagascar, Malawi, Malaysia, Maldives, Mali, Marshall Islands, Mauritius, Mexico, Mongolia, Morocco, Mozambique, Myanmar, Namibia, Nauru, Nepal, New Zealand, Nicaragua, Niger, Nigeria, Oman, Pakistan, Panama, Papua New Guinea, Paraguay, Peru, Philippines, Qatar, Russian Federation, Rwanda, Saint Lucia, Sao Tome and Principe, Saudi Arabia, Senegal, Seychelles, Sierra Leone, Solomon Islands, Somalia, South Africa, Sri Lanka, Sudan, Suriname, Swaziland, Syrian Arab Republic, Tajikistan, Thailand, Timor-Leste, Togo, Tonga, Trinidad and Tobago, Tunisia, Turkmenistan, Uganda, Ukraine, United Arab Emirates, United Republic of Tanzania, Venezuela, Viet Nam, Yemen, Zambia, Zimbabwe.

Against: Israel, Micronesia, Palau, United States.

Abstaining: Albania, Andorra, Argentina, Armenia, Australia, Austria, Azerbaijan, Belgium, Bolivia, Bosnia and Herzegovina, Bulgaria, Canada, Croatia, Cyprus, Czech Republic, Denmark, Estonia, Fiji, Finland, France, Georgia, Germany, Greece, Haiti, Honduras, Hungary, Iceland, Ireland, Italy, Japan, Latvia, Liberia, Liechtenstein, Lithuania, Luxembourg, Malta, Monaco, Netherlands, Norway, Poland, Portugal, Republic of Korea, Republic of Moldova, Romania, Saint Vincent and the Grenadines, Samoa, San Marino, Serbia and Montenegro, Singapore, Slovakia, Slovenia, Spain, Sweden, Switzerland, The former Yugoslav Republic of Macedonia, Turkey, Tuvalu, United Kingdom, Uruguay, Uzbekistan.

Also on 3 December [meeting 66], the General Assembly, on the recommendation of the First Committee [A/59/459 & Corr.1], adopted **resolution 59/91** by recorded vote (161-2-15) [agenda item 65].

The Hague Code of Conduct against Ballistic Missile Proliferation

The General Assembly,

Concerned about the increasing regional and global security challenges caused, inter alia, by the ongoing proliferation of ballistic missiles capable of delivering weapons of mass destruction,

Bearing in mind the purposes and principles of the United Nations and its role and responsibility in the field of international peace and security in accordance with the Charter of the United Nations,

Emphasizing the significance of regional and international efforts to prevent and curb comprehensively the proliferation of ballistic missile systems capable of delivering weapons of mass destruction, as a contribution to international peace and security,

Convinced that the Hague Code of Conduct against Ballistic Missile Proliferation will contribute to enhancing transparency and confidence among States,

Confirming its commitment to the Declaration on International Cooperation in the Exploration and Use of Outer Space for the Benefit and in the Interest of All States, Taking into Particular Account the Needs of Developing Countries, as contained in the annex to its resolution 51/122 of 13 December 1996,

Recognizing that States should not be excluded from utilizing the benefits of space for peaceful purposes, but that in reaping such benefits and in conducting related cooperation they must not contribute to the proliferation of ballistic missiles capable of carrying weapons of mass destruction,

Mindful of the need to combat the proliferation of weapons of mass destruction and their means of delivery,

1. *Welcomes* the adoption of the Hague Code of Conduct against Ballistic Missile Proliferation on 25 November 2002 at The Hague as a practical step against the proliferation of weapons of mass destruction and their means of delivery;

2. *Notes with satisfaction* that one hundred and seventeen States already have subscribed to the Code of Conduct;

3. *Invites* all States that have not yet subscribed to the Code of Conduct to do so;

4. *Encourages* the exploration of further ways and means to deal effectively with the problem of the proliferation of ballistic missiles capable of delivering weapons of mass destruction;

5. *Decides* to include in the provisional agenda of its sixtieth session an item entitled "The Hague Code of Conduct against Ballistic Missile Proliferation".

RECORDED VOTE ON RESOLUTION 59/91:

In favour: Afghanistan, Albania, Andorra, Angola, Antigua and Barbuda, Argentina, Armenia, Australia, Austria, Azerbaijan, Bahamas, Barbados, Belarus, Belgium, Belize, Benin, Bhutan, Bolivia, Bosnia and Herzegovina, Botswana, Brunei Darussalam, Bulgaria, Burkina Faso, Burundi, Cambodia, Cameroon, Canada, Cape Verde, Central African Republic, Chile, China, Colombia, Comoros, Congo, Costa Rica, Côte d'Ivoire, Croatia, Cyprus, Czech Republic, Denmark, Dominica, Dominican Republic, Ecuador, El Salvador, Equatorial Guinea, Eritrea, Estonia, Ethiopia, Fiji, Finland, France, Gabon, Gambia, Georgia, Germany, Ghana, Greece, Grenada, Guatemala, Guinea-Bissau, Guyana, Haiti, Honduras, Hungary, Iceland, Ireland, Israel, Italy, Jamaica, Japan, Jordan, Kazakhstan, Kenya, Kuwait, Kyrgyzstan, Latvia, Lesotho, Liberia, Libyan Arab Jamahiriya, Liechtenstein, Lithuania, Luxembourg, Madagascar, Malawi, Maldives, Mali, Malta, Marshall Islands, Micronesia, Monaco, Mongolia, Morocco, Mozambique, Myanmar, Namibia, Nauru, Nepal, Netherlands, New Zealand, Nicaragua, Niger, Nigeria, Norway, Oman, Palau, Panama, Papua New Guinea, Paraguay, Peru, Philippines, Poland, Portugal, Qatar, Republic of Korea, Republic of Moldova, Romania, Russian Federation, Rwanda, Saint Kitts and Nevis, Saint Lucia, Saint Vincent and the Grenadines, Samoa, San Marino, Sao Tome and Principe, Senegal, Serbia and Montenegro, Seychelles, Sierra Leone, Singapore, Slovakia, Slovenia, Solomon Islands, Somalia, South Africa, Spain, Sri Lanka, Sudan, Suriname, Swaziland, Sweden, Switzerland, Tajikistan, Thailand, The former Yugoslav Republic of Macedonia, Timor-Leste, Togo, Trinidad and Tobago, Tunisia, Turkey, Tuvalu, Uganda, Ukraine, United Kingdom, United Republic of Tanzania, United States, Uruguay, Uzbekistan, Vanuatu, Venezuela, Zambia, Zimbabwe.

Against: Egypt, Iran.

Abstaining: Algeria, Bahrain, Bangladesh, Brazil, Cuba, Djibouti, India, Indonesia, Malaysia, Mauritius, Mexico, Pakistan, Syrian Arab Republic, United Arab Emirates, Yemen.

Comprehensive Nuclear-Test-Ban Treaty

Status

As at 31 December, 174 States had signed the 1996 Comprehensive Nuclear-Test-Ban Treaty (CTBT) adopted by General Assembly resolution 50/245 [YUN 1996, p. 454], and 120 had ratified it. During the year, instruments of ratification were deposited by Bahrain, Belize, the Democratic Republic of the Congo, the Libyan Arab Jamahiriya, Liechtenstein, Rwanda, Serbia and Montenegro,

Seychelles, the Sudan, Togo, Tunisia and the United Republic of Tanzania. In accordance with article XIV, CTBT would enter into force 180 days after the 44 States possessing nuclear reactors, listed in annex 2 of the Treaty, had deposited their instruments of ratification. By year's end, 33 of those States had ratified the Treaty.

On 1 November [A/59/550], Australia, Finland, Japan and the Netherlands transmitted a Joint Ministerial Statement (New York, 23 September), signed by a total of 66 Foreign Ministers, reaffirming their support for CTBT, which was intended to rid the world of nuclear-weapons test explosions and to contribute to the progressive reduction of nuclear weapons and the prevention of nuclear proliferation. They called on States that had not done so to ratify CTBT, in particular those whose ratification was needed for its entry into force. States were urged to maintain a moratorium on nuclear-weapon test explosions or any other nuclear explosions.

GENERAL ASSEMBLY ACTION

On 3 December [meeting 66], the General Assembly, on the recommendation of the First Committee [A/59/465], adopted **resolution 59/109** by recorded vote (177-2-4) [agenda item 71].

Comprehensive Nuclear-Test-Ban Treaty

The General Assembly,

Reiterating that the cessation of nuclear-weapon test explosions or any other nuclear explosions constitutes an effective nuclear disarmament and non-proliferation measure,

Recalling that the Comprehensive Nuclear-Test-Ban Treaty, adopted by its resolution 50/245 of 10 September 1996, was opened for signature on 24 September 1996,

Stressing that a universal and effectively verifiable Comprehensive Nuclear-Test-Ban Treaty constitutes a fundamental instrument in the field of nuclear disarmament and non-proliferation,

Encouraged by the signing of the Treaty by one hundred and seventy-three States, including forty-one of the forty-four needed for its entry into force, and welcoming the ratification of one hundred and nineteen States, including thirty-three of the forty-four needed for its entry into force, among which there are three nuclear-weapon States,

Recalling its resolution 58/71 of 8 December 2003,

Welcoming the Joint Ministerial Statement reaffirming support for the Comprehensive Nuclear-Test-Ban Treaty, signed in New York on 23 September 2004,

1. *Stresses* the importance and urgency of signature and ratification, without delay and without conditions, to achieve the earliest entry into force of the Comprehensive Nuclear-Test-Ban Treaty;

2. *Welcomes* the contributions by the States signatories to the work of the Preparatory Commission for the Comprehensive Nuclear-Test-Ban Treaty Organization, in particular its efforts to ensure that the Treaty's verification regime will be capable of meeting the verification requirements of the Treaty upon its entry into force, in accordance with article IV of the Treaty;

3. *Underlines* the need to maintain momentum towards completion of the verification regime;

4. *Calls upon* all States to maintain their moratoriums on nuclear-weapons test explosions or any other nuclear explosions and to refrain from acts that would defeat the object and purpose of the Treaty;

5. *Calls upon* all States that have not yet signed the Treaty to sign and ratify it as soon as possible;

6. *Calls upon* all States that have signed but not yet ratified the Treaty, in particular those whose ratification is needed for its entry into force, to accelerate their ratification processes with a view to their earliest successful conclusion;

7. *Urges* all States to remain seized of the issue at the highest political level;

8. *Requests* the Secretary-General, in consultation with the Preparatory Commission for the Comprehensive Nuclear-Test-Ban Treaty Organization, to prepare a report on the efforts of States that have ratified the Treaty towards its universalization and possibilities for providing assistance on ratification procedures to States that so request it, and to submit such a report to the General Assembly at its sixtieth session;

9. *Decides* to include in the provisional agenda of its sixtieth session the item entitled "Comprehensive Nuclear-Test-Ban Treaty".

RECORDED VOTE ON RESOLUTION 59/109:

In favour: Afghanistan, Albania, Algeria, Andorra, Angola, Antigua and Barbuda, Argentina, Armenia, Australia, Austria, Azerbaijan, Bahamas, Bahrain, Bangladesh, Barbados, Belarus, Belgium, Belize, Benin, Bhutan, Bolivia, Bosnia and Herzegovina, Botswana, Brazil, Brunei Darussalam, Bulgaria, Burkina Faso, Burundi, Cambodia, Cameroon, Canada, Cape Verde, Central African Republic, Chile, China, Comoros, Congo, Costa Rica, Côte d'Ivoire, Croatia, Cuba, Cyprus, Czech Republic, Denmark, Djibouti, Dominica, Dominican Republic, Ecuador, Egypt, El Salvador, Equatorial Guinea, Eritrea, Estonia, Ethiopia, Fiji, Finland, France, Gabon, Gambia, Georgia, Germany, Ghana, Greece, Grenada, Guatemala, Guinea-Bissau, Guyana, Haiti, Honduras, Hungary, Iceland, Indonesia, Iran, Iraq, Ireland, Israel, Italy, Jamaica, Japan, Jordan, Kazakhstan, Kenya, Kuwait, Kyrgyzstan, Lao People's Democratic Republic, Latvia, Lesotho, Liberia, Libyan Arab Jamahiriya, Liechtenstein, Lithuania, Luxembourg, Madagascar, Malawi, Malaysia, Maldives, Mali, Malta, Marshall Islands, Mexico, Micronesia, Monaco, Mongolia, Morocco, Mozambique, Myanmar, Namibia, Nauru, Nepal, Netherlands, New Zealand, Nicaragua, Niger, Nigeria, Norway, Oman, Pakistan, Panama, Papua New Guinea, Paraguay, Peru, Philippines, Poland, Portugal, Qatar, Republic of Korea, Republic of Moldova, Romania, Russian Federation, Rwanda, Saint Lucia, Saint Vincent and the Grenadines, Samoa, San Marino, Sao Tome and Principe, Saudi Arabia, Senegal, Serbia and Montenegro, Seychelles, Sierra Leone, Singapore, Slovakia, Slovenia, Solomon Islands, Somalia, South Africa, Spain, Sri Lanka, Sudan, Suriname, Swaziland, Sweden, Switzerland, Tajikistan, Thailand, The former Yugoslav Republic of Macedonia, Timor-Leste, Togo, Tonga, Trinidad and Tobago, Tunisia, Turkey, Turkmenistan, Tuvalu, Uganda, Ukraine, United Arab Emirates, United Kingdom, United Republic of Tanzania, Uruguay, Uzbekistan, Vanuatu, Venezuela, Viet Nam, Yemen, Zambia, Zimbabwe.

Against: Palau, United States.

Abstaining: Colombia, India, Mauritius, Syrian Arab Republic.

Preparatory Commission for the CTBT Organization

The Preparatory Commission for the Comprehensive Nuclear-Test-Ban Treaty Organization (CTBTO), established in 1996 [YUN 1996, p. 452], continued to develop the Treaty's verification regime. Significant progress was made in establishing the International Monitoring System (IMS) [YUN 1999, p. 472], the global network of 337 facilities in 90 countries designed to track and detect nuclear explosions prohibited by CTBT via a global satellite communication system, and to transmit relevant information to the International Data Centre (IDC) in Vienna. At year's end, 204 stations (64 per cent) were either certified as meeting the technical requirements of the Preparatory Commission or were installed and substantially met specifications. Over 55 per cent of all the stations were operational and the entire IMS network was scheduled to be completed within three to four years. The current phase of testing and evaluation of the system had good results and it was providing global coverage by transmitting raw data to IDC, which was connected to 82 national data centres through a satellite-based global communications infrastructure. Other activities of the Commission included training courses for IMS station operators and international workshops to enhance participation in the Commission's work.

The Preparatory Commission held its twenty-second (22-24 June) [CTBT/PC-22/1] and twenty-third (15-19 November) [CTBT /PC-23/1] sessions, both in Vienna, to consider the reports of its working groups and to discuss organizational, budgetary and other matters. The Commission adopted its 2005 programme budget in the combined amounts of $51,047,250 and 42,540,900 euros, of which approximately $30 million and 12 million euros were earmarked for the IMS network.

GENERAL ASSEMBLY ACTION

On 22 October [meeting 40], the General Assembly adopted **resolution 59/6** [draft A/59/L.7 & Add.1] by recorded vote (104-1) [agenda item 56 (r)].

Cooperation between the United Nations and the Preparatory Commission for the Comprehensive Nuclear-Test-Ban Treaty Organization

The General Assembly,

Taking note of the note by the Secretary-General on cooperation between the United Nations and the Preparatory Commission for the Comprehensive Nuclear-Test-Ban Treaty Organization,

Taking note also of the report of the Executive Secretary of the Preparatory Commission for the Comprehensive Nuclear-Test-Ban Treaty Organization,

Decides to include in the provisional agenda of its sixty-first session the sub-item entitled "Cooperation between the United Nations and the Preparatory Commission for the Comprehensive Nuclear-Test-Ban Treaty Organization".

RECORDED VOTE ON RESOLUTION 59/6:

In favour: Afghanistan, Argentina, Armenia, Austria, Azerbaijan, Bahrain, Bangladesh, Bolivia, Bosnia and Herzegovina, Botswana, Brazil, Brunei Darussalam, Bulgaria, Central African Republic, Chile, China, Colombia, Congo, Croatia, Cuba, Cyprus, Czech Republic, Denmark, El Salvador, Equatorial Guinea, Estonia, Ethiopia, Finland, Georgia, Greece, Guatemala, Guinea, Guinea-Bissau, Guyana, Hungary, Iceland, India, Indonesia, Iran, Ireland, Israel, Italy, Japan, Kazakhstan, Kenya, Kuwait, Lao People's Democratic Republic, Latvia, Lebanon, Libyan Arab Jamahiriya,

Liechtenstein, Lithuania, Madagascar, Malaysia, Marshall Islands, Mauritius, Mexico, Monaco, Mongolia, Morocco, Mozambique, Myanmar, Namibia, Netherlands, New Zealand, Nicaragua, Nigeria, Norway, Oman, Peru, Philippines, Poland, Portugal, Republic of Korea, Republic of Moldova, Romania, Russian Federation, San Marino, Saudi Arabia, Senegal, Serbia and Montenegro, Slovakia, Slovenia, Spain, Sri Lanka, Sudan, Suriname, Swaziland, Sweden, Syrian Arab Republic, Thailand, Timor-Leste, Trinidad and Tobago, Tunisia, Turkey, Ukraine, United Arab Emirates, United Kingdom, United Republic of Tanzania, Uruguay, Venezuela, Viet Nam, Yemen, Zambia.

Against: United States.

Prohibition of the use of nuclear weapons

In 2004, as in previous years, the Conference on Disarmament was not able to undertake negotiations on a convention on the prohibition of the use of nuclear weapons, as called for in General Assembly resolution 58/64 [YUN 2003, p. 551].

GENERAL ASSEMBLY ACTION

On 3 December [meeting 66], the General Assembly, on the recommendation of the First Committee [A/59/460], adopted **resolution 59/102** by recorded vote (125-48-12) [agenda item 66].

Convention on the Prohibition of the Use of Nuclear Weapons

The General Assembly,

Convinced that the use of nuclear weapons poses the most serious threat to the survival of mankind,

Bearing in mind the advisory opinion of the International Court of Justice of 8 July 1996 on the *Legality of the Threat or Use of Nuclear Weapons,*

Convinced that a multilateral, universal and binding agreement prohibiting the use or threat of use of nuclear weapons would contribute to the elimination of the nuclear threat and to the climate for negotiations leading to the ultimate elimination of nuclear weapons, thereby strengthening international peace and security,

Conscious that some steps taken by the Russian Federation and the United States of America towards a reduction of their nuclear weapons and the improvement in the international climate can contribute towards the goal of the complete elimination of nuclear weapons,

Recalling that, in paragraph 58 of the Final Document of the Tenth Special Session of the General Assembly, it is stated that all States should actively participate in efforts to bring about conditions in international relations among States in which a code of peaceful conduct of nations in international affairs could be agreed upon and that would preclude the use or threat of use of nuclear weapons,

Reaffirming that any use of nuclear weapons would be a violation of the Charter of the United Nations and a crime against humanity, as declared in its resolutions 1653(XVI) of 24 November 1961, 33/71 B of 14 December 1978, 34/83 G of 11 December 1979, 35/152 D of 12 December 1980 and 36/92 I of 9 December 1981,

Determined to achieve an international convention prohibiting the development, production, stockpiling and use of nuclear weapons, leading to their ultimate destruction,

Stressing that an international convention on the prohibition of the use of nuclear weapons would be an important step in a phased programme towards the complete elimination of nuclear weapons, with a specified framework of time,

Noting with regret that the Conference on Disarmament, during its 2004 session, was unable to undertake negotiations on this subject as called for in General Assembly resolution 58/64 of 8 December 2003,

1. *Reiterates its request* to the Conference on Disarmament to commence negotiations in order to reach agreement on an international convention prohibiting the use or threat of use of nuclear weapons under any circumstances;

2. *Requests* the Conference on Disarmament to report to the General Assembly on the results of those negotiations.

RECORDED VOTE ON RESOLUTION 59/102:

In favour: Afghanistan, Algeria, Angola, Antigua and Barbuda, Bahamas, Bahrain, Bangladesh, Barbados, Belize, Benin, Bhutan, Bolivia, Botswana, Brazil, Brunei Darussalam, Burkina Faso, Burundi, Cambodia, Cameroon, Cape Verde, Central African Republic, Chile, China, Colombia, Comoros, Congo, Costa Rica, Côte d'Ivoire, Cuba, Democratic People's Republic of Korea, Djibouti, Dominica, Dominican Republic, Ecuador, Egypt, El Salvador, Equatorial Guinea, Eritrea, Ethiopia, Fiji, Gabon, Gambia, Ghana, Grenada, Guatemala, Guinea-Bissau, Guyana, Haiti, Honduras, India, Indonesia, Iran, Iraq, Jamaica, Jordan, Kenya, Kuwait, Lao People's Democratic Republic, Lebanon, Lesotho, Liberia, Libyan Arab Jamahiriya, Madagascar, Malawi, Malaysia, Maldives, Mali, Marshall Islands, Mauritius, Mexico, Mongolia, Morocco, Mozambique, Myanmar, Namibia, Nauru, Nepal, Nicaragua, Niger, Nigeria, Oman, Pakistan, Panama, Papua New Guinea, Paraguay, Peru, Philippines, Qatar, Rwanda, Saint Lucia, Saint Vincent and the Grenadines, Samoa, Sao Tome and Principe, Saudi Arabia, Senegal, Seychelles, Sierra Leone, Singapore, Solomon Islands, Somalia, South Africa, Sri Lanka, Sudan, Suriname, Swaziland, Syrian Arab Republic, Thailand, Timor-Leste, Togo, Tonga, Trinidad and Tobago, Tunisia, Turkmenistan, Tuvalu, Uganda, United Arab Emirates, United Republic of Tanzania, Uruguay, Vanuatu, Venezuela, Viet Nam, Yemen, Zambia, Zimbabwe.

Against: Albania, Andorra, Australia, Austria, Belgium, Bosnia and Herzegovina, Bulgaria, Canada, Croatia, Cyprus, Czech Republic, Denmark, Estonia, Finland, France, Georgia, Germany, Greece, Hungary, Iceland, Ireland, Israel, Italy, Latvia, Liechtenstein, Lithuania, Luxembourg, Malta, Micronesia, Monaco, Netherlands, New Zealand, Norway, Palau, Poland, Portugal, Romania, San Marino, Serbia and Montenegro, Slovakia, Slovenia, Spain, Sweden, Switzerland, The former Yugoslav Republic of Macedonia, Turkey, United Kingdom, United States.

Abstaining: Argentina, Armenia, Azerbaijan, Japan, Kazakhstan, Kyrgyzstan, Republic of Korea, Republic of Moldova, Russian Federation, Tajikistan, Ukraine, Uzbekistan.

Advisory opinion of the International Court of Justice

Pursuant to General Assembly resolution 58/46 [YUN 2003, p. 552] on the advisory opinion of the International Court of Justice that the threat or use of nuclear weapons was contrary to the UN Charter [YUN 1996, p. 461], the Secretary-General presented information received from six States (China, Cuba, Guatemala, Mexico, Syrian Arab Republic, Venezuela) on measures they had taken to implement the resolution and towards nuclear disarmament [A/59/136].

GENERAL ASSEMBLY ACTION

On 3 December [meeting 66], the General Assembly, on the recommendation of the First Committee [A/59/459 & Corr.1], adopted **resolution 59/83** by recorded vote (132-29-24) [agenda item 65].

Follow-up to the advisory opinion of the International Court of Justice on the
Legality of the Threat or Use of Nuclear Weapons
The General Assembly,

Recalling its resolutions 49/75 K of 15 December 1994, 51/45 M of 10 December 1996, 52/38 O of 9 December 1997, 53/77 W of 4 December 1998, 54/54 Q of 1 December 1999, 55/33 X of 20 November 2000, 56/24 S of 29 November 2001, 57/85 of 22 November 2002 and 58/46 of 8 December 2003,

Convinced that the continuing existence of nuclear weapons poses a threat to all humanity and that their use would have catastrophic consequences for all life on Earth, and recognizing that the only defence against a nuclear catastrophe is the total elimination of nuclear weapons and the certainty that they will never be produced again,

Reaffirming the commitment of the international community to the goal of the total elimination of nuclear weapons and the creation of a nuclear-weapon-free world,

Mindful of the solemn obligations of States parties, undertaken in article VI of the Treaty on the Non-Proliferation of Nuclear Weapons, particularly to pursue negotiations in good faith on effective measures relating to cessation of the nuclear-arms race at an early date and to nuclear disarmament,

Recalling the principles and objectives for nuclear non-proliferation and disarmament adopted at the 1995 Review and Extension Conference of the Parties to the Treaty on the Non-Proliferation of Nuclear Weapons,

Emphasizing the unequivocal undertaking by the nuclear-weapon States to accomplish the total elimination of their nuclear arsenals leading to nuclear disarmament, adopted at the 2000 Review Conference of the Parties to the Treaty on the Non-Proliferation of Nuclear Weapons,

Recalling the adoption of the Comprehensive Nuclear-Test-Ban Treaty in its resolution 50/245 of 10 September 1996, and expressing its satisfaction at the increasing number of States that have signed and ratified the Treaty,

Recognizing with satisfaction that the Antarctic Treaty and the treaties of Tlatelolco, Rarotonga, Bangkok and Pelindaba are gradually freeing the entire southern hemisphere and adjacent areas covered by those treaties from nuclear weapons,

Stressing the importance of strengthening all existing nuclear-related disarmament and arms control and reduction measures,

Recognizing the need for a multilaterally negotiated and legally binding instrument to assure non-nuclear-weapon States against the threat or use of nuclear weapons,

Reaffirming the central role of the Conference on Disarmament as the single multilateral disarmament negotiating forum, and regretting the lack of progress in disarmament negotiations, particularly nuclear disarmament, in the Conference during its 2004 session,

Emphasizing the need for the Conference on Disarmament to commence negotiations on a phased programme for the complete elimination of nuclear weapons with a specified framework of time,

Expressing its deep concern at the lack of progress in the implementation of the thirteen steps to implement article VI of the Treaty on the Non-Proliferation of Nuclear Weapons agreed to at the 2000 Review Conference of the Parties to the Treaty on the Non-Proliferation of Nuclear Weapons,

Desiring to achieve the objective of a legally binding prohibition of the development, production, testing, deployment, stockpiling, threat or use of nuclear weapons and their destruction under effective international control,

Recalling the advisory opinion of the International Court of Justice on the *Legality of the Threat or Use of Nuclear Weapons*, issued on 8 July 1996,

Taking note of the relevant portions of the report of the Secretary-General relating to the implementation of resolution 58/46,

1. *Underlines once again* the unanimous conclusion of the International Court of Justice that there exists an obligation to pursue in good faith and bring to a conclusion negotiations leading to nuclear disarmament in all its aspects under strict and effective international control;

2. *Calls once again upon* all States immediately to fulfil that obligation by commencing multilateral negotiations leading to an early conclusion of a nuclear weapons convention prohibiting the development, production, testing, deployment, stockpiling, transfer, threat or use of nuclear weapons and providing for their elimination;

3. *Requests* all States to inform the Secretary-General of the efforts and measures they have taken on the implementation of the present resolution and nuclear disarmament, and requests the Secretary-General to apprise the General Assembly of that information at its sixtieth session;

4. *Decides* to include in the provisional agenda of its sixtieth session the item entitled "Follow-up to the advisory opinion of the International Court of Justice on the *Legality of the Threat or Use of Nuclear Weapons*".

RECORDED VOTE ON RESOLUTION 59/83:

In favour: Afghanistan, Algeria, Angola, Antigua and Barbuda, Argentina, Bahamas, Bahrain, Bangladesh, Barbados, Belize, Benin, Bhutan, Bolivia, Botswana, Brazil, Brunei Darussalam, Burkina Faso, Burundi, Cambodia, Cameroon, Cape Verde, Central African Republic, Chile, China, Colombia, Comoros, Congo, Costa Rica, Côte d'Ivoire, Cuba, Democratic People's Republic of Korea, Djibouti, Dominica, Dominican Republic, Ecuador, Egypt, El Salvador, Equatorial Guinea, Eritrea, Ethiopia, Fiji, Gabon, Gambia, Ghana, Grenada, Guatemala, Guinea-Bissau, Guyana, Haiti, Honduras, India, Indonesia, Iran, Iraq, Ireland, Jamaica, Jordan, Kenya, Kuwait, Kyrgyzstan, Lao People's Democratic Republic, Lebanon, Lesotho, Liberia, Libyan Arab Jamahiriya, Madagascar, Malawi, Malaysia, Maldives, Mali, Malta, Marshall Islands, Mauritius, Mexico, Mongolia, Morocco, Mozambique, Myanmar, Namibia, Nauru, Nepal, New Zealand, Nicaragua, Niger, Nigeria, Oman, Pakistan, Panama, Papua New Guinea, Paraguay, Peru, Philippines, Qatar, Rwanda, Saint Lucia, Saint Vincent and the Grenadines, Samoa, San Marino, Sao Tome and Principe, Saudi Arabia, Senegal, Seychelles, Sierra Leone, Singapore, Solomon Islands, Somalia, South Africa, Sri Lanka, Sudan, Suriname, Swaziland, Sweden, Syrian Arab Republic, Thailand, Timor-Leste, Togo, Tonga, Trinidad and Tobago, Tunisia, Turkmenistan, Tuvalu, Uganda, Ukraine, United Arab Emirates, United Republic of Tanzania, Uruguay, Vanuatu, Venezuela, Viet Nam, Yemen, Zambia, Zimbabwe.

Against: Albania, Belgium, Bulgaria, Czech Republic, Denmark, France, Germany, Greece, Hungary, Iceland, Israel, Italy, Latvia, Lithuania, Luxembourg, Monaco, Netherlands, Norway, Palau, Poland, Portugal, Romania, Russian Federation, Slovakia, Slovenia, Spain, Turkey, United Kingdom, United States.

Abstaining: Andorra, Armenia, Australia, Austria, Azerbaijan, Belarus, Bosnia and Herzegovina, Canada, Croatia, Cyprus, Estonia, Finland, Georgia, Japan, Kazakhstan, Liechtenstein, Micronesia, Republic of Korea, Republic of Moldova, Serbia and Montenegro, Switzerland, Tajikistan, The former Yugoslav Republic of Macedonia, Uzbekistan.

Radioactive waste

In response to a 2003 request of the IAEA General Conference [YUN 2003, p. 553], the Agency's Board of Governors approved in March the Action Plan for the Safety of Transport of Radioactive Material, which provided direction for the Agency's transport safety activities over the next five years. The Action Plan was based on the outcome of the 2003 International Conference on the Safety of Transport of Radioactive Material [ibid.]. In September [GC(48)/RES/10], the General Conference, welcoming the Board's approval of the Action Plan, encouraged member States to cooperate in implementing it. Recognizing the potential for damage in the event of an accident while transporting radioactive materials by sea, the General Conference urged member States that did not have national regulatory documents governing the transport of those materials to adopt them.

Non-proliferation issues

Non-Proliferation Treaty

Status

In 2004, the number of States party to the 1968 Treaty on the Non-Proliferation of Nuclear Weapons (NPT), adopted by the General Assembly in resolution 2373(XXII) [YUN 1968, p. 17], remained at 189. NPT entered into force on 5 March 1970.

2005 review conference

Quinquennial review conferences, as called for under article VIII, paragraph 3, of the Treaty, were held in 1975 [YUN 1975, p. 27], 1980 [YUN 1980, p. 51], 1985 [YUN 1985, p. 56], 1990 [YUN 1990, p. 50], 1995 [YUN 1995, p. 189] and 2000 [YUN 2000, p. 487].

In accordance with the decision of the NPT parties in 2002 [YUN 2002, p. 507], the Preparatory Committee for the 2005 Review Conference held its third session (New York, 26 April–7 May) [NPT/CONF.2005/1], at which it considered the implementation of the Treaty's provisions relating to the non-proliferation of nuclear weapons, disarmament and international peace and security; safeguards and nuclear-weapon-free zones; and the right of States parties to research, produce and use nuclear energy for peaceful purposes. The Committee also considered its decision on principles and objectives for nuclear non-proliferation and disarmament, and its resolution on the Middle East, both adopted at the 1995

Review Conference, as well as related aspects of the Final Document of the 2000 Review Conference, and the safety and security of peaceful nuclear programmes. On 7 May, the Committee adopted its final report, reaffirming that the 2005 Review Conference of the NPT parties would be held in New York from 2 to 27 May 2005. The Committee considered questions relating to the organization and work of the Conference, but was not able to reach agreement on its provisional agenda and decided to defer consideration of the final outcome document to the Conference.

Documents considered by the Committee included reports by 27 States on implementation of NPT and of the 1995 decision [NPT/CONF.2005/PC.III/1, 5, 7, 9, 10, 12, 13, 14, 16, 18, 20, 22, 23, 24, 25, 28, 29, 31, 33, 34, 36, 37, 38, 39, 41, 44, 45]; reports by 12 States on steps or measures taken to promote the establishment of the Middle East as a zone free of nuclear weapons, particularly within the context of the 1995 resolution [NPT/CONF.2005/PC.III/2, 3, 6, 8, 15, 19, 21, 26, 32, 35, 40, 47, 48]; a report by CTBTO updating the report of its Preparatory Commission [NPT/CONF.2005/PC.III/4]; recommendations submitted by the New Agenda Coalition [NPT/CONF.2005/PC.III/11] and by Iran [NPT/CONF.2005/PC.III/42]; the Havana Declaration relating to the Treaty for the Prohibition of Nuclear Weapons in Latin America and the Caribbean (Treaty of Tlatelolco) (see p. 552), submitted by Cuba [NPT/CONF.2005/PC.III/17]; a report on NPT by New Zealand [NPT/CONF.2005/PC.III/27]; a position paper on the final outcome of the session by the Non-Aligned States and other States parties of NPT [NPT/CONF.2005/PC.III/43]; a document on the contemporary crisis of compliance submitted by the United States [NPT/CONF.2005/PC.III/46]; and numerous working papers.

Communication. The Ministers of the Non-Aligned Movement, at their Fourteenth Ministerial Conference (Durban, 17-19 August), called for firm commitment by all States parties to the implementation of NPT. Reaffirming the right of developing countries to use nuclear energy for peaceful purposes, the Ministers expressed concern that undue restrictions on exports to developing countries of material, equipment and technology for peaceful purposes persisted.

Non-proliferation of weapons of mass destruction

The High-level Panel on Threats, Challenges and Change, a group of eminent persons established by the Secretary-General to assess threats to international peace and security and to recommend ways of strengthening the collective security capacity of the United Nations (see p. 54), in its December report [A/59/565 & Corr.1], described the threat posed by the proliferation of nuclear, radiological, chemical and biological weapons and made recommendations for stopping it. The Panel determined that the threat posed by nuclear proliferation arose from countries, even NPT signatories, covertly and illegally developing full-scale weapons programmes or acquiring the materials and expertise needed for weapons programmes. The Panel remarked on the erosion and possible collapse of the NPT regime. Chemical and biological materials also posed a growing threat, as they were capable of inflicting mass casualties and were relatively easy to acquire and weaponize.

Among its proposals to restart disarmament, the Panel suggested that the nuclear-weapon States honour their NPT commitments and reaffirm commitments not to use nuclear weapons against non-nuclear-weapon States. The United States and the Russian Federation, other nuclear-weapon States and States not party to NPT should adopt practical measures to reduce the risk of accidental nuclear war, including a schedule for de-alerting their strategic nuclear weapons. The Security Council should pledge to take collective action in response to a nuclear attack or the threat of such attack on a non-nuclear-weapon State, and should act in cases of serious non-compliance with IAEA non-proliferation and safeguards standards. States not party to NPT should pledge commitment to non-proliferation and disarmament, ratify the Comprehensive Nuclear-Test-Ban Treaty and support negotiations for a fissile material cut-off treaty. Negotiations should begin on enabling IAEA to act as guarantor for the supply of fissile material to civilian nuclear users. All States were encouraged to join the voluntary Proliferation Security Initiative to interdict the illicit trade in components for nuclear programmes. The Panel called for efforts in the Middle East and South Asia to launch nuclear disarmament talks that could lead to the establishment of nuclear-weapon-free zones similar to those established in other parts of the world. It proposed a scheduled destruction of all chemical weapons stockpiles by 2012. Urging the resumption of negotiations by the States parties to the Convention on the Prohibition of the Development, Production and Stockpiling of Bacteriological (Biological) and Toxin Weapons and on Their Destruction on a verification protocol, the Panel also called on those States to negotiate a new bio-security protocol to classify dangerous biological agents and establish binding international standards for their export.

Establishment of Security Council Committee

The Security Council, in resolution 1540 (2004) (see below), affirming that the proliferation of nuclear, chemical and biological weapons and their means of delivery constituted a threat to international peace and security, established a Committee consisting of all Council members to monitor Member States' efforts to combat the problem.

SECURITY COUNCIL ACTION

On 28 April [meeting 4956], the Security Council unanimously adopted **resolution 1540(2004)**. The draft [S/2004/326] was prepared in consultations among Council members.

The Security Council,

Affirming that proliferation of nuclear, chemical and biological weapons, as well as their means of delivery[1], constitutes a threat to international peace and security,

Reaffirming, in this context, the statement by its President adopted at the Council's meeting at the level of heads of State and Government on 31 January 1992, including the need for all Member States to fulfil their obligations in relation to arms control and disarmament and to prevent proliferation in all its aspects of all weapons of mass destruction,

Recalling that the statement underlined the need for all Member States to resolve peacefully, in accordance with the Charter of the United Nations, any problems in that context threatening or disrupting the maintenance of regional and global stability,

Affirming its resolve to take appropriate and effective action against any threat to international peace and security caused by the proliferation of nuclear, chemical and biological weapons and their means of delivery, in conformity with its primary responsibilities, as provided for in the Charter,

Affirming also its support for the multilateral treaties whose aim is to eliminate or prevent the proliferation of nuclear, chemical or biological weapons and the importance for all States parties to those treaties to implement them fully in order to promote international stability,

Welcoming efforts in this context by multilateral arrangements which contribute to non-proliferation,

Affirming that prevention of the proliferation of nuclear, chemical and biological weapons should not hamper international cooperation in materials, equipment and technology for peaceful purposes, while goals of peaceful utilization should not be used as a cover for proliferation,

Gravely concerned by the threat of terrorism and the risk that non-State actors[1] such as those identified in the United Nations list established and maintained by the Committee established under Security Council resolution 1267(1999) of 15 October 1999 and those to whom resolution 1373(2001) of 28 September 2001 applies, may acquire, develop, traffic in or use nuclear, chemical and biological weapons and their means of delivery,

Gravely concerned also by the threat of illicit trafficking in nuclear, chemical, or biological weapons and their means of delivery, and related materials,[1] which adds a new dimension to the issue of proliferation of such weapons and also poses a threat to international peace and security,

Recognizing the need to enhance coordination of efforts on national, subregional, regional and international levels in order to strengthen a global response to this serious challenge and threat to international security,

Recognizing also that most States have undertaken binding legal obligations under treaties to which they are parties, or have made other commitments aimed at preventing the proliferation of nuclear, chemical or biological weapons, and have taken effective measures to account for, secure and physically protect sensitive materials, such as those required by the Convention on the Physical Protection of Nuclear Materials and those recommended by the Code of Conduct on the Safety and Security of Radioactive Sources of the International Atomic Energy Agency,

Recognizing further the urgent need for all States to take additional effective measures to prevent the proliferation of nuclear, chemical or biological weapons and their means of delivery,

Encouraging all Member States to implement fully the disarmament treaties and agreements to which they are party,

Reaffirming the need to combat by all means, in accordance with the Charter, threats to international peace and security caused by terrorist acts,

Determined to facilitate henceforth an effective response to global threats in the area of non-proliferation,

Acting under Chapter VII of the Charter,

1. *Decides* that all States shall refrain from providing any form of support to non-State actors that attempt to develop, acquire, manufacture, possess, transport, transfer or use nuclear, chemical or biological weapons and their means of delivery;

2. *Decides also* that all States, in accordance with their national procedures, shall adopt and enforce appropriate effective laws which prohibit any non-State actor to manufacture, acquire, possess, develop, transport, transfer or use nuclear, chemical or biological weapons and their means of delivery, in particular for terrorist purposes, as well as attempts to engage in any of the foregoing activities, participate in them as an accomplice, assist or finance them;

3. *Decides further* that all States shall take and enforce effective measures to establish domestic controls to prevent the proliferation of nuclear, chemical, or biological weapons and their means of delivery, including by establishing appropriate controls over related materials, and to this end shall:

(*a*) Develop and maintain appropriate effective measures to account for and secure such items in production, use, storage or transport;

(*b*) Develop and maintain appropriate effective physical protection measures;

(*c*) Develop and maintain appropriate effective border controls and law enforcement efforts to detect, deter, prevent and combat, including through international cooperation when necessary, the illicit trafficking and brokering in such items in accordance with their national legal authorities and legislation and consistent with international law;

(*d*) Establish, develop, review and maintain appropriate effective national export and trans-shipment controls over such items, including appropriate laws and regulations to control export, transit, trans-shipment and re-export, and controls on providing funds and services related to such export and trans-shipment, such as financing, and transporting, that would contribute to proliferation, as well as establishing end-user controls; and establishing and enforcing appropriate criminal or civil penalties for violations of such export control laws and regulations;

4. *Decides* to establish, in accordance with rule 28 of its provisional rules of procedure, for a period of no longer than two years, a Committee of the Security Council, consisting of all members of the Council, which will, calling as appropriate on other expertise, report to the Council for its examination, on the implementation of the present resolution, and to this end calls upon States to present a first report to the Committee, no later than six months from the adoption of the present resolution, on steps they have taken or intend to take to implement the present resolution;

5. *Decides also* that none of the obligations set forth in the present resolution shall be interpreted so as to conflict with or alter the rights and obligations of State parties to the Treaty on the Non-Proliferation of Nuclear Weapons, the Convention on the Prohibition of the Development, Production, Stockpiling and Use of Chemical Weapons and on Their Destruction, and the Convention on the Prohibition of the Development, Production and Stockpiling of Bacteriological (Biological) and Toxin Weapons and on Their Destruction or alter the responsibilities of the International Atomic Energy Agency or the Organization for the Prohibition of Chemical Weapons;

6. *Recognizes* the utility, in implementing the present resolution, of effective national control lists, and calls upon all Member States, when necessary, to pursue at the earliest opportunity the development of such lists;

7. *Recognizes also* that some States may require assistance in implementing the provisions of the present resolution within their territories, and invites States in a position to do so to offer assistance as appropriate, in response to specific requests, to the States lacking the legal and regulatory infrastructure, implementation experience and/or resources for fulfilling the above provisions;

8. *Calls upon* all States:

(a) To promote the universal adoption and full implementation and, where necessary, strengthening of multilateral treaties to which they are parties, whose aim is to prevent the proliferation of nuclear, biological or chemical weapons;

(b) To adopt national rules and regulations, where it has not yet been done, to ensure compliance with their commitments under the key multilateral non-proliferation treaties;

(c) To renew and fulfil their commitment to multilateral cooperation, in particular within the framework of the International Atomic Energy Agency, the Organization for the Prohibition of Chemical Weapons and the Convention on the Prohibition of the Development, Production and Stockpiling of Bacteriological (Biological) and Toxin Weapons and on Their Destruction, as important means of pursuing and achieving their common objectives in the area of non-proliferation and of promoting international cooperation for peaceful purposes;

(d) To develop appropriate ways to work with and inform industry and the public regarding their obligations under such laws;

9. *Also calls upon* all States to promote dialogue and cooperation on non-proliferation so as to address the threat posed by the proliferation of nuclear, chemical, or biological weapons and their means of delivery;

10. *Further calls upon* all States, as a means to further counter that threat, to take cooperative action, in accordance with their national legal authorities and legislation and consistent with international law, to prevent illicit trafficking in nuclear, chemical or biological weapons, their means of delivery, and related materials;

11. *Expresses its intention* to monitor closely the implementation of the present resolution and, at the appropriate level, to take further decisions which may be required to this end;

12. *Decides* to remain seized of the matter.

---

[1]Definitions for the purpose of the present resolution only:

Means of delivery: missiles, rockets and other unmanned systems capable of delivering nuclear, chemical, or biological weapons, that are specially designed for such use.

Non-State actor: individual or entity, not acting under the lawful authority of any State in conducting activities which come within the scope of the present resolution.

Related materials: materials, equipment and technology covered by relevant multilateral treaties and arrangements, or included on national control lists, which could be used for the design, development, production or use of nuclear, chemical and biological weapons and their means of delivery.

Committee activities. On 8 December [S/2004/958 & Corr.1], the Chairman of the Security Council Committee established pursuant to resolution 1540(2004) (above) reported on the Committee's activities since its establishment. Efforts had focused on making the Committee fully operational in preparation for its consideration of reports from Member States, as requested by the Council. The Committee adopted guidelines for the conduct of its work, for the preparation of national reports and for hiring experts who would facilitate consideration of those reports, and established three subcommittees to review national reports. On 1 December, the Committee approved the recruitment of four experts, which enabled it to enter the substantive stage of its work and invited further nominations of experts in the necessary areas of expertise, particularly from Asia and Africa. As at 7 December, 87 States and one organization (the EU) had submitted reports. Annexed to the Committee's report were a list of those States and another of the 104 countries which had not submitted reports.

On 20 December [S/2004/985], the Secretary-General informed the Council of the four experts he intended to appoint to assist the Committee in its work.

Multilateralism in disarmament and non-proliferation

Pursuant to General Assembly resolution 58/44 [YUN 2003, p. 581], the Secretary-General, in a July report with a later addendum [A/59/128 & Add.1], presented replies received from eight Governments regarding the promotion of multilateralism in the area of disarmament and non-proliferation.

In a press release of 14 May [A/58/807-S/2004/407], Cuba expressed objections to the United States Proliferation Security Initiative (see below), a May 2003 proposal by President George W. Bush, which built on existing treaties, agreements and export controls to prevent proliferation of weapons of mass destruction (WMDs) [YUN 2003, p. 536]. Cuba stated that the Initiative weakened the disarmament and arms control efforts of the United Nations and of related international treaties, and it was not in line with principles of the UN Charter and of international law. Cuba said that Security Council resolution 1540(2004) (see p. 544) was ambiguous, as it made it possible for States to claim that actions promoted by the Initiative were legitimized by the Council. Furthermore, the establishment of the Council Committee seemed to imply the foundation of a separate non-proliferation regime that would erode or replace the current regimes established by existing international treaties, including IAEA and the Organization (OPCW) for the Prohibition of Chemical Weapons (see p. 558).

A meeting marking the first anniversary of the launching of the Initiative (Krakow, Poland, 31 May–1 June) [CD/1737], which was designed as a network for intercepting shipments of WMDs and related materials worldwide, considered ways to promote cooperation and identify the tools and assets needed to combat proliferation.

The G-8 (major industrialized countries) (Sea Island, Georgia, United States, 8-10 June), adopted an action plan on non-proliferation to reinforce the global regime and reaffirmed commitment to fulfilling their arms control, disarmament and non-proliferation obligations. They expressed support for Council resolution 1540 (2004) and recommitted themselves to the Proliferation Security Initiative and their 2002 Global Partnership Against the Spread of Weapons and Materials of Mass Destruction [YUN 2002, p. 494]. A number of other related challenges were also addressed by the G-8 leaders.

The United States and the EU, following a summit meeting (Shannon, Ireland, 26 June), issued a declaration on the non-proliferation of WMDs in which they emphasized the threat to international peace and security posed by the spread of those weapons and listed joint actions aimed at preventing, containing and reversing proliferation. They agreed on the need to tackle the problem individually and collectively, working with other partners, especially UN institutions. While expressing concern about the nuclear programmes of Iran and the Democratic People's Republic of Korea (DPRK), they ap-

plauded the resolve of the Libyan Arab Jamahiriya to abandon its pursuit of WMDs and promised to assist it to implement its non-proliferation commitments.

In a communiqué issued after a meeting in New York on 28 September [A/59/425-S/2004/808], the Foreign Ministers of member States of the Organization of the Islamic Conference noted that the scope of resolution 1540(2004) was limited to preventing the acquisition of WMDs by non-State actors. The meeting underscored that the resolution was a temporary arrangement to fill a gap in international rules. The Council could not assume responsibility for non-proliferation since the States seeking to perpetuate the monopoly of nuclear weapons also wielded veto power in the Council. The meeting called for a non-discriminatory and universally negotiated treaty on the threat of WMD proliferation by non-State actors to replace the temporary arrangements assumed by the Council under resolution 1540(2004).

During the year, an independent commission on WMDs, launched in 2003 by Sweden and tasked with developing proposals for reducing dangers posed by those weapons, received a variety of expert studies and held three international meetings. Its final report was expected to be presented to the Secretary-General in 2006.

GENERAL ASSEMBLY ACTION

On 3 December [meeting 66], the General Assembly, on the recommendation of the First Committee [A/59/459 & Corr.1], adopted **resolution 59/69** by recorded vote (125-9-49) [agenda item 65 (n)].

Promotion of multilateralism in the area of disarmament and non-proliferation

The General Assembly,

Determined to foster strict respect for the purposes and principles enshrined in the Charter of the United Nations,

Recalling its resolution 56/24 T of 29 November 2001 on multilateral cooperation in the area of disarmament and non-proliferation and global efforts against terrorism and other relevant resolutions, as well as its resolutions 57/63 of 22 November 2002 and 58/44 of 8 December 2003 on promotion of multilateralism in the area of disarmament and non-proliferation,

Recalling also the purpose of the United Nations to maintain international peace and security and, to that end, to take effective collective measures for the prevention and removal of threats to the peace and for the suppression of acts of aggression or other breaches of the peace, and to bring about by peaceful means, and in conformity with the principles of justice and international law, adjustment or settlement of international disputes or situations which might lead to a breach of the peace, as enshrined in the Charter,

Recalling further the United Nations Millennium Declaration, which states, inter alia, that the responsibility for managing worldwide economic and social development, as well as threats to international peace and security, must be shared among the nations of the world and should be exercised multilaterally and that, as the most universal and most representative organization in the world, the United Nations must play the central role,

Convinced that, in the globalization era and with the information revolution, arms regulation, non-proliferation and disarmament problems are more than ever the concern of all countries in the world, which are affected in one way or another by these problems and, therefore, should have the possibility to participate in the negotiations that arise to tackle them,

Bearing in mind the existence of a broad structure of disarmament and arms regulation agreements resulting from non-discriminatory and transparent multilateral negotiations with the participation of a large number of countries, regardless of their size and power,

Aware of the need to advance further in the field of arms regulation, non-proliferation and disarmament on the basis of universal, multilateral, non-discriminatory and transparent negotiations with the goal of reaching general and complete disarmament under strict international control,

Recognizing the complementarity of bilateral, plurilateral and multilateral negotiations on disarmament,

Recognizing also that the proliferation and development of weapons of mass destruction, including nuclear weapons, are among the most immediate threats to international peace and security which need to be dealt with, with the highest priority,

Considering that the multilateral disarmament agreements provide the mechanism for States parties to consult one another and to cooperate in solving any problems which may arise in relation to the objective of, or in the application of, the provisions of the agreements and that such consultations and cooperation may also be undertaken through appropriate international procedures within the framework of the United Nations and in accordance with the Charter,

Stressing that international cooperation, the peaceful settlement of disputes, dialogue and confidence-building measures would contribute essentially to the creation of multilateral and bilateral friendly relations among peoples and nations,

Being concerned at the continuous erosion of multilateralism in the field of arms regulation, non-proliferation and disarmament, and recognizing that a resort to unilateral actions by Member States in resolving their security concerns would jeopardize international peace and security and undermine confidence in the international security system as well as the foundations of the United Nations itself,

Reaffirming the absolute validity of multilateral diplomacy in the field of disarmament and non-proliferation, and determined to promote multilateralism as an essential way to develop arms regulation and disarmament negotiations,

1. *Reaffirms* multilateralism as the core principle in negotiations in the area of disarmament and non-proliferation with a view to maintaining and strengthening universal norms and enlarging their scope;

2. *Also reaffirms* multilateralism as the core principle in resolving disarmament and non-proliferation concerns;

3. *Urges* the participation of all interested States in multilateral negotiations on arms regulation, non-proliferation and disarmament in a non-discriminatory and transparent manner;

4. *Underlines* the importance of preserving the existing agreements on arms regulation and disarmament, which constitute an expression of the results of international cooperation and multilateral negotiations in response to the challenges facing mankind;

5. *Calls once again upon* all Member States to renew and fulfil their individual and collective commitments to multilateral cooperation as an important means of pursuing and achieving their common objectives in the area of disarmament and non-proliferation;

6. *Requests* the States parties to the relevant instruments on weapons of mass destruction to consult and cooperate among themselves in resolving their concerns with regard to cases of non-compliance as well as on implementation, in accordance with the procedures defined in those instruments, and to refrain from resorting or threatening to resort to unilateral actions or directing unverified non-compliance accusations against one another to resolve their concerns;

7. *Takes note* of the report of the Secretary-General containing the replies of Member States on the promotion of multilateralism in the area of disarmament and non-proliferation, submitted pursuant to resolution 58/44;

8. *Requests* the Secretary-General to seek the views of Member States on the issue of the promotion of multilateralism in the area of disarmament and non-proliferation and to submit a report thereon to the General Assembly at its sixtieth session;

9. *Decides* to include in the provisional agenda of its sixtieth session the item entitled "Promotion of multilateralism in the area of disarmament and non-proliferation".

RECORDED VOTE ON RESOLUTION 59/69:

In favour: Afghanistan, Algeria, Angola, Antigua and Barbuda, Azerbaijan, Bahamas, Bahrain, Bangladesh, Barbados, Belarus, Belize, Benin, Bhutan, Bolivia, Botswana, Brazil, Brunei Darussalam, Burkina Faso, Burundi, Cambodia, Cameroon, Cape Verde, Central African Republic, Chile, China, Colombia, Comoros, Congo, Costa Rica, Côte d'Ivoire, Cuba, Democratic People's Republic of Korea, Djibouti, Dominica, Dominican Republic, Ecuador, Egypt, El Salvador, Equatorial Guinea, Eritrea, Ethiopia, Fiji, Gabon, Gambia, Ghana, Greece, Grenada, Guatemala, Guinea-Bissau, Guyana, Haiti, Honduras, India, Indonesia, Iran, Iraq, Jamaica, Jordan, Kazakhstan, Kenya, Kuwait, Kyrgyzstan, Lao People's Democratic Republic, Lebanon, Lesotho, Liberia, Libyan Arab Jamahiriya, Madagascar, Malawi, Malaysia, Maldives, Mali, Mauritius, Mexico, Mongolia, Morocco, Mozambique, Myanmar, Namibia, Nepal, Nicaragua, Niger, Nigeria, Oman, Pakistan, Panama, Papua New Guinea, Paraguay, Peru, Philippines, Qatar, Russian Federation, Rwanda, Saint Lucia, Saint Vincent and the Grenadines, Sao Tome and Principe, Saudi Arabia, Senegal, Seychelles, Sierra Leone, Singapore, Solomon Islands, Somalia, South Africa, Sri Lanka, Sudan, Suriname, Swaziland, Syrian Arab Republic, Tajikistan, Thailand, Togo, Trinidad and Tobago, Tunisia, Turkmenistan, Uganda, United Arab Emirates, United Republic of Tanzania, Uruguay, Vanuatu, Venezuela, Viet Nam, Yemen, Zambia, Zimbabwe.

Against: Albania, Israel, Latvia, Marshall Islands, Micronesia, Palau, Poland, United Kingdom, United States.

Abstaining: Andorra, Argentina, Armenia, Australia, Austria, Belgium, Bosnia and Herzegovina, Bulgaria, Canada, Croatia, Cyprus, Czech Republic, Denmark, Estonia, Finland, France, Georgia, Germany, Hungary, Iceland, Ireland, Italy, Japan, Liechtenstein, Lithuania, Luxembourg, Malta, Monaco, Nauru, Netherlands, New Zealand, Norway, Portugal, Republic of Korea, Republic of Moldova, Romania, Samoa, San Marino, Serbia and Montenegro, Slovakia, Slovenia, Spain, Sweden, Switzerland, The former Yugoslav Republic of Macedonia, Turkey, Tuvalu, Ukraine, Uzbekistan.

On 22 April [meeting 4949], the Security Council considered the decision of the Libyan Arab Jamahiriya to abandon its WMD programmes. At the meeting, following consultations among Council members, the President made statement **S/PRST/2004/10** on behalf of the Council:

The Security Council takes note of resolution 2004/18 of 10 March 2004 of the Board of Governors of the International Atomic Energy Agency regarding the implementation of the safeguards agreement of the Socialist People's Libyan Arab Jamahiriya, a State party to the Treaty on the Non-proliferation of Nuclear Weapons, by which the Board requested the Director General of the International Atomic Energy Agency to report a case of non-compliance to the Security Council for information purposes only, while commending the Socialist People's Libyan Arab Jamahiriya for the actions it has taken to date and those it has proposed to take to remedy it.

The Council welcomes the decision by the Socialist People's Libyan Arab Jamahiriya to abandon its programmes for developing weapons of mass destruction and their means of delivery and the positive steps taken to fulfil its commitments and obligations, including its active cooperation with the International Atomic Energy Agency and the Organization for the Prohibition of Chemical Weapons.

The Council takes note that in its resolution 2004/18 the Board of Governors of the International Atomic Energy Agency recognized the decision of the Socialist People's Libyan Arab Jamahiriya as a step towards the realization of the goal of an Africa and a Middle East free of weapons of mass destruction and at peace.

The Council reaffirms the need to seek to resolve proliferation problems by peaceful means through political and diplomatic channels.

The Council welcomes existing and future efforts to assist the Socialist People's Libyan Arab Jamahiriya in this task, and expresses the hope that the steps taken by the Socialist People's Libyan Arab Jamahiriya would facilitate and improve international cooperation with and enhance the security of that country.

The Council encourages the Socialist People's Libyan Arab Jamahiriya to ensure the verified elimination of all of its weapons of mass destruction programmes. It welcomes the roles played in that regard by the International Atomic Energy Agency and the Organization for the Prohibition of Chemical Weapons in facilitating the fulfilment of the commitments of the Socialist People's Libyan Arab Jamahiriya, demonstrating the importance and usefulness of existing international treaty regimes.

The Council expresses the hope that resolution 2004/18 will be implemented in the spirit of continued cooperation.

IAEA safeguards

As at 31 December, the Model Protocol Additional to Safeguards Agreements strengthening the safeguards regime of the International Atomic Energy Agency (IAEA), approved by the Agency's Board of Governors in 1997 [YUN 1997, p. 486], had been signed by 100 States, including the five nuclear-weapon States, and was in force or being provisionally applied in 62 States.

The IAEA General Conference [GC(48)/RES/14], as in previous years, requested concerned States and other parties to safeguards agreements, including nuclear-weapon States, that had not done so to sign the additional protocols promptly and to bring them into force as soon as possible, in conformity with their national legislation. The Conference called for cooperation among member States to facilitate the exchange of equipment, material and scientific and technological information for implementing those protocols. It commended member States, notably Japan, that had implemented elements of the plan of action outlined in a 2000 resolution of the Conference [YUN 2000, p. 504] and recommended that other member States consider such action to facilitate the entry into force of comprehensive safeguards agreements and additional protocols.

In 2004, IAEA continued to be unable to verify that the DPRK was following Agency safeguards; therefore it could not provide assurance that nuclear material was not being diverted, owing to the DPRK's refusal to permit IAEA inspectors to carry out verification activities in the country. On 24 September [GC(48)/RES/15], the General Conference, deploring the DPRK's non-compliance with its NPT safeguards agreement and its unwillingness to discuss the issue with IAEA, urged it to reconsider its actions, to dismantle completely any nuclear weapons programme and to accept comprehensive IAEA safeguards.

IAEA made progress in gaining a comprehensive understanding of Iran's nuclear programme, but a number of issues remained outstanding [GOV/2004/34]. Iran provided access to locations requested by the Agency, which was able to verify that Iran had suspended enrichment and reprocessing activities. However, some discrepancies subsequently emerged in information concerning centrifuge components provided by Iran. The IAEA Board of Governors urged Iran to cooperate fully in the verification process.

The IAEA mandate under various Security Council resolutions on inspections of Iraq's nuclear programme remained in effect, although the Agency was not able to carry out that mandate during the year. At the time IAEA was asked to cease its activities in Iraq in March 2003 [YUN 2003, p. 549], it had found no evidence of nuclear activities prohibited by the Council, a finding that had since been validated. The Council, in **resolution 1546(2004)** (see p. 348), reaffirmed its intention to revisit the mandate, which the Agency expected to guide its future work. IAEA remained concerned about the dismantlement of sites previously used in Iraq's nuclear programme that had been subject to IAEA safeguards. In June, the United States informed IAEA that it had removed most of the nuclear material in Iraq under those safeguards and, in August, the Agency verified the removal of the material and carried out an annual physical inventory verification of the remaining nuclear material under the NPT safeguards agreement between Iraq and IAEA.

On 10 March, Libya signed the IAEA Additional Protocol to the NPT safeguards agreement, which gave IAEA inspectors greater authority in verifying Libya's nuclear programme. On the same date [GOV/2004/18], the IAEA Board of Governors, welcoming Libya's decision to sign the Protocol and to dismantle weapons-related programmes, called for its continuing cooperation and full disclosure in order to facilitate the Agency's completion of its mandated tasks. In September [GOV/2004/59], the IAEA Director General, acknowledging Libya's cooperation, reported that the Agency's assessment of Libya's declarations on its uranium conversion and enrichment programmes and other nuclear-related activities appeared consistent with information available to the Agency. However, further investigation was needed to fully verify the completeness and correctness of Libya's declarations.

During the year, IAEA considered undeclared activities and/or material in the Republic of Korea and in Egypt. At year's end, the Agency was still in the process of determining whether declarations made by both countries were correct and complete.

Note by Secretary-General. In August [A/59/295], the Secretary-General informed the General Assembly of the availability of the forty-eighth report of IAEA [GC(48)/3] covering 2003.

Communication. In May [A/58/816], Cuba announced that it had ratified the comprehensive safeguards agreement with IAEA and the Additional Protocol thereto, in demonstration of its commitment to fulfil its obligations as a State party to NPT and the Treaty for the Prohibition of Nuclear Weapons in Latin America and the Caribbean (Treaty of Tlatelolco) (see p. 552).

Middle East

In 2004, the General Assembly (see below) and the IAEA General Conference [GC(48)/RES/16] took action regarding the risk of nuclear proliferation in the Middle East. While the Assembly continued to call on the non-party in the region to place all its nuclear facilities under IAEA safeguards, IAEA reaffirmed the need for States in the region to accept the full application of Agency safeguards to all their nuclear activities.

Pursuant to Assembly resolution 58/68 [YUN 2003, p. 550], the Secretary-General reported in October [A/59/165 (Part II)] that, apart from the IAEA resolution on the application of IAEA safeguards in the Middle East, which was annexed to his report, he had not received any additional information since his 2003 report.

GENERAL ASSEMBLY ACTION

On 3 December [meeting 66], the General Assembly, on the recommendation of the First Committee [A/59/462], adopted **resolution 59/106** by recorded vote (170-5-9) [agenda item 68].

**The risk of nuclear proliferation
in the Middle East**

The General Assembly,

Bearing in mind its relevant resolutions,

Taking note of the relevant resolutions adopted by the General Conference of the International Atomic Energy Agency, the latest of which is resolution GC(48)/RES/16, adopted on 24 September 2004,

Cognizant that the proliferation of nuclear weapons in the region of the Middle East would pose a serious threat to international peace and security,

Mindful of the immediate need for placing all nuclear facilities in the region of the Middle East under full-scope safeguards of the International Atomic Energy Agency,

Recalling the decision on principles and objectives for nuclear non-proliferation and disarmament adopted by the 1995 Review and Extension Conference of the Parties to the Treaty on the Non-Proliferation of Nuclear Weapons on 11 May 1995, in which the Conference urged universal adherence to the Treaty as an urgent priority and called upon all States not yet parties to the Treaty to accede to it at the earliest date, particularly those States that operate unsafeguarded nuclear facilities,

Recognizing with satisfaction that, in the Final Document of the 2000 Review Conference of the Parties to the Treaty on the Non-Proliferation of Nuclear Weapons, the Conference undertook to make determined efforts towards the achievement of the goal of universality of the Treaty on the Non-Proliferation of Nuclear Weapons, called upon those remaining States not parties to the Treaty to accede to it, thereby accepting an international legally binding commitment not to acquire nuclear weapons or nuclear explosive devices and to accept International Atomic Energy Agency safeguards on all their nuclear activities, and underlined the necessity of universal adherence to the Treaty and of strict compliance by all parties with their obligations under the Treaty,

Recalling the resolution on the Middle East adopted by the 1995 Review and Extension Conference of the Parties to the Treaty on the Non-Proliferation of Nuclear Weapons on 11 May 1995, in which the Conference noted with concern the continued existence in the Middle East of unsafeguarded nuclear facilities, reaffirmed the importance of the early realization of universal adherence to the Treaty and called upon all

States in the Middle East that had not yet done so, without exception, to accede to the Treaty as soon as possible and to place all their nuclear facilities under full-scope International Atomic Energy Agency safeguards,

Noting that Israel remains the only State in the Middle East that has not yet become party to the Treaty on the Non-Proliferation of Nuclear Weapons,

Concerned about the threats posed by the proliferation of nuclear weapons to the security and stability of the Middle East region,

Stressing the importance of taking confidence-building measures, in particular the establishment of a nuclear-weapon-free zone in the Middle East, in order to enhance peace and security in the region and to consolidate the global non-proliferation regime,

Emphasizing the need for all parties directly concerned to consider seriously taking the practical and urgent steps required for the implementation of the proposal to establish a nuclear-weapon-free zone in the region of the Middle East in accordance with the relevant resolutions of the General Assembly and, as a means of promoting this objective, inviting the countries concerned to adhere to the Treaty on the Non-Proliferation of Nuclear Weapons and, pending the establishment of the zone, to agree to place all their nuclear activities under International Atomic Energy Agency safeguards,

Noting that one hundred and seventy-three States have signed the Comprehensive Nuclear-Test-Ban Treaty, including a number of States in the region,

1. *Welcomes* the conclusions on the Middle East of the 2000 Review Conference of the Parties to the Treaty on the Non-Proliferation of Nuclear Weapons;

2. *Reaffirms* the importance of Israel's accession to the Treaty on the Non-Proliferation of Nuclear Weapons and placement of all its nuclear facilities under comprehensive International Atomic Energy Agency safeguards, in realizing the goal of universal adherence to the Treaty in the Middle East;

3. *Calls upon* that State to accede to the Treaty on the Non-Proliferation of Nuclear Weapons without further delay and not to develop, produce, test or otherwise acquire nuclear weapons, and to renounce possession of nuclear weapons, and to place all its unsafeguarded nuclear facilities under full-scope International Atomic Energy Agency safeguards as an important confidence-building measure among all States of the region and as a step towards enhancing peace and security;

4. *Requests* the Secretary-General to report to the General Assembly at its sixtieth session on the implementation of the present resolution;

5. *Decides* to include in the provisional agenda of its sixtieth session the item entitled "The risk of nuclear proliferation in the Middle East".

RECORDED VOTE ON RESOLUTION 59/106:

In favour: Afghanistan, Albania, Algeria, Andorra, Angola, Antigua and Barbuda, Argentina, Armenia, Austria, Azerbaijan, Bahamas, Bahrain, Bangladesh, Barbados, Belarus, Belgium, Belize, Benin, Bhutan, Bolivia, Bosnia and Herzegovina, Botswana, Brazil, Brunei Darussalam, Bulgaria, Burkina Faso, Burundi, Cambodia, Canada, Cape Verde, Central African Republic, Chile, China, Colombia, Comoros, Congo, Costa Rica, Côte d'Ivoire, Croatia, Cuba, Cyprus, Czech Republic, Democratic People's Republic of Korea, Denmark, Djibouti, Dominica, Dominican Republic, Ecuador, Egypt, El Salvador, Equatorial Guinea, Eritrea, Estonia, Fiji, Finland, France, Gabon, Gambia, Georgia, Germany, Ghana, Greece, Grenada, Guatemala, Guinea-Bissau, Guyana, Haiti, Honduras, Hun-

gary, Iceland, Indonesia, Iran, Iraq, Ireland, Italy, Jamaica, Japan, Jordan, Kazakhstan, Kenya, Kuwait, Kyrgyzstan, Lao People's Democratic Republic, Latvia, Lebanon, Lesotho, Liberia, Libyan Arab Jamahiriya, Liechtenstein, Lithuania, Luxembourg, Madagascar, Malawi, Malaysia, Maldives, Mali, Malta, Mauritius, Mexico, Monaco, Mongolia, Morocco, Mozambique, Myanmar, Namibia, Nepal, Netherlands, New Zealand, Nicaragua, Niger, Nigeria, Norway, Oman, Pakistan, Panama, Paraguay, Peru, Philippines, Poland, Portugal, Qatar, Republic of Korea, Republic of Moldova, Romania, Russian Federation, Saint Lucia, Saint Vincent and the Grenadines, Samoa, San Marino, Sao Tome and Principe, Saudi Arabia, Senegal, Serbia and Montenegro, Seychelles, Sierra Leone, Singapore, Slovakia, Slovenia, Solomon Islands, Somalia, South Africa, Spain, Sri Lanka, Sudan, Suriname, Swaziland, Sweden, Switzerland, Syrian Arab Republic, Tajikistan, Thailand, The former Yugoslav Republic of Macedonia, Timor-Leste, Togo, Tunisia, Turkey, Turkmenistan, Tuvalu, Uganda, Ukraine, United Arab Emirates, United Kingdom, United Republic of Tanzania, Uruguay, Uzbekistan, Venezuela, Viet Nam, Yemen, Zambia, Zimbabwe.

Against: Israel, Marshall Islands, Micronesia, Palau, United States.

Abstaining: Australia, Cameroon, Ethiopia, India, Nauru, Papua New Guinea, Tonga, Trinidad and Tobago, Vanuatu.

The First Committee adopted the sixth preambular paragraph by a separate recorded vote (154-3-4). The Assembly retained the paragraph by recorded vote (169-6-4).

Nuclear-weapon-free zones

Africa

As at 31 December, 22 States had ratified the African Nuclear-Weapon-Free Zone Treaty (Treaty of Pelindaba) [YUN 1995, p. 203], which was opened for signature in 1996 [YUN 1996, p. 486]. China, France and the United Kingdom had ratified Protocols I and II thereto, and France had also ratified Protocol III. The Russian Federation and the United States had signed Protocols I and II. The Treaty had 55 signatories. By the terms of the Treaty, ratification by 28 States was required for its entry into force.

The General Assembly, in **resolution 59/85** (see p. 553), welcomed efforts towards completion of the ratification process and called on States that had not done so to ratify the Treaty so as to facilitate its entry into force.

Asia

Central Asia

With assistance from the Department for Disarmament Affairs, in particular its Regional Centre for Peace and Disarmament in Asia and the Pacific (see p. 587), the five Central Asian States (Kazakhstan, Kyrgyzstan, Tajikistan, Turkmenistan, Uzbekistan) continued efforts to conclude a Central Asian nuclear-weapon-free zone treaty. During the year, the Regional Centre organized several consultation sessions in New York for regional States to help them reach agreement on a text.

On 3 December, the General Assembly decided to include in the provisional agenda of its sixtieth (2005) session the item entitled "Establishment of a nuclear-weapon-free zone in Central Asia" (**decision 59/513**).

Mongolia

Report of Secretary-General. The Secretary-General, in response to General Assembly resolution 57/67 [YUN 2002, p. 513], reviewed in a September report [A/59/364] new developments and UN assistance to Mongolia to strengthen its nuclear-weapon-free status. The report also covered non-nuclear aspects of Mongolia's international security. The Secretary-General remarked that the UN system would continue to assist that country in coping with economic and ecological vulnerabilities, in particular those identified in recent UN studies. He hoped that UN assistance would contribute to sustainable development and balanced growth in Mongolia, reinforcing its efforts at achieving the Millennium Development Goals [YUN 2000, p. 51]. He welcomed the international community's support in strengthening the non-nuclear aspects of international security in Mongolia.

GENERAL ASSEMBLY ACTION

On 3 December [meeting 66], the General Assembly, on the recommendation of the First Committee [A/59/459 & Corr.1], adopted **resolution 59/73** without vote [agenda item 65 (*f*)].

Mongolia's international security and nuclear-weapon-free status

The General Assembly,

Recalling its resolutions 53/77 D of 4 December 1998, 55/33 S of 20 November 2000 and 57/67 of 22 November 2002,

Recalling also the purposes and principles of the Charter of the United Nations, as well as the Declaration on Principles of International Law concerning Friendly Relations and Cooperation among States in accordance with the Charter of the United Nations,

Bearing in mind its resolution 49/31 of 9 December 1994 on the protection and security of small States,

Proceeding from the fact that nuclear-weapon-free status is one of the means of ensuring the national security of States,

Convinced that the internationally recognized status of Mongolia will contribute to enhancing stability and confidence-building in the region as well as promote Mongolia's security by strengthening its independence, sovereignty and territorial integrity, the inviolability of its borders and the preservation of its ecological balance,

Taking note of the adoption by the Mongolian parliament of legislation defining and regulating its nuclear-weapon-free status as a concrete step towards promoting the aims of nuclear non-proliferation,

Bearing in mind the joint statement of the five nuclear-weapon States on security assurances to Mongolia in connection with its nuclear-weapon-free status as a contribution to implementing resolution 53/77 D as well as their commitment to Mongolia to cooperate

in the implementation of the resolution, in accordance with the principles of the Charter,

Noting that the joint statement has been transmitted to the Security Council by the five nuclear-weapon States,

Mindful that at the Thirteenth Conference of Heads of State or Government of Non-Aligned Countries, held in Kuala Lumpur, from 20 to 25 February 2003, the Heads of State or Government reiterated their support for Mongolia's nuclear-weapon-free status and considered that the institutionalization of that status would be an important measure towards strengthening the non-proliferation regime in the region,

Noting other measures taken to implement resolution 57/67 at the national and international levels,

Welcoming Mongolia's active and positive role in developing peaceful, friendly and mutually beneficial relations with the States of the region and other States,

Having considered the report of the Secretary-General on Mongolia's international security and nuclear-weapon-free status,

1. *Takes note* of the report of the Secretary-General on the implementation of resolution 57/67;

2. *Expresses its appreciation* to the Secretary-General for the efforts to implement resolution 57/67, in particular the completion of the two studies on the non-nuclear aspects of Mongolia's international security;

3. *Endorses and supports* Mongolia's good-neighbourly and balanced relationship with its neighbours as an important element of strengthening regional peace, security and stability;

4. *Welcomes* the efforts made by Member States to cooperate with Mongolia in implementing resolution 57/67, as well as the progress made in consolidating Mongolia's international security;

5. *Invites* Member States to continue to cooperate with Mongolia in taking the necessary measures to consolidate and strengthen Mongolia's independence, sovereignty and territorial integrity, the inviolability of its borders, its independent foreign policy, its economic security, and its ecological balance, as well as its nuclear-weapon-free status;

6. *Appeals* to the Member States of the Asia and Pacific region to support Mongolia's efforts to join the relevant regional security and economic arrangements;

7. *Requests* the Secretary-General and relevant United Nations bodies to continue to provide assistance to Mongolia in taking the necessary measures mentioned in paragraph 5 above;

8. *Requests* the Secretary-General to report to the General Assembly at its sixty-first session on the implementation of the present resolution;

9. *Decides* to include in the provisional agenda of its sixty-first session the item entitled "Mongolia's international security and nuclear-weapon-free status".

South-East Asia

In 2004, the States parties to the Treaty on the South-East Asia Nuclear-Weapon-Free Zone (Bangkok Treaty), which opened for signature in 1995 [YUN 1995, p. 207] and entered into force in 1997 [YUN 1997, p. 495], continued to focus on establishing an institutional framework to implement the Treaty. At the tenth summit of the Association of Southeast Asian Nations (Vientiane, Lao People's Democratic Republic, 29-30 November), leaders adopted the Vientiane Action Programme, in which they expressed determination to resolve outstanding issues, thereby ensuring that the nuclear-weapon States would sign the protocols to the Treaty.

Latin America and the Caribbean

During the year, States parties to the Treaty for the Prohibition of Nuclear Weapons in Latin America and the Caribbean (Treaty of Tlatelolco) [YUN 1967, p. 13] continued efforts to consolidate the treaty regime. The General Assembly of the Organization of American States (OAS), at its thirty-fourth regular session (Quito, Ecuador, 6-8 June) [AG/RES.2009(XXXIV-O/04)], urged regional States that had not done so to sign or ratify the amendments to the Treaty. It called on the OAS Permanent Council to hold, within the framework of the Committee on Hemispheric Security, a meeting on the consolidation of the treaty regime, with the support of the Agency for the Prohibition of Nuclear Weapons in Latin America and the Caribbean and the participation of the United Nations and other relevant international organizations.

Middle East

In response to General Assembly resolution 58/34 on the establishment of a nuclear-weapon-free zone in the Middle East [YUN 2003, p. 556], the Secretary-General, in a July report with a later addendum [A/59/165 (Part I) & Corr.1, Add.1], provided information on the resolution's implementation. He stated that he continued to consult with concerned parties within and outside the region on ways to establish such a zone, and he urged them to resume dialogue, with a view to creating stable security conditions and an eventual settlement that would facilitate the establishment of a nuclear-weapon-free zone in the Middle East. The report included the replies of China, Egypt, Guatemala, Ireland (on behalf of the EU), Israel, Lebanon, Mexico, Oman, the Syrian Arab Republic and Venezuela to his request for the views of concerned States.

In September, the IAEA General Conference, in a resolution on the Middle East [GC(48)/RES/16], called on all parties directly concerned to take the steps required for implementing the proposal to establish a mutually and effectively verifiable nuclear-weapon-free zone in the region.

GENERAL ASSEMBLY ACTION

On 3 December [meeting 66], the General Assembly, on the recommendation of the First Com-

mittee [A/59/456], adopted **resolution 59/63** without vote [agenda item 62].

Establishment of a nuclear-weapon-free zone in the region of the Middle East

The General Assembly,

Recalling its resolutions 3263(XXIX) of 9 December 1974, 3474(XXX) of 11 December 1975, 31/71 of 10 December 1976, 32/82 of 12 December 1977, 33/64 of 14 December 1978, 34/77 of 11 December 1979, 35/147 of 12 December 1980, 36/87 A and B of 9 December 1981, 37/75 of 9 December 1982, 38/64 of 15 December 1983, 39/54 of 12 December 1984, 40/82 of 12 December 1985, 41/48 of 3 December 1986, 42/28 of 30 November 1987, 43/65 of 7 December 1988, 44/108 of 15 December 1989, 45/52 of 4 December 1990, 46/30 of 6 December 1991, 47/48 of 9 December 1992, 48/71 of 16 December 1993, 49/71 of 15 December 1994, 50/66 of 12 December 1995, 51/41 of 10 December 1996, 52/34 of 9 December 1997, 53/74 of 4 December 1998, 54/51 of 1 December 1999, 55/30 of 20 November 2000, 56/21 of 29 November 2001, 57/55 of 22 November 2002 and 58/34 of 8 December 2003 on the establishment of a nuclear-weapon-free zone in the region of the Middle East,

Recalling also the recommendations for the establishment of such a zone in the Middle East consistent with paragraphs 60 to 63, and in particular paragraph 63 *(d)*, of the Final Document of the Tenth Special Session of the General Assembly,

Emphasizing the basic provisions of the above-mentioned resolutions, which call upon all parties directly concerned to consider taking the practical and urgent steps required for the implementation of the proposal to establish a nuclear-weapon-free zone in the region of the Middle East and, pending and during the establishment of such a zone, to declare solemnly that they will refrain, on a reciprocal basis, from producing, acquiring or in any other way possessing nuclear weapons and nuclear explosive devices and from permitting the stationing of nuclear weapons on their territory by any third party, to agree to place their nuclear facilities under International Atomic Energy Agency safeguards and to declare their support for the establishment of the zone and to deposit such declarations with the Security Council for consideration, as appropriate,

Reaffirming the inalienable right of all States to acquire and develop nuclear energy for peaceful purposes,

Emphasizing the need for appropriate measures on the question of the prohibition of military attacks on nuclear facilities,

Bearing in mind the consensus reached by the General Assembly since its thirty-fifth session that the establishment of a nuclear-weapon-free zone in the Middle East would greatly enhance international peace and security,

Desirous of building on that consensus so that substantial progress can be made towards establishing a nuclear-weapon-free zone in the Middle East,

Welcoming all initiatives leading to general and complete disarmament, including in the region of the Middle East, and in particular on the establishment therein of a zone free of weapons of mass destruction, including nuclear weapons,

Noting the peace negotiations in the Middle East, which should be of a comprehensive nature and represent an appropriate framework for the peaceful settlement of contentious issues in the region,

Recognizing the importance of credible regional security, including the establishment of a mutually verifiable nuclear-weapon-free zone,

Emphasizing the essential role of the United Nations in the establishment of a mutually verifiable nuclear-weapon-free zone,

Having examined the report of the Secretary-General on the implementation of resolution 58/34,

1. *Urges* all parties directly concerned to consider seriously taking the practical and urgent steps required for the implementation of the proposal to establish a nuclear-weapon-free zone in the region of the Middle East in accordance with the relevant resolutions of the General Assembly, and, as a means of promoting this objective, invites the countries concerned to adhere to the Treaty on the Non-Proliferation of Nuclear Weapons;

2. *Calls upon* all countries of the region that have not done so, pending the establishment of the zone, to agree to place all their nuclear activities under International Atomic Energy Agency safeguards;

3. *Takes note* of resolution GC(48)/RES/16, adopted on 24 September 2004 by the General Conference of the International Atomic Energy Agency at its forty-eighth regular session, concerning the application of Agency safeguards in the Middle East;

4. *Notes* the importance of the ongoing bilateral Middle East peace negotiations and the activities of the multilateral Working Group on Arms Control and Regional Security in promoting mutual confidence and security in the Middle East, including the establishment of a nuclear-weapon-free zone;

5. *Invites* all countries of the region, pending the establishment of a nuclear-weapon-free zone in the region of the Middle East, to declare their support for establishing such a zone, consistent with paragraph 63 (*d*) of the Final Document of the Tenth Special Session of the General Assembly, and to deposit those declarations with the Security Council;

6. *Also invites* those countries, pending the establishment of the zone, not to develop, produce, test or otherwise acquire nuclear weapons or permit the stationing on their territories, or territories under their control, of nuclear weapons or nuclear explosive devices;

7. *Invites* the nuclear-weapon States and all other States to render their assistance in the establishment of the zone and at the same time to refrain from any action that runs counter to both the letter and the spirit of the present resolution;

8. *Takes note* of the report of the Secretary-General;

9. *Invites* all parties to consider the appropriate means that may contribute towards the goal of general and complete disarmament and the establishment of a zone free of weapons of mass destruction in the region of the Middle East;

10. *Requests* the Secretary-General to continue to pursue consultations with the States of the region and other concerned States, in accordance with paragraph 7 of resolution 46/30 and taking into account the evolving situation in the region, and to seek from those States their views on the measures outlined in chapters III and IV of the study annexed to his report

of 10 October 1990 or other relevant measures, in order to move towards the establishment of a nuclear-weapon-free zone in the Middle East;

11. *Also requests* the Secretary-General to submit to the General Assembly at its sixtieth session a report on the implementation of the present resolution;

12. *Decides* to include in the provisional agenda of its sixtieth session the item entitled "Establishment of a nuclear-weapon-free zone in the region of the Middle East".

South Pacific

In 2004, the number of States that had ratified the 1985 South Pacific Nuclear-Free Zone Treaty (Treaty of Rarotonga) [YUN 1985, p. 58] remained at 17. China and the Russian Federation had ratified Protocols 2 and 3, and France and the United Kingdom had ratified all three Protocols. The heads of State and Government of countries of the Pacific Islands Forum, in a communiqué issued after their thirty-fifth session (Apia, Samoa, 5-7 August), called on the United States, as the remaining nuclear-weapon State to ratify the Treaty's protocols, to do so as a means of enhancing global and regional peace and security, including global nuclear non-proliferation.

Under Protocol 1, the States internationally responsible for territories situated within the zone would undertake to apply the relevant prohibitions of the Treaty to those territories; under Protocol 2, the five nuclear-weapon States would provide security assurances to parties or territories within the same zone; and under Protocol 3, the five would not carry out nuclear tests in the zone.

Southern hemisphere and adjacent areas

On 3 December [meeting 66], the General Assembly, on the recommendation of the First Committee [A/59/459 & Corr.1], adopted **resolution 59/85** by recorded vote (171-4-8) [agenda item 65 (*s*)].

Nuclear-weapon-free southern hemisphere and adjacent areas

The General Assembly,

Recalling its resolutions 51/45 B of 10 December 1996, 52/38 N of 9 December 1997, 53/77 Q of 4 December 1998, 54/54 L of 1 December 1999, 55/33 I of 20 November 2000, 56/24 G of 29 November 2001, 57/73 of 22 November 2002 and 58/49 of 8 December 2003,

Recalling also the adoption by the Disarmament Commission at its 1999 substantive session of a text entitled "Establishment of nuclear-weapon-free zones on the basis of arrangements freely arrived at among the States of the region concerned",

Determined to pursue the total elimination of nuclear weapons,

Determined also to continue to contribute to the prevention of the proliferation of nuclear weapons in all its aspects and to the process of general and complete disarmament under strict and effective international control, in particular in the field of nuclear weapons and other weapons of mass destruction, with a view to strengthening international peace and security, in accordance with the purposes and principles of the Charter of the United Nations,

Recalling the provisions on nuclear-weapon-free zones of the Final Document of the Tenth Special Session of the General Assembly, the first special session devoted to disarmament,

Stressing the importance of the treaties of Tlatelolco, Rarotonga, Bangkok and Pelindaba establishing nuclear-weapon-free zones, as well as the Antarctic Treaty, to, inter alia, achieve a world entirely free of nuclear weapons,

Underlining the value of enhancing cooperation among the nuclear-weapon-free-zone treaty members by means of mechanisms such as joint meetings of States parties, signatories and observers to those treaties,

Welcoming the announcement of the organization of an international conference of States parties signatories to the nuclear-weapon-free-zone treaties in Mexico, in 2005, to support the common goals envisaged in those treaties,

Recalling the applicable principles and rules of international law relating to the freedom of the high seas and the rights of passage through maritime space, including those of the United Nations Convention on the Law of the Sea,

1. *Welcomes* the continued contribution that the Antarctic Treaty and the treaties of Tlatelolco, Rarotonga, Bangkok and Pelindaba are making towards freeing the southern hemisphere and adjacent areas covered by those treaties from nuclear weapons;

2. *Also welcomes* the ratification by all original parties of the Treaty of Rarotonga, and calls upon eligible States to adhere to the treaty and the protocols thereto;

3. *Further welcomes* the efforts towards the completion of the ratification process of the Treaty of Pelindaba, and calls upon the States of the region that have not yet done so to sign and ratify the treaty, with the aim of its early entry into force;

4. *Calls upon* all concerned States to continue to work together in order to facilitate adherence to the protocols to nuclear-weapon-free-zone treaties by all relevant States that have not yet done so;

5. *Welcomes* the steps taken to conclude further nuclear-weapon-free-zone treaties on the basis of arrangements freely arrived at among the States of the region concerned, and calls upon all States to consider all relevant proposals, including those reflected in its resolutions on the establishment of nuclear-weapon-free zones in the Middle East and South Asia;

6. *Affirms its conviction* of the important role of nuclear-weapon-free zones in strengthening the nuclear non-proliferation regime and in extending the areas of the world that are nuclear-weapon-free, and, with particular reference to the responsibilities of the nuclear-weapon States, calls upon all States to support the process of nuclear disarmament and to work for the total elimination of all nuclear weapons;

7. *Calls upon* the States parties and signatories to the treaties of Tlatelolco, Rarotonga, Bangkok and Pelindaba, in order to pursue the common goals envisaged in those treaties and to promote the nuclear-weapon-free status of the southern hemisphere and adjacent areas, to explore and implement further ways

and means of cooperation among themselves and their treaty agencies;

8. *Welcomes* the vigorous efforts being made among States parties and signatories to those treaties to promote their common objectives, and encourages the competent authorities of the nuclear-weapon-free-zone treaties to provide assistance to the States parties and signatories to those treaties so as to facilitate the accomplishment of these goals;

9. *Decides* to include in the provisional agenda of its sixtieth session the item entitled "Nuclear-weapon-free southern hemisphere and adjacent areas".

RECORDED VOTE ON RESOLUTION 59/85:

In favour: Afghanistan, Albania, Algeria, Andorra, Angola, Antigua and Barbuda, Argentina, Armenia, Australia, Austria, Azerbaijan, Bahamas, Bahrain, Bangladesh, Barbados, Belarus, Belgium, Belize, Benin, Bolivia, Bosnia and Herzegovina, Botswana, Brazil, Brunei Darussalam, Bulgaria, Burkina Faso, Burundi, Cambodia, Cameroon, Canada, Cape Verde, Central African Republic, Chile, China, Colombia, Comoros, Congo, Costa Rica, Côte d'Ivoire, Croatia, Cuba, Cyprus, Czech Republic, Democratic People's Republic of Korea, Denmark, Djibouti, Dominica, Dominican Republic, Ecuador, Egypt, El Salvador, Equatorial Guinea, Eritrea, Estonia, Ethiopia, Fiji, Finland, Gabon, Gambia, Georgia, Germany, Ghana, Greece, Grenada, Guatemala, Guinea-Bissau, Guyana, Haiti, Honduras, Hungary, Iceland, Indonesia, Iran, Iraq, Ireland, Italy, Jamaica, Japan, Jordan, Kazakhstan, Kenya, Kuwait, Kyrgyzstan, Lao People's Democratic Republic, Latvia, Lebanon, Lesotho, Liberia, Libyan Arab Jamahiriya, Liechtenstein, Lithuania, Luxembourg, Madagascar, Malawi, Malaysia, Maldives, Mali, Malta, Mauritius, Mexico, Mongolia, Morocco, Mozambique, Myanmar, Namibia, Nauru, Nepal, Netherlands, New Zealand, Nicaragua, Niger, Nigeria, Norway, Oman, Panama, Papua New Guinea, Paraguay, Peru, Philippines, Poland, Portugal, Qatar, Republic of Korea, Republic of Moldova, Romania, Rwanda, Saint Lucia, Saint Vincent and the Grenadines, Samoa, San Marino, Sao Tome and Principe, Saudi Arabia, Senegal, Serbia and Montenegro, Seychelles, Sierra Leone, Singapore, Slovakia, Slovenia, Solomon Islands, Somalia, South Africa, Sri Lanka, Sudan, Suriname, Swaziland, Sweden, Switzerland, Syrian Arab Republic, Tajikistan, Thailand, The former Yugoslav Republic of Macedonia, Timor-Leste, Togo, Tonga, Tunisia, Turkey, Turkmenistan, Tuvalu, Uganda, Ukraine, United Arab Emirates, United Republic of Tanzania, Uruguay, Uzbekistan, Vanuatu, Venezuela, Viet Nam, Yemen, Zambia, Zimbabwe.

Against: France, Palau, United Kingdom, United States.

Abstaining: Bhutan, India, Israel, Marshall Islands, Micronesia, Pakistan, Russian Federation, Spain.

The First Committee adopted the last three words of operative paragraph 5 "and South Asia", then paragraph 5 as a whole, by two separate recorded votes (139-2-9 and 144-1-8, respectively). The Assembly followed the same procedure, adopting them by recorded votes (158-4-7 and 166-3-7, respectively).

Bacteriological (biological) and chemical weapons

Bacteriological (biological) weapons

In 2004, increasing concern about the potential acquisition by terrorists of chemical and biological weapons and related materials and technology continued to motivate calls for further strengthening of the Convention on the Prohibition of the Development, Production and Stockpiling of Bacteriological (Biological) and Toxin Weapons and on Their Destruction (BWC) and the

Convention on the Prohibition of the Development, Production, Stockpiling and Use of Chemical Weapons and on Their Destruction, and for States parties to implement measures that would respond to those calls. The need for action in that regard was underscored by the Security Council in **resolution 1540(2004)** (see p. 544).

Meeting of States parties

As decided by the BWC States parties in 2003 [YUN 2003, p. 559], the second annual meeting of those States was convened (Geneva, 6-10 December) [BWC/MSP/2004/3]. Participants considered strengthening and broadening national and international institutional efforts and existing mechanisms for the surveillance, detection, diagnosis and combating of infectious diseases affecting humans, animals and plants, as well as enhancing international capabilities for responding to alleged use of biological or toxin weapons or suspicious outbreaks of disease. The States parties agreed on the value of: supporting existing networks of international organizations dealing with aspects of infectious diseases; enhancing national and regional disease surveillance capabilities and communication on the issue among international organizations and States; and developing national capacities for response, investigation and mitigation, in cooperation with international and regional organizations. They also agreed that the Sixth Review Conference, scheduled for 2006, should consider, among other things, the further development of procedures for assisting States parties in cases of alleged use of biological weapons or suspicious outbreaks of disease. Participants were encouraged to inform the Sixth Review Conference of any steps they had taken on the basis of discussions at the 2004 meetings of States parties or experts (see below). The States parties considered a number of working papers, presentations and statements, a list of which was annexed to the meeting's report, as was a synthesis of the issues considered, perspectives, recommendations, conclusions and proposals drawn from statements and working papers presented to the meeting, and prepared by the Chairman. The States parties decided that their next meeting would be held in Geneva from 5 to 9 December 2005.

Expert meeting. In accordance with a decision of the Fifth Review Conference of the BWC States parties [YUN 2002, p. 516], the 2004 meeting of States parties (see above) was preceded by a preparatory meeting of experts (Geneva, 19-30 July) [BWC/MSP/2004/MX/3], which discussed issues relevant to the topics taken up by the States parties' meeting. The expert meeting reviewed a number of working papers and heard statements and thematic presentations from delegates. On 30 July, the meeting adopted its report, which listed background papers prepared by the secretariat and other working papers, presentations and contributions considered.

GENERAL ASSEMBLY ACTION

On 3 December [meeting 66], the General Assembly, on the recommendation of the First Committee [A/59/466], adopted **resolution 59/110** without vote [agenda item 72].

Convention on the Prohibition of the Development, Production and Stockpiling of Bacteriological (Biological) and Toxin Weapons and on Their Destruction

The General Assembly,

Recalling its previous resolutions relating to the complete and effective prohibition of bacteriological (biological) and toxin weapons and to their destruction,

Noting with satisfaction that there are one hundred and fifty-two States parties to the Convention on the Prohibition of the Development, Production and Stockpiling of Bacteriological (Biological) and Toxin Weapons and on Their Destruction, including all of the permanent members of the Security Council,

Bearing in mind its call upon all States parties to the Convention to participate in the implementation of the recommendations of the Review Conferences, including the exchange of information and data agreed to in the Final Declaration of the Third Review Conference of the Parties to the Convention on the Prohibition of the Development, Production and Stockpiling of Bacteriological (Biological) and Toxin Weapons and on Their Destruction, and to provide such information and data in conformity with standardized procedure to the Secretary-General on an annual basis and no later than 15 April,

Welcoming the reaffirmation made in the Final Declaration of the Fourth Review Conference that under all circumstances the use of bacteriological (biological) and toxin weapons and their development, production and stockpiling are effectively prohibited under article I of the Convention,

Recalling the decision reached at the Fifth Review Conference to hold three annual meetings of the States parties of one week's duration each year commencing in 2003 until the Sixth Review Conference and to hold a two-week meeting of experts to prepare for each meeting of the States parties,

1. *Notes with satisfaction* the increase in the number of States parties to the Convention on the Prohibition of the Development, Production and Stockpiling of Bacteriological (Biological) and Toxin Weapons and on Their Destruction, reaffirms the call upon all signatory States that have not yet ratified the Convention to do so without delay, and calls upon those States that have not signed the Convention to become parties thereto at an early date, thus contributing to the achievement of universal adherence to the Convention;

2. *Welcomes* the information and data provided to date, and reiterates its call upon all States parties to the Convention to participate in the exchange of informa-

tion and data agreed to in the Final Declaration of the Third Review Conference of the Parties to the Convention;

3. *Recalls* the decision reached at the Fifth Review Conference to discuss and promote common understanding and effective action in 2003 on the two topics of the adoption of necessary national measures to implement the prohibitions set forth in the Convention, including the enactment of penal legislation, and national mechanisms to establish and maintain the security and oversight of pathogenic micro-organisms and toxins; in 2004 on the two topics of enhancing international capabilities for responding to, investigating and mitigating the effects of cases of alleged use of biological or toxin weapons or suspicious outbreaks of disease, and strengthening and broadening national and international institutional efforts and existing mechanisms for the surveillance, detection, diagnosis and combating of infectious diseases affecting humans, animals and plants; and in 2005 on the topic of the content, promulgation and adoption of codes of conduct for scientists; and calls upon the States parties to the Convention to participate in its implementation;

4. *Requests* the Secretary-General to continue to render the necessary assistance to the depositary Governments of the Convention and to provide such services as may be required for the implementation of the decisions and recommendations of the Review Conferences, including all necessary assistance to the annual meetings of the States parties and the meetings of experts;

5. *Decides* to include in the provisional agenda of its sixtieth session the item entitled "Convention on the Prohibition of the Development, Production and Stockpiling of Bacteriological (Biological) and Toxin Weapons and on Their Destruction".

1925 Geneva Protocol

In response to General Assembly resolution 57/62 [YUN 2002, p. 517], the Secretary-General reported in July [A/59/179] that France, as the depositary of the Protocol for the Prohibition of the Use in War of Asphyxiating, Poisonous or Other Gases, and of Bacteriological Methods of Warfare (the 1925 Geneva Protocol), had received notice of three withdrawals of reservations (Portugal, Republic of Korea, United Kingdom) since the Assembly's adoption of the resolution.

GENERAL ASSEMBLY ACTION

On 3 December [meeting 66], the General Assembly, on the recommendation of the First Committee [A/59/459 & Corr.1], adopted **resolution 59/70** by recorded vote (179-0-5) [agenda item 65 (*d*)].

Measures to uphold the authority of the 1925 Geneva Protocol

The General Assembly,

Recalling its previous resolutions on the subject, in particular resolution 57/62 of 22 November 2002,

Determined to act with a view to achieving effective progress towards general and complete disarmament under strict and effective international control,

Recalling the long-standing determination of the international community to achieve the effective prohibition of the development, production, stockpiling and use of chemical and biological weapons as well as the continuing support for measures to uphold the authority of the Protocol for the Prohibition of the Use in War of Asphyxiating, Poisonous or Other Gases, and of Bacteriological Methods of Warfare, signed at Geneva on 17 June 1925, as expressed by consensus in many previous resolutions,

Emphasizing the necessity of easing international tension and strengthening trust and confidence between States,

Welcoming the recent initiatives by three more States Parties to withdraw their reservations to the 1925 Geneva Protocol,

1. *Takes note* of the note by the Secretary-General;

2. *Renews its previous call* to all States to observe strictly the principles and objectives of the Protocol for the Prohibition of the Use in War of Asphyxiating, Poisonous or Other Gases, and of Bacteriological Methods of Warfare, and reaffirms the vital necessity of upholding its provisions;

3. *Calls upon* those States that continue to maintain reservations to the 1925 Geneva Protocol to withdraw them;

4. *Requests* the Secretary-General to submit to the General Assembly at its sixty-first session a report on the implementation of the present resolution.

RECORDED VOTE ON RESOLUTION 59/70:

In favour: Afghanistan, Albania, Algeria, Andorra, Angola, Antigua and Barbuda, Argentina, Armenia, Australia, Austria, Azerbaijan, Bahamas, Bahrain, Bangladesh, Barbados, Belarus, Belgium, Belize, Benin, Bhutan, Bolivia, Bosnia and Herzegovina, Botswana, Brazil, Brunei Darussalam, Bulgaria, Burkina Faso, Burundi, Cambodia, Cameroon, Canada, Cape Verde, Central African Republic, Chile, China, Colombia, Comoros, Congo, Costa Rica, Côte d'Ivoire, Croatia, Cuba, Cyprus, Czech Republic, Democratic People's Republic of Korea, Denmark, Djibouti, Dominica, Dominican Republic, Ecuador, Egypt, El Salvador, Equatorial Guinea, Eritrea, Estonia, Ethiopia, Fiji, Finland, France, Gabon, Gambia, Georgia, Germany, Ghana, Greece, Grenada, Guatemala, Guinea-Bissau, Guyana, Haiti, Honduras, Hungary, Iceland, India, Indonesia, Iran, Ireland, Italy, Jamaica, Japan, Jordan, Kazakhstan, Kenya, Kuwait, Kyrgyzstan, Lao People's Democratic Republic, Latvia, Lebanon, Lesotho, Liberia, Libyan Arab Jamahiriya, Liechtenstein, Lithuania, Luxembourg, Madagascar, Malawi, Malaysia, Maldives, Mali, Malta, Mauritius, Mexico, Monaco, Mongolia, Morocco, Mozambique, Myanmar, Namibia, Nauru, Nepal, Netherlands, New Zealand, Nicaragua, Niger, Nigeria, Norway, Oman, Pakistan, Panama, Papua New Guinea, Paraguay, Peru, Philippines, Poland, Portugal, Qatar, Republic of Korea, Republic of Moldova, Romania, Russian Federation, Rwanda, Saint Lucia, Saint Vincent and the Grenadines, Samoa, San Marino, Sao Tome and Principe, Saudi Arabia, Senegal, Serbia and Montenegro, Seychelles, Sierra Leone, Singapore, Slovakia, Slovenia, Solomon Islands, Somalia, South Africa, Spain, Sri Lanka, Sudan, Suriname, Swaziland, Sweden, Switzerland, Syrian Arab Republic, Tajikistan, Thailand, The former Yugoslav Republic of Macedonia, Timor-Leste, Togo, Tonga, Trinidad and Tobago, Tunisia, Turkey, Turkmenistan, Tuvalu, Uganda, Ukraine, United Arab Emirates, United Kingdom, United Republic of Tanzania, Uruguay, Uzbekistan, Vanuatu, Venezuela, Viet Nam, Yemen, Zambia, Zimbabwe.

Against: None.

Abstaining: Israel, Marshall Islands, Micronesia, Palau, United States.

Chemical weapons

Chemical weapons convention

In 2004, Chad, Madagascar, the Marshall Islands, Rwanda, Saint Kitts and Nevis and Sierra Leone ratified the Convention on the Prohibition of the Development, Production, Stockpiling and

Use of Chemical Weapons and on Their Destruction (CWC), and the Libyan Arab Jamahiriya, Solomon Islands and Tuvalu acceded to it, bringing the total number of States parties to 167. The number of signatories stood at 165. The Convention was adopted by the Conference on Disarmament in 1992 [YUN 1992, p. 65] and entered into force in 1997 [YUN 1997, p. 499].

The ninth session of the Conference of the States Parties (The Hague, Netherlands, 29 November–2 December) [C-9/6] considered the status of CWC implementation, fostering international cooperation for peaceful purposes in the field of chemical activities, ensuring the Convention's universality, and administrative and budgetary matters. The Conference adopted decisions on action needed for further implementation of the obligations in article VII of the Convention on national implementation measures; the inclusion of an additional item on the list of approved equipment; an understanding of the concept of "captive use" in connection with declarations of production and/or consumption under the Convention's verification annex; extension of deadlines for the destruction of Category 1 chemical weapons stockpiles; a request for conversion of chemical weapons production facilities for purposes not prohibited under the Convention; submission of information regarding national programmes related to protective purposes; and administrative, financial and oversight matters, including the programme and budget of the Organization for the Prohibition of Chemical Weapons (OPCW) for 2005. The Conference approved requests by Albania and Libya for extensions of the intermediate deadlines for the destruction of their Category 1 chemical weapons and a further request by Libya to convert its chemical weapons production facilities into a pharmaceuticals plant for producing low-cost vaccines to be distributed in Africa for treating HIV/AIDS, malaria and tuberculosis. The Conference decided to hold its tenth session in November 2005.

GENERAL ASSEMBLY ACTION

On 3 December [meeting 66], the General Assembly, on the recommendation of the First Committee [A/59/459 & Corr.1], adopted **resolution 59/72** without vote [agenda item 65 (u)].

Implementation of the Convention on the Prohibition of the Development, Production, Stockpiling and Use of Chemical Weapons and on Their Destruction

The General Assembly,

Recalling its previous resolutions on the subject of chemical weapons, in particular resolution 58/52 of 8 December 2003, adopted without a vote, in which it noted with appreciation the ongoing work to achieve the objective and purpose of the Convention on the Prohibition of the Development, Production, Stockpiling and Use of Chemical Weapons and on Their Destruction,

Determined to achieve the effective prohibition of the development, production, acquisition, transfer, stockpiling and use of chemical weapons and their destruction,

Noting with satisfaction that, since the adoption of resolution 58/52, nine additional States have ratified the Convention or acceded to it, bringing the total number of States parties to the Convention to one hundred and sixty-seven,

Reaffirming the importance of the outcome of the First Special Session of the Conference of the States Parties to Review the Operation of the Chemical Weapons Convention, including the Political Declaration, in which the States parties reaffirmed their commitment to achieving the objective and purpose of the Convention, and the final report, which addressed all aspects of the Convention and made important recommendations on its continued implementation,

1. _Emphasizes_ that the universality of the Convention on the Prohibition of the Development, Production, Stockpiling and Use of Chemical Weapons and on Their Destruction is fundamental to the achievement of its objective and purpose, and acknowledges progress made in the implementation of the action plan for the universality of the Convention, and calls upon all States that have not yet done so to become parties to the Convention without delay;

2. _Underlines_ that the Convention and its implementation contribute to enhancing international peace and security, and emphasizes that its full, universal and effective implementation will contribute further to that purpose by excluding completely, for the sake of all humankind, the possibility of the use of chemical weapons;

3. _Stresses_ that the full and effective implementation of all provisions of the Convention is in itself an important contribution to the efforts of the United Nations in the global fight against terrorism in all its forms and manifestations;

4. _Also stresses_ the importance to the Convention that all possessors of chemical weapons, chemical weapons production facilities or chemical weapons development facilities, including previously declared possessor States, should be among the States parties to the Convention, and welcomes progress to that end;

5. _Notes_ that the effective application of the verification system builds confidence in compliance with the Convention by States parties;

6. _Stresses_ the importance of the Organization for the Prohibition of Chemical Weapons in verifying compliance with the provisions of the Convention as well as in promoting the timely and efficient accomplishment of all its objectives;

7. _Urges_ all States parties to the Convention to meet in full and on time their obligations under the Convention and to support the Organization for the Prohibition of Chemical Weapons in its implementation activities;

8. _Reaffirms_ the undertaking of the States parties to foster international cooperation for peaceful purposes in the field of chemical activities of the States parties

and the importance of that cooperation and its contribution to the promotion of the Convention as a whole;

9. *Notes with appreciation* the ongoing work of the Organization for the Prohibition of Chemical Weapons to achieve the objective and purpose of the Convention, to ensure the full implementation of its provisions, including those for international verification of compliance with it, and to provide a forum for consultation and cooperation among States parties, and also notes with appreciation progress made in the implementation of the plan of action regarding the implementation of article VII obligations;

10. *Welcomes* the cooperation between the United Nations and the Organization for the Prohibition of Chemical Weapons within the framework of the Relationship Agreement between the United Nations and the Organization, in accordance with the provisions of the Convention;

11. *Decides* to include in the provisional agenda of its sixtieth session the item entitled "Implementation of the Convention on the Prohibition of the Development, Production, Stockpiling and Use of Chemical Weapons and on Their Destruction".

Organization for the Prohibition of Chemical Weapons

In 2004, OPCW continued efforts to achieve the objective and purpose of CWC, particularly regarding the complete elimination of chemical weapons. In the seven years since the Convention's entry into force in 1997, OPCW as at year's end had inspected over 750 facilities in 66 States parties. By October, over 71,000 tonnes of chemical agents and approximately 8.7 million munitions and containers were identified by the six declared chemical weapons possessor States, and approximately 10,048 tonnes of chemical warfare agents, accounting for more than 14 per cent of the total stockpiles declared, were destroyed by four of those States under OPCW verification. With the accession of Libya to CWC (see above) and its declaration that it possessed chemical weapons, the total number of declared possessor States rose to six. Out of 64 chemical weapons production facilities (CWPFs) worldwide, 35 were certified as destroyed, and 13 were converted to other uses or were scheduled to be destroyed by April 2007.

Progress was made towards realizing the plan of action on national implementation of the Convention, adopted at the eighth session of the Conference of the States Parties in 2003 [YUN 2003, p. 560]. The States parties set November 2005 as the deadline for evaluating progress made in developing and enacting national legislation mandated by the Convention and in establishing the required internal mechanisms.

The OPCW Executive Council addressed a variety of issues at its thirty-sixth (23-26 March), thirty-seventh (29 June–2 July), thirty-eighth (12-

15 October) and thirty-ninth (14-17 December) sessions. During the year, the Council considered Secretariat reports on the status of the Convention's implementation, including verification activities and the Convention's articles X and XI on protection against chemical weapons and on economic and technological development, respectively. It adopted recommendations on implementation-related action and on changing the Convention regarding conditions for converting CWPFs for purposes not prohibited under the Convention. The Council also adopted decisions on the destruction of chemical weapons and/or conversion of CWPFs, and on issues relating to the chemical industry and financial matters.

By an August note [A/59/297], the Secretary-General submitted to the General Assembly the 2002 report of OPCW, in accordance with the Agreement concerning the Relationship between the United Nations and OPCW, which was signed in 2000 [YUN 2000, p. 516] and entered into force in 2001 [YUN 2001, p. 495].

GENERAL ASSEMBLY ACTION

On 22 October [meeting 40], the General Assembly adopted **resolution 59/7** [draft: A/59/L.8 & Add.1] without vote [agenda item 56 (*m*)].

Cooperation between the United Nations and the Organization for the Prohibition of Chemical Weapons

The General Assembly,

Recalling its resolution 57/45 of 21 November 2002 on cooperation between the United Nations and the Organization for the Prohibition of Chemical Weapons,

Having received the annual report for 2002 of the Organization for the Prohibition of Chemical Weapons on the implementation of the Convention on the Prohibition of the Development, Production, Stockpiling and Use of Chemical Weapons and on Their Destruction,

1. *Takes note* of the annual report for 2002 of the Organization for the Prohibition of Chemical Weapons submitted on its behalf by its Director-General;

2. *Decides* to include in the provisional agenda of its sixty-first session the sub-item entitled "Cooperation between the United Nations and the Organization for the Prohibition of Chemical Weapons".

Conventional weapons

Programme of Action on illicit trade in small arms

In 2004, the international community continued to make progress in efforts to address problems relating to the spread of small arms and light weapons, particularly regarding the implementation of the Programme of Action to Prevent, Combat and Eradicate the Illicit Trade in Small Arms and Light Weapons in All Its Aspects [YUN 2001, p. 499]. The open-ended working group established by the General Assembly in resolution 58/241 [YUN 2003, p. 564] to negotiate an international instrument to help identify and trace illicit small arms and light weapons began its work. Other broad-based consultations were undertaken to enhance international cooperation in combating the small arms problem. In January, the Security Council called for international cooperation to prevent the diversion of small arms and light weapons to terrorist groups, particularly Al-Qaida (see below). The General Assembly, in **resolutions 59/74** (see p. 560) and **59/86** (see p. 561), called for strengthening the capacity of civil society to combat the illicit trade in small arms and for regional measures to tackle the problem. In further action, the Assembly, in **resolution 59/90** (see p. 566), urged Member States to support efforts to prevent the illicit transfer and use of man-portable air defence systems. National, regional and subregional initiatives undertaken in regard to small arms and light weapons increased significantly during the year, including the establishment of coordinating bodies in many countries, the adoption and strengthening of national laws, regulations and controls, weapons collection and destruction activities, and the establishment of arrangements for cooperation, networking and exchange of information at the regional and subregional levels.

SECURITY COUNCIL ACTION

On 19 January [meeting 4896], following consultations among Security Council members, the President made statement **S/PRST/2004/1** on behalf of the Council:

The Security Council welcomes the report of the Secretary-General of 31 December 2003 on the implementation of his recommendations to the Council on small arms, and reaffirms the statements by its President of 24 September 1999 (S/PRST/1999/28), 31 August 2001 (S/PRST/2001/21) and 31 October 2002 (S/PRST/2002/30).

The Council recalls its primary responsibility under the Charter of the United Nations for the maintenance of international peace and security, in view of which its attention is drawn inevitably to the illicit trade of small arms and light weapons, as such weapons are the most frequently used in armed conflicts. The Council reaffirms the inherent right of individual or collective self-defence in accordance with Article 51 of the Charter and, subject to the Charter, the right of each State to import, produce and retain small arms and light weapons for its self-defence and security needs.

The Council welcomes all efforts already undertaken by Member States, and calls upon them to fully implement at the national, regional and international levels the recommendations contained in the Programme of Action to Prevent, Combat and Eradicate the Illicit Trade in Small Arms and Light Weapons in All Its Aspects, adopted on 20 July 2001 by the United Nations Conference on the Illicit Trade in Small Arms and Light Weapons in All Its Aspects.

The Council welcomes General Assembly resolution 58/241 of 23 December 2003 by which, among other things, it decided to establish an open-ended working group to negotiate an international instrument to enable States to identify and trace, in a timely and reliable manner, illicit small arms and light weapons, and calls upon all Member States to support all efforts aimed at this purpose.

The Council encourages the arms-exporting countries to exercise the highest degree of responsibility in small arms and light weapons transactions. It also encourages international and regional cooperation in the consideration of the origin and transfers of small arms and light weapons in order to prevent their diversion to terrorist groups, in particular, Al-Qaida. The Council welcomes the significant steps that have been taken by Member States in this regard. The obligation of Member States to enforce the arms embargo should be coupled with enhanced international and regional cooperation concerning arms exports.

The Council reiterates its call upon all Member States to effectively implement arms embargoes and other sanction measures imposed by the Council in its relevant resolutions, and urges Member States in a position to do so to provide assistance to interested States in strengthening their capacity to fulfil their obligations in this regard. The Council encourages Member States to undertake vigorous actions aimed at restricting the supply of small arms, light weapons and ammunitions to areas of instability. The Council further encourages Member States to provide the Sanctions Committees with available information on alleged violations of arms embargoes, and also calls upon Member States to give due consideration to the recommendations of the related reports.

The Council continues to recognize the need to engage the relevant international organizations, non-governmental organizations, business and financial institutions and other actors at the international, regional and local levels to contribute to the implementation of arms embargoes.

The Council reiterates the importance of carrying out disarmament, demobilization and reintegration programmes, an increasingly essential component of peacekeeping mandates, as comprehensively and effectively as possible in post-conflict situations under its consideration.

The Council takes note of the inclusion of man-portable air defence systems, on an exceptional basis, in the United Nations Register on Conventional Arms.

The Council requests the Secretary-General to update the Council for its next meeting on the subject on the further implementation of the recommendations contained in his report on small arms of 20 September 2002.

Working Group activities. The Open-ended Working Group to Negotiate an International Instrument to Enable States to Identify and Trace, in a Timely and Reliable Manner, Illicit Small Arms and Light Weapons, established by General Assembly resolution 58/241 [YUN 2003, p. 564], held an organizational session (3 February) and its first substantive session (14-25 June), both in New York. In June, the Working Group, in addition to holding a general debate, organized thematic discussions of the three main elements of tracing—marking, record-keeping and international cooperation. The Working group used as a basis for its discussions the report of the Group of Governmental Experts that had examined the feasibility of developing the proposed instrument [YUN 2003, p. 562] and the Protocol against the Illicit Manufacturing of and Trafficking in Firearms, Their Parts and Components and Ammunition, supplementing the United Nations Convention against Transnational Organized Crime [YUN 2001, p. 1036]. Divergent views were expressed on several issues, including the scope and nature of the instrument, marking small arms and light weapons at the time of import, the right to initiate a request for tracing, and the role of the United Nations and other international organizations in supporting the operation of the proposed instrument. The Working Group agreed that its Chairman would produce the first draft of an instrument before the convening of the second session in January 2005. The Chairman, on 20 October, held informal consultations with States on elements of a draft instrument.

Other consultations. In response to General Assembly resolution 58/241 [YUN 2003, p. 564], which called for further steps to enhance international cooperation in preventing, combating and eradicating illicit brokering in small arms and light weapons, the Department for Disarmament Affairs (DDA) organized a number of informal consultations for Member States, international organizations and civil society groups. DDA ensured that the issue of illicit brokering was included in the agenda of the regional meetings it organized during the year. The key issues of concern raised during the consultations were the definition of "brokering" and whether related activities, such as financing, transport and export controls, should be included in the definition. Other matters of concern were the need to strengthen an international regime on brokering and the need for a set of minimum standards and controls to be adopted by Member States. The participants agreed that the consultations had been useful and should be continued, particularly at the regional level.

Report of Secretary-General. Pursuant to General Assembly resolutions 58/58 [YUN 2003, p. 563] and 58/241 [ibid., p. 564], the Secretary-General, in a report covering July 2003 to July 2004 [A/59/181], summarized national, subregional and regional activities undertaken in Africa in response to States' requests for UN assistance in curbing the illicit trade in small arms and to collect and dispose of them. He also reviewed action by the UN system and by States to implement the Programme of Action to combat illicit trade. The Secretary-General concluded that the implementation of the Programme of Action gained momentum as States, the United Nations and other organizations had consolidated previous activities and developed new ones, often involving civil society and non-governmental organizations (NGOs). The establishment of the Open-ended Working Group (see above) was a significant step in the development of international norms to fight the scourge of illicit small arms and light weapons. However, the consultations on illicit brokering highlighted the complex nature of the small arms challenge and the need to develop States' capacity to address its many facets. The initiatives undertaken by UN departments, specialized agencies and funds under the auspices of the Coordinating Action on Small Arms mechanism [YUN 1998, p. 525] illustrated that assistance to States and development of capacity to implement the Programme of Action remained a priority of the United Nations in its efforts to prevent, combat and eradicate the illicit trade in small arms and light weapons.

GENERAL ASSEMBLY ACTION

On 3 December [meeting 66], the General Assembly, on the recommendation of the First Committee [A/59/459 & Corr.1], adopted **resolution 59/74** without vote [agenda item 65 (y)].

Assistance to States for curbing the illicit traffic in small arms and collecting them

The General Assembly,

Recalling its resolution 58/58 of 8 December 2003 on assistance to States for curbing the illicit traffic in small arms and collecting them,

Considering that the illicit proliferation and circulation of and traffic in small arms impede development, constitute a threat to populations and to national and regional security and are a factor contributing to the destabilization of States,

Deeply disturbed by the magnitude of the illicit proliferation and circulation of and traffic in small arms in the States of the Sahelo-Saharan subregion,

Noting with satisfaction the conclusions of the United Nations advisory missions dispatched by the Secretary-General to the affected countries of the subregion to study the most appropriate way of halting the illicit circulation of small arms and collecting them,

Welcoming the designation of the Department for Disarmament Affairs of the Secretariat as a centre for the coordination of all activities of United Nations bodies concerned with small arms,

Congratulating the Secretary-General for his report on the causes of conflict and the promotion of durable peace and sustainable development in Africa, and bearing in mind the statement on small arms made by the President of the Security Council on 24 September 1999,

Welcoming the recommendations resulting from the meetings of the States of the subregion held at Banjul, Algiers, Bamako, Yamoussoukro and Niamey to establish close regional cooperation with a view to strengthening security,

Welcoming also the decision taken by the Economic Community of West African States to renew the Declaration of a Moratorium on the Importation, Exportation and Manufacture of Small Arms and Light Weapons in West Africa, adopted by the Heads of State and Government of the Economic Community at Abuja on 31 October 1998,

Recalling the Algiers Declaration adopted by the Assembly of Heads of State and Government of the Organization of African Unity at its thirty-fifth ordinary session, held at Algiers from 12 to 14 July 1999,

Emphasizing the need to advance efforts towards wider cooperation and better coordination in the struggle against the illicit proliferation of small arms through the common understanding reached at the meeting on small arms held at Oslo on 13 and 14 July 1998 and the Brussels Call for Action adopted by the International Conference on Sustainable Disarmament for Sustainable Development, held at Brussels on 12 and 13 October 1998,

Bearing in mind the Bamako Declaration on an African Common Position on the Illicit Proliferation, Circulation and Trafficking of Small Arms and Light Weapons, adopted at Bamako on 1 December 2000,

Recalling the millennium report of the Secretary-General,

Welcoming the Programme of Action to Prevent, Combat and Eradicate the Illicit Trade in Small Arms and Light Weapons in All Its Aspects, adopted by the United Nations Conference on the Illicit Trade in Small Arms and Light Weapons in All Its Aspects, and calling for its expeditious implementation,

Recognizing the important role that the organizations of civil society play in detection, prevention and raising public awareness, in efforts to curb the illicit traffic in small arms,

Welcoming the convening of the Open-ended Working Group to Negotiate an International Instrument to Enable States to Identify and Trace, in a Timely and Reliable Manner, Illicit Small Arms and Light Weapons, which held its first session in New York from 14 to 25 June 2004,

1. *Notes with satisfaction* the Declaration of the Ministerial Conference on Security, Stability, Development and Cooperation in Africa, held at Abuja on 8 and 9 May 2000, and encourages the Secretary-General to pursue his efforts in the context of the implementation of General Assembly resolution 49/75 G of 15 December 1994 and the recommendations of the United Nations advisory missions, aimed at curbing the illicit circulation of small arms and collecting such arms in the affected States that so request, with the support of the United Nations Regional Centre for Peace and Disarmament in Africa and in close cooperation with the African Union;

2. *Encourages* the international community to support the implementation of the moratorium on the importation, exportation and manufacture of small arms and light weapons in West Africa;

3. *Encourages* the establishment in the countries of the Sahelo-Saharan subregion of national commissions to combat the illicit proliferation of small arms, and invites the international community to lend its support wherever possible to ensure the smooth functioning of the commissions;

4. *Also encourages* the involvement of organizations and associations of civil society in the efforts of the national commissions to combat the illicit traffic in small arms and their participation in the implementation of the moratorium on the importation, exportation and manufacture of small arms and light weapons in West Africa as well as in the implementation of the Programme of Action to Prevent, Combat and Eradicate the Illicit Trade in Small Arms and Light Weapons in All Its Aspects;

5. *Further encourages* cooperation among State organs, international organizations and civil society in combating the illicit traffic in small arms and supporting operations to collect the said arms in the subregions;

6. *Calls upon* the international community to provide technical and financial support to strengthen the capacity of civil organizations to take action to combat the illicit trade in small arms;

7. *Takes note* of the conclusions of the meeting of Ministers for Foreign Affairs of the Economic Community of West African States, held at Bamako on 24 and 25 March 1999, on the modalities for the implementation of the Programme for Coordination and Assistance for Security and Development, and welcomes the adoption by the meeting of a plan of action;

8. *Takes note also* of the conclusions of the African Conference on the Implementation of the United Nations Programme of Action on Small Arms: Needs and Partnerships, held at Pretoria from 18 to 21 March 2002;

9. *Invites* the Secretary-General and those States and organizations that are in a position to do so to provide assistance to States for curbing the illicit traffic in small arms and collecting them;

10. *Requests* the Secretary-General to continue to consider the matter and to report to the General Assembly at its sixtieth session on the implementation of the present resolution;

11. *Decides* to include in the provisional agenda of its sixtieth session the item entitled "Assistance to States for curbing the illicit traffic in small arms and collecting them".

Also on 3 December [meeting 66], the Assembly, on the recommendation of the First Committee [A/59/459 & Corr.1], adopted **resolution 59/86** without vote [agenda item 65 (z)].

The illicit trade in small arms and light weapons in all its aspects

The General Assembly,

Recalling its resolutions 56/24 V of 24 December 2001, 57/72 of 22 November 2002 and 58/241 of 23 December 2003,

Emphasizing the importance of early and full implementation of the Programme of Action to Prevent, Combat and Eradicate the Illicit Trade in Small Arms and Light Weapons in All Its Aspects, adopted by the United Nations Conference on the Illicit Trade in Small Arms and Light Weapons in All Its Aspects,

Welcoming the efforts by Member States to submit, on a voluntary basis, national reports on their implementation of the Programme of Action,

Noting with satisfaction regional and subregional efforts being undertaken in support of the implementation of the Programme of Action, and commending the progress that has already been made in this regard,

Taking note of the report of the Secretary-General on the implementation of resolution 58/241,

Welcoming the convening of the Open-ended Working Group to Negotiate an International Instrument to Enable States to Identify and Trace, in a Timely and Reliable Manner, Illicit Small Arms and Light Weapons, which held its first two-week substantive session in New York from 14 to 25 June 2004,

Welcoming also the broad-based consultations held by the Secretary-General with all Member States, interested regional and subregional organizations, international agencies and experts in the field on further steps to enhance international cooperation in preventing, combating and eradicating illicit brokering in small arms and light weapons, and noting the report of the Secretary-General in this regard,

1. *Decides* that the United Nations conference to review progress made in the implementation of the Programme of Action to Prevent, Combat and Eradicate the Illicit Trade in Small Arms and Light Weapons in All Its Aspects shall be held in New York for a period of two weeks, from 26 June to 7 July 2006;

2. *Also decides* that the preparatory committee for the conference shall hold a two-week session in New York from 9 to 20 January 2006, and reiterates that, if necessary, a subsequent session of up to two weeks in duration may be held;

3. *Further decides* that the second biennial meeting of States, as stipulated in the Programme of Action, to consider the national, regional and global implementation of the Programme of Action shall be held in New York from 11 to 15 July 2005;

4. *Expresses its appreciation* for the efforts undertaken by the Chair of the Open-ended Working Group to Negotiate an International Instrument to Enable States to Identify and Trace, in a Timely and Reliable Manner, Illicit Small Arms and Light Weapons, encourages the continued active participation of delegations in the remaining sessions of the Open-ended Working Group, and stresses the importance of making every effort to ensure that a positive outcome is achieved by the Open-ended Working Group;

5. *Requests* the Secretary-General, while seeking the views of States, to continue to hold broad-based consultations, within available financial resources, with all Member States and interested regional and subregional organizations on further steps to enhance international cooperation in preventing, combating and eradicating illicit brokering in small arms and light weapons, with a view to establishing, after the 2006 review conference and no later than 2007, and after the conclusion of the work of the Open-ended Working Group, a group of governmental experts, appointed

by him on the basis of equitable geographical representation, to consider further steps to enhance international cooperation in preventing, combating and eradicating illicit brokering in small arms and light weapons, and requests the Secretary-General to report to the General Assembly at its sixtieth session on the outcome of his consultations;

6. *Reaffirms* the importance of ongoing efforts at the regional and subregional levels in support of the implementation of the Programme of Action, and invites all Member States that have not yet done so to examine the possibility of developing and adopting regional and subregional measures, as appropriate, to combat the illicit trade in small arms and light weapons in all its aspects;

7. *Continues to encourage* all initiatives to mobilize resources and expertise to promote the implementation of the Programme of Action and to provide assistance to States in its implementation;

8. *Requests* the Secretary-General to continue to collate and circulate data and information provided by States on a voluntary basis, including national reports, on the implementation by those States of the Programme of Action, and encourages Member States to submit such reports;

9. *Also requests* the Secretary-General to report to the General Assembly at its sixtieth session on the implementation of the present resolution, including any outcome of the work of the Open-ended Working Group;

10. *Decides* to include in the provisional agenda of its sixtieth session the item entitled "The illicit trade in small arms and light weapons in all its aspects".

(For regional initiatives regarding implementation of the Programme of Action, see pp. 570-576).

Convention on excessively injurious conventional weapons and Protocols

As at 31 December, the accessions of Paraguay, Sri Lanka and Turkmenistan and the ratification by Sierra Leone brought to 97 the number of States parties to the 1980 Convention on Prohibitions or Restrictions on the Use of Certain Conventional Weapons Which May Be Deemed to Be Excessively Injurious or to Have Indiscriminate Effects [YUN 1980, p. 76] and its annexed Protocols on Non-Detectable Fragments (Protocol I); on Prohibitions or Restrictions on the Use of Mines, Booby Traps and Other Devices, as amended on 3 May 1996 (Protocol II) [YUN 1996, p. 484]; and on Prohibitions or Restrictions on the Use of Incendiary Weapons (Protocol III). The 1995 Additional Protocol on Blinding Laser Weapons (Protocol IV) [YUN 1995, p. 221], which took effect on 30 July 1998 [YUN 1998, p. 530], had 79 parties, after Malta, Poland, Sierra Leone and Sri Lanka gave consent in 2004 to be bound by the Protocol.

The Group of Governmental Experts established by the Second Review Conference of the

States Parties to the Convention [YUN 2001, p. 504] to consider the issues of explosive remnants of war, mines other than anti-personnel mines, small-calibre weapons and ammunition, and promotion of compliance with the Convention and its annexed Protocols, held its seventh (8-12 March) [CCW/GGE/VII/3 & Add.1], eighth (5-16 July) [CCW/GGE/VIII/3] and ninth (8-16 November) [CCW/GGE/IX/2 & Corr.1, 2] sessions in Geneva. The Group discussed issues relating to the weapons under consideration and promoting compliance with the Convention, and in that context, considered working papers and presentations from delegations, international organizations and other participants, including military experts. On 16 November, the Group endorsed the recommendations of its working groups on explosive remnants of war and on mines other than anti-personnel mines, which were annexed to the report on its ninth session. The Group agreed that the intersessional work of up to five weeks would be undertaken in three sessions during 2005, and it recommended that follow-up work arising from the 2004 Meeting of the States Parties (see below) should be overseen by the Chairman-designate of the 2005 Meeting, scheduled to be held in conjunction with the Seventh (2005) Annual Conference of the States Parties to Amended Protocol II.

The Sixth Annual Conference of the States Parties to Amended Protocol II (Geneva, 17 November) [CCW/AP.II/CONF.6/3] reviewed the operation and status of the Protocol, considered related issues and examined national reports received from 50 States parties. The Conference adopted conclusions, recommendations and an appeal to States to accede to Amended Protocol II. It recommended that the Secretary-General, as depositary, and the President of the Conference exercise their authority to achieve the goal of universality of the Protocol and called on the States parties to promote wider adherence in their respective regions.

The Meeting of the States Parties (Geneva, 18-19 November) [CCW/MSP/2004/2 & Corr.1] considered the work of the Group of Governmental Experts and decided that the Group should continue its work in 2005 in three sessions. The working group on explosive remnants of war was mandated to continue its consideration of the implementation of existing principles of international humanitarian law and possible preventive measures, aimed at improving the design of certain types of munitions, with a view to minimizing the risk of their becoming explosive remnants of war. The working group on mines other than anti-personnel mines was asked to consider all proposals put forward. The Meeting decided that

the Seventh Annual Conference of the States Parties to Amended Protocol II would be held in November 2005 in Geneva, and that its Chairperson-designate should undertake consultations on options to promote compliance with the Convention and its annexed Protocols.

GENERAL ASSEMBLY ACTION

On 3 December [meeting 66], the General Assembly, on the recommendation of the First Committee [A/59/463], adopted **resolution 59/107** without vote [agenda item 69].

Convention on Prohibitions or Restrictions on the Use of Certain Conventional Weapons Which May Be Deemed to Be Excessively Injurious or to Have Indiscriminate Effects

The General Assembly,

Recalling its resolution 58/69 of 8 December 2003,

Recalling with satisfaction the adoption and the entry into force of the Convention on Prohibitions or Restrictions on the Use of Certain Conventional Weapons Which May Be Deemed to Be Excessively Injurious or to Have Indiscriminate Effects, and the Protocol on Non-Detectable Fragments (Protocol I), the Protocol on Prohibitions or Restrictions on the Use of Mines, Booby Traps and Other Devices (Protocol II) and its amended version, the Protocol on Prohibitions or Restrictions on the Use of Incendiary Weapons (Protocol III) and the Protocol on Blinding Laser Weapons (Protocol IV),

Recalling the decision by the Second Review Conference of the States Parties to the Convention on Prohibitions or Restrictions on the Use of Certain Conventional Weapons Which May Be Deemed to Be Excessively Injurious or to Have Indiscriminate Effects to establish an open-ended group of governmental experts with two separate coordinators on explosive remnants of war and on mines other than anti-personnel mines,

Recalling also the role played by the International Committee of the Red Cross in the elaboration of the Convention and the Protocols thereto, and welcoming the particular efforts of various international, non-governmental and other organizations in raising awareness of the humanitarian consequences of explosive remnants of war,

1. *Calls upon* all States that have not yet done so to take all measures to become parties, as soon as possible, to the Convention on Prohibitions or Restrictions on the Use of Certain Conventional Weapons Which May Be Deemed to Be Excessively Injurious or to Have Indiscriminate Effects and the Protocols thereto, as amended, with a view to achieving the widest possible adherence to these instruments at an early date, and so as to ultimately achieve their universality;

2. *Calls upon* all States parties to the Convention that have not yet done so to express their consent to be bound by the Protocols to the Convention and the amendment extending the scope of the Convention and the Protocols thereto to include armed conflicts of a non-international character;

3. *Welcomes with satisfaction* the adoption of the Protocol on Explosive Remnants of War (Protocol V) at the Meeting of the States Parties held at Geneva on 27 and

28 November 2003, and calls upon the States parties to express their consent to be bound by the Protocol and to notify the depositary at an early date of their consent;

4. *Notes* the decision of the Meeting of the States Parties that the Working Group on Explosive Remnants of War would continue its work in 2004 with the mandate to continue to consider the implementation of existing principles of international humanitarian law and to further study, on an open-ended basis, and initially with particular emphasis on meetings of military and technical experts, possible preventive measures aimed at improving the design of certain specific types of munitions, including sub-munitions, with a view to minimizing the humanitarian risk of these munitions becoming explosive remnants of war;

5. *Also notes* the decision of the Meeting of the States Parties that the Working Group on Mines Other Than Anti-Personnel Mines would continue its work in 2004 with the mandate to consider all proposals on mines other than anti-personnel mines put forward since the establishment of the Group of Governmental Experts;

6. *Further notes* the decision of the Meeting of the States Parties that the Chairman-designate should continue to undertake consultations during the intersessional period on possible options to promote compliance with the Convention and the Protocols thereto, taking into account proposals put forward;

7. *Expresses support* for the work conducted by the Group of Governmental Experts, and encourages the Chairman-designate and the Group to conduct work, in accordance with the mandate for 2004, with the aim of elaborating appropriate recommendations on mines other than anti-personnel mines, for submission to the Meeting of the States Parties on 18 and 19 November 2004, and to report on the work done on compliance, as well as on the implementation of existing principles of international humanitarian law and on possible preventive technical measures in relation to explosive remnants of war;

8. *Recalls* the decision of the Second Review Conference of the States Parties to the Convention on Prohibitions or Restrictions on the Use of Certain Conventional Weapons Which May Be Deemed to Be Excessively Injurious or to Have Indiscriminate Effects to convene a further conference not later than 2006, with preparatory meetings starting as early as 2005, if necessary, and requests the Meeting of the States Parties on 18 and 19 November 2004 to consider this issue;

9. *Requests* the Secretary-General to render the necessary assistance and to provide such services, including summary records, as may be required for the Meeting of the States Parties on 18 and 19 November 2004, as well as for any possible continuation of work after the Meeting, should the States parties deem it appropriate;

10. *Also requests* the Secretary-General, in his capacity as depositary of the Convention and the Protocols thereto, to continue to inform the General Assembly periodically, by electronic means, of ratifications and acceptances of and accessions to the Convention and the Protocols thereto;

11. *Decides* to include in the provisional agenda of its sixtieth session the item entitled "Convention on Prohibitions or Restrictions on the Use of Certain Conventional Weapons Which May Be Deemed to Be Excessively Injurious or to Have Indiscriminate Effects".

Practical disarmament

The Group of Interested States, established in 1998 [YUN 1998, p. 531] to examine and support concrete projects of practical disarmament, met three times during 2004 to assess current and new project proposals and recent requests for assistance by Governments. It provided support for practical disarmament efforts of countries of the League of Arab States and of the Economic Community of West African States, particularly within the context of their fight against the proliferation of small arms and light weapons. The Group also considered other projects to assist Member States in tackling the small arms problem and reviewed related requests from Burundi, Nigeria and Tajikistan.

The General Assembly invited the Group to continue to analyse lessons learned from previous disarmament and peace-building projects, and to promote new practical disarmament measures to consolidate peace, especially as undertaken or designed by affected States themselves, regional and subregional organizations and UN agencies (see below).

Disarmament Commission action. In 2004 [A/59/42], the Disarmament Commission, while deliberating on possible agenda items, considered a number of proposals relating to practical disarmament measures. However, owing to disagreements among delegations, the Commission was not able to reach consensus on its substantive agenda and decided to continue deliberations on the issue in 2005.

GENERAL ASSEMBLY ACTION

On 3 December [meeting 66], the General Assembly, on the recommendation of the First Committee [A/59/459 & Corr.1], adopted **resolution 59/82** without vote [agenda item 65].

Consolidation of peace through practical disarmament measures

The General Assembly,

Recalling its resolutions 51/45 N of 10 December 1996, 52/38 G of 9 December 1997, 53/77 M of 4 December 1998, 54/54 H of 1 December 1999, 55/33 G of 20 November 2000, 56/24 P of 29 November 2001 and 57/81 of 22 November 2002 and its decision 58/519 of 8 December 2003, entitled "Consolidation of peace through practical disarmament measures",

Convinced that a comprehensive and integrated approach towards certain practical disarmament measures often is a prerequisite to maintaining and consolidating peace and security and thus provides a basis for effective post-conflict peace-building; such measures include: collection and responsible disposal, preferably through destruction, of weapons obtained through illicit trafficking or illicit manufacture as well as of weapons and ammunition declared by competent national authorities to be surplus to requirements, particularly with regard to small arms and light weapons, unless another form of disposition or use has been officially authorized and provided that such weapons have been duly marked and registered; confidence-building measures; disarmament, demobilization and reintegration of former combatants; demining; and conversion,

Noting with satisfaction that the international community is more than ever aware of the importance of such practical disarmament measures, especially with regard to the growing problems arising from the excessive accumulation and uncontrolled spread of small arms and light weapons, which pose a threat to peace and security and reduce the prospects for economic development in many regions, particularly in post-conflict situations,

Stressing that further efforts are needed in order to develop and effectively implement programmes of practical disarmament in affected areas as part of disarmament, demobilization and reintegration measures so as to complement, on a case-by-case basis, peacekeeping and peace-building efforts,

Taking note with appreciation of the report of the Secretary-General on prevention of armed conflict, which, inter alia, refers to the role which the proliferation and the illicit transfer of small arms and light weapons play in the context of the build-up and sustaining of conflicts,

Taking note of the statement by the President of the Security Council of 31 August 2001 underlining the importance of practical disarmament measures in the context of armed conflicts, and, with regard to disarmament, demobilization and reintegration programmes, emphasizing the importance of measures to contain the security risks stemming from the use of illicit small arms and light weapons,

Also taking note of the report of the Secretary-General prepared with the assistance of the Group of Governmental Experts on Small Arms and, in particular, the recommendations contained therein, as an important contribution to the consolidation of the peace process through practical disarmament measures,

Welcoming the work of the Coordinating Action on Small Arms, which was established by the Secretary-General to bring about a holistic and multidisciplinary approach to this complex and multifaceted global problem and to cooperate with non-governmental organizations in the implementation of practical disarmament measures,

Welcoming also the report of the First Biennial Meeting of States to Consider the Implementation of the Programme of Action to Prevent, Combat and Eradicate the Illicit Trade in Small Arms and Light Weapons in All Its Aspects, held in New York from 7 to 11 July 2003, as well as the convening of the open-ended working group to negotiate an international instrument to enable States to identify and trace, in a timely and reliable manner, illicit small arms and light weapons,

1. *Stresses* the particular relevance of the "Guidelines on conventional arms control/limitation and disarmament, with particular emphasis on consolidation of peace in the context of General Assembly resolution

51/45 N", adopted by the Disarmament Commission by consensus at its 1999 substantive session;

2. *Takes note* of the report of the Secretary-General on the consolidation of peace through practical disarmament measures, submitted pursuant to resolution 51/45 N, and once again encourages Member States as well as regional arrangements and agencies to lend their support to the implementation of recommendations contained therein;

3. *Emphasizes* the importance of including in United Nations–mandated peacekeeping missions, as appropriate and with the consent of the host State, practical disarmament measures aimed at addressing the problem of the illicit trade in small arms and light weapons in conjunction with disarmament, demobilization and reintegration programmes aimed at former combatants, with a view to promoting an integrated comprehensive and effective weapons management strategy that would contribute to a sustainable peace-building process;

4. *Welcomes* the activities undertaken by the Group of Interested States, and invites the Group to continue to analyse lessons learned from previous disarmament and peace-building projects, as well as to promote new practical disarmament measures to consolidate peace, especially as undertaken or designed by affected States themselves, regional and subregional organizations as well as United Nations agencies;

5. *Encourages* Member States, including the Group of Interested States, to lend their support to the Secretary-General, relevant international, regional and subregional organizations, in accordance with Chapter VIII of the Charter of the United Nations, and non-governmental organizations in responding to requests by Member States to collect and destroy small arms and light weapons in post-conflict situations;

6. *Welcomes* the synergies within the multi-stakeholder process, including Governments, the United Nations system, regional and subregional organizations and institutions as well as non-governmental organizations in support of practical disarmament measures and the Programme of Action to Prevent, Combat and Eradicate the Illicit Trade in Small Arms and Light Weapons in All Its Aspects, in particular, inter alia through the Coordinating Action on Small Arms;

7. *Thanks* the Secretary-General for his report on the implementation of resolution 57/81, taking into consideration the activities of the Group of Interested States in this regard;

8. *Welcomes* the report of the Secretary-General on disarmament and non-proliferation education, as well as his report on the United Nations Disarmament Information Programme;

9. *Requests* the Secretary-General to submit to the General Assembly at its sixty-first session a report on the implementation of practical disarmament measures, taking into consideration the activities of the Group of Interested States in this regard;

10. *Decides* to include in the provisional agenda of its sixty-first session the item entitled "Consolidation of peace through practical disarmament measures".

Transparency

Conference on Disarmament. In 2004, the Conference on Disarmament [A/59/27] was not able to establish or re-establish any mechanism to deal with seven issues on its agenda, including transparency in armaments, owing to the deadlock over a substantive programme of work. Consequently, the item was considered at plenary meetings, during which delegates reaffirmed or further elaborated their respective positions on the issue.

GENERAL ASSEMBLY ACTION

On 3 December [meeting 66], the General Assembly, on the recommendation of the First Committee [A/59/459 & Corr.1], adopted three resolutions and a decision relating to transparency in conventional arms transfers. The Assembly adopted **resolution 59/66** without vote [agenda item 65 (*l*)].

National legislation on transfer of arms, military equipment and dual-use goods and technology

The General Assembly,

Recognizing that disarmament, arms control and non-proliferation are essential for the maintenance of international peace and security,

Recalling that effective national control of the transfer of arms, military equipment and dual-use goods and technology, including those transfers that could contribute to proliferation activities, is an important tool for achieving those objectives,

Recalling also that the States parties to the international disarmament and non-proliferation treaties have undertaken to facilitate the fullest possible exchange of materials, equipment and technological information for peaceful purposes, in accordance with the provisions of those treaties,

Considering that the exchange of national legislation, regulations and procedures on the transfer of arms, military equipment and dual-use goods and technology contributes to mutual understanding and confidence among Member States,

Convinced that such an exchange would be beneficial to Member States that are in the process of developing such legislation,

Reaffirming the inherent right of individual or collective self-defence in accordance with Article 51 of the Charter of the United Nations,

1. *Invites* Member States that are in a position to do so, without prejudice to the provisions contained in Security Council resolution 1540(2004) of 28 April 2004, to enact or improve national legislation, regulations and procedures to exercise effective control over the transfer of arms, military equipment and dual-use goods and technology, while ensuring that such legislation, regulations and procedures are consistent with the obligations of States parties under international treaties;

2. *Encourages* Member States to provide, on a voluntary basis, information to the Secretary-General on their national legislation, regulations and procedures on the transfer of arms, military equipment and dual-use goods and technology, as well as the changes therein, and requests the Secretary-General to make this information accessible to Member States;

3. *Decides* to remain attentive to the matter.

The Assembly adopted **resolution 59/90** without vote [agenda item 65].

Prevention of the illicit transfer and unauthorized access to and use of man-portable air defence systems

The General Assembly,

Recalling its resolutions 58/42 and 58/54 of 8 December 2003 and 58/241 of 23 December 2003,

Recognizing that disarmament, arms control and non-proliferation are essential for the maintenance of international peace and security,

Acknowledging the authorized trade in man-portable air defence systems between Governments and the legitimate right of Governments to possess such weapons in the interests of their national security,

Recognizing the threat posed to civil aviation, peacekeeping, crisis management and security by the illicit transfer and unauthorized access to and use of man-portable air defence systems,

Taking into account that man-portable air defence systems are easily carried, concealed, fired and, in certain circumstances, obtained,

Recognizing that effective control over man-portable air defence systems acquires special importance in the context of the intensified international fight against global terrorism,

Convinced of the importance of effective national control of transfers of man-portable air defence systems and the safe and effective management of stockpiles of such weapons,

Welcoming the ongoing efforts of various international and regional forums to enhance transport security and to strengthen management of man-portable air defence systems stockpiles in order to prevent the illicit transfer and unauthorized access to and use of such weapons,

Noting the importance of information exchange and transparency in the trade in man-portable air defence systems to build confidence and security among States and to prevent the illicit trade in and unauthorized access to such weapons,

1. *Emphasizes* the importance of the full implementation of the Programme of Action to Prevent, Combat and Eradicate the Illicit Trade in Small Arms and Light Weapons in All Its Aspects, adopted by the United Nations Conference on the Illicit Trade in Small Arms and Light Weapons in All Its Aspects;

2. *Urges* Member States to support current international, regional and national efforts to combat and prevent the illicit transfer of man-portable air defence systems and unauthorized access to and use of such weapons;

3. *Stresses* the importance of effective and comprehensive national controls on the production, stockpiling, transfer and brokering of man-portable air defence systems to prevent the illicit trade in and unauthorized access to and use of such weapons;

4. *Encourages* Member States to enact or improve legislation, regulations, procedures and stockpile management practices to exercise effective control over access to and transfer of man-portable air defence systems so as to prevent the illicit transfer and unauthorized access to and use of such weapons;

5. *Also encourages* Member States to enact or improve legislation, regulations and procedures to ban the transfer of man-portable air defence systems to

non-State end-users and to ensure that such weapons are exported only to Governments or agents authorized by a Government;

6. *Encourages* initiatives to exchange information and to mobilize resources and technical expertise to assist States, at their request, in enhancing national controls and stockpile management practices to prevent unauthorized access to and use and transfer of man-portable air defence systems and to destroy excess or obsolete stockpiles of such weapons, as appropriate;

7. *Decides* to include in the provisional agenda of its sixtieth session an item entitled "Prevention of the illicit transfer and unauthorized access to and use of man-portable air defence systems".

The Assembly adopted **resolution 59/92** without vote [agenda item 65].

Information on confidence-building measures in the field of conventional arms

The General Assembly,

Guided by the purposes and principles enshrined in the Charter of the United Nations,

Bearing in mind the contribution of confidence-building measures in the field of conventional arms, adopted on the initiative and with the agreement of the States concerned, to the improvement of the overall international peace and security situation,

Convinced that the relationship between the development of confidence-building measures in the field of conventional arms and the international security environment can also be mutually reinforcing,

Considering the important role that confidence-building measures in the field of conventional arms can also play in creating favourable conditions for progress in the field of disarmament,

Recognizing that the exchange of information on confidence-building measures in the field of conventional arms contributes to mutual understanding and confidence among Member States,

1. *Welcomes* all confidence-building measures in the field of conventional arms already undertaken by Member States as well as the information on such measures voluntarily provided;

2. *Encourages* Member States to continue to adopt confidence-building measures in the field of conventional arms and to provide information in that regard;

3. *Also encourages* Member States to engage in a dialogue on confidence-building measures in the field of conventional arms;

4. *Requests* the Secretary-General to establish, with the financial support of States in a position to do so, an electronic database containing information provided by Member States and to assist them, at their request, in the organization of seminars, courses and workshops aimed at enhancing the knowledge of new developments in this field;

5. *Decides* to include in the provisional agenda of its sixtieth session an item entitled "Information on confidence-building measures in the field of conventional arms".

Also on 3 December, the Assembly decided to include in the provisional agenda of its sixtieth (2005) session an item entitled "Problems arising from the accumulation of conventional ammunition stockpiles in surplus" (**decision 59/515**).

UN Register of Conventional Arms

In response to General Assembly resolution 58/54 [YUN 2003, p. 568], the Secretary-General submitted the twelfth annual report on the United Nations Register of Conventional Arms [A/59/193 & Corr.1, Add.1], established in 1992 [YUN 1992, p. 75] to promote enhanced transparency on arms transfers.

The report presented information provided by 114 Governments on imports and exports in 2003 in the seven categories of conventional arms (battle tanks, armoured combat vehicles, large-calibre artillery systems, attack helicopters, combat aircraft, warships and missiles and missile launchers). Governments also provided information on procurement from national production and military holdings, on the continuing operation of the Register and its further development and on transparency measures related to WMDs. The report indicated a reduction in the number of submissions from 119 in 2002.

Regarding the recommendations contained in the 2003 report of the Group of Governmental Experts on the operation and development of the Register [YUN 2003, p. 568], the Secretary-General's report stated that the scope of the Register had been adapted in conformity with those recommendations and described the adjustments made to reporting requirements. His report also highlighted the variety of activities undertaken by the Secretariat during the year, through DDA, in collaboration with Governments and regional organizations, to enhance awareness of the Register and to encourage greater participation in it.

Transparency of military expenditures

In response to General Assembly resolution 58/28 [YUN 2003, p. 570], the Secretary-General, in a July report and later addendum, presented reports from 79 Member States on military expenditures for the latest fiscal year for which data were available [A/59/192 & Add.1]. The reporting instrument was that recommended by the Assembly in resolution 35/142 B [YUN 1980, p. 88].

The report also described activities undertaken by the Secretariat, through DDA, to promote the standardized instrument for reporting military expenditures, which included DDA's participation in a meeting of the OAS Committee on Hemispheric Security (Washington, D.C., 23 March); progress of reporting through that instrument and the UN Register of Conventional Arms was addressed. DDA, with the financial assistance of Sweden and the United Kingdom, organized a subregional workshop (Nairobi, Kenya, 18-20 May) covering the Horn of Africa and the Great Lakes region, which discussed the technical operation and procedures of both instruments.

The Assembly, in **decision 59/512** of 3 December, took note of the First Committee's report [A/59/451] on the reduction of military budgets.

Verification

On 3 December [meeting 66], the General Assembly, on the recommendation of the First Committee [A/59/453], adopted **resolution 59/60** without vote [agenda item 59].

Verification in all its aspects, including the role of the United Nations in the field of verification

The General Assembly,

Noting the critical importance of and the vital contribution that has been made by effective verification measures in non-proliferation, arms limitation and disarmament agreements and other similar obligations,

Reaffirming its support for the sixteen principles of verification drawn up by the Disarmament Commission,

Recalling its resolutions 40/152 O of 16 December 1985, 41/86 Q of 4 December 1986, 42/42 F of 30 November 1987, 43/81 B of 7 December 1988, 45/65 of 4 December 1990, 47/45 of 9 December 1992, 48/68 of 16 December 1993, 50/61 of 12 December 1995, 52/31 of 9 December 1997, 54/46 of 1 December 1999 and 56/15 of 29 November 2001, as well as its decision 58/515 of 8 December 2003,

Recalling also the reports of the Secretary-General of 11 July 1986, 28 August 1990, 16 September 1992, 26 July 1993, 22 September 1995, 6 August 1997, 9 July 1999, 10 September 2001 and 10 July 2003, and the addenda thereto,

1. *Reaffirms* the critical importance of and the vital contribution that has been made by effective verification measures in non-proliferation, arms limitation and disarmament agreements and other similar obligations;

2. *Requests* the Secretary-General to report to the General Assembly at its sixtieth session on further views received from Member States;

3. *Also requests* the Secretary-General, with the assistance of a panel of government experts to be established in 2006 on the basis of equitable geographic distribution, to explore the question of verification in all its aspects, including the role of the United Nations in the field of verification, and to transmit the report of the panel of experts to the General Assembly for consideration at its sixty-first session;

4. *Decides* to include in the provisional agenda of its sixty-first session the item entitled "Verification in all its aspects, including the role of the United Nations in the field of verification".

Anti-personnel mines

1997 Convention

The number of States parties to the Convention on the Prohibition of the Use, Stockpiling, Production and Transfer of Anti-personnel Mines and on Their Destruction (Mine-Ban Convention or Ottawa Convention), which was adopted in 1997 [YUN 1997, p. 503] and entered into force in 1999 [YUN 1999, p. 498], totalled 144 as at 31 December. During the year, three States adhered to the Convention.

Review Conference

In accordance with article 12 of the Mine-Ban Convention, which provided for a Review Conference five years after the Convention's entry into force, and as decided by the Fifth Meeting of the States Parties [YUN 2003, p. 571], the Convention's First Review Conference was convened (Nairobi, 29 November–3 December) [APLC/CONF/2004/5]. Participants reviewed the operation and status of the Convention and a plan of action to overcome challenges that remained in ending suffering caused by anti-personnel mines, among other issues.

The Conference's final report comprised five main parts, the first of which addressed organizational matters. The other parts contained the following outcome documents: "Review of the operation and status of the Convention on the Prohibition of the Use, Stockpiling, Production and Transfer of Anti-personnel Mines and on Their Destruction: 1999-2004", which emphasized that although great progress had been made in ending the suffering caused by anti-personnel mines, much more needed to be done; "Ending the suffering caused by anti-personnel mines: Nairobi Action Plan 2005-2009", which urged States parties and all others who shared the States parties' aims to take steps to implement the action plan; "Towards a mine-free world: the 2004 Nairobi Declaration", which renewed the States parties' commitment to achieving a world free of anti-personnel mines, in which there were no more new victims; and a "Programme of meetings and related matters to facilitate implementation 2005-2009", which contained the Conference's decision to hold annually, until the Second Review Conference, a Meeting of the States parties. The Conference also decided to convene annually, until 2009, informal intersessional meetings of the Standing Committees in the first half of the year in Geneva; to convene the Second Review Conference in 2009; and to review, as warranted, decisions regarding their 2005-2009 programme of meetings. The Conference decided to hold the next Meeting of the States Parties in Croatia from 28 November to 2 December 2005, and meetings of the Standing Committees in June 2005. Documents before the Conference included information from Governments on the implementation of the Convention [APLC/CONF/

2004/MISC.3, 4, 8, 9] and national and regional perspectives on how to address the problems posed by anti-personnel mines [APLC/CONF/2004/MISC.5/Rev.1, 6, 7].

The Review Conference was preceded by two preparatory meetings, on 13 February [APLC/CONF/2004/PM.1/2] and on 28-29 June [APLC/CONF/2004/PM.2/2], which made and revised recommendations on the provisional agenda, programme of work, cost estimates and draft rules of procedure of the Conference, among other organizational matters.

Communications. The United States, on 17 March [CD/1730], announced a new policy of commitment to eliminate persistent landmines of all types from its arsenal. It would continue to develop non-persistent anti-personnel and anti-tank mines with self-destruct or self-deactivate capabilities. Reaffirming its position that it would not join the Mine-Ban Convention because it would require that needed military capability be given up, the United States said that the new policy markedly reduced the danger posed to civilians from unexploded landmines left behind after military conflicts.

On 6 February [CD/1727], Romania transmitted the report of a workshop it hosted (Bucharest, 2-3 February), which assessed progress and challenges in South-Eastern Europe to clear mined areas, assist victims, destroy stockpiled mines, establish national implementation measures, exchange information and generate resources in complying with the Mine-Ban Convention.

Other relevant conferences or workshops during the year took place in Dushanbe, Tajikistan (15-16 April) [A/58/773], on progress towards the Convention's aims in Central Asia, and in Kunming City, China (26-28 April) [A/58/812], on humanitarian mine/unexploded ordnance clearance technology and cooperation. In Vilnius, Lithuania (8-9 June) [A/58/861], a seminar was held on advancing the Convention in Northern and Eastern Europe, which took stock of the progress made and the challenges that remained in the pursuit of the Convention's aims.

GENERAL ASSEMBLY ACTION

On 3 December [meeting 66], the General Assembly, on the recommendation of the First Committee [A/59/459 & Corr.1], adopted **resolution 59/84** by recorded vote (157-0-22) [agenda item 65 (v)].

Implementation of the Convention on the Prohibition of the Use, Stockpiling, Production and Transfer of Anti-personnel Mines and on Their Destruction

The General Assembly,

Recalling its resolutions 54/54 B of 1 December 1999, 55/33 V of 20 November 2000, 56/24 M of 29 November 2001, 57/74 of 22 November 2002 and 58/53 of 8 December 2003,

Reaffirming its determination to put an end to the suffering and casualties caused by anti-personnel mines, which kill or maim hundreds of people every week, mostly innocent and defenceless civilians and especially children, obstruct economic development and reconstruction, inhibit the repatriation of refugees and internally displaced persons and have other severe consequences for years after emplacement,

Believing it necessary to do the utmost to contribute in an efficient and coordinated manner to facing the challenge of removing anti-personnel mines placed throughout the world and to assure their destruction,

Wishing to do the utmost in ensuring assistance for the care and rehabilitation, including the social and economic reintegration, of mine victims,

Welcoming the entry into force, on 1 March 1999, of the Convention on the Prohibition of the Use, Stockpiling, Production and Transfer of Anti-personnel Mines and on Their Destruction, and noting with satisfaction the work undertaken to implement the Convention and the substantial progress made towards addressing the global landmine problem,

Recalling the first to fifth meetings of the States parties to the Convention held in Maputo (1999), Geneva (2000), Managua (2001), Geneva (2002) and Bangkok (2003), and the reaffirmation of a commitment to the total elimination of anti-personnel mines and to pursue, with renewed vigour, efforts to clear mined areas, assist victims, destroy stockpiled anti-personnel mines and promote universal adherence to the Convention,

Recalling also the preparatory process for the First Review Conference of the Convention, to be held in Nairobi from 29 November to 3 December 2004, and the two preparatory meetings held in Geneva on 13 February and on 28 and 29 June 2004 pursuant to the decisions of the Fifth Meeting of the States Parties,

Welcoming the regional seminars that have been held in different parts of the world during 2003 and 2004, which contributed to the exchange of information, experiences and best practices in mine action as well as to preparations for the First Review Conference, and recalling the efforts to enhance cooperation in the regional context and promote synergies between different regions,

Noting with interest the increased recognition of the need to integrate mine action into international and national development programmes and strategies, and, in this respect, welcoming the developments since the Fifth Meeting of the States Parties, including the meeting between the President of the Fifth Meeting of the States Parties and the President of the World Bank on 20 September 2004, which contributed to possible partnership between the mine action community and the World Bank,

Noting with satisfaction that additional States have ratified or acceded to the Convention, bringing the total number of States that have formally accepted the obligations of the Convention to one hundred and forty-three,

Emphasizing the desirability of attracting the adherence of all States to the Convention, and determined to work strenuously towards the promotion of its universalization,

Noting with regret that anti-personnel mines continue to be used in conflicts around the world, causing human suffering and impeding post-conflict development,

1. *Invites* all States that have not signed the Convention on the Prohibition of the Use, Stockpiling, Production and Transfer of Anti-personnel Mines and on Their Destruction to accede to it without delay;

2. *Urges* all States that have signed but not ratified the Convention to ratify it without delay;

3. *Stresses* the importance of the full and effective implementation of and compliance with the Convention;

4. *Urges* all States parties to provide the Secretary-General with complete and timely information as required under article 7 of the Convention in order to promote transparency and compliance with the Convention;

5. *Invites* all States that have not ratified the Convention or acceded to it to provide, on a voluntary basis, information to make global mine action efforts more effective;

6. *Renews its call upon* all States and other relevant parties to work together to promote, support and advance the care, rehabilitation and social and economic reintegration of mine victims, mine risk education programmes and the removal of anti-personnel mines and stockpiles throughout the world and the assurance of their destruction;

7. *Invites and encourages* all interested States, the United Nations, other relevant international organizations or institutions, regional organizations, the International Committee of the Red Cross and relevant non-governmental organizations to attend the First Review Conference at the highest possible level and, pending a decision to be taken at the First Review Conference, to maintain the high level of participation in the subsequent meetings of the States parties, including their intersessional work programme;

8. *Requests* the Secretary-General to undertake the preparations necessary to convene the next meeting of the States parties, pending a decision to be taken at the First Review Conference, and to invite States not parties to the Convention, as well as the United Nations, other relevant international organizations or institutions, regional organizations, the International Committee of the Red Cross and relevant non-governmental organizations to attend the meeting as observers;

9. *Decides* to include in the provisional agenda of its sixtieth session the item entitled "Implementation of the Convention on the Prohibition of the Use, Stockpiling, Production and Transfer of Anti-personnel Mines and on Their Destruction".

RECORDED VOTE ON RESOLUTION 59/84:

In favour: Afghanistan, Albania, Algeria, Andorra, Angola, Antigua and Barbuda, Argentina, Armenia, Australia, Austria, Bahamas, Bahrain, Bangladesh, Barbados, Belarus, Belgium, Belize, Benin, Bhutan, Bolivia, Bosnia and Herzegovina, Botswana, Brazil, Brunei Darussalam, Bulgaria, Burkina Faso, Burundi, Cambodia, Cameroon, Canada, Cape Verde, Central African Republic, Chile, Colombia, Comoros, Congo, Costa Rica, Côte d'Ivoire, Croatia, Cyprus, Czech Republic, Denmark, Djibouti, Dominica, Dominican Republic, Ecuador, El Salvador, Equatorial Guinea, Eritrea, Estonia, Ethiopia, Fiji, Finland, France, Gabon, Gambia, Georgia, Germany, Ghana, Greece, Grenada, Guatemala, Guinea-Bissau, Guyana, Haiti, Honduras, Hungary, Iceland, Indonesia, Iraq, Ireland, Italy, Jamaica, Japan, Jordan, Kenya, Latvia, Lesotho, Liberia, Liechtenstein, Lithuania, Luxembourg, Madagascar, Malawi, Malaysia, Maldives, Mali, Malta, Mauritius, Mexico, Monaco, Mongolia, Morocco, Mozambique, Namibia, Netherlands, New Zealand, Nicaragua, Niger, Nigeria, Norway, Oman, Panama, Papua New Guinea, Paraguay, Peru, Philippines, Poland, Portugal, Qatar, Republic of Moldova, Romania, Rwanda, Saint Lucia, Saint Vincent and the Grenadines, Samoa, San Marino, Sao Tome

and Principe, Senegal, Serbia and Montenegro, Seychelles, Sierra Leone, Singapore, Slovakia, Slovenia, Solomon Islands, Somalia, South Africa, Spain, Sri Lanka, Sudan, Suriname, Swaziland, Sweden, Switzerland, Tajikistan, Thailand, The former Yugoslav Republic of Macedonia, Timor-Leste, Togo, Tonga, Trinidad and Tobago, Tunisia, Turkey, Turkmenistan, Tuvalu, Uganda, Ukraine, United Arab Emirates, United Kingdom, United Republic of Tanzania, Uruguay, Vanuatu, Venezuela, Yemen, Zambia, Zimbabwe.

Against: None.

Abstaining: Azerbaijan, China, Cuba, Egypt, India, Iran, Israel, Kazakhstan, Kyrgyzstan, Lebanon, Libyan Arab Jamahiriya, Marshall Islands, Micronesia, Myanmar, Pakistan, Palau, Republic of Korea, Russian Federation, Syrian Arab Republic, United States, Uzbekistan, Viet Nam.

Regional and other approaches to disarmament

Reports of Secretary-General. Pursuant to General Assembly resolution 58/39 [YUN 2003, p. 578], the Secretary-General, in June [A/59/118], presented the views of 11 Member States (Argentina, El Salvador, Honduras, Lebanon, Mexico, New Zealand, Panama, Philippines, Qatar, Russian Federation, Venezuela) and the Holy See regarding conventional arms control at the regional and subregional levels.

The Secretary-General, in response to Assembly resolution 58/43 [YUN 2003, p. 578], submitted a July report with a later addendum [A/59/127 & Corr.1, & Add.1] containing the views of 11 Member States (China, India, Israel, Lebanon, Mexico, Nicaragua, Panama, Philippines, Poland, Qatar, Venezuela) and the Holy See on the possibilities of furthering efforts towards confidence-building measures in the regional and subregional context, particularly in regions of tension.

Africa

In 2004, African States, through the African Union (AU) and subregional organizations, continued efforts to combat small arms proliferation on the continent, particularly within the framework of implementing the 2001 Programme of Action to Prevent, Combat and Eradicate the Illicit Trade in Small Arms and Light Weapons in All Its Aspects [YUN 2001, p. 499]. The Second Extraordinary Session of the AU Assembly (Sirte, Libyan Arab Jamahiriya, 28 February) adopted the Common African Defence and Security Policy, which identified the illicit proliferation, circulation and trafficking in small arms and light weapons as one of the factors threatening continental security and called for coordinated action in addressing it. Efforts were made during the year to operationalize the AU Peace and Security Council, designed to foster coordinated continental cooperation in responding to threats to security, including the small arms scourge.

On the subregional level, member States of the Economic Community of West African States (ECOWAS) maintained efforts to implement their 1998 Moratorium on the Importation, Exportation and Manufacture of Small Arms and Light Weapons in West Africa [YUN 1998, p. 537], which was renewed in 2001 [YUN 2001, p. 511]. They began the process of transforming the Moratorium into a convention and circulated a draft text entitled "Protocol Regarding the Fight against the Proliferation of Small Arms and Light Weapons, Their Munitions and Other Related Material". An ECOWAS conference on combating illicit small arms brokering and trafficking (Abuja, Nigeria, 22-24 March) reinforced the call for a convention to stem the flow of those weapons in West Africa and to address loopholes in the ECOWAS Moratorium, particularly regarding brokering controls. At the Second Ministerial Review Conference (Nairobi, 20-21 April) of the Nairobi Declaration on the Problem of the Proliferation of Illicit Small Arms and Light Weapons in the Great Lakes Region and the Horn of Africa [YUN 2000, p. 518], Ministers signed the Nairobi Protocol for the Prevention, Control and Reduction of Small Arms and Light Weapons in the Great Lakes Region and the Horn of Africa. The Protocol was designed to prevent, combat and eradicate the illicit manufacture, possession and use of those weapons in the subregion, among other objectives, and participating States pledged to ratify it by year's end. A seminar on developing West African and international arms control (Dakar, Senegal, 19-23 July), organized by Oxfam and supported by the UN Regional Centre for Peace and Disarmament in Africa (see p. 585), considered ways of raising awareness of initiatives to advance recommendations contained in the 2001 Programme of Action. ECOWAS member States adopted a successor project document to the Programme for Coordination and Assistance on Security and Development in Africa, a mechanism charged with assisting in the Moratorium's implementation. In Southern Africa, a joint ministerial meeting of the Southern African Development Community (SADC) and the EU (Netherlands, 20 October) agreed to strengthen bilateral collaboration in subregional security, including peace support, peacekeeping training, postconflict reconstruction, demining and small arms and light weapons. On 8 November, the Protocol on the Control of Firearms, Ammunition and Other Related Materials, which SADC adopted in 2001, entered into force, enhancing subregional efforts to address the influx of small arms and light weapons into the region.

Standing Advisory Committee

In response to General Assembly resolution 58/65 [YUN 2003, p. 574], the Secretary-General, in July [A/59/182], described the activities of the Standing Advisory Committee on Security Questions in Central Africa, which remained the only forum for States members of the Economic Community of Central African States (ECCAS) to meet regularly to examine political and security developments in the subregion. However, despite the establishment of the Council for Peace and Security in Central Africa (COPAX) [YUN 1999, p. 500], the Council, designed to prevent, manage and settle subregional conflicts, had yet to meet on relevant developments. As the Central African region was facing new security challenges requiring a collective and robust involvement of the regional States, the Secretary-General said it was imperative for COPAX to become operational, particularly its early warning mechanism. That demanded the commitment of ECCAS member States and international cooperation and support. The United Nations remained determined to assist the subregion's efforts in promoting confidence- and security-building measures.

At its twenty-first ministerial meeting (Malabo, Equatorial Guinea, 21-25 June) [A/59/154-S/2004/576], the Standing Advisory Committee reviewed the geopolitical and security situation in some of its member States and cooperation between the United Nations and ECCAS. It assessed its own work, with a view to becoming more responsive to the needs of the Central African region. The Committee condemned attempts to forcibly overthrow the democratically elected Governments of Chad and Equatorial Guinea, and, reflecting on the magnitude of mercenary activities in that context, decided to consider the issue of mercenaries at its twenty-second (2005) ministerial meeting.

GENERAL ASSEMBLY ACTION

On 3 December [meeting 66], the General Assembly, on the recommendation of the First Committee [A/59/460], adopted **resolution 59/96** without vote [agenda item 66 (h)].

Regional confidence-building measures: activities of the United Nations Standing Advisory Committee on Security Questions in Central Africa

The General Assembly,

Bearing in mind the purposes and principles of the United Nations and its primary responsibility for the maintenance of international peace and security in accordance with the Charter of the United Nations,

Recalling its resolutions 43/78 H and 43/85 of 7 December 1988, 44/21 of 15 November 1989, 45/58 M of 4 December 1990, 46/37 B of 6 December 1991, 47/53 F of 15 December 1992, 48/76 A of 16 December 1993, 49/76 C of 15 December 1994, 50/71 B of 12 December 1995, 51/46 C of 10 December 1996, 52/39 B of 9 December 1997, 53/78 A of 4 December 1998, 54/55 A of 1 December 1999, 55/34 B of 20 November 2000, 56/25 A of 29 November 2001, 57/88 of 22 November 2002 and 58/65 of 8 December 2003,

Considering the importance and effectiveness of confidence-building measures taken at the initiative and with the participation of all States concerned and taking into account the specific characteristics of each region, since such measures can contribute to regional stability and to international peace and security,

Convinced that the resources released by disarmament, including regional disarmament, can be devoted to economic and social development and to the protection of the environment for the benefit of all peoples, in particular those of the developing countries,

Recalling the guidelines for general and complete disarmament adopted at its tenth special session, the first special session devoted to disarmament,

Convinced that development can be achieved only in a climate of peace, security and mutual confidence both within and among States,

Bearing in mind the establishment by the Secretary-General on 28 May 1992 of the United Nations Standing Advisory Committee on Security Questions in Central Africa, the purpose of which is to encourage arms limitation, disarmament, non-proliferation and development in the subregion,

Recalling the Brazzaville Declaration on Cooperation for Peace and Security in Central Africa, the Bata Declaration for the Promotion of Lasting Democracy, Peace and Development in Central Africa and the Yaoundé Declaration on Peace, Security and Stability in Central Africa,

Bearing in mind resolutions 1196(1998) and 1197 (1998), adopted by the Security Council on 16 and 18 September 1998 respectively, following its consideration of the report of the Secretary-General on the causes of conflict and the promotion of durable peace and sustainable development in Africa,

Emphasizing the need to strengthen the capacity for conflict prevention and peacekeeping in Africa,

Recalling the decision of the fourth ministerial meeting of the Standing Advisory Committee in favour of establishing, under the auspices of the Office of the United Nations High Commissioner for Human Rights, a subregional centre for human rights and democracy in Central Africa at Yaoundé,

1. *Takes note* of the report of the Secretary-General on regional confidence-building measures, which deals with the activities of the United Nations Standing Advisory Committee on Security Questions in Central Africa in the period since the adoption by the General Assembly of resolution 58/65;

2. *Reaffirms its support* for efforts aimed at promoting confidence-building measures at the regional and subregional levels in order to ease tensions and conflicts in Central Africa and to further peace, stability and sustainable development in the subregion;

3. *Also reaffirms its support* for the programme of work of the Standing Advisory Committee adopted at the organizational meeting of the Committee, held at Yaoundé from 27 to 31 July 1992;

4. *Notes with satisfaction* the progress made by the States members of the Standing Advisory Committee in implementing the programme of activities for the period 2003-2004, in particular by holding the twenty-first ministerial meeting of the Standing Advisory Committee in Malabo from 21 to 25 June 2004;

5. *Emphasizes* the importance of providing the States members of the Standing Advisory Committee with the essential support they need to carry out the full programme of activities which they adopted at their ministerial meetings;

6. *Welcomes* the creation of a mechanism for the promotion, maintenance and consolidation of peace and security in Central Africa, known as the Council for Peace and Security in Central Africa, by the Conference of Heads of State and Government of the member countries of the Economic Community of Central African States, held at Yaoundé on 25 February 1999, and requests the Secretary-General to give his full support to the effective realization of that important mechanism;

7. *Emphasizes* the need to make the early warning mechanism in Central Africa operational so that it will serve, on the one hand, as an instrument for analysing and monitoring political situations in the States members of the Standing Advisory Committee with a view to preventing the outbreak of future armed conflicts and, on the other hand, as a technical body through which the member States will carry out the programme of work of the Committee, adopted at its organizational meeting held at Yaoundé in 1992, and requests the Secretary-General to provide it with the assistance necessary for it to function properly;

8. *Requests* the Secretary-General and the United Nations High Commissioner for Human Rights to continue to provide their full assistance for the proper functioning of the Subregional Centre for Human Rights and Democracy in Central Africa;

9. *Requests* the Secretary-General, pursuant to Security Council resolution 1197(1998), to provide the States members of the Standing Advisory Committee with the necessary support for the implementation and smooth functioning of the Council for Peace and Security in Central Africa and the early warning mechanism;

10. *Also requests* the Secretary-General to support the establishment of a network of parliamentarians with a view to the creation of a subregional parliament in Central Africa;

11. *Requests* the Secretary-General and the United Nations High Commissioner for Refugees to continue to provide increased assistance to the countries of Central Africa for coping with the problems of refugees and displaced persons in their territories;

12. *Thanks* the Secretary-General for having established the Trust Fund for the United Nations Standing Advisory Committee on Security Questions in Central Africa;

13. *Appeals* to Member States and to governmental and non-governmental organizations to make additional voluntary contributions to the Trust Fund for the implementation of the programme of work of the Standing Advisory Committee;

14. *Thanks* the Secretary-General for sending a multidisciplinary mission from 8 to 22 June 2003 for the purpose of undertaking an assessment of the priority needs of the region and challenges confronting it in the areas of peace, security, economic development, human rights, HIV/AIDS and humanitarian questions;

15. *Requests* the Secretary-General to continue to provide the States members of the Standing Advisory Committee with assistance to ensure that they are able to carry on their efforts;

16. *Also requests* the Secretary-General to submit to the General Assembly at its sixtieth session a report on the implementation of the present resolution;

17. *Decides* to include in the provisional agenda of its sixtieth session the item entitled "Regional confidence-building measures: activities of the United Nations Standing Advisory Committee on Security Questions in Central Africa".

Asia and the Pacific

In 2004, disarmament and non-proliferation issues in Asia and the Pacific were addressed by the regional States through national initiatives and the frameworks of subregional organizations, notably the Association of Southeast Asian Nations, its Regional Forum (ARF) and the Shanghai Cooperation Organization (SCO) (China, Kazakhstan, Kyrgyzstan, Russian Federation, Tajikistan, Uzbekistan). SCO, founded in 2001 to address mutual concerns, including regional security, at its fourth summit (Tashkent, Uzbekistan, 17 June), adopted the Tashkent Declaration, in which the member States, expressing concern over rising terrorism and extremism, affirmed their readiness to construct a new security architecture to counter global and regional security threats through cooperation with other States and international mechanisms, primarily the United Nations. The eleventh ARF Ministerial Meeting (Jakarta, Indonesia, 2 July) underlined the importance of close collaboration among member States in efforts to prevent the proliferation of WMDs and the need to eliminate small arms trafficking, particularly to non-State actors.

Europe

During the year, security and disarmament issues were addressed within several European institutional frameworks. The Organization for Security and Cooperation in Europe adopted decisions to enhance the control of small arms, light weapons and other conventional arms exports. It helped members combat trafficking of small arms and light weapons through border management assistance and began projects to assist countries in destroying excess weapons and improving stockpile security. The EU pursued conventional disarmament and arms control through the implementation of its 1998 Code of Conduct on Arms Exports [YUN 1998, p. 540], which was expanded by the admission of 10 additional States to EU membership. The South-Eastern Europe

Clearinghouse for the Control of Small Arms and Light Weapons (SEESAC), established in 2002 [YUN 2002, p. 534], provided regional States with operational and technical assistance for control and reduction of those weapons. A conference on countering trafficking in those weapons in the Black Sea subregion (Chisinau, Moldova, 4-5 March), organized jointly by SEESAC, Moldova, the Netherlands and Switzerland, discussed measures for small arms control in the region and explored cross-border cooperation to curb related threats. In April, SEESAC, in collaboration with the Regional Arms Control Verification and Implementation Assistance Centre, held a training course for civil society on the monitoring, collection and destruction of small arms and light weapons. A similar SEESAC initiative during the year trained journalists in the subregion on small arms and light weapons reporting, and at the second Regional Arms Law Roundtable (Belgrade, Serbia and Montenegro, 25-26 May), Ministers from eight States discussed legislative developments on small arms and light weapons. The heads of State and Government of member States of the NATO (Istanbul, Turkey, 28-29 June) adopted the "Istanbul Declaration: Our security in a new era" and a summit communiqué, by which they renewed commitment to collective defence in addressing security challenges, particularly terrorism (see p. 576) and the proliferation of WMDs. They launched a Partnership Action Plan on Defence Institution Building to support partners in building democratically responsible defence institutions. The NATO Verification Coordinating Committee, at its annual seminar on the implementation of conventional arms control agreements (Brussels, Belgium, 6-8 October), discussed the practical aspects of the ongoing implementation of the 1990 Treaty on Conventional Armed Forces in Europe [YUN 1990, p. 79], considered the cornerstone of European security.

Latin America

The Organization of American States (OAS) maintained its involvement in regional disarmament and non-proliferation initiatives. At the Special Summit of the Americas (Monterrey, Mexico, 12-13 January), 34 heads of State and Government adopted the Declaration of Nuevo León, by which they resolved to work together to address common needs and challenges, including new security threats, such as terrorism, organized crime and trafficking in arms. The thirty-fourth regular session of the OAS General Assembly (Quito, Ecuador, 6-8 June) adopted resolutions relating to disarmament and non-proliferation. The First Conference of the States

Parties (Bogotá, Colombia, 8-9 March) to the Inter-American Convention against the Illicit Manufacturing of and Trafficking in Firearms, Ammunition, Explosives, and Other Related Materials [YUN 1997, p. 519] adopted the Declaration of Bogotá on the Convention's functioning and application, in which they agreed to exchange relevant information and experiences. A seminar organized by the OAS General Secretariat, the Inter-American Defense College and Nicaragua (Managua, Nicaragua, 12-13 May) considered the identification, collection, stockpile management and destruction of small arms and light weapons. Also during the year, the Sixth Conference of Ministers of Defense of the Americas (Quito, 16-21 November) issued a declaration reaffirming commitment to disarmament agreements and expressing support for the establishment of national controls for exporting and importing materials that could contribute to the production of WMDs.

GENERAL ASSEMBLY ACTION

On 3 December [meeting 66], the General Assembly, on the recommendation of the First Committee [A/59/459 & Corr.1], adopted **resolution 59/89** without vote [agenda item 65 (i)].

Regional disarmament

The General Assembly,

Recalling its resolutions 45/58 P of 4 December 1990, 46/36 I of 6 December 1991, 47/52 J of 9 December 1992, 48/75 I of 16 December 1993, 49/75 N of 15 December 1994, 50/70 K of 12 December 1995, 51/45 K of 10 December 1996, 52/38 P of 9 December 1997, 53/77 O of 4 December 1998, 54/54 N of 1 December 1999, 55/33 O of 20 November 2000, 56/24 H of 29 November 2001, 57/76 of 22 November 2002 and 58/38 of 8 December 2003 on regional disarmament,

Believing that the efforts of the international community to move towards the ideal of general and complete disarmament are guided by the inherent human desire for genuine peace and security, the elimination of the danger of war and the release of economic, intellectual and other resources for peaceful pursuits,

Affirming the abiding commitment of all States to the purposes and principles enshrined in the Charter of the United Nations in the conduct of their international relations,

Noting that essential guidelines for progress towards general and complete disarmament were adopted at the tenth special session of the General Assembly,

Taking note of the guidelines and recommendations for regional approaches to disarmament within the context of global security adopted by the Disarmament Commission at its 1993 substantive session,

Welcoming the prospects of genuine progress in the field of disarmament engendered in recent years as a result of negotiations between the two superpowers,

Taking note of the recent proposals for disarmament at the regional and subregional levels,

Recognizing the importance of confidence-building measures for regional and international peace and security,

Convinced that endeavours by countries to promote regional disarmament, taking into account the specific characteristics of each region and in accordance with the principle of undiminished security at the lowest level of armaments, would enhance the security of all States and would thus contribute to international peace and security by reducing the risk of regional conflicts,

1. *Stresses* that sustained efforts are needed, within the framework of the Conference on Disarmament and under the umbrella of the United Nations, to make progress on the entire range of disarmament issues;

2. *Affirms* that global and regional approaches to disarmament complement each other and should therefore be pursued simultaneously to promote regional and international peace and security;

3. *Calls upon* States to conclude agreements, wherever possible, for nuclear non-proliferation, disarmament and confidence-building measures at the regional and subregional levels;

4. *Welcomes* the initiatives towards disarmament, nuclear non-proliferation and security undertaken by some countries at the regional and subregional levels;

5. *Supports and encourages* efforts aimed at promoting confidence-building measures at the regional and subregional levels to ease regional tensions and to further disarmament and nuclear non-proliferation measures at the regional and subregional levels;

6. *Decides* to include in the provisional agenda of its sixtieth session the item entitled "Regional disarmament".

Also on 3 December [meeting 66], the General Assembly, on the recommendation of the First Committee [A/59/459 & Corr.1], adopted **resolution 59/88** by recorded vote (178-1-1) [agenda item 65 (j)].

Conventional arms control at the regional and subregional levels

The General Assembly,

Recalling its resolutions 48/75 J of 16 December 1993, 49/75 O of 15 December 1994, 50/70 L of 12 December 1995, 51/45 Q of 10 December 1996, 52/38 Q of 9 December 1997, 53/77 P of 4 December 1998, 54/54 M of 1 December 1999, 55/33 P of 20 November 2000, 56/24 I of 29 November 2001, 57/77 of 22 November 2002 and 58/39 of 8 December 2003,

Recognizing the crucial role of conventional arms control in promoting regional and international peace and security,

Convinced that conventional arms control needs to be pursued primarily in the regional and subregional contexts, since most threats to peace and security in the post-cold-war era arise mainly among States located in the same region or subregion,

Aware that the preservation of a balance in the defence capabilities of States at the lowest level of armaments would contribute to peace and stability and should be a prime objective of conventional arms control,

Desirous of promoting agreements to strengthen regional peace and security at the lowest possible level of armaments and military forces,

Noting with particular interest the initiatives taken in this regard in different regions of the world, in particular the commencement of consultations among a number of Latin American countries and the proposals for conventional arms control made in the context of South Asia, and recognizing, in the context of this subject, the relevance and value of the Treaty on Conventional Armed Forces in Europe, which is a cornerstone of European security,

Believing that militarily significant States and States with larger military capabilities have a special responsibility in promoting such agreements for regional security,

Believing also that an important objective of conventional arms control in regions of tension should be to prevent the possibility of military attack launched by surprise and to avoid aggression,

1. *Decides* to give urgent consideration to the issues involved in conventional arms control at the regional and subregional levels;

2. *Requests* the Conference on Disarmament to consider the formulation of principles that can serve as a framework for regional agreements on conventional arms control, and looks forward to a report of the Conference on this subject;

3. *Requests* the Secretary-General, in the meantime, to seek the views of Member States on the subject and to submit a report to the General Assembly at its sixtieth session;

4. *Decides* to include in the provisional agenda of its sixtieth session the item entitled "Conventional arms control at the regional and subregional levels".

RECORDED VOTE ON RESOLUTION 59/88:

In favour: Afghanistan, Albania, Algeria, Andorra, Angola, Antigua and Barbuda, Argentina, Armenia, Australia, Austria, Azerbaijan, Bahamas, Bahrain, Bangladesh, Barbados, Belarus, Belgium, Belize, Benin, Bolivia, Bosnia and Herzegovina, Botswana, Brazil, Brunei Darussalam, Bulgaria, Burkina Faso, Burundi, Cambodia, Cameroon, Canada, Cape Verde, Central African Republic, Chile, China, Colombia, Comoros, Congo, Costa Rica, Côte d'Ivoire, Croatia, Cyprus, Czech Republic, Denmark, Djibouti, Dominica, Dominican Republic, Ecuador, Egypt, El Salvador, Equatorial Guinea, Eritrea, Estonia, Ethiopia, Fiji, Finland, France, Gabon, Gambia, Georgia, Germany, Ghana, Greece, Grenada, Guatemala, Guinea-Bissau, Guyana, Haiti, Honduras, Hungary, Iceland, Indonesia, Iran, Ireland, Israel, Italy, Jamaica, Japan, Jordan, Kazakhstan, Kenya, Kuwait, Kyrgyzstan, Latvia, Lebanon, Lesotho, Liberia, Libyan Arab Jamahiriya, Liechtenstein, Lithuania, Luxembourg, Madagascar, Malawi, Malaysia, Maldives, Mali, Malta, Marshall Islands, Mauritius, Mexico, Micronesia, Monaco, Mongolia, Morocco, Mozambique, Myanmar, Namibia, Nauru, Nepal, Netherlands, New Zealand, Nicaragua, Niger, Nigeria, Norway, Oman, Pakistan, Palau, Panama, Papua New Guinea, Paraguay, Peru, Philippines, Poland, Portugal, Qatar, Republic of Korea, Republic of Moldova, Romania, Russian Federation, Rwanda, Saint Lucia, Saint Vincent and the Grenadines, Samoa, San Marino, Sao Tome and Principe, Saudi Arabia, Senegal, Serbia and Montenegro, Seychelles, Sierra Leone, Singapore, Slovakia, Slovenia, Solomon Islands, Somalia, South Africa, Spain, Sri Lanka, Sudan, Suriname, Swaziland, Sweden, Switzerland, Syrian Arab Republic, Tajikistan, Thailand, The former Yugoslav Republic of Macedonia, Timor-Leste, Togo, Tonga, Trinidad and Tobago, Tunisia, Turkey, Turkmenistan, Tuvalu, Uganda, Ukraine, United Arab Emirates, United Kingdom, United Republic of Tanzania, United States, Uruguay, Uzbekistan, Vanuatu, Venezuela, Yemen, Zambia, Zimbabwe.

Against: India

Abstaining: Bhutan.

On 3 December [meeting 66], the General Assembly, on the recommendation of the First Committee [A/59/459 & Corr.1], adopted **resolution 59/87** without vote [agenda item 65 (*m*)].

Confidence-building measures in the regional and subregional context

The General Assembly,

Guided by the purposes and principles enshrined in the Charter of the United Nations,

Recalling its resolution 58/43 of 8 December 2003,

Recalling also its resolution 57/337 of 3 July 2003, entitled "Prevention of armed conflict", in which it called upon Member States to settle their disputes by peaceful means, as set out in Chapter VI of the Charter, inter alia, by any procedures adopted by the parties,

Recalling further the resolutions and guidelines adopted by consensus by the General Assembly and the Disarmament Commission relating to confidence-building measures and their implementation at the global, regional and subregional levels,

Considering the importance and effectiveness of confidence-building measures taken at the initiative and with the agreement of all States concerned and taking into account the specific characteristics of each region, since such measures can contribute to regional stability,

Convinced that resources released by disarmament, including regional disarmament, can be devoted to economic and social development and to the protection of the environment for the benefit of all peoples, in particular those of the developing countries,

Recognizing the need for meaningful dialogue among States concerned to avert conflict,

Welcoming the peace processes already initiated by States concerned to resolve their disputes through peaceful means bilaterally or through mediation, inter alia, by third parties, regional organizations or the United Nations,

Recognizing that States in some regions have already taken steps towards confidence-building measures at the bilateral, subregional and regional levels in the political and military fields, including arms control and disarmament, and noting that such confidence-building measures have improved peace and security in those regions and contributed to progress in the socio-economic conditions of their people,

Concerned that the continuation of disputes among States, particularly in the absence of an effective mechanism to resolve them through peaceful means, may contribute to the arms race and endanger the maintenance of international peace and security and the efforts of the international community to promote arms control and disarmament,

1. *Calls upon* Member States to refrain from the use or threat of use of force, in accordance with the purposes and principles of the Charter of the United Nations;

2. *Reaffirms its commitment* to the peaceful settlement of disputes under Chapter VI of the Charter, in particular Article 33, which provides for a solution by negotiation, enquiry, mediation, conciliation, arbitration, judicial settlement, resort to regional agencies or arrangements or other peaceful means chosen by the parties;

3. *Reaffirms* the ways and means regarding confidence- and security-building measures set out in the report of the Disarmament Commission on its 1993 session;

4. *Calls upon* Member States to pursue those ways and means through sustained consultations and dia-

logue, while at the same time avoiding actions which may hinder or impair such a dialogue;

5. *Urges* States to comply strictly with all bilateral, regional and international agreements, including arms control and disarmament agreements, to which they are party;

6. *Emphasizes* that the objective of confidence-building measures should be to help to strengthen international peace and security and be consistent with the principle of undiminished security at the lowest level of armament;

7. *Encourages* the promotion of bilateral and regional confidence-building measures, with the consent and participation of the parties concerned, to avoid conflict and prevent the unintended and accidental outbreak of hostilities;

8. *Requests* the Secretary-General to submit a report to the General Assembly at its sixtieth session containing the views of Member States on confidence-building measures in the regional and subregional context;

9. *Decides* to include in the provisional agenda of its sixtieth session the item entitled "Confidence-building measures in the regional and subregional context".

Other disarmament issues

Terrorism

In 2004, the United Nations continued to develop and promote global action to combat international terrorism in collaboration with Member States and international, regional and subregional organizations. In a January report [S/2004/70], the Counter-Terrorism Committee, established by Security Council resolution 1373 (2001) [YUN 2001, p. 61], described States' difficulties in implementing that resolution, which dealt with threats to international peace and security through terrorist acts. In particular, the report covered the financing of terrorism, the competence of courts to deal with those threats, ratification of related international conventions without enforcement measures, links between terrorism and organized crime, and links between terrorism and the illegal movement of nuclear, chemical, biological and other potentially deadly materials. In general, the Committee found that implementation of resolution 1373(2001) was facing serious difficulties. In April, the Council, in resolution 1540(2004) on the non-proliferation of WMDs (see p. 544), expressed grave concern about the risk that non-State actors might acquire, develop, traffic in or use WMDs. In October, by resolution 1566(2004) (see p. 74), the Council called for strengthened international cooperation in the fight against terrorism and established a working group to recommend practical measures against those involved with terrorist activities. The General Assembly, in resolution

59/80 (see p. 577), urged Member States to strengthen national measures to prevent terrorists from acquiring WMDs. Progress was maintained during the year in the work of the Ad Hoc Committee established by Assembly resolution 51/210 [YUN 1996, p. 1208] to elaborate international conventions for the suppression of terrorist bombings and nuclear terrorism (see p. 1310). The Advisory Board on Disarmament Matters (see p. 583) recommended that State action to combat terrorism by WMDs, including preventive action, be embedded in a multilateral legal framework within the ambit of the United Nations [A/59/361].

IAEA continued work on its action plan for nuclear security to enhance its capacity and that of Member States to respond to terrorist acts involving nuclear and other radiological materials. In September [GC(48)/RES/11], the IAEA General Conference, in a resolution on protection measures against such acts, appealed to States that had not done so to accede to the Convention on the Physical Protection of Nuclear Material [YUN 1980, p. 161], and to apply the related protection objectives endorsed by the IAEA Board of Governors. The Conference had before it a report of the Director General on nuclear security: measures to protect against nuclear terrorism [GOV/2004/50-GC(48)/6], which described IAEA action on protection against nuclear and radiological terrorism.

Report of Secretary-General. Pursuant to General Assembly resolution 58/48 [YUN 2003, p. 580], the Secretary-General, in a July report with a later addendum [A/59/156 & Add.1], presented the views of eight Member States and 10 international organizations, including UN agencies, on measures they had taken to prevent terrorists from acquiring WMDs.

Report of High-level Panel. In a December report [A/59/565 & Corr.1], the High-level Panel on Threats, Challenges and Change, a group of eminent persons established to assess threats to international peace and security and to recommend ways of strengthening the UN collective security capacity, described the threats that terrorism posed (see p. 71). In the Panel's view, meeting the prevention challenge called for a comprehensive strategy that incorporated more than coercive measures, better counter-terrorism instruments, assistance to States in confronting the terrorist threat and a consensus definition of terrorism within the General Assembly so that it could complete a comprehensive convention on terrorism.

Communications. The Ministers of States members of the Non-Aligned Movement, at its Fourteenth Ministerial Conference (Durban, 17-19 August), emphasized that terrorism could not be attributed to religion, race, nationality or civilization, and condemned international terrorism in all its forms as a criminal act. At the same time, they rejected attempts to equate terrorism with the legitimate struggle of peoples under colonial or alien domination and foreign occupation for self-determination and national liberation.

Similar beliefs were expressed by the Foreign Ministers of States members of the Organization of the Islamic Conference (New York, 28 September) [A/59/425-S/2004/808].

GENERAL ASSEMBLY ACTION

On 3 December [meeting 66], the General Assembly, on the recommendation of the First Committee [A/59/459 & Corr.1], adopted **resolution 59/80** without vote [agenda item 65].

Measures to prevent terrorists from acquiring weapons of mass destruction

The General Assembly,

Recalling its resolution 58/48 of 8 December 2003,

Recognizing the determination of the international community to combat terrorism, as evident in relevant General Assembly and Security Council resolutions,

Deeply concerned by the growing risk of linkages between terrorism and weapons of mass destruction, and in particular by the fact that terrorists may seek to acquire weapons of mass destruction,

Taking note of Security Council resolution 1540 (2004) on the non-proliferation of weapons of mass destruction, adopted on 28 April 2004,

Noting the support expressed in the Final Document of the Thirteenth Conference of Heads of State or Government of Non-Aligned Countries, which was held in Kuala Lumpur from 20 to 25 February 2003, and in the Final Document of the Fourteenth Ministerial Conference of the Movement of Non-Aligned Countries, which was held in Durban, South Africa, from 17 to 19 August 2004, for measures to prevent terrorists from acquiring weapons of mass destruction,

Noting also that the Group of Eight, the European Union, the Regional Forum of the Association of Southeast Asian Nations and others have taken into account in their deliberations the dangers posed by the acquisition by terrorists of weapons of mass destruction, and the need for international cooperation in combating it,

Acknowledging the consideration of issues relating to terrorism and weapons of mass destruction by the Advisory Board on Disarmament Matters,

Taking note of resolution GC(48)/RES/11, adopted on 24 September 2004 by the General Conference of the International Atomic Energy Agency at its forty-eighth regular session, and the setting up of an Advisory Group on Security in the Agency to advise the Director General on the Agency's activities relating to nuclear security,

Taking note also of the report of the Policy Working Group on the United Nations and Terrorism,

Taking note further of the report of the Secretary-General, submitted pursuant to paragraphs 2 and 4 of resolution 58/48,

Mindful of the urgent need for addressing, within the United Nations framework and through international cooperation, this threat to humanity,

Emphasizing that progress is urgently needed in the area of disarmament and non-proliferation in order to help to maintain international peace and security and to contribute to global efforts against terrorism,

1. *Calls upon* all Member States to support international efforts to prevent terrorists from acquiring weapons of mass destruction and their means of delivery;

2. *Urges* all Member States to take and strengthen national measures, as appropriate, to prevent terrorists from acquiring weapons of mass destruction, their means of delivery and materials and technologies related to their manufacture, and invites them to inform the Secretary-General, on a voluntary basis, of the measures taken in this regard;

3. *Encourages* cooperation among and between Member States and relevant regional and international organizations for strengthening national capacities in this regard;

4. *Requests* the Secretary-General to compile a report on measures already taken by international organizations on issues relating to the linkage between the fight against terrorism and the proliferation of weapons of mass destruction, to seek the views of Member States on additional relevant measures for tackling the global threat posed by the acquisition by terrorists of weapons of mass destruction, and to report to the General Assembly at its sixtieth session;

5. *Decides* to include in the provisional agenda of its sixtieth session the item entitled "Measures to prevent terrorists from acquiring weapons of mass destruction".

New types of weapons of mass destruction

In 2004, the persisting lack of consensus over an overall programme of work again prevented the Conference on Disarmament [A/59/27] from establishing an ad hoc committee to address the agenda item "New types of weapons of mass destruction and new systems of such weapons; radiological weapons".

Prevention of an arms race in outer space

During the year, the Conference on Disarmament was unable to establish a subsidiary body to deal with the issue of the prevention of an arms race in outer space, owing to the continuing deadlock on a programme of work. Delegates, nonetheless, devoted a plenary meeting to discussion of the item. China and the Russian Federation, as they had done in 2002 [YUN 2002, p. 540] and 2003 [YUN 2003, p. 582], collaborated on working papers on the issue, and, in 2004, circulated two informal papers, one on the verification aspects of the prevention of an arms race in outer space, and the other on existing international legal instruments and prevention of the weaponization of outer space. While the majority of delegations supported the re-establishment of an ad hoc committee to address the item, others countered that there was first a need to avoid an arms race on the ground. Delegates remained deadlocked on how to deal with the issue.

GENERAL ASSEMBLY ACTION

On 3 December [meeting 66], the General Assembly, on the recommendation of the First Committee [A/59/458], adopted **resolution 59/65** by recorded vote (178-0-4) [agenda item 64].

Prevention of an arms race in outer space

The General Assembly,

Recognizing the common interest of all mankind in the exploration and use of outer space for peaceful purposes,

Reaffirming the will of all States that the exploration and use of outer space, including the Moon and other celestial bodies, shall be for peaceful purposes and shall be carried out for the benefit and in the interest of all countries, irrespective of their degree of economic or scientific development,

Reaffirming also the provisions of articles III and IV of the Treaty on Principles Governing the Activities of States in the Exploration and Use of Outer Space, including the Moon and Other Celestial Bodies,

Recalling the obligation of all States to observe the provisions of the Charter of the United Nations regarding the use or threat of use of force in their international relations, including in their space activities,

Reaffirming paragraph 80 of the Final Document of the Tenth Special Session of the General Assembly, in which it is stated that in order to prevent an arms race in outer space, further measures should be taken and appropriate international negotiations held in accordance with the spirit of the Treaty,

Recalling its previous resolutions on this issue, and taking note of the proposals submitted to the General Assembly at its tenth special session and at its regular sessions, and of the recommendations made to the competent organs of the United Nations and to the Conference on Disarmament,

Recognizing that prevention of an arms race in outer space would avert a grave danger for international peace and security,

Emphasizing the paramount importance of strict compliance with existing arms limitation and disarmament agreements relevant to outer space, including bilateral agreements, and with the existing legal regime concerning the use of outer space,

Considering that wide participation in the legal regime applicable to outer space could contribute to enhancing its effectiveness,

Noting that the Ad Hoc Committee on the Prevention of an Arms Race in Outer Space, taking into account its previous efforts since its establishment in 1985 and seeking to enhance its functioning in qualitative terms, continued the examination and identification of various issues, existing agreements and existing proposals, as well as future initiatives relevant to the prevention of an

arms race in outer space, and that this contributed to a better understanding of a number of problems and to a clearer perception of the various positions,

Noting also that there were no objections in principle in the Conference on Disarmament to the re-establishment of the Ad Hoc Committee, subject to re-examination of the mandate contained in the decision of the Conference on Disarmament of 13 February 1992,

Emphasizing the mutually complementary nature of bilateral and multilateral efforts in the field of preventing an arms race in outer space, and hoping that concrete results will emerge from those efforts as soon as possible,

Convinced that further measures should be examined in the search for effective and verifiable bilateral and multilateral agreements in order to prevent an arms race in outer space, including the weaponization of outer space,

Stressing that the growing use of outer space increases the need for greater transparency and better information on the part of the international community,

Recalling, in this context, its previous resolutions, in particular resolutions 45/55 B of 4 December 1990, 47/51 of 9 December 1992 and 48/74 A of 16 December 1993, in which, inter alia, it reaffirmed the importance of confidence-building measures as a means conducive to ensuring the attainment of the objective of the prevention of an arms race in outer space,

Conscious of the benefits of confidence- and security-building measures in the military field,

Recognizing that negotiations for the conclusion of an international agreement or agreements to prevent an arms race in outer space remain a priority task of the Ad Hoc Committee and that the concrete proposals on confidence-building measures could form an integral part of such agreements,

1. *Reaffirms* the importance and urgency of preventing an arms race in outer space and the readiness of all States to contribute to that common objective, in conformity with the provisions of the Treaty on Principles Governing the Activities of States in the Exploration and Use of Outer Space, including the Moon and Other Celestial Bodies;

2. *Reaffirms its recognition*, as stated in the report of the Ad Hoc Committee on the Prevention of an Arms Race in Outer Space, that the legal regime applicable to outer space does not in and of itself guarantee the prevention of an arms race in outer space, that the regime plays a significant role in the prevention of an arms race in that environment, that there is a need to consolidate and reinforce that regime and enhance its effectiveness and that it is important to comply strictly with existing agreements, both bilateral and multilateral;

3. *Emphasizes* the necessity of further measures with appropriate and effective provisions for verification to prevent an arms race in outer space;

4. *Calls upon* all States, in particular those with major space capabilities, to contribute actively to the objective of the peaceful use of outer space and of the prevention of an arms race in outer space and to refrain from actions contrary to that objective and to the relevant existing treaties in the interest of maintaining international peace and security and promoting international cooperation;

5. *Reiterates* that the Conference on Disarmament, as the single multilateral disarmament negotiating forum, has the primary role in the negotiation of a multilateral agreement or agreements, as appropriate, on the prevention of an arms race in outer space in all its aspects;

6. *Invites* the Conference on Disarmament to complete the examination and updating of the mandate contained in its decision of 13 February 1992 and to establish an ad hoc committee as early as possible during its 2005 session;

7. *Recognizes*, in this respect, the growing convergence of views on the elaboration of measures designed to strengthen transparency, confidence and security in the peaceful uses of outer space;

8. *Urges* States conducting activities in outer space, as well as States interested in conducting such activities, to keep the Conference on Disarmament informed of the progress of bilateral and multilateral negotiations on the matter, if any, so as to facilitate its work;

9. *Decides* to include in the provisional agenda of its sixtieth session the item entitled "Prevention of an arms race in outer space".

RECORDED VOTE ON RESOLUTION 59/65:

In favour: Afghanistan, Albania, Algeria, Andorra, Angola, Antigua and Barbuda, Argentina, Armenia, Australia, Austria, Azerbaijan, Bahamas, Bahrain, Bangladesh, Barbados, Belarus, Belgium, Belize, Benin, Bhutan, Bolivia, Bosnia and Herzegovina, Brazil, Brunei Darussalam, Bulgaria, Burkina Faso, Burundi, Cambodia, Cameroon, Canada, Cape Verde, Central African Republic, Chile, China, Colombia, Comoros, Congo, Costa Rica, Côte d'Ivoire, Croatia, Cuba, Cyprus, Czech Republic, Democratic People's Republic of Korea, Denmark, Djibouti, Dominica, Dominican Republic, Ecuador, Egypt, El Salvador, Equatorial Guinea, Eritrea, Estonia, Ethiopia, Fiji, Finland, France, Gabon, Gambia, Germany, Ghana, Greece, Grenada, Guatemala, Guinea-Bissau, Guyana, Honduras, Hungary, Iceland, India, Indonesia, Iran, Iraq, Ireland, Italy, Jamaica, Japan, Jordan, Kazakhstan, Kenya, Kuwait, Kyrgyzstan, Lao People's Democratic Republic, Latvia, Lebanon, Lesotho, Liberia, Libyan Arab Jamahiriya, Liechtenstein, Lithuania, Luxembourg, Madagascar, Malawi, Malaysia, Maldives, Mali, Malta, Marshall Islands, Mauritius, Mexico, Micronesia, Monaco, Mongolia, Morocco, Mozambique, Myanmar, Namibia, Nauru, Nepal, Netherlands, New Zealand, Nicaragua, Niger, Nigeria, Norway, Oman, Pakistan, Panama, Paraguay, Peru, Philippines, Poland, Portugal, Qatar, Republic of Korea, Republic of Moldova, Romania, Russian Federation, Rwanda, Saint Kitts and Nevis, Saint Lucia, Saint Vincent and the Grenadines, Samoa, San Marino, Sao Tome and Principe, Saudi Arabia, Senegal, Serbia and Montenegro, Seychelles, Sierra Leone, Singapore, Slovakia, Slovenia, Solomon Islands, Somalia, South Africa, Spain, Sri Lanka, Sudan, Suriname, Swaziland, Sweden, Switzerland, Syrian Arab Republic, Tajikistan, Thailand, The former Yugoslav Republic of Macedonia, Timor-Leste, Togo, Tonga, Trinidad and Tobago, Tunisia, Turkey, Turkmenistan, Tuvalu, Ukraine, United Arab Emirates, United Kingdom, United Republic of Tanzania, Uruguay, Uzbekistan, Vanuatu, Venezuela, Viet Nam, Yemen, Zambia, Zimbabwe.

Against: None.

Abstaining: Haiti, Israel, Palau, United States.

Seabed Treaty

Pursuant to General Assembly resolution 44/116 O [YUN 1989, p. 81], the Secretary-General, in a June report with a later addendum [A/59/117 & Add.1], presented the replies of four Governments in response to his request for information on technological developments relevant to the Treaty on the Prohibition of the Emplacement of Nuclear Weapons and Other Weapons of Mass Destruction on the Seabed and the Ocean Floor and in the Subsoil Thereof, adopted by the Assembly in resolution 2660(XXV) [YUN 1970, p. 18],

and to the verification of compliance with the Treaty.

Disarmament and development

In 2004, disagreement persisted over the question of the relationship between disarmament and development. While the majority of Member States, mostly non-aligned countries, continued to call for the implementation of the action programme adopted by the 1987 International Conference that examined the relationship in all its aspects [YUN 1987, p. 82], a number of other States, including the United States and EU members, maintained the argument that there was no automatic link between the two concepts.

Expert group. By a June note [A/59/119], the Secretary-General transmitted the report of the Group of Governmental Experts he had established as requested by the General Assembly in resolution 57/65 [YUN 2002, p. 542], charged to review the relationship between disarmament and development in the current international context. Taking into account major international changes since the 1987 Conference, the report addressed the pivotal role of security, the costs and consequences of military expenditure, the release of resources for development, the importance of multilateralism and the role of the United Nations and other international organizations. The experts determined that disarmament and development were two distinct, yet mutually reinforcing processes that were linked by security in all its aspects. They reaffirmed the finding of the 1987 Conference that progress in one area could create a conducive environment for the other. The Group recommended that the Secretary-General strengthen the high-level Steering Group on Disarmament and Development [YUN 1999, p. 506] in order that relevant departments and agencies could share best practices and increase cooperation. Other recommendations advocated meeting disarmament and development commitments; assessing Member States' security needs; mainstreaming the disarmament and development relationship and increasing awareness of it; facilitating research and dialogue on issues relating to the relationship between disarmament, development and security; promoting security through openness, transparency and confidence; converting and destroying surplus weapons; and preventing conflict and promoting peace.

GENERAL ASSEMBLY ACTION

On 3 December [meeting 66], the General Assembly, on the recommendation of the First Committee [A/59/459 & Corr.1], adopted **resolution 59/78** by recorded vote (180-2-2) [agenda item 65 (*e*)].

Relationship between disarmament and development

The General Assembly,

Recalling that the Charter of the United Nations envisages the establishment and maintenance of international peace and security with the least diversion for armaments of the world's human and economic resources,

Recalling also the provisions of the Final Document of the Tenth Special Session of the General Assembly concerning the relationship between disarmament and development, as well as the adoption on 11 September 1987 of the Final Document of the International Conference on the Relationship between Disarmament and Development,

Recalling further its resolutions 49/75 J of 15 December 1994, 50/70 G of 12 December 1995, 51/45 D of 10 December 1996, 52/38 D of 9 December 1997, 53/77 K of 4 December 1998, 54/54 T of 1 December 1999, 55/33 L of 20 November 2000, 56/24 E of 29 November 2001 and 57/65 of 22 November 2002, and its decision 58/520 of 8 December 2003,

Bearing in mind the Final Document of the Twelfth Conference of Heads of State or Government of Non-Aligned Countries, held in Durban, South Africa, from 29 August to 3 September 1998, and the Final Document of the Thirteenth Ministerial Conference of the Movement of Non-Aligned Countries, held in Cartagena, Colombia, on 8 and 9 April 2000,

Mindful of the changes in international relations that have taken place since the adoption on 11 September 1987 of the Final Document of the International Conference on the Relationship between Disarmament and Development, including the development agenda that has emerged over the past decade,

Bearing in mind the new challenges for the international community in the field of development, poverty eradication and the elimination of the diseases that afflict humanity,

Stressing the importance of the symbiotic relationship between disarmament and development and the important role of security in this connection, and concerned at increasing global military expenditure, which could otherwise be spent on development needs,

1. *Welcomes* the report of the Group of Governmental Experts on the relationship between disarmament and development and its reappraisal of this significant issue in the current international context;

2. *Stresses* the central role of the United Nations in the disarmament-development relationship, and requests the Secretary-General to strengthen further the role of the Organization in this field, in particular the high-level Steering Group on Disarmament and Development, in order to assure continued and effective coordination and close cooperation between the relevant United Nations departments, agencies and subagencies;

3. *Requests* the Secretary-General to continue to take action, through appropriate organs and within available resources, for the implementation of the action programme adopted at the 1987 International Conference on the Relationship between Disarmament and Development;

4. *Urges* the international community to devote part of the resources made available by the implementation of disarmament and arms limitation agreements to economic and social development, with a view to reducing the ever widening gap between developed and developing countries;

5. *Encourages* the international community to achieve the Millennium Development Goals and to make reference to the contribution that disarmament could provide in meeting them when it reviews its progress towards this purpose in 2005, as well as to make greater efforts to integrate disarmament, humanitarian and development activities;

6. *Encourages* the relevant regional and subregional organizations and institutions, non-governmental organizations and research institutes to incorporate issues related to the relationship between disarmament and development in their agendas and, in this regard, to take into account the report of the Group of Governmental Experts;

7. *Requests* the Secretary-General to report to the General Assembly at its sixtieth session on the implementation of the present resolution;

8. *Decides* to include in the provisional agenda of its sixtieth session the item entitled "Relationship between disarmament and development".

RECORDED VOTE ON RESOLUTION 59/78:

In favour: Afghanistan, Albania, Algeria, Andorra, Angola, Antigua and Barbuda, Argentina, Armenia, Australia, Austria, Azerbaijan, Bahamas, Bahrain, Bangladesh, Barbados, Belarus, Belgium, Belize, Benin, Bhutan, Bolivia, Bosnia and Herzegovina, Botswana, Brazil, Brunei Darussalam, Bulgaria, Burkina Faso, Burundi, Cambodia, Cameroon, Canada, Cape Verde, Central African Republic, Chile, China, Colombia, Comoros, Congo, Costa Rica, Côte d'Ivoire, Croatia, Cuba, Cyprus, Czech Republic, Democratic People's Republic of Korea, Denmark, Djibouti, Dominica, Dominican Republic, Ecuador, Egypt, El Salvador, Equatorial Guinea, Eritrea, Estonia, Ethiopia, Fiji, Finland, Gabon, Gambia, Georgia, Germany, Ghana, Greece, Grenada, Guatemala, Guinea-Bissau, Guyana, Haiti, Honduras, Hungary, Iceland, India, Indonesia, Iran, Iraq, Ireland, Italy, Jamaica, Japan, Jordan, Kazakhstan, Kenya, Kuwait, Kyrgyzstan, Lao People's Democratic Republic, Latvia, Lebanon, Lesotho, Liberia, Libyan Arab Jamahiriya, Liechtenstein, Lithuania, Luxembourg, Madagascar, Malawi, Malaysia, Maldives, Mali, Malta, Marshall Islands, Mauritius, Mexico, Micronesia, Monaco, Mongolia, Morocco, Mozambique, Myanmar, Namibia, Nauru, Nepal, Netherlands, New Zealand, Nicaragua, Niger, Nigeria, Norway, Oman, Pakistan, Panama, Papua New Guinea, Paraguay, Peru, Philippines, Poland, Portugal, Qatar, Republic of Korea, Republic of Moldova, Romania, Russian Federation, Rwanda, Saint Lucia, Saint Vincent and the Grenadines, Samoa, San Marino, Sao Tome and Principe, Saudi Arabia, Senegal, Serbia and Montenegro, Seychelles, Sierra Leone, Singapore, Slovakia, Slovenia, Solomon Islands, Somalia, South Africa, Spain, Sri Lanka, Sudan, Suriname, Swaziland, Sweden, Switzerland, Syrian Arab Republic, Tajikistan, Thailand, The former Yugoslav Republic of Macedonia, Timor-Leste, Togo, Tonga, Trinidad and Tobago, Tunisia, Turkey, Tuvalu, Uganda, Ukraine, United Arab Emirates, United Kingdom, United Republic of Tanzania, Uruguay, Uzbekistan, Vanuatu, Venezuela, Viet Nam, Yemen, Zambia, Zimbabwe.

Against: Palau, United States.

Abstaining: France, Israel.

Arms limitation and disarmament agreements

The Secretary-General, in response to General Assembly resolution 58/45 [YUN 2003, p. 584], submitted a July report with later addendum [A/59/129 & Add.1] containing information from five Member States on measures they had taken to ensure the application of scientific and technological progress in the context of international security, disarmament and related areas, without detriment to the environment or to its contribution to attaining sustainable development.

GENERAL ASSEMBLY ACTION

On 3 December [meeting 66], the General Assembly, on the recommendation of the First Committee [A/59/459 & Corr.1], adopted **resolution 59/68** by recorded vote (175-2-3) [agenda item 65 (*o*)].

Observance of environmental norms in the drafting and implementation of agreements on disarmament and arms control

The General Assembly,

Recalling its resolutions 50/70 M of 12 December 1995, 51/45 E of 10 December 1996, 52/38 E of 9 December 1997, 53/77 J of 4 December 1998, 54/54 S of 1 December 1999, 55/33 K of 20 November 2000, 56/24 F of 29 November 2001, 57/64 of 22 November 2002 and 58/45 of 8 December 2003,

Emphasizing the importance of the observance of environmental norms in the preparation and implementation of disarmament and arms limitation agreements,

Recognizing that it is necessary to take duly into account the agreements adopted at the United Nations Conference on Environment and Development, as well as prior relevant agreements, in the drafting and implementation of agreements on disarmament and arms limitation,

Taking note of the report of the Secretary-General,

Mindful of the detrimental environmental effects of the use of nuclear weapons,

1. *Reaffirms* that international disarmament forums should take fully into account the relevant environmental norms in negotiating treaties and agreements on disarmament and arms limitation and that all States, through their actions, should contribute fully to ensuring compliance with the aforementioned norms in the implementation of treaties and conventions to which they are parties;

2. *Calls upon* States to adopt unilateral, bilateral, regional and multilateral measures so as to contribute to ensuring the application of scientific and technological progress within the framework of international security, disarmament and other related spheres, without detriment to the environment or to its effective contribution to attaining sustainable development;

3. *Welcomes* the information provided by Member States on the implementation of the measures they have adopted to promote the objectives envisaged in the present resolution;

4. *Invites* all Member States to communicate to the Secretary-General information on the measures they have adopted to promote the objectives envisaged in the present resolution, and requests the Secretary-General to submit a report containing this information to the General Assembly at its sixtieth session;

5. *Decides* to include in the provisional agenda of its sixtieth session the item entitled "Observance of environmental norms in the drafting and implementation of agreements on disarmament and arms control".

RECORDED VOTE ON RESOLUTION 59/68:

In favour: Afghanistan, Albania, Algeria, Andorra, Angola, Antigua and Barbuda, Argentina, Armenia, Australia, Austria, Azerbaijan, Bahamas, Bahrain, Bangladesh, Barbados, Belarus, Belgium, Belize, Benin, Bhutan, Bolivia, Bosnia and Herzegovina, Botswana, Brazil, Brunei Darussalam, Bulgaria, Burkina Faso, Burundi, Cambodia, Cameroon, Cape Verde, Central African Republic, Chile, China, Colombia, Comoros, Congo, Costa Rica, Côte d'Ivoire, Croatia, Cuba, Cyprus, Democratic People's Republic of Korea, Denmark, Djibouti, Dominica, Dominican Republic, Ecuador, Egypt, El Salvador, Equatorial Guinea, Eritrea, Estonia, Ethiopia, Fiji, Finland, Gabon, Gambia, Georgia, Germany, Ghana, Greece, Grenada, Guatemala, Guinea-Bissau, Guyana, Haiti, Honduras, Hungary, Iceland, India, Indonesia, Iran, Ireland, Italy, Jamaica, Japan, Jordan, Kazakhstan, Kenya, Kuwait, Kyrgyzstan, Lao People's Democratic Republic, Lebanon, Lesotho, Liberia, Libyan Arab Jamahiriya, Liechtenstein, Lithuania, Luxembourg, Madagascar, Malawi, Malaysia, Maldives, Mali, Malta, Marshall Islands, Mexico, Micronesia, Monaco, Mongolia, Morocco, Mozambique, Myanmar, Namibia, Nauru, Nepal, Netherlands, New Zealand, Nicaragua, Niger, Nigeria, Norway, Oman, Pakistan, Panama, Papua New Guinea, Paraguay, Peru, Philippines, Poland, Portugal, Qatar, Republic of Korea, Republic of Moldova, Romania, Russian Federation, Rwanda, Saint Lucia, Saint Vincent and the Grenadines, Samoa, San Marino, Sao Tome and Principe, Saudi Arabia, Senegal, Serbia and Montenegro, Seychelles, Sierra Leone, Singapore, Slovakia, Slovenia, Solomon Islands, Somalia, South Africa, Spain, Sri Lanka, Sudan, Suriname, Swaziland, Sweden, Switzerland, Syrian Arab Republic, Tajikistan, Thailand, The former Yugoslav Republic of Macedonia, Timor-Leste, Togo, Tonga, Trinidad and Tobago, Tunisia, Turkey, Turkmenistan, Tuvalu, Uganda, Ukraine, United Arab Emirates, United Republic of Tanzania, Uruguay, Uzbekistan, Vanuatu, Venezuela, Viet Nam, Yemen, Zimbabwe.

Against: Palau, United States.

Abstaining: France, Israel, United Kingdom.

Studies, information and training

Disarmament studies programme

As requested by the General Assembly in resolution 57/60 [YUN 2002, p. 545], the Secretary-General, in a July report with later addenda [A/59/178 & Add.1,2], provided information on the implementation of the recommendations contained in the 2002 report [YUN 2002, p. 544] of the Group of Governmental Experts established by the Assembly in resolution 55/33 E [YUN 2000, p. 535] to undertake a study on disarmament and non-proliferation education. The 2004 report included information provided by seven Member States, six UN bodies and other international organizations and seven NGOs on their activities to promote disarmament and non-proliferation education related to the 34 recommendations contained in the Group's report. The Secretary-General concluded that in the two years since the study's publication, international developments, relating especially to war and WMDs, had opened up opportunities for discussions and lessons that could enrich the knowledge of those dealing with the issue, and the need for teacher-training and curriculum development in the field was great. The study helped to advance disarmament education and training in non-proliferation among Member States and encouraged partnerships between Governments and NGOs, especially academic institutions. It also enhanced information exchange and project collaboration within the UN system and spurred on partnerships between the Organization and non-proliferation educators. Unfortunately, the funding environment for education in that area had not been positive.

GENERAL ASSEMBLY ACTION

On 3 December [meeting 66], the General Assembly, on the recommendation of the First Committee [A/59/459 & Corr.1], adopted **resolution 59/93** without vote [agenda item 65 (c)].

United Nations study on disarmament and non-proliferation education

The General Assembly,

Recalling its resolution 55/33 E of 20 November 2000 and 57/60 of 22 November 2002,

Welcoming the report of the Secretary-General on disarmament and non-proliferation education, in which the Secretary-General reported on the implementation of the recommendations contained in the United Nations study on disarmament and non-proliferation education,

Desirous of stressing the urgency of promoting concerted international efforts at disarmament and non-proliferation, in particular in the field of nuclear disarmament and non-proliferation, with a view to strengthening international security and enhancing sustainable economic and social development,

Conscious of the need to combat the negative effects of cultures of violence and complacency in the face of current dangers in this field through long-term programmes of education and training,

Remaining convinced that the need for disarmament and non-proliferation education has never been greater, especially on the subject of weapons of mass destruction, but also in the field of small arms and light weapons, terrorism and other challenges to international security and the process of disarmament, as well as on the relevance of implementing the recommendations contained in the United Nations study,

Recognizing the importance of the role of civil society, including non-governmental organizations, in the promotion of disarmament and non-proliferation education,

1. *Expresses its appreciation* to the Member States, the United Nations and other international and regional organizations, civil society and non-governmental organizations, which, within their purview, implemented the recommendations made in the United Nations study, as discussed in the report of the Secretary-General reviewing the implementation of the recommendations;

2. *Conveys once again* those recommendations to Member States, the United Nations and other international and regional organizations, civil society and non-governmental organizations, and encourages them to report to the Secretary-General on steps taken to implement them;

3. *Requests* the Secretary-General to prepare a report reviewing the results of the implementation of the recommendations and possible new opportunities for promoting disarmament and non-proliferation education, and to submit it to the General Assembly at its sixty-first session;

4. *Also requests* the Secretary-General to utilize electronic means to the fullest extent possible in the dissemination, in as many official languages as feasible, of information related to that report and any other information that the Department for Disarmament Affairs gathers on an ongoing basis in regard to the implementation of the recommendations of the United Nations study;

5. *Decides* to include in the provisional agenda of its sixty-first session an item entitled "Disarmament and non-proliferation education".

Disarmament Information Programme

In response to General Assembly resolution 57/90 [YUN 2002, p. 545], the Secretary-General, in July [A/59/171], reported on the activities of the Disarmament Information Programme during the previous two years and those planned for the forthcoming two years. The report described efforts by the Department for Disarmament Affairs (DDA) and the Department of Public Information (DPI) to raise awareness and understanding of UN work regarding disarmament and related issues, focusing on WMDs and conventional weapons, particularly small arms and light weapons, and on international terrorism, the UN Register of Conventional Arms and other transparency and confidence-building measures. The programme was carried out through publications, website access (disarmament.un.org), exhibits, information activities, cooperation with civil society, and radio and television broadcasts. Surveys conducted by DPI and DDA indicated that the DDA flagship publication—*The United Nations Disarmament Yearbook*—should continue. DDA, in collaboration with DPI, would continue to facilitate the access of civil society organizations at important disarmament-related events.

Annexed to the report was a financial statement of the Voluntary Trust Fund for the United Nations Disarmament Information Programme, which supported DDA information and outreach activities. At the end of the 2002-2003 biennium, the Fund's available balance was $472,481.

GENERAL ASSEMBLY ACTION

On 3 December [meeting 66], the General Assembly, on the recommendation of the First Committee [A/59/460], adopted **resolution 59/103** without vote [agenda item 66 (a)].

United Nations Disarmament Information Programme

The General Assembly,

Recalling its decision taken in 1982 at its twelfth special session, the second special session devoted to disarmament, by which the World Disarmament Campaign was launched,

Bearing in mind its resolution 47/53 D of 9 December 1992, in which it decided, inter alia, that the World Disarmament Campaign should be known thereafter as the "United Nations Disarmament Information Programme" and the World Disarmament Campaign Voluntary Trust Fund as the "Voluntary Trust Fund for the United Nations Disarmament Information Programme",

Recalling its resolutions 51/46 A of 10 December 1996, 53/78 E of 4 December 1998, 55/34 A of 20 November 2000 and 57/90 of 22 November 2002,

Welcoming the report of the Secretary-General on the United Nations Disarmament Information Programme,

1. *Takes note with appreciation* of the report of the Secretary-General on the United Nations Disarmament Information Programme;

2. *Commends* the Secretary-General for his efforts to make effective use of the limited resources available to him in disseminating as widely as possible, including by electronic means, information on arms limitation and disarmament to Governments, the media, non-governmental organizations, educational communities and research institutes, and in carrying out a seminar and conference programme;

3. *Stresses* the importance of the Programme as a significant instrument in enabling all Member States to participate fully in the deliberations and negotiations on disarmament in the various United Nations bodies, in assisting them in complying with treaties, as required, and in contributing to agreed mechanisms for transparency;

4. *Notes* the results of the survey of users of *The United Nations Disarmament Yearbook*;

5. *Notes with appreciation* the cooperation of the Department of Public Information of the Secretariat and its information centres in pursuit of the objectives of the Programme;

6. *Recommends* that the Programme continue to inform, educate and generate public understanding of the importance of multilateral action and support for it, including action by the United Nations and the Conference on Disarmament, in the field of arms limitation and disarmament, in a factual, balanced and objective manner, and that it focus its efforts:

(a) To continue to publish in all official languages *The United Nations Disarmament Yearbook* and to increase its dissemination by posting the 2002 and 2003 English editions on the Internet;

(b) To continue to maintain the Disarmament web site as a part of the United Nations web site and to produce versions of the site in as many official languages as feasible;

(c) To continue to intensify United Nations interaction with the public, principally non-governmental organizations and research institutes, to help further an informed debate on topical issues of arms limitation, disarmament and security;

(d) To continue to organize discussions on topics of interest in the field of arms limitation and disarmament with a view to broadening understanding and facilitating an exchange of views and information among Member States and civil society;

7. *Invites* all Member States to make contributions to the Voluntary Trust Fund for the United Nations Disarmament Information Programme with a view to sustaining a strong outreach programme;

8. *Takes note* of the recommendations contained in the report of the Secretary-General, which reviews the implementation of the recommendations made in the 2002 study on disarmament and non-proliferation education;

9. *Requests* the Secretary-General to submit to the General Assembly at its sixty-first session a report covering both the implementation of the activities of the Programme by the United Nations system during the previous two years and the activities of the Programme contemplated by the system for the following two years;

10. *Decides* to include in the provisional agenda of its sixty-first session the item entitled "United Nations Disarmament Information Programme".

Advisory Board on Disarmament Matters

The Advisory Board on Disarmament Matters, which advised the Secretary-General on the disarmament studies programme and implementation of the Disarmament Information Programme and served as the Board of Trustees of the United Nations Institute for Disarmament Research (UNIDIR) (see below), held its forty-second and forty-third sessions (New York, 4-6 February; Geneva, 30 June–2 July) [A/59/361]. The Board deliberated on terrorism and WMDs and their delivery systems; disarmament and reconciliation in conflict prevention; export controls; and its contribution to the work of the High-level Panel on Threats, Challenges and Change (see p. 54). It recommended that the proliferation of WMDs be made punishable under international law and that perpetrators, whether in State service or private, be held personally accountable. State action to combat terrorism by WMDs, including preventive action, should be embedded in a multilateral legal framework and within the ambit of the United Nations. The Security Council should consider widening the mandate of future peacekeeping operations to include disarmament and reconciliation aspects of conflict resolution. Regarding export control, the Board recommended strengthening the UN role in fostering cooperation and coordination among Member States and establishing working groups on States' export control obligations under disarmament and non-proliferation treaties. The Nuclear Suppliers Group and other export control regimes should provide input on possible items to be listed, experiences and models for export control structures, and licensing criteria. Concerning its contribution to the High-level Panel, the Board made recommendations to it on WMDs, missiles, small arms and light weapons, landmines and export controls, and the role of the United Nations in strengthening multilateral disarmament, arms control and non-proliferation regimes (see p. 522).

In its capacity as the Board of Trustees of UNIDIR (see below), the Board made recommendations concerning the Institute's 2005 work programme and budget.

UN Institute for Disarmament Research

The Secretary-General transmitted to the General Assembly the report of the UNIDIR Director covering the period from August 2003 to July 2004, as well as the report of the UNIDIR Board of Trustees on the proposed 2004-2005 programme of work and budget [A/59/168]. The Institute's research activities continued to focus on global security, regional security and human security, addressing the full range of substantive disarmament issues, from small arms to weapons in space. The report drew attention to the scope of UNIDIR's research activities worldwide, which included conferences, seminars and discussion meetings, and to its networking initiatives with specialized agencies and UN organizations and institutions. Contained in the report was a list of UNIDIR publications issued during the reporting period.

The Board of Trustees recommended a subvention of $227,600 from the UN regular budget for 2005, which the Assembly approved on 23 December (**resolution 59/276**, section V) (see p. 1383).

Disarmament fellowship, training and advisory services

In 2004, 30 fellows participated in the UN disarmament fellowship, training and advisory services programme, which began in Geneva on 30 August and terminated in New York on 3 November, as the Secretary-General reported in July [A/59/177]. The programme comprised study sessions in Geneva and New York and study visits to intergovernmental organizations in The Hague and Vienna working in the field of disarmament, and to Germany and Japan.

GENERAL ASSEMBLY ACTION

On 3 December [meeting 66], the General Assembly, on the recommendation of the First Committee [A/59/460], adopted **resolution 59/97** without vote [agenda item 66 *(b)*].

United Nations disarmament fellowship, training and advisory services

The General Assembly,

Having considered the report of the Secretary-General,

Recalling its decision, contained in paragraph 108 of the Final Document of the Tenth Special Session of the General Assembly, the first special session devoted to disarmament, to establish a programme of fellowships on disarmament, as well as its decisions contained in annex IV to the Concluding Document of the Twelfth Special Session of the General Assembly, the second special session devoted to disarmament, in which it decided, inter alia, to continue the programme,

Noting that the programme continues to contribute significantly to developing greater awareness of the importance and benefits of disarmament and better understanding of the concerns of the international community in the field of disarmament and security, as well as to enhancing the knowledge and skills of fellows, allowing them to participate more effectively in efforts in the field of disarmament at all levels,

Noting with satisfaction that the programme has trained a large number of officials from Member States throughout its twenty-six years of existence, many of whom hold positions of responsibility in the field of disarmament within their own Governments,

Recognizing the need for Member States to take into account gender equality when nominating candidates to the programme,

Recalling all the annual resolutions on the matter since the thirty-seventh session of the General Assembly, in 1982, including resolution 50/71 A of 12 December 1995,

Believing that the forms of assistance available to Member States, in particular to developing countries, under the programme will enhance the capabilities of their officials to follow ongoing deliberations and negotiations on disarmament, both bilateral and multilateral,

1. *Reaffirms* its decisions contained in annex IV to the Concluding Document of the Twelfth Special Session of the General Assembly and the report of the Secretary-General approved by the Assembly in its resolution 33/71 E of 14 December 1978;

2. *Expresses its appreciation* to all Member States and organizations that have consistently supported the programme throughout the years, thereby contributing to its success, in particular to the Governments of Germany and Japan for the continuation of extensive and highly educative study visits for the participants in the programme, and to the Government of the United States of America for organizing a presentation to the fellows in the area of disarmament;

3. *Expresses its appreciation* to the International Atomic Energy Agency, the Organization for the Prohibition of Chemical Weapons, the Preparatory Commission for the Comprehensive Nuclear-Test-Ban Treaty Organization and the Monterey Institute of International Studies for having organized specific study programmes in the field of disarmament in their respective areas of competence, thereby contributing to the objectives of the programme;

4. *Commends* the Secretary-General for the diligence with which the programme has continued to be carried out;

5. *Requests* the Secretary-General to continue to implement annually the Geneva-based programme within existing resources and to report thereon to the General Assembly at its sixty-first session;

6. *Decides* to include in the provisional agenda of its sixty-first session the item entitled "United Nations disarmament fellowship, training and advisory services".

Regional centres for peace and disarmament

On 3 December [meeting 66], the General Assembly, on the recommendation of the First Committee [A/59/460], adopted **resolution 59/98** without vote [agenda item 66 *(f)*].

United Nations regional centres for peace and disarmament

The General Assembly,

Recalling its resolution 58/63 of 8 December 2003 regarding the maintenance and revitalization of the three United Nations regional centres for peace and disarmament,

Recalling also the reports of the Secretary-General on the United Nations Regional Centre for Peace and Disarmament in Africa, the United Nations Regional Centre for Peace and Disarmament in Asia and the Pacific and the United Nations Regional Centre for Peace, Disarmament and Development in Latin America and the Caribbean,

Reaffirming its decision, taken in 1982 at its twelfth special session, to establish the United Nations Disarmament Information Programme, the purpose of which is to inform, educate and generate public understanding and support for the objectives of the United Nations in the field of arms control and disarmament,

Bearing in mind its resolutions 40/151 G of 16 December 1985, 41/60 J of 3 December 1986, 42/39 D of 30 November 1987 and 44/117 F of 15 December 1989 on the regional centres for peace and disarmament in Nepal, Peru and Togo,

Recognizing that the changes that have taken place in the world have created new opportunities as well as posed new challenges for the pursuit of disarmament, and, in this regard, bearing in mind that the regional centres for peace and disarmament can contribute substantially to understanding and cooperation among States in each particular region in the areas of peace, disarmament and development,

Noting that in paragraph 146 of the Final Document of the Twelfth Conference of Heads of State or Government of the Non-Aligned Countries, held at Durban, South Africa, from 29 August to 3 September 1998, the Heads of State or Government welcomed the decision adopted by the General Assembly on maintaining and revitalizing the three regional centres for peace and disarmament in Nepal, Peru and Togo,

1. *Reiterates* the importance of the United Nations activities at the regional level to increase the stability and security of its Member States, which could be promoted in a substantive manner by the maintenance and revitalization of the three regional centres for peace and disarmament;

2. *Reaffirms* that, in order to achieve positive results, it is useful for the three regional centres to carry out dissemination and educational programmes that promote regional peace and security and that are aimed at changing basic attitudes with respect to peace and security and disarmament so as to support the achievement of the purposes and principles of the United Nations;

3. *Appeals* to Member States in each region and those that are able to do so, as well as to international governmental and non-governmental organizations and foundations, to make voluntary contributions to the regional centres in their respective regions to strengthen their activities and initiatives;

4. *Emphasizes* the importance of the activities of the regional branch of the Department for Disarmament Affairs of the Secretariat;

5. *Requests* the Secretary-General to provide all necessary support, within existing resources, to the regional centres in carrying out their programmes of activities;

6. *Decides* to include in the provisional agenda of its sixtieth session the item entitled "United Nations regional centres for peace and disarmament".

Africa

Pursuant to General Assembly resolution 58/61 [YUN 2003, p. 587], the Secretary-General described the activities of the United Nations Regional Centre for Peace and Disarmament in Africa, covering July 2003 to June 2004 [A/59/209]. The Centre was established in Lomé, Togo, in 1986 [YUN 1986, p. 85].

During the reporting period, the Centre focused its activities on support for peace processes and related initiatives in Africa; practical disarmament and arms control; information, research and publications; and advocacy and resource mobilization. Maintaining consultations with ECOWAS on the situation in Côte d'Ivoire, the Centre hosted related briefings in Lomé with high-level officials. Working with the UN peacebuilding support offices in Africa, it facilitated the collection and destruction of surplus weapons and helped harmonize civil-military relations in the Central African Republic, Guinea-Bissau and Liberia. To facilitate programmes of disarmament, demobilization and reintegration of ex-combatants, the Centre launched a pilot consultative process on training for peace operations with ECOWAS and initiated a partnership in that field with the Norwegian Institute of International Affairs. In January and February, the Centre provided technical support to the AU in formulating an African common defence and security policy and an African standby force. The Centre supported Member States' efforts to establish and strengthen national mechanisms to combat the proliferation of small arms and light weapons, by organizing, with financial support from France, a capacity-building workshop (9-10 February) for 16 Togolese officials. To address that problem in other parts of the continent, the Centre cooperated with concerned regional and subregional organizations, including the Nairobi Secretariat overseeing the implementation of the Nairobi Declaration on the Problem of the Proliferation of Illicit Small Arms and Light Weapons in the Great Lakes Region and the Horn of Africa [YUN 2000, p. 518]; ECOWAS, within the context of its 1998 Moratorium on the Importation, Exportation and Manufacture of Small Arms and Light Weapons in West Africa [YUN 1998, p. 537]; the

Southern African Development Community (SADC), whose Protocol on the Control of Firearms, Ammunition and Other Related Materials entered into force during the year; and the Economic Community of Central African States (ECCAS), with which the Centre explored ways of supporting civil society efforts regarding the implementation of the Programme of Action adopted by the 2001 UN Conference on small arms [YUN 2001, p. 499].

Concerning other disarmament issues, the Centre made efforts to promote nuclear nonproliferation in Africa, and collaborated with IAEA to organize subregional seminars on a strengthened safeguards system for member States of ECOWAS (Ouagadougou, Burkina Faso, 26-27 February) and of SADC (Windhoek, Namibia, 29-31 March). Both seminars aimed at promoting implementation of the Treaty on the Non-Proliferation of Nuclear Weapons (see p. 542) and the entry into force of the African Nuclear-Weapon-Free-Zone Treaty (Treaty of Pelindaba) (see p. 550). The Centre collaborated with the AU, ECOWAS and a number of NGOs to convene a regional workshop (Lomé, 21-24 April) to help build the capacity of ECOWAS member States in modern techniques for control of military institutions, among other things. The Centre provided support to the United Nations Standing Advisory Committee on Security Questions in Central Africa (see p. 571), and undertook activities to build civil-military relations, including training workshops and sensitization campaigns on crisis prevention and resolution. It made efforts to promote compliance with, and the signing and ratification of, international disarmament and arms control instruments and norms, and maintained its information, research and publications activities on security issues in the region.

GENERAL ASSEMBLY ACTION

On 3 December [meeting 66], the General Assembly, on the recommendation of the First Committee [A/59/460], adopted **resolution 59/101** without vote [agenda item 66 (d)].

United Nations Regional Centre for Peace and Disarmament in Africa

The General Assembly,

Mindful of the provisions of Article 11, paragraph 1, of the Charter of the United Nations stipulating that a function of the General Assembly is to consider the general principles of cooperation in the maintenance of international peace and security, including the principles governing disarmament and arms limitation,

Recalling its resolutions 40/151 G of 16 December 1985, 41/60 D of 3 December 1986, 42/39 J of 30 November 1987 and 43/76 D of 7 December 1988 on the United Nations Regional Centre for Peace and Dis-

armament in Africa, and its resolutions 46/36 F of 6 December 1991 and 47/52 G of 9 December 1992 on regional disarmament, including confidence-building measures,

Recalling also its resolutions 48/76 E of 16 December 1993, 49/76 D of 15 December 1994, 50/71 C of 12 December 1995, 51/46 E of 10 December 1996, 52/220 of 22 December 1997, 53/78 C of 4 December 1998, 54/55 B of 1 December 1999, 55/34 D of 20 November 2000, 56/25 D of 29 November 2001, 57/91 of 22 November 2002 and 58/61 of 8 December 2003,

Aware of the widespread support for the activities of the Regional Centre and the important role that the Centre can play in the present context in promoting confidence-building and arms-limitation measures at the regional level, thereby promoting progress in the area of sustainable development,

Taking note of the report of the Secretary-General, in which it was stated that the Regional Centre received an increasing number of requests from Member States in the African region for substantive support for several peace initiatives and conflict resolution activities in the region,

Taking note also of the fact that, as noted in the report of the Secretary-General, very limited financial contributions were made to the Regional Centre despite continued fund-raising efforts,

Concerned that the continuing financial difficulties faced by the Regional Centre have impaired its ability to realize its full potential and to fulfil its mandate adequately,

Bearing in mind the efforts undertaken to mobilize the necessary resources for the operational costs of the Regional Centre,

Taking into account the need to establish close cooperation between the Regional Centre and the Mechanism for Conflict Prevention, Management and Resolution of the African Union, in conformity with the decision adopted by the Assembly of Heads of State and Government of the Organization of African Unity at its thirty-fifth ordinary session, held at Algiers from 12 to 14 July 1999,

1. *Commends* the activities that the United Nations Regional Centre for Peace and Disarmament in Africa is continuing to carry out, in particular in support of the efforts made by the African States in the areas of peace and security;

2. *Reaffirms its strong support* for the Regional Centre, and emphasizes the need to provide it with the necessary resources to enable it to strengthen its activities and carry out its programmes;

3. *Appeals once again* to all States, as well as to international governmental and non-governmental organizations and foundations, to make voluntary contributions in order to strengthen the programmes and activities of the Regional Centre and facilitate their implementation;

4. *Requests* the Secretary-General to continue to provide the necessary support to the Regional Centre for better achievements and results;

5. *Also requests* the Secretary-General to facilitate close cooperation between the Regional Centre and the African Union, in particular in the areas of peace, security and development, and to continue to assist the Director of the Regional Centre in his efforts to stabilize the financial situation of the Centre;

6. *Appeals in particular* to the Regional Centre, in cooperation with the African Union, regional and sub-regional organizations and the African States, to take steps to promote the consistent implementation of the Programme of Action to Prevent, Combat and Eradicate the Illicit Trade in Small Arms and Light Weapons in All Its Aspects;

7. *Requests* the Secretary-General to report to the General Assembly at its sixtieth session on the implementation of the present resolution;

8. *Decides* to include in the provisional agenda of its sixtieth session the item entitled "United Nations Regional Centre for Peace and Disarmament in Africa".

Asia and the Pacific

As requested by the General Assembly in resolution 58/62 [YUN 2003, p. 589], the Secretary-General reported on the activities of the United Nations Regional Centre for Peace and Disarmament in Asia and the Pacific from August 2003 to July 2004 [A/59/169]. The Centre was inaugurated in Kathmandu, Nepal, in 1989 [YUN 1989, p. 88].

During the period under review, the Centre continued to promote disarmament and security through the organization of meetings and conferences (Osaka, Japan, 19-22 August 2003; Jeju Island, Republic of Korea, 3-5 December, 2003; Almaty, Kazakhstan, 16-18 March 2004). In a final communiqué adopted by the Almaty meeting, the regional States, particularly the five Central Asian States, expressed their resolve for joint action in stemming the spread of small arms and light weapons in the subregion. The Centre assisted the five Central Asian States in finalizing a draft treaty on the establishment of a nuclear-weapon-free zone in Central Asia. It made efforts to strengthen Mongolia's nuclear-weapon-free status, and to that end held consultations with the Central Asian States, the five nuclear-weapon States and Mongolia. As a means of promoting cooperation with relevant regional organizations, the Centre provided support to the United Nations Association of Japan in organizing the tenth Kanazawa Symposium on North-East Asia (Kanazawa, Japan 7-9 June), which addressed, among other things, conflict prevention, crisis management, nuclear disarmament and other security questions. The Centre helped organize a UN conference on disarmament (Sapporo, Japan, 26-29 July), which considered mounting challenges and international response to nuclear non-proliferation and related issues. It facilitated discussion of small arms and light weapons issues at a regional seminar (Nadi, Fiji, 18-20 August).

Consultations were maintained during the year with the host country on the relocation of the Centre, and in that context, DDA and the Nepalese authorities continued to pursue agreement on outstanding issues, with a view to finalizing the host country agreement and memorandum of understanding.

On 3 December [meeting 66], the General Assembly, on the recommendation of the First Committee [A/59/460], adopted **resolution 59/100** without vote [agenda item 66 *(e)*].

United Nations Regional Centre for Peace and Disarmament in Asia and the Pacific

The General Assembly,

Recalling its resolutions 42/39 D of 30 November 1987 and 44/117 F of 15 December 1989, by which it established the United Nations Regional Centre for Peace and Disarmament in Asia and renamed it the United Nations Regional Centre for Peace and Disarmament in Asia and the Pacific, with headquarters in Kathmandu and with the mandate of providing, on request, substantive support for the initiatives and other activities mutually agreed upon by the Member States of the Asia-Pacific region for the implementation of measures for peace and disarmament, through appropriate utilization of available resources,

Welcoming the report of the Secretary-General, in which he expresses his belief that the mandate of the Regional Centre remains valid and that the Centre has been a useful instrument for fostering a climate of cooperation for peace and disarmament in the region,

Noting that trends in the post-cold-war era have emphasized the function of the Regional Centre in assisting Member States as they deal with new security concerns and disarmament issues emerging in the region,

Commending the useful activities carried out by the Regional Centre in encouraging regional and sub-regional dialogue for the enhancement of openness, transparency and confidence-building, as well as the promotion of disarmament and security through the organization of regional meetings, which has come to be widely known within the Asia-Pacific region as "the Kathmandu process",

Expressing its appreciation to the Regional Centre for its organization of meetings and conferences in the region, held in Osaka, Japan, from 19 to 22 August 2003, on Jeju Island, Republic of Korea, from 3 to 5 December 2003, in Almaty, Kazakhstan, from 16 to 18 March 2004, in Kanazawa, Japan, from 7 to 9 June 2004 and in Sapporo, Japan, from 26 to 29 July 2004,

Welcoming the idea of the possible creation of an educational and training programme for peace and disarmament in Asia and the Pacific for young people with different backgrounds, to be financed from voluntary contributions,

Noting the important role of the Regional Centre in assisting region-specific initiatives of Member States, including its continued assistance in finalizing a treaty related to the establishment of a nuclear-weapon-free zone in Central Asia, as well as to Mongolia's international security and nuclear-weapon-free status, including the organization of an informal consultation among relevant United Nations bodies in January and June 2004 to discuss the status of implementation of the non-nuclear aspects of Mongolia's status,

Appreciating highly the overall support that Nepal has extended as the host nation of the headquarters of the Regional Centre,

1. *Reaffirms its strong support* for the forthcoming operation and further strengthening of the United Nations Regional Centre for Peace and Disarmament in Asia and the Pacific;

2. *Underlines* the importance of the Kathmandu process as a powerful vehicle for the development of the practice of region-wide security and disarmament dialogue;

3. *Expresses its appreciation* for the continuing political support and voluntary financial contributions to the Regional Centre, which are essential for its continued operation;

4. *Appeals* to Member States, in particular those within the Asia-Pacific region, as well as to international governmental and non-governmental organizations and foundations, to make voluntary contributions, the only resources of the Regional Centre, to strengthen the programme of activities of the Centre and the implementation thereof;

5. *Requests* the Secretary-General, taking note of paragraph 6 of General Assembly resolution 49/76 D of 15 December 1994, to provide the Regional Centre with the necessary support, within existing resources, in carrying out its programme of activities;

6. *Urges* the Secretary-General to ensure the physical operation of the Regional Centre from Kathmandu within six months of the date of signature of the host country agreement and to enable the Centre to function effectively;

7. *Requests* the Secretary-General to report to the General Assembly at its sixtieth session on the implementation of the present resolution;

8. *Decides* to include in the provisional agenda of its sixtieth session the item entitled "United Nations Regional Centre for Peace and Disarmament in Asia and the Pacific".

Latin America and the Caribbean

As requested by the General Assembly in resolution 58/60 [YUN 2003, p. 590], the Secretary-General reported on the activities of the United Nations Regional Centre for Peace, Disarmament and Development in Latin America and the Caribbean from July 2003 to June 2004 [A/59/157]. The Centre was inaugurated in Lima, Peru, in 1987 [YUN 1987, p. 88].

During the period under review, the Centre focused on consolidating its programme of activities and organizational structure, and on strengthening its human resources capacity. It continued to organize and participate in a growing number of activities such as seminars, training courses, weapons and ammunition destruction events, technical advisory missions and dissemination of information. Those activities related to confidence- and security-building, such as support for conventional weapons methodology studies; practical disarmament, including the destruction of firearms, ammunition and

explosives and the improvement of stockpile management practices; and capacity-building, such as training courses for the law enforcement community and NGOs. The Centre also supported efforts to strengthen the Treaty for the Prohibition of Nuclear Weapons in Latin America and the Caribbean (Treaty of Tlatelolco) (see p. 552) and to promote the ratification and implementation of existing multilateral agreements relating to WMDs. Having completed the development of its Small Arms and Light Weapons Administration system, the Centre presented it to the States parties to the Inter-American Convention against the Illicit Manufacturing of and Trafficking in Firearms, Ammunition, Explosives, and Other Related Materials at their first Conference on the Convention (Bogotá, Colombia, 9 March). The system was intended to accelerate information flow among those countries regarding the Convention's implementation. Among training courses, the Centre held one (Brasilia, Brazil, 3-21 May) which educated 85 law enforcement officials from 15 regional countries in a wide range of security-related issues, including drugs, terrorism and money-laundering. In continuing cooperation with NGOs in strengthening the regional network on the control of firearms trafficking, the Centre held a similar training course for NGO representatives (San Salvador, El Salvador, 1-2 April), at which gender issues constituted an important aspect. In May, the Centre began coordinating with country offices of the United Nations Development Programme (UNDP) in planning firearms-related activities, particularly in Central America, and discussions were held on extending such cooperation to members of the Coordinating Action on Small Arms mechanism, established in 1998 [YUN 1998, p. 525]. The Centre undertook a variety of activities aimed at consolidating its Regional Clearinghouse Programme on Firearms, Ammunition and Explosives, which was developed to support States in implementing regional firearms instruments. On 25 May, DDA and UNDP's Small Arms and Demobilization Unit signed a memorandum of understanding to facilitate cooperation, through the Centre, in providing assistance to States in firearms collection, weapons destruction and stockpile management. The Centre and the Unit formalized cooperation in several areas, such as joint activities to assist States in reporting on implementation of the 2001 Programme of Action to counter small arms trafficking [YUN 2001, p. 499] and training courses on relevant issues, particularly disarmament and development. In other efforts to aid the implementation of the Programme of Action, the Centre created a software database containing information on the manufacture of firearms, ammunition and explosives and the legal trade of those weapons, which served as an information resource to manufacturers and brokers. The Centre collaborated with OAS and the Swedish Fellowship for Reconciliation, an NGO, to produce a book on legal norms and instruments on firearms, ammunition and explosives in Latin America and the Caribbean, for use by members of parliament and legal experts in harmonizing and improving firearms legislation and control mechanisms.

GENERAL ASSEMBLY ACTION

On 3 December [meeting 66], the General Assembly, on the recommendation of the First Committee [A/59/460], adopted **resolution 59/99** without vote [agenda item 66 (c)].

United Nations Regional Centre for Peace, Disarmament and Development in Latin America and the Caribbean

The General Assembly,

Recalling its resolutions 41/60 J of 3 December 1986, 42/39 K of 30 November 1987 and 43/76 H of 7 December 1988 on the United Nations Regional Centre for Peace, Disarmament and Development in Latin America and the Caribbean, with headquarters in Lima,

Recalling also its resolutions 46/37 F of 9 December 1991, 48/76 E of 16 December 1993, 49/76 D of 15 December 1994, 50/71 C of 12 December 1995, 52/220 of 22 December 1997, 53/78 F of 4 December 1998, 54/55 F of 1 December 1999, 55/34 E of 20 November 2000, 56/25 E of 29 November 2001, 57/89 of 22 November 2002 and 58/60 of 8 December 2003,

Underlining the revitalization of the Regional Centre, the efforts made by the Government of Peru and other countries to that end, as well as the important work done by the Director of the Centre,

Recognizing that the Regional Centre has continued to act as an instrument for the implementation of regional initiatives and has intensified its contribution to the coordination of United Nations efforts towards peace and security,

Welcoming the report of the Secretary-General, which concludes that the Regional Centre has continued to act as a facilitator for the implementation of regional initiatives by identifying regional security needs and new areas of cooperation with States and organizations in the region, and to provide more in-depth information on weapons-related matters, weapons destruction and stockpile management, including the initiation of a series of training courses for the law enforcement community, members of parliament, representatives of ministries of foreign affairs and nongovernmental organizations on such matters,

Welcoming also the fact that the report stresses that the Regional Centre has placed more emphasis on the inclusion of a gender perspective in its planned activities and the relationship between disarmament and development,

Welcoming further the report of the Group of Governmental Experts on the relationship between disarmament and development, established pursuant to General Assembly resolution 57/65 of 22 November 2002, which is of utmost interest with regard to the role that the Regional Centre plays in promoting the issue in the region in pursuit of its mandate to promote economic and social development related to peace and disarmament,

Noting that security and disarmament issues have always been recognized as significant topics in Latin America and the Caribbean, the first inhabited region in the world to be declared a nuclear-weapon-free zone,

Welcoming the support provided by the Regional Centre to strengthening the nuclear-weapon-free zone established by the Treaty for the Prohibition of Nuclear Weapons in Latin America and the Caribbean (Treaty of Tlatelolco), as well as to promoting and assisting the ratification and implementation of existing multilateral agreements related to weapons of mass destruction and to promoting peace and disarmament education projects during the period under review,

Bearing in mind the important role that the Regional Centre can play in promoting confidence-building measures, arms control and limitation, disarmament and development at the regional level,

Bearing in mind also the importance of information, research, education and training for peace, disarmament and development in order to achieve understanding and cooperation among States,

Recognizing the need to provide the three United Nations regional centres for peace and disarmament with sufficient financial resources and cooperation for the planning and implementation of their programmes of activities,

1. *Reiterates its strong support* for the role of the United Nations Regional Centre for Peace, Disarmament and Development in Latin America and the Caribbean in the promotion of United Nations activities at the regional level to strengthen peace, stability, security and development among its member States;

2. *Expresses its satisfaction and congratulates* the Regional Centre for the expansion of the vast range of activities carried out in the last year in the fields of peace, disarmament and development, and requests the Regional Centre to take into account the proposals to be submitted by the countries of the region in promoting confidence-building measures, arms control and limitation, transparency, disarmament and development at the regional level;

3. *Expresses its appreciation* for the political support and financial contributions to the Regional Centre, which are essential for its continued operation;

4. *Invites* all States of the region to continue to take part in the activities of the Regional Centre, proposing items for inclusion in its programme and making greater and better use of the potential of the Centre to meet the current challenges facing the international community with a view to fulfilling the aims of the Charter of the United Nations in the fields of peace, disarmament and development;

5. *Recognizes* that the Regional Centre has an important role in the promotion and development of regional initiatives agreed upon by the countries of Latin America and the Caribbean in the field of weapons of mass destruction, in particular nuclear weapons, conventional arms, including small arms and light weapons, as well as the relationship between disarmament and development;

6. *Encourages* the Regional Centre to further develop activities in the important area of disarmament and development;

7. *Highlights* the conclusion contained in the report of the Secretary-General that the vast regional co-operation undertaken by the Regional Centre during the reporting period was evidence of the important role of the Organization as a viable regional actor in assisting countries in the region to advance the cause of peace, disarmament and development in Latin America and the Caribbean;

8. *Appeals* to Member States, in particular those within the Latin American and Caribbean region, as well as to international governmental and non-governmental organizations and foundations, to make and to increase voluntary contributions to strengthen the Regional Centre, its programme of activities and the implementation thereof;

9. *Requests* the Secretary-General to provide the Regional Centre with all necessary support, within existing resources, so that it may carry out its programme of activities in accordance with its mandate;

10. *Also requests* the Secretary-General to report to the General Assembly at its sixtieth session on the implementation of the present resolution;

11. *Decides* to include in the provisional agenda of its sixtieth session the item entitled "United Nations Regional Centre for Peace, Disarmament and Development in Latin America and the Caribbean".

Chapter VIII

Other political and security questions

The United Nations continued in 2004 to consider political and security questions relating to its efforts to support democratization worldwide, the promotion of decolonization, public information activities and the peaceful uses of outer space.

The General Assembly, in February, welcomed Qatar's proposal to host the Sixth International Conference of New or Restored Democracies in November 2006. In December, it welcomed the Declaration of San Francisco de Quito by the five member States of the Andean Community, establishing the Andean Zone of Peace.

The Special Committee on the Situation with regard to the Implementation of the Declaration on the Granting of Independence to Colonial Countries and Peoples continued to review progress in implementing the 1960 Declaration, particularly the exercise of self-determination by the remaining Non-Self-Governing Territories. The Assembly requested the Special Committee to continue to seek suitable means for the immediate and full implementation of the Declaration and to carry out actions approved by the Assembly regarding the International Decade for the Eradication of Colonialism (1990-2000) and the Second International Decade (2001-2010).

The Committee on Information continued to review the management and operation of the Department of Public Information (DPI), based on reports submitted by the Secretary-General. As part of its continuing departmental reorientation process, DPI introduced the concept of the Secretariat departments as clients, which identified their own priorities, and DPI as service provider. It redoubled its efforts to bring UN system members within a common communications framework, and continued to promote and refine a culture of evaluation, with a first annual programme impact review completed in January. The first regional United Nations information centre, in Brussels, Belgium, became operational on 1 January, and the Secretary-General set out the proposed strategy and modalities for implementing the regionalization of information centres around hubs in other regions.

In a December resolution on developments in information and telecommunications, the Assembly called on Member States to promote the consideration of existing and potential threats in the field of information security. Regarding the role of science and technology in the context of international security, the Assembly, in another December resolution, encouraged UN bodies to contribute, within existing mandates, to promoting the application of science and technology for peaceful purposes.

Of the 12 action teams established to implement the recommendations of the Third (1999) United Nations Conference on the Exploration and Peaceful Uses of Outer Space (UNISPACE III), 9 had submitted final reports to the Committee on the Peaceful Uses of Outer Space and its Scientific and Technical Subcommittee; two other teams reported on progress in their work. The Committee submitted a plan of action to the Assembly proposing further specific actions for implementing the UNISPACE III recommendations, which the Assembly endorsed in October. In a December resolution on the application of the concept of a "launching State", the Assembly requested the Committee to continue to provide States, at their request, with relevant information and assistance in developing national space laws based on the relevant treaties.

The United Nations Scientific Committee on the Effects of Atomic Radiation held its fifty-second session in April.

General aspects of international security

Support for democracies

Sixth International Conference (2006)

In February, the General Assembly welcomed Qatar's offer, made during the Fifth International Conference of New or Restored Democracies [YUN 2003, p. 593], to host the Sixth Conference in Doha in 2006 (see below).

In addition to the 2003 Conference, four earlier conferences on the subject had been held, in 1988, 1994 [YUN 1994, p. 250], 1997 [YUN 1997, p. 530] and 2000 [YUN 2000, p. 544].

On 9 February [meeting 80], the General Assembly adopted **resolution 58/281** [draft: A/58/L.57 & Add.1] without vote [agenda item 20].

Sixth International Conference of New or Restored Democracies, to be held in Doha in 2006

The General Assembly,

Bearing in mind the indissoluble links between the principles enshrined in the Universal Declaration of Human Rights and the foundations of any democratic society,

Recognizing that the United Nations has an important role to play in providing timely, appropriate and coherent support to the efforts of Governments to achieve democratization within the context of their development efforts,

Recalling the offer by the Government of Qatar to host the Sixth International Conference of New or Restored Democracies in 2006,

Expressing once again its deep appreciation for the support provided by Member States, the United Nations system, including the specialized agencies, and other intergovernmental organizations to the Government of Mongolia for the holding of the Fifth International Conference of New or Restored Democracies in Ulaanbaatar,

1. *Welcomes* the proposal of the Government of Qatar to hold the Sixth International Conference of New or Restored Democracies from 13 to 15 November 2006 in Doha;

2. *Invites* the Secretary-General, Member States, the relevant specialized agencies and bodies of the United Nations system, as well as other intergovernmental and non-governmental organizations, to support and collaborate in the holding of the Sixth International Conference of New or Restored Democracies;

3. *Encourages* the intergovernmental follow-up mechanism of the Ulaanbaatar Conference to cooperate actively in the preparatory process for the Sixth International Conference of New or Restored Democracies.

Regional aspects of international peace and security

Andean region

By a 12 October letter [A/59/235], Bolivia, Colombia, Ecuador, Peru and Venezuela—the member countries of the Andean Community—transmitted to the Secretary-General the Declaration of San Francisco de Quito on the Establishment and Development of the Andean Zone of Peace, adopted on 12 July by the Presidents of those countries at the fifteenth meeting of the Andean Presidential Council held in Quito, Ecuador. The Andean Zone of Peace was intended to promote friendship and cooperation for all-around development, the culture of peace,

efforts to prevent and combat threats to security and a more fair and equitable international order for the Andean countries. Annexed to the letter was a draft resolution for consideration by the General Assembly (see below).

On 2 December [meeting 65], the General Assembly adopted **resolution 59/54** [draft: A/59/L.20/Rev.1, orally revised] without vote [agenda item 161].

Andean Zone of Peace

The General Assembly,

Aware of the determination of the States members of the Andean Community to preserve their independence, sovereignty and territorial integrity, promote peaceful coexistence in the Andean region and develop their relations in conditions of peace, self-determination and freedom,

Bearing in mind the commitment of the States members of the Andean Community to promote political, economic, social and cultural integration and cooperation in order to contribute to the sustainable long-term peace, security and balanced and harmonious development of the Andean region,

Noting its resolution 58/317 of 5 August 2004, by which it reaffirmed the central role of the United Nations in the maintenance of international peace and security and the promotion of international cooperation,

Recognizing the Declaration of San Francisco de Quito on the Establishment and Development of the Andean Zone of Peace, adopted in Quito on 12 July 2004 by the Heads of State of the member countries of the Andean Community within the framework of the fifteenth Andean Presidential Council, which sets forth the purpose of establishing a zone of peace within the geographical area comprising the territories, airspace and waters under the sovereignty and jurisdiction of Bolivia, Colombia, Ecuador, Peru and Venezuela (Bolivarian Republic of), as a nuclear, chemical and biological weapons–free zone, as well as the objective of definitively eradicating anti-personnel mines in the Andean Community, by which the necessary conditions will be developed to permit the peaceful and agreed resolution of conflicts of any nature whatsoever, as well as the causes thereof,

Noting with satisfaction that the Andean Zone of Peace is based on the responsible exercise by citizens of democratic values, principles and practices, the rule of law, human rights, social justice, human development, eradicating poverty, social exclusion and inequity, national sovereignty and non-interference in internal affairs, as well as on Andean identity, the promotion of relations of friendship and cooperation for all-round development, the culture of peace, joint efforts to prevent and counteract both conventional and new threats to security, and the joint quest for a fairer and more equitable international order,

Stressing that the Andean Zone of Peace represents a continuous and participatory effort of the States members of the Andean Community aimed at promoting growing commonality among Governments, public opinion, political parties and civil society with regard to widely shared objectives and values,

Also stressing the progress achieved by the States that comprise the Andean Community in matters of security, peace and confidence-building on the basis of a democratic and non-offensive conception of external security through the adoption, on 10 July 2004, of decision 587, containing the Andean Common External Security Policy Guidelines, as well as Andean norms to promote cooperation and coordination in regard to initiatives for fostering efforts to combat the global problem of drugs and associated crimes, and to prevent, combat and eradicate the illicit trade in small arms and light weapons in all its aspects,

Noting that decision 552, entitled "Andean plan to prevent, combat and eradicate the illicit trade in small arms and light weapons in all its aspects", adopted on 25 June 2003, is the first binding subregional instrument derived from the Programme of Action to Prevent, Combat and Eradicate the Illicit Trade in Small Arms and Light Weapons in All Its Aspects, adopted in 2001,

Considering that peace, security and mutual trust are essential requirements for achieving sustainable and long-term political, economic, social and cultural development,

Persuaded of the need to contribute to the maintenance of the Andean Community as a region free of weapons of mass destruction—nuclear, chemical, biological and toxin—as well as to the definitive eradication of anti-personnel mines in the Andean Community,

Recognizing the importance of promoting peace, security and cooperation in the Andean Community for the benefit of the entire human race and, in particular, the peoples of the Andean Community,

Convinced that the establishment of the Andean Zone of Peace will contribute considerably to the strengthening of international peace, security and trust and to the promotion of the purposes and principles on which the Charter of the United Nations and international law are based,

1. *Welcomes with satisfaction* the Declaration of San Francisco de Quito on the Establishment and Development of the Andean Zone of Peace, which establishes the geographical area comprising the territories, airspace and waters under the sovereignty and jurisdiction of the States members of the Andean Community as the Andean Zone of Peace, to be pursued in accordance with the Treaty for the Prohibition of Nuclear Weapons in Latin America and the Caribbean (Treaty of Tlatelolco) and other international conventions on the matter;

2. *Calls upon* all States to support the States that comprise the Andean Community in promoting the principles and purposes provided for by the Declaration of San Francisco de Quito;

3. *Encourages* the States members of the Andean Community to make every effort to ensure the early fulfilment of the commitments arising from the Declaration of San Francisco de Quito.

Decolonization

The General Assembly's Special Committee on the Situation with regard to the Implementa-

tion of the Declaration on the Granting of Independence to Colonial Countries and Peoples (Special Committee on decolonization) held its annual session in New York in two parts—11 February and 6 April (first part); and 7-8, 14, 16-18 and 21-22 June (second part). It considered various aspects of the implementation of the 1960 Declaration, adopted by the Assembly in resolution 1514(XV) [YUN 1960, p. 49], including general decolonization issues and the situation of individual Non-Self-Governing Territories (NSGTs). In accordance with Assembly resolution 57/140 [YUN 2002, p. 557], the Special Committee transmitted to the Assembly the report on its 2004 activities [A/59/23].

By **decision 59/520** of 10 December, the Assembly increased the Special Committee's membership from 25 to 27.

Decade for the Eradication of Colonialism

Pacific regional seminar

As part of its efforts to implement the plan of action for the Second International Decade for the Eradication of Colonialism (2001-2010) [YUN 2001, p. 530], declared by the General Assembly in resolution 55/146 [YUN 2000, p. 548], the Special Committee on decolonization [A/59/23] organized a Pacific regional seminar (Madang, Papua New Guinea, 18-20 May) on advancing the decolonization process in the Pacific region.

The seminar recommended that the Special Committee, the administering Powers and NSGTs discuss expediting the implementation of the goals of the Second Decade, and that the General Assembly conduct in 2005 a midterm review of the implementation of the Decade's plan of action. The Special Committee should continue to monitor actively the evolution of NSGTs towards self-determination, include them, on a case-by-case basis, in consultations on the discussions between the Special Committee and the administering Powers, and develop a mechanism to review annually the implementation of the recommendations on decolonization.

Affirming the need for the Special Committee to embark on a public awareness campaign aimed at fostering an understanding among the peoples of the Territories of their self-determination options, the seminar recommended that the Special Committee, with the UN Department of Public Information (DPI) and other UN bodies, develop a programme to disseminate information and raise public awareness in the Territories in order to heighten understanding of the legitimate political status options available. UN information centres should be directed to disseminate information on decolonization to the Territories and to the administering Powers, and the Electoral Unit of the UN Department of Political Affairs (DPA) should be asked to support and assist any consultation process regarding self-determination to be held in an NSGT.

Participants confirmed the need for periodic visiting missions to NSGTs to assess the situation in those Territories and ascertain the wishes and aspirations of the peoples thereof regarding their future status, and called on the administering Powers to cooperate in facilitating such missions.

Subject to Economic and Social Council approval, NSGTs should be given access to relevant UN economic and social programmes, including those emanating from the plans of action of UN world conferences, in furtherance of capacity-building and consistent with the preparation for the attainment of full internal self-government. The Special Committee should continue to explore ways to strengthen support for and formulate assistance programmes to the remaining NSGTs and seek proposals for the full implementation of the relevant resolutions by the specialized agencies. Participants recommended that the Special Committee establish closer ties with the Pacific Islands Forum, including through its observer status at the United Nations, and by encouraging Pacific region NSGTs to develop closer contacts with the Forum's secretariat.

Participants recommended that the Special Committee call on the United States, as the administering Power for Guam, to work with Guam's Commission on Decolonization for the Implementation and Exercise of Chamorro Self-Determination with a view to facilitating the decolonization of Guam, to keep the Secretary-General informed of progress towards that end, and to cooperate with Guam to develop and promote political education for the indigenous Chamorros on their right to self-determination. The Special Committee should engage the administering Power and the representatives of Guam in developing a specific work programme for that Territory. (For more information on Guam, see p. 613.)

Participants welcomed New Zealand's presence at Special Committee meetings, and that of France and the United Kingdom as observers at the seminar, and the United Kingdom's statement regarding its intention to continue to engage with the Special Committee with a view to enhancing cooperation. They reiterated their call on other administering Powers to engage the Special Committee in constructive dialogue in the future, and recommended that the Special Committee integrate the recommendations of the seminar into its relevant resolutions on decolonization.

GENERAL ASSEMBLY ACTION

On 10 December [meeting 71], the General Assembly, on the recommendation of the Fourth (Special Political and Decolonization) Committee [A/59/478], adopted **resolution 59/136** by recorded vote (167-2-4) [agenda item 20].

Implementation of the Declaration on the Granting of Independence to Colonial Countries and Peoples

The General Assembly,

Having examined the report of the Special Committee on the Situation with regard to the Implementation of the Declaration on the Granting of Independence to Colonial Countries and Peoples,

Recalling its resolution 1514(XV) of 14 December 1960, containing the Declaration on the Granting of Independence to Colonial Countries and Peoples, and all its subsequent resolutions concerning the implementation of the Declaration, the most recent of which was resolution 58/111 of 9 December 2003, as well as the relevant resolutions of the Security Council,

Bearing in mind its resolution 55/146 of 8 December 2000, by which it declared the period 2001-2010 the Second International Decade for the Eradication of Colonialism, and the need to examine ways to ascertain the wishes of the peoples of the Non-Self-Governing Territories on the basis of resolution 1514(XV) and other relevant resolutions on decolonization,

Recognizing that the eradication of colonialism has been one of the priorities of the United Nations and continues to be one of its priorities for the decade that began in 2001,

Reconfirming the need to take measures to eliminate colonialism before 2010, as called for in its resolution 55/146,

Reiterating its conviction of the need for the eradication of colonialism, as well as racial discrimination and violations of basic human rights,

Noting with satisfaction the achievements of the Special Committee in contributing to the effective and complete implementation of the Declaration and other relevant resolutions of the United Nations on decolonization,

Stressing the importance of the participation of the administering Powers in the work of the Special Committee,

Noting with satisfaction the cooperation and active participation of some administering Powers in the work of the Special Committee, and encouraging the others also to do so,

Taking note of the fact that the Special Committee held a Pacific regional seminar on advancing the decolonization process in the Pacific region at Madang, Papua New Guinea, from 18 to 20 May 2004,

1. *Reaffirms* its resolution 1514(XV) and all other resolutions and decisions on decolonization, including its resolution 55/146, by which it declared the period 2001-2010 the Second International Decade for the Eradication of Colonialism, and calls upon the administering Powers, in accordance with those resolutions, to take all necessary steps to enable the peoples of the

Non-Self-Governing Territories concerned to exercise fully as soon as possible their right to self-determination, including independence;

2. *Reaffirms once again* that the existence of colonialism in any form or manifestation, including economic exploitation, is incompatible with the Charter of the United Nations, the Declaration on the Granting of Independence to Colonial Countries and Peoples and the Universal Declaration of Human Rights;

3. *Reaffirms its determination* to continue to take all steps necessary to bring about the complete and speedy eradication of colonialism and the faithful observance by all States of the relevant provisions of the Charter, the Declaration on the Granting of Independence to Colonial Countries and Peoples and the Universal Declaration of Human Rights;

4. *Affirms once again its support* for the aspirations of the peoples under colonial rule to exercise their right to self-determination, including independence, in accordance with relevant resolutions of the United Nations on decolonization;

5. *Approves* the report of the Special Committee on the Situation with regard to the Implementation of the Declaration on the Granting of Independence to Colonial Countries and Peoples covering its work during 2004, including the programme of work envisaged for 2005;

6. *Calls upon* the administering Powers to cooperate fully with the Special Committee to finalize before the end of 2005 a constructive programme of work on a case-by-case basis for the Non-Self-Governing Territories to facilitate the implementation of the mandate of the Special Committee and the relevant resolutions on decolonization, including resolutions on specific Territories;

7. *Welcomes* the progress made in the ongoing consultations between the Special Committee and New Zealand, as administering Power for Tokelau, with the participation of representatives of the people of Tokelau, as evidenced by the decision of the General Fono of Tokelau in November 2003 to actively explore with New Zealand the option of self-government in free association;

8. *Requests* the Special Committee to continue to seek suitable means for the immediate and full implementation of the Declaration and to carry out the actions approved by the General Assembly regarding the International Decade for the Eradication of Colonialism and the Second International Decade for the Eradication of Colonialism in all Territories that have not yet exercised their right to self-determination, including independence, and in particular:

(a) To formulate specific proposals to bring about an end to colonialism and to report thereon to the General Assembly at its sixtieth session;

(b) To continue to examine the implementation by Member States of resolution 1514(XV) and other relevant resolutions on decolonization;

(c) To continue to examine the political, economic and social situation in the Non-Self-Governing Territories, and to recommend, as appropriate, to the General Assembly the most suitable steps to be taken to enable the populations of those Territories to exercise their right to self-determination, including independence, in accordance with relevant resolutions on de-

colonization, including resolutions on specific Territories;

(d) To finalize before the end of 2005 a constructive programme of work on a case-by-case basis for the Non-Self-Governing Territories to facilitate the implementation of the mandate of the Special Committee and the relevant resolutions on decolonization, including resolutions on specific Territories;

(e) To continue to dispatch visiting missions to the Non-Self-Governing Territories in accordance with relevant resolutions on decolonization, including resolutions on specific Territories;

(f) To conduct seminars, as appropriate, for the purpose of receiving and disseminating information on the work of the Special Committee, and to facilitate participation by the peoples of the Non-Self-Governing Territories in those seminars;

(g) To take all necessary steps to enlist worldwide support among Governments, as well as national and international organizations, for the achievement of the objectives of the Declaration and the implementation of the relevant resolutions of the United Nations;

(h) To observe annually the Week of Solidarity with the Peoples of Non-Self-Governing Territories;

9. *Calls upon* all States, in particular the administering Powers, as well as the specialized agencies and other organizations of the United Nations system, to give effect within their respective spheres of competence to the recommendations of the Special Committee for the implementation of the Declaration and other relevant resolutions of the United Nations;

10. *Calls upon* the administering Powers to ensure that the economic activities in the Non-Self-Governing Territories under their administration do not adversely affect the interests of the peoples but instead promote development, and to assist them in the exercise of their right to self-determination;

11. *Urges* the administering Powers concerned to take effective measures to safeguard and guarantee the inalienable rights of the peoples of the Non-Self-Governing Territories to their natural resources, including land, and to establish and maintain control over the future development of those resources, and requests the administering Powers to take all necessary steps to protect the property rights of the peoples of those Territories;

12. *Urges* all States, directly and through their action in the specialized agencies and other organizations of the United Nations system, to provide moral and material assistance to the peoples of the Non-Self-Governing Territories, and requests the administering Powers to take steps to enlist and make effective use of all possible assistance, on both a bilateral and a multilateral basis, in the strengthening of the economies of those Territories;

13. *Reaffirms* that the United Nations visiting missions to the Territories are an effective means of ascertaining the situation in the Territories, as well as the wishes and aspirations of their inhabitants, and calls upon the administering Powers to continue to cooperate with the Special Committee in the discharge of its mandate and to facilitate visiting missions to the Territories;

14. *Calls upon* the administering Powers that have not participated formally in the work of the Special Committee to do so at its session in 2005;

15. *Requests* the Secretary-General, the specialized agencies and other organizations of the United Nations system to provide economic, social and other assistance to the Non-Self-Governing Territories and to continue to do so, as appropriate, after they exercise their right to self-determination, including independence;

16. *Requests* the Secretary-General to provide the Special Committee with the facilities and services required for the implementation of the present resolution, as well as the other resolutions and decisions on decolonization adopted by the General Assembly and the Special Committee.

RECORDED VOTE ON RESOLUTION 59/136:

In favour: Afghanistan, Albania, Algeria, Andorra, Angola, Antigua and Barbuda, Argentina, Armenia, Australia, Austria, Azerbaijan, Bahamas, Bahrain, Bangladesh, Barbados, Belarus, Belize, Benin, Bolivia, Bosnia and Herzegovina, Botswana, Brazil, Brunei Darussalam, Bulgaria, Burkina Faso, Burundi, Cambodia, Cameroon, Canada, Cape Verde, Central African Republic, Chile, China, Colombia, Comoros, Congo, Costa Rica, Côte d'Ivoire, Croatia, Cuba, Cyprus, Czech Republic, Democratic People's Republic of Korea, Democratic Republic of the Congo, Denmark, Djibouti, Dominica, Dominican Republic, Ecuador, Egypt, El Salvador, Equatorial Guinea, Eritrea, Estonia, Ethiopia, Fiji, Finland, Gabon, Georgia, Ghana, Greece, Grenada, Guatemala, Guinea, Guinea-Bissau, Guyana, Honduras, Hungary, Iceland, India, Indonesia, Iran, Ireland, Italy, Jamaica, Japan, Jordan, Kazakhstan, Kenya, Kuwait, Kyrgyzstan, Lao People's Democratic Republic, Latvia, Lebanon, Lesotho, Liberia, Libyan Arab Jamahiriya, Liechtenstein, Lithuania, Luxembourg, Madagascar, Malaysia, Maldives, Malta, Marshall Islands, Mauritius, Mexico, Monaco, Mongolia, Morocco, Mozambique, Myanmar, Namibia, Nauru, Nepal, Netherlands, New Zealand, Nicaragua, Nigeria, Norway, Oman, Pakistan, Panama, Papua New Guinea, Paraguay, Peru, Philippines, Poland, Portugal, Qatar, Republic of Korea, Republic of Moldova, Romania, Russian Federation, Rwanda, Saint Lucia, Saint Vincent and the Grenadines, Samoa, San Marino, Sao Tome and Principe, Saudi Arabia, Senegal, Serbia and Montenegro, Seychelles, Sierra Leone, Singapore, Slovakia, Slovenia, Solomon Islands, Somalia, South Africa, Spain, Sri Lanka, Sudan, Suriname, Swaziland, Sweden, Switzerland, Syrian Arab Republic, Tajikistan, Thailand, The former Yugoslav Republic of Macedonia, Timor-Leste, Togo, Trinidad and Tobago, Tunisia, Turkey, Tuvalu, Uganda, Ukraine, United Arab Emirates, United Republic of Tanzania, Uruguay, Venezuela, Yemen, Zambia, Zimbabwe.

Against: United Kingdom, United States.

Abstaining: Belgium, France, Germany, Israel.

Speaking after the vote, the United Kingdom said that it continued to find some elements of the resolution unacceptable. However, it remained committed to modernizing its relationship with the overseas Territories, taking fully into account the views of the peoples of those Territories, and was continuing to further the process of informal dialogue with the Special Committee.

By **decision 59/552** of 23 December, the Assembly decided that the agenda item on the implementation of the Declaration would remain for consideration during its resumed fifty-ninth (2005) session.

Implementation by international organizations

In a March report [A/59/64], the Secretary-General stated that he had brought General Assembly resolution 58/104 [YUN 2003, p. 602] to the attention of the specialized agencies and other international organizations associated with the United Nations and invited them to submit information regarding the implementation of activi-

ties in support of NSGTs. Replies received from 10 agencies or organizations were summarized in an April report of the Economic and Social Council President on consultations held with the Chairman of the Special Committee on decolonization [E/2004/47]. According to the information provided, a number of specialized agencies and organizations continued to extend programmes of assistance to NSGTs from within their own budgetary resources, in addition to their respective contributions as executing agencies of projects funded by the United Nations Development Programme.

ECONOMIC AND SOCIAL COUNCIL ACTION

On 23 July [meeting 50], the Economic and Social Council adopted **resolution 2004/53** [draft: E/2004/L.23] by recorded vote (33-1-19) [agenda item 9].

Implementation of the Declaration on the Granting of Independence to Colonial Countries and Peoples by the specialized agencies and the international institutions associated with the United Nations

The Economic and Social Council,

Having examined the report of the Secretary-General and the report of the President of the Economic and Social Council containing the information submitted by the specialized agencies and the international institutions associated with the United Nations on their activities with regard to the implementation of the Declaration on the Granting of Independence to Colonial Countries and Peoples,

Having heard the statement by the representative of the Special Committee on the Situation with regard to the Implementation of the Declaration on the Granting of Independence to Colonial Countries and Peoples,

Recalling General Assembly resolutions 1514(XV) of 14 December 1960 and 1541(XV) of 15 December 1960, the resolutions of the Special Committee and other relevant resolutions and decisions, including, in particular, Economic and Social Council resolution 2003/51 of 24 July 2003,

Bearing in mind the relevant provisions of the final documents of the successive Conferences of Heads of State or Government of Non-Aligned Countries and of the resolutions adopted by the Assembly of Heads of State and Government of the African Union, the Pacific Islands Forum and the Caribbean Community,

Conscious of the need to facilitate the implementation of the Declaration,

Welcoming the participation, in the capacity of observer, of those Non-Self-Governing Territories that are associate members of the regional commissions in world conferences in the economic and social sphere, subject to the rules of procedure of the General Assembly and in accordance with relevant United Nations resolutions and decisions, including resolutions and decisions of the General Assembly and the Special Committee on specific Territories,

Noting that only some specialized agencies and organizations of the United Nations system have been involved in providing assistance to Non-Self-Governing Territories,

Welcoming the assistance extended to Non-Self-Governing Territories by certain specialized agencies and other organizations of the United Nations system, in particular the United Nations Development Programme,

Stressing that, because the development options of the small island Non-Self-Governing Territories are limited, there are special challenges to planning for and implementing sustainable development and that those Territories will be constrained in meeting the challenges without the continued cooperation and assistance of the specialized agencies and other organizations of the United Nations system,

Stressing also the importance of securing the resources necessary to fund expanded programmes of assistance for the peoples concerned and the need to enlist the support of all the major funding institutions within the United Nations system in that regard,

Reaffirming the mandate of the specialized agencies and other organizations of the United Nations system to take all appropriate measures, within their respective spheres of competence, to ensure the full implementation of resolution 1514(XV) and other relevant resolutions,

Expressing its appreciation to the African Union, the Pacific Islands Forum, the Caribbean Community and other regional organizations for the continued cooperation and assistance they have extended to the specialized agencies and other organizations of the United Nations system in this regard,

Expressing its conviction that closer contacts and consultations between and among the specialized agencies and other organizations of the United Nations system and regional organizations help to facilitate the effective formulation of programmes of assistance for the peoples concerned,

Mindful of the imperative need to keep under continuous review the activities of the specialized agencies and other organizations of the United Nations system in the implementation of the various United Nations decisions related to decolonization,

Bearing in mind the extremely fragile economies of the small island Non-Self-Governing Territories and their vulnerability to natural disasters, such as hurricanes, cyclones and sea-level rise, and recalling the relevant resolutions of the General Assembly,

Recalling General Assembly resolution 58/104 of 9 December 2003, entitled "Implementation of the Declaration on the Granting of Independence to Colonial Countries and Peoples by the specialized agencies and the international institutions associated with the United Nations",

1. *Takes note* of the report of the President of the Economic and Social Council, and endorses the observations and suggestions arising therefrom;

2. *Also takes note* of the report of the Secretary-General;

3. *Recommends* that all States intensify their efforts in the specialized agencies and other organizations of the United Nations system to ensure the full and effective implementation of the Declaration on the Granting of Independence to Colonial Countries and Peoples contained in resolution 1514(XV), and other relevant resolutions of the United Nations;

4. *Reaffirms* that the specialized agencies and other organizations and institutions of the United Nations system should continue to be guided by the relevant resolutions of the United Nations in their efforts to contribute to the implementation of the Declaration and all other relevant General Assembly resolutions;

5. *Also reaffirms* that the recognition by the General Assembly, the Security Council and other United Nations organs of the legitimacy of the aspirations of the peoples of the Non-Self-Governing Territories to exercise their right to self-determination entails, as a corollary, the extension of all appropriate assistance to those peoples;

6. *Expresses its appreciation* to those specialized agencies and other organizations of the United Nations system that have continued to cooperate with the United Nations and the regional and subregional organizations in the implementation of General Assembly resolution 1514(XV) and other relevant resolutions of the United Nations, and requests all the specialized agencies and other organizations of the United Nations system to implement the relevant provisions of those resolutions;

7. *Requests* the specialized agencies and other organizations of the United Nations system and international and regional organizations to examine and review conditions in each Territory so as to take appropriate measures to accelerate progress in the economic and social sectors of the Territories;

8. *Requests* the specialized agencies and other organizations and bodies of the United Nations system and regional organizations to strengthen existing measures of support and to formulate appropriate programmes of assistance to the remaining Non-Self-Governing Territories, within the framework of their respective mandates, in order to accelerate progress in the economic and social sectors of those Territories;

9. *Recommends* that the executive heads of the specialized agencies and other organizations of the United Nations system formulate, with the active cooperation of the regional organizations concerned, concrete proposals for the full implementation of the relevant resolutions of the United Nations and submit the proposals to their governing and legislative organs;

10. *Also recommends* that the specialized agencies and other organizations of the United Nations system continue to review, at the regular meetings of their governing bodies, the implementation of resolution 1514(XV) and other relevant resolutions of the United Nations;

11. *Welcomes* the continuing initiative exercised by the United Nations Development Programme in maintaining close liaison among the specialized agencies and other organizations of the United Nations system, including the Economic Commission for Latin America and the Caribbean and the Economic and Social Commission for Asia and the Pacific, and in providing assistance to the peoples of the Non-Self-Governing Territories;

12. *Encourages* Non-Self-Governing Territories to take steps to establish and/or strengthen disaster preparedness and management institutions and policies;

13. *Requests* the administering Powers concerned to facilitate, when appropriate, the participation of appointed and elected representatives of Non-Self-Governing Territories in the meetings and conferences of the specialized agencies and other organizations of the United Nations system, in accordance with relevant United Nations resolutions and decisions, in-

cluding resolutions and decisions of the General Assembly and the Special Committee on the Situation with regard to the Implementation of the Declaration on the Granting of Independence to Colonial Countries and Peoples related to specific Territories, so that the Territories may benefit from the related activities of those agencies and organizations;

14. *Recommends* that all Governments intensify their efforts in the specialized agencies and other organizations of the United Nations system of which they are members to accord priority to the question of providing assistance to the peoples of the Non-Self-Governing Territories;

15. *Draws the attention* of the Special Committee to the present resolution and to the discussion held on the subject at the substantive session of 2004 of the Economic and Social Council;

16. *Welcomes* the adoption by the Economic Commission for Latin America and the Caribbean of its resolution 574(XXVII) of 16 May 1998 calling for the mechanisms necessary for its associate members, including small island Non-Self-Governing Territories, to participate in the special sessions of the General Assembly, subject to the rules of procedure of the Assembly, to review and assess the implementation of the plans of action of those United Nations world conferences in which the Territories originally participated in the capacity of observer, and in the work of the Economic and Social Council and its subsidiary bodies;

17. *Requests* the President of the Council to continue to maintain close contact on these matters with the Chairman of the Special Committee and to report thereon to the Council;

18. *Requests* the Secretary-General to follow the implementation of the present resolution, paying particular attention to cooperation and integration arrangements for maximizing the efficiency of the assistance activities undertaken by various organizations of the United Nations system, and to report thereon to the Council at its substantive session of 2005;

19. *Decides* to keep these questions under continuous review.

RECORDED VOTE ON RESOLUTION 2004/53:

In favour: Azerbaijan, Bangladesh, Belize, Benin, Bhutan, Burundi, Chile, China, Colombia, Congo, Cuba, Ecuador, El Salvador, Ghana, Guatemala, India, Indonesia, Jamaica, Kenya, Libyan Arab Jamahiriya, Malaysia, Mauritius, Mozambique, Namibia, Nicaragua, Nigeria, Panama, Qatar, Saudi Arabia, Tunisia, United Arab Emirates, United Republic of Tanzania, Zimbabwe.

Against: Belgium.

Abstaining: Armenia, Australia, Canada, Finland, France, Germany, Greece, Hungary, Italy, Japan, Poland, Republic of Korea, Russian Federation, Senegal, Sweden, Turkey, Ukraine, United Kingdom, United States.

GENERAL ASSEMBLY ACTION

On 10 December [meeting 71], the General Assembly, on the recommendation of the Fourth Committee [A/59/476], adopted **resolution 59/129** by recorded vote (121-0-57) [agenda item 81].

Implementation of the Declaration on the Granting of Independence to Colonial Countries and Peoples by the specialized agencies and the international institutions associated with the United Nations

The General Assembly,

Having considered the item entitled "Implementation of the Declaration on the Granting of Independence to

Colonial Countries and Peoples by the specialized agencies and the international institutions associated with the United Nations",

Having also considered the report of the Secretary-General and the report of the Economic and Social Council on the item,

Having examined the chapter of the report of the Special Committee on the Situation with regard to the Implementation of the Declaration on the Granting of Independence to Colonial Countries and Peoples relating to the item,

Recalling General Assembly resolutions 1514(XV) of 14 December 1960 and 1541(XV) of 15 December 1960 and the resolutions of the Special Committee, as well as other relevant resolutions and decisions, including in particular Economic and Social Council resolution 2003/51 of 24 July 2003,

Bearing in mind the relevant provisions of the final documents of the successive Conferences of Heads of State or Government of Non-Aligned Countries and of the resolutions adopted by the Assembly of Heads of State and Government of the African Union, the Pacific Islands Forum and the Caribbean Community,

Conscious of the need to facilitate the implementation of the Declaration on the Granting of Independence to Colonial Countries and Peoples, contained in resolution 1514(XV),

Noting that the large majority of the remaining Non-Self-Governing Territories are small island Territories,

Welcoming the assistance extended to Non-Self-Governing Territories by certain specialized agencies and other organizations of the United Nations system, in particular the United Nations Development Programme,

Also welcoming the current participation in the capacity of observers of those Non-Self-Governing Territories that are associate members of regional commissions in the world conferences in the economic and social sphere, subject to the rules of procedure of the General Assembly and in accordance with relevant United Nations resolutions and decisions, including resolutions and decisions of the Assembly and the Special Committee on specific Territories,

Noting that only some specialized agencies and other organizations of the United Nations system have been involved in providing assistance to Non-Self-Governing Territories,

Stressing that, because the development options of the small island Non-Self-Governing Territories are limited, there are special challenges to planning for and implementing sustainable development and that those Territories will be constrained in meeting the challenges without the continuing cooperation and assistance of the specialized agencies and other organizations of the United Nations system,

Stressing also the importance of securing the necessary resources for funding expanded programmes of assistance for the peoples concerned and the need to enlist the support of all major funding institutions within the United Nations system in that regard,

Reaffirming the mandates of the specialized agencies and other organizations of the United Nations system to take all appropriate measures, within their respective spheres of competence, to ensure the full implementation of General Assembly resolution 1514(XV) and other relevant resolutions,

Expressing its appreciation to the African Union, the Pacific Islands Forum, the Caribbean Community and other regional organizations for the continued cooperation and assistance they have extended to the specialized agencies and other organizations of the United Nations system in this regard,

Expressing its conviction that closer contacts and consultations between and among the specialized agencies and other organizations of the United Nations system and regional organizations help to facilitate the effective formulation of programmes of assistance to the peoples concerned,

Mindful of the imperative need to keep under continuous review the activities of the specialized agencies and other organizations of the United Nations system in the implementation of the various United Nations decisions relating to decolonization,

Bearing in mind the extremely fragile economies of the small island Non-Self-Governing Territories and their vulnerability to natural disasters, such as hurricanes, cyclones and sea-level rise, and recalling the relevant resolutions of the General Assembly,

Recalling General Assembly resolution 58/104 of 9 December 2003 on the implementation of the Declaration by the specialized agencies and the international institutions associated with the United Nations,

1. *Takes note* of the report of the Secretary-General;

2. *Recommends* that all States intensify their efforts in the specialized agencies and other organizations of the United Nations system to ensure the full and effective implementation of the Declaration on the Granting of Independence to Colonial Countries and Peoples, contained in General Assembly resolution 1514(XV), and other relevant resolutions of the United Nations;

3. *Reaffirms* that the specialized agencies and other organizations and institutions of the United Nations system should continue to be guided by the relevant resolutions of the United Nations in their efforts to contribute to the implementation of the Declaration and all other relevant General Assembly resolutions;

4. *Reaffirms also* that the recognition by the General Assembly, the Security Council and other United Nations organs of the legitimacy of the aspirations of the peoples of the Non-Self-Governing Territories to exercise their right to self-determination entails, as a corollary, the extension of all appropriate assistance to those peoples;

5. *Expresses its appreciation* to those specialized agencies and other organizations of the United Nations system that have continued to cooperate with the United Nations and the regional and subregional organizations in the implementation of General Assembly resolution 1514(XV) and other relevant resolutions of the United Nations, and requests all the specialized agencies and other organizations of the United Nations system to implement the relevant provisions of those resolutions;

6. *Requests* the specialized agencies and other organizations of the United Nations system and international and regional organizations to examine and review conditions in each Territory so as to take appropriate measures to accelerate progress in the economic and social sectors of the Territories;

7. *Urges* those specialized agencies and organizations of the United Nations system that have not yet provided assistance to Non-Self-Governing Territories to do so as soon as possible;

8. *Requests* the specialized agencies and other organizations and institutions of the United Nations system and regional organizations to strengthen existing measures of support and formulate appropriate programmes of assistance to the remaining Non-Self-Governing Territories, within the framework of their respective mandates, in order to accelerate progress in the economic and social sectors of those Territories;

9. *Requests* the specialized agencies and other organizations of the United Nations system concerned to provide information on:

(*a*) Environmental problems facing the Non-Self-Governing Territories;

(*b*) The impact of natural disasters, such as hurricanes and volcanic eruptions, and other environmental problems, such as beach and coastal erosion and droughts, on those Territories;

(*c*) Ways and means to assist the Territories to fight drug trafficking, money-laundering and other illegal and criminal activities;

(*d*) The illegal exploitation of the marine resources of the Territories and the need to utilize those resources for the benefit of the peoples of the Territories;

10. *Recommends* that the executive heads of the specialized agencies and other organizations of the United Nations system formulate, with the active cooperation of the regional organizations concerned, concrete proposals for the full implementation of the relevant resolutions of the United Nations and submit the proposals to their governing and legislative organs;

11. *Also recommends* that the specialized agencies and other organizations of the United Nations system continue to review at the regular meetings of their governing bodies the implementation of General Assembly resolution 1514(XV) and other relevant resolutions of the United Nations;

12. *Welcomes* the continuing initiative exercised by the United Nations Development Programme in maintaining close liaison among the specialized agencies and other organizations of the United Nations system, including the Economic Commission for Latin America and the Caribbean and the Economic and Social Commission for Asia and the Pacific, and in providing assistance to the peoples of the Non-Self-Governing Territories;

13. *Encourages* Non-Self-Governing Territories to take steps to establish and/or strengthen disaster preparedness and management institutions and policies;

14. *Requests* the administering Powers concerned to facilitate, when appropriate, the participation of appointed and elected representatives of Non-Self-Governing Territories in the relevant meetings and conferences of the specialized agencies and other organizations of the United Nations system, in accordance with relevant United Nations resolutions and decisions, including resolutions and decisions of the General Assembly and the Special Committee on the Situation with regard to the Implementation of the Declaration on the Granting of Independence to Colonial Countries and Peoples on specific Territories, so

that the Territories may benefit from the related activities of those agencies and organizations;

15. *Recommends* that all Governments intensify their efforts in the specialized agencies and other organizations of the United Nations system of which they are members to accord priority to the question of providing assistance to the peoples of the Non-Self-Governing Territories;

16. *Requests* the Secretary-General to continue to assist the specialized agencies and other organizations of the United Nations system in working out appropriate measures for implementing the relevant resolutions of the United Nations and to prepare for submission to the relevant bodies, with the assistance of those agencies and organizations, a report on the action taken in implementation of the relevant resolutions, including the present resolution, since the circulation of his previous report;

17. *Commends* the Economic and Social Council for its debate and resolution on this question, and requests it to continue to consider, in consultation with the Special Committee, appropriate measures for the coordination of the policies and activities of the specialized agencies and other organizations of the United Nations system in implementing the relevant resolutions of the General Assembly;

18. *Requests* the specialized agencies to report periodically to the Secretary-General on the implementation of the present resolution;

19. *Requests* the Secretary-General to transmit the present resolution to the governing bodies of the appropriate specialized agencies and international institutions associated with the United Nations so that those bodies may take the necessary measures to implement the resolution, and also requests the Secretary-General to report to the General Assembly at its sixtieth session on the implementation of the present resolution;

20. *Requests* the Special Committee to continue to examine the question and to report thereon to the General Assembly at its sixtieth session.

RECORDED VOTE ON RESOLUTION 59/129:

In favour: Afghanistan, Algeria, Angola, Antigua and Barbuda, Argentina, Bahamas, Bahrain, Bangladesh, Barbados, Belarus, Belize, Benin, Bolivia, Botswana, Brazil, Brunei Darussalam, Burkina Faso, Burundi, Cambodia, Cameroon, Cape Verde, Central African Republic, Chile, China, Colombia, Comoros, Congo, Costa Rica, Côte d'Ivoire, Cuba, Democratic People's Republic of Korea, Democratic Republic of the Congo, Djibouti, Dominica, Ecuador, Egypt, El Salvador, Equatorial Guinea, Eritrea, Ethiopia, Fiji, Gabon, Ghana, Grenada, Guatemala, Guinea, Guinea-Bissau, Guyana, Honduras, India, Indonesia, Iran, Jamaica, Jordan, Kenya, Kuwait, Kyrgyzstan, Lao People's Democratic Republic, Lebanon, Lesotho, Liberia, Libyan Arab Jamahiriya, Madagascar, Malaysia, Maldives, Mali, Marshall Islands, Mauritania, Mauritius, Mexico, Mongolia, Morocco, Mozambique, Myanmar, Namibia, Nauru, Nepal, New Zealand, Nicaragua, Nigeria, Oman, Pakistan, Panama, Papua New Guinea, Paraguay, Peru, Philippines, Qatar, Saint Lucia, Saint Vincent and the Grenadines, Samoa, Sao Tome and Principe, Saudi Arabia, Senegal, Seychelles, Sierra Leone, Singapore, Solomon Islands, Somalia, South Africa, Sri Lanka, Sudan, Suriname, Syrian Arab Republic, Thailand, Timor-Leste, Togo, Tonga, Trinidad and Tobago, Tunisia, Tuvalu, Uganda, United Arab Emirates, United Republic of Tanzania, Uruguay, Vanuatu, Venezuela, Viet Nam, Yemen, Zambia, Zimbabwe.

Against: None.

Abstaining: Albania, Andorra, Armenia, Australia, Austria, Azerbaijan, Belgium, Bosnia and Herzegovina, Bulgaria, Canada, Croatia, Cyprus, Czech Republic, Denmark, Estonia, Finland, France, Georgia, Germany, Greece, Haiti, Hungary, Iceland, Ireland, Israel, Italy, Japan, Kazakhstan, Latvia, Liechtenstein, Lithuania, Luxembourg, Malta, Micronesia, Monaco, Netherlands, Norway, Palau, Poland, Portugal, Republic of Korea, Republic of Moldova, Romania, Russian Federation, San Marino, Serbia and Montenegro, Slovakia, Slovenia, Spain, Sweden, Switzerland, Tajikistan, The former Yugoslav Republic of Macedonia, Turkey, Ukraine, United Kingdom, United States.

Military activities and arrangements in colonial countries

In working papers on Bermuda [A/AC.109/2004/14], Guam [A/AC.109/2004/5] and the United States Virgin Islands [A/AC.109/2004/17], the Secretariat presented information on, among other subjects, military activities and arrangements by the administering colonial Powers in those Territories.

Economic and other activities affecting the interests of NSGTs

The Special Committee on decolonization continued consideration of economic and other activities affecting the interests of the peoples of NSGTs. It had before it Secretariat working papers containing information on, among other things, economic conditions, with particular reference to foreign economic activities, in Anguilla [A/AC.109/2004/10], Bermuda [A/AC.109/2004/14], the British Virgin Islands [A/AC.109/2004/3], the Cayman Islands [A/AC.109/2004/15], Montserrat [A/AC.109/2004/13], New Caledonia [A/AC.109/2004/11], the Turks and Caicos Islands [A/AC.109/2004/16] and the United States Virgin Islands [A/AC.109/2004/17].

GENERAL ASSEMBLY ACTION

On 10 December [meeting 71], the General Assembly, on the recommendation of the Fourth Committee [A/59/475], adopted **resolution 59/128** by recorded vote (173-3-3) [agenda item 80].

Economic and other activities which affect the interests of the peoples of the Non-Self-Governing Territories

The General Assembly,

Having considered the item entitled "Economic and other activities which affect the interests of the peoples of the Non-Self-Governing Territories",

Having examined the chapter of the report of the Special Committee on the Situation with regard to the Implementation of the Declaration on the Granting of Independence to Colonial Countries and Peoples relating to the item,

Recalling its resolution 1514(XV) of 14 December 1960, as well as all other relevant resolutions of the General Assembly, including, in particular, resolutions 46/181 of 19 December 1991 and 55/146 of 8 December 2000,

Reaffirming the solemn obligation of the administering Powers under the Charter of the United Nations to promote the political, economic, social and educational advancement of the inhabitants of the Territories under their administration and to protect the human and natural resources of those Territories against abuses,

Reaffirming also that any economic or other activity that has a negative impact on the interests of the peoples of the Non-Self-Governing Territories and on the exercise of their right to self-determination in conformity with the Charter of the United Nations and General Assembly resolution 1514(XV) is contrary to the purposes and principles of the Charter,

Reaffirming further that the natural resources are the heritage of the peoples of the Non-Self-Governing Territories, including the indigenous populations,

Aware of the special circumstances of the geographical location, size and economic conditions of each Territory, and bearing in mind the need to promote the economic stability, diversification and strengthening of the economy of each Territory,

Conscious of the particular vulnerability of the small Territories to natural disasters and environmental degradation,

Conscious also that foreign economic investment, when undertaken in collaboration with the peoples of the Non-Self-Governing Territories and in accordance with their wishes, could make a valid contribution to the socio-economic development of the Territories and also to the exercise of their right to self-determination,

Concerned about any activities aimed at exploiting the natural and human resources of the Non-Self-Governing Territories to the detriment of the interests of the inhabitants of those Territories,

Bearing in mind the relevant provisions of the final documents of the successive Conferences of Heads of State or Government of Non-Aligned Countries and of the resolutions adopted by the Assembly of Heads of State and Government of the African Union, the Pacific Islands Forum and the Caribbean Community,

1. *Reaffirms* the right of peoples of Non-Self-Governing Territories to self-determination in conformity with the Charter of the United Nations and with General Assembly resolution 1514(XV), containing the Declaration on the Granting of Independence to Colonial Countries and Peoples, as well as their right to the enjoyment of their natural resources and their right to dispose of those resources in their best interest;

2. *Affirms* the value of foreign economic investment undertaken in collaboration with the peoples of the Non-Self-Governing Territories and in accordance with their wishes in order to make a valid contribution to the socio-economic development of the Territories;

3. *Reaffirms* the responsibility of the administering Powers under the Charter of the United Nations to promote the political, economic, social and educational advancement of the Non-Self-Governing Territories, and reaffirms the legitimate rights of the peoples of those Territories over their natural resources;

4. *Reaffirms its concern* about any activities aimed at the exploitation of the natural resources that are the heritage of the peoples of the Non-Self-Governing Territories, including the indigenous populations, in the Caribbean, the Pacific and other regions, and of their human resources, to the detriment of their interests, and in such a way as to deprive them of their right to dispose of those resources;

5. *Affirms* the need to avoid any economic and other activities that adversely affect the interests of the peoples of the Non-Self-Governing Territories;

6. *Calls once again upon* all Governments that have not yet done so to take, in accordance with the relevant

provisions of General Assembly resolution 2621(XXV) of 12 October 1970, legislative, administrative or other measures in respect of their nationals and the bodies corporate under their jurisdiction that own and operate enterprises in the Non-Self-Governing Territories that are detrimental to the interests of the inhabitants of those Territories, in order to put an end to such enterprises;

7. *Reiterates* that the damaging exploitation and plundering of the marine and other natural resources of the Non-Self-Governing Territories, in violation of the relevant resolutions of the United Nations, are a threat to the integrity and prosperity of those Territories;

8. *Invites* all Governments and organizations of the United Nations system to take all possible measures to ensure that the permanent sovereignty of the peoples of the Non-Self-Governing Territories over their natural resources is fully respected and safeguarded in accordance with the relevant resolutions of the United Nations on decolonization;

9. *Urges* the administering Powers concerned to take effective measures to safeguard and guarantee the inalienable right of the peoples of the Non-Self-Governing Territories to their natural resources and to establish and maintain control over the future development of those resources, and requests the administering Powers to take all necessary steps to protect the property rights of the peoples of those Territories in accordance with the relevant resolutions of the United Nations on decolonization;

10. *Calls upon* the administering Powers concerned to ensure that no discriminatory working conditions prevail in the Territories under their administration and to promote in each Territory a fair system of wages applicable to all the inhabitants without any discrimination;

11. *Requests* the Secretary-General to continue, through all means at his disposal, to inform world public opinion of any activity that affects the exercise of the right of the peoples of the Non-Self-Governing Territories to self-determination in conformity with the Charter of the United Nations and General Assembly resolution 1514(XV);

12. *Appeals* to the mass media, trade unions and non-governmental organizations, as well as individuals, to continue their efforts to promote the economic well-being of the peoples of the Non-Self-Governing Territories;

13. *Decides* to follow the situation in the Non-Self-Governing Territories so as to ensure that all economic activities in those Territories are aimed at strengthening and diversifying their economies in the interest of their peoples, including the indigenous populations, and at promoting the economic and financial viability of those Territories;

14. *Requests* the Special Committee on the Situation with regard to the Implementation of Declaration on the Granting of Independence to Colonial Countries and Peoples to continue to examine this question and to report thereon to the General Assembly at its sixtieth session.

RECORDED VOTE ON RESOLUTION 59/128:

In favour: Afghanistan, Albania, Algeria, Andorra, Angola, Antigua and Barbuda, Argentina, Armenia, Australia, Austria, Azerbaijan, Bahamas, Bahrain, Bangladesh, Barbados, Belarus, Belgium, Belize, Benin, Bolivia,

Bosnia and Herzegovina, Botswana, Brazil, Brunei Darussalam, Bulgaria, Burkina Faso, Burundi, Cambodia, Cameroon, Canada, Cape Verde, Central African Republic, Chile, China, Colombia, Comoros, Congo, Costa Rica, Côte d'Ivoire, Croatia, Cuba, Cyprus, Czech Republic, Democratic People's Republic of Korea, Democratic Republic of the Congo, Denmark, Djibouti, Dominica, Dominican Republic, Ecuador, Egypt, El Salvador, Equatorial Guinea, Eritrea, Estonia, Ethiopia, Fiji, Finland, Gabon, Georgia, Germany, Ghana, Greece, Grenada, Guatemala, Guinea, Guinea-Bissau, Guyana, Honduras, Hungary, Iceland, India, Indonesia, Iran, Ireland, Italy, Jamaica, Japan, Jordan, Kazakhstan, Kenya, Kuwait, Kyrgyzstan, Lao People's Democratic Republic, Latvia, Lebanon, Lesotho, Liberia, Libyan Arab Jamahiriya, Liechtenstein, Lithuania, Luxembourg, Madagascar, Malaysia, Maldives, Mali, Malta, Marshall Islands, Mauritania, Mauritius, Mexico, Mongolia, Morocco, Mozambique, Myanmar, Namibia, Nauru, Nepal, Netherlands, New Zealand, Nicaragua, Nigeria, Norway, Oman, Pakistan, Panama, Papua New Guinea, Paraguay, Peru, Philippines, Poland, Portugal, Qatar, Republic of Korea, Republic of Moldova, Romania, Russian Federation, Rwanda, Saint Lucia, Saint Vincent and the Grenadines, Samoa, San Marino, Sao Tome and Principe, Saudi Arabia, Senegal, Serbia and Montenegro, Seychelles, Sierra Leone, Singapore, Slovakia, Slovenia, Solomon Islands, Somalia, South Africa, Spain, Sri Lanka, Sudan, Suriname, Sweden, Switzerland, Syrian Arab Republic, Tajikistan, Thailand, The former Yugoslav Republic of Macedonia, Timor-Leste, Togo, Tonga, Trinidad and Tobago, Tunisia, Turkey, Turkmenistan, Tuvalu, Uganda, Ukraine, United Arab Emirates, United Republic of Tanzania, Uruguay, Vanuatu, Venezuela, Viet Nam, Yemen, Zambia, Zimbabwe.

Against: Israel, Palau, United States.

Abstaining: France, Haiti, United Kingdom.

Dissemination of information

The Special Committee on decolonization held consultations in June with representatives of DPA and DPI of the Secretariat on the dissemination of information on decolonization. It also considered a report of the Secretary-General on DPI activities on the topic from June 2003 to May 2004 [A/AC.109/2004/18].

GENERAL ASSEMBLY ACTION

On 10 December [meeting 71], the General Assembly, on the recommendation of the Fourth Committee [A/59/478], adopted **resolution 59/135** by recorded vote (170-3-1) [agenda item 20].

Dissemination of information on decolonization

The General Assembly,

Having examined the chapter of the report of the Special Committee on the Situation with regard to the Implementation of the Declaration on the Granting of Independence to Colonial Countries and Peoples relating to the dissemination of information on decolonization and publicity for the work of the United Nations in the field of decolonization,

Recalling General Assembly resolution 1514(XV) of 14 December 1960, containing the Declaration on the Granting of Independence to Colonial Countries and Peoples, and other resolutions and decisions of the United Nations concerning the dissemination of information on decolonization, in particular Assembly resolution 58/110 of 9 December 2003,

Recognizing the need for flexible, practical and innovative approaches to reviewing the options of self-determination for the peoples of Non-Self-Governing Territories with a view to achieving the goals of the Second International Decade for the Eradication of Colonialism,

Reiterating the importance of dissemination of information as an instrument for furthering the aims of the Declaration, and mindful of the role of world public opinion in effectively assisting the peoples of Non-Self-Governing Territories to achieve self-determination,

Recognizing the role played by the administering Powers in transmitting information to the Secretary-General in accordance with the terms of Article 73 *e* of the Charter of the United Nations,

Aware of the role of non-governmental organizations in the dissemination of information on decolonization,

1. *Approves* the activities in the field of dissemination of information on decolonization undertaken by the Department of Public Information and the Department of Political Affairs of the Secretariat, in accordance with the relevant resolutions of the United Nations on decolonization;

2. *Considers it important* to continue its efforts to ensure the widest possible dissemination of information on decolonization, with particular emphasis on the options for self-determination available to the peoples of Non-Self-Governing Territories;

3. *Requests* the Department of Political Affairs and the Department of Public Information to take into account the suggestions of the Special Committee on the Situation with regard to the Implementation of the Declaration on the Granting of Independence to Colonial Countries and Peoples to continue their efforts to take measures through all the media available, including publications, radio and television, as well as the Internet, to give publicity to the work of the United Nations in the field of decolonization and, inter alia:

(*a*) To continue to collect, prepare and disseminate, particularly to the Territories, basic material on the issue of self-determination of the peoples of Non-Self-Governing Territories;

(*b*) To seek the full cooperation of the administering Powers in the discharge of the tasks referred to above;

(*c*) To maintain a working relationship with the appropriate regional and intergovernmental organizations, particularly in the Pacific and Caribbean regions, by holding periodic consultations and exchanging information;

(*d*) To encourage the involvement of non-governmental organizations in the dissemination of information on decolonization;

(*e*) To report to the Special Committee on measures taken in the implementation of the present resolution;

4. *Requests* all States, including the administering Powers, to continue to extend their cooperation in the dissemination of information referred to in paragraph 2 above;

5. *Requests* the Special Committee to follow the implementation of the present resolution and to report thereon to the General Assembly at its sixtieth session.

RECORDED VOTE ON RESOLUTION 59/135:

In favour: Afghanistan, Albania, Algeria, Andorra, Angola, Antigua and Barbuda, Argentina, Armenia, Australia, Austria, Azerbaijan, Bahamas, Bahrain, Bangladesh, Barbados, Belarus, Belgium, Belize, Benin, Bolivia, Bosnia and Herzegovina, Botswana, Brazil, Brunei Darussalam, Bulgaria, Burkina Faso, Burundi, Cambodia, Cameroon, Canada, Cape Verde, Central African Republic, China, Colombia, Comoros, Congo, Costa Rica, Côte d'Ivoire, Croatia, Cuba, Cyprus, Czech Republic, Democratic People's Republic of Korea, Democratic Republic of the Congo, Denmark, Djibouti, Dominica, Dominican Republic, Ecuador, Egypt, El Salvador, Equatorial Guinea, Eritrea, Estonia, Ethiopia, Fiji, Finland, Gabon, Georgia, Germany, Ghana, Greece, Grenada, Guatemala, Guinea, Guinea-Bissau, Guyana, Haiti, Honduras, Hungary, Iceland, India, Indonesia, Iran, Ireland, Italy, Jamaica, Japan, Jordan, Kazakhstan, Kenya, Kuwait, Kyrgyzstan, Lao People's Democratic Republic, Latvia, Lebanon, Lesotho, Liberia, Libyan Arab Jamahiriya, Liechtenstein, Lithuania, Luxembourg, Madagascar, Malaysia, Maldives, Malta, Marshall Islands, Mauritius, Mexico, Monaco, Mongolia, Morocco, Mozambique, Myanmar, Namibia, Nauru, Nepal, Netherlands, New Zealand, Nicaragua, Nigeria, Norway, Oman, Pakistan, Panama, Papua New Guinea, Paraguay, Peru, Philippines, Poland, Portugal, Qatar, Republic of Korea, Republic of Moldova, Romania, Russian Federation, Rwanda, Saint Lucia, Saint Vincent and the Grenadines, Samoa, San Marino, Sao Tome and Principe, Saudi Arabia, Senegal, Serbia and Montenegro, Sierra Leone, Singapore, Slovakia, Slovenia, Solomon Islands, Somalia, South Africa, Spain, Sri Lanka, Sudan, Suriname, Swaziland, Sweden, Switzerland, Syrian Arab Republic, Tajikistan, Thailand, The former Yugoslav Republic of Macedonia, Timor-Leste, Togo, Trinidad and Tobago, Tunisia, Turkey, Tuvalu, Uganda, Ukraine, United Arab Emirates, United Republic of Tanzania, Uruguay, Vanuatu, Venezuela, Viet Nam, Yemen, Zambia, Zimbabwe.

Against: Israel, United Kingdom, United States.

Abstaining: France.

Speaking after the vote, the United Kingdom said that it continued to view the obligation the text placed on the Secretariat to publicize decolonization issues as an unwarranted drain on scarce UN resources.

Information on Territories

In response to General Assembly resolution 58/102 [YUN 2003, p. 607], the Secretary-General submitted an April report [A/59/71] showing the dates of transmittal of information on economic, social and educational conditions in NSGTs for the years 1999-2004, under Article 73 *e* of the Charter of the United Nations.

GENERAL ASSEMBLY ACTION

On 10 December [meeting 71], the General Assembly, on the recommendation of the Fourth Committee [A/59/474], adopted **resolution 59/127** by recorded vote (172-0-6) [agenda item 79].

Information from Non-Self-Governing Territories transmitted under Article 73 *e* of the Charter of the United Nations

The General Assembly,

Recalling its resolution 1970(XVIII) of 16 December 1963, in which it requested the Special Committee on the Situation with regard to the Implementation of the Declaration on the Granting of Independence to Colonial Countries and Peoples to study the information transmitted to the Secretary-General in accordance with Article 73 *e* of the Charter of the United Nations and to take such information fully into account in examining the situation with regard to the implementation of the Declaration, contained in General Assembly resolution 1514(XV) of 14 December 1960,

Recalling also its resolution 58/102 of 9 December 2003, in which it requested the Special Committee to continue to discharge the functions entrusted to it under resolution 1970(XVIII),

Stressing the importance of timely transmission by the administering Powers of adequate information under Article 73 *e* of the Charter, in particular in relation to the preparation by the Secretariat of the working papers on the Territories concerned,

Having examined the report of the Secretary-General,

1. *Reaffirms* that, in the absence of a decision by the General Assembly itself that a Non-Self-Governing

Territory has attained a full measure of self-government in terms of Chapter XI of the Charter of the United Nations, the administering Power concerned should continue to transmit information under Article 73 *e* of the Charter with respect to that Territory;

2. *Requests* the administering Powers concerned to transmit or continue to transmit to the Secretary-General the information prescribed in Article 73 *e* of the Charter, as well as the fullest possible information on political and constitutional developments in the Territories concerned, within a maximum period of six months following the expiration of the administrative year in those Territories;

3. *Requests* the Secretary-General to continue to ensure that adequate information is drawn from all available published sources in connection with the preparation of the working papers relating to the Territories concerned;

4. *Requests* the Special Committee on the Situation with regard to the Implementation of the Declaration on the Granting of Independence to Colonial Countries and Peoples to continue to discharge the functions entrusted to it under General Assembly resolution 1970(XVIII), in accordance with established procedures.

RECORDED VOTE ON RESOLUTION 59/127:

In favour: Afghanistan, Albania, Algeria, Andorra, Angola, Antigua and Barbuda, Argentina, Armenia, Australia, Austria, Azerbaijan, Bahrain, Bangladesh, Barbados, Belarus, Belgium, Belize, Benin, Bolivia, Bosnia and Herzegovina, Botswana, Brazil, Brunei Darussalam, Bulgaria, Burkina Faso, Burundi, Cambodia, Cameroon, Canada, Cape Verde, Central African Republic, China, Colombia, Comoros, Congo, Costa Rica, Côte d'Ivoire, Croatia, Cuba, Cyprus, Czech Republic, Democratic People's Republic of Korea, Democratic Republic of the Congo, Denmark, Djibouti, Dominica, Dominican Republic, Ecuador, Egypt, El Salvador, Equatorial Guinea, Eritrea, Estonia, Ethiopia, Fiji, Finland, Gabon, Georgia, Germany, Ghana, Greece, Grenada, Guatemala, Guinea, Guinea-Bissau, Guyana, Haiti, Honduras, Hungary, Iceland, India, Indonesia, Iran, Ireland, Italy, Jamaica, Japan, Jordan, Kazakhstan, Kenya, Kuwait, Kyrgyzstan, Lao People's Democratic Republic, Latvia, Lebanon, Lesotho, Liberia, Libyan Arab Jamahiriya, Liechtenstein, Lithuania, Luxembourg, Madagascar, Malaysia, Maldives, Mali, Malta, Marshall Islands, Mauritania, Mauritius, Mexico, Mongolia, Morocco, Mozambique, Myanmar, Namibia, Nauru, Nepal, Netherlands, New Zealand, Nicaragua, Nigeria, Norway, Oman, Pakistan, Panama, Papua New Guinea, Peru, Philippines, Poland, Portugal, Qatar, Republic of Korea, Republic of Moldova, Romania, Russian Federation, Rwanda, Saint Lucia, Saint Vincent and the Grenadines, Samoa, San Marino, Sao Tome and Principe, Saudi Arabia, Senegal, Serbia and Montenegro, Seychelles, Sierra Leone, Singapore, Slovakia, Slovenia, Solomon Islands, Somalia, South Africa, Spain, Sri Lanka, Sudan, Suriname, Swaziland, Sweden, Switzerland, Syrian Arab Republic, Tajikistan, Thailand, The former Yugoslav Republic of Macedonia, Timor-Leste, Togo, Tonga, Trinidad and Tobago, Tunisia, Turkey, Turkmenistan, Tuvalu, Uganda, Ukraine, United Arab Emirates, United Republic of Tanzania, Uruguay, Vanuatu, Venezuela, Viet Nam, Yemen, Zambia, Zimbabwe.

Against: None.

Abstaining: France, Israel, Micronesia, Palau, United Kingdom, United States.

Study and training

In response to General Assembly resolution 58/105 [YUN 2003, p. 608], the Secretary-General reported on offers of study and training scholarships for inhabitants of NSGTs during the period 2 April 2003 to 15 April 2004 by the following Member States: Antigua and Barbuda, Argentina, Cuba, Japan, Mexico, New Zealand, Sweden, Switzerland, Trinidad and Tobago and the United States [A/59/74]. Fifty-six Member States and one non-member State had made such offers over the years.

GENERAL ASSEMBLY ACTION

On 10 December [meeting 71], the General Assembly, on the recommendation of the Fourth Committee [A/59/477], adopted **resolution 59/130** without vote [agenda item 82].

Offers by Member States of study and training facilities for inhabitants of Non-Self-Governing Territories

The General Assembly,

Recalling its resolution 58/105 of 9 December 2003,

Having examined the report of the Secretary-General on offers by Member States of study and training facilities for inhabitants of Non-Self-Governing Territories, prepared pursuant to its resolution 845(IX) of 22 November 1954,

Conscious of the importance of promoting the educational advancement of the inhabitants of Non-Self-Governing Territories,

Strongly convinced that the continuation and expansion of offers of scholarships is essential in order to meet the increasing need of students from Non-Self-Governing Territories for educational and training assistance, and considering that students in those Territories should be encouraged to avail themselves of such offers,

1. *Takes note* of the report of the Secretary-General;

2. *Expresses its appreciation* to those Member States that have made scholarships available to the inhabitants of Non-Self-Governing Territories;

3. *Invites* all States to make or continue to make generous offers of study and training facilities to the inhabitants of those Territories that have not yet attained self-government or independence and, wherever possible, to provide travel funds to prospective students;

4. *Urges* the administering Powers to take effective measures to ensure the widespread and continuous dissemination in the Territories under their administration of information relating to offers of study and training facilities made by States and to provide all the necessary facilities to enable students to avail themselves of such offers;

5. *Requests* the Secretary-General to report to the General Assembly at its sixtieth session on the implementation of the present resolution;

6. *Draws the attention* of the Special Committee on the Situation with regard to the Implementation of the Declaration on the Granting of Independence to Colonial Countries and Peoples to the present resolution.

Visiting missions

In June, the Special Committee on decolonization considered the question of sending visiting missions to NSGTs [A/59/23]. It adopted a resolution in which it stressed the need to dispatch periodic visiting missions to facilitate the full implementation of the 1960 Declaration on decolonization and called on administering Powers to receive those missions in the Territories under their administration.

The Committee recommended to the General Assembly for adoption draft resolutions on 11 small NSGTs (see p. 610) and on Tokelau (see p. 609). In its draft resolutions, the Committee endorsed a number of conclusions and recommendations concerning the sending of visiting missions to the Territories.

Puerto Rico

In accordance with the Special Committee's 2003 resolution concerning the self-determination and independence of Puerto Rico [YUN 2003, p. 609], the Committee's Rapporteur, in an April report [A/AC.109/2004/L.3], provided information on Puerto Rico, including recent political, military and economic developments, and on UN action.

Following its usual practice, the Committee acceded to requests for hearings from representatives of a number of organizations, who presented their views on 14 June [A/59/23]. The Committee adopted a resolution without vote, by which it reaffirmed the inalienable right of the people of Puerto Rico to self-determination and independence; called on the United States to assume its responsibility of expediting a process to allow the Puerto Rican people to exercise that right; urged the United States to return the occupied land and installations on Vieques Island and at the Roosevelt Roads Naval Station to the people of Puerto Rico; and requested the Rapporteur to report in 2005 on the resolution's implementation.

Territories under review

Falklands Islands (Malvinas)

The Special Committee on decolonization considered the question of the Falkland Islands (Malvinas) on 18 June [A/59/23]. It examined a Secretariat working paper on constitutional and political developments, mine clearance, and economic and social conditions in the Territory [A/AC.109/2004/12], and adopted a resolution requesting Argentina and the United Kingdom to consolidate current dialogue and cooperation by resuming negotiations to find a peaceful solution to the sovereignty dispute.

Argentina, on 5 January [A/58/671], transmitted to the Secretary-General a 3 January press release recalling its objective to recover full sovereignty over the Malvinas, South Georgia and South Sandwich Islands and surrounding maritime areas through peaceful means. It reiterated the need to comply with UN resolutions and Organization of American States declarations calling for a resumption of bilateral negotiations in order to find a just and lasting solution to the sovereignty dispute; recalled its readiness to resume such negotiations immediately; and exhorted the United Kingdom to do likewise. The United Kingdom, in a 13 January response [A/58/681], stated that it had no doubt about its sovereignty over the Falkland Islands, South Georgia and South Sandwich Islands, and rejected as unfounded Argentina's claim to sovereignty.

On 8 June [A/58/840], Argentina formally protested the recent upgrading of the British military base in the Malvinas, as a violation of Assembly resolution 31/49 [YUN 1976, p. 747], which called on the two parties to refrain from introducing unilateral modifications in the situation while the islands were going through the process recommended in relevant Assembly resolutions. Argentina believed that the expansion of the military occupation in the disputed area was incompatible with the letter and spirit of the provisional understandings under the sovereignty formula regarding practical aspects of the South Atlantic, particularly in relation to measures aimed at building and strengthening mutual confidence. On 28 July [A/58/860], the United Kingdom rejected Argentina's claims that the change in titles to Headquarters British Forces South Atlantic Islands and Commander British Forces South Atlantic Islands reflected changes in administrative structures. There had been no change in the mission or role of the United Kingdom's armed forces providing security for the Falkland Islands, South Georgia and South Sandwich Islands.

Addressing the General Assembly during the general debate on 21 September [A/59/PV.4], Argentina's President, Néstor Kirchner, reaffirmed his country's willingness to reach a just, peaceful and lasting solution to the sovereignty dispute and urged the United Kingdom to resume negotiations. In exercise of its right of reply, the United Kingdom, in a 30 September letter to the Assembly President [A/59/406], stated that the elected representatives of the Falkland Islands again asked the Committee on decolonization to recognize that they, like any other people, were entitled to exercise the right of self-determination, and reiterated that the people of the Falkland Islands did not wish for any change in the status of the islands. There could be no negotiations on sovereignty unless and until the islanders so wished.

Gibraltar

The Special Committee on decolonization considered the question of Gibraltar on 8 June [A/59/23]. Before it was a Secretariat working paper describing political developments and economic and social conditions in the Territory, and setting forth the positions of the United Kingdom (the administering Power), Gibraltar and Spain concerning Gibraltar's future status [A/AC.109/2004/7].

Gibraltar's Chief Minister, Peter Caruana, in his New Year message, said that it was important that Gibraltarians pursued the constitutional modernization proposals submitted to the British Secretary of State for Foreign and Commonwealth Affairs in 2003 [YUN 2003, p. 611] and political routes based on development of and respect for their political rights. A later Secretariat working paper [A/AC.109/2005/11] reported that the Foreign Secretary, Jack Straw, had acknowledged the importance of the proposals to Gibraltar and said that they would receive careful consideration. Preliminary talks were held between the Foreign Secretary and Gibraltar's Chief Minister on 26 May on constitutional reform and how to move the process forward. The first meeting to discuss the reform proposals took place on 1 December.

The Chief Minister, speaking before the Special Committee on 8 June, reiterated Gibraltar's calls for the Special Committee to visit the Territory and to recommend to the Fourth Committee that the case be referred to the International Court of Justice (ICJ) for an advisory opinion. Gibraltar also proposed that the annual draft decision on the issue reflect a call for the Government of Gibraltar to be present at any talks affecting the Territory.

On 21 September, Spain's Prime Minister, José Luis Rodríguez Zapatero, speaking before the General Assembly, said that his country remained willing to negotiate a solution that benefited the region as a whole and to listen to Gibraltar's voice. On 6 October, Spain's representative, speaking before the Fourth Committee, referred to a statement by Spain's Minister for Foreign Affairs and Cooperation, Miguel Angel Moratinos, who said that Spain was willing to facilitate the establishment of close and fruitful cooperation between Gibraltar and the surrounding area. Spain's policy towards Gibraltar needed to include a significant person-to-person dimension, with contacts between civil societies. Spain, while preferring dialogue to confrontation, would continue to defend its positions based on reason and justice. Regarding the suggestion that the Assembly request an advisory opinion from ICJ, the representative said that the issue was political and had to be settled at that level.

Gibraltar's Chief Minister, speaking before the Fourth Committee on the same date, rejected Spain's argument that, because of Spain's sovereignty claim, the principle of self-determination could not apply to the decolonization of Gibraltar, stating that nowhere in the UN Charter, in UN doctrine or in international law was it written that a neighbour's sovereignty claim overrode, let alone extinguished, the inalienable right to self-determination of a colonial people. He welcomed the statement by the Spanish Prime Minister (see p. 605) as a constructive step in the right direction; emphasized that Gibraltarians were entitled to be heard and their wishes respected; and that only they could decide Gibraltar's future. He welcomed statements by the Spanish Foreign Minister concerning Gibraltar (see p. 605) and Spain's offer of dialogue on issues of local cooperation with no sovereignty implications for either side. The Chief Minister said that Gibraltar would engage constructively and amicably in such a process and emphasized that sovereignty was a different matter for which concessions would not be made.

In a joint communiqué issued on 16 December, Gibraltar, Spain and the United Kingdom confirmed their earlier agreement reached in Madrid on 27 October to establish a new, three-sided forum for dialogue on Gibraltar, separate from the Brussels Process [YUN 1984, p. 1075], and the work modalities for the forum, including the creation of working groups on specific issues. The forum would adopt an open agenda, with each party having its own voice and participating on an equal basis. The parties would try to create a constructive atmosphere of mutual confidence and cooperation and refrain from making public statements which distorted or misrepresented the basis, purpose or modalities of the forum.

After hearing statements by the Chief Minister of Gibraltar, the Leader of the Opposition in Gibraltar and the representative of Spain, the Special Committee decided to continue consideration of the question in 2005.

GENERAL ASSEMBLY ACTION

In December, the General Assembly, on the recommendation of the Fourth Committee [A/59/478], adopted **decision 59/519** without vote [agenda item 20].

Question of Gibraltar

At its 71st plenary meeting, on 10 December 2004, the General Assembly, on the recommendation of the Special Political and Decolonization Committee (Fourth Committee), recalling its decision 58/526 of 9 December 2003, and recalling at the same time that the statement agreed to by the Governments of Spain and the United Kingdom of Great Britain and Northern Ireland at Brussels on 27 November 1984 stipulated, inter alia, the following:

"The establishment of a negotiating process aimed at overcoming all the differences between them over Gibraltar and at promoting cooperation on a mutually beneficial basis on economic, cultural, touristic, aviation, military and environmental matters. Both sides accept that the issues of sovereignty will be discussed in that process. The British Government will fully maintain its commitment to honour the wishes of the people of Gibraltar as set out in the preamble of the 1969 Constitution",

urged both Governments, while listening to the interests and aspirations of Gibraltar, to reach in the spirit of that statement a definitive solution to the question of Gibraltar, in the light of relevant resolutions of the General Assembly and in the spirit of the Charter of the United Nations.

New Caledonia

The Special Committee on decolonization considered the question of New Caledonia on 16 June [A/59/23]. Before it was a Secretariat working paper describing the political situation and economic data and developments in the Territory [A/AC.109/2004/11].

A later Secretariat working paper [A/AC.109/2005/13] reported that, according to France, the administering Power, uneasiness about one political party dominating the system culminated just months prior to the Caledonian general elections on 9 May, with the emergence of a new party, Avenir Ensemble (AE), which was opposed to complete independence from France and was viewed as more consensus-oriented with the indigenous Kanak movement and supportive of full implementation of the 1998 Nouméa Accord on New Caledonia's future status [YUN 1998, p. 574]. The elections ended the 25-year domination of the Caledonian Government led by the pro-integration Rassemblement pour la Calédonie dans la République (RPCR), with AE obtaining 16 of the 54 seats in Congress, on a par with RPCR. The pro-independence coalition party, the Front de Libération national kanak socialiste (FLNKS) won nine seats, the Union Calédonienne (UC) seven seats, the Front National four, and two smaller parties one seat each. The anti-independence alliance therefore increased its representation from 31 to 36 seats. At the provincial level, AE won 19 of the 40 seats in the South Province, while the North Province remained in the hands of FLNKS and UC, normally one of the FLNKS parties. The independence alliance was the strongest performer in the Loyalty Islands, holding 6 of 14 seats.

Following the May elections, the Government elected Marie-Noëlle Thémereau of AE, President, and re-elected FLNKS member, Déwé Gorodey, Vice-President. However, Mrs. Thémereau's Government had to resign when RPCR withdrew from the Cabinet, claiming that it was entitled to four seats instead of three. After RPCR was promised one more seat at the expense of AE, Mrs. Thémereau and Mrs. Gorodey, on 29 June, finally received the required votes to be elected President and Vice-President, respectively, marking the first time the Territorial Government was headed by two women.

In view of the election results and subsequent events, former President Pierre Frogier of RPCR predicted, in a 9 November speech to the French National Assembly, a new period of instability, stating that his party was systematically excluded from all responsibilities by a heterogeneous coalition. However, his successor, Mrs. Thémereau, stressed in her Déclaration de politique générale in August that the absence of an absolute majority both in Congress and in the Government reflected the nature of the Nouméa Accord, which stipulated that power should not be monolithic, but shared.

The Customary Senate, considered the guarantor of Kanak identity, selected a new chief, Paul Jewine. In her Déclaration, the President suggested that the Senate's renewal in 2005 could be an occasion to tackle certain reforms, specifying that it was up to the Kanak society to decide on its representation.

During the period under review, 10 country laws (lois du pays), which had the full force of law and could be contested only before the Constitutional Council, were adopted, the most recent relating to social, finance and customs issues and taxes. According to France, the competencies that could be transferred from the State to the Government of New Caledonia under the Nouméa Accord in the period 2004-2009, which corresponded to the length of office of the current New Caledonian Congress, were those related to the police and security in air and sea traffic, private primary education, civil and commercial law and civil security. Upon the approval of an additional organic law, transfer would also be possible for rules regarding the administration of the provinces and municipalities, higher education and audio-visual communication. France stressed that, since the New Caledonian Government did not ask for the transfer of those powers during the first six months following the May elections, as called for in the Nouméa Accord, no powers were likely to be transferred until 2009, when the next Congress was to be elected.

GENERAL ASSEMBLY ACTION

On 10 December [meeting 71], the General Assembly, on the recommendation of the Fourth Committee [A/59/478], adopted **resolution 59/132** without vote [agenda item 20].

Question of New Caledonia

The General Assembly,

Having considered the question of New Caledonia,

Having examined the chapter of the report of the Special Committee on the Situation with regard to the Implementation of the Declaration on the Granting of Independence to Colonial Countries and Peoples relating to New Caledonia,

Reaffirming the right of peoples to self-determination as enshrined in the Charter of the United Nations,

Recalling General Assembly resolutions 1514(XV) of 14 December 1960 and 1541(XV) of 15 December 1960,

Noting the importance of the positive measures being pursued in New Caledonia by the French authorities, in cooperation with all sectors of the population, to promote political, economic and social development in the Territory, including measures in the area of environmental protection and action with respect to drug abuse and trafficking, in order to provide a framework for its peaceful progress to self-determination,

Noting also, in this context, the importance of equitable economic and social development, as well as continued dialogue among the parties involved in New Caledonia in the preparation of the act of self-determination of New Caledonia,

Noting with satisfaction the intensification of contacts between New Caledonia and neighbouring countries of the South Pacific region,

1. *Welcomes* the significant developments that have taken place in New Caledonia as exemplified by the signing of the Nouméa Accord of 5 May 1998 by the representatives of New Caledonia and the Government of France;

2. *Urges* all the parties involved, in the interest of all the people of New Caledonia, to maintain, in the framework of the Nouméa Accord, their dialogue in a spirit of harmony;

3. *Notes* the relevant provisions of the Nouméa Accord aimed at taking more broadly into account the Kanak identity in the political and social organization of New Caledonia, and also those provisions of the Accord relating to control of immigration and protection of local employment;

4. *Also notes* the relevant provisions of the Nouméa Accord to the effect that New Caledonia may become a member or associate member of certain international organizations, such as international organizations in the Pacific region, the United Nations, the United Nations Educational, Scientific and Cultural Organization and the International Labour Organization, according to their regulations;

5. *Further notes* the agreement between the signatories of the Nouméa Accord that the progress made in the emancipation process shall be brought to the attention of the United Nations;

6. *Welcomes* the fact that the administering Power invited to New Caledonia, at the time the new institutions were established, a mission of information which comprised representatives of countries of the Pacific region;

7. *Calls upon* the administering Power to transmit information regarding the political, economic and social situation of New Caledonia to the Secretary-General;

8. *Invites* all the parties involved to continue promoting a framework for the peaceful progress of the Territory towards an act of self-determination in which all options are open and which would safeguard the rights and identity of all the sectors of the population, according to the letter and the spirit of the Nouméa Accord, which is based on the principle that it is for the populations of New Caledonia to choose how to control their destiny;

9. *Welcomes* measures that have been taken to strengthen and diversify the New Caledonian economy in all fields, and encourages further such measures in accordance with the spirit of the Matignon and Nouméa Accords;

10. *Also welcomes* the importance attached by the parties to the Matignon and Nouméa Accords to greater progress in housing, employment, training, education and health care in New Caledonia;

11. *Acknowledges* the contribution of the Melanesian Cultural Centre to the protection of the indigenous Kanak culture of New Caledonia;

12. *Notes* the positive initiatives aimed at protecting the natural environment of New Caledonia, notably the "Zonéco" operation designed to map and evaluate marine resources within the economic zone of New Caledonia;

13. *Acknowledges* the close links between New Caledonia and the peoples of the South Pacific and the positive actions being taken by the French and territorial authorities to facilitate the further development of those links, including the development of closer relations with the countries members of the Pacific Islands Forum;

14. *Welcomes*, in this regard, the accession by New Caledonia to the status of observer in the Pacific Islands Forum, continuing high-level visits to New Caledonia by delegations from countries of the Pacific region and high-level visits by delegations from New Caledonia to countries members of the Pacific Islands Forum;

15. *Decides* to keep under continuous review the process unfolding in New Caledonia as a result of the signing of the Nouméa Accord;

16. *Requests* the Special Committee on the Situation with regard to the Implementation of the Declaration on the Granting of Independence to Colonial Countries and Peoples to continue to examine the question of the Non-Self-Governing Territory of New Caledonia and to report thereon to the General Assembly at its sixtieth session.

Tokelau

On 16 June, the Special Committee on decolonization considered the question of Tokelau (the three small atolls of Nukunonu, Fakaofo and Atafu in the South Pacific), administered by New Zealand [A/59/23]. Before it was a Secretariat working paper covering constitutional and political developments and economic and social conditions in the Territory, and setting out the positions of New Zealand and Tokelau on the Territory's future status [A/AC.109/2004/8].

A later Secretariat working paper [A/AC.109/2005/3] reported that, in January, Atafu's Faipule

(the representative of each village/atoll), Patuki Isaako, took over as Ulu o Tokelau (titular head of the Territory), a position that was rotated annually among the three Faipule.

In January, the General Fono (Tokelau's national representative body) adopted the recommendations of a Commission of Inquiry, established by the Territory's New Zealand–appointed Administrator, on the future shape and functioning of Tokelau's public services. At the June General Fono, the Administrator formally delegated his responsibilities to the taupulega (village councils) of the three villages, which in turn, subdelegated to the General Fono responsibility for specified subjects to be handled at the national level, thus completing the devolution of public services in line with the new political structure based on the three villages. The arrangement, which represented the realization of the Modern House of Tokelau approach [YUN 1998, p. 575], put the villages squarely at the heart of Tokelau's system of government and reaffirmed the "pule" (traditional authority) of the three village councils.

Also in January, the General Fono agreed on the steps to be taken to give effect to its 2003 decision to endorse self-government in free association with New Zealand [YUN 2003, p. 614]. Those included discussions of senior officials in Wellington, New Zealand, in April, and of the Special Committee on decolonization during the Pacific regional seminar in May (see p. 593); consultations during the Special Committee's meetings in New York in June; and an official visit to Tokelau by Prime Minister Helen Clark of New Zealand in August, during which she welcomed Tokelau's recent decisions on its future political status and assured Tokelau of New Zealand's ongoing friendship and support as it moved towards an act of self-determination.

The issue of representation within the General Fono, previously reviewed in 2003 [YUN 2003, p. 613], was again reviewed at a meeting of the Special Constitutional Committee during the October General Fono, which decided on the method of appointment of the Chairperson of the General Fono and on the role and responsibilities of the six-person Council for Ongoing Government [ibid., p. 614]. The General Fono also took decisions on Tokelau's draft constitution and legislative framework; law-making procedures; the role of the Kau Hauatea (the constitutional advisory body); the judicial system; and Tokelau's International Trust Fund, which was formally established in November.

In November, at the invitation of New Zealand's Prime Minister, the Council for Ongoing Government visited New Zealand for high-level discussions on Tokelau's further political evolution. The Council met with the Governor-General, the Prime Minister, the Minister for Foreign Affairs and Trade, the Leader of the Opposition and the main Tokelauan communities in New Zealand. Agreement was reached on the principal elements to be included in a draft Treaty of Free Association. It was noted that, if Tokelau agreed to undertake an act of self-determination, the United Nations would be invited to provide electoral assistance.

Speaking before the Special Committee on decolonization on 16 June, the Administrator of Tokelau said that Tokelau had made good progress in its discussions with New Zealand about the decolonization option of self-government in free association and had pushed ahead with its draft constitution, anthem and flag. It had firm assurances of ongoing New Zealand support, including an enhanced multi-year economic support agreement and the joint statement of the principles of partnership, which were drafted in 2002 [YUN 2002, p. 574] and signed in 2003 [YUN 2003, p. 614].

At a 4 October meeting of the Fourth Committee, New Zealand outlined recent developments and noted that the previous 12 months had seen considerable movement, both in New Zealand and in Tokelau, towards an act of self-determination.

At a 16 June meeting of the Special Committee on decolonization, the Ulu o Tokelau said that positive engagement had taken place with New Zealand on Tokelau's future political status. Noting the establishment of Tokelau's International Trust Fund, the Ulu appealed for support from the international community as Tokelau moved to take on greater responsibility for its own affairs. He extended an invitation to the Special Committee to attend the workshop of the Special Constitutional Committee in October.

GENERAL ASSEMBLY ACTION

On 10 December [meeting 71], the General Assembly, on the recommendation of the Fourth Committee [A/59/478], adopted **resolution 59/133** without vote [agenda item 20].

Question of Tokelau

The General Assembly,

Having considered the question of Tokelau,

Having examined the chapter of the report of the Special Committee on the Situation with regard to the Implementation of the Declaration on the Granting of Independence to Colonial Countries and Peoples relating to Tokelau,

Noting with appreciation the continuing exemplary cooperation of New Zealand as the administering Power with regard to the work of the Special Committee relating to Tokelau and its readiness to permit access by United Nations visiting missions to the Territory,

Noting also with appreciation the collaborative contribution to the development of Tokelau by New Zealand and the specialized agencies and other organizations of the United Nations system, in particular the United Nations Development Programme,

Recalling the inauguration in 1999 of a national legislative body, the General Fono, based on village elections by universal adult suffrage and the assumption by that body in June 2003 of full responsibility for the Tokelau budget,

Recalling also the report of the United Nations mission dispatched in August 2002 to Tokelau at the invitation of the Government of New Zealand and the representatives of Tokelau,

Noting that, as a small island Territory, Tokelau exemplifies the situation of most remaining Non-Self-Governing Territories and that, as a case study pointing to successful cooperation for decolonization, Tokelau has wider significance for the United Nations as it seeks to complete its work in decolonization,

Recalling that New Zealand and Tokelau signed in November 2003 a document entitled "Joint statement of the principles of partnership", which sets out in writing, for the first time, the rights and obligations of the two partner countries,

Recalling also the decision of the General Fono at its meeting in November 2003, following extensive consultations undertaken in all three villages, to explore formally with New Zealand the option of self-government in free association,

1. *Notes* that Tokelau remains firmly committed to the development of self-government and to an act of self-determination that would result in Tokelau assuming a status in accordance with the options on future status for Non-Self-Governing Territories contained in principle VI of the annex to General Assembly resolution 1541(XV) of 15 December 1960;

2. *Welcomes* the substantial progress made in the past year towards the devolution of power to the three taupulega (village councils), in particular the delegation of the Administrator's powers to the three taupulega with effect from 1 July 2004 and the assumption by each taupulega from that date of full responsibility for the management of all its public services;

3. *Notes in particular* the decision of the General Fono in November 2003, following extensive consultations in all three villages and a meeting of the Special Committee on the Constitution of Tokelau, to explore formally with New Zealand the option of self-government in free association, and the discussions now under way between Tokelau and New Zealand pursuant to the General Fono decision;

4. *Notes* that the General Fono has endorsed a series of recommendations of the workshop of the Special Committee on the Constitution held in Tokelau in October 2003 with the support of the United Nations Development Programme relating to Tokelau's Constitution, the role and functioning of the General Fono, the judicial system and international human rights conventions;

5. *Acknowledges* Tokelau's initiative in devising a strategic economic development plan for the period 2002-2004 to advance its capacity for self-government;

6. *Also acknowledges* the continuing assistance that New Zealand has committed to promoting Tokelau's self-government as well as the cooperation of the United Nations Development Programme;

7. *Further acknowledges* Tokelau's need for continued reassurance, given the cultural adjustments that are taking place with the strengthening of its capacity for self-government and, since local resources cannot adequately cover the material side of self-determination, the ongoing responsibility of Tokelau's external partners to assist Tokelau in balancing its desire to be self-reliant to the greatest extent possible with its need for external assistance;

8. *Welcomes* the establishment of an international trust fund to support Tokelau's future development needs, and urges all Member States and international and regional agencies to contribute to the fund and thereby lend practical support to assist this emerging country in overcoming the problems of smallness, isolation and lack of resources;

9. *Welcomes* the assurance of the Government of New Zealand that it will meet its obligations to the United Nations with respect to Tokelau and abide by the freely expressed wishes of the people of Tokelau with regard to their future status;

10. *Also welcomes* the cooperative attitude of the other States and territories in the region towards Tokelau, its economic and political aspirations and its increasing participation in regional and international affairs;

11. *Further welcomes* Tokelau's associate membership in the United Nations Educational, Scientific and Cultural Organization and its recent accession to membership in the Forum Fisheries Agency;

12. *Calls upon* the administering Power and United Nations agencies to continue to provide assistance to Tokelau as it further develops its economy and governance structures in the context of its ongoing constitutional evolution;

13. *Notes with satisfaction* the invitation of the Ulu o Tokelau to the Chairman of the Special Committee on the Situation with regard to the Implementation of the Declaration on the Granting of Independence to Colonial Countries and Peoples to attend the workshop of the Special Committee on the Constitution to be held in October 2004 in the Tokelau Islands;

14. *Requests* the Special Committee to continue to examine the question of the Non-Self-Governing Territory of Tokelau and to report thereon to the General Assembly at its sixtieth session.

Western Sahara

The Special Committee on decolonization considered the question of Western Sahara on 7 June [A/59/23]. A Secretariat working paper [A/AC.109/2004/4] detailed the Secretary-General's good offices with the parties concerned and actions taken by the General Assembly and Security Council (see p. 274). The Special Committee transmitted the relevant documentation to the Assembly's fifty-ninth (2004) session to facilitate the Fourth Committee's consideration of the question. The Secretary-General's report was submitted to the Assembly in July [A/59/134].

By a 30 August letter to the Secretary-General [A/59/314-S/2004/704], Namibia transmitted a memorandum by the Frente Popular para la Liberación de Saguía el-Hamra y de Río de Oro on the question of Western Sahara.

Island Territories

In June, the Special Committee on decolonization [A/59/23] considered working papers on American Samoa [A/AC.109/2004/6], Anguilla [A/AC.109/2004/10], Bermuda [A/AC.109/2004/14], the British Virgin Islands [A/AC.109/2004/3], the Cayman Islands [A/AC.109/2004/15], Guam [A/AC.109/2004/5], Montserrat [A/AC.109/2004/13], Pitcairn [A/AC.109/2004/2], Saint Helena [A/AC.109/2004/9], the Turks and Caicos Islands [A/AC.109/2004/16] and the United States Virgin Islands [A/AC.109/2004/17], describing political developments and economic and social conditions in each of those 11 island Territories. On 17 June, the Committee approved a two-part consolidated draft resolution for adoption by the General Assembly (see below).

GENERAL ASSEMBLY ACTION

On 10 December [meeting 71], the General Assembly, on the recommendation of the Fourth Committee [A/59/478], adopted **resolutions 59/134 A** and **B** without vote [agenda item 20].

Questions of American Samoa, Anguilla, Bermuda, the British Virgin Islands, the Cayman Islands, Guam, Montserrat, Pitcairn, Saint Helena, the Turks and Caicos Islands and the United States Virgin Islands

A

General

The General Assembly,

Having considered the questions of the Non-Self-Governing Territories of American Samoa, Anguilla, Bermuda, the British Virgin Islands, the Cayman Islands, Guam, Montserrat, Pitcairn, Saint Helena, the Turks and Caicos Islands and the United States Virgin Islands, hereinafter referred to as "the Territories",

Having examined the relevant chapter of the report of the Special Committee on the Situation with regard to the Implementation of the Declaration on the Granting of Independence to Colonial Countries and Peoples,

Recalling all resolutions and decisions of the United Nations relating to those Territories, including, in particular, the resolutions adopted by the General Assembly at its fifty-eighth session on the individual Territories covered by the present resolution,

Recognizing that all available options for self-determination of the Territories are valid as long as they are in accordance with the freely expressed wishes of the peoples concerned and in conformity with the clearly defined principles contained in General Assembly resolutions 1514(XV) of 14 December 1960, 1541(XV) of 15 December 1960 and other resolutions of the Assembly,

Recalling General Assembly resolution 1541(XV), containing the principles that should guide Member States in determining whether or not an obligation exists to transmit the information called for under Article 73 *e* of the Charter of the United Nations,

Expressing its concern that more than forty-three years after the adoption of the Declaration there still remain a number of Non-Self-Governing Territories,

Conscious of the importance of continuing effective implementation of the Declaration, taking into account the target set by the United Nations to eradicate colonialism by 2010 and the plan of action for the Second International Decade for the Eradication of Colonialism,

Recognizing that the specific characteristics and the sentiments of the peoples of the Territories require flexible, practical and innovative approaches to the options of self-determination, without any prejudice to territorial size, geographical location, size of population or natural resources,

Taking note of the stated position of the Government of the United Kingdom of Great Britain and Northern Ireland on the Non-Self-Governing Territories under its administration,

Taking note also of the stated position of the Government of the United States of America on the Non-Self-Governing Territories under its administration,

Noting the constitutional developments in some Non-Self-Governing Territories about which the Special Committee has received information,

Aware of the usefulness both to the Territories and to the Special Committee of the participation of elected and appointed representatives of the Territories in the work of the Special Committee,

Convinced that the wishes and aspirations of the peoples of the Territories should continue to guide the development of their future political status and that referendums, free and fair elections and other forms of popular consultation play an important role in ascertaining the wishes and aspirations of the people,

Convinced also that any negotiations to determine the status of a Territory must take place with the active involvement and participation of the people of that Territory, under the supervision of the United Nations, on a case-by-case basis, and that the views of the peoples of the Non-Self-Governing Territories in respect of their right to self-determination should be ascertained,

Aware of the importance of international financial services for the economies of some of the Non-Self-Governing Territories,

Noting the continued cooperation of the Non-Self-Governing Territories at the local and regional levels, including their participation in the work of regional organizations,

Mindful that United Nations visiting missions provide an effective means of ascertaining the situation in the Territories, that some Territories have not received a United Nations visiting mission for a long time and that no visiting missions have been sent to some of the Territories, and considering the possibility of sending further visiting missions to the Territories at an appropriate time and in consultation with the administering Powers,

Mindful also that, in order for the Special Committee to enhance its understanding of the political status of the peoples of the Territories and to fulfil its mandate effectively, it is important for it to be apprised by the administering Powers and to receive information from other appropriate sources, including the representatives of the Territories, concerning the wishes and aspirations of the peoples of the Territories,

Recognizing the need for the Special Committee to embark actively on a public awareness campaign aimed at assisting the peoples of the Territories in gaining an understanding of the options of self-determination,

Mindful, in this connection, that the holding of regional seminars in the Caribbean and Pacific regions and at Headquarters and other venues, with the active participation of representatives of the Non-Self-Governing Territories, provides a helpful means for the Special Committee to fulfil its mandate, and that the regional nature of the seminars, which alternate between the Caribbean and the Pacific, is a crucial element in their success, while recognizing the need for reviewing the role of those seminars in the context of a United Nations programme for ascertaining the political status of the Territories,

Mindful also that, by holding a Pacific regional seminar in Madang, Papua New Guinea, from 18 to 20 May 2004, the Special Committee was able to hear the views of the representatives of the Territories and Member States as well as organizations and experts in the region, in order to review the political, economic and social conditions in the Territories,

Conscious of the particular vulnerability of the Territories to natural disasters and environmental degradation and, in this connection, bearing in mind the programmes of action of the United Nations Conference on Environment and Development, the World Conference on Natural Disaster Reduction, the Global Conference on the Sustainable Development of Small Island Developing States, the International Conference on Population and Development, the United Nations Conference on Human Settlements (Habitat II), the World Summit on Sustainable Development and other relevant world conferences,

Noting with appreciation the contribution to the development of some Territories by the specialized agencies and other organizations of the United Nations system,

Recalling the ongoing efforts of the Special Committee in carrying out a critical review of its work with the aim of making appropriate and constructive recommendations and decisions to attain its objectives in accordance with its mandate,

1. *Reaffirms* the inalienable right of the peoples of the Territories to self-determination, in conformity with the Charter of the United Nations and with General Assembly resolution 1514(XV), containing the Declaration on the Granting of Independence to Colonial Countries and Peoples;

2. *Reaffirms also* that, in the process of decolonization, there is no alternative to the principle of self-determination, which is also a fundamental human right, as recognized under the relevant human rights conventions;

3. *Reaffirms further* that it is ultimately for the peoples of the Territories themselves to determine freely

their future political status in accordance with the relevant provisions of the Charter, the Declaration and the relevant resolutions of the General Assembly, and in that connection reiterates its long-standing call for the administering Powers, in cooperation with the territorial Governments, to promote political education in the Territories in order to foster an awareness among the people of their right to self-determination in conformity with the legitimate political status options, based on the principles clearly defined in General Assembly resolution 1541(XV);

4. *Requests* the administering Powers to continue to transmit to the Secretary-General information called for under Article 73 *e* of the Charter;

5. *Stresses* the importance of the Special Committee on the Situation with regard to the Implementation of the Declaration on the Granting of Independence to Colonial Countries and Peoples being apprised of the views and wishes of the peoples of the Territories and enhancing its understanding of their conditions, including the nature and scope of the existing political and constitutional arrangements between the Non-Self-Governing Territories and their respective administering Powers;

6. *Reaffirms* the responsibility of the administering Powers under the Charter to promote the economic and social development and to preserve the cultural identity of the Territories, and recommends that priority continue to be given, in consultation with the territorial Governments concerned, to the strengthening and diversification of their respective economies;

7. *Requests* the Special Committee to continue to follow closely the developments in legislation in the area of international financial services and its impact on the economy in some of the Territories;

8. *Requests* the Territories and the administering Powers to take all necessary measures to protect and conserve the environment of the Territories under their administration against any environmental degradation, and once again requests the specialized agencies concerned to continue to monitor environmental conditions in those Territories;

9. *Welcomes* the participation of the Non-Self-Governing Territories in regional activities, including the work of regional organizations;

10. *Stresses* the importance of implementing the plan of action for the Second International Decade for the Eradication of Colonialism, in particular by expediting the application of the work programme for the decolonization of each Non-Self-Governing Territory, on a case-by-case basis;

11. *Invites* the administering Powers to participate fully in the work of the Special Committee in order to implement the provisions of Article 73 *e* of the Charter and the Declaration;

12. *Urges* Member States to contribute to the efforts of the United Nations to usher in a world free of colonialism within the Second International Decade for the Eradication of Colonialism, and calls upon them to continue to give their full support to the Special Committee in its endeavours towards that noble goal;

13. *Notes* that some Non-Self-Governing Territories have expressed concern at the procedure followed by one administering Power, contrary to the wishes of the Territories themselves, namely, of amending or enacting legislation for the Territories

through Orders in Council, in order to apply to the Territories the international treaty obligations of the administering Power;

14. *Takes note* of the constitutional reviews in the Territories administered by the United Kingdom of Great Britain and Northern Ireland and led by the territorial Governments;

15. *Reiterates its requests* to the Secretary-General to report to the General Assembly on the implementation of decolonization resolutions since the proclamation of the Second International Decade for the Eradication of Colonialism for the purpose of a midterm review in 2005;

16. *Requests* the Special Committee to continue to examine the question of the Non-Self-Governing Territories and to report thereon to the General Assembly at its sixtieth session with recommendations on appropriate ways to assist the peoples of the Territories in exercising their right to self-determination.

B

Individual Territories

The General Assembly,

Referring to resolution A above,

I

American Samoa

Taking note of the report by the administering Power that most American Samoan leaders express satisfaction with the Territory's present relationship with the United States of America, as reflected in statements made by those leaders in the regional seminars held in Havana, Cuba, Nadi, Fiji, and Madang, Papua New Guinea, in 2001, 2002 and 2004, respectively,

Noting that the Government of the Territory continues to take steps to increase revenue and decrease government expenditure,

Noting also that the Territory, similar to isolated communities with limited funds, continues to experience a lack of adequate medical and other infrastructural facilities,

1. *Notes* that the Department of the Interior of the United States of America provides that the Secretary of the Interior has administrative jurisdiction over American Samoa;

2. *Calls upon* the administering Power to continue to assist the territorial Government in the economic and social development of the Territory, including measures to rebuild financial management capabilities and strengthen other governmental functions of the Government of the Territory, and welcomes the assistance from the administering Power to the Territory in its recovery efforts following the recent floods;

3. *Welcomes* the invitation extended to the Special Committee on the Situation with regard to the Implementation of the Declaration on the Granting of Independence to Colonial Countries and Peoples by the Governor of American Samoa at the Pacific regional seminar held in Madang, Papua New Guinea, from 18 to 20 May 2004, to send a visiting mission to the Territory, calls upon the administering Power to facilitate such a mission and requests the Chairman of the Special Committee to take all the necessary steps to that end;

II

Anguilla

Taking note of the constitutional review process led by the territorial Government,

Recalling the holding of the 2003 Caribbean regional seminar in Anguilla, the first time that the seminar has been held in a Non-Self-Governing Territory,

Noting the desire of the territorial Government and the people of Anguilla for a visiting mission by the Special Committee,

Aware of the efforts of the Government of Anguilla to continue to develop the Territory as a viable offshore centre and well-regulated financial centre for investors by enacting modern company and trust laws, as well as partnership and insurance legislation, and computerizing the company registry system,

1. *Welcomes* the constitutional review process led by the Government of Anguilla in cooperation with the administering Power;

2. *Recalls* the cooperation of the territorial Government of Anguilla and the United Kingdom of Great Britain and Northern Ireland in holding the 2003 Caribbean regional seminar in Anguilla, and notes that the staging of the seminar in a Non-Self-Governing Territory for the first time, as well as a town hall meeting between the people of Anguilla and the Special Committee during the seminar, contributed to its success;

III

Bermuda

Noting the results of the independence referendum held on 16 August 1995, and conscious of the different viewpoints of the political parties of the Territory on the future status of the Territory,

1. *Welcomes* the agreement reached in June 2002 between the United States of America, the United Kingdom of Great Britain and Northern Ireland and the Territory formally transferring the former military base lands to the territorial Government, and the provision of financial resources to address some of the environmental problems;

2. *Decides* to closely follow the territorial consultations on the future status of Bermuda and to facilitate assistance to the Territory in a public educational programme, if requested, as well as to hold consultations and to make all necessary arrangements to have a visiting mission to the Territory;

IV

British Virgin Islands

Taking note of the constitutional review process led by the territorial Government,

Noting that the Territory continues to emerge as one of the world's leading offshore financial centres,

Welcomes the constitutional review process led by the Government of the British Virgin Islands in cooperation with the administering Power;

V

Cayman Islands

Taking note of the constitutional review process led by the territorial Government,

Noting the approval by the Cayman Islands Legislative Assembly of the Territory's Vision 2008 Development Plan, which aims to promote development that is consistent with the aims and values of Caymanian society,

Welcomes the continuing constitutional review process led by the Government of the Cayman Islands in cooperation with the administering Power;

VI

Guam

Recalling that, in a referendum held in 1987, the registered and eligible voters of Guam endorsed a draft Guam Commonwealth Act that would establish a new framework for relations between the Territory and the administering Power, providing for a greater measure of internal self-government for Guam and recognition of the right of the Chamorro people of Guam to self-determination for the Territory,

Recalling also the requests by the elected representatives and non-governmental organizations of the Territory that Guam not be removed from the list of the Non-Self-Governing Territories with which the Special Committee is concerned, pending the self-determination of the Chamorro people and taking into account their legitimate rights and interests,

Aware that negotiations between the administering Power and the territorial Government on the draft Guam Commonwealth Act are no longer continuing and that Guam has established the process for a self-determination vote by the eligible Chamorro voters,

Cognizant that the administering Power continues to implement its programme of transferring surplus federal land to the Government of Guam,

Noting that the people of the Territory have called for reform in the programme of the administering Power with respect to the thorough, unconditional and expeditious transfer of land property to the people of Guam,

Conscious that immigration into Guam has resulted in the indigenous Chamorros becoming a minority in their homeland,

Aware of the potential for diversifying and developing the economy of Guam through commercial fishing and agriculture and other viable activities,

Recalling the dispatch in 1979 of a United Nations visiting mission to the Territory, and noting the recommendation of the 1996 Pacific regional seminar for sending a visiting mission to Guam,

1. *Calls upon* the administering Power to take into consideration the expressed will of the Chamorro people as supported by Guam voters in the plebiscite of 1987 and as provided for in Guam law, encourages the administering Power and the territorial Government of Guam to enter into negotiations on the matter, and requests the administering Power to inform the Secretary-General of progress to that end;

2. *Requests* the administering Power to continue to assist the elected territorial Government in achieving its political, economic and social goals;

3. *Also requests* the administering Power, in cooperation with the territorial Government, to continue to transfer land to the original landowners of the Territory;

4. *Further requests* the administering Power to continue to recognize and respect the political rights and the cultural and ethnic identity of the Chamorro people of Guam, and to take all necessary measures to re-

spond to the concerns of the territorial Government with regard to the question of immigration;

5. *Requests* the administering Power to cooperate in establishing programmes specifically intended to promote the sustainable development of economic activities and enterprises, noting the special role of the Chamorro people in the development of Guam;

6. *Also requests* the administering Power to continue to support appropriate measures by the territorial Government aimed at promoting growth in commercial fishing and agricultural and other viable activities;

VII

Montserrat

Taking note with interest of the statements made and the information on the political and economic situation in Montserrat provided by the Chief Minister of the Territory to the Caribbean regional seminar, held at The Valley, Anguilla, from 20 to 22 May 2003,

Noting with concern the dire consequences of the volcanic eruption, which led to the evacuation of three quarters of the Territory's population to safe areas of the island and to areas outside the Territory, in particular Antigua and Barbuda and the United Kingdom of Great Britain and Northern Ireland, and which continues to have enduring consequences for the economy of the island,

Welcoming the continued assistance provided to the Territory by States members of the Caribbean Community, in particular Antigua and Barbuda, which has offered safe refuge and access to educational and health facilities, as well as employment for thousands who have left the Territory,

Noting the continuing efforts of the administering Power to deal with the consequences of the volcanic eruption,

Noting with concern that a number of the inhabitants of the Territory continue to live in shelters because of volcanic activity,

Taking note of the constitutional review process led by the territorial Government,

1. *Calls upon* the administering Power, the specialized agencies and other organizations of the United Nations system, as well as regional and other organizations, to continue to provide assistance to the Territory in alleviating the consequences of the volcanic eruption;

2. *Welcomes* the continuing constitutional review process led by the Government of Montserrat in cooperation with the administering Power;

VIII

Pitcairn

Taking into account the unique nature of Pitcairn in terms of population and area,

Welcoming the participation of a representative of the Mayor of Pitcairn in the Pacific regional seminar, held in Madang, Papua New Guinea, from 18 to 20 May 2004, and taking note of the positive developments in the Territory,

Requests the administering Power to continue its assistance for the improvement of the economic, social, educational and other conditions of the population of the Territory and to continue its discussions with the representatives of Pitcairn on how best to support their economic security;

IX

Saint Helena

Taking into account the unique character of Saint Helena, its population and its natural resources,

Taking note of the constitutional review process led by the territorial Government,

Aware of the efforts of the administering Power and the territorial authorities to improve the socio-economic conditions of the population of Saint Helena, in particular in the sphere of food production, continuing high unemployment and limited transport and communications,

Noting with concern the problem of unemployment on the island and the joint action of the administering Power and the territorial Government to deal with it,

1. *Welcomes* the continuing constitutional review process led by the Government of Saint Helena in cooperation with the administering Power;

2. *Requests* the administering Power and relevant international organizations to continue to support the efforts of the territorial Government to address the socio-economic development challenges, including the high unemployment and the limited transport and communications problems;

X

Turks and Caicos Islands

Noting the results of the general elections held in April 2003,

Noting with concern the vulnerability of the Territory to drug trafficking and related activities, as well as its problems caused by illegal immigration and the need for continued cooperation between the administering Power and the territorial Government in countering drug trafficking and money-laundering,

Taking note of the constitutional review process led by the territorial Government,

Welcomes the continuing constitutional review process led by the Government of the Turks and Caicos Islands in cooperation with the administering Power;

XI

United States Virgin Islands

Noting the continuing interest of the territorial Government in seeking associate membership in the Organization of Eastern Caribbean States and observer status in the Caribbean Community and the pending request by the Territory to the administering Power for the delegation of authority to proceed, as well as the 2003 resolution of the territorial legislature in support of that request,

Noting also the necessity of further diversifying the economy of the Territory,

Noting further the efforts of the Government of the Territory to promote the Territory as an offshore financial services centre,

Recalling that the Territory has not received a United Nations visiting mission since 1977, and bearing in mind the formal request of the Territory for such a mission in 1993 to assist the Territory in its political education process and to observe the Territory's only referendum on political status options in its history,

Noting the ongoing cooperation between the territorial Government and Denmark on the exchange of artefacts and archives,

1. *Requests* the administering Power to continue to assist the territorial Government in achieving its political, economic and social goals;

2. *Once again requests* the administering Power to facilitate the participation of the Territory, as appropriate, in various organizations, in particular the Organization of Eastern Caribbean States, the Caribbean Community and the Association of Caribbean States;

3. *Calls for* the inclusion of the Territory in regional programmes of the United Nations Development Programme, consistent with the participation of other Non-Self-Governing Territories;

4. *Notes* the economic difficulties being experienced by the territorial Government and the fiscal austerity measures being implemented, and others proposed, to relieve the Territory's cash flow shortage, and calls upon the administering Power to continue to provide every assistance required by the Territory to further alleviate the difficult economic situation, including, inter alia, the provision of debt relief and loans;

5. *Notes also* the position of the territorial Government, including its articulation in resolution 1609 of 9 April 2001 of the 24th Legislature of the United States Virgin Islands, opposing the assumption by the administering Power of submerged land in territorial waters, having regard to relevant resolutions of the General Assembly on the ownership and control of natural resources, including marine resources, by the people of the Non-Self-Governing Territories, and its calls for the return of those marine resources within its jurisdiction.

Information

UN public information

The General Assembly's Committee on Information, at its twenty-sixth session (New York, 26 April–7 May) [A/59/21], continued to consider UN information policies and activities and to evaluate and follow up efforts made and progress achieved in information and communications. The major report before the Committee dealt with the reorientation of UN activities in public information and communications. Other reports covered the rationalization of the network of UN information centres (UNICs), modernization and integrated management of UN libraries and in-depth review of library activities, the activities of the United Nations Communications Group (UNCG), activities of the UN Department of Public Information (DPI) to publicize the Assembly's work and decisions, and the proposed 2006-2007 strategic framework for DPI.

Those reports and the Secretary-General's report on questions relating to information [A/59/221 & Corr.1] are discussed in the relevant sections below.

By **decision 59/518** of 10 December, the Assembly increased the Committee's membership from 102 to 107.

GENERAL ASSEMBLY ACTION

On 10 December [meeting 71], the General Assembly, on the recommendation of the Fourth Committee [A/59/473], adopted resolutions **59/126 A** and **B** without vote [agenda item 78].

Questions relating to information

A

Information in the service of humanity

The General Assembly,

Taking note of the comprehensive and important report of the Committee on Information,

Also taking note of the report of the Secretary-General on questions relating to information,

Urges all countries, organizations of the United Nations system as a whole and all others concerned, reaffirming their commitment to the principles of the Charter of the United Nations and to the principles of freedom of the press and freedom of information, as well as to those of the independence, pluralism and diversity of the media, deeply concerned by the disparities existing between developed and developing countries and the consequences of every kind arising from those disparities that affect the capability of the public, private or other media and individuals in developing countries to disseminate information and communicate their views and their cultural and ethical values through endogenous cultural production, as well as to ensure the diversity of sources and their free access to information, and recognizing the call in this context for what in the United Nations and at various international forums has been termed "a new world information and communication order, seen as an evolving and continuous process":

(a) To cooperate and interact with a view to reducing existing disparities in information flows at all levels by increasing assistance for the development of communication infrastructures and capabilities in developing countries, with due regard for their needs and the priorities attached to such areas by those countries, and in order to enable them and the public, private or other media in developing countries to develop their own information and communication policies freely and independently and increase the participation of media and individuals in the communication process, and to ensure a free flow of information at all levels;

(b) To ensure for journalists the free and effective performance of their professional tasks and condemn resolutely all attacks against them;

(c) To provide support for the continuation and strengthening of practical training programmes for broadcasters and journalists from public, private and other media in developing countries;

(d) To enhance regional efforts and cooperation among developing countries, as well as cooperation between developed and developing countries, to strengthen communication capacities and to improve the media infrastructure and communication technol-

ogy in the developing countries, especially in the areas of training and dissemination of information;

(*e*) To aim at, in addition to bilateral cooperation, providing all possible support and assistance to the developing countries and their media, public, private or other, with due regard to their interests and needs in the field of information and to action already adopted within the United Nations system, including:

(i) The development of the human and technical resources that are indispensable for the improvement of information and communication systems in developing countries and support for the continuation and strengthening of practical training programmes, such as those already operating under both public and private auspices throughout the developing world;

(ii) The creation of conditions that will enable developing countries and their media, public, private or other, to have, by using their national and regional resources, the communication technology suited to their national needs, as well as the necessary programme material, especially for radio and television broadcasting;

(iii) Assistance in establishing and promoting telecommunication links at the subregional, regional and interregional levels, especially among developing countries;

(iv) The facilitation, as appropriate, of access by the developing countries to advanced communication technology available on the open market;

(*f*) To provide full support for the International Programme for the Development of Communication of the United Nations Educational, Scientific and Cultural Organization, which should support both public and private media.

B

United Nations public information policies and activities

The General Assembly,

Reiterating its decision to consolidate the role of the Committee on Information as its main subsidiary body mandated to make recommendations to it relating to the work of the Department of Public Information of the Secretariat,

Concurring with the view of the Secretary-General that the fundamental premise underlying the reorientation efforts of the Department of Public Information remains General Assembly resolution 13(I) of 13 February 1946, establishing the Department, which states in paragraph 2 of annex I that "the activities of the Department should be so organized and directed as to promote to the greatest possible extent an informed understanding of the work and purposes of the United Nations among the peoples of the world",

Concurring also with the view of the Secretary-General that the contents of public information and communications should be placed at the heart of the strategic management of the United Nations and that a culture of communications should permeate all levels of the Organization, as a means of fully informing the peoples of the world of the aims and activities of the United Nations, in accordance with the purposes and principles enshrined in the Charter of the United Nations, in order to create broad-based global support for the United Nations,

Stressing that the primary mission of the Department of Public Information is to provide, through its outreach activities, accurate, impartial, comprehensive and timely information to the public on the tasks and responsibilities of the United Nations in order to strengthen international support for the activities of the Organization with the greatest transparency,

Noting that the comprehensive review of the work of the Department of Public Information, requested by the General Assembly in its resolution 56/253 of 24 December 2001, and the implementation of its second phase, described in the report of the Secretary-General on reorientation of United Nations activities in the field of public information and communications to the Committee on Information at its twenty-fifth session, as well as the report of the Secretary-General entitled "Strengthening of the United Nations: an agenda for further change", and Assembly resolutions 57/300 of 20 December 2002 and 58/101 B of 9 December 2003, as they apply to the Department of Public Information, provide an opportunity to take further steps to rationalize the work of the Department in order to enhance its efficiency and effectiveness, and to maximize the use of its resources,

Expressing its concern that the gap in the information and communication technologies between the developed and the developing countries has continued to widen and that vast segments of the population in developing countries are not benefiting from the present information and technology revolution, and, in this regard, underlining the necessity of rectifying the imbalances of the global information and technology revolution in order to make it more just, equitable and effective,

Recognizing that developments in the information and communication technology revolution open vast new opportunities for economic growth and social development and can play an important role in the eradication of poverty in developing countries, and, at the same time, emphasizing that the revolution also poses challenges and risks and could lead to the further widening of disparities between and within countries,

Recalling its resolution 56/262 of 15 February 2002 on multilingualism, and emphasizing the importance of making appropriate use of the official languages of the United Nations in the activities of the Department of Public Information, aiming to eliminate the disparity between the use of English and the five other official languages,

Welcoming Saint Vincent and the Grenadines, Suriname and Switzerland to membership in the Committee on Information,

I

Introduction

1. *Reaffirms* its resolution 13(I), in which it established the Department of Public Information, and all other relevant General Assembly resolutions related to the activities of the Department;

2. *Calls upon* the Secretary-General, in respect of the public information policies and activities of the United Nations, to continue to implement fully the recommendations contained in paragraph 2 of General Assembly resolution 48/44 B of 10 December 1993 and other mandates as established by the Assembly;

3. *Notes* that the medium-term plan for the period 2002-2005 continues to serve as a guideline that sets out the overall orientation of the public information programme for the Organization's goals through effective communication, and recalls its resolution 58/269 of 23 December 2003, entitled "Strengthening of the United Nations: an agenda for further change", in which it requested the Secretary-General to prepare, on a trial basis, for submission to the General Assembly at its fifty-ninth session, a strategic framework to replace the current four-year medium-term plan;

4. *Reaffirms* that the United Nations remains the indispensable foundation of a peaceful and just world and that its voice must be heard in a clear and effective manner, and emphasizes the essential role of the Department of Public Information in this context;

5. *Stresses* the importance of clear and timely provision of information by the Secretariat to Member States, upon their request, within the framework of existing mandates and procedures, and encourages the Department of Public Information to continue to do so;

6. *Reaffirms* the central role of the Committee on Information in United Nations public information policies and activities, including the restructuring process of the Department of Public Information, and the prioritization of its activities, and welcomes the continued constructive interaction between the Department and the members of the Committee;

7. *Calls upon* Member States to ensure, to the extent possible, that recommendations relating to the programme of the Department of Public Information originate and are considered in the Committee on Information;

8. *Requests* the Department of Public Information, following the priorities laid down by the General Assembly in the medium-term plan and using the United Nations Millennium Declaration as its guide, to pay particular attention to such major issues as the eradication of poverty, conflict prevention, sustainable development, human rights, the human immunodeficiency virus/acquired immunodeficiency syndrome (HIV/AIDS) epidemic, combating terrorism in all its forms and manifestations and the needs of the African continent;

9. *Also requests* the Department of Public Information to pay attention to all major issues addressed in the United Nations Millennium Declaration and the Millennium Development Goals in carrying out its activities;

10. *Concurs* with the Secretary-General on the need to enhance the technological infrastructure of the Department of Public Information in order to widen its outreach and improve the United Nations web site;

11. *Recognizes* the important work carried out by the United Nations Educational, Scientific and Cultural Organization and its collaboration with news agencies and broadcasting organizations in developing countries in disseminating information on priority issues, and encourages a continued collaboration between the Department of Public Information and the United Nations Educational, Scientific and Cultural Organization in the promotion of culture and in the fields of education and communication;

II

General activities of the Department of Public Information

12. *Notes* the proposals and actions of the Secretary-General to improve the effective and targeted delivery of public information activities, including the restructuring of the Department of Public Information, in accordance with the relevant resolutions and decisions of the General Assembly, and requests the Secretary-General to report to the Committee on Information in this regard at its twenty-seventh session;

13. *Reaffirms* that the Department of Public Information is the focal point for information policies of the United Nations and the primary news centre for information about the United Nations, its activities and those of the Secretary-General, and encourages a closer integration of functions between the Department and the office providing spokesman services for the Secretary-General;

14. *Welcomes* the recommendations of the Department of Public Information for developing a communications strategy to publicize the work and decisions of the General Assembly, encourages the Department to establish a closer working relationship with the Office of the President of the General Assembly, and requests the Secretary-General to report further on the progress achieved in, and the remaining challenges to, the implementation of those recommendations to the Committee on Information at its twenty-seventh session;

15. *Emphasizes* the central role of the Committee on Information in making recommendations to the General Assembly on the mandate of the Department of Public Information, takes note of the reorientation exercise in enhancing the performance and effectiveness of the Department, which should be in accordance with the mandates established by the Assembly, and requests the Secretary-General to report on progress achieved in this regard to the Committee at its twenty-seventh session;

16. *Requests* the Secretary-General, in the context of the reorientation process, to continue to exert all efforts to ensure that publications and other information services of the Secretariat, including the United Nations web site and the United Nations News Service, contain comprehensive, objective and equitable information about the issues before the Organization and that they maintain editorial independence, impartiality, accuracy and full consistency with resolutions and decisions of the General Assembly;

17. *Reiterates* that all printed materials of the Department of Public Information, in accordance with existing mandates, should not duplicate other publications of the United Nations system and should be produced in a cost-effective manner;

18. *Welcomes* the reconstitution of the Publications Board, in accordance with existing legislative mandates, by the Department of Public Information;

19. *Urges* the Department of Public Information to continue to exhibit transparency to the greatest extent possible, so as to increase awareness of the impact of its programmes and activities;

20. *Emphasizes* that, through its reorientation, the Department of Public Information should maintain and improve its activities in the areas of special interest

to developing countries and, where appropriate, other countries with special needs, including countries in transition, and that such reorientation contributes to bridging the existing gap between the developing and the developed countries in the crucial field of public information and communications;

21. *Encourages* the Secretary-General to strengthen the coordination between the Department of Public Information and other departments of the Secretariat, including the designation of focal points to work with substantive departments, in the context of its client-oriented approach, to identify target audiences and develop information programmes and media strategies for priority issues, and emphasizes that public information capacities and activities in other departments should function under the guidance of the Department;

22. *Welcomes* the initiatives that have been taken by the Department of Public Information to strengthen the public information system of the United Nations, and, in this regard, stresses the importance of a coherent and results-oriented approach being taken by the United Nations, the specialized agencies and the programmes and funds of the United Nations system involved in public information activities, as well as the provision of resources for their implementation, and that feedback from Member States on the relevance and effectiveness of its programme delivery should be taken into account;

23. *Appreciates* the continued efforts of the Department of Public Information in issuing daily press releases, and requests the Department to continue providing this invaluable service to both Member States and representatives of the media, while considering possible means of improving their production process and streamlining their format, structure and length, keeping in mind the views of Member States;

24. *Requests* that during the deliberations on the item entitled "Questions relating to information" in the Special Political and Decolonization Committee (Fourth Committee) during the successive regular sessions of the General Assembly, an informal interaction between the Secretariat and members of the Fourth Committee take place after the presentation by the Under-Secretary-General for Communications and Public Information on the substance of that oral briefing, within existing resources;

Multilingualism and public information

25. *Welcomes* the ongoing efforts of the Department of Public Information to enhance multilingualism in its activities, and encourages the Department to continue its endeavours in this regard;

26. *Emphasizes* the importance of ensuring the full, equitable treatment of all the official languages of the United Nations in all activities of the Department of Public Information, and stresses the importance of fully implementing its resolution 52/214 of 22 December 1997, in section C of which it requested the Secretary-General to ensure that the texts of all new public documents, in all six official languages, and information materials of the United Nations are made available daily through the United Nations web site and are accessible to Member States without delay;

27. *Recognizes* the fact that the integration of the Official Document System with the United Nations web site, scheduled to take place during the fourth

quarter of 2004, will significantly enhance the multilingual nature of the site by providing free, public access to all United Nations parliamentary documents in the six official languages;

28. *Reaffirms its request* to the Secretary-General to ensure that the Department of Public Information has appropriate staffing capacity in all official languages of the United Nations to undertake all its activities;

29. *Reminds* the Secretary-General of the need to include in future programme budget proposals for the Department of Public Information the importance of using all six official languages in its activities;

Bridging the digital divide

30. *Welcomes* the holding of the Geneva phase of the World Summit on the Information Society from 10 to 12 December 2003, and looks forward to the second phase, to be held in Tunis from 16 to 18 November 2005;

31. *Calls upon* the Department of Public Information to contribute to raising the awareness of the international community of the importance of the World Summit on the Information Society and the need to join efforts to make it a success;

32. *Recalls* paragraph 32 of its resolution 58/101 B, welcomes the contribution of the Department of Public Information in publicizing the efforts of the Secretary-General to close the digital divide as a means of spurring economic growth and as a response to the continuing gulf between developed and developing countries, and, in this context, requests the Department to further enhance its role;

III

New programmatic priorities for the Department of Public Information

33. *Takes note* of the note by the Secretary-General on the proposed strategic framework for the period 2006-2007 concerning the programmatic aspects for the Department of Public Information;

34. *Notes* that the proposed strategic framework does not include the first part;

35. *Notes also* that the executive direction and management elements of the programme, as well as the details of performance measures (baselines and targets), external factors and outputs, together with resource requirements, will be reflected in the proposed programme budget for the biennium 2006-2007;

36. *Stresses* the need to include in the proposed programme budget for the biennium 2006-2007, to the fullest extent possible, quantifiable and verifiable indicators for measuring expected accomplishments, so as to give a clear indication of the progress towards the accomplishment of objectives set;

37. *Also stresses* the importance of full compliance with all legislative mandates when preparing the proposed programme budget for the biennium 2006-2007;

38. *Recommends* that, in the last sentence of paragraph 1 in the Overall orientation section in the annex to the note by the Secretary-General on the proposed strategic framework for the period 2006-2007, the words "in particular, the legislative mandates included in the present biennial programme plan, as well as those of" be inserted after the words "General Assembly" and the word "and" be deleted;

39. *Acknowledges* that the Department of Public Information, with the assistance of the Office of Internal

Oversight Services of the Secretariat, has developed an annual programme impact review to systematically evaluate its products and activities and that, as an initial step in a three-year project between the Department and the Office, the first annual programme impact review was completed in January 2004, as requested by the General Assembly in its resolution 57/300 of 20 December 2002, and requests the Secretary-General to report further on the progress made to the Committee on Information at its twenty-seventh session;

40. *Reaffirms* that the Department of Public Information must prioritize its work programme while respecting existing mandates and in line with regulation 5.6 of the Regulations and Rules Governing Programme Planning, the Programme Aspects of the Budget, the Monitoring of Implementation and the Methods of Evaluation, to focus its message and concentrate its efforts better and, as a function of performance management, to match its programmes with the needs of its target audiences, on the basis of improved feedback and evaluation mechanisms;

United Nations information centres

41. *Reaffirms* paragraph 15 of its resolution 57/300, in which it took note of the proposal of the Secretary-General contained in action 8 of his report, to rationalize the network of United Nations information centres around regional hubs, where appropriate, in consultation with concerned Member States, starting with the creation of a Western European hub, followed by a similar approach in other high-cost developed countries, and requests the Secretary-General to submit a progress report on the implementation of the proposal with the objective of applying this initiative in other regions, in consultation with Member States, where this initiative will strengthen the flow and exchange of information in developing countries;

42. *Welcomes* the agreement between the Department of Public Information and the Western European countries to establish a regional United Nations information centre in Brussels;

43. *Takes note* of the report of the Secretary-General on the rationalization of the network of United Nations information centres, stresses that the report could not, at the time it was written, fully address all aspects of the implementation of the rationalization of United Nations information centres in Western Europe and other high-cost developed countries, and, in this regard, requests the Secretary-General to report in detail to the Committee on Information at its twenty-seventh session;

44. *Stresses* that the United Nations information centres and services and information components or regional hubs, as applicable, should play a significant role in disseminating information about the work of the Organization to the peoples of the world, including in the areas outlined in the United Nations Millennium Declaration, and emphasizes that the information centres, or regional hubs, as applicable, as the "field voice" of the Department of Public Information, should promote public awareness of and mobilize support for the work of the United Nations at the local level, bearing in mind that information in the local languages has the strongest impact on the local populations;

45. *Also stresses* the importance of taking into account the special needs and requirements of developing countries in the field of information and communications technology for the effective flow of information in those countries;

46. *Affirms* that the measures highlighted and objectives expressed in paragraphs 41 to 45 above are central to future rationalization of United Nations information centres, which must be carried out in consultation, on a case-by-case basis, with all concerned Member States in which existing information centres are located, the countries served by those information centres and other interested countries in the region, taking into consideration the distinctive characteristics of each region;

47. *Requests* the Secretariat, within the framework of the rationalization process, to extend the services of the United Nations information centres and regional United Nations information centres, where applicable, to those Member States currently outside the scope of the field information capacity of the Department of Public Information;

48. *Requests* the Secretary-General, within the framework of the rationalization process, to take into account the needs of Portuguese-speaking African countries and the offer made by the Government of Angola;

49. *Recalls* paragraph 39 of its resolution 58/270 of 23 December 2003, and welcomes, in this context, the ongoing efforts of the Department of Public Information to review the allocation of both staff and financial resources to the United Nations information centres with a view to transferring resources from information centres in developed countries to United Nations information activities in developing countries, emphasizing the needs of the least developed countries, and to any other activities of high priority, such as multilingualism on the web site and evaluation of services, in consultation with Member States concerned;

50. *Encourages* United Nations information centres and regional United Nations information centres, as applicable, to develop web pages in local languages, also encourages the Department of Public Information to provide resources and technical facilities, in particular to those information centres whose web pages are not yet operational, and further encourages host countries to respond to the needs of the information centres;

51. *Recalls* the appeal made by the Secretary-General to host countries of United Nations information centres to facilitate the work of the centres in their countries by providing rent-free or rent-subsidized premises, while taking into account the economic condition of the host countries and bearing in mind that such support should not be a substitute for the full allocation of financial resources for the information centres in the context of the programme budget of the United Nations;

52. *Notes* the continuing support of the Department of Public Information in the consolidation of the United Nations field presences into United Nations houses, and requests the Secretary-General to report in detail on the progress made to the Committee on Information at its twenty-seventh session;

53. *Requests* the Secretary-General to continue to submit progress reports on the implementation of the rationalization process to the Committee on Information at its successive sessions and to include in these re-

ports information on the functioning of the Department's field capacity, including newly established regional United Nations information centres, where applicable, and United Nations information centres that have undergone the rationalization process;

IV

Strategic communications services

54. *Notes* paragraph 6 of the report of the Secretary-General on the continuing reorientation of United Nations activities in the field of public information and communications, and, in this context, reaffirms that the Department of Public Information is the principal department responsible for the implementation of information strategies, as mandated;

55. *Affirms* the role of the strategic communications services in devising and disseminating United Nations messages by developing communications strategies, in close collaboration with the substantive departments, United Nations funds and programmes and the specialized agencies, in full compliance with the legislative mandates;

Promotional campaigns

56. *Recognizes* that promotional campaigns aimed at supporting special sessions and international conferences of the United Nations are part of the core responsibility of the Department of Public Information, and welcomes the efforts of the Department to examine creative ways in which it can organize and implement these campaigns in partnership with the substantive departments concerned, using the United Nations Millennium Declaration as its guide;

57. *Supports* the efforts of the Department of Public Information, while ensuring respect for the priorities established by the General Assembly, to also focus its promotional campaigns on the major issues identified by the Secretary-General;

58. *Appreciates* the work of the Department of Public Information in promoting, through its campaigns, issues of importance to the international community, such as sustainable development, children, HIV/AIDS, malaria and other diseases and decolonization, as well as the dialogue among civilizations, culture of peace and tolerance and the consequences of the Chernobyl disaster, and encourages the Department, in cooperation with the countries concerned and with the relevant organizations and bodies of the United Nations system, to continue to take appropriate measures to enhance world public awareness of these and other important global issues;

59. *Encourages* the Department of Public Information to continue to work within the United Nations Communications Group to coordinate the implementation of communication strategies with the heads of information of the agencies, funds and programmes of the United Nations system, and requests the Secretary-General to report to the Committee on Information at successive sessions on the activities of the Group;

60. *Stresses* the need for the renewed emphasis in support of Africa's development, in particular by the Department of Public Information, in order to promote awareness in the international community of the nature of the critical economic and social situation in Africa and of the priorities of the New Partnership for Africa's Development;

Role of the Department of Public Information in United Nations peacekeeping

61. *Commends* the efforts of the Secretary-General to strengthen the public information capacity of the Department of Public Information for the establishment and functioning of the information components of peacekeeping operations and of political and peace-building missions of the United Nations, including its promotional efforts and other information support activities, and requests the Secretariat to continue to ensure the involvement of the Department from the planning stage of future operations through interdepartmental consultations and coordination with other departments of the Secretariat, in particular with the Department of Peacekeeping Operations;

62. *Stresses* the importance of enhancing the public information capacity of the Department of Public Information in the field of peacekeeping operations and its role in the selection process of spokespersons for United Nations peacekeeping operations or missions, and, in this regard, encourages the Department to second spokespersons who have the necessary skills to fulfil the tasks of the operations or missions, taking into account the principle of equitable geographical distribution in accordance with Chapter XV, Article 101, paragraph 3, of the Charter of the United Nations, and to consider views expressed, especially by host countries, when appropriate, in this regard;

63. *Welcomes* the actions taken by the Department of Public Information to increase its involvement in the planning stage of new or expanding peacekeeping operations, as well as the deployment of public information components in new missions, and also welcomes the improvements made to the peacekeeping portal on the United Nations web site;

64. *Encourages* the Department of Public Information to continue its efforts in supporting the peacekeeping missions to further develop their web sites;

65. *Regrets* the information gap between the new realities and successes of peacekeeping operations, especially multidimensional and complex ones, and the public perceptions, as stated by the Secretary-General in his report on the implementation of the recommendations of the Special Committee on Peacekeeping Operations, and stresses the need for a comprehensive public information strategy on peacekeeping operations, undertaken in close coordination with other relevant departments, in order to overcome this gap and ensure a positive public impact;

66. *Emphasizes* the need for interdepartmental cooperation between the Department of Peacekeeping Operations and the Department of Public Information in order to develop the strategy requested in paragraph 65 above;

67. *Requests* the Secretary-General to continue to report to the Committee on Information at its successive sessions on the role of the Department of Public Information in United Nations peacekeeping;

Role of the Department of Public Information in strengthening dialogue among civilizations and the culture of peace as means of enhancing understanding among nations

68. *Recalls* its resolutions 53/22 of 4 November 1998 and 55/23 of 13 November 2000 on the United Nations Year of Dialogue among Civilizations, 52/15

of 20 November 1997, by which it proclaimed 2000 the International Year for the Culture of Peace, 53/25 of 10 November 1998, by which it proclaimed the period 2001-2010 the International Decade for a Culture of Peace and Non-Violence for the Children of the World, and 56/6 of 9 November 2001 on the Global Agenda for Dialogue among Civilizations, encourages the Department of Public Information to provide the necessary support, within existing resources, for the dissemination of information pertaining to dialogue among civilizations and the culture of peace and to take due steps in fostering the culture of dialogue among civilizations via all mass media, such as the Internet, print, radio and television, and requests the Secretary-General to submit a report in this regard to the Committee on Information at its twenty-seventh session;

V

News services

69. *Stresses* that the central objective of the news services, implemented by the News and Media Division, is the timely delivery of accurate, objective and balanced news and information emanating from the United Nations system in all four mass media—print, radio, television and Internet—to the media and other audiences worldwide with the overall emphasis on multilingualism;

Traditional means of communication

70. *Also stresses* that radio remains one of the most cost-effective and far-reaching traditional media available to the Department of Public Information and an important instrument in United Nations activities, including development and peacekeeping, with a view to achieving a broad client base around the world;

71. *Notes* that the international radio broadcasting capacity for the United Nations has been made an integral part of the activities of the Department of Public Information, and requests the Secretary-General to make every effort to ensure its success and to report on its activities to the Committee on Information at its twenty-seventh session;

72. *Requests* the Secretary-General to pay full attention to the parity of the six official languages in expanding the international radio broadcasting capacity;

73. *Notes* the efforts being made by the Department of Public Information to disseminate programmes directly to broadcasting stations all over the world in the six official languages, with the addition of Portuguese, as well as in other languages, where possible, and, in this regard, stresses the need for impartiality and objectivity concerning information activities of the United Nations;

74. *Encourages* the Department of Public Information to continue building partnerships with local, national and regional broadcasters to extend the United Nations message to all the corners of the world in an accurate and impartial way;

75. *Emphasizes* that the United Nations Radio and Television Service should take full advantage of the technological infrastructure made available in recent years, including satellite platforms, information and communication technologies and the Internet, and requests the Secretary-General, as a part of the reorientation of the Department of Public Information, to

consider a global strategy for broadcasting, taking into account existing technologies;

United Nations web site

76. *Reiterates its appreciation* for the efforts of the Department of Public Information in creating a high-quality, user-friendly and cost-effective web site, noting that this is especially noteworthy considering the scope of the undertaking, the budget constraints within the United Nations and the remarkably rapid expansion of the World Wide Web, and reaffirms that the web site remains a very useful tool for the media, non-governmental organizations, educational institutions, Member States and the general public;

77. *Stresses* the need for the Department of Public Information to take further necessary measures to ensure accessibility to the United Nations web site by persons with disabilities, including visual and hearing disabilities, calls upon the Department, as a first step, to make further efforts for all new and revised pages to adhere to the obligatory level of compliance with recognized industry standards regarding such accessibility and, within existing resources, to work towards compliance with all other levels of such standards, and requests the Secretary-General to report to the Committee on Information at its twenty-seventh session on progress made in this regard;

78. *Notes* that the multilingual development and enrichment of the United Nations web site has improved, although at a slower rate than expected owing to several constraints that need to be addressed, and, in this regard, encourages the Department of Public Information, in coordination with content-providing offices, to improve the actions undertaken to achieve parity among the six official languages on the United Nations web site;

79. *Stresses* the need to adopt a decision on the multilingual development, maintenance and enrichment of the United Nations web site, considering, inter alia, the possibility of organizational restructuring towards separate language units for each of the six official languages within the Department of Public Information, in order to achieve full parity among the official languages of the United Nations;

80. *Reaffirms its request* to the Secretary-General to ensure, until such a decision has been taken and implemented, to the extent possible and while maintaining an up-to-date and accurate web site, the equitable distribution of financial and human resources within the Department of Public Information allocated to the United Nations web site among all official languages on a continuous basis, and to make every possible effort to ensure also that all materials contained on the web site that do not change and do not need regular maintenance are made available in all six official languages;

81. *Reaffirms* the need to achieve full parity among the six official languages on the United Nations web sites, and, in this regard, takes note of the proposal of the Secretary-General to translate all English materials and databases posted on the United Nations web sites by the respective content-providing offices of the Secretariat into all official languages, and reiterates its request to the Secretary-General to report to the Committee on Information at its twenty-seventh session on

the most practical, efficient and cost-effective means of implementing this proposal;

82. *Requests* the Secretary-General to include in his report to the Committee on Information at its twenty-seventh session proposals relating to the designation of a date by which all supporting arrangements would be in place for the implementation of this concept, after which date parity would continue, as well as proposals relating to the exemption from translation of specific items on the United Nations web site;

83. *Stresses* the importance of access for the public to the United Nations Treaty Collection and United Nations parliamentary documentation;

84. *Encourages* the Department of Public Information to implement an e-mail service to inform subscribers of recent additions to the United Nations web site;

85. *Encourages* the Secretary-General, through the Department of Public Information, to continue to take full advantage of recent developments in information technology in order to improve, in a cost-effective manner, the expeditious dissemination of information on the United Nations, in accordance with the priorities established by the General Assembly and taking into account the linguistic diversity of the Organization;

86. *Notes* the gap among different official languages on United Nations web sites, and recognizes that some official languages use non-Latin and bidirectional scripts;

87. *Recognizes* that technological infrastructures and supportive applications in the United Nations are based on Latin script, which leads to difficulties in processing non-Latin and bidirectional scripts, and encourages the Department of Public Information to continue its efforts, to the extent possible, to ensure that technological infrastructures and supportive applications in the United Nations fully support Latin, non-Latin and bidirectional scripts so as to enhance the equality of all official languages on the United Nations web site;

88. *Notes with satisfaction* that access to the Official Document System of the United Nations will be provided free to the public by the end of 2004, and requests the Secretary-General to report on progress to the Committee on Information at its twenty-seventh session;

89. *Commends* the Information Technology Services Division of the Office of Central Support Services of the Secretariat on its efforts to ensure that the required technological infrastructure is in place to accommodate the linkage of the Official Document System to the United Nations web site, and also commends the Department of Public Information for addressing issues of content management relating to that System;

90. *Takes note* of paragraph 56 of its resolution 58/270, in which it reaffirmed that the Official Document System of the United Nations, as an archival and retrieval system of official documents, should cover the entire Organization, and requests the Secretary-General to transmit the report requested in this regard to the Committee on Information at its twenty-seventh session;

91. *Welcomes* the electronic mail-based United Nations News Service, distributed worldwide through e-mail by the Department of Public Information, and requests the Department to provide this service in all official languages, ensuring that news-breaking stories and news alerts are accurate, impartial and free of bias;

92. *Also welcomes* the inclusion of news e-mail services in the English and French languages and the Secretary-General's intention to include the other official languages in these services by 2004;

93. *Calls upon* the Secretary-General to continue to work within the United Nations System Chief Executives Board for Coordination and other appropriate inter-agency bodies to establish a United Nations portal, an inter-agency search facility encompassing the public web sites of all United Nations system organizations, and requests the Secretary-General to report on this matter to the Committee on Information at its twenty-seventh session;

94. *Reiterates its request* to the Department of Public Information to encourage all United Nations system entities to participate in the United Nations system search pilot project, and requests the Secretary-General to report to the Committee on Information at its twenty-seventh session on the activities of the High-Level Committee on Management in this regard;

95. *Reaffirms* paragraph 42 of its resolution 58/270, in which it requested the Secretary-General to strengthen the web site through further redeployment to the required language posts;

VI

Library services

96. *Welcomes* the progress reported by the Secretary-General in his report on the modernization and integrated management of United Nations libraries and in-depth review of library activities, in particular the efforts to fill gaps in the Official Document System of the United Nations, establish common standards for indexing, cataloguing and collection development, produce a common list of serials, eliminate duplication in the acquisition of electronic information, create joint web pages and assess the needs of the smaller libraries of the Organization;

97. *Also welcomes* the creation of the Steering Committee for the Modernization and Integrated Management of United Nations Libraries, and commends the Steering Committee for its coordinating role and initial organizational efforts and for reaching agreement on an impressive programme of work;

98. *Acknowledges* that the Dag Hammarskjöld Library, as part of the Outreach Division of the Department of Public Information, endeavours to facilitate access to timely and up-to-date library products and services for use by delegates, permanent missions of Member States, the Secretariat, researchers and depository libraries worldwide, notes the continuing efforts of the Secretary-General to make the Library a virtual library with world outreach, reiterates the need to enable the provision of hard copies to Member States, subject to the relevant provisions of its resolution 57/283 B of 15 April 2003, and also notes the efforts of the Secretary-General to enrich, on a multilingual basis, the stock of books and journals in the Library, including publications on peace and security and development-related issues, in order to ensure that the Library continues to be a broadly accessible resource for information about the United Nations and its activities;

99. *Calls upon* the Department of Public Information to continue to lead the Steering Committee, encourages the member libraries of the Steering Committee to coordinate closely and to establish time frames for fulfilment of its programme of work, and requests the Secretary-General to report to the Committee on Information at its successive sessions on the activities of the Dag Hammarskjöld Library and the work of the Steering Committee;

100. *Takes note* of paragraph 50 of its resolution 58/270, in which it requested the Secretary-General to conduct, through the Office of Internal Oversight Services, a review of the operation and management of United Nations libraries, with a view to assessing staffing requirements for those libraries in the light of technological advances in the delivery of information services, and to report thereon to the General Assembly at its fifty-ninth session, and requests the Secretary-General to transmit that report to the Committee on Information at its twenty-seventh session;

101. *Recognizes* the importance of the depository libraries in disseminating information and knowledge about United Nations activities, and, in this connection, urges the Dag Hammarskjöld Library, in its capacity as the focal point, to take the initiatives necessary to strengthen such libraries by providing regional training and other assistance;

102. *Notes* the holding of training courses conducted by the Dag Hammarskjöld Library for the representatives of Member States and Secretariat staff on the use of Cyberseek, web search, the Intranet, United Nations documentation, United Nations Info Quest and the Official Document System of the United Nations;

103. *Recalls* paragraph 44 of its resolution 56/64 B of 24 December 2001, in which it welcomed the role of the Department of Public Information in fostering increased collaboration among libraries of the United Nations system, particularly in establishing one central system-wide online catalogue that would allow for the searching of the bibliographic records of all print holdings of all United Nations system libraries, commends the International Computing Centre for developing the United Nations System Shared Cataloguing and Public Access System, which provides a single point of access to library catalogues, indexes and abstract databases, library holdings, links to full-text resources and archives, also commends the Department for its role in the development of the United Nations System Shared Cataloguing and Public Access System, requests the Department to encourage all United Nations system organizations to participate in the System, and requests the Secretary-General to report to the Committee on Information at its twenty-seventh session in this regard;

104. *Notes with appreciation* the operation of a common library in Nairobi within existing resources, in line with the approach set out in paragraph 37 of the Secretary-General's report on the modernization and integrated management of United Nations libraries and in-depth review of library activities, and urges all United Nations offices in Nairobi to participate in and support this venture;

VII

Outreach services

105. *Acknowledges* that the outreach services, implemented by the Outreach Division of the Department of Public Information, continue to work towards promoting awareness of the role and work of the United Nations on priority issues;

106. *Notes* the importance of the continued implementation by the Department of Public Information of the ongoing programme for broadcasters and journalists from developing countries and countries in transition, as mandated by the General Assembly, and encourages the Department to consider how best to maximize the benefits derived from the programme by reviewing, inter alia, its duration and the number of its participants;

107. *Recognizes* the need for the Department of Public Information to increase its outreach services in all regions, and reiterates the need to include, in the reorientation of United Nations activities in the field of public information and communications, an analysis of the present reach and scope of the activities of the Department, identifying the widest possible spectrum of audiences and geographical areas that are not covered adequately and that may require special attention, including the appropriate means of communication and bearing in mind local language requirements;

108. *Welcomes* the movement towards educational outreach and the orientation of the *UN Chronicle*, both print and online editions, to this end;

109. *Calls upon* the Department of Public Information to strengthen its role as a focal point for two-way interaction with civil society relating to the priorities and concerns of the Organization;

110. *Congratulates* the United Nations Correspondents Association on its Dag Hammarskjöld Memorial Scholarship Fund, which sponsors journalists from developing countries to come to the United Nations Headquarters and report on the activities during the General Assembly, and urges donors to extend financial support to the Fund so that it may increase the number of such scholarships to journalists in this context;

111. *Notes* that the sixtieth anniversary of the founding of the United Nations will be observed in 2005, and requests the Department of Public Information to take necessary measures to publicize the occasion in every way possible, stressing the purposes and principles enshrined in the Charter of the United Nations and highlighting the accomplishments of the Organization in the past six decades;

VIII

Final remarks

112. *Requests* the Secretary-General to report to the Committee on Information at its twenty-seventh session and to the General Assembly at its sixtieth session on the activities of the Department of Public Information and on the implementation of the recommendations contained in the present resolution;

113. *Requests* the Committee on Information to report to the General Assembly at its sixtieth session;

114. *Decides* to include in the provisional agenda of its sixtieth session the item entitled "Questions relating to information".

Reorientation of information and communications activities

In response to General Assembly resolution 58/101 B [YUN 2003, p. 623], the Secretary-General submitted a February report to the Committee on Information [A/AC.198/2004/2] detailing the steps taken since his previous report [YUN 2003, p. 630] towards the continuing reorientation of DPI.

DPI introduced the concept of the Secretariat departments as clients, identifying their own priorities, and DPI as service provider, working along clear guidelines provided by the departments. The client-consultation process was led by the Strategic Communications Division, created in 2003 [ibid.]. To facilitate that process, each client department was assigned to one of the four sections within the Division's Communications Campaign Service. Formal working arrangements had been established with 24 clients, and more than 30 strategies were prepared. Eighteen reports on the effectiveness of those strategies were sent to the client departments, seeking their feedback.

DPI strengthened its efforts to bring UN system members within a common communications framework, with UNCG being key to that objective. In terms of system-wide coordination, UNIC heads had become full-fledged members of UN country teams in developing countries and countries with economies in transition, and chaired or co-chaired nearly 80 per cent of the theme groups on public information and communications in the field. Cooperation with the country team had been further strengthened with the implementation of the recommendation of the Office of Internal Oversight Services (OIOS) that all field offices should produce annual work plans. Eighty-four per cent of UNICs submitted new work plans in 2003, containing client department information strategies aimed at giving field offices strategic guidance on UN priorities and helping them to focus their outreach activities. The rationalization of the UNIC network around regional hubs, an important element in the DPI reorientation process, started with the creation of a Western European hub, the Regional United Nations Information Centre in Brussels, Belgium, which began operations in 1 January. (For further information on UNIC regionalization, see p. 628.)

In response to Assembly resolutions 57/300 [YUN 2002, p. 1353] and 58/101 B [YUN 2003, p. 623], DPI, with OIOS support, developed an annual programme impact review of its products and services, the first of which was completed in January as an initial step in the three-year DPI/OIOS project. The review first sought to establish baseline data to track future performance. By the end of 2003, DPI had formulated 170 performance indicators. Over 30 performance indicators were designed to help link DPI's products and ac-

tivities more precisely to the needs of target audiences through user feedback. Evaluation results would also be used by programme managers to direct the reallocation of resources based on programme performance. In recognition of DPI's efforts, the United Nations Foundation (see p. 892) established an award for the best research on the effectiveness and impact of UN public information and communications activities.

In continuing efforts to meet new communications challenges, including those resulting from the situation in Iraq (see p. 339) and UN strategic priorities, DPI undertook issue-specific communications campaigns and reached out to the public and the media in the Arab world, including through the designation of a focal point for Arab media.

DPI's support for peacekeeping focused on helping deploy public information components in new missions, including the development of their communications strategies and alignment of their work with strategic goals. It was building a strategy to publicize new peacekeeping activities, particularly in Africa, in order to garner support among key decision makers, in particular with regard to troop contributions and other assistance. DPI had also made a concerted effort to publicize UN counter-terrorism measures (see p. 76).

The Secretary-General described DPI's efforts to reach out to the media, build partnerships with the public and, led by the Dag Hammarskjöld Library, manage information and respond to the growing needs of delegations, Secretariat staff, scholars, depository libraries and the general public for library services. (For information on UN libraries, see p. 626.)

The report concluded that the reorientation and restructuring of DPI had helped the United Nations to move closer to achieving a key goal of the Secretary-General's reform proposals, namely, enhancing public information [YUN 2002, p. 1352]. A clearer conception of the Department's role and a more coherent elaboration of its functions had been established. With its activities aligned with its overall priorities, a more effective client consultation mechanism in place and system-wide coordination at all levels, DPI was better equipped to achieve its mandate. DPI sought to revitalize public confidence in the Organization by bringing the United Nations closer to the people.

DPI activities

In response to General Assembly resolution 58/101 B [YUN 2003, p. 623], the Secretary-General submitted an August report [A/59/221 & Corr.1] covering DPI's activities from July 2003 to June 2004 and the implementation of the resolution's recommendations. The report also included an overview of DPI's continuing efforts to promote and refine a culture of evaluation and performance management.

The Department's activities were organized within its four subprogrammes: strategic communications services, news services, library services and outreach services. A March note submitted by the Secretary-General to the Committee on Information [A/AC.198/2004/7] set out the proposed 2006-2007 strategic framework for DPI under programme 24, public information, covering the four subprogrammes.

Building international support for the most vulnerable countries remained a priority for DPI, and the Department worked to publicize the situation of least developed countries and other economic and social development issues. DPI, with the Millennium Campaign Office, strategized a system-wide effort to promote and boost implementation of the UN Millennium Development Goals [YUN 2000, p. 51], in preparation for the high-level Assembly event on the outcome of the 2000 Millennium Summit in September 2005. The situation in Africa and its needs continued to be a major focus of the Department's news-gathering and reporting activities.

During the year, DPI continued to initiate and coordinate multimedia activities on human rights, and assisted the UNIC network in promoting the commemoration of the tenth anniversary of the Rwanda genocide (see p. 159). It increased interdepartmental collaboration and production of targeted information materials on decolonization and maintained its focus on the question of Palestine.

Guided by the priorities of the UN Department of Peacekeeping Operations (DPKO), a major client department, DPI emphasized UN peacekeeping operations worldwide (see p. 81). It conducted assessment missions to plan for the public information aspects of UN operations in Côte d'Ivoire, Haiti and Liberia, and composed budgets, staffing tables and operational concepts for the information components of missions in those countries, as well as in Burundi, Iraq and the Sudan. A week-long training programme for 25 public information officers, organized with DPKO (Brindisi, Italy, June), focused on how to deploy full public information components during a mission's initial phase. DPI also placed special emphasis on promoting UN counter-terrorism work, convening an interdepartmental/inter-agency group to prepare a system-wide communications strategy to coordinate with and complement the revitalized Counter-Terrorism Committee (see p. 76). It continued to work

closely with the Department for Disarmament Affairs to promote disarmament-related issues on the UN agenda. It also worked to explain and promote the UN political and humanitarian roles in Iraq.

DPI introduced a new electronic multimedia production system to streamline the work of its radio and photo services for more efficient delivery of radio programmes and photographs. United Nations Television continued to provide coverage of meetings, press conferences and special events at Headquarters. During the year, DPI expanded considerably its co-production efforts with major television broadcasters worldwide. As to United Nations Radio, the Assembly, in **resolution 59/277 A** (see p. 1381) of 23 December, approved the regular budget funding for the live radio project for the 2004-2005 biennium.

The UN web site had become a premier tool for reaching target audiences, including the media, non-governmental organizations (NGOs), academia and people worldwide. An ever-increasing number of visitors was using the official language sites, but the overall level of resources for the web site section would continue to constrain the pace of progress towards full parity across all languages. DPI was encouraging and assisting other Secretariat departments to make their information materials available on the web site in all official languages, and it expanded its partnership with the academic community worldwide to translate information materials. In an important step towards linguistic parity, DPI made the UN News Centre online portal and the associated UN News Service available in all official languages, and was working to further enhance the Centre's English and French e-mail service and to make it available in other official languages. Webcasts of General Assembly and Security Council meetings, daily press briefings, most press conferences and other public events were provided. The technical guidelines on web-site development issued by the Working Group on Internet Matters were being revised to incorporate requirements for access to the site by users with disabilities.

DPI continued to provide an intensive information programme for NGOs. During the year, it associated 62 new NGOs and disassociated 77 organizations that no longer met the criteria for association, bringing the total number of associated NGOs to 1,501 as at July 2004.

DPI offered information and activities for students of all ages, including through the Cyber-schoolbus web site of its Global Learning and Teaching Project, which was aimed at school-age children. The *UN Chronicle* strengthened its targeting of educators and institutions of higher education by featuring thematic clusters that could also be used as part of curricula. The UN Chronicle Feature Service continued to redisseminate, through UNICs, articles from eminent contributors to newspapers and magazines worldwide.

Library services

As at June 2004, there were 396 active UN depository libraries. During the period under review, 11 libraries converted from paper to electronic deposit, increasing the total number of electronic deposit recipients to 127. The Dag Hammarskjöld Library (DHL) conducted more than 100 training sessions for some 800 trainees, including Secretariat staff, mission personnel, government officials, interns, NGO representatives, depository librarians and visitors. It continued to expand its web-based services in the six official languages, the most significant change being the creation of automated daily updated linkages to all of the documentation of the Official Document System for all language versions. The Library set up focal points for the multilingual United Nations Bibliographic Information System (UNBIS) thesaurus in offices away from Headquarters to encourage their staff's participation in thesaurus development and to ensure that the terminology remained relevant to users. It brought high-quality commercial information resources to the desktops of official users. Acquisition of those services was coordinated by the United Nations System Electronic Information Acquisitions Consortium.

The Steering Committee for the Modernization and Integrated Management of United Nations Libraries, established in 2003 [YUN 2003, p. 635] and chaired by DPI, held five meetings from January 2003 to June 2004, covering a variety of technical and organizational issues. The Committee completed several initiatives, including the online UNBIS reference manuals and guides to cataloguing and indexing standards, which were made available on the UN Intranet. The Committee encouraged support for the creation of a common library in Nairobi, resulting in the redesignation of the United Nations Environment Programme Library—renamed the Sergio Vieira de Mello Library in June—as a common library for the United Nations Office at Nairobi.

Management of UN libraries

In response to General Assembly resolution 56/253 [YUN 2001, p. 1297], the Secretary-General submitted a February report to the Committee on Information on the modernization and integrated management of UN libraries and in-depth review of library activities [A/AC.198/

2004/4]. It provided background information on the mission of DHL and other UN libraries and on library services for permanent missions and Secretariat departments, the depository library system, reference services of UNICs and the relationship among the various UN libraries.

The survey indicated that services to departments, permanent missions and other clients could be improved or enhanced by launching regular electronic alerts of new information sources, services and acquisitions; increasing purchases of monographs and some serials on subjects related to substantive work; increasing specialized online services; disseminating information selectively from online databases; and increasing technical cooperation with departments in cataloguing, digitization and other areas.

Regarding the relationship among DHL, UNICs and depository libraries, the survey found that, despite the achievements of individual libraries, UN libraries had been operating independently, with limited coordination or common direction and costly modernization being undertaken by each library. While the Internet and other communication technologies provided opportunities for greater synergy and integration among UN libraries, closer coordination might allow them to share knowledge more effectively, promote knowledge sharing within the Secretariat, provide better library services to delegates and staff, enhance multilingualism, achieve greater outreach to the public and contribute to bridging the digital divide in Member States. Although better coordination would lead to some savings, a significant investment would be required to enhance online services and create a more electronic environment. The survey made clear that cooperation between Headquarters and the field and among the libraries at the various duty stations could be improved and identified areas of further collaboration.

The report provided information on recent achievements of the Steering Committee for the Modernization and Integrated Management of United Nations Libraries in all major areas of library activity, including an initial research gateway web page in the six official languages; a common list of serial holdings; a manual for bibliographic description posted on the Intranet; and the identification of additional online services to be acquired through the United Nations System Electronic Information Acquisition Consortium. To serve library users more effectively, however, the member libraries and the Steering Committee needed to, among other efforts, increase print acquisitions; substantially increase access to commercial online services; promote the acquisition of software to permit the generation of automatic electronic alerts from databases; and hold regional training courses for depository librarians, videoconferences and annual meetings of the Steering Committee. The objective was to move further in the direction of a virtual library network, with resources that could be shared across duty stations, while not neglecting the print resources required by local users.

At the inter-agency level, the Acquisition Consortium needed to be expanded to include a richer menu of products and services. The United Nations Libraries Shared Cataloguing and Public Access System should be expanded and re-engineered, and funding needed to be identified for that purpose.

The report recommended that UN libraries and those of the UN system agencies, working in concert, should bring their expertise in information management to bear in the development of knowledge-sharing initiatives.

OIOS report. Pursuant to resolution 58/270 [YUN 2003, p. 1399], the Secretary-General, in September, transmitted the OIOS report on the review of the operations and management of UN libraries [A/59/373]. The review assessed the staffing requirements for UN libraries in the light of technological advances in the delivery of information services, focusing on DHL and the Library of the United Nations Office at Geneva (UNOG Library), which together accounted for 75 per cent of UN library staff. OIOS also surveyed six other UN libraries. The report covered the organization and current levels of automation of UN libraries, additional automation needed for specific operations and staffing requirements in the light of advanced technologies. The draft report was discussed with DPI and UNOG Library officials, and their comments were included in the final report.

OIOS reported that an accurate assessment of the staffing requirements of UN libraries was not possible at the time of the review because the libraries had not fully adapted their operations to the use of advanced technologies and the Internet. DHL and the UNOG Library had implemented state-of-the-art automation systems and were providing electronic access to their bibliographic databases to users worldwide, but most of the other libraries generally lagged behind in introducing more advanced technology, owing to their small size and budgetary constraints. The review found that a comprehensive automation strategy that encouraged harmonization and resource-sharing would ensure quicker and more efficient implementation of advanced technology by the other UN system libraries.

The review also found that the weakness of the performance management systems impeded an assessment of the staffing requirements of UN libraries. Common workload and productivity standards and data for assessing staffing requirements were not properly developed, and there were large disparities in productivity levels between DHL and the UNOG Library, indicating the need for harmonization of working methods and performance management.

In the view of OIOS, the Steering Committee for the Modernization and Integrated Management of United Nations Libraries could be entrusted with the preparation of a new UN library policy. However, to achieve its goals, the Steering Committee needed to prepare a timetable of expected results in its action plan, supported by the necessary resources. The libraries of the UN specialized agencies should be invited to participate in the work of the Steering Committee in order to attain a more comprehensive modernization and integration of UN libraries.

The report concluded that the functioning of the Steering Committee could be made more effective, thereby strengthening cooperation among UN libraries. The use of advanced technology in the delivery of information services was limited by the number of documents available in electronic formats, and the transfer of the old catalogues and documents to those formats could be expedited through more robust project management. The full extent of those tasks should be accurately determined, a timetable and strategy for completing them formulated, and the amount of required resources determined and mobilized. A concrete and comprehensive automation strategy should be developed with specific goals in terms of improved services and the level of resources required. To support new DHL and UNOG Library strategies for delivering information services, the assessment of resource requirements should be based on realistic workload indicators for major library functions.

The Secretary-General, in his transmittal note, said that he concurred with the recommendations, which would contribute to more comprehensive cooperation among UN libraries and increased efficiency.

UN information centres

In line with the Secretary-General's reform plans [YUN 2002, p. 585], DPI took the first step to rationalize the network of information centres by closing nine offices in Western Europe and establishing the Regional United Nations Information Centre in Brussels on 1 January. The legacies of the closed centres were transferred to the new regional centre, enabling it to continue servicing its audiences in Western Europe.

During the year, the ability of UNICs to maintain outreach services and sustain regular activities was severely limited by the significant reduction in operational funds, resulting from the cut of $2 million from the 2004-2005 biennial budget by the General Assembly in resolution 58/270 [YUN 2003, p. 1399]. However, they continued to strengthen their partnerships with UN country teams. During the period under review, UNICs reported 170 instances of providing support to the country launches of major UN reports, and UNIC staff chaired or co-chaired more than 70 per cent of the theme groups on public information established by country teams. To further strengthen their partnership at the country level, DPI and the United Nations Development Programme (UNDP) consulted regularly at Headquarters, and resident coordinators were briefed by the Department when they visited Headquarters. DPI also resumed its participation in the inter-agency Working Group on Common Premises and Services, in order to play an active role in decisions taken in the field. UNICs continued to work intensively to brief media representatives and involve them in a dialogue on priority UN issues.

By **decision 58/564 B** of 8 April, the General Assembly decided to defer until its fifty-ninth (2004) session consideration of the 2003 OIOS report on the review of the structure and operations of UNICs [YUN 2003, p. 636].

Regionalization of UN information centres

Pursuant to General Assembly resolutions 57/300 [YUN 2002, p. 1353] and 58/101 B [YUN 2003, p. 623], the Secretary-General submitted to the Committee on Information a February report on the regionalization of the UNIC network [A/AC.198/2004/3]. The report detailed progress made in the implementation of the UNIC regionalization initiative in Western Europe [YUN 2003, p. 637] and in other high-cost developed countries, and set out the proposed strategy and modalities for implementation in other regions. It also followed up on the 2003 OIOS recommendations to streamline and revitalize UNIC operations [YUN 2003, p. 636]. An annex to the report contained information on UNICs and UN houses.

On 1 January, DPI established a regional UNIC in Brussels. The UN information services in Geneva and Vienna, which supported the UN Offices in those cities, were not affected. Under the terms of an agreement concluded with the Secretary-General, Belgium would provide rent-free premises to the centre and an annual cash contribution of $50,000 for the next four years for the translation of information materials into local languages. As the regional centre had only been in operation for two months at the time of the submission of the report, it was too early to evaluate the success of the regionalization initiative in Western Europe and its impact on DPI's work.

Reporting on the implementation of a similar approach in other high-cost developed countries, as requested in resolution 58/101 B, the Secretary-General said that DPI had successfully negotiated an agreement with Australia to relocate the UNIC in Sydney to rent-free premises in Canberra, thereby releasing funds for programme activities in the Pacific region, including seven developing countries, and enabling the centre to better fulfil its role as a regional information centre. As to the UNIC in Tokyo, DPI saw no advantage in changing the current arrangements in view of Japan's role in international affairs, including as a major donor, and its financial support to the centre. As the Secretariat considered the liaison work undertaken in the host country by the UNIC in Washington, D.C., to be vital, the Secretary-General intended to pursue other cost-saving measures, including a reduction in rented office space.

With regard to centres in countries with economies in transition, the Secretary-General said that the well-established UNIC in Moscow was a natural candidate to become a regional centre. In due course and after consultations with the Governments concerned, DPI expected to make proposals regarding the future of the UNICs in Bucharest, Romania; Prague, Czech Republic; Warsaw, Poland; and Ankara, Turkey.

An analysis of the situation of UNICs in other regions showed that the existing network of information centres could not, within available resources, meet the outreach challenges for which it was established and therefore needed to be reconfigured. Regionalization in developing countries would strengthen the flow and exchange of information and improve access to information on the United Nations for people not currently well served by the UNICs, without reducing service to countries that found the current arrangements satisfactory. To meet those objectives and to make the most effective use of scarce resources, the Secretary-General said that resources should be distributed on the basis of a new model that would include a number of strategically located regional hubs.

As a preliminary step towards implementation of the new model, DPI would use the three senior posts released with the establishment of the regional hub in Brussels to strengthen the capacity of UNICs in cities that were regional media hubs in the Middle East and Arab region (Cairo, Egypt), Latin America and the Caribbean (Mexico City) and Africa (Addis Ababa, Ethiopia), though further resources would be needed for the latter to function effectively. Pending consultations with Member States on further regionalization, those UNICs would not, for the time being, be formally designated as regional centres, but they would be asked to develop strategies for strengthening the UN regional information capacity and outreach programmes for their respective regions.

Under the new model, DPI proposed establishing regional information centres in key media hubs in developing countries, using the guidelines and criteria for the regionalization of UNICs, which were annexed to the Secretary-General's report. Unlike the Western European model, the developing country model would consist of a significant number of small hubs, located so as to ensure that distance and linguistic diversity did not inhibit their operation. UNICs in the regions covered by the hubs would, for the most part, be closed, but DPI's national information staff would remain in the country, working out of the offices of the resident coordinators, serving as an integral part of the country team. The proposed model would take full advantage of the resident coordinator infrastructure and allow collaboration with the United Nations Development Group. The regional hub would, among other duties, develop and implement region-wide communications campaigns and provide programme and administrative support to the national information staff. It was proposed that the model be applied to all the countries currently served by UNICs. Details concerning the division of responsibilities between the regional information centres and national information staff were provided in an annex to the report.

DPI intended to tailor the regionalization concept to the diverse geographic and cultural characteristics of each region. The Secretary-General's report provided preliminary proposals for the possible locations of regional centres in the League of Arab States region and in the Asian, Latin American and Caribbean, and African States regions.

Development of UN websites

The Secretary-General, responding to General Assembly resolution 58/270 [YUN 2003, p. 1399] and decision 57/579 [YUN 2002, p. 589], submitted a September report [A/59/336] on strengthening DPI, within existing capacity, to support and enhance the UN website in all official languages: status of implementation. The Secretary-General said that DPI was continuing to make all efforts to strengthen the UN website in all official languages, being mindful of the need to strike a balance between other mandated activities competing for re-

sources. Progress had been made through staff redeployment and other innovative measures to expand the volume of material in languages other than English, such as expanding the UN News Service web page into all official languages, undertaking major technological improvements to enhance productivity and facilitate the availability of materials in all official languages and putting into place other arrangements, such as agreements with universities for translations of information materials free of cost. Those efforts had resulted in a significant increase in the number of pages processed for posting in each of the languages. DPI was also facing expanded responsibilities and an increase in the workload required to ensure continued maintenance of the website, severely challenging its current resources. However, it was not in a position to redeploy more resources to meet that increasing challenge without adversely affecting other mandated programmes and activities.

The Advisory Committee on Administrative and Budgetary Questions (ACABQ), in November [A/59/558], recommended that the Assembly take note of the Secretary-General's report.

The Assembly, in section IX of **resolution 59/276** of 23 December (see p. 1383), took note of the Secretary-General's report and that of ACABQ, and requested the Secretary-General to submit proposals for strengthening the UN web site within the context of the 2006-2007 proposed programme budget.

UN Communications Group

The United Nations Communications Group (UNCG), established in 2002 [YUN 2002, p. 589], at its third annual meeting (Nairobi, Kenya, 24-25 June) [A/AC.198/2005/5], discussed information strategies to be adopted and tools to be used for their implementation in the evolving political and media environment. It agreed that one of the key communications challenges facing the UN system was drawing world attention to the many untold or underreported stories relating to the work of the United Nations, and that the Group should continue to be used as the common UN system platform for that purpose. An initiative launched by the Under-Secretary-General for Communications and Public Information on World Press Freedom Day 2004 (3 May)—"Top Ten Stories the World Should Hear More About"—was a useful tool that should be continued and strengthened.

With regard to Africa and the New Partnership for Africa's Development (NEPAD) (see p. 629), UNCG agreed that UN communicators should convey clear, simple and consistent messages that would help the African people to understand their responsibilities in shaping their future. It decided that a proposed advocacy and communications strategy being developed by the NEPAD secretariat and the UN Office of the Special Adviser on Africa would form the general framework for a common UN system communications strategy for NEPAD. The meeting considered a communications strategy for the Millennium Development Goals (MDGs) Campaign, which, it agreed, was to generate awareness and mobilization around the MDGs [YUN 2000, p. 51] globally and nationally, and build support for the 2005 follow-up to the outcome of the 2000 Millennium Summit [ibid., p. 47]. The Campaign should have a visual identity and common slogan, and a clearing house would be established within DPI to maintain a central list and calendar of UN system events and promotional initiatives. UNCG agreed to promote the Fifteenth International AIDS Conference in Bangkok (11-16 July) and other activities of the Global Media AIDS Initiative, which grew out of a meeting of high-level media executives and the Secretary-General (New York, 15 January). UNCG would introduce a new calendar of media events before the end of 2004. The UNCG Consultative Group for Expo 2005, to be held in Aichi, Japan, from 25 March to 25 September 2005, would remain the principal forum for consultation and coordination for the Expo. The Group agreed to examine ways to increase its contributions to the United Nations Non-Governmental Liaison Service and asked the Service to pursue alternative sources of funding.

The meeting agreed that global public opinion polls could serve to evaluate the impact of past UN communications efforts and that the work of the UNCG task force on public opinion surveys, led by UNDP, should be strengthened. It recommended that the task force contact internationally known pollsters, in addition to those that had already been approached, for pro bono surveys on UN-related questions. It also agreed to support the promotion of the United Nations Environment Programme International Photographic Competition on the Environment 2004-2005 and the Summit on a Mine-Free World (Nairobi, 29 November–3 December). Other decisions dealt with the development and adoption of common UN system guidelines on the use and distribution of UN photos, and media accreditation at UN meetings. UNCG agreed to hold its next annual meeting in Geneva in July 2005.

During its 2004 session, the Committee on Information [A/59/21] considered the Secretary-General's report on UNCG's 2003 activities [A/AC.198/2004/5].

Publicizing the work of the General Assembly

In response to General Assembly resolution 58/126 [YUN 2003, p. 1389], the Secretary-General, in a February report [A/AC.198/2004/6], described current DPI activities for publicizing the Assembly's work and decisions and presented recommendations for developing a communications strategy to further publicize the activities, addressing issues of staffing, the website of the Assembly President and media relations. The report called for a closer working relationship between the Office of the Assembly President and DPI.

Information and communications in the context of international security

In response to General Assembly resolution 58/32 [YUN 2003, p. 639], the Secretary-General, in a June report and later addendum [A/59/116 & Add.1], transmitted the views of 10 Member States on the general appreciation of the issues of information security; the definition of basic notions related to information security, including unauthorized interference with or misuse of information and telecommunication systems and information resources; and the context of relevant international concepts aimed at strengthening the security of global information and telecommunication systems. Pursuant to resolution 58/32, the Secretary-General appointed the Group of Governmental Experts on Developments in the Field of Information and Telecommunications in the Context of International Security to assist in a study of existing and potential threats in the sphere of information security and possible cooperative measures to address them. The Group held its first session in New York from 12 to 16 July; it would meet twice more in 2005 and submit a report to the sixtieth (2005) session of the Assembly.

GENERAL ASSEMBLY ACTION

On 3 December [meeting 66], the General Assembly, on the recommendation of the First (Disarmament and International Security) Committee [A/59/454], adopted **resolution 59/61** without vote [agenda item 60].

Developments in the field of information and telecommunications in the context of international security

The General Assembly,

Recalling its resolutions 53/70 of 4 December 1998, 54/49 of 1 December 1999, 55/28 of 20 November 2000, 56/19 of 29 November 2001, 57/53 of 22 November 2002 and 58/32 of 8 December 2003,

Recalling also its resolutions on the role of science and technology in the context of international security, in which, inter alia, it recognized that scientific and technological developments could have both civilian and military applications and that progress in science and technology for civilian applications needed to be maintained and encouraged,

Noting that considerable progress has been achieved in developing and applying the latest information technologies and means of telecommunication,

Affirming that it sees in this process the broadest positive opportunities for the further development of civilization, the expansion of opportunities for co-operation for the common good of all States, the enhancement of the creative potential of humankind and additional improvements in the circulation of information in the global community,

Recalling, in this connection, the approaches and principles outlined at the Information Society and Development Conference, held in Midrand, South Africa, from 13 to 15 May 1996,

Bearing in mind the results of the Ministerial Conference on Terrorism, held in Paris on 30 July 1996, and the recommendations that it made,

Noting that the dissemination and use of information technologies and means affect the interests of the entire international community and that optimum effectiveness is enhanced by broad international co-operation,

Expressing its concern that these technologies and means can potentially be used for purposes that are inconsistent with the objectives of maintaining international stability and security and may adversely affect the integrity of the infrastructure of States to the detriment of their security in both civil and military fields,

Considering that it is necessary to prevent the use of information resources or technologies for criminal or terrorist purposes,

Noting the contribution of those Member States that have submitted their assessments on issues of information security to the Secretary-General pursuant to paragraphs 1 to 3 of resolutions 53/70, 54/49, 55/28, 56/19, 57/53 and 58/32,

Taking note of the reports of the Secretary-General containing those assessments,

Welcoming the initiative taken by the Secretariat and the United Nations Institute for Disarmament Research in convening an international meeting of experts in Geneva in August 1999 on developments in the field of information and telecommunications in the context of international security, as well as its results,

Considering that the assessments of the Member States contained in the reports of the Secretary-General and the international meeting of experts have contributed to a better understanding of the substance of issues of international information security and related notions,

1. *Calls upon* Member States to promote further at multilateral levels the consideration of existing and potential threats in the field of information security, as well as possible measures to limit the threats emerging in this field, consistent with the need to preserve the free flow of information;

2. *Considers* that the purpose of such measures could be served through the examination of relevant international concepts aimed at strengthening the security of global information and telecommunications systems;

3. *Invites* all Member States to continue to inform the Secretary-General of their views and assessments on the following questions:

(*a*) General appreciation of the issues of information security;

(*b*) Definition of basic notions related to information security, including unauthorized interference with or misuse of information and telecommunications systems and information resources;

(*c*) The content of the concepts mentioned in paragraph 2 above;

4. *Notes with satisfaction* that the Secretary-General is considering existing and potential threats in the sphere of information security and possible cooperative measures to address them, and is conducting a study on the concepts referred to in paragraph 2 above, with the assistance of the group of governmental experts, established in 2004 pursuant to resolution 58/32, and will submit a report on the outcome of the study to the General Assembly at its sixtieth session;

5. *Also notes with satisfaction* that the group of governmental experts established by the Secretary-General held its first session from 12 to 16 July 2004 in New York and that it intends to convene two more sessions in 2005 to fulfil its mandate specified in resolution 58/32;

6. *Decides* to include in the provisional agenda of its sixtieth session the item entitled "Developments in the field of information and telecommunications in the context of international security".

Science and technology in international security and disarmament

On 3 December [meeting 66], the General Assembly, on the recommendation of the First Committee [A/59/455], adopted **resolution 59/62** by recorded vote (106-48-21) [agenda item 61].

Role of science and technology in the context of international security and disarmament

The General Assembly,

Recognizing that scientific and technological developments can have both civilian and military applications and that progress in science and technology for civilian applications needs to be maintained and encouraged,

Concerned that military applications of scientific and technological developments can contribute significantly to the improvement and upgrading of advanced weapons systems and, in particular, weapons of mass destruction,

Aware of the need to follow closely the scientific and technological developments that may have a negative impact on international security and disarmament, and to channel scientific and technological developments for beneficial purposes,

Cognizant that international transfers of dual-use as well as high-technology products, services and know-how for peaceful purposes are important for the economic and social development of States,

Also cognizant of the need to regulate such transfers of dual-use goods and technologies and high technology with military applications through multilaterally negotiated, universally applicable, non-discriminatory guidelines,

Expressing its concern about the growing proliferation of ad hoc and exclusive export control regimes and arrangements for dual-use goods and technologies, which tend to impede the economic and social development of developing countries,

Recalling that in the Final Document of the Thirteenth Conference of Heads of State or Government of Non-Aligned Countries, held in Kuala Lumpur from 20 to 25 February 2003, and in the Final Document of the Fourteenth Ministerial Conference of the Movement of Non-Aligned Countries, held in Durban, South Africa, from 17 to 19 August 2004, it was again noted with concern that undue restrictions on exports to developing countries of material, equipment and technology for peaceful purposes persisted,

Emphasizing that internationally negotiated guidelines for the transfer of high technology with military applications should take into account the legitimate defence requirements of all States and the requirements for the maintenance of international peace and security, while ensuring that access to high-technology products and services and know-how for peaceful purposes is not denied,

1. *Affirms* that scientific and technological progress should be used for the benefit of all mankind to promote the sustainable economic and social development of all States and to safeguard international security, and that international cooperation in the use of science and technology through the transfer and exchange of technological know-how for peaceful purposes should be promoted;

2. *Invites* Member States to undertake additional efforts to apply science and technology for disarmament-related purposes and to make disarmament-related technologies available to interested States;

3. *Urges* Member States to undertake multilateral negotiations with the participation of all interested States in order to establish universally acceptable, non-discriminatory guidelines for international transfers of dual-use goods and technologies and high technology with military applications;

4. *Encourages* United Nations bodies to contribute, within existing mandates, to promoting the application of science and technology for peaceful purposes;

5. *Decides* to include in the provisional agenda of its sixtieth session the item entitled "Role of science and technology in the context of international security and disarmament".

RECORDED VOTE ON RESOLUTION 59/62:

In favour: Afghanistan, Algeria, Angola, Antigua and Barbuda, Bahamas, Bahrain, Bangladesh, Barbados, Belize, Benin, Bhutan, Bolivia, Brazil, Brunei Darussalam, Burkina Faso, Burundi, Cambodia, Cameroon, Cape Verde, Central African Republic, China, Colombia, Comoros, Congo, Costa Rica, Côte d'Ivoire, Cuba, Democratic People's Republic of Korea, Djibouti, Dominican Republic, Ecuador, Egypt, El Salvador, Equatorial Guinea, Eritrea, Ethiopia, Fiji, Gabon, Gambia, Ghana, Grenada, Guatemala, Guinea-Bissau, Guyana, Honduras, India, Indonesia, Iran, Iraq, Jamaica, Jordan, Kenya, Kuwait, Lao People's Democratic Republic, Lebanon, Lesotho, Liberia, Libyan Arab Jamahiriya, Madagascar, Malaysia, Maldives, Mali, Mauritius, Mexico, Mongolia, Morocco, Mozambique, Myanmar, Namibia, Nepal, Nicaragua, Nigeria, Oman, Pakistan, Panama, Peru, Philippines, Qatar, Rwanda, Saint Kitts and Nevis, Saint Lucia, Saint Vincent and the Grenadines, Sao Tome and Principe, Saudi Arabia, Senegal, Sierra Leone, Singapore, Somalia, Sri Lanka, Sudan,

Suriname, Syrian Arab Republic, Thailand, Timor-Leste, Togo, Trinidad and Tobago, Tunisia, Turkmenistan, Tuvalu, Uganda, United Arab Emirates, Venezuela, Viet Nam, Yemen, Zambia, Zimbabwe.

Against: Albania, Andorra, Australia, Austria, Belgium, Bosnia and Herzegovina, Bulgaria, Canada, Croatia, Cyprus, Czech Republic, Denmark, Estonia, Finland, France, Germany, Greece, Hungary, Iceland, Ireland, Israel, Italy, Liechtenstein, Lithuania, Luxembourg, Malta, Micronesia, Monaco, Netherlands, New Zealand, Norway, Palau, Poland, Portugal, Republic of Korea, Republic of Moldova, Romania, San Marino, Serbia and Montenegro, Slovakia, Slovenia, Spain, Sweden, Switzerland, The former Yugoslav Republic of Macedonia, Turkey, United Kingdom, United States.

Abstaining: Argentina, Armenia, Azerbaijan, Belarus, Chile, Haiti, Japan, Kazakhstan, Kyrgyzstan, Marshall Islands, Nauru, Paraguay, Russian Federation, Samoa, South Africa, Tajikistan, Tonga, Ukraine, Uruguay, Uzbekistan, Vanuatu.

Peaceful uses of outer space

The Committee on the Peaceful Uses of Outer Space (Committee on Outer Space), at its forty-seventh session (Vienna, 2-11 June) [A/59/20], discussed ways to maintain outer space for peaceful purposes, the spin-off benefits of space technology, space and society, and space and water. It examined the implementation of the recommendations of the Third (1999) United Nations Conference on the Exploration and Peaceful Uses of Outer Space (UNISPACE III) [YUN 1999, p. 556], and reviewed the work of its two subcommittees, one dealing with scientific and technical issues (see p. 638) and the other with legal questions (see p. 641).

GENERAL ASSEMBLY ACTION

On 10 December [meeting 71], the General Assembly, on the recommendation of the Fourth Committee [A/59/469], adopted **resolution 59/116** without vote [agenda item 74].

International cooperation in the peaceful uses of outer space

The General Assembly,

Recalling its resolutions 51/122 of 13 December 1996, 54/68 of 6 December 1999 and 58/89 of 9 December 2003,

Deeply convinced of the common interest of mankind in promoting and expanding the exploration and use of outer space, as the province of all mankind, for peaceful purposes and in continuing efforts to extend to all States the benefits derived therefrom, and also of the importance of international cooperation in this field, for which the United Nations should continue to provide a focal point,

Reaffirming the importance of international cooperation in developing the rule of law, including the relevant norms of space law and their important role in international cooperation for the exploration and use of outer space for peaceful purposes, and of the widest possible adherence to international treaties that promote the peaceful uses of outer space in order to meet emerging new challenges, especially for developing countries,

Seriously concerned about the possibility of an arms race in outer space, and bearing in mind the importance of article IV of the Treaty on Principles Governing the Activities of States in the Exploration and Use of Outer Space, including the Moon and Other Celestial Bodies,

Recognizing that all States, in particular those with major space capabilities, should contribute actively to the goal of preventing an arms race in outer space as an essential condition for the promotion and strengthening of international cooperation in the exploration and use of outer space for peaceful purposes,

Considering that space debris is an issue of concern to all nations,

Noting the progress achieved in the further development of peaceful space exploration and applications as well as in various national and cooperative space projects, which contributes to international cooperation, and the importance of further developing the legal framework to strengthen international cooperation in this field,

Convinced of the importance of the recommendations in the resolution entitled "The Space Millennium: Vienna Declaration on Space and Human Development", adopted by the Third United Nations Conference on the Exploration and Peaceful Uses of Outer Space (UNISPACE III), held at Vienna from 19 to 30 July 1999, and the need to promote the use of space technology towards implementing the United Nations Millennium Declaration,

Convinced also that the use of space science and technology and their applications, in such areas as telemedicine, tele-education and disaster management, and environmental protection as well as other Earth observation applications, contribute to achieving the objectives of the global conferences of the United Nations that address various aspects of economic, social and cultural development, inter alia, poverty eradication,

Having considered the report of the Committee on the Peaceful Uses of Outer Space on the work of its forty-seventh session,

1. *Endorses* the report of the Committee on the Peaceful Uses of Outer Space on the work of its forty-seventh session;

2. *Urges* States that have not yet become parties to the international treaties governing the uses of outer space to give consideration to ratifying or acceding to those treaties as well as incorporating them in their national legislation;

3. *Notes* that, at its forty-third session, the Legal Subcommittee of the Committee on the Peaceful Uses of Outer Space continued its work, as mandated by the General Assembly in its resolution 58/89;

4. *Requests* the Secretary-General to send to the Ministers for Foreign Affairs of States that have not yet become parties to the above-mentioned international treaties, the letter and document, as endorsed by the Legal Subcommittee, encouraging their States to participate in those treaties, and to send a similar letter to intergovernmental organizations that have not yet declared their acceptance of the rights and obligations under those treaties;

5. *Endorses* the recommendation of the Committee that the Legal Subcommittee, at its forty-fourth session, taking into account the concerns of all countries, in particular those of developing countries:

(*a*) Consider the following as regular agenda items:
(i) General exchange of views;
(ii) Status and application of the five United Nations treaties on outer space;
(iii) Information on the activities of international organizations relating to space law;
(iv) Matters relating to:
    a. The definition and delimitation of outer space;
    b. The character and utilization of the geostationary orbit, including consideration of ways and means to ensure the rational and equitable use of the geostationary orbit without prejudice to the role of the International Telecommunication Union;

(*b*) Consider the following single issues/items for discussion:
(i) Review and possible revision of the Principles Relevant to the Use of Nuclear Power Sources in Outer Space;
(ii) Examination of the preliminary draft protocol on matters specific to space assets to the Convention on International Interests in Mobile Equipment, opened for signature at Cape Town, South Africa, on 16 November 2001:
    a. Considerations relating to the possibility of the United Nations serving as supervisory authority under the future protocol;
    b. Considerations relating to the relationship between the terms of the future protocol and the rights and obligations of States under the legal regime applicable to outer space;

(*c*) Consider the practice of States and international organizations in registering space objects in accordance with the work plan adopted by the Committee;

6. *Notes* that the Legal Subcommittee, at its forty-fourth session, will submit its proposals to the Committee for new items to be considered by the Subcommittee at its forty-fifth session in 2006;

7. *Also notes* that, in the context of paragraph 5 (*a*) (ii) above, the Legal Subcommittee at its forty-fourth session will reconvene its Working Group and review the need to extend the mandate of the Working Group beyond that session of the Subcommittee;

8. *Further notes* that, in the context of paragraph 5 (*a*) (iv) *a.* above, the Legal Subcommittee will reconvene its Working Group on the item only to consider matters relating to the definition and delimitation of outer space;

9. *Notes* that the Legal Subcommittee will reconvene its Working Group to consider the questions reflected in paragraphs 5 (*b*) (ii) *a.* and *b.* above separately;

10. *Endorses* the recommendation of the Legal Subcommittee, in the context of paragraph 5 (*b*) (ii) *a.* above, to establish an open-ended ad hoc working group to continue between the forty-third and forty-fourth sessions of the Subcommittee, the consideration of the question of the appropriateness of the United Nations acting as supervisory authority, and notes that the working group would prepare a report, including the text of a draft resolution, to be submitted to the Subcommittee for consideration at its forty-fourth session;

11. *Agrees* that, in the context of paragraph 5 (*c*) above, the Legal Subcommittee should establish a working group in accordance with the work plan adopted by the Committee;

12. Notes that the Scientific and Technical Sub-committee, at its forty-first session, continued its work as mandated by the General Assembly in its resolution 58/89;

13. *Endorses* the recommendation of the Committee that the Scientific and Technical Subcommittee, at its forty-second session, taking into account the concerns of all countries, in particular those of developing countries:

(a) Consider the following items:

(i) General exchange of views and introduction to reports submitted on national activities;

(ii) United Nations Programme on Space Applications;

(iii) Implementation of the recommendations of the Third United Nations Conference on the Exploration and Peaceful Uses of Outer Space (UNISPACE III);

(iv) Matters relating to remote-sensing of the Earth by satellite, including applications for developing countries and monitoring of the Earth's environment;

(b) Consider the following items in accordance with the work plans adopted by the Committee:

(i) Space debris;

(ii) Use of nuclear power sources in outer space;

(iii) Space-system-based telemedicine;

(iv) Near-Earth objects;

(v) Space-system-based disaster management support;

(c) Consider the following single issues/items for discussion:

(i) Examination of the physical nature and technical attributes of the geostationary orbit and its utilization and applications, including, inter alia, in the field of space communications, as well as other questions relating to developments in space communications, taking particular account of the needs and interests of developing countries;

(ii) Support to proclaim the year 2007 the International Geophysical and Heliophysical Year;

14. *Notes* that the Scientific and Technical Subcommittee at its forty-second session will submit its proposal to the Committee for a draft provisional agenda for the forty-third session of the Subcommittee, in 2006;

15. *Endorses* the recommendation of the Committee that the Committee on Space Research and the International Astronautical Federation, in liaison with member States, be invited to arrange a symposium to address high-resolution and hyperspectral satellite data integration for precision farming, environmental monitoring and possible new applications, with as wide a participation as possible, to be held during the first week of the forty-second session of the Scientific and Technical Subcommittee;

16. *Agrees* that, in the context of paragraphs 13 (a) (ii) and (iii) and 14 above, the Scientific and Technical Subcommittee at its forty-second session should reconvene the Working Group of the Whole;

17. *Also agrees* that, in the context of paragraph 13 (b) (i) above, the Scientific and Technical Subcommittee, at its forty-second session, should reconvene the Working Group on Space Debris to consider, as necessary, the proposals of the Inter-Agency Space Debris Coordination Committee on space debris mitigation and any related comments that might be received;

18. *Further agrees* that, in the context of paragraph 13 (b) (ii) above, the Scientific and Technical Subcommittee at its forty-second session, should reconvene its Working Group on the Use of Nuclear Power Sources in Outer Space;

19. *Endorses* the United Nations Programme on Space Applications for 2005, as proposed to the Committee by the Expert on Space Applications and endorsed by the Committee;

20. *Notes with satisfaction* that, in accordance with paragraph 30 of General Assembly resolution 50/27 of 6 December 1995, the African regional centres for space science and technology education, in the French language and in the English language, located in Morocco and Nigeria, respectively, as well as the Centre for Space Science and Technology Education in Asia and the Pacific and the Regional Centre for Space Science and Technology Education for Latin America and the Caribbean, continued their education programmes in 2004, that all the above regional centres have entered into an affiliation agreement with the Office for Outer Space Affairs of the Secretariat, and that the Office is providing technical support to the Government of Jordan for the establishment of the regional centre for space science and technology education for Western Asia;

21. *Welcomes* the memorandum of understanding between the Office for Outer Space Affairs of the Secretariat and the Pro Tempore Secretariat of the Fourth Space Conference of the Americas, under which the parties demonstrated their intention to collaborate in promoting and implementing joint activities, and invites the Pro Tempore Secretariat to inform the Committee of the work accomplished;

22. *Notes with satisfaction* that the Government of Ecuador is considering positively hosting the Fifth Space Conference of the Americas, to be held in Quito in the second half of 2005 or in 2006, and that the convening of the Conference will be in accordance with the desire of Member States in the Latin American and Caribbean region to institutionalize the Space Conference of the Americas;

23. *Also notes with satisfaction* that concerning the report on the review of the implementation of the recommendations of UNISPACE III, the Committee, at its forty-seventh session, approved the draft report of the Committee as finalized by the Working Group which was reconvened at that session to prepare the report, and submitted the report to the General Assembly for use in its review and appraisal of the implementation of the recommendations of UNISPACE III at its fifty-ninth session;

24. *Recommends* that more attention be paid and political support be provided to all matters relating to the protection and the preservation of the outer space environment, especially those potentially affecting the Earth's environment;

25. *Considers* that it is essential that Member States pay more attention to the problem of collisions of space objects, including those with nuclear power sources, with space debris, and other aspects of space debris, calls for the continuation of national research on this question, for the development of improved technology for the monitoring of space debris and for the compilation and dissemination of data on space debris, also considers that, to the extent possible, infor-

mation thereon should be provided to the Scientific and Technical Subcommittee, and agrees that international cooperation is needed to expand appropriate and affordable strategies to minimize the impact of space debris on future space missions;

26. *Urges* all States, in particular those with major space capabilities, to contribute actively to the goal of preventing an arms race in outer space as an essential condition for the promotion of international cooperation in the exploration and use of outer space for peaceful purposes;

27. *Emphasizes* the need to increase the benefits of space technology and its applications and to contribute to an orderly growth of space activities favourable to sustained economic growth and sustainable development in all countries, including mitigation of the consequences of disasters, in particular in the developing countries;

28. *Notes* that space science and technology and their applications could make important contributions to economic, social and cultural development and welfare as indicated in the resolution entitled "The Space Millennium: Vienna Declaration on Space and Human Development", notes with satisfaction the convening of a conference entitled "International Conference on Space and Water: Towards Sustainable Development and Human Security" in the context of the International Air and Space Fair, held at Santiago de Chile from 29 March to 4 April 2004, and also notes that the next Fair will be held in 2006;

29. *Notes with satisfaction* the convening of the International Seminar on Satellite Technology Applications in Communications and Remote Sensing in Tehran, Islamic Republic of Iran, in October 2004 in cooperation with the Inter-Islamic Network on Space Sciences and Technology;

30. *Agrees* that the benefits of space technology and its applications should be prominently brought to the attention of conferences organized within the United Nations system to address global issues relating to social, economic and cultural development and that the use of space technology should be promoted towards achieving the objectives of those conferences and implementing the United Nations Millennium Declaration;

31. *Notes with satisfaction* the increased efforts of the Committee and its Scientific and Technical Subcommittee as well as the Office for Outer Space Affairs and the Inter-Agency Meeting on Outer Space Activities to promote the use of space science and technology and their applications in carrying out actions recommended in the Plan of Implementation of the World Summit on Sustainable Development ("Johannesburg Plan of Implementation") and the joint initiative taken by the Committee and the Inter-Agency Meeting to compile a list of space-related initiatives and programmes that correspond to recommendations contained in the Johannesburg Plan of Implementation;

32. *Notes* that space technology could play a central role in disaster reduction and that both the Committee and its Scientific and Technical Subcommittee could contribute to the follow-up to the World Conference on Disaster Reduction to be held in Kobe, Japan, in January 2005;

33. *Urges* entities of the United Nations system, particularly those participating in the Inter-Agency Meeting on Outer Space Activities, to examine, in cooperation with the Committee, how space science and

technology and their applications could contribute to implementing the United Nations Millennium Declaration, particularly in the areas relating to, inter alia, food security and increasing opportunities for education;

34. *Invites* the Inter-Agency Meeting on Outer Space Activities to continue to contribute to the work of the Committee and to report to the Committee and its Scientific and Technical Subcommittee on the work conducted at its annual session;

35. *Requests* the Committee to continue to consider, as a matter of priority, ways and means of maintaining outer space for peaceful purposes and to report thereon to the General Assembly at its sixtieth session, and agrees that during its consideration of the matter, the Committee could consider ways to promote regional and interregional cooperation based on experiences stemming from the Space Conference of the Americas and the role space technology could play in the implementation of recommendations of the World Summit on Sustainable Development;

36. *Agrees* that the Committee should continue to consider a report on the activities of the International Satellite System for Search and Rescue as a part of its consideration of the United Nations Programme on Space Applications under the agenda item entitled "Report of the Scientific and Technical Subcommittee", and invites Member States to report on their activities regarding the System;

37. *Requests* the Committee to continue to consider, at its forty-eighth session, its agenda item entitled "Spin-off benefits of space technology: review of current status";

38. *Also requests* the Committee to continue to consider, at its forty-eighth session, its agenda item entitled "Space and society" under the special theme for the focus of discussions for the period 2004-2006 entitled "Space and education", in accordance with the work plan adopted by the Committee;

39. *Agrees* that the Committee should continue to consider, at its forty-eighth session, its agenda item entitled "Space and water" and urges entities of the United Nations system and invites other intergovernmental entities dealing with issues relating to the use and management of water resources as well as space agencies to contribute to the work of the Committee by, inter alia, sharing their experience in the use of space-related technology for water resources management;

40. *Also agrees* that a symposium on space and archaeology should be held during the forty-eighth session of the Committee;

41. *Notes* that in accordance with the agreement reached by the Committee at its forty-sixth session on the measures relating to the future composition of the bureaux of the Committee and its subsidiary bodies, on the basis of the measures relating to the working methods of the Committee and its subsidiary bodies, the Group of African States, the Group of Latin American and Caribbean States and the Group of Western European and Other States nominated their candidates for the offices of Second Vice-Chairman/Rapporteur of the Committee, Chairman of the Legal Subcommittee and Chairman of the Committee, respectively, for the period 2006-2007, at the forty-seventh session of the Committee, for its consideration;

42. *Urges* the Group of Asian States and the Group of Eastern European States to reach a consensus agree-

ment on their candidates for the offices of Chairman of the Scientific and Technical Subcommittee and the First Vice-Chairman of the Committee, respectively, before the forty-eighth session of the Committee;

43. *Agrees* that the Committee should reach agreement on all the officers of the bureaux of the Committee and its subsidiary bodies for the period 2006-2007 and that, for this purpose, the Committee should include in the agenda of its forty-eighth session an item on the composition of the bureaux of the Committee and its subsidiary bodies for that period;

44. *Decides* that the Libyan Arab Jamahiriya and Thailand shall become members of the Committee;

45. *Requests* the Committee to consider ways to improve participation in its work by member States and entities with observer status, with a view to agreeing on specific recommendations in that regard at its forty-eighth session;

46. *Notes* that each of the regional groups has responsibility to actively promote the participation in the work of the Committee and its subsidiary bodies of the member States of the Committee that are also members of the respective regional group, and agrees that the regional groups should consider this Committee-related matter among their members;

47. *Invites* the Inter-Agency Meeting on Outer Space Activities to consider at its twenty-fifth session, in 2005, the question of the enhancement of the participation of the entities of the United Nations system in the work of the Committee and its Subcommittees, and requests the Office for Outer Space Affairs, in its capacity as the secretariat of the Inter-Agency Meeting, to report to the Scientific and Technical Subcommittee and the Legal Subcommittee, at their sessions in 2005, on the outcome of the discussions of the Inter-Agency Meeting;

48. *Agrees* that the Legal Subcommittee should, at its forty-fourth session, address the level of participation of the entities having permanent observer status with the Committee and report to the Committee, at its forty-eighth session, on means of enhancing their participation in the work of the Legal Subcommittee;

49. *Urges* the Committee to expand the scope of international cooperation relating to the social, economic, ethical and human dimension in space science and technology applications;

50. *Requests* entities of the United Nations system and other international organizations to continue and, where appropriate, to enhance their cooperation with the Committee and to provide it with reports on the issues dealt with in the work of the Committee and its subsidiary bodies;

51. *Requests* the Committee to identify and consider new areas and mechanisms of international cooperation in the peaceful uses of outer space to strengthen multilateralism, in accordance with the preamble to the present resolution, and to submit a report to the General Assembly at its sixtieth session, including its views on which subjects should be studied in the future.

Implementation of UNISPACE III recommendations

In accordance with General Assembly resolution 58/89 [YUN 2003, p. 646], the Committee on Outer Space reconvened the working group established in 2002 [YUN 2002, p. 598] to prepare a report to enable the Assembly to review and appraise, at its fifty-ninth (2004) session, the implementation of the UNISPACE III recommendations and to consider further actions and initiatives. The Committee endorsed the working group's recommendations, which were annexed to the Committee's report [A/59/20], and approved the draft report on the implementation of the UNISPACE III recommendations as finalized by the working group.

The Committee noted that 9 of the 12 action teams established in 2001 [YUN 2001, p. 568] and 2003 [YUN 2003, p. 641] to initiate the process of implementing the UNISPACE III recommendations had submitted their final reports to the forty-first (2004) session of the Committee's Scientific and Technical Subcommittee (see p. 638), including the reports of the Action Teams for the Development of a Comprehensive Worldwide Environmental Monitoring Strategy [A/AC.105/C.1/L.275] and on Increasing Awareness [A/AC.105/L.252], and those of the Action Teams on the Management of Natural Resources and on Capacity-building, which were submitted to the Subcommittee as conference room papers. The Committee also noted that the Action Team on Near-Earth Objects and the Action Team on Knowledge-Sharing had reported on progress in their work. The Committee agreed that the action teams were a successful and innovative mechanism and the inputs received from them could guide the Committee's work. Some of the action teams could further define and implement action plans and inform the Scientific and Technical Subcommittee in 2005 accordingly.

Also in accordance with resolution 58/89, the Scientific and Technical Subcommittee reconvened the Working Group of the Whole to consider, among other issues, the implementation of the UNISPACE III recommendations.

Report of Committee on Outer Space. Pursuant to General Assembly resolutions 56/51 [YUN 2001, p. 571], 57/116 [YUN 2002, p. 602] and 58/90 [YUN 2003, p. 642], the Secretary-General, in July, transmitted to the Assembly the report of the Committee on Outer Space on the implementation of the UNISPACE III recommendations [A/59/174]. The report discussed the various mechanisms for implementing the recommendations, including revised agenda structures of the Scientific and Technical and Legal Subcommittees, the 2000 plan of action of the Office for Outer Space Affairs [YUN 2000, p. 584] and the establishment of action teams. It described progress made in implementing the recommendations in the Committee and its subsidiary bodies, through national and regional efforts, and by UN system entities, intergovernmental organizations and NGOs. The report also examined the synergies between implementation of the UNISPACE III recommendations and the results of the 2000 Millennium Summit [YUN 2000, p. 47], the 2002 World Summit on Sustainable Development [YUN 2002, p. 821], the first phase of the World Summit on the Information Society in 2003 [YUN 2003, p. 857] and other global initiatives, and assessed the implementation process.

The report presented a plan of action, which proposed further specific actions for implementing the UNISPACE III recommendations and identified entities to undertake some of those actions, as well as expected benefits. The proposed actions dealt with the use of space to support overarching global agendas for sustainable development, as well as specific agendas to meet human development needs at the global level; developing coordinated, global space capabilities; and capacity development.

Among the actions proposed was a study on the possibility of creating an international entity to coordinate and optimize the effectiveness of space-based services for use in disaster management. The study, to be prepared by an ad hoc expert group, should be completed for consideration by the Committee in 2005. The Committee agreed that the Office for Outer Space Affairs should coordinate the preparation of the study and called on Member States to provide support through voluntary contributions.

The Committee also proposed that Global Navigation Satellite System (GNSS) and augmentation providers should establish an international committee on GNSS for, among other things, optimizing compatibility and interoperability and providing training opportunities in GNSS, in particular in developing countries. Member States should provide support, including financial resources, to implement the World Meteorological Organization Space Programme and its Long-term Strategy, initiated by the fourteenth World Meteorological Conference in 2003 [YUN 2003, p. 1527]. The report also contained measures for strengthening the role of the Committee, its subcommittees and its secretariat in implementing the UNISPACE III recommendations. The Committee sought the endorsement and the participation of Member States in the activities recommended in its report.

Annexed to the report were summaries of the proposed actions, entities to carry out those actions and expected benefits.

GENERAL ASSEMBLY ACTION

On 20 October [meeting 37], the General Assembly adopted **resolution 59/2** [draft: A/59/L.4 & Add.1, orally revised] without vote [agenda item 23].

Review of the implementation of the recommendations of the Third United Nations Conference on the Exploration and Peaceful Uses of Outer Space

The General Assembly,

Recalling its resolutions 54/68 of 6 December 1999, 55/122 of 8 December 2000, 56/51 of 10 December 2001, 57/116 of 11 December 2002 and 58/90 of 9 December 2003, concerning the review and appraisal by the General Assembly at its fifty-ninth session of the implementation of the recommendations of the Third United Nations Conference on the Exploration and Peaceful Uses of Outer Space (UNISPACE III), held in Vienna from 19 to 30 July 1999,

Reaffirming the importance of international cooperation in increasing benefits of the exploration and use of outer space to enhance human development,

Stressing the importance of implementing the resolution adopted by UNISPACE III entitled "The Space Millennium: Vienna Declaration on Space and Human Development", which contains a strategy to address global challenges through the use of space science and technology and their applications,

Recalling the unique organizational aspects of UNISPACE III, which allowed for active contributions by non-governmental organizations, industry and youth to the outcome of UNISPACE III while organizing the Conference within existing resources,

Recognizing that responsibility for implementing the recommendations of UNISPACE III rests with Member States, the Office for Outer Space Affairs of the Secretariat, under the guidance of the Committee on the Peaceful Uses of Outer Space and its subsidiary bodies, intergovernmental organizations for multilateral cooperation and other entities with space-related activities, including non-governmental entities, and the young generation,

Having considered the report of the Committee on the Peaceful Uses of Outer Space on the review of the implementation of the recommendations of UNISPACE III,

Noting with interest that the structure of the agendas of the Scientific and Technical Subcommittee and Legal Subcommittee as revised by the Committee at its forty-second session, as well as the action teams established by the Committee at its forty-fifth and forty-seventh sessions, under voluntary leadership by Member States, served as unique mechanisms to revitalize the work of the Committee and its subsidiary bodies and to implement the recommendations of UNISPACE III,

Expressing its appreciation to the Member States and organizations that participated in the action teams, in particular to the chairpersons of the action teams,

Noting that the establishment of action teams to implement the recommendations of UNISPACE III could be considered by other bodies of the United Nations as a very useful mechanism for implementing results of other major conferences held within the United Nations system,

Noting with satisfaction that the implementation of the recommendations of UNISPACE III contributes to the implementation of the results of global conferences held within the United Nations system, in particular the Millennium Summit, the World Summit on Sustainable Development and the World Summit on the Information Society,

1. *Takes note with satisfaction* of the report of the Committee on the Peaceful Uses of Outer Space on

the review of the implementation of the recommendations of the Third United Nations Conference on the Exploration and Peaceful Uses of Outer Space (UNISPACE III);

2. *Expresses its appreciation* for the work conducted by the Committee and its subsidiary bodies as well as the Office for Outer Space Affairs in the five years since the holding of UNISPACE III to implement the recommendations of the Conference;

3. *Notes with appreciation* the work of the working group established by the Committee in preparing and finalizing the above-mentioned report;

4. *Endorses* the Plan of Action as proposed by the Committee in its report;

5. *Urges* all Governments, entities of the United Nations system as well as intergovernmental and non-governmental entities conducting space-related activities to carry out the actions contained in the Plan of Action, mentioned in paragraph 4 above, on a priority basis for the further implementation of the recommendations of UNISPACE III, in particular its resolution entitled "The Space Millennium: Vienna Declaration on Space and Human Development";

6. *Notes* that the Committee will implement some of the actions contained in the Plan of Action through the consideration of items of the agendas of the Committee or its subsidiary bodies and through those action teams that will continue their work as endorsed by the Committee;

7. *Requests* the Committee to examine the contributions that could be made by space science and technology and their applications to one or more of the issues selected by the Commission on Sustainable Development as a thematic cluster and to provide substantive inputs for consideration by the Commission;

8. *Also requests* the Committee to include items in the agendas of its future sessions, starting from its forty-ninth session, in 2006, to consider its contributions to the work of those entities that are responsible for convening United Nations conferences and/or for implementing their outcomes;

9. *Agrees* that a study should be conducted on the possibility of creating an international entity to provide for coordination and the means of realistically optimizing the effectiveness of space-based services for use in disaster management and that the study should be prepared by an ad hoc expert group, with experts to be provided by interested Member States and relevant international organizations, and requests the Committee to review progress in the work of the ad hoc expert group, at its forty-eighth session, in 2005;

10. *Calls upon* Member States to make contributions to the Trust Fund for the United Nations Programme on Space Applications before the end of 2004 for the purpose of preparing the study by the ad hoc expert group mentioned in paragraph 9 above;

11. *Invites* Global Navigation Satellite System (GNSS) and augmentation providers to consider establishing an international committee on GNSS as proposed in the Plan of Action in order to maximize the benefits of the use and applications of GNSS to support sustainable development;

12. *Encourages* Member States to provide support to implement the Space Programme of the World Meteorological Organization and its Long-term Strategy, as proposed in the Plan of Action, in order to expand international cooperation in meteorological satellite applications to enhance weather and climate forecasting;

13. *Requests* the Secretary-General to undertake necessary measures to strengthen the role of the Office for Outer Space Affairs in implementing the recommendations of UNISPACE III, particularly with a view to achieving the following objectives:

(a) Strengthening the capacity-building activities of the Office in space law by, inter alia, continuing to organize the series of workshops on space law and developing a model education curriculum for a short-term course on space law;

(b) Strengthening the technical advisory services of the Office to support the operational use of space technologies, in particular in response to actions called for in the Plan of Action;

(c) Requesting the Committee to undertake further implementation of UNISPACE III recommendations with a view to enhancing the capacity of developing countries to initiate space application programmes;

14. *Agrees* that the activities of the United Nations Programme on Space Applications should be clustered, to the extent feasible, to address a few priority themes to be selected by the Committee for each year;

15. *Also agrees* that the Office for Outer Space Affairs should review the activities that are included in the Plan of Action for implementation by the Office and submit its proposal to the Committee at its forty-eighth session, in 2005, on how those activities could be included in its programme of work;

16. *Requests* the Secretary-General to implement activities of the Office for Outer Space Affairs as contained in the Plan of Action and to ensure that those activities are included in the programme of work for the biennium 2006-2007;

17. *Encourages* all Member States and space-related intergovernmental and non-governmental entities to contribute to the Trust Fund for the United Nations Programme on Space Applications while allowing full flexibility for the Office for Outer Space Affairs to carry out the activities of the Programme in accordance with the priorities set by the Committee;

18. *Agrees* that the Committee should continue to consider, in its future sessions, starting with its forty-eighth session, the implementation of the recommendations of UNISPACE III until the Committee considers that concrete results are achieved.

Scientific and Technical Subcommittee

The Scientific and Technical Subcommittee of the Committee on Outer Space, at its forty-first session (Vienna, 16-27 February) [A/AC.105/823], considered the United Nations Programme on Space Applications and the implementation of the UNISPACE III recommendations. It also dealt with matters relating to the remote sensing of the Earth by satellite, including applications for developing countries and monitoring of the Earth's environment; space debris; the use of nuclear power sources in outer space; space-system-based telemedicine; the examination of the physical nature and technical attributes of the geostationary orbit and its utilization and applications; implementation of an integrated, space-based global natural disaster management system; and solar-terrestrial physics.

UN Programme on Space Applications

The United Nations Programme on Space Applications, as mandated by General Assembly resolution 37/90 [YUN 1982, p. 163], continued to assist developing countries and countries with economies in transition to establish or strengthen their capacity in space science and technology through long-term training fellowships, technical advisory services, regional and international training courses and conferences, and to promote co-operation between developed and developing countries.

The United Nations Expert on Space Applications [A/AC.105/840] stated that the Programme continued to emphasize cooperation with Member States at the regional and international levels in support of UN-affiliated regional centres for space science and technology education. Under the Programme's priority area of space technology and disaster management, which aimed at supporting developing countries' use of space technology to deal with natural disasters, a fifth regional workshop was held in Saudi Arabia and a final international workshop, which built on the results of previous regional workshops, was held in Germany. The Programme also conducted the United Nations/United States Training Course on Satellite-Aided Search and Rescue (Miami, Florida, United States) for the benefit of countries in the Latin American and Caribbean region, and organized the fourteenth United Nations/International Astronautical Federation Workshop on Capacity-Building in Space Technology for the Benefit of Developing Countries, with Emphasis on Natural Disaster Management (Vancouver, Canada, October). A number of workshops were held in support of the priority thematic area of natural resource management and environmental monitoring, including a United Nations/European Space Agency (ESA)/Sudan regional workshop on the subject (Khartoum, April); the United Nations/Iran Regional Workshop on the Use of Space Technology for Environmental Security, Disaster Rehabilitation and Sustainable Development (Tehran, 8-12 May); and the United Nations/ESA/Switzerland/Austria Workshop on Remote Sensing in the Service of Sustainable Development in Mountain Areas (Kathmandu, Nepal, 15-19 November). The Programme also promoted the use of enabling technologies, including GNSS for social and economic benefits, and the use of space science and technology and their applications to support sustainable development. In October, the Programme organized a meeting of UN agencies and members of

the Charter on Cooperation to Achieve the Coordinated Use of Space Facilities in the Event of Natural or Technological Disasters (the International Charter on Space and Major Disasters), of which the UN Office for Outer Space Affairs became an operating body in 2003 [YUN 2003, p. 643], to assess the first year of activities and to revise the "common vision" for the second year; participants agreed on a strategy for consolidating a network of partnerships in each country. The Programme held 14 workshops, training courses and conferences in 2004 and provided technical advisory services to activities promoting regional cooperation.

Following consideration of the report of the Expert on Space Applications [A/AC.105/815], describing 2003 Programme activities, those scheduled for 2004, and activities of UN-affiliated regional centres for space science and technology education for 2003, 2004 and 2005, the Subcommittee reiterated its concern over the Programme's limited financial resources and appealed to Member States for voluntary contributions.

The General Assembly, in **resolution 59/116** (see p. 632), endorsed the Programme on Space Applications for 2005, as proposed by the Expert.

Cooperation

The Inter-Agency Meeting on Outer Space Activities, at its twenty-fourth session (Geneva, 21-23 January) [A/AC.105/818], discussed the coordination of plans and programmes in the practical application of space technology and related areas, involvement of UN entities in the International Charter on Space and Major Disasters and the space-related outcomes of the 2002 World Summit on Sustainable Development [YUN 2002, p. 821]. It also considered electronic information networking in the UN system, the implementation of the UNISPACE III recommendations, and a draft revised brochure on the use of space technology by the UN system for sustainable development.

The Meeting noted the primary areas of satellite technology applications that required inter-agency coordination, and that, although the use of such technology in support of aeronautical applications was growing steadily, it was not progressing as fast as anticipated. It also noted that the work of the International Civil Aviation Organization in that area would continue to be coordinated with relevant agencies.

The Meeting revised the draft of the Secretary-General's report on the coordination of space-related activities within the UN system: direction and anticipated results for the period 2004-2005 [A/AC.105/822], and agreed that a separate report should be prepared on new and emerging space-

related technologies for inter-agency cooperation for submission to the Scientific and Technical Subcommittee in 2005.

The Meeting agreed to create, with the participation of the Committee on Outer Space, inventories of equipment, education and training
materials, satellite data sets and other capacity-
building resources provided by UN entities that
carried out national or regional technical cooperation projects, so that future projects or
other development activities might build on
existing capacity. An inventory of all satellite
data acquired by UN entities should be carried
out on a yearly basis. The Meeting agreed to discuss further the establishment of inventories at
its next session.

The Meeting agreed to promote the use of the
International Charter on Space and Major Disasters by more UN system entities and to examine
the possibility of establishing non-UN focal
points, that it be kept informed of developments
with the Charter and the involvement of UN entities, and that the item on the Charter be retained
on the agenda for its next session.

The Meeting agreed to submit to the Scientific
and Technical Subcommittee at its 2004 session a
list, prepared by the Office for Outer Space Affairs, of space-related initiatives and programmes within the UN system that responded
to recommendations contained in the Plan of Implementation of the 2002 World Summit on Sustainable Development and to review that list
again in 2005.

The Meeting agreed that its focal points
should provide the Office for Outer Space
Affairs with updated information on their space-
related programmes and activities and the relevant web-site addresses, and on upcoming activities to be posted on the Office's web site. Regarding the implementation of the UNISPACE III
recommendations, the Meeting noted that the
work of the action teams could help support the
programmes and activities of UN system entities,
and agreed that those entities should consider actively participating in the action teams that had
relevance to their mandates and activities.

Scientific and technical issues

In 2004, the Scientific and Technical Subcommittee [A/AC.105/823] continued to emphasize
the importance of the provision of non-
discriminatory access to state-of-the-art remote
sensing data and to derive information at reasonable cost and in a timely manner; capacity-
building, in particular to meet the needs of developing countries; and Earth observation satellite
data to support key development activities. It encouraged further international cooperation in

the use of remote sensing satellites, in particular
by sharing experience and technologies through
bilateral, regional and international collaborative
efforts.

The Subcommittee noted that the Inter-
Agency Space Debris Coordination Committee
(IADC) continued to achieve progress in the technical understanding of issues related to space debris. It agreed that Member States, in particular
space-faring countries, should pay more attention to the problem of collision of space objects,
including those with nuclear power sources on
board, with space debris, and to other aspects of
space debris, and that they should make available
the results of national research on space debris,
including information on minimizing its creation. Pursuant to General Assembly resolution
58/89 [YUN 2003, p. 646], the Subcommittee established a working group to consider comments
from States members of the Committee on Outer
Space on the proposals on debris mitigation presented by IADC in 2003 [ibid., p. 644] and endorsed
the working group's report, which was annexed
to the Subcommittee's report.

Also in accordance with that resolution, the
Subcommittee reconvened its Working Group on
the Use of Nuclear Power Sources in Outer
Space. It noted progress made by the Working
Group on the development of options for establishing an international, technically based framework of goals and recommendations for the
safety of space nuclear power source applications. It also noted that the Working Group's proposed options for establishing cooperation between the Committee and the International
Atomic Energy Agency, contained in the Group's
working paper [A/AC.105/C.1/L.271/Rev.1]. The
Subcommittee endorsed the Working Group's
report, which was annexed to the Subcommittee's report, and the recommendation that it continue intersessional work on topics described in
the 2003-2006 multi-year work plan on the use of
nuclear power sources in outer space, adopted in
2003 [YUN 2003, p. 644].

The Subcommittee agreed that the recommendation to establish a disaster management
international space coordination organization
within the UN framework, made by the
UNISPACE III Action Team on Disaster Management should be further studied. The Subcommittee was of the view that every national and
international organization involved in disaster response should have free access to and possess
readily deployable mobile communication termi-
nals, compatible with different communication
satellite systems, and that Member States should
facilitate such access.

The Committee on Outer Space [A/59/20] hoped that IADC would further develop its space debris mitigation guidelines, taking into account comments submitted by Member States. In 2004, only one Member State [A/AC.105/820/Add.1] responded to the Committee's 2003 request [YUN 2003, p. 645] that its members study the IADC proposals on space debris mitigation and provide their comments to the Office for Outer Space Affairs.

The Committee agreed that the Action Team on Disaster Management should undertake further study to establish, within the UN framework, an international organization for the coordination of space activities for disaster management. It noted that both the Committee and its Scientific and Technical Subcommittee could contribute to the World Conference on Disaster Reduction, to be held in 2005 in Kobe, Japan, and its follow-up, ensuring that space technologies would be an integral part of the solutions put forward in the Conference's plan of implementation. The Committee reported that, in accordance with resolution 58/89, a workshop on satellites for disaster communications: saving lives from natural disasters was held on 7 June 2004.

In response to the Subcommittee's request that Member States and regional space agencies continue to report on national research concerning the safety of space objects with nuclear power sources, the Secretariat submitted replies received from three States [A/AC.105/838].

Also submitted to the Scientific and Technical Subcommittee were a Secretariat note [A/AC.105/832 & Add.1] and a series of addenda [A/AC.105/816/Add.1-4] to a 2003 note [YUN 2003, p. 645] containing information received from 15 Member States on their space activities.

Legal Subcommittee

The Legal Subcommittee, at its forty-third session (Vienna, 29 March–8 April) [A/AC.105/826], reconvened its working group on the examination of the preliminary draft protocol on matters specific to space assets to the Convention on International Interests in Mobile Equipment, which was opened for signature in 2001 [YUN 2001, p. 570]. The working group considered separately the possibility of the United Nations serving as supervisory body under the preliminary draft protocol and the relationship between the terms of the draft protocol and the rights and obligations of States, under the legal regime applicable to outer space. It agreed that, as a number of both practical and fundamental issues remained to be resolved before the Subcommittee could decide on the appropriateness of the United Nations act-

ing as supervisory authority, to establish an open-ended ad hoc working group to continue consideration of the question. The ad hoc working group would prepare a report, including the text of a draft resolution, to be submitted to the Subcommittee in 2005.

The Subcommittee also reconvened its working group established on the status and application of the five UN treaties on outer space [YUN 2001, p. 570]. Having considered a working paper [A/AC.105/C.2/L.251] submitted by a group of ESA States and those that had concluded cooperation agreements with it, a draft resolution on the application of the legal concept of the "launching State", the working group agreed on the text of a draft resolution for consideration by the Assembly. It also approved the text of a model letter, together with the information material to be attached thereto, for the Secretary-General to send to the ministers for foreign affairs of States that had not become parties to UN treaties on outer space, and to intergovernmental organizations that had not declared their acceptance of the rights and obligations under those treaties. The Subcommittee endorsed the working group's report and the recommendation that its mandate be extended until 2005, when it would be reviewed. The text of the letter and its attachment were annexed to the Subcommittee's report.

The Subcommittee reconvened its working group on the definition and delimitation of outer space to consider an analytical summary of the replies to a questionnaire on possible legal issues with regard to aerospace objects [A/AC.105/C.2/L.249 & Corr.1]. It agreed that the Secretariat should compile all the replies to the questionnaire received from Member States in a single document, which should be made available to the members of the Committee on Outer Space and others, and used as a working document for establishing a technical or legal basis for the consideration of possible legal issues with regard to aerospace objects and matters relating to the definition and delimitation of outer space. The Subcommittee could continue its consideration of the analytical summary in 2005, and Member States that had not replied to the questionnaire should be invited to do so.

The Subcommittee, noting that various international organizations had been invited by the Secretariat to report on their activities relating to space law, considered a Secretariat note [A/AC.105/C.2/L.248] and a conference room paper containing reports from five international organizations on their activities in that regard. It agreed that international intergovernmental organizations conducting space activities could enhance the legal framework applicable to those activities by encouraging their member States, if they had not already done so, to become parties to the international treaties governing outer space.

The Subcommittee was informed of the practices of 12 Member States and ESA [A/AC.105/C.2/L.250 & Corr.1 & Add.1,2] in registering space objects and implementing the 1974 Convention on the Registration of Objects Launched into Outer Space, contained in General Assembly resolution 3235(XXIX) [YUN 1974, p. 63]. It requested the Secretariat to prepare a background document on the Register of Objects Launched into Outer Space maintained by the Secretary-General under the Convention to facilitate the work of the working group to be established by the Subcommittee in 2005.

The Committee on Outer Space [A/59/20] endorsed the recommendations of the Subcommittee and its working groups.

GENERAL ASSEMBLY ACTION

On 10 December [meeting 71], the General Assembly, on the recommendation of the Fourth Committee [A/59/469], adopted **resolution 59/115** without vote [agenda item 74].

Application of the concept of the "launching State"

The General Assembly,

Recalling the Convention on International Liability for Damage Caused by Space Objects and the Convention on Registration of Objects Launched into Outer Space,

Bearing in mind that the term "launching State" as used in the Liability Convention and the Registration Convention is important in space law, that a launching State shall register a space object in accordance with the Registration Convention and that the Liability Convention identifies those States which may be liable for damage caused by a space object and which would have to pay compensation in such a case,

Taking note of the report of the Committee on the Peaceful Uses of Outer Space on its forty-second session and the report of the Legal Subcommittee on its forty-first session, in particular the conclusions of the Working Group on the agenda item entitled "Review of the concept of the 'launching State'" annexed to the report of the Legal Subcommittee,

Noting that nothing in the conclusions of the Working Group or in the present resolution constitutes an authoritative interpretation of or a proposed amendment to the Registration Convention or the Liability Convention,

Noting also that changes in space activities since the Liability Convention and the Registration Convention entered into force include the continuous development of new technologies, an increase in the number of States carrying out space activities, an increase in international cooperation in the peaceful uses of outer space and an increase in space activities carried out by non-governmental entities, including activities carried out jointly by government agencies and non-governmental entities, as well as partnerships formed by non-governmental entities from one or more countries,

Desirous of facilitating adherence to and the application of the provisions of the United Nations treaties on outer space, in particular the Liability Convention and the Registration Convention,

1. *Recommends* that States conducting space activities, in fulfilling their international obligations under the United Nations treaties on outer space, in particular the Treaty on Principles Governing the Activities of States in the Exploration and Use of Outer Space, including the Moon and Other Celestial Bodies, the Convention on International Liability for Damage Caused by Space Objects and the Convention on Registration of Objects Launched into Outer Space, as well as other relevant international agreements, consider enacting and implementing national laws authorizing and providing for continuing supervision of the activities in outer space of non-governmental entities under their jurisdiction;

2. *Also recommends* that States consider the conclusion of agreements in accordance with the Liability Convention with respect to joint launches or cooperation programmes;

3. *Further recommends* that the Committee on the Peaceful Uses of Outer Space invite Member States to submit information on a voluntary basis on their current practices regarding on-orbit transfer of ownership of space objects;

4. *Recommends* that States consider, on the basis of that information, the possibility of harmonizing such practices as appropriate with a view to increasing the consistency of national space legislation with international law;

5. *Requests* the Committee on the Peaceful Uses of Outer Space, in making full use of the functions and resources of the Secretariat, to continue to provide States, at their request, with relevant information and assistance in developing national space laws based on the relevant treaties.

Effects of atomic radiation

At its fifty-second session (Vienna, 26-30 April) [A/59/46], the United Nations Scientific Committee on the Effects of Atomic Radiation continued the development of new documents on the sources and effects of ionizing radiation, last reviewed by the Committee in 2003 [YUN 2003, p. 650]. It held detailed technical discussions that resulted in clear instructions to the Secretariat as to the content and form of future scientific annexes and considered new information relevant to assessing sources of radiation, the exposures that those sources gave rise to and the resulting effects. The Committee reviewed Secretariat documents on important topics, including exposure of workers and the public to various sources of radiation; sources-to-effects assessment for radon in homes and workplaces; radioecology, methodologies for dose assessment and effects of radiation on non-human biota; non-targeted and delayed effects of exposure to ionizing radiation; health effects due to radiation from the 1986 Chernobyl accident [YUN 1986, p. 584]; evaluation of new epidemiological studies of radiation and cancer; epidemiological evaluation and dose response of diseases other than cancer that might be related to radiation exposure; medical radiation exposure; effects of radiation on the immune system; and summary documents on the health effects of radiation and the sources of ionizing radiation exposure. Internet access was provided to published Committee documents for the period 2003-2004 to allow the Committee's findings to reach a broader audience.

The provision of an adequate operating budget to allow the Committee to fulfil its General Assembly mandate, most recently expressed in resolutions 57/115 [YUN 2002, p. 606] and 58/88 [YUN 2003, p. 650], remained a concern. The Committee's anticipation that adequate funds to hold its annual meetings would be restored for the biennium 2004-2005 were only partially realized. In the circumstances, the Committee would only be able to continue the current, approved programme of work by holding its fifty-third session at a lower level of effectiveness. The Committee decided to hold that session in Vienna from 30 May to 3 June 2005.

GENERAL ASSEMBLY ACTION

On 10 December [meeting 71], the General Assembly, on the recommendation of the Fourth Committee [A/59/468], adopted **resolution 59/114** without vote [agenda item 73].

Effects of atomic radiation

The General Assembly,

Recalling its resolution 913(X) of 3 December 1955, by which it established the United Nations Scientific Committee on the Effects of Atomic Radiation, and its subsequent resolutions on the subject, including resolution 58/88 of 9 December 2003, in which, inter alia, it requested the Scientific Committee to continue its work,

Taking note with appreciation of the work of the Scientific Committee,

Reaffirming the desirability of the Scientific Committee continuing its work,

Concerned about the potentially harmful effects on present and future generations resulting from the levels of radiation to which mankind and the environment are exposed,

Noting the views expressed by Member States at its fifty-ninth session with regard to the work of the Scientific Committee,

Noting with satisfaction that some Member States have expressed particular interest in becoming members of the Scientific Committee, and expressing its intention to consider the issue further at its next session,

Conscious of the continuing need to examine and compile information about atomic and ionizing radiation and to analyse its effects on mankind and the environment,

1. *Commends* the United Nations Scientific Committee on the Effects of Atomic Radiation for the valuable contribution it has been making in the course of the past forty-nine years, since its inception, to wider knowledge and understanding of the levels, effects and risks of ionizing radiation, and for fulfilling its original mandate with scientific authority and independence of judgement;

2. *Reaffirms* the decision to maintain the present functions and independent role of the Scientific Committee;

3. *Requests* the Scientific Committee to continue its work, including its important activities to increase knowledge of the levels, effects and risks of ionizing radiation from all sources, and invites the Scientific Committee to submit its programme of work to the General Assembly;

4. *Endorses* the intentions and plans of the Scientific Committee for its future activities of scientific review and assessment on behalf of the General Assembly;

5. *Requests* the Scientific Committee to continue at its next session the review of the important problems in the field of ionizing radiation and to report thereon to the General Assembly at its sixtieth session;

6. *Requests* the United Nations Environment Programme to continue providing support for the effective conduct of the work of the Scientific Committee and for the dissemination of its findings to the General Assembly, the scientific community and the public;

7. *Expresses its appreciation* for the assistance rendered to the Scientific Committee by Member States, the specialized agencies, the International Atomic Energy Agency and non-governmental organizations, and invites them to increase their cooperation in this field;

8. *Invites* the Scientific Committee to continue its consultations with scientists and experts from interested Member States in the process of preparing its future scientific reports;

9. *Welcomes*, in this context, the readiness of Member States to provide the Scientific Committee with relevant information on the effects of ionizing radiation in affected areas, and invites the Scientific Committee to analyse and give due consideration to such information, particularly in the light of its own findings;

10. *Invites* Member States, the organizations of the United Nations system and non-governmental organizations concerned to provide further relevant data about doses, effects and risks from various sources of radiation, which would greatly help in the preparation of future reports of the Scientific Committee to the General Assembly;

11. *Urges* the United Nations Environment Programme to review and strengthen the present funding of the Scientific Committee, pursuant to paragraph 6 of resolution 58/88, so that the Committee can discharge the responsibilities and mandate entrusted to it by the General Assembly;

12. *Emphasizes* the need for the Scientific Committee to hold regular sessions on an annual basis so that its report can reflect the latest developments and findings in the field of ionizing radiation and thereby provide updated information for dissemination among all States.

PART TWO

Human rights

Chapter I

Promotion of human rights

In 2004, human rights were promoted through initiatives regarding legally binding instruments and the Commission on Human Rights and its subsidiary body, the Subcommission on the Promotion and Protection of Human Rights. The Office of the United Nations High Commissioner for Human Rights continued its coordination and implementation activities, and provided advisory services and a technical cooperation programme.

The Committee on the Protection of the Rights of All Migrant Workers and Members of Their Families, the monitoring body of the International Convention on the Protection of the Rights of All Migrant Workers and Members of Their Families, which was adopted by the General Assembly in 1990 and entered into force in 2003, at its first session, elected its officers and adopted its rules of procedure. Other monitoring bodies of human rights instruments promoted civil, political, economic, social and cultural rights, and aimed to eliminate racial discrimination and discrimination against women, to protect children and to end the practice of torture and other cruel, inhuman or degrading treatment or punishment.

On 10 December, the annual observance of Human Rights Day, the General Assembly dedicated its plenary meeting to a review of the achievements of the United Nations Decade for Human Rights Education (1995-2004), which it proclaimed in 1994. On the same day, the Assembly proclaimed the World Programme for Human Rights Education, structured in consecutive phases and scheduled to begin on 1 January 2005, in order to advance the implementation of human rights education programmes in all sectors.

During the year, the Assembly appointed Louise Arbour (Canada) as United Nations High Commissioner for Human Rights. Her term of office would be from 1 July 2004 to 30 June 2008.

UN machinery

Commission on Human Rights

The Commission on Human Rights held its sixtieth session in Geneva from 15 March to 23 April [E/2004/23], during which it adopted 88 resolutions and 28 decisions. It recommended 47 draft decisions for adoption by the Economic and Social Council. The Council took note of the Commission's report on 23 July (**decision 2004/317**).

Pursuant to a 2000 Commission decision on enhancing the effectiveness of its mechanisms [YUN 2000, p. 595], the Commission Chairperson convened a one-day informal meeting on 28 September to facilitate the exchange of information in preparation for the General Assembly's fifty-ninth (2004) session [E/CN.4/IM/2004/1]. In a September note [E/CN.4/IM/2004/2], the Secretariat summarized the post-sessional meetings and activities of the Commission's Expanded Bureau.

Organization of work

Note by Secretariat. The Commission had before it a note by the Secretariat [E/CN.4/2004/11] containing statistical data on its 2003 session to assist with the organization of the Commission's work in 2004.

In response to a 2003 Commission decision [YUN 2003, p. 656] on ways to improve the organization of the Commission's work, a 12 January note of the Secretariat [E/CN.4/2004/109] summarized the views received from Member States, regional groups and non-governmental organizations (NGOs) and considered by the Expanded Bureau. A March note by the Secretariat [E/CN.4/2004/110/Rev.1] transmitted a report containing recommendations on improving the Commission's work, as proposed by the Expanded Bureau.

On 15 March [dec. 2004/101], the Commission invited special representatives, special rapporteurs, chairpersons and chairpersons/rapporteurs of various working groups and experts to participate in its meetings.

An April note of the Secretary-General [E/CN.4/2004/124] contained the proposed strategic framework for the 2006-2007 biennium of the Office of the United Nations High Commissioner for Human Rights (OHCHR), which would replace the current four-year medium-term plan.

On 21 April [dec. 2004/125], the Commission decided that the first meeting of its sixty-first (2005) session would take place in January to elect its officers and that the session would be held from 14

March to 22 April. The Council approved the Commission's decision on 22 July (**decision 2004/282**).

On 23 April [dec. 2004/127], the Commission recommended that the Council authorize six additional meetings for its sixty-first session and requested the Chairperson of that session to organize the session's work within the time normally allotted so that the additional meetings would be utilized only if necessary.

ECONOMIC AND SOCIAL COUNCIL ACTION

In July, the Economic and Social Council, on the recommendation of the Commission on Human Rights [E/2004/23], adopted **decision 2004/283** by recorded vote (53-1) [agenda item 14 (g)].

Organization of work of the sixty-first session of the Commission on Human Rights

At its 49th plenary meeting, on 22 July 2004, the Economic and Social Council took note of Commission on Human Rights decision 2004/127 of 23 April 2004 and authorized six fully serviced additional meetings, including summary records, in accordance with rules 29 and 31 of the rules of procedure of the functional commissions of the Council, for the sixty-first session of the Commission.

The Council also requested the Chairperson of the sixty-first session of the Commission to make every effort to organize the work of the session within the time normally allotted so that the additional meetings that the Council might authorize would be utilized only if they proved to be absolutely necessary.

RECORDED VOTE ON DECISION 2004/283:

In favour: Armenia, Australia, Azerbaijan, Bangladesh, Belgium, Belize, Benin, Bhutan, Burundi, Canada, Chile, China, Colombia, Congo, Cuba, Ecuador, El Salvador, Finland, France, Germany, Ghana, Greece, Guatemala, Hungary, India, Indonesia, Ireland, Italy, Jamaica, Japan, Kenya, Libyan Arab Jamahiriya, Malaysia, Mauritius, Mozambique, Namibia, Nicaragua, Nigeria, Panama, Poland, Qatar, Republic of Korea, Russian Federation, Saudi Arabia, Senegal, Sweden, Tunisia, Turkey, Ukraine, United Arab Emirates, United Kingdom, United Republic of Tanzania, Zimbabwe.

Against: United States.

Thematic procedures

In January, the Secretary-General provided a list of the thematic and country-specific procedures and other Commission mechanisms for 2004 [E/CN.4/2004/Add.1 & Corr.1], and in March [E/CN.4/2004/97] he submitted a report containing references to the conclusions and recommendations of thematic special rapporteurs and working groups, pursuant to a 2002 Commission resolution [YUN 2002, p. 613]. The eleventh meeting of special rapporteurs/representatives, independent experts and chairpersons of working groups of the special procedures of the Commission and of the advisory services programme was held in June [E/CN.4/2005/5] (see p. 669).

Commission action. On 21 April [res. 2004/76], by a recorded vote of 35 to none, with 18 abstentions, the Commission urged Governments to co-operate with it through its special procedures and requested those procedures to make recommendations to prevent human rights violations; follow progress made by Governments; continue close cooperation with relevant treaty bodies and with each other; focus resources on ways that best advanced their mandates; provide comprehensive reports; report on follow-up action by Governments; include in their reports gender-disaggregated data and address women's human rights and violations of the rights of children and other vulnerable groups; and maintain dialogue with Governments. The High Commissioner was requested to continue to organize periodic meetings; facilitate the implementation of special procedures' recommendations; update electronic compilation of special procedures' recommendations by country; support the work of all special procedures; intensify coordination and enhance further the quality, consistency and independence of the work of special procedures; and report on the implementation of recommendations contained in the Commission's current resolution. The Secretary-General was asked to issue annually the conclusions and recommendations of the special procedures; present annually a list of all persons mandated to carry out special procedures; convene periodic meetings among special procedures; and ensure the availability of resources to support the special procedures' mandates.

Subcommission on the Promotion and Protection of Human Rights

The Subcommission on the Promotion and Protection of Human Rights, at its fifty-sixth session (Geneva, 26 July–13 August) [E/CN.4/2005/2], adopted 30 resolutions and 23 decisions, and recommended one draft resolution and 11 draft decisions for adoption by the Commission.

On 12 August [dec. 2004/122], the Subcommission approved the composition of its working groups for 2005. On the same date [dec. 2004/120], it decided to entrust Françoise Hampson (United Kingdom) with the preparation, without financial implications, of a working paper on the organization, content and outcome of its work under agenda item 2 on the question of human rights and fundamental freedoms, which would enable it to focus attention on a situation not otherwise before a human rights body, taking into account Commission resolution 2004/60 (see p. 649). The working paper was to be submitted by the end of April 2005 and translated into the UN official languages, posted on the OHCHR website not later than May, and sent to Subcommission members. NGOs, national human rights institutions, the Commission's special procedures, OHCHR, States and other interested parties should be invited to submit comments no later than the end of June. The working paper was to be presented during the first meeting of the Subcommission's fifty-seventh (2005) session, with at least one meeting devoted to a general discussion of the report as a whole in a public forum.

Also on 12 August [dec. 2004/121], the Subcommission decided to entrust Emmanuel Decaux (France) with preparing, without financial implications, a working paper, for submission in 2005, on the Subcommission's methods of work relating to the choice of subject and preparation of reports and on how it should organize its work to ensure full consideration of reports by its members, NGOs, national delegations and other interested parties.

Report of Subcommission Chairperson. The Commission had before it a report [E/CN.4/2004/83] of the Subcommission's 2003 Chairperson, Halima Embarek Warzazi (Morocco), which summarized the Subcommission's work in 2003.

Commission action. On 20 April [res. 2004/60], the Commission decided that the Subcommission should continue to debate country situations not being dealt with in the Commission, but should not adopt country-specific resolutions, decisions or Chairperson's statements. It further decided that the Subcommission could best assist it by providing it with independent expert studies and working papers by its members or their alternates; recommendations based on the studies; and studies, research and expert advice at the Commission's request. It recommended that the Subcommission continue holding annual closed meetings with the Commission's Expanded Bureau; streamlining its agenda; holding closed meetings on its working rules, procedures and timetables; drafting as many of its resolutions as possible in closed session; and using a question-and-answer format and expert panel discussions. The Commission also recommended that the Subcommission further improve its work methods by focusing on its primary role as the Commission's advisory body; giving attention to studies recommended by the Commission or proposals suggested by treaty bodies or other UN human rights bodies; respecting the highest standards of impartiality and expertise, and avoiding acts that would affect confidence in its members' independence; facilitating the participation of NGOs; considering studies and working papers by special rapporteurs and its members before sending them to the Commission; taking further steps to accomplish its work within a

three-week session; making proposals to the Commission on how to assist the Subcommission to improve its work and vice versa; focusing on human rights questions relating to its mandate; avoiding duplication of its work with that of other bodies and mechanisms; and giving appropriate regard to legal opinions addressed to it. The Commission requested States to consider a number of criteria when nominating and electing Subcommission members and alternates.

The Secretary-General was asked to support the Subcommission by making documentation available in good time before each session in UN official languages and by assisting it in requests for information from Governments, intergovernmental organizations and NGOs. The Commission recommended that the Subcommission Chairperson or his/her representative attend the meeting of special rapporteurs/representatives, experts and chairpersons of working groups of the Commission's special procedures and the meeting of chairpersons of treaty bodies (see p. 660) to facilitate coordination between the Subcommission and other relevant UN bodies and procedures. The Chairperson of the Subcommission's 2004 session was asked to report in 2005 on how recent enhancements of the Subcommission had worked in practice.

Notes by Secretary-General. A note of the Secretary-General [E/CN.4/2004/82 & Add.1 & Add.1/Corr.1] contained the nominations and biographical data of candidates for election to the 26-member Subcommission and the corresponding alternates, as the term of office of half the membership was due to expire.

A June note of the Secretary-General [E/CN.4/Sub.2/2004/33] reviewed developments between 1 June 2003 and 1 June 2004 in areas with which the Subcommission had been concerned.

A July note of the Secretary-General [E/CN.4/Sub.2/2004/3] contained a proposal by an NGO for inclusion in the Subcommission's provisional agenda of an item concerning the rule of law in Sri Lanka.

Working paper. In an August working paper [E/CN.4/Sub.2/2004/46], Subcommission member Gudmundur Alfredsson (Iceland) presented research and study topic proposals for consideration by the Subcommission.

Office of the High Commissioner for Human Rights

Reports of Acting High Commissioner and High Commissioner. The Acting High Commissioner for Human Rights, in a June report [E/2004/89] to the Economic and Social Council, described UN system initiatives to assist Member

States in building their national systems of human rights promotion and protection. The report also detailed the efforts of UN bodies and programmes and specialized agencies to integrate human rights into their activities. The Acting High Commissioner recommended a number of measures to the Council, including a periodic review of progress achieved in integrating human rights as an essential part of the work of UN bodies and programmes. The Council took note of the report on 23 July (**decision 2004/317**).

The High Commissioner's report to the General Assembly [A/59/36] covered urgent reporting by the Acting High Commissioner to the Commission on the conflict situations in the Darfur region of the Sudan (see p. 803) and in Iraq (see pp. 339 and 809); the 2004 activities of the Commission, the Subcommission, treaty bodies and special procedures established to deal with alleged human rights violations; standard-setting activities; and human rights and development. The report also described OHCHR activities at the country level, its support to peace missions and role in the area of humanitarian action. The Office continued to devote efforts to the development and strengthening of national human rights protection systems, implement the Secretary-General's reform agenda (see p. 1360) and develop strategies for its field activities. Specific human rights issues reviewed concerned racism, racial discrimination, xenophobia and related intolerance; globalization; the right to adequate food; poverty reduction; human trafficking; women's rights; the rule of law and democracy; indigenous peoples; minorities; and human rights education.

On 20 December, the General Assembly took note of a report of the Third (Social, Humanitarian and Cultural) Committee [A/59/503/Add.5] regarding the High Commissioner's report (**decision 59/530**).

Appointment. Following a 20 February note of the Secretary-General [A/58/718] proposing Louise Arbour (Canada) as United Nations High Commissioner for Human Rights, the General Assembly approved her appointment on 25 February (**decision 58/417**). In May [A/58/718/Add.1], the Secretary-General informed the Assembly that her term of office would be from 1 July 2004 to 30 June 2008.

Strengthening the functioning of OHCHR

Report of High Commissioner. A February report of the High Commissioner [E/CN.4/2004/12/Add.1] highlighted OHCHR activities designed to implement the Secretary-General's

2002 proposals for strengthening the UN system [YUN 2002, p. 1352], particularly regarding measures to enhance human rights–related UN actions at the country level and to improve the effectiveness of treaty bodies and special procedures.

Commission action. On 8 April [res. 2004/2], by a recorded vote of 51 to none, with 2 abstentions, the Commission asked the High Commissioner to continue to emphasize the promotion and protection of economic, social and cultural rights; to continue to strengthen OHCHR's management structure; to enhance international cooperation for human rights promotion and protection; and to engage in dialogue with Governments to secure respect for all human rights. The Commission recommended that the Economic and Social Council and the General Assembly provide OHCHR with means commensurate with its increasing tasks and more resources for special rapporteurs.

ECONOMIC AND SOCIAL COUNCIL ACTION

In July, the Economic and Social Council, on the recommendation of the Commission on Human Rights [E/2004/23], adopted **decision 2004/247** by recorded vote (52-0-2) [agenda item 14 (*g*)].

Strengthening of the Office of the United Nations High Commissioner for Human Rights

At its 48th plenary meeting, on 22 July 2004, the Economic and Social Council took note of Commission on Human Rights resolution 2004/2 of 8 April 2004 and endorsed the Commission's recommendation that the Council and the General Assembly provide the Office of the United Nations High Commissioner for Human Rights with ways and means commensurate with its increasing tasks, as well as more resources for special rapporteurs.

RECORDED VOTE ON DECISION 2004/247:

In favour: Armenia, Azerbaijan, Bangladesh, Belgium, Belize, Benin, Bhutan, Burundi, Canada, Chile, China, Colombia, Congo, Cuba, Ecuador, El Salvador, Finland, France, Germany, Ghana, Greece, Guatemala, Hungary, India, Indonesia, Ireland, Italy, Jamaica, Japan, Kenya, Libyan Arab Jamahiriya, Malaysia, Mauritius, Mozambique, Namibia, Nicaragua, Nigeria, Panama, Poland, Qatar, Republic of Korea, Russian Federation, Saudi Arabia, Senegal, Sweden, Tunisia, Turkey, Ukraine, United Arab Emirates, United Kingdom, United Republic of Tanzania, Zimbabwe.

Against: None.

Abstaining: Australia, United States.

Management review

Report of JIU. By a 10 March note [A/59/65-E/2004/48], the Secretary-General transmitted a report of the Joint Inspection Unit (JIU) on a management and administrative review of OHCHR, as requested by the Commission in 2002 [YUN 2002, p. 615]. JIU recommended that the High Commissioner create a post of Chief of Staff and review the grading of branch chiefs to ensure streamlined management, optimal leadership and consistency of structures. The organigram of the proposed Capacity-building and Field Operations Branch should be revised by integrating the National Institutions Team within various geographical teams. Field operations conducted exclusively by OHCHR should be minimal and limited to cases where no alternative existed, and OHCHR might consider drawing up an action plan detailing measures to develop cooperation with different partners. Further recommendations advocated the establishment of an accounting system for the assets of field representations, the development of a field administrative procedures manual and the formulation of a clear information technology strategy. Regarding human resources management, JIU proposed that the Office should review the mandate of the Advisory Panel on Personnel Issues, compile annually a list of countries which were either unrepresented or underrepresented within OHCHR, align its recruitment and contractual policies with those of the Secretariat and align its post-classification criteria with those of the Secretariat before advertising any post. The High Commissioner should prepare an action plan aimed at reducing the current imbalance in the geographical distribution of staff.

Note by Secretary-General. By a 12 March note [A/59/65/Add.1-E/2004/48/Add.1], the Secretary-General transmitted his comments on JIU's recommendations, indicating that some of the recommendations were under implementation, while others would be further studied.

On 23 July, the Economic and Social Council took note of the Secretary-General's notes transmitting the JIU report and his comments thereon (**decision 2004/317**).

Note by Secretariat. A 5 April note of the Secretariat [E/CN.4/2004/95] drew the Commission's attention to the JIU report and to the Secretary-General's comments thereon.

Composition of staff

Report of High Commissioner. In response to a 2003 Commission request [YUN 2003, p. 659], the High Commissioner submitted a report on the composition of OHCHR staff by nationality, grade and gender as at 1 December 2003 [E/CN.4/2004/100].

Commission action. On 21 April [res. 2004/73], by a recorded vote of 35 to 14, with 4 abstentions, the Commission considered it necessary to change the prevailing geographical distribution of OHCHR staff and requested the Secretary-General to ensure that particular attention was paid to recruiting personnel from unrepresented and underrepresented Member States, particularly from developing countries and countries

with economies in transition. The High Commissioner was requested to prepare an action plan aimed at reducing the current staff imbalance, indicating specific targets and deadlines to be achieved, to avoid duplication of functions and to work towards the goal of increased effectiveness and improved management, and to report in 2005. JIU was asked to assist the Commission to monitor the implementation of its current resolution and to submit to the General Assembly in 2006 and to the Commission in 2007 a review of the implementation of the decisions of the Commission and other UN intergovernmental bodies regarding the management, programmes and administration of OHCHR. Annexed to the Commission's resolution was tabular information on the geographical distribution of OHCHR's staff between 2000 and 2004.

ECONOMIC AND SOCIAL COUNCIL ACTION

In July, the Economic and Social Council, on the recommendation of the Commission on Human Rights [E/2004/23], adopted **decision 2004/269** by recorded vote (32-18-3) [agenda item 14 (g)].

Composition of the staff of the Office of the United Nations High Commissioner for Human Rights

At its 48th plenary meeting, on 22 July 2004, the Economic and Social Council took note of Commission on Human Rights resolution 2004/73 of 21 April 2004 and drew the attention of the General Assembly to the resolution in the context of the consideration of the agenda item on human resources management.

The Council further endorsed the Commission's:

(a) Invitation to the General Assembly and its appropriate subsidiary bodies, inter alia, the Advisory Committee on Administrative and Budgetary Questions, the Committee for Programme and Coordination and the Fifth Committee, to give due consideration to Commission resolution 2004/73 and to the report of the Joint Inspection Unit entitled "Management review of the Office of the United Nations High Commissioner for Human Rights", transmitted to the Assembly in a note by the Secretary-General, in particular to any other organization, management, executive direction, structure, administrative, financial and more technical human resources management issues and recommendations contained therein and not addressed in Commission resolution 2004/73;

(b) Request to the Joint Inspection Unit to assist the Commission to monitor systematically the implementation of Commission resolution 2004/73 and to submit a follow-up comprehensive review of the implementation of the decisions of the Commission and other United Nations intergovernmental bodies regarding the management, programmes and administration of the Office of the United Nations High Commissioner for Human Rights, in particular with regard to their impact on the recruitment policies and the composition of the staff, to the Commission at its sixty-third session and to the General Assembly at its sixty-first session, containing any concrete proposals for corrective action, if required, for the implementation of the relevant intergovernmental bodies' resolutions, including Commission resolution 2004/73.

RECORDED VOTE ON DECISION 2004/269:

In favour: Armenia, Azerbaijan, Bangladesh, Belize, Benin, Bhutan, Burundi, Chile, China, Colombia, Cuba, Ecuador, El Salvador, Ghana, India, Indonesia, Jamaica, Kenya, Libyan Arab Jamahiriya, Malaysia, Mauritius, Mozambique, Namibia, Nigeria, Panama, Qatar, Russian Federation, Saudi Arabia, Tunisia, United Arab Emirates, United Republic of Tanzania, Zimbabwe.

Against: Australia, Belgium, Canada, Finland, France, Germany, Greece, Hungary, Ireland, Italy, Japan, Poland, Republic of Korea, Sweden, Turkey, Ukraine, United Kingdom, United States.

Abstaining: Guatemala, Nicaragua, Senegal.

Annual Appeal 2004

During the year, OHCHR received $60 million in voluntary contributions from donors towards activities outlined in the 2004 Annual Appeal, representing an increase of $16 million over 2003. The UN regular budget provided $32.7 million in 2004.

Strengthening action to promote human rights

In response to General Assembly resolutions 56/153 [YUN 2001, p. 582], 57/203 [YUN 2002, p. 616] and 58/168 [YUN 2003, p. 660], the Secretary-General, in a September report [A/59/327], submitted the proposals of three Member States to strengthen UN action in human rights through the promotion of international cooperation based on the principles of non-selectivity, impartiality and objectivity.

GENERAL ASSEMBLY ACTION

On 20 December [meeting 74], the General Assembly, on the recommendation of the Third Committee [A/59/503/Add.2], adopted **resolution 59/190** without vote [agenda item 105 (b)].

Strengthening United Nations action in the field of human rights through the promotion of international cooperation and the importance of non-selectivity, impartiality and objectivity

The General Assembly,

Bearing in mind that among the purposes of the United Nations are those of developing friendly relations among nations based on respect for the principle of equal rights and self-determination of peoples and taking other appropriate measures to strengthen universal peace, as well as achieving international cooperation in solving international problems of an economic, social, cultural or humanitarian character and in promoting and encouraging respect for human rights and fundamental freedoms for all without distinction as to race, sex, language or religion,

Desirous of achieving further progress in international cooperation in promoting and encouraging respect for human rights and fundamental freedoms,

Considering that such international cooperation should be based on the principles embodied in international law, especially the Charter of the United Nations, as well as the Universal Declaration of Human

Rights, the International Covenants on Human Rights and other relevant instruments,

Deeply convinced that United Nations action in the field of human rights should be based not only on a profound understanding of the broad range of problems existing in all societies but also on full respect for the political, economic and social realities of each of them, in strict compliance with the purposes and principles of the Charter and for the basic purpose of promoting and encouraging respect for human rights and fundamental freedoms through international cooperation,

Recalling its previous resolutions in this regard,

Reaffirming the importance of ensuring the universality, objectivity and non-selectivity of the consideration of human rights issues, as affirmed in the Vienna Declaration and Programme of Action adopted by the World Conference on Human Rights on 25 June 1993,

Affirming the importance of the objectivity, independence and discretion of the special rapporteurs and representatives on thematic issues and on countries, as well as of the members of the working groups, in carrying out their mandates,

Underlining the obligation that Governments have to promote and protect human rights and to carry out the responsibilities that they have undertaken under international law, especially the Charter, as well as various international instruments in the field of human rights,

1. _Reiterates_ that, by virtue of the principle of equal rights and self-determination of peoples enshrined in the Charter of the United Nations, all peoples have the right freely to determine, without external interference, their political status and to pursue their economic, social and cultural development, and that every State has the duty to respect that right within the provisions of the Charter, including respect for territorial integrity;

2. _Reaffirms_ that it is a purpose of the United Nations and the task of all Member States, in cooperation with the Organization, to promote and encourage respect for human rights and fundamental freedoms and to remain vigilant with regard to violations of human rights wherever they occur;

3. _Calls upon_ all Member States to base their activities for the promotion and protection of human rights, including the development of further international cooperation in this field, on the Charter of the United Nations, the Universal Declaration of Human Rights, the International Covenant on Economic, Social and Cultural Rights, the International Covenant on Civil and Political Rights and other relevant international instruments, and to refrain from activities that are inconsistent with that international framework;

4. _Considers_ that international cooperation in this field should make an effective and practical contribution to the urgent task of preventing mass and flagrant violations of human rights and fundamental freedoms for all and to the strengthening of international peace and security;

5. _Reaffirms_ that the promotion, protection and full realization of all human rights and fundamental freedoms, as a legitimate concern of the world community, should be guided by the principles of non-selectivity, impartiality and objectivity and should not be used for political ends;

6. _Requests_ all human rights bodies within the United Nations system, as well as the special rappor-

teurs and representatives, independent experts and working groups, to take duly into account the contents of the present resolution in carrying out their mandates;

7. *Expresses its conviction* that an unbiased and fair approach to human rights issues contributes to the promotion of international cooperation as well as to the effective promotion, protection and realization of human rights and fundamental freedoms;

8. *Stresses*, in this context, the continuing need for impartial and objective information on the political, economic and social situations and events of all countries;

9. *Invites* Member States to consider adopting, as appropriate, within the framework of their respective legal systems and in accordance with their obligations under international law, especially the Charter, and international human rights instruments, the measures that they may deem appropriate to achieve further progress in international cooperation in promoting and encouraging respect for human rights and fundamental freedoms;

10. *Requests* the Commission on Human Rights to take duly into account the present resolution and to consider further proposals for the strengthening of United Nations action in the field of human rights through the promotion of international cooperation and the importance of non-selectivity, impartiality and objectivity;

11. *Takes note* of the report of the Secretary-General, and requests the Secretary-General to invite Member States and intergovernmental and non-governmental organizations to present further practical proposals and ideas that would contribute to the strengthening of United Nations action in the field of human rights through the promotion of international cooperation based on the principles of non-selectivity, impartiality and objectivity, and to submit a comprehensive report on the question to the General Assembly at its sixtieth session;

12. *Decides* to consider the matter at its sixty-first session under the item entitled "Human rights questions".

On 23 December, the Assembly decided that the item on human rights questions, including alternative approaches for improving the effective enjoyment of human rights and fundamental freedoms, would remain for consideration during its resumed fifty-ninth (2005) session (**decision 59/552**).

International cooperation in the field of human rights

On 21 April [res. 2004/63], the Commission called on Member States, specialized agencies and intergovernmental organizations to continue constructive dialogue and consultations to enhance the understanding and promotion and protection of all human rights and fundamental freedoms. States and relevant UN human rights mechanisms and procedures were asked to continue to pay attention to the importance of mutual cooperation in ensuring human rights promotion and protection.

GENERAL ASSEMBLY ACTION

On 20 December [meeting 74], the General Assembly, on the recommendation of the Third Committee [A/59/503/Add.2], adopted **resolution 59/187** without vote [agenda item 105 (*b*)].

Enhancement of international cooperation in the field of human rights

The General Assembly,

Reaffirming its commitment to promoting international cooperation, as set forth in the Charter of the United Nations, in particular Article 1, paragraph 3, as well as relevant provisions of the Vienna Declaration and Programme of Action, adopted by the World Conference on Human Rights on 25 June 1993, for enhancing genuine cooperation among Member States in the field of human rights,

Recalling its adoption of the United Nations Millennium Declaration on 8 September 2000 and its resolution 58/170 of 22 December 2003, and taking note of Commission on Human Rights resolution 2004/63 of 21 April 2004 on the enhancement of international cooperation in the field of human rights,

Recalling also the World Conference against Racism, Racial Discrimination, Xenophobia and Related Intolerance, held at Durban, South Africa, from 31 August to 8 September 2001, and its role in the enhancement of international cooperation in the field of human rights,

Recognizing that the enhancement of international cooperation in the field of human rights is essential for the full achievement of the purposes of the United Nations, including the effective promotion and protection of all human rights,

Reaffirming that dialogue among religions, cultures and civilizations in the field of human rights could contribute greatly to the enhancement of international cooperation in this field,

Emphasizing the need for further progress in the promotion and encouragement of respect for human rights and fundamental freedoms through, inter alia, international cooperation,

Underlining the fact that mutual understanding, dialogue, cooperation, transparency and confidence-building are important elements in all the activities for the promotion and protection of human rights,

Recalling the adoption of resolution 2000/22 of 18 August 2000, on the promotion of dialogue on human rights issues, by the Subcommission on the Promotion and Protection of Human Rights at its fifty-second session,

1. *Reaffirms* that it is one of the purposes of the United Nations and the responsibility of all Member States to promote, protect and encourage respect for human rights and fundamental freedoms through, inter alia, international cooperation;

2. *Recognizes* that, in addition to their separate responsibilities to their individual societies, States have a collective responsibility to uphold the principles of human dignity, equality and equity at the global level;

3. *Reaffirms* that dialogue among cultures and civilizations facilitates the promotion of a culture of tolerance and respect for diversity, and welcomes in this regard the holding of conferences and meetings at the national, regional and international levels on dialogue among civilizations;

4. *Urges* all actors on the international scene to build an international order based on inclusion, justice, equality and equity, human dignity, mutual understanding and promotion of and respect for cultural diversity and universal human rights, and to reject all doctrines of exclusion based on racism, racial discrimination, xenophobia and related intolerance;

5. *Reaffirms* the importance of the enhancement of international cooperation for the promotion and protection of human rights and for the achievement of the objectives of the fight against racism, racial discrimination, xenophobia and related intolerance;

6. *Considers* that international cooperation in the field of human rights, in conformity with the purposes and principles set out in the Charter of the United Nations and international law, should make an effective and practical contribution to the urgent task of preventing violations of human rights and fundamental freedoms;

7. *Reaffirms* that the promotion, protection and full realization of all human rights and fundamental freedoms should be guided by the principles of universality, non-selectivity, objectivity and transparency, in a manner consistent with the purposes and principles set out in the Charter;

8. *Calls upon* Member States, specialized agencies and intergovernmental organizations to continue to carry out a constructive dialogue and consultations for the enhancement of understanding and the promotion and protection of all human rights and fundamental freedoms, and encourages non-governmental organizations to contribute actively to this endeavour;

9. *Invites* States and relevant United Nations human rights mechanisms and procedures to continue to pay attention to the importance of mutual cooperation, understanding and dialogue in ensuring the promotion and protection of all human rights;

10. *Decides* to continue its consideration of the question at its sixtieth session.

At the same meeting, the Assembly, also on the recommendation of the Third Committee [A/59/503/Add.2], adopted **resolution 59/204** by recorded vote (118-55-13) [agenda item 105 *(b)*].

Respect for the purposes and principles contained in the Charter of the United Nations to achieve international cooperation in promoting and encouraging respect for human rights and for fundamental freedoms and in solving international problems of a humanitarian character

The General Assembly,

Recalling that, in accordance with Article 56 of the Charter of the United Nations, all Member States have pledged themselves to take joint and separate action in cooperation with the Organization for the achievement of the purposes set forth in Article 55, including universal respect for and observance of human rights and fundamental freedoms for all without distinction as to race, sex, language or religion,

Recalling also the Preamble to the Charter, in particular the determination to reaffirm faith in fundamental human rights, in the dignity and worth of the human person and in the equal rights of men and women and of nations large and small,

Reaffirming that the promotion and protection of all human rights and fundamental freedoms must be considered a priority objective of the United Nations in accordance with its purposes and principles, in particular the purpose of international cooperation, and that, within the framework of these purposes and principles, the promotion and protection of all human rights is a legitimate concern of the international community,

Considering the major changes taking place on the international scene and the aspirations of all peoples to an international order based on the principles enshrined in the Charter, including promoting and encouraging respect for human rights and fundamental freedoms for all and respect for the principle of equal rights and self-determination of peoples, peace, democracy, justice, equality, the rule of law, pluralism, development, better standards of living and solidarity,

Recognizing that the international community should devise ways and means to remove current obstacles and meet the challenges to the full realization of all human rights and to prevent the continuation of human rights violations resulting therefrom throughout the world, and should continue to pay attention to the importance of mutual cooperation, understanding and dialogue in ensuring the promotion and protection of all human rights,

Reaffirming that the enhancement of international cooperation in the field of human rights is essential for the full achievement of the purposes of the United Nations and that human rights and fundamental freedoms are the birthright of all human beings, the promotion and protection of such rights and freedoms being the first responsibility of Governments,

Reaffirming also that all human rights are universal, indivisible, interdependent and interrelated and that the international community must treat human rights globally in a fair and equal manner, on the same footing and with the same emphasis,

Reaffirming further the various Articles of the Charter setting out the respective powers and functions of the General Assembly, the Security Council and the Economic and Social Council, as the paramount framework for the achievement of the purposes of the United Nations,

Reaffirming the commitment of all States to fulfil their obligations under other important instruments of international law, in particular those of international human rights law and international humanitarian law,

Bearing in mind that, in accordance with Article 103 of the Charter, in the event of a conflict between the obligations of the Members of the United Nations under the Charter and their obligations under any other international agreement, their obligations under the Charter shall prevail,

Recalling all its previous resolutions on the question, including resolution 58/188 of 22 December 2003,

1. *Reiterates* the solemn commitment of all States to enhance international cooperation in the field of human rights and in the solution to international problems of a humanitarian character in full compliance with the Charter of the United Nations, inter alia, by the strict observance of all the purposes and principles set forth in Articles 1 and 2 thereof;

2. *Stresses* the vital role of the work of the United Nations and regional arrangements, acting consistently with the purposes and principles enshrined in

the Charter, in promoting and encouraging respect for human rights and fundamental freedoms, as well as in solving international problems of a humanitarian character, and affirms that all States, in these activities, must fully comply with the principles set forth in Article 2 of the Charter, in particular respecting the sovereign equality of all States and refraining from the threat or use of force against the territorial integrity or political independence of any State, or acting in any other manner inconsistent with the purposes of the United Nations;

3. *Reaffirms* that the United Nations shall promote universal respect for and observance of human rights and fundamental freedoms for all without distinction as to race, sex, language or religion;

4. *Reaffirms also* that the responsibility for managing worldwide economic and social development, the promotion and protection of human rights and threats to international peace and security must be shared among the nations of the world and should be exercised multilaterally and that, as the most universal and most representative organization in the world, the United Nations must play the central role;

5. *Calls upon* Member States to refrain from enacting or enforcing unilateral coercive measures as tools of political, military or economic pressure against any country, in particular against developing countries, which would prevent those countries from exercising their right to decide of their own free will their own political, economic and social systems;

6. *Calls upon* all States to cooperate fully, through constructive dialogue, to ensure the promotion and protection of all human rights for all and in promoting peaceful solutions to international problems of a humanitarian character and, in their actions towards that purpose, to comply strictly with the principles and norms of international law, inter alia, by fully respecting international human rights law and international humanitarian law;

7. *Requests* the Secretary-General to bring the present resolution to the attention of Member States, organs, bodies and other components of the United Nations system and intergovernmental and non-governmental organizations, and to disseminate it as widely as possible;

8. *Decides* to consider the question at its sixty-first session under the item entitled "Human rights questions".

RECORDED VOTE ON RESOLUTION 59/204:

In favour: Algeria, Angola, Antigua and Barbuda, Azerbaijan, Bahamas, Bahrain, Bangladesh, Barbados, Belarus, Belize, Benin, Bhutan, Bolivia, Botswana, Brunei Darussalam, Burkina Faso, Burundi, Cambodia, Cameroon, Cape Verde, Central African Republic, Chad, China, Colombia, Comoros, Costa Rica, Côte d'Ivoire, Cuba, Democratic People's Republic of Korea, Democratic Republic of the Congo, Djibouti, Dominica, Dominican Republic, Ecuador, Egypt, El Salvador, Equatorial Guinea, Eritrea, Ethiopia, Fiji, Gabon, Gambia, Ghana, Grenada, Guatemala, Guinea, Guinea-Bissau, Guyana, Haiti, Honduras, India, Indonesia, Iran, Iraq, Jamaica, Jordan, Kazakhstan, Kenya, Kuwait, Kyrgyzstan, Lao People's Democratic Republic, Lebanon, Lesotho, Liberia, Libyan Arab Jamahiriya, Madagascar, Malawi, Malaysia, Maldives, Mali, Mauritania, Mauritius, Mexico, Mongolia, Morocco, Mozambique, Myanmar, Namibia, Nepal, Nicaragua, Niger, Nigeria, Oman, Pakistan, Panama, Papua New Guinea, Philippines, Qatar, Russian Federation, Rwanda, Saint Lucia, Saint Vincent and the Grenadines, Sao Tome and Principe, Saudi Arabia, Senegal, Sierra Leone, Somalia, South Africa, Sri Lanka, Sudan, Suriname, Swaziland, Syrian Arab Republic, Tajikistan, Timor-Leste, Togo, Trinidad and Tobago, Tunisia, Turkmenistan, Uganda, United Arab Emirates, United Republic of Tanzania, Uzbekistan, Venezuela, Viet Nam, Yemen, Zambia, Zimbabwe.

Against: Albania, Andorra, Armenia, Australia, Austria, Belgium, Bosnia and Herzegovina, Bulgaria, Canada, Croatia, Cyprus, Czech Republic, Denmark, Estonia, Finland, France, Georgia, Germany, Greece, Hungary, Iceland, Ireland, Israel, Italy, Japan, Latvia, Liechtenstein, Lithuania, Luxembourg, Malta, Marshall Islands, Micronesia, Monaco, Netherlands, New Zealand, Norway, Palau, Poland, Portugal, Republic of Korea, Republic of Moldova, Romania, Samoa, San Marino, Serbia and Montenegro, Slovakia, Slovenia, Spain, Sweden, Switzerland, The former Yugoslav Republic of Macedonia, Turkey, Ukraine, United Kingdom, United States.

Abstaining: Argentina, Brazil, Chile, Nauru, Paraguay, Peru, Singapore, Solomon Islands, Thailand, Tonga, Tuvalu, Uruguay, Vanuatu.

Right to promote and protect human rights

Human rights defenders

Reports of Special Representative. In a January report [E/CN.4/2004/94], the Secretary-General's Special Representative on human rights defenders, Hina Jilani (Pakistan), described her activities and analysed alleged violations of the 1998 Declaration on the Right and Responsibility of Individuals, Groups and Organs of Society to Promote and Protect Universally Recognized Human Rights and Fundamental Freedoms (Declaration on human rights defenders), adopted by the General Assembly in resolution 53/144 [YUN 1998, p. 608]. She also analysed trends in Governments' responses to her communications and made a series of recommendations for strengthening support for the role of human rights defenders and for promoting the implementation of human rights standards.

The Special Representative noted that she had taken up 266 cases, representing a small proportion of what was occurring, which revealed allegations that defenders had been victims of killings, attacks, death threats, torture, arbitrary arrest and detention, and numerous other forms of mistreatment, including the targeting of their family members. She therefore urged States to adopt, publish and implement a policy on defenders, ensure domestic legislation conformed with the rights recognized in the 1998 Declaration and in other international human rights instruments and the Charter of the United Nations, and investigate promptly complaints and allegations brought to their attention. NGOs were encouraged to create and strengthen coalitions and networks to enhance defenders' protection and to accord priority to training defenders on the national, regional and international protection instruments and on ways to invoke them. A March addendum to the report [E/CN.4/2004/94/Add.3] summarized communications sent to and received from Governments.

The Special Representative visited Angola (16-24 August) to assess the situation and role of human rights defenders in the country [E/CN.4/2005/101/Add.2]. She described the legal and institutional environment in which human rights defenders worked in Angola, and examined the defenders' capacity to raise human rights issues, which, she observed, remained weak. State authorities continued to consider human rights defenders with hostility, and as a result, human rights defenders often practised self-censorship, leaving many important issues unaddressed. The absence of an independent media hindered the defenders' capacity to publicize their concerns and to conduct their activities. Defenders also continued to face serious obstacles to the creation and operation of NGOs, and their limited access to justice adversely affected their work. The Special Representative urged the Government to review existing legislation and ensure its compatibility with the 1998 Declaration; review the process for registering human rights defenders' associations; ensure full respect for the freedom of expression; improve access to information for human rights defenders and ensure that they had timely and regular access to State officials; establish an environment conducive to free and fair elections; and consider inviting OHCHR to increase the capacity of its presence in Angola. Human rights defenders were urged to seek training, strengthen their network and consider publishing an annual human rights report for Angola. The United Nations was asked to consider ways to contribute to the implementation of the Declaration, and OHCHR to consider seeking a broadening of its mandate and an increase in its personnel to monitor and raise concerns affecting human rights defenders.

In Turkey (11-20 October) [E/CN.4/2005/101/ Add.3 & Corr.1], the Special Representative welcomed a significant improvement in the situation of human rights defenders over the past four years, but noted that they continued to face obstacles, particularly in the area of publicizing human rights concerns, forming NGOs and accessing information and funding. She expressed concern about the number of prosecutions and heavy fines inflicted on defenders and about the fact that some authorities perceived them as adversaries. The Government was called on to fully guarantee freedom of expression and of assembly; review laws regulating trade unions and collective bargaining to ensure that defenders could freely defend social and labour rights; simplify administrative procedures for establishing NGOs; and end practices that stigmatized human rights defenders. The Government was urged to ensure that harassment of human rights defenders was not perpetuated by new means.

In an October note [A/59/401], the Secretary-General transmitted a report of the Special Representative, in accordance with Assembly resolu-

tion 58/178 [YUN 2003, p. 665]. The Special Representative discussed the several levels of responsibility in applying the 1998 Declaration and presented examples of the most common violations against human rights defenders, including arbitrary arrest and detention, prosecution and pre-trial detention, violation of their physical integrity and harassment. The factors that encouraged those violations included, among other things, weaknesses in the legal system, limitations on the competence and independence of the judiciary, the lack of awareness or accountability among local authorities for the respect of international human rights standards and weaknesses in civil society. Actions needed to overcome the problem included a much wider dissemination and use of the Declaration, strengthened training on the Declaration for the judiciary, legislative reform, wider citizen participation, greater oversight by parliamentary bodies and better interministerial coordination. The report accorded special attention to the freedom of association, owing to various restrictions on the right and its centrality to the effective work of defenders. The obstacles facing the defenders in that regard included the criminalization of non-registered human rights groups; unnecessarily burdensome and lengthy registration procedures; limits on the creation of networks; inappropriate denial of registration; limited independence of registration authorities; requirements to re-register when new legislation was introduced; State scrutiny of and interference with an organization's management, objectives and activities; administrative and judicial harassment; and restrictions on cooperation with international human rights partners. The report concluded with examples of good practices and recommendations in conformity with the Declaration, relating in particular to registration, the objectives and activities of human rights NGOs, the suspension and closure of NGOs and access to funds.

On 20 December, the General Assembly took note of the Secretary-General's note (**decision 59/528**).

Commission action. On 21 April [res. 2004/68], the Commission, condemning all human rights violations committed against persons promoting and defending human rights and fundamental freedoms, called on States to protect human rights defenders and asked the Special Representative to report on her activities to the General Assembly and to the Commission. The Secretary-General and concerned UN agencies and organizations were requested to assist her.

On 20 December [meeting 74], the General Assembly, on the recommendation of the Third Committee [A/59/503/Add.2], adopted **resolution 59/192** without vote [agenda item 105 (b)].

Declaration on the Right and Responsibility of Individuals, Groups and Organs of Society to Promote and Protect Universally Recognized Human Rights and Fundamental Freedoms

The General Assembly,

Recalling its resolution 53/144 of 9 December 1998, by which it adopted by consensus the Declaration on the Right and Responsibility of Individuals, Groups and Organs of Society to Promote and Protect Universally Recognized Human Rights and Fundamental Freedoms annexed to that resolution, and reiterating the importance of the Declaration and its wide dissemination,

Recalling also all previous resolutions on this subject, in particular its resolution 58/178 of 22 December 2003 and Commission on Human Rights resolution 2004/68 of 21 April 2004,

Noting with deep concern that, in many countries, persons and organizations engaged in promoting and defending human rights and fundamental freedoms are facing threats, harassment and insecurity as a result of those activities,

Gravely concerned by the continuing high level of human rights violations committed against persons engaged in promoting and defending human rights and fundamental freedoms around the world and by the fact that, in a number of countries in all regions of the world, impunity for threats, attacks and acts of intimidation against human rights defenders persists and that this has a negative impact on their work and safety,

Recalling that human rights defenders are entitled to equal protection of the law, and deeply concerned about any abuse of civil or criminal proceedings against them because of their activities for the promotion and protection of human rights and fundamental freedoms,

Concerned by the considerable number of communications received by the Special Representative of the Secretary-General on the situation of human rights defenders that, together with the reports submitted by some of the special procedure mechanisms, indicate the serious nature of the risks faced by human rights defenders,

Emphasizing the important role that individuals, groups and organs of society play in the promotion and protection of all human rights and fundamental freedoms for all,

Recalling that, in accordance with article 4 of the International Covenant on Civil and Political Rights, certain rights are recognized as non-derogable in any circumstances and that any measures derogating from other provisions of the Covenant must be in accordance with that article in all cases, and underlining the exceptional and temporary nature of any such derogations, as stated in General Comment No. 29, on states of emergency, adopted by the Human Rights Committee on 24 July 2001,

Gravely concerned that, in some instances, national security and counter-terrorism legislation and other measures have been misused to target human rights defenders or have hindered their work and safety in a manner contrary to international law,

Acknowledging the significant work conducted by the Special Representative, and welcoming the cooperation between the Special Representative and other special procedures of the Commission on Human Rights,

Welcoming regional initiatives for the promotion and protection of human rights and the cooperation between international and regional mechanisms for the protection of human rights defenders, and encouraging further development in this regard,

Welcoming also the steps taken by some States towards adopting national policies and legislation for the protection of human rights defenders,

Recalling that the primary responsibility for promoting and protecting human rights rests with the State, and noting with deep concern that the activities of some non-State actors pose a major threat to the security of human rights defenders,

Emphasizing the need for strong and effective measures for the protection of human rights defenders,

1. *Calls upon* all States to promote and give full effect to the Declaration on the Right and Responsibility of Individuals, Groups and Organs of Society to Promote and Protect Universally Recognized Human Rights and Fundamental Freedoms, including by taking, as appropriate, practical steps to that end;

2. *Welcomes* the reports of the Special Representative of the Secretary-General on the situation of human rights defenders and her contribution to the effective promotion of the Declaration and the improvement of the protection of human rights defenders worldwide;

3. *Encourages* all States to ensure and maintain an environment conducive to the work of human rights defenders;

4. *Condemns* all human rights violations committed against persons engaged in promoting and defending human rights and fundamental freedoms around the world, and urges States to take all appropriate action, consistent with the Declaration and all other relevant human rights instruments, to eliminate such human rights violations;

5. *Calls upon* all States to take all necessary measures to ensure the protection of human rights defenders, at both the local and the national levels;

6. *Also calls upon* all States to ensure, protect and respect the freedom of expression and association of human rights defenders and, where registration is required, to facilitate registration, including through the establishment of effective and transparent criteria and non-discriminatory procedures under domestic law;

7. *Urges* States to ensure that any measures to combat terrorism and preserve national security comply with their obligations under international law, in particular under international human rights law, and do not hinder the work and safety of human rights defenders;

8. *Emphasizes* the importance of combating impunity, and in this regard urges States to take appropriate measures to address the question of impunity for threats, attacks and acts of intimidation against human rights defenders;

9. *Urges* States to ensure that complaints from human rights defenders are investigated and addressed

in a transparent, independent and accountable manner;

10. *Urges* all Governments to cooperate with and assist the Special Representative in the performance of her tasks and to furnish all information in the fulfilment of her mandate upon request;

11. *Calls upon* Governments to give serious consideration to responding favourably to the requests of the Special Representative to visit their countries, and urges them to enter into a constructive dialogue with the Special Representative with respect to the follow-up and implementation of her recommendations, so as to enable her to fulfil her mandate even more effectively;

12. *Urges* those Governments that have not yet responded to the communications transmitted to them by the Special Representative to answer without further delay;

13. *Invites* Governments to translate the Declaration into national languages and to take measures to improve its dissemination;

14. *Encourages* States to promote awareness and training in regard to the Declaration in order to enable officials, agencies, authorities and the judiciary to observe the provisions of the Declaration and thus to promote better understanding and respect for human rights defenders;

15. *Requests* all concerned United Nations agencies and organizations, within their mandates, to provide all possible assistance and support to the Special Representative in the implementation of her programme of activities;

16. *Invites* relevant United Nations bodies, including at the country level, within their mandates and working in cooperation with States, to give due consideration to the Declaration and to the reports of the Special Representative, and requests the Office of the United Nations High Commissioner for Human Rights to draw the attention of all relevant United Nations bodies, including at the country level, to the reports of the Special Representative;

17. *Encourages* all Governments to investigate expeditiously urgent appeals and allegations brought to their attention by the Special Representative and to take timely action to prevent violations of the rights of human rights defenders;

18. *Requests* the Secretary-General to provide the Special Representative with all necessary human, material and financial resources in order to enable her to continue to carry out her mandate effectively, including through country visits;

19. *Requests* the Special Representative to continue to report on her activities to the General Assembly and to the Commission on Human Rights in accordance with her mandate;

20. *Decides* to consider the question at its sixtieth session under the item entitled "Human rights questions".

Human rights and human responsibilities

On 21 April [dec. 2004/117], by a recorded vote of 26 to 25, with 2 abstentions, the Commission asked OHCHR to circulate to Member States and to intergovermental organizations and NGOs the pre-draft declaration on human social responsibilities [YUN 2003, p. 667], requesting their views on

it, and to submit in 2005 a compilation of the replies received.

Other aspects

Good governance

Note by Secretariat. The Commission had before it a Secretariat note [E/CN.4/2004/92] informing members about the activities undertaken to prepare the seminar on good governance practices for the promotion of human rights (below), pursuant to a 2003 Commission resolution [YUN 2003, p. 667].

Commission action. On 21 April [res. 2004/70], the Commission called on States to provide responsible government, responsive to the needs of the people, to achieve human rights. The High Commissioner was requested to compile ideas and practices arising from the seminar (see below) and material provided by States, intergovernmental organizations and NGOs for consultation by interested States and to report in 2005 on the outcome of the seminar.

Seminar. In response to Commission resolution 2004/70 (see above), OHCHR, in collaboration with the United Nations Development Programme (UNDP) and the Government of the Republic of Korea, convened a seminar on good governance practices for the promotion of human rights (Seoul, 15-16 September) [E/CN.4/2005/97]. The purpose was to discuss illustrative governance practices that had had an impact on the promotion of human rights and to draw lessons from them. Eight case studies were discussed during four sessions on the rule of law, strengthening the delivery of services contributing to the realization of human rights, strengthening democratic institutions and participation, and combating corruption in the public and private sectors. The seminar concluded that, although there was a mutually reinforcing relationship between good governance and human rights, there was no exhaustive definition of the notion of good governance. However, common elements could be identified, such as participation, accountability, transparency, and State responsibility and accessibility, in particular to marginalized groups. Participants also concluded that there was a need for greater awareness of good governance and its relationship to human rights, particularly from the perspective of political will and public participation.

Protection systems

A February report of the High Commissioner [E/CN.4/2004/12/Add.3] summarized Governments' replies to a national human rights protection systems questionnaire. While all States indicated that they had constitutional human rights provisions, in the majority of responding States, judicial organs, including Constitutional Courts, were empowered to review the compatibility of domestic law with the human rights norms of international instruments to which the State concerned was party. A number of States noted that national courts referred to human rights instruments and took into account international human rights law when interpreting national law in cases before them. All responding States reported that they had taken or were taking measures relating to human rights/civic rights education or human rights awareness-raising, both in the primary and secondary school curricula and in the training of professional groups, such as the police, civil servants, the judiciary and religious groups. The majority indicated that they had some form of national human rights institution which monitored human rights compliance.

The report also described action taken pursuant to the Secretary-General's programme on strengthening of the United Nations, as contained in his 2002 report [YUN 2002, p. 1352], which required the High Commissioner to develop and implement a plan, in cooperation with the United Nations Development Group and the Executive Committee for Humanitarian Affairs, to strengthen human rights–related UN action at the country level. In that regard, various UN system entities were combining their efforts to provide support to Member States, at their request, in strengthening their national protection systems, with the key goal of enhancing the capacity of UN country teams to help strengthen national systems for human rights promotion and protection.

Human rights instruments

General aspects

In 2004, seven UN human rights instruments were in force that required their implementation to be monitored by expert bodies. The instruments and their treaty bodies were: the 1965 International Convention on the Elimination of All Forms of Racial Discrimination [YUN 1965, p. 440, GA res. 2106 A (XX)] (Committee on the Elimination of Racial Discrimination); the 1966 International Covenant on Civil and Political Rights and the Optional Protocol thereto [YUN 1966, p. 423, GA res. 2200 A (XXI)] and the Second Optional Protocol, aiming at the abolition of the death penalty [YUN 1989, p. 484, GA res. 44/128] (Human Rights Commit-

tee); the 1966 International Covenant on Economic, Social and Cultural Rights [YUN 1966, p. 419, GA res. 2200 A (XXI)] (Committee on Economic, Social and Cultural Rights); the 1979 Convention on the Elimination of All Forms of Discrimination against Women [YUN 1979, p. 895, GA res. 34/180] and Optional Protocol [YUN 1999, p. 1100, GA res. 54/4] (Committee on the Elimination of Discrimination against Women); the 1984 Convention against Torture and Other Cruel, Inhuman or Degrading Treatment or Punishment [YUN 1984, p. 813, GA res. 39/46] and 2002 Optional Protocol [YUN 2002, p. 631, GA res. 57/199] (Committee against Torture); the 1989 Convention on the Rights of the Child [YUN 1989, p. 560, GA res. 44/25] and Optional Protocols on the involvement of children in armed conflict and on the sale of children, child prostitution and child pornography [YUN 2000, pp. 616 & 618, GA res. 54/263] (Committee on the Rights of the Child); and the 1990 International Convention on the Protection of the Rights of All Migrant Workers and Members of Their Families [YUN 1990, p. 594, GA res. 45/158] (Committee on the Protection of the Rights of All Migrant Workers and Migrants and Their Families).

Commission action. On 21 April [dec. 2004/123], the Commission, taking note of a 2003 Subcommission resolution [YUN 2003, p. 668], approved the Subcommission's decision to appoint Emmanuel Decaux (France) as Special Rapporteur to conduct a detailed study of the universal implementation of international human rights treaties based on his working paper [ibid.]. It decided to ask him to submit a preliminary report to the Subcommission in 2004, an interim report in 2005 and a final report in 2006. The Secretary-General was asked to assist him.

On 22 July, the Economic and Social Council approved the Commission's decision to appoint the Special Rapporteur and its requests to him to report; it also endorsed the Commission's request to the Secretary-General to assist him (**decision 2004/281**).

Preliminary report. In a July preliminary report [E/CN.4/Sub.2/2004/8], the Special Rapporteur defined the scope of the study and spelled out the legal aspects of the universal implementation of human rights treaties in the context of international public law. Noting that he intended to devote the study to the universal ratification of treaties and the universal implementation of international human rights instruments, the Special Rapporteur indicated that the study should take into account parallel efforts to improve the human rights treaty system undertaken in close cooperation with all interested parties. In that regard, it might be useful to convene a seminar, with a view to creating a grid for use in organizing dialogue with States regarding the ratification of universal treaties. Annexed to the report were tables listing the principal universal instruments, including those deposited with the Secretary-General; a quantitative overview of ratifications of instruments that had a monitoring mechanism; and the status of ratification of the International Covenants (see pp. 662 and 663) and Optional Protocols to the International Covenant on Civil and Political Rights (see p. 662).

Subcommission action. On 12 August [res. 2004/26], the Subcommission asked the Secretary-General to continue to assist the Special Rapporteur and the Special Rapporteur to submit an interim report in 2005.

Human rights treaty body system

Note by OHCHR. A February note by OHCHR [E/CN.4/2004/98] described developments in the human rights treaty body system, in response to a 2002 Commission request to the Secretary-General [YUN 2002, p. 623]. During the reporting period, further ratification of and accession to key human rights instruments were recorded among Member States, and the treaty bodies continued to develop their working methods and to streamline reporting procedures. Technical assistance was provided to facilitate reporting by States parties to those instruments, and delays in processing individual complaints were reduced significantly. Efforts also continued to develop and harmonize electronic databases concerning the treaty bodies, and to strengthen the web sites of OHCHR and the UN Division for the Advancement of Women.

Commission action. On 21 April [res. 2004/78], the Commission encouraged continuing efforts by human rights treaty bodies and the Secretary-General to improve the effectiveness of the treaty body system, with a view to a more coordinated approach to its activities and standardized reporting. It requested the Secretary-General to provide the resources necessary to give the treaty bodies adequate administrative support and better access to technical expertise and relevant information, and to report in 2006.

Meeting of chairpersons. A May note by the Secretary-General [HRI/MC/2004/1] contained the provisional agenda and annotations for the sixteenth meeting of chairpersons of human rights treaty bodies (see below), and by an August note [A/59/254], he submitted the report of the meeting (Geneva, 23-25 June). The meeting considered follow-up to the recommendations of the fifteenth meeting [YUN 2003, p. 669] and reviewed developments relating to the work of the treaty bodies. In that context, the chairpersons considered the issues of strengthening support to the treaty bodies, enhancing their effectiveness and streamlining their reporting procedures and requirements. Background information for discussions was provided by a Secretariat report [HRI/MC/2004/3] on guidelines on an expanded core document and treaty-specific targeted reports and harmonized guidelines on reporting under the international human rights treaties. Also held was the sixth joint meeting of treaty body chairpersons, special rapporteurs/representatives, independent experts and chairpersons of working groups of the Commission's special procedures, including a meeting with the Chairperson of the Board of the Voluntary Fund for Technical Cooperation. The meeting adopted recommendations relating to technical cooperation; cooperation with special procedures mandate-holders, field presences, UN agencies and other entities, the African Commission on Human and Peoples' Rights, and the Commission; NGO participation; ratification of the International Convention on the Protection of the Rights of All Migrant Workers and Members of Their Families (see below); participation in the inter-committee meeting; and the approach to be adopted by treaty bodies when addressing States parties' last-minute requests for postponement of the consideration of their reports, as well as when delegations did not attend to present reports as scheduled. The chairpersons requested the Secretariat to consider a means of presenting the corpus of treaty body jurisprudence in an accessible way, along with commentaries, to allow it to be used more effectively by all treaty bodies and others. Annexed to the report was the report of the third inter-committee meeting of human rights treaty bodies (Geneva, 21-22 June), which adopted recommendations on reporting guidelines and support for national human rights institutions, among other relevant issues.

On 20 December, the General Assembly took note of the report on the chairpersons' meeting (**decision 59/528**).

Report of Secretary-General. An August report of the Secretary-General [A/59/308] described efforts to implement General Assembly resolution 57/202 [YUN 2002, p. 623] on the effective implementation of international human rights instruments, including reporting obligations under those instruments. The report focused on the meetings of persons chairing human rights treaty bodies and the inter-committee meetings on the methods of work of treaty bodies relating to reporting.

On 20 December, the Assembly took note of the report (**decision 59/528**).

GENERAL ASSEMBLY ACTION

On 20 December [meeting 74], the General Assembly, on the recommendation of the Third Committee [A/59/503/Add.1], adopted **resolution 59/181** by recorded vote (128-52-4) [agenda item 105 (a)].

Equitable geographical distribution in the membership of the human rights treaty bodies

The General Assembly,

Recalling its resolution 56/146 of 19 December 2001,

Reaffirming the importance of the goal of universal ratification of the United Nations human rights instruments,

Welcoming the significant increase in the number of ratifications of United Nations human rights instruments, which has especially contributed to their universality,

Reiterating the importance of the effective functioning of treaty bodies established pursuant to United Nations human rights instruments for the full and effective implementation of those instruments,

Recalling that, with regard to the election of the members of the human rights treaty bodies, the Commission on Human Rights and the General Assembly have recognized the importance of giving consideration in their membership to equitable geographical distribution, gender balance and representation of the principal legal systems and of bearing in mind that the members shall be elected and shall serve in their personal capacity, and shall be of high moral character, acknowledged impartiality and recognized competence in the field of human rights,

Reaffirming the significance of national and regional particularities and various historical, cultural and religious backgrounds, as well as of different political, economic and legal systems,

Recognizing that the United Nations pursues multilingualism as a means of promoting, protecting and preserving diversity of languages and cultures globally and that genuine multilingualism promotes unity in diversity and international understanding,

Recalling that the Commission on Human Rights and the General Assembly have encouraged States parties to United Nations human rights treaties, individually and through meetings of States parties, to consider how to give better effect, inter alia, to the principle of equitable geographical distribution in the membership of treaty bodies,

Expressing concern at the regional imbalance in the current composition of the membership of some of the human rights treaty bodies,

Noting in particular that the status quo tends to be particularly detrimental to the election of experts from some regional groups,

Convinced that the goal of equitable geographical distribution in the membership of human rights treaty bodies is perfectly compatible and can be fully realized and achieved in harmony with the need to ensure gender balance and the representation of the principal legal systems in those bodies and the high moral character, acknowledged impartiality and recognized competence in the field of human rights of their members,

1. *Encourages* the States parties to the United Nations human rights instruments to adopt concrete actions, inter alia, the possible establishment of quota distribution systems by geographical region for the election of the members of the treaty bodies, thereby ensuring the paramount objective of equitable geographical distribution in the membership of those human rights bodies;

2. *Calls upon* the States parties to the United Nations human rights instruments to include, as an agenda item at their forthcoming meetings, a debate on ways and means to ensure equitable geographical distribution in the membership of the human rights treaty bodies, based on the recommendations of the Commission on Human Rights and the Economic and Social Council and the provisions of the present resolution;

3. *Recommends*, when considering the possible establishment of a quota by region for the election of the membership of each treaty body, the introduction of flexible procedures that encompass the following criteria:

(a) Each of the five regional groups established by the General Assembly must be assigned a quota of the membership of each treaty body in equivalent proportion to the number of States parties to the instrument that it represents;

(b) There must be provision for periodic revisions that reflect the relative changes in the geographical distribution of States parties;

(c) Automatic periodic revisions should be envisaged in order to avoid amending the text of the instrument when the quotas are revised;

4. *Stresses* that the process needed to achieve the goal of equitable geographical distribution in the membership of human rights treaty bodies can contribute to raising awareness of the importance of gender balance, the representation of the principal legal systems and the principle that the members of the treaty bodies shall be elected and shall serve in their personal capacity, and shall be of high moral character, acknowledged impartiality and recognized competence in the field of human rights;

5. *Requests* the chairpersons of the human rights treaty bodies to consider at their next meeting the content of the present resolution and to submit, through the United Nations High Commissioner for Human Rights, specific recommendations for the achievement of the goal of equitable geographical distribution in the membership of the human rights treaty bodies;

6. *Requests* the United Nations High Commissioner for Human Rights to submit concrete recommendations on the implementation of the present resolution to the General Assembly at its sixtieth session;

7. *Decides* to continue its consideration of the question at its sixtieth session under the sub-item entitled "Implementation of human rights instruments".

RECORDED VOTE ON RESOLUTION 59/181:

In favour: Afghanistan, Algeria, Angola, Antigua and Barbuda, Argentina, Azerbaijan, Bahamas, Bahrain, Bangladesh, Barbados, Belarus, Belize, Benin, Bhutan, Bolivia, Botswana, Brunei Darussalam, Burkina Faso, Burundi, Cambodia, Cameroon, Cape Verde, Central African Republic, Chad, China, Colombia, Comoros, Costa Rica, Côte d'Ivoire, Cuba, Democratic People's Republic of Korea, Democratic Republic of the Congo, Djibouti, Dominica, Dominican Republic, Ecuador, Egypt, El Salvador, Eritrea, Ethiopia, Fiji, Gabon, Gambia, Ghana, Grenada, Guatemala, Guinea, Guinea-Bissau, Guyana, Haiti, Honduras, India, Indonesia,

Iran, Iraq, Jamaica, Jordan, Kazakhstan, Kenya, Kuwait, Kyrgyzstan, Lao People's Democratic Republic, Lesotho, Liberia, Libyan Arab Jamahiriya, Madagascar, Malawi, Malaysia, Maldives, Mali, Marshall Islands, Mauritania, Mauritius, Mexico, Mongolia, Morocco, Mozambique, Myanmar, Namibia, Nauru, Nepal, Nicaragua, Niger, Nigeria, Oman, Pakistan, Panama, Papua New Guinea, Peru, Philippines, Qatar, Russian Federation, Rwanda, Saint Lucia, Saint Vincent and the Grenadines, Samoa, Sao Tome and Principe, Saudi Arabia, Senegal, Seychelles, Sierra Leone, Singapore, Solomon Islands, Somalia, South Africa, Sri Lanka, Sudan, Suriname, Swaziland, Syrian Arab Republic, Tajikistan, Thailand, Timor-Leste, Togo, Trinidad and Tobago, Tunisia, Turkmenistan, Tuvalu, Uganda, United Arab Emirates, United Republic of Tanzania, Uruguay, Uzbekistan, Venezuela, Viet Nam, Yemen, Zambia, Zimbabwe.

Against: Albania, Andorra, Armenia, Australia, Austria, Belgium, Bosnia and Herzegovina, Bulgaria, Canada, Chile, Croatia, Cyprus, Czech Republic, Denmark, Estonia, Finland, France, Georgia, Germany, Greece, Hungary, Iceland, Ireland, Israel, Italy, Japan, Latvia, Liechtenstein, Lithuania, Luxembourg, Malta, Monaco, Netherlands, New Zealand, Norway, Palau, Poland, Portugal, Republic of Korea, Republic of Moldova, Romania, San Marino, Serbia and Montenegro, Slovakia, Slovenia, Spain, Sweden, Switzerland, The former Yugoslav Republic of Macedonia, Turkey, United Kingdom, United States.

Abstaining: Brazil, Equatorial Guinea, Paraguay, Ukraine.

Reservations to human rights treaties

Working paper. In July [E/CN.4/Sub.2/2004/42], Françoise Hampson (United Kingdom) submitted a final working paper on reservations to human rights treaties. She had submitted previous working papers in 1999 [YUN 1999, p. 574] and 2002 [YUN 2002, p. 625] and an expanded report in 2003 [YUN 2003, p. 669]. She concluded that there was a need to consider the relationship between a reserving State and another State party and between a reserving State and the treaty monitoring mechanism. Generally, the validity or effectiveness of a reservation was not decisive. However, the issue of validity might become decisive when/if a treaty body was called on to reach an opinion in an inter-State case or an individual application. Ms. Hampson recommended that the Subcommission suspend further consideration of the question of reservations to human rights treaties, pending the publication of the next report of the Special Rapporteur of the International Law Commission (ILC) (see p. 1298) on reservations to treaties, particularly, his examination of how to determine whether a reservation was compatible with the objects and purposes of a human rights treaty and the consequences of such a finding.

Subcommission action. On 12 August [dec. 2004/110], the Subcommission decided to transmit Ms. Hampson's working paper to the Commission (see above), the Committee on the Elimination of Racial Discrimination (CERD), which originally requested the study, and other human rights treaty monitoring bodies and ILC.

Covenant on Civil and Political Rights and Optional Protocols

Accessions and ratifications

As at 31 December 2004, parties to the International Covenant on Civil and Political Rights and the Optional Protocol thereto, adopted by the General Assembly in resolution 2200 A (XXI) [YUN 1966, p. 423], numbered 154 and 104, respectively. During the year, Liberia, Mauritania and Swaziland became parties to the Covenant.

The Second Optional Protocol, aiming at the abolition of the death penalty, adopted by the Assembly in resolution 44/128 [YUN 1989, p. 484], was acceded to by the Czech Republic and Estonia and ratified by San Marino, bringing the total number of States parties to 54 as at 31 December.

Implementation

Monitoring body. The Human Rights Committee, established under article 28 of the Covenant, held three sessions in 2004: its eightieth from 15 March to 2 April in New York, and its eighty-first from 5 to 30 July [A/59/40, vol. I] and eighty-second from 18 October to 5 November [A/60/40, vol. I] in Geneva. In 2004, the Committee considered reports from 15 States—Albania, Belgium, Benin, Colombia, Finland, Germany, Liechtenstein, Lithuania, Morocco, Namibia, Poland, Serbia and Montenegro, Suriname, Tajikistan and Uganda—under article 40. It adopted views on communications from individuals alleging violations of their rights under the Covenant, and decided that other such communications were inadmissible. Those views and decisions were annexed to the Committee's reports [A/59/40, vol. II; A/60/40, vol. II].

On 29 March, the Committee adopted General Comment No. 31 on the nature of the general legal obligation imposed on States parties to the Covenant. A June note [E/2004/87] by the Secretary-General contained the texts of the Committee's General Comments Nos. 29 [YUN 2001, p. 590], 30 [YUN 2002, p. 626] and 31 (above).

On 23 July, the Economic and Social Council took note of the Secretary-General's note (**decision 2004/317**).

By notifications of 27 January, 30 March, 12 April, 3, 4 and 13 May and 2 June, Peru stated that it had extended the state of emergency in different provinces and parts of the country. On 5 August, it notified other States parties, through the intermediary of the Secretary-General, of the further extension of the state of emergency for 60 days. By further notifications of 28 October and 16 and 23 November, Peru again extended the state of emergency in different parts of the country. On 28 September, Jamaica notified other States parties, through the intermediary of the Secretary-General, of the declaration of a state of emergency for an initial period of 30 days; on 27 October, it informed the Secretary-General that the possible derogation from the rights guaranteed by various articles of the Covenant ceased on 8 October.

The twenty-third meeting of States parties to the Covenant (New York, 9 September) [CCPR/SP/62 & Add.1] was held to elect nine Committee members to replace those whose terms were due to expire on 31 December.

Commission action. On 21 April [res. 2004/69], the Commission, welcoming the Secretary-General's initiative to give more publicity to the work of the Human Rights Committee, requested him to ensure that OHCHR assisted the Committee to implement its mandate and to submit in 2005 and 2006 a report on the status of the Covenant and its Optional Protocols.

Covenant on Economic, Social and Cultural Rights

Accessions and ratifications

As at 31 December 2004, there were 151 parties to the International Covenant on Economic, Social and Cultural Rights, adopted by the General Assembly in resolution 2200 A (XXI) [YUN 1966, p. 419]. Liberia, Mauritania and Swaziland became parties during the year.

On 21 April [res. 2004/69] (see also above), the Commission asked the Secretary-General to report on the status of the Covenant in 2005 and 2006.

Draft optional protocol

In response to a 2003 Commission request [YUN 2003, p. 670], the open-ended Working Group to consider options regarding the elaboration of an optional protocol to the Covenant held its first session (Geneva, 23 February–5 March) [E/CN.4/2004/44]. The optional protocol would be designed to establish a formal complaints procedure for individuals or groups who felt that their rights under the Covenant had been violated.

After considering preliminary views on options by States, delegations and representatives of intergovernmental organizations and NGOs, the Working Group held an interactive dialogue with the Commission's special rapporteurs whose mandates addressed economic, social and cultural rights, and with experts of the Human Rights Committee, the Committee on Economic, Social and Cultural Rights and CERD. The Group also discussed issues related to the nature and scope of States parties' obligations under the Covenant, the justiciability of economic, social and cultural rights and the benefits of an optional protocol to the Covenant and its complementarity with other mechanisms. Thereafter, the Group's Chairperson-Rapporteur recom-

mended renewing the Group's mandate for two years; authorizing the Group to meet for 10 working days prior to the Commission's 2005 and 2006 sessions; and inviting a representative of the Committee on Economic, Social and Cultural Rights to attend the Group's meetings. It was proposed that the Commission identify experts who could be invited to future Working Group sessions and request as background documentation for its next session a report of the Secretary-General providing the Group at its second session with a comparative summary of existing communications and enquiry procedures and practices under international human rights instruments and the UN system.

Commission action. On 19 April [res. 2004/29], by a recorded vote of 48 to none, with 5 abstentions, the Commission decided to renew the Group's mandate for a two-year period; authorized it to meet for 10 working days prior to the Commission's 2005 and 2006 sessions; invited a representative of the Committee on Economic, Social and Cultural Rights to attend the meetings; and requested the Chairperson-Rapporteur to identify experts who could be invited to the Group's future sessions. The Group was requested to report in 2005. The Secretary-General was asked to submit to the Group, at its second session, a report containing a comparative summary of existing communications and enquiry procedures and practices under international human rights instruments and under the UN system, and to report to the Commission in 2005.

ECONOMIC AND SOCIAL COUNCIL ACTION

In July, the Economic and Social Council, on the recommendation of the Commission on Human Rights [E/2004/23], adopted **decision 2004/256** by recorded vote (49-1-4) [agenda 14 (g)].

Question of the realization in all countries of the economic, social and cultural rights contained in the Universal Declaration of Human Rights and in the International Covenant on Economic, Social and Cultural Rights, and study of special problems which the developing countries face in their efforts to achieve these human rights

At its 48th plenary meeting, on 22 July 2004, the Economic and Social Council took note of Commission on Human Rights resolution 2004/29 of 19 April 2004 and approved the decision of the Commission to renew for a period of two years the mandate of the open-ended Working Group of the Commission with a view to considering options regarding the elaboration of an optional protocol to the International Covenant on Economic, Social and Cultural Rights, pursuant to Commission resolution 2002/24 of 22 April 2002, and authorized the Working Group to meet for ten working days prior to the sixty-first and the sixty-second sessions of the Commission.

In favour: Armenia, Azerbaijan, Bangladesh, Belgium, Belize, Benin, Bhutan, Burundi, Canada, Chile, China, Colombia, Congo, Cuba, Ecuador, El Salvador, Finland, France, Germany, Ghana, Greece, Guatemala, Hungary, India, Indonesia, Ireland, Italy, Jamaica, Japan, Kenya, Libyan Arab Jamahiriya, Malaysia, Mauritius, Mozambique, Namibia, Nicaragua, Nigeria, Panama, Poland, Republic of Korea, Russian Federation, Senegal, Sweden, Tunisia, Turkey, Ukraine, United Kingdom, United Republic of Tanzania, Zimbabwe.

Against: Australia.

Abstaining: Qatar, Saudi Arabia, United Arab Emirates, United States.

Implementation

Monitoring body. The Committee on Economic, Social and Cultural Rights held its thirty-second (26 April–14 May) and thirty-third (8-26 November) sessions, both in Geneva [E/2005/22]. Its pre-sessional working group met in Geneva from 29 November to 3 December to identify issues to be discussed with reporting States.

On 23 July, the Economic and Social Council took note of the Committee's report on its thirtieth and thirty-first sessions, held in 2003 [YUN 2003, p. 671] (**decision 2004/317**).

In 2004, the Committee examined reports under articles 16 and 17 of the Covenant submitted by Azerbaijan, Chile, Denmark, Ecuador, Greece, Italy, Kuwait, Lithuania, Malta and Spain.

The Committee, as a follow-up to its 2002 day of general discussion [YUN 2002, p. 627] on the equal right of men and women to the enjoyment of all economic, social and cultural rights (article 3 of the Covenant), continued to discuss the draft general comment on article 3, and, as follow-up to its 2003 day of general discussion [YUN 2003, p. 671] on the right to work (article 6), it continued its discussions on the draft general comment on article 6.

Convention against racial discrimination

Accessions and ratifications

As at 31 December, the number of parties to the International Convention on the Elimination of All Forms of Racial Discrimination, adopted by the General Assembly in resolution 2106 A (XX) [YUN 1965, p. 440], rose to 170, with ratification by Comoros.

On 22 April [res. 2004/88], by a recorded vote of 38 to 1, with 14 abstentions, the Commission reiterated the call made in the Durban Plan of Action, adopted at the World Conference against Racism, Racial Discrimination, Xenophobia and Related Intolerance [YUN 2001, p. 615], to achieve universal ratification of the Convention by 2005 and for all States to consider making the declaration provided for in article 14 (see below).

The Secretary-General reported on the status of the Convention as at 1 July [A/59/275].

Implementation

Monitoring body. The Committee on the Elimination of Racial Discrimination (CERD), established under article 8 of the Convention, held its sixty-fourth (23 February–12 March) and sixty-fifth (2-20 August) sessions [A/59/18], both in Geneva.

The Committee considered reports submitted by Argentina, the Bahamas, Belarus, Brazil, Kazakhstan, Lebanon, the Libyan Arab Jamahiriya, Madagascar, Mauritania, Nepal, the Netherlands, Portugal, Slovakia, Spain, Suriname, Sweden and Tajikistan. It adopted a decision on Guyana, regretting the State party's inability to submit its initial to fourteenth periodic reports, combined in one document, in time for consideration in 2004. On 20 August, CERD made public its concluding observations relating to the Convention's implementation by Saint Lucia, in the absence of any indication as to when the initial to seventh periodic reports would be submitted.

Under article 14 of the Convention, CERD considered communications from individuals or groups of individuals claiming violation of their rights enumerated in the Convention by a State party. Forty-five States parties had recognized CERD's competence to do so (Algeria, Australia, Austria, Azerbaijan, Belgium, Brazil, Bulgaria, Chile, Costa Rica, Cyprus, Czech Republic, Denmark, Ecuador, Finland, France, Germany, Hungary, Iceland, Ireland, Italy, Liechtenstein, Luxembourg, Malta, Mexico, Monaco, Netherlands, Norway, Peru, Poland, Portugal, Republic of Korea, Romania, Russian Federation, Senegal, Serbia and Montenegro, Slovakia, Slovenia, South Africa, Spain, Sweden, Switzerland, The former Yugoslav Republic of Macedonia, Ukraine, Uruguay, Venezuela).

Pursuant to article 15, the Committee was empowered to consider petitions, reports and other information relating to Trust and Non-Self-Governing Territories. The Committee noted, as it had in the past, the difficulty in fulfilling its functions in that regard, owing to the lack of copies of relevant petitions and to the fact that reports received contained scant information relating directly to the Convention's principles and objectives.

CERD also considered follow-up to the World Conference against Racism, Racial Discrimination, Xenophobia and Related Intolerance [YUN 2001, p. 615] and the Third Decade to Combat Racism and Racial Discrimination (1993-2003), proclaimed by the General Assembly in resolution 48/91 [YUN 1993, p. 853] (see p. 686).

The Committee adopted decisions under the early warning and urgent procedures regarding the situation in Darfur, Sudan [dec. 1(65)], and on

Israel [dec. 2(65)]. It also adopted general recommendation XXX on discrimination against non-citizens.

An August report [A/59/276] of the Secretary-General on CERD's financial situation indicated that States parties' arrears outstanding to the Committee as at 1 July totalled $151,052.52. As at 31 December, 39 States parties had accepted an amendment to article 8 of the Convention regarding the financing of CERD [YUN 1992, p. 714]. The amendment was to enter into force when accepted by a two-thirds majority of States parties, comprising approximately 113 of the 170 States parties to the Convention. A meeting of the States parties (New York, 14 January) [CERD/SP/66 & Add.1-3] considered the biographical data of candidates for election to replace Committee members whose terms of office were to expire on 19 January.

As the Committee Chairperson was unable to attend the Commission's session, he submitted the text of an oral report [E/CN.4/2004/126] on the Committee's work.

GENERAL ASSEMBLY ACTION

On 20 December [meeting 74], the General Assembly, on the recommendation of the Third Committee [A/59/501], adopted **resolution 59/176** without vote [agenda item 103 (a)].

International Convention on the Elimination of All Forms of Racial Discrimination

The General Assembly,

Recalling its previous resolutions on the International Convention on the Elimination of All Forms of Racial Discrimination, most recently resolution 57/194 of 18 December 2002,

Bearing in mind the Vienna Declaration and Programme of Action adopted by the World Conference on Human Rights on 25 June 1993, in particular section II.B of the Declaration, relating to equality, dignity and tolerance,

Reiterating the need to intensify the struggle to eliminate all forms of racism, racial discrimination, xenophobia and related intolerance throughout the world,

Reiterating also the importance of the Convention, which is one of the most widely accepted human rights instruments adopted under the auspices of the United Nations,

Reaffirming that universal adherence to and full implementation of the Convention are of paramount importance for promoting equality and non-discrimination in the world, as stated in the Durban Declaration and Programme of Action adopted by the World Conference against Racism, Racial Discrimination, Xenophobia and Related Intolerance on 8 September 2001,

Mindful of the importance of the contributions of the Committee on the Elimination of Racial Discrimination to the effective implementation of the Convention and to the efforts of the United Nations to combat racism, racial discrimination, xenophobia and related intolerance,

Emphasizing the obligation of all States parties to the Convention to take legislative, judicial and other measures in order to secure full implementation of the provisions of the Convention,

Recalling its resolution 47/111 of 16 December 1992, in which it welcomed the decision, taken on 15 January 1992 by the Fourteenth Meeting of States Parties to the International Convention on the Elimination of All Forms of Racial Discrimination, to amend paragraph 6 of article 8 of the Convention and to add a new paragraph, as paragraph 7 of article 8, with a view to providing for the financing of the Committee from the regular budget of the United Nations, and reiterating its deep concern that the amendment to the Convention has not yet entered into force,

Stressing the importance of enabling the Committee to function smoothly and to have all necessary facilities for the effective performance of its functions under the Convention,

I

Reports of the Committee on the Elimination of Racial Discrimination

1. *Takes note* of the reports of the Committee on the Elimination of Racial Discrimination on its sixty-second and sixty-third and its sixty-fourth and sixty-fifth sessions;

2. *Commends* the Committee for its contributions to the effective implementation of the International Convention on the Elimination of All Forms of Racial Discrimination, especially through the examination of reports under article 9 of the Convention, action on communications under article 14 of the Convention and thematic discussions, which contribute to the prevention and elimination of racism, racial discrimination, xenophobia and related intolerance;

3. *Calls upon* States parties to fulfil their obligation, under article 9, paragraph 1, of the Convention, to submit their periodic reports on measures taken to implement the Convention in due time;

4. *Expresses its concern* at the fact that a great number of reports are overdue and continue to be overdue, in particular initial reports, which constitutes an obstacle to the full implementation of the Convention;

5. *Encourages* States parties to the Convention whose reports are seriously overdue to avail themselves of the advisory services and technical assistance that the Office of the United Nations High Commissioner for Human Rights can provide, upon their request, for the preparation of the reports;

6. *Encourages* the Committee to continue to cooperate and exchange information with United Nations bodies and mechanisms, in particular with the Subcommission on the Promotion and Protection of Human Rights and the Special Rapporteur of the Commission on Human Rights on contemporary forms of racism, racial discrimination, xenophobia and related intolerance, and with intergovernmental organizations, as well as with non-governmental organizations;

7. *Encourages* States parties to continue to include a gender perspective in their reports to the Committee, and invites the Committee to take into account a gender perspective in the implementation of its mandate;

8. *Notes with appreciation* the engagement of the Committee in the follow-up to the Durban Declaration and Programme of Action;

9. *Expresses its appreciation* for the efforts made so far by the Committee to improve the efficiency of its working methods, and encourages the Committee to continue its activities in this regard;

10. *Encourages* the continued participation of members of the Committee in the annual inter-committee meetings and meetings of chairpersons of the human rights treaty bodies, especially with a view to a more co-ordinated approach to the activities of the treaty body system and standardized reporting;

II

Financial situation of the Committee on the Elimination of Racial Discrimination

11. *Takes note* of the report of the Secretary-General on the financial situation of the Committee on the Elimination of Racial Discrimination;

12. *Expresses its profound concern* at the fact that a number of States parties to the International Convention on the Elimination of All Forms of Racial Discrimination have still not fulfilled their financial obligations, as shown in the report of the Secretary-General, and strongly appeals to all States parties that are in arrears to fulfil their outstanding financial obligations under article 8, paragraph 6, of the Convention;

13. *Strongly urges* States parties to the Convention to accelerate their domestic ratification procedures with regard to the amendment to the Convention concerning the financing of the Committee and to notify the Secretary-General expeditiously in writing of their agreement to the amendment, as decided upon at the Fourteenth Meeting of States Parties to the International Convention on the Elimination of All Forms of Racial Discrimination on 15 January 1992, endorsed by the General Assembly in its resolution 47/111 and further reiterated at the Sixteenth Meeting of States Parties on 16 January 1996;

14. *Requests* the Secretary-General to continue to ensure adequate financial arrangements and to provide the necessary support, including an adequate level of Secretariat assistance, in order to ensure the functioning of the Committee and to enable it to cope with its increasing amount of work;

15. *Also requests* the Secretary-General to invite those States parties to the Convention that are in arrears to pay the amounts in arrears, and to report thereon to the General Assembly at its sixty-first session;

III

Status of the International Convention on the Elimination of All Forms of Racial Discrimination

16. *Takes note* of the report of the Secretary-General on the status of the International Convention on the Elimination of All Forms of Racial Discrimination;

17. *Expresses its satisfaction* at the number of States that have ratified or acceded to the Convention, which now stands at one hundred and seventy;

18. *Urges* States parties to comply fully with their obligations under the Convention and to take into consideration the concluding observations and general recommendations of the Committee;

19. *Reaffirms its conviction* that ratification of or accession to the Convention on a universal basis and the implementation of its provisions are necessary for the effectiveness of the fight against racism, racial discrimination, xenophobia and related intolerance and for the implementation of the commitments undertaken under the Durban Declaration and Programme of Action;

20. *Urges* all States that have not yet become parties to the Convention to ratify or accede to it as a matter of urgency, with a view to achieving universal ratification by 2005;

21. *Urges* States to limit the extent of any reservation they lodge to the Convention and to formulate any reservation as precisely and as narrowly as possible in order to ensure that no reservation is incompatible with the object and purpose of the Convention, to review their reservations on a regular basis with a view to withdrawing them, and to withdraw reservations that are contrary to the object and purpose of the Convention;

22. *Notes* that the number of States parties to the Convention that have made the declaration provided for in article 14 of the Convention now stands at forty-five, and requests the States parties that have not yet done so to consider making that declaration;

23. *Decides* to consider, at its sixty-first session, under the item entitled "Elimination of racism and racial discrimination", the reports of the Committee on the Elimination of Racial Discrimination on its sixty-sixth and sixty-seventh and its sixty-eighth and sixty-ninth sessions, the report of the Secretary-General on the financial situation of the Committee and the report of the Secretary-General on the status of the Convention.

Convention against torture

Accessions and ratifications

As at 31 December, 139 States were parties to the 1984 Convention against Torture and Other Cruel, Inhuman or Degrading Treatment or Punishment, adopted by the General Assembly in resolution 39/46 [YUN 1984, p. 813]. Liberia, Maldives, Mauritania, Swaziland and the Syrian Arab Republic acceded to the Convention during the year. The Optional Protocol to the Convention, which was adopted in resolution 57/199 [YUN 2002, p. 631] and opened for signature on 4 February 2003, had 31 signatories and six States parties (Albania, Argentina, Denmark, Liberia, Malta, United Kingdom). The Protocol would enter into force 30 days following the deposit of the twentieth instrument of ratification or accession. As at 15 July, 52 parties had made the required declarations under articles 21 and 22 (under which a party recognized the competence of the Committee against Torture to receive and consider communications to the effect that a party claimed that another was not fulfilling its obligations under the Convention, and to receive communications from or on behalf of individuals who claimed to be victims of a violation of the Convention by a

State party) and four had made the declaration only under article 21, bringing the total of declarations under that article to 56; four parties had made the declaration only under article 22, also bringing the total of declarations under that article to 56. Amendments to articles 17 and 18, adopted in 1992 [YUN 1992, p. 735], had been accepted by 25 parties at year's end.

On 19 April [res. 2004/41], the Commission urged States to become parties to the Convention and to limit the extent of their reservations. Ratifying or acceding States were invited to make the declarations provided for in articles 21 and 22 and to comply with their obligations pursuant to article 19, including their reporting obligations.

The Secretary-General reported on the status of the Convention, its Optional Protocol and the declarations provided for in articles 21 and 22 as at 15 July [A/59/310]. On 20 December, the Assembly took note of the report (**decision 59/528**).

Implementation

Monitoring body. The Committee against Torture, established as a monitoring body under the Convention, held its thirty-second and thirty-third sessions in Geneva from 3 to 21 May [A/59/44] and from 6 to 26 November [A/60/44], respectively. Under article 19, it considered reports submitted by Argentina, Bulgaria, Chile, Croatia, the Czech Republic, Germany, Greece, Monaco, New Zealand and the United Kingdom.

In accordance with article 20, the Committee studied reliable information that appeared to contain well-founded indications that torture was systematically practised in a State party. Also under article 20, the Committee, after consultations with the State party concerned (Serbia and Montenegro), decided to include a summary account of the results of proceedings, begun in 1998, in its May report. Under article 22, the Committee considered communications submitted by individuals who claimed that their rights under the Convention had been violated by a State party and who had exhausted all available domestic remedies.

An April report [E/CN.4/2004/125] of the Committee's Acting Chairman summarized the Committee's activities since its 2003 sessions [YUN 2003, p. 675].

Convention on elimination of discrimination against women and Optional Protocol

(For details on the status of the Convention and on the Optional Protocol, see p. 1169.)

Convention on the Rights of the Child

Accessions and ratifications

As at 31 December, the number of States parties to the 1989 Convention on the Rights of the Child, adopted by the General Assembly in resolution 44/25 [YUN 1989, p. 560], remained at 192. States parties to the Optional Protocol to the Convention on the involvement of children in armed conflict, adopted by the Assembly in resolution 54/263 [YUN 2000, p. 615], rose to 91 with ratification during the year by Botswana, Brazil, Cambodia, Ecuador, Germany, Japan, Luxembourg, Madagascar, Maldives, Mongolia, the Republic of Korea, the Republic of Moldova, Senegal, Slovenia, The former Yugoslav Republic of Macedonia and Turkey, and accession by Bahrain, Bolivia, Kuwait, the Libyan Arab Jamahiriya, Mozambique, Oman, Timor-Leste and the United Republic of Tanzania. The Optional Protocol to the Convention on the sale of children, child prostitution and child pornography, also adopted by resolution 54/263, had 89 States parties, with ratification in 2004 by Austria, Brazil, Ecuador, El Salvador, Estonia, Lebanon, Madagascar, the Niger, the Republic of Korea, Slovakia, Slovenia and Togo, and accession by Bahrain, Kuwait, the Libyan Arab Jamahiriya, Lithuania, Nicaragua, Oman, the Sudan and Yemen.

The Secretary-General reported on the status of the Convention and Optional Protocols as at 22 June [A/59/190] and 7 December [E/CN.4/2005/73].

On 20 April [res. 2004/48], by a recorded vote of 52 to 1, the Commission urged States that had not done so to sign and ratify or accede to the Convention and the Optional Protocols, and to strengthen cooperation with the Committee on the Rights of the Child (CRC). The Secretary-General was requested to assist the Committee, while OHCHR, UN mechanisms and relevant UN system organs were asked to incorporate a strong child rights perspective in all activities in the fulfilment of their mandates, and to ensure that their staff was trained in child protection matters.

On 23 December, the Assembly urged States that had not done so to sign and ratify or accede to the Convention and the Optional Protocols, and called on them to strengthen cooperation with CRC (**resolution 59/261**) (see p. 779).

Implementation

Monitoring body. In 2004, CRC held its thirty-fifth (12-30 January) [CRC/C/137], thirty-sixth (17 May–4 June) [CRC/C/140] and thirty-seventh (13 September–1 October [CRC/C/143] sessions, all in Geneva. Each session was preceded by a working group meeting to review State party reports and identify the main questions to be discussed with representatives of the reporting States.

Under article 44 of the Convention, CRC considered initial or periodic reports submitted by Angola, Antigua and Barbuda, Armenia, Botswana, Brazil, Croatia, the Democratic People's Republic of Korea, Dominica, El Salvador, Equatorial Guinea, France, Germany, Guyana, India, Indonesia, Japan, Kyrgyzstan, Liberia, Myanmar, the Netherlands (including Aruba), Panama, Papua New Guinea, Rwanda, Sao Tome and Principe and Slovenia.

In January, the Committee held a day of general discussion on implementing child rights in early childhood.

CRC reports covering its thirtieth to thirty-fifth sessions were issued in a consolidated report [A/59/41 & Corr.1 & Add.1]. On 20 December, the Assembly took note of the report (**decision 59/525**).

Convention on migrant workers

Accessions and ratifications

As at 31 December, the number of States parties to the International Convention on the Protection of the Rights of All Migrant Workers and Members of Their Families, adopted by the General Assembly in resolution 45/158 [YUN 1990, p. 594] and which entered into force in 2003 [YUN 2003, p. 676], totalled 27. During the year, Turkey ratified the Convention and the Libyan Arab Jamahirya and Timor-Leste acceded to it.

The Secretary-General reported on the status of the Convention as at 20 August [A/59/306]; the Assembly took note of the report on 20 December (**decision 59/528**).

On 20 April [res. 2004/56], the Commission called on States that had not done so to sign and ratify or accede to the Convention. It asked the Secretary-General to assist the promotion of the Convention through the programme of advisory services and technical cooperation (see p. 670) and to report in 2006 on the Convention's status and on the Secretariat's efforts to promote the Convention and protect migrant workers' rights.

Implementation. The Committee on the Protection of the Rights of All Migrant Workers and Members of Their Families held its first session from 1 to 5 March in Geneva [A/59/48], at which it elected its officers, discussed ways to organize its future work, adopted its rules of procedure and decided to request the Secretary-General to arrange two Committee sessions in 2005. It noted that the reports of 22 States parties would become due on 1 July.

The Committee had held the first meeting of the States parties to the Convention in December 2003 [YUN 2003, p. 677] to elect 10 Committee members, of which five were elected for a two-year term and five for four years.

GENERAL ASSEMBLY ACTION

On 23 December [meeting 76], the General Assembly, on the recommendation of the Third Committee [A/59/503/Add.1], adopted **resolution 59/262** without vote [agenda item 105 (a)].

International Convention on the Protection of the Rights of All Migrant Workers and Members of Their Families

The General Assembly,

Guided by the basic instruments regarding the international protection of human rights, in particular the Universal Declaration of Human Rights and other relevant human rights instruments, and reaffirming the obligation of States to promote and protect human rights and fundamental freedoms,

Recalling its resolution 45/158 of 18 December 1990, by which it adopted and opened for signature, ratification and accession the International Convention on the Protection of the Rights of All Migrant Workers and Members of Their Families,

Recalling also the entry into force of the International Convention on the Protection of the Rights of All Migrant Workers and Members of Their Families on 1 July 2003,

Considering that, in the Vienna Declaration and Programme of Action adopted by the World Conference on Human Rights on 25 June 1993, all States are urged to guarantee the protection of the human rights of all migrant workers and their families and are invited to consider the possibility of signing and ratifying the Convention at the earliest possible time,

Bearing in mind the principles and norms established within the framework of the International Labour Organization and the importance of the work done in connection with migrant workers and members of their families in other specialized agencies and in various organs of the United Nations, as well as in the International Organization for Migration,

Conscious of the marked increase in migratory movements that has occurred, especially in certain parts of the world,

Deeply concerned at the manifestations of violence, racism, racial discrimination, xenophobia and other forms of intolerance and inhuman and degrading treatment directed against migrants in various parts of the world,

Recognizing the urgent need to make further efforts worldwide to improve the situation and to guarantee respect for the human rights and dignity of all migrant workers and members of their families, and aware of the important contribution of the Convention in this regard,

1. *Welcomes* the increasing number of signatures, ratifications or accessions to the International Convention on the Protection of the Rights of All Migrant Workers and Members of Their Families, calls upon States parties to undertake the necessary measures for the implementation of the Convention, and takes note

of the report of the Secretary-General on the status of the Convention;

2. *Calls upon* all Member States that have not yet done so to consider urgently signing and ratifying or acceding to the Convention, with the aim of achieving a broader participation by Member States in the Convention;

3. *Welcomes* the establishment of the Committee on the Protection of the Rights of All Migrant Workers and Members of Their Families, as well as the report on its first session, held in Geneva from 1 to 5 March 2004, and takes note of the rules of procedure adopted by the Committee;

4. *Requests* the Secretary-General to continue to provide all the necessary facilities and assistance for the effective functioning of the Committee on the Protection of the Rights of All Migrant Workers and Members of Their Families, making efficient use of available resources;

5. *Invites* the Committee to take into account the work done by other human rights treaty bodies and special procedures of the Commission on Human Rights to promote and protect the human rights of migrant workers, as well as the work of other international forums and other parts of the United Nations system in addressing issues of international migration;

6. *Also invites* the Committee to take into account the efforts by the other human rights treaty bodies and the Secretary-General aimed at improving the effectiveness of the treaty body system;

7. *Calls upon* States parties to the Convention to submit in due time their first periodic report, as requested in article 73 of the Convention;

8. *Invites* States parties to the Convention to consider making the declarations foreseen in articles 76 and 77 of the Convention;

9. *Requests* the Secretary-General to provide all the facilities and assistance necessary for the active promotion of the Convention through the programme of advisory services and technical cooperation in the field of human rights;

10. *Welcomes* the increasing activities undertaken by the organizations and bodies of the United Nations system and intergovernmental and non-governmental organizations to disseminate information on and promote understanding of the importance of the Convention, and invites them to intensify further their efforts in this regard;

11. *Also welcomes* the work of the Special Rapporteur of the Commission on Human Rights on the human rights of migrants in relation to the Convention, and encourages her to persevere in her efforts;

12. *Requests* the Secretary-General to submit an updated report on the status of the Convention and on the implementation of the present resolution to the General Assembly at its sixty-first session.

Convention on genocide

As at 31 December, 136 States were parties to the 1948 Convention on the Prevention and Punishment of the Crime of Genocide, adopted by the General Assembly in resolution 260 A (III) [YUN 1948-49, p. 959]. During the year, the Comoros acceded to the Convention.

Note by Secretariat. A note by the Secretariat [E/CN.4/2005/46] presented the views of 10 States parties, the European Union and the Secretary-General's Special Adviser on the Prevention of Genocide (see p. 730) as at 26 November, in response to the Secretary-General's proposal to establish a committee on the prevention of genocide. While the majority of replies indicated support for the initiative, two States parties opposed it. The report concluded that the limited number of replies did not provide a sufficiently large basis upon which final conclusions might be reached. It was suggested that further views be sought and that the Secretariat report to the Commission in 2006.

Other activities

Follow-up to 1993 World Conference

Report of High Commissioner. In a March report [E/CN.4/2004/12] on follow-up to the World Conference on Human Rights [YUN 1993, p. 908], the High Commissioner described the current state of human rights in the world, the potential pillars of international cooperation for the universal realization of human rights, the state of protection at all levels and measures to strengthen it. The High Commissioner appealed to the Commission to take action regarding trafficking in young women, possibly by establishing a mechanism to study and analyse the problem and present findings and recommendations to the Commission. The High Commissioner also asked the Commission to take urgent action to protect those at risk and to lead an international campaign against trafficking in humans. Addenda to the report focused on the Secretary-General's UN system reform proposals [E/CN.4/2004/12/Add.1] (see p. 650), the promotion of tolerance and pluralism [E/CN.4/2004/12/Add.2] (see p. 709) and strengthening national human rights protection systems [E/CN.4/2004/12/Add.3] (see p. 658).

Annual meeting. In July, the High Commissioner transmitted the report of the eleventh meeting of special rapporteurs/representatives, independent experts and chairpersons of working groups of the Commission's special procedures and advisory services programme (Geneva, 21-25 June) [E/CN.4/2005/5]. Participants discussed, among other things, measures to enhance the effectiveness of the special procedures system and ways of integrating their work into OHCHR activities through its field presences, technical cooperation activities and the work of its National Institutions Team, and into the wider

UN system, in accordance with the Secretary-General's reform agenda (see p. 1360). They also held a thematic discussion on mainstreaming child rights. The meeting decided to enhance coordination in preparing fact-finding missions and in publishing statements relating to situations of grave human rights concerns, and requested the Secretariat to prepare country assessments, develop a LISTSERV to facilitate communication and information exchange between special procedures mandate-holders, compile electronically country-specific recommendations prior to each Commission session, and reflect on effective means for follow-up of special procedures recommendations. It also decided to include on the agenda for the special procedures annual meeting a new item on a thematic issue and on coordination and possible information exchange with the Security Council's Counter-Terrorism Committee (see p. 76) and the Secretary-General's Special Adviser on the Prevention of Genocide and to prepare a joint report on the world human rights situation, in the light of the respective experiences of the mandate-holders.

On 20 December, the Assembly took note of the Third Committee's report [A/59/503/Add.4] on the implementation of and follow-up to the Vienna Declaration and Programme of Action adopted at the 1993 World Conference (**decision 59/529**).

Advisory services and technical cooperation

Commission action. On 21 April [res. 2004/81], the Commission, recognizing the usefulness of advisory services and technical cooperation for all countries, called on OHCHR to continue to develop its potential for human rights promotion and protection. The Secretary-General was requested to ensure the efficient management of the Voluntary Fund for Technical Cooperation in the Field of Human Rights and to hold information meetings for Member States and organizations involved in the programme of advisory services and technical cooperation; to assist the Fund's Board of Trustees and to ensure that the conclusions of Board meetings were reflected in the annual report to the Commission regarding technical cooperation; and to report in 2006 on the progress and achievements made and on the obstacles encountered in implementing the programme of advisory services and technical cooperation.

Report of Secretary-General. In accordance with Commission resolution 2004/81 (see above), the Secretary-General, in a December report

[E/CN.4/2005/110], described the OHCHR technical cooperation programme, which provided assistance for building national and regional human rights infrastructure, focusing on incorporating international human rights standards in national laws and policies and on the establishment or strengthening of national institutions capable of promoting and protecting human rights and democracy under the rule of law. In addition to projects implemented from Geneva, technical cooperation activities were carried out through field presences, including by technical cooperation project offices, regional representatives and senior human rights advisers to UN country teams. Technical cooperation activities were also undertaken in collaboration with UN peacekeeping and peace-building missions and UN country teams. OHCHR implemented related projects in cooperation with other UN agencies and programmes, particularly UNDP.

In 2004, the Voluntary Fund for Technical Cooperation in the Field of Human Rights funded 31 projects; 17 were completed during the year, while 29 new requests were received. As at 31 December, the Fund had received approximately $9.3 million against expenditure of some $12.8 million. The Fund's Board of Trustees, at its twenty-first (8-11 June) and twenty-second (23-26 November) sessions reviewed the programme's regional activities, discussed follow-up to the 2003 global review of the programme [YUN 2003, p. 679] and examined financial and administrative matters. In November, the Board held a joint meeting with the heads of OHCHR field presences on ensuring one UN human rights programme with three interlinked components—treaty bodies, special procedures and technical cooperation. As at 31 December, the Fund's income amounted to $17.4 million for 2004, including carry-over from previous years; commitments totalled $12.8 million, leaving a balance of $4.6 million.

During the year, OHCHR initiated an internal review of its regional presences and approaches, which demonstrated that such presence was a good strategic choice for the Office. The review process would continue in 2005, with evaluations of several regional presences planned.

Subcommission action. On 12 August [dec. 2004/115], the Subcommission requested Gudmundur Alfredsson (Iceland) and Ibrahim Salama (Egypt) to prepare, without financial implications, for 2005, a working paper on the evaluation of the content and delivery of human rights technical cooperation for the purpose of seeking possible improvements.

Afghanistan

Note by Secretariat. A January note by the Secretariat [E/CN.4/2004/102] informed the Commission that the independent expert, whose appointment it had requested in 2003 [YUN 2003, p. 679], had not yet been appointed.

In April, the Commission appointed M. Cherif Bassiouni (Egypt) as independent expert.

Commission action. The Commission Chairperson, in a 21 April statement on technical cooperation in the field of human rights in Afghanistan, which the Commission adopted by consensus, stated that the Commission welcomed the adoption of the new Afghan Constitution by the Constitutional Loya Jirga on 5 January and its provisions, which stated that all citizens were equal before the law and that at least two women were to be elected to the Wolesi Jirga from each province. It also welcomed the Constitution's recognition of the status of the Afghan Independent Human Rights Commission and encouraged the Transitional Authority (TA) and the international community to assist the Independent Commission. Noting improvements in the TA's institutional capacity to deal with human rights, the Commission encouraged it to maintain focus on the promotion and protection of human rights and fundamental freedoms, as described in the Universal Declaration of Human Rights, adopted by the General Assembly in resolution 217 A (III) [YUN 1948-49, p. 535]. The Commission, recalling that continued attention to the protection and promotion of women's and children's rights were of paramount importance, requested the independent expert on the situation of human rights in Afghanistan (see below) to report to the Assembly in 2004 and to the Commission in 2005. The Secretary-General was asked to extend the expert's mandate for a further year, to assist the expert and to report in 2005. OHCHR was requested to continue and expand, in collaboration with the TA, its human rights programme of advisory services and technical cooperation. The Economic and Social Council endorsed the Commission's requests to the Secretary-General and to the expert on 22 July (**decision 2004/284**).

Reports of independent expert. An April note by the Secretariat [E/CN.4/2004/102/Add.1] contained the expert's oral statement before the Commission, in which he presented his views regarding his future work.

A September note of the Secretary-General [A/59/370] transmitted the expert's report on the current human rights situation in Afghanistan, following his visit to the country (14-22 August), during which he was briefed on the work of the Afghan Independent Human Rights Commission and met with 32 Afghan human rights or-ganizations and individual human rights activists. The expert also inspected a prison and a women's detention facility, and identified gross violations of fundamental human rights, such as extrajudicial execution, torture, rape, arbitrary arrest and detention, inhumane conditions of detention, illegal and forceful seizure of property, child abduction and trafficking, and various forms of abuse against women, minorities, returning refugees, poor people and handicapped persons. Most of the violations were committed by warlords, local commanders, drug traffickers and other actors who exercised varying degrees of authority in the provinces and districts. The Coalition forces, which could have marginalized the warlords, did not do so, and even worked with them to combat the Taliban regime and to pursue Al-Qaida. That situation helped to entrench the warlords. Thus, the paramount factor affecting human rights was security. The expert noted that, although the Government's accomplishments during the last two years were impressive, more was still needed, and made recommendations to the Government and the international community regarding security issues, the rule of law, improvements in detention facilities and due process, women and children, land disputes and housing, education, the development of a policy for transitional or post-conflict justice, strengthening civil society and the establishment of status-of-forces agreements with the Coalition forces and the International Security Assistance Force.

The General Assembly took note of the expert's report on 20 December (**decision 59/528**).

Burundi

Commission action. On 21 April [res. 2004/82], the Commission, condemning all acts of violence and violations of human rights and international humanitarian law in Burundi, decided to appoint an independent expert to back the Government's efforts to improve the country's human rights situation. The expert was requested to submit an interim report to the General Assembly in 2004 and to report to the Commission in 2005. The Economic and Social Council endorsed the Commission's decision and its request to the expert on 15 June (**decision 2004/224**).

In July, Akich Okola (Kenya) was appointed independent expert.

Report of independent expert. During his first mission to Burundi (4-13 October) [E/CN.4/2005/118], the independent expert met with officials from all political parties and several national institutions, NGOs, diplomatic missions, UN agencies and international organizations. He also visited an internally displaced people camp in the commune of Kabezi, Bujumbura Rural province, the site of Gatumba, where some 160 Congolese refugees were massacred, and a central prison in the same province. He noted that since the mission did not take place until October, he was unable to submit the interim report requested by the Commission.

The expert observed that, despite continuous efforts by national and international actors, human rights violations persisted, and because most of the violations remained unpunished, a climate conducive to further abuses arose, particularly regarding sexual violence. The principal violations related to the right to life, liberty, security and inviolability of the person, and to freedom of movement, of the right to chose a place of residence and of opinion, expression and peaceful assembly, as well as the rights of women and children. Frequent looting resulting from armed conflict and displacement dispossessed whole communities of the few resources they had, including housing, land and cattle, and access to basic health and education services was constrained by various factors. Despite some improvement, the prisons remained overcrowded, exerting a negative impact on health, nutrition and sanitary conditions. In his recommendations, the expert addressed an urgent appeal to all belligerents in the country to respect civilians' rights; encouraged the initiation of judicial proceedings to ensure that the perpetrators of the killings at Gatumba (see p. 149) and those that aided and abetted them were brought to justice; and urged the Government to combat increasing sexual violence against women. He also recommended that the international community support the Government's efforts to promote human rights and secure lasting peace, and that additional funding be made available to enable him to better discharge his mandate.

Cambodia

Commission action. On 21 April [res. 2004/79], the Commission welcomed Cambodia's improvement on its human rights situation, while still expressing concern about continuing violations, including torture, excessive pre-trial detention, land reform issues, violence against activists, and problems relating to the rule of law, impunity and corruption. The Commission invited the Secretary-General and the international community to continue to assist the Government in improving democracy and protecting human rights, and requested the Secretary-General to report in 2005.

Report of Special Representative. The Secretary-General's Special Representative for human rights in Cambodia, Peter Leuprecht (Austria), during his visit to Cambodia (7-14 November) [E/CN.4/2005/116] focused on land management and natural resources, impunity and corruption. He also addressed the general political climate following the establishment of a new coalition Government in July, and examined issues of justice sector reform, the freedoms of association and assembly, indigenous land rights and issues relating to the trials of senior Khmer Rouge leaders (see p. 380). The Special Representative found that Cambodian society was still suffering from poverty, violence, corruption and lawlessness. He pointed to corrupt and opaque power structures, inequality before the law, impunity, collusion and lack of transparency and accountability as the main obstacles to genuine democracy, rule of law and respect for human rights. Endemic corruption also remained a recurring obstacle to the rule of law and economic and social development. The Special Representative recommended a series of measures to the Government regarding democratic institutions; the need to investigate human rights violations and to bring those responsible to justice; steps to end executive interference in the judiciary; steps to ensure respect for the rights to the freedom of expression, of association, of assembly, of non-violent demonstration and of movement; and the need to address land and natural resources management issues and to end forced evictions, investigate and prosecute cases of corruption and ensure the Government met its obligations under international human rights treaties to which it was party.

OHCHR/Cambodia

Report of Secretary-General. A December report [E/CN.4/2005/111] of the Secretary-General described the role and achievements of OHCHR/Cambodia in 2004 in assisting the Cambodian Government and people to promote and protect human rights. During the year, the Office continued to monitor the overall human rights situation, to investigate reports of human rights violations and to document their pattern. It regularly brought its concerns to the authorities' attention and requested their intervention. OHCHR/Cambodia also continued to contribute to justice sector reform and the administration of justice, by facilitating discussion on legal policy issues, observing trials in the courts, analysing key developments and patterns of violations in the criminal justice system, acting as a legal resource, and providing comments on draft laws. The Office actively advocated for freedom of information legislation and monitored developments related to the forthcoming trials of senior Khmer Rouge leaders. Regarding the development of land management and natural resource policies, the Office continued its work to protect local communities affected by land and forest concessions. In December, the High Commissioner and the Government signed a new memorandum of understanding for the implementation of a technical cooperation programme on human rights for a two-year period.

Chad

Commission action. On 21 April [res. 2004/85], the Commission, expressing concern at violence in Chad, the dependence of the judiciary on the Government, the country's culture of impunity, the scarcity of resources in the judicial and prison sectors, and the weakness of national human rights structures and institutions, decided to appoint an independent expert for a one-year period to facilitate cooperation between the Government and OHCHR and to report in 2005. The Economic and Social Council endorsed the Commission's decision on 15 June (**decision 2004/226**).

In July, Mónica Pinto (Argentina) was appointed independent expert.

Report of independent expert. The expert visited Chad (7-17 October) [E/CN.4/2005/121], where she examined human rights concerns and observed that national identity was secondary to ethnic or clan identity. The current focus was on dichotomies, particularly between northerners and southerners, Muslims and Christians, nomads and sedentary people, Arabs and Africans, and such differences were manipulated to exacerbate tensions among different groups. The expert characterized the country as one in which no one had confidence in national institutions; national legislation took second place to local customs; people exerted pressure on one another, with the most powerful prevailing; refugees enjoyed a better quality of life than local people; and there was no deliberate policy for addressing persistent human rights violations. The expert recommended the establishment of a transparent, accountable and participatory government; the need for the State to embrace the rule of law; and the necessity for judicial reform and for the rehabilitation of prisoners. She also advocated, among other things, the protection of vulnerable groups and of civil society, an intensive literacy campaign, sustainable development efforts and the overall development of society.

Democratic Republic of the Congo

Commission action. On 21 April [res. 2004/84], the Commission, expressing concern at persistent reports of serious violations of human rights and international humanitarian law in the eastern part of the Democratic Republic of the Congo (DRC), particularly in North and South Kivu, northern Katanga and Ituri, decided to appoint an independent expert to assist the Government in the field of human rights and to study the evolving human rights situation and verify that the country's obligations were being fulfilled. The expert was asked to report to the General Assembly in 2004 and to the Commission in 2005, and the Secretary-General was requested to provide the DRC with human rights advisory services. The Economic and Social Council approved the Commission's decision on 15 June (**decision 2004/225**).

In July, Titinga Frédéric Pacéré (Burkina Faso) was appointed independent expert.

Note by Secretariat. A September note by the Secretariat [A/59/378] stated that the expert, owing to his late appointment, would not be able to submit a report to the General Assembly as requested by the Commission, but would report orally (see below).

Reports of independent expert. In an oral report to the General Assembly's Third Committee [A/C.3/59/SR.29] on 28 October, the independent expert said grave violations of human rights and other crimes continued, especially in the eastern regions, and that the justice system was underfunded, understaffed and unable to cope with the situation. He recommended setting up an international criminal tribunal for the DRC, with its modus operandi determined by the Congolese Government. The Assembly took note of the report on 20 December (**decision 59/528**).

The expert undertook two missions to the DRC [E/CN.4/2005/120], the first to Kinshasa and Kisangani (22 August–2 September), and the second to Kinshasa, Bukavu and Goma (9-19 November). The expert noted that, as in previous years, the current year was characterized by constructive efforts, but also by massive human rights violations, inter-ethnic intolerance, violence, massacres, the abuse of women and children, various kinds of atrocities perpetrated by armed groups against civilians and endless political crises. Congolese women and children were the main victims of the armed violence and of the most atrocious and destructive forms of sexual violence. The expert called on the transitional Government and all parties to the conflict to end the violence, arrest the perpetrators and hand them over to Congolese and international justice; to dismiss from the Government, institutions and armed forces those found guilty of crimes against humanity and serious human rights violations; to launch a national human rights campaign; to set up a compensation fund for victims of crimes against humanity; to enhance women's status and stop the abuse of women and children; and to practice good governance, manage the country's resources properly and combat corruption. Recommendations addressed to the international community highlighted the need to provide political, financial, military and diplomatic support and assistance for the country's process of transition, reconstruction and pacification, and requested that it cooperate with the country to end the illegal exploitation of natural resources and arms-trafficking; place the protection of the population and respect for human rights at the core of the Security Council's next resolution on the situation in the country; strengthen the mandates and resources of the Human Rights and Child Protection Sections of the United Nations Organization Mission in the Democratic Republic of the Congo; grant OHCHR the resources necessary to enable it to accord priority to the situation in the DRC; and establish, by decision of the Security Council, an international criminal tribunal to try crimes committed during the successive conflicts in the DRC.

GENERAL ASSEMBLY ACTION

On 20 December [meeting 74], the General Assembly, on the recommendation of the Third Committee [A/59/503/Add.3], adopted **resolution 59/207** by recorded vote (76-2-100) [agenda item 105 (c)].

Situation of human rights in the Democratic Republic of the Congo

The General Assembly,

Reaffirming that all States Members of the United Nations have an obligation to promote and protect human rights and fundamental freedoms, and the duty to fulfil the obligations they have undertaken under the various instruments in this field,

Noting that the Democratic Republic of the Congo is a party to several international and regional human rights instruments and to several instruments pertaining to international humanitarian law,

Recalling all its previous resolutions, as well as those of the Commission on Human Rights, on the situation of human rights in the Democratic Republic of the Congo,

Noting the special report of the Secretary-General on the events in Ituri between January 2002 and December 2003 that was drafted by the Human Rights and Child Protection Sections of the United Nations Organization Mission in the Democratic Republic of the Congo,

Recalling Security Council resolutions 1493(2003) of 28 July 2003, 1522(2004) of 15 January 2004, 1533 (2004) of 12 March 2004 and 1565(2004) of 1 October 2004,

1. *Welcomes:*

(a) The nomination of the independent expert on the situation of human rights in the Democratic Re-

public of the Congo in July 2004, as well as his visit to the Democratic Republic of the Congo in August 2004;

(b) In particular the extended mandate of the United Nations Organization Mission in the Democratic Republic of the Congo regarding the promotion and protection of human rights in accordance with Security Council resolution 1565(2004), and expresses its support for the work of the Special Representative of the Secretary-General for the Democratic Republic of the Congo and for the Mission;

(c) The work accomplished by the human rights field office in the Democratic Republic of the Congo, and encourages the office to pursue and enhance its cooperation with the relevant agencies of the United Nations and the Mission in the fulfilment of its mandate;

(d) The measures taken by the transitional institutions in order to implement the Global and All-Inclusive Agreement on the Transition in the Democratic Republic of the Congo signed in Pretoria on 17 December 2002 and to restore the authority of the State, such as the appointment of provincial governors, the establishment of the Independent Electoral Commission, the appointment of the High Command of the Integrated National Police and the setting up of the Supreme Defence Council;

(e) The adoption of the Declaration of Principles by the Heads of State who participated in the International Conference on Peace, Security, Democracy and Development in the Great Lakes Region, which took place in Dar es Salaam, United Republic of Tanzania, on 19 and 20 November 2004;

2. *Calls upon* the United Nations High Commissioner for Human Rights to keep it informed of the consultations between her Office and the Secretary-General concerning the ways in which to assist the transitional Government of the Democratic Republic of the Congo in tackling the problem of impunity;

3. *Takes note* of the decision by the Office of the Prosecutor of the International Criminal Court, based upon the referral of the Democratic Republic of the Congo, to commence an investigation into crimes allegedly committed in the territory of the Democratic Republic of the Congo since the entry into force of the Rome Statute of the International Criminal Court on 1 July 2002;

4. *Condemns* the continuing violations of human rights and international humanitarian law in the Democratic Republic of the Congo, while remaining concerned about the prevalence of grave violations and the rise in ethnic tensions throughout the Democratic Republic of the Congo and, in particular, in Ituri, North and South Kivu and other areas in the eastern part of the country;

5. *Urges* all parties to the conflict in the Democratic Republic of the Congo:

(a) To respect and further implement the Global and All-Inclusive Agreement;

(b) To adhere fully to the Principles on Good-neighbourly Relations and Cooperation between the Democratic Republic of the Congo and Burundi, Rwanda and Uganda signed in New York on 25 September 2003, to engage firmly for the full success of the joint verification mechanism agreed upon by the Presidents of the Democratic Republic of the Congo and Rwanda in Abuja on 25 June 2004, and to take part constructively in the International Conference on Peace, Security, Democracy and Development in the Great Lakes Region of Africa;

(c) To cease immediately all military activity that impedes the consolidation of the sovereignty, unity and territorial integrity of the Democratic Republic of the Congo, including support for the armed groups allied to the parties to the conflict;

(d) To support the transitional Government and its institutions in order to allow for the re-establishment of political and economic stability and for the gradual reinforcement of state structures over the entire territory of the Democratic Republic of the Congo, in accordance with their obligations under the Transitional Constitution;

(e) To put an immediate end to the recruitment and use of child soldiers, which is contrary to international law and to the African Charter on the Rights and Welfare of the Child, with the understanding that, under the Convention on the Rights of the Child and the Optional Protocol thereto on the involvement of children in armed conflict, and in accordance with Security Council resolution 1539(2004) of 22 April 2004 on children and armed conflict, persons under the age of 18 are entitled to special protection, and to provide information without delay on measures taken to discontinue such practices;

(f) To take special measures to protect women and children from the appalling violence, including sexual violence, which has been and continues to be prevalent throughout the country, in particular in Ituri, North and South Kivu and other areas in the eastern part of the country, and condemns in particular the widespread use of sexual violence as a means of warfare;

(g) To promote the full enjoyment of all human rights by women and children and to meet the special needs of women and girls in post-conflict reconstruction, as well as to ensure the full participation of women in all aspects of conflict resolution and peace processes, including peacekeeping, conflict management and peace-building, as a matter of priority, in accordance with Security Council resolution 1325(2000) of 31 October 2000 on women and peace and security;

(h) To ensure the rights and well-being of internally displaced persons, returnees and refugee populations;

(i) To respect international humanitarian law, in particular on the protection of civilians by ensuring the safety, security and freedom of movement of all civilians and United Nations and associated personnel, and the unhindered access of humanitarian personnel to all of the affected population throughout the territory of the Democratic Republic of the Congo in accordance with Security Council resolutions 1265(1999) of 17 September 1999 and 1296(2000) of 19 April 2000;

(j) To promote the full enjoyment of all human rights and to protect the safety, security and freedom of movement of all human rights defenders;

6. *Calls upon* the Government of National Unity and Transition to take specific measures:

(a) To achieve the objectives of the transitional period as laid down in the Global and All-Inclusive Agreement, in particular the holding of free and transparent elections at all levels, enabling the establishment of a democratic constitutional regime, and the formation of a restructured and integrated na-

tional army; and also the formation of an integrated and adequately resourced national police force;

(b) To strengthen the transitional institutions, in particular to set up effectively the Independent Electoral Commission, the Truth and Reconciliation Commission and the Human Rights Monitoring Centre, and to re-establish stability and the rule of law over the entire territory of the Democratic Republic of the Congo, thereby returning peace and progress to its people;

(c) To comply fully with its obligations under international human rights instruments and, accordingly, to continue to cooperate with United Nations mechanisms for the protection of human rights and further strengthen its cooperation with the Office of the United Nations High Commissioner for Human Rights in the Democratic Republic of the Congo;

(d) To put an end to impunity and to ensure, as it is duty-bound to do, that those responsible for human rights violations and grave breaches of international humanitarian law are brought to justice in accordance with due process, and to carry out urgently a comprehensive reform of the judicial system;

(e) To put an end to the use of the death penalty in a manner contrary to its obligations assumed under the relevant provisions of the International Covenant on Civil and Political Rights and other human rights instruments, while recalling its commitment to progressively abolish the death penalty and not to impose it on juvenile offenders;

(f) To continue to cooperate with the International Criminal Court and with the International Criminal Tribunal for Rwanda;

(g) To prevent the use of the media to incite hatred or tensions among communities, while respecting freedom of expression and of the press;

(h) To continue its programme to demobilize, disarm and reintegrate former combatants, taking into account the special needs of women and children, including girls, associated with those combatants;

(i) To put an end to the illegal exploitation of the natural resources of the Democratic Republic of the Congo, in view of the link between that exploitation and the continuation of the conflict;

7. *Encourages* the international community to continue to support the transition in the Democratic Republic of the Congo and its institutions and, in particular, to provide assistance in the reform of national judicial institutions;

8. *Decides* to continue to examine the situation of human rights in the Democratic Republic of the Congo, and requests the independent expert on the situation of human rights in the Democratic Republic of the Congo to report to the General Assembly at its sixtieth session.

Haiti

Commission action. On 21 April [E/2004/23], the Commission Chairperson, in a statement concerning technical cooperation and the situation of human rights in Haiti, stated that the Commission condemned the human rights violations in the country and called on all sectors and actors in national life to protect and promote human dignity. The Commission called for the swift restoration of security, particularly to improve the situation of the country's citizens, and emphasized the urgency of OHCHR's establishing an office there and contributing towards UN human rights activities. The independent expert on Haiti's human rights was asked to include in his 2005 report information on progress made to combat impunity and on the administration of justice.

Report of independent expert. Independent expert Louis Joinet (France) visited Haiti twice in 2004 (3-11 April, 6-17 November) [E/CN.4/2005/123], where he found persistent human rights violations, including armed assaults, reprisals, rapes, murders, summary executions, looting and arson. Mostly responsible were two groups of armed adversaries, one of which comprised supporters of the previous Government, and the other, former soldiers demobilized during the disbandment of the army in 1995, who felt that their social rights had not been recognized. Although all social classes were affected, the most vulnerable victims of the violations were the poor populations in shanty towns, women and children, and there were also reports of intimidation against the press. Overall, human rights violations in the country were exacerbated by the shortcomings of the judicial system, and, after examining the main obstacles to the reform of the system and the difficulties in combating impunity, the expert observed that most of his previous recommendations remained valid. In addition, however, he proposed that high priority be accorded to the reconstruction or rehabilitation of the judicial system, including in particular the courts and related infrastructure, the police and the prison administration. He also proposed numerous reform measures for adoption.

Liberia

Commission action. On 21 April [res. 2004/83], the Commission expressed concern at the continued existence of paramilitary groups in Liberia; serious human rights violations against civilians; sexual violence against women and girls; the country's persistent insecurity; and the culture of impunity. The international community was asked to support the Government in the process of disarmament, demobilization and reintegration of former combatants and to mobilize the resources needed to enable the National Transitional Government to implement relief and recovery programmes. The independent expert on the human rights situation in Liberia was requested to report in 2005, and the High Commissioner was asked to assist her.

Report of independent expert. The independent expert on the human rights situation in Li-

beria, Charlotte Abaka (Ghana), visited the country (23 May–13 June) [E/CN.4/2005/119], where she found that improved security conditions had led to increased access by humanitarian workers and provided the context for human rights activities. State-sponsored human rights violations had ceased, and, although institutions to address abuses and ensure the rule of law were lacking, national bodies provided for in the Comprehensive Peace Agreement, signed in 2003 [YUN 2003, p. 185], had been established and were in varying stages of operation. The expert recommended measures to facilitate the process of disarmament, demobilization, rehabilitation and reintegration, and to end impunity, establish a national law reform commission to ensure that domestic laws were brought in line with international instruments to which Liberia was a party, and ensure that adequate resources were provided for the Human Rights and Protection Component of the United Nations Mission in Liberia.

Nepal

On 21 April [E/2004/23], the Commission Chairperson, in a statement on behalf of the Commission, said the Commission was concerned at the human rights situation in Nepal and at the growing number of civilian victims as a result of ongoing violence. It condemned the indiscriminate violence perpetrated by the Communist Party of Nepal-Maoist, including the use of children in armed conflict. Welcoming Nepal's submission of periodic reports to the various human rights treaty bodies, the Commission encouraged the Government to follow up adequately their recommendations. The Commission asked OHCHR to report in 2005 on its activities in Nepal.

(For information on a visit to Nepal by the Working Group on Enforced and Involuntary Disappearances, see p. 731.)

Sierra Leone

Commission action. On 21 April [res. 2004/86], the Commission urged the Government of Sierra Leone to promote and protect human rights, give priority attention to the special needs of mutilated victims, facilitate the effective functioning of the National Commission for War-Affected Children and reconsider the issue of resettlement and reintegration of Sierra Leonean combatants who were being demobilized and repatriated from Côte d'Ivoire and Liberia. It requested the High Commissioner to report to the General Assembly in 2004 and to the Commission in 2005 on assistance to Sierra Leone in the field of human rights.

The Economic and Social Council endorsed the Commission's request on 22 July (**decision 2004/271**).

Report of High Commissioner. In a September report [A/59/340] to the General Assembly, submitted in response to Commission resolution 2004/86 (see above), the High Commissioner examined the human rights situation in Sierra Leone and UN activities and the status of transitional justice in the country. The High Commissioner observed that there had been significant improvements in the area of civil and political rights during the seven-year presence of the United Nations in Sierra Leone, despite a weak national human rights protection system. Important transitional justice mechanisms had been established with UN assistance. The Truth and Reconciliation Commission had concluded its public activities and the Special Court had commenced trials of some accused war criminals. However, there were serious concerns about the prolonged pre-trial detention of some 97 ex-combatants, and the situation of amputees and war wounded had not improved. Regarding children, the scars of war were seen in the traumatic conditions of some teenagers and young adults. School enrolment was low, especially among girls, and the country's endemic problem of child labour was exacerbated by extreme poverty. There were also concerns regarding child trafficking, early and forced marriages and children in conflict with the law, and although progress had been made regarding awareness of women's rights among the police, discrimination against women continued, resulting in various forms of violence such as deprivation, psychological abuse and physical assault. Also, progress in implementing civil and political rights had not been matched by advances in the realization of economic, social and cultural rights, with rising inflation pushing the price of basic commodities and foodstuffs beyond the reach of many citizens. The expert called for continuous capacity-building for local human rights NGOs, support for the Government's work in the review of women's status in the country and implementation of the recommendations of the Truth and Reconciliation Commission.

The General Assembly took note of the High Commissioner's report on 20 December (**decision 59/528**).

Somalia

Commission action. On 21 April [res. 2004/80], the Commission, welcoming steps towards last-ing peace and reconciliation in Somalia, condemned those who obstructed the peace process and the widespread violations and abuses of human rights and humanitarian law in the country. The Commission decided to extend the independent expert's mandate for a further year, asked him to report in 2005 and requested the Secretary-General to continue to assist him.

On 22 July, the Economic and Social Council approved the Commission's request to the Secretary-General (**decision 2004/270**).

Timor-Leste

On 21 April [E/2004/23], the Commission Chairperson, in a statement on behalf of the Commission, said the Commission underlined the importance of a continuing UN human rights presence in Timor-Leste following the end of the mandate of the United Nations Mission of Support in East Timor, in order to ensure an effective transition to the post-Mission phase. It also emphasized the need for continuing international assistance to strengthen the country's justice system and asked the international community to continue to support its fight against impunity. The Commission requested the High Commissioner to report in 2005.

Human rights education

UN Decade for Human Rights Education (1995-2004)

Report of High Commissioner. A February report [E/CN.4/2004/93] of the High Commissioner highlighted the achievements, shortcomings and future activities of the United Nations Decade for Human Rights Education (1995-2004), proclaimed by the General Assembly in resolution 49/184 [YUN 1994, p. 1039]. The report was based on replies received from 29 Governments and two national commissions for the United Nations Educational, Scientific and Cultural Organization (UNESCO) to a questionnaire prepared jointly by OHCHR and UNESCO. Most respondents reported increased human rights education activities within or outside the Decade's framework, but noted that human rights education remained a priority because specific issues had not been dealt with and appropriate coordination mechanisms for human rights education were not in place. The majority also supported the proclamation of a second Decade (2005-2014) and the establishment of a voluntary fund for human rights education. The report suggested that the Commission reflect on the desirability of an international convention on human rights education.

General Assembly consideration. On 10 December [meeting 70], the General Assembly, in commemoration of the annual observance of Human Rights Day, dedicated its plenary meeting to a review of the achievements of the Decade.

Follow-up to Decade

Commission action. On 21 April [res. 2004/71], the Commission recommended that the Economic and Social Council recommend that the General Assembly proclaim at its fifty-ninth (2004) session a world programme for human rights education, to begin on 1 January 2005 and structured in consecutive phases, in order to maintain and develop the implementation of human rights education programmes in all sectors. OHCHR was requested to prepare, in cooperation with UNESCO and other relevant actors, a plan of action for the first phase (2005-2007) of the proposed world programme, focusing on the primary and secondary school systems, and to submit it to the Assembly. The Office was further requested to report in 2005. The Commission recommended that the Secretary-General ensure that human rights education was supported by adequate UN assistance, provided at Member States' request, to develop their national systems of human rights promotion and protection.

On the same date [dec. 2004/121], the Commission decided to recommend to the Council that it recommend to the Assembly the proclamation of a world programme for human rights education to begin on 1 January 2005.

On 22 July, the Council endorsed the Commission's recommendation regarding the Assembly's proclamation of a world programme for human rights education and the Commission's request regarding the submission of a plan of action for the programme's first phase (**decision 2004/268**).

Plan of action. In accordance with Commission resolution 2004/71 (see above), the Secretary-General, in an October note [A/59/525], transmitted a draft plan of action for the first phase (2005-2007) of the proposed world programme for human rights education, focusing on the primary and secondary school systems, prepared by OHCHR and UNESCO and other governmental and non-governmental actors. The plan aimed to promote the inclusion and practice of human rights in the primary and secondary school systems; support the development, adoption and implementation of comprehensive, effective and sustainable national human rights education strategies in school systems, and/or the review and improvement of existing initiatives; provide guidelines on key components of

human rights education in the school system; facilitate the provision of support to Member States by international, regional, national and local organizations; and support networking and cooperation among local, national, regional and international institutions. The plan provided a definition of human rights education in the school system, based on internationally agreed principles, a user-friendly guide to developing and/or improving human rights education and a flexible guide, which could be adapted to different contexts and situations. The report also outlined a strategy for implementing the plan and for coordinating the implementation process, sources of international cooperation and support, as well as steps for evaluating actions implemented under the plan. Annexed to the report was information on components of human rights education in the primary and secondary school systems.

Subcommission action. On 12 August [res. 2004/18], the Subcommission, welcoming the recommendation of the Commission and the Economic and Social Council that the General Assembly proclaim a world programme for human rights education to begin on 1 January 2005, recommended that human rights treaty bodies, when examining reports of States parties, devote attention to human rights education and that it be included in the agenda of the annual meeting of the persons chairing the treaty bodies.

GENERAL ASSEMBLY ACTION

On 10 December [meeting 70], the General Assembly adopted **resolution 59/113** [draft: A/59/L.43 & Add.1] without vote [agenda item 105 (*b*)].

World Programme for Human Rights Education

The General Assembly,

Recalling the relevant resolutions adopted by the General Assembly and the Commission on Human Rights concerning the United Nations Decade for Human Rights Education, 1995-2004,

Recalling also its resolution 58/181 of 22 December 2003, in which it decided to dedicate a plenary meeting during the fifty-ninth session of the General Assembly, on the occasion of Human Rights Day, 10 December 2004, to review the achievements of the Decade and to discuss possible future activities for the enhancement of human rights education,

Taking note of Commission on Human Rights resolution 2004/71 of 21 April 2004, in which the Commission recommended that the General Assembly proclaim at its fifty-ninth session a world programme for human rights education, to begin on 1 January 2005,

Reaffirming the need for continued actions at the international level to support national efforts to achieve the internationally agreed development goals, including those contained in the United Nations Millennium Declaration, in particular, universal access to basic education for all, by 2015,

Convinced that human rights education is a long-term and lifelong process by which everyone learns tolerance and respect for the dignity of others and the means and methods of ensuring that respect in all societies,

Believing that human rights education is essential to the realization of human rights and fundamental freedoms and contributes significantly to promoting equality, preventing conflict and human rights violations and enhancing participation and democratic processes, with a view to developing societies in which all human beings are valued and respected, without discrimination or distinction of any kind, such as race, colour, sex, language, religion, political, or other opinion, national or social origin, property, birth or other status,

1. *Takes note* of the views expressed in the report of the United Nations High Commissioner for Human Rights on the achievements and shortcomings of the United Nations Decade for Human Rights Education, 1995-2004, and on future United Nations activities in this area concerning the need to continue a global framework for human rights education beyond the Decade in order to ensure a priority focus on human rights education within the international agenda;

2. *Proclaims* the World Programme for Human Rights Education, structured in consecutive phases, scheduled to begin on 1 January 2005, in order to advance the implementation of human rights education programmes in all sectors;

3. *Notes with appreciation* the draft plan of action for the first phase (2005-2007) of the World Programme for Human Rights Education, prepared jointly by the Office of the United Nations High Commissioner for Human Rights and the United Nations Educational, Scientific and Cultural Organization, as contained in the note by the Secretary-General, and invites States to submit comments thereon to the Office of the High Commissioner, with a view to its early adoption.

Children and a culture of peace

In response to General Assembly resolution 58/11 [YUN 2003, p. 689] on the International Decade for a Culture of Peace and Non-Violence for the Children of the World (2001-2010) proclaimed in 1998 [YUN 1998, p. 639], an August note of the Secretary-General [A/59/223] transmitted a report of the UNESCO Director-General covering the implementation of the 1999 Programme of Action on a Culture of Peace [YUN 1999, p. 594]. The report was an interim contribution to the mid-term progress report of the Secretary-General, to be submitted in 2005, on the observance of the Decade.

The report described activities carried out by UNESCO, as the lead agency for the Decade, with the participation of other UN bodies and Governments, to foster a culture of peace through education, promote sustainable economic and social development, promote respect for human rights, ensure equality between women and men, foster democratic participation, advance under-

standing, tolerance and solidarity, support participatory communication and the free flow of information and knowledge, and promote international peace and security. The report also reviewed the role of civil society and UNESCO communication and networking arrangements. To further advance the "culture of peace" concept, the Director-General recommended closer inter-agency cooperation, resource mobilization to sustain the momentum and renewing commitment to the Decade, as well as enhancing the online network underpinning current efforts as an effective tool for information sharing and mobilization.

GENERAL ASSEMBLY ACTION

On 15 December [meeting 72], the General Assembly adopted **resolution 59/143** [draft: A/59/L.21 & Add.1] without vote [agenda item 35].

International Decade for a Culture of Peace and Non-Violence for the Children of the World, 2001-2010

The General Assembly,

Bearing in mind the Charter of the United Nations, including the purposes and principles contained therein, and especially the dedication to saving succeeding generations from the scourge of war,

Recalling the Constitution of the United Nations Educational, Scientific and Cultural Organization, which states that, "since wars begin in the minds of men, it is in the minds of men that the defences of peace must be constructed",

Recalling also its previous resolutions on a culture of peace, in particular resolution 52/15 of 20 November 1997 proclaiming 2000 the International Year for the Culture of Peace, resolution 53/25 of 10 November 1998 proclaiming the period 2001-2010 the International Decade for a Culture of Peace and Non-Violence for the Children of the World, and resolutions 56/5 of 5 November 2001, 57/6 of 4 November 2002 and 58/11 of 10 November 2003,

Reaffirming the Declaration and Programme of Action on a Culture of Peace, recognizing that they serve, inter alia, as the basis for the observance of the Decade, and convinced that the effective and successful observance of the Decade throughout the world will promote a culture of peace and non-violence that benefits humanity, in particular future generations,

Recalling the United Nations Millennium Declaration, which calls for the active promotion of a culture of peace,

Taking note of Commission on Human Rights resolution 2000/66 of 26 April 2000, entitled "Towards a culture of peace",

Taking note also of the report of the Secretary-General on the International Decade for a Culture of Peace and Non-Violence for the Children of the World, including paragraph 28 thereof, which indicates that each of the ten years of the Decade will be marked with a different priority theme related to the Programme of Action,

Noting the relevance of the World Summit on Sustainable Development, held in Johannesburg, South

Africa, from 26 August to 4 September 2002, the International Conference on Financing for Development, held in Monterrey, Mexico, from 18 to 22 March 2002, the special session of the General Assembly on children, held in New York from 8 to 10 May 2002, the World Conference against Racism, Racial Discrimination, Xenophobia and Related Intolerance, held in Durban, South Africa, from 31 August to 7 September 2001, and the United Nations Decade for Human Rights Education, 1995-2004, for the International Decade for a Culture of Peace and Non-Violence for the Children of the World, 2001-2010, as well as the need to implement, as appropriate, the relevant decisions agreed upon therein,

Recognizing that all efforts made by the United Nations system in general and the international community at large for peacekeeping, peace-building, the prevention of conflicts, disarmament, sustainable development, the promotion of human dignity and human rights, democracy, the rule of law, good governance and gender equality at the national and international levels contribute greatly to the culture of peace,

Noting that its resolution 57/337 of 3 July 2003 on the prevention of armed conflict could contribute to the further promotion of a culture of peace,

Taking into account the "Manifesto 2000" initiative of the United Nations Educational, Scientific and Cultural Organization promoting a culture of peace, which has so far received over seventy-five million signatures of endorsement throughout the world,

Taking note with appreciation of the report of the Director-General of the United Nations Educational, Scientific and Cultural Organization on the implementation of General Assembly resolution 58/11,

1. *Reiterates* that the objective of the International Decade for a Culture of Peace and Non-Violence for the Children of the World, 2001-2010, is to strengthen further the global movement for a culture of peace following the observance of the International Year for the Culture of Peace in 2000;

2. *Invites* Member States to continue to place greater emphasis on and expand their activities promoting a culture of peace and non-violence, in particular during the Decade, at the national, regional and international levels and to ensure that peace and non-violence are fostered at all levels;

3. *Commends* the United Nations Educational, Scientific and Cultural Organization for recognizing the promotion of a culture of peace as the expression of its fundamental mandate, and encourages it, as the lead agency for the Decade, to strengthen further the activities it has undertaken for promoting a culture of peace, including the dissemination of the Declaration and Programme of Action on a Culture of Peace and related materials in various languages across the world;

4. *Also commends* the relevant United Nations bodies, in particular the United Nations Children's Fund, the United Nations Development Fund for Women and the University for Peace, for their activities in further promoting a culture of peace and non-violence, including the promotion of peace education and activities related to specific areas identified in the Programme of Action on a Culture of Peace, and encour-

ages them to continue and further strengthen and expand their efforts;

5. *Encourages* the appropriate authorities to provide education, in children's schools, that includes lessons in mutual understanding, tolerance, active citizenship, human rights and the promotion of a culture of peace;

6. *Encourages* civil society, including non-governmental organizations, to strengthen its efforts in furtherance of the objectives of the Decade, inter alia, by adopting its own programme of activities to complement the initiatives of Member States, the organizations of the United Nations system and other international and regional organizations;

7. *Encourages* the involvement of the mass media in education for a culture of peace and non-violence, with particular regard to children and young people, including through the planned expansion of the Culture of Peace News Network as a global network of Internet sites in many languages;

8. *Welcomes* the efforts made by the United Nations Educational, Scientific and Cultural Organization to continue the communication and networking arrangements established during the International Year for providing an instant update of developments related to the observance of the Decade;

9. *Invites* Member States to observe 21 September each year as the International Day of Peace, as a day of global ceasefire and non-violence, in accordance with General Assembly resolution 55/282 of 7 September 2001;

10. *Invites* Member States as well as civil society, including non-governmental organizations, to provide information to the Secretary-General on the observance of the Decade and the activities undertaken to promote a culture of peace and non-violence;

11. *Emphasizes* the significance of the plenary meetings on the item planned for its sixtieth session, and in that regard encourages participation at a high level, and decides to consider, at an appropriate time, the possibility of organizing those meetings as close as possible to the general debate;

12. *Requests* the Secretary-General to submit to the General Assembly at its sixtieth session a report on the implementation of the present resolution;

13. *Decides* to include in the provisional agenda of its sixtieth session the item entitled "Culture of peace".

National institutions and regional arrangements

National institutions for human rights promotion and protection

Commission action. On 21 April [res. 2004/75], the Commission welcomed the role of the International Coordinating Committee of National Institutions for the Promotion and Protection of Human Rights (for which OHCHR served as secretariat) in assessing conformity with the principles relating to the status of national institutions for the promotion and protection of human rights (Paris Principles), adopted in General Assembly resolution 48/134 [YUN 1993, p. 899]. The

Secretary-General was requested to assist the meetings of the Coordinating Committee and international and regional meetings of national institutions, and to report in 2005.

Report of Secretary-General. A report of the Secretary-General [E/CN.4/2005/106], covering January to December 2004, contained information on the activities undertaken by OHCHR to establish and strengthen national institutions, the measures taken by Governments and national institutions in that regard, and cooperation between those institutions and international mechanisms to promote and protect human rights.

During the year, at the request of Governments, OHCHR provided advice and information on activities and issues which might assist national institutions in Afghanistan, Albania, Angola, Burundi, China, Colombia, the Comoros, the Congo, Côte d'Ivoire, Cyprus, the Democratic Republic of the Congo, Djibouti, Egypt, Greece, Iraq, Japan, Jordan, Kenya, Lesotho, Maldives, Nepal, the Netherlands, the Niger, Norway, Pakistan, Qatar, Saudi Arabia, Serbia and Montenegro, Sierra Leone, Sri Lanka, the Sudan, The former Yugoslav Republic of Macedonia, Turkey and Uzbekistan. The national institutions of Afghanistan, Mongolia, Nepal, the Occupied Palestinian Territory, Rwanda and Zambia benefited from the support programmes provided by the National Institutions Unit of OHCHR's Capacity-Building and Field Operations Branch. During its 2004 sessions (Geneva, 14-16 April; Seoul, Republic of Korea, 14 September), the International Coordinating Committee held thematic discussions on human rights and disabilities and human rights education, and also discussed best practices of cooperation between NGOs and national institutions and a paper on early warning mechanisms. Support was given to regional initiatives, including the eighth Annual Meeting of the Asia Pacific Forum (Kathmandu, Nepal, 16-18 February), the twelfth Workshop on Regional Cooperation for the Promotion and Protection of Human Rights in the Asia-Pacific Region (Doha, Qatar, 1-4 March) (see p. 684), the third General Assembly of the Network of National Institutions of the Americas (Buenos Aires, Argentina 9-11 June), the ninth Annual Meeting of the Asia Pacific Forum (Seoul, 13 September), the seventh International Conference of National Human Rights Institutions (Seoul, 14-17 September) and the first African Union Conference of National Human Rights Institutions (Addis Ababa, Ethiopia, 18-21 October). OHCHR also supported the international race relations round table (Auckland, New Zealand, 2-5 February) and various initiatives of national institutions on migration, the advancement of women,

good governance, the rights of persons with disabilities, indigenous peoples, minorities, HIV/AIDS prevention and related discrimination, the prevention of conflict and of torture, and the Paris Principles. Annexed to the report were the Seoul Declaration, adopted at the Seventh International Conference for National Institutions for the Promotion and Protection of Human Rights in September; issues emerging from the international race relations round table in New Zealand and the Zacatecas Declaration, adopted at the International Workshop of National Institutions for the Promotion and Protection of Human Rights: Causes, Effects and Consequences of the Migratory Phenomenon and Human Rights Protection (Zacatecas, Mexico, 14-15 October); and a statement outlining challenges and recommendations regarding women's rights, adopted at the round table of national human rights institutions and national machineries for the advancement of women (Ouarzazate, Morocco, 15-19 November).

Regional arrangements

Report of Secretary-General. A September report [A/59/323] of the Secretary-General, submitted pursuant to General Assembly resolution 57/210 [YUN 2002, p. 655], focused on OHCHR regional strategies. In order to maximize the impact of UN activities at the national level, OHCHR had pursued a regional and subregional approach through various complementary methods, including supporting the establishment of regional frameworks for human rights promotion and protection; adopting a subregional focus wherever appropriate; outposting regional and subregional representatives; and concluding cooperative agreements with UN agencies and regional institutions undertaking joint regional projects, and sponsoring or organizing consultations and dialogues.

In Africa, OHCHR's regional arrangement was to support the African Union to strengthen its human rights system and to ensure subregional representation to strengthen national and subregional human rights capacities. In the Arab region, the OHCHR Regional Office in Beirut undertook activities aimed at enabling OHCHR to respond better to the human rights needs of respective Arab countries. Within the framework of cooperation with the League of Arab States, considerable emphasis was placed on the progress of the Arab Charter on Human Rights, the final text of which was adopted by the Arab Summit in May. The work of the Regional Office had also enabled OHCHR to strengthen partnerships outside the UN system; relevant activities in that regard included workshops on the Convention on the Elimination of All Forms of Discrimination against Women and on violence against women (Beirut, 26-27 January), as well as on the role of civil society in the reform process in the Arab world, which took place in Alexandria, Egypt, in June.

In Asia and the Pacific, OHCHR organized a Subregional Workshop on Human Rights Education in School Systems, held in Doha, Qatar, in February. Also held in Doha was the twelfth Workshop on Regional Cooperation for the Promotion and Protection of Human Rights in the Asia-Pacific Region. Intersessional activities included a Subregional Workshop for Judges and Lawyers on the Justiciability of Economic, Social and Cultural Rights (Ulaanbaatar, Mongolia, 26-28 January); a February study on popular and non-formal human rights education in the Asia-Pacific region; and the eighth Annual Meeting of the Asia-Pacific Forum (Kathmandu, Nepal, 16-18 February).

In Europe, Central Asia and the Caucasus, OHCHR further intensified cooperation with regional organizations, including the Council of Europe, the Organization for Security and Cooperation in Europe and the European Union. The Office particularly maintained close contact with regional organizations in Europe on the issue of respect of human rights in the context of counter-terrorism. In Central Asia, OHCHR began to implement a four-year regional project, covering Kazakhstan, Kyrgyzstan, Tajikistan and Uzbekistan; the project aimed at raising broad public understanding of human rights.

In Latin America and the Carribean, the Office, in coordination with the Latin American Institute for the Prevention of Crime and the Treatment of Offenders, organized a workshop on prison conditions for women in Central America (Costa Rica, 24-26 February), which adopted a declaration and a follow-up action plan. OHCHR also continued to strengthen cooperation with the Organization of American States and the Inter-American Commission on Human Rights, and supported the establishment and strengthening of the Network of National Human Rights Institutions of the Americas.

GENERAL ASSEMBLY ACTION

On 20 December [meeting 74], the General Assembly, on the recommendation of the Third Committee [A/59/203/Add.2], adopted **resolution 59/196** without vote [agenda item 105 (*b*)].

Regional arrangements for the promotion and protection of human rights

The General Assembly,

Recalling its resolution 32/127 of 16 December 1977 and its subsequent resolutions concerning regional ar-

rangements for the promotion and protection of human rights,

Recalling also Commission on Human Rights resolution 1993/51 of 9 March 1993 and its subsequent resolutions in this regard,

Bearing in mind the relevant resolutions of the Commission on Human Rights concerning advisory services and technical cooperation in the field of human rights, including its most recent on that subject, resolution 2004/81 of 21 April 2004,

Bearing in mind also the Vienna Declaration and Programme of Action adopted by the World Conference on Human Rights on 25 June 1993, which reiterates, inter alia, the need to consider the possibility of establishing regional and subregional arrangements for the promotion and protection of human rights where they do not already exist,

Recalling that the World Conference recommended that more resources should be made available for the strengthening of regional arrangements for the promotion and protection of human rights under the programme of technical cooperation in the field of human rights of the Office of the United Nations High Commissioner for Human Rights,

Reaffirming that regional arrangements play an important role in promoting and protecting human rights and should reinforce universal human rights standards, as contained in international human rights instruments,

Noting the progress achieved thus far in the promotion and protection of human rights at the regional level under the auspices of the United Nations, the specialized agencies and the regional intergovernmental organizations,

Considering that cooperation between the United Nations and regional arrangements in the field of human rights continues to be both substantive and supportive and that possibilities exist for increased cooperation,

Welcoming the fact that the Office of the High Commissioner has been systematically pursuing a regional and subregional approach through a variety of complementary means and methods, in order to maximize the impact of the activities of the United Nations at the national level,

1. *Takes note with satisfaction* of the report of the Secretary-General;

2. *Welcomes* the continuing cooperation and assistance of the Office of the United Nations High Commissioner for Human Rights in the further strengthening of the existing regional arrangements and regional machinery for the promotion and protection of human rights, in particular through technical cooperation aimed at national capacity-building, public information and education, with a view to exchanging information and experience in the field of human rights;

3. *Also welcomes*, in that respect, the close cooperation of the Office of the High Commissioner in the organization of regional and subregional training courses and workshops in the field of human rights, high-level governmental expert meetings and regional conferences of national human rights institutions, aimed at creating greater understanding in the regions of issues concerning the promotion and protection of human rights, improving procedures and examining

the various systems for the promotion and protection of universally accepted human rights standards and identifying obstacles to ratification of the principal international human rights treaties and strategies to overcome them;

4. *Recognizes*, therefore, that progress in promoting and protecting all human rights depends primarily on efforts made at the national and local levels, and that the regional approach should imply intensive cooperation and coordination with all partners involved, while bearing in mind the importance of international cooperation;

5. *Stresses* the importance of the programme of technical cooperation in the field of human rights, renews its appeal to all Governments to consider making use of the possibilities offered by the United Nations under this programme of organizing information or training courses at the national level for government personnel on the application of international human rights standards and the experience of relevant international bodies, and notes with satisfaction, in that respect, the establishment of technical cooperation projects with Governments of all regions;

6. *Welcomes* the growing exchanges between the United Nations and the United Nations human rights treaty bodies, on the one hand, and regional organizations and institutions, including the Council of Europe, the Organization for Security and Cooperation in Europe, the League of Arab States, the Inter-American Commission on Human Rights and the African Commission on Human and Peoples' Rights, on the other;

7. *Also welcomes* the placement by the Office of the High Commissioner of regional representatives in subregions and in regional commissions;

8. *Further welcomes* the progress achieved in the establishment of regional and subregional arrangements for the promotion and protection of human rights, and, in this regard, notes with interest:

(a) The positive experience of the regional and subregional presence of the Office of the High Commissioner in southern, central and eastern Africa aimed at strengthening national and subregional human rights capacities;

(b) The support provided by the Office of the High Commissioner to the African Union for the strengthening of its human rights system, and welcomes in this regard the entry into force of the Protocol to the African Charter on Human and Peoples' Rights, and the establishment of an African Court on Human and Peoples' Rights;

(c) The increased, valuable sharing of concrete national experiences at the eleventh and twelfth Workshops on Regional Cooperation for the Promotion and Protection of Human Rights in the Asian and Pacific Region, held in Islamabad from 25 to 27 February 2003 and in Doha from 2 to 4 March 2004, respectively, regarding the implementation of the Framework of Regional Technical Cooperation for the Asia-Pacific Region, which contributes to the enhancement of the promotion and protection of human rights in the region;

(d) Activities undertaken within the framework of the regional project of the Office of the High Commissioner for the promotion and protection of human rights in the Latin American and Caribbean region and the strengthening of the cooperation between the Office of the High Commissioner, the Organization of American States and the Inter-American Commission on Human Rights;

(e) Activities undertaken within the framework of cooperation between the Office of the High Commissioner and the League of Arab States and the intention to develop a broader technical cooperation programme in cooperation with the League of Arab States following the recent adoption of the Arab Charter on Human Rights;

(f) The continued cooperation between the Office of the High Commissioner and regional organizations in Europe and Central Asia, namely the Organization for Security and Cooperation in Europe, the Council of Europe and the European Union, in particular for activities at the country level, as well as the agreements between the European Commission and the Office of the High Commissioner for financing technical cooperation projects;

9. *Invites* States in areas in which regional arrangements in the field of human rights do not yet exist to consider concluding agreements with a view to establishing, within their respective regions, suitable regional machinery for the promotion and protection of human rights;

10. *Requests* the Secretary-General, as foreseen in programme 19, Human rights, of the revised medium-term plan for the period 2002-2005, to continue to strengthen exchanges between the United Nations and regional intergovernmental organizations dealing with human rights and to make available adequate resources from within the regular budget of technical cooperation to the activities of the Office of the High Commissioner to promote regional arrangements;

11. *Requests* the Office of the High Commissioner to continue to pay special attention to the most appropriate ways of assisting countries of the various regions, at their request, under the programme of technical cooperation and to make, where necessary, relevant recommendations, and in this regard welcomes the decision of the Office to strengthen national protection systems in accordance with action 2 of the reform programme of the Secretary-General;

12. *Invites* the Secretary-General to provide, in the report that he will submit to the Commission on Human Rights at its sixty-first session, information on progress made since the adoption of the Vienna Declaration and Programme of Action on reinforcing the exchange of information and extending collaboration between the organs of the United Nations dealing with human rights and regional organizations in the field of the promotion and protection of human rights;

13. *Requests* the Secretary-General to submit to the General Assembly at its sixty-first session a report on the state of regional arrangements for the promotion and protection of human rights, formulating concrete proposals and recommendations on ways and means to strengthen cooperation between the United Nations and regional arrangements in the field of human rights, and to include therein the results of action taken in pursuance of the present resolution;

14. *Decides* to consider the question further at its sixty-first session.

Africa

An October report of the Secretary-General [A/59/403] described the activities of the Subregional Centre for Human Rights and Democracy in Central Africa, based in Yaoundé, Cameroon. The Centre held workshops on civil society, human rights and the rule of law (Kribi, Cameroon, 2-4 February) and on women's rights and national legislation in Central Africa (Kigali, Rwanda, 17-19 March), in partnership with the United Nations Development Fund for Women. It also organized a training seminar on women journalists, human rights and the rule of law (Brazzaville, Congo, 29-30 March) and, in collaboration with the OHCHR Anti-Discrimination Unit, the Centre organized a training seminar on the role of civil society in the implementation of the Durban Declaration and Programme of Action (Yaoundé, 12-14 July). Furthermore, a two-day working session was held at the Centre with the UN Resident Coordinator in Equatorial Guinea on the design of projects for a human rights training project for implementation during 2004-2006. During 2003 and 2004, 24 interns were trained. The Centre also carried out activities related to democracy, including training workshops on the rights-based approach to lobbying and advocacy on human rights and democracy issues (Bamenda, Cameroon, 19-20 April) and on the rights-based approach in general terms (Yaoundé, 10-11 June). During the year, the Centre continued to provide technical cooperation to Governments, NGOs and national institutions, upon request. The report concluded that, taking into account the increasing number of requests for technical assistance submitted to the Centre, strengthening its structure and the allocation of additional funds should be envisaged to enable it to respond effectively.

The General Assembly took note of the report on 20 December (**decision 59/528**).

GENERAL ASSEMBLY ACTION

On 20 December [meeting 74], the General Assembly, on the recommendation of the Third Committee [A/59/503/Add.2], adopted **resolution 59/183** without vote [agenda item 105 (b)].

Subregional Centre for Human Rights and Democracy in Central Africa

The General Assembly,

Recalling its resolution 55/105 of 4 December 2000, concerning regional arrangements for the promotion and protection of human rights,

Recalling also its resolution 58/176 of 22 December 2003 on the Subregional Centre for Human Rights and Democracy in Central Africa,

Recalling further its resolutions 55/34 B of 20 November 2000 and 55/233 of 23 December 2000 and section III of its resolution 55/234 of 23 December 2000,

Recalling that the World Conference on Human Rights recommended that more resources be made available for the strengthening of regional arrangements for the promotion and protection of human rights under the programme of technical cooperation in the field of human rights of the Office of the United Nations High Commissioner for Human Rights,

Recalling also the report of the United Nations High Commissioner for Human Rights,

Taking note of the holding of the twenty-first ministerial meeting of the United Nations Standing Advisory Committee on Security Questions in Central Africa in Malabo from 21 to 25 June 2004,

1. *Welcomes* the activities of the Subregional Centre for Human Rights and Democracy in Central Africa at Yaoundé;

2. *Notes with satisfaction* the support provided for the establishment of the Centre by the host country;

3. *Requests* the Secretary-General and the United Nations High Commissioner for Human Rights to provide adequate assistance for the proper functioning of the Centre;

4. *Requests* the Secretary-General to submit to the General Assembly at its sixtieth session a report on the implementation of the present resolution.

Asia and the Pacific

Report of Secretary-General. A March report [E/CN.4/2004/89] of the Secretary-General highlighted the key points made at the twelfth Workshop on Regional Cooperation for the Promotion and Protection of Human Rights in the Asia-Pacific Region (Doha, 2-4 March), which adopted the 2004-2006 Programme of Action for the Asia-Pacific Framework on Regional Cooperation for the Promotion and Protection of Human Rights. It adopted conclusions regarding national human rights plans of action and national capacity-building; human rights education; national human rights institutions; and the realization of the right to development and economic, social and cultural rights. The Programme of Action and conclusions were annexed to the Secretary-General's report.

Commission action. On 21 April [res. 2004/74], the Commission, endorsing the conclusions of the Workshop, noted its discussions on obstacles to the effective realization of economic, social and cultural rights and the right to development, as well as the need for international cooperation to support the efforts of countries to overcome those obstacles. The Secretary-General was requested to report in 2005 on the conclusions of the thirteenth workshop.

Cooperation with human rights bodies

Report of Secretary-General. A January report of the Secretary-General [E/CN.4/2004/29] described situations in which persons or NGO members had allegedly suffered intimidation or reprisals for having cooperated with UN human rights bodies regarding human rights violations.

Commission action. On 15 April [res. 2004/15], the Commission urged Governments to refrain from intimidation against persons who sought to cooperate or had cooperated with representatives of UN human rights bodies; persons who availed themselves of UN procedures and who had provided legal assistance to them for that purpose; those who submitted communications under procedures established by human rights instru-ments; and relatives of victims of human rights violations. It requested representatives of UN human rights bodies and treaty bodies monitoring human rights to help prevent such intimidation and to include in their reports allegations of intimidation or reprisal and of hampering access to UN human rights procedures, as well as an account of the action they had taken. The Secretary-General was asked to draw the attention of UN human rights treaty bodies to the Commission's resolution and to report in 2005.

Chapter II

Protection of human rights

In 2004, the protection of human rights—civil and political, as well as economic, social and cultural—remained a major focus of UN activities. Follow-up activities advanced during the year to implement the Durban Declaration and Programme of Action (DDPA), adopted by the 2001 World Conference against Racism, Racial Discrimination, Xenophobia and Related Intolerance. The Intergovernmental Working Group mandated to make recommendations for effective implementation of DDPA proposed measures to promote tolerance and combat discrimination, and considered ways to strengthen the implementation of existing international human rights instruments and to prepare complementary standards. To further strengthen international cooperation for protecting indigenous peoples' rights, the General Assembly, while welcoming the achievements made during the International Decade of the World's Indigenous Peoples (1995-2004), proclaimed a second International Decade, with effect from 1 January 2005.

In April, the Security Council, in its continuing effort to protect children affected by armed conflict, called for an action plan for a systematic and comprehensive monitoring mechanism that would provide timely and reliable information on the recruitment of child soldiers. In related action, the Council, in December, continued to consider ways to enhance the protection of civilians in armed conflict and urged parties to armed conflict to end the use of the media to incite hatred and violence.

In 2004, the Commission on Human Rights and its subsidiary body, the Subcommission on the Promotion and Protection of Human Rights, established new mandates for special rapporteurs to undertake studies on discrimination based on work and descent, non-discrimination, the difficulties of establishing guilt and/or responsibilities with regard to crimes of sexual violence, and to address the human rights aspects of the rights of victims of trafficking in persons. Further mandates were created for an independent expert on impunity, a special adviser on the prevention of genocide, an independent expert on terrorism and a representative of the Secretary-General on the human rights of internally displaced persons.

Special rapporteurs, special representatives and independent experts of the Commission and the Subcommission examined, among other issues, contemporary forms of racism; the rights of migrants; freedom of religion or belief; mercenary activity; the independence of the judiciary; extra-legal executions; allegations of torture; freedom of expression; human rights and terrorism; the prevention of human rights violations committed with small arms and light weapons; the right to development; the effects of structural adjustment programmes and foreign debt on human rights; corruption and its impact on the enjoyment of human rights; the question of human rights and extreme poverty; the right to food; the right to adequate housing; the right to education; illicit practices related to toxic and dangerous products and wastes; the right to physical and mental health; human rights and the human genome; violence against women; violence against children; the sale of children, child prostitution and child pornography; children affected by armed conflict; internally displaced persons; and the human rights and fundamental freedoms of indigenous people.

Working groups considered problems of racial discrimination affecting people of African descent, recommendations for effective implementation of DDPA and complementary standards to strengthen related international instruments, discrimination against minorities, arbitrary detention, enforced or involuntary disappearances, the right to development, working methods and activities of transnational corporations, contemporary forms of slavery and the rights of indigenous peoples.

Racism and racial discrimination

Follow-up to 2001 World Conference

Intergovernmental Working Group. The Intergovernmental Working Group established in 2002 [YUN 2002, p. 661] to make recommendations for the effective implementation of the Durban Declaration and Programme of Action (DDPA), adopted by the World Conference against Racism, Racial Discrimination, Xenophobia and Related Intolerance [YUN 2001, p. 615], and to prepare complementary standards to strengthen related international instruments, held its second (26 January–6 February) [E/CN.4/2004/20] and third (11-22 October) [E/CN.4/2005/20] sessions, both in Geneva.

In January/February, the Group focused on education, poverty and complementary standards, within the context of efforts to combat racism and racial discrimination. It considered a number of background papers on those themes, as well as a Secretariat note on existing focal points for DDPA implementation within the UN system [E/CN.4/2004/WG.21/4], a report of the United Nations High Commissioner for Human Rights on complementary standards [E/CN.4/2004/WG.21/3], submitted in response to a 2003 Commission request [YUN 2003, p. 697], and a related note by the Office of the High Commissioner (OHCHR) [E/CN.4/2004.WG.21/5] containing a compendium of international and regional standards for combating racism and racial discrimination. The Group recommended, among other measures, the establishment of educational plans or guidelines to promote tolerance, cultural interaction, respect for diversity and human rights; it urged States to implement the education-related provisions of DDPA. The Group encouraged States to strengthen their national programmes for eradicating poverty and reducing social exclusion. It decided to undertake a dialogue on substantive issues relating to its mandate to prepare complementary standards to update and strengthen existing instruments concerning the elimination of racism, and requested OHCHR to invite the Committee on the Elimination of Racial Discrimination (CERD) and other treaty bodies to submit their views on the effectiveness and implementation of the 1965 International Convention on the Elimination of All Forms of Racial Discrimination (see p. 665). OHCHR was requested to facilitate the compilation of those views and their circulation to Group members before its next session, while UN entities and international financial, trade and development institutions were invited to exchange information and coordinate their activities with the Group, with a view to mainstreaming the effective implementation of DDPA in their policies, programmes and actions.

In October, the Group discussed racism and health, racism and the Internet, and issues relating to the preparation of complementary standards. It had before it the views of CERD [E/CN.4/2004/WG.21/10 & Add.1] and the contribution of other intergovernmental organizations [E/CN.4/2004/WG.21/11] regarding the implementation of the 1965 Convention. The Group recom-

mended measures to combat discrimination in health policies and to counter the incitement of hatred or acts of violence through the media and new information and communication technologies, including the Internet, as well as the organization by OHCHR of a high-level seminar on the Internet and racism, racial discrimination, xenophobia and related intolerance. The Group also considered strengthening the implementation of existing instruments by identifying gaps in international human rights law, with a view to preparing complementary standards. The process would involve an in-depth assessment and evaluation of the implementation of existing instruments, including suggestions to enhance the effectiveness of the fight against racism. The Group requested OHCHR to organize a four- to five-day high-level seminar during its fourth session to address work relating to the Group's recommendations.

Report of High Commissioner. Pursuant to General Assembly resolution 56/266 [YUN 2002, p. 659], the High Commissioner, in a March report on the implementation of and follow-up to the 2001 World Conference [E/CN.4/2004/17 & Corr.1], described the activities taken by States, special procedures and other Commission mechanisms, UN agencies, international and regional organizations, national human rights institutions and non-governmental organizations (NGOs) to implement DDPA.

Commission action. On 22 April [E/2004/23 (res. 2004/88)], the Commission, by a recorded vote of 38 to 1, with 14 abstentions, underlining the importance of mainstreaming non-discrimination, equality, human dignity and human solidarity into the UN system, welcomed the recommendations of the Intergovernmental Working Group (see above) and called on OHCHR to implement them and to report in 2005. Taking note of the outcome of the 2003 inaugural meeting of the independent eminent experts appointed to follow up the implementation of DDPA provisions [YUN 2003, p. 698], the Commission asked the High Commissioner to examine the possibility of developing a racial equality index, as proposed by the experts, and to report in 2005.

CERD action. In 2004 [A/59/18], the Committee on the Elimination of Racial Discrimination (see p. 665) considered follow-up to the World Conference, focusing on the work of the Intergovernmental Working Group in relation to the development of complementary standards to the International Convention on the Elimination of Racial Discrimination (see p. 664).

Report of Secretary-General. Pursuant to General Assembly resolution 58/160 [YUN 2003, p. 699], the Secretary-General, in a September report [A/59/375], described activities undertaken by States, OHCHR, UN bodies, specialized agencies, international and regional organizations, national human rights institutions, NGOs and youth organizations to implement DDPA. He observed that, despite increasing involvement by different actors in the implementation process, further efforts were needed to combat racism and racial discrimination, given the frequent manifestations of the phenomena.

On 20 December, the Assembly took note of the Secretary-General's report (**decision 59/527**).

Working Group on people of African descent. The Working Group of Experts on People of African Descent, established in accordance with DDPA in 2002 [YUN 2002, p. 661] to consider problems of racial discrimination affecting people of African descent, held its fourth session (Geneva, 25 October–5 November) [E/CN.4/2005/21]. The Group examined the themes of racism and employment, racism and health and racism and housing, and discussed related challenges affecting people of African descent. Also discussed was the Group's mandate as it related to the definition of the term "people of African descent", which was central to the discharge of its mandate. The Group had before it a September note [E/CN.4/2004/WG.20/2] by the Secretariat containing an analysis of the themes under consideration. The Group made recommendations on the collection of reliably disaggregated data to measure inequalities among specific social groups, the implementation of anti-discrimination laws and measures aimed at overcoming underrepresentation and to ensure an equitable redistribution of resources and power. Further recommendations proposed measures to ensure equality of peoples of African descent in employment and the labour market, health care and housing. The Group said that country visits were necessary for the effective discharge of its mandate, as that would facilitate an in-depth understanding of the situation of people of African descent in various regions.

Regional seminars. OHCHR, in collaboration with the UN Subregional Centre for Human Rights and Democracy in Central Africa, organized a training seminar on the role of civil society in implementing DDPA (Yaoundé, Cameroon, 12-14 July), which aimed at highlighting threats to peace posed by racist practices and the need for the urgent implementation of DDPA; the seminar adopted a declaration and plans of action.

OHCHR, in collaboration with the Pan-American Health Organization, a UN system public health agency, organized a regional workshop for Latin America and the Caribbean on efforts to ensure that the Millennium Development Goals (MDGs)

contained in the UN Millennium Declaration [YUN 2000, p. 49] contributed to overcoming discrimination based on race, colour, descent and national and ethnic origin (Brasília, Brazil, 1-3 December) [E/CN.4/2005/22].

GENERAL ASSEMBLY ACTION

On 20 December [meeting 74], the General Assembly, on the recommendation of the Third (Social, Humanitarian and Cultural) Committee [A/59/501], adopted **resolution 59/177** by recorded vote (183-3-2) [agenda item 103].

Global efforts for the total elimination of racism, racial discrimination, xenophobia and related intolerance and the comprehensive implementation of and follow-up to the Durban Declaration and Programme of Action

The General Assembly,

Recalling its resolution 58/160 of 22 December 2003, in which it decided to place emphasis on the concrete implementation of the Durban Declaration and Programme of Action, adopted by the World Conference against Racism, Racial Discrimination, Xenophobia and Related Intolerance, held in Durban, South Africa, from 31 August to 8 September 2001, as a solid foundation for a broad-based consensus for further actions and initiatives towards the total elimination of the scourge of racism,

Recalling also its resolution 57/195 of 18 December 2002, in which it outlined the important roles and responsibilities of the various organs of the United Nations and other stakeholders at the international, regional and national levels, including, in particular, the Commission on Human Rights,

Recalling further its resolution 56/266 of 27 March 2002, in which it endorsed the Durban Declaration and Programme of Action as constituting a solid foundation for further action and initiatives towards the total elimination of the scourge of racism,

Reiterating that all human beings are born free and equal in dignity and rights and have the potential to contribute constructively to the development and well-being of their societies, and that any doctrine of racial superiority is scientifically false, morally condemnable, socially unjust and dangerous and must be rejected, together with theories that attempt to determine the existence of separate human races,

Convinced that racism, racial discrimination, xenophobia and related intolerance manifest themselves in a differentiated manner for women and girls and may be among the factors leading to a deterioration in their living conditions, poverty, violence, multiple forms of discrimination and the limitation or denial of their human rights, and recognizing the need to integrate a gender perspective into relevant policies, strategies and programmes of action against racism, racial discrimination, xenophobia and related intolerance in order to address multiple forms of discrimination,

Taking note of Commission on Human Rights resolutions 2002/68 of 25 April 2002, 2003/30 of 23 April 2003 and 2004/88 of 22 April 2004, by which the international community put into effect mechanisms for the effective implementation of the Durban Declaration and Programme of Action,

Reaffirming its commitment to a global drive for the total elimination of racism, racial discrimination, xenophobia and related intolerance,

Reaffirming that universal adherence to and full implementation of the International Convention on the Elimination of All Forms of Racial Discrimination are of paramount importance for the promotion of equality and non-discrimination in the world,

Underlining the primacy of political will, international cooperation and adequate funding at the national, regional and international levels for the successful implementation of the Durban Programme of Action,

Alarmed at the increase in racist violence and xenophobic ideas in many parts of the world, in political circles, in the sphere of public opinion and in society at large, inter alia, as a result of the resurgent activities of associations established on the basis of racist and xenophobic platforms and charters, and the persistent use of those platforms and charters to promote or incite racist ideologies,

Underlining the importance of urgently eliminating continuing and violent trends involving racism and racial discrimination, and conscious that any form of impunity for crimes motivated by racist and xenophobic attitudes plays a role in weakening the rule of law and democracy, tends to encourage the recurrence of such crimes and requires resolute action and cooperation for its eradication,

Welcoming all the regional initiatives being undertaken to implement the Durban commitments and, in this context, expressing its appreciation to the Governments of Mexico, Kenya, the Czech Republic and Belgium for hosting the regional expert seminars with a view to the implementation of the Durban Declaration and Programme of Action within their respective regions, and encouraging the remaining region to take the necessary action in this regard,

Welcoming also the determination of the United Nations High Commissioner for Human Rights to profile and increase the visibility of the struggle against racism, racial discrimination, xenophobia and related intolerance and her intention to make this a cross-cutting issue in the activities and programmes of her Office,

I
Basic general principles

1. *Acknowledges* that no derogation from the prohibition of racial discrimination, genocide, the crime of apartheid or slavery is permitted, as defined in the obligations under the relevant human rights instruments;

2. *Expresses its profound concern about and its unequivocal condemnation* of all forms of racism and racial discrimination, including related acts of racially motivated violence, xenophobia and intolerance, as well as propaganda activities and organizations that attempt to justify or promote racism, racial discrimination, xenophobia and related intolerance in any form;

3. *Stresses* that States and international organizations have a responsibility to ensure that measures taken in the struggle against terrorism do not discriminate in purpose or effect on grounds of race, colour, descent or national or ethnic origin, and urges all States to rescind or refrain from all forms of racial profiling;

4. *Recognizes* that States should implement and enforce appropriate and effective legislative, judicial, regulatory and administrative measures to prevent and protect against acts of racism, racial discrimination, xenophobia and related intolerance, thereby contributing to the prevention of human rights violations;

5. *Emphasizes* that it is the responsibility of States to adopt effective measures to combat criminal acts motivated by racism, racial discrimination, xenophobia and related intolerance, including measures to ensure that such motivations are considered an aggravating factor for the purposes of sentencing, to prevent those crimes from going unpunished and to ensure the rule of law;

6. *Urges* all States to review and, where necessary, revise their immigration laws, policies and practices so that they are free of racial discrimination and compatible with their obligations under international human rights instruments;

7. *Condemns* the misuse of print, audio-visual and electronic media and new communication technologies, including the Internet, to incite violence motivated by racial hatred, and calls upon States to take all necessary measures to combat this form of racism in accordance with the commitments that they have undertaken under the Durban Declaration and Programme of Action, in particular paragraph 147 of the Programme of Action, in accordance with existing international and regional standards of freedom of expression and taking all necessary measures to guarantee the right to freedom of opinion and expression;

8. *Encourages* all States to include in their educational curricula and social programmes at all levels, as appropriate, knowledge of and tolerance and respect for foreign cultures, peoples and countries;

9. *Stresses* the responsibility of States to mainstream a gender perspective in the design and development of prevention, education and protection measures aimed at the eradication of racism, racial discrimination, xenophobia and related intolerance at all levels, to ensure that they effectively target the distinct situations of women and men;

II
International Convention on the Elimination of All Forms of Racial Discrimination

10. *Reiterates* the call made by the World Conference against Racism, Racial Discrimination, Xenophobia and Related Intolerance in paragraph 75 of the Durban Programme of Action to achieve universal ratification of the International Convention on the Elimination of All Forms of Racial Discrimination by 2005 and for all States to consider making the declaration envisaged under article 14 of the Convention, and endorses the concern expressed by the Commission on Human Rights in its resolution 2004/88 to the effect that, at the current pace, with one hundred and seventy ratifications and only forty-five declarations, the deadline of 2005 for universal ratification decided by the World Conference will, regrettably, not be realized;

11. *Urges*, in that context, the Office of the United Nations High Commissioner for Human Rights to maintain and issue regular updates on its web site of a list of countries that have not yet ratified the Convention, and to encourage such countries to demonstrate

their practical commitment to meet the deadline for universal ratification as decided upon by the World Conference;

12. *Invites* States parties to the Convention to ratify the amendment to article 8 of the Convention, on the financing of the Committee on the Elimination of Racial Discrimination, and calls for adequate additional resources from the regular budget of the United Nations to enable the Committee to discharge its mandate fully;

13. *Urges* all States parties to the Convention to intensify their efforts to implement the obligations that they have accepted under article 4 of the Convention, with due regard to the principles of the Universal Declaration of Human Rights and article 5 of the Convention;

14. *Notes* that the Committee holds that the prohibition of the dissemination of ideas based on racial superiority or racial hatred is compatible with the right to freedom of opinion and expression as outlined in article 19 of the Universal Declaration of Human Rights and in article 5 of the Convention;

15. *Welcomes* the emphasis placed by the Committee on the importance of follow-up to the World Conference and the measures recommended to strengthen the implementation of the Convention as well as the functioning of the Committee;

III
Comprehensive implementation of and follow-up to the Durban Declaration and Programme of Action

16. *Emphasizes* that the basic responsibility for effectively combating racism, racial discrimination, xenophobia and related intolerance lies with States, and to this end stresses that States have the primary responsibility to ensure full and effective implementation of all commitments and recommendations contained in the Durban Declaration and Programme of Action;

17. *Also emphasizes*, in that context, the fundamental and complementary role of national human rights institutions, regional bodies or centres and civil society, working jointly with States towards the achievement of the objectives of the Durban Declaration and Programme of Action;

18. *Calls upon* States to elaborate action plans, in consultation with national human rights institutions, other institutions created by law to combat racism, and civil society, and to provide the United Nations High Commissioner for Human Rights with such action plans and other relevant materials on measures taken to implement the provisions of the Durban Declaration and Programme of Action;

19. *Calls upon* all States to formulate and implement without delay, at the national, regional and international levels, policies and plans of action to combat racism, racial discrimination, xenophobia and related intolerance, including their gender-based manifestations;

20. *Urges* States to support the activities of existing regional bodies or centres that combat racism, racial discrimination, xenophobia and related intolerance in their respective regions, and recommends the establishment of such bodies or centres in all regions where they do not exist;

21. *Recognizes* the fundamental role of civil society in the fight against racism, racial discrimination, xeno-phobia and related intolerance, in particular in assisting States to develop regulations and strategies, in taking measures and action against such forms of discrimination and through follow-up implementation;

22. *Emphasizes* that, in accordance with the Durban Declaration and Programme of Action, States have a shared responsibility, at the international level and within the framework of the United Nations system, to determine modalities for the overall review of the implementation of the Declaration and Programme of Action;

23. *Decides* that the General Assembly, through its role in policy formulation, the Economic and Social Council, through its role in overall guidance and coordination, in accordance with their respective roles under the Charter of the United Nations and Assembly resolution 50/227 of 24 May 1996, and the Commission on Human Rights shall constitute a three-tiered intergovernmental process for the comprehensive implementation of and follow-up to the Durban Declaration and Programme of Action;

24. *Stresses and reaffirms* its role as the highest intergovernmental mechanism for the formulation and appraisal of policy on matters related to the economic, social and related fields, in accordance with Chapter IX of the Charter, including in the comprehensive implementation of and follow-up to the goals and targets set at all the major United Nations conferences, summits and special sessions;

25. *Acknowledges* that the outcome of the World Conference against Racism, Racial Discrimination, Xenophobia and Related Intolerance is on an equal footing with the outcomes of all the major United Nations conferences, summits and special sessions in the human rights and social fields;

26. *Decides* that the Economic and Social Council shall oversee system-wide coordination of the implementation of the Durban Declaration and Programme of Action;

27. *Also decides* that the Commission on Human Rights, as a functional commission of the Economic and Social Council, shall have a central role in the monitoring of the implementation of the Durban Declaration and Programme of Action within the United Nations system and in advising the Council thereon;

28. *Expresses its appreciation* for the continuing work of the Intergovernmental Working Group on the Effective Implementation of the Durban Declaration and Programme of Action and the Working Group of Experts on People of African Descent, and looks forward to the consideration of the outcomes of their third sessions by the Commission on Human Rights at its sixty-first session;

29. *Acknowledges* that the World Conference against Racism, Racial Discrimination, Xenophobia and Related Intolerance, held in Durban, South Africa, from 31 August to 8 September 2001, which was the third world conference against racism, was significantly different from the previous two conferences, as evidenced by the inclusion in its title of two important components relating to contemporary forms of racism, namely, xenophobia and related intolerance;

30. *Welcomes* the work of the Committee on the Elimination of Racial Discrimination in applying the International Convention on the Elimination of All

Forms of Racial Discrimination to the new and contemporary forms of racism and racial discrimination;

31. *Underlines* the importance of the elaboration of complementary standards with a view to strengthening and updating international instruments against racism, racial discrimination, xenophobia and related intolerance, taking into account issues discussed during the previous sessions of the Intergovernmental Working Group on the Effective Implementation of the Durban Declaration and Programme of Action, as well as issues identified by the high-level seminar to be convened during the next session of the Intergovernmental Working Group;

32. *Underlines also* the importance of considering progress made in the implementation of the provisions of the Durban Declaration and Programme of Action related to the media and racism, including the use of the Internet, with the participation of all stakeholders, inter alia, States, the World Summit on the Information Society, international and regional organizations, non-governmental organizations, the private sector and the media;

33. *Takes note* of the recommendation of the Intergovernmental Working Group on the Effective Implementation of the Durban Declaration and Programme of Action, in that context, to request the Office of the United Nations High Commissioner for Human Rights to convene a high-level seminar, the format of which should be agreed among Member States, assisted by the Office of the High Commissioner, and which could include, but would not necessarily be limited to, a core group of ministers responsible for human rights and/or equivalent participants from all regions as panellists;

34. *Strongly recommends* that no intersessional meetings of the working groups of the Commission on Human Rights in follow-up to the World Conference and the implementation of the Durban Declaration and Programme of Action be scheduled in a manner that clashes or overlaps with the sessions of the General Assembly, and in this regard calls upon the Commission to address this issue and to ensure that the future sessions of the Working Group of Experts on People of African Descent are scheduled to precede those of the Intergovernmental Working Group on the Effective Implementation of the Durban Declaration and Programme of Action;

35. *Requests* the Secretary-General to reflect the outcome of the high-level seminar in his report to the General Assembly at its sixty-first session on the follow-up to the World Conference;

36. *Acknowledges* the centrality of resource mobilization, effective global partnership and international cooperation in the context of paragraphs 157 and 158 of the Durban Programme of Action for the successful realization of commitments undertaken at the World Conference, and to this end emphasizes the central role to be played by the group of independent eminent experts on the implementation of the Durban Declaration and Programme of Action in mobilizing the necessary political will required for the successful implementation of the Declaration and Programme of Action;

37. *Requests* the Secretary-General to provide the necessary resources for the effective fulfilment of the mandates of the Intergovernmental Working Group on the Effective Implementation of the Durban Declaration and Programme of Action, the Working Group of Experts on People of African Descent and the group of independent eminent experts on the implementation of the Durban Declaration and Programme of Action;

38. *Condemns* the resurgence of xenophobia, and underlines the fact that, while anchoring human rights in legal instruments is a fundamental way of expressing their universality, it is no longer capable of eliminating the underlying causes of discriminatory culture and mentalities, and that action on human rights must henceforth include discussion of the deep cultural roots of racism;

39. *Expresses its concern* at the increasing incidence of racism in various sporting events, while noting with appreciation the efforts made by some sporting governing bodies to combat racism;

40. *Invites* Member States to adopt measures to counter the dissemination of discriminatory, racist and xenophobic messages on the Internet, in accordance with paragraphs 144 to 147 of the Durban Programme of Action, and to promote a positive use of the Internet to foster social harmony and to combat racism;

41. *Requests* the Office of the United Nations High Commissioner for Human Rights to convene the second meeting of the group of independent eminent experts on the implementation of the Durban Declaration and Programme of Action before the sixty-first session of the Commission on Human Rights to produce a concrete programme of action related to their mandate, based on the core values of racial equality and dignity as elaborated in the outcome document of their first meeting, held in Geneva from 16 to 18 September 2003;

IV
Special Rapporteur of the Commission on Human Rights on contemporary forms of racism, racial discrimination, xenophobia and related intolerance and follow-up to his visits

42. *Expresses its full support and appreciation* for the work of the Special Rapporteur of the Commission on Human Rights on contemporary forms of racism, racial discrimination, xenophobia and related intolerance, and encourages its continuation;

43. *Reiterates its call* to all Member States, intergovernmental organizations, relevant organizations of the United Nations system and non-governmental organizations to cooperate fully with the Special Rapporteur;

44. *Requests* the Special Rapporteur to continue his exchange of views with Member States and relevant mechanisms and treaty bodies within the United Nations system in order to enhance further their effectiveness and mutual cooperation;

45. *Recognizes with deep concern* the increase in anti-Semitism, Christianophobia and Islamophobia in various parts of the world, as well as the emergence of racial and violent movements based on racism and discriminatory ideas directed against Arab, Christian, Jewish and Muslim communities, communities of people of African descent, communities of people of Asian descent and other communities;

46. *Requests* the Special Rapporteur to collect information from all concerned, to respond effectively to reliable information that becomes available to him, to

follow up on communications and country visits and to seek the views and comments of Governments and reflect them, as appropriate, in his reports;

47. *Calls upon* States to cooperate with the Special Rapporteur and to give serious consideration to his requests to visit their countries so as to enable him to fulfil his mandate fully and effectively;

48. *Encourages* closer collaboration between the Special Rapporteur and the Office of the United Nations High Commissioner for Human Rights, in particular the Anti-Discrimination Unit;

49. *Urges* the United Nations High Commissioner for Human Rights to provide States, at their request, with advisory services and technical assistance to enable them to implement fully the recommendations of the Special Rapporteur;

50. *Requests* the Secretary-General to provide the Special Rapporteur with all the necessary human and financial assistance to carry out his mandate efficiently, effectively and expeditiously and to enable him to submit an interim report to the General Assembly at its sixtieth session;

51. *Takes note* of the recommendations contained in the interim report of the Special Rapporteur, and encourages the continuation of his work;

52. *Urges* Member States to consider implementing the recommendations contained in the reports of the Special Rapporteur, and invites other relevant stakeholders to implement those recommendations;

V

General

53. *Requests* the Secretary-General to submit a report on the implementation of the present resolution to the General Assembly at its sixtieth session;

54. *Decides* to remain seized of this important matter at its sixtieth session under the item entitled "Elimination of racism and racial discrimination".

RECORDED VOTE ON RESOLUTION 59/177:

In favour: Afghanistan, Albania, Algeria, Andorra, Angola, Antigua and Barbuda, Argentina, Armenia, Austria, Azerbaijan, Bahamas, Bahrain, Bangladesh, Barbados, Belarus, Belgium, Belize, Benin, Bhutan, Bolivia, Bosnia and Herzegovina, Botswana, Brazil, Brunei Darussalam, Bulgaria, Burkina Faso, Burundi, Cambodia, Cameroon, Cape Verde, Central African Republic, Chad, Chile, China, Colombia, Comoros, Costa Rica, Côte d'Ivoire, Croatia, Cuba, Cyprus, Czech Republic, Democratic People's Republic of Korea, Democratic Republic of the Congo, Denmark, Djibouti, Dominica, Dominican Republic, Ecuador, Egypt, El Salvador, Equatorial Guinea, Eritrea, Estonia, Ethiopia, Fiji, Finland, France, Gabon, Gambia, Georgia, Germany, Ghana, Greece, Grenada, Guatemala, Guinea, Guinea-Bissau, Guyana, Haiti, Honduras, Hungary, Iceland, India, Indonesia, Iran, Iraq, Ireland, Italy, Jamaica, Japan, Jordan, Kazakhstan, Kenya, Kuwait, Kyrgyzstan, Lao People's Democratic Republic, Lebanon, Lesotho, Liberia, Libyan Arab Jamahiriya, Liechtenstein, Lithuania, Luxembourg, Madagascar, Malawi, Malaysia, Maldives, Mali, Malta, Marshall Islands, Mauritania, Mauritius, Mexico, Micronesia, Monaco, Mongolia, Morocco, Mozambique, Myanmar, Namibia, Nauru, Nepal, Netherlands, New Zealand, Nicaragua, Niger, Nigeria, Norway, Oman, Pakistan, Panama, Papua New Guinea, Paraguay, Peru, Philippines, Poland, Portugal, Qatar, Republic of Korea, Republic of Moldova, Romania, Russian Federation, Rwanda, Saint Lucia, Saint Vincent and the Grenadines, Samoa, San Marino, Sao Tome and Principe, Saudi Arabia, Senegal, Serbia and Montenegro, Seychelles, Sierra Leone, Singapore, Slovakia, Slovenia, Solomon Islands, Somalia, South Africa, Spain, Sri Lanka, Sudan, Suriname, Swaziland, Sweden, Switzerland, Syrian Arab Republic, Tajikistan, Thailand, The former Yugoslav Republic of Macedonia, Timor-Leste, Togo, Tonga, Trinidad and Tobago, Tunisia, Turkey, Turkmenistan, Tuvalu, Uganda, Ukraine, United Arab Emirates, United Kingdom, United Republic of Tanzania, Uruguay, Uzbekistan, Vanuatu, Venezuela, Viet Nam, Yemen, Zambia, Zimbabwe.

Against: Israel, Palau, United States.

Abstaining: Australia, Canada.

Contemporary forms of racism

Reports of Special Rapporteur. In January [E/CN.4/2004/18], the Special Rapporteur on contemporary forms of racism, racial discrimination, xenophobia and related intolerance, Doudou Diène (Senegal), described activities he had undertaken since his 2003 report [YUN 2003, p. 704]. His activities focused on fieldwork and dialogue with Governments, UN agencies, national human rights institutions and NGOs, with particular attention accorded to racism in sport and to countries mostly affected by increasing racism relating to immigration and other factors. He considered contemporary manifestations of the phenomenon related to isolationism and the rejection of ethnic and cultural diversity; racial profiling; discrimination against the Roma/Gypsies/Sinti/Travellers; and anti-Semitism and Islamophobia. The Special Rapporteur discussed measures taken by Governments to address those issues and summarized allegations of racial discrimination received from individuals in seven countries. Based on the information he had gathered, the Special Rapporteur pointed to a resurgence of contemporary forms of racism, discrimination and xenophobia. He recommended national programmes, based on international instruments and DDPA, to combat those scourges; the promotion of pluralism; measures to deal with the rise of racism in sport; and an appeal to Member States concerned for cooperation with him for the recognition and treatment of the question of castes.

In response to a 2003 Commission request [YUN 2003, p. 704], the Special Rapporteur submitted a February progress report [E/CN.4/2004/19] regarding his study [YUN 2003, p. 703] of the situation of Muslim and Arab peoples in various parts of the world in the aftermath of the terrorist attacks of 11 September 2001 in the United States [YUN 2001, p. 60]. The Special Rapporteur said there had been an increase in Islamophobia, manifested through intellectual legitimization of hostility towards Islam and its followers by influential figures in society and tolerance of such hostility in many countries. The trend was particularly prevalent in France and the United States, both of which had large Arab and Muslim communities, and in other countries such as Australia, Belgium and Canada. In that regard, aspects of the behaviour of Muslims viewed as fundamentalists were being questioned, and Islam itself was openly and publicly attacked. The trend was further complicated by the overlap between Islamophobia and other phenomena of rejection, such as anti-Semitism. The Special Rapporteur recommended that the Commission appeal urgently to Member States to recognize the reality and seriousness of Islamophobia and to develop the necessary strategy to combat it. The Commission should recommend the establishment by OHCHR of a centre, which should be mandated to monitor the contemporary phenomena of racism, anti-Semitism and Islamophobia; develop a scientific methodology for measuring the phenomena; and, in collaboration with the Special Rapporteur, report annually to the Commission and the General Assembly.

The Special Rapporteur visited Côte d'Ivoire (9-21 February) [E/CN.4/2004/18/Add.4, E/CN.4/2005/18/Add.3] to assess the role of ethnic factors in the crisis facing the country since the outbreak of armed conflict there in 2002. He had received reports of increasing xenophobia and the information he gathered during the visit highlighted many allegations of serious human rights violations and critical shortcomings in the judicial system, which fostered a climate of impunity and perpetuated a cycle of violence. Alleged xenophobia stemmed from the fact that certain communities were especially targeted, notably persons from the northern part of the country or from neighbouring countries, and the victims reportedly suffered violations of the rights to life and the freedom of expression and of movement, arbitrary detention and arrests, enforced disappearances, torture and inhuman or degrading treatment, and attacks on property. The Special Rapporteur concluded that Côte d'Ivoire had no tradition of xenophobia, given that the society had developed a deep-rooted multi-ethnicity and a peaceful coexistence based on intercultural values. However, the crisis currently facing the country exposed it to the dynamic of xenophobia, stemming from a variety of factors that should be analysed and addressed to avert the emergence of real xenophobia. The Special Rapporteur recommended measures to strengthen the values of tolerance and coexistence in the society, to ensure a lasting political solution to the crisis afflicting the country and to improve the rule of law and the enjoyment of human rights. On the regional level, he proposed that, under the aegis of the Economic Community of West African States, regional States promote jointly intercultural dialogue and cultural pluralism.

Commission action. By a recorded vote of 36 to 13, with 4 abstentions, the Commission, on 16 April [res. 2004/16], alarmed at the spread in many parts of the world of various extremist political parties, movements and groups, including neo-Nazis and skinheads, stressed that the practices of such organizations fuelled contemporary forms of racism and were incompatible with Member States' obligations under the UN Charter and detrimental to the Organization's goals

and principles. Emphasizing the need for measures to put an end to those practices, the Commission asked the Special Rapporteur to reflect on the issue, make relevant recommendations and report in 2005, taking into account the views of Governments and NGOs.

On 22 April [res. 2004/88], the Commission, by a recorded vote of 38 to 1, with 14 abstentions, urged Member States to consider implementing the recommendations contained in the Special Rapporteur's reports and invited the High Commissioner to provide States, at their request, with advisory services and technical assistance in that regard. The Special Rapporteur was asked to submit an interim report to the General Assembly in 2004 and to the Commission in 2005. The Secretary-General was asked to assist him.

By **decision 2004/272** of 22 July, the Economic and Social Council endorsed the Commission's request to the Secretary-General to assist the Special Rapporteur.

Further reports of Special Rapporteur. The Special Rapporteur visited Guatemala (26 June–2 July) [E/CN.4/2005/18/Add.2] as part of a regional mission to Central America, during which he also went to Honduras and Nicaragua (see below). The mission was prompted by the need to shed light on two significant factors relating to the problem of racism in the region: the historical legacy of racial discrimination underpinning the era of slavery and colonial systems and the impact of the political violence that had marked the region's recent history. The three countries visited were of particular interest with respect to the structuring and management of ethnic, racial and cultural pluralism because they shared similar ethnic and demographic features and common historical and political legacies. Other common trends in the three countries that revealed the existence of racial discrimination included a troubling correlation between poverty-stricken areas and places inhabited by communities of indigenous people and people of African descent; the marginal involvement of representatives of those communities in power structures—government, parliament, the judiciary and the media; and their treatment as objects of folklore. To varying degrees, the authorities in the three countries also lacked an awareness of how extensive and deeply rooted discrimination was, contrary to information obtained from the affected communities.

In Guatemala, which had a population of 11.2 million, comprising four main ethnic groups, the Special Rapporteur found that the process of strengthening democracy and peace-building had progressed considerably in the 10 years following peace agreements that ended

36 years of conflict between the Government and insurgents. That process had involved the amendment of the criminal code through the incorporation of provisions banning racial discrimination. Although Guatemala's constitution and leadership recognized its ethnic diversity, the country overwhelmingly accorded precedence to its Hispanic identity, marginalizing a large proportion of the population. The Special Rapporteur, believing that combating racial discrimination should be the cornerstone of the process of building peace and democracy in Guatemala, recommended that the Government demonstrate its determination to tackle the phenomenon by recognizing its existence and related consequences and by expressing the commitment to eliminate them, and take an integrated approach by establishing a national programme to combat racism, based on DDPA and involving NGO participation. He also recommended, among other measures, moral and material redress for victims of racial discrimination and their families, strengthening national and international human rights mechanisms and action at the regional level against the phenomenon.

In Nicaragua (26 June–13 July) [E/CN.4/2005/18/Add.6], the Special Rapporteur said that the Government considered that there was neither racism nor racial discrimination in the country, as the complex ethnic and racial make-up of the population resulting from intermarriage was said to make manifestations of those phenomena improbable. By contrast, representatives of indigenous peoples and people of African descent considered themselves victims of racism and racial discrimination. The grievances of the affected ethnic groups included the infringement of their cultural identities and land rights, low levels of State investment in regions where they lived and their insignificant representation in power structures. Nicaragua comprised two main regions: the Pacific and Atlantic (Atlántico Norte and Atlántico Sur) regions, with the latter inhabited mostly by indigenous peoples and people of African descent, who were isolated and lacked basic infrastructure. Under a 1987 constitution, the two Atlantic subregions were granted autonomy, thereby establishing the institutional framework for their inhabitants to plan and assume responsibility for their own development and for protecting their collective ethnic rights. Other constitutional provisions were also designed to protect Nicaraguans, especially the indigenous community, from discrimination based on language, culture or origin, while various institutions ensured the protection of human rights. Those measures, although constituting a major step towards multiculturalism and the manage-

ment of ethnic and racial pluralism, had not yielded the desired results owing to the lack of the requisite resources for related operations. Moreover, there was no general law containing provisions for combating discriminatory acts committed by State officials or private individuals. The Special Rapporteur recommended measures to maintain the momentum of planned reforms and to open up new prospects for enhanced participation by Nicaragua's various ethnic groups in the process. The Government should make a firmer commitment to combating racial discrimination by developing a programme of action for that purpose and for building a multicultural, egalitarian, democratic and interactive society inspired by DDPA. Its efforts in that regard should be supported by the activities of UN entities operating in Nicaragua and by the Organization of American States.

In Honduras (2-8 July) [E/CN.4/2005/18/Add.5], the Special Rapporteur found that the situation regarding racial discrimination was largely consistent with what he saw in Guatemala and Nicaragua, particularly in terms of the victims. Of an estimated population of 6.5 million, mestizos or Ladinos (people of mixed race) accounted for 90 per cent. Indigenous communities and people of African descent accounted for just 9 per cent of the population and allegedly suffered marginalization and discriminatory policies and practices that undermined their ethnic identity, cultural traditions and land rights. The Special Rapporteur recommended measures for strengthening the entire judicial system and government programmes and policies to better combat racism and racial discrimination and to remedy the situation of the affected communities. He advocated actions at the regional level similar to those he had proposed in Guatemala and Nicaragua.

Pursuant to General Assembly resolution 58/160 [YUN 2003, p. 699], the Secretary-General, in September [A/59/329], transmitted an interim report of the Special Rapporteur on the fight against racism, racial discrimination, xenophobia and related intolerance. The report summarized the Special Rapporteur's activities during the year and drew the Assembly's attention to related developments, including an upsurge of xenophobia and the weakening of protection against certain forms of discrimination, the persistence of racist propaganda on the Internet, racism in sports and racism connected with anti-Semitism and Islamophobia, as well as action taken or planned by Governments, judicial authorities and other entities. The Special Rapporteur recommended that the Assembly alert Member States to the need for measures to counter those developments, for an intellectual strategy against racism and racial discrimination, and for legislative and judicial action to ensure that the legitimate struggle against terrorism did not breed new forms of discrimination. The Assembly, in contemplating future measures against racism, discrimination and xenophobia, should consider the complication resulting from the fact that contemporary forms of racism conflated religion and culture with ethnicity and race, and should advocate a set of ethics to fight racism.

Communication. In March [E/CN.4/2004/G/35], Trinidad and Tobago, referring to the Special Rapporteur's 2003 visit to the country [YUN 2003, p. 704], regretted that it was not provided with an English language version of the Special Rapporteur's report on that visit in good time, which prevented it from giving its comments or views.

(For General Assembly action regarding the Special Rapporteur, see resolution 59/177 (p. 688).)

Study of political platforms

Reports of Special Rapporteur. In response to a 2003 Commission request [YUN 2003, p. 705], the Special Rapporteur on contemporary forms of racism, racial discrimination, xenophobia and related intolerance submitted a January report [E/CN.4/2004/61] updating a 2001 study on political platforms which promoted or incited racial discrimination [YUN 2001, p. 616], which his predecessor had presented to the Preparatory Committee for the World Conference against Racism, Racial Discrimination, Xenophobia and Related Intolerance [ibid.]. The report defined such platforms as political ideologies, discourses, programmes or strategies advocating racial discrimination or hatred in order to gain political power and marginalize certain groups in a given country. It also reviewed political parties and other organizations that promoted racism, and highlighted the rising tide of the phenomenon in Europe, the United States, South America, Asia, the Middle East and Africa. Observing that the persistence or resurgence of racism, ethnocentrism and xenophobia demanded the adoption of multiple strategies at the national, regional and global levels, the Special Rapporteur recommended that the phenomenon be recognized and acknowledged as a major threat to peace, security and human development. He advocated the establishment of monitoring, reporting, documentation and information-processing institutions and procedures and emphasized the need for an intellectual and ethical strategy to complement political and legal strategies in combating racism, and for political vigilance

against the racist agenda of the extreme right in individual States.

Pursuant to Assembly resolution 58/159 [YUN 2003, p. 705], the Secretary-General, in October [A/59/330], transmitted the Special Rapporteur's updated and expanded report on the study of political platforms that promoted or incited racism, racial discrimination, xenophobia and related intolerance worldwide, which replicated the findings and recommendations contained in his January report to the Commission (see above).

Communications. In March [E/CN.4/2004/G/39] and October [A/C.3/59/4], Italy, responding to the Special Rapporteur's reports (see above), objected that the two political parties comprising the country's coalition Government had been included in the list of openly racist and xenophobic political groups in Europe. Its Government, it noted, had made the fight against racism a priority and was engaged in the implementation of DDPA, and no reference to fascist or hate ideologies was in the political programme of either of the two parties.

Commission action. On 19 April [res. 2004/38], the Commission, condemning political platforms and organizations based on racism, xenophobia or doctrines of racial superiority and related discrimination, recommended the creation, where they did not exist, of monitoring, reporting, documentation and information- processing institutions and procedures in order to contribute to preventing and reducing racial, ethnic or religious tensions. OHCHR, in collaboration with the Special Rapporteur, was invited to continue efforts to further analyse the issue of incitement and promotion of racism, racial discrimination, xenophobia and related intolerance in the political debate.

GENERAL ASSEMBLY ACTION

On 20 December [meeting 74], the General Assembly, on the recommendation of the Third Committee [A/59/501], adopted **resolution 59/175** without vote [agenda item 103 (a)].

Measures to be taken against political platforms and activities based on doctrines of superiority and violent nationalist ideologies which are based on racial discrimination or ethnic exclusiveness and xenophobia, including neo-Nazism

The General Assembly,

Recalling that the United Nations emerged from the struggle against Nazism, fascism, aggression and foreign occupation, and that the people expressed their resolve in the Charter of the United Nations to save succeeding generations from the scourge of war,

Aware of the determination proclaimed by the peoples of the world in the Charter to reaffirm faith in fundamental human rights, in the dignity and worth of the human person, in the equal rights of men and women and of nations large and small and to promote social progress and better standards of life in larger freedom,

Convinced that any doctrine of superiority based on racial differentiation is scientifically false, morally condemnable, socially unjust and dangerous, and that there is no justification for racial discrimination, in theory or in practice, anywhere,

Recognizing the fact that the World Conference against Racism, Racial Discrimination, Xenophobia and Related Intolerance, held at Durban, South Africa, from 31 August to 8 September 2001, condemned political platforms and organizations based on racism, xenophobia or doctrines of racial superiority and related discrimination, as well as legislation and practices based on racism, racial discrimination, xenophobia and related intolerance, as incompatible with democracy and transparent and accountable governance,

Reaffirming in this regard that everyone has the right to freedom of opinion and expression as well as the right to freedom of peaceful assembly and association,

Underlining the key role that politicians and political parties can and ought to play in combating racism, racial discrimination, xenophobia and related intolerance,

Noting with regret that, in the contemporary world, there continue to exist various manifestations of neo-Nazi activities, as well as other political platforms and activities based on doctrines of superiority and violent nationalist ideologies which are based on racial discrimination or ethnic exclusiveness and xenophobia, which entail contempt for the individual or a denial of the intrinsic dignity and equality of all human beings and of equality of opportunity in the civil, political, economic and social and cultural spheres and in social justice,

Deeply alarmed at the persistence and resurgence of these phenomena, and stating that they can never be justified in any instance or under any circumstances,

Noting with concern the widening misuse by such groups and organizations of the opportunities provided by scientific and technological progress, including the Internet, to promote racist and xenophobic propaganda aimed at inciting racial hatred and to collect funds to sustain violent campaigns against multiethnic societies throughout the world,

Noting that the use of such technologies can also contribute to combating racism, racial discrimination, xenophobia and related intolerance,

Expressing serious concern at the persistence in many parts of the world of doctrines of superiority and violent nationalist ideologies which are based on racial discrimination or ethnic exclusiveness and xenophobia,

Particularly alarmed at the persistence of such ideas in political circles, in the sphere of public opinion and in society at large,

Recognizing the important role that relevant regional bodies, including regional associations of national human rights institutions, can play in combating racism, racial discrimination, xenophobia and related intolerance, and the key role that they can play in monitoring and raising awareness about intolerance and discrimination at the regional level, reaffirming support for

such bodies where they exist, and encouraging their establishment,

Recalling its previous resolutions, in particular resolutions 55/82 of 4 December 2000 and 56/268 of 27 March 2002,

Taking into consideration the report of the Special Rapporteur of the Commission on Human Rights on contemporary forms of racism, racial discrimination, xenophobia and related intolerance to the Commission on Human Rights and, in particular, his study on the question of political platforms which promote or incite racial discrimination,

1. *Remains convinced* that political platforms and activities based on doctrines of superiority and violent nationalist ideologies which are based on racial discrimination or ethnic exclusiveness and xenophobia, including neo-Nazism, must be condemned as incompatible with democracy and accountable governance;

2. *Expresses its determination* to resist such political platforms and activities which can undermine the enjoyment of human rights and fundamental freedoms and of equality of opportunity;

3. *Urges* States to take all available measures in accordance with their obligations under international human rights instruments to combat political platforms and activities based on doctrines of superiority and violent nationalist ideologies which are based on racial discrimination or ethnic exclusiveness and xenophobia, inter alia, through the dissemination of human rights principles at all levels of society through education, as well as by other means;

4. *Takes note* of the recommendations of the Special Rapporteur of the Commission on Human Rights on contemporary forms of racism, racial discrimination, xenophobia and related intolerance, including on the need for States to exercise greater control over racist and xenophobic statements, especially when they are expressed by representatives of political parties or other ideological movements, and emphasizes in this regard that measures taken to combat racism must be in accordance with the commitments they have undertaken under the Durban Declaration and Programme of Action and with international standards of freedom of expression;

5. *Calls upon* States to undertake and facilitate activities aimed at educating young people in human rights and democratic citizenship and instilling values of solidarity, respect and appreciation of diversity, including respect for different groups, and affirms that a special effort to inform and sensitize young people with regard to democratic values and human rights should be undertaken or developed to fight against ideologies based on the fallacious theory of racial superiority;

6. *Urges* all States to consider the adoption, as a matter of high priority, of appropriate measures, consistent with their national legal systems and in accordance with the provisions of the Universal Declaration of Human Rights, the International Covenants on Human Rights and the International Convention on the Elimination of All Forms of Racial Discrimination, to eradicate activities that lead to violence based on racial discrimination or ethnic exclusiveness and xenophobia, including neo-Nazism, and to condemn all propaganda and all organizations which are based on ideas and theories of superiority;

7. *Expresses support* for the activities of the Special Rapporteur, and calls upon all States to cooperate with him in all aspects with a view to enabling him to fulfil his mandate;

8. *Requests* the Secretary-General to bring the present resolution to the attention of the Member States and relevant human rights bodies and mechanisms of the United Nations system.

Protection of migrants

Report of Special Rapporteur. The Special Rapporteur on the human rights of migrants, Gabriela Rodríguez Pizarro (Costa Rica), in a report covering her 2003 activities [E/CN.4/2004/76], analysed the situation of migrant domestic workers in the context of State legislation and practices and in the light of international human rights standards, based on responses to a questionnaire she had circulated and on her personal observations. Specific violations perpetrated against them included cases of death or disappearance, sexual abuse, infringement of privacy rights, false accusation of theft or other crimes, inadequate representation when charged, religious intolerance, slavery-like working hours, and denial of medical attention, food and telephone access to their families. Factors rendering migrant domestic workers vulnerable in that regard included the fact that host country legislation and recruitment methods often made them heavily dependent on their employer, especially when legal residence depended on the work contract. The Special Rapporteur addressed a series of recommendations to both States of origin and destination of large-scale flows of migrant domestic workers on steps to ensure the protection of their rights and to eliminate factors which made them vulnerable to abuse at all phases of migration, from recruitment to their return home.

An addendum to the report [E/CN.4/2004/76/Add.1] summarized the communications the Special Rapporteur had sent to 26 Governments and responses thereto, regarding individual cases of alleged violations of migrants' human rights and general situations concerning their rights in specific countries.

Commission action. On 20 April [res. 2004/53], the Commission, strongly condemning racism, racial discrimination, xenophobia and related intolerance against migrants, asked States to promote and protect their rights. It encouraged the Special Rapporteur to examine ways of overcoming existing obstacles in that regard and requested her to report to the General Assembly in 2004 and to the Commission in 2005. The Secretary-General was asked to assist her.

On 22 July (**decision 2004/262**), the Economic and Social Council endorsed the Commission's request to the Special Rapporteur to submit reports.

Further reports of Special Rapporteur. At the invitation of the Government, the Special Rapporteur visited Iran (22-29 February) [E/CN.4/2004/76/Add.4, E/CN.4/2005/85/Add.2], where she found that the majority of migrants were refugees who were essentially being cared for by the Government, placing an economic and social burden on the country. Those registered in Iran comprised mostly Afghans, numbering about 1.5 million. Hundreds of thousands of other Afghans residing in the country were unregistered. Iraqi migrants numbered about 202,000, of whom some 70,000 had repatriated spontaneously. The Special Rapporteur said there was often a tendency to equate the situation of irregular migrants with that of refugees, and the confusion might jeopardize efforts to protect the rights of both migrants and asylum-seekers. Other issues of concern were the exploitation of irregular migrants, difficulties in curbing irregular migration, the delimitation of responsibilities among offices dealing with migration issues, obstacles to the integration of migrants, a lack of knowledge of the guarantees and rights that international human rights law accorded to migrants and the lack of national NGOs dealing with migrants' issues. She recommended the implementation of a national policy of assistance and protection for migrants, and pointed to the need to initiate and encourage more domestic research on and evaluation of the presence and working conditions of foreign migrant workers and their impact on the Iranian economy and society. Futher recommendations emphasized Iran's need to adhere to international legal instruments for securing migrants' interests and action to protect irregular migrants.

In Italy (7-18 June) [E/CN.4/2005/85/Add.3], which faced considerable migratory pressure and was home to an estimated 2.5 million migrants, the Special Rapporteur addressed border security and the administration of undocumented immigrants, and assessed the impact of recent reforms of the country's immigration legislation relating to efforts to integrate its immigrant population. While acknowledging government efforts to improve relations with countries of origin and transit as a means of checking illegal migration, to regularize the situation of gainfully employed illegal immigrants and to combat trafficking in persons, the Special Rapporteur expressed concern that measures to combat illegal immigration were also restricting the entry of foreigners and the rights of immigrants in the country. Further issues of concern related to the lack of coordination between employment and migration policies, the status and management of reception and identification centres, the high percentage of foreigners in prisons and the fact that discrimination against migrants was not addressed directly either in political spheres or by civil society. The Special Rapporteur recommended that the Government bring its migration policy in line with the employment situation; promote legal migration; ensure health assistance for arriving immigrants; develop for foreign prisoners alternatives to the deprivation of liberty, arrangements for sentences to be served in countries of origin and opportunities for rehabilitation; and arrange voluntary return programmes.

In Peru (20-30 September) [E/CN.4/2005/85/ Add.4], the Special Rapporteur addressed the migration of an estimated 1.8 million Peruvian citizens to other countries, particularly to neighbouring Ecuador, Chile, Brazil and Colombia. She assessed the country's reform of its policy of consular assistance to those affected and investigated the situation of foreigners deprived of their liberty in Peruvian jails. The Special Rapporteur found that broad sectors of the population, young people in particular, saw emigration as the only solution to unemployment and poverty, given that Peru's recent economic growth had not resulted in any significant improvement in the labour market. The Special Rapporteur encouraged the Government to be proactive in defending the rights of Peruvian emigrants abroad and of foreigners in Peru, and to request UN support in doing so. She considered inadequate the country's efforts to deal with the smuggling of migrants and trafficking in persons, noting that there was a need for an institutional structure capable of combating such crimes and ensuring that the perpetrators were brought to justice. Another cause for concern was the prison conditions of foreigners in Peru, which violated human rights principles and standards. It was important to ensure that those affected had access to essential medical and legal assistance, among other services.

In response to General Assembly resolution 58/190 [YUN 2003, p. 708] and to Commission resolution 2004/53 (see p. 697), the Secretary-General, in September [A/59/377], transmitted a report of the Special Rapporteur, which further described her activities and issues of concern. Noting a continuing deterioration of migrants' human rights, the Special Rapporteur observed that the most frequent abuses against them included discriminatory, xenophobic and racist practices, the administrative detention of undocumented immigrants and exploitation of migrant workers. The Special Rapporteur said that

traditional ways of managing migratory flows had become obsolete given that immigration currently took place in the context of globalization. The Special Rapporteur proposed that migration management should be stronger from a human rights perspective and based on the shared responsibility of States to fulfil their obligations towards migrants. States needed to ensure that their migration policies and domestic immigration laws were in line with the principles of international human rights law and with related commitments they had made at the international level. The Special Rapporteur urged the Assembly to continue its work on the codification of draft articles on the responsibility of States for internationally wrongful acts submitted by the International Law Commission (see p. 1298). She urged the Commission to do likewise on the Basic Principles and Guidelines on the Right to a Remedy and Reparation for Victims of Violations of International Human Rights and Humanitarian Law.

On 20 December, the Assembly took note of the Special Rapporteur's report (**decision 59/528**).

Report of Secretary-General. Pursuant to General Assembly resolution 58/190 [YUN 2003, p. 708], the Secretary-General, in a September report [A/59/328], summarized communications received from 12 States providing information on legal provisions, programmes, campaigns and policies established to protect migrants. The Secretary-General was encouraged by the increasing number of bilateral, regional and international consultations on migration, including the question of the protection of migrants, and by States' efforts in that regard. He welcomed the establishment of the Committee on the Protection of the Rights of All Migrant Workers and Members of Their Families, which would monitor the compliance of States parties with the provisions of the 1990 International Convention on the Protection of the Rights of All Migrant Workers and Members of Their Families (see p. 668). The Secretary-General encouraged States to implement their national action plans, particularly regarding aspects relating to migrants, in follow-up action to the 2001 World Conference against Racism, Racial Discrimination, Xenophobia and Related Intolerance [YUN 2001, p. 615].

By **decision 59/528** of 20 December, the Assembly took note of the Secretary-General's report.

Communication. In February [E/CN.4/2004/G/ 17], Spain, referring to the Special Rapporteur's report on her 2003 visit to the country [YUN 2003, p. 707], stated that it disagreed with a number of statements and interpretations contained in the report, which, among other things, implied the existence of gender and racial discrimination against nationals of some countries.

GENERAL ASSEMBLY ACTION

On 20 December [meeting 74], the General Assembly, on the recommendation of the Third Committee [A/59/503/Add.2], adopted **resolution 59/194** without vote [agenda item 105 (b)].

Protection of migrants

The General Assembly,

Recalling its resolution 58/190 of 22 December 2003 and Commission on Human Rights resolution 2004/53 of 20 April 2004,

Recalling also its resolution 40/144 of 13 December 1985, by which it adopted the Declaration on the Human Rights of Individuals Who are not Nationals of the Country in which They Live,

Reaffirming that the Universal Declaration of Human Rights proclaims that all human beings are born free and equal in dignity and rights and that everyone is entitled to all the rights and freedoms set out therein, without distinction of any kind, in particular as to race, colour or national origin,

Considering that every State party to the International Covenant on Civil and Political Rights must ensure to all individuals within its territory and subject to its jurisdiction the rights recognized in the Covenant,

Bearing in mind that every State party to the International Covenant on Economic, Social and Cultural Rights has undertaken to guarantee the exercise of all rights enunciated in that Covenant without discrimination of any kind, including, in particular, on the basis of national origin,

Reaffirming the provisions concerning migrants adopted by the World Conference on Human Rights, the International Conference on Population and Development, the World Summit for Social Development and the Fourth World Conference on Women,

Reaffirming also the provisions on the human rights of migrants contained in the Durban Declaration and Programme of Action, adopted by the World Conference against Racism, Racial Discrimination, Xenophobia and Related Intolerance on 8 September 2001, and expressing its satisfaction at the important recommendations made for the development of international and national strategies for the protection of migrants and for the design of migration policies that fully respect the human rights of migrants,

Welcoming the renewed commitment made in the United Nations Millennium Declaration to take measures to ensure respect for and protection of the human rights of migrants, migrant workers and their families, to eliminate the increasing acts of racism and xenophobia in many societies and to promote greater harmony and tolerance in all societies,

Taking note with appreciation of the report of the Special Rapporteur of the Commission on Human Rights on the human rights of migrants, especially the work she has undertaken on the human rights of migrants, and taking note of the conclusions and recommendations contained therein,

Taking note of advisory opinion OC-16/99, issued by the Inter-American Court of Human Rights on 1 October 1999, on The Right to Information on Consular

Assistance in the Framework of the Guarantees of the Due Process of Law,

Taking note also of the Judgment of the International Court of Justice of 31 March 2004 in the case concerning *Avena and Other Mexican Nationals,* and recalling the obligations of States reaffirmed therein,

Taking note further of advisory opinion OC-18/03, issued by the Inter-American Court of Human Rights on 17 September 2003, on The Juridical Condition and Rights of Undocumented Migrants,

Aware of the increasing number of migrants worldwide, and bearing in mind the situation of vulnerability in which migrants and their families frequently find themselves, owing, inter alia, to their absence from their States of origin and to the difficulties they encounter because of differences of language, custom and culture, as well as the economic and social difficulties and obstacles to the return to their States of origin of migrants who are non-documented or in an irregular situation,

Recognizing the positive contributions that migrants frequently make, including through their eventual integration into their host society, and the efforts that some host countries undertake to integrate migrants and their families,

Underlining the importance of the creation of conditions that foster greater harmony, tolerance and respect between migrants and the rest of society in the States in which they reside in order to eliminate manifestations of racism and xenophobia against migrants,

Encouraged by the increasing interest of the international community in the effective and full protection of the human rights of all migrants, and underlining the need to make further efforts to ensure respect for the human rights and fundamental freedoms of all migrants,

Bearing in mind the need for a focused and consistent approach towards migrants as a specific vulnerable group, in particular migrant women and children,

Resolved to ensure respect for the human rights and fundamental freedoms of all migrants,

1. *Strongly condemns* the manifestations and acts of racism, racial discrimination, xenophobia and related intolerance against migrants and the stereotypes often applied to them, and urges States to apply the existing laws when xenophobic or intolerant acts, manifestations or expressions against migrants occur, in order to eradicate impunity for those who commit xenophobic and racist acts;

2. *Also strongly condemns* all forms of racial discrimination and xenophobia related to access to employment, vocational training, housing, schooling, health services and social services, as well as services intended for use by the public, and welcomes the active role played by governmental and non-governmental organizations in combating racism and xenophobia and in assisting individual victims of racist acts, including migrant victims;

3. *Requests* all Member States, in conformity with their respective constitutional systems, effectively to promote and protect the human rights of all migrants, in conformity with the Universal Declaration of Human Rights and the international instruments to which they are party, which may include the International Covenants on Human Rights, the Convention against Torture and Other Cruel, Inhuman or Degrad-

ing Treatment or Punishment, the International Convention on the Elimination of All Forms of Racial Discrimination, the International Convention on the Protection of the Rights of All Migrant Workers and Members of Their Families, the Convention on the Elimination of All Forms of Discrimination against Women, the Convention on the Rights of the Child and other relevant international human rights instruments;

4. *Welcomes* the increasing number of signatures and ratifications or accessions to the International Convention on the Protection of the Rights of All Migrant Workers and Members of Their Families, and calls upon States that have not done so to consider urgently signing and ratifying or acceding to the Convention;

5. *Also welcomes* the entry into force of the United Nations Convention against Transnational Organized Crime, the Protocol to Prevent, Suppress and Punish Trafficking in Persons, Especially Women and Children, supplementing the United Nations Convention against Transnational Organized Crime, and the Protocol against the Smuggling of Migrants by Land, Sea and Air, supplementing the United Nations Convention against Transnational Organized Crime, and calls upon States that have not done so to consider urgently signing and ratifying or acceding to them;

6. *Reaffirms emphatically* the duty of States parties to ensure full respect for and observance of the Vienna Convention on Consular Relations of 1963, in particular with regard to the right of all foreign nationals to communicate with a consular official of the sending State in the case of arrest, imprisonment, custody or detention, and the obligation of the receiving State to inform without delay the foreign national of his or her rights under the Convention;

7. *Calls upon* States to promote and protect fully the human rights of migrants, as set out in the Durban Declaration and Programme of Action, through, inter alia, the adoption of national plans of action as recommended by the World Conference against Racism, Racial Discrimination, Xenophobia and Related Intolerance;

8. *Also calls upon* all States to consider reviewing and, where necessary, revising immigration policies with a view to eliminating all discriminatory practices against migrants and their families, and to provide specialized training for government policy-making, law enforcement, migration and other concerned officials, including in cooperation with non-governmental organizations and civil society, thus underlining the importance of effective action to create conditions that foster greater harmony and tolerance within societies;

9. *Welcomes* immigration programmes, adopted by some countries, that allow migrants to integrate fully into the host countries, facilitate family reunification and promote a harmonious and tolerant environment, and encourages States to consider the possibility of adopting these types of programmes;

10. *Requests* all States, in conformity with national legislation and applicable international legal instruments to which they are party, firmly to prosecute violations of labour law with regard to the conditions of work of migrant workers, including those related to, inter alia, their remuneration and the conditions of health and safety at work;

11. *Encourages* all States to remove obstacles that may prevent the safe, unrestricted and expeditious transfer of earnings, assets and pensions of migrants to their country of origin or to any other countries, in conformity with applicable legislation, and to consider, as appropriate, measures to solve other problems that may impede such transfers;

12. *Urges* all States to adopt effective measures to put an end to the arbitrary arrest and detention of migrants and to take action to prevent and punish any form of illegal deprivation of liberty of migrants by individuals or groups;

13. *Calls upon* States to observe national legislation and applicable international legal instruments to which they are party when enacting national security measures in order to respect the human rights of migrants;

14. *Requests* States to adopt concrete measures to prevent the violation of the human rights of migrants while in transit, including in ports and airports and at borders and migration checkpoints, to train public officials who work in those facilities and in border areas to treat migrants and their families respectfully and in accordance with the law, and to prosecute, in conformity with applicable law, any act of violation of the human rights of migrants and their families, such as arbitrary detention, torture and violations of the right to life, including extrajudicial executions, during their transit from their country of origin to the country of destination and vice versa, including their transit through national borders;

15. *Encourages* Member States that have not yet done so to enact domestic legislation and to take further effective measures to combat international trafficking in and smuggling of migrants, recognizing that these crimes may endanger the lives of migrants or subject them to harm, servitude or exploitation, which may include debt bondage, slavery, sexual exploitation or forced labour, and also encourages Member States to strengthen international cooperation to combat such trafficking and smuggling;

16. *Encourages* States, in cooperation with non-governmental organizations, to undertake information campaigns aimed at clarifying opportunities, limitations and rights in the event of migration so as to enable everyone, in particular women, to make informed decisions and to prevent them from becoming victims of trafficking and utilizing dangerous means of access that put their lives and physical integrity at risk;

17. *Calls upon* States to facilitate family reunification in an expeditious and effective manner, with due regard to applicable laws, as such reunification has a positive effect on the integration of migrants;

18. *Calls upon* all States to protect and promote all human rights of migrant children, in particular unaccompanied migrant children, ensuring that the best interests of the children are a primary consideration, underlines the importance of reuniting them with their parents, when possible, and encourages the relevant United Nations bodies, within the framework of their respective mandates, to pay special attention to the conditions of migrant children in all States and, where necessary, to put forward recommendations for strengthening their protection;

19. *Encourages* States of origin to promote and protect the human rights of those families of migrant workers which remain in the countries of origin, paying particular attention to children and adolescents whose parents have emigrated, and encourages international organizations to consider supporting States in this regard;

20. *Encourages* States to consider participating in international and regional dialogues on migration that include countries of origin and destination, as well as countries of transit, and invites them to consider negotiating bilateral and regional agreements on migrant workers within the framework of applicable human rights law and designing and implementing programmes with States of other regions to protect the rights of migrants;

21. *Requests* all Governments to cooperate fully with the Special Rapporteur of the Commission on Human Rights on the human rights of migrants in the performance of the tasks and duties mandated, to furnish all information requested and to respond appropriately and expeditiously to her urgent appeals and to give serious consideration to her requests to visit their countries, and welcomes in this regard the standing invitations extended by some Member States to all special procedures, including the Special Rapporteur;

22. *Encourages* States to review and examine the conclusions and recommendations contained in the report of the Special Rapporteur and to consider their re-implementation;

23. *Invites* States and intergovernmental and non-governmental organizations to observe, on 18 December of each year, International Migrants Day, proclaimed by the General Assembly, through, inter alia, the dissemination of information on the human rights and fundamental freedoms of migrants and on their economic, social and cultural contributions to their host and home countries, the sharing of experience and the design of actions to ensure their protection, and to promote greater harmony between migrants and the societies in which they live;

24. *Requests* the Secretary-General to submit to the General Assembly at its sixtieth session a report on the implementation of the present resolution under the sub-item entitled "Human rights questions, including alternative approaches for improving the effective enjoyment of human rights and fundamental freedoms", and requests the Special Rapporteur to submit to the Assembly at its sixtieth session an interim report on the fulfilment of her mandate;

25. *Decides* to examine the question further at its sixtieth session under the sub-item.

Also on 20 December [meeting 74], the Assembly, on the recommendation of the Third Committee [A/59/503/Add.2], adopted **resolution 59/203** by recorded vote (122-3-61) [agenda item 105 (*b*)].

Respect for the right to universal freedom of travel and the vital importance of family reunification

The General Assembly,

Recalling its resolution 57/227 of 18 December 2002,

Reaffirming that all human rights and fundamental freedoms are universal, indivisible, interdependent and interrelated,

Recalling the provisions of the Universal Declaration of Human Rights, as well as article 12 of the International Covenant on Civil and Political Rights,

Stressing that, as stated in the Programme of Action of the International Conference on Population and Development, family reunification of documented migrants is an important factor in international migration and that remittances by documented migrants to their countries of origin often constitute a very important source of foreign exchange and are instrumental in improving the well-being of relatives left behind,

Noting that while some positive developments occurred during the past two years in the accomplishment of the objectives highlighted in resolution 57/227, in particular the commitment made on 9 June 2004 at the summit meeting of the Group of Eight, held at Sea Island, United States of America, to facilitate the flow of remittances across international borders to help families, in certain cases it has been reported that measures have been adopted that have increased the restrictions imposed on documented migrants in relation to family reunification and the possibility of sending remittances to their relatives in the country of origin,

Recalling that the family is the basic unit of society and, as such, should be strengthened, and that it is entitled to receive comprehensive protection and support,

1. *Once again calls upon* all States to guarantee the universally recognized freedom of travel to all foreign nationals legally residing in their territory;

2. *Reaffirms* that all Governments, in particular those of receiving countries, must recognize the vital importance of family reunification and promote its incorporation into national legislation in order to ensure protection of the unity of families of documented migrants;

3. *Calls upon* all States to allow, in conformity with international legislation, the free flow of financial remittances by foreign nationals residing in their territory to relatives in the country of origin;

4. *Also calls upon* all States to refrain from enacting, and to repeal if it already exists, legislation intended as a coercive measure that discriminates against individuals or groups of legal migrants by adversely affecting family reunification and the right to send financial remittances to relatives in the country of origin;

5. *Decides* to continue its consideration of the question at its sixty-first session under the item entitled "Human rights questions".

RECORDED VOTE ON RESOLUTION 59/203:

In favour: Afghanistan, Algeria, Angola, Antigua and Barbuda, Argentina, Armenia, Azerbaijan, Bahamas, Bahrain, Bangladesh, Barbados, Belarus, Belize, Benin, Bhutan, Bolivia, Botswana, Brazil, Burkina Faso, Burundi, Cambodia, Cameroon, Cape Verde, Central African Republic, Chad, Chile, China, Colombia, Comoros, Costa Rica, Côte d'Ivoire, Cuba, Democratic People's Republic of Korea, Democratic Republic of the Congo, Djibouti, Dominica, Dominican Republic, Ecuador, Egypt, El Salvador, Equatorial Guinea, Eritrea, Ethiopia, Fiji, Gabon, Gambia, Ghana, Grenada, Guatemala, Guinea, Guinea-Bissau, Guyana, Haiti, Honduras, India, Indonesia, Iran, Iraq, Jamaica, Jordan, Kazakhstan, Kenya, Kuwait, Kyrgyzstan, Lao People's Democratic Republic, Lebanon, Lesotho, Liberia, Libyan Arab Jamahiriya, Madagascar, Mali, Mauritania, Mauritius, Mexico, Mongolia, Morocco, Mozambique, Myanmar, Namibia, Nepal, Nicaragua, Niger, Nigeria, Oman, Pakistan, Panama, Papua New Guinea, Peru, Philippines, Qatar, Russian Federation, Rwanda, Saint Lucia, Saint Vincent and the Grenadines, Sao Tome and Principe, Saudi Arabia, Senegal, Seychelles, Sierra Leone, Somalia, South Africa, Sri Lanka, Sudan, Suriname, Swaziland, Syrian Arab Republic, Tajikistan, Timor-Leste, Togo, Trinidad and Tobago, Tunisia, Turkmenistan, Tuvalu, Uganda,

United Arab Emirates, United Republic of Tanzania, Uruguay, Venezuela, Viet Nam, Yemen, Zambia, Zimbabwe.

Against: Israel, Palau, United States.

Abstaining: Albania, Andorra, Australia, Austria, Belgium, Bosnia and Herzegovina, Brunei Darussalam, Bulgaria, Canada, Croatia, Cyprus, Czech Republic, Denmark, Estonia, Finland, France, Georgia, Germany, Greece, Hungary, Iceland, Ireland, Italy, Japan, Latvia, Liechtenstein, Lithuania, Luxembourg, Malawi, Malaysia, Maldives, Malta, Marshall Islands, Micronesia (Federated States of), Monaco, Nauru, Netherlands, New Zealand, Norway, Paraguay, Poland, Portugal, Republic of Korea, Republic of Moldova, Romania, Samoa, San Marino, Serbia and Montenegro, Singapore, Slovakia, Slovenia, Solomon Islands, Spain, Sweden, Switzerland, Thailand, The former Yugoslav Republic of Macedonia, Turkey, Ukraine, United Kingdom, Uzbekistan.

Other forms of intolerance

On 9 August [E/CN.4/2005/2 (dec. 2004/108)], the Subcommission asked Soli Sorabjee (India) to submit, without financial implications, a working paper on the impact of intolerance on the enjoyment and exercise of human rights and measures to counter it, for consideration in 2005.

Cultural prejudice

Report of High Commissioner. In response to the Commission's 2002 [YUN 2002, p. 677] and 2003 [YUN 2003, p. 710] requests to the High Commissioner to consult with States, intergovernmental organizations and NGOs on the possibility of appointing a special rapporteur to implement the Commission's resolutions on cultural rights, the High Commissioner submitted a report [E/CN.4/2004/41 & Corr.1 & Add.1] summarizing replies received from seven Governments and two UN system agencies on the appointment of a special rapporteur and on steps they had taken to promote the full enjoyment of cultural rights.

Commission action. By a recorded vote of 38 to 1, with 14 abstentions, the Commission, on 16 April [res. 2004/20], reaffirming that cultural rights were an integral part of human rights, recognized that States had the responsibility to promote the full enjoyment of cultural rights and to enhance respect for different cultural identities. The Commission called on States, intergovernmental organizations and NGOs to implement its resolution and asked the High Commissioner to consult with them on the possibility of establishing a thematic procedure, whose mandate would be the comprehensive implementation of the resolution, and to report in 2005.

Discrimination against minorities

Report of High Commissioner. In response to a 2003 Commission request [YUN 2003, p. 712], a February report of the High Commissioner [E/CN.4/2004/75] reviewed existing human rights norms and mechanisms for protecting persons belonging to minorities, identified structural and functional gaps and considered how proposals made by legislative or advisory bodies might contribute to strengthening the promotion and protection of minorities' rights. Particular attention was accorded to the work of the Working Group on Minorities (see below), human rights treaty bodies and the Commission's special procedures. The High Commissioner concluded that, owing to structural or functional reasons, the challenges facing minorities had not been appropriately covered by existing mandates, and that the potential of those mandates had not been fully exploited. The High Commissioner said there were no procedures for dealing swiftly with violations of minorities' rights and with individual or group communications, and there was also no mandate to follow up minority issues in a systematic and specialized way through contacts with Governments and societies. Several proposals had been made, mostly by the Working Group (see below), regarding the better exploitation of the potential of existing mechanisms and other arrangements, including the appointment of a special rapporteur of the Commission and a special representative of the Secretary-General on minority-related problems, the creation of a voluntary fund for minorities and the proclamation of an international year for the world's minorities. It was important that the debate on such new arrangements be undertaken in the context of the reform of human rights mechanisms. Drawing on the existing mechanisms, enhancing their impact through greater involvement in minority issues and making any new ones fully complementary could strengthen the ability of the UN human rights machinery to effectively address problems faced by minorities.

Referring to the Commission's request to the Secretary-General to report on recent developments with regard to the promotion and protection of persons belonging to minorities [YUN 2003, p. 712], the High Commissioner drew the Commission's attention to the 2003 report of the Secretary-General [ibid., p. 713], which provided relevant information.

Commission action. On 20 April [res. 2004/51], the Commission urged States to promote and protect the rights of persons belonging to national or ethnic, religious and linguistic minorities, to accord special attention to protecting their children's rights and to take measures to protect their cultural and religious sites. The Working Group on Minorities (see p. 703) was invited to strengthen its role as a platform for interactive dialogue between representatives of Governments and minority groups, while the Secretary-General and the High Commissioner were asked to assist in strengthening OHCHR's capacity to deal with minority issues and to seek voluntary contributions to facilitate the participation of NGO and minority representatives in the Group's work. The High Commissioner was asked to study options for the timely identification of minority issues and related measures through the compilation of the views of Member States, relevant parts of the UN system, regional and international organizations and NGOs regarding their analysis of the activities of the Working Group and the results it achieved, and to report in 2005. The High Commissioner was further requested to report in 2005 on the implementation of the Commission's resolution.

Also on 20 April [dec. 2004/114], the Commission endorsed the 2003 recommendation of the Subcommission [YUN 2003, p. 713] that a voluntary fund on minority-related activities be established to facilitate participation in the Working Group and its related activities of representatives and experts from developing countries and for the organization of other activities relating to the implementation of the rights of persons belonging to minorities, with Working Group members acting as a virtual decision-making board.

On 22 July, the Economic and Social Council endorsed the establishment of the fund and recommended that the General Assembly consider it favourably (**decision 2004/278**).

Further on 20 April [dec. 2004/115], the Commission, taking note of the Subcommission's 2003 recommendation [YUN 2003, p. 713] to proclaim an international year for the world's minorities, followed by a decade, with a view to advancing the implementation of the 1992 Declaration on the Rights of Persons Belonging to National or Ethnic, Religious and Linguistic Minorities [YUN 1992, p. 723], called for greater cooperation among specialized agencies and other organizations of the UN system in order to contribute to the full realization of the rights and principles set forth in the Declaration.

Working Group activities. The five-member Working Group on Minorities, at its tenth session (Geneva, 1-5 March) [E/CN.4/Sub.2/2004/29], reviewed the promotion of the 1992 Declaration, examined possible solutions to problems involving minorities, including the promotion of mutual understanding between and among minorities and Governments, and recommended further measures to promote and protect minority rights. The Group also discussed its future role.

The Group had before it working papers on minorities and self-determination [E/CN.4/Sub.2/ AC.5/2004/WP.1], international and national action for the protection of the rights of minorities [E/CN.4/Sub.2/AC.5/2004/WP.3], an examination of approaches by international development agencies to minority issues in development [E/CN.4/ Sub.2/AC.5/2004/WP.5] and integration of and autonomy for minorities in Côte d'Ivoire [E/CN.4/ Sub.2/ AC.5/2004/WP.8].

In its decisions and recommendations, the Group addressed issues relating to the promotion and realization of the 1992 Declaration and decided to continue consideration of the item in 2005, beginning with important developments concerning minority situations around the world and effective enforcement mechanisms and remedies. It decided to focus on minorities and development, including conflicts over development, and action taken by Governments and international agencies for incorporating minority issues into activities designed to realize the MDGs, and the elaboration of general comments, regarding which the Group decided to endorse the commentary on the Declaration prepared in 2001 [YUN 2001, p. 623] by Asbjørn Eide (Norway). The commentary was to be reissued as the commentary of the Group as a whole and distributed widely. The Group decided to develop more specific commentaries on particular issues, including the protection of minorities from forced assimilation, of their places of worship and sacred places, and of their rights in the areas of education, land deprivation and exclusion, and on autonomy vis-à-vis self-determination. The Group encouraged regional or subregional meetings/ seminars/workshops, in cooperation with regional mechanisms, and recommended for discussion at the seminars the development of regional codes of conduct or guidelines based on universal norms and international minority rights standards. It also recommended the organization of a seminar on the Roma population. The Group considered issues relating to the promotion of constructive dialogue between and among minorities and Governments, emphasized the importance of establishing a voluntary fund to support the participation of minority representatives, particularly from developing countries, in its meetings, and recommended that a special representative of the Secretary-General on minority issues be appointed. It also recommended that the Subcommission entrust one of its members to prepare a working paper, without financial implications, on the advisability of drafting an additional protocol (containing minority rights and remedies for violations thereof) to the 1966 International Covenant on Civil and Political Rights, adopted by the General Assembly in resolution 2200 A (XXI) [YUN 1966, p. 423].

The Group further recommended that Governments ratify relevant international instruments and take measures to protect minorities' rights, that OHCHR continue to organize training on universal and regional standards and mechanisms in order to strengthen minority representatives' cooperation with human rights procedures, and that the technical cooperation programme of the Office assist with the sensitization and awareness- raising of all sectors of society, particularly law enforcement agencies, on minorities' needs and rights. The High Commissioner/OHCHR was invited to prepare, for inclusion in the *United Nations Guide for Minorities,* pamphlets on regional conflict-prevention initiatives and development matters, including with respect to the work of the United Nations Development Programme (UNDP) in integrating minority issues in its work. OHCHR was also asked to organize, in cooperation with development agencies, a meeting between the Working Group, representatives of international and bilateral development agencies, Minority Rights Group International (London) and minority representatives to examine further the integration of minority issues in development programming. The Group addressed a number of other recommendations aimed at promoting and protecting minorities' rights to regional mechanisms and to international, regional and national development agencies and UN system bodies.

At the invitation of the Government, four Working Group members visited Finland (17-20 January) [E/CN.4/Sub.2/2004/29/Add.1]. In the Aland autonomous Province, the Group focused on the legislation and implementation of autonomy, particularly as a mechanism for conflict resolution, and in the capital city, Helsinki, reviewed the participation and integration of all communities in political and social life and the issues of languages and cultures. The Group found that the autonomous Aland Islands and the State had developed a common ground for peaceful conflict resolution and for achieving balance between minority protection and the sovereignty and territorial integrity of the State. The Group welcomed the willingness of both sides to share their experiences in international forums as an inspiration for other parts of the world. In Helsinki, the Group found a comprehensive legislative framework and a monitoring mechanisms for minority protection, which was in conformity with international and European standards of human rights and minority rights. Noting that new minorities, composed mainly of some 30,000 Ingrians (a Russian-speaking community) and an estimated 4,000 Somalis, suffered stereotyping in the media and racism and discrimination in the labour market and social services, the Group recommended that the Government establish an advisory body to examine integration issues affecting the Russian-speaking community and invited the minority communities it did not meet to send it information. Regarding the indigenous Sami people in the country, the Group recommended that the Government ratify the International Labour Organization (ILO) Convention No. 169 concerning Indigenous and Tribal Peoples in Independent Countries [YUN 1989, p. 917].

Note by Secretariat. By a 29 July note [E/CN.4/Sub.2/2004/32], the Secretariat, referring to a 2003 Subcommission request [YUN 2003, p. 713] to Mr. Eide to submit the final report updating his 1993 study on peaceful and constructive approaches to situations involving minorities [YUN 1993, p. 869], informed the Subcommission that Mr. Eide instead intended to prepare a draft report for consideration in 2005, which would contain a synthesis of the experience of the first decade of the Working Group.

Subcommission action. On 9 August [E/CN.4/2005/2 (res. 2004/13)], the Subcommission, endorsing the Working Group's recommendations and decisions, invited OHCHR to consider organizing training workshops at the national level on the implementation of minorities' rights; to organize, in cooperation with development agencies, a meeting between the Working Group, representatives of international and bilateral development agencies, Minority Rights Group International and minority representatives to examine further the integration of minority issues in development programming; and to prepare additional pamphlets for inclusion in the *United Nations Guide for Minorities,* particularly on the work of conflict-prevention mechanisms for the promotion and protection of minorities' rights. The Subcommission recommended that the High Commissioner, when inviting Governments and others to submit their views on how best to protect the rights of persons belonging to minorities, to request them to provide the names of experts, with a view to facilitating their participation in regional and international meetings and in advisory services, and to consider providing information about recent cases relating to minority rights. The Subcommission also recommended the preparation of a working paper by one of its members on the advisability of drafting an additional protocol to the International Covenant on Civil and Political Rights containing remedies for violations, for presentation in 2006, and the nomination of a special representative of the Secretary-General on minority issues, which it recommended that the Commission endorse.

Subregional seminars. Subregional seminars on minority rights were held, dealing with cultural diversity and development in Central Asia (Bishkek, Kyrgyzstan, 27-30 October) [E/CN.4/Sub.2/AC.5/2005/5] and in South Asia (Kandy, Sri Lanka, 21-24 November) [E/CN.4/Sub.2/AC.5/2005/4].

Leprosy victims

On 9 August [res. 2004/12], the Subcommission asked Yozo Yokota (Japan) to prepare, without financial implications, a preliminary working paper on discrimination against leprosy victims and their families, for consideration in 2005, under the agenda item "Prevention of discrimination and protection of minorities".

Discrimination based on work and descent

Working paper. In response to a 2003 Subcommission request [YUN 2003, p. 715], Messrs. Eide and Yokota submitted, in July, an expanded working paper on discrimination based on work and descent [E/CN.4/Sub.2/2004/31], which supplemented earlier papers considered in 2001 [YUN 2001, p. 625] and 2003 [YUN 2003, p. 715]. The current paper compiled information submitted by 12 Governments on legal, judicial, administrative and educational measures they had taken to address such discrimination. It also identified communities suffering such discrimination, noting that diaspora communities whose original cultures and traditions included aspects of inherited social exclusion had been mostly affected. The paper focused on the South Asian diaspora in the United States and the United Kingdom and highlighted the discrimination they suffered with regard to intermarriages, commensality (the practice of eating/drinking together), access to and organization of places of worship, employment opportunities, participation in politics, projection in the media and violent activities. The paper concluded that the elimination of discrimination based on work and descent was an important global human rights challenge, which had not always received the attention it deserved at the international level. It proposed a framework for draft principles and guidelines for the elimination of the phenomenon and recommended that the Subcommission appoint a special rapporteur to study it further.

Subcommission action. On 12 August [res. 2004/17], the Subcommission decided to appoint Mr. Yokota and Chin Sung Chung (Republic of Korea) as Special Rapporteurs with the task of preparing a comprehensive study on discrimination based on work and descent, and to submit a preliminary report in 2005, a progress report in

2006 and a final report in 2007. They were asked to focus on the finalization of a set of draft principles and guidelines for the effective elimination of the phenomenon and to obtain more comprehensive information on constitutional, legislative, judicial, administrative and educational measures taken to address the problem, for the purpose of identifying best practices. The Secretary-General and the High Commissioner were asked to assist them.

Rights of non-citizens

On 20 April [dec. 2004/113], the Commission, welcoming the 2003 final report of the Special Rapporteur on the rights of non-citizens [YUN 2003, p. 715], together with his 1999 working paper [YUN 1999, p. 611], 2001 preliminary report [YUN 2001, p. 625] and 2002 progress report [YUN 2002, p. 680], requested the Special Rapporteur to compile and update all his reports, addenda and questionnaire replies into a single report. The Economic and Social Council, by **decision 2004/277** of 22 July, decided that the 2003 updated and consolidated report on the rights of non-citizens should be published in all UN official languages and distributed widely.

Also on 20 April [dec. 2004/112], the Commission, by a recorded vote of 33 to 10, with 10 abstentions, decided not to recommend that the Council authorize the Special Rapporteur to undertake the task of furthering the study of the rights of non-citizens.

Non-discrimination

In response to a 2003 Subcommission request [YUN 2003, p. 717], Emmanuel Decaux (France) submitted a June working paper on non-discrimination [E/CN.4/Sub.2/2004/24], as enshrined in article 2, paragraph 2, of the International Covenant on Economic, Social and Cultural Rights, adopted by the General Assembly in resolution 2200 A (XXI) [YUN 1966, p. 419]. The paper concluded that issues deserving further attention included the scope of the principle of non-discrimination set forth in article 2, paragraph 2, of the Covenant; the relationship between general and specific clauses in relevant instruments, focusing on neglected categories of discrimination; the practical application of article 2, paragraph 2, in different areas of economic, social and cultural rights, as defined in the Covenant, in order to identify "blind spots" regarding discrimination; State responsibility for filling gaps, where necessary, in the international and domestic legal framework and for ensuring effective legal application of the principle; identification of good practices to promote respect for article 2, paragraph 2, in relations between private persons and between corporations and individuals; and development of the role of national institutions for the promotion and protection of human rights, particularly ombudsmen or independent administrative authorities.

Subcommission action. On 9 August [res. 2004/5], the Subcommission decided to appoint Marc Bossuyt (Belgium) as Special Rapporteur to undertake a study on non-discrimination as enshrined in article 2, paragraph 2, of the Covenant, based on the working paper prepared by Mr. Decaux (see above), on comments received thereto and on Subcommission discussions. He was requested to submit a preliminary report in 2005, a progress report in 2006 and a final report in 2007; the Secretary-General was asked to assist him.

Religious intolerance

Report of Special Rapporteur. In January [E/CN.4/2004/63], the Special Rapporteur on freedom of religion or belief, Abdelfattah Amor (Tunisia), summarized 69 communications he had sent to 42 States and the replies received from 15 States, regarding incidents and governmental action inconsistent with the provisions of the 1981 Declaration on the Elimination of All Forms of Intolerance and of Discrimination Based on Religion or Belief, adopted in General Assembly resolution 36/55 [YUN 1981, p. 881]. As his mandate neared conclusion, the Special Rapporteur took stock of his activities since 1993. Noting that he had accorded the greatest importance to the prevention of intolerance and discrimination in freedom of religion or belief, he described related activities in the fields of education and inter-religious dialogue and highlighted cooperation with the Commission, UN human rights mechanisms, specialized agencies and NGOs. The Special Rapporteur concluded that, although anti-religious policies or policies for the total control of religious matters by States had declined progressively, non-State entities had often failed to respect freedom of religion and extremism in that regard affected practically all religions. States had not met their human rights obligations regarding freedom of religion. The Special Rapporteur, drawing attention to the fact that women continued to be the main victims of violations, encouraged States to take decisive measures. He noted that extremists increasingly used religion for unrelated purposes, particularly the extremism claiming to be rooted in Islam, which had grown markedly since the 11 September 2001 terrorist attacks in the United States [YUN 2001, p. 60]. Addressing inter-religious

dialogue and education as a means of combating intolerance and discrimination based on religion or belief, the Special Rapporteur highlighted the difficulties encountered and advocated related measures.

Report of High Commissioner. In response to a 2003 Commission request [YUN 2003, p. 717], the High Commissioner submitted a February report [E/CN.4/2004/16] summarizing information received from two Governments on steps they had taken to promote religious and cultural diversity, and describing relevant activities of Commission mechanisms and of OHCHR.

Commission action. On 13 April [res. 2004/6], the Commission, by a recorded vote of 29 to 16, with 7 abstentions, called on the High Commissioner to promote and include human rights aspects in the dialogue among civilizations, by integrating them into topical seminars and special debates on the positive contributions of cultures and religious and cultural diversity, to hold joint conferences with other international organizations to promote understanding of the universality of human rights and their implementation, and to report in 2005.

On 19 April [res. 2004/36], the Commission decided to extend the Special Rapporteur's mandate for three years and asked him to submit an interim report to the General Assembly in 2004 and to report to the Commission in 2005. The Secretary-General was asked to assist him.

On 22 July, the Economic and Social Council approved the Commission's decision to extend the Special Rapporteur's mandate, its requests regarding the submission of reports to the Assembly and the Commission and its request to the Secretary-General (**decision 2004/258**).

In July, the Commission appointed Asma Jahangir (Pakistan) as the new Special Rapporteur.

Further report of Special Rapporteur. Pursuant to General Assembly resolution 58/184 [YUN 2003, p. 718], the Secretary-General, by a September note [A/59/366], transmitted the interim report of the Special Rapporteur, which contained 39 additional communications transmitted to 29 States and replies received from 15 States. The Special Rapporteur observed growing tensions between and within religious communities in a number of countries, which could degenerate into violent confrontations. The challenge for Governments was to resist interference through legislation and actions that could restrict the right to freedom of religion or belief, further aggravating the situation. Governments should avoid administrative measures restricting the freedom to practise religious ceremonies or rites, as such measures would be counterproductive and a violation of relevant international norms. They should also remain neutral in the face of tension between different religious communities.

By **decision 59/528** of 20 December, the Assembly took note of the interim report.

Communications. On 13 February [E/CN.4/2004/G/18], China responded to letters it had received from the Special Rapporteur relating to circumstances of alleged infringement of the freedom of religion or belief of a number of persons.

On 18 May [A/58/808], Turkmenistan transmitted the text of the country's law abolishing criminal responsibility for the violation of laws on religious organizations, and the text of the decree signed by its President repealing a previous decree on control and use of charitable aid in religious groups and organizations in the country.

The Foreign Ministers of member States of the Organization of the Islamic Conference (New York, 28 September) [A/59/425-S/2004/808] underscored the need for a viable strategy, which should aim at creating and promoting tolerance and harmony among different religions and civilizations.

GENERAL ASSEMBLY ACTION

On 20 December [meeting 74], the General Assembly, on the recommendation of the Third Committee [A/59/503/Add.2], adopted **resolution 59/199** by recorded vote (186-0) [agenda item 105 (b)].

Elimination of all forms of religious intolerance

The General Assembly,

Recalling that all States have pledged themselves, under the Charter of the United Nations, to promote and encourage universal respect for and observance of human rights and fundamental freedoms for all without distinction as to race, sex, language or religion,

Reaffirming that discrimination against human beings on the grounds of religion or belief constitutes an affront to human dignity and a disavowal of the principles of the Charter,

Recalling article 18 of the Universal Declaration of Human Rights, article 18 of the International Covenant on Civil and Political Rights and paragraph 4 of the United Nations Millennium Declaration,

Reaffirming its resolution 36/55 of 25 November 1981, by which it proclaimed the Declaration on the Elimination of All Forms of Intolerance and of Discrimination Based on Religion or Belief,

Noting the provisions of the Durban Declaration and Programme of Action adopted by the World Conference against Racism, Racial Discrimination, Xenophobia and Related Intolerance, held in Durban, South Africa, from 31 August to 8 September 2001, aimed at combating religious intolerance,

Emphasizing that the right to freedom of thought, conscience, religion and belief is far-reaching and profound and that it encompasses freedom of thought on all matters, personal conviction and the commitment to religion or belief, whether manifested individually or in community with others, and in public or in private,

Reaffirming the call, made eleven years ago in Vienna at the World Conference on Human Rights, for all Governments to take all appropriate measures in compliance with their international obligations and with due regard to their respective legal systems to counter intolerance and related violence based on religion or belief, including practices of discrimination against women and the desecration of religious sites, recognizing that every individual has the right to freedom of thought, conscience, expression and religion,

Underlining the important role of education in the promotion of tolerance, which involves the acceptance of and respect for diversity, and underlining also that education, in particular at school, should contribute in a meaningful way to the promotion of tolerance and the elimination of discrimination based on religion or belief,

Alarmed that serious instances of intolerance and discrimination on the grounds of religion or belief, including acts of violence, intimidation and coercion motivated by religious intolerance, continue to occur in many parts of the world and threaten the full enjoyment of human rights and fundamental freedoms,

Profoundly concerned at acts and situations of violence and discrimination resulting from religious intolerance that affect many women,

Deeply concerned at the overall rise in intolerance and discrimination on the grounds of religion or belief, including restrictive legislation, administrative regulations and discriminatory registration and the arbitrary application of these and other measures,

Seriously concerned at all attacks upon religious places, sites and shrines, including any deliberate destruction of relics and monuments,

Believing that further intensified efforts are therefore required to promote and protect the right to freedom of thought, conscience, religion or belief and to eliminate all forms of hatred, intolerance and discrimination based on religion or belief, as emphasized also at the World Conference against Racism, Racial Discrimination, Xenophobia and Related Intolerance,

1. *Reaffirms* that freedom of thought, conscience, religion or belief is a human right derived from the inherent dignity of the human person and guaranteed to all without discrimination;

2. *Urges* States to ensure that their constitutional and legal systems provide effective guarantees of freedom of thought, conscience, religion or belief, including the provision of effective remedies in cases where the right to freedom of thought, conscience, religion or belief is violated;

3. *Also urges* States to ensure, in particular, that no one within their jurisdiction is, because of their religion or belief, deprived of the right to life, liberty and security of person, the right to freedom of expression, the right not to be subjected to torture or other cruel, inhuman or degrading treatment or punishment and the right not to be arbitrarily arrested or detained, and to protect their physical integrity and bring to justice all perpetrators of violations of these rights;

4. *Further urges* States, in conformity with international standards of human rights, to take all necessary action to combat hatred, intolerance and acts of violence, intimidation and coercion motivated by intoler-

ance based on religion or belief, with particular regard to persons belonging to religious minorities;

5. *Urges* States to devote particular attention to combating all practices motivated by religion or belief which lead, directly or indirectly, to human rights violations and to discrimination against women;

6. *Emphasizes* that, as underlined by the Human Rights Committee, restrictions on the freedom to manifest religion or belief are permitted only if those limitations are prescribed by law, are necessary to protect public safety, order, health or morals or the fundamental rights and freedoms of others, and are applied in a manner that does not vitiate the right to freedom of thought, conscience and religion;

7. *Urges* States to ensure that all public officials and civil servants, including members of law enforcement bodies, the military and educators, in the course of their official duties, respect different religions and beliefs and do not discriminate on the grounds of religion or belief, and to ensure that all necessary and appropriate education or training is provided;

8. *Calls upon* all States to recognize, as provided for in the Declaration on the Elimination of All Forms of Intolerance and of Discrimination Based on Religion or Belief, the right of all persons to worship or assemble in connection with a religion or belief and to establish and maintain places for those purposes;

9. *Recognizes with deep concern* the overall rise in instances of intolerance and violence directed against members of many religious communities in various parts of the world, including cases motivated by Islamophobia, anti-Semitism and Christianophobia;

10. *Further urges* States to exert their utmost efforts, in accordance with their national legislation and in conformity with international human rights standards, to ensure that religious places, sites and shrines are fully respected and protected, and to take additional measures in cases where they are vulnerable to desecration or destruction;

11. *Recognizes* that legislation alone is not enough to prevent violations of human rights, including the right to freedom of religion or belief, and that the exercise of tolerance and non-discrimination by persons and groups is necessary for the full realization of the aims of the Declaration, and in this regard invites States, religious bodies and civil society to undertake dialogue at all levels to promote greater tolerance, respect and understanding of freedom of religion or belief and to encourage and promote, through the educational system and by other means, understanding, tolerance and respect in matters relating to freedom of religion or belief;

12. *Emphasizes* the importance of a continued and strengthened dialogue among religions or beliefs, including as encompassed in the dialogue among civilizations, to promote greater tolerance, respect and mutual understanding;

13. *Takes note with appreciation* of the interim report of the Special Rapporteur of the Commission on Human Rights on freedom of religion or belief, and encourages her continued efforts to examine incidents and governmental actions in all parts of the world that are incompatible with the provisions of the Declaration and to recommend remedial measures as appropriate;

14. *Urges* all States to cooperate fully with the Special Rapporteur, including by considering favourably her requests to visit their countries so as to enable her to fulfil her mandate even more effectively, welcomes the initiatives of States to collaborate with the Special Rapporteur, and encourages civil society to continue its active collaboration with her;

15. *Urges* States to make all appropriate efforts to encourage those engaged in education to cultivate respect for all religions or beliefs, thereby promoting mutual understanding and tolerance;

16. *Encourages* Governments, when seeking the assistance of the United Nations Programme of Advisory Services and Technical Assistance in the Field of Human Rights, to consider, where appropriate, including requests for assistance in the field of the promotion and protection of the right to freedom of thought, conscience, religion or belief;

17. *Welcomes and encourages* the continuing efforts of non-governmental organizations and religious bodies and groups to promote the implementation and dissemination of the Declaration, and further encourages their work in relation to promoting freedom of religion or belief and in highlighting cases of religious intolerance, discrimination and persecution;

18. *Requests* the Commission on Human Rights to continue its consideration of measures to implement the Declaration;

19. *Requests* the Secretary-General to ensure that the Special Rapporteur receives the necessary resources to enable her to discharge her mandate fully;

20. *Decides* to consider the question of the elimination of all forms of religious intolerance at its sixtieth session under the item entitled "Human rights questions", and requests the Special Rapporteur to submit an interim report to the General Assembly on the question.

RECORDED VOTE ON RESOLUTION 59/199:

In favour: Afghanistan, Albania, Algeria, Andorra, Angola, Antigua and Barbuda, Argentina, Armenia, Australia, Austria, Azerbaijan, Bahamas, Bahrain, Bangladesh, Barbados, Belarus, Belgium, Belize, Benin, Bhutan, Bolivia, Bosnia and Herzegovina, Botswana, Brazil, Brunei Darussalam, Bulgaria, Burkina Faso, Burundi, Cambodia, Cameroon, Canada, Cape Verde, Central African Republic, Chad, Chile, China, Colombia, Comoros, Costa Rica, Côte d'Ivoire, Croatia, Cuba, Cyprus, Czech Republic, Democratic People's Republic of Korea, Democratic Republic of the Congo, Denmark, Djibouti, Dominica, Dominican Republic, Ecuador, Egypt, El Salvador, Equatorial Guinea, Eritrea, Estonia, Ethiopia, Fiji, Finland, France, Gabon, Gambia, Georgia, Germany, Ghana, Greece, Grenada, Guatemala, Guinea, Guinea-Bissau, Guyana, Haiti, Honduras, Hungary, Iceland, India, Indonesia, Iran, Iraq, Ireland, Israel, Italy, Jamaica, Japan, Jordan, Kazakhstan, Kenya, Kuwait, Kyrgyzstan, Lao People's Democratic Republic, Latvia, Lebanon, Lesotho, Liberia, Libyan Arab Jamahiriya, Liechtenstein, Lithuania, Luxembourg, Madagascar, Malawi, Malaysia, Maldives, Mali, Malta, Marshall Islands, Mauritania, Mauritius, Mexico, Micronesia, Monaco, Mongolia, Morocco, Mozambique, Myanmar, Namibia, Nauru, Nepal, Netherlands, New Zealand, Nicaragua, Niger, Nigeria, Norway, Oman, Pakistan, Palau, Panama, Papua New Guinea, Paraguay, Peru, Philippines, Poland, Portugal, Qatar, Republic of Korea, Republic of Moldova, Romania, Russian Federation, Rwanda, Saint Lucia, Saint Vincent and the Grenadines, Samoa, San Marino, Sao Tome and Principe, Saudi Arabia, Senegal, Serbia and Montenegro, Seychelles, Sierra Leone, Singapore, Slovakia, Slovenia, Solomon Islands, Somalia, South Africa, Spain, Sri Lanka, Sudan, Suriname, Swaziland, Sweden, Switzerland, Syrian Arab Republic, Tajikistan, Thailand, The former Yugoslav Republic of Macedonia, Timor-Leste, Togo, Trinidad and Tobago, Tunisia, Turkey, Turkmenistan, Tuvalu, Uganda, Ukraine, United Arab Emirates, United Kingdom, United Republic of Tanzania, United States, Uruguay, Uzbekistan, Venezuela, Viet Nam, Yemen, Zambia, Zimbabwe.

Against: None.

The Third Committee adopted paragraph 9 by a separate recorded vote of 99 to 33, with 21 abstentions. The Assembly retained the paragraph by a recorded vote of 105 to 35, with 19 abstentions.

Tolerance and pluralism

Report of OHCHR. In response to its 2002 request [YUN 2002, p. 684], the Commission had before it a report [E/CN.4/2004/12/Add.2] on activities undertaken by OHCHR to promote tolerance and pluralism in the two-year period since the Commission's request. Activities were undertaken within the context of the United Nations Decade for Human Rights Education (1995-2004) (see p. 677), the International Decade of the World's Indigenous People (1995-2004) (see p. 796), the Third Decade to Combat Racism and Racial Discrimination (1993-2002) (see p. 664) and OHCHR's programme of advisory services and technical cooperation. The report provided information on the activities of special procedures, mechanisms and treaty monitoring bodies, whose work was also important for preventing human rights violations and for promoting tolerance and pluralism.

Commission action. On 20 April [res. 2004/54], the Commission, condemning all violent activities that undermined tolerance and pluralism, called on the High Commissioner to: include in OHCHR's work programme the promotion of tolerance and assist countries in their national programmes; undertake educational and public-awareness activities to promote tolerance and pluralism within the programmes and activities being implemented by the United Nations; and to advise or assist countries, upon request, through the programme of advisory services and technical cooperation, to put in place effective safeguards, including appropriate legislation, against intolerance and discrimination. The High Commissioner was called on to include in her 2006 report details of activities undertaken by OHCHR to implement the resolution. The Commission's relevant mechanisms were called on to accord priority to promoting democracy, pluralism and tolerance, to study conditions that promoted intolerance and to identify commonly accepted principles and best practices to promote tolerance and pluralism.

Civil and political rights

Right to self-determination

Report of Secretary-General. In response to General Assembly resolution 58/161 [YUN 2003, p. 720], the Secretary-General submitted a September report [A/59/376] summarizing Commission discussions of the right of peoples to self-determination and its application to peoples under colonial or alien domination or foreign occupation and the advisory opinion of the International Court of Justice regarding the construction of a wall in the Occupied Palestinian Territory (see p. 465).

GENERAL ASSEMBLY ACTION

On 20 December [meeting 74], the General Assembly, on the recommendation of the Third Committee [A/59/502], adopted **resolution 59/180** without vote [agenda item 104].

Universal realization of the right of peoples to self-determination

The General Assembly,

Reaffirming the importance, for the effective guarantee and observance of human rights, of the universal realization of the right of peoples to self-determination enshrined in the Charter of the United Nations and embodied in the International Covenants on Human Rights, as well as in the Declaration on the Granting of Independence to Colonial Countries and Peoples contained in General Assembly resolution 1514(XV) of 14 December 1960,

Welcoming the progressive exercise of the right to self-determination by peoples under colonial, foreign or alien occupation and their emergence into sovereign statehood and independence,

Deeply concerned at the continuation of acts or threats of foreign military intervention and occupation that are threatening to suppress, or have already suppressed, the right to self-determination of peoples and nations,

Expressing grave concern that, as a consequence of the persistence of such actions, millions of people have been and are being uprooted from their homes as refugees and displaced persons, and emphasizing the urgent need for concerted international action to alleviate their condition,

Recalling the relevant resolutions regarding the violation of the right of peoples to self-determination and other human rights as a result of foreign military intervention, aggression and occupation, adopted by the Commission on Human Rights at its sixtieth and previous sessions,

Reaffirming its previous resolutions on the universal realization of the right of peoples to self-determination, including resolution 58/161 of 22 December 2003,

Reaffirming also its resolution 55/2 of 8 September 2000, containing the United Nations Millennium Declaration, which, inter alia, upholds the right to self-determination of peoples under colonial domination and foreign occupation,

Taking note of the report of the Secretary-General on the right of peoples to self-determination,

1. *Reaffirms* that the universal realization of the right of all peoples, including those under colonial, foreign and alien domination, to self-determination is a fundamental condition for the effective guarantee and observance of human rights and for the preservation and promotion of such rights;

2. *Declares its firm opposition* to acts of foreign military intervention, aggression and occupation, since these have resulted in the suppression of the right of peoples to self-determination and other human rights in certain parts of the world;

3. *Calls upon* those States responsible to cease immediately their military intervention in and occupation of foreign countries and territories and all acts of repression, discrimination, exploitation and maltreatment, in particular the brutal and inhuman methods reportedly employed for the execution of those acts against the peoples concerned;

4. *Deplores* the plight of millions of refugees and displaced persons who have been uprooted as a result of the aforementioned acts, and reaffirms their right to return to their homes voluntarily in safety and honour;

5. *Requests* the Commission on Human Rights to continue to give special attention to the violation of human rights, especially the right to self-determination, resulting from foreign military intervention, aggression or occupation;

6. *Requests* the Secretary-General to report on the question to the General Assembly at its sixtieth session under the item entitled "Right of peoples to self-determination".

Right of Palestinians

Commission action. By a recorded vote of 52 to 1, the Commission, on 8 April [res. 2004/3], reaffirming the right of the Palestinian people to self-determination, requested the Secretary-General to transmit its resolution to Israel and other Governments, to disseminate it widely and to make available to the Commission before its 2005 session information pertaining to its implementation by Israel.

Report of Secretary-General. The Commission had before it a report of the Secretary-General [E/CN.4/2004/14] stating that he had received no reply from Israel to his request for information regarding the implementation of the Commission's 2003 resolution on the situation in occupied Palestine [YUN 2003, p. 721]. However, the United Nations Department of Public Information (DPI) had undertaken relevant activities by disseminating information on the work of the Special Committee to Investigate Israeli Practices Affecting the Human Rights of the Palestinian People and Other Arabs of the Occupied Territories (see p. 476), through the Internet, the media, publications and direct outreach to the public and NGOs. DPI continued to distribute its publication *The Question of Palestine and the United Nations* in all official languages at Headquarters and through the UN information centres, services and offices.

GENERAL ASSEMBLY ACTION

On 20 December [meeting 74], the General Assembly, on the recommendation of the Third Committee [A/59/502], adopted **resolution 59/179** by recorded vote (179-5-3) [agenda item 104].

The right of the Palestinian people to self-determination

The General Assembly,

Aware that the development of friendly relations among nations, based on respect for the principle of equal rights and self-determination of peoples, is among the purposes and principles of the United Nations, as defined in the Charter,

Recalling, in this regard, its resolution 2625(XXV) of 24 October 1970 entitled "Declaration on Principles of International Law concerning Friendly Relations and Cooperation among States in accordance with the Charter of the United Nations",

Bearing in mind the International Covenants on Human Rights, the Universal Declaration of Human Rights, the Declaration on the Granting of Independence to Colonial Countries and Peoples and the Vienna Declaration and Programme of Action adopted at the World Conference on Human Rights on 25 June 1993,

Recalling the Declaration on the Occasion of the Fiftieth Anniversary of the United Nations,

Recalling also the United Nations Millennium Declaration,

Recalling further the advisory opinion rendered on 9 July 2004 by the International Court of Justice on the *Legal Consequences of the Construction of a Wall in the Occupied Palestinian Territory*, and noting in particular the reply of the Court, including on the right of peoples to self-determination, which is a right *erga omnes*,

Recalling the conclusion of the Court, in its advisory opinion of 9 July 2004, that the construction of the wall by Israel, the occupying Power, in the Occupied Palestinian Territory, including East Jerusalem, along with measures previously taken, severely impedes the right of the Palestinian people to self-determination,

Expressing the urgent need for the resumption of negotiations within the Middle East peace process on its agreed basis and for the speedy achievement of a final settlement between the Palestinian and Israeli sides,

Recalling its resolution 58/292 of 6 May 2004,

Affirming the right of all States in the region to live in peace within secure and internationally recognized borders,

1. *Reaffirms* the right of the Palestinian people to self-determination, including the right to their independent State of Palestine;

2. *Urges* all States and the specialized agencies and organizations of the United Nations system to continue to support and assist the Palestinian people in the early realization of their right to self-determination.

RECORDED VOTE ON RESOLUTION 59/179:

In favour: Afghanistan, Albania, Algeria, Andorra, Angola, Antigua and Barbuda, Argentina, Armenia, Austria, Azerbaijan, Bahamas, Bahrain, Bangladesh, Barbados, Belarus, Belgium, Belize, Benin, Bhutan, Bolivia, Bosnia and Herzegovina, Botswana, Brazil, Brunei Darussalam, Bulgaria, Burkina Faso, Burundi, Cambodia, Cameroon, Canada, Cape Verde, Central African Republic, Chad, Chile, China, Colombia, Comoros, Costa Rica, Côte d'Ivoire, Croatia, Cuba, Cyprus, Czech Republic, Democratic People's Republic of Korea, Democratic Republic of the Congo, Denmark, Djibouti, Dominica, Dominican Republic, Ecuador, Egypt, El Salvador, Equatorial Guinea, Eritrea, Estonia, Ethiopia, Fiji, Finland, France, Gabon, Gambia, Georgia, Germany, Ghana, Greece, Grenada, Guatemala, Guinea, Guinea-Bissau, Guyana, Haiti, Honduras, Hungary, Iceland, India, Indonesia, Iran, Iraq, Ireland, Italy, Jamaica, Japan, Jordan, Kazakhstan, Kenya, Kuwait, Kyrgyzstan, Lao People's Democratic Republic, Latvia, Lebanon, Lesotho, Liberia, Libyan Arab Jamahiriya, Liechtenstein, Lithuania, Luxembourg, Madagascar, Malawi, Malaysia, Maldives, Mali, Malta, Mauritania, Mauritius, Mexico, Monaco, Mongolia, Morocco, Mozambique, Myanmar, Namibia, Nauru, Nepal, Netherlands, New Zealand, Nicaragua, Niger, Nigeria, Norway, Oman, Pakistan, Panama, Paraguay, Peru, Philippines, Poland, Portugal, Qatar, Republic of Korea, Republic of Moldova, Romania, Russian Federation, Rwanda, Saint Lucia, Saint Vincent and the Grenadines, Samoa, San Marino, Sao Tome and Principe, Saudi Arabia, Senegal, Serbia and Montenegro, Seychelles, Sierra Leone, Singapore, Slovakia, Slovenia, Solomon Islands, Somalia, South Africa, Spain, Sri Lanka, Sudan, Suriname, Swaziland, Sweden, Switzerland, Syrian Arab Republic, Tajikistan, Thailand, The former Yugoslav Republic of Macedonia, Timor-Leste, Togo, Trinidad and Tobago, Tunisia, Turkey, Turkmenistan, Tuvalu, Uganda, Ukraine, United Arab Emirates, United Kingdom, United Republic of Tanzania, Uruguay, Uzbekistan, Venezuela, Viet Nam, Yemen, Zambia, Zimbabwe.

Against: Israel, Marshall Islands, Micronesia, Palau, United States.

Abstaining: Australia, Papua New Guinea, Vanuatu.

Western Sahara

On 8 April [res. 2004/4], the Commission, reaffirming the responsibility of the United Nations towards the people of Western Sahara, supported the efforts of the Secretary-General and his Personal Envoy to achieve a mutually acceptable political solution to the dispute over Western Sahara and called on Morocco, the Frente Popular para la Liberación de Saguía el-Hamra y de Río de Oro and the regional States to cooperate with them. The parties were further called on to cooperate with the International Committee of the Red Cross (ICRC) in its efforts to solve the problem of the fate of people unaccounted for and to abide by their obligation under international humanitarian law to release without further delay all those being held.

Mercenaries

Report of Special Rapporteur. In response to a 2003 Commission request [YUN 2003, p. 722], the Special Rapporteur on the question of the use of mercenaries, Enrique Bernales Ballesteros (Peru), submitted his final report [E/CN.4/2004/15]. He summarized replies received from States in response to his request for information on mercenary activities, described developments in mercenary activities in Africa, reviewed the evolution of such activities and of his mandate, and discussed the link between terrorism and mercenary activities. The Special Rapporteur said that one of the greatest problems in combating mercenary activities was the absence of a clear and comprehensive legal definition of a mercenary and recommended that the Commission support the circulation among States of a new proposal for a legal definition as presented in the report. He proposed strengthening UN bodies and regional organizations to consider the link between mercenaries and terrorism, and the participation of mercenaries in organized crime and illicit trafficking in persons. Further recommendations were that the Commission reaffirm its condemnation of mercenary activities and em-

phasize its appeal to States to maintain vigilance against the threat posed by the phenomenon. There was an urgent need to regulate private military assistance, consultancy and security companies, and to establish criminal liability for members of such companies.

Commission action. On 8 April [res. 2004/5], the Commission, by a recorded vote of 36 to 14, with 3 abstentions, decided to extend the mandate of the Special Rapporteur for three years and asked the new Special Rapporteur (see below) to circulate to and consult with States on the new proposal for a legal definition of a mercenary drafted by the outgoing Special Rapporteur, and to report to the Commission. The new Special Rapporteur was further asked to take into account in the discharge of the mandate that mercenary activities were continuing in many parts of the world and were taking new forms; to pay particular attention to the impact on the exercise of the right of peoples to self-determination of the activities of private companies offering military assistance, consultancy and security services on the international market; to consult States, intergovernmental organizations and NGOs in the implementation of the Commission's resolution; and to report in 2005. OHCHR was asked to convene a third meeting of experts on traditional and new forms of mercenary activities as a means of violating human rights and impeding the exercise of the right of peoples to self-determination, whose main objectives would be to consider the proposed new legal definition of a mercenary, propose possible means of regulating and supervising the activities of private companies offering military assistance, consultancy and security services, and to study and evaluate mercenary activities in Africa. OHCHR was also asked to publicize the adverse effects of mercenary activities on the right to self-determination, provide advisory services to affected States when requested and assist the Special Rapporteur.

In July, Shaista Shameem (Fiji) was appointed Special Rapporteur.

ECONOMIC AND SOCIAL COUNCIL ACTION

In July, the Economic and Social Council, on the recommendation of the Commission on Human Rights [E/2004/23], adopted **decision 2004/248** by recorded vote (34-17-3) [agenda item 14 (g)].

Use of mercenaries as a means of violating human rights and impeding the exercise of the right of peoples to self-determination

At its 48th plenary meeting, on 22 July 2004, the Economic and Social Council took note of Commission on Human Rights resolution 2004/5 of 8 April 2004 and approved the decision of the Commission to extend for a period of three years the mandate of the

Special Rapporteur on the use of mercenaries as a means of impeding the exercise of the right of peoples to self-determination.

The Council also approved the request to the Office of the United Nations High Commissioner for Human Rights to convene a third meeting of experts on traditional and new forms of mercenary activities as a means of violating human rights and impeding the exercise of the right of peoples to self-determination, whose main objectives would be:

(a) To give further consideration to the proposed new legal definition of a mercenary as contained in paragraph 47 of the report of the Special Rapporteur;

(b) To make proposals on possible means of regulation and international supervision of the activities of private companies offering military assistance, consultancy and security services on the international market;

(c) To study and evaluate recent activities of mercenaries in Africa.

RECORDED VOTE ON DECISION 2004/248:

In favour: Armenia, Azerbaijan, Bangladesh, Belize, Benin, Bhutan, Burundi, Chile, China, Colombia, Congo, Cuba, Ecuador, El Salvador, Ghana, Guatemala, India, Indonesia, Jamaica, Kenya, Libyan Arab Jamahiriya, Malaysia, Mauritius, Mozambique, Namibia, Nigeria, Panama, Qatar, Russian Federation, Senegal, Tunisia, United Arab Emirates, United Republic of Tanzania, Zimbabwe.

Against: Australia, Belgium, Canada, Finland, France, Germany, Greece, Hungary, Ireland, Italy, Japan, Poland, Sweden, Turkey, Ukraine, United Kingdom, United States.

Abstaining: Nicaragua, Republic of Korea, Saudi Arabia.

Report of OHCHR. Pursuant to a General Assembly resolution 58/162 [YUN 2003, p. 723], which had asked the Special Rapporteur to report to the Assembly in 2004, the Secretary-General, by a 30 July note [A/59/191], transmitted a report of OHCHR instead, in view of the expiry of the Special Rapporteur's term of office. The report drew on the Special Rapporteur's report to the Commission (see above) and updated information therein as warranted.

Expert meeting. In accordance with Economic and Social Council decision 2004/248 (above), OHCHR organized a third expert meeting (Geneva, 6-10 December) [E/CN.4/2005/23] on traditional and new forms of mercenary activities as a means of violating human rights and impeding the exercise of the right of peoples to self-determination, building on the work of the first [YUN 2001, p. 631] and second [YUN 2002, p. 687] expert meetings. The objectives were set out in Council decision 2004/248 (see above). The experts held thematic discussions on relevant issues. Among their conclusions and recommendations was that, from a legal perspective, there was difficulty with the notion of self-determination as contained in the preamble to the International Convention against the Recruitment, Use, Financing and Training of Mercenaries (see below), insofar as there might be a contradiction in defining a mercenary as a person recruited for the purpose of denying self-determination and also undermin-

ing the territorial integrity of a State. Instead of referring to self-determination, reference could be made to acts that violated fundamental rights, which would include the right to self-determination. The words "or legal personality" should be added in order to attach liability to private companies and persons engaging in those activities, and the illegal acts mentioned in the Special Rapporteur's proposal should be redrafted in order to cover all illegal acts performed by mercenaries. That could be done by adding the words "or other nefarious activities" to the clause. The experts determined that an important way to regulate private military companies was to set thresholds for permissible activity, systems of registration and oversight mechanisms. They further proposed that professional codes of conduct for such companies be encouraged and that any structures of international supervision of the companies should be instituted under the Economic and Social Council. To counter mercenary activities in Africa, the meeting recommended a combination of international, regional and national legislation that specifically targeted mercenarism, and that such legislation should be punitive and attempt to close the loopholes regarding how mercenaries acquired arms.

1989 International Convention

As at 31 December, 26 States had become parties to the 1989 International Convention against the Recruitment, Use, Financing and Training of Mercenaries, adopted by the General Assembly in resolution 44/34 [YUN 1989, p. 825], with New Zealand acceding in 2004. The Convention entered into force in 2001 [YUN 2001, p. 632].

GENERAL ASSEMBLY ACTION

On 20 December [meeting 74], the General Assembly, on the recommendation of the Third Committee [A/59/502], adopted **resolution 59/178** by recorded vote (129-46-13) [agenda item 104].

Use of mercenaries as a means of violating human rights and impeding the exercise of the right of peoples to self-determination

The General Assembly,

Recalling its resolution 58/162 of 22 December 2003, and taking note of Commission on Human Rights resolution 2004/5 of 8 April 2004,

Recalling also all of its relevant resolutions, in which, inter alia, it condemned any State that permitted or tolerated the recruitment, financing, training, assembly, transit and use of mercenaries with the objective of overthrowing the Governments of States Members of the United Nations, especially those of developing countries, or of fighting against national liberation movements, and recalling further the relevant resolutions and international instruments adopted by the

General Assembly, the Security Council, the Economic and Social Council and the Organization of African Unity, inter alia, the Organization of African Unity Convention for the elimination of mercenarism in Africa, as well as the African Union,

Reaffirming the purposes and principles enshrined in the Charter of the United Nations concerning the strict observance of the principles of sovereign equality, political independence, the territorial integrity of States, the self-determination of peoples, the non-use of force or of the threat of use of force in international relations and non-interference in affairs within the domestic jurisdiction of States,

Reaffirming also that, by virtue of the principle of self-determination, all peoples have the right freely to determine their political status and to pursue their economic, social and cultural development, and that every State has the duty to respect this right in accordance with the provisions of the Charter,

Reaffirming further the Declaration on Principles of International Law concerning Friendly Relations and Cooperation among States in accordance with the Charter of the United Nations,

Alarmed and concerned at the danger that the activities of mercenaries constitute to peace and security in developing countries, in particular in Africa and in small States,

Deeply concerned at the loss of life, the substantial damage to property and the negative effects on the policy and economies of affected countries resulting from criminal mercenary activities,

Extremely alarmed and concerned about recent mercenary activities in Africa and the threat they pose to the integrity of and respect for the constitutional order of those countries,

Convinced that, notwithstanding the way in which they are used or the form that they take to acquire some semblance of legitimacy, mercenaries or mercenary-related activities are a threat to peace, security and the self-determination of peoples and an obstacle to the enjoyment of human rights by peoples,

1. *Takes note* of the brief report prepared by the Office of the United Nations High Commissioner for Human Rights on the question of the use of mercenaries as a means of violating human rights and impeding the exercise of the right of peoples to self-determination;

2. *Welcomes* the appointment of Shaista Shameem as Special Rapporteur of the Commission on Human Rights on the use of mercenaries as a means of impeding the exercise of the right of peoples to self-determination, and encourages her to continue and further advance the valuable work done and the important contributions made by Enrique Bernales Ballesteros in the sixteen years of his mandate;

3. *Reaffirms* that the use of mercenaries and their recruitment, financing and training are causes for grave concern to all States and violate the purposes and principles enshrined in the Charter of the United Nations;

4. *Recognizes* that armed conflict, terrorism, arms trafficking and covert operations by third Powers, inter alia, encourage the demand for mercenaries on the global market;

5. *Urges* all States to take the necessary steps and to exercise the utmost vigilance against the menace posed by the activities of mercenaries and to take legislative measures to ensure that their territories and other territories under their control, as well as their nationals, are not used for the recruitment, assembly, financing, training and transit of mercenaries for the planning of activities designed to impede the right of peoples to self-determination, to destabilize or overthrow the Government of any State or to dismember or impair, totally or in part, the territorial integrity or political unity of sovereign and independent States conducting themselves in compliance with the right of peoples to self-determination;

6. *Requests* all States to exercise the utmost vigilance against any kind of recruitment, training, hiring or financing of mercenaries by private companies offering international military consultancy and security services, as well as to impose a specific ban on such companies intervening in armed conflicts or actions to destabilize constitutional regimes;

7. *Welcomes* the entry into force of the International Convention against the Recruitment, Use, Financing and Training of Mercenaries, and calls upon all States that have not yet done so to consider taking the necessary action to accede to or ratify the Convention;

8. *Welcomes also* the cooperation extended by those countries that have received visits from the Special Rapporteur and the adoption by some States of national legislation that restricts the recruitment, assembly, financing, training and transit of mercenaries;

9. *Condemns* recent mercenary activities in Africa, and commends the African Governments on their collaboration in thwarting those illegal actions, which posed a threat to the integrity of and respect for the constitutional order of those countries and the exercise of the right of their peoples to self-determination;

10. *Calls upon* States to investigate the possibility of mercenary involvement whenever and wherever criminal acts of a terrorist nature occur and to bring to trial those found responsible or to consider their extradition, if so requested, in accordance with domestic law and applicable bilateral or international treaties;

11. *Condemns* any form of impunity granted to perpetrators of mercenary activities and to those responsible for the use, recruitment, financing and training of mercenaries, and urges all States, in accordance with their obligations under international law, to bring them, without distinction, to justice;

12. *Requests* the new Special Rapporteur to circulate to States and consult with them on the new proposal for a legal definition of a mercenary drafted by the former Special Rapporteur and to report her findings to the Commission on Human Rights and the General Assembly;

13. *Requests* the Office of the High Commissioner, as a matter of priority, to publicize the adverse effects of the activities of mercenaries on the right of peoples to self-determination and, when requested and where necessary, to render advisory services to States that are affected by those activities;

14. *Also requests* the Office of the High Commissioner to convene a third meeting of experts on traditional and new forms of mercenary activities as a means of violating human rights and impeding the exercise of the right of peoples to self-determination, respecting the main objectives defined in paragraph 16 of Commission on Human Rights resolution 2004/5;

15. *Requests* the Special Rapporteur to continue to take into account, in the discharge of her mandate, the fact that mercenary activities continue to occur in many parts of the world and are taking on new forms, manifestations and modalities, and, in this regard, requests her to pay particular attention to the impact of the activities of private companies offering military assistance, consultancy and security services on the international market on the exercise of the right of peoples to self-determination;

16. *Urges* all States to cooperate fully with the Special Rapporteur in the fulfilment of her mandate;

17. *Requests* the Secretary-General and the United Nations High Commissioner for Human Rights to provide the Special Rapporteur with all the necessary assistance and support for the fulfilment of her mandate, both professional and financial, including through the promotion of cooperation between the Special Rapporteur and other components of the United Nations system that deal with countering mercenary-related activities;

18. *Requests* the Special Rapporteur to consult States and intergovernmental and non-governmental organizations in the implementation of the present resolution and to report, with specific recommendations, to the General Assembly at its sixtieth session her findings on the use of mercenaries to undermine the right of peoples to self-determination;

19. *Decides* to consider at its sixtieth session the question of the use of mercenaries as a means of violating human rights and impeding the exercise of the right of peoples to self-determination under the item entitled "Right of peoples to self-determination".

RECORDED VOTE ON RESOLUTION 59/178:

In favour: Afghanistan, Algeria, Angola, Antigua and Barbuda, Argentina, Armenia, Azerbaijan, Bahamas, Bahrain, Bangladesh, Barbados, Belarus, Belize, Benin, Bhutan, Bolivia, Botswana, Brazil, Brunei Darussalam, Burkina Faso, Burundi, Cambodia, Cameroon, Cape Verde, Central African Republic, Chad, Chile, China, Colombia, Comoros, Costa Rica, Côte d'Ivoire, Cuba, Democratic People's Republic of Korea, Democratic Republic of the Congo, Djibouti, Dominica, Dominican Republic, Ecuador, Egypt, El Salvador, Equatorial Guinea, Eritrea, Ethiopia, Fiji, Gabon, Gambia, Ghana, Grenada, Guatemala, Guinea, Guinea-Bissau, Guyana, Haiti, Honduras, India, Indonesia, Iran, Iraq, Jamaica, Jordan, Kenya, Kuwait, Kyrgyzstan, Lao People's Democratic Republic, Lebanon, Lesotho, Liberia, Libyan Arab Jamahiriya, Madagascar, Malaysia, Maldives, Mali, Mauritania, Mauritius, Mexico, Mongolia, Morocco, Mozambique, Myanmar, Namibia, Nepal, Nicaragua, Niger, Nigeria, Oman, Pakistan, Panama, Papua New Guinea, Paraguay, Peru, Philippines, Qatar, Russian Federation, Rwanda, Saint Lucia, Saint Vincent and the Grenadines, Samoa, Sao Tome and Principe, Saudi Arabia, Senegal, Seychelles, Sierra Leone, Singapore, Solomon Islands, Somalia, South Africa, Sri Lanka, Sudan, Suriname, Swaziland, Syrian Arab Republic, Tajikistan, Thailand, Timor-Leste, Togo, Trinidad and Tobago, Tunisia, Turkmenistan, Tuvalu, Uganda, United Arab Emirates, United Republic of Tanzania, Uruguay, Venezuela, Viet Nam, Yemen, Zambia, Zimbabwe.

Against: Albania, Andorra, Austria, Belgium, Bosnia and Herzegovina, Bulgaria, Canada, Croatia, Cyprus, Czech Republic, Denmark, Estonia, Finland, France, Georgia, Germany, Greece, Hungary, Iceland, Ireland, Israel, Italy, Japan, Latvia, Lithuania, Luxembourg, Malta, Marshall Islands, Micronesia, Monaco, Netherlands, Norway, Palau, Poland, Portugal, Republic of Moldova, Romania, Serbia and Montenegro, Slovakia, Slovenia, Spain, Sweden, The former Yugoslav Republic of Macedonia, Turkey, United Kingdom, United States.

Abstaining: Australia, Kazakhstan, Liechtenstein, Malawi, Nauru, New Zealand, Republic of Korea, San Marino, Switzerland, Tonga, Ukraine, Uzbekistan, Vanuatu.

Administration of justice

Report of Secretary-General. As requested by the Commission in 2002 [YUN 2002, p. 689], the Secretary-General, in a February report [E/CN.4/2004/51], described measures taken by UN human rights mechanisms to implement international human rights standards with respect to the administration of justice, particularly regarding the rebuilding and strengthening of structures and capacities for the administration of justice in post-conflict situations and in juvenile justice. The report also highlighted the role of the UN system technical assistance in that context.

Commission action. On 19 April [res. 2004/43], the Commission called on the High Commissioner to reinforce advisory services and technical assistance relating to national capacity-building in the field of the administration of justice, particularly juvenile justice, and to develop an action programme to facilitate the exchange of experience among judges as regards their role in protecting and promoting human rights. It recommended that the Eleventh (2005) United Nations Congress on Crime Prevention and Criminal Justice (see p. 1108) pay attention to applying UN standards and norms on human rights in the administration of justice. The Commission's special procedures were called on to give special attention to questions relating to the effective protection of human rights in the administration of justice, while the Secretary-General was asked to report in 2007 on practical measures taken and activities planned to assist countries in strengthening their systems of administration of justice. Other aspects of the Commission's resolution dealt with juvenile justice.

Working group activities. Established by the Subcommission on 26 July [dec. 2004/101], the five-member sessional working group on the administration of justice met on 26 and 28 July and in August [E/CN.4/Sub.2/2004/6]. The group discussed criminalization, investigation and prosecution of acts of serious sexual violence and guidelines on criminalization, investigation and prosecution of acts of serious sexual violence occurring in the context of an armed conflict or committed as part of a widespread or systematic attack directed against civilians, as well as the provision of remedies. Under the item on witnesses and rules of evidence, it considered medical secrecy and problems in prosecuting rape and sexual assault, especially the problem of gender discrimination. Also discussed was the obligation to provide domestic remedies.

Pursuant to a 2003 Subcommission request [YUN 2003, p. 725], the group had before it a June report on the administration of justice through military tribunals [E/CN.4/Sub.2/2004/7], prepared by Emmanual Decaux (France), updating his 2003 report [YUN 2003, p. 725]. The June report presented a set of principles governing the administration of justice through military tribunals and called for the broadest possible consultation on the principles. Noting that an expert seminar on human rights and the administration of justice through military tribunals (Geneva, 26-28 January), organized by the International Commission of Jurists, had considered the recommendations in the 2003 report, Mr. Decaux called for a further seminar to be organized by the International Commission.

As requested by the Subcommission [YUN 2003, p. 725], the group considered a July working paper on women in prison [E/CN.4/Sub.2/2004/9], prepared by Florizell O'Connor (Jamaica), which found that imprisoned women suffered gross violations of almost all human rights principles. It recommended that non-custodial options for women be given more consideration and that training in professional and childcare skills be incorporated in women's prison programmes.

In response to a further Subcommission request [YUN 2003, p. 725], the group had before it a July working paper on the difficulties of establishing guilt and/or responsibilities with regard to crimes of sexual violence [E/CN.4/Sub.2/2004/11], submitted by Lalaina Rakotoarisoa (Madagascar), which expanded the scope of her 2003 paper [YUN 2003, p. 724]. The July paper focused on the forms and causes of sexual violence and abuse, on the increasing number of investigations and statements by victims and witnesses of sexual abuse and on gathering evidence. The paper concluded that the process of gathering evidence regarding the crime needed to be reviewed and that there was a need to strengthen international judicial cooperation, particularly in the area of extraterritorial judicial competence and cyber-criminality. Better coordination among UN bodies was warranted, in order to increase efficiency in combating the problem.

The group also considered a July working paper on the criminalization, investigation and prosecution of acts of serious sexual violence [E/CN.4/Sub.2/2004/12], prepared by Françoise Hampson (United Kingdom), pursuant to a further Subcommission request [YUN 2003, p. 777], which explored the definitions of rape and other forms of sexual violence, described the circumstances under which those crimes might constitute torture, a crime against humanity, a war crime or genocide, and addressed related questions to the group. Ms. Hampson submitted additional papers on human rights issues in the enforcement of international criminal law by national courts and on respect for human rights norms by international and mixed criminal tribunals, produced by academics of the Human

Rights Centre at the University of Essex (United Kingdom).

Secretariat note. A 15 June Secretariat note [E/CN.4/Sub.2/2004/5], referring to a 2002 Subcommission request [YUN 2002, p. 689], announced that Leïla Zerrougui (Algeria) would not be able to submit her progress report on discrimination in the criminal justice system. A preliminary report on the subject was considered by the group in 2003 [YUN 2003, p. 724].

Subcommission action. On 12 August [res. 2004/30], the Subcommission, taking note of the discussions of the sessional working group (see above), reaffirmed the importance of the full and effective implementation of all UN standards on human rights in the administration of justice and invited States, competent UN bodies, specialized agencies, intergovernmental organizations and NGOs to provide information to the group at its future sessions.

Also on 12 August [res. 2004/24], the Subcommission, regretting that Ms. Zerrougui was unable to submit her report on discrimination in the criminal justice system, asked her to submit the report in 2005. The Secretary-General was asked to assist her.

On the same date [res. 2004/27], the Subcommission asked Mr. Decaux to continue his work on the draft principles governing the administration of justice through military tribunals and to submit an updated report in 2005.

In further action on 12 August [res. 2004/28], the Subcommission, concerned that historically discriminatory practices might sometimes lead to disproportionate numbers of the poor and minorities in a criminal justice system, urged States to examine their treatment of convicted persons after they had served their punishment. It requested the sessional working group to examine the question and suggest types of information that could be collected to better understand the extent of discrimination against convicted persons who had served their sentences and the relevant international human rights standards applicable in such situations.

Also on 12 August [res. 2004/29], the Subcommission appointed Ms. Rakotoarisoa as Special Rapporteur entrusted with preparing a detailed study on the difficulties of establishing guilt and/or responsibilities with regard to crimes of sexual violence and asked her to submit a preliminary report in 2005, an interim report in 2006 and a final report in 2007. The Secretary-General was asked to assist her and to invite Governments, UN bodies, specialized agencies and NGOs to provide her with information.

On the same date [dec. 2004/118], the Subcommission asked Ms. Hampson and Ibrahim

Salama (Egypt) to prepare, without financial implications, a working paper on human rights law and international humanitarian law, their enforcement systems and the scope of the obligation of States and to submit it in 2005 to the working group.

On 12 August [dec. 2004/117], the Subcommission entrusted Mohamed Habib Cherif (Tunisia) with the preparation, without financial implications, of a working paper on the right to an effective remedy in criminal proceedings and asked him to submit it in 2005 to the working group.

Also on 12 August [dec. 2004/119], the Subcommission asked Ms. Hampson to prepare, without financial implications, a working paper on the implementation in domestic law of the right to an effective remedy in civil matters against violations of human rights by State agents and to submit it in 2005 to the working group.

Compensation for victims

Commission action. On 19 April [res. 2004/34], the Commission, taking note of the second consultative meeting on basic principles and guidelines on the right to a remedy and reparation for victims of violations of international human rights and humanitarian law [YUN 2003, p. 727], asked the Chairperson-Rapporteur to prepare, in consultation with independent experts Theo van Boven (Netherlands) and Cherif Bassiouni (Egypt/United States), a revised version of the text, taking into account opinions and commentaries of States, intergovernmental organizations and NGOs and the results of previous consultative meetings. The High Commissioner was asked to hold a third consultative meeting (see below), with a view to finalizing the principles and guidelines, and, if appropriate, to consider their adoption, and to report in 2005.

ECONOMIC AND SOCIAL COUNCIL ACTION

In July, the Economic and Social Council, on the recommendation of the Commission on Human Rights [E/2004/23], adopted **decision 2004/257** by recorded vote (52-1) [agenda item 14 (g)].

The right to restitution, compensation and rehabilitation for victims of grave violations of human rights and fundamental freedoms

At its 48th plenary meeting, on 22 July 2004, the Economic and Social Council took note of Commission on Human Rights resolution 2004/34 of 19 April 2004 and approved the Commission's request to the United Nations High Commissioner for Human Rights to hold, with the cooperation of interested Governments, a third consultative meeting for all interested Member States, intergovernmental organizations and non-governmental organizations in consultative status with the Council, using available resources, with

a view to finalizing the "Basic principles and guidelines on the right to a remedy and reparation for victims of violations of international human rights and humanitarian law", and, if appropriate, to consider all options for the adoption of those principles and guidelines.

RECORDED VOTE ON DECISION 2004/257:

In favour: Armenia, Australia, Azerbaijan, Bangladesh, Belgium, Belize, Benin, Bhutan, Burundi, Canada, Chile, China, Colombia, Congo, Cuba, Ecuador, Finland, France, Germany, Ghana, Greece, Guatemala, Hungary, India, Indonesia, Ireland, Italy, Jamaica, Japan, Kenya, Libyan Arab Jamahiriya, Malaysia, Mauritius, Mozambique, Namibia, Nicaragua, Nigeria, Panama, Poland, Qatar, Republic of Korea, Russian Federation, Saudi Arabia, Senegal, Sweden, Tunisia, Turkey, Ukraine, United Arab Emirates, United Kingdom, United Republic of Tanzania, Zimbabwe.

Against: United States.

Consultative meeting. In accordance with Commission resolution 2004/34 (see above), OHCHR, in cooperation with Chile, convened a third international consultation (Geneva, 29 September–1 October) [E/CN.4/2005/59] to finalize the draft basic principles and guidelines. Participants considered the revised text, principle by principle, and provided comments on the text. Subsequently, the Chairperson-Rapporteur summarized the main issues addressed and declared the text finalized. Delegates were urged to examine the revised text and to consult with their capitals. The Chairperson-Rapporteur announced that he planned to convene an additional informal consultation prior to the Commission's 2005 session to discuss ideas on how to proceed on the issue.

Rule of law

Pursuant to General Assembly resolution 57/221 [YUN 2002, p. 690], the Secretary-General, in an October report [A/59/402], described efforts by OHCHR to coordinate UN system activities regarding human rights and the rule of law. As at 30 April, of 36 ongoing human rights technical cooperation projects, at least 20 supported activities relating to strengthening the rule of law. Support was provided for developing and implementing national action plans; establishing and strengthening national human rights institutions; assisting with constitutional and legislative reforms, the administration of justice, elections and national parliaments; and training for police, judges and other legal professionals, prison personnel and the armed forces. OHCHR was in the final phase of implementing a project to develop guidelines that would help ensure the centrality of human rights in the administration of justice in post-conflict and post-crisis countries. It was also reinforcing its capacity to address the relationship between international human rights law, international humanitarian law and international criminal law, and planned to focus on issuing additional digests of jurisprudence that might be useful to judges and other legal professionals. In 2005, OHCHR would issue a number of new rule of law policy tools and would convene technical meetings to collect and analyse relevant experiences. In the UN system, it would continue to focus on providing greater support and advice to its key partners on rule of law–related issues, particularly within the context of UN peace operations and the administration of transitional justice in post-conflict situations.

By **decision 59/528** of 20 December, the General Assembly took note of the Secretary-General's report.

Non-State actors

On 12 August [dec. 2004/114], the Subcommission asked Gáspár Bíró (Hungary) and Antoanella-Iulia Motoc (Romania) to prepare, without financial implications, a working paper on human rights and non-State actors, in order to approach in a systematic way the question of accountability under international human rights law, and to submit it in 2005.

Humanitarian standards

Report of Secretary-General. In response to a 2002 Commission request [YUN 2002, p. 691], the Secretary-General, in consultation with ICRC, submitted a February report [E/CN.4/2004/90] highlighting developments between 1998 and 2003 that had contributed to the clarification of problems relating to the interpretation and application of relevant standards of humanity. The report described recent developments in international humanitarian and international criminal law, as well as relevant rulings of regional human rights bodies that had helped clarify the law. It presented examples of recent developments contributing to the development of fundamental principles, particularly with regard to the challenges posed by the implementation of international human rights and humanitarian law during situations of internal conflict. The report, while emphasizing that there was no apparent need to develop new standards, concluded that there was a need to secure respect for existing rules of international law aimed at ensuring the protection of persons in all circumstances and by all actors. Despite the progress achieved, some issues remained to be further considered and clarified, including the question of how to secure better compliance with fundamental standards of international human rights and humanitarian law by non State actors. An ICRC study on customary rules of international humanitarian law, which was in the final stage of preparation, was expected to contribute to the process by clarify-

ing international humanitarian law rules applicable in non-international armed conflict.

Commission action. On 21 April [dec. 2004/118], the Commission requested the Secretary-General, in consultation with ICRC, to submit in 2006 a further report consolidating and updating previous reports and studies.

Civilians in armed conflict

A May report [S/2004/431] of the Secretary-General on the protection of civilians in armed conflict reviewed progress made since his previous report [YUN 2002, p. 695], as well as continuing shortfalls, and discussed the way forward in ensuring protection. The Secretary-General said that in the five years since the initiation of the framework to strengthen the protection of civilians in armed conflict, the system of public international order had been under unprecedented strain, and the fundamentals of international humanitarian law and human rights had been under severe pressure. There were also concerns that counter-terrorism measures had not always complied with human rights obligations. Noting that the issues examined in his current report were key to developing a 10-point plan to strengthen the protection of civilians in armed conflict, the Secretary-General said it was urgent for the international community to deliver on the commitments it had made on the issue. Urging the Security Council to engage fully with relevant issues in order to address important new challenges to the environment for protecting civilians, the Secretary-General observed that, as the nature of warfare continued to change, the evolving environment and diversity of new actors created new circumstances where certain groups might evade responsibility entirely. That situation warranted better regulation and standards of accountability for armed forces, and for private sector groups actively engaged with or working in support of militaries. The international community needed to recommit itself to the principles of international law based on justice, the peaceful settlement of disputes and respect for human dignity.

SECURITY COUNCIL ACTION

On 14 December [meeting 5100], the Security Council discussed the protection of civilians in armed conflict. Its President made statement **S/PRST/2004/46** on behalf of the Council:

The Security Council has considered the matter of protection of civilians in armed conflict. The Council recalls all its relevant resolutions, in particular resolutions 1265(1999) of 17 September 1999 and 1296(2000) of 19 April 2000 on the protection of civilians in armed conflict as well as statements by its

Presidents, and reiterates its commitment to address the widespread impact of armed conflict on civilians.

The Council reaffirms its strong condemnation of all acts of violence targeting civilians or other protected persons under international law. The Council is gravely concerned that civilians are increasingly targeted by combatants and armed elements during armed conflict, in particular women, children and other vulnerable groups, including refugees and internally displaced persons, and recognizes the negative impact this will have on durable peace and national reconciliation. The Council also reaffirms its condemnation of all incitements to violence against civilians in situations of armed conflict, in particular the use of media to incite hatred and violence. The Council urges all parties to armed conflict, including non-State parties, to put an end to such practices.

The Council reiterates its call to all parties to armed conflict, including non-State parties, to comply fully with the provisions of the Charter of the United Nations and with rules and principles of international law, in particular international humanitarian law, and, as applicable, human rights and refugee law, and to implement fully the relevant decisions of the Council. The Council recalls the obligations of all States to ensure respect for international humanitarian law, including the four Geneva Conventions of 12 August 1949, and emphasizes the responsibility of States to end impunity and to prosecute those responsible for genocide, war crimes, crimes against humanity and serious violations of humanitarian law. It further calls upon all States which have not already done so to consider ratifying or acceding to major instruments of international humanitarian, human rights and refugee law, and to take appropriate measures to implement them.

The Council underlines the importance of safe and unhindered access of humanitarian personnel and assistance to civilians in armed conflict in accordance with international law. The Council reiterates its call to all parties to armed conflict, including non-State parties, to take all necessary measures to ensure security and freedom of movement of United Nations and associated personnel as well as personnel of humanitarian organizations. The Council condemns all attacks targeting United Nations personnel and other humanitarian workers, and underlines the fact that the perpetrators of such attacks must be held accountable as outlined in its resolution 1502(2003) of 26 August 2003. The Council underscores the importance for humanitarian organizations to uphold the principles of the neutrality, impartiality and humanity of their humanitarian activities and the independence of their objectives.

The Council recognizes the importance of a comprehensive, coherent and action-oriented approach, including early planning, to the protection of civilians in situations of armed conflict. It stresses, in this regard, the need to adopt a broad strategy of conflict prevention, which addresses the root causes of armed conflict in a comprehensive manner in order to enhance the protection of civilians on a long-term basis, including by promoting sustainable development, poverty eradication, national reconciliation,

good governance, democracy, the rule of law and respect for and protection of human rights. It encourages further cooperation and coordination between Member States and the United Nations system. The Council, moreover, recognizes the needs of civilians under foreign occupation, and stresses further, in this regard, the responsibilities of the occupying Power.

The Council, recognizing the regional dimensions of certain armed conflict, stresses the need for regional cooperation in order to address cross-border issues such as disarmament, demobilization, reintegration and rehabilitation, cross-border movement of refugees and combatants, human trafficking, illicit flow of small arms and illegal exploitation of natural resources and post-conflict situations. It encourages regional and subregional organizations to develop, as appropriate, a regional protection strategy and provide for a coherent and strong framework for addressing protection issues. The Council welcomes the steps taken by regional organizations in this regard and requests the United Nations system and other international organizations to provide them with the necessary support, and to consider means for the reinforcement of national capacities. The Council takes into account, in this regard, the Secretary-General's recommendation regarding the establishment of a framework within which the United Nations could engage with regional organizations more systematically on humanitarian issues related to protection and access and better address those issues at the regional intergovernmental level.

The Council strongly condemns the increased use of sexual and gender-based violence as a weapon of war as well as the recruitment and use of child soldiers by parties to armed conflict in violation of international obligations applicable to them. The Council underlines the vulnerability of women and children in situations of armed conflict, bearing in mind in this regard its resolutions 1325(2000) on women and peace and security and 1539(2004) as well as all other resolutions on children and armed conflict, and recognizes their special needs, in particular those of the girl child. It stresses the importance of developing strategies aimed at preventing and responding to sexual and gender-based violence, through the improvement in the design of peacekeeping and assessment missions by, inter alia, the inclusion of gender and child protection advisers. It stresses also the importance for women and children subject to exploitation and sexual violence to receive adequate assistance and support.

Mindful of the particular vulnerability of refugees and internally displaced persons, the Council reaffirms the primary responsibility of States to ensure their protection, in particular, by preserving the civilian character of camps of refugees and internally displaced persons, and to take effective measures to protect them from infiltration by armed groups, abduction and forced military recruitment.

The Council reaffirms its readiness to ensure that peacekeeping missions are given suitable mandates and adequate resources so as to enable them to better protect civilians under imminent threat of physical danger, including by strengthening the ability of the

United Nations to plan and rapidly deploy peace-keeping and humanitarian personnel, utilizing the United Nations stand-by arrangements system, as appropriate.

The Council considers that a coherent and integrated approach to the disarmament, demobilization, reintegration and rehabilitation of ex-combatants, which takes into account the special needs of child soldiers and women combatants, is of crucial importance for a sustained peace and stability. The Council reaffirms the need for the inclusion of these activities in the mandates of United Nations peacekeeping operations, and emphasizes the importance of resources being made available for such activities.

The Council is concerned by the growing problem of humanitarian emergency situations while funding and resources do not match requirements. It urges the international community to ensure adequate and timely funding in response to humanitarian need across crises, so as to provide sufficient humanitarian assistance in alleviating the suffering of civilian populations, in particular those in areas affected by armed conflict or emerging from a situation of conflict.

The Council expresses its appreciation for the efforts of the United Nations agencies, regional organizations, international humanitarian organizations and other relevant actors aimed at raising international awareness of the suffering of civilians in armed conflicts, including refugees and internally displaced persons, and considers such efforts as a key element for the promotion of a culture of protection and for the building of international solidarity with the victims of armed conflict.

The Council invites the Secretary-General to continue to refer to it relevant information and analysis, where he believes that such information or analysis could contribute to the improvement of its work on the protection of civilians in armed conflict, and to continue to include in his written reports to the Council on matters of which it is seized, as appropriate, observations relating to the protection of civilians in armed conflict. In this context, the Security Council reiterates the importance of the aide-memoire annexed to the statement by its President (S/PRST/2002/6) as well as the road map for the protection of civilians in armed conflict as a practical tool for dealing with protection issues.

The Council notes the submission of the report of the Secretary-General of 28 May 2004 on the protection of civilians in armed conflict, which examines the ten-point platform, and requests him to submit his next report by 28 November 2005, and to include in this report information on the implementation of Council resolutions previously adopted on this subject as well as any additional recommendations on ways the Council and other organs of the United Nations, acting within their respective spheres of responsibility, could further improve the protection of civilians in situations of armed conflict.

Missing persons

Note by Secretariat. A 17 March note [E/CN.4/2004/72] by the Secretariat, referring to a 2002 Commission resolution on missing persons in connection with armed conflict [YUN 2002, p. 696], informed the Commission that the Secretary-General's report on the resolution's implementation was under preparation and would be submitted in 2005. Meanwhile, information was being sought from Governments, competent UN bodies, specialized agencies, and regional intergovernmental and international humanitarian organizations.

Commission action. On 20 April [res. 2004/50], the Commission, by a recorded vote of 52 to none, with 1 abstention, called on States that were parties to an armed conflict to take measures to prevent persons from going missing in connection with the conflict, to determine the identity of those reported missing and to cooperate with ICRC in establishing their fate and to develop a comprehensive approach to the issue. The Secretary-General was asked to bring the Commission's resolution to the attention of Governments, competent UN bodies, specialized agencies, regional intergovernmental organizations and international humanitarian entities, and to report in 2006 on its implementation.

GENERAL ASSEMBLY ACTION

On 20 December [meeting 74], the General Assembly, on the recommendation of the Third Committee [A/59/503/Add.2], adopted **resolution 59/189** without vote [agenda item 105 (*b*)].

Missing persons

The General Assembly,

Guided by the purposes, principles and provisions of the Charter of the United Nations,

Guided also by the principles and norms of international humanitarian law, in particular the Geneva Conventions of 12 August 1949 and the Additional Protocols thereto, of 1977, as well as international standards of human rights, in particular the Universal Declaration of Human Rights, the International Covenant on Economic, Social and Cultural Rights, the International Covenant on Civil and Political Rights, the Convention on the Rights of the Child and the Vienna Declaration and Programme of Action adopted by the World Conference on Human Rights on 25 June 1993,

Recalling its resolution 57/207 of 18 December 2002 and Commission on Human Rights resolutions 2002/60 of 25 April 2002 and 2004/50 of 20 April 2004,

Noting with deep concern that armed conflicts are continuing in various parts of the world, often resulting in serious violations of international humanitarian law and human rights law,

Recognizing that great technological progress has been achieved in the field of DNA forensic sciences with regard to missing persons, such as the work done by the International Commission on Missing Persons, based in Sarajevo, which could significantly assist efforts to identify missing persons from other conflict areas in the world,

Noting, in this regard, that the issue of persons reported missing in connection with international armed conflicts, in particular those who are victims of serious violations of international humanitarian law and human rights law, continues to have a negative impact on efforts to put an end to those conflicts,

Welcoming the convening in Geneva, from 19 to 21 February 2003, by the International Committee of the Red Cross, of the International Conference of Governmental and Non-Governmental Experts on the theme "The missing: action to resolve the problem of people unaccounted for as a result of armed conflict or internal violence and to assist their families" and the observations and recommendations of the Conference for addressing the problem of missing persons and their families,

Welcoming also the undertakings by the participants at the Twenty-eighth International Conference of the Red Cross and Red Crescent, held in Geneva from 2 to 6 December 2003, through their adoption of the Agenda for Humanitarian Action, in particular general objective 1, to respect and restore the dignity of persons missing as a result of armed conflicts or other situations of armed violence and of their families,

1. *Urges* States strictly to observe and respect and ensure respect for the rules of international humanitarian law, as set out in the Geneva Conventions of 12 August 1949 and in the Additional Protocols thereto, of 1977;

2. *Calls upon* States that are parties to an armed conflict to take all appropriate measures to prevent persons from going missing in connection with armed conflict and to account for persons reported missing as a result of such a situation;

3. *Reaffirms* the right of families to know the fate of their relatives reported missing in connection with armed conflicts;

4. *Also reaffirms* that each party to an armed conflict, as soon as circumstances permit and, at the latest, from the end of active hostilities, shall search for the persons who have been reported missing by an adverse party;

5. *Calls upon* States which are parties to an armed conflict to take all necessary measures, in a timely manner, to determine the identity and fate of persons reported missing in connection with the armed conflict;

6. *Requests* States to pay the utmost attention to cases of children reported missing in connection with armed conflicts and to take appropriate measures to search for and identify those children;

7. *Invites* States which are parties to an armed conflict to cooperate fully with the International Committee of the Red Cross in establishing the fate of missing persons and to adopt a comprehensive approach to this issue, including all practical and coordination mechanisms that may be necessary, based on humanitarian considerations only;

8. *Urges* States and encourages intergovernmental and non-governmental organizations to take all necessary measures at the national, regional and international levels to address the problem of persons reported missing in connection with armed conflicts and to provide appropriate assistance as requested by the States concerned;

9. *Invites* relevant human rights mechanisms and procedures, as appropriate, to address the problem of persons reported missing in connection with armed conflicts in their forthcoming reports to the General Assembly;

10. *Requests* the Secretary-General to bring the present resolution to the attention of all Governments, the competent United Nations bodies, the specialized agencies, regional intergovernmental organizations and international humanitarian organizations;

11. *Also requests* the Secretary-General to submit a comprehensive report on the implementation of the present resolution to the Commission on Human Rights at its sixty-second session and to the General Assembly at its sixty-first session;

12. *Decides* to consider the question at its sixty-first session.

Security of UN staff

Note by Secretariat. A March note by the Secretariat [E/CN.4/2004/96], recalling the Commission's 2002 request [YUN 2002, p. 697] to the Secretary-General to submit a report on the situation of UN and associated personnel carrying out activities in fulfilment of the mandate of a UN operation who were imprisoned, missing or held in a country against their will, referred the Commission to his 2003 reports on the scope of legal protection under the Convention on the Safety of United Nations and Associated Personnel [YUN 2003, p. 1341] and on the safety and security of humanitarian personnel and the protection of UN personnel [ibid., p. 922]. The Secretary-General had initiated a number of measures to meet the increasing risks that staff faced while carrying out UN programmes, the most notable of which included the reorganization of the Office of the UN Security Coordinator, changes to the method of financing security needs, the introduction of minimum operating security standards (MOSS) and the establishment of a framework for accountability for security management. The UN System Chief Executives Board for Coordination had deliberated on the need to improve staff security and the Deputy Secretary-General had been asked to lead the process, which would build on improvements already made in mandatory staff security awareness training, threat analysis and risk management, the development of enhanced and headquarters MOSS, security clearance procedures and staff tracking procedures. Nonetheless, the key to improving the protection of all UN staff, property and programmes was the support of Member States in recognizing issues of privileges and immunities and the provision of the necessary resources.

Commission action. On 21 April [res. 2004/77], the Commission called on States to consider becoming parties to the 1994 Convention on the Safety of United Nations and Associated Personnel, adopted by the General Assembly in resolution 49/59 [YUN 1994, p. 1289] and the Rome Statute of the International Criminal Court [YUN 1998, p. 1209]. States and others were called on, among other things, to ensure the safety and security of UN and associated personnel carrying out activities in fulfilment of a UN operation mandate and to adopt and/or enforce domestic legislation and judicial and administrative measures to ensure that perpetrators of unlawful acts against them were held accountable. The Secretary-General was asked to ensure respect for the human rights, privileges and immunities of the personnel, to improve safeguards for the security and safety of locally recruited personnel, to ensure the inclusion in headquarters and other mission agreements of the applicable principles and rules on protection contained in the 1994 Convention and related instruments, to ensure that security matters were an integral part of the planning for existing and newly mandated UN operations and to take further measures to ensure that personnel were properly aware of the conditions under which they were called to operate, and that adequate training in security, human rights and humanitarian law was provided to enhance their security.

Arbitrary detention

Commission action. On 19 April [res. 2004/39], the Commission encouraged Governments to consider the recommendations of the Working Group on Arbitrary Detention and to ensure that their legislation, regulations and practices conformed with international standards and instruments. The Secretary-General was asked to assist Governments, special rapporteurs and working groups to ensure the promotion and observance of guarantees relating to states of emergency embodied in international instruments and to assist the Group. The Group was asked to report in 2005.

Working Group activities. The Working Group on Arbitrary Detention held its thirty-ninth (24-28 May), fortieth (13-17 September) and forty-first (17-26 November) sessions, all in Geneva [E/CN.4/2005/6]. During the year, the Group adopted 25 opinions concerning 51 persons in 17 countries; the text of the opinions were contained in a separate report [E/CN.4/2005/6/Add.1]. The Group also transmitted 202 urgent appeals to 56 Governments concerning 770 individuals, of which 196 were issued jointly by the Group and thematic or geographical special rapporteurs. In 35 cases, the Governments concerned informed the Group that they had taken measures to remedy the situation of the detainees.

The Group examined issues related to psychiatric detention, developments concerning deprivation of liberty as a measure in countering terrorism, hostage-taking and arbitrary detention, and the negative impact on the right to defence of inadequate conditions of detention. In November, the Group adopted deliberation No. 7 concerning the rights and protection of persons held in detention in relation to their mental disability and encouraged Governments to consider the criteria it had set out when deciding on measures involving the deprivation of liberty of those affected and their placement in closed psychiatric establishments. The Group also recommended that measures restricting resort to judicial control of detainees suspected of terrorism-related activity should be proportionate to the legitimate need to combat terrorism, as unreasonably harsh restrictions easily became counterproductive and might compromise the rule of law. The Group was of the opinion that the right not to be detained incommunicado over prolonged periods of time could not be derogated from, and recommended that States review their legislation and practice in the light of that principle. In other recommendations, it advocated affording guarantees applicable to criminal proceedings to persons suspected of criminal activity and liable to the deprivation of liberty under domestic law, introducing an effective remedy for any form of unlawful or arbitrary deprivation of liberty and the right to defend oneself in the area of criminal law when coercive measures were imposed.

Three Working Group members visited Latvia, at the invitation of the Government (23-28 February) [E/CN.4/2005/6/Add.2], where they reviewed the criminal justice system, particularly the rules applying to the deprivation of liberty. The Group, while noting efforts being made to guarantee respect for human rights and to improve the treatment of persons deprived of their liberty in the country, expressed concern at the length and frequency of pre-trial detention, the harshness of the regime and its implications for the presumption of innocence; the lack of real access to assigned counsel; the failure to allow evidence to be challenged; the unbalanced powers of the prosecution and defence; and shortcomings in the imposition of punishments and alternatives to detention. The situation of minors in detention constituted a particular cause for concern, as did issues relating to the administrative detention of illegal aliens. The Group recommended that the Government bring its legislation and practice into line with standards of international law and take steps to ensure that those deprived of their liberty had appropriate defence; pay particular attention to the situation of children and to involuntary committals to psychiatric hospitals other than when ordered by a court; and address problems relating to the detention of non-nationals.

In Belarus (16-26 August) [E/CN.4/2005/6/Add.3], the Group, acknowledging efforts to improve the conditions of persons deprived of their liberty, expressed concern about the excessive powers granted to prosecutors and investigators during the pre-trial detention phase and the lack of effective proceedings to challenge the legality of such detention, the lack of independence of the judiciary, the pre-trial detention regime, detention as a means of repressing the freedom of expression, the jurisdiction of military courts over civilians, unsatisfactory protection of vulnerable detainees, and the lack of safeguards regarding detention in psychiatric hospitals. The Group recommended that the Government reconsider the role and place of the actors in a criminal procedure in order to ensure their independence, establish a balance between parties at trial and ensure the effective protection of the rights of persons deprived of their liberty. It should consider priority measures to guarantee the independence of judges and lawyers, and amendments to the provisions of internal criminal laws in the light of international and constitutional norms, to bring to an end the arrest of persons for peaceful demonstrations, for distributing information or for exercising their right to the freedom of expression.

In China (18-30 September) [E/CN.4/2005/6/Add.4], the Group focused on developments since its 1997 visit to the country [YUN 1997, p. 653]. While acknowledging a number of positive developments, the Group found that none of its previous recommendations had been followed, particularly regarding the definition of such ambiguous terms as "endangering national security" in criminal law, legislative measures exempting from criminal responsibility those who peacefully exercised their rights as guaranteed in the Universal Declaration of Human Rights, adopted by the General Assembly in resolution 217 A (III) [YUN 1948-49, p. 535], and judicial control over the procedure to commit someone to re-education through labour. Also, the rules and practice concerning judicial deprivation of liberty were still not in keeping with international law and standards and there existed no genuine right to challenge administrative detention. As no law provided a clear definition of "State secrets", the Group was concerned about possible restriction on the right to defence in circumstances involving State security or secrets. The Group recommended, among other things, that the authorities examine the possibility of instituting a simplified

emergency procedure to allow persons detained to be brought before a judge and not only a procurator. All conduct subject to sanction should be described in detail and persons deprived of their liberty on account of administrative offences should be guaranteed due process. Persons placed against their will in a psychiatric hospital or detoxification centre should enjoy an effective remedy and there was a need to amend all legal provisions that could be used to sanction the peaceful exercise of rights and freedoms enshrined in the Universal Declaration of Human Rights.

Communication. On 1 November [A/C.3/59/6], Belarus drew attention to its cooperation with the Working Group during the Group's visit to the country (see above).

Impunity

Note by Secretary-General. In response to a 2003 Commission request [YUN 2003, p. 734], the Secretary-General, by a 27 February note [E/CN.4/2004/88], transmitted the independent study conducted by Diane Orentlicher (United States) on best practices to assist States in strengthening their domestic capacity to combat impunity, taking into account the application of the 1997 set of principles for the protection and promotion of human rights through action to combat impunity [YUN 1997, p. 655]. The report, which was based on information provided by 20 Governments, reviewed recent developments regarding the 1997 principles under the themes of the right to know the truth, the right to justice and the right to reparation. A recurring theme in the study was that domestic efforts to combat impunity had been significantly enhanced by States' adherence to human rights treaties and their acceptance of optional complaint procedures. The study observed that, although some aspects of the principles, notably those pertaining to the creation of an international criminal court, might need to be updated, recent developments in international law had strongly affirmed the principles as a whole. The principles had provided an influential framework for domestic measures aimed at combating impunity. The study recommended that the Commission appoint an independent expert to update the principles with a view to their adoption.

Commission action. On 21 April [res. 2004/72], the Commission asked the Secretary-General to invite States, intergovernmental organizations and NGOs to provide information on steps taken to combat impunity for human rights violations and on remedies available to victims, and to appoint an independent expert to update the 1997 set of principles to reflect developments in international law and practice, taking into account the independent study (above) and comments received pursuant to the resolution, for consideration in 2005.

On 15 June (**decision 2004/223**), the Economic and Social Council approved the Commission's request to the Secretary-General to appoint an independent expert.

Ms. Orentlicher was appointed independent expert in September.

Independence of the judicial system

Report of Special Rapporteur. The Special Rapporteur on the independence of judges and lawyers, Leandro Despouy (Argentina), submitted his first report [E/CN.4/2004/60], which provided an overview of his activities, his understanding of the mandate and his methodology for approaching relevant issues. He had transmitted 70 urgent appeals, communications and press releases to 40 Governments and the Palestinian Authority, replies to which were received from 5 countries. An addendum to the report [E/CN.4/2004/60/Add.1] contained summaries of the communications sent and replies thereto. The Special Rapporteur observed that the number of allegations received indicated the extent to which the independence of the judiciary, the legal profession and their members continued to be threatened in many countries. He was persuaded that the institutional weaknesses and functional problems affecting the work of judges and lawyers were a direct cause of violations of the right to a fair trial and, in addressing that, he recommended the allocation of adequate resources to the justice system, and hoped to develop fruitful cooperation with Governments.

Commission action. On 19 April [res. 2004/32], the Commission called on States that used military courts to try criminal offenders to ensure that such courts were an integral part of the general judicial system and that they applied internationally recognized due process procedures.

Also on 19 April [res. 2004/33], the Commission called on Governments to respect and uphold the independence of judges and lawyers and asked the High Commissioner to continue to provide technical assistance to train them. The Special Rapporteur was asked to report in 2005 and the Secretary-General was asked to assist him.

Further reports of Special Rapporteur. The Special Rapporteur visited Kazakhstan (11-17 June) [E/CN.4/2005/60/Add.2] at the invitation of the Government, following increasing allegations that the judiciary was compromised by political pressure, administrative directives and corruption. The Special Rapporteur found that Kazakhstan, since achieving independence in 1991, had taken steps to move from a situation where the administration of justice was governed by political priorities and administrative instructions, and even by personal connections, but the executive continued to play a dominant role in the judiciary. The Special Rapporteur observed that if Kazakhstan was to be considered a truly democratic State, it needed to introduce legal adjustments that might include constitutional reforms, in order to achieve a fairer balance of power between the branches of Government and to increase the independence of the judiciary. Crucial issues in that regard included the process of nominating judges, the powers of the prosecutor, the composition and functioning of the Higher Judicial Council and the weakness of the Constitutional Council. Further recommendations addressed related issues undermining human rights and the justice system.

In Brazil (13-25 October) [E/CN.4/2005/60/Add.3 & Corr.1], the Special Rapporteur aimed to examine the independence of the judicial system and to determine whether justice was properly served and whether the most needy members of the population had access to justice. The visit, which took place as the country prepared to adopt major judicial reforms, enabled the Special Rapporteur to comment on the feasibility of those reforms. He found that the system was plagued by such structural problems as delays in the administration of justice, the lack of access to justice—particularly for poor or marginalized groups in society—impunity, especially for crimes against young people, discriminatory practices that often resulted in the further victimization of certain groups and a marked trend towards the criminalization of social movements. The justice system was also undermined by very low representation of women at top levels, threats and acts of violence against judges, lawyers and defence attorneys working on cases that involved social issues concerning indigenous, environmental and land questions, insufficient resources and a lack of transparency in the mechanisms that regulated key aspects of the functioning of the judiciary. The Special Rapporteur recommended strengthening the Office of the Public Defender; establishing special courts to deal with crimes against children and young persons; limiting the jurisdiction of military justice to military offences; addressing discrimination against vulnerable groups; monitoring the effectiveness of judicial services in order to measure the impact of the changes introduced by the reforms; and implementing international human rights instruments ratified by Brazil.

Communication. In February [E/CN.4/2004/G/ 26], Austria transmitted "The Vienna Declaration on the Role of Judges in the Promotion and Protection of Human Rights and Fundamental Freedoms", adopted at an international symposium (Vienna, 24 November 2003) organized jointly by Austria, OHCHR and the United Nations Office on Drugs and Crime. The symposium highlighted the pivotal role of judges in human rights and drew attention to their need for support regarding their independence, impartiality, competence and integrity.

Capital punishment

Report of Secretary-General. In response to a 2003 Commission request [YUN 2003, p. 735], the Secretary-General, in a January report [E/CN.4/ 2004/86], supplemented information in his sixth quinquennial report [YUN 2000, p. 672] on capital punishment and implementation of the safeguards guaranteeing protection of the rights of those facing the death penalty, covering the period from January to December 2003. The report summarized information received from 12 countries relating to the use of capital punishment, changes in law and practice concerning the death penalty and implementation of the safeguards, with special attention to the imposition of the death penalty against persons younger than 18 years of age at the time of the offence. Additional information was provided by eight intergovernmental organizations and NGOs. During the reporting period, no country abolished the death penalty for all crimes, one ratified an international instrument abolishing it in peacetime, one limited its use, 26 acceded to or ratified instruments that abolished it, three established a moratorium and one reintroduced the death penalty. The only figures available suggested that at least 3,248 persons were sentenced to death in 67 countries and at least 1,526 people were executed in 31 countries during 2002. The Secretary-General concluded that the trend towards abolition had continued, as the number of countries that could be considered de facto abolitionist rose from 33 to 37, while the total number of retentionist countries decreased from 71 to 66. The number of countries that had ratified international instruments abolishing the death penalty also increased markedly. However, during the reporting period, Amnesty International reported three executions of juveniles in one country. The report also highlighted initiatives by the Commission and its mechanisms regarding relevant international developments and the implementation of safeguards.

Commission action. By a recorded vote of 29 to 19, with 5 abstentions, the Commission, on 21 April [res. 2004/67], called on States parties to the International Covenant on Civil and Political Rights that had not done so to consider acceding to or ratifying the Second Optional Protocol thereto on the abolition of the death penalty (see p. 662). Among other measures, States that maintained the death penalty were urged not to impose it for crimes committed by persons below 18 years of age; to exclude pregnant women and mothers with dependent infants; not to impose it on a person suffering from mental disorder; to establish a moratorium on executions; to restrict the number of offences for which the death penalty might be imposed; and to provide the Secretary-General and relevant UN bodies with information relating to the use of capital punishment and the observance of the safeguards guaranteeing the rights of those facing the death penalty, as contained in Economic and Social Council resolution 1984/50 [YUN 1984, p. 709]. The Secretary-General was asked to submit his quinquennial report, paying special attention to the imposition of the death penalty against persons younger than 18 years of age at the time of the offence.

Communication. On 21 April [E/CN.4/2004/ G/54], Saudi Arabia, also on behalf of 63 other States, dissociated itself from the Commission's resolution.

Subcommission action. On 12 August [res. 2004/25], the Subcommission, by a roll-call vote of 20 to 1, with 3 abstentions, called on States in which the death penalty had been imposed on a civilian tried by military tribunal or a tribunal whose composition included one or more members of the armed forces to re-try the suspect before a competent, independent and impartial tribunal. They were further called on to refuse requests for extradition or other form of transfer to any State where there was a risk that civilians could be tried by a military court.

Right to democracy

Report of High Commissioner. In response to a 2003 Commission request [YUN 2003, p. 736], the High Commissioner submitted a February report [E/CN.4/2004/54], which summarized the views of three UN departments, two UN system organizations, two regional organizations and two intergovernmental organizations on the role they had played in promoting and consolidating democracy.

Commission action. On 19 April [res. 2004/30], the Commission, by a recorded vote of 45 to none, with 8 abstentions, called on OHCHR to stimulate dialogue and interaction within the UN system and between the system and interested intergovernmental regional, subregional and other organizations and arrangements on the means of promoting democratic values and principles, and to report in 2005. The High Commissioner was asked to continue promoting and consolidating democracy, in collaboration with other organizations, by strengthening programmes for assistance to countries seeking technical advice, by continuing to cooperate with Member States, with a view to identifying challenges to democratic governance at the country level, and by designating a focal point in OHCHR to that effect.

Note by Secretariat. A July note [E/CN.4/Sub.2/2004/10] of the Secretariat stated that, as at 23 July, it had not received from Manuel Rodríguez Cuadros (Peru) the extended working paper on measures to promote and consolidate democracy, requested by the Subcommission in 2003 [YUN 2003, p. 736].

GENERAL ASSEMBLY ACTION

On 20 December [meeting 74], the General Assembly, on the recommendation of the Third Committee [A/59/503/Add.2], adopted **resolution 59/201** by recorded vote (172-0-15) [agenda item 105 (b)].

Enhancing the role of regional, subregional and other organizations and arrangements in promoting and consolidating democracy

The General Assembly,

Reaffirming the purposes and principles set forth in the Charter of the United Nations,

Recalling its resolution 55/96 of 4 December 2000 and all relevant resolutions of the Commission on Human Rights, in particular resolutions 1999/57 of 27 April 1999, 2000/47 of 25 April 2000, 2001/41 of 23 April 2001, 2002/46 of 23 April 2002, 2003/36 of 23 April 2003 and 2004/30 of 19 April 2004,

Recalling also that all peoples have the right to self-determination, by virtue of which they can freely determine their political status and freely pursue their economic, social and cultural development,

Reaffirming its resolve, expressed, inter alia, in the United Nations Millennium Declaration, to implement the principles and practices of democracy, and recognizing the diverse nature of the community of the world's democracies,

1. *Declares* that the essential elements of democracy include respect for human rights and fundamental freedoms, inter alia, freedom of association and peaceful assembly and of expression and opinion, and the right to take part in the conduct of public affairs, directly or through freely chosen representatives, to vote and to be elected at genuine periodic free elections by universal and equal suffrage and by secret ballot guaranteeing the free expression of the will of the people, as well as a pluralistic system of political parties and organizations, respect for the rule of law, the separation of powers, the independence of the judiciary, transparency and accountability in public administration, and free, independent and pluralistic media;

2. *Reaffirms* that the promotion and protection of all human rights is a basic prerequisite for the existence of a democratic society, and recognizes the importance of the continuous development and strengthening of the United Nations human rights mechanisms for the consolidation of democracy;

3. *Recognizes* the importance of all actions taken at the regional and subregional levels that are aimed at facilitating the establishment, development and consolidation of democratic institutions, based on democratic values and principles and capable of responding to the specific needs of the countries in each region;

4. *Acknowledges* the importance of better awareness of democratic values and principles in all regions and for all people;

5. *Reaffirms* that democracy, development and respect for all human rights and fundamental freedoms are interdependent and mutually reinforcing, that democracy is based on the freely expressed will of the people to determine their own political, economic, social and cultural systems and their full participation in all aspects of their lives and, in that context, that the promotion and protection of human rights and fundamental freedoms at the national, regional and international levels should be universal and conducted without conditions attached; the international community should support the strengthening and promoting of democracy, development and respect for human rights and fundamental freedoms in the entire world;

6. *Acknowledges* that democracy contributes substantially to preventing violent conflict, to accelerating reconciliation and reconstruction in post-conflict peacebuilding and, in peacetime, to resolving disputes that may impede economic and social progress;

7. *Recognizes* the need for Member States to pay further special attention and contribute to democratic institution-building by including relevant objectives to this effect in the mandates of peacemaking, peacekeeping and post-conflict peacebuilding operations and by providing adequate resources in that regard;

8. *Invites* intergovernmental regional, subregional and other organizations and arrangements, as well as non-governmental organizations, to engage actively in work at the local, national, subregional and regional levels for the constant promotion and consolidation of democracy and to initiate exchanges with the United Nations system on their experiences, inter alia, by:

(a) Identifying and disseminating best practices and experiences at the regional, subregional and cross-regional levels in promoting and protecting democratic processes;

(b) Establishing and supporting regional, subregional and national civic education programmes that provide access to information on democratic governance and stimulate dialogue on the functioning of democracy;

(c) Encouraging the study, in schools and universities, of democracy, human rights, good governance and the functioning of public administration, political institutions and civil society organizations;

(d) Elaborating and widely distributing reports, assessments, training material, handbooks, case studies and documentation on alternative types of democratic constitutions, electoral systems and administration so as to assist populations in making more informed choices;

(e) Encouraging the use of democratic consultative mechanisms in disputes as an opportunity for the parties involved to advance their interests within institutional frameworks;

(f) Working with the focal point for democracy of the Office of the United Nations High Commissioner for Human Rights;

9. *Invites* States members of intergovernmental regional organizations and arrangements to include or reinforce the provisions of the constitutive acts of the organizations and arrangements that are aimed at promoting democratic values and principles and protecting and consolidating democracy in their respective societies;

10. *Welcomes* the adoption by various regional, subregional and other organizations and arrangements of institutional rules designed to prevent situations that threaten democratic institutions;

11. *Invites* intergovernmental regional organizations and arrangements to institutionalize dialogue among themselves on joint actions to promote and consolidate democracy and democratic practices in all areas;

12. *Encourages* Member States and intergovernmental regional and cross-regional organizations and arrangements, as well as non-governmental organizations, to initiate networks and partnerships with a view to assisting the Governments and civil society in their respective regions in disseminating knowledge and information about the role of democratic institutions and mechanisms in meeting the political, economic, social and cultural challenges in their respective societies;

13. *Urges* the continuation and expansion of activities carried out by the United Nations system, intergovernmental organizations and Member States to promote and consolidate democracy within the framework of international cooperation;

14. *Invites* the United Nations system to identify, develop and coordinate effective policies of assistance in the field of democracy and, in this context, to support programmes of technical assistance to States, upon their request, aimed at:

(a) Developing a competent, independent and impartial judiciary and accountable government institutions;

(b) Strengthening political party systems, free and independent media and civil society organizations;

(c) Fostering a democratic culture;

15. *Calls upon* the Office of the United Nations High Commissioner for Human Rights to stimulate dialogue and interaction within the United Nations system and between the United Nations system and interested intergovernmental regional, subregional and other organizations and arrangements on the ways and means of promoting democratic values and principles, on the basis of the present resolution and other relevant resolutions of the General Assembly and of the Commission on Human Rights, and, to this end, to invite, inter alia, the Department of Political Affairs of the Secretariat, including its Electoral Assistance Division, and the Department of Economic and Social Affairs of the Secretariat, the United Nations Development Programme, the International Labour Organization, the United Nations Educational, Scientific and Cultural Organization and regional organizations to

inform the Commission on Human Rights, at its sixty-first session, of action taken to promote and consolidate democracy;

16. *Requests* the Secretary-General to bring the present resolution to the attention of Member States.

RECORDED VOTE ON RESOLUTION 59/201:

In favour: Afghanistan, Albania, Algeria, Andorra, Angola, Antigua and Barbuda, Argentina, Armenia, Australia, Austria, Azerbaijan, Bahamas, Bahrain, Bangladesh, Barbados, Belgium, Belize, Benin, Bolivia, Bosnia and Herzegovina, Botswana, Brazil, Brunei Darussalam, Bulgaria, Burkina Faso, Burundi, Cambodia, Cameroon, Canada, Cape Verde, Central African Republic, Chad, Chile, Colombia, Comoros, Costa Rica, Côte d'Ivoire, Croatia, Cyprus, Czech Republic, Democratic Republic of the Congo, Denmark, Djibouti, Dominica, Dominican Republic, Ecuador, Egypt, El Salvador, Equatorial Guinea, Eritrea, Estonia, Ethiopia, Fiji, Finland, France, Gabon, Gambia, Georgia, Germany, Ghana, Greece, Grenada, Guatemala, Guinea, Guinea-Bissau, Guyana, Haiti, Honduras, Hungary, Iceland, India, Indonesia, Iran, Iraq, Ireland, Israel, Italy, Jamaica, Japan, Jordan, Kazakhstan, Kenya, Kuwait, Kyrgyzstan, Latvia, Lebanon, Lesotho, Liberia, Liechtenstein, Lithuania, Luxembourg, Madagascar, Malawi, Malaysia, Maldives, Mali, Malta, Marshall Islands, Mauritania, Mauritius, Mexico, Micronesia, Monaco, Mongolia, Morocco, Mozambique, Namibia, Nauru, Nepal, Netherlands, New Zealand, Nicaragua, Niger, Nigeria, Norway, Oman, Pakistan, Palau, Panama, Papua New Guinea, Paraguay, Peru, Philippines, Poland, Portugal, Qatar, Republic of Korea, Republic of Moldova, Romania, Russian Federation, Rwanda, Saint Lucia, Saint Vincent and the Grenadines, Samoa, San Marino, Sao Tome and Principe, Senegal, Serbia and Montenegro, Seychelles, Sierra Leone, Singapore, Slovakia, Slovenia, Solomon Islands, Somalia, South Africa, Spain, Sri Lanka, Sudan, Suriname, Swaziland, Sweden, Switzerland, Tajikistan, Thailand, The former Yugoslav Republic of Macedonia, Timor-Leste, Togo, Trinidad and Tobago, Tunisia, Turkey, Tuvalu, Uganda, Ukraine, United Kingdom, United Republic of Tanzania, United States, Uruguay, Uzbekistan, Vanuatu, Yemen, Zambia.

Against: None.

Abstaining: Belarus, Bhutan, China, Cuba, Democratic People's Republic of Korea, Lao People's Democratic Republic, Libyan Arab Jamahiriya, Myanmar, Saudi Arabia, Syrian Arab Republic, Turkmenistan, United Arab Emirates, Venezuela, Viet Nam, Zimbabwe.

Electoral processes

By a recorded vote of 28 to 14, with 11 abstentions, the Commission, on 19 April [res. 2004/31], urged States to foster a democracy that promoted people's welfare and invited Commission mechanisms and human rights treaty bodies to continue taking into account, in the discharge of their respective mandates, the question of strengthening popular participation, equity, social justice and non-discrimination as foundations of democracy.

Other issues

Extralegal executions

Reports of Special Rapporteur. The Special Rapporteur on extrajudicial, summary or arbitrary executions, Asma Jahangir (Pakistan), in her annual report [E/CN.4/2004/7 & Corr.1 & Add.1], updated developments since her 2003 report [YUN 2003, p. 739]. Between 2 December 2002 and 1 December 2003, she transmitted 97 urgent appeals to 35 countries and the Palestinian Authority, of which 45 were transmitted jointly with other Commission mechanisms. In addition, she transmitted 61 communications containing allegations of violations of the right to life of a large number of individuals and groups to 43 countries. The report summarized the cases transmitted and the replies received. The Special Rapporteur expressed concern at the lack of improvement in the situation relating to extrajudicial, summary or arbitrary executions. Governments were using excessive force on the justification of defending security, and a pattern of extrajudicial executions had emerged, carried out mainly in conflict and post-conflict situations; under authoritarian regimes; in situations of transition from dictatorship to democracy; in circumstances of serious lapses in governance, particularly in countries with a high crime rate; in corrupt government institutions; and in countries with weak and inefficient judicial systems. In addition to the recommendations contained in her 2003 report, the Special Rapporteur proposed that the UN strengthen early warning mechanisms against genocide and crimes against humanity, and that Governments not resort to aerial bombing, the use of snipers or pre-emptive strikes against people, but should review their policies and withdraw "shoot on sight" orders to security forces. She further recommended, among other things, that all deaths in custody be investigated, that law enforcement officials receive human rights training and that all retentionist Governments impose a moratorium on executions.

The Special Rapporteur visited the Sudan (1-13 June) [E/CN.4/2005/7/Add.2] following reports of alleged violations of the right to life in the country. As part of the mission, she also visited Cairo and Nairobi, where she met with interlocutors on developments in the Sudan. The mission took place at a time when, despite ongoing peace negotiations in southern Sudan to end a protracted civil war between the Government and opposition forces, most notably the Sudan People's Liberation Movement/Army (see p. 233), escalating conflict in the Darfur region in the west resulted in a humanitarian crisis in which an estimated 1 million civilians were displaced, of whom many were allegedly targeted and killed extrajudicially by government agents. Further allegations of extrajudicial killings were reported elsewhere in the country. Against that background, the Special Rapporteur focused on problem areas in order to investigate the reported killings and on the application of the death penalty. She found evidence that extrajudicial killings of civilians had occurred in Darfur, and that the scale of the violations of the right to life could be termed a crime against humanity. Moreover, the manner in which the death penalty was imposed and carried out did not conform to the safeguards and restrictions under international customary law. The Special Rapporteur recom-

mended that the Government accord priority to ensuring effective humanitarian assistance and protection of the rights of the vulnerable population in Darfur and in southern Sudan, in order to safeguard their right to life; that all militias be disarmed and that the actions of the Popular Defence Forces remain under control. The Government should, in addition, maintain accountability in the peace process, end the culture of impunity and revise the national legislation concerning the death penalty to ensure that it conformed to international standards.

In September [A/59/319], the Secretary-General transmitted the interim report of the Special Rapporteur, pursuant to General Assembly resolution 57/214 [YUN 2002, p. 706]. The report focused on activities she had undertaken between 1 July 2002 and 1 June 2004 and on issues of concern requiring urgent attention. The Special Rapporteur transmitted 115 communications containing allegations of violations of the right to life of a large number of individuals and groups, of which 64 were transmitted to 63 Governments jointly with other special rapporteurs. The report also summarized the activities undertaken by the Special Rapporteur, situations involving violations of the right to life of special groups and issues of special focus. She had transmitted communications to Governments or taken other forms of action in relation to violations of the right to life regarding: non-implementation of existing international standards on safeguards and restrictions relating to the imposition of capital punishment; genocide and crimes against humanity; violations of the right to life during armed conflicts; deaths due to excessive use of force by law enforcement officials; deaths in custody; death threats and violations of the right to life of persons carrying out peaceful activities in defence of human rights; expulsion and return of persons to a country or place where their lives were in danger (refoulement); and impunity. The Special Rapporteur concluded that there was no indication that violations of the right to life decreased during the reporting period and that the increasing number of communications relating to alleged violations indicated the magnitude of the incidence of extrajudicial, summary and arbitrary executions worldwide. She recommended that retentionist States impose a moratorium on executions and establish national commissions to report on the situation to enable States to ensure that applicable standards and guarantees were observed, and encouraged Governments to ratify relevant international instruments.

Commission action. On 19 April [res. 2004/37], the Commission, by a recorded vote of 39 to none, with 12 abstentions, strongly condemning all extrajudicial, summary or arbitrary executions, demanded that States end the practice in all its forms. The Commission asked the Secretary-General and High Commissioner to use their best endeavours in cases where the minimum standard of legal safeguards provided for in the International Covenant on Civil and Political Rights (see p. 662) appeared not to be respected. The Secretary-General was also asked to provide the Special Rapporteur with adequate resources, and to ensure that personnel specialized in human rights and humanitarian law formed part of UN missions, in order to deal with extrajudicial, summary or arbitrary executions. The Commission decided to extend the Special Rapporteur's mandate for three years.

In July, the Commission appointed Philip Alston (Australia) as Special Rapporteur.

ECONOMIC AND SOCIAL COUNCIL ACTION

In July, the Economic and Social Council, on the recommendation of the Commission on Human Rights [E/2004/23], adopted **decision 2004/259** by recorded vote (45-0-9) [agenda item 14 (g)].

Extrajudicial, summary or arbitrary executions

At its 48th plenary meeting, on 22 July 2004, the Economic and Social Council took note of Commission on Human Rights resolution 2004/37 of 19 April 2004 and endorsed the decision of the Commission to extend for three years the mandate of the Special Rapporteur on extrajudicial, summary or arbitrary executions and approved the Commission's request to the Secretary-General to provide the Special Rapporteur with adequate human, financial and material resources in order to enable her or him to continue to carry out her or his mandate effectively.

RECORDED VOTE ON DECISION 2004/259:

In favour: Armenia, Australia, Azerbaijan, Belgium, Belize, Benin, Bhutan, Burundi, Canada, Chile, Colombia, Congo, Cuba, Ecuador, El Salvador, Finland, France, Germany, Ghana, Greece, Guatemala, Hungary, India, Indonesia, Ireland, Italy, Jamaica, Japan, Mauritius, Mozambique, Namibia, Nicaragua, Panama, Poland, Republic of Korea, Russian Federation, Senegal, Sweden, Tunisia, Turkey, Ukraine, United Kingdom, United Republic of Tanzania, United States, Zimbabwe.

Against: None.

Abstaining: Bangladesh, China, Kenya, Libyan Arab Jamahiriya, Malaysia, Nigeria, Qatar, Saudi Arabia, United Arab Emirates.

Subcommission action. On 9 August [dec. 2004/103], the Subcommission adopted a statement recalling that the extrajudicial, summary or arbitrary execution of a human being was unlawful in all circumstances.

Communications. In March [E/CN.4/2004/G/33], Brazil transmitted information on measures of investigation and protection it had adopted regarding witnesses interviewed by the Special Rapporteur during her 2003 visit to the country [YUN 2003, p. 739].

In April [E/CN.4/2004/G/51], Jamaica, commenting on the Special Rapporteur's report following her visit to the country [YUN 2003, p. 739], stated that it was committed to ensuring that the rights of its citizens were protected in accordance with its obligations under the country's Constitution and under international agreements.

GENERAL ASSEMBLY ACTION

On 20 December [meeting 74], the General Assembly, on the recommendation of the Third Committee [A/59/503/Add.2], adopted **resolution 59/197** by recorded vote (142-0-43) [agenda item 105 (b)].

Extrajudicial, summary or arbitrary executions
The General Assembly,

Recalling the Universal Declaration of Human Rights, which guarantees the right to life, liberty and security of person, and the relevant provisions of the International Covenant on Civil and Political Rights,

Having regard to the legal framework of the mandate of the Special Rapporteur of the Commission on Human Rights on extrajudicial, summary or arbitrary executions, including the provisions contained in Commission on Human Rights resolutions 1992/72 of 5 March 1992 and 2001/45 of 23 April 2001, as well as General Assembly resolution 47/136 of 18 December 1992,

Noting its resolutions on the subject of extrajudicial, summary or arbitrary executions and the resolutions of the Commission on Human Rights on the subject,

Recalling Economic and Social Council resolution 1984/50 of 25 May 1984 and the safeguards guaranteeing protection of the rights of those facing the death penalty, annexed thereto, and Council resolution 1989/64 of 24 May 1989 on their implementation, as well as the Declaration of Basic Principles of Justice for Victims of Crime and Abuse of Power adopted by the General Assembly in its resolution 40/34 of 29 November 1985,

Recalling also Economic and Social Council resolution 1989/65 of 24 May 1989, in which the Council recommended the Principles on the Effective Prevention and Investigation of Extra-legal, Arbitrary and Summary Executions,

Convinced of the need for effective action to combat and to eliminate the abhorrent practice of extrajudicial, summary or arbitrary executions, which represent a flagrant violation of the right to life,

1. *Strongly condemns once again* all the extrajudicial, summary or arbitrary executions that continue to occur throughout the world;

2. *Demands* that all Governments ensure that the practice of extrajudicial, summary or arbitrary executions is brought to an end and that they take effective action to combat and eliminate the phenomenon in all its forms;

3. *Notes with grave concern* that situations of extrajudicial, summary or arbitrary executions may, under certain circumstances, result in genocide or crimes against humanity, as defined in the Convention on the Prevention and Punishment of the Crime of Genocide and other relevant international instruments;

4. *Notes with deep concern* that impunity continues to be a major cause of the perpetuation of violations of human rights, including extrajudicial, summary or arbitrary executions;

5. *Reiterates* the obligation of all Governments to conduct exhaustive and impartial investigations into all suspected cases of extrajudicial, summary or arbitrary executions, to identify and bring to justice those responsible, while ensuring the right of every person to a fair and public hearing by a competent, independent and impartial tribunal established by law, to grant adequate compensation within a reasonable time to the victims or their families, and to adopt all necessary measures, including legal and judicial measures, to put an end to impunity and to prevent the further occurrence of such executions;

6. *Acknowledges* the establishment of the International Criminal Court as an important contribution to ending impunity concerning extrajudicial, summary or arbitrary executions and the fact that ninety-seven States have already ratified or acceded to and one hundred and thirty-nine States have signed the Rome Statute, and calls upon all other States to consider becoming parties to the Statute;

7. *Calls upon* all States in which the death penalty has not been abolished to comply with their obligations under relevant provisions of international human rights instruments, including in particular articles 6, 7 and 14 of the International Covenant on Civil and Political Rights and articles 37 and 40 of the Convention on the Rights of the Child, bearing in mind the safeguards and guarantees set out in Economic and Social Council resolutions 1984/50 and 1989/64;

8. *Urges* all Governments:

(a) To take all necessary measures to prevent the occurrence of extrajudicial, summary or arbitrary executions, including those occurring in custody;

(b) To take all necessary and possible measures, in conformity with international human rights law and international humanitarian law, to prevent loss of life, in particular that of children, during public demonstrations, internal and communal violence, civil unrest and public emergencies or armed conflicts, and to ensure that the police, law enforcement agents and security forces act with restraint and in conformity with international human rights law and international humanitarian law;

(c) To ensure the effective protection of the right to life of all persons under their jurisdiction and to investigate promptly and thoroughly all killings, including those targeted at specific groups of persons, such as racially motivated violence leading to the death of the victim, killings of members of national, ethnic, religious or linguistic minorities, of refugees, internally displaced persons, migrants, street children or members of indigenous communities, killings of persons for reasons related to their peaceful activities as human rights defenders, lawyers, journalists or demonstrators, killings committed in the name of passion or in the name of honour, all killings committed for any discriminatory reason, including sexual orientation, as well as all other cases where a person's right to life has been violated, and to bring those responsible to justice before a competent, independent and impartial judiciary and to ensure that such killings, including those committed by security forces, police and law enforce-

ment agents, paramilitary groups or private forces, are neither condoned nor sanctioned by State officials or personnel;

9. *Encourages* Governments and intergovernmental and non-governmental organizations to organize training programmes and to support projects with a view to training or educating military forces, law enforcement officers and government officials in human rights and humanitarian law issues connected with their work and to include a gender perspective in such training, and appeals to the international community and requests the Office of the United Nations High Commissioner for Human Rights to support endeavours to that end;

10. *Reaffirms* Economic and Social Council decision 2004/259 of 22 July 2004, by which the Council endorsed the decision of the Commission on Human Rights to extend the mandate of the Special Rapporteur of the Commission on Human Rights on extrajudicial, summary or arbitrary executions for three years;

11. *Takes note* of the interim report of the Special Rapporteur to the General Assembly;

12. *Commends* the important role that the Special Rapporteur plays towards the elimination of extrajudicial, summary or arbitrary executions, and encourages the Special Rapporteur to continue, within his mandate, to collect information from all concerned, to respond effectively to reliable information that comes before him, to follow up on communications and country visits and to seek the views and comments of Governments and to reflect them, as appropriate, in his reports;

13. *Urges* the Special Rapporteur to continue, within his mandate, to bring to the attention of the United Nations High Commissioner for Human Rights and, as appropriate, the Special Adviser to the Secretary-General on the Prevention of Genocide, situations of extrajudicial, summary or arbitrary executions that are of particularly serious concern or in which early action might prevent further deterioration;

14. *Welcomes* the cooperation established between the Special Rapporteur and other United Nations mechanisms and procedures relating to human rights, as well as with medical and forensic experts, and encourages the Special Rapporteur to continue efforts in that regard;

15. *Urges* all Governments, in particular those that have not yet done so, to respond in a timely manner to the communications and requests for information transmitted to them by the Special Rapporteur, and urges them and all others concerned to cooperate with and assist the Special Rapporteur so that he may carry out his mandate effectively, including, where appropriate, by issuing invitations to the Special Rapporteur when he so requests;

16. *Expresses its appreciation* to those Governments that have invited the Special Rapporteur to visit their countries, asks them to examine carefully the recommendations made by the Special Rapporteur, invites them to inform the Special Rapporteur of the actions taken on those recommendations, and requests other Governments to cooperate in a similar way;

17. *Again requests* the Secretary-General to continue to use his best endeavours in cases where the minimum standards of legal safeguards provided for in articles 6, 9, 14 and 15 of the International Covenant on

Civil and Political Rights appear not to have been respected;

18. *Requests* the Secretary-General to provide the Special Rapporteur with adequate human, financial and material resources to enable him to carry out his mandate effectively, including through country visits;

19. *Also requests* the Secretary-General to continue, in close collaboration with the High Commissioner, in conformity with the mandate of the High Commissioner established by the General Assembly in its resolution 48/141 of 20 December 1993, to ensure that personnel specialized in human rights and humanitarian law issues form part of United Nations missions, where appropriate, in order to deal with serious violations of human rights, such as extrajudicial, summary or arbitrary executions;

20. *Requests* the Special Rapporteur to submit an interim report to the General Assembly at its sixty-first session on the situation worldwide in regard to extrajudicial, summary or arbitrary executions and his recommendations for more effective action to combat this phenomenon.

RECORDED VOTE ON RESOLUTION 59/197:

In favour: Afghanistan, Albania, Algeria, Andorra, Angola, Antigua and Barbuda, Argentina, Armenia, Australia, Austria, Azerbaijan, Bahamas, Barbados, Belgium, Belize, Benin, Bhutan, Bolivia, Bosnia and Herzegovina, Botswana, Brazil, Bulgaria, Burkina Faso, Burundi, Cambodia, Cameroon, Canada, Cape Verde, Central African Republic, Chile, Costa Rica, Côte d'Ivoire, Croatia, Cuba, Cyprus, Czech Republic, Democratic Republic of the Congo, Denmark, Dominica, Dominican Republic, Ecuador, El Salvador, Equatorial Guinea, Eritrea, Estonia, Fiji, Finland, France, Gabon, Gambia, Georgia, Germany, Ghana, Greece, Grenada, Guatemala, Guinea, Guinea-Bissau, Guyana, Haiti, Honduras, Hungary, Iceland, India, Ireland, Israel, Italy, Jamaica, Japan, Jordan, Kyrgyzstan, Latvia, Lesotho, Liberia, Liechtenstein, Lithuania, Luxembourg, Madagascar, Malawi, Mali, Malta, Marshall Islands, Mauritius, Mexico, Micronesia, Monaco, Mongolia, Mozambique, Namibia, Nauru, Nepal, Netherlands, New Zealand, Nicaragua, Niger, Nigeria, Norway, Palau, Panama, Paraguay, Peru, Philippines, Poland, Portugal, Republic of Korea, Republic of Moldova, Romania, Russian Federation, Rwanda, Saint Lucia, Saint Vincent and the Grenadines, Samoa, San Marino, Sao Tome and Principe, Serbia and Montenegro, Seychelles, Sierra Leone, Slovakia, Slovenia, Solomon Islands, Somalia, South Africa, Spain, Sri Lanka, Suriname, Swaziland, Sweden, Switzerland, Tajikistan, Thailand, The former Yugoslav Republic of Macedonia, Timor-Leste, Togo, Trinidad and Tobago, Turkey, Ukraine, United Kingdom, United States, Uruguay, Uzbekistan, Venezuela, Zambia

Against: None.

Abstaining: Bahrain, Bangladesh, Belarus, Brunei Darussalam, China, Colombia, Comoros, Democratic People's Republic of Korea, Djibouti, Egypt, Ethiopia, Indonesia, Iran, Iraq, Kazakhstan, Kenya, Kuwait, Lao People's Democratic Republic, Lebanon, Libyan Arab Jamahiriya, Malaysia, Maldives, Mauritania, Morocco, Myanmar, Oman, Pakistan, Papua New Guinea, Qatar, Saudi Arabia, Senegal, Singapore, Sudan, Syrian Arab Republic, Tunisia, Turkmenistan, Tuvalu, Uganda, United Arab Emirates, United Republic of Tanzania, Viet Nam, Yemen, Zimbabwe.

The Third Committee adopted, by separate recorded votes, paragraph 7 by 84 to 41, with 39 abstentions, and the words "including sexual orientation" after the words "for any discriminatory reason" in paragraph 8 *(c)*, by 93 to 42, with 29 abstentions. The Assembly retained that paragraph and those words by recorded votes of 86 to 44, with 39 abstentions, and 95 to 41, with 26 abstentions, respectively.

Prevention of genocide

In accordance with Security Council resolution 1366(2001) [YUN 2001, p. 50], the Secretary-General, in July [S/2004/567], appointed Juan Méndez as his Special Adviser on the Prevention of Genocide, with a mandate to: collect information on massive and serious violations of human rights and humanitarian law of ethnic and racial origin that, if not prevented or halted, might lead to genocide; act as an early warning mechanism to the Secretary-General, and through him to the Council, by bringing to their attention potential situations that could result in genocide; make recommendations to the Council on actions to halt genocide; liaise with the UN system on activities to prevent genocide; and work to enhance the Organization's capacity to analyse and manage information regarding genocide or related crimes. The Special Adviser would not be required to make a determination on whether genocide had occurred, within the definition of the 1948 Convention on the Prevention and Punishment of the Crime of Genocide (see p. 669). His activities would be intended to enable the United Nations to act in a timely fashion and would help the Secretary-General define steps necessary to prevent the deterioration of existing situations into genocide.

Disappearance of persons

Draft instrument. Pursuant to a 2003 Commission request [YUN 2003, p. 740], the intersessional open-ended working group established to prepare a draft legally binding instrument for the protection of all persons from enforced disappearance held its second (12-23 January) [E/CN.4/2004/59] and third (4-8 October) [E/CN.4/2005/66] sessions, both in Geneva. In January, the group reviewed the Chairman's working paper containing a draft preamble and articles, which took into account observations made at the group's first session [YUN 2003, p. 740] and incorporated the language of international instruments. Relevant issues discussed included the definition of enforced disappearance, the phenomenon as a crime against humanity, offences and penalties, protection against impunity, prosecution in domestic courts, international cooperation, prevention of enforced disappearances, victims of enforced disappearance, children of disappeared persons, a monitoring body and the final provisions of the draft instrument. The group, having considered that it made major progress in January, considered in October a revised version of the Chairman's working paper, which it decided to continue discussing at its fourth (2005) session.

Commission action. On 19 April [res. 2004/40], the Commission urged States to promote and give full effect to the 1992 Declaration on the Protection of All Persons from Enforced Disappearance, adopted by the General Assembly in resolution 47/133 [YUN 1992, p. 744], and to cooperate with the Working Group on Enforced or Involuntary Disappearances (see below). The Commission decided to extend the Group's mandate for three years and asked it to report in 2005. States were invited to provide the Group with information on preventive measures and in giving effect to the Declaration. The Secretary-General was asked to assist it, to provide the requisite resources to update the database on cases of enforced disappearance and to inform the Commission of steps taken to disseminate and promote the Declaration. The Commission asked the intersessional working group (see above) to meet for 15 working days before the Commission's 2005 session and to report at that session.

On 22 July, the Economic and Social Council approved the Commission's decision to extend the Group's mandate for three years, as well as its request to the intersessional working group to meet (**decision 2004/260**).

Working Group activities. The five-member Working Group on Enforced or Involuntary Disappearances held three sessions in 2004: its seventy-second (24-28 May), seventy-third (16-20 August) and seventy-fourth (8-15 November), all in Geneva [E/CN.4/2005/65]. In addition to its original mandate, which was to act as a channel of communication between families of disappeared persons and the Governments concerned, with a view to ensuring that sufficiently documented individual cases were investigated, the Working Group monitored States' compliance with the 1992 Declaration. Cases under active consideration by the Group totalled 41,909, while countries with outstanding cases of alleged disappearance numbered 79. During the period under review, up to 15 November, the last day of its seventy-fourth session, the Group transmitted 595 new cases of disappearance to 20 States, 131 of which allegedly occurred in 2004. It also sent 152 urgent action appeals to 12 countries and clarified 23 cases. The Group's report summarized information regarding disappearances received from 51 countries. The Group, regretting that the phenomenon of enforced disappearances had continued in many States, expressed concern that in a number of cases children had been affected. While in the past the phenomenon was mainly associated with the State policies of authoritarian regimes, it currently occurred in the context of much more complex situations of internal conflict or tensions generating violence, humanitarian crisis and human rights violations. The Group called on Governments to comply with their obligations under relevant provisions of the 1992 Declaration.

Two Working Group members visited Nepal (6-14 December) [E/CN.4/2005/65/Add.1] to examine alleged cases of enforced or involuntary disappearance, following reports of a marked increase in the number of such incidents and of other human rights violations, within the context of the conflict between the Government and the Communist Party of Nepal (Maoist). There were currently some 267 outstanding cases of disappearances in the country reported to the Group, which occurred between 1998 and 2004, and the perpetrators, which included Maoist insurgents and Nepalese security forces, were often shielded by political and legal impunity. Among the reported victims were women, students, businessmen, farmers, workers, journalists and human rights defenders. The Group concluded that resolving the underlying conflict in the country was the best means to guarantee a reduction in human rights and humanitarian law violations, including disappearances, and recommended, among other measures, amending the Nepalese criminal law, to create a specific crime of enforced and involuntary disappearance, and the Army Act, to ensure that security forces personnel accused of the crime against a civilian would be tried in civilian courts. The Government and the security forces were asked to keep up-to-date lists of detainees and ensure that human rights defenders were protected from persecution for their work.

Report of Secretary-General. In response to General Assembly resolution 57/215 [YUN 2002, p. 710], the Secretary-General, in a September report [A/59/341], presented replies received from six Governments in response to his request for information on steps they had taken to combat enforced or involuntary disappearance. The report highlighted the 2003 activities of the Working Group on the phenomenon [YUN 2003, p. 740], and of the UN Secretariat, including efforts by DPI and OHCHR to promote the 1992 Declaration.

GENERAL ASSEMBLY ACTION

On 20 December [meeting 74], the General Assembly, on the recommendation of the Third Committee [A/59/503/Add.2], adopted **resolution 59/200** without vote [agenda item 105 (b)].

Question of enforced or involuntary disappearances

The General Assembly,

Guided by the purposes and principles set forth in the Charter of the United Nations, the Universal Declaration of Human Rights, the International Covenants on Human Rights and the other relevant international human rights instruments,

Recalling its resolution 33/173 of 20 December 1978 concerning disappeared persons and its resolutions on the question of enforced or involuntary disappearances, in particular resolution 57/215 of 18 December 2002,

Recalling also its resolution 47/133 of 18 December 1992 proclaiming the Declaration on the Protection of All Persons from Enforced Disappearance as a body of principles for all States,

Bearing in mind Commission on Human Rights resolution 2004/40 of 19 April 2004,

Deeply concerned, in particular, by the intensification of enforced disappearances, including arrest, detention and abduction, where these are part of or amount to enforced disappearances, in various regions of the world and by the growing number of reports concerning the harassment, ill-treatment and intimidation of witnesses of disappearances or relatives of persons who have disappeared,

Taking note with interest of the initiatives taken at the national and international levels in order to end impunity,

Acknowledging the fact that acts of enforced disappearance, as defined in the Rome Statute of the International Criminal Court, come within the jurisdiction of the Court as crimes against humanity,

Convinced that further efforts are needed to promote wider awareness of and respect for the Declaration, and taking note in this regard of the report of the Secretary-General,

Taking note of the report of the Working Group on Enforced or Involuntary Disappearances of the Commission on Human Rights,

1. *Reaffirms* that any act of enforced disappearance is an offence to human dignity and a grave and flagrant violation of the human rights and fundamental freedoms proclaimed in the Universal Declaration of Human Rights and reaffirmed and developed in other international instruments in this field, as well as a violation of the rules of international law; and that no State shall practise, permit or tolerate enforced disappearances as proclaimed in the Declaration on the Protection of All Persons from Enforced Disappearance;

2. *Urges* all Governments to take appropriate legislative or other steps to prevent and suppress the practice of enforced disappearances, in keeping with the Declaration, and to take action to that end at the national and regional levels and in cooperation with the United Nations, including through the provision of technical assistance;

3. *Calls upon* Governments to take steps to ensure that, when a state of emergency is introduced, the protection of human rights is ensured, in particular with regard to the prevention of enforced disappearances;

4. *Reminds* Governments that impunity with regard to enforced disappearances contributes to the perpetuation of this phenomenon and constitutes one of the obstacles to the elucidation of its manifestations, and in this respect also reminds them of the need to ensure that their competent authorities conduct prompt and impartial inquiries in all circumstances in which there is a reason to believe that an enforced disappearance has occurred in territory under their jurisdiction, and that, if allegations are confirmed, perpetrators should be prosecuted;

5. *Expresses its appreciation* to those Governments that are investigating, are cooperating at the international and bilateral levels, have developed or are developing appropriate mechanisms to investigate any cases of enforced disappearances that are brought to their attention and to prevent any such occurrences, and urges all the Governments concerned to expand their efforts in this area;

6. *Once again urges* the Governments concerned:

(a) To take steps to protect witnesses of enforced disappearances, human rights defenders acting against enforced disappearances, and the lawyers and families of disappeared persons against any intimidation or ill-treatment to which they may be subjected;

(b) To continue their efforts to elucidate the fate of disappeared persons;

(c) To make provision in their legal systems for machinery for victims of enforced or involuntary disappearances or their families to seek fair and adequate reparation;

7. *Reaffirms* that all persons deprived of liberty must be released in a manner permitting reliable verification that they have actually been released and, further, have been released in conditions in which their physical integrity and ability to exercise their rights are assured;

8. *Encourages* States, as some have already done, to provide concrete information on measures taken to give effect to the Declaration, as well as obstacles encountered;

9. *Requests* all States to consider the possibility of disseminating the text of the Declaration in their respective national languages and to facilitate its dissemination in local languages;

10. *Notes* the action taken by non-governmental organizations to encourage implementation of the Declaration, and invites them to continue to facilitate its dissemination;

11. *Stresses* the importance of the work of the Working Group on Enforced or Involuntary Disappearances of the Commission on Human Rights, and encourages it in the execution of its mandate to continue to promote communication between the families of disappeared persons and the Governments concerned, in particular when ordinary channels have failed, with a view to ensuring that sufficiently documented and clearly identified individual cases are investigated and to ascertaining whether such information falls under its mandate and contains the required elements;

12. *Invites* the Working Group to continue to seek the views and comments of all concerned, including Member States, in preparing its reports;

13. *Also invites* the Working Group to identify obstacles to the realization of the provisions of the Declaration, to recommend ways of overcoming those obstacles and, in this regard, to continue a dialogue with Governments and relevant intergovernmental and non-governmental organizations;

14. *Encourages* the Working Group to continue to consider the question of impunity, in the light of the relevant provisions of the Declaration;

15. *Requests* the Working Group to pay the utmost attention to cases of children subjected to enforced disappearance and children of disappeared persons and to cooperate closely with the Governments concerned to search for and identify those children;

16. *Appeals* to the Governments concerned, in particular those that have not yet replied to the communications transmitted by the Working Group, to cooperate fully with it and, in particular, to reply

promptly to its requests for information so that, while respecting its working methods based on discretion, it may perform its strictly humanitarian role;

17. *Encourages* the Governments concerned to give serious consideration to requests for visits to their countries by the Working Group so as to enable the Group to fulfil its mandate even more effectively;

18. *Expresses its profound thanks* to the many Governments that have cooperated with the Working Group and replied to its requests for information and to the Governments that have invited the Group to visit their countries, requests them to give all necessary attention to the recommendations of the Group, and invites them to inform the Group of any action they take on those recommendations;

19. *Calls upon* the Commission on Human Rights to continue to study this question as a matter of priority and to take any steps it may deem necessary to the pursuit of the task of the Working Group and to the follow-up to its recommendations when it considers the report to be submitted by the Group to the Commission at its sixty-first session;

20. *Renews its requests* to the Secretary-General to continue to provide the Working Group with all of the facilities it requires to perform its functions, especially for carrying out missions and following them up;

21. *Recalls* Economic and Social Council decision 2001/221 of 4 June 2001, in which the Council endorsed the decision of the Commission on Human Rights to create an intersessional open-ended working group, with the mandate to prepare a draft legally binding normative instrument for the protection of all persons from enforced disappearance;

22. *Welcomes* the decision of the Commission on Human Rights to convene the intersessional working group before its sixty-first session, with a view to the prompt completion of its work and the submission of its report to the Commission at its sixty-first session;

23. *Requests* the Secretary-General to keep it informed of the steps he takes to secure the widespread dissemination and promotion of the Declaration;

24. *Also requests* the Secretary-General to submit to it at its sixty-first session a report on the steps taken to implement the present resolution;

25. *Decides* to consider the question of enforced disappearances, in particular the implementation of the Declaration, at its sixtieth session, under the sub-item entitled "Human rights questions, including alternative approaches for improving the effective enjoyment of human rights and fundamental freedoms".

Torture and cruel treatment

Reports of Special Rapporteur. In response to a 2003 Commission request [YUN 2003, p. 741], the Special Rapporteur on torture, Theo van Boven (Netherlands), described his activities from 15 December 2002 to 15 December 2003 [E/CN.4/2004/56]. He had sent 154 letters to 76 countries on alleged torture of individuals, 71 letters reminding Governments of a number of cases transmitted in previous years and 369 urgent appeals to 80 Governments on behalf of individuals who, it was feared, might suffer torture and other forms of ill-treatment. A summary of the communications sent by the Special Rapporteur and of replies received were contained in an addendum to the report [E/CN.4/2004/56/Add.1]. The Special Rapporteur drew attention to a number of guarantees for individuals deprived of their liberty, with a view to protecting them from the risk of torture and other forms of ill-treatment, examined the question of HIV/AIDS and the right to freedom from cruel, inhuman and degrading treatment or punishment, and provided information on the follow-up to his 2003 preliminary study [YUN 2003, p. 741] on the situation of trade in and production of equipment specifically designed to inflict torture or other cruel, inhuman or degrading treatment, its origin, destination and forms. Annexed to the report was a list of issues of particular concern regarding torture and other forms of ill-treatment examined by the Special Rapporteur and his predecessors between 1986 and 2004.

In a further report [E/CN.4/2005/62/Add.2], the Special Rapporteur summarized follow-up to recommendations made regarding visits to Azerbaijan [YUN 2000, p. 682], Chile [YUN 1995, p. 756], Mexico [YUN 1997, p. 666], the Russian Federation [YUN 1994, p. 1016], Spain [YUN 2003, p. 742], Turkey [YUN 1998, p. 681] and Uzbekistan [YUN 2002, p. 712].

Commission action. On 19 April [res. 2004/41], the Commission, condemning all forms of torture, urged States to become parties to the 1984 Convention against Torture and Other Cruel, Inhuman or Degrading Treatment or Punishment (see p. 666). Governments were called on to eliminate the practice and to prevent and prohibit the production, trade, export and use of equipment specifically designed to inflict torture. The Commission decided to extend for three years the Special Rapporteur's mandate and called on States and NGOs to provide the information requested by the Special Rapporteur and to combat the proliferation of torture equipment; the Special Rapporteur was asked to report on the proliferation of the equipment and to submit an interim report to the General Assembly in 2004 and a report to the Commission in 2005.

On 22 July, the Economic and Social Council endorsed the Commission's decision to extend the Special Rapporteur's mandate for three years (**decision 2004/261**).

In November, the Commission appointed Manfred Nowak (Austria) as Special Rapporteur.

Subcommission action. On 9 August [res. 2004/1], the Subcommission recommended that all States develop independent and effective domestic mechanisms as concrete means of combating torture and other cruel, inhuman or degrading treatment or punishment.

Further report of Special Rapporteur. Pursuant to General Assembly resolution 58/164 [YUN 2003, p. 742] and to Commission resolution 2004/41 (see p. 733), the Secretary-General, in September, transmitted the interim report of the Special Rapporteur [A/59/324], which further described his activities from 16 December 2003 to 31 July 2004 and covered issues of special concern to him. In addition to communications contained in his report to the Commission (see above), the Special Rapporteur had transmitted 94 letters concerning allegations of torture to 42 Governments and 237 urgent appeals to 58 Governments on behalf of persons who might be at risk of torture or other forms of ill-treatment. As a follow-up to his previous reports to the Assembly on the prohibition of torture and other forms of cruel, inhuman or degrading treatment or punishment in the context of anti-terrorism measures, the Special Rapporteur drew attention to attempts to circumvent the absolute and non-derogable nature of the prohibition. The report also discussed the principle of non-refoulement, highlighting the jurisprudence underlying it and increasing efforts to undermine it. Also examined was the impact of torture on victims. Noting that the consequences of torture went beyond the damage caused to victims and also affected their families and community at large, the Special Rapporteur advocated a holistic understanding of the impact on victims, so as to develop adequate assistance.

Communications. In January [E/CN.4/2004/G/19], Spain stated that the provisional report of the Special Rapporteur on his 2003 visit [YUN 2003, p. 742] contained factual errors that undermined the report's conclusions.

In May [A/59/96], Uzbekistan transmitted the text of the action plan it had adopted to comply with the 1984 Convention (see p. 666).

Voluntary fund for torture victims

Commission action. On 19 April [res. 2004/41], the Commission, recognizing the need for international assistance to victims of torture, appealed to Governments, organizations and individuals to contribute annually to the United Nations Voluntary Fund for Victims of Torture and, if possible, to increase their contributions. The Secretary-General was asked to continue to include the Fund among the programmes receiving donations at the annual UN Pledging Conference for Development Activities and to ensure adequate staffing and technical facilities for UN bodies and mechanisms dealing with torture. The Fund's Board of Trustees was asked to report in 2005.

Report of Secretary-General. In response to a 2003 Commission resolution [YUN 2003, p. 742], the Secretary-General submitted a report [E/CN.4/2004/53], which supplemented and updated information contained in his previous report on the Fund's operation [YUN 2003, p. 742].

An addendum to the report [E/CN.4/2004/53/Add.1] described progress made on the evaluation of the Fund. The UN Office of Internal Oversight Services (OIOS) had finalized the terms of reference for the evaluation and recruited two consultants for the project. The evaluation team visited Geneva (23-27 February) and was to conduct on-site evaluations of projects from March to May (see below).

Note by Secretariat. A September note of the Secretariat [A/59/353] stated that the Secretary-General would not submit his annual report on the activities of the Fund to the General Assembly at its fifty-ninth (2004) session because the Board's meeting had been postponed. A comprehensive report would be submitted in 2005.

Further report of Secretary-General. A November report of the Secretary-General [E/CN.4/2005/54 & Corr.1] provided information on the recommendations of the Fund's Board of Trustees at its twenty-third session (4-8 October). Contributions received during the year totalled $7,763,701 from 32 States, three individuals and three NGOs. The total available for new grants to assist victims of torture amounted to some $165,376 against requests amounting to $13.2 million. The Board recommended a total of $6.7 million in grants to 172 organizations in 61 countries, which were approved on 11 October by the High Commissioner on behalf of the Secretary-General. New grants totalling $6,765,668 were also allocated to 179 projects in numerous countries. The Board estimated that $14 million would be needed to cover new requests at its next session. Annexed to the report was a list of organizations and activities financed by the Fund in 2004.

OIOS report. By a November note [E/CN.4/2005/55], the Secretariat transmitted an OIOS report on its review of the Fund's functioning, in accordance with a 2003 Commission request [YUN 2003, p. 742]. The report said that the Fund was fulfilling its mandate and having a positive impact on victims of torture. OIOS stated that it was encouraged by the work of 16 projects financed by the Fund, which it had reviewed in Austria, Bangladesh, Canada, Chile, Rwanda and the United States. Opportunities existed for enhancing and expanding the Fund; currently it was inadequately financed in relation to the needs it met and the requests it received. Many of its existing management systems were no longer adequate, and its impact was not well communicated to stakeholders, including donors. With additional funding, the Fund had a great potential to increase its impact. Further measures recommended for improving the Fund's functioning related to its policy and mode of operation, staffing status, management system and funding.

GENERAL ASSEMBLY ACTION

On 20 December [meeting 74], the General Assembly, on the recommendation of the Third Committee [A/59/503/Add.1], adopted **resolution 59/182** without vote [agenda item 105 (*a*)].

Torture and other cruel, inhuman or degrading treatment or punishment

The General Assembly,

Recalling that freedom from torture and other cruel, inhuman or degrading treatment or punishment is a non-derogable right that must be protected under all circumstances, including in times of internal or international disturbance or armed conflict, and that the prohibition of torture is explicitly affirmed in all relevant international instruments,

Recalling also that a number of international, regional and domestic courts, including the International Tribunal for the Prosecution of Persons Responsible for Serious Violations of International Humanitarian Law Committed in the Territory of the Former Yugoslavia since 1991, have recognized that the prohibition of torture is a peremptory norm of international law,

Recalling further the definition of torture contained in article 1 of the Convention against Torture and Other Cruel, Inhuman or Degrading Treatment or Punishment,

Recalling the recommendation contained in the Vienna Declaration and Programme of Action adopted by the World Conference on Human Rights on 25 June 1993 that high priority be given to providing the necessary resources to assist victims of torture and effective remedies for their physical, psychological and social rehabilitation, inter alia, through additional contributions to the United Nations Voluntary Fund for Victims of Torture, and noting with satisfaction the existence of a considerable international network of centres for the rehabilitation of victims of torture,

Commending the persistent efforts by non-governmental organizations to combat torture and to alleviate the suffering of victims of torture,

1. *Condemns* all forms of torture and other cruel, inhuman or degrading treatment or punishment, including through intimidation, which are and shall remain prohibited at any time and in any place whatsoever and can thus never be justified, and calls upon all Governments to implement fully the prohibition of torture and other cruel, inhuman or degrading treatment or punishment;

2. *Condemns in particular* any action or attempt by States or public officials to legalize or authorize torture and other cruel, inhuman or degrading treatment or punishment under any circumstances, including on grounds of national security or through judicial decisions, and calls upon Governments to eliminate any practices of torture and other cruel, inhuman or degrading treatment or punishment;

3. *Urges* Governments to take effective measures to prevent torture and other cruel, inhuman or degrading treatment or punishment, including their gender-based manifestations;

4. *Stresses* that all allegations of torture or other cruel, inhuman or degrading treatment or punishment must be promptly and impartially examined by the competent national authority, that those who encourage, order, tolerate or perpetrate acts of torture must be held responsible and severely punished, including the officials in charge of the place of detention where the prohibited act is found to have been committed, and takes note in this respect of the Principles on the Effective Investigation and Documentation of Torture and Other Cruel, Inhuman or Degrading Treatment or Punishment (the Istanbul Principles) as a useful tool in efforts to combat torture;

5. *Stresses also* that all acts of torture must be made offences under domestic criminal law, and emphasizes that acts of torture are serious violations of international humanitarian law and can constitute crimes against humanity and war crimes and that the perpetrators of all acts of torture must be prosecuted and punished;

6. *Urges* States to ensure that any statement that is established to have been made as a result of torture shall not be invoked as evidence in any proceedings, except against a person accused of torture as evidence that the statement was made;

7. *Stresses* that States must not punish personnel who are involved in the custody, interrogation or treatment of any individual subjected to any form of arrest, detention or imprisonment for not obeying orders to commit or conceal acts amounting to torture or other cruel, inhuman or degrading treatment or punishment;

8. *Recalls* that States shall not expel, return ("refouler") or extradite a person to another State where there are substantial grounds for believing that the person would be in danger of being subjected to torture;

9. *Stresses* that national legal systems must ensure that victims of torture and other cruel, inhuman or degrading treatment or punishment obtain redress, are awarded fair and adequate compensation and receive appropriate social and medical rehabilitation, urges Governments to take effective measures to this end, and in this regard encourages the development of rehabilitation centres;

10. *Calls upon* all Governments to take appropriate effective legislative, administrative, judicial and other measures to prevent and prohibit the production, trade, export and use of equipment that is specifically designed to inflict torture or other cruel, inhuman or degrading treatment;

11. *Notes with appreciation* that one hundred and thirty-nine States have become parties to the Convention against Torture and Other Cruel, Inhuman or Degrading Treatment or Punishment, and urges all States that have not yet done so to become parties to the Convention as a matter of priority;

12. *Invites* all States parties to the Convention that have not yet done so to consider making the declarations provided for in articles 21 and 22 of the Conven-

tion and to consider the possibility of withdrawing their reservations to article 20, and urges all States parties to notify the Secretary-General of their acceptance of the amendments to articles 17 and 18 of the Convention as soon as possible;

13. *Urges* States parties to comply strictly with their obligations under the Convention, including, in view of the high number of reports not submitted, their obligation to submit reports in accordance with article 19 of the Convention, and invites States parties to incorporate a gender perspective and information concerning children and juveniles when submitting reports to the Committee against Torture;

14. *Calls upon* States parties to give early consideration to signing and ratifying the Optional Protocol to the Convention against Torture and Other Cruel, Inhuman or Degrading Treatment or Punishment, which was adopted on 18 December 2002 by the General Assembly in its resolution 57/199 and which provides further measures for use in the fight against and prevention of torture, and notes in this context that ratifications by twenty States parties are required for the Optional Protocol to enter into force;

15. *Welcomes* the work of the Committee against Torture and the report of the Committee, submitted in accordance with article 24 of the Convention;

16. *Calls upon* the United Nations High Commissioner for Human Rights, in conformity with her mandate established by the General Assembly in its resolution 48/141 of 20 December 1993, to continue to provide, at the request of Governments, advisory services for the preparation of national reports to the Committee and for the prevention of torture, as well as technical assistance in the development, production and distribution of teaching material for this purpose;

17. *Urges* States parties to take fully into account the conclusions and recommendations made by the Committee after its consideration of their reports;

18. *Notes with appreciation* the interim report of the Special Rapporteur of the Commission on Human Rights on torture and other cruel, inhuman or degrading treatment or punishment on the overall trends and developments with regard to his mandate, and encourages the Special Rapporteur to continue to include in his recommendations proposals on the prevention and investigation of torture, including its gender-based manifestations;

19. *Requests* the Special Rapporteur to continue to consider including in his report information on the follow-up by Governments to his recommendations, visits and communications, including progress made and problems encountered;

20. *Calls upon* all Governments to cooperate with and assist the Special Rapporteur in the performance of his task, to supply all necessary information requested by the Special Rapporteur, to respond appropriately and expeditiously to his urgent appeals and to give serious consideration to responding favourably to requests by the Special Rapporteur to visit their countries, and urges them to enter into a constructive dialogue with the Special Rapporteur with respect to the follow-up to his recommendations;

21. *Stresses* the need for the continued regular exchange of views among the Committee, the Special Rapporteur and other relevant United Nations mechanisms and bodies, as well as for the pursuance of co-operation with relevant United Nations programmes, notably the United Nations Crime Prevention and Criminal Justice Programme, with a view to enhancing further their effectiveness and cooperation on issues relating to torture, inter alia, by improving their coordination;

22. *Expresses its gratitude and appreciation* to the Governments, organizations and individuals that have already contributed to the United Nations Voluntary Fund for Victims of Torture;

23. *Stresses* the importance of the work of the Board of Trustees of the Fund, and appeals to all Governments and organizations to contribute annually to the Fund, preferably by 1 March before the annual meeting of the Board, if possible with a substantial increase in the level of contributions;

24. *Requests* the Secretary-General to transmit to all Governments the appeals of the General Assembly for contributions to the Fund, to continue to include the Fund on an annual basis among the programmes for which funds are pledged at the United Nations Pledging Conference for Development Activities and to assist the Board of Trustees of the Fund in its appeal for contributions and in its efforts to make better known the existence of the Fund;

25. *Also requests* the Secretary-General to ensure, within the overall budgetary framework of the United Nations, the provision of adequate staff and facilities for the bodies and mechanisms involved in combating torture and assisting victims of torture, commensurate with the strong support expressed by Member States for combating torture and assisting victims of torture;

26. *Further requests* the Secretary-General to submit to the Commission on Human Rights at its sixty-first session and to the General Assembly at its sixtieth session a report on the status of the Convention and a report on the operations of the Fund;

27. *Calls upon* all Governments, the Office of the United Nations High Commissioner for Human Rights and other United Nations bodies and agencies, as well as relevant intergovernmental and non-governmental organizations, to commemorate, on 26 June, the United Nations International Day in Support of Victims of Torture;

28. *Decides* to consider at its sixtieth session the reports of the Secretary-General, including the report on the United Nations Voluntary Fund for Victims of Torture, the report of the Committee against Torture and the interim report of the Special Rapporteur of the Commission on Human Rights on torture and other cruel, inhuman or degrading treatment or punishment.

Freedom of expression

Reports of Special Rapporteur. In accordance with a 2002 Commission request [YUN 2002, p. 716], the Special Rapporteur on the promotion and protection of the right to freedom of opinion and expression, Ambeyi Ligabo (Kenya), described his 2003 activities [E/CN.4/2004/62]. He had sent allegation letters and urgent appeals to 99 countries, on behalf of numerous individuals whose right to the freedom of opinion and expression was reportedly threatened or violated. The texts of the communications he sent and replies received from Governments were summarized in an addendum [E/CN.4/2004/62/Add.1]. The Special Rapporteur updated information contained in his previous report [YUN 2003, p. 745] relating to access to information, particularly regarding the prevention of HIV/AIDS, and the safeguard of human rights, especially the right to freedom of opinion and expression while adopting and implementing counter-terrorism measures. The Special Rapporteur concluded that, although positive measures had been taken in a number of countries to better protect and promote the right to freedom of opinion and expression, the situation remained grim, as violations continued. Of particular concern were continuing attacks against journalists and media practitioners in many countries, including killings, for which perpetrators were often not punished adequately. Urging Governments to take measures to protect journalists from attacks and to end the impunity of the perpetrators, the Special Rapporteur said an in-depth study on the security of journalists, particularly in situations of armed conflict, was necessary, and he would welcome a request from the Commission to undertake the study. Also, in the legitimate effort to prevent and eliminate terror, the right to information was vulnerable and susceptible to restrictions. Thus, he would consider reporting annually on the subject. The Special Rapporteur, cautioning against the concentration of large media groups in the hands of a few business corporations, advocated a pluralistic approach to information, as well as a survey of the scope of accessible information held by parliaments and the development of initiatives aimed at monitoring the implementation of the right to information. He would welcome the opportunity of gathering information on proposals to enhance the right by the adoption of a global and/or regional binding instrument.

The Special Rapporteur visited Côte d'Ivoire (28 January–5 February) [E/CN.4/2004/62/Add.3, E/CN.4/2005/64/Add.2] at the invitation of the Government, where he determined that the main obstacle to the right to freedom of opinion and expression was the conflict that had plagued the country since 2002 (see p. 170). Human rights violations, including violence against women, children and migrants, had reached an intolerable level, as had attacks and death threats against journalists and media offices, which hampered the circulation of publications and impeded the exercise of the right to freedom of opinion and expression. Highlighting the negative role played by the media in the conflict, the Special Rapporteur noted that, owing to the lack of regulatory mechanisms entailing obligations, responsibility

and discipline among newspaper publishers and editors, journalists tended to write without following their professional ethics. With little or no professional training, they remained vulnerable to the pressure of political power. The Special Rapporteur recommended that the Government accord priority to the fight against impunity and abide by the decisions in the Linas-Marcoussis Agreement [YUN 2003, p. 166], particularly with regard to the disarmament process and national reconciliation and reconstruction, as well as the establishment of national human rights mechanisms. As decided in the Agreement, article 35 of the Constitution should be reformulated in order to guarantee the right to freedom of expression and the right to vote in a pluralistic environment. The Government should join efforts with civil society to reactivate and reinforce existing media institutions and professional associations, which had been overwhelmed by the political conflict.

In Colombia (22-29 February) [E/CN.4/2005/ 64/Add.3], the Special Rapporteur found that the 40-year civil war between the Government and rebel groups had created a highly violent environment that undermined freedom of opinion and expression. The most common targets included human rights defenders, trade union leaders, church dignitaries and media representatives, as well as women, children, indigenous people and all those who, in the exercise of their right to freedom of opinion and expression, were perceived to be against one of the parties to the conflict. Infringement of the right had been encouraged by such government strategies as the "democratic security" policy, under which government forces arrested and detained persons accused of terrorism or criticisms and remarks interpreted as an attack on the State, and by related anti-terrorism legislation. Other factors included the existence of paramilitary groups who impinged on people's lives and rights, the stigmatization of persons and the concentration of the media in the hands of a few owners. The Special Rapporteur recommended that the Government and all parties to the conflict restart the process of national reconciliation and reconstruction; prepare and implement a national plan on human rights; and ensure the protection of journalists, trade unionists, human rights defenders and teachers. All ethnic groups should be granted access to comprehensive and impartial information and the opportunity of expressing themselves freely.

During his visit to Serbia and Montenegro (10-20 October) [E/CN.4/2005/64/Add.4], the Special Rapporteur found that, in the aftermath of past conflicts, the polarization of opinions, stigmatization of ethnic groups and the use of hate speech had continued to aggravate instability and to undermine the development of freedom of opinion and expression. The situation was particularly difficult in the province of Kosovo, where, despite the work of the United Nations Interim Administration Mission in Kosovo (see p. 404), much remained to be done to achieve sustainable peaceful coexistence and tolerance among all the ethnic groups and to create an environment where freedom of opinion and expression could be fully exercised. The media, in particular, faced numerous difficulties relating to hostile and restrictive legislation, among other things. The Special Rapporteur recommended a series of measures, including the establishment of a mechanism to monitor regularly the status of minorities' freedom of opinion and expression and a consistent strategy against the dissemination of hatred and hate speech.

The Special Rapporteur visited Italy (20-29 October) [E/CN.4/2005/64/Add.5], where he found that the concentration of media control in the hands of government officials, and the related issue of conflict of interest, constituted the most worrisome challenge to the full enjoyment of the right to freedom of opinion and expression. The problem was illustrated by several incidents in which media professionals were dismissed or relieved of their jobs for criticizing the Government. Also of concern were the situation of migrants and children, and potential problems relating to the role of ombudspersons in monitoring abuses and deficiencies in provincial and municipal public administrations. The Special Rapporteur, noting the need for the Government to review its policy and facilitate professionalism and independence of the media, recommended that it take measures to ensure the full enjoyment of the right to freedom of opinion and expression and work closely with civil society in that regard. There was a need for the Government to ensure the participation of multiple actors in television broadcasting, depoliticize the media sector, address the issue of conflict of interest, particularly concerning the President of the Council of Ministers, facilitate migrants' access to information and establish a national institution for human rights protection.

Commission action. On 19 April [res. 2004/42], the Commission called on States to ensure respect for the right to freedom of opinion and expression; end violations of the right and create conditions to prevent such violation; ensure that victims of violations had an effective remedy and that persons exercising the right were not discriminated against, particularly in employment, housing, the justice system, social services and education; respect freedom of expression in the

media; encourage a diverse ownership of media and information sources; create an enabling environment for the training and professional development of the media; and refrain from the use of imprisonment or imposition of fines for offences relating to the media and from using counter-terrorism as a pretext to restrict the right to freedom of opinion and expression. The Commission stressed the importance of the active participation of the Special Rapporteur and the High Commissioner in the second phase of the World Summit on the Information Society, scheduled for 2005 (see p. 845), in order to provide information and expertise on matters relating to the right to freedom of opinion and expression. The Special Rapporteur was asked to report in 2005, and the Secretary-General was asked to assist him.

Conscientious objection

Report of High Commissioner. A February report of the High Commissioner [E/CN.4/ 2004/55], submitted in response to a 2002 Commission request [YUN 2002, p. 716], summarized information regarding conscientious objection to military service received from 22 Governments, 10 national human rights institutions, one intergovernmental organization and six NGOs. The report identified trends in national laws regulating conscientious objection and described the development of the right and the jurisprudence of various international human rights bodies. The High Commissioner said that the report indicated that the right to conscientious objection to military service was grounded in existing human rights norms guaranteeing the right to freedom of conscience and religion, and there were indications that an increasing number of Member States were continuing to develop or improve provisions for the right.

Commission action. On 19 April [res. 2004/35], the Commission called on States to review their laws and practices relating to conscientious objection to military service and asked OHCHR to prepare an analytical report providing supplementary information on best practices regarding the right, for consideration in 2006.

Terrorism

Reports of Secretary-General. In response to a 2003 Commission request [YUN 2003, p. 746], the Secretary-General, in a January report [E/CN.4/ 2004/50], presented replies received from two Governments in response to an OHCHR questionnaire seeking the views of Member States on the implications of terrorism in all its forms and manifestations for the full enjoyment of human rights and fundamental freedoms, the possible establishment of a voluntary fund for victims of terrorism and ways to rehabilitate them.

Also in response to a 2003 Commission request [YUN 2003, p. 746], the Secretary-General, in a March report [E/CN.4/2004/91], summarized comments received from four Governments on the protection of human rights and fundamental freedoms while countering terrorism, as well as action taken in that regard by the Security Council and its Counter-Terrorism Committee, UN human rights special procedures, treaty bodies and OHCHR. The report reviewed the OHCHR publication *Digest of Jurisprudence of the United Nations and Regional Organizations on the Protection of Human Rights while Countering Terrorism*, which compiled relevant excerpts from the jurisprudence of UN human rights bodies and others in Europe, Africa and the Americas. In accordance with General Assembly resolution 58/187 [YUN 2003, p. 748], requesting the High Commissioner to submit a study on the extent to which human rights special procedures and treaty-monitoring bodies were able to address the compatibility of national counter-terrorism measures with international human rights obligations (see p. 740), the report summarized the replies of five Governments, in response to an OHCHR communication seeking Member States' views on the subject. The Secretary-General concluded that international concern remained high over the continuing menace of terrorism and the importance of protecting human rights while countering it. Although international law and Security Council resolutions had set out Governments' obligations in countering terrorism, international cooperation, involving regional organizations, was essential, and OHCHR had initiated important cooperation with key partners. Regarding possibilities for future action by the Commission, two options could be considered: the designation of an independent expert to gather and analyse information and provide recommendations or the appointment of a special rapporteur or representative to examine the question.

Commission action. By a recorded vote of 31 to 14, with 8 abstentions, the Commission, on 19 April [res. 2004/44], urged States to enhance cooperation in the fight against terrorism and asked human rights mechanisms and procedures to address the consequences of the acts, methods and practices of terrorist groups in their reports. The Secretary-General was asked to assist the Special Rapporteur to consult with competent UN system bodies in finalizing her report. OHCHR was asked to respond to requests from interested Governments for assistance and advice regarding compliance with international human rights standards when undertaking measures to

combat terrorism, and to circulate in all official UN languages the Special Rapporteur's reports on terrorism and human rights.

On 21 April [res. 2004/87], the Commission asked the High Commissioner to examine the question of the protection of human rights and fundamental freedoms while countering terrorism, to make general recommendations to States and provide them with assistance and advice upon their request, to complete the study requested in General Assembly resolution 58/187 [YUN 2003, p. 748] and to report to the Assembly in 2004 and to the Commission in 2005. The Commission decided to designate for a one-year period an independent expert to assist the High Commissioner and to report in 2005 on ways of strengthening the promotion and protection of human rights and fundamental freedoms while countering terrorism.

On 15 June, the Economic and Social Council endorsed the Commission's decision to designate an independent expert and its request to the expert to report in 2005 (**decision 2004/227**).

In July, Robert Goldman (United States) was appointed independent expert.

Reports of Special Rapporteur. In response to a 2003 Subcommission request [YUN 2003, p. 746], the Special Rapporteur on terrorism and human rights, Kalliopi K. Koufa (Greece), submitted a June final report [E/CN.4/Sub.2/2004/40], which built on a 1999 preliminary report [YUN 1999, p. 642] and 2001 [YUN 2001, p. 648], 2002 [YUN 2002, p. 717] and 2003 [YUN 2003, p. 746] progress reports. The final report discussed previously identified issues that needed further consideration and clarification, notably, the problem of a clear and precise definition of terrorism, and related human rights and humanitarian law concerns. Also addressed were issues that had not been developed, such as accountability for acts of terrorism, focusing on the questions of State-sponsored terrorism (State actors) and the applicability of human rights norms to non-State terrorist operatives. The Special Rapporteur concluded that, owing to the complexity of the issue of terrorism and human rights, there was a need to draw on disciplines other than international law to better understand the phenomenon and to design responses to it. As the most important issues to address in that regard, said the Special Rapporteur, were an examination of the many root causes of terrorism and a review of strategies for reducing or preventing it, she recommended that the Subcommission undertake a study of those questions. In her conclusions and recommendations, she addressed issues relating to extradition, impunity, the periodic review of national counter-terrorism measures, undue fear of terrorism, the distinction between armed conflict and terrorism, and between terrorism and other criminal activities, bringing perpetrators of terrorist acts to justice, the work of the Counter-Terrorism Committee, and international guidelines for counter-terrorism measures. The Special Rapporteur recommended that the Subcommission consider requesting her to draw up a comprehensive document based on her work.

An August working paper of the Special Rapporteur [E/CN.4/Sub.2/2004/47] contained a preliminary framework draft of principles and guidelines concerning human rights and terrorism, in accordance with a 2003 Subcommission resolution [YUN 2003, p. 747].

Note by Secretariat. By a July note [E/CN.4/Sub.2/2004/39], the Secretariat stated that the final report of the Special Rapporteur (see above) had exceeded the maximum page limit allowed for such reports, as did her 2003 progress report. Owing to the fact that a waiver was granted for the final report, but not for the progress report, it was not possible to proceed with the translation of both into all UN official languages, as requested in Commission resolution 2004/44 (see above). Consequently, only the final report was being issued in all official languages as a document.

Subcommission action. On 12 August [res. 2004/21], the Subcommission asked OHCHR to transmit and ensure the distribution of the Special Rapporteur's final report (see above) to the Commission in 2005. The Secretary-General was asked to ensure that the final report and all previous reports and documents submitted by the Special Rapporteur could be accessed by those seeking information on the activities of the Economic and Social Council on the website "UN action against terrorism". The Special Rapporteur was asked to compile all her reports in one study, reflecting important points, aspects and recommendations contained therein. The Subcommission recommended that the Commission recommend to the Council that a compilation into a comprehensive document of all reports and documents submitted by the Special Rapporteur be published as a UN publication as part of the human rights study series.

On the same date [dec. 2004/109], the Subcommission decided to establish in 2005 a sessional working group with the mandate to develop detailed principles and guidelines, with relevant commentary, regarding human rights promotion and protection when combating terrorism, based on, among other things, the preliminary framework draft of principles and guidelines contained in the working paper prepared by the Special Rapporteur (see above).

Report of Secretary-General. Pursuant to General Assembly resolution 58/187 [YUN 2003, p. 748], the Secretary-General, in October [A/59/404], provided an overview of UN action to implement the resolution. The report described activities to counter terrorism undertaken by the Security Council's Counter-Terrorism Committee, OHCHR, special procedures and treaty bodies. The Secretary-General said that UN human rights mechanisms, treaty bodies and the High Commissioner had further clarified the international human rights foundation on which counter-terrorism action must be based, including full respect for the principles of necessity and proportionality, for the non-derogability of certain rights even in time of national emergency, and for the role of the courts and national human rights institutions in ensuring the compatibility of counter-terrorism measures with national and international human rights obligations. He hoped that the Commission's appointment of an independent expert (see above) to assist the High Commissioner in addressing the issue would lead to a more integrated and coherent understanding of it.

Report of High Commissioner. Pursuant to General Assembly resolution 58/187 and Commission resolution 2004/87 (see p. 739), the High Commissioner submitted an October report [A/59/428] containing the completed study on the extent to which human rights special procedures and treaty monitoring bodies were able, within their existing mandates, to address the compatibility of national counter-terrorism measures with international human rights obligations. The report presented the views of 13 States on the issue, which, together with earlier views summarized in the Secretary-General's interim report (see p. 738), indicated that States strongly condemned terrorist acts but also agreed that counter-terrorism measures should respect human rights. New proposals put forward included the idea of a code for the protection of human rights against terrorism. However, varying views were expressed on the question of the extent to which special procedures and treaty monitoring bodies were able to address the subject. Some States were open to considering new ways of dealing with the matter, while others considered that the existing mechanisms were adequate for the task and the establishment of a new mechanism could lead to duplication. The report described national counter-terrorism measures and the related activities of the Commission's special procedures and of the Subcommission and treaty monitoring bodies, as well as the work of the Counter-Terrorism Committee. The High Commissioner concluded that, owing to the wide range of rights under pressure from counter-terrorism measures, the analysis provided by special procedures was fragmented rather than being a coherent and integrated treatment of the compatibility of those measures with international human rights obligations. Also, the capacity of treaty monitoring bodies to address the issue was limited by several factors, including the fact that many States had not ratified the treaties most directly relevant to counter-terrorism, and that the treaty bodies, in the course of a year, were often able to address only a fraction of national counter-terrorism measures taken worldwide. Thus, there were significant gaps in the consideration of national counter-terrorism measures by the UN human rights system. Effective measures might require steps that affected mandates, processes and resources.

GENERAL ASSEMBLY ACTION

On 20 December [meeting 74], the General Assembly, on the recommendation of the Third Committee [A/59/503/Add.2], adopted **resolution 59/191** without vote [agenda item 105 (*b*)].

Protection of human rights and fundamental freedoms while countering terrorism

The General Assembly,

Reaffirming the purposes and principles of the Charter of the United Nations,

Reaffirming also the fundamental importance, including in response to terrorism and the fear of terrorism, of respecting all human rights and fundamental freedoms and the rule of law,

Recalling that States are under the obligation to protect all human rights and fundamental freedoms of all persons, and deploring violations of human rights and fundamental freedoms in the context of the fight against terrorism,

Recognizing that the respect for human rights, the respect for democracy and the respect for the rule of law are interrelated and mutually reinforcing,

Noting the declarations, statements and recommendations of a number of human rights treaty monitoring bodies and special procedures on the question of the compatibility of counter-terrorism measures with human rights obligations,

Recalling its resolutions 57/219 of 18 December 2002 and 58/187 of 22 December 2003 as well as Commission on Human Rights resolutions 2003/68 of 25 April 2003 and 2004/87 of 21 April 2004 and other relevant resolutions of the General Assembly and the Commission on Human Rights,

Recalling also its resolution 48/141 of 20 December 1993 and, inter alia, the responsibility of the United Nations High Commissioner for Human Rights to promote and protect the effective enjoyment of all human rights,

Reaffirming that acts, methods and practices of terrorism in all its forms and manifestations are activities aimed at the destruction of human rights, fundamental freedoms and democracy, threatening the territorial integrity and the security of States and destabilizing legitimately constituted Governments, and that the international community should take the necessary steps to enhance cooperation to prevent and combat terrorism,

Noting the declaration on the issue of combating terrorism contained in the annex to Security Council resolution 1456(2003) of 20 January 2003, in particular the statement that States must ensure that any measures taken to combat terrorism comply with all their obligations under international law and should adopt such measures in accordance with international law, in particular international human rights, refugee and humanitarian law,

Reaffirming its unequivocal condemnation of all acts, methods and practices of terrorism in all its forms and manifestations, wherever and by whomsoever committed, regardless of their motivation, as criminal and unjustifiable, and renewing its commitment to strengthen international cooperation to prevent and combat terrorism,

Deploring the suffering caused by terrorism to the victims and their families, and expressing its profound solidarity with them,

Stressing that everyone is entitled to all the rights and freedoms recognized in the Universal Declaration of Human Rights without distinction of any kind, including on the grounds of race, colour, sex, language, religion, political or other opinion, national or social origin, property, birth or other status,

1. *Reaffirms* that States must ensure that any measure taken to combat terrorism complies with their obligations under international law, in particular international human rights, refugee and humanitarian law;

2. *Also reaffirms* the obligation of States, in accordance with article 4 of the International Covenant on Civil and Political Rights, to respect certain rights as non-derogable in any circumstances, recalls, in regard to all other Covenant rights, that any measures derogating from the provisions of the Covenant must be in accordance with that article in all cases, and underlines the exceptional and temporary nature of any such derogations;

3. *Calls upon* States to raise awareness about the importance of these obligations among national authorities involved in combating terrorism;

4. *Welcomes* the report of the Secretary-General submitted pursuant to resolution 58/187, in which it is stated that it is imperative that all States work to uphold and protect the dignity of individuals and their fundamental freedoms, as well as democratic practices and the rule of law, while countering terrorism;

5. *Takes note with appreciation* of the study of the United Nations High Commissioner for Human Rights submitted pursuant to resolution 58/187;

6. *Encourages* States to make available to relevant national authorities the "Digest of Jurisprudence of the United Nations and Regional Organizations on the Protection of Human Rights while Countering Terrorism" and to take into account its content, and requests the High Commissioner to update and publish it periodically;

7. *Welcomes* the ongoing dialogue established in the context of the fight against terrorism between the Security Council and its Counter-Terrorism Committee and the relevant bodies for the promotion and protection of human rights, and encourages the Security

Council and its Counter-Terrorism Committee to strengthen the links and to continue to develop cooperation with relevant human rights bodies, in particular with the Office of the United Nations High Commissioner for Human Rights, giving due regard to the promotion and protection of human rights in the ongoing work pursuant to relevant Security Council resolutions relating to terrorism;

8. *Requests* all relevant special procedures and mechanisms of the Commission on Human Rights, as well as the United Nations human rights treaty bodies, to consider, within their mandates, the protection of human rights and fundamental freedoms in the context of measures to combat terrorism, and encourages them to coordinate their efforts where appropriate, in order to promote a consistent approach on this subject;

9. *Encourages* States, while countering terrorism, to take into account relevant United Nations resolutions and decisions on human rights, and encourages them to consider the recommendations of the special procedures and mechanisms of the Commission on Human Rights and the relevant comments and views of United Nations human rights treaty bodies;

10. *Notes with appreciation* the appointment of an independent expert on the protection of human rights and fundamental freedoms while countering terrorism pursuant to Commission on Human Rights resolution 2004/87, and encourages States to cooperate fully with him;

11. *Requests* the High Commissioner, making use of existing mechanisms, to continue:

(a) To examine the question of the protection of human rights and fundamental freedoms while countering terrorism, taking into account reliable information from all sources;

(b) To make general recommendations concerning the obligation of States to promote and protect human rights and fundamental freedoms while taking actions to counter terrorism;

(c) To provide assistance and advice to States, upon their request, on the protection of human rights and fundamental freedoms while countering terrorism, as well as to relevant United Nations bodies;

12. *Requests* the independent expert to take into account the debate held during the fifty-ninth regular session of the General Assembly in finalizing the report mandated by the Commission on Human Rights in its resolution 2004/87, to be presented through the High Commissioner to the Commission on Human Rights at its sixty-first session;

13. *Requests* the Secretary-General to submit a report on the implementation of the present resolution to the Commission on Human Rights at its sixty-first session and to the General Assembly at its sixtieth session.

Also on 20 December [meeting 74], the General Assembly, on the recommendation of the Third Committee [A/59/503/Add.2], adopted **resolution 59/195** by recorded vote (127-50-8) [agenda item 105 (b)].

Human rights and terrorism

The General Assembly,

Guided by the Charter of the United Nations, the Universal Declaration of Human Rights, the Declaration on Principles of International Law concerning Friendly Relations and Cooperation among States in accordance with the Charter of the United Nations and the International Covenants on Human Rights,

Recalling the Declaration on the Occasion of the Fiftieth Anniversary of the United Nations, as well as the Declaration on Measures to Eliminate International Terrorism,

Recalling also the Vienna Declaration and Programme of Action adopted by the World Conference on Human Rights on 25 June 1993, in which the Conference reaffirmed that the acts, methods and practices of terrorism in all its forms and manifestations, as well as its linkage in some countries to drug trafficking, are activities aimed at the destruction of human rights, fundamental freedoms and democracy, threatening the territorial integrity and the security of States and destabilizing legitimately constituted Governments, and that the international community should take the necessary steps to enhance cooperation to prevent and combat terrorism,

Recalling further the United Nations Millennium Declaration adopted by the General Assembly,

Recalling, in this regard, the reference in the report of the Secretary-General on the implementation of the Millennium Declaration to the fact that terrorism itself is a violation of human rights and must be combated as such and that efforts at combating it must be pursued, however, in full compliance with established international norms,

Recalling also its resolutions 48/122 of 20 December 1993, 49/185 of 23 December 1994, 50/186 of 22 December 1995, 52/133 of 12 December 1997, 54/109 and 54/110 of 9 December 1999, 54/164 of 17 December 1999, 55/158 of 12 December 2000, 56/160 of 19 December 2001, 57/219 and 57/220 of 18 December 2002 and 58/174 of 22 December 2003,

Recalling in particular that, in its resolution 52/133, it requested the Secretary-General to seek the views of Member States on the implications of terrorism in all its forms and manifestations for the full enjoyment of human rights and fundamental freedoms,

Recalling previous resolutions of the Commission on Human Rights on the issue of human rights and terrorism, as well as on hostage-taking,

Bearing in mind all other relevant General Assembly resolutions,

Bearing in mind also relevant Security Council resolutions,

Aware that, at the dawn of the twenty-first century, the world is witness to historic and far-reaching transformations, in the course of which forces of aggressive nationalism and religious and ethnic extremism continue to produce fresh challenges,

Alarmed that acts of terrorism in all its forms and manifestations aimed at the destruction of human rights have continued despite national and international efforts,

Convinced that terrorism in all its forms and manifestations, wherever and by whomever committed, can never be justified in any instance, including as a means to promote and protect human rights,

Concerned that, despite the efforts of the international community, acts of hostage-taking in different forms and manifestations, inter alia, committed by terrorists and armed groups, continue to take place and have even increased in many regions of the world,

Bearing in mind that the right to life is the basic human right, without which a human being can exercise no other right,

Bearing in mind also that terrorism creates an environment that destroys the right of people to live in freedom from fear,

Reiterating that all States have an obligation to promote and protect all human rights and fundamental freedoms and to ensure effective implementation of their obligations under international law,

Seriously concerned about the gross violations of human rights perpetrated by terrorist groups,

Expressing its deepest sympathy and condolences to all the victims of terrorism and their families,

Alarmed in particular at the possibility that terrorist groups may exploit new technologies to facilitate acts of terrorism, which may cause massive damage, including huge loss of human life,

Emphasizing the need to intensify the fight against terrorism at the national level, to enhance effective international cooperation in combating terrorism in conformity with international law, including relevant State obligations under international human rights and international humanitarian law, and to strengthen the role of the United Nations in this respect,

Emphasizing also that States shall deny safe haven to those who finance, plan, support or commit terrorist acts or provide safe havens,

Reaffirming that all measures to counter terrorism must be in strict conformity with international law, including international human rights standards and obligations,

Mindful of the need to protect the human rights of and guarantees for the individual in accordance with the relevant human rights principles and instruments, in particular the right to life,

Noting the growing consciousness within the international community of the negative effects of terrorism in all its forms and manifestations on the full enjoyment of human rights and fundamental freedoms and on the establishment of the rule of law and democratic freedoms as enshrined in the Charter of the United Nations and the International Covenants on Human Rights,

Concerned by the tendencies to link terrorism and violence with religion,

Noting the developments that have occurred since its fifty-eighth session on addressing the issue of human rights and terrorism at the national, regional and international levels,

1. *Reiterates its unequivocal condemnation* of the acts, methods and practices of terrorism in all its forms and manifestations as activities aimed at the destruction of human rights, fundamental freedoms and democracy, threatening the territorial integrity and the security of States, destabilizing legitimately constituted Governments, undermining pluralistic civil society and having adverse consequences for the economic and social development of States;

2. *Strongly condemns* the violations of the right to life, liberty and security;

3. *Rejects* the identification of terrorism with any religion, nationality or culture;

4. *Profoundly deplores* the increasing number of innocent persons, including women, children and the elderly, killed, massacred and maimed by terrorists in indiscriminate and random acts of violence and terror, which cannot be justified in any circumstances;

5. *Expresses its solidarity* with the victims of terrorism;

6. *Reaffirms* the decision of the Heads of State and Government, as contained in the United Nations Millennium Declaration, to take concerted action against international terrorism and to accede as soon as possible to all the relevant regional and international conventions;

7. *Urges* the international community to enhance cooperation at the regional and international levels in the fight against terrorism in all its forms and manifestations, in accordance with relevant international instruments, including those relating to human rights, with the aim of its eradication;

8. *Calls upon* States to take all necessary and effective measures, in accordance with relevant provisions of international law, including international human rights standards, to prevent, combat and eliminate terrorism in all its forms and manifestations, wherever and by whomever it is committed, and also calls upon States to strengthen, where appropriate, their legislation to combat terrorism in all its forms and manifestations;

9. *Urges* all States to deny safe haven to terrorists;

10. *Calls upon* States to take appropriate measures, in conformity with relevant provisions of national and international law, including international human rights standards, before granting refugee status, for the purpose of ensuring that an asylum-seeker has not planned, facilitated or participated in the commission of terrorist acts, including assassinations, and to ensure, in conformity with international law, that refugee status is not abused by the perpetrators, organizers or facilitators of terrorist acts and that claims of political motivation are not recognized as grounds for refusing requests for the extradition of alleged terrorists;

11. *Urges* States and the Office of the United Nations High Commissioner for Refugees to review, with full respect for legal safeguards, the validity of a refugee status decision in an individual case if credible and relevant evidence comes to light which indicates that the person in question has planned, facilitated or participated in the commission of terrorist acts;

12. *Condemns* the incitement to ethnic hatred, violence and terrorism;

13. *Stresses* that every person, regardless of nationality, race, sex, religion or any other distinction, has a right to protection from terrorism and terrorist acts;

14. *Expresses concern* about the growing connection between terrorist groups and other criminal organizations engaged in the illegal traffic in arms and drugs at the national and international levels, as well as the consequent commission of serious crimes such as murder, extortion, kidnapping, assault, the taking of hostages and robbery, and requests the relevant United Nations bodies to continue to give special attention to this question;

15. *Requests* the Secretary-General to continue to seek the views of Member States on the implications of terrorism in all its forms and manifestations for the full enjoyment of all human rights and fundamental freedoms and on the possible establishment of a voluntary fund for the victims of terrorism, as well as on ways and means to rehabilitate the victims of terrorism

and to reintegrate them into society, with a view to incorporating his findings in his report to the General Assembly;

16. *Takes note* of the work of the Subcommission on the Promotion and Protection of Human Rights on the issue of terrorism and the final report of the Special Rapporteur of the Subcommission on terrorism and human rights;

17. *Requests* the Office of the United Nations High Commissioner for Human Rights, in the course of the examination of the question and in the conduct of any study on terrorism that may be mandated, and in its activities relating to the issue of terrorism, to adopt a comprehensive approach, in particular by giving full and equal attention to the issues raised in the present resolution with relation to the grave impact of terrorism on the enjoyment of the human rights of individuals;

18. *Decides* to consider the question at its sixtieth session under the item entitled "Human rights questions".

RECORDED VOTE ON RESOLUTION 59/195:

In favour: Algeria, Angola, Antigua and Barbuda, Azerbaijan, Bahamas, Bahrain, Bangladesh, Barbados, Belarus, Belize, Benin, Bhutan, Bolivia, Botswana, Brunei Darussalam, Burkina Faso, Burundi, Cambodia, Cameroon, Cape Verde, Central African Republic, Chad, China, Colombia, Comoros, Costa Rica, Côte d'Ivoire, Cuba, Democratic People's Republic of Korea, Democratic Republic of the Congo, Djibouti, Dominica, Dominican Republic, Ecuador, Egypt, El Salvador, Equatorial Guinea, Eritrea, Ethiopia, Gabon, Gambia, Ghana, Grenada, Guatemala, Guinea, Guinea-Bissau, Guyana, Haiti, Honduras, India, Indonesia, Iran, Iraq, Jamaica, Jordan, Kazakhstan, Kenya, Kuwait, Kyrgyzstan, Lao People's Democratic Republic, Lebanon, Lesotho, Liberia, Libyan Arab Jamahiriya, Madagascar, Malaysia, Maldives, Mali, Mauritania, Mauritius, Mexico, Mongolia, Morocco, Mozambique, Myanmar, Namibia, Nepal, Nicaragua, Niger, Nigeria, Oman, Pakistan, Panama, Papua New Guinea, Paraguay, Peru, Philippines, Qatar, Russian Federation, Rwanda, Saint Lucia, Saint Vincent and the Grenadines, Samoa, Sao Tome and Principe, Saudi Arabia, Senegal, Seychelles, Sierra Leone, Singapore, Somalia, South Africa, Sri Lanka, Sudan, Suriname, Swaziland, Tajikistan, Thailand, Timor-Leste, Togo, Tonga, Trinidad and Tobago, Tunisia, Turkey, Turkmenistan, Tuvalu, Uganda, Ukraine, United Arab Emirates, United Republic of Tanzania, Uruguay, Uzbekistan, Vanuatu, Venezuela, Viet Nam, Yemen, Zambia, Zimbabwe.

Against: Albania, Andorra, Australia, Austria, Belgium, Bosnia and Herzegovina, Bulgaria, Canada, Croatia, Cyprus, Czech Republic, Denmark, Estonia, Finland, France, Georgia, Germany, Greece, Hungary, Iceland, Ireland, Israel, Italy, Japan, Latvia, Liechtenstein, Lithuania, Luxembourg, Malta, Marshall Islands, Micronesia, Monaco, Netherlands, New Zealand, Norway, Palau, Poland, Portugal, Republic of Korea, Romania, San Marino, Serbia and Montenegro, Slovakia, Slovenia, Spain, Sweden, Switzerland, The former Yugoslav Republic of Macedonia, United Kingdom, United States.

Abstaining: Argentina, Armenia, Brazil, Chile, Fiji, Malawi, Nauru, Syrian Arab Republic.

Peace and security

By a recorded vote of 32 to 15, with 6 abstentions, the Commission, on 21 April [res. 2004/65], affirming that States should promote international peace and security, urged them to respect and put into practice the principles and purposes of the UN Charter in their relations with other States.

Small arms

Commission action. By a recorded vote of 49 to 2, with 2 abstentions, the Commission, on 21 April [dec. 2004/124], approved the Subcommission's 2003 request [YUN 2003, p. 752] to the Secretary-General to transmit a questionnaire drawn up by the Special Rapporteur on the pre-

vention of human rights violations committed with small arms and light weapons (see below) to Governments, national human rights institutions and NGOs to solicit information in connection with her study.

Report of Special Rapporteur. In response to a 2002 Subcommission request [YUN 2002, p. 720] and to a 2003 Commission decision [YUN 2003, p. 752], the Special Rapporteur on the prevention of human rights violations committed with small arms and light weapons, Barbara Frey (United States), submitted a June progress report [E/CN.4/Sub.2/2004/37], which addressed the humanitarian consequences of small arms in situations of armed conflict, international law protections regarding the availability, misuse and transfer of those weapons, and the gender implications of small arms availability and use. The Special Rapporteur concluded that the international community had not taken the necessary steps to keep small arms out of the hands of those who used them to violate human rights and international humanitarian law. As such, the human rights community, including the Subcommission, should call for human security and human rights to be at the centre of international action regarding small arms. It was critical for States to provide training to their armed forces on basic principles of international human rights and humanitarian law, particularly with regard to the use of small arms. The international community needed to strengthen the design and enforcement of arms embargoes, and States should enforce criminal sanctions against violators of those embargoes. Those who knowingly supplied small arms used to commit genocide, war crimes and crimes against humanity should be investigated and prosecuted, and women should be involved in policy-making regarding the availability and use of the weapons.

An addendum to the report [E/CN.4/Sub.2/2004/37/Add.1] presented draft principles on the prevention of human rights violations committed with small arms and commentary thereto.

Subcommission action. On 13 August [dec. 2004/123], the Subcommission asked the Special Rapporteur to report in 2005.

Economic, social and cultural rights

Right to development

Reports of Secretary-General. The Commission had before it a report of the Secretary-General [E/CN.4/2004/38], submitted in accordance with a 2003 Commission request [YUN 2003,

p. 670], describing activities undertaken by the Committee on Economic, Social and Cultural Rights (see p. 663), the Committee on the Rights of the Child (see p. 667), the Commission's special procedures and OHCHR, which contributed to the realization of economic, social and cultural rights. The Secretary-General concluded that progress continued to increase understanding of those rights, marked by higher levels of cooperation among UN agencies and a greater focus on the rights in technical cooperation and in the follow-up to the World Conference against Racism, Racial Discrimination, Xenophobia and Related Intolerance [YUN 2001, p. 615].

An August report of the Secretary-General [A/59/255] updated and complemented information contained in the High Commissioner's report (see below). OHCHR had organized, in February, a high-level seminar on global partnership for development (see p. 746). The Office was providing support to the Working Group on the Right to Development to establish a high-level task force for a one-year period to help the Group fulfil its mandate.

On 20 December, the Assembly took note of the Secretary-General's report (**decision 59/528**).

Report of High Commissioner. In response to a 1998 Commission request [YUN 1998, p. 683], the High Commissioner submitted a January report [E/CN.4/2004/22], which summarized the activities undertaken by OHCHR to implement the right to development and provided information on the implementation of related General Assembly and Commission resolutions, as well as inter-agency cooperation within the UN system to implement Commission resolutions.

In response to General Assembly resolution 58/172 [YUN 2003, p. 754], the Secretary-General, in a January note of the Secretariat [E/CN.4/2004/116], drew attention to the High Commissioner's report.

Reports of independent expert. In response to a 2003 Commission request [YUN 2003, p. 753], the independent expert on the right to development, Arjun Sengupta (India), submitted his sixth report [E/CN.4/2004/WG.18/2] in February to the Working Group on the Right to Development, which considered the impact of international economic and financial issues on the enjoyment of the right. Building on his 2003 preliminary study on the topic [YUN 2003, p. 752], the expert outlined the characteristics of the current phase of globalization and discussed how it had impacted on the desired development outcomes and the methods of realizing them. Related issues discussed in that context were growth performance and prospects, poverty incidence and distributional inequalities, technology trans-

fer and intellectual property rights, capital mobility and financial instability, globalization and the implications for policy-making, the loss of policy autonomy, the constraints of institutional capacity, the speed of adjustment and the need for coordinated policies. The expert observed that globalization had not always resulted in increased economic growth for developing countries, and where it had, it had not always been associated with increased equity and social justice, nor with reduced poverty. Thus, there was a need to regulate and guide the market to make the production of goods and services correspond to the desired outcomes consistent with the realization of the right to development. States needed to adopt appropriate policies that harnessed the opportunity provided by the global economy, and a development policy framework that would enable them to realize all human rights and fundamental freedoms progressively and sustainably. The expert outlined policy measures and steps at the national and international levels that could help in managing the process of globalization, with a view to realizing human rights, including the right to development. In that context, he revisited his proposal of a development compact [YUN 2001, p. 657] as a possible means of implementing a country-level right to development programme.

The independent expert visited Argentina, Brazil and Chile [E/CN.4/2004/WG.18/3] to assess progress in implementing the right to development. He focused on identifying and evaluating constraints and elements conducive to realizing the right, and on assessing the role of development cooperation in complementing national development initiatives. In that connection, he studied the interplay of national and international economic and financial developments affecting the development process, the institutional framework for planning and policy formulation, and mechanisms for implementing and monitoring development outcomes consistent with the realization of human rights. The expert found that the three South American economies, although they had common developmental concerns and a similar policy approach, experienced different outcomes from the liberal model of economic reform. Each of them had something to offer in terms of a human rights perspective on development: the success of the social safety net in Argentina, the rights-based approach to social protection in Brazil and the long-term perspective on the social development strategy and its anchoring in a sound macroeconomic balance and fiscal prudence in Chile. Yet, none of them offered complete working models for implementing the right to development.

Seminar. In response to a 2003 Commission request [YUN 2003, p. 753], OHCHR organized a high-level seminar on global partnerships for development (Geneva, 9-10 February) [E/CN.4/2004/23/Add.1], which addressed the contribution of UN agencies and programmes to the right to development, country experience in operationalizing the right, partnership for development, international trade and development, and national perspectives on the right. The seminar adopted points for consideration by the Working Group on the Right to Development (see below), which emphasized, among other things, the need to focus deliberations relating to the right on operational steps more than on general debate, building and strengthening effective partnerships, ensuring that free trade was fair trade and improving the well-being of the vulnerable, the marginalized, minorities, the disadvantaged, women and children.

Working Group activities. The open-ended Working Group on the Right to Development, at its fifth session (Geneva, 11-20 February) [E/CN.4/2004/23 & Corr.1], considered the High Commissioner's report (see p. 745), the independent expert's study and report on country visits (see p. 745), and information provided jointly by the NGOs Europe–Third World Centre and the American Association of Jurists [E/CN.4/2004/WG.18/CRP.1]. The Group agreed on the importance of establishing partnerships between the Commission, UN agencies, funds and programmes, multilateral financial and development institutions and the World Trade Organization (WTO) for implementing the right to development. It held that its focus and follow-up would be on mainstreaming and implementing the right as established in the Declaration on the Right to Development, adopted by the General Assembly in resolution 41/128 [YUN 1986, p. 717]. The Group adopted a series of conclusions, noting, among other things, that there was an emerging consensus among Member States and development institutions regarding the need to strengthen the global partnership for development, taking into account the principles of accountability, transparency, non-discrimination, equal participation, the rule of law, good governance and international cooperation. The Group recommended that the Commission consider renewing the Group's mandate for one year, and establish a high-level task force on the implementation of the right, for an initial period of one year, to assist the Group to fulfil its mandate. The participation of the Group's Chair would ensure continuity between the task force and the Group, and Member States would participate as observers. The task force would meet for five days and

submit a report of its findings and recommendations for the Group's consideration. For its first report, the task force would consider obstacles and challenges to the implementation of the Millennium Development Goals [YUN 2000, p. 51] in relation to the right to development; social impact assessments in the areas of trade and development at the national and international levels; and best practices in implementing the right.

Commission action. By a recorded vote of 49 to 3, the Commission, on 13 April [res. 2004/7], referring to its 2003 request to the Subcommission to prepare a concept document for its consideration in 2005, asked OHCHR to continue to support the Subcommission in its work on the document and to provide support to the proposed high-level task force on the implementation of the right to development, established within the framework of the Working Group (see above). The High Commissioner was asked to undertake effective activities aimed at strengthening the global partnership for development between Member States, development agencies and international development, financial and trade institutions, and to reflect those activities in her 2005 report to the Commission. Endorsing the conclusions and recommendations of the Working Group, the Commission decided to renew the Group's mandate for one year and to convene its sixth session before the Commission's 2005 session to consider the findings and recommendations of the task force. The Commission decided to consider the renewal of the mandate of the independent expert in 2005.

On 19 April [res. 2004/29], by a recorded vote of 48 to none, with 5 abstentions, the Commission called on States to guarantee economic, social and cultural rights without discrimination of any kind; to secure through national development policies and with international assistance, full realization of those rights, giving particular attention to the most vulnerable and disadvantaged, most often women and children, especially girls, and communities living in extreme poverty; and to promote the effective participation of civil society in decision-making processes related to those rights. The Secretary-General was asked to report in 2005 on the implementation of the Commission's resolution.

Notes by Secretariat. In a June Secretariat note [E/CN.4/Sub.2/2004/13], the Secretary-General drew the Subcommission's attention to the High Commissioner's report (see p. 745) containing information on OHCHR activities relating to the implementation of the right to development, and to his 2003 report to the General Assembly on the right [YUN 2003, p. 754].

By a July note [E/CN.4/Sub.2/2004/14], the Secretariat, referring to a 2003 Subcommission request [YUN 2003, p. 754], noted that Florizelle O'Connor (Jamaica) was unable to submit the working paper identifying and analysing possible alternatives that would enable the Subcommission to respond to a 2003 Commission request [YUN 2003, p. 753].

Additional notes by the Secretariat transmitted, for consideration by the Subcommission, studies on existing bilateral and multilateral programmes and policies for development partnership [E/CN.4/Sub.2/2004/15 & Corr.1]; on the legal nature of the right to development and enhancement of its binding nature [E/CN.4/Sub.2/2004/16]; on mainstreaming the right to development into international trade law and policy at WTO [E/CN.4/Sub.2/2004/17]; on policies for development in a globalizing world: what can the human rights approach contribute? [E/CN.4/Sub.2/2004/18]; and on a human rights approach to development: concepts and implications [E/CN.4/Sub.2/2004/19], all commissioned by OHCHR, in accordance with a 2003 Commission request to the Subcommission to prepare a concept document, and to OHCHR to assist it [YUN 2003, p. 753].

ECONOMIC AND SOCIAL COUNCIL ACTION

In July, the Economic and Social Council, on the recommendation of the Commission on Human Rights [E/2004/23], adopted **decision 2004/249** by recorded vote (51-3) [agenda item 14 (g)].

The right to development

At its 48th plenary meeting, on 22 July 2004, the Economic and Social Council took note of Commission on Human Rights resolution 2004/7 of 13 April 2004 and approved the decision of the Commission to extend for one year the mandate of the Working Group on the Right to Development and to convene its sixth session before the sixty-first session of the Commission for a period of ten working days; of those ten working days, five should be allocated to the high-level task force established within the framework of the Working Group to hold its meetings and submit its findings and recommendations to the Working Group well in advance of its session; the Working Group in turn would meet for a period of five working days to consider the findings and recommendations of the task force and further initiatives in accordance with its mandate.

RECORDED VOTE ON DECISION 2004/249:

In favour: Armenia, Azerbaijan, Bangladesh, Belgium, Belize, Benin, Bhutan, Burundi, Canada, Chile, China, Colombia, Congo, Cuba, Ecuador, El Salvador, Finland, France, Germany, Ghana, Greece, Guatemala, Hungary, India, Indonesia, Ireland, Italy, Jamaica, Kenya, Libyan Arab Jamahiriya, Malaysia, Mauritius, Mozambique, Namibia, Nicaragua, Nigeria, Panama, Poland, Qatar, Republic of Korea, Russian Federation, Saudi Arabia, Senegal, Sweden, Tunisia, Turkey, Ukraine, United Arab Emirates, United Kingdom, United Republic of Tanzania, Zimbabwe.

Against: Australia, Japan, United States.

Subcommission action. On 9 August [dec. 2004/104], the Subcommission recommended that the Commission ask Ms. O'Connor to submit in 2005 the working paper requested by the Subcommison in 2003 [YUN 2003, p. 754].

GENERAL ASSEMBLY ACTION

On 20 December [meeting 74], the General Assembly, on the recommendation of the Third Committee [A/59/503/Add.2], adopted **resolution 59/185** by recorded vote (181-2-4) [agenda item 105 (b)].

The right to development

The General Assembly,

Guided by the Charter of the United Nations, which expresses, in particular, the determination to promote social progress and better standards of life in larger freedom, as well as to employ international mechanisms for the promotion of the economic and social advancement of all peoples,

Recalling that the Declaration on the Right to Development, adopted by the General Assembly in its resolution 41/128 of 4 December 1986, confirmed that the right to development is an inalienable human right and that equality of opportunity for development is a prerogative both of nations and of individuals who make up nations, and that the individual is the central subject and beneficiary of development,

Stressing that the Vienna Declaration and Programme of Action reaffirmed the right to development as a universal and inalienable right and an integral part of fundamental human rights, and the individual as the central subject and beneficiary of development,

Reaffirming the objective of making the right to development a reality for everyone, as set out in the United Nations Millennium Declaration, adopted by the General Assembly on 8 September 2000,

Welcoming the framework modalities agreed at the General Council meeting of the World Trade Organization in Geneva on 1 August 2004 in key areas such as agriculture, market access for non-agricultural products, trade facilitation, development and services,

Welcoming also the outcome of the eleventh session of the United Nations Conference on Trade and Development, held at São Paulo, Brazil, from 13 to 18 June 2004, on the theme "Enhancing the coherence between national development strategies and global economic processes towards economic growth and development, particularly of developing countries",

Recalling all its previous resolutions and those of the Commission on Human Rights on the right to development, in particular Commission resolution 1998/72 of 22 April 1998, on the urgent need to make further progress towards the realization of the right to development as set out in the Declaration on the Right to Development,

Recalling also the Thirteenth Conference of Heads of State or Government of Non-Aligned Countries, held at Kuala Lumpur from 20 to 25 February 2003, and the Fourteenth Ministerial Conference of the Movement of Non-Aligned Countries, held at Durban, South Africa, from 17 to 19 August 2004,

Reiterating its continuing support for the New Partnership for Africa's Development as a development framework for Africa,

Recognizing that historical injustices have undeniably contributed to the poverty, underdevelopment, marginalization, social exclusion, economic disparity, instability and insecurity that affect many people in different parts of the world, in particular in developing countries,

Stressing that poverty eradication is one of the critical elements in the promotion and realization of the right to development and that poverty is a multifaceted problem that requires a multifaceted and integrated approach in addressing economic, political, social, environmental and institutional dimensions at all levels, especially in the context of the millennium development goal of halving, by 2015, the proportion of the world's people whose income is less than one dollar a day and the proportion of people who suffer from hunger,

1. *Endorses* the agreed conclusions and recommendations adopted by the Working Group on the Right to Development at its fifth session, and calls for their immediate, full and effective implementation by the Office of the United Nations High Commissioner for Human Rights and other relevant actors;

2. *Welcomes* the establishment of a high-level task force on the implementation of the right to development within the framework of the Working Group to assist the Working Group to fulfil its mandate, and looks forward to the consideration by the Working Group of its concrete recommendations at its next session;

3. *Calls upon* the Working Group and, through it, its high-level task force, to contribute actively towards the mainstreaming of the right to development at the high-level event to be held in New York at the commencement of the sixtieth session of the General Assembly, at which a comprehensive review will be undertaken of the progress made in the fulfilment of all the commitments contained in the United Nations Millennium Declaration, including the internationally agreed development goals and the global partnership required for their achievement;

4. *Stresses* the importance of the core principles contained in the conclusions of the Working Group at its third session, congruent with the purpose of international human rights instruments, such as equality, non-discrimination, accountability, participation and international cooperation, as critical to mainstreaming the right to development at the national and international levels, and underlines the importance of the principles of equity and transparency;

5. *Notes with concern* that the Subcommission on the Promotion and Protection of Human Rights at its fifty-sixth session did not consider the working paper identifying and analysing possible alternatives, and requests the Subcommission, without further delay, to submit to the Commission on Human Rights at its sixty-second session the concept document establishing options for the implementation of the right to development and their feasibility;

6. *Takes note* of the convening and outcome of the second Social Forum held at Geneva on 22 and 23 July 2004 on the theme "Poverty, rural poverty and human rights" and the strong support extended to it by the Subcommission on the Promotion and Protection of Human Rights, and invites all stakeholders, including Member States, to participate actively in its subsequent sessions;

7. *Reaffirms* the commitment to implement the goals and targets set out in all the outcome documents of the major United Nations conferences and summits and their review processes, in particular those relating to the realization of the right to development, recognizing that the realization of the right to development is critical to achieving the objectives, goals and targets set in those outcome documents;

8. *Also reaffirms* that the realization of the right to development is essential to the implementation of the Vienna Declaration and Programme of Action, which regards all human rights as universal, indivisible, interdependent and interrelated, places the human person at the centre of development and recognizes that, while development facilitates the enjoyment of all human rights, the lack of development may not be invoked to justify the abridgement of internationally recognized human rights;

9. *Stresses* that the basic responsibility for the promotion and protection of all human rights lies with the State, and reaffirms that States have the primary responsibility for their own economic and social development and that the role of national policies and development strategies cannot be overemphasized;

10. *Reaffirms* that States have the primary responsibility for the creation of national and international conditions favourable to the realization of the right to development and their commitment to cooperating with each other to that end;

11. *Also reaffirms* the need for an international environment that is conducive to the realization of the right to development;

12. *Stresses* the need to strive for greater acceptance, operationalization and realization of the right to development at the international and national levels, and calls upon States to institute the measures required for the implementation of the right to development as a fundamental human right;

13. *Emphasizes* the critical importance of identifying and analysing obstacles impeding the full realization of the right to development at both the national and the international levels;

14. *Affirms* that, while globalization offers both opportunities and challenges, the process of globalization remains deficient in achieving the objectives of integrating all countries into a globalized world, and stresses the need for policies and measures at the national and global levels to respond to the challenges and opportunities of globalization if this process is to be made fully inclusive and equitable;

15. *Recognizes* that, despite continuous efforts on the part of the international community, the gap between developed and developing countries remains unacceptably wide, that developing countries continue to face difficulties in participating in the globalization process and that many risk being marginalized and effectively excluded from its benefits;

16. *Underlines* the fact that the international community is far from meeting the target set in the Millennium Declaration of halving the number of people living in poverty by 2015, reaffirms the commitment made to meet that target, and emphasizes the principle

of international cooperation, including partnership and commitment, between developed and developing countries towards achieving the goal;

17. *Urges* developed countries that have not yet done so to make concrete efforts towards meeting the targets of 0.7 per cent of their gross national product for official development assistance to developing countries and 0.15 to 0.2 per cent of their gross national product to least developed countries, and encourages developing countries to build on the progress achieved in ensuring that official development assistance is used effectively to help to meet development goals and targets;

18. *Recognizes* the need to address market access for developing countries, including in agriculture, services and non-agricultural products, in particular those of interest to developing countries;

19. *Calls for* the implementation of a desirable pace of meaningful trade liberalization, including in areas under negotiation; implementation of commitments on implementation-related issues and concerns; review of special and differential-treatment provisions, with a view to strengthening them and making them more precise, effective and operational; avoidance of new forms of protectionism; and capacity-building and technical assistance for developing countries as important issues in making progress towards the effective implementation of the right to development;

20. *Recognizes* the important link between the international economic, commercial and financial spheres and the realization of the right to development, stresses, in this regard, the need for good governance and broadening the base of decision-making at the international level on issues of development concern and the need to fill organizational gaps, as well as strengthen the United Nations system and other multilateral institutions, and also stresses the need to broaden and strengthen the participation of developing countries and countries with economies in transition in international economic decision-making and norm-setting;

21. *Also recognizes* that good governance and the rule of law at the national level assist all States in the promotion and protection of human rights, including the right to development, and agrees on the value of the ongoing efforts being made by States to identify and strengthen good governance practices, including transparent, responsible, accountable and participatory government, that are responsive and appropriate to their needs and aspirations, including in the context of agreed partnership approaches to development, capacity-building and technical assistance;

22. *Further recognizes* the important role and the rights of women and the application of a gender perspective as a cross-cutting issue in the process of realizing the right to development, and notes in particular the positive relationship between women's education and their equal participation in the civil, cultural, economic, political and social activities of the community and the promotion of the right to development;

23. *Stresses* the need for the integration of the rights of children, girls and boys alike, in all policies and programmes, and for ensuring the promotion and protection of those rights, especially in areas relating to health, education and the full development of their capacities;

24. *Also stresses* that further and additional measures must be taken at the national and international levels to fight HIV/AIDS and other communicable diseases, taking into account ongoing efforts and programmes, and reiterates the need for international assistance in this regard;

25. *Recognizes* the need for strong partnerships with civil society organizations and the private sector in pursuit of poverty eradication and development, as well as for corporate social responsibility;

26. *Emphasizes* the urgent need for taking concrete measures to fight against all forms of corruption at the national and international levels, to prevent, detect and deter in a more effective manner international transfers of illicitly acquired assets and to strengthen international cooperation in asset recovery, stresses the importance of a genuine political commitment on the part of all Governments through a firm legal framework, and in this context urges States to sign and ratify as soon as possible, and States parties to implement effectively, the United Nations Convention against Corruption;

27. *Also emphasizes* the need to strengthen further the activities of the Office of the United Nations High Commissioner for Human Rights in the promotion and realization of the right to development, including ensuring effective use of the financial and human resources necessary to fulfil its mandate, and calls upon the Secretary-General to provide the Office of the High Commissioner with the necessary resources;

28. *Reaffirms* the request to the High Commissioner, in mainstreaming the right to development, to undertake effectively activities aimed at strengthening the global partnership for development between Member States, development agencies and the international development, financial and trade institutions, and to reflect those activities in detail in her report to the Commission on Human Rights at its sixty-first session;

29. *Calls upon* the United Nations agencies, funds and programmes, as well as the specialized agencies, to mainstream the right to development in their operational programmes and objectives, and stresses the need for the international financial and multilateral trading systems to mainstream the right to development in their policies and objectives;

30. *Requests* the Secretary-General to bring the present resolution to the attention of Member States, United Nations organs and bodies, specialized agencies, funds and programmes, international development and financial institutions, in particular the Bretton Woods institutions, and non-governmental organizations;

31. *Also requests* the Secretary-General to submit a report to the General Assembly at its sixtieth session and an interim report to the Commission on Human Rights at its sixty-first session on the implementation of the present resolution, including efforts undertaken at the national, regional and international levels in the promotion and realization of the right to development, and invites the Chairperson of the Working Group on the Right to Development to present a verbal update to the General Assembly at its sixtieth session.

RECORDED VOTE ON RESOLUTION 59/185:

In favour: Afghanistan, Albania, Algeria, Andorra, Angola, Antigua and Barbuda, Argentina, Armenia, Austria, Azerbaijan, Bahamas, Bahrain, Bangladesh, Barbados, Belarus, Belgium, Belize, Benin, Bhutan, Bolivia,

Bosnia and Herzegovina, Botswana, Brazil, Brunei Darussalam, Bulgaria, Burkina Faso, Burundi, Cambodia, Cameroon, Cape Verde, Central African Republic, Chad, Chile, China, Colombia, Comoros, Costa Rica, Côte d'Ivoire, Croatia, Cuba, Cyprus, Czech Republic, Democratic People's Republic of Korea, Democratic Republic of the Congo, Denmark, Djibouti, Dominica, Dominican Republic, Ecuador, Egypt, El Salvador, Equatorial Guinea, Eritrea, Estonia, Ethiopia, Fiji, Finland, France, Gabon, Gambia, Georgia, Germany, Ghana, Greece, Grenada, Guatemala, Guinea, Guinea-Bissau, Guyana, Haiti, Honduras, Hungary, Iceland, India, Indonesia, Iran, Iraq, Ireland, Italy, Jamaica, Jordan, Kazakhstan, Kenya, Kuwait, Kyrgyzstan, Lao People's Democratic Republic, Latvia, Lebanon, Lesotho, Liberia, Libyan Arab Jamahiriya, Liechtenstein, Lithuania, Luxembourg, Madagascar, Malawi, Malaysia, Maldives, Mali, Malta, Marshall Islands, Mauritania, Mauritius, Mexico, Micronesia, Monaco, Mongolia, Morocco, Mozambique, Myanmar, Namibia, Nauru, Nepal, Netherlands, New Zealand, Nicaragua, Niger, Nigeria, Norway, Oman, Pakistan, Panama, Papua New Guinea, Paraguay, Peru, Philippines, Poland, Portugal, Qatar, Republic of Korea, Republic of Moldova, Romania, Russian Federation, Rwanda, Saint Lucia, Saint Vincent and the Grenadines, Samoa, San Marino, Sao Tome and Principe, Saudi Arabia, Senegal, Serbia and Montenegro, Seychelles, Sierra Leone, Singapore, Slovakia, Slovenia, Solomon Islands, Somalia, South Africa, Spain, Sri Lanka, Sudan, Suriname, Swaziland, Switzerland, Syrian Arab Republic, Tajikistan, Thailand, The former Yugoslav Republic of Macedonia, Timor-Leste, Togo, Tonga, Trinidad and Tobago, Tunisia, Turkey, Turkmenistan, Tuvalu, Uganda, Ukraine, United Arab Emirates, United Kingdom, United Republic of Tanzania, Uruguay, Uzbekistan, Vanuatu, Venezuela, Viet Nam, Yemen, Zambia, Zimbabwe.

Against: Israel, United States.

Abstaining: Australia, Canada, Japan, Sweden.

Human rights and international solidarity

Note by Secretariat. A note by the Secretariat [E/CN.4/2004/84], referring to a 2002 Commission request [YUN 2002, p. 722] to the Subcommission to undertake a study on the implementation of the Commission's resolution, noted that the Subcommission, by a 2003 decision [YUN 2003, p. 754], had asked Rui Baltazar Dos Santos Alves (Mozambique) to prepare a working paper on human rights and international solidarity, for consideration in 2004 (see below).

Commission action. By a recorded vote of 37 to 15, with 1 abstention, the Commission, on 21 April [res. 2004/66], urged the international community to consider concrete measures to promote and consolidate international assistance to developing countries in their endeavours for development and for the promotion of conditions that made possible the full realization of human rights. It recognized that the "third-generation rights" or "right to solidarity" needed further progressive development within the UN human rights machinery to respond to the increasing challenges to international cooperation in that area.

Further note by Secretariat. A June Secretariat note [E/CN.4/Sub.2/2004/43] transmitted a preliminary report on human rights and international solidarity prepared by Mr. Dos Santos Alves. The paper pointed out that one of the greatest challenges currently facing humanity was the widening gulf between the developed and the developing countries. International solidarity as an instrument for the attainment of human rights needed new development, with the objective of building a more just and equitable

international order that favoured human rights. To facilitate a better understanding of the principle, the paper proposed a preliminary work plan for the Subcommission's consideration.

Subcommission action. On 12 August [dec. 2004/111], the Subcommission asked Mr. Dos Santos Alves to prepare, without financial implications, an expanded version of his working paper for consideration in 2005.

Democratic and equitable international order

By a recorded vote of 31 to 15, with 7 abstentions, the Commission, on 21 April [res. 2004/64], urged States to continue efforts to establish a democratic and equitable international order. The Commission asked human rights treaty bodies, OHCHR and Commission and Subcommission mechanisms to contribute to the implementation of its resolution. The Secretary-General was asked to bring the resolution to the attention of Member States, UN organs and bodies, intergovernmental organizations and NGOs and to disseminate it widely.

GENERAL ASSEMBLY ACTION

On 20 December [meeting 74], the General Assembly, on the recommendation of the Third Committee [A/59/503/Add.2], adopted **resolution 59/193** by recorded vote (125-55-6) [agenda item 105 (b)].

Promotion of a democratic and equitable international order

The General Assembly,

Recalling its resolution 57/213 of 18 December 2002, and taking note of Commission on Human Rights resolution 2004/64 of 21 April 2004,

Reaffirming the commitment of all States to fulfil their obligations to promote universal respect for, and observance and protection of, all human rights and fundamental freedoms for all, in accordance with the Charter of the United Nations, other instruments relating to human rights and international law,

Affirming that the enhancement of international cooperation for the promotion and protection of all human rights should continue to be carried out in full conformity with the purposes and principles of the Charter and international law as set forth in Articles 1 and 2 of the Charter and, inter alia, with full respect for sovereignty, territorial integrity, political independence, the non-use of force or the threat of force in international relations and non-intervention in matters that are essentially within the domestic jurisdiction of any State,

Recalling the Preamble to the Charter, in particular the determination to reaffirm faith in fundamental human rights, in the dignity and worth of the human person and in the equal rights of men and women and of nations large and small,

Reaffirming that everyone is entitled to a social and international order in which the rights and freedoms set forth in the Universal Declaration of Human Rights can be fully realized,

Reaffirming also the determination expressed in the Preamble to the Charter to save succeeding generations from the scourge of war, to establish conditions under which justice and respect for the obligations arising from treaties and other sources of international law can be maintained, to promote social progress and better standards of life in larger freedom, to practice tolerance and good-neighbourliness, and to employ international machinery for the promotion of the economic and social advancement of all peoples,

Considering the major changes taking place on the international scene and the aspirations of all peoples for an international order based on the principles enshrined in the Charter, including promoting and encouraging respect for human rights and fundamental freedoms for all and respect for the principle of equal rights and self-determination of peoples, peace, democracy, justice, equality, the rule of law, pluralism, development, better standards of living and solidarity,

Considering also that the Universal Declaration of Human Rights proclaims that all human beings are born free and equal in dignity and rights and that everyone is entitled to all the rights and freedoms set out therein, without distinction of any kind, such as race, colour, sex, language, religion, political or other opinion, national or social origin, property, birth or other status,

Reaffirming that democracy, development and respect for human rights and fundamental freedoms are interdependent and mutually reinforcing, and that democracy is based on the freely expressed will of the people to determine their own political, economic, social and cultural systems and their full participation in all aspects of their lives,

Emphasizing that democracy is not only a political concept but that it also has economic and social dimensions,

Recognizing that democracy, respect for all human rights, including the right to development, transparent and accountable governance and administration in all sectors of society, and effective participation by civil society are an essential part of the necessary foundations for the realization of social and people-centred sustainable development,

Noting with concern that racism, racial discrimination, xenophobia and related intolerance may be aggravated by, inter alia, inequitable distribution of wealth, marginalization and social exclusion,

Underlining the fact that it is imperative for the international community to ensure that globalization becomes a positive force for all the world's people, and that only through broad and sustained efforts, based on common humanity in all its diversity, can globalization be made fully inclusive and equitable,

Stressing that efforts to make globalization fully inclusive and equitable must include policies and measures, at the global level, that correspond to the needs of developing countries and countries with economies in transition and are formulated and implemented with their effective participation,

Having listened to the peoples of the world, and recognizing their aspirations to justice, to equality of opportunity for all, to the enjoyment of their human rights, including the right to development, to live in peace and freedom and to equal participation without discrimination in economic, social, cultural, civil and political life,

Resolved to take all measures within its power to secure a democratic and equitable international order,

1. *Affirms* that everyone is entitled to a democratic and equitable international order;

2. *Also affirms* that a democratic and equitable international order fosters the full realization of all human rights for all;

3. *Calls upon* all Member States to fulfil their commitment expressed in Durban, South Africa, during the World Conference against Racism, Racial Discrimination, Xenophobia and Related Intolerance to maximize the benefits of globalization through, inter alia, the strengthening and enhancement of international cooperation to increase equality of opportunities for trade, economic growth and sustainable development, global communications through the use of new technologies, and increased intercultural exchange through the preservation and promotion of cultural diversity, and reiterates that only through broad and sustained efforts to create a shared future based upon our common humanity and all its diversity can globalization be made fully inclusive and equitable;

4. *Affirms* that a democratic and equitable international order requires, inter alia, the realization of the following:

(*a*) The right of all peoples to self-determination, by virtue of which they can freely determine their political status and freely pursue their economic, social and cultural development;

(*b*) The right of peoples and nations to permanent sovereignty over their natural wealth and resources;

(*c*) The right of every human person and all peoples to development;

(*d*) The right of all peoples to peace;

(*e*) The right to an international economic order based on equal participation in the decision-making process, interdependence, mutual interest, solidarity and cooperation among all States;

(*f*) Solidarity, as a fundamental value, by virtue of which global challenges must be managed in a way that distributes costs and burdens fairly, in accordance with basic principles of equity and social justice, and ensures that those who suffer or benefit the least receive help from those who benefit the most;

(*g*) The promotion and consolidation of transparent, democratic, just and accountable international institutions in all areas of cooperation, in particular through the implementation of the principles of full and equal participation in their respective decision-making mechanisms;

(*h*) The right to equitable participation of all, without any discrimination, in domestic and global decision-making;

(*i*) The principle of equitable regional and gender-balanced representation in the composition of the staff of the United Nations system;

(*j*) The promotion of a free, just, effective and balanced international information and communications order, based on international cooperation for the establishment of a new equilibrium and greater reciprocity in the international flow of information, in particular correcting the inequalities in the flow of information to and from developing countries;

(k) Respect for cultural diversity and the cultural rights of all, since this enhances cultural pluralism, contributes to a wider exchange of knowledge and understanding of cultural backgrounds, advances the application and enjoyment of universally accepted human rights across the world and fosters stable, friendly relations among peoples and nations worldwide;

(l) The right of every person and all peoples to a healthy environment;

(m) The promotion of equitable access to benefits from the international distribution of wealth through enhanced international cooperation, in particular in economic, commercial and financial international relations;

(n) The enjoyment by everyone of ownership of the common heritage of mankind;

(o) The shared responsibility of the nations of the world for managing worldwide economic and social development as well as threats to international peace and security that should be exercised multilaterally;

5. *Stresses* the importance of preserving the rich and diverse nature of the international community of nations and peoples, as well as respect for national and regional particularities and various historical, cultural and religious backgrounds in the enhancement of international cooperation in the field of human rights;

6. *Also stresses* that all human rights are universal, indivisible, interdependent and interrelated and that the international community must treat human rights globally in a fair and equal manner, on the same footing and with the same emphasis, and reaffirms that, while the significance of national and regional particularities and various historical, cultural and religious backgrounds must be borne in mind, it is the duty of States, regardless of their political, economic and cultural systems, to promote and protect all human rights and fundamental freedoms;

7. *Urges* all actors on the international scene to build an international order based on inclusion, justice, equality and equity, human dignity, mutual understanding and promotion of and respect for cultural diversity and universal human rights, and to reject all doctrines of exclusion based on racism, racial discrimination, xenophobia and related intolerance;

8. *Reaffirms* that all States should promote the establishment, maintenance and strengthening of international peace and security and, to that end, should do their utmost to achieve general and complete disarmament under effective international control, as well as to ensure that the resources released by effective disarmament measures are used for comprehensive development, in particular that of the developing countries;

9. *Recalls* the proclamation by the General Assembly of its determination to work urgently for the establishment of an international economic order based on equity, sovereign equality, interdependence, common interest and cooperation among all States, irrespective of their economic and social systems, which shall correct inequalities and redress existing injustices, make it possible to eliminate the widening gap between the developed and the developing countries, and ensure steadily accelerating economic and social development and peace and justice for present and future generations;

10. *Reaffirms* that the international community should devise ways and means to remove the current obstacles and meet the challenges to the full realization of all human rights and to prevent the continuation of human rights violations resulting therefrom throughout the world;

11. *Urges* States to continue their efforts, through enhanced international cooperation, towards the promotion of a democratic and equitable international order;

12. *Requests* the Commission on Human Rights, the human rights treaty bodies, the Office of the United Nations High Commissioner for Human Rights and the mechanisms of the Commission on Human Rights and the Subcommission on the Promotion and Protection of Human Rights to pay due attention, within their respective mandates, to the present resolution and to make contributions towards its implementation;

13. *Calls upon* the Office of the High Commissioner to build upon the issue of the promotion of a democratic and equitable international order, to take into account the present resolution in the preparations and development of the expert seminar to examine the interdependence between democracy and human rights that it will convene in February 2005, and to invite all Governments, specialized agencies, United Nations funds and programmes and interested non-governmental organizations to attend that seminar;

14. *Requests* the Secretary-General to bring the present resolution to the attention of Member States, United Nations organs, bodies and components, intergovernmental organizations, in particular the Bretton Woods institutions, and non-governmental organizations, and to disseminate it on the widest possible basis;

15. *Decides* to continue consideration of the matter at its sixty-first session under the item entitled "Human rights questions".

RECORDED VOTE ON RESOLUTION 59/193:

In favour: Algeria, Angola, Antigua and Barbuda, Azerbaijan, Bahamas, Bahrain, Bangladesh, Barbados, Belarus, Belize, Benin, Bhutan, Bolivia, Botswana, Brazil, Brunei Darussalam, Burkina Faso, Burundi, Cambodia, Cameroon, Cape Verde, Central African Republic, Chad, China, Colombia, Comoros, Costa Rica, Côte d'Ivoire, Cuba, Democratic People's Republic of Korea, Democratic Republic of the Congo, Djibouti, Dominica, Dominican Republic, Ecuador, Egypt, El Salvador, Equatorial Guinea, Eritrea, Ethiopia, Gabon, Gambia, Ghana, Grenada, Guatemala, Guinea, Guinea-Bissau, Guyana, Haiti, Honduras, India, Indonesia, Iran, Iraq, Jamaica, Jordan, Kazakhstan, Kenya, Kuwait, Kyrgyzstan, Lao People's Democratic Republic, Lebanon, Lesotho, Liberia, Libyan Arab Jamahiriya, Madagascar, Malawi, Malaysia, Maldives, Mali, Mauritania, Mauritius, Mongolia, Morocco, Mozambique, Myanmar, Namibia, Nepal, Nicaragua, Niger, Nigeria, Oman, Pakistan, Panama, Papua New Guinea, Paraguay, Philippines, Qatar, Russian Federation, Rwanda, Saint Lucia, Saint Vincent and the Grenadines, Sao Tome and Principe, Saudi Arabia, Senegal, Seychelles, Sierra Leone, Singapore, Solomon Islands, Somalia, South Africa, Sri Lanka, Sudan, Suriname, Swaziland, Syrian Arab Republic, Tajikistan, Thailand, Timor-Leste, Togo, Trinidad and Tobago, Tunisia, Turkmenistan, Tuvalu, Uganda, United Arab Emirates, United Republic of Tanzania, Uruguay, Uzbekistan, Vanuatu, Venezuela, Viet Nam, Yemen, Zambia, Zimbabwe.

Against: Albania, Andorra, Australia, Austria, Belgium, Bosnia and Herzegovina, Bulgaria, Canada, Chile, Croatia, Cyprus, Czech Republic, Denmark, Estonia, Finland, France, Georgia, Germany, Greece, Hungary, Iceland, Ireland, Israel, Italy, Japan, Latvia, Liechtenstein, Lithuania, Luxembourg, Malta, Marshall Islands, Micronesia, Monaco, Netherlands, New Zealand, Norway, Palau, Poland, Portugal, Republic of Korea, Republic of Moldova, Romania, Samoa, San Marino, Serbia and Montenegro, Slovakia, Slovenia, Spain, Sweden, Switzerland, The former Yugoslav Republic of Macedonia, Turkey, Ukraine, United Kingdom, United States.

Abstaining: Argentina, Armenia, Fiji, Mexico, Nauru, Peru.

Globalization

Report of High Commissioner. In response to a 2003 Commission request [YUN 2003, p. 757], the

High Commissioner submitted a January analytical study [E/CN.4/2004/40], which considered how globalization had brought new attention to the principle of non-discrimination—on the one hand providing opportunities for increasing commercial and cultural exchange, while on the other highlighting inequalities within and between countries. The prohibition of discrimination therefore provided an essential principle for globalization. The report focused on the interaction between the principle in human rights and trade law, and addressed the question of clarifying the principle and other key issues concerning government procurement, agricultural trade and social labelling. It concluded that respect for the principle was a fundamental means of promoting a more inclusive globalization that reduced inequalities within and between nations. To better integrate and implement the principle in the debate on globalization, the High Commissioner recommended measures relating to the human rights implications of general exceptions to trade rules, agricultural trade, the need to promote institutional coordination and human rights impact assessments.

Commission action. By a recorded vote of 38 to 15, the Commission, on 16 April [res. 2004/24], reaffirmed the commitment to create an environment conducive to development and to the elimination of poverty through good governance, transparency in the financial, monetary and trading systems and commitment to an open, equitable, rule-based, predictable and non-discriminatory multilateral trading and financial system. The High Commissioner was asked to bring her analytical report (see above) to the attention of WTO and other relevant international organizations, with a view to operationalizing its conclusions and recommendations. The High Commissioner was further asked to study and clarify the fundamental principle of participation and its application at the global level, with a view to recommending measures for its integration and effective implementation in the debate on globalization and to submit a comprehensive analytical study in 2005.

By a recorded vote of 51 to none, with 2 abstentions, the Commission, on 16 April [dec. 2004/107], approved the Subcommission's 2003 request [YUN 2003, p. 758] to publish in UN official languages the Special Rapporteur's preliminary report [YUN 2000, p. 696], progress report [YUN 2001, p. 663] and final report [YUN 2003, p. 757].

ECONOMIC AND SOCIAL COUNCIL ACTION

In July, the Economic and Social Council, on the recommendation of the Commission on Human Rights [E/2004/23], adopted **decision 2004/275** by recorded vote (49-1-1) [agenda item 14 (g)].

Globalization and its impact on the full enjoyment of human rights

At its 49th plenary meeting, on 22 July 2004, the Economic and Social Council took note of Commission on Human Rights decision 2004/107 of 16 April 2004 and endorsed the Commission's request that the reports of the Special Rapporteurs on globalization and its impact on the full enjoyment of human rights be published in the official languages of the United Nations.

RECORDED VOTE ON DECISION 2004/275:

In favour: Armenia, Azerbaijan, Bangladesh, Belgium, Belize, Benin, Bhutan, Burundi, Canada, Chile, China, Colombia, Congo, Cuba, Ecuador, El Salvador, Finland, France, Germany, Ghana, Greece, Guatemala, Hungary, India, Indonesia, Ireland, Italy, Jamaica, Japan, Kenya, Libyan Arab Jamahiriya, Malaysia, Mauritius, Mozambique, Namibia, Panama, Poland, Qatar, Republic of Korea, Russian Federation, Saudi Arabia, Sweden, Tunisia, Turkey, Ukraine, United Arab Emirates, United Kingdom, United Republic of Tanzania, Zimbabwe.

Against: United States.

Abstaining: Australia.

Report of Secretary-General. In response to General Assembly resolution 58/193 [YUN 2003, p. 758], the Secretary-General, in September [A/59/320], submitted a report summarizing the views of seven Governments on globalization and its impact on human rights.

GENERAL ASSEMBLY ACTION

On 20 December [meeting 74], the General Assembly, on the recommendation of the Third Committee [A/59/503/Add.2], adopted **resolution 59/184** by recorded vote (129-53-4) [agenda item 105 (b)].

Globalization and its impact on the full enjoyment of all human rights

The General Assembly,

Guided by the purposes and principles of the Charter of the United Nations, and expressing in particular the need to achieve international cooperation in promoting and encouraging respect for human rights and fundamental freedoms for all without distinction,

Recalling the Universal Declaration of Human Rights, as well as the Vienna Declaration and Programme of Action adopted by the World Conference on Human Rights on 25 June 1993,

Recalling also the International Covenant on Civil and Political Rights and the International Covenant on Economic, Social and Cultural Rights,

Recalling further the Declaration on the Right to Development adopted by the General Assembly in its resolution 41/128 of 4 December 1986,

Recalling the United Nations Millennium Declaration and the outcome documents of the twenty-third and twenty-fourth special sessions of the General Assembly, held in New York from 5 to 10 June 2000 and in Geneva from 26 June to 1 July 2000, respectively,

Recalling also its resolution 58/193 of 22 December 2003,

Recalling further Commission on Human Rights resolution 2004/24 of 16 April 2004 on globalization and its impact on the full enjoyment of all human rights,

Recognizing that all human rights are universal, indivisible, interdependent and interrelated and that the international community must treat human rights globally in a fair and equal manner, on the same footing and with the same emphasis,

Realizing that globalization affects all countries differently and makes them more exposed to external developments, positive as well as negative, inter alia, in the field of human rights,

Realizing also that globalization is not merely an economic process, but that it also has social, political, environmental, cultural and legal dimensions, which have an impact on the full enjoyment of all human rights,

Realizing further the need to undertake a thorough, independent and comprehensive assessment of the social, environmental and cultural impact of globalization on societies,

Recognizing in each culture a dignity and value that deserve recognition, respect and preservation, convinced that, in their rich variety and diversity and in the reciprocal influences that they exert on one another, all cultures form part of the common heritage belonging to all humankind, and aware that the risk of a global monoculture poses more of a threat if the developing world remains poor and marginalized,

Recognizing also that multilateral mechanisms have a unique role to play in meeting the challenges and opportunities presented by globalization,

Expressing concern at the negative impact of international financial turbulence on social and economic development and on the full enjoyment of all human rights,

Deeply concerned that the widening gap between the developed and the developing countries, and within countries, has contributed, inter alia, to deepening poverty and has adversely affected the full enjoyment of all human rights, in particular in developing countries,

Noting that human beings strive for a world that is respectful of human rights and cultural diversity and that, in this regard, they work to ensure that all activities, including those affected by globalization, are consistent with those aims,

1. *Recognizes* that, while globalization, by its impact on, inter alia, the role of the State, may affect human rights, the promotion and protection of all human rights is first and foremost the responsibility of the State;

2. *Reaffirms* that narrowing the gap between rich and poor, both within and between countries, is an explicit goal at the national and international levels, as part of the effort to create an enabling environment for the full enjoyment of all human rights;

3. *Reaffirms also* the commitment to create an environment at both the national and the global levels that is conducive to development and to the elimination of poverty through, inter alia, good governance within each country and at the international level, transparency in the financial, monetary and trading systems and commitment to an open, equitable, rule-based, predictable and non-discriminatory multilateral trading and financial system;

4. *Recognizes* that, while globalization offers great opportunities, the fact that its benefits are very unevenly shared and its costs unevenly distributed represents an aspect of the process that affects the full enjoyment of all human rights, in particular in developing countries;

5. *Welcomes* the report of the United Nations High Commissioner for Human Rights on globalization and its impact on the full enjoyment of human rights, which focuses on the liberalization of agricultural trade and its impact on the realization of the right to development, including the right to food, and takes note of the conclusions and recommendations contained therein;

6. *Calls upon* Member States, relevant agencies of the United Nations system, intergovernmental organizations and civil society to promote equitable and environmentally sustainable economic growth for managing globalization so that poverty is systematically reduced and the international development targets are achieved;

7. *Recognizes* that only through broad and sustained efforts, including policies and measures at the global level to create a shared future based upon our common humanity in all its diversity, can globalization be made fully inclusive and equitable and have a human face, thus contributing to the full enjoyment of all human rights;

8. *Underlines* the urgent need to establish an equitable, transparent and democratic international system in which poor people and countries have a more effective voice;

9. *Affirms* that globalization is a complex process of structural transformation, with numerous interdisciplinary aspects, which has an impact on the enjoyment of civil, political, economic, social and cultural rights, including the right to development;

10. *Affirms also* that the international community should strive to respond to the challenges and opportunities posed by globalization in a manner that ensures respect for the cultural diversity of all;

11. *Underlines*, therefore, the need to continue to analyse the consequences of globalization for the full enjoyment of all human rights;

12. *Takes note* of the report of the Secretary-General, and requests the Secretary-General to seek further the views of Member States and relevant agencies of the United Nations system and to submit a substantive report on this subject to the General Assembly at its sixtieth session.

RECORDED VOTE ON RESOLUTION 59/184:

In favour: Afghanistan, Algeria, Angola, Antigua and Barbuda, Argentina, Armenia, Azerbaijan, Bahamas, Bahrain, Bangladesh, Barbados, Belarus, Belize, Benin, Bhutan, Bolivia, Botswana, Brunei Darussalam, Burkina Faso, Burundi, Cambodia, Cameroon, Cape Verde, Central African Republic, Chad, China, Colombia, Comoros, Costa Rica, Côte d'Ivoire, Cuba, Democratic People's Republic of Korea, Democratic Republic of the Congo, Djibouti, Dominica, Dominican Republic, Ecuador, Egypt, El Salvador, Equatorial Guinea, Eritrea, Ethiopia, Fiji, Gabon, Gambia, Ghana, Grenada, Guatemala, Guinea, Guinea-Bissau, Guyana, Haiti, Honduras, India, Indonesia, Iran, Iraq, Jamaica, Jordan, Kazakhstan, Kenya, Kuwait, Kyrgyzstan, Lao People's Democratic Republic, Lebanon, Lesotho, Liberia, Libyan Arab Jamahiriya, Madagascar, Malaysia, Maldives, Mali, Mauritania, Mauritius, Mexico, Mongolia, Morocco, Mozambique, Myanmar, Namibia, Nauru, Nepal, Nicaragua, Niger, Nigeria, Oman, Pakistan, Panama, Papua New Guinea, Paraguay, Peru, Philippines, Qatar, Russian Federation, Rwanda, Saint Lucia, Saint Vincent and the Grenadines, Samoa, Sao Tome and Principe, Saudi Arabia, Senegal, Sierra Leone, Solomon Islands, Somalia, South Africa, Sri Lanka, Sudan, Suriname, Syrian Arab Republic, Tajikistan, Thailand, Timor-Leste, Togo,

Tonga, Trinidad and Tobago, Tunisia, Turkmenistan, Tuvalu, Uganda, United Arab Emirates, United Republic of Tanzania, Uruguay, Uzbekistan, Vanuatu, Venezuela, Viet Nam, Yemen, Zambia, Zimbabwe.
Against: Albania, Andorra, Australia, Austria, Belgium, Bosnia and Herzegovina, Bulgaria, Canada, Croatia, Cyprus, Czech Republic, Denmark, Estonia, Finland, France, Georgia, Germany, Greece, Hungary, Iceland, Ireland, Israel, Italy, Japan, Latvia, Liechtenstein, Lithuania, Luxembourg, Malta, Marshall Islands, Micronesia, Monaco, Netherlands, New Zealand, Norway, Palau, Poland, Portugal, Republic of Korea, Republic of Moldova, Romania, San Marino, Serbia and Montenegro, Slovakia, Slovenia, Spain, Sweden, Switzerland, The former Yugoslav Republic of Macedonia, Turkey, Ukraine, United Kingdom, United States.
Abstaining: Brazil, Chile, Malawi, Singapore.

Structural adjustment policies

Report of independent expert. The Commission considered a February report [E/CN.4/2004/47] of the independent expert on the effects of structural adjustment policies and foreign debt on human rights, Bernards Mudho (Kenya). The report reviewed progress made in implementing the heavily indebted poor countries (HIPCs) initiative, explored the integration of human rights into national budgeting processes and analysed the impact of structural adjustment policies and foreign debt on the enjoyment of those rights, pointing out the need to examine interlinkages with such economic and social issues as multilateral trade and global initiatives to achieve the MDGs. The expert advocated increased support to the HIPC initiative, consideration to the role that national human rights institutions could play in monitoring the public expenditure performance and the implementation of the HIPC initiative, poverty reduction strategy papers and other initiatives and further cooperation between the International Monetary Fund and the World Bank. The Commission should encourage the expert to further explore the interlinkages with other issues, contribute to the follow-up process of the 2002 International Conference on Financing for Development [YUN 2002, p. 953] and cooperate with other Commission mechanisms and human rights treaty bodies in further reviewing the effects of the foreign debt burden and related policies on the capacity of developing countries to adopt programmes for the enjoyment of economic, social and cultural rights.

Note by Secretariat. The Commission had before it a note by the Secretariat [E/CN.4/2004/47/Add.2], which stated that the expert's visit to Kyrgyzstan had been postponed to an undetermined date.

Commission action. By a recorded vote of 29 to 14, with 10 abstentions, the Commission, on 16 April [res. 2004/18], asked the independent expert to explore further the interlinkages with trade and other issues, including HIV/AIDS, when examining the impact of structural adjustment and foreign debt, and to contribute to the follow-up to the International Conference on Financing for Development, with a view to bringing to the

Commission's attention the effects of structural adjustment and foreign debt on the enjoyment of human rights. The expert was requested to draft general guidelines to be followed by States and by private, public, national and international financial institutions in the decision-making on and execution of debt repayments and structural reform programmes, to ensure that compliance with the commitments related to foreign debt would not undermine the obligations for the realization of fundamental economic, social and cultural rights, and to present a preliminary draft in 2005 and a final draft in 2006. The Secretary-General was asked to assist him.

Adverse effects of debt

Working paper. A July working paper, prepared by El-Hadji Guissé (Senegal) in response to a 2003 Subcommission request [YUN 2003, p. 760], highlighted the adverse effects of the debt owed by developing countries, evoking its origins and legal aspects and emphasizing ways in which it had contributed to extreme poverty and constituted an obstacle to human development. The debt burden, the paper concluded, rendered insurmountable problems affecting third world countries, including disease, famine, underdevelopment and lack of education and employment opportunities, among others. Thus, it constituted a serious impediment to the realization of all human rights.

Subcommission action. On 9 August [dec. 2004/106], the Subcommission asked Mr. Guissé to prepare, without financial implications, an expanded working paper on the effects of debt on human rights and to submit it in 2005.

Social Forum

Note by OHCHR. In June [E/CN.4/Sub.2/SF/2004/2], OHCHR presented the organizational details of the 2004 Social Forum, held in accordance with Economic and Social Council **decision 2004/217.**

Social Forum session. At its second session (Geneva, 22-23 July) [E/CN.4/Sub.2/2004/26 & Corr.1], the Social Forum held panel discussions on the empowerment of people living in poverty; the voice of affected groups on rural poverty and extreme poverty; the role of human rights in the development of operational strategies to address poverty; and recommendations on elements for incorporating human rights into poverty reduction strategies. It adopted conclusions on the first three discussion topics. Regarding the challenge of extreme poverty, it recommended that Governments and international institutions recognize that poverty needed to be addressed from a human rights perspective, which emphasized the importance of empowerment and non-discrimination involving the poor. Other recommendations advocated measures for empowering the poor and for national-level responsibility and national ownership in overcoming poverty. At the international level, the Forum recommended that all human rights bodies and mechanisms include in their studies and reports the examination of situations of poverty and poverty eradication programmes implemented by States and other actors. There was a growing need to include the human rights dimension in international economic decisions, such as those relating to debt cancellation, commodity price regulation or multilateral and bilateral free trade treaties and other economic arrangements as a way of preventing the occurrence of poverty. The Forum proposed a stronger focus on poverty prevention, through a more systematic and rigorous assessment of the human rights impacts of economic policies, and that poverty impact assessment processes and mechanisms be made compulsory. It adopted recommendations regarding its activities and methodology for fulfilling its role as the "intellectual antechamber" to the Subcommission in matters within its competence.

Subcommission action. On 9 August [res. 2004/3], the Subcommission, noting that the selection of issues relating to economic, social and cultural rights had to be restricted because of the two-day limitation to the Social Forum's meeting, recommended that the Commission study the possibility of extending the Forum's annual intersessional meeting.

Also on 9 August [res. 2004/8], the Subcommission decided that the next meeting of the Forum would be held in 2005 in Geneva and that the theme would be "Poverty and economic growth: challenges to human rights", to be addressed within the context of the five-year assessment of the goals set in the Millennium Declaration [YUN 2000, p. 49]. The Forum was invited to submit in 2005 a separate report containing a summary of the discussions, including recommendations and draft resolutions. Governments, NGOs, international organizations, UN bodies and specialized agencies were invited to submit to the High Commissioner their views on the theme, and to submit to OHCHR information about best practices in poverty-eradication policies and programmes incorporating a human rights perspective. The High Commissioner was asked to maintain a database of those practices in the Forum's web page. UN bodies and specialized agencies, relevant functional commissions of the Economic and Social Council, regional commis-

sions, international financial institutions, the Committee on Economic, Social and Cultural Rights, special rapporteurs and independent experts, NGOs, scholars and workers' associations were invited to submit studies to the Forum. Governments were asked to consider submitting reports to it on the obstacles encountered in their efforts to eradicate poverty. Gudmundur Alfredsson (Iceland), José Bengoa (Chile) and Antoanella-Iulia Motoc (Romania) were each asked to prepare a working paper for consideration in 2005. The Subcommission asked the Commission to recommend to the Economic and Social Council the establishment of a voluntary fund to facilitate the participation of grass-roots groups and disadvantaged organizations in the Forum. The Secretary-General was asked to disseminate information about the Forum, invite relevant individuals and organizations to attend it and to take practical measures for its success.

Transnational corporations

Commission action. On 20 April [dec. 2004/116], the Commission, taking note of a 2003 Subcommission resolution [YUN 2003, p. 761] and document on norms on the responsibilities of transnational corporations (TNCs) and other business enterprises with regard to human rights [ibid.], adopted recommendations relating to the activities of those corporations and the work of the Subcommission, which it submitted to the Economic and Social Council for approval (see below).

ECONOMIC AND SOCIAL COUNCIL ACTION

On 22 July (**decision 2004/279**), the Council confirmed the importance and priority it accorded to the question of the responsibilities of TNCs with regard to human rights; and requested OHCHR to compile a report setting out the scope and legal status of existing initiatives and standards relating to the responsibility of TNCs and related business enterprises regarding human rights, including the draft norms, and to submit the report to the Commission in 2005. It affirmed that the draft norms [YUN 2003, p. 761] had not been requested by the Commission and, as a draft proposal, had no legal standing, and that the Subcommission should not perform any monitoring function in that regard.

Working group activities. The working group on the working methods and activities of TNCs, at its sixth session (Geneva, 29-30 July) [E/CN.4/ Sub.2/2004/21], continued to work on the draft norms on the responsibilities of TNCs and other business enterprises, towards the elaboration of a binding instrument. The group had before it a number of relevant background documents, including the draft norms approved by the Subcommission in 2003 [YUN 2003, p. 761] and commentary thereto [ibid., p. 762]. The group considered current standards and standard-setting activities and comments by its members, Subcommission experts, Member States and NGOs. It adopted recommendations on its future work.

Subcommission action. On 26 July [dec. 2004/102], the Subcommission decided to establish a sessional working group to examine the working methods and activities of TNCs (see above).

On 12 August [res. 2004/16], the Subcommission decided to extend the mandate of the group for a three-year period, to enable it to fulfil its mandate, and asked it to report on its seventh (2005) session.

Coercive economic measures

Commission action. By a recorded vote of 36 to 14, with 3 abstentions, the Commission, on 16 April [res. 2004/22], requested the open-ended working group established to monitor and review progress made in the promotion and implementation of the right to development (see p. 744) to consider the question of human rights and the negative impact of unilateral coercive economic measures. The Commission decided to consider the negative impact of such measures in its work regarding the implementation of the right to development, and asked the High Commissioner to give urgent consideration to its resolution and the Secretary-General to bring the resolution to the attention of States, to seek their views on the implications and negative effects of those measures and to report in 2005.

Reports of Secretary-General. In response to a 2003 Commission request [YUN 2003, p. 762], the Secretary-General summarized information received from one State (Cuba) on the implications and negative effects of unilateral coercive economic measures [E/CN.4/2004/37].

Pursuant to General Assembly resolution 58/171 [YUN 2003, p. 762], the Secretary-General, in an October report [A/59/436], presented further information received from five States regarding such measures.

On 20 December, the Assembly took note of the Secretary-General's report (**decision 59/528**).

GENERAL ASSEMBLY ACTION

On 20 December [meeting 74], the General Assembly, on the recommendation of the Third Committee [A/59/503/Add.2], adopted **resolution 59/188** by recorded vote (132-53) [agenda item 105 (b)].

Human rights and unilateral coercive measures
The General Assembly,

Recalling all its previous resolutions, the most recent of which was resolution 58/171 of 22 December 2003, and Commission on Human Rights resolution 2004/22 of 16 April 2004,

Reaffirming the pertinent principles and provisions contained in the Charter of Economic Rights and Duties of States proclaimed by the General Assembly in its resolution 3281(XXIX) of 12 December 1974, in particular article 32 thereof, in which it declared that no State may use or encourage the use of economic, political or any other type of measures to coerce another State in order to obtain from it the subordination of the exercise of its sovereign rights,

Taking note of the report of the Secretary-General, submitted pursuant to Commission on Human Rights resolution 1999/21 of 23 April 1999, and the reports of the Secretary-General on the implementation of resolutions 52/120 of 12 December 1997 and 55/110 of 4 December 2000,

Recognizing the universal, indivisible, interdependent and interrelated character of all human rights, and, in this regard, reaffirming the right to development as an integral part of all human rights,

Recalling that the World Conference on Human Rights, held at Vienna from 14 to 25 June 1993, called upon States to refrain from any unilateral coercive measure not in accordance with international law and the Charter of the United Nations that creates obstacles to trade relations among States and impedes the full realization of all human rights,

Bearing in mind all the references to this question in the Copenhagen Declaration on Social Development, adopted by the World Summit for Social Development on 12 March 1995, the Beijing Declaration and Platform for Action, adopted by the Fourth World Conference on Women on 15 September 1995, the Istanbul Declaration on Human Settlements and the Habitat Agenda, adopted by the second United Nations Conference on Human Settlements (Habitat II) on 14 June 1996, and their five-year reviews,

Expressing its concern about the negative impact of unilateral coercive measures on international relations, trade, investment and cooperation,

Expressing its grave concern that, in some countries, the situation of children is adversely affected by unilateral coercive measures not in accordance with international law and the Charter that create obstacles to trade relations among States, impede the full realization of social and economic development and hinder the well-being of the population in the affected countries, with particular consequences for women and children, including adolescents,

Deeply concerned that, despite the recommendations adopted on this question by the General Assembly and recent major United Nations conferences, and contrary to general international law and the Charter, unilateral coercive measures continue to be promulgated and implemented with all their negative implications for the social-humanitarian activities and economic and social development of developing countries, including their extraterritorial effects, thereby creating additional obstacles to the full enjoyment of all human rights by peoples and individuals under the jurisdiction of other States,

Bearing in mind all the extraterritorial effects of any unilateral legislative, administrative and economic measures, policies and practices of a coercive nature against the development process and the enhancement of human rights in developing countries, which create obstacles to the full realization of all human rights,

Noting the continuing efforts of the open-ended Working Group on the Right to Development of the Commission on Human Rights, and reaffirming in particular its criteria, according to which unilateral coercive measures are one of the obstacles to the implementation of the Declaration on the Right to Development,

1. *Urges* all States to refrain from adopting or implementing any unilateral measures not in accordance with international law and the Charter of the United Nations, in particular those of a coercive nature with all their extraterritorial effects, which create obstacles to trade relations among States, thus impeding the full realization of the rights set forth in the Universal Declaration of Human Rights and other international human rights instruments, in particular the right of individuals and peoples to development;

2. *Also urges* all States to take steps to avoid and to refrain from adopting any unilateral measures not in accordance with international law and the Charter that impede the full achievement of economic and social development by the population of the affected countries, in particular children and women, that hinder their well-being and that create obstacles to the full enjoyment of their human rights, including the right of everyone to a standard of living adequate for their health and well-being and their right to food, medical care and the necessary social services, as well as to ensure that food and medicine are not used as tools for political pressure;

3. *Invites* all States to consider adopting administrative or legislative measures, as appropriate, to counteract the extraterritorial applications or effects of unilateral coercive measures;

4. *Rejects* unilateral coercive measures with all their extraterritorial effects as tools for political or economic pressure against any country, in particular against developing countries, because of their negative effects on the realization of all the human rights of vast sectors of their populations, in particular children, women and the elderly;

5. *Calls upon* Member States that have initiated such measures to commit themselves to their obligations and responsibilities arising from the international human rights instruments to which they are party by revoking such measures at the earliest possible time;

6. *Reaffirms*, in this context, the right of all peoples to self-determination, by virtue of which they freely determine their political status and freely pursue their economic, social and cultural development;

7. *Urges* the Commission on Human Rights to take fully into account the negative impact of unilateral coercive measures, including the enactment of national laws and their extraterritorial application, in its task concerning the implementation of the right to development;

8. *Requests* the United Nations High Commissioner for Human Rights, in discharging her functions relating to the promotion, realization and protection of the right to development and bearing in mind the continuing impact of unilateral coercive measures on the population of developing countries, to give priority to the present resolution in her annual report to the General Assembly;

9. *Requests* the Secretary-General to bring the present resolution to the attention of all Member States, to continue to collect their views and information on the implications and negative effects of unilateral coercive measures on their populations and to submit an analytical report thereon to the General Assembly at its sixtieth session, highlighting the practical and preventive measures in this respect;

10. *Decides* to examine the question on a priority basis at its sixtieth session under the sub-item entitled "Human rights questions, including alternative approaches for improving the effective enjoyment of human rights and fundamental freedoms".

RECORDED VOTE ON RESOLUTION 59/188:

In favour: Algeria, Angola, Antigua and Barbuda, Argentina, Armenia, Azerbaijan, Bahamas, Bahrain, Bangladesh, Barbados, Belarus, Belize, Benin, Bhutan, Bolivia, Botswana, Brazil, Brunei Darussalam, Burkina Faso, Burundi, Cambodia, Cameroon, Cape Verde, Central African Republic, Chad, Chile, China, Colombia, Comoros, Costa Rica, Côte d'Ivoire, Cuba, Democratic People's Republic of Korea, Democratic Republic of the Congo, Djibouti, Dominica, Dominican Republic, Ecuador, Egypt, El Salvador, Equatorial Guinea, Eritrea, Ethiopia, Fiji, Gabon, Gambia, Ghana, Grenada, Guatemala, Guinea, Guinea-Bissau, Guyana, Haiti, Honduras, India, Indonesia, Iran, Iraq, Jamaica, Jordan, Kazakhstan, Kenya, Kuwait, Kyrgyzstan, Lao People's Democratic Republic, Lebanon, Lesotho, Liberia, Libyan Arab Jamahiriya, Madagascar, Malawi, Malaysia, Mali, Mauritania, Mauritius, Mexico, Mongolia, Morocco, Mozambique, Myanmar, Namibia, Nauru, Nepal, Nicaragua, Niger, Nigeria, Oman, Pakistan, Panama, Papua New Guinea, Paraguay, Peru, Philippines, Qatar, Russian Federation, Rwanda, Saint Lucia, Saint Vincent and the Grenadines, Samoa, Sao Tome and Principe, Saudi Arabia, Senegal, Sierra Leone, Singapore, Solomon Islands, Somalia, South Africa, Sri Lanka, Sudan, Suriname, Swaziland, Syrian Arab Republic, Tajikistan, Thailand, Timor-Leste, Togo, Tonga, Trinidad and Tobago, Tunisia, Turkmenistan, Tuvalu, Uganda, United Arab Emirates, United Republic of Tanzania, Uruguay, Uzbekistan, Vanuatu, Venezuela, Viet Nam, Yemen, Zambia, Zimbabwe.

Against: Albania, Andorra, Australia, Austria, Belgium, Bosnia and Herzegovina, Bulgaria, Canada, Croatia, Cyprus, Czech Republic, Denmark, Estonia, Finland, France, Georgia, Germany, Greece, Hungary, Iceland, Ireland, Israel, Italy, Japan, Latvia, Liechtenstein, Lithuania, Luxembourg, Malta, Marshall Islands, Micronesia, Monaco, Netherlands, New Zealand, Norway, Palau, Poland, Portugal, Republic of Korea, Republic of Moldova, Romania, San Marino, Serbia and Montenegro, Slovakia, Slovenia, Spain, Sweden, Switzerland, The former Yugoslav Republic of Macedonia, Turkey, Ukraine, United Kingdom, United States.

Corruption

Commission action. On 16 April [dec. 2004/106], the Commission endorsed the Subcommission's 2003 decision [YUN 2003, p. 764] to appoint Christy Mbonu (Nigeria) as Special Rapporteur with the task of preparing a comprehensive study on corruption and its impact on the enjoyment of human rights, and the request to her to submit reports and to the Secretary-General to assist her.

On 22 July, the Economic and Social Council endorsed the Commission's decision (**decision 2004/274**).

Report of Special Rapporteur. In response to a 2003 Subcommission request [YUN 2003, p. 764], the Special Rapporteur submitted a July preliminary report [E/CN.4/Sub.2/2004/23], which built on her 2003 working paper. The report explored some of the manifestations of corruption and identified the victims, the poor being the most vulnerable. It discussed the consequences of corruption in human rights terms and considered the campaign against impunity for perpetrators of corruption, covering national and international mechanisms relating to the subject. The Special Rapporteur found that all organizations worldwide lost about 6 per cent of their annual revenue to fraud and corruption and concluded that the first step in tackling the problem lay in realizing that it existed, and that it posed serious threats to peaceful coexistence among nations and violated people's rights embodied in international instruments. The Special Rapporteur emphasized the importance of the political will of leaders in combating corruption and encouraged States to sign and ratify the United Nations Convention against Corruption, adopted in General Assembly resolution 58/4 [YUN 2003, p. 1128]. She proposed the establishment and enforcement of national anti-corruption mechanisms; cooperation between States, including with regard to the role of the International Criminal Police Organization; and safety net mechanisms to protect citizens from corporate corruption resulting in bankruptcy and the collapse of companies.

Subcommission action. On 9 August [res. 2004/4], the Subcommission called on OHCHR, in cooperation with specialized agencies, to organize periodic high-level meetings, under the auspices of the Subcommission, to create greater awareness on the part of the international community, particularly States, of the importance of eliminating corruption. It asked the Secretary-General to facilitate the Special Rapporteur's work by enabling her to attend the meetings of the "Friends of the Convention".

Extreme poverty

Report of independent expert. In accordance with a 2002 Commission request [YUN 2002, p. 732], the independent expert on the question of human rights and extreme poverty, Anne-Marie Lizin (Belgium), submitted a February final report [E/CN.4/2004/43], which stated that extreme poverty was still a long way from being overcome and that numerous initiatives by the international community and development bodies could not hide the fact that the phenomenon continued to pose enormous problems. She recommended measures relating to the responsibility of affected States; effective legislation; restructuring of States and public governance; minimum income and employment opportunities; access to schools and health care; the role of women; microcredit as a policy component to combat extreme poverty; and continuing dialogue with affected populations. The expert said that it was vital for the

Commission to remain attentive to the question of extreme poverty in connection with human rights, recommended the renewal of her mandate and advocated the idea of decentralization for the benefit of the poorest, first evaluated in 1999 [YUN 1999, p. 660] and in 2002 [YUN 2002, p. 732].

Commission action. On 16 April [res. 2004/23], the Commission asked OHCHR to give high priority to the relationship between extreme poverty and human rights and to pursue further work in that area, notably with regard to the draft guidelines on the integration of human rights into poverty reduction strategies (see below). It called on States, intergovernmental organizations and NGOs to take into account, in activities carried out under the United Nations Decade for the Eradication of Poverty (1997-2006), proclaimed by the General Assembly in resolution 50/107 [YUN 1995, p. 844] (see p. 833), the links between human rights and extreme poverty, and efforts to empower people living in poverty to participate in decision-making processes on policies affecting them. The United Nations was called on to strengthen poverty eradication as a priority throughout the system. The Commission decided to extend for a period of two years the independent expert's mandate and asked her to report in 2005.

On 22 July, the Economic and Social Council approved the Commission's decision to extend the expert's mandate and its request to her to report (**decision 2004/253**).

Working paper. In response to a 2003 Subcommission request [YUN 2003, p. 761], José Bengoa (Chile) submitted a working paper [E/CN.4/Sub.2/2004/44], which discussed poverty, particularly extreme poverty resulting in social exclusion, as a violation of human rights. The paper examined a number of current initiatives and advocated a conception of poverty as the absence or underdevelopment of human capabilities and freedoms. It emphasized the need to empower the poor as a poverty-reduction human rights strategy.

International declaration

Ad hoc group of experts. In response to a 2003 Subcommission request [YUN 2003, p. 765], Mr. Bengoa, in his capacity as coordinator of the ad hoc group of experts to prepare a study on the draft of an international declaration on extreme poverty and human rights, presented a June progress report [E/CN.4/Sub.2/2004/25] on the need to develop guiding principles on the implementation of human rights norms and standards in the context of the fight against extreme poverty. The report considered the challenge of poverty eradication and summarized discussions emanating from the International Experts Meeting on Women and Justice (Pune, India, 26-30 January), which covered draft guidelines on women and justice, presentations and discussions on women and poverty, and the need to develop guiding principles on human rights and extreme poverty within the framework of the ad hoc group's mandate. Based on those discussions, the group's previous work and consultations with people living in poverty, the group agreed on the need to draft a text on human rights and extreme poverty, which would serve as an empowerment tool for people living in poverty and those working with them. The group, recognizing that a number of outstanding issues needed to be more closely examined and resolved, recommended, for consideration by the Subcommission, broad consultations with regional and international organizations, NGOs, grass-roots organizations, academics and others to consider possible elements of a text, with particular efforts made to include in the process people living in poverty. It further recommended clarification of such outstanding issues as the nature of the document, the definition of poverty, the distinction between poverty and extreme poverty, the indivisibility of human rights versus the prioritization of certain rights in the context of poverty eradication or reduction, and a careful examination of a possible right-by-right approach. The group proposed to submit a final report in 2005. Annexed to the report was the outcome document of the Experts Meeting on Women.

A July addendum [E/CN.4/Sub.2/2004/25/Add.1] contained draft initial elements for discussion on possible guiding principles on human rights, poverty and extreme poverty, as well as preliminary comments received thereto from various counterparts.

Subcommission action. On 9 August [res. 2004/7], the Subcommission asked Ms. Motoc, Mr. Decaux, Mr. Yokota, Mr. Guissé and Mr. Bengoa to prepare, without financial implications, a progress report in 2005 and a final report in 2006 on the need to develop guiding principles on the implementation of existing human rights norms and standards in the context of the fight against extreme poverty. They were also asked to study the application of the human rights covenants and conventions in the context of poverty, in order to identify gaps and obstacles to their implementation; to consider situations of poverty in various parts of the world, as well as the policies of the World Bank, WTO, the International Monetary Fund and other international bodies for fighting poverty; to adopt an approach towards extreme poverty that strengthened bonds of solidarity and social inclusion mechanisms; and,

with the assistance of the population groups concerned, to identify a range of indicators for keeping track of situations of extreme poverty and changes therein, pinpointing related needs. Governments and regional specialized bodies in Africa, Asia, Europe and Latin America, as well as international agencies, such as the United Nations Conference on Trade and Development, UNDP and the United Nations Educational, Scientific and Cultural Organization (UNESCO), were asked to provide the experts with information. NGOs were asked to contribute to the study and OHCHR was asked to support it.

GENERAL ASSEMBLY ACTION

On 20 December [meeting 74], the General Assembly, on the recommendation of the Third Committee [A/59/503/Add.2], adopted **resolution 59/186** without vote [agenda item 105 *(b)*].

Human rights and extreme poverty

The General Assembly,

Reaffirming the Universal Declaration of Human Rights, the International Covenant on Civil and Political Rights, the International Covenant on Economic, Social and Cultural Rights and other human rights instruments adopted by the United Nations,

Recalling its resolution 47/196 of 22 December 1992, by which it declared 17 October the International Day for the Eradication of Poverty, and its resolution 50/107 of 20 December 1995, by which it proclaimed the first United Nations Decade for the Eradication of Poverty (1997-2006), as well as its resolution 57/211 of 18 December 2002 and its previous resolutions on human rights and extreme poverty, in which it reaffirmed that extreme poverty and exclusion from society constitute a violation of human dignity and that urgent national and international action is therefore required to eliminate them,

Recalling also its resolution 52/134 of 12 December 1997, in which it recognized that the enhancement of international cooperation in the field of human rights was essential for the understanding, promotion and protection of all human rights,

Deeply concerned that extreme poverty persists in all countries of the world, regardless of their economic, social and cultural situation, and that its extent and manifestations, such as hunger, trafficking in human beings, disease, lack of adequate shelter, illiteracy and hopelessness, are particularly severe in developing countries, while acknowledging the significant progress made in several parts of the world in combating extreme poverty,

Recalling Commission on Human Rights resolution 2004/23 of 16 April 2004, as well as resolution 2004/7 of 9 August 2004 of the Subcommission on the Promotion and Protection of Human Rights,

Welcoming the Summit of World Leaders for Action against Hunger and Poverty of 20 September 2004, convened in New York by the Presidents of Brazil, Chile and France and the Prime Minister of Spain with the support of the Secretary-General,

Recognizing that the eradication of extreme poverty is a major challenge within the process of globalization and requires coordinated and continued policies through decisive national action and international cooperation,

Reaffirming that, since the existence of widespread extreme poverty inhibits the full and effective enjoyment of human rights and might, in some situations, constitute a threat to the right to life, its immediate alleviation and eventual eradication must remain a high priority for the international community,

Reaffirming also that democracy, development and the full and effective enjoyment of human rights and fundamental freedoms are interdependent and mutually reinforcing and contribute to the eradication of extreme poverty,

Noting with interest the extension for a period of two years of the mandate of the independent expert on the question of human rights and extreme poverty,

1. *Reaffirms* that extreme poverty and exclusion from society constitute a violation of human dignity and that urgent national and international action is therefore required to eliminate them;

2. *Also reaffirms* that it is essential for States to foster participation by the poorest people in the decision-making process in the societies in which they live, in the promotion of human rights and in efforts to combat extreme poverty, and that it is essential for people living in poverty and vulnerable groups to be empowered to organize themselves and to participate in all aspects of political, economic and social life, in particular the planning and implementation of policies that affect them, thus enabling them to become genuine partners in development;

3. *Emphasizes* that extreme poverty is a major issue to be addressed by Governments, civil society and the United Nations system, including international financial institutions, and in this context reaffirms that political commitment is a prerequisite for the eradication of poverty;

4. *Reaffirms* that the existence of widespread absolute poverty inhibits the full and effective enjoyment of human rights and renders democracy and popular participation fragile;

5. *Recognizes* the need to promote respect for human rights and fundamental freedoms in order to address the most pressing social needs of people living in poverty, including through the design and development of appropriate mechanisms to strengthen and consolidate democratic institutions and governance;

6. *Reaffirms* the commitments contained in the United Nations Millennium Declaration, in particular the commitments to spare no effort to fight against extreme poverty and to achieve development and poverty eradication, including the commitment to halve, by 2015, the proportion of the world's people whose income is less than one United States dollar a day and the proportion of people who suffer from hunger;

7. *Invites* the United Nations High Commissioner for Human Rights, within the framework of the implementation of the United Nations Decade for the Eradication of Poverty, to continue to give appropriate attention to the question of human rights and extreme poverty;

8. *Welcomes* the efforts of entities throughout the United Nations system to incorporate the Millennium Declaration and the internationally agreed development goals set out therein into their work;

9. *Requests* the independent expert on the question of human rights and extreme poverty to forward his reports on his activities, which he will submit to the Commission on Human Rights at its sixty-first and sixty-second sessions, to the General Assembly at its sixty-first session;

10. *Calls upon* States, United Nations bodies, in particular the Office of the United Nations High Commissioner for Human Rights and the United Nations Development Programme, intergovernmental organizations and non-governmental organizations to continue to give appropriate attention to the links between human rights and extreme poverty;

11. *Decides* to consider the question further at its sixty-first session under the sub-item entitled "Human rights questions, including alternative approaches for improving the effective enjoyment of human rights and fundamental freedoms".

Right to food

Reports of Special Rapporteur. In response to a 2003 Commission request [YUN 2003, p. 766], the Special Rapporteur on the right to food, Jean Ziegler (Switzerland), in a February report [E/CN.4/2004/10], reviewed his 2003 activities to promote and monitor the right. During the year, he transmitted a number of communications regarding alleged violations of the right to seven countries and received responses from three of them. The report described the Special Rapporteur's efforts to further develop the conceptual background to the right and considered the emerging concept of food sovereignty, which emphasized national and individual ability to determine food and agricultural policies. Addressing the concept in relation to trade and the right to food, the Special Rapporteur reviewed the reasons why international trade in food and agriculture was not benefiting the vast majority of poor and marginalized people, but was instead worsening marginalization and inequality. He concluded that it was time to examine new and alternative models for agriculture and trade, and to develop binding legal norms that held TNCs to human rights standards and prevented potential abuses of their growing power. The Special Rapporteur recommended that Governments take action to meet commitments made at the 1996 World Food Summit [YUN 1996, p. 1129] to realize the right to food, and in the Millennium Declaration [YUN 2000, p. 49] to halve the number of hunger victims by 2015. Efforts should be made to ensure the livelihoods of poor peasant farmers who made up 75 per cent of the world's 1.2 billion poorest people, and States should monitor the activities of TNCs to ensure that they did not violate the right to food. The Commission should adopt the Subcommission's draft norms on the responsibilities of TNCs and other business enterprises with regard to human rights (see p. 756).

The Special Rapporteur visited Ethiopia (16-27 February) [E/CN.4/2005/47/Add.1], where he sought to understand the persistent hunger, malnutrition and famine that afflicted the country. The Special Rapporteur reviewed the sources, nature and impact of famine, food insecurity, hunger and malnutrition in the country, examined the legal framework governing the right to food, and evaluated government policies and programmes for realizing the right. He said Ethiopia remained one of the world's poorest countries and that half of its people continued to be affected by hunger. Food shortages struck regularly, and an estimated 5-6 million people depended on food aid yearly, regardless of the rains or harvest. During the 2003 famine, the number needing food aid had increased markedly to 13 million. Although the Government was making progress in realizing the right to food, through programmes and policies that sought to increase availability and access to food and water, it was not acceptable that nearly half of the population still did not get enough to eat daily and that more than two thirds of Ethiopians lacked access to safe clean water, said the Special Rapporteur. He recommended that a shift from an emergency to a development perspective be made a priority for food security and for realizing the right to food, and advocated, among other measures, increased donor funding support to the Government for long-term development in both rural and urban sectors.

In Mongolia (14-24 August) [E/CN.4/2005/47/Add.2], which, according to the statistics of the Food and Agriculture Organization of the United Nations (FAO), had the highest level of undernourishment in Asia, the Special Rapporteur examined the impact of severe winters and other natural disasters, and reviewed the situation of hunger and poverty in the country, and the legal and policy frameworks governing the right to food. Although he was encouraged by the Government's efforts to improve food supply and quality, he believed that the lack of access to food and consequent undernourishment deserved more attention, as did early warning mechanisms and preventive measures against natural disasters. The Special Rapporteur was particularly concerned that chronic undernourishment appeared to have increased over the past decade, with over a third of the population chronically undernourished. Other areas of concern related to violations of the right to food, including reports of people having starved to death, and to obstacles affecting the Government's capacity to guarantee the progressive realization of the right.

The Special Rapporteur recommended a comprehensive study of the situation of food insecurity and chronic undernourishment in the country to determine the urgency of the problem, and proposed a series of measures to strengthen protection of the right and to reverse the apparent regression in efforts to realize it.

Commission action. By a recorded vote of 51 to 1, with 1 abstention, the Commission, on 16 April [res. 2004/19], considering it intolerable that there were some 840 million undernourished people in the world, asked States, private actors and international organizations to promote the effective realization of the right to food for all. The Commission encouraged the Special Rapporteur to continue mainstreaming a gender perspective in his work and asked him to report to the General Assembly in 2004 and to the Commission in 2005. The High Commissioner was asked to assist him, while Governments, UN agencies, funds and programmes, treaty bodies and NGOs were invited to cooperate with him by submitting suggestions on ways to realize the right to food.

ECONOMIC AND SOCIAL COUNCIL ACTION

In July, the Economic and Social Council, on the recommendation of the Commission on Human Rights [E/2004/23], adopted **decision 2004/252** by recorded vote (52-1-1) [agenda item 14 (g)].

The right to food

At its 48th plenary meeting, on 22 July 2004, the Economic and Social Council took note of Commission on Human Rights resolution 2004/19 of 16 April 2004 and approved the request to the Special Rapporteur on the right to food to submit a report to the General Assembly at its fifty-ninth session and to report to the Commission at its sixty-first session on the implementation of resolution 2004/19.

RECORDED VOTE ON DECISION 2004/252:

In favour: Armenia, Azerbaijan, Bangladesh, Belgium, Belize, Benin, Bhutan, Burundi, Canada, Chile, China, Colombia, Congo, Cuba, Ecuador, El Salvador, Finland, France, Germany, Ghana, Greece, Guatemala, Hungary, India, Indonesia, Ireland, Italy, Jamaica, Japan, Kenya, Libyan Arab Jamahiriya, Malaysia, Mauritius, Mozambique, Namibia, Nicaragua, Nigeria, Panama, Poland, Qatar, Republic of Korea, Russian Federation, Saudi Arabia, Senegal, Sweden, Tunisia, Turkey, Ukraine, United Arab Emirates, United Kingdom, United Republic of Tanzania, Zimbabwe.

Against: United States.

Abstaining: Australia.

Subcommission action. On 9 August [dec. 2004/105], the Subcommission, reiterating the recommendations contained in its 2003 resolution [YUN 2003, p. 766] and welcoming progress made in elaborating voluntary guidelines to support the progressive realization of the right to food under FAO auspices, called on Governments and interested parties to continue the drafting process and to renew efforts to reach consensus on outstanding issues, to make it possible to complete and adopt the guidelines.

Further report of Special Rapporteur. Pursuant to General Assembly resolution 58/186 [YUN 2003, p. 767] and to Commission resolution 2004/19 (above), the Secretary-General, in September, transmitted a report of the Special Rapporteur [A/59/385], which further described his activities and considered situations of concern in the Darfur region of western Sudan, the Democratic People's Republic of Korea, Cuba and the Occupied Palestinian Territory. The report also updated information regarding the drafting of voluntary guidelines to assist Governments in implementing the right to food and examined the increasing dependence of communities in Africa, Asia and Latin America on fish and fishery resources for food and livelihood, which was a newly emerging issue in the struggle for food security. The Special Rapporteur said hunger levels were rising and had increased every year since the 1996 World Food Summit when Governments promised to reduce the level. Hunger killed more people than any contemporary war or terrorist attack, and one child below the age of 5 died from a hunger-related disease every five seconds. He recommended measures to reverse the trend of increasing world hunger and undernourishment, to address alleged violations of the right to food of people in some countries and to complete negotiations on the voluntary guidelines and ensure that they would be an enabling tool for the realization of the right to food. Governments should not implement policies countering their legal obligations to realize the right, and should ensure that their activities did not impact negatively on the capacity of people in other countries to realize the right, particularly regarding those reliant on fish and fishery products.

GENERAL ASSEMBLY ACTION

On 20 December [meeting 74], the General Assembly, on the recommendation of the Third Committee [A/59/503/Add.2], adopted **resolution 59/202** by recorded vote (182-3) [agenda item 105 (*b*)].

The right to food

The General Assembly,

Recalling its resolution 58/186 of 22 December 2003, as well as all Commission on Human Rights resolutions in this regard, in particular resolution 2004/19 of 16 April 2004,

Recalling also the Universal Declaration of Human Rights, which provides that everyone has the right to a standard of living adequate for her or his health and well-being, including food, the Universal Declaration on the Eradication of Hunger and Malnutrition, and the United Nations Millennium Declaration,

Recalling further the provisions of the International Covenant on Economic, Social and Cultural Rights, in which the fundamental right of every person to be free from hunger is recognized,

Bearing in mind the Rome Declaration on World Food Security and the World Food Summit Plan of Action and the Declaration of the World Food Summit: five years later, adopted in Rome on 13 June 2002,

Reaffirming that all human rights are universal, indivisible, interdependent and interrelated,

Reaffirming also that a peaceful, stable and enabling political, social and economic environment, at both the national and the international levels, is the essential foundation that will enable States to give adequate priority to food security and poverty eradication,

Reiterating, as in the Rome Declaration on World Food Security and the Declaration of the World Food Summit: five years later, that food should not be used as an instrument of political or economic pressure, and reaffirming in this regard the importance of international cooperation and solidarity, as well as the necessity of refraining from unilateral measures that are not in accordance with international law and the Charter of the United Nations and that endanger food security,

Convinced that each State must adopt a strategy consistent with its resources and capacities to achieve its individual goals in implementing the recommendations contained in the Rome Declaration on World Food Security and the World Food Summit Plan of Action and, at the same time, cooperate regionally and internationally in order to organize collective solutions to global issues of food security in a world of increasingly interlinked institutions, societies and economies where coordinated efforts and shared responsibilities are essential,

Recognizing that the problems of hunger and food insecurity have global dimensions and that they are likely to persist and even to increase dramatically in some regions unless urgent, determined and concerted action is taken, given the anticipated increase in the world's population and the stress on natural resources,

Expressing its concern about the adverse impact on the realization of the right to food caused by many humanitarian emergencies, including plagues and natural disasters,

Stressing the importance of reversing the continuing decline of official development assistance devoted to agriculture, both in real terms and as a share of total official development assistance,

1. *Reaffirms* that hunger constitutes an outrage and a violation of human dignity and therefore requires the adoption of urgent measures at the national, regional and international levels for its elimination;

2. *Also reaffirms* the right of everyone to have access to safe and nutritious food, consistent with the right to adequate food and the fundamental right of everyone to be free from hunger, so as to be able to fully develop and maintain their physical and mental capacities;

3. *Considers it intolerable* that there are about 842 million undernourished people in the world, that every five seconds a child under the age of 5 dies from hunger-related diseases and that more than 2 billion people throughout the world suffer from "hidden hunger" or micronutrient malnutrition when, according to the Food and Agriculture Organization of the United Nations, the world produces more than enough food to feed its entire population;

4. *Expresses its concern* that women are disproportionately affected by hunger, food insecurity and poverty, in part as a result of gender inequality, that in many countries, girls are twice as likely as boys to die from malnutrition and preventable childhood diseases, and that it is estimated that almost twice as many women as men suffer from malnutrition;

5. *Encourages* all States to take steps with a view to achieving progressively the full realization of the right to food, including steps to promote the conditions for everyone to be free from hunger and, as soon as possible, to enjoy fully the right to food, and to create and adopt national plans to combat hunger;

6. *Requests* all States and private actors, as well as international organizations within their respective mandates, to take fully into account the need to promote the effective realization of the right to food for all, including in the ongoing negotiations in different fields;

7. *Encourages* all States to take action to address discrimination against women, particularly where it contributes to the malnutrition of women and girls, including measures to ensure the realization of the right to food and ensuring that women have equal access to resources, including income, land and water, to enable them to feed themselves;

8. *Stresses* the need to make efforts to mobilize and optimize the allocation and utilization of technical and financial resources from all sources, including external debt relief for developing countries, and to reinforce national actions to implement sustainable food security policies;

9. *Welcomes* the meeting of world leaders for action against hunger and poverty, convened by the Presidents of Brazil, Chile and France and the Prime Minister of Spain, with the support of the Secretary-General, and the resulting New York Declaration on Action against Hunger and Poverty, which has been supported by one hundred and ten countries to date, and recommends the continuation of efforts aimed at identifying additional sources of financing for the fight against hunger and poverty;

10. *Recognizes* that the promises made at the World Food Summit in 1996 to halve the number of persons who are undernourished are not being fulfilled, and invites once again all international financial and developmental institutions, as well as the relevant United Nations agencies and funds, to give priority to and provide the necessary funding to realize the aim of halving by 2015 the proportion of people who suffer from hunger, as well as the right to food as set out in the Rome Declaration on World Food Security and the United Nations Millennium Declaration;

11. *Urges* States to give adequate priority in their development strategies and expenditures to the realization of the right to food;

12. *Takes note* of the interim report of the Special Rapporteur of the Commission on Human Rights on the right to food, and commends the Special Rapporteur for his valuable work in the promotion of the right to food;

13. *Supports* the realization of the mandate of the Special Rapporteur as extended by the Commission on Human Rights in its resolution 2003/25 of 22 April 2003;

14. *Expresses its appreciation* to the Special Rapporteur for his effective contribution to the medium-term review of the implementation of the Rome Declaration on World Food Security and the World Food Summit Plan of Action through the submission to the United Nations High Commissioner for Human Rights of his recommendations on all aspects of the right to food, and his participation in and contribution to the proceedings of that event;

15. *Encourages* the Special Rapporteur to continue mainstreaming a gender perspective in the activities relating to his mandate;

16. *Requests* the Secretary-General and the High Commissioner to provide all the necessary human and financial resources for the effective fulfilment of the mandate of the Special Rapporteur;

17. *Welcomes* the work already done by the Committee on Economic, Social and Cultural Rights in promoting the right to adequate food, in particular its general comment No. 12 (1999) on the right to adequate food (article 11 of the International Covenant on Economic, Social and Cultural Rights), in which the Committee affirmed, inter alia, that the right to adequate food is indivisibly linked to the inherent dignity of the human person and is indispensable for the fulfilment of other human rights enshrined in the International Bill of Human Rights, and is also inseparable from social justice, requiring the adoption of appropriate economic, environmental and social policies, at both the national and the international levels, oriented to the eradication of poverty and the fulfilment of all human rights for all;

18. *Takes note* of general comment No. 15 (2002) of the Committee on Economic, Social and Cultural Rights on the right to water (articles 11 and 12 of the Covenant), in which the Committee noted, inter alia, the importance of ensuring sustainable water resources for human consumption and agriculture in realization of the right to adequate food;

19. *Welcomes* the adoption by the Intergovernmental Working Group, as mandated by the Council of the Food and Agriculture Organization of the United Nations, of a set of voluntary guidelines to support the progressive realization of the right to adequate food in the context of national food security, as well as the endorsement by the Committee on World Food Security of the voluntary guidelines as submitted and its decision to transmit them to the Council for final adoption, and in this regard encourages States members of the Council to adopt the voluntary guidelines;

20. *Also welcomes* the continued cooperation of the High Commissioner, the Committee on Economic, Social and Cultural Rights and the Special Rapporteur, and encourages them to continue their cooperation in this regard;

21. *Requests* the Special Rapporteur to submit a comprehensive report to the Commission on Human Rights at its sixty-first session and an interim report to the General Assembly at its sixtieth session on the implementation of the present resolution;

22. *Invites* Governments, relevant United Nations agencies, funds and programmes, treaty bodies, civil society actors, including non-governmental organizations, as well as the private sector, to cooperate fully with the Special Rapporteur in the fulfilment of his mandate, inter alia, through the submission of comments and suggestions on ways and means of realizing the right to food;

23. *Decides* to continue the consideration of the question at its sixtieth session under the item entitled "Human rights questions".

RECORDED VOTE ON RESOLUTION 59/202:

In favour: Afghanistan, Albania, Algeria, Andorra, Angola, Antigua and Barbuda, Argentina, Armenia, Australia, Austria, Azerbaijan, Bahamas, Bahrain, Bangladesh, Barbados, Belarus, Belgium, Belize, Benin, Bhutan, Bolivia, Bosnia and Herzegovina, Botswana, Brazil, Brunei Darussalam, Bulgaria, Burkina Faso, Burundi, Cambodia, Cameroon, Canada, Cape Verde, Central African Republic, Chad, Chile, China, Colombia, Comoros, Costa Rica, Côte d'Ivoire, Croatia, Cuba, Cyprus, Czech Republic, Democratic Republic of the Congo, Denmark, Djibouti, Dominica, Dominican Republic, Ecuador, Egypt, El Salvador, Equatorial Guinea, Eritrea, Estonia, Ethiopia, Fiji, Finland, France, Gabon, Gambia, Georgia, Germany, Ghana, Greece, Grenada, Guatemala, Guinea, Guinea-Bissau, Guyana, Haiti, Honduras, Hungary, Iceland, India, Indonesia, Iran, Iraq, Ireland, Italy, Jamaica, Japan, Jordan, Kazakhstan, Kenya, Kuwait, Kyrgyzstan, Lao People's Democratic Republic, Latvia, Lebanon, Lesotho, Liberia, Libyan Arab Jamahiriya, Liechtenstein, Lithuania, Luxembourg, Madagascar, Malawi, Malaysia, Maldives, Mali, Malta, Marshall Islands, Mauritania, Mauritius, Mexico, Monaco, Mongolia, Morocco, Mozambique, Myanmar, Namibia, Nauru, Nepal, Netherlands, New Zealand, Nicaragua, Niger, Nigeria, Norway, Oman, Pakistan, Panama, Papua New Guinea, Paraguay, Peru, Philippines, Poland, Portugal, Qatar, Republic of Korea, Republic of Moldova, Romania, Russian Federation, Rwanda, Saint Lucia, Saint Vincent and the Grenadines, Samoa, San Marino, Sao Tome and Principe, Saudi Arabia, Senegal, Serbia and Montenegro, Seychelles, Sierra Leone, Singapore, Slovakia, Slovenia, Solomon Islands, Somalia, South Africa, Spain, Sri Lanka, Sudan, Suriname, Swaziland, Sweden, Switzerland, Syrian Arab Republic, Tajikistan, Thailand, The former Yugoslav Republic of Macedonia, Timor-Leste, Togo, Tonga, Trinidad and Tobago, Tunisia, Turkey, Turkmenistan, Tuvalu, Uganda, Ukraine, United Arab Emirates, United Kingdom, Uruguay, Uzbekistan, Vanuatu, Venezuela, Viet Nam, Yemen, Zambia, Zimbabwe.

Against: Israel, Palau, United States.

Right to adequate housing

Reports of Special Rapporteur. The Special Rapporteur on the right to adequate housing, Miloon Kothari (India), in a March report [E/CN.4/2004/48], focused on forced evictions, a priority issue that had emerged with respect to the question of adequate housing as a component of the right to an adequate standard of living. The report examined the legal basis for protection against forced evictions at the international, regional and national levels, considered the causes and impact of the practice and discussed strategies to counter it. Despite efforts by treaty bodies, special procedures, UN agencies and programmes and civil society organizations to counter forced evictions, the phenomenon continued, resulting in displacement, loss of livelihood, property and belongings, and physical and psychological injury to those affected, which often included persons already living in extreme poverty. The Special Rapporteur recommended that the Commission call for an expert seminar to develop guidelines or principles for States on forced evictions, based on general comment No. 7 on forced evictions, adopted in 1997 [YUN 1997, p. 599] by the Committee on Economic, Social and Cultural Rights, and other relevant international instruments. Although existing instruments provided useful guidance for States and the international community, new standards were required

to capture comprehensive preventive and compensatory measures that needed to be taken to tackle forced evictions. The Special Rapporteur also urged the Commission to include forced evictions more explicitly in his mandate, to enable him to respond to related problems effectively, to request OHCHR to develop indicators on the phenomenon based on existing indicators from the UN housing rights programme, developed jointly with the United Nations Programme on Human Settlements (UN-Habitat), to support the programme, and to urge States to adopt policies and legislation on forced evictions based on the provisions of international human rights instruments. Further recommendations addressed measures to protect women from forced evictions.

The Special Rapporteur visited Kenya (9-22 February) [E/CN.4/2005/48/Add.2] to examine the status of the realization of the right to adequate housing and related rights in the country, with particular attention to gender equality and non-discrimination. He found that previous Kenyan Governments had failed to protect the right to adequate housing and access to related services, such as potable water, electricity, sanitation and land, particularly with respect to the poorest segments of society, and that failure had been accentuated by corruption, resource mismanagement, land-grabbing, increasing poverty and growing slums. He recommended the integration of a human rights perspective in sectoral policies and housing programmes, and a government review of existing programmes, policies and laws, in order to orient them towards the poorest, vulnerable and marginalized segments of the population, including indigenous peoples, persons living with HIV/AIDS or disabilities, destitute persons and forest dwellers. A comprehensive approach was needed to address the issues of forced evictions, security of tenure, legalization of informal settlements and slum upgrading, and to ensure close consultation with those affected.

In Brazil (29 May–13 June) [E/CN.4/2005/48/Add.3], the Special Rapporteur focused on women with regard to the realization of the right to adequate housing, highlighting positive developments implemented by the Government, while noting that the challenges facing the country in the housing and land sector were overwhelming. The failure to realize the land rights of the poor was driven by widespread poverty, inequalities, an enormous housing deficit and historical discrimination against indigenous peoples and Afro-Brazilians. The country's housing deficit was estimated at 7 million housing units and some 6.6 million Brazilian families had nowhere to live. The Special Rapporteur pointed to an urgent need for a comprehensive national housing policy encompassing both urban and rural considerations, and equally comprehensive national housing legislation binding together existing laws and programmes. Further recommendations related to the convening of an expert seminar to develop guidelines on forced evictions, the development of a new national housing policy, the reconciliation of macroeconomic and social objectives, the reorientation of existing housing finance programmes to meet the needs of the poor, legislation to harmonize and simplify the issuing of title deeds and increased inter-ministerial cooperation on such issues as indigenous peoples' rights.

Commission action. On 16 April [res. 2004/21], the Commission asked the Special Rapporteur to emphasize practical solutions regarding the right to adequate housing as a component of the right to an adequate standard of living, facilitate the provision of technical assistance, pay specific attention to the needs of persons with disabilities, further review the interrelatedness of adequate housing and other human rights, continue to apply a gender perspective in his work and report in 2005 and 2006. OHCHR and UN-Habitat were asked to strengthen cooperation, to continue developing a joint UN housing rights programme and to cooperate with the Special Rapporteur. States were called on to give full effect to housing rights, paying particular attention to those living in extreme poverty, most often women and children; to ensure indigenous peoples and other minorities non-discriminatory access to adequate housing; and to cooperate with the Special Rapporteur and submit to him information on national experiences, notably on best practices.

Also on 16 April [res. 2004/28], the Commission, by a recorded vote of 45 to 1, with 7 abstentions, reaffirming that the practice of forced eviction violated a broad range of human rights, particularly the right to adequate housing, recommended that Governments provide restitution, compensation or sufficient alternative accommodation to persons forcibly evicted. The High Commissioner was asked to give attention to the practice and States were invited to study the Comprehensive Human Rights Guidelines on Development-based Displacement, adopted at the 1997 expert seminar on the practice of forced evictions [YUN 1997, p. 676], with a view to considering further action.

Right to education

Report of Special Rapporteur. The Special Rapporteur on the right to education, Katarina Tomasevski (Croatia), in January, submitted her final report [E/CN.4/2004/45], which focused on the financial obstacles to the realization of the right to education, the elimination of gender discrimination in and through education, and the content of education. It summarized the lessons learned in the past five years of the Special Rapporteur's mandate, noting that there was an urgent need for a contribution by UN human rights actors. The report presented tabular information regarding countries with school fees in public primary education, by region; key obstacles to girls' education: marriage and pregnancy; and adolescent childbearing: births per 1,000 girls aged 15-19. The Special Rapporteur recommended that the Commission not renew her mandate.

Commission action. On 16 April [res. 2004/25], the Commission urged States to give full effect to the right to education and to guarantee that the right was recognized and exercised without discrimination. The Commission decided to extend the Special Rapporteur's mandate for three years and invited him/her to intensify efforts aimed at identifying ways to overcome obstacles and difficulties in realizing the right, to apply a gender perspective in his/her work and to report in 2005. The Secretary-General was asked to assist the Special Rapporteur.

On 22 July, the Economic and Social Council approved the Commission's decision to extend the Special Rapporteur's mandate and its requests to him/her to report and to the Secretary-General to assist him/her (**decision 2004/254**).

In August, the Commission appointed Vernor Muñoz Villalobos (Costa Rica) as Special Rapporteur.

Environmental and scientific concerns

Toxic wastes

Reports of Special Rapporteur. In response to a 2003 Commission request [YUN 2003, p. 771], the Special Rapporteur on the adverse effects of the illicit movement and dumping of toxic and dangerous products and wastes on the enjoyment of human rights, Fatma-Zohra Ouhachi-Vesely (Algeria), submitted a report [E/CN.4/2004/46 & Corr.1] describing her activities. The report also described new national, regional and international developments and trends in the illicit traffic and dumping of those wastes, the role of TNCs and the human rights impact of the phenomenon.

An addendum to the report [E/CN.4/2004/46/Add.1] summarized general observations and information received from Governments on the adverse effects of the phenomenon on the enjoyment of human rights, new allegations transmitted to the Special Rapporteur and replies thereto, and updates on cases contained in previous reports.

The Special Rapporteur concluded that the nature of the problem had not changed, despite efforts by the international community to combat it. Countries of the Organisation for Economic Co-operation and Development continued to be the main producers and exporters of those wastes, as the stringent legislation they adopted had increased the costs of waste-processing within their own countries and given rise to transboundary movements to other countries. The communications she received illustrated the adverse impact of the practice and the difficulties the victims faced in obtaining justice and reparation. The Special Rapporteur recommended stringent laws to control the phenomenon and that domestic and international regulations be provided with effective monitoring and implementation mechanisms. She addressed a series of further recommendations to Governments, including administrative, civil and criminal penalties for individuals, enterprises and TNCs involved in illicit trafficking. She proposed strengthening cooperation between OHCHR, the United Nations Environment Programme (UNEP) and the secretariats of multilateral environmental conventions in order to give impetus to the environmental approach to human rights and the human rights dimension of environmental standards.

The Special Rapporteur visited Turkey (10-20 March) [E/CN.4/2005/44] to review, among other matters, relevant laws and practice, governmental policy and the impact on human rights of multilateral agreements on the transbounday movement of toxic waste and hazardous materials. While encouraged by legislative reforms undertaken by the Government, the Special Rapporteur expressed concern regarding numerous attempts of illegal transfers of dangerous waste and products to Turkey and advocated that the countries of origin accept the return of the products. She recommended that the secretariat of the 1989 Basel Convention on the Control of Transboundary Movements of Hazardous Wastes and their Disposal [YUN 1989, p. 420] continue to assist Turkey to find solutions to the situation. Further concern related to the issue of ship dismantling, which, although it had some economic advantages, also carried social, human and environmental costs and posed health hazards. The Special Rapporteur recommended that the Government maintain prohibition on the entry and demolition of contaminated ships for as long as the country lacked the capacity to ensure optimal protection of workers and rational ecological

management during the dismantling and final disposal of toxic wastes recovered. Countries of origin should decontaminate ships before exporting them for dismantling, and, on the multilateral level, States should develop binding norms managing and controlling related activities.

Commission action. By a recorded vote of 38 to 13, with 2 abstentions, the Commission, on 16 April [res. 2004/17], welcoming the entry into force in February of the 1998 Rotterdam Convention on the Prior Informed Consent Procedure for Certain Hazardous Chemicals and Pesticides in International Trade [YUN 1998, p. 997] (see p. 767), called on countries that had not done so to consider ratifying it. The Governments of developed countries and international financial institutions were asked to provide financial assistance for the implementation of the Programme of Action adopted at the First Continental Conference for Africa on the Environmentally Sound Management of Unwanted Stocks of Hazardous Wastes and Their Prevention [YUN 2001, p. 972]. The Commission decided to extend the Special Rapporteur's mandate and asked him/her to study existing problems of and solutions to illicit trafficking, particularly in developing countries, and to report in 2005. The Secretary-General was asked to assist him/her.

In July, the Commission appointed Okechukwu Ibeanu (Nigeria) as Special Rapporteur.

Communication. In March [E/CN.4/2004/G/27], the United Kingdom transmitted its response to enquiries received from the Special Rapporteur regarding the Baku-Tbilisi-Ceyhan pipeline and the issue of human rights and the environment.

ECONOMIC AND SOCIAL COUNCIL ACTION

In July, the Economic and Social Council, on the recommendation of the Commission on Human Rights [E/2004/23], adopted **decision 2004/251** by recorded vote (35-17-2) [agenda item 14 (g)].

Adverse effects of the illicit movement and dumping of toxic and dangerous products and wastes on the enjoyment of human rights

At its 48th plenary meeting, on 22 July 2004, the Economic and Social Council took note of Commission on Human Rights resolution 2004/17 of 16 April 2004 and endorsed the decision of the Commission to extend for a further three years the mandate of the Special Rapporteur on the adverse effects of the illicit movement and dumping of toxic and dangerous products and wastes on the enjoyment of human rights.

RECORDED VOTE ON DECISION 2004/251:

In favour: Azerbaijan, Bangladesh, Belize, Benin, Bhutan, Burundi, Chile, China, Colombia, Congo, Cuba, Ecuador, El Salvador, Ghana, Guatemala, India, Indonesia, Jamaica, Kenya, Libyan Arab Jamahiriya, Malaysia, Mauritius, Mozambique, Namibia, Nicaragua, Nigeria, Panama, Qatar, Republic of Korea, Russian Federation, Saudi Arabia, Tunisia, United Arab Emirates, United Republic of Tanzania, Zimbabwe.

Against: Australia, Belgium, Canada, Finland, France, Germany, Greece, Hungary, Ireland, Italy, Japan, Poland, Senegal, Sweden, Turkey, United Kingdom, United States.
Abstaining: Armenia, Ukraine.

Environmental protection and sustainable development

Report of Secretary-General. In response to a 2003 Commission request [YUN 2003, p. 772], the Secretary-General submitted a February report [E/CN.4/2004/87], which summarized information received from Governments, UN bodies, specialized agencies, intergovernmental organizations and NGOs on their consideration of the relationship between the environment and human rights as part of sustainable development. The report took into consideration the views expressed at the 2002 expert seminar organized jointly by OHCHR and UNEP [YUN 2002, p. 741], and also identified links between the environment and human rights in a number of international and regional documents and instruments, including the International Covenant on Economic, Social and Cultural Rights (see p. 663).

Commission action. On 21 April [dec. 2004/119], the Commission asked the High Commissioner and UNEP to continue to coordinate their efforts in capacity-building activities, in cooperation with other relevant bodies and organizations. The Secretary-General was asked to update his report (see above). The Commission decided to continue consideration of the issue in 2005.

Disappearance of States for environmental reasons

Commission action. On 21 April [dec. 2004/122], the Commission called on the Subcommission to prepare a report on the legal implications of the disappearance of States for environmental reasons, including the implications for the human rights of their residents, with particular reference to the rights of indigenous people.

Working paper. In accordance with a 2003 Subcommission [YUN 2003, p. 772] resolution and with Commission decision 2004/122 (see above), Françoise Hampson (United Kingdom) submitted a July working paper [E/CN.4/Sub.2/AC.4/2004/CRP.1] on the human rights implications, particularly for indigenous populations, of the disappearance of States for environmental reasons. The paper determined that potentially affected States included States that might disappear totally; those that might lose a significant part of their territory, with the remainder unable to sustain the surviving population; and those that might lose portions of their territory with serious implications for the population. The paper focused on the category most likely to disappear entirely, among them being the Bahamas,

Kiribati, Maldives, Nauru and Tuvalu, all of which were islands or groups of islands with a combined total population of 0.5 million. The paper discussed legal issues which might arise from the disappearance of such States, highlighted current efforts to address the problem in the international community and raised questions regarding the scope and analysis of a proposed study on the subject.

Subcommission action. On 9 August [res. 2004/10], the Subcommission invited Ms. Hampson to update her working paper (above) and to submit it in 2005. It asked the Secretary-General to assist her and recommended that the Commission endorse its requests.

Right to physical and mental health

Note by Secretariat. A Secretariat note [E/CN.4/2004/42], referring to a 2003 Commission resolution [YUN 2003, p. 772] and to Economic and Social Council resolution 2003/45 [ibid.], drew attention to the fact that the General Assembly had taken no action during its fifty-eighth (2003) session regarding the Council's recommendation that it declare 2007 the United Nations Year for Violence Prevention. OHCHR had transmitted communications to Governments, NGOs and UN bodies soliciting proposals on possible activities to be undertaken during the year, to which replies were received from five Governments, one UN body and three NGOs.

Reports of Special Rapporteur. The Special Rapporteur on the right to the highest attainable standard of physical and mental health, Paul Hunt (New Zealand), in a February report [E/CN.4/2004/49], described his activities. Between 1 December 2003 and 1 December 2004, he transmitted 36 communications, including urgent appeals, to 21 Governments regarding alleged violations of the right to physical and mental health. The communications sent and replies received were summarized in a separate document [E/CN.4/2005/51/Add.1]. In the February report, the Special Rapporteur reviewed the right to sexual and reproductive health; poverty and the right to health, illustrated with a case study of the Niger's poverty reduction strategy; neglected diseases; and the right to health and violence prevention. Regarding the human rights dimensions of neglected diseases, he wished to explore international assistance and cooperation, which were needed to develop new drugs, vaccines and diagnostic tools. The Special Rapporteur concluded that the right to health, like all human rights, was governed by a set of global norms or standards giving rise to governmental obligations, which required effective monitoring and accountability mechanisms. The combination of globally legitimized norms, obligations, monitoring and accountability empowered disadvantaged and marginalized individuals and communities. Policies that were based on human rights norms, including the right to health, were more likely to be effective.

Subsequent to his preliminary report [YUN 2003, p. 773] regarding his visit to Mozambique in 2003, the Special Rapporteur submitted a further report [E/CN.4/2005/51/Add.2]. He addressed, among other issues, access to health services and facilities, user fees, the role of donors and intergovernmental organizations, the situation of health professionals, access to water and sanitation, sexual and reproductive health, HIV/AIDS, tuberculosis and malaria. Noting Mozambique's legacies of colonization, civil war and natural disasters that had destroyed part of the country's health infrastructure, the Special Rapporteur concluded that, although the situation was improving, health indicators remained weak. He recommended that the Government integrate the right to health into all its national and international policies, with particular attention to such key human rights principles as non-discrimination, equality, access to information, transparency, monitoring and accountability. The Government needed to develop an integrated and coordinated approach to the health sector that was comprehensive, simple and efficient, and to increase health resources, including more health professionals and improved terms and conditions of work.

Commission action. By a recorded vote of 52 to 1, the Commission, on 16 April [res. 2004/27], recommended that States establish effective mechanisms to ensure that they took account of the realization of the right to the enjoyment of the highest standard of physical and mental health in formulating their national and international policies. The Commission invited the Special Rapporteur to explore how efforts to realize the right could reinforce poverty reduction strategies; to continue analysis of the human rights dimensions of neglected diseases, particularly those affecting developing countries; and to submit annually a report to the Commission and an interim report to the General Assembly on his activities. The High Commissioner was asked to assist him and Governments were called on to cooperate with him, provide him with information and respond promptly to his communications.

ECONOMIC AND SOCIAL COUNCIL ACTION

On 22 July, the Economic and Social Council, on the recommendation of the Commission on

Human Rights [E/2004/23], adopted **decision 2004/255** by recorded vote (53-1) [agenda item 14 (g)].

The right of everyone to the enjoyment of the highest attainable standard of physical and mental health

At its 48th plenary meeting, on 22 July 2004, the Economic and Social Council took note of Commission on Human Rights resolution 2004/27 of 16 April 2004 and approved the Commission's request to the Special Rapporteur on the right of everyone to the enjoyment of the highest attainable standard of physical and mental health to submit annually a report to the Commission and an interim report to the General Assembly on the activities performed under his mandate.

RECORDED VOTE ON DECISION 2004/255:

In favour: Armenia, Australia, Azerbaijan, Bangladesh, Belgium, Belize, Benin, Bhutan, Burundi, Canada, Chile, China, Colombia, Congo, Cuba, Ecuador, El Salvador, Finland, France, Germany, Ghana, Greece, Guatemala, Hungary, India, Indonesia, Ireland, Italy, Jamaica, Japan, Kenya, Libyan Arab Jamahiriya, Malaysia, Mauritius, Mozambique, Namibia, Nicaragua, Nigeria, Panama, Poland, Qatar, Republic of Korea, Russian Federation, Saudi Arabia, Senegal, Sweden, Tunisia, Turkey, Ukraine, United Arab Emirates, United Kingdom, United Republic of Tanzania, Zimbabwe.

Against: United States.

Further reports of Special Rapporteur. The Special Rapporteur visited Peru (6-15 June) [E/CN.4/2005/51/Add.3], where he found significant obstacles to the realization of the right to health, despite the commitment of the Ministry of Health and of related public institutions and civil society organizations to promote and protect the right. Many health-related problems were linked to problems of poverty and discrimination. Issues of particular concern were the potential impact of a trade agreement with the United States on access to essential medicines in Peru; environmental health problems arising from the lack of access to safe water, inadequate sanitation and industrial pollution; health care for people with mental disabilities and the mental health legacy of two decades of internal armed conflict; inadequate access to sexual and reproductive health facilities; and disparities in access to health services for marginalized groups, including indigenous peoples and ethnic minorities. The Special Rapporteur recommended measures to resolve those concerns and to improve the prospects for realizing the right to health, including that the Government formulate a comprehensive pro-poor and equity-based health policy underpinned by the right to health and that the international community cancel a significant portion of Peru's foreign debt, on the understanding that the funds released would be reallocated towards the implementation of the proposed policy.

In Romania (23-27 August) [E/CN.4/2005/51/Add.4], the Special Rapporteur found that the transition from communism to democracy and to a market economy, as well as preparations for accession to the European Union in 2007, were affecting the prospects for realizing the right to health. Notable problems in Romania included the highest prevalence of HIV/AIDS and tuberculosis in Europe, corruption, inadequate budgetary allocations to the health sector, low level of participation of the population in health policy-making and increasing poverty levels. Other issues of concern related to access to sexual, reproductive and mental health care, environmental health problems arising from limited access to safe drinking water, inadequate sanitation, air pollution, the contamination of water by industrial effluents and the situation of the Roma ethnic group. In addition to recommendations targeting those problem areas, the Special Rapporteur urged the Government to ensure the implementation of the health policies and programmes it had adopted, according particular attention to realizing the right to health of marginalized groups, to accountability and to remedies regarding related abuses.

Pursuant to Commission resolution 2004/27 (above), the Secretary-General, by an October note [A/59/422], transmitted the Special Rapporteur's interim report, which discussed the health-related MDGs and illustrated how the right to health could contribute to the achievement of those goals, by ensuring that vertical health interventions strengthened health systems and by reinforcing the goal for a global partnership for development. The report highlighted the disparities between the health situation of indigenous peoples and non-indigenous peoples in many countries and called for urgent efforts to reverse the trend. It addressed issues relating to the right to health, child survival and indicators, and applied in that context the methodology for the use of the right to health indicators and benchmarks, a concept first introduced in the Special Rapporteur's previous interim report to the Assembly [YUN 2003, p. 773].

By **decision 59/528** of 20 December, the Assembly took note of the Special Rapporteur's report.

Access to medication

Report of Secretary-General. In response to a 2003 Commission request [YUN 2003, p. 807], the Commission had before it a report of the Secretary-General [E/CN.4/2004/39], which summarized information received from Governments, one UN body and NGOs on steps they had taken to promote access to medication in the context of pandemics, such as HIV/AIDS, tuberculosis and malaria.

Commission action. On 16 April [res. 2004/26], the Commission recognized that access to medi-

cation in the context of pandemics such as HIV/AIDS, tuberculosis and malaria was fundamental to achieving the full realization of the right of everyone to the enjoyment of the highest attainable standard of physical and mental health. It called on States to effectively deliver prevention, treatment, care and support to respond to the pandemics. The Secretary-General was asked to solicit comments from Governments, UN organs, programmes and specialized agencies, international organizations and NGOs on steps they had taken to implement the Commission's resolution, and to report in 2005.

Water and sanitation services

Report of Special Rapporteur. As requested by the Subcommission in 2001 [YUN 2001, p. 674] and the Commission in 2002 [YUN 2002, p. 743], the Special Rapporteur on the right to adequate water and sanitation, El-Hadji Guissé (Senegal), submitted a July final report [E/CN.4/Sub.2/2004/20] on a study of the relationship between the enjoyment of economic, social and cultural rights and the promotion of the realization of the right to drinking water supply and sanitation. The report summarized information received from Governments, UN bodies and international organizations on steps taken to realize the right, examined the right's legal basis and analysed related implementation issues. The report found that, although there was sufficient water to meet the needs of people in almost all countries, some 1.1 billion persons worldwide did not have access to safe drinking water and about 2.4 billion lacked adequate means of personal sanitation. The main challenges related to distribution and insufficient water infrastructure to carry water inside or close to households. The Special Rapporteur proposed measures to advance the realization of the right to drinking water and sanitation, including the establishment by States of a plan of action and programme to promote, realize and protect the right, and to avoid action that impeded it. In order to ensure availability without discrimination, public authorities should facilitate access for deprived persons by improving the quality of water and establishing reasonable pricing for household supplies. There was also a need for States, international organizations and civil society to jointly develop tools to implement the right.

Subcommission action. On 9 August [res. 2004/6], the Subcommission asked the Secretary-General to bring to the attention of States, NGOs and international organizations the recommendations contained in the Special Rapporteur's final report (above) and in general comment No. 15 on the right to water, adopted in 2002 by the Committee on Economic, Social and Cultural Rights [YUN 2002, p. 628]. The Subcommission recommended that the Commission approve its request to issue the Special Rapporteur's 2002 preliminary report [YUN 2002, p. 743], 2003 progress report [YUN 2003, p. 775] and 2004 final report in the UN official languages.

Also on 9 August [dec. 2004/107], the Subcommission asked Mr. Guissé to prepare, without financial implications, a set of draft guidelines for the realization of the right to drinking water supply and sanitation, for submission in 2005.

Bioethics

Commission action. By a recorded vote of 50 to 2, with 1 abstention, the Commission, on 21 April [dec. 2004/120], approved the Subcommission's appointment of Iulia-Antoanella Motoc (Romania) [YUN 2003, p. 775] as Special Rapporteur to undertake a study on human rights and the human genome, based on her 2003 working paper [ibid.], and asked her to submit a preliminary report to the Subcommission in 2004 and a final report to the Commission in 2005. The Secretary-General was asked to assist her.

ECONOMIC AND SOCIAL COUNCIL ACTION

In July, the Economic and Social Council, on the recommendation of the Commission on Human Rights [E/2004/23], adopted **decision 2004/280** by recorded vote (52-1) [agenda item 14 (g)].

Human rights and bioethics

At its 49th plenary meeting, on 22 July 2004, the Economic and Social Council took note of Commission on Human Rights decision 2004/120 of 21 April 2004 and approved the decision of the Commission to appoint Iulia-Antoanella Motoc as special rapporteur to undertake a study on human rights and the human genome, based on her working paper; the Special Rapporteur was requested to submit her preliminary report to the Subcommission on the Promotion and Protection of Human Rights at its fifty-sixth session and her final report to the Commission at its sixty-first session.

The Council also approved the Commission's request to the Secretary-General to provide the Special Rapporteur with the necessary assistance to enable her to carry out her study.

RECORDED VOTE ON DECISION 2004/280:

In favour: Armenia, Australia, Azerbaijan, Bangladesh, Belgium, Belize, Benin, Bhutan, Burundi, Canada, Chile, China, Colombia, Congo, Cuba, Ecuador, El Salvador, Finland, France, Germany, Ghana, Greece, Guatemala, Hungary, India, Indonesia, Ireland, Italy, Jamaica, Japan, Kenya, Libyan Arab Jamahiriya, Malaysia, Mauritius, Mozambique, Namibia, Nigeria, Panama, Poland, Qatar, Republic of Korea, Russian Federation, Saudi Arabia, Senegal, Sweden, Tunisia, Turkey, Ukraine, United Arab Emirates, United Kingdom, United Republic of Tanzania, Zimbabwe.
Against: United States.

Report of Special Rapporteur. In response to Commission decision 2004/120 (above), the Spe-

cial Rapporteur on human rights and the human genome, Ms. Motoc, submitted a July preliminary report [E/CN.4/Sub.2/2004/38], which considered the question of discrimination in genetics. The report explored the definition of genetic discrimination and examined the phenomenon in international and domestic instruments, as well as the right to privacy over medical information, employment and insurance questions, and the interests of vulnerable groups, including indigenous peoples and persons with disabilities. The Special Rapporteur concluded that the possible use of personal genetic information against individuals might stifle acceptance of further genetic inquiry. Therefore, failure to protect privacy and prevent discrimination threatened to diminish the potential for genetics to improve health care. The key to benefiting from genetic information while avoiding its negative aspects lay in determining how information would be used beyond the health-care needs of the person to whom the information pertained. The Special Rapporteur advocated regulation and/or prohibition of secondary uses of personal genetic information, legislation to address specific issues relating to genetic testing and public education to protect genetic privacy and prevent discrimination. Governments had a duty to explain to the public and researchers the uses of genetic information, their possible impact on society and the precise meaning of the results of genetic studies.

Subcommission action. On 12 August [dec. 2004/112], the Subcommission asked the Special Rapporteur to submit an interim report in 2005 and a final report in 2006. The Secretary-General was asked to assist her.

Genetic privacy

Report of Secretary-General. Pursuant to Economic and Social Council decision 2003/232 [YUN 2003, p. 776], the Secretary-General submitted an April report [E/2004/56] containing information from Governments and OHCHR on measures taken to promote the development and implementation of standards relating to genetic privacy and to support research in human genetics and biotechnology. The report supplemented information contained in the Secretary-General's 2003 report on the subject [YUN 2003, p. 775].

On 23 July, the Economic and Social Council took note of the Secretary-General's report (**decision 2004/317**).

ECONOMIC AND SOCIAL COUNCIL ACTION

On 21 July [meeting 46], the Economic and Social Council adopted **resolution 2004/9** [draft: E/2004/L.13/Rev.1] without vote [agenda item 14 (i)].

Genetic privacy and non-discrimination

The Economic and Social Council,

Guided by the purposes and principles set forth in the Charter of the United Nations and also by the Universal Declaration of Human Rights, the International Covenants on Human Rights and the other relevant international human rights instruments,

Recalling the Universal Declaration on the Human Genome and Human Rights adopted on 11 November 1997 by the General Conference of the United Nations Educational, Scientific and Cultural Organization, and General Assembly resolution 53/152 of 9 December 1998 endorsing the Declaration,

Recalling also the Programme of Action of the World Conference against Racism, Racial Discrimination, Xenophobia and Related Intolerance adopted in Durban, South Africa, on 8 September 2001,

Welcoming the International Declaration on Human Genetic Data adopted on 16 October 2003 by the General Conference of the United Nations Educational, Scientific and Cultural Organization, which, inter alia, considers discrimination based on genetic characteristics as acts intended to infringe or to have the effect of infringing the human rights, fundamental freedoms or human dignity of an individual or for purposes that lead to stigmatization of an individual, a family or a group or communities,

Recalling its resolution 2001/39 of 26 July 2001, as well as its decision 2003/232 of 22 July 2003,

Recalling also Commission on Human Rights resolution 2003/69 of 25 April 2003 on human rights and bioethics,

Recalling further the decision taken on 7 May 1998 whereby the Executive Board of the United Nations Educational, Scientific and Cultural Organization established the International Bioethics Committee, which is carrying out work on confidentiality and genetic data,

Reiterating that the life and health of individuals are inevitably related to developments in life sciences and social areas,

Acknowledging the importance of advances in genetic research, which have led to the identification of strategies for the early detection, prevention and treatment of diseases,

Bearing in mind that the genetic revolution has far-reaching implications and consequences for all humankind and that its evaluation and applications should therefore be conducted in an open, ethical and participatory manner,

Recognizing the contribution that civil society involved in this matter can make to the protection of genetic privacy and to the fight against discrimination based on genetic information,

Reaffirming that the information obtained from genetic tests, which is personal, should be held confidential, based on the conditions set by law,

Recognizing that genetic data associated with an identifiable person can in some instances be relevant to other members of the individual's family or to other persons and that the rights and interests of such persons must also be taken into account in the handling of such data,

Stressing the fact that revealing genetic information belonging to individuals without their consent may cause harm and discrimination against them in such areas as employment, insurance, education and other areas of social life,

Recalling that, in order to protect human rights and fundamental freedoms, the limitations to the principles of consent and confidentiality may be prescribed only by law, for compelling reasons consistent with international law, including international human rights law,

1. *Takes note* of the reports of the Secretary-General on information and comments received from Governments and relevant international organizations and functional commissions pursuant to Economic and Social Council resolution 2001/39;

2. *Expresses its appreciation* to the Governments, relevant international organizations and functional commissions that have responded to the request for information formulated by the Council in its resolution 2001/39;

3. *Urges* States to ensure that no one shall be subjected to discrimination based on genetic information;

4. *Also urges* States to protect the privacy of those subject to genetic testing and to ensure that genetic testing and the subsequent processing, use and storage of human genetic data is done with the prior, free, informed and express consent of the individual or authorization obtained in the manner prescribed by law consistent with international law, including international human rights law, and to ensure that limitations on the principle of consent are prescribed only for compelling reasons, such as forensic medicine and related legal proceedings, by domestic law consistent with international law, including international human rights law;

5. *Calls upon* States to take appropriate specific measures, including through legislation, to prevent the misuse of genetic information leading to discrimination against, or stigmatization of, individuals, members of their families or groups in all areas, particularly in insurance, employment, education and other areas of social life, whether in the public or the private sector, and in this respect calls upon States to take all appropriate measures to ensure that the results and interpretations of population-based genetic studies are not used for purposes that discriminate against the individual or group concerned;

6. *Also calls upon* States to promote, as appropriate, the development and implementation of standards providing appropriate protection with regard to the collection, storage, disclosure and use of genetic information taken from genetic tests that might lead to discrimination, stigmatization or invasion of privacy;

7. *Urges* States to continue to support research in the area of human genetics, subject to accepted scientific and ethical standards and to the potential benefit of all people, emphasizing that such research and its applications should fully respect human rights, fundamental freedoms and human dignity, as well as the prohibition of all forms of discrimination based on genetic characteristics;

8. *Recognizes,* in this context, that international efforts to ensure non-discrimination on genetic grounds need to be pursued and that, in the context of international cooperation, States should endeavour to assist developing countries to build their capacity to participate in generating and sharing scientific know-

ledge concerning human genetic data and the related know-how, with full respect for all human rights;

9. *Decides* to continue considering the various implications of the question of genetic privacy and non-discrimination for ethical, legal, medical, employment, insurance-related and other aspects of social life, consistent with public international law and international human rights law;

10. *Requests* the Secretary-General to bring the present resolution to the attention of all Governments, relevant international organizations and functional commissions, to collect the comments received pursuant to it, and other relevant information, and to submit a report to the Council at its substantive session of 2007.

Slavery and related issues

Working group activities. The five-member Working Group on Contemporary Forms of Slavery, at its twenty-ninth session (Geneva, 28 June–2 July) [E/CN.4/Sub.2/2004/36 & Corr.1], reviewed developments in contemporary forms of slavery and measures to prevent and repress all its forms, including corruption and international debt as factors that promoted the phenomenon. It devoted priority attention to forced labour, in the light of the ILO Programme of Action on forced labour [YUN 2001, p. 1404], and co-organized with ILO a discussion on various aspects of the phenomenon, particularly the challenges associated with new manifestations of forced labour in the light of globalization and technological change. Further issues considered related to the activities of the United Nations Voluntary Trust Fund on Contemporary Forms of Slavery (see p. 774), the status of slavery conventions (see below), the Programme of Action for the Prevention of the Sale of Children, Child Prostitution and Child Pornography (see p. 785) and the activities of the Special Rapporteur on that issue, the Programme of Action for the Elimination of the Exploitation of Child Labour, migrant and domestic workers, bonded labour and debt bondage, and child labour (see below). Also considered were sexual exploitation, trafficking in persons and the exploitation of the prostitution of others, including children, forced and child marriage, the activities of the Special Rapporteur on violence against women, its causes and consequences (see p. 775), illegal activities of certain religious and other sects, trafficking in organs and tissues of children and slavery-like practices related to armed conflicts. The Group observed that the treaties forbidding slavery and slavery-like practices and other instruments relevant to its work had not been universally ratified and recommended that States ratify them. It adopted recommendations on the issues it considered during the session and decided to focus in 2005 on a review of the status

of ratification of relevant treaties and the identification of gaps and challenges remaining in areas covered by its mandate. Also in 2005, it would assess its activities since its creation in 1975 [YUN 1975, p. 639]. It would devote priority attention in 2006 to the impact of the media and the Internet on contemporary forms of slavery.

Documents considered by the Group included May notes by the Secretary-General [E/CN.4/Sub.2/AC.2/2004/2, E/CN.4/Sub.2/AC.2/2004/3] updating the status of the slavery conventions (1956 Supplementary Convention on the Abolition of Slavery, the Slave Trade and Institutions and Practices Similar to Slavery [YUN 1956, p. 228] and 1949 Convention for the Suppression of the Traffic in Persons and of the Exploitation of the Prostitution of Others, adopted by the General Assembly in resolution 317(IV) [YUN 1948-49, p. 613]) and a June report of the Secretary-General [E/CN.4/Sub.2/AC.2/2004/4] containing information submitted by Governments, UN bodies and specialized agencies on measures they had taken to prevent and repress all forms of slavery.

Subcommission action. On 12 August [res. 2004/19], the Subcommission recommended States' ratification of treaties on slavery-related issues and closer international cooperation for the prevention, punishment and suppression of corruption and money-laundering resulting from trafficking and sexual exploitation, particularly of women and children. It called on the United Nations Children's Fund (UNICEF), the World Health Organization (WHO), ILO, UNDP and other competent UN organs, specialized agencies, development banks and intergovernmental agencies to develop programmes in order to break the cycle of poverty, social exclusion and discrimination which made people vulnerable to exploitation through forced labour. UN human rights bodies were called on to address violations relating to sexual exploitation and trafficking in persons, while UN bodies and NGOs were called on to develop and implement codes of conduct that prohibited all forms of sexual exploitation by UN employees and contract workers and humanitarian aid workers. The Subcommission welcomed ILO's participation in the Working Group on Contemporary Forms of Slavery (see above) and invited Governments, international organizations, national institutions and NGOs that had information relating to the Group's agenda to assist it by providing it with information.

Trafficking in human organs

On 20 December, the General Assembly, in **resolution 59/156** (see p. 1127), alarmed at the potential growth of trafficking in human organs, encouraged Member States to exchange experience in and information on preventing, combating and punishing the practice.

1993 Programme of Action

In response to a 2003 Subcommission request [YUN 2003, p. 776], the Secretary-General, in a June report [E/CN.4/Sub.2/2004/34], presented information received from Governments and UN agencies on action they had taken to implement the 1993 Programme of Action for the Elimination of the Exploitation of Child Labour [YUN 1993, p. 965].

Sexual exploitation during armed conflict

Report of High Commissioner. The High Commissioner, in a June report [E/CN.4/Sub.2/2004/35], supplemented information contained in a previous report [YUN 2003, p. 776] regarding steps taken by human rights treaty bodies, the Commission and its mechanisms, the International Tribunal for the Former Yugoslavia (ICTY) and the International Criminal Tribunal for Rwanda (ICTR) to address the problem of systematic rape, sexual slavery and slavery-like practices during armed conflicts. The High Commissioner concluded that the problem remained widespread, despite legal advances, exemplified by judgements by ICTY, ICTR, the Special Court for Sierra Leone, the Rome Statute of the International Criminal Court, and the adoption of Security Council resolution 1325(2000) [YUN 2000, p. 1113] on women, peace and security, sexual gender-based violence, systematic rape and various forms of enslavement. Constraints included women's poor representation at decision-making levels; the persistence of violence against women, which hindered many of them from reaching their potential; the lack of access to resources, including finances and information; and persistent stereotypes on the roles and expected behaviour of women. As the situation of women could be improved only through concrete and effective policies and programmes addressing prevailing gender relations and persistent gender-based stereotypes, a key challenge concerned the effective implementation of Council resolution 1325 (2000) and general recommendation No. 25 of the Committee on the Elimination of Discrimination against Women (see p. 1169). To end the cycle of violence and prevent armed conflicts, the equal rights of women to participate fully in all aspects of life needed to be promoted and protected.

Working paper. In response to a 2003 Subcommission request [YUN 2003, p. 777], Françoise Hampson (United Kingdom) submitted a July working paper [E/CN.4/Sub.2/2004/12] on the criminalization, investigation and prosecution of acts of serious sexual violence, which was considered by the sessional working group on the administration of justice (see p. 714). The paper, which addressed the definition of relevant international crimes and charging practice, explored the definitions of rape and other forms of sexual violence and raised questions relating to the scope of the subject.

Subcommission action. On 12 August [res. 2004/22], the Subcommission asked the High Commissioner to submit an updated report in 2005 on the issues of systematic rape, sexual slavery and slavery-like practices during armed conflicts. States were encouraged to promote human rights education on those issues.

Fund on slavery

Reports of Secretary-General. In February [E/CN.4/2004/78/Add.1] and August [A/59/309], the Secretary-General reported on the status of the United Nations Voluntary Trust Fund on Contemporary Forms of Slavery.

The Fund's Board of Trustees, at its ninth session (Geneva, 26-30 January), recommended 20 project grants amounting to $150,700 to assist NGOs in 15 countries in Africa, the Americas, Asia and Europe, and nine travel grants amounting to $30,000 to enable NGO representatives to participate in the deliberations of the Working Group on Contemporary Forms of Slavery (see p. 773). The Board estimated that, in order to fulfil its mandate satisfactorily, the Fund would need at least $325,000 before its tenth session, scheduled for January 2005. On 23 February, the High Commissioner, on behalf of the Secretary-General, approved the Board's recommendations. The Secretary-General reported that contributions available to the Fund as at 2 November 2004 stood at $93,295 [E/CN.4/2005/86].

On 20 December, the General Assembly took note of the Secretary-General's August report (**decision 59/528**).

Subcommission action. On 12 August [res. 2004/20], the Subcommission urged Governments, NGOs and other private or public entities to contribute to the Fund.

Vulnerable groups

In an August report [A/59/282] on progress made to implement the UN Millennium Declaration [YUN 2000, p. 49] (see also p. 1362), the Secretary-General drew attention to efforts to protect vulnerable people in emergency situations, such as disasters resulting from and during conflicts. He noted that increased attention had been paid to ensuring local preparedness and building response capacities to natural hazards. Although some progress had been made to stabilize some of the countries affected by conflicts, much remained to be done. There was a need for the international community to harmonize its transition planning and fund-raising tools, address more coherently needs assessments and construct more local institutions to enable national actors to be involved in their own transition from the beginning. Increased levels of timely, predictable and flexible funding were also required to ensure adequate and equitable financial assistance when necessary.

Women

Violence against women

Report of Secretary-General. Pursuant to General Assembly resolution 50/166 [YUN 1995, p. 1188], the Secretary-General submitted in January to the Commission on Human Rights and the Commission on the Status of Women the report of the United Nations Development Fund for Women regarding the Fund's activities to eliminate violence against women [E/CN.6/2004/8-E/CN.4/2004/117] (see p. 1170).

Reports of Special Rapporteur. The Special Rapporteur on violence against women, its causes and consequences, Yakin Ertürk (Turkey), in her annual report [E/CN.4/2004/66], assessed developments of the past decade and focused on violence against women as manifested within a broad spectrum from the domicile to the transnational arena. She discussed gaps and challenges relating to the problem, considered the connection between HIV/AIDS infection and sexual violence against women and elaborated guidelines for developing strategies for the effective implementation of international standards to end the violence. The Special Rapporteur proposed a three-tiered intervention strategy involving the State, the community and the individual woman; while the State was bound by international human rights law, it was suggested that the human rights discourse at the level of the community and the individual woman needed to be complemented by a culture and an empowerment discourse, respectively. The Special Rapporteur identified critical issues that required further attention, including measures to address the adverse impact of religious extremism on women's rights, further research to understand how sexual violence against women related to the HIV/AIDS pandemic, the adoption of a gender perspective in policy-making to help protect women's rights, an analysis of the obstacles to

women's access to justice at all levels of social experience, further exploration of gender budgeting as a means of monitoring States' compliance with international law to eliminate violence against women, and the development of indices and States' accountability to serve as frameworks for monitoring violence against women and State initiatives to tackle it globally.

An addendum to the report [E/CN.4/2004/66/Add.1] summarized communications and urgent appeals on alleged cases of violence or threats of violence against women, which the Special Rapporteur had transmitted to 30 Governments, and the replies received thereto, and on cases transmitted by her predecessor.

The Special Rapporteur visited El Salvador (2-8 February) [E/CN.4/2005/72/Add.2], at the invitation of the Government, following allegations of an emerging pattern of murders of young women in the Central American region. She found that socio-economic pressures, a weak legal sector that fostered impunity and male dominance had combined to reinforce a general state of violence against women and girls. The most pervasive included murder, domestic violence and sexual abuse of girls, violence and sexual harassment in the workplace, police-related violence and violence relating to commercial sexual exploitation. The Special Rapporteur recommended measures to the Government relating to the need to create an information and knowledge base; ensure legislative, investigative and judicial reforms; strengthen institutional infrastructure; initiate training and awareness-raising programmes; and enforce and monitor international labour standards. Recommendations were addressed to the international community and civil society, including women's NGOs, human rights groups and the media.

In Guatemala (9-14 February) [E/CN.4/2005/72/Add.3], the Special Rapporteur found that violence against women was widespread and that the impunity enjoyed by the perpetrators sustained structures of power, resulting in fear and the lack of confidence in State apparatuses. The major problem confronting the State was its inability to provide women with legal, judicial and institutional protection. The Special Rapporteur recommended measures to the Government, civil society and the international community, including the need to end impunity for violence against women through legal reforms; provide protection and support services to women facing actual or potential violence; create a gender-sensitive information and knowledge base; strengthen institutional infrastructure; and promote training and operational and awareness-raising programmes.

Commission action. On 20 April [res. 2004/46], the Commission stressed the importance of efforts to eliminate impunity for violence against women and girls in situations of armed conflict, including by prosecuting gender-related crimes and crimes of sexual violence, providing protective measures, counselling and other appropriate assistance to victims and witnesses in international and internationally supported courts and tribunals, and integrating a gender perspective into all efforts to eliminate impunity. The Special Rapporteur was invited to report, as appropriate, on those mechanisms, and the Secretary-General was asked to assist her and to ensure that her reports were brought to the attention of the Commission on the Status of Women in 2005 and the Committee on the Elimination of Discrimination against Women. Relevant UN bodies, States, the Special Rapporteur and NGOs were called on to cooperate in the preparation of the Secretary-General's in-depth study on all forms of violence against women, called for in General Assembly resolution 58/185 [YUN 2003, p. 1172].

Further reports of Special Rapporteur. The Special Rapporteur visited the Occupied Palestinian Territory (13-18 June) [E/CN.4/2005/72/Add.4], where she reviewed the impact of the conflict and occupation on violence against women. She found that women suffered violence from Israeli security forces and from the family and the community. Security measures enforced included restrictions on freedom of movement, house demolitions, detention and injuries and loss of lives. Regarding violence within the family and the community, the Special Rapporteur focused on how violence against women was justified and sustained under the occupation. She highlighted how the situation had placed women at the centre of the conflict, the legitimization of violence against them as a weapon of patriarchy and the impact of culturally inherited values, under which women were killed or threatened with death for tarnishing family honour. The Special Rapporteur, in a series of recommendations, asked the Government of Israel and the Palestinian Authority (PA) to take measures to end the conflict and occupation and to ensure that women's needs and interests were addressed in the negotiations. Israel should observe international human rights and humanitarian law in undertaking security measures and include in its reports to treaty bodies on compliance with obligations in the occupied territories information on the protection and promotion of women's rights. The PA, on its part, should adopt legislation to punish and redress the situation of women subjected to violence, adopt the bill of rights for women, eliminate structural discrimination against women and increase their representation in the PA.

In the Darfur region of the Sudan (25-26 September) [E/CN.4/2005/72/Add.5], which had witnessed intense fighting in civil war for over two decades, the Special Rapporteur found that women and girls had suffered and continued to suffer multiple forms of violence during attacks on their villages, including rape, killings, the burning of homes and pillaging of livestock, allegedly perpetrated by government-backed militia and security forces (see p. 233). The atrocities were also inflicted on women in camps and victims faced numerous obstacles in access to justice and health care. The Special Rapporteur recommended that the Government facilitate the full involvement of women in peace efforts and ensure that their needs and interests were addressed in all negotiations; ensure the security of civilians and introduce protection measures to reduce women's risk of rape, beatings and abduction; investigate allegations of violence against women and prosecute perpetrators; and initiate dialogue for improving the legal protection of women's rights and effectively implement current obligations under international law.

Communication. On 22 July [E/CN.4/Sub.2/2004/G/1], Iraq transmitted a study it had undertaken on follow-up to the implementation of the Beijing Declaration and Platform for Action [YUN 1995, p. 1170], which highlighted its experience.

Security Council action. On 28 October, the Security Council President, in statement **S/PRST/2004/40** (see p. 1152), stated that the Council strongly condemned the continued acts of gender-based violence and violations of women's and girls' rights in situations of armed conflict and urged the cessation by all parties of such acts.

General Assembly action. On 20 December, the General Assembly, in **resolution 59/167** (see p. 0000), invited the Special Rapporteur to devote further attention to all forms of violence against women, including crimes identified in the outcome document of the Assembly's twenty-third special session on women [YUN 2000, p. 1082].

Also on 20 December, the Assembly, in **resolution 59/165** (see p. 1150), expressing concern that women continued to be victims of crimes committed in the name of honour and at the continuing occurrence in all regions of such violence, called on States to prevent and eliminate the practice and invited relevant UN human rights treaty bodies and the Special Rapporteur to address the issue.

Women migrant workers

Note by Secretary-General. In response to a 2002 Commission request [YUN 2002, p. 746], the Commission had before it a note by the Secretary-General [E/CN.4/2004/71] drawing the Commission's attention to his 2003 report on violence against women migrant workers [YUN 2003, p. 1172]. The Commission's attention was also drawn to the report of the Special Rapporteur on the human rights of migrants (see p. 668), which reviewed the situation of women migrant domestic workers and trafficking in persons, particularly women.

Commission action. On 20 April [res. 2004/49], the Commission called on Governments to ensure the full enjoyment of human rights by women migrant workers and to establish penal sanctions to punish perpetrators of violence against women migrant workers and to assist victims. States, particularly countries of origin and destination, were invited to adopt legal measures against intermediaries who deliberately encouraged the clandestine movement of workers and who exploited women migrant workers.

Traditional practices affecting the health of women and girls

Commission action. On 20 April [dec. 2004/111], the Commission, taking note of a 2003 Subcommission resolution [YUN 2003, p. 778], decided to approve the Subcommission's decision to renew the mandate of the Special Rapporteur on traditional practices affecting the health of women and the girl child and its request to her to report.

On 22 July (**decision 2004/276**), the Economic and Social Council endorsed the Commission's decision.

Report of Special Rapporteur. In response to a 2003 Subcommission request [YUN 2003, p. 778], the Special Rapporteur on traditional practices affecting the health of women and the girl child, Halima Warzazi (Morocco), in a June report [E/CN.4/Sub.2/2004/41], described progress made to implement the 1994 Plan of Action for the Elimination of Harmful Traditional Practices Affecting the Health of Women and Children [YUN 1994, p. 1123]. She noted that the year was marked by activities focusing on the elimination of female genital mutilation, culminating in the observance of 6 February as the international day of zero tolerance of the practice. The report summarized measures taken by Governments to ensure the criminal prosecution of perpetrators and by UN system organizations to promote action against the practice. Further initiatives included training, workshops, seminars, information-sharing and cultural exchange programmes designed to raise public awareness about the harmful effects of the practice. The Special Rapporteur concluded that harmful traditional practices were persistent owing to respect for tradition, particularly when affected communities did not have contact with the outside world and suffered from illiteracy and ignorance. Policies and actions aimed at eradicating harmful practices should be directed towards strengthening the status of women in society from the earliest age.

Subcommission action. On 12 August [res. 2004/23], the Subcommission called on Governments to give full attention to the implementation of the 1994 Plan of Action and asked the Secretary-General to invite them to submit information regularly to the Subcommission on the situation regarding harmful traditional practices in their countries. The Subcommission reiterated its 2003 proposal [YUN 2003, p. 778] that three seminars be held in Africa, Asia and Europe to review progress achieved and to explore ways of overcoming obstacles in implementing the Plan of Action, and asked the High Commissioner to help raise funds to organize the seminars. The Special Rapporteur was asked to report in 2005 and the High Commissioner was asked to assist her.

Women and girls in Afghanistan

On 21 July, the Economic and Social Council, in **resolution 2004/10** (see p. 1163), urged the Afghan Transitional Administration and future Government to enable the full, equal and effective participation of women and girls in civil, cultural, economic, political and social life throughout the country at all levels, and to strengthen efforts to prevent and eliminate violence against them. The Council encouraged continuing efforts of the United Nations and its agencies, donors and civil society, guided by Security Council resolution 1325(2000) [YUN 2000, p. 1113], to support capacity-building for Afghan women to enable them to participate in all sectors, particularly in the 2004 electoral process.

The girl child

On 20 April [res. 2004/48], the Commission called on States to take measures, including legal reforms, to ensure girls' enjoyment of human rights and fundamental freedoms and to eliminate discrimination against them, and all forms of violence, harmful traditional practices, the root causes of son preference and forced and early marriages.

(See also p. 782.)

Mainstreaming women's rights

Reports of Secretary-General. Pursuant to a 2003 Commission request [YUN 2003, p. 780], the Secretary-General, in a March report [E/CN.4/2004/64], described measures to integrate a gender perspective into the UN system, taken by Commission mechanisms and procedures, human rights treaty bodies, OHCHR and UN human rights field presences. The report noted continuing progress in efforts to improve the integration of gender and women's rights issues into the UN human rights system, but that those efforts remained uneven. An assessment of technical cooperation activities by OHCHR and human rights field presence agents indicated a wide diversity in terms of efforts and achievements. The Secretary-General stated that systematic monitoring of the integration of gender and women's rights into technical cooperation activities was essential and asked the Commission to consider that possibility. He proposed similar preliminary assessment of efforts in other areas and consideration of the results by the Commission. Given that women experts had often led treaty body efforts to integrate gender perspectives into their work, the Secretary-General said the Commission might wish to emphasize the importance of the relevant provisions of the Beijing Platform for Action [YUN 1995, p. 1170] and of Commission resolutions, and to ask him to bring gender trends to the attention of States parties when inviting their nominations for the election of treaty bodies' members. The Secretary-General further suggested that the Commission consider ways to ensure greater attention to gender balance and relevant expertise in the designation of experts. Increased participation of women in human rights activities could be an effective way to improve attention to women's rights, and relevant actors, including Governments, UN agencies, OHCHR and NGOs, should be encouraged to work for more gender-balanced participation in human rights activities.

A further report [E/CN.4/2004/65-E/CN.6/2004/7] of the Secretary-General presented the joint work plan of the UN Division for the Advancement of Women and OHCHR in 2004. Both entities would continue to cooperate to advance women's human rights and the mainstreaming of gender perspectives in all activities, particularly regarding support for human rights treaty bodies and for intergovernmental bodies and special procedures, technical cooperation, advisory services and meetings, awareness-raising and outreach, and inter-agency cooperation. They planned to continue cooperation in the exchange of documents, reports and the results of the work of treaty bodies and the circulation of those documents; in the exchange of information and collaboration among their staff regarding communications and inquiry procedures; in supporting mutual participation of the Chairpersons of the Commission on the Status of Women and of the Commission on Human Rights in each other's work, and the participation of the Chairperson of the Committee on the Elimination of Discrimination against Women; in the preparation of reports on similar issues; in efforts to improve early information exchange and coordination in technical cooperation activities; and in preparing and piloting training packages on international human rights instruments. Cooperation would continue in convening a proposed joint meeting of the bureaux of the Commission on the Status of Women and the Commission on Human Rights, in organizing a workshop on the integration of gender perspectives into the work of thematic mandates and in organizing a joint meeting of the Division and OHCHR on national human rights institutions and machineries for the advancement of women regarding strategies to eliminate sexual discrimination. Joint efforts would focus on ensuring that the electronic database covering the main human rights treaty bodies was updated, operational and accessible, and on updating and improving their web sites to enhance information about human rights, particularly women's. They would collaborate in publishing materials on the gender dimensions of racial discrimination, and prepare a guide on human rights and legislative practices to combat trafficking in women.

Commission action. On 19 April [dec. 2004/108], the Commission decided to consider in 2005 the issue of integrating the human rights of women throughout the UN system on a biennial basis, and asked the Secretary-General to update his March report (see above).

Trafficking in women and girls

Commission action. On 19 April [res. 2004/45], the Commission invited Governments, donors, OHCHR, international and regional organizations and NGOs to consider the need for comprehensive anti-trafficking strategies, greater allocation of resources and better coordination of activities in tackling the problem of trafficking in persons, particularly women and children. Governments were further encouraged, in cooperation with intergovernmental organizations and NGOs, to study the vulnerable situation of potential victims and to undertake information campaigns targeted at them, especially women and girls, aimed at clarifying opportunities, limitations and rights in the event of migration, to enable them to make informed decisions to prevent them from becoming trafficking victims. The High Commissioner was invited, in cooperation with participating organizations of the Intergovernmental Organization Contact Group on Human Trafficking and Migrant Smuggling, to brief delegations and other interested parties on OHCHR's trafficking programme and the Contact Group's activities during the Commission's 2006 session.

Also on 19 April [dec. 2004/110], the Commission decided to appoint for a period of three years a Special Rapporteur whose mandate would focus on the human rights aspects of the rights of victims of trafficking in persons, especially women and children. The Commission requested that the Special Rapporteur report annually, starting in 2005, with recommendations on measures to uphold the rights of victims and cooperate with other relevant special rapporteurs, particularly the Special Rapporteur on violence against women (see p. 775) and with relevant UN bodies, regional organizations and victims and their representatives. The Special Rapporteur might, as appropriate, respond to reliable information on possible violations, with a view to protecting the rights of actual or potential victims. Governments and international organizations were asked to cooperate with the Special Rapporteur and the Secretary-General was asked to assist in fulfilling the mandate.

On 15 June, the Economic and Social Council endorsed the Commission's decision to appoint the Special Rapporteur and its requests to the Special Rapporteur and the Secretary-General (**decision 2004/228**).

In October, Sigma Huda (Bangladesh) was appointed Special Rapporteur on trafficking in persons, especially women and children.

General Assembly action. On 20 December, the General Assembly, in **resolution 59/166** (see p. 1160), urged Governments to devise, enforce and strengthen effective measures to combat and eliminate all forms of trafficking in women and girls, including for sexual exploitation, as part of a comprehensive anti-trafficking strategy that integrated a gender and human rights perspective, and to draw up national action plans in that regard.

Children

By a recorded vote of 52 to 1, the Commission, on 20 April [res. 2004/48], called on States to ensure children's registration immediately after birth; to respect children's rights and preserve their identity; and to ensure children's right to know and be cared for by their parents and not be separated from their parents against their will, except when competent authorities determined that such separation was in the best interests of the child. Among other things, States were also called on to support and participate in global poverty eradication efforts and to promote the rights of the child in that context; ensure children's access, without discrimination, to health; support and rehabilitate children and their families affected by HIV/AIDS and ensure the prevention of HIV infections; ensure that children had access, without discrimination, to quality education; protect children from violence and ensure they did not suffer discrimination; protect the rights of minority children, and those of children with disabilities, migrant children, street children and refugee and internally displaced children; eliminate child labour; and ensure children were not deprived of their liberty except as a last resort, and ensure that those arrested, detained or imprisoned were provided legal assistance and not sentenced to forced labour, corporal punishment or deprived of access to health care.

(Other aspects of the Commission's resolution—child labour, the prevention and eradication of the sale of children, child prostitution and child pornography, the protection of children affected by armed conflict and violence against children—are covered below.)

GENERAL ASSEMBLY ACTION

On 23 December [meeting 76], the General Assembly, on the recommendation of the Third Committee [A/59/499], adopted **resolution 59/261** by recorded vote (166-2-1) [agenda item 101].

Rights of the child

The General Assembly,

Recalling its previous resolutions on the rights of the child, the most recent of which is resolution 58/157 of 22 December 2003, as well as Commission on Human Rights resolution 2004/48 of 20 April 2004,

Emphasizing that the Convention on the Rights of the Child must constitute the standard in the promotion and protection of the rights of the child, and bearing in mind the importance of the Optional Protocols to the Convention on the Rights of the Child on the involvement of children in armed conflict and on the sale of children, child prostitution and child pornography, as well as other relevant human rights instruments,

Welcoming the entry into force on 25 December 2003 of the Protocol to Prevent, Suppress and Punish Trafficking in Persons, Especially Women and Children, supplementing the United Nations Convention against Transnational Organized Crime,

Reaffirming the outcome documents of the special session of the General Assembly on children, entitled "A world fit for children", and the commitments contained therein to promote and protect the rights of each child, every human being below the age of 18 years, including adolescents, and of all major United Nations conferences, and the integration of child rights issues into the outcome documents of all major

United Nations conferences, special sessions and summits,

Welcoming the reports of the Secretary-General on the status of the Convention on the Rights of the Child and on progress achieved in realizing the commitments set out in the document entitled "A world fit for children",

Welcoming also the work of the Committee on the Rights of the Child in examining the progress made by States parties to the Convention in implementing the obligations undertaken in the Convention and in providing recommendations to States parties on the implementation of the Convention and, in cooperation with the Office of the United Nations High Commissioner for Human Rights, in enhancing awareness of the principles and provisions of the Convention,

Profoundly concerned that the situation of children in many parts of the world remains critical as a result of the persistence of poverty, social inequality, inadequate social and economic conditions in an increasingly globalized economic environment, pandemics, in particular HIV/AIDS, malaria and tuberculosis, environmental damage, natural disasters, armed conflict, displacement, exploitation, illiteracy, hunger, intolerance, discrimination, gender inequality, disability and inadequate legal protection, and convinced that urgent and effective national and international action is called for,

Underlining the need to mainstream a gender perspective in all policies and programmes relating to children,

Implementation of the Convention on the Rights of the Child and the Optional Protocols thereto on the involvement of children in armed conflict and on the sale of children, child prostitution and child pornography

1. *Reaffirms* that the general principles of, inter alia, the best interests of the child, non-discrimination, participation and survival and development provide the framework for all actions concerning children, including adolescents;

2. *Urges* States that have not yet done so to sign and ratify or accede to the Convention on the Rights of the Child as a matter of priority, and urges States parties to implement it fully, while stressing that the implementation of the Convention and the achievement of the goals of the World Summit for Children and the special session of the General Assembly on children are mutually reinforcing;

3. *Expresses its concern* about the great number of reservations to the Convention, and urges States parties to withdraw reservations that are incompatible with the object and purpose of the Convention and to consider reviewing other reservations with a view to withdrawing them;

4. *Urges* States that have not yet done so to consider signing and ratifying or acceding to the Optional Protocols to the Convention on the Rights of the Child on the involvement of children in armed conflict and on the sale of children, child prostitution and child pornography, and urges States parties to implement them fully;

5. *Urges* States parties to take all appropriate measures for the implementation of the rights recognized in the Convention by, inter alia, putting in place effective national legislation, policies and action plans, by strengthening relevant governmental structures for children and by ensuring adequate and systematic training in the rights of the child for professional groups working with and for children;

6. *Encourages* States to strengthen their national statistical capacities and to use statistics disaggregated, inter alia, by age, gender and other relevant factors that may lead to disparities and other statistical indicators at the national, subregional, regional and international levels to develop and assess social policies and programmes so that economic and social resources are used efficiently and effectively for the full realization of the rights of the child;

7. *Also encourages* States to strengthen their partnership with United Nations organs, within their respective mandates, the Bretton Woods institutions and other multilateral agencies, and affirms the important role of international cooperation for the purposes of the promotion and protection of the rights of the child, in particular with regard to economic, social and cultural rights;

8. *Calls upon* States to strengthen their cooperation with the Committee on the Rights of the Child, to comply in a timely manner with their reporting obligations under the Convention and the Optional Protocols thereto, in accordance with the guidelines elaborated by the Committee, and to take into account the recommendations made by the Committee in the implementation of the provisions of the Convention;

9. *Welcomes* the efforts of the Committee to reform its working methods so as to consider the reports of States parties in a timely manner, including its proposal to work in two chambers, as an exceptional and temporary measure, for a period of two years, in order to clear the backlog of reports, taking due account of equitable geographical distribution, urges the Committee to continue to review its working methods in order to enhance its efficiency, and requests it to assess the progress made after two years, taking into account the wider context of treaty body reform;

10. *Calls upon* all States and relevant actors concerned to continue to cooperate with the special rapporteurs and special representatives of the United Nations system in the implementation of their mandates;

11. *Requests* all relevant organs of the United Nations system, the Office of the United Nations High Commissioner for Human Rights and United Nations mechanisms regularly and systematically to incorporate a strong child rights perspective as well as a gender perspective throughout all activities in the fulfilment of their mandates, as well as to ensure that their staff is trained in child protection matters, and calls upon States to cooperate closely with them;

Promoting and protecting the rights of children and non-discrimination against children, including children in particularly difficult situations

Identity, family relations and birth registration

12. *Urges* all States to intensify their efforts in order to ensure the implementation of the right of the child to birth registration, preservation of identity, including nationality, and family relations, as recognized by law, by:

(*a*) Providing, at minimal cost, simplified, expeditious and effective procedures for birth registration;

(*b*) Raising awareness at the national, regional and local levels, whenever necessary, of the importance of birth registration;

(*c*) Guaranteeing, to the extent consistent with each State's obligations, the right of a child whose parents reside in different States to maintain, on a regular basis, save in exceptional circumstances, personal relations and direct contact with both parents by providing means of access and visitation in both States and by respecting the principle that both parents have common responsibilities for the upbringing and development of their children;

(*d*) Where alternative care is necessary, promoting family and community-based care in preference to placement in institutions;

13. *Calls upon* States to take all necessary measures to prevent and combat illegal adoptions;

14. *Calls upon* all States to adopt and enforce laws and improve the implementation of policies and programmes to protect children growing up without parents and caregivers, in particular orphaned and other vulnerable children, from all forms of violence, neglect, abuse and exploitation, and to ensure their access to education, health and social services;

15. *Calls upon* States to take all necessary measures to ensure the full enjoyment of all human rights and fundamental freedoms by orphaned and other vulnerable children and to take effective measures against violations of those rights;

16. *Calls upon* all States to address cases of international abduction of children, and encourages States to engage in multilateral and bilateral cooperation so as to facilitate, inter alia, the return of the child to the country in which he or she resided immediately before the removal or retention and, in this respect, to pay particular attention to cases of international abduction of children by a parent or by other relatives;

Poverty

17. *Calls upon* States and the international community to cooperate, support and participate in the global efforts for poverty eradication at the global, regional and country levels, recognizing that strengthened availability and effective allocation of resources are required at all of these levels, in order to ensure that all the internationally agreed development and poverty eradication goals, including those set out in the United Nations Millennium Declaration, are realized within their time framework, and reaffirms that investments in children and the realization of their rights are among the most effective ways to eradicate poverty;

Health

18. *Calls upon* all States to take all necessary measures to ensure the right of the child, without discrimination, to the enjoyment of the highest attainable standard of health and to develop sustainable health systems and social services, to ensure access to such systems and services without discrimination and to pay particular attention to adequate food and nutrition to prevent disease and malnutrition, to prenatal and postnatal health care, to the special needs of adolescents and to reproductive and sexual health;

19. *Urges* all States to assign priority to activities and programmes aimed at preventing the abuse of narcotic drugs, psychotropic substances and inhalants as well as preventing other addictions, in particular addiction to alcohol and tobacco, among children and young people, especially those in vulnerable situations, and to counter the use of children and young people in the illicit production of and trafficking in narcotic drugs and psychotropic substances;

20. *Calls upon* all States to give support and rehabilitation to children and their families affected by HIV/AIDS and to involve children and their caregivers, as well as the private sector, to ensure the effective prevention of HIV infections through correct information and access to voluntary and confidential care, treatment and testing, including pharmaceutical products and medical technologies, affordable to all, giving due importance to the prevention of mother-to-child transmission of the virus;

Education

21. *Also calls upon* all States:

(*a*) To recognize the right to education on the basis of equal opportunity and non-discrimination by making primary education compulsory and available free to all children, by ensuring that all children have access to education of good quality, as well as by making secondary education generally available and accessible to all, in particular by the progressive introduction of free education, bearing in mind that special measures to ensure equal access, including affirmative action, contribute to achieving equal opportunity and combating exclusion;

(*b*) To design and implement programmes to provide social services and support to pregnant adolescents and adolescent mothers, in particular by enabling them to continue and complete their education;

(*c*) To take all appropriate measures to prevent racism and discriminatory and xenophobic attitudes and behaviour through education, keeping in mind the important role that children play in changing those practices;

(*d*) To ensure that children, from an early age, benefit from education programmes, materials and activities that develop respect for human rights and reflect fully the values of peace, non-violence against oneself and others, tolerance and gender equality;

(*e*) To harness the rapidly evolving information and communication technologies to support education at an affordable cost, including open and distance education, while reducing inequality in access and quality;

(*f*) To enable children, including adolescents, to exercise their right to express their views freely, according to their evolving capacity, and build self-esteem, acquire knowledge and skills, such as those for conflict resolution, decision-making and communication, to meet the challenges of life;

22. *Invites* the United Nations Educational, Scientific and Cultural Organization to continue to implement its mandated role in coordinating Education for All, as a means of reaching the commitments contained in the Millennium Declaration in this regard;

23. *Urges* States:

(*a*) To take measures to protect schoolchildren from violence, injury or abuse, including sexual abuse and intimidation or maltreatment in schools, to establish complaint mechanisms that are age-appropriate and accessible to children and to undertake thorough and prompt investigations of all acts of violence and discrimination;

(b) To take measures to eliminate the use of corporal punishment in schools;

Freedom from violence

24. *Calls upon* States:

(a) To take all appropriate measures to prevent and protect children from all forms of violence, including physical, mental and sexual violence, torture, child abuse, domestic violence, and abuse by police, other law enforcement authorities and employees and officials in detention centres or welfare institutions, including orphanages;

(b) To investigate and submit cases of torture and other forms of violence against children to the competent authorities for the purpose of prosecution and to impose appropriate disciplinary or penal sanctions against those responsible for such practices;

25. *Calls upon* all States to end impunity for perpetrators of crimes committed against children, recognizing in this regard the contribution of the establishment of the International Criminal Court as a way to prevent violations of human rights and international humanitarian law, in particular when children are victims of serious crimes, including the crime of genocide, crimes against humanity and war crimes, to bring perpetrators of such crimes to justice and not grant amnesties for these crimes and to strengthen international cooperation towards the goal of ending impunity;

26. *Requests* all relevant human rights mechanisms, in particular special rapporteurs and working groups, within their mandates, to pay attention to the special situations of violence against children, reflecting their experiences in the field;

27. *Invites* the independent expert for the United Nations study on violence against children to report to the General Assembly at its sixtieth session;

Non-discrimination

28. *Calls upon* all States to ensure that children are entitled to their civil, political, economic, social and cultural rights without discrimination of any kind;

29. *Notes with concern* the large number of children, particularly girls and children belonging to minorities, who are among the victims of racism, racial discrimination, xenophobia and related intolerance, stresses the need to incorporate special measures, in accordance with the principle of the best interests of the child and respect for his or her views, in programmes to combat racism, racial discrimination, xenophobia and related intolerance, and calls upon States to provide special support and ensure equal access to services for all children;

The girl child

30. *Calls upon* all States to take all necessary measures, including legal reforms where appropriate:

(a) To ensure the full and equal enjoyment by girls of all human rights and fundamental freedoms, to take effective actions against violations of those rights and freedoms and to base programmes and policies on the rights of the child, taking into account the special situation of girls;

(b) To eliminate all forms of discrimination against girls and all forms of violence, including female infanticide and prenatal sex selection, rape, sexual abuse and harmful traditional or customary practices, including female genital mutilation, the root causes of son preference, marriages without free and full consent of the intending spouses, early marriages and forced sterilization, by enacting and enforcing legislation and, where appropriate, formulating comprehensive, multidisciplinary and coordinated national plans, programmes or strategies protecting girls;

Children with disabilities

31. *Also calls upon* all States to take the necessary measures to ensure the full and equal enjoyment of all human rights and fundamental freedoms by children with disabilities in both the public and the private spheres, including access to good quality education and health care and protection from violence, abuse and neglect, and to develop and, where it already exists, to enforce legislation to prohibit discrimination against them to ensure their dignity, promote their self-reliance and facilitate their active participation and integration in the community, taking into account the particularly difficult situation of children with disabilities living in poverty;

32. *Encourages* the Ad Hoc Committee on a Comprehensive and Integral International Convention on the Protection and Promotion of the Rights and Dignity of Persons with Disabilities to continue to consider the issue of children with disabilities in its deliberations;

Migrant children

33. *Calls upon* all States to ensure, for migrant children, the enjoyment of all human rights as well as access to health care, social services and education of good quality and to ensure that migrant children, and especially those who are unaccompanied, in particular victims of violence and exploitation, receive special protection and assistance;

Children working and/or living on the street

34. *Also calls upon* all States to prevent violations of the rights of children working and/or living on the street, including discrimination, arbitrary detention and extrajudicial, arbitrary and summary executions, torture, all kinds of violence and exploitation, and to bring the perpetrators to justice, to adopt and implement policies for the protection, social and psychosocial rehabilitation and reintegration of these children and to adopt economic, social and educational strategies to address the problems of children working and/or living on the street;

Refugee and internally displaced children

35. *Further calls upon* all States to protect refugee, asylum-seeking and internally displaced children, in particular those who are unaccompanied, who are particularly exposed to risks in connection with armed conflict, such as recruitment, sexual violence and exploitation, to pay particular attention to programmes for voluntary repatriation and, wherever possible, local integration and resettlement, to give priority to family tracing and reunification and, where appropriate, to cooperate with international humanitarian and refugee organizations, including by facilitating their work;

Child labour

36. *Calls upon* all States to translate into concrete action their commitment to the progressive and effective elimination of child labour that is likely to be hazardous to or interfere with the child's education or to be harmful to the child's health or physical, mental, spiritual, moral or social development, to eliminate immediately the worst forms of child labour, to promote education as a key strategy in this regard, including the creation of vocational training and apprenticeship programmes and the integration of working children into the formal education system, and to examine and devise economic policies, where necessary, in cooperation with the international community, that address factors contributing to these forms of child labour;

37. *Urges* all States that have not yet done so to consider ratifying the Convention concerning Minimum Age for Admission to Employment, 1973 (Convention No. 138) and the Convention concerning the Prohibition and Immediate Action for the Elimination of the Worst Forms of Child Labour, 1999 (Convention No. 182) of the International Labour Organization, and calls upon States parties to those instruments to implement them fully and to comply in a timely manner with their reporting obligations;

Children alleged to have infringed or
recognized as having infringed penal law

38. *Calls upon:*

(a) All States, in particular States in which the death penalty has not been abolished, to comply with their obligations as assumed under relevant provisions of international human rights instruments, including, in particular, articles 37 and 40 of the Convention on the Rights of the Child and articles 6 and 14 of the International Covenant on Civil and Political Rights, keeping in mind the safeguards guaranteeing protection of the rights of those facing the death penalty and the guarantees set out in Economic and Social Council resolutions 1984/50 of 25 May 1984 and 1989/64 of 24 May 1989, and calls upon those States to abolish by law, as soon as possible, the death penalty for those below the age of 18 years at the time of the commission of the offence;

(b) All States to ensure that no child in detention is sentenced to forced labour or corporal punishment or deprived of access to and provision of health-care services, hygiene and environmental sanitation, education, basic instruction and vocational training, taking into consideration the special needs of children with disabilities in detention, in accordance with their obligations under the Convention;

Recovery and social reintegration

39. *Encourages* States to promote actions, including through bilateral and multilateral technical cooperation and financial assistance, for the social reintegration of children in difficult situations, considering, inter alia, views, skills and capacities that these children have developed in the conditions in which they lived and, where appropriate, with their meaningful participation;

40. *Recognizes* that children affected by the severe impact of natural disasters must be provided with access to basic social services;

Prevention and eradication of the sale of children, child prostitution and child pornography

41. *Calls upon* all States:

(a) To criminalize and penalize effectively all forms of sexual exploitation and sexual abuse of children, including all acts of paedophilia, including within the family or for commercial purposes, child pornography and child prostitution, child sex tourism, trafficking in children, the sale of children and their organs and the use of the Internet for these purposes, and to take effective measures against the criminalization of children who are victims of exploitation;

(b) To ensure the prosecution of offenders, whether local or foreign, by the competent national authorities, either in the country in which the crime was committed, or in the country of which the offender is a national or resident, or in the country of which the victim is a national, or on any other basis permitted under domestic law in accordance with due process of law, and for these purposes, to afford one another the greatest measure of assistance in connection with investigations or criminal or extradition proceedings;

(c) To increase cooperation at all levels to prevent and dismantle networks trafficking in children;

(d) To consider ratifying or acceding to the Protocol to Prevent, Suppress and Punish Trafficking in Persons, Especially Women and Children, supplementing the United Nations Convention against Transnational Organized Crime;

(e) In cases of trafficking in children, the sale of children, child prostitution and child pornography, to address effectively the needs of victims, including their safety and protection, physical and psychological recovery and full reintegration into their family and society;

(f) To combat the existence of a market that encourages such criminal practices against children, including through the adoption, effective application and enforcement of preventive, rehabilitative and punitive measures targeting customers or individuals who sexually exploit or sexually abuse children, as well as by ensuring public awareness;

(g) To contribute to the elimination of the sale of children, child prostitution and child pornography by adopting a holistic approach, addressing the contributing factors, including underdevelopment, poverty, economic disparities, inequitable socio-economic structures, dysfunctional families, lack of education, urban-rural migration, gender discrimination, irresponsible adult sexual behaviour, harmful traditional practices, armed conflicts and trafficking in children;

Children affected by armed conflict

42. *Reaffirms* the essential roles of the General Assembly, the Economic and Social Council and the Commission on Human Rights in promoting and protecting the rights and welfare of children, notes the importance of the debates held by the Security Council on children and armed conflict and its resolutions, and takes note of other recent documents on this issue and of the importance of the undertaking by the Council to give special attention to the protection, welfare and rights of children in armed conflict when taking action aimed at maintaining peace and security, including provisions for the protection of children in the mandates of peacekeeping operations, as well as the in-

clusion of child protection advisers in those operations;

43. *Takes note* of the report of the Secretary-General on the comprehensive assessment of the United Nations system response to children affected by armed conflict;

44. *Also takes note* of the report of the Special Representative of the Secretary-General for Children and Armed Conflict;

45. *Recognizes* the inclusion in the Rome Statute of the International Criminal Court, as a war crime, of crimes involving sexual violence and crimes of conscripting or enlisting children under the age of 15 years or using them to participate actively in hostilities in both international and non-international armed conflicts;

46. *Strongly condemns* any recruitment and use of children in armed conflict contrary to international law, and urges all States and other parties to armed conflict that are engaged in such practices to end them;

47. *Recognizes* the efforts of States, the United Nations system and civil society to end the recruitment and use of children in armed conflict;

48. *Calls upon* States:

(a) When ratifying the Optional Protocol to the Convention on the Rights of the Child on the involvement of children in armed conflict, to raise the minimum age for voluntary recruitment of persons into the national armed forces from that set out in article 38, paragraph 3, of the Convention, bearing in mind that under the Convention persons under 18 years of age are entitled to special protection, and to adopt safeguards to ensure that such recruitment is not forced or coerced;

(b) To take all feasible measures to ensure the demobilization and effective disarmament of children used in armed conflicts and to implement effective measures for their rehabilitation, physical and psychological recovery and reintegration into society, taking into account the rights and the specific needs and capacities of girls;

(c) To take all feasible measures, as a matter of priority, to prevent the recruitment and use of children by armed groups, as distinct from the armed forces of a State, including the adoption of legal measures necessary to prohibit and criminalize such practices;

(d) To protect children affected by armed conflict, in particular from violations of international humanitarian law and human rights law and to ensure that they receive timely, effective humanitarian assistance in accordance with the Geneva Conventions of 12 August 1949 and international humanitarian law;

49. *Calls upon* the United Nations system and the international community to cooperate with States in the development of projects to build capacity and to educate and train demobilized children in order to reintegrate them into society;

Follow-up

50. *Urges* those States that have not yet done so to complete as soon as possible a national action plan incorporating the goals agreed at the special session of the General Assembly on children, as reflected in its outcome document entitled "A world fit for children", and to place those goals within the framework of the Convention on the Rights of the Child;

51. *Decides:*

(a) To request the Secretary-General to prepare an updated report on the progress achieved in realizing the commitments set out in the document entitled "A world fit for children", with a view to identifying new challenges and making recommendations on the action needed to achieve further progress;

(b) To request the Secretary-General to submit to the General Assembly at its sixtieth session a report on the rights of the child, containing information on the status of the Convention and the issues addressed in the present resolution;

(c) To request the Special Representative of the Secretary-General for Children and Armed Conflict to continue to submit reports to the General Assembly and the Commission on Human Rights and to ensure that they contain relevant, accurate and objective information on the situation of children affected by armed conflict, taking into account the views of Member States and the outcome document adopted by the General Assembly at its special session on children and bearing in mind existing mandates and reports of relevant bodies;

(d) To invite the Chairman of the Committee on the Rights of the Child to present an oral report on the work of the Committee to the General Assembly at its sixtieth session;

(e) To focus its general debate regarding the promotion of the rights of the child, at future sessions, on specific challenges, beginning, at its sixtieth session, with the contribution that the implementation of the Convention on the Rights of the Child can make to the eradication of poverty and hunger;

(f) To continue its consideration of the question at its sixtieth session under the item entitled "Promotion and protection of the rights of children".

RECORDED VOTE ON RESOLUTION 59/261:

In favour: Albania, Algeria, Andorra, Antigua and Barbuda, Argentina, Armenia, Australia, Austria, Azerbaijan, Bahamas, Bahrain, Bangladesh, Barbados, Belarus, Belgium, Belize, Benin, Bhutan, Bolivia, Bosnia and Herzegovina, Brazil, Brunei Darussalam, Bulgaria, Burkina Faso, Burundi, Cambodia, Cameroon, Canada, Cape Verde, Central African Republic, Chad, Chile, China, Colombia, Comoros, Congo, Costa Rica, Croatia, Cuba, Cyprus, Czech Republic, Democratic People's Republic of Korea, Democratic Republic of the Congo, Denmark, Djibouti, Dominica, Dominican Republic, Ecuador, Egypt, El Salvador, Eritrea, Estonia, Fiji, Finland, France, Gabon, Georgia, Germany, Ghana, Greece, Grenada, Guatemala, Guinea, Guyana, Haiti, Honduras, Hungary, Iceland, Indonesia, Iran, Iraq, Ireland, Israel, Italy, Japan, Jordan, Kazakhstan, Kenya, Kuwait, Kyrgyzstan, Lao People's Democratic Republic, Latvia, Lebanon, Lesotho, Liberia, Libyan Arab Jamahiriya, Liechtenstein, Lithuania, Luxembourg, Madagascar, Malaysia, Maldives, Mali, Malta, Mauritius, Mexico, Micronesia, Monaco, Mongolia, Morocco, Mozambique, Myanmar, Namibia, Nepal, Netherlands, New Zealand, Nicaragua, Niger, Nigeria, Norway, Oman, Pakistan, Panama, Papua New Guinea, Paraguay, Peru, Philippines, Poland, Portugal, Qatar, Republic of Korea, Republic of Moldova, Romania, Russian Federation, Rwanda, Saint Lucia, Saint Vincent and the Grenadines, San Marino, Saudi Arabia, Senegal, Serbia and Montenegro, Sierra Leone, Singapore, Slovakia, Slovenia, Solomon Islands, Somalia, South Africa, Spain, Sri Lanka, Sudan, Suriname, Sweden, Switzerland, Syrian Arab Republic, Thailand, The former Yugoslav Republic of Macedonia, Timor-Leste, Togo, Tonga, Trinidad and Tobago, Tunisia, Turkey, Turkmenistan, Uganda, Ukraine, United Arab Emirates, United Kingdom, United Republic of Tanzania, Uruguay, Uzbekistan, Venezuela, Viet Nam, Yemen, Zambia, Zimbabwe.

Against: Marshall Islands, United States.

Abstaining: India.

The Third Committee adopted by separate recorded votes paragraph 9 by 114 to 30, with 14 abstentions; paragraph 23 (*b*) by 123 to 7, with 32 abstentions; and the words "corporal punishment" in paragraph 38 (*b*) by 130 to 4, with 33 abstentions. The Assembly retained those paragraphs by recorded votes, respectively, of 110 to 26, with 12 abstentions; 116 to 4, with 33 abstentions; and 115 to 3, with 34 abstentions.

Violence against children

Report of Secretary-General. In response to a 2003 Commission request [YUN 2003, p. 780], the Secretary-General submitted a January progress report [E/CN.4/2004/68] on the study on violence against children, pursuant to General Assembly resolution 56/138 [YUN 2001, p. 681]. He noted that the independent expert appointed to lead the study, Paulo Sérgio Pinheiro (Brazil), had undertaken a number of related activities, including the development of a concept paper, which was annexed to the report and outlined the scope of the study. In addition, a questionnaire had been circulated requesting Governments to submit information on the issue of violence against children. As the lead UN bodies designated to support the study, OHCHR, UNICEF and WHO had agreed to establish a secretariat in Geneva, headed by a Director, to support the expert. The Director had been hired, but since no provision was made in the regular budget for the study, the secretariat and other aspects of the study would be financed through voluntary contributions. UNICEF regional directors had been invited to consider modalities for regional consultations that would provide input for the study, and NGOs had also taken steps to facilitate their input.

Oral report of independent expert. As called for in General Assembly resolution 58/157 [YUN 2003, p. 781], the independent expert leading the study on violence against children, Mr. Pinheiro, in an October oral report to the Third Committee [A/C.3/59/SR.17], discussed the work he had undertaken to provide an in-depth, global picture of violence against children, documenting its causes, magnitude, incidence and consequences. He had focused on gathering information on measures to prevent and respond to the problem, and, in that regard, he was working to identify best practices, including those developed by children themselves. The objective was to heighten attention at the national, regional and international levels to the problem, and to put forward recommendations to improve national legislation, policy and programmes, and for consideration by the Assembly, the UN system and civil society. In accordance with the definition of a child contained in the 1989 Convention on the Rights of the Child [YUN 1989, p. 561] (see p. 667), the study would be concerned with violence against girls and boys under 18 years of age and would take a broad view of violence, covering physical and mental violence, injury and abuse, maltreatment or exploitation, including sexual abuse. He would focus on children as both victims and perpetrators of violence and would address violence that was less visible, such as that in the family and community, including schools, care and residential institutions, detention facilities, prisons and in the administration of justice. Existing knowledge, documentation and research would form the basis of the study, and inputs were expected from Governments, regional mechanisms, NGOs, other parts of civil society and children themselves. It was hoped that the study, scheduled for submission in 2006, would provide concrete tools to prevent and combat all forms of violence against children.

Commission action. On 20 April [res. 2004/48], by a recorded vote of 52 to 1, the Commission invited Member States, UN bodies and organizations and relevant intergovernmental organizations to provide financial support, including through voluntary contributions, for the conduct of the study on violence against children. NGOs were invited to contribute to the study, while the independent expert was encouraged to seek children's participation. The Secretary-General was asked to submit a progress report in 2005 and a final in-depth study in 2006.

Sale of children, child prostitution and child pornography

Reports of Special Rapporteur. In response to a 2003 Commission request [YUN 2003, p. 780], the Special Rapporteur on the sale of children, child prostitution and child pornography, Juan Miguel Petit (Uruguay), submitted a January report [E/CN.4/2004/9] on the prevention of child sexual exploitation, based on information received from Governments, international organizations and NGOs, in response to a questionnaire he had circulated. The report focused on international instruments, programmes and measures aimed at identifying strategies to prevent child sexual exploitation. Using as a basis the 1996 Stockholm Agenda for Action against Commercial Sexual Exploitation of Children, adopted by the first World Congress against Commercial Sexual Exploitation of Children [YUN 1996, p. 660], the Special Rapporteur described initiatives relating to international instruments, legislation, enforcement mechanisms, institutions and networks, national plans of action, programmes and projects, the role of the media, sex tourism: the business sector and codes of conduct, the right to education, peer education, participation and empowerment, gender issues, and groups discriminated against and exposed to higher risks. The Special Rapporteur concluded that child sexual exploitation was a multifaceted and evolving phenomenon and that targeted measures were necessary to address its various manifestations. He recommended better programmes and policies for intervention, particularly regarding the areas discussed in the report. He further recommended, among other things, the development of monitoring tools and indicators to set benchmarks and measure achievements, encouraging behavioural change by persons who engaged in child sexual exploitation, and policies and programmes to prevent commercial sexual exploitation of children, including through the Internet.

Between 1 January and 31 December, the Special Rapporteur sent 47 communications to 30 Governments regarding alleged cases relating to the sale of children, child prostitution and child pornography, of which over 60 per cent were sent jointly with other special rapporteurs. Of those, replies were received from 18 Governments. The communications sent and replies received were summarized in a separate report [E/CN.4/2005/78/Add.3].

The Special Rapporteur visited Paraguay (23 February–5 March) [E/CN.4/2005/78/Add.1] at the invitation of the Government, where he found that, against the backdrop of poverty and inequality, the sexual exploitation of children and young persons had grown to alarming levels. Information he had received suggested that about two out of every three sex workers in the country were minors, who began working in the sex trade between the ages of 12 and 13, and that girls as young as 8 years of age were involved. The nonregistration of children at birth raised cause for concern, as children without birth certificates accounted for a large proportion of people deprived of an identity or rights and who were vulnerable to exploitation. The Special Rapporteur, pointing to limited progress in efforts to protect children's rights, determined that new social programmes and preventive measures were required, and proposed that the State and civil society pool their resources to build a system to protect children's rights in situations of social risk. Priority should be accorded the full implementation of the Government's Code on Children and Young Persons, care for victims of sexual exploitation and the eradication of the system of servant girls.

In Romania (1-10 September) [E/CN.4/2005/78/Add.2], the Special Rapporteur found that, despite some achievements regarding some child protection issues, other problems affecting children had not been addressed adequately, including internal trafficking and child prostitution. The Special Rapporteur pointed out that internal trafficking opened doors to international trafficking and that anti-trafficking strategies would work only if the problem was also addressed internally. He found that social exclusion, discrimination and stigmatization were the root causes of vulnerability to trafficking and sexual exploitation, and that those at risk included street children, Roma children, victims of sexual abuse and domestic violence, children in institutions and children with dysfunctional and poor families. The Special Rapporteur recommended measures relating to relevant legislation, law enforcement, the protection of migrants' interests, anti-trafficking programmes and the transformation of residential institutions for children.

Commission action. On 20 April [res. 2004/48], the Commission, by a recorded vote of 52 to 1, called on States to take measures to prevent and combat the trafficking and sale of children and to criminalize and penalize all forms of sexual exploitation and abuse of children, child pornography and child prostitution, child trafficking and child sex tourism, the sale of children and their organs and the use of the Internet for those purposes, and to address the needs of victims. The Special Rapporteur was asked to report in 2005.

On 22 July, the Economic and Social Council, noting the Commission's resolution, decided to extend the Special Rapporteur's mandate for a further three years (**decision 2004/285**).

Child labour

By a recorded vote of 52 to 1, the Commission, on 20 April [res. 2004/48], called on States to eliminate child labour that was hazardous, interfered with a child's education or was harmful to the child's health, and to promote education as a key strategy. It also called on them to consider ratifying and implementing ILO Convention No. 182 concerning the prohibition and elimination of the worst forms of child labour (Worst Forms of Child Labour Convention), adopted in 1999 [YUN 1999, p. 1388], and Convention No. 138 concerning the minimum age for admission to employment (Minimum Age Convention), adopted in 1973 [YUN 1973, p. 885].

Children and armed conflict

Report of Special Representative. In accordance with General Assembly resolution 51/77 [YUN 1996, p. 665], the Secretary-General's Special Representative for Children and Armed Conflict, Olara A. Otunnu (Côte d'Ivoire), in a January report [E/CN.4/2004/70], updated information on violations against children in situations of armed conflict, which supplemented his 2003 report and that of the Secretary-General on the subject [YUN 2003, p. 790]. Annexed to the report were lists of parties to armed conflict that recruited and used children in combat. Violations discussed in the report included abduction, maiming and killing, sexual and gender-based violence, denial of humanitarian access, attacks on schools and hospitals and the recruitment and use of children in armed conflict. The Special Representative concluded that, at the level of application and enforcement, the international community possessed the means and influence that could be brought to bear on parties to conflict to ensure their compliance with international standards. The most pressing challenge facing the international community was to galvanize and unify the two assets of normative tools and the power of collective influence into a coherent and concerted project: an effective regime of protection for war-affected children. That was the purpose of the "era of application" campaign and agenda for action proposed in the Secretary-General's 2003 report [ibid.]. The Commission had an important role to play with regard to monitoring and reporting on violations against children's rights in situations of armed conflict and should review the information in the Secretary-General's report and take action in accordance with its mandate, procedures and mechanisms.

Commission action. By a recorded vote of 52 to 1, the Commission, on 20 April [res. 2004/48], called on States to end the use of children in armed conflicts and, together with parties to armed conflict, to respect international humanitarian law. It asked States, UN bodies and agencies and regional organizations to integrate the rights of the child into all activities in conflict and post-conflict situations and to support national and international mine action efforts. It recommended that the impact on children of sanctions imposed in the context of armed conflict be assessed and monitored, in order to address possible adverse effects.

SECURITY COUNCIL ACTION

On 22 April [meeting 4948], the Security Council unanimously adopted **resolution 1539(2004)**. The draft [S/2004/314] was prepared in consultations among Council members.

The Security Council,

Reaffirming its resolutions 1261(1999) of 25 August 1999, 1314(2000) of 11 August 2000, 1379(2001) of 20 November 2001 and 1460(2003) of 30 January 2003, which provide a comprehensive framework for addressing the protection of children affected by armed conflict,

Recalling its resolution 1308(2000) of 17 July 2000 on the responsibility of the Security Council in the maintenance of international peace and security: HIV/AIDS and international peacekeeping operations, and its resolution 1325(2000) of 31 October 2000 on women and peace and security,

Noting the advances made for the protection of children affected by armed conflict, particularly in the areas of advocacy and the development of norms and standards, while remaining deeply concerned over the lack of overall progress on the ground, where parties to conflict continue to violate with impunity the relevant provisions of applicable international law relating to the rights and protection of children in armed conflict,

Recalling the responsibilities of States to end impunity and to prosecute those responsible for genocide, crimes against humanity, war crimes and other egregious crimes perpetrated against children,

Reiterating its primary responsibility for the maintenance of international peace and security and, in this connection, its commitment to address the widespread impact of armed conflict on children,

Underlining the importance of the full, safe and unhindered access of humanitarian personnel and goods and the delivery of humanitarian assistance to all children affected by armed conflict,

Noting the fact that the conscription or enlistment of children under the age of 15, or using them to participate actively in hostilities in both international and non-international armed conflict, is classified as a war crime by the Rome Statute of the International Criminal Court, and noting also that the Optional Protocol to the Convention on the Rights of the Child on the involvement of children in armed conflict requires States parties to set a minimum age of 18 for compulsory recruitment and participation in hostilities and to raise the minimum age for voluntary recruitment from that set out in article 38, paragraph 3, of the Convention on the Rights of the Child and to take all feasible measures to ensure that members of their armed forces who have not attained the age of 18 years do not take a direct part in hostilities,

Stressing its determination to ensure respect for its resolutions and other international norms and standards for the protection of children affected by armed conflict,

Having considered the report of the Secretary-General of 10 November 2003 submitted pursuant to paragraph 16 of its resolution 1460(2003), and stressing that the present resolution does not seek to make any legal determination as to whether situations referred to in the report of the Secretary-General are or are not armed conflicts within the context of the Geneva Conventions of 1949 and the Additional Protocols thereto, of 1977,nor does it prejudge the legal status of the non-State parties involved in those situations,

1. *Strongly condemns* the recruitment and use of child soldiers by parties to armed conflict in violation of international obligations applicable to them, the killing and maiming of children, rape and other sexual violence mostly committed against girls, abduction and forced displacement, denial of humanitarian access to children, attacks against schools and hospitals, as well as trafficking, forced labour and all forms of slavery and all other violations and abuses committed against children affected by armed conflict;

2. *Requests* the Secretary-General, taking into account the proposals contained in his report as well as any other relevant elements, to devise urgently, and preferably within three months, an action plan for a systematic and comprehensive monitoring and reporting mechanism, which utilizes expertise from the United Nations system and the contributions of national Governments,

regional organizations, non-governmental organizations in their advisory capacity and various civil society actors, in order to provide timely, objective, accurate and reliable information on the recruitment and use of child soldiers in violation of applicable international law and on other violations and abuses committed against children affected by armed conflict, for consideration in taking appropriate action;

3. *Expresses its intention* to take appropriate measures, in particular while considering subregional and cross-border activities, to curb linkages between illicit trade in natural and other resources, illicit trafficking in small arms and light weapons, cross-border abduction and recruitment, and armed conflict, which can prolong armed conflict and intensify its impact on children, and consequently requests the Secretary-General to propose effective measures to control this illicit trade and trafficking;

4. *Calls upon* all parties concerned to abide by the international obligations applicable to them relating to the protection of children affected by armed conflict, as well as the concrete commitments they have made to the Special Representative of the Secretary-General for Children and Armed Conflict, the United Nations Children's Fund and other United Nations agencies, and to cooperate fully with the United Nations peacekeeping missions and United Nations country teams, where appropriate in the context of the cooperation framework between the United Nations and the concerned Government, in the follow-up to and implementation of those commitments;

5. *Takes note with deep concern* of the continued recruitment and use of children, by parties mentioned in the report of the Secretary-General, in situations of armed conflict on the agenda of the Council, in violation of applicable international law relating to the rights and protection of children and, in this regard:

(*a*) Calls upon those parties to prepare, within three months, concrete time-bound action plans to halt the recruitment and use of children in violation of the international obligations applicable to them, in close collaboration with United Nations peacekeeping missions and United Nations country teams, consistent with their respective mandates;

(*b*) Requests the Secretary-General, in order to promote an effective and coordinated follow-up to the present resolution, to ensure that compliance by those parties is reviewed regularly, within existing resources, through a process involving all stakeholders at the country level, including Government representatives, and coordinated by a focal point to be designated by the Secretary-General and who would be in charge of engaging parties in dialogue leading to time-bound action plans, so as to report to the Secretary-General through his Special Representative by 31 July 2004, bearing in mind lessons learned from past dialogues as contained in paragraph 77 of the report of the Secretary-General;

(*c*) Expresses its intention to consider imposing targeted and graduated measures, through country-specific resolutions, such as, inter alia, a ban on the export or supply of small arms and light weapons and other military equipment and on military assistance, against those parties if they refuse to enter into dialogue, fail to develop an action plan or fail to meet the commitments included in their action plan, bearing in mind the report of the Secretary-General;

6. *Also takes note with deep concern* of the continued recruitment and use of children by parties in other situations of armed conflict mentioned in the report of the Secretary-General, in violation of applicable international law relating to the rights and protection of children, calls upon those parties to halt immediately their recruitment or use of children, and expresses, on the basis of timely, objective, accurate and reliable information received from relevant stakeholders, its intention to consider taking appropriate steps to further address this issue, in accordance with the Charter of the United Nations, its resolutions 1379(2001) and 1460(2003) and the present resolution;

7. *Decides* to continue the inclusion of specific provisions for the protection of children in the mandates of United Nations peacekeeping operations, including, on a case-by-case basis, the deployment of child protection advisers, and requests the Secretary-General to ensure that the need for and the number and roles of child protection advisers are systematically assessed during the preparation for each United Nations peacekeeping operation;

8. *Reiterates its request* to all parties concerned, including United Nations agencies, funds and programmes as well as financial institutions, to continue to ensure that all children associated with armed forces and groups, as well as issues related to children, are systematically included in every disarmament, demobilization and reintegration process, taking into account the specific needs and capacities of girls, with a particular emphasis on education, including the monitoring through, inter alia, schools, of children demobilized, in order to prevent re-recruitment, and bearing in mind the assessment of best practices, including those contained in paragraph 65 of the report of the Secretary-General;

9. *Calls upon* States and the United Nations system to recognize the important role of education in conflict areas in halting and preventing recruitment and re-recruitment of children contrary to the obligations of parties to conflict;

10. *Notes with concern* all the cases of sexual exploitation and abuse of women and children, especially girls, in situations of humanitarian crisis, including those cases involving humanitarian workers and peacekeepers, requests contributing countries to incorporate the six core principles of the Inter-Agency Standing Committee on emergencies into pertinent codes of conduct for peacekeeping personnel and to develop appropriate disciplinary and accountability mechanisms, and welcomes the promulgation of the Secretary-General's bulletin on special measures for protection from sexual exploitation and sexual abuse;

11. *Requests* the agencies, funds and programmes of the United Nations, with support from contributing countries, to implement HIV/AIDS education and offer HIV testing and counselling services for all United Nations peacekeepers, police and humanitarian personnel;

12. *Welcomes* recent initiatives by regional and subregional organizations and arrangements for the protection of children affected by armed conflict, and in this regard notes the adoption by the Economic Community of West African States of a peer review frame-

work on the protection of children and the adoption of "Guidelines on Children and Armed Conflict" by the European Union, and encourages such organizations and arrangements, in cooperation with the United Nations, to pursue their efforts, by, inter alia:

(a) Mainstreaming the protection of children affected by armed conflict into their advocacy, policies and programmes, paying special attention to girls;

(b) Developing peer review and monitoring and reporting mechanisms;

(c) Establishing, within their secretariats, child protection mechanisms;

(d) Including child protection staff and training in their peace and field operations;

(e) Undertaking subregional and interregional initiatives to end activities harmful to children in times of conflict, in particular, cross-border recruitment and abduction of children, illicit movement of small arms, and illicit trade in natural resources;

13. *Encourages* support for the development and strengthening of capacities of national and regional institutions and local and regional civil society networks to ensure the sustainability of local initiatives for the advocacy, protection and rehabilitation of children affected by armed conflict;

14. *Reiterates its request* to the Secretary-General to ensure that, in all his reports on country-specific situations, the protection of children is included as a specific aspect of the report, expresses its intention to give its full attention to the information provided therein when dealing with those situations on its agenda, and in this regard stresses the primary responsibility of United Nations peacekeeping missions and United Nations country teams, consistent within their respective mandates, to ensure effective follow-up to the present resolution and the other resolutions;

15. *Requests* the Secretary-General to submit a report by 31 October 2004 on the implementation of the present resolution and its resolutions 1379(2001) and 1460(2003) which would include, inter alia:

(a) Information on compliance and progress made by parties mentioned in his report in situations of armed conflict on the agenda of the Security Council, in accordance with paragraph 5 above, as well as by parties in other situations of armed conflict mentioned in his report, in accordance with paragraph 6 above, in ending the recruitment or use of children in armed conflict in violation of applicable international law relating to the rights and protection of children, bearing in mind all other violations and abuses committed against children affected by armed conflict;

(b) Information on progress made regarding the action plan requested in paragraph 2 above that calls for a systematic and comprehensive monitoring and reporting mechanism;

(c) The incorporation of best practices for disarmament, demobilization and reintegration programmes outlined in his report;

16. *Decides* to remain actively seized of this matter.

Report of Secretary-General. Pursuant to General Assembly resolution 57/190 [YUN 2002, p. 749], the Secretary-General, in September [A/59/331], reported on a comprehensive assessment of the scope and effectiveness of the UN system response to the issue of children and armed conflict. The assessment, undertaken by the Office of Internal Oversight Services, had focused on the development and application of international standards relating to children affected by armed conflict; the degree of mainstreaming of those issues within relevant UN entities; and the effectiveness of coordination within the United Nations of concerns relating to children affected by armed conflict. Guidance was provided by the 1996 study [YUN 1996, p. 663] by Graça Machel (Mozambique/South Africa) on the impact of armed conflict on children. Pointing out that significant progress had been made in efforts to strengthen international standards and to protect affected children, the Secretary-General noted that the inclusion of related concerns on the agendas of the Assembly and Security Council had enhanced child protection initiatives, while the Office of the Special Representative had helped in raising the profile of the problem. UNICEF and NGOs had also contributed to the development of a robust framework for norms and standards addressing children affected by armed conflict. Nonetheless, more needed to be done, particularly regarding the application of accepted norms and standards and to put in place an effective monitoring and reporting mechanism. The Secretary-General made recommendations for improving and sustaining efforts for children affected by armed conflict, through continued advocacy, the development of an effective and credible monitoring and reporting system on child rights violations, enhanced mainstreaming and improved coordination of the issue in the UN system.

Further report of Special Representative. In an October report [A/59/426], the Special Representative assessed progress made in mainstreaming the concerns of war-affected children in the UN system. The report examined the integration of the issue into the work of: the Security Council, UN peacekeeping operations, relevant thematic activities, UN executive coordination mechanisms, key UN-led institutional processes, and relevant UN entities and offices, including at the country level. The report noted that, although some progress had been made, particularly in mainstreaming the issue in the peace and security sector, conspicuous gaps existed and the gains made remained fragile and might dissipate if not consolidated and institutionalized. To ensure that the question of children affected by armed conflict became a consistent cross-cutting issue in UN policies and programmes, system-wide commitment and action were necessary, as were the commitment of the leaders of key UN entities and the mobilization of the requisite resources.

Communication. On 26 July [A/59/184-S/2004/602], Colombia, Myanmar, Nepal, the Philippines, Sri Lanka, the Sudan and Uganda, referring to the Secretary-General's 2003 report [YUN 2003, p. 790], expressed concern about the corrigenda to the report, particularly the use of the Geneva Conventions of 12 August 1949 relating to the protection of victims of armed conflict and the two 1977 Additional Protocols [YUN 1977, p. 706] thereto in the definition of "armed conflict" when those legal instruments did not provide for an internationally agreed definition of armed conflict.

Abduction of children in Africa

Commission action. On 20 April [res. 2004/47], the Commission, deeply alarmed at the spread of the practice of abduction of children during armed conflict in many African countries, demanded the immediate demobilization and disarmament of all child soldiers and the unconditional release and safe return of those abducted. The Commission called on African States to prohibit and criminalize such practices, and asked them, in cooperation with UN agencies, to assist the victims and their families and to support sustainable rehabilitation and reintegration programmes for them, taking into account the special needs of abducted girls. OHCHR was asked to organize subregional consultations to provide a framework for gathering research, expertise and information from each subregion, and for sensitizing political actors and networking among public authorities and civil society, including NGOs, and to report in 2005. States were urged to submit observations on the implementation of the resolution, while relevant intergovernmental organizations were called on to submit reports on the issue to OHCHR.

Subregional consultations. In response to Commission resolution 2004/47 (above), OHCHR participated in two conferences which discussed the abduction of children in Africa [E/CN.4/2005/74]. The first, the International Conference on the Transatlantic Slave Trade: Landmarks, Legacies and Expectations (Ghana, 30 August–2 September), considered, among other things, the links to slavery and how abductions could be addressed. The second, the Arab-African Conference on exploitation, violence and sexual abuse against children (Rabat, Morocco, 14-16 December), discussed issues relating to the vulnerability of children in situations of armed conflict. In further consultations, OHCHR circulated a questionnaire among NGOs to collect data.

Internally displaced persons

Reports of Secretary-General's Representative. In March [E/CN.4/2004/77], the Secretary-General's Representative, Francis M. Deng (Sudan), updated developments regarding the promotion, dissemination and application of the Guiding Principles on Internal Displacement [YUN 1998, p. 675] and efforts to develop an institutional framework for internally displaced persons (IDPs). He reviewed persisting challenges and the successes achieved in the past 10 years, noting that despite progress in the areas of norm-setting, institutional arrangements and operational responses to internal displacement, there remained a significant gap between those areas and the needs of displaced populations for protection and assistance. Although the estimated number of the displaced remained at about 25 million, internal displacement posed a continuing crisis in 2004, as millions of those affected were unable to return home owing to protracted conflicts, and millions of returnees continued to face hardships. There was a need to reinvigorate efforts to overcome both pessimism and complacency in confronting the challenge of internal displacement. Together with Governments, UN agencies had a key role to play in addressing internal displacement, and a consensus was currently emerging that indicated a readiness to increase efforts to make the collaborative approach work and to better protect and assist IDPs worldwide. The United Nations would need to demonstrate its capacity to improve the operational response to the issue, which would depend on adequate financial support from donor countries and the political backing of all States.

In accordance with a 2003 Commission request [YUN 2003, p. 793], the Representative summarized the deliberations of a regional seminar (Mexico City, 18-20 February) [E/CN.4/2005/124] he had organized, in collaboration with Mexico and the Brookings Institution–Johns Hopkins project on internal displacement. The seminar examined current trends in internal displacement in the region and responses thereto. Participants adopted a Framework for Action, which outlined issues for improved national response and steps to be taken at the regional and international levels to reinforce national responsibility.

In the Sudan (25 July–1 August) [E/CN.4/2005/8], the Representative focused on the internal displacement crisis in Darfur, where an estimated 1.2 million people had been displaced and 200,000 others were forced to flee to neighbouring Chad as refugees. He said the crisis in Darfur remained acute, and issues needing urgent attention included the security situation and the protection of IDPs and the civilian population at large; the provision of humanitarian assistance (see p. 235); and political issues, especially the challenges posed by armed groups, particularly the Janjaweed. Also warranting attention were the linkages of the Darfur crisis to the war in southern Sudan, the impending peace agreement between the Government and the Sudan People's Liberation Movement and Army, and the options open to the international community for responding to the situation in Darfur. The Representative recommended according priority to the security situation, and advocated cooperation on security and protection to create the requisite environment for humanitarian activities, facilitate access by UN and other humanitarian workers, and encourage the donor community to provide adequate financial support. Other recommendations addressed the political dimension, particularly with regard to dealing with the threat posed by armed groups, and the need for sustainable peace and security in the Darfur region and for effectively addressing the root causes of the conflict as a whole.

Commission action. On 20 April [res. 2004/55], the Commission called on the High Commissioner, in cooperation with Governments, the Representative and other relevant entities of the UN system, to promote the rights of internally displaced persons, enhance their protection and develop projects to address their plight as part of the programme of technical cooperation and advisory services, and to provide information thereon. The Secretary-General was asked to establish a mechanism that would address internal displacement, particularly by mainstreaming the rights of IDPs into all relevant parts of the UN system; to assist the mechanism and ensure the support of OHCHR and cooperation with the offices of the Emergency Relief Coordinator and the United Nations High Commissioner for Refugees; to review the mechanism's performance and effectiveness two years after its inception and report in 2006; and to ensure that the mechanism reported annually to the Commission and the General Assembly. The Commission recommended that the mechanism work towards strengthening the international response to internal displacement and engage in coordinated international advocacy and action for improving protection and respect for the rights of IDPs.

On 22 July, the Economic and Social Council endorsed the Commission's requests to the Secretary-General to establish a mechanism and to ensure that the mechanism reported annually (**decision 2004/263**).

In September [A/59/389], the Secretary-General appointed Walter Kälin (Switzerland) as his new Representative on the human rights of IDPs. He would report to the Commission and to the Assembly in 2005.

Communication. On 25 March [E/CN.4/2004/G/32], the Russian Federation transmitted its comments regarding the Representative's report on his visit to the country [YUN 2003, p. 794], stating that the report's recommendations were one-sided and did not fully cover the latest trends.

Housing and property restitution

Reports of Special Rapporteur. In response to a 2002 Subcommission request [YUN 2002, p. 761], the Special Rapporteur on housing and property restitution in the context of the return of refugees and IDPs, Paulo Sérgio Pinheiro (Brazil), submitted a June progress report [E/CN.4/Sub.2/2004/22]. The report contained draft principles designed to provide guidance on international standard setting and to guide States seeking to implement restitution programmes, and intergovernmental organizations and NGOs addressing issues of population displacement, post-conflict peace-building and restitution. The draft principles, developed in consultation with various agencies and organizations involved in restitution processes, reflected the view that a human rights–based approach to return and restitution would achieve equitable and sustainable results in restoring housing and property rights for refugees and displaced persons and in creating long-term stability. They addressed key universal principles regarding the right to housing and property restitution; the rights necessary to ensure protection from displacement; the protection of the rights of refugees and displaced persons, including the right to safe, voluntary and dignified return and to a remedy in cases of human rights violations; policy guidelines for housing and property restitution; guidance on strengthening restitution procedures, institutions, mechanisms and legal frameworks in order to facilitate the restitution process; and the role of international organizations.

An addendum to the report [E/CN.4/Sub.2/2004/22/Add.1] contained a commentary designed to guide the interpretation of the draft principles and to identify the international legal basis for the standards articulated in the principles. The Special Rapporteur hoped to expand consultations to benefit from the experience and knowledge of relevant UN agencies and organs, Governments and NGOs, in order to facilitate the development of the draft principles, and suggested convening an international meeting in 2005 to discuss them.

Subcommission action. On 9 August [res. 2004/2], the Subcommission urged States to ensure the free and fair exercise of the right to return to one's home and place of habitual residence by all refugees and IDPs and to develop effective and expeditious legal, administrative and other procedures to ensure the exercise of the right. The Subcommission, welcoming the Special Rapporteur's progress report (see p. 791), asked OHCHR to circulate the draft principles widely among NGOs, Governments, specialized agencies and other interested parties for comment. The Special Rapporteur was asked to take the comments into account in preparing his final report in 2005.

Indigenous people

Reports of Special Rapporteur. In response to a 2003 Commission request [YUN 2003, p. 798], the Special Rapporteur on the situation of human rights and fundamental freedoms of indigenous people, Rodolfo Stavenhagen (Mexico), submitted a January report [E/CN.4/2004/80] on the obstacles, gaps and challenges faced by indigenous peoples in the administration of justice and the relevance of indigenous customary law in national legal systems. He noted that the major concerns involving indigenous rights related to land, territory, the environment, natural resources, language, culture and education, and examined the situation in the courts and indigenous peoples' rights, discrimination and the justice system, the criminalization of indigenous protest activities and indigenous law and culture and alternative dispute resolution mechanisms. The Special Rapporteur found that a human rights protection gap with regard to indigenous peoples was evident in various communities around the world, particularly in the area of criminal justice. In many countries, indigenous peoples did not have equal access to the justice system and often suffered discrimination, partly due to racism and to the non-acceptance of indigenous law and customs. He recommended that States review and, if possible, reform their justice systems to better protect indigenous peoples' rights, and invited the Commission to take up the issue with Member States. Judicial reform should include respect for indigenous legal customs, language and culture in the courts and the administration of justice; indigenous peoples' participation in the reform process; and the establishment of alternative justice mechanisms.

A separate report of the Special Rapporteur [E/CN.4/2005/88/Add.1] summarized communications, including urgent appeals, he had sent to 17 Governments on alleged violations of indigenous peoples's rights between 15 December 2003 and 31 December 2004, and the responses received.

The Special Rapporteur visited Colombia (8-17 March) [E/CN.4/2005/88/Add.2], home to an estimated 1 million indigenous peoples, comprising 90 ethnic groups. He found that, although its 1991 Constitution recognized Colombia's multi-ethnic composition and established an institutional framework for protecting indigenous peoples' rights, enormous challenges remained. He heard alleged violations of indigenous peoples' rights within the context of the ongoing armed conflict affecting Colombia, including reports of murder and torture, mass displacement, forced disappearance, forced recruitment into combat units, the rape of women and the militarization of indigenous communities (see p. 805). A particular cause for concern was the situation of small indigenous communities that were at the brink of extinction owing to the murder of their leaders, massacres, threats and the forced dispersal of their members. The Special Rapporteur recommended the establishment of an independent commission to ensure that the State and armed groups fulfilled their obligations to comply with international humanitarian law and respect human rights. He advocated that priority be given to indigenous peoples' demand that all armed groups respect their neutral and demilitarized zones, and proposed the creation of indigenous peace zones free from all military operations and subject to international supervision. Further recommendations were addressed to the Government, armed groups, the country's indigenous population and the international community.

Commission action. On 21 April [res. 2004/62], the Commission decided to extend the Special Rapporteur's mandate for a further period of three years and asked him to request, receive and exchange information on violations of indigenous people's rights from Governments, UN human rights treaty bodies, specialized agencies, Commission and Subcommission special mechanisms, international organizations, relevant UN system organizations and civil society, and to respond to the information; to consider the recommendations of the World Conference against Racism, Racial Discrimination, Xenophobia and Related Intolerance [YUN 2001, p. 615], of the Permanent Forum on Indigenous Issues (see p. 798) and of the Working Group on Indigenous Populations (see p. 793); to continue working on the topics included in his first report [YUN 2002, p. 762]; and to report to the General Assembly in 2004 and to the Commission in 2005. The Secretary-General and the High Commissioner were asked to assist him. The Commission noted OHCHR's intention to organize, with the participation of indigenous and governmental and non-governmental experts, a seminar on indigenous education (see p. 793) to assist the Special Rapporteur in examining the main topic of his annual report for 2005. The World Summit on the Information Society was encouraged to take indigenous issues into account in its declaration of principles and action plan and in all other relevant programmes to be adopted by the Summit in its second phase in 2005 (see p. 844).

On 22 July, the Economic and Social Council approved the Commission's decision to extend the Special Rapporteur's mandate and its requests to him to submit reports, and to the Secretary-General and High Commissioner to assist him (**decision 2004/267**).

Further reports of Special Rapporteur. The Special Rapporteur visited Canada (21 May–4 June) [E/CN.4/2005/88/Add.3 & Corr.1], where Aboriginal people accounted for some 4.4 per cent of the total population of 30 million. He observed that Canada's indigenous people had been progressively dispossessed of their lands, resources and culture, a process that led them into destitution, deprivation and dependency and generated an assertive and occasionally militant social movement in defence of their rights. While encouraged by Canada's commitment to ensuring that the country's prosperity was shared by Aboriginal people, the Special Rapporteur noted that economic, social and human indicators of well being, quality of life and development were consistently lower among them than other Canadians. He recommended that the Government enact new legislation on Aboriginal rights and adopt measures to close the human development indicator gaps between Aboriginal and non-Aboriginal Canadians in the areas of health care, housing, education, welfare and social services. The Special Rapporteur emphasized the need to secure Aboriginal rights with regard to treaties and other constructive arrangements, lands and resources, human rights promotion and protection, sustainable economic development, the welfare of Aboriginal women, the administration of justice, and international policy on indigenous peoples.

In response to Commission resolution 2004/62 (see above), the Secretary-General, by an August note [A/59/258], transmitted a report of the Special Rapporteur, which reviewed activities he had undertaken between 10 August 2001 and 10 August 2004 and highlighted issues of concern he viewed as requiring urgent attention. The report described the progress made and the major human rights problems affecting indigenous peoples, regarding the rights to land, territory and access to natural resources; social organization and local government; the conflict between legislation and customary law in the administration of justice; poverty and access to basic services; political representation, autonomy and self-determination; education and culture; and indigenous women and girls. The Special Rapporteur concluded that, although the problem of violations of indigenous peoples' rights was being ad-

dressed through specific programmes and proposals, rhetoric often failed to result in action, leaving their needs neglected, particularly those relating to protection. He recommended that Governments take steps to combat discrimination against indigenous people; end impunity; explore cooperation with native peoples to resolve ongoing conflicts regarding land, territory and access to natural resources; adopt specific measures to benefit indigenous women and their families; and protect the lives and dignity of indigenous children.

On 20 December, the General Assembly took note of the Secretary-General's August note (**decision 59/526**).

Expert seminar. The Special Rapporteur transmitted to the Commission the report of an expert seminar on indigenous peoples and education (Paris, 18-20 October) [E/CN.4/2005/88/Add.4], organized by OHCHR in cooperation with UNESCO, pursuant to Commission resolution 2004/62 (see p. 792). The experts discussed issues relating to indigenous peoples' access to quality education and participatory approaches and higher education. They identified, among other issues, a range of concerns relating to indigenous peoples' access to quality education and some of the barriers they faced, and emphasized that indigenous peoples' cultural diversity was not always respected and that discrimination and xenophobia remained the main impediment to their enjoyment of the right to education in all regions of the world. The experts proposed recommendations to Governments, UN bodies, specialized agencies and human rights mechanisms and indigenous peoples.

Communications. On 11 March [E/CN.4/2004/G/22], Mexico, referring to the Special Rapporteur's visit to the country [YUN 2003, p. 797], described action it would take to implement the Special Rapporteur's recommendations, measures aimed at resolving high priority conflicts related to agricultural land, its policy regarding IDPs and information pertaining to a national public hearing for indigenous peoples.

On 7 April [E/CN.4/2004/G/47], Chile transmitted its comments regarding the Special Rapporteur's report on his visit to the country [YUN 2003, p. 797].

Working Group on Indigenous Populations

Commission action. By a recorded vote of 38 to 15, the Commission, on 20 April [res. 2004/57], taking into account that, in accordance with Economic and Social Council decision 2003/307 [YUN 2003, p. 804], the Council would consider in 2004 the review mandated in Council resolution 2000/22 [YUN 2000, p. 731] regarding all existing mechanisms, procedures and programmes with-

in the United Nations concerned with indigenous issues, including the Working Group on
Indigenous Populations, reaffirmed its 2003 recommendation [YUN 2003, p. 798] that the Council
take into account the contents of the Commission's 2003 resolution [ibid.], which considered
the continuing need for the Working Group.

Also on 20 April [res. 2004/58], by a recorded
vote of 38 to 2, with 13 abstentions, the Commission recommended that the Council authorize
the Group to meet for five working days prior to
the Subcommission's 2004 session.

ECONOMIC AND SOCIAL COUNCIL ACTION

In July, the Economic and Social Council, on the
recommendation of the Commission on Human
Rights [E/2004/23], adopted **decision 2004/264**
by recorded vote (35-2-17) [agenda item 14 (g)].

**Working Group on Indigenous Populations of the
Subcommission on the Promotion and Protection of
Human Rights, and the International Decade
of the World's Indigenous People**
At its 48th plenary meeting, on 22 July 2004, the
Economic and Social Council took note of Commission on Human Rights resolution 2004/58 of 20 April
2004 and endorsed the Commission's recommendation that the Working Group on Indigenous Populations be authorized to meet for five working days prior
to the fifty-sixth session of the Subcommission on the
Promotion and Protection of Human Rights.

RECORDED VOTE ON DECISION 2004/264:

In favour: Armenia, Azerbaijan, Belize, Benin, Bhutan, Burundi, Can-
ada, Chile, China, Colombia, Congo, Cuba, Ecuador, El Salvador, Ghana,
Guatemala, India, Indonesia, Jamaica, Kenya, Libyan Arab Jamahiriya,
Mauritius, Mozambique, Namibia, Nicaragua, Panama, Qatar, Russian
Federation, Saudi Arabia, Senegal, Tunisia, Ukraine, United Arab
Emirates, United Republic of Tanzania, Zimbabwe.
Against: Australia, United States.
Abstaining: Bangladesh, Belgium, Finland, France, Germany, Greece,
Hungary, Ireland, Italy, Japan, Malaysia, Nigeria, Poland, Republic of Ko-
rea, Sweden, Turkey, United Kingdom.

Working Group activities. The Working Group
on Indigenous Populations held its twenty-
second session (Geneva, 19-23 July) [E/CN.4/Sub.2/
2004/28] to review developments pertaining to the
promotion and protection of human rights and
fundamental freedoms of indigenous populations and to give special attention to the evolution
of the relevant standards. In annotations to the
provisional agenda [E/CN.4/Sub.2/AC.4/2004/1/
Add.1], the Secretariat presented background information on indigenous peoples and conflict
resolution, the principal theme of the Group's
session; globalization and indigenous peoples;
cooperation with other UN bodies in the sphere
of indigenous issues; follow-up to the World Conference against Racism, Racial Discrimination,
Xenophobia and Related Intolerance [YUN 2001,
p. 615]; the International Decade of the World's Indigenous People (1995-2004) (see p. 796); and
standard-setting activities.

The Group had before it June working papers
on globalization and indigenous peoples [E/CN.4/
Sub.2/AC.4/2004/3], prepared by Mr. Guissé, and
on guidance regarding the review of the draft
principles and guidelines on the heritage of indigenous peoples [E/CN.4/Sub.2/AC.4/2004/5], submitted by Mr. Yokota and the Saami Council
(an NGO concerned with indigenous peoples' interests), as well as July working papers on the
principle of free, prior and informed consent of
indigenous peoples in relation to development
affecting their lands and natural resources [E/CN.4/
Sub.2/AC.4/2004/4], prepared by Ms. Motoc and the
Tebtebba Foundation (an indigenous peoples'
organization), and on indigenous peoples' rights
in States and territories threatened with extinction for environmental reasons [E/CN.4/Sub.2/AC.4/
2004/CRP.1], submitted by Ms. Hampson (see also
p. 795). Regarding the session's principal theme,
the Group considered a July working paper [E/CN.4/
Sub.2/AC.4/2004/2 & Corr.1], submitted by Miguel
Alfonso Martínez (Cuba), which examined the
character of conflict and conflict resolution and
prevention within the context of indigenous peoples' rights and put forth recommendations for
the Group's consideration.

In its recommendations, the Group decided to
maintain on its agenda for 2005 a sub-item on indigenous peoples and conflict prevention and resolution; asked Mr. Alfonso Martínez to submit in
2005 a working paper on indigenous peoples and
the prevention and resolution of conflict; and requested OHCHR to organize a workshop on indigenous peoples and conflict resolution in 2005 and a
seminar on the implementation of treaties, agreements and other constructive arrangements between States and indigenous peoples in 2006.
OHCHR was also asked to continue to organize further seminars and workshops on indigenous issues
in Africa, Asia and Latin America. The Group accepted an invitation by representatives of indigenous peoples in Canada to hold a seminar on the
implementation of treaties, agreements and constructive arrangements in 2006. In other action,
the Group recommended that Mr. Yokota and the
Saami Council prepare, without financial implications, a further working paper containing proposals on the draft principles and guidelines relating
to indigenous peoples' heritage, for consideration in
2005, and that OHCHR facilitate consultation with
them and other interested parties on the principles
and guidelines; that Ms. Motoc, the Tebtebba
Foundation and other interested indigenous
sources prepare guidelines on the principle of
free, prior and informed consent, for submission
in 2005; and that OHCHR request information on
standard-setting activities from Governments, indigenous organizations, the UN system and NGOs,

and invite UN system representatives to recommend ways of improving cooperation. The Group further recommended that the High Commissioner, in her capacity as Coordinator of the International Decade of the World's Indigenous People, take steps to ensure submission to the General Assembly in 2005 of a substantive programme of action for a possible second Decade; that OHCHR organize a second workshop on indigenous peoples, mining companies and human rights, the first having been held in 2001 [YUN 2001, p. 688]; and that Ms. Hampson prepare another working paper, developing further the information and ideas contained in her first paper on the human rights of indigenous peoples in States and territories threatened with extinction for environmental reasons (see p. 794). The Group decided to adopt as the principal theme for its 2005 session indigenous peoples and the international and domestic protection of traditional knowledge, and invited Governments, indigenous peoples, the UN system and NGOs to provide relevant information on the theme. In particular, the Group asked the World Intellectual Property Organization and UNESCO to contribute to the debate.

Subcommission action. On 9 August [res. 2004/15], the Subcommission asked the Secretary-General to transmit the Working Group's report on its 2004 session to the High Commissioner, indigenous organizations, Governments, intergovernmental organizations, concerned NGOs, treaty bodies and all thematic rapporteurs, special representatives, independent experts and working groups, and asked that it be made available to the Commission in 2005. It recommended that the Group, upon request, assist the open-ended intersessional working group to elaborate further the draft UN declaration on the rights of indigenous peoples (see p. 798). The Subcommission decided that the Group, in 2005, should adopt as its principal theme "Indigenous peoples and the international and domestic protection of traditional knowledge" and review the revised draft principles and guidelines on the heritage of indigenous people [YUN 1995, p. 780]. It decided on the Group's agenda for 2005 and asked the Secretary-General to prepare an annotated agenda for the 2005 session. The Subcommission endorsed the Group's request to OHCHR to organize, possibly in 2005, a workshop on indigenous peoples and conflict resolution and prevention, and a seminar, preferably in 2006, on possible ways to implement treaties, agreements and other constructive arrangements between States and indigenous peoples. The Subcommission called for working papers in 2005 by: Mr. Yokota, in cooperation with the Saami Council, on the draft principles and guidelines related to indigenous peoples' heritage; Ms. Motoc, in cooperation with the Tebtebba

Foundation and other interested indigenous sources, on guidelines to govern the practice of implementation of the principle of free, prior and informed consent; Ms. Hampson, on the human rights implications, especially for indigenous populations, of the disappearance of States for environmental reasons; and Mr. Alfonso Martínez, on the issue of indigenous peoples and conflict prevention and resolution. OHCHR was asked to organize, as a matter of priority and in consultation with the Group's Chairperson/Rapporteur, a second workshop on indigenous peoples' mining and other private sector companies and human rights. The Subcommission emphasized that the Economic and Social Council, in reviewing all UN mechanisms relating to indigenous peoples, should take into account the fact that the mandates of the Group, the Special Rapporteur and the Permanent Forum were distinct and complementary. It requested the Commission to endorse that view and the participation of the Group's Chairperson/Rapporteur at the Forum's fourth (2005) session, and recommended that the Council approve that participation and that the Commission request the Council to authorize the Group to meet for five working days prior to the Subcommission's 2005 session.

Also on 9 August [res. 2004/11], the Subcommission asked the Secretary-General to ensure that the Special Adviser for the Prevention of Genocide, appointed under the Action Plan to Prevent Genocide (see p. 730), took into consideration the need to protect indigenous peoples and their territories; that forces present under a UN mandate protected vulnerable indigenous peoples, their territories and objects indispensable to their survival; and that the mandates of UN authorized operations included a requirement to protect indigenous populations and their territories. The Special Rapporteur on the human rights and fundamental principles of indigenous people (see p. 792) was asked to liaise with the Special Adviser regarding the protection of indigenous peoples from genocide and to develop an emergency response mechanism as part of his mandate.

Voluntary Fund for Indigenous Populations

The Board of Trustees of the United Nations Voluntary Fund for Indigenous Populations, at its seventeenth session (Geneva, 11-19 March) [E/CN.4/Sub.2/AC.4/2004/8], recommended travel grants totalling $154,212 to enable 47 representatives of indigenous communities and organizations to attend the Working Group on Indigenous Populations (see p. 794), $249,700 to allow 46 indigenous representatives to attend the Permanent Forum on Indigenous Issues (see p. 798), and $56,316 to enable 13 other representatives of indigenous communities to attend the working group on the draft UN declaration on the rights of indigenous peoples (see p. 798). The Board's recommendations were approved by the High Commissioner on the Secretary-General's behalf on 22 April.

An August note [A/59/257] of the Secretary-General presented an overview of the Fund's activities in 2003 and 2004. The Board had approved its revised cost plan for 2005 and envisaged expenditure amounting to $777,000. It expressed concern that there was a discrepancy with the figures that appeared in the OHCHR annual appeal for 2004 and hoped that its cost plan would be reflected in the appeal. The Board discussed the future direction of the Fund. Taking note of the review of UN mechanisms relating to indigenous issues, to be undertaken by the Economic and Social Council (see p. 800), the Board underlined the importance of the Fund as an independent body that provided direct assistance to indigenous peoples and allowed them to participate in UN activities. The Board further underlined the fact that all its current members were indigenous representatives, expressed its commitment to the Fund, requested that any proposed changes be discussed with its members before implementation, and emphasized the need to prioritize indigenous peoples' interests. The Board scheduled its eighteenth session for 21 to 25 February 2005 to discuss the allocation of travel grants to attend the Permanent Forum.

On 20 December, the General Assembly took note of the Secretary-General's note (**decision 59/526**).

Subcommission action. On 9 August [res. 2004/15], the Subcommission appealed to Governments, organizations, NGOs, indigenous groups and other potential donors in a position to do so to contribute to the Fund.

International Decade of the World's Indigenous People

Commission action. By a recorded vote of 38 to 2, with 13 abstentions, the Commission, on 20 April [res. 2004/58], invited the Working Group to continue its review of activities undertaken during the International Decade of the World's Indigenous People (1995-2004), proclaimed by the General Assembly in resolution 48/163 [YUN 1993, p. 865]. The High Commissioner, in her capacity as Coordinator of the Decade, was asked to submit in 2005 a final report reviewing activities within the UN system under the Decade's programme of activities, to ensure that OHCHR's indigenous people's unit was adequately staffed and resourced, and to give due regard to developing human rights training for indigenous people. UN financial

and development institutions, operational programmes and specialized agencies were asked to give increased priority and resources to improving the conditions of indigenous people and to launch special projects to strengthen their community-level initiatives and facilitate information exchange and expertise among indigenous people and other relevant experts. The Secretary-General was requested to begin implementing the evaluation of the Decade, as called for by the World Conference against Racism, Racial Discrimination, Xenophobia and Related Intolerance [YUN 2001, p. 615].

Report of Secretary-General. Pursuant to Economic and Social Council decision 2003/306 [YUN 2003, p. 804], the Secretary-General submitted a June report [E/2004/82] on the preliminary review of the Decade. The report summarized OHCHR activities undertaken between 1995 and 2004 to implement the Decade, and related information received from departments and organizations of the UN system, Member States, indigenous peoples and NGOs. The Secretary-General noted positive developments during the Decade, including an increase in programmes, projects and activities relating to indigenous peoples in some UN organizations and agencies. Indigenous peoples had been better integrated into UN system operational activities; information about the work of the UN system regarding them was more widely available through increased publications and particularly on web sites. Seminars and workshops undertaken within the context of the Decade had placed lesser-known indigenous issues on the international agenda. Furthermore, the Decade had witnessed advances in inter-agency cooperation on indigenous issues, and positive institutional developments, including the establishment of the mandate of the Special Rapporteur on indigenous peoples and the growing jurisprudence of the treaty bodies on indigenous peoples' rights. It was also evident that indigenous representatives were better aware of the wider system of human rights protection and were increasingly using the opportunities available to them in that regard. However challenges remained, particularly the lack of implementation of human rights standards at the national level and the failure to adopt the draft declaration on the rights of indigenous peoples (see below), as recommended in the Decade's programme of activities. A further challenge related to the implementation by Member States of programmes that promoted the development and rights of indigenous peoples and the UN role in assisting them. Whether or not Member States decided to establish a second decade, it would be important to maintain the momentum generated, establish an operational framework for further international action and, in countries where indigenous people lived, set out realizable targets for the medium term.

On 23 July, the Economic and Social Council took note of the Secretary-General's report (**decision 2004/317**).

Note by Secretary-General. In an August note [A/59/277], the Secretary-General summarized implementation of the Decade's programme of activities undertaken by OHCHR during the period from August 2003 to July 2004. Of particular note were the third session of the Permanent Forum on Indigenous Issues (see p. 798), the twenty-second (2004) session of the Working Group (see p. 794) and the activities undertaken by the Special Rapporteur (see p. 792). OHCHR continued to promote inter-agency cooperation within the Decade's framework, through participation in inter-agency consultations, cooperation in human rights training and joint activities. Other ongoing programmes included the Indigenous Fellowship Programme.

On 20 December, the General Assembly took note of the Secretary-General's note (**decision 59/526**).

Subcommission action. On 9 August [res. 2004/14], the Subcommission, welcoming the observance in 2004 of the International Day of the World's Indigenous People (22 July), recommended that it be held on the fourth day of the Working Group's 2005 session to ensure as large a participation of indigenous peoples as possible. It recommended that the Decade's Coordinator appeal to Governments and other donors to contribute to the Voluntary Fund for the Decade and stressed the need to give particular attention to improving the extent of indigenous peoples' participation in planning and implementing the Decade's activities. It also recommended that the High Commissioner, in consultation with interested Governments and indigenous peoples and organizations, organize meetings, particularly in Africa, Asia, Oceania and Latin America, in order to raise public awareness about indigenous issues. Welcoming the proposal for a second international decade of the world's indigenous peoples contained in Economic and Social Council decision 2004/290 (see p. 799), the Subcommission invited the High Commissioner, in her capacity as Coordinator of the first Decade, to organize early in 2005 consultations with the purpose of developing a preliminary draft programme of activities for a possible second decade, for consideration by the General Assembly.

Report of High Commissioner. A final report of the High Commissioner [E/CN.4/2005/87], which completed the review of activities undertaken within the context of the Decade, provided information on the Indigenous Fellowship Programme in 2004 (3 May–1 October), in which 13 fellows

participated. As part of the practical work experience in the UN system, five fellows from Greenland, Kenya, Myanmar, the Solomon Islands and Ukraine assisted the Working Group (see p. 796). OHCHR, in cooperation with the University of Deusto (Bilbao, Spain), provided training for four fellows from Argentina, Brazil, Colombia and Mexico, and, in collaboration with the University of Burgundy (Dijon, France), similar training was offered to four other fellows from Canada, France (New Caledonia), Mali and Morocco.

In August, OHCHR undertook an independent evaluation of the Programme as part of the overall assessment of the Decade. The evaluation, aimed at assessing how the fellowship had helped promote indigenous peoples' human rights, was undertaken during the Barcelona Cultural Forum (9 May–26 September), attended by 43 former fellows to whom questionnaires were distributed. The evaluation concluded that the Programme was greatly appreciated by indigenous peoples and organizations, and provided evidence of individual initiatives which the fellows had attributed to new knowledge, experience and confidence obtained through the Programme.

The report also described activities regarding inter-agency cooperation on indigenous issues and the work of the Voluntary Fund for the Decade (see below) and the Voluntary Fund for Indigenous Populations (see p. 795).

The High Commissioner concluded that progress was made during the Decade, particularly regarding the considerable increase in UN system activities relating to indigenous peoples, greater opportunities for participation by indigenous organizations in international and regional processes and positive institutional developments, such as the establishment of the Special Rapporteur's mandate and the Permanent Forum. In her capacity as Coordinator for the Decade, she urged that the momentum generated be maintained and recommended that the Commission request a further six weeks of meetings over a two-year period to complete negotiations on a draft UN declaration on the rights of indigenous peoples (see p. 798). The goals during a second decade should be the rapid adoption of the declaration and of a binding legal instrument.

Voluntary Fund for International Decade

The Advisory Group of the United Nations Voluntary Fund for the International Decade of the World's Indigenous People, at its ninth session (Geneva, 22-26 March) [E/CN.4/Sub.2/AC.4/2004/9], recommended 35 project grants, which were approved for a total of $243,500. It recommended the allocation of $92,800 to activities of the High Commissioner as the Decade's Coordinator, of which $56,800 would be spent on a publication entitled _The International Decade of the World's Indigenous People: 10 Years of Partnership in Action_, designed to disseminate the results of Decade projects financed by the Fund and OHCHR activities. The remainder would fund three community-led human rights training courses, at $12,000 each. The Group proposed holding a seminar during 2004 to assess the impact of the Fund and of the Voluntary Fund for Indigenous Populations (see p. 797), and recommended that $30,788 be allocated for that purpose. Regarding the Fund's future in the light of developments within the context of the Secretary-General's reform agenda and of the planned review of UN mechanisms relating to indigenous issues (see p. 800), the Group requested that any changes be discussed with its members.

Seminar. As requested by the Advisory Group (see above), OHCHR organized a technical seminar (Geneva, 15-16 July) [E/CN.4/Sub.2/AC.4/2005/CRP.1], which evaluated the impact of the Fund for the Decade and the Voluntary Fund for Indigenous Populations (see p. 797) in achieving the Decade's goals. Participants concluded that both Funds had made a contribution by empowering indigenous peoples and promoting and protecting their rights through support for relevant activities and projects. The seminar recommended that the High Commissioner encourage the General Assembly to proclaim a second international decade, that both Funds continue to function separately and that the High Commissioner ensure that their activities did not overlap.

Draft declaration

Commission action. On 20 April [res. 2004/59], the Commission recommended that the working group established to consider a draft declaration on the rights of indigenous peoples (see p. 794) meet for 10 working days prior to the Commission's 2005 session and asked the group to report in 2005.

On 22 July, the Economic and Social Council authorized the group to meet (**decision 2004/265**).

Subcommission action. On 9 August [res. 2004/14], the Subcommission recommended the adoption of the draft declaration as early as possible, in accordance with General Assembly resolution 50/157 [YUN 1995, p. 772], and appealed to participants in the working group and others concerned to accelerate the draft's preparation.

Working group activities. The working group established to consider a draft declaration on the rights of indigenous peoples, at its tenth session (Geneva, 13-24 September, 29 November–3 December) [E/CN.4/2005/89], discussed proposed amendments to articles of the draft declaration relating to lands, territories and natural resources, self-determination and treaties, agreements and constructive arrangements with States, as well as the provisional adoption of articles and cross-cutting issues. Addenda to the report contained a list of the documentation and communications considered by the group, and of Governments and NGOs that participated in its meetings [E/CN.4/2005/89/Add.1], and proposals by the group's Chairperson/Rapporteur relating to the draft and a summary of the status of all provisions of the draft [E/CN.4/2005/89/Add.2]. The meeting ended on the understanding that the group had made substantial progress towards consensus. The Chairperson/Rapporteur would recommend that the Commission allocate additional time in order to conclude the process in 2005.

Permanent Forum on Indigenous Issues

Report of Permanent Forum. The 16-member Permanent Forum on Indigenous Issues, established by Economic and Social Council resolution 2000/22 [YUN 2000, p. 731] to address indigenous issues relating to economic and social development, the environment, health, education and culture, and human rights, at its third session (New York, 10-21 May) [E/2004/43], considered as its theme "Indigenous women" and recommended five draft decisions for adoption by the Council (see below). Matters brought to the Council's attention related to indigenous women, education, culture, human rights, economic and social development, environment, health and the Forum's future work.

ECONOMIC AND SOCIAL COUNCIL ACTION

On 22 July, the Council took note of the Forum's report and asked it to take into account in its work the concerns and reservations on paragraph 52 of document [E/2004/SR.48], which covered voting records within the Council on the use of mercenaries as a means of violating human rights and impeding the exercise of the right to self-determination (**decision 2004/291**); authorized a three-day pre-sessional meeting of the Forum in 2005 to prepare for its fourth (2005) session (**decision 2004/286**); authorized a technical three-day workshop on free, prior and informed consent and asked the workshop to report to the Forum in 2005 (**decision 2004/287**); decided that the Forum's fourth session would be held in New York from 16 to 27 May 2005 (**decision 2004/288**) and approved that session's provisional agenda and documentation (**decision 2004/289**); and decided to transmit to the General Assembly the Forum's recommendation for a second international decade of the world's indigenous people, to begin in January 2005, recommending that the Assembly, in considering the item, identify goals and a coordinator of activities for the decade and also address the question of human and financial resources to be made available to support those activities (**decision 2004/290**).

GENERAL ASSEMBLY ACTION

On 20 December [meeting 74], the General Assembly, on the recommendation of the Third Committee [A/59/500], adopted **resolution 59/174** without vote [agenda item 102].

Second International Decade of the World's Indigenous People

The General Assembly,

Bearing in mind that, in the Vienna Declaration and Programme of Action, the 1993 World Conference on Human Rights recognized the inherent dignity and the unique contribution of indigenous people to the development and plurality of society and strongly reaffirmed the commitment of the international community to their economic, social and cultural well-being and their enjoyment of the fruits of sustainable development,

Reaffirming that States should, in accordance with international law, take concerted positive steps to ensure respect for all human rights and fundamental freedoms of indigenous people, on the basis of equality and non-discrimination, and recognizing the value and diversity of their distinctive identities, cultures and social organization,

Recalling its resolution 48/163 of 21 December 1993, in which it proclaimed the International Decade of the World's Indigenous People, commencing on 10 December 1994, with the goal of strengthening international cooperation for the solution of problems faced by indigenous people in such areas as human rights, the environment, development, education and health,

Recalling also its resolution 58/158 of 22 December 2003 and all previous resolutions on the International Decade of the World's Indigenous People,

Welcoming all achievements during the Decade, in particular the establishment of the Permanent Forum on Indigenous Issues, and the contributions to the realization of the goals of the Decade made by the Permanent Forum, the Working Group on Indigenous Populations of the Subcommission on the Promotion and Protection of Human Rights and the Special Rapporteur of the Commission on Human Rights on the situation of human rights and fundamental freedoms of indigenous people, such as the comprehensive work programme that the Permanent Forum is carrying out for the benefit of indigenous peoples in the areas of culture, education, environment, health, human rights and social and economic development,

Taking due note of Commission on Human Rights resolution 2004/62 of 21 April 2004, in which the Commission expressed its deep concern about the precarious economic and social situation that indigenous people continue to endure in many parts of the world in comparison to the overall population and the persistence of grave violations of their human rights, and reaffirmed the urgent need to recognize, promote and protect more effectively their rights and freedoms,

Recalling that in its resolution 49/214 of 23 December 1994 it expressly put on record its expectation of achieving the adoption of a declaration on indigenous rights within the International Decade and that in its resolution 50/157 of 21 December 1995 it decided that the adoption by the General Assembly of a declaration on the rights of indigenous people constituted a major objective of the Decade, and noting the progress made in the recent rounds of negotiations in the open-ended intersessional working group of the Commission on Human Rights charged with elaborating a draft declaration on the rights of indigenous people, established pursuant to Commission resolution 1995/32 of 3 March 1995,

Recognizing the importance of consultation and cooperation with indigenous people in planning and implementing the programme of activities for the Decade and the need for adequate financial support from the international community,

1. *Proclaims* the Second International Decade of the World's Indigenous People, commencing on 1 January 2005;

2. *Decides* that the goal of the Second Decade shall be the further strengthening of international cooperation for the solution of problems faced by indigenous people in such areas as culture, education, health, human rights, the environment and social and economic development, by means of action-oriented programmes and specific projects, increased technical assistance and relevant standard-setting activities;

3. *Requests* the Secretary-General to appoint the Under-Secretary-General for Economic and Social Affairs as the Coordinator for the Second Decade;

4. *Requests* the Coordinator to fulfil the mandate in full cooperation and consultation with Governments, the Permanent Forum on Indigenous Issues and other relevant bodies and mechanisms of the United Nations system, the Office of the United Nations High Commissioner for Human Rights, other members of the Inter-Agency Support Group on Indigenous Issues and indigenous and non-governmental organizations;

5. *Invites* Governments to ensure that activities and objectives for the Second Decade are planned and implemented on the basis of full consultation and collaboration with indigenous people;

6. *Appeals* to the specialized agencies, regional commissions, financial and development institutions and other relevant organizations of the United Nations system to increase their efforts to take special account of the needs of indigenous people in their budgeting and in their programming;

7. *Requests* the Secretary-General to establish a voluntary fund for the Second Decade, which to all juridical purposes and effects should be set up and should discharge its functions as a successor to the already existing voluntary fund established for the present Decade pursuant to General Assembly resolutions 48/163, 49/214 and 50/157;

8. *Authorizes* the Secretary-General to accept and administer voluntary contributions from Governments, intergovernmental and non-governmental organizations, indigenous organizations and private institutions and individuals for the purpose of funding projects and programmes during the Second Decade;

9. *Urges* Governments, intergovernmental and non-governmental organizations to contribute to the voluntary fund for the Second Decade established by

the Secretary-General, and invites indigenous organizations and private institutions and individuals to do likewise;

10. *Urges* the competent United Nations organs, programmes and specialized agencies, in planning activities for the Second Decade, to examine how existing programmes and resources might be utilized to benefit indigenous people more effectively, including through the exploration of ways in which indigenous perspectives and activities can be included or enhanced;

11. *Decides* to continue observing in New York, Geneva and other offices of the United Nations every year during the Second Decade the International Day of Indigenous People, to request the Secretary-General to support the observance of the Day from within existing resources, and to encourage Governments to observe the Day at the national level;

12. *Urges* all parties involved in the process of negotiation to do their utmost to carry out successfully the mandate of the open-ended intersessional working group established by the Commission on Human Rights in its resolution 1995/32 and to present for adoption as soon as possible a final draft United Nations declaration on the rights of indigenous peoples;

13. *Requests* the Secretary-General to give all the assistance necessary to ensure the success of the Second Decade;

14. *Also requests* the Secretary-General to submit a report to the General Assembly at its sixtieth session on a comprehensive programme of action for the Second Decade based on the achievements of the first Decade;

15. *Decides* to include in the provisional agenda of its sixtieth session an item entitled "Indigenous issues".

Review of existing mechanisms on indigenous issues

Pursuant to Economic and Social Council decision 2003/307 [YUN 2003, p. 804], the Secretary-General, in July [E/2004/85], summarized information received from three Governments, seven indigenous NGOs and three UN system bodies in response to his request for information on the Council's planned review of all existing UN mechanisms, procedures and programmes concerning indigenous issues. Based on the information received, the Secretary-General reviewed those mechanisms, of which the most notable were the Working Group on Indigenous Populations (see p. 793), the Special Rapporteur on the situation of human rights and fundamental freedoms of indigenous people (see p. 792), the working group on the draft declaration on the rights of indigenous peoples (see p. 798) and the Permanent Forum on Indigenous Issues (see p. 795). The Secretary-General concluded that, although views differed on the various mechanisms, it was clear that every effort should be made to ensure coordination among them, while recognizing the specific task that each was mandated to perform. It was also crucial that the scarce resources of indigenous peoples and organizations and the voluntary contributions by Member States were utilized with maximum efficiency and effectiveness. The United Nations should continue to mainstream indigenous issues and to expand its programmes and activities for the benefit of indigenous peoples in a coordinated manner. The Economic and Social Council should play a leading role in ensuring greater coherence, improved coordination and effectiveness in the various mechanisms, and UN efforts in that regard should be consistent with the broader reform objectives endorsed by the General Assembly in resolution 57/300 [YUN 2002, p. 1353]. Reflecting on ongoing work on the draft declaration and on support for a second international decade (see p. 799), the Secretary-General acknowledged the importance of the current period in the history of indigenous peoples. They were often among the most disadvantaged people in the world and 1994 was a pivotal year in their struggle to end marginalization. They hoped for full UN support in that struggle and the international community should endeavour to respond to their expectations.

On 23 July, the Council took note of the Secretary-General's report (**decision 2004/317**).

Indigenous peoples' permanent sovereignty over natural resources

Report of Special Rapporteur. As requested by the Subcommission in 2002 [YUN 2002, p. 771], the Special Rapporteur on indigenous peoples' permanent sovereignty over natural resources, Erica-Irene A. Daes (Greece), submitted a July final report [E/CN.4/Sub.2/2004/30], which discussed the history of the concept of permanent sovereignty over natural resources within the UN system, considered the trend in international law and practice and analysed the nature and scope of indigenous peoples' right to own, use, control and manage their lands, territories and resources. The report built on a 2001 working paper of the Special Rapporteur [YUN 2001, p. 693]. It concluded that, although indigenous peoples' permanent sovereignty over resources had not been explicitly recognized in international legal instruments, the right existed, nonetheless, owing to the recognition of a broad range of indigenous rights, most notably the right to own property, to ownership of the lands they historically or traditionally used or occupied, to self-determination or autonomy, to development and to be free from discrimination, among other rights. The right might therefore be articulated as a collective right by virtue of which States were obligated to respect, protect and promote the governmental and property interests of indigenous peoples. However, further studies of the issue were needed. She recommended, among a series of measures, that States, in consultation with indigenous peoples, take necessary legislative and administrative action to ensure that indigenous peoples enjoyed ownership of and benefits from the natural resources on, under or otherwise pertaining to the land they historically occupied and used. The Subcommission should recommend the establishment of an ad hoc committee to study, implement and promote indigenous peoples' rights in that context, and to monitor States' progress in recognizing and implementing them. In addition, the Subcommission should request the Special Rapporteur to prepare an updated and consolidated study on the subject, for submission in 2005. The Special Rapporteur further recommended that the Secretariat convene an expert seminar to give further attention to related issues that needed to be adequately researched and considered, and that the Permanent Forum also accord the issue regular attention.

An addendum to the report [E/CN.4/Sub.2/2004/30/Add.1] provided examples of legal regimes regarding indigenous peoples and natural resources in various parts of the world, an analysis of international law concerning permanent sovereignty over natural resources and indigenous peoples, relevant conclusions, guiding principles and recommendations contained in the 2001 working paper of the Special Rapporteur and select bibliography, UN resolutions, relevant cases and legal standards concerning indigenous peoples' permanent sovereignty.

Subcommission action. On 9 August [res. 2004/9], the Subcommission decided to submit the Special Rapporteur's report (see above) to the Commission in 2005 and recommended that the Commission and the Economic and Social Council authorize OHCHR to convene an expert seminar to further address the many political, legal, economic, social and cultural questions relating to the topic and to the Special Rapporteur's 2001 working paper. The Subcommission further recommended that the studies entitled "Indigenous peoples and their relationship to land" and "Indigenous peoples' permanent sovereignty over natural resources" be issued as UN publications as part of the human rights study series.

Persons with disabilities

Report of OHCHR. In accordance with a 2003 Commission request [YUN 2003, p. 806], a report of OHCHR [E/CN.4/2004/74] provided information on progress made to implement the recommendations contained in the 2002 study on *Human Rights and Disability: The Current Use and Future Potential of United Nations Human Rights Instruments in the Context of Disability* [YUN 2002, p. 771]. The report exam-

ined efforts by States, treaty bodies, the Commission, national human rights institutions and civil society, and also assessed progress made on OHCHR's programme of work relating to the human rights of persons with disabilities. The report concluded that, despite encouraging developments in the way in which disability issues were addressed within the human rights treaty system, more needed to be done to ensure the equal and effective enjoyment by persons with disabilities of the protection afforded by existing human rights treaties. As recommended by the 2002 study, OHCHR supported the idea of drafting a new convention on the human rights of persons with disabilities, which would represent an additional tool for promoting and protecting their rights. Thus, the Office welcomed the decision by the Ad Hoc Committee to establish a working group to prepare a draft text (see below), pledged support to the Committee and the group and encouraged national human rights institutions and civil society organizations to participate in discussions on the new treaty.

Commission action. On 20 April [res. 2004/52], the Commission asked the Secretary-General to make the OHCHR report available to the Ad Hoc Committee and to include in relevant reports to the General Assembly information on progress made to ensure the full recognition and enjoyment of the human rights of persons with disabilities. OHCHR was called on to report to the Commission in 2005 on progress made to implement the recommendations contained in the study on *Human Rights and Disability* and on the objectives set forth in its programme of work. The Special Rapporteur on disability of the Commission for Social Development was invited to address the Commission on Human Rights in 2005 on the human rights dimension gained through monitoring the Standard Rules on the Equalization of Opportunities for Persons with Disabilities, adopted by the General Assembly in resolution 48/96 [YUN 1993, p. 978]. The Commission urged Governments to cover the human rights of persons with disabilities in their reporting obligations under relevant UN human rights instruments, and called on UN organizations and agencies and intergovernmental institutions for development cooperation to integrate disability measures into their activities and to reflect that in their reports.

Report of Ad Hoc Committee. Pursuant to General Assembly resolution 58/246 [YUN 2003, p. 1108], the Secretary-General, in September [A/59/360], transmitted the report of the Ad Hoc Committee on a Comprehensive and Integral International Convention on the Protection and Promotion of the Rights and Dignity of Persons with Disabilities, established in Assembly resolution

56/168 [YUN 2001, p. 1012], on its fourth session (New York, 23 August–3 September). The Committee, mandated to consider proposals for the convention, recommended that it continue its work in 2005.

In **resolution 59/198**, the General Assembly invited Member States and observers to participate actively in the Committee, in order to present to the Assembly the draft text of a convention (see p. 1100).

Chapter III

Human rights violations

Alleged violations of human rights and international humanitarian law in a number of countries were examined in 2004 by the General Assembly, the Economic and Social Council, the Commission on Human Rights and its Subcommission on the Promotion and Protection of Human Rights, as well as by special rapporteurs, special representatives of the Secretary-General and independent experts appointed to examine the allegations.

General aspects

In accordance with a procedure established by Economic and Social Council resolution 1503 (XLVIII) (1503 procedure) [YUN 1970, p. 530] to deal with communications alleging denial or violation of human rights, the Working Group on Situations of the Commission on Human Rights, in closed meetings during March, examined the human rights situations in Bolivia, Djibouti, Honduras and Uzbekistan to decide whether or not to refer any of those situations to the Commission. The Commission decided to discontinue consideration of the situation of human rights in Bolivia, Djibouti and Honduras. Regarding Uzbekistan, it decided to keep the situation in the country under review and to appoint an independent expert to report in accordance with the 1503 procedure and Council resolution 2000/3 [YUN 2000, p. 596].

The Commission, on 31 March [E/2004/23 (dec. 2004/103)], made public a decision regarding Paraguay, which recommended to the Council that relevant documentation the Commission had examined between 1978 and 1990 should no longer be considered confidential, as requested by the Government.

On 22 July, the Council took note of the Commission's decision and endorsed its recommendation (**decision 2004/273**).

Africa

(For information on the human rights situation in Burundi, see p. 671; Chad, p. 673; the Democratic Republic of the Congo, p. 673; Liberia, p. 676; Sierra Leone, p. 676; and Somalia, p. 677.)

Sudan

Commission action. On 23 April [E/2004/23 (dec. 2004/128)], the Commission on Human Rights, by a recorded vote of 50 to 1, with 2 abstentions, expressing deep concern about the situation in the Sudan and particularly in Darfur, shared the Secretary-General's concern regarding the scale of reported human rights abuses and the humanitarian situation in Darfur, and welcomed his decision to send a high-level team there (see p. 233). The Commission requested its Chairman to appoint an independent expert on the situation of human rights in the Sudan for a one-year period and asked the expert to submit an interim report to the General Assembly in 2004 and a report to the Commission in 2005. The Secretary-General was asked to assist the expert.

On 15 June, the Economic and Social Council endorsed the Commission's request to appoint an independent expert and for the Secretary-General to assist the expert (**decision 2004/229**).

In July, Emmanuel Akwei Addo (Ghana) was appointed independent expert.

Report of Acting High Commissioner. A May report [E/CN.4/2005/3] of the Acting United Nations High Commissioner for Human Rights summarized the findings of two missions dispatched by the Office of the United Nations High Commissioner for Human Rights (OHCHR) in response to reports of allegations of serious human rights violations in the Darfur region of western Sudan. The first mission (5-15 April) visited the border areas with Chad where refugees had fled the violence; the same team visited Khartoum and Darfur (21 April–2 May), where it met with government officials, UN agencies and non-governmental organizations (NGOs), and interviewed displaced persons. In response to actions by rebel forces, notably the Sudan Liberation Army and the Justice and Equality Movement, who demanded that the Khartoum authorities address the marginalization and underdevelopment to which the region was reportedly subjected, the Government sponsored a militia composed of a loose collection of fighters, including an Arab militia known as the Janjaweed. With the support of the regular army, the Janjaweed attacked villages, targeting those suspected of supporting the rebels and committing numerous human rights violations. While it appeared that the Government employed different tactics to counter the rebellion, the mission found consistent allegations that government and militia forces carried out indiscriminate attacks against civilians; rape and other serious forms of sexual violence; destruction of property and pillage; forced displacements; disappearances; and persecution and discrimination. The mission recommended disarming and disbanding the Janjaweed and other militias; a government policy of national reconciliation, the end of impunity, the rule of law and the protection of minorities; the voluntary return of refugees and displaced persons to their lands and homes with restitution or fair compensation for their losses; and the establishment of an international commission of inquiry to identify the crimes that had been committed, assess the responsibility of the authorities and recommend measures for securing accountability.

Communication. On 13 May [E/CN.4/2005/G/3], the Sudan said that its President had issued a decree establishing a Commission of Inquiry into the allegations of human rights violations by armed groups in Darfur. (See also p. 235.)

Reports of independent expert. In a 29 October oral report [A/C.3/59/SR.30] to the General Assembly's Third (Social, Humanitarian and Cultural) Committee, the expert said there were strong indications that war crimes had been committed in Darfur, including murder, torture, rape and intentional attacks against civilians, and that crimes against humanity had also been committed, comprising killings, forcible displacements and rapes as part of a systematic attack on civilians. He said that the Government was unable or unwilling to disarm the militias and was therefore unable to protect displaced persons and civilians. Consideration should be given to broadening the mandate of the troops deployed so as to allow them to disarm the militias, which could be done with the backing of the United Nations and the entire international community. The Sudan said it took exception to the expert's report, which it found to be an oversimplified presentation of the situation, giving too much weight to the political dimensions of the problems.

On 20 December, the Assembly took note of the oral report (**decision 59/528**).

In a later report [E/CN.4/2005/11] covering his visit to the Sudan (19-29 August) and Nairobi, Kenya (30 and 31 August), the independent ex-

pert focused on the ongoing crisis in the Sudan's Darfur region and on human rights related developments in Kassala and Upper Nile states.

The expert stated that following attacks by the Sudanese Liberation Movement/Army against government forces, reportedly in protest at what they perceived as their marginalization, the intensity of the conflict increased. To flush out the rebel groups from their stronghold in Darfur, the Government deployed the military, the Popular Defence Forces and the Janjaweed militia, against civilians belonging to the same tribal groups as the rebels. The militia's indiscriminate attacks against civilians resulted in widespread killing and incidents of rape. There were strong indications that war crimes and crimes against humanity had occurred. The rebels had grown more intransigent and security on the ground had worsened. The peace process between the Government and the Sudan People's Liberation Movement/Army (SPLM/A) continued (see p. 233), with the two parties pledging to end the war by 31 December. On that day, the Government and SPLM/A signed the final two protocols of the peace accord, paving the way for the signing in January 2005 of a comprehensive peace agreement. The expert recommended repeal of the National Security Forces Act, which allowed up to nine months' detention outside the control of the judiciary, and of immunity from prosecution of the national security forces; independent investigation of reports of detainees held incommunicado and holding those responsible accountable; and ratification by the Sudan of the 1984 Convention against Torture and Other Cruel, Inhuman or Degrading Treatment or Punishment, adopted by the Assembly in resolution 39/46 [YUN 1984, p. 813]. He called for compensation to victims of torture, the end of incommunicado detention and prompt notification to families of detainees of their arrest and place of detention. Annexed to the expert's report was the text of his statement before the Assembly's Third Committee (see above).

(See pp. 727 and 776 respectively for information on visits to the Sudan by the Special Rapporteurs on extrajudicial, summary or arbitrary executions and on violence against women.)

(For the report of the Representative of the Secretary-General on internally displaced persons on his mission to the Darfur region, see p. 790.)

Zimbabwe

During the sixtieth session of the Commission on Human Rights [E/2004/23], the Congo, on behalf of the Group of African States, moved that the Commission take no action on a draft resolution on the human rights situation in Zimbabwe, which would have expressed deep concern at the continuing human rights violations in the country and requested the relevant special rapporteurs and special representatives to examine alleged human rights violations and to report thereon. The motion was carried by a vote of 27 to 24, with 2 abstentions.

Americas

(For information on the human rights situation in Haiti, see p. 675.)

Colombia

The Commission Chairperson, in a 23 April statement, said the Commission appreciated the priority placed by the Government of Colombia on the development of a fully functioning democratic State that was more capable of protecting the most basic human rights of its citizens [E/2004/23]. Welcoming the conviction and sentencing of senior army officers for complicity in a massacre, the Commission called for stepping up the fight against impunity. It also called for further progress regarding the investigation of collusion between members of the public service and illegal armed groups. The Commission condemned all breaches of international humanitarian law arising from the conflict in Colombia, terrorism and other criminal attacks committed by illegal armed groups, the recruitment of a large number of children by those groups and kidnapping. Although the situation of some vulnerable groups had improved, trade unionists, human rights defenders, journalists, departmental officials, community leaders and local government officials continued to be particularly affected by the armed conflict. The Commission deplored the increase in selective violence against Afro-Colombian communities and violations of the right to life of large numbers of children. The High Commissioner was asked to report in 2005.

Report of High Commissioner. The High Commissioner reported on the 2004 human rights situation in Colombia, based on information gathered by OHCHR/Bogotá [E/CN.4/2005/10 & Corr.1].

In 2004, the Office carried out 226 field missions and received 1,211 complaints, of which 827 were admitted as referring to conduct in violation of human rights and/or breaches of international humanitarian law. The Office maintained an ongoing dialogue with civil society organizations and issued several publications. It was engaged in developing a national plan of action on human rights, institutional strengthening and human rights training. On 30 March, OHCHR/Bucaramanga, covering the north-eastern part of the country, was inaugurated to complement the offices in Bogotá, Cali and Medellín.

The High Commissioner stated that during 2004, the human rights situation continued to be critical. Violations continued to be recorded of the rights to life, personal integrity, freedom and security, due process and privacy, as well as of the fundamental freedoms of movement, residence, opinion and expression. No significant progress was observed regarding economic, social and cultural rights. Reports of extrajudicial executions attributed to the security forces and other public officials increased, and high levels of torture and forced disappearances continued, as did reports of arrests and mass searches carried out without an appropriate legal basis by the army and the Attorney-General's Office. The downward trend of various indicators of breaches of international humanitarian law continued, particularly multiple homicides and hostage-taking, although their incidence remained high. Illegal armed groups, particularly the Fuerzas Armadas Revolucionarias de Colombia–Ejército del Pueblo (FARC-EP) and the paramilitaries, continued to commit serious and numerous breaches such as attacks on civilians, indiscriminate attacks, homicides, massacres, hostage-taking, terrorist acts, forced displacements, the use of anti-personnel mines, the recruitment of minors and acts of sexual violence against women and girls. Allegations against members of the security forces, particularly the army, included homicides, indiscriminate attacks, forced displacements and attacks on the personal integrity and dignity of women. The vulnerability of human rights defenders continued. The number of newly displaced persons continued to decrease, although the total number of internally displaced persons increased. The indigenous and Afro-Colombian communities continued to be threatened by the illegal armed groups.

The High Commissioner proposed 27 recommendations addressed to the Government, the supervisory bodies responsible for human rights promotion and protection, representative sectors of civil society, the international community and the illegal armed groups, regarding prevention and protection, the internal armed conflict, the rule of law and impunity, economic and social policies, the promotion of a culture of human rights, and technical cooperation and advisory services provided by OHCHR.

Communication. Colombia, in observations on the High Commissioner's report [E/CN.4/2005/G/29], presented its comments regarding the evolution of the armed conflict, public policy and implementation of the High Commissioner's recommendations, economic and social policies, and the situation of human rights and international humanitarian law.

(See pp. 737 and 792 respectively for details of visits to Colombia by the Special Rapporteurs on the right to freedom of opinion and expression and on the situation of human rights and fundamental freedoms of indigenous peoples.)

Cuba

Commission action. On 15 April [res. 2004/11], by a recorded vote of 22 to 21, with 10 abstentions, the Commission stated that Cuba should refrain from adopting measures that could jeopardize the fundamental rights, the freedom of expression and the right to due process of its citizens, and, in that regard, deplored the events which occurred in 2003 relating to verdicts pronounced against certain political dissidents and journalists. It urged the Government to cooperate with the Personal Representative of the High Commissioner.

Report of Personal Representative. A report of the High Commissioner's Personal Representative [E/CN.4/2005/33 & Corr.1], Christine Chanet (France), reviewed the factors hindering the realization of human rights in Cuba, particularly in terms of the impact of the economic, trade and financial embargo (see p. 305) on economic, social and cultural rights. She said the difficulties the population had encountered as a result of the embargo were compounded in 2004, particularly as a result of tighter economic and financial restrictions imposed by the United States in May. Despite an unfavourable environment, the Government maintained a sound health system and school success rates, and made improvements in combating discrimination against women and in the exercise of freedom of religion. Subjects of concern were the arrest of some 80 persons, in March/April 2003, while working as journalists, writers, members of associations, human rights defenders or members of political parties and opposition trade unions. Moreover, in 2004 more people were arrested and convicted for openly expressing dissident political opinions. Although the Government had released 18 prisoners on humanitarian grounds, the releases did not signify the end of the period of repression which began in 2003, nor an improvement in civil and political

rights. According to the Working Group on Arbitrary Detention (see p. 721), 61 people were still in arbitrary detention. The Personal Representative was alarmed at the allegations of ill-treatment in detention made by prisoners' families. She recommended that the Government release detainees who had not committed violent acts against individuals or property; review laws which led to criminal prosecutions of persons exercising their freedom of expression, demonstration, assembly and association; uphold the moratorium on the application of the death penalty introduced in 2000; establish an independent body to receive complaints from persons claiming violation of their fundamental rights; review the regulations relating to travel into and out of the country; authorize NGOs to enter Cuba; foster pluralism in respect of associations, trade unions, organs of the press and political parties; and accede to the International Covenant on Civil and Political Rights and the Optional Protocol thereto and the International Covenant on Economic, Social and Cultural Rights, adopted by the General Assembly in resolution 2200 A (XXI) [YUN 1966, pp. 423 & 419], as well as the Second Optional Protocol of the Covenant on Civil and Political Rights, relating to the abolition of the death penalty, adopted by Assembly resolution 44/128 [YUN 1989, p. 484]. Annexed to the report was a list of civilians arrested in March/April 2003 and still imprisoned.

Communications. During the course of the year, Cuba submitted to the Commission a series of documents regarding human rights and fundamental freedoms [E/CN.4/2004/G/30, E/CN.4/2004/G/41, E/CN.4/2004/G/46, E/CN.4/2005/G/4, E/CN.4/2005/G/6, E/CN.4/2005/G/8, E/CN.4/2005/G/10].

Asia

(For information on the human rights situation in Afghanistan, see p. 671; Cambodia, p. 672; and Timor-Leste, p. 675.)

China

On 15 April [E/2004/23], China motioned that the Commission take no action on a draft resolution on the human rights situation in China that would have expressed concern at continuing reports regarding severe restrictions of the freedoms of assembly, association, expression, conscience and religion, legal processes that continued to fall short of international norms of due process and transparency, and arrests and other severe sentences for those seeking to exercise their fundamental rights, including those in Tibet and Xinjiang. The motion was carried by 28 votes to 16, with 9 abstentions.

(For information on a visit to China by the Working Group on Arbitrary Detention, see p. 722.)

Democratic People's Republic of Korea

Commission action. On 15 April [res. 2004/13], by a recorded vote of 29 to 8, with 16 abstentions, the Commission, expressing deep concern about continuing reports of systemic, widespread and grave human rights violations in the Democratic People's Republic of Korea (DPRK), regretted that the DPRK authorities had not permitted the international community to examine the reports in an independent manner and called on the Government to do so. The Commission Chairperson was requested to appoint a Special Rapporteur on the situation of human rights in the DPRK. The Special Rapporteur was asked to establish direct contact with the Government and people of the DPRK, report on the human rights situation in the country, seek and receive reliable information, including through country visits, and report to the General Assembly in 2004 and to the Commission in 2005. The Secretary-General was requested to assist the Special Rapporteur and the High Commissioner to engage in a dialogue with the DPRK authorities with a view to establishing human rights technical cooperation programmes and to report thereon. Relevant special rapporteurs and special representatives were requested to examine alleged human rights violations in the DPRK and to report in 2005; the Secretary-General was asked to assist them.

The Economic and Social Council, on 15 June, approved the Commission's request to its Chairperson to appoint a Special Rapporteur and to the Secretary-General to assist him/her (**decision 2004/221**).

In July, Vitit Muntarbhorn (Thailand) was appointed Special Rapporteur.

Notes by Secretariat. A February note by the Secretariat [E/CN.4/2004/31] described efforts to provide human rights advisory services and technical cooperation to the DPRK and provided information on the broad range of recommendations that the Commission addressed to the Government. Annexed to the note was a note verbale of 4 February from the DPRK to OHCHR, in which it objected to the Commission's 2003 resolution [YUN 2003, p. 816], which, it said, lacked fairness and objectivity, and contained wording designed to impair its image.

A September Secretariat note [A/59/316] stated that, owing to his late appointment, the Special Rapporteur was unable to provide a written report to the General Assembly; instead he would present an oral statement.

Report of Special Rapporteur. On 28 October, in an oral report to the General Assembly's Third Committee [A/C.3/59/SR.29], the Special Rapporteur said there were key human rights challenges in the DPRK regarding implementation of the right to food and the right to life. He pointed to the continuing debates on how much of the food aid provided to the country from abroad actually reached the target population. There were alleged violations of the right to security of person, humane treatment, non-discrimination and access to justice. The right to freedom of movement was also of concern, as were the rights to the freedom of information, expression and opinion, association and religion. The Special Rapporteur recommended that the Government abide by international human rights standards to which it was party and reform laws and practices inconsistent with those standards. He called for respect for the rule of law, and for measures addressing the root causes of displacement and ensuring humanitarian assistance.

Responding to the Special Rapporteur's report, the DPRK said it was the ultimate manifestation of prejudice, unfairness and interference in the internal affairs of the country. The report was the result of a political plot on the part of Western countries to isolate the DPRK under the pretext of human rights protection.

On 20 December, the Assembly took note of the report (**decision 59/528**).

Iran

(For details of the visit to Iran by the Special Rapporteur on the human rights of migrants, see p. 697.)

GENERAL ASSEMBLY ACTION

On 20 December [meeting 74], the General Assembly, on the recommendation of the Third Committee [A/59/503/Add.3], adopted **resolution 59/205** by recorded vote (71-54-55) [agenda item 105 (c)].

Situation of human rights in the Islamic Republic of Iran

The General Assembly,

Guided by the Charter of the United Nations, the Universal Declaration of Human Rights, the International Covenants on Human Rights and other international human rights instruments,

Reaffirming that all Member States have an obligation to promote and protect human rights and fundamental freedoms and to fulfil the obligations they have undertaken under the various international instruments in this field,

Mindful that the Islamic Republic of Iran is a party to the International Covenant on Civil and Political Rights, the International Covenant on Economic, Social and Cultural Rights, the International Convention on the Elimination of All Forms of Racial Discrimination and the Convention on the Rights of the Child,

Recalling its previous resolutions on the subject, the most recent of which is resolution 58/195 of 22 December 2003, and recalling also Commission on Human Rights resolution 2001/17 of 20 April 2001,

Noting the commitment made by the Government of the Islamic Republic of Iran to strengthen respect for human rights in the country and to promote the rule of law,

1. *Welcomes:*

(a) The open invitation extended by the Government of the Islamic Republic of Iran to all human rights thematic monitoring mechanisms in April 2002;

(b) The visit of the Working Group on Arbitrary Detention of the Commission on Human Rights to the Islamic Republic of Iran in February 2003 and its subsequent report;

(c) The visit of the Special Rapporteur of the Commission on Human Rights on the promotion and protection of the right to freedom of opinion and expression to the Islamic Republic of Iran in November 2003 and his subsequent report;

(d) The visit of the Special Rapporteur of the Commission on Human Rights on the human rights of migrants to the Islamic Republic of Iran in February 2004;

(e) The recommendation by the head of the judiciary of the Islamic Republic of Iran to judges in December 2002 that they choose alternative punishment in cases where the sentence of stoning would otherwise be imposed;

(f) The announcement by the head of the judiciary in April 2004 of the ban on torture and the subsequent passage of related legislation by the Parliament, which was approved by the Guardian Council in May 2004;

(g) The efforts of the elected Government to foster the growth of civil society;

(h) The human rights dialogues between the Islamic Republic of Iran and a number of countries;

(i) The cooperation with United Nations agencies in developing programmes in the field of human rights, good governance and the rule of law;

2. *Expresses its serious concern* at:

(a) The continuing violations of human rights in the Islamic Republic of Iran;

(b) The worsening situation with regard to freedom of opinion and expression and freedom of the media, especially the increased persecution for the peaceful expression of political views, including arbitrary arrest and detention without charge or trial; crackdowns by the judiciary and security forces against journalists, parliamentarians, students, clerics and academics; the unjustified closure of newspapers and blocking of Internet sites; the targeted disqualification of large numbers of prospective candidates in the Majlis elections as well as the intimidation and harassment of opposition activists in the run-up to the elections held in February 2004;

(c) The continuing executions in the absence of respect for internationally recognized safeguards, and in particular deplores the execution of persons below 18 years of age, contrary to the obligations of the Islamic Republic of Iran under article 37 of the Convention on the Rights of the Child and article 6 of the International Covenant on Civil and Political Rights, as well as public executions;

(d) The use of torture and other forms of cruel, inhuman and degrading punishment, in particular the practice of amputation and flogging, noting in this context the rejection by the Guardian Council in August 2003 of the proposal of the elected parliament to accede to the Convention against Torture and Other Cruel, Inhuman or Degrading Treatment or Punishment;

(e) The continued restrictions on free assembly and the forcible dissolution of political parties;

(f) The failure to comply fully with international standards in the administration of justice, the absence of due process of law, the refusal to provide fair and public hearings and right to counsel, the use of national security laws to deny the rights of the individual and the lack of respect for internationally recognized legal safeguards, inter alia, with respect to persons belonging to religious minorities, officially recognized or otherwise;

(g) The systemic discrimination against women and girls in law and in practice, despite some minor legislative improvements, and the refusal of the Guardian Council to take steps to address this systematic discrimination, noting in this context its rejection, in August 2003, of the proposal of the elected parliament to accede to the Convention on the Elimination of All Forms of Discrimination against Women;

(h) The continuing discrimination against persons belonging to minorities, including Christians, Jews and Sunnis, and the increased discrimination against the Baha'is, including cases of arbitrary arrest and detention, the denial of free worship or of publicly carrying out communal affairs, the disregard of property rights, the destruction of sites of religious importance, the suspension of social, educational and community-related activities and the denial of access to higher education, employment, pensions and other benefits;

(i) The continuing persecution, including through the systematic and arbitrary use of prolonged solitary confinement, and arbitrary sentencing to prison of human rights defenders, political opponents, religious dissenters and reformists;

(j) The postponement of the visit of the Working Group on Enforced or Involuntary Disappearances of the Commission on Human Rights to the Islamic Republic of Iran;

3. *Calls upon* the Government of the Islamic Republic of Iran:

(a) To abide by its obligations freely undertaken under the International Covenants on Human Rights and other international human rights instruments, including provisions relating to freedom of opinion and expression, the use of torture and other forms of cruel, inhuman and degrading treatment or punishment, the promotion and protection of the human rights of women and girls and the rights of the child, and to continue its efforts to consolidate respect for human rights and the rule of law;

(b) To implement the recommendations of the Working Group on Arbitrary Detention, the Special Rapporteur on the promotion and protection of the right to freedom of opinion and expression and the Special Rapporteur of the Commission on Human Rights on freedom of religion or belief;

(c) To cooperate with United Nations mechanisms, including by setting a date for a visit by the Working Group on Enforced or Involuntary Disappearances, and to respond fully to their recommendations;

(d) To implement fully the ban on torture, announced in April 2004 by the head of the judiciary, and the related parliamentary legislation of May 2004;

(e) To expedite judicial reform, to guarantee the dignity of the individual and to ensure the full application of due process of law and fair and transparent procedures by an independent and impartial judiciary, and in this context to ensure respect for the rights of the defence and the equity of verdicts in all instances, including for members of religious minority groups, officially recognized or otherwise;

(f) To appoint an impartial prosecutor and to expedite the creation of offices of the Prosecutor in all provinces, in keeping with the decision taken in November 2002 for their re-establishment;

(g) To eliminate all forms of discrimination based on religious grounds or against persons belonging to minorities, including the Baha'is, Christians, Jews and Sunnis, and to address this matter in an open manner, with the full participation of the minorities themselves, and to ensure respect for the freedom of religion or belief of all persons;

(h) To end amputation and flogging and all other forms of punishment that are cruel, inhuman or degrading;

(i) To abolish the punishment of execution by stoning and, in the meantime, to end the practice of stoning, as recommended by the head of the judiciary;

(j) To comply with its obligations under article 37 of the Convention on the Rights of the Child and article 6 of the International Covenant on Civil and Political Rights not to impose the sentence of death for offences committed by persons below 18 years of age;

(k) To vigorously pursue penitentiary reform;

4. *Encourages* the thematic mechanisms of the Commission on Human Rights, including the Special Rapporteur on extrajudicial, summary or arbitrary executions, the Special Rapporteur on torture and other cruel, inhuman or degrading treatment or punishment, the Special Rapporteur on the independence of judges and lawyers, the Special Rapporteur on freedom of religion or belief and the Special Representative of the Secretary-General on the situation of human rights defenders to visit the Islamic Republic of Iran, and encourages the Government of the Islamic Republic of Iran to cooperate with these special mechanisms and to respond fully to their subsequent recommendations;

5. *Decides* to continue its examination of the situation of human rights in the Islamic Republic of Iran at its sixtieth session, under the item entitled "Human rights questions", in the light of additional elements provided by the Commission on Human Rights.

RECORDED VOTE ON RESOLUTION 59/205:

In favour: Albania, Andorra, Australia, Austria, Belgium, Belize, Bolivia, Bosnia and Herzegovina, Bulgaria, Canada, Chile, Costa Rica, Croatia, Cyprus, Czech Republic, Denmark, El Salvador, Estonia, Finland, France, Germany, Greece, Grenada, Haiti, Hungary, Iceland, Ireland, Israel, Italy, Japan, Jordan, Kiribati, Latvia, Liechtenstein, Lithuania, Luxembourg, Malawi, Malta, Marshall Islands, Mexico, Micronesia, Monaco, Nauru, Netherlands, New Zealand, Nicaragua, Norway, Palau, Panama, Papua New Guinea, Paraguay, Peru, Poland, Portugal, Republic of Moldova, Romania, Saint Vincent and the Grenadines, Samoa, San Marino, Serbia and Montenegro, Slovakia, Slovenia, Solomon Islands, Spain, Sweden, Switzerland, The former Yugoslav Republic of Macedonia, Timor-Leste, Tuvalu, United Kingdom, United States.

Against: Algeria, Armenia, Azerbaijan, Bahrain, Bangladesh, Belarus, Brunei Darussalam, Chad, China, Comoros, Cuba, Democratic People's Republic of Korea, Democratic Republic of the Congo, Djibouti, Egypt, Gambia, Guinea, India, Indonesia, Iran, Iraq, Kazakhstan, Kuwait, Kyrgyzstan, Lebanon, Libyan Arab Jamahiriya, Malaysia, Maldives, Mauritania, Morocco, Myanmar, Niger, Nigeria, Oman, Pakistan, Qatar, Russian Federation, Saudi Arabia, Senegal, Somalia, South Africa, Sri Lanka, Sudan, Syrian Arab Republic, Tajikistan, Togo, Tunisia, Turkmenistan, Ukraine, Uzbekistan, Venezuela, Viet Nam, Yemen, Zimbabwe.

Abstaining: Angola, Antigua and Barbuda, Argentina, Bahamas, Barbados, Benin, Bhutan, Botswana, Brazil, Burkina Faso, Burundi, Cambodia, Cameroon, Cape Verde, Central African Republic, Colombia, Côte d'Ivoire, Dominica, Dominican Republic, Ecuador, Equatorial Guinea, Eritrea, Ethiopia, Fiji, Ghana, Guatemala, Guinea-Bissau, Guyana, Honduras, Jamaica, Kenya, Lao People's Democratic Republic, Lesotho, Liberia, Madagascar, Mauritius, Mozambique, Namibia, Nepal, Philippines, Republic of Korea, Rwanda, Saint Lucia, Sao Tome and Principe, Sierra Leone, Singapore, Suriname, Swaziland, Thailand, Trinidad and Tobago, Uganda, United Arab Emirates, United Republic of Tanzania, Uruguay, Zambia.

Iraq

Report of Special Rapporteur. A March report [E/CN.4/2004/36/Add.1] of the Special Rapporteur on the situation of human rights in Iraq, Andreas Mavrommatis (Cyprus), covered the situation in the country from 10 February to 7 March. Its findings were based mainly on substantive consultations he had held in Amman, Jordan, with eyewitnesses and high-level officials of the Iraqi Ministries of Human Rights, of Immigration and of Justice, and the Minister for Human Rights of the Kurdistan Regional Government. The consultations focused on oppression, discrimination, religious persecution, mass executions of persons belonging to the majority Shi'ah community, expulsions, mass executions of Faili (Shi'ah Iraqi Kurds) and misappropriation of their properties, eyewitness evidence on the Anfal campaigns and the Halabcha bombings in 1988, and the draining of the Marshes, including the consequent violations of a wide range of rights of the Marsh people. The Special Rapporteur urged all concerned to accelerate criminal investigations regarding grave human rights violations and to prosecute those responsible; to secure all mass graves and accelerate the identification of remains; and to continue and enhance cooperation with him. He called on all countries of asylum not to press refugees to return to Iraq and called on the Iraqi authorities to ensure that all laws and practices adopted were consistent with the country's international obligations. The Special Rapporteur urged the Iraqi authorities to ratify the Convention against Torture and Other Cruel, Inhuman or Degrading Treatment or Punishment, adopted by the General Assembly in resolution 39/46 [YUN 1984, p. 813].

Report of Acting High Commissioner. A June report of the Acting High Commissioner [E/CN.4/2005/4] focused on the human rights situation in Iraq. He said that human rights gains had been made during the period since Coalition forces took control of the country, including an internal debate on a constitutional architecture mindful of international human rights norms; the establishment of an Iraqi Ministry of Human Rights; enhanced freedoms for ordinary Iraqis; increased participation of women in public life; and greater freedom of opinion and expression. Nevertheless, serious human rights problems were evidenced by the fact that large numbers of people were incarcerated without public knowledge of their number, nor the reasons for, place of and conditions of their detention. Ordinary Iraqis suffered privations in respect of basic economic and social rights, but that situation had improved. The treatment of Iraqi detainees was, as recognized by Coalition leaders at the highest levels, a stain on the effort to bring freedom to Iraq. The Acting High Commissioner recommended regular inspections of places of detention, the appointment of an international ombudsman or commissioner, the establishment of an independent Iraqi national human rights commission, bringing to justice members of the Coalition forces responsible for serious human rights violations and the creation by the Coalition authorities of a human rights fund for Iraq. Recommendations to the Iraqi Interim Government included promulgating a human rights policy for Iraq, establishing an Iraqi legal and judicial reform commission, developing a strategy for addressing the legacy of brutal authoritarian rule and massive human rights abuses, and reviewing the statute of the Iraq Special Tribunal. Recommendations were also made for consideration to be given to the need to establish an Iraqi truth and reconciliation commission, for designating a reparations commission for past crimes, ensuring the effective security of legal actors, defendants, victims and witnesses, supporting human rights civil society organizations and supporting the Ministry of Human Rights. The United Nations should continue to provide human rights training for government officials, judges, prosecutors, lawyers, and representatives of NGOs and civil society. Annexed to the report were submissions by the Coalition Provisional Authority, the United Kingdom and the United States; and a list of documents used to prepare the report.

Communication. In a July note [E/CN.4/2005/G/12], Iraq, responding to a 6 May letter of the Acting High Commissioner addressed to Iraqi senior officials regarding the situation of human rights and humanitarian law in the country, described aspects of the functioning of the Iraqi Interim Government, the situation of women and children, health concerns, education enrolment, the economic, social and cultural situation, and civil and political rights.

Myanmar

Commission action. On 21 April [res. 2004/61], the Commission, while welcoming some positive developments regarding human rights in Myanmar, expressed grave concern at the ongoing systematic human rights violations in the country. It called on the Government to restore the independence of the judiciary and due process of law, and to further reform the justice system; eradicate the practice of forced labour; ensure safe and unhindered access for the United Nations and international humanitarian organizations; cooperate with the Secretary-General's Special Envoy for Myanmar and the Special Rapporteur; consider becoming party to international human rights instruments; suspend and permanently end conflict with ethnic groups; conclude a ceasefire agreement with the Karen National Union (KNU) and ensure that the rights of ethnic nationalities were respected fully; and establish a national human rights commission in accordance with the Principles relating to the establishment of national institutions for the promotion and protection of human rights (the Paris Principles), adopted in General Assembly resolution 48/134 [YUN 1993, p. 899]. The Commission decided to extend the Special Rapporteur's mandate for a further year and asked him to report to the Assembly in 2004 and to the Commission in 2005 and to integrate a gender perspective in his work. The Secretary-General was asked to assist him.

On 22 July, the Economic and Social Council endorsed the Commission's decision to extend the Special Rapporteur's mandate and its request to him to submit reports (**decision 2004/266**).

Reports of Secretary-General. In response to General Assembly resolution 58/247 [YUN 2003, p. 820], the Secretary-General submitted a March report [E/CN.4/2004/30] on his good offices efforts and those of his Special Envoy, Razali Ismail, in facilitating national reconciliation and democratization in Myanmar. Discussions focused on the reconvening of the Government's National Convention in order to draft a new constitution, with the participation of representatives of other political parties. The Secretary-General called for the release of those detained for engaging in peaceful political activities and took note of the peace talks that had resumed between the Government and KNU, the largest armed opposition group. He urged the Government to start dialogue with Daw Aung San Suu Kyi, leader of the National League for Democracy (NLD), and representatives of Myanmar's other political parties.

In an August report [A/59/269], the Secretary-General said that his Special Envoy visited Myanmar (1-4 March) where he stressed to all parties that a democratic transition in Myanmar should be all-inclusive, open and transparent. Following the Envoy's visit, several NLD Central Executive Committee (CEC) members were released from house arrest, the NLD headquarters in Yangon were reopened and several meetings between Daw Aung San Suu Kyi and NLD CEC members were allowed to take place at her residence. Optimism dissipated on 14 May when the Government informed CEC members that the remaining restrictions on Daw Aung San Suu Kyi and NLD would not be lifted. NLD announced that it would not participate in the National Convention. The National Convention reconvened on 17 May with the participation of ethnic nationality ceasefire groups but without NLD and some other ethnic nationality political parties, including the Shan National League for Democracy. On 22 May, meetings of the groups began to prepare proposals on the draft chapters of the constitution on the legislature, executive and judiciary already laid down at the previous Convention. In plenary sessions (24 June–9 July), delegates put forward proposals for sharing power in the legislative, executive and judicial sectors to be included in the new constitution. The National Convention was adjourned on 9 July with no firm date for reconvening. A government statement of 10 July affirmed that when the Convention resumed, detailed basic principles on the legislature, executive and judiciary, as well as the sharing and distribution of legislative power and the formation of a financial commission, would be laid down with the consent of a majority of the delegates.

Reports of Special Rapporteur. In response to Commission resolution 2004/61 and Economic and Social Council decision 2004/266 (above), the Secretary-General, by an August note [A/59/311], transmitted a report of Special Rapporteur Paulo Sérgio Pinheiro (Brazil) on the human rights situation in Myanmar, based on information received by him up to 30 July.

Regarding civil and political rights, the Special Rapporteur said that the situation in Myanmar had not substantially changed. There remained large numbers (over 1,300) of security detainees and there were no indications as to when Daw Aung San Suu Kyi would be released. Since the beginning of 2004, he had received reports about continuing arrests and harsh sentences for peaceful political activities. There were still restrictions on political activity, with all NLD party offices remaining shut except for its headquarters in Yangon. Regarding the situation in the border areas, the resumption of peace talks between the Government and KNU was a significant development. The two sides planned to meet in August for a fourth round of negotiations aimed at ending the armed conflict. The Special Rapporteur received credible reports of human rights violations in certain counter-insurgency areas. As to children's rights, the Committee for the Prevention of the Recruitment of Child Soldiers was established in January, and the Government had invited a delegation of the Committee on the Rights of the Child to visit Myanmar.

A December report [E/CN.4/2005/36] of the Special Rapporteur, based on information received by him up to 29 November, said there was a change of Prime Minister on 19 October. The Government, under the new Prime Minister, had given public assurances that all commitments made under the previous Government would be honoured. Regarding the human rights situation, the Special Rapporteur reported that there had been no change in the situation of fundamental rights and freedoms. Recent cases of arrests, trials and prison sentences for peaceful political activity had been brought to his attention. The Special Rapporteur expressed concern that the number of persons imprisoned for exercising their fundamental rights to freedom of expression, opinion, information, religion, association and assembly had remained unchanged during the reporting period, and political prisoners had been detained beyond the expiry of their sentences. With the recent leadership changes, the 1983 law on the National Intelligence Bureau was repealed on 22 October. The Special Rapporteur remained disturbed by continuing allegations of human rights violations in ethnic minority areas, where civilians had witnessed widespread violations of economic, social and cultural rights. There continued to be credible reports about the recruitment and use of minors by the Myanmar armed forces and a range of non-State armed opposition groups. The Special Rapporteur recommended the unconditional release of political prisoners, the restoration of freedom for political parties and ceasefire partners to operate and pursue peaceful political activity, the establishment by the Government of mechanisms for determining the accountability of army personnel for human rights violations, the coordination of political, humanitarian and human rights initiatives by UN and international community actors and agencies, and that priority be given to the ratification of human rights instruments.

On 23 December [meeting 76], the General Assembly, on the recommendation of the Third Committee [A/59/503/Add.3], adopted **resolution 59/263** without vote [agenda item 105 (c)].

Situation of human rights in Myanmar

The General Assembly,

Reaffirming that all States Members of the United Nations have an obligation to promote and protect human rights and fundamental freedoms and the duty to fulfil the obligations they have undertaken under the various international instruments in this field,

Reaffirming also its previous resolutions on the human rights situation in Myanmar, the most recent of which is resolution 58/247 of 23 December 2003, those of the Commission on Human Rights, the most recent of which is resolution 2004/61 of 21 April 2004, and the conclusions of the special sitting of the Committee on the Application of Standards of the International Labour Conference of 5 June 2004,

Bearing in mind Security Council resolutions 1460 (2003) of 30 January 2003 and 1539(2004) of 22 April 2004,

Recognizing that good governance, democracy, the rule of law and respect for human rights are essential to achieving sustainable development and economic growth,

1. *Welcomes:*

(a) The report of the Secretary-General and the interim report of the Special Rapporteur of the Commission on Human Rights on the situation of human rights in Myanmar;

(b) The personal engagement of the Secretary-General with the situation in Myanmar and his statement of 17 August 2004, in which he calls upon the Government of Myanmar to release Daw Aung San Suu Kyi immediately and to engage in substantive dialogue with the National League for Democracy and other political parties;

(c) The establishment by the Government of a committee for the prevention of military recruitment of underage children and its discussions with the United Nations Children's Fund towards concluding a plan of action, and stresses the need for the Government to work closely with the Fund;

(d) The resumption of peace talks between the Government of Myanmar and the Karen National Union;

(e) The access to the eastern part of Myanmar of the International Committee of the Red Cross and the United Nations High Commissioner for Refugees;

2. *Expresses its grave concern* at:

(a) The ongoing systematic violation of the human rights, including civil, political, economic, social and cultural rights, of the people of Myanmar, in particular as outlined in previous resolutions concerning the situation of human rights in Myanmar, the most recent of which are General Assembly resolution 58/247 and Commission on Human Rights resolution 2004/61;

(b) The events of 30 May 2003 and the continuing detention and house arrest of Daw Aung San Suu Kyi and members of the National League for Democracy;

(c) The fact that the Myanmar authorities have yet to implement recommendations contained in the aforementioned resolutions adopted by the General Assembly and the Commission on Human Rights;

(d) The fact that the Myanmar authorities have not permitted the Special Envoy of the Secretary-General for Myanmar to visit for over six months, or the Special Rapporteur to visit for almost twelve months, despite repeated requests;

(e) The continuing restrictions placed on the National League for Democracy and other political parties which prevented them from participating in the National Convention;

3. *Calls upon* the Government of Myanmar:

(a) To end the systematic violations of human rights in Myanmar, including extrajudicial killings, the use of torture, the use of rape and other forms of sexual violence persistently carried out by members of the armed forces, discrimination and violations suffered in particular by persons belonging to ethnic minorities, women and children and violations of the right to an adequate standard of living; to ensure full respect for all human rights and fundamental freedoms; to end impunity; and to investigate and bring to justice any perpetrators of human rights violations, including members of the military and other government agents in all circumstances;

(b) To ensure that the next session of the National Convention is fully inclusive of all political parties and representatives and all major ethnic nationalities not represented by a political party, and that participants are guaranteed freedom of association and freedom of expression, including freedom of the media and unlimited access to information for the people of Myanmar, and guarantees the safety of all participants;

(c) To restore democracy and respect the results of the 1990 elections by, inter alia, releasing immediately and unconditionally the leadership of the National League for Democracy, including Daw Aung San Suu Kyi, and members of the League detained on or after 30 May 2003, as well as other prisoners of conscience, and to cease the ongoing harassment of the League and other political parties and allow the reopening of the offices of the League throughout the country;

(d) To release immediately and unconditionally all detained or imprisoned political prisoners;

(e) To initiate a full and independent inquiry, with international cooperation, into the Depayin incident of 30 May 2003, as called for by the General Assembly at its fifty-eighth session;

(f) To cooperate fully with the Special Envoy and the Special Rapporteur in order to help to bring Myanmar towards a transition to civilian rule and to ensure that they are both granted without further delay full, free and unimpeded access to Myanmar and that no person cooperating with the Special Envoy, the Special Rapporteur or any international organization is subjected to any form of intimidation, harassment or punishment, and to review as a matter of urgency the case of those undergoing punishment in this regard;

(g) To consider as a matter of high priority becoming a party to all relevant human rights instruments;

(*h*) To take immediate action to implement fully concrete legislative, executive and administrative measures to eradicate the practice of forced labour by all organs of Government, including the armed forces, to cooperate with the International Labour Organization, and to implement fully the recommendations of the Commission of Inquiry established to examine the observance by Myanmar of the Convention concerning Forced or Compulsory Labour, 1930 (Convention No. 29), of the International Labour Organization;

(*i*) To put an immediate end to the recruitment and use of child soldiers and to extend full cooperation to relevant international organizations in order to ensure the demobilization of child soldiers, their return home and their rehabilitation in accordance with recommendations of the Committee on the Rights of the Child;

(*j*) To end the policy of the systematic enforced displacement of persons and other policies leading to displacement within Myanmar and refugee flows to neighbouring countries, to provide the necessary protection and assistance to internally displaced persons and to respect the right of refugees to voluntary, safe and dignified return monitored by appropriate international agencies;

(*k*) To immediately ensure the safe and unhindered access to all parts of Myanmar of the United Nations and international humanitarian organizations so as to ensure the provision of humanitarian assistance and to guarantee that it reaches the most vulnerable groups of the population, including internally displaced persons and returnees;

(*l*) To pursue through dialogue and peaceful means an immediate end to conflict with all remaining ethnic groups with which ceasefire agreements have not yet been signed;

(*m*) To formulate a clear and detailed plan for the transition to democracy, which includes concrete timing and the involvement of all political groups and ethnic nationalities in a way that ensures the process is transparent and inclusive;

4. *Requests* the Secretary-General:

(*a*) To continue to provide his good offices and to pursue his discussions on the situation of human rights and the restoration of democracy with the Government and people of Myanmar, including all relevant parties to the national reconciliation process in Myanmar;

(*b*) To give all necessary assistance to enable his Special Envoy and the Special Rapporteur to discharge their mandate fully and effectively;

(*c*) To report to the General Assembly at its sixtieth session and to the Commission on Human Rights at its sixty-first session on the progress made in the implementation of the present resolution;

5. *Decides* to continue the consideration of the question at its sixtieth session.

Turkmenistan

Commission action. On 15 April [res. 2004/12], by a recorded vote of 25 to 11, with 17 abstentions, the Commission expressed grave concern at the Government of Turkmenistan's policy based on the repression of political opposition activities; abuse of the legal system through arbitrary detention, imprisonment and surveillance of those who tried to exercise their freedoms of thought, expression, assembly and association, and harassment of their families; restrictions on the freedoms of information and expression, thought, conscience, religion and belief; employment and education discrimination against ethnic Russian, Uzbek and other minorities; and poor prison conditions. The Government was urged to ensure full respect for all human rights and fundamental freedoms, end forced displacement and guarantee freedom of movement, remove new restrictions on the activities of public associations, develop further a constructive dialogue with OHCHR and submit reports to relevant UN treaty bodies and ensure full implementation of their recommendations. The Commission requested the Special Rapporteurs on the independence of judges and lawyers, on torture and other cruel, inhuman or degrading treatment or punishment, on extrajudicial, summary or arbitrary executions, on the right to freedom of opinion and expression and on freedom of religion or belief, the Working Group on Arbitrary Detention, the Representative of the Secretary-General on internally displaced persons and the Special Representative of the Secretary-General on the situation of human rights defenders to consider visiting the country, and called on the Government of Turkmenistan to facilitate the visits.

Communication. On 20 April [E/CN.4/2004/ G/53], Turkmenistan said that the Commission's resolution (above) did not correspond to reality and it felt it necessary to present information regarding the implementation of guarantees of personal, political, economic, social and other rights of its citizens.

GENERAL ASSEMBLY ACTION

On 20 December [meeting 74], the General Assembly, on the recommendation of the Third Committee [A/59/503/Add.3], adopted **resolution 59/206** by recorded vote (69-47-63) [agenda item 105 (*c*)].

Situation of human rights in Turkmenistan

The General Assembly,

Reaffirming that all States Members of the United Nations have the obligation to promote and protect human rights and fundamental freedoms and the duty to fulfil the obligations that they have undertaken under the various international instruments in this field,

Recalling its resolution 58/194 of 22 December 2003,

1. *Welcomes:*

(*a*) The limited increase in the ability of members of certain religious minority groups, including members of the Baha'i faith, the Baptist church, the Hare Krishna movement and the Seventh Day Adventist church, to practise their religion;

(*b*) The release in June 2004 of a number of Jehovah's Witnesses who had made conscientious objections to undertaking military service, but notes with concern that other Jehovah's Witnesses continue to be jailed on the same charge;

(c) The comments of the Government of Turkmenistan in May 2004 that interested representatives of the international community were welcome to visit Turkmen prisons, and notes with satisfaction that the Government has begun preliminary discussions with representatives of the International Committee of the Red Cross regarding prison access;

(d) The fact that the Personal Envoy of the Chairman-in-Office of the Organization for Security and Cooperation in Europe for Participating States in Central Asia has been given the opportunity for further dialogue with the Government of Turkmenistan, and expresses the hope that a constructive dialogue on human rights issues is to be continued soon;

(e) The submission of the national report under the International Convention on the Elimination of All Forms of Racial Discrimination to the Office of the United Nations High Commissioner for Human Rights and the recent submission of the report under the Convention on the Elimination of All Forms of Discrimination against Women to the Division for the Advancement of Women of the Department of Economic and Social Affairs of the Secretariat and the announcement by the Government of Turkmenistan that it intends to submit the reports due under the Convention on the Rights of the Child by the end of 2004;

(f) The amendment of 2 November 2004 to the Criminal Code of Turkmenistan rescinding article 223/1, which stipulated criminal penalties for unregistered activities of public associations, including non-governmental organizations;

(g) The invitation by the Government of Turkmenistan to the High Commissioner on National Minorities of the Organization for Security and Cooperation in Europe, which was extended on 16 November 2004, to visit the country by the end of 2004;

2. *Expresses its grave concern* at the continuing and serious human rights violations occurring in Turkmenistan, in particular:

(a) The persistence of a governmental policy based on the repression of all political opposition activities;

(b) The continuing abuse of the legal system through arbitrary detentions, imprisonment and surveillance of persons who try to exercise their freedom of expression, assembly and association, and by harassment of their families;

(c) Further restrictions on the freedom of expression and opinion, including the loss of local retransmissions of Russian language programmes on Radio Mayak, and serious harassment endured by local correspondents and collaborators of Radio Liberty;

(d) Continued restrictions on the exercise of the freedom of thought, conscience, religion and belief;

(e) Continued discrimination by the Government of Turkmenistan against ethnic minorities in the fields of education and employment and by forced displacements, despite assurances by the Government that it will stop this discrimination;

(f) Constraints faced by civil society organizations, including the slow progress in the registration of non-governmental organizations;

3. *Regrets* the decision of the Government of Turkmenistan not to renew the accreditation for the Head of the Centre of the Organization for Security and Cooperation in Europe at Ashgabat, but hopes that the Turkmen authorities will cooperate fully with her successor;

4. *Calls upon* the Government of Turkmenistan:

(a) To ensure full respect for all human rights and fundamental freedoms and, in this regard, to implement fully the measures set out in Commission on Human Rights resolutions 2003/11 of 16 April 2003 and 2004/12 of 15 April 2004;

(b) To work closely with the Office of the United Nations High Commissioner for Human Rights with regard to the areas of concern and to cooperate fully with all the mechanisms of the Commission on Human Rights and all the relevant United Nations treaty bodies;

(c) To implement fully the recommendations outlined in the report of the Rapporteur of the Moscow Mechanism of the Organization for Security and Cooperation in Europe and to work constructively with the various institutions of the Organization, in particular following the visit of the Personal Envoy of the Chairman-in-Office of the Organization for Participating States in Central Asia, to work towards implementation of those recommendations and to make the necessary arrangements to facilitate fully a visit by the High Commissioner on National Minorities of the Organization by the end of 2004;

(d) To release immediately and unconditionally all prisoners of conscience;

(e) To give real substance to the May 2004 offer of the Government of Turkmenistan for interested representatives of the international community to visit Turkmen prisons by providing appropriate independent bodies, including the International Committee of the Red Cross, with full access to all places of detention in accordance with the usual modalities for those organizations and ensuring that lawyers and relatives have full and repeated access to all those in detention, including those convicted of involvement in the attempted coup d'état of 25 November 2002;

(f) To ensure that the forthcoming parliamentary elections will be held consistent with the commitments of the Organization for Security and Cooperation in Europe and other international standards for democratic elections;

(g) To remove the remaining restrictions on the activities of public associations, including non-governmental organizations, and to enable those organizations, in particular human rights organizations, and other civil society actors to carry out their activities without hindrance, building upon the amendment of 2 November 2004 to the Criminal Code of Turkmenistan abolishing criminal penalties for unregistered activities of public associations;

5. *Requests* the Secretary-General to submit a report to the General Assembly at its sixtieth session on the implementation of the present resolution.

RECORDED VOTE ON RESOLUTION 59/206:

In favour: Albania, Andorra, Argentina, Australia, Austria, Belgium, Bolivia, Bosnia and Herzegovina, Brazil, Bulgaria, Canada, Chile, Costa Rica, Croatia, Cyprus, Czech Republic, Denmark, Dominican Republic, El Salvador, Estonia, Finland, France, Germany, Greece, Guatemala, Guinea-Bissau, Haiti, Honduras, Hungary, Iceland, Ireland, Israel, Italy, Japan, Latvia, Liechtenstein, Lithuania, Luxembourg, Malawi, Malta, Marshall Islands, Mexico, Micronesia, Monaco, Nauru, Netherlands, New Zealand, Nicaragua, Norway, Palau, Panama, Paraguay, Peru, Poland, Portugal, Republic of Korea, Romania, Samoa, San Marino, Serbia and Montenegro, Slovakia, Slovenia, Spain, Sweden, Switzerland, The former Yugoslav Republic of Macedonia, Timor-Leste, United Kingdom, United States.

Against: Algeria, Azerbaijan, Bahrain, Bangladesh, Belarus, Brunei Darussalam, Chad, China, Comoros, Cuba, Democratic People's Republic of Korea, Egypt, Gambia, India, Indonesia, Iran, Jordan, Kazakhstan, Kuwait, Kyrgyzstan, Lebanon, Libyan Arab Jamahiriya, Malaysia, Maldives, Mauritania, Morocco, Myanmar, Nepal, Niger, Nigeria, Oman, Pakistan, Qatar, Saudi Arabia, Somalia, Sudan, Syrian Arab Republic, Tajikistan, Tunisia, Turkmenistan, Ukraine, United Arab Emirates, Uzbekistan, Venezuela, Viet Nam, Yemen, Zimbabwe.

Abstaining: Angola, Antigua and Barbuda, Armenia, Bahamas, Barbados, Belize, Benin, Bhutan, Botswana, Burkina Faso, Burundi, Cambodia, Cameroon, Cape Verde, Central African Republic, Colombia, Côte d'Ivoire, Democratic Republic of the Congo, Djibouti, Dominica, Ecuador, Equatorial Guinea, Eritrea, Ethiopia, Fiji, Ghana, Grenada, Guinea, Guyana, Jamaica, Kenya, Lao People's Democratic Republic, Lesotho, Liberia, Madagascar, Mali, Mauritius, Mozambique, Namibia, Papua New Guinea, Philippines, Republic of Moldova, Russian Federation, Rwanda, Saint Lucia, Saint Vincent and the Grenadines, Sao Tome and Principe, Senegal, Sierra Leone, Singapore, South Africa, Sri Lanka, Suriname, Swaziland, Thailand, Togo, Trinidad and Tobago, Tuvalu, Uganda, United Republic of Tanzania, Uruguay, Vanuatu, Zambia.

Europe

Belarus

Commission action. On 15 April [res. 2004/14], by a recorded vote of 23 to 13, with 17 abstentions, the Commission expressed deep concern at reports from credible sources implicating senior Belarus government officials in the forced disappearance and/or summary execution of three political opponents of the incumbent authorities and of a journalist; the electoral process and legislative framework in Belarus, which remained fundamentally flawed; continued reports of arbitrary arrest and detention; persistent reports of harassment and closure of NGOs, national minority organizations, independent media outlets, opposition political parties and independent trade unions, and the harassment of those engaged in democratic activities; increased restrictions on the activities of religious organizations; reports of harassment of independent and internationally oriented educational establishments; the failure of the Government to cooperate with the Commission's mechanisms; and the criminal prosecution of a leading opposition figure. The Commission decided to appoint a special rapporteur to report in 2005.

On 15 June, the Economic and Social Council approved that decision (**decision 2004/222**).

In July, Adrian Severin (Romania) was appointed Special Rapporteur.

Report of Special Rapporteur. The Special Rapporteur submitted a report on the human rights situation in Belarus, based on his missions to Poland, Lithuania and Latvia (30 November–4 December) [E/CN.4/2005/35].

The Special Rapporteur said that the regime in Belarus was of an authoritarian nature. It was also a bureaucratic State, lacking a strong civil society and a well-developed middle class. The Special Rapporteur said that Belarus still imposed the death penalty and, while it was not illegal under international law, the practice potentially was linked with other human rights violations, such as abuses of the right to a fair trial and of torture and ill-treatment used to extract confessions; certain convictions resulting in the death penalty might be unsound owing to judicial errors or due process violations. He expressed concern about reports of disappearances; torture used routinely to extract confessions and used systematically on prisoners on death row; detention; irregularities in the judicial system; allegations of violations of the freedom of expression; attacks on human rights defenders and political opposition members; allegations of violations of workers' rights; violations of freedom of religion and the principle of equality of religions; and irregularities regarding a referendum to change the Constitution with a view to eliminating limits to the term of office of the President.

The Special Rapporteur called for a deep reform of the political system and a dramatic restructuring of the society in order to promote human rights in the country, a programme of public education and public awareness regarding human rights, and the creation of an international fund for human rights education in Belarus, under the supervision of the Commission on Human Rights. The High Commissioner should convene an international conference on the human rights situation in Belarus.

Communications. Referring to Commission resolution 2004/14 (above), Belarus, in a December communication [E/CN.4/2005/G/11], said it had always been committed to the cause of human rights protection and rejected the resolution, including the Special Rapporteur's mandate. In further communications, Belarus, in view of the Special Rapporteur's report (above), submitted information on measures it had taken to strengthen international security, arms control and disarmament [E/CN.4/2005/G/27] and on social and economic developments in the country [E/CN.4/2005/G/28].

(For information about a visit to Belarus by the Working Group on Arbitrary Detention, see p. 722.)

Cyprus

Report of Secretary-General. Pursuant to a 2003 request of the Commission [YUN 2003, p. 824], the Secretary-General transmitted an April OHCHR report [E/CN.4/2004/27], which gave an overview of human rights issues in Cyprus covering the period up to 2 April 2004.

Human rights concerns stemmed predominantly from the persisting division of the island and the political situation, which had consequences for the enjoyment of the freedoms of movement, association and expression, property rights and religion and the rights to education and health. Also affected were voting rights and the human rights issues pertaining to missing persons. The report said that, although there were some positive developments, the persisting de facto partition of the island constituted a major obstacle to human rights enjoyment throughout the island.

Commission action. On 21 April [dec. 2004/126], the Commission retained the item on Cyprus on its agenda, on the understanding that previous resolutions would continue to remain operative, including its request to the Secretary-General to report on their implementation.

(See also p. 434.)

Russian Federation

A draft resolution [E/2004/23], introduced in the Commission on 15 April, would have expressed deep concern about human rights, the humanitarian situation and security in Chechnya. It would have called on the Russian Federation to cooperate with human rights mechanisms; facilitate the delivery of humanitarian aid; stop and prevent violations of human rights and international humanitarian law; and ensure free, unimpeded and secure access to Chechnya for international organizations, NGOs and the media. By a recorded vote of 23 votes to 12, with 18 abstentions, taken at the request of the Russian Federation, the draft was rejected.

Middle East

Lebanon

Report of Secretary-General. In response to a 2003 Commission resolution on the human rights situation of Lebanese detainees in Israel [YUN 2003, p. 825], the Secretary-General said he had asked Israel for information on the status of implementation of the resolution but had received no reply [E/CN.4/2004/28].

A March addendum to the Secretary-General's report [E/CN.4/2004/28/Add.1] stated that, on 29 January, 23 Lebanese detainees were released. He had further requested information on the extent of the implementation of the Commission's 2003 resolution but had received no reply.

Communications. On 24 March [E/CN.4/2004/G/36], Israel said that it was not holding any Lebanese detainees as so-called hostages or for bargaining purposes. It submitted a list of those currently held in Israel and the reasons for their detention. On 25 March [E/CN.4/2004/G/37], Israel submitted a list of names of some Lebanese detainees and those reorded as missing.

Commission action. On 15 April [dec. 2004/105], the Commission decided to defer to its 2005 session consideration of a draft resolution on the human rights situation of Lebanese detainees in Israel.

Territories occupied by Israel

During 2004, the question of human rights violations in the territories occupied by Israel as a result of the 1967 hostilities in the Middle East was again considered by the Commission on Human Rights. Political and other aspects were considered by the General Assembly, its Special Committee to Investigate Israeli Practices Affecting the Human Rights of the Palestinian People and Other Arabs of the Occupied Territories (Committee on Israeli Practices) and other bodies (see PART ONE, Chapter VI).

Reports of Secretary-General. In response to a 2003 Commission request [YUN 2003, p. 826], the Secretary-General reported that he had brought the Commission's resolution on the occupied Syrian Golan to the attention of all Governments, the specialized agencies, regional intergovernmental organizations and international humanitarian organizations [E/CN.4/2004/24]. It was also communicated to the Committee on Israeli Practices, the Committee on the Exercise of the Inalienable Rights of the Palestinian People (Committee on Palestinian Rights) and the United Nations Relief and Works Agency for Palestine Refugees in the Near East (UNRWA).

The Secretary-General, in a further report [E/CN.4/2004/25], submitted in response to a 2003 Commission request [YUN 2003, p. 826], said he had brought the Commission's resolution on the violation of human rights in the occupied Arab territories to the attention of the Government of Israel and all other Governments, UN organs, the specialized agencies, regional intergovernmental organizations and international humanitarian organizations, the Committee on Israeli Practices, the Committee on Palestinian Rights and UNRWA. He had received no reply from Israel.

A note of the Secretary-General [E/CN.4/2004/26] listed all General Assembly reports issued since 25 April 2003 on the situation of the population living in the occupied Arab territories.

Commission action. On 23 March [dec. 2004/102], the Commission, by a recorded vote of 34 to 3, with 14 abstentions, called for an urgent special sitting to consider the situation in the Occupied Palestinian Territory resulting from the assassination of Sheikh Ahmed Yassin on 22 March (see p. 457). At the special sitting [E/CN.4/2004/SR.18], on 24 March [res. 2004/1], by a recorded vote of 31 to 2, with 18 abstentions, the Commission strongly condemned the continuing grave human rights violations in the Territory, particularly the assassination of Sheikh Yassin. Noting with grave concern the implications of such targeted assassinations, liquidation and murder of political leadership by the Israeli occupation forces, the Commission called on Israel to respect the principles of international humanitarian law and to desist from all forms of human rights violation in the Territory.

On 15 April [res. 2004/8], by a recorded vote of 31 to 1, with 21 abstentions, the Commission called on Israel to comply with UN resolutions on the Syrian Golan and demanded that it rescind its decision to impose its laws, jurisdiction and administration on the occupied territory. It also called on Israel to desist from changing the physical character, demographic composition, institutional structure and legal status of the area and to desist from imposing Israeli citizenship and identity cards on the Syrian citizens of the Syrian Golan and from its repressive measures against them. The Secretary-General was requested to bring the Commission's resolution to the attention of all Governments, UN organs, the specialized agencies, regional intergovernmental organizations and international humanitarian organizations, to widely publicize the resolution and to report in 2005.

On 15 April [res. 2004/9], by a recorded vote of 27 to 2, with 24 abstentions, the Commission, expressing grave concern at the continued escalation of the Israeli-Palestinian conflict (see p. 453), Israeli settlement activities in the occupied territories, the restriction of freedom of movement of the Palestinians and the construction of the so-called security fence, and condemning all violent acts, including terrorist attacks, urged Israel to comply with the Commission's previous resolutions, reverse its settlement policy, prevent any new installation of settlers, implement the High Commissioner's recommendations [YUN 2000, p. 777] and guarantee the safety and protection of Palestinian civilians. The Commission demanded that Israel stop and reverse the construction of the so-called security fence. The parties

were urged to resume negotiations on a political settlement in accordance with UN resolutions.

On the same date [res. 2004/10], by a recorded vote of 31 to 7, with 15 abstentions, the Commission condemned the human rights violations of the Israeli occupation authorities in the Occupied Palestinian Territory, including East Jerusalem; the war launched by the Israeli army against Palestinian towns and camps; the practice of liquidation or extrajudicial executions carried out by the Israeli army against Palestinians; torture against Palestinians during interrogation; and the mass killing of Palestinians by the occupation authorities. The Secretary-General was asked to bring the Commission's resolution to the attention of all Governments, competent UN organs, the specialized agencies, regional intergovernmental organizations and international humanitarian organizations, to disseminate it widely and to report on its implementation by Israel in 2005. He was also asked to provide the Commission with all UN reports issued between the Commission's sessions that dealt with the conditions of the Palestinian and other Arab territories under Israeli occupation. The Special Rapporteur was requested to report to the General Assembly in 2004 and to the Commission in 2005.

On 22 July, the Economic and Social Council took note of Commission resolution 2004/10 and approved the Commission's request to the Special Rapporteur (**decision 2004/250**).

Reports of Special Rapporteur. In a February addendum [E/CN.4/2004/6/Add.1] to a report submitted in 2003 [YUN 2003, p. 826], Special Rapporteur John Dugard (South Africa), following his visit to the Occupied Palestinian Territory and Israel (8-15 February), focused on the wall being built by Israel in the West Bank, which had resulted in the creation of a zone between the Green Line (the de facto border between Israel and Palestine) and the wall inside the Occupied Palestinian Territory. He concluded that, based on evidence made available to him and the benefit of on-site inspection, the wall did not serve a legitimate security purpose when it entered into Palestinian land. Thus, it had to be seen as an instrument of annexation, in violation of international law. The wall interfered with the Palestinian right of self-determination as it substantially reduced the size of the self-determination unit within which the right was to be exercised; violated the right to freedom of movement and the rights to family life, to work, to health, to an adequate standard of living and to education; violated principles of international humanitarian law; and constituted de facto annexation of Palestinian territory by forcible means. He recommended that the Commission call on States to respond to such violations by explicit non-recognition of the acquisition of territory by forcible means occasioned by the wall and by condemning the ensuing violation of human rights and international humanitarian law. He also proposed expanding OHCHR's mandate in the region to include monitoring of human rights violations in addition to technical assistance.

An August note of the Secretary-General [A/59/256] transmitted a report of the Special Rapporteur, in response to Commission resolution 2004/10 (above), based on his visit to the Occupied Palestinian Territory (Gaza and the West Bank, 18-25 June). The report focused on the consequences of military incursions into the Gaza Strip, violations of human rights and humanitarian law arising from the construction of the wall and the pervasiveness of restrictions on freedom of movement. The Special Rapporteur pointed out that the International Court of Justice held that the wall was contrary to international law (see p. 1272). Thus, the unlawfulness of the wall was now made clear under international law. Israel was legally and morally obliged to bring its practices and policies into line with international law, said the Special Rapporteur. He reminded States of their obligation not to recognize the illegal situation resulting from the construction of the wall and not to render aid or assistance in maintaining the situation created by its construction.

On 20 December, the General Assembly took note of the report (**decision 59/528**).

(For information on a visit to the Occupied Palestinian Territory by the Special Rapporteur on violence against women, see p. 776)

Communications. Israel, in a 29 March letter [E/CN.4/2004/G/42], responding to the Special Rapporteur's February report (above), said that his allegations were based almost entirely on rumour and speculation. The report was rife with unsubstantiated and unattributed reports and made no mention of Israel's efforts to ease the impact of the wall on the lives of affected Palestinians. Referring to the Special Rapporteur's August report (above), Israel, on 25 October [E/CN.4/2005/G/9], said it distorted both fact and law, all in the service of a narrow and extreme political agenda. Israel made a number of general observations on the report.

The Commission also received communications from Palestine regarding alleged violations of human rights and the principles of international law and international humanitarian law [E/CN.4/2004/G/20, E/CN.4/2004/G/21, E/CN.4/2005/G/5].

PART THREE

Economic and social questions

Chapter I

Development policy and international economic cooperation

Global economic growth in 2004, at 4 per cent, was not only the highest for many years, but was also unusually widespread and well balanced. The broadening of the economic recovery was reflected in the fact that almost half the developing countries, accounting for over 80 per cent of the developing world's population, increased per capita output by more than 3 per cent. Per capita output also increased by more than 3 per cent in all the economies in transition except one. Among the developed countries, performance was more varied. Growth was strong in North America, moderate in Japan but weak in Europe.

Achieving the Millennium Development Goal (MDG), adopted by the General Assembly in 2000, of halving by 2015 the proportion of the world's people living in extreme poverty was a major focus of the work of several UN bodies in 2004. The high-level segment of the Economic and Social Council was devoted to the question of resource mobilization and enabling environment for poverty eradication in the context of the implementation of the Programme of Action for the Least Developed Countries (LDCs) for the Decade 2001-2010, and a ministerial declaration on the subject was adopted. The Council's coordination segment considered the promotion of rural development in developing countries, with due consideration to LDCs, for poverty eradication and sustainable development. After considering the role of microcredit and microfinance in the eradication of poverty, the Assembly adopted a December resolution in which it recognized that access to microcredit and microfinance could contribute to the achievement of the goals and targets of major UN conferences and summits in the economic and social fields, including the MDGs, and decided to devote one plenary meeting at its sixty-first (2006) session to the outcome of and follow-up to the International Year of Microcredit, 2005. The Assembly also adopted a resolution on the implementation of the first United Nations Decade for the Eradication of Poverty (1997-2006).

Reaffirming that information and communication technologies were powerful tools to foster socio-economic development and contribute to the realization of the MDGs, the Assembly endorsed the Declaration of Principles and the Plan of Action adopted at the first phase of the World Summit on the Information Society in 2003. It also took note of progress in the preparations for the second phase, to be held in 2006. The Commission on Science and Technology for Development, in May, had as its main theme the question of promoting the application of science and technology to meet the MDGs.

The Commission on Sustainable Development, in overseeing the follow-up to the 2002 World Summit on Sustainable Development, which reviewed progress in implementing Agenda 21, the action plan on sustainable development adopted by the 1992 United Nations Conference on Environment and Development, focused on the thematic cluster of water, sanitation and human settlements. It also continued preparations for the International Meeting to Review the Implementation of the 1994 Programme of Action for the Sustainable Development of Small Island Developing States (SIDS). The International Meeting, which had been scheduled to take place in 2004, was postponed until January 2005.

In addition to SIDS, other groups of countries in special situations that were of concern to the Organization during 2004 included LDCs, landlocked developing countries, economies in transition and poor mountain countries. The need for a smooth transition for countries graduating from the list of LDCs so that the graduation would not result in a disruption of development plans, programmes and projects was addressed by the Assembly, the Council and the Committee for Development Policy.

International economic relations

Development and international economic cooperation

A number of UN bodies addressed development and international economic cooperation issues during 2004, including the General Assembly and the Economic and Social Council.

On 22 December, the Assembly took note of the report of the Second (Economic and Financial) Committee on its discussion of macroeconomic policy questions [A/59/481] (**decision 59/533**).

Economic and Social Council consideration. On 26 April, the Economic and Social Council held its seventh special high-level meeting with the Bretton Woods institutions (the World Bank Group and the International Monetary Fund) and the World Trade Organization [A/59/3/Rev.1]. It had before it an 8 April note [E/2004/50] by the Secretary-General on coherence, coordination and cooperation in the context of the implementation of the Monterrey Consensus, adopted at the 2002 International Conference on Financing for Development [YUN 2002, p. 953] (see p. 978).

At its high-level segment (28-30 June and 6 July) [A/59/3/Rev.1], the Council considered resource mobilization and enabling environment for poverty eradication in the context of the implementation of the Programme of Action for the Least Developed Countries for the Decade 2001-2010 (see p. 855).

During its coordination segment (1, 2, 6, 7 and 23 July) [A/59/3/Rev.1], the Council considered a coordinated and integrated UN system approach to promoting rural development in developing countries, with due consideration to LDCs, for poverty eradication and sustainable development (see p. 839).

Globalization and interdependence

In response to General Assembly resolution 58/225 [YUN 2003, p. 832], the Secretary-General submitted a 31 August report on globalization and interdependence [A/59/312], which focused on ways to forge greater coherence in order to advance the internationally agreed development goals, including those contained in the United Nations Millennium Declaration [YUN 2000, p. 49]. The report attempted to identify the impact of globalization on various dimensions of the development goals and the areas that required greater policy coherence, and explored ways of forging policy coherence at the national, regional and global levels to address the challenges of integrating the three dimensions of development and managing the uneven impact of globalization. It was noted that the report should be read in conjunction with the reports of the Secretary-General on the implementation of the Millennium Declaration [A/59/282 & Corr.1] (see p. 1362), the international financial system and development [A/59/218] (see p. 973), the external debt crisis and development [A/59/219] (see p. 977), the state of implementation of the Monterrey Consensus [A/59/270] (see p. 979) and international trade and development and developments in the multilateral trading system [A/59/305] (see p. 959).

In the report's conclusions and recommendations, the Secretary-General observed that there were two main aspects for forging coherence in advancing the development goals in a globalizing world economy—promoting coherence among the economic, social and environmental dimensions of the goals and achieving harmony and consistency between those goals and the policies for integration into the global economy while managing the risks involved. At the national level, the challenges needed to be addressed by building stronger institutions, enhancing coordination among various parts of government, investing in economic and social infrastructure, including education and health, generating employment, providing opportunities for training and skill acquisition, addressing environmental sustainability concerns and promoting broader participation. At the regional level, the Secretary-General proposed broadening and deepening regional integration and fostering coherence through greater coordination of policies and through peer reviews. At the global level, there was a need to strengthen multilateral institutions and to enhance coordination and dialogue among them, promote consistency in aid, trade, external debt and development cooperation policies, launch policy coherence initiatives and provide policy space for developing countries, provide a forum for dialogue among policy makers dealing with the economic, social and environmental aspects of development, and facilitate broad-based participation in international decision-making.

The Assembly also had before it for consideration the reports of the World Commission on the Social Dimension of Globalization, established by the International Labour Organization (ILO), entitled *A Fair Globalization: Creating Opportunities for All* [A/59/98-E/2004/79], which it took note of by **resolution 59/57** of 2 December (see p. 1091), and of the Commission on the Private Sector and Development, established by the United Nations Development Programme (UNDP), entitled *Unleashing Entrepreneurship: Making Business Work for the Poor* [Sales No. E.04.III.B.4].

GENERAL ASSEMBLY ACTION

On 22 December [meeting 75], the General Assembly, on the recommendation of the Second Committee [A/59/485/Add.1], adopted **resolution 59/240** without vote [agenda item 87 (a)].

Role of the United Nations in promoting development in the context of globalization and interdependence

The General Assembly,

Recalling its resolutions 53/169 of 15 December 1998, 54/231 of 22 December 1999, 55/212 of 20 December 2000, 56/209 of 21 December 2001, 57/274 of 20 December 2002 and 58/225 of 23 December 2003 on the role of the United Nations in promoting development in the context of globalization and interdependence,

Recalling also its resolution 58/291 of 6 May 2004,

Reaffirming the resolve expressed in the United Nations Millennium Declaration to ensure that globalization becomes a positive force for the people of the world,

Recognizing that globalization and interdependence have opened new opportunities for the growth of the world economy and development, that globalization offers new perspectives for the integration of developing countries into the world economy and that it can improve the overall performance of the economies of developing countries by opening up market opportunities for their exports, by promoting the transfer of information, skills and technology and by increasing the financial resources available for investment in physical and intangible assets, acknowledging that globalization has also brought new challenges for growth and sustainable development and that developing countries have been facing special difficulties in responding to them, recognizing that some countries have successfully adapted to the changes and benefited from globalization but that many others, especially the least developed countries, have remained marginalized in the globalizing world economy, and recognizing also that, as stated in the Millennium Declaration, the benefits and costs of globalization are very unevenly distributed,

Recognizing also that a universal, rule-based, open, non-discriminatory and equitable multilateral trading system, as well as meaningful trade liberalization, can substantially stimulate development worldwide, benefiting countries at all stages of development, reaffirming its commitment to trade liberalization and to ensuring that trade plays its full part in promoting economic growth, employment and development for all, welcoming in that regard the decisions taken by the World Trade Organization to place the needs and interests of developing countries at the heart of its work programme, and committing itself to their implementation,

Recognizing further that all human rights are universal, indivisible, interdependent and interrelated,

Noting that an overall commitment to multiculturalism helps to provide an environment preventing and combating discrimination and promoting solidarity and tolerance in our societies,

Recognizing that an enabling economic environment should, inter alia, foster a dynamic and well-functioning business sector and include efforts to further promote good corporate and public sector governance, to combat corruption in the public and private sectors and to promote the strengthening of and respect for the rule of law,

Noting that particular attention must be given, in the context of globalization, to the objective of protecting, promoting and enhancing the rights and welfare of women and girls, as stated in the Beijing Declaration and Platform for Action,

Taking note of the report of the World Commission on the Social Dimension of Globalization entitled *A Fair Globalization: Creating Opportunities for All* as a contribution to the international dialogue towards a fully inclusive and equitable globalization,

Noting the report of the Commission on the Private Sector and Development entitled *Unleashing Entrepreneurship: Making Business Work for the Poor,*

1. *Takes note* of the report of the Secretary-General;

2. *Reaffirms* that the United Nations has a central role in promoting international cooperation for development and in promoting policy coherence on global development issues, including in the context of globalization and interdependence;

3. *Reaffirms also* that each country has primary responsibility for its own economic and social development and that the role of national policies and development strategies cannot be overemphasized;

4. *Invites* the international community, including all Member States, to devote special attention to improving resource flows for development, including public and private, foreign and domestic, to assist the developing countries, particularly the least developed countries, to achieve the internationally agreed development goals, including those contained in the United Nations Millennium Declaration;

5. *Stresses* that, in the common pursuit of growth, poverty eradication and sustainable development, a critical challenge is to ensure the necessary internal conditions for mobilizing domestic savings, both public and private, sustaining adequate levels of productive investment and increasing human capacity, while a crucial task is to enhance the efficacy, coherence and consistency of macroeconomic policies and an enabling domestic environment is vital for mobilizing domestic resources, increasing productivity, reducing capital flight, encouraging the private sector and attracting and making effective use of international investment and assistance, and in this regard stresses also that efforts to create such an environment should be supported by the international community;

6. *Underlines* the fact that, in addressing the linkages between globalization and sustainable development, particular focus should be placed on identifying and implementing mutually reinforcing policies and practices that promote sustained economic growth, social development and environmental protection and that this requires efforts at both the national and international levels;

7. *Reiterates* that success in meeting the objectives of development and poverty eradication depends, inter alia, on good governance, both within individual countries and at the international level, sound economic policies, solid democratic institutions that are responsive to the needs of the people and improved infrastructure, which are the basis for sustained growth, poverty eradication and employment creation, and that transparency in financial, monetary and trading systems and commitment to an open, equitable, rule-based, predictable and non-discriminatory multilateral trading and financial system are equally essential;

8. *Stresses* that improved coherence between national and international efforts and between the international monetary, financial and trading systems is fundamental for sound global economic governance; in this context reaffirms the commitment to improving the coherence between those systems in order to enhance their capacities to better respond to the needs of development and recognizes that the institutional di-

mension in terms of development is central; emphasizes that development should be at the centre of the international economic agenda and that coherence between national development strategies, on the one hand, and international obligations and commitments, on the other, contributes to the creation of an enabling economic environment for development; and stresses the need to broaden and strengthen the participation of developing countries and countries with economies in transition in international economic decision-making and norm-setting;

9. *Stresses also* that development strategies have to be formulated with a view to minimizing the negative social impact of globalization and maximizing its positive impact, while ensuring that all groups of the population, in particular the poorest, benefit from it, and that at the international level, efforts have to converge on the means to achieve the internationally agreed development goals, including those contained in the Millennium Declaration;

10. *Underlines* the fact that the increasing interdependence of national economies in a globalizing world and the emergence of rule-based regimes for international economic relations have meant that the space for national economic policy, i.e., the scope for domestic policies, especially in the areas of trade, investment and industrial development, is now often framed by international disciplines, commitments and global market considerations, that it is for each Government to evaluate the trade-off between the benefits of accepting international rules and commitments and the constraints posed by the loss of policy space and that it is particularly important for developing countries, bearing in mind development goals and objectives, that all countries take into account the need for appropriate balance between national policy space and international disciplines and commitments;

11. *Reaffirms* that education, employment creation and improvement of working conditions, which are some of the indispensable elements of poverty eradication, social integration, gender equality and overall development, should be at the centre of development strategies and international cooperation in support of national policies, and recognizes the need to promote employment that takes into account labour standards as defined in the relevant instruments of the International Labour Organization and other international instruments;

12. *Urges* all Governments to ensure women's equal rights with men and their full and equal access to education, training, employment, technology and economic and financial resources, including credit, in particular for rural women and women in the informal sector, and to facilitate, where appropriate, the transition of women from the informal to the formal sector;

13. *Stresses* the importance of migration as a phenomenon accompanying increased globalization, including its impact on economies, and underlines further the need for greater coordination and cooperation among countries as well as relevant regional and international organizations;

14. *Recognizes* the special needs of the least developed countries, the small island developing States and the landlocked developing countries within a new global framework for transit transport cooperation for landlocked and transit developing countries, and reaf-

firms continued support and assistance for their endeavours, particularly in their efforts to achieve the internationally agreed development goals, including those contained in the Millennium Declaration, and the implementation of the Programme of Action for the Least Developed Countries for the Decade 2001-2010, the Programme of Action for the Sustainable Development of Small Island Developing States, and the Almaty Programme of Action;

15. *Emphasizes* the importance of recognizing and addressing the specific concerns of countries with economies in transition so as to help them to benefit from globalization, with a view to their full integration into the world economy;

16. *Invites* all relevant agencies of the United Nations system, through, inter alia, the United Nations System Chief Executives Board for Coordination, within existing resources, to continue to review the impact of their work on the achievement of the internationally agreed development goals, including those contained in the Millennium Declaration;

17. *Welcomes* the decision taken by the General Council of the World Trade Organization on 1 August 2004, which rededicates and recommits members to fulfilling the development dimensions of the Doha Development Agenda, which places the needs of developing and least developed countries at the heart of the Doha work programme;

18. *Stresses* the need to build an inclusive information society, which is intrinsically global in nature, and that therefore national efforts need to be supported by effective international and regional cooperation among Governments, the private sector, civil society and other stakeholders, including the international financial institutions, in order, inter alia, to assist in bridging the digital divide, promoting access to information and communication technologies, creating digital opportunities and harnessing the potential of information and communication technologies for development, and invites the World Summit on the Information Society to encourage all stakeholders in this regard;

19. *Requests* the Secretary-General to submit to the General Assembly at its sixtieth session a report on globalization and interdependence;

20. *Decides* to include in the provisional agenda of its sixtieth session the item entitled "Globalization and interdependence".

Also on 22 December, the Assembly, by **decision 59/535**, took note of the report of the Second Committee on its consideration of the agenda item on globalization and interdependence [A/59/485].

New global human order

On 18 August [A/59/283], Guyana, in response to General Assembly resolution 57/12 [YUN 2002, p. 817], submitted a memorandum on the role of the United Nations in promoting a new global human order.

By **decision 59/543** of 23 December, the Assembly deferred consideration of the item on the role of the United Nations in promoting a new global human order and included it in the provisional agenda of its sixty-first (2006) session.

Industrial development

In response to General Assembly resolution 57/243 [YUN 2002, p. 819], the Secretary-General transmitted a July report of the Director-General of the United Nations Industrial Development Organization (UNIDO) on industrial development cooperation [A/59/138]. The report focused on the critical role of productivity factors and industrial development for the achievement of the MDGs [YUN 2000, p. 51], contained in the Millennium Declaration adopted by Assembly resolution 55/2 [ibid., p. 49], and emphasized the fact that productivity enhancement was a main factor in promoting sustained growth, which was essential for poverty alleviation. It described UNIDO's response to the challenges posed by the MDGs and how the services offered by UNIDO covered a wide range of activities related to the Goals. The report provided information on UNIDO's cooperation with other parts of the UN system in working towards the MDGs and on its programmes for Africa and LDCs, which remained at the core of UNIDO's priorities. In addition, the report summarized some of the findings of the *Industrial Development Report, 2004*, which focused on sub-Saharan Africa, and described the work of UNIDO's field offices.

The report concluded, among other things, that the poorest countries, especially in sub-Saharan Africa, posed the greatest challenges in terms of required growth rates in order to achieve the MDGs. Industrial development had a critical role to play in helping to raise growth rates and was the motivating force for applying new technologies to production and the most important source and diffuser of technological innovation. Successful industrialization helped to create the employment that poor economies needed as they released labour from agriculture. Given the critical role of industrial development for achieving the MDGs, there was a stronger need for an intergovernmental body like UNIDO to provide international public goods that promoted productivity growth. UNIDO had made a comprehensive review of its services to ensure their alignment with the requirements of the MDGs, thus enhancing the impact of its activities and their contribution to the achievement of the Goals.

Annexed to the report was an information note on the Global Biotechnology Forum, held in Concepción, Chile, in March.

GENERAL ASSEMBLY ACTION

On 22 December [meeting 75], the General Assembly, on the recommendation of the Second Committee [A/59/487/Add.3], adopted **resolution 59/249** without vote [agenda item 89 *(c)*].

Industrial development cooperation

The General Assembly,

Recalling its resolutions 46/151 of 18 December 1991, 49/108 of 19 December 1994, 51/170 of 16 December 1996, 53/177 of 15 December 1998, 55/187 of 20 December 2000 and 57/243 of 20 December 2002 on industrial development cooperation,

Recalling also the United Nations Millennium Declaration adopted by Heads of State and Government on 8 September 2000,

Reaffirming the outcomes of the Fourth Ministerial Conference of the World Trade Organization, held in Doha from 9 to 14 November 2001, the Third United Nations Conference on the Least Developed Countries, held in Brussels from 14 to 20 May 2001, the International Conference on Financing for Development, held in Monterrey, Mexico, from 18 to 22 March 2002, and the World Summit on Sustainable Development, held in Johannesburg, South Africa, from 26 August to 4 September 2002,

Recognizing the role of the business community, including the private sector, in enhancing the dynamic process of the development of the industrial sector, and underlining the importance of the benefits of foreign direct investment in that process,

Recognizing also the importance of the transfer of technology to the developing countries and countries with economies in transition as an effective means of international cooperation in the pursuit of poverty eradication and sustainable development,

Taking note of the corporate strategy of the United Nations Industrial Development Organization, which aims at, inter alia, promoting productivity growth as a means of supporting the achievement of the internationally agreed development goals, including those contained in the Millennium Declaration, and the measures being taken to operationalize this strategy,

Taking note also of the signing of the cooperation agreement between the United Nations Industrial Development Organization and the United Nations Development Programme on 23 September 2004 and that the agreement should lead to the improvement of the field presence of the United Nations Industrial Development Organization and a better fulfilment of its primary objective, which is to promote and accelerate industrial development in the developing countries while retaining its identity, visibility and core competencies, and noting that it establishes, inter alia, a basis for both institutions to develop joint technical cooperation programmes in support of private-sector development in developing countries,

Taking note further of the signing of a memorandum of technical cooperation between the United Nations Industrial Development Organization and the World Trade Organization, at Cancun, Mexico, on 10 September 2003, aiming at the joint development and implementation of trade-related technical cooperation programmes,

1. *Takes note* of the report of the Secretary-General, and welcomes the conclusions and recommendations contained therein;

2. *Reaffirms* that industrialization is an essential factor in the sustained economic growth, sustainable de-

velopment and eradication of poverty of developing countries and countries with economies in transition as well as in the creation of productive employment, income generation and the facilitation of social integration, including the integration of women into the development process;

3. *Stresses* the critical role of productive capacity-building and industrial development for the achievement of the internationally agreed development goals, including those contained in the United Nations Millennium Declaration;

4. *Takes note* of the comprehensive review of the activities of the United Nations Industrial Development Organization conducted in line with its corporate strategy, which has enabled it to become a more focused, effective and efficient organization, especially for developing countries and countries with economies in transition, capable of delivering concrete outcomes and providing valuable contributions to the achievement of the internationally agreed development goals, including those contained in the Millennium Declaration;

5. *Emphasizes* the necessity of favourable national and international measures for the industrialization of developing countries, and urges all Governments to adopt and to implement development policies and strategies to unleash the productivity growth potential through private-sector development, the diffusion of environmentally sound and emerging technologies, investment promotion, enhanced access to markets and the effective use of official development assistance to enable developing countries to achieve the internationally agreed development goals, including those contained in the Millennium Declaration, and to make this process sustainable;

6. *Underlines* the importance of industrial development cooperation and of a positive investment and business climate at the international, regional, subregional and national levels in promoting the expansion, diversification and modernization of productive capacities in developing countries, in particular the least developed countries, landlocked developing countries and countries with economies in transition;

7. *Takes note with appreciation* of the organization of the Global Biotechnology Forum, held in Concepción, Chile, from 2 to 5 March 2004, which was organized jointly by the United Nations Industrial Development Organization and the Government of Chile, with support from the International Centre for Genetic Engineering and Biotechnology, and takes note of decision IDB.28/Dec.6 of the Industrial Development Board of the United Nations Industrial Development Organization;

8. *Confirms* the contribution of industry to social development, especially in the context of the linkages between industry and agriculture, and notes that, within the totality of these interlinkages, industry serves as a powerful source of employment generation, income creation and social integration required for the eradication of poverty;

9. *Calls for* the continuing use of official development assistance for industrial development in the developing countries and countries with economies in transition, calls upon donor countries and recipient countries to continue to cooperate in their efforts to achieve greater efficiency and effectiveness of the offi-

cial development assistance resources devoted to industrial development cooperation and to support the efforts of developing countries and countries with economies in transition to promote industrial development cooperation among themselves, and underlines the importance of mobilizing funds for industrial development at the country level, including private funding and funds from relevant development finance institutions;

10. *Also calls for*, in this regard, the continuing use of all other resources, including private and public, foreign and domestic resources, for industrial development in the developing countries and countries with economies in transition;

11. *Reiterates* the importance of cooperation and coordination within the United Nations system in providing effective support for the sustainable industrial development of developing countries and countries with economies in transition, and calls upon the United Nations Industrial Development Organization to continue to carry out its central role in the field of industrial development according to its mandate;

12. *Encourages* the United Nations Industrial Development Organization to continue to enhance its effectiveness, relevance and development impact by, inter alia, strengthening its cooperation with other institutions of the United Nations system at all levels;

13. *Calls upon* the United Nations Industrial Development Organization to participate actively in coordination at the field level through the common country assessment and the United Nations Development Assistance Framework processes and sector-wide approaches;

14. *Emphasizes* the need to promote the development of microenterprises and small and medium-sized enterprises, including by means of training, education and skills enhancement, with a special focus on agroindustry as a provider of livelihoods for rural communities;

15. *Stresses* the need for the United Nations Industrial Development Organization to promote, within its mandate, the development of competitive industries in developing countries and countries with economies in transition, as well as in landlocked developing countries;

16. *Reaffirms* the need to support the survival and expansion of industrial manufacturing activity in developing countries, and in this regard calls upon the United Nations Industrial Development Organization to continue to improve its technical cooperation activities through, inter alia, the areas of technology diffusion and capacity-building for market access and development;

17. *Welcomes* the active role played by the United Nations Industrial Development Organization in the High-Level Committee on Programmes of the United Nations System Chief Executives Board for Coordination, and encourages it to continue promoting enhanced coordination and coherence within the United Nations system with a view to reinforcing the quality and relevance of the United Nations in the field of economic development;

18. *Requests* the United Nations Industrial Development Organization to facilitate industrial development with emphasis on the priority areas outlined in its medium-term programme framework, 2004-2007;

19. *Encourages* the United Nations Industrial Development Organization to increase its contributions to achieve the objectives of the New Partnership for Africa's Development with a view to further strengthening the industrialization process in Africa;

20. *Also encourages* the United Nations Industrial Development Organization to develop further its global forum capacity according to its mandate, with the aim of enhancing, in the context of the globalization process, a common understanding of global and regional industrial sector issues and their impact on poverty eradication and sustainable development, and calls for further strengthening of the demand-driven integrated programme approach at the field level.

21. *Requests* the Secretary-General to submit to the General Assembly at its sixty-first session a report on the implementation of the present resolution.

Coercive economic measures

In response to General Assembly resolution 57/5 [YUN 2002, p. 832], the Secretary-General submitted a 16 August report [A/59/266] containing replies received from 10 Governments in response to his request for information on the elimination of unilateral extraterritorial coercive economic measures as a means of political and economic compulsion.

On 23 December, the Assembly decided that the item on elimination of unilateral extraterritorial coercive economic measures as a means of political and economic compulsion would remain for consideration during its resumed fifty-ninth (2005) session (**decision 59/552**).

Economic rights and duties of States

In an 18 June report [A/59/99-E/2004/83], the Secretary-General suggested to the General Assembly and the Economic and Social Council that they consider whether the mandated quinquennial review of the implementation of the 1974 Charter of Economic Rights and Duties of States, adopted by the Assembly in resolution 3281(XXIX) [YUN 1974, p. 403], should be implicit in the overall framework of the integrated and coordinated implementation of the outcomes of, and follow-up to, major UN conferences and summits, in particular as part of the biennial high-level dialogue to monitor the implementation of the Monterrey Consensus of the 2002 International Conference on Financing for Development [YUN 2002, p. 953].

By **decision 2004/312** of 23 July, the Council deferred consideration of the Secretary-General's report to a resumed session. On 16 September, the Council took note of the Secretary-General's report and referred it to the Assembly's fifty-ninth session for action (**decision 2004/319**).

Sustainable development

Implementation of Agenda 21, the Programme for the Further Implementation of Agenda 21 and the Johannesburg Plan of Implementation

In 2004, several UN bodies, including the General Assembly, the Economic and Social Council and the Commission on Sustainable Development, considered the implementation of the outcomes of the 2002 World Summit on Sustainable Development [YUN 2002, p. 821], particularly the Johannesburg Declaration and the Plan of Implementation, which outlined actions and targets for stepping up implementation of Agenda 21—a programme of action for sustainable development worldwide, adopted at the 1992 United Nations Conference on Environment and Development [YUN 1992, p. 672]—and of the Programme for the Further Implementation of Agenda 21, adopted by the Assembly at its nineteenth special session in 1997 [YUN 1997, p. 792].

CEB consideration. In a 23 February report [E/2004/12], the Secretary-General described the work being carried out within the framework of the United Nations System Chief Executives Board for Coordination (CEB) to enhance inter-agency cooperation and coordination in the follow-up to the World Summit on Sustainable Development, focusing on collaborative arrangements relating to freshwater, water and sanitation, energy, oceans and coastal areas, and changing unsustainable patterns of consumption and production.

While the arrangements were being tailored to the different requirements of each thematic area, the key cross-cutting objectives included strengthening inter-agency participation and involvement, and enhancing system-wide synergy in support of the follow-up to the Summit and the work of the Commission on Sustainable Development. CEB's High-Level Committee on Programmes (HLCP) would keep under review the overall contribution of the UN system to Summit follow-up and would seek to ensure mutual reinforcement between that effort and inter-agency processes in the follow-up to other global conferences and the Millennium Declaration [YUN 2000, p. 49].

HLCP reviewed the Summit follow-up at its seventh (Beirut, Lebanon, 26-27 February) [CEB/2004/4] and eighth (Florence, Italy, 15-17 September) [CEB 2004/7] sessions and at an intersessional meeting (Frascati, Italy, 31 May–1 June) [CEB/2004/5].

Commission on Sustainable Development consideration. As the main body responsible for coordinating and monitoring implementation of the Summit outcomes, the Commission on Sustainable Development, at its twelfth session (New York, 14-30 April) [E/2004/29], discussed, in line with the multi-year programme adopted by the Economic and Social Council in resolution 2003/61 [YUN 2003, p. 842], the thematic cluster for the 2004-2005 implementation cycle—water; sanitation; and human settlements (see below).

The Commission had before it a February report of the Secretary-General [E/CN.17/2004/2] that provided an overview of progress towards sustainable development: a review of the implementation of Agenda 21, the Programme for the Further Implementation of Agenda 21 and the Johannesburg Plan of Implementation. It was noted that, since the World Summit in 2002, progress had been made mostly in terms of process, including capacity-building in developing countries, development of action plans and refinement of the framework for global environmental governance. However, only halting progress had been made at the international level towards addressing challenges such as that of climate change, though regional, national and local initiatives were numerous.

There were very mixed outcomes in terms of social and economic progress. On the one hand, the world's two largest countries by population had made significant strides in poverty reduction and in improving various social indicators. On the other, many other developing countries had stagnated or even experienced periods of economic crisis. Outside Asia, few were on track to meet the MDGs concerning poverty reduction, and in parts of sub-Saharan Africa, hunger remained a very serious problem. That subregion was also heavily burdened by the HIV/AIDS epidemic, which had multiple, profound implications for its socio-economic development prospects. Child mortality had fallen in the 1990s, but only accelerated progress would achieve the relevant MDGs, and maternal mortality had seen little improvement. In education, some regions had made significant progress in expanding enrolments, particularly at the secondary level, and in moving towards gender parity.

Progress had been especially slow in the international economic arena, as evidenced by the stalling of international trade negotiations (see p. 958). Also, while foreign direct investment had been considered a relatively stable source of financing to developing countries at the height of the financial crises of the late 1990s, more recently some regions had experienced sharp declines in inflows, while overseas remittances had proved more stable—at least for countries with large populations resident abroad. Bright spots were the recent increases in real official development assistance flows from member countries of the Development Assistance Committee of the Organisation for Economic Co-operation and Development, and substantially increased funding for the fight against HIV/AIDS.

A further report of the Secretary-General [E/CN.17/2004/16] discussed partnerships for sustainable development—voluntary, multi-stakeholder initiatives that were specifically linked to the implementation of commitments outlined in the Johannesburg Plan of Implementation, Agenda 21 and/or the Programme for the Further Implementation of Agenda 21. It summarized information on the 266 partnerships for sustainable development registered with the secretariat of the Commission on Sustainable Development and provided more detailed information on partnerships focusing on water, sanitation and human settlements.

In a review of the thematic issues, the Commission Chairman summarized the opening statements and the oral reports by delegations on the outcomes of seven intersessional events held in preparation for the session.

Intersessional events. The Commission had before it reports on the following intersessional events that were held in preparation for its twelfth session: International Expert Meeting on a 10-Year Framework of Programmes for Sustainable Consumption and Production (Marrakech, Morocco, 16-19 June 2003) [E/CN.17/2004/11]; International Freshwater Forum (Dushanbe, Tajikistan, 29 August–1 September 2003) [A/58/362]; Workshop on Governance for World Summit on Sustainable Development Implementation in Countries with Economies in Transition (Istanbul, Turkey, 16-18 September 2003) [E/CN.17/2004/13]; international conference on the theme "Water for the poorest" (Stavanger, Norway, 4-5 November 2003) [E/CN.17/2004/14]; International Forum on Partnerships for Sustainable Development (Rome, Italy, 4-6 March 2004) [E/CN.17/2004/15]; United Nations Asia-Pacific Leadership Forum: Sustainable Development for Cities (Hong Kong, China, 25-26 February 2004) [E/CN.17/2004/19]; and the eighth special session of the United Nations Environment Programme Governing Council and the Global Ministerial Environment Forum (Jeju, Republic of Korea, 29-31 March 2004) [A/59/25] (see p. 1036).

Thematic issues. For its consideration of the thematic issues to be considered in 2004 and 2005 (water, sanitation and human settlements), as established in the multi-year programme of work adopted by the Economic and Social Council in resolution 2003/61 [YUN 2003, p. 842], the Commission on Sustainable Development had before it reports of the Secretary-General on progress in meeting the goals, targets and commitments of Agenda

21, the Programme for the Further Implementation of Agenda 21 and the Johannesburg Plan of Implementation covering freshwater management [E/CN.17/2004/4], sanitation [E/CN.17/2004/5] and human settlements [E/CN.17/2004/6]. It also considered discussion papers reflecting the views of major groups (youth and children; business and industry; the scientific and technological community; indigenous people; farmers' organizations; non-governmental organizations (NGOs); workers and trade unions; local authorities; women) on the status of implementation of commitments made related to the thematic areas [E/CN.17/2004/10 & Add.1-9]. The Commission also considered reports on the outcomes of regional implementation meetings [E/CN.17/2004/7 & Add.1-5], organized by the five UN regional commissions, to contribute to advancing the implementation of Agenda 21, the Programme for the Further Implementation of Agenda 21 and the Johannesburg Plan of Implementation, focusing on the thematic cluster of issues: African Regional Implementation Meeting (Addis Ababa, Ethiopia, 8-12 December 2003); Regional Implementation Meeting for Asia and the Pacific (Bangkok, Thailand, 27-28 October 2003); Regional Implementation Forum on Sustainable Development within the Economic Commission for Europe region (Geneva, 15-16 January 2004); three regional meetings in the Latin America and the Caribbean region (La Paz, Bolivia, 5-7 November 2003; Santiago, Chile, 17-18 November 2003; Panama City, 20-25 November 2003); and the Joint Committee on Environment and Development in the Arab World (Cairo, Egypt, 19-21 October 2003).

Implementation activities

In response to General Assembly resolution 58/218 [YUN 2003, p. 840], the Secretary-General submitted an August report on the implementation of Agenda 21, the Programme for the Further Implementation of Agenda 21 and the outcomes of the World Summit on Sustainable Development [A/59/220], which provided an update on actions taken by Governments, organizations and bodies of the UN system and major groups to ensure the effective implementation of and follow-up to the commitments and time-bound goals and targets in the area of sustainable development, including through partnerships for sustainable development.

The report showed that there was encouraging progress at all levels in pursuing sustainable development. At the intergovernmental level, the Commission on Sustainable Development, at its twelfth session, carried out an in-depth review of water, sanitation and human settlements, and en-

hanced the understanding of priority concerns by identifying key constraints and obstacles in implementation. Within the UN system, efforts to ensure a coordinated follow-up to the World Summit were bearing concrete results. At the regional level, there was great support for a regional implementation track to complement global action and, at the national level, the sharper focus on implementation established at the Summit was inspiring Governments to take renewed action in various areas. Over 50 countries had submitted national information on such action to the Commission's twelfth session and the composite picture emerging from those updates pointed to a strong commitment to implementation.

The report concluded that the challenge ahead was to sustain the momentum by tackling the policy options and possible actions required to address constraints and obstacles in implementation. The international community needed to transform the mutual accountability and the spirit of global partnership between developed and developing countries into concrete results. To that end, the Secretary-General made a number of recommendations for action by the Assembly (see below).

GENERAL ASSEMBLY ACTION

On 22 December [meeting 75], the General Assembly, on the recommendation of the Second Committee [A/59/483/Add.1], adopted **resolution 59/227** without vote [agenda item 85 *(a)*].

Implementation of Agenda 21, the Programme for the Further Implementation of Agenda 21 and the outcomes of the World Summit on Sustainable Development

The General Assembly,

Recalling its resolutions 55/199 of 20 December 2000, 56/226 of 24 December 2001, 57/253 of 20 December 2002 and 57/270 A and B of 20 December 2002 and 23 June 2003, respectively, as well as its resolution 58/218 of 23 December 2003,

Recalling also the Rio Declaration on Environment and Development, Agenda 21, the Programme for the Further Implementation of Agenda 21, the Johannesburg Declaration on Sustainable Development and the Plan of Implementation of the World Summit on Sustainable Development ("Johannesburg Plan of Implementation"),

Reaffirming the commitment to implement Agenda 21, the Programme for the Further Implementation of Agenda 21, the Johannesburg Plan of Implementation, including the time-bound goals and targets, and the other internationally agreed development goals, including those contained in the United Nations Millennium Declaration,

Recalling the outcomes of the major United Nations conferences and summits, including the Monterrey Consensus of the International Conference on Financing for Development,

Reaffirming the continuing need to ensure a balance between economic development, social development and environmental protection as interdependent and mutually reinforcing pillars of sustainable development,

Reaffirming also that eradicating poverty, changing unsustainable patterns of production and consumption and protecting and managing the natural resource base of economic and social development are overarching objectives of and essential requirements for sustainable development,

Recognizing that good governance within each country and at the international level is essential for sustainable development,

Noting with satisfaction that the Commission on Sustainable Development at its twelfth session undertook an in-depth evaluation of progress in implementing Agenda 21, the Programme for the Further Implementation of Agenda 21 and the Johannesburg Plan of Implementation, focusing on the thematic cluster of issues on water, sanitation and human settlements, and identified best practices, constraints and obstacles in the process of implementation,

Noting that the organization of work of the twelfth session of the Commission included plenary sessions, an interactive plenary dialogue and regional meetings, as well as a partnership fair, learning centres and side events,

Recalling the decision of the Commission at its eleventh session, endorsed by the Economic and Social Council in its resolution 2003/61 of 25 July 2003, that the Commission, at its policy sessions, to be held in April/May of the second year of the cycle, would take policy decisions on practical measures and options to expedite implementation in the selected thematic cluster of issues, taking account of the discussions of the intergovernmental preparatory meeting, the reports of the Secretary-General and other relevant inputs,

Recalling also the decision of the Commission at its eleventh session that the discussions of the intergovernmental preparatory meeting would be based on the outcome of the review session and reports of the Secretary-General, as well as other relevant inputs, and that, on the basis of those discussions, the Chair would prepare a draft negotiating document for consideration at the policy session,

Looking forward to the upcoming cycles of the work programme of the Commission as adopted at its eleventh session and their contributions to the further implementation of Agenda 21, the Programme for the Further Implementation of Agenda 21 and the outcomes of the World Summit on Sustainable Development,

1. *Takes note* of the report of the Secretary-General on the activities undertaken in the implementation of Agenda 21, the Programme for the Further Implementation of Agenda 21 and the outcomes of the World Summit on Sustainable Development;

2. *Reiterates* that sustainable development is a key element of the overarching framework for United Nations activities, in particular for achieving the internationally agreed development goals, including those contained in the United Nations Millennium Declaration and in the Johannesburg Plan of Implementation;

3. *Calls upon* Governments, all relevant international and regional organizations, the Economic and Social Council, the United Nations funds and pro-grammes, the regional commissions and specialized agencies, the international financial institutions, the Global Environment Facility and other intergovernmental organizations, in accordance with their respective mandates, as well as major groups, to take action to ensure the effective implementation of and follow-up to the commitments, programmes and time-bound targets adopted at the World Summit on Sustainable Development, and encourages them to report on concrete progress in that regard;

4. *Calls for* the implementation of the commitments, programmes and time-bound targets adopted at the Summit and, to that end, for the fulfilment of the provisions relating to the means of implementation, as contained in the Johannesburg Plan of Implementation;

5. *Encourages* Governments to participate, at the appropriate level, with representatives from the relevant departments and agencies in water, sanitation and human settlements, as well as finance, in the intergovernmental preparatory meeting and the thirteenth session of the Commission on Sustainable Development;

6. *Recalls* the decision of the Commission at its eleventh session to invite the regional commissions, in collaboration with the secretariat of the Commission, to consider organizing regional implementation meetings in order to contribute to the work of the Commission, and in this regard urges the regional commissions to take into account the relevant thematic clusters contained in the programme of work of the Commission and to provide inputs as specified by the Commission at its eleventh session;

7. *Recalls also* the decision of the Commission at its eleventh session that activities during Commission meetings should provide for the balanced involvement of participants from all regions, as well as for gender balance;

8. *Welcomes* the contributions of the regional commissions to the work of the Commission at its twelfth session, including the regional meetings focusing on the thematic cluster of issues on water, sanitation and human settlements, and their inputs to the reports of the Secretary-General;

9. *Invites* donor countries to consider supporting the participation of experts from the developing countries in the areas of water, sanitation and human settlements in the thirteenth session of the Commission;

10. *Takes note with interest* of the establishment of the Advisory Board on Water and Sanitation by the Secretary-General, and looks forward to its contribution to the mobilization of efforts and resources towards the implementation of the commitments, goals and targets agreed upon in these areas;

11. *Requests* the Secretary-General, in reporting to the Commission at its thirteenth session on the state of the implementation of Agenda 21, the Programme for the Further Implementation of Agenda 21 and the Johannesburg Plan of Implementation, on the basis of appropriate inputs from all levels, to submit thematic reports on each of the three issues contained in the thematic cluster of issues on water, sanitation and human settlements, taking into account their interlinkages, while addressing the cross-cutting issues identified by the Commission at its eleventh session;

12. *Requests* the Commission, in accordance with General Assembly resolution 47/191 of 22 December

1992 and as specified by the Commission at its eleventh session, to examine the cross-cutting issues related to the thematic cluster of issues on water, sanitation and human settlements;

13. *Stresses* the importance of the success of the Commission at its thirteenth session in:

(a) Taking policy decisions on practical measures and options to expedite implementation in the thematic cluster of issues on water, sanitation and human settlements;

(b) Mobilizing further action by all implementation actors to overcome obstacles and constraints in the implementation of Agenda 21, the Programme for the Further Implementation of Agenda 21 and the Johannesburg Plan of Implementation;

14. *Takes note* of the report of the Secretary-General on inter-agency cooperation, and requests him to continue his efforts to strengthen system-wide inter-agency cooperation and coordination for the implementation of Agenda 21, the Programme for the Further Implementation of Agenda 21 and the Johannesburg Plan of Implementation, and in this regard to report on such inter-agency cooperation and coordination activities and their terms of reference to the Economic and Social Council in 2005;

15. *Recalls* its resolution 58/291 of 6 May 2004 and Economic and Social Council resolutions 2004/44 of 22 July 2004 and 2004/63 of 23 July 2004, and in this regard requests the Commission, without prejudice to the decisions adopted at its eleventh session, to contribute through the Council to the high-level plenary meeting of the General Assembly in 2005, in accordance with the modalities to be set out by the Assembly at its fifty-ninth session;

16. *Requests* the secretariat of the Commission to make arrangements to facilitate the balanced representation of major groups from developed and developing countries in the sessions of the Commission;

17. *Notes* the convening of the second international expert meeting on a ten-year framework of programmes for sustainable consumption and production, to be held in Costa Rica in September 2005, and in this regard, while acknowledging their ongoing support, urges Member States to consider further support for those activities;

18. *Encourages* Governments and organizations at all levels, as well as major groups, including the scientific community and educators, to undertake results-oriented initiatives and activities to support the work of the Commission and to promote and facilitate the implementation of Agenda 21, the Programme for the Further Implementation of Agenda 21 and the Johannesburg Plan of Implementation, including through voluntary multi-stakeholder partnership initiatives;

19. *Decides* to include in the provisional agenda of its sixtieth session the item entitled "Implementation of Agenda 21, the Programme for the Further Implementation of Agenda 21 and the outcomes of the World Summit on Sustainable Development", and requests the Secretary-General, at that session, to submit a report on the implementation of the present resolution.

Commission on Sustainable Development

The Commission on Sustainable Development held its twelfth session in New York on 9 May

2003 and from 14 to 30 April 2004 [E/2004/29]. On 30 April, the Commission held the first meeting of its thirteenth session, at which it elected the members of its Bureau [E/2005/29]. The high-level segment of the twelfth session focused on the thematic cluster for the implementation cycle of Agenda 21, the Programme for the Further Implementation of Agenda 21 and the Johannesburg Plan of Implementation, 2004-2005: water; sanitation; and human settlements (see p. 828). The Commission discussed preparations for the International Meeting to Review the Implementation of the Programme of Action for the Sustainable Development of Small Island Developing States (SIDS) (see p. 858). A partnerships fair was held during the session, during which six interactive discussion sessions took place.

In addition to the reports on the review of Agenda 21 and preparations for the International Meeting on SIDS, the Commission had before it a report of the Secretary-General on progress in implementing its decisions related to improvements in national reporting and further work on indicators of sustainable development [E/CN.17/2004/17] and a note by the Secretary-General on the proposed strategic framework for 2006-2007 [E/CN.17/2004/18]. By a 13 April note [E/CN.17/2004/20], the Secretary-General drew the Commission's attention to his report on human rights and the environment as part of sustainable development, which was submitted to the Commission on Human Rights [E/CN.4/2004/87] (see p. 768).

ECONOMIC AND SOCIAL COUNCIL ACTION

On 6 February, by **decision 2004/212**, the Economic and Social Council decided that, subject to their approval by the Council, NGOs and other major groups accredited to the 2002 World Summit on Sustainable Development [YUN 2002, p. 821] could participate in the first two-year implementation cycle of the Commission on Sustainable Development in accordance with the rules of procedure of the Council's functional commissions. The Council emphasized that the decision was taken on an exceptional basis and that it applied to those NGOs that had submitted their applications for consultative status with the Council or that expressed their wish to participate in the first two-year implementation cycle. The Council decided that the established UN rules of procedure on the accreditation and participation of NGOs and other major groups in the work of the Council and its subsidiary bodies would apply to NGOs and other major groups accredited to the World Summit that wished to participate in future sessions of the Commission beyond the first two-year cycle, stressing, in that context, that early submission of applications to the Committee on Non-Governmental Organizations would enhance the possibility of their review in time for the Commission's future sessions. The Committee on Non-Governmental Organizations was invited to consider such applications, in accordance with the rules of procedure, as expeditiously as possible, and the Secretary-General was asked to make the Council's decision widely known in order to facilitate the involvement of NGOs from all regions and areas of the world.

On 13 February (**decision 2004/216**), the Council adopted the list of NGOs and other major groups accredited to the World Summit for participation in the Commission's twelfth and thirteenth sessions, in accordance with the provisions set forth in decision 2004/212.

Also on 13 February (**decision 2004/214**), the Council took note of the decision adopted by the Commission on Sustainable Development in 2003 [YUN 2003, p. 842], by which it asked the Council to consider the term of the Commission's Bureau for future sessions, taking into account the Commission's two-year work cycle, and decided to give further consideration to the term of the Bureau for future sessions after the completion of the first two-year implementation cycle in 2005.

The Council, on 20 July, took note of the report of the Commission on its twelfth session [E/2004/29] and approved the provisional agenda for the thirteenth (2005) session (**decision 2004/234**).

Education for sustainable development

In accordance with resolution 58/219 [YUN 2003, p. 848], the General Assembly, in the Second Committee, considered the question of the United Nations Decade of Education for Sustainable Development (2005-2014), proclaimed by the Assembly in resolution 57/254 [YUN 2002, p. 826]. The Committee, on 18 October [A/C.2/59/SR.14], heard an oral report by the Assistant Director-General for Education of the United Nations Educational, Scientific and Cultural Organization (UNESCO)—the lead agency for promoting the Decade—regarding preparations. It also considered the report of the Secretary-General on implementation of the International Strategy for Disaster Reduction [A/59/228], adopted in 1999 [YUN 1999, p. 859], particularly with reference to the need to focus on education and awareness (see also p. 945).

GENERAL ASSEMBLY ACTION

On 22 December [meeting 75], the General Assembly, on the recommendation of the Second Committee [A/59/483/Add.7], adopted **resolution 59/237** without vote [agenda item 85 (g)].

United Nations Decade of Education for Sustainable Development

The General Assembly,

Recalling chapter 36 of Agenda 21, on promoting education, public awareness and training, adopted at the United Nations Conference on Environment and Development, held in Rio de Janeiro, Brazil, from 3 to 14 June 1992,

Recalling also the work programme on education, public awareness and training initiated by the Commission on Sustainable Development at its fourth session in 1996 and elaborated upon at its sixth session in 1998,

Recalling further the relevant provisions of the Plan of Implementation of the World Summit on Sustainable Development ("Johannesburg Plan of Implementation") on education to promote sustainable development, in particular its provision 124,

Recalling its resolutions 57/254 of 20 December 2002 and 58/219 of 23 December 2003,

Underlining in this regard the fact that the United Nations Decade of Education for Sustainable Development will begin on 1 January 2005,

Welcoming the fact that the Commission on Sustainable Development, at its eleventh session, identified education as one of the cross-cutting issues of its multiyear programme of work,

Reaffirming the internationally agreed development goal of achieving universal primary education, in particular that by 2015 children everywhere, boys and girls alike, will be able to complete a full course of primary schooling and that boys and girls will have equal access to all levels of education,

Taking note of the oral report presented on 18 October 2004 at the fifty-ninth session of the General Assembly by the Assistant Director-General for Education of the United Nations Educational, Scientific and Cultural Organization regarding its preparations for the Decade,

Taking note also of the report of the Secretary-General on the implementation of the International Strategy for Disaster Reduction, in particular the reference to the issue "Learning to live with risk", as regards the need to focus on education and awareness, linked with the Decade, to be considered at the World Conference on Disaster Reduction, to be held in Kobe, Japan, from 18 to 22 January 2005,

Emphasizing that education is an indispensable element for achieving sustainable development,

1. *Reaffirms* that education for sustainable development is critical for promoting sustainable development;

2. *Requests* the United Nations Educational, Scientific and Cultural Organization, as the designated lead agency, to promote the United Nations Decade of Education for Sustainable Development, in coordination with other relevant United Nations organizations and programmes, while taking into account the special needs of developing countries;

3. *Requests* the Secretary-General to call upon the United Nations Educational, Scientific and Cultural Organization to finalize the draft international implementation scheme for the Decade as soon as possible,

preferably by the beginning of the Decade, in consultation with Governments, the United Nations and relevant international organizations, non-governmental organizations and other stakeholders, while clarifying its relationship with the existing educational processes, in particular the Dakar Framework for Action adopted at the World Education Forum and the United Nations Literacy Decade;

4. *Also requests* the Secretary-General to call upon the Director-General of the United Nations Educational, Scientific and Cultural Organization to submit the draft international implementation scheme to the governing bodies of the United Nations Educational, Scientific and Cultural Organization for their final consideration and adoption;

5. *Encourages* Governments to consider the inclusion, especially upon completion and adoption of the international implementation scheme, of measures to implement the Decade in their respective educational systems and strategies and, where appropriate, national development plans;

6. *Invites* Governments to promote public awareness of and wider participation in the Decade, inter alia, through cooperation with and initiatives engaging civil society and other relevant stakeholders, especially at the beginning of the Decade;

7. *Requests* the Secretary-General to invite the Director-General of the United Nations Educational, Scientific and Cultural Organization to prepare a mid-term review of the implementation of the Decade, for submission to the General Assembly at its sixty-fifth session under the sub-item entitled "United Nations Decade of Education for Sustainable Development".

Tourism

On 13 September, the General Assembly decided to consider the report of the Secretary-General on the implementation of resolution 56/212 [YUN 2001, p. 752] on the Global Code of Ethics for Tourism, which was adopted by the General Assembly of the World Tourism Organization in 1999, at its sixtieth (2005) session, instead of at its fifty-ninth session (**decision 58/573**).

Triennial review

By a March note [E/AC.51/2004/4], the Secretary-General transmitted to the Committee for Programme and Coordination (CPC) the report of the Office of Internal Oversight Services (OIOS) on the triennial review of the implementation of the recommendations made by CPC in 2001 [YUN 2001, p. 748] on the in-depth evaluation of sustainable development.

OIOS concluded that progress had been made over the preceding three years towards promoting and strengthening the sustainable development agenda. The Division for Sustainable Development of the Department of Economic and Social Affairs, together with the Department of Public Information, had increased access to information by both government representatives and the public. The quality of that information had also improved. Through its regional and global meetings, the Division had facilitated the exchange of national experiences and provided guidance for national sustainable development strategies. It had also provided technical assistance to countries. However, greater efforts were needed to address a number of issues, including continuing dissemination of the concept of sustainable development, efforts to streamline national reporting, further facilitation and support of national Governments' monitoring of their own sustainable development strategies and strengthening of the Division's technical cooperation programme. The Secretary-General concurred with those recommendations.

At its forty-fourth session (New York, 7 June–2 July) [A/59/16], CPC recommended approval of the triennial review's recommendations. It stressed the need for the Division for Sustainable Development to enhance efforts to ensure that a common understanding of sustainable development, incorporating its social, economic and environmental pillars, was achieved in accordance with General Assembly resolution 57/253 [YUN 2002, p. 825]. CPC emphasized that the Division should focus on promoting multisectoral approaches in the area of sustainable development and stressed that achieving sustainable development objectives depended on the effective collection and analysis of data on national progress towards goals in the social, economic and environmental areas.

Eradication of poverty

UN Decade for Eradication of Poverty

In response to General Assembly resolution 58/222 [YUN 2003, p. 849], the Secretary-General submitted a September report and October addendum [A/59/326 & Add.1] on the implementation of the first United Nations Decade for the Eradication of Poverty (1997-2006) and on preparations for the International Year of Microcredit, 2005 (see p. 837).

In view of the upcoming International Year of Microcredit, the report discussed the implementation of the Decade through the lens of microcredit and microfinance, highlighting the increasing recognition of the important role that they could play in poverty eradication strategies. It provided a brief overview of the contribution of microcredit and microfinance to poverty reduction and the achievement of the MDGs. The report also examined the challenges to the future growth, expansion and outreach of the microfinance sector, while discussing the policies and programmes needed to provide greater access by poor people to microcredit and microfinance and to promote sustainable microfinance institutions.

For its consideration of the implementation of the Decade, the Assembly also had before it the report of the Commission on the Private Sector and Development entitled *Unleashing Entrepreneurship: Making Business Work for the Poor* [Sales No. E.04.III.B.4].

GENERAL ASSEMBLY ACTION

On 22 December [meeting 75], the General Assembly, on the recommendation of the Second Committee [A/59/487/Add.1], adopted **resolution 59/247** without vote [agenda item 89 *(a)*].

Implementation of the first United Nations Decade for the Eradication of Poverty (1997-2006)

The General Assembly,

Recalling its resolutions 47/196 of 22 December 1992, 48/183 of 21 December 1993, 50/107 of 20 December 1995, 56/207 of 21 December 2001, 57/265 and 57/266 of 20 December 2002 and 58/222 of 23 December 2003,

Recalling also the United Nations Millennium Declaration, adopted by Heads of State and Government on the occasion of the Millennium Summit, and their commitment to eradicate extreme poverty and to halve, by 2015, the proportion of the world's people whose income is less than one dollar a day and the proportion of people who suffer from hunger,

Underlining the priority and urgency given by the Heads of State and Government to the eradication of poverty, as expressed in the Monterrey Consensus of the International Conference on Financing for Development and in the outcomes of the World Summit on Sustainable Development,

Recalling the outcomes of the major United Nations conferences and summits in the economic and social fields,

Bearing in mind the outcomes of the World Summit for Social Development and the twenty-fourth special session of the General Assembly,

Expressing its deep concern that the number of people living in extreme poverty in many countries continues to increase, with women and children constituting the majority and the most affected groups, in particular in the least developed countries and in sub-Saharan Africa,

Welcoming the initiative launched by the Presidents of Brazil, Chile and France and the Prime Minister of Spain, with the support of the Secretary-General, to convene in New York on 20 September 2004 the Summit of World Leaders for Action against Hunger and Poverty,

Noting the report of the Commission on Private Sector and Development entitled *Unleashing Entrepreneurship: Making Business Work for the Poor,*

Reiterating the need to strengthen the leadership role of the United Nations in promoting development,

1. *Takes note* of the report of the Secretary-General;

2. *Reiterates* that eradicating poverty is the greatest global challenge facing the world today and an indispensable requirement for sustainable development, in particular for developing countries;

3. *Underlines* the fact that each country has the primary responsibility for its own sustainable development and poverty eradication, that the role of national policies and development strategies cannot be overemphasized, and that concerted and concrete measures are required at all levels to enable developing countries to eradicate poverty and achieve sustainable development;

4. *Acknowledges* that sustained economic growth, supported by rising productivity and a favourable environment, including for private investment and entrepreneurship, is necessary to eradicate poverty, achieve the internationally agreed development goals, including those contained in the United Nations Millennium Declaration, and realize a rise in living standards;

5. *Reaffirms* the importance of the contributions and assistance of developing countries to the other developing countries in the context of South-South cooperation in order to achieve development and eradicate poverty;

6. *Recognizes* that, for developing countries to reach the targets set in the context of national development strategies for the achievement of the internationally agreed development goals, including those contained in the Millennium Declaration, in particular the goal on the eradication of poverty, and for such poverty eradication strategies to be effective, it is imperative that developing countries be integrated into the world economy and share equitably in the benefits of globalization;

7. *Reaffirms* that, within the context of overall action for the eradication of poverty, special attention should be given to the multidimensional nature of poverty and the national and international conditions and policies that are conducive to its eradication, fostering, inter alia, the social and economic integration of people living in poverty and the promotion and protection of all human rights and fundamental freedoms for all, including the right to development;

Global response for the eradication of poverty

8. *Stresses* the importance of the follow-up to the outcome of the International Conference on Financing for Development, and calls for the full and effective implementation of the Monterrey Consensus;

9. *Reaffirms* that good governance at the international level is fundamental for achieving poverty eradication and sustainable development; that, in order to ensure a dynamic and enabling international economic environment, it is important to promote global economic governance through addressing the international finance, trade, technology and investment patterns that have an impact on the development prospects of developing countries; that, to that end, the international community should take all necessary and appropriate measures, including ensuring support for structural and macroeconomic reform, a comprehensive solution to the external debt problem and increasing market access for developing countries; that efforts to reform the international financial architecture need to be sustained, with greater transparency and the effective participation of developing countries in

decision-making processes; and that a universal, rule-based, open, non-discriminatory and equitable multilateral trading system, as well as meaningful trade liberalization, can substantially stimulate development worldwide, benefiting countries at all stages of development;

10. *Also reaffirms* that good governance at the national level is essential for poverty eradication and sustainable development; that sound economic policies, solid democratic institutions responsive to the needs of the people and improved infrastructure are the basis for sustained economic growth, poverty eradication and employment creation; and that freedom, peace and security, domestic stability, respect for human rights, including the right to development, and the rule of law, gender equality, market-oriented policies and an overall commitment to just and democratic societies are also essential and mutually reinforcing;

11. *Welcomes* the outcomes of the eleventh session of the United Nations Conference on Trade and Development, held in São Paulo, Brazil, from 13 to 18 June 2004, and the adoption of The Spirit of São Paulo and the São Paulo Consensus;

12. *Recognizes* the major role that trade plays as an engine of growth and development and in eradicating poverty, and welcomes the adoption by the General Council of the World Trade Organization of its decision of 1 August 2004, in which the members rededicated and recommitted themselves to fulfilling the development dimensions of the Doha Development Agenda, which places the needs and interests of developing and least developed countries at the heart of the Doha work programme;

13. *Also recognizes* that fighting corruption at all levels is a priority and that corruption is a serious barrier to effective resource mobilization and allocation and diverts resources from activities that are vital for poverty eradication, the fight against hunger and economic and sustainable development;

14. *Underlines* the fact that, together with coherent and consistent domestic policies, international cooperation is essential in supplementing and supporting the efforts of developing countries to utilize their domestic resources for development and poverty eradication and in ensuring that they will be able to achieve the development goals as envisioned in the Millennium Declaration;

15. *Welcomes* the recent increase in official development assistance, and reiterates that a substantial increase in official development assistance and other resources will be required if developing countries, in particular the least developed countries, are to achieve the internationally agreed development goals and objectives, including those contained in the Millennium Declaration, and that to build support for official development assistance, cooperation is necessary to further improve policies and development strategies to enhance aid effectiveness, both nationally and internationally;

16. *Stresses* the importance of enhanced and predictable financing to ensure the sustainability of the development and poverty eradication efforts of developing countries;

17. *Urges* developed countries that have not done so to make concrete efforts to reach the targets of 0.7 per cent of their gross national product as official development assistance to developing countries and 0.15 to 0.20 per cent of their gross national product to least developed countries, as reconfirmed at the Third United Nations Conference on the Least Developed Countries, held in Brussels from 14 to 20 May 2001, encourages developing countries to build on progress achieved in ensuring that official development assistance is used effectively to help to achieve development goals and targets, acknowledges the efforts of all donors, commends those donors whose official development assistance contributions exceed, reach or are increasing towards the targets, and underlines the importance of undertaking to examine the means and time frames for achieving the targets and goals;

18. *Recalls* the decision to give further consideration to the subject of possible innovative and additional sources of financing for development from all sources, public and private, domestic and external, taking into account international efforts, contributions and discussions, within the overall inclusive framework of the follow-up to the International Conference on Financing for Development;

19. *Recognizes* that an enabling domestic environment is vital for mobilizing domestic resources, increasing productivity, reducing capital flight, encouraging the private sector and attracting and making effective use of international investment and assistance, and that efforts to create such an environment should be supported by the international community;

20. *Also recognizes* that creditors and debtors must share the responsibility for preventing and resolving unsustainable debt situations and that debt relief can play a key role in liberating resources that should be directed towards activities consistent with attaining poverty eradication, sustainable economic growth and sustainable development and achieving the internationally agreed development goals, including those contained in the Millennium Declaration, and in this regard urges countries to direct those resources freed through debt relief, in particular through debt cancellation and reduction, towards these objectives;

21. *Calls upon* the developed countries, by means of intensified and effective cooperation with developing countries, to promote capacity-building and facilitate access to and transfer of technologies and corresponding knowledge, in particular to developing countries, on favourable terms, including concessional and preferential terms, as mutually agreed, taking into account the need to protect intellectual property rights, as well as the special needs of developing countries;

22. *Recognizes* the crucial role that microfinance and microcredit could play in the eradication of poverty, the promotion of gender equality, the empowerment of vulnerable groups and the development of rural communities, invites Member States to consider undertaking policies to facilitate the expansion of microfinance and microcredit institutions in order to service the large unmet demand among poor people for financial services, including the identification and development of mechanisms to promote sustainable access to financial services, the removal of institutional and regulatory obstacles and the provision of incentives to microfinance institutions that meet national standards for delivering such financial services to the poor;

23. *Also recognizes* the potential of information and communication technologies to serve as a powerful tool for development and poverty eradication and to help the international community to maximize the benefits of globalization, and welcomes in this regard the holding of the first phase of the World Summit on the Information Society from 10 to 12 December 2003 in Geneva and the offer of Tunisia to host the second phase in Tunis from 16 to 18 November 2005;

Policies for the eradication of poverty

24. *Reaffirms* that the eradication of poverty should be addressed in an integrated way, as set out in the Plan of Implementation of the World Summit on Sustainable Development ("Johannesburg Plan of Implementation"), taking into account the importance of the need for the empowerment of women and sectoral strategies in such areas as education, the development of human resources, health, human settlements, rural, local and community development, productive employment, population, environment and natural resources, water and sanitation, agriculture, food security, energy and migration and the specific needs of disadvantaged and vulnerable groups in such a way as to increase opportunities and choices for people living in poverty and to enable them to build and to strengthen their assets so as to achieve development, security and stability, and in that regard encourages countries to develop their national poverty reduction policies in accordance with their national priorities, including, where appropriate, through poverty reduction strategy papers;

25. *Underlines*, in this context, the importance of further integration of the internationally agreed development goals, including those contained in the Millennium Declaration, in the national development strategies and plans, including the poverty reduction strategy papers where they exist, and calls upon the international community to continue to support developing countries in the implementation of these development strategies and plans;

26. *Recognizes* the importance of disseminating best practices for the reduction of poverty in its various dimensions, taking into account the need to adapt those best practices to suit the social, economic, cultural and historical conditions of each country;

27. *Reaffirms* that all Governments and the United Nations system should promote an active and visible policy of mainstreaming a gender perspective in all policies and programmes aimed at the eradication of poverty, at both the national and international levels, and encourages the use of gender analysis as a tool for the integration of a gender dimension into planning the implementation of policies, strategies and programmes for the eradication of poverty;

28. *Also reaffirms* that poverty eradication, changing unsustainable patterns of production and consumption and protecting and managing the natural resource base of economic and social development are overarching objectives of, and essential requirements for, sustainable development;

29. *Emphasizes* the critical role of both formal and non-formal education, in particular basic education and training, especially for girls, in empowering those living in poverty, reaffirms in that context the Dakar Framework for Action adopted at the World Education Forum, and recognizes the importance of the United Nations Educational, Scientific and Cultural Organization strategy for the eradication of poverty, especially extreme poverty, in supporting the Education For All programmes as a tool to achieve the Millennium Development Goal on universal primary education by 2015;

30. *Recognizes* the devastating effect of HIV/AIDS, malaria, tuberculosis and other infectious, contagious diseases on human development, economic growth, food security and poverty reduction efforts in all regions, in particular in sub-Saharan Africa, and urges Governments and the international community to give urgent priority to combating those diseases;

31. *Also recognizes* that HIV/AIDS continues to exact a devastating toll on individuals and families, in particular women and girls, and that in the hardest-hit countries it threatens decades of health, economic and social progress, reducing life expectancy, slowing economic growth, deepening poverty and contributing to chronic food shortages; that urgent action is needed to address gender inequality and economic dependency and poverty; and that addressing HIV/AIDS is therefore an important component of poverty eradication and a key requisite when working to achieve the internationally agreed development goals, including those contained in the Millennium Declaration;

32. *Emphasizes* the link between poverty eradication and improving access to safe drinking water, and stresses in that regard the objective to halve, by 2015, the proportion of people who are unable to reach or to afford safe drinking water and the proportion of people who do not have access to basic sanitation, as reaffirmed in the Johannesburg Plan of Implementation;

33. *Recognizes* that the lack of adequate housing remains a pressing challenge in the fight to eradicate extreme poverty, particularly in the urban areas in developing countries, expresses its concern at the rapid growth in the number of slum-dwellers in the urban areas of developing countries, particularly in Africa, stresses that, unless urgent and effective measures and actions are taken at the national and international levels, the number of slum-dwellers, who constitute one third of the world's urban population, will continue to increase, and emphasizes the need for increased efforts with a view to significantly improving the lives of at least 100 million slum-dwellers by 2020;

34. *Encourages* Governments to support the Global Campaign for Secure Tenure and the Global Campaign for Urban Governance of the United Nations Human Settlements Programme as important tools for, inter alia, promoting administration of land and property rights, in accordance with national circumstances, and enhancing access to affordable credit by the urban poor;

35. *Recognizes* that the eradication of rural poverty and hunger is crucial for the achievement of the internationally agreed development goals, including those contained in the Millennium Declaration, and that rural development should be an integral part of national and international development policies;

Specific initiatives in the fight against poverty

36. *Recognizes* the important potential contribution of the World Solidarity Fund to the achievement of the internationally agreed development goals, including

those contained in the Millennium Declaration, in particular the objective to halve, by 2015, the proportion of people living on less than one dollar a day and the proportion of the people who suffer from hunger;

37. *Takes note* of efforts to define the strategy of the World Solidarity Fund and to mobilize resources to enable it to start its activities, and invites Member States, international organizations, the private sector, relevant institutions, foundations and individuals to contribute to the Fund;

38. *Recalls* that in the Millennium Declaration, the Heads of State and Government, inter alia, identified solidarity as one of the fundamental and universal values that should underlie relations between peoples in the twenty-first century, and in this regard decides to consider at the sixtieth session of the General Assembly the issue of proclaiming 20 December of each year International Human Solidarity Day;

39. *Invites* Governments and relevant stakeholders to utilize entrepreneurship, taking fully into account national interests, development strategies and priorities to contribute to poverty eradication;

Africa, least developed countries, landlocked developing countries and small island developing States

40. *Stresses*, as recognized in the Millennium Declaration, the importance of meeting the special needs of Africa, where poverty remains a major challenge and where most countries have not benefited fully from the opportunities of globalization, which has further exacerbated the continent's marginalization;

41. *Reaffirms its support* for the New Partnership for Africa's Development, encourages further efforts in the implementation of the commitments contained therein in the political, economic and social fields, and calls upon the Member States and the international community, and invites the United Nations system, to continue to support the implementation of the Partnership, the primary objective of which is to eradicate poverty and promote sustainable development on the basis of African ownership and leadership and enhanced partnerships with the international community, in accordance with the principles, objectives and priorities of the Partnership;

42. *Takes note* of the Plan of Action for Promotion of Employment and Poverty Alleviation in Africa adopted at the extraordinary summit of the African Union on employment and poverty alleviation, held in Ouagadougou from 3 to 9 September 2004, and notes the role of the International Labour Organization in assisting the African countries in implementing the Plan of Action adopted at the summit;

43. *Calls upon* the Governments of the least developed countries and their development partners to implement fully the commitments contained in the Brussels Declaration and the Programme of Action for the Least Developed Countries for the Decade 2001-2010, adopted at the Third United Nations Conference on the Least Developed Countries, held in Brussels from 14 to 20 May 2001;

44. *Stresses* the vulnerabilities of the small island developing States, reiterates the importance of international support for the full implementation of the Programme of Action for the Sustainable Development of Small Island Developing States, supports in this regard the holding of the International Meeting to

Review the Implementation of the Programme of Action for the Sustainable Development of Small Island Developing States in Mauritius from 10 to 14 January 2005, and looks forward to its outcomes;

45. *Recognizes* the special problems and needs of the landlocked developing countries within a new global framework for transit transport cooperation for landlocked and transit developing countries, calls, in this regard, for the full and effective implementation of the Almaty Programme of Action: Addressing the Special Needs of Landlocked Developing Countries within a New Global Framework for Transit Transport Cooperation for Landlocked and Transit Developing Countries, and stresses the need for the implementation of the São Paulo Consensus, adopted in São Paulo, Brazil, on 18 June 2004 at the eleventh session of the United Nations Conference on Trade and Development, in particular paragraphs 66 and 84 thereof, by the relevant international organizations and donors in a multi-stakeholder approach;

The United Nations and the fight against poverty

46. *Calls for* the full implementation of General Assembly resolution 57/270 B of 23 June 2003 on the integrated and coordinated implementation of and follow-up to the outcomes of the major United Nations conferences and summits in the economic and social fields, which provides a comprehensive basis for the follow-up to the outcomes of those conferences and summits and contributes to the achievement of the internationally agreed development goals, including those contained in the Millennium Declaration, in particular the eradication of poverty, and stresses the importance of the 2005 high-level event to be held at the commencement of the sixtieth session of the General Assembly, as decided by the Assembly in its resolution 58/291 of 6 May 2004;

47. *Reaffirms* the role of United Nations funds and programmes, in particular the United Nations Development Programme and its associated funds, in assisting the national efforts of developing countries, inter alia, in the eradication of poverty, and the need for their funding in accordance with the relevant resolutions of the United Nations;

48. *Requests* the Secretary-General to submit a report to the General Assembly at its sixtieth session on the implementation of the present resolution;

49. *Decides* to include in the provisional agenda of its sixtieth session the item entitled "Implementation of the first United Nations Decade for the Eradication of Poverty (1997-2006)".

Also on 22 December, the Assembly took note of the report of the Second Committee [A/59/487] on its discussion of the eradication of poverty and other development issues (**decision 59/538**).

International Year of Microcredit, 2005

In response to General Assembly resolution 58/221 [YUN 2003, p. 854], the Secretary-General submitted a September report and October addendum [A/59/326 & Add.1], in which he described the preparations for the International Year of Microcredit, 2005, which was declared by the Assembly in resolution 53/197 [YUN 1998, p. 785]. The report provided information on the preparations at the national, regional and international levels for the observance of the Year, taking into account information received from 25 Member States, 11 organizations of the UN system and two NGOs.

GENERAL ASSEMBLY ACTION

On 22 December [meeting 75], the General Assembly, on the recommendation of the Second Committee [A/59/487/Add.1], adopted **resolution 59/246** without vote [agenda item 89 (a)].

Role of microcredit and microfinance in the eradication of poverty

The General Assembly,

Recalling its resolutions 52/193 and 52/194 of 18 December 1997, 53/197 of 15 December 1998 and 58/221 of 23 December 2003,

Recognizing that microcredit and microfinance programmes have succeeded in generating productive self-employment and proved to be an effective tool in assisting people to overcome poverty and reducing their vulnerability to crisis, and have led to their growing participation, in particular the participation of women, in the mainstream economic and political processes of society,

Welcoming the efforts made in the field of property rights, and noting that an enabling environment at all levels, including transparent regulatory systems and competitive markets, foster the mobilization of resources and access to finance for people living in poverty,

Bearing in mind the importance of microfinance instruments, such as credit, savings and other financial products and services, in providing access to capital for people living in poverty,

Recognizing the need to create inclusive financial sectors in order to facilitate access for people living in poverty, especially women, to microcredit and microfinance so as to enable them to undertake microenterprises to generate employment and contribute to achieving self-empowerment, and to enhance their ability to increase income, build assets and mitigate vulnerability in times of hardship,

Noting that the availability of microcredit and microfinance to people living in poverty, especially women, can support entrepreneurship and spur the development of microenterprises, providing goods, services and income to the poor, thus raising incomes and fostering equitable growth,

Recalling its resolution 53/197, by which it proclaimed 2005 the International Year of Microcredit and requested that the observance of the Year be a special occasion for giving impetus to microcredit and microfinance programmes in all countries, particularly the developing countries,

Encouraging the holding and supporting of regional, subregional and national events on the observance of the International Year of Microcredit, 2005,

Noting the ongoing efforts by the Department of Economic and Social Affairs of the Secretariat and the United Nations Capital Development Fund in jointly coordinating the activities of the United Nations system regarding the preparation and observance of the Year, and noting also the ongoing efforts of public and private development agencies, including the Consultative Group to Assist the Poor, on microcredit and microfinance,

Noting also that the international community is observing the period 1997-2006 as the first United Nations Decade for the Eradication of Poverty,

1. *Takes note* of the report of the Secretary-General on the implementation of the first United Nations Decade for the Eradication of Poverty (1997-2006) and preparations for the International Year of Microcredit, 2005;

2. *Welcomes* the launching of the International Year of Microcredit, 2005;

3. *Emphasizes* that the observance of 2005 as the International Year of Microcredit will provide a significant opportunity to raise awareness of the importance of microcredit and microfinance in the eradication of poverty, to share good practices and to further enhance financial sectors that support sustainable pro-poor financial services in all countries;

4. *Recognizes* the importance of scaling up microcredit and other microfinance instruments, using the Year as a platform to find ways of enhancing development impact and sustainability through the increased dissemination of data and sharing of best practices and lessons learned among microcredit and microfinance institutions, and welcomes the ongoing efforts of United Nations regional organizations, funds, programmes and specialized agencies responsible for operational activities related to development in promoting microcredit and microfinance institutions, inter alia, supporting the development of entrepreneurship;

5. *Reiterates its invitation* to Member States, relevant organizations of the United Nations system, nongovernmental organizations, the private sector and civil society to collaborate, including through making voluntary contributions, in observing the Year, to raise public awareness and knowledge about microcredit and microfinance;

6. *Recognizes* that access to microcredit and microfinance can contribute to the achievement of the goals and targets of major United Nations conferences and summits in the economic and social fields, including those contained in the United Nations Millennium Declaration, in particular the goals relating to poverty eradication, gender equality and the empowerment of women;

7. *Invites* Member States to consider undertaking policies to facilitate the expansion of microcredit and microfinance institutions in order to service the large unmet demand among poor people for financial services, including the identification and development of mechanisms to promote sustainable access to financial services, the removal of institutional and regulatory obstacles and the provision of incentives to microfinance institutions that meet national standards for delivering such financial services to the poor;

8. *Also invites* Member States to consider developing and promoting regulatory guidance and standards to ensure effectiveness in management, financial reporting, internal auditing, domestic supervision and accountability among microfinance institutions;

9. *Decides* to devote one plenary meeting at its sixty-first session to the consideration of the outcome of and follow-up to the International Year of Microcredit, with a view to broadening and deepening the discussion about microcredit and microfinance;

10. *Requests* the Secretary-General to prepare a report on the observance of the International Year of Microcredit, 2005, and on the implementation of the present resolution, and to submit it to the General Assembly at its sixty-first session under the item entitled "Implementation of the first United Nations Decade for the Eradication of Poverty (1997-2006)".

Rural development

In accordance with Economic and Social Council decision 2003/290 [YUN 2003, p. 853], the Council, at the coordination segment of its 2004 substantive session, considered the theme of a coordinated and integrated UN system approach to promote rural development in developing countries, with due consideration to LDCs, for poverty eradication and sustainable development [A/59/3/Rev.1]. It had before it a report of the Secretary-General [E/2004/58], which analysed the role of the UN system in promoting a coordinated and integrated approach to rural development and made proposals on how to improve policy coherence at the international, regional and country levels.

The report noted that the potential contribution of rural development in the realization of the internationally agreed development goals, including the MDGs, was being increasingly acknowledged. However, there were certain issues that needed to be taken into account while assimilating the goal of integrated rural development in the broader framework of the MDGs: how to ensure complementarity between the strategies to achieve the MDGs and rural development–related activities, and how to promote efficient allocation of resources and optimal utilization of capacities of various organizations and actors. In addressing those issues, the UN system, Governments and other relevant actors were trying to develop an integrated approach for their activities, which contained three important elements—the integration of various dimensions of rural development and the development goals, based on a coherent strategy, a clear division of labour and mutually reinforcing programmes; a coherent framework for capacity-building activities and projects in rural development; and regional cooperation.

On 1 July, the Council held a panel discussion entitled "Working together to promote integrated rural development in developing countries, particularly the least developed countries".

ECONOMIC AND SOCIAL COUNCIL ACTION

On 23 July [meeting 50], the Economic and Social Council adopted **resolution 2004/48** [draft: E/2004/L.18] without vote [agenda item 4 (b)].

Coordinated and integrated United Nations system approach to promoting rural development in developing countries, with due consideration to least developed countries, for poverty eradication and sustainable development

The Economic and Social Council,

Recalling its decision 2003/287 of 24 July 2003, in which it decided to consider, during its coordination segment in 2004, the theme "Coordinated and integrated United Nations system approach to promoting rural development in developing countries, with due consideration to least developed countries, for poverty eradication and sustainable development",

Reaffirming the ministerial declaration of the high-level segment of the Economic and Social Council adopted on 2 July 2003,

Recalling the internationally agreed development goals, including those contained in the United Nations Millennium Declaration, and the outcomes of the major United Nations conferences, summits and relevant special sessions of the General Assembly,

Recalling also the Declaration of the World Food Summit: five years later, adopted in Rome on 13 June 2002,

Reaffirming the Programme of Action for the Least Developed Countries for the Decade 2001-2010,

Reiterating that the eradication of rural poverty and hunger is crucial for the achievement of internationally agreed development goals, including those contained in the Millennium Declaration, and that rural development should be pursued through an integrated approach, which encompasses the economic, social and environmental dimensions, takes into account the gender perspective and consists of mutually reinforcing policies and programmes, and which should be balanced, targeted, situation specific, locally owned, include local synergies and initiatives and be responsive to the needs of rural populations,

Recognizing that rural development is the responsibility of each country and is predicated on an enabling national environment, and reaffirming that an enabling international economic environment is important for the support of effective national development efforts, including rural development efforts, that it should combine effective and coherent policies, good governance and accountable institutions at the national and international levels as well as the promotion of gender equality and the promotion and protection of human rights and fundamental freedoms, including the right to development, and that robust, broad-based and equitable economic growth as well as human resources development are needed to fight rural poverty,

1. *Takes note* of the report of the Secretary-General;

2. *Notes* the efforts made by United Nations organizations to assist developing countries, upon their request, in integrating rural development into their national development strategies, urges them to promote further the integration of this approach into their operational and other activities, to enhance further the efficiency of resources utilization and to continue to work, within their mandates, to this end, and, in this

regard, emphasizes the need for relevant United Nations agencies to be provided with appropriate resources to promote integrated rural development;

3. *Calls* for enhanced coordination and cooperation among the agencies of the United Nations system, including among the Rome-based agencies, especially at the country level, on the basis of the common country assessment and the United Nations Development Assistance Framework, in support of national development strategies as well as in enhancing their cooperation with the World Bank and the regional development banks;

4. *Acknowledges* the recent increase in official development assistance allocations to rural development and agriculture, urges developed countries that have not done so to make concrete efforts to reach the target of providing 0.7 per cent of their gross national product as official development assistance to developing countries and 0.15 to 0.20 per cent of their gross national product to least developed countries, as reconfirmed at the Third United Nations Conference on the Least Developed Countries, held in Brussels from 14 to 20 May 2001, encourages developing countries to build on progress achieved in ensuring that official development assistance is used effectively to help achieve development goals and targets, acknowledges the efforts of all donors, commends those donors whose official development assistance contributions exceed, reach or are increasing towards the targets, and underlines the importance of undertaking an examination of the means and time frames for achieving the targets and goals;

5. *Invites* the international and regional financial institutions to continue to enhance their support for national efforts for poverty eradication and rural development in developing countries, including the mobilization of public and private investment as well as improved access to credit for the development of rural infrastructure in order to enhance productivity and increase access to markets and information, calls for actions to facilitate the establishment and strengthening of rural financial institutions, including microcredit/microfinancing, savings and insurance facilities and co-operative ventures for rural development, as well as the development of microenterprises and small and medium-sized enterprises, and in this regard underlines the importance of the International Year of Microcredit, 2005, as a platform to promote these goals;

6. *Recognizes* that, despite serious efforts to achieve progress, important issues in the implementation of the Ministerial Declaration adopted at the Fourth Ministerial Conference of the World Trade Organization, held in Doha from 9 to 14 November 2001, are still outstanding, in particular regarding the commitments for, inter alia, comprehensive negotiations aimed at substantial improvements in market access; that in the agricultural sector, without prejudging the outcome of negotiations, reductions of, with a view to phasing out, all forms of export subsidies, substantial reduction in trade-distorting domestic support and enhanced market access are needed; that special and differential treatment for developing countries shall be an integral part of all elements of the negotiations, taking development needs fully into account, in a manner consistent with the Doha mandate, including food security and rural development; and that non-trade concerns of countries will also be taken into account, as provided for in the Agreement on Agriculture, in accordance with paragraph 13 of the Doha Ministerial Declaration, and urges the United Nations system, including the Food and Agriculture Organization of the United Nations and the United Nations Conference on Trade and Development, to provide further trade-related technical assistance and capacity-building for developing countries, in particular the least developed countries;

7. *Also recognizes* the vulnerability of the commodity-dependent developing countries, in particular the least developed countries, to market fluctuations, and calls upon the United Nations system to support their efforts towards diversification of exports and value-added through processing as a means of increasing export earnings, including through support to enable developing countries to put in place measures that are appropriate and necessary for meeting standards consistent with the provisions of the World Trade Organization and improving terms of trade, and to address the impact of the instability of commodity prices;

8. *Stresses* the need to enhance and expand access by developing countries to appropriate technologies that are pro-poor and raise productivity, underlines the need for measures to increase investment in agricultural research, including modern technologies, as well as in natural resources management and capacity-building, and encourages the United Nations system to strengthen support for the Consultative Group on International Agricultural Research;

9. *Reaffirms* that sustainable agriculture and rural development are essential to the implementation of an integrated approach to food security and safety in an environmentally sustainable way, recognizes the important role of the rural population in sustainably managing natural resources, and calls for enhanced coordination and cooperation among the agencies of the United Nations system in supporting national efforts to promote environmentally sound and sustainable natural resources management;

10. *Also reaffirms* the need to improve access to reliable, affordable, economically viable, socially acceptable and environmentally sound energy services and resources, taking into account national specificities and circumstances, through various means, such as enhanced rural electrification and decentralized energy systems, increased use of renewables, cleaner liquid and gaseous fuels and enhanced energy efficiency, as well as by intensifying regional and international cooperation and enhancing coordination and cooperation among agencies of the United Nations system in support of national efforts, including through capacity-building, financial and technological assistance and innovative financing mechanisms, inter alia at the micro- and meso-levels, recognizing the specific factors for providing access to the poor;

11. *Expresses its serious concern* regarding the severe food shortages and hunger facing millions of people, especially in Africa, recognizes that food security is a global concern, and stresses the importance of improving famine prevention mechanisms and long-term food security, as well as of responding to emergency food aid needs;

12. *Invites* the United Nations system to support further the implementation of the United Nations

Convention to Combat Desertification in Those Countries Experiencing Serious Drought and/or Desertification, Particularly in Africa and to address the causes of desertification and land degradation in order to maintain and restore land, as well as addressing poverty resulting from land degradation;

13. *Realizes* that bridging the digital divide will require strong commitment by all stakeholders at the national and international levels, and encourages all efforts by agencies, funds and programmes of the United Nations system to assist developing countries in overcoming the digital divide and promoting the use of information and communication technologies to foster economic and social development, particularly in rural areas;

14. *Recognizes* the devastating impact of HIV/AIDS and other infectious diseases on societies, and calls for measures by United Nations bodies, especially the Joint United Nations Programme on HIV/AIDS co-sponsoring agencies, and development partners to further mainstream HIV/AIDS concerns into rural development planning, including poverty eradication and food security strategies and multisectoral development activities covering economic and social aspects, including the gender perspective;

15. *Invites* the relevant organizations of the United Nations system dealing with issues of development to strengthen their cooperation in addressing and supporting the empowerment and the specific needs of rural women in their programmes and strategies;

16. *Stresses* that the United Nations system should improve its coordination in support of national efforts to increase the school enrolment rate, especially of the girl child, and to provide quality education for the rural poor, inter alia, through mobilizing the financial and technical resources necessary, including the full utilization of modern methodologies and technologies as well as the establishment of distance learning education systems;

17. *Recognizes* the importance of employment for pro-poor growth in rural areas, and encourages the United Nations system and development partners to assist countries, upon their request, in mainstreaming employment into investment policy and poverty reduction strategies, including those focused on rural area development;

18. *Invites* the United Nations system to further assist developing countries in their efforts to enhance access by the rural poor to productive assets, especially land and water, in order to promote social and economic development;

19. *Calls upon* the United Nations system to further support capacity-building programmes for, and exchanges of experience on, rural development through enhanced coordination and information exchange mechanisms such as the United Nations System Network on Rural Development and Food Security;

20. *Stresses* that the United Nations system should further support regional and subregional initiatives, where appropriate, in order to promote an integrated approach to rural development, and requests the United Nations regional commissions to further enhance regional and interregional cooperation, in particular for sharing best practices;

21. *Calls upon* the United Nations system and regional organizations to undertake measures to further promote South-South cooperation, including triangular cooperation, in the area of rural development, and in this regard underlines the need for increased cooperation among bodies of the United Nations system to promote South-South cooperation;

22. *Notes* the work of the United Nations system on partnerships, welcomes the establishment of a multitude of partnerships for sustainable rural development at the field level entered into by various United Nations agencies, Member States, the private sector, non-governmental organizations and civil society in general, and encourages the United Nations system to continue to promote partnerships at the national and international levels in accordance with relevant General Assembly resolutions.

United Nations Alliance

On 23 July [meeting 50], the Economic and Social Council adopted **resolution 2004/49** [draft: E/2004/L.32] without vote [agenda item 4 (*b*)].

United Nations Public-Private Alliance for Rural Development

The Economic and Social Council,

Recalling the ministerial declaration of the high-level segment of the Economic and Social Council adopted on 2 July 2003, which underlined the importance of alliances and partnerships among actors in different sectors for the promotion of integrated rural development,

Underlining the importance of the contribution of the private sector, non-governmental organizations and civil society in general to the implementation of the outcomes of United Nations conferences in the economic, social and related fields,

Recalling the central role and responsibility of Governments in national and international policy-making,

Bearing in mind General Assembly resolution 58/129 of 19 December 2003, entitled "Towards global partnerships", in which the Assembly, inter alia, identified the principles and objectives of such partnerships and welcomed the establishment of a multitude of partnerships at the field level, entered into by various United Nations organizations, Member States and other stakeholders, such as the United Nations Public-Private Alliance for Rural Development (the United Nations Alliance),

1. *Welcomes* the initiative of the Government of Madagascar to serve as the pilot country for the United Nations Public-Private Alliance for Rural Development (the United Nations Alliance);

2. *Invites* all Member States, the funds, programmes and agencies of the United Nations system, the Bretton Woods institutions, civil society, the private sector and other relevant stakeholders to support the programmes and activities of the United Nations Alliance in its mission to promote sustainable rural development, consistent with General Assembly resolution 58/129 and other relevant resolutions and decisions of the Assembly and the Economic and Social Council;

3. *Stresses* that activities of the funds, programmes and specialized agencies of the United Nations system at the country level in support of the United Nations Alliance should take into account the implementation

of the United Nations Development Assistance Framework;

4. *Requests* the Secretary-General to report to the Economic and Social Council at its substantive session of 2006 on the work of the United Nations Alliance.

Science and technology for development

Commission on Science and Technology for Development

The Commission on Science and Technology for Development held its seventh session in Geneva from 24 to 28 May [E/2004/31]. It considered as its main substantive theme "Promoting the application of science and technology to meet the development goals contained in the Millennium Declaration" (see below). It also discussed an April note by the Secretariat on implementation of and progress made on decisions taken at the Commission's sixth (2003) session [E/CN.16/2004/3], and heard national country reports on information and communication technology (ICT) policies from a number of countries.

The Commission recommended a draft resolution and two draft decisions for adoption by the Economic and Social Council. It brought to the Council's attention a decision by which it took note of the Secretary-General's report on the main substantive theme [E/2004/31 (dec. 7/101)] (see below).

By **decision 2004/314** of 23 July, the Economic and Social Council took note, during its consideration at its high-level segment of the theme "Resources mobilization and enabling environment for poverty eradication in the context of the implementation of the Programme of Action for the Least Developed Countries for the Decade 2001-2010" (see p. 855), of the Commission's contribution, which was addressed under the substantive theme at its seventh session. The Council encouraged all stakeholders to consider the Commission's recommendations thereon.

On the same date, by **decision 2004/315**, the Council took note of the Commission's report on its seventh session and approved the provisional agenda and documentation for the eighth (2005) session.

Promoting the application of science and technology to meet the development goals

The Commission had before it an April report by the Secretary-General on promoting the application of science and technology to meet the development goals contained in the Millennium Declaration [E/CN.16/2004/2] that sought to identify approaches for the effective promotion and use of science and technology to meet the MDGs [YUN 2000, p. 51].

The report examined strategies for promoting the application of science and technology to meeting the MDGs, including improving the policy environment for the application of science and technology to development; strengthening basic and applied research in developing countries and promoting international scientific networking; and promoting universal Internet access and building strategic partnerships for development and competitiveness. It found that most developing countries were unlikely to meet the MDGs without making science and technology top priorities in their development agenda. Achieving the MDGs, therefore, would require a reorientation of national science, technology and innovation policies to ensure that they served the needs of development effectively. In particular, a solid national science and technology base would have to be built to enable the generation, use and diffusion of scientific and technological knowledge. Academia/government/industry partnerships were essential in building scientific and technological capabilities and fostering market-oriented policies and developments. Also essential was access to new and emerging technologies, which required technology transfer, technical cooperation and building a scientific and technological capacity to participate in the development, mastery and adaptation of those technologies to local conditions.

The report concluded by directing a number of recommendations to Governments, the Commission and the UN system.

ECONOMIC AND SOCIAL COUNCIL ACTION

By **decision 2004/313** of 23 July, the Economic and Social Council deferred consideration of the draft resolution on promoting the application of science and technology to meeting the development goals contained in the Millennium Declaration, contained in the report of the Commission on Science and Technology for Development, to a resumed session.

On 5 November [meeting 53], the Council, on the recommendation of the Commission [E/2004/31, orally amended], adopted **resolution 2004/68** without vote [agenda item 13 (*b*)].

Science and technology for development

The Economic and Social Council,

I

Promoting the application of science and technology to meet the development goals contained in the United Nations Millennium Declaration

Welcoming the work of the Commission on Science and Technology for Development on its theme "Promoting the application of science and technology to meet the development goals contained in the United Nations Millennium Declaration" and taking note of the findings, which include, inter alia, the following:

1. Most developing countries are unlikely to meet the internationally agreed development goals, including those contained in the United Nations Millennium Declaration, without a clear political commitment to making science and technology top priorities in their development agenda;

2. Many developing countries lack solid science and technology bases. Science and technology institutions and national innovation systems in many developing countries are fragmented and uncoordinated and links between them and the private business sector are poorly developed. Review and analysis of national science, technology and innovation policies and institutional and legal frameworks, including advisory bodies and mechanisms, are urgently needed to ensure that they serve the needs of development effectively;

3. The lack of a solid science and technology base not only results from poor human and capital resources, but also stems from a lack of appreciation of the critical role of science and technology in development, as well as from an incoherent methodology for establishing such a base and the absence of a coherent policy addressing national needs and human and capital resources;

4. For developing countries to meet the internationally agreed development goals, including those contained in the Millennium Declaration, they need access to new and emerging technologies, which requires technology transfer, technical cooperation and the building and nurturing of a scientific and technological capacity to participate in the development and adaptation of these technologies to local conditions;

5. Promoting the development and application of new and emerging technologies, most notably biotechnology and information and communication technologies as well as biomedical and environmental technologies, will both reduce the cost and increase the likelihood of attaining the internationally agreed development goals, including those contained in the Millennium Declaration;

6. Academia/government/industry partnerships and networking are essential in building scientific and technological capabilities and fostering policies and developments. Science and technology parks, business incubators and support organizations for innovation are effective mechanisms for promoting academia/ government/industry partnerships and entrepreneurship;

7. The current North-South gap in respect of the generation and application of new and emerging technologies and their contribution to economic and social development constitutes a "technological divide" which must be bridged if developing countries are to participate effectively in a global inclusive knowledge society;

8. States need to invest in publicly funded universities and research institutions to improve infrastructure, quality of education and human resources. To enhance the impact of investment, Governments should consider linking funding of universities to performance in teaching and research;

9. Despite the efforts of various development agencies, poverty still persists in many parts of the world. There is a need to coordinate technical cooperation programmes and to monitor progress so as to ensure policy coherence and socio-economic benefits for the poor;

10. In recent years, there has been a rapid rise in the number of open and collaborative projects to create public goods. These projects are extremely important, as they affect the ability of countries to achieve the development goals contained in the Millennium Declaration;

Decides to make the following recommendations for consideration by national Governments and the Commission on Science and Technology for Development:

(a) Governments are encouraged to undertake the following actions:

(i) Demonstrate their political commitment by increasing research and development expenditure in science and technology to at least 1 per cent of gross domestic product and encourage research and development, engineering and design, inter alia, in areas involving the assimilation of existing knowledge that address the needs of national development;

(ii) Establish and/or enhance national advisory bodies and their linkages to provide systematic and institutionalized science and technology advice to various branches of government responsible for coordinating and implementing development strategies;

(iii) Implement fiscal and other incentives to encourage research and development in the private sector and joint projects between private companies and public research and development institutes;

(iv) Strengthen universities and research institutions and develop centres of excellence in the fields of science and technology and encourage them to contribute to national development;

(v) Increase investment in scientific and technical education, particularly at tertiary and vocational levels, and adopt concrete measures to increase the enrolment of girls and women in scientific and engineering disciplines and ensure their representation in science and technology, particularly in decision-making positions;

(vi) Adopt special measures to attract and retain young and talented scientists and technologists, and establish close ties with expatriate scientists and engineers and encourage their participation in national development;

(vii) Strengthen the diffusion and commercialization of technology by encouraging venture capital and other forms of financial intermediaries supporting innovation from both public and private sources and establishing facilitatory institutions such as science parks and technology incubators;

(viii) Explore the potential of openly available public development projects for the enhancement of science and technology infrastructure;

(ix) Raise public awareness on the importance of science and technology in development and, in particular, the benefits, opportunities and risks of new and emerging technologies;

(b) The Commission on Science and Technology for Development, within existing resources and within the framework of its role in coordinating science and technology activities in the United Nations system, is requested to:

(i) Forge links between itself and national science and technology bodies in each country, in order to promote networking, share national experiences, facilitate information flows and increase the impact of the work of the Commission. In this regard, the Commission is invited to establish an international network of science and technology institutions, including national science and technology commissions and other stakeholders in development such as the international research centres of the Trieste System. The new association would meet annually in conjunction with the regular sessions of the Commission;

(ii) Establish, in collaboration with the United Nations Development Programme and other institutions dealing with the use of science, technology and innovation in achieving the Millennium Development Goals, mechanisms for the ongoing review, evaluation and analysis of national strategies for achieving the internationally agreed development goals, including those contained in the Millennium Declaration, to ensure that science and technology play a central role. To this end, the Commission is invited to consider the feasibility of developing a reliable tool to monitor implementation and benchmark progress;

(iii) Explore the possibility of establishing new initiatives involving important development partners, such as the New Partnership for Africa's Development, with a view to enhancing closer South-South and North-South collaboration in the area of science and technology;

(iv) Explore the feasibility of preparing and producing an annual world technology for development report that would include technology achievement indicators and benchmarks and a review of emerging technologies and related policies, as well as best practices and case studies on the application of science and technology towards the achievement of the internationally agreed development goals, including those contained in the Millennium Declaration;

(v) Provide a forum within the Science and Technology for Development Network within which success stories and lessons learned could be shared in respect of national efforts to apply science and technology to serve the needs of development;

(vi) Interact closely with the United Nations Information and Communication Technologies Task Force, the International Telecommunication Union and regional commissions in order to assist developing countries in the implementation of national action plans to support the fulfilment of the goals indicated in the Declaration of Principles and the Plan of Action adopted at the first phase of the World Summit on the Information Society, held in Geneva from 10 to 12 December 2003, and contribute to the preparation of the second phase of the Summit, to be held in Tunis from 16 to 18 November 2005.

II

New substantive theme and other activities

Endorses the following decision taken by the Commission on Science and Technology for Development at its seventh session:

The Commission on Science and Technology for Development, recognizing that the implementation of the development goals contained in the United Nations Millennium Declaration entails significant reorientation in the use of science, technology and innovation policies to ensure that they serve the needs of development, especially for poverty reduction, recognizing also that national advisory bodies are essential in providing systematic and institutionalized science and technology advice to the executive and other branches of government responsible for coordinating and implementing development strategies, and taking note of the Declaration of Principles and the Plan of Action adopted at the first phase of the World Summit on the Information Society, held in Geneva from 10 to 12 December 2003, decides to select as its substantive theme for the intersessional period 2004-2005 "Science and technology promotion, advice and application for the achievement of the internationally agreed development goals contained in the United Nations Millennium Declaration", and considers that specific emphasis should be placed on at least three key areas: the mutual interaction and dependency of science and technology education and research and development; infrastructure-building as a foundation for scientific and technological development; and promoting gainful employment, in general, and enterprise development, in particular, through the use of existing and emerging technologies, especially information and communication technologies and biotechnologies.

Information and communication technologies

During 2004, the United Nations continued to consider how the benefits of new technologies, especially ICT, could contribute to development and preparations for the second phase of the World Summit on the Information Society; the first phase was held in 2003. The UN ICT Task Force continued its substantive work as a global forum on integrating information on ICT into development programmes.

World Summit on the Information Society

By **decision 58/569** of 1 July, the General Assembly, on the proposal of its President, decided to consider the report of the World Summit on the Information Society (first phase, Geneva, 10-12 December 2003 [YUN 2003, p. 857]; second phase, Tunis, Tunisia, 16-18 November 2005) in plenary meeting at its sixtieth (2005) session, notwithstanding the fact that the item entitled "Information and communication technologies for development" would be allocated to the Second Committee pursuant to Assembly resolution 58/316 (see p. 1374).

Report of ITU Secretary-General. In response to General Assembly resolution 57/238 [YUN 2002, p. 836], the Secretary-General submitted to the Assembly and the Economic and Social Council a May report by the Secretary-General of the International Telecommunication

Union (ITU) [A/59/80-E/2004/61 & Corr.1] on the first phase [YUN 2003, p. 857] and progress in the preparations for the second phase (2005) of the World Summit on the Information Society. The report noted that the core outputs of the first phase were the Declaration of Principles, "Building the information society: a global challenge in the new Millennium", and the Plan of Action. The Council took note of the ITU report by **decision 2004/301** of 23 July. The Declaration and Plan of Action were transmitted to the Secretary-General by Switzerland on 7 October [A/C.2/59/3].

In preparation for the second phase, an informal brainstorming meeting was organized (Hammamet, Tunisia, 2-3 March) and the Preparatory Committee held its first session (Hammamet, 24-26 June) [WSIS-II/PC-1/DOC/6-E]. Regional conferences were held, including the Second Bishkek-Moscow Regional Conference on the Information Society (Bishkek, Kyrgyzstan, 16-18 November) and the West Asia Regional Conference (Damascus, Syrian Arab Republic, 22-23 November). Other preparatory activities included the ITU workshop on Internet governance (Geneva, 26-27 February) and the establishment by the United Nations Secretary-General of the Task Force on Financial Mechanisms for ICT for Development, which produced a report on the subject in December.

CEB consideration. In the context of its consideration of the question of bridging the digital divide, CEB/HLCP discussed the outcome of the first phase of the World Summit on the Information Society at both its seventh session (Beirut, 26-27 February) [CEB/2004/4] and its intersessional meeting (Frascati, Italy, 31 May–1 June) [CEB/2004/5]. It considered the preparations for the second phase of the Summit at its eighth session (Florence, Italy, 15-17 September) [CEB/2004/7].

At CEB's second regular session of 2004 (New York, 29-30 October) [CEB/2004/2], the ITU Secretary-General provided an update on preparations for the second phase.

GENERAL ASSEMBLY ACTION

On 22 December [meeting 75], the General Assembly, on the recommendation of the Second Committee [A/59/480], adopted **resolution 59/220** without vote [agenda item 44].

World Summit on the Information Society

The General Assembly,

Recalling its resolutions 56/183 of 21 December 2001 and 57/238 of 20 December 2002,

Reaffirming the potential of information and communication technologies as powerful tools to foster socio-economic development and contribute to the realization of the internationally agreed development goals, including those contained in the United Nations Millennium Declaration,

1. *Expresses its gratitude* to the Government of Switzerland for having hosted the first phase of the World Summit on the Information Society in Geneva from 10 to 12 December 2003 and for the support and arrangements put at the disposal of the Summit;

2. *Renews with gratitude its acknowledgement* of the generous offer of the Government of Tunisia to host the second phase of the Summit, which will take place in Tunis from 16 to 18 November 2005;

3. *Takes note* of the note by the Secretary-General transmitting the report of the Secretary-General of the International Telecommunication Union on the first phase and progress in the preparations for the second phase of the World Summit on the Information Society;

4. *Endorses* the Declaration of Principles and the Plan of Action adopted by the Summit on 12 December 2003, and welcomes, in this regard, the strong development orientation of both documents, encourages developing and developed countries in partnership to continue to identify how information technologies can further contribute to achieving the internationally agreed development goals, including those contained in the United Nations Millennium Declaration, and stresses the importance of the effective and timely implementation of the Plan of Action;

5. *Welcomes* the contribution of Member States, relevant United Nations bodies, including the Information and Communication Technologies Task Force, and other intergovernmental organizations, non-governmental organizations, civil society and the private sector to the success of the Geneva phase of the Summit;

6. *Urges* Member States, relevant United Nations bodies, including the Information and Communication Technologies Task Force, and other intergovernmental organizations, non-governmental organizations, civil society and the private sector to contribute actively to the implementation of the outcome of the Geneva phase and to the preparatory process of the Tunis phase of the Summit as well as to the Summit itself in order to ensure its overall success;

7. *Takes note* of the results and decisions of the first meeting of the Preparatory Committee, held in Hammamet, Tunisia, from 24 to 26 June 2004, concerning the structure and output of the second phase of the Summit;

8. *Welcomes* the establishment of the Working Group on Internet Governance and the Task Force on Financial Mechanisms, set up in accordance with the decisions of the first phase of the Summit;

9. *Invites* countries to be represented at the highest possible political level at the second phase of the Summit, to be held in Tunis in 2005;

10. *Reiterates its call* to the international community to make voluntary contributions to the special fund established by the International Telecommunication Union to support the preparations for and holding of the Summit;

11. *Invites* the Secretary-General of the International Telecommunication Union to transmit to the General Assembly, as soon as it is available, the report of the World Summit on the Information Society.

UN role

ICT Task Force. In May, the Secretary-General submitted to the Economic and Social Council the second annual report [E/2004/62 & Corr.1] of the Information and Communication Technologies Task Force, which was established in 2001 [YUN 2001, p. 763] to provide a global forum on integrating ICT into development programmes and a platform for promoting public and private partnerships to help bridge the digital divide and foster digital opportunity. The first report was submitted to the Council in 2003 [YUN 2003, p. 859].

In its second year, the Task Force, through its core activities, working groups and regional nodes, successfully served as a multi-stakeholder mechanism to facilitate and promote collaborative initiatives at the regional, subregional and national levels and to mobilize new public and private resources to support ICT-for-development programmes and projects. The Task Force facilitated the pooling of relevant experience of both developed and developing countries and the sharing of lessons learned in introducing and promoting ICT.

In addition to assessing progress made by the Task Force during its second year (December 2002–February 2004) and outlining its major activities and accomplishments, the report outlined a strategy for the Task Force's activities until the end of 2005.

By **decision 2004/296** of 23 July, the Council welcomed the valuable contribution of the Task Force to harnessing the potential of ICT for advancing development and encouraged the Task Force to continue promoting ICT for development worldwide, including through contributing to the World Summit on the Information Society process.

CEB consideration. The issue of the digital divide and its implications for the UN system was discussed by CEB/HLCP at its seventh [CEB/2004/4] and eighth [CEB/2004/7] sessions and at its intersessional meeting [CEB/2004/5].

At its second regular session of 2004 [CEB/2004/2], CEB recommended that HLCP, in close consultation with the High-Level Summit Organizing Committee, should undertake a work programme for mainstreaming and integrating ICT into the broader MDG agenda, including through the development of system-wide approaches and guidelines for use by country representatives and by the resident coordinator system; and, working closely with the CEB High-Level Committee on Management (HLCM) and its ICT Network, to focus on developing a clear vision of a UN system-wide knowledge management system, its optimum functionality and implementation options. The UN system ICT strat-egy had to be pursued as an essential component of the overall effort to enhance cost-effectiveness, strengthen system-wide knowledge management and enhance the capacity to support countries in using ICT for achieving the MDGs. HLCM and its ICT Network had to work closely with HLCP to continue to develop the business cases for the strategy, its resource implications and measures to address constraints in its implementation for consideration and decision by CEB.

Report of Secretary-General. In response to General Assembly resolution 57/295 [YUN 2002, p. 836], the Secretary-General, in a November report [A/59/563], described activities undertaken to develop a comprehensive ICT strategy for the UN system. The activities related to devising a comprehensive and coherent response to the broad issues of harnessing the potential of ICT for promoting development and were focused on: the coherence of the policy advice that UN system organizations provided to countries in setting comprehensive, forward-looking strategies to harness ICT for economic and social progress; and the unprecedented opportunities that ICT offered for system-wide knowledge management and knowledge creation.

Annexed to the report were the text of the United Nations Information and Communication Technologies Charter, which defined the principles and framework for coordination and collaboration within the organizations of the UN system, and the strategy that underpinned the Charter, comprising a set of 15 initiatives in ICT for development, ICT governance, information security, practical applications and capacity-building.

By **decision 59/531** of 22 December, the Assembly took note of the Secretary-General's report and requested him to submit a further report on the implementation of the ICT strategy to the Assembly's sixtieth (2005) session.

Communication for UN development programmes

In response to General Assembly resolution 50/130 [YUN 1995, p. 1438], the Secretary-General, in August [A/59/207], transmitted the report of the Director-General of UNESCO, which described the inter-agency collaborative mechanisms for effective and integrated follow-up to that resolution. The recommendations of the seven UN agencies, funds and programmes that contributed to the review of existing coordination arrangements and of the eighth Inter-Agency Round Table on Communication for Development (Managua, Nicaragua, 26-28 November 2001) were: creation of an international consortium on HIV/AIDS communication strategies; collection and sharing of tools from key agencies/

implementers to identify and improve access to proven tools and reduce duplication; improvement of training for journalists by reinforcing learning institutions; and encouragement of the production and dissemination of local media content while keeping a calculated balance between local, national and international contributions. The report called for increased resources for more effective communication programmes, enhanced synergy among all partners and intensified efforts to address the digital divide.

By **decision 59/532** of 22 December, the Assembly took note of the UNESCO Director-General's report.

Economic and social trends

The *World Economic and Social Survey 2004* [Sales No. E.04.II.C.1], prepared in mid-2004 by the UN Department of Economic and Social Affairs (DESA), stated that, after a mediocre performance for some three years, world economic growth began to improve in 2003 and continued to do so in early 2004. Gross world product grew by 2.7 per cent in 2003, compared with 1.8 per cent in 2002; it was expected to grow by 3.7 per cent in 2004.

Although economic performance and outlook improved for most countries, differences in economic strength across regions and economies persisted. The economy of the United States expanded apace in 2003 and early 2004 and remained a key engine for the world economy. However, its large fiscal and trade deficits continued to be major concerns, not only for the United States economy but also for the rest of the world because of the downside risks those deficits posed. Economic activity in Western Europe, apart from the United Kingdom, was sluggish but the gradual recovery was expected to continue. Japan was expected to grow by about 3 per cent in 2004, with the resurgence being driven mainly by exports, particularly to other Asian economies. As to the other developed economies, the substantial appreciation of their currencies vis-à-vis the United States dollar had an adverse impact on Australia, Canada and New Zealand.

Developing countries were again growing faster than the developed countries in 2004, with more of them than in any year since 2000 expected to achieve an increase in their per capita income. The extended periods of rapid growth of the two most populous developing countries— China and India—were good not only for the countries themselves and the large number of poor within them, but also for other countries.

Many developing countries had benefited from China's growing appetite for energy and raw materials and from the resulting higher prices of oil and other commodities. Gross domestic product (GDP) growth in Africa was expected to accelerate in 2004-2005 as many countries achieved an increase in agricultural and industrial output. Higher consumer spending, increasing investment, including more foreign direct investment (FDI) in several countries, and expanded, though cautious, government expenditure in a growing number of countries were expected to support domestic demand. The accelerating economic growth in East Asia was fuelled by the region's traditional source of dynamism—international trade. Demand from the United States strengthened in the second half of 2003 and there was an upturn in global information and communication technologies (ICT) product markets. The impetus from powerful growth in China continued to increase and a better-than-anticipated recovery in Japan added new strength to the region's growth. After a rebound in 2003, growth in South Asia was expected to solidify further in 2004, with more balance across countries and sectors. While the surge in Pakistan's exports in 2003 had moderated as the one-off effects of increased textile quotas waned, India's exports and imports both increased sharply, with exports driven by ICT-related products and services. International tourism to the region also improved and recovery in the agricultural sector (except for Sri Lanka) contributed to higher incomes. Western Asia's economic prospects were still heavily conditioned by geopolitical developments, particularly the situation in Iraq, whose economic improvement had been dilatory, and the escalating conflict between Israel and Palestine. The only propitious sign for the region was the higher dollar price of petroleum, a benefit that was discounted by the depreciation of the United States dollar. GDP growth for the region was expected to decelerate to 2.8 per cent in 2004. The short-term economic outlook for Latin America and the Caribbean continued to improve, with stronger demand from North America, Japan and China and the substantial rise in commodity prices boosting the growth of exports. Depreciation of the United States dollar and more flexible exchange-rate regimes had allowed most countries to ease monetary policy; interest rates in many economies were at multi-year lows. For the first time in decades, the region had registered a current-account surplus.

The economies in transition were the most rapidly growing of the three major groups of countries in 2003 as they continued to recover from the setbacks of the 1990s. The economies of the Commonwealth of Independent States (CIS) accelerated to over 7 per cent in 2003 and were expected to remain robust for 2004-2005, with the Russian Federation in the lead. Their economic vigour was bolstered by improved domestic fundamentals; higher production, exports and prices of petroleum and gas; and increased foreign investment. Improved consumer and investor confidence also continued to support growth. The prospects for Central and Eastern Europe continued to improve, mostly due to the performance of the Polish economy, with the momentum of growth shifting to South-Eastern Europe. Growth in the Baltic States was expected to remain robust in 2004-2005, reflecting success in broad-based structural policies and gains in macroeconomic stability. Membership of the European Union (EU) was expected to be beneficial for those economies in the long run, but uncertainties associated with EU entry could pose some short-term risks.

The second volume of the *World Economic and Social Survey 2004* [Sales No. E.04.II.C.3] dealt with the subject of international migration (see p. 1077).

The *Trade and Development Report, 2004* [Sales No. E.04.II.D.29], published by the United Nations Conference on Trade and Development (UNCTAD), stated that the outlook for a sustained economic recovery was more clouded and uncertain than at the beginning of the 1990s. Large disparities in the strength of domestic demand persisted among the major industrial countries, and increasing trade imbalances between the major economic blocks could lead to new protectionist pressures and increase instability in currency and financial markets, with adverse implications for developing countries. The sharp increase in oil prices, uncertainty about their future development and their possible impact on inflation and interest rates were an additional reason for concern. Moreover, income growth was unequally distributed both among developed countries, where the euro area continued to lag behind, and among developing countries, where fast and sustained growth continued to be concentrated in East and South Asia. At the same time, per capita income in most of sub-Saharan Africa was stagnating, and the basis for sustained growth in Latin America was still very fragile. The improvement in the global economy was the result of exceptionally good performance in a small number of countries, with great variations in the spillover effects on other economies.

A report on the world economic situation and prospects [Sales No. E.05.II.C.2], prepared jointly by DESA and UNCTAD, stated that global growth was not only the highest for many years (4 per cent),

but was also unusually widespread and well balanced. Growth in the developing countries was the fastest for more than two decades, while output in the remaining economies in transition continued to increase more rapidly than in the other major country groups. The high aggregate rate of growth in 2004 reflected the fact that every region except South Asia and CIS grew more rapidly in 2004 than in 2003. In those two exceptional cases, growth slipped from previous high levels but remained above 6 per cent and 7 per cent respectively. Even the higher price of oil did not have the discriminating effects that might have been assumed. In Latin America, with its large number of oil-importing countries, growth surged to over 5 per cent after six years of weak performance. In Africa, the impact of higher oil prices was offset for many oil-importing countries by higher non-oil commodity prices; non-oil prices rose less than oil prices, but non-oil commodities often accounted for a higher proportion of exports than oil did of imports. Asia, despite also being predominantly an oil-importing region, received an even greater stimulus than other regions from the rapid growth in China and the large increase in trade that it generated.

On a per capita basis, output increased by more than 3 per cent in almost half the developing countries, but those countries accounted for over 80 per cent of the developing world's population. Per capita output also increased by more than 3 per cent in all the economies in transition except one.

Of the 107 developing countries for which data were available, per capita output fell in only 13 cases, and those countries accounted for less than 3 per cent of the population. Of those 13 countries, 9 were in Africa and accounted for almost one quarter of that region's population. On the other hand, almost half the countries in Africa (but accounting for 40 per cent of the region's population) increased per capita output by more than 3 per cent. Those cases demonstrated that it was possible to achieve rates of growth in Africa that, if sustained, would slowly reduce poverty in the region. In South and East Asia, only four countries, accounting for less than 3 per cent of the region's population, failed to achieve 3 per cent growth of per capita output in 2004. In Western Asia, two of the four countries that experienced a decline in per capita output in 2003 achieved positive growth in 2004, but only half the countries in the region—the same number as in 2003—increased per capita output by more than 3 per cent. The largest turnaround was in Latin America: in 2003, one third of the 24 countries in the region for which data were available (accounting for over 60 per cent of the region's population) experienced a decline in per capita output; in 2004, the same number of countries, accounting for over half the region's population, increased per capita output by more than 3 per cent. Among the developed countries performance was more varied. Growth was strong in North America, moderate in Japan but weak in Europe. With the exception of its new members and a few other countries, the EU had replaced Japan as the lagging economy.

Human Development Report 2004

The *Human Development Report 2004* [Sales No. E.04.III.B.I], prepared by UNDP, discussed the question of cultural liberty in a diverse world (see p. 1101).

In addition to providing a critical analysis of a different theme each year, the *Report* assessed the state of human development across the globe, involving country data that focused on human well-being, not just economic trends. In 2004, it ranked 177 countries in its human development index by combining indicators of life expectancy, educational attainment and adjusted per capita income, among other factors. Of the 177 countries listed, 55 were in the high human development category, 86 were in the medium category and 36 were in the low category.

UNDP consideration. In response to General Assembly resolution 57/264 [YUN 2002, p. 841], the Executive Board of UNDP/United Nations Population Fund included in its agenda an item on the *Human Development Report* for the purpose of improving the consultation process with Member States regarding the *Report*, in order to enhance its quality and accuracy without compromising its editorial independence. The UNDP Administrator's first report on the subject was submitted in 2003 [YUN 2003, p. 864]. In an April 2004 update, it was stated that for the *Human Development Report 2004*, UNDP had held consultations with the members of the Executive Board on five occasions and was committed to maintaining that level of consultation in future years.

In June [E/2004/35 (dec. 2004/25)], the Executive Board took note of the update.

Development policy and public administration

Committee for Development Policy

The Committee for Development Policy (CDP), at its sixth session (New York, 29 March–2 April) [E/2004/33], considered three major themes:

measures to improve resources mobilization for the implementation of the Programme of Action for the Least Developed Countries for the Decade 2001-2010 (see p. 855); evaluation of progress towards good governance in the context of the implementation of the MDGs; and matters related to the 2003 triennial review of the list of LDCs (see p. 852).

The Committee considered that good governance could be instrumental in achieving the goals of poverty reduction only if the process of measurement and assessment was not biased in favour of external criteria relevant to the donors, investors and international monitoring bodies, as opposed to the internal perspective of the country. In designing institutions and mechanisms for good governance in developing countries, an interactive process between donors and recipient countries was thus essential. On the one hand, measures imposed by donors had often lacked success when they failed to pay due consideration to the culture and history of recipient countries. On the other, recipient countries needed assistance from donors to bring their institutions and social, political and economic processes closer to those required by good governance. CDP proposed that LDCs be invited to participate in the deliberations of institutions where global norms and standards for aspects of good governance were established.

Public administration

Committee of Experts on Public Administration. The Committee of Experts on Public Administration, at its third session (New York, 29 March–2 April) [E/2004/44], had before it Secretariat reports on: revitalizing public administration as a strategic action for sustainable human development [E/C.16/2004/2]; the role of human resources in revitalizing public administration [E/C.16.2004/3]; the role of the public sector in advancing the knowledge society [E/C.16/2004/4]; strengthening public administration for the MDGs: a partnership-building approach [E/C.16/2004/5]; developing institutions of governance and public administration in Africa [E/C.16/2004/6]; basic data on government expenditure and taxation [E/C.16/2004/7]; and a proposed strategic framework for the period 2006-2007 [E/C.16/2004/8].

The Committee recommended that the Economic and Social Council: reaffirm the role of the public service in fulfilling the specific national goals for socio-economic development, as they were key indicators of Member States' attainment of the MDGs, devoting one of its future high-level segments to the changing role of a public administration geared to development; propose to the General Assembly three options relating to the commemoration of the tenth anniversary of the Assembly's resumed fiftieth session on public administration and development [YUN 1996, p. 750]—host the Global Forum on Reinventing Government in 2006, devote the Council's 2006 high-level segment to "A service-oriented public administration for the achievement of the MDGs", or celebrate the United Nations Public Service Day (23 June) and the awarding of the United Nations Public Service Awards in a more visible manner; consider how to leverage and integrate the work of the Committee of Experts in intergovernmental processes, particularly the deliberations of the commissions that considered development issues; recommend to international organizations and the donor community that they should increase financial, material and technical support to African States to strengthen governance and public administration; and decide that the next session of the Committee of Experts should be devoted to revitalizing public administration: strategic directions for the future, development of a methodology for a bottom-up participatory approach in identifying public administration foundations and principles, and enhancement of the celebration of the United Nations Public Service Day and of the competition for the United Nations Public Service Awards.

The Committee of Experts recommended to Member States that they should: focus the reform of their public administration systems on achieving conditions that would ensure and facilitate the attainment of the MDGs; adopt a holistic national strategy to strengthen the management of human capital in the public sector; have national public administrations act as the major facilitating factor in transition to the knowledge society and perceive themselves as e-governments; pursue the issue of partnerships through South-South cooperation; with UN assistance, if necessary, develop approaches, methodologies and tools for and knowledge on citizen-based policy formulation and performance monitoring; pay attention to low ratios of tax revenues to GDP; and disseminate available data on the public sector. Specific recommendations to African Governments were that they should: implement the African Union's Governance and Public Administration Programme under the aegis of the New Partnership for Africa's Development [YUN 2001, p. 900]; institute mechanisms for implementing and disseminating the Charter for the Public Service in Africa [ibid., p. 847]; adopt methods and systems that fostered opportunities for popular participation in the governance and develop-

ment process; strengthen the law-making, oversight and budget review capacities of the legislature; depoliticize the public service and transform it into a professional and non-partisan agent; and strengthen the judiciary to ensure predictability and peaceful resolution of disputes arising out of trade, industrial and international relations.

With regard to the United Nations, the Committee of Experts recommended that: the UN programme on public administration, finance and development should continue to focus on the reform/revitalization of the practice of public administration; the Secretariat should carry out policy research and technical cooperation on the role of human resources in revitalizing public administration and build on the successful outcomes of the Global Forum on Reinventing Government (see p. 851) by assisting in developing regional and national strategies to reinvent government; the UN Online Network in Public Administration and Finance (UNPAN) should be continuously enhanced; the Secretariat should continue studying the knowledge society and develop innovative tools, such as the code of accountability, engaged governance norms and a data base of best practices and indicators; the UN system should continue providing substantive technical and advisory support aimed at strengthening governance and public administration institutions in African States; and the Secretariat should assist Governments in their efforts to produce better data related to the measurement of public sector efficiency. The Committee of Experts advised the Secretariat to narrow the focus of the subprogramme's involvement and concentrate more on key priorities. In that respect, it regretted that resources for that purpose were again reduced. The Committee underscored the need for better dissemination of the Secretariat's outputs and promotion of its activities in the area of public administration and indicated that the promotion of successful practices of selected applicants for the United Nations Public Service Awards would increase the visibility of both the Economic and Social Council and the Secretariat. The Committee emphasized the importance of synergy between normative and technical cooperation work and that the Secretariat should continue implementing technical cooperation as an essential feeding mechanism into the deliberations of the policy-making organs of the United Nations.

Economic and Social Council action. By decision 2004/302 of 23 July, the Economic and Social Council took note of the report of the Committee of Experts on its third session and decided that its fourth (2005) session should be devoted to: revitalizing public administration, including by improving transparency, competence and accountability: strategic directions for the future; development of a methodology for a bottom-up participatory approach in identifying public administration foundations and principles; and enhancement of the celebration of United Nations Public Service Day and of the competition for United Nations Public Service Awards. The Council also decided to discuss the Council's recommendations further during its resumed substantive session.

By **decision 2004/325** of 11 November, the Council deferred consideration of the recommendations contained in the report of the Committee of Experts on its third session to its organizational session in January 2005.

Report of Secretary-General. In response to General Assembly resolution 58/231 [YUN 2003, p. 866], the Secretary-General submitted a 9 September report on public administration and development [A/59/346]. He outlined proposals for commemorating, during the Assembly's sixty-first (2006) session, the tenth anniversary of the Assembly's resumed fiftieth session on public administration and development [YUN 1996, p. 750], suggesting that the commemoration could be an opportune time to evaluate progress made in revitalizing public administration and to share successful experiences that had contributed to achieving the MDGs. The report recalled the recommendations made by the Committee of Experts on Public Administration (see p. 849) and drew the Assembly's attention to recommendations on preparatory and supporting actions that could be taken in connection with the observance of the anniversary, including hosting the Global Forum on Reinventing Government in New York in 2006; devoting the high-level segment of the Economic and Social Council in 2006 to the changing role of administration; and celebrating United Nations Public Service Day and the presentation of the United Nations Public Service Awards in a more visible manner.

The report also described activities under way to promote information exchange, research and the dissemination of successful practices and advisory services in public administration, and to support e-government initiatives in the African, Asian, Central American and Caribbean regions as a tool for development.

The report noted that the Global Forum on Reinventing Government, which was supported technically and substantively by the UN programme on public administration, finance and development, had been held five times since its launch in 1999 by the United States and was to hold its sixth session in the Republic of Korea in

2005 on the theme "Towards participatory and transparent governance". The seventh Global Forum could be hosted at United Nations Headquarters in 2006.

On 2 December [meeting 65], the General Assembly adopted **resolution 59/55** [draft: A/59/L.27/Rev.1 & Add.1, orally revised], without vote [agenda item 12].

Public administration and development

The General Assembly,

Recalling all pertinent resolutions, in particular its resolution 58/231 of 23 December 2003 on public administration and development,

Recalling also the historic resumed fiftieth session of the General Assembly, devoted to the subject of the strengthening of public administration and development,

Stressing the need for capacity-building and e-Government initiatives as tools to promote development,

Recognizing that efficient, accountable, effective and transparent public administration at both the national and the international levels constitutes a key factor in development,

Recognizing also the importance of strengthening public administration institutions, improving public sector human resources capacity and fostering knowledge creation and innovation and the utilization of information technology for development in public administration and in the implementation of internationally agreed development goals, including those contained in the United Nations Millennium Declaration,

Welcoming the adoption of the United Nations Convention against Corruption,

1. *Takes note* of the report of the Secretary-General;

2. *Stresses* the importance of United Nations Public Service Day and the United Nations Public Service Awards in the process of revitalizing public administration by building a culture of innovation, partnership and responsiveness;

3. *Also stresses* the valuable contribution that the Global Forum on Reinventing Government has made to the exchange of lessons learned in public administration reform, and reiterates its appreciation to the Government of the Republic of Korea for hosting the Sixth Global Forum on Reinventing Government in 2005;

4. *Encourages* the Secretary-General to make arrangements for the implementation of the proposals made for the commemoration of the tenth anniversary of the resumed fiftieth session of the General Assembly, on public administration and development;

5. *Takes note* of the important analytical and operational contribution that the *World Public Sector Report* provides to policy makers responsible for public administration in Member States;

6. *Requests* the Secretary-General to continue to facilitate, through the United Nations Online Network in Public Administration and Finance, the dissemination of valuable practices in public administration;

7. *Also requests* the Secretary-General to focus the work on public administration along the lines of Eco-

nomic and Social Council decision 2004/302 of 23 July 2004 and General Assembly resolution 58/231;

8. *Further requests* the Secretary-General to submit a report to the General Assembly at its sixtieth session on progress made in Member States by revitalizing public administration during the last ten years, since the resumed fiftieth session of the Assembly, on public administration and development, and to ensure that the findings are brought to the attention of Member States on the occasion of the special event in 2005.

In-depth evaluation

By a 16 March note [E/AC.51/2004/3], the Secretary-General transmitted to CPC the OIOS report on the in-depth evaluation of the UN programme on public administration, finance and development. The report recommended: rationalizing the scope and focus of DESA's Division for Public Administration and Development Management; ensuring support to international cooperation in tax matters and to public finance management work; enhancing the repertoire of best practices; developing an information strategy; enhancing UNPAN; enhancing linkages and synergies between functions and across themes; and strengthening collaboration among UN entities. The Secretary-General concurred with the report's recommendations.

At its forty-fourth session (New York, 7 June–2 July) [A/59/16], CPC reworded the recommendation on support to international cooperation in tax matters, and recalled the General Assembly's request in resolution 58/270 [YUN 2003, p. 1399] that the Secretary-General undertake a review of the regular programme of technical cooperation and make proposals to the Assembly at its fifty-ninth session. It recommended the approval of the other recommendations contained in the evaluation.

Groups of countries in special situations

On 17 September, the General Assembly, on the recommendation of the General Committee, included in the agenda of its fifty-ninth session the item entitled "Groups of countries in special situations", covering LDCs and landlocked and transit developing countries.

By **decision 59/537** of 22 December, the Assembly took note of the report of the Second Committee on groups of countries in special situations [A/59/486].

Least developed countries

The special problems of the officially designated LDCs were considered in several UN forums in 2004, especially through the implementation of the Brussels Declaration and the Programme of Action for LDCs for the Decade 2001-2010, adopted at the Third UN Conference on LDCs in 2001 [YUN 2001, p. 770] and endorsed by the General Assembly in resolution 55/279 in July of that year [ibid., p. 771]. Of major concern in 2004 was the question of a smooth transition strategy for countries graduating from the list of LDCs.

LDC list

The number of countries officially designated as LDCs remained at 50. Although Cape Verde and Maldives were recommended for graduation from the list, that process would take place over a three-year period, as decided by the General Assembly in **resolution 59/209** (see p. 854).

The full list of LDCs comprised: Afghanistan, Angola, Bangladesh, Benin, Bhutan, Burkina Faso, Burundi, Cambodia, Cape Verde, Central African Republic, Chad, Comoros, Democratic Republic of the Congo, Djibouti, Equatorial Guinea, Eritrea, Ethiopia, Gambia, Guinea, Guinea-Bissau, Haiti, Kiribati, Lao People's Democratic Republic, Lesotho, Liberia, Madagascar, Malawi, Maldives, Mali, Mauritania, Mozambique, Myanmar, Nepal, Niger, Rwanda, Samoa, Sao Tome and Principe, Senegal, Sierra Leone, Solomon Islands, Somalia, Sudan, Timor-Leste, Togo, Tuvalu, Uganda, United Republic of Tanzania, Vanuatu, Yemen, Zambia.

Smooth transition strategy

CDP consideration. At its sixth session (New York, 29 March–2 April) [E/2004/33], CDP, which was responsible for adding countries to or graduating them from the LDC list, confirmed at the conclusion of its fifth (2003) session [YUN 2003, p. 868] that Cape Verde and Maldives qualified for graduation from the list and recommended that they be graduated from the LDC category. However, CDP stressed the need for a smooth transition strategy to be put in place by both the countries themselves and the international community. Among the measures to ensure a smooth transition, the Committee proposed that the United Nations convene an ad hoc country advisory group, in which the graduated country, in cooperation with its development partners, would identify measures to ensure that its development was maintained. The guiding principle of that initiative was that specific transition support measures, monitoring arrangements and the period of transition would be decided on a case-by-case basis so that the development progress of graduated countries was not interrupted or reversed.

On 3 June [meeting 13], the Economic and Social Council adopted **resolution 2004/3** [draft: E/2004/L.10] without vote [agenda item 2].

Report of the Committee for Development Policy

The Economic and Social Council,

Recalling General Assembly resolution 46/206 of 20 December 1991,

Expressing its conviction that no country graduating from the least developed country category should have its positive development disrupted or reversed but should be able to continue and sustain its progress and development,

Emphasizing the need for putting in place a process for smooth transition of countries graduating out of the group of least developed countries,

1. *Takes note* of chapter IV of the report of the Committee for Development Policy on its fifth session and the conclusions contained therein, inter alia, that Cape Verde and Maldives qualified for graduation from the list of least developed countries;

2. *Requests* the Secretary-General, in consultation with Member States, to submit to the Economic and Social Council at its substantive session of 2004 a report including recommendations on how to formulate a smooth transition strategy for countries graduating from least developed country status;

3. *Also requests* the Secretary-General to prepare the report in an inclusive and transparent manner with the involvement of Member States, in particular the least developed countries, as well as bilateral and multilateral donors and relevant international organizations;

4. *Decides* to take a decision on a smooth transition strategy for countries graduating from least developed country status and on the graduation of Cape Verde and Maldives from the list of least developed countries at its substantive session of 2004.

Report of Secretary-General. In response to Economic and Social Council resolution 2004/3 (above), the Secretary-General submitted to the Council's substantive session a report on formulating a smooth transition strategy for countries graduating from LDC status [E/2004/94]. The report took into account CDP's recommendations (see p. 852), information provided to the Committee by a number of international organizations and information supplied by Governments. It described the benefits associated with LDC status, such as preferential market access, special treatment regarding World Trade Organization (WTO)–related obligations, development financing and technical cooperation, and suggested possible elements for a smooth transition strategy that involved a graduating country retaining some existing benefits so that its development prospects would not be adversely affected.

The report concluded that the success of a smooth transition strategy would depend on cooperation between graduated LDCs and the international community. However, as with all development strategies, the graduated LDCs themselves had to play the central role in formulating and implementing their transition strategy and to ensure that the strategy was attuned to national conditions and circumstances. At the same time, the continued support of development partners was critical to ensuring success. Given that WTO provisions granting differential treatment to LDCs constituted a multilateral instrument outside the purview of the Council and the General Assembly, WTO member States would need to take the initiative to ensure that graduated countries continued to benefit from LDC trade preferences for a transition period after graduation. The international community was encouraged to strengthen efforts to foster private sector development in, and to increase credit guarantees for, graduated countries.

In July, the Economic and Social Council adopted **decision 2004/299** [draft: E/2004/L.45] without vote [agenda item 13 *(a)*].

Report of the Committee for Development Policy

At its 50th plenary meeting, on 23 July 2004, the Economic and Social Council, recalling its resolution 2004/3 of 3 June 2004 on the report of the Committee for Development Policy:

(a) Took note of the progress achieved so far in the consideration of the report of the Secretary-General on formulating a smooth transition strategy for countries graduating from least developed country status and of the report of the Committee for Development Policy on its sixth session;

(b) Decided to revert to this matter at its resumed substantive session of 2004, building further on the elements for draft resolutions under agenda item 13 *(a)* contained in the annex to the present decision.

Annex

Elements for draft resolutions under agenda item 13 *(a)*

The Economic and Social Council will adopt simultaneously two different resolutions:

- One on the report of the Secretary-General on formulating a smooth transition strategy for countries graduating from least developed country status

- One on the report of the Committee for Development Policy on its sixth session, including its recommendation to graduate Maldives and Cape Verde

Elements for a draft resolution on a smooth transition strategy

1. Reconfirmation of general principles related to a smooth transition

2. Definition of the time sequence of a transition process, building on General Assembly resolution

46/206 of 20 December 1991 and subsequent resolutions of the Economic and Social Council:

- A first phase (I), of a three-year duration, beginning with the first identification of a country by
  the Committee for Development Policy and
  ending with the validation of the findings at the
  second review and the recommendation by the
  Committee to graduate the country

- A second phase (II), following the endorsement
  by the General Assembly of the recommendation by the Committee for Development Policy,
  lasting for a period of three years, during which
  the graduating country keeps its least developed
  country status and the advantages associated
  with it and activates, in a dialogue with its main
  partners at the country level, the preparations
  for the third phase, when it will have lost its least
  developed country status

- A third phase (III), following the expiration of
  phase II, of an undetermined duration, during
  which the graduated country, in line with the
  strategy elaborated with its partners in phase II,
  phases out advantages associated with its earlier
  least developed country status

3. Definition of the mechanisms and content of the
transition process, building on the recommendations in the report of the Secretary-General:

- Invite the graduating country to envisage action
  during phase I and initiate a process at the
  country level and, especially during phase II,
  build on the existing mechanism for coordination with donors

- Invite the partners of the graduating country
  (bilateral and multilateral) to engage in the elaboration in phase II and implementation in
  phase III of a country-specific transition strategy

4. Definition of a monitoring mechanism:

- Follow-up of the implementation of the smooth
  transition strategy at the country level during
  phase III under the overall responsibility of the
  Government

- Specific monitoring of the country, beginning
  at the end of phase II, during a series of triennial reviews by the Committee for Development
  Policy

- Invitation to the national Government to keep
  the Committee informed of evolution at the
  country level

5. Specific requests to the Secretary-General and
United Nations agencies:

- The issue of the vulnerability profile in phase I

- Assistance through the resident coordinator
  system during phase II (convening a country-
  based mechanism; assisting the Government in
  the identification of critical areas, etc.)

6. Recommendation to the General Assembly to endorse the resolution

**Elements for a draft resolution on the
report of the Committee for Development Policy**

Take note of the report, including its recommendation to graduate Maldives and Cape Verde.

On 5 November [meeting 53], the Council
adopted **resolution 2004/66** [draft: E/2004/L.56]
without vote [agenda item 13 (*a*)].

**Smooth transition strategy for countries graduating
from the list of least developed countries**

The Economic and Social Council

Recommends to the General Assembly the adoption of
the following draft resolution:

[For text, see General Assembly resolution 59/209 below.]

On 20 December [meeting 74], the General Assembly adopted **resolution 59/209** [draft: A/59/
L.47 & Add.1] without vote [agenda item 12].

**Smooth transition strategy for countries graduating
from the list of least developed countries**

The General Assembly,

Recalling its resolution 46/206 of 20 December 1991,

Recalling also Economic and Social Council resolution 2004/66 of 5 November 2004,

Reconfirming Economic and Social Council resolutions 2000/34 of 28 July 2000, 2001/43 of 24 October
2001, 2002/36 of 26 July 2002 and 2004/3 of 3 June
2004,

1. *Re-emphasizes* the need for a smooth transition for
countries graduating from the list of least developed
countries;

2. *Reconfirms* that graduating from the list of least
developed countries should not result in a disruption
of development plans, programmes and projects;

3. *Decides* that the process to ensure a smooth transition of countries graduating from the list of least developed countries shall be as follows:

(*a*) When the Committee for Development Policy,
in its triennial review of the list of least developed
countries, identifies a country that meets the criteria
for graduation for the first time, it will submit its findings to the Economic and Social Council;

(*b*) After a country has met the criteria for graduation for the first time, the Secretary-General of the
United Nations will invite the Secretary-General of the
United Nations Conference on Trade and Development to prepare a vulnerability profile on the identified country, as described in paragraph 3 (*a*) above, to
be taken into account by the Committee for Development Policy at its subsequent triennial review;

(*c*) At the subsequent triennial review undertaken
by the Committee for Development Policy, referred to
in paragraph 3 (*b*) above, the qualification for graduation of the country will be reviewed and, if reconfirmed, the Committee will submit a recommendation, in accordance with the established procedures, to
the Economic and Social Council;

(*d*) The Economic and Social Council, in turn, will
take action on the recommendation of the Committee
for Development Policy at its first substantive session
following the triennial review of the Committee and
will transmit its decision to the General Assembly;

(*e*) Three years following the decision of the General Assembly to take note of the recommendation of
the Committee for Development Policy to graduate a
country from the list of least developed countries,
graduation will become effective; during the three-

year period, the country will remain on the list of least developed countries and will maintain the advantages associated with membership on that list;

4. *Invites* the graduating country, in cooperation with its bilateral and multilateral development and trading partners and with the support of the United Nations system, to prepare, during the three-year period, a transition strategy to adjust to the phasing out, over a period appropriate to the development situation of the country, of the advantages associated with its membership on the list of least developed countries, and to identify actions to be taken by the graduating country and its bilateral and multilateral development and trading partners to that end;

5. *Recommends* that the graduating country establish, in cooperation with its bilateral and multilateral development and trading partners, a consultative mechanism to facilitate the preparation of the transition strategy and the identification of the associated actions;

6. *Requests* the Administrator of the United Nations Development Programme, in his capacity as Chair of the United Nations Development Group, to assist countries graduating from the list of least developed countries by providing, if requested, the support of the United Nations Resident Coordinator and the United Nations Country Team to the consultative mechanism;

7. *Urges* all development partners to support the implementation of the transition strategy and to avoid any abrupt reductions in either official development assistance or technical assistance provided to the graduated country;

8. *Invites* development and trading partners to consider extending to the graduated country trade preferences previously made available as a result of least developed country status, or reducing them in a phased manner in order to avoid their abrupt reduction;

9. *Invites* all members of the World Trade Organization to consider extending to a graduated country, as appropriate, the existing special and differential treatment and exemptions available to least developed countries for a period appropriate to the development situation;

10. *Recommends* that the continued implementation of technical assistance programmes under the Integrated Framework for Trade-related Technical Assistance to Least Developed Countries be considered for the graduated country over a period appropriate to the development situation of the country;

11. *Invites* the Government of the graduated country to closely monitor, with the support of the consultative mechanism, the implementation of the transition strategy and to keep the Secretary-General informed on a regular basis;

12. *Requests* the Committee for Development Policy to continue to monitor the development progress of the graduated country as a complement to its triennial review of the list of least developed countries, with the assistance and support of other relevant entities, and to report thereon to the Economic and Social Council.

Graduation of Cape Verde and Maldives

On 5 November [meeting 53], the Economic and Social Council adopted **resolution 2004/67** [draft: E/2004/L.57] without vote [agenda item 13 (a)].

Report of the Committee for Development Policy on its sixth session

The Economic and Social Council,

Recalling its decision 2004/299 of 23 July 2004 on the report of the Committee for Development Policy,

Taking into account its resolution 2004/66 of 5 November 2004 on a smooth transition strategy for countries graduating from the list of least developed countries,

1. *Endorses* the recommendation of the Committee for Development Policy that Cape Verde and Maldives be graduated from the least developed country category, as contained in the report of the Committee on its sixth session;

2. *Recommends* that the General Assembly take note of the recommendation of the Committee for Development Policy that Cape Verde and Maldives be graduated from the least developed country category.

On 20 December [meeting 74], the General Assembly adopted **resolution 59/210** [draft: A/59/L.48 & Add.1] without vote [agenda item 12].

Report of the Committee for Development Policy on its sixth session

The General Assembly,

Recalling Economic and Social Council resolution 2004/67 of 5 November 2004 on the report of the Committee for Development Policy,

Taking into account its resolution 59/209 of 20 December 2004 on a smooth transition strategy for countries graduating from the list of least developed countries,

Takes note of the recommendation of the Committee for Development Policy that Cape Verde and Maldives be graduated from the group of least developed countries.

Programme of Action (2001-2010)

UNCTAD XI action. The eleventh session of the United Nations Conference on Trade and Development (UNCTAD XI) (São Paulo, Brazil, 13-18 June) [TD/412] (see p. 954) adopted the São Paulo Consensus in which it called for special measures to assist LDCs. In view of the increasing marginalization of LDCs in the global economy, the Consensus called for UNCTAD to play a leading role in the substantive and technical implementation of the Brussels Programme of Action, stating that it should continue to examine the causes of decline in the share of LDCs in world trade and the linkages between trade, growth and poverty reduction with a view to identifying long-term solutions to those problems.

During UNCTAD XI, on 13 June, the Ministers of the LDCs met and adopted the Declaration of the LDCs Ministerial Meeting at UNCTAD XI [TD/408], which was included in the UNCTAD XI report.

Economic and Social Council ministerial declaration. In accordance with decision 2003/287

[YUN 2003, p. 869], the high-level segment of the Economic and Social Council in 2004 (New York, 28-30 June and 6 July) [A/59/3/Rev.1] considered the theme "Resources mobilization and enabling environment for poverty eradication in the context of the implementation of the Programme of Action for the Least Developed Countries for the Decade 2001-2010". It had before it an April report of the Secretary-General on the subject [E/2004/54], which stated that improving the domestic and global environment was crucial to enabling the development of LDCs and that global, regional and national partnerships, including with civil society and the private sector, should be explored to that end.

During the segment, five high-level round tables were held on: local private sector development: the role of microfinance/microcredit; attracting foreign direct investment (FDI) in LDCs; the role of trade preferences for LDCs in promoting investment; unleashing entrepreneurship: the role of partnerships in mobilizing resources for LDCs; and investment in urban water, sanitation and sustainable human settlements development in LDCs.

Also during the segment, the ILO Director-General made a presentation on the report of the World Commission on the Social Dimension of Globalization entitled *A Fair Globalization: Creating Opportunities for All* [A/59/98-E/2004/79] (see p. 1091) as it related to the successful implementation of the Programme of Action.

On 6 July, the Council adopted a ministerial declaration in which the ministers and heads of delegations participating in the high-level segment affirmed their commitment to the implementation of the goals and objectives set out in the Brussels Programme of Action. They recognized the need for creating an overall enabling environment for national and international actions to eradicate poverty, promote sustainable development of LDCs and for the implementation of the Programme of Action, and addressed the specific issues of good governance; the significance of food security, fighting the HIV/AIDS pandemic, malaria and tuberculosis, improving access to health care, education and other social services, particularly for women, the poor and other vulnerable groups, and protecting the environment; and the need for international support for LDCs and for the implementation of the actions contained in the Programme of Action. National and/or international action was encouraged in the areas of improving the enabling environment for the private sector; enhancing the agricultural sector; promoting an inclusive financial sector; removing obstacles preventing the transfer of assets of migrant workers from

LDCs to their countries of origin; reaching the official development assistance (ODA) target of contributing 0.2 per cent of gross national product to LDCs; solving the debt problems of LDCs; trade preferences in favour of LDCs; FDI; and the special need of LDCs emerging from conflict situations.

ECONOMIC AND SOCIAL COUNCIL ACTION

On 5 November [meeting 53], the Economic and Social Council adopted **resolution 2004/65** [draft: E/2004/L.55] without vote [agenda item 6 (b)].

Implementation of the Programme of Action for the Least Developed Countries for the Decade 2001-2010

The Economic and Social Council,

Recalling the Brussels Declaration and the Programme of Action for the Least Developed Countries for the Decade 2001-2010,

Recalling also its decision 2001/320 of 24 October 2001, in which it decided to establish, under the regular agenda item entitled "Integrated and coordinated implementation of and follow-up to the major United Nations conferences and summits", a regular sub-item entitled "Review and coordination of the implementation of the Programme of Action for the Least Developed Countries for the Decade 2001-2010",

Recalling further its resolution 2003/17 of 22 July 2003 and its decision 2003/287 of 24 July 2003, as well as the ministerial declaration of the high-level segment of its substantive session of 2004 on the theme "Resources mobilization and enabling environment for poverty eradication in the context of the implementation of the Programme of Action for the Least Developed Countries for the Decade 2001-2010",

Acknowledging the presentation made by the Director-General of the International Labour Organization during the 2004 high-level segment of the Economic and Social Council on the report of the World Commission on the Social Dimension of Globalization entitled *A Fair Globalization: Creating Opportunities for All* as it relates to the successful implementation of the Programme of Action,

Taking note of the report of the Secretary-General,

1. *Expresses its concern* over the still weak implementation of the Programme of Action for the Least Developed Countries for the Decade 2001-2010;

2. *Urges* the least developed countries and their bilateral and multilateral development partners to undertake increased efforts and to adopt speedy measures, with a view to creating an overall enabling environment for the implementation of the Programme of Action and to meeting its goals and targets in a timely manner;

3. *Reiterates* the critical importance of the participation of government representatives from the least developed countries in the annual assessment of the Programme of Action by the Economic and Social Council, and in this regard requests the Secretary-General to take concrete measures for the full implementation of the provision of paragraph 8 of General Assembly resolution 58/228 of 23 December 2003;

4. *Calls upon* the Secretary-General, while stressing the central role of the Economic and Social Council in

the coordination of actions in the United Nations system for the implementation of the Programme of Action, to take appropriate measures to strengthen the efficiency and effectiveness of the Office of the High Representative for the Least Developed Countries, Landlocked Developing Countries and Small Island Developing States so that it can fulfil its functions in accordance with General Assembly resolution 56/227 of 24 December 2001;

5. *Reiterates* that the review of the Programme of Action and the evaluation of the performance of the least developed countries and their development partners in implementing their various commitments should be based on the goals and targets set out in the Programme of Action;

6. *Requests* the Secretary-General to submit an annual progress report on the implementation of the Programme of Action in a more analytical and results-oriented manner by placing greater emphasis on concrete results and indicating the progress achieved in its implementation, which could include the use of a matrix of achievements;

7. *Also requests* the Secretary-General to ensure that the report takes into consideration the broader development agenda and existing reporting mechanisms in order to avoid duplication.

Trade and Development Board action. The UNCTAD Trade and Development Board (TDB), at its fifty-first session (Geneva, 4-15 October), adopted agreed conclusions [A/59/15 (agreed conclusions 479(LI))] on the review of progress in the implementation of the Brussels Programme of Action. Having considered *The Least Developed Countries Report 2004: Linking International Trade with Poverty Reduction* [Sales No. E.04.II.D.27], the Board noted with concern the lack of progress in LDCs towards achieving the international development goals, including those contained in the United Nations Millennium Declaration [YUN 2000, p. 49] and the Programme of Action. It stressed the urgent need for development strategies that responded to the development needs of LDCs, including debt relief, enhanced ODA and investment flows, improved market access and a more conducive international trading regime, in addition to a conducive domestic macroeconomic framework in order to make international trade work for poverty reduction in LDCs. TDB emphasized the necessity for capacity-building in LDCs and recommended that, in order to enable the UNCTAD Special Programme on the Least Developed Countries, Landlocked Developing Countries and Small Island Developing States to discharge effectively the tasks assigned to it, due consideration should be given to the outcomes of UNCTAD XI in the allocation of resources for the Programme for the 2006-2007 biennium.

Report of Secretary-General. In response to Economic and Social Council resolution 2003/17 [YUN 2003, p. 868] and General Assembly resolution 58/228 [ibid., p. 870], the Secretary-General submitted a June report on the implementation of the Programme of Action for the LDCs for the Decade 2001-2010 [A/59/94-E/2004/77]. He described the overall situation in the LDCs and provided an overview of the implementation of the Programme of Action, including by the Office of the High Representative for the LDCs, Landlocked Developing Countries and Small Island Developing States (SIDS).

The Secretary-General said all LDCs that had not done so should articulate their strategy and programme for poverty reduction and sustainable growth and should expeditiously set up national forums to guide and monitor the implementation of the Brussels Programme of Action. LDCs should give special attention to infrastructure development and policies for the development of manufacturing and focus on selected sectors for expansion of their productive capacity and beneficial integration into the global economy. Developed countries should expedite the process of opening up markets for LDC products, and all development partners, particularly the donor countries, should endeavour to focus on the category of LDCs in their ODA policy and development support.

GENERAL ASSEMBLY ACTION

On 22 December [meeting 75], the General Assembly, on the recommendation of the Second Committee [A/59/486/Add.1], adopted **resolution 59/244** without vote [agenda item 88 *(a)*].

Third United Nations Conference on the Least Developed Countries

The General Assembly,

Recalling its resolution 55/279 of 12 July 2001, in which it endorsed the Brussels Declaration and the Programme of Action for the Least Developed Countries for the Decade 2001-2010, and its resolutions 57/276 of 20 December 2002 and 58/228 of 23 December 2003 on the Third United Nations Conference on the Least Developed Countries,

Reaffirming its resolution 55/2 of 8 September 2000, by which it adopted the United Nations Millennium Declaration, in particular paragraph 15 thereof, in which the Heads of State and Government undertook to address the special needs of the least developed countries,

Recognizing the importance of the review of the progress achieved towards meeting the goals and targets contained in the Programme of Action, as well as other internationally agreed development goals, including those contained in the Millennium Declaration, as they address the special needs of the least developed countries,

Taking note of the ministerial declaration of the high-level segment of the substantive session of 2004 of the Economic and Social Council on the theme "Resources mobilization and enabling environment for poverty eradication in the context of the implementation of the Programme of Action for the Least Developed Countries for the Decade 2001-2010",

Taking note also of Economic and Social Council resolutions 2004/66 of 5 November 2004 on the smooth transition strategy for countries graduating from the list of least developed countries and 2004/67 of 5 November 2004 on the report of the Committee for Development Policy on its sixth session,

Taking note further of the *Least Developed Countries Report, 2004,*

Recognizing that the eradication of poverty in the least developed countries will require, inter alia, steps to empower the poor, unleash their entrepreneurial skills and allow them to access, develop and use their assets,

Taking note of the report of the Secretary-General,

1. *Reiterates its deep concern* over the weak implementation of the Programme of Action for the Least Developed Countries for the Decade 2001-2010;

2. *Urges* the least developed countries and their bilateral and multilateral development partners to increase concerted efforts and speedy measures for meeting the goals and targets of the Programme of Action in a timely manner;

3. *Reiterates its request* to the Secretary-General to ensure at the secretariat level the full mobilization and coordination of all parts of the United Nations system to facilitate coordinated implementation as well as coherence in the follow-up to and monitoring of the Programme of Action at the national, regional, subregional and global levels, and in this context requests the Secretary-General to engage the United Nations Development Group's team leaders, consistent with their respective mandates, in the coordinated implementation of activities of the Programme of Action;

4. *Invites* the 2005 high-level event, in accordance with the modalities to be set by the General Assembly at its fifty-ninth session, to address the special needs of the least developed countries, while reviewing the progress made in the achievement of internationally agreed development goals, including those contained in the United Nations Millennium Declaration;

5. *Decides* to hold the comprehensive review of the Programme of Action in 2006 within the General Assembly during its sixty-first session, in accordance with paragraph 114 of the Programme of Action, bearing in mind the provisions of General Assembly resolution 57/270 B of 23 June 2003, with modalities to be decided upon;

6. *Decides also* to consider at its sixtieth session the modalities for conducting such a comprehensive review;

7. *Reiterates* the critical importance of the participation of government representatives from the least developed countries in the annual review of the Programme of Action by the Economic and Social Council, and in this regard requests the Secretary-General to establish a specific trust fund for the travel and subsistence of two representatives from each least developed country to attend the annual review of the Programme of Action; the trust fund should be funded by voluntary contributions;

8. *Calls upon* Member States, and invites intergovernmental and non-governmental organizations and the private sector, to make voluntary contributions to the trust fund;

9. *Welcomes* the decision of the United Nations Conference on Trade and Development at its eleventh session to conduct analyses through the *Least Developed Countries Report, 2004* on the causes of the decline in the share of least developed countries in world trade and the linkages between trade, growth and poverty reduction, with a view to identifying long-term solutions to the problem, as expressed in paragraph 34 of the São Paulo Consensus, and invites the United Nations Conference on Trade and Development to conduct an analysis of the role that enterprise development can play in alleviating poverty in least developed countries and to recommend measures the Governments of least developed countries can take to promote the development of their private sector;

10. *Emphasizes* the importance of the effective implementation of Economic and Social Council resolution 2004/66 in order to support countries graduating from the list of least developed countries;

11. *Requests* the Secretary-General to submit an annual progress report on the implementation of the Programme of Action in an analytical and results-oriented way by placing emphasis on concrete results and indicating the progress achieved in its implementation.

Island developing States

During 2004, UN bodies continued to review progress in the implementation of the Programme of Action for the Sustainable Development of Small Island Developing States (Barbados Programme of Action), adopted at the 1994 Global Conference on the subject [YUN 1994, p. 783]. Also, preparations proceeded for the International Meeting to Review the Implementation of the Programme of Action for the Sustainable Development of Small Island Developing States. The International Meeting, originally scheduled to be held in Mauritius from 30 August to 3 September 2004, was deferred to 10 to 14 January 2005, at the request of the Government of Mauritius.

Commission on Sustainable Development action. The Commission on Sustainable Development, acting as the preparatory meeting for the International Meeting to Review the Implementation of the Programme of Action for the Sustainable Development of SIDS, met in New York from 14 to 16 April [A/CONF.207/3].

In response to General Assembly resolutions 57/262 [YUN 2002, p. 848] and 58/213 A [YUN 2003, p. 873], the Secretary-General submitted an 11 March report on review of progress in the implementation of the Barbados Programme of Action [E/CN.17/2004/8], which offered an overall assessment of progress achieved through the efforts of SIDS, with the support of regional and international organizations, including UN agencies and the donor community. It concluded that progress in implementing the Programme of Action had been mixed and that SIDS still faced major challenges to their sustainable development, some of long standing and others of more recent origin. Key emerging challenges included those related to the implementation of effective strategies for poverty eradication and the pursuit of people-centred development, coping with the effects and the cost of international security threats on travel and tourism, the development of cultural industries and addressing urgently the growing problem of HIV/AIDS. Sustainable development financing mechanisms were needed, including through regional development banks, to cover the provision of energy and capacity development investments; direct assistance programmes for poverty alleviation; collective insurance in the face of climate change and increased vulnerability to natural disasters; technology transfer; programmes to assist the development and protection of traditional and indigenous knowledge; and the active exploration of ways to make more productive use of the natural and indigenous endowments of SIDS.

Also before the Commission was a March note by the Secretariat on accreditation of NGOs and other major groups to the International Meeting [E/CN.17/2004/9], to which a list of recommended NGOs and other major groups was appended. The Commission approved the requests for accreditation of the listed groups on 14 April. Additions to that list were submitted to the General Assembly by the Secretariat in a 4 October note [A/59/409 & Corr.1].

By a 26 March letter [E/CN.17/2004/12], Qatar transmitted to the Secretary-General the Alliance of Small Island States Strategy for the Further Implementation of the Barbados Programme of Action, adopted by the Interregional Preparatory Meeting of SIDS for the International Meeting (Nassau, Bahamas, 26-30 January).

The Commission adopted two decisions by which it authorized the New Zealand Ambassador to continue his consultations with a view to reaching agreement on remaining pending issues for the preparations for the International Meeting [dec. 2004/1] and agreed to hold two-day informal consultations in Mauritius prior to the International Meeting [dec. 2004/2].

Communication. By a letter of 16 January [A/58/686], Seychelles transmitted the final report of the second Small Island Developing States of the Atlantic, Indian Ocean, Mediterranean and South China Seas Regional Meeting to Review the Implementation of the Programme of Action, held in Mahé, Seychelles, from 8 to 10 January.

GENERAL ASSEMBLY ACTION

On 10 June [meeting 90], the General Assembly adopted **resolution 58/213 B** [draft: A/58/L.63] without vote [agenda items 8 & 94 *(d)*].

Further implementation of the Programme of Action for the Sustainable Development of Small Island Developing States

The General Assembly,

Recalling its resolution 58/213 A of 23 December 2003, in which it decided to convene the International Meeting to Review the Implementation of the Programme of Action for the Sustainable Development of Small Island Developing States from 30 August to 3 September 2004,

Recalling also the offer of the Government of Mauritius to host the International Meeting,

Taking note of the request by the Government of Mauritius to reschedule the International Meeting due to logistical considerations,

1. *Decides* to convene the International Meeting to Review the Implementation of the Programme of Action for the Sustainable Development of Small Island Developing States from 10 to 14 January 2005;

2. *Also decides* to hold, if deemed necessary and taking into account paragraph 7 of its resolution 58/213 A, two days of informal consultations in Mauritius, on 8 and 9 January 2005, to facilitate the effective preparation of the International Meeting;

3. *Takes note* of the appointment of a Facilitator for the process of informal consultations, who will report progress thereon to the Bureau of the International Meeting, when constituted.

On 22 December [meeting 75], the Assembly, on the recommendation of the Second Committee [A/59/483/Add.2], adopted **resolution 59/229** without vote [agenda item 85 *(b)*].

Further implementation of the Programme of Action for the Sustainable Development of Small Island Developing States

The General Assembly,

Recalling the Declaration of Barbados and the Programme of Action for the Sustainable Development of Small Island Developing States, adopted by the Global Conference on the Sustainable Development of Small Island Developing States, and recalling also its resolution 49/122 of 19 December 1994 on the Global Conference,

Recalling also its resolutions 58/213 A of 23 December 2003 and 58/213 B of 10 June 2004,

Recalling with appreciation the offer by the Government of Mauritius to host the International Meeting to Review the Implementation of the Programme of Action for the Sustainable Development of Small Island Developing States,

Welcoming the preparatory activities undertaken at the national, regional and international levels for the International Meeting,

1. *Recalls* its decision, in resolution 58/213 B, to convene the International Meeting to Review the Implementation of the Programme of Action for the Sustainable Development of Small Island Developing States from 10 to 14 January 2005;

2. *Decides* to hold two days of informal consultations in Mauritius, on 8 and 9 January 2005, to facilitate the effective preparation of the International Meeting;

3. *Urges* that representation and participation at the International Meeting be at the highest possible level;

4. *Takes note* of the report of the Commission on Sustainable Development, acting as the preparatory meeting for the International Meeting;

5. *Expresses its appreciation* for the contributions made to the voluntary trust fund established for the purpose of assisting small island developing States to participate fully and effectively in the International Meeting and its preparatory process, as approved by the Economic and Social Council in its resolution 2003/55 and decision 2003/283, and urges all Member States and organizations to contribute generously to the fund;

6. *Decides* that non-governmental organizations whose work is relevant to the subject of the International Meeting, which are not currently accredited to the Economic and Social Council and which submitted applications to participate as observers in the International Meeting by 31 October 2004, may participate as observers in the International Meeting, subject to the approval of the General Assembly at its fifty-ninth session, and in this regard recalls that the participation of major groups, including non-governmental organizations, in the International Meeting shall be in accordance with rule 65 of the provisional rules of procedure of the International Meeting;

7. *Stresses* that strengthening of the Small Island Developing States Unit of the Department of Economic and Social Affairs of the Secretariat has yet to take place, and in this regard reiterates its request to the Secretary-General, made in General Assembly resolution 57/262 of 20 December 2002 and resolution 58/213 A, to strengthen the Unit without delay and, within existing resources, to enable the Unit, including the Small Island Developing States Network, to undertake its broad range of mandated functions with a view to facilitating the full and effective implementation of the Declaration of Barbados and the Programme of Action for the Sustainable Development of Small Island Developing States and the outcomes of the International Meeting;

8. *Invites* the International Meeting to consider fully the modalities for strengthening the Small Island Developing States Unit, including the Small Island Developing States Network, to enable it to assist effectively in the implementation of the outcomes of the International Meeting;

9. *Requests* the Secretary-General to submit to the General Assembly at its fifty-ninth session the report of the International Meeting, and decides to include in the provisional agenda of its sixtieth session, under the item entitled "Sustainable development", a sub-item entitled "Further implementation of the outcome of the Global Conference on the Sustainable Development of Small Island Developing States and follow-up to the outcomes of the International Meeting to Review the Implementation of the Barbados Programme of Action".

In other action, the Assembly, by **decision 59/534** of 22 December, approved the participation of NGOs listed in the 4 October note by the Secretariat (see p. 859) as observers to the International Meeting. On 23 December, the Assembly decided that the agenda item on further implementation of the Programme of Action would remain for consideration during its resumed fifty-ninth (2005) session (**decision 59/552**).

Landlocked developing countries

Report of Secretary-General. In response to General Assembly resolution 58/201 [YUN 2003, p. 877], the Secretary-General submitted a 5 August report [A/59/208] on the implementation of the Almaty Programme of Action: Addressing the Special Needs of Landlocked Developing Countries within a New Global Framework for Transit Transport Cooperation for Landlocked and Transit Developing Countries. The Programme of Action was adopted by the International Ministerial Conference of Landlocked and Transit Developing Countries and Donor Countries and International Financial and Development Institutions on Transit Transport Cooperation (Almaty, Kazakhstan) in 2003 [YUN 2003, p. 875].

The report noted that UN system organizations had made concerted efforts to operationalize coordination and monitoring mechanisms for the implementation of the Programme of Action. One of the main results was the preparation of the road map towards the implementation of the Programme of Action, which would provide guidance to organizations within the UN system and other international, regional and subregional organizations in undertaking necessary actions in a focused and well-coordinated manner. The report stated that, since landlocked developing countries depended on their transit neighbours for access to and from the sea, the establishment of efficient transit systems required closer and more effective collaboration between those countries and their transit neighbours. Transit policy reforms aimed at enhancing the efficiency of transit operations and reducing transport costs, including the commercialization and liberalization of transport services and efforts to improve institutional, procedural, regulatory and managerial systems, should be further encouraged, as should competition between different modes of transport and between different transit corridors. A strong case could be made in respect of landlocked developing countries for giving high priority to financial and technical assistance for the improvement of the transport infrastructure and to the management and maintenance of existing facilities. Given the relative poverty and related development handicaps characteristic of landlocked developing countries, it was important that financial assistance to those countries be extended under the most generous terms possible. The international community should provide greater market access for goods originating in landlocked developing countries, taking into consideration the high transport costs associated with their remoteness from major world markets, their lack of access to the sea and their dependence on a very limited number of commodities.

The report recommended that UN system organizations and bodies and relevant international, regional and subregional organizations provide greater financial and technical assistance to landlocked and transit developing countries. UN organizations should take action to pool together their expertise and resources to better address the issue. Donor countries and international financial and development institutions were invited to make contributions to the trust fund established to facilitate the implementation of and follow-up to the Almaty conference.

Ministerial communiqués. On the occasion of UNCTAD XI (São Paulo, 13-18 June), the ministers of landlocked developing countries issued a communiqué [TD/409] in which they stressed that excessive transport costs created a major barrier to foreign markets and observed that the share of landlocked developing countries in international trade was on the decline. They invited UN system organizations and other international organizations to take measures to implement the Almaty Programme of Action. On 15 July [A/59/158], the Lao People's Democratic Republic called the attention of UN Member States to the communiqué.

On 1 October [A/C.2/59/2], the Lao People's Democratic Republic, as Chairman of the Group of Landlocked Developing Countries, transmitted to the Secretary-General the ministerial communiqué adopted at the Fifth Annual Ministerial Meeting of Landlocked Developing Countries (New York, 27 September).

GENERAL ASSEMBLY ACTION

On 22 December [meeting 75], the General Assembly, on the recommendation of the Second Committee [A/59/486/Add.2], adopted **resolution 59/245** without vote [agenda item 88 (*b*)].

Specific actions related to the particular needs and problems of landlocked developing countries: outcome of the International Ministerial Conference of Landlocked and Transit Developing Countries and Donor Countries and International Financial and Development Institutions on Transit Transport Cooperation

The General Assembly,

Recalling its resolutions 56/180 of 21 December 2001, 57/242 of 20 December 2002 and 58/201 of 23 December 2003,

Recalling also the United Nations Millennium Declaration, in which Heads of State and Government recognized the particular needs and problems of landlocked developing countries and urged both bilateral and multilateral donors to increase financial and technical assistance to this group of countries to meet their particular development needs and to help them to overcome the impediments of geography by improving their transit transport systems, and resolved to create an environment, at the national and global levels alike, that is conducive to development and to the elimination of poverty,

Recognizing that the lack of territorial access to the sea, aggravated by remoteness from world markets, and prohibitive transit costs and risks impose serious constraints on export earnings, private capital inflow and domestic resource mobilization of landlocked developing countries and therefore adversely affect their overall growth and socio-economic development,

Recognizing also that landlocked developing countries, with their small and vulnerable economies, are among the poorest of developing countries, and noting that, of the thirty-one landlocked developing countries, sixteen are also classified by the United Nations as least developed countries,

Recalling the Almaty Declaration and the Almaty Programme of Action: Addressing the Special Needs of Landlocked Developing Countries within a New Global Framework for Transit Transport Cooperation for Landlocked and Transit Developing Countries,

Recalling also the New Partnership for Africa's Development (NEPAD), an initiative for accelerating regional economic cooperation and development as most landlocked and transit developing countries are located in Africa,

Taking note of the ministerial communiqué adopted at the Fifth Annual Ministerial Meeting of Landlocked Developing Countries, held on 27 September 2004 at United Nations Headquarters,

1. *Takes note* of the report of the Secretary-General on the implementation of the Almaty Programme of Action;

2. *Reaffirms* the right of access of landlocked countries to and from the sea and freedom of transit through the territory of transit countries by all means of transport, in accordance with applicable rules of international law;

3. *Reaffirms also* that transit countries, in the exercise of their full sovereignty over their territory, have the right to take all measures necessary to ensure that the rights and facilities provided for landlocked countries in no way infringe upon their legitimate interests;

4. *Invites* Member States, organizations of the United Nations system as well as other relevant international, regional and subregional organizations and multilateral financial and development institutions to implement the specific actions in the five priorities agreed upon in the Almaty Programme of Action;

5. *Invites* donor countries, the United Nations Development Programme and multilateral financial and development institutions to provide landlocked and transit developing countries with appropriate financial and technical assistance in the form of grants or concessional loans for the construction, maintenance and improvement of their transport, storage and other transit-related facilities, including alternative routes

and improved communications, to promote sub-regional, regional and interregional projects and pro-grammes, and, in this regard, to consider, inter alia, improving the availability and optimal use of different transport modes and intermodal efficiency along transport corridors;

6. *Recognizes* that most transit countries are them-selves developing countries often of broadly similar economic structure and beset by similar scarcity of re-sources, including the lack of adequate transit trans-port infrastructure;

7. *Emphasizes* that assistance for the improvement of transit transport facilities and services should be in-tegrated into the overall economic development strate-gies of the landlocked and transit developing countries and that donor countries should consequently take into account the requirements for the long-term re-structuring of the economies of the landlocked devel-oping countries;

8. *Stresses* the need for the implementation of the São Paulo Consensus adopted at the eleventh session of the United Nations Conference on Trade and Develop-ment, held in São Paulo, Brazil, from 13 to 18 June 2004, in particular paragraphs 66 and 84 thereof, by the rele-vant international organizations and donors in a multi-stakeholder approach, and emphasizes, in this regard, that the examination of issues relating to the trade of small, vulnerable economies, and the framing of re-sponses to these trade-related issues to facilitate their fuller integration into the multilateral trading system should be actively pursued consistent with the Doha work programme, taking into consideration the particu-lar needs of landlocked developing countries within a new global framework for transit transport cooperation for landlocked and transit developing countries;

9. *Invites* the relevant organizations of the United Nations system and other international organizations, including the regional commissions, the United Nations Conference on Trade and Development, the World Bank, the World Customs Organization, the World Trade Organization and the International Mari-time Organization, to integrate the Almaty Pro-gramme of Action into their relevant programmes of work, and encourages them to continue their support to the landlocked and transit developing countries, in-ter alia, through well-coordinated and coherent tech-nical assistance programmes in transit transport;

10. *Encourages* the United Nations Conference on Trade and Development, in particular the Division for Services Infrastructure for Development and Trade Efficiency and the Special Programme on the Least Developed Countries, Landlocked Developing Coun-tries and Small Island Developing States to continue its technical assistance activities and analytical work re-lated to transit transport cooperation between land-locked and transit developing countries;

11. *Requests* the Office of the High Representative for the Least Developed Countries, Landlocked Devel-oping Countries and Small Island Developing States of the Secretariat, in accordance with the mandate given by the General Assembly in its resolution 56/227 of 24 December 2001 and in the Almaty Programme of Action and the Almaty Declaration, to continue its co-operation and coordination with organizations within the United Nations system, particularly those engaged in operational activities on the ground in landlocked

and transit developing countries to ensure effective im-plementation of the Almaty Programme of Action in line with General Assembly resolution 57/270 B of 23 June 2003, and also requests the Office to continue to carry out advocacy work to mobilize international awareness and focus attention on the implementation of the Almaty Programme of Action;

12. *Requests*, in this regard, the Secretary-General to take the necessary measures, within existing re-sources, to provide the Office with adequate resources so as to allow it to effectively carry out its added man-date as stipulated in the Almaty Programme of Action;

13. *Invites* donor countries and the international fi-nancial and development institutions to make volun-tary contributions to the trust fund established by the Secretary-General to support the activities related to the follow-up to the implementation of the outcome of the Almaty International Ministerial Conference;

14. *Invites* the 2005 high-level event to address the special needs of the landlocked developing countries, within a new global framework for transit transport co-operation for landlocked and transit developing coun-tries, in accordance with the modalities to be set by the General Assembly at its fifty-ninth session, while as-sessing the progress achieved in the implementation of the internationally agreed development goals, includ-ing those contained in the United Nations Millennium Declaration;

15. *Decides* to include in the provisional agenda of its sixtieth session the item entitled "Specific actions related to the particular needs and problems of land-locked developing countries: outcome of the Interna-tional Ministerial Conference of Landlocked and Transit Developing Countries and Donor Countries and International Financial and Development Institu-tions on Transit Transport Cooperation";

16. *Requests* the Secretary-General to submit to the General Assembly at its sixtieth session a report on the progress made in the implementation of the Almaty Programme of Action.

Economies in transition

In response to General Assembly resolution 57/247 [YUN 2002, p. 852], the Secretary-General submitted a 26 August report [A/59/301] on pro-gress made in integrating the economies in tran-sition into the world economy. It examined the challenges that they faced and the advances made over the preceding two years, and analysed the current process of integration by tracing the pro-gress of the economies in transition through the channels of trade in goods and services, and capi-tal and labour flows, with particular attention to the role that the enlargement of the EU had played in some of those countries. It also pro-vided a brief overview of recent macroeconomic developments.

The report concluded that the economies in transition had further integrated themselves into the global economy, which had, in turn, contrib-uted to an acceleration of their transformation from planned to market economies. Progress had been achieved across all the dimensions of transition: liberalization of markets, institution-building, and upgrade of industrial capacity through trade and FDI, factor movements and the communication of economically useful knowledge and technology. However, progress was uneven across countries: in the Central European and Baltic States, integration of the eight countries into the EU had been a major success and a manifestation of their advancement. However, many countries in South-Eastern Europe and the smaller, low-income countries of CIS continued to experience difficulties and still needed international assistance to support growth and balance their resources in respect of achieving functioning structures.

Since integration was a political process, as well as an economic one, further progress required coordinated efforts among Governments, institutions, societies in those countries and international organizations, in order to ensure that the economies in transition increased their capacities to utilize their human, technological and natural resources.

GENERAL ASSEMBLY ACTION

On 22 December [meeting 75], the General Assembly, on the recommendation of the Second Committee [A/59/485/Add.5], adopted **resolution 59/243** without vote [agenda item 87 *(e)*].

Integration of the economies in transition into the world economy

The General Assembly,

Reaffirming its resolutions 47/187 of 22 December 1992, 48/181 of 21 December 1993, 49/106 of 19 December 1994, 51/175 of 6 December 1996, 53/179 of 15 December 1998, 55/191 of 20 December 2000 and 57/247 of 20 December 2002,

Reaffirming also the need for the full integration of the countries with economies in transition into the world economy,

Welcoming the progress made in those countries towards market-oriented reforms and achieving macroeconomic and financial stability and economic growth, inter alia, through sound macroeconomic policies, good governance and the rule of law, and noting the need to sustain those positive trends,

Noting that in some economies in transition this progress has been slower, resulting in lower aggregate development levels and lower per capita income,

Stressing the importance of continued international assistance to countries with economies in transition to support their efforts towards market-oriented reforms, institution-building, infrastructure development and achieving macroeconomic and financial stability and economic growth, and to ensure that they are fully integrated into the world economy,

Recognizing, in particular, the need to enhance the capacity of those countries to utilize effectively the benefits of globalization, including those in the field of information and communication technologies, and to respond more adequately to its challenges,

Recognizing also the continuing need for favourable conditions for market access of exports from countries with economies in transition, in accordance with multilateral trade agreements,

Recognizing further the important role that foreign direct investment should play in those countries, and stressing the need to create an enabling environment, both domestically and internationally, to attract more foreign direct investment to those countries,

Recognizing the role that the private sector can play in the socio-economic development of those countries and their integration into the world economy, and stressing the importance of fostering a favourable environment for private investment and entrepreneurship,

Noting the aspiration of the countries with economies in transition towards the further development of regional and interregional cooperation,

Taking note with appreciation of the report of the Secretary-General,

1. *Welcomes* the measures taken by the organizations of the United Nations system to implement General Assembly resolutions on the integration of the economies in transition into the world economy;

2. *Calls upon* the organizations of the United Nations system, including the regional commissions, and invites the Bretton Woods institutions, in collaboration with relevant non–United Nations multilateral and regional institutions, to continue to conduct analytical activities and provide policy advice and targeted and substantial technical assistance to the Governments of the countries with economies in transition aimed at strengthening the social, legal and political framework for completing market-oriented reforms, supporting national development priorities with a view to sustaining the positive trends and reversing any declines in the economic and social development of those countries;

3. *Emphasizes* in this regard the importance of the further integration of the countries with economies in transition into the world economy, taking into account, inter alia, the relevant provisions of the Monterrey Consensus of the International Conference on Financing for Development, the Johannesburg Declaration on Sustainable Development and the Plan of Implementation of the World Summit on Sustainable Development ("Johannesburg Plan of Implementation");

4. *Stresses* the need to focus international assistance to countries with economies in transition on those facing particular difficulties in socio-economic development, implementing market-oriented reforms and meeting internationally agreed development goals, including those contained in the United Nations Millennium Declaration, and welcomes efforts made by countries with economies in transition to improve governance and institutional capabilities in order to use aid more effectively;

5. *Welcomes* the efforts made by countries with economies in transition in implementing policies that promote sustained economic growth and sustainable development, including, inter alia, by promoting competition, regulatory reform, respect for property rights and expeditious contract enforcement, and calls upon the United Nations system to highlight the successful models as good practices;

6. *Requests* the Secretary-General to submit to the General Assembly at its sixty-first session a report on the implementation of the present resolution.

Poor mountain countries

On 22 December [meeting 75], the General Assembly, on the recommendation of the Second Committee [A/59/483/Add.8], adopted **resolution 59/238** without vote [agenda item 85 (*h*)].

Rendering assistance to poor mountain countries to overcome obstacles in socio-economic and ecological areas

The General Assembly,

Recalling its resolution 53/24 of 10 November 1998, by which it proclaimed 2002 the International Year of Mountains,

Recalling also its resolutions 55/189 of 20 December 2000, 57/245 of 20 December 2002 and 58/216 of 23 December 2003,

Recalling further the United Nations Millennium Declaration adopted on 8 September 2000,

Recalling chapter 13 of Agenda 21 and all relevant paragraphs of the Plan of Implementation of the World Summit on Sustainable Development ("Johannesburg Plan of Implementation"), in particular paragraph 42 thereof, as the overall policy frameworks for sustainable development in mountain regions,

Decides to consider at its sixtieth session, under the item entitled "Sustainable development", a sub-item entitled "Rendering assistance to poor mountain countries to overcome obstacles in socio-economic and ecological areas", bearing in mind its resolution 58/216.

Chapter II

Operational activities for development

In 2004, the UN system continued to provide development assistance to developing countries and countries with economies in transition through the United Nations Development Programme (UNDP), the central UN funding body for technical assistance. UNDP income in 2004 amounted to $4.2 billion, a 24 per cent increase over 2003. Total expenditure for all programme activities and support costs in 2004 was $3.6 billion, compared with $3.1 billion the previous year. Technical cooperation funded through other sources included $48.9 million provided through the programme executed by the Department of Economic and Social Affairs, $76.8 million through the United Nations Fund for International Partnerships, and $27.6 million through the United Nations Capital Development Fund.

The United Nations completed a triennial comprehensive policy review of UN system operational activities for development, which assessed the capacity of the UN development system to assist developing countries in pursuing poverty eradication, economic growth and sustainable development in the context of the follow-up to the 2000 United Nations Millennium Summit and major UN conferences and summits. Following the review, the Secretary-General called for actions to enhance the effectiveness of UN system development cooperation. In December, the General Assembly adopted a broad outline for future UN system development activities.

UNDP activities were organized under five practice areas: poverty reduction, fostering democratic governance, crisis prevention and recovery, energy and the environment, and responding to HIV/AIDS. UNDP made progress in gender mainstreaming and implemented a joint plan of action with the United Nations Development Fund for Women to achieve gender equality.

The United Nations Office for Project Services (UNOPS) had a project delivery of $495.3 million, exceeding the amount forecasted for the year by 2 per cent. As part of an ongoing change management process, the UNDP/United Nations Population Fund (UNFPA) Executive Board, in January, approved the expansion of the UNOPS mandate to allow it to cooperate directly with regional and subregional development banks on a pilot basis.

The United Nations Volunteer programme, administered by UNDP, expanded for the eighth consecutive year, with 7,300 volunteers carrying out 7,772 assignments in 139 countries.

In September, the UNDP/UNFPA Executive Board considered options for a future strategic niche and business model for the United Nations Capital Development Fund.

System-wide activities

Operational activities segment of Economic and Social Council

The Economic and Social Council, at its 2004 substantive session [A/59/3], considered the question of operational activities of the United Nations for international development cooperation at meetings from 7 to 9 July, as decided by the Council on 4 February (**decision 2004/205**), and on 12 July. As also decided by the Council on 4 February (**decision 2004/206**), the theme for the operational activities segment was "Triennial comprehensive policy review of the operational activities for development of the United Nations system and the implementation of General Assembly resolution 56/201 and Council resolution 2003/3". The Council held discussions on the follow-up to the policy recommendations of the Assembly and the Council, including a high-level panel discussion on the international development agenda and the improvements of the operational activities of the UN system at the country level: effectiveness and challenges; and the reports of the Executive Boards of the United Nations Development Programme (UNDP)/United Nations Population Fund (UNFPA), the United Nations Children's Fund (UNICEF) and the World Food Programme (WFP).

Among the documents before the Council were the Secretary-General's reports on comprehensive statistical data on operational activities for development for 2002 [A/59/84-E/2004/53], the triennial comprehensive policy review of operational activities for development of the UN system [A/59/85-E/2004/68], and assessment of the value added of the joint meetings of the

UNDP/UNFPA, UNICEF and WFP Executive Boards [E/2004/60] (see sections below).

On 8 July, the Council held a panel discussion on the role of the common country assessment (CCA) and the United Nations Development Assistance Framework (UNDAF) and a dialogue with the heads of UN funds and programmes on key policy issues for the triennial comprehensive policy review.

Triennial policy review

A May report of the Secretary-General [A/59/85-E/2004/68] reviewed the implementation of General Assembly resolution 56/201 [YUN 2001, p. 784] on the triennial policy review of operational activities for development of the UN system, focusing on the assessment of the capacity of the UN development system to assist developing countries to pursue their national priorities and needs in relation to poverty eradication, economic growth and sustainable development within the framework of the follow-up to major UN conferences and summits. To assist in the review, the Secretary-General would submit policy recommendations to the Assembly, following consideration of the report by the Economic and Social Council (see p. 867), drawing on the Council's deliberations.

The report stated that the 2004 triennial comprehensive policy review should take into account the reform measures undertaken by the Secretary-General in 1997 [YUN 1997, p. 1390] and 2002 [YUN 2002, p. 1352] to increase the coherence and effectiveness of UN development cooperation by enhancing coordination and improving management practices, take stock of the shifting global trends and overall development dynamics affecting UN development cooperation, and provide guidance to the system to enable it to adjust to changes. The principal focus of the analysis contained in the report was on assessing the performance and effectiveness of UN development cooperation. The report discussed the effectiveness of and current challenges to UN development cooperation; challenges and new perspectives in funding UN development cooperation; UN reforms and field-level coordination; country-level capacity of the UN development system and development of national capacities; UN system operational activities for development in countries in transition from crisis to development; and partnership between the UN system and national development stakeholders and partners.

The report indicated that substantial progress had been made in bringing cohesion to the system at the country level and in aligning its operations with the development agenda emerging from major UN conferences and summits and, in particular, with the Millennium Development Goals (MDGs) [YUN 2000, p. 51]. The system increasingly served as a catalyst for national dialogue among all stakeholders for implementing the MDGs, including within the framework of the UNDP poverty reduction strategy papers (PRSPs). The United Nations helped to build partnerships for action and devised accountability and monitoring instruments, including the MDG country reports. The evaluation of diagnostic and programming tools, including CCA and UNDAF, showed their potential, especially in terms of increased coherence, and highlighted the importance of a more integrated approach to national poverty reduction strategy frameworks. The UN reform processes created strong imperatives to work together, especially among the members of the United Nations Development Group (UNDG) and its Executive Committee. In many countries, the resident coordinator system increasingly functioned as a vibrant instrument with a common set of goals. Clear guidelines were issued on joint programming, and actual joint programmes were developed in such areas as HIV/AIDS, the protection of children and the advancement of women, while the adoption of results-based programming and management by a majority of organizations was helping to create a new culture of efficiency, effectiveness and accountability. Significant progress was also made in integrating reconstruction, rehabilitation and long-term development within a single strategic framework for peace-building and development.

Efforts to simplify and harmonize processes between organizations had yielded limited efficiencies, however, forcing UNDG to formulate a new work programme to accelerate those efforts, the implementation of which depended on further institutional changes and funding. The critical capacity of the system to make available relevant technical resources at the country and regional levels was constrained by the lack of real incentives and institutional reward systems to encourage the various entities to make their knowledge and expertise available to the resident coordinator system. A stronger commitment by all UN system organizations involved in operational activities for development to system-wide collaboration and the effective participation of all, including entities with no country offices, were key requirements for progress. In addition, stable, predictable funding commensurate with the programme priorities identified in CCA/UNDAF was needed. Efforts to improve internal coherence, simplification and efficiency within the UN system would not succeed without Member States reforming their funding practices to limit fragmentation, inconsistency and unnecessary competition for scarce resources. As long as funding arrangements for UN development activities remained inadequate, unstable and unpredictable, the UN development system would not be able to fully play its role in advancing comprehensive, durable development. The mismatch among funding levels, mechanisms and sustained efforts required to support countries in their implementation of the MDGs needed to be addressed.

The Secretary-General, in an April report [A/59/84-E/2004/53], issued to complement his report on progress in implementing resolution 56/201, provided detailed statistical data on resources channelled through the UN system organizations for 2002, which the Council noted on 12 July (**decision 2004/232**).

ECONOMIC AND SOCIAL COUNCIL ACTION

On 12 July [meeting 33], the Economic and Social Council adopted **resolution 2004/5** [draft: E/2004/L.15] without vote [agenda item 3 (*a*)].

Triennial comprehensive policy review of operational activities for development of the United Nations system

The Economic and Social Council,

Recalling the United Nations Millennium Declaration, which set out priorities and goals to be reached by the international community by 2015,

Recalling also General Assembly resolutions 47/199 of 22 December 1992, 50/120 of 20 December 1995, 53/192 of 15 December 1998 and 56/201 of

21 December 2001 on the triennial policy review of operational activities for development of the United Nations system,

Recalling further General Assembly resolution 58/291 of 6 May 2004 entitled "Follow-up to the outcome of the Millennium Summit and integrated and coordinated implementation of and follow-up to the outcomes of the major United Nations conferences and summits in the economic and social fields",

Recalling Economic and Social Council resolutions 2002/29 of 25 July 2002 and 2003/3 of 11 July 2003,

Having considered the reports of the Secretary-General on the triennial comprehensive policy review of operational activities for development of the United Nations system and on the assessment of the value added of the joint meetings of the Executive Boards of the United Nations Development Programme/United Nations Population Fund, the United Nations Children's Fund and the World Food Programme,

Noting the importance of ensuring that the 2004 triennial comprehensive policy review of operational activities for development of the United Nations system contributes to the review of progress made in the achievement of the internationally agreed development goals, including those contained in the Millennium Declaration and the outcomes of other United Nations summits and conferences,

1. *Requests* the Secretary-General, when finalizing his report on the triennial comprehensive policy review for submission to the General Assembly at its

fifty-ninth session, to take into account the views and comments of Member States on the issues relating to the operational activities for development discussed during the operational activities segment of the substantive session of 2004 of the Economic and Social Council and to make appropriate recommendations;

2. *Invites* the Secretary-General, in accordance with the coordination, guidance and oversight roles of the Council in the implementation by the United Nations system of the triennial policy review of operational activities, to make recommendations, when finalizing his report on the triennial comprehensive policy review, on the possible themes that could be discussed at the operational activities segment of the substantive sessions of the Council in 2005 and 2006, taking into account the necessary preparatory work for the following triennial policy review;

3. *Invites* the General Assembly to consider a concise and action-oriented resolution on the triennial comprehensive policy review, focusing on priority areas as determined by Member States.

Report of Secretary-General. In a September report [A/59/387], the Secretary-General provided a synopsis of the detailed analysis of the implementation of resolution 56/201 contained in his May report on the triennial comprehensive policy review (see p. 866). It took into account the views and comments of Member States at the operational activities segment of the Council's substantive session of 2004, as well as additional information provided by UN system organizations. The report was complemented by the reports of the Secretary-General on the comprehensive statistical data on operational activities for development for 2002 (see p. 865) and the preliminary statistical data for the year 2003 [A/59/386] (see p. 875). It also took into account the report of the Secretary-General on assessment of the value added of the joint meetings of the Executive Boards of UNDP/UNFPA, UNICEF, and WFP [E/2004/60] (see p. 878) and provided an overall analysis of progress on the 1997 and 2002 reform measures undertaken by the Secretary-General regarding UN development cooperation.

The report called for actions to enhance the effectiveness of the UN system development cooperation, strengthen coherence within a unified, nationally-owned development framework, ensure adequate use of all relevant capacities available, place greater emphasis on results and their evaluation, and translate internationally agreed development goals into national terms. It called for adequate funding and further reflection on funding arrangements, and for organizational and structural changes, including strengthening of the resident coordinator system. The system's country-level presence should be responsive to national priorities and needs, ensuring comprehensive support to dimensions that were key to a sustained and sustainable development effort. Intensified field-level coordination and participation of all relevant parts of the system, including those entities without country-level representation, were essential. Greater consideration should be given to the regional dimensions of development cooperation and to developing national capacities, as one of its key functions. Added emphasis should be placed on gender mainstreaming.

By **decision 59/539** of 22 December, the General Assembly took note of the report of the Second (Economic and Financial) Committee on operational activities for development [A/59/488].

GENERAL ASSEMBLY ACTION

On 22 December [meeting 75], the General Assembly, on the recommendation of the Second Committee [A/59/488/Add.1], adopted **resolution 59/250** without vote [agenda item 90 (b)].

Triennial comprehensive policy review of operational activities for development of the United Nations system

The General Assembly,

Recalling its resolutions 44/211 of 22 December 1989, 47/199 of 22 December 1992, 50/120 of 20 December 1995, 52/203 of 18 December 1997, 52/12 B of 19 December 1997, 53/192 of 15 December 1998 and 56/201 of 21 December 2001, as well as Economic and Social Council resolutions 2002/29 of 25 July 2002, 2003/3 of 11 July 2003 and 2004/5 of 12 July 2004, and other relevant resolutions,

Reaffirming the importance of the triennial comprehensive policy review of operational activities, through which the General Assembly establishes key system-wide policy orientations for the development cooperation and country-level modalities of the United Nations system,

Recalling the role of the Economic and Social Council in providing coordination and guidance to the United Nations system to ensure that those policy orientations are implemented on a system-wide basis in accordance with Assembly resolutions 48/162 of 20 December 1993, 50/227 of 24 May 1996 and 57/270 B of 23 June 2003,

Recalling also the United Nations Millennium Declaration of 8 September 2000, including the development and poverty eradication goals contained therein, and recalling further the International Conference on Financing for Development, held in Monterrey, Mexico, from 18 to 22 March 2002, and the World Summit on Sustainable Development, held in Johannesburg, South Africa, from 26 August to 4 September 2002 and other major United Nations conferences and summits in the economic, social and related fields, and their importance for international development cooperation, in particular for the operational activities for development of the United Nations system,

Noting, in this context, the activities of the United Nations funds and programmes aimed at providing technical assistance to recipient countries, in response to their national economic and social needs and priorities, including poverty eradication and the promotion of all human rights, including the right to develop-

ment, for achieving sustained economic growth and sustainable development in accordance with relevant General Assembly resolutions and recent United Nations conferences, and stressing the need for those activities to be undertaken at the request of interested recipient Governments strictly within the respective mandates of the United Nations funds and programmes, which should receive increased contributions from donor countries,

Recognizing that the transition from relief to development represents a complex challenge as regards the universal achievement of the MDGs,

Reiterating that developing countries are responsible for their own development processes, and in this context stressing the responsibility of the international community, in partnership, in assisting developing countries in their national development efforts,

Recognizing that the United Nations development system should take into account the specific needs and requirements of the countries with economies in transition and other recipient countries,

Recognizing also that new technologies, including information and communication technologies, present an opportunity to accelerate development, especially in developing countries, and noting that the access to those technologies is uneven and that a digital divide still prevails,

Reaffirming the need to ensure, in a coherent and timely manner, the full implementation of all the elements of its resolutions 44/211, 47/199, 50/120, 53/192 and 56/201 and the parts of its resolution 52/12 B relevant to operational activities for development, which should be considered an integral part of the present resolution,

Reiterating the importance of the development of national capacities to eradicate poverty and pursue sustained economic growth and sustainable development as a central goal of the development cooperation of the United Nations system,

Recognizing that new trends in development assistance, including sector-wide approaches and budget support, pose challenges to the United Nations, and stressing that the United Nations has a role to play in assisting developing countries to manage the new aid modalities,

Noting the advances that the United Nations development system is making in the area of coordination, including in the implementation of resolution 56/201,

Encouraging the governing bodies of United Nations agencies, funds and programmes to ensure that gender perspectives are integrated into all aspects of their monitoring functions in relation to policies and strategies, medium-term plans, multi-year funding frameworks and operational activities, including those relating to the implementation of the Millennium Declaration and the outcomes of major United Nations conferences and summits in the economic and social fields,

I

Introduction

1. *Takes note with appreciation* of the reports of the Secretary-General on the triennial comprehensive policy review of operational activities for development of the United Nations system;

2. *Reaffirms* that the fundamental characteristics of the operational activities for development of the United Nations system should be, inter alia, their universal, voluntary and grant nature, their neutrality and their multilateralism, as well as their ability to respond to the development needs of recipient countries in a flexible manner, and that the operational activities are carried out for the benefit of recipient countries, at the request of those countries and in accordance with their own policies and priorities for development;

3. *Urges* all Member States to pursue the full implementation of the internationally agreed development goals, including those contained in the United Nations Millennium Declaration, and recognizes the positive contribution that these can make in providing direction to the operational activities for development of the United Nations system in accordance with national development efforts and priorities;

4. *Recognizes* that the strength of the United Nations operational system lies in its legitimacy, at the country level, as a neutral, objective and trusted partner for both recipient countries and donor countries;

5. *Stresses* that national Governments have the primary responsibility for their countries' development, and recognizes the importance of national ownership of development programmes;

6. *Emphasizes* that recipient Governments have the primary responsibility for coordinating, on the basis of national strategies and priorities, all types of external assistance, including that provided by multilateral organizations, in order to integrate effectively such assistance into their development process;

7. *Emphasizes also* that the operational activities for development of the United Nations system should be valued and assessed on the basis of their impact on the recipient countries as contributions to enhance their capacity to pursue poverty eradication, sustained economic growth and sustainable development;

8. *Calls upon* the United Nations development system to highlight best practices, where these can inform national efforts to implement policies that promote sustained economic growth and sustainable development, inter alia, through the rule of law and the strengthening of effective, efficient, transparent and accountable systems for mobilizing resources;

9. *Decides* that, with the agreement of the host country, the United Nations development system should assist national Governments in creating an enabling environment in which the links between national Governments, the United Nations development system, civil society, national non-governmental organizations and the private sector that are involved in the development process are strengthened, with a view to seeking new and innovative solutions to development problems in accordance with national policies and priorities;

10. *Stresses* that the purpose of reform is to make the United Nations development system more efficient and effective in its support to developing countries to achieve the internationally agreed development goals, on the basis of their national development strategies, and stresses also that reform efforts should enhance organizational efficiency and achieve concrete development results;

11. *Requests* the organizations of the United Nations system to continue their efforts to respond to national development plans, policies and priorities, which constitute the only viable frame of reference for programming their operational activities at the country level, and to pursue full integration of the operational activities for development at the country-level with national planning and programming, under the leadership of national Governments, at all stages of the process, while ensuring the full involvement of all relevant stakeholders at the national level;

12. *Welcomes* the efforts of the Secretary-General, through the members of the United Nations Development Group and the United Nations System Chief Executives Board for Coordination, as appropriate, to enhance the coherence, effectiveness and efficiency of the United Nations development system at the country level;

13. *Recognizes* that strengthening the role and capacity of the United Nations development system to assist countries in achieving their development goals requires continuing improvement in its effectiveness, efficiency, coherence and impact, along with a significant increase in resources and an expansion of its resource base on a continuous, more predictable and assured basis;

II
Funding for operational activities for development of the United Nations system

14. *Emphasizes* that increasing financial contributions to the United Nations development system is key to achieving the MDGs, and in this regard recognizes the mutually reinforcing links between increased effectiveness, efficiency and coherence of the United Nations development system, achieving concrete results in assisting developing countries to eradicate poverty and achieve sustained economic growth and sustainable development through operational activities for development and the overall resourcing of the United Nations development system;

15. *Emphasizes also* that funding of operational activities for development of the United Nations system should focus on long-term development challenges based on national development strategies;

16. *Notes with concern* that the United Nations development system has not benefited commensurately from recent increases in official development assistance, despite the additional tasks entrusted to the United Nations system in the implementation of and follow-up to internationally agreed goals;

17. *Stresses* that core resources, because of their untied nature, continue to be the bedrock of the operational activities for development of the United Nations system, and in this regard notes with appreciation that core contributions to United Nations funds and programmes have begun to increase again over the last three years;

18. *Calls upon* donor countries and other countries in a position to do so to substantially increase their contributions to the core/regular budgets of the United Nations development system, in particular its funds and programmes, and wherever possible, to contribute on a multi-year basis;

19. *Urges* developed countries that have not yet done so to make concrete efforts to reach the targets of 0.7 per cent of their gross national product as official development assistance to developing countries and

0.15 to 0.20 per cent of their gross national product to least developed countries, as reconfirmed at the Third United Nations Conference on Least Developed Countries, held in Brussels from 14 to 20 May 2001, encourages developing countries to build on progress achieved in ensuring that official development assistance is used effectively to help to achieve development goals and targets, acknowledges the efforts of all donors, commends those donors whose official development assistance contributions exceed, reach or are increasing towards the targets, and underlines the importance of undertaking to examine the means and time frames for achieving the targets and goals;

20. *Notes* the increase in non-core resources as a mechanism to supplement the means of operational activities for development of the United Nations system, which contributes to an increase in total resources, while recognizing that non-core resources are not a substitute for core resources and that unearmarked contributions are vital for the coherence and harmonization of the operational activities for development;

21. *Invites* the governing bodies of all organizations of the United Nations development system to address systematically the funding of their operational activities and to explore, within the context of their multi-year planning and related financial frameworks, where appropriate, additional sources of financial support and alternative funding modalities so as to secure, on a predictable, continuous and sustained basis, the critical mass of resources required to ensure adequate functioning and pursuit of long-term development objectives;

22. *Requests* the Secretary-General to improve his annual statistical compendium to the operational activities segment of the Economic and Social Council by adding a multi-year perspective, fully incorporating available information and statistics;

23. *Requests* the Economic and Social Council to undertake triennially, as of 2006, a comprehensive review of trends and perspectives in funding for development cooperation;

24. *Requests* the Secretary-General, in consultation with Member States, to explore various funding options for increasing financing for operational activities for development of the United Nations system and to examine ways to enhance the predictability, long-term stability, reliability and adequacy of funding for the operational activities for development, including through the identification of possible new funding sources, as a follow-up to his report, while preserving the advantages of the current funding modalities, and to submit a report to the General Assembly through the Economic and Social Council at its substantive session in 2005;

25. *Recognizes* the urgent and specific needs of low-income countries, in particular the least developed countries, and stresses the need to continue to assist those countries through the existing institutions and funding mechanisms of the United Nations development system;

III
Capacity-building

26. *Recognizes* that capacity development and ownership of national development strategies are essential for the achievement of the MDGs, and calls upon United Nations organizations to provide further support to the efforts of developing countries to establish and/or maintain effective national institutions and to support the implementation and, as necessary, the devising of national strategies for capacity-building;

27. *Urges* all organizations of the United Nations development system to intensify inter-agency sharing of information at the system-wide level on good practices and experiences gained, results achieved, benchmarks and indicators, monitoring and evaluation criteria concerning their capacity-building activities;

28. *Encourages* all organizations of the United Nations development system to include reporting on their capacity-building activities in their annual reports to their respective governing bodies;

29. *Requests* the United Nations System Chief Executives Board for Coordination to analyse the capacity development efforts of the United Nations development system and to make recommendations on measures necessary to enhance their effectiveness, including through the improvement of the assessment and measurement of results;

30. *Calls upon* United Nations organizations to further strengthen the capacity of developing countries to better utilize the various aid modalities, including system-wide approaches and budget support;

31. *Also calls upon* United Nations organizations to adopt measures that ensure sustainability in capacity-building activities, and reiterates that the United Nations development system should use, to the fullest extent possible, national execution and available national expertise and technologies as the norm in the implementation of operational activities;

32. *Stresses* that developing countries, in order to meet the internationally agreed development goals, including those contained in the Millennium Declaration, should have access to new and emerging technologies, including information and communication technologies, which requires technology transfer, technical cooperation and the building and nurturing of scientific and technological capacity to participate in the development and adaptation of these technologies to local conditions, and in this regard urges Member States and the United Nations system to ensure the promotion and transfer of new and emerging technologies to developing countries;

33. *Encourages* the United Nations development system to support the national development strategies and plans of countries with economies in transition that face continuing difficulties in economic and social development, specifically to assist them in addressing the challenges of achieving the internationally agreed development goals, including those contained in the Millennium Declaration;

IV
Transaction costs and efficiency

34. *Invites* the governing bodies of all organizations of the United Nations system actively involved in development cooperation activities and their respective management to adopt harmonization and simplification measures, with a view to achieving a significant reduction in the administrative and procedural burden on the organizations and their national partners that derives from the preparation and implementation of operational activities;

35. *Notes* the progress achieved in the area of simplification and harmonization as defined in section VI of resolution 56/201, with the assistance of the United Nations Development Group, and calls upon the funds, programmes and the specialized agencies of the United Nations system to continue to implement the simplification and harmonization agenda by taking further steps to enhance and ensure the sustainability of that process;

36. *Requests* the funds, programmes and specialized agencies of the United Nations system to examine ways to further simplify their rules and procedures and, in this context, to accord the issue of simplification and harmonization high priority and to take concrete steps in the following areas: rationalization of country presence through common premises and co-location of members of United Nations country teams; implementation of the joint office model; common shared support services, including security, information technology, telecommunications, travel, banking and administrative and financial procedures, including for procurement; harmonization of the principles of cost recovery policies, including that of full cost recovery; alignment of the regional technical support structures and regional bureaux at headquarters level, including their regional coverage; as well as further simplification and harmonization measures;

37. *Requests* the Secretary-General, in full consultation with all members of the United Nations Development Group, through the Executive Committee of the Development Group, to submit to the Economic and Social Council, at its substantive session of 2005, a programme of work for the full implementation of the above-mentioned actions, to be completed before the end of 2007, including benchmarks, responsibilities and provisions to phase out redundant rules and procedures, as well as a timetable to monitor the progress made towards meeting these targets;

38. *Invites* the executive boards and governing bodies of the funds, programmes and specialized agencies to assess regularly the progress achieved in the area of simplification and harmonization of rules and procedures;

39. *Requests* the funds and programmes to provide, in their annual reports to the Economic and Social Council, specific information on the progress achieved in implementing the above-mentioned agenda;

40. *Requests* the United Nations Development Group to consult regularly with the United Nations System Chief Executives Board for Coordination on all activities undertaken to implement the above;

V

Coherence, effectiveness and relevance of operational activities for development

A. Common country assessment/United Nations Development Assistance Framework

41. *Requests* the United Nations system to conduct the common country assessment and the United Nations Development Assistance Framework processes as efforts to improve the support for national development priorities and policies, and stresses that full governmental ownership, participation and leadership is required at all stages of those processes;

42. *Welcomes* the efforts made so far by the United Nations system in the context of the improved func-

tioning of the resident coordinator system, including through the common country assessment and the Framework, in order to achieve greater country-level programmatic coherence within the system and to foster teamwork among the organizations of the system, in particular those represented at the country level;

43. *Recognizes* that, in spite of these efforts, participation of the funds, programmes and agencies of the United Nations development system in country-level operational activities for development and coordination mechanisms still differs in level, quality and intensity, and that for some organizations it is inadequate, and in this context calls upon the United Nations development system to improve its country-level coordination so as to optimize its support to national development efforts, at the request of national authorities;

44. *Calls upon* the United Nations system to draw from its accumulated experience in all pertinent economic, social and other domains and to facilitate the access of developing countries to the services available within the system on the basis of its comparative advantages and expertise;

45. *Calls upon* the United Nations development system to foster an inclusive approach in promoting inter-agency collaboration, both at the country and headquarters levels, and requests the United Nations System Chief Executives Board for Coordination, in collaboration with the United Nations Development Group, to take the necessary steps to secure a more participatory involvement of the United Nations development system in the country-level operations and their coordination mechanisms, including through promotion, decentralization, the delegation of authority and multi-year programming, which will facilitate their participation in country-level coordination mechanisms;

46. *Stresses* the importance of the common country assessment as the common analytical tool of the United Nations system at the country level, including the specialized agencies, the regional commissions and other United Nations agencies with no country representation or limited country-level presence, which should contribute their accumulated analytical and normative experience so as to enable the use of all capacities available within the United Nations system;

47. *Notes* the progress made by the United Nations operational system in developing and using the common country assessment, and stresses that the formulation of the assessment is meant to be short, light and flexible;

48. *Underlines* the complementarity of the common country assessment to other analytical processes, and urges all funds, programmes and agencies to avoid duplication by utilizing, to the maximum extent possible, the common country assessment as their own country-level analytical tool;

49. *Reiterates* that the ownership and full participation of national authorities in the preparation and development of the Framework are key to guaranteeing that it responds to the national development plans and poverty reduction strategies of the countries concerned, and requests the Secretary-General to develop the Framework and its results matrix where applicable, as the common programming tool for country-level contributions of the funds and programmes towards

achieving the MDGs, to be fully endorsed and counter-signed by the national authorities;

50. *Notes* the potential of the Framework and its results matrix as the collective, coherent and integrated programming and monitoring framework for the operations of the United Nations development system at the country level, bringing increased opportunities for joint initiatives, including joint programming, and urges the United Nations development system to fully utilize such opportunities in the interest of enhancing aid efficiency and aid effectiveness;

51. *Requests* the Secretary-General, through the Executive Committee of the United Nations Development Group, in consultation with the United Nations System Chief Executives Board for Coordination, to ensure that United Nations Development Group agencies with multi-year programmes as well as the entities of the Secretariat that carry out operational activities in pursuit of the MDGs, fully align their respective programming and monitoring with the Framework, as well as take further steps to harmonize their programming cycles and to synchronize them as far as possible with the national programming instruments, in particular the national poverty reduction strategies, including poverty reduction strategy papers, where they exist;

52. *Invites* the United Nations system and the Bretton Woods institutions to explore further ways to enhance cooperation, collaboration and coordination, including through the greater harmonization of strategic frameworks, instruments, modalities and partnership arrangements, in full accordance with the priorities of the recipient Governments, and in this regard emphasizes the importance of ensuring, under the leadership of national authorities, greater consistency between the strategic frameworks developed by the United Nations funds and programmes, agencies and the Bretton Woods institutions, while maintaining the institutional integrity and organizational mandates of each organization and the national poverty reduction strategies, including poverty reduction strategy papers, where they exist;

**B. Resident coordinator system
and United Nations country teams**

53. *Reaffirms* that the resident coordinator system, within the framework of national ownership, has a key role to play in the effective and efficient functioning of the United Nations system at the country level, including in the formulation of the common country assessment and the United Nations Development Assistance Framework, and is a key instrument for the efficient and effective coordination of the operational activities for development of the United Nations system, and requests the United Nations system, including the funds and programmes, the specialized agencies and the Secretariat, to enhance support to the resident coordinator system;

54. *Urges* the United Nations system to provide further financial, technical and organizational support for the resident coordinator system, and requests the Secretary-General, in consultation with the members of the United Nations Development Group to ensure that resident coordinators have the necessary resources to fulfil their role effectively;

55. *Welcomes* the improvements in the selection process and training of the resident coordinators, and urges the members of the Executive Committee of the United Nations Development Group, in full consultation with the members of the Development Group, to develop a procedure for the common assessment of the performance of resident coordinators by all members of the United Nations country teams;

56. *Notes* that coordination activities, while beneficial, represent transaction costs that are borne by both recipient countries and the organizations of the United Nations system, and emphasizes the need for their continuous evaluation and for an analysis and assessment of costs compared with the total programme expenditures for operational activities for development in order to ensure maximum efficiency and feasibility;

57. *Reaffirms* that the utilization of advanced information and communication technologies by the United Nations system could contribute to enhanced information-sharing and knowledge management, resulting in more effective delivery of development cooperation by the United Nations system, and encourages United Nations organizations to intensify their efforts to expand the use of information and communication technologies and to further harmonize their information technology platforms;

58. *Requests* the Secretary-General, in full consultation with all agencies of the United Nations Development Group and the United Nations System Chief Executives Board for Coordination, as appropriate, to develop, by the end of 2005, a comprehensive accountability framework for resident coordinators to exercise oversight of the design and implementation of the Framework, in a fully participatory manner, in support and under the leadership of national Governments;

59. *Underscores* the fact that the resident coordinator system is owned by the United Nations development system as a whole and that its functioning should be participatory, collegial and accountable;

60. *Also underscores* the fact that the management of the resident coordinator system continues to be firmly anchored in the United Nations Development Programme, while recognizing that many resident coordinators, especially in countries with large country teams, complex coordination situations or in situations of complex emergencies, lack the capacity to address equally well all tasks inherent to their functions, and in this regard requests that in such cases the United Nations Development Programme appoint, within the existing programming arrangement, a country director to run its core activities, including fund-raising, so as to assure that resident coordinators are fully available for their tasks;

61. *Requests* that, when raising funds, resident coordinators concentrate on raising funds for the whole of the United Nations at the country level;

VI

Country-level capacity of the United Nations system

62. *Reaffirms* the principle, as contained in resolutions 44/211 and 47/199, that the country-level presence of the United Nations system should be tailored to meet the specific development needs of recipient countries, as required by their country programmes;

63. *Emphasizes* the need for the range and level of skills and expertise assembled by the United Nations system at the country level to be commensurate with that needed to deliver on the priorities specified in each country's United Nations Development Assistance Framework, in line with the national development strategies and plans, including poverty reduction strategy papers, where they exist, and to correspond to the technical backstopping and capacity-building needs and requirements of the developing countries;

64. *Stresses* the principle that no core function of the Secretariat can be outsourced to operational bodies, in particular at the field level, without proper financial compensation;

65. *Invites* the governing bodies of the organizations of the United Nations development system to consider means to strengthen their country-level capacities, including through complementary measures at their headquarters;

VII
Evaluation of operational activities for development

66. *Requests* the Secretary-General to continue to assess the effectiveness of the operational activities for development of the United Nations system, including, in particular, by assessing the effective use of all capacities available to provide a comprehensive and flexible response to the demand of developing countries for development support, and to report on the results of this assessment in the context of the next triennial policy review at its sixty-second session;

67. *Reaffirms* that the effectiveness of operational activities should be assessed by their impact on the poverty eradication efforts, economic growth and sustainable development of recipient countries;

68. *Underlines* the fact that future assessments of the effectiveness of the operational activities for development of the United Nations system should make full use of the data and expertise available within the system and from national authorities in full collaboration with national stakeholders and United Nations entities;

69. *Recognizes* the need to optimize the linking of evaluation to performance in the achievement of development goals, and encourages the United Nations development system to strengthen its evaluation activities, with particular focus on development results, including through the effective use of the results matrix of the United Nations Development Assistance Framework, the systematic use of monitoring and evaluation approaches at the system-wide level and the promotion of collaborative approaches to the evaluation, including joint evaluations, and further encourages the United Nations Evaluation Group, under the aegis of the United Nations System Chief Executives Board for Coordination, to make further progress in system-wide collaboration on evaluation, in particular harmonization and simplification of methodologies, norms, standards and cycles of evaluation;

70. *Strongly encourages* country-level evaluations of the Framework at the end of the programming cycle, based on the results matrix of the Framework, with full participation and leadership of the recipient Government;

71. *Recognizes* that national Governments have primary responsibility for coordinating external assistance, including that from the United Nations system, and evaluating the impact of its contribution to national priorities;

72. *Requests* the United Nations development system to conduct evaluations of its operations at the country level, in close consultation with national Governments, and in this context stresses the need to assist Governments in the development of national evaluation capacities through, inter alia, better use of lessons learned from past activities at the country level;

73. *Also requests* the United Nations development system to consider, where appropriate, applying lessons learned in the course of monitoring and evaluation to programming processes;

74. *Stresses* the need for all organizations of the United Nations development system to implement their global, regional and country-level activities in accordance with their mandates and the priorities of the recipient countries, urges their governing bodies to ensure that the activities, responsibilities and operational strategies of each fund and programme are consistent with their mandates and the overall policy guidance set forth by the General Assembly and the Economic and Social Council and to report on these issues within the context of the annual reports submitted to the Council, and requests the Secretary-General to include an assessment of these issues in the report on the triennial comprehensive policy review prepared for the sixty-second session of the General Assembly;

75. *Requests* that the United Nations Development Programme conduct full consultation with the Member States prior to issuing global and regional flagship reports, in accordance with, inter alia, the principles contained in General Assembly resolution 57/264 of 20 December 2002;

VIII
Regional dimensions

76. *Calls upon* the organizations of the United Nations development system, its regional commissions and other regional and subregional entities, as appropriate and consistent with their mandates, to intensify their cooperation and adopt more collaborative approaches to support country-level development initiatives at the request of recipient countries, in particular through closer collaboration within the resident coordinator system and by improving mechanisms for access to the technical capacities of the United Nations system at the regional and subregional levels;

77. *Invites* the governing bodies of the organizations of the United Nations development system to give greater and more systematic consideration to the regional and subregional dimensions of development cooperation and to promote measures for more intensive inter-agency collaboration at the regional and subregional levels, facilitating inter-country exchanges of experience and promoting both intraregional and interregional cooperation, as appropriate;

78. *Encourages* development agencies of the United Nations system to seek to maximize the opportunity to address development challenges on a regional or subregional basis, where appropriate, recognizing the important contribution of regional cooperation to national and regional development;

IX
South-South cooperation and development of national capacities

79. *Welcomes* the growing importance of South-South cooperation and its adoption as a driver of development effectiveness within the multi-year funding framework of the United Nations Development Programme;

80. *Urges* organizations and bodies of the United Nations system to mainstream, in their programmes and through their country-level activities and country offices, modalities to support South-South cooperation that would promote identification and dissemination of best practices, promote indigenous knowledge, know-how and technology in the South and facilitate networking among experts and institutions in developing countries;

81. *Invites* Member States and the organizations of the United Nations development system to celebrate the United Nations Day for South-South Cooperation in a befitting and comprehensive manner every year;

82. *Emphasizes* the need to mobilize additional resources for enhancing South-South cooperation, including from both the United Nations system and donors, and through triangular cooperation;

83. *Urges* all Member States and the organizations of the United Nations development system to actively participate in the High-Level Committee on the Review of South-South Cooperation with a view to formulating and reviewing the strategies as well as sharing information and their experience;

84. *Encourages,* in this regard, United Nations funds and programmes, the specialized agencies as well as centres of excellence in the South to contribute to the periodic updating of the Web of Information for Development, the electronic databank operated by the Special Unit for South-South Cooperation of the United Nations Development Programme in coordination with Governments, allowing for the wide diffusion of and access to the information contained therein, including experiences, best practices and potential partners in South-South cooperation;

85. *Highlights* the fact that, in spite of progress achieved in this area, further efforts are required to better understand the approaches and potential of South-South cooperation to enhance development effectiveness, including through national capacity development, and in this context calls upon all the organizations of the system to further enhance their support for national capacity development in the context of South-South cooperation;

X
Gender

86. *Calls upon* all organizations of the United Nations system, within their organizational mandates, to mainstream a gender perspective and to pursue gender equality in their country programmes, planning instruments and sector-wide programmes and to articulate specific country-level goals and targets in this field in accordance with the national development strategies;

87. *Urges* all organizations of the system to collaborate with the resident coordinator system to provide gender specialist resources in support of gender mainstreaming in country-level activities in all sectors where they operate, working closely with relevant national counterparts in generating the gender disaggregated, quantitative and qualitative information required to produce better analysis of gender-related issues of development;

88. *Requests* all entities of the United Nations system to enhance the effectiveness of gender specialist resources, gender focal points and gender theme groups by establishing clear mandates, by ensuring adequate training, access to information and to adequate and stable resources, and by increasing the support and participation of senior staff;

89. *Calls upon* the United Nations development system to avail itself of the technical experience of the United Nations Development Fund for Women on gender issues;

90. *Encourages* the continuing efforts to achieve gender balance in appointments within the United Nations system at the headquarters and country levels in positions that affect operational activities, including resident coordinator appointments, with due regard to representation of women from developing countries and keeping in mind the principle of equitable geographic representation;

91. *Requests* the Secretary-General to ensure that the annual report on resident coordinators includes adequate and concise information on progress on the above;

XI
Transition from relief to development

92. *Takes note* of the ongoing work within the United Nations on the complex issue of transition from relief to development;

93. *Recognizes* that the United Nations development system has a vital role to play in situations of transition from relief to development;

94. *Requests* the organizations of the system to strengthen interdepartmental and inter-agency coordination to ensure an integrated, coherent and coordinated approach to assistance at the country level, which takes account of the complexity of challenges that countries in those circumstances face and the country-specific character of those challenges;

95. *Recognizes,* in this regard, the important role that the effective resident coordinator/humanitarian coordinator system can play in situations of transition from relief to development;

96. *Stresses,* in this regard, the need for such transitional activities to be undertaken under national ownership through the development of national capacities at all levels to manage the transition process;

97. *Recognizes* the benefits of sharing experience and expertise, and encourages the development of South-South cooperation modalities, including triangular cooperation modalities, to assist the transition from relief to development through, inter alia, the use of information technologies and knowledge management systems, as well as exchange of expertise to enable countries in that situation to benefit from the experience of other developing countries;

98. *Urges* the donor countries and other countries in a position to do so to consider more coordinated and flexible approaches to funding operational activities for development in situations of transition from relief to development, making use of multiple resource mo-

bilization instruments, and stresses that contributions to humanitarian assistance should not be provided at the expense of development assistance and that sufficient resources for humanitarian assistance should be made available by the international community;

99. *Urges* United Nations agencies and the donor community, in coordination with the national authorities, to begin planning the transition to development and taking measures supportive of that transition, such as institutional and capacity-building, from the beginning of the relief phase;

XII
Follow-up

100. *Reaffirms* that the governing bodies of the funds, programmes and specialized agencies of the United Nations system should take appropriate actions for the full implementation of the present resolution, in line with paragraphs 91 and 92 of resolution 56/201;

101. *Requests* the Secretary-General, after consultation with the funds, programmes and specialized agencies of the United Nations system, to submit a report to the Economic and Social Council, at its substantive session of 2005, on an appropriate management process, containing clear guidelines, targets, benchmarks and time frames for the full implementation of the present resolution;

102. *Invites* the Economic and Social Council, during the operational activities segment of its substantive session of 2006, to examine the operational activities of the United Nations system in order to evaluate the implementation of the present resolution with a view to ensuring its full implementation;

103. *Requests* the Secretary-General to submit to the General Assembly at its sixty-second session, through the Economic and Social Council, a comprehensive analysis of the implementation of the present resolution in the context of the triennial policy review, inter alia, by making use of relevant documentation, and to make appropriate recommendations.

Financing of operational activities in 2003

Expenditures of the UN system on operational activities, excluding loans through the World Bank Group, totalled $9.7 billion in 2003 [A/59/386], the most recent year for which figures were available (compared with $7.3 billion in 2002). Of that amount, $2,411.5 million was distributed in development grants by UNDP and UNDP-administered funds, $1,992.1 million by specialized agencies and other organizations from extrabudgetary sources, $3,275.3 million by WFP, $1,208.1 million by UNICEF, $518.2 million by specialized agencies and other organizations from regular budgets, and $272.9 million from UNFPA.

The UNDP Administrator, in an August report on UN system technical cooperation expenditures in 2003 [DP/2004/37 & Add.1], said that the unprecedented $9.7 billion in technical cooperation to the developing world, a 31.7 per cent increase over 2002, was the highest level of expenditure in

the last decade, attributable to, among other factors, the response to the humanitarian situation in Iraq in 2003 [YUN 2003, p. 936]. Expenditure increases were posted by WFP of 105.7 per cent (at $3.3 billion); UNICEF, 15.7 per cent (at $1.3 billion); and specialized agencies, funds and programmes, 11.5 per cent (at $2.5 billion). Only UNFPA registered a decline of 12.7 per cent (at $273 million).

By region, Africa was the largest recipient (28.2 per cent, or $2.7 billion), followed by the Arab States (27.5 per cent, or $2.6 billion), Asia and the Pacific (17.2 per cent, or $1.7 billion), Latin America and the Caribbean (15.6 per cent, or $1.5 billion), and Europe and the Commonwealth of Independent States (CIS) (4.6 per cent, or $446 million). Other global and interregional activities received 6.9 per cent, or $669 million. Four countries received one quarter of the total technical cooperation expenditure: Iraq ($1.5 billion), Afghanistan ($359 million), Ethiopia ($323 million) and Brazil ($258 million). The health and humanitarian assistance sectors together accounted for 48.1 per cent of total, or $4.6 billion. Humanitarian assistance alone increased 97.6 per cent, to $2.9 billion, from $1.5 billion in 2002.

On 24 September [E/2004/35 (dec. 2004/41)], the UNDP/UNFPA Executive Board took note of the Administrator's report on technical cooperation expenditure for 2003.

At the 2004 United Nations Pledging Conference for Development Activities (New York, 11 November) [A/CONF.208/2004/3], Governments made pledges to UN programmes and funds concerned with development. The Conference noted that several Governments would communicate their pledges to the Secretary-General as soon as they were able to do so.

The Secretary-General provided a statement of contributions pledged or paid at the 2003 Pledging Conference, as at 30 June 2004, to 21 funds and programmes [A/CONF.208/2004/2]. The total amounted to some $1.5 billion.

World Solidarity Fund

On 8 July, during the operational activities segment of the Economic and Social Council's substantive session for 2004 [meeting 29], the UNDP Administrator updated delegations on developments with regard to the World Solidarity Fund, established in 2003 [YUN 2003, p. 889] as a UNDP trust fund for the eradication of poverty and the promotion of social and human development in developing countries. He reported that Tunisia and UNDP had invited prospective members of the High-level Committee established for the Fund and had received seven acceptances. At the time of the meeting, however, the Fund had as yet no financial resources, and he counted on the High-level Committee to provide assistance in that regard.

Technical cooperation through UNDP

The report of UNDP on its performance and results for 2004 in implementation of the multi-year funding framework (MYFF) for 2004-2007 [DP/2005/16] described the key messages and conclusions on performance that emerged from analysis of reports on country office results and other data on activities. It provided analysis against strategic performance indicators; qualitative analysis of results by practice; a summary of results in building organizational capacities, promoting efficiency and enhancing accountability; and aggregate information on the use of financial resources. The report also presented two aspects of UNDP contributions to development: the rates of achievement of annual targets set by country offices towards intended programme outcomes and the extent to which UNDP promoted the drivers of development effectiveness.

By four key performance measures, the report assessed the extent of UNDP strategic focus. It indicated that demand for UNDP support and concentration of activity, as measured by intended outcomes, centred on five practices: reducing human poverty; fostering democratic governance; energy and environment for sustainable development; crisis prevention and recovery; and responding to HIV/AIDS. More than 90 per cent of programme countries sought support for the first three practices, 71 per cent for the fourth and 59 per cent for the fifth. At the regional level, the largest areas of UNDP support across all regions continued to be in poverty reduction and democratic governance. Almost 90 per cent of countries in Asia and the Pacific benefited from support in crisis prevention and recovery, compared to 50 to 60 per cent for other regions, while support in HIV/AIDS response was highest in Africa, followed by Asia and the Pacific. As to strategic interventions, the number of intended outcomes being pursued per country varied from 12 to 17; country programmes concentrated on 11 service lines on average, indicating that, of 30 such lines provided to respond to country demands across five regions, country offices focused on just one third of possible thematic options available in the MYFF. The degree of convergence of programme outcomes with core

results was found to be strong in 91 country offices, moderate in 12 and weak in 24. Total programme expenditure within thematic priorities as a proportion of all programme expenditures was just over $2.43 billion, of which about 92 per cent (or about $2.23 billion) was spent in pursuing results within the practices and service lines of the MYFF, 2004-2007—in marked contrast to the 79 per cent spent within the focus areas of the MYFF, 2000-2003. Less than 4 per cent fell within the practices not associated with specific service lines or core results.

An analysis of the rates of achievement of targets set by country offices in 2004 showed that, on average, 50 per cent of targets were fully achieved, 42 per cent partially achieved and 8 per cent were not. The targets that were fully achieved were highest in HIV/AIDS response (57 per cent) and lowest in support to energy and environment for sustainable development (45 per cent). As to achievement by service lines, six of the 10 top-performing lines fell under reducing poverty and fostering governance, the two practices at the core of the UNDP profile as a development partner; the other four fell under crisis prevention and recovery, and HIV/AIDS response. Three service lines in two practices (access to sustainable energy services and part of crisis prevention and recovery) failed to achieve 40 per cent or more of annual targets, due mainly to over-ambitious targets and to the need for realigning annual budget targets to government policy and for clarifying national policy.

Analysis of the promotion of the six elements or drivers identified by UNDP for effective development suggested that, in 2004, a UNDP that had become more outward-looking relied heavily on creating an enabling policy environment, thereby influencing country-level policies for effective development, and on forging partnerships for results, which was strong in all five regions. Developing national capacities proved more effective than policy advocacy in enabling national ownership over the development agenda. The promotion of gender equality and South-South solutions appeared not to have been sufficiently incorporated into the design of all programmes.

The UNDP Administrator stated in his annual report [E/2005/4-DP/2005/13] to the Economic and Social Council that, in December 2003, UNDP adopted a two-pronged strategy for its engagement in trade, following the Fifth (2003) Ministerial Conference of the World Trade Organization [YUN 2003 p. 1535], to help developing countries prepare for the resumption of trade negotiations stalled at that Conference and to enhance developing-country competitiveness and capacity-building for trade through the removal of supply-side constraints. The strategy was to ensure the linkage of trade policies to human development concerns and outcomes, while strengthening developing-country capacity for integrating trade policies into national anti-poverty strategies.

UNDP implemented its 2003 decision to mainstream information and communication technologies (ICT) into other practice areas [YUN 2003, p. 891] by bridging dedicated "ICT for development" expertise into the poverty reduction and democratic governance practices. It focused on ICT for the poor and e-governance-related programmes, especially in Eastern Europe and the Arab States, and was working closely with the Department of Economic and Social Affairs (DESA) to support the implementation of country-level e-governance programmes.

UNDP streamlined its practice areas to five (see p. 879), with 30 clear-cut service lines that structured activities under each practice, with direct links to the MDGs and an integrated emphasis on gender mainstreaming. It strengthened the implementation of strategic, comprehensive initiatives in support of the empowerment of women and the promotion of gender equality (see p. 883).

The Millennium Project, an independent advisory body launched in 2002 [YUN 2002, p. 863], posted in September 2004 its draft *Global Plan to Achieve the Millennium Development Goals*, together with background research, on its website for public comment; it would present the final version to the Secretary-General in 2005. In 2004, the Project initiated country-level advisory work in Cambodia, the Dominican Republic, Ethiopia, Ghana, Kenya, Senegal, Tajikistan and Yemen. By the end of September, 84 MDG country reports had been produced. The Millennium Campaign continued to expand its assistance to national campaigns, focusing on advocacy of issues related to the MDG goal of developing a global partnership for development. It was working closely with the United Nations Communications Group on a joint strategy for 2005 to leverage the UN system's communications infrastructure.

UNDP/UNFPA Executive Board

In 2004, the UNDP/UNFPA Executive Board held its first (23-30 January) and second (20-24 September) regular sessions and an annual session (14-23 June), all in New York [E/2004/35].

At the first regular session, the Board adopted 12 decisions, including one giving an overview of the Board's actions taken at that session [E/2004/35 (dec. 2004/12)]. Other decisions dealt with reporting on the UNDP MYFF, 2004-2007 (see p. 887); as-

sistance to Myanmar (see p. 878); the United Nations Office for Project Services (UNOPS) (see p. 894); the implementation of the recommendations of the Board of Auditors by UNDP and UNFPA (see p. 890); the follow-up to the fourteenth (2003) meeting of the Programme Coordinating Board of the Joint United Nations Programme on HIV/AIDS (UNAIDS) [YUN 2003, p. 1248] (see p. 1220); the reports of the UNDP Administrator and the UNFPA Executive Director to the Economic and Social Council (see p. 878); the UNFPA MYFF, 2004-2007 and its intercountry programme, 2004-2007 (see PART THREE, Chapter VIII); the Evaluation Office report *Millennium Development Goal reports: an assessment* (see p. 886); the United Nations Development Fund for Women (UNIFEM) MYFF, 2004-2007 (see p. 1171); and the World Health Organization (WHO)/UNICEF/UNFPA Coordinating Committee on Health (see p. 1224).

At its annual session, the Executive Board adopted 13 decisions. In addition to an overview decision that summarized the action taken at that session [dec. 2004/25], it adopted decisions regarding the United Nations Capital Development Fund (UNCDF) (see p. 899); funding commitments to UNDP (see p. 888); UNOPS (see p. 895); the United Nations Volunteers (UNV) programme (see p. 897); internal audit and oversight for UNDP, UNFPA and UNOPS (see p. 890); joint UNDP/UNFPA/UNIFEM proposals for MYFF reporting (see p. 887); the management response to the UNDP assessment report "Transforming the Mainstream: Gender in UNDP" (see p. 883) and gender balance in UNDP (see p. 884); the report of the UNFPA Executive Director for 2003 and funding commitments to UNFPA (see PART THREE, Chapter VIII); and the report on the implementation of a 2001 Board decision [YUN 2001, p. 799] on the UNDP/UNFPA programming process and joint UNDP/UNFPA programming (see p. 884).

At its second regular session, the Board adopted 16 decisions, including an overview decision [dec. 2004/41]. The other decisions concerned the 2003 UNFPA annual financial review, additional security requirements to safeguard UNFPA personnel and premises globally, and the report on the midterm review of the Technical Advisory Programme (see PART THREE, Chapter VIII); the annual review of the UNDP financial situation (see p. 888); the UNDP strategic cost management and implications for cost recovery (see p. 890); the report of the Inter-Agency Procurement Services Office for the 2002-2003 biennium (see p. 891); the third cooperation framework for South-South cooperation (see p. 898); the UNDP Administrator's annual report on evaluation (see p. 885); the second global cooperation framework (see p. 886); assistance to Somalia (see p. 879); UNOPS (see pp. 895 & 896); the progress report on options for a future business model for UNCDF (see p. 899); gender in UNDP (see p. 884); internal audit and oversight (see p. 891); and UNDP and UNFPA follow-up to the fifteenth UNAIDS Programme Coordinating Board meeting (see p. 1220).

The Economic and Social Council, by **decision 2004/232** of 12 July, took note of the reports of the UNDP/UNFPA Executive Board on its work in 2003 [YUN 2003, p. 891], the report on its 2004 first regular session and the decisions adopted by the Board at its 2004 annual session.

UNDP/UNFPA reports

In January [dec. 2004/6], the UNDP/UNFPA Executive Board took note of the reports of the UNDP Administrator [E/2004/4-DP/2004/12] and UNFPA Executive Director [E/2004/5-DP/FPA/2004/2] to the Economic and Social Council and requested the secretariat to transmit them to the Council, together with a summary of the discussion at the January session.

In June [dec. 2004/24], the Board took note of the UNDP Administrator's 2003 annual report [YUN 2003, p. 890] and addenda [DP/2004/16/Add.1,2]. The Council, by **decision 2004/232** of 12 July, also took note of the Administrator's annual report.

The Executive Board, at its annual session in June, had before it an April update on the *Human Development Report* consultations [DP/2004/22], submitted in response to General Assembly resolution 57/264 [YUN 2002, p. 841]. UNDP maintained the frequency of consultations as in 2003 [YUN 2003, p. 892]. The Human Development Report Office, charged with preparing the report (see p. 849), held consultations with the Board members on five occasions on the report's theme, outline, structure, statistics and messages. The Board took note of the update in June [dec. 2004/25].

In accordance with Council resolution 2003/3 [YUN 2003, p. 883], the Secretary-General submitted a May report [E/2004/60], which assessed the value added of the joint meetings of the Executive Boards of UNDP/UNFPA, UNICEF and WFP and their impact on the Council's operational activities segment, and made suggestions for further consideration by the Council. The annual joint meetings, organized in response to Assembly resolution 52/12 B [YUN 1997, p. 1392], were to take into account the respective mandates of the individual Boards. Members of the UNDG Executive Committee were of the view that the joint meetings provided a useful addition to the ongoing dialogue facilitating discussion of oper-

ational issues facing all four agencies, and addressed the gap between single agency discussions on operational and policy issues in individual Boards and the more general global policy dialogue in the Council and Assembly. However, several shortcomings remained. It had proved impractical for the entire WFP Board to be in New York, so it was being represented at the meetings by its Bureau, and many of the cross-cutting programme issues addressed also applied to one or more of the specialized agencies whose views could only be heard in the Council or Assembly, leading to duplication of discussions. Members of the Executive Committee believed it would be useful for member States and the concerned funds and programmes to discuss a more formal approach to the joint meetings, in particular one that would involve formal decision-making authority. The key consideration should be the contribution of current or alternative arrangements in advancing the basic policy objective of greater system-wide coherence in support of countries' development priorities and agreed development goals that were guiding the Council's work and the 2004 triennial policy review of operational activities (see p. 866).

UNDP operational activities

Country and regional programmes

The UNDP/UNFPA Executive Board, at its January session [dec. 2004/12], approved country programmes for Benin, the Central African Republic, the Congo, Croatia, Djibouti, Ecuador, Kenya, Lithuania, Niger, Pakistan, Poland, the Russian Federation, Sierra Leone and Thailand. It approved a two-year extension of the second country cooperation framework (CCF) for Guyana; took note of the one-year extensions of the second CCFs for the Democratic People's Republic of Korea and the Republic of Korea, and of the first one-year extension of the first subregional cooperation framework for the countries of the Organisation of Eastern Caribbean States and Barbados [DP/2004/9]; and approved a two-year extension of the second cooperation framework for technical cooperation among developing countries [DP/CF/TCDC/2/EXTENSION I].

Also at the January session [dec. 2004/2], the Board took note of the UNDP Administrator's note on assistance to Myanmar [DP/2004/8] and the report by the independent assessment mission to that country, in particular the strategic challenges and recommendations mentioned therein. The Board requested the Administrator to take account of the mission's findings during phase IV of the Human Development Initiative.

At its annual session in June [dec. 2004/25], the Board took note of draft country programme documents and the comments made thereon for Angola, Argentina, Armenia, Azerbaijan, Burundi, Bosnia and Herzegovina, Iran, Kazakhstan, Kyrgyzstan, Lesotho, Madagascar, the Philippines, Romania, Serbia and Montenegro, Tajikistan, The former Yugoslav Republic of Macedonia, Turkmenistan, and Uzbekistan. It approved a second one-year extension of the second CCFs for Chile and Uruguay and a two-year extension of the second CCF for Zimbabwe. The Board also took note of the one-year extensions of the second CCFs for Belarus, Hungary, Latvia and Slovakia [DP/2004/21].

At its second regular session in September [dec. 2004/41], the Board took note of the draft country programme documents and the comments made thereon for the Democratic People's Republic of Korea, Guatemala, Mauritius, and the Republic of Korea. It adopted extensions of the CCFs for the British Overseas Territory of Saint Helena, and for Senegal and Paraguay [DP/2004/44].

Also in September, the Board had before it the Administrator's note on assistance to Somalia (2005-2006) [DP/2004/43 & Corr.1]. On 24 September [dec. 2004/35], the Board took note of the situation in Somalia and its implications for the delivery of humanitarian and development assistance to the Somali people; endorsed the UNDP strategic approach to promoting peace and security by concentrating on security and the rule of law, poverty reduction, and governance, public administration and civil society; encouraged UNDP to continue to mobilize resources and develop strategic partnerships, and to cooperate with the Intergovernmental Authority on Development Partner's Forum on international assistance and coordination arrangements in support of the future Somali transitional federal institutions; and authorized the Administrator to approve projects consistent with the strategic approach on a case-by-case basis.

UNDP programme results

The establishment and implementation by UNDP of its practice approach were an important element of its strategy to provide knowledge services and part of its objective to develop its ability to provide high-quality support to programme countries. UNDP activities were organized under five practice areas: poverty reduction, fostering democratic governance, crisis prevention and recovery, energy and environment, and responding to HIV/AIDS.

Poverty reduction

UNDP work in the poverty practice remained largely concentrated in local-level initiatives and monitoring and reporting, particularly around country targets related to the MDGs [YUN 2000, p. 51]. Country office reports indicated a rapid increase in the number of initiatives to support MDG reporting and continued progress on the development and use of national human development reports (NHDRs). Together with NHDRs, MDG reporting accounted for around one quarter of all initiatives. However, the effect of MDG reports and NHDRs on national policy-making or poverty reduction strategies needed further examination, and the biggest challenge for UNDP support was to help lay the foundation for influencing the policy content of national poverty reduction strategies. The downside of the increasing emphasis on reporting and monitoring was the relatively slower progress in providing policy advisory services to countries on poverty reduction strategies, which had become a major priority of UNDP. Nevertheless, several policy-related initiatives continued to support participatory processes and took up the challenge of linking PRSP indicators with the MDGs through global or regional programmes.

UNDP continued to support diverse local poverty reduction initiatives, which accounted for 17 per cent of all poverty practice activities over a broad range of disparate interventions, among which microfinance remained the most coherent and the most closely linked to national policy, accounting for about one third of all activities. The main challenge to UNDP for activities in that area was to consolidate efforts, in line with the microfinance model within a more limited set of corporate priorities, build up systematic bodies of practice and give greater attention to influencing national policy frameworks.

UNDP support to civil society organizations (CSOs) for achieving the MDGs and reducing poverty, while progressing, remained disconnected from work in other poverty service lines. Activities needed to concentrate more on developing the capacities of CSOs and empowering them to engage substantively in the PRSPs and MDGs. Support to ICT for development was also making progress, with country offices reporting significant success in achieving outcomes. However, that area of work remained limited in scope and was not yet well integrated into the poverty practice.

Private sector development was the newest service line for the poverty practice, accounting for only 7 per cent of all activities, most of which related to micro, small and medium-sized enterprises or microfinance. In March, UNDP globally launched the report of the Commission on the Private Sector and Development, entitled *Unleashing Entrepreneurship: Making Business Work for the Poor*, an independent publication by UNDP. By May, UNDP had facilitated policy dialogue around the report in more than 25 countries.

Representing over 1,100 practitioners and 467 registered resource persons, the poverty reduction practice was the largest thematic practice. The global network of poverty reduction practitioners enabled professionals from every region, country office and service line to share knowledge and lessons learned, to contribute substantively and to backstop each other's work.

UNDP role in PRSP process

A May report [DP/2004/25 & Corr.1] followed up on the 2003 evaluation of the role of UNDP in the PRSP process [YUN 2003, p. 894] and the UNDP management response to that evaluation [ibid., p. 895]. UNDP launched an array of global and regional programmes to address the objectives recommended in the management response report, including championing equity as an integral component of growth strategies, helping link long-term development policies to the causes of poverty and promoting a healthy national dialogue by fostering greater policy choice, especially on economic policies. It initiated the Macroeconomics of Poverty Reduction, a nine-country Asia-Pacific programme aimed at translating the concept of pro-poor growth into practical policy recommendations at the county level, fostering greater consistency between economic policies and poverty reduction strategies, and promoting broader dialogue on policy options. Similar policy-oriented research and capacity development programmes were undertaken in Latin America and the Caribbean, Eastern Europe and CIS, and the Arab States; another programme was planned for Africa. Such programmes were designed to strengthen national policy autonomy in the formulation and implementation of poverty reduction strategies, particularly the PRSPs.

UNDP initiated several new global programmes in 2004, based largely on financing by the Thematic Trust Fund for Poverty Reduction. They included initiatives on pro-poor public investment, the effect on poverty of the privatization of public services and utilities, land reform and poverty reduction, and pro-poor domestic resource mobilization. UNDP had also reached an agreement with the International Labour Organization (ILO) on a global programme on employment and poverty. As recommended in the management response, UNDP was upgrading its in-house capacity by, among other means, training and consolidation of expertise at the sub-regional level through the new regional centres of policy specialists. The challenge was to help link the MDGs and PRSPs by making short-term reforms fit into long-term comprehensive development plans.

The UNDP/UNFPA Executive Board took note of the report at its annual session in June [dec. 2004/25].

Democratic governance

The democratic governance practice was the second largest thematic practice for UNDP, and it continued to grow, making UNDP the leading provider of democratic governance services worldwide. Africa remained at the core of UNDP governance work, with 85 per cent of the countries reporting activity. The greatest concentration was in decentralization and local governance, with UNDP support sustaining both the central government agendas towards devolution and local capacity-development efforts. The strategy of localizing the MDGs was aimed at providing service delivery through democratic participatory processes, blending the governance aspects of local capacity- and institution-building to address the HIV/AIDS pandemic, and ensuring a sustainable environment while promoting local development.

Country office reporting for 2004 reflected a shift in the overall governance portfolio towards increased demand for services where UNDP had comparative strengths at the supranational, national and subnational levels. For example, at the supranational level, UNDP, in partnership with the European Union, launched the report *Democracy in Latin America: towards a citizen's democracy*, which offered a comprehensive analysis on the state of democracy in 18 Latin American countries and proposals for guiding the debate on democratic governance in the region. At the national level, UNDP support in Liberia put into place an institutional framework for the operation of the Truth and Reconciliation Commission (see p. 196). At the subnational level, community-based policing was initiated in Albania.

UNDP was recognized as one of the key providers of technical cooperation in support of elections and parliaments, supporting one out of every three parliaments and, on average, one election every two weeks somewhere in the world. Notable support was provided to Afghanistan, Egypt and Liberia. UNDP was a leading provider of technical advice in public administration reform, and in recent years that support had increased significantly. UNDP reoriented its position and identified types of support to programme country governments that could improve the prospects of lasting impact, resulting in a greater emphasis on capacity development for policy making and anti-corruption initiatives. E-governance and access to information activities were consolidated in 2004, with over 30 country offices reporting core results where the use of ICT in government functions had a strategic value in terms of increased access to information, transparency of operations and improved accountability. In that regard, UNDP's effort was to ensure that its support remained focused on the policy and governance aspects of ICT, rather than on the provision of hardware.

A main challenge for the democratic governance practice was to build on ongoing efforts and raise the emphasis on gender equality. Policy guidance and toolkits for mainstreaming gender were being developed or implemented, and the governance trust fund was introducing incentives to mainstream gender into fund-approved projects.

Crisis prevention and recovery

The commitment to eradicating poverty and empowering the poorest and most vulnerable groups placed conflict prevention and recovery at the core of the UNDP development agenda. In 2004, 80 countries sought UNDP support under that practice (compared to 54 in 2000); the actual number was even higher, as some countries reported their crisis prevention and recovery work under other practices. The year saw a series of conflicts and natural disasters afflicting a growing percentage of the countries in which UNDP worked, and the crisis prevention and recovery practice saw consolidation, growth and a steep increase in demand. Forty countries specifically sought UNDP support for natural disaster reduction. Of the service lines dealing with conflict and its aftermath, UNDP worked with 31 countries on recovery, 25 on conflict prevention and peace-building, 21 on small arms reduction, disarmament and demobilization, 18 on mine action, and 7 on special initiatives for countries in transition. In Africa, UNDP participated in the Mano River Union Initiative involving Côte d'Ivoire, Guinea, Liberia, and Sierra Leone, which helped with the exchange of experiences and lessons learned, and examined common challenges in a post-conflict environment.

UNDP developed tools for mainstreaming conflict prevention into development strategies in pre- and post-conflict countries; deepened collaboration and programming in crisis situations with the Departments of Political Affairs and of Peacekeeping Operations; worked with 13 other UN organizations to revise and update the UN inter-agency policy on mine action; and issued policy recommendations on mainstreaming mine action into development. It also worked with other UN partners to make the Inter-department Framework for Coordination a more effective mechanism for supporting UN country teams in developing strategies for early conflict prevention and, with UNDG and the World Bank, to develop the post-conflict needs assessment, a joint methodology to coordinate analysis of and response to a country's post-crisis recovery needs. It contributed to the UNDG–Executive Committee on Humanitarian Assistance (ECHA) working group on transitions and produced a disaster risk index.

However, country office reporting for 2004 on the integration of drivers of development into crisis prevention and recovery work indicated some serious shortcomings, such as giving the least attention to developing national capacity, enhancing national ownership, advocating and fostering an enabling policy environment, seeking South-South solutions and forging partnerships for results. A possible explanation might be the political nature of crisis prevention and recovery programmes, which made promoting specific drivers, like national ownership, difficult. In contrast, 25 countries reported high emphasis on the gender driver in the context of the crisis prevention and recovery practice.

To strengthen crisis prevention and recovery capacities in Africa, 85 practitioners from across the continent were brought together in two workshops to discuss common approaches, share challenges and experiences and learn about the latest programmatic and operational policies and procedures for crisis prevention and recovery.

Environment and energy

One hundred and twenty-eight countries, representing more than 90 per cent of programme countries across all regions, were engaged with UNDP in managing energy and the environment for sustainable development. The greatest concentration of work was on frameworks and strategies for sustainable development, representing 29 per cent of all reported practice outcomes. In 47 countries, support to biodiversity initiatives resulted in specific progress in integrating biodiversity into one or more of their sector strategies in agriculture, forestry, rangeland and grazing, coastal management, fisheries, and wildlife, while 66 countries made progress in adjusting their legal frameworks to incorporate biodiversity.

The UNDP focus on energy-poverty linkages was strengthened to integrate the role of energy into national MDG frameworks and poverty reduction strategies. While there was considerable effort on policy and strategic planning of resources and a broad recognition of poverty-environment linkages, there had not yet been sufficient demonstrated results on delivery of community water and energy services to contribute significantly to progress on MDGs; only a quarter of total outcomes in water governance and energy access was devoted to service delivery.

In 2004, the energy and environment practice was reoriented towards the new realities of development cooperation. In terms of integrating security concerns, some of the key areas for the practice were climate change, natural disaster prevention and recovery, and transboundary environmental cooperation. The UNDP transboundary portfolio with the Global Environment Facility (GEF) (see p. 1046), under the focal areas of international waters and biodiversity, continued to build frameworks for cooperation and dialogue between countries. Work on climate risk assessment resulted in a large body of guidance to assist national Governments.

The majority of outcomes in the energy and environment practice demonstrated a significant emphasis on partnerships for results. Partnership agreements included local private-sector and community action in Zimbabwe; support to environmental management in the decentralization process in Rwanda; and partnerships among non-governmental organizations (NGOs), national Governments and research institutions in Azerbaijan, the Dominican Republic, Kuwait and Romania. Partnerships with GEF and the Multilateral Fund for the Implementation of the Montreal Protocol on Substances that Deplete the Ozone Layer (see p. 1052) [YUN 1987, p. 686] supported the majority of activities in energy and the environment.

The practice initiated cross-practice initiatives with a view to improving gender equality. Both the sustainable energy and water governance service lines worked with the UNDP gender team to develop guidelines for mainstreaming gender into programmes and projects in those areas. In terms of encouraging South-South cooperation, the practice supported a mission from Latin America in response to a request from Europe and CIS to learn from southern knowledge and experiences on debt swaps.

Five regional workshops covering Africa were held on building cross-practice linkages to advance the MDG related to poverty reduction, safe drinking water and improving the lives of slum dwellers, and financing for sustainable development. Workshops on the theme of sustainable livelihoods were held in Asia and the Pacific, and in Europe and CIS.

Response to HIV/AIDS

Demand for UNDP support under the HIV/AIDS practice continued to grow rapidly, nearly doubling from 55 countries in 2000 to 97 in 2004, an 85 per cent increase in country engagement. Development planning and implementation remained the most active service line (76 outcomes reported), followed by leadership and capacity development (71 outcomes). In terms of leadership and capacity development to address HIV/AIDS, initiatives focused primarily on the development of critical multi-stakeholder leadership capacities at the individual, institutional and societal levels to generate breakthrough responses for reversing the course of the pandemic. In the Arab States, more outcomes were reported that sought to influence individual and community responses to address attitudes and practices influencing the spread of HIV/AIDS. Most activities also focused on developing advocacy and communications strategies to develop a deeper understanding of the pandemic and its underlying causes, and address issues of vulnerability, stigma and discrimination.

In several regions, HIV/AIDS programmes worked across service lines to create a synergistic response and action, notably in Cambodia, Ethiopia and Ukraine. The programme in Ethiopia aimed at scaling up the multisectoral response with a view to developing leadership for local and national action to combat the disease. Cambodia reported breakthrough results under all service lines for HIV/AIDS and indicated interest in sharing its expertise in implementing a nationwide response to the epidemic with other countries in the region. Countries implementing activities under all service lines were able to strengthen programmes at national and district levels, take ownership of initiatives and engage in multi-stakeholder partnerships to address the pandemic.

Joint action in the HIV/AIDS and poverty reduction practices project was aimed at building developing country capacity to access HIV/AIDS drugs sustainability in the context of the 1994 World Trade Organization Agreement on Trade-related Aspects of Intellectual Property Rights [YUN 1994, p. 1475] and other bilateral and multilateral intellectual property and trade agreements.

UNDP was increasingly seen as credible and effective in multi-partner initiatives to respond to HIV/AIDS, as evidenced by its role in relation to the Global Fund to Fight AIDS, Tuberculosis and Malaria, established in 2002 [YUN 2002, p. 1217]. Several African Governments called on UNDP to provide medium-term operational support by performing the functions of principal recipient for the Fund and to help them build their own capacities to eventually take over those functions. UNDP support was also helping to bring anti-retroviral drugs to HIV-infected patients; provide mosquito nets to prevent the propagation of malaria; and increase the availability of drugs to cure tuberculosis.

A key feature of all country action in HIV/AIDS was the strong emphasis on forging partnerships for results, with actors ranging from Government, civil society and the private sector to donors and the international community at large. Emphasis was being placed on the enhancement of national ownership in the design and implementation of HIV/AIDS initiatives. While overall support to the driver on gender equity in HIV/AIDS programmes was relatively high compared to other practices, it appeared to be given a lower priority when compared to the other drivers of development. Concerted efforts needed to be made to generate a comprehensive approach that integrated gender concerns into HIV/AIDS strategies.

In 2004, the HIV/AIDS practice had policy advisers in all regions, 50 per cent of whom were women. At the end of the year, the practice had 132 registered practitioners within the organization, of whom 54 per cent were women.

Programme planning and management

Gender issues

The UNDP/UNFPA Executive Board, at its January session, considered a conference room paper on efforts to strengthen the partnership between UNDP and UNIFEM to achieve gender equality [DP/2004/CRP.2]. The paper was an initial step towards the formulation of a results-based strategy for strengthening UNDP-UNIFEM partnership for 2004-2007.

Also in January, UNDP shared with the Board an assessment of gender mainstreaming efforts entitled "Transforming the mainstream: gender in UNDP", featuring major achievements and key challenges in gender mainstreaming drawn from UNDP experience and the shared concerns of other partners. It highlighted issues requiring particular attention in UNDP, including integrated approaches to ways of working; ensuring women-specific strategic programmes; poverty and the environment; measurement of results; and in-house gender expertise. UNDP's gender mainstreaming efforts were analysed within the context of achieving the MDGs and reducing human poverty, fostering democratic governance, energy and the environment for sustainable development, and crisis prevention and recovery. The assessment underscored that, although the

macroeconomic framework was a strategic arena for engagement to transform the mainstream, it was still a relatively neglected area; it thus called for investments in specific programme tools to provide practitioners with the necessary technical skills and expertise. The assessment highlighted successful approaches supported by UNDP to increase women's participation in Government and to mainstream gender in governance interventions. It underscored three areas for future work: more support to gender responsiveness; strengthening women's capacities to participate in government; and development of staff capacities. It also emphasized the need for UNDP to bring women's voices into national strategies for sustainable development; ensure women's involvement in participatory resource planning; and strengthen policy and regulatory frameworks to protect women's access to natural resources. UNDP was in a critical position at the country level, where it was able to promote a multifaceted approach to address gender issues in conflict and post-conflict reconstruction.

UNDP management, responding to the assessment in June [DP/2004/31], described its efforts to strengthen strategic programming and accountability in gender mainstreaming, as well as arrangements to increase mainstreaming capacities, commitment and resources. An independent evaluation of gender mainstreaming was initiated under the leadership of the Evaluation Office, and an organizational scorecard was being developed to monitor progress at all levels and build managers' responsibility for the implementation of the UNDP policy on gender balance in management and in the work-life policy. In 2005, UNDP would produce a 10-year review of gender and development and gender empowerment indicators. A UNDP-UNIFEM joint plan of action incorporated features to improve coherence between the two organizations and bring their work closer together. UNIFEM regional programmes and UNDP regional centres would become regional hubs for expanded knowledge and action on gender equality. There would be a unity of leadership on the gender issue between UNDP and UNIFEM, under the strategic direction and policy guidance of the UNDP Administrator.

In June [dec. 2004/21], the Executive Board took note of the assessment report and management response, and the January conference room paper. It stressed that UNDP should implement its strategy for gender mainstreaming rigorously and requested that it prepare a detailed plan of action on gender mainstreaming, with concrete targets and measurable actions, for review by the Board no later than at its first regular session in January 2005. The Board requested further clarification, at its September 2004 session, of the UNDP-UNIFEM joint plan of action and, at the January 2005 session, an elaboration of how UNDP could scale up operations based on lessons learned in UNIFEM pilot projects.

The Board also requested that the organizational scorecard mentioned in the management response (see p. 883) be presented at its June 2005 meeting [dec. 2004/22].

A September report, submitted in response to Board decision 2004/21, described UNDP progress in gender mainstreaming and the joint plan of action with UNIFEM [DP/2004/47], including internal steps already under implementation. In July, the Senior Management Team endorsed a plan of action that called for the creation of a gender task force; discussions with facilitators on all networks; a strategic planning workshop in November to review and endorse the final UNDP plan of action and the UNDP-UNIFEM joint action plan; and a final report to be presented to the Executive Board in January 2005. UNDP made considerable progress in: the identification of specific gender indicators of the MYFF performance indicators; the development of gender mainstreaming strategies, a gender scorecard and a toolkit to build the capacities of gender thematic groups within UN country teams; a joint UNDP-UNIFEM gender analysis of their programme portfolio; and an evaluation of gender in UNDP. The report also discussed progress in strengthening the UNDP-UNIFEM partnership on gender equality.

In September [dec. 2004/38], the Executive Board took note of the report on UNDP progress in gender mainstreaming and the joint plan of action with UNIFEM. It requested UNDP to submit to the Board at its January 2005 session more detailed information on specific gender indicators and gender drivers in the MYFF and in the Atlas information management system, and to provide an update on progress achieved in the UNDP-UNIFEM partnership.

Programming arrangements

Joint programming

In response to a 2003 Executive Board decision [YUN 2003, p. 898], the UNDP Administrator and the UNFPA Executive Director submitted an April report [DP/2004/30-DP/FPA/2004/8] analysing joint programming between UN organizations, based on evidence provided during the revision of the current Guidance Note on Joint Programming. The revised Guidance Note 2004 addressed deficiencies and clarified the difference between joint programming and joint programmes. It was

meant to avoid duplication, reduce transaction costs and maximize synergies among national partners and different contributions of UN system organizations. The revised Guidance Note provided programmatic and administrative guidance for seizing joint programming opportunities. It introduced detailed guidance on three fund management options to be applied on the basis of a programmatic rationale and a new mechanism for passing funds through one UN organization to another; clarified the value added to joint programming; and included standard legal agreements for the pooling and pass-through fund management options. Efforts were under way to internalize the Guidance Note into the organizations' procedures. The Note suggested the development of a common work plan consisting of shared objectives, actions, time frames, resource requirements and clear delineation of responsibilities, and included communication activities to publicize joint programme activities. The report stated that the Note should be seen as an instrument to identify areas for further harmonization.

A group of financial experts from different UN organizations was working on a common format for high-level reporting to donors for use in joint programmes.

Also in April [DP/2004/29-DP/FPA/2004/7], the UNDP Administrator and the UNFPA Executive Director reported on progress in the implementation of a 2001 Executive Board decision that called for modifying the UNDP/UNFPA two-step programming process [YUN 2001, p. 799]. Following that decision, UNDP and UNFPA agreed on a harmonized format for country programme outlines and documents aimed at the formulation of brief, concise and focused outlines; the UNICEF and WFP Executive Boards adopted a similar process in 2002. Country programme documents (CPDs) replaced draft country outlines and programmes; draft CPDs were discussed and reviewed by the UNDP/UNFPA Executive Board during its annual session, the final versions of which were approved by the Board at the first regular session of the following year. While country office staff welcomed the more focused document limiting resources and outputs to the UNDAF outcomes, they expressed concern that the new two-step approval process had increased the time frame for developing country programmes, and that the process might not be sufficiently flexible.

In June [dec. 2004/19], the Executive Board took note of the report on joint programming and deferred consideration of a decision to its first regular session in 2005. In a separate decision [dec. 2004/18], the Board took note of the report on the UNDP and UNFPA programming process and the concerns expressed in that report regarding the increased time frame for developing country programmes; it requested UNDP and UNFPA to consult with their UNDG partners on how to address that concern in a harmonized way and report to the Board in 2005.

Monitoring and evaluation

In July [DP/2004/40], the UNDP Administrator, in his annual report on evaluation covering the period from July 2003 to June 2004, examined the progress made by UNDP in contributing to global and national development results and identified organizational lessons distilled from strategic assessments. Key thematic and country evaluations pointed to some achievements in influencing policy and stimulating national debate on human development. UNDP was an effective broker between Government and external agencies, successfully piloting and feeding lessons and experiences from downstream work into upstream dialogue. However, it needed to do more to position itself strategically as a major global upstream policy advisor and in building on niches that it often created successfully.

There had been some success, as noted in the evaluations of UNDP support to the PRSP process and to reporting on the MDGs [YUN 2000, p. 51] (see below). However, UNDP and its associated funds and programmes still had some way to go in building awareness and capacity to support evaluative evidence-based decision-making. Several outcomes and country evaluations revealed UNDP failures to seize opportunities to build on existing work, how a lack of clear focus prevented it from establishing or retaining a strategic role, and that results-based management tools had not been sufficiently internalized to sharpen focus and direct efforts towards achieving development outcomes.

The Executive Board, in a September decision on the Administrator's annual evaluation report [dec. 2004/33], urged UNDP to continue to give high priority to training key staff in results-based planning, monitoring, evaluation and reporting, in the light of the finding that results-based management tools were not sufficiently internalized in the organization. Recalling its January decision on reporting on the UNDP MYFF, 2004-2007 (see p. 887), the Board stressed that the assessment of development results (ADR) should be a priority of the Evaluation Office. It encouraged UNDP to give continued high priority to the work of the United Nations Evaluation Group and stressed that UN entities, especially UNDP, UNICEF and UNFPA, could benefit significantly from strengthening further their cooperation in support of UNDAF evaluation. The Board asked UNDP to include in its next annual evaluation report an annex containing an overview of all the evaluations undertaken by the Evaluation Office and by UNDP at the local level.

In November [E/2005/4-DP/2005/13], the Administrator said that continual improvements had been made to align the evaluation architecture to corporate goals, review and update methodologies and strengthen assessment capacities in UNDP and its partners. After two years of implementation, the architecture and its instrumentation were under review. The third Development Effectiveness Report successfully advanced the conceptual understanding of development effectiveness by identifying key drivers underpinning the MYFF, 2004-2007 (see p. 887). The utility of strategic and thematic evaluations as effective instruments of corporate relevance had been demonstrated through the evaluation of UNDP support to the PRSP process and to national MDG reports. The Evaluation Office was exploring how to expand annual ADR coverage to validate UNDP results at the country level. In 2004, the second global cooperation framework of UNDP was evaluated comprehensively (see p. 886), which led to a number of key lessons to inform the development of the UNDP global programme, 2005-2007. Alignment with the evaluation policies and procedures of the UNDP-associated funds was also enhanced.

Assessing MDG reports

The Executive Board, at its January session, considered a note [DP/2004/3] summarizing the response of UNDP management to the seven challenges (communication, participation, reporting, statistical, campaign, evaluation, global cooperation) identified in the 2003 assessment of the MDG reports [YUN 2003, pp. 899-890].

Management had since revised the Guidance Note for MDG reporting to emphasize national ownership and participation in the preparation of those reports; better use of disaggregated data to identify development gaps and help set resource allocation priorities; capacity development to promote active participation of key development actors; and advocacy and campaigning, with the reports serving as tools to build consensus around development priorities.

In pursuit of the twofold purpose of the MDG report on public information and social mobilization, the revised note defined mechanisms for closer consultation to improve coordination so that each report was accompanied by a clearly defined communication and advocacy campaign.

Management drew attention to the recommendation not to mistake government participation in the preparation of the MDG report for national ownership. It emphasized the importance of customizing targets through broad-based, inclusive dialogue and debate, and that close collaboration with civil society organizations was essential for widening support and consensus around the MDGs. It was also reinforcing UNDP participation in existing mechanisms for inter-agency coordination to strengthen countries' statistical capacity as the basis for improving global data sources.

In January [dec. 2004/9], the Executive Board took note of the 2003 assessment of the MDG reports, together with the UNDP management response, and asked UNDP to provide further substantive information on the assessment at its June session. The Board decided to include the topic "UNDP cooperation with Member States in the preparation of the MDG reports" in the agenda of its 2005 annual session and requested UNDP to report on the topic, taking into account the triennial comprehensive policy review (see p. 866) during the fifty-ninth (2004) session of the General Assembly.

As requested by the Board, UNDP issued a May report [DP/2004/25 & Corr.1] providing further information on steps taken by management in response to the assessment challenges (see p. 885). Among those steps were the closer collaboration between the monitoring and campaign units to address the communication and campaign challenges; the publication by UNDG of the *Indicators for Monitoring the Millennium Development Goals: Definitions, Rationale, Concepts and Sources* to promote a better understanding of the MDG indicators; and a closer UNDG focus on statistical capacity. To address global cooperation, a seminar was organized (Bergen, Norway) for donor and developing countries to discuss mutual accountability. With UNDP support, a common format for developed country reporting on the MDG on global partnership for development was prepared with the secretariat of the Development Assistance Committee (DAC) of the Organisation for Economic Co-operation and Development (OECD) and a group of bilateral donors.

UNDP was helping to improve the management and accessibility of country-level data produced through administrative reporting systems, surveys and censuses and, in close collaboration with relevant UN organizations and the World Bank, was intensifying its operational support in capacity development for MDG monitoring and basic statistical literacy, with a focus on making MDG-related data more accessible, using disaggregated data by sex, level of education, ethnicity, rural-urban location, region and socioeconomic status.

Second global cooperation framework

An August report [DP/2004/41] summarized the findings of an independent evaluation of the second global cooperation framework (GCF-II), approved in 2001 [YUN 2001, p. 793] and extended in 2003 [YUN 2003, p. 893], for one year, until December 2004. The evaluation's main objectives were to: assess the overall performance and the degree to which the intended organizational goals and development results had been achieved; ascertain how GCF-II had contributed strategically to positioning UNDP as a major upstream policy advisor for poverty reduction and sustainable human development, and as a knowledge-based organization; and make recommendations for the third GCF phase.

In line with UNDP's objectives, GCF-II had contributed to the UNDP development and transformation goals, notably in turning UNDP into a learning, knowledge-sharing organization. However, lingering questions on the meaning and quality of upstream policy advice and the noted weaknesses in governance and management might combine to generate a perception that GCF served as an exclusive facility for internal purposes only. If GCF-III was to serve UNDP corporate goals further, changes would be needed in the design, programming and management of the GCF facility. More fundamentally, it should sharply define its niche for addressing truly global development issues of strategic importance to UNDP and provide a clear strategy for enhancing the quality and effectiveness of UNDP work at the country level through its global programmes.

UNDP management, responding to the GCF-II evaluation in an August report [DP/2004/42], acknowledged the weaknesses in execution, oversight and reporting, but also pointed out that significant progress had been made on certain challenges, and that problems in execution, oversight and reporting were being tackled aggressively. UNDP would use GCF-III to continue to strengthen its promotion of global advocacy and analysis; knowledge networking and sharing; and policy support, consistency and advice. It would further strengthen the links among those three services, particularly the management mechanisms for carrying them out. The GCF-III programming cycle, starting in 2005, would seek to consolidate the gains achieved during GCF-II and delineate a more focused strategy than that of GCF-II. Its central organizing framework would be the priority areas and service lines of the MYFF, 2004-2007 (see p. 887).

In September [dec. 2004/34], the Executive Board noted with concern the findings of the GCF-II evaluation and the related UNDP management response. It requested UNDP, in consultation with Member States, to implement the evaluation recommendations in elaborating the proposed GCF-III, which the Board would consider at its January 2005 session.

Funding strategy

Multi-year funding framework, 2004-2007

In response to a 2003 Executive Board decision that endorsed the MYFF, 2004-2007 [YUN 2003, p. 901], UNDP, in January [DP/2004/4], submitted proposals for reporting on the MYFF. UNDP would continue to report to the Board on progress under the MYFF through the results-oriented annual report (ROAR) covering results achieved in 2004 and 2005. The ROAR for each year would be presented for consideration at the Board's annual session immediately following each year. Results for 2004 to 2006 would be presented in an MYFF report to the Board at its 2007 annual session. The structure and format of the two reports would correspond to the elements of organizational effectiveness identified in the MYFF, while the ROAR would serve as an integrated report. The analysis of results achieved in both reporting documents would be presented under the following categories: summary overview of performance against key MYFF strategic objectives; and analyses of substantive results by MYFF goal and service line, of results in building organizational capacity for development effectiveness, and of programme and operational resources and expenditure.

The proposals envisaged the elimination of a number of reports submitted concurrently to the Board, including reporting on the thematic trust funds, and incorporated conceptual and methodological advances to help UNDP respond to the challenges of attribution and aggregation in the attempt to monitor its contribution to development change. The specific indicators and benchmarks to measure progress, if endorsed by the Board, could serve to inform the entire range of management and oversight processes in use, thus strengthening accountability and results orientation at all levels of the organization.

On 30 January [dec. 2004/1], the Executive Board took note of the strategically designed approach to the ROAR presented by UNDP and looked forward to discussing that matter at the Board's annual session in June. The Board stressed that ROAR reporting should provide Member States with factual analysis of the development effectiveness of UNDP activities and institutional effectiveness, and that UNDP evaluation

functions should support the ROAR process by focusing on UNDP activities and effectiveness. It requested the Administrator, in collaboration with the UNFPA and UNIFEM Executive Directors and in consultation with Member States, to explore options for harmonized reporting and to report on the issue, also at the Board's annual session in June.

In response to the Executive Board's January request (see above), UNDP, UNFPA and UNIFEM submitted in May [DP/2004/CRP.6-DP/FPA/2004/CRP.2] a joint proposal for reporting on MYFF results following a harmonized schedule and time frame. The Board adopted the proposal in June [dec. 2004/20].

Financing

The UNDP Administrator, in his annual review of the financial situation for 2004 [DP/2005/33 & Add.1], said that consistent growth in resource contributions continued, reaching $4 billion, a 20 per cent increase over the 2003 level of $3.2 billion. Compared to 2003, regular resources also continued an upward trend, increasing by 9 per cent to $842 million, with a weakening United States dollar and resulting exchange rate fluctuations accounting for more than two thirds of the increase. The positive developments in the volume of contributions to regular resources also reflected the strong political endorsement by donors of the UNDP reform process and UNDP's impact in the countries it served. Expenditures under regular resources increased by 12 per cent to $836 million. The resource balance, exclusive of operational reserves but including after-service health insurance reserves, increased by 17 per cent. Contributions received from the top 15 non-programme country donors (Belgium, Canada, Denmark, Finland, France, Germany, Ireland, Italy, Japan, the Netherlands, Norway, Sweden, Switzerland, United Kingdom, United States) increased by 11 per cent.

Programme expenditure, including programme support to the resident coordinator system, increased by 19 per cent, from $404 million to $483 million. By appropriation group, 55 per cent of expenditure went to programme support activities, 21 per cent to management and administration and 23 per cent to operational activities. In terms of the percentage share of programme expenditure among regions, Latin America and the Caribbean continued to record the highest share of programme delivery ($27 million or 6 per cent and $1.1 billion or 47 per cent for regular and other expenditures, respectively), followed by Asia and the Pacific ($131 million or 27 per cent and $558 million or

23 per cent, respectively), Africa ($188 million or 39 per cent and $214 million and 9 per cent, respectively), the Arab States ($38 million or 8 per cent and $201 million or 8 per cent, respectively), and Europe and CIS ($43 million or 9 per cent and $159 million or 6 per cent, respectively).

The percentage share for execution modalities showed that national execution represented 60 per cent overall; UNDP, 21 per cent; UNOPS, 10 per cent; the "big five" entities (DESA, the Food and Agriculture Organization of the United Nations, ILO, the United Nations Educational, Scientific and Cultural Organization, the United Nations Industrial Development Organization), 3 per cent; other agencies, 4 per cent; and NGOs, 2 per cent.

The growth of UNDP expenditure was mainly in crisis countries, representing 70 per cent of the total execution.

As at 31 December, the balance of unexpended regular resources stood at $171 million, an increase of 11 per cent over the $154 million in 2003. UNDP held cash and investments for regular resources totalling $272 million, excluding the operational reserve.

For other resources activities—local resources (government cost-sharing and cash-counterpart contributions), donor cost-sharing, trust funds, the United Nations Volunteers (UNV) programme (see p. 896), management services agreements, the Junior Professional Officer programme and the reserve for field accommodation—overall income increased by $752 million, from $2.5 billion in 2003 to $3.3 billion in 2004. Overall expenditure also increased by 15 per cent ($345 million). Net contributions received totalled $3.0 billion, of which 38 per cent ($1.2 billion) accounted for local resources. Contributions from the OECD/DAC countries increased 59 per cent, from $569 million in 2003 to $900 million in 2004.

In September [dec. 2004/29], the Executive Board took note of the Administrator's annual review of the financial situation for 2003 [YUN 2003, p. 902]. The Board encouraged all Member States to increase their funding and to give priority to regular resources (core contributions) over other resources (non-core contributions). It called on all contributing countries to make early payments to, among other things, avoid liquidity constraints, and on Member States in a position to do so to announce and adhere to multi-year pledges and payment schedules. The Board stressed the need for UNDP to build on its successes in results-oriented management and to continue to improve administrative and financial management practices in key areas.

Regular funding commitments to UNDP

In May [DP/2004/20], UNDP submitted a report on the status of regular funding commitments to UNDP and its associated funds and programmes for 2004 and onward. According to the provisional data for 2003, total net income reached $769 million, a 15 per cent ($99 million) increase over the $670 million reached in 2002. Current projections suggested that, based on the official UN exchange rate as at 1 May, contributions would exceed $800 million for the first time since 1997. Eleven OECD/DAC members increased or resumed their contributions in local currency terms in 2003. One donor's contribution increased by 43 per cent, while another increased by 28.4 per cent. In contrast to previous years, all OECD/DAC donors paid their 2003 contributions in full. Current estimates for 2004 indicated that all OECD/DAC donors would either maintain or increase their contributions. Nine such donors indicated that they would increase their contribution in local currency terms, while two committed to increasing their contributions regularly over the full period of the 2004-2007 MYFF (see p. 887). Five of the programme countries made contributions in excess of $1 million to UNDP regular resources, demonstrating the high value such countries were placing on UNDP and its work. Indications were that some donors might be in a position to make additional pledges and contributions to regular resources during the year, which was particularly important since the 2004 income levels continued to be far below requirements. A total of 11 OECD/DAC donor countries provided fixed payment schedules in 2003, compared to 14 in 2002. While fewer donors had provided schedules over the previous four years, those who had provided them, increasingly deviated from the schedules. Of the 11 OECD/DAC donors that provided payment schedules in 2003, many did not pay as pledged. Although a number of donors paid significant portions of their pledges only in the last quarter of the year, the operational reserves did not have to be used in 2003.

In June [dec. 2004/14], the Executive Board took note of the report on the status of regular resources funding commitments to UNDP for 2004 and onward. It also noted that UNDP was within reach of being provided with a stable and adequate resource base, but that achieving that goal would require all Member States, developed countries in particular, to sustain and increase their funding efforts over the MYFF period. It encouraged all countries that had not yet done so to provide contributions to core resources for 2004 and those that had already contributed to consider supplementing their 2004 contributions so as to accelerate the rebuilding of UNDP's regular resource base.

Strategic cost management and cost recovery

In accordance with a 2003 Executive Board decision [YUN 2003, p. 903], the UNDP Administrator, in a May report [DP/2004/35], provided a framework for strategic cost management and an update on UNDP cost recovery. In a series of meetings in the context of the High-level Committee on Management of the United Nations System Chief Executives Board for Coordination (CEB) (see p. 1449), UN organizations had agreed on a common definition of principles for the purpose of cost recovery to facilitate comparability of cost-recovery policies and practices across UN organizations. They had agreed on common definitions of cost categories, including various elements of direct, fixed and variable costs, and that cost recovery would generally apply to variable indirect cost.

UNDP had adapted the harmonized principles and definitions to fit its business model, covering the provision of development services, advocacy and advisory services and support to UN system coordination. All costs linked to activities under those business lines were considered direct costs on programme budgets. As part of its 2004-2005 biennial support budget, UNDP introduced a base structure concept for headquarters and country offices, which was linked to UNDP's core mandated activities and statutory functions, particularly as custodian of the resident coordinator system. Costs attributable to the base structure were considered fixed costs, covered exclusively from regular resources. Country office costs for all management and operational services outside the base structure were considered variable indirect costs, of which each fund source was charged its proportional share.

Notwithstanding the alignment of UNDP cost management with the common principles, particularly regarding the recovery of variable indirect costs, determination of a single programme support cost or cost recovery rate across multiple UN organizations was not feasible due to differences in mandates, business models and structures. Owing to system limitations, further disaggregate analysis of recovery income and the necessary structures were unattainable—a circumstance being remedied with the introduction, in January 2004, of the new Atlas enterprise resource planning system. UNDP's ultimate objective was the true attribution of all costs to their proper fund source, which was also a prerequisite for results-based budgeting. The delineation between fixed and variable costs would be reviewed and further defined, taking into account

structural changes resulting from the implementation of the Atlas system and would be presented to the Executive Board as part of the 2006-2007 biennial support budget.

To achieve a proportional burden sharing of all variable indirect costs, UNDP determined a percentage fee chargeable to all programmes funded from other resources for those costs. The general management service fee (GMS) had been set at a range of 5 to 7 per cent for third-party cost sharing and trust funds. As per the calculation presented in an annex to the report, UNDP should ideally recover about 7.6 per cent from other resources, but had decided to increase its GMS rate gradually to that level. The GMS fee for programme country cost-sharing was set at an average of 3 per cent measured over the country-specific programme portfolio. Owing to its different nature, programme country cost-sharing was excluded from the GMS rate calculation, which was instead based on donor resources. UNDP also assessed an implementation support service (ISS) fee as a direct cost for services provided during programme implementation, either to programme country governments in support of national execution or to other UN organizations in the implementation of their own programmes. ISS fees were calculated based on cost surveys conducted in over 60 country offices grouped into four cost bands. The table of average prices for each standard transaction under each of the cost bands, referred to as the Universal Price List, ensured that the cost of country-based operations units were fully recovered. Annexed to the report were: common definitions of different types of costs; information on the calculation of the cost recovery rate; a comparison of cost recovery practices in UNDG organizations; and an overview of all UNDP cost recovery mechanisms.

In May [DP/2004/36], the Advisory Committee on Administrative and Budgetary Questions (ACABQ), having considered the UNDP Administrator's report on strategic cost management and implications for cost recovery, noted that the comparison of cost recovery practices in UNDG organizations annexed to the report was not meaningful, because the basis for the calculation of the indirect support rates was quite different for each organization. All entities concerned needed to follow the same template to achieve a meaningful comparison. UN funds and programmes should continue consultations for further harmonization of cost recovery principles, clearly identifying common elements under each cost category and differences resulting from different mandates and operating modalities. ACABQ encouraged all UN organizations concerned to continue cost recovery harmonization, taking into account the specific issues raised in its report. It intended to monitor progress within the context of the UNDP 2006-2007 biennial support budget and trusted that a means could be found to increase transparency in the setting of cost recovery rates.

In September [dec. 2004/30], the Executive Board took note of the harmonized cost recovery principles contained in the Administrator's report and encouraged UNDP to intensify consultations for further harmonization. It endorsed, on an interim basis, the UNDP-specific implementation of the harmonized principles, and their application in the cost recovery policy, particularly regarding the proportional sharing of variable indirect cost among all sources of funds. The Board stressed that UNDP ensure full recovery, at an aggregate level, of all actual costs for implementing activities financed from UNDP third-party cost sharing, trust fund contributions and programme country cost sharing. It should report at the first regular session in 2005 on options for transparent reporting on income from cost recovery, including the possibility of including such income in calculating the next biennial support budget. UNDP should submit to the Board, with a view to considering the rates under that policy, at its June 2005 session, a detailed proposal containing clear criteria that encouraged incentives for un-earmarked, timely and flexible contributions to trust funds, third-party cost sharing and programme country cost sharing in order to reach that aggregate level, and to develop the report in close consultation with interested Member States. The Board stressed that new rates under that policy should only be applied subject to a decision by the Board. UNDP was asked to review its cost-recovery policy after two years and to report to the Board at its September 2007 session on the lessons learned, including the aggregate cost recovery rate in time for the 2008 MYFF. It should continue monitoring the level of cost recovered from other (non-core) resources, and refining its strategic cost management system, including through the implementation of the Atlas system, introduced in January, in order to better attribute indirect cost to programmes and projects. The Board reiterated that regular resources remained the bedrock of contributions to UNDP.

Also in September [dec. 2004/41], the Executive Board took note of the related ACABQ report.

Audit reports

The Executive Board, at its January session, considered the Administrator's report [DP/2004/11] on implementation of the recommendations of the Board of Auditors for the 2000-2001 biennium [YUN 2002, p. 1388], which contained an update of actions taken by UNDP on the Board's recommendations, including the status of any follow-up action and the target date for completion. The Administrator said progress had already been achieved in most areas and outstanding issues were being addressed.

In January [dec. 2004/4], the Executive Board took note of the Administrator's report and stressed the importance of adequate follow-up to the recommendations by the Board of Auditors.

In April [DP/2004/27], the Administrator submitted the annual report on the internal audit and oversight services provided by the UNDP Office of Audit and Performance Review (OAPR) for 2003. Key recommendations regarding the new approach to audit and the repositioning exercise initiated in 2002 [YUN 2003, p. 904], including the elimination of Control Self Assessment workshops and discontinuation of the use of public accounting firms to perform internal audits of country offices, were implemented, and changes were made to the OAPR organizational structure to achieve the other key recommendations for strengthening investigation, quality assurance and ICT functions, and enhancing the multidisciplinary character of audit teams. A revised scope was introduced that reduced the number of audit areas from 15 to 12.

The number of UNDP audits/reviews issued in 2003 was 18, down from 56 in 2002, while assessments of national execution of audit reports were relatively unchanged at 1,660. The decline reflected the large number of vacant posts resulting from OAPR's repositioning exercise and the discontinuation of routinely contracting out internal audits of country offices. OAPR issued a total of 15 internal audit reports of country offices, containing 346 recommendations, virtually all of which were accepted by management and were being implemented.

In June [dec. 2004/17], the Executive Board took note of the reports of the Administrator, of OAPR to the UNOPS Executive Director [DP/2004/28] (see p. 896) and of the UNFPA Executive Director on internal audit and oversight (see p. 1083) and the comments made thereon. It urged the Administrator and the UNOPS and UNFPA Executive Directors to address the issues raised in those reports and report to the Board at its annual session in 2005. They should develop a framework containing concrete objectives and a time-path and indicators for resolving those issues and report to the Board at its second regular session in September. UNDP should also report at that session on a periodic review of its policy on universal prices for its services, with clear measures for improving cost recovery, including a timetable (see p. 889). The Board noted with concern that UNDP routinely provided a variety of services to UN organizations, sometimes based on a memorandum of understanding and sometimes not.

As requested, UNDP, UNFPA, and UNOPS submitted an August joint report [DP/2004/CRP.8-DP/FPA/2004/CRP.5] outlining their current practices for ensuring implementation of audit recommendations and proposing a framework for resolving issues contained in internal audit reports. They also proposed that, starting from 2004, the report on internal audit and oversight activities be revised to present findings in a schematic format instead of the current narrative presentation. In September [dec. 2004/39], the Executive Board took note of the joint report and welcomed the proposed framework for future reports.

Procurement

According to the 2003 annual statistical report in procurement [DP/2004/39], total procurement for goods and services under UNDP funding in 2003 was $825.6 million, of which the share from developing countries was 78.3 per cent, an increase of 4.2 per cent. Total procurement by the UN system under all sources of funding was $5.08 billion, of which the share from developing countries was 45.1 per cent.

The Administrator, in his update of the activities of the Inter-Agency Procurement Services Office (IAPSO) from June 2002 to June 2004 [DP/2004/38], reported that the volume of procurement handled by IAPSO fell by 7.9 per cent, from $185.6 million in 2000-2001 to $171 million in 2002-2003. Having brought costs under control and achieved self-financing status [YUN 2002, p. 873], IAPSO shifted its focus to diversifying and strengthening its revenue sources in the 2002-2003 biennium. Total turnover during 2002 was $81.3 million with an average fee of 3.9 per cent; corresponding figures for 2003 were $89.7 million and 4.7 per cent. The net operating surplus was about 0.33 per cent of the turnover in 2002, which tripled in 2003. IAPSO continued to develop its e-procurement system, United Nations Web Buy, launched in 2002 [ibid.] with the introduction of its e-tendering module. In 2003, it launched the first web-based tender in the UN system, thereby reducing the resources needed for managing complex tenders by 90 per cent. IAPSO supported implementation of the UNDP Atlas system by developing content for the contract, asset and procurement management modules in the online Atlas learning tool.

In September [dec. 2004/31], the Executive Board took note of the report on the activities of

IAPSO and its continuing self-financed status. The Board encouraged IAPSO to continue raising the professional standards of procurement within the UN system by developing a procurement curriculum for professional certification and recommended that it continue to research collaborative purchasing system-wide as requested by the inter-agency procurement working group.

Other technical cooperation

Review of UN regular programme of technical cooperation and Development Account

UN technical cooperation

As requested by General Assembly resolution 58/270 [YUN 2003, p. 1399], the Secretary-General submitted an October report [A/59/397] reviewing the UN regular programme of technical cooperation and the Development Account. The report examined the full range of operations of both, with analyses of the similarities and differences between them.

Specific proposals were made for improving the two programmes (see below), including two options for the future of the regular programme of technical cooperation. One option was to eliminate section 23, Regular programme of technical cooperation, of the 2004-2005 programme budget [YUN 2003, p. 1399] and to allocate, on a pro rata basis, its resources to technical cooperation subprogrammes within each programme section, while ensuring that the resources were protected for the use of developing countries. The second option was to retain the regular programme by maintaining section 23, while updating its objective, criteria, management responsibilities and reporting arrangements. The second option was considered the most suitable, since implementing the first could prove complex, and it was not evident that restructuring into the individual programmes would result in more effective management.

The review proposed that the objective for the regular programme be rewritten to better reflect its role within the UN system and include wording based on the Secretary-General's statement on technical cooperation contained in his 2002 report [YUN 2002, p. 860] on the delivery of advisory services to Member States. It also suggested criteria to govern the programme as a whole and to be applied by implementing entities.

Proposals for reporting arrangements called for designating the Under-Secretary-General for Economic and Social Affairs as programme coordinator and the executive head of each implementing entity as programme manager for the funds allocated to it; using the budget fascicle to present the request for new programme funding and to report on the previous biennium, linking budget approval to reporting on past performance, or to report separately (outside of the UN programme performance report), as in the case for the Development Account; and the performance report to be submitted, in addition to the bodies involved in budget approval, to the Economic and Social Council and the Second Committee. Also proposed was an audit of the regular programme of technical cooperation, which could be considered in 2008 or later.

The review found the Development Account to be well managed and operating in a manner fully consistent with its General Assembly–approved directions. However, it would be useful to ensure a clear ongoing mandate for the Account through the agreed criteria and an approved statement of objective. As to arrangements for its funding, Assembly resolution 54/15 [YUN 1999, p. 1307] had provided that the savings identified from reductions in administrative and overhead costs and transferred to the Account formed the base level of funding for future years, with future verifiable and sustainable savings to be added to the Account. Since no further savings had been identified, the provision should be rescinded by the Assembly. Any future increase in funding levels for the Account should be considered in the light of competing priorities for the use of the overall UN programme budget.

It was further suggested that the Assembly consider combining sections 23 and 35 (Development Account) of the 2004-2005 programme budget [YUN 2003, p. 1399] into one budget section with two separate parts.

UN activities

Department of Economic and Social Affairs

During 2004, the Department of Economic and Social Affairs (DESA) had approximately 500 technical cooperation projects under execution in a dozen substantive sectors, with a total project expenditure of $48.9 million. Projects financed by UNDP represented $12.8 million; those by trust funds, $36 million; and those by UNFPA, $0.1 million.

On a geographical basis, DESA's technical cooperation programme included expenditures of $29.6 million for interregional and global pro-

grammes; $11.6 million in Africa; $4 million in Asia and the Pacific; $2.6 million in the Middle East; $0.9 million in the Americas; and $0.2 million in Europe.

Distribution of expenditures by substantive sectors was as follows: associate expert programme, $22 million; socio-economic governance management, $10.3 million; governance and public administration, $8.1 million; energy, $2.4 million; water, $2 million; ICT task force, $1.2 million; programme support, $1 million; knowledge management, $0.8 million; social development, $0.5 million; infrastructure, $0.4 million; statistics $0.1 million; and the United Nations Forum on Forests, $0.1 million. Of the total delivery of $48.9 million, the associate expert programme comprised 45 per cent; socio-economic governance management, 21 per cent; and governance and public administration, 16 per cent.

On a component basis, DESA's delivery in 2004 included $39.4 million for project personnel; $4.5 million for sub-contracts; $2.6 million for training; $1.5 million for equipment; and $0.9 million for miscellaneous expenses.

Total expenditure for DESA against the UN regular programme of technical cooperation was $5.1 million. Distribution of expenditures by division was as follows: sustainable development, $1.4 million; public administration and development management, $1.9 million; social policy and development, $0.7 million; statistics, $0.9 million; advancement of women, $0.1 million; and administrative support, $0.1 million. On a component basis, expenditure for the year included $3.7 million for advisory services; $0.6 million for meetings; $0.5 million for travel; and $0.3 million for consultancy services.

UN Fund for International Partnerships

The Secretary-General, in his report on the 2004 activities of the United Nations Fund for International Partnerships (UNFIP) [A/60/327], established in 1998 [YUN 1998, p. 1297] to manage the process of grant allocations through the United Nations Foundation, a public charity founded by Robert E. Turner to channel his gift to the United Nations of stock valued at some $1 billion, provided data on the fifteenth and sixteenth funding cycles, progress in each programme area, and a review of UNFIP activities in advocacy and partnership-building. A total of $76.8 million was programmed for 2004, including $11.4 million in the fifteenth funding cycle and $44.3 million in the sixteenth. Of the total, $46.5 million was for 12 projects related to children's health; $22.6 million for 13 projects for the environment; $3.5 million for six projects for population and women; $2.2 million for nine projects for peace, security and human rights; and $2 million for seven strategic initiative projects. Since 1998, a total of $639 million had been allocated to fund 324 projects in 122 countries involving 37 UN organizations.

UN Office for Project Services

The United Nations Office for Project Services (UNOPS), established in 1995 [YUN 1995, p. 900] in accordance with General Assembly decision 48/501 [YUN 1994, p. 806] as a separate and self-financing entity of the UN system to act as a service provider to UN organizations, offered a broad range of services, from overall project management to the provision of single inputs.

2004 activities

The Executive Director, in his annual report on UNOPS activities for 2004 [DP/2005/23], stated that the Office achieved further transition and recovery during the year. Project delivery exceeded the forecast submitted to the Executive Board in January (see p. 895) by 2 per cent, or $10 million, reaching $495.3 million.

In 2004, UNOPS generated $45.5 million in total revenue, exceeding the 2004 approved estimates of $44 million by $1.5 million (see p. 895). Project services continued to provide the largest percentage of total UNOPS revenue ($35.4 million, or 78 per cent), including $17.6 million from UNDP core and trust funds, $5.3 million from UNDP management service agreements, and $12.6 million from other UN organizations. Service revenue totalled $8.6 million, including $7.0 million from the International Fund for Agricultural Development (IFAD), $1.4 million from reimbursable service agreements, and $200,000 from the Programme of Assistance to the Palestinian People. Interest and rental income totalled $1.5 million.

By UNOPS geographic/service division, income was generated from global/interregional projects ($10.7 million), and from projects in Afghanistan ($9.6 million); Europe, North Africa and Central Asia ($7.6 million); Latin America and the Caribbean ($4.7 million); East and Southern Africa ($4.2 million); Asia and the Pacific ($4 million); and West and Central Africa ($2.7 million). Revenues also included $600,000 from the UNOPS finance division, $200,000 from its procurement division, and $1.5 million from other sources.

Administrative expenditures totalled $57.4 million in 2004, $9.6 million over the 2003 figure, but spending on staff costs declined to $25.8 million from $27.9 million in 2003. Contractual services, equipment, communications, travel and general operating expenses in 2004 equalled $15.2 million. UNOPS paid $6.4 million in reimbursements to UNDP and the United Nations for a range of central and operational support services.

UNOPS spent $3.5 million, or 7 per cent of its total expenditure base, on the wave I rollout of the Atlas system, exceeding the budgeted provision of $2.5 million by 40 per cent. It also paid $4.1 million related to its ongoing change management programme (see below), including the recruitment and installation of a new senior management team and the alignment of its client service divisions.

As at 31 December, UNOPS had a fund balance of $14.5 million, including $6 million in operational reserve and $17.2 million in working capital.

Change management process

The Executive Board, at its January session, considered a report [DP/2004/7] issued in response to a 2003 Board decision [YUN 2003, p. 908] on the implementation of the UNOPS change management process. The report provided a full response to the recommendations set out in the final report of the independent review of the UNOPS business model and related issues [ibid., p. 907]. It reviewed the current status of consultations with stakeholders on the UNOPS mandate and governance mechanisms and its vision as the service provider of choice within the UN system. It summarized measures under way to develop additional business portfolios, strengthen existing client relationships and build new ones.

Concerning the financial viability of UNOPS, the anticipated balance at the end of 2003 and the 2004 projected income would enable the Office to meet its 2004 budget obligations, including the planned change management implementation, and raise the operational reserve, from which it would not have to draw down further. To ensure the realization of income projections and sustained long-term viability, UNOPS identified priority countries for portfolio development in early 2004 and consulted with current and potential clients to consolidate portfolios under negotiation and identify new opportunities. In the event that portfolio growth and the budgetary situation in 2004 did not support that intent, the UNOPS Executive Director would propose to the Executive Board a financing alternative for the change management implementation.

The UNDP Administrator and the UNOPS Executive Director collaborated to improve relations between their two organizations and established a joint, senior-level task force to examine expanded possibilities for partnership. An interdivisional strategic advisory team within UNOPS was drafting a framework for client relationship management and a longer-term strategy for management of business acquisition and portfolio development. UNOPS would also establish a regular and systematic review and consolidation of its pipeline opportunities and of changing market trends. Other change management initiatives included establishing a new fee-setting mechanism and restructuring UNOPS to eliminate interdivisional competition. Recommendations on a new vision, mission and value statement for UNOPS, submitted in 2003 by a cross-functional strategic advisory team, were being refined. Linked to that were ongoing consultations on changing the UNOPS mandate to allow it to implement donor-funded programmes and projects on behalf of recipient Governments and for its long-term sustainability. It was proposed that where UNOPS was judged by regional development banks and their recipient Governments as the best entity to provide required services in areas of its mandated competence, it should be allowed to enter directly into service relationships with those multilateral entities.

Concerning business improvement, the strategic advisory team on project pricing and cost estimating made initial recommendations on how UNOPS could become more transparent in its pricing practices, introduce standard rate sheets for project implementation services and improve its internal capabilities for understanding the costs of delivering its services. An initial standard rate sheet was developed and was expected to be implemented in 2004. A UNOPS team was developing project management standards, common tools and templates for internal use to support the entire life cycle of a project. UNOPS had piloted a new appraisal and reward system—the Performance Management and Development System—in its Copenhagen (Denmark) and Kuala Lumpur (Malaysia) offices since early 2003, and its organization-wide introduction was planned for 2004.

The first wave of the Atlas system began operations in January 2004, and successive waves would be introduced in midyear and in 2005. UNOPS would also change its outmoded e-mail systems and systems used to maintain and update its Internet and intranet sites, and would invest in staff training and capacity development programmes in 2004.

A strategic advisory team conducted a criteria-based analysis of the UNOPS organizational structure and client interactions, and made recommendations for change. Following a review by the

UNOPS Management Coordination Committee (MCC), the Executive Director approved a series of structural and organizational changes to facilitate a strong client focus at corporate and service delivery levels; enhance portfolio development, management and delivery; ensure clear lines of accountability; and promote capacity development, knowledge networking and team spirit. UNOPS headquarters would remain in New York, and its mix of thematic and geographic operational divisions would be replaced by five geographic and one global/interregional divisions, directly overseen by the Director of Operations/Deputy Executive Director. All geographic regional offices would be located in the regions they served, necessitating the decentralization of some divisions headquartered in New York. The report contained the 2004 timetable for major components of the change process and an annotated budget for the 2004 change plan, totalling $8.4 million.

In January 2004 [dec. 2004/3], the UNDP/UNFPA Executive Board took note of the full response to the recommendations set out in the 2003 report of the independent review [YUN 2003, p. 907], the strategy for business acquisition, progress in implementing internal change, the comprehensive timetable and benchmarks for monitoring progress. It approved the detailed budget for the longer-term change process and the modalities for meeting its cost, and the expansion of the UNOPS mandate to allow it to cooperate directly with regional and subregional development banks on a pilot basis. The Board encouraged UNOPS to ensure close consultation with the resident coordinators and requested its Executive Director to provide an update on progress in his report to the Board at its annual session in June 2004.

In a September progress report on UNOPS activities [DP/2004/45], the Executive Director provided an update on the change management process. A new management team was installed on 1 August. Client service offices were established for the Asia and the Pacific region (Bangkok, Thailand), Europe, North Africa and Western/Central Asia (Geneva), Western and Central Africa (Dakar, Senegal), and Eastern and Southern Africa (Nairobi, Kenya); the Latin America and the Caribbean office was to be established in 2005. The Division for the Global and Interregional Programme was established in New York. The realignment of the procurement and the client services divisions was completed on 31 August. Given the experience of the first phase of the change management process and taking into account the recommendations of the Board of Auditors (see p. 896), the change process was re-focused on six turnaround initiatives: corporate strategy redefinition; Atlas wave I rollout; imprest accounting; management reporting, budget and planning; client reporting; and project proposal tracking and acceptance. The initiatives were estimated to cost some $5 million over the 2004-2005 period. Initial gains in client reporting were expected to be achieved by the end of September 2004 and a comprehensive reporting system to be fully operational by April 2005, and the prior years' imprest account reconciliations to be completed by June 2005. To facilitate those improvements, the Executive Board was informed at its June 2004 session that resources approved at the January 2004 session for change initiatives (see p. 894) had been reallocated to the adjusted priority tasks.

At its regular session in September [dec. 2004/36], the Executive Board urged the Executive Director to redouble his efforts towards implementing the change management process and ensure financial accountability in UNOPS.

Budget estimates

Revised 2003 budget and 2004 forecast

In January [DP/2004/6], the Executive Director, reporting on the implementation of the UNOPS 2003 budget, indicated that, as at 31 October 2003, total project delivery would be $460 million, or 95 per cent of the $484.4 million target; $63.5 million in total projected income, including $31.3 million from the implementation of project portfolios; $11.6 million in service income; $19.5 million in non-recurring income from contract amendments under the United Nations Office for the Iraq Programme; and $1.1 million in other miscellaneous income. As at 31 December 2003, total expenditure was estimated to be $49.2 million, of which $44 million pertained to recurring administrative expenditure and $5.2 million for non-recurring expenses. The 2003 year-end fund balance was projected to be $18.5 million, comprising an operational reserve of $4.2 million and a $14.3 million working capital fund.

As at January, the indicative figure for project delivery in 2004 was $485 million. Total income was estimated at $44 million, comprising $35 million in portfolio implementation income, $8 million in service income, and $1 million in rental income, while indicative 2004 expenditures totalled $56.7 million, pending finalization of the restructuring implementation plan.

The Executive Board, at its January session [dec. 2004/3], took note of the Executive Director's report on the 2003 UNOPS budget and the en-

couraging estimated financial results. It also took note of the 2004-2005 revised budget estimates and requested the Executive Director to submit to the Board at its annual session in June an update on the budget estimates, including a critical assessment of the 2004-2005 business projections.

In response to the Executive Board's request, the Executive Director, in his annual report [DP/2004/23], stated that a conservative projection of the 2004 revenue and expenditure data indicated a revised gross project delivery of $429 million. At a revised average income rate of 6.9 per cent, annual revenue generated under the project portfolio would amount to $29.4 million. Additional revenue of $9 million was generated through the IFAD loan portfolio, rental income, and other miscellaneous income, bringing the revised total income projection for 2004 to $38.4 million. Recurrent expenditures, exclusive of change management and Atlas-related expenditures, were projected to be $43.7 million, which would exceed revenues by $5.4 million. The deficit was expected to be reduced through the strict curtailment and monitoring of expenditures, combined with further business acquisition generating additional income in 2004.

In June [dec. 2004/15], the Executive Board took note of the Executive Director's annual report and stressed the importance of the short- and long-term financial viability of UNOPS. It endorsed the proposal of the Executive Director and MCC to extend the UNOPS mandate to allow it to work directly with Governments in providing infrastructure and public works services. The Board asked the Executive Director to keep it informed of the progress and challenges in implementing the expanded mandate. It noted the progress made by UNOPS in its change management process (see p. 893) and looked forward to a furtherance of the process in 2004 and 2005. The Board encouraged all UN entities, particularly UNDP, to work closely with UNOPS, especially in the field of common services, in situations where UNOPS was cost effective and had comparative advantages. It requested the Executive Director to prepare, in consultations with MCC, a progress report for the Board's September session.

In September [DP/2004/45], the Executive Director submitted a progress report on UNOPS activities covering business projections for 2004 and beyond, initiatives to overcome potential obstacles in business acquisition and diversification, and updates on change management. UNOPS proceeded with the realignment of its existing portfolio of projects to reflect the new client service structure and revised the functions and structure of its procurement division.

At the same time, it embarked on a major financial data reconciliation and clean-up exercise.

The project revenue forecast for the end of 2004 was $29.5 million, based on a projected level of delivery of $429 million. Additional revenue for services delivered of at least $9.7 million was projected to be generated through the IFAD loan portfolio; services to the Global Alliance on Improved Nutrition and the Global Fund for HIV/AIDS, Tuberculosis and Malaria; and rental income. Total revenue for 2004 was projected at $39.2 million, which was subject to changes due to additions and corrections in the data entered into the Atlas system, business acquisition initiatives, and initiatives in support of UN system activities in Burundi, Haiti and the Sudan.

As at 30 June, actual administrative expenditures stood at $21.4 million, comprising some $11.9 million in salaries and entitlements and $9.5 million in general and administrative expenditures. Expenditures estimated to 31 December totalled $44.6 million, including the estimated annual $5 million in UNOPS payments for services bought from UNDP, the United Nations and the Board of Auditors. The end-2004 fund balance was projected at $8 million, including the $6 million operational reserve. New project portfolios acquired to date stood at $408.2 million, with 34.9 per cent of funds attributable to World Bank loan-funded activities, 59.4 per cent to UN programmes, and the remaining 5.6 per cent to other sources. With a projected 2004 delivery of $429 million, the UNOPS 2005 project portfolio budget would amount to some $431 million.

The report also discussed UNOPS governance and mandate. UNOPS intended to explore the case for enlarging MCC to better reflect the UNOPS client structure and to consult with MCC on options for its functioning and composition, and make proposals to the Executive Board in January 2005. The role and service scope of UNOPS would be re-examined within the overall corporate strategy initiative and through intensive stakeholder, client and staff consultations.

At its second regular session in September [dec. 2004/36], the Executive Board noted with concern the financial projections and the fund balance projection in the Executive Director's report. It asked MCC to report to the Board in January 2005 on its assessment of progress in UNOPS and the guidance it provided to the Office. The Board stressed that it was important for UNOPS to increase its business volume through cooperation with other UN entities, particularly UNDP, and requested the UNDP Administrator, in his capacity as MCC chairman, to communicate the Board's view to CEB as soon as possible.

Audit reports

The Executive Board, at its January session [dec. 2004/12], took note of the Executive Director's report [DP/2004/10] on the implementation of the recommendations of the Board of Auditors [YUN 2002, p. 1388] for the 2001-2002 biennium.

In June [DP/2004/28], the UNDP Office of Audit and Performance Review (OAPR) and the UNOPS Project Services Audit Section reported on internal audit services for UNOPS operations in 2003. OAPR initiated and conducted 21 internal audits covering operational activities at headquarters and in the field, including those under management and support services arrangements. Of the 21 final reports, 18 were on audits started and finalized in 2003 and three on audits begun in 2002 and completed in 2003. Together, the reports contained 149 recommendations, of which 48 were in finance, 35 in administration, 25 in programme, 23 in organization and structure, 10 in policy, 6 in personnel and 2 in office automation. The organizational units concerned provided written comments on the contents of the draft audit reports. UNOPS disagreed with only one of the recommendations; in general the comments indicated that actions had been taken or were being taken to address the audit issues and recommendations.

In response to the recommendations and concerns expressed in the Board of Auditors report on UNOPS for the biennium ended 31 December 2003 [A/59/5/Add.10] (see p. 1397), the Executive Director, in a September progress report [DP/2004/45], stated that UNOPS concurred with the recommendations, which called for more efficient financial procedures, improved internal controls, and strengthened administrative and management processes. UNOPS would present its action plan to address the recommendations, including an update on progress in implementing the plan, at the Executive Board's January 2005 session.

The Executive Board, in September [dec. 2004/36], took note of the preliminary comments of UNOPS to the report of the Board of Auditors and deferred further consideration of the matter to its January 2005 session, when the report would be formally presented, together with ACABQ's recommendations.

UN Volunteers

In 2004, the number of volunteers working for the UNDP-administered United Nations Volunteers (UNV) programme increased to 7,300 from 5,635 in 2003. The volunteers, from 163 countries, carried out 7,772 assignments in 139 countries. Seventy-seven per cent of them were from developing countries. Women accounted for 35 per cent of all volunteers in 2004, compared to 37 per cent in 2003. By region, 41.8 per cent of assignments were carried out in Africa, 26 per cent in Asia and the Pacific, 18.2 per cent in Latin America and the Caribbean, 8.5 per cent in Europe and CIS, and 5.5 per cent in the Arab States.

The UNDP Administrator, in his annual report on the UNV financial situation in 2004 [DP/2005/33 & Add.1], indicated that, excluding funds for UN peacekeeping operations, income recorded for UNV in 2004 amounted to $22.7 million, an increase of $7.6 million compared to $15.1 million in 2003. Programme expenditure in 2004, excluding UN peacekeeping operations, decreased by $800,000 to $17.7 million from $18.5 million in 2003. The balance of the operational reserve as at 31 December 2004 was $1 million.

At its June session [dec. 2004/25], the Executive Board took note of the report of the UNDP Administrator [DP/2004/24] on UNV activities during 2002-2003. On 18 June [dec. 2004/16], the Board recognized UNV achievements in articulating and advocating the importance of the contributions of volunteerism, particularly in its role towards the attainment of the MDGs [YUN 2000, p. 51]. It welcomed initiatives to extend opportunities for volunteerism by expanding the forms of affiliation with the programme and called for relevant UN system organizations and bodies to continue to integrate volunteerism into their policies, programmes and reports, including those relating to the achievement of the MDGs. The Board encouraged Governments to contribute to the Special Voluntary Fund to enable UNV to further explore, expand and strengthen the role of volunteerism and volunteer contributions to development, reconfirmed its support for UNV as the focal point for follow-up to the International Year of Volunteers (2001) [YUN 2001, p. 814], and supported the further development of its future role in the report of the Secretary-General to the General Assembly's sixtieth (2005) session. It encouraged UNV to enhance analysis in future annual reports so as to provide the Board with an in-depth understanding of UNV activities and their impact.

The Assembly, by **decision 58/567** of 8 April, deferred until its fifty-ninth (2004) session consideration of the Secretary-General's 2000 report on the participation of UNVs in peacekeeping operations [YUN 2001, p. 814] and the related ACABQ report [ibid., p. 94].

Economic and technical cooperation among developing countries

South-South cooperation

The UNDP/UNFPA Executive Board considered a report on the implementation of South-South cooperation [DP/2004/26] at its June session. The report highlighted opportunities for enhancing South-South cooperation based on lessons learned and recommendations made to the Special Unit for South-South Cooperation, which was in the process of formulating the third South-South cooperation framework (2005-2007). It indicated that developing countries were placing renewed emphasis on South-South cooperation efforts to reduce gaps between rich and poor countries. It was envisaged that South-South relations would enable countries not benefiting from globalization to learn winning strategies through the exchange of ideas, resources, skills and knowledge with countries that had successfully adjusted to globalization and raised living standards. A number of institutions had been established by developing countries to coordinate South-South initiatives, but the implementation of their agreed action plans remained slower than desired so that only a limited number of programmes were contributing to demonstrable socio-economic transformation. Measures to overcome obstacles and scale up the volume of exchanges among developing countries were the prime concern of the Special Unit as it formulated the third cooperation framework, whose main thrust hinged on marshalling South-South efforts towards meeting the MDGs. To overcome its resource limitations, the Special Unit sought new and larger coalitions among the more advanced developing countries.

On 23 June, the Executive Board took note of the report on South-South cooperation [dec. 2004/25].

The Board considered the third cooperation framework for South-South cooperation (2005-2007) [DP/CF/SSC/3] at its September session. The framework detailed a forward-looking agenda for the use of resources under the UNDP MYFF, 2004-2007 (see p. 887) and elaborated on the context, strategy and directions for broadening South-South cooperation through policy support to global efforts to enhance it, backstopping country initiatives, and mainstreaming South-South cooperation in UNDP's work. The framework would focus on areas of cooperation where the demand expressed by developing countries was greatest; where the commitment to work in multilateral arrangements to achieve agreed objectives was strongest; and where the involvement of and support by State, civil society and private sector partners were likeliest. The Special Unit would work to bring potential partners together by establishing lines of communication, facilitating the sharing of information and best practices, and fostering practical relationships that contributed to human development objectives. The framework would serve as the Special Unit's main instrument for mobilizing financial, technical, institutional social and intellectual resources to pursue growth and development through South-South cooperation, in addition to those required for supporting the Unit's core functions and catalytic efforts in the 2005-2007 period.

The total resource mobilization target for the framework during the 2005-2007 period was $31.4 million, comprising $14.4 million in core resources and $17 million in non-core resources.

In September [dec. 2004/32], the Executive Board requested the Special Unit for South-South cooperation, in close cooperation with Member States, to update the third cooperation framework in the light of the Board's comments for final consideration by the Board in January 2005. To ensure the effective implementation of the framework, it encouraged the UNDP Administrator to appoint a new head of the Special Unit before that session. The Board decided that South-South cooperation be considered as a driver of development effectiveness and incorporated in the MYFF.

UN Capital Development Fund

Contributions to the United Nations Capital Development Fund (UNCDF) regular resources in 2004 decreased by $9.7 million, or 36 per cent, bringing the total to $17.2 million, from $26.9 million in 2003 [DP/2005/33]. Contributions to other resources were $6.3 million in 2004, down from $10.7 million in 2003. Overall expenditure increased by almost $5 million, from $22.9 million in 2003 to $27.6 million in 2004. Expenditure against regular resources increased to $19.7 million, from $17 million in 2003. Other resources expenditures increased from $5.9 million in 2003 to $6.6 million in 2004. Unexpended resources at the end of 2004 totalled $48 million, including an operational reserve of $22.6 million.

In April [DP/2004/17 & Corr.1], UNCDF submitted to the UNDP/UNFPA Executive Board its 2003 results-oriented annual report (ROAR), which assessed results achieved by its 2000-2003 strategic results framework.

In 2003, UNCDF operational activities continued to be severely affected by the lower-than-expected level of contributions to its core re-

sources, although the downward trend of income in 2000-2002 was reversed. Core contributions increased from $22.2 million in 2002 to $26.9 million in 2003, 10 per cent short of the $30 million target. Despite that increase, the long-term financial viability of UNCDF remained a concern. It thus reduced its core expenditures significantly in 2003 to align programme expenditures with available resources to ensure the Fund's integrity, resulting in programme expenditures from core resources of $16.7 million, down about a third from 2002. The situation also required a significant reduction of new project approvals, from $9.1 million in 2002 to $5.1 million in 2003, and a write-off of more than $55 million in outstanding commitments, involving programme cuts and closures. Total expenditures in 2003 were at a low of $27.8 million, down from $48.5 million in 2000. However, the 2003 portfolio clean-up, combined with an improving core resource situation, would allow for increased expenditures in 2004. Between 2000 and 2003, UNCDF partially achieved its operational targets in local governance and microfinance while achieving its targets in organizational strengthening.

In 2003, UNCDF had an active portfolio of 74 projects, valued at some $21.6 million, of which 50 met the criteria for reporting (projects lasting more than five months and with expenditure of over $50,000). The majority consisted of local development programmes, followed by programmes in microfinance investments, eco-development projects, and infrastructure projects.

UNCDF impact assessment

An April report [DP/2004/18] summarized the independent impact assessment of UNCDF, mandated by the Executive Board in 1999 [YUN 1999, p. 822]. Keeping in mind its objectives, the assessment concluded that UNCDF was effectively carrying out its mandate to reduce poverty in the least developed countries (LDCs). It had, for the most part, organized its existing portfolio according to the 1995 policy shift that narrowed the Fund's focus to local governance and microfinance programmes, and had responded to the recommendations of the 1999 independent external evaluation [ibid., p. 821]. Through its two programmes, the Fund had contributed to significant results in poverty reduction, policy impact and replication of its projects by donors. Overall, it had generally achieved positive results and remained a relatively efficient organization with a balanced budget in 2003. However, its financial viability after 2004 was questionable, a situation resulting from the mismatch between UNCDF's niche and international donor funding trends, its governance structure, and the need for a clarification of its role in the UNDP group.

The assessment recommendations called on the UNDP Administrator and the UNCDF Management Team to clarify UNCDF's role and responsibilities within UNDP and its associated funds, and to work with the Executive Board to identify a new Executive Secretary; on the UNCDF Senior Management Team to establish a team to review and analyse the Fund's business model and corporate governance arrangements, their strengths and weaknesses, and to propose alternatives on the Fund's future; and on UNCDF to make significant reductions in administrative costs or find alternative sources of funding for that budget item should its programme funding continue to decline. The assessment further recommended improving specific areas of the local governance and microfinance programmes, a clearer UNCDF mission statement, symbols, templates and logos, substantive knowledge sharing within and across programmes and creating a monitoring team to oversee implementation of the various Atlas clusters and modules being deployed.

UNCDF management, in a May report [DP/2004/19], welcomed the findings of the independent impact assessment, which were in line with the self-assessment contained in the 2003 cumulative ROAR (see p. 898). The report addressed two key assessment recommendations: UNCDF's positioning, niche and relationship to UNDP; and the development of a new business model. The report proposed several options that could contribute to the funding base for a new UNCDF business model; namely, voluntary core contributions, non-core resource mobilization, fees from technical services, capital lending and concessional loan funding of some elements of UNCDF capital assistance to private enterprise and LDC Governments. Management concluded that the Fund would have to undergo urgent transformation to become more market-oriented in its programmes and financially viable as an institution, while preserving and capitalizing on gains made in its support of local development and microfinance activities.

In June [dec. 2004/13], the UNDP/UNFPA Executive Board took note of the 2003 ROAR, the executive summary of the independent impact assessment of UNCDF and the management response to the assessment. The Board recognized that a number of the assessment recommendations had potentially wide-ranging implications in terms of, among others, a future closer relationship with UNDP, programming arrangements within the context of the MYFF, governance structures, and funding arrangements. In that regard, the Board asked the UNDP Administrator to report to

it at its second regular session in September on possible options, including for future closer relationships with UNDP and their implications for governance, programming, funding arrangements, and the possibilities for UNCDF to contribute to pro-poor local private sector development. The Board noted with concern that UNCDF, despite efforts to broaden the donor base, was still unable to meet the annual core resource target of $30 million called for by the Board in 2002 [YUN 2002, p. 884]. It asserted that, pending the submission of the requested proposals, UNCDF had a clear role to play in achieving the MDGs at the local level, particularly in local governance and microfinance in LDCs, and called on Member States and other institutions to further strengthen their contributions to its core funding in the light of the significant results achieved.

UNCDF future business model

A September progress report [DP/2004/46] proposed a framework for evaluating strategic options for a UNCDF future business model, including key guiding principles for identifying those options, and described existing strategic opportunities.

The report outlined two options for a future strategic niche and business model for UNCDF. The first was an official development assistance (ODA)-based model, with a UNCDF specialized in retail microfinance funded by voluntary contributions. The second was a private sector–based model, with a UNCDF specialized in channelling and utilizing private capital for high social impact investments in support of the MDGs. Under that option, UNDCF would focus on identifying high-impact investment opportunities and establish preconditions to attract and channel private capital to fund such opportunities. Under both models, the UNCDF local governance programmes would be transferred to a new UNDP unit: the Centre for Local Development. In the Administrator's view, the private sector–based model embodied a more innovative approach and a longer-term vision than the ODA-based model, which called for more radical adjustments in the UNCDF philosophy, approach and organizational culture.

In September [dec. 2004/37], the Executive Board took note of the progress report and the proposal it contained for integrating UNCDF activities and personnel dealing with local development within UNDP's Centre for Local Development, operating primarily in LDCs. To facilitate a final decision on the proposal, the UNDP Administrator was asked to elaborate, in close consultation with Board members and other key stakeholders and partners, a detailed proposal on the business plan for the future Centre for the Board's consideration in January 2005.

The Board noted the different options proposed for UNCDF to support local private sector development and stressed the need for a continued focus on LDCs. It requested the Administrator, in close consultation with UNCDF and Member States, to elaborate further on the viability and feasibility of both the ODA- and the private sector-based model options, taking into account the Board's concerns. The Administrator, in close consultation with UNCDF and Member States, particularly LDCs, should elaborate on other options, including maintaining an independent UNCDF, focusing on practice areas in accordance with its current mandate, and on the possibility for UNDP to strengthen its assistance to UNCDF in its advocacy efforts to mobilize the necessary resources. He should also elaborate on the option of integrating UNCDF microfinance activities in UNDP, taking into account the Board's June decision (see p. 899) and views expressed in the Board, for consideration by the Board in January 2005. The Board called on UNDP to assist UNCDF in mobilizing the resources to sustain its current local governance and microfinance activities.

Chapter III

Humanitarian and special economic assistance

In 2004, the United Nations, through the Office for the Coordination of Humanitarian Affairs (OCHA), continued to mobilize and coordinate humanitarian assistance to respond to international emergencies. During the year, consolidated inter-agency appeals were launched for Angola, Bangladesh, Bolivia, Burundi, the Central African Republic, Chad, Chechnya and neighbouring republics of the Russian Federation, Côte d'Ivoire + 3 (Burkina Faso, Ghana, Mali), the Democratic Republic of the Congo, the Democratic People's Republic of Korea, Eritrea, the Great Lakes region (Burundi, the Democratic Republic of the Congo, Rwanda, Uganda, the United Republic of Tanzania), Grenada, Guinea, Haiti, Indonesia, Iran, Kenya, Liberia, Madagascar, the Occupied Palestinian Territory, the Philippines, Sierra Leone, Somalia, Sudan, Tajikistan, the United Republic of Tanzania, Uganda, the West Africa subregion (Burkina Faso, Côte d'Ivoire, Ghana, Guinea, Liberia, Mali, Sierra Leone) and Zimbabwe. The appeals sought 3.4 billion, of which 2.2 billion was made available, meeting 64 per cent of requirements. Excluding contributions in kind and services not costed, OCHA recorded contributions for natural disaster assistance totalling $597.3 million.

At the request of Haiti, an ad hoc advisory group to develop a long-term programme of assistance was established. The groups created in 2002 on Guinea-Bissau and 2003 on Burundi continued their work.

The Preparatory Committee for the World Conference on Disaster Reduction, to be held in Kobe, Japan, in 2005, was established. It held its first and second sessions in Geneva, in May and October 2004, respectively.

Humanitarian assistance

Coordination

Humanitarian affairs segment of the Economic and Social Council

The humanitarian affairs segment of the Economic and Social Council (12-14 and 23 July) considered the strengthening of the coordination of humanitarian assistance of the United Nations: present and future challenges; it convened panels on strengthening preparedness and response to natural disasters, with an emphasis on capacity-building, and on field-level coordination for the purpose of continuing the presence and operation of UN humanitarian assistance missions in higher-risk environments (**decision 2004/219**). On 3 June (**decision 2004/220**), the Council decided to hold an informal event on 12 July to consider the issue of the transition from relief to development.

The Council considered the Secretary-General's June report [A/59/93-E/2004/74] on strengthening the coordination of emergency humanitarian assistance, submitted in response to General Assembly resolutions 46/182 [YUN 1991, p. 421], 57/153 [YUN 2002, p. 889] and 58/114 [YUN 2003, p. 919], and Council resolution 2003/5 [ibid., p. 916]. The report summarized humanitarian developments over the preceding year, and addressed the theme of the Council's humanitarian affairs segment (see above), including issues related to natural disaster management and the challenges in obtaining sustainable humanitarian access to populations affected by conflict. It also highlighted key humanitarian policy initiatives, including updates on efforts to strengthen policies and actions related to the transition from relief to development, gender and humanitarian action, humanitarian financing, and protection from sexual exploitation and abuse in humanitarian crises.

The number of countries requiring humanitarian assistance as a result of complex emergencies remained constant, as was the overall level of requirements, which totalled some $2.86 billion. However, the uneven pattern of funding of humanitarian activities left some countries substantially underfinanced. An important development in the provision of humanitarian assistance was the increase in the diversity of actors providing such assistance, including regional peacekeeping operations with mandated humanitarian support tasks, private contractors, who were increasingly used in the management and distribution of relief assistance, and armed forces, which were directly involved in relief and reconstruction activities, highlighting the need for clearer guidance on civil-military relations and coordination. Unfortunately, there was a shift in the perception and acceptance of humanitarian organizations by belligerent groups, as evidenced by the 2003 bombing of the UN headquarters in Iraq [YUN 2003, p. 346] and attacks on other humanitarian organizations and workers, suggesting that the emblematic protection traditionally afforded those organizations was no longer recognized, thus forcing them to re-examine their approaches to security and their ability to maintain an effective, impartial presence.

The reporting period also highlighted a serious crisis of protection with widespread and interrelated humanitarian consequences, especially in the West Africa subregion, where (see p. 108) the interrelated nature of the situation in Sierra Leone, Liberia and Côte d'Ivoire underlined the importance of a regional response to better address regional cross-border issues that were of a humanitarian, political, economic and protection nature. The Inter-Agency Standing Committee—a mechanism for the coordination of humanitarian assistance—had formulated preparedness and contingency planning strategies to take into account the importance of dealing with the regional dimensions of and challenges to the effective delivery of humanitarian aid in the West Africa region. Other humanitarian concerns included the plight of internally displaced persons and refugees as a result of conflict situations worldwide; the increasing use of sexual abuse and sexual violence as weapons of war; the interrelated nature of humanitarian problems, such as the combination of food insecurity, HIV/AIDS and weakened capacity for governance, which kept some 6.5 million people in Southern Africa in need of emergency assistance and natural disasters; and environmental emergencies, especially among the world's poorest, which reinforced the need to develop national preparedness and response capacities in disaster-prone countries.

Under the Good Humanitarian Donorship Initiative, which promoted best practice among donors and facilitated improved humanitarian coordination, a commonly agreed definition of humanitarian assistance and its component elements was near completion to allow for better-informed resource allocation and review of humanitarian assistance. UN agencies developed the CAP Needs Assessment Framework and Matrix (NAFM) to analyze, compare and present needs assessments consistently across emergencies. NAFM was being piloted in Burundi and the Democratic Republic of the Congo (DRC). To improve UN response to the transition of countries emerging from conflict, the standing mechanism for transition planning established in 2003 [YUN 2003, p. 916]—the secretariats of the Executive Committee on Humanitarian Affairs (ECHA), the United Nations Development Group (UNDG) and the Executive Committee on Peace and Security—was exploring programming approaches, including the repatriation, reintegration, rehabilitation and reconstruction (the "4Rs"), to assist persons displaced by conflict make the transition from relief to development and to ensure the smooth handover of humanitarian coordination functions to national and international actors in those countries. Renewed efforts were made to strengthen gender analysis in common humanitarian action plans and to ensure that projects included in the Consolidated Appeals Process (CAP) were in line with agreed analysis of priority needs and response. Also, gender issues were integrated into NAFM.

The report noted that, in many of the world's complex emergencies, access by humanitarian agencies remained limited and sporadic. Over 10 million people in 20 countries affected by such emergencies were estimated to be inaccessible by humanitarian agencies, owing to lack of security, which was the major obstacle to the delivery of aid and a threat to the security of humanitarian personnel, physical impediments that reduced access to vulnerable populations and political, procedural and administrative obstacles. To deal with the question of the changing perceptions and misperceptions of humanitarian actors by local governments and populations, the report suggested that the humanitarian community had to better communicate its purpose and objectives to local populations, while addressing the growth of military involvement in humanitarian operations. That would require agreement on and communication concerning the respective roles and responsibilities of military and humanitarian actors, better assessment of the role of military engagement in relief activities and its impact on the perception of humanitarian operations, addressing the way humanitarian relief workers engaged and interacted with populations and improving collaboration among humanitarian agencies to deal with the perceptions influencing their safety and security.

The report also described efforts to build capacity for natural disaster preparedness and response, including assistance and support to national response capacity and the promotion of disaster management and risk capacity. The 2005 World Conference on Disaster Reduction (see p. 946) was expected to produce new and specific mechanisms to assist countries and the international community to implement improvements in risk reduction and disaster management.

The Secretary-General observed that as humanitarian challenges evolved into peace-building challenges, strong coordination and effective planning among UN development, humanitarian, peacekeeping and political actors became more critical. The international humanitarian community should strengthen its awareness and understanding of local dynamics and work to reassure recipient communities concerning the principles that guided humanitarian action. It was essential to ensure that disaster-risk reduction was more explicitly integrated into development planning. Member States and the United Nations should strengthen efforts to identify more practical ways of channelling resources to support national and regional disaster management capacities.

The Secretary-General made a number of recommendations concerning humanitarian financing, transition from relief to development, gender, HIV/AIDS in emergencies, protection from sexual exploitation and abuse, internally displaced persons, UN humanitarian presence and natural disasters.

ECONOMIC AND SOCIAL COUNCIL ACTION

On 23 July [meeting 50], the Economic and Social Council adopted **resolution 2004/50** [draft: E/2004/L.35, orally corrected] without vote [agenda item 5].

Strengthening of the coordination of emergency humanitarian assistance of the United Nations

The Economic and Social Council,

Reaffirming General Assembly resolution 46/182 of 19 December 1991, recalling that humanitarian assistance should be provided in accordance with and with due respect for the guiding principles contained in the annex to that resolution, and recalling also other relevant resolutions of the Assembly and resolutions and agreed conclusions of the Economic and Social Council,

Recalling its resolution 2003/5 of 15 July 2003 and General Assembly resolution 58/114 of 17 December 2003,

Welcoming the fact that at the humanitarian affairs segment of 2004 the Economic and Social Council considered the theme strengthening of the coordination of humanitarian assistance of the United Nations: present and future challenges and that the Council held two panels, on strengthening preparedness and response to natural disasters, with an emphasis on capacity-building and field-level coordination for the purpose of continuing the presence and operation of United Nations humanitarian assistance missions in higher-risk environments

Recognizing that the affected State has the primary role in the initiation, organization, coordination and implementation of humanitarian assistance within its territory and in the facilitation of the work of humanitarian organizations,

Emphasizing the importance of continued international cooperation in support of the efforts of affected States in dealing with natural disasters and complex emergencies in all their phases, and recognizing that the magnitude and duration of many emergencies may

be beyond the response capacity of many affected countries,

Reaffirming that humanitarian assistance is of cardinal importance for the victims of natural disasters and other emergencies,

Reaffirming also the importance of the principles of neutrality, humanity and impartiality for the provision of humanitarian assistance,

Reaffirming further that independence, meaning the autonomy of humanitarian objectives from the political, economic, military or other objectives that any actor may hold with regard to areas where humanitarian action is being implemented, is also an important guiding principle for the provision of humanitarian assistance, and should be applied in full respect for and compliance with international humanitarian law,

Welcoming positive developments towards the resolution of some long-standing complex emergencies, while remaining deeply concerned about the outbreak of new complex emergencies and the protracted nature of other complex emergencies,

Noting the increase in the number and nature of organizations engaged in humanitarian action, and mindful of the need to ensure that this multiplication of actors does not detract from the effectiveness of the humanitarian response and the neutrality and independence of humanitarian assistance,

Expressing profound regret and grave concern at the tragic loss of the lives of humanitarian staff while providing humanitarian assistance and the increased insecurity encountered by humanitarian staff as well as the acts of violence committed against them, in particular deliberate attacks, and mindful of the need to provide the fullest possible protection for their security, and, in this regard, bearing in mind General Assembly resolution 58/122 of 17 December 2003 and Security Council resolution 1502(2003) of 26 August 2003,

Gravely concerned that, in some of the world current complex emergencies, access by humanitarian agencies to affected civilian populations remains limited, sporadic and sometimes restricted,

Bearing in mind that success in peace negotiation, among other processes, could lead to a significant increase in voluntary repatriation of refugees and in the possible reintegration of internally displaced persons, and expressing its belief that the United Nations system should give due consideration to these developments in the planning of its response,

Noting with grave concern the growing intensity and recurrence of natural disasters, and reaffirming the importance of sustainable measures to reduce the vulnerability of societies to natural hazards using an integrated, multi-hazard and participatory approach to addressing vulnerability, risk assessment and disaster prevention, mitigation, preparedness, response and recovery,

Noting the grave humanitarian and development implications of the HIV/AIDS pandemic and other widespread major infectious diseases prevalent in humanitarian contexts, such as malaria, tuberculosis and cholera, for the affected countries,

Gravely concerned that violence, including sexual abuse and sexual and other violence against women, girls and boys, continues to be, in many emergency situations, deliberately directed against civilian populations, and reiterating that acts of sexual violence in situations of armed conflict can constitute serious violations or grave breaches of international humanitarian law and constitute, in defined circumstances, a crime against humanity and/or a war crime, and recalling the relevant provisions of the Rome Statute of the International Criminal Court,

Reiterating that humanitarian assistance should be provided in a way that is not to the detriment of resources made available for international cooperation for development,

1. *Takes note* of the report of the Secretary-General;
2. *Calls upon* all parties to armed conflict to comply with their obligations under international humanitarian law, human rights law and refugee law;
3. *Reaffirms* the obligation of all States and parties to armed conflict to protect civilians in armed conflict in accordance with international humanitarian law, and invites States to promote a culture of protection, taking into account the particular needs of women, children, older persons and persons with disabilities;
4. *Notes* that some of the issues affecting the protection of civilians in armed conflict could also be effectively addressed at a regional level, and welcomes in this context the fact that States and some regional organizations, within their mandates, have increasingly taken measures to address these and related protection concerns;
5. *Strongly encourages* the United Nations to address more systematically the protection of civilians and other humanitarian issues with regional organizations, in accordance with their respective mandates, including through continued dialogue;
6. *Calls* for enhanced collaboration within the United Nations system and among various United Nations bodies, including the General Assembly and the Economic and Social Council, within their respective mandates, in the area of the protection of civilians in armed conflict;
7. *Calls upon* States to comply fully with the provisions of international humanitarian law, in particular as provided in the Geneva Conventions of 12 August 1949 for the protection of victims of war, in order to protect and assist civilians in occupied territories;
8. *Urges* the international community and the relevant organizations of the United Nations system, in this regard, to strengthen humanitarian and other assistance to civilians under foreign occupation;
9. *Calls upon* all Governments and parties in complex humanitarian emergencies, in particular in armed conflict and in post-conflict situations, in countries in which humanitarian personnel are operating, in conformity with the relevant provisions of international law and national laws, to cooperate fully with the United Nations and other humanitarian agencies and organizations and to ensure the safe and unhindered access of humanitarian personnel, as well as supplies and equipment, in order to allow them to perform efficiently their task of assisting the affected civilian population, including refugees and internally displaced persons;
10. *Strongly urges* all States to take the measures necessary to ensure the safety and security of humanitarian personnel and United Nations and associated personnel;
11. *Also strongly urges* States to ensure that those responsible for attacks against humanitarian personnel and United Nations and associated personnel are promptly brought to justice, as provided by national law and obligations under international law, and notes the need for States to end impunity for such acts;

12. *Stresses* the importance of continued collaboration among all parts of the United Nations system on staff safety and security issues, mindful of the ongoing efforts of the Secretary-General on measures to further improve the United Nations security management system;
13. *Encourages* United Nations organizations and other humanitarian actors to address security risks posed to humanitarian staff, inter alia, by promoting accountability at all levels and by promoting and enhancing collaborative actions, in accordance with the relevant provisions of international humanitarian law and national laws, where applicable;
14. *Stresses* the importance of ensuring that humanitarian personnel and United Nations and associated personnel remain sensitive to national and local customs and traditions in their countries of assignment, communicate better their purpose and objectives to local populations and observe and respect the laws of the country in which they are operating, in accordance with international law and the Charter of the United Nations;
15. *Takes note with appreciation* of the continued efforts of the Office for the Coordination of Humanitarian Affairs of the Secretariat to strengthen the coordination of United Nations humanitarian assistance;
16. *Encourages* the Office for the Coordination of Humanitarian Affairs to continue engaging in dialogue with States on humanitarian assistance, including through the Economic and Social Council, in order to enhance its coordinating role for all United Nations humanitarian activities with a view to enhancing comprehensive intergovernmental support and guidance to the United Nations system;
17. *Supports* the efforts of the Office for the Coordination of Humanitarian Affairs to ensure that the design and implementation of United Nations integrated missions take into account the principles of neutrality, humanity and impartiality as well as the independence of humanitarian objectives for the provision of humanitarian assistance;
18. *Encourages* the United Nations Secretariat, in strengthening the coordination of humanitarian work and assistance, to engage in a dialogue with States and United Nations humanitarian entities to clarify the respective roles of, and complementarity among, relevant entities of the United Nations operating in the framework of United Nations multidimensional missions, invites the Secretariat to consult with relevant humanitarian organizations in that regard, and requests the Secretary-General to report thereon to the General Assembly, through the Economic and Social Council;
19. *Reaffirms* the leading role of civilian organizations in implementing humanitarian assistance, particularly in areas affected by conflict, and also affirms the need, in situations where military capacity and assets are used to support the implementation of humanitarian assistance, for their use to be in conformity with international humanitarian law and humanitarian principles;
20. *Encourages* United Nations humanitarian organizations and other relevant United Nations entities to

carry out jointly an in-depth examination of the extent to which current developments in international peace and security have affected the understanding and acceptance of the United Nations humanitarian organizations by local populations, as well as the understanding and acceptance of other humanitarian organizations, and the ability of humanitarian organizations to operate in the context of an international military presence, and to provide advice to these organizations on how they may respond better to these new developments;

21. *Stresses* the value of the use of the 2003 Guidelines on the Use of Military and Civil Defence Assets to Support United Nations Humanitarian Activities in Complex Emergencies and the 1994 Guidelines on the Use of Military and Civil Defence Assets in Disaster Relief and also stresses the value of the development by the United Nations, in consultation with States and other relevant actors, of further guidance on civil-military relations in the context of humanitarian activities and transition situations;

22. *Encourages* the Office for the Coordination of Humanitarian Affairs, in close collaboration with the United Nations Development Group Office, to improve further the training and capacity of Humanitarian and Resident Coordinators so that they can respond to the full range of humanitarian issues in a given context, including protection and assistance needs;

23. *Encourages* the channelling of increased resources to capacity-building activities in disaster-prone areas, in particular to address the dynamics and disproportionate risks that natural disasters pose in urban and rural environments;

24. *Emphasizes* the importance of building effective and inclusive partnerships, including in risk planning, with populations that live in disaster-prone and disaster-affected areas;

25. *Recalls* General Assembly resolution 57/150 of 16 December 2002 on strengthening the effectiveness and coordination of international urban search and rescue assistance, and welcomes the work that is being undertaken to strengthen further the effectiveness and coordination of international urban search and rescue assistance;

26. *Invites* States, as appropriate, to give priority to disaster risk reduction strategies and to integrate them fully into all relevant legal, policy and planning instruments in order to address the social, economic and environmental dimensions that influence vulnerability to natural hazards, bearing in mind the International Strategy for Disaster Reduction;

27. *Recommends* that the General Assembly raise the maximum limit for an emergency cash grant to 100,000 United States dollars per country in the case of any one disaster, from within existing resources available in the regular budget;

28. *Strongly encourages* States, relevant agencies and institutions as well as major groups as identified in Agenda 21 to participate in the World Conference on Disaster Reduction, in accordance with the rules of procedure agreed upon by the Preparatory Committee for the Conference, and invites them to contribute inputs to the ongoing preparations for the Conference, to be held in Kobe, Japan, from 18 to 22 January 2005, and to ensure that the opportunity is used to reaffirm

and to strengthen disaster reduction policy and its implementation at all levels;

29. *Encourages* States that have not done so to consider ratifying or acceding to the Tampere Convention on the Provision of Telecommunication Resources for Disaster Mitigation and Relief Operations, adopted at Tampere, Finland, on 18 June 1998;

30. *Emphasizes* the importance of integrating further HIV/AIDS responses into the planning, programming and implementation of humanitarian action by ensuring linkages between humanitarian, development and HIV/AIDS mechanisms and activities and by using the Inter-Agency Standing Committee Guidelines on HIV/AIDS Interventions in Emergency Settings, and encourages the United Nations system to improve its guidance to ensure a comprehensive approach to prevention, care and treatment in the context of humanitarian action;

31. *Recognizes* the important role of humanitarian agencies in addressing other major infectious diseases, such as malaria, tuberculosis and cholera, in emergencies, and urges them to factor considerations pertaining to these major infectious diseases into their planning and coordination efforts, including in the areas of early warning and contingency planning;

32. *Stresses* the continued need and relevance of integrating, through implementation of all relevant resolutions, agreed conclusions, policies, commitments and guidelines on gender mainstreaming, a gender perspective into the planning, programming and implementation of humanitarian assistance activities, and calls upon the Inter-Agency Standing Committee to undertake a review of its 1999 policy statement on the integration of a gender perspective into humanitarian assistance;

33. *Strongly condemns* all violence committed in situations of humanitarian crisis, especially against women, girls and boys, including sexual violence and abuse, and calls upon States to adopt preventive measures and effective responses to these acts as well as to ensure that those responsible for these acts are promptly brought to justice, as provided for by national law and obligations under international law;

34. *Invites* the organizations of the United Nations system to enhance geographical balance in terms of humanitarian personnel employed by them, in a manner consistent with Article 101, paragraph 3, of the Charter;

35. *Encourages* humanitarian agencies to ensure, to the extent possible, the participation and perspective of all those affected by humanitarian situations, at both the local and national levels, in the design, implementation and evaluation of humanitarian assistance activities, while respecting the role of authorities of affected countries;

36. *Encourages* the United Nations system to continue to develop and implement internal tools and to take effective measures for protection from sexual exploitation and sexual abuse, and, in this respect, notes with interest the Secretary-General Bulletin on special measures for protection from sexual exploitation and sexual abuse;

37. *Encourages* Governments as well as international humanitarian organizations, as appropriate, to take further initiatives to prevent, address and follow up on allegations of sexual exploitation and abuse in human-

itarian emergencies, and emphasizes that the highest standards of conduct and accountability are required of all personnel serving in humanitarian and peace-keeping operations;

38. *Encourages*, in this regard, the United Nations system and its Member States to urge international humanitarian organizations and implementing partners serving within the framework of United Nations humanitarian and other relevant operations to live up to the highest standards of conduct and accountability;

39. *Encourages* Member States with internally displaced persons to develop or to strengthen, as appropriate, national laws, policies and minimum standards on internal displacement, inter alia, taking into account the Guiding Principles on Internal Displacement, and to continue to work with humanitarian agencies in endeavours to provide a more predictable response to the needs of internally displaced persons, and in this regard calls for international support, upon request, to capacity-building efforts of Governments;

40. *Calls upon* the relevant United Nations entities, under the coordination mandate of the Office for the Coordination of Humanitarian Affairs, to improve the development of common needs assessments and to work towards more effective prioritization, including reviewing the Consolidated Appeals Process Needs Assessment Framework and Matrix;

41. *Encourages* the donor community to provide humanitarian assistance in proportion to needs and on the basis of needs assessments, with a view to ensuring a more equitable distribution of humanitarian assistance across humanitarian emergencies, including those of a protracted nature, as well as fuller coverage of the needs of all sectors, and to this end requests the organizations of the United Nations system, including through the United Nations country teams, to continue developing and applying transparent needs assessment mechanisms;

42. *Also encourages* the donor community to establish reliable, predictable and timely funding to meet humanitarian needs, and to consider increasing the flexibility of funding and the share of non-earmarked contributions to United Nations organizations in response to humanitarian emergencies, including within the consolidated appeals, and notes with interest the progress being made by donors in improving their policies and practices of good donorship, inter alia under the Good Humanitarian Donorship initiative;

43. *Emphasizes* the need for a more inclusive dialogue with States on the complex issue of transition from relief to development, and requests the Secretary-General to submit a report to the General Assembly, through the Economic and Social Council, taking into account the range of views expressed by States at the event held by the Council during its substantive session of 2004 to discuss the issue of transition from relief to development, and with the participation of United Nations entities, including the United Nations Development Group and the Executive Committee on Humanitarian Affairs, with the aim of improving the international community efforts to respond better to transition situations, in support of the efforts of affected States, bearing in mind the uniqueness of each transition situation;

44. *Welcomes* the collaborative effort of the United Nations and the World Bank on the development and implementation of post-emergency programming tools

and needs assessment with the full participation of affected States, and underlines the need for further work to enhance coordination;

45. *Encourages* States to support, including through the allocation of funds, the development and implementation of the 4Rs (repatriation, reintegration, rehabilitation and reconstruction and of other programming tools, to facilitate the transition from relief to development;

46. *Requests* the Secretary-General to reflect the progress made in the implementation of and follow-up to the present resolution and to Economic and Social Council resolutions 2002/32 of 26 July 2002 and 2003/5 in his next report to the Council and the General Assembly on the coordination of emergency humanitarian assistance of the United Nations.

GENERAL ASSEMBLY ACTION

On 15 December [meeting 72], the General Assembly adopted **resolution 59/141** [draft: A/59/L.49 & Add.1] without vote [agenda item 39 (a)].

Strengthening of the coordination of emergency humanitarian assistance of the United Nations

The General Assembly,

Recalling its resolution 46/182 of 19 December 1991 and the guiding principles contained in the annex thereto, other relevant General Assembly and Economic and Social Council resolutions and agreed conclusions of the Council,

Taking note of the report of the Secretary-General,

Reaffirming the principles of humanity, neutrality and impartiality for the provision of humanitarian assistance,

Recognizing that independence, meaning the autonomy of humanitarian objectives from the political, economic, military or other objectives that any actor may hold with regard to areas where humanitarian action is being implemented, is also an important guiding principle for the provision of humanitarian assistance,

Gravely concerned that violence, including sexual abuse and sexual and other violence against women, girls and boys, continues to be, in many emergency situations, deliberately directed against civilian populations,

Gravely concerned also about the lack of access by humanitarian personnel to victims of humanitarian emergencies, in particular in armed conflict and in post-conflict situations, in many regions of the world,

Reaffirming the responsibility first and foremost of States to take care of the victims of humanitarian emergencies within their own borders, while recognizing that the magnitude and duration of many emergencies may be beyond the response capacity of many affected countries,

Reaffirming also that States whose populations are in need of humanitarian assistance are called upon to facilitate the work of humanitarian organizations and that States in proximity to humanitarian emergencies are urged to facilitate, to the extent possible, the transit of humanitarian assistance,

Concerned about the need to mobilize adequate support, including financial resources, for emergency humanitarian assistance at all levels, including at national, regional and international levels,

Emphasizing that the Office for the Coordination of Humanitarian Affairs of the Secretariat should benefit from adequate and more predictable funding, while stressing the importance for the Office to continue to make efforts to broaden its donor base,

Reiterating that contributions for humanitarian assistance should be provided in a way that is not to the detriment of resources made available for international cooperation for development,

Recognizing the importance of humanitarian assistance in ensuring the effective transition from conflict to peace and the positive effect it may have in preventing the recurrence of armed conflict, and that humanitarian assistance must be provided in ways that will be supportive of recovery and long-term development,

Noting with grave concern the growing intensity and recurrence of natural disasters, and reaffirming the importance of sustainable measures to reduce the vulnerability of societies to natural hazards using an integrated, multi-hazard and participatory approach to addressing vulnerability, risk assessment and disaster prevention, mitigation, preparedness, response and recovery,

1. *Takes note with appreciation* of the outcome of the seventh humanitarian affairs segment of the Economic and Social Council, during its substantive session of 2004;

2. *Encourages* the Emergency Relief Coordinator to continue his efforts to strengthen the coordination of humanitarian assistance, and calls upon relevant United Nations organizations as well as other humanitarian and development actors to work with the Office for the Coordination of Humanitarian Affairs of the Secretariat in enhancing the coordination, effectiveness and efficiency of humanitarian assistance;

3. *Recognizes* the importance of secure and predictable funding to the coordinated, appropriate and timely delivery of humanitarian assistance, stresses the need to increase in an incremental way, in the normal course of the budget process, the share of the budget of the Office for the Coordination of Humanitarian Affairs borne by the regular budget of the United Nations, and requests the Secretary-General to give this matter full consideration;

4. *Emphasizes* the importance of the discussion of humanitarian policies and activities in the General Assembly and in the Economic and Social Council and that these discussions should be further revitalized by Member States;

5. *Calls upon* Governments, relevant organizations of the United Nations system, other relevant international organizations and non-governmental organizations to cooperate with the Secretary-General and the Emergency Relief Coordinator to ensure timely implementation of and follow-up to resolutions of the General Assembly and resolutions of the Economic and Social Council adopted at the humanitarian affairs segment of its substantive sessions;

6. *Strongly encourages* the United Nations to address more systematically protection of civilians and other humanitarian issues with regional organizations, in accordance with their respective mandates, inter alia, through dialogue;

7. *Decides* to raise the maximum limit of an emergency cash grant to 100,000 United States dollars per country in the case of any one disaster, within existing resources available from the regular budget of the United Nations;

8. *Encourages* the Office for the Coordination of Humanitarian Affairs, in close collaboration with the United Nations Development Group Office, to improve further the training and capacity of humanitarian and resident coordinators so that they can respond to the full range of humanitarian issues and those related to transition from relief to development in a given context, including protection and assistance needs;

9. *Calls upon* the Secretary-General to ensure that the design and implementation of United Nations integrated missions take into account the principles of humanity, neutrality and impartiality as well as independence for the provision of humanitarian assistance;

10. *Welcomes* the ongoing work within the United Nations on the complex issue of transition from relief to development, and takes note of the request by the Economic and Social Council to the Secretary-General to prepare a report on the issue for further consideration by the Council and the General Assembly;

11. *Emphasizes* the fundamentally civilian character of humanitarian assistance, reaffirms the leading role of civilian organizations in implementing humanitarian assistance, particularly in areas affected by conflicts, and affirms the need, in situations where military capacity and assets are used to support the implementation of humanitarian assistance, for their use to be in conformity with international humanitarian law and humanitarian principles;

12. *Recalls* the 2003 "Guidelines on the Use of Military and Civil Defence Assets to Support United Nations Humanitarian Activities in Complex Emergencies", as well as the 1994 "Guidelines on the Use of Military and Civil Defence Assets in Disaster Relief", and stresses the value of their use and of the development by the United Nations in consultation with States and other relevant actors of further guidance on civil-military relations in the context of humanitarian activities and transition situations;

13. *Strongly condemns* all acts of violence committed against civilian populations in situations of humanitarian crisis, especially against women, girls and boys, including sexual violence and abuse, and reiterates that such acts can constitute serious violations or grave breaches of international humanitarian law and constitute, in defined circumstances, a crime against humanity and/or a war crime;

14. *Calls upon* States to adopt preventive measures and effective responses to acts of violence committed against civilian populations as well as to ensure that those responsible are promptly brought to justice, as provided for by national law and obligations under international law;

15. *Reaffirms* the obligation of all States and parties to an armed conflict to protect civilians in armed conflicts in accordance with international humanitarian law, and invites States to promote a culture of protection, taking into account the particular needs of women, children, older persons and persons with disabilities;

16. *Encourages* Member States with internally displaced persons to develop or strengthen, as appropriate, national laws, policies and minimum standards on internal displacement, inter alia, taking into account the Guiding Principles on Internal Displacement, and to continue to work with humanitarian agencies in endeavours to provide a more predictable response to the needs of internally displaced persons, and in this

regard calls for international support, upon request, to the capacity-building efforts of Governments;

17. *Strongly condemns* all forms of violence to which humanitarian personnel and United Nations and its associated personnel are increasingly subjected, as well as any act or failure to act, contrary to international law that obstructs or prevents humanitarian personnel and United Nations and its associated personnel from discharging their humanitarian functions;

18. *Calls upon* all Governments and parties in complex humanitarian emergencies, in particular in armed conflicts and in post-conflict situations, in countries in which humanitarian personnel are operating, in conformity with the relevant provisions of international law and national laws, to cooperate fully with the United Nations and other humanitarian agencies and organizations and to ensure the safe and unhindered access of humanitarian personnel as well as supplies and equipment in order to allow them to perform efficiently their task of assisting the affected civilian population, including refugees and internally displaced persons;

19. *Expresses concern* about the continued occurrence of sexual exploitation and abuse in humanitarian crises, emphasizes that the highest standards of conduct and accountability are required of all personnel serving in humanitarian and peacekeeping operations, and requests the Secretary-General to report on measures to follow up, inter alia, the Plan of Action on Protection from Sexual Exploitation and Abuse in Humanitarian Crises developed by the Inter-Agency Standing Committee and the application of the bulletin of the Secretary-General on special measures for protection from sexual exploitation and sexual abuse;

20. *Takes note with interest* of the progress being made by donors to improve their policies and practices of good donorship, including under the Good Humanitarian Donorship initiative, and calls upon donors to take further steps to improve their policies and practices with respect to humanitarian assistance;

21. *Calls upon* relevant United Nations organizations to continue to improve transparency and reliability of humanitarian needs assessments;

22. *Encourages* the Secretary-General to continue to improve his reporting on emergency humanitarian assistance, including with respect to natural disasters;

23. *Requests* the Secretary-General to report to the General Assembly at its sixtieth session, through the Economic and Social Council at its substantive session of 2005, on progress made in strengthening the coordination of emergency humanitarian assistance of the United Nations.

UN and other humanitarian personnel

In response to General Assembly resolution 58/122 [YUN 2003, p. 1453], the Secretary-General, in a September report [A/59/332], described threats against humanitarian and UN personnel over the preceding year. He strongly urged all States to take stronger actions to ensure that threats or acts of violence committed against humanitarian personnel and UN and associated personnel on their territory were investigated fully and that the perpetrators were brought to justice.

The Assembly, in **resolution 59/211** of 20 December, called on Governments and parties in complex humanitarian emergencies to ensure the safe and unhindered access of humanitarian personnel (see p. 1435).

Defining UNHCR's administrative functions

The Committee for Programme and Coordination (CPC), at its forty-fourth session (7 June–2 July) [A/59/16], during consideration of programme 22, Humanitarian assistance, of the programme outline of the 2006-2007 proposed strategic framework (see p. 1401), recognized that the effective implementation of UNHCR's mandate involved ongoing functions at UN Headquarters, including humanitarian coordination, policy development and advocacy, information analysis and dissemination, field support and the management of relevant inter-agency and interdepartmental mechanisms. It recommended that the General Assembly request the Secretary-General to make recommendations at its sixtieth session (2005) on how to ensure the ongoing discharge of those key functions.

Responding to Assembly resolution 58/270 [YUN 2003, p. 1399] and to CPC's concerns (above), the Secretary-General submitted a November report [A/59/562], which described the mandate, funding history and coordination role of the UN Office for the Coordination of Humanitarian Affairs and the benefits of secure and predictable funding of its work and that of the United Nations. It also proposed a conceptual framework and definition of the Office's administrative functions, and identified the standing functions that were critical to the discharge of its mandate. According to the Secretary-General, the report outlined a framework that could serve as a basis for the Assembly to consider the coordination of humanitarian assistance in the strategic planning and programming activities of the United Nations as a whole, as well as in the programme budgeting process.

The Assembly, in **resolution 59/275** of 23 December (see p. 1401), requested the Secretary-General to make recommendations by the end of the Assembly's fifty-ninth session on how to ensure the ongoing discharge of key UNHCR functions as defined by CPC, at Headquarters.

Resource mobilization

Central Emergency Revolving Fund

In 2004, the Central Emergency Revolving Fund, established in 1992 [YUN 1992, p. 584] as a cash-flow mechanism for the initial phase of humanitarian emergencies, granted 13 advances, amounting to $27.8 million.

Consolidated appeals

The consolidated appeals process (CAP), an inclusive and coordinated programme cycle for analysing context, assessing needs and planning prioritized humanitarian response, was the humanitarian sector's main strategic planning and programming tool. In 2004, the United Nations and its humanitarian partners issued consolidated appeals seeking $3.4 billion in assistance to Angola, Bangladesh, Bolivia, the Central African Republic, Chad, Chechnya and neighbouring republics of the Russian Federation, the Democratic People's Republic of Korea, Eritrea, the Great Lakes region (Burundi, the Democratic Republic of the Congo (DRC), Rwanda, Uganda, the United Republic of Tanzania), Grenada, Haiti, Indonesia, Iran, Kenya, Madagascar, the Occupied Palestinian Territory, the Philippines, Somalia, Sudan, Tajikistan, the West Africa Subregion (Burkina Faso, Côte d'Ivoire, Ghana, Guinea, Liberia, Mali, Sierra Leone), and Zimbabwe. Separate appeals were issued for Burundi, Côte d'Ivoire + 3 (Burkina Faso, Ghana, Mali), DRC, Guinea, Liberia, Sierra Leone, Uganda and the United Republic of Tanzania.

The latest available data indicated that 64 per cent ($2.2 billion) of requirements had been met.

Mine clearance

In response to General Assembly resolution 58/127 [YUN 2003, p. 924], the Secretary-General, in an August report [A/59/284], described progress in implementing the goals and objectives of the UN mine-action strategy for the period 2001-2005 [YUN 2001, p. 828]. A review of the six strategic goals identified progress in each goal as follows: improved assessment of situations in mine-affected countries, including assessment missions conducted in Liberia, Malawi, Senegal and Uganda (goal 1); improved capacity to respond to emergencies, through the UN rapid response plan tested in Iraq, which was being revised (goal 2); ongoing efforts to build national mine action capacity through new capacity-building programmes such as in Afghanistan, Colombia, Iraq, Jordan and the Sudan (goal 3); strengthened quality management through the approval and dissemination of international mine action standards for mine risk education (goal 4); increased availability of resources and initiatives to encourage mine action participation by international financial institutions (goal 5); and improved advocacy coordination and implementation through the approval of a UN mine action strategy (goal 6) (see below).

The Secretary-General concluded that efforts to raise the visibility of mine-related issues throughout the United Nations had resulted in the systematic integration of mine action into planning and operations in peacekeeping, humanitarian affairs and development at national and international levels. UN efforts had strengthened the capacities of mine-affected States to effectively manage mine action policy planning, coordination and operations, and encouraged strengthened cooperation among those States. He recommended that Member States continue to support implementation of the UN mine action strategy for 2001-2005 and that the United Nations present a new strategy for the period 2006-2010. The rapid response plan should be further integrated into the planning processes of UN humanitarian and peacekeeping operations and activated in emergency situations, political developments permitting, and in the absence of other national capacity to address the landmine problem. Member States should continue to strengthen national capacities to address the problem of landmines and explosive remnants of war, and mine-affected Member States should include mine action in poverty reduction strategy papers and national development plans. International financial institutions should assist mine-affected developing States to meet targets and treaty obligations and to advance the Millennium Development Goals (MDGs) [YUN 2000, p. 51], while mine action donors should refer to the portfolio of mine action projects and provide data to the donor investments database. Member States should be represented at the highest possible level at the Summit on a Mine-Free World (Nairobi, Kenya, 29 November-3 December), which would be the first review conference of the 1997 Convention on the Prohibition of the Use, Stockpiling, Production and Transfer of Anti-personnel Mines and on Their Destruction [YUN 1997, p. 503] (see p. 568); mine affected States should submit comprehensive national plans for consideration at the Summit.

An addendum to the report [A/59/284/Add.1] presented the UN mine action advocacy strategy for 2004-2005, which was endorsed by the Inter-Agency Coordination Group on Mine Action in April.

The General Assembly, by **decision 59/516** of 10 December, decided to include in the provisional agenda of its sixtieth (2005) session the item entitled "Assistance in mine action".

New international humanitarian order

In response to General Assembly resolution 57/184 [YUN 2002, p. 893], the Secretary-General, in a November report [A/59/554], presented the views of three Member States and the Independent Bureau for Humanitarian Issues on the promotion of a new international humanitarian order. The report recommended that the Assembly urge Governments to share their views regarding the constituent elements of an agenda for humanitarian action, and call on Member States to make available to the Secretary-General the expertise and means for developing and implementing the proposed agenda. It also recommended that the Assembly strengthen the role of non-governmental organizations (NGOs) and the private sector in the humanitarian field, and recommend that measures be identified to strengthen the nexus between human rights and humanitarian issues, and between emergency assistance and development aid.

GENERAL ASSEMBLY ACTION

On 20 December [meeting 74], the General Assembly, on the recommendation of the Third (Social, Humanitarian and Cultural) Committee [A/59/498], adopted **resolution 59/171** without vote [agenda item 100].

New international humanitarian order

The General Assembly,

Recalling its resolution 57/184 of 18 December 2002 and all previous resolutions concerning the promotion of a new international humanitarian order as well as all relevant resolutions, in particular resolution 46/182 of 19 December 1991 on the strengthening of the coordination of humanitarian emergency assistance of the United Nations, and the annex thereto,

Reaffirming the fundamental importance of adherence to and implementation of international humanitarian law, refugee law and human rights law as well as internationally accepted norms and principles, in particular the principles of humanity, neutrality and impartiality for the provision of humanitarian assistance,

Recognizing the importance of action at the national and regional levels and the role that regional organizations can play in certain cases to prevent humanitarian crises, and noting with appreciation the complementary role played in this regard by the United Nations entities, including the agencies, funds and programmes,

Aware of the important role that international organizations, intergovernmental and non-governmental organizations and the private sector can play, within their respective mandates, in the humanitarian context,

Concerned by the increasingly difficult context in which humanitarian assistance takes place in some areas, in particular the continuous erosion, in many cases, of respect for the principles and rules of international humanitarian law,

Emphasizing the importance of continued international cooperation in support of the efforts of affected States in dealing with natural disasters and complex emergencies in all their phases,

Reiterating that humanitarian assistance should be provided in a way which is not to the detriment of resources made available for international cooperation for development,

Taking note of the report of the Secretary-General,

1. *Expresses its appreciation* for the continuing efforts of the Secretary-General in the humanitarian field, and urges Governments to assist him in promoting a new international humanitarian order that corresponds to new realities and challenges, including the development of an agenda for humanitarian action, in accordance with international law;

2. *Reaffirms* the obligation of all States and parties to armed conflicts to protect civilians in armed conflicts in accordance with international humanitarian law, and invites States to promote a culture of protection, taking into account the particular needs of women, children, older persons and persons with disabilities;

3. *Calls upon* all Governments and parties in complex humanitarian emergencies, in particular armed conflicts and post-conflict situations, in countries in which humanitarian personnel are operating, in conformity with the relevant provisions of international law and national laws, to cooperate fully with the United Nations and other humanitarian agencies and organizations and to ensure the safe and unhindered access of humanitarian personnel in order to allow them to perform efficiently their task of assisting the affected civilian population, including refugees and internally displaced persons;

4. *Urges* Governments, intergovernmental and non-governmental organizations and others concerned to extend cooperation and provide support to the efforts of the Secretary-General, inter alia, through the relevant United Nations agencies and organizational mechanisms set up to address the assistance and protection needs of victims of complex emergencies as well as the safety and security of United Nations and other humanitarian workers;

5. *Invites* the Secretary-General to continue to promote strict adherence to refugee law, international humanitarian law, human rights law and internationally accepted norms and principles in situations of humanitarian emergency;

6. *Recognizes* the complementarity between humanitarian assistance and human rights;

7. *Encourages* the international community to improve its response to humanitarian emergencies, including those of a protracted nature, including efforts by donors with regard to policies and practices of good donorship;

8. *Encourages* intergovernmental and non-governmental organizations as well as the private sector to assist and support national and international efforts to respond to humanitarian challenges and alleviate human suffering;

9. *Recognizes* the important need to address more effectively the transition from relief to development, and welcomes in this regard the request made by the Economic and Social Council to the Secretary-General to prepare a report on the issue for further consideration by the Council and the General Assembly;

10. *Invites* Member States, the Secretary-General and the United Nations system, within their respective mandates, to strengthen the capacities of regional and subregional organizations, where applicable, in the context of the response to humanitarian crises;

11. *Invites* Member States, the Office for the Coordination of Humanitarian Affairs of the Secretariat, relevant entities of the United Nations system, and intergovernmental and non-governmental organizations, including the Independent Bureau for Humanitarian Issues, to reinforce activities and cooperation so as to continue to develop an agenda for humanitarian action;

12. *Requests* the Secretary-General to support the process of developing an agenda for humanitarian action and to report to the General Assembly at its sixty-first session on the overall progress made.

Humanitarian activities

Africa

Angola

An August consolidated report of the Secretary-General [A/59/293], prepared in response to General Assembly resolution 57/102 [YUN 2002, p. 913], provided information on humanitarian and rehabilitation assistance given to nine countries, including Angola, undergoing or emerging from humanitarian crises induced by conflict or natural causes. According to the report, some 133,000 Angolan refugees returned home in 2003, including 76,000 under the voluntary repatriation operation of the Office of the United Nations High Commissioner for Refugees (UNHCR). UNHCR estimated that, of the 240,000 Angolan refugees still in Botswana, the DRC, Namibia, the Republic of the Congo, South Africa and Zambia, some 145,000 were expected to return in 2004. Refugees continued to return spontaneously, mainly in the eastern province of Moxico.

In the country itself, the situation was still of concern for an estimated 1.2 million people in difficult-to-access areas, as the war-devastated infrastructure and the presence of landmines posed major impediments to humanitarian operations and the return to normal life. Key humanitarian coordination functions were being handed over to government ministries and UN agencies in conjunction with an ongoing capacity-building programme. To facilitate the transition period, the United Nations used a consolidated appeal for transition for 2004 and a flexible United Nations Development Assistance Framework (UNDAF) for the period 2005-2008. The Consolidated Inter-Agency Appeal for Angola sought $136 million in 2004, of which 130 million (96 per cent) had been received.

(See also p. 926 under "Special economic assistance".)

Central African Republic

The Consolidated Inter-Agency Appeal for the Central African Republic sought $7.6 million for 2004, of which $2.9 million (38 per cent) had been received.

During 2004, the combined burdens of physical insecurity, poor health and economic vulnerability weighed heavily on the daily lives of Central Africans, particularly those in the north western regions of the country, which were hit hardest by the civil war of October 2002–March 2003. A year after the armed rebellion had ended, its devastating effects remained in evidence at the political, military and social levels. The few existing public infrastructures, particularly health centres and schools, had been subjected to almost systematic pillage and destruction. The response by humanitarian agencies was severely limited by both the lack of donor resources and diminished capacity for intervention. However, the country was entering an electoral period due to culminate in presidential elections in March 2005, which, if successful, would herald a return to constitutional legality and thereby open the path to normalized relations with international financial institutions.

Eritrea

The UN Consolidated Inter-Agency Appeal for Eritrea, launched for a total of $126 million to assist 1.9 million beneficiaries during 2004, received 60 per cent ($75 million) of requirements.

The cumulative effects of drought, underperformance of the economy, and lack of funding for a post-conflict recovery programme in Eritrea led to a further deterioration of the humanitarian situation. More than 66 per cent of the population was threatened by direct hunger, extreme poverty and poor access to clean water, while scarce resources limited the Government's ability to purchase food commercially. The stalemate in the peace process with Ethiopia (see p. 265) constrained demobilization activities, thus creating a marked workforce shortage in the public and private sectors, and prevented the resettlement of a high number of internally displaced persons (IDPs), who remained in camps.

Great Lakes region

The UN Consolidated Inter-Agency Appeal for the Great Lakes region, launched for a total of $85.5 million to cover 2004, received 96 per cent ($82.1 million) of that amount. In addition to the Great Lakes regional appeal, individual country appeals were made for the other countries of the region, except Rwanda, for which other mechanisms were used.

The key thematic priorities for 2004 were violence against children; assistance for internally displaced persons; transmission of HIV/AIDS during emergencies; prevention and support to survivors of sexual violence; and the integration of humanitarian principles into all aspects of demobilization, disarmament and reintegration.

Burundi

The UN Consolidated Inter-Agency Appeal for Burundi sought $119 million, of which 47 per cent ($56 million) was received.

In 2004, widespread changes in the security conditions throughout Burundi led to expanded and sustained humanitarian access to Burundian populations, including in those communities living in remote areas. However, forced displacement, instability and armed conflict continued to affect some regions. Access to basic health and education services was seriously constrained, but the improved security situation in rural areas and the continuous provision of food aid and emergency agricultural assistance contributed to a reduction in the scope of food insecurity that had plagued the country.

Democratic Republic of the Congo

The UN Consolidated Inter-Agency Appeal for the DRC sought $163 million in assistance in 2004, of which 73 per cent ($119 million) was received.

Improved security, active advocacy, better risk management and a relative improvement in geographic accessibility in the DRC in 2004 led to expanded humanitarian access, thus saving thousands of lives. The malnutrition rate among the most vulnerable groups was stabilized due to the establishment of feeding centres and technical standards, and coordination was optimized. By mid-August, more than 725,000 internally displaced persons out of an estimated 2.3 million returned to their place of origin in a period of 12 months. However, those achievements still warranted improvement and were outweighed by events that altered or prevented humanitarian action, the main constraint being the lack of land and maritime infrastructure.

(See also p. 928 under "Special economic assistance".)

United Republic of Tanzania

The UN Consolidated Inter-Agency Appeal for the United Republic of Tanzania, launched for a total of $38.8 million to cover 2004, received 83 per cent ($32.3 million) of that amount.

In Tanzania, the ongoing repatriation of Burundian refugees lessened government criticism of the presence of refugees in the country, but restrictions on refugee movement around the camps and the policy of vetting new arrivals from the DRC remained in place. A substantially reduced maize harvest in the northern highland areas led to maize price increases and limited availability. Water and pasture availability was likely to decline further if drought conditions continued.

Uganda

The UN Consolidated Inter-Agency Appeal for Uganda, launched for a total of $143 million to cover 2004, received 79 per cent ($122.3 million) of that amount.

In 2004, more than 1.6 million internally displaced persons (IDPs) lived in more than 180 camps and temporary shelters set up as much as eight years earlier and never intended for long-term use. All camps were highly congested and over-crowded, with squalid living conditions. Limited water supply and low sanitation led to disease outbreaks, contributing to increased morbidity and mortality. Children and women, the most vulnerable groups, comprised 80 per cent of those internally displaced. From January to June, the security situation worsened seriously, as the rebel Lord's Resistance Army (LRA) intensified their attacks on displaced people in Gulu, Kitgum, Pader and Lira districts. However, the general security situation improved markedly beginning in July, following high LRA desertion. Humanitarian access then improved in Teso, Lira and Gulu, but remained difficult in Kitgum and Pader. A number of aid agencies reached the IDP camps with military escorts from the Uganda People's Defence Force.

Somalia

In response to General Assembly resolution 58/115 [YUN 2003, p. 928], the Secretary-General, in his August consolidated report [A/59/293], provided information on relief and rehabilitation assistance provided by the United Nations and its partners in Somalia in 2004.

Insecurity continued to prevail in many parts of Somalia in the period 2003-2004, especially in the Galguduud region, the Belet Weyne district, Kismaayo, the Northern Gedo, Sool and Sanaag regions and in Mogadishu. The United Nations and many NGOs enhanced their security measures in response to the increase in threats and attacks on international and national aid workers. Over four years of consecutive drought in northern Somalia led to massive livestock deaths and, in some cases, the collapse of pastoralism as a viable means of making a living. The drought also triggered unprecedented water and food price increases, which had an impact on the purchasing power of affected populations. UN agencies and NGOs responded with short-term interventions from November 2003 to June 2004. To improve the international humanitarian community's response capacity, the UN Office for the Coordination of Humanitarian Affairs (OCHA) established a humanitarian response fund in April 2004, with support from the United Kingdom, and five projects totalling $550,000 were funded. The Food and Agriculture Organization of the United Nations (FAO) provided returnees and internally displaced persons, women, children and minorities in the most food insecure areas with staple food crop seeds and farming hand tools; small-scale irrigation pumps, animal traction equipment and processing equipment would be distributed during the remainder of 2004. To improve further the economic situation, the United Nations was supporting the establishment of a credible and recognized animal health certification for the export of livestock and the formation of a livestock products system, to be known as the Somali Livestock Board.

The UN Consolidated Inter-Agency Appeal for Somalia sought $120 million in 2004, of which 60 per cent ($71.7 million) was received.

GENERAL ASSEMBLY ACTION

On 22 December [meeting 75], the General Assembly, on the recommendation of the Second (Economic and Financial) Committee [A/59/479 & Corr.1], adopted **resolution 59/218** without vote [agenda item 39 (b)].

Assistance for humanitarian relief and the economic and social rehabilitation of Somalia

The General Assembly,

Recalling its resolution 47/160 of 18 December 1992 and subsequent relevant resolutions, in particular resolutions 56/106 of 14 December 2001, 57/154 of 16 December 2002 and 58/115 of 17 December 2003,

Noting with serious concern that the current drought in some parts of Somalia threatens the lives of Somali nomads as well as livestock,

Noting with grave concern the high mortality rate of over 80 per cent of livestock in the worst-affected areas of the Sool, Sanaag and Togdheer plateaux of Somalia and the high risk of starvation of Somali nomads,

Noting with serious concern the threat, as a result of this drought, of a serious negative impact on the Somali economy, and in particular on the pastoral economy and social support systems,

Underlining the urgent need for humanitarian assistance, relief and reconstruction,

Noting the linkage between the search for peace and reconciliation and the alleviation of the humanitarian crisis in Somalia,

Welcoming the continued focus of the United Nations, in partnership with civil society at the grassroots level, on programmes of assistance, including both humanitarian and development approaches, taking into consideration the conditions on the ground,

Recalling the statements by the President of the Security Council of 31 October 2001 and 28 March

2002, by which the Council condemned attacks on humanitarian personnel and called upon all parties in Somalia to respect fully the security and safety of personnel of the United Nations, the International Committee of the Red Cross and non-governmental organizations, and to guarantee their complete freedom of movement and access throughout Somalia,

Re-emphasizing the importance of the further implementation of its resolutions 47/160, 56/106, 57/154 and 58/115 to rehabilitate basic social and economic services throughout the country,

Taking note of the reports of the Secretary-General,

1. *Expresses its appreciation* to the Secretary-General for his continued and tireless efforts to mobilize assistance for the Somali people;

2. *Welcomes with great satisfaction* the progress made in the last two years of the reconciliation process in Kenya, in particular the elections of the Somali Transitional Federal Parliament, the Speaker of Parliament and the President, the appointment of the Prime Minister and the formation of the Cabinet, and urges all Somali parties and States members of the Intergovernmental Authority on Development to fully support the new Transitional Federal Government of Somalia;

3. *Expresses the need* for continued engagement and commitment to a structured support, based on joint principles and structures of coordination and monitoring, as endorsed in Stockholm on 29 October 2004, to be agreed upon with the future transitional national federal institutions;

4. *Welcomes* the strategy of the United Nations focusing on the implementation of community-based interventions aimed at rebuilding local infrastructures and increased self-reliance of the local population, and the ongoing efforts by the United Nations agencies, their Somali counterparts and their partner organizations to establish and maintain close coordination and cooperation mechanisms for the implementation of the relief, rehabilitation and reconstruction programme in line with the priorities of the new Transitional Federal Government;

5. *Notes* the incremental and prioritized approach of the United Nations system to addressing the continuing crisis and needs in Somalia while maintaining long-term commitments to rehabilitation, recovery and development activities;

6. *Commends* the Office for the Coordination of Humanitarian Affairs of the Secretariat, the funds and programmes of the United Nations as well as other humanitarian organizations for their response, and underlines the urgent need for putting into place practical measures aimed at the alleviation of the consequences of the drought in the most affected areas in Somalia;

7. *Urges* all States and intergovernmental and non-governmental organizations concerned to continue to implement further its resolutions 47/160, 56/106, 57/154 and 58/115 in order to assist the Somali people in embarking on the rehabilitation of basic social and economic services, as well as institution-building aimed at the restoration of structures of civil governance at all levels in all parts of the country wherever possible;

8. *Calls upon* the Secretary-General to continue to mobilize international humanitarian, rehabilitation and reconstruction assistance for Somalia;

9. *Calls upon* all Somali parties to respect the security and safety of the personnel of the United Nations, the specialized agencies and non-governmental organizations and to guarantee their complete freedom of movement and safe access throughout Somalia;

10. *Urges* the international community to provide:

(*a*) Political support to the new Transitional Federal Government;

(*b*) Significant financial and technical support for the rehabilitation and reconstruction of Somalia;

(*c*) Full support to the need for peacebuilding measures and the speedy implementation of programmes for the disarmament, demobilization and reintegration of militias throughout Somalia in order to stabilize the entire country and thereby ensure the effectiveness of the new Transitional Federal Government;

11. *Urges* the Transitional Federal Government, in coordination with the Intergovernmental Authority on Development and the African Union, to develop a strategy and timetable outlining its functional priorities;

12. *Urges* the international community to provide as a matter of urgency humanitarian assistance and relief to the Somali people to alleviate in particular the consequences of the prevailing drought;

13. *Calls upon* the international community to provide continuing and increased assistance in response to the United Nations 2004 Consolidated Inter-Agency Appeal for relief, rehabilitation and reconstruction assistance for Somalia;

14. *Commends* the Secretary-General for the establishment of the Trust Fund for Peacebuilding in Somalia, welcomes the contributions made thus far to the Fund, and appeals to Member States to contribute to it;

15. *Requests* the Secretary-General, in view of the critical situation in Somalia, to take all necessary and practicable measures for the implementation of the present resolution and to report thereon to the General Assembly at its sixtieth session.

Sudan

The UN Consolidated Inter-Agency Appeal for the Sudan Assistance Programme (ASAP), including the Revised ASAP 2004: Darfur Crisis and the appeal for remaining humanitarian requirements for the Sudan until 31 December, sought a total of $726.6 million to cover assistance needs in 2004. Of that amount, 76 per cent ($553.7 million) was received.

At the end of 2004, peace talks in the Sudan had not yet led to agreement on a comprehensive peace agreement for ending 38 years of North-South conflict and rebuilding the country. At the same time, conflict in the Darfur region continued, with an increase in security incidents against aid workers and abuses against civilians. The Darfur crisis displaced 1.6 million people, with 200,000 refugees fleeing to Chad, and caused severe hardship for several hundred thousand other conflict-affected people. Despite the large humanitarian effort, an average of 30 to 50 per cent of the needy did not yet have access to assistance. The crisis threatened security across the region, and risked further detracting from the North-South peace process. In addition, the Sudan as a whole continued to suffer from widespread poverty and inequitable development.

(For more information on the crisis in Darfur, see p. 235).

Chad

The UN Consolidated Inter-Agency Appeal for Chad sought $165.5 million in assistance for 2004, of which 88 per cent ($145.4 million) was received.

The conflict in western Sudan profoundly impacted the situation in Chad, especially its eastern region, to which an estimated 200,000 people had fled to escape the crisis in the Sudan's Darfur region (see p. 235). The resulting demographic pressure on an already fragile environment destabilized the local economic and social situation. To overcome logistical constraints and reach beneficiaries, humanitarian organizations had to establish alternative transportation routes and add air capacity, which translated into higher programming cost. In addition, Chad was plagued by internal and external security problems, including political-military instability, cross-border raids from the Sudanese rebels and tensions between refugees and host communities.

West Africa

The UN Consolidated Inter-Agency Appeal for the West Africa subregion, launched in 2004 for $97.3 million to assist beneficiaries in Burkina Faso, Côte d'Ivoire, Ghana, Guinea, Liberia, Mali and Sierra Leone, received 59 per cent ($57.5 million) of that amount.

The subregion continued to experience the impact of various complex emergencies and natural disasters. While Liberia made initial steps towards recovery, Côte d'Ivoire struggled with the implementation of the Linas Marcoussis Accord (see p. 170). Both peace processes proved fragile, and large populations continued to be displaced. Arms and combatants, as well as epidemics including HIV/AIDS, moved swiftly across the region. Poor host communities remained overburdened by refugees and returning migrants. In addition, locust swarm invasions resulted in the infestation of cropping and grassland areas of the Sahelian countries, and damage to pasture cereals and vegetable crops became widespread.

Côte d'Ivoire + 3

The UN Consolidated Inter-Agency Appeal for Côte d'Ivoire and the three neighbouring countries of Burkina Faso, Ghana and Mali, launched in 2004, sought $64.2 million to assist 1 million beneficiaries. Of the total amount, 32 per cent ($20.5 million) was received from the donor community.

In 2004, there were serious setbacks in the consolidation of peace in Côte d'Ivoire, with serious humanitarian consequences. The humanitarian response varied from zone to zone. Humanitarian needs were the most urgent in the West, where security remained precarious. In the North, although the humanitarian situation remained relatively stable, multi-assessment reports indicated that, depending on the harvest, food scarcity could be a problem in early 2005. In the centre of the country, around Yamoussoukro, humanitarian agencies continued to grapple with the needs of IDPs, as Government resources to respond to those needs diminished greatly. The humanitarian situation was also characterized by the limited return of civil servants to run health clinics, schools and other services in the west and north; increased intra-community tensions and clashes, particularly in the West; decreased food production; the proliferation of small arms and the presence of militia in various parts of the country; and increased violation of human rights and international humanitarian law.

The situation in Côte d'Ivoire continued to affect Burkina Faso, one of the world's least developed countries. The return of some 360,000 Burkina nationals from Côte d'Ivoire demonstrated the country's capacity to coordinate emergency aid and absorb large population groups. However, a renewed mass influx of returning nationals living in Côte d'Ivoire, combined with the consequences of the subregional locust invasion could have a devastating impact on social cohesiveness, social services, economic performance and subregional peace. The proliferation of small arms and light weapons across Burkina Faso's borders increased insecurity significantly in various regions, especially along the border with Côte d'Ivoire and could further erode an already fragile situation.

As the crisis in Côte d'Ivoire continued to affect the economy in Mali, another least developed country, basic social services, particularly along the border areas, deteriorated. Furthermore, the subregional locust invasion was expected to destroy up to 440,000 tons (14 per cent) of the total harvest in Mali, which relied heavily on agricultural production. While some 3,000 refugees were living in Mali, around 10,000 transiting migrants and 120,000-150,000 returning Malian residents from Côted'Ivoire put pressure on the already fragile delivery of basic social services. The influx of small arms and light weapons had also increased insecurity in areas along the border with Algeria, Mauritania and Niger.

Ghana remained affected by the situation in Côte d'Ivoire. Though it only received some 4,500 refugees during the Côte d'Ivoire crisis, it had temporarily accommodated a large number of transiting populations on their way home to Burkina Faso and Mali.

Guinea

The UN Consolidated Inter-Agency Appeal for Guinea, launched for a total of $36 million in 2004, received 65 per cent ($23.4 million) of the requirement.

The deterioration of the socio-economic and political situation in Guinea, the inability of the local authorities to provide basic social services to the populations, combined with inadequate funding levels and the lack of consolidated and verifiable vulnerability data were major humanitarian challenges in 2004. However, significant progress was made with regard to refugee assistance, with the last group of 92,920 Sierra Leonean refugees repatriated and a memorandum of understanding provided for the integration of the remaining caseload of 1,814 Sierra Leoneans. The repatriation of 73,026 Liberians started in October, and about 1,385 separated or unaccompanied children were assisted. Assistance was also provided to host communities and indirectly to returnees and IDPs.

Liberia

The UN Consolidated Inter-Agency Appeal for Liberia sought $138 million for 2004 and received 58 per cent ($80.2 million) of that amount from the donor community.

Liberia saw significant improvements in security, stability and access. However, a climate of political instability and relative insecurity remained in certain areas of the country. The progressive deployment of UN peacekeeping forces substantially increased access to vulnerable groups, thus allowing humanitarian actors to increase efforts to meet the most critical needs, but new challenges were emerging with the imminent return of hundreds of thousands of IDPs, ex-combatants and refugees.

(See also p. 929 under "Special economic assistance".)

Sierra Leone

The UN Transitional Appeal for Relief and Recovery for Sierra Leone sought some $60 million in 2004. Of that amount, 62 per cent ($38 million) was received from the donor community.

Voluntary repatriation to Sierra Leone was completed in June, and the country continued its reconstruction efforts. The disarmament, demobilization and rehabilitation process was relatively successful, with a few exceptions regarding the integration of female combatants. The reintegration of former fighters would continue to pose challenges in Sierra Leone, with its fragile economy that offered few prospects for young and unemployed people.

Malawi

The Secretary-General, in his August consolidated report [A/59/293], provided information on humanitarian and rehabilitation assistance to Malawi. As the consolidated appeal for Southern Africa covering the period from July 2003 to June 2004 [YUN 2003, p. 931] came to an end, the UN system would continue to work with the Government of Malawi to address the triple threat of HIV/AIDS, food insecurity and weakened capacity for governance through both humanitarian and development interventions. The UN system would support the Government in its disaster management efforts, including the development of a national disaster management plan and operations manual; the preparation of contingency plans for vulnerable districts; the elaboration of an emergency recovery programme integrating issues related to HIV/AIDS and other diseases; and the promotion of bilateral and other funding partner involvement to address vulnerability in an integrated and comprehensive manner.

Zimbabwe

The UN Consolidated Inter-Agency Appeal for Zimbabwe sought $90 million for 2004. Of that amount, 11 per cent ($10.1 million) was received from the donor community.

Zimbabwe was experiencing a multi-dimensional decline, which resulted from a number of inter-related factors, including increased vulnerability to climatic fluctuations and the shock of drought, the HIV/AIDS pandemic and a constrained policy environment. Those factors were eroding household self-reliance, economic productivity and the quality of public services. In addition, coping mechanisms increasingly relied on the unsustainable use of natural resources. The cumulative effect left the country in a serious humanitarian situation.

Asia

Afghanistan

In response to resolution 58/27 B [YUN 2003, p. 934], the Secretary-General, in a November report covering the period from 1 December 2003 to 22 November 2004 [A/59/581-S/2004/925], described key political and humanitarian developments in Afghanistan. (For political aspects, see p. 311.)

The Afghan Government's capacity remained weak in terms of public administration, institutions, its ability to extend its development plans to provincial governments and the delivery of essential services. The uncertain security situation and the development of a parallel and illicit narco-economy exacerbated that weakness and seriously challenged further economic and institutional development. The core development budget of $609 million was fully financed and, in addition to national priority programmes, new programmes were being developed for the urban, justice and private sectors and for skills development. The UN country team, with the Government, NGOs, donor communities and international financial institutions, conducted Afghanistan's first common country assessment, an in-depth analysis of the country's development challenges and their root causes, covering institutional development and governance; peace, security and justice; economic development and growth; and social well-being.

The year 2004 marked the sixth year of below-average rainfall and snowfall in Afghanistan, exacerbating the country's chronic water shortage, and resulting in reduced crop yields and increased grain costs. Vulnerable populations, totalling an estimated 4 million people, were identified in localized pockets in at least 27 provinces. In line with the strategy prepared by the Ministry of Health, the United Nations Children's Fund (UNICEF) and other UN agencies, the international community was supporting the Government in rebuilding the primary health-care system, with a particular focus on obstetric care and reproductive and child health. In education, the Government's strategic focus in 2004 was on improving the quality and content of the education package, with significant UNICEF support. The net enrolment rate for Afghan children between the ages of 7 and 13 increased to 54 per cent (67 per cent for boys, 37 per cent for girls), but a number of factors continued to impede larger enrolment. Ongoing rural infrastructure development, coordinated by the Ministry of Rural Rehabilitation and Development and supported by the Untied Nations Development Programme (UNDP), included the construction of houses for returning refugees and internally displaced persons; road, school and clinic construction; agricultural development; and economic reintegration projects.

Between January and October 2004, some 740,000 people returned to Afghanistan under the voluntary and assisted repatriation programme supported by the Ministry of Refugees and Repatriation and UNHCR. However, lack of employment and slow progress in reconstruction in rural areas posed a continuing challenge to the sustainable reintegration of returnees, and the increased returns to urban areas placed an additional burden on the already stretched infrastructure capacity of major cities. The UN Mine Action Centre for Afghanistan facilitated the transfer of responsibility for mine action in Afghanistan from the United Nations to a national mine-action coordination agency. Since January 2003, 33 square kilometres of minefields and 69 square kilometres of battlefields had been cleared, and a total of 2,354,244 mines and pieces of unexploded ordnance had been destroyed.

GENERAL ASSEMBLY ACTION

On 8 December [meeting 69], the General Assembly adopted **resolution 59/112 B** [draft: A/59/L.44 & Add.1] without vote [agenda items 27 & 39 (d)].

Emergency international assistance for peace, normalcy and reconstruction of war-stricken Afghanistan

The General Assembly,

Recalling its resolution 58/27 B of 5 December 2003 and its previous relevant resolutions,

Recalling also the agreement reached among various Afghan groups in Bonn, Germany, on 5 December 2001, the International Conference on Reconstruction Assistance to Afghanistan, held in Tokyo on 21 and 22 January 2002, and the International Conference on Afghanistan, held in Berlin on 31 March and 1 April 2004,

Welcoming the adoption of a new constitution for Afghanistan on 4 January 2004 and the historic presidential elections held on 9 October 2004,

Welcoming also the continuing and growing ownership of the rehabilitation and reconstruction efforts by the Government of Afghanistan through the National Development Framework, the "Securing Afghanistan's future" exercise and the national budget, and emphasizing the crucial need to achieve ownership in all fields of governance and to improve institutional capabilities in order to use aid more effectively,

Welcoming further the efforts of the Government of Afghanistan to develop a poverty reduction strategy paper as an integrated part of the national development plans,

Welcoming, in this regard, the guarantee of human rights and fundamental freedoms for all Afghans in the new Constitution as a significant step towards an improved situation of human rights and fundamental freedoms, in particular for women and children,

Noting, at the same time, reports about incidents of violations of human rights and of international humanitarian law and violent or discriminatory practices in parts of the country,

Alarmed by continued attacks on Afghan civilians, United Nations staff, national and international humanitarian personnel and the International Security Assistance Force,

Noting with concern that the lack of security in certain areas has caused some organizations to cease or curtail humanitarian and development operations in some parts of Afghanistan because limited access and inadequate security conditions for the delivery of aid hampered their work substantially,

Welcoming the continuous return of refugees and internally displaced persons, while noting with concern that conditions in parts of Afghanistan are not yet conducive to safe and sustainable returns to places of origin,

Remaining deeply concerned about the problem of millions of anti-personnel landmines and unexploded ordnance, which constitute a great danger for the civilian population and a major obstacle for the return of refugees and displaced populations and for the resumption of agricultural and other economic activities, the provision of humanitarian assistance and rehabilitation and reconstruction efforts,

Aware of the high vulnerability of Afghanistan to natural disasters, and mindful in particular that the Afghan people continue to suffer from a severe multi-year drought that affects more than half of the provinces of the country,

Underlining the coordinating role of the Special Representative of the Secretary-General for Afghanistan and of the United Nations Assistance Mission in Afghanistan in ensuring a seamless transition, under Afghan leadership, from humanitarian relief to the reconstruction of Afghanistan, including the cooperation of the United Nations system with other actors in the international community, in particular with the international financial institutions,

Welcoming the establishment of an executive steering committee of the provincial reconstruction teams, a high-level decision-making and consultative body that provides guidance on the management of provincial reconstruction teams and on the interaction of civilian and military actors within the framework of development and reconstruction,

Expressing its appreciation to the United Nations system and to all States and international and non-governmental organizations whose international and local staff continue to respond positively to the humanitarian needs of Afghanistan, as well as to the Secretary-General and his Emergency Relief Coordinator for mobilizing and coordinating the delivery of appropriate humanitarian assistance,

1. *Welcomes* the report of the Secretary-General and the recommendations contained therein;

2. *Urges* the Government of Afghanistan and local authorities to take all possible steps to ensure the safety, security and free movement of all United Nations and humanitarian personnel, as well as their safe and unimpeded access to all affected populations, and to protect the property of the United Nations and of humanitarian organizations, including non-governmental organizations, and calls upon the international community to continue to support the efforts of the Government of Afghanistan in the area of security in a coordinated manner;

3. *Strongly condemns* all acts of violence and intimidation directed against humanitarian personnel and United Nations and associated personnel, regrets the loss of life and physical harm, and urges the Government of Afghanistan to make every effort to identify and to bring to justice the perpetrators of attacks;

4. *Welcomes* the progress of the disarmament, demobilization and reintegration process for ex-combatants, including child soldiers, by the Government of Afghanistan and the efforts of the international community to assist in this process, and urges all Afghan parties to continue their efforts in this regard; recognizing the efforts of the Government of Afghanistan, reiterates the importance of ending the use of children contrary to international law, while welcoming the recent accession by Afghanistan to the Convention on the Rights of the Child and the Optional Protocol thereto on the involvement of children in armed conflict; and stresses the importance of the demobilization and reintegration of child soldiers and care for other war-affected children, and notes in this regard the value of preparing an action plan to address this issue;

5. *Reiterates* the importance of providing Afghan children with educational and health facilities in all parts of the country, recognizing the special needs of girls, and encourages the Government of Afghanistan, with the assistance of the international community, to expand those facilities and to promote full and equal access to them by all members of Afghan society;

6. *Welcomes* the initiative of the Government of Afghanistan to formulate a national plan of action on combating child trafficking, encourages the Government, in the formulation of the plan of action, to be guided by the Protocol to Prevent, Suppress and Punish Trafficking in Persons, Especially Women and Children, supplementing the United Nations Convention against Transnational Organized Crime, and stresses the importance of considering becoming party to this Protocol;

7. *Reminds* all Afghan parties of their commitment to the Bonn Agreement and the Berlin Declaration, and calls for the full respect of the human rights and fundamental freedoms of all, without discrimination of any kind, including on the basis of gender, ethnicity or religion, in accordance with obligations under the Afghan Constitution and international law, and commends the commitment of the Government of Afghanistan in this respect;

8. *Emphasizes again* the necessity of investigating allegations of current and past violations of human rights and of international humanitarian law, including violations committed against persons belonging to ethnic and religious minorities, as well as against women and girls, of facilitating the provision of efficient and effective remedies to the victims and of bringing the perpetrators to justice in accordance with international law;

9. *Reiterates* the important role of the Afghan Independent Human Rights Commission in the promotion and protection of human rights and fundamental freedoms, and stresses the need to expand its range of operation in all parts of Afghanistan in accordance with the Afghan Constitution;

10. *Commends* the efforts of the Government of Afghanistan to mainstream gender issues and to protect and promote the equal rights of women and men as guaranteed, inter alia, by the Convention on the Elimination of All Forms of Discrimination against Women, ratified by Afghanistan on 5 March 2003, and the Afghan Constitution, in this context welcomes the high level of participation of Afghan women in the recent presidential election, and reiterates the continued importance of the full and equal participation of women in all spheres of Afghan life;

11. *Strongly condemns* incidents of discrimination and violence against women and girls, welcomes the significant efforts by the Government of Afghanistan to counter discrimination, urges the Government to actively involve all elements of Afghan society, in particular women, in the development and implementation of relief, rehabilitation and reconstruction programmes, and encourages the collection and use of statistical data on a sex-disaggregated basis to accurately track the progress of the full integration of women into the political, economic and social life of Afghanistan;

12. *Notes with concern* that opium poppy cultivation and the related drug production and trafficking pose a serious threat to security, the rule of law and development in Afghanistan, and urges the Government of Afghanistan, in cooperation with the international community, to implement its comprehensive national drug control strategy, aimed at eliminating illicit poppy cultivation, supporting increased law enforcement, interdiction, demand reduction, eradication of illicit crops, crop substitution and other alternative livelihood and development programmes, increasing public awareness and building the capacity of drug control institutions, and to promote the development of sustainable livelihoods in the formal production sector as well as other sectors, thus improving substantially the lives, health and security of the people, particularly in rural areas;

13. *Expresses its appreciation* to those Governments that continue to host Afghan refugees, acknowledging the huge burden they have so far shouldered in this regard, and reminds them of their obligations under international refugee law with respect to the protection of refugees and the right to seek asylum and to allow international access for their protection and care;

14. *Calls upon* the Government of Afghanistan, acting with the support of the international community, to continue its efforts to create the conditions for the voluntary, safe, dignified and sustainable return of the remaining Afghan refugees and internally displaced persons;

15. *Stresses* the need for further progress on judicial reform in Afghanistan, and urges the Government of Afghanistan and the international community to devote resources also to the reconstruction and reform of the prison sector in order to improve the respect for the rule of law and human rights therein, while reducing physical and mental health risks to inmates;

16. *Urges* the Government of Afghanistan to meet its responsibilities under the Convention on the Prohibition of the Use, Stockpiling, Production and Transfer of Anti-personnel Mines and on Their Destruction, to cooperate fully with the mine action programme coordinated by the United Nations, and to execute the destruction of all existing stocks of anti-personnel landmines;

17. *Welcomes* the generous commitments made in Berlin at the International Conference on Afghanistan, and urges donors to follow through on their pledges;

18. *Urges* the international community to channel assistance through the national budget, including by contributing to the Afghanistan Reconstruction Trust Fund and the Law and Order Trust Fund, which are not adequately funded, and to generously support the national priority programmes of the Government of Afghanistan in order to strengthen ownership, transparency and the functioning of basic State institutions;

19. *Urges* the Government of Afghanistan to continue to effectively reform the public administration sector and to ensure good governance, the rule of law and accountability at all levels, both national and local;

20. *Welcomes* the initiative taken by the Government of Afghanistan in setting out priorities and development programmes and in national development, reconstruction and regional integration, and calls upon the international community to support Afghanistan in this regard;

21. *Urgently appeals* to all States, the United Nations system and international and non-governmental organizations to continue to provide, in close coordination with the Government of Afghanistan and in accordance with its national development strategy, all possible and necessary humanitarian, financial, technical and material assistance for Afghanistan;

22. *Emphasizes* the need to establish, maintain and strengthen civil-military relations among international actors, as appropriate, at all levels in order to ensure complementarity of action based on the different mandates and comparative advantages of humanitarian, development, law enforcement and military actors in Afghanistan;

23. *Invites* all States and intergovernmental and non-governmental organizations providing assistance to Afghanistan to emphasize capacity-building, institution-building and local employment generation in their work and to ensure that such work complements and contributes to the development of an economy characterized by sound macroeconomic policies, the development of a financial sector that provides services, inter alia, to microenterprises, small and medium-sized enterprises and households, transparent business regulations, accountability, good governance and the rule of law;

24. *Requests* that existing capacity-building programmes and projects be sufficiently funded in order to strengthen, inter alia, the capacity of Afghanistan to respond to natural disasters, in particular long-term drought;

25. *Requests* the Secretary-General to report to the General Assembly every six months during its fifty-ninth session on developments in Afghanistan, including, after parliamentary elections, on the future role of the United Nations Assistance Mission in Afghanistan, and to report to the Assembly at its sixtieth session on the progress made in the implementation of the present resolution;

26. *Decides* to include in the provisional agenda of its sixtieth session the sub-item entitled "Emergency international assistance for peace, normalcy and reconstruction of war-stricken Afghanistan".

In **resolution 59/112 A** of the same date, the Assembly called on the international community to assist Afghanistan in the implementation of its comprehensive national drug control strategy. It also called for continued international assistance to Afghan refugees and IDPs.

Democratic People's Republic of Korea

The UN Consolidated Inter-Agency Appeal for the Democratic People's Republic of Korea (DPRK), launched for a total of $208.8 million to cover assistance in 2004, received 73 per cent ($151.5 million).

On 22 April, two train wagons exploded in Ryongchon, DPRK, killing 161 people and injuring 1,300. The explosion caused major damage to housing and infrastructure, including schools and medical facilities, and destroyed or rendered unsafe 1,850 dwellings, leaving an estimated 8,000 people homeless. The impact of the disaster was magnified by continuing economic difficulties and ongoing deficiencies in the health sector. Large segments of the population were confronted with a serious reduction in purchasing power, resulting in increased food insecurity. At the same time, the quality and quantity of basic social services continued to diminish, and food aid contributions became erratic. Funding shortfalls caused major interruptions in food aid, resulting in the World Food Programme (WFP) having to remove up to 3 million beneficiaries from its assistance programme. In August, the Government announced that it would not support the consolidated appeal for 2005.

Indonesia

The UN Consolidated Inter-Agency Appeal for Indonesia, which sought $40.4 million in 2004, received 30 per cent ($12.1 million) of the requirements.

In Indonesia, the Indian Ocean earthquake and resulting tsunami of 26 December (see p. 952) affected primarily the Aceh region, destroying homes and buildings up to 5 kilometres inland, and damaging roads and bridges, telecommunications, water and electricity supplies, crops, irrigation and fishery infrastructure, food and fuel outlets. Some 80,000 Indonesians lost their lives, and an estimated 2 million people were in need as a result of the wider impact of the disaster.

Palestine

The UN Consolidated Inter-Agency Appeal for the Occupied Palestinian Territory, which sought $300.5 million in 2004, received 58 per cent ($174 million) of the requirements.

Palestinian living standards continued to deteriorate in 2004. The decline in consumption, and educational and health standards was caused primarily by Israel's imposition of heavy movement restrictions, known as closures, which severely impeded economic activity and prevented many Palestinians from accessing essential services. The humanitarian crisis was characterized by poverty, malnutrition, a collapse in output, and widespread destruction of infrastructure.

Tajikistan

In response to General Assembly resolution 57/103 [YUN 2002, p. 903], the Secretary-General, in his August consolidated report [A/59/293], provided information on humanitarian and rehabilitation assistance to Tajikistan.

The Secretary-General stated that, despite the overall improvement in security and positive economic growth indicators for the country as a whole, disparities in Tajikistan were not diminishing, and there had been little recent change in the humanitarian context for the most vulnerable groups. The coping mechanisms of communities had been stretched far beyond their limits, and most of the population continued to live in poverty. The goal of improving food security was being addressed through a multifaceted, inter-agency approach. Closer ties were forged between agencies providing relief-oriented aid and those involved in development, community mobilization and credit initiatives.

The Secretary-General observed that the crisis situation that gave rise to the provision of special economic assistance in Tajikistan and three other countries covered in the consolidated report, namely Comoros (see p. 282), Mozambique (see p. 281) and Serbia and Montenegro (see p. 404), had essentially stabilized. Accordingly, he recommended that, following the debate on special economic assistance to individual countries or regions at the Assembly's fifty-ninth (2004) session, the Assembly no longer consider the situation in those countries under that agenda item.

The UN Consolidated Inter-Agency Appeal for Tajikistan, which sought $39.2 million in 2004, received 55 per cent ($21.5 million) of that amount.

Europe

North Caucasus (Russian Federation)

The UN Consolidated Inter-Agency Appeal for Chechnya and Neighbouring Republics (North Caucasus–Russian Federation) sought $61.4 million in 2004. Of that amount, 75 per cent ($45.8 million) was received.

The situation in Chechnya and neighbouring republics continued to be complex and unstable. An unpredictable series of violent confrontations and acts of terror hit the North Caucasus, leaving hundreds of people killed and injured, including civilians, law enforcement officials and non-State combatants. Human rights organizations and eyewitnesses in Chechnya continued to report human rights violations, including arbitrary arrests, extra-judicial executions and torture. The unstable environment limited improvements to the humanitarian situation. Unemployment and poverty remained high. The most significant humanitarian development in 2004 was the increased rate of the return of IDPs to Chechnya.

Special economic assistance

African economic recovery and development

New Partnership for Africa's Development

The General Assembly, by resolution 57/7 [YUN 2002, 910], endorsed the Secretary-General's recommendation [ibid., p. 909] that the New Partnership for Africa's Development (NEPAD), adopted in 2001 by the Assembly of Heads of State and Government of the Organization of African Unity (AU) [YUN 2001, p. 900], should be the framework within which the international community should concentrate its efforts for Africa's development.

Report of Secretary-General. The Secretary-General, responding to a 2003 request of the Committee for Programme and Coordination (CPC) [YUN 2003, p. 939], submitted a March report [E/AC.51/2004/6] on UN system support for NEPAD, which detailed the individual and collective activities undertaken by UN system entities. It also described recent efforts at resource mobilization for NEPAD priorities, and challenges and constraints faced by the UN system in supporting the Partnership. UN system support for NEPAD was organized around six clusters that broadly corresponded to the Partnership's priorities: infrastructure development; governance, peace and security; agriculture, trade and market access; environment, population and urbanization; human resources development, employment and HIV/AIDS; and science and technology. The Secretary-General concluded that, in order to ensure the effectiveness of continued UN system support to NEPAD, the UN system should use the existing coordination mechanisms at the global, regional and country levels to strengthen policy coherence in support of the Partnership; UN system entities should deepen their collaboration to achieve operational coherence of their programmes in support of NEPAD; and additional resources should be made available to the system to better support the Partnership.

CPC action. CPC, at its forty-fourth session (7 June–2 July) [A/59/16], noted the Secretary-General's report on UN system support for NEPAD. CPC recommended that the UN system use existing coordination at all levels to strengthen policy coherence in support of NEPAD, and mobilize sufficient resources to fund activities to support it. CPC further recommended that the General Assembly request the Secretary-General to report to the Committee at its forty-fifth session on further future engagement of the UN system with NEPAD.

ECONOMIC AND SOCIAL COUNCIL ACTION

On 21 July [meeting 47], the Economic and Social Council, on the recommendation of the Commission for Social Development [E/2004/26], adopted **resolution 2004/16** without vote [agenda item 14 (*b*)].

Implementation of the social objectives of the New Partnership for Africa's Development

The Economic and Social Council,

Recalling the World Summit for Social Development, held in Copenhagen from 6 to 12 March 1995, and the twenty-fourth special session of the General Assembly, entitled "World Summit for Social Development and beyond: achieving social development for all in a globalizing world", held in Geneva from 26 June to 1 July 2000,

Recalling also General Assembly resolution 56/218 of 21 December 2001, by which the Assembly established the Ad Hoc Committee of the Whole of the General Assembly for the Final Review and Appraisal of the Implementation of the United Nations New Agenda for the Development of Africa in the 1990s to conduct, during the fifty-seventh session of the Assembly, the final review and appraisal of the New Agenda and related initiatives on the basis of the report of the Secretary-General on the independent high-level quality evaluation, as well as on the basis of proposals by the Secretary-General on the modalities of the future engagement of the United Nations with the New Partnership for Africa's Development, and Assembly resolution 56/508 of 27 June 2002,

Reaffirming the United Nations Millennium Declaration of 8 September 2000, the United Nations Declaration on the New Partnership for Africa's Development of 16 September 2002 and General Assembly resolution 57/7 of 4 November 2002 on the final review and appraisal of the United Nations New Agenda for the Development of Africa in the 1990s and support for the New Partnership for Africa's Development,

Recalling General Assembly resolution 58/233 of 23 December 2003 entitled "New Partnership for Africa's Development: progress in implementation and inter-

national support", in which the Assembly, inter alia, welcomed the creation of the Office of the Special Adviser on Africa and requested the Secretary-General to continue to take measures to strengthen the Office to enable it to effectively fulfil its mandate,

Welcoming the adoption of chapter VIII entitled "Sustainable development for Africa" of the Johannesburg Plan of Implementation adopted at the World Summit on Sustainable Development, held in Johannesburg, South Africa, from 26 August to 4 September 2002,

Cognizant of the link between the priorities of the New Partnership and the Millennium Declaration, in which the international community committed itself to addressing the special needs of Africa, and of the need to achieve the internationally agreed development goals, including those set out in the Millennium Declaration,

Bearing in mind the reports of the Secretary-General of 20 June 1995 and 12 June 2001 submitted to the high-level segments of the Economic and Social Council devoted to the consideration of the development of Africa,

Bearing in mind also that, while the primary responsibility for the development of Africa remains with African countries, the international community has a stake in it and in supporting the efforts of those countries in that regard,

Noting with appreciation the commitment of the international community in its support of the New Partnership, and welcoming in this regard the outcome of the third Tokyo International Conference on African Development, held in Tokyo from 29 September to 1 October 2003,

Underlining the fact that international cooperation based on a spirit of partnership and solidarity among all countries contributes to the creation of an enabling environment for the achievement of the goals of social development,

Recognizing the urgent need to continue to assist African countries in their efforts to diversify their economies as well as enhance capacity-building and promote regional cooperation, and noting in this context the outcome of the fourth Pan-African Conference of Ministers of Public Service, held in Stellenbosch, South Africa, from 4 to 7 May 2003,

Recognizing also the serious challenges facing social development in Africa, in particular illiteracy, poverty and HIV/AIDS, the scourge of malaria and other major communicable diseases,

1. *Emphasizes* that economic development, social development and environmental protection are interdependent and mutually reinforcing components of sustainable development;

2. *Recognizes* that, while social development is primarily the responsibility of Governments, international cooperation and assistance are essential for the full achievement of that goal;

3. *Reiterates* the importance of all human rights and fundamental freedoms, including the right to development;

4. *Reaffirms* the need to strengthen, in a spirit of partnership, inter alia, international, regional and subregional cooperation for social development and the implementation of the outcome of the World Summit for Social Development and the twenty-fourth special

session of the General Assembly, entitled "World Summit for Social Development and beyond: achieving social development for all in a globalizing world";

5. *Also reaffirms* the need for effective partnership and cooperation between Governments and the relevant actors of civil society for the achievement of social development;

6. *Welcomes* the New Partnership for Africa's Development as a socio-economic programme of the African Union that embodies the vision and commitment of all African Governments and peoples;

7. *Also welcomes* the commitment of African countries to peace, security, democracy, good governance, human rights and sound economic management, as well as their commitment to taking concrete measures to strengthen the mechanism for conflict prevention, management and resolution, as embodied in the New Partnership, as an essential basis for sustainable development in Africa, and in this context welcomes the ongoing efforts of African countries to develop further the African peer review mechanism, which is an important and innovative feature of the New Partnership;

8. *Notes* the progress made with respect to the African peer review mechanism, in particular the accession of a number of member States of the African Union to the mechanism, as well as the appointment of the Panel of Eminent Persons;

9. *Stresses* the need for renewed political will at the national, regional and international levels to invest in people and their well-being in order to achieve the objectives of social development;

10. *Emphasizes* that democracy, respect for all human rights and fundamental freedoms and transparent and accountable governance and administration in all sectors of society, as well as effective participation by civil society, are among the indispensable foundations for the realization of social and people-centred sustainable development;

11. *Also emphasizes* the objectives of the New Partnership to eradicate poverty in Africa and to place African countries, both individually and collectively, on a path of sustainable growth and development, thus facilitating Africa's participation in the globalization process;

12. *Underlines* the need for effective partnership and cooperation between Governments and the relevant actors of civil society, including non-governmental organizations and the private sector, in the implementation of and follow-up to the Copenhagen Declaration on Social Development and the Programme of Action of the World Summit for Social Development and the twenty-fourth special session of the General Assembly, and the need for ensuring, within the framework of the New Partnership, their involvement in the planning, elaboration, implementation and evaluation of social policies at the national, regional and international levels;

13. *Welcomes with appreciation* actions already under way at the regional level to organize the activities of the United Nations system around thematic clusters covering the priority areas of the New Partnership, and in that regard urges the strengthening of that process as a means of enhancing the coordinated response of the United Nations system in support of the New Partnership;

14. *Stresses*, in that context, the vital need for the United Nations in assisting Member States to achieve the development objectives and targets of the United Nations Millennium Declaration and to mainstream them in an integrated and coordinated manner in United Nations development activities;

15. *Recognizes* that illiteracy, poverty, HIV/AIDS, the scourge of malaria and other major communicable diseases add challenges to Africa's development, and urges the international community to continue to increase its assistance to African countries in their efforts to address these challenges;

16. *Notes* the African Union declaration on the implementation of the New Partnership for Africa's Development of July 2003, in which the African Union recognized the need for the formal integration of the New Partnership into its structures and processes, as well as the need to sustain the momentum, genuine interest, support and solidarity created by the New Partnership;

17. *Urges* the international community and the United Nations system to organize support for African countries in accordance with the principles, objectives and priorities of the New Partnership in the new spirit of partnership;

18. *Invites* the international financial institutions to ensure that their support for Africa is compatible with the principles, objectives and priorities of the New Partnership in the new spirit of partnership;

19. *Urges* the United Nations system, in coordinating its activities at the national, regional and global levels, to foster a coherent response, including through close collaboration with bilateral donors in the implementation of the New Partnership, in response to the needs of individual countries within its larger framework;

20. *Welcomes* the decision of the General Assembly to invite the Economic and Social Council, pursuant to its role in respect of system-wide coordination, to consider how to support the objectives of Assembly resolution 57/7;

21. *Calls upon* the Secretary-General, in his efforts to harmonize current initiatives on Africa, to enhance coordination between the United Nations and its specialized agencies, programmes and funds;

22. *Acknowledges* the reflection by the Secretary-General of the social dimensions of the New Partnership in his report on the priority theme "National and international cooperation for social development" to the Commission for Social Development at its forty-first session, and invites him to continue to reflect those dimensions in future reports submitted to the Commission on its priority themes;

23. *Invites* all development partners, including regional and international development partners and the United Nations system, to support the governance and public administration programme and the Pan-African Conference of Ministers of Public Service through the provision of critical resources and collaboration in building the capacity of local institutions and their staff to ensure sustainability into the future, as outlined in the Stellenbosch Declaration;

24. *Acknowledges* the linkage between the work of the Committee of African Ministers of Public Service and the programmatic thrust of the New Partnership;

25. *Recommends* that the Commission for Social Development continue to give prominence to the social

dimensions of the New Partnership in its future priority themes;

26. *Decides* to bring the present resolution to the attention of the General Assembly at its fifty-ninth session during its consideration of the agenda item entitled "New Partnership for Africa's Development: progress in implementation and international support".

Report of Secretary-General. In response to General Assembly resolution 58/233 [YUN 2003, p. 941], the Secretary-General, in August, submitted to the Assembly the second consolidated report [A/59/206] on progress made to implement and support NEPAD, highlighting policy measures and actions taken by African countries and organizations and the response of the international community and UN system support.

According to the report, many countries faced severe fiscal constraints in implementing NEPAD in the short to medium term, suggesting that external support would be needed to achieve the established expenditure targets on NEPAD priorities. Implementation in the infrastructure sector was impeded by long project-approval cycles in partner institutions, limited grant resources and severe technical capacity constraints at the national and regional levels. In agriculture, despite progress in the implementation of the Comprehensive Africa Agriculture Development Programme, many countries would not meet the target of allocating 10 per cent of budgetary resources to agriculture in the next five years. The health sector was afflicted by the twofold crisis of the migration of highly trained professionals to developed countries, and health professionals in the front line of HIV/AIDS care and treatment themselves falling victim to the pandemic. In varying degrees, and in some countries, the education sector was experiencing a severe loss of professionals for the same reasons as was the health sector. In addition, the AU Commission and subregional organizations, which were required to play an important role in NEPAD implementation were also constrained financially.

On the positive side, the NEPAD Heads of State and Government Implementation Committee approved 20 top-priority short-term action plan projects in infrastructure development and capacity-building, at an estimated cost of $8.12 billion, half of which was to be financed by the private sector. The African Development Bank (ADB), which provided broad financial, institutional and programme development support for infrastructure development and other aspects of NEPAD, was preparing nine investment projects, three capacity-building projects and five studies for ABD Group financing at an estimated cost of $580 million.

In the education sector, NEPAD identified eight priority areas to address educational challenges: meeting the MDGS on basic education [YUN 2000, p. 51]; improving the quality of education; achieving gender equality in education; developing effective feeding and nutrition programmes in schools; promoting open learning, distance education for teacher development, and capacity-building in the public sector; improving mathematics and science education; assisting in the reconstruction of the educational system in post-conflict environments; and supporting member States in developing a comprehensive educational response to prevent the spread of HIV/AIDS. Its e-schools project aimed at developing a sustainable knowledge-based society in Africa by turning 600,000 primary and secondary schools into e-schools. A pilot project was launched for 6 schools in 15 countries.

A regional strategy for disaster reduction and the NEPAD Tourism Action Plan were endorsed by the AU at its third ordinary session (Addis Ababa, Ethiopia, 6-8 July). Under the Comprehensive Africa Agriculture Development Programme, the NEPAD secretariat was developing a tracking mechanism to help countries account for and evaluate their expenditures and budgetary provisions in the agricultural sector. The First NEPAD Ministerial Conference on Science and Technology (Johannesburg, South Africa, 6-7 November 2003) adopted a declaration and agreed on the outline of a plan of action to promote the development and application of science and technology and to guide the development of a coherent business plan. The African Productive Capacity Initiative, adopted by the sixteenth Conference of African Ministers of Industry [YUN 2003, p. 1005], was evolving into the policy framework of Africa's industrialization effort, and the African investment initiative was launched.

Progress was made in advancing the African Peer Review Mechanism, an instrument for African self-monitoring established by the AU in 2003 [YUN 2003, p. 938]. The work programme and rules of procedure for the African peer review panel of eminent personalities were adopted in February 2004, a separate secretariat and a trust fund for the Mechanism were established, and a schedule for the peer review of participating countries agreed upon.

The international community's response in support of NEPAD included the establishment of the African Partnership Forum for deepening the policy dialogue on support for Africa's development, which held its inaugural (Paris, France, November, 2003) and second (Maputo, Mozambique, April 2004) meetings; the establishment, in February 2004, by the Prime Minster of the United Kingdom of the Commission for Africa (see p. 993), which sought, among other things, to generate increased support for NEPAD; the extension by the 2004 G-8 summit (Sea Island, Georgia, United States, 8-10 June 2004) of the Heavily Indebted Poor Countries (HIPC) Initiative until 31 December 2006 to provide financing to complete HIPC and help the poorest countries address the sustainability of debt relief, the pledge of additional official development assistance (ODA) by Africa's developed country partners to support NEPAD implementation; the adoption by the Second International Round Table on Managing for Development Results (Marrakech, Morocco, 4-6 February 2004) of an action plan on harmonization and simplification to improve aid effectiveness; and the ongoing work of the ECA/OECD secretariat on joint review of development effectiveness. In the area of trade liberalization, China signed bilateral agreements with 40 African countries, providing reciprocal most-favoured-nation status, and awarded duty-free status to some goods exported by the least developed African countries; Canada extended the Least Developed Country Tariff for an additional 10 years by providing duty-free access to the Canadian market, with the exception of dairy products, poultry and eggs; and the United States extended its African Growth and Opportunity Act through 2015 (see p. 993). However, a fundamental challenge in international support for NEPAD was the achievement of policy coherence, which was highlighted by the lack of complementarities in debt, aid and trade policies.

In terms of UN support to NEPAD, the Secretary-General set up the Advisory Panel on International Support for NEPAD, which would review and assess the scope and adequacy of international support to the Partnership; conduct a dialogue with Africa's development partners, including the UN system, with a view to promoting support for NEPAD; and make recommendations to the Secretary-General on actions to be taken by the international community to enhance support for NEPAD implementation. UN system support also included technical assistance for institutional development, capacity-building, project development, resource mobilization and advocacy. However, that support was constrained by a lack of financial resources, which limited the scope and prospect of joint activities.

The Secretary-General concluded that a strengthened partnership was needed, in which African countries deepened their commitments to NEPAD priorities and NEPAD development partners targeted measures and actions to give the Partnership a major impetus. Africa's devel-opment partners could give further practical expression to their support of the efforts of African countries by creating an enabling environment that was supportive of growth and development, bringing much-needed coherence to trade, aid and foreign debt policies, and accelerating NEPAD's implementation by making significant financial outlays to fund its key sectoral priorities.

GENERAL ASSEMBLY ACTION

On 23 December [meeting 76], the General Assembly adopted **resolution 59/254** [draft: A/59/L.33/Rev.1 & Add.1] without vote [agenda item 38 (a)].

New Partnership for Africa's Development: progress in implementation and international support

The General Assembly,

Recalling its resolution 57/2 of 16 September 2002 on the United Nations Declaration on the New Partnership for Africa's Development,

Recalling also its resolution 57/7 of 4 November 2002 on the final review and appraisal of the United Nations New Agenda for the Development of Africa in the 1990s and support for the New Partnership for Africa's Development and resolution 58/233 of 23 December 2003 entitled "New Partnership for Africa's Development: progress in implementation and international support",

Bearing in mind that African countries have primary responsibility for their own economic and social development and that the role of national policies and development strategies cannot be overemphasized, also the need for their development efforts to be supported by an enabling international economic environment, and in this regard recalling the support given by the International Conference on Financing for Development to the New Partnership,

Having considered the report of the Secretary-General entitled "New Partnership for Africa's Development: second consolidated report on progress in implementation and international support",

1. *Takes note* of the report of the Secretary-General;

2. *Reaffirms its full support* for the implementation of the New Partnership for Africa's Development;

3. *Also reaffirms its full support* for the implementation of the Declaration of Commitment on HIV/AIDS, adopted at the twenty-sixth special session of the General Assembly on 27 June 2001;

4. *Recognizes* the progress made in the implementation of the New Partnership as well as regional and international support for the New Partnership, while acknowledging that much needs to be done in the implementation of the New Partnership;

5. *Welcomes* the establishment of a Peace and Security Council within the African Union, stresses that conflict prevention, management and resolution and post-conflict consolidation are essential for the achievement of the objectives of the New Partnership, and welcomes, in this regard, the cooperation and support granted by the United Nations and development partners to the African regional and subregional organizations in the implementation of the New Partnership;

I
Actions by African countries and organizations

6. *Welcomes* the progress made by the African countries in fulfilling their commitments in the implementation of the New Partnership to deepen democracy, human rights, good governance and sound economic management, and encourages African countries, with the participation of stakeholders, including civil society and the private sector, to continue their efforts in this regard by developing and strengthening institutions for governance and the development of the region;

7. *Also welcomes* the progress that has been achieved in implementing the African Peer Review Mechanism, including through the establishment of a trust fund to support the activities of the Mechanism, to which participating countries will make financial contributions, and the launching of support missions to several African countries;

8. *Further welcomes* the efforts made by African countries in developing sectoral policy frameworks and implementing specific programmes of the New Partnership, including by establishing expenditure targets in sectoral priority areas of the New Partnership, and encourages them to continue to integrate the priorities of the New Partnership into their national development plans and frameworks, including poverty reduction strategies, where they exist;

9. *Emphasizes* the importance for African countries of continuing to coordinate, on the basis of national strategies and priorities, all types of external assistance, including that provided by multilateral organizations, in order to integrate effectively such assistance into their development processes;

10. *Welcomes* the commitment of African countries to advance the implementation of the New Partnership, acknowledges, in this regard, the role of the Heads of State and Government Implementation Committee of the New Partnership in furthering the implementation of the New Partnership, and welcomes the New Partnership summits held so far, as well as the upcoming summits;

11. *Also welcomes* the approval by the Heads of State and Government Implementation Committee of the New Partnership of priority infrastructural and capacity-building projects to be implemented by the regional economic communities;

12. *Encourages* the further integration of the priorities and objectives of the New Partnership into the programmes of the regional structures and organizations, as well as programmes for the African least developed countries;

13. *Appreciates* the increasing efforts of African countries in mainstreaming a gender perspective and empowerment of women in the implementation of the New Partnership, and in this regard welcomes the Solemn Declaration on Gender Equality in Africa, adopted by the African Union at its third ordinary session in Addis Ababa from 6 to 8 July 2004, and encourages the African countries to track progress in the full integration of women into African social, political and economic life;

14. *Emphasizes* that progress in the implementation of the New Partnership depends also on a favourable national and international environment for Africa's growth and development, including, inter alia, measures to promote a policy environment conducive to private sector development and entrepreneurship;

II
Response of the international community

15. *Welcomes* the efforts by development partners to strengthen cooperation with the New Partnership;

16. *Acknowledges* the importance of various initiatives, such as the Tokyo International Conference on African Development process, the Africa Action Plan of the Group of Eight, initiated at Genoa, Italy, as developed at the Summit of the Group held in Kananaskis, Canada, in 2002, and furthered at their subsequent Summits held in Evian, France, in 2003, and at Sea Island, United States of America, in 2004, as well as the Africa Partnership Forum in support of the implementation of the New Partnership, emphasizes, in this regard, the importance of effective coordination of such initiatives for Africa, and looks forward to the forthcoming report of the Commission for Africa;

17. *Welcomes* the contribution made by Member States to the implementation of the New Partnership in the context of South-South cooperation;

18. *Stresses* the need to mobilize additional resources for Africa's development through promoting South-South cooperation and trade and investment as discussed at various forums, including the Asia-Africa Trade and Investment Conference, held in Tokyo on 1 and 2 November 2004, under the auspices of the Tokyo International Conference on African Development;

19. *Welcomes* the financial support extended by many of the development partners to the various programmes of the New Partnership, and in this regard notes with satisfaction that some developed countries have committed resources for the infrastructure project preparation facility of the New Partnership and have provided resources for institutional strengthening activities at the secretariat of the New Partnership and in some regional economic communities;

20. *Recalls* that regional economic communities have a critical role to play in the implementation of the New Partnership, and encourages development partners to increase their support to enhance the capacities of these communities;

21. *Urges* continued attention to the need to continue to take measures to address the challenges of poverty eradication and sustainable development in Africa, including, as appropriate, debt relief, improved market access, support for the private sector and entrepreneurship, enhanced official development assistance and increased flows of foreign direct investment, as well as transfer of technology;

22. *Reiterates* the need for the international community, relevant multilateral institutions and developed countries to enhance coherence in their trade, investment, aid and debt policies towards African countries;

23. *Stresses* the need to find comprehensive solutions for the debt problems of African countries, and in this regard welcomes the decision to extend the sunset clause of the Heavily Indebted Poor Countries Initiative until 31 December 2006 and the ongoing work by the International Monetary Fund and the World Bank to develop a forward-looking debt sustainability

framework for heavily indebted poor countries and low-income countries;

24. *Welcomes* the recent increase in official development assistance by many of the development partners, and urges all development partners to make continued efforts to increase the flows of all resources, public and private, to support the development of African countries and to improve the effectiveness of aid;

25. *Also welcomes* efforts by development partners to align their financial and technical support to Africa more closely to the priorities of the New Partnership, as reflected in national poverty reduction strategies or in similar strategies, and encourages development partners to increase their efforts in this regard;

26. *Acknowledges* the activities of the Bretton Woods institutions and the African Development Bank in African countries, and invites those institutions to continue their support for the implementation of the priorities and objectives of the New Partnership;

27. *Requests* the United Nations system to continue to provide assistance to the secretariat of the New Partnership and to African countries in developing projects and programmes within the scope of the priorities of the New Partnership;

28. *Notes* that the entities of the United Nations system have been actively using the regional consultation mechanism as a vehicle for fostering collaboration and coordination at the regional level, and encourages them to intensify their efforts in developing and implementing joint programmes in support of the New Partnership at the regional level;

29. *Encourages* the United Nations funds, programmes and specialized agencies to continue to strengthen further their existing coordination and programming mechanisms, as well as the simplification and harmonization of planning, disbursement and reporting procedures, as a means of enhancing support for African countries in the implementation of the New Partnership;

30. *Notes* the growing collaboration among the entities of the United Nations system in support of the New Partnership, and requests the Secretary-General to promote greater coherence in the work of the United Nations system in support of the New Partnership, on the basis of the agreed clusters;

31. *Invites* the High-level Plenary Meeting, which is to be held at the commencement of the sixtieth session of the General Assembly, in accordance with the modalities set by the Assembly at its fifty-ninth session, to address the special needs of African countries;

32. *Urges* the Commission for Social Development and the Commission on the Status of Women to give prominence to the New Partnership in future priority themes;

33. *Welcomes* the establishment of the Secretary-General's Advisory Panel on International Support for the New Partnership for Africa's Development, and looks forward to its recommendations on the actions to be taken to enhance support for the implementation of the New Partnership;

34. *Requests* the Secretary-General to continue to take measures to strengthen the Office of the Special Adviser on Africa in order to enable it to effectively fulfil its mandate;

35. *Also requests* the Secretary-General to submit a comprehensive report on the implementation of the present resolution to the General Assembly at its sixtieth session on the basis of inputs from Governments, organizations of the United Nations system and other stakeholders in the New Partnership, such as the private sector and civil society.

Angola

In response to General Assembly resolution 57/102 [YUN 2002, p. 913], the Secretary-General, in his August consolidated report [A/59/293], provided information on humanitarian and rehabilitation assistance to Angola.

Social indicators in Angola remained very low, with the under-five mortality rate (250 per 1,000 live births) the second highest in the world, the fertility rate (7.2) one of the three highest, and adult literacy (33 per cent) comparable with the average for sub-Saharan Africa (38 per cent). As part of the drive to improve education, and in a step towards achievement of the MDG on education [YUN 2000, p. 51], the Government recruited 29,154 teachers in 2003 to support the return of some 1 million children to school.

The prevalence rate for HIV/AIDS was officially estimated at about 5.5 per cent, but the lack of statistical data and the limited number of surveillance centres meant that the true rate was probably much higher. With UN support, the Government undertook, in 2004, the first national seroprevalence survey and approved its National Law and Strategic Plan to Fight against HIV/AIDS, which aimed to strengthen national-level coordination among governmental, civil society and international partners.

Economic growth in Angola had not yet been translated into better lives for its people. According to the poverty reduction strategy paper (PRSP), 68 per cent of the population lived below the poverty line and 26 per cent was extremely poor. The defence and security ministries and general administrative services consumed the largest share of public resources (41.8 per cent), debt 27 per cent of the budget, while expenditures on health and education (6 and 11 per cent, respectively) remained low. In January, the Government approved its PRSP outlining 10 priority areas for reconstruction to be addressed by 2006. The UN system was focusing on fostering the Government's efforts towards a transition to sustainable development.

The Secretary-General concluded that, while the level of international assistance to Angola since the coming of peace remained inadequate, and donor support needed to be increased, the Government should review the way resources were being used. He recommended that: the Government's capacity be strengthened to ensure that it provided leadership in all development-oriented interventions; Member States give to Angola generously; and the United Nations continue to build alliances among civil society, government, the private sector and the donor community so that development responses were coordinated and strategically harmonized.

GENERAL ASSEMBLY ACTION

On 22 December [meeting 75], the General Assembly, on the recommendation of the Second Committee [A/59/479 & Corr.1] adopted **resolution 59/216** without vote [agenda item 39 (*b*)].

International assistance for the economic rehabilitation of Angola

The General Assembly,

Recalling all its previous resolutions in which it called upon the international community to continue to render material, technical and financial assistance for the economic rehabilitation of Angola, including resolution 57/102, adopted by consensus on 25 November 2002,

Recalling also that the Security Council, in resolution 922(1994) of 31 May 1994 and in subsequent resolutions adopted as from 2001, the President of the Security Council, in statements on Angola, and the General Assembly, in all of its resolutions on international assistance for the economic rehabilitation of Angola, have, inter alia, called upon the international community to provide economic assistance to Angola,

Bearing in mind that the main responsibility for improving the humanitarian situation and creating the conditions for long-term development and poverty reduction in Angola lies with the Government of Angola, together with, where appropriate, the participation of the international community,

Noting the importance of international engagement for the consolidation of peace in Angola,

Noting with concern that, although there are unprecedented opportunities to tackle the country's problems and achieve international and national development goals, recovery will take years as the war has had a devastating economic and social impact,

Recognizing that there is a clear relationship between emergency relief and rehabilitation and development and that in order to ensure a smooth transition from relief to rehabilitation and development, emergency assistance should be provided in ways supportive of recovery and long-term development,

Concerned about the need to mobilize adequate financial resources for emergency humanitarian assistance at all levels,

Welcoming the efforts made by the Government of Angola to improve governance, transparency and institutional capabilities and to use aid more effectively, in cooperation with the United Nations system, and encouraging continued efforts in this regard,

Noting with satisfaction the successful implementation of and effective compliance with the provisions of the Lusaka Protocol,

Taking into account the initiatives taken by the Government of Angola to allocate the human, material and financial resources to improve the social and economic situation of the population and to address the humanitarian situation, and stressing the need to allo-

cate more means towards reconstruction, rehabilitation and social and economic stabilization, with the cooperation of the international community,

Recognizing the urgent need to address as well as to increase national efforts and international support for the resettlement and reintegration of internally displaced persons as well as for the return of refugees and vulnerable groups and for their care in all parts of Angola,

Recognizing also the urgent need to address as well as to increase national efforts and international support for mine-action activities in order to enable the country to tackle the social, economic and humanitarian crises,

Noting that an economically revived and democratic Angola will contribute to regional stability,

Recalling the first Round-Table Conference of Donors, held in Brussels from 25 to 27 September 1995,

Welcoming the efforts made by donors and United Nations agencies, funds and programmes to provide humanitarian, economic and financial assistance to Angola,

1. *Takes note* of the report of the Secretary-General;

2. *Welcomes* the successful implementation of the Memorandum of Understanding additional to the Lusaka Protocol, which ended hostilities in the country and created unprecedented conditions for the re-establishment and consolidation of peace in Angola;

3. *Recognizes* the efforts undertaken by the Government of Angola, with the support of the international community, to facilitate the delivery of humanitarian assistance and to continue to work towards ensuring the maintenance of the peace and national security so necessary for the reconstruction, rehabilitation and economic stabilization of the country, and in this context encourages the Government, with the support of the international community, to continue its efforts, including the increase of budgetary allocations to the development sectors, for poverty reduction and the achievement of sustained economic growth and sustainable development;

4. *Welcomes* the adoption by the Government of Angola of the poverty reduction strategy paper, and in this regard calls upon the Government of Angola, the World Bank and the international community to remain engaged, with a view to its early endorsement by the World Bank and the Board of the International Monetary Fund, as well as the continued support of the international community to the efforts of the Government of Angola for its implementation;

5. *Recognizes* the primary responsibility of the Government of Angola for the welfare of all its citizens, including returning refugees and internally displaced persons, and calls upon Member States, in particular the donor community, including through South-South cooperation and triangular cooperation, to continue to support the remaining humanitarian needs in Angola and to assist with the return and resettlement of refugees and internally displaced persons;

6. *Welcomes* the approval of the National Law and Strategic Plan to Fight against HIV/AIDS, which aims to strengthen national coordination among governmental, civil society and international partners, encourages continued international support to assist in implementing concrete actions to help meet the goals laid out in the Declaration of Commitment on HIV/

AIDS, and in this regard notes with satisfaction the successful conclusion of the first national seroprevalence survey by the Government of Angola with the support of the international community;

7. *Requests* all national and international, regional and subregional financial institutions to provide their support to the Government of Angola in its efforts to alleviate poverty, consolidate peace and democracy and contribute to economic stability throughout the country and to implement successfully the economic development programmes and strategies;

8. *Welcomes* the continued commitment of the Government of Angola to improve governance, transparency and accountability in the management of public resources, including natural resources, encourages the Government of Angola to continue its efforts to that end, calls upon international organizations and others in a position to do so to assist the Government of Angola in this endeavour, including through the promotion of responsible business practices, and welcomes in this regard the decision of Angola to accede to the African Peer Review Mechanism;

9. *Recognizes* the progress towards the adoption of a programme to be monitored by the International Monetary Fund, and encourages the Government and the International Monetary Fund to continue to negotiate actively with a view to reaching an early agreement;

10. *Welcomes* the commitment of the Government of Angola to the strengthening of its democratic institutions, takes note in this regard of the efforts undertaken by the Government of Angola to hold elections in 2006, looks forward to the early adoption by the National Assembly of a timetable to prepare such elections, and calls upon Members States, international, regional and subregional organizations to provide financial and technical support in this regard;

11. *Requests* the Government of Angola and the United Nations, and invites the international financial institutions, to take all necessary steps for the preparation and successful organization of an international donors conference for long-term development and reconstruction, including special economic assistance;

12. *Expresses its appreciation* to the international community, the United Nations system, funds and programmes, and the governmental and non-governmental organizations that are participating in humanitarian assistance programmes in Angola, including mine-action activities, and appeals for their continued contribution to humanitarian mine-action activities in a manner complementary to that of the Government;

13. *Expresses its gratitude* to donors and United Nations agencies, funds and programmes for the assistance provided to Angola in support of initiatives and programmes for the alleviation of the humanitarian crisis and poverty eradication;

14. *Requests* the Secretary-General to submit to the General Assembly, at its sixty-first session, a report on the implementation of the present resolution.

Democratic Republic of the Congo

The Secretary-General, in his August consolidated report [A/59/293], provided information on humanitarian and rehabilitation assistance to the DRC, focusing on economic recovery, national reconstruction and the fight against HIV/AIDS.

Although the DRC's positive economic growth continued in 2003, based mainly on the extractive, transport and communications industries, the social situation scarcely improved. Seventy-three per cent of the population were in a situation of food insecurity, children suffered from malnutrition and primary school enrolment rate was just over 50 per cent. An already alarming health situation was aggravated by the HIV/AIDS pandemic which continued to spread. The DRC continued to face the challenge of overhauling its basic socio-economic structures, which were totally dilapidated and insufficient. In response, it intended implementing an expanded Emergency Multisector Rehabilitation and Reconstruction Project costing some $7 billion, and for which partner support was needed. At the same time, its institutional and human resources weaknesses, in particular in public administration and the judicial system, hindered national productivity.

The UN system helped to rehabilitate social and community infrastructures, promote income-generating activities in rural areas, develop microcredit and distribute equipment for the resumption of trade between provinces. It also helped to draw up DRC's poverty reduction strategy paper (PRSP). The Bretton Woods institutions (the World Bank Group and IMF) supported the improvement of the macroeconomic framework, the administration of public funds and the promotion of the private sector. The UN system intensified its multifaceted support for the national programme to fight HIV/AIDS, including the development of catalytic initiatives to promote safe sex among young people, prevent mother-to-child transmission, and contain the spread of HIV/AIDS within the uniformed services and among refugees.

The Secretary-General said that, despite recent growth, the DRC's economy was not strong enough to generate the resources for national reconstruction. The low level of public investment did not permit the construction of a suitable base to relaunch the economy, and foreign/private sector investment would prove ineffectual without basic economic infrastructure. Public investment should be substantially increased, while the elements that limited the country's ability to absorb it were reduced. In addition, job creation had to be put at the centre of the investment policy to revitalize domestic demand. External debt would continue to weigh heavily on national resources.

Liberia

Information on humanitarian and rehabilitation assistance to Liberia, provided by the Secretary-General, in his August consolidated report [A/59/293], revealed that an estimated 1.7 million people in the country still needed humanitarian assistance, of whom some 300,000 were living in 21 IDP camps. Since December 2003, more than 50,000 Liberian refugees had returned spontaneously, many of whom ended up in IDP camps or in returnee camps administered by UNHCR around the capital, Monrovia. UNICEF continued to work with the Ministry of Education to return 750,000 children to school, and since June 2003, UNICEF and its partners had immunized more than 1.24 million children between the ages of 6 months and 15 years. UNDP, the World Health Organization (WHO) and the United Nations Population Fund (UNFPA) supported education campaigns and communication and dissemination initiatives aimed at creating awareness of the HIV/AIDS pandemic, including among ex-combatants who were taking part in the disarmament, demobilization and reintegration process. The United Nations Human Settlements Programme (UN-Habitat) led an initiative to improve water and sanitation facilities in Liberia. The protracted conflict had severely affected agricultural production. It was estimated that food production would be considerably less than that required.

The Secretary-General stated that, if not addressed urgently and decisively, the serious security, humanitarian and development challenges facing Liberia could endanger efforts to bring sustainable peace and regional stability. The restoration of lasting peace also required that special attention be paid to other major cross-cutting problems, including the lack of economic opportunity and the disruption of livelihoods as a result of population displacement. Job opportunities had to be created for the large number of unemployed, often illiterate young men who were vulnerable to recruitment by armed groups.

GENERAL ASSEMBLY ACTION

On 22 December [meeting 75], the General Assembly, on the recommendation of the Second Committee [A/59/479 & Corr.1], adopted **resolution 59/219** without vote [agenda item 39 *(b)*].

Assistance for the rehabilitation and reconstruction of Liberia

The General Assembly,

Recalling its resolutions 45/232 of 21 December 1990, 46/147 of 17 December 1991, 47/154 of 18 December 1992, 48/197 of 21 December 1993, 49/21 E of 20 December 1994, 50/58 A of 12 December 1995,

51/30 B of 5 December 1996, 52/169 E of 16 December 1997, 53/1 I of 16 November 1998, 55/176 of 19 December 2000 and 57/151 of 16 December 2002,

Having considered the report of the Secretary-General,

Commending the Economic Community of West African States and the International Contact Group on Liberia for facilitating the signing of the Comprehensive Peace Agreement in Accra on 18 August 2003, which, inter alia, provided for the formation of the National Transitional Government of Liberia and the holding of democratic elections in October 2005, and for continuing their collaborative efforts with the transitional authority in peacebuilding and security in Liberia,

Welcoming the establishment of the United Nations Mission in Liberia in accordance with Security Council resolution 1509(2003) of 19 September 2003, whereby an enabling environment for the restoration of peace and stability in the country was created,

Also welcoming the formal completion of the disarmament and demobilization operations of the Mission on 31 October 2004 and the subsequent official dissolution of factions on 3 November 2004,

Considering that the holding of free and fair presidential and general elections in October 2005 is a vital undertaking for ensuring national unity, peacebuilding and reconstruction,

Deeply concerned about the recent violence in the city of Monrovia and its environs, which poses a serious threat to the peace process,

Recognizing the importance of a thriving private sector, employment generation, good governance and the rule of law to sustainable economic growth,

1. *Expresses its gratitude* to the Economic Community of West African States, the African Union, donor countries, specialized agencies of the United Nations system and non-governmental organizations for their valuable support in the provision of humanitarian assistance and their adoption of a comprehensive approach to peacebuilding in Liberia and the subregion;

2. *Also expresses its gratitude* to all donor countries, specialized agencies of the United Nations system and governmental and non-governmental organizations for their participation in the International Reconstruction Conference on Liberia, held at United Nations Headquarters in New York on 5 and 6 February 2004, at which the National Transitional Government presented the results-focused transition framework, and urges those who have not yet honoured their pledges and commitments to do so;

3. *Calls upon* all signatories to the Comprehensive Peace Agreement of 18 August 2003 to uphold the spirit and letter of its provisions, to seek to promote socio-economic development and a culture of sustained peace in the country, including a commitment to the rule of law, national reconciliation and human rights and to refrain from actions that may jeopardize the work of the National Transitional Government;

4. *Invites* all States and intergovernmental and non-governmental organizations to provide assistance to Liberia to facilitate the creation of an enabling environment for the promotion of peace, socio-economic development and regional security, including by emphasizing capacity-building, institution-building and employment generation in their work and ensuring

that such work complements and contributes to the development of an economy characterized by an investment climate conducive to entrepreneurship, good governance and the rule of law;

5. *Urges* the National Transitional Government to create an environment conducive to the promotion of socio-economic development, peace and security in the country, including a commitment to upholding the rule of law, national reconciliation and human rights, establishing inclusive processes that will ensure free and fair presidential and general elections in October 2005 with maximum participation of the citizenry, as well as a commitment to ensuring transparency in the management of government expenditures and donor funds;

6. *Invites* the international community to provide financial and technical assistance to the National Transitional Government to facilitate free and fair presidential and general elections in October 2005;

7. *Urges* the National Transitional Government and all States to facilitate and support the return and reintegration of ex-combatants into their home communities, with special attention to children;

8. *Commends* the Secretary-General for his continuing efforts to mobilize international assistance for the development and reconstruction of Liberia, and requests him to continue his efforts to mobilize all possible assistance within the United Nations system to help in the reconstruction and development of Liberia and in the return and reintegration of refugees, displaced persons and demobilized soldiers;

9. *Requests* the Secretary-General to report to the General Assembly at its sixty-first session on the implementation of the present resolution;

10. *Decides* to consider at its sixty-first session the question of international assistance for the rehabilitation and reconstruction of Liberia.

Mozambique

In response to General Assembly resolutions 55/167 [YUN 2000, p. 859], the Secretary-General, in a May report [A/59/86-E/2004/69], described follow-up initiatives undertaken in Mozambique in response to the drought of 2002 and 2003, preparation for and response to the spread of the HIV/AIDS pandemic, and other UN assistance initiatives in support of the Government.

Mozambique, the sixth poorest country in the world, was suffering from the compounding effects of HIV/AIDS and repeated natural disasters, including the current drought, which significantly increased the vulnerability of an already impoverished population. HIV/AIDS constituted a threat to sustainable agriculture and rural development and food security. Throughout 2003, the United Nations responded to the Government's's requests for assistance in the areas of agriculture, capacity-building, education and child protection, food supplies, health and nutrition, and water, sanitation and hygiene promotion. Following a request from the Government, the UN Country Team in Mozambique decided that

the MDGs would be the centre stage of all UN activities in 2004 and would focus on progress made under the national plan towards their achievement. In addition, the national contingency plan for 2004 was launched, with a budget of $35 million to deal with the drought, the risk of cyclones and floods. It comprised the prepositioning of stocks, building a disaster preparedness and early warning capacity, and disaster prevention. The United Nations Inter-Agency Emergency Preparedness and Response Plan for 2004 was intended to support the National Disaster Management Institute in the implementation of the national contingency plan. In light of the poor rainfall in late 2003 and early 2004, the Southern African Development Community (SADC), at a strategic assessment and disaster preparedness meeting (Maputo, Mozambique, February), made a series of recommendations, endorsed by the Mozambique Government, which called for, among other things: refined assessments to better understand the levels of vulnerability; the use of second season and winter cropping; improved emergency response by member States, the United Nations and other multilateral agencies; increased emphasis on disaster prevention, mitigation and preparedness by member States and cooperating partners; strengthening the institutional capacities of the SADC secretariat and member States in disaster management structures and functions; and the promotion of trade and markets.

The Secretary-General said that the UN Country Team in Mozambique shared the concerns and recommendations of the SADC meeting, and should continue to implement 2003 recommendations made by the Special Envoy of the Secretary-General for Humanitarian Needs in Southern Africa. In particular, the Team would, during the mid-term review of the United Nations Development Assistance Framework (UNDAF), address the severe impact of HIV/AIDS on women, girls and orphaned children, including vulnerability. A national plan for disaster management was crucial for Mozambique, and the National Institute for Disaster Management should go beyond preparing annual contingency plans and develop a national plan.

On 23 July (**decision 2004/293**), the Economic and Social Council took note of the report.

GENERAL ASSEMBLY ACTION

On 22 December [meeting 75], the General Assembly, on the recommendation of the Second Committee [A/59/479 & Corr.1], adopted **resolution 59/214** without vote [agenda item 39 (b)].

Assistance to Mozambique

The General Assembly,

Recalling Security Council resolution 386(1976) of 17 March 1976 and all relevant General Assembly resolutions, in which it urged the international community to respond effectively and generously to the call for assistance to Mozambique,

Reaffirming the principles for humanitarian assistance contained in the annex to its resolution 46/182 of 19 December 1991,

Recalling its resolutions 48/7 of 19 October 1993, 49/215 of 23 December 1994, 50/82 of 14 December 1995, 51/149 of 13 December 1996 and 52/173 of 18 December 1997 on assistance in mine action,

Recognizing that Mozambique is prone to natural disasters which can have a negative impact upon its development efforts,

Aware that, to prevent and manage natural disasters, strategies at the local, national and regional levels are required, in addition to international assistance,

Recognizing that the devastating impact of HIV/AIDS and other endemic diseases is undoing decades of economic and social development and contributing to food insecurity and the increased vulnerability of the population in Mozambique,

Recognizing also that the main responsibility for improving the humanitarian situation and creating conditions for long-term development lies with the Government of Mozambique, while bearing in mind the important role that the international community plays,

Recognizing further the efforts of the Government of Mozambique to promote peace and stability, democracy and national reconciliation as well as economic growth and socio-economic development, including the mainstreaming of internationally agreed development goals, including those contained in the United Nations Millennium Declaration, the Action Plan for the Reduction of Absolute Poverty(2001–2005) and national development plans,

Bearing in mind the Brussels Declaration and the Programme of Action for the Least Developed Countries for the Decade 2001–2010, adopted by the Third United Nations Conference on the Least Developed Countries, held in Brussels from 14 to 20 May 2001, and the mutual commitments entered into on that occasion,

Noting with appreciation the mobilization and allocation of resources by States, relevant organizations of the United Nations system and intergovernmental and non-governmental organizations to assist national development efforts,

Having considered the reports of the Secretary-General on assistance to Mozambique, and humanitarian assistance and rehabilitation for countries and regions,

1. *Takes note* of the reports of the Secretary-General and the recommendations contained therein;

2. *Commends* the Government of Mozambique for its efforts in the maintenance of peace, stability, economic growth and development and for the enhancement of democracy and the consolidation of national reconciliation in the country, and stresses the importance of further consolidation and enhancement of those efforts;

3. *Takes note* of the launching by the Government of Mozambique of the national contingency plan for natural disasters to improve disaster prevention, mitigation, preparedness and management, and invites the international community to support this initiative;

4. *Encourages* the Government of Mozambique to continue its efforts to fight HIV/AIDS, malaria and tuberculosis and to implement the Action Plan for the Reduction of Absolute Poverty(2001–2005) and national development plans, with a view to achieving internationally agreed development goals, including those contained in the United Nations Millennium Declaration, fighting absolute poverty, improving national capacity for education and governance, reducing the vulnerability of the population and promoting economic growth and sustainable development, and invites the international community to continue to support such efforts;

5. *Stresses* the importance of international assistance for the development programmes in Mozambique, and expresses its gratitude to the development partners that have supported the Government of Mozambique;

6. *Requests* the Secretary-General to make all necessary arrangements to continue to mobilize and coordinate, with a view to supporting the efforts of the Government of Mozambique:

(*a*) Humanitarian assistance from the specialized agencies, organizations and bodies of the United Nations system;

(*b*) International assistance for the national reconstruction and development of Mozambique;

7. *Also requests* the Secretary-General to report to it at its sixty-first session on the implementation of the present resolution.

African countries emerging from conflict

In response to Economic and Social Council resolution 2003/50 [YUN 2003, p. 947], the Secretary-General submitted a June report [E/2004/86] assessing the Council's ad hoc advisory groups on African countries emerging from conflict. Two such groups had been established thus far, on Guinea-Bissau [YUN 2002, p. 920] and Burundi [YUN 2003, p. 947]. The report highlighted the positive role played by the groups in the post-conflict reconstruction efforts of those countries by mobilizing donor support, while encouraging national authorities to create a conducive environment for increased assistance. To those ends, a partnership approach was fostered between national authorities and international stakeholders. The groups promoted enhanced coordination, in particular between the United Nations and the Bretton Woods institutions (the World Bank Group and IMF) and between the Security Council and the Economic and Social Council, which had advanced a holistic approach that addressed both security and economic issues in the transition and recovery phase.

On 3 May, the Economic and Social Council held an informal meeting to assess the work of the ad hoc groups. The meeting agreed that the overall experience had been positive. The discussions helped identify lessons learned, and a number of suggestions and ideas were put forward for future action.

The Secretary-General concluded that the ad hoc advisory groups had proved to be innovative, non-bureaucratic and flexible mechanisms in bringing the attention of the international community to the necessity of supporting the transition from conflict to peace and development in two African countries emerging from conflicts. Having fulfilled their core mandate of identifying short- and long-term recommendations for further support, the Groups were focusing on advocacy to ensure that their recommendations were being implemented and that adequate and coordinated assistance was provided to Burundi and Guinea-Bissau. The groups were also effective in shaping the comprehensive approach to peace and stability called for by the United Nations, and fostered genuine collaboration among international stakeholders. The groups were an example of how the intergovernmental machinery could enhance its impact in relation to post-conflict countries, and the Council might wish to build on their experiences in its response to requests for the creation of new groups. The Secretary-General clarified that the groups should not be seen as continuing mechanisms and should conclude their mandate within a reasonable time. Their experience should be taken into account in the ongoing discussions within the United Nations on promoting coherent international responses to countries in crisis.

Annexed to the report was an overview of the activities carried out by the ad hoc advisory groups on Burundi and Guinea-Bissau.

ECONOMIC AND SOCIAL COUNCIL ACTION

On 23 July [meeting 51], the Economic and Social Council adopted **resolution 2004/59** [draft: E/2004/L.53] by recorded vote (53-1) [agenda item 7 (*f*)].

Assessment of the ad hoc advisory groups of the Economic and Social Council on African countries emerging from conflict

The Economic and Social Council,

Recalling General Assembly resolution 55/217 of 21 December 2000 on the causes of conflict and the promotion of durable peace and sustainable development in Africa, in which the Assembly requested the Economic and Social Council to consider creating ad hoc advisory groups on African countries emerging from conflict, with a view to assessing their needs and elaborating a long-term programme of support that begins with the integration of relief into development,

Recalling also the ministerial declaration adopted at the high-level segment of the Economic and Social Council on 18 July 2001 on the role of the United Nations in support of the efforts of African countries to achieve sustainable development, in which the im-

portance of efforts for integrating peace and development was emphasized, and its resolution 2002/1 of 15 July 2002, in which the Council, having taken note of the report of the Secretary-General on this matter, decided to consider creating, at the request of any African country emerging from conflict, an ad hoc advisory group,

Recalling further its decision 2002/304 of 25 October 2002 and its resolutions 2003/1 of 31 January 2003, 2003/53 of 24 July 2003 and 2004/1 of 3 May 2004 related to the establishment and the work of the Ad Hoc Advisory Group on Guinea-Bissau,

Recalling its resolution 2003/16 of 21 July 2003, its decision 2003/311 of 22 August 2003 and its resolution 2004/2 of 3 May 2004 related to the establishment and the work of the Ad Hoc Advisory Group on Burundi,

Recalling also its resolution 2003/50 of 24 July 2003, in which the Council reiterated the need to undertake an assessment of the lessons learned from the ad hoc advisory groups at its substantive session of 2004, and stressed the need to assess also progress made in the implementation of recommendations made by the ad hoc advisory groups,

1. *Takes note with appreciation* of the report of the Secretary-General;

2. *Recognizes* that the composition of the groups, in particular the participation of the countries concerned, which led to their strong ownership of the process, and the presence of African countries, other developing countries and donor countries as members, assisted in ensuring balanced positions and contributing to constructive outcomes;

3. *Commends* the ad hoc advisory groups for their innovative and constructive work in support of the countries concerned, in particular as it relates to:

(*a*) The open, transparent and participatory approach adopted by the ad hoc advisory groups and the broad consultations carried out at United Nations Headquarters, in the countries concerned and in other places, with a wide range of actors, including from civil society and the private sector;

(*b*) The promotion of a comprehensive approach to peace and development by recognizing the complexity and specificity of the situations in the countries concerned and contributing to the development of a framework within which longer-term development activities are planned;

(*c*) The promotion of an integrated approach to relief, rehabilitation, reconstruction and development, as a follow-up to the Council's agreed conclusions 1998/1 of 31 July 1998, by, inter alia, linking short- and medium-term humanitarian assistance to the need for longer-term rehabilitation of communities;

(*d*) The close and fruitful collaboration engaged in with the organizations of the United Nations system, the World Bank and the International Monetary Fund, thus creating a constructive and mutually beneficial dynamic among the key players, in support of the countries concerned;

(*e*) The advocacy role played by the ad hoc advisory groups for long-term international support to the countries concerned, particularly through their partnership approach aimed at establishing a shared understanding of the development challenges and providing recommendations towards concrete solutions, including a long-term development strategy, outlining the respective responsibilities of national authorities and international partners;

4. *Urges* the ad hoc advisory groups to take into account the following areas for enhancing the effectiveness of their work, within their respective mandates:

(a) Fostering the creation of practical recommendations or strategic advice on how to make the transition from relief to development and increasing relationships with the United Nations Development Group/Executive Committee on Humanitarian Affairs working group on transition issues by exploring the complementary nature of their work;

(b) Entering into closer contacts and collaboration with regional and subregional organizations, such as the African Union, the regional economic communities and regional financial organizations, such as the African Development Bank, whose activities are key to the transition processes of the countries concerned;

(c) Continuing to strengthen their advice on how to ensure that the assistance of the international community in supporting the countries concerned is adequate, coherent, well-coordinated and effective and promotes synergy, including through exploring modalities to further mobilize additional resources, building on relevant mechanisms of coordination at the country level and at the international level;

(d) Ensuring the groups' early contribution to and participation in donor conferences on the countries concerned in order to maximize the impact of their advocacy work;

(e) Promoting a further increase in the interaction between the Economic and Social Council and the Security Council on the situation in the countries concerned, within their respective mandates;

5. *Invites* the Bretton Woods institutions to continue to cooperate with the ad hoc advisory groups and identify areas of convergence, in support of the post-conflict recovery phase that these countries are going through;

6. *Decides* to have a substantive debate on the reports of the ad hoc advisory groups as soon as it is appropriate;

7. *Stresses* the need to conclude the mandate of the ad hoc advisory groups, taking into account all aspects of the situation in each case, and decides to assess progress made towards that end on a semi-annual basis;

8. *Expresses its appreciation* to the Secretary-General for the support provided to the ad hoc advisory groups, and requests the Secretary-General to ensure adequate human and technical resources, within existing resources, to provide substantive secretariat support while making maximum use of existing mechanisms and coordination structures, and to ensure the provision of financial resources to cover the operating costs in order to enable the groups to function in a smooth and optimal manner;

9. *Decides* to undertake a further assessment of lessons learned from the experience of the ad hoc advisory groups, including progress made in the implementation of their mandate, during its substantive session of 2006, and requests the Secretary-General to submit a report to the Economic and Social Council in this regard;

10. *Reaffirms* that each ad hoc advisory group should be specific to the situation prevailing in each country and that further decisions and resolutions should take into account the specific circumstances of any other African country emerging from conflict that requests the establishment of an ad hoc advisory group.

RECORDED VOTE ON RESOLUTION 2004/59:

In favour: Armenia, Australia, Azerbaijan, Bangladesh, Belgium, Belize, Benin, Bhutan, Burundi, Canada, Chile, China, Colombia, Congo, Cuba, Ecuador, El Salvador, Finland, France, Germany, Ghana, Greece, Guatemala, Hungary, India, Indonesia, Ireland, Italy, Jamaica, Japan, Kenya, Libyan Arab Jamahiriya, Malaysia, Mauritius, Mozambique, Namibia, Nicaragua, Nigeria, Panama, Poland, Qatar, Republic of Korea, Russian Federation, Saudi Arabia, Senegal, Sweden, Tunisia, Turkey, Ukraine, United Arab Emirates, United Kingdom, United Republic of Tanzania, Zimbabwe.

Against: United States.

Burundi

On 19 January [S/2004/49], Burundi transmitted to the Security Council the Final Communiqué of the fourth Forum of Burundi's Development Partners (Brussels, 13-14 January). At the close of the Forum, Burundi's international partners announced their intention to finance a total of $1.03 billion to cover the priority programme for the second phase of the political transition in Burundi (see p. 141), which included economic recovery; capacity-building for good governance; repatriation of refugees and rehabilitation of "sinistrés" (survivors); and establishment of a new defence and security force. Burundi requested the Council's support in ensuring that the amounts pledged were actually disbursed.

On 29 January [E/2004/9], Burundi informed the Economic and Social Council that the IMF Executive Board had approved a $104 million line of credit for the country under the Poverty Reduction and Growth Facility.

ECONOMIC AND SOCIAL COUNCIL ACTION

On 3 May [meeting 10], the Economic and Social Council, having considered the 2003 report of the Ad Hoc Advisory Group on Burundi [YUN 2003, p. 948], adopted **resolution 2004/2** [draft: E/2004/L.6] without vote [agenda item 2].

Ad Hoc Advisory Group on Burundi

The Economic and Social Council,

Recalling its resolution 2002/1 of 15 July 2002 on the establishment of ad hoc advisory groups on African countries emerging from conflict, in which it decided to consider creating, at the request of any African country emerging from conflict, an ad hoc advisory group,

Recalling also its resolution 2003/16 of 21 July 2003, in which it decided to establish the Ad Hoc Advisory Group on Burundi and entrusted the President of the Economic and Social Council with the task of holding consultations and making recommendations on the composition, terms of reference and relevant modalities for the Advisory Group,

Recalling further its decision 2003/311 of 22 August 2003, in which it decided on the terms of reference and composition of the Advisory Group and requested the Advisory Group to submit a report on its recommendations to the Council by mid-January 2004,

Recalling its resolution 2003/50 of 24 July 2003, in which it reiterated the need to undertake an assessment of the lessons learned from the ad hoc advisory groups at its substantive session of 2004 and stressed the need to undertake an assessment of the progress made in the implementation of the recommendations made by the ad hoc advisory groups,

1. *Takes note with appreciation* of the report of the Ad Hoc Advisory Group on Burundi, and welcomes its recommendations;

2. *Welcomes* the efforts of the Transitional Government of Burundi to maintain the momentum and consolidate the peace process and the promotion of stability, and encourages the Transitional Government to strengthen its efforts in implementing the recommendations of the Advisory Group as it addresses the economic and social challenges faced by the people of Burundi;

3. *Welcomes also* the support provided by the international community for the efforts of the Transitional Government, stresses the need for further emergency assistance as well as support for Burundi in embarking on the path of sustainable development, welcomes in this regard the outcome of the fourth Forum of Burundi Development Partners, held in Brussels on 13 and 14 January 2004, and stresses the importance of translating, as a matter of priority, the commitments made into tangible assistance;

4. *Requests* the Advisory Group to continue to follow closely the humanitarian situation and economic and social conditions, to examine the transition from relief to development in Burundi and the way in which the international community supports the process and to report, as appropriate, to the Economic and Social Council at its substantive session in July 2004;

5. *Decides* that the Advisory Group should contribute to the assessment of the ad hoc advisory groups in relation to lessons learned during the application of its mandate and the implementation of its recommendations;

6. *Decides also* that the Advisory Group shall invite the participation in its work of the President of the Economic and Social Council for 2004 and the Chairperson of the Ad Hoc Working Group on Conflict Prevention and Resolution in Africa of the Security Council;

7. *Requests* the Secretary-General, the United Nations Development Group, as well as other relevant United Nations funds and programmes and the specialized agencies to continue to assist the Ad Hoc Advisory Group on Burundi in accomplishing its mandate, and invites the Bretton Woods institutions to continue to cooperate to that end.

Advisory Group activities. On 16 July [E/2004/98], South Africa, Chairman of the Advisory Group, transmitted to the Economic and Social Council its 15 July statement made before the Council regarding the Group's activities. The Chairman reported that the Group continued to interact with a wide range of stakeholders and the international community, but support for Burundi's dire humanitarian, economic and social needs continued to be insufficient. Following the announcement of commitment by the Forum of Burundi's Development Partners (see p. 933), a follow-up committee was established, which met

monthly in Burundi. Other developments included significant debt relief by the African Development Bank, Belgium, France and Italy; approval by the UNDP Executive Board of the country programme for Burundi for 2005-2007; the deployment of the United Nations Operation in Burundi, the finalization of the UN Development Assistance Framework; and adoption by the UNICEF Executive Board of the country programme for Burundi and approval of a global indicative budget of $37 million. The Group reiterated its call to the donor community to be more forthcoming in providing support to Burundi, including by contributing to the multilateral debt trust fund established by the World Bank.

ECONOMIC AND SOCIAL COUNCIL

On 23 July [meeting 51], the Economic and Social Council adopted **resolution 2004/60** [draft: E/2004/L.31] without vote [agenda item 7 (*f*)].

Ad Hoc Advisory Group on Burundi

The Economic and Social Council,

Recalling its resolutions 2002/1 of 15 July 2002, 2003/16 of 21 July 2003, 2003/50 of 24 July 2003 and 2004/2 of 3 May 2004, and its decision 2003/311 of 22 August 2003,

Welcoming the efforts of the African Mission in Burundi as an expression of ownership by the African Union and the establishment of the United Nations Operation in Burundi, in accordance with Security Council resolution 1545(2004) of 21 May 2004,

1. *Welcomes* the report of the Ad Hoc Advisory Group on Burundi;

2. *Reiterates* the importance of maintaining the momentum in consolidating the peace process, calls upon donor countries to follow up on the outcome of the fourth Forum of Burundi Development Partners, held in Brussels on 13 and 14 January 2004, and encourages disbursement of funds announced during that meeting;

3. *Requests* the Advisory Group to continue to follow closely the humanitarian situation and economic and social conditions, to examine the transition from relief to development in Burundi and the way in which the international community supports the process, and to report, as appropriate, to the Economic and Social Council at its organizational session of 2005;

4. *Requests* the Secretary-General, the United Nations Development Group, the Office for the Coordination of Humanitarian Affairs of the Secretariat and other relevant United Nations funds and programmes and the specialized agencies to continue to assist the Ad Hoc Advisory Group on Burundi in accomplishing its mandate, and invites the Bretton Woods institutions to continue to cooperate to that end.

Guinea-Bissau

In February [E/2004/10], the Ad Hoc Advisory Group on Guinea-Bissau, established by the Economic and Social Council in decision 2002/304 [YUN 2002, p. 920], reported on its activities since its last report [YUN 2003, p. 949].

On 17 November 2003, the Advisory Group organized an informal dialogue on Guinea-Bissau in New York, which discussed support to the Transitional Government.

The World Bank, IMF and the African Development Bank sent a joint mission to Guinea-Bissau in late 2003 to assess the situation and to make recommendations. Together with UNDP, they provided assistance to the Government in elaborating the Emergency Economic Management Plan and the budget for 2004. The transitional authorities presented their development strategy and announced that they had approved the Plan at an informal meeting of donors organized by the World Bank (Paris, 18 December 2003). At the time of the report, contributions amounted to $5.5 million, but it was estimated that $10.3 million would be needed through June 2004 to enable public institutions to operate and ensure that hospitals and schools remained open. A further $8 to $9 million would be needed for the rest of 2004. UNDP established an Emergency Economic Management Fund (EEMF) to receive funds to address the country's social and economic challenges.

The Advisory Group concluded that a fully fledged dialogue on development priorities would benefit from the return to constitutional order and the holding of elections, primarily the legislative elections scheduled to be held on 28 March 2004. International assistance should focus on emergency support, including electoral assistance. The Advisory Group recommended that the Economic and Social Council further appeal to the donor community to increase emergency assistance to Guinea-Bissau through contributions to the UNDP-managed EEMF.

ECONOMIC AND SOCIAL COUNCIL ACTION (May)

On 3 May [meeting 10], the Economic and Social Council adopted **resolution 2004/1** [draft: E/2004/L.5] without vote [agenda item 2].

Ad Hoc Advisory Group on Guinea-Bissau

The Economic and Social Council,

Recalling its resolution 2002/1 of 15 July 2002, in which it decided to consider creating, at the request of any African country emerging from conflict, an ad hoc advisory group, and its decision 2002/304 of 25 October 2002, in which it decided to establish such an Ad Hoc Advisory Group on Guinea-Bissau,

Recalling also its resolution 2003/1 of 31 January 2003, in which it took note with appreciation of the report of the Ad Hoc Advisory Group on Guinea-Bissau, welcomed its recommendations, endorsed the partnership approach it set out and decided to extend the mandate of the Advisory Group until the substantive session of the Council in July 2003,

Recalling further its resolution 2003/53 of 24 July 2003, in which it took note with appreciation of the supplementary report of the Advisory Group and de-

cided to extend the mandate of the Advisory Group until the organizational session of the Council in January 2004, with the request that it submit a report,

Recalling its resolution 2003/50 of 24 July 2003, in which it reiterated the need to undertake an assessment of the lessons learned from the ad hoc advisory groups at its substantive session of 2004 and stressed the need to undertake an assessment of the progress made in the implementation of the recommendations made by the ad hoc advisory groups,

1. *Takes note with appreciation* of the report of the Ad Hoc Advisory Group on Guinea-Bissau, and welcomes its recommendations;

2. *Welcomes* the continued interaction and cooperation between the Economic and Social Council and the Security Council, within their respective mandates, on the situation in Guinea-Bissau;

3. *Welcomes also* the steps taken by the Transitional Government in Guinea-Bissau to give effect to the partnership approach proposed by the Advisory Group and the continued support provided by the international community to the Transitional Government and its efforts towards achieving sustainable development, welcomes further the recent parliamentary elections as an important step towards the restoration of democratic government, and appeals to donor countries to contribute further to these efforts;

4. *Welcomes further* the establishment of an Emergency Economic Management Fund, managed by the United Nations Development Programme, as recommended by the Advisory Group in its initial report, as well as the contributions made to the Fund, and invites donor countries to provide further emergency assistance through the Fund;

5. *Decides* to extend the mandate of the Advisory Group until the substantive session of the Economic and Social Council in July 2004, with the purpose of monitoring the implementation of its recommendations, following closely the humanitarian situation and the economic and social conditions unfolding in the country and reporting, as appropriate, to the Council at its substantive session in July 2004;

6. *Decides also* that the Advisory Group should contribute to the assessment of the ad hoc advisory groups in relation to lessons learned during the application of its mandate and the implementation of its recommendations;

7. *Decides further* that the Advisory Group shall invite the participation in its work of the President of the Economic and Social Council for 2004, the Chairperson of the Group of Friends of Guinea-Bissau and the Chairperson of the Ad Hoc Working Group on Conflict Prevention and Resolution in Africa of the Security Council;

8. *Requests* the Secretary-General, the United Nations Development Group as well as other relevant United Nations funds and programmes and the specialized agencies to continue to assist the Ad Hoc Advisory Group on Guinea-Bissau in accomplishing its mandate, and invites the Bretton Woods institutions to continue to cooperate to that end.

On 2 July, South Africa, in its capacity as Chairman of the Advisory Group, transmitted a supplementary report [E/2004/92] updating the information on the Group's activities. The Group visited Guinea-Bissau from 25 to 28 June and held discussions with government officials, representatives of IMF and the European Commission (EC). It was joined on 27 and 28 June by the Security Council mission to West Africa (see p. 164). The joint mission assured the Government that the international community would continue to support its efforts by recommending that international partners, the Bretton Woods institutions and donors provide resources to address the country's social and economic priorities. It was convinced that the Government had met key conditions of the partnership and that the substantial improvements in economic management should be rewarded with additional resources. The joint mission called on the Bretton Woods institutions to continue providing technical assistance, with a view to formulating a comprehensive technical assistance plan.

While the Group was impressed with the new rigour in public administration and finance, those improvements needed to be backed up by resources. The EEMF attracted $4.9 million in contributions, of which $2.5 million was disbursed to pay the salaries of some 11,000 civil servants from January to April. The Fund had proved to be an efficient and transparent mechanism for supporting the Government in covering part of the gap in its emergency budget for 2004. The Group was concerned over a $14 million funding gap during the remainder of 2004.

The Advisory Group called for urgent and immediate assistance for a comprehensive restructuring package required for the armed forces, including a review of salaries, career structures, working conditions and infrastructure, as well as a reformulation of their respective roles in a fragile democratic State. It was of the view that there should be no further delay in re-engagement of the international community with Guinea-Bissau to assist the country in meeting its short- and long-term needs. The Group called the attention of the Economic and Social Council to the recommendations made in its first report [YUN 2003, p. 948] regarding the agriculture sector, in particular the fisheries and rice subsectors. The Group urged the Council to call on IMF to resume a programme for the country, and on donors to participate in a round table organized by UNDP and scheduled for November (see p. 937).

ECONOMIC AND SOCIAL COUNCIL ACTION (July)

On 23 July [meeting 51], the Economic and Social Council adopted **resolution 2004/61** [draft: E/2004/L.43] without vote [agenda item 7 (*f*)].

Ad Hoc Advisory Group on Guinea-Bissau

The Economic and Social Council,

Recalling its resolutions 2002/1 of 15 July 2002, 2003/1 of 31 January 2003, 2003/50 of 24 July 2003, 2003/53 of 24 July 2003 and 2004/1 of 3 May 2004, and its decision 2002/304 of 25 October 2002,

1. *Takes note with appreciation* of the supplementary report of the Ad Hoc Advisory Group on Guinea-Bissau and its recommendations;

2. *Welcomes* the interaction and cooperation that has taken place between the Economic and Social Council and the Security Council, within their respective mandates, on the situation in Guinea-Bissau;

3. *Welcomes also* the promising developments that have taken place with regard to the economic, social and political situation in Guinea-Bissau following the legislative elections in March 2004, as well as the reforms initiated by the Government to improve the management of public finances;

4. *Welcomes further* the recommitment of the Government of Guinea-Bissau to the partnership approach, endorsed by the Economic and Social Council in its resolution 2003/1, calls upon donor countries to support the development efforts of the Government of Guinea-Bissau, including through contributions to the Emergency Economic Management Fund, managed by the United Nations Development Programme, and urges the international community, in particular the donor countries, to increase their assistance to the country in meeting its short-term needs and to implement a long-term programme of support;

5. *Encourages* the Government of Guinea-Bissau to hold presidential elections by May 2005, and, in this regard, calls upon the international community to support Guinea-Bissau in holding the elections in order to complete the second phase of the Transition Charter;

6. *Encourages* the International Monetary Fund to consider all possible forms of further support to Guinea-Bissau, and calls upon the donor community to participate in the round table being organized by the United Nations Development Programme, tentatively scheduled for November 2004, which would further the partnership approach;

7. *Decides* to extend the mandate of the Advisory Group until the organizational session of the Economic and Social Council of 2005, with the purpose of monitoring the implementation of its recommendations, following closely the humanitarian situation and the economic and social conditions unfolding in the country and reporting, as appropriate, to the Council at its organizational session of 2005;

8. *Requests* the Secretary-General, the United Nations Development Group, the Office for the Coordination of Humanitarian Affairs of the Secretariat as well as the relevant United Nations funds and programmes and the specialized agencies to continue to assist the Ad Hoc Advisory Group on Guinea-Bissau in accomplishing its mandate, and invites the Bretton Woods institutions to continue to cooperate to that end.

A December report [E/2005/8] described the activities of the Ad Hoc Advisory Group since its July report (see p. 935); reviewed those undertaken by other international partners; and addressed challenges and constraints impacting the country's transition from crisis to sustainable development.

Following an army mutiny on 6 October (see p. 228), the Ad Hoc Advisory Group in an 11 October communiqué called on the international community to provide urgent and immediate assistance for the restructuring of the armed forces, with a view to professionalizing the army, and renewed its call for budgetary assistance to meet the salary arrears for civil servants and the armed forces. International donor support continued to be critical in helping the Government meet its short-, medium- and long-term priorities. However, the donors round table scheduled for 15 December was postponed, partly as a result of the 6 October events and delays in the finalization of the background documents, including the PRSP, the principal technical document for the round table. The Policy Charter on Infrastructure Development and the National Good Governance Programme were being finalized. The IMF Executive Board (Guinea-Bissau, 19 November) agreed to re-engage with the country on the basis of the Emergency Post-Conflict Assistance programme, provided there were demonstrated international support and political stability.

Concerned at the economic and social situation of the country and the Government's difficulty in meeting the basic needs of the people, the Group supported the Secretary-General's call, made in his December report to the Security Council on Guinea-Bissau (see p. 229) for a special fund to facilitate the planning and implementation of the process of reform of the armed forces, and called on the international community to contribute to the funding of that effort. The Group called on the country's partners to participate actively in the donors round table once a new date was set.

(For more information on the situation in Guinea-Bissau, see p. 225.)

Other economic assistance

Comoros

The Secretary-General, in his August consolidated report on humanitarian assistance [A/59/293], provided information on assistance to the Comoros. The Comoros economic difficulties over the past two decades, including low growth of its gross domestic product, falling investment, arrears in domestic and foreign payments and major macroeconomic imbalances, resulted in an estimated 60 per cent of the population living below the poverty line. The high level of cash poverty went hand in hand with poor human development performance; a situation further aggravated by a constitutional crisis leading to jurisdictional disputes. The institutional instability

and political turbulence prevented the country from drawing up a coherent development policy, causing donors to adopt a wait and see attitude. That resulted in a downward trend in development aid to the country. Following the signing by the Comorian parties on 20 December 2003 of the Moroni Agreement, which laid down the interim provisions for governing the Comorian entity until the establishment of the national assembly, the international community met in Paris on 21 January 2004 and established a trust fund of just over $5 million to be managed by UNDP in support of the transition. That allowed the country to formulate a consolidated budget in 2004, with a view to reopening negotiations on a formal IMF programme. The UN system supported the launch of a national process to draw up a PRSP for the Comoros, which should open the door to a number of mechanisms for financing the economy and prepare the country for the next donor round table on funding for national development.

The Secretary-General concluded that the long and multifaceted crisis in the Comoros had left the country economically bereft, socially vulnerable and institutionally fragile. The Comorian national report for 2003 on the MDGs [YUN 2000, p. 51] showed that the Comoros was not advancing towards the agreed goals, but was actually falling behind. Among its greatest challenges were the creation of a new and viable institutional framework, and the re-establishment of effective cooperation with the Bretton Woods institutions, so that the country could access development financing mechanisms. The Comoros needed multifaceted support from the international community to pursue national reconciliation and reconstruction.

Haiti

In response to Economic and Social Council resolution 2003/46 [YUN 2003, p. 952], the Secretary-General submitted a June report [E/2004/80] on progress achieved in implementing the long-term programme of support for Haiti. Over the past year, Haiti's critical economic condition was related to the political situation, with a direct negative effect on public sector efficiency and domestic investments, including increasing inflation as a result of unsustainable fiscal deficits. In April 2004, the Prime Minister, calling for pluri-annual commitments by donors in support of Haiti in order to achieve sustainable results, announced his Government's priorities in relation to the MDGs, including modernization of State institutions, public security, infrastructure, education, the environment, the economy and finance. The suspension of most external assistance to Haiti continued into early 2004, but with the new political situation (see p. 288), major development partners announced their intention to resume support to Haiti. At a meeting convened by the World Bank (Washington, D.C., 23 March), donor Governments, international financial institutions and international and regional organizations decided to ensure a coordinated response to Haiti's pressing and medium-term needs. In partnership with the Transitional Government, the meeting agreed to initiate a joint Government/multi-donor assessment stressing the country's economic, social and institutional needs. On 22 April, Haiti's development partners met to consider the Transitional Government's policy priorities (see above) and to elaborate a plan of action. UNDP and the World Bank decided to lead the assessment process for the preparation of the Interim Cooperation Framework for Haiti, and a donor round table was scheduled for July.

The Prime Minister of the Transitional Government of Haiti, in a meeting with the President of the Economic and Social Council on 14 June, requested the Council to set up an ad hoc advisory group on Haiti to help coordinate the development of a long-term programme of assistance to the country and the activities being carried out or planned with the donor community and the Government for that purpose.

The Secretary-General concluded that a long-term effort and international commitment were needed to rebuild the economic and social structures, and support the Government and people of Haiti in building democratic institutions. In the light of the changes in the political environment in Haiti, and taking into account the experience gained through the work of the Council's ad hoc advisory groups on Guinea-Bissau and Burundi (see pp. 935 and 933, respectively), the Economic and Social Council might wish to consider establishing an ad hoc advisory group on Haiti.

(For information on the human rights situation in Haiti, see p. 675.)

The UN Consolidated Inter-Agency Flash Appeal for Haiti, launched on 9 March, sought $35.8 million to meet urgent humanitarian needs and establish the basis for recovery for the Haitian people over a six-month period. Of the total, 43 per cent ($15.4 million) was received. A separate flash appeal was launched to address emergency relief and recovery needs following floods in Haiti on 17 and 18 September (see p. 952).

ECONOMIC AND SOCIAL COUNCIL ACTION

On 23 July [meeting 50], the Economic and Social Council adopted **resolution 2004/52** [draft: E/2004/L.44] without vote [agenda item 7 (d)].

Long-term programme of support for Haiti

The Economic and Social Council,

Recalling its resolution 1999/4 of 7 May 1999, in which the Council decided to create an Ad Hoc Advisory Group on Haiti, and its subsequent resolutions 1999/11 of 27 July 1999, 2001/25 of 26 July 2001, 2002/22 of 24 July 2002 and 2003/46 of 23 July 2003, and its decisions 2000/235 of 27 July 2000 and 2001/290 of 24 July 2001, adopted with a view to the development of a long-term programme of support for Haiti,

Recalling also Security Council resolutions 1529 (2004) of 29 February 2004 and 1542(2004) of 30 April 2004, in which it decided to establish the United Nations Stabilization Mission in Haiti and supported the establishment of a Core Group to be chaired by the Special Representative of the Secretary-General for Haiti in order, inter alia, to facilitate the implementation of the mandate of the Stabilization Mission,

Recalling further paragraphs 13 and 14 of Security Council resolution 1542(2004), which emphasized the need for Member States, organs, bodies and agencies of the United Nations system and other international organizations to continue to contribute to the promotion of the social and economic development of Haiti, in particular over the long term, in order to achieve and sustain stability and to combat poverty,

Taking note of the request made by the Transitional Government of Haiti to reactivate the Ad Hoc Advisory Group on Haiti,

1. *Welcomes* the report of the Secretary-General;

2. *Stresses* the need for renewed efforts at the local, national, regional and international levels to secure long-term support for Haiti, together with a sustained commitment at all levels to rebuild the economic and social structures of the country, combat poverty and build institutional capacity in support of the efforts of the Government and people of Haiti;

3. *Calls upon* the international community to provide substantial contributions to relief and assistance programmes carried out by the United Nations system and other relevant partners to improve the living conditions of the population in Haiti;

4. *Underscores* the need for a long-term development strategy to promote socio-economic recovery and stability and to ensure coherence and sustainability in international support for Haiti;

5. *Decides* to reactivate the Ad Hoc Advisory Group on Haiti established by its resolution 1999/4 and to consider the mandate and modalities of the Advisory Group at its resumed substantive session of 2004, in close consultation with the Transitional Government of Haiti and with the participation of the Special Representative of the Secretary-General for Haiti, based on long-term national development needs and taking into account the need to avoid overlap and duplication with existing mechanisms;

6. *Also decides* to entrust the President of the Economic and Social Council with the task of holding consultations on the composition of the Advisory Group with the participation of all regional groups and the Transitional Government of Haiti, ensuring that it is limited, representative, at the ambassadorial level and drawn from the membership of the Council and its observer States, including representation from Haiti, taking into account the need to include countries that can

make a positive contribution to the objectives of the Advisory Group, and with the task of making recommendations on the composition of the Advisory Group for a decision by the Council at its resumed substantive session of 2004.

On 11 November, the Council adopted **decision 2004/322** [draft E/2004/L.58/Rev.1] without vote [agenda item 7 (d)].

Ad Hoc Advisory Group on Haiti

At its 54th plenary meeting, on 11 November 2004, the Economic and Social Council, recalling its resolution 2004/52 of 23 July 2004 on the long-term programme of support for Haiti, and in order to reactivate the Ad Hoc Advisory Group on Haiti, decided:

(a) To appoint the Permanent Representatives of Benin, Brazil, Canada, Chile, Haiti, Spain and Trinidad and Tobago to the United Nations as the members of the Advisory Group;

(b) That the Advisory Group would invite the participation of the President of the Economic and Social Council and the Special Representative of the Secretary-General in Haiti, also acting as Chairman of the core group, in the work of the Advisory Group;

(c) That the Advisory Group would follow closely and provide advice on Haiti's long-term development strategy to promote socio-economic recovery and stability, with particular attention to the need to ensure coherence and sustainability in international support for Haiti, based on the long-term national development priorities, building upon the Interim Cooperation Framework and stressing the need to avoid overlap and duplication with respect to existing mechanisms;

(d) That the Advisory Group would work with Member States, the Core Group, the Security Council, other United Nations organs, bodies and specialized agencies and, in particular, the United Nations Development Programme, the Bretton Woods institutions, regional organizations and institutions, including the Organization of American States and the Caribbean Community, the Inter-American Development Bank and other major stakeholders;

(e) To request the Advisory Group to submit a report on its work, with recommendations, as appropriate, to the Economic and Social Council at its substantive session of 2005.

Serbia and Montenegro

The Secretary-General, in his August consolidated report on humanitarian assistance and rehabilitation [A/59/293], provided information on humanitarian and rehabilitation assistance to Serbia and Montenegro. Serbia and Montenegro witnessed a steady decline in humanitarian aid, as the country was no longer in a humanitarian crisis situation but had moved towards stabilization and economic development. The most significant component of that assistance continued to be basic food aid provided by WFP and UNHCR to vulnerable refugees and by the International Committee of the Red Cross (ICRC) to internally displaced persons (IDPs). As that assistance was phased out, the remaining eligible beneficiaries were integrated into the local social welfare system, with international agencies providing residual support to the most vulnerable. Although significant progress was made in finding durable solutions for refugees, focusing mostly on repatriation to Bosnia and Herzegovina and Croatia, and on local integration through housing, income-generation and vocational training programmes, national policies for comprehensive durable solutions for IDPs had not yet been developed. Ethnic violence against the Serb and other non-Albanian populations in the province of Kosovo in March 2004 (see p. 405) posed additional threats to returnees. In the wake of the disturbances, UN agencies in Kosovo addressed urgent humanitarian needs through the provision of food and temporary accommodation assistance and some reconstruction activities.

The United Nations Development Assistance Framework (UNDAF) for 2005-2009 incorporated remaining humanitarian issues into development objectives. The UN country team was implementing a strategic plan for Kosovo, devised according to the Government's comments and priorities. While solutions for refugees, IDPs and other marginalized groups were sought within broad community development, poverty reduction and social assistance strategies, governments at the republican and local levels were unable to meet their needs without the support of the international community. Outside support would enable domestic bodies to assume a greater share of the rehabilitation, reconstruction and development burden. More coordination was required between international development actors and government ministries to ensure that medium-term and longer-term solutions for the most vulnerable populations were addressed comprehensively as humanitarian programmes ended.

GENERAL ASSEMBLY ACTION

On 22 December [meeting 75], the General Assembly, on the recommendation of the Second Committee [A/59/479 & Corr.1], adopted **resolution 59/215** without vote [agenda item 39 (b)].

Humanitarian and special economic assistance to Serbia and Montenegro

The General Assembly,

Recalling its resolution 46/182 of 19 December 1991, and reaffirming that humanitarian assistance should be provided in accordance with the guiding principles contained in the annex to that resolution,

Recalling also its resolutions 54/96 F of 15 December 1999, 55/169 of 14 December 2000, 56/101 of 14 December 2001 and 57/148 of 16 December 2002,

Deeply appreciative of the humanitarian assistance and the rehabilitation support rendered by a number of States, in particular major contributors, international agencies and organizations and non-governmental organizations to alleviate the humanitarian needs of the affected population in Serbia and Montenegro, in particular emergency assistance provided by the European Union and various countries,

Recognizing the role of the Stability Pact for South-Eastern Europe and the stabilization and association process for the western Balkans in assisting Serbia and Montenegro in its efforts in further promoting democratic and economic reforms and in intensifying regional cooperation,

Recognizing also the need to ensure the effective and smooth transition from humanitarian to development efforts in Serbia and Montenegro, including with respect to the humanitarian and rehabilitation needs of refugees and internally displaced persons, in particular the most vulnerable,

Aware of the weakness of the economy and basic services, which exacerbates further the situation of socially and economically vulnerable segments of the population, including refugees and internally displaced persons, and which is coupled with limited basic social services capacity, especially in the health sector,

Acknowledging that still a large number of refugees and internally displaced persons remain in Serbia and Montenegro and that assistance requirements will include local integration, whenever refugees and internally displaced persons are not willing to return to their places of origin,

Recognizing the role of the United Nations in helping Serbia and Montenegro to achieve a successful transition from humanitarian assistance to development assistance and in coordinating the efforts of the international community in that regard,

Acknowledging the support of the Office of the United Nations High Commissioner for Refugees, the United Nations Development Programme and the Office for the Coordination of Humanitarian Affairs of the Secretariat to the Council of Ministers of Serbia and Montenegro in the implementation of the National Strategy for Resolving Problems of Refugees and Internally Displaced Persons in Serbia and Montenegro, as well as international support for the development of a Roma integration and empowerment strategy and poverty reduction strategies in Serbia and Montenegro and the adoption of a poverty reduction strategy paper,

Recognizing a continued decrease in humanitarian assistance in 2004, in line with an understanding that, as stressed in the report of the Secretary-General, the country was no longer in a humanitarian crisis situation but had moved towards stabilization and economic development,

Recognizing also the importance of the rule of law, good governance, a vibrant private sector, as well as effective social sectors, including education and health, to achieve sustainable development,

Taking note of the report of the Secretary-General,

1. *Calls upon* all States, regional organizations, intergovernmental and non-governmental organizations and other relevant bodies to continue to provide assistance to alleviate the needs of refugees and internally displaced persons, bearing in mind in particular the special situation of women, children, the elderly and other vulnerable groups, and to assist financially and otherwise in seeking durable solutions for a safe return of refugees and internally displaced persons to their places of origin, or for settlement at their place of refuge for those who want to integrate locally, in cooperation with the local authorities, with a successive transition to development projects aimed at durable solutions to those questions;

2. *Encourages* the Council of Ministers of Serbia and Montenegro in its efforts to ensure a smooth transition from relief to long-term development, and calls upon all States, regional organizations, intergovernmental and non-governmental organizations and other relevant bodies to offer support for those efforts;

3. *Welcomes* the adoption of the United Nations Development Assistance Framework for Serbia and Montenegro as a strategic document for the operational activities of the United Nations system in Serbia and Montenegro and as a basis for the entire development assistance programme in the period 2005-2009 and the adoption of the United Nations Development Programme country programme outline for Serbia and Montenegro for the period 2005-2009 and the United Nations Children's Fund country programme document for Serbia and Montenegro for the period 2005-2009, and calls upon all States, regional organizations, intergovernmental and non-governmental organizations and other relevant bodies to support their implementation;

4. *Recognizes* that the main responsibility for improving the humanitarian situation and creating conditions for long-term development lies with the Council of Ministers of Serbia and Montenegro, while bearing in mind the important role played by the international community;

5. *Welcomes* the continued commitment of Serbia and Montenegro and encourages it to cooperate further with the United Nations system as well as development and humanitarian organizations to address the needs of the affected population, including refugees and internally displaced persons, and urges the relevant authorities and the international community to support and stimulate development assistance for the implementation of the National Strategy for Resolving Problems of Refugees and Internally Displaced Persons, national strategies for poverty reduction and other programmes that will ensure that the needs of the vulnerable refugees and internally displaced persons in Serbia and Montenegro are met and to pursue durable solutions to their plight, in particular voluntary repatriation and reintegration, stresses the need to create conditions that are conducive to their safe return, and emphasizes in this regard the importance of regional cooperation in the search for solutions to the plight of refugees;

6. *Urges* the relevant government authorities in Serbia and Montenegro to develop, with the assistance of the United Nations system, national policies for comprehensive durable solutions for internally displaced persons based on the Guiding Principles on Internal Displacement, and in that regard invites the United Nations Interim Administration Mission in Kosovo to strengthen its efforts, within its mandate, in coordination with relevant government authorities in Serbia and Montenegro, for the establishment of the necessary conditions for the safe and sustainable return of internally displaced persons;

7. *Calls upon* the Secretary-General, as well as development agencies, to continue to mobilize the timely provision of international development assistance to Serbia and Montenegro, and welcomes efforts by Serbia and Montenegro to improve governance and institutional capabilities in order to use aid more effectively;

8. *Emphasizes* the importance of the increased donor coordination of assistance to Serbia and Montenegro, inter alia, through the mechanism of the United Nations resident coordinator system;

9. *Urges* development partners to assist in capacity-building, institution-building and local employment generation in their programmes and to train and employ local staff to the maximum extent possible, welcomes work by Serbia and Montenegro to create an enabling environment for its private sector, including the development of a financial sector that provides services, inter alia, to microenterprises and to small and medium-sized enterprises and to their households, and encourages continued work on regulatory reform, transparency, accountability, good governance and the rule of law, all of which support sustainable development;

10. *Also urges* Serbia and Montenegro and its development partners to support and strengthen initiatives that contribute to the enhancement of social capital in areas such as health and education, emphasizing, inter alia, the development of capacity to improve the quality of and access to health care and education;

11. *Requests* the United Nations and the specialized agencies to continue their efforts to assess needs, in cooperation with the Council of Ministers of Serbia and Montenegro, relevant international and regional organizations and bodies and interested States, with a view to ensuring an effective and smooth transition from relief to longer-term development assistance to Serbia and Montenegro, taking into account the work already carried out in this field and the need to avoid duplication and the overlapping of efforts;

12. *Requests* the Secretary-General, bearing in mind the recommendation contained in his report, to submit to it at its sixty-first session, under the item entitled "Strengthening of the coordination of humanitarian and disaster relief assistance of the United Nations, including special economic assistance", a final report on the implementation of the present resolution.

Third States affected by sanctions

In response to General Assembly resolution 58/80 [YUN 2003, p. 1367], the Secretary-General submitted a September report [A/59/334] highlighting measures for further improvement of the procedures and working methods of the Security Council and its sanctions committees related to assistance to third States affected by the application of sanctions. It reviewed the Secretariat's capacity and modalities for implementing the intergovernmental mandates and for addressing the main findings, including recommendations of the ad hoc expert group meeting on assistance to third States affected by the application of sanctions [YUN 1998, p. 1235]. It also reviewed recent developments related to the role of the Assembly, the Economic and Social Council and the Committee for Programme and Coordination in the area of assistance to third States.

The Assembly took action with regard to the Secretary-General's report in **resolution 59/45** (see p. 1346).

Disaster relief

In 2004, an estimated 360 disasters affected approximately 145 million people, causing more than $130 billion in material damage. The most significant was the massive earthquake that occurred off the coast of Indonesia on 26 December and the resulting tsunami (see p. 952), which unleashed a series of major disasters across more than 12 nations, killing more than 240,000 persons and displacing over 1 million.

In Africa, Eritrea was experiencing worsening drought conditions, with over 66 per cent of the population threatened by hunger, extreme poverty and poor access to safe water. Over 7 million people in Ethiopia were still unable to meet their basic needs following the drought of 2003. Floods and cyclones affected over 1 million people in the Southern Africa region, and erratic, dry weather conditions affected the crop production of over 6 million people in six countries. In the Central and East Africa region, 40 million people were chronically vulnerable from successive years of drought and natural and man-made disasters. In the latter half of 2004, locust swarms invaded the Sahelian zone of the West Africa region, with detrimental consequences for food security. The continuing drought in Somalia affected 700,000 people.

More natural disasters struck Asia than any other continent, and South Asia was particularly prone to floods, landslides, earthquakes, cyclones and droughts. Severe floods hit South Asia and China, affecting 80 million people. In July, floods in Bangladesh affected more than 30 million people, of which 5 million were in urgent need of food and other relief items (see p. 950) . Floods also occurred in Bangladesh, India and Nepal, and a storm killed more than 140 people in Myanmar in May.

The Pacific region was hit by three cyclones in 2004. In January, Cyclone Heta impacted the Cook Islands, Niue, Samoa and Tokelau. Cyclone Ivy caused heavy damage to Vanuatu in February, and Typhoon Sudal swept through the Federated

States of Micronesia in April. The Philippines was also struck by four typhoons and tropical storms (see p. 952).

Political unrest in Haiti was compounded by floods in May (see p. 952) and Tropical Storm Jeanne in September. It was estimated that natural disasters in the Caribbean in 2003 and 2004 affected millions of people and caused more than $65 billion worth of material damage. Hurricanes Charley, Frances, Ivan and Jeanne in 2004 were the strongest chain of storms to hit the region in a decade, and their paths of destruction included small, developing islands, many of which were unprepared for the level of devastation brought by those storms. A prolonged drought in Bolivia affected an estimated 180,000 people (see p. 950).

Excluding contributions in kind and services not costed, the United Nations Office for the Coordination of Humanitarian Affairs (OCHA) recorded contributions totalling $592 million for natural disaster assistance.

International cooperation

In response to General Assembly resolution 58/25 [YUN 2003, p. 955], the Secretary-General, in a September report [A/59/374], highlighted key activities undertaken in response to natural disasters, with an emphasis on disaster response, recovery and transition efforts and global initiatives to reduce risk. In response to resolution 57/150 [YUN 2002, p. 926], the report also updated the activities of the International Search and Rescue Advisory Group (INSARAG), an intergovernmental network established in 1991 [YUN 1991, p. 413] for international cooperation and coordination in earthquake response.

The United Nations assisted countries and regions affected by more than 50 natural disasters, in response to 20 international appeals launched by Member States. Efforts to coordinate the UN system response to natural disasters included the launch of four UN inter-agency flash appeals. The United Nations Disaster Assessment and Coordination (UNDAC), a network of 180 disaster management professionals from 57 countries, coordinated the responses in 10 disasters, with WFP support. The United Nations was also trying to expand Member States participation in its disaster response networks and to foster a regional approach to natural disaster response, particularly among low-income countries. UNDAC expanded its network, including the holding of an induction course for new African emergency managers. To address local and regional capacity-building for response to disasters, several capacity-building programmes were initiated worldwide.

To improve local response, UNDAC teams visited Colombia and the Philippines to introduce new on-site coordination methodologies to disaster-prone countries and to train national authorities in international response coordination. At the regional level, the network of UN regional disaster response advisers focused on strengthening regional mechanisms to address all phases of disaster management.

INSARAG organized lessons-learned meetings with Governments and international, national and local response teams to evaluate earthquake response and to make recommendations for inclusion in the INSARAG guidelines, which were being revised. It also organized regional meetings in Japan (November 2003), Tunisia (April 2004), Peru (August 2004) and Singapore (September 2004) to discuss regional cooperation, emphasizing national capacity-building for emergency response preparedness, and meetings of all international urban search-and-rescue team leaders in Seoul (November 2003) and Singapore (September 2004) on technical and operational collapsed structure rescue issues, in order to improve performance standards.

The Secretary-General concluded that, without focused efforts to improve preparedness and response, and to address risk and vulnerability, the effects of disasters on people and human settlements would become more deadly and costly. The situation called for more concerted and comprehensive approaches to disaster management, aimed at building national and regional capacity and emphasizing risk reduction as a core principle. The lack of systematic policies and practices to support local and national responses and risk reduction capacities called for institutional and financial commitments to ensure that disaster risk reduction was more explicitly integrated into development planning, and that the more difficult political and structural elements of risk reduction policies were seriously addressed.

The Secretary-General made recommendations for strengthening international assistance, dealing with disaster response; building local and regional disaster management capacity; information management; risk reduction and sustainable development; disaster funding; and monitoring and evaluation. Member States were encouraged to support the World Conference on Disaster Reduction, to be held in Japan, in 2005 (see p. 946), and to use the opportunity to reaffirm and strengthen the implementation of disaster-reduction policy and practices.

On 20 December [meeting 74], the General Assembly adopted **resolution 59/212** [draft: A/59/L.26/Rev.1 & Add.1] without vote [agenda item 39 (*a*)].

International cooperation on humanitarian assistance in the field of natural disasters, from relief to development

The General Assembly,

Reaffirming its resolution 46/182 of 19 December 1991, the annex to which contains the guiding principles for the strengthening of the coordination of emergency humanitarian assistance of the United Nations system, as well as all its resolutions on international cooperation on humanitarian assistance in the field of natural disasters, from relief to development, and recalling the resolutions of the humanitarian segments of the substantive sessions of the Economic and Social Council,

Recognizing the importance of the principles of neutrality, humanity and impartiality for the provision of humanitarian assistance,

Emphasizing that the affected State has the primary responsibility in the initiation, organization, coordination and implementation of humanitarian assistance within its territory and in the facilitation of the work of humanitarian organizations in mitigating the consequences of natural disasters,

Emphasizing also the importance of integrating risk reduction into all phases of disaster management, development planning and post-disaster recovery,

Emphasizing further, in this context, the important role of development organizations in supporting national efforts to mitigate the consequences of natural disasters,

Emphasizing the responsibility of all States to undertake disaster preparedness, response and mitigation efforts in order to minimize the impact of natural disasters, while recognizing the importance of international cooperation in support of the efforts of affected countries which may have limited capacities to fulfil this requirement,

Welcoming the International Strategy for Disaster Reduction,

Stressing that national authorities need to enhance the resilience of populations to disasters through, inter alia, implementation of the International Strategy for Disaster Reduction so as to reduce risks to people, their livelihoods, the social and economic infrastructure and environmental resources,

Taking into account the outcome of the Second International Conference on Early Warning, held in Bonn, Germany, from 16 to 18 October 2003, under the auspices of the United Nations,

Welcoming the efforts undertaken in preparation for the World Conference on Disaster Reduction, to be held in Kobe, Japan, from 18 to 22 January 2005, and underlining the importance of this conference in the promotion of new efforts in the field of disaster risk reduction,

Noting the critical role played by local resources, as well as by existing in-country capacities, in natural disaster response and risk management,

Recognizing the significant role played by national Red Cross and Red Crescent societies, as part of the International Red Cross and Red Crescent Movement, in disaster preparedness and risk reduction, disaster response, rehabilitation and development,

Emphasizing the importance of raising awareness among developing countries of the capacities existing at the national, regional and international levels that could be deployed to assist them,

Noting the lack of progress made in finalizing the establishment of the Directory of Advanced Technologies for Disaster Response as a new part of the Central Register of Disaster Management Capacities as requested in its resolution 58/25 of 5 December 2003,

Emphasizing the importance of international cooperation in support of the efforts of the affected States in dealing with natural disasters in all their phases, including prevention, preparedness, mitigation and recovery and reconstruction, and of strengthening the response capacity of affected countries,

Recognizing that efforts to achieve economic growth, sustainable development and internationally agreed development goals, including the Millennium Development Goals, can be adversely affected by natural disasters, and noting the positive contribution that those efforts can make in strengthening the resilience of populations to such disasters,

Welcoming the efforts of Member States, with facilitation by the Office for the Coordination of Humanitarian Affairs of the Secretariat and in cooperation with the International Search and Rescue Advisory Group, to improve efficiency and effectiveness in the provision of international urban search and rescue assistance, and, in this context noting its resolution 57/150 of 16 December 2002 entitled "Strengthening the effectiveness and coordination of international urban search and rescue assistance",

Encouraging, in this regard, efforts aimed at strengthening the International Search and Rescue Advisory Group and its regional groups, particularly through the participation in their activities of representatives of a larger number of countries,

Mindful of the effects that shortfalls in resources can have on the preparedness for and response to natural disasters, and underscoring, in this regard, the need to gain a more precise understanding of the impact of levels of funding on natural disaster response,

Underlining the need for further improvement in information and analyses available regarding needs, responses and funding related to natural disasters,

1. *Takes note* of the reports of the Secretary-General entitled "International cooperation on humanitarian assistance in the field of natural disasters, from relief to development" and "Strengthening the coordination of emergency humanitarian assistance of the United Nations";

2. *Expresses its deep concern* at the high number and the scale of natural disasters and their increasing impact, resulting in massive losses of life and property worldwide, in particular in vulnerable societies lacking adequate capacity to mitigate effectively the long-term negative social, economic and environmental consequences of natural disasters;

3. *Calls upon* all States to adopt, where required, and to continue to implement effectively necessary legislative and other appropriate measures to mitigate the effects of natural disasters and integrate disaster risk reduction strategies into development planning, inter alia, by disaster prevention, including appropriate

land-use and building regulations, as well as disaster preparedness and capacity-building in disaster response and mitigation, and requests the international community to continue to assist developing countries as well as countries with economies in transition, bearing in mind their vulnerability to natural hazards, in this regard;

4. *Stresses,* in this context, the importance of strengthening international cooperation, particularly through the effective use of multilateral mechanisms, in the provision of humanitarian assistance through all phases of a disaster, from relief and mitigation to development, including the provision of adequate resources;

5. *Also stresses* that humanitarian assistance for natural disasters should be provided in accordance with and with due respect for the guiding principles contained in the annex to resolution 46/182 and should be determined on the basis of the human dimension and needs arising out of the particular natural disasters;

6. *Recognizes* that economic growth and sustainable development contribute to improving the capacity of States to mitigate, respond to and prepare for natural disasters;

7. *Reaffirms* that disaster risk analysis and vulnerability reduction form an integral part of humanitarian assistance, poverty eradication and sustainable development strategies and need to be considered in the development plans of all vulnerable countries and communities, including, where appropriate, in plans relating to post-disaster recovery and the transition from relief to development, and affirms that within such preventive strategies, disaster preparedness and early warning systems must be further strengthened at the country and regional levels, inter alia, through better coordination among relevant United Nations bodies and cooperation with Governments of affected countries and regional and other relevant organizations with the aim of maximizing the effectiveness of natural disaster response and reducing the impact of natural disasters, particularly in developing countries;

8. *Emphasizes* the importance of the outcome of the Twenty-eighth International Conference of the Red Cross and Red Crescent, held in Geneva from 2 to 6 December 2003;

9. *Also emphasizes* the importance of enhanced international cooperation, including through the United Nations and regional organizations, to assist developing countries in their efforts to build local and national capacities and to effectively and efficiently predict, prepare for and respond to natural disasters;

10. *Stresses* the need for partnerships among Governments, organizations of the United Nations system, relevant humanitarian organizations and specialized companies to promote training to strengthen preparedness for and response to natural disasters;

11. *Calls upon* States, the United Nations and other relevant actors, as appropriate, to assist in addressing knowledge gaps in disaster management and risk reduction by identifying ways of improving systems and networks for the collection and analysis of information on disasters, vulnerability and risk to facilitate informed decision-making;

12. *Stresses* the need to promote the access to and transfer of technology and knowledge related to early warning systems and to mitigation programmes to developing countries affected by natural disasters;

13. *Encourages* the further use of space-based and ground-based remote-sensing technologies for the prevention, mitigation and management of natural disasters, where appropriate;

14. *Also encourages* in such operations the sharing of geographical data, including remotely sensed images and geographic information system and global positioning system data, among Governments, space agencies and relevant international humanitarian and development organizations, as appropriate, and notes in that context initiatives such as those undertaken by the International Charter on Space and Major Disasters and the Global Disaster Information Network;

15. *Stresses* that particular international cooperation efforts should be undertaken to enhance and broaden further the utilization of national and local capacities, including within the framework of the International Search and Rescue Advisory Group, and, where appropriate, of regional and subregional capacities of developing countries for disaster preparedness and response, which may be made available in closer proximity to the site of a disaster, more efficiently and at lower cost;

16. *Recognizes,* in this regard, that the United Nations Disaster Assessment and Coordination system continues to be a valuable tool by which disaster management expertise is made available by Member States to respond to the sudden onset of emergencies;

17. *Urges* Member States, with the support of relevant bodies of the United Nations system, to strengthen efforts to identify practical ways to channel resources to and strengthen support for national disaster management capacities in disaster-prone countries;

18. *Welcomes* the role of the Office for the Coordination of Humanitarian Affairs of the Secretariat as the focal point within the overall United Nations system for the promotion and coordination of disaster responses among United Nations humanitarian agencies and other humanitarian partners;

19. *Takes note with interest* of the initiatives taken by the Office for the Coordination of Humanitarian Affairs and the United Nations Development Programme for the establishment of regional positions of disaster response advisers and disaster reduction advisers to assist developing countries in capacity-building for disaster prevention, preparedness, mitigation and response in a coordinated and complementary manner;

20. *Encourages* further cooperation between the United Nations system and regional organizations in order to increase the capacity of these organizations to respond to natural disasters;

21. *Encourages* States that have not acceded to or ratified the Tampere Convention on the Provision of Telecommunication Resources for Disaster Mitigation and Relief Operations, adopted at Tampere, Finland, on 18 June 1998, to consider doing so;

22. *Reiterates its request* that the Secretary-General, in collaboration with the relevant organizations and partners, finalize the establishment of, and then update periodically, the Directory of Advanced Technologies for Disaster Response as a new part of the Central Register of Disaster Management Capacities;

23. *Encourages* donors to consider the importance of ensuring that assistance in the case of higher-profile natural disasters does not come at the expense of those that may have a relatively lower profile, bearing in mind that the allocation of resources should be driven by needs, as well as the importance of making efforts to increase the level of assistance for disaster reduction and preparedness programmes and for disaster response and mitigation activities;

24. *Requests* the Secretary-General to examine ways to further improve the assessment of needs and responses and to enhance the availability of data regarding funding in response to natural disasters and to consider concrete recommendations to improve the international response to natural disasters, as necessary, based on his examination, keeping in mind also the need to address any geographical and sectoral imbalances and shortfalls in such responses, where they exist, as well as the more effective use of national emergency response agencies, and to report thereon to the General Assembly at its sixtieth session.

International Strategy for Disaster Reduction

In response to General Assembly resolution 58/214 [YUN 2003, p. 958], the Secretary-General, in an August report [A/59/228], described UN activities to implement the International Strategy for Disaster Reduction (ISDR), which was adopted by the programme forum of the International Decade for Natural Disaster Reduction (1990-2000) in 1999 [YUN 1999, p. 859] and endorsed by the Assembly in resolution 54/219 [ibid., p. 861]. The Inter-Agency Task Force for Disaster Reduction and the ISDR secretariat served as the main mechanisms for the Strategy's implementation by the UN system.

Preliminary findings of the 10-year review, initiated in 2003 [YUN 2003, p. 958], of the Yokohama Strategy for a Safer World: Guidelines for Natural Disaster Prevention, Preparedness and Mitigation and its Plan of Action [YUN 1994, p. 851], showed that it remained a powerful guide for disaster risk reduction and that significant progress had been made in some areas, especially in integrating disaster risk management into development sectors. However, progress was still seriously handicapped by a lack of systematic implementation and the progressive increase in risk factors. More systematic approaches and greater commitment by Governments were required to build national and community resilience to natural hazards and to protect lives and livelihoods. Regional and thematic meetings held in 2003 and 2004 in the Asia, Africa, South Pacific and Latin America and Caribbean regions provided inputs relevant to the review and the programme outcome of the 2005 World Conference on Disaster Reduction.

The Inter-Agency Task Force on Disaster Reduction continued to evolve, adapting its programme to current policy requirements and addressing emerging issues, following the recommendations made in the 2003 implementation report [YUN 2003, p. 958]. The aim was to strengthen the Task Force as a global mechanism for devising strategies and policies and enhancing coordination. Priority areas of the 2004 work programme included guidance and assistance on current major policy processes; strengthening disaster risk reduction in Africa; adaptation to climate change and extreme weather events; data on impacts, risk and vulnerability; and urban risk and vulnerability. The ninth meeting of the Task Force (Geneva, 4-5 May) established a working group to provide specific guidance on the substantive work of the Conference.

Through collaborative partnerships and national and local support, the UN system specialized agencies and programmes, regional bodies and civil society organizations made substantial contributions to ISDR implementation in the areas of governance, inter-agency knowledge management, community-based risk reduction and preparedness, science, risk assessment, monitoring and early warning, and the reduction of underlying risk factors. The ISDR secretariat contributed to the two-year review cycle on water, sanitation and human settlements by the Commission on Sustainable Development (see p. 827), resulting in disaster risk being recognized as a cross-cutting issue in those areas. In cooperation with UNDP, it developed a framework setting out the key elements for systematic disaster risk reduction, and was promoting the use of national platforms for advancing the implementation of disaster risk reduction. With support from Germany, the ISDR secretariat made progress in developing the early warning platform recommended by the Second (2003) International Conference in Early Warning [YUN 2003, p. 957]. The revised version of its flagship publication, *Living with Risk: a Global Review of Disaster Reduction Initiatives*, was launched in July 2004. An institutional internal review of the tripartite arrangement between OCHA, UNDP and the ISDR secretariat was underway. ISDR funding, provided by a small number of donors, remained unpredictable, and insufficient.

The Secretary-General encouraged all parties to contribute to the 2005 World Conference on Disaster Reduction and to the development of a substantive international programme for guiding action and investments. Member States and regional organizations were urged to follow the example of the Assembly of the African Union and the Pacific Forum in developing disaster reduction strategies and programmes to enable all countries to integrate disaster reduction into national development processes. In follow-up to the request made by the General Assembly in resolution 58/215 [YUN 2003, p. 960], the Secretary-General stated that progress had been made in developing linkages between disaster reduction and adaptation to climate change. The initiatives undertaken under the Strategy demonstrated the capacity of ISDR and its secretariat to deal effectively and quickly with emerging and cross-cutting issues. Those efforts should be pursued, particularly within the processes of the United Nations Framework Convention on Climate Change (see p. 1051) and the Intergovernmental Panel on Climate Change.

As requested by the Assembly in resolution 58/214 [YUN 2003, p. 958], the Secretary-General was looking into allocating adequate financial and administrative resources for the effective functioning of the ISDR secretariat. Meanwhile, the international community was encouraged to provide the necessary financial support to the Trust Fund for the Strategy.

World Conference on Disaster Reduction (2005). The Preparatory Committee for the World Conference on Disaster Reduction, to be held in Kobe, Japan, from 18 to 22 January 2005, held its first (Geneva, 6-7 May) [A/CONF.206/PC(I)/6 & Corr.1], and second (Geneva, 11-12 October) [A/CONF.206/PC(II)/10] sessions. The Committee reviewed the procedural and organizational aspects of the Conference preparations and a draft programme outcome document entitled "Building the resilience of nations and communities to disasters: elements for a programme of action", prepared by the ISDR secretariat [A/CONF.206/PC(II)/4]. It also considered a draft review [A/CONF.206/PC(II)/3] of the 1994 Yokohama Strategy and Plan of Action [YUN 1994, p. 851].

The themes of the Conference, corresponding to the major findings of the review of the Yokohama Strategy and its Plan of Action, would be: governance: institutional and policy frameworks for risk reduction; risk identification, assessment, monitoring and early warning; knowledge management and education: building a culture of resilient communities; reducing the underlying risk factors; and preparedness for effective response. The thematic segment would focus on good practices and implementation and would include a regional session for the exchange of experience and lessons learned in different regions. Three high-level round tables would focus on disaster risk: the next development challenge; learning to live with risk; and emerging risks. Governments, civil society organizations, technical and academic institutions and the private sec-

tor would disseminate information and present exhibits at a public forum. A conference unit was established within the ISDR secretariat to coordinate preparations. Japan pledged $2.5 million to cover Conference costs.

GENERAL ASSEMBLY ACTION

On 22 December [meeting 75], the General Assembly, on the recommendation of the Second Committee [A/59/483/Add.3], adopted **resolution 59/231** without vote [agenda item 85 (c)].

International Strategy for Disaster Reduction

The General Assembly,

Recalling its resolutions 44/236 of 22 December 1989, 49/22 A of 2 December 1994, 49/22 B of 20 December 1994, 53/185 of 15 December 1998, 54/219 of 22 December 1999, 56/195 of 21 December 2001, 57/256 of 20 December 2002 and 58/214 of 23 December 2003 and Economic and Social Council resolutions 1999/63 of 30 July 1999 and 2001/35 of 26 July 2001, and taking into due consideration its resolution 57/270 B of 23 June 2003 on integrated and coordinated implementation of and follow-up to the outcomes of the major United Nations conferences and summits in the economic and social fields,

Recalling also the inclusion of the item entitled "Disaster management and vulnerability" in the multi-year programme of work of the Commission on Sustainable Development,

Reiterating that, although natural disasters damage the social and economic infrastructure of all countries, the long-term consequences of natural disasters are especially severe for developing countries and hamper the achievement of their sustainable development,

Recognizing the urgent need to further develop and make use of the existing scientific and technical knowledge to build resilience to natural disasters, and emphasizing the need for developing countries to have access to technology so as to tackle natural disasters effectively,

Expressing its deep concern at the number and scale of natural disasters and their increasing impact within recent years, which have resulted in massive loss of life and long-term negative social, economic and environmental consequences for vulnerable societies throughout the world, in particular in developing countries,

Recognizing the need to continue to develop an understanding of, and to address, socio-economic activities that exacerbate the vulnerability of societies to natural disasters and to build and further strengthen community capability to cope with disaster risks,

Emphasizing that disaster reduction, including reducing vulnerability to natural disasters, is an important element that contributes to the achievement of sustainable development,

Stressing the importance of advancing the implementation of the Plan of Implementation of the World Summit on Sustainable Development, and its relevant provisions on vulnerability, risk assessment and disaster management,

Noting the ongoing work of all the working groups established by the Inter-Agency Task Force for Disaster Reduction, namely the Working Group on Climate Change and Disaster Risk Reduction, the Working

Group on Disaster Reduction in Africa, the Working Group on Risk, Vulnerability and Disaster Impact Assessment and the Working Group on the World Conference on Disaster Reduction,

1. *Takes note* of the report of the Secretary-General on the implementation of the International Strategy for Disaster Reduction;

2. *Invites* Governments and relevant international organizations to consider disaster risk assessment as an integral component of development plans and poverty eradication programmes;

3. *Welcomes* the work of the ongoing preparatory process for the World Conference on Disaster Reduction, to be held in Kobe, Japan, from 18 to 22 January 2005;

4. *Notes with appreciation* the generous pledge made by the Government of Japan to cover costs of the World Conference, and welcomes the voluntary contributions already made to facilitate the participation of representatives of developing countries, in particular the least developed countries, in that event, and invites those States that have not yet done so to make such voluntary contributions;

5. *Reiterates its invitation* to Member States, all United Nations bodies and the specialized agencies and other relevant intergovernmental agencies and organizations, in particular the members of the Inter-Agency Task Force for Disaster Reduction, to participate actively in the World Conference;

6. *Encourages* major groups, as identified in Agenda 21, to contribute further to and actively participate in the World Conference, according to the rules of procedure agreed upon by its Preparatory Committee;

7. *Stresses* the importance of close cooperation and coordination between the relevant institutions, in particular within the United Nations system and with other relevant international organizations, in both the preparation of and follow-up to the World Conference, within their mandate and taking into account their comparative advantages and the need to avoid any duplication of work;

8. *Also stresses* that continued cooperation and coordination among Governments, the United Nations system, other organizations, regional organizations, non-governmental organizations and other partners, as appropriate, are considered essential to address effectively the impact of natural disasters;

9. *Recognizes* the importance of linking disaster risk management with regional frameworks, as appropriate, such as with the New Partnership for Africa's Development, to address issues of poverty eradication and sustainable development;

10. *Also recognizes* the importance of integrating a gender perspective as well as of engaging women in the design and implementation of all phases of disaster management, particularly in the disaster reduction stage;

11. *Stresses* the importance of identifying, assessing and managing risks prior to the occurrence of disasters, for which it is necessary to combine the efforts at all levels of the development, humanitarian, scientific and environmental communities, as well as the importance of integrating disaster reduction, as appropriate, into development plans and poverty eradication programmes;

12. *Also stresses* the need to foster better understanding and knowledge of the causes of disasters, as well as to build and strengthen coping capacities through, inter alia, the transfer and exchange of experiences and technical knowledge, access to relevant data and information and the strengthening of institutional arrangements, including community-based organizations;

13. *Recognizes* the importance of early warning as an essential element of disaster reduction, recommends the implementation of the outcome of the Second International Conference on Early Warning, held in Bonn, Germany, from 16 to 18 October 2003, and takes note of further work done in this regard, including the establishment of the Platform for the Promotion of Early Warning in Bonn;

14. *Calls upon* Governments to establish national platforms or focal points for disaster reduction, encourages the platforms to share relevant information on standards and practices, encourages Governments to strengthen platforms where they already exist, urges the United Nations system to provide appropriate support for those mechanisms, and invites the Secretary-General to strengthen the regional outreach of the inter-agency secretariat for the International Strategy for Disaster Reduction in order to ensure such support;

15. *Requests* the Under-Secretary-General for Humanitarian Affairs, in his capacity as Chairman of the Inter-Agency Task Force for Disaster Reduction, to continue reviewing annually the work carried out by its working groups in order to ensure their effective contribution to the attainment of the objectives of the Strategy;

16. *Expresses its appreciation* to those countries that have provided financial support for the activities of the Strategy by making voluntary contributions to the Trust Fund for the International Strategy for Disaster Reduction;

17. *Encourages* the international community to provide the necessary financial resources to the Trust Fund for the Strategy and to provide the necessary scientific, technical, human and other resources to ensure adequate support for the activities of the inter-agency secretariat for the Strategy and the Inter-Agency Task Force for Disaster Reduction and its working groups;

18. *Requests* the Secretary-General to allocate adequate financial and administrative resources, within existing resources, for the effective functioning of the inter-agency secretariat for the Strategy;

19. *Also requests* the Secretary-General to submit to the General Assembly at its sixtieth session a report on the implementation of the present resolution, in particular on the outcome of the World Conference on Disaster Reduction, under the item entitled "Sustainable development".

GENERAL ASSEMBLY ACTION

On 22 December [meeting 75], the Assembly, also on the recommendation of the Second Committee [A/59/483/Add.3], adopted **resolution 59/233** without vote [agenda item 85 *(c)*].

Natural disasters and vulnerability

The General Assembly,

Recalling its decision 57/547 of 20 December 2002 and its resolution 58/215 of 23 December 2003,

Taking into account the Johannesburg Declaration on Sustainable Development and the Plan of Implementation of the World Summit on Sustainable Development, adopted by the World Summit, held in Johannesburg, South Africa, from 26 August to 4 September 2002,

Recognizing the need to continue to develop an understanding of, and to address, socio-economic activities that exacerbate the vulnerability of societies to natural disasters, to build and further strengthen community capacity to cope with disaster risks and to enhance resilience against hazards associated with disasters,

Noting that the global environment continues to suffer degradation, adding to economic and social vulnerabilities, in particular in developing countries,

Taking into account the various ways and forms in which all countries, in particular the more vulnerable countries, are affected by severe natural hazards such as earthquakes and volcanic eruptions and extreme weather events such as heat waves, severe droughts, floods and storms, and the El Niño/La Niña events, which have global reach,

Recognizing that the impact of natural disasters upon vulnerable countries is, among others, a significant obstacle to the achievement of the internationally agreed development goals, including those contained in the United Nations Millennium Declaration, in particular those relating to poverty eradication and environmental sustainability,

Expressing deep concern at the recent increases in the frequency and intensity of extreme weather events and associated natural disasters in some regions of the world and their substantial economic, social and environmental impacts, in particular upon developing countries in those regions,

Taking into account that extreme weather events and associated natural disasters and their reduction must be dealt with in a coherent and effective manner,

Expressing deep concern at the increasing negative impact of severe natural hazards, including earthquakes, extreme weather events and associated natural disasters, which continues to hinder social and economic progress, in particular in developing countries,

Stressing the need to develop and implement risk-reduction strategies, including disaster preparedness, mitigation and early warning systems at all levels, and to integrate them, where appropriate, into national development plans, in particular through the implementation of the International Strategy for Disaster Reduction, so as to enhance the resilience of populations to disasters and reduce the risks to them, their livelihoods, the social and economic infrastructure and environmental resources,

Recognizing that the development of stronger institutions, mechanisms and capacities, including at the community level, that can systematically build resilience to hazards and disasters is essential to reducing the risks and vulnerability of populations to disasters,

Noting the need for international cooperation to increase the capacity of countries to respond to the negative impacts of all natural hazards, including earthquakes, extreme weather events and associated natural disasters, particularly in developing countries,

1. *Takes note* of the report of the Secretary-General on the implementation of the International Strategy for Disaster Reduction, in particular section II, on natural disasters and vulnerability;

2. *Urges* the international community to continue to address ways and means, including through cooperation and technical assistance, to reduce the adverse effects of natural disasters, including those caused by extreme weather events, in particular in vulnerable developing countries, through the implementation of the International Strategy for Disaster Reduction, and encourages the Inter-Agency Task Force for Disaster Reduction to continue its work in this regard;

3. *Stresses* the importance for the World Conference on Disaster Reduction to conclude the review of the Yokohama Strategy for a Safer World: Guidelines for Natural Disaster Prevention, Preparedness and Mitigation and its Plan of Action, with a view to updating the guiding framework on disaster reduction for the twenty-first century, and to identify specific activities aimed at ensuring the implementation of relevant provisions of the Plan of Implementation of the World Summit on Sustainable Development on vulnerability, risk assessment and disaster management, bearing in mind the vital importance of addressing the adverse effects of natural disasters in efforts to achieve the internationally agreed development goals, including those contained in the United Nations Millennium Declaration;

4. *Emphasizes* that the World Conference on Disaster Reduction should, within its mandate as set out in General Assembly resolution 58/214 of 23 December 2003, make concrete recommendations to reduce the risks and vulnerabilities of all countries, in particular developing countries, in relation to disasters, including through the provision of technical and financial assistance, as well as through the strengthening of International Strategy for Disaster Reduction national platforms for disaster reduction or the establishment of institutional mechanisms, including at the regional level, where appropriate;

5. *Encourages* Governments, through their respective International Strategy for Disaster Reduction national platforms and national focal points for disaster reduction, in cooperation with the United Nations system and other stakeholders, to strengthen capacity-building in the most vulnerable regions, to enable them to address the socio-economic factors that increase vulnerability, and to develop measures that will enable them to prepare for and cope with natural disasters, including those associated with earthquakes and extreme weather events, and encourages the international community to provide effective assistance to developing countries in this regard;

6. *Also encourages* the Inter-Agency Task Force for Disaster Reduction to continue to enhance the coordination of activities to promote disaster reduction and to make available to the relevant United Nations entities information on options for natural disaster reduction, including severe natural hazards and extreme weather-related disasters and vulnerabilities;

7. *Stresses* the importance of close cooperation and coordination among Governments, the United Nations system, other organizations, regional organizations, non-governmental organizations and other partners as appropriate, taking into account the need for the development of disaster management strategies, including the effective establishment of early warning systems, where appropriate, while taking advantage of all available resources and expertise for that purpose;

8. *Encourages* the Conference of the Parties to the United Nations Framework Convention on Climate Change and the parties to the Kyoto Protocol to the United Nations Framework Convention on Climate Change to continue to address the adverse effects of climate change, especially in developing countries that are particularly vulnerable, in accordance with the provisions of the Convention, and also encourages the Intergovernmental Panel on Climate Change to continue to assess the adverse effects of climate change on the socio-economic and natural disaster reduction systems of developing countries;

9. *Requests* the Secretary-General to report to the General Assembly at its sixtieth session on the implementation of the present resolution in a separate section of his report on the implementation of the International Strategy for Disaster Reduction, and decides to consider the issue of natural disasters and vulnerability at that session, under the sub-item entitled "International Strategy for Disaster Reduction" of the item entitled "Sustainable development".

El Niño

In response to General Assembly resolution 57/255 [YUN 2002, p. 930], the Secretary-General, in August [A/59/228], provided information on international cooperation to reduce the impact of the El Niño phenomenon—a disruption of the ocean-atmosphere system in the tropical Pacific that had important consequences for weather and climate worldwide.

The international community continued to improve capacities to predict and respond to future events of El Niño and La Niña—the cool phase of the El Niño cycle. Seasonal forecasts of climatic anomalies could be used for disaster management, even when no El Niño or La Niña event was present. The International Research Centre on the El Niño phenomenon in Guayaquil, Ecuador, established in 2003 [YUN 2003, p. 961], developed an international board, a fund-raising strategy and specific projects. The Andean Disaster Prevention Programme of the Andean Development Bank was conducting a study to help the Centre structure its organizational basis and links with other initiatives and organizations working in the field of El Niño, in particular in the Andean countries.

GENERAL ASSEMBLY ACTION

On 22 December [meeting 75], the General Assembly, on the recommendation of the Second Committee [A/59/483/Add.3], adopted **resolution 59/232** without vote [agenda item 85 (c)].

International cooperation to reduce the impact of the El Niño phenomenon

The General Assembly,

Recalling its resolutions 52/200 of 18 December 1997, 53/185 of 15 December 1998, 54/220 of 22 December 1999, 55/197 of 20 December 2000, 56/194 of 21 December 2001 and 57/255 of 20 December 2002 and Economic and Social Council resolutions 1999/46 of 28 July 1999, 1999/63 of 30 July 1999 and 2000/33 of 28 July 2000,

Noting that the El Niño phenomenon has a recurring character and that it can lead to extensive natural hazards with the potential to seriously affect humankind,

Reaffirming the importance of developing strategies at the national, subregional, regional and international levels that aim to prevent, mitigate and repair the damage caused by natural disasters that result from the El Niño phenomenon,

Noting that technological developments and international cooperation have enhanced the capabilities for the prediction of the El Niño phenomenon and thereby the potential for the preventive actions that may be taken to reduce its negative impacts,

Taking into account the Johannesburg Declaration on Sustainable Development and the Plan of Implementation of the World Summit on Sustainable Development ("Johannesburg Plan of Implementation"), in particular paragraph 37 (*i*) thereof,

1. *Takes note* of the report of the Secretary-General on the implementation of the International Strategy for Disaster Reduction, in particular the section entitled "International cooperation to reduce the impact of the El Niño phenomenon";

2. *Welcomes* the efforts of the Government of Ecuador, the World Meteorological Organization and the inter-agency secretariat for the International Strategy for Disaster Reduction which led to the establishment of the International Centre for the Study of the El Niño Phenomenon at Guayaquil, Ecuador, and to its opening in February 2003, and encourages those parties to continue their efforts for the advancement of the Centre;

3. *Calls upon* the Secretary-General and the relevant United Nations organs, funds and programmes, in particular those taking part in the International Strategy for Disaster Reduction, encourages the international community to adopt, as appropriate, the necessary measures to support the development of the International Centre for the Study of the El Niño Phenomenon, and invites the international community to provide scientific, technical and financial assistance and cooperation for this purpose, as well as to strengthen, as appropriate, other centres devoted to the study of the El Niño phenomenon;

4. *Encourages* the Centre to strengthen its links, as appropriate, with national meteorological and hydrological services of the Latin American region, the Permanent Commission for the South Pacific, the Inter-American Institute for Global Change Research and the International Research Institute for Climate Prediction, as well as with other relevant regional and global organizations that study climate, such as the European Centre for Medium-Range Weather Forecasts, the African Centre of Meteorological Applications for Development, the Drought Monitoring Centre and the Asia-Pacific Network for Global Change Research, and other relevant centres, as appropriate, in order to ensure the effective and efficient use of the available resources;

5. *Underscores* the importance of maintaining the El Niño/Southern Oscillation observation system, continuing research into extreme weather events, improving forecasting skills and developing appropriate

policies for reducing the impact of the El Niño phenomenon and other extreme weather events and emphasizes the need to further develop and strengthen these institutional capacities in all countries, in particular in developing countries;

6. *Requests* the Secretary-General to report to the General Assembly at its sixty-first session on the implementation of the present resolution, under the item entitled "Sustainable development".

Disaster assistance

Bangladesh

Heavy monsoon rains in Bangladesh in late June, combined with torrential flows from India, Nepal, China (Tibet) and Bhutan, and snow melt from the Himalayas led to floods that devastated large areas of Bangladesh in July, affecting 33 million people. Gastro-enteric and other diseases were rife as millions of clean water sources were contaminated and sanitation facilities were disrupted. Hundreds of thousands of homes were completely washed away or damaged, and other buildings, including schools, clinics and small businesses were severely affected. Roads between communities were submerged, as well as over 2,000,000 acres of agricultural land.

The UN Consolidated Inter-Agency Flash Appeal for Bangladesh, covering the period from August 2004 to January 2005, was launched for the immediate relief and early recovery needs of the poorest and most vulnerable victims of the floods. The Flash Appeal sought $209.9 million, of which 31 per cent ($65 million) was received.

Bolivia

A prolonged drought severely threatened the food security, health and nutritional status of children and adults in the El Chaco region of Bolivia. The cumulative effects of past years and the acute nature of the 2004 drought put the region at risk of a major humanitarian crisis. According to assessments conducted by FAO, UNICEF, WFP and the Government in July and August, the drought affected an estimated 180,000 people, including 26,000 children under five years of age. Food availability was expected to worsen until the next harvest in May 2005.

Following the 5 October declaration by the Bolivian Government of the drought-affected El Chaco region as a national disaster area, the UN Consolidated Inter-Agency Flash Appeal for Bolivia was launched to respond to immediate needs of approximately 55,000 of the most affected population. The Flash Appeal, which covered the period from 1 November 2004 to 31 May 2005, sought $1.8 million; it received 51 per cent ($930,368) of that amount.

Ethiopia

In response to General Assembly resolution 58/24 [YUN 2003, p. 961], the Secretary-General, in his August consolidated report [A/59/293], provided information on humanitarian and rehabilitation assistance to Ethiopia.

Ethiopia continued to be affected by the 2002 drought which caused widespread acute food insecurity by late 2002 and 2003, and required the mobilization of a huge humanitarian effort. Although the rains in 2003 were significantly better than in 2002, resulting in a crop surplus, many pockets of chronic and acute food insecurity remained in Ethiopia, requiring a further appeal for humanitarian assistance in 2004. Consequently, in December 2003, the Government, the United Nations and humanitarian partners appealed for $85 million of non-food assistance and 871,000 tons of food to meet humanitarian needs in 2004 for an estimated 7.2 million people. As at the end of June, the net food requirements were 79.1 per cent funded, with additional pledges under discussion. However, non-food items were only 38 per cent funded.

The Secretary-General stated that the success of the 2003 relief operation in preventing widespread death and suffering was recognized as a major achievement, which was accredited to donor commitment; effective early warning systems; effective coordination at the federal, regional and *weredas* (district) levels; early response of the Government, which contributed 45,000 metric tons of wheat; and improved logistics capacity. Drought had become a chronic hazard in Ethiopia that was related to the erosion of the natural resource base caused by high population growth, deforestation, desiccation of water resources, insufficient family farming plots and climate change. Recurrent droughts increased the vulnerability of the population.

Group of Eight initiative. The Group of Eight (G-8) countries (Canada, France, Germany, Italy, Japan, Russian Federation, United Kingdom, United States), during their 2004 summit (Sea Island, Georgia, United States, 8-10 June), launched an initiative to end famine in the Horn of Africa by improving worldwide emergency assessment; raising agricultural productivity; and helping 5 million people in Ethiopia attain food security by 2009.

GENERAL ASSEMBLY ACTION

On 22 December [meeting 75], the General Assembly, on the recommendation of the Second Committee [A/59/479 & Corr.1], adopted **resolution 59/217** without vote [agenda item 39 (*b*)].

Humanitarian assistance and rehabilitation for Ethiopia

The General Assembly,

Recalling its resolution 58/24 of 5 December 2003 on emergency humanitarian assistance to Ethiopia,

Recalling also the initiatives of the Secretary-General to improve food security, including the appointment of the Special Envoy for the Humanitarian Crisis in the Horn of Africa,

Concerned by the recurrent drought, which still affects millions owing to the serious crop failures in drought-prone parts of the country and the pastoralist areas that have weak infrastructures and low development capacities,

Bearing in mind the joint 2005 appeal of the United Nations and the Government of Ethiopia for emergency assistance for Ethiopia, to respond to the food and non-food requirements of households in need so as to prevent the worsening of the current humanitarian crisis,

Noting with serious concern the significant and persistent humanitarian needs in such areas as health, water and acute malnutrition that still exist in parts of the country,

Also noting with serious concern the dire humanitarian situation and its long-term socio-economic and environmental impacts,

Recognizing that the persistent problem of food insecurity is linked to inadequate progress in achieving and sustaining rural growth at levels required to build the household and community assets needed to manage through the various shocks that induce food crises,

Emphasizing the need to address the crisis, bearing in mind the importance of the transition from relief to development, and acknowledging the underlying structural causes of recurrent drought in Ethiopia,

Recognizing that the main responsibility for improving the humanitarian situation and creating conditions for long-term development lies with the Government of Ethiopia, while bearing in mind the important role played by the international community,

Emphasizing the importance of establishing a strong early warning system for both food and non-food needs in order to predict better and respond as early as possible to disasters and to minimize their consequences,

1. *Takes note* of the report of the Secretary-General;

2. *Welcomes* the coordinated and collaborative efforts of the Government of Ethiopia, agencies, funds and programmes of the United Nations system, the donor community, non-governmental organizations and other entities for their timely and generous response to the joint 2004 appeal;

3. *Calls upon* the international community to respond in a timely manner to the joint 2005 appeal of the United Nations and the Government of Ethiopia for emergency assistance for Ethiopia, covering food and non-food needs;

4. *Welcomes* the efforts of the Government of Ethiopia, the international community and civil society, including non-governmental organizations, to strengthen mechanisms already in place to respond to such emergency situations, appreciates their endeavours to increase the availability of food through the procurement of local produce and to ensure access of

households in need to food, health and water facilities, sanitation, seeds and veterinary services, and strongly encourages the Government of Ethiopia to continue such efforts;

5. *Stresses* the need to address the underlying causes of food insecurity, and issues of recovery, asset protection and the sustainable development of the affected areas, welcomes in this regard the programme prepared by the Coalition for Food Security in Ethiopia, and encourages the international community to support the Coalition in realizing its main objective, namely, breaking the cycle of food aid dependency within the next three to five years, thereby enabling fifteen million vulnerable people to engage in sustainable productive activities;

6. *Welcomes* the Group of Eight action plan on ending the cycle of famine in the Horn of Africa, and looks forward to its full implementation;

7. *Encourages* the Government of Ethiopia to continue to strengthen its efforts to address the underlying structural causes of recurrent threats of drought as part of its overall economic development programme;

8. *Calls upon* all development partners, in cooperation with the Government of Ethiopia, to integrate relief efforts with recovery, asset protection and long-term development, including the structural and productive options needed to stimulate accelerated rural growth, and to address the underlying causes of recurrent drought in Ethiopia in a way that is, inter alia, in line with the poverty reduction strategy paper, including strategies that are aimed at preventing such crises in the future and that improve the resilience of the population;

9. *Welcomes* the initiative taken by the Secretary-General in appointing a Special Envoy for the Humanitarian Crisis in the Horn of Africa, with the objective of mobilizing resources to address the root causes of food insecurity as well as the sustainable development of the affected areas;

10. *Invites* the Office for the Coordination of Humanitarian Affairs of the Secretariat to continue its efforts to coordinate and develop a strategic response to recurrent humanitarian needs in Ethiopia and to consider ways to enhance the mobilization of emergency relief assistance to cover the remaining humanitarian needs in Ethiopia;

11. *Takes note* of the report on evaluation of the response to the 2002-2003 emergency in Ethiopia prepared jointly by the Government of Ethiopia and humanitarian partners, and urges the Government of Ethiopia, donors and all other stakeholders to implement its recommendations;

12. *Requests* the Secretary-General to report to the General Assembly at its sixtieth session on the implementation of the present resolution.

Grenada

On 7 September, Hurricane Ivan, a category 4 storm, hit Grenada, leaving some 37 people dead, and most of the population of 102,000 affected. Four of the island nation's six parishes—St. Andrew, St. David, St. Georges and St. John—were completely devastated. Approximately 90 per cent of the houses were damaged or destroyed and, according to Government statistics, some 50 per cent of the population were left homeless. Food shortages and distribution were a major challenge. It was estimated that over 60 per cent of employment in the tourism industry was likely lost, and the agriculture sector was decimated.

The UN Consolidated Inter-Agency Flash Appeal for Grenada, intended to respond to the urgent humanitarian needs and quickly establish the foundation for rehabilitation of social services and economic recovery, sought $27.6 million for the period 1 October 2004 to 31 March 2005, of which 24 per cent ($6.6 million) was received.

Haiti

On 18 September, the passage of Tropical Storm Jeanne brought heavy rains to Haiti and caused violent flash floods in the Artibonite and North West departments of the country, particularly affecting the towns of Gonaïves and Port-de-Paix. According to the Haitian Civil Protection Directorate, 1,514 people died as a result of the floods, 952 were missing and 2,600 were injured. The total number of people affected was estimated at 298,926.

The UN Consolidated Inter-Agency Haiti Floods Flash Appeal sought $37.4 million for emergency relief and the early recovery needs of the Haitian people affected by the floods, of which 47 per cent ($17.5 million) was received.

Iran

The UN Consolidated Inter-Agency Flash Appeal for Iran sought $32.7 million to address the relief, recovery and immediate rehabilitation requirements in the Bam region of Iran, which, on 26 December 2003 [YUN 2003, p. 962], was struck by an earthquake measuring 6.5 on the Richter scale, killing more than 30,000 people and rendering more than 75,000 homeless. Of the total amount required, 56 per cent ($18.4 million) was received.

Kenya

In 2004, drought-like conditions hit arid and semi-arid areas in Kenya, while erratic rainfall patterns caused crop failure on a massive scale in some of the fertile areas. Maize stocks in some areas of the country were contaminated with Aflatoxin, a toxin created by grain mold. Food shortages and the fear of famine resulted in abnormal grain price increases, which in turn had a negative impact on trade for vulnerable populations and on food security in general. Up to 2.3 million people were extremely food-insecure

and in need of emergency relief assistance, including 1.8 million requiring general food distribution and 0.5 million school children, for whom assistance under the school feeding programme was required

The UN Consolidated Inter-Agency Flash Appeal for Kenya sought $83.2 million covering the period from August 2004 to February 2005. Of that amount, 57 per cent ($47.4 million) was received.

Madagascar

Between 26 January and 4 February, tropical cyclone Elita hit Madagascar several times, leaving 29 people dead, 100 injured and 44,190 homeless. On 7 March, the intense tropical cyclone Gafilo hit the country killing 74 people. Of the estimated 774,000 people affected, 309,500 were in need of relief supplies.

The UN Consolidated Inter-Agency Flash Appeal for Madagascar sought $15.7 million to cover the period 19 March to 19 June. It received 47 per cent ($7.4 million) of the required amount.

The Philippines

During a three-week period in November and December, landslides and flash floods resulting from four consecutive typhoons and tropical storms caused widespread destruction in the Philippines, particularly on the eastern coast of the main island of Luzon. As at 13 December, the Government reported 1,060 dead, 1,023 injured and 559 missing. Houses, infrastructure, and crops were wiped out. The Government, with the assistance of the international community, mounted an immediate relief operation. Continued relief assistance was needed, and emergency rehabilitation activities required immediate support to restore life-sustaining services.

The UN Consolidated Inter-Agency Flash Appeal for the Philippines sought $6.4 million to meet the relief and emergency rehabilitation needs of the most vulnerable for the period from mid-December 2004 to mid-March 2005. Of the required amount, 23 per cent ($1.5 million) was received.

Indian Ocean tsunami

On 26 December, an earthquake off the coast of Indonesia registering 9.0 on the Richter scale created a massive tsunami, which struck Indonesia, Thailand, Sri Lanka, the Maldives, and the western coast of Africa in Somalia and Kenya. The earthquake and tsunami caused unprecedented destruction in terms of scale and geographic distribution, primarily affecting poor coastal communities in 12 countries. An estimated 240,000 people died and over 1 million were displaced. OCHA, working with Government officials, organized relief through coordinated sectoral working groups, created databases and websites to manage information, facilitated contributions to relief projects and resolved bottlenecks at major ports and hubs. It deployed four UN Disaster Assessment and Coordination (UNDAC) teams to Indonesia, the Maldives, Sri Lanka and Thailand, the most severely affected States, to liaise with Government authorities, organize inter-agency assessments and jump-start sectoral coordination meetings. OCHA established the Tsunami Task Force and chaired Inter-Agency Standing Committee (IASC) Tsunami Task Force video conferences between New York and Geneva.

Chapter IV

International trade, finance and transport

In 2004, international trade continued to grow, with the volume of world merchandise trade increasing markedly by an estimated 10.5 per cent, from 6.2 per cent in 2003. As manufacturing gathered pace and domestic demand improved in more economies, the brisk economic environment further raised the prices of commodities and manufactures, resulting in a nearly 19 per cent increase in the dollar value of global trade, to $8.6 trillion. Although developed countries, particularly North American States and Japan, accounted for much of the growth, many developing countries and economies in transition also experienced remarkable trade performance.

In June, the United Nations Conference on Trade and Development (UNCTAD) held its eleventh session, UNCTAD XI, in São Paulo, Brazil. The Conference concluded with the adoption of The Spirit of São Paulo, a declaration by which member States reaffirmed their commitment to support UNCTAD in fulfilling its mandate as the UN focal point for the integrated treatment of trade and development and for improving the coherence of the international monetary, financial and trading systems in order to respond better to development needs. The Conference also adopted the São Paulo Consensus, a policy statement and analysis confirming the 2000 Plan of Action adopted by UNCTAD X, as the guide to the future work of UNCTAD. The General Assembly stressed the need to implement the Consensus, and invited UNCTAD to analyse the role of enterprise development in alleviating poverty in the least developed countries.

Unprecedented diplomatic efforts during the year enabled the resumption of multilateral trade negotiations under the Doha (Qatar) work programme adopted at the 2001 World Trade Organization (WTO) Ministerial Conference. The talks culminated on 1 August in the adoption by the WTO General Council of a decision setting out frameworks for future negotiations in the areas of agriculture, non-agricultural market access, development issues, services and trade facilitation.

In April, the high-level meeting between the Economic and Social Council and the Bretton Woods institutions (the World Bank Group and the International Monetary Fund) discussed coherence, coordination and cooperation in the context of the implementation of the Monterrey Consensus, adopted at the 2002 International Conference on Financing for Development. Also during the year, a study commissioned by the United Nations proposed innovative sources of financing for development.

The Trade and Development Board, the governing body of UNCTAD, adopted agreed conclusions on the review of progress in the implementation of the Programme of Action for the Least Developed Countries for the Decade 2001-2010 and recommended that the outcomes of UNCTAD XI be considered when allocating resources to the Programme for the 2006-2007 biennium. The Board adopted further agreed conclusions on economic development in Africa: issues relating to Africa's debt sustainability, and a decision on the review of UNCTAD technical cooperation activities.

UNCTAD XI

The eleventh session of the United Nations Conference on Trade and Development, designated UNCTAD XI, was held in São Paulo, Brazil, from 13 to 18 June [TD/412], in accordance with General Assembly resolutions 1995(XIX) [YUN 1964, p. 210] and 57/235 [YUN 2002, p. 934]. Attended by 155 States and the Permanent Observer of Palestine, UN system bodies and numerous intergovernmental and non-governmental organizations, the Conference had as its theme "Enhancing coherence between national development strategies and global economic processes towards economic growth and development, particularly of developing countries". The focus on coherence was examined under four sub-themes: development strategies in a globalizing world economy; building productive capacity and international competitiveness; assuring development gains from the international trading system and trade negotiations; and partnership for development.

The Conference established a Committee of the Whole to consider and report on specific substantive items referred to it, and the draft negotiated text and annex for the Conference [TD/L.368 & Add.1], prepared and approved by the Trade and Development Board (TDB), acting as the Preparatory Committee for the Conference (see p. 956). The main Conference events were a high-level panel (13 June) on creative industries and development [TD/L.379]; a high-level segment (14 June) on the new geography of trade: South-South cooperation in an increasingly interdependent world [TD/404]; and a high-level round table (14 June) on trade and poverty [TD/L.384]. Parallel meetings included a civil society forum and a series of interactive thematic sessions on topics related to the Conference sub-themes. The Committee of Participants of the Global System of Trade Preferences (GSTP) among Developing Countries, at a special ministerial-level session (16 June), launched the third round of GSTP negotiations.

Declaration and Consensus

The Conference [TD/412] concluded on 18 June with the adoption of The Spirit of São Paulo, a political declaration by which UNCTAD member States affirmed their continuing commitment to support UNCTAD in fulfilling its mandate as the focal point within the United Nations for the integrated treatment of trade and development and to joint efforts towards the attainment of the international development goals set forth in previously adopted instruments and initiatives, including the United Nations Millennium Declaration [YUN 2000, p. 49]. They further committed themselves to eradicating poverty and hunger, and to improving coherence among the international monetary, financial and trading systems in order to respond better to development needs, giving utmost attention to the plight of the least developed countries (LDCs).

Also adopted was the São Paulo Consensus, an analytical, policy action and programmatic statement, which reaffirmed the two-part Plan of Action (Bangkok Plan of Action) adopted at UNCTAD X [YUN 2000, p. 891] as the continuing guide to UNCTAD's future work, and described UNCTAD XI as an opportunity to identify new trade and development issues. Its overarching goal was to generate greater understanding of the interface and coherence between international processes and negotiations on the one hand, and development strategies and policies that developing countries needed to pursue on the other. Under each of the four Conference sub-themes, the Consensus identified problems, formulated appropriate national and international responses and specified actions to be undertaken by UNCTAD.

Regarding the first sub-theme on development strategies in a globalizing world economy, the Consensus noted that the central challenge was how globalization could improve living standards for all people. In that regard, UNCTAD should maintain its role of delivering policy analysis and identifying policy options at the global

and national levels and of examining and analysing, through the annual report on LDCs (see p. 857), the causes of decline in their share of world trade and the linkages among trade, growth and poverty reduction, with a view to identifying long-term solutions.

As to the second sub-theme on building productive capacities and international competitiveness, the Consensus noted that an enabling international environment was essential for developing countries and economies in transition to integrate successfully into the world economy and stressed the need to harness domestic resources for investment in productive capacity and technological upgrading, to be complemented by external capital flows, particularly in LDCs. UNCTAD was to assist developing countries to design and implement policies in that regard.

Addressing the third sub-theme on assuring development gains from the international trading system and trade negotiations, the Consensus pointed to the dependence of over 50 developing countries on exports of three or fewer commodities for more than half of their export earnings, and to the decline and instability of world commodity prices and consequent terms-of-trade losses that had reduced economic growth in many of those countries and had increased poverty and indebtedness. UNCTAD was to build on and strengthen the implementation of the Bangkok Plan of Action through measures to assist developing countries to integrate trade and development concerns into their national development plans and poverty reduction strategies.

Regarding the fourth sub-theme on partnership for development, the Consensus noted that efforts to meet the challenges and opportunities of globalization could benefit from enhanced cooperation among all relevant partners, including developing countries from all geographic regions. Noting the specific partnerships launched at the Conference—in information and communication technology (ICT) for development, commodities, investment and capacity-building, and training (the UNCTAD Virtual Institute on Trade and Development)—the Consensus called on TDB to review the implementation of partnerships annually for their funding and continued relevance. The Conference report [TD/412] contained information on UNCTAD XI multi-stakeholder partnership activities to be built around the objective of "ICT applications for improving the economic competitiveness of developing countries", and on future partnerships in the other fields named above.

Annexed to the report were: a ministerial declaration on the occasion of the fortieth anniversary of the Group of 77; a declaration by the parliamentary meeting on the occasion of UNCTAD XI; a declaration of the LDC ministerial meeting; a ministerial communiqué of landlocked developing countries; and the Civil Society Forum declaration. In addition, the report contained two resolutions (below) and statements of position on the outcome of the Conference.

Other action. On 18 June, the Conference adopted two resolutions: one expressing gratitude to the Government and people of Brazil for hosting the Conference [res. 177(XI)] and the other approving the Credentials Committee report [res. 178(XI)].

The Conference called on TDB to conduct in 2006 a mid-term review of the implementation of the Bangkok Plan of Action and the São Paulo Consensus, based on the framework established by General Assembly resolution 58/269 [YUN 2003, p. 1395].

Preparatory process

At the twenty-first special session (Geneva, 14 May) of TDB [A/59/15] (see below), its President, acting also as Chairman of the UNCTAD XI Preparatory Committee, reported on the results of the Committee's work on the draft negotiated text for the Conference [TD/L.368 & Add.1], which TDB transmitted to the Conference following amendments to the text.

UNCTAD XI follow-up

At its fifty-first session (Geneva, 4-5 October) [A/59/15], TDB discussed the follow-up to UNCTAD XI: new developments in international economic relations. Before it were UNCTAD secretariat background notes on the new geography of international trade [TD/404] and on international economic relations [TD/B/51/6]. It considered three key interlinked determinants shaping the new trade geography: the developing countries' increasing role to drive trade and growth; the vigorous growth of South-South trade and economic cooperation; and the changing context of North-South interdependence and terms of engagement. Other matters considered concerned: policy options and complementary measures by the North for enhancing South-South trade; official development assistance flows to help build supply capacity and competitiveness; policy space; corporate responsibility; and the restrictive impact of security-related measures on the ability of developing countries to trade in goods and services.

UNCTAD, in its continuing analysis and interpretation of the evolving new trade geography from a development standpoint, was encouraged to take a disaggregated view of differential performance and to further elaborate strategic approaches to enhancing South-South trade; a challenge would be to determine whether current developments portended a decisive or qualitative change in the economic situation of the South. UNCTAD was to examine the impact of the multiplicity of free trade agreements on North-to-South investment flows, contribute to confidence-building between developed and developing countries, and play a complementary role in technical assistance.

In **resolution 59/245** (see p. 861), the General Assembly stressed the need to implement the São Paulo Consensus and, in that regard, to pursue actively the examination of and responses to issues relating to the trade of small vulnerable economies to facilitate their full integration into the multilateral trading system. In **resolution 59/244** (see p. 857), the Assembly welcomed the UNCTAD XI decision to examine the causes of the decline in the share of LDCs in world trade and invited UNCTAD to analyse the role that enterprise development could play in alleviating poverty in LDCs and to recommend measures to develop their private sector.

International trade

The *Trade and Development Report, 2004* [Sales No. E.04.II.D.29] stated that global trade increased significantly in 2003, after sluggish growth in 2002 and a slight contraction in 2001. Import volumes rose by 6 per cent and export volumes by 4.9 per cent (compared to increases of 2.7 per cent and 2.6 per cent, respectively, in 2002). The growth rate in 2003 was characterized by a surge in the unit value of both manufactures and commodities, due mainly to the depreciation of the United States dollar vis-à-vis other major currencies. The origins of most global exports shifted in 2003 from developed to developing countries, with the latter accounting for 66 per cent of the increase in the volume of world exports, while developed countries accounted for about 21 per cent and transition economies for some 12 per cent. The shift was attributable to sluggish exports in most developed countries and the rapid expansion of export volumes in the developing regions of East and South Asia and in the transition economies of Central and Eastern Europe and the Commonwealth of Independent States (CIS).

The contribution of developed and developing countries to the growth of world imports by volume was more balanced, at about 40 per cent and

50 per cent, respectively. In Western Europe, the low growth of export volumes was due to faltering domestic demand within the region. In the United States, where both exports and imports were affected by the economic downturn in 2001 and the global slowdown of growth, relative recovery could not contain a widening trade deficit equivalent to 5 per cent of gross domestic product (GDP). Japan's trade surplus continued to grow as its import volumes picked up following the yen's appreciation and improved domestic economic conditions. In the developing economies, East and South Asia experienced rapid growth of both imports and exports, continuing their strong growth trend of recent years. In Africa, both exports and imports rose by almost 8 per cent each in volume, and by 22 per cent and 17 per cent in value, respectively. Much of the export expansion came from a few oil exporters (Algeria, Angola, Egypt, the Libyan Arab Jamahiriya and Nigeria), which accounted for approximately 60 per cent of the growth in regional export value. In Latin America, trade continued to recover from its downturn of 2001 and 2002, although the situation differed by country and subregion. In transition economies, both imports and exports expanded by 27 per cent at current values. For the Central and Eastern European countries that acceded to the European Union (EU) in May 2004, expectations from accession generated additional trade flows between them and the EU.

According to the *World Economic and Social Survey 2004* [Sales No. E.04.II.C.1], after a tentative beginning brought about by the build-up of tensions over Iraq and the outbreak of severe acute respiratory syndrome, international trade resumed its recovery. Growth in the volume of world trade more than doubled to almost 6 per cent in real terms in 2003, with developing countries accounting for most of the increase. It was even higher in nominal terms (almost 15 per cent), owing to the depreciation of the United States dollar, a factor partly responsible for increases in the international prices of many commodities, notably the surge in the price of oil.

The *World Economic Situation and Prospects 2005* [Sales No. E.05.II.C.2], jointly issued by UNCTAD and the UN Department of Economic and Social Affairs (DESA), stated that, in 2004, international merchandise trade grew markedly at an estimated 10.5 per cent (up from 6.2 per cent in 2003), reflecting the cyclical strength of the global economic recovery, as manufacturing picked up pace in the first half of the year and domestic demand improved in more economies. The brisk global economic environment further raised the prices of commodities and, to a lesser extent, of manufactures, leading to an increase in the dollar value of global trade of almost 19 per cent, to $8.6 trillion.

Much of the growth originated in developed countries, supported by their faster economic growth, particularly in North America and Japan, and the continued expansion of China's economy. After a lull in United States exports around mid-year, largely due to a slowdown in some Asian economies and a deceleration in ICT exports, its exports rebounded in the last quarter, and the annual growth of real exports for the year was about 10 per cent. Exports from Canada rebounded from a 2003 decline in volume terms. In the EU, strong external demand offset the decrease in competitiveness stemming from the euro's appreciation since 2000. Despite some slowdown during the second half of 2004, real export growth in the region accelerated to an estimated 6.9 per cent (from 1.5 per cent in 2003). EU import demand also accelerated, boosted in part by the appreciation of the euro and an increase in investment spending. Japan continued to experience an exceptionally strong real export growth, which reached over 15 per cent in the first half of 2004 before decelerating in the third quarter to an annual rate of 1.5 per cent. Australia and New Zealand both achieved import growth of over 10 per cent due to robust domestic demand, as well as export recovery, despite a continuing trade deficit in both of about 5 per cent of GDP.

The surge in world commodity prices, particularly oil and gas, and the upturn in the global economy boosted the value of exports of resource-rich CIS countries. In the Russian Federation, real export growth was estimated at 10 per cent, led by oil and gas, ferrous and non-ferrous metals and chemicals. Meanwhile, robust domestic demand and exchange-rate appreciation led to fast import growth.

Developing economies also maintained a remarkable trade performance; Africa's exports continued to grow, although at a slower pace than in 2003. In East Asia, merchandise trade expanded by over 18 per cent in real terms, with merchandise exports driven by the positive global economic environment and strong demand from China. In South Asia, the larger countries recorded double-digit growth of both exports and imports. Western Asia's exports grew by 6.7 per cent, driven by increased oil production by the region's oil-exporting countries. Non-fuel exports also expanded due to strong performances by Israel, Jordan and Turkey. In Latin America and the Caribbean, trade gained strength as both exports and imports experienced a broad-based recovery.

Multilateral trading system

Report of Secretary-General. In response to General Assembly resolution 58/197 [YUN 2003, p. 968], the Secretary-General submitted an August report [A/59/305] on international trade and development, prepared in collaboration with UNCTAD. The report reviewed recent trends in international trade, the outcome of UNCTAD XI (see p. 955), developments in the multilateral trading system in the context of the WTO trade negotiations under the Doha work programme and developments in regional trade arrangements, a major component of the evolving international trading system. The decision adopted by the WTO General Council on 1 August was also examined (see below).

The report noted several positive trends in developing countries, among them the trend towards diversification, indicated by the fact that manufactures currently represented nearly three quarters of their exports. Growth in the share of the South in world trade, currently at 30 per cent, signalled the emergence of a trade geography in which developing countries were increasingly important to the trade of developed countries, especially the United States and Japan. South-South trade, which accounted for just over one tenth of total world trade, was growing significantly: over 40 per cent of developing-country exports were destined for other developing countries and trade among them was increasing at the rate of 11 per cent a year; trade in services was also on the rise. That transformation was further underlined by intraregional and interregional investment, transfer of technology and enterprise-level interaction. Perhaps the most important trend was the continuing rise of oil prices, which was largely due to the economic recovery and increasing demand from such countries as the United States, China and some newly industrialized countries.

The report noted that, during the past decade, a major development in the expansion of regional trade agreements was the emergence of such agreements between North and South. The challenge to developing countries in that regard was to design the appropriate degree and pacing of regional liberalization and to retain policy space and differential treatment.

The report concluded that the positive outcomes of UNCTAD XI and recent developments in WTO negotiations underscored the shared interests of the international community in advancing multilateral trade negotiations under the Doha work programme and in identifying practical inputs for achieving the MDGs, the objectives of the Monterrey Consensus of the International Conference on Financing for Development [YUN 2002, p. 953] and the Plan of Implementation of the World Summit on Sustainable Development [ibid., p. 821].

Negotiating frameworks

As noted in the Secretary-General's August report [A/59/305], unprecedented diplomatic efforts were mounted to resume the multilateral trade negotiations under the Doha work programme that were stalled at the WTO Fifth Ministerial Conference [YUN 2003, p. 1535]. Negotiations resumed in July, culminating in the WTO General Council's adoption, on 1 August, of a decision setting out frameworks for a future negotiating package in five core areas: agriculture, market access of non-agricultural products, services, development issues and trade facilitation (improving the movement, release and clearance of goods, including goods in transit).

The General Council reiterated calls for completing the review of the WTO provisions on all categories of special and differential treatment in favour of developing countries, agreed that special attention would be given to their specific trade and development-related needs, and affirmed that developing countries and low-income countries in transition should be provided with enhanced trade-related technical assistance and capacity-building. It also extended the moratorium on imposing customs duties on electronic transmissions until the WTO conference in 2005.

The General Council reaffirmed the commitment to progress in the negotiating areas of rules, trade and environment; trade-related aspects of intellectual property rights; and dispute settlement. It agreed that the decision and its annexes should not be used in any dispute settlement proceeding under the WTO Dispute Settlement Understanding or for interpreting existing WTO agreements. It further agreed to continue the Doha round of negotiations beyond the January 2005 time frame set in the Doha declaration [YUN 2001, p. 1432], leading to the Sixth Ministerial Conference, scheduled for December 2005.

UNCTAD consideration. TDB, in October [A/59/15], discussed UNCTAD secretariat background notes on developments and issues in the post-Doha work programme of particular concern to developing countries from a post-UNCTAD XI perspective [TD/B/51/4], and on assuring development gains from trade negotiations with respect to the implications of the termination on 31 December 2004 of the Agreement on Textiles and Clothing (ATC) [TD/B/51/CRP.1].

The President noted that a fundamental lesson of the most recent trade negotiations was that negotiators had to ensure that WTO agreements addressed the trade-related concerns of its members, and that they had to place the development needs of developing countries at the heart of the Doha work programme if the current round of multilateral trade negotiations was to conclude successfully. While it might prove impossible to conclude negotiations by the time of the Sixth Ministerial Conference in December 2005, the prospects were good for their conclusion by 2006. Addressing development issues required a concerted effort by all parties to incorporate special and differential treatment in all areas of negotiations and to address implementation-related issues and concerns; it would also require finding appropriate solutions to specific trade and development needs. It was particularly important that the multilateral trading system be sensitive to the special needs of LDCs, small island developing States, and landlocked and transit developing countries. The specific trade and development concerns of commodity-dependent countries needed to be addressed, as they remained marginalized in international trade.

Also noted were: the recommendations and modalities of the 1 August decision for negotiations on trade in services and on trade facilitation; the complete phase-out effective 1 January 2005 of the quotas in the textile and clothing sector as required by ATC; negotiations on WTO rules; and accelerating the accession of all developing countries and transition economies to WTO.

In pointing to the mutually supportive relationship between the UNCTAD and WTO processes, the President encouraged both organizations to strengthen their cooperation to assist countries to derive development gains from related agreements.

GENERAL ASSEMBLY ACTION

On 22 December [meeting 75], the General Assembly, on the recommendation of the Second (Economic and Financial) Committee [A/59/481/Add.1], adopted **resolution 59/221** by recorded vote (166-2-6) [agenda item 83 (*a*)].

International trade and development

The General Assembly,

Recalling its resolutions 56/178 of 21 December 2001, 57/235 of 20 December 2002 and 58/197 of 23 December 2003 on international trade and development,

Recalling also the provisions of the United Nations Millennium Declaration pertaining to trade and related development issues, as well as the outcomes of the International Conference on Financing for Development, held in Monterrey, Mexico, from 18 to 22 March 2002 and the World Summit on Sustainable Development, held in Johannesburg, South Africa, from 26 August to 4 September 2002,

Noting the Ministerial Declaration and decisions adopted at the Fourth Ministerial Conference of the World Trade Organization, held in Doha from 9 to 14 November 2001, and the full commitment of all members of the World Trade Organization to give effect to them, in accordance with the decision of 1 August 2004 of the General Council of the World Trade Organization,

Reaffirming the role of the United Nations Conference on Trade and Development as focal point within the United Nations for the integrated treatment of trade and development and the interrelated issues in the areas of finance, technology, investment and sustainable development,

Recalling its resolutions 57/250 of 20 December 2002 and 57/270 B of 23 June 2003, in which it invited the United Nations Conference on Trade and Development, as well as the Trade and Development Board, to contribute, within its mandate, to the implementation and to the review of the progress made in the implementation of the outcomes of the major United Nations conferences and summits and invited the President of the Trade and Development Board to present the outcomes of such reviews to the Economic and Social Council,

Recalling also that, to benefit fully from trade, which in many cases is the single most important external source of development financing, the establishment and the enhancement of appropriate institutions and policies in developing countries, as well as in countries with economies in transition, are needed and that, in this context, enhanced market access, balanced rules and well-targeted, sustainably financed technical assistance and capacity-building programmes for developing countries also play an important role,

Noting the significant contribution of the multilateral trading system to economic growth, development and employment and the importance of maintaining the process of reform and liberalization of trade policies, as well as the importance of rejecting the use of protectionism, so that the system plays its full part in promoting recovery, growth and development, in particular of developing countries, bearing in mind paragraph 10 of General Assembly resolution 55/182 of 20 December 2000,

Reaffirming that agriculture remains a key sector for the overwhelming majority of developing countries, and stressing the importance of the successful conclusion of the World Trade Organization Doha work programme in accordance with the decision of 1 August 2004 of the General Council of the World Trade Organization,

Reaffirming also the urgency, subject to national legislation, of recognizing the rights of local and indigenous communities that are holders of traditional knowledge, innovations and practices and, with the approval and involvement of the holders of such knowledge, innovations and practices, of developing and implementing benefit-sharing mechanisms on mutually agreed terms for the use of such knowledge, innovations and practices,

Recalling that it is particularly important for developing countries, bearing in mind development goals and objectives, that all countries take into account the need for an appropriate balance between national policy space and international disciplines and commitments,

Bearing in mind the special needs of the least developed countries, the small island developing States and the landlocked developing countries, as identified, respectively, in the Brussels Programme of Action and the Barbados Programme of Action and within a new global framework for transit transport cooperation for landlocked and transit developing countries as set out in the Almaty Programme of Action,

Noting with concern that a number of developing countries, in particular the least developed countries and commodity-dependent developing countries, have not fully benefited from the global economy and trade liberalization,

Recognizing that countries must take appropriate and necessary security measures, but also underlining the importance of taking these measures in the manner that is least disruptive of normal trade and related practices,

Taking note of the review undertaken by the Trade and Development Board at its fifty-first session of developments and issues in the post-Doha work programme of particular concern to developing countries following the eleventh session of the United Nations Conference on Trade and Development, and its contribution to an understanding of the actions required to help developing countries integrate, in a beneficial and meaningful manner, into the multilateral trading system and the global economy and to achieve a balanced, development-oriented and successful conclusion of the Doha negotiations,

Taking note also of the report of the Trade and Development Board and the report of the Secretary-General,

1. *Recognizes* that a universal, rule-based, open, non-discriminatory and equitable multilateral trading system, as well as meaningful trade liberalization, can substantially stimulate development worldwide, benefiting countries at all stages of development, thereby promoting economic growth and sustainable development necessary to achieve the internationally agreed development goals, including those contained in the United Nations Millennium Declaration;

2. *Reaffirms* the value of multilateralism to the global trading system, and in this regard welcomes the progress achieved in the Doha work programme, with the adoption by the General Council of the World Trade Organization of its decision of 1 August 2004 on frameworks for further negotiations, which re-energizes the Doha round of the multilateral trade negotiations and recommits the members of the World Trade Organization to fulfilling the development dimension of the Doha work programme;

3. *Welcomes* the eleventh session of the United Nations Conference on Trade and Development, held in São Paulo, Brazil, from 13 to 18 June 2004, and the adoption of The Spirit of São Paulo and the São Paulo Consensus, which, building upon the Plan of Action adopted at its tenth session, held in Bangkok from 12 to 19 February 2000, reaffirm the continued commitment of the international community to supporting the United Nations Conference on Trade and Development in fulfilling its mandate in consensus-building, research and policy analysis, and in technical assistance on trade and development;

4. *Welcomes also* the commitment made at the Fourth Ministerial Conference of the World Trade Organization, held in Doha from 9 to 14 November 2001, and in the decision of 1 August 2004 of the General Council of the World Trade Organization, to place development at the heart of the Doha work programme and to continue to make positive efforts to ensure that developing countries, especially the least developed among them, secure a share in the growth of world trade commensurate with the needs of their economic development;

5. *Reaffirms* that all countries have a shared interest in the success of the Doha work programme, which aims both at further increasing trading opportunities and reducing barriers to trade among nations and at making the trading system more development-friendly, which would contribute to the objective of upholding and safeguarding an open, equitable, rule-based, predictable and non-discriminatory multilateral trading system, and recalls that a major contribution of the Doha Ministerial Declaration was to place the needs and interests of developing countries at the heart of the Doha work programme and that this important objective needs to be pursued with a view to bringing about concrete development-oriented outcomes from the multilateral trade negotiations;

6. *Looks forward* to the early development of the frameworks outlined in the decision of 1 August 2004 of the General Council of the World Trade Organization, in an inclusive and transparent manner, into concrete, detailed and specific modalities for the early and successful conclusion of the negotiations, while ensuring balance and parallel progress within and between areas under negotiation bearing in mind the needs and concerns of developing countries, and ensuring a fair and development-oriented outcome of the Doha work programme based on a broad agenda, including enhanced market access, balanced rules and well-targeted, sustainably financed technical assistance and capacity-building programmes;

7. *Recognizes*, in regard to the decision of 1 August 2004 of the General Council of the World Trade Organization and consistent with the Doha work programme, the following issues of particular interest and concern to developing countries:

(a) Reviewing special and differential treatment provisions with a view to making them more precise, effective and operational and, in this regard, expeditiously completing the review of the outstanding agreement-specific proposals and cross-cutting issues, and finding appropriate solutions to outstanding implementation issues, by July 2005, as provided for in paragraph 1 (d) of the decision;

(b) The elaboration of modalities under the framework on agriculture, as contained in annex A to the decision, for negotiations, in accordance with paragraph 13 of the Doha Ministerial Declaration, noting that reforms in all three pillars of market access, domestic support and export competition form an interconnected whole and must be approached in a balanced and equitable manner with operationally effective and meaningful special and differential treatment for developing countries, and recalling that agriculture is of critical importance to the economic development of developing country members of the World Trade Organization, particularly to the least developed countries and the net food-importing developing countries, and that they must be able to pursue agricultural policies that are supportive of their development goals, poverty reduction strategies and food security and livelihood concerns, and that non-trade concerns will be taken into account;

(c) Implementing concretely the commitment to address cotton issues ambitiously, expeditiously and specifically within the agriculture negotiations, as provided for in annex A to the decision;

(d) The elaboration of modalities on market access for non-agricultural products pursuant to annex B to the decision, with the aim of reducing or, as appropriate, eliminating tariffs, including the reduction or elimination of tariff peaks, high tariffs and tariff escalation, as well as non-tariff barriers, in particular on products of export interest to developing countries, with a comprehensive product coverage and without a priori exclusions, and recalling also the importance of special and differential treatment and less than full reciprocity in reduction commitments for developing countries as integral parts of the modalities;

(e) Negotiations on trade in services, as provided for in annex C to the decision, with a view to providing effective market access to all members of the World Trade Organization; in order to ensure a substantive outcome, members shall strive to ensure a high quality of offers by May 2005, particularly in sectors and modes of supply of export interest to developing countries, giving special attention to the least developed countries, and aiming to achieve progressively higher levels of liberalization with no a priori exclusion of any service sector or mode of supply; special attention shall be given to sectors and modes of supply of export interest to developing countries, noting the interest of developing countries, as well as other members, in mode 4;

(f) Enhancing trade-related technical assistance and capacity-building to increase the effective participation of developing countries in the negotiations, to facilitate their implementation of World Trade Organization rules and to enable them to adjust and diversify their economies;

(g) Advancing the negotiations aimed at clarifying and improving disciplines under the agreements in the areas of anti-dumping, subsidies and countervailing measures, while preserving the basic concepts, principles and effectiveness of those agreements, taking into account the needs of developing countries, in accordance with paragraph 1 (f) of the decision;

(h) Advancing negotiations under the review of the dispute settlement understanding, in accordance with paragraph 1 (f) of the decision;

(i) Negotiations on trade facilitation, the results of which should take fully into account the principle of special and differential treatment for developing and least developed countries, in accordance with annex D to the decision;

8. *Reaffirms* the importance of market access, and in this context recalls the importance of respect for World Trade Organization disciplines, including in the area of anti-dumping, inter alia, to avoid the abusive application of anti-dumping and other trade-distorting measures;

9. *Reaffirms also* the importance of the full implementation of the Agreement on Textiles and Clothing of the World Trade Organization, which provides for the complete phase-out of the quotas on textiles and clothing by 31 December 2004;

10. *Reaffirms further* the importance of the development dimension of the Agreement on Trade-related Aspects of Intellectual Property Rights;

11. *Invites* all members of the World Trade Organization to effectively implement the decision adopted by the General Council of the World Trade Organization on 30 August 2003 on the implementation of paragraph 6 of the Doha Declaration on the Agreement on Trade-related Aspects of Intellectual Property Rights and Public Health to address the problems faced bycountries with insufficient or no manufacturing capacity in the pharmaceutical sector in accessing medicines at affordable prices when combating serious public health problems afflicting many developing and least developed countries, especially those resulting from HIV/AIDS, tuberculosis, malaria and other epidemics, and, as agreed by the World Trade Organization Council for Trade-related Aspects of Intellectual Property Rights on 16 June 2004, to expeditiously establish a permanent solution by amending the Agreement on Trade-related Aspects of Intellectual Property Rights on the basis of the recommendations by the Council to be presented by March 2005;

12. *Invites* the World Intellectual Property Organization to continue further its development activities and to continue to cooperate with relevant international organizations;

13. *Stresses* that the adoption or enforcement of any measures necessary to protect human, animal or plant life or health should not be applied in a manner that would constitute arbitrary or unjustified discrimination or a disguised restriction on international trade, while recognizing the rights of members of the World Trade Organization to determine their own appropriate level of sanitary and phyto-sanitary protection in accordance with World Trade Organization rules, and recognizes the need to facilitate the increased participation of the developing countries in the work of relevant international standard-setting organizations as well as the importance of providing financial and technical assistance and capacity-building efforts to enable them to respond adequately to the introduction of any new measures;

14. *Emphasizes* that issues related to trade, debt and finance and transfer of technology duly covered in the Doha work programme should be addressed as a high priority in accordance with the Doha work programme and the World Trade Organization General Council decision of 1 August 2004;

15. *Recalls* the commitment of the members of the World Trade Organization, in line with the Doha mandates, to progress in the areas of rules, trade and environment, and trade-related aspects of intellectual property rights, as stated in the World Trade Organization General Council decision of 1 August 2004;

16. *Stresses* the importance of an open, transparent, inclusive and democratic process and of procedures for the effective functioning of the multilateral trading system that allow for internal transparency and the effective participation of members, including in the decision-making process, and that enable them to have their vital interests duly reflected in the outcome of trade negotiations;

17. *Also stresses* the importance of facilitating the accession of all developing countries, in particular the least developed countries, as well as countries with

economies in transition, that apply for membership in the World Trade Organization, consistent with its criteria, bearing in mind paragraph 21 of resolution 55/182 and subsequent developments, and calls for the effective and faithful application of the World Trade Organization guidelines on accession of the least developed countries;

18. *Invites* members of the international community to consider the interests of non-members of the World Trade Organization in the context of trade liberalization;

19. *Emphasizes* that bilateral and regional trade arrangements should complement the goals of the multilateral trading system, and in this context stresses the importance of clarifying and improving disciplines and procedures under the existing provisions of the World Trade Organization applying to regional trade agreements in accordance with paragraph 29 of the Doha Ministerial Declaration, taking into account the developmental aspects of regional trade agreements, and urges the United Nations Conference on Trade and Development, in accordance with its mandate, to provide technical inputs in this respect;

20. *Notes with appreciation* the autonomous steps taken by some countries in providing trade-related assistance and by simplifying administrative procedures to facilitate access to their markets for exports from developing countries;

21. *Reaffirms* the commitments made at the Fourth Ministerial Conference of the World Trade Organization, and at the Third United Nations Conference on the Least Developed Countries, held in Brussels from 14 to 20 May 2001, in this regard calls upon developed countries that have not already done so to work towards the objective of duty-free, quota-free market access for all least developed country exports, and notes that the consideration of proposals for developing countries to contribute to improved market access for the least developed countries would also be helpful;

22. *Welcomes* the commitment to actively pursue the work programme of the World Trade Organization with respect to addressing the trade-related issues and concerns affecting the fuller integration of countries with small, vulnerable economies into the multilateral trading system in a manner commensurate with their special circumstances and in support of their efforts towards sustainable development, in accordance with paragraph 35 of the Doha Ministerial Declaration;

23. *Recognizes* the special problems and needs of the landlocked developing countries within a new global framework for transit transport cooperation for landlocked and transit developing countries, in this regard calls for the full and effective implementation of the Almaty Programme of Action, and stresses the need for the implementation of the São Paulo Consensus, adopted on 18 June 2004 at the eleventh session of the United Nations Conference on Trade and Development in São Paulo, Brazil, in particular paragraphs 66 and 84 thereof, by the relevant international organizations and donors in a multi-stakeholder approach;

24. *Recognizes also* the importance of addressing seriously the concerns of commodity-dependent developing countries, owing to the continuing volatility of world commodity prices and other factors, and of supporting the efforts of such countries to restructure, diversify and strengthen the competitiveness of their commodity sectors, and in this regard notes the forma-

tion of an international task force on commodities by the United Nations Conference on Trade and Development;

25. *Emphasizes* the importance of addressing the concerns of a number of developing countries in respect of the erosion of preferences and the impact of liberalization on their tariff revenues;

26. *Stresses* the importance of enhancing South-South trade and cooperation in the context of an emerging new trade geography that complements North-South trade and cooperation, and takes note of the decision, adopted in June 2004, to launch the third round of negotiations on the Global System of Trade Preferences among Developing Countries;

27. *Recognizes* that it is important for developing countries and countries with economies in transition to consider reducing trade barriers among themselves;

28. *Expresses its concern* about the adoption of a number of unilateral actions that are not consistent with the rules of the World Trade Organization, harm the exports of all countries, in particular those of developing countries, and have a considerable bearing on the ongoing World Trade Organization negotiations and on the achievement and further enhancement of the development dimension of the trade negotiations;

29. *Emphasizes* the importance of developing human, institutional, regulatory and research and development capacities and infrastructures aimed at enhanced supply-side capacity and competitiveness, as well as ensuring a conducive international environment for the full and effective integration of developing countries and countries with economies in transition into the international trading system;

30. *Stresses* the importance of strengthening and enabling the trade, investment and business environments through the adoption of appropriate domestic measures and conditions to encourage local, regional and international investment and efforts to prevent and dismantle anti-competitive practices and promote responsibility and accountability of corporate actors at both the international and the national levels, thereby enabling developing countries' producers, enterprises and consumers to take advantage of trade liberalization, and encourages developing countries to consider establishing competition laws and frameworks best suited to their development needs, complemented by technical and financial assistance for capacity-building, taking fully into account national policy objectives and capacity constraints;

31. *Notes* that the outcome documents of the eleventh session of the United Nations Conference on Trade and Development emphasized the importance for all countries of enhancing coherence between national development strategies and global economic processes towards economic growth and development, in particular of developing countries, and, in that context, reinforced the consensus that trade is a means to growth and development and that the international trading system and trade negotiations should facilitate development gains;

32. *Also notes* the important and unique mandate of the United Nations Conference on Trade and Development, which was reaffirmed at its eleventh session, and supports the continued work of the United Nations Conference on Trade and Development in support of the effective and beneficial integration of developing countries and countries with economies in transition

into the global economy in cooperation with relevant international organizations;

33. *Invites* the United Nations Conference on Trade and Development, in accordance with its mandate, to monitor and assess the evolution of the international trading system and of trends in international trade from a development perspective, and in particular to analyse issues of concern to developing countries and countries with economies in transition, supporting them in the formulation, implementation and review of national trade and trade-related policies and options with a view to maximizing their share of world trade;

34. *Reiterates* the importance of supporting the programmes and technical cooperation and capacity-building activities of the United Nations Conference on Trade and Development that assist developing countries, especially the least developed countries and countries with economies in transition, in international trade and trade negotiations, in particular in support of their participation in the Doha work programme, including the Integrated Framework for Trade-related Technical Assistance to Least Developed Countries and the Joint Integrated Technical Assistance Programme;

35. *Requests* the Secretary-General, in collaboration with the secretariat of the United Nations Conference on Trade and Development, to report to the General Assembly at its sixtieth session on the implementation of the present resolution and on developments in the multilateral trading system under the sub-item entitled "International trade and development".

RECORDED VOTE ON RESOLUTION 59/221:

In favour: Afghanistan, Albania, Algeria, Andorra, Angola, Antigua and Barbuda, Argentina, Armenia, Austria, Azerbaijan, Bahamas, Bahrain, Bangladesh, Barbados, Belarus, Belgium, Belize, Benin, Bolivia, Bosnia and Herzegovina, Botswana, Brazil, Brunei Darussalam, Bulgaria, Burkina Faso, Burundi, Cambodia, Cameroon, Central African Republic, Chile, China, Colombia, Comoros, Congo, Costa Rica, Côte d'Ivoire, Croatia, Cuba, Cyprus, Czech Republic, Democratic People's Republic of Korea, Denmark, Djibouti, Dominica, Dominican Republic, Ecuador, Egypt, El Salvador, Eritrea, Estonia, Ethiopia, Fiji, Finland, France, Gabon, Georgia, Germany, Ghana, Greece, Grenada, Guatemala, Guyana, Haiti, Hungary, Iceland, India, Indonesia, Iran, Iraq, Ireland, Italy, Jamaica, Jordan, Kazakhstan, Kenya, Kuwait, Lao People's Democratic Republic, Latvia, Lebanon, Lesotho, Liberia, Libyan Arab Jamahiriya, Liechtenstein, Lithuania, Luxembourg, Madagascar, Malaysia, Maldives, Mali, Malta, Marshall Islands, Mauritius, Mexico, Micronesia (Federated States of), Monaco, Mongolia, Morocco, Mozambique, Myanmar, Namibia, Nauru, Nepal, Netherlands, Nicaragua, Niger, Nigeria, Norway, Oman, Pakistan, Panama, Papua New Guinea, Paraguay, Peru, Philippines, Poland, Portugal, Qatar, Republic of Moldova, Romania, Russian Federation, Rwanda, Saint Kitts and Nevis, Saint Lucia, Saint Vincent and the Grenadines, Samoa, San Marino, Sao Tome and Principe, Saudi Arabia, Senegal, Serbia and Montenegro, Sierra Leone, Singapore, Slovakia, Slovenia, Solomon Islands, Somalia, South Africa, Spain, Sri Lanka, Sudan, Suriname, Sweden, Switzerland, Syrian Arab Republic, Thailand, The former Yugoslav Republic of Macedonia, Timor-Leste, Togo, Tonga, Trinidad and Tobago, Tunisia, Turkey, Turkmenistan, Tuvalu, Uganda, Ukraine, United Arab Emirates, United Kingdom, United Republic of Tanzania, Uruguay, Vanuatu, Venezuela (Bolivarian Republic of), Viet Nam, Yemen, Zambia, Zimbabwe.

Against: Palau, United States.

Abstaining: Australia, Canada, Israel, Japan, New Zealand, Republic of Korea.

Trade policy

Trade in goods and services, and commodities

The Commission on Trade in Goods and Services, and Commodities, at its eighth session (Geneva, 9-13 February) [TD/B/COM.1/67 & Corr.1],

had before it the following: a note by the UNCTAD secretariat on access, market entry and competitiveness [TD/B/COM.1/65]; the report of the Expert Meeting on Market Entry Conditions Affecting Competitiveness and Exports of Goods and Services of Developing Countries: Large Distribution Networks, Taking into Account the Special Needs of LDCs [YUN 2003, p. 973]; an UNCTAD secretariat note on trade in services and development implications [TD/B/COM.1/62]; the report of the Expert Meeting on Market Access Issues in Mode 4 (Movement of Natural Persons to Supply Services) and Effective Implementation of Article IV on Increasing the Participation of Developing Countries [YUN 2003, p. 973]; an UNCTAD secretariat note on trade, environment and development [TD/B/COM.1/63]; the report of the Expert Meeting on Definitions and Dimensions of Environmental Goods and Services in Trade and Development [YUN 2003, p. 972]; and a progress report on the implementation of agreed conclusions and recommendations of the Commission, including the post-Doha follow-up [TD/B/COM.1/61].

In agreed recommendations adopted on 13 February, the Commission underscored the significance of interrelationships among market access, market entry and competitiveness in shaping the pace and scope of gains accruing to developing countries from international trade and trade negotiations, and emphasized the importance of UNCTAD's work in that regard.

The Commission recommended that UNCTAD continue its development-oriented policy analysis, confidence and consensus building, exchange of experience and information, and capacity development activities, focusing on, among other issues, market entry and market access conditions facing developing-country exports, including commodities; examine tariff and non-tariff barriers, including technical barriers and other market entry conditions that obstructed international trade, with special attention to those affecting developing-country exports; continue its work on factors shaping developing countries' competitiveness; and deepen its work on preferences, South-South trade (including GSTP among developing countries) and the interface between regional and global trade agreements and processes, together with their implications for trade and development.

The Commission further recommended that UNCTAD continue to enhance its work on international commodity markets, policies and measures to improve the contribution of the commodity sector to development, focusing on: the relationship between poverty reduction and commodity production and trade; enhancing the competitiveness of the commodity sector in developing countries; the strategic positioning of developing-country producers in value chains; diversifying the commodity sector in developing countries towards activities generating higher development gains; further work on the concentration of commodity distribution chains and their impact on commodity sectors; and financing and risk management mechanisms for commodity sector development. UNCTAD was to maintain its role in building effective partnerships among relevant stakeholders to find viable solutions to commodity problems. It was also to contribute to greater coherence between policies on poverty reduction, trade, commodities and financial flows; support development-oriented follow-up to the Doha work programme; promote implementation of the United Nations Millennium Declaration [YUN 2000, p. 49]; and maintain technical assistance to developing countries on their accession to WTO. UNCTAD should contribute to assuring development gains to developing countries accruing from international trade and trade negotiations in: the assessment of trade in services; sector-specific studies of interest to developing countries; identifying opportunities in new and dynamic services sectors and through outsourcing; assisting developing countries in implementing the General Agreement on Trade in Services (GATS); analysing approaches to further commitments in GATS Mode 4; identifying opportunities for integrating developing countries into regional trade arrangements; enhancing analytical work on cross-cutting issues of special interest to them; and analysing the economic implications of security measures on trade in services.

At its thirty-fourth executive session (Geneva, 10 March) [A/59/15], TDB took note of the Commission's report and endorsed its recommendations.

Subsidiary body. During the year, the Expert Meeting on Financing Commodity-Based Trade and Development: Innovative Financing Mechanisms was held (Geneva, 16-17 November) [TD/B/COM.1/EM.24/3]. Before it was an UNCTAD report providing an overview of innovative mechanisms for agricultural finance [TD/B/COM.1/EM.24/2]. The Meeting proceeded from the premise that lack of financing was a major impediment to the development of the agriculture sector in developing countries and that available finance was provided mostly to larger borrowers to the exclusion of the majority of small producers from the formal credit system.

Noting the integration of farmers, processors and traders in the national or global supply chain, the experts felt that financiers could use that chain to strengthen their financing mecha-

nisms by providing credits to farmers, processors, service and infrastructure providers on the basis not of their individual credit risk but of their position in the supply chain. The experts viewed the supply chain approach as the safest way to provide pre-harvest finance; after harvest, warehouse receipt finance and collateral management could provide solutions.

Other potential financing mechanisms discussed called for a credit framework to provide farmers credit cards or passbooks with credit lines based on the size of their holdings; a joint venture (a corporative) between farmers and banks, with the banks providing management expertise, research and development, extension services and marketing support; and linking farmers directly to the capital market through their country's commodity exchange for their agricultural crops, livestock and poultry.

The experts called on the private sector to take the lead in designing agricultural financing products; on UNCTAD to enhance its support across the board, targeting Governments, banks, agricultural borrowers and other key players; and on donors and international agencies to support those activities to enable UNCTAD to respond better to requests for assistance from developing countries, especially from LDCs.

Interdependence and global economic issues

TDB in October [A/59/15] considered interdependence and global economic issues from a trade and development perspective: policy coherence, development strategies and integration into the world economy. Participants agreed that, while increased interdependence could benefit the global economy, a simultaneous slowdown in the United States and Asia, if not counterbalanced by growth in other major economic centres, would seriously threaten global growth. Recent developments in the world oil market had illustrated the negative reverberations that actions or events in one country could have in a highly interdependent world economy. The economic and social transformations unleashed by globalization were a major challenge for many developing countries, which were not always capable of handling their consequences. While improvements in national governance were important to remedy the situation, current global rules could reduce developing countries' options to manage liberalization and integration processes effectively.

Multilateral and domestic policy solutions were thus required to make the trading environment truly supportive of rapid development. A comprehensive approach in that regard should be people-centred, respect the need for adequate economic policy space at the national level, and comprise good governance of globalization with inclusive and transparent structures of international economic decision-making. The *Trade and Development Report 2004* (see p. 957) provided useful data, analyses and ideas regarding the interplay among trade, monetary and financial factors shaping trade performance. However, a collective approach was needed to foster coherence among those factors. TDB stated that UNCTAD could contribute to the debate towards that end and, in addition to examining successful strategies in certain parts of the world, should also present alternative scenarios, including possible action by the international community.

Trade promotion and facilitation

In 2004, UN bodies maintained assistance to developing countries and transition economies in promoting their exports and facilitating their integration into the multilateral trading system. The main originator of technical cooperation projects in that area was the International Trade Centre, under the joint sponsorship of UNCTAD and WTO.

International Trade Centre

In 2004, the UNCTAD/WTO International Trade Centre (ITC) increased its delivery of technical assistance by 5 per cent to $21.1 million, from $20.1 million in 2003 [ITC/AG(XXXVIII)/202]. Between 2000 and 2004, total delivery rose by 82 per cent.

In addition to providing assistance to 133 countries, ITC established new strategic alliances and programmes so as to contribute better to the achievement of the MDGs, refining business processes, and servicing inspection and evaluation activities. Against the background of global trade growth and resumed trade negotiations under the Doha work programme, the need for supply-side responses became more critical to ensure that benefits from growth in global trade did not bypass developing countries. In that context, ITC focused on providing small and medium-sized enterprises (SMEs) with comprehensive business support services, including targeted business information; access to analytical and operational tools; and training in identifying market opportunities, adapting products and services to demand and developing capabilities for converting business opportunities into actual trade.

ITC focused its activities on its five corporate goals. Under the first goal, facilitating the integration of enterprises into the multilateral trading system, ITC increased its field activities in 67 countries and provided specific country-level assistance on WTO agreements and initiatives, promoted business advocacy, held interactive workshops on a number of trade topics, and conducted business analyses for the textile and clothing industry.

On the second goal, supporting the design of trade development strategies, although significant results were achieved at the national level, ITC attempted to ensure that its tools and back-stopping capacities were adequate to meet the high demand in that area. However, national capacities needed to be improved and capacity-building integrated into ITC country-level programmes.

As to the third goal, strengthening key trade support services (both public and private), ITC helped trade support institutions (TSIs) deliver high-quality services; TSIs in over 100 countries benefited from ITC partnerships. The challenge for ITC was to provide the TSI community with locally adaptable capacity-building tools and services in a timely and efficient manner to enable it to be proactive in its response to quickly changing business requirements.

Under the fourth goal, improving sector performance, ITC provided product sector-specific assistance to 27 LDCs and assisted 17 others in the area of services. New export opportunities were created through buyers-sellers meetings in nine product areas, including publishing and printing, pharmaceuticals, leather and the aid procurement market across Africa. Those meetings resulted in new business worth more than $22 million for over 500 SME exporters from 66 countries.

With regard to the fifth goal, building enterprise competitiveness, ITC delivered 80 projects to improve the competitiveness of SMEs through access to key information, human, financial and network resources. Its programmes helped companies to identify and realize market opportunities in growing markets, such as herbal medicines, cosmetics, tourism, services and creative industries. Over 1,300 SMEs in 20 services subsectors benefited from a direct training programme held in 17 countries.

In 2004, its fortieth anniversary year, ITC consolidated its achievements in terms of rapid delivery, established the basis for better attaining its goals and sharpened its vision for the future.

JAG action. The ITC Joint Advisory Group (JAG), at its thirty-seventh session (Geneva, 26-30 April) [ITC/AG(XXXVII)/200], considered the reports of ITC on its 2003 activities [YUN 2003, p. 974] and on its technical cooperation projects in 2003 [ITC/AG(XXXVII)/197/Add.1,2], the report of the Consultative Committee of the ITC Global Trust Fund [ITC/AG(XXXVII)/198] and the ITC proposed strategic framework for the 2006-2007 biennium [ITC/AG(XXXVII)/199].

The Group endorsed the overall orientation of ITC, encouraged it to continue its activities in accordance with the 2006-2007 proposed strategic framework and welcomed its focus on human and institutional trade capacity-building. Noting that ITC had increased its delivery target by a further 20 per cent in 2004 and maintained double-digit growth in its 2004-2006 Business Plan, the Group expressed concern over the implications that such an ambitious growth rate might have for the quality of ITC field assistance; in that regard, it endorsed the principle of growth through intensification rather than diversification of activity. It also endorsed ITC's unique approach to supporting national, sectoral and enterprise competitiveness through specialized, practical technical assistance targeting SMEs and TSIs servicing them.

In terms of the value of the enterprise-level programme in support of South-South trade, the Group encouraged ITC to expand the programme within the region to cover additional sectors and to include cross-regional trade. It urged ITC to pay increased attention to the supply-side aspects of competitiveness, particularly regarding product adaptation and development issues, and recommended that it broaden its focus to include future industries and subsectors of untapped potential. It encouraged ITC to be proactive in consolidating partnerships with multilateral and bilateral organizations and in pursuing new technical relationships with specialized technical organizations. The Group endorsed ITC's focus on the needs of the business sector and individual SMEs and recommended that it expand its field activities under both its Export-led Poverty Reduction Programme and projects funded under the Integrated Framework for Trade-related Technical Assistance to LDCs Trust Fund. Concerned about the falling share of ITC field support to LDCs, particularly those in Africa, and to Arab, Eastern European and CIS countries, the Group encouraged ITC to increase its development activities on behalf of all stakeholders.

Pledges of trust fund contributions to ITC were announced by Canada, Denmark, Finland, France, Germany, India, Norway, Switzerland, United Kingdom and the United States.

In October [A/59/15], TDB took note of JAG's report on its thirty-seventh session.

ITC administrative arrangements

OIOS report. Pursuant to General Assembly resolution 54/244 [YUN 1999, p. 1274], the Secretary-General transmitted an August report [A/59/229] of the Office of Internal Oversight

Services (OIOS) on the inspection of ITC's programme management and administrative practices. The inspection, which focused on assessing the efficiency and effectiveness of ITC's operations, examined programme planning and delivery, and arrangements for monitoring and evaluating programme implementation and for managing financial and human resources.

OIOS found that ITC had successfully established its niche and strengthened its comparative advantages in enhancing the capacity of the business community in developing countries and in countries with economies in transition, especially of their SMEs, for successful participation in international trade. Its services to beneficiaries were relevant and of high quality and its contribution to trade development was increasingly recognized by member States. The inspection highlighted good practices, such as the Global Trust Fund, established in 1995 for financing multi-donor, multi-country and multi-year projects. For many countries, the Fund was the sole source of funding for ITC assistance, and OIOS believed it was an effective mechanism, ensuring adequate operational flexibility in the use of technical cooperation resources while maintaining control by recipient and donor countries over the parameters of their use. Other good practices included the projects portal, an online database designed to improve project monitoring and evaluation; the Senior Management Committee, which played a key role in directing ITC activities; and the effective use of information technology.

OIOS ascertained that ITC products and services, in respect of product and market development, trade support services, and information and promotion met the needs of clients and were considered of high quality. Nonetheless, enhanced horizontal communication and strengthened interdivisional and intersectional cooperation in project development and implementation would further increase the value of ITC activities to developing and transition economies. While acknowledging ITC's success in expanding and intensifying its specialized trade-related technical assistance, OIOS recommended measures to further enhance programme performance monitoring and reporting, increase internal cohesion and strengthen human resources management.

Report of Secretary-General. Pursuant to General Assembly decision 57/572 [YUN 2002, p. 942], the Secretary-General submitted an October report [A/59/405] on the ITC administrative arrangements. Prepared in consultation with WTO and ITC, the report made recommendations to simplify those arrangements and adapt them to recent changes in the budgetary processes of the ITC parent organizations: in the case of the

United Nations, the replacement of the four-year medium-term plan by a biennium-based strategic framework; and at WTO, the replacement of the annual budget, in force until the end of 2003, by a biennium budget cycle coinciding with that of the United Nations.

Instead of the budget outline required under the current administrative arrangements, ITC would submit a simplified fascicle to both the UN General Assembly and the WTO General Council for them to take note of, with a full proposal to be submitted for decision by both in the fall. The ITC 2006-2007 strategic framework, in the UN format, would be reviewed by JAG in the spring of the first year of a financial period. The amended framework would be submitted to the Committee for Programme and Coordination (CPC). The JAG report would be submitted for review to TDB and the WTO Committee on Trade and Development. The CPC-approved version of the framework would be sent to WTO for information. ITC should continue to prepare two budget fascicles with the same financial and substantive information in different formats, and endeavour to harmonize the two fascicles in consultation with the UN and WTO secretariats.

Annexed to the report was a detailed time line of the current and proposed simplified procedures for the review of the ITC proposed budget by the United Nations and WTO.

In October [A/59/543], the Advisory Committee on Administrative and Budgetary Questions (ACABQ) recommended that the Assembly take note of the Secretary-General's report and endorse its recommendations.

In **resolution 59/276** of 23 December (see p. 1383), the Assembly took note of the report of the Secretary-General and of the related ACABQ report. It also took note of the OIOS report (see p. 966) and requested the Secretary-General to ensure the expeditious implementation of its recommendations.

Enterprise, business facilitation and development

The Commission on Enterprise, Business Facilitation and Development, at its eighth session (Geneva, 12-15 January) [TD/B/COM.3/64], had before it UNCTAD secretariat documents on policy options for strengthening SME competitiveness [TD/B/COM.3/58 & Corr.1]; efficient transport and trade facilitation to improve developing countries' participation in international trade [TD/B/COM.3/60]; e-commerce and ICT for development: selected issues [TD/B/COM.3/62]; a progress report [TD/B/COM.3/63] on the implementation of the Commission's 2003 agreed recommendations [YUN 2003, p. 976]; the report of the 2003 Expert Meeting on Policies and Programmes for Technology Development and Mastery, including the Role of Foreign Direct Investment [TD/B/COM.3/56]; and a number of other 2003 expert meeting reports [YUN 2003, p. 977].

The Commission requested the UNCTAD secretariat to continue its policy analysis, technical assistance and capacity development to enhance the export competitiveness of SMEs.

On efficient transport and trade facilitation, it asked UNCTAD to continue implementing the Commission's 2003 recommendations related to the topic with respect to: analysing developments, transferring technological and managerial capabilities and examining their implications for developing countries; providing guidance and assistance to those countries on ICT use; analysing the impact of security measures; cooperating with other intergovernmetal organizations engaged in the development of international legal instruments affecting international transport and trade facilitation, disseminating information on their implications for developing countries and providing negotiating assistance with regard to ongoing work related to the Doha work programme; and analysing trade facilitation developments, with particular attention to the Almaty Plan of Action [YUN 2003, p. 875] and to identifying the related needs and priorities of developing countries.

Recommendations on electronic commerce for development called for UNCTAD research on and policy-oriented analysis of the economic implications for developing countries of ICT trends and business applications, and for the dissemination of information on international discussions of the technological, commercial, legal and/or financial aspects of ICT, e-business and e-commerce. UNCTAD was asked to assist developing countries in building their capacity to formulate and implement the economic components of their national e-strategies for development; to be actively involved in the implementation of the Action Plan and follow-up to the Declaration of Principles adopted at the first phase of the World Summit on the Information Society [ibid., p. 857]; to continue its work in the statistical measurement of ICT use by enterprises and households and to contribute to the establishment of a set of internationally comparable ICT statistical indicators designed for monitoring progress between the first and second phases of the Summit; and to continue to provide a forum for the discussion of ICT-related policy issues relevant to economic development, facilitate the exchange of experiences in the economic applications of ICT and ensure inclusion of the development dimension in international discussions on such matters.

In March [A/59/15], TDB took note of the Commission's report and endorsed its recommendations.

Subsidiary bodies. A number of expert meetings were held in Geneva during the year. The Expert Meeting on Free and Open-Source Software: Policy and Development Implications (22-24 September) [TD/B/COM.3/EM.21/3] had before it an UNCTAD secretariat paper on the subject [TD/B/COM.3/EM.21/2]. The meeting discussed the question of free and open-source software (FOSS) from a public and ICT-for-development policy perspective and advanced the notion that it promoted digital inclusion and provided a good foundation for an ICT software industry, as future programmers could learn from the best source code by freely inspecting, modifying and including it in their own work. The experts were fully reassured that a number of prominent global ICT industry players had embraced some or all of the principles and processes of FOSS and that any doubts about its suitability for economic activities were unfounded. However, the UN system and UNCTAD needed to address it further from many other perspectives. UNCTAD, in particular, would pursue the implementation of an ICT-for-development partnership so as to promote human-capacity development and awareness-building with regard to FOSS.

The Expert Meeting on the Design and Implementation of Transit Transport Arrangements (24-26 November) [TD/B/COM.3/EM.22/3] had before it an UNCTAD secretariat note on the subject [TD/B/COM.3/EM.22/2]. The meeting discussed the constraints confronting countries depending on transit trade, notably the landlocked countries, that increased the logistics costs of their international trade. Those constraints related to border and customs procedures, different sets of administrative regimes and commercial practices of transit countries, poor and inadequate transit infrastructure, insufficient use of information systems, and commercial risks from broken container seals and aged fleets.

Transit arrangements aimed at diminishing those constraints needed to take account of new developments, such as the recent trade facilitation negotiations regarding articles V (free transit of goods), VIII (trade fees and formalities) and X (transparency of information about trade regulations) of the General Agreement on Tariffs and Trade; the customs transit regime known as the Transport International Routier applicable to intermodal containerized transport, whereby goods could not be removed without leaving traces or breaking customs seals; the Automated System for Customs Data whose transit module included forgery-proof electronic documents, electronic signature and registration of all transactions; and new security and trade facilitation initiatives in the form of cargo tracking based on radio frequency identification devices and smart and secure trade lanes.

In order to develop effective solutions to transit trade, the meeting called for national and regional cooperation in the planning, organization and administration of transit transport arrangements; appropriate coordination mechanisms; and international community support.

The Expert Meeting on Promoting the Export Competitiveness of SMEs (8-10 December) [TD/B/COM.3/EM.23/3] had before it an UNCTAD secretariat note on the subject [TD/B/COM.3/EM.23/2]. The meeting examined different patterns of internationalizing SMEs through exports and discussed policies and measures that could help to strengthen their export competitiveness in developing countries. Special attention was devoted to possible link-ups with transnational corporations (TNCs), perceived as a way for SMEs to solve their traditional problem of access to the critical resources of finance, technology, managerial skills and new markets. While reaffirming the important role of Governments in enhancing the productive capacity of SMEs, the sustainability of government interventions emerged as a common concern among the experts. Difficulties in creating and strengthening the domestic supplier base were noted, and it was argued that, while TNCs could play a role in upgrading technological capabilities, their interests were not always in alignment with those of host countries. National policies were therefore important for solving and preventing problems that could arise from that conflict of interests.

Commodities

The UNCTAD/DESA report *World Economic Situation and Prospects 2005* [Sales No. E.05.II.C.2] stated that, due mainly to the global economic recovery, particularly the rapidly increasing demand in Asia, notably China, and the concurrent depreciation of the United States dollar, prices of non-oil commodities rose by an average of 10 per cent in 2004, continuing the upward trend that had emerged in 2003 [YUN 2003, p. 977]. That did not, however, offset the setback recorded for 1980-2002, when prices fell by 40 per cent. At the end of 2004, for example, the price index for all food products remained almost 20 per cent below the average for 1995. Developing countries exporting agricultural commodities thus continued to face prices that were low by historical standards. Oil prices also increased and remained volatile throughout 2004, driven by a strong demand in a context of low and declining inventories and limited spare capacity, an unsettled security situation, speculative movements and natural disasters that disrupted production in the Gulf of Mexico. Despite some slowdown in the second quarter of the year, world oil demand increased by 3.3 per cent to 81.8 million barrels a day, the fastest growth rate and the largest absolute increase since 1977.

Report of Secretary-General. In keeping with General Assembly resolution 57/236 [YUN 2002, p. 945], the Secretary-General, in an August report [A/59/304], provided an overview of world commodity trends and prospects and discussed converting opportunities for increased commodity exports into development and poverty reduction. The report addressed progress in implementing Assembly resolution 58/204 on commodities [YUN 2003, p. 978], which called for actions by Governments and international financial institutions to continue assessing the effectiveness of the systems for compensatory financing of export-earnings shortfalls, by the Secretary-General to undertake open discussions on enhancing the impact of existing instruments to support efforts of commodity-dependent developing countries to diversify their exports, and by UNCTAD and other relevant UN system bodies to strengthen their capacity-building and technical cooperation activities.

The report concluded that, in the past several decades, commodities had not been an engine of growth; however, with an expected demand increase resulting from rapid growth, especially in developing countries, prospects might improve and lead to increased commodity exports from those countries. For the resultant benefits to be shared equitably and to reach the poorest developing countries and their poorest population segments, national and international policies and action were required. At the national level, productivity needed to be improved, especially in LDCs and African countries, through such measures as improved extension services, the rational use of inputs and adoption of better yielding plant varieties and better farming practices. Improvements in the quality of products and quality control were also necessary; the role of Governments in that regard was to establish an enabling environment for producers, processors and traders.

At the international level, the international trading system needed to be reformed so as to offer substantially improved opportunities to developing-country agricultural exporters. Also needed were financial and technical assistance to support developing countries' efforts to participate more effectively in international commodity trade, and international support to mitigate the consequences of price instability through user-friendly and operational approaches to schemes intended to address earnings shortfalls.

GENERAL ASSEMBLY ACTION

On 22 December [meeting 75], the General Assembly, on the recommendation of the Second Committee [A/59/481/Add.4], adopted **resolution 59/224** without vote [agenda item 83 (*d*)].

Commodities

The General Assembly,

Recalling its resolutions 57/236 of 20 December 2002 and 58/204 of 23 December 2003, and stressing the urgent need to ensure their full implementation,

Recalling also the United Nations Millennium Declaration adopted by Heads of State and Government on 8 September 2000,

Taking note of the Monterrey Consensus of the International Conference on Financing for Development,

Taking note also of the Plan of Implementation of the World Summit on Sustainable Development,

Taking note further of the Programme of Action for the Least Developed Countries for the Decade 2001-2010 and the *Least Developed Countries Report, 2004,*

Recalling the Doha work programme adopted at the Fourth Ministerial Conference of the World Trade Organization, on 14 November 2001, and welcoming the decision adopted in this context by the General Council of the World Trade Organization on 1 August 2004,

Taking note of the São Paulo Consensus adopted at the eleventh session of the United Nations Conference on Trade and Development, particularly the paragraphs relating to commodities,

Taking note also of the report of the Trade and Development Board on its fifty-first session,

Recognizing that commodity prices are an important element for heavily indebted poor countries that are dependent on commodities for maintaining long-term debt sustainability,

Taking note of the targets set out in the Rome Declaration on World Food Security and the Plan of Action of the World Food Summit and the outcome document of the World Food Summit: five years later, which reaffirms the pledge to end hunger and poverty,

Recognizing that structural changes in international commodity markets, particularly the increasing concentration in trade and distribution, constitute new challenges for small farmers, commodity producers and exporters in developing countries,

Expressing its concern about the difficulties experienced by the developing countries in financing and implementing viable diversification programmes, which are essential for sustainable development and for attaining access to markets for their commodities,

1. *Takes note* of the report of Secretary-General on world commodity trends and prospects, including the fact that while prices have improved for some commodities, the real prices of others remain on a declining trend;

2. *Recognizes* that many developing countries are highly dependent on primary commodities as their principal source of export revenues, employment, income generation and domestic savings and as the driv-

ing force of investment, economic growth and social development;

3. *Reiterates* the importance of maximizing the contribution of the commodity sector to sustained economic growth and sustainable development, while continuing diversification efforts in commodity-dependent developing countries;

4. *Emphasizes* the need for efforts by the developing countries that are heavily dependent on primary commodities to continue to promote a domestic policy and an institutional environment that encourage diversification and liberalization of the trade and export sectors and enhance competitiveness;

5. *Reaffirms* that each country has primary responsibility for its own economic and social development, and recognizes that an effective enabling environment at the national and international levels entails, inter alia, a sound macroeconomic framework, competitive markets, clearly defined property rights, an attractive investment climate, good governance, an absence of corruption and well-designed regulatory policies that protect the public interest and generate public confidence in market operations;

6. *Encourages* developing countries, with the necessary support of donor countries and the international community, to formulate specific commodity policies so as to contribute to the facilitation of trade expansion, the reduction of vulnerability and the improvement of livelihood and food security, by:

(a) Creating an enabling environment that encourages the participation of rural producers and small farmers;

(b) Continuing the diversification of the commodity sector and enhancing its competitiveness in developing countries that are heavily dependent on commodities;

(c) Increasing technology development and improving information systems, institutions and human resources;

7. *Notes* that the supply capacity and adaptability of many countries is constrained by weak institutional and technical capacity, and invites the international community to support commodity-dependent developing countries in addressing the loss of competitiveness and negative commodity production and trade trends and in taking the measures necessary to improve livelihoods and food security in commodity-dependent developing countries by supporting the design and implementation of commodity chain strategies, and welcomes initiatives taken in this regard;

8. *Emphasizes* the importance of official development assistance for agriculture and rural development, and invites developing countries to prioritize agriculture and rural development in their national development strategies and programmes, inter alia, in the New Partnership for Africa's Development, and in this regard invites developed countries and the donor community to further reinforce their assistance to those sectors in developing countries by providing financial and technical support for activities aimed at addressing commodity issues, particularly the needs and problems of commodity-dependent developing countries;

9. *Welcomes* the decision taken by members of the World Trade Organization on 1 August 2004, and

stresses the importance of a successful conclusion of the Doha work programme;

10. *Reiterates* the importance of expanded South-South trade and investment in commodities;

11. *Recalls* the potential of regional integration and cooperation to improve the effectiveness of traditional commodity sectors and support diversification efforts;

12. *Calls upon* developed countries that have not already done so to work towards the objective of providing duty-free and quota-free market access for all least developed country products, and encourages developing countries in a position to do so to contribute to improved market access for the least developed countries;

13. *Recognizes* that developed countries account for two thirds of world non-fuel commodity imports, and expresses the urgent need for supportive international policies and measures to improve the functioning of the commodity markets through efficient and transparent price-formation mechanisms, including commodity exchanges, and through the use of viable and effective commodity price risk-management instruments;

14. *Also recognizes* that market exigencies can constitute formidable challenges to developing country commodity producers and exporters, in particular small farmers, and urges both developing and developed countries to take appropriate steps to enable those producers to enter global supply chains and to facilitate their effective participation in supply chains, and invites the private sector to promote partnerships that contribute to the effective participation of small producers in supply chains;

15. *Encourages* the United Nations Conference on Trade and Development, the Food and Agriculture Organization of the United Nations, the World Bank and other relevant international organizations, within their respective mandates, to enhance their efforts to facilitate access to market-based instruments, with prudential oversight for managing commodity risks due to price fluctuation and natural disasters, so as to address the commodity problems in developing countries;

16. *Regrets* that schemes to mitigate earnings shortfalls have not reached the originally envisaged goals, and urges Governments and invites international financial organizations to continue to assess the effectiveness, including the operationalization and user-friendliness, of the systems for compensatory financing of shortfalls in export earnings, and in this regard stresses the importance of empowering developing country commodity producers to insure themselves against risk, including natural disasters;

17. *Reiterates* the role of the United Nations Conference on Trade and Development in addressing commodities issues in a comprehensive way in accordance with relevant General Assembly resolutions and the provisions of the São Paulo Consensus, and in this regard invites development partners to provide the resources required to enable the United Nations Conference on Trade and Development to undertake those activities;

18. *Notes with concern* that the real prices of some commodities are still on a declining trend, and requests the United Nations Conference on Trade and Development and the Food and Agriculture Organization of the United Nations, within their respective

mandates, to explore appropriate ways of addressing this problem and identifying best practices for dealing with persistent oversupply situations;

19. *Calls upon* the United Nations Conference on Trade and Development to continue to work, in cooperation with all interested stakeholders, including donor countries and organizations, for the effective operation of the International Task Force on Commodities launched at the eleventh session of the United Nations Conference on Trade and Development, and invites interested parties to provide voluntary financial support for its effective operation;

20. *Underlines* the need to strengthen the Common Fund for Commodities, and encourages it, in cooperation with the International Trade Centre UNCTAD/ WTO, the United Nations Conference on Trade and Development and other relevant bodies, to continue to strengthen the activities covered by its Second Account in developing countries with its supply chain concept of improving access to markets and reliability of supply, enhancing diversification and addition of value, improving the competitiveness of commodities, strengthening the market chain, improving market structures, broadening the export base and ensuring the effective participation of all stakeholders;

21. *Invites* all relevant stakeholders, including the United Nations Conference on Trade and Development, the Common Fund for Commodities and the Food and Agriculture Organization of the United Nations, within their respective mandates, and other donors to intensify their support for the financing of commodity diversification, focusing on developing private sector capacity, strengthening market institutions, developing strong producer associations for commodities with a proper role for producers, including women and small farmers, developing key infrastructure and stimulating investments;

22. *Requests* the Secretary-General of the United Nations, in collaboration with the Secretariat of the United Nations Conference on Trade and Development, to report on the implementation of the present resolution and on world commodity trends and prospects to the General Assembly at its sixty-first session;

23. *Decides* to include in the provisional agenda of its sixty-first session, under the item entitled "Macroeconomic policy questions", the sub-item entitled "Commodities".

Individual commodities

Timber. The United Nations Conference for the Negotiation of a Successor Agreement to the International Tropical Timber Agreement, 1994 [YUN 1994, p. 887] reconvened in 2004 (Geneva, 26-30 July). It had before it proposals prepared by the Chairperson and Vice-Chairperson of the Preparatory Committee [TD/TIMBER.3/4] and an UNCTAD secretariat note containing a review of related work of the International Tropical Timber Organization [TD/TIMBER.3/3]. The Conference adopted a resolution [TD/TIMBER.3/L.2] requesting the UNCTAD Secretary-General, in cooperation with the Executive Director of the International Tropical Timber Organization, to

prepare the working document resulting from the current Conference session, to maintain contact with producing and consuming countries with a view to assisting the Conference in reaching a successful conclusion, and to make arrangements to reconvene the Conference from 14 to 18 February 2005.

As requested, UNCTAD, in October [TD/ TIMBER.3/L.3], presented the working document resulting from the July Conference session. During the year, Mexico acceded to the Agreement, bringing the number of parties to 60. The signatories numbered 49.

Olive oil and table olives. The International Olive Oil Council (29 November–2 December) extended, with effect from 1 January 2005, the International Agreement on Olive Oil and Table Olives, 1986, as amended and extended, 1993 [YUN 1993, p. 760], until 31 December 2005. It also extended until 30 June 2005 the time limit for depositing the instrument of accession by Turkey. In 2004, Iran acceded to the Agreement, bringing the total number of parties to 16.

Sugar. As at 31 December, the International Sugar Agreement, 1992 [YUN 1992, p. 625] had 22 signatories and 49 parties. During the year, the International Sugar Council (29 November) extended until 31 December 2005 the time limit for the deposit by signatories of their instrument of ratification, acceptance or approval.

Coffee. As at 31 December, the International Coffee Agreement 2001 [YUN 2001, p. 880] had 35 signatories and 60 parties. During the year, Colombia, the Dominican Republic, Greece, Paraguay, Venezuela and Zimbabwe became parties. The International Coffee Council (19-21 May) extended until 31 May 2005 the time limit for the deposit of instruments of ratification, acceptance or approval or accession, including by States applying the Agreement provisionally.

Cocoa. As at 31 December, the International Cocoa Agreement, 2001 [YUN 2001, p. 880] had 11 signatories and 15 parties, including Brazil, Papua New Guinea and Trinidad and Tobago, which became parties during the year.

Common Fund for Commodities

The 1980 Agreement establishing the Common Fund for Commodities [YUN 1980, p. 621], a mechanism intended to stabilize the commodities market by helping to finance buffer stocks of specific commodities and such commodity development activities as research and marketing, entered into force in 1989, and the Fund became operational later that year. As at 31 December 2004, the number of parties to the Agreement stood at 110.

Finance

Financial policy

The *World Economic and Social Survey 2004*
[Sales No. E.04. II.C.1] stated that macroeconomic
policies had played a crucial role in stimulating
global recovery in 2003 and 2004, and that the
current challenge was to transform the cyclical
upturn into sustained long-run growth that generated additional employment. That required
striking a balance between accommodating
strong growth and at the same time managing potential risks for the escalation of inflation. Additional actions, which would vary from country to
country, were necessary to accelerate growth and
development beyond the cyclical recovery. Net financial flows to developing countries had increased in 2003, when official development assistance (ODA) rose from 0.23 per cent to a record
0.25 per cent of developed countries' gross national income, although still far short of the target of 0.7 per cent. For countries with access to international capital markets, private capital flows
increased markedly, despite a decline in inflows
of foreign direct investment (FDI). In that regard,
low interest rates and ample liquidity in developed economies encouraged international
investors to search for higher returns and thus to
purchase higher-risk financial instruments, including the high-yield corporate bonds of developed countries and bonds and stocks of
emerging markets. Despite the encouraging
prospects in international commodity and financial markets, both commodity prices and capital
market conditions were highly volatile so that a
possible tightening of monetary policy or a mar-
ket-driven correction in the United States posed
risks for developing countries heavily dependent
on international capital flows or with substantial
amounts of dollar- denominated debt. Thus, although the expansion in 2003 and 2004 of the
United States economy remained a key locomo-
tive for the world economy, its large fiscal and
trade deficits continued to be of major concern
for the downside risks they posed for the United
States itself and for the rest of the world.

The UNCTAD/DESA report *World Economic Situation and Prospects 2005* [Sales No. E.05.II.C.2], based
on information available as at 30 November 2004,
stated that macroeconomic policy stimulus was
reduced in many developed countries as recovery
gained momentum in 2004. Many central banks
began to raise interest rates, gradually reversing
the monetary easing they had adopted following
the slowdown in 2001; nevertheless, the process

was incremental, as policy makers recognized the
fragility of the recovery in some countries. In the
United States, for example, the Federal Reserve
raised the Federal Funds rate five times in the
second half of 2004, but by a total of only 125
basis points. In developing economies, monetary
policy was mixed: some countries tightened policy modestly in response to emerging inflationary pressures; a few others—the Republic of Korea, Hungary, South Africa and Turkey—reduced
interest rates because of weakening growth, currency appreciation or diminished inflationary
pressures, notwithstanding higher oil and commodity prices. Barring a supply-side shock that
would raise inflation substantially, such as a further surge in oil prices, monetary policy in 2005
was expected to remain generally accommodative
in most developing countries across all regions.

Financial flows

According to the UNCTAD/DESA report on the
world economic situation and prospects, the net
outward financial transfers from developing
countries continued to increase in 2004, reaching
some $312.7 billion. Net transfers from East and
South Asia moderated but remained at a high
level. Due to external surpluses, countries in that
region continued to accumulate large holdings of
foreign exchange reserves, mainly low-risk securities of developed countries. While the majority
of those reserves continued to be invested in
United States securities, there was evidence of
Asian central banks and oil-exporting countries
increasing the diversification of their reserve
holdings to include more euro-denominated securities. Net financial transfers from Latin America also increased, reflecting the region's improved trade and current-account surpluses. The
financial outflows were used to make debt
repayments, but there was also an increase in
official reserves for precautionary purposes.

In terms of inflows, developing countries received $59.6 billion in net private financial flows,
$4.9 billion less than they received in 2003. FDI,
the largest source of net private financial inflows
in 2004, began to recover from the depressed levels of recent years. Net financial flows to countries with economies in transition turned negative in 2004, owing to sharply lower net private
financial flows to the Russian Federation.

International financial system

Report of Secretary-General. In response to
General Assembly resolution 58/202 [YUN 2003,
p. 981], the Secretary-General submitted an August report [A/59/218 & Corr.1], which reviewed recent developments in the international financial

system, with particular relevance to developing countries, provided estimates of the net transfer of financial resources of regional groups of developing countries in 2003 and updated developments in international financial reform since his 2003 report on the subject [YUN 2003, p. 981].

The Secretary-General concluded that, although developing countries had taken wide-ranging measures to strengthen financial regulation and supervision, they remained highly vulnerable to global uncertainties and risks. To help lessen their susceptibility to shocks, the international community needed to promote policies and measures to reduce their exposure to external developments. It was also important to continue exploring measures to better assist them in reducing the high volatility of their external payment positions and to make their debt structures less vulnerable to crisis; in that regard, there might be a need for more appropriate regulatory instruments that recognized the close connection between macroeconomic cycles and risk-taking by financial institutions. It was essential to continue work on crisis prevention and resolution; in that connection, there was a need for more effective and less intrusive surveillance, backed by lending facilities offering emerging markets some form of contingent insurance that could be mobilized quickly and on a sufficiently large scale if necessary. There was broad recognition that international financial governance structures had to evolve in order to broaden and strengthen the participation of developing countries and countries with economies in transition in international economic decision-making and norm-setting; however, the political will to address that issue comprehensively was still lacking. The international community should continue the search for acceptable solutions towards a breakthrough in that area.

IMF/World Bank Development Committee. The joint International Monetary Fund (IMF)/ World Bank Development Committee, in a communiqué issued following its 2 October meeting (Washington, D.C.), expressed concern that most Millennium Development Goals (MDGs) [YUN 2000, p. 51]would not be met by many developing countries and recommitted itself to supporting efforts by those countries to pursue sustainable growth, sound macroeconomic policies, debt sustainability, open trade, job creation, poverty reduction and good governance. Reforms undertaken by many countries and private-sector-driven growth were critical to the success of country-led efforts to reduce global poverty. The Committee stated that success in the Doha Development Agenda [YUN 2001, p. 1432] could only complement those efforts and stressed the impor-

tance of translating into tangible results the agreed frameworks for further negotiations, as contained in the 1 August decision of the WTO General Council (see p. 958). It urged the IMF and World Bank to support efforts towards that end, to help developing countries assess the impact of negotiations and to provide them with additional support to address potential adjustment costs.

To address needs for additional stable and predictable financing to help developing countries undertake investment plans to meet the MDGs and to finance associated recurrent costs where appropriate, the Committee reviewed proposals to complement increased aid flows and commitments with innovative mechanisms. It welcomed the World Bank and IMF analysis of those options, notably the international finance facility, global taxes and voluntary contributions, including the analysis of their technical feasibility.

In an earlier communiqué, following a 25 April meeting (Washington, D.C.), the Committee, welcoming World Bank and IMF actions to promote trade facilitation and support developing countries as they integrated further into the global trading system, urged continued efforts to tailor Bank lending to support capacity-building and country-owned trade initiatives.

GENERAL ASSEMBLY ACTION

On 22 December [meeting 75], the General Assembly, on the recommendation of the Second Committee [A/59/481/Add.2], adopted **resolution 59/222** without vote [agenda item 83 (b)].

International financial system and development
The General Assembly,

Recalling its resolutions 55/186 of 20 December 2000 and 56/181 of 21 December 2001, both entitled "Towards a strengthened and stable international financial architecture responsive to the priorities of growth and development, especially in developing countries, and to the promotion of economic and social equity", as well as its resolutions 57/241 of 20 December 2002 and 58/202 of 23 December 2003,

Recalling also the United Nations Millennium Declaration and its resolution 56/210 B of 9 July 2002, in which it endorsed the Monterrey Consensus of the International Conference on Financing for Development, and the Plan of Implementation of the World Summit on Sustainable Development ("Johannesburg Plan of Implementation"),

Emphasizing that the international financial system should further sustain economic growth and support sustainable development and poverty eradication, while allowing for the coherent mobilization of all sources of financing for development, including the mobilization of domestic resources, international investment flows, official development assistance and external debt relief, and an open, equitable, rule-based, predictable and non-discriminatory global trading system,

Reiterating that success in meeting the objectives of development and poverty eradication depends on good governance within each country and at the international level, and stressing that sound economic policies, solid democratic institutions responsive to the needs of the people and improved infrastructure are the basis for sustained economic growth, poverty eradication and employment creation,

Recognizing that an enabling economic environment should, inter alia, foster a dynamic and well-functioning business sector and include efforts to further promote good corporate and public sector governance, to combat corruption in the private and public sectors, and to promote the strengthening of and respect for the rule of law,

Encouraging further progress on the issue of participation of developing countries in international economic decision-making and norm-setting processes, including those in the Bretton Woods institutions and other economic and financial institutions and ad hoc groupings, while welcoming the steps that have been taken with a view to strengthening the capacity of developing countries to participate effectively in the international financial institutions,

Recognizing the urgent need to enhance the coherence, governance and consistency of the international monetary, financial and trading systems, and the importance of ensuring their openness, fairness and inclusiveness in order to complement national development efforts to ensure sustained economic growth and the achievement of the internationally agreed development goals, including those contained in the United Nations Millennium Declaration,

Emphasizing the need for additional stable and predictable financing to help developing countries undertake investment plans to achieve internationally agreed development goals,

Welcoming the initiative launched by the Presidents of Brazil, Chile and France and the Prime Minister of Spain, with the support of the Secretary-General, to convene in New York on 20 September 2004 the Summit of World Leaders for Action against Hunger and Poverty,

Taking note of the note by the Secretary-General on innovative sources of financing for development,

Reiterating the need to strengthen the leadership role of the United Nations in promoting development,

1. *Takes note* of the report of the Secretary-General;

2. *Notes* that the global economy is recovering, supported by growth in some developing countries, and that economic growth should be further strengthened and sustained, and stresses the importance of cooperative efforts by all countries and institutions to cope with the risks of financial instability and to ensure a strong and steady recovery, as a means of achieving greater financial stability, and in this regard acknowledges recent efforts at regional monetary cooperation;

3. *Also notes* the continued net outward transfer of financial resources from developing to developed countries, acknowledging the outward investment from some developing countries as an indication of their integration into the world economy, underscores the need for appropriate measures at the national and international levels to address this issue, and further notes the efforts that have been made thus far to this end and the fact that, for some developing countries, those transfers, at the present time, indicate positive developments in the trade balance, which are required, inter alia, for debt repayment and allow for the purchase of foreign assets;

4. *Underlines* the importance of promoting international financial stability and sustainable growth, and welcomes the efforts undertaken to this end by the International Monetary Fund and the Financial Stability Forum, as well as the consideration by the International Monetary and Financial Committee of ways to sharpen tools designed to promote international financial stability and enhance crisis prevention, inter alia, through an even-handed implementation of surveillance, including at the regional level, and a sharpening of surveillance of capital markets and systemically and regionally important countries, with a view, inter alia, to the early identification of problems and risks, integrating debt sustainability analysis, the fostering of appropriate policy responses, the possible provision of financing and other instruments designed to prevent the emergence or spread of financial crises, and further improvements in the transparency of macroeconomic data and statistical information on international capital flows;

5. *Also underlines* the importance of efforts at the national level to increase resilience to financial risk, stresses in this regard the importance of better assessment of a country's debt burden and its ability to service that debt in both crisis prevention and resolution, and welcomes the ongoing work of the International Monetary Fund on assessing debt sustainability;

6. *Reiterates* in this regard that measures to mitigate the impact of excessive volatility of short-term capital flows and to improve transparency of and information about financial flows are important and must be considered;

7. *Notes* the impact of financial crisis or risk of contagion in developing countries and countries with economies in transition, regardless of their size, and in this regard welcomes the efforts of the international financial institutions, in their support to countries, to continuously adapt their array of financial facilities and resources, drawing on a full range of policies, taking into account the effects of economic cycles, as and where appropriate, having due regard to sound fiscal management and the specific circumstances of each case, so as to prevent and respond to such crises in a timely and appropriate way;

8. *Stresses* the importance of strong domestic institutions in promoting business activities and financial stability for the achievement of growth and development, inter alia, through sound macroeconomic policies and policies aimed at strengthening the regulatory systems of the corporate, financial and banking sectors, and also stresses that international cooperation initiatives in those areas should encourage flows of capital to developing countries;

9. *Notes* that building an environment that encourages development of the domestic business sector requires that countries undertake appropriate policies to minimize the risk of and respond to external shocks and their impact, inter alia, on growth and employment, and encourages the International Monetary Fund and the World Bank to take into account the spe-

cific conditions of developing countries in determining their guidance to them in this area;

10. *Stresses* the importance of advancing in respect of the efforts to reform the international financial architecture, as envisaged in the Monterrey Consensus of the International Conference on Financing for Development, and in this regard encourages the International Monetary Fund and the World Bank to continue examining the issues of the voice and effective participation of developing countries and countries with economies in transition in their decision-making processes;

11. *Welcomes* the ongoing work of the International Monetary Fund on quotas, and notes the conclusion of the Fund's Twelfth General Review of Quotas, the report on which indicated the adequacy of the current level of Fund resources and the intention of the Executive Board, during the period of the Thirteenth General Review, to monitor closely and assess the adequacy of Fund resources, to consider measures to achieve a distribution of quotas that reflects developments in the world economy and to consider measures to strengthen the governance of the Fund;

12. *Notes* the ongoing analysis by the World Bank and the International Monetary Fund, as mentioned in the communiqué of the Development Committee of 2 October 2004, of proposals on financing modalities to complement increased aid flows and commitments with innovative mechanisms, and their technical feasibility;

13. *Looks forward* to further consideration of the subject of possible innovative and additional sources of financing for development from all sources, public and private, domestic and external, taking into account international efforts, contributions and discussions, within the overall framework of the follow-up to the International Conference on Financing for Development;

14. *Reaffirms* the need to adopt policies and undertake measures to reduce the cost of the transfer of migrant remittances to developing countries, and welcomes the efforts of Governments and stakeholders in this regard;

15. *Emphasizes* that it is essential to ensure the effective and equitable participation of developing countries in the formulation of financial standards and codes, underscores the need to ensure their implementation, on a voluntary and progressive basis, as a contribution to reducing vulnerability to financial crisis and contagion, and notes that more than one hundred countries participated or agreed to participate in a joint World Bank–International Monetary Fund financial sector assessment programme;

16. *Invites* the multilateral and regional development banks and development funds to continue to play a vital role in serving the development needs of developing countries and countries with economies in transition, including through coordinated action, as appropriate, and stresses that strengthened regional development banks and subregional financial institutions add flexible financial support to national and regional development efforts, thus enhancing their ownership and overall efficiency, and are an essential source of knowledge and expertise for their developing-country members;

17. *Calls for* the continued effort of the multilateral financial institutions, in providing policy advice, technical assistance and financial support to member countries, to work on the basis of nationally owned reform and development strategies, to pay due regard to the special needs and implementing capacities of developing countries and countries with economies in transition, and to minimize the negative impacts of the adjustment programmes on the vulnerable segments of society, while taking into account the importance of gender-sensitive employment and poverty eradication policies and strategies;

18. *Stresses* the need to continuously improve standards of corporate and public sector governance, including accounting, auditing and measures to ensure transparency, noting the disruptive effects of inadequate policies;

19. *Acknowledges* the ongoing work towards a more comprehensive approach to sovereign debt restructurings, supports the increasing inclusion of collective action clauses in international bond issuing, and strongly encourages leading bond issuing countries and the private sector to make substantial progress on the preparation of an effective code of conduct, bearing in mind the need not to preclude emergency financing in times of crisis, to promote fair burden-sharing and minimize moral hazard, which will engage debtors and creditors to come together to restructure unsustainable debts in a timely and efficient manner;

20. *Welcomes* the ongoing efforts, including those of the Bretton Woods institutions, to improve the assessment of debt sustainability in low- and middle-income countries through, inter alia, the development of better tools to deal with exogenous shocks and the need to take country-specific factors into account;

21. *Requests* the Secretary-General to report to the General Assembly at its sixtieth session on the implementation of the present resolution;

22. *Decides* to include in the provisional agenda of its sixtieth session, under the item entitled "Macroeconomic policy questions", the sub-item entitled "International financial system and development".

Debt problems of developing countries

Report of Secretary-General. In response to General Assembly resolution 58/203 [YUN 2003, p. 984], the Secretary-General submitted an August report [A/59/219] on external debt crisis and development, which complemented his report on the follow-up to and implementation of the outcome of the International Conference on Financing for Development (see p. 978). The report analysed the evolution of debt indicators of developing countries and countries with economies in transition in the context of recent developments in international trade and payments, and in international capital markets. It discussed official debt relief under the Heavily Indebted Poor Countries (HIPC) Initiative, launched in 1996 [YUN 1996, p. 867], and official development assistance in the form of debt restructuring at the Paris Club (a group of creditor countries); debt management in developing countries and technical assistance; and developments in internationally agreed mechanisms for solving problems related to sovereign debt to private creditors.

The report concluded that a further extension of the HIPC Initiative appeared appropriate so as to allow all eligible countries to benefit. Implementation of the Initiative could be enhanced by a further streamlining of conditionality, particularly the elimination of structural and microconditions not essential to growth and poverty alleviation, while poverty reduction strategy papers (PRSPs) should be integrated into wider national development programmes focused on export diversification into the production of higher value-added products. In the light of the emerging consensus that full implementation of the Initiative would not remove the debt overhang in all beneficiary countries, renewed efforts by the international community would be required to help those countries attain debt sustainability and the MDGs. Increased grants to the poorest countries would be needed, in addition to debt forgiveness. For the heavily indebted low- and middle-income countries not eligible for debt relief under the HIPC Initiative, a satisfactory solution remained to be found. In that connection, the new Evian Approach of the Paris Club aimed at introducing greater flexibility in addressing the debt problems of non-HIPC countries should be explored. Continued efforts were needed to find an internationally agreed mechanism to address that problem, help prevent future financial crises and lead to more equitable burden sharing between debtors and creditors in crisis situations.

Other actions. The joint IMF/World Bank Development Committee (Washington, D.C., 25 April), in its review of the implementation of the HIPC Initiative, noted that 11 countries, several of them affected by conflict and some burdened with protracted arrears, had yet to reach the "decision point", which would make them eligible for interim debt relief under the Initiative, or to begin establishing a track record under an IMF-supported programme. It urged the Bank and the Fund to help facilitate those countries' rapid access to HIPC debt relief when their outstanding issues were addressed, and suggested that careful consideration be given to options to deal with the HIPC sunset clause scheduled to take effect at year's end.

In October, the Committee reviewed progress under the enhanced HIPC Initiative, welcomed the recent decision to extend its sunset clause to the end of December 2006, urged full creditor participation and welcomed the development of a forward-looking debt sustainability framework aimed at helping low-income countries manage their borrowings and avoid a build-up of unsustainable debt, while pursuing the MDGs.

The UNCTAD/DESA report on the world economic situation and prospects recorded that, as at December 2004, 15 countries qualified for debt relief under the HIPC Initiative, and another 12 reached their "decision points". Progress in implementing the Initiative was slow, owing mainly to the difficulty of eligible countries in complying with the conditions for receiving debt relief; in addition, maintaining macroeconomic stability remained a challenge for those in the interim phase of the programme.

Africa's debt sustainability

In accordance with the São Paulo Consensus adopted at UNCTAD XI (see p. 954), which mandated UNCTAD to continue to address developing countries' problems arising from debt sustainability, UNCTAD conducted a study on economic development in Africa—debt sustainability: oasis or mirage [UNCTAD/GDS/AFRICA/2004/1], a summary of which was issued in July by the UNCTAD secretariat [TD/B/51/3 & Corr.1]. The study analysed issues relating to Africa's debt overhang and HIPC debt relief, the eligibility and debt sustainability criteria of the HIPC Initiative and the sustainability of Africa's HIPC debt after debt relief. It explored new approaches to attaining sustainable debt levels.

The study concluded that Africa's debt burden had been a major obstacle to the region's economic growth and poverty reduction. It had frustrated public investment in physical and social infrastructure, including in health and human resource development, and deterred private investment. The consensus was that, for a permanent solution to the external debt crisis, African countries would need to pursue prudent debt management, economic diversification and sustained economic growth, which would require greater policy space; the international community had to support those policies with concerted and coherent actions in trade and finance through increased market access and major reductions, and eventually elimination, of agricultural subsidies, combined with international action on commodities and increased ODA. The study illustrated the weaknesses of the HIPC approach to finding a permanent exit solution to the debt crisis of African HIPCs, and highlighted the fact that several other equally poor African countries had been left out of the process. It examined the possible write-off of the debt of the poorest countries and, in the absence of the political will for debt cancellation, stated that the international community could consider applying the principles of bankruptcy codes to international debt work-outs corresponding to the notion of insolvency under such codes.

TDB [A/59/15], in agreed conclusions adopted on 15 October [agreed conclusions 480 (LI)], noted with concern that African HIPCs still faced daunting challenges, including high levels of poverty, and that in some cases progress in implementing the HIPC Initiative had been slow and funding had not always matched the estimated total costs of debt relief. It underscored the shared responsibility of both creditors and debtors in preventing and resolving unsustainable debt situations and agreed that UNCTAD should continue to provide analysis and advice on African development and to support African countries in their endeavour to implement the programmes of the New Partnership for Africa's Development (NEPAD) (see p. 920) and to attain international development goals, including those contained in the Millennium Declaration [YUN 2000, p. 49].

GENERAL ASSEMBLY ACTION

On 22 December [meeting 75], the General Assembly, on the recommendation of the Second Committee [A/59/481/Add.3], adopted **resolution 59/223** without vote [agenda item 83 *(c)*].

External debt crisis and development

The General Assembly,

Recalling its resolution 58/203 of 23 December 2003 on the external debt crisis and development,

Reaffirming the Monterrey Consensus of the International Conference on Financing for Development, which recognizes sustainable debt financing as an important element for mobilizing resources for public and private investment,

Recalling the United Nations Millennium Declaration adopted on 8 September 2000, which reaffirms the need to deal comprehensively and effectively with the debt problems of low- and middle-income developing countries,

Recalling also its resolution 57/270 B of 23 June 2003,

Concerned that a number of developing countries have not sufficiently benefited from the current global economic recovery in their efforts to attain the internationally agreed development goals, in particular the heavily indebted poor countries, where continuing debt and debt-servicing obligations could adversely affect their sustainable development,

Welcoming the further extension of the sunset clause of the Heavily Indebted Poor Countries Initiative, noting that the Initiative aims to promote debt sustainability in the poorest countries and that its implementation could be enhanced by streamlining conditionalities, emphasizing in this regard the need to ensure that debt relief does not replace other sources of financing, acknowledging furthermore the progress in the implementation of the Initiative, and welcoming the call in the communiqué issued by the joint International Monetary Fund/World Bank Development Committee on 2 October 2004 urging all creditors to participate in the Initiative,

1. *Takes note* of the report of the Secretary-General;

2. *Emphasizes* that creditors and debtors must share responsibility for preventing and resolving unsustainable debt situations in a timely and efficient manner, stresses the need to continue to bring them together in relevant international forums, and in this regard reiterates that the international financial system, along with enhanced official and private external financing and foreign direct investment, are key elements for a durable solution;

3. *Stresses* that debt relief can play a key role in liberating resources that should be directed towards activities consistent with poverty eradication, sustained economic growth and sustainable development and the achievement of the internationally agreed development goals, including those contained in the United Nations Millennium Declaration, and in this regard urges countries to direct those resources freed through debt relief, in particular through debt cancellation and reduction, towards these objectives;

4. *Also stresses* that debt sustainability depends on a confluence of many factors at the international and national levels, underscores the fact that no single indicator should be used to make definitive judgements about debt sustainability, and in this regard, while acknowledging the need to use transparent and comparable indicators, emphasizes that country-specific circumstances and the impact of external shocks should be taken into account in debt sustainability analyses and invites the International Monetary Fund and the World Bank, in their assessment of debt sustainability, to take into account fundamental changes caused by, inter alia, natural disasters, conflicts and changes in global growth prospects or in the terms of trade, especially for commodity-exporting developing countries;

5. *Notes with concern* that, in spite of the progress achieved, some countries that have reached the completion point of the Heavily Indebted Poor Countries Initiative have not been able to achieve lasting debt sustainability, stresses the importance of promoting responsible lending and borrowing and the need to help these countries manage their borrowings and avoid a build-up of unsustainable debt, including through the use of grants, and in this regard welcomes the ongoing work by the International Monetary Fund and the World Bank to develop a forward-looking debt sustainability framework for heavily indebted poor countries and low-income countries, as well as the current discussion on other initiatives aimed at ensuring long-term debt sustainability, including through debt reduction or cancellation, while stressing the need to maintain the financial integrity of the multilateral financial institutions;

6. *Stresses* the need for the World Bank and the International Monetary Fund to keep the overall implications of the framework for low-income countries under review, calls for transparency in the computation of the country policy and institutional assessments, and welcomes the intention to disclose the International Development Association country performance ratings that form part of the framework;

7. *Reaffirms* the need to pursue, where appropriate, debt relief measures vigorously and expeditiously, by all creditors, including within the Paris and London Clubs and other relevant forums, and welcomes other bilateral initiatives that have been undertaken to re-

duce outstanding indebtedness, so as to contribute to debt sustainability and facilitate sustainable development;

8. *Reiterates* the call upon developed countries, as expressed in the Millennium Declaration, to complete the enhanced programme of debt relief for the Heavily Indebted Poor Countries Initiative and to ensure that it is fully financed;

9. *Recognizes and encourages* the efforts of the heavily indebted poor countries, and calls upon them to continue to improve their domestic policies and economic management, inter alia, through poverty reduction strategies, and to create a domestic environment conducive to private sector development, economic growth and poverty reduction, including a stable macroeconomic framework, transparent and accountable systems of public finance, a sound business climate and a predictable investment climate, and in this regard invites all creditors, both private and public, to encourage those efforts, for example, through further participation in the delivery of debt relief in the framework of the enhanced Heavily Indebted Poor Countries Initiative and continued provision of adequate and sufficiently concessional financing by international financing institutions and the donor community;

10. *Stresses* the importance of continued flexibility with regard to the eligibility criteria for the enhanced Heavily Indebted Poor Countries Initiative, in particular for countries in post-conflict situations, and the need to keep the computational procedures and assumptions underlying debt sustainability analysis under review;

11. *Also stresses* the need to find a solution for the debt problems of heavily indebted low- and middle-income developing countries that are not eligible for debt relief under the Heavily Indebted Poor Countries Initiative, and in this regard continues to encourage the exploration of mechanisms to comprehensively address the debt problems of those countries, which may include debt-for-sustainable-development swaps or multicreditor debt swap arrangements, as appropriate;

12. *Takes note* of the acceptance that the debt of some non-HIPC debtor countries is unsustainable and that prudent and appropriate steps are needed to deal with these problems, in this regard welcomes the Evian Approach of the Paris Club, and calls upon creditor countries to ensure that a more tailored response to debt restructuring is granted only in case of imminent default and is not considered by debtor countries as an alternative to more expensive sources of financing and that the debt of such countries is treated in a way that reflects their financial vulnerabilities and the objective of enhancing long-lasting debt sustainability;

13. *Invites* donor countries, taking into account country-specific debt sustainability analyses, to continue their efforts to increase bilateral grants to developing countries, which could contribute to debt sustainability in the medium to long term, recognizes the need for countries to be able to invest, inter alia, in health and education while maintaining debt sustainability, and in this regard stresses the need to take steps to ensure that resources provided for debt relief do not detract from official development assistance resources;

14. *Welcomes* the efforts of the international community to provide flexibility, and stresses the need to continue those efforts in helping post-conflict developing countries, especially those that are heavily indebted and poor, to achieve initial reconstruction for economic and social development;

15. *Acknowledges* the ongoing work towards a more comprehensive approach to sovereign debt restructuring, supports the increasing inclusion of collective action clauses in international bond issuing, and strongly encourages leading bond-issuing countries and the private sector to make substantial progress in the preparation of an effective code of conduct, bearing in mind the need not to preclude emergency financing in times of crisis, to promote fair burden-sharing and to minimize moral hazard, which will engage debtors and creditors to come together to restructure unsustainable debts in a timely and efficient manner;

16. *Welcomes* the efforts of, and further calls upon, the international community to support institutional capacity-building in developing countries and countries with economies in transition for the management of financial assets and liabilities and to enhance sustainable debt management as an integral part of national development strategies;

17. *Invites* the United Nations Conference on Trade and Development, the International Monetary Fund and the World Bank, in cooperation with the regional commissions, development banks and funds and other multilateral institutions, to continue to study the possibility of creating a consultative group on external debt management aimed at developing best practices, promoting coherence and strengthening the institutional capacity of developing countries in debt management, taking into account work that has already been done;

18. *Calls upon* all Member States as well as the United Nations system, and invites the Bretton Woods institutions as well as the private sector to take appropriate measures and actions for the implementation of the commitments, agreements and decisions of the major United Nations conferences and summits, in particular those relating to the question of the external debt problem of developing countries;

19. *Requests* the Secretary-General to submit to the General Assembly at its sixtieth session a report on the implementation of the present resolution and to include in that report a comprehensive and substantive analysis of the external debt and debt-servicing problems of developing countries;

20. *Decides* to include in the provisional agenda of its sixtieth session, under the item entitled "Macroeconomic policy questions", the sub-item entitled "External debt crisis and development".

Financing for development

Follow-up to International Conference on Financing for Development

High-level meeting of Economic and Social Council, Bretton Woods institutions and WTO. In accordance with General Assembly resolution 50/227 [YUN 1996, p. 1249] and Economic and Social Council resolution 2003/47 [YUN 2003, p. 987], the Council, the Bretton Woods institutions (the World Bank Group and IMF) and WTO met for their seventh special high-level meeting (New York, 26 April). Before it was an April note by the Secretary-General [E/2004/50] providing background information and raising a number of questions. The meeting's overall theme was "Coherence, coordination and cooperation in the context of the implementation of the Monterrey Consensus". The discussions focused on three sub-themes: the impact of private investment and trade-related issues on financing for development; the role of multilateral institutions in reaching the MDGs; and debt sustainability and debt relief.

The Council President, in his summary of the proceedings [A/59/92-E/2004/73], noted the participants' emphasis on the key role of good governance in encouraging local and overseas investments; that a dynamic private sector was critical for economic growth and poverty alleviation; and that, to thrive, the sector required sound legal and regulatory systems, transparency and accountability of private and public institutions, macroeconomic stability, and peace and security. The key role of small and medium-sized enterprises as engines of growth was emphasized, as was the importance of effective progress in multilateral trade negotiations with a view to promoting development worldwide and achieving the MDGs. Although the MDGs had become the core business of several international organizations, concern was expressed about insufficient coordination of their activities and the lack of clarity in the division of labour, a problem often compounded by weak coordination with bilateral donors. The joint World Bank/IMF publication *Global Monitoring Report 2004: Policies and Actions for Achieving the Millennium Development Goals and Related Outcomes*, which reported on progress and gaps in achieving the MDGs, pointed to the critical need for more and better aid, which was especially important to Sub-Saharan Africa if it was to achieve the MDGs. In noting the significant progress being made in implementing the HIPC Initiative, the meeting considered it important that the debt sustainability framework take into account the imperative of reaching the MDGs, which could be addressed by linking poverty reduction strategies with national budgets and, through the budgets, with macroeconomic programmes and debt sustainability analyses.

Report of Secretary-General. In response to the Monterrey Consensus [YUN 2002, p. 953] and as requested by General Assembly resolution 58/230 [YUN 2003, p. 989], the Secretary-General submitted an August report [A/59/270] on follow-up to and implementation of the outcome of the International Conference on Financing for Development [YUN 2002, p. 953]. Prepared in collabo-

ration with major institutional stakeholders, the report provided an account of initiatives and commitments undertaken by Governments and stakeholders since the Secretary-General's 2003 report [YUN 2003, p. 989]. It reflected uneven progress towards achieving the goals set out in the Monterrey Consensus, and suggested that strengthening implementation efforts in all areas of the Consensus continued to be essential and that previous recommendations remained valid.

ECONOMIC AND SOCIAL COUNCIL ACTION

On 16 September [meeting 52], the Economic and Social Council adopted **resolution 2004/64** [draft: E/2004/L.47] without vote [agenda item 6 (a)].

International Conference on Financing for Development

The Economic and Social Council,

Recalling General Assembly resolutions 56/210 B of 9 July 2002, 57/250, 57/272 and 57/273 of 20 December 2002, 57/270 B of 23 June 2003 and 58/230 of 23 December 2003,

Recalling also its resolutions 2002/34 of 26 July 2002 and 2003/47 of 24 July 2003,

Recalling further General Assembly resolution 58/291 of 6 May 2004, entitled "Follow-up to the outcome of the Millennium Summit and integrated and coordinated implementation of and follow-up to the outcomes of the major United Nations conferences and summits in the economic and social fields",

Reaffirming its commitment to contribute to the implementation of the Monterrey Consensus of the International Conference on Financing for Development,

Stressing the importance of staying fully engaged, nationally, regionally and internationally, in order to ensure both proper follow-up to and implementation of commitments made and agreements reached at the International Conference on Financing for Development and to continue to build bridges between development, finance and trade organizations and initiatives, within the framework of the holistic agenda of the Conference,

Taking note of the interactive discussions among all stakeholders during the special high-level meeting of the Economic and Social Council with the Bretton Woods institutions and the World Trade Organization, held in New York on 26 April 2004, in which the President of the Trade and Development Board of the United Nations Conference on Trade and Development participated for the first time, as mandated by the General Assembly in its resolution 57/270 B, and welcoming the increased participation of high-level governmental representatives as well as senior intergovernmental and management officials from the major institutional stakeholders in the Monterrey process,

Encouraging the continued participation of non-governmental organizations and the business sector in the Monterrey process, and expressing its readiness to continue its work in the innovative and participatory spirit that characterized the International Conference on Financing for Development, strengthening the role of the Economic and Social Council in its interaction with non-governmental organizations and the business sector, in accordance with paragraph 9 of Council resolution 2003/47,

1. *Emphasizes* the link between financing for development and the achievement of the internationally agreed development goals, including those contained in the United Nations Millennium Declaration;

2. *Takes note* of the note by the Secretary-General on coherence, coordination and cooperation in the context of the implementation of the Monterrey Consensus of the International Conference on Financing for Development, prepared in collaboration with the major institutional stakeholders and other relevant organizations of the United Nations system, and of the summary by the President of the Economic and Social Council of the special high-level meeting of the Council with the Bretton Woods institutions and the World Trade Organization, held in New York on 26 April 2004;

3. *Looks forward* to the contribution to the 2005 high-level event of the next special high-level spring meeting of the Economic and Social Council on financing for development, in accordance with the modalities to be set out by the General Assembly at its fifty-ninth session;

4. *Encourages* the Financing for Development Office of the Department of Economic and Social Affairs of the Secretariat, in accordance with resolution 58/230, to continue supporting the intergovernmental process entrusted with the follow-up to the International Conference on Financing for Development, as well as to continue, within its mandate, and with the participation of all stakeholders, including the private sector, civil society and academia, to organize consultations and workshops to examine issues related to the mobilization of resources for financing development and poverty eradication and to organize workshops, panel discussions and other activities to promote best practices and exchange information on the implementation of the commitments made and agreements reached at the Conference;

5. *Decides* that the Department of Economic and Social Affairs, in collaboration with the secretariats of the Bretton Woods institutions, the World Trade Organization, the United Nations Conference on Trade and Development and other institutional stakeholders, shall prepare the documentation necessary for the special high-level spring meetings of the Economic and Social Council, and also decides to invite all institutional stakeholders to provide the Secretary-General with interim reports during the first quarter of the year on the work undertaken and planned in their respective areas of competence regarding implementation of the different components of the Monterrey Consensus, with the understanding that those reports shall constitute essential inputs to the preparation of the meetings;

6. *Encourages* the regional commissions, with the support of regional development banks, as appropriate, and in cooperation with the United Nations funds and programmes, to continue to strengthen their efforts in addressing regional and interregional aspects of the follow-up to the International Conference on Financing for Development, in the context of resolution 58/230, and to provide inputs to the High-level Dialogue on Financing for Development as well as to the spring meeting of the Economic and Social Council;

7. *Encourages* the President of the Economic and Social Council, in consultation with all major institutional stakeholders, to focus the special high-level spring meeting on specific issues, under the overall theme of coherence, coordination and cooperation in the context of the implementation of the Monterrey Consensus, within the holistic integrated approach of the Consensus, and to report thereon to the Council well in advance of the meeting, and, in this regard, underlines the importance of transparency and openness with respect to Member States;

8. *Stresses* the importance of pursuing appropriate policy and regulatory frameworks at the national level and in a manner consistent with national laws so as to foster a dynamic and well-functioning business sector able to increase economic growth and reduce poverty, while recognizing that the appropriate role of government in market-oriented economies will vary from country to country;

9. *Takes note* of the outcomes of the eleventh session of the United Nations Conference on Trade and Development, held in São Paulo, Brazil, from 13 to 18 June 2004, namely, the São Paulo Consensus and The Spirit of São Paulo, which contain relevant provisions with respect to the follow-up process of the International Conference on Financing for Development, and requests the United Nations Conference on Trade and Development to continue to contribute to the implementation of that process;

10. *Requests* the Secretary General to submit a report on financing for development pertaining to the role of the private sector, taking into consideration the report entitled *Unleashing Entrepreneurship: Making Business Work for the Poor*, for consideration by the General Assembly, under the relevant agenda items, at its fifty-ninth session.

Prior to the adoption of the above resolution, the Council, on 23 July, had deferred consideration of the draft [E/2004/L.47] to its resumed session in September (**decision 2004/310**).

Innovative sources of financing for development

As requested by the General Assembly in resolution 58/230 [YUN 2003, p. 989] and by the Monterrey Consensus [YUN 2002, p. 953], the Secretary-General submitted an August note [A/59/272] providing background information on a study conducted by the World Institute for Development Economic Research of the United Nations University, entitled *New Sources of Development Finance*. A summary of the study, entitled "New sources of development finance: funding the Millennium Development Goals", was annexed to the Secretary-General's note. It presented an analytical framework; seven proposed sources of funding, namely, global environmental taxes (carbon-use taxes), a tax on currency transactions to combat financial volatility referred to as the Tobin tax, creation of new special drawing rights, an international finance facility, increased private donations for development, a global lottery and global premium bond, and increased remittances from emigrants. Also presented was an overview of the key findings and some conclusions. The objective was to determine new funding sources to finance the achievement of the MDGS by the target date of 2015, in addition to a major effort by developing countries and the international community to mobilize additional financial resources.

The study concluded that the two global taxes proposed could yield revenue of the magnitude required (carbon-use tax), or at least half of the requirement (Tobin tax at a rate of 0.02 per cent). The double dividend of increased revenue plus improved functioning of the economy to be derived from the former might fall short on the second dimension; the much more modest Tobin tax rates were more acceptable and less likely to have disruptive economic consequences. As to the alternatives to global taxation, as listed above, the extent of additionality in each case had to be considered. In practice, each of the seven proposed sources of funding ran a distinct risk of crowding out existing sources. Overcoming the obstacles to each was primarily a matter for political action. Developing countries could do much to facilitate the effective enactment of the proposals and to take the necessary dialogue forward.

GENERAL ASSEMBLY ACTION

On 22 December [meeting 75], the General Assembly, on the recommendation of the Second Committee [A/59/482], adopted **resolution 59/225** without vote [agenda item 84].

Follow-up to and implementation of the outcome of the International Conference on Financing for Development

The General Assembly,

Recalling the International Conference on Financing for Development, held in Monterrey, Mexico, from 18 to 22 March 2002, and its resolutions 56/210 B of 9 July 2002, 57/250 of 20 December 2002, 57/270 B of 23 June 2003, 57/272 and 57/273 of 20 December 2002 and 58/230 of 23 December 2003, as well as Economic and Social Council resolutions 2002/34 of 26 July 2002, 2003/47 of 24 July 2003 and 2004/64 of 16 September 2004,

Taking note of the report of the Secretary-General on the follow-up to and implementation of the outcome of the International Conference on Financing for Development, prepared in collaboration with the major institutional stakeholders, and the note by the Secretary-General on innovative sources of financing for development,

Having considered the summary by the President of the Economic and Social Council of the special high-level meeting of the Council with the Bretton Woods institutions and the World Trade Organization, held in New York on 26 April 2004,

Recognizing the progress made in the implementation of the commitments made and agreements reached at the International Conference on Financing for Development and that more remains to be done,

Determined to continue to implement and build further on these commitments and agreements and to strengthen the coordinated and coherent engagement of all relevant stakeholders in the financing for development process,

Recalling the invitation to the World Trade Organization to strengthen its institutional relationship with the United Nations, in the context of the follow-up to the International Conference on Financing for Development,

Noting international efforts, contributions and discussions aimed at identifying possible innovative and additional sources of financing for development from all sources, public and private, domestic and external, within the context of the follow-up to the International Conference on Financing for Development, recognizing that some of the sources and their use fall within the realm of sovereign action,

Welcoming in this regard the initiative launched by the Presidents of Brazil, Chile and France and the Prime Minister of Spain, with the support of the Secretary-General, to convene in New York on 20 September 2004 the Summit of World Leaders on Action against Hunger and Poverty,

Noting the report of the Commission on the Private Sector and Development entitled *Unleashing Entrepreneurship: Making Business Work for the Poor,*

Noting also the ongoing analysis by the World Bank and the International Monetary Fund, mentioned in the communiqué of the Development Committee of 2 October 2004, of proposals on financing modalities to complement increased aid flows and commitments with innovative mechanisms, and their technical feasibility,

Welcoming the support of Member States for the Financing for Development Office of the Secretariat for organizing multi-stakeholder consultations within its mandate, and in accordance with resolution 58/230,

Recognizing the strong link between financing for development and the achievement of the internationally agreed development goals, including those contained in the United Nations Millennium Declaration,

1. *Reiterates* the call to implement fully and build further on the commitments made and agreements reached at the International Conference on Financing for Development;

2. *Stresses* the importance of the full involvement of all relevant stakeholders in the implementation of the Monterrey Consensus of the International Conference on Financing for Development at all levels, and stresses also the importance of their full participation in the Monterrey follow-up process, in accordance with the rules of procedure of the United Nations, in particular the accreditation procedures and modalities of participation utilized at the Conference and in its preparatory process;

3. *Underlines,* in accordance with the Monterrey Consensus:

(*a*) The importance of the implementation of the commitment to sound policies, good governance at all levels and the rule of law;

(*b*) The importance of the implementation of the commitment to create an enabling environment for mobilizing domestic resources and the importance of sound economic policies, solid democratic institutions responsive to the needs of the people and improved infrastructure as a basis for sustained economic growth, poverty eradication and employment creation;

(c) The importance, in order to complement national development efforts, of the implementation of the commitment to enhance the coherence and consistency of international monetary, financial and trading systems;

4. *Requests* the Secretary-General to consult with the Director-General of the World Trade Organization in order to expand existing cooperation between the two organizations on issues related to financing for development and to build on the ad hoc modality of interaction between the United Nations and the World Trade Organization in the preparations for the International Conference on Financing for Development by making better use of the possibilities offered by the existing framework of cooperation;

5. *Recognizes* the issues of particular concern to developing countries and countries with economies in transition acknowledged in paragraph 28 of the Monterrey Consensus, and the importance and critical role that a universal, rule-based, open, non-discriminatory and equitable multilateral trading system, as well as meaningful trade liberalization, can play in stimulating economic growth and development, benefiting countries at all stages of development, particularly in the case of the developing countries, where trade continues to be one of the most important sources of development financing, and in this regard welcomes the decision taken by the General Council of the World Trade Organization on 1 August 2004, which rededicates and recommits members to fulfilling the development dimensions of the Doha Development Agenda, which places the needs of developing and least developed countries at the heart of the Doha work programme;

6. *Notes* the recognition by the World Bank and the International Monetary Fund of the need to pursue efforts to increase fiscal space for public infrastructure investment within limits of fiscal prudence and debt sustainability;

7. *Decides* to give further consideration to the subject of possible innovative and additional sources of financing for development from all sources, public and private, domestic and external, taking into account international efforts, contributions and discussions, within the overall inclusive framework of the follow-up to the International Conference on Financing for Development;

8. *Acknowledges* the role that the private sector can play in generating new financing for development, and stresses the importance of pursuing appropriate policy and regulatory frameworks at the national level, in a manner consistent with national laws, to foster a dynamic and well-functioning business sector so as to increase economic growth and reduce poverty, while recognizing that the appropriate role of Government in market-oriented economies will vary from country to country;

9. *Reaffirms* the need to adopt policies and undertake measures to reduce the cost of transfer of migrant remittances to developing countries, and welcomes efforts by Governments and stakeholders in this regard;

10. *Notes* that, while foreign direct investment is a major source of financing development, the flow of such funds to developing countries and countries with economies in transition remains uneven, and in this regard calls upon developed countries to continue to devise source-country measures to encourage and facilitate the flow of foreign direct investment, inter alia, through the provision of export credits and other lending instruments, risk guarantees and business development services, and calls upon developing countries and countries with economies in transition to continue their efforts to create a conducive domestic environment for attracting investments by, inter alia, achieving a transparent, stable and predictable investment climate with proper contract enforcement and respect for property rights;

11. *Recalls* the commitments made at the International Conference on Financing for Development to increase the levels and effectiveness of official development assistance, in this regard welcomes the recent increase in official development assistance, which represents progress towards the target of 0.7 per cent of gross national product, as well as the progress announced by some countries, including in some cases the setting of clear timetables to achieve this objective, urges developed countries that have not yet done so to make concrete efforts to achieve the target of 0.7 per cent of gross national product as official development assistance to developing countries and 0.15 to 0.20 per cent of gross national product to least developed countries, and encourages developing countries to continue to build on progress achieved in ensuring that official development assistance is used effectively to help achieve development goals and targets;

12. *Notes* the efforts of donor countries and recipient countries to improve aid effectiveness, based on national development needs and priorities, including through sound policies at all levels, and stresses the need to intensify the efforts of multilateral and bilateral financial and development institutions in accordance with the Monterrey Consensus;

13. *Stresses* that debt relief can play a key role in liberating resources that should be directed towards activities consistent with poverty eradication, achieving sustained economic growth and sustainable development, as well as in the achievement of the internationally agreed development goals, including those contained in the United Nations Millennium Declaration; in this regard notes with concern that, in spite of some progress, some countries that have reached the completion point of the Heavily Indebted Poor Countries Initiative have not been able to achieve lasting debt sustainability; stresses the importance of promoting responsible lending and borrowing and the need to help these countries manage their borrowings and avoid a build-up of unsustainable debt, including through the use of grants; and in this regard welcomes the ongoing work by the International Monetary Fund and the World Bank to develop a forward-looking debt-sustainability framework for heavily indebted poor countries and low-income countries, as well as the current discussion on other initiatives aimed at ensuring long-term debt sustainability, including through debt reduction or cancellation, while stressing the need to maintain the financial integrity of the multilateral financial institutions;

14. *Stresses also* the importance of advancing in the efforts to reform the international financial architec-

ture, as envisaged in the Monterrey Consensus, and in this regard encourages the International Monetary Fund and the World Bank to continue examining the issues of the voice and effective participation of developing countries and countries with economies in transition in their decision-making processes;

15. *Emphasizes* that corruption at all levels is a serious barrier to development and to effective resource mobilization and allocation, reaffirms the commitment expressed in the Monterrey Consensus to make the fight against corruption at all levels a priority, welcomes actions taken in that regard at the national and international levels, and invites all Governments that have not yet done so to sign and ratify the United Nations Convention against Corruption;

16. *Decides* to consider, by the first part of 2005, the appropriate modalities for holding the High-Level Dialogue on Financing for Development, taking into account developments in the preparation for the high-level event of the General Assembly to be held in 2005, and in this context stresses the importance of financing for development for the comprehensive review of the progress made in the implementation of the Millennium Declaration and the outcomes of the major United Nations conferences and summits in the economic, social and related fields;

17. *Decides also* to consider in 2005 the timing and modalities for a follow-up conference to review the implementation of the Monterrey Consensus, as called for in paragraph 73 of the Consensus;

18. *Emphasizes* the importance of an effective intergovernmental follow-up to the International Conference on Financing for Development, in this regard recalls paragraph 69 of the Monterrey Consensus as well as resolution 58/230, reiterates the need to continue to explore ways of strengthening the follow-up, and decides to keep the issue under review;

19. *Decides* to include in the provisional agenda of its sixtieth session the item entitled "Follow-up to and implementation of the outcome of the International Conference on Financing for Development", and requests the Secretary-General to submit under this item an annual analytical assessment of the state of implementation of the Monterrey Consensus and of the present resolution, to be prepared in full collaboration with the major institutional stakeholders.

On 23 December, the Assembly decided that the agenda item on the follow-up to and implementation of the outcome of the International Conference on Financing for Development would remain for consideration at its resumed fifty-ninth (2005) session (**decision 59/552**).

Investment, technology and related financial issues

The UNCTAD Commission on Investment, Technology and Related Financial Issues held its eighth session (Geneva, 26-30 January), the report on which [TD/B/COM.2/60 & Corr.1] and the recommendations it contained were taken note of and endorsed, respectively, by TDB in March [A/59/15].

Investment and development. For its consideration of policy issues related to investment and development, the Commission had before it an UNCTAD secretariat note on the effectiveness of foreign direct investment (FDI) policy measures [TD/B/COM.2/EM.13/2]; the report of the Expert Meeting on the subject [YUN 2003, p. 991]; an UNCTAD secretariat note on FDI and development: the case of privatization-related services FDI—trends, impact and policy issues [TD/B/COM.2/EM.14/2]; the report of the Expert Meeting on FDI and Development [YUN 2003, p. 991]; an UNCTAD secretariat note on FDI and development: policy issues related to the growth of FDI services [TD/B/COM.2/55]; and the World Investment Report 2003: FDI Policies for Development: National and International Perspectives [UNCTAD/WIR/2003]. The Commission recommended that UNCTAD continue its work on investment, technology and enterprise development through research and policy analysis, technical assistance and capacity and consensus building; and, in particular, to examine the impact of FDI on development, with a view to helping developing countries attract FDI, maximize its positive effects and face challenges deriving from it. Particular attention should be paid to FDI in services, given the increasing importance of that sector in the world economy, and to how to foster FDI at the regional level and the need to strengthen human and institutional capacity-building efforts at the subnational level to help developing countries attract FDI.

Investment arrangements. For its consideration of issues related to investment arrangements, the Commission had before it the UNCTAD secretariat's note on the subject [TD/B/COM.2/54] and a progress report on the implementation of post-Doha technical assistance work in the area of investment [UNCTAD/ITE/IIT/2003/3].

The Commission recommended that UNCTAD continue its work on international arrangements, with emphasis on the bilateral and regional dimensions, including in the context of North-South and especially South-South cooperation, and of the needs of member countries. It should also continue to facilitate the ongoing exchange of information and experiences in that area, especially at the intergovernmental level.

Investment policy reviews. For its consideration of the topic of investment policy reviews (IPRs): exchange of national experiences, the Commission had before it the Investment Policy Review of Algeria [UNCTAD/ITE/IPC/2003/9] and the summary of the deliberations of the Investment Policy Reviews of Lesotho and Nepal [TD/B/COM.2/59].

The Commission recommended that UNCTAD disseminate information on country experiences related to FDI policies and to the interaction between foreign and domestic investment; continue the preparation of IPRs and strengthen the process for implementing their recommendations; complement its analytical work in the context of IPRs with technical assistance and capacity-building; and encourage linkages between foreign and local firms.

Subsidiary body. The Expert Meeting on Good Governance in Investment Promotion (Geneva, 1-3 November) [TD/B/COM.2/EM.15/3] had before it an UNCTAD secretariat note on the subject [TD/B/COM.2/EM.15/2]. The Meeting discussed what constituted good governance in investment promotion, examined national efforts to increase transparency and accountability in the public sector and to promote high standards of corporate governance, and considered ways to further strengthen those efforts. Special attention was given to the role of stakeholders, including business groups and civil society, in improving governance in investment.

The Meeting recognized that efforts to implement legislation to reform the investment climate in some developing countries were obstructed by resource constraints, corruption and the abuse of discretionary authority, which undermined the rule of law and the credibility of the host country. The Meeting suggested that international organizations assist developing countries in implementing measures to improve good governance in investment promotion, and that UNCTAD continue to support host Governments through its related programme and include many more developing countries, especially LDCs, in the programme.

Other suggestions called for the further examination and exchange of experiences in dispute and grievance resolution between foreign investors and host countries; encouraging host Governments to strengthen their mandates in policy advocacy; continued support by international agencies for the further development of corporate governance frameworks in developing countries; and encouraging investment promotion agencies to integrate and supply online client services to create transparent and predictable "single window systems". A further suggestion was for UNCTAD and other international organizations to provide technical assistance through such programmes as the Investment Gateway, an electronic system to help Governments gather and share online information on investment formalities and opportunities.

Competition law and policy

The Intergovernmental Group of Experts on Competition Law and Policy, at its sixth session (Geneva, 8-10 November) [TD/B/COM.2/CLP/48], held consultations and discussions regarding peer reviews on competition law and policy; review of the Model Law on Competition and studies related to the provisions of the 1980 Set of Multilaterally Agreed Equitable Principles and Rules for the Control of Restrictive Business Practices (known as the Set) [YUN 1980, p. 626]; the UNCTAD work programme, including capacity-building and technical assistance on competition law and policy; and the provisional agenda of the Fifth United Nations Conference to Review all Aspects of the Set, scheduled for 2005. It had before it UNCTAD secretariat reports on: experiences gained in international cooperation on competition policy issues and the mechanisms used [TD/B/COM.2/CLP/21/Rev.2]; roles of possible dispute mediation mechanisms and alternative arrangements, including voluntary peer reviews, in competition law and policy [TD/B/COM.2/CLP/37/Rev.1]; a handbook on competition legislation [TD/B/COM.2/CLP/41]; the Directory of Competition Authorities [TD/B/COM.2/CLP/42, TD/B/COM.2/CLP/49]; review of capacity-building and technical assistance on competition law and policy [TD/B/COM.2/CLP/43]; best practices for defining respective competences and settling of cases which involved joint action of competition authorities and regulatory bodies [TD/B/COM.2/CLP/44]; preliminary assessment of the Set [TD/B/COM.2/CLP/45]; ways in which possible international agreements on competition might apply to developing countries, including through preferential or different treatment, with a view to enabling those countries to introduce and enforce competition law and policy consistent with their level of economic development [TD/B/COM.2/CLP/46]; and recent competition cases [TD/B/COM.2/CLP/47].

Among the agreed conclusions adopted by the Group was the recommendation that, in order to better implement the Set, the Fifth (2005) UN Conference to review the Set should consider the following: an ad hoc voluntary peer review during the Conference; techniques for gathering evidence on cartels; the role of economic analysis and of the judiciary in competition law enforcement; the application of competition law and policy to the informal sector; and how to operationalize special and differential treatment for developing countries in competition law and policy. UNCTAD was to prepare, for the consideration of the Conference, studies on closer international cooperation in competition policy for the development objectives of developing countries and LDCs, in particular, an assessment of the application and implementation of the Set; a presentation of types of common provisions to be found in international cooperation agreements on competition policy and their application, particularly in bilateral and regional cooperation;

and a synthesis of recent, publicly available cartel investigations. It was also to prepare an updated review of capacity-building and technical assistance, taking into account information to be submitted by member States and international organizations; a further revised and updated version of the Model Law on Competition; and an information note on recent important cases, with special reference to competition cases involving more than one country. UNCTAD was to continue to prepare regularly and make available on the Internet further issues of the *Handbook on Competition Legislation,* including regional and international instruments, and an updated version of the *Directory of Competition Authorities.*

The Group invited member States to continue their voluntary assistance to UNCTAD for its capacity-building and technical cooperation activities in the form of experts, training facilities and financial resources. UNCTAD should expand those activities, taking into account the Group's deliberations and consultations at the current session, and provide updated information about its forthcoming events on its website.

The Commission on Investment, Technology and Related Financial Issues, in January [TD/B/COM.2/60], took note of the report of the fifth (2003) session of the Intergovernmental Group of Experts [YUN 2003, p. 991] and endorsed its agreed conclusions.

International standards of accounting and reporting

The Intergovernmental Working Group of Experts on International Standards of Accounting and Reporting, at its twenty-first session (Geneva, 27-29 October) [TD/B/COM.2/ISAR/26], had before it UNCTAD secretariat reports on: the review of the comparability and relevance of existing indicators on corporate social responsibility [TD/B/COM.2/ISAR/24]; the review of the implementation status of corporate governance disclosures and the role of such disclosures in adding sustainable value [TD/B/COM.2/ISAR/25]; and transparency and disclosure requirements for corporate governance, first considered in 2002 [YUN 2002, p. 967].

In its agreed conclusions, the Working Group noted that UNCTAD XI had provided a broader context for addressing corporate responsibility and agreed with suggestions for further improving the relevance and comparability of social reporting to encourage disclosure, which could constitute part of enterprise annual reporting to supplement financial information and provide a broader view of corporate activities and their impact on society. On the issue of corporate governance disclosure, the Working Group agreed that

further efforts were needed to reassert the development benefits to host countries of good corporate governance, as well as its impact on company performance. Having considered the results of the UNCTAD secretariat survey of corporate governance disclosure, based on its 2002 report on transparency and disclosure requirements for corporate governance, the Working Group agreed that an annual study to assess the state of reporting on corporate governance would be useful. It also agreed that the 2002 report needed updating to reflect best practices that had since evolved.

As to the mandate provided by the São Paulo Consensus (see p. 955) on corporate responsibility and other issues relevant to its work, the Group asked the UNCTAD secretariat to consider the related implications and report to its 2005 session. It also asked that the secretariat continue to disseminate the Accounting and Financial Reporting Guidelines for Small and Medium-Sized Enterprises Guidance, and to monitor and compile feedback on its implementation. The Working Group recommended that work on environmental accounting and eco-efficiency indicators continue to be disseminated, and that UNCTAD, in that context, coordinate its work on reporting with other initiatives, including the United Nations Environment Programme, the Global Reporting Initiative and other bodies engaged in environmental accounting and reporting. With regard to the Model Curriculum, the Working Group requested the UNCTAD secretariat to continue efforts on defining national, regional and international requirements for the qualification of professional accountants, in coordination with the Education Committee of the International Federation of Accountants.

The Commission on Investment, Technology and Related Financial Issues, in January [TD/B/COM.2/60], took note of the Intergovernmental Working Group's report on its twentieth (2003) session [YUN 2003, p. 992] and endorsed its agreed conclusions.

Taxation

The Economic and Social Council, by **decision 2004/316** of 23 July, deferred consideration of the agenda item on international cooperation in tax matters until its resumed (2004) session.

On 11 November [meeting 54], the Council adopted **resolution 2004/69** [drafts: E/2004/L.60 & E/2004/L.61] without vote [agenda item 13 (h)].

Committee of Experts on International Cooperation in Tax Matters

The Economic and Social Council,

Recalling General Assembly resolution 58/230 of 23 December 2003, in which the Assembly requested the

Economic and Social Council, in its examination of the report of the Ad Hoc Group of Experts on International Cooperation in Tax Matters at its next substantive session to give consideration to the institutional framework for international cooperation in tax matters,

Reaffirming its resolutions 1273(XLIII) of 4 August 1967, 1980/13 of 28 April 1980 and 1982/45 of 27 July 1982,

Taking note of the report of the Secretary-General on the eleventh meeting of the Ad Hoc Group of Experts on International Cooperation in Tax Matters,

Recognizing the call made in the Monterrey Consensus of the International Conference on Financing for Development, for the strengthening of international tax cooperation through enhanced dialogue among national tax authorities and greater coordination of the work of the concerned multilateral bodies and relevant regional organizations, giving special attention to the needs of developing countries and countries with economies in transition,

Taking note of the report of the Secretary-General on the implementation of and follow-up to commitments and agreements made at the International Conference on Financing for Development and the recommendations contained therein,

Recognizing the need for an inclusive, participatory and broad-based dialogue on international cooperation in tax matters,

Noting the activities developing within the concerned multilateral bodies and relevant regional organizations, including the international tax dialogue,

Decides that:

(a) The Ad Hoc Group of Experts on International Cooperation in Tax Matters shall be renamed the Committee of Experts on International Cooperation in Tax Matters;

(b) The Committee shall comprise twenty-five members nominated by Governments and acting in their expert capacity, who are to be drawn from the fields of tax policy and tax administration and who are to be selected to reflect an adequate equitable geographical distribution, representing different tax systems. The members shall be appointed by the Secretary-General, after notification is given to the Economic and Social Council. The term of office shall be four years;

(c) The Committee as of 2005 shall meet in Geneva on a yearly basis for not more than five days, within existing resources;

(d) The Committee shall:

(i) Keep under review and update as necessary the *United Nations Model Double Taxation Convention between Developed and Developing Countries* and the *Manual for the Negotiation of Bilateral Tax Treaties between Developed and Developing Countries*;

(ii) Provide a framework for dialogue with a view to enhancing and promoting international tax cooperation among national tax authorities;

(iii) Consider how new and emerging issues could affect international cooperation in tax matters and develop assessments, commentaries and appropriate recommendations;

(iv) Make recommendations on capacity-building and the provision of technical assistance to developing countries and countries with economies in transition;

(v) Give special attention to developing countries and countries with economies in transition in dealing with all the above issues;

(e) The Committee shall submit its report to the Economic and Social Council at its substantive session of July 2005, to be considered under the sub-item entitled "International cooperation in tax matters";

(f) The Committee shall be serviced by a small technical staff, which shall, inter alia, within existing resources, help collect and disseminate information on tax policies and practices, in collaboration with concerned multilateral bodies and relevant international organizations.

Transport

Maritime transport

The *Review of Maritime Transport, 2004* [Sales No. E.04.II.D.34] reported that world seaborne trade continued to grow in 2003, reaching a record high of 6.17 billion tons. The annual growth rate increased to 3.7 per cent, well above the 1.0 per cent increase for 2002. The world merchant fleet expanded to 857 million deadweight tons (dwt) at the beginning of 2004, a 1.5 per cent increase. New building deliveries increased marginally to 49.2 million dwt and tonnage broken up and lost declined by 16.1 per cent to 25.6 million dwt, leaving a net gain of 23.6 million dwt.

The fleet of oil tankers and dry bulk carriers, which together made up 72.9 per cent of the total world fleet, increased by 4.1 per cent and 2.5 per cent, respectively. There was a 9.3 per cent increase from 82.8 to 90.5 million dwt in the container ship fleet and a 7.6 per cent increase from 19.5 to 20.9 million dwt in the liquefied gas carriers fleet. Registration of ships by developed market economies and major open-registry countries accounted for 26.9 and 46.6 per cent of the world fleet, respectively. Open registries increased their tonnage marginally, and two thirds of that beneficially owned fleet was owned by market economies and developing countries. Developing countries' share reached 5.9 per cent, or 181.4 million dwt, of which 136 million dwt was registered in Asia.

Transport of dangerous goods

The Committee of Experts on the Transport of Dangerous Goods and on the Globally Harmonized System of Classification and Labelling of Chemicals, at its second session (Geneva, 10 December) [ST/SG/AC.10/32 & Add.1], considered the reports of the Subcommittee of Experts on the

Transport of Dangerous Goods on its twenty-fifth (5-14 July) [ST/SG/AC.10/C.3/50 & Add.1-3 & Add.3/Corr.1] and twenty-sixth (29 November–7 December) [ST/SG/AC.10/C.3/52] sessions; and of the Subcommittee of Experts on the Globally Harmonized System of Classification and Labelling of Chemicals on its seventh (14-16 July) [ST/SG/AC.10/C.4/14] and eighth (7-9 December) [ST/SG/AC.10/C.4/16] sessions, all held in Geneva.

The Committee endorsed the reports of the Subcommittee on the transport of dangerous goods, together with its recommended draft amendments to the thirteenth revised edition of the *Model Regulations* and to the fourth revised edition of the *Manual of Tests and Criteria*. The Committee likewise endorsed the reports of the Subcommittee on the Globally Harmonized System and the draft amendments to the first edition of the *Globally Harmonized System of Classification and Labelling of Chemicals*, adopted by the Committee in 2003 [YUN 2003, p. 993]. The amendments were annexed to the Committee report. The Committee also approved the Subcommittees' work programmes and meeting schedules for 2005-2006, and adopted a draft resolution for consideration by the Economic and Social Council in 2005.

UNCTAD institutional and organizational questions

In 2004, the Trade and Development Board, the governing body of UNCTAD, held the following sessions, all in Geneva: thirty-fourth executive session (10 March); twenty-first special session (14 May); thirty-fifth (21 September) and second part of thirty-third (30 September) executive sessions; and fifty-first session (4-15 October) [A/59/15].

In March, TDB took note of the reports of its subsidiary bodies and took action relating to the participation of its members in the high-level meeting of the Economic and Social Council with the Bretton Woods institutions, WTO and UNCTAD.

In May, TDB considered preparations, including the draft negotiated text, for UNCTAD XI (see p. 954), approved proposed amendments to the certificate of origin of the generalized system of preferences, considered the UNCTAD strategic framework for the 2006-2007 biennium and adopted the draft calendar for the remainder of 2004 and part of 2005.

In September, TDB considered the activities undertaken by UNCTAD in favour of Africa. It also continued its consideration of the financing of the participation of experts from developing countries and countries with economies in transition.

In October, TDB adopted agreed conclusions [agreed conclusions 479(LI 479(I))] on the review of progress in the implementation of the Programme of Action for the Least Developed Countries for the Decade 2001-2010 (see p. 857) and on economic development in Africa: issues relating to Africa's debt sustainability [agreed conclusions 480(L1)] (see p. 976), as well as a decision on the review of UNCTAD technical cooperation activities and their financing (see below). It took note of: the reports on UNCTAD assistance to the Palestinian people and on multi-stakeholder partnerships for UNCTAD XI; the TDB President's summary of discussions on a hearing with civil society and the private sector; and the reports of the Working Party (see p. 988) on the UNCTAD medium-term plan and programme budget for the 2004-2005 biennium, of the June session of the United Nations Commission on International Trade Law [A/59/17] (see p. 1352), of JAG on its April session (see p. 965) and of the Advisory Body on the implementation of courses by the secretariat in 2003-2004 and their impact, in accordance with the Bangkok Plan of Action [YUN 2000, p. 891].

Working Party. The UNCTAD Working Party on the Medium-term Plan and Programme Budget (the Working Party) held two sessions in 2004, both in Geneva: the forty-second (4 June and 6 July) [TD/B/WP/173] and the forty-third (13-17 September) [TD/B/WP/176 & Corr.1].

Technical cooperation

As described by the UNCTAD Secretary-General in his July report [TD/B/WP/172 & Corr.1 & Add.1, 2], the main features of UNCTAD technical cooperation activities in 2003 were an increased emphasis on capacity development, a focus on LDCs, and an increased level of contributions and delivery. Activities continued to focus on responding to the priorities identified by beneficiary countries and regions and supported the implementation of recommendations of the Bangkok Plan of Action. In 2003, trust fund contributions, the main source of financing for UNCTAD operational activities, increased by 28.6 per cent to $26.6 million, the highest contribution ever.

Expenditures rose sharply to $27.8 million, a 25.5 per cent increase over 2002, attributable to a 30 per cent increase in trust funds expenditures amounting to $19.9 million, and an increase of $1.5 million in UNDP-financed projects, amounting to $4.9 million. Expenditures on technical cooperation from the regular budget were unchanged.

By region, $3.8 million went to Africa, $5.5 million to Asia and the Pacific, $2.2 million to Latin America and the Caribbean, $0.9 million to Europe, and $15.3 million to interregional projects. LDCs' share of technical cooperation expenditures increased slightly, to 31.5 per cent, from 29 per cent in 2002.

By programme, services infrastructure for development and trade efficiency accounted for 32.6 per cent of total expenditures; international trade in goods and services, and commodities, 24.8 per cent; investment, technology and enterprise development, 19.2 per cent; and globalization and development strategies, 11.5 per cent. The balance of 11.9 per cent went to programmes for executive direction and management and support services (4.8 per cent), cross-divisional advisory services (4.2 per cent) and least developed, landlocked and island developing countries (2.9 per cent).

Major technical assistance programmes in order of expenditures included the Automated System for Customs Data ($6 million); investment policies and capacity-building ($4 million); the Debt Management and Financial Analysis System ($3 million); trade negotiations and commercial diplomacy ($2.8 million); trade, environment and development ($2 million); trade logistics ($1.4 million); and competition law and policy and consumer protection ($1.2 million).

Technical cooperation strategy

The July report on UNCTAD technical cooperation activities in 2003 (see above) was considered by the Working Party on the Medium-term Plan and the Programme Budget at its forty-third session (13-17 September) [TD/B/WP/176 & Corr.1], following which it adopted a draft decision for TDB action.

On 14 October [A/59/15 (dec. 481 (LI)], TDB took note of the information on the implementation of the new technical cooperation strategy adopted by TDB in 2003 [YUN 2003, p. 996] and requested the secretariat to further improve the presentation of the information on the allocation of trust fund contributions to different regions and thematic areas. It highlighted the need to ensure a more equitable distribution of resources among developing-country regions in the overall delivery of technical cooperation, and reaffirmed the importance of further implementing the strategy, in accordance with the related 2003 TDB decision and the São Paulo Consensus (see p. 955). TDB asked the secretariat to continue disseminating the strategy and to consider the implications of UNCTAD XI for the strategy.

Evaluation

An August UNCTAD secretariat note transmitted a progress report [TD/B/WP/175] detailing the actions UNCTAD had taken to implement the nine recommendations arising from the 2003 evaluation [YUN 2003, p. 996] of the UNCTAD technical cooperation/capacity-building (TC/CB) programme on trade, environment and development.

The report stated that UNCTAD had outlined the elements of the vision and strategy of its TC/CB programme and communicated them to its stakeholders; devised a communication strategy encompassing a website, a mailing list database, a newsletter launched in 2004, the publication of the *Trade and Environment Review*, reports to relevant intergovernmental bodies, briefings/meetings for key target audiences and information for the press; developed logical frameworks and objectively verifiable indicators for its main projects; pursued training opportunities to enhance staff capacities to develop and manage projects; consulted with beneficiary countries to identify target core institutions and individuals to be invited to activities; and stepped up efforts to ensure follow-up and hand-over of projects with individual participants and institutions. UNCTAD agreed to focus on trade-related aspects of the value chain and strengthen its partnerships with other organizations with competence in production and infrastructure. It was endeavouring to include a broad range of stakeholders in project activities, including companies and organizations operating at the grassroots level; was discussing project hand-over and follow-up with beneficiaries; and would incorporate end-of-project hand-over arrangements into future project design. It was also extending the coverage of its TC/CB programme to all regions, particularly Africa.

The Working Party, in September [TD/B/WP/176 & Corr.1], took note of the steps taken by UNCTAD, asked the secretariat to keep the evaluators and member States informed of follow-up to the evaluation, and noted the need for continued funding to secure the continuation of the programme's activities and the expansion of its geographical coverage. It requested that, in the implementation of the evaluation plan proposed by the secretariat, provision be made in 2005 for training courses on key issues on the international economic agenda, in accordance with the Bangkok Plan of Action [YUN 2000, p. 891], for accession to WTO in 2006 and for investment advisory services in 2007. TDB in October [A/59/15] endorsed Working Party's conclusions.

Participation in expert meetings

TDB in March [A/59/15] resumed its consideration of the financing of the participation of experts from developing countries and countries with economies in transition in UNCTAD expert meetings. The UNCTAD Deputy Secretary-General stated that the UNCTAD secretariat had tried without success to provide for the item in the proposed UN regular budget and that, if the Group of 77 wished to recommend the use of the regular budget, a proposal to that effect would have to be submitted to the General Assembly. He added, however, that such a proposal was unlikely to meet with success.

TDB returned to the issue in September, when Brazil, on behalf of the Group of 77 and China, pointed out that the participation of experts from various regions had had a significant positive effect on the quality of the meetings, and that, unfortunately, financial resources were inadequate for the full number of experts for 2004, and the outlook for 2005 was even bleaker. As financing through extrabudgetary resources was uncertain, it reiterated that the use of the regular budget represented a reliable and long-term solution.

TDB requested its President to hold consultations with regional coordinators and interested delegations with a view to finding a solution by year's end for predictable financing and to report to it with recommendations at an executive or special session.

Medium-term plan and programme budget

The Working Party on 6 July [TD/B/WP/173] considered the draft UNCTAD section of the proposed UN strategic framework for the period 2006-2007, on the basis of the final outcome of UNCTAD XI (see p. 954). In agreed conclusions adopted on the subject, the Working Party concurred with the UNCTAD section and recommended that TDB transmit to the General Assembly at its fifty-ninth (2004) session the proposed strategic framework for Programme 10: Trade and development for the period 2006-2007.

TDB in September [A/59/15] took note of the Working Party's report, endorsed its agreed conclusions and decided to transmit the proposed strategic framework for Programme 10 to the Assembly at its fifty-ninth session.

The Working Party, in September [TD/B/WP/176 & Corr.1], approved draft agreed conclusions on the review of the UNCTAD programme of work for the 2004-2005 biennium in the light of the outcomes of UNCTAD XI, a draft decision on the review of technical cooperation activities for consideration by TDB (see p. 988) and draft agreed conclusions on the evaluation of UNCTAD technical cooperation activities. The Working Party also approved the provisional agenda for its forty-fourth (2005) session.

TDB in October [A/59/15] took note of the Working Party's report and endorsed its agreed conclusions.

On 22 December, the Assembly took note of the report of the Second Committee [A/59/610], which considered and approved the proposed strategic framework for the period 2006-2007 (**decision 59/542**).

UNCTAD Secretary-General

By **decision 58/574** of 13 September, the General Assembly decided to defer consideration of the item entitled "Confirmation of the appointment of the Secretary-General of the United Nations Conference on Trade and Development" and to include it in the draft agenda of its fifty-ninth (2004) session. By **decision 59/552** of 23 December, the Assembly decided that the item would remain for consideration during its resumed fifty-ninth (2005) session.

Chapter V

Regional economic and social activities

The five regional commissions continued in 2004 to provide technical cooperation, including advisory services, to their member States, promote programmes and projects and provide training to enhance national capacity-building in various sectors. Four of them—the Economic Commission for Africa (ECA), the Economic Commission for Europe (ECE), the Economic Commission for Asia and the Pacific (ESCAP), and the Economic Commission for Latin America and the Caribbean (ECLAC)—held regular sessions during the year. The Economic and Social Commission for Western Asia (ESCWA) did not meet in 2004 but was scheduled to meet in 2005.

The executive secretaries of the commissions continued to exchange views and coordinate activities and positions on major development issues and on preparations for and follow-up to UN conferences. The Economic and Social Council decided to hold annually a dialogue with the executive secretaries immediately after the high-level segment of its substantive session. The Secretary-General forwarded to the General Assembly the findings and recommendations of the Office of Internal Oversight Services on its audit of the regional commissions, which evaluated the efficiency and effectiveness of their programmes and administrative management.

During the year, ECA placed emphasis on mainstreaming trade policy in national development strategies and reaffirmed its commitment to economic growth and poverty eradication as well as to support for sustainable development. ECE focused mainly on economic policies, in particular on those designed to stimulate competitive growth within the region. ESCAP adopted the Shanghai Declaration, by which it reaffirmed the importance of focusing its work on the three thematic areas of poverty reduction, managing globalization and addressing emerging issues, and, in that connection, set forth the actions ESCAP members would strive to undertake. Through the efforts of ESCAP, the Intergovernmental Agreement on the Asian Highway Network was adopted. The Council endorsed the Declaration and welcomed the adoption of the Agreement; it additionally recognized the work of ESCAP in implementing its technical cooperation projects. The Council adopted the San Juan resolution, in which it welcomed the ECLAC docu-

ment on productive development in open economies and the proactive agenda proposed by ECLAC for meeting the challenges of the productive development process. It also instructed the ECLAC Executive Secretary to evaluate the modalities of ESCAP collaboration with the United Nations Stabilization Mission in Haiti.

The General Assembly adopted resolutions on cooperation between the United Nations and several regional organizations.

Regional cooperation

In 2004, the United Nations continued to strengthen cooperation among its regional commissions, between them and other UN entities, and with regional and international organizations.

By **decision 2004/213** of 13 February, the Economic and Social Council decided that the theme for the agenda item on regional cooperation of its 2004 substantive session would be "Information technology for development: a regional perspective".

Meetings of executive secretaries. The executive secretaries of the five regional commissions met on 17-19 February (New York), 26 April (Shanghai, China), 18 June (Santiago, Chile), 14 and 17 July (New York) and 20-22 October (New York) [E/2004/15, E/2005/15].

At the 2004 meetings and at those held in the second half of 2003, the executive secretaries exchanged views on: global issues and activities of their respective commissions in response to the related development challenges within the regions, particularly on the regional dimensions of the work of the United Nations; ways to further strengthen coherence of UN activities at the regional level; interregional and horizontal cooperation among the commissions in given areas; and the commissions' participation in the eleventh session of the United Nations Conference on Trade and Development (UNCTAD XI) (see p. 954). They also reviewed the commissions' activities on: regional follow-up to the 2002 International Conference on Financing for Development [YUN 2002, p. 953]; resources mobilization and enabling environment for poverty eradication in the context of the implementation of the Brussels Programme of Action for the Least Developed Countries for the Decade 2001-2010 [YUN 2001, p. 770] (see p. 852); follow-up to the 2002 World Summit on Sustainable Development [YUN 2002, p. 821]; and preparations for the twelfth session of the Commission on Sustainable Development, for the first [YUN 2003, p. 857] and second (see p. 827) phases of the World Summit on the Information Society, and for UNCTAD XI (see p. 845).

Concerning measures taken by the Executive Committee on Economic and Social Affairs to involve the regional commissions more closely in the central policy work of the Secretariat, the executive secretaries agreed that there should be an improved two-way flow of information between global programmes, departments and offices, and the commissions to reflect more systematically the regional perspective in policy discussions at Headquarters and to ensure functional linkages between Headquarters and commission activities. The commissions should be more closely involved in the preparation of the Secretary-General's reports to global bodies, and the thematic groups established by the Executive Committee for the preparation of the 2004-2005 programme budget should remain active in support of that objective. Cooperation and joint work should be further pursued and clearly reflected in the work programme and budget of each of the commissions and the departments and offices concerned.

At the intergovernmental level, the Economic and Social Council, at its substantive sessions, should consider the item on regional cooperation at a separate segment to be held immediately after the high-level segment; it should be devoted to the interface between the commissions and the Council so as to ensure a more effective mainstreaming of their contributions to the Council's overall policy work and facilitate their provision of regional perspectives on global issues under consideration. That would enable the Council to better assess the commissions' response to its directives regarding policy coherence in the economic and social sectors. The executive secretaries further agreed on the need to hold yearly informal meetings at Headquarters to brief commission delegations on socio-economic policies, perspectives and outlooks in their respective regions and to encourage a more effective two-way flow of information and substantive exchange, including on the findings of the economic surveys of the five regions, thereby eliminating the need for their simultaneous launching at Headquarters.

To strengthen coherence of UN regional activities, the executive secretaries felt that there should be a framework for cooperation with regional and subregional organizations, with the commissions having the lead role. The relevant regional commissions should also be involved in initiatives undertaken by such entities as the Department of Economic and Social Affairs (DESA), UNCTAD, the United Nations Development Programme (UNDP), the United Nations Environment Programme (UNEP) and the offices of the Special Representative for Africa and of the High Representative for the Least Developed Countries, Landlocked Countries and Small Island Developing States.

As to the increasing need to bring more coherence to operational activities at the regional and subregional levels, the Millennium Development Goals (MDGs) [YUN 2000, p. 51] provided a sound basis for coordination and cooperation between the commissions and the United Nations Development Group.

The executive secretaries agreed that the regional commissions should align their technical cooperation work within the framework of the common country assessments/United Nations Development Assistance Framework (CCA/UNDAF) and poverty reduction strategy papers (PRSPs). To further support that approach, there should be a strong two-way communication between the commissions and the resident coordinators/UN country teams, including information flows on the commissions' country-level activities and their capacities.

The executive secretaries noted that the first phase of the World Summit on the Information Society [YUN 2003, p. 857] (see p. 845) had brought into focus the need for cooperation among relevant organizations within and outside the UN system to develop methodology for measuring selected indicators and for benchmarking and monitoring progress in the implementation of the Summit outcomes. They emphasized also the need for interregional and horizontal cooperation among their respective secretariats in that area. They recommended information and communication technologies (ICT) as the interregional theme for consideration by the Economic and Social Council in 2004 and identified ICT as an important area for a joint project by the commissions, to be funded from the Development Account. They also agreed to participate in a high-level panel organized by ESCAP, in connection with its sixtieth session, on "ICT and knowledge-economy development: a regional perspective".

By **decision 2004/323** of 11 November, the Economic and Social Council decided to hold a dialogue with the executive secretaries of the regional commissions immediately after the high-level segment of its substantive session, and requested the Secretariat to ensure that that decision was reflected in the programme of work for the Council's 2005 substantive session. It would assess the implementation of that decision in 2008, in the context of Council resolution 1998/46 [YUN 1998, p. 1262] on the restructuring and revitalization of the United Nations and General Assembly resolution 57/270 B [YUN 2003, p. 1468] on follow-up to major UN conferences.

Review and reform of regional commissions

In a May report [E/2004/15], the Secretary-General updated the Economic and Social Council on the two cross-cutting issues related to the regional commissions: mainstreaming the regional dimension in UN work and enhancing the coherence of UN activities at the regional level, in accordance with the guidance provided for in Council resolution 1998/46 [YUN 1998, p. 1262] on restructuring and revitalizing the United Nations. In response to decision 2004/213 (see p. 990), the report also explored the theme "Information technology for development: a regional perspective".

In addenda to the report [E/2004/15/Add.1, 2], the Secretary-General submitted resolutions and decisions adopted at recent meetings of the regional commissions calling for action by or brought to the attention of the Council.

The Secretary-General also submitted the summaries of the overview of the economic report on Africa 2004: unlocking Africa's potential in the global economy [E/2004/17]; the economic and social survey of Asia and the Pacific [E/2004/18]; the economic survey of Europe [E/2004/16]; the economic survey of Latin America and the Caribbean, 2003 [E/2004/19]; and the survey of economic and social developments in the ESCWA region 2004 [E/2004/20].

The Council adopted resolutions on the Shanghai Declaration (resolution 2004/6), the work of ESCAP in implementing its technical cooperation projects (resolution 2004/7), the Intergovernmental Agreement on the Asian Highway Network (resolution 2004/8), the San Juan resolution on productive development in open economies (resolution 2004/45), support for the reconstruction of Haiti and the United Nations Stabilization Mission in Haiti (resolution 2004/46), and on the venue of the next session of ECLAC (resolution 2004/47). It also adopted decisions on the implementation of resolutions concerning the participation of associate member countries of ECLAC in the follow-up to UN world conferences and in the Council's work (decision 2004/324), the United Nations Framework Classification for Fossil Energy and Mineral Resources (decision 2004/233), and the venue and dates of ESCWA's twenty-third session (decision 2004/320).

(For the summaries of the surveys and texts of the resolutions, see the relevant sections of this chapter.)

Audit of regional commissions

In May [A/58/785], the Secretary-General submitted the report of the Office of Internal Oversight Services (OIOS) on its audit of the five regional commissions, which evaluated the efficiency and effectiveness of programme and administrative management and made a series of recommendations.

Overall, OIOS found the financial and administrative controls in the commissions adequate. The reforms and restructuring implemented in the past few years had resulted in more relevant and appropriate substantive programmes, with an implementation rate during 2002-2003 that ranged from 87 per cent to 94 per cent. However, OIOS noted inconsistencies and weaknesses in the planning, selection, scope, methodology, conclusions, timing and costs of the self-evaluation exercises carried out by most of the commissions, and the absence of a systematic monitoring of recommendations emerging from those exercises to determine if specific process improvements had been achieved. The management of regional advisers was ineffective due to problems in coordinating and integrating their activities with the work programmes of the substantive divisions.

OIOS recommended that, to support the Economic and Social Council's discussion of the linkages among the work of the regional commissions and other UN entities in the economic and social sectors, the commissions' New York office should write its annual report more succinctly and begin with the section summarizing the executive secretaries' discussions on common issues. The Council should move its discussions relating to the commissions from the general segment to a special segment, with a day dedicated to incorporating the regional perspectives into the wide-ranging issues under consideration.

The overall coherence and effectiveness of intergovernmental bodies needed constant review for adherence to rules and procedures, for functionality and timely reporting, and for follow-up of recommendations. The calendars of the commissions' annual/biennial sessions should be harmonized with the submissions of the biennial programme plan and the proposed programme budgets to the Office of Programme Planning, Budget and Accounts at Headquarters.

ESCWA and ECA should review the need for a separate statistics division, with a minimum critical mass of statisticians to strengthen their statistical strategy and outputs and to better guarantee methodological standards in their regions. The regional commissions should establish mechanisms for: assessing the quality of publications; categorizing a publication as a "flagship"one and harmonizing the issuance of such publications; conducting peer-review exercises; and assessing the composition of the readership. Policies on access and downloading of publications from websites also needed to be standardized.

The General Assembly, in **resolution 59/271** of 23 December (see p. 1369), took note of the OIOS report on its audit of the regional commissions and requested the Secretary-General to report to the Assembly in 2005 on actions taken by the commissions' legislative bodies on the OIOS recommendations.

Africa

The Economic Commission for Africa (ECA) held its thirty-seventh session/Conference of African Ministers of Finance, Planning and Economic Development (Kampala, Uganda, 21-22 May) [E/2004/38] under the theme "Mainstreaming trade policy in national development strategies". It considered an overview report on recent economic and social conditions in Africa [E/ECA/CM.37/6], a paper on mainstreaming trade policy in national development strategies [E/ECA/CM.37/2], a progress report on the work of the ECA/Organisation for Economic Co-operation and Development (OECD) on monitoring mutual reviews of development effectiveness, a report of the Expert Group Meeting on Africa's External Debt Problem [E/ECA/CM.37/8], the annual report on the work of ECA, 2004 [E/ECA/CM.37/4], a report on the external review of ECA's work since 1996 [E/ECA/CM.37/5], a note on proposals for enhancing the effectiveness of the United Nations Trust Fund for African Development [E/ECA/CM.37/7] and the proposed ECA 2006-2007 programme plan [E/ECA/CM.37/3].

The Conference of African Ministers adopted a statement [E/ECA/CM.37/10] by which the Ministers reaffirmed their commitment to achieving sustained economic growth and eradicating poverty, and to promoting sustainable development as they advanced towards an inclusive and equitable global economic system; expressed concern that, unlike other developing regions, Africa had not reaped the gains of global integration; underscored the importance of successfully concluding the Doha Development Round of trade negotiations launched in 2001 at the Fourth Ministerial Conference of the World Trade Organization (WTO) [YUN 2001, p. 1432] to better integrate Africa into the global trading system; strongly urged renewal beyond 2008 of the African Growth and Opportunity Act (AGOA), enacted by the United States to promote African exports and due to expire in September 2004; also urged trading partners to reduce cotton subsidies, with a view to eliminating them; and recommended that development partners correct the tariff escalation maintained by industrial countries.

The Ministers noted the establishment of the Commission for Africa by Prime Minister Anthony Blair of the United Kingdom to galvanize efforts to achieve the MDGs in Africa and believed that it had an important role to play in supporting the implementation of the New Partnership for Africa's Development (NEPAD) [YUN 2001, p. 899] and advancing Africa's agenda in international forums; recognized ECA's key role in promoting Africa's economic and social development and urged member States to support its efforts by contributing to the United Nations Trust Fund for Africa; and, noting the progress of reform achieved by ECA over the past eight years, believed that the way forward, proposed in the report on the external review of ECA's work since 1996, would enable ECA to deepen the relevance of its contribution to Africa's development agenda. Finally, the Ministers endorsed the ECA programme plan for the 2006-2007 biennium [E/2004/38 (res. 842 (XXXVII))].

The Conference was preceded by the twenty-third meeting of the Committee of Experts of the Conference of African Ministers of Finance, Planning, and Economic Development (Kampala, Uganda, 18-20 May), which discussed the agenda items of the Conference. Its report [E/ECA/CM.37/9] was adopted by the Conference.

On 13 July, President George W. Bush of the United States signed into law the AGOA Acceleration Act of 2004, extending AGOA long into the future.

Economic trends

In 2004, Africa's gross domestic product (GDP) grew by 4.6 per cent, the highest growth rate in almost a decade, up from the final 2003 figure of 4.3 per cent. Underpinning the improvement were higher commodity prices, good macroeconomic management, better performance in agriculture, an improved political situation in many African countries, and increased aid and debt relief, according to the Overview of the Economic Report for Africa 2005: Meeting the Challenges of Unemployment and Poverty in Africa [E/2005/17]. Central Africa led the improved performance, with a 7.3 per cent growth rate, followed by East Africa at 5.8 per cent, North Africa at 4.8 per cent, West Africa at 4.3 per cent and Southern Africa at 3.5 per cent. At the country level, the fastest growing economies were those of Chad, Equatorial Guinea, Liberia, Ethiopia, Angola and Mozambique, while the slowest were those of Zimbabwe, Seychelles, Côte d'Ivoire, Central African Republic, Guinea-Bissau, Gabon, Kenya, Malawi, the Comoros, and Somalia.

On average, inflation declined from 10.3 per cent to 8.4 per cent due to prudent monetary and fiscal policies, good harvests and relatively stable exchange rates. Fiscal deficits also declined, with 32 countries recording either fiscal surpluses or declines in fiscal deficit. Current account performance was also favourable, with roughly one half of African countries (26 out of 51) showing improvement.

Overall, exports grew at 23.5 per cent as a result of both volume and price increases. Import growth averaged 16.9 per cent, reflecting higher incomes and rising oil and food prices.

Activities in 2004

ECA activities in 2004 were undertaken in seven subprogrammes: facilitating economic and social policy analysis; fostering sustainable development; strengthening development management; harnessing information for development; promoting trade and regional integration; promoting the advancement of women; and supporting subregional activities for development [E/2004/38, E/ECA/CM.38/2].

Development policy and regional economic development

African recovery and development

ECA continued in 2004 to strengthen the capacity of member States to design and implement policies for economic growth and poverty reduction, in line with the priorities of the Millennium Declaration [YUN 2000, p. 49] and NEPAD [YUN 2001, p. 899]. Particular emphasis was placed on economic policy analysis, development issues related to social policy and poverty analysis, issues related to financing for development and statistical development. To follow up the implementation of the Monterrey Consensus, adopted by the International Conference on Financing for Development [YUN 2002, p. 953], an ad hoc expert group meeting on financial systems and resource mobilization for economic development in Africa was held (Nairobi, Kenya, November) to identify the challenges constraining the emergence of well-functioning capital markets in the continent. The meeting called for the establishment of an African Monetary Fund, improvement and streamlining of regulatory and supervisory infrastructure, transparency, regional harmonization of laws and regulations, and adoption of policies for attracting remittances and mobilizing foreign resources through capital markets.

ECA hosted the fourth meeting of the ECA Big Table (Addis Ababa, Ethiopia, October) on the theme "Stimulating private sector investments in Africa", which proposed the creation of an investment climate facility to improve the policy environment for private sector growth. ECA also played a key role in the Strategic Partnership with Africa, a bilateral and multilateral donor group established to mobilize support for Africa and ensure the alignment of donor support with national poverty reduction strategies, including the tracking of results. It organized the first annual meeting of the Advisory Board on Statistics in Africa (Addis Ababa, May), which reviewed the objectives, scope, institutional arrangements and governance structure, including the future direction of ECA work in statistics.

New Partnership for Africa's Development

ECA continued to support the implementation of NEPAD, a programme initiated by African leaders in 2001 [YUN 2001, p. 900] for the development of Africa. The programme's African Peer Review Mechanism (APRM) became operational in 2004, with the roll-out of country support missions to Ghana, Kenya, Mauritius and Rwanda to assess the processes in those countries for self-assessment and drafting programmes of action that would be reviewed by the APRM Panel. ECA helped in the development of some APRM codes and standards, provided country economic and governance data to its secretariat, participated in all four support missions and collaborated with UN system agencies and other partners in supporting NEPAD infrastructure development. It worked with the OECD secretariat in developing a framework for mutual accountability and policy coherence, which would form the basis of a new partnership between African countries and their development partners.

ECA convened the Sixth Annual Regional Consultations of UN agencies working in Africa (Addis Ababa, July) to review progress made by the thematic clusters around which UN support for NEPAD was organized [YUN 2002, p. 977], consider immediate UN assistance to advance progress, address challenges and concerns, and chart the way forward. The consultations found that, although significant progress had been made in all the thematic clusters, the United Nations faced a number of constraints in supporting NEPAD at the regional level: increased financial commitment by the UN entities was dependent on their receiving additional resources for NEPAD programmes, without which the scope and flexibility for undertaking additional joint activities were limited. Thus, if further progress was to be made, UN entities would need to deepen their collaboration to achieve greater operational coherence in their various NEPAD support programmes using existing coordination mechanisms.

In **resolution 59/254** of 23 December (see p. 924), the General Assembly urged UN system entities to intensify their efforts in developing and implementing joint programmes in support of NEPAD at the regional level.

(For detailed information on NEPAD, see p. 920.)

Illicit diamond transactions and development

In 2004, the General Assembly and the Security Council considered the role that illegal transactions of diamonds played in fuelling conflict (see p. 57), particularly in Africa.

GENERAL ASSEMBLY ACTION

On 15 December [meeting 72], the General Assembly adopted resolution 59/144 [draft: A/59/L.46 & Add.1] without vote [agenda item 21].

The role of diamonds in fuelling conflict: breaking the link between the illicit transaction of rough diamonds and armed conflict as a contribution to prevention and settlement of conflicts

The General Assembly,

Recognizing that the trade in conflict diamonds is a matter of serious international concern, which can be directly linked to the fuelling of armed conflict, the activities of rebel movements aimed at undermining or overthrowing legitimate Governments and the illicit traffic in and proliferation of armaments, especially small arms and light weapons,

Recognizing also the devastating impact of conflicts fuelled by the trade in conflict diamonds on the peace, safety and security of people in affected countries, and the systematic and gross human rights violations that have been perpetrated in such conflicts,

Noting the negative impact of such conflicts on regional stability and the obligations placed upon States by the Charter of the United Nations regarding the maintenance of international peace and security,

Recognizing, therefore, that continued action to curb the trade in conflict diamonds is imperative,

Recognizing also the positive benefits of the legitimate diamond trade to producing countries, and underlining the need for continued international action

to prevent the problem of conflict diamonds from negatively affecting the trade in legitimate diamonds, which makes a critical contribution to the economies of many of the producing, exporting and importing States, especially developing States,

Noting that the vast majority of rough diamonds produced in the world are from legitimate sources,

Recalling the Charter and all the relevant resolutions of the Security Council related to conflict diamonds, and determined to contribute to and support the implementation of the measures provided for in those resolutions,

Recalling also Security Council resolution 1459(2003) of 28 January 2003, in which the Council strongly supported the Kimberley Process Certification Scheme as a valuable contribution against trafficking in conflict diamonds,

Welcoming the important contribution of the Kimberley Process, which was initiated by African diamond-producing countries,

Believing that the implementation of the Kimberley Process Certification Scheme should substantially reduce the opportunity for conflict diamonds to play a role in fuelling armed conflict and should help to protect legitimate trade and ensure the effective implementation of the relevant resolutions on trade in conflict diamonds,

Recalling its resolutions 55/56 of 1 December 2000, 56/263 of 13 March 2002, 57/302 of 15 April 2003 and 58/290 of 14 April 2004, in which it called for the development and implementation of proposals for a simple, effective and pragmatic international certification scheme for rough diamonds,

Welcoming, in this regard, the implementation of the Kimberley Process Certification Scheme in such a way that it does not impede the legitimate trade in diamonds or impose an undue burden on Governments or industry, particularly smaller producers, and does not hinder the development of the diamond industry,

Welcoming also the decision of countries and one regional economic integration organization to address the problem of conflict diamonds by participating in the Kimberley Process and to implement the Kimberley Process Certification Scheme,

Welcoming further the important contribution made by the diamond industry, in particular the World Diamond Council, as well as civil society, to assist international efforts to stop the trade in conflict diamonds,

Welcoming the voluntary self-regulation initiatives for the diamond industry announced by the World Diamond Council, and recognizing that a system of such voluntary self-regulation will contribute, as described in the Interlaken Declaration of 5 November 2002 on the Kimberley Process Certification Scheme for Rough Diamonds, to ensuring the effectiveness of national systems of internal control for rough diamonds,

Noting with appreciation that the Kimberley Process has pursued its deliberations on an inclusive basis, involving concerned stakeholders, including producing, exporting and importing States, the diamond industry and civil society,

Recognizing that State sovereignty should be fully respected and that the principles of equality, mutual benefits and consensus should be adhered to,

Recognizing also that the Kimberley Process Certification Scheme, which came into effect on 1 January 2003, will be credible only if all participants have established internal systems of control designed to eliminate the presence of conflict diamonds in the chain of producing, exporting and importing rough diamonds within their own territories, while taking into account that differences in production methods and trading practices, as well as differences in institutional controls thereof, may require different approaches to meet minimum standards,

1. *Reaffirms its strong and continuing support* for the Kimberley Process Certification Scheme;

2. *Recognizes* that the Kimberley Process Certification Scheme can help to ensure the effective implementation of relevant resolutions of the Security Council containing sanctions on the trade in conflict diamonds, and calls for the full implementation of existing Council measures targeting the illicit trade in rough diamonds that play a role in fuelling conflict;

3. *Also recognizes* the important contributions that the international efforts to address the problem of conflict diamonds, including the Kimberley Process Certification Scheme, have made to the settlement of conflicts in Angola, the Democratic Republic of the Congo, Liberia and Sierra Leone, and the ongoing value of the Certification Scheme as a mechanism for the prevention of future conflicts;

4. *Stresses* that the widest possible participation in the Kimberley Process Certification Scheme is essential and should be encouraged, and urges all Member States to participate actively in the Certification Scheme by complying with its undertakings;

5. *Notes with appreciation* the report of the Chair of the Kimberley Process submitted pursuant to resolution 58/290, and congratulates the Governments, regional economic integration organization representatives, the organized diamond industry and civil society participating in the Kimberley Process for contributing to the development and implementation of the Kimberley Process Certification Scheme;

6. *Takes note* of the decision of the General Council of the World Trade Organization of 15 May 2003 granting a waiver with respect to the measures taken to implement the Kimberley Process Certification Scheme, effective from 1 January 2003 to 31 December 2006;

7. *Welcomes* the progress achieved at the plenary meeting of the Kimberley Process held in Gatineau, Canada, from 27 to 29 October 2004, expanding the mandate of the Participation Committee to advise the Chair on matters of non-compliance by participants;

8. *Also welcomes* the important progress made towards the implementation of the peer review mechanism, including the submission of annual reports by all participants and the completion of eleven voluntary review visits, and encourages all remaining participants to receive voluntary review visits;

9. *Encourages* all participants in the Kimberley Process Certification Scheme to collate and submit relevant statistical data on the production of and international trade in rough diamonds as a tool for effective implementation and as envisaged by the Certification Scheme;

10. *Acknowledges with great appreciation* the important contribution that Canada, as Chair of the Kimberley Process in 2004, has made to the efforts to curb the trade in conflict diamonds, and welcomes the succession of the Russian Federation as Chair and Botswana as Vice-Chair of the Process for 2005;

11. *Requests* the Chair of the Kimberley Process to submit a report on the implementation of the Process to the General Assembly at its sixtieth session;

12. *Decides* to include in the provisional agenda of its sixtieth session the item entitled "The role of diamonds in fuelling conflict".

Information technology

ECA activities under the subprogramme on harnessing information for development was focused on assisting member States in strengthening national capacities for the utilization of information and communication technologies (ICTs), including strengthening capacities in the development and use of information knowledge systems as decision-support tools for socio-economic development. Activities were undertaken to promote the growth of the information society in Africa and the harnessing of ICTs to achieve broad development goals, including the MDGs. A major achievement was the increase in the number of African countries that had developed national information and communication infrastructure plans and policies. ECA assisted the Comoros, Ghana, Mali and Niger in developing strategies for the adoption and use of ICTs. The Gambia and Malawi received support for integrating their ICT policies with poverty reduction strategies and the MDGs, and in building capacity for application in social sectors, such as health and education. ECA also began to implement a pilot project on the development of e-strategy at the village level, with the development of village information and communication infrastructure policies, and developed plans for Ghana, aimed at making ICTs accessible to rural communities.

As follow-up to the first phase of the World Summit on the Information Society [YUN 2003, p. 857], ECA organized a meeting (Addis Ababa, February) to discuss preparations for the second phase in 2005. It also organized two workshops (Addis Ababa, February); the first reviewed achievements under the first phase of its benchmarking initiative, the SCAN-ICT project, a multi-donor project aimed at building capacity for gathering information and data in support of investment in ICT; the second reviewed progress in the formulation and implementation of national ICT infrastructure plans and strategies.

Transport and communications

An important objective of ECA's work in infrastructure development was to help establish an efficient, integrated and affordable transport and communications system and to facilitate national and international traffic. ECA continued to assist member States and regional economic communities in the implementation of the Yamoussoukro Declaration on air transport liberalization [YUN 1988, p. 273], particularly in strengthening their capacity to implement the Declaration and incorporate it into their national policies. ECA and the Sub-Saharan Africa Transport Programme (SSATP), in collaboration with Ethiopia, organized the SSATP annual general meetings (September), which highlighted improvements in collaboration between regional economic communities and SSATP, the increased participation of countries (33 countries joined SSATP in 2004), and the inclusion of road safety in the SSATP action plan. The meeting identified priority activities to be implemented as part of corridor development and increased movement of people and goods.

Other notable activities in the area of transport included a study on the development of multi-modal transport in Africa, which was endorsed by an expert group meeting on the subject, and a study on best practices for the commercialization and privatization of rail, air, road and maritime transport, highlighting the importance of private sector involvement in the development of infrastructure and services. ECA also contributed to a NEPAD short-term action plan on infrastructure. It organized a forum (Yaoundé, Cameroon, December) on transport infrastructure and regional integration for the Central Africa subregion.

Food security and sustainable development

ECA's work under the subprogramme of fostering sustainable development focused on assisting member States in defining their environmental challenges and priorities, and identifying strategies for addressing them.

As a contribution to the 10-year review of the Dakar/Ngor Declaration on Population, Family and Sustainable Development [YUN 1992, p. 476] and the Programme of Action of the 1994 International Conference on Population and Development (ICPD) [YUN 1994, p. 955], ECA prepared a regional review which was adopted by the Regional Ministerial Review Conference on Implementation of the Dakar/Ngor Declaration and the Programme of Action of ICPD-10 (Dakar, Senegal, June 10-11) (see p. 1078), together with a ministerial declaration constituting a blueprint for the further implementation the Dakar/Ngor Declaration and the ICPD Programme of Action. ECA studied the role of National Councils for Sustainable Development in achieving sustainable development in Africa, as part of efforts to ensure integrated follow-up and implementation of the

outcomes of the 2002 World Summit on Sustainable Development [YUN 2002, p. 821]. It prepared studies to create awareness of the potential of science and technology in achieving food security and sustainable development, including the study on emerging issues in science and technology—principles, methodology and strategy for promoting the African Green Revolution. It was also developing an African Green Revolution Design and Training Manual as a contribution to the African Green Revolution and as a tool for achieving MDG sustainable development targets in Africa.

ECA supported member States in promoting an integrated approach to national policy-making that included issues related to mineral resources development and assisted several regional organizations in elaborating their programmes in that field. Under the NEPAD regional consultations of UN agencies on the sub-cluster on water, the ECA secretariat organized three regional workshops for decision makers and technical personnel in Geo-Water Information Development and Management for Central African countries (Yaoundé, June), East Africa (Accra, Ghana, September) and East Africa (Mombassa, Kenya, October) to facilitate the development of an African Regional Water Clearinghouse for strengthening cooperation in integrated water resources management. ECA also launched the publication of the African Water Journal.

Development management

ECA activities under the subprogramme on strengthening development management were aimed at improving and sustaining good governance practices for broad stakeholder participation in the development process to strengthen the foundations for sustainable development in Africa. ECA organized the Fourth African Development Forum (Addis Ababa, 11-15 October) under the theme "Governance for a progressing Africa" to address key issues related to the challenges of achieving good governance. Before it were the findings of an ECA secretariat project on the development of indicators for measuring and monitoring progress towards that objective. The Forum focused on conflict prevention and sustainable economic development, strategies for fighting corruption, strengthening the judiciary, and ensuring effective political parties and a strong civil society. It adopted a Consensus Statement containing major policy recommendations and time-bound actions for follow-up at the country level, including for the enhancement of the role and participation of youth and civil society in the governance process in Africa.

Promoting trade and regional integration

The Trade and Regional Integration Division of ECA continued to promote the integration and participation of African countries in the global economy. Its office in Geneva, established in 2003, provided assistance and technical support to the African WTO Geneva Group in preparing its negotiating positions within the framework of the Doha Development Agenda, adopted by the Fourth WTO Ministerial Conference [YUN 2001, p. 1432], and its proposals and submissions on various WTO issues under negotiation. Following the failure of the 2003 Fifth WTO Ministerial Conference [YUN 2003, p. 967], ECA organized a number of meetings to assist the region's countries in developing strategies for further negotiations, including a high-level brainstorming meeting of African trade negotiators (Addis Ababa, November) to evaluate the implications for African countries of the so-called July Framework Agreements at WTO.

ECA's work of building sustainable trade capacities of African countries was enhanced by the Africa Trade Policy Centre, recently established to strengthen Africa's trading capacity in line with the trade-related objectives of NEPAD. It supported African capacity-building efforts through policy research and training activities.

ECA increased its support to member States in building a strategy for the ongoing negotiations on Economic Partnership Agreements (EPAs) between the African, Caribbean and Pacific States and European Union countries, by undertaking an impact assessment of EPAs and organizing four subregional expert group meetings to examine the main challenges of the negotiations and the potential implications of the EPAs for subregional economies.

A major accomplishment was the launch in July of a publication entitled "Assessment of Regional Integration in Africa", produced in collaboration with the AU and the African Development Bank, which provided the first comprehensive assessment of progress towards regional integration in Africa.

Integration of women in development

Promoting the advancement of women in Africa remained a major priority of ECA's work programme, involving the continuing elaboration of tools and mechanisms for monitoring progress towards the goal of gender equality set in global and regional platforms of action and for mainstreaming gender into national planning instruments. Those objectives were being achieved through the African Gender and Development Index, which entered an expanded phase with field trials in 12 countries. The Index would provide tools for measuring the performance of ECA member States in addressing gender equality, promote political awareness of gender issues and help streamline reporting on gender-related human rights issues, the MDGs and NEPAD.

The seventh African Regional Conference on Women (Addis Ababa, October), organized as the regional review of the Beijing Platform for Action [YUN 1995, p. 1170] (Beijing +10), endorsed the Index. The Conference adopted an outcome document on the way forward, which reviewed progress achieved and major constraints to the advancement of women in Africa and highlighted further actions to accelerate progress in the implementation of the Beijing Platform for Action, especially in such critical areas as poverty reduction, HIV/AIDS, human rights of women, health, education, the girl-child and women's participation in peace-building and reconstruction.

To promote the collection of gender-aggregated data, ECA produced and disseminated 53 country gender profiles based on secondary data collected in a number of thematic areas. It produced a guidebook entitled "Mainstreaming Gender Perspectives and Household Production in National Accounts, Budgets and Policies in Africa" to improve the skills of statisticians, national accountants and policy analysis experts in collecting, analysing and integrating gender-disaggregated micro- and macro-economic statistics into national planning instruments. ECA also prepared the first National Satellite Accounts of Household Production for South Africa and developed a gender-aware macro-economic model to evaluate the impact of policies on poverty reduction and welfare, using the South African economy as a pilot case.

Subregional offices

The five subregional offices (SROS), located in Central, East, North, Southern and West Africa, strengthened policy dialogue by sharing information with African experts principally through meetings of ad hoc expert groups and intergovernmental expert committees. They continued to collaborate with the UN system through the UN Resident Coordinator system and the CCA/UNDAF, a major outcome of which was the publication of a joint report assessing progress towards meeting the MDGs. The SROS helped to facilitate a better understanding of trade issues in the context of the Doha work programme (see p. 958) and of current negotiations on economic partnership agreements between Africa and Europe. They supported member States and subregional economic communities in translating NEPAD priorities and objectives into concrete country-level projects and programmes, including formulation of subregional strategies for infrastructure development and the assessment of progress in implementation.

Construction of office facilities at ECA

In October [A/59/444], the Secretary-General, in response to General Assembly resolution 56/270 [YUN 2002, p. 1459], reported to the Assembly on progress in the construction of additional office facilities at ECA headquarters in Addis Ababa, including activities related to the preliminary design. Also submitted to the Assembly were the related comments and recommendations of the Advisory Committee on Administrative and Budgetary Questions [A/59/572]. (For details on this subject, see p. 1364.)

Regional cooperation

Cooperation between UN and ECCAS

The Secretary-General, in his consolidated report on cooperation between the United Nations and regional and other organizations [A/59/303], submitted pursuant to General Assembly resolution 58/316 (see p. 1374), provided information on cooperation between the UN system and the Economic Community of Central African States (ECCAS).

The Assembly, by **decision 59/552** of 23 December, decided that the item on cooperation between the United Nations and ECCAS would remain for consideration at its resumed (2005) fifty-ninth session.

Cooperation between UN and SADC

The Secretary-General, in his consolidated report on cooperation between the United Nations and regional and other organizations [A/59/303], provided information on cooperation between the UN system and the Southern African Development Community (SADC).

On 2 December, the General Assembly, by **resolution 59/49** (see p. 1459), invited SADC to participate in its sessions in the capacity of observer.

GENERAL ASSEMBLY ACTION

On 15 December [meeting 72], the General Assembly adopted **resolution 59/140** [draft: A/59/L.42 & Add.1] without vote [agenda item 56 (s)].

Cooperation between the United Nations and the Southern African Development Community

The General Assembly,

Recalling its resolution 37/248 of 21 December 1982 and all other relevant General Assembly resolutions and decisions on the promotion of cooperation between the United Nations and the Southern African Development Community, including resolution 57/44 of 21 November 2002 and decision 56/443 of 21 December 2001,

Welcoming the adoption of its resolution 59/49 of 2 December 2004, in which it decided to invite the Community to participate in its sessions and its work in the capacity of observer,

Commending States members of the Community for demonstrating continued commitment to deeper and more formal arrangements for cooperation among themselves towards regional integration,

Recognizing the continued efforts to strengthen democracy, good governance, sound economic management, human rights and the rule of law and the consolidation of peace, including the adoption at the annual summit of the Community, held in Mauritius on 16 and 17 August 2004, of the Principles and Guidelines Governing Democratic Elections,

Noting with concern the HIV/AIDS pandemic, which has reached crisis proportions in the region, and the high prevalence of communicable diseases such as malaria and tuberculosis, which are having far-reaching social and economic consequences,

Noting the continued efforts of the Community to make Southern Africa a landmine-free zone,

Expressing concern about the very difficult humanitarian situation in countries of the region,

Welcoming the launch by the Community of the Strategic Indicative Plan for the Organ on Politics, Defence and Security Cooperation in August 2004 as an enabling instrument for the implementation of the development agenda embodied in the Regional Indicative Strategic Development Plan of the Community,

Recognizing the important role that women play in the development of the region,

Recognizing also the important role of civil society and the private sector in the development of the region,

1. *Takes note* of the report of the Secretary-General on cooperation between the United Nations and regional and other organizations;

2. *Expresses its appreciation* to the United Nations funds and programmes as well as the international community for the financial, technical and material support given to the Southern African Development Community;

3. *Expresses its support* for the economic reforms being implemented by States members of the Community, in pursuance of their shared vision of creating a strengthened regional economic community through deeper economic integration;

4. *Calls upon* the international community to strengthen support for the measures taken by the Community in addressing HIV/AIDS, including commitments on the outcome of the special session of the General Assembly on HIV/AIDS, as well as support for the implementation of the Maseru Declaration on the Fight against HIV/AIDS;

5. *Appeals* to the United Nations, its related bodies and the international community to assist and support the Community in its efforts against landmines;

6. *Appeals* to the international community and to relevant organizations and bodies of the United Nations system to continue providing financial, technical and material assistance to the Community to support its efforts to fully implement the Regional In-

dicative Strategic Development Plan and the New Partnership for Africa's Development as well as towards the achievement of the Millennium Development Goals;

7. _Calls upon_ the international community to support the efforts of the Community in capacity-building and in addressing the new challenges, opportunities and consequences presented to the economies in the region arising from the process of globalization and liberalization;

8. _Requests_ the Secretary-General, in consultation with the Executive Secretary of the Community, to enhance contacts aimed at promoting and harmonizing further cooperation between the United Nations and the Community;

9. _Also requests_ the Secretary-General to submit to the General Assembly at its sixty-first session a report on cooperation between the United Nations and the Southern African Development Community.

Asia and the Pacific

The Economic and Social Commission for Asia and the Pacific (ESCAP) held its sixtieth session (Shanghai, China, 26-28 April) [E/2004/39], preceded by a senior officials segment (22-24 April), under the theme "Meeting the challenges in an era of globalization by strengthening regional development cooperation". The High-level Visionary Meeting for Asia and the Pacific 2020 was held in place of the traditional Ministerial Round Table. The Commission reviewed policy issues for the ESCAP region; emerging issues and developments at the regional level; least developed, landlocked and island developing countries; programme planning and evaluation; ESCAP technical cooperation activities; activities of the Advisory Committee of Permanent Representatives and Other Representatives Designated by Members of the Commission; and reports of regional intergovernmental bodies.

Economic trends

According to the summary of the economic and social survey of Asia and the Pacific, 2005 [E/2005/18], economic performance in the ESCAP region for 2004 was marked by an impressive 7.2 per cent estimated GDP growth rate, the highest since 2000, and low inflation, which was supported by robust export growth, higher commodity prices and strong domestic demand driven by low interest rates.

Overall growth in East and North-East Asia climbed to 7.5 per cent, 1.3 percentage point higher than in 2003, led by China, with a real GDP growth rate of 9.5 per cent. North and Central Asia also enjoyed another year of buoyant growth, although marginally lower than that of 2003, with the economies of Tajikistan, Azerbaijan and Armenia maintaining their dominant positions. The energy sector was the main driver of growth, accounting for some one third of GDP and one half of exports in Kazakhstan and the Russian Federation.

Real GDP growth continued at the modest pace of 3 per cent in the Pacific island economies, supported by higher prices for commodity exports and increased tourism. Improved economic management reduced budget deficits and lowered public debt, leading to greatly improved inflation performance. However, macroeconomic stability had not resulted in faster economic growth owing to the absence of an investor-friendly environment brought on by political instability, poor governance, corruption and law-and-order problems.

In the developed economies of South and South-West Asia, the already high economic growth improved slightly, from 7.2 per cent to 7.4 per cent. Rates of inflation picked up in Pakistan and Sri Lanka, but fell somewhat in India and Iran and more sharply in Turkey. Among the least developed countries (LDCs) of South Asia, economic growth improved modestly, although Afghanistan and Bangladesh were affected by bad weather, and the Maldives was devastated by the December 2004 tsunami (see p. 952). Inflation was generally lower, partly owing to currency appreciation, which offset the rise in petroleum prices.

GDP growth in South-East Asia increased to 6.4 per cent, compared to 4.9 per cent the previous year. That growth was broadly-based, with manufacturing particularly benefiting from the upturn in the electronics cycle and strong export demand. Higher food and energy prices put upward pressure on price levels in the subregion but were partly offset by fuel subsidies in some countries. In the LDCs of South-East Asia, economic growth continued to vary widely from year to year, depending on developments in the agricultural sector. With the exception of Myanmar, inflation tended to be lower in all of those countries, owing to greater exchange-rate stability and prudent monetary policies, although higher oil prices were beginning to affect the general price level.

In the developed countries of the region, recently revised economic data from Japan indicated that, after years of stagnation, growth was much stronger, reaching a high of 2.6 per cent, compared to 1.3 per cent the previous year. Growth accelerated in New Zealand to 4.8 per cent, while remaining substantially unchanged in Australia at 3.5 per cent, supported by buoyant domestic demand and high commodity prices. Deflationary pressures eased in Japan, but the fiscal deficit continued to present a daunting challenge. The fiscal position in Australia and New Zealand remained strong, but monetary policy in the latter was tightened in the face of price-pressure build-up. The boom in the Australian housing market appeared to have passed its peak and inflation was subdued.

Policy issues

Among the issues with significant policy implications for ESCAP Governments in the near term was the exacerbation of an already volatile economic situation by higher oil prices, which were likely to remain under upward pressure for some time, posing a significant threat of inflation that would discourage investment. There was also the possibility that the external environment could deteriorate in the coming months. Those developments, together with a weakening dollar, posed a major challenge to the maintenance of growth and macroeconomic stability.

Several long-term development policy issues faced the ESCAP region. The tsunami disaster (see p. 952) illustrated the lack of a systematic disaster management framework, including disaster mitigation measures, in many countries and highlighted the importance of handling vulnerability to achieve a sustainable reduction in poverty in line with the MDG of halving by 2015 the proportion of the world's people whose income was less than a dollar a day [YUN 2000, p. 52]. While most countries in the region were making progress towards that goal, they nevertheless were likely to miss many of the other non-income-related goals. Reaching the targets within and across countries would require more national and international resources, and a radical shift in attitudes, priorities and policies to ensure equitable and sustainable basic services. Meeting the twin challenges of sustaining growth and reducing inequality was high on the region's policy agenda. Some of the most important issues were employment opportunities, especially for the young; access to productive assets; public spending on basic social services; gender equality; and population policy and good governance.

At its 2004 session, the Commission considered a report on the current economic situation in the region and related policy issues [E/ESCAP/ 1304] and a paper on meeting the challenges in an era of globalization by strengthening regional development cooperation [E/ESCAP/1305]. The Commission recognized that the most pressing long-term challenge facing the region was poverty, and its eradication had to be given the highest priority, requiring not just economic growth but also good

governance, increased regional cooperation, and integrated national strategies that focused on generating additional employment, creating productive assets, imparting technical and entrepreneurial skills, and raising the income levels of the poor on a targeted basis and providing them with wider educational facilities. Recognizing that economic indicators did not always reflect the reality of people's lives or explain the reasons for underdevelopment, ESCAP encouraged its secretariat to study alternative standard measures of poverty and assist in the design of more effective indicators of development.

ESCAP agreed that many LDCs lacked the necessary human and financial capital and institutions to enable them to reap the benefits of globalization, and that technical assistance would be useful in the restructuring and institutional development of those countries. ESCAP should use its comparative advantage and enhance its ability to assist countries within its thematic areas through technical assistance and capacity-building activities. In particular, it should strengthen coordination and partnership with other organizations to assist member countries in achieving greater cooperation by analysing and providing access to relevant cross-country experiences.

Activities in 2004

Strengthening regional development cooperation

ESCAP had before it a report on policy issues for the ESCAP region: meeting the challenges in an era of globalization by strengthening regional development cooperation [E/ESCAP/1305] and a publication on the subject [E/ESCAP/2319]. By a resolution of 28 April [E/2004/39 (res. 60/1)], it adopted the Shanghai Declaration, which it hoped would be a milestone for deepening cooperation among the countries and territories of the Asian and Pacific region, and recommended the Declaration for adoption by the Economic and Social Council (see below).

ECONOMIC AND SOCIAL COUNCIL ACTION

On 16 July [meeting 42], the Economic and Social Council, on the recommendation of ESCAP [E/2004/15/Add.1], adopted **resolution 2004/6** without vote [agenda item 10].

Shanghai Declaration

The Economic and Social Council,

Endorses the Shanghai Declaration adopted on 28 April by the Economic and Social Commission for Asia and the Pacific at its sixtieth session, as set out in the annex to the present resolution.

Annex

Shanghai Declaration

I. General provisions

1. We, members and associate members of the Economic and Social Commission for Asia and the Pacific, on the occasion of the historic sixtieth session of the Commission, express our deep appreciation to the Government and citizens of the People's Republic of China for hosting the present session in Shanghai, the birthplace of the Commission, and to the government and citizens of Shanghai municipality.

2. We reiterate our commitment to multilateralism and to addressing global issues through dialogue, consultation and cooperation.

3. We reaffirm that the United Nations has a central role in promoting international cooperation for development and in promoting policy coherence on global development issues, including in the context of globalization and interdependence.

4. We support further reform of the United Nations with a view to promoting its important role in peace and development and in establishing a cohesive and effective system for responding to global threats and challenges, as well as enhancing the effectiveness of the United Nations through increased coordination and cooperation between the various agencies and their programmes within the United Nations system.

5. We note the diversity in the levels of development of countries and areas of the Asian and Pacific region and the special needs of the least developed economies, landlocked and island developing economies, and economies in transition.

6. We emphasize the unique role of the Commission as the most representative body for the Asian and Pacific region and its mandate as the main general economic and social development centre within the United Nations system for the Asian and Pacific region.

7. We reaffirm our determination to strengthen further the role, capacity and efficiency of the Economic and Social Commission for Asia and the Pacific to respond more effectively to the needs of its members and associate members and to existing and new global challenges.

8. We welcome the achievements of the region in economic and social development, including progress made in achieving the internationally agreed development goals, including those contained in the United Nations Millennium Declaration, adopted by the General Assembly in its resolution 55/2 of 8 September 2000, and the outcomes and final documents of major United Nations summits and international conferences.

9. We renew our commitment to enhancing subregional and regional cooperation and remain conscious of the need to further improve national capacities in order to promote sustainable development in the Asian and Pacific region.

10. In this context, we acknowledge the importance of the main theme of the Shanghai session, "Meeting the challenges in an era of globalization by strengthening regional development cooperation".

11. We reaffirm that South-South cooperation, South-North cooperation and triangular cooperation play important roles in promoting development and contribute to the achievement of the internationally agreed development goals, including those contained in the Millennium Declaration.

12. We note that globalization offers opportunities and challenges to the world, particularly for the developing countries, and that it is only through greater economic growth coupled with broad, sustained and collaborative efforts that globalization can be made fully inclusive and equitable so that the poor are not left behind. At the same time, the benefits of globalization can be realized only when environmental pressure from the impact of globalization is properly addressed through strengthened common strategies in the Asian and Pacific region.

13. We welcome the conclusion and holding of the signing ceremony of the Intergovernmental Agreement on the Asian Highway Network and the inaugural session of the Asia-Pacific Business Forum, and look forward to the first meeting of the Ministerial Council of the Asia-Pacific Trade Agreement as part of the efforts to strengthen the development of infrastructure and foster closer trade relations within the region. We reaffirm the importance of focusing the work of the Economic and Social Commission for Asia and the Pacific on its three thematic areas: poverty reduction, managing globalization and addressing emerging social issues.

II. Poverty reduction

14. In the area of poverty reduction, we will strive:

(a) To maximize the contribution of economic growth in reducing poverty and hunger, by consolidating successes and facilitating the sharing of best practices, with a view to halving, by 2015, the proportion of people suffering from poverty and hunger, thus making the region a forerunner in the global campaign against poverty;

(b) To implement policies aimed at engendering confidence in the operation of markets to assist in the creation of a favourable business environment;

(c) To emphasize the importance of according priority to the fight against hunger and poverty and, in this context, put in place the necessary policy and institutional framework and implement programmes that are designed to overcome hunger and poverty;

(d) To encourage the efficient utilization of existing financial, physical and human resources and the involvement of all stakeholders, including Governments, international organizations, international and regional development and financial institutions, donors and civil society, to achieve the internationally agreed sustainable development goals, including those contained in the Millennium Declaration;

(e) To eliminate corruption at all levels, welcoming in that regard the adoption of the United Nations Convention against Corruption and inviting all member States to sign and ratify it as soon as possible in order to ensure its rapid entry into force.

III. Managing globalization

15. In the area of managing globalization, we will strive:

(a) To address the regional and interregional aspects of the follow-up to the Monterrey Consensus of the International Conference on Financing for Development;

(b) To revitalize the multilateral trading system, taking into account the importance of promoting the objectives set out in the Millennium Declaration of ensuring an open, equitable, rule-based, predictable and non-discriminatory multilateral trading system;

(c) To work towards a successful, timely and development-oriented conclusion of the Doha negotiations;

(d) To take action to enable those countries in the region that are not yet members of the World Trade Organization to accede to it in order to participate more effectively in the multilateral trading system;

(e) To strengthen national capacities to negotiate, conclude and implement multilateral and regional agreements designed to promote interregional and intraregional trade and investment flows;

(f) To implement, in a timely fashion, the various regional and subregional economic cooperation initiatives in promoting trade and investment, with a view to expanding economic interaction and promoting stable growth and prosperity for the entire region;

(g) To mobilize investment from domestic and foreign resources by strengthening and developing domestic financial systems and creating an enabling environment;

(h) To advance current efforts to reform the international financial architecture as envisaged in the Monterrey Consensus and promote the effective participation of developing countries and countries with economies in transition in those efforts;

(i) To take action at the regional level to ensure the effective implementation of and follow-up to the outcomes of the World Summit on Sustainable Development, including the Johannesburg Plan of Implementation, in which some of the salient features of the Phnom Penh Regional Platform on Sustainable Development for Asia and the Pacific were reflected, to move the region towards a more sustainable path to development, with the developed countries taking the lead and with all countries benefiting from the process, taking into account the principles of common but differentiated responsibilities, while taking note of the recent follow-up activities, including the Kyoto Ministerial Declaration and the Jeju Initiative;

(j) To make the next ten years a decade of economic growth and sustainable development in the region, striving to meet the various internationally agreed goals;

(k) To undertake regular studies and analyses of regional environmental trends, strengthen national capacities for protecting the environment consistent with national commitments and support regional and subregional environmental cooperation;

(l) To assist in capacity-building and the formulation and implementation of strategies and action plans for the sustainable use of water resources, with a special focus on problems of water quality and access to safe drinking water for the poor;

(m) To promote capacity-building in sustainable energy development, enhanced utilization of renewable energy and energy efficiency improvement and to support subregional cooperation in energy sector development;

(n) To develop an integrated intermodal transport network in Asia and the Pacific as well as Asia-Europe transport corridors;

(o) To implement the Plan of Action adopted at the first phase of the World Summit on the Information Society, held in Geneva from 10 to 12 December 2003, and take action to achieve the objectives of the World Summit as enunciated in the Declaration of Principles and the Plan of Action adopted at the first phase, and to prepare for the second phase in 2005, paying special attention to least developed countries, landlocked developing countries, small island developing States and countries with economies in transition;

(p) To promote regional cooperation and effective integration of satellite-based information and communication technology applications with other information technologies for informed sustainable economic and social development planning and management and improved quality of life;

(q) To promote the development of transport and tourism in the region so as to provide opportunities for increased national, regional and international trade and better access to health and education services, and to promote cultural exchanges.

IV. Emerging social issues

16. In the area of emerging social issues, we will strive:

(a) To promote social policy development and the mainstreaming of social dimensions in national development programmes;

(b) To improve the development and delivery of basic social services, such as education, health and nutrition, focusing on vulnerable population groups;

(c) To enhance cooperation in capacity-building in public health, inter alia, through the exchange of information and the sharing of experience, as well as research and training programmes focusing on surveillance, prevention, control, response, care and treatment in respect of infectious diseases;

(d) To coordinate a more effective and comprehensive response to HIV/AIDS and other serious diseases in the region by prioritizing effective strategies against them in national development planning, committing sufficient resources, mobilizing the private sector and civil society, enhancing sustained and comprehensive intervention and strengthening regional cooperation in establishing preventive measures and increasing the availability of affordable quality drugs;

(e) To foster an integrated social safety net and, particularly, to establish a social safety net which provides necessary assistance to the unemployed, the poor and senior citizens, as well as other vulnerable groups;

(f) To promote and support gender equality and eliminate discrimination against women;

(g) To promote human security in the region through greater regional cooperation, especially for vulnerable people;

(h) To support and encourage the active participation of all relevant stakeholders, including the business community, for the promotion of social development.

V. Overarching issues

17. On overarching issues, we will strive:

(a) To fully implement the Monterrey Consensus;

(b) To promote regional cooperation by inviting the United Nations regional commissions, in collaboration with other regional and subregional organizations and processes, as appropriate, to contribute, within their mandates, to the review of progress made towards achieving the internationally agreed development goals contained in the Millennium Declaration, which synthesizes and prioritizes the key elements of major international conferences held in prior years, and to provide input to the discussions of the Economic and Social Council on the cross-sectoral thematic issues to be addressed during the coordination segment of its substantive session, in accordance with the rules of procedure of the Council;

(c) To intensify our efforts to implement effectively in the Asian and Pacific region the International Plan of Action for the United Nations Literacy Decade;

(d) To implement the Programme of Action for the Least Developed Countries for the Decade 2001-2010 and the Almaty Plan of Action: Addressing the Special Needs of Landlocked Developing Countries within a New Global Framework for Transit Transport Co-operation for Landlocked and Transit Developing Countries;

(e) To promote initiatives for the least developed countries in the context of South-South cooperation by implementing projects that address the special needs of those countries;

(f) To support the Programme of Action for the Sustainable Development of Small Island Developing States and work towards a positive outcome at the review of the implementation of the Programme of Action in Mauritius;

(g) To strengthen and support the implementation of the United Nations Special Programme for the Economies of Central Asia;

(h) To encourage the establishment of a regional network of research institutions and universities in the Economic and Social Commission for Asia and the Pacific region by 2006 in order to promote education, technical skills development and technology transfer through the exchange of programmes, students and academics.

VI. Strengthening of the Economic and Social Commission for Asia and the Pacific

18. We reaffirm the vital role of the Economic and Social Commission for Asia and the Pacific in fostering sustainable economic and social development in Asia and the Pacific.

19. We request the Executive Secretary to design programmes, within the existing mandate and resources of the Economic and Social Commission for Asia and the Pacific, that reflect the overall vision contained in the present Declaration, to present the programme of work for endorsement by the Commission and to report on these matters to the Commission at future sessions.

20. We resolve, therefore, to support efforts by the Executive Secretary to mobilize and make effective use of additional financial and in-kind resources in support of activities of the Economic and Social Commission for Asia and the Pacific and for its further revitalization in line with the needs and priorities of its members and associate members.

21. We also request the Commission to review on a regular basis the progress made in implementing the provisions of the present Declaration.

Poverty reduction

ESCAP endorsed the report of the Committee on Poverty Reduction on its first session [YUN 2003, p. 1009]. The Committee had urged ESCAP, at the Economic and Social Council's June high-level segment, to present the true scope of poverty in Asia and the Pacific in order to attract the attention of donor countries and forge partnerships. Noting that poverty reduction required an enabling international economic environment, ESCAP requested the secretariat to organize a high-level meeting with the Bretton Woods institutions (the World Bank Group and the International Monetary Fund) to engage in policy dialogue and explore practicable cooperative arrangements, and to encourage countries to meet their commitments as set out in the Monterrey Consensus [YUN 2002, p. 953].

ESCAP urged countries of the region and their development partners, including ESCAP, to strengthen their efforts to accelerate the pace of achieving the MDGs, including developing national plans for that purpose. It called for the adoption of a comprehensive approach with greater emphasis on better access to financial and non-financial resources, human security, increased investments in health and education, empowerment of women, better governance, rural development, environmental protection, social protection, enhanced participation of all stakeholders and more effective partnerships between Governments, non-governmental organizations (NGOs), the private sector and other civil society entities. It also called for strengthening ESCAP's capacity to address poverty reduction and for fostering regional cooperation in that regard. The secretariat should assist developing countries and LDCs in mobilizing resources and in making them more accessible to the poor. The Commission welcomed the secretariat's work to promote the use of ICT for rural poverty reduction, especially for enhancing market access by the poor, improving social service delivery in remote areas and for lifelong learning. It recommended the promotion of public-private partnerships for the provision of basic services as an approach to poverty alleviation.

ESCAP endorsed the recommendations of the Committee on Poverty Reduction on poverty measurement and concurred with its view that sound poverty measurement at the country level depended on the national statistical system. It supported the formulation of a regional action plan to improve poverty statistics and monitoring in the region. The Commission urged the secretariat to ensure that all information was available to different users and to continue playing an active role in implementing a wide range of statistical capacity-building measures. The secretariat should also contribute to the UN Statistics Division handbook on poverty statistics and take advantage of ICT initiatives to enhance statistical capabilities. It should also collaborate in producing more accurate and objective data for measuring the MDGs, study alternative measures of poverty, and assist in designing more effective indicators of development.

In adopting the Shanghai Declaration (see p. 1002), ESCAP reaffirmed its commitments to reduce poverty (see p. 1004), as set out in the Declaration.

The Subcommittee on Poverty Reduction Practices, at its first session (Bangkok, Thailand, 30 June–2 July) [E/ESCAP/SCPRP/Rep.], discussed creating an enabling environment for successful poverty reduction initiatives, implementing ESCAP's poverty reduction strategies, evaluating the impact of targeted poverty reduction programmes, and selected policy issues in poverty reduction.

Statistics

ESCAP noted the report of the Governing Board of the Statistical Institute for Asia and the Pacific (SIAP) [E/ESCAP/1319], which highlighted the Institute's accomplishments and the factors and strategies that guided the implementation of its activities, the 2004 work programme, the 2005-2009 long-term work programme approved by the Board at its ninth session (Chiba, Japan, 14-15 November 2003), and the Institute's financial status.

The Commission noted that additional contributions and technical assistance were required to place the Institute on a sound financial footing to enable it to respond effectively to the evolving needs of ESCAP members and associate members. It supported the Board's recommendation that a three-year, rather than a five-year, strategic plan be adopted as a more effective way to adjust programmes to changing needs and situations; it recommended that the secretariat formulate measures to implement the suggestion made in the 2003 independent evaluation [YUN 2003, p. 1015] that the Institute play a coordinating role in regional statistical training activities.

The Subcommittee on Statistics of the Committee on Poverty Reduction, at its first session (Bangkok, 18-20 February) [E/ESCAP/CRP(2)/4], conducted an overview of significant global and regional issues in official statistics and examined ESCAP activities in social, poverty and economic statistics, statistical training including the Institute's role, reports for the Subcommittee's attention and programme matters. It noted that the draft Regional Action Plan on Poverty Statistics

submitted in 2003 to the Committee on Poverty Reduction [YUN 2003, p. 1009] was broad and ambitious, and whose viability rested on the financing of the activities called for and coordination of regional efforts. The Subcommittee decided that the ESCAP secretariat should revise the Regional Action Plan on Poverty Statistics and clearly identify priority activities.

The Expert Group Meeting on Population and Housing Censuses (Bangkok, 9-10 December), held in preparation for the 2010 Round of Population and Housing Censuses, requested ESCAP to facilitate communication between the regional and global census programmes and ensure their full coordination and mutual support. The Meeting recommended that ESCAP establish a forum for census stakeholders to discuss issues of concern and share experiences. It identified a number of priorities for establishing activities to be carried out in the coming years.

Managing globalization

ESCAP endorsed the report of the Committee on Managing Globalization on its first session [YUN 2003, p. 1010], including its recommendations, and expressed satisfaction with the progress made in implementing six ESCAP resolutions relating to the theme of managing globalization, as described in a March note by the secretariat [E/ESCAP/1308].

In its consideration of selected cross-cutting issues, ESCAP encouraged its members to establish national trade and transport committees to address the high cost of trade and transport transactions and asked the secretariat to provide support and guidance in that regard. The Commission also asked the secretariat: to provide training and advisory services to countries undertaking corridor studies in applying the ESCAP cost/time-distance model and the Trade Facilitation Framework; to accord priority to bridging the digital divide through sharing of best practices, capacity-building and pilot projects; and to promote e-centres in order to bring the benefits of globalization to rural areas. The Commission recognized that ICT had a high impact on the flow of capital, goods, services and knowledge, thus becoming one of the main driving forces of globalization.

ESCAP noted the common understanding and strategies developed at regional expert meetings for mapping out a 10-year plan for revising current consumption and production patterns and for translating international commitments into reality.

Least developed, landlocked and island developing countries

Special Body on Pacific Island Developing Countries

ESCAP endorsed the recommendation of the eighth session (Shanghai, 20-21 April) [E/ESCAP/1312] of the Special Body on Pacific Island Developing Countries on urban management issues in Pacific island developing countries and on the revitalization of the ESCAP Pacific Operations Centre. On 28 April, ESCAP adopted a resolution on the Centre's revitalization (see p. 1011).

ESCAP also adopted a resolution [E/2004/39 (res. 60/7)] endorsing the Pacific Urban Agenda developed by an ESCAP workshop (Nadi, Fiji, 1-4 December 2003) on the urban governance initiative of UNDP, the United Nations Human Settlements Programme and the Pacific Islands Forum secretariat. It requested the Executive Secretary to accord priority to the implementation of the Agenda and called on Pacific members and associate members to address the actions outlined therein; it invited partner agencies to provide technical and financial support, and members and associate members to coordinate implementation. It also asked the Executive Secretary to convene a workshop in 2006 for the exchange of experience and capacity-building and to report to ESCAP at its sixty-second (2006) session.

Economic and technical cooperation

In 2004, ESCAP received $11.5 million for technical cooperation activities [E/ESCAP/1351], significantly less than the $13.6 million for 2003, but that did not include additional multimillion dollar contributions, which would be deferred to 2005. Of the 2004 amount, $5.7 million (49.2 per cent) was contributed by the UN system and $5.8 million from individual countries. Contributions from three developed countries (Japan, Finland, United States) provided over 50 per cent ($3.3 million) of the total bilateral assistance, with Japan contributing the most. Among the developing countries, the Republic of Korea, China and India were the largest contributors. In addition to cash contributions, donor countries provided some 113 work-months of expert services on a non-reimbursable basis.

ESCAP adopted a resolution [E/2003/39 (res. 60/3)] on its work in implementing technical cooperation projects, which it recommended to the Economic and Social Council for adoption (see below).

ECONOMIC AND SOCIAL COUNCIL ACTION

On 16 July [meeting 42], the Economic and Social Council, on the recommendation of ESCAP [E/2004/15/Add.1], adopted **resolution 2004/7** without vote [agenda item 10].

Work of the Economic and Social Commission for Asia and the Pacific in implementing its technical cooperation projects

The Economic and Social Council,

Recalling its resolution 37(IV) of 28 March 1947, by which it established the Economic and Social Commission for Asia and the Pacific, and in particular paragraphs 1 *(d)* and *(e)* of the terms of reference of the Commission, regarding advisory services and technical assistance,

Recalling also General Assembly resolution 32/197 of 20 December 1977, through which the Commission was mandated to serve as the main general economic and social development centre within the United Nations system for the Asian and Pacific region and as an executing agency for intersectoral, subregional, regional and interregional projects,

Cognizant of the scope of the responsibilities of the Commission, the domain of which comprises the largest region in the world in geographical coverage and contains 62 per cent of the world's population, as well as the majority of the world's poor,

Aware of the focus of the work of the Commission on three key thematic areas, namely, poverty reduction, managing globalization and addressing emerging social issues,

1. *Recognizes with appreciation* that the Economic and Social Commission for Asia and the Pacific has been implementing a number of technical cooperation projects that strengthen the capacity of Commission members and associate members in the development and implementation of policies and programmes in the economic and social fields;

2. *Expresses its appreciation* to those traditional donors which have made significant voluntary contributions to the technical cooperation activities of the Commission, and invites non-traditional donors to increase their contributions;

3. *Welcomes* the efforts of the Executive Secretary of the Economic and Social Commission for Asia and the Pacific to focus on high-priority, results-oriented and demand-based projects, and requests him to implement such projects in an effective and efficient manner;

4. *Recognizes* the need for the technical cooperation activities of the Commission to be guided by the internationally agreed development goals contained in the United Nations Millennium Declaration, adopted by the General Assembly in its resolution 55/2 of 8 September 2000, and the outcomes of United Nations summits and conferences, including the Doha Development Agenda, the Johannesburg Plan of Implementation, the Monterrey Consensus, the Almaty Programme of Action and the Plan of Action of the World Summit on the Information Society;

5. *Also recognizes* that the Commission has comparative strengths and advantages in certain technical cooperation activities in the Asian and Pacific region, and requests the Executive Secretary, in carrying out the technical cooperation activities of the Commission, to continue to attach high priority to the following areas:

(a) Capacity-building for members and associate members to plan and implement effective policies and programmes in the economic and social fields through training activities, such as organizing seminars, workshops and the exchange of experts;

(b) Provision of advisory services, at the request of members or associate members, to strengthen their capacity to respond effectively to the challenges of globalization in the region;

(c) Identification of existing good practices in the region and promotion of their introduction in places where feasibility studies yield positive results;

(d) Enhancement of awareness among members and associate members and facilitation of the dissemination of relevant information;

6. *Urges* the Executive Secretary to implement the projects in close cooperation with the participating Governments and relevant international organizations and bodies, as well as in partnership with the private sector and relevant non-governmental organizations;

7. *Also urges* the Executive Secretary to pay particular attention to the special needs of socially vulnerable groups and to the gender dimension when implementing projects;

8. *Further urges* the Executive Secretary to pay particular attention to the special needs of least developed countries, landlocked and Pacific island developing countries, and countries with economies in transition when implementing projects;

9. *Expresses its appreciation* to the Executive Secretary for actively monitoring and evaluating the projects of the Commission, and urges him to continue to do so in order to determine the effectiveness of those projects and to draw lessons therefrom for improved planning and implementation of future projects of the Commission;

10. *Requests* the Executive Secretary to include the following in his report to the Commission at its sixty-first session under the agenda item on technical cooperation activities of the Commission and announcement of intended contributions:

(a) His efforts to mobilize resources in areas such as broadening the donor base, cost-sharing, private sector funding and other innovative means in view of the trend towards declining voluntary contributions for technical cooperation activities;

(b) His strategy paper and action plan for technical cooperation activities for the year 2005 and thereafter, taking into account the priorities of the Commission and recognizing that the implementation of projects is subject to the availability of extrabudgetary resources;

(c) The results of the monitoring and evaluation of ongoing and recently completed projects for the purposes mentioned in paragraph 9 above.

Transport, communications, tourism and infrastructure development

ESCAP, having considered the report on the outcome of the International Ministerial Conference of Landlocked and Transit Developing Countries and Donor Countries and International Financial and Development Institutions on Transit Transport Cooperation [YUN 2003, p. 1010], requested the secretariat to continue to

work with member countries to realize the vision of an integrated, international intermodal transport system that supported mobility, trade and tourism both domestically and across international borders. It endorsed the strategy on transport infrastructure and facilitation proposed by the Committee on Managing Globalization at its first session [ibid.].

Noting the progress made in the accession by member States to international conventions, and also noting that numerous agreements on transport and facilitation were already in place but that problems with implementation remained, ESCAP requested the secretariat to conduct workshops at the national and regional levels to enhance understanding and assist the implementation of existing agreements, including those listed in its resolution 48/11 [YUN 1992, p. 485]. It endorsed the convening in 2006 of a ministerial conference on transport to review the implementation of the New Delhi Action Plan on Infrastructure Development in Asia and the Pacific, 1997-2006 [YUN 1995, p. 1012] and to develop a strategy for the further development of reliable and efficient, integrated, intermodal international transport that facilitated international trade and tourism and economic integration processes.

In a resolution on the Intergovernmental Agreement on the Asian Highway Network [E/2004/39 (res. 60/4)], ESCAP welcomed the unanimous adoption in 2003 of that Agreement [YUN 2003, p. 1010], which the Economic and Social Council also welcomed in resolution 2004/8 (see p. 1008). ESCAP endorsed the development of an intergovernmental agreement on the Trans-Asian Railway and urged the secretariat to focus on additional land and land-cum-sea corridors, including the North-South and Southern Corridors.

In the context of Asia-Europe transport corridors, ESCAP underscored the importance of the joint ECE-ESCAP programme of work and noted the First Expert Group Meeting on Developing Euro-Asian Transport Linkages convened by those two regional commissions (Almaty, Kazakhstan, March). ESCAP requested the secretariat to focus on the implementation of the Almaty Programme of Action: Addressing the Special Needs of Landlocked Developing Countries within a New Global Framework for Transit Transport Cooperation for Landlocked and Transit Developing Countries [YUN 2003, p. 875].

ESCAP noted the secretariat's work in transport facilitation and assistance to the Greater Mekong subregion in preparation for the negotiation of facilitation agreements in collaboration with the Asian Development Bank. It requested the secretariat to continue to provide guidance to the

Shanghai Cooperation Organization countries (China, Kazakhstan, Kyrgyzstan, Russian Federation, Tajikistan, Uzbekistan) in the hope that that would lead to the development of a multilateral road transport facilitation agreement among them.

ESCAP endorsed the convening of an intergovernmental meeting on sustainable tourism development in 2005 to review the implementation of the Plan of Action for Sustainable Tourism Development in the Asian and Pacific Region [YUN 1999, p. 929] and to consider launching a second phase of the Plan, focusing on the promotion of transport linkages from a tourism perspective and the promotion of tourism as a means of reducing poverty. It encouraged the secretariat to assist member countries in accelerating the use of ICT in tourism, including the creation of mechanisms for preventing its abuse.

The Subcommittee on Transport Infrastructure and Facilitation and Tourism, at its first session (Bangkok, 24-26 November) [E/ESCAP/STIFT/Rep.], noted that 27 ESCAP member States had signed the Intergovernmental Agreement on the Asian Highway Network (see above) and that seven had become parties to it. Noting the progress made at a regional meeting (Bangkok, 22-23 November) to initiate negotiation of an intergovernmental agreement on the Trans-Asian Railway network, the Subcommittee recommended that an intergovernmental meeting be organized in 2005 to finalize and adopt the draft agreement for recommendation to ESCAP in 2006.

ECONOMIC AND SOCIAL COUNCIL ACTION

On 16 July [meeting 42], the Economic and Social Council, on the recommendation of ESCAP [E/2004/15/Add.1], adopted **resolution 2004/8** without vote [agenda item 10].

Intergovernmental Agreement on the Asian Highway Network

The Economic and Social Council,

Recognizing the importance of international road transport to the development of the economy, trade and tourism in the Economic and Social Commission for Asia and the Pacific region,

Recognizing also that an intergovernmental agreement on the Asian Highway network would play a catalytic role in the coordinated development of international highways in the region and between Asia and Europe,

Recalling the establishment of a working group to develop an intergovernmental agreement on the Asian Highway network, as recommended by the Ministerial Conference on Infrastructure, held in Seoul from 12 to 17 November 2001, and endorsed by the Commission at its fifty-eighth session,

Recalling also the decision of the Commission at its fifty-ninth session to convene an ad hoc intergovernmental meeting to consider and adopt the agreement in the second half of 2003 and its hope that the agreement could be concluded at the meeting in November 2003,

Welcoming the unanimous adoption of the Intergovernmental Agreement on the Asian Highway Network by the Intergovernmental Meeting to Develop an Intergovernmental Agreement on the Asian Highway Network, held in Bangkok on 17 and 18 November 2003,

Recalling the priority area of infrastructure development and maintenance identified in the Almaty Programme of Action: Addressing the Special Needs of Landlocked Developing Countries within a New Global Framework for Transit Transport Cooperation for Landlocked and Transit Developing Countries, adopted at the International Ministerial Conference of Landlocked and Transit Developing Countries and Donor Countries and International Financial and Development Institutions on Transit Transport Cooperation, held in Almaty, Kazakhstan, on 28 and 29 August 2003, and acknowledging that the Asian Highway network provides transit transport opportunities,

Expressing its appreciation to the Government of Japan for its valuable support for the development and formalization of the Asian Highway network and for the assistance which it provided in preparing for and convening the Intergovernmental Meeting,

Also expressing its appreciation also to the Government of China for hosting the signing ceremony for the Agreement in Shanghai on 26 April 2004,

Convinced that the Agreement will strengthen relations between member countries, promote international trade and tourism through coordinated development of the Asian Highway network and have a substantial positive impact on the region by achieving internationally agreed development goals, including those contained in the United Nations Millennium Declaration adopted by the General Assembly in its resolution 55/2 of 8 September 2000,

1. *Invites* all the relevant members of the Economic and Social Commission for Asia and the Pacific to become parties to the Intergovernmental Agreement on the Asian Highway Network in order to ensure the speedy entry into force of the Agreement;

2. *Invites* the international and regional financing institutions and multilateral and bilateral donors to provide financial and technical support for the development of the Asian Highway network and related infrastructure, particularly taking into account the special needs of landlocked developing countries;

3. *Invites* subregional organizations to promote the Agreement and accord priority to the development of the Asian Highway network in their respective subregions;

4. *Encourages* landlocked developing countries and their transit neighbours that are members of the Commission to enter into bilateral or subregional transit traffic facilitation agreements which will enable the Asian Highway network to provide further tangible transit transport opportunities within the scope of the Almaty Programme of Action;

5. *Requests* the Executive Secretary of the Economic and Social Commission for Asia and the Pacific:

(a) To assist member countries in becoming parties to the Agreement;

(*b*) To accord priority to the development of the Asian Highway network, within the programme of work of the Commission;

(*c*) To collaborate effectively with international and regional financing institutions, multilateral and bilateral donors and subregional organizations for the development of the Asian Highway network;

(*d*) To discharge effectively the functions of the secretariat of the Agreement;

(*e*) To report to the Commission at its sixty-first session on the implementation of the present resolution.

Science and technology

ESCAP took note of the report of the Asian and Pacific Centre for Transfer of Technology (APCTT) on its 2003 activities [E/ESACP/1317 & Corr.1], to which was annexed the report of the APCTT Governing Board at its eighteenth session (Manila, Philippines, 6-7 February). The Commission urged its members and associate members to consider increasing their annual contributions to the Centre to enable it to deliver its technology transfer services in a more effective, regular and sustainable manner.

ESCAP, in its consideration of the report of the Coordinating Committee for Geoscience Programmes in East and Southeast Asia [E/ESCAP/1323], noted that the Committee had carried out most of its planned activities to enhance coordination of geoscience programmes of member countries. ESCAP agreed that the Space Applications Programme for Sustainable Development in Asia and the Pacific should be strengthened to help its members and associate members to meet the MDGs.

Environment and sustainable development

ESCAP, in noting the importance of the secretariat's activities to enhance the capacity of countries in the implementation of multilateral environmental agreements, environmental monitoring, biodiversity conservation, energy efficiency, enhanced utilization of renewable energy and water resources management, requested the secretariat to take cognizance of issues and problems at the subregional and national levels in its studies and projects in those areas. It noted that the achievements under the Johannesburg Plan of Implementation of the World Summit on Sustainable Development [YUN 2002, p. 822] were well below the desired level and suggested that the secretariat, in support of the UN Commission on Sustainable Development, ensure that regional inputs were effectively integrated into that body's work programme.

In other action, ESCAP endorsed the preparations [E/ESCAP/1329] for the fifth Ministerial Conference on Environment and Development in Asia and the Pacific in 2005 and recommended that it focus on translating the Johannesburg Plan of Implementation into concrete activities. It supported the recommendations adopted by the Ninth Senior Officials Meeting (Moscow, Russian Federation, March) on the North-East Asian Subregional Programme of Environmental Cooperation. To ensure sustainable development in that subregion, it requested the secretariat to facilitate dialogue towards promoting energy cooperation. It encouraged the development of integrated water resources management and water efficiency plans, and the establishment of strategies and policies for regional and national disaster mitigation and preparedness. For that purpose, it was suggested that a research network be considered, with the cooperation of international organizations under ESCAP guidance, to deal with floods and earthquakes.

Agriculture and development

ESCAP considered the report of the Regional Coordination Centre for Research and Development of Coarse Grains, Pulses, Roots and Tuber Crops in the Humid Tropics of Asia and the Pacific (CGPRT) [E/ESCAP/1318], which also covered the proceedings of the twenty-second meeting (Bangor, Indonesia, 15-16 January) of the Centre's Governing Board. Besides adopting the Centre's 2004 programme of work and planned 2004 expenditures, the Board agreed to meet in March to deliberate on changing the mandate and name of the Centre. Subsequently, ESCAP took note of the recommendation of the Board at its extraordinary session (22 March) that the Centre's name be changed to the "Centre for Alleviation of Poverty through Secondary Crops Development in Asia and the Pacific" (CAPSA) and that its statute be revised to reflect the realignment of its work. By its resolution on CGPRT [E/2004/39 (res. 60/5)], ESCAP agreed to the name change and granted the Centre the status of a subsidiary body, with a Governing Council, a Director and a Technical Committee.

ESCAP noted the report of the Asian and Pacific Centre for Agricultural Engineering and Machinery (APCAEM) [YUN 2003, p. 1012], in particular the establishment of its headquarters in Beijing, China. Noting the many challenges facing any new institution, ESCAP looked forward to increasing programme and fund-raising support from the secretariat to make APCAEM self-sustainable as soon as possible.

Social development

ESCAP endorsed the report of the Committee on Emerging Social Issues on its first session [YUN 2003, p. 1013]. It requested the secretariat to continue to support national efforts to promote social development and to assist members and associate members in implementing the Biwako Millennium Framework for Action towards an Inclusive, Barrier-free and Rights-based Society for Persons with Disabilities in Asia and the Pacific [ibid., p. 1014]. It further requested its members and associate members to continue their support for and active participation in the drafting of an international convention on promoting and protecting the rights and dignity of persons with disabilities.

ESCAP concurred with the analysis and recommendations contained in the document entitled "Emerging social issues: trends, issues and strategies" [E/ESCAP/1311], which demonstrated how the rights-based approach was applied to the formulation of policies and programmes in the areas of population, ageing, disability, migration, gender and health. ESCAP called upon the secretariat to analyse the causes and consequences of international migration, in particular labour migration, including projecting future trends and assessing the use and impact of remittances. Concerned about the region's increasing trafficking in women and children, it called for improving existing mechanisms to combat such trafficking and for strengthening domestic legislative frameworks to complement multinational and bilateral initiatives. It called on the secretariat to assist in fostering regional cooperation in promoting investment in health for development and in providing capacity-building programmes for allocating, managing and utilizing funds. Noting the slow overall progress in achieving the HIV/AIDS-related targets in the Millennium Declaration, it urged the international community to increase its resources and action in order to strengthen national AIDS programmes. It urged its members and associate members to accord priority to combating the spread of HIV/AIDS and to advocate the full mobilization of all sectors and levels of government to integrate HIV/AIDS issues into national development planning.

In its resolution on a regional call for action to enhance capacity-building in public health [E/2004/39 (res. 60/2)], ESCAP urged members and associate members to implement domestic measures to counter the impact of avian influenza on human health, livestock production and economic development, in particular to strengthen reporting and surveillance systems; participate in the Global Fund to Fight AIDS, Tuberculosis and Malaria and encourage the private sector to contribute to the Fund; further integrate public health into their economic and social development strategies; raise professional and public awareness of the importance of public health and mobilize the participation of educational institu-

tions, civil society and the mass media in promoting good public health practices; and improve regional public health preparedness and response systems to better cope with major diseases, such as global or regional outbreaks of new diseases.

By the same resolution, ESCAP encouraged donors to continue to support the Asian and Pacific countries in combating infectious diseases and epidemics. It requested the Executive Secretary to coordinate with the World Health Organization (WHO) and other organizations, to assist members and associate members in mainstreaming health concerns into development sectors in support of attaining internationally agreed development goals; to promote coordinated regional action in strengthening capacity-building in public health, including through the Subcommittee on Health and Development, which held its first session (Bangkok, 1-3 December), and in facilitating the exchange of information and the sharing of experience; and to report to ESCAP in 2005 on the implementation of the resolution.

In its resolution on the Shanghai Declaration (see p. 1002), ESCAP reaffirmed the measures it would strive to carry out to address emerging social issues.

The High-level Intergovernmental Meeting to Review Regional Implementation of the Beijing Platform for Action and its Regional and Global Outcomes (Bangkok, 7-10 September) [E/ESCAP/1341] reviewed achievements, identified challenges and addressed strategies for an enabling environment to achieve gender equality. It adopted the Bangkok Communiqué, which acknowledged gaps in the implementation of the Beijing Platform for Action [YUN 1995, p. 1170] and recognized a number of challenges to be addressed. The Meeting's outcome would serve as the Asian and Pacific contribution to the global review and appraisal of the implementation of the Beijing Platform for Action at the 2006 session of the Commission on the Status of Women.

Natural disasters

ESCAP considered and took note of the reports of three regional intergovernmental bodies highlighting activities in 2003 and progress achieved in the implementation of their respective programmes related to natural disasters.

The Mekong River Commission [E/ESCAP/1324] reported its approval of two procedures of its water utilization programme; the navigation programme to address important shortcomings in the regional navigation sector; and the flood management and mitigation programme, which made up the fourth in the Commission's core programmes. The flood programme was approved as a core programme, together with three current programmes—the Mekong Basin development plan, the water utilization programme and the environment programme.

The Typhoon Committee [E/ESCAP/1325] evaluated the activities undertaken by ESCAP members related to the meteorological and hydrological components of its regional cooperation programme implementation plan, including flood forecasting and warnings, natural disaster prevention and mitigation, and enhancement of public awareness of cyclone and water-related hazards. It reviewed activities under the disaster prevention and preparedness, training and research components. It set up a working group to review the Committee's operations and structure.

The Panel on Tropical Cyclones [E/ESCAP/1326] evaluated its activities under the meteorological, hydrological, natural disaster prevention and preparedness, training and research components of its work programme. It highlighted significant improvements in flood forecasting techniques and modelling, real-time monitoring of water levels and rainfall, risk mapping and participation of stakeholders in flood-warning systems in Bangladesh, India, Maldives, Pakistan, Sri Lanka and Thailand. It further underscored the modernization of observation and telecommunication networks and forecasting systems aimed at improving tropical cyclone monitoring, forecasting and warning services.

Programme and organizational questions

ESCAP congratulated the secretariat on the production of the programme performance report for 2002-2003 [E/ESCAP/1414], reflecting for the first time the results-based approach. It endorsed the proposed programme changes for the 2004-2005 programme of work [E/ESCAP/1315], which reflected mandates adopted in 2003 and emerging global priorities identified by the Economic and Social Council and the General Assembly. It also endorsed the draft strategic framework for 2006-2007 [E/ESCAP/1313/Rev.1]. It supported efforts to align the activities of the regional institutions (APCTT, CGPRT, SIAP, APCAEM) [E/ESCAP/1316] with ESCAP's programme of work and to ensure that their governance structures were consistent with UN processes for intergovernmental review.

ESCAP reform

Revitalization of Pacific Operations Centre

In its resolution on the revitalization of the ESCAP Pacific Operations Centre [E/2004/39 (res.

60/6)], ESCAP expressed appreciation for progress in implementing the key institutional changes in that regard in line with the recommendations of the independent evaluation carried out in 2003 [YUN 2003, p. 1015]. It welcomed the revised mission statement clarifying the Centre's role, noted the preparations under way for its relocation from Port Vila, Vanuatu, to Suva, Fiji, and also noted the establishment of an Advisory Council to advise it on work programme priorities. ESCAP requested the Executive Secretary to mobilize the resources required to relocate the Centre in 2004, increase its Professional staff in the 2006-2007 biennium, and use the Pacific Trust Fund for its revitalization, including capacity-development activities in support of the Pacific region and to carry out needs assessment and evaluations.

ESCAP further requested the Executive Secretary to prepare amendments to the terms of reference of the Special Body on Pacific Island Developing Countries to provide for the possible convening of its sessions prior to Commission sessions, in alternate years with the Special Body on Least Developed and Landlocked Developing Countries, and alternately between Bangkok and the location of the Centre. It welcomed the Executive Secretary's decision to establish subprogramme 3, on the development of Pacific island countries, with the objective of building policy and management capacity in Pacific island developing countries and territories.

Date and venue of ESCAP sixty-first session

The Commission decided that its sixty-first session would be held in Bangkok on 21-27 April 2005 under the theme "Implementing the Monterrey Consensus in the Asia and Pacific region: achieving coherence and consistency".

Subregional activities

Cooperation with Economic Cooperation Organization

In response to General Assembly resolution 57/38 [YUN 2002, p. 1001], the Secretary-General reported on cooperation between the United Nations, its programmes and organizations, and the Economic Cooperation Organization [A/59/303].

GENERAL ASSEMBLY ACTION

On 22 October [meeting 40], the General Assembly adopted **resolution 59/4** [draft: A/59/L.3 & Add.1] without vote [agenda item 56 *(h)*].

Cooperation between the United Nations and the Economic Cooperation Organization

The General Assembly,

Recalling its resolution 48/2 of 13 October 1993, by which it granted observer status to the Economic Cooperation Organization,

Recalling also its previous resolutions on cooperation between the United Nations and the Economic Cooperation Organization, and inviting various specialized agencies as well as other organizations and programmes of the United Nations system and relevant international financial institutions to join in their efforts towards realization of the goals and objectives of the Economic Cooperation Organization,

Welcoming the efforts of the Economic Cooperation Organization with regard to consolidating ties with the United Nations system and relevant international and regional organizations,

1. *Takes note with appreciation* of the report of the Secretary-General on the implementation of resolution 57/38 of 21 November 2002, and expresses satisfaction at the enhanced cooperation between the United Nations and the Economic Cooperation Organization;

2. *Takes note* of the Dushanbe Declaration, adopted at the eighth Economic Cooperation Organization summit on 14 September 2004, following the fourteenth meeting of the Council of Ministers in Dushanbe on 12 September 2004;

3. *Stresses* the importance of cooperation between the United Nations and the Economic Cooperation Organization with regard to the provision of financial and technical cooperation for pre-feasibility and feasibility studies of projects of the Economic Cooperation Organization, consultancy services, information on drug control, training courses on trade and investment by the specialized agencies of the United Nations, including the United Nations Development Programme, the Economic and Social Commission for Asia and the Pacific, the Food and Agriculture Organization of the United Nations, the United Nations Office on Drugs and Crime, the United Nations Conference on Trade and Development, the International Trade Centres UNCTAD/WTO and the United Nations Industrial Development Organization, in the ongoing and future activities of the Economic Cooperation Organization;

4. *Notes with appreciation* the implementation of the ongoing project of the Economic Cooperation Organization and the International Trade Centres on expanding intraregional trade, and stresses the importance of the continuation of the second phase of the project;

5. *Also notes with appreciation* the signing of the Economic Cooperation Organization Trade Agreement in Islamabad in July 2003, and stresses its importance in the accomplishment of the goal of establishing a free trade area in the region;

6. *Further notes with appreciation* the holding of the second Economic Cooperation Organization Regional Trade and Investment Conference, and the seventh General Assembly Meeting of Economic Cooperation Organization Chambers of Commerce and Industry, in Kabul, from 18 to 20 April 2004, and stresses the close interaction in the field of trade and investment between the Economic Cooperation Organization and trade-related agencies and bodies of the United Nations;

7. *Notes with appreciation* the memorandum of understanding signed by the Economic Cooperation Organization and the World Customs Organization on 17 March 2003 in Brussels with a view to establishing and maintaining effective and regular consultations, cooperation and exchanges of information between the two organizations;

8. *Notes with satisfaction* the holding of a workshop on multimodal transport and trade facilitation, in Tehran in May 2004, sponsored by the Economic Cooperation Organization, in which the Islamic Development Bank, the United Nations Conference on Trade and Development and the Economic and Social Commission for Asia and the Pacific participated, and hopes that efforts will be made to bring about the successful completion of the multimodal transport project as soon as possible;

9. *Expresses its appreciation* for the importance the Economic Cooperation Organization attaches to the smooth running of container trains on the Trans-Asian Railway main line and to the fine-tuning of a draft action plan for revitalizing and operating the China-Middle East-Europe corridor, as well as for the organization of meetings in Tehran in May 2004 to discuss these issues;

10. *Notes with satisfaction* the efforts of the Economic Cooperation Organization to implement United Nations programmes for the development of transit transport facilities in the landlocked countries of the region;

11. *Recognizes* the importance of removing barriers to transport and trade development in the region, and welcomes the joint project of the Economic Cooperation Organization and the United Nations Development Programme to prepare a comprehensive report on the subject;

12. *Takes note with satisfaction* of the decisions of the first Economic Cooperation Organization Ministerial Meeting on Industry, held in Tehran from 25 to 27 January 2004, and notes the importance of the adoption of the Tehran Declaration and the Plan of Action for Industrial Cooperation in the Economic Cooperation Organization Region, which pave the way for consolidating regional efforts to promote industrial cooperation in the region through the mobilization of regional and international resources and the industrial potential of the member States, and to that end encourages the United Nations Industrial Development Organization to actively contribute to the activities of the Economic Cooperation Organization in the field of industry;

13. *Also takes note with satisfaction* of the decisions of the first Economic Cooperation Organization Ministerial Meeting on Finance/Economy, held on 29 and 30 January 2004, and the Islamabad Joint Communiqué for Cooperation on Finance/Economy, especially in the areas of: (*a*) macroeconomic management and global capital markets; (*b*) promotion of banking, investment, transit and trade from legal and financial aspects; (*c*) securities and capital market regulations and stock/commodity exchanges; (*d*) privatization of public enterprises; and (*e*) cost of economic adjustment and the need for social safety nets;

14. *Appreciates* the efforts of the Economic Cooperation Organization to implement the Millennium Development Goals, especially its attempts to reduce pov-

erty and food insecurity in the region, takes note with satisfaction of the implementation of the technical cooperation programme of the Food and Agriculture Organization of the United Nations and the regional programme for food security in the member States of the Economic Cooperation Organization, and urges the relevant financial institutions to support the ideas to be outlined within the programme;

15. *Welcomes* the initiative of the Economic Cooperation Organization to establish institutional cooperation among its member States and relevant international organizations on agriculture-related matters of the World Trade Organization, and encourages the Food and Agriculture Organization of the United Nations, the United Nations Conference on Trade and Development and other international organizations and institutions to support the activities of the Economic Cooperation Organization in this regard;

16. *Notes with satisfaction* the adoption of the Tehran Declaration on Environmental Cooperation among member States of the Economic Cooperation Organization and the Plan of Action for Cooperation among the States members of the Economic Cooperation Organization on Environment (2003-2007) at the first Ministerial Meeting of the Economic Cooperation Organization on Environment, held in Tehran, from 13 to 15 December 2002, and the revision of the Plan of Action by the member States at the first meeting of the Working Group on Environment, held in Ankara on 7 and 8 April 2004;

17. *Also notes with satisfaction* the adoption by the United Nations Environment Programme of decision 22/14 of 7 February 2003 on the role of the Programme in strengthening regional activities and cooperation in the Economic Cooperation Organization region, at the twenty-second session of the United Nations Environment Programme Governing Council/Global Ministerial Environment Forum;

18. *Welcomes* the signing of the memorandum of understanding on cooperation in the field of environment between the Economic Cooperation Organization and the United Nations Environment Programme, in Tehran on 18 August 2004;

19. *Also welcomes* the growing cooperation between the Economic Cooperation Organization, the Economic and Social Commission for Asia and the Pacific and the United Nations Environment Programme in the field of environment, and encourages their active collaboration with the Economic Cooperation Organization;

20. *Notes with satisfaction* the ongoing cooperation between the Economic Cooperation Organization and the Islamic Development Bank concerning the project of the Economic Cooperation Organization on the interconnection and parallel functioning of power systems in the region, as well as the assistance provided by the Bank to the Economic Cooperation Organization in convening meetings on power trading as well as on legal and fiscal aspects of the promotion of foreign direct investment in the mineral sector, held in 2002 and 2003, respectively;

21. *Takes note* of the decision to hold ministerial meetings in the areas of transport and communications, energy/petroleum, environment, agriculture and information technology in 2004 and 2005;

22. *Requests* the Secretary-General to submit to the General Assembly at its sixty-first session a report on the implementation of the present resolution;

23. *Decides* to include in the provisional agenda of its sixty-first session the sub-item entitled "Cooperation between the United Nations and the Economic Cooperation Organization".

Cooperation with Pacific Islands Forum

On 4 June [A/59/95], New Zealand transmitted to the Secretary-General the Auckland Declaration, adopted by the Special Leaders' Retreat of the Pacific Islands Forum (Auckland, 6 April), in which they agreed to a Pacific Vision statement on enhanced regional cooperation, to be elaborated through the development of a Pacific Plan. The leaders confirmed the key goals of the Forum as economic growth, sustainable development, good governance and security.

The Secretary-General, in his 1 September consolidated report on cooperation between the United Nations and regional and other organizations [A/59/303], described cooperation activities between the United Nations, its programmes and organizations and the Pacific Islands Forum.

On 8 November, the General Assembly adopted **resolution 59/20** (see p. 387) on cooperation between the United Nations and the Pacific Islands Forum.

Observer status

On 2 December, the General Assembly, by **resolution 59/53** (see p. 1460), granted observer status to the South Asian Association for Regional Cooperation in the work of the Assembly.

Europe

The Economic Commission for Europe (ECE), at its fifty-ninth session (Geneva, 24-26 February) [E/2004/37], considered economic developments and policies of the ECE region on the basis of the *Economic Survey of Europe 2004 No. 1* [Sales No. E.04.II.E.7]. It convened two round tables to discuss policies to stimulate competitive growth: the first identified best practices and national policies that had proved successful in increasing competitiveness and growth; the second focused on regional initiatives and cooperation and ECE's role in stimulating competitiveness.

ECE discussed its work on the basis of a December 2003 report of the Executive Secretary [E/ECE/1412] on ECE achievements, constraints and perspectives. It considered preparations for, and follow-up to, global and regional conferences. It endorsed proposals for ECE participation in the second phase of the World Summit on the Information Society (see p. 845) and for the Executive Secretary to help organize two subregional meetings to promote implementation of the information society in the countries concerned and for them to benefit from the exchange of best practices and policies. Noting the success of the first Regional Implementation Forum on Sustainable Development, ECE endorsed the Executive Secretary's proposal that, as a follow-up to the International Ministerial Conference of Landlocked and Transit Developing Countries and Donor Countries and International Financial and Development Institutions on Transit Transport Cooperation [YUN 2003, p. 875], ECE should continue or undertake the specific activities outlined in his 19 December 2003 note on follow-up to world and regional conferences [E/ECE/1413]. It also endorsed the proposals for organizing a regional preparatory meeting regarding follow-up to the special session of the General Assembly on women (Beijing+10) (see p. 1145), and the Executive Secretary's proposal that ECE devote a high-level policy segment of its sixtieth (2005) session to follow up the results of the International Conference on Financing for Development [YUN 2002, p. 953]. It recommended financing for development as a thematic orientation for a seminar in 2005.

Also considered were: an overview of ECE technical cooperation activities in 2003 [E/ECE/1414], which, ECE pointed out, needed to be supported by additional resources and thus urged the secretariat to make additional efforts to attract extrabudgetary resources, particularly from the private sector; and ECE reform [E/ECE/1411], regarding which ECE decided to commission a review of possible changes to its role, mandate and functions in the light of changes in the European institutional architecture since ECE's inception almost 60 years earlier. The review, also covering the mandate of the Group of Experts on the Programme of Work (GEPW) with a view to strengthening its role as an intergovernmental supervisory body within ECE, would be considered by ECE in 2005.

In connection with the review, ECE endorsed the secretariat proposals and GEPW recommendations with regard to intergovernmental structures, its principal subsidiary bodies and a priority-setting mechanism for technical cooperation activities. It requested the secretariat and GEPW to revise the work programme planning process for endorsement at ECE's next ad hoc informal session. ECE endorsed, as well as urged the secretariat to implement, the technical cooperation strategy contained in the Executive Secretary's

note of 17 December 2003 [E/ECE/1411/Add.1] identifying measures to address the new challenges faced by ECE in technical cooperation, to facilitate priority setting, coordination, monitoring, reporting and evaluation, and to strengthen coordination and fund-raising.

ECE welcomed a proposed formalization of relations between it and the Organization for Security and Cooperation in Europe [E/ECE/1410] in the form of a memorandum of understanding that should not duplicate the work under other cooperation agreements. It endorsed the proposals on best practice for the evaluation of ECE work programmes as outlined by GEPW [E/ECE/1415 & Add.1].

Economic trends

According to the ECE summary [E/2005/16] of the *Economic Survey of Europe 2005 No. 1* [Sales No. E.05.II.E.7] covering the economic situation in and forecasts for Europe and the Commonwealth of Independent States (CIS) in 2004 and 2005 [E/2005/16], global economic recovery maintained strong momentum in 2004, with the United States and China remaining the principal engines of growth. In Europe, the CIS countries registered rapid growth due largely to the boom in commodity prices, and, in most of Central and Eastern Europe, economic activity continued at high momentum. However, as in 2003, the euro area lagged behind in the global recovery.

In the United States, GDP rose to 4.4 per cent, led by strong domestic demand and increased exports helped by a weaker dollar, but the country's trade and current-account deficit surged to record levels. Although the Federal Reserve started to gradually raise the target for the federal funds rate, monetary policy remained strongly supportive of economic growth.

In the euro area, real GDP rose by some 2 per cent, compared to 0.6 per cent the previous year, masking variations in the growth performance of individual countries; however, that ranged from a little more than 1 per cent in Italy, the Netherlands and Portugal, to a buoyant 4 per cent and more in Ireland and Luxembourg. Germany, the major euro economy, witnessed a return to positive growth of 1.7 per cent, following two years of virtual stagnation. In the non-euro European Union (EU) area, the United Kingdom maintained relatively strong momentum, with real GDP rising by 3.2 per cent, compared to 2.2 per cent the previous year, and economic growth recovered strongly in Denmark and Sweden.

In Central and Eastern Europe, economic activity in the eight new EU member States (EU-8) picked up noticeably, their aggregate GDP growing by some 5 per cent, led by a strengthened recovery in Poland. That growth was driven by robust consumption, investment expenditures and strong external demand; import growth was dynamic, reflecting strong domestic demand and exports. All Baltic economies continued to grow at a brisk pace. Economic growth in South-East Europe likewise accelerated considerably, underpinned by strong domestic demand and exports. Aggregate GDP rose by some 8 per cent, led by Romania and Turkey.

The CIS region, including the Russian Federation, continued to benefit from the surge in world commodity prices, increasing its aggregate GDP by almost 8 per cent. The rapid growth of commodity exports (particularly oil and natural gas) was the main factor behind the output growth in the most resource-rich CIS countries, leading to a surge in domestic demand, especially private consumption. The expansionary macroeconomic policy in many CIS economies further boosted economic activity.

Activities in 2004

Trade, industry and enterprise development

The Committee for Trade, Industry and Enterprise Development, at its eighth session (Geneva, 10 and 14 May) [ECE/TRADE/340], approved its consolidated procedures and guidelines, including procedures for an intersessional decision-making process and for its subgroups. It renewed the mandates of the Real Estate Advisory Group, the Advisory Group on the Protection and Implementation of Intellectual Property Rights for Investment, and of the teams of specialists on industrial restructuring, quality management systems, youth entrepreneurship, women's entrepreneurship and Internet enterprise development.

Also approved were the establishment of a telecom task force and terms of reference for the Advisory Group on Market Surveillance; new terms of reference for the Working Party on Technical Harmonization and Standardization Policies (WP.6), renamed the Working Party for Regulatory Cooperation and Standardization Policies; and a proposal by the Working Party on Agricultural Quality Standards to abolish the Specialized Section on Standardization of Early and Ware Potatoes and combining its work with that of the Specialized Section on Standardization of Fresh Fruit and Vegetables. The Committee agreed that the title of its 2005 forum would be "After fifteen years of market reforms in transition economies: new challenges and perspectives for the industrial sector", and for 2006,

"Regulatory cooperation in support of international trade".

In addition, the Committee held an interactive policy discussion on priority activities for the Committee for Trade, Industry and Enterprise Development in order to promote its objectives [ECE/TRADE/340/Add.1].

Timber

The Timber Committee, at its sixty-second session (Geneva, 5-9 October) [ECE/TIM/2004/2], held jointly with the thirty-second session of the European Forestry Commission of the Food and Agriculture Organization of the United Nations (FAO), convened a policy forum to discuss long-term challenges for forest and timber policies and institutions in a wider Europe; forest law enforcement and governance; the future of the Timber Committee and the European Forestry Commission in the international forest policy dialogue; and forest products market developments and prospects and links between forest policy and market policy.

The joint session approved a statement on links between forest policy and market policy for publication and wide dissemination. It recommended that ECE/FAO contribute to regional efforts to improve forest law compliance in the region and that the secretariat, in consultation with partners, submit proposals on their areas of comparative advantage. It adopted the 2005-2008 integrated ECE/FAO programme of work [TIM/2004/7] resulting from the 2003-2004 strategic review process.

Transport

The Inland Transport Committee, at its sixty-sixth session (Geneva, 17-19 February) [ECE/TRANS/156 & Add.1], reviewed, among other subjects, its strategic objectives, intersectoral activities, the transport situation in ECE member countries and emerging development trends, transport security, assistance to countries with economies in transition, and the status of the application of international ECE transport agreements and conventions. The Committee also considered transport trends and economics, road transport, road traffic safety and safety in tunnels, harmonization of vehicle regulations, rail and inland water transport, intermodal transport logistics, border crossing facilitation, transport of dangerous goods and perishable foodstuffs, and transport statistics.

The Committee adopted its strategic objectives, focusing on the creation, improvement and unification of international transport legislation and the monitoring of its implementation; the development of road infrastructure; increased facilitation of transport operations; and elimination of barriers to cross-border transport. It adopted resolutions on a global coordinating role for the ECE Working Party on Road Traffic Safety; a 2005 combined census of road traffic and inventory of standards and parameters on international traffic arteries in Europe; and a 2005 e-rail traffic census in Europe.

Energy

In 2004, in response to calls for greater energy security, the Energy Security Forum, launched in 2003 [YUN 2003, p. 1018], examined emerging energy security risks and risk mitigation, including the contribution of the Caspian Sea region to promoting energy security. The Forum's Executive Board held discussions in Geneva (March) and Moscow (June) with representatives of Governments, the financial community and energy industries on how oil price rises could be affected by energy security risk. ECE also established the Ad Hoc Group of Experts on the Supply of Fossil Fuels to promote worldwide application of the United Nations Framework Classification for Fossil Energy and Mineral Resources, which had been approved by the Committee on Sustainable Energy at its thirteenth session [YUN 2003, p. 1018]; its endorsement by ECE was welcomed by the Economic and Social Council in its decision 2004/233 (see p. 1032).

In January, the Gas Centres set up a new Task Force on Company and Market Structure to examine gas markets and industries and the implications for countries in Central and Eastern Europe. Under regional advisory services, the CIS countries began the second phase of the energy efficiency and energy security projects in the region. A new technical assistance project was initiated on coal mine methane in Central and Eastern Europe and the CIS.

Environment

The Committee on Environment Policy, at its eleventh session (Geneva, 13-15 October) [ECE/CEP/124 & Add.1], requested the secretariat to prepare the next regional implementation forum on sustainable development in 2005 or 2006, pending a decision by ECE. It reviewed the environmental performance of Bosnia and Herzegovina and of Tajikistan, adopting recommendations for those countries, and took note of the interim reports on the reviews of the environmental performance of Armenia, the Republic of Moldova and Ukraine. It extended the mandate of the Ad Hoc Expert Group on Environmental Performance for a further two years, adopted its terms of

reference and elected its members. It decided to convene a High-level Meeting of Environment and Education Ministries in 2005 for the final consideration of the strategy on education for sustainable development.

In other action, the Committee provided guidance for further work on developing a communication strategy to raise awareness of the "Environment for Europe" process; supported the cross-sectoral activities on sustainable energy, environment and health, and transport, health and environment; and established a working group of senior officials for the sixth Ministerial Conference "Environment for Europe" and adopted its mandate.

Human settlements

The Committee on Human Settlements, at its sixty-fifth session (Geneva, 20-22 September) [ECE/HBP/134], agreed to submit a paper on challenges and policy options for human settlements in the ECE region to the regional preparatory meeting for the 2005 session of the UN Commission on Sustainable Development (see p. 827). It also agreed that, at its next session, the Committee and its Working Party on Land Administration would assess, in the context of the preparations for the World Urban Forum in Canada in 2006, the implementation of the ECE Strategy for a Sustainable Quality of Life in Human Settlements in the Twenty-first Century, adopted in 2000 [YUN 2000, p. 946]. The Committee noted the activities of the Working Party, in particular its reviews and studies on real estate units and identifiers, and public/private partnerships in land administration. It undertook to strengthen the linkage between the country profile programme and the land administration reviews whenever they took place in the same country. It would also strengthen its activities in urban and regional planning and study spatial planning at the local level in cooperation with the Council of Europe. It stressed the need to cooperate with the Conference of European Statisticians in preparation for the new round of housing censuses.

The Committee adopted its 2005-2006 programme of work and confirmed the high priority of the country profile programme for the housing sector.

Statistics

The Conference of European Statisticians, at its fifty-second session (Paris, 8-10 June) [ECE/CES/66], considered the implications of the meetings of its parent bodies—the February session of ECE (see p. 1013) and the March session of the UN Statistical Commission (see p. 1255). It agreed that the Conference itself, its Bureau and the Statistical Division secretariat should continue to work towards strengthening ECE. It asked the Bureau to review its intergovernmental structure and the work programme of the Conference biennially; it also asked the ECE Statistical Division to find ways to increase its technical assistance, and regularly draw the attention of Conference members to those statistical areas where the less developed statistical offices in the region needed technical assistance but were currently underfunded.

The Conference reviewed the Integrated Presentation (IP), a unique document crucial to the coordination of international statistical work in the ECE region, and agreed that its improvement was an ongoing process and that several changes were expected with regard to its structure and procedures for its review updating. A Task Force was created to review the classification of IP statistical activities. The Conference approved the issues agreed to by its Bureau for the future development of the IP, the Annual Statistical Programme for 2004, and guidelines for establishing teams of specialists.

Operational activities

Operational activities in 2003, as described in a note by the Executive Secretary [E/ECE/1414], were carried out through capacity-building workshops, seminars, study tours, policy advisory services and field projects. Those activities were funded from the UN regular budget, with a value of $1,210,648, of which 46.3 per cent went to trade, industry and enterprise development, 15.4 per cent to the environment sector, 14.9 per cent to transport, 11.8 per cent to energy and 11.6 per cent to statistics. ECE technical cooperation activities financed from extra-budgetary sources (general trust funds, local trust funds and other sources) totalled $5,880,199.

ECE noted that, while cooperation with other organizations in implementing technical cooperation activities was appreciated, there was a need for stepping up inter-agency coordination.

Subregional activities

Pursuant to General Assembly resolution 57/34 [YUN 2002, p. 1008], the Secretary-General, in his consolidated report on cooperation between the United Nations and regional and other organizations [A/59/303], described cooperation between the United Nations and the Black Sea Economic Cooperation Organization, in the areas of transport, promotion of entrepreneurship, and support and development of small and medium-

sized enterprises. Negotiations were ongoing to extend cooperation to trade facilitation and sustainable energy.

GENERAL ASSEMBLY ACTION

On 23 December [meeting 76], the General Assembly adopted **resolution 59/259** [draft: A/59/L.57 & Add.1] without vote [agenda item 56 (*d*)].

Cooperation between the United Nations and the Black Sea Economic Cooperation Organization

The General Assembly,

Recalling its resolution 54/5 of 8 October 1999, by which it granted observer status to the Black Sea Economic Cooperation Organization, as well as its resolutions 55/211 of 20 December 2000 and 57/34 of 21 November 2002, on cooperation between the United Nations and the Black Sea Economic Cooperation Organization,

Recalling also that one of the purposes of the United Nations is to achieve international cooperation in solving international problems of an economic, social or humanitarian nature,

Recalling further the Articles of the Charter of the United Nations that encourage activities through regional cooperation for the promotion of the purposes and principles of the United Nations,

Recalling its Declaration on the Enhancement of Cooperation between the United Nations and Regional Arrangements or Agencies in the Maintenance of International Peace and Security of 9 December 1994,

Pointing out the fact that since its transformation into a regional economic organization with an international legal identity as from 1 May 1999, the Black Sea Economic Cooperation Organization has established itself as a reliable partner in boosting economic cooperation in the Black Sea region,

Recognizing that any dispute or conflict in the region impedes cooperation, and stressing the need to solve such a dispute or conflict on the basis of the norms and principles of international law,

Convinced that the strengthening of cooperation between the United Nations and other organizations contributes to the promotion of the purposes and principles of the United Nations,

Recalling the report of the Secretary-General submitted pursuant to resolution 57/34,

1. *Welcomes* the statement issued in Istanbul, Turkey, on 25 June 2004 by the Council of Ministers for Foreign Affairs of the States members of the Black Sea Economic Cooperation Organization on the contribution of the Organization to security and stability, and encourages the ongoing process of considering ways and means of enhancing the contribution of the Organization to security and stability in the region;

2. *Takes note* of the entry into force of the Additional Protocol to the Agreement among the Governments of the Black Sea Economic Cooperation Organization Participating States on Cooperation in Combating Crime, in Particular in its Organized Forms, done in Kyiv on 15 March 2002, as well as the imminent signature of the Additional Protocol on Combating Terrorism to the same Agreement;

3. *Welcomes* the activities of the Black Sea Economic Cooperation Organization aimed at strengthening regional cooperation in various fields, such as trade and economic development, banking and finance, communications, energy, transport, agriculture and agro-industry, health care and pharmaceuticals, environmental protection, tourism, science and technology, exchange of statistical data and economic information, collaboration among Customs services, and combating organized crime and the illicit trafficking of drugs, weapons and radioactive material, all acts of terrorism and illegal migration, or in any other related area;

4. *Also welcomes* the adoption of the Baku Declaration on energy cooperation in the region of the Black Sea Economic Cooperation Organization by the Ministers of Energy of the States members of the Organization on 19 September 2003 and the Joint Declaration by the Ministers of Transport from countries of the Black Sea and Caspian Sea region on 3 October 2003;

5. *Further welcomes* the operationalization and financing of the first projects by the Project Development Fund of the Black Sea Economic Cooperation Organization to the benefit of the sustainable development of the Black Sea region;

6. *Takes note* of the positive contribution of the Parliamentary Assembly of the Black Sea Economic Cooperation Organization, the Business Council, the Black Sea Trade and Development Bank and the International Centres for Black Sea Studies to the strengthening of multifaceted regional cooperation in the Black Sea area;

7. *Welcomes* the Cooperation Agreement between the Economic Commission for Europe and the Black Sea Economic Cooperation Organization, signed on 2 July 2001, and the support given by the Commission to the activities of the Organization in the fields provided for in the Agreement, notably in small and medium-sized enterprises, energy and transportation policy development;

8. *Also welcomes* the collaboration between the Black Sea Economic Cooperation Organization and the United Nations Environment Programme based on the Cooperation Agreement signed in Istanbul on 20 February 2002;

9. *Further welcomes* the cooperation between the Food and Agriculture Organization of the United Nations and the Black Sea Economic Cooperation Organization, as well as the financial support provided by the Food and Agriculture Organization in implementing the project on institutional strengthening to facilitate intraregional and interregional agricultural trade among States members of the Black Sea Economic Cooperation Organization and other projects on trade promotion;

10. *Takes note* of the cooperation between the Black Sea Economic Cooperation Organization and the World Bank and the World Trade Organization and the working contacts with the World Tourism Organization, aimed at the sustainable development of the Black Sea region;

11. *Also takes note* of the importance attached by the Black Sea Economic Cooperation Organization to the strengthening of relations with the European Union, and supports the efforts of the Organization to take concrete steps to advance this cooperation;

12. *Further takes note* of the cooperation established between the Black Sea Economic Cooperation Organization and other regional organizations and initiatives;

13. *Invites* the Secretary-General to strengthen dialogue with the Black Sea Economic Cooperation Organization with a view to promoting cooperation and coordination between the two secretariats;

14. *Invites* the specialized agencies and other organizations and programmes of the United Nations system to cooperate with the Black Sea Economic Cooperation Organization in order to continue programmes with the Organization and its associated institutions for the achievement of their objectives;

15. *Requests* the Secretary-General to submit to the General Assembly at its sixty-first session a report on the implementation of the present resolution;

16. *Decides* to include in the provisional agenda of its sixty-first session the sub-item entitled "Cooperation between the United Nations and the Black Sea Economic Cooperation Organization".

Latin America and the Caribbean

At its thirtieth session (San Juan, Puerto Rico, 28 June–2 July), the Economic Commission for Latin America and the Caribbean (ECLAC) [LC/G.2267] considered a document [LC/G.2234 (SES.30/3)] analysing the strategies in Latin America and the Caribbean for furthering productive development in open economies in pursuit of the region's integration into the global economy. ECLAC adopted a number of resolutions, among them the San Juan resolution on productive development in open economies [LC/G.2267 (res. 612(XXX))], which it recommended to the Economic and Social Council for adoption (see p. 1019), and a resolution on support for the United Nations Stabilization Mission in Haiti (see p. 296).

The remaining resolutions were on support for the work of the Latin American and Caribbean Institute for Economic and Social Planning [res. 597(XXX)]; implementation of resolutions concerning the participation of ECLAC associate member countries in the follow-up to UN world conferences and in the work of the Council [res. 598(XXX)], consideration of which the Council deferred to its January 2005 organizational session (**decision 2004/324**); ECLAC Statistical Conference of the Americas [res. 599(XXX)]; ECLAC Caribbean Development and Cooperation Committee [res. 600(XXX)]; modalities for the introduction of amendments to the work programme of ECLAC's subregional headquarters for the Caribbean [res. 601(XXX)]; monitoring sustainable development in Latin America and the Caribbean [res. 602 (XXX)]; the 2004-2006 calendar of conferences [res. 603(XXX)]; priority activities for 2004-2006 in population and development [res. 604(XXX)]; the Regional Conference on Women in Latin America and the Caribbean [res. 605(XXX)]; ECLAC programme of work for 2006-2007 [res. 607(XXX)]; promotion of coordination in studies and activities concerning South America [res. 608(XXX)]; financing and management for education [res. 609(XXX)]; follow-up to the World Summit on the Information Society [res. 610(XXX)]; cooperation among developing countries and regions [res. 611(XXX)]; and the place (Uruguay) of the next session [res. 613(XXX)].

ECONOMIC AND SOCIAL COUNCIL ACTION

On 22 July [meeting 48], the Economic and Social Council, on the recommendation of ECLAC [E/2004/15/Add.2], adopted **resolution 2004/45** without vote [agenda items 10].

San Juan resolution on productive development in open economies

The Economic and Social Council,

Bearing in mind resolution 595(XXIX) of 10 May 2002, adopted by the Economic Commission for Latin America and the Caribbean at its twenty-ninth session, in which it urged the secretariat to analyse the relationship existing between the liberalization agendas of the countries of the region and the associated productive development policies including, in particular, their links with trade, national and international financing and social and environmental issues, in order to ensure that those policies take into account the interests of the countries of Latin America and the Caribbean,

Recognizing that progress has been made in the gradual dissemination of economic and social reforms in countries of the Economic Commission for Latin America and the Caribbean region but that this has not been manifested in high, stable rates of growth that would create the necessary conditions to provide the individual and shared resources that would meet the inherent need for economic, social and cultural rights, as is emphasized, in particular, in the United Nations Millennium Declaration,

Noting that the emergence of signs of growing interdependence among countries of the region in a number of areas, such as trade, international finance and the environment, opens up new opportunities but also hinders the policy-making autonomy of national authorities,

Aware of the profound processes of productive, trade and financial restructuring now taking place worldwide, with the active participation of transnational corporations at the helm of internationally integrated production systems into which some countries of the region are being incorporated,

Observing that the expansion of trade has not resulted in rapid worldwide economic growth, that the inflow of capital to the region, including foreign direct investment, has declined and that this has been a factor in widening the gap in knowledge and technological innovation between the region and the industrialized countries,

Noting that a trend towards income disparities across countries of the region persists; that, within those countries, the low density of the processes involved in changing production patterns has exacerbated the heterogeneity of the production structure, with some sectors displaying differing patterns; and that, through their impact on the composition and quality of employment, those sectors have an influence on the disparity among households in levels of well-being,

Underlining, in sum, that the current phase of access to international markets offers a range of opportunities for productive development, some of which have been fully utilized by some sectors in developing countries, but that it also has negative consequences owing to the structural change required to adapt to changing conditions in terms of competitiveness,

Underlining also the tradition and vitality of sub-regional integration schemes and the potential for deepening them within a framework of open regionalism, along with the rich pool of regional institutions present in Latin America and the Caribbean,

Aware of the various means demonstrated by countries of the region of expanding their trade both within and outside the region and the difficult conditions under which they attract financial resources, including resources in the form of foreign direct investment, and the fact that in many cases the procyclical behaviour of capital flows to the region has led to unsustainable indebtedness,

Highlighting the progress achieved by many countries of the region in the area of macroeconomic management, especially with regard to the control of public finances and inflation; the strides made towards a more effective incorporation of the sustainable development agenda; the expansion, in many cases, of public expenditure on education, which has made it possible to increase the coverage of basic and intermediate education and to launch activities aimed at giving the population access to computerized information networks and audio-visual media; the efforts being devoted to making the labour market more adaptable by introducing new worker training arrangements and unemployment insurance; the participation of the private sector in the modernization of various infrastructure sectors and in interacting with the public sector to develop innovative approaches in the area of social security; and the fact that, nonetheless, efforts should be made to place greater emphasis on devoting attention to the difficulties that the implementation of pension reforms has raised in some countries,

Observing that obstacles to the process of changing production patterns with social equity and environmental sustainability in the region persist; that poverty levels regrettably persist; that economic growth has been insufficient and volatile; that the increase in productivity has not narrowed the gap with the developed world; that the linkages of export activities and foreign direct investment with other economic activities remain insufficient; that institutions for sustainable development have few instruments and scant resources at their disposal; that the insufficient creation of quality jobs continues to impede a reduction in open unemployment and informal employment; that the educational gap with the developed world persists in terms of both coverage (secondary and higher education) and learning outcomes; and that increased demands are being made for social security systems to cover traditional risks (health care, old age and illness) and new risks associated with the increased employment and income vulnerability,

1. *Welcomes* the document prepared by the secretariat of the Economic Commission for Latin America and the Caribbean, entitled "Productive development in open economies", considering that, thanks to the concepts it explores, the information it contains and the proposals it sets forth regarding international linkages, productive development and social vulnerability, it makes a significant contribution to the current phase of trade liberalization, levels of competitiveness and development of labour markets, education and training;

2. *Welcomes* the proactive agenda proposed by the secretariat of the Commission for meeting the challenges posed by the current phase of the productive development process, in particular the reaffirmation of national strategies for improving linkages with the world economy as pillars of the process of strengthening competitiveness; the region's potential contribution to building cohesive societies that can mitigate social vulnerability and give the countries greater room for manoeuvre in restructuring production systems; and the stress laid on the importance of an integral approach in which macroeconomic solvency is consistent with productive development and social cohesion policies;

3. *Requests* the secretariat of the Commission to ensure the wide dissemination of the document entitled "Productive development in open economies" and to encourage its consideration in the following areas:

   (i) Political, social, academic and business spheres and civil-society organizations in the region, through national, subregional and regional dialogues on the chief components of the proposed agenda;

   (ii) International organizations dealing with the various dimensions of economic development, with a view, in particular, to fostering an exchange of ideas regarding proposals for correcting asymmetries and gaps in the international agenda, especially with the International Labour Organization in relation to employment and social cohesion policies and the creation of decent jobs for a just form of globalization;

4. *Requests* the Executive Secretary of the Economic Commission for Latin America and the Caribbean to undertake a more in-depth analysis of the following issues:

   (i) Education, science and technology, highlighting the development of national and regional innovation systems that unite the efforts of the public and private sectors;

   (ii) Social protection and active labour-market policies aimed at achieving complementarity between public and private mechanisms in order to broaden coverage and adopt solidarity-based approaches, as part of a major effort to enhance social cohesion;

   (iii) Countercyclical macroeconomic management, adding national, subregional and regional measures to complement the changes required at the international level;

   (iv) Production linkages, defining policies for developing and deepening them and for forming production clusters;

   (v) Sustainable development and competitiveness, devoting special attention to the economic valuation of environmental goods and services and to the improvement of their market access conditions;

   (vi) Financing for development, placing special emphasis on the financial development needed to replace intermediation systems dominated by banks with systems that include large capital markets; strengthening of development banks with a view to promoting the institutional changes needed to capture and extend long-term financing and to design risk management instruments to give different types of enterprises easier access to financing; reliance on subregional financial institutions to provide countercyclical financing, correct situations of illiquidity and support investment programmes for sustainable development; and the role of infrastructure in productive development and competitiveness;

   (vii) Trade integration and development, paying special attention to trade in agricultural goods and access to markets that can enable the region's economies to capitalize on their competitive advantages and use appropriate technology;

5. *Calls upon* the secretariat of the Commission to pursue its examination of the development strategies of the Latin American and Caribbean countries in the context of globalization, based on an integrated approach to economic, social and environmental issues which also incorporates gender analysis, and to identify the measures that should be adopted at the national, regional and international levels.

Economic trends

In 2004, the Latin American and Caribbean economy grew by 5.8 per cent, with per capita GDP expanding by some 4.2 per cent, accompanied by a surplus on the balance-of-payments current account, according to the summary of the economic survey of Latin America and the Caribbean, 2004 [E/2005/19]. With the exception of Haiti, all the countries of the region recorded positive growth rates, led by Venezuela, which achieved the highest growth rate, at 17.3 per cent, followed by Uruguay at 11.8 per cent, Argentina at 9.0 per cent, Ecuador at 6.6 per cent, Chile at 5.8 per cent and Brazil at 5.2 per cent.

The strong economic performance of the region was tied to the expansion in world economic activity and trade. The combination of higher export prices and larger volumes gave rise to an unprecedented boom in merchandise trade. Exports expanded by 23 per cent while imports climbed by 20.9 per cent. Improved terms of trade brought an additional $24.2 billion in foreign exchange into the region.

For the second year in a row, the region posted a surplus in the balance-of-payments current account, reaching $18 billion in 2004. The macroeconomic performance of the region resulted in a significant improvement in the countries' fiscal accounts. The financial surplus made it possible to reduce debt-to-GDP ratios, which remained very high, averaging 50 per cent. Monetary policy supported the recovery of domestic demand by lowering the cost of financing, and real interest rates generally followed a downward trend and were actually negative in some cases.

Job creation picked up in 2004, although labour supply expansion was slower than in 2003. The unemployment rate declined from 10.7 per cent in 2003 to 10 per cent in 2004, the largest region-wide decrease since 1986. The rate of inflation also continued its downward trend, declining to a region-wide average of 7.4 per cent, compared to 8.5 per cent in 2003.

Activities in 2004

Development policy and regional economic performance

The Economic Development Division of ECLAC continued to report on the macroeconomic performance of the region as a whole and individual countries in the ECLAC publications entitled *Economic Survey of Latin and the Caribbean 2003-2004, Preliminary Overview of the Economies of Latin America and the Caribbean 2004* and *Macroeconomic of Development Series.* Two of the Division's projects, on the integration of young people into the labour market and on international mobility of talent, were in the process of implementation; six others were awaiting approval. Its inter-divisional activities included providing technical assistance to Brazil's Ministries of Finance and of Planning on matters of public spending and their implications for fiscal policy, technical cooperation with Bolivia, preparing a project on social public spending in Latin America, and organizing a workshop on the role of legislative power in the budgetary process in Latin America (Santiago, Chile, 12 July).

The Latin American and Caribbean Institute for Economic and Social Planning (ILPES) focused its activities on public administration and regulation; decentralization, territorial planning, management and development; programming and investment projects; and cooperation among Latin American and Caribbean organizations. It organized meetings and international and national seminars, among them the sixteenth regional seminar on fiscal policy (Santiago, 26-29 January); 11 international seminars,

attended by a total of 343 representatives from 18 countries; 10 national courses attended by 297 participants; and one subregional course for 28 representatives from Latin America and the Caribbean. It provided consultancy services to the Honduran municipalities association to assist in the preparation of local economic development policy for its institutional development plan. The ECLAC/ILPES agreement with the German Agency for Technical Cooperation on State reform, productive development and sustainable use of natural resources enabled a series of technical support missions to be carried out in several countries of the region.

The meeting of the Presiding Officers of the Regional Council for Planning (San Juan, 29 June), the intergovernmental body directing the work of the Institute, reviewed its activities in the 2002-2003 biennium and considered its 2004-2005 work programme. The Regional Council adopted a resolution expressing support for the Institute's work and requested ECLAC to organize a meeting to explore opportunities for implementing economic instruments as a complement to instruments for environmental regulation. ECLAC took note of the resolutions adopted at the June meeting of the Presiding Officers, reiterated to the Regional Council members the importance of their contributions to the regular system of government financing, and requested the Executive Secretary to continue to provide resources to support ILPES [res. 597(XXX)].

The Committee on Cooperation among Developing Countries and Regions (San Juan, 30 June) reviewed the ECLAC secretariat report entitled "Activities of the ECLAC system to promote and support technical cooperation among developing countries and regions during the 2002-2003 biennium" [LC/G.2242(SES.30/18)] and discussed opportunities and challenges for international cooperation in Latin America and the Caribbean. ECLAC, in its resolution relating to that review [res. 611(XXX)], took note of the report and stressed the need to broaden South-South cooperation in areas related to strategies for productive development in open economies; to support activities for extending the use of South-South mechanisms and modalities in the priority areas of economic and social development policy; and to arrange for greater financial participation by countries and agencies to strengthen cooperation for development.

ECLAC requested the Executive Secretary to modernize its strategic approaches to international cooperation for development, including South-South, North-South and multilateral cooperation; intensify the incorporation of South-South cooperation modalities into the secretariat's 2006-2007 programme of work; strengthen strategic partnerships with donors to increase North-South and South-South cooperation; disseminate, through the new ECLAC Internet site, activities promoting South-South cooperation; request the international community to support Latin American and Caribbean countries in responding to globalization; strengthen collaboration with UN development bodies to foster interregional cooperation in the context of globalization; participate in regional coordination activities for South-South cooperation in the areas of ECLAC competence; and support UNDP and the Latin American Economic System activities to promote South-South cooperation in UN regional work. In addition, ECLAC decided to change the name of the Committee on Cooperation among Developing Countries to the Committee on South-South Cooperation.

In the resolution on follow-up to the first phase of the World Summit on the Information Society [YUN 2003, p. 857], ECLAC requested the secretariat to prepare regional countries for the second phase by, among other actions, developing and updating indicators for the ongoing assessment of progress; supporting a regional preparatory meeting to define goals for the second phase; and developing a work plan aimed at building an inclusive information society [res. 610(XXX)].

International trade and integration

The International Trade and Integration Division of ECLAC undertook several projects, the most important of which was a comparative study of East Asian and Latin American information technology industries, which resulted in an international seminar that provided a useful exchange of ideas on best practices for using information and communication technology (ICT) in those two regions. Among other projects were: a UNDP-funded project with the other four regional commissions on interregional partnership for promoting trade as an engine of growth through knowledge management and for taking advantage of ICT; and an international collaboration project to assess the overall impact of free trade agreements.

The Division continued to offer technical assistance, taking part in more than 30 talks, courses and seminars for government officials, university officials, students and technicians throughout the region. It issued a series of papers and studies on international trade and finance, among other publications.

Social development and equity

The Social Development Division of ECLAC prepared a framework document defining aspects for a regional report on progress made by countries of the region towards achievement of the MDGs [YUN 2000, p. 51]. An inter-institutional meeting (6-7 October) supported the initiative and decided to contribute to the preparation of that report. The Division launched the 2004 edition of the *Social Panorama of Latin America* on 30 November, which focused on poverty and distribution of income, demographic changes, the social situation of young people, changes within families and the social agenda of programmes for young people. A document on poverty, hunger and food security was also published. The second stage of an ECLAC/World Food Programme agreement was implemented, with an analysis of hunger and inequality in the Andean countries, which was considered at a Hunger Forum of the Andean Nations (Quito, Ecuador, 22-23 November). The Forum ended with a declaration on investing in programmes for hunger eradication in Andean countries.

The Division conducted and published five national studies (Argentina, Chile, Costa Rica, Mexico, Uruguay) on the processes of construction and application of public policies, the management of reforms and the role of political actors. A regional seminar of experts was held (August, 10-12) on the improvement of the institutionalization of social policies and the constitution of a social authority. In October, ECLAC signed an agreement with the United Nations Children's Fund (UNICEF) for the evaluation of the costs of implementing goals on children's rights.

ECLAC held a seminar on education financing and management in Latin America and the Caribbean, at which it considered an ECLAC/United Nations Educational, Scientific and Cultural Organization (UNESCO) document on the subject [LC/G.2253(SES.30/15)]. As a result, ECLAC decided [res. 609(XXX)] to undertake with UNESCO an analysis of options for financing and managing education and to promote the formulation of public policy agendas to help countries to meet their education targets, as well as an analysis of the causes of educational inequality in the region, and to stimulate the formulation of regional strategies for reducing inequalities in economic, social and educational development. It also undertook to follow up the fulfilment of the education-related MDGs; help mobilize stakeholders to uphold the principle of social responsibility for education; promote interaction among education and finance authorities with a view to arriving at agreements on management and financing options; and promote activities with other UN bodies and multilateral agencies to follow up on financing and management of education. ECLAC agreed to support UNESCO in the fulfilment of its mandate to follow up on the educational goals agreed upon in international forums.

Sustainable development and human settlements

In 2004, the Sustainable Development and Human Settlements Division of ECLAC completed a number of projects, including a training programme to improve environmental management in Latin America and the Caribbean; an action-oriented strategy to strengthen the capacity of urban governments and institutions to craft policies and manage programmes for the reduction of urban poverty at the national and local levels; consulting services for drawing up a model for sustainable development by integrating environmental policies with social and economic policies; the development of an economic sector through cooperative alliances and agreements that benefited from market opportunities created by the growing demand for environmental services and technologies; and assistance for organizing an editorial group and coordinating the writing of a book on science and technology for sustainable development. The Division also carried out a number of interdivisional activities in the areas of energy and climate change, and of water, sanitation and human settlements for the Commission on Sustainable Development.

ECLAC commended the secretariat for organizing a special meeting within the framework of its session to analyse the challenges and opportunities that sustainable development represented for the region; agreed to proceed with a regional forum on sustainable development for the implementation of decisions adopted at the World Summit on Sustainable Development [YUN 2002, p. 821], to be convened by the Executive Secretary; and invited the international community and ECLAC member countries to collaborate in organizing those meetings to ensure their regularity and permanence as a forum for dialogue and consensus-building [res. 602(XXX)].

Population and development

In 2004, ECLAC's Latin American and Caribbean Demographic Centre (CELADE) provided technical assistance to regional countries in drawing up policies and programmes related to the elderly to meet the requirements of the International Plan of Action on Ageing, 2002 (the Madrid Plan of Action) [YUN 2002, p. 1194] and

those of the regional strategy approved by the Regional Intergovernmental Conference on Ageing [YUN 2003, p. 1022]. CELADE continued to update and disseminate a database on international migration, which proved of assistance to the Statistical Information System on Migrations in Central America, established by CELADE and the International Office for Migration. CELADE participated in national and regional seminars, intergovernmental forums on migration in the region and meetings related to the UN Global Commission for International Migration. It also convened a meeting of experts to discuss the relation between migration, regional integration and human rights. It developed specific studies on the interrelation of the demographic dynamic and development.

The open-ended meeting of the Presiding Officers of the sessional Ad Hoc Committee on Population and Development (Santiago, 10-11 March) [LC/L.2141] adopted a Declaration in commemoration of the tenth anniversary of the International Conference on Population and Development (ICPD) [YUN 1994, p. 955] and requested the Committee Chair to present the results of the meeting to the Commission on Population and Development at its thirty-seventh session in March and to the Ad Hoc Committee at its next meeting. The Declaration urged countries to intensify their efforts in a number of areas and requested ECLAC and the United Nations Population Fund (UNFPA) to prepare a regional strategy for meeting the need for trained human resources in population and development for submission to the Ad Hoc Committee.

The Ad Hoc Committee, at its meeting (San Juan, 29-30 June), adopted conclusions that were reflected in the ECLAC resolution on population and development covering priority activities for 2004-2006 [res. 604(XXX)]. By that resolution, ECLAC endorsed the Declaration, urged regional countries to intensify efforts to implement the CPD Programme of Action, and adopted the recommendation that the Committee assume responsibility for monitoring the regional strategy for implementing the Madrid Plan of Action. ECLAC recommended that the Ad Hoc Committee analyse in 2006 international migration, human rights and development, and prepare relevant documents. It requested the Presiding Officers, during the intersessional period and in coordination with UNFPA, to examine the issues related to indigenous peoples and other ethnic groups, ageing, and human resources development in preparation for the Committee's 2006 session. It called on the region's countries to provide resources for the implementation of the ICPD Programme of Action and the key actions it specified and to ensure their inclusion in policies aimed at reducing social inequalities, eliminating gender inequality and eradicating poverty; it urged the international community to increase technical and financial cooperation for fulfilling those objectives.

Integration of women in development

The Regional Conference on Women in Latin America and the Caribbean (ninth session, Mexico City, 10-12 June) [LC/G.2256(CRM.9/6)] adopted the Mexico City Consensus, by which participating Governments reaffirmed their determination to, among other actions, adopt measures to ensure the full development and advancement of women of all ages, with a view to guaranteeing their access to justice and their enjoyment of all human rights. The Conference welcomed the research agenda proposed in the document entitled "Roads towards gender equity in Latin America and the Caribbean" [LC/L.2114(CRM.9/3)] and requested the ECLAC secretariat to put it into practice, in collaboration with regional Governments and other international organizations. It declared that the Mexico City Consensus should constitute the region's contribution to the work of the 2005 session of the Commission on the Status of Women and asked the Chairman to submit it to ECLAC at its thirtieth session.

ECLAC took note of the report of the Regional Conference and reaffirmed the Mexico City Consensus [res. 605(XXX)].

The thirty-seventh meeting of the Presiding Officers of the Regional Conference on Women in Latin America and the Caribbean (Santiago, 29-30 November) agreed on a regional strategy for participation in UN system activities related to the tenth anniversary of the Fourth World Conference on Women (Beijing +10) (see p. 1144), the special session of the Economic and Social Council on the analysis of cross-cutting of gender issues in the UN system, and the charting of the objective of the Millennium Declaration on the promotion of gender equality [YUN 2000, p. 52] and of the cross-cutting of other goals.

ECLAC organized a meeting of experts (Quito, Ecuador, 25 August) on policies and programmes for overcoming poverty from the perspective of democratic governance and gender. It also organized the twelfth meeting (Santiago, 30 November) of UN system bodies on the advancement of women in the region.

Economic statistics and technical cooperation

The ECLAC Statistics and Economic Projection Division published, in addition to the *Statistical Yearbook*, various technical documents designed to offer methodological tools in the production and analysis of social and economic statistics, and prepared a Cuaderno Estadístico on the classification of international statistics, including a framework for the economic analysis of tourism information. As an initial response to the growing demand from member States for the improvement of the institutional and organizational aspects of national statistics systems, the Division translated into Spanish the UN manual on the organization of statistical institutions. It redesigned the *Statistical Yearbook* and the Cuadernos Estadísticos, as well as its online databases and website.

The Division carried out a number of projects, such as those for the creation of a network of institutions and experts in social and environmental statistics (REDESA project), the improvement of surveys and measurement of living conditions in Latin America and the Caribbean (MECOVI project), and the International Comparison Programme (ICP project), a global initiative to obtain statistics of the parities of purchasing power. It also played a central role in coordinating information, documents and data for monitoring the MDGs.

ECLAC [res. 599(XXX)] endorsed the agreements adopted by the second meeting of the Executive Committee of the ECLAC Statistical Conference of the Americas [YUN 2002, p. 1014] and the Conference's resolution [YUN 2003, p. 1023].

Natural resources and infrastructure

The ECLAC Division of Natural Resources and Infrastructure focused on productive development based on the exploitation of natural resources and a conceptual review of the development of infrastructure and economic growth. It conducted studies on sustainable management and natural resources, on the integration of regional infrastructure, and on the regulation of infrastructure and public utility services and its impact on competitiveness, economic growth and social equality. It carried out projects on sustainable management of natural resources and on the regulation of infrastructure and public utility services. It cooperated with other Divisions, UN agencies and regional organizations, in particular with the Inter-American Development Bank and the World Bank, and assisted 12 countries in drawing up regulations for infrastructure and energy services and legislation for water and mining resources. The Division presented the study "Renewable energy resources in Latin America and the Caribbean: the situation and policy proposals" at the World Conference on Renewable Energies.

Subregional activities

Caribbean

The ECLAC subregional headquarters for the Caribbean—the Caribbean Development and Co-operation Committee (CDCC) in Port of Spain, Trinidad and Tobago—held its twentieth meeting (St. Croix, United States Virgin Islands, 22-23 April) [LC/CAR/L.15]. The meeting reviewed the implementation of its work programmes for 2002-2003 and for 2004-2005 up to March 2004, and considered the draft 2006-2007 work programme. It also considered the draft revised text of the CDCC Constituent Declaration and Rules of Procedure [LC/G.2251(SES.30/9)], preparations for the international meeting to review the implementation of the Barbados Programme of Action for the Sustainable Development of Small Island Developing States [YUN 1994, p. 783], recent developments in relation to the proposal for securing international recognition of the Caribbean Sea as a special area in the context of sustainable development, obstacles to the implementation of the Plan of Action of the World Summit on the Information Society [YUN 2003, p. 857], the challenges of the Free Trade Area of the Americas and of social development in the Caribbean small island developing States, and measurements of social and economic trends in the Caribbean.

ECLAC noted the report of CDCC's twentieth session, endorsed its resolutions and approved its Constituent Declaration and Functions and Rules of Procedure [res. 600(XXX)]. It requested that the amendments proposed by the Monitoring Committee or adopted by the CDCC ministerial session with respect to the CDCC work programme be incorporated into any revision of the ECLAC work programme, and that the Executive Secretary establish a time frame for the submission of proposed amendments [res. 601(XXX)].

ECLAC also adopted a resolution [res. 606(XXX)] on support for the United Nations Stabilization Mission in Haiti (see p. 288), which it recommended for adoption by the Economic and Social Council (see below).

ECONOMIC AND SOCIAL COUNCIL ACTION

On 22 July [meeting 48], the Economic and Social Council, on the recommendation of ECLAC [E/2004/15/Add.2], adopted **resolution 2004/46** without vote [agenda item 10].

Support for the United Nations Stabilization Mission in Haiti

The Economic and Social Council,

Recalling resolution 503(XXIII) of 9 May 1990, adopted by the Economic Commission for Latin America and the Caribbean, on support for Haiti,

Recalling also General Assembly resolution 57/337 of 3 July 2003 on the prevention of armed conflict, and in particular the role assigned to the Economic and Social Council in that connection,

Bearing in mind Security Council resolution 1542 (2004) of 30 April 2004, in which the Council decided to establish the United Nations Stabilization Mission in Haiti and considered its various aspects, including the promotion of the social and economic development of Haiti and the need to design a long-term development strategy to that effect,

Bearing in mind also that Security Council resolution 1542(2004) underscores the need for Member States, in particular those in the region, and bodies of the United Nations system, among other actors, to provide appropriate support for these actions,

Highlighting the role that the Economic and Social Council can play in a long-term programme of support for Haiti,

Highlighting also the fact that these economic and social efforts will make an important contribution to the longer-term peace and security objectives of the Mission, which are currently the most immediate priority on the ground,

Considering the content of the Programme of Action for the Least Developed Countries for the Decade 2001-2010,

1. *Welcomes* the commitments undertaken by the countries of the region in connection with the efforts towards the reconstruction of Haiti;

2. *Trusts* that these commitments will be extended to all the spheres envisaged in the mandate of the United Nations Stabilization Mission in Haiti, with special emphasis on economic and social development, in accordance with the spirit of Security Council resolution 1542(2004);

3. *Requests* the secretariat of the Economic Commission for Latin America and the Caribbean to support the countries of the region in the context of this effort, in full cooperation with the transitional Government of Haiti and in close coordination with the Mission, with a view to optimizing the actions they seek to carry out under the terms of reference of the Mission;

4. *Instructs* the Executive Secretary of the Economic Commission for Latin America and the Caribbean to evaluate, in coordination with the transitional Government of Haiti, the Secretary-General and the Mission, the timing and modalities of such collaboration;

5. *Expresses its satisfaction* with the assistance being provided by the Governments participating in the Mission, and urges other Governments in the region, to the extent of their abilities, to join in this manifestation of solidarity.

Mexico and Central America

In 2004, the ECLAC subregional headquarters in Mexico, at the request of those member States that faced a particularly intense cycle of hurricanes and torrential rains, undertook seven evaluations of the socio-economic and environmental impact of natural phenomena: two on floods in Mexico and five on hurricanes in the Caribbean. It also held five training courses on the methodology used for such evaluations.

The subregional headquarters provided consultancy services to 18 member States and held one meeting of experts and 14 training courses. A total of 19 projects were carried out at a cost of some $1.2 million from extra-budgetary sources. It conducted a number of interdivisional activities, including coordination with CDCC for technical cooperation with Haiti's provisional Government and the United Nations Stabilization Mission in Haiti, joint preparation with the ECLAC office in Washington, D.C. of an extra-budgetary project proposal on the strengthening of capacities related to trade, and provision of technical assistance to Andean nations for negotiating a free-trade agreement with the United States.

South America

ECLAC, in taking account of the interest of the South American countries in strengthening the coherence of studies and projects concerning the subregion, recommended that the various ECLAC national offices and organs carry out joint integrated and complementary studies and activities, focusing in depth on the subregion; in that connection, it highlighted the need to guarantee coordination and unity in their work, especially with respect to physical integration, international trade and the analysis of macroeconomic convergence in South America, without prejudice to issues relating to the social sphere and sustainable development [res. 608(XXX)].

Programme and organizational questions

ECLAC approved the draft 2006-2007 programme of work of the ECLAC system [LC/G.2238 (SES.30/6)], including ILPES, and endorsed the proposed priorities, which encompassed the promotion of a broader vision of macroeconomic stability to fuel growth and reduce volatility, the importance of regional affairs and integration into the rest of the world, an increase in the region's production potential and in social cohesion, improvements in global institutions, and the importance of migration, sustainable development and financing for development. It asked the Executive Secretary to strengthen the structure of its national and liaison offices, to submit proposals for the execution of the programme of work, and to convene the Committee of the Whole in between Commission sessions so as to strengthen and broaden the dialogue between member States and the secretariat [res. 607(XXX)]. In other action, ECLAC approved its calendar of conferences [LC/G.2248(SES.30/7)] for 2004-2006 [res. 603(XXX)].

Venue of and participation in ECLAC thirty-first session

On 22 July [meeting 48], the Economic and Social Council, on the recommendation of ECLAC [E/2004/15/Add.2], adopted **resolution 2004/47** without vote [agenda item 10].

Place of the next session of the Economic Commission for Latin America and the Caribbean

The Economic and Social Council,

Bearing in mind paragraph 15 of the terms of reference and rules 1 and 2 of the rules of procedure of the Economic Commission for Latin America and the Caribbean,

Considering the invitation of the Government of Uruguay to host the thirty-first session of the Commission,

1. *Expresses its appreciation* to the Government of Uruguay for its generous invitation;

2. *Notes* the acceptance by the Economic Commission for Latin America and the Caribbean of this invitation with pleasure;

3. *Endorses* the decision of the Commission to hold its thirty-first session in Uruguay in 2006.

Also on 22 July, the Council, by **decision 2004/246**, deferred consideration of a draft resolution recommended by ECLAC on the participation of ECLAC associate member countries in the follow-up to UN world conferences and in the Council's work.

Cooperation with regional organizations

Cooperation between United Nations and Latin American Economic System

In accordance with General Assembly resolution 57/39 [YUN 2002, p. 1016], the Secretary-General, in his consolidated report on cooperation between the United Nations and regional and other organizations [A/59/303], provided information on cooperation between the various programmes and agencies of the UN system and the Latin American Economic System (SELA).

GENERAL ASSEMBLY ACTION

On 23 December [meeting 76], the General Assembly adopted **resolution 59/258** [draft: A/59/L.55], as orally revised, without vote [agenda item 56 (k)].

Cooperation between the United Nations and the Latin American Economic System

The General Assembly,

Recalling its resolution 57/39 of 21 November 2002 on cooperation between the United Nations and the Latin American Economic System,

Having considered the report of the Secretary-General on cooperation between the United Nations and regional and other organizations,

Bearing in mind the Agreement between the United Nations and the Latin American Economic System, in which the parties agree to strengthen and expand their cooperation in matters that are of common concern in the fields of their respective competence pursuant to their constitutional instruments,

Noting that cooperation between the Latin American Economic System and the United Nations has been evolving, strengthening and diversifying over the years with regard to its areas of cooperation,

Welcoming the changes in the treatment of topics relating to the United Nations system, in close contact with the delegations of the Member States participating in such deliberations,

1. *Takes note* of the holding of the thirtieth regular meeting of the Latin American Council of the Latin American Economic System from 22 to 24 November 2004;

2. *Takes note with satisfaction* of the report of the Secretary-General;

3. *Urges* the Economic Commission for Latin America and the Caribbean to continue deepening its coordination and mutual support activities with the Latin American Economic System;

4. *Urges* the specialized agencies and other organizations, funds and programmes of the United Nations system to continue and intensify their support for and to strengthen their cooperation with activities of the Latin American Economic System and to contribute to joint actions to achieve the internationally agreed development objectives, including those contained in the United Nations Millennium Declaration, in Latin America and the Caribbean;

5. *Reiterates its request* to the Secretary-General of the United Nations and the Permanent Secretary of the Latin American Economic System to assess, at the appropriate time, the implementation of the Agreement between the United Nations and the Latin American Economic System and to report thereon to the General Assembly at its sixty-first session;

6. *Requests* the Secretary-General to submit to the General Assembly at its sixty-first session a report on the implementation of the present resolution.

Cooperation with Caribbean Community and OAS

The General Assembly, on 10 December, adopted **resolution 59/138** on cooperation between the United Nations and the Caribbean Community (see p. 306). On 23 December, the Assembly adopted **resolution 59/257** on cooperation between the United Nations and the Organization of American States (see p. 307).

Western Asia

The Economic and Social Commission for Western Asia (ESCWA) did not meet in 2004. Its twenty-third meeting was scheduled to be held in 2005.

Economic and social trends

Economic trends

Despite the situations in Iraq and Palestine, 2004 was another positive year for the overall economic growth of Western Asia. GDP, which grew by 4.8 per cent, compared to 5.7 per cent in 2003, still represented a considerable improvement over the growth of recent years, according to the summary of the survey of economic and social developments in the ESCWA region, 2005 [E/2005/20]. That was due to a combination of high oil prices and production, low interest rates, ample liquidity in the public and private sectors and an expansion of domestic demand. With average population growth estimated at 2.4 per cent, per capita GDP, excluding Iraq and Palestine, increased by 2.3 per cent in real terms.

In the Gulf Cooperation Council States (GCC) (Bahrain, Kuwait, Oman, Qatar, Saudi Arabia, United Arab Emirates), real growth was only 4.7 per cent, as compared with a final figure of 6.6 per cent in 2003, largely due to high oil and natural gas production and revenues. Non-oil sectors performed well, particularly transport, telecommunications, real estate, banking and finance, as well as high domestic liquidity and low, albeit gently rising, interest rates. Among the GCC countries, Qatar achieved the highest GDP growth rate (6.0 per cent), followed by Saudi Arabia (5.3 per cent) and Bahrain (5.0 per cent).

In the more diversified economies (Egypt, Jordan, Lebanon, Syrian Arab Republic, Yemen), favourable external factors, including low dollar interest rates, the expansion of regional tourism, a sustained increase in worker remittances and other income transfers, resulted in healthy domestic demand, which drove the real GDP up to 4.9 per cent, the highest since 2000. Egypt and Jordan each had the highest growth rate, at 5.5 per cent, followed by Lebanon at 5.0 per cent.

Tensions and political instability continued to overshadow prospects for steady economic growth and development in the conflict zones of Iraq and Palestine, leading to falling levels of per capita income and widespread poverty. However, the Iraqi economy showed signs of recovery from a very low base, with an improvement of per capita GDP, reversing the decline of preceding years, although not enough to achieve self-sustaining economic growth. The Palestinian economy registered a real GDP growth rate of 1.6 per cent, down from the 6.1 per cent rate in 2003.

Oil

In 2004, the average basket price of crude oil of the Organization of Petroleum Exporting Countries (OPEC) was $36.05 per barrel. Oil production in the ESCWA region expanded by 6 per cent from its 2003 level, with ESCWA's OPEC members (Kuwait, Qatar, Saudi Arabia, United Arab Emirates) producing an average of 4 per cent more than in 2003, while production in non-OPEC ESCWA countries (Bahrain, Egypt, Oman, the Syrian Arab Republic, Yemen) declined by 5 per cent as they struggled to maintain output. All ESCWA oil-exporting countries experienced a boost in oil export revenue, which rose to an estimated $213 billion, a 29 per cent increase over 2003.

Trade

In 2004, total merchandise exports of ESCWA member countries reached $297 billion, while that of merchandise imports reached $194 billion. The GCC countries accounted for 86 per cent of those exports and 70 per cent of all imports. Total gross exports from the region increased by 24 per cent, largely as a result of increased oil export values. Exports from the more diversified economies, notably Egypt, Jordan and Lebanon, also rose significantly, as did imports, which increased by 22 per cent due to an expansion in domestic demand.

Social trends

In the social sphere, the region remained trapped in a vicious circle of poverty, unemployment and violent conflict, each reinforcing the other and interacting with other negative parameters, including weak and/or waning social protection systems, non-participatory modes of governance, segmentation, modest growth and a shock therapy approach to economic reform, resulting in worsening social conditions for large parts of the population. Poverty was a serious challenge to both policy makers and decision makers. Household surveys revealed clear symptoms of widespread poverty. Non-money metric measures of poverty provided a different perspective on living conditions other than the income measure. Most ESCWA member countries performed quite well when judged by life expectancy at birth and by infant and under-five mortality rates. However, the region still experienced

literacy rates of only 67 per cent for its adult population and 75 per cent for its youth population.

Activities in 2004

During 2004, ESCWA activities under its 2004-2005 work programme [YUN 2003, p. 1028] focused on the four pivotal priorities: water and energy resources, social policies, globalization, and technology; and on the interdisciplinary issues of the empowerment and advancement of women, national statistical capacity-building, especially in monitoring the attainment of the MDGs [YUN 2000, p. 51], and the special needs of countries emerging from conflict.

Economic development and cooperation

The Economic Analysis Division of ESCWA focused on increasing the capacity of ESCWA member countries to coordinate their economic policies and achieve economic development by providing a quantitative assessment of economic and financial data and trends. Activities included the provision to end-users of in-depth analyses showing macroeconomic variables and trends, workshops, studies, and dialogue with regional stakeholders. A workshop on the role of indebtedness in regional economic development was held (Beirut, Lebanon, 6-7 December) and a study on the impact of economic variables was published.

The Globalization and Regional Integration Division concentrated its activities on, among other aspects of its work, facilitating transboundary flows of goods, services, people and capital; increasing awareness of ESCWA member countries to new developments in the multilateral trading system and familiarity with WTO negotiations and agreements and their implications; and disseminating knowledge and capacity-building through expert group meetings, seminars and workshops. To that end, an expert group meeting was organized (Beirut, 11-12 May) to follow up the results of the Fifth WTO Ministerial Conference [YUN 2003, p. 1535], as were six seminars/workshops, including two regional seminars in Beirut on trade facilitation (1-3 June) and on trade in services for the Arab countries (7-9 December). Briefing notes on recent developments in respect of the WTO Doha round of WTO trade negotiations (see p. 958) and an Arabic translation of the 2004 framework agreement were prepared.

Transportation

The Committee on Transport, at its fifth session (Beirut, 2-4 March) [E/ESCWA/GRID/2004/IG.1/7], recommended that the draft action plan

[E/ESCWA/GRID/2004/1] for the implementation of the Agreement on International Roads in the Arab Mashreq [YUN 2001, p. 928] be adopted to allow implementation to begin; that member States accelerate implementation of the action plan before the expiry of the maximum period allowed for under the Agreement; and that countries that had not yet done so, sign and ratify the Agreement. They should likewise sign and ratify the Agreement on International Railways in the Arab Mashreq [YUN 2003, p. 1026]. Noting the efforts made by member countries to establish and activate national committees for the facilitation of transport and trade, the Committee urged the ESCWA secretariat to provide those countries with technical assistance to enable them to accelerate measures for doing so.

The Committee further recommended that member States approve by 30 June the amended memorandum of understanding on cooperation in maritime transport in the Arab Mashreq, with a view to submitting it to ESCWA in 2005, and, by that date, complete and update data on the regional road transport information system and on international road network connections. ESCWA was to submit the collected data to the Committee in 2005.

Statistics

The Statistical Committee, at its sixth session (Beirut, 6-8 October) [E/ESCWA/SCU/2004/IG.1/6], called on ESCWA member countries to strengthen human and material capacities of central statistical offices and units; communicate with one another through ESCWA in order to develop national capacities; submit proposals on the modification of the Statistical Committee's internal organization and enhancement of its performance by the end of 2004; and exchange expertise and experts in various statistical fields with a view to raising the level of statistical activities and reducing implementation costs.

The Committee called on ESCWA to form a task force to coordinate the region's work on population and housing censuses with a view to harmonizing national censuses. Regarding drafting a strategy for national statistical development, the Committee proposed that the Paris 21 Consortium (Partnership for Statistics) assist ESCWA member countries in preparing national statistical strategies by the end of 2006 and provide the necessary funding. It recommended that ESCWA member countries take a number of measures to fulfil the statistical requirements related to the MDGs and asked ESCWA to establish a joint regional technical task force of UN agencies to coordinate efforts related to the United Nations Millennium Declaration [YUN 2000, p. 49]. It fur-

ther recommended that ESCWA strengthen the partnership between its member countries and the UN Statistical Department with regard to support for and development of activities related to population censuses, as part of the 2010 World Programme on Population and Housing Censuses and Related Surveys.

Natural resources, energy and environment

The Committee on Water Resources, at its sixth session (Beirut, 2-4 December) [E/ESCAP/SDPD/2004/IG.2/6], recommended that water resources in ESCWA member countries be developed and their management assured by realistic goals and feasible national policies based on integrated management. Approval should be given for the adoption of a mechanism for consolidating regional cooperation, proposed in the ESCWA study on the principles for formulating guidelines for groundwater management. Through effective coordination and cooperation with all relevant parties, greater effort should be exerted to protect water resources from contamination, maintain water quality, formulate and develop indicators on the quality of surface water and groundwater, rainwater and water from springs feeding aquifers, and formulate comprehensive monitoring programmes for water quality management at basin level. The Committee urged ESCWA to continue efforts to build national capacities, especially in strengthening integrated water resource management; assist countries in developing their national plans with a view to achieving the MDGs and the goals of the Plan of Implementation of the 2002 World Summit on Sustainable Development [YUN 2002, p. 821], and, in that regard, assist countries in formulating policies and mechanisms for improving water supplies and sanitation services; convene a preparatory meeting in 2005 to coordinate the countries' positions; and develop a regional stance on water issues for the Fourth World Water Forum to be held in 2006 (see p. 1039).

The Committee on Energy, at its fifth session (Beirut, 11-12 October) [E/ESCWA/SDPD/2004/IG.1/7], recommended that member countries formulate national strategies, implement policies and programmes for energy conservation and efficiency in production and use, use clean fossil fuel technologies, exploit renewable energy resources, and formulate national strategies for sustainable development in energy. The Committee recommended to ESCWA that it include in its programme of work studies on policies involving social, economic and environmental aspects of energy resources management, with a view to achieving sustainable development, and continue the development of an energy database, which should be updated to include use for sustainable development.

Quality of life

The Committee on Women, at its first session (Beirut, 4-5 December 2003) [E/ESCWA/WOM/2003/IG.1/9], reviewed achievements for the advancement of Arab women 10 years after the 1995 Fourth World Conference on Women [YUN 1995, p. 1169], the tasks before the Committee and the programme of work of the Centres for Women in that regard. It identified country needs concerning the empowerment of women in preparation for the 2006-2007 strategic framework and programme of work of the Centres. It adopted recommendations directed at Governments and ESCWA, focusing on commitment to the formulation of a comprehensive programme for Beijing +10 (see p. 1144), the provision of technical assistance to Arab countries in the preparation of national reports and the review, and revision and testing of an indicator for measuring the status of Arab women.

The Committee, at its second session (Beirut, 8-10 July 2004) [E/ESCWA/WOM/2004/IG.1/6], convened in conjunction with the Arab Regional Conference Ten Years after Beijing: Call for Peace, adopted the Beirut Declaration on Arab Women Ten Years After Beijing: Call for Peace, which was issued by the Arab Regional Conference. The Declaration appealed to the international community to take action to end wars and find a just and lasting solution for the occupied territories in the Arab region, called on all Governments to implement the Beirut Declaration, and urged them to strengthen national machineries for women. It requested ESCWA to provide advisory services in the areas of empowerment and the advancement of women, and called for the allocation of human and material resources to the Centres for Women to enable it to assume its expanded tasks.

The Committee also adopted the subprogramme on the empowerment and advancement of women within the 2006-2007 proposed strategic framework.

In other developments, ESCWA was preparing the first draft of the integrated social policies report and issued a booklet providing a comparative analysis of and guidelines for formulating such policies in the ESCWA region. It assisted the Palestinian Authority, the Palestinian private sector and civil society in articulating a coordinated vision for rehabilitation and development and in establishing socio-economic needs and priorities. It organized, in coordination with the League of Arab States, the Arab-International Forum on Rehabilitation and Development in the Occupied Palestinian Territory (Beirut, 11-14 October).

ESCWA also focused on advocacy for empowering youth and disabled persons, providing them with opportunities for employment, and on maintaining gender perspectives in such activities. It convened the Regional Expert Group Meeting on Information and Communication Technologies for Persons with Disabilities (Beirut, 25-26 May) and launched a website entitled "Net Forum for the Blind" and another for the Arab Youth Directory.

Programme and organizational questions

Venue and dates of ESCWA twenty-third session

By **decision 2004/320** of 5 November, the Economic and Social Council approved the ESCWA request to accept the invitation of the Government of the Syrian Arab Republic to hold its twenty-third session in Damascus in April/May 2005.

Chapter VI

Energy, natural resources and cartography

The conservation and use of energy and natural resources continued to be considered by several UN bodies in 2004, including the Commission for Sustainable Development.

During the year, the Commission reviewed progress towards realizing the commitments and meeting the targets agreed to in the 1992 Agenda 21 and the 2002 Johannesburg Plan of Implementation, both of which called for sustainable access to and affordability of environmentally sound energy. The use of nuclear energy as an environmentally clean source of electricity was also considered by the General Assembly in November.

The natural resource water, considered together with sanitation and human settlements, was the focus of discussion at the Commission's twelfth session in 2004, the first year of its thematic two-year work cycle (2004-2005). The Assembly, reiterating that water was critical for sustainable development, including environmental integrity and the eradication of poverty and hunger, and indispensable for human health and well-being, invited the Secretary-General to organize the International Decade for Action, "Water for Life" (2005-2015).

On the World Day for Water (22 March), the Secretary-General announced the establishment of a high-level Advisory Board on Water and Sanitation, which aimed to galvanize global action on the related issues of water, sanitation and human settlements as part of the international effort to eradicate poverty and achieve sustainable development.

The recommendations of the Sixteenth United Nations Regional Cartographic Conference for Asia and the Pacific and the twenty-second session of the United Nations Group of Experts on Geographical Names were endorsed by the Economic and Social Council in July.

Energy and natural resources

The Commission on Sustainable Development, which assumed the work of the Committee on Energy and Natural Resources for Development following the latter's termination by Economic and Social Council decision 2002/303 [YUN 2002, p. 1022], held its twelfth session (New York, 14-30 April 2004) [E/2004/29] (see p. 827).

The Commission, at its high-level segment (28-30 April), discussed a series of reports of the Secretary-General on various aspects of implementation of Agenda 21 (the 1992 action plan for sustainable development) [YUN 1992, p. 672], and subsequent intergovernmental meetings related to sustainable development, including a report providing an overview of implementation and the related challenges and opportunities [E/CN.17/2004/2]. The reports contained a detailed review of implementation in a selected thematic cluster of issues, among which was a report on water management [E/CN.17/2004/4]. In his summary of the issues before the high-level segment, the Chairman stated that this was the first non-negotiating session, the purpose of which was to analyse the reasons for successes and failures, and to identify constraints, achievements and best practices in respect to the thematic cluster for 2004-2005—water, sanitation and human settlements. He noted that water was key to economic growth and that meeting the targets on water was a prerequisite for progress in poverty eradication, reduction of child mortality, health and environmental sustainability.

Energy

The Secretary-General, in his February overview report [E/CN.17/2004/2] on progress towards sustainable development, noted that Agenda 21 and the two major follow-up documents—the Programme for the Further Implementation of Agenda 21 [YUN 1997, p. 792] and the Johannesburg Plan of Implementation [YUN 2002, p. 821]—stressed the importance of access to and affordability of environmentally sound energy. The report briefly discussed energy, which would be dealt with in depth by the Commission for Sustainable Development at its fourteenth (2006) session. It noted that approximately 1.6 billion people, one quarter of the world's population, remained without access to electricity, and that the share of renewable energy, excluding hydroelectricity, in global electricity generation was 1.7 per cent.

Initiatives to promote access to reliable and affordable energy were carried out by the United

Nations Development Programme (UNDP) and the World Bank, among others. The UNDP-World Bank Global Village Energy Partnership launched in 2002 continued to bring together public and private stakeholders to ensure access to modern energy services by the poor. A UNDP-led World Summit on Sustainable Development partnership worked to improve access to liquefied petroleum gas (LPG) in rural areas, in a programme known as the LPG Challenge. Ongoing forums such as the World Bank's Energy Forum and the Global Forum on Sustainable Energy continued to serve as catalysts for action. To increase the share of renewables in energy supply, some countries promoted renewable energy for the production of electricity with tax and subsidy incentives as well as legislation, and some took steps to encourage the use of ethanol in gasoline. A number of World Summit on Sustainable Development partnerships were established to promote energy efficiency and cleaner energy technologies. For example, the Partnership for Clean Fuels and Vehicles was aimed at eliminating lead in gasoline and reducing emissions, and the Collaborative Labelling and Appliance Standards Programme promoted cost-effective energy-efficiency standards and labels for appliances, equipment and lighting. In addition, the UN Department of Economic and Social Affairs (DESA) worked with States to develop a mechanism that developing countries could use in attracting clean energy investments. The Secretary-General affirmed that development and transfer of cleaner energy technologies by developed countries were crucial to addressing climate change.

The Secretary-General reported in February [E/2004/12-E/CN.17/2004/3] on the efforts of the United Nations System Chief Executives Board for Coordination (CEB) to enhance inter-agency cooperation in the follow-up to the World Summit on Sustainable Development [YUN 2002, p. 821] (see p. 827), focusing on efforts in several areas, including water (see p. 1034) and energy. CEB found there was wide recognition throughout the UN system that energy use and efficiency were closely linked to climate change. It identified gaps in the programmatic reach of the institutions and the financial resources available to them to implement their mandates on energy. No single entity in the system had primary responsibility for energy, and independent approaches had been taken; as a result, a system-wide approach to addressing energy issues had not emerged. Adequate joint action on energy by the United Nations and other stakeholders would require more inclusive and broad-based arrangements than were in place. Other development actors, particularly the private sector, had compara-

tive advantages in that area and should be engaged in the follow-up efforts.

By **decision 2004/233** of 16 July, the Economic and Social Council welcomed the endorsement by the Economic Commission for Europe of the United Nations Framework Classification for Fossil Energy and Mineral Resources and decided to invite the Member States of the United Nations, international organizations and the regional commissions to ensure its worldwide application. The new classification included energy commodities such as natural gas, oil and uranium, among others, and was an extension of the earlier framework developed for solid fuels and mineral commodities.

Nuclear energy

By an August note [A/59/295], the Secretary-General transmitted to the General Assembly the 2003 report of the International Atomic Energy Agency (IAEA). Presenting the report to the Assembly on 1 November [A/59/PV.47], the IAEA Director General said that, during the past year, increasing attention was paid to the benefits of nuclear energy as an environmentally clean source of electricity, while concerns remained about waste disposal, safety and security, despite overall improvements. With 439 nuclear reactors worldwide, nuclear energy accounted for about 16 per cent of the world's electricity production, keeping pace with the steady growth in the global electricity market. Asia and Eastern Europe remained the largest centres of expansion in nuclear capacity owing to demand for electricity, existence of a well-developed industrial infrastructure and lack of indigenous alternatives in some countries.

The Agency continued to improve its ability to implement safeguards and to encourage and stimulate technological innovation related to nuclear fuel. The development and adoption of legally binding international agreements had proved to be a powerful mechanism for enhancing safety. Work progressed on amending and broadening the scope of the 1979 Convention on the Physical Protection of Nuclear Material [YUN 1979, p. 1239], to include transport, storage and use, and on the Agency's revision and updating of international nuclear safety standards, all part of IAEA efforts to enhance protection against nuclear and radiological terrorism. In services to member States, IAEA undertook more than 50 advisory and evaluation missions and convened more than 60 training courses and seminars. Despite increased attention to the security of radioactive sources, deficiencies remained and a market existed for such sources for malicious purposes.

The Director General reported that the situation in the Democratic People's Republic of Korea (DPRK) continued to pose a serious challenge to the nuclear non-proliferation regime. Since December 2002, no verification activities were performed in the DPRK and the Agency could not provide any level of assurance about the non-diversion of nuclear material. Over the course of the year, the IAEA's verification activities in the Libyan Arab Jamahiriya confirmed that the country had pursued an undeclared nuclear programme for many years. However, in December 2003, Libya renounced its programmes for nuclear weapons and other weapons of mass destruction (see p. 280) and actively cooperated with IAEA's efforts on verification. Regarding the implementation of the Treaty on the Non-Proliferation of Nuclear Weapons (NPT) safeguards agreements in Iran (see p. 548), the IAEA Board of Governors adopted several resolutions on Iran's undeclared nuclear programme and its failure to meet many of its obligations under its safeguard agreement, and urged Iran to cooperate fully with the Agency in the verification process. In 2003, IAEA had begun its verification of Iran's undeclared programme. As for Iraq, the Agency's mandate in that country remained in effect, although it was requested in March 2003 to cease its verification activities there. At that time, IAEA had found no evidence of the revival of nuclear activities (see p. 363). No progress had resulted from the Director General's consultations with the Middle East States on the application of full-scope safeguards for all nuclear activities. He also raised the possibility of the development of model agreements on establishing a nuclear-weapon-free zone in that region. The Agency continued its technical cooperation programme, including support for nuclear applications in such areas as human health, water resources management and mutation breeding of major food crops. The year 2004 marked the fiftieth anniversary of civilian nuclear power.

GENERAL ASSEMBLY ACTION

On 1 November [meeting 48], the General Assembly adopted **resolution 59/18** [draft: A/59/L.18 & Add.1] by recorded vote (123-1-67) [agenda item 14].

Report of the International Atomic Energy Agency

The General Assembly,

Having received the report of the International Atomic Energy Agency for 2003,

Taking note of the statement of the Director General of the International Atomic Energy Agency, in which he provided additional information on the main developments in the activities of the Agency during 2004,

Recognizing the importance of the work of the Agency,

Recognizing also the cooperation between the United Nations and the Agency and the Agreement governing the relationship between the United Nations and the Agency as approved by the General Conference of the Agency on 23 October 1957 and by the General Assembly in the annex to its resolution 1145(XII) of 14 November 1957,

1. *Takes note with appreciation* of the report of the International Atomic Energy Agency;

2. *Takes note* of resolutions GC(48)/RES/10A on measures to strengthen international cooperation in nuclear, radiation and waste safety, GC(48)/RES/10B on international nuclear and radiological emergency preparedness and response, GC(48)/RES/10C on transport safety, GC(48)/RES/10D on the safety and security of radioactive sources, GC(48)/RES/11 on progress on measures to protect against nuclear and radiological terrorism, GC(48)/RES/12 on strengthening of the Agency's technical cooperation activities, GC(48)/RES/13A on strengthening the Agency's activities related to nuclear science, technology and applications, GC(48)/RES/13B on support to the African Union's Pan-African Tsetse and Trypanosomosis Eradication Campaign, GC(48)/RES/13C on development of the sterile insect technique for the control or eradication of malaria-transmitting mosquitoes, GC(48)/RES/13D on a programme of action for cancer therapy, GC(48)/RES/13E on nuclear knowledge, GC(48)/RES/13F on Agency activities in the development of innovative nuclear technology, GC(48)/RES/14 on strengthening the effectiveness and improving the efficiency of the safeguards system and application of the Model Additional Protocol, GC(48)/RES/15 on implementation of the Agreement between the Agency and the Democratic People's Republic of Korea for the application of safeguards in connection with the Treaty on the Non-Proliferation of Nuclear Weapons, GC(48)/RES/16 on the application of Agency safeguards in the Middle East and decision GC(48)/DEC/10 on Israeli nuclear capabilities and threat, adopted on 24 September 2004 by the General Conference of the Agency at its forty-eighth regular session;

3. *Affirms its support* for the indispensable role of the Agency in encouraging and assisting the development and practical application of atomic energy for peaceful uses, in technology transfer to developing countries and in nuclear safety, verification and security;

4. *Appeals* to Member States to continue to support the activities of the Agency;

5. *Requests* the Secretary-General to transmit to the Director General of the Agency the records of the fifty-ninth session of the General Assembly relating to the activities of the Agency.

RECORDED VOTE ON RESOLUTION 59/18:

In favour: Algeria, Andorra, Angola, Argentina, Armenia, Austria, Azerbaijan, Bahrain, Bangladesh, Belarus, Benin, Bolivia, Bosnia and Herzegovina, Brazil, Brunei Darussalam, Bulgaria, Burkina Faso, Cameroon, Canada, Central African Republic, Chile, China, Colombia, Côte d'Ivoire, Croatia, Cuba, Cyprus, Czech Republic, Democratic Republic of the Congo, Denmark, Djibouti, Dominican Republic, Ecuador, El Salvador, Ethiopia, Finland, France, Germany, Ghana, Greece, Guatemala, Guyana, Honduras, Hungary, Iceland, India, Indonesia, Iran, Ireland, Israel, Italy, Jamaica, Japan, Jordan, Kazakhstan, Kenya, Kuwait, Lao People's Democratic Republic, Latvia, Lebanon, Libyan Arab Jamahiriya, Liechtenstein, Lithuania, Luxembourg, Malaysia, Maldives, Malta, Marshall Islands, Mexico, Monaco, Mongolia, Morocco, Mozambique, Myanmar, Nepal, Netherlands, New Zealand, Nicaragua, Nigeria, Norway, Oman, Pakistan, Panama, Paraguay, Peru, Philippines, Poland, Portugal, Qatar, Republic of Korea, Romania, Russian Federation, San Marino, Saudi Arabia, Senegal, Serbia and Montenegro, Seychelles, Singapore, Slovakia, Slovenia, South Africa, Spain, Sri Lanka, Sudan, Swaziland, Sweden, Switzerland, Syrian Arab Republic, Thailand, Timor-Leste, Togo, Tonga, Tunisia, Turkey, Ukraine, United Arab Emirates, United Kingdom, United Republic of Tanzania, United States, Vanuatu, Venezuela, Yemen, Zambia

Against: Democratic People's Republic of Korea

Abstaining: None

Natural resources

Water resources

In preparation for the twelfth session of the Commission for Sustainable Development, the Secretary-General issued a February report on freshwater management [E/CN.17/2004/4] in which he linked the issue to the goals on water set in Agenda 21 and the Millennium Declaration (MDG) [YUN 2000, p. 49]. Meeting the MDG of halving the number of people without access to safe drinking water by 2015 would require providing access to an additional 1.6 billion people by that date, estimated to require a doubling of spending in drinking water supply. That goal appeared to be attainable in many Asian countries, but not in most countries in other regions. In developing countries, most freshwater was used for agricultural irrigation, while in developed countries the largest user was industry. In both sectors, there was potential for increased efficiency in use, as well as reduction in pollution. Many countries had strengthened their integrated water resource management processes, with decentralization of some aspects of water management and increased participation of local users or water user associations and other stakeholders, frequently resulting in improved water allocations, greater efficiency of use and greater cost recovery.

The Secretary-General, in his February report [E/2004/12-E/CN.17/2004/3] on CEB efforts to coordinate UN system activities on sustainable development, covered freshwater and water and sanitation, among other things. He noted the formation in 2002 of UN-Water, bringing together the senior managers of the water-related programmes of 24 UN system entities, which provided global water assessment and policy advice. UN-Water was preparing to manage new external partnerships such as with the Global Water Partnership, the World Water Council, the Water Supply and Sanitation Council, the International Union for the Conservation of Nature, and the private sector. CEB endorsed UN-Water as the inter-agency mechanism for follow-up of the water-related decisions reached at the World Summit on Sustainable Development and the MDGs concerning freshwater. It requested UN-Water to finalize its terms of reference and modalities of work, including arrangements for participation of non-UN actors in the Summit follow-up.

The Commission also considered: the report of the African Regional Implementation Review Meeting on water, sanitation and human settlements (Addis Ababa, Ethiopia, 8-12 December 2003) [E/CN.17/2004/7/Add.1]; the report of the Regional Implementation Meeting on water, sanitation and human settlements for Asia and the Pacific [E/CN.17/2004/7/Add.2]; and discussion papers on water, sanitation and human settlements submitted by major groups [E/CN.17/2004/10 & Add.1].

Communication. On 13 February [E/CN.17/2004/14], Norway transmitted the report of an international conference on the theme "Water for the poorest", held in Stavanger, Norway, on 4 and 5 November 2003. The conference made recommendations for priority actions that could expand and accelerate the MDG and the World Summit's water and poverty agenda.

GENERAL ASSEMBLY ACTION

On 22 December [meeting 75], the General Assembly, on the recommendation of the Second (Economic and Social) Committee [A/59/483/Add.1], adopted **resolution 59/228** without vote [agenda item 85(*a*)].

Activities undertaken during the International Year of Freshwater, 2003, preparations for the International Decade for Action, "Water for Life", 2005-2015, and further efforts to achieve the sustainable development of water resources

The General Assembly,

Recalling its resolution 55/196 of 20 December 2000, by which it proclaimed 2003 the International Year of Freshwater, and its resolution 58/217 of 23 December 2003, by which it proclaimed that the International Decade for Action, "Water for Life", 2005-2015, would commence on World Water Day, 22 March 2005,

Emphasizing that water is critical for sustainable development, including environmental integrity and the eradication of poverty and hunger, and is indispensable for human health and well-being,

Recalling the provisions of Agenda 21, the Programme for the Further Implementation of Agenda 21 adopted at its nineteenth special session, the Plan of Implementation of the World Summit on Sustainable Development ("Johannesburg Plan of Implementation") and the decisions of the Economic and Social Council and of the Commission on Sustainable Development at its sixth session relating to freshwater,

Reaffirming the internationally agreed development goals on water and sanitation, including those contained in the United Nations Millennium Declaration, and determined to achieve the goal to halve, by 2015, the proportion of people who are unable to reach or to afford safe drinking water, and the goals set out in the Johannesburg Plan of Implementation to halve the proportion of people without access to basic sanitation as well as to develop integrated water resources management and water efficiency plans by 2005, with support to developing countries,

Taking note of the Ministerial Declaration, entitled "Message from the Lake Biwa and Yodo River Basin", adopted on 23 March 2003 at the Ministerial Conference of the Third World Water Forum, held in Kyoto, Japan, and the Dushanbe Water Appeal, proclaimed on 1 September 2003 at the International Freshwater Forum, held in Dushanbe from 29 August to 1 September 2003,

Noting that the Fourth World Water Forum will take place in Mexico in March 2006,

Taking note with interest of the establishment of the Advisory Board on Water and Sanitation by the Secretary-General, and looking forward to its contribution to the mobilization of efforts and resources towards the implementation of the commitments, goals and targets agreed upon in those areas,

1. *Takes note* of the report of the Secretary-General;

2. *Welcomes* the activities related to freshwater undertaken by Member States, the United Nations Secretariat and the organizations of the United Nations system, inter alia, through inter-agency work, as well as contributions from major groups, for the observance of the International Year of Freshwater, 2003;

3. *Encourages* Member States, the Secretariat, organizations of the United Nations system and major groups to continue their efforts to achieve the internationally agreed water-related goals contained in Agenda 21, the Programme for the Further Implementation of Agenda 21, the United Nations Millennium Declaration and the Johannesburg Plan of Implementation;

4. *Welcomes* the work of the twelfth session of the Commission on Sustainable Development, and looks forward to the upcoming thirteenth session of the Commission on the thematic cluster of issues on water, sanitation and human settlements;

5. *Invites* the Secretary-General to take appropriate actions in organizing the activities of the International Decade for Action, "Water for Life", 2005-2015, taking into account the results of the International Year of Freshwater and the work of the Commission on Sustainable Development at its twelfth and thirteenth sessions;

6. *Calls upon* the relevant United Nations bodies, the specialized agencies, regional commissions and other organizations of the United Nations system to step up their efforts to deliver a coordinated response in order to make the Decade a decade of delivering promises through the use of existing resources and voluntary funds;

7. *Notes with interest* the partnership initiatives on water and sanitation undertaken within the framework of the World Summit on Sustainable Development and in the follow-up to the Summit and in accordance with the criteria and guidelines adopted by the Commission on Sustainable Development at its eleventh session;

8. *Requests* the Secretary-General to report to the General Assembly at its sixtieth session on the implementation of the present resolution, as well as on the activities planned by the Secretary-General and other relevant organizations of the United Nations system for the Decade;

9. *Decides* to consider, at its sixtieth session, the future arrangements for the review of the implementation of the Decade, including the possibility of a review on a biennial or triennial basis or a mid-term review.

Cartography

UN Regional Cartographic Conference for Asia and the Pacific

The Economic and Social Council, by **decision 2004/301** of 23 July, took note of the Secretary-General's report on the Sixteenth United Nations Regional Cartographic Conference for Asia and the Pacific (Okinawa, Japan, 14-18 July 2003) [YUN 2003, p. 1035]. On the same date, the Council endorsed the Conference's recommendation (**decision 2004/304**) that the Seventeenth United Nations Regional Cartographic Conference for Asia and the Pacific be convened for five working days in 2006, with a primary focus on the contribution of cartography and geographic information in support of the implementation of Agenda 21. The Council requested the Secretary-General to implement the other recommendations made by the sixteenth conference, in particular, that the United Nations continue to support surveying, mapping and spatial data infrastructure activities in the Asian and Pacific region and facilitate the participation of the least developed countries and the small island developing States of the region.

Standardization of geographical names

In accordance with Economic and Social Council decision 2003/294 [YUN 2003, p. 1035], the Secretary-General reported on the twenty-second session of the UN Group of Experts on Geographical Names (New York, 20-29 April) [E/2004/64, GEGN/22]. The Group of Experts considered the reports of the nine working groups and 18 linguistic/geographical divisions on their regions and on progress made in the standardization of geographical names since the Eighth UN Conference on the Standardization of Geographical Names [YUN, 2002, p. 1029]. The Group of Experts addressed organizational matters for the Ninth Conference (2007), and commenced planning for implementing its recommendations. The Group proposed that the Council endorse its recommendation that its twenty-third session be held for six days in 2006 to prepare for the ninth Conference and requested the Secretary-General to implement that recommendation.

The Council, by **decision 2004/301** of 23 July, took note of the report on the twenty-second session of the Group of Experts and by **decision 2004/303**, endorsed its recommendation that the twenty-third (2006) session be held in Vienna.

Chapter VII

Environment and human settlements

In 2004, the United Nations and the international community continued to protect the environment through legally binding instruments and the activities of the United Nations Environment Programme (UNEP).

The UNEP Governing Council/fifth Global Ministerial Environment Forum held its eighth special session on the theme of the environmental dimensions of water, sanitation and human settlements, as part of its follow-up to the 2002 World Summit on Sustainable Development. The summary of its consultations—the Jeju Initiative—addressed key environmental dimensions and concepts for meeting the water-related targets of the 2000 Millennium Declaration. The meeting also adopted decisions relating to international environmental governance; small island developing States; regional implementation of UNEP's work programme; and waste management.

The High-level Open-ended Intergovernmental Working Group on an Intergovernmental Strategic Plan for Technology Support and Capacity-building, established by GC/GMEF in March, adopted in December the Bali Strategic Plan for Technology Support and Capacity-building, designed to provide targeted long- and short-term measures for support in those areas to developing countries and economies in transition. The first Global Women's Assembly on Environment: Women as the Voice for the Environment, held in October, adopted a manifesto calling for urgent action to achieve sustainable development and made recommendations for action, among others, on gender issues with regard to global environmental change.

The Conference of the Parties to the 1992 United Nations Framework Convention on Climate Change adopted the Buenos Aires programme of work on measures dealing with adaptation and response to climate change. The seventh meeting of the Conference of the Parties to the 1992 Convention on Biological Diversity adopted the Addis Ababa Principles and Guidelines for the Sustainable Use of Biodiversity. The 1998 Rotterdam Convention on the Prior Informed Consent Procedure for Certain Hazardous Chemicals and Pesticides in International Trade, which entered into force on 24 February, held its first Conference of the Parties to the Convention in September. The 2001 Stockholm Convention on Persistent Organic Pollutants also entered into force on 17 May.

The United Nations Human Settlements Programme (UN-Habitat) continued to support the implementation of the 1996 Habitat Agenda; the 2000 UN Millennium Declaration; the 2001 Declaration on Cities and Other Human Settlements in the New Millennium; and the human settlements-related elements of the Johannesburg Plan of Implementation of the 2002 World Summit on Sustainable Development. It convened the second session of the World Urban Forum in September. In 2004, UN-Habitat had 95 technical cooperation programmes and projects under execution in 56 countries.

Environment

UN Environment Programme

Governing Council/Ministerial Forum

The fifth Global Ministerial Environment Forum (GMEF), also serving as the eighth special session of the Governing Council (GC) of the United Nations Environment Programme (UNEP), was held at Jeju, Republic of Korea, from 29 to 31 March [A/59/25].

GC/GMEF discussed the follow-up to the 2002 World Summit on Sustainable Development [YUN 2002, p. 821]: UNEP's contribution to the twelfth (2004) session of the Commission on Sustainable Development (see p. 827) in the form of ministerial consultations on the theme "Environmental dimensions of water, sanitation and human settlements". The theme was addressed through three focus areas: integrated ecosystem approaches by the year 2005; water and sanitation; and water, health and poverty. A summary of the consultations, entitled the Jeju Initiative (see p. 1044), was annexed to the GC/GMEF report.

The Committee of the Whole (29-31 March) considered assessment, monitoring and early warning: the state of the environment (see p. 1041); outcomes of intergovernmental meetings of relevance to GC/GMEF [UNEP/GCSS.VII/3]; and international environmental governance: implementation of decisions of the World Summit and the seventh (2002) special session of GC/GMEF [YUN 2002, p. 1030] on the 2002 report of the Open-ended Intergovernmental Group of Ministers or Their Representatives on International Environmental Governance [ibid., p. 1032] (see p. 1038). The Committee's report was annexed to the Governing Council's report.

On 23 July, the Economic and Social Council took note of the Governing Council's report on its eighth special session (**decision 2004/301**).

Subsidiary body

In 2004, the Committee of Permanent Representatives, which was open to representatives of all UN Member States and members of specialized agencies, held an extraordinary meeting on 26 February and regular meetings on 15 April, 1 July, 1 September [UNEP/GC.23/INF/4], and 7 December [UNEP/CPR/90/2]. The Committee discussed, among other matters, preparations for and the outcome of the Governing Council's eighth (2004) special session, implementation of UNEP's programme of work and the relevant decisions of the Governing Council's twenty-first [YUN 2002, p. 1030] and twenty-second [YUN 2003, p. 1036] sessions, UNEP relations with the United Nations Office at Nairobi (UNON), and the status of the Environment Fund.

GENERAL ASSEMBLY ACTION

On 22 December [meeting 75], the General Assembly, on the recommendation of the Second (Economic and Financial) Committee [A/59/483], adopted **resolution 59/226** without vote [agenda item 85].

Report of the Governing Council of the United Nations Environment Programme on its eighth special session

The General Assembly,

Recalling its resolutions 2997(XXVII) of 15 December 1972, 53/242 of 28 July 1999, 56/193 of 21 December 2001, 57/251 of 20 December 2002 and 58/209 of 23 December 2003,

Taking into account Agenda 21 and the Plan of Implementation of the World Summit on Sustainable Development ("Johannesburg Plan of Implementation"),

Reaffirming the role of the United Nations Environment Programme as the principal body within the United Nations system in the field of environment, which should take into account, within its mandate, the sustainable development needs of developing countries as well as countries with economies in transition,

Recalling the provisions of the Johannesburg Plan of Implementation on the full implementation of the outcomes of the decision on international environmental governance adopted by the Governing Council of the United Nations Environment Programme at its seventh special session,

Reiterating the need to ensure that capacity-building and technology support to developing countries, as

well as countries with economies in transition, in environment-related fields, remain important components of the work of the United Nations Environment Programme, and noting in this regard the ongoing work of the High-level Open-ended Intergovernmental Working Group to prepare an intergovernmental strategic plan for technology support and capacity-building,

Recalling its resolutions 57/251 and 58/209, by which Member States, the Governing Council and the relevant bodies of the United Nations system were encouraged to submit their comments, in a timely manner, on the important but complex issue of establishing universal membership of the Governing Council/ Global Ministerial Environment Forum, including its legal, political, institutional, financial and system-wide implications, in order to contribute to the report of the Secretary-General to be submitted to the General Assembly for consideration before its sixtieth session,

1. *Takes note* of the report of the Governing Council of the United Nations Environment Programme on its eighth special session and the decisions contained therein;

2. *Also takes note* of the report of the Secretary-General submitted pursuant to its resolutions 57/251 and 58/209;

3. *Notes* that the Governing Council, at its eighth special session, discussed all components of the recommendations on international environmental governance, as contained in its decision SS.VII/1, and notes the continued discussion scheduled for its twenty-third session;

4. *Emphasizes* the need for the United Nations Environment Programme, within its mandate, to further contribute to sustainable development programmes, the implementation of Agenda 21 and the Johannesburg Plan of Implementation at all levels and to the work of the Commission on Sustainable Development, bearing in mind the mandate of the Commission on Sustainable Development;

5. *Calls upon* all countries to further engage in the negotiations of the intergovernmental strategic plan for technology support and capacity-building with a view to its adoption at the twenty-third session of the Governing Council, in February 2005;

6. *Notes* the differences in the views expressed so far on the important but complex issue of establishing universal membership for the Governing Council/ Global Ministerial Environment Forum, notes also the upcoming consideration of the question of universal membership by the Council/Forum at its twenty-third session, encourages Member States, the Governing Council and the relevant bodies of the United Nations system that have not yet done so to submit their comments to the Secretariat on the important but complex issue of establishing universal membership for the Council/Forum, including the legal, political, institutional, financial and system-wide implications, as their contribution to the report of the Secretary-General and requests the Secretary-General to submit a report incorporating those views to the Assembly for consideration at its sixty-first session;

7. *Emphasizes* the need to further enhance coordination and cooperation among the relevant United Nations organizations in the promotion of the environmental dimension of sustainable development, and in

this respect welcomes the continued participation of the United Nations Environment Programme in the United Nations Development Group;

8. *Calls upon* the United Nations Environment Programme to continue to contribute, within its mandate and as a member of the Inter-Agency Task Force, to the preparations for the International Meeting to Review the Implementation of the Programme of Action for the Sustainable Development of Small Island Developing States, to be held in Mauritius from 10 to 14 January 2005;

9. *Notes* the decision of the Governing Council to discuss at its twenty-third session issues related to domestic, industrial and hazardous waste management, in particular regarding capacity-building and technology support, and, in that context, to consider innovative ways of mobilizing financial resources from all appropriate sources to support the efforts of developing countries and countries with economies in transition in this area;

10. *Also notes* the decision of the Governing Council to review at its twenty-third session the implementation of the conclusions and recommendations contained in the report of the intergovernmental consultation on the strengthening of the scientific base of the United Nations Environment Programme;

11. *Reiterates* the need for stable, adequate and predictable financial resources for the United Nations Environment Programme, and in accordance with resolution 2997(XXVII) underlines the need to consider the adequate reflection of all administrative and management costs of the Environment Programme in the context of the United Nations regular budget;

12. *Welcomes* the progress made in the implementation of the provisions of section III.B. of the appendix to decision SS.VII/1 of the Governing Council on strengthening the role and financial situation of the United Nations Environment Programme, including the significant broadening of the donor base and increasing total contributions to the Environment Fund, and, in this regard, notes that the Governing Council will review the implementation of those provisions at its twenty-third session;

13. *Requests* the Secretary-General to keep the resource needs of the United Nations Environment Programme and the United Nations Office at Nairobi under review so as to permit the delivery, in an effective manner, of necessary services to the Environment Programme and to the other United Nations organs and organizations in Nairobi.

International environmental governance

In response to 2002 [YUN 2002, p. 1033] and 2003 [YUN 2003, p. 1039] Governing Council decisions, the Executive Director, in a February overview report on international governance [UNEP/GCSS.VIII/5], detailed progress achieved on the issues of universal membership for GC/GMEF (see below); strengthening UNEP's scientific base (see p. 1041); the development of an intergovernmental strategic plan for technology support and capacity-building (see p. 1039); strengthening UNEP financing (see p. 1049); multilateral environmental agreements (see p. 1050); and en-

hanced coordination across the UN system and the Environmental Management Group (see below).

He also submitted, pursuant to General Assembly resolution 57/251 [YUN 2002, p. 1031] and the above-mentioned 2003 Council decision, in March [UNEP/GCSS.VIII/INF/6], a synthesis of the views of Governments concerning the question of universal membership of GC/GMEF. Of the 19 replies received as of 1 March, including one representing the 25 members and acceding States of the European Union, 13 expressed their support for universal membership, 3 were opposed, 2 others had not yet decided their positions, and one indicated that the matter was being positively pursued. The views and comments presented in the note focused on the legality, legitimacy and practical and financial implications of universal membership.

On 31 March [A/59/25 (dec. SS.VIII/1, section I)], the Council requested the Executive Director to continue to invite views on the universal membership of GC/GMEF and to convey them to the Secretary-General as an input for his report requested by the Assembly in resolutions 57/251 and 58/209 [YUN 2003, p. 1037]. He should report on the matter at the twenty-third (2005) GC/GMEF session.

Report of Secretary-General. In response to Assembly resolutions 57/251 and 58/209, the Secretary-General submitted his report in August [A/59/262] on establishing universal membership for GC/GMEF, which outlined consideration of the issue by GC/GMEF. The Secretary-General recommended that the Assembly encourage Member States, the Governing Council and the relevant UN system bodies to submit their comments on the issue to the UNEP Executive Director, including its legal, political, institutional, financial and system-wide implications, for incorporation in the Secretary-General's report to be submitted to the Assembly for consideration at its sixtieth (2005) session.

The Assembly took action on the report in resolution 59/226 (see p. 1037).

Environmental Management Group

The Environmental Management Group (EMG), an inter-agency advisory group set up in 1999 to coordinate UN system activities in addressing the major challenges in the UNEP work programme [YUN 1999, p. 974], held its sixth (Geneva, 6 February), seventh (New York, 20 April), eighth (Nairobi, Kenya, 1 September) and ninth (Geneva, 8 November) meetings in 2004.

A February report of the Executive Director [UNEP/GCSS.VIII/5/Add.2] summarized EMG's work from mid-2003 to February 2004, covering activities relating to its contribution to major intergovernmental processes, including international environmental governance, implementation of the outcomes of the 2002 World Summit on Sustainable Development [YUN 2002, p. 821] in the areas of water, sanitation and human settlements (see p. 1044) and strengthening of UNEP's scientific base (see p. 1041). The report also discussed planned activities; links with intergovernmental forums and other UN system coordination mechanisms; and the functioning of the EMG secretariat. The work of EMG's issue management group on the harmonization of information management and reporting for biodiversity-related conventions, established in 2001, were detailed in an annex to the report. In February, EMG established an issue management group on environmental capacity-building to discuss the issue further and to develop a specific, time-bound programme of work, which would consider, as its immediate focus, the development of an environmental capacity-building resource library.

A February note by the Executive Director [UNEP/GCSS.VIII/INF/5] contained information on the activities of EMG members in the field of water, focusing on environmental aspects and the ecosystem approach, as a contribution to the eighth (2004) special session of GC/GMEF and the twelfth (2004) session of the Commission on Sustainable Development (see p. 827).

Governing Council action. On 31 March [dec. SS.VIII/1, section VI], the Governing Council requested the Executive Director to continue to promote UN-system coordination of environmental activities, in particular those relevant to UN system operations, through EMG's work. It decided to convey the report on EMG's work to the General Assembly as an annex to the 2004 report of GC/GMEF. The Executive Director was requested to submit a report to GC/GMEF in 2005, including a comprehensive assessment of the location of the EMG secretariat, taking into account, among other things, current efforts to strengthen UNON—the headquarters of UNEP and the United Nations Human Settlements Programme (UN-Habitat)—and EMG's mandate and membership.

Reports of Executive Director. In response to Governing Council decision [SS.VIII/1, section VI] (above), the Executive Director, in a December report [UNEP/GC.23/7], summarized EMG's work under its 2004-2005 work programme and outlined its 2006-2007 work programme.

Environmental capacity-building and sustainable procurement for the UN system constituted the bulk of EMG's programme of work for 2004. With regard to environmental capacity-building, EMG focused on defining its role as a facilitator for more coordinated exchange of information and data on lessons learned, experiences and

methodologies within the UN system, and on the possibility of establishing a resource library. Two pilot situation/needs analyses in biodiversity and chemicals management capacity-building, prepared in cooperation with the UNEP World Conservation Monitoring Centre (see p. 1063) and the United Nations Institute for Training and Research, constituted EMG's contribution to the third meeting (Bali, Indonesia, 2-4 December) of the High-level Open-ended Intergovernmental Working Group on an Intergovernmental Strategic Plan for Technology Support and Capacity-building (see p. 1040). The main findings of both studies were discussed in the report, as were EMG's contributions to the development of a strategic plan on technology support and capacity-building (see below).

On the question of sustainable procurement, EMG discussed how it could best assist in the development of sustainable procurement policies and environmental management programmes throughout the UN system. It established an issue management group with the UNEP Division of Technology, Industry and Economics as the task manager, with other agencies, to survey current regulations and activities and address the development of supplier codes of conduct and training.

Among its future activities, EMG would support the implementation of the internationally agreed goals of the UN Millennium Declaration, adopted in General Assembly resolution 55/2 [YUN 2000, p. 49], in the areas of its mandate; continue work on environment-related capacity-building; and address specific issues related to urban poverty and environment, as requested by UN-Habitat.

Strategic plan on technology support and capacity-building

In response to a 2003 Governing Council decision [YUN 2003, p. 1038], the Executive Director submitted in February [UNEP/GCSS.VIII/5/Add.1 & Corr.1] the elements for an intergovernmental strategic plan on technology support and capacity-building, as called for in a 2002 decision of the Council [YUN 2002, p. 1033].

On 31 March [dec. SS.VIII/I, section III], the Governing Council established a high-level, open-ended intergovernmental working group of GC/GMEF to prepare an intergovernmental strategic plan for technology support and capacity-building, for its consideration in 2005. The group would consider, among other things, the draft elements for the plan submitted by the Executive Director (see above). The Council requested the Executive Director to seek additional financial resources to facilitate the participation of developing countries in the Group's meetings. It invited Governments, relevant organizations and stakeholders, in particular the United Nations Development Programme (UNDP) and the Global Environment Facility (GEF) (see p. 1046), other relevant bodies and UN system organizations, international financial institutions and the secretariats of multilateral environmental agreements, to contribute to the group's work; and regional and subregional ministerial environmental forums to submit for the group's consideration, views on their technology support and capacity-building needs. The Executive Director would make available reports, including an inventory of UNEP's capacity-building and technology support activities, to assist the working group.

Intergovernmental working group. The High-level Open-ended Intergovernmental Working Group on an Intergovernmental Strategic Plan for Technology Support and Capacity-building held its first (New York, 25 June) [UNEP/IEG/IGSP/1/5], second (Nairobi, 2-4 September) [UNEP/IEG/IGSP/2/4], and third (Bali, Indonesia, 2-4 December) [UNEP/IEG/IGSP/3/4] sessions.

The working group had before it the Executive Director's June report [UNEP/IEG/IGSP/1/3/Rev.1] on perspectives on needs and gaps to be taken into account in the development of the intergovernmental strategic plan for technology support and capacity-building, which presented a set of issues to be addressed; the report of meetings of the working group of the Committee of Permanent Representatives (5 and 19 May and 2 June) [UNEP/IEG/IGSP/1/2] to consider the Committee's contribution to the intergovernmental working group; outcomes of the expert consultation (Geneva, 17-18 June) and civil society consultation (Nairobi, 21-22 June) [UNEP/IEG/IGSP/1/4]; the report of the civil society consultation [UNEP/IEG/IGSP/ CS/1/2]; an inventory of UNEP capacity-building and technology support activities [UNEP/IEG/ IGSP/2/3]; and a compilation of proposals by Governments [UNEP/IEG/IGSP/3/2].

The working group also considered notes by the Executive Director on an overview of UNEP activities relating to technology support and capacity-building in the fields of technology, industry and economics [UNEP/IEG/IGSP/1/INF/2] and environmental law [UNEP/IEG/IGSP/1/INF/3]; and secretariat notes on the submission by the African Ministerial Conference on the Environment (AMCEN) to the working group [UNEP/IEG/ IGSP/2/INF/1], the strategic approach to enhance capacity-building prepared by GEF and approved by the GEF Council in 2003 [UNEP/IEG/IGSP/ 1/INF/4], and the Chair's summary of a meeting hosted by UNEP and the Republic of Korea on

capacity-building for integrated policy design and implementation for sustainable development (Jeju, Republic of Korea, 27-28 March) [UNEP/IEG/IGSP/1/INF/5].

The Chair of the working group proposed a draft framework for the plan [UNEP/IEG/IGSP/2/2] based on the elements contained in the Executive Director's February paper (see p. 1039), the discussions at the working group's first session and inputs from related processes, including the consultations of the Committee of Permanent Representatives, and of experts and civil society held in June (see above).

Bali Strategic Plan. The Bali Strategic Plan for Technology Support and Capacity-building [UNEP/GC.23/6/Add.1 & Corr.1], adopted by the High-level Open-ended Intergovernmental Working Group on an Intergovernmental Strategic Plan for Technology Support and Capacity-building, at its third session on 4 December, was intended as an intergovernmentally agreed approach to strengthen technology support and capacity-building in developing countries and countries with economies in transition, including reinforcing UNEP's role and building on areas where it had comparative advantage and expertise. Its objectives were to: strengthen the capacity of Governments of developing countries and countries with economies in transition; provide systematic, targeted, short- and long-term measures for technology support and capacity-building; ensure the participation of developing countries and countries with economies in transition in the negotiations on multilateral environmental agreements; ensure that principles of transparency and accountability were integrated in all activities; integrate gender-mainstreaming strategies and education and training for women in formulating relevant policies, and promote women's participation in environmental decision-making; enable collaboration with stakeholders and provide a basis for a comprehensive approach to developing partnerships; emphasize the identification and dissemination of best practices and the fostering of entrepreneurship and partnerships; enhance UNEP's delivery of technology support and capacity-building to developing countries and countries with economies in transition; strengthen cooperation among UNEP, multilateral environmental agreement secretariats, and other bodies engaged in environmental capacity-building, including UNDP and GEF; and promote, facilitate and finance access to and support of environmentally sound technologies and know-how, especially for developing countries and countries with economies in transition.

The Plan included measures for implementation at the national, regional and global levels, including the strengthening of regional UNEP offices to facilitate its effective support. It included a list of cross-cutting issues and thematic areas to be addressed, among which were the strengthening of national and regional environmental or environment-related institutions; development of national environmental law; and strengthening civil society and private sector cooperation. The Plan also supported South-South cooperation and the implementation of the outcomes of the intergovernmental consultation on strengthening UNEP's scientific base (see below). It provided for the reporting of its implementation to GC/GMEF and outlined coordination and evaluation mechanisms. A strategic partnership between UNEP and GEF would be developed to further the goals of the plan and submitted to GC/GMEF for adoption. Activities under the plan would be implemented through the Environmental Fund and resources mobilized from other sources, including public-private partnerships.

UNEP activities

A March policy statement of the Executive Director [UNEP/GCSS.VII/7] outlined UNEP's efforts with regard to the follow-up to the 2002 World Summit on Sustainable Development [YUN 2002, p. 821]; strengthening its work in environmental assessment and early warning; enabling countries to meet their commitments made at the 2000 Millennium Summit [YUN 2000, p. 47] and the World Summit; and international environmental governance. The challenge before the eighth (2004) GC/GMEF special session was to provide a substantive environmental perspective on the implementation of the environmental pillar of sustainable development in the fields of water, sanitation and human settlements; sustain momentum of implementation required to meet the goals and targets of the Millennium Declaration [ibid., p. 49] and World Summit; and implement measures related to international environmental governance.

Monitoring and assessment

Responding to a 2003 Governing Council decision [YUN 2003, p. 1039] initiating a consultative process on strengthening UNEP's scientific base, also known as the Science Initiative, the Executive Director submitted to the Council a synthesis [UNEP/SI/IGC/2] of 122 substantive responses received as at 12 November 2003 from Governments, intergovernmental organizations, NGOs and scientific institutions on the likely gaps and types of assessment needs with respect to the environment, how UNEP and other organizations were meeting those needs, and current options

for meeting any unfulfilled needs within UNEP's mandate. The synthesis report identified gaps and types of needs including: assessment of existing international intergovernmental challenges and of inter-linkages; scientific credibility, legitimacy and relevance in the assessment process; cost-effectiveness, cooperation and strengthening of existing institutions; and developing country participation and capacity-building. Options for meeting the needs within UNEP's mandate included strengthening UNEP cooperation with scientific institutions and academia, the operations of inter-agency cooperation mechanisms, and local and regional capacities for integrated environmental assessment and enhanced capacity-building, technology transfer and increased financial support.

On 26 January [UNEP/GCSS.VIII/5/Add.3], the Executive Director updated his earlier synthesis report and in February [UNEP/GCSS.VIII/INF.8] submitted a draft report, prepared by consultants, analysing the additional questions regarding the strengthening of UNEP's scientific base posed by its secretariat.

Governing Council action. On 31 March [dec. SS.VIII/1, section II], the Governing Council requested the Executive Director to evaluate the conclusions and recommendations contained in the report of the intergovernmental consultation and report to GC/GMEF in 2005, at which time it would review also their implementation. It invited both developed and developing countries in a position to do so and other partners active in development to provide additional funding for implementing the conclusions and recommendations, in particular those related to participation by, capacity-building in and support to subglobal assessments in developing countries and countries with economies in transition.

Post-conflict assessments

In November [UNEP/GC.23/3/Add.2], the Executive Director described progress by the UNEP Post-Conflict Assessment Unit in implementing the 2003 Governing Council decision on post-conflict assessment [YUN 2003, p. 1039] in Afghanistan, Bosnia and Herzegovina, Haiti, Iraq, Liberia, Serbia and Montenegro and the Sudan. In Afghanistan, the Unit was implementing a comprehensive capacity- and institution-building programme. It participated in a United Nations Development Group (UNDG)/World Bank assessment mission to Haiti, and, in Iraq, it conducted a desk study on the environment and organized six round tables to coordinate activities among key stakeholders. It was also the focal point for cross-cutting issues on the environment within the context of the joint United Nations/World

Bank mission to assess rehabilitation and transitional recovery needs in the Sudan. UNEP was developing a proposal to strengthen environmental administration in Liberia.

In support of the United Nations Compensation Commission, UNEP provided eight review reports of environmental studies by claimant countries. A December note by the Executive Director [UNEP/GC.23/INF/20] contained additional information on UNEP's post-conflict assessment activities.

Support to Africa

In response to a 2003 Governing Council decision [YUN 2003, p. 1040], the Executive Director, in a November report on meeting substantial environmental challenges in Africa and other regions [UNEP/GC.23/3/Add.7], stated that UNEP provided institutional support for the establishment of the interim secretariat of the environment initiative of the New Partnership for Africa's Development (NEPAD) [YUN 2002, p. 1035], which targeted desertification, wetland conservation, invasive alien species, coastal management, global warming, transboundary conservation areas, environmental governance and financing. It also initiated the implementation phase of the capacity-building programme of the Action Plan for the implementation of the NEPAD environment initiative.

UNEP continued to support the African Ministerial Conference on the Environment (AMCEN), especially the organization of its tenth regular session (Sirte, Libyan Arab Jamahiriya, 26-30 June), which provided policy guidance on the environment in Africa. UNEP gave support to the Bureau of the African Ministers' Council on Water (AMCOW), which was part of the NEPAD environment initiative, the consultative processes of its Technical Advisory Committee and the organization of AMCOW's fourth ordinary session (Kampala, Uganda, 4-6 November). Through a memorandum of understanding signed between UNEP and Kenya's National Environmental Management Authority, support was given to the establishment of the NEPAD office in Kenya, in the coordination of coastal and marine sub-theme of the NEPAD environment initiative.

UNEP conducted several reviews and assessments of land-based sources of pollution and their impacts on the physical environment and human lives. It also provided support to Africa for the implementation of a number of multilateral environmental agreements and participation in international forums. It supported sectoral and cross-cutting activities in Africa including in the areas of trade and environment; cleaner production and sustainable consumption; environmental law; post-conflict efforts, including a desk study on Liberia; integrated water resources management; the ecosystem approach to dryland management; and the Great Apes Survival Project Partnership.

Pursuant to another 2003 Governing Council decision [YUN 2003, p. 1040], the Executive Director's report included information on poverty and the environment in Africa. UNEP developed a four-year project aimed at increasing African countries' capacities to mainstream environmental and ecosystem considerations in their development plans, thereby creating an enabling environment for poverty eradication. The project was initiated in Kenya, Mozambique, Rwanda, Uganda and the United Republic of Tanzania, and was scheduled to begin in Mali and Mauritania in 2005. UNEP developed a global partnership on the issue in cooperation with the UNDP Poverty and Environment Initiative. At the national level, UNEP also worked with UNDP country offices and with the World Bank's ongoing country assessment strategies and the establishment of its poverty reduction credits.

In 2004, 20 UNEP/GEF projects devoted exclusively to Africa were approved, with total funding of $64.6 million, including $20.4 million in GEF resources. UNEP continued to support African countries in the development of the Action Plan for implementation of the NEPAD environment initiative through a GEF-funded medium-sized project.

Water policy and strategy

UNEP's updated water policy and strategy, whose overall goals were: improved assessment and awareness of environmental water issues, environmental management of basins, coastal and marine waters and cooperation and coordination between UNEP and others in the international water sector, was submitted by the Executive Director in a November report [UNEP/GC.23/3/Add.5], pursuant to a 2003 Governing Council decision [YUN 2003, p. 1041]. The updated policy and strategy also included a revitalized environmentally sound management of inland waters programme, developed in 1985 [YUN 1985, p. 814], to be known as the Programme for the Environmentally Sound Management of Freshwater (EMWA). The water policy and strategy was designed to yield results in, among other areas, global and regional assessments of the state of major priority aquatic ecosystems, with a view to developing appropriate policy responses, and strengthened integrated management of internationally shared basins, marine and costal areas, using multisectoral approaches. The Governing Council would conduct regular reviews to gauge progress in the stated objectives under the three key components of the policy and strategy: assessment, management and coordination.

A November note by the Executive Director [UNEP/GC.23/INF/25] presented the key policy issues, developments and processes that were taken into account in updating the water policy and strategy, and EMWA. The Council was to review the policy and strategy in 2005.

The atmosphere

UNEP was engaged in a number of national-level activities to reduce the vulnerability of least developed countries and small island developing States to climate change. Under the Assessment of Impacts and Adaptation to Climate Change, a global initiative of UNEP, the World Meteorological Organization, and the Intergovernmental Panel on Climate Change (see p. 1057) for advancing scientific understanding of climate change vulnerabilities and adaptation options in developing countries, 24 regional studies were under way in 46 developing countries. Other projects included integrating vulnerability and adaptation to climate change into sustainable development planning in Southern and Eastern Africa.

Under its Energy Programme, UNEP addressed the environmental consequences of energy production and use, including global climate change and local air pollution, focusing on promoting policies that placed energy and transport within a broader sustainable development context.

Environment and sustainable development

In response to a 2003 Governing Council decision on the sustainable development of Small Island Developing States (SIDS) [YUN 2003, p. 1042], a report of the Executive Director [UNEP/GCSS.VIII/6] outlined modalities to: strengthen the institutional capacity of SIDS; increase funding for UNEP's SIDS-related activities during the 2004-2005 biennium; and provide focused support for the development and execution of partnership initiatives. The modalities, which were framed within the context of UNEP's substantive programmes and projects consisted of, among other things, the organization of thematic workshops, the elaboration and dissemination of technical papers and the provision of technical assistance.

On 31 March [dec. SS.VIII/2], the Governing Council requested the Executive Director to prepare a report on the outcome of the upcoming international meeting (Mauritius, 10-14 January 2005) for a ten-year review of the 1994 Barbados Programme of Action for the Sustainable Development of Small Island Developing States [YUN 1994, p. 783] (see p. 858) for review in 2005 in the context of UNEP's mandate.

In response to the decision, the Executive Director in November, submitted a preliminary report [UNEP/GC.23/3/Add.6] describing UNEP's mandate for SIDS-related activities, background on the international meeting, and UNEP's contributions. An updated report would be issued following the meeting's conclusion.

Follow-up to World Summit on Sustainable Development (2002)

Pursuant to a 2003 Governing Council decision [YUN 2003, p. 1043], a December report of the Executive Director [UNEP/GC.23/5] provided an overview of UNEP activities to implement the Johannesburg Plan of Implementation, adopted at the World Summit on Sustainable Development [YUN 2002, p. 821], in the areas of water, sanitation and human settlements (see p. 1044); poverty, gender and the environment; technology support and capacity-building (see p. 1039); regional support; international environmental governance (see p. 1038); and other cross-cutting and thematic areas.

In other areas, a November report of the Executive Director [UNEP/GC.23/3/Add.7] included information on UNEP's role in strengthening regional activities and cooperation in the Economic Cooperation Organization (ECO) region (Western and Central Asia). The report described UNEP's activities in the areas identified for cooperation with ECO in a memorandum of understanding signed between the two organizations on 18 August, namely, environmentally sound and renewable energy services and resources; capacity-building services in environmental law, environmental education and ecotourism; and environmental assessment services.

Also in November [UNEP/GC.23/INF/23], the Executive Director reported on the implementation of a 2003 Governing Council decision on environment and cultural diversity [YUN 2003, p. 1043]. The report contained the results of the survey on the subject, which was undertaken in cooperation with UNESCO and the secretariat of the 1992 Convention on Biological Diversity (CBD) [YUN 1992, p. 638]. Among the objectives of the survey were to understand if safeguarding cultural diversity was a prerequisite to preserving the environment, and to reveal the level of diversity and interlinkages between the environment and culture and their role in programmes and activities. The survey concluded that it was becoming clear that the link between cultural and biological diversity was often an inextricable one, and that it was necessary to think of preserving the world's biological and cultural diversity as an integrated goal. Fostering a convergence of perspectives required strengthening the links among various fields of research and applied work involved in diversity conservation. As a way forward, the report identified possible short-term activities, including organizing a workshop on cultural, environmental and social impact assessments and regional workshops on ethics, customs and traditions on environmental protection. However, in the longer term, a deeper analysis in the form of a comprehensive desk study in collaboration with other agencies, in particular UNESCO and CBD, could highlight concrete, implementable steps to demonstrate the interlinkages between environment and cultural diversity, and would culminate in a final report. Annexed to the report were a legal analysis of interlinkages between environment and cultural diversity and the results of a questionnaire on women, cultural diversity and sustainable development distributed at the first Global Women's Assembly on Environment in October (see p. 1048).

CEB consideration. The United Nations Chief Executives Board for Coordination (CEB), in its annual overview report for 2003 [E/2004/67], stated that, in follow-up to the 2002 World Summit on Sustainable Development [YUN 2002, p. 821], it had, through its High-level Committee on Programmes (HLCP), established or strengthened collaborative arrangements in the areas of freshwater, energy, water and sanitation, oceans and coastal areas, and patterns of consumption and production. Specifically, UN-Water, an informal arrangement for coordinating the activities of senior managers of UN water programmes, was confirmed as the inter-agency mechanism for follow-up on the Summit's water-related decisions and the Millennium Development Goals (MDGs) concerning freshwater [YUN 2000, p. 52]. UN-Water's terms of reference and modalities of work were to include an inter-agency plan for addressing water and sanitation issues and mechanisms for interacting with non-UN system stakeholders. CEB established the Oceans and Coastal Areas Network (UN-Oceans) to ensure information-sharing and enhance coherence in the system's policies and activities relating to oceans and coastal areas. HLCP, at its eighth session (Florence, Italy, 15-17 September) [CEB/2004/7], noted the adoption of UN-Water's terms of reference.

Jeju Initiative

GC/GMEF, at its eighth special session [A/59/25] (see p. 1036), considered follow-up to the 2002 World Summit on Sustainable Development [YUN 2002, p. 821]: UNEP's contribution to the twelfth (2004) session of the Commission on Sustainable Development [E/2004/29] (see p. 827) on the theme of the environmental dimensions of water, sanitation and human settlements. The theme was addressed through the focus areas of integrated ecosystems approaches by 2005; water and sanitation; and water health and poverty. The Chair's summary of the consultations—the Jeju Initiative—identified key environmental dimensions and concepts for addressing the functions and needs of the natural environment, particularly water, in local, national and international efforts to achieve the water-related targets stemming from the 2000 Millennium Declaration [YUN 2000, p. 49] and the World Summit, and examples of partnerships and best practices. The Initiative emphasized the need for the international community and Governments to make substantive progress in implementing the integrated water resource management target to develop integrated water resources management by 2005, the need for an environmentally sound approach to the Summit's target of halving the proportion of people without access to safe drinking water and basic sanitation; and the need to address water and sanitation issues in poverty reduction efforts. It also addressed the role of UNEP and other UN agencies.

While there was widespread agreement on many of the points contained in the Initiative, there was no consensus on a number of other issues. Nevertheless, the ministers and other delegation heads agreed that the Initiative should be transmitted to the Commission as UNEP's contribution to its 2004 session, at which it would review progress on the implementation of the goals, targets and commitments on freshwater, sanitation and human settlements in Agenda 21, adopted by the United Nations Conference on Environment and Development [YUN 1992, p. 672]; the Programme for the Further Implementation of Agenda 21, adopted by the nineteenth special session of the General Assembly in resolution S/19-2 [YUN 1997, p. 792]; and the Johannesburg Plan of Implementation of the World Summit [YUN 2002, p. 821].

As background papers for the ministerial consultations, GC/GMEF had before it summaries submitted by Governments on innovative practices [UNEP/GCSS.VIII/INF/17]; a discussion paper by the Executive Director on water, sanitation and human settlements [UNEP/GCSS.VIII/4]; and a January note [UNEP/GCSS.VIII/INF/4] on financing wastewater and treatment in relation to the MDGs, and the Summit's water and sanitation targets.

Policy and advisory services

Trade and the environment

A November note by the Executive Director [UNEP/GC.23/INF/5] contained information on UNEP's activities in trade and the environment. With the United Nations Conference on Trade and Development (UNCTAD), UNEP convened the Capacity-building Task Force on Trade, Environment and Development Training Workshop on Integrated Assessment for African Countries (Nairobi, Kenya, 19-20 July). UNEP also convened national stakeholders workshops to launch a pilot project on integrated assessment and planning for sustainable development (Kampala, Uganda, 7-8 September) and a pilot project on integrated assessment and planning to analyse the impacts of trade policy on the Colombian agriculture sector, with special emphasis on biodiversity and poverty reduction. The note also discussed UNEP's activities with respect to the use of environmental impact assessments, economic instruments and natural resource accounting, which included the convening, in cooperation with the United Nations Statistical Division, of a meeting on integrated environmental and economic accounting (Copenhagen, Denmark, 20-21 September).

Institution-building

In November [UNEP/GC.23/3/Add.3], the Executive Director reported on the implementation of a 2003 Governing Council decision [YUN 2003, p. 1044] on enhancing the application of principle 10 of the 1992 Rio Declaration on Environment and Development [YUN 1992, p. 670], which related to public awareness and access to information held by public authorities, public participation in decision-making and access to justice in environmental matters. UNEP carried out consultations with Governments and relevant civil society organizations to determine the value of initiating an intergovernmental process for preparing global guidelines on the application of Principle 10. Responses received so far favoured the development of a "soft-law" international instrument, in the form of global guidelines. UNEP would continue to work with other organizations to enhance implementation of the Principle, preparing and disseminating information to raise awareness on the issue.

Coordination and cooperation

Business and industry

As requested by the Governing Council in 2003 [YUN 2003, p. 1044], the Executive Director, in a November note [UNEP/GC.23/INF/5], reported on the development of guidelines on cooperation between UNEP and the business sector. Taking into account the proposed elements contributed by Governments, and based on the Secretary-General's 2000 Guidelines on Cooperation between the United Nations and the Business Community, the "Guidelines on Cooperation between the United Nations Environment Programme and Business" were finalized in March and were appended to the Executive Director's note. The Guidelines were based on UNEP's ongoing work with business and industry and aimed to ensure greater private sector commitment to a new culture of environmental accountability and responsibility.

UNEP continued working with individual business entities and business associations to create greater environmental and social responsibility, mainly through its annual consultative meeting with industry associations. Other UNEP activities aimed at engaging businesses and industries included strengthening voluntary initiatives. Its Finance Initiative, involving more than 270 banks and insurance companies, was taking the lead in monitoring follow-up to undertakings made by major brokerage firms on corporate responsibility and sustainability at the first summit of leaders of the Global Compact (New York, 24 June), which was launched in 2000 [YUN 2000, p. 989] to engage the business community in advancing basic values in human rights, labour and the environment. The Global Reporting Initiative (GRI), a multi-stakeholder process and independent institution, was launched in 2002 [YUN 2002, p. 1038] to develop and disseminate globally applicable sustainable reporting guidelines. With UNEP's support, the GRI secretariat was gathering feedback from all regions, and assessing and making amendments to the GRI guidelines, originally released in 2002 [ibid.], with a view to releasing version 3 in 2006.

Environmental emergencies

In response to a 2003 Governing Council decision [YUN 2003, p. 1045], the Executive Director, in November [UNEP/GC.23/3/Add.2], reported on environmental emergency prevention, preparedness, assessment, response and mitigation. UNEP continued to strengthen its capacity to address natural disasters with significant environmental impacts, including by enhancing the global network of environment and disaster experts that supported its response activities. It was assisted in those efforts by the Environmental Emergencies Partnership, a UNEP/ UN Office for the Coordination of Humanitarian Affairs (OCHA) global mechanism for reducing the frequency and severity of environmental emergencies, through the strengthening of collaboration and information-sharing among environmental emergency stake-holders. UNEP's capacity-building and training activities included the development, in May, of profiles of institutions working on disaster and environmental risk reduction in Africa and a March publication on environmental and flood management, targeting children. To strengthen capacities and promote regional perspectives in disaster reduction and management, UNEP organized a workshop (Lesotho, February) on national legislation and institutions for environmental disaster in selected countries in Southern Africa.

Among other activities, UNEP, as requested by the Governing Council in 2003 [YUN 2003, p. 1045], put in place a process for reviewing the 2001 Strategic Framework on Environmental Emergency Prevention, Preparedness, Assessment, Mitigation and Response [YUN 2001, p. 950]. With support from Norway, and in cooperation with the International Federation of Red Cross and Red Crescent Societies and the Office of the United Nations High Commissioner for Refugees, UNEP was implementing a project on strengthening capacities for integration of environmental dimensions in the management of refugee settlements and flows in Angola, Liberia and Sierra Leone. It was also implementing, in cooperation with a number of African organizations and institutions, a project to promote the harnessing, use and application of indigenous knowledge in environmental conservation and coping mechanisms for flood and drought disasters in Kenya, South Africa, Swaziland, and the United Republic of Tanzania.

In 2004, the Joint UNEP/OCHA Environment Unit coordinated responses to the environmental aspects of emergencies resulting from the 26 December Indian Ocean earthquake and subsequent tsunami (see p. 952) in Indonesia, Maldives and Sri Lanka (see p. 914); the humanitarian crisis in the Darfur region of the Sudan (see p. 942); hurricanes Ivan and Jeanne in the Dominican Republic, Grenada and Haiti; uranium mining in the Democratic Republic of the Congo; and the outbreak of neurological disease in Tanzania.

Global Environment Facility

The Global Environment Facility (GEF), a joint programme of UNDP, UNEP and the World Bank, established in 1991 [YUN 1991, p. 505] to help solve global environmental problems, was the designated financial mechanism for the 1992 Convention on Biological Diversity [YUN 1992, p. 683] (see p. 1053), the 1992 United Nations Framework Convention on Climate Change [ibid., p. 681] (see p. 1051), and the 1994 United Nations Convention to Combat Desertification [YUN 1994, p. 944] (see p. 1055), and served as the interim financial mechanism for the 2001 Stockholm Convention on Persistent Organic Pollutants (POPs) [YUN 2001, p. 971] (see p. 1066), pending that Convention's entry into force.

At year's end, the cumulative UNEP/GEF work programme was financed to $865 million, including $444 million in GEF resources, involving activities in 153 countries. Through GEF enabling activities related to biodiversity, climate change, POPs, and capacity-building needs assessment for global environmental management, UNEP assisted 138 countries to meet their obligations to the global environmental conventions and to build capacity to implement them.

Fifty-three new UNEP/GEF initiatives were approved in 2004, with funding of $258 million, including $80 million in GEF grant financing.

A December note by the Executive Director [UNEP/GC.23/INF/24] contained information on the activities of UNEP as a GEF implementing agency.

Memorandums of understanding

In 2004, UNEP signed memorandums of understanding (MOUs) with: the Organizing Committee for the 2004 Olympic Games and Paralympic Games, to collaborate on environmental awareness-raising during the games (Athens, Greece, 13-29 August and 17-28 September, respectively); the World Organization of the Scout Movement, to promote environmental activities among its members and support the implementation of UNEP's long-term (Tunza) strategy on the engagement and involvement of young people in environmental issues [YUN 2002, p. 1040] (see below); the University of New South Wales (Sydney, Australia), to expand sustainability programmes in the Asia-Pacific region; the Economic Cooperation Organization (ECO), to cooperate in strengthening environmental management in the ECO region (Western and Central Asia); the European Commission, to strengthen cooperation to fight global threats to the environment more effectively; and the Barbados Ministry of Housing, Lands and the Environment, to cooperate on the establishment of an association to develop, implement and monitor a license system to import and export ozone depleting substances in that country.

Participation of civil society

In December [UNEP/GC.23/INF/14], the Executive Director reported on the implementation of UNEP's Tunza strategy (2003-2008) for the engagement and involvement of young people in environmental issues [YUN 2002, p. 1040], endorsed by the Governing Council in 2003 [YUN 2003, p. 1046]. The report described activities in the four focus areas of information exchange, awareness-building, youth in decision-making processes and capacity-building. UNEP launched a new illustrated environmental series for children, a new website for children and youth and a video encouraging children to protect themselves better from ozone-related problems. A version of the African Environment Outlook (AEO) was being prepared by leaders of African youth organizations in collaboration with UNEP's Division of Early Warning and Assessment. UNEP's network for children and youth organizations continued to grow, with over 10,000 organizations in over 150 countries regularly receiving environmental information from UNEP, including electronic networks for information sharing with children and youth organizations. Despite an annual contribution of 1 million euros by the German-based chemical and health-care company, Bayer AG, full implementation of the Tunza strategy was still hampered by inadequate financial resources.

The 2004 Tunza International Children's Conference (New London, Connecticut, United States, 19-23 July) agreed to a set of commitments and challenges for protecting the environment. Annexed to a December note by the Executive Director [UNEP/GC.23/INF/27], was a statement by the Tunza Youth Advisory Council to the 2005 GC/GMEF session, proposing key priorities for action to meet the goals of the 2000 United Nations Millennium Summit [YUN 2000, p. 47] and the 2002 World Summit on Sustainable Development [YUN 2002, p. 821].

Another December note by the Executive Director [UNEP/GC.23/INF/28] contained a report on activities to implement UNEP's long-term strategy on sport and the environment, endorsed by the Governing Council in 2003 [YUN 2003, p. 1046]. Those activities included participation in the Secretary-General's initiative on sport, including the work of his Task Force on Sport for Development and Peace [YUN 2003, p. 1111], efforts to commemorate the International Year for Sport and Physical Education (2005), proclaimed by the General Assembly in resolution 58/5 [ibid.] and UNEP's efforts to strengthen its work with sports organizations. UNEP, in cooperation with the World Federation of the Sporting Goods Industry and the sporting goods industry in Pakistan, organized the 2004 Global Forum for Sport and the Environment (Lahore, Pakistan, 25-26 November), which adopted the Lahore/Sialkot Declaration on Corporate Environmental Responsibility.

The main challenge for the full implementation of the strategy was the urgent need to raise the required financial resources. Given the lack of Government support, UNEP was increasingly looking to the private sector to provide those resources. The report encouraged Governments to engage sport federations and associations to promote environmental awareness and action, and to use the opportunity of the International Year for Sport and Physical Education (2005) to promote the use of sport for the enhancement of the sustainable development agenda and achieving the internationally agreed goals of the Millennium Declaration [YUN 2000, p. 49].

The Fifth Global Civil Society Forum (Jeju, Republic of Korea, 27-28 March) [UNEP/GCS/5/1] considered environmental issues on the Korean peninsula and in North-East Asia, Asia and the Pacific and West Asia, Latin America and the Caribbean and Africa, and Europe and North America. It discussed the global approach to issues raised by the regions and heard civil society statements [UNEP/GCSS.VIII/INF/10 & Add.1]. The Forum's conclusions and recommendations were contained in the Jeju statement adopted by the eighth (2004) GC/GMEF special session (see p. 1044).

Four earlier Global Civil Society Forums were held in 2000, 2001, 2002, and 2003 [UNEP/GCS/4/2].

Gender and the environment

Consultative seminar. UNEP's Division of Policy Development and Law convened a consultative seminar (Nairobi, Kenya, 25-26 February) [UNEP/DPDL/CSGE/1] to deal with substantive and strategic challenges regarding gender and environment. Seminar working groups made recommendations on women, poverty and the environment; the ten-year review of the Beijing Declaration and Platform for Action [YUN 1995, p. 1170], adopted by the Fourth (1995) World Conference on Women [ibid., p. 1169], and the MDGs [YUN 2000, p. 51]; the establishment of a mentoring programme on women and youth; better incorporation of gender in UNEP's work; biodiversity, water and indigenous knowledge at the core of sustainable and equitable development; and planning the upcoming UNEP Global Women's Assembly on Environment (see p. 1048). The recommendations called for an audit of UNEP's gender mainstreaming strategy; the establishment of a gender task force and a mechanism for monitoring gender mainstreaming; and a global review of indigenous knowledge, biodiversity and water as they related to women and of the impact of water privatization policies on communities and on women.

Global Women's Assembly. The first Global Women's Assembly on Environment: women as the voice for the environment (WAVE) (Nairobi, 10-13 October) [UNEP/DPDL/WAVE/1], discussed gender-sensitive policies on sustainable livelihoods in the context of world conflict and peace; the development of a draft manifesto and action plan on women and the environment (see below); women's rights, environment, poverty and health; female leadership and starting a mentorship programme; and recommendations by women ministers for the environment. The manifesto, adopted by the Assembly and annexed to its report, called for urgent action by all stakeholders, in particular the UN system, to achieve sustainable development. Through their global partnership, Assembly participants would use and promote non-violent approaches, eliminate destructive practices and build a sustainable, just and valuable life for all current and future generations. The manifesto contained recommendations for action on the issues discussed during the Assembly (see above), as well as on gender issues with regard to global environmental change and urban challenges and the environment. Further recommendations dealt with the implementation of the 2002 World Summit on Sustainable Development [YUN 2002, p. 821]; the 10-year review in 2005 of the 1995 Beijing Declaration and Platform for Action [YUN 1995, p. 1170]; the 1979 Convention on the Elimination of all Forms of Discrimination against Women, adopted by the General Assembly in resolution 34/180 [YUN 1979, p. 895]; and the MDGs. The manifesto also included a number of project ideas, corresponding to its recommendations, for implementation by UNEP.

General Assembly issues

In January [UNEP/GCSS.VIII/INF/7], the Executive Director provided information on the issues arising from resolutions adopted by the General Assembly in 2003 that called for action by, or were of relevance to, UNEP.

Global Environment Outlook Yearbook

In response to a 2003 Governing Council decision [YUN 2003, p. 1039], a December note by the Executive Director [UNEP/GC.23/INF/2] contained UNEP's Global Environmental Outlook (GEO), *GEO Yearbook 2004/5*, which presented a global and regional overview of the state of the environment, including the Indian Ocean tsunami disaster of 26 December (see p. 952); gender and the environment (see p. 1047); changes in ocean salinity; environmental indicators; and emerging infectious diseases. The *GEO Yearbook 2004/5* would be published in 2005. Future yearbooks

would be dated according to the years in which they were published.

UNEP secretariat

OIOS audit and inspection services

The tenth annual report of the Office of Internal Oversight Services (OIOS), transmitted by the Secretary-General in October [A/59/359] (see p. 1368), included the results of an audit of UNEP's Division of Technology, Industry and Economics. The audit showed that, while the Division had improved its handling of administrative matters, it lacked basic data to establish an overall picture of its advisory bodies and how they contributed to its work. The mandate and rationale for the current organizational structure were still unclear and in need of review. UNEP needed a mechanism to provide an overview of the mandates and missions of its divisions, and to strengthen the administrative arrangements for its Nairobi-based divisions in management information, budget control and asset management.

Administrative and budgetary matters

Environment Fund

A February note by the Executive Director [UNEP/GCSS.VIII/INF/9] contained information on the execution of UNEP's 2002-2003 biennial budget, showing total projected income for the biennium, including from the UN regular budget, the Environment Fund, trust funds, trust fund support and earmarked contributions, amounting to $334.20 million and expenditures totalling $237.15 million. The balance in the funds as at 31 December 2003 was projected at $97.05 million.

Pursuant to 2003 Governing Council decisions on UNEP's 2004-2005 biennial programme and support budget [YUN 2003, p. 1047] and regional implementation of UNEP's programme of work [ibid., p. 1043], a report of the Executive Director [UNEP/GCSS.VIII/6] provided information on progress in the development of preliminary data and a format for the regional annexes of UNEP's 2006-2007 programme of work based on the 2004-2005 programme of work of subprogramme 1 of the Division of Early Warning and Assessment. It provided a synopsis by region of the area of work of the Division and a format for presenting the resource plan. The annex indicating the Environment Fund resources allocated and the percentage to be implemented at the regional level per subprogramme, was to be included as part of the work programme for the 2006-2007 biennium, and starting from that biennium, the synopsis by region and by division would be submitted to the GC/GMEF sessions as a separate document.

The Governing Council, on 31 March [dec. SS.VIII/3], reiterated its 2003 request [YUN 2003, p. 1047] to the Executive Director to include in the work programme, beginning with the 2006-2007 biennium, regional annexes identifying the percentage of the Environment Fund budget from each division to be implemented at the regional level and to present that information for a decision in 2005. The UNEP secretariat should prepare, as a separate document, a synopsis by region of the area of work of each division for presentation to the Council at its regular sessions, starting from the 2006-2007 biennium.

Responding to the Council's decision, the Executive Director submitted the requested regional synopses in a November note [UNEP/GC.23/INF/9].

Board of Auditors report

A December note by the Executive Director [UNEP/GC.23/INF/7] contained the report of the Board of Auditors, which included the financial report and audited financial statements for the 2002-2003 biennium [A/59/5/Add.6]. UNEP's financial statements covered the major funds, including the Environment Fund, general trust funds, the Multilateral Fund for the Implementation of the Montreal Protocol on Substances that Deplete the Ozone Layer (see p. 1052), Technical Cooperation Trust Funds and other trust funds. The Environment Fund reported a total income of $98.79 million against expenditures of $109.97 million, showing a net shortfall of $11.18 million (11 per cent), as compared with a net shortfall of income over expenditures of $11.23 million in 2000-2001. The general trust funds showed a shortfall of income relative to expenditure of $8.59 million, compared to a net excess of $24.48 million for 2000-2001. The Multilateral Fund reported a net excess of income over expenditures of $16.15 million, compared with a net shortfall of income relative to expenditures of $32.24 million for 2000-2001.

The Board made recommendations for establishing and reviewing obligations in accordance with UN regulations; recovering outstanding advances paid to staff members and "other persons"; enforcing agreement in respect of the timely liquidation of advances to implementing agencies; and disclosing, in the notes to the financial statements, the amount of non-expendable property "pending write-off".

Strengthening UNEP's financing

In February [UNEP/GCSS.VIII/5], the Executive Director reported on measures taken to strengthen UNEP's financing, including implementation of the voluntary indicative scale of contributions, a pilot phase of which began in 2003 [YUN 2003, p. 1048]. The pilot phase revealed a significant widening of the base for voluntary contributions, with 118 countries having pledged or contributed to the Environment Fund in 2003, compared to the annual average of 74 countries, and an increase in payments by countries to the Fund. By the end of 2003, over 70 Governments had pledged or paid higher contributions than in the previous year, and over 50 had increased budget allocations for contributions to UNEP. Taking into account the feedback from Governments during the pilot phase, UNEP developed a new indicative scale for the 2004-2005 biennium, which was supported by 61 countries as at the end of 2003, 43 of which had paid or pledged amounts for 2004, the highest number ever before the start of the calendar year to which the pledges related. The report also discussed the more efficient and effective use of available resources and the possibility of utilizing external management review mechanisms; a strong focus on agreed UNEP priorities and ongoing review of previous priorities; and greater mobilization of resources from the private sector and other major groups.

Data on the implementation of the 2003 pilot phase of the voluntary indicative scale of contributions and the new 2004-2005 scale were submitted by the Executive Director in a March note [UNEP/GCSS.VIII/INF/12].

On 31 March [dec. SS.VIII/1, section IV], the Governing Council requested the Executive Director to continue efforts to increase funding from all sources for strengthening UNEP's financial base and to implement its 2002 decision [YUN 2002, p. 1032] with respect to the recommendations on financing the Programme, including through resources approved for UNEP by the General Assembly from the UN regular budget. The Council decided to review all aspects of the strengthening of UNEP's financing in 2005 and requested the Executive Director to report thereon.

The General Assembly, in resolution 59/226 (see p. 1037) of 23 December, welcomed the progress made in strengthening UNEP's role and financial situation, including the significant broadening of its donor base and increasing total contributions to the Environmental Fund, and which would be reviewed by the Governing Council in 2005.

International conventions and mechanisms

MEAs

A February report of the Executive Director [UNEP/GCSS.VIII/5] discussed issues concerning multilateral environmental agreements (MEAs), whose implementation was supported through a significant proportion of UNEP activities. UNEP was striving to enhance complementarity and communication between conventions at the national level in capacity-building and reporting, among other areas. It continued to identify programmatic synergies between the conventions and improve cooperation between convention secretariats and respective UNEP programmes. UNEP, through its World Conservation Monitoring Centre, was facilitating pilot projects in Ghana, Indonesia, Panama and Seychelles to test information management and harmonization concepts in the context of national reporting to global biodiversity-related conventions, including the 1992 Convention on Biological Diversity [YUN 1992, p. 683] (see p. 1053); the 1973 Convention on International Trade in Endangered Species of Wild Fauna and Flora (CITES), the 1979 Convention on the Conservation of Migratory Species of Wild Animals, and the 1971 Ramsar Convention on Wetlands of International Importance, Especially as Waterfowl Habitat. UNEP was launching a major project on achieving synergies between conventions in Africa, and was organizing a series of regional and subregional workshops to promote the coordinated national implementation of the 1989 Basel Convention on the Control of Transboundary Movements of Hazardous Wastes and their Disposal [YUN 1989, p. 420] (see p. 1066), the 1998 Rotterdam Convention on the Prior Informed Consent Procedure for Certain Hazardous Chemicals and Pesticides in International Trade [YUN 1998, p. 997] (see p. 1063) and the 2001 Stockholm Convention on Persistent Organic Pollutants [YUN 2001, p. 971] (see p. 1066).

On 31 March [dec. SS.VIII/1, section V] the Governing Council requested the Executive Director to continue to promote the implementation of the Council's recommendations with respect to coordination between and effectiveness of multilateral environmental agreements, in pursuance of a 2002 Council decision on international environmental governance [YUN 2002, p. 1032], taking into account the autonomous decision-making authority of the conferences of the parties to those conventions.

A November report of the Executive Director [UNEP/GC.23/3/Add.4] contained information on UNEP support for MEAs and a progress report on the implementation of a 2002 Governing Council decision on compliance with and enforcement of multilateral environmental agreements [YUN 2002, p. 1042]. The tenth meeting of MEA secretariats (Nairobi, Kenya, 8-9 March) suggested that systematic contact between UNEP and the MEA secretariats be established, as well as a UNEP focus areas on MEA-related issues. UNEP should provide political and practical support to MEAs; strengthen regional delivery through capacity-building and training; and improve coherence among MEAs. As a follow-up to the meeting, UNEP established an interdivisional task force to coordinate the work of all UNEP divisions in support of MEAs, and was asked to help develop a database to monitor the implementation of decisions of conferences of the parties.

The report also discussed an issue-based modular approach project for implementing biodiversity-related MEAs decisions at the national level; efforts to harmonize national reporting; the results of an expert workshop on promoting cooperation and synergy between CITES and the Convention on Biological Diversity (Vilm, Germany, 21-24 April); coordinated national implementation of the Basel, Rotterdam and Stockholm Conventions; and the OzonAction Programme, established by the UNEP Division of Technology, Industry and Economics to help developing countries and countries with economies in transition improve their ability to comply with the 1987 Montreal Protocol on Substances that Deplete the Ozone Layer [YUN 1987, p. 686] of the 1985 Vienna Convention for the Protection of the Ozone Layer [YUN 1985, p. 804] (see p. 1052). The report also dealt with issues related to biodiversity and biosafety among others.

The 2002 Guidelines on Compliance and Enforcement of Multilateral Environmental Agreements [YUN 2002, p. 1042] were translated into all official UN languages and disseminated to Governments and international organizations, MEA conferences of parties and other stakeholders. UNEP developed a manual for implementing the guidelines, which was tested in regional workshops held in 2003 and 2004. The report described ongoing activities for the implementation of the guidelines and the development of national laws for the implementation of the Rio conventions taking into account poverty reduction (Convention on Biological Diversity, the 1992 United Nations Framework Convention on Climate Change [YUN 1992, p. 681], the 1994 United Nations Convention to Combat Desertification in Those Countries Experiencing Serious Drought and/or Desertification, Particularly in Africa [YUN 1994, p. 944]).

Report of Secretary-General. In response to General Assembly resolutions 58/243 [YUN 2003, p. 1049], 58/242 [ibid., p. 1053] and 58/212 [ibid., p. 1052], the Secretary-General, by an August note [A/59/197], transmitted reports submitted by the secretariats of the United Nations Framework Convention on Climate Change (see below), the United Nations Convention to Combat Desertification in Those Countries Experiencing Serious Drought and/or Desertification, Particularly in Africa (see p. 1055), and the Convention on Biological Diversity (see p. 1053), respectively. The note also contained a joint submission on cooperative activities of the three secretariats.

Climate change convention

As at 31 December, the number of parties to the United Nations Framework Convention on Climate Change (UNFCCC), which was opened for signature in 1992 [YUN 1992, p. 681] and entered into force in 1994 [YUN 1994, p. 938], stood at 188 States and the European Community (EC). During the year, the Convention was acceded to by Turkey.

At year's end, 132 States and the EC were parties to the Kyoto Protocol to the Convention [YUN 1997, p. 1048]. During the year, seven States ratified the Protocol and six acceded to it.

Conference of Parties

The tenth session of the Conference of the Parties to UNFCCC (Buenos Aires, Argentina, 6-18 December) [FCCC/CP/2004/10 & Add.1-2] adopted decisions on the Buenos Aires programme of work on measures dealing with adaptation and response to climate change, and simplified modalities and procedures for small-scale afforestation and reforestation project activities under the Kyoto Protocol's clean development mechanism (CDM) (see below). Other decisions related to: capacity-building for developing countries not included in the Convention's annex I list of industrialized countries and countries with economies in transition; the work of the Least Developed Countries Expert Group; implementation of the global observing system for climate; the development and transfer of technology; the status of, and ways to enhance, implementation of the New Delhi work programme, adopted in 2002 [YUN 2002, p. 1042], on article 6 of the Convention relating to education, training and public awareness; the continuation of pilot phase activities implemented jointly by the Subsidiary Body for Scientific and Technological Advice and the Subsidiary Body for Implementation; and issues related to the technical review of greenhouse gas inventories from UNFCCC parties included in an-

nex I and the implementation of article 8 of the Kyoto Protocol. The Conference adopted decisions on a standard electronic format for reporting emission reduction units under the Protocol; the incorporation of modalities and procedures for afforestation and reforestation project activities under the CDM and measures to facilitate their implementation; good practice guidance for land use, land-use change and forestry activities under the Protocol's article 3; and issues relating to registry systems under article 7. Further decisions dealt with the Convention's financial mechanism; the assessment of funding to assist developing countries in fulfilling their commitments under the Convention, a report which [FCCC/SBI/2004/18] was prepared by the secretariat in collaboration with GEF; and other administrative and financial matters.

In October, the CDM Executive Board issued its third annual report [FCCC/CP/2004/2 & Add.1], covering the period from November 2003 to December 2004. At its tenth session, the Conference of the Parties adopted a decision on guidance relating to CDM.

The Subsidiary Body for Scientific and Technological Advice (SBSTA) [FCCC/SBSTA/2004/6 & Add.1, 2] and the Subsidiary Body for Implementation (SBI) [FCCC/SBI/2004/10] held their twentieth sessions (Bonn, Germany, 16-25 June). SBSTA [FCCC/SBSTA/2004/13 & Corr.1] and SBI [FCCC/SBI/2004/19] also held their twenty-first sessions in 2004 (Buenos Aires, Argentina, 6-14 December).

GENERAL ASSEMBLY ACTION

On 22 December [meeting 75] the General Assembly, on the recommendation of the Second Committee [A/59/483/Add.4], adopted **resolution 59/234** without vote [agenda item 85(d)].

Protection of global climate for present and future generations of mankind

The General Assembly,

Recalling its resolution 54/222 of 22 December 1999, its decision 55/443 of 20 December 2000 and its resolutions 56/199 of 21 December 2001, 57/257 of 20 December 2002 and 58/243 of 23 December 2003 and other resolutions relating to the protection of the global climate for present and future generations of mankind,

Recalling also the provisions of the United Nations Framework Convention on Climate Change, including the acknowledgement that the global nature of climate change calls for the widest possible cooperation by all countries and their participation in an effective and appropriate international response, in accordance with their common but differentiated responsibilities and respective capabilities and their social and economic conditions,

Recalling further the Johannesburg Declaration on Sustainable Development, the Plan of Implementation of the World Summit on Sustainable Development

("Johannesburg Plan of Implementation"), the Delhi Ministerial Declaration on Climate Change and Sustainable Development, adopted by the Conference of the Parties to the United Nations Framework Convention on Climate Change at its eighth session, held in New Delhi from 23 October to 1 November 2002, and the outcome of the ninth session of the Conference of the Parties held in Milan, Italy, from 1 to 12 December 2003,

Noting the review of the Programme of Action for the Sustainable Development of Small Island Developing States,

Remaining deeply concerned that all countries, in particular developing countries, including the least developed countries and small island developing States, face increased risks from the negative impacts of climate change,

Noting that one hundred and eighty-nine States and one regional economic integration organization have ratified the Convention,

Noting also that, to date, the Kyoto Protocol to the United Nations Framework Convention on Climate Change has attracted one hundred and twenty-eight ratifications, including from parties mentioned in annex I to the Convention, which account for 61.6 per cent of emissions,

Noting further the work of the Intergovernmental Panel on Climate Change and the need to build and enhance scientific and technological capabilities, inter alia, through continuing support to the Panel for the exchange of scientific data and information, especially in developing countries,

Recalling the United Nations Millennium Declaration, in which Heads of State and Government resolved to make every effort to ensure the entry into force of the Kyoto Protocol, preferably by the tenth anniversary of the United Nations Conference on Environment and Development in 2002, and to embark on the required reduction in emissions of greenhouse gases,

Taking note of the report of the Executive Secretary of the United Nations Framework Convention on Climate Change on the work of the Conference of the Parties to the Convention,

1. *Calls upon* States to work cooperatively towards achieving the ultimate objective of the United Nations Framework Convention on Climate Change;

2. *Notes* that States that have ratified the Kyoto Protocol to the United Nations Framework Convention on Climate Change strongly urge States that have not yet done so to ratify it in a timely manner;

3. *Notes also* that States that have ratified the Kyoto Protocol welcome its ratification by the Russian Federation, which satisfies the requirements for the Kyoto Protocol to enter into force;

4. *Encourages* States that have ratified the Kyoto Protocol to continue their preparations for its entry into force;

5. *Notes with interest* the preparations undertaken for the implementation of the flexible mechanisms established by the Kyoto Protocol;

6. *Takes note* of the decisions adopted by the Conference of the Parties at its ninth session, and calls for their implementation;

7. *Notes* the ongoing work of the liaison group of the secretariats and offices of the relevant subsidiary bodies of the United Nations Framework Convention on Climate Change, the United Nations Convention to Combat Desertification in Those Countries Experiencing Serious Drought and/or Desertification, Particularly in Africa, and the Convention on Biological Diversity, and encourages cooperation to promote complementarities among the three secretariats while respecting their independent legal status;

8. *Invites* the Executive Secretary of the United Nations Framework Convention on Climate Change to report to the General Assembly at its sixtieth session on the work of the Conference of the Parties;

9. *Invites* the conferences of the parties to the multilateral environmental conventions, when setting the dates of their meetings, to take into consideration the schedule of meetings of the General Assembly and the Commission on Sustainable Development so as to ensure the adequate representation of developing countries at those meetings;

10. *Decides* to include in the provisional agenda of its sixtieth session the sub-item entitled "Protection of global climate for present and future generations of mankind".

Vienna Convention and Montreal Protocol

As at 31 December, 188 States and the EC were parties to the 1985 Vienna Convention for the Protection of the Ozone Layer [YUN 1985, p. 804], which entered into force in 1998 [YUN 1998, p. 810]. In 2004, Afghanistan and Bhutan acceded to the Convention and to the Montreal Protocol on Substances that Deplete the Ozone Layer.

Parties to the Montreal Protocol, which was adopted in 1987 [YUN 1987, p. 686], numbered 187 States and the EC; to the 1990 Amendment to the Protocol, 174 and the EC; to the 1992 Amendment, 163 and the EC; to the 1997 Amendment, 123 and the EC; and to the 1999 Amendment, 85 and the EC.

The first Extraordinary Meeting of the Parties to the Montreal Protocol (Montreal, Canada, 24-26 March) [UNEP/OzL.Pro.ExMP/1/3], addressed unresolved issues related to methyl bromide [YUN 2003, p. 1050] and adopted a double-cap concept, which distinguished between use and production for critical use exemptions for methyl bromide for 2005. It established an ad hoc working group to review the working procedures and terms of reference of the Methyl Bromide Technical Options Committee, and adopted other decisions relating to reductions in and accelerated phase-out of methyl bromide by parties operating under article 5 of the Protocol (developing countries) and conditions for granting and reporting critical-use exemptions.

The Sixteenth Meeting of the Parties (Montreal, Canada, 22-26 November) [UNEP/OzL.Pro.16/17] adopted decisions on: critical use exemptions for methyl bromide for 2005 and 2006; a review of the working procedures and terms of reference of, and financial assistance to, the Methyl Bromide Technical Options Committee; the adoption of an accounting framework; trade in products and commodities treated with methyl bromide; technical and financial support relating to alternatives and flexibility in their use; and reporting of information on quarantine and pre-shipment uses of the substance and coordination among UN bodies on such uses. Other decisions dealt with essential use nominations for 2005 and 2006 of chloroflourocarbons (CFCs) for metered-dose inhalers; an assessment of the portion of the refrigeration service sector made up by chillers and the identification of incentives and impediments to the transition to non-CFC equipment; sources of carbon tetrachloride emissions and opportunities for reductions; a review of approved destruction technologies; the establishment of licensing systems; illegal trade in ozone-depleting substances; cooperation between the Protocol's secretariat and other related conventions and international organizations; terms of reference for a study on the 2006-2008 replenishment of the Multilateral Fund for the Implementation of the Montreal Protocol; the 2004 evaluation and review of the Fund [UNEP/ OzL.Pro.16/11]; and compliance issues. The Meeting declared 2007 the "International Year of the Ozone Layer" and decided to hold a second extraordinary meeting in 2005 to complete work on methyl bromide exemptions for 2006.

Convention on air pollution

As at 31 December, the number of parties to the 1979 Convention on Long-Range Trans-boundary Air Pollution [YUN 1979, p. 710], which entered into force in 1983 [YUN 1983, p. 645], remained at 48 States and the EC. Eight protocols to the Convention dealt with the programme for monitoring and evaluation of the pollutants in Europe (1984), the reduction of sulphur emissions or their transboundary fluxes by at least 30 percent (1985), the control of emissions of nitrogen oxides or their transboundary fluxes (1988), the control of volatile organic compounds or their transboundary fluxes (1991), further reduction of sulphur emissions (1984), heavy metals (1998), persistent organic pollutants (POPs) (1998) and the abatement of acidification, eutrophication and ground-level ozone (1999).

The twenty-second session of the Executive Body for the Convention (Geneva, 29 November–3 December) [ECE/EB.AIR/83 & Add.1, 2] established task forces on heavy metals and hemispheric transport of air pollution, and an expert group on particulate matter. It adopted decisions on compliance and the implementation of the Cooperative Programme for Monitoring and Eval-

uation of the Long-range Transmission of Air Pollutants in Europe (EMEP) monitoring strategy, which was approved by the Executive Body during the session, and its 2005 work plan.

Convention on Biological Diversity

As at 31 December, the number of parties to the 1992 Convention on Biological Diversity [YUN 1992, p. 638], which entered into force in 1993 [YUN 1993, p. 210], remained at 187 States and the EC.

At year's end, 110 States and the EC were parties to the Cartagena Protocol on Biosafety, which was adopted in 2000 [YUN 2000, p. 973] and entered into force in 2003 [YUN 2003, p. 1051]. During the year, 20 States ratified the Protocol, 11 States acceded to it and Portugal accepted it.

The seventh meeting of the Conference of the Parties to the Convention (Kuala Lumpur, Malaysia, 9-20 and 27 February) [UNEP/CBD/COP/7/21] adopted the Addis Ababa Principles and Guidelines for the Sustainable Use of Biodiversity, which were developed during the Fourth Open-Ended Workshop for the Sustainable Use of Biological Diversity (Addis Ababa, Ethiopia, 6-8 May 2003). In a decision on the Strategic Plan for the Convention (2002-2010), adopted in 2002 [YUN 2002, p. 1045], the Meeting established an Ad Hoc Open-ended Working Group on Review of Implementation of the Convention. It took action on the Global Strategy for Plant Conservation, also adopted in 2002 [ibid.], and on the Global Taxonomy Initiative. The Meeting adopted decisions on forest and mountain biological diversity; the biological diversity of inland water ecosystems, marine and coastal ecosystems, and dry and sub-humid lands; agricultural biological diversity; biological diversity and tourism; and biodiversity and climate change. Further decisions dealt with, the ecosystem approach for addressing the Convention objectives; issues related to article 8(j) of the Convention on traditional knowledge; implementation of the Bonn Guidelines on Access to Genetic Resources and Fair and Equitable Sharing of the Benefits Arising out of their Utilization, adopted in 2002 [ibid.]; and administrative and budgetary and other matters. A ministerial segment of the meeting adopted the Kuala Lumpur Ministerial Declaration, which, among other things, reaffirmed the significant role of indigenous and local communities in the conservation and sustainable use of biological resources and committed Governments to integrating biodiversity conservation and sustainable use into socio-economic development.

Cartagena Protocol on Biosafety

The first meeting of the Conference of the Parties to the Convention serving as the Meeting of the Parties to the Cartagena Protocol on Biosafety (Kuala Lumpur, Malaysia, 23-27 February) [UNEP/CBD/BS/COP-MOP/1/15] adopted an action plan for building capacities for the effective implementation of the Protocol; approved the transition of the pilot phase of the Biosafety Clearing-House to the fully operational phase; and adopted procedures and mechanisms on compliance under the Protocol and established the Compliance Committee. In a decision on the handling, transport, packaging and identification of living modified organisms, the meeting established an open-ended technical expert group on identification requirements of living modified organisms intended for direct use as food or feed, or for processing. It also established the Open-ended Ad Hoc Working Group of Legal and Technical Experts on Liability and Redress and adopted a medium-term programme of work for the Conference of the Parties serving as the meeting of the Parties to the Protocol from the second to fifth meetings. Other decisions dealt with monitoring and reporting under the Protocol and administrative and budgetary matters.

GENERAL ASSEMBLY ACTION

On 22 December [meeting 75], the General Assembly, on the recommendation of the Second Committee [A/59/483/Add.6], adopted **resolution 59/236** without vote [agenda item 85(*f*)].

Convention on Biological Diversity

The General Assembly,

Recalling its resolutions 55/201 of 20 December 2000, 56/197 of 21 December 2001, 57/253 and 57/260 of 20 December 2002 and 58/212 of 23 December 2003,

Reiterating that the Convention on Biological Diversity is the key international instrument for the conservation and sustainable use of biological resources and the fair and equitable sharing of benefits arising from the use of genetic resources,

Recalling the commitments of the World Summit on Sustainable Development to pursue a more efficient and coherent implementation of the three objectives of the Convention and the achievement by 2010 of a significant reduction in the current rate of loss of biological diversity, which will require action at all levels, including the implementation of national biodiversity strategies and action plans and the provision of new and additional financial and technical resources to developing countries,

Taking note of the entry into force of the International Treaty on Plant Genetic Resources for Food and Agriculture, the objectives of which are the conservation and sustainable use of plant genetic resources for food and agriculture and the fair and equitable sharing of the benefits arising from their use, in harmony with the Convention on Biological Diversity, for sustainable agriculture and food security,

Expressing its deep appreciation to the Government of Malaysia for hosting the seventh meeting of the Con-

ference of the Parties to the Convention on Biological Diversity and the first meeting of the Conference of the Parties to the Convention serving as the Meeting of the Parties to the Cartagena Protocol on Biosafety, held in Kuala Lumpur from 9 to 20 and on 27 February, and from 23 to 27 February 2004, respectively,

Expressing its deep appreciation also to the Government of Brazil for its offer to host the eighth meeting of the Conference of the Parties to the Convention on Biological Diversity and the third meeting of the Conference of the Parties to the Convention serving as the Meeting of the Parties to the Cartagena Protocol on Biosafety, to be held in the first half of 2006,

Noting the efforts of the Government of France to organize a biodiversity-related conference in Paris in 2005,

1. *Takes note* of the report of the Executive Secretary of the Convention on Biological Diversity, transmitted by the Secretary-General to the General Assembly at its fifty-ninth session;

2. *Takes note also* of the outcome of the seventh meeting of the Conference of Parties to the Convention on Biological Diversity and the outcome of the first meeting of the Conference of the Parties to the Convention on Biological Diversity serving as the Meeting of the Parties to the Cartagena Protocol on Biosafety, and urges all parties to these respective agreements to implement their decisions;

3. *Notes* the recent progress made with respect to the achievement of the three objectives set out in the Convention on Biological Diversity;

4. *Notes also* the progress made at the first meeting of the Conference of the Parties to the Convention serving as the Meeting of the Parties to the Cartagena Protocol on Biosafety in establishing an operational framework for the implementation of the Protocol, and reiterates that the effective implementation of the Protocol will require the full support of parties and of relevant international organizations, in particular with regard to the provision of assistance to developing countries as well as countries with economies in transition in capacity-building for biosafety;

5. *Invites* the countries that have not yet done so to ratify or to accede to the Convention on Biological Diversity;

6. *Invites* the parties to the Convention that have not yet ratified or acceded to the Cartagena Protocol on Biosafety to the Convention on Biological Diversity to consider doing so;

7. *Invites* countries to consider ratifying or acceding to the International Treaty on Plant Genetic Resources for Food and Agriculture;

8. *Encourages* developed countries parties to the Convention to contribute to the relevant trust funds of the Convention, in particular so as to enhance the full participation of the developing countries parties in all of its activities;

9. *Urges* parties to the Convention on Biological Diversity to facilitate the transfer of technology for the effective implementation of the Convention in accordance with its provisions;

10. *Takes note* of the ongoing work of the liaison group of the secretariats and offices of the relevant subsidiary bodies of the United Nations Framework Convention on Climate Change, the United Nations Convention to Combat Desertification in Those Coun-

tries Experiencing Serious Drought and/or Desertification, Particularly in Africa, and the Convention on Biological Diversity, and further encourages continuing cooperation in order to promote complementarities among the secretariats, while respecting their independent legal status;

11. *Stresses* the importance of harmonizing the reporting requirements of the biodiversity-related conventions while respecting their independent legal status;

12. *Invites* the Executive Secretary of the Convention on Biological Diversity to continue reporting to the General Assembly on the ongoing work regarding the Convention, including its Cartagena Protocol;

13. *Decides* to include in the provisional agenda of its sixtieth session, under the item entitled "Sustainable development", the sub-item entitled "Convention on Biological Diversity".

Convention to combat desertification

As at 31 December, the total number of parties to the 1994 United Nations Convention to Combat Desertification in Those Countries Experiencing Serious Drought and/or Desertification, particularly in Africa (UNCCD) [YUN 1994, p. 944], which entered into force in 1996 [YUN 1996, p. 958], remained at 190 States and the EC.

Following a meeting of the Bureau of the Conference of the Parties to the Convention (Bonn, Germany, 9 June) and consultations with the President of the Committee for the Review of the Implementation of the Convention (CRIC), it was agreed that the third CRIC session, originally planned for 2004, would be held in Bonn in May 2005. The seventh session of the Conference of the Parties and the Committee on Science and Technology, a Conference subsidiary body, were scheduled to take place in Nairobi, Kenya, in October 2005.

To commemorate the tenth anniversary of the adoption of the Convention (17 June), the Convention secretariat published "Preserving our common ground: UNCCD 10 years on", which included articles on the work of the Convention since its inception.

GENERAL ASSEMBLY ACTION

On 22 December [meeting 75], the General Assembly, on the recommendation of the Second Committee [A/59/483/Add.5], adopted **resolution 59/235** without vote [agenda item 85 (*e*)].

Implementation of the United Nations Convention to Combat Desertification in Those Countries Experiencing Serious Drought and/or Desertification, Particularly in Africa

The General Assembly,

Recalling its resolution 58/242 of 23 December 2003 and other resolutions relating to the United Nations Convention to Combat Desertification in Those Countries Experiencing Serious Drought and/or Desertification, Particularly in Africa,

Recalling also its resolution 58/211 of 23 December 2003, in which it declared 2006 the International Year of Deserts and Desertification,

Reaffirming that desertification constitutes a serious obstacle to sustainable development and contributes to food insecurity, famine and poverty, which are factors that can give rise to social, economic and political tensions, including forced migration and conflicts, and that the Convention is an important tool for poverty eradication,

Reaffirming also the universal membership of the Convention, and acknowledging that desertification and drought are problems of a global dimension in that they affect all regions of the world,

Noting that timely and effective implementation of the Convention would help to achieve the internationally agreed development goals, including those contained in the United Nations Millennium Declaration,

Emphasizing the need for the provision of adequate resources for the focal area of land degradation, primarily desertification and deforestation, of the Global Environment Facility,

Stressing the need for further diversification of funding sources to address land degradation, in accordance with articles 20 and 21 of the Convention,

1. *Takes note* of the note by the Secretary-General;

2. *Stresses* the importance of the implementation of the United Nations Convention to Combat Desertification in Those Countries Experiencing Serious Drought and/or Desertification, Particularly in Africa, for meeting the internationally agreed development goals, including those contained in the United Nations Millennium Declaration, and in this regard invites all Governments to take further measures to strengthen the implementation of the Convention;

3. *Invites* the Secretary-General to give due consideration to the role and place of the Convention in ongoing work in the context of the preparations for the high-level plenary meeting of the General Assembly in 2005, including the report of the Millennium Project;

4. *Invites* the Global Environment Facility to strengthen the focal area of land degradation, primarily desertification and deforestation;

5. *Takes note with interest* of ongoing efforts to diversify the availability of financial resources to support activities aimed at combating desertification and poverty;

6. *Invites* the donor community to increase its support to the Convention with a view to bringing greater international attention to bear on the issue of land degradation and desertification, which will contribute to the improvement of the sustainable development of drylands and the global environment;

7. *Invites* the secretariat of the Global Environment Facility and the secretariat of the Convention to finalize the draft memorandum of understanding in an expeditious way and to submit it, as mandated by Conference of the Parties decision 6/COP.6 of 3 September 2003, for the consideration of and adoption by the Conference of the Parties to the Convention and the Council of the Global Environment Facility;

8. *Takes note* of Conference of the Parties decision 23/COP.6 of 5 September 2003 on the programme and budget for the biennium 2004–2005, as an ongoing process of the Conference of the Parties to undertake a comprehensive review of the activities of the secretariat, as

defined in article 23, paragraph 2, of the Convention, and looks forward to the review at the seventh session of the Conference of the Parties to the Convention;

9. *Urges* United Nations funds and programmes, the Bretton Woods institutions, the donor countries and other development agencies to integrate actions in support of the Convention into their strategies to support the achievement of the internationally agreed development goals, including those contained in the Millennium Declaration;

10. *Calls upon* Governments, where appropriate, in collaboration with relevant multilateral organizations, including the Global Environment Facility implementation agencies, to integrate desertification into their plans and strategies for sustainable development;

11. *Encourages* countries to undertake special initiatives in observance of the International Year of Deserts and Desertification and, as they are able, to contribute to its preparatory process;

12. *Reiterates* the invitation to all parties to pay promptly and in full the contributions required for the core budget of the Convention for the biennium 2004–2005, and urges all parties that have not yet paid their contributions for 1999 and/or the bienniums 2000–2001 and 2002–2003 to do so as soon as possible in order to ensure continuity in the cash flow required to finance the ongoing work of the Conference of the Parties, the secretariat and the Global Mechanism;

13. *Calls upon* Governments, and invites multilateral financial institutions, regional development banks, regional economic integration organizations and all other interested organizations, as well as non-governmental organizations and the private sector, to contribute generously to the General Fund, the Supplementary Fund and the Special Fund, in accordance with the relevant paragraphs of the financial rules of the Conference of the Parties, and welcomes the financial support already provided by some countries;

14. *Takes note* of the ongoing work of the liaison group of the secretariats and offices of the relevant subsidiary bodies of the United Nations Framework Convention on Climate Change, the United Nations Convention to Combat Desertification in Those Countries Experiencing Serious Drought and/or Desertification, Particularly in Africa, and the Convention on Biological Diversity, and further encourages continuing cooperation in order to promote complementarities among the secretariats, while respecting their independent legal status;

15. *Requests* the Secretary-General to report to the General Assembly at its sixtieth session on the implementation of the present resolution;

16. *Decides* to include in the provisional agenda of its sixtieth session the sub-item entitled "Implementation of the United Nations Convention to Combat Desertification in Those Countries Experiencing Serious Drought and/or Desertification, Particularly in Africa".

Environmental activities

Follow-up to the Millennium Summit

The Secretary-General, in his August report [A/59/282 & Corr.1] on the implementation of the Millennium Declaration, adopted by the General Assembly in resolution 55/2 [YUN 2000, p. 49], including progress toward the MDG on ensuring environmental sustainability, stated that protected areas had increased in all regions, but there was a loss of forest cover in some parts of the world, notably those with tropical forests. Energy use and per capita carbon dioxide had increased in developing countries but fell in the countries with economies in transition as industrial production declined in the 1990s. The use of ozone-depleting chlorofluorocarbons had been almost eliminated globally. The 1997 Kyoto Protocol [YUN 1997, p. 1048] to the 1992 United Nations Framework Convention on Climate Change [YUN 1992, p. 681] (see p. 1051) still required ratification by either the Russian Federation or the United States in order to come into force, and implementation of the 1994 United Nations Convention to Combat Desertification in Countries Experiencing Serious Drought and/or Desertification, Particularly in Africa [YUN 1994, p. 944] was limited by a lack of financial resources. However, progress was made towards the full implementation of the 1992 Convention on Biological Diversity [YUN 1992, p. 638], with the adoption of measurable indicators and specific goals to reduce the current rate of biodiversity loss by 2010 [YUN 2002, p. 1045] and the entry into force of the Cartagena Protocol on Biosafety in 2003 [YUN 2003, p. 1051]. As to deforestation and forest degradation (see p. 1057), nine international processes involving 150 countries encompassing 85 per cent of the world's forests made progress in developing criteria and indicators for sustainable forest management.

Millennium Ecosystem Assessment

A November note by the Executive Director [UNEP/GC.23/INF/18 & Corr.1] contained information on the Millennium Ecosystem Assessment (MA), a four-year international assessment launched in 2001 [YUN 2001, p. 961] to evaluate the state of major ecosystems and their links with human well-being. During 2004, draft assessment reports underwent expert and Government reviews, and synthesis reports for specific audiences, including the Convention on Biological Diversity (see p. 1053), the United Nations Convention to Combat Desertification in Those Countries Experiencing Serious Drought and/or Desertification, Particularly in Africa (see p. 1055), the Ramsar Convention on Wetlands of International Importance, Especially as Waterfowl Habitat, and for business and industry were being prepared. A plan for outreach activities would be implemented through the end of 2005. The southern African sub-global assessment (SAfMA) was largely completed, and the SAfMA integrated report, the regional assessment report and the Gariep River basin report were published. MA partners were examining how best to make use of its findings, including in strengthening the ecosystem aspects of sub-global environmental research, assessment and management.

The atmosphere

Intergovernmental Panel on Climate Change

The Intergovernmental Panel on Climate Change (IPCC), at its twenty-second session (New Delhi, India, 9-11 November), discussed the scope, content and process for its Fourth Assessment Synthesis Report; Fourth Assessment Report products; outreach; and administrative matters. It approved a process for developing the Fourth Assessment Report, which was to be adopted and approved by IPCC in October 2007, and adopted a decision on its programme and budget for 2005 to 2008.

Report of Executive Director. Pursuant to a 2003 Governing Council decision [YUN 2003, p. 1056], the Executive Director, in November [UNEP/GC.23/3/Add.4], gave a progress report on IPCC's work.

Terrestrial ecosystems

With an estimated 135 million people worldwide at risk of being displaced as a consequence of desertification, UNEP's strategy for dryland environmental management involved working with Governments and other stakeholders to implement, test and further develop an ecosystems approach, integrating the management of land, water and living resources and promoting conservation and sustainable use. UNEP was testing the approach through a drylands policy initiative aimed at restoring degraded drylands, preventing further desertification and promoting sustainable land management as an integral part of intergovernmental and national development policies, strategies and plans. UNEP and FAO began the Global Land Cover Network cooperative programme and were developing a Land Degradation Assessment for Drylands to provide a policy tool for the implementation of national and subregional action programmes of the 1994 United Nations Convention to Combat Desertification in Those Countries Experiencing Serious Drought and/or Desertification, Particularly in Africa (UNCCD) [YUN 1994, p. 944] (see p. 1055). UNEP and the Consultative Group for International Agricultural Research completed the first two-year phase of the Desert Margins Programme and began a second phase. UNEP was also helping African countries to formulate re-

gional, subregional and national action plans and to develop environmental legislation and institutions to combat desertification.

Note by Executive Director. A February note by the Executive Director [UNEP/GCSS.VIII/INF/3] contained a summary of progress made in the implementation of a joint project among China, Japan, Mongolia and the Republic of Korea, and the Asian Development Bank, the Economic and Social Commission for Asia and the Pacific, the UNCCD secretariat and UNEP to tackle the problem of dust and sandstorms in North-East Asia.

Deforestation and forest degradation

United Nations Forum on Forests

The United Nations Forum on Forests (UNFF), at its fourth session (Geneva, 3-14 May) [E/2004/42 & Corr.1], adopted four resolutions and three decisions, which were brought to the attention of the Economic and Social Council. The resolutions pertained to forest-related scientific knowledge [res. 4/1]; social and cultural aspects of forests [res. 4/2]; forest-related monitoring, assessment and reporting: criteria and indicators for sustainable forest management [res. 4/3]; and a process to facilitate the review of the effectiveness of the international arrangement on forests at UNFF's fifth (2005) session [res. 4/4]. The Forum encouraged member States, Collaborative Partnership on Forests members, and other relevant international, regional and subregional organizations, bodies and processes to take action on the recommendations of the Ad Hoc Expert Group on Finance and Transfer of Environmentally Sound Technologies [YUN 2003, p. 1062]. It decided to further consider in its work programme the issues of finance and transfer of environmentally sound technologies, including the Expert Group's recommendations. The Forum took note of documents before it [dec. 4/3] (see below) and invited the Association of Southeast Asian Nations (ASEAN) to participate in its deliberations [dec. 4/1].

The Forum had before it reports of the Secretary-General on traditional forest-related knowledge [E/CN.18/2004/7]; social and cultural aspects of forests [E/CN.18/2004/8]; forest-related scientific knowledge [E/CN.18/2004/9]; monitoring, assessment and reporting, concepts, terminology and definitions [E/CN.18/2004/10]; and criteria and indicators of sustainable forest management [E/CN.18/2004/11]. The Secretary-General also provided information on the Forum's third multi-stakeholder dialogue [E/CN.18/2004/4 & Add.1-5], which took place during UNFF's fourth session; enhanced cooperation and policy and programme coordination to effectively promote and implement Intergovernmental Panel/Forum on Forests (IPF/IFF) proposals and achieve sustainable forest management [E/CN.18/2004/13]; and the proposed UNFF strategic framework for the 2006-2007 biennium [E/CN.18/2004/14]. Secretariat notes described the activities and status of the UNFF secretariat during the 2002-2003 biennium, focusing on 2003 activities [E/CN.18/2004/3]; preparations for the meeting of the Ad Hoc Expert Group on Consideration with a View to Recommending the Parameters of a Mandate for Developing a Legal Framework on All Types of Forests [E/CN.18/2004/6], established by Economic and Social Council decision 2003/299 [YUN 2003, p. 1058] (see below); and a proposal to facilitate the review of the effectiveness of international arrangement on forests, established by Council resolution 2000/35 [YUN 2000, p. 979], at the fifth (2005) UNFF session [E/CN.18/2004/12]. A further Secretariat note dealt with ASEAN's request to participate in UNFF's deliberations [E/CN.18/2004/16] (see p. 1057). Also before the Forum was the Collaborative Partnership on Forests Framework 2004 [E/CN.18/2004/INF/1]; a 5 March letter from Indonesia and Switzerland concerning the convening of an international meeting (Interlaken, Switzerland, 27-30 April) on forestry and national forest programmes in support of UNFF, known as the Interlaken Workshop [E/CN.18/2004/15]; and the reports of the Ad Hoc Expert Groups on Approaches and Mechanisms for Monitoring, Assessment and Reporting, and on Finance and Transfer of Environmentally Sound Technology [YUN 2003, p. 1062].

On 20 July, the Economic and Social Council took note of the Forum's report on its fourth session and approved the provisional agenda for the fifth session (**decision 2004/235**).

Expert group meeting. The Ad Hoc Expert Group on Consideration with a View to Recommending the Parameters of a Mandate for Developing a Legal Framework on All Types of Forests (New York, 7-10 September) [E/CN.18/2005/2] addressed, under the tasks assigned to it by the Council in decision 2003/299 [YUN 2003, p. 1058], complementarities, gaps and duplications and a review of relevant experiences of existing regional and international binding and non-binding instruments and processes relevant to forests; other outcomes of the international arrangement on forests; and options for the parameters of a mandate for developing a legal framework on all types of forests. In carrying out its tasks, the Group considered reports by member States and organizations of the Collaborative Partnership on Forests and the Forum secretariat, and the outcomes of UNFF sessions. It also considered an overview of catalysts and obstacles in implementing IPF/IFF proposals for action [YUN 1997, p. 1057] and UNFF resolutions and decisions [E/CN.18/AC.3/2004/3], and background information to facilitate its deliberations [E/CN.18/AC.3/2004/2].

The Group recommended that the fifth (2005) UNFF session consider and build upon the discussions and exchange of views of the Group, as reflected in its report.

Marine ecosystems

Oceans and seas

The fifth meeting of the United Nations Open-ended Informal Consultative Process in Oceans and the Law of the Sea (New York, 7-11 June) [A/59/122] (see p. 1333) discussed new sustainable uses of the oceans, including the conservation and management of the biological diversity of the seabed in areas beyond national jurisdiction. It proposed that the General Assembly welcome the establishment of the Oceans and Coastal Areas Network (UN-Oceans), a new inter-agency coordination mechanism (see p. 1044), and urge the close and continuous involvement in the Network of all UN programmes, funds, specialized agencies and organizations, which the Assembly did, in section XV of **resolution 59/24** of 17 November (see p. 1340).

Global waters assessment

The Global International Waters Assessment (GIWA), inaugurated in 2000 [YUN 2000, p. 982] to assess international waters and causes of environmental problems in 66 water regions, focusing on the aquatic environment in transboundary waters, published a number of regional assessment reports in 2004, including reports on environmental conditions of international waters in three regions of South America and on Lake Chad in Africa. Other GIWA reports highlighted the problems of solid wastes on Indian Ocean islands and threats to the ecosystems of the Barents and Baltic Seas.

A November note by the Executive Director [UNEP/GC.23/INF/18 & Corr.1] included further information on GIWA. By the end of 2004, GIWA would have published 22 regional reports and 20 more would be ready for publishing, covering 98 per cent of all regions eligible for assessment under GEF funding. With the GIWA project nearing completion, a proposal for the further use of GIWA networks and assessment methodologies was put forward.

Report of Secretary-General. The Secretary-General, in July [A/59/126], reported on the results of the Global Marine Assessment (GMA) International Workshop (New York, 8-11 June), held in accordance with General Assembly resolution 58/240 [YUN 2003, p. 1355], and convened in conjunction with the fifth meeting of the UN Open-ended Informal Consultative Process on Oceans and the Law of the Sea (see p. 1333). The Workshop considered a draft document [A/AC.271/WP.1], prepared by a Group of Experts established in compliance with resolution 58/240, covering the scope, general framework and outline of GMA, and other matters. The Workshop discussed an "Assessment of Assessments" as a first step in the implementation of the start-up phase of GMA, a proposed task force for launching the "Assessment of Assessments", and GMA's scope. The Workshop concluded that, since no consensus was reached on launching GMA, it would be premature to hold the intergovernmental meeting mandated in resolution 58/240 and planned for Reykjavik, Iceland, in October, to formally establish it. The draft conclusions of the Workshop were annexed to the report.

The Assembly, in section XII of **resolution 59/24** (p. 1339), took note of the report, and recognizing the urgent need to initiate the start-up phase (the Assessment of Assessments) for establishing GMA, requested the Secretary-General to convene another workshop in 2005 and to report thereon.

Note by Executive Director. A November note by the Executive Director [UNEP/GC.23/INF/18 & Corr.1] reported that the Group of Experts (New York, 23-26 March), convened pursuant to resolution 58/240, concluded that GMA should: produce regular, integrated global syntheses of the status and trends of marine ecosystems, including their socio-economic aspects; be built on integrated regional assessments conducted by regional affiliates; and facilitate continuous access to information on the status and trends of marine ecosystems on diverse geographic scales. Negotiations on the establishment of the GMA process were to continue up to the Assembly's fifty-ninth (2004) session, with the hope that a consensus would be reached that would allow the start-up of the initial, "Assessment of Assessments" phase.

UNEP continued to work on the development of policy summary reports based on the findings of its coastal and marine assessment projects, particularly GIWA (see p. 1058) and the Millennium Ecosystem Assessment (see p. 1056). It also developed modules for the assessments of coastal and marine environments, in partnership with key institutions and collaborators, which would contribute to the GMA process once it was established.

Global Programme of Action

In response to a 2003 Governing Council decision [YUN 2003, p. 1066], a November report of the

Executive Director [UNEP/GC.23/3/Add.5] contained information on the implementation of the Global Programme of Action (GPA) for the Protection of the Marine Environment from Land-based Activities [YUN 1995, p. 1081]. UNEP continued to implement the GPA 2002-2006 work programme, endorsed by the Governing Council [YUN 2002, p. 1054], and strived to ensure that the 2001 Montreal Declaration on the implementation of GPA [YUN 2001, p. 965], the 2002 Monterrey Consensus, adopted by the International Conference on Financing for Development [YUN 2002, p. 953], and the outcomes of the 2002 World Summit on Sustainable Development [YUN 2002, p. 821] were addressed in GPA implementation efforts.

At the global level, UNEP hosted the inaugural Global Hilltops-2-Oceans (H2O) Partnership Conference (Cairns, Australia, 11-14 May), which resulted in the Cairns Communiqué [UNEP/GC.23/INF/17] on the integration of water resource and coastal area management from hilltops to oceans through multi-stakeholder partnerships. During the Conference, UNEP and the Water Supply and Sanitation Collaborative Council launched the Wastewater Emissions Targets: Water and Sanitation for All (WET-WASH) campaign. UNEP finalized guidelines on municipal wastewater management, related checklists and 10 Keys for Local and National Action on Municipal Wastewater, which were annexed to a January note by the Executive Director [UNEP/GCSS.VIII/INF/4]. It also helped develop a training course on improving municipal wastewater management in coastal cities and cooperated with the Regional Seas Programme on regional GPA activities.

UNEP's national-level activities included support for the development of national programmes of action and the implementation of a strategic plan on municipal wastewater; programmes dealing with the physical alteration and destruction of coastal and marine habitats and integrated coastal area and river basin management; the development of national legislation to address marine pollution from land-based activities and innovative financial arrangements to secure GPA implementation.

In section X of **resolution 59/24** of 17 November (see p. 1338), the General Assembly called on States to advance the implementation of GPA and the 2001 Montreal Declaration on the implementation of GPA [YUN 2001, p. 965].

Coral reefs

A November report of the Executive Director [UNEP/GC.23/3/Add.5] described progress in the implementation of a 2003 Governing Council decision regarding coral reefs [YUN 2003, p. 1067], led by UNEP's Coral Reef Unit. The Unit, which operated under UNEP's Division of Environmental Policy Implementation, provided programme support and policy analysis on the conservation, management and sustainable use of coral reef resources. The Unit furthered the subject of cold-water coral reefs and raised the issue of dredging in coral reef regions. It was developing relationships with coral reef stakeholders from private and industrial sectors, including the dredging industry, and initiated a project, with the International Association for Dredging Companies and the Central Dredging Association, on reducing the environmental impact of dredging operations in areas with corals. A UNEP initiative, established in collaboration with Ireland, Norway, the United Kingdom and the World Wide Fund for Nature, commissioned a report on a comprehensive and up-to-date baseline on cold-water coral reefs from around the world. The report, "Cold-water corals: out of sight—no longer out of mind", was released on 28 June at the International Coral Reef Symposium in Okinawa, Japan.

In February, the International Coral Reef Action Network (ICRAN) Mesoamerican Reef Alliance project, providing for the establishment and strengthening of private sector alliances, was signed in Belize City, Belize. In preparation for the expansion of ICRAN into additional coral reef areas as announced at the World Summit, UNEP supported an assessment of the needs, priorities and opportunities for coral reef work in a number of regions. In September, the World Resources Institute, with support from ICRAN, the UNEP regional coordinating unit for the Caribbean and the United States Agency for International Development, published an analysis of threats to Caribbean coral reefs, entitled "Reefs at Risk in the Caribbean". The joint ICRAN board and steering committee meeting (Washington, D.C., 21-23 January) adopted a new ICRAN framework document which emphasized a regional focus. The Executive Director's report also described UNEP's efforts to realize the Johannesburg Plan of Implementation [YUN 2002, p.821] with respect to coral reefs; collaborative efforts in coral-related activities with multilateral environmental agreements; collaboration with UN agencies to address the urgency of achieving sustainability in the management and use of coral reefs; and efforts to engage international financial institutions.

Regional Seas Programme

A November note by the UNEP secretariat [UNEP/GC.23/INF/26] provided information on the implementation of the Governing Council's 2003 decisions on regional seas conventions and action plans [YUN 2003, p. 1067] and UNEP's activities in marine safety and protection of the marine environment from accidental pollution. With regard to regional seas strategies for sustainable development, the note summarized progress relating to the global strategic directions/guidelines agreed upon by the Fifth (2003) Global Meeting of Regional Seas Conventions and Action Plans [YUN 2003, p. 1068]. The directions/ guidelines were finalized at the Sixth Global Meeting (Istanbul, Turkey, 29 November–3 December) [UNEP(DEC)/RS.6]. Based on the report of a feasibility study, UNEP planned developing a global initiative on the sustainable management of marine litter through regional pilot projects.

UNEP finalized host country agreements with Japan and the Republic of Korea to co-host the regional coordinating unit offices (Toyama, Japan and Busan, Republic of Korea) of the Action Plan for the Protection, Management and Development of the Marine and Coastal Environment of the North-West Pacific Region (NOWPAP), established in 2001 [YUN 2001, p. 966], which were to become operational in November. NOWPAP's ninth intergovernmental meeting was held in Busan (2-4 November).

With support from the Swedish International Development Agency (SIDA), UNEP assisted in institutionalizing the Action Plan of the Convention for Cooperation in the Protection and Sustainable Development of the Marine and Coastal Environment of the North-East Pacific, first signed in 2002 [YUN 2002, p. 1055]. Informal consultations were taking place on institutional arrangements, including a host country for the secretariat and its programme of work.

UNEP continued to support the 1981 Abidjan Convention for Cooperation in the Protection and Development of the Marine and Coastal Environment of the West and Central African Region [YUN 1981, p. 840] and the 1985 Nairobi Convention for the Protection, Management and Development of the Marine and Coastal Environment of the Eastern African Region [YUN 1985, p. 816], and assisted in mobilizing a major Global Environment Facility project in the Abidjan Convention region.

The Regional Seas and GPA Coordinating Offices, in collaboration with the Comisión Permanente del Pacífico Sudeste, organized workshops and supported expert meetings in the region of the South-East Pacific Action Plan and Convention for the Protection of the Marine Environment and Coastal Area of the South-East Pacific, both established in 1981 [YUN 1981, p. 833], including on integrated coastal area and river basin management, and marine mammals.

Regarding marine safety and protection of the marine environment from accidental pollution,

UNEP and the International Maritime Organization (IMO) finalized a report of a joint IMO/UNEP forum on regional arrangements in emergency response to marine pollution and held a joint workshop on marine pollution prevention and environmental management in ports in East Africa (Mombassa, Kenya, 26-30 April). Collaboration between UNEP, IMO and other partners on the development of related activities also continued.

Caribbean Sea management

In response to General Assembly resolution 57/261 [YUN 2002, p. 1056], the Secretary-General submitted a July report [A/59/173] assessing progress made in promoting an integrated management approach to the Caribbean Sea in the context of sustainable development. It described activities undertaken by the Association of Caribbean States (ACS), the Economic Commission for Latin America and the Caribbean, UNDP, UNEP, GEF, UNESCO, and various States. The Secretary-General's report contained an ACS report, which included information on the first meeting of the Technical Advisory Group on the Caribbean Sea Initiative (Port of Spain, Trinidad and Tobago, 26 May 2003).

GENERAL ASSEMBLY ACTION

On 22 December [meeting 75], the General Assembly, on the recommendation of the Second Committee [A/59/483/Add.2], adopted **resolution 59/230** without vote [agenda item 85(b)].

Promoting an integrated management approach to the Caribbean Sea area in the context of sustainable development

The General Assembly,

Reaffirming the principles and commitments enshrined in the Rio Declaration on Environment and Development and the principles embodied in the Declaration of Barbados and the Programme of Action for the Sustainable Development of Small Island Developing States, as well as other relevant declarations and international instruments,

Recalling the Declaration and review document adopted by the General Assembly at its twenty-second special session,

Taking into account all other relevant General Assembly resolutions, including resolutions 54/225 of 22 December 1999, 55/203 of 20 December 2000 and 57/261 of 20 December 2002,

Taking into account also the Johannesburg Declaration on Sustainable Development and the Plan of Implementation of the World Summit on Sustainable Development ("Johannesburg Plan of Implementation"),

Noting with interest the respective partnership initiatives voluntarily undertaken by Governments, international organizations and major groups and announced at the Summit,

Reaffirming the United Nations Convention on the Law of the Sea, which provides the overall legal framework for ocean activities, and emphasizing its fundamental character, conscious that the problems of ocean space are closely interrelated and need to be considered as a whole through an integrated, interdisciplinary and intersectoral approach,

Emphasizing the importance of national, regional and global action and cooperation in the marine sector as recognized by the United Nations Conference on Environment and Development in chapter 17 of Agenda 21,

Recalling the Convention for the Protection and Development of the Marine Environment of the Wider Caribbean Region, signed at Cartagena de Indias, Colombia, on 24 March 1983, which contains the definition of the wider Caribbean region of which the Caribbean Sea is part,

Welcoming the adoption, on 6 October 1999 in Aruba, of the Protocol Concerning Pollution from Land-based Sources and Activities to the Convention for the Protection and Development of the Marine Environment of the Wider Caribbean Region,

Welcoming also the entry into force, on 18 June 2000, of the Protocol Concerning Specially Protected Areas and Wildlife to the Convention for the Protection and Development of the Marine Environment of the Wider Caribbean Region and the establishment by the United Nations Environment Programme of the Regional Activities Centre in Guadaloupe to assist in the implementation of the Protocol,

Recalling the relevant work done by the International Maritime Organization,

Considering that the Caribbean Sea area includes a large number of States, countries and territories, most of which are developing countries and small island developing States that are ecologically fragile, structurally weak and economically vulnerable and are also affected, inter alia, by their limited capacity, narrow resource base, need for financial resources, high levels of poverty and the resulting social problems and the challenges and opportunities of globalization and trade liberalization,

Recognizing that the Caribbean Sea has a unique biodiversity and highly fragile ecosystem,

Emphasizing that the Caribbean countries have a high degree of vulnerability occasioned by climate change, climate variability and associated phenomena, such as the rise in sea level, the El NiZo phenomenon and the increase in the frequency and intensity of natural disasters caused by hurricanes, floods and droughts, and that they are also subject to natural disasters, such as those caused by volcanoes, tsunamis and earthquakes,

Expressing deep concern over the severe destruction and devastation caused to several countries by heightened hurricane activity in the Caribbean region in 2004,

Recognizing national and regional efforts to undertake disaster preparedness, response and mitigation efforts to minimize the impact of natural disasters, and reiterating the responsibility of all States in that regard,

Bearing in mind the heavy reliance of most of the Caribbean economies on their coastal areas, as well as on the marine environment in general, to achieve their sustainable development needs and goals,

Recognizing the Caribbean Environment Outlook process currently being undertaken by the United Nations Environment Programme, and welcoming the support being provided by the Caribbean Environment Programme of the United Nations Environment Programme towards its implementation,

Acknowledging that the intensive use of the Caribbean Sea for maritime transport, as well as the considerable number and interlocking character of the maritime areas under national jurisdiction where Caribbean countries exercise their rights and duties under international law, present a challenge for the effective management of the resources,

Noting the problem of marine pollution caused, inter alia, by land-based sources and the continuing threat of pollution from ship-generated waste and sewage, as well as from the accidental release of hazardous and noxious substances in the Caribbean Sea area,

Taking note of the relevant resolutions of the General Conference of the International Atomic Energy Agency on safety of transport of radioactive materials,

Mindful of the diversity and dynamic interaction and competition among socio-economic activities for the use of the coastal areas and the marine environment and their resources,

Mindful also of the efforts of the Caribbean countries to address in a more holistic manner the sectoral issues relating to the management of the Caribbean Sea area and, in so doing, to promote an integrated management approach to the Caribbean Sea area in the context of sustainable development, through a regional cooperative effort among Caribbean countries,

Noting the importance of the ongoing work of the Working Group on climate change and disaster risk reduction, established by the Inter-Agency Task Force for Disaster Reduction,

Noting also the efforts of the Caribbean countries, within the framework of the Association of Caribbean States, to develop further support for their concept of the Caribbean Sea as an area of special importance, in the context of sustainable development and in conformity with the United Nations Convention on the Law of the Sea,

Welcoming the decision by the Association of Caribbean States to establish the Technical Advisory Group to further advance the Caribbean Sea Initiative and the implementation of resolutions 55/203 and 57/261, inter alia, through the preparation of a technical report,

Cognizant of the importance of the Caribbean Sea to present and future generations and to the heritage and the continuing economic well-being and sustenance of people living in the area, and the urgent need for the countries of the region to take appropriate steps for its preservation and protection, with the support of the international community,

1. *Takes note* of the report of the Secretary-General;

2. *Takes note also* of the report of the Association of Caribbean States, pursuant to General Assembly resolution 57/261;

3. *Recognizes* the importance of adopting an integrated management approach to the Caribbean Sea area in the context of sustainable development;

4. *Encourages* the further promotion of an integrated management approach to the Caribbean Sea area in the context of sustainable development, in accordance with the recommendations contained in resolution 54/225, as well as the provisions of Agenda 21, the Programme of Action for the Sustainable Development of Small Island Developing States, the outcome of the twenty-second special session of the General Assembly, the Johannesburg Declaration on Sustainable Development, the Johannesburg Plan of Implementation and the work of the Commission on Sustainable Development, and in conformity with relevant international law, including the United Nations Convention on the Law of the Sea;

5. *Also encourages* the continued efforts of the Caribbean countries to develop further an integrated management approach to the Caribbean Sea area in the context of sustainable development and, in this regard, to continue to develop regional cooperation in the management of their ocean affairs in the context of sustainable development, in order to address such issues as land-based pollution, pollution from ships, physical impacts on coral reefs and the diversity and dynamic interaction of, and competition among, socio-economic activities for the use of the coastal areas and the marine environment and their resources;

6. *Welcomes* the wide range of activities being implemented within the scope of the mandate of resolution 57/261, with a view to promoting an integrated management approach to the Caribbean Sea area in the context of sustainable development;

7. *Recognizes* the efforts of Caribbean countries to create conditions leading to sustainable development aimed at combating poverty and inequality, and in this regard notes with interest the initiatives of the Association of Caribbean States in the focal areas of sustainable tourism, trade, transport and natural disasters;

8. *Calls upon* States to continue to prioritize action on marine pollution from land-based sources as part of their national sustainable development strategies and programmes, in an integrated and inclusive manner, and also calls upon them to advance the implementation of the Global Programme of Action for the Protection of the Marine Environment from Land-based Activities and the Montreal Declaration on the Protection of the Marine Environment from Land-based Activities;

9. *Calls upon* the United Nations system and the international community to assist, as appropriate, Caribbean countries and their regional organizations in their efforts to ensure the protection of the Caribbean Sea from degradation as a result of pollution from ships, in particular through the illegal release of oil and other harmful substances, and from illegal dumping or accidental release of hazardous waste, including radioactive materials, nuclear waste and dangerous chemicals, in violation of relevant international rules and standards, as well as pollution from land-based activities;

10. *Calls upon* all relevant States to take the necessary steps to bring into force, and to support the implementation of, the Protocol Concerning Pollution from Land-based Sources and Activities to the Convention for the Protection and Development of the Marine Environment of the Wider Caribbean Region in order to protect the marine environment of the Caribbean Sea from land-based pollution and degradation;

11. *Calls upon* the international community to continue to support the efforts of the Association of Caribbean States to further implement resolutions 55/203

and 57/261, and invites the Association to submit a report on its progress to the Secretary-General for consideration during the sixty-first session of the General Assembly;

12. *Calls upon* all States to become contracting parties to relevant international agreements to enhance maritime safety and promote the protection of the marine environment of the Caribbean Sea from pollution, damage and degradation from ships and ship-generated waste;

13. *Supports* the efforts of Caribbean countries to implement sustainable fisheries management programmes by strengthening the Caribbean Regional Fisheries Mechanism;

14. *Calls upon* States, taking into consideration the Convention on Biological Diversity, to develop national, regional and international programmes for halting the loss of marine biodiversity in the Caribbean Sea, in particular fragile ecosystems, such as coral reefs;

15. *Invites* intergovernmental organizations within the United Nations system to continue their efforts to assist Caribbean countries in becoming parties to the relevant conventions and protocols and in implementing them effectively;

16. *Calls upon* the international community, the United Nations system and the multilateral financial institutions, and invites the Global Environment Facility, within its mandate, to support actively national and regional activities towards the above-mentioned approach;

17. *Urges* the United Nations system and the international community to continue to provide aid and assistance to the countries of the Caribbean region in the implementation of their long-term programmes of disaster prevention, preparedness, mitigation, management, relief and recovery, based on their development priorities, through the integration of relief, rehabilitation and reconstruction into a comprehensive approach to sustainable development;

18. *Calls upon* Member States to improve as a matter of priority their emergency response capabilities and the containment of environmental damage, particularly in the Caribbean Sea, in the event of natural disasters or of an accident or incident relating to maritime navigation;

19. *Requests* the Secretary-General to report to it at its sixty-first session, under the sub-item entitled "Further implementation of the Programme of Action for the Sustainable Development of Small Island Developing States" of the item entitled "Sustainable development", on the implementation of the present resolution, taking into account the views expressed by relevant regional organizations.

Conservation of wildlife

As at 31 December, the number of parties to the 1994 Lusaka Agreement on Cooperative Enforcement Operations Directed at Illegal Trade in Wild Fauna and Flora [YUN 1994, p. 951], which entered into force in 1996 [YUN 1996, p. 970], remained at six States (Congo, Kenya, Lesotho, Uganda, United Republic of Tanzania, Zambia). The Agreement aimed to reduce, and ultimately eliminate, illegal trafficking in African wildlife.

Reports of Executive Director. In November [UNEP/GC.23/3/Add.4], the Executive Director, in line with a 2003 decision of the Governing Council of the Parties to the Agreement [YUN 2003, p. 1068], reported that UNEP had completed a draft report reviewing and evaluating the Agreement's work since its adoption. A revised report would be submitted to the UNEP Governing Council in 2005. The Executive Director's report also provided an overview of UNEP involvement in the Great Apes Survival Project.

Also in November [UNEP/GC.23/INF/5], the Executive Director, reporting on the implementation of a 2003 Governing Council decision on the UNEP World Conservation Monitoring Centre (WCMC) [YUN 2003, p. 1068], stated that UNEP established a process to strengthen the Centre, including consultations with key stakeholders and the development of a review process. It completed a study on a network for enhancing the work of WCMC and other organizations concerned with biodiversity, particularly biodiversity assessment and information management; finalized a report on the state of the world's protected areas to be launched at the third World Conservation Union World Conservation Congress (Bangkok, Thailand, 17-25 November); continued to strengthen the World Database on Protected Areas (WDPA); and initiated discussions with the relevant partners on the renewed mandate for the United Nations List of Protected Areas (UN List) process, the latest (2003) edition of which was released during the fifth World Parks Congress (Durban, South Africa, 8-17 September 2003).

Protection against harmful products and waste

Chemical safety

As at 31 December, 72 States and the EC had signed and 79 States and the EC were parties to the 1998 Rotterdam Convention on the Prior Informed Consent (PIC) Procedure for Certain Hazardous Chemicals and Pesticides in International Trade [YUN 1998, p. 997]. During the year, 14 States ratified the Convention, two accepted it, one approved it, and nine acceded to it. The Convention entered into force on 24 February, 90 days after the deposit of the fiftieth instrument of ratification.

Prior to the entry into force of the Convention, the PIC Procedure was applied voluntarily by Governments.

The 29-member Interim Chemical Review Committee, a subsidiary body of the Intergovernmental Negotiating Committee (INC) for an International Legally Binding Instrument for the Application of the PIC Procedure, established in 1999 [YUN 1999, p. 997] to make recommendations on specific chemicals or hazardous pesticide formulations for inclusion in the PIC procedure, held its fifth session (Geneva, 2-5 February) [UNEP/FAO/PIC/ICRC.5/15], at which it made a number of recommendations on chemicals to INC.

The eleventh and final session of INC (Geneva, 18 September) [UNEP/FAO/PIC/INC.11/7] extended the period for inclusion of any additional chemicals under the interim PIC procedure from the date of entry into force of the Convention until the date of the opening of the first meeting of the Conference of the Parties (see below) and agreed to decide on the inclusion of any additional chemicals to the interim PIC procedure in accordance with articles 5, 6, 7 and 22 of the Convention. On the recommendation of the Interim Chemical Review Committee (see above), INC made tetraethyl lead and tetramethyl lead (gasoline additives) subject to the interim PIC procedure, along with the pesticide parathion. INC did not reach a consensus on the inclusion of chrysotile asbestos in the voluntary PIC procedure.

Conference of Parties. The first meeting of the Conference of the Parties to the Rotterdam Convention (Geneva, 20-24 September) [UNEP/FAO/RC/COP.1/33] adopted its rules of procedure and financial rules and requested the secretariat to propose options on a financial mechanism. It established a 31 member Chemical Review Committee as a subsidiary body and rules and procedures for preventing and dealing with conflicts of interest relating to the activities of the Committee. The Conference invited the UNEP Executive Director and the FAO Director-General to make proposals on a Convention secretariat for consideration and approval at its second meeting and to continue to perform those functions in the interim, and to appoint an Executive Director in consultation with the parties. It accepted the offer of Italy and Switzerland to host the secretariat jointly in Rome and Geneva and decided that developing countries should be adequately represented at senior grades in the secretariat. It also approved an operational budget for 2005 and an indicative budget for 2006.

The Conference adopted the regions and listing of countries as PIC regions for the purposes of article 5, paragraph 5 of the Convention; amendments to annex III to the Convention; and annex VI to the Convention setting out procedures for the settlement of disputes. It also adopted procedures for banned or severely restricted chemicals, and established a period of transition (24 February 2004 to 24 February 2006) from the interim to the Convention PIC procedure. The Conference encouraged the World Customs Organization to assign specific Harmonized System codes to the chemicals listed in annex III of the Convention. It decided to convene an open-ended ad hoc working group to consider the issue of non-compliance under article 17. Decisions were also adopted on regional delivery of technical assistance and on cooperation with the World Trade Organization.

International chemicals management

Report of Executive Director. A November report of the Executive Director [UNEP/GC.23/3/Add.1], outlined progress in the development of the strategic approach to international chemicals management (SAICM), pursuant to a 2002 Governing Council decision [YUN 2002, p. 1063]. Intersessional regional consultations, following the first (2003) session of the Preparatory Committee of the Development of SAICM [YUN 2003, p. 1071], were held by the African Group (Abuja, Nigeria, 24-26 May) and the Latin American and Caribbean Group (Nairobi, Kenya, 2-3 May). The second session of the Preparatory Committee (Nairobi, 4-8 October) [SAICM/PREPCOM.2/4] agreed on a tripartite structure for SAICM, comprising a high-level declaration, an overarching policy statement and a global plan of action. The Committee's president and secretariat were to continue intersessional work, and regional consultations were expected to take place in February and March 2005. Following one further Preparatory Committee meeting in 2005, the final international conference on chemicals management was planned to take place in 2006.

Lead

The Executive Director reported [UNEP/GC.23/3/Add.1] that activities for implementing the 2003 Governing Council decision on lead [YUN 2003, p. 1071] were constrained by lack of funding and staff resources. Concerning the phasing out of lead in gasoline, 65 bodies, drawn from Governments, the private sector, NGOs, and international organizations had joined the Partnership for Clean Fuels and Vehicles, launched at the 2002 World Summit on Sustainable Development [YUN 2002, p. 821]. In Africa, UNEP was supporting national-level activities, including workshops, training sessions for gasoline attendants, the formation of country task teams and public awareness campaigns. A regional conference on progress made in leaded gasoline phase-out in sub-Saharan Africa (Nairobi, Kenya, 5-7 May) reconfirmed the phase-out date of the end of 2005 set by African Governments and their partners, including UNEP, in 2001, and proposed actions to ensure that the target was met. The conference outcomes were adopted by the tenth regular session of the African Ministerial Conference on the Environment (Sirte, Libya, 26-30 June). To date, 50 per cent of gasoline sold in Africa was unleaded; nine countries had completely phased out leaded gasoline, 12 had fixed phase-out dates by December 2005, 16 introduced unleaded gasoline, and 20 had action plans to phase out leaded gasoline.

Mercury programme

Responding to a 2003 Governing Council decision on mercury [YUN 2003, p. 1071], the Executive Director, in November [UNEP/GC.23/3/Add.1], reported on the UNEP mercury programme, whose long-term objective was to facilitate national, regional and global action to reduce or eliminate as far as possible anthropogenic uses and releases of mercury and mercury compounds. Its immediate objective was to encourage all countries to adopt goals, identify at-risk populations and ecosystems and reduce anthropogenic mercury releases. The report described capacity-building and technical activities; programme funding; technical and financial assistance activities; and further activities.

A December note by the Executive Director [UNEP/GC.23/INF/19], provided an analysis of the views and options submitted by 25 Governments and regional economic organizations as at 1 October, in response to his 23 February request to them to report on progress in implementing the Governing Council's 2003 decision on mercury, especially with regard to any goals or national action taken, and to provide views on further measures to address significant global adverse impacts of mercury and further action on other heavy metals.

Harmful products

In May [A/59/81-E/2004/63], the Secretary-General submitted a report covering the seventh triennial review of the Consolidated List of Products Whose Consumption and/or Sale Have Been Banned, Withdrawn, Severely Restricted or Not Approved by Governments. The report updated developments since the submission of the Secretary-General's last report in 2001 [YUN 2001, p. 970].

Significant progress had been made since the previous review, particularly the coming into force of the Rotterdam (see p. 1063) and the Stockholm Conventions (see p. 1066). The Secretary-General made recommendations to the Economic and Social Council relating to the permanent online availability of the List and printing updates in all UN official languages;

strengthening capacity-building and technical assistance in developing countries and providing financial resources in support of national efforts to improve the environmentally sound management of toxic chemicals; and full participation by Member States in the process to successfully develop the strategic approach to international chemicals management (see p. 1064) by 2005.

ECONOMIC AND SOCIAL COUNCIL ACTION

On 23 July [meeting 50], the Economic and Social Council adopted **resolution 2004/55** [draft: E/2004/L.46] without vote [agenda item 13(e)].

Protection against products harmful to health and the environment

The Economic and Social Council,

Recalling General Assembly resolutions 37/137 of 17 December 1982, 38/149 of 19 December 1983, 39/229 of 18 December 1984 and 44/226 of 22 December 1989, Assembly decisions 47/439 of 22 December 1992 and 50/431 of 20 December 1995, and Economic and Social Council resolutions 1998/41 of 30 July 1998 and 2001/33 of 26 July 2001,

Having considered the report of the Secretary-General on products harmful to health and the environment, which contains a review of the Consolidated List of Products Whose Consumption and/or Sale Have Been Banned, Withdrawn, Severely Restricted or Not Approved by Governments,

Taking note of the fact that an increasing number of countries participate in the preparation of the Consolidated List,

Noting with satisfaction the continued close collaboration among the United Nations, the Food and Agriculture Organization of the United Nations, the World Health Organization and the United Nations Environment Programme in the preparation and dissemination of the Consolidated List,

Taking note of commitments made and targets established regarding environmentally sound management of chemicals in the Plan of Implementation of the World Summit on Sustainable Development ("Johannesburg Plan of Implementation"), adopted by the Summit on 4 September 2002,

Noting the entry into force, in early 2004, of the Rotterdam Convention on the Prior Informed Consent Procedure for Certain Hazardous Chemicals and Pesticides in International Trade and the Stockholm Convention on Persistent Organic Pollutants,

1. *Takes note* of the report of the Secretary-General, and notes that the Consolidated List of Products Whose Consumption and/or Sale Have Been Banned, Withdrawn, Severely Restricted or Not Approved by Governments is available online;

2. *Expresses its appreciation* for the cooperation extended by Governments in the preparation of the Consolidated List, and urges all Governments, in particular those that have not yet done so, to provide the information necessary to relevant organizations for inclusion in future issues of the Consolidated List;

3. *Requests* the Secretary-General to continue to update the electronic version of the Consolidated List, alternating between chemicals and pharmaceuticals

every year, while printing only new data to complement previously printed issues for the benefit of those, particularly in developing countries, who may not have easy access to the electronic version;

4. *Urges* all Governments to participate fully in the process of developing a strategic approach to international chemicals management by 2005, in order to achieve the 2020 target of the World Summit on Sustainable Development, as set out in paragraph 23 of the Johannesburg Plan of Implementation, pursuant to which chemicals would be used and produced in ways that lead to the minimization of significant adverse effects on human health and the environment, using transparent science-based risk assessment procedures and science-based risk management procedures, taking into account the precautionary approach, as set out in principle 15 of the Rio Declaration on Environment and Development, and support developing countries in strengthening their capacity for the sound management of chemicals and hazardous wastes by providing technical and financial assistance, and calls for a more coordinated use of existing international instruments in this field, taking into account the work undertaken by the United Nations system in this regard;

5. *Encourages* countries to implement the new Globally Harmonized System of Classification and Labelling of Chemicals, as agreed in paragraph 23 *(c)* of the Johannesburg Plan of Implementation, as soon as possible, with a view to having the system fully operational by 2008;

6. *Urges* all Governments that have not yet done so to consider ratifying the Rotterdam Convention on the Prior Informed Consent Procedure for Certain Hazardous Chemicals and Pesticides in International Trade and the Stockholm Convention on Persistent Organic Pollutants and to fully implement them;

7. *Invites* multilateral and bilateral agencies to continue to strengthen and coordinate their activities for improving the capacity-building of developing countries, in particular the least developed countries, as well as countries with economies in transition, including through technical assistance in the area of the sound management of hazardous chemicals and dangerous pharmaceutical products;

8. *Emphasizes* the need to continue to utilize the work being undertaken by relevant organizations of the United Nations system and other intergovernmental organizations in this area, as well as that being carried out under international agreements and conventions in related areas, in updating the Consolidated List;

9. *Requests* the Secretary-General to continue to report every three years, in accordance with resolution 39/229, on the implementation of the present resolution, taking into account previous Assembly resolutions on the same subject, as appropriate.

Persistent organic pollutants

As at 31 December, 88 States and the EC were parties to the 2001 Stockholm Convention on Persistent Organic Pollutants (POPs) [YUN 2001, p. 971]. During the year, 34 States ratified the Convention, one accepted it, one State and the EC approved it, and 10 acceded to it. The Convention entered into force on 17 May, 90 days after the deposit of the fiftieth instrument of approval. The first Conference of the Parties to the Convention was scheduled to be held in Punta del Este, Uruguay, in May 2005.

The Expert Group on Best Available Techniques and Best Environmental Practices, established in 2002 by the Intergovernmental Negotiating Committee for an International Legally Binding Instrument for Implementing International Action on Certain POPs [YUN 2002, p. 1064], at its third session (Tokyo, Japan, 11-16 October) [UNEP/POPS/EGB.3/3], endorsed the draft guidelines on best available techniques and provisional guidance on best environmental practices and agreed to forward them to the Conference of Parties to the Stockholm Convention.

Hazardous wastes

As at 31 December, the number of parties to the 1989 Basel Convention on the Control of Transboundary Movements of Hazardous Wastes and their Disposal [YUN 1989, p. 420], which entered into force in 1992 [YUN 1992, p. 685], rose to 163 with the accession of Chad, the Cook Islands, Liberia, Rwanda and Togo. The 1995 amendment to the Convention [YUN 1995, p. 1333], not yet in force, had been ratified, accepted or approved by 55 parties. During the year, Botswana, the Syrian Arab Republic and Togo acceded to the 1999 Basel Protocol on Liability and Compensation for Damage resulting from Transboundary Movements of Hazardous Wastes and their Disposal [YUN 1999, p. 998], bringing the total number of parties to four.

The third session of the Open-ended Working Group of the Convention (26-30 April) [UNEP/CHW/OEWG/3/34 & Corr.1], adopted the 2004 work plan of the Basel Convention Partnership Programme. Other decisions dealt with the selection of project proposals under the Strategic Plan for the Implementation of the Convention to 2010, adopted by the Conference of the Parties to the Convention in 2002 [YUN 2002, p. 1065]; legal aspects of the dismantling of ships; a proposed decision on the Joint Working Group of ILO, the International Maritime Organization (IMO) and the Convention (see p. 1067); issues related to annex VII to the Convention; the Basel Protocol on Liability and Compensation [YUN 1999, p. 998]; establishment of a mechanism for implementation and compliance; technical guidelines on POPs; implementation of existing technical guidelines; work on hazard characteristics; India's application regarding plastic-coated cable scrap; the import of wastes contained in annex IX to the Convention; and illegal traffic in hazardous wastes.

The seventh meeting of the Conference of the Parties to the Basel Convention (Geneva, 25-

29 October) [UNEP/CHW.7/33] adopted amendments to annexes VIII and IX to the Convention; a standardized format for reporting under article 3 of the Convention on national definitions of hazardous wastes; and technical guidelines on POPs and on the environmentally sound recycling/reclamation of metals and metal compounds. The meeting asked the Open-ended Working Group to finalize technical guidelines on the environmentally sound management of wastes resulting from surface treatment of metals and plastics and invited Parties to provide comments on the implementation of existing technical guidelines. It also adopted the 2005-2006 work plan of the Basel Convention Partnership Programme and that of the Convention's Open-ended Working Group. It requested the secretariat to conclude a framework agreement with Iran to establish a Regional Centre for Training and Technology Transfer in Tehran. The meeting incorporated modifications into the French language version of the lists of wastes contained in annexes VIII and IX to the Convention. Other decisions related to the implementation of the Strategic Plan for the Implementation of the Convention [YUN 2002, p. 1065]; hazardous waste minimization; the Mobile Phone Partnership Initiative; implementation of the 1994 Barbados Programme of Action for the Sustainable Development of Small Island Developing States [YUN 1994, p. 783]; the implementation of the environment initiative of the New Partnership for Africa's Development [YUN 2002, p. 907]; follow-up to the 2002 World Summit on Sustainable Development [YUN 2002, p. 821]; regional centres for training and technology transfer; designation of competent authorities and focal points; work on hazard characteristics; the disposal of polyvinyl chloride (PVC) wastes; the import of wastes contained in annex IX to the Convention; harmonization of lists of wastes and related procedures; the Joint Working Group of ILO, IMO and the Basel Convention on Ship Scrapping; the environmentally sound management of ship dismantling and the abandonment of ships; the Basel Protocol [YUN 1999, p. 998]; the Trust Fund to Assist Developing Countries and Other Countries in Need of Technical Assistance in the Implementation of the Basel Convention; the mechanism established in 2002 [YUN 2002, p. 1065] to promote implementation and compliance; a checklist for the preparation of national legislation for the implementation of the Convention; illegal traffic in hazardous wastes and other wastes; the transmission of information; bilateral, multilateral or regional agreements; international cooperation, including with WTO and the Global Environment Facility; sustainable financing; and administrative, financial and other matters. (For information on the human rights aspects of the illicit movement and dumping of toxic and dangerous products and wastes, see p. 766).

Cleaner production and sustainable consumption patterns

The Executive Director, reporting in November [UNEP/GC.23/INF/5] on the implementation of a 2003 Governing Council decision on the promotion of sustainable consumption and production [YUN 2003, p. 1073], described UNEP's activities in cooperation with the UN Department of Economic and Social Affairs (DESA), activities undertaken through UNEP's cleaner production and sustainable consumption programmes, and training and capacity-building programmes.

The Global Compact, an initiative launched in 2000 [YUN 2000, p. 989] with the aim of engaging the business community in advancing basic values in human rights, and UNEP, held a policy dialogue on sustainable consumption: marketing and communications (Paris, 5-6 April). The First African Expert Meeting on Sustainable Consumption and Production (Casablanca, Morocco, 19-20 May) adopted the Casablanca Statement on Sustainable Consumption and Production, which, among other things, called on the UN system, including UNEP, the United Nations Industrial Development Organization, and DESA to strengthen their support to national, subregional and regional efforts in Africa to promote sustainable consumption and production, as part of the 10-year Framework of Programmes for Sustainable Consumption and Production—the Marrakech Process—agreed to in 2003 [YUN 2003, p. 840]. The Statement was to be submitted to the tenth regular session of the African Ministerial Conference on the Environment (Sirte, Libya, 29-30 June). Other meetings held were: the Third African Roundtable on Sustainable Consumption and Production (Casablanca, 17-20 May); and the European stakeholder meeting on sustainable consumption and production (Ostend, Belgium, 25-26 November), organized by UNEP and the EC.

UNEP held its eighth International High-level Seminar on Sustainable Consumption and Production (Monterrey, Mexico, 15-16 November) to select methodologies, approaches, projects and funding mechanisms to be replicated and used to change unsustainable patterns of production and consumption; build new partnerships to share and leverage resources and facilitate the implementation process; and identify priority activities for UNEP and other organizations mandated to implement the sustainability agenda. Seminar participants agreed on 16 recommendations relating to water; energy; consumption; resource use, technology and products; and other issues for consideration by the Governing Council in 2005, which would review progress on the sustainable consumption and production agenda.

Governing Council action. On 31 March [dec. SS.VIII/4], the Governing Council decided to discuss, in 2005, domestic, industrial and hazardous waste management, in particular capacity-building and technology support, and to consider innovative ways of mobilizing financial resources to support developing countries and countries with economies in transition in that regard.

Other matters

Environmental law

In response to a 2003 Governing Council decision [YUN 2003, p. 1073], the Executive Director, in November [UNEP/GC.23/3/Add.3], reported on follow-up to the 2002 Global Judges Symposium on the Role of Law and Sustainable Development [YUN 2002, p. 1065], focusing on capacity-building in the area of environmental law. The report summarized the results of activities conducted pursuant to the decision, including the creation of a UNEP alliance of chief justices; the establishment of a global training centre for judges in Cairo, Egypt, as a centre of excellence for the implementation of UNEP's global judges capacity-building programme; the creation of judges forums on environmental law in Europe, the Pacific, southern Africa, the Arab States, the Caribbean and francophone African countries; the development of a UNEP Judges Handbook on Environmental Law for common law, civil law and the Arab States; the convening of regional chief justices needs-assessment and planning meetings; the implementation of the capacity-building programme for judges and other legal stakeholders; and systematic and sustained capacity-building activities at the national level in several countries. Future activities would focus on intensifying national judicial training in environmental law through national judicial training institutes, supported by UNEP and its partner agencies; dissemination of the UNEP Judges Handbook on Environmental Law to judges worldwide; and further strengthening networking among chief justices through a UNEP global alliance of chief justices for environmental law.

In response to a further 2003 Governing Council decision [YUN 2003, p. 1073], the Executive Director reported on the implementation of the Programme for the Development and Periodic Review of Environmental Law for the First Decade of the Twenty-first Century (Montevideo Programme III), adopted by the Governing Council in 2001 [YUN 2001, p. 972]. The report listed UNEP achievements in the implementation of Montevideo Programme III, including the launch of its environmental law website and the joint UNEP-FAO-World Conservation Union database—ECOLEX—and the publication of environmental law materials and training manuals. Montevideo Programme III programme areas warranting special attention in the second half of the decade included implementation, compliance and enforcement; strengthening and development of international environmental law; freshwater resources; coastal and marine ecosystems; and trade and environment. UNEP activities in those areas would continue to be aligned with, and directed towards achieving the internationally agreed goals of the 2000 Millennium Declaration, adopted by the General Assembly in resolution 55/2 [YUN 2000, p. 49]. Further information on the implementation of Montevideo Programme III for the period 2000-2005 was provided in a December note by the Executive Director [UNEP/GC.23/INF/10].

Occupied Palestinian and other Arab territories

In response to a 2003 Governing Council decision on the environment in the Occupied Palestinian Territories [YUN 2003, p. 1073] the Executive Director, reported in November [UNEP/GC.23/3/Add.2] that UNEP's Post-Conflict Assessment Unit convened a trilateral technical meeting on environmental issues to discuss implementation of the decision, including the recommendations contained in the 2002 UNEP Desk Study on the Environment in the Occupied Palestinian Territories [YUN 2003, p. 1073]. The meeting considered the next steps to be undertaken by UNEP under eight jointly agreed priority desk study recommendations. The Unit subsequently held capacity-building training seminars for Palestinian officials, including on communications and the environment, environmental quality standards on wastewater and air pollution, environmental impact assessment, environmental policy-making and environmental laboratory analysis.

Human settlements

Follow-up to the 1996 UN Conference on Human Settlements (Habitat II) and the 2001 General Assembly special session

In August [A/59/198], the Secretary-General, in response to General Assembly resolution 58/226 [YUN 2003, p. 1076], reported on follow-up to the

Assembly's twenty-fifth (2001) special session [YUN 2001, p. 973] to review and appraise the implementation of the Habitat Agenda [YUN 1996, p. 994], adopted by the 1996 United Nations Conference on Human Settlements (Habitat II) [ibid., p. 992], and on the strengthening of the United Nations Human Settlements Programme (UN-Habitat). As a result of a positive response by Governments to the Assembly's calls in resolution 58/226 [YUN 2003, p. 1076] for increased contributions to the United Nations Habitat and Human Settlements Foundation (see p. 1076), general-purpose funds from Governments rose from $6 million in 2002 to $8.3 million in 2003, and special-purpose contributions from Governments and other donors increased from $30 million in 2002 to $37.8 million in 2003. The UN-Habitat Executive Director appealed to member States for multi-year funding, to enable more effective support of programme implementation. There were also promising signs of commitments from other sources.

Implementation of the Special Human Settlements Programme for the Palestinian People and the Technical Cooperation Trust Fund, the establishment of which was endorsed by the UN-Habitat Governing Council in 2003 [YUN 2003, p. 1083], began with a programme definition phase (March to December). The UN-Habitat Global Urban Observatory (GUO) was strengthened as a worldwide monitoring and learning network to assist countries and cities in collecting, analysing and using urban indicators and statistical data. UN-Habitat was providing technical assistance to Governments through GUO and technical cooperation projects with partners to promote the development of city performance monitoring systems and the development and implementation of indicator systems for monitoring the Habitat Agenda, the Millennium Development Goals (MDGs) [YUN 2000, p. 52] and national and local development targets. Joint initiatives were established with ongoing urban projects in Bangladesh, Cambodia, China, Georgia, India, Indonesia, Latvia, Mexico, South Africa and Yemen. With the World Bank, UN-Habitat produced operational guidelines for municipal performance measurement and introduced a programme on the monitoring of urban inequities, whose overarching global goal was to influence urban policies by providing knowledge support to Governments. An ongoing dialogue on the improvement of slum-dwellers' conditions was also initiated.

UN-Habitat established a Partners and Youth Section to provide an integrated approach and promote cooperation with Habitat Agenda partners. Cooperation and collaboration with NGOs

and other Habitat Agenda partners centred on the implementation of UN-Habitat's Global Campaigns for Secure Tenure and Urban Governance, launched in 2000 [YUN 2000, p. 995], and on the global monitoring of urbanization trends. UN-Habitat was working towards increasing the number of women's organizations and women's affairs ministries working in the area of human settlement in order to bring human settlement issues into the mainstream agenda and the 10-year review, in 2005, of the implementation of the 1995 Beijing Platform for Action [YUN 1995, p. 1170], adopted at the Fourth World Conference on Women [ibid., p. 1169] (see p. 1145). It conducted studies on women's rights to land and property as part of a larger study in Latin America, the findings of which would be published during the year.

UN-Habitat was cooperating with member States to address issues facing young people. Together with the UN Secretariat's Department of Economic and Social Affairs (DESA) and ILO, UN-Habitat organized an expert group meeting on urban youth employment (Nairobi, Kenya, June). A global partnership initiative on urban youth development in Africa was to be launched at the second session of the World Urban Forum (see p. 1073). UN-Habitat was also cooperating with various UN agencies in youth-related initiatives.

Initiatives of the Cities Alliance partnership between the World Bank and UN-Habitat included a state-wide slum upgrading programme in Bahia, Brazil. The MDGs were integrated into new guidelines for the common country assessment and the United Nations Development Assistance Framework (UNDAF), and linkages between the common country assessment and UNDAF, the MDGs and poverty reduction strategy papers were clarified. UN-Habitat began assigning programme managers to selected UNDP country offices, with 33 programme managers expected to be in place by the end of the year.

The Secretary-General said that multilateral and bilateral assistance for housing and urban infrastructure, which amounted to some $4 billion annually, had not increased in recent years and played a limited supporting role in view of the magnitude of the housing and basic services needs in developing countries. While major gains were registered during the period 2000-2003 in implementing the Programme, human and financial resource constraints limited the achievement of better results in partnership activities. The Secretary-General encouraged Governments to: include water, sanitation and human settlements in their national development plans and to integrate urban poverty in national poverty reduction strategy documents; increase the non-earmarked component of their contribution to facilitate the implementation of the Habitat Agenda, the 2001 Declaration on Cities and Other Human Settlements in the New Millennium, adopted by the twenty-fifth special session of the General Assembly in resolution S-25/2 [YUN 2001, p. 974], and the relevant commitments of the Millennium Declaration, in particular the MDG target of significantly improving the lives of at least 100 million slum dwellers by 2020 [YUN 2000, p. 52]; and support the participation of partner groups from developing countries at the second (2004) session of the World Urban Forum (see p. 1073). He encouraged Governments and financial institutions to contribute generously to the Technical Cooperation Trust Fund and the Special Human Settlements Programme for the Palestinian people. He also encouraged Governments and international agencies to review and promote the role of cities in sustainable development as the engines of economic growth and to assess their social risk and opportunity, as well as their potential assets in relation to rural hinterlands.

Coordinated implementation of Habitat Agenda

In May [E/2004/70], the Secretary-General reported on the implementation of Economic and Social Council resolution 2003/62 [YUN 2003, p. 1075] regarding the coordinated implementation of the Habitat Agenda. The report discussed the continued increase in contributions to the United Nations Habitat and Human Settlements Foundation, a campaign to widen the donor base, the Special Human Settlements Programme for the Palestinian people and the Technical Cooperation Trust Fund. It described cooperation and collaboration with NGOs and other Habitat Agenda partners, including civil society representatives, women's organizations, and member States and UN agencies working on youth-related initiatives. It also described the work of the Habitat Agenda task manager system, the establishment of which was supported by the General Assembly in the 2001 Declaration on Cities and Other Human Settlements [YUN 2001, p. 974]; coordination efforts through the United Nations Development Group, UNDAF and UNDP; and the inclusion of shelter and urbanization issues in national development strategies.

The Secretary-General encouraged Governments to increase their contributions for the implementation of the Habitat Agenda, the 2001 Declaration and the MDGs; facilitate partnerships at the national and local levels with civil society organizations, local authorities and the business sector; and support the participation of partner groups from developing countries in the second (2004) World Urban Forum (see p. 1073).

On 23 July, the Economic and Social Council, by **decision 2004/300**, took note of the Secretary-General's report; decided to transmit it to the Assembly for consideration at its fifty-ninth (2004) session; and requested the Secretary-General to submit a further report for consideration by the Council in 2005.

Pursuant to the Council's decision, the Secretary-General, by a September note [A/59/382], transmitted his May report on the coordinated implementation of the Habitat Agenda (see above) to the Assembly.

GENERAL ASSEMBLY ACTION

On 22 December [meeting 75], the General Assembly, on the recommendation of the Second Committee [A/59/484], adopted **resolution 59/239** without vote [agenda item 86].

Implementation of the outcome of the United Nations Conference on Human Settlements (Habitat II) and strengthening of the United Nations Human Settlements Programme (UN-Habitat)

The General Assembly,

Recalling its resolutions 3327(XXIX) of 16 December 1974, 32/162 of 19 December 1977, 34/115 of 14 December 1979, 56/205 and 56/206 of 21 December 2001, 57/275 of 20 December 2002 and 58/226 and 58/227 of 23 December 2003,

Taking note of Economic and Social Council resolutions 2002/38 of 26 July 2002 and 2003/62 of 25 July 2003 and Council decision 2004/300 of 23 July 2004,

Recalling the Habitat Agenda and the Declaration on Cities and Other Human Settlements in the New Millennium,

Taking into account the Johannesburg Declaration on Sustainable Development and the Plan of Implementation of the World Summit on Sustainable Development ("Johannesburg Plan of Implementation"), as well as the Monterrey Consensus of the International Conference on Financing for Development,

Recalling the goal contained in the United Nations Millennium Declaration of achieving a significant improvement in the lives of at least 100 million slum-dwellers by 2020, as proposed in the Cities Without Slums Initiative, and recalling further the goal contained in the Johannesburg Plan of Implementation to halve, by 2015, the proportion of people who are unable to reach or afford safe drinking water and the proportion of people who do not have access to basic sanitation,

Recognizing that the overall thrust of the strategic vision of the United Nations Human Settlements Programme (UN-Habitat) and its emphasis on the two global campaigns on secure tenure and urban governance are strategic points of entry for the effective implementation of the Habitat Agenda, especially for guiding international cooperation in respect of adequate shelter for all and sustainable human settlements development,

Conscious of the need to achieve greater coherence and effectiveness in the implementation of the Habitat Agenda, the Declaration on Cities and Other Human Settlements in the New Millennium and the relevant internationally agreed development goals, including those contained in the Millennium Declaration,

Recognizing the continued urgent need for increased and predictable financial contributions to the United Nations Habitat and Human Settlements Foundation to ensure timely, effective and concrete global implementation of the Habitat Agenda, the Declaration on Cities and Other Human Settlements in the New Millennium and the relevant internationally agreed development goals, including those contained in the Millennium Declaration and the Johannesburg Declaration and Plan of Implementation,

Reiterating the call to the Executive Director of UN-Habitat to increase the efforts to strengthen the Foundation in order to achieve its primary operative objective of supporting the implementation of the Habitat Agenda, including supporting shelter, related infrastructure-development programmes and housing-finance institutions and mechanisms, particularly in developing countries,

Recognizing that humanitarian assistance in the field of human settlements must be provided in ways that will be supportive of reconstruction and long-term development,

Noting the convening of the second session of the World Urban Forum, organized by UN-Habitat in cooperation with the Government of Spain, the Autonomous Government of Catalonia and the Municipality of Barcelona, in Barcelona, from 13 to 17 September 2004,

Expressing its appreciation to the Government of Canada and the city of Vancouver for their willingness to host the third session of the World Urban Forum in 2006,

Emphasizing the importance of access to basic services for the urban poor, and in this regard noting the decision of the Governing Council of UN-Habitat at its nineteenth session on water and sanitation in cities,

Noting the commitment to integrate urban planning and management in relation to housing, transport, employment opportunities, environmental conditions and community facilities, and further noting the commitment to promote, where appropriate, the upgrading of informal settlements and urban slums as an expedient measure and pragmatic solution to the urban shelter deficit,

1. *Takes note* of the report of the Secretary-General;

2. *Recognizes* that Governments have the primary responsibility for the sound and effective implementation of the Habitat Agenda and the Declaration on Cities and Other Human Settlements in the New Millennium, and stresses that the international community should fully implement its commitments to support the Governments of developing countries as well as countries with economies in transition in their efforts, through the provision of the requisite resources, capacity-building, the transfer of technology and the creation of an international enabling environment;

3. *Calls for* continued financial support to UN-Habitat through increased voluntary contributions to the United Nations Habitat and Human Settlements Foundation, and invites Governments to provide multi-year funding to support programme implementation;

4. *Also calls for* increased, non-earmarked contributions to the Foundation;

5. *Requests* the Executive Director to continue to work with the World Bank Group, regional development banks, other development banks, the private sector and other relevant partners to field-test approaches through pilot projects and to develop longer-term programmes to mobilize resources to increase the supply of affordable credit for slum upgrading and other pro-poor human settlements development in developing countries as well as countries with economies in transition;

6. *Calls upon* the international donor community and financial institutions to contribute generously to the Technical Cooperation Trust Fund and other operational activities of UN-Habitat for the effective implementation of its field programmes;

7. *Recognizes* the important role of regional offices and personnel of UN-Habitat in providing operational support to developing countries, and in this regard calls upon Governments to strengthen and support financially the regional offices of UN-Habitat in order to expand operational support to developing countries and countries with economies in transition;

8. *Calls upon* UN-Habitat to continue to work closely with the other organizations of the United Nations system, integrating UN-Habitat staff as appropriate into existing United Nations country offices;

9. *Requests* the Secretary-General to keep the resource needs of UN-Habitat and the United Nations Office at Nairobi under review so as to permit the delivery, in an effective manner, of necessary services to UN-Habitat and the other United Nations organs and organizations in Nairobi;

10. *Encourages* Governments to establish local, national and regional urban observatories and to provide financial and substantive support to UN-Habitat for the further development of methodologies for data collection, analysis and dissemination;

11. *Encourages* Member States as well as Habitat Agenda partners to provide support for the preparation of the UN-Habitat flagship reports, the *Global Report on Human Settlements* and the *State of the World's Cities* report, on a biennial basis so as to raise awareness of human settlements and to provide information on urban conditions and trends around the world;

12. *Encourages* Governments to support the UN-Habitat Global Campaign for Secure Tenure and the Global Campaign on Urban Governance as important tools for, inter alia, promoting administration of land and property rights, in accordance with national circumstances, and enhancing access to affordable credit by the urban poor;

13. *Invites* Governments to continue to promote linkages between urban and rural areas in line with the Habitat Agenda, which recognized that cities and rural areas are interdependent economically, socially and environmentally;

14. *Encourages* Governments and UN-Habitat to continue to promote partnerships with local authorities, non-governmental organizations, the private sector and other Habitat Agenda partners, including women's groups and academic and professional groups, in order to empower them, within the legal framework and conditions of each country, to play a more effective role in the provision of adequate shelter

for all and sustainable human settlements development in an urbanizing world;

15. *Also encourages* Governments to support and enable the participation of youth in the implementation of the Habitat Agenda through social, cultural and economic activities at the city level and other national- and local-level activities;

16. *Further encourages* Governments to include issues pertaining to shelter, sustainable human settlements and urban poverty in their national development strategies, including poverty reduction strategy papers, where they exist;

17. *Urges* the donor community to support the efforts of developing countries to make pro-poor investments in services and infrastructure in order to improve living environments, in particular in slums and informal settlements;

18. *Requests* UN-Habitat, within its mandate, to continue to support the efforts of countries affected by natural disasters and complex emergencies to develop prevention, rehabilitation and reconstruction programmes for the transition from relief to development, and encourages UN-Habitat to continue to work closely with the members of the Inter-Agency Standing Committee and other relevant agencies in the United Nations system in this field;

19. *Invites* the Secretary-General to incorporate the assessment of progress made towards the target of achieving a significant improvement in the lives of at least 100 million slum-dwellers by 2020 in his report on the review in 2005 of the implementation of the United Nations Millennium Declaration;

20. *Calls upon* UN-Habitat and the Division for Sustainable Development of the Department of Economic and Social Affairs of the Secretariat to work together closely in the preparations for the thirteenth session of the Commission on Sustainable Development in order to ensure a fruitful policy discussion of the thematic cluster of issues on water, sanitation and human settlements;

21. *Requests* the Secretary-General to submit a report to the General Assembly at its sixtieth session on the implementation of the present resolution;

22. *Decides* to include in the provisional agenda of its sixtieth session an item entitled "Implementation of the outcome of the United Nations Conference on Human Settlements (Habitat II) and strengthening of the United Nations Human Settlements Programme (UN-Habitat)".

UN Human Settlements Programme

Governing Council

In accordance with General Assembly resolution 56/206 [YUN 2001, p. 987], the Governing Council of the United Nations Human Settlements Programme (UN-Habitat) met biennially. It did not meet in 2004. The Governing Council's twentieth session would take place in 2005.

Committee of Permanent Representatives

The Committee of Permanent Representatives, the intersessional body of UN-Habitat's Governing Council, met three times in 2003 (4 June, 4 September, 11 December) and four times in 2004 (3 March, 30 June, 30 September and 9 December) [HSP/GC/20/3]. The Committee discussed follow-up to the decisions of the nineteenth (2003) session of the Governing Council [YUN 2003, p. 1078]; implementation of the UN-Habitat work programme, and of UN-Habitat's Global Campaigns for Secure Tenure and Urban Governance [YUN 2000, p. 995]; UN-Habitat's operational activities; preparations for the second session of the World Urban Forum (Barcelona, Spain, 13-17 September) (see p. 1073); UN-Habitat's financial status; the outcome of the twelfth session of the Commission on Sustainable Development (see p. 827); implementation of the MDG on slums; the programme on water and sanitation for cities; strengthening the role and status of local authorities and promoting effective decentralization; mainstreaming gender issues in UN-Habitat's work; and the UN-Habitat budget for the 2006-2007 biennium.

UN-Habitat activities

UN-Habitat's work in 2004, within its four-pillar strategy for attaining the goal of cities without slums, consisted of advocacy of global norms, analysis of information, field testing of solutions and financing. Its shelter, urban development, research and finance programmes, and its Global Campaigns on Secure Tenure and Urban Governance [YUN 2000, p. 995], were revised to contribute to the strategic vision adopted by the Governing Council in 1999 [YUN 1999, p. 1003] and updated in 2003 [YUN 2003, p. 1081]. The Global Campaign for Secure Tenure was launched in three countries in West Africa and an international task force created to facilitate negotiated policy alternatives to unlawful eviction. Regional and country consultations were conducted under the Water for African Cities and the Water for Asian Cities programmes, and community-led initiatives for improving water and sanitation for the urban poor were supported. Consultations started on a new Water for Eastern European Cities programme. Training and capacity-building for pursuing the Habitat Agenda and achieving the MDGs were conducted in eight countries. In Latin America and the Caribbean, technical support was provided to the capacity-building component in urban safety and youth-at-risk. The United Cities and Local Governments, an association advocating democratic local self-government worldwide, was launched during a meeting of its Founding Congress (Paris, 2-5 May), and the Global Campaign on Urban Governance was launched in Morocco, Senegal and Burkina Faso. New field operations in disaster management and response were identified in fifteen countries and several islands, and work on the strategy for addressing shelter problems for women and orphans afflicted by HIV/AIDS in informal settlements was ongoing in East Africa.

UN-Habitat's monitoring systems were strengthened to enable effective tracking of the MDG on slums [YUN 2000, p. 52], with Urban Inequities Surveys implemented in selected cities. UN-Habitat made considerable progress in preparing its Global Urban Indicators Database Version 3, including by revising urban indicators in line with the MDGs. The 2004-2005 edition of one of UN-Habitat's flagship publications, *The State of the World's Cities 2004/05: Globalization and Urban Culture*, was launched at the World Urban Forum's second session (see below).

In 2004, UN-Habitat had 95 technical programmes and projects under execution in 56 countries. It executed 36 technical cooperation projects, including 12 regional programmes, in 31 countries in Africa and the Arab States, and published 5 reports on the state of human settlements. In Asia and the Pacific, 23 projects worth $15.9 million were executed. New projects were undertaken in Afghanistan, China, Indonesia, Mongolia, Nepal, Sri Lanka, and the Philippines, and projects covering a range of priority issues from urban upgrading to urban governance were implemented in 13 countries. UN-Habitat started a new Urban and Housing Rehabilitation Programme for Iraq (UHRP), working within the UN strategic planning framework for Iraq (see p. 354), and served as the Deputy Task Manager for Cluster 4 of the Plan on infrastructure and housing. Large programmes, including reconstruction projects, were implemented in Africa, the Arab States, Asia and Europe. The Regional and Technical Cooperation Division also provided advisory services and implemented technical programmes and projects within the Global Campaigns [YUN 2000, p. 995], assisted several countries with post-war reconstruction and recovery and worked on training programmes and capacity-building in disaster prevention and management. Considerable progress was made in establishing the Slum Upgrading Facility, with $1.8 million raised for the design phase, and $10 million for the Facility's three-year pilot phase.

UN Habitat convened the second session of the World Urban Forum (Barcelona, Spain, 13-17 September) [HSP/GC/20/2/Add.2] on the theme "Cities: Crossroads of Cultures, Inclusiveness and Integration". It focused on urban cultures, realities, governance and renaissance, and thematic dialogues on urban poor, resources, sustainability, services, and disasters and reconstruction. The third Forum session would be held in Vancouver, Canada, in 2006.

Through the Cities Alliance, UN-Habitat and the World Bank collaborated to strengthen local government authorities, help in the emergency reconstruction of urban infrastructure, initiate and sustain labour intensive municipal public works, formulate city development strategies, and set up urban indicators databases, among other objectives, in Afghanistan, East Asia, Egypt, Latvia, Tanzania, and Yemen. UN-Habitat continued to publish its flagship quarterly magazine *Habitat Debate*. In collaboration with UNDP, UN-Habitat established a worldwide network of Habitat Programme Managers to enhance normative work with respect to implementation of the Habitat Agenda and the MDGs on water and sanitation and on slums [YUN 2000, p. 52]. UN-Habitat's disaster recovery activities related to the Indian Ocean tsunami of 26 December (see p. 952) were bringing a long-term, community-oriented perspective to the rapid recovery efforts of agencies and NGOs in Indonesia, Maldives, Sri Lanka and Thailand.

UN-Habitat's main focus with regard to urban environment was on assisting local authorities in better planning and managing their environmental resources towards more sustainable growth and development. Expert group meetings were held in Burkina Faso, Kenya and Sri Lanka on basic urban services and sustainable urban mobility. UN-Habitat continued in-country activities to achieve the MDG on slums. Activities of the Cities Without Slums subregional programme for Eastern and Southern Africa were initiated and consolidated. The Best Practices and Local Leadership Programme finalized the pilot phase of the initiative to document and review good urban policies and enabling legislation; evaluations were conducted in Brazil, Burkina Faso, Colombia, Mexico, Peru, the Philippines, Senegal, Uganda and the United Republic of Tanzania.

Cooperation with UNEP

A December report [HSP/GC/20/10] prepared jointly by the Executive Directors of UN-Habitat and UNEP described cooperation between the two organizations in the areas of assessment, policy development and implementation of joint initiatives; cooperation in Africa, Europe, and the Asia-Pacific and Latin America and Caribbean regions; and opportunities for future cooperation.

Decentralization and strengthening local authorities

In response to a 2003 Governing Council resolution [YUN 2003, p. 1079], the Executive Director submitted a November report [HSP/GC/20/7] on decentralization and the strengthening of local authorities. The report discussed, among other issues, the establishment by UN-Habitat of the Advisory Group of Experts on Decentralization (AGRED). AGRED's inaugural meeting (Ville de Gatineau, Canada, 9-10 March) reviewed the status of decentralization legislation of selected countries and the basic principles of decentralization policies, including subsidiarity, administrative and financial capacities of local authorities, governance and democracy at the local level, with the aim of developing best practices. AGRED members prepared draft guidelines on decentralization, which were discussed during its second meeting (Barcelona, Spain, 14 September) and presented to the tenth meeting (Barcelona, 12 September) of the Advisory Committee of Local Authorities, established in 2000 [YUN 2000, p. 990]. The draft guidelines were annexed to the Executive Director's report. AGRED members also agreed on the format for documenting best practices. Given the interconnection between the promotion of decentralization and the monitoring of local democracy, UN-Habitat and the newly established United Cities and Local Governments (see p. 1072) agreed to establish a global observatory of local democracy and decentralization. A special AGRED meeting on the guidelines and best practices was scheduled to take place in conjunction with the twentieth (2005) Governing Council session. A dialogue session on decentralization would also form part of the Council's deliberations.

UN Habitat and Human Settlements Foundation

Biennial financial audit

Allocations and expenditures in respect of project activities and programme support cost amounted to $59 million and $48 million, respectively, leaving an unexpended allocation of $11 million. The UN Board of auditors, in its report on UN-Habitat financial reports and audited financial statements for the year ended 31 December 2003 [A/59/5/Add.8], found that only $175,000 of the invalid unliquidated obligations of $775,000 (that remained outstanding as of 31 December 2002) was cancelled in 2003, leaving an outstanding balance of $600,000 or 5 per cent of the total unliquidated obligations of $11,827,356 as at 31 December 2003. Operationally completed projects had not been financially closed or completed within 12 months of the date of their operational completion, as required and adequate assurance on the accuracy and completeness of non-expendable property was not obtained. Of 24 contracts reviewed, seven (29 per cent) did not comply with the six-month evaluation requirement, and the database on consultants at the Regional Office for Asia and the Pacific did not include information on their performance.

Chapter VIII

Population

In 2004, the world population reached 6.4 billion, as compared with 6.3 billion in 2003. While the number of people was greater, the actual rate of increase declined, an indication that the world was beginning to witness the end of rapid population growth.

United Nations population activities continued to be guided by the Programme of Action adopted at the 1994 International Conference on Population and Development (ICPD). The year 2004 also marked the tenth anniversary of ICPD, and through various events, including the commemoration by the United Nations of the anniversary on 14 October, the international community reaffirmed its commitment to the ICPD Programme of Action.

The issue of international migration was considered by a number of organizations, both within and outside the UN system, as the Secretary-General reported, and the General Assembly recognized that they could contribute to the high-level dialogue on international migration and development. The Assembly encouraged countries of origin, transit and destination to increase cooperation on migration issues.

The United Nations Population Fund (UNFPA) maintained its focus on goals in the areas of reproductive health, population development and poverty, and gender equality and women's empowerment, as well as on HIV/AIDS, humanitarian assistance and adolescent and youth needs. UNFPA established an International Youth Advisory Board and launched the Global Coalition on Women and AIDS. Among other publications, it issued the results of its global survey, *Investing in People: National Progress in Implementing the ICPD Programme of Action 1994-2004*. In 2004, UNFPA's donor base grew to a record 166 countries, and the Fund's income from all sources totalled $506.1 million, compared to $397.9 million in 2003.

The Commission on Population and Development, at its 2004 session, reviewed, as its special theme, progress made in achieving the goals and objectives of the ICPD Programme of Action. Other matters discussed by the Commission included financial resources to implement the Programme of Action, world population monitoring and the activities of the UN Population Division. The Population Division continued to analyse and report on world demographic trends and policies and to make its findings available in publications and on the Internet.

Follow-up to 1994 Conference on Population and Development

Implementation of the Programme of Action

Commission on Population and Development action. In follow-up to the recommendations of the 1994 International Conference on Population and Development (ICPD) [YUN 1994, p. 955], the Commission on Population and Development, at its thirty-seventh session (New York, 22–26 March and 6 May) [E/2004/25], considered as its special theme "Review and appraisal of the progress made in achieving the goals and objectives of the Programme of Action of the ICPD". The Commission also discussed the flow of financial resources for assisting in the implementation of the Programme of Action.

Review of progress towards Programme of Action goals

The General Assembly, in its 1994 resolution 49/128 [YUN 1994, p. 963], had named the Commission on Population and Development as the body responsible for monitoring, reviewing and assessing the implementation of the Programme of Action. In January 2004, pursuant to Economic and Social Council decision 2003/229 [YUN 2003, p. 1094], the Secretary-General submitted [E/CN.9/2004/3] the second quinquennial review and appraisal of progress made in achieving the goals and objectives of the Programme of Action. The report provided an overview of population levels and trends; population growth, structure and distribution globally and by major regions; reproductive rights and reproductive health; health and mortality; international migration; and population programmes. The first quinquennial review on that subject was presented to the Commission in 1999 [E/CN.9/1999/PC/2].

The report stated that, with a world population of 6.4 billion, nearly all countries experienced in 2004 some reduction of fertility—the main source of population growth—and that world population was increasing at a declining rate. Between 1994 and 2004, the average annual growth rate was 1.3 per cent, with the less developed regions growing more rapidly than the more developed regions (at annual rates of 1.6 per cent and 0.3 per cent, respectively), and the least developed countries at an even faster pace (2.4 per cent per year). By 2015, the world population was projected to reach 7.2 billion at an annual average growth rate of 1.1 per cent. During the 2004-2015 period, 104 countries, accounting for 41 per cent of the world population, were expected to exhibit growth rates lower than 1 per cent per year, and 52 countries, accounting for 14 per cent of the total population, were expected to experience growth rates above 2 per cent per year, of which 31 were less developed countries. Six developing countries accounted for about half of the annual population growth: India (21 per cent); China (13 per cent); and Pakistan, Nigeria, Bangladesh and Indonesia (about 4 per cent each). In 2004, the five most populous countries were China (1.3 billion), India (1 billion), the United States (297 million), Indonesia (223 million) and Brazil (181 million).

Population statistics indicated that the distribution of the world population was shifting towards the less developed regions and that rates of growth varied considerably. Africa was the fastest growing region, at a rate of 2.3 per cent annually, followed by Latin America and the Caribbean (1.5 per cent), Asia (1.4 per cent), Oceania (1.4 per cent), North America (1.0 per cent) and Europe (negative 0.02 per cent). The world fertility rate declined from over 3 children per woman in 1990-1995 to 2.7 children in 2000-2005. Among other trends, the report noted an increased world life expectancy, currently 66 years of age; an increased number of international migrants; rising school enrollment at all educational levels and declining illiteracy; increased growth of the older population, at a much faster rate than that of the child population; increased growth of urban agglomerations, with 49 per cent of the world's population living in urban areas; and an increased number of internally displaced persons, the fastest growing group of uprooted persons in the world, largely as a result of environmental degradation, natural disasters, armed conflict and forced resettlement.

In regard to reproductive health issues, the report indicated that contraceptive use among couples had risen, indicating greater access to family planning; awareness of sexually transmitted infections as a threat to public health had increased, but incidences remained high with 340 million new cases worldwide in 1999; the HIV/AIDS epidemic continued to expand throughout the world; and more and more pregnant women sought antenatal care. It was expected that 65 per cent of the world population would achieve the Programme of Action goal of a rate below 50 deaths per 1,000 live births by 2000-2005. A total of 100 countries, representing 47 per cent of the world population in 2003, had met the goal of a life expectancy at birth greater than 70 years.

The report concluded that although much progress had been made in the implementation of the Programme of Action during the decade, it had not been universal, and, based on current trends, many countries might fall short of the agreed goals. Continued efforts to mobilize resources, strengthen institutional capacities and nurture partnerships would be required to achieve them.

Financial resources

In accordance with General Assembly resolution 50/124 [YUN 1995, p. 1094], the Secretary-General submitted to the Commission a report [E/CN.9/2004/4], coveirng ten years, on the flow of financial resources for assisting in the implementation of the ICPD Programme of Action. The report examined trends in bilateral, multilateral and foundation/non-governmental assistance for population activities in developing countries from 1994 to 2002, and domestic expenditures reported by developing countries from 1997 to 2001. Although international population assistance rose in 2002 to $3 billion, up from $2.5 billion in 2001, and was expected to increase slightly in 2003, the ICPD goal of reaching $18.5 billion by 2005 appeared unlikely. The consequences of resource shortfalls included increases in unintended pregnancies, abortions, maternal morbidity and mortality and infant and child mortality, as well as the likelihood that ICPD goals would not be met.

International migration and development

As requested by the General Assembly in resolution 58/208 [YUN 2003, p. 1087], the Secretary-General, in September [A/59/325], submitted a report on international migration and development, providing an update on activities relating to international migration undertaken by organizations within the UN system and involving UN cooperation with relevant intergovernmental organizations. Those included the International Organization for Migration (IOM) and the Geneva Migration Group (GMG), an informal mechanism for the exchange of information among organizations, established in 2003 by the heads of the International Labour Organization

(ILO), IOM, the Office of the United Nations High Commissioner for Human Rights (OHCHR), the United Nations High Commissioner for Refugees (UNHCR), the United Nations Conference on Trade and Development (UNCTAD) and the United Nations Office on Drugs and Crime (UNODC). Among 2004 activities were a high-level panel discussion on "International migration and migrants from a social perspective", held by the Commission for Social Development (10 February, New York); the selection by the UN Department of Economic and Social Affairs (DESA) of international migration as the special topic for its *World Economic and Social Survey, 2004,* a publication that provided an annual analysis of the state of the world economy and emerging policy issues; and the first session (1–5 March, Geneva) of the Committee on the Protection of the Rights of Migrant Workers and Members of Their Families (see p. 668), established in 2003 [YUN 2003, p. 676] to monitor implementation of the International Convention on those rights [YUN 1990, p. 594]. The report also reviewed Member States' initiatives to create a multilateral framework of cooperation for improving migration management and proposed action-oriented options of the United Nations for addressing the issue of international migration and development.

The report concluded that the response by the international community to the significant increase in international migration since the 1990s had been swift, and the UN system, in collaboration with relevant institutions and organizations, including IOM and GMG, had addressed a wide array of relevant issues. In addition, a number of government initiatives had given rise to several regional consultative processes, and the work of the United Nations on international migration would benefit from closer ties with those processes, particularly in obtaining inputs that would be useful in preparatory activities for the General Assembly's high-level dialogue on international migration scheduled for 2006. The findings of the Global Commission on International Migration (GCIM), which met for the first time (Stockholm, Sweden, 26-27 February) and was expected to issue its report in mid-2005, would also benefit from consideration of international migration issues at the United Nations.

Communication. In a letter dated 5 April [A/59/73], El Salvador welcomed the Secretary-General's initiative in December 2003 to launch GCIM, an independent body comprised of 19 Commissioners which was given the mandate to provide a framework for the formulation of a comprehensive and global response to the issue of international migration. El Salvador ex-

pressed its support for the work to be done by the Commission.

GENERAL ASSEMBLY ACTION

On 22 December [meeting 75], the General Assembly, on the recommendation of the Second (Economic and Financial) Committee [A/59/485/Add.2], adopted **resolution 59/241** without vote [agenda item 87 (*b*)].

International migration and development

The General Assembly,

Recalling the Programme of Action of the International Conference on Population and Development adopted at Cairo, in particular chapter X on international migration, and the key actions for the further implementation of the Programme of Action, set out in the annex to General Assembly resolution S-21/2 of 2 July 1999, in particular section II.C on international migration, as well as the relevant provisions contained in the Copenhagen Declaration on Social Development, the Programme of Action of the World Summit for Social Development, the Platform for Action adopted by the Fourth World Conference on Women and the outcome documents of the twenty-fourth and twenty-fifth special sessions of the General Assembly,

Recalling also its relevant resolutions, in particular resolutions 57/270 B of 23 June 2003, 58/190 of 22 December 2003 and 58/208 of 23 December 2003, in which it decided to devote a high-level dialogue to international migration and development during its sixty-first session, bearing in mind that the purpose of the high-level dialogue is to discuss the multidimensional aspects of international migration and development in order to identify appropriate ways and means to maximize its development benefits and minimize its negative impacts,

Reaffirming the obligations of all States to promote and protect all human rights and fundamental freedoms, reaffirming also the Universal Declaration of Human Rights, and recalling the International Convention on the Elimination of All Forms of Racial Discrimination, the Convention on the Elimination of All Forms of Discrimination against Women and the Convention on the Rights of the Child,

Noting the work undertaken under the International Migration Policy Programme by the United Nations Institute for Training and Research, the International Organization for Migration and the United Nations Population Fund, in partnership with the International Labour Office, the Office of the United Nations High Commissioner for Refugees, the Office of the United Nations High Commissioner for Human Rights and other relevant international and regional institutions, with a view to strengthening the capacity of Governments to manage migration flows at the national and regional levels and thus foster greater cooperation among States towards orderly migration,

Noting also the ongoing efforts and recent activities within the United Nations system and the other intergovernmental activities and multilateral initiatives on international migration and development being undertaken, as well as the exchanges of information on the subject,

Recalling the International Convention on the Protection of the Rights of All Migrant Workers and Members of Their Families, which entered into force in July 2003,

Welcoming the adoption of the special theme of the thirty-ninth session of the Commission on Population and Development in 2006, which will be "International migration and development",

Taking note of the views of the Member States on the question of convening a United Nations conference on international migration, its scope, form and agenda, noting the low number of respondents to the survey of the Secretariat, and in this context inviting the Secretary-General to continue considering the issue,

Acknowledging the important contribution provided by migrants and migration to development as well as the complex interrelationship between migration and development,

Aware of the fact that all countries are impacted by international migration, and hence stressing the crucial importance of dialogue and cooperation so as to better understand the international migration phenomenon, including its gender perspective, and to identify appropriate ways and means to maximize its development benefits and minimize its negative impacts,

Realizing the benefits that international migration can bring to migrants, their families, the receiving societies and their communities of origin and the need for countries of origin, transit and destination to ensure that migrants, including migrant workers, are not subject to exploitation of any kind and the need to ensure that the human rights and dignity of all migrants and their families, in particular of women migrant workers, are respected and protected,

Noting that an overall commitment to multiculturalism helps to provide a context for the effective integration of migrants, preventing and combating discrimination and promoting solidarity and tolerance in receiving societies,

Aware that, among other important factors, both domestic and international, the widening economic and social gap between and among many countries and the marginalization of some countries in the global economy, due in part to the uneven impact of the benefits of globalization and liberalization, have contributed to large flows of people between and among countries and to the intensification of the complex phenomenon of international migration,

Recognizing that countries can be concurrently any combination of origin, transit and/or destination,

1. *Takes note* of the report of the Secretary-General;

2. *Reconfirms* that the Secretary-General will report to the General Assembly at its sixtieth session on the organizational details of the 2006 high-level dialogue;

3. *Recognizes* the important contributions that international and regional efforts, including by the regional commissions, can provide to the high-level dialogue on international migration and development;

4. *Invites* appropriate regional consultative processes and other major initiatives undertaken by Member States in the field of international migration to contribute to the high-level dialogue;

5. *Takes note* of the establishment of the Global Commission on International Migration;

6. *Calls upon* all relevant bodies, agencies, funds and programmes of the United Nations system and other relevant intergovernmental, regional and subregional organizations, within their continuing mandated activities, to continue to address the issue of international migration and development, with a view to integrating migration issues, including a gender perspective and cultural diversity, in a more coherent way within the broader context of the implementation of agreed economic and social development goals and respect for all human rights;

7. *Encourages* Governments of countries of origin, countries of transit and countries of destination to increase cooperation on issues related to migration, and notes with appreciation the numerous meetings and conferences convened relating to migration and development, in particular in the context of regional cooperation;

8. *Invites* Governments, with the assistance of the international community, where appropriate, to seek to make the option of remaining in one's own country viable for all people, in particular through efforts to achieve sustainable development, leading to a better economic balance between developed and developing countries;

9. *Reaffirms* the need to adopt policies and undertake measures to reduce the cost of the transfer of migrant remittances to developing countries, and welcomes the efforts of Governments and stakeholders in this regard;

10. *Requests* the Secretary-General, within existing resources, to prepare a comprehensive overview of studies and analyses on the multidimensional aspects of migration and development, including the effects of migration on economic and social development in developed and developing countries, and on the effects of the movements of highly skilled migrant workers and those with advanced education;

11. *Also requests* the Secretary-General to submit a report to the General Assembly at its sixty-first session on the implementation of the present resolution.

UN Population Fund

2004 activities

In 2004, the international community celebrated a decade of steady progress towards implementation of ICDP goals since the 1994 conference in Cairo, Egypt [YUN 1994, p. 955]. Those goals were linked to the programme priorities of the United Nations Population Fund (UNFPA). To mark the anniversary, government and civil society leaders reaffirmed their commitment to the ICPD Programme of Action at such events as the "Commemoration of the tenth anniversary of ICPD" (New York, 14 October), held in accordance with General Assembly decision 58/529, which called for an event during its fifty-ninth session [YUN 2003, p. 1085], and the second International Parliamentarians' Conference on the Implementation of the ICPD Programme of Action (Strasbourg, France, 18-19 October), following which parliamentarians and ministers from 90 countries issued the Strasbourg Statement of Commitment. Support for ICPD and the UNFPA mandate was also expressed by countries at regional meetings and at the 2004 sessions of the Commission on Population and Development and the General Assembly.

UNFPA published a global survey, *Investing in People: National Progress in Implementing the ICPD Programme of Action 1994-2004*, which confirmed progress towards ICPD goals. Among its findings, the survey noted that the percentage of couples in the developing world able to choose contraception had increased from 55 to 60 since the implementation of the ICPD Programme of Action in 1994; infant mortality rates had dropped from 71 to 61 out of every 1,000 babies born; life expectancy in the developing world had risen from 61 to 63 years of age; and women and men in ever greater numbers had stood up against female genital cutting, rape, gender violence and other human rights violations. The survey identified areas for future action and the major challenge of UNFPA—to secure the political will and funding required to achieve the ICPD and Millennium Development Goals (MDGs) [YUN 2000, p. 51].

Report of Executive Director. As requested by the Executive Board of the United Nations Development Programme (UNDP)/UNFPA [YUN 2003, p. 1090], the UNFPA Executive Director submitted her report covering 2004 [DP/FPA/2005/7 (Part I & Add.1, Part II)] in a new format, merging various parts of the annual report into a single performance- and results-oriented annual report that reflected the goals and outputs of the multi-year funding framework (MYFF). The report discussed implementation of the 2004-2007 MYFF (see p. 1083), the context in which UNFPA operated, and the strengthening of UNFPA's effectiveness. It described progress towards achieving three goals identified in the MYFF—universal access to reproductive health, the inclusion of population dynamics to promote development, and gender equality (see below).

The implementation of country and sub-regional programmes continued as the Fund's core work during 2004. By programme area, the largest share of resources, 62.8 per cent, went to reproductive health activities; 21.6 per cent to population and development strategies; 9.6 per cent to programme coordination and assistance; and 6.0 per cent to gender equality and the empowerment of women. The highest priority for allocation of assistance, 66.7 per cent, was for Group A countries, which included all the least developed countries (see p. 852). By region, sub-Saharan Africa accounted for 35.2 per cent of programme assistance; Asia and the Pacific for 29.7 per cent; the Arab States and Europe for 12.9 per cent; and Latin America and the Caribbean for 9.5 per cent; interregional activities accounted for 12.7 per cent

The Executive Director noted that UNFPA was operating in a changing environment. Many countries had implemented elements of the ICPD Programme of Action and, increasingly, population factors were being integrated into national development frameworks. Efforts were made to strengthen reproductive health policies, promote gender equality, and address reproductive health needs and rights. At the regional and country levels, UNFPA cooperated with other members of the UN country team in joint programmes and increasingly with other partners, bringing to the common agenda key population, reproductive health and rights, and gender equality issues. The March issuance of the United Nations Development Group (UNDG) Guidelines on Joint Programmes resulted in an increased number of UNFPA country offices engaging in joint programmes—activities with a common work plan among two or more UN agencies. Conflict, political crisis and natural disasters continued to affect the work of UNFPA, with new crisis situations emerging in eight countries during 2004, including those affected by the 26 December tsunami in the Indian Ocean (see p. 952). In those situations, UNFPA focused its assistance on ensuring access to reproductive health, prevention of violence against women and girls, and psychological counselling.

The Fund's main publication, *State of World Population 2004* [Sales No. E.04.III.H.1], also took stock of achievements and challenges in implementing the ICPD Programme of Action. While noting that many developing countries had made great strides in putting the ICPD recommendations into action, it stated that inadequate resources and persistent gaps in serving the poorest populations were impeding progress, particularly in halting the spread of HIV/AIDS and providing family planning and reproductive health.

In 2004, the level of regular source mobilization for UNFPA reached an all-time high of $331.6 million and a record of 166 donor countries was achieved. Membership in the "million dollar club"—country offices that mobilized over $1 million for country programmes—almost doubled, rising to 17 members.

The Executive Director reported [DP/FPA/2005/7 (Part II)] that UNFPA had provided inputs for the preparation of a number of Joint Inspection Unit (JIU) reports and reviews. Of the seven reports issued by JIU in 2004, five were of interest for UNFPA operations, mostly dealing with administrative issues, and were shared with UNFPA managers for their information and consideration.

On 23 June [E/2004/35 (dec. 2004/23)], the UNDP/UNFPA Executive Board welcomed the 2003 report of the Executive Director [YUN 2003, p. 1089].

By **decision 2004/232** of 12 July, the Economic and Social Council took note of the reports of the UNDP/UNFPA Executive Board on its work during 2003 [E/2003/35] and at its first regular session of 2004 [E/2004/35]. The Council also noted the annual report of the UNFPA Executive Director [E/2004/5-DP/FPA/2004/2], which addressed the implementation of the Secretary-General's reform programme, the provisions of the triennial comprehensive policy review and follow-up to international conferences and the MDGs.

Communication. In a letter of 17 February [A/59/61], Switzerland transmitted the summary of deliberations of the "European Population Forum 2004", a high-level expert meeting (Geneva, 12–14 January) jointly organized by the Economic Commission for Europe (ECE) and UNFPA, which focused on the theme "Population Challenges and Policy Responses" and discussed, among other things, newly emerging population challenges.

Reproductive health

UNFPA, as it had done over the previous decade, invested more than two thirds of its financial resources in reproductive health. Appraisal of the ICPD goal of universal access to reproductive health showed varying progress both among countries and among population groups within countries. While the use of modern contraceptive methods was around 54 per cent in developing countries, such methods remained unavailable to large numbers of couples. Adolescent reproductive health emerged as a global concern, and the HIV/AIDS crisis worsened the mortality and morbidity situation in 53 of the most affected countries.

Increased numbers of UNFPA country offices were involved in various national partnerships, working to incorporate reproductive health in poverty reduction strategy paper (PRSP) processes, sector-wide approaches (SWAps) and MDG reporting. An analysis of 60 MDG reports and 29 PRSPs showed increased attention to the issues of reproductive health and gender. However, closer examination of the PRSPs revealed a lack of attention to adolescent sexual and reproductive health, gender-based violence and emergency obstetric care, a key strategy for averting maternal deaths. Among other signs of progress, 14 countries approved policies to increase adolescents' access to services and 87 countries reported

a legal minimum age for marriage, viewed as a means to reduce maternal mortality as young women were statistically at a higher risk of dying during pregnancy. UNFPA's strategy also focused on addressing family planning and preventing sexually transmitted infections (STIs), including HIV/AIDS. In its response to the epidemic, the Fund focused on the prevention of HIV infection among young people, the prevention of infection in pregnant women, and comprehensive condom programming, including advocating for increased condom use by sexually active young people. UNFPA also joined an existing partnership to work on the television company MTV's "Staying Alive Campaign", the largest global HIV/AIDS awareness-and-prevention campaign for young people. (For further information on UNFPA's activities on HIV/AIDS, see Chapter XIII of this section.)

Population development and poverty

The UNFPA Executive Director, in her report covering 2004 [DP/FPA/2005/7 (part I)], stated that attempts to reduce poverty by addressing interactions between population dynamics, sustainable development and poverty had made only modest progress since 1990. The gap between rich and poor nations remained unacceptably wide.

In 2004, a number of countries in Africa, Asia and Latin America were at various stages of implementing population and housing censuses. As it had determined that the availability of relevant data was vital for planning poverty reduction strategies, UNFPA provided assistance for conducting censuses and for planning, mobilizing resources, analysing the data and disseminating the results in at least 13 countries. The number of country offices reporting national sex-disaggregated population-related databases rose from 50 in 2002 to 74 in 2004, with another 15 developing them. UNFPA intensified its advocacy efforts for incorporating population dimensions into national development plans, including PRSPs, and 43 country offices reported undertaking interventions to make population and poverty linkages. The Fund also continued to support the formulation, operationalization and implementation of national population policies.

Gender equality and empowerment of women

The UNFPA Executive Director stated that there had been notable progress in the last decade in female education, literacy and participation in civic life, in many countries and regions, but discrimination remained high in certain regions and countries, or in pockets of poverty or social marginalization within countries. In 2004,

UNFPA offices in 56 countries reported the existence of mechanisms to monitor and reduce gender-based violence, and 55 country offices reported the existence of protocols for managing the health consequences of gender-based violence, as compared to 19 offices in 2002. Civil society became more involved in promoting gender equality and the empowerment of women, with a diversity of movements, alliances, coalitions, networks and multisectoral committees functioning in over 80 per cent of the countries where UNFPA had programmes. Many UNFPA country offices reported significant involvement in supporting efforts to eliminate discrimination against women and girls, particularly through training and building the capacity of non-governmental organizations (NGOs) for advocacy.

Country and intercountry programmes

In January, the UNDP/UNFPA Executive Board considered the proposed UNFPA intercountry programme for 2004-2007 [DP/FPA/2004/3], which was designed to help countries to implement the ICPD Programme of Action. The programme was consistent with the goals of the MYFF and was aligned with the new strategic direction of UNFPA that emerged from the Fund's transition process, and focused on three programme areas— reproductive health, population and development strategies, and gender. The objective of the programme was to strengthen policy dialogue, development frameworks and programming processes in population.

On 30 January [E/2004/35 (dec. 2004/8)], the UNDP/UNFPA Executive Board approved the proposed 2004-2007 intercountry programme, in the amount of $226 million, and requested UNFPA to develop a results-based management system for planning, monitoring and evaluating the programme. On the same date [dec. 2004/12], the Board took note of the review of the UNFPA intercountry programme for 2000-2003 [DP/FPA/2004/3/Add.1].

Report of Executive Director. UNFPA's provisional project expenditures for country and intercountry (regional and interregional) programmes in 2004 totalled $221.9 million, compared to $176.4 million in 2003, according to the Executive Director's statistical overview report [DP/FPA/2005/7 (Part I, Add.1)]. The 2004 figure included $181.6 million for country programmes and $40.3 million for intercountry programmes. Costs for administrative and operational services amounting to $6.4 million were included in programme expenditures. In accordance with the Board's procedure for allocating resources according to its categorization of countries laid down in 1996 [YUN 1996, p. 989], total expenditures

in 2004 for Group A countries (see p. 1079) amounted to $121.1 million, compared to $92.1 million in 2003.

Africa. Provisional expenditures for UNFPA programmes in sub-Saharan Africa totalled $78.1 million in 2004, compared to $63.5 million in 2003. Most of that amount (54.7 per cent) went to reproductive health and family planning, followed by population and development strategies (30.6 per cent), programme coordination and assistance (8.8 per cent) and gender equality and women's empowerment (5.9 per cent).

On 30 January [E/2004/35 (dec. 2004/12)], the UNDP/UNFPA Executive Board approved UNFPA country programmes for Benin, the Republic of the Congo, Kenya, the Central African Republic, the Niger and Sierra Leone. On 23 June [dec. 2004/25], the Board took note of the draft country programme documents for Angola, Burundi and Madagascar, and approved a two-year extension of the fourth country programme for Zimbabwe [DP/FPA/2004/13].

Arab States and Europe. Provisional expenditures for UNFPA programmes in the Arab States and Europe totalled $28.7 million in 2004, compared to $23 million in 2003. Most (64.8 per cent) was spent on reproductive health and family planning, followed by population and development strategies (18.8 per cent), programme assistance (11 per cent) and gender equality and women's empowerment (5.5 per cent). On 23 June [dec. 2004/25], the Board took note of the draft country programmes for Armenia, Azerbaijan, Kazakhstan, Kyrgyzstan, Romania, Tajikistan, Turkmenistan and Uzbekistan.

Asia and the Pacific. Provisional expenditures for UNFPA programmes in Asia and the Pacific amounted to $65.9 million in 2004, compared to $53.3 million in 2003. Most of those expenditures (69.2 per cent) went to reproductive health, followed by population and development strategies (18.6 per cent), programme coordination and assistance (7.3 per cent) and gender equality and women's empowerment (4.9 per cent).

On 30 January [dec. 2004/12], the UNDP/UNFPA Executive Board approved UNFPA country programmes for Afghanistan and Pakistan. On 23 June [dec. 2004/25], the Board took note of the draft country programme documents for Iran and the Philippines, and took note of the report on the implementation of UNFPA's special programme of assistance to Myanmar [DP/FPA/2004/11].

Latin America and the Caribbean. Provisional expenditures for UNFPA programmes in Latin America and the Caribbean totalled $21.1 million in 2004, compared to $13.5 million in 2003. As in the other regions, most of the total (52.4 per cent) went to reproductive health and family planning, followed by population and development strategies (22.8 per cent), gender equality and women's empowerment (13.7 per cent) and programme coordination and assistance (11.1 per cent).

On 30 January [dec. 2004/12], the UNDP/UNFPA Executive Board approved country programmes for Cuba and Ecuador.

Interregional programmes. Provisional expenditures for UNFPA's interregional and global programmes totalled $28.1 million in 2004, compared to $23.2 million in 2003. Of that total, 76.0 per cent went to reproductive health and family planning, 14.7 per cent to programme coordination and assistance, 5.2 per cent to population and development strategies and 4.0 per cent to gender equality and women's empowerment.

Financial and management questions

Financing

UNFPA's income from all sources totalled $506.1 million in 2004, compared to $397.9 million in 2003 [DP/FPA/2005/7 (Part I, Add.1)], and comprised $331.6 million in regular resources and $174.5 million from other resources. Expenditures totalled $451.5 million in 2004, up from $380 million in 2003, comprising $318.6 million from regular resources and $132.9 million from other resources, resulting in an excess of $54.6 million.

Contributions to regular resources from donor Governments and a private contribution from the Mars Trust totalled $322.5 million in 2004, an increase of 11.8 per cent over 2003. Interest and other income brought the total of regular resources to $331.6 million. Contributions to trust funds, cost-sharing arrangements and other sources totalled $171.4 million, and interest income another $3.1 million.

On 21 September [E/2004/35 (dec. 2004/26)], the UNDP/UNFPA Executive Board took note of the 2003 UNFPA financial review [YUN 2003, p. 1091] and recognized the significance of increasing predictability in contributions to regular resources.

Revision of financial regulations and recovery of indirect costs

In November [DP/FPA/2005/3], the Executive Director submitted a report on the revision of UNFPA financial regulations. The revisions, which reflected the introduction of the MYFF and UN simplification and harmonization initiatives, were the result of a review of financial regulations necessitated by the January introduction of the PeopleSoft financial system (known as Atlas). The report proposed new regulations to permit electronic signatures, approvals and authorizations in lieu of signed paper copies.

In another November report [DP/FPA/2005/5] on recovery of indirect costs for co-financing, the Executive Director proposed revisions to the recovery policy for indirect costs, by which the existing structure of multiple rates would be replaced with a single rate of 7 per cent charged to all non-core expenditures. The report proposed confirmation of the rate of 5 per cent for third-party procurement expenditures.

ACABQ report. In December [DP/FPA/2005/4], the Advisory Committee on Administrative and Budgetary Questions (ACABQ) considered the November reports of the UNFPA Executive Director (see above). It noted that the revisions of the financial regulations included the replacement of the "certifying" function by the "committing" function, establishing the approval to spend against a budget source; the replacement of the "approving" function by the "verifying" function, ensuring controls were in place before disbursing of funds; and the replacement of the "allocation" concept by the "budget" concept, used to control expenditures. Also, as authority had been delegated to UNFPA on managerial, financial and staff issues [YUN 2003, p. 1093], references to the UNDP Administrator had been removed from the regulations. ACABQ recommended that the Executive Board approve the revisions to the regulations and the proposed new regulations.

In regard to the Executive Director's proposals on the recovery of indirect costs for co-financing, ACABQ noted that the basis for the review included the JIU recommendation that all organizations of the UN system review their indirect cost rates in order to harmonize whenever possible. The Committee further noted that in reviewing the cost-recovery rates, UNFPA examined the rates for the reimbursement of third party procurement services, calculated at 5 per cent of the value of goods procured, and confirmed its appropriateness. The Committee agreed that the rate of 7 per cent—proposed to be the one rate to be used to recover indirect costs for co-financed activities—was reasonable, and that the UNFPA Executive Director should be allowed to keep the indirect cost-recovery rate under review and propose amendments to avoid cross-subsidization, if necessary.

Audit reports

The Executive Director submitted to the UNDP/UNFPA Executive Board a report [DP/FPA/2004/1] on follow-up action by UNFPA to recommendations by the Board of Auditors for the 2000-2001 biennium [YUN 2002, p. 1093]. On 30 January [E/2004/35 (dec. 2004/4)], the Executive Board took note of the report.

In a March report [DP/FPA/2004/6], the Executive Director described UNFPA's internal audit and oversight activities carried out in 2003, including management audits of 16 country offices and one functional area at Headquarters; follow-up on the implementation of previous audit recommendations concerning two divisions at Headquarters; and contracted audits of nine country offices. In addition, 473 audit reports covering 2002 activities for projects executed by government and NGOs were reviewed. Of the 23 reports issued in 2003, the level of internal controls and the compliance with financial and administrative requirements were found to be satisfactory in seven offices. Eleven offices were rated partially satisfactory and four deficient. One report did not include a rating. The report also summarized the activities of the three new organizational committees, established to improve oversight and accountability: the Oversight Committee; the Management Committee; and the Programme Committee.

On 18 June [E/2004/35 (dec. 2004/17)], the Executive Board urged the Executive Director to take the necessary steps to address the issues contained in the report on internal audit and oversight and to report to the Board in 2005. On 24 September [ibid., dec. 2004/39], the Board welcomed the proposed framework for future reports, as proposed in an August report on a framework for resolution of issues contained in internal audit reports [DP/2004/CRP.8-DP/FPA/2004/CRP.5].

Multi-year funding commitments

In May [DP/FPA/2004/10], the Executive Director submitted to the UNDP/UNFPA Executive Board updated estimates of regular and other resources for 2004 and future years, in the multi-year funding framework (MYFF). As at 1 April, 60 countries had submitted written pledges to UNFPA for 2004, of which only 19 were multi-year pledges.

In 2003, UNFPA received regular contributions from a record 149 donor Governments. Total contributions received from donor Governments in 2003 amounted to $293 million, of which 16 major donors provided approximately 96 per cent. It was estimated that 17 major donors would account for approximately 97 per cent of total contributions of $322 million in 2004. Discussions were ongoing with donors to increase their regular contributions in order to broaden the base of support of the Fund's regular resources.

The report concluded that the Fund's 2003 income level increased substantially in comparison to 2002 due to the larger contributions from five major donors (Canada, Finland, Ireland, Norway and Sweden) and favourable exchange rates of the euro and other currencies against the US dollar. As resource requirements for regular resources for 2004-2007 amounted to $1.2 billion and UNFPA's regular resources would need to exceed $300 million annually, it stressed that UNFPA should focus its resource mobilization efforts on increasing regular resources. UNFPA urged countries to increase their contributions and make timely payment of pledges to ensure a more predictable cash flow and stable income base.

On 23 June [E/2004/35 (dec. 2004/24)], the UNDP/UNFPA Executive Board, taking note of the report, encouraged countries to commit to multi-year pledges and make early payments, and encouraged UNFPA to reduce its dependency on a few large donors and broaden its donor base.

Assessment of the 2004-2007 MYFF

At its January session, the UNDP/UNFPA Executive Board had before it the UNFPA Executive Director's report [DP/FPA/2004/4] on the Fund's second multi-year funding framework (MYFF), covering 2004-2007. The report provided background information on the MYFF as the Fund's medium-term strategic plan, lessons learned implementing the first MYFF, and the process used to develop the second MYFF. It described the two major components: the strategic results framework (SRF) that outlined the MYFF development goals, outcomes, indicators and strategies; and the integrated resources framework (IRF) that set out resource requirements for 2004-2007. The report also outlined how the Fund would monitor its progress in managing for results, and how it would report on results.

On 30 January [E/2004/35 (dec. 2004/7)], the UNDP/UNFPA Executive Board endorsed the proposed 2004-2007 MYFF and welcomed the report's focus on the three results areas of reproductive health, population and development, and gender as key requirements for poverty eradication. It affirmed that the MYFF was to serve as the main policy document of UNFPA, as well as a strategic resource and management tool. Approving the proposed IRF, the Board urged countries to make multi-year pledges. It requested the Executive Director to explore options for reporting on results in a harmonized manner. On 18 June [ibid., dec. 2004/20], the Board adopted the joint UNDP/UNFPA/United Nations Development Fund for Women (UNIFEM) proposal for harmonized reporting on results under the MYFF process.

Report of Executive Director. In her report on implementation of the 2004-2007 MYFF [DP/FPA/2005/7 (Part I)], the UNFPA Executive Director indicated an overall positive assessment of UNFPA's contribution to achieve MYFF results. The Fund had been engaged in policy work and had strengthened partnerships with Governments, UN agencies, donors and civil society organizations. UNFPA country offices had increasingly participated in poverty reduction strategy paper (PRSPs) processes and sector-wide approaches (SWAps) to incorporate reproductive health and gender issues. However, obtaining updated data for most of the quantitative goal and outcome indicators had been a challenge. Due to issues of attribution and aggregation, the contributions of UNFPA and other partners and the results obtained from countries could not be combined to provide a meaningful measure of overall progress. Lack of up-to-date and comparable data had also limited the discussion of progress on indicators. To improve the Fund's capacity to track and report on results, UNFPA revised its annual reporting mechanisms and established an MYFF impact tracking system (i-track) to allow country office annual reporting to be done online.

In 2004, country offices aimed to achieve 557 outputs in different programme areas, with 60 per cent in reproductive health, 29 per cent in population and development and 11 per cent in gender equality and women's empowerment. Other progress included implementation of a new performance appraisal and development system; development of a website or web pages by 55 per cent of country offices in programme countries; implementation of a country office typology piloted in 2003; the launching of "DocuShare", a UNFPA electronic document and publication repository; development of a reproductive health website; and the launching of an electronic financial and resources system to improve the Fund's accountability. To assess progress in managing for results, UNFPA identified 11 lead indicators that reflected five key managing-for-results dimensions presented in the 2004-2007 MYFF. The report also presented the 2004 baselines for those indicators.

Programming process

In response to a 2001 Executive Board decision [YUN 2001, p. 1000], the UNDP Administrator and the UNFPA Executive Director submitted an April report [DP/2004/29-DP/FPA/2004/7] on progress in implementing decision 2001/11 on the UNDP/UNFPA programming process (see p. 884). On 18 June [E/2004/35 (dec. 2004/18)], the Executive Board requested UNDP and UNFPA to determine how to address the issue of the increased time frame for developing country programmes in a harmonized way and to report back to the Execu-

tive Board in 2005. On the same date [ibid., dec. 2004/19], the Board took note of the report on UNDP/UNFPA experiences in joint programming [DP/2004/30-DP/FPA/2004/8] and deferred consideration of a decision to 2005.

Evaluation

In an April report [DP/FPA/2004/12], the Executive Director provided an overview of UNFPA's evaluation activities, including progress during the 2002-2003 biennium in conducting and using the results of evaluations and evaluative activities, and in institutionalizing evaluation recommendations. It also described initiatives taken to establish results-based planning, monitoring and evaluation systems and to develop related national capacities.

On 23 June [E/2004/35 (dec. 2004/25)], the Executive Board took note of the periodic report on evaluation.

Technical Advisory Programme

In response to a 2002 Executive Board request [YUN 2002, p. 1083], the Executive Director submitted in August [DP/FPA/2004/16] a mid-term review of the UNFPA Technical Advisory Programme (TAP), an inter-agency arrangement for providing UNFPA assistance to countries for population and development activities. TAP constituted the UNFPA strategy to increase the efficiency, effectiveness and impact of its technical support in reproductive health, population and development, and gender empowerment, and was composed of nine multi-disciplinary Country Technical Services Teams (CSTs).

The report indicated that despite the brief period of operation in 2003 and 2004 of the new TAP programme, it was clear that the system was changing in the intended direction and that the CSTs were moving away from demand-driven and project-oriented technical support towards more strategic mission and non-mission support focused on capacity-building, regional and institutional-level analyses, and policy dialogue. Progress was also made towards implementation of the strategic partnerships programme, which represented a departure from past inter-agency arrangements, and the implementation by the World Health Organization (WHO) of a project on family planning, sexually transmitted infections and safe motherhood. However, the changeover had not been complete. The report summarized actions taken to address the issues raised in the midterm review, including the establishment of a working group to review the work planning process and make recommendations to modify current practices; adoption of a two-year timetable for programmable and time-bound activities in order to expand participation of the CSTs in key exercises; and the revision of previously defined parameters to standardize the operational definition of strategic support.

On 23 September [E/2004/35 (dec. 2004/28)], the Executive Board took note of the report and requested UNFPA to provide a further review in 2005 of the impact of the TAP programme against strategic goals as contained in the MYFF.

Security of personnel

The Executive Director submitted in July [DP/FPA/2004/14] a proposal to the UNDP/UNFPA Executive Board on additional security requirements to safeguard UNFPA personnel and premises globally. Citing the attack on the UN office in Baghdad, Iraq, in August 2003 [YUN 2003, p. 346], the Executive Director stated that the security threat levels for UN operations worldwide had significantly increased. Consequently, she requested that the Executive Board grant her authority to access up to 4 per cent of the approved gross 2004-2005 regular biennial support budget in additional funding, i.e., a maximum of $6.8 million for additional protective measures, including: relocating UNFPA country offices to safer premises; enforcing compliance with the enhanced minimum operating security standards (MOSS); increasing the number of field security officers; meeting the increased malicious acts insurance policy premium and other insurance requirements; and establishing a security structure with four security advisers.

ACABQ consideration. In September [DP/FPA/2004/17], ACABQ considered the Executive Director's request. The Committee indicated that such requests should not be based on a piecemeal approach, but preceded by a comprehensive and complete review of security arrangements. It endorsed all the measures proposed in the report, except the establishment of a basic security structure, which the Committee advised should await the submission of a comprehensive review of security arrangements to be submitted by the Secretary-General (see p. 1478) and any relevant decision by the General Assembly.

On 22 September [E/2004/35 (dec. 2004/27)], the UNDP/UNFPA Executive Board endorsed the Executive Director's proposal to grant her authority to access up to a maximum of $6.8 million and noted that the amount would be recorded as a reserve, disclosed in the financial statement and reported to the Board in the annual financial review. The Board took note [ibid., dec. 2004/41] of the ACABQ report.

UN Population award

The 2004 United Nations Population Award was presented to John C. Caldwell (Australia), Professor Emeritus of Demography of the Australian National University, in the individual category, and to the Addis Ababa Fistula Hospital in the institutional category. Professor Caldwell was selected for his significant contributions to demographic research, including demographic transition theory, the study of culture and mortality decline, family formation, sexual networking and the spread of HIV/AIDS; anthropological and qualitative approaches to demographic techniques of analysis; and the interaction of culture, managerial practice and family planning programme success. The Addis Ababa Fistula Hospital was selected for its achievements in providing services for women suffering from childbirth and related injuries and in offering a holistic package of rehabilitation services with the objective of reintegrating patients into society in a dignified manner.

The Award was established by General Assembly resolution 36/201 [YUN 1981, p. 792], to be presented annually to individuals or institutions for outstanding contributions to increasing awareness of population problems and to their solutions. In July, the Secretary-General transmitted to the Assembly the report of the UNFPA Executive Director on the Population Award [A/59/160].

Other population activities

Commission on Population and Development

The Commission on Population and Development, at its thirty-seventh session (New York, 22-26 March and 6 May) [E/2004/25], considered as its special theme "Review and appraisal of the progress made in achieving the goals and objectives of the Programme of Action of the ICPD", which was discussed in the context of the follow-up to the 1994 ICPD (see p. 1075). Documents before the Commission included the Secretary-General's report reviewing progress in achieving ICPD goals [E/CN.9/2004/3] (see p. 1075); the report of the Commission's Bureau on its intersessional meeting (Vilnius, Lithuania, November 2003) [E/CN.9/2004/2] [YUN 2003, p. 1094]; the Secretary-General's report on the flow of financial resources for implementation of the ICPD Programme of Action [E/CN.9/2004/4] (see p. 1076); the Secretary-General's report on programme implementation and progress of work in the field of population in 2003 [YUN 2003, p. 1094] and the

Secretary-General's note on the proposed strategic framework for 2006-2007 [E/CN.9/2004/6].

The Commission adopted and brought to the Economic and Social Council's attention resolutions on the work programme in the field of population [E/2004/25 (res. 2004/1)] and on follow-up to the ICPD Programme of Action [res. 2004/2]. The Commission also reaffirmed that the special theme for its thirty-eighth (2005) session would be "Population, development and HIV/AIDS, with particular emphasis on poverty" [dec. 2004/1]; decided to consider its methods of work at its 2005 session [dec. 2004/2]; and took note of the documents it had considered [dec. 2004/3]. It also decided that the special theme for its thirty-ninth (2006) session would be "International migration and development".

By **decision 2004/237** of 20 July, the Economic and Social Council took note of the Commission's report on its thirty-seventh session and approved the provisional agenda for its thirty-eighth (2005) session.

In preparation for the thirty-eighth session, the Commission's Bureau held an intersessional meeting (Lima, Peru, 16-19 October) [E/CN.9/2005/2].

2004 UN activities

In a report on programme implementation and progress of work of the UN Population Division in 2004 [E/CN.9/2005/9], the Secretary-General described the Division's activities dealing with the analysis of fertility, mortality and migration; world population estimates and projections; population policies and population ageing; population and development; monitoring, coordination and dissemination of population information; and technical cooperation in population.

The Division's work in fertility and family planning analysis included the issuance of a wallchart entitled *World Fertility Pattern 2004*, which presented data on selected fertility indicators. According to the data, the number of countries with total fertility below replacement level increased fourfold between 1970 and 2000, with fertility levels below replacement in all developed countries, and the fertility decline accompanied by shifts in the timing of childbearing. In most developing countries, the mean age at childbearing declined as the fertility of older women fell, and in developed countries, the mean age at childbearing was rising as women postponed the beginning of childbearing. The Division also issued a CD-ROM entitled "World Contraceptive Use 2003", and undertook a study on the prevalence of childlessness among women nearing the end of the reproductive lifespan.

On mortality and health, the Population Division developed a database and issued a CD-ROM containing key mortality indicators for two periods—the early 1970s and the most recent period for each country, according to data availability. The Division also prepared a report of the Workshop on HIV/AIDS and Adult Mortality in Developing Countries, held in 2003 [YUN 2003, p. 1094], which combined a technical meeting and a training activity for African officials working in the area of HIV/AIDS.

In the area of international migration, the Population Division organized the Third Coordination Meeting on International Migration (New York, 27-28 October), which focused on issues that might be considered by the High-Level Dialogue on International Migration and Development, scheduled by the General Assembly for 2006. Participants exchanged information on recent activities of their organizations in the area of international migration and development. In addition to the issuance of a database, *Trends in Total Migrant Stock: The 2003 Revision*, and its contribution to part two of the *World Economic and Social Survey, 2004*, published by DESA, the Population Division prepared and submitted to the General Assembly the Secretary-General's report on international migration and development (see p. 1076).

With regard to population projections, the Division issued the third and final volume of the 2002 revision of its biennial *World Population Prospects,* entitled *Analytical Report.* That volume analysed the results of the demographic estimates and projections for 228 countries and provided a view on demographic trends between 1950 and 2050. It predicted that the world population would grow from 6.1 billion in 2000 to 8.9 billion in 2050, with the population in the less developed regions rising at six times the rate of the developed regions (0.25 per cent annually). The Division published the results of the 2003 revision of world urbanization prospects [YUN 2003, p. 1095], in a publication and a CD-ROM, and made them available on the Division's website (www.unpopulation.org). The final report of the Division's new set of long-range projections, *World Population to 2300*, was also issued and made available online.

In the area of population policies, the Division published *World Population Policies, 2003*, which revealed that the most significant demographic concern of Governments was HIV/AIDS. Other concerns included low fertility and population ageing, in developed countries; and rapid population growth and infant, child and maternal mortality in developing countries. Evaluation and analysis of the United Nations Ninth Inquiry among Governments on Population and Development were under way. Responses had been received from some 80 countries representing 80 per cent of the world population and the results of the quinquennial Inquiry would be incorporated into *World Population Policies, 2005*.

Population ageing was another area of research. The Division's study on living arrangements of older persons around the world was due to appear in 2005. Based on census and survey data from more than 130 countries, the study provided comparative analysis of patterns and trends of the living arrangements of people aged 60 years or over. It showed that the majority of older persons in developed countries lived alone or with a spouse only, while in most developing countries, a large majority lived with children or other relatives. A new wallchart, Population Ageing 2005, was prepared for publication, which showed numbers of the older population, proportions currently married, living alone and in the labour force, the sex ratio of those aged 60 and over and aged 80 or older, and life expectancy at age 60 for men and women.

The Division issued the report entitled *The Impact of AIDS* and finalized the fourth version of the database on *Population, Resources, Environment and Development*. During the year, it prepared the latest edition of its annual monitoring report, which focused on population, development and HIV/AIDS, and continued to expand and update its website and to develop the Population Information Network (POPIN), a major channel for information dissemination. The Division's automatic e-mail announcement service, established in 2003 [YUN 2003, p. 1095], had over 1,000 subscribers in 2004, and the Division continued to produce and distribute a software package for demographic estimation.

Internal oversight

In conformity with General Assembly resolution 54/244 [YUN 1999, p. 1274], the Secretary-General transmitted an April report [E/AC.51/2004/5] of the Office of Internal Oversight Services (OIOS) on the triennial review of the implementation of the recommendations made by the Committee for Programme and Coordination (CPC) on the in-depth evaluation of the population programme. The review concluded that there had been significant progress towards implementing the CPC recommendations [YUN 2001, p. 1328], including the dissemination of information through the Internet, improvements in the design and navigation of the POPIN website, the discussion in its reports of the Division's technical procedures and methods, and consolidation of population activities into larger social and development subprogrammes. However, the report also indicated that there had been a decline in basic research and data collection in regional population data, and it stressed the need for financial support to the UN population research agenda.

Chapter IX

Social policy, crime prevention and human resources development

In 2004, the United Nations continued to promote social, cultural and human resources development, and to strengthen its crime prevention and criminal justice programme.

The Commission for Social Development considered as its priority theme improving public sector effectiveness, and adopted agreed conclusions on that topic. Preparations continued for the ten-year review by the Commission in 2005 of the 1995 World Summit for Social Development and the five-year review of the General Assembly's twenty-fourth (2000) special session. The Assembly endorsed the conclusions of the World Commission on the Social Dimension of Globalization, entitled *A Fair Globalization: Creating Opportunities For All*, which called for a people-centred globalization process. The Assembly stressed the importance of supporting the efforts of developing countries to achieve economic growth, sustainable development, poverty reduction and the strengthening of their democratic systems.

In December, the tenth anniversary of the International Year of the Family was observed at UN Headquarters. Also observed during the year were the second World Day for Cultural Diversity for Dialogue and Development in May and the Olympic Truce during the twenty-eighth Olympic Games in August.

On the issue of persons with disabilities, work continued by the Ad Hoc Committee on the Comprehensive and Integral International Convention on the Protection and Promotion of the Rights and Dignity of Persons with Disabilities, while consideration by the Assembly of the proposed supplement to the Standard Rules on the Equalization of Opportunities for Persons with Disabilities was postponed until its sixty-first (2006) session. Also during the year, efforts to promote religious and cultural understanding continued under the guidance of the United Nations Educational, Scientific and Cultural Organization, and preparations were made to usher in the International Year of Sport and Physical Education and the International Year of Physics in 2005.

In the area of crime prevention, the Commission on Crime Prevention and Criminal Justice considered crimes against cultural property, preparations for the Eleventh United Nations Congress on Crime Prevention and Criminal Justice, the rule of law, implementation of technical assistance projects in Africa, strengthening the technical cooperation capacity of the United Nations Crime Prevention and Criminal Justice Programme, promoting the implementation of the universal conventions and protocols related to terrorism, corruption, transnational organized crime, kidnapping, trafficking in human organs, money laundering, fraud, urban crime, UN norms and standards in crime prevention, the second World Summit of Attorneys General and General Prosecutors, and the Commission's functioning.

The Secretary-General reported on activities undertaken to implement the International Plan of Action for the United Nations Literacy Decade (2003-2012). Concerned about meeting the goals of the Decade, the Assembly appealed to Governments to mobilize enough resources to achieve those goals and called for increased investments in education. The Secretary-General also reported on the work of the United Nations Institute for Training and Research and the United Nations University.

Social policy and cultural issues

Social development

Follow-up to the 1995 World Summit and to the General Assembly special session

In response to General Assembly resolution 58/130 [YUN 2003, p. 1097], the Secretary-General submitted a June report [A/59/120] on the implementation of the Copenhagen Declaration on Social Development and the Programme of Action adopted at the 1995 World Summit for Social Development [YUN 1995, p. 1113] and of the further initiatives for social development adopted by the Assembly's twenty-fourth (2000) special session [YUN 2000, p. 1012]. The report discussed, in preparation for the ten-year review of the Summit and review of the Assembly's special session, the various priority themes considered by the Commission for Social Development from 1996 to 2004, a list of which was annexed to the report. It also analysed the agreed conclusions adopted by the Commission on those themes in 2002, 2003 and 2004 and selected issues which appeared to be of particular importance ten years later.

According to the report, although the Summit emphasized the placing of people at the centre of development efforts, a people-centred approach to national and international public affairs remained too much of an abstract concept. Progress towards achieving the main goals of the Summit—reduction of poverty and elimination of extreme poverty, full employment and integration in stable, safe and just societies—was at best uneven. Achieving social development continued to be characterized by a gap between intentions and actions, and between proclaimed objectives and the actual orientation of national and international affairs. While the acute problems of society, such as extreme poverty and insecurity, were receiving increased attention, as evidenced by the visibility of the Millennium Development Goals [YUN 2000, p. 51], their means of implementation left much to be desired, including that of resources. Three issues selected from the work of the Commission on follow-up to the Summit appeared to be of general relevance for countries—the social aspects of globalization, the compatibility and contribution of macroeconomic policies with and to social development goals and the capacity of national Governments to define and implement their own social policies—which were at the core of the search for equity and the reduction of poverty and inequality. The Secretary-General proposed that the Assembly recommend that, in the context of the ten-year review to take place in 2005, particular attention be given to the principle of a people-centred approach and its realization in public policies and development strategies.

GENERAL ASSEMBLY ACTION

On 20 December [meeting 74], the General Assembly, on the recommendation of the Third (Social, Humanitarian and Cultural) Committee [A/59/491], adopted **resolution 59/146** without vote [agenda item 93].

Implementation of the outcome of the World Summit for Social Development and of the twenty-fourth special session of the General Assembly

The General Assembly,

Recalling the World Summit for Social Development, held at Copenhagen from 6 to 12 March 1995, and the twenty-fourth special session of the General Assembly, entitled "World Summit for Social Development and beyond: achieving social development for all in a globalizing world", held at Geneva from 26 June to 1 July 2000,

Reaffirming that the Copenhagen Declaration on Social Development and the Programme of Action and the further initiatives for social development adopted by the General Assembly at its twenty-fourth special session constitute the basic framework for the promotion of social development for all at the national and international levels,

Recalling the United Nations Millennium Declaration and the development goals contained therein, as well as the commitments made at major United Nations summits, conferences and special sessions,

Considering that, despite the efforts made and the progress achieved in some areas of economic and social development, vast sectors of our societies, in particular in developing countries, especially the least developed countries, are still facing serious challenges, including financial crises, insecurity, poverty, exclusion and inequality in income growth and distribution, education and health, as well as environmental degradation,

Recalling the commitment to promote national and global economic systems based on the principles of justice, equity, democracy, participation, transparency, accountability and inclusion,

Recalling also its resolution 57/270 B of 23 June 2003 on the integrated and coordinated implementation of and follow-up to the outcomes of the major United Nations conferences and summits in the economic and social fields,

1. *Takes note with appreciation* of the report of the Secretary-General;

2. *Welcomes* the contribution of the Commission for Social Development in the follow-up to and review of the further implementation of the commitments made at the World Summit for Social Development and the further initiatives agreed upon at the twenty-fourth special session of the General Assembly, reaffirms that the Commission will continue to have the primary responsibility in this regard, and encourages Governments, the relevant specialized agencies, funds and programmes of the United Nations system and civil society to enhance their support to its work;

3. *Underlines* the significance of the forty-third session of the Commission for Social Development, which will mark the tenth anniversary of the World Summit for Social Development and at which the Commission will undertake a review of the implementation of the Copenhagen Declaration on Social Development and the Programme of Action and the outcome of the twenty-fourth special session of the General Assembly, and recommends that the Commission reflect the outcome of its review, on an exceptional basis, in a short declaration to be elaborated during its forty-third session, reaffirming the agreed commitments and the need for continued implementation of the outcome of the World Summit for Social Development and of the twenty-fourth special session;

4. *Welcomes* the decision by the Economic and Social Council, in its resolution 2004/58 of 23 July 2004, that the Commission for Social Development at its forty-third session should convene high-level plenary meetings, open to the participation of all States Members of

the United Nations and observers, on the implementation of the Copenhagen Declaration and the Programme of Action and the outcome of the twenty-fourth special session of the General Assembly, and also welcomes the request of the Council to the Chairman of the Commission at its forty-third session to transmit the outcome, through the Council, to the Assembly at its sixtieth session, including to the high-level event of the Assembly on the review of the United Nations Millennium Declaration in 2005;

5. *Recommends* that the Commission for Social Development, at its forty-third session and in undertaking the review of the implementation of the Copenhagen Declaration and the Programme of Action and the outcome of the twenty-fourth special session of the General Assembly, give particular attention to the people-centred approach and to its concrete implementation, as set out in the Copenhagen Declaration and the Programme of Action and the outcome of the twenty-fourth special session, and that it emphasize the sharing of experiences and good practices in overcoming challenges to the implementation of the Copenhagen Declaration and the Programme of Action and the outcome of the twenty-fourth special session;

6. *Reaffirms* that the aim of social integration is to create a society for all, in which every individual, each with rights and responsibilities, has an active role to play, and that such an inclusive society must be based on respect for all human rights and fundamental freedoms, cultural and religious diversity, social justice and the special needs of vulnerable and disadvantaged groups, democratic participation and the rule of law;

7. *Recognizes* the need to promote respect for human rights and fundamental freedoms in order to address the most pressing social needs of people living in poverty, including through the design and development of appropriate mechanisms to strengthen and consolidate democratic institutions and governance;

8. *Reaffirms* the commitment to gender equality and to strengthening policies and programmes that improve, ensure and broaden the full participation of women in all spheres of political, economic, social and cultural life, as equal partners, and to improving their access to all resources needed for the full exercise of all their human rights and fundamental freedoms by removing persistent barriers;

9. *Stresses* the vital importance of achieving social development for all and of integrating social development objectives, as set out in the Copenhagen Declaration and the Programme of Action and in the further initiatives for social development, into economic policy-making, including into policies that influence domestic and global market forces and the global economy;

10. *Recognizes* that globalization and interdependence are opening new opportunities through trade, investment and capital flows and advances in technology, including information technology, for the growth of the world economy and the development and improvement of living standards around the world, while at the same time there remain serious challenges, including serious financial crises, insecurity, poverty, exclusion and inequality within and among societies and considerable obstacles to further integration and full participation in the global economy for developing countries, and that unless the benefits of social and economic development are extended to all countries, a growing number of people in all countries and even entire regions will remain marginalized from the global economy, and in this regard reiterates the need for further action in order to overcome those obstacles affecting peoples and countries and to realize the full potential of opportunities presented for the benefit of all;

11. *Looks forward,* in this context, to further consideration of the impact of globalization on social development at the forty-third session of the Commission for Social Development, taking note of the report of the World Commission on the Social Dimension of Globalization;

12. *Reaffirms* the need to place people at the centre of all our development policies in order to eradicate poverty, promote full and productive employment and foster social integration so as to promote stable, safe and just societies for all;

13. *Underlines* the importance of adopting effective measures, including new financial mechanisms, as appropriate, to support the efforts of developing countries to achieve sustained economic growth, sustainable development, poverty reduction and the strengthening of their democratic systems, while reaffirming that each country has primary responsibility for its own economic and social development and that national policies have the leading role in the development process;

14. *Emphasizes* the importance of integrating economic and social policies in promoting human resources development and enhancing the process of development, invites the Economic and Social Council and the Commission for Social Development to continue to give particular attention to this issue at their forthcoming sessions, and invites the various entities of the United Nations system, within their respective mandates, to take into account the integration of economic and social policies in their respective domains;

15. *Recognizes* that, while action taken to implement the outcomes of the major United Nations summits, conferences and special sessions in the economic, social and related fields held during the past ten years will further promote social development, strengthened and effective international and regional cooperation and assistance for development and progress towards increased participation, greater social justice and improved equity in societies will also be required;

16. *Recognizes also* that achieving the internationally agreed development goals, including those contained in the Millennium Declaration, demands a new partnership between developed and developing countries, and in this context stresses the importance of achieving sound policies, good governance at all levels and the rule of law, as well as mobilizing domestic resources, attracting international flows, promoting international trade as an engine for development, increasing international and financial and technical cooperation for development, sustainable debt financing and external debt relief and enhancing the coherence and consistency of the international monetary, financial and trading systems;

17. *Stresses* the necessity of ensuring the effective involvement of developing countries in the international economic decision-making process through, inter alia, greater participation in international economic forums, thereby ensuring the transparency and account-

ability of international financial institutions with respect to according a central position to social development in their policies and programmes;

18. *Reaffirms* the call of the Economic and Social Council for enhanced coordination within the United Nations system and the ongoing efforts to harmonize the current initiatives on Africa, and requests the Commission for Social Development to continue to give due prominence in its work to the social dimension of the New Partnership for Africa's Development;

19. *Reaffirms also* that education, employment creation and improvement in working conditions, which are some of the indispensable elements of poverty eradication, social integration, gender equality and overall development, should be at the centre of development strategies and international cooperation in support of national policies, and recognizes the need to promote employment that meets labour standards as defined in relevant instruments of the International Labour Organization and other international instruments;

20. *Encourages*, in this context, current initiatives of the United Nations system on the elaboration of comprehensive employment strategies and measures to foster youth employment, bearing in mind relevant international instruments pertaining to youth;

21. *Reaffirms* that social development requires the active involvement of all actors in the development process, including civil society organizations, corporations and small businesses, and that partnerships among all relevant actors are increasingly becoming part of national and international cooperation for social development, reaffirms also that, within countries, partnerships among the Government, civil society and the private sector can contribute effectively to the achievement of social development goals, and underlines the fact that, at the international level, the recent initiatives towards building voluntary partnerships for social development should be encouraged and discussed further at, inter alia, the intergovernmental level;

22. *Underlines* the responsibility of the private sector, at both the national and the international levels, including small and large companies and transnational corporations, regarding not only the economic and financial, but also the development, social, gender and environmental implications of their activities, their obligations towards their workers and their contributions to achieving sustainable development, including social development, and emphasizes the need to take concrete actions within the United Nations system and through the participation of all relevant stakeholders on corporate responsibility and accountability;

23. *Invites* the Secretary-General, the Economic and Social Council, the Commission for Social Development, the regional commissions, the relevant specialized agencies, funds and programmes of the United Nations system and other intergovernmental forums, within their respective mandates, to continue to integrate into their work programmes and give priority attention to the commitments and undertakings set out in the Copenhagen Declaration and the Programme of Action and in the further initiatives for social development, to continue to be actively involved in their follow-up and to monitor the achievement of those commitments and undertakings;

24. *Decides* to include in the provisional agenda of its sixtieth session the item entitled "Implementation

of the outcome of the World Summit for Social Development and of the twenty-fourth special session of the General Assembly", and requests the Secretary-General to submit a report on this question to the Assembly at that session.

World Commission on the Social Dimensions of Globalization

In June [A/59/98-E/2004/79], Finland and the United Republic of Tanzania transmitted to the General Assembly and the Economic and Social Council the report of the World Commission on the Social Dimension of Globalization entitled *A Fair Globalization: Creating Opportunities for All*, which focused on governance and accountability and recommended coordinated measures at the national and international levels in the areas of trade, investment, finance, migration and labour.

GENERAL ASSEMBLY ACTION

On 2 December [meeting 65], the General Assembly adopted **resolution 59/57** [draft: A/59/L.38 & Add.1] without vote [agenda item 55].

A Fair Globalization: Creating Opportunities for All- report of the World Commission on the Social Dimension of Globalization

The General Assembly,

Reaffirming the resolve expressed in the United Nations Millennium Declaration to ensure that globalization becomes a positive force for the people of the entire world,

Recalling the commitment in the Millennium Declaration to ensure greater policy coherence and better cooperation between the United Nations, its agencies, the Bretton Woods institutions and other multilateral bodies, with a view to achieving a fully coordinated approach to the problems of peace and development,

Recalling also its resolution 58/225 of 23 December 2003, in which it stressed the need for the United Nations to continue to address the social dimension of globalization and took note of the work of the World Commission on the Social Dimension of Globalization,

Recognizing the support expressed at the International Conference on Financing for Development and the World Summit on Sustainable Development for the work of the International Labour Organization on the social dimension of globalization,

Acknowledging the work of the World Commission on the Social Dimension of Globalization, co-chaired by the President of Finland and the President of the United Republic of Tanzania and facilitated by the International Labour Organization,

Recognizing the contribution of the implementation of the commitments agreed in the outcomes of the major United Nations conferences and summits, including the important contributions of the Monterrey Consensus, adopted by the International Conference on Financing for Development, and the World Summit on Sustainable Development to eradicating poverty, achieving sustained economic growth and promoting sustainable development, as well as advancing towards a fully inclusive and equitable globalization,

Recalling its resolutions 58/291 of 6 May 2004 and 57/270 B of 23 June 2003 on the follow-up to the outcome of the Millennium Summit of the United Nations and the integrated and coordinated follow-up to the outcomes of the major United Nations conferences and summits in economic and social fields,

1. *Takes note* of the report of the World Commission on the Social Dimension of Globalization entitled *A Fair Globalization: Creating Opportunities for All*, as a contribution to the international dialogue towards a fully inclusive and equitable globalization;

2. *Decides* to consider the wider challenges and opportunities linked to the issue of globalization, including those in the report of the World Commission, within the framework of the comprehensive review of the implementation of the United Nations Millennium Declaration, under resolution 58/291, and the ten-year review of the further implementation of the outcome of the World Summit for Social Development by the Commission for Social Development in 2005;

3. *Calls upon* the organs and bodies of the United Nations, and invites the organizations of the United Nations system, to consider within their mandates the report of the World Commission, and also calls upon Member States to consider the report;

4. *Invites* relevant organizations of the United Nations system and other relevant multilateral bodies to provide information to the Secretary-General on their activities to promote an inclusive and equitable globalization;

5. *Requests* the Secretary-General to take into account, inter alia, the report of the World Commission in his comprehensive report for the high-level review of 2005 at the sixtieth session of the General Assembly, within the follow-up to the outcome of the Millennium Summit of the United Nations.

Commission for Social Development

The Commission for Social Development, at its forty-second session (New York, 4-13 and 20 February) [E/2004/26], adopted agreed conclusions on its priority theme, "Improving public sector effectiveness" (see p. 1093). The Commission made recommendations for action by the Economic and Social Council on: the drafting of a comprehensive and integral international convention on protection and promotion of the rights and dignity of persons with disabilities (see p. 1098); further promotion of equalization of opportunities by, for and with persons with disabilities, and protection of the human rights of persons with disabilities (see p. 1097); and implementation of the social objectives of the New Partnership for Africa's Development (see p. 920). A text on the celebration of the tenth anniversary of the International Year of the Family was recommended to the Council for adoption by the General Assembly (see p. 1095). The Commission also adopted a resolution [E/2004/26 (res. 42/1)] on modalities for reviewing the 2002 Ma-

drid International Plan of Action on Ageing [YUN 2002, p. 1194] (see p. 1192).

In consideration of emerging trends in social development, the Commission heard a presentation on the findings of the Third International Forum for Social Development (New York, October 2003) held under the theme "International migration and migrants from a social perspective" and held a panel discussion on the subject.

The Commission considered the Secretary-General's report [E/CN.5/2004/2] on the review of the methods of its work, submitted in accordance with Assembly resolution 57/270 B [YUN 2003, p. 1468], and decided to continue consideration of the item at its forty-third session. The Commission also agreed to provide comments on the Secretary-General's proposed strategic framework for the 2006-2007 biennium in social policy and development [E/CN.5/2004/7].

On 21 July, the Council took note of the Commission's report on its forty-second session and approved the provisional agenda and documentation for its forty-third (2005) session (**decision 2004/241**).

In **resolution 2004/16** of 21 July on the implementation of the social objectives of the New Partnership for Africa's Development (see p. 921), the Economic and Social Council reaffirmed the need to strengthen, in the spirit of partnership, international, regional and subregional cooperation for social development and for the implementation of the outcome of the 1995 World Summit for Social Development and the twenty-fourth special session of the General Assembly. It invited the Secretary-General to continue to reflect social dimensions in future reports submitted to the Commission for Social Development on its priority theme of national and international cooperation for social development.

Preparations for the forty-third session of the Commission for Social Development

ECONOMIC AND SOCIAL COUNCIL ACTION

On 23 July [meeting 51], the Economic and Social Council adopted **resolution 2004/58** [draft: E/2004/L.27] without vote [agenda item 14 (*b*)].

Preparations for the forty-third session of the Commission for Social Development

The Economic and Social Council,

Underlining the significance of the forty-third session of the Commission for Social Development, which will mark the tenth anniversary of the adoption of the Copenhagen Declaration on Social Development and the Programme of Action of the World Summit for Social Development,

Noting that the Commission will undertake, at its forty-third session, a review of the implementation of the Copenhagen Programme of Action and the outcome of the twenty-fourth special session of the General Assembly, entitled "World Summit for Social Development and beyond: achieving social development for all in a globalizing world", held in Geneva from 26 June to 1 July 2000, which constitute the basic framework for the promotion of social development for all at the national and international levels,

Building upon Economic and Social Council resolution 1996/7 of 22 July 1996 and also taking into account General Assembly resolutions 50/161 of 22 December 1995, 57/270 B of 23 June 2003 and 58/291 of 6 May 2004,

Considering the special nature of the task before the Commission for Social Development at its forty-third session,

1. *Decides* to focus on the implementation of the Copenhagen Declaration on Social Development and the Programme of Action of the World Summit for Social Development and the outcome of the twenty-fourth special session of the General Assembly through the expanded use of interactive dialogue, and with broad-based participation of governmental delegations at the highest level of responsibility and expertise, and of civil society and organizations within the United Nations system, bearing in mind the need to integrate the social development perspective in the comprehensive review of the progress made in the fulfilment of all the commitments contained in the United Nations Millennium Declaration;

2. *Also decides* the Commission for Social Development at its forty-third session, should emphasize the sharing of experiences and good practices on overcoming challenges to the implementation of the Copenhagen Declaration and Programme of Action and the outcome of the twenty-fourth special session of the General Assembly;

3. *Further decides* that the Commission for Social Development should convene, during its forty-third session, high-level plenary meetings, open to all States Members of the United Nations and observers, on the implementation of the Copenhagen Declaration and Programme of Action and the outcome of the twenty-fourth special session of the General Assembly, and requests the Chairman of the forty-third session of the Commission to transmit the outcome, through the Economic and Social Council, to the General Assembly at its sixtieth session, including to the high-level event of the Assembly on the review of the Millennium Declaration in 2005;

4. *Requests* the Bureau of the Commission for Social Development, in its preparations for the forty-third session of the Commission, to take into account the views expressed by representatives at the forty-second session of the Commission and to convene informal consultative meetings with the participation of all interested member States and observers, with a view to facilitating the work of the Commission at its forthcoming forty-third session.

Improving public sector effectiveness

The Secretary-General, in response to Economic and Social Council decision 2003/230 [YUN 2003, p. 1099], submitted a report on its priority theme: improving public sector effectiveness [E/CN.5/2004/5]. The report explored the notion of "public sector" in the context of UN activities, and particularly the mandate of the Commission; described the context of the call for improving public sector effectiveness; analysed what constituted an effective public sector; and discussed means for improving its effectiveness, including through adequate financing, improved delivery, privatization, increased social dialogue and participation, and maintaining high standards among public servants.

The report proposed policy recommendations for the Commission's consideration.

ECONOMIC AND SOCIAL COUNCIL ACTION

On 21 July [meeting 47], the Economic and Social Council, on the recommendation of the Commission on Social Development [E/2004/26], adopted **resolution 2004/240** without vote [agenda item 14 (b)].

Agreed conclusions of the Commission for Social Development on improving public sector effectiveness

At its 47th plenary meeting, on 21 July 2004, the Economic and Social Council, endorsed the following agreed conclusions adopted by the Commission for Social Development with respect to its priority theme at its forty-second session:

1. Governments have the primary responsibility for the provision of social services in order to enhance social development and contribute to the achievement of the internationally agreed development goals, including those contained in the Copenhagen Declaration on Social Development and the Programme of Action of the World Summit for Social Development, the outcome document adopted at the twenty-fourth special session of the General Assembly, entitled World Summit for Social Development and Beyond: Achieving Social Development for All in a Globalizing World, and the Millennium Declaration. In this regard, national priorities and policies have the leading role in the development process. At the same time, national efforts need to be supported by an enabling international environment. The Commission emphasizes the crucial role of the public sector in, inter alia, the provision of equitable, adequate and accessible social services for all to meet the essential needs of the entire population, in particular those excluded from social services and those most in need. Governments should constantly strive to improve the public sector, taking into account the level of economic and social development of each country.

2. The Commission reiterates that sound social and economic development policies at the national and international levels should be part of the framework for the improvement of the effectiveness of the public sector. This requires long-term planning, well-defined priorities and coherent policies, effective implementation and capacity-building. Those policies should be formulated and implemented by Governments, with the participation of all relevant stakeholders, as appro-

priate, and should be supported by the international community.

3. The Commission acknowledges that improvement of public sector effectiveness can be achieved through, inter alia, dialogue, partnership and cooperation at all levels. The Commission encourages Governments to strengthen the exchanges of experience and methods of effective delivery of public services. The United Nations system and international financial, trade and economic institutions and bilateral donors are invited to play an important role, through an integrated and coherent approach, in assisting Governments, in particular those of developing countries, least developed countries and countries with economies in transition, in this endeavour, specifically in exchanging and disseminating good practices and capacity-building activities aimed at improving public sector effectiveness.

4. The Commission acknowledges that developing countries, in particular the least developed countries, need to have a sufficient level of financial resources in order to provide social services commensurate with the needs of their citizens.

5. The Commission recognizes that a substantial increase in official development assistance and other resources will be required if developing countries are to achieve the internationally agreed development goals and objectives, including those contained in the Millennium Declaration. In order to build support for official development assistance, heads of State and Government have pledged to further improve policies and development strategies, both nationally and internationally, to enhance aid effectiveness.

6. Achieving the internationally agreed development goals, including those contained in the Millennium Declaration, demands a new partnership between developed and developing countries. In this context, the Commission stresses the importance of the commitment recently made by heads of State and Government to achieving sound policies, good governance at all levels and the rule of law, as well as to mobilizing domestic resources, attracting international flows, promoting international trade as an engine for development, increasing international financial and technical cooperation for development, sustainable debt financing and external debt relief and enhancing the coherence and consistency of the international monetary, financial and trading systems.

7. Each country has the primary responsibility for its own economic and social development, within which the role of national policies and development strategies cannot be overemphasized. In this context, the Commission reaffirms that international cooperation has an essential role in assisting developing countries, including the least developed countries, in the strengthening of their human, institutional and technological capacity and that the improvement of the effectiveness of the public sector is one of the conditions for social development requiring strengthened international cooperation.

8. The Commission stresses that in making recommendations on macroeconomic policies and implementing various programmes related to development and poverty eradication, the international financial institutions are invited to take full account of the role and specificity of the public sector, notably public social services.

9. At the international level, the Commission has the primary responsibility in the follow-up to and review of the implementation of the commitments made at the World Summit for Social Development and the further initiatives agreed upon at the twenty-fourth special session of the General Assembly. In this regard, the Commission is a forum where countries can participate in an exchange of views and assessment of efforts, including through best practices aimed, inter alia, at promoting public sector effectiveness and seeking optimal ways of ensuring equitable delivery of social services in order to enhance social cohesion and accelerate social development.

10. The Commission recommends that, when making decisions about the allocation of public resources, Governments, with the contribution of relevant stakeholders, should consider the social development goals when developing or strengthening, inter alia, their national poverty eradication policies and strategies, taking into account that the financing of effective social services is an investment in economic growth and should be evaluated in the context of their impact on social development goals as well as on public expenditures and finances.

11. The Commission, while noting that economic hardship has in some cases led to reduced public social expenditures, recognizes that social and economic development policies and programmes should be complementary and that effective spending on strengthening public social services, including human capital development, social equity enhancement and social protection, contributes to long-term economic development and the development of society as a whole.

12. The Commission invites Governments to consider complementary and alternative approaches to the delivery of social services, including decentralization, privatization and public-private partnerships or, where appropriate, the introduction of competitive market-based structures. In general, social services can be delivered most effectively and efficiently by entities that are most appropriate and closest to local communities and are therefore more aware of their needs. While services can be provided by private entities, the fundamental objectives of those services and the ultimate responsibility of the State remain unchanged. The Commission reaffirms that any reform of public service delivery should aim at promoting and attaining the goals of universal and equitable access to those services by all, without discrimination, and at eradicating poverty and at the promotion and protection of all human rights, promoting full and productive employment and fostering social integration. In this regard, factors such as the rule of law, good governance, sound financial management at all levels, gender equality and strengthened international cooperation are important elements for success in meeting these objectives.

13. The Commission underlines that improvement of public sector effectiveness requires, inter alia, that all countries strive to eliminate corruption at all levels and welcomes the adoption by the General Assembly of the United Nations Convention against Corruption.

14. The Commission emphasizes the importance of dialogue and inclusive stakeholder participation, as appropriate, in the formulation, implementation and evaluation of social development policies, including policies on social services, to increase the efficiency, ef-

fectiveness, accessibility, affordability and flexibility of such services, and the importance of the sense of ownership among all relevant stakeholders, including civil society, as well as entities that provide social services.

15. The Commission underscores the importance of the principles of transparency, accountability, integrity, efficiency and equality for improving the effectiveness of the public sector. In addition, the Commission considers that when Governments address the monitoring and evaluation of the delivery and impact of social services, equitable access to and quality of such services as well as the attainment of their initial objectives should be taken into account.

UN Research Institute for Social Development

During 2004, the United Nations Research Institute for Social Development (UNRISD) continued to conduct research on the social dimensions of the development process, within a holistic and multidisciplinary framework, focusing on decision-making processes and the social impact of development policies.

A November report of the UNRISD Board [E/CN.5/2005/3] described activities in 2003-2004, among which were the release of UNRISD's *Research for Social Change* at a conference on social knowledge and international policy-making: exploring the linkages (Geneva, 20-21 April), which marked the Institute's fortieth anniversary. UNRISD also held conferences on corporate social responsibility and development: towards a new agenda (17-18 November), and on the ethnic structure, inequality and governance of the public sector (Riga, Latvia, 25-27 March, 2004). It launched new projects on the development impacts of HIV/AIDS: politics and political economy of HIV/AIDS and community responses to HIV/AIDS, and on civil society engagement and global civil society movements: dynamics in international campaigns and national implementation. The Institute also launched a new series of research and policy briefs aimed at improving dialogue on development. In 2003-2004, eighteen scholars from thirteen countries worked at the Institute.

Observance of tenth anniversary of International Year of the Family (1994)

In accordance with General Assembly resolution 58/15 [YUN 2003, p. 1103], the Secretary-General submitted in February an interim report [E/CN.5/2004/3] to the Commission for Social Development on preparations for and observance of the tenth anniversary of the International Year of the Family, to be celebrated on 6 December 2004. The report provided an overview of preparations for the anniversary at the national, regional and international levels. According to the report, na-

tional coordination mechanisms for the tenth anniversary were established and long-standing national priorities for family policies were given new impetus, with initiatives to address those priorities launched in many countries. The tenth anniversary was seen as an opportunity to update, refine or develop legislation concerning families and to address the broad spectrum of family-related issues. Numerous Governments mainstreamed a family dimension in decision-making and administrative processes, and established infrastructure and policy instruments to strengthen and support families and promote an enabling environment for them. At the regional level, the UN regional commissions interacted with various national authorities and civil society organizations on family issues. At the international level, coordination between the Department of Economic and Social Affairs (DESA) and the UN information centres was strengthened to enhance dissemination and exchange of information on issues relating to the family. In January, DESA, as part of the observance, organized a policy workshop on HIV/AIDS and family well-being to explore the effects of HIV/AIDS on the family unit and family network, identify coping mechanisms, review existing policies and programmes, develop a policy framework and recommendations for addressing family issues and identify further capacity-building needs.

The report recommended the strengthening of cooperation and mechanisms for consultation and advocacy to promote greater consensus on policy content, concepts and an integrated perspective on the family, enhance international cooperation in research, promote training and advisory services, and continue support to the United Nations Trust Fund on Family Activities to assist in national capacity-building.

ECONOMIC AND SOCIAL COUNCIL ACTION

On 21 July [meeting 47], the Economic and Social Council, on the recommendation of the Commission for Social Development [E/2004/26], adopted **resolution 2004/13** without vote [agenda item 14 (*b*)].

Celebration of the tenth anniversary of the International Year of the Family and beyond

The Economic and Social Council,

Recommends to the General Assembly the adoption of the following draft resolution:

[For text, see General Assembly resolution 59/147 on p. 1096.]

Report of Secretary-General. Also in response to Assembly resolution 58/15, the Secretary-General submitted a July report [A/59/176] to the Assembly, which provided additional information and analysis of the situation of families worldwide, and approaches undertaken, primarily at the national level, on policy in support of families, derived from experience gained in the preparation of the tenth anniversary. It suggested the need for regular national surveys of the situation of families, and proposed actions for national coordination of family policies and programmes and other national actions, such as legal reforms, legislation and related measures, public awareness, research, service provision and support to non-governmental organizations (NGOs). It proposed several recommendations to the Assembly, including that DESA provide technical assistance to national coordination mechanisms; support diagnostic studies, research and data collection; exchange expertise and experiences on family issues; disseminate information; support networking at all levels; and encourage policy and programme coordination within the UN system. The United Nations Programme on the Family should highlight advocacy, capacity-building and technical support to Governments on the issue of the family.

By **decision 59/522** of 20 December, the Assembly took note of the Secretary-General's report.

Doha International Conference for the Family. Qatar transmitted to the Assembly in December the final report of the Doha International Conference for the Family to commemorate the tenth anniversary of the Year (29-30 November) [A/59/599], and the Doha Declaration adopted at that Conference [A/59/592]. The Declaration reaffirmed international commitments to the family and called upon Governments, international organizations and members of civil society at all levels to take action to protect the family. The Conference welcomed the announcement by Qatar of the creation of an International Institute for Study of the Family.

GENERAL ASSEMBLY ACTION

On 6 December [meeting 67], the General Assembly adopted **resolution 59/111** [draft: A/59/L.29 & Add. 1] without vote [agenda item 94].

Celebrating the tenth anniversary of the International Year of the Family

The General Assembly,

Recalling its resolution 44/82 of 8 December 1989 concerning the proclamation of, preparations for and observance of the International Year of the Family in 1994, and resolutions 50/142 of 21 December 1995, 52/81 of 12 December 1997 and 54/124 of 17 December 1999 concerning the follow-up to the International Year of the Family,

Recalling also its resolutions 56/113 of 19 December 2001, 57/164 of 18 December 2002 and 58/15 of 3 December 2003 concerning the preparations for and observance of the tenth anniversary of the International Year of the Family in 2004,

Taking note with appreciation of the report of the Secretary-General on the preparations for and observance of the tenth anniversary of the International Year of the Family in 2004,

1. *Reaffirms* its resolution 58/15;

2. *Welcomes* the celebration of the tenth anniversary of the International Year of the Family on 6 December 2004 at Headquarters;

3. *Commends* the important contributions made by Governments at the international, national, regional and local levels to observe the tenth anniversary of the International Year of the Family;

4. *Welcomes* the hosting of the Regional Conference on the Family in Africa on 27 and 28 July 2004 by the Government of Benin, and also welcomes the hosting of the Doha International Conference for the Family on 29 and 30 November 2004 by the State of Qatar, and takes note of their outcomes;

5. *Encourages* Governments to make every possible effort to realize the objectives of the tenth anniversary of the International Year of the Family and to integrate a family perspective in the planning process;

6. *Notes with appreciation* the contribution of the non-governmental organizations through local and regional meetings, as well as the programmes and activities throughout civil society undertaken in support of the celebration of the tenth anniversary of the International Year of the Family;

7. *Recommends* that all relevant agencies of the United Nations system, civil society organizations, the media, religious and community-based organizations as well as the private sector contribute to developing strategies and programmes aimed at strengthening the livelihood of families;

8. *Encourages* United Nations agencies and bodies, including the regional commissions, as well as intergovernmental and non-governmental organizations and research and academic institutions, to work closely with the Department of Economic and Social Affairs of the Secretariat in a coordinated manner on family-related issues, inter alia, by sharing experience and findings, in recognition of their valuable role in family policy development at all levels;

9. *Decides* to celebrate the anniversary of the International Year of the Family on a ten-year basis.

On 20 December [meeting 74], the General Assembly, on the recommendation of the Third Committee [A/59/492], adopted **resolution 59/147** without vote [agenda item 94 (a)].

Celebration of the tenth anniversary of the International Year of the Family and beyond

The General Assembly,

Recalling its resolutions 44/82 of 8 December 1989, 45/133 of 14 December 1990, 46/92 of 16 December 1991, 47/237 of 20 September 1993, 50/142 of 21 December 1995, 52/81 of 12 December 1997, 54/124 of 17 December 1999, 56/113 of 19 December 2001, 57/164 of 18 December 2002 and 58/15 of 3 December 2003 concerning the proclamation of, preparations for and observance of the International Year of the Family in 1994 and its tenth anniversary in 2004,

Recalling also that relevant United Nations instruments on human rights as well as relevant global plans and programmes of action call for the widest possible protection and assistance to be accorded to the family, bearing in mind that in different cultural, political and social systems various forms of the family exist,

Recalling further that the family is the basic unit of society and, as such, should be strengthened, and that it is entitled to receive comprehensive protection and support,

Noting that the family-related provisions of the outcomes of the major United Nations conferences and summits of the 1990s and their follow-up processes continue to provide policy guidance on ways to strengthen family-centred components of policies and programmes as part of an integrated comprehensive approach to development,

Recognizing that the preparations for and observance of the tenth anniversary of the International Year of the Family provided a useful opportunity for drawing further attention to the objectives of the Year for increasing cooperation at all levels on family issues,

Recognizing also the commendable efforts made by Governments at the local and national levels in carrying out specific programmes concerning families,

Emphasizing that equality between women and men and respect for all the human rights and fundamental freedoms of all family members are essential to family well-being and to society at large, noting the importance of reconciliation of work and family life, and recognizing the principle that both parents have common responsibilities for the upbringing and development of the child,

Aware that families are affected by social and economic changes, manifested as observable worldwide trends, and that the causes and consequences of those trends concerning families have to be identified and analysed,

Noting with concern the devastating effects of the HIV/AIDS pandemic on family life, as well as the devastating effects on family life of other infectious diseases, such as malaria and tuberculosis,

Noting with concern also the devastating effects of difficult social and economic conditions, armed conflicts and natural disasters on family life,

Recognizing the important role of non-governmental organizations, at both the local and the national levels, working in the interest of families,

Aware that there is a need for continued inter-agency cooperation on the family in order to generate greater awareness of family issues among the governing bodies of the United Nations system,

Recalling that the tenth anniversary of the International Year of the Family will be observed and celebrated during the fifty-ninth session of the General Assembly,

Having considered the report of the Secretary-General,

1. *Notes* that the follow-up to the tenth anniversary of the International Year of the Family is an integral part of the agenda and the multi-year programme of work of the Commission for Social Development until 2006;

2. *Urges* Governments to continue to take sustained action at all levels concerning family issues, including applied studies and research, in order to promote the role of families in development and develop concrete measures and approaches to address national priorities in dealing with family issues;

3. *Urges* the international community to address family-related concerns within the framework of the commitments undertaken at relevant major United Nations conferences and their follow-up processes, including those agreed to in the Declaration of Commitment on HIV/AIDS adopted by the General Assembly at its twenty-sixth special session on 27 June 2001;

4. *Encourages* more inter-agency cooperation within the United Nations system on issues relating to the family;

5. *Encourages* the regional commissions of the United Nations, within existing resources, to promote further the exchange of experiences at the regional level through the provision of technical assistance, including advisory services, to Governments upon request;

6. *Emphasizes* that the Secretariat should continue its important role in the programme of work on family issues within the United Nations system, and, in this regard, encourages the Department of Economic and Social Affairs, within existing resources, to continue to cooperate with Governments, the United Nations system and civil society in strengthening national capacities through the implementation of the mandated objectives of the International Year of the Family, including through:

   (a) The provision of policy guidance on emerging issues and trends affecting the family through the preparation of studies and research papers aimed, in particular, at enhancing the role of the family in society;

   (b) The provision of technical assistance to countries, upon request, to enhance, where appropriate, their national capacities in the area of family-related work;

7. *Invites* the Secretary-General, within existing resources, to disseminate a compilation of existing development cooperation activities of the United Nations system in the field of the family for the benefit of the Department of Economic and Social Affairs, other relevant United Nations bodies, Member States and observers by the time of the holding of the forty-fourth session of the Commission for Social Development;

8. *Requests* the Secretary-General:

   (a) To give appropriate consideration to the tenth anniversary of the International Year of the Family by preparing for the observance of the International Day of Families on 15 May 2004 and by taking appropriate steps for the celebration of the tenth anniversary of the International Year of the Family;

   (b) To continue to utilize the United Nations Trust Fund on Family Activities to provide financial assistance for activities specific to the family and for projects of direct benefit to it, with special focus on least developed and developing countries;

9. *Also requests* the Secretary-General to report on the implementation of the present resolution to the General Assembly at its sixtieth session.

Persons with disabilities

Standard Rules on the Equalization of Opportunities for Persons with Disabilities

The Secretary-General, in accordance with Economic and Social Council resolution 2002/26 [YUN 20002, p.1091], transmitted to the Commission for Social Development the views of 15 Governments and the European Union, on behalf of its 15 members and 10 accessing countries, on the proposals of the Special Rapporteur on Disability [ibid.], especially on the suggested supplement to the Standard Rules on the Equalization of Opportunities for Persons with Disabilities [E/CN.5/2004/4].

ECONOMIC AND SOCIAL COUNCIL ACTION

On 21 July [meeting 47], the Economic and Social Council, on the recommendation of the Commission for Social Development [E/2004/26], adopted **resolution 2004/15** without vote [agenda item 14 (*b*)].

Further promotion of equalization of opportunities by, for and with persons with disabilities, and protection of the human rights of persons with disabilities

The Economic and Social Council,

Recalling the purposes and principles of the Charter of the United Nations, and reaffirming the obligations contained in relevant human rights instruments,

Recalling also General Assembly resolution 37/52 of 3 December 1982, by which the Assembly adopted the World Programme of Action concerning Disabled Persons, resolution 48/96 of 20 December 1993, by which it adopted the Standard Rules on the Equalization of Opportunities for Persons with Disabilities, and resolution 58/132 of 22 December 2003,

Recalling further General Assembly resolution 56/168 of 19 December 2001, by which the Assembly established the Ad Hoc Committee on a Comprehensive and Integral International Convention on the Protection and Promotion of the Rights and Dignity of Persons with Disabilities, resolution 57/229 of 18 December 2002, in which it sought views on proposals for a convention, and resolution 58/246 of 23 December 2003, in which it decided that the Ad Hoc Committee should start negotiations on a draft convention at its third session,

Recalling Economic and Social Council resolution 2002/26 of 24 July 2002 on further promotion of equalization of opportunities by, for and with persons with disabilities and protection of their human rights, Commission on Human Rights resolution 2003/49 of 23 April 2003 on the human rights of persons with disabilities and other relevant resolutions of the General Assembly, the Economic and Social Council and its functional commissions,

Noting with satisfaction that the Standard Rules play an increasingly important role in the equalization of opportunities for persons with disabilities,

1. *Takes note* of the views of Governments on the proposals contained in the report of the former Special Rapporteur on disability of the Commission for Social Development, especially on the proposed supplement to the Standard Rules on the Equalization of Opportunities for Persons with Disabilities contained in the annex to the report, as well as the views expressed during the forty-second session of the Commission;

2. *Welcomes* the work of the Special Rapporteur undertaken in accordance with section IV of the Standard Rules;

3. *Recommends* that the General Assembly consider the proposed supplement to the Standard Rules con-

tained in the annex to the report of the former Special Rapporteur, with a view to completing its consideration at its fifty-ninth session;

4. *Also recommends* that the General Assembly, in considering the proposed supplement to the Standard Rules, take into account the work of the Ad Hoc Committee on a Comprehensive and Integral International Convention on the Protection and Promotion of the Rights and Dignity of Persons with Disabilities;

5. *Invites* the Special Rapporteur to contribute to the consideration by the General Assembly of the proposed supplement to the Standard Rules, and requests the Secretary-General to make the contributions of the Special Rapporteur available to all Member States and observers;

6. *Encourages* Governments, as well as non-governmental organizations and the private sector, to continue to contribute to the United Nations Voluntary Fund on Disability in order to support the activities of the Special Rapporteur, as well as new and expanded initiatives to strengthen national capacities for the equalization of opportunities by, for and with persons with disabilities;

7. *Requests* the Special Rapporteur to submit a report on the monitoring of the implementation of the Standard Rules to the Commission for Social Development at its forty-third session.

GENERAL ASSEMBLY ACTION

By **decision 59/521** of 20 December, the General Assembly took note of Council resolution 2004/15 (see above), postponed until its sixty-first (2006) session consideration of the proposed supplement to the Standard Rules on the Equalization of Opportunities for Persons with Disabilities, and requested the Special Rapporteur on disability of the Commission for Social Development to take into account the ideas contained in the proposed supplement to the Standard Rules in accomplishing her mandate.

International convention on the rights of persons with disabilities

In accordance with General Assembly resolution 58/246 [YUN 2003, p. 1108], the Ad Hoc Committee on a Comprehensive and Integral International Convention on the Protection and Promotion of the Rights and Dignity of Persons with Disabilities, established by General Assembly resolution 56/168 [YUN 2001, p. 1012], held its third (24 May–4 June) and fourth (23 August–3 September) sessions in 2004, both in New York.

At its third session [A/AC.265/2004/5], the Ad Hoc Committee conducted a first reading of the draft text of the convention as contained in the report of its Working Group [A/AC.265/2004/WORKING GROUP.1, annex I]. It considered articles 1 to 24 on issues of international cooperation and the preamble. It considered articles 1 to 24 on issues of international cooperation and the preamble. It deferred to its fourth session consideration of the title, structure, part of the preamble, definitions (article 3) and monitoring (article 25), and the compilation of proposed revisions and amendments to the draft text made by Committee members, which was annexed to the report. It also recommended that the Secretary-General implement measures to facilitate access to UN premises, technology and documents and invited, among others, persons with disabilities and experts to present proposals in that regard.

At its fourth session [A/59/360], the Committee concluded the first reading of the draft text, adopted the organization of work and conducted reviews of articles 1 to 15 and 24 bis. The Ad Hoc Committee recommended that it meet in January 2005 to continue its work. It invited the General Assembly, at its fifty-ninth (2004) session, to examine in greater detail the provision of reasonable accommodation for persons with disabilities to facilitate accessibility to UN premises, technology and documents.

ECONOMIC AND SOCIAL COUNCIL ACTION

On 21 July [meeting 47], the Economic and Social Council, on the recommendation of the Commission for Social Development [E/2004/26], adopted **resolution 2004/14** without vote [agenda item 14(b)].

Comprehensive and integral international convention on the protection and promotion of the rights and dignity of persons with disabilities

The Economic and Social Council,

Recalling General Assembly resolution 56/168 of 19 December 2001, by which the Assembly established an Ad Hoc Committee, open to the participation of all Member States and observers of the United Nations, to consider proposals for a comprehensive and integral international convention to promote and protect the rights and dignity of persons with disabilities, based on the holistic approach in the work carried out in the fields of social development, human rights and non-discrimination and taking into account the recommendations of the Commission on Human Rights and the Commission for Social Development,

Recalling also Economic and Social Council resolution 2003/12 of 21 July 2003 on a comprehensive and integral international convention to promote and protect the rights and dignity of persons with disabilities,

Recalling further General Assembly resolution 58/246 of 23 December 2003, in which the Assembly decided that the Ad Hoc Committee on a Comprehensive and Integral International Convention on the Promotion and Protection of the Rights and Dignity of Persons with Disabilities should start the negotiations on a draft convention at its third session,

Welcoming the important contributions made so far to the work of the Ad Hoc Committee by all stakeholders,

Welcoming the progress made in the working group established by the Ad Hoc Committee in preparing a draft text that will form the basis for negotiations on a draft convention in the Ad Hoc Committee, taking into account all contributions,

Encouraging Member States and observers to participate actively in the Ad Hoc Committee in order to present to the General Assembly, as a matter of priority, a draft text of a convention,

Reaffirming the universality, indivisibility and interdependence of all human rights and fundamental freedoms and the need for their full enjoyment to be guaranteed to persons with disabilities, without discrimination,

Recognizing the positive steps taken by Governments, including continued collaboration at the regional and international levels, to promote and protect the rights and dignity of persons with disabilities,

Encouraged by the increased support of the international community for the promotion and protection of the rights and dignity of persons with disabilities under a comprehensive and integral approach,

1. *Requests* the Commission for Social Development to continue to contribute to the process of negotiation of a draft international convention by, inter alia, providing its views regarding the social development perspective, bearing in mind the experience in the implementation of the Standard Rules on the Equalization of Opportunities for Persons with Disabilities and the World Programme of Action concerning Disabled Persons;

2. *Welcomes* the contributions of the Special Rapporteur on disability of the Commission to the process of elaboration of a draft convention, and requests the Special Rapporteur to contribute further to the work of the Ad Hoc Committee, drawing from her experience in the monitoring of the Standard Rules on the Equalization of Opportunities for Persons with Disabilities and in collaboration with the Secretariat, by, inter alia, providing her views on the elements to be considered in drawing up a draft international convention;

3. *Requests* the Department of Economic and Social Affairs of the Secretariat, through its Division for Social Policy and Development, to continue to support the work of the Ad Hoc Committee, in collaboration with the Special Rapporteur and other relevant United Nations bodies and agencies, through, inter alia, the provision of information on issues related to a draft international convention and the promotion of awareness of the work of the Ad Hoc Committee, from within existing resources;

4. *Underlines* the importance of strengthening cooperation and coordination between the Office of the United Nations High Commissioner for Human Rights and the Department of Economic and Social Affairs in order for them to jointly support the work of the Ad Hoc Committee;

5. *Invites* bodies, organs and entities of the United Nations system, including the funds and programmes, in particular those working in the fields of social and economic development and human rights, within their respective mandates, as well as non-governmental organizations, national disability and human rights institutions and independent experts with an interest in the matter, to continue to make available to the Ad Hoc Committee suggestions about elements to be considered in a draft international convention;

6. *Encourages* the relevant bodies of the United Nations to continue to promote and support the active participation of civil society, including non-governmental organizations, in the work of the Ad Hoc Committee, in accordance with General Assembly resolutions

56/510 of 23 July 2002 and 57/229 of 18 December 2002, and requests the Secretary-General to disseminate widely to non-governmental organizations all available information on accreditation procedures, modalities and supportive measures for their participation in the work of the Ad Hoc Committee;

7. *Invites* Governments, civil society and the private sector to contribute to the voluntary fund established by the General Assembly to support the participation of non-governmental organizations and experts from developing countries, in particular from least developed countries, in the work of the Ad Hoc Committee;

8. *Stresses* the need for additional efforts to ensure reasonable accessibility to facilities and documentation at the United Nations for all persons with disabilities, in accordance with General Assembly decision 56/474 of 23 July 2002;

9. *Requests* the Secretary-General and the Special Rapporteur to report, as part of their presentations to the Commission for Social Development at its forty-third session, on the implementation of the present resolution.

GENERAL ASSEMBLY ACTION

On 20 December [meeting 74], the General Assembly, on the recommendation of the Third Committee [A/59/503/Add. 2], adopted **resolution 59/198** without vote [agenda item 105 *(b)*].

Ad Hoc Committee on a Comprehensive and Integral International Convention on the Protection and Promotion of the Rights and Dignity of Persons with Disabilities

The General Assembly,

Recalling its resolution 56/168 of 19 December 2001, by which it decided to establish an Ad Hoc Committee, open to the participation of all Member States and observers to the United Nations, to consider proposals for a comprehensive and integral international convention to promote and protect the rights and dignity of persons with disabilities, based on a holistic approach in the work done in the fields of social development, human rights and non-discrimination and taking into account the recommendations of the Commission on Human Rights and the Commission for Social Development,

Recalling also its resolution 58/246 of 23 December 2003, as well as relevant resolutions of the Commission for Social Development and the Commission on Human Rights,

Reaffirming the universality, indivisibility and interdependence of all human rights and fundamental freedoms and the need for persons with disabilities to be guaranteed their full enjoyment without discrimination,

Convinced of the contribution that a convention can make in this regard, and encouraged by the increased support of the international community for such a convention,

Stressing the importance of the active participation of intergovernmental and non-governmental organizations and national human rights institutions in the work of the Ad Hoc Committee, and their valuable contribution to the promotion of the full enjoyment of all human rights and fundamental freedoms by persons with disabilities,

Underlining the importance of the participation of the Special Rapporteur on disability of the Commission for Social Development in the work of the Ad Hoc Committee,

Recognizing the important contributions made thus far to the Ad Hoc Committee by all stakeholders,

1. *Welcomes* the report of the Ad Hoc Committee on a Comprehensive and Integral International Convention on the Protection and Promotion of the Rights and Dignity of Persons with Disabilities;

2. *Requests* the Secretary-General to transmit the report of the Ad Hoc Committee to the Commission for Social Development at its forty-third session and to the Commission on Human Rights at its sixty-first session, and further requests both Commissions to continue to contribute to the work of the Ad Hoc Committee;

3. *Welcomes with satisfaction* the beginning of the negotiations on a draft convention by the Ad Hoc Committee at its third session, as requested by the General Assembly in resolution 58/246, and the progress achieved so far in the negotiation of a draft convention;

4. *Invites* Member States and observers to continue to participate actively and constructively in the Ad Hoc Committee with a view to the early conclusion of a draft text of a convention, in order to present it to the General Assembly, as a matter of priority, for its adoption;

5. *Decides* that the Ad Hoc Committee shall hold, within existing resources, prior to the sixtieth session of the General Assembly, two sessions in 2005, of ten working days each, to be held, respectively, from 24 January to 4 February and in July/August;

6. *Underlines* the importance of further strengthening the cooperation and coordination between the Office of the United Nations High Commissioner for Human Rights and the Department of Economic and Social Affairs of the Secretariat in order to provide technical support to the work of the Ad Hoc Committee, and in this regard invites them to provide, in advance of the meetings of the Ad Hoc Committee, background documentation to assist Member States and observers in the negotiation of a draft convention, and to organize, in close connection and timing with the meetings and venue of the Ad Hoc Committee, meetings of experts and seminars in relation to the draft convention, within existing resources;

7. *Requests* the Secretary-General to continue to provide the Ad Hoc Committee with the facilities necessary for the performance of its work, and in this context invites the Secretary-General to reallocate resources to the United Nations Programme on Disability so as to provide support to the negotiations on a draft convention;

8. *Stresses* the need for additional efforts to ensure accessibility at the United Nations, with reasonable accommodation regarding facilities and documentation, for all persons with disabilities, in accordance with General Assembly decision 56/474 of 23 July 2002;

9. *Encourages* Member States to continue to include in their delegations to the Ad Hoc Committee persons with disabilities and/or other experts in the field;

10. *Urges* Member States, observers, civil society and the private sector to contribute to the voluntary fund established pursuant to its resolution 57/229 of 18 December 2002 to support the participation of non-governmental organizations and experts from developing countries, in particular least developed countries, in the work of the Ad Hoc Committee;

11. *Requests* the Secretary-General to disseminate widely to non-governmental organizations all available information on accreditation procedures, modalities and supportive measures for their participation in the work of the Ad Hoc Committee, as well as the criteria for the financial assistance that is available through the voluntary fund;

12. *Also requests* the Secretary-General to transmit a comprehensive report of the Ad Hoc Committee and to report on the implementation of paragraphs 6, 7, 8 and 11 of the present resolution to the General Assembly at its sixtieth session.

Cultural development

Culture and development

In response to General Assembly resolution 57/249 [YUN 2002, p. 1097], the Secretary-General transmitted in August the report of the United Nations Educational, Scientific and Cultural Organization (UNESCO) Director-General on culture and development [A/59/202], which reviewed progress in the implementation of that resolution. The report discussed UNESCO's programmes for culture and development, aimed at furthering dialogue and action-oriented ideas from all sectors of society to, among other things, clarify the current understanding of cultural diversity and its links to dialogue and development, and deliver better policies for creative partnerships to build upon the relationship between cultural diversity and development. Activities in 2004 included initiation of the elaboration of a convention on the protection of the diversity of cultural content and artistic expression, the draft of which was to be submitted to the UNESCO General Conference in October 2005, and the celebration of the second World Day for Cultural Diversity for Dialogue and Development on 21 May. The report proposed the establishment of functional linkages, with a view to reviewing the role of culture in the development process and providing a more adequate response to the challenges of globalization. The review should cover the various fields of the cultural sector as they related to the components of development policies, such as education, science and technology, communication, health, tourism, environment, land use, fresh water and the sea.

By **decision 59/536** of 22 December, the Assembly took note of the Secretary-General's note transmitting the UNESCO Director-General's report.

Culture of peace

Religious and cultural understanding

In August, the Secretary-General, in accordance with resolution 58/128 [YUN 2003, p.1110], transmitted the UNESCO Director-General's report [A/59/201] on the promotion of religious and cultural understanding, harmony and cooperation. The report discussed UNESCO's role in that regard, including the use of education as a means of promoting sustainable tolerance and peace; activities for promoting interreligious dialogue; and implementation of activities in support of the dialogue among civilizations. UNESCO activities to promote religious and cultural understanding and harmony through education were aimed at helping countries to mainstream mutual and intercultural understanding, and integrating a culture of peace values into their national education systems, through teacher training and the production of educational materials. In that regard, it helped to revise textbooks in Israel, Palestine and Iraq to reflect religious and cultural tolerance in schools. UNESCO was also developing guidelines on intercultural education to guide Member States when considering educational policies in multicultural contexts.

As the concept of a dialogue among civilizations assumed greater salience in the face of new and multidimensional threats to global peace and security, the UNESCO General Conference (16 October 2003), in its resolution 47, set out new perspectives on and concrete action for the organization's work in that regard. To translate agreed principles and agreements that inspired a dialogue among civilizations and cultures into concrete activities and action, UNESCO activities were to focus on: education; science and technology, including the role of traditional and local knowledge systems; cultural diversity; and media, information and communication technologies.

The UNESCO programme on interreligious dialogue, launched in 1995, had gained fresh impetus since the events of 11 September 2001 [YUN 2001, p. 60], with many activities undertaken to promote reciprocal knowledge and understanding among cultures and religions, stressing mutual respect and recognition. As part of the geo-strategic coverage of the interreligious dialogue, UNESCO organized a series of regional meetings on conflict resolution, the HIV/AIDS pandemic and the role that religious community leaders might play in easing tensions. Its 2004 meeting (Sydney, Australia, November) focused on religions in peace and conflict. To strengthen religious and cultural understanding, UNESCO established a university twinning network (UNITWIN) of 13 Chairs on comparative studies of religions in centres of academic excellence in almost all continents to build a common programme of research and learning and to facilitate teacher and student exchange. A meeting on intercultural education (Oslo, Norway, 2-5 September) under the UNITWIN umbrella, would identify best practices and the focal points for each region, with the aim of examining the role of education in overcoming stereotyped images and other obstacles to dialogue, and interdisciplinary approaches to overcoming those barriers.

In related developments, the Assembly also had before it the text of the declaration of the participants at the First Congress of Leaders of World and Traditional Religions (Astana, Kazakhstan, 23-24 September 2003) [A/58/390-S/2003/916]. The Fifth Asia-Europe Meeting (ASEM) (Hanoi, Viet Nam, 7-9 October 2004) adopted the ASEM Declaration on Dialogue among Cultures and Civilizations.

GENERAL ASSEMBLY ACTION

On 11 November [meeting 52], the General Assembly adopted **resolution 59/23** [draft: A/59/L.15/Rev. 1 & Add.1] without vote [agenda item 35].

Promotion of interreligious dialogue

The General Assembly,

Reaffirming the purposes and principles enshrined in the Charter of the United Nations,

Recalling its resolutions 56/6 of 9 November 2001, on dialogue among civilizations, 57/6 of 4 November 2002, concerning the promotion of a culture of peace and non-violence, 57/337 of 3 July 2003, on the prevention of armed conflict, and 58/128 of 19 December 2003, on the promotion of religious and cultural understanding, harmony and cooperation,

Recalling also the conclusions and recommendations contained in the report of the Director-General of the United Nations Educational, Scientific and Cultural Organization, transmitted by the Secretary-General to the General Assembly in accordance with resolution 58/128,

Taking note of the various initiatives and efforts to organize interreligious dialogues, including the First Congress of Leaders of World and Traditional Religions, held in Astana on 23 and 24 September 2003, and the interreligious dialogue initiative adopted by the Fifth Asia-Europe Meeting, held in Hanoi from 7 to 9 October 2004,

Recognizing the commitment of all religions to peace,

1. *Affirms* that mutual understanding and interreligious dialogue constitute important dimensions of the dialogue among civilizations and of the culture of peace;

2. *Takes note with appreciation* of the work of the United Nations Educational, Scientific and Cultural

Organization on interreligious dialogue, and encourages relevant bodies of the United Nations to work closely with the Organization and coordinate their efforts in this regard;

3. *Invites* the Secretary-General to bring the promotion of interreligious dialogue to the attention of all Governments and relevant international organizations and to submit a report thereon, including all views received, to the General Assembly at its sixtieth session.

On 15 December [meeting 72], the General Assembly adopted **resolution 59/142** [draft: A/59/L.17/Rev.1 & Add.1, as orally revised] without vote [agenda item 35].

Promotion of religious and cultural understanding, harmony and cooperation

The General Assembly,

Reaffirming the purposes and principles enshrined in the Charter of the United Nations and the Universal Declaration of Human Rights, in particular the rights to freedom of thought, conscience and religion,

Underlining the importance of promoting understanding, tolerance and friendship among human beings in all their diversity of religion, belief, culture and language, and recalling that all States have pledged themselves under the Charter to promote and encourage universal respect for and observance of human rights and fundamental freedoms for all, without distinction as to race, sex, language or religion,

Affirming that interreligious dialogue is an integral part of the efforts to translate shared values, as reflected in the United Nations Millennium Declaration, into actions, in particular the efforts to promote a culture of peace and dialogue among civilizations,

Recalling its resolution 58/128 of 19 December 2003 as well as its resolution 57/6 of 4 November 2002, in which it invited Member States to expand their activities promoting a culture of peace and non-violence at the national, regional and international levels, and other relevant resolutions,

Taking note of different initiatives aimed at promoting religious and cultural understanding, harmony and cooperation, and noting that at its tenth session, held at Putrajaya, Malaysia, from 16 to 18 October 2003, the Islamic Summit Conference endorsed the concept of "enlightened moderation", which contained the principles of enhancing human welfare, freedom and progress everywhere, of forging harmony and understanding among all peoples and of seeking the peaceful resolution of conflicts and disputes,

Recalling with satisfaction the proclamation of the Global Agenda for Dialogue among Civilizations, bearing in mind the valuable contribution that dialogue among civilizations can make to an improved awareness and understanding of the common values shared by all humankind,

Recalling the Universal Declaration on Cultural Diversity of the United Nations Educational, Scientific and Cultural Organization and the principles contained therein,

Emphasizing the need, at all levels of society and among nations, for strengthening freedom, justice, democracy, tolerance, solidarity, cooperation, pluralism, respect for diversity of culture and religion or belief, dialogue and understanding, which are important elements for peace, and convinced that the guiding principles of democratic society need to be actively promoted by the international community,

Reaffirming that freedom of expression, media pluralism, multilingualism, equal access to art and to scientific and technological knowledge, including in digital form, and the possibility for all cultures to have access to the means of expression and dissemination are the guarantees of cultural diversity, and that in ensuring the free flow of ideas by word and image, care should be exercised that all cultures can express themselves and make themselves known,

Recognizing all efforts made by the United Nations system and other international and regional organizations to promote understanding, tolerance and friendship among human beings in all their diversity of culture, religion, belief and language, including the initiative of the United Nations Educational, Scientific and Cultural Organization to proclaim 2006 the International Year of Global Consciousness and the Ethics of Dialogue among Peoples,

Alarmed that serious instances of intolerance and discrimination on the grounds of religion or belief, including acts of violence, intimidation and coercion motivated by religious intolerance, are on the increase in many parts of the world and threaten the enjoyment of human rights and fundamental freedoms,

Considering that tolerance for cultural, ethnic, and religious and linguistic diversities, as well as dialogue among and within civilizations, is essential for peace, understanding and friendship among individuals and people of different cultures and nations of the world, while manifestations of cultural prejudice, intolerance and xenophobia towards different cultures and religions generate hatred and violence among peoples and nations throughout the world,

Emphasizing that combating hatred, prejudice, intolerance and stereotyping on the basis of religion or culture represents a significant global challenge that requires further action,

1. *Takes note* of the report transmitted by the Secretary-General in accordance with resolution 58/128;

2. *Acknowledges* that respect for the diversity of religions and cultures, tolerance, dialogue and cooperation in a climate of mutual trust and understanding can contribute to the combating of ideologies and practices based on discrimination, intolerance and hatred and help to reinforce world peace, social justice and friendship among peoples;

3. *Reaffirms* the solemn commitment of all States to fulfil their obligations to promote universal respect for, and observance and protection of, all human rights and fundamental freedoms for all in accordance with the Charter of the United Nations, other instruments relating to human rights, and international law; the universal nature of these rights and freedoms is beyond question;

4. *Also reaffirms* the importance for all peoples and nations to hold, develop and preserve their cultural heritage and traditions in a national and international atmosphere of peace, tolerance and mutual respect;

5. *Recognizes* that respect for religious and cultural diversity in an increasingly globalizing world contributes to international cooperation, promotes enhanced

dialogue among religions, cultures and civilizations, and helps to create an environment conducive to the exchange of human experience;

6. *Also recognizes* that all cultures and civilizations share a common set of universal values;

7. *Further recognizes* that, while the significance of national and regional particularities and various historical, cultural and religious backgrounds must be borne in mind, it is the duty of States, regardless of their political, economic and cultural systems, to promote and protect all human rights and fundamental freedoms;

8. *Reaffirms* that the promotion and protection of the rights of persons belonging to national or ethnic, religious and linguistic minorities contribute to political and social stability and peace and enrich the cultural diversity and heritage of society as a whole in the States in which such persons live, and urges States to ensure that their political and legal systems reflect the multicultural diversity within their societies and, where necessary, to improve democratic and political institutions, organizations and practices so that they are more fully participatory and avoid the marginalization and exclusion of, and discrimination against, specific sectors of society;

9. *Encourages* Governments to promote, including through education, as well as the development of progressive curricula and text books, understanding, tolerance and friendship among human beings in all their diversity of religion, belief, culture and language, which will address the cultural, social, economic, political and religious sources of intolerance, and to apply a gender perspective while doing so, in order to promote understanding, tolerance, peace and friendly relations among nations and all racial and religious groups, recognizing that education at all levels is one of the principal means to build a culture of peace;

10. *Calls upon* all States to exert their utmost efforts to ensure that religious and cultural sites are fully respected and protected in compliance with their international obligations and in accordance with their national legislation, and to adopt adequate measures aimed at preventing acts or threats of damage to and destruction of these sites;

11. *Urges* States, in compliance with their international obligations, to take all necessary action to combat incitement to or acts of violence, intimidation and coercion motivated by hatred and intolerance based on culture, religion or belief, which may cause discord and disharmony within and among societies;

12. *Also urges* States to take effective measures to prevent and eliminate discrimination on the grounds of religion or belief in the recognition, exercise and enjoyment of human rights and fundamental freedoms in all fields of civil, economic, political, social and cultural life and to make all efforts to enact or rescind legislation, where necessary, to prohibit any such discrimination, and to take all appropriate measures to combat intolerance on the grounds of religion or beliefs;

13. *Further urges* States to ensure that, in the course of their official duties, members of law enforcement bodies and the military, civil servants, educators and other public officials respect different religions and beliefs and do not discriminate against persons professing other religions or beliefs, and that any ne-

cessary and appropriate education or training is provided;

14. *Welcomes* the efforts of States, relevant entities of the United Nations system and other intergovernmental organizations, civil society, including religion-based and other non-governmental organizations, and the media in developing a culture of peace, and encourages them to continue such efforts, including the promotion of interreligious and intercultural interaction within and among societies through, inter alia, congresses, conferences, seminars, workshops, research work and related processes;

15. *Requests* the Secretary-General to ensure the widest dissemination of the relevant United Nations material related to the present resolution in as many different languages as possible through the United Nations system, including the United Nations information centres, within available resources;

16. *Also requests* the Secretary-General, in the context of his report to the General Assembly at its sixtieth session under the item entitled "Culture of peace", to include information on the implementation of the present resolution.

Sport for development and peace

International Year of Sport and Physical Education (2005)

In response to its resolution 58/5 [YUN 2003, p. 1111], in which the General Assembly proclaimed 2005 as the International Year of Sport and Physical Education, the Secretary-General reported in August 2004 [A/59/268] on activities planned for the observance of the Year and on the status of the drafting of an international convention against doping in sport.

The objectives of the International Year were: to broaden the perception of sport from "elite sport" to "sport for all"; to underline the need for physical education as part of a balanced education; to create interest, and to facilitate partnerships in human development within the sports industry, sport federations, sports media and among athletes; to encourage initiatives where sport could assist in creating a platform for intercultural, post-conflict, peace-building dialogue; and to integrate sport into development activities by disseminating information about the value of sport and physical education.

To assist in the preparations for the International Year, the small office establishment in Geneva, led by the Special Adviser to the Secretary-General on Sport for Development and Peace, worked in cooperation with the United Nations Fund for International Partnerships (UNFIP) and UNESCO, the lead agency for the Year. Other activities included the convening of an inter-agency meeting on sport (Geneva, July) to discuss coordination, cooperation and consistency to maximize the impact of the celebrations

for the International Year. The meeting drew up a list of complementary activities and projects to be implemented on a voluntary basis by the UN system. UNESCO organized the Fourth International Conference of Ministers and Senior Officials Responsible for Physical Education and Sport (Athens, Greece, 6-8 December) to discuss development-related themes of sport. During the High-level segment of the Economic and Social Council, UNFIP and the United Nations Children's Fund co-hosted a ministerial round table entitled "Common ground: sport as an innovative tool for development and peace". The international sports NGO Right to Play organized a round table (Athens, Greece, August) entitled "Harnessing the power of sport for development and peace".

A public information strategy was being formulated by UN system public information units and the Department of Public Information of the Secretariat, a logo for the Year had been approved by the Publications Board, and a UN stamp designed, in conjunction with the International Olympic Committee and the Swiss Postal services. Several UN journals and other development-related publications on international cooperation and peace-building issues would be used for promoting the Year.

Concerning the elaboration of an international anti-doping convention in all sporting activities, a preliminary draft prepared as a result of three ad hoc meetings of experts and two sessions of the intergovernmental meeting was sent to Member States for comment in mid-July. The Fourth International Conference of Ministers and Senior Officials responsible for Physical Education and Sport would consider inputs to the draft and agree on pending issues.

A later addendum [A/59/268/Add.1] contained information provided by UN agencies, funds and programmes on their plans to integrate elements of sport and physical education into their core activities.

GENERAL ASSEMBLY ACTION

On 27 October [meeting 42], the General Assembly adopted **resolution 59/10** [draft: A/59/L.9 & Add 1] without vote [agenda item 47].

Sport as a means to promote education, health, development and peace

The General Assembly,

Recalling its resolution 58/5 of 3 November 2003 and its decision to proclaim 2005 the International Year for Sport and Physical Education, as a means to promote education, health, development and peace,

Considering the role of sport and physical education as a means to promote education, health, development and peace,

Acknowledging the major role of the United Nations, its funds and programmes and the United Nations Educational, Scientific and Cultural Organization and other specialized agencies, in promoting human development through sport and physical education, through its country programmes,

Noting that sport and physical education in many countries face increasing marginalization within education systems even though they are a major tool not only for health and physical development but also for acquiring values necessary for social cohesion and intercultural dialogue,

Recalling the Convention on the Rights of the Child and the outcome document of the special session of the General Assembly on children, entitled "A world fit for children", stressing that education shall be directed to the development of children's personality, talents and mental and physical abilities to their fullest potential,

Acknowledging with concern the dangers faced by sportsmen and sportswomen, in particular young athletes, including child labour, violence, doping, early specialization, over-training and exploitative forms of commercialization, as well as less visible threats and deprivations, such as the premature severance of family bonds and the loss of sporting, social and cultural ties,

Recognizing the need for greater coordination of efforts at the international level to facilitate a more effective fight against doping, and noting in this regard the Anti-Doping Convention established by the Council of Europe, the Copenhagen Declaration on Anti-doping in Sport, adopted during the World Conference on Doping in Sport, held from 3 to 5 March 2003, and any other relevant international instrument,

1. *Takes note* of the report of the Secretary-General entitled "Sport for peace and development: International Year of Sport and Physical Education";

2. *Decides* to launch, on 5 November 2004, the International Year for Sport and Physical Education, as a means to promote education, health, development and peace;

3. *Invites* Governments, the United Nations, its funds and programmes, the specialized agencies, where appropriate, and sport-related institutions to organize events to underline their commitment and to seek the assistance of sports personalities in this regard;

4. *Also invites* Governments, the United Nations, its funds and programmes, the specialized agencies, where appropriate, and sport-related institutions:

(a) To promote the role of sport and physical education for all when furthering their development programmes and policies, to advance health awareness, the spirit of achievement and cultural bridging and to entrench collective values;

(b) To include sport and physical education as a tool to contribute towards achieving the internationally agreed development goals, including those contained in the United Nations Millennium Declaration and the broader aims of development and peace;

(c) To work collectively so that sport and physical education can present opportunities for solidarity and cooperation in order to promote a culture of peace and social and gender equality and to advocate dialogue and harmony;

(d) To recognize the contribution of sport and physical education towards economic and social development and to encourage the building and restoration of sports infrastructures;

(e) To further promote sport and physical education, on the basis of locally assessed needs, as a tool for health, education, social and cultural development and environmental sustainability;

(f) To strengthen cooperation and partnership between all actors, including family, school, clubs/leagues, local communities, youth sports associations and decision makers as well as the public and private sectors, in order to ensure complementarities and to make sport and physical education available to everyone;

(g) To ensure that young talents can develop their athletic potential without any threat to their safety and physical and moral integrity;

5. *Encourages* Governments, international sports bodies and sport-related organizations to elaborate and implement partnership initiatives and development projects compatible with the education provided at all levels of schooling to help to achieve the Millennium Development Goals;

6. *Invites* Governments and international sports bodies to assist developing countries, in particular the least developed countries and small island developing States, in their capacity-building efforts in sport and physical education;

7. *Encourages* the United Nations to develop strategic partnerships with the range of stakeholders involved in sport, including sports organizations, sports associations and the private sector, to assist in the implementation of sport for development programmes;

8. *Encourages* Governments and the United Nations system to seek new and innovative ways to use sport for communication and social mobilization, particularly at the national, regional and local levels, engaging civil society through active participation and ensuring that target audiences are reached;

9. *Acknowledges* that the Olympic Games contribute to understanding between peoples and civilizations, and welcomes in this regard the contribution of the 2004 Olympic Games organized in Athens;

10. *Stresses* the need for all parties to cooperate closely with international sports bodies to elaborate a "code of good practice";

11. *Invites* Governments to accelerate the elaboration of an international anti-doping convention in all sports activities, and requests the United Nations Educational, Scientific and Cultural Organization, in cooperation with other relevant international and regional organizations, to coordinate the elaboration of such a convention;

12. *Requests* the Secretary-General to report to the General Assembly at its sixtieth session on the implementation of the present resolution and on the events organized at the national, regional and international levels to celebrate the year 2005, under the item entitled "International Year of Sport and Physical Education".

Olympic Truce and ideal

On 4 August, just prior to the Games of the XXVIII Olympiad held in Athens, Greece (13-29 August), the President of the General Assembly made a solemn appeal [A/58/863] to Member

States to demonstrate their commitment to peace in the world by observing the Olympic Truce during the Games, as the Assembly had earlier urged in the unanimously co-sponsored text of resolution 58/6 [YUN 2003, p. 1112].

By **decision 58/570** of 5 August, the Assembly took note of the solemn appeal of its President in connection with the observance of the Olympic Truce.

Cultural property

Prevention of crimes against cultural heritage

The Secretary-General, in his March report [E/CN.15/2004/10 & Add. 1] on prevention of crimes that infringed on the cultural heritage of peoples in the form of movable property, submitted in response to Economic and Social Council resolution 2003/29 [YUN 2003, p. 1115], provided an analysis of the comments received from 14 Governments and the European Commission on the implementation of resolution 2003/39. The report also gave an overview of multilateral legal and institutional frameworks for the protection of cultural property at the international and regional levels, and described the role of organized criminal groups in trafficking in stolen cultural property.

The report stated that international trade in looted, stolen or smuggled art was estimated at $4.5 billion per year. Trafficking in cultural property was not only a lucrative business for traders but a source of additional income for populations living in poverty. The illicit market was populated by a mixture of sophisticated criminal organizations, individual thieves, small-time dealers and unscrupulous collectors. Only 5 per cent of stolen art was ever recovered. The law enforcement community had recognized that illicit trade in cultural objects was a major category of international crime, and Interpol was working as a clearing house for information and circulated information about cultural objects reported to member police forces as stolen or as found in suspicious circumstances. A number of other organizations, including the International Council of Museums, also collected and disseminated information about stolen cultural objects. The entry into force of the United Nations Convention against Transnational Organized Crime in 2003 [YUN 2003, p. 1125] was expected to assist in dealing with various manifestations of transnational crimes, including trafficking in movable cultural property. The International Conference celebrating the fiftieth anniversary of the 1954 Hague Convention for the Protection of Cultural Property in the Event of Conflict (Cairo, Egypt,

14-16 February) adopted the Cairo Declaration on the Protection of Cultural Property, which urged the Commission on Crime Prevention and Criminal Justice to accord special attention to the protection of cultural property.

ECONOMIC AND SOCIAL COUNCIL ACTION

On 21 July [meeting 47], the Economic and Social Council, on the recommendation of the Commission for Crime Prevention and Criminal Justice [E/2004/30], adopted **resolution 2004/34** without vote [agenda item 14 (c)].

Protection against trafficking in cultural property

The Economic and Social Council,

Emphasizing the importance for States of protecting and preserving their cultural heritage in accordance with the Convention on the Means of Prohibiting and Preventing the Illicit Import, Export and Transfer of Ownership of Cultural Property, adopted by the United Nations Educational, Scientific and Cultural Organization on 14 November 1970, and other relevant instruments such as the 1995 Unidroit Convention on Stolen or Illegally Exported Cultural Objects and the 1954 Convention for the Protection of Cultural Property in the Event of Armed Conflict and its two Protocols,

Reaffirming its resolution 2003/29 of 22 July 2003, entitled "Prevention of crimes that infringe on the cultural heritage of peoples in the form of movable property",

Recalling General Assembly resolution 58/17 of 3 December 2003, entitled "Return or restitution of cultural property to the countries of origin",

Recalling also the model treaty for the prevention of crimes that infringe on the cultural heritage of peoples in the form of movable property, adopted by the Eighth United Nations Congress on the Prevention of Crime and the Treatment of Offenders, which was welcomed by the General Assembly in its resolution 45/121 of 14 December 1990,

Noting with appreciation the Cairo Declaration on the Protection of Cultural Property, made at the international conference celebrating the fiftieth anniversary of the 1954 Convention for the Protection of Cultural Property in the Event of Armed Conflict, held in Cairo from 14 to 16 February 2004, as well as its relevant recommendations,

Alarmed that organized criminal groups are involved in trafficking in stolen cultural property and that the international trade in looted, stolen or smuggled cultural property is estimated at several billion United States dollars per year,

Stressing that the entry into force of the United Nations Convention against Transnational Organized Crime is expected to create a new impetus in international cooperation to counter and curb transnational organized crime, which will in turn lead to innovative and broader approaches to dealing with the various manifestations of such crime, including trafficking in movable cultural property,

Expressing the need to enhance or to establish, as appropriate, standards for the restitution and return of movable property forming part of the cultural heritage of peoples after it has been stolen or trafficked and for its protection and preservation;

1. *Takes note with appreciation* of the report of the Secretary-General on the prevention of crimes that infringe on the cultural heritage of peoples in the form of movable property;

2. *Welcomes* international, regional and national initiatives for the protection of cultural property, in particular the work of the United Nations Educational, Scientific and Cultural Organization and its Intergovernmental Committee for Promoting the Return of Cultural Property to its Countries of Origin or its Restitution in Case of Illicit Appropriation;

3. *Requests* the Secretary-General to direct the United Nations Office on Drugs and Crime, in close cooperation with the United Nations Educational, Scientific and Cultural Organization and subject to the availability of extrabudgetary resources, to convene an expert group meeting to submit relevant recommendations to the Commission on Crime Prevention and Criminal Justice at its fifteenth session on protection against trafficking in cultural property, including ways of making more effective the model treaty for the prevention of crimes that infringe on the cultural heritage of peoples in the form of movable property;

4. *Encourages* Member States asserting state ownership of cultural property to consider means of issuing statements of such ownership with a view to facilitating the enforcement of property claims in other States;

5. *Urges* Member States to continue to strengthen international cooperation and mutual assistance in the prevention and prosecution of crime against movable property that forms part of the cultural heritage of peoples, as well as to ratify and implement the Convention on the Means of Prohibiting and Preventing the Illicit Import, Export and Transfer of Ownership of Cultural Property and the other relevant conventions;

6. *Requests* the Secretary-General to report to the Commission on Crime Prevention and Criminal Justice at its fifteenth session on the implementation of the present resolution.

Crime prevention and criminal justice

Commission on Crime Prevention and Criminal Justice

The Commission on Crime Prevention and Criminal Justice, at its thirteenth session (Vienna, 11-20 May) [E/2004/30], recommended to the Economic and Social Council 7 draft resolutions for adoption by the General Assembly and 12 draft resolutions and 2 draft decisions for adoption by the Council. The draft resolutions related to preparations for the Eleventh United Nations Congress on Crime Prevention and Criminal Justice, participation of least developed

countries in the work of the Commission and its conferences of States parties, technical assistance, kidnapping, corruption, trafficking in human organs, transnational organized crime, a draft agreement on disposal of confiscated proceeds of crime, strengthening the rule of law, punishment of fraud and misuse and falsification of identity, child victims and witnesses of crime, UN standards and norms, money-laundering, the Second World Summit of Attorneys General and General Prosecutors, Chief Prosecutors and Ministers of Justice, urban crime, technical assistance and technical cooperation, and trafficking in cultural property (see headings below).

A discussion was held on the rule of law and development: the contribution of operational activities in crime prevention and criminal justice, on the basis of a note submitted by the Secretary-General. The Commission also considered strategic management and programme questions and the provisional agenda for its 2005 session.

On 21 July, the Council took note of the Commission's report on its thirteenth session, approved the provisional agenda and documentation for the fourteenth (2005) session, and decided that the prominent themes for the 2005 session should be conclusions and recommendations of the Eleventh United Nations Congress on Crime Prevention and Criminal Justice (**decision 2004/242**). The Council also endorsed the Commission's appointment of two new members to the Board of Trustees of the United Nations Interregional Crime and Justice Research Institute (**decision 2004/243**).

Participation in Commission sessions and those of conferences of States parties

On 21 July [meeting 47], the Economic and Social Council, on the recommendation of the Commission on Crime Prevention and Criminal Justice [E/2004/30], adopted **resolution 2004/18** without vote [agenda item 14 (c)].

Assistance to least developed countries to ensure their participation in the sessions of the Commission on Crime Prevention and Criminal Justice and the sessions of conferences of States parties

The Economic and Social Council

Recommends to the General Assembly the adoption of the following draft resolution:

[For text, see General Assembly resolution 59/152, below.]

GENERAL ASSEMBLY ACTION

On 20 December [meeting 74], the General Assembly, on the recommendation of the Third Committee [A/59/494], adopted **resolution 59/152** [draft: A/C.3/59/L.4] without vote [agenda item 96].

**Assistance to least developed countries
to ensure their participation in the sessions of the
Commission on Crime Prevention and
Criminal Justice and the sessions of
conferences of States parties**

The General Assembly,

Recalling its resolution 55/2 of 8 September 2000, by which it adopted the United Nations Millennium Declaration, and in particular paragraph 15 of the Millennium Declaration, in which the Heads of State and Government undertook to address the special needs of the least developed countries,

Recalling also its resolution 58/228 of 23 December 2003, in particular paragraph 9 thereof, in which it requested the Secretary-General to take appropriate measures, within existing resources and with the full participation of the regional commissions and relevant United Nations bodies, to support the participation of the least developed countries in international meetings, as well as in their preparation and consultation processes,

Stressing the need for the effective and timely ratification of the United Nations conventions and protocols relating to transnational organized crime, corruption and terrorism and their subsequent implementation,

Recognizing the critical significance of those instruments, which provide a legal framework for strengthening international cooperation, based on mutual commitments by the least developed countries and their development partners to undertake specific action to ensure the full implementation of the provisions of the instruments,

Welcoming the contributions already made by multilateral and bilateral donors to ensure the participation of representatives of least developed countries in the negotiation of the United Nations Convention against Transnational Organized Crime and the Protocols thereto, as well as the United Nations Convention against Corruption,

Emphasizing the importance of the effective participation of all relevant stakeholders from the least developed countries, developing countries and countries with economies in transition in the sessions of the Commission on Crime Prevention and Criminal Justice and in the sessions of the Conference of the Parties to the United Nations Convention against Transnational Organized Crime and the Conference of the States Parties to the United Nations Convention against Corruption,

1. *Calls upon* Member States, international organizations and funding institutions to redouble their efforts to increase their voluntary contributions to assist the Secretary-General in covering the cost of travel and daily subsistence allowance for the participation of representatives of least developed countries in the sessions of the Commission on Crime Prevention and Criminal Justice and in the sessions of the Conference of the Parties to the United Nations Convention against Transnational Organized Crime and the Conference of the States Parties to the United Nations Convention against Corruption, and requests the Executive Director of the United Nations Office on Drugs and Crime to intensify efforts to ensure the increased participation of representatives of least developed countries in those meetings;

2. *Requests* the Secretary-General to report to the Commission on Crime Prevention and Criminal Justice at its fourteenth session on the implementation of the present resolution.

Preparations for Eleventh Crime Congress

The Commission on Crime Prevention and Criminal Justice considered a March report [E/CN.15/2004/11] by the Secretary-General on preparations for the Eleventh United Nations Congress on Crime Prevention and Criminal Justice, scheduled for 2005 in Thailand. The report presented the views of States, specialized agencies, UN programmes, intergovernmental organizations and NGOs on agenda items and workshop topics planned for the Congress and on documentation and public information activities.

The Commission also had before it a discussion guide [A/CONF.203/PM.1 & Corr.1], prepared in response to Assembly resolution 58/138 [YUN 2003, p. 1117], for stimulating discussions on the substantive items of the Congress with a view to identifying the main policy options for consideration and action by the Congress, as well as discussion of the topics covered by the workshops to be conducted within the framework of the Congress.

In July [A/59/123-E/2004/90], the Secretary-General updated the information contained in his March report and included the recommendations from regional preparatory meetings held in Africa (Addis Ababa, Ethiopia, 1-3 March); Asia and the Pacific (Bangkok, Thailand, 29-31 March); Latin America and the Caribbean (San Jose, Costa Rica, 19-21 April); and Western Asia (Beirut, Lebanon, 28-30 April).

On 20 December, the General Assembly took note of the Secretary-General's report (**decision 59/523**).

ECONOMIC AND SOCIAL COUNCIL ACTION

On 21 July, [meeting 47], the Economic and Social Council, on the recommendation of the Commission for Crime Prevention and Criminal Justice [E/2004/30], adopted **resolution 2004/17** without vote [item 14(*c*)].

**Preparations for the Eleventh United Nations
Congress on Crime Prevention and Criminal Justice**

The Economic and Social Council

Recommends to the General Assembly the adoption of the following draft resolution:

[For text, see General Assembly resolution 59/151 below.]

GENERAL ASSEMBLY ACTION

On 20 December [meeting 74], the General Assembly, on the recommendation of the Third (Social, Humanitarian and Cultural) Committee [A/59/494], adopted **resolution 59/151** without vote [agenda item 96].

Preparations for the Eleventh United Nations Congress on Crime Prevention and Criminal Justice

The General Assembly,

Recalling its resolution 56/119 of 19 December 2001 on the role, function, periodicity and duration of the United Nations congresses on the prevention of crime and the treatment of offenders, in which it stipulated the guidelines in accordance with which, beginning in 2005, the congresses, pursuant to paragraphs 29 and 30 of the statement of principles and programme of action of the United Nations Crime Prevention and Criminal Justice Programme, should be held,

Recalling also its resolution 57/170 of 18 December 2002 on the follow-up to the plans of action for the implementation of the Vienna Declaration on Crime and Justice: Meeting the Challenges of the Twenty-first Century,

Recalling further its resolution 57/171 of 18 December 2002, in which it decided that the main theme of the Eleventh United Nations Congress on Crime Prevention and Criminal Justice should be "Synergies and responses: strategic alliances in crime prevention and criminal justice",

Recalling its resolution 58/138 of 22 December 2003, in which it requested the Commission on Crime Prevention and Criminal Justice to accord sufficient time at its thirteenth session to reviewing the progress made in the preparations for the Eleventh Congress, to finalize in good time all the necessary organizational and substantive arrangements and to make its final recommendations, through the Economic and Social Council, to the General Assembly,

Recognizing the significant contributions of the congresses in promoting the exchange of experience in research, law and policy development and the identification of emerging trends and issues in crime prevention and criminal justice among States, intergovernmental and non-governmental organizations and individual experts representing various professions and disciplines,

Recognizing also the efforts already made by the Government of Thailand to prepare for the hosting of the Eleventh Congress in Bangkok from 18 to 25 April 2005,

Stressing the importance of undertaking all the preparatory activities for the Eleventh Congress in a timely and concerted manner,

1. *Takes note with appreciation* of the report of the Secretary-General;

2. *Also takes note with appreciation* of the discussion guide prepared by the Secretary-General, in cooperation with the institutes of the United Nations Crime Prevention and Criminal Justice Programme network, for the regional preparatory meetings for the Eleventh United Nations Congress on Crime Prevention and Criminal Justice;

3. *Acknowledges* the relevance of the regional preparatory meetings, which have examined the substantive items of the agenda and the workshop topics of the Eleventh Congress and made action-oriented recommendations to serve as a basis for the draft declaration to be adopted by the Eleventh Congress;

4. *Requests* the Commission on Crime Prevention and Criminal Justice to begin preparation of a draft declaration at intersessional meetings to be held following its thirteenth session, for submission to the Eleventh Congress at least one month prior to its commencement, taking into account the recommendations of the regional preparatory meetings;

5. *Approves* the draft programme of work for the Eleventh Congress and the documentation relating thereto;

6. *Reiterates* its decision, contained in its resolution 58/138, that the high-level segment of the Eleventh Congress shall be held during the last three days of the Congress in order to allow Heads of State or Government or government ministers to focus on the main substantive agenda items of the Congress;

7. *Emphasizes* the importance of the workshops to be held during the Eleventh Congress, and invites Member States, intergovernmental and non-governmental organizations and other relevant entities to provide financial, organizational and technical support to the United Nations Office on Drugs and Crime and to the institutes of the United Nations Crime Prevention and Criminal Justice Programme network for the preparations for the workshops, including the preparation and circulation of relevant background material;

8. *Invites* donor countries to cooperate with developing countries to ensure their full participation in the workshops, and encourages States, other entities concerned and the Secretary-General to work together in order to ensure that the workshops focus on the respective issues and achieve practical results, leading to technical cooperation ideas, projects and documents related to enhancing bilateral and multilateral efforts in technical assistance activities in crime prevention and criminal justice;

9. *Reiterates its invitation* to Governments and relevant intergovernmental and non-governmental organizations to inform the Eleventh Congress about their activities aimed at putting into practice the plans of action for the implementation of the Vienna Declaration on Crime and Justice: Meeting the Challenges of the Twenty-first Century, with a view to providing guidance in the formulation of legislation, policies and programmes in the field of crime prevention and criminal justice at the national and international levels, and, to that end, requests the Secretary-General to compile that information and to prepare a report on the subject to be submitted to the Eleventh Congress for consideration;

10. *Reiterates its request* to the Secretary-General to make available the resources necessary to ensure the participation of the least developed countries in the Eleventh Congress, in accordance with past practice;

11. *Encourages* Governments to make preparations for the Eleventh Congress at an early stage by all appropriate means, including, where appropriate, the establishment of national preparatory committees, with a view to contributing to a focused and productive discussion on the topics and to participating actively in the organization and conduct of the workshops, the submission of national position papers on the various substantive items of the agenda and the encouragement of contributions from the academic community and relevant scientific institutions;

12. *Reiterates its invitation* to Member States to be represented at the Eleventh Congress at the highest possible level, for example by Heads of State or Government or government ministers and attorneys gen-

eral, and to participate actively in the high-level segment;

13. *Requests* the Secretary-General to facilitate
the organization of ancillary meetings of non-
governmental and professional organizations participating in the Eleventh Congress, in accordance with
past practice, as well as meetings of professional and
geographical interest groups, and to take appropriate
measures to encourage the participation of the academic and research community in the Congress;

14. *Encourages* the relevant specialized agencies
and programmes of the United Nations system and
inter-governmental and non-governmental organizations, as well as other professional organizations, to cooperate with the United Nations Office on Drugs and
Crime in the preparations for the Eleventh Congress;

15. *Requests* the Secretary-General to ensure, in
collaboration with Member States, a wide and effective
programme of public information relating to the preparations for the Eleventh Congress, to the Congress itself and to the follow-up to and implementation of its
recommendations;

16. *Welcomes* the appointment, by the Secretary-
General, of a Secretary-General and an Executive
Secretary of the Eleventh Congress, to perform their
functions under the rules of procedure for United
Nations congresses on crime prevention and criminal
justice;

17. *Requests* the Secretary-General to prepare an
overview of the state of crime and criminal justice
worldwide for presentation at the Eleventh Congress,
in accordance with past practice;

18. *Calls upon* the Eleventh Congress to formulate
concrete proposals for further follow-up and action,
paying particular attention to practical arrangements
relating to the effective implementation of the international legal instruments pertaining to transnational organized crime, terrorism and corruption and technical
assistance activities relating thereto;

19. *Requests* the Commission on Crime Prevention
and Criminal Justice at its fourteenth session to give
high priority to considering the conclusions and recommendations of the Eleventh Congress, with a view
to recommending, through the Economic and Social
Council, appropriate follow-up by the General Assembly at its sixtieth session;

20. *Requests* the Secretary-General to ensure proper
follow-up to the present resolution and to report
thereon, through the Commission on Crime Prevention and Criminal Justice, to the General Assembly at
its sixtieth session.

Crime prevention programme

In February, the Commission on Crime Prevention and Criminal Justice [E/CN.15/2004/2]
considered the report of the Executive Director
of the United Nations Office on Drugs and
Crime (UNODC) entitled "Development, security
and justice for all", examining UNODC's strategy
in 2003 to counter the problems of terrorism,
crime, corruption, drug abuse and trafficking,
which constituted threats to peace and stability.
It highlighted UNODC's work in the areas of

peace and security, poverty eradication, and the
rule of law and good governance. UNODC assisted States to comply with international conventions on international drug control, transnational
organized crime and corruption through the provision of legal assistance and law enforcement
support in the context of its Global Programme
against Organized Crime and Global Programme against Money Laundering (see p. 1117).
Emphasis was placed on the special needs of Africa in combating organized crime, corruption,
terrorism and the spread of HIV/AIDS, which
were impediments to the region's sustainable
development. UNODC helped African Governments to strengthen judicial integrity and develop multisectoral programmes to tackle those
issues. It also helped to improve seaport and airport law enforcement capabilities in Eastern and
Southern Africa and in the adoption and implementation of an action plan to counter trafficking in human beings.

UNODC advised Governments in enhancing
their capacities to administer criminal law and
reduce crime by promoting the treatment of offenders, juvenile justice reform, prison improvement, victim support and urban security.

Contributions and pledges to the United
Nations Crime Prevention and Criminal Justice
Fund from January 2003 to June 2004 totalled
$13,626,894, a 43 per cent increase over the pre-
vious year. Some 95 per cent of contributions
were earmarked for specific projects.

The Commission also considered an April
note by the Secretary-General entitled "Thematic discussion on the rule of law and development: the contribution of operational activities in
crime prevention and criminal justice" [E/CN.15/
2004/3]. The report stated that development agencies had increasingly recognized the importance
of fair and effective criminal justice systems, but
noted that significant achievements in development had often been undermined by lawlessness
and criminal behaviour. There was a close relationship between institutional failure in the justice sector and the extent of organized crime in
many countries. Recognition of that relationship
was not always matched by sufficient funding for
justice sector projects. The report discussed international cooperation in criminal justice to
strengthen the rule of law, including combating
corruption and new types of crime, and strengthening the rule of law in post-conflict reconstruction, including reform of criminal justice institutions, with emphasis on technical assistance.

ECONOMIC AND SOCIAL COUNCIL ACTION

On 21 July [meeting 47], the Economic and Social
Council, on the recommendation of the Commis-

sion on Crime and Criminal Justice [E/2004/30], adopted **resolution 2004/32** without vote [agenda item 14 *(c)*].

Implementation of technical assistance projects in Africa by the United Nations Office on Drugs and Crime

The Economic and Social Council,

Recalling the United Nations Millennium Declaration, in which Heads of State and Government pledged to support the consolidation of democracy in Africa and to assist Africans in their struggle for lasting peace, poverty eradication and sustainable development, thereby bringing Africa into the mainstream of the world economy,

Concerned at the fact that Africa has in recent years become a significant zone of transit, trafficking and abuse of drugs and trafficking in firearms and human beings, and bearing in mind that a number of African countries are facing post-conflict instability,

Welcoming the report of the Executive Director of the United Nations Office on Drugs and Crime entitled "Development, security and justice for all", in which it was underlined that drug abuse and trafficking, organized crime, corruption, terrorism and the spread of HIV/AIDS had all impeded sustainable development in Africa,

Mindful of the difficulties encountered by the United Nations Office on Drugs and Crime in the implementation of its projects in Africa,

1. *Reaffirms* that recent developments in Africa call for particular attention, especially in the fight against drugs and crime;

2. *Expresses its appreciation* to donor countries that have supported projects related to drug and crime issues on the African continent through their voluntary contributions to the United Nations Office on Drugs and Crime and invites them to continue their efforts, and invites other potential donor countries to provide similar support;

3. *Welcomes* the efforts of the United Nations Office on Drugs and Crime to improve the implementation of its projects in Africa, both at headquarters and in the field, and encourages the Office to continue those efforts;

4. *Requests* the United Nations Office on Drugs and Crime to produce a concept paper to analyse the current situation with respect to major drug and crime issues affecting the African continent and to propose policy directives, strategies and priority focus to gain support for assistance to Africa;

5. *Also requests* the United Nations Office on Drugs and Crime, in coordination with the African Union and interested Member States and subject to the availability of extrabudgetary resources, to promote an exchange of views, based on the results of the concept paper, by organizing an appropriate special event among interested Member States, relevant agencies and institutes providing technical assistance to Africa, as well as those promoting South-South cooperation, in order:

(a) To discuss ways of reducing impediments to economic growth and sustainable development caused by widespread criminality, such as drug trafficking, organized crime and corruption;

(b) To ensure that appropriate responses to drug and crime issues are incorporated as core elements within bilateral and multilateral development assistance policies in the context of the New Partnership for Africa's Development and other relevant initiatives;

(c) To explore ways of maximizing existing resources, including official development assistance, that could lead to improvements in the tackling of drug and crime issues and to the strengthening of criminal justice institutions;

6. *Requests* Member States in the African region where projects are being implemented to mobilize national stakeholders and to make every effort to facilitate the implementation of such projects;

7. *Invites* Member States to promote synergies between technical assistance provided by the United Nations Office on Drugs and Crime and bilateral and regional cooperation activities in the African region, in particular in the context of the New Partnership for Africa's Development;

8. *Requests* the Secretary-General to report to the Commission on Crime Prevention and Criminal Justice at its fourteenth session on the implementation of the present resolution.

Also on 21 July [meeting 47], the Economic and Social Council, on the recommendation of the Commission on Crime Prevention and Criminal Justice [E/2004/30], adopted **resolution 2004/25** without vote [agenda item 14 *(c)*].

The rule of law and development: strengthening the rule of law and the reform of criminal justice institutions, with emphasis on technical assistance, including in post-conflict reconstruction

The Economic and Social Council,

Bearing in mind that one of the fundamental purposes of the United Nations, as enshrined in the Preamble to the Charter of the United Nations, is to establish conditions under which justice and respect for the obligations arising from treaties and other sources of international law can be maintained,

Recalling the ministerial-level discussion of the Security Council held in September 2003, during which the Council invited all Member States to contribute to enhancing the role of the United Nations in establishing justice and the rule of law in post-conflict societies,

Fully aware that the international community is confronted with the problem of conflict and war in certain parts of the world, especially in Africa, Asia and Latin America and the Caribbean,

Concerned about the activities of organized criminal groups engaged in trafficking in human beings, drug trafficking and money-laundering at the national and international levels, and in particular about the destabilizing impact of those activities on national security and peacekeeping and reconstruction efforts,

Recalling the United Nations Millennium Declaration, in which heads of State and Government expressed their resolve to strengthen respect for the rule of law in international as in national affairs, and stated that they would spare no effort to strengthen respect for all internationally recognized human rights and fundamental freedoms, including the right to development, and would support the consolidation of democracy in Africa and assist Africans in their struggle for lasting peace, poverty eradication and sustainable development, thereby bringing Africa into the mainstream of the world economy,

Bearing in mind that, in the Vienna Declaration on Crime and Justice: Meeting the Challenges of the Twenty-first Century, Member States emphasized that it was the responsibility of each State to establish and maintain a fair, responsible, ethical and efficient criminal justice system and that effective action for crime prevention and criminal justice required the involvement, as partners and actors, of Governments, national, regional, interregional and international institutions, intergovernmental and non-governmental organizations and various segments of civil society,

Recalling the plans of action for the implementation of the Vienna Declaration on Crime and Justice, in particular the actions against transnational organized crime, corruption, money-laundering, terrorism and high-technology and computer-related crime and the actions on crime prevention, witnesses and victims of crime, prison overcrowding and alternatives to incarceration, juvenile justice, special needs of women in the criminal justice system, standards and norms and restorative justice,

Recalling also the Basic Principles on the Independence of the Judiciary,

Stressing that the participants in the Symposium on the Role of Judges in the Promotion and Protection of Human Rights, held in Vienna on 24 November 2003, called upon States to ensure that the rule of law and the independence of the judicial system and its functioning were to be preserved, to the extent possible, in conflict situations and that judges and their staff were to be protected from unlawful pressure, which might hinder them from exercising their functions,

Noting the thematic discussions on the "Rule of law and development: the contribution of operational activities in crime prevention and criminal justice" held at the thirteenth session of the Commission on Crime Prevention and Criminal Justice,

Recalling Commission on Human Rights resolution 2004/43, entitled "Human rights in the administration of justice, in particular juvenile justice", in which the Commission encouraged all relevant parts of the United Nations system, as well as relevant regional and international intergovernmental and non-governmental organizations, including professional associations, to continue to develop and coordinate their activities in promoting human rights in the administration of justice, in particular juvenile justice, addressing as a matter of priority the needs of judges,

Bearing in mind that, in its resolution 2004/39 entitled "Drug control and related crime prevention assistance for countries emerging from conflict", recommended by the Commission on Narcotic Drugs for adoption by the Economic and Social Council, in which the Council would urge Member States emerging from conflict to give adequate priority to addressing the drug problem and related crime in their post-conflict reconstruction efforts,

Noting with satisfaction the steady progress being made towards restoring peace in a number of conflict zones throughout the world, especially in Africa, Asia and Latin America and the Caribbean,

Noting with appreciation the progress made by the United Nations Office on Drugs and Crime in the implementation of the criminal justice reform programme in Afghanistan, aimed at restoring the rule of law in that post-conflict society,

Recognizing the importance of the rule of law in post-conflict reconstruction and the consolidation of peace,

Noting the leading role of the Department of Peacekeeping Operations of the Secretariat, among other entities, in providing assistance to countries in post-conflict situations,

1. *Requests* the United Nations Office on Drugs and Crime, in coordination with the Department of Peacekeeping Operations of the Secretariat and other relevant entities charged with providing assistance to countries in post-conflict situations, to consider specific practical strategies to assist in promoting the rule of law, especially in countries emerging from conflict, paying particular attention to the most affected countries in Africa and taking an integrated approach to crime prevention and criminal justice reform, with particular emphasis on protecting vulnerable groups, subject to the availability of extrabudgetary resources;

2. *Encourages* the United Nations Office on Drugs and Crime to continue to provide technical assistance and advisory services to Member States upon request in support of criminal justice reform and to incorporate elements concerning the rule of law into such assistance, wherever possible, including in the framework of peacekeeping and post-conflict reconstruction, in coordination with the Department of Peacekeeping Operations and other relevant entities charged with providing assistance to countries in post-conflict situations, drawing on United Nations standards and norms in crime prevention and criminal justice, the United Nations Convention against Transnational Organized Crime and the Protocols thereto and the United Nations Convention against Corruption;

3. *Invites* the United Nations Office on Drugs and Crime to develop assessment tools for criminal justice reform, including in the framework of peacekeeping and post-conflict reconstruction;

4. *Urges* Member States providing development assistance to countries emerging from conflict to increase, where relevant, their bilateral assistance in crime prevention and criminal justice to those countries;

5. *Invites* the global and regional intergovernmental financial and development institutions, including the World Bank and the International Monetary Fund, to strengthen collaboration with the Department of Peacekeeping Operations, the United Nations Office on Drugs and Crime and other providers of technical assistance in the area of the rule of law and to provide adequate funding for projects in the justice sector;

6. *Invites* the institutes of the United Nations Crime Prevention and Criminal Justice Programme network to include in their work programmes the question of the rule of law, with a view to contributing to a better understanding of the links between the rule of law and development, and to develop appropriate training materials;

7. *Urges* the Eleventh United Nations Congress on Crime Prevention and Criminal Justice, to be held in Bangkok from 18 to 25 April 2005, to incorporate matters related to the rule of law in its programme of work, where relevant;

8. *Requests* the Secretary-General to report to the Commission on Crime Prevention and Criminal Justice at its fifteenth session on the implementation of the present resolution.

In response to General Assembly resolution 58/140 [YUN 2003, p. 1120], the Secretary-General published an August report [A/59/205] on strengthening the United Nations Crime Prevention and Criminal Justice Programme, in particular its technical cooperation capacity. The report discussed the role of the Commission, the entry into force of the United Nations Convention on Transnational Organized Crime and its Supplementary Protocols, which entered into force in 2003 [YUN 2003, p. 1126], the convening of the High-level Political Conference for the Purpose of Signing the United Nations Convention against Corruption (see p. 1119), and preparations for the Eleventh Congress on Crime Prevention and Criminal Justice (see p. 1108). The report also covered technical cooperation and operational activities, as well as implementation of UN standards and norms, research and dissemination of information and coordination activities.

The Programme's technical cooperation activities supported 150 States during the 2003-2004 biennium and trained 2,600 officials, including 800 women, through its technical cooperation activities on combating terrorism, organized crime, trafficking in human beings and corruption. Those activities were implemented within the framework of the four global programmes (against terrorism, organized crime, trafficking in human beings and corruption), and in the areas of reconstruction of criminal justice systems, justice reform and crime prevention.

ECONOMIC AND SOCIAL COUNCIL ACTION

On 21 July [meeting 47], the Economic and Social Council, on the recommendation of the Commission on Crime and Criminal Justice [E/2004/30], adopted **resolution 2004/33** without vote [agenda item 14 (c)].

Strengthening the technical cooperation capacity of the crime prevention and criminal justice programme of the United Nations Office on Drugs and Crime

The Economic and Social Council,

Recalling the United Nations Millennium Declaration, in which heads of State and Government resolved to take concerted action against international terrorism and to accede as soon as possible to all the relevant international conventions, as well as to intensify efforts to fight transnational crime in all its dimensions, including trafficking as well as smuggling of migrants and money-laundering,

Reaffirming the values and principles enshrined in the United Nations Millennium Declaration, thereby emphasizing the importance of international cooperation and coordination among Member States in the fight against crime, in order to achieve sustainable development, improved quality of life, democracy and human rights,

Recalling the Vienna Declaration on Crime and Justice: Meeting the Challenges of the Twenty-first Century, adopted by the Tenth United Nations Congress on the Prevention of Crime and the Treatment of Offenders and endorsed by the General Assembly in its resolution 55/59 of 4 December 2000, as well as the plans of action for its implementation,

Recalling also General Assembly resolution 58/140 of 22 December 2003, on strengthening the United Nations Crime Prevention and Criminal Justice Programme, in particular its technical cooperation capacity,

Recalling further its resolution 2003/25 of 23 July 2003, on international cooperation, technical assistance and advisory services in crime prevention and criminal justice,

Welcoming the entry into force of the United Nations Convention against Transnational Organized Crime, as well as the Protocol to Prevent, Suppress and Punish Trafficking in Persons, Especially Women and Children, supplementing the United Nations Convention against Transnational Organized Crime and the Protocol against the Smuggling of Migrants by Land, Sea and Air, supplementing the United Nations Convention against Transnational Organized Crime,

Recognizing the importance of the entry into force of the Protocol against the Illicit Manufacturing of and Trafficking in Firearms, Their Parts and Components and Ammunition, supplementing the United Nations Convention against Transnational Organized Crime,

Welcoming the adoption and opening for signature of the United Nations Convention against Corruption,

Recognizing that these important new instruments of international cooperation require the United Nations Office on Drugs and Crime to respond to an increasing number of requests for technical assistance in the area of crime prevention and criminal justice reform,

Expressing its appreciation to those Member States which have provided extrabudgetary funds in 2003, thus allowing the United Nations Office on Drugs and Crime to carry out a large number of advisory services and technical assistance activities in least developed countries, developing countries, countries with economies in transition and countries in post-conflict situations,

1. *Commends* the United Nations Office on Drugs and Crime for assisting Member States by responding to an increasing number of requests for advisory services and technical assistance in the implementation of projects, including with respect to the strengthening of institutional capacity, training in drafting of legislation and of law enforcement and criminal justice personnel and awareness-raising activities, in particular for parliamentarians, as well as in the development of national policies and promotion of legislative reform;

2. *Recognizes* the expansion of the technical assistance activities of the United Nations Office on Drugs and Crime, including additional interregional advisory services, and encourages international, regional and national funding agencies, as well as international financial institutions, to support the technical co-

operation activities and interregional advisory services of the United Nations Office on Drugs and Crime;

3. *Encourages* relevant entities of the United Nations system, including the United Nations Development Programme, the World Bank and the International Monetary Fund, as well as other international and regional organizations, to strengthen their cooperation with the United Nations Office on Drugs and Crime, in order to ensure that, as appropriate, technical assistance activities in the field of crime prevention and criminal justice, in particular to combat organized crime, corruption, trafficking in persons and terrorism and its financing, are properly brought into the mainstream of their respective programmes, so as to ensure that expertise available at the Office relating to crime prevention and criminal justice is fully utilized and that duplication of efforts is avoided;

4. *Reiterates* the need to have adequate resources available to further operationalize the activities of the United Nations Office on Drugs and Crime, taking into account the recently adopted integrated approach to drugs and crime;

5. *Invites* Member States to cooperate at the bilateral level with the least developed and developing countries and at the multilateral level with the United Nations and other international organizations within the framework of the United Nations Convention against Transnational Organized Crime;

6. *Also invites* Member States to make or increase voluntary contributions, as appropriate, to the United Nations Crime Prevention and Criminal Justice Fund, as well as contributions in direct support of activities and projects of the United Nations Office on Drugs and Crime, in order to strengthen further the capacity of the Office to provide advisory services and technical assistance;

7. *Encourages* recipient Member States that are in a position to do so to contribute to the activities of the United Nations Office on Drugs and Crime by providing the necessary infrastructure, as well as human and financial resources, for projects to be implemented in partnership with the Office;

8. *Requests* the Secretary-General to enhance further the resources available within the existing overall budgetary framework of the United Nations for operational activities and, in particular, the interregional advisory services of the United Nations Office on Drugs and Crime under section 23, Regular programme of technical cooperation, of the regular budget of the United Nations;

9. *Also requests* the Secretary-General to make all possible efforts, including appeals to donors in the private sector, mobilization of resources and fundraising, to increase extrabudgetary resources, including general-purpose funds, bearing in mind the need to safeguard the independence and international character of the United Nations Office on Drugs and Crime.

GENERAL ASSEMBLY ACTION

On 20 December [meeting 74], the General Assembly, on the recommendation of the Third Committee [A/59/494], adopted **resolution 59/159** without vote [agenda item 96].

Strengthening the United Nations Crime Prevention and Criminal Justice Programme, in particular its technical cooperation capacity

The General Assembly,

Recalling its resolution 46/152 of 18 December 1991 on the creation of an effective United Nations crime prevention and criminal justice programme, in which it approved the statement of principles and programme of action annexed to that resolution,

Recalling also its resolution 58/140 of 22 December 2003 on strengthening the United Nations Crime Prevention and Criminal Justice Programme, in particular its technical cooperation capacity,

Bearing in mind the United Nations Millennium Declaration, as well as the Vienna Declaration on Crime and Justice: Meeting the Challenges of the Twenty-first Century and the plans of action for its implementation,

Emphasizing the role of the United Nations in the field of crime prevention and criminal justice, specifically the reduction of criminality, more efficient and effective law enforcement and administration of justice, respect for human rights and the rule of law and promotion of the highest standards of fairness, humanity and professional conduct,

Recognizing that action against global crime is a common and shared responsibility,

Convinced of the need for closer coordination and cooperation among States in combating crime in all its forms and manifestations, including criminal activities carried out for the purpose of furthering terrorism, and bearing in mind the role that is played by both the United Nations and regional organizations in this respect,

Recognizing existing efforts at the regional level that complement the work of the United Nations Crime Prevention and Criminal Justice Programme in combating corruption, the smuggling of migrants and trafficking in persons, especially women and children, and noting in this context the ongoing work of the Bali and Puebla Processes,

Looking forward to the Eleventh United Nations Congress on Crime Prevention and Criminal Justice, to be held in Bangkok in 2005, which will provide an important opportunity to exchange views and experiences and to identify emerging trends and issues in the field of crime prevention and criminal justice,

Welcoming the entry into force in 2003 of the Protocol to Prevent, Suppress and Punish Trafficking in Persons, Especially Women and Children, supplementing the United Nations Convention against Transnational Organized Crime, and in 2004 of the Protocol against the Smuggling of Migrants by Land, Sea and Air, supplementing the United Nations Convention against Transnational Organized Crime,

Welcoming also the opening for signature, at the High-level Political Conference, held in Merida, Mexico, from 9 to 11 December 2003, of the United Nations Convention against Corruption,

Bearing in mind all its relevant resolutions, in particular those related to the urgent need to strengthen international cooperation and technical assistance in promoting and facilitating the ratification and implementation of the United Nations Convention against Transnational Organized Crime and the Protocols thereto and the United Nations Convention against

Corruption, as well as the universal instruments against terrorism,

Bearing in mind also all Economic and Social Council resolutions on strengthening international cooperation, technical assistance and advisory services in crime prevention and criminal justice, as well as on strengthening the rule of law and the reform of criminal justice institutions, including in post-conflict reconstruction, the technical cooperation capacity of the United Nations Crime Prevention and Criminal Justice Programme of the United Nations Office on Drugs and Crime and on the implementation of technical assistance in Africa by the Office,

Acknowledging the role of United Nations standards and norms in crime prevention and criminal justice and their development, as reflected in Economic and Social Council resolution 2004/28 of 21 July 2004,

Recalling its relevant resolutions in which it requested the Secretary-General, as a matter of urgency, to provide the United Nations Crime Prevention and Criminal Justice Programme with sufficient resources for the full implementation of its mandate, in conformity with the high priority attached to the Programme,

Aware of the continued increase in requests for technical assistance forwarded to the United Nations Office on Drugs and Crime by least developed countries, developing countries, countries with economies in transition and countries emerging from conflict, and recognizing the need to maintain a balance in the technical cooperation capacity of the Office between all priorities identified by the General Assembly and the Economic and Social Council,

Expressing its appreciation for the funding provided by certain Member States, which in recent years has permitted the United Nations Office on Drugs and Crime and the United Nations Interregional Crime and Justice Research Institute and institutes of the United Nations Crime Prevention and Criminal Justice Programme network and other relevant bodies to enhance their capacity to execute an increased number of projects in the field of crime prevention and criminal justice,

1. *Takes note with appreciation* of the report of the Secretary-General on the progress made in the implementation of General Assembly resolution 58/140;

2. *Reaffirms* the importance of the United Nations Crime Prevention and Criminal Justice Programme in promoting effective action to strengthen international cooperation in crime prevention and criminal justice, in responding to the needs of the international community in the face of both national and transnational criminality and in assisting Member States in achieving the goals of preventing crime within and among States and improving the response to crime;

3. *Reiterates its appreciation* of the work of the Commission on Crime Prevention and Criminal Justice to coordinate international cooperation efforts, and requests that a gender perspective continue to be integrated into all activities of the United Nations Office on Drugs and Crime;

4. *Reaffirms* the importance of the work of the United Nations Office on Drugs and Crime in the fulfilment of its mandate in crime prevention and criminal justice, including to prevent and combat terrorism in coordination with and complementing the work of the Security Council Committee established pursuant to resolution 1373(2001) concerning counter-terrorism, in particular in strengthening international cooperation and providing technical assistance, upon request;

5. *Reaffirms also* the role of the United Nations Office on Drugs and Crime in providing to Member States, upon request and as a matter of high priority, technical cooperation, advisory services and other forms of assistance in the field of crime prevention and criminal justice, including in the areas of prevention and control of transnational organized crime, corruption and terrorism as well as in the area of reconstruction of national criminal justice systems, and stresses the need to enhance its operational activities to assist, in particular, least developed countries, developing countries, countries with economies in transition and countries emerging from conflict;

6. *Recognizes* the progress made in the implementation of the global programmes addressing trafficking in human beings, corruption, organized crime and terrorism, and calls upon the Secretary-General to enhance further the visibility of those programmes and to strengthen the United Nations Office on Drugs and Crime by providing it with the resources necessary for the full implementation of its mandate in crime prevention and criminal justice, including the preparation of an updated publication on world crime trends;

7. *Invites* all States to support the operational activities of the United Nations Crime Prevention and Criminal Justice Programme, through voluntary contributions to the United Nations Crime Prevention and Criminal Justice Fund or through voluntary contributions in direct support of such activities, including for the provision of technical assistance for the implementation of the commitments entered into at the Tenth United Nations Congress on the Prevention of Crime and the Treatment of Offenders, including the measures outlined in the plans of action for the implementation of the Vienna Declaration on Crime and Justice: Meeting the Challenges of the Twenty-first Century;

8. *Also invites* all States to support, through voluntary contributions, the activities carried out by the United Nations Interregional Crime and Justice Research Institute and institutes of the United Nations Crime Prevention and Criminal Justice Programme network and other relevant bodies;

9. *Encourages* relevant programmes, funds and organizations of the United Nations system, in particular the United Nations Development Programme, and invites the international financial institutions, in particular the World Bank and regional and national funding agencies, to support the operational activities of the United Nations Office on Drugs and Crime in the field of crime prevention and criminal justice;

10. *Urges* States and relevant international organizations to develop national, regional and international strategies and other necessary measures to complement the work of the United Nations Crime Prevention and Criminal Justice Programme in addressing effectively the significant problems posed by the smuggling of migrants and trafficking in persons and related criminal activities, such as kidnapping;

11. *Urges* States and funding agencies to review, as appropriate, their funding policies for development

assistance and to include a crime prevention and criminal justice component in such assistance;

12. *Welcomes* the efforts undertaken by the Commission on Crime Prevention and Criminal Justice to exercise more vigorously its mandated function of resource mobilization, and calls upon the Commission to strengthen further its activities in this direction;

13. *Notes with appreciation* the outcome of the senior-level discussion held during the thirteenth session of the Commission on Crime Prevention and Criminal Justice on progress made with regard to the criminal justice aspects of terrorism and international cooperation and to the universal conventions and protocols related to terrorism;

14. *Expresses its appreciation* to non-governmental organizations and other relevant sectors of civil society for their support for the United Nations Crime Prevention and Criminal Justice Programme;

15. *Invites* relevant entities of the United Nations system, including the United Nations Development Programme as well as the World Bank and other international funding agencies, to increase further their interaction with the United Nations Office on Drugs and Crime in order to benefit from synergies and avoid duplication of effort and to ensure that, as appropriate, activities on crime prevention and criminal justice, including activities related to the prevention of corruption and the promotion of the rule of law, are considered in their sustainable development agenda and that the expertise of the Office is fully utilized;

16. *Requests* the Secretary-General to take all necessary measures to provide adequate support to the Commission on Crime Prevention and Criminal Justice, as the principal policy-making body in this field, in performing its activities, including cooperation and coordination with the institutes of the United Nations Crime Prevention and Criminal Justice Programme network and other relevant bodies;

17. *Urges* all States and regional economic organizations that have not yet done so to ratify or accede to the United Nations Convention against Transnational Organized Crime (Palermo Convention) and the Protocols thereto;

18. *Emphasizes* the importance of the expeditious entry into force of the Protocol against the Illicit Manufacturing of and Trafficking in Firearms, Their Parts and Components and Ammunition, supplementing the United Nations Convention against Transnational Organized Crime, adopted by its resolution 55/255 of 31 May 2001;

19. *Welcomes* the voluntary contributions already made, and encourages States to make adequate and regular voluntary contributions for the implementation of the Convention and the Protocols thereto, through the United Nations funding mechanism specifically designed for that purpose in the Convention or in direct support of implementation activities and initiatives;

20. *Urges* all States and competent regional economic integration organizations that have not yet done so to sign, ratify or accede to the United Nations Convention against Corruption;

21. *Requests* the Secretary-General to take all necessary measures and provide adequate support to the United Nations Office on Drugs and Crime so as to en-

able it to promote the speedy entry into force of the United Nations Convention against Corruption;

22. *Encourages* States to make adequate and regular voluntary contributions for the entry into force of the United Nations Convention against Corruption, through the United Nations funding mechanism specifically designed for that purpose in the Convention or in direct support of implementation activities and initiatives;

23. *Requests* the Secretary-General to submit a report on the implementation of the present resolution to the General Assembly at its sixtieth session.

Crime Prevention and Criminal Justice Programme

A March report [E/CN.15/2004/4] of the Secretary-General summarized the activities of the institutions comprising the United Nations Crime Prevention and Criminal Justice Programme network: the United Nations Interregional Crime and Justice Research Institute (UNRCRI); 11 regional and affiliated institutes; and the International Scientific and Professional Advisory Council.

UN African crime prevention institute

In a July report [A/59/175], submitted in response to General Assembly resolution 58/139 [YUN 2003, p. 1124], the Secretary-General highlighted activities of the African Institute for the Prevention of Crime and the Treatment of Offenders (UNAFRI) and discussed funding and support for the Institute, its future and strategies for sustaining it, including its main focus of studying and developing remedial action to address crime problems by conducting advisory missions in Africa and holding follow-up workshops. The main focus of the activities of the Institute was on the individual needs of member States and the growing awareness of the necessity of making crime prevention strategies a component of sustainable socio-economic development. It worked to complete the extradition and mutual legal conventions assistance projects, and implemented, with assistance from the United States, a project on trafficking in firearms and ammunition in Africa.

UNAFRI operated against a backdrop of financial difficulty arising from poor financial support from member States. As at 31 December 2003, only $1,011,565 in contributions had been received out of total assessed contributions of $3,594,766 for the 1998-2003 period, leaving an outstanding balance of $2,583,201. For the period January to June 2004, only $25,375 had been received. The Institute's Governing Board, at its ninth session (Kampala, Uganda, 21-22 June), directed the secretariat to ascertain from members their continuing interest in membership in the

Institute and requested an external review to evaluate the Institute's performance in relation to mandated objectives. The review would examine the structure, objectives and operations, with a view to upgrading its relevance, performance and acceptability.

GENERAL ASSEMBLY ACTION

On 20 December [meeting 74], the General Assembly, on the recommendation of the Third Committee [A/59/494], adopted **resolution 59/158** without vote [agenda item 96].

United Nations African Institute for the Prevention of Crime and the Treatment of Offenders

The General Assembly,

Recalling its resolution 58/139 of 22 December 2003 and all other relevant resolutions,

Taking note of the report of the Secretary-General,

Bearing in mind the urgent need to establish effective crime prevention strategies for Africa, as well as the importance of law enforcement agencies and the judiciary at the regional and subregional levels,

Noting that the financial situation of the United Nations African Institute for the Prevention of Crime and the Treatment of Offenders has greatly affected its capacity to deliver its services to African Member States in an effective and comprehensive manner,

1. *Commends* the United Nations African Institute for the Prevention of Crime and the Treatment of Offenders for its efforts to promote and coordinate regional technical cooperation activities related to crime prevention and criminal justice systems in Africa;

2. *Commends* the Secretary-General for his efforts to mobilize the financial resources necessary to provide the Institute with the core professional staff required to enable it to function effectively in the fulfilment of its mandated obligations;

3. *Reiterates* the need to strengthen further the capacity of the Institute to support national mechanisms for crime prevention and criminal justice in African countries;

4. *Urges* the States members of the Institute to make every possible effort to meet their obligations to the Institute;

5. *Calls upon* all Member States and nongovernmental organizations to adopt concrete practical measures to support the Institute in the development of the requisite capacity and to implement its programmes and activities aimed at strengthening crime prevention and criminal justice systems in Africa;

6. *Requests* the Secretary-General to intensify efforts to mobilize all relevant entities of the United Nations system to provide the necessary financial and technical support to the Institute to enable it to fulfil its mandate;

7. *Also requests* the Secretary-General to continue his efforts to mobilize the financial resources necessary to maintain the Institute with the core professional staff required to enable it to function effectively in the fulfilment of its mandated obligations;

8. *Calls upon* the United Nations Crime Prevention and Criminal Justice Programme and the United Nations Office on Drugs and Crime to work closely with the Institute;

9. *Requests* the Secretary-General to enhance the promotion of regional cooperation, coordination and collaboration in the fight against crime, especially in its transnational dimension, which cannot be dealt with adequately by national action alone;

10. *Also requests* the Secretary-General to make concrete proposals, including the provision of additional core professional staff, to strengthen the programmes and activities of the Institute and to report to the General Assembly at its sixtieth session on the implementation of the present resolution.

Transnational organized crime

International convention

Following the entry into force on 29 September 2003 [YUN 2003, 1125] of the United Nations Convention against Transnational Organized Crime and the Protocols thereto, the Protocol against the Smuggling of Migrants by Land, Sea and Air entered into force on 28 January 2004. As at 31 December, there were 97 parties and 147 signatories to the Convention, 77 parties and 117 signatories to the Protocol to Prevent, Suppress and Punish Trafficking in Persons, Especially Women and Children, 65 parties and 112 signatories to the Protocol on Smuggling of Migrants by Land, Sea and Air, and 31 Parties and 52 signatories to the Protocol against the Illicit Manufacturing of and Trafficking in Firearms.

Reports of Secretary-General. In response to General Assembly resolution 58/135 [YUN 2003, p. 1126], the Secretary-General submitted a March report [E/CN.15/2004/5], updated in July [A/59/204], on the Convention and its Protocols. The Ad Hoc Committee on the Elaboration of a Convention against Transnational Organized Crime, at its thirteenth and final session (Vienna, 2-6 February), approved the draft rules of procedure of the Conference of the Parties to the Convention. The Conference, at its first session (28 June–8 July), endorsed a work plan for its second session on the themes of adaptation of national legislation in accordance with the Convention and its Protocols; criminalization legislation and difficulties encountered in the implementation of the instruments; and international cooperation and technical assistance. The Conference also endorsed the draft questionnaires prepared by the Secretariat to help identify needs and concerns of States in ratifying and implementing the Convention and its Protocols, responses to which would be submitted by the Secretariat at the second session of the Conference. It requested the Secretariat to submit the full text of notifications, declarations and reservations by States parties to the Convention and its Protocols and to prepare a working paper on technical assistance provided by the Secretariat and by other relevant international and regional organizations.

CEB consideration. At its April [CEB/2004/1] session (Vienna, 2-3 April), the United Nations System Chief Executive Board (CEB) for Coordination addressed the issue of curbing transnational organized crime. The Board endorsed measures outlined in a note prepared by UNODC entitled "Organized crime and corruption are threats to security and development: the role of the United Nations system", aimed at building a response to curbing transnational crime in the short and medium term.

On 20 December, the General Assembly took note of the Secretary-General's report on international cooperation in the fight against transnational organized crime (**decision 59/523**).

ECONOMIC AND SOCIAL COUNCIL ACTION

On 21 July [meeting 47], the Economic and Social Council, on the recommendation of the Commission on Crime Prevention and Criminal Justice [E/2004/30], adopted **resolution 2004/23** without vote [agenda item 14 *(c)*].

International cooperation in the fight against transnational organized crime: assistance to States in capacity-building with a view to facilitating the implementation of the United Nations Convention against Transnational Organized Crime and the Protocols thereto

The Economic and Social Council

Recommends to the General Assembly the adoption of the following draft resolution:

[For text, see General Assembly resolution 59/157 below.]

GENERAL ASSEMBLY ACTION

On 20 December [meeting 74], the General Assembly, on the recommendation of the Third Committee [A/49/494], adopted **resolution 59/157** without vote [agenda item 96].

International cooperation in the fight against transnational organized crime: assistance to States in capacity-building with a view to facilitating the implementation of the United Nations Convention against Transnational Organized Crime and the Protocols thereto

The General Assembly,

Recalling its resolution 55/25 of 15 November 2000, by which it adopted the United Nations Convention against Transnational Organized Crime, the Protocol to Prevent, Suppress and Punish Trafficking in Persons, Especially Women and Children, supplementing the United Nations Convention against Transnational Organized Crime, and the Protocol against the Smuggling of Migrants by Land, Sea and Air, supplementing the United Nations Convention against Transnational Organized Crime,

Recalling also its resolution 55/255 of 31 May 2001, by which it adopted the Protocol against the Illicit Manufacturing of and Trafficking in Firearms, Their Parts and Components and Ammunition, supplementing the United Nations Convention against Transnational Organized Crime,

Recalling further its resolution 58/135 of 22 December 2003 on international cooperation in the fight against transnational organized crime: assistance to States in capacity-building with a view to facilitating the implementation of the United Nations Convention against Transnational Organized Crime and the Protocols thereto,

Reaffirming its deep concern at the impact of transnational organized crime on the political, social and economic stability and development of societies,

Reaffirming that the adoption of the Convention and the Protocols thereto is a significant development in international criminal law and that they constitute important instruments for effective international cooperation against transnational organized crime,

1. *Takes note with appreciation* of the report of the Secretary-General on the United Nations Convention against Transnational Organized Crime and the Protocols thereto;

2. *Welcomes* the entry into force of the United Nations Convention against Transnational Organized Crime, of the Protocol to Prevent, Suppress and Punish Trafficking in Persons, Especially Women and Children, supplementing the United Nations Convention against Transnational Organized Crime, and of the Protocol against the Smuggling of Migrants by Land, Sea and Air, supplementing the United Nations Convention against Transnational Organized Crime;

3. *Commends* the United Nations Office on Drugs and Crime for its work in promoting the ratification of the Convention and the Protocols thereto, including, in particular, the preparation of legislative guides designed to facilitate the ratification and subsequent implementation of those instruments, and invites the Office to finalize the legislative guides and to disseminate them as widely as possible;

4. *Urges* all States and relevant regional economic integration organizations that have not done so to consider ratifying or acceding to the Protocol against the Illicit Manufacturing of and Trafficking in Firearms, Their Parts and Components and Ammunition, supplementing the United Nations Convention against Transnational Organized Crime, as soon as possible;

5. *Also urges* all States and relevant regional economic integration organizations to take all necessary measures to improve international cooperation in criminal matters, especially extradition and mutual legal assistance, in accordance with the Convention;

6. *Welcomes* the financial support provided by several donors to promote the entry into force and implementation of the Convention and the Protocols thereto, and encourages Member States to make sufficient voluntary contributions to the United Nations Crime Prevention and Criminal Justice Fund, as well as contributions in direct support of activities and projects of the United Nations Office on Drugs and Crime, including through contributions to the institutes of the United Nations Crime Prevention and Criminal Justice Programme network, for the provision of technical assistance to developing countries and countries with economies in transition for the implementation of those international legal instruments;

7. *Requests* the Secretary-General to continue to provide the United Nations Office on Drugs and Crime with the resources necessary to enable it to promote, in an effective manner, the implementation of the Convention and the Protocols thereto and to discharge its functions as the secretariat of the Conference of the Parties in accordance with its mandate;

8. *Requests* the United Nations Office on Drugs and Crime to continue to assist States, upon request, with capacity-building in the area of international cooperation in criminal matters, in particular extradition and mutual legal assistance;

9. *Requests* the Secretary-General to report on the implementation of the present resolution in his report on the work of the United Nations Office on Drugs and Crime to be submitted to the General Assembly at its sixtieth session.

Draft model agreement on disposal of confiscated proceeds of crime

ECONOMIC AND SOCIAL COUNCIL ACTION

On 21 July [meeting 47], the Economic and Social Council, on the recommendation of the Commission on Crime Prevention and Criminal Justice [E/2004/30], adopted **resolution 2004/24** without vote [agenda item 14(c)].

Establishment of an intergovernmental expert group to prepare a draft model bilateral agreement on disposal of confiscated proceeds of crime covered by the United Nations Convention against Transnational Organized Crime and the United Nations Convention against Illicit Traffic in Narcotic Drugs and Psychotropic Substances of 1988

The Economic and Social Council,

Recalling article 13, paragraph 2, of the United Nations Convention against Transnational Organized Crime, which obliges States parties to the Convention, when requested by other States parties, to take measures to identify, trace and freeze or seize proceeds of crime, property, equipment or other instrumentalities referred to in article 12, paragraph 1, of the Convention for the purpose of eventual confiscation, and recalling also article 14, paragraph 3, of the Convention, according to which States parties may give special consideration to concluding agreements on sharing with other States parties such confiscated proceeds of crime,

Recalling also article 5, paragraph 4 (b), of the United Nations Convention against Illicit Traffic in Narcotic Drugs and Psychotropic Substances of 1988, which provides for such measures as well,

Aware that requesting States, in pursuing property subject to confiscation located beyond their borders, and States executing requests from other States relating to confiscation often incur substantial expenses in investigations, prosecutions or judicial proceedings,

Mindful that an increasing number of States have concluded agreements on sharing confiscated proceeds of crime in order to foster cooperation in matters involving confiscation, for example by defraying case-related expenses,

Determined to strengthen international cooperation in the confiscation and disposal of the proceeds of crime covered by the United Nations Convention against Transnational Organized Crime and the United Nations Convention against Illicit Traffic in Narcotic Drugs and Psychotropic Substances,

Recognizing that a model bilateral agreement on sharing confiscated proceeds of crime could facilitate greater international cooperation in this matter and could contribute to the achievement of the objectives of the United Nations Convention against Transnational Organized Crime and the United Nations Convention against Illicit Traffic in Narcotic Drugs and Psychotropic Substances, and that such a model agreement should not prejudice the principles set forth in the United Nations Convention against Corruption or the development, at a later stage, of any appropriate mechanism to facilitate the implementation of that Convention,

1. *Requests* the Secretary-General to convene, subject to the availability of extrabudgetary resources, an open-ended intergovernmental expert group, the composition of which should reflect an equitable geographical representation and a diversity of legal systems, to prepare a draft model bilateral agreement on sharing confiscated proceeds of crime covered by the United Nations Convention against Transnational Organized Crime and the United Nations Convention against Illicit Traffic in Narcotic Drugs and Psychotropic Substances of 1988;

2. *Accepts with gratitude* the offer of the Government of the United States of America to host the meeting of the open-ended intergovernmental expert group;

3. *Requests* the open-ended intergovernmental expert group, in carrying out its work, to take into account, where appropriate, existing agreements on sharing confiscated proceeds of crime and other relevant instruments developed in multilateral forums;

4. *Requests* the Secretary-General to submit the results of the meeting of the open-ended intergovernmental expert group to the Conference of the Parties to the United Nations Convention against Transnational Organized Crime and the Commission on Crime Prevention and Criminal Justice at its fourteenth session for their consideration.

Strategies for crime prevention

Corruption

UN Convention against Corruption

The Secretary-General, by an April note [A/59/77], submitted to the General Assembly the report of the High-level Political Conference for the Purpose of Signing the United Nations Convention against Corruption [YUN 2003, p. 1147], which was adopted by Assembly resolution 58/4 [ibid., p. 1127].

As at 31 December, the Convention had been signed by 116 countries and ratified by 15 countries.

On 21 July [meeting 47], the Economic and Social Council, on the recommendation of the Commission on Crime Prevention and Criminal Justice [E/2004/30], adopted **resolution 2004/21** without vote [agenda item 14 (*c*)].

Action against corruption: assistance to States in capacity-building with a view to facilitating the entry into force and subsequent implementation of the United Nations Convention against Corruption

The Economic and Social Council

Recommends to the General Assembly the adoption of the following draft resolution:

[For text, see General Assembly **resolution 59/155** below.]

On 20 December [meeting 74], the General Assembly, on the recommendation of the Third Committee [A/59/494], adopted **resolution 59/155** without vote [agenda item 96].

Action against corruption: assistance to States in capacity-building with a view to facilitating the entry into force and subsequent implementation of the United Nations Convention against Corruption

The General Assembly,

Deeply concerned about the impact of corruption on the political, social and economic stability and development of societies,

Bearing in mind that the prevention and combating of corruption is a common and shared responsibility of the international community, necessitating cooperation at the bilateral and multilateral levels,

Bearing in mind also that the prevention and eradication of corruption is a responsibility of all States and that they must cooperate with one another, with the support and involvement of individuals and groups outside the public sector, such as civil society, nongovernmental organizations and community-based organizations, if their efforts to prevent and combat corruption are to be effective,

Reaffirming its support and commitment to the goals of the United Nations in the field of crime prevention and criminal justice, in particular the objectives set forth in the Vienna Declaration on Crime and Justice: Meeting the Challenges of the Twenty-first Century,

Recalling its resolution 58/4 of 31 October 2003, in which it adopted the United Nations Convention against Corruption and urged all States and competent regional economic integration organizations to sign and ratify it,

Noting with appreciation the High-level Political Conference for the Purpose of Signing the United Nations Convention against Corruption, held in Merida, Mexico, from 9 to 11 December 2003,

Noting with appreciation also the initiative of those States which have pledged financial contributions to the United Nations Crime Prevention and Criminal Justice Fund in order to enable developing countries and countries with economies in transition to initiate measures to implement the Convention,

1. *Welcomes* the signing of the United Nations Convention against Corruption by a large number of Member States, which reflects the high level of commitment on the part of the international community to the purpose of the Convention;

2. *Urges* Member States to consider signing and ratifying the Convention as soon as possible, in order to allow its early entry into force and subsequent implementation;

3. *Encourages* Member States to make adequate voluntary contributions, where appropriate, to the United Nations Crime Prevention and Criminal Justice Fund to provide developing countries and countries with economies in transition with the technical assistance they may require to implement the Convention, including assistance for the preparatory measures required for implementation, taking into account article 62 of the Convention;

4. *Requests* the Secretary-General to provide the United Nations Office on Drugs and Crime with the resources necessary to enable it to promote, in an effective manner, the entry into force and implementation of the Convention, inter alia, through the provision of assistance to developing countries and countries with economies in transition for building capacity in the areas covered by the Convention;

5. *Also requests* the Secretary-General to report to the Commission on Crime Prevention and Criminal Justice at its fourteenth session on the implementation of the present resolution.

On the same date, the General Assembly took note of the Secretary-General's note transmitting the report of the High-level Political Conference for the Purpose of Signing the United Nations Convention against Corruption (see p. 1119) (**decision 59/523**).

Funds of illicit origin

In response to General Assembly resolution 58/205 [YUN 2003, p. 1148], the Secretary-General submitted in July [A/59/203 & Add.1] a report on preventing and combating corrupt practices and transfer of assets of illicit origin and returning such assets to the countries of origin, which contained a summary of the responses received from 19 States on corruption issues, and of a legal framework of asset recovery under the United Nations Convention against Corruption, and highlighted international initiatives in that area.

The G-8 (the eight most industrialized countries), at its 2004 Summit (Sea Island, Georgia, United States, 8-10 June), recommended that throughout Africa, targeted assistance should fund anti-corruption units, public expenditure transparency systems, democracy-building activities and civil society participation in key decisions.

On 20 December, the General Assembly took note of the Secretary-General's report (**decision 59/523**).

On 22 December [meeting 75], the General Assembly, on the recommendation of the Second (Economic and Financial) Committee [A/59/485/Add.3] adopted **resolution 59/242** without vote [agenda item 87 (c)].

Preventing and combating corrupt practices and transfer of assets of illicit origin and returning such assets to the countries of origin

The General Assembly,

Recalling its resolutions 54/205 of 22 December 1999, 56/186 of 21 December 2001 and 57/244 of 20 December 2002, and recalling also its resolution 58/205 of 23 December 2003 on preventing and combating corrupt practices and transfer of assets of illicit origin and returning such assets to the countries of origin,

Recalling also the Monterrey Consensus of the International Conference on Financing for Development, which underlined that fighting corruption at all levels is a priority, and the Plan of Implementation of the World Summit on Sustainable Development ("Johannesburg Plan of Implementation"),

Emphasizing the need for solid democratic institutions responsive to the needs of the people and the need to improve the efficiency, transparency and accountability of domestic administration and public spending and the rule of law, to ensure full respect for human rights, including the right to development, and to eradicate corruption and build sound economic and social institutions,

Recognizing that fighting corruption at all levels is a priority and that corruption is a serious barrier to effective resource mobilization and allocation and diverts resources away from activities that are vital for poverty eradication, the fight against hunger, and economic and sustainable development,

Noting the particular concern of developing countries and countries with economies in transition regarding the return of assets of illicit origin derived from corruption to the countries from which they originated, consistent with the principles of the United Nations Convention against Corruption, in particular chapter V, in view of the importance that such assets can have to their sustainable development,

Recognizing the concern over the transfer and/or transaction of assets of illicit origin, and stressing the need to address this concern consistent with the principles of chapter V of the United Nations Convention against Corruption,

Recognizing also that the illicit acquisition of wealth can be particularly damaging to democratic institutions, national economies and the rule of law,

Convinced that a stable and transparent environment for national and international commercial transactions in all countries is essential for the mobilization of investment, finance, technology, skills and other important resources, and recognizing that effective efforts at all levels to combat and avoid corruption in all its forms in all countries are essential elements of an improved national and international business environment,

Concerned about the links between corruption in all its forms, including bribery, money-laundering and the transfer of assets of illicit origin, and other forms of crime, in particular organized crime and economic crime,

Reiterating its concern about the seriousness of problems and threats posed by corruption to the stability and security of societies, undermining the institutions and the values of democracy, ethical values and justice and jeopardizing sustainable development and the rule of law, in particular when an inadequate national and international response leads to impunity,

Welcoming the initiatives taken by the Commonwealth Secretariat and the Group of Eight with regard to fighting corruption and improving transparency, including the initiative of the Group of Eight to support with bilateral technical assistance those countries committed to a partnership to increase transparency, good governance and the rule of law, and welcoming also the efforts of those Member States that have entered into "Compacts to Promote Transparency and Combat Corruption" with the Group of Eight,

Noting with appreciation the holding of the High-level Political Conference for the Purpose of Signing the United Nations Convention against Corruption in Merida, Mexico, from 9 to 11 December 2003,

Recalling its resolution 58/4 of 31 October 2003, by which it adopted the United Nations Convention against Corruption and urged all States and competent regional economic organizations to sign and ratify it,

1. *Condemns* corruption in all its forms, including bribery, money-laundering and the transfer of assets of illicit origin;

2. *Takes note* of the report of the Secretary-General;

3. *Welcomes* the adoption of the United Nations Convention against Corruption;

4. *Reiterates its invitation* to all Member States and competent regional economic integration organizations to sign, ratify and fully implement the United Nations Convention against Corruption as soon as possible in order to ensure its rapid entry into force;

5. *Welcomes* the efforts of Member States that have enacted laws and taken other positive measures in the fight against corruption in all its forms, including, inter alia, in accordance with the United Nations Convention against Corruption, and in this regard encourages Member States that have not yet done so to enact such laws;

6. *Encourages* all Governments to prevent, combat and penalize corruption in all its forms, including bribery, money-laundering and the transfer of illicitly acquired assets, and to work for the prompt return of such assets through asset recovery consistent with the principles of the United Nations Convention against Corruption, particularly chapter V;

7. *Further encourages* subregional and regional cooperation, where appropriate, in the efforts to prevent and combat corrupt practices and the transfer of assets of illicit origin as well as for asset recovery consistent with the principles of the United Nations Convention against Corruption, particularly chapter V;

8. *Calls for* further international cooperation, inter alia, through the United Nations system, in support of national, subregional and regional efforts to prevent and combat corrupt practices and the transfer of assets of illicit origin, as well as for asset recovery consistent with the principles of the United Nations Convention against Corruption, particularly chapter V;

9. *Encourages* Member States to provide adequate financial and human resources to the United Nations

Office on Drugs and Crime, and further encourages the Office to give high priority to technical cooperation, upon request, inter alia, to promote and facilitate the signing and ratification, acceptance, approval or accession and the implementation of the United Nations Convention against Corruption, including the early finalization, in cooperation with the United Nations Interregional Crime and Justice Research Institute, of the legislative guide for the ratification and implementation of the Convention;

10. *Reiterates its request* to the international community to provide, inter alia, technical assistance to support national efforts to strengthen human and institutional capacity aimed at preventing and combating corrupt practices and the transfer of assets of illicit origin as well as for asset recovery consistent with the principles of the United Nations Convention against Corruption, particularly chapter V, and formulating strategies for mainstreaming and promoting transparency and integrity in both the public and the private sectors;

11. *Urges* all Member States, consistent with the United Nations Convention against Corruption, to abide by the principles of proper management of public affairs and public property, fairness, responsibility and equality before the law and the need to safeguard integrity and to foster a culture of transparency, accountability and rejection of corruption;

12. *Calls upon* the private sector, at both the international and the national levels, including small and large companies and transnational corporations, to remain fully engaged in the fight against corruption, welcomes the agreement to add anti-corruption as the tenth principle of the Global Compact, and emphasizes the need for all relevant stakeholders, including within the United Nations system, as appropriate, to continue to promote corporate responsibility and accountability;

13. *Encourages* all Member States that have not yet done so to require financial institutions to properly implement comprehensive due diligence and vigilance programmes, consistent with the principles of the United Nations Convention against Corruption and other applicable instruments, that could facilitate transparency and prevent the placement of illicitly acquired funds;

14. *Also encourages* Member States, relevant international organizations and the United Nations Office on Drugs and Crime to give prominence to 9 December as International Anti-Corruption Day, as established by the General Assembly in its resolution 58/4;

15. *Requests* the Secretary-General to submit to the General Assembly at its sixtieth session a report on the implementation of the present resolution and on the impact of corruption in all its forms, including on the scale of transfers of assets of illicit origin and the impact of corruption and such outflows on economic growth and sustainable development.

Money laundering

ECONOMIC AND SOCIAL COUNCIL ACTION

On 21 July [meeting 47], the Economic and Social Council, on the recommendation of the Commission on Crime Prevention and Criminal Justice

[E/2004/30], adopted **resolution 2004/29** without vote [agenda item 14 *(c)*].

Strengthening international cooperation and technical assistance in combating money laundering

The Economic and Social Council,

Bearing in mind the United Nations Convention against Illicit Traffic in Narcotic Drugs and Psychotropic Substances of 1988, the International Convention for the Suppression of the Financing of Terrorism, the United Nations Convention against Transnational Organized Crime and the United Nations Convention against Corruption,

Taking into account the activities of the Financial Action Task Force on Money Laundering, in particular its Forty Recommendations and eight Special Recommendations on Terrorist Financing, and those of similar regional bodies, such as the Egmont Group of Financial Intelligence Units,

Considering that multilateral action against the contemporary global phenomenon of transnational organized crime and its unlawful activities, including in particular trafficking in drugs, arms and human beings, money-laundering, corruption and the financing of terrorism, is important and involves shared responsibility and coordinated action by States in order to obtain greater coherence in conformity with relevant multilateral instruments,

Recognizing that the laundering of the proceeds of crime has spread internationally and in that way has become a worldwide threat to the stability and security of financial and commercial systems, including governmental structures, and that finding a solution to the problems stemming from organized crime and the proceeds of crime requires joint measures on the part of the international community,

Stressing the need for sufficient harmonization of the legislation of States so as to allow for a satisfactory level of coordination of their efforts for the prevention, control, investigation and suppression of money-laundering, including money-laundering related to the financing of terrorism and other criminal activities,

Recognizing that effective action against money-laundering requires strengthened international cooperation and the use of systems that facilitate collaboration and the exchange of information among the competent authorities in the States concerned,

Recognizing also the strategic need for States to possess an infrastructure suited to the conduct of financial analyses and investigations for a coordinated fight against money-laundering and the financing of transnational organized crime and of terrorism, using national, regional and international strategies,

Recognizing further the work carried out by the United Nations Office on Drugs and Crime, especially the Global Programme against Money-Laundering, as a centre for the coordination and provision of technical assistance in that regard,

Reiterating the importance of establishing national plans or strategies for combating the laundering of the proceeds of crime,

1. *Urges* Member States that have not yet done so to strengthen their capacity to prevent, control, investigate and suppress serious crimes related to money-laundering, including money-laundering related to

the financing of terrorism and, in general, any criminal action connected with transnational organized crime;

2. *Also urges* Member States that have not yet done so to establish financial intelligence units or to strengthen those already in existence and to provide them with the administrative, legal and technical resources needed to make progress in their work, with a view to enhancing their capacity to prevent, detect and control money-laundering, including money-laundering related to the financing of terrorism;

3. *Recommends* to Member States that they hold consultations with the United Nations Office on Drugs and Crime and other relevant bodies when drafting legislation against money-laundering in order to ensure that it is in conformity with applicable international instruments and relevant standards;

4. *Requests* the United Nations Office on Drugs and Crime to continue its work against money-laundering, subject to the availability of extrabudgetary resources and in cooperation with relevant regional and international organizations participating in activities designed to give effect to applicable international instruments and relevant standards for combating money-laundering, through the provision to Member States, upon request, of training, advisory assistance and long-term technical assistance, bearing in mind, inter alia, the Forty Recommendations and eight Special Recommendations on Terrorist Financing of the Financial Action Task Force on Money Laundering and the work of similar regional bodies;

5. *Encourages* Member States and the relevant international organizations to contribute to the mobilization of resources in order to strengthen the capacity of the United Nations Office on Drugs and Crime to provide technical assistance.

International commercial fraud

ECONOMIC AND SOCIAL COUNCIL ACTION

On 21 July [meeting 47], the Economic and Social Council, on the recommendation of the Commission on Crime Prevention and Criminal Justice [E/2004/30], adopted **resolution 2004/26** without vote [agenda item 14(c)].

International cooperation in the prevention, investigation, prosecution and punishment of fraud, the criminal misuse and falsification of identity and related crimes

The Economic and Social Council,

Concerned at the proliferation of national and transnational cases of fraud and related economic crimes and the involvement of organized criminal groups, modern technologies and the criminal misuse and falsification of identity in such cases,

Convinced that forms of criminal misuse and falsification of identity such as the taking and criminal misuse of personal identifying information and the assumption of false identities constitute a significant and increasing problem related to fraud,

Convinced also that the criminal misuse and falsification of identity is commonly associated with other illicit activities, including money-laundering, of organized criminal groups, corruption and terrorism and

that the proceeds of fraud are used to finance such activities,

Concerned that the spread of modern information and communication technologies creates a vast range of new opportunities for fraud and the criminal misuse and falsification of identity, which in turn jeopardizes the legitimate use of such technologies and represents a threat to States seeking to use such technologies for development,

Recalling chapter XI of the report of the United Nations Commission on International Trade Law on its thirty-sixth session, in which the Commission considered that it would be useful to conduct a study of forms of commercial fraud and that it might be possible for the Commission on Crime Prevention and Criminal Justice to conduct such a study,

Recalling also the report on the Colloquium on International Commercial Fraud, convened by the United Nations Commission on International Trade Law and held in Vienna from 14 to 16 April 2004,

1. *Condemns* the perpetration of fraud, the criminal misuse and falsification of identity and other illicit activities supported thereby;

2. *Encourages* Member States that have not already done so:

(*a*) To prevent, detect, investigate, prosecute and punish fraud and the criminal misuse and falsification of identity through criminal law and other measures;

(*b*) To take into account the need to prevent and combat fraud and the criminal misuse and falsification of identity in the development and regulation of relevant domestic commercial, financial or other institutions and systems;

(*c*) To facilitate the identification, tracing, freezing, seizure and confiscation of the proceeds of fraud and the criminal misuse and falsification of identity;

3. *Encourages* Member States to cooperate with one another in efforts to prevent and combat fraud and the criminal misuse and falsification of identity, including through the United Nations Convention against Transnational Organized Crime and other appropriate international instruments, and to consider the review of domestic laws on fraud and the criminal misuse and falsification of identity, where necessary and appropriate, to facilitate such cooperation;

4. *Requests* the Secretary-General to convene, in consultation with regional groups and subject to the availability of extrabudgetary resources, an intergovernmental expert group, with representation based on the regional composition of the Commission on Crime Prevention and Criminal Justice and reflecting the diversity of legal systems and open to any Member State wishing to participate as an observer, to prepare a study on fraud and the criminal misuse and falsification of identity, including:

(*a*) The nature and extent of fraud and the criminal misuse and falsification of identity;

(*b*) Domestic and transnational trends in fraud and the criminal misuse and falsification of identity;

(*c*) The relationship between fraud, other forms of economic crime, the criminal misuse and falsification of identity and other illicit activities, including organized crime, money-laundering and terrorism;

(*d*) The prevention and control of fraud and the criminal misuse and falsification of identity using commercial and criminal law, criminal justice and other means, and how these can be harmonized;

(e) The particular problems posed by fraud and the criminal misuse and falsification of identity for developing countries and countries with economies in transition;

5. *Requests* the intergovernmental expert group to use the information gained by the study for the purpose of developing useful practices, guidelines or other materials in the prevention, investigation and prosecution of fraud and the criminal misuse and falsification of identity;

6. *Also requests* the intergovernmental expert group, in carrying out its work, to take into consideration the relevant work of the United Nations Commission on International Trade Law and other bodies where relevant and appropriate, bearing in mind the need to avoid duplication;

7. *Invites* Member States to cooperate with and assist the intergovernmental expert group in its work, including by the provision of relevant and appropriate policy, legislative, research and other materials and by the provision of data about the nature and scope of fraud, the criminal misuse and falsification of identity and related problems in each country;

8. *Also invites* Member States to make voluntary contributions in order to support the work of the intergovernmental expert group and to facilitate the participation of experts from developing countries therein;

9. *Invites* the Eleventh United Nations Congress on Crime Prevention and Criminal Justice, under the substantive item entitled "Economic and financial crimes: challenges to sustainable development" and at its Workshop on Measures to Combat Economic Crime, including Money-Laundering, to consider and discuss the issues of fraud and the criminal misuse and falsification of identity, and invites the intergovernmental expert group to take into account the results of those discussions in carrying out its work;

10. *Recommends* that the Secretary-General designate the United Nations Office on Drugs and Crime to serve as the secretariat for the intergovernmental expert group, in consultation with the secretariat of the United Nations Commission on International Trade Law;

11. *Requests* the Secretary-General to submit a progress report on the work of the intergovernmental expert group and the plan of work for the study to the Commission on Crime Prevention and Criminal Justice at its fourteenth session and to submit, in a timely manner, a substantive report containing the results of the study to the Commission at its fifteenth session or, if necessary, at its sixteenth session, for its consideration;

12. *Also requests* the Secretary-General to circulate, in advance, the report on the work of the intergovernmental expert group and the results of the study, including any useful practices, guidelines or other materials, to all Member States in all official languages, in order to seek their views on the results of the study and to reflect any views or concerns expressed in the final report to the Commission on Crime Prevention and Criminal Justice.

Terrorism

In March [E/CN.15/2004/8 & Add.1], the Secretary-General submitted a report on strengthening in-

ternational cooperation and technical assistance in preventing and combating terrorism, in response to General Assembly resolution 58/136 [YUN 2003, p. 1149]. The report reviewed the technical assistance activities of the Terrorism Prevention Branch of the Division for Treaty Affairs of UNODC, under its Global Programme against Terrorism, whose main focus was facilitating the ratification and implementation of 12 international conventions and protocols related to terrorism [YUN 2001, p. 69]. Assistance was provided to 73 countries through country-specific activities or regional workshops, benefiting more than 500 law makers and criminal justice officials. Two projects to strengthen the legal regime against terrorism were also implemented. UNODC, in cooperation with the International Centre for Criminal Law and Reform and Criminal Justice Policy, convened a meeting of experts (Cape Town, South Africa, 24-25 February) to consider the compilation of international legal instruments, declarations and models pertaining to terrorism, related forms of crime and international cooperation. The experts proposed guidelines for UNODC in the provision of technical assistance aimed at promoting implementation of the universal conventions and protocols related to terrorism. They suggested that the Secretariat should develop an implementation guide to update the legislative guide on the universal anti-terrorism conventions and protocols.

The Secretary-General also reported on the responses received as at 9 March from 38 countries and territories and 3 international organizations on the links between international terrorism and other forms of crime, including money-laundering, fraud, trafficking in illicit goods, corruption, falsification of official documents and the smuggling of migrants. UNODC also organized a meeting of experts (Cape Town, 26-27 February) on increasing synergy in the delivery of technical assistance to address terrorist involvement in other forms of crime.

On 11-12 March (Vienna), the Organization for Security and Cooperation in Europe, in cooperation with UNODC, hosted a follow-up meeting (see p. 76) to the Counter-Terrorism Committee meeting of 6 March 2003 [YUN 2003, p. 67]. In its declaration, annexed to the report, participants committed themselves to undertaking joint initiatives to strengthen cooperation.

In July [A/59/187], the Secretary-General, in response to General Assembly resolution 58/136 [YUN 2003, p. 1149], submitted a report on international cooperation and technical assistance in preventing and combating terrorism. The report reviewed the status of technical assistance activities of the Terrorism Prevention Branch of the

UNODC Division for Treaty Affairs and included an update on efforts to initiate joint activities with other relevant role players, and on information-sharing and awareness-raising. It also provided an overview of the responses received from Member States and international organizations on the nature of the links between terrorism and other forms of crime.

The main focus of technical cooperation projects on strengthening the legal regime against terrorism was on the provision of direct legal advisory services to States on the incorporation of the relevant provisions contained in the 12 anti-terrorism conventions and protocols, carried out in close consultation with the Counter-Terrorism Committee. Specific national actions developed with Governments and legislative drafting committees were established to study the provisions of the instruments and to make recommendations regarding ratification and implementation of the legislation. As at July 2004, direct country-specific assistance had been delivered to 43 countries. A number of regional and subregional workshops were held to allow countries to compare progress, share experiences and harmonize legislative efforts.

ECONOMIC AND SOCIAL COUNCIL ACTION

On 21 July [meeting 47], the Economic and Social Council, on the recommendation of the Commission on Crime Prevention and Criminal Justice [E/2004/30], adopted **resolution 2004/19** without vote [agenda item 14 (c)].

Strengthening international cooperation and technical assistance in promoting the implementation of the universal conventions and protocols related to terrorism within the framework of the activities of the United Nations Office on Drugs and Crime

The Economic and Social Council

Recommends to the General Assembly the adoption of the following draft resolution:

[For text, see General Assembly resolution 59/153 below.]

GENERAL ASSEMBLY ACTION

On 20 December [meeting 74], the General Assembly, on the recommendation of the Third Committee [A/59/494], adopted **resolution 59/153** without vote [agenda item 96].

Strengthening international cooperation and technical assistance in promoting the implementation of the universal conventions and protocols related to terrorism within the framework of the activities of the United Nations Office on Drugs and Crime

The General Assembly,

Recalling its relevant resolutions on the prevention and suppression of terrorism, as well as Security Council resolutions 1269(1999) of 19 October 1999, 1373 (2001) of 28 September 2001, 1377(2001) of 12 November 2001 and 1456(2003) of 20 January 2003,

Recalling also its resolution 56/1 of 12 September 2001, in which it strongly condemned the heinous acts of terrorism of 11 September 2001 and urgently called for international cooperation to prevent and eradicate acts of terrorism, and its resolution 57/27 of 19 November 2002, in which it also condemned those in Bali and Moscow, as well as Security Council resolutions 1450(2002) of 13 December 2002, 1465(2003) of 13 February 2003, 1516(2003) of 20 November 2003 and 1530(2004) of 11 March 2004 condemning in the strongest terms the bomb attacks in Kikambala, Kenya, in Bogotá, in Istanbul, Turkey, and in Madrid, respectively, and expressing its deepest sympathy and condolences to the victims of terrorist attacks and their families,

Condemning the acts of violence perpetrated in many parts of the world against humanitarian personnel and United Nations and associated personnel, in particular deliberate attacks, which are in violation of international humanitarian law as well as other international law that may be applicable, such as the attack against the headquarters of the United Nations Assistance Mission for Iraq in Baghdad on 19 August 2003,

Recalling its resolutions 58/136 and 58/140 of 22 December 2003, in which it, inter alia, encouraged the activities of the United Nations Office on Drugs and Crime within its mandates in the area of preventing terrorism by providing Member States, upon request, with technical assistance, specifically to implement the universal conventions and protocols related to terrorism, thereby strengthening international cooperation in preventing and combating terrorism, working in close coordination with the Security Council Committee established pursuant to resolution 1373(2001) concerning counter-terrorism (the Counter-Terrorism Committee) and the Office of Legal Affairs of the Secretariat, as well as with international, regional and subregional organizations and specialized agencies,

Mindful of its resolution 58/81 of 9 December 2003, in which it welcomed the efforts of the Terrorism Prevention Branch of the United Nations Office on Drugs and Crime to enhance, through its mandate, the capabilities of the United Nations in the prevention of terrorism and recognized, in the context of Security Council resolution 1373(2001), the role of the Branch in assisting States to become parties to and implement the relevant international conventions and protocols related to terrorism,

Recalling Security Council resolution 1535(2004) of 26 March 2004 concerning enhancement of the ability of the Counter-Terrorism Committee to monitor the implementation of Council resolution 1373(2001),

Recalling also the Vienna Declaration on Crime and Justice: Meeting the Challenges of the Twenty-first Century, which emanated from the Tenth United Nations Congress on the Prevention of Crime and the Treatment of Offenders, held in Vienna from 10 to 17 April 2000,

Noting with appreciation the issuance, in all the official languages of the United Nations, of the *Legislative Guide to the Universal Anti-Terrorism Conventions and Protocols*, which was reviewed by an expert group hosted by the International Institute of Higher Studies in Criminal Sciences in Siracusa, Italy, from 3 to 5 December 2002,

Noting with appreciation also the guidelines for technical assistance within the framework of international cooperation against terrorism, which were formulated and reviewed during an expert group meeting held in Cape Town, South Africa, from 24 to 27 February 2004,

Deeply concerned that acts of international terrorism continue to be perpetrated, endangering the lives and well-being of individuals worldwide, as well as the peace and security of all States,

Reaffirming its unequivocal condemnation of terrorism in all its forms and manifestations, wherever and by whomsoever committed, in accordance with the principles of the Charter of the United Nations, international law and the relevant international conventions,

Recalling that Member States must ensure that any measures taken to combat terrorism comply with all their obligations under international law and that such measures are adopted in accordance with international law, in particular international human rights, refugee and humanitarian law,

Mindful of the essential need to strengthen international, regional and subregional cooperation aimed at enhancing the national capacity of States to prevent and suppress effectively international terrorism in all its forms and manifestations,

1. *Commends* the United Nations Office on Drugs and Crime for its work in preventing and combating terrorism through the provision of technical assistance, in close consultation with the Counter-Terrorism Committee, for the implementation of Security Council resolution 1373(2001), in particular for the promotion of the ratification of, accession to and implementation of the universal conventions and protocols related to terrorism;

2. *Also commends* the United Nations Office on Drugs and Crime for its efforts to reinforce close cooperation with international, regional and subregional organizations, such as the Council of Europe, the International Monetary Fund, the Organization of American States, the Organization for Security and Cooperation in Europe and the World Bank, and the Counter-Terrorism Committee in preventing and combating terrorism, an example of which was the meeting held in follow-up to the Counter-Terrorism Committee special meeting of 6 March 2003, with participants from international, regional and subregional organizations, organized by the Organization for Security and Cooperation in Europe, in close cooperation with the United Nations Office on Drugs and Crime, in Vienna on 11 and 12 March 2004, which resulted in the Vienna Declaration of 12 March 2004;

3. *Welcomes* the regional and subregional workshops held in Antalya, Turkey, and in Bamako, Khartoum, London, San José and Vilnius to familiarize national experts and criminal justice officials with the requirements of Security Council resolution 1373 (2001) and the requirements for becoming parties to and implementing the universal conventions and protocols related to terrorism and international cooperation agreements, and encourages the Terrorism Prevention Branch of the United Nations Office on Drugs and Crime, in coordination with the Counter-Terrorism Committee and subject to the availability of extrabudgetary resources, to ensure proper follow-up

to those workshops, in cases where such follow-up is indicated by the participating States;

4. *Calls upon* Member States that have not yet done so to become parties to and to implement the universal conventions and protocols related to terrorism as soon as possible and, where appropriate, to request assistance to that end from the United Nations Office on Drugs and Crime, in coordination with the Counter-Terrorism Committee;

5. *Invites* Member States that are not yet parties to those instruments to make use of the *Legislative Guide to the Universal Anti-Terrorism Conventions and Protocols* in their efforts to incorporate the provisions of those instruments in their national legislation, and requests the Secretariat, subject to the availability of extrabudgetary resources, to develop the *Legislative Guide* further as a tool for the provision of technical assistance aimed at the implementation of the universal conventions and protocols related to terrorism;

6. *Requests* the Secretariat to submit the guidelines for technical assistance that were formulated and reviewed during the expert group meeting held in Cape Town, South Africa, from 24 to 27 February 2004 to the Eleventh United Nations Congress on Crime Prevention and Criminal Justice for discussion, with a view to consideration of the guidelines by the Commission on Crime Prevention and Criminal Justice at its subsequent session;

7. *Requests* the United Nations Office on Drugs and Crime to continue to work with international organizations, in particular specialized agencies and other relevant United Nations entities that undertake work that is complementary to that of the Office, in order to enhance synergies;

8. *Urges* Member States to continue working together, including on a regional and bilateral basis and in close cooperation with the United Nations, to prevent and combat acts of terrorism by strengthening international cooperation and technical assistance within the framework of Security Council resolutions 1373 (2001), 1377(2001) and 1456(2003), as well as the universal conventions and protocols related to terrorism, Council resolutions 1267(1999) of 15 October 1999, 1333(2000) of 19 December 2000, 1390(2002) of 16 January 2002, 1455(2003) of 17 January 2003, 1526 (2004) of 30 January 2004 and 1535(2004) and other relevant United Nations resolutions, and in accordance with the Charter of the United Nations and international law;

9. *Invites* Member States to examine ways and means to reinforce international cooperation in criminal justice matters pertaining to terrorism prevention during the Eleventh United Nations Congress on Crime Prevention and Criminal Justice with a view to enhancing global efforts in the fight against terrorism;

10. *Requests* the United Nations Office on Drugs and Crime, subject to the availability of extrabudgetary resources, to intensify its efforts to provide technical assistance, upon request, in preventing and combating terrorism through the implementation of the universal conventions and protocols related to terrorism, with particular emphasis on the need to coordinate its work with the Counter-Terrorism Committee and its Executive Directorate, including training of judicial and prosecutorial personnel, where appropri-

ate, in the proper implementation of the universal conventions and protocols related to terrorism;

11. *Also requests* the United Nations Office on Drugs and Crime to pursue an integrated, synergistic approach in the delivery of technical assistance to requesting States, taking into account the links that exist between terrorism and other forms of crime;

12. *Expresses its appreciation* to donor countries that have supported the Global Programme against Terrorism, through voluntary contributions to the United Nations Crime Prevention and Criminal Justice Fund or the United Nations Crime Prevention and Criminal Justice Programme network, and invites all Member States to make voluntary contributions to the Fund in order to allow the United Nations Office on Drugs and Crime to provide technical assistance to requesting Member States;

13. *Calls upon* Member States to strengthen, to the greatest extent possible, international cooperation in order to combat terrorism, including, when necessary, entering into bilateral treaties on extradition and mutual legal assistance;

14. *Recognizes* the need for the United Nations Office on Drugs and Crime, subject to the availability of extrabudgetary resources, to provide Member States, upon request, and in coordination with the Counter-Terrorism Committee, with technical assistance to strengthen international cooperation, including in international, national, regional and subregional forums, in terrorism-related criminal justice matters within the framework of the universal conventions and protocols and the relevant Security Council resolutions related to terrorism;

15. *Requests* the Secretary-General to convene, subject to the availability of extrabudgetary resources, an expert workshop, taking into account the need for adequate and equitable geographical representation, and open to any Member State wishing to participate as an observer, to examine and analyse problems encountered by criminal justice practitioners in affording mutual legal assistance and granting extradition for terrorist offences, with a view to identifying proven and promising practices and possible ways of facilitating international cooperation, taking into account information that Member States may wish to provide;

16. *Also requests* the Secretary-General to report to the General Assembly at its sixtieth session on the implementation of the present resolution.

On the same date, the General Assembly took note of the Secretary-General's report on strengthening international cooperation and technical assistance in preventing and combating terrorism (see p. 1125) (**decision 59/523**).

Trafficking in human organs

ECONOMIC AND SOCIAL COUNCIL ACTION

On 21 July [meeting 47], the Economic and Social Council, on the recommendation of the Commission on Crime Prevention and Criminal Justice [E/2004/30], adopted resolution **2004/22** without vote [agenda item 14 *(c)*].

Preventing, combating and punishing trafficking in human organs

The Economic and Social Council

Recommends to the General Assembly the adoption of the following draft resolution:

[For text, see General Assembly resolution 59/156 below.]

GENERAL ASSEMBLY ACTION

On 20 December [meeting 74], the General Assembly, on the recommendation of the Third Committee [A/59/494], adopted **resolution 59/156** without vote [agenda item 96].

Preventing, combating and punishing trafficking in human organs

The General Assembly,

Recalling its resolution 53/111 of 9 December 1998, by which it established an open-ended intergovernmental ad hoc committee for the purpose of elaborating a comprehensive international convention against transnational organized crime and of discussing the elaboration, as appropriate, of international instruments addressing trafficking in women and children, combating illicit manufacturing of and trafficking in firearms, their parts and components and ammunition, and illegal trafficking in and transporting of migrants, including by sea,

Recalling also its resolution 55/25 of 15 November 2000, by which it adopted the United Nations Convention against Transnational Organized Crime, the Protocol to Prevent, Suppress and Punish Trafficking in Persons, Especially Women and Children, supplementing the United Nations Convention against Transnational Organized Crime, and the Protocol against the Smuggling of Migrants by Land, Sea and Air, supplementing the United Nations Convention against Transnational Organized Crime,

Recalling further its resolution 55/255 of 31 May 2001, by which it adopted the Protocol against the Illicit Manufacturing of and Trafficking in Firearms, Their Parts and Components and Ammunition, supplementing the United Nations Convention against Transnational Organized Crime,

Concerned about the negative economic and social implications of the activities of organized crime and the possible expansion of such crime, such as trafficking in human organs,

Alarmed at the potential growth of exploitation by criminal groups of human needs, poverty and destitution for the purpose of trafficking in human organs, using violence, coercion and kidnapping, especially kidnapping of children, with a view to exploiting them by means of organ transplant operations,

Noting with concern that trafficking in human organs, wherever it occurs, constitutes a gross violation of the human rights, including the integrity, of its victims,

Convinced of the need to strengthen local, regional and international cooperation in effective prevention and combating of such activities wherever they occur,

Determined to prevent the provision of safe haven to those who participate in or profit from transnational organized crime and to prosecute such persons for the crimes they commit,

Deploring the commercialization of the human body,

1. *Urges* Member States, should they ascertain that such a phenomenon exists in their country, to adopt the necessary measures to prevent, combat and punish the illicit removal of and trafficking in human organs;

2. *Encourages* Member States to exchange experience in and information on preventing, combating and punishing the illicit removal of and trafficking in human organs;

3. *Requests* the Eleventh United Nations Congress on Crime Prevention and Criminal Justice to pay attention to the issue of the illicit removal of and trafficking in human organs;

4. *Requests* the Secretary-General, in collaboration with the States and organizations concerned and subject to the availability of extrabudgetary resources, to prepare a study on the extent of the phenomenon of trafficking in human organs for submission to the Commission on Crime Prevention and Criminal Justice at its fifteenth session.

Kidnapping

In March [E/CN.15/2004/7 & Add.1], the Secretary-General, in response to Economic and Social Council resolution 2003/28 [YUN 2003, p. 1153], submitted a report on "international cooperation in the prevention, combating and elimination of kidnapping and in providing assistance to victims". The report summarized the replies received from an additional eight Member States to a survey on the practice and extent of kidnapping, which related to legal provisions, types and extent of kidnapping and measures adopted to counter it. It also outlined the key findings of a consultative meeting on best practices (Mexico City, October 2003).

The Secretary-General recommended that attempts should be made to: harmonize the definition of kidnapping used in various jurisdictions; monitor global levels of kidnapping and its connection to organized crime; increase the debate between States as to measures that had proved successful in combating the problem; and develop a law enforcement manual on prevention and counter-kidnapping techniques and its promotion through the Internet. The Secretariat should be authorized to prepare the manual and submit proposals to the Eleventh United Nations Congress on Crime Prevention and Criminal Justice in 2005 (see p. 1108).

ECONOMIC AND SOCIAL COUNCIL ACTION

On 21 July [meeting 47], the Economic and Social Council, on the recommendation of the Commission on Crime Prevention and Criminal Justice [E/2004/30], adopted **resolution 2004/20** without vote [agenda item 14 (c)].

International cooperation in the prevention, combating and elimination of kidnapping and in providing assistance to victims

The Economic and Social Council

Recommends to the General Assembly the adoption of the following draft resolution:

[For text, see General Assembly resolution 59/154 below.]

GENERAL ASSEMBLY ACTION

On 20 December [meeting 74], the General Assembly, on the recommendation of the Third Committee [A/59/494], adopted **resolution 59/154** without vote [agenda item 96].

International cooperation in the prevention, combating and elimination of kidnapping and in providing assistance to victims

The General Assembly,

Concerned at the increase in the practice of kidnapping in various countries of the world and at the harmful effects of that crime on victims and their families, and determined to support measures to assist and protect them and to promote their recovery,

Reiterating that the kidnapping of persons under any circumstances and for any purpose constitutes a serious crime and a violation of individual freedom and undermines human rights,

Noting the transnational nature of organized crime and the tendency of organized criminal groups and terrorist groups to expand their illegal operations,

Concerned at the growing tendency of organized criminal groups and terrorist groups to resort to kidnapping, especially for the purpose of extortion, as a method of accumulating capital with a view to consolidating their criminal operations and undertaking other illegal activities, such as trafficking in firearms and drugs, money-laundering and crimes related to terrorism,

Convinced that the links between various illegal activities, including terrorism, and organized crime pose an additional threat to security and the quality of life, hindering economic and social development,

Convinced also that the United Nations Convention against Transnational Organized Crime provides the legal framework necessary for international cooperation in the fight against kidnapping,

Recalling Economic and Social Council resolution 2003/28 of 22 July 2003 entitled "International cooperation in the prevention, combating and elimination of kidnapping and in providing assistance to victims", in which the Council requested the Secretary-General, drawing on extrabudgetary funds or voluntary contributions, to provide technical assistance to States, upon request, to enable them to strengthen their capacity to combat kidnapping, and to submit a progress report on that topic to the Commission on Crime Prevention and Criminal Justice at its thirteenth session,

1. *Vigorously condemns and rejects once again* the practice of kidnapping, under any circumstances and for any purpose, especially when it is carried out by organized criminal groups and terrorist groups;

2. *Reiterates* that organized criminal groups and terrorist groups, as well as all perpetrators, are responsible for any harm or death that may result from a kid-

napping for which they are responsible and should be punished accordingly;

3. *Takes note with appreciation* of the report of the Secretary-General and of the recommendations presented therein, submitted pursuant to Economic and Social Council resolutions 2002/16 of 24 July 2002 and 2003/28;

4. *Encourages* Member States to continue to foster international cooperation, especially extradition, mutual legal assistance, collaboration between law enforcement authorities and exchange of information, with a view to preventing, combating and eradicating kidnapping;

5. *Calls upon* Member States that have not yet done so, in furtherance of the fight against kidnapping, to strengthen their measures against money-laundering and to engage in international cooperation and mutual assistance in, inter alia, the tracing, detection, freezing and confiscation of proceeds of kidnapping in order to combat organized criminal groups and terrorist groups;

6. *Urges* Member States that have not yet done so to pay special attention to the considerable psychological, social and economic damage associated with kidnapping by adopting legislative, administrative or any other measures to provide appropriate support and assistance to victims and their families;

7. *Requests* the United Nations Office on Drugs and Crime, subject to the availability of extrabudgetary resources, to prepare a handbook, for use by competent authorities, of proven and promising practices in the fight against kidnapping, including:

(a) Measures to prevent the crime of kidnapping that are directed at potential victims;

(b) Preventive measures aimed at disbanding organized criminal groups and terrorist groups;

(c) Cooperation or strategic alliances with the private sector;

(d) Response to and management of crises;

(e) Identification of the minimum elements that would help States to make adjustments to their domestic legislation with a view to having a common understanding of the crime of kidnapping, which would also help to ascertain reliable trends from a global perspective;

(f) Development of specialized measures for providing support and assistance to victims and their families;

(g) Information on national authorities responsible for preventing and combating kidnapping;

(h) Reporting procedures, rescue operations, information systems and prosecutions;

8. *Also requests* the United Nations Office on Drugs and Crime, subject to the availability of extrabudgetary resources, to provide technical assistance to States, upon request, to enable them to strengthen their capacity to combat kidnapping, including:

(a) Training of judges, prosecutors and other law enforcement officials in mechanisms for disbanding criminal organizations and in the use of special investigative techniques for the rescue of kidnapped persons, bearing in mind the particular need to safeguard and protect the victims;

(b) Review of trends and greater understanding of the problem in order to create a basis for developing policies and strategies against kidnapping.

Urban crime

In response to Economic and Social Council resolution 2003/26 [YUN 2003, p. 1154], the Secretary-General submitted a March report [E/CN.15/2004/12 & Add.1] on good practices in crime prevention, which discussed the preparation of a UN manual on the use and application of the Guidelines for the Prevention of Crime, accepted by the Council in resolution 2002/13, annex [YUN 2002, p. 1126], the modalities of which were agreed at a meeting of experts (Durban, South Africa, 28 November 2003). The experts agreed that every effort should be made to finalize the draft for discussion at a workshop on crime prevention at the Eleventh Congress on Crime Prevention and Criminal Justice in 2005.

Under the project approved by the General Assembly in resolution 58/271 A [YUN 2003, p. 1414], on South-South regional cooperation for promoting good practices for crime prevention in the developing world, the first meeting of crime prevention experts from South Africa and the Southern African Regional Police Chiefs Cooperation organization with their Caribbean counterparts was held (Kingston, Jamaica, 13-14 February) in conjunction with the Third Caribbean Conference on Crime and Criminal Justice (Kingston, 11-14 February). Participants discussed community policing, prevention of violence, conflict resolution and reintegration of offenders. They agreed to set up a website to be hosted and maintained by the Institute for Security Studies, in Pretoria, South Africa, for the exchange of information. UNODC also organized, with the Permanent Mission of Hungary to the United Nations (Vienna), a workshop (February) to discuss the Hungarian National Strategy for Social Crime Prevention.

The report also contained replies from eight Member States and two organizations on the implementation of resolution 2003/26.

ECONOMIC AND SOCIAL COUNCIL ACTION

On 21 July [meeting 47], the Economic and Social Council, on the recommendation of the Commission on Crime Prevention and Criminal Justice [E/2004/30], adopted **resolution 2004/31** without vote [item 14 (c)].

Prevention of urban crime

The Economic and Social Council,

Recalling its resolution 2003/26 of 22 July 2003 on the prevention of urban crime, in which it called upon all relevant United Nations organizations and bodies and international financial institutions to give appropriate consideration to the inclusion of urban crime prevention and law enforcement projects in their assistance programmes,

Recalling also the Declaration on Cities and Other Human Settlements in the New Millennium adopted by the General Assembly in its resolution S-25/2 of 9 June 2001, in which the Assembly reaffirmed that the Istanbul Declaration on Human Settlements and the Habitat Agenda would remain the basic framework for sustainable human settlement development in the years to come,

Concerned about the seriousness of violent crimes in cities all over the world, which generates a fear of crime and has an impact on sustainable economic development, the quality of life and human rights,

Recalling that it had requested the United Nations Office on Drugs and Crime and the United Nations Human Settlements Programme (UN-Habitat) to prepare proposals for the provision of technical assistance in the area of crime prevention in accordance with the Guidelines for the Prevention of Crime, including through capacity-building and training,

Recalling also that the United Nations Human Settlements Programme and the United Nations Office on Drugs and Crime have explored areas of mutual interest in order to collaborate in the betterment of good urban governance with a view to achieving the goals and targets of the United Nations Millennium Declaration, including linking urban safety and urban governance, developing a conceptual understanding and tools in relation to the role of local authorities in crime prevention, examining local manifestations of transnational organized crime and developing new forms of justice, policing and policies targeting groups at risk, in particular children, youth and women,

Taking note of the memorandum of understanding between the United Nations Office on Drugs and Crime and the United Nations Human Settlements Programme aimed at establishing a framework for collaboration, and noting that bilateral consultations have taken place and a programme of work has been developed,

Noting the progress made by Member States in establishing effective policies and programmes in urban crime prevention, and encouraging increased sharing of experience,

1. *Welcomes* the initiative of the United Nations Human Settlements Programme (UN-Habitat) to collaborate with the United Nations Office on Drugs and Crime on technical assistance in relation to crime prevention, including the links between local and transnational organized crime, through operational projects, joint workshops and the compilation of useful practices and guidelines;

2. *Also welcomes* the fact that due attention will be given to the issue of urban crime at the Eleventh United Nations Congress on Crime Prevention and Criminal Justice in the Workshop on Strategies and Best Practices for Crime Prevention, in particular in relation to Urban Crime and Youth at Risk;

3. *Takes note* of the Safer Cities Programme of the United Nations Human Settlements Programme, and encourages municipalities to join the related network;

4. *Welcomes* the initiative of the United Nations Office on Drugs and Crime to establish, for developing countries, a database of good and promising practices in the area of urban crime prevention, in coordination with the United Nations Human Settlements Programme and the relevant institutes of the United Nations Crime Prevention and Criminal Justice Programme network;

5. *Encourages* the United Nations Office on Drugs and Crime to develop its knowledge and tools pertaining to the role of local authorities in the prevention of crime through the development of specific measures targeting groups at risk, in particular children and youth;

6. *Invites* Member States to make or increase voluntary contributions, as appropriate, to the United Nations Crime Prevention and Criminal Justice Fund, as well as to make or increase contributions in direct support of activities and projects, including through contributions to the institutes of the United Nations Crime Prevention and Criminal Justice Programme network, in order to strengthen further the capacity of the United Nations Office on Drugs and Crime to provide technical assistance;

7. *Requests* the United Nations Office on Drugs and Crime, subject to the availability of extrabudgetary resources, to provide technical assistance to States, upon request, in collaboration with other relevant entities, in the area of urban crime prevention;

8. *Calls once again upon* all relevant United Nations organizations and bodies and international financial institutions to give appropriate consideration to the inclusion of urban crime prevention and law enforcement projects in their programmes of assistance.

UN standards and norms

The Intergovernmental Expert Group Meeting on United Nations Standards and Norms in Crime Prevention and Criminal Justice (Vienna, 23-25 March) [E/CN.15/2004/9/Add.1], convened pursuant to Economic and Social Council resolution 2003/30 [YUN 2003, p. 1155], adopted a draft resolution on standards and norms in crime prevention and criminal justice, which it recommended to the Commission on Crime Prevention and Criminal Justice. The meeting reviewed the four draft instruments for gathering information on standards and norms primarily related to persons in custody, non-custodial sanctions, and juvenile and restorative justice, and adopted the revised instruments for submission to the Commission at its 2004 session (see p. 1110). It also reviewed the standards and norms related to legal, institutional and practical arrangements for international cooperation and concluded that because they took the form of model treaties they could not be effectively assessed through information-gathering instruments. However, the meeting stressed the importance of keeping the development of those instruments under review.

The Secretary-General submitted to the Commission an April report [A/CN.15/2004/9] on UN standards and norms in crime prevention and criminal justice, in response to Council resolution 2003/30. The report summarized the replies from Member States and non-governmental organizations relating to the implementation of that resolution and the outcome of the intergovernmental expert group meeting (see above). It provided an overview of activities undertaken to disseminate UN standards and norms in crime prevention and criminal justice and described advisory services and technical cooperation delivered.

ECONOMIC AND SOCIAL COUNCIL ACTION

On 21 July [meeting 47], the Economic and Social Council, on the recommendation of the Commission on Crime Prevention and Criminal Justice [E/2004/30], adopted **resolution 2004/28** without vote [agenda 14 (*c*)].

United Nations standards and norms in crime prevention and criminal justice

The Economic and Social Council,

Recalling the United Nations Millennium Declaration, contained in General Assembly resolution 55/2 of 8 September 2000, in which the Assembly resolved to strengthen respect for the rule of law in international as in national affairs and to make the United Nations more effective in maintaining peace and security by giving it the resources and tools it needed for conflict prevention, peaceful resolution of disputes, peacekeeping, post-conflict peace-building and reconstruction,

Mindful of the report of 21 August 2000 of the Panel on United Nations Peace Operations and the discussions on justice and the rule of law held by the Security Council,

Noting the leading role of the Department of Peacekeeping Operations of the Secretariat, among other entities, in providing assistance to countries in post-conflict situations,

Recognizing the critical importance of incorporating crime prevention and criminal justice components in post-conflict reconstruction, poverty alleviation and socio-economic development programmes in order to ensure economic progress and good governance,

Mindful of the importance for Member States and intergovernmental and non-governmental organizations to use and apply United Nations standards and norms in crime prevention and criminal justice as important international principles in developing an efficient and fair criminal justice system, in particular in circumstances where the basic tenets of the rule of law are ineffective or absent or in post-conflict reconstruction,

Recalling its resolution 1993/34 of 27 July 1993, in particular section III, paragraph 7 (*c*) thereof, in which it requested the Secretary-General to commence without delay a process of information-gathering to be undertaken by means of surveys, such as reporting systems, and contributions from other sources,

Recalling also its resolution 2002/15 of 24 July 2002, in which it reaffirmed the importance of United Nations standards and norms in crime prevention and criminal justice, including in the framework of peacekeeping and post-conflict reconstruction,

Recalling further its resolution 2003/30 of 22 July 2003, in which it decided to group United Nations standards and norms in crime prevention and criminal

justice into four categories for the purpose of targeted collection of information, in order to better identify the specific needs of Member States and to provide an analytical framework with a view to improving technical cooperation,

Reaffirming the important role of intergovernmental and non-governmental organizations in contributing to the effective use and application of United Nations standards and norms in crime prevention and criminal justice,

Desirous of reforming and streamlining the current process of information-gathering with regard to the application of United Nations standards and norms in crime prevention and criminal justice, in order to make it more efficient and cost-effective,

Wishing to streamline the provision of technical assistance in the use and application of United Nations standards and norms in crime prevention and criminal justice,

1. *Takes note* of the report of the Secretary-General on United Nations standards and norms in crime prevention and criminal justice;

2. *Also takes note* of the report of the Intergovernmental Expert Group Meeting on United Nations Standards and Norms in Crime Prevention and Criminal Justice held in Vienna from 23 to 25 March 2004;

3. *Notes* the work undertaken by the Intergovernmental Expert Group Meeting on United Nations Standards and Norms in Crime Prevention and Criminal Justice;

4. *Expresses its gratitude* to the Government of Canada for its financial support in the organization of the Intergovernmental Expert Group Meeting and to the European Institute for Crime Prevention and Control, affiliated with the United Nations, for assisting in the preparation of the information-gathering instruments for the first category of United Nations standards and norms in crime prevention and criminal justice;

5. *Takes note* of the instruments for gathering information on United Nations standards and norms related primarily to persons in custody, non-custodial sanctions and juvenile and restorative justice, as revised by the Intergovernmental Expert Group Meeting;

6. *Requests* the Secretary-General to forward the information-gathering instruments referred to in paragraph 5 above to Member States, intergovernmental and non-governmental organizations and the institutes of the United Nations Crime Prevention and Criminal Justice Programme network and other United Nations entities for their comments;

7. *Also requests* the Secretary-General to review the information-gathering instruments referred to in paragraph 5 above on the basis of the comments received and, following that review, to submit the revised instruments to an intersessional meeting of the Commission on Crime Prevention and Criminal Justice for approval;

8. *Invites* Member States to reply concerning the information-gathering instruments and to indicate their needs for technical assistance in the areas covered by the standards and norms referred to in paragraph 5 above;

9. *Requests* the Secretary-General to report to the Commission on Crime Prevention and Criminal Justice at its fifteenth session on the use and application of

the United Nations standards and norms referred to in paragraph 5 above, in particular as regards:

(*a*) The difficulties encountered in the application of the United Nations standards and norms in crime prevention and criminal justice;

(*b*) Ways in which technical assistance can be provided to overcome those difficulties;

(*c*) Useful practices in addressing persisting and emerging challenges in crime prevention and criminal justice;

10. *Invites* Member States to strengthen the human and financial resources available to the United Nations Office on Drugs and Crime in order to enable the Office to better assist States in conducting seminars, workshops, training programmes and other activities aimed at promoting the use and application of the United Nations standards and norms in crime prevention and criminal justice;

11. *Requests* the Secretary-General to assist Member States, upon request, subject to the availability of extrabudgetary resources, in the use and application of United Nations standards and norms in crime prevention and criminal justice through the development and implementation of technical assistance projects aimed at criminal justice reform;

12. *Requests* the United Nations Office on Drugs and Crime to continue to work with the Department of Peacekeeping Operations of the Secretariat and other relevant entities responsible for providing assistance to countries in post-conflict situations and, subject to the availability of extrabudgetary resources, to strengthen its capacity to provide technical assistance and advisory services to post-conflict reconstruction efforts by utilizing the instruments for gathering information on United Nations standards and norms in crime prevention and criminal justice to obtain data that will assist in integrating a crime prevention and criminal justice component into those activities;

13. *Requests* the Secretary-General to keep the development of legal, institutional and practical arrangements for international cooperation under review, through appropriate mechanisms such as, subject to the availability of extrabudgetary resources, the revision of the manuals on extradition and mutual legal assistance and preparation of model laws, in order to make international cooperation and technical assistance more effective;

14. *Invites* the Eleventh United Nations Congress on Crime Prevention and Criminal Justice, to be held in Bangkok from 18 to 25 April 2005, under the agenda item "Making standards work: fifty years of standard-setting in crime prevention and criminal justice", to address the issues raised in the present resolution with a view to consolidating and making more effective the action of United Nations and other intergovernmental and non-governmental organizations in this field;

15. *Requests* the Secretary-General to convene a meeting of intergovernmental experts, with representation based on the regional composition of the Commission on Crime Prevention and Criminal Justice and open to observers, subject to the availability of extrabudgetary resources, in cooperation with the institutes of the United Nations Crime Prevention and Criminal Justice Programme network, to design information-gathering instruments on the following categories of United Nations standards and norms:

(*a*) Standards and norms related to legal, institutional and practical arrangements for international cooperation, wherever feasible;

(*b*) Standards and norms related primarily to crime prevention and victim issues;

16. *Also requests* the Secretary-General to forward the information-gathering instruments referred to in paragraph 15 above to Member States, intergovernmental and non-governmental organizations and the institutes of the United Nations Crime Prevention and Criminal Justice Programme network and other United Nations entities for their comments;

17. *Further requests* the Secretary-General to review the information-gathering instruments referred to in paragraph 15 above, on the basis of the comments received, and to present those instruments, together with his report on progress made in their preparation, to the Commission on Crime Prevention and Criminal Justice at its sixteenth session.

Guidelines on justice for child victims and witnesses

On 21 July [meeting 47], the Economic and Social Council, on the recommendation of the Commission on Crime Prevention and Criminal Justice [E/2004/30], adopted **resolution 2004/27** without vote [agenda item 14 (*c*)].

Guidelines on justice for child victims and witnesses of crime

The Economic and Social Council,

Recalling General Assembly resolution 40/34 of 29 November 1985, by which the Assembly adopted the Declaration of Basic Principles of Justice for Victims of Crime and Abuse of Power,

Recalling also the provisions of the Convention on the Rights of the Child, adopted by the General Assembly in its resolution 44/25 of 20 November 1989, in particular articles 3 and 39 thereof, as well as the provisions of the Optional Protocol to the Convention on the Rights of the Child on the sale of children, child prostitution and child pornography, adopted by the Assembly in its resolution 54/263 of 25 May 2000, in particular article 8 thereof,

Bearing in mind the relevant provisions of the Vienna Declaration on Crime and Justice: Meeting the Challenges of the Twenty-first Century, annexed to General Assembly resolution 55/59 of 4 December 2000, as well as the plans of action for the implementation of the Vienna Declaration, annexed to Assembly resolution 56/261 of 31 January 2002, in particular the plans of action on witnesses and victims of crime and juvenile justice,

Bearing in mind also the document entitled "A world fit for children", adopted by the General Assembly in its resolution S-27/2 of 10 May 2002,

Recalling its resolution 1996/16 of 23 July 1996, in which it requested the Secretary-General to continue to promote the use and application of United Nations standards and norms in crime prevention and criminal justice,

Mindful of the serious physical, psychological and emotional consequences of various forms of crime for the victims, especially child victims,

Recognizing that the participation of child victims and witnesses of crime in the criminal justice process is essential in order to prosecute effectively various forms of crime, including in cases of sexual exploitation of children, trafficking in children and other forms of transnational organized crime where children are often the only witnesses,

Mindful of the public interest in a fair trial based on reliable evidence and also of the susceptibility of child witnesses and victims to suggestion or coercion,

Mindful also of the fact that child victims and witnesses of crime require special protection, assistance and support appropriate to their age, level of maturity and individual special needs in order to prevent additional hardship caused to them as a result of their participation in the criminal justice process,

Emphasizing that United Nations standards and norms in crime prevention and criminal justice contribute to the body of declarations, treaties and other instruments spearheading criminal justice reform in Member States aimed at dealing effectively and humanely with any form of crime and its prevention worldwide,

Noting with appreciation the efforts of the International Bureau for Children's Rights in drawing up guidelines on justice for child victims and witnesses of crime, drafted together with a steering/drafting committee of renowned international experts in the area of child rights, criminal law and victimology,

1. *Requests* the Secretary-General to convene an intergovernmental expert group, with representation based on the regional composition of the Commission on Crime Prevention and Criminal Justice and open to any Member State wishing to participate as an observer, subject to the availability of extrabudgetary resources, in order to develop guidelines on justice in matters involving child victims and witnesses of crime;

2. *Requests* the intergovernmental expert group, within the context of its meeting, to take into consideration any relevant material, including the guidelines on justice for child victims and witnesses of crime drawn up by the International Bureau for Children's Rights, annexed to the present resolution;

3. *Invites* the Eleventh United Nations Congress on Crime Prevention and Criminal Justice, under the substantive item entitled "Making standards work: fifty years of standard-setting in crime prevention and criminal justice", during the Workshop on Enhancing Criminal Justice Reform, including Restorative Justice, and during the ancillary meetings of non-governmental and professional organizations, to consider and discuss the issue of guidelines on justice for child victims and witnesses of crime, and invites the intergovernmental expert group to take into account the results of those discussions in carrying out its work;

4. *Requests* the Secretary-General to submit to the Commission on Crime Prevention and Criminal Justice at its fifteenth session for its consideration and action a report on the results of the meeting of the intergovernmental expert group.

Annex

Guidelines on justice for child victims and witnesses of crime drawn up by the International Bureau for Children's Rights

I. Objectives and preamble

A. Objectives

1. The present guidelines on justice for child victims and witnesses of crime set forth good practice based on the consensus of contemporary knowledge and relevant international and regional norms, standards and principles.

2. The guidelines provide a practical framework to achieve the following objectives:

(a) To guide professionals and, where appropriate, volunteers working with child victims and witnesses of crime in their day-to-day practice in the adult and juvenile justice process at the national, regional and international levels, consistent with the Declaration of Basic Principles of Justice for Victims of Crime and Abuse of Power;

(b) To assist in the review of national and domestic laws, procedures and practices so that these ensure full respect for the rights of child victims and witnesses of crime and fully implement the Convention on the Rights of the Child;

(c) To assist Governments, international organizations, public agencies, non-governmental and community based organizations and other interested parties in designing and implementing legislation, policy, programmes and practices that address key issues related to child victims and witnesses of crime;

(d) To assist and support those caring for children in dealing sensitively with child victims and witnesses of crime.

3. Each jurisdiction will need to implement the present guidelines consistent with its legal, social, economic, cultural and geographical conditions. However, the jurisdiction should constantly endeavour to overcome practical difficulties in their application, as the guidelines are, in their entirety, a set of minimum acceptable principles and standards.

4. In implementing the guidelines, each jurisdiction must ensure that adequate training, selection and procedures are put in place to meet the special needs of child victims and witnesses of crime, where the nature of the victimization affects categories of children differently, such as sexual assault of girl children.

5. The guidelines cover a field in which knowledge and practice are growing and improving. They are neither intended to be exhaustive nor to preclude further development, provided it is in harmony with their underlying objectives and principles.

6. The guidelines should also be applied to processes in informal and customary systems of justice such as restorative justice and in non-criminal fields of law including, but not limited to, custody, divorce, adoption, child protection, mental health, citizenship, immigration and refugee law.

B. Considerations

7. The guidelines were developed:

(a) Cognizant that millions of children throughout the world suffer harm as a result of crime and abuse of power and that the rights of those children have not been adequately recognized and that they may suffer additional hardship when assisting in the justice process;

(b) Reaffirming that every effort must be made to prevent victimization of children, particularly through implementation of the Guidelines for the Prevention of Crime;

(c) Recalling that the Convention on the Rights of the Child sets forth requirements and principles to secure effective recognition of the rights of children and that the Declaration of Basic Principles of Justice for Victims of Crime and Abuse of Power sets forth principles to provide victims with the right to information, participation, protection, reparation and assistance;

(d) Stressing that all States parties to international and regional instruments have a duty to fulfil their obligations, including the implementation of the Convention on the Rights of the Child and its Protocols;

(e) Recalling international and regional initiatives that implement the principles of the Declaration of Basic Principles of Justice for Victims of Crime and Abuse of Power, including the *Handbook on Justice for Victims* and the *Guide for Policy Makers on the Declaration of Basic Principles*, both issued by the United Nations Office for Drug Control and Crime Prevention in 1999;

(f) Recognizing that children are vulnerable and require special protection appropriate to their age, level of maturity and individual special needs;

(g) Considering that improved responses to child victims and witnesses of crime can make children and their families more willing to disclose instances of victimization and more supportive of the justice process;

(h) Recalling that justice for child victims and witnesses of crime must be assured while safeguarding the rights of accused and convicted offenders, including those that focus on children in conflict with the law, such as the United Nations Standard Minimum Rules for the Administration of Juvenile Justice (the Beijing Rules);

(i) Bearing in mind the variety of legal systems and traditions, and noting that crime is increasingly transnational in nature and that there is a need to ensure that child victims and witnesses of crime receive equivalent protection in all countries.

C. Principles

8. In order to ensure justice for child victims and witnesses of crime, professionals and others responsible for the well-being of those children must respect the following cross-cutting principles as stated in other international instruments and in particular the Convention on the Rights of the Child, as reflected in the work of the Committee on the Rights of the Child:

(a) *Dignity*. Every child is a unique and valuable human being and as such his or her individual dignity, special needs, interests and privacy should be respected and protected;

(b) *Non-discrimination*. Every child has the right to be treated fairly and equally, regardless of his or her or the parent or legal guardian's race, ethnicity, colour, gender, language, religion, political or other opinion, national, ethnic or social origin, property, disability and birth or other status;

(c) *Best interests of the child*. Every child has the right to have his or her best interests given primary consideration. This includes the right to protection and to a chance for harmonious development:

(i) *Protection*. Every child has the right to life and survival and to be shielded from any form of hardship, abuse or neglect, including physical, psychological, mental and emotional abuse and neglect;

(ii) *Harmonious development*. Every child has the right to a chance for harmonious development and to a standard of living adequate for physical, mental, spiritual, moral and social growth. In the case of a child who has been traumatized, every step should be taken to enable the child to enjoy healthy development;

(d) *Right to participation*. Every child has the right to express his or her views, opinions and beliefs freely in all matters, in his or her own words, and to contribute especially to the decisions affecting his or her life, including those taken in any judicial processes, and to have those views taken into consideration.

D. Definitions

9. Throughout the present guidelines, the following definitions apply:

(a) "Child victims and witnesses" denotes children and adolescents, under the age of 18, who are victims of crime or witnesses to crime regardless of their role in the offence or in the prosecution of the alleged offender or groups of offenders;

(b) "Professionals" refers to persons who, within the context of their work, are in contact with child victims and witnesses of crime and for whom the present guidelines are applicable. This includes, but is not limited to, the following: child and victim advocates and support persons; child protection service practitioners; child welfare agency staff; prosecutors and defence lawyers; diplomatic and consular staff; domestic violence programme staff; judges; law enforcement officials; medical and mental health professionals; and social workers;

(c) "Justice process" encompasses detection of the crime, making of the complaint, investigation, prosecution and trial and post-trial procedures, regardless of whether the case is handled in a national, international or regional criminal justice system for adults or juveniles, or in a customary or informal system of justice;

(d) "Child-sensitive" denotes an approach that takes into account the child's individual needs and wishes.

II. Guidelines on justice for child victims and witnesses of crime

A. The right to be treated with dignity and compassion

10. Child victims and witnesses should be treated in a caring and sensitive manner throughout the justice process, taking into account their personal situation and immediate needs, age, gender, disability and level of maturity and fully respecting their physical, mental and moral integrity.

11. Every child should be treated as an individual with his or her individual needs, wishes and feelings. Professionals should not treat any child as a typical child of a given age or as a typical victim or witness of a specific crime.

12. Interference in the child's private life should be limited to the minimum needed at the same time as high standards of evidence collection are maintained in order to ensure fair and equitable outcomes of the justice process.

13. In order to avoid further hardship to the child, interviews, examinations and other forms of investigation should be conducted by trained professionals who proceed in a sensitive, respectful and thorough manner.

14. All interactions described in the present guidelines should be conducted in a child-sensitive and empathetic manner in a suitable environment that accommodates the special needs of the child. They should also take place in a language that the child uses and understands.

B. The right to be protected from discrimination

15. Child victims and witnesses should have access to a justice process that protects them from discrimination based on the child, parent or legal guardian's race, colour, sex, language, religion, political or other opinion, national, ethnic or social origin, property, disability and birth or other status.

16. The justice process and support services available to child victims and witnesses and their families should be sensitive to the child's age, wishes, understanding, gender, sexual orientation, ethnic, cultural, religious, linguistic and social background, caste, socio-economic condition and immigration or refugee status, as well as to the special needs of the child, including health, abilities and capacities. Professionals should be trained and educated about such differences.

17. In many cases, special services and protection will need to be instituted to take account of the different nature of specific offences against children, such as sexual assault involving girl children.

18. Age should not be a barrier to a child's right to participate fully in the justice process. Every child has the right to be treated as a capable witness and his or her testimony should be presumed valid and credible at trial unless proven otherwise and as long as his or her age and maturity allow the giving of intelligible testimony, with or without communication aids and other assistance.

C. The right to be informed

19. Child victims and witnesses, their families and their legal representatives, from their first contact with the justice process and throughout that process, have the right to be promptly informed of:

(*a*) The availability of health, psychological, social and other relevant services as well as the means of accessing such services along with legal or other advice or representation, compensation and emergency financial support, where applicable;

(*b*) The procedures for the adult and juvenile criminal justice process, including the role of child victims and witnesses, the importance, timing and manner of testimony, and ways in which "questioning" will be conducted during the investigation and trial;

(*c*) The progress and disposition of the specific case, including the apprehension, arrest and custodial status of the accused and any pending changes to that status, the prosecutorial decision and relevant post-trial developments and the outcome of the case;

(*d*) The existing support mechanisms for the child when making a complaint and participating in the investigation and court proceedings;

(*e*) The specific places and times of hearings and other relevant events;

(*f*) The availability of protective measures;

(*g*) The existing opportunities to obtain reparation from the offender or from the State through the justice process, through alternative civil proceedings or through other processes;

(*h*) The existing mechanisms for review of decisions affecting child victims and witnesses;

(*i*) The relevant rights for child victims and witnesses pursuant to the Convention on the Rights of the Child and the Declaration of Basic Principles of Justice for Victims of Crime and Abuse of Power.

D. The right to express views and concerns and to be heard

20. Professionals should make every effort to enable child victims and witnesses to express their views and concerns related to their involvement in the justice process.

21. Professionals should:

(*a*) Ensure that child victims and witnesses are consulted on the matters set forth in paragraph 19 above;

(*b*) Ensure that child victims and witnesses are enabled to express freely and in their own manner their views and concerns regarding their involvement in the justice process, their concerns regarding safety in relation to the accused, the manner in which they prefer to provide testimony and their feelings about the conclusions of the process.

22. Professionals should give due regard to the child's views and concerns and, if they are unable to accommodate them, should explain the reasons to the child.

E. The right to effective assistance

23. Child victims and witnesses and, where appropriate, family members should have access to assistance provided by professionals who have received relevant training as set out in paragraphs 41-43 below. This includes assistance and support services such as financial, legal, counselling, health and social services, physical and psychological recovery services, and other services necessary for the child's reintegration. All such assistance should address the child's needs and enable them to participate effectively at all stages of the justice process.

24. In assisting child victims and witnesses, professionals should make every effort to coordinate support so that the child is not subjected to excessive interventions.

25. Child victims and witnesses should receive assistance from support persons, such as child victim/witness specialists, commencing at the initial report and continuing until such services are no longer required.

26. Professionals should develop and implement measures to make it easier for children to give evidence and to improve communication and understanding at the pre-trial and trial stages. These measures may include:

(*a*) Child victim and witness specialists to address the child's special needs;

(*b*) Support persons, including specialists and appropriate family members to accompany the child during testimony;

(*c*) Guardians ad litem to protect the child's legal interests.

F. The right to privacy

27. Child victims and witnesses should have their privacy protected as a matter of primary importance.

28. Any information relating to a child's involvement in the justice process should be protected. This can be achieved through maintaining confidentiality and restricting disclosure of information that may lead to identification of a child who is a victim or witness in the justice process.

29. Where appropriate, measures should be taken to exclude the public and the media from the courtroom during the child's testimony.

G. The right to be protected from hardship during the justice process

30. Professionals should take measures to prevent hardship during the detection, investigation and prosecution process in order to ensure that the best interests and dignity of child victims and witnesses are respected.

31. Professionals should approach child victims and witnesses with sensitivity, so that they:

(a) Provide support for child victims and witnesses, including accompanying the child throughout his or her involvement in the justice process, when it is in his or her best interests;

(b) Provide certainty about the process, including providing child victims and witnesses with clear expectations as to what to expect in the process, with as much certainty as possible. The child's participation in hearings and trials should be planned ahead of time and every effort should be made to ensure continuity in the relationships between children and the professionals in contact with them throughout the process;

(c) Ensure speedy trials, unless delays are in the child's best interest. Investigation of crimes involving child victims and witnesses should also be expedited and there should be procedures, laws or court rules that provide for cases involving child victims and witnesses to be expedited;

(d) Use child-sensitive procedures, including interview rooms designed for children, interdisciplinary services for child victims integrated under one roof, modified court environments that take child witnesses into consideration, recesses during a child's testimony, hearings scheduled at times of day appropriate to the age and maturity of the child, an on-call system to ensure the child goes to court only when necessary and other appropriate measures to facilitate the child's testimony.

32. Professionals should also implement measures:

(a) To limit the number of interviews. Special procedures for collection of evidence from child victims and witnesses should be implemented in order to reduce the number of interviews, statements, hearings and, specifically, unnecessary contact with the justice process, such as through use of pre-recorded videos;

(b) To avoid unnecessary contacts with the alleged perpetrator, his or her defence team and other persons not directly related to the justice process. Professionals should ensure that child victims and witnesses are protected, if compatible with the legal system and with due respect for the rights of the defence, from being cross-examined by the alleged perpetrator. Wherever possible, and as necessary, child victims and witnesses should be interviewed, and examined in court, out of sight of the alleged perpetrator, and separate courthouse waiting rooms and private interview areas should be provided;

(c) To use testimonial aids to facilitate the child's testimony. Judges should give serious consideration to permitting the use of testimonial aids to facilitate the child's testimony and to reduce potential for intimidation of the child, as well as exercise supervision and take appropriate measures to ensure that child victims and witnesses are questioned in a child-sensitive manner.

H. The right to safety

33. Where the safety of a child victim or witness may be at risk, appropriate measures should be taken to require the reporting of those safety risks to appropriate authorities and to protect the child from such risk before, during and after the justice process.

34. Child-focused facility staff, professionals and other individuals who come into contact with children should be required to notify appropriate authorities if they suspect that a child victim or witness has been harmed, is being harmed or is likely to be harmed.

35. Professionals should be trained in recognizing and preventing intimidation, threats and harm to child victims and witnesses. Where child victims and witnesses may be the subject of intimidation, threats or harm, appropriate conditions should be put in place to ensure the safety of the child. Such safeguards could include:

(a) Avoiding direct contact between child victims and witnesses and the alleged perpetrators at any point in the justice process;

(b) Using court-ordered restraining orders supported by a registry system;

(c) Ordering pre-trial detention of the accused and setting special "no contact" bail conditions;

(d) Placing the accused under house arrest;

(e) Wherever possible, giving child victims and witnesses protection by the police or other relevant agencies and safeguarding their whereabouts from disclosure.

I. The right to reparation

36. Child victims and witnesses should, wherever possible, receive reparation in order to achieve full redress, reintegration and recovery. Procedures for obtaining and enforcing reparation should be readily accessible and child-sensitive.

37. Provided the proceedings are child-sensitive and respect the present guidelines, combined criminal and reparations proceedings should be encouraged, together with informal and community justice procedures such as restorative justice.

38. Reparation may include restitution from the offender ordered in the criminal court, aid from victim compensation programmes administered by the State and damages ordered to be paid in civil proceedings. Where possible, costs of social and educational reintegration, medical treatment, mental health care and legal services should be addressed. Procedures should be instituted to ensure automatic enforcement of reparation orders and payment of reparation before fines.

J. The right to special preventive measures

39. In addition to preventive measures that should be in place for all children, special strategies are re-

quired for child victims and witnesses who are particularly vulnerable to repeat victimization or offending.

40. Professionals should develop and implement comprehensive and specially tailored strategies and interventions in cases where there are risks that child victims may be victimized further. These strategies and interventions should take into account the nature of the victimization, including victimization related to abuse in the home, sexual exploitation, abuse in institutional settings and trafficking. The strategies may include those based on government, neighbourhood and citizen initiatives.

III. Implementation

A. Professionals should be trained and educated in the present guidelines in order to deal effectively and sensitively with child victims and witnesses

41. Adequate training, education and information should be made available to front-line professionals, criminal and juvenile justice officials, justice system practitioners and other professionals working with child victims and witnesses with a view to improving and sustaining specialized methods, approaches and attitudes.

42. Professionals should be selected and trained to meet the needs of child victims and witnesses, including in specialized units and services.

43. This training should include:

(a) Relevant human rights norms, standards and principles, including the rights of the child;

(b) Principles and ethical duties of their office;

(c) Signs and symptoms that point to evidence of crimes against children;

(d) Crisis assessment skills and techniques, especially for making referrals, with an emphasis placed on the need for confidentiality;

(e) Impact, consequences and trauma of crimes against children;

(f) Special measures and techniques to assist child victims and witnesses in the justice process;

(g) Cross-cultural and age-related linguistic, religious, social and gender issues;

(h) Appropriate adult-child communication skills;

(i) Interviewing and assessment techniques that minimize any trauma to the child while maximizing the quality of information received from the child;

(j) Skills to deal with child victims and witnesses in a sympathetic, understanding, constructive and reassuring manner;

(k) Methods to protect and present evidence and to question child witnesses;

(l) Roles of, and methods used by, professionals working with child victims and witnesses.

B. Professionals should cooperate in the implementation of the present guidelines so that child victims and witnesses are dealt with efficiently and effectively

44. Professionals should make every effort to adopt an interdisciplinary approach in aiding children by familiarizing themselves with the wide array of available services, such as victim support, advocacy, economic assistance, counselling, health, legal and social services. This approach may include protocols for the different stages of the justice process to encourage cooperation among entities that provide services to child victims and witnesses, as well as other forms of multi-

disciplinary work that includes police, prosecutor, medical, social services and psychological personnel working in the same location.

45. International cooperation should be enhanced between States and all sectors of society, both at the national and international levels, including mutual assistance for the purpose of facilitating collection and exchange of information and the detection, investigation and prosecution of transnational crimes involving child victims and witnesses.

C. The implementation of the guidelines should be monitored

46. Professionals should utilize the present guidelines as a basis for developing laws and written policies, standards and protocols aimed at assisting child victims and witnesses involved in the justice process.

47. Professionals should periodically review and evaluate their role, together with other agencies in the justice process, in ensuring the protection of the rights of the child and the effective implementation of the present guidelines.

Other crime prevention and criminal justice issues

HIV/AIDS in criminal justice

ECONOMIC AND SOCIAL COUNCIL ACTION

On 21 July [meeting 47], the Economic and Social Council, on the recommendation of the Commission on Crime and Criminal Justice [E/2004/30], adopted **resolution 2004/35** without vote [agenda item 14 (c)].

Combating the spread of HIV/AIDS in criminal justice pre-trial and correctional facilities

The Economic and Social Council,

Alarmed at the continuing spread of the HIV/AIDS epidemic in pre-trial and correctional facilities,

Recalling its resolution 1997/36 of 21 July 1997 on international cooperation for the improvement of prison conditions and its resolution 1999/27 of 28 July 1999 on penal reform,

Reaffirming its resolution 2002/15 of 24 July 2002 on United Nations standards and norms in crime prevention and criminal justice, in section II of which it invited Member States to undertake the necessary efforts to solve the problem of prison overcrowding,

Recalling General Assembly resolution 56/261 of 31 January 2001 on the plans of action for the implementation of the Vienna Declaration on Crime and Justice: Meeting the Challenges of the Twenty-first Century, in particular the plans of action on crime prevention, on prison overcrowding and alternatives to incarceration, on juvenile justice and on the special needs of women in the criminal justice system,

Recalling also the objectives related to HIV/AIDS contained in the United Nations Millennium Declaration,

Welcoming the Declaration of Commitment on HIV/AIDS adopted by the General Assembly at its twenty-sixth special session, on HIV/AIDS, in June 2001,

Acknowledging that HIV/AIDS is primarily, but not exclusively, a public health issue governed by the World

Health Organization and coordinated by the Joint United Nations Programme on HIV/AIDS, combining the efforts of the nine co-sponsoring agencies and programmes within the United Nations system, which formulate and coordinate policy responses to this global problem,

Taking into account that, within that framework, specific vulnerable groups, such as prisoners, merit particular attention and, as such, the United Nations Office on Drugs and Crime has an important role within the framework of its mandate in questions of standards and norms related to pre-trial and correctional facilities,

Recalling Commission on Narcotic Drugs resolutions 45/1 and 46/2 on strengthening strategies regarding the prevention of HIV/AIDS in the context of drug abuse, as well as its resolution 47/2 on prevention of HIV/AIDS among drug users,

Recalling also Commission on Human Rights resolution 2003/47 on the protection of human rights in the context of HIV/AIDS, in which the Commission urged Member States to ensure that their prison policies and practices respect human rights in the context of HIV/AIDS, prohibit HIV/AIDS-related discrimination and promote effective programmes for the prevention of HIV/AIDS in pre-trial and correctional facilities,

Recalling further the concerns of the Commission on Human Rights, reflected in its resolution 2004/26 on access to medication in the context of pandemics such as HIV/AIDS, tuberculosis and malaria,

Mindful that the physical and social conditions associated with imprisonment may facilitate the spread of HIV/AIDS in pre-trial and correctional facilities, and thus in society,

Deeply concerned at the potential role of pre-trial and correctional facilities as multipliers or "incubators" of the HIV/AIDS epidemic, as the findings of the report of the United Nations Development Programme entitled *Reversing the Epidemic: Facts and Policy Options* suggest,

Underlining the importance of the Standard Minimum Rules for the Treatment of Prisoners as guidelines for operating secure, safe and orderly pre-trial and correctional facilities, providing meaningful activities for prisoners, monitoring general prison conditions, ensuring an effective complaint system and providing for basic prisoner rights, including the right to adequate health care,

1. *Recognizes* that measures are needed to address overcrowding and to curb violence in pre-trial and correctional facilities;

2. *Invites* Member States to consider, where appropriate and in accordance with national legislation, the use of alternatives to imprisonment, as well as early release for prisoners with advanced AIDS;

3. *Recognizes* that effective HIV/AIDS prevention, care and treatment strategies require behavioural changes and increased availability of and non-discriminatory access to HIV/AIDS prevention, care and treatment, as well as increased research and development;

4. *Also recognizes* that prisoners have the right to adequate health care and that access to qualified medical personnel should be ensured;

5. *Suggests* that appropriate training should be given to managers and warders of pre-trial and correc-

tional facilities to enable them to deal better with HIV/AIDS;

6. *Requests* the United Nations Office on Drugs and Crime, subject to the availability of extrabudgetary resources, to work in coordination with the United Nations Joint Programme on HIV/AIDS, the World Health Organization and other relevant United Nations entities to collect information and analyse the situation of HIV/AIDS in pre-trial and correctional facilities, with a view to providing Governments with programmatic and policy guidance, within its mandate in relation to standards and norms concerning such facilities, building on lessons learned and taking into account existing guidelines and recommendations from previous and ongoing activities in various regions of the world;

7. *Encourages* the United Nations Office on Drugs and Crime, within its mandate in relation to standards and norms concerning pre-trial and correctional facilities, to offer advice and expertise to the United Nations Joint Programme on HIV/AIDS, the World Health Organization and other relevant United Nations entities in order to ensure that the particular problems of HIV/AIDS in such facilities are adequately addressed;

8. *Invites* Member States to make voluntary contributions to the United Nations Crime Prevention and Criminal Justice Fund, in direct support of activities and projects of the United Nations Office on Drugs and Crime related to prevention of HIV/AIDS in pre-trial and correctional facilities;

9. *Requests* the Secretary-General to report to the Commission on Crime Prevention and Criminal Justice at its fifteenth session on the implementation of the present resolution.

Second World Summit of Attorneys General and General Prosecutors, Chief Prosecutors and Ministers of Justice

ECONOMIC AND SOCIAL COUNCIL ACTION

On 21 July [meeting 47], the Economic and Social Council, on the recommendation of the Commission on Crime Prevention and Criminal Justice [E/2004/30], adopted **resolution 2004/30** without vote [agenda item 14 (*c*)].

Second World Summit of Attorneys General and General Prosecutors, Chief Prosecutors and Ministers of Justice

The Economic and Social Council,

Recalling its resolutions on the use and application of United Nations standards and norms in crime prevention and criminal justice, especially in relation to the Guidelines on the Role of Prosecutors,

Stressing the important role that law enforcement and criminal justice professionals, in particular prosecutors, should play in the implementation of the United Nations Convention against Transnational Organized Crime and the Protocols thereto, the United Nations Convention against Corruption and the twelve international legal instruments against terrorism,

Emphasizing the significance of promoting international cooperation in criminal matters, to which prosecutors can make a major contribution,

Aware of the outcome of the first World Summit of Attorneys General and General Prosecutors, Chief Prosecutors and Ministers of Justice, held in Guatemala from 2 to 5 February 2004, and the adoption of its declaration, which contains important recommendations for future action,

1. *Welcomes* the initiative of Qatar to act as host to the second World Summit of Attorneys General and General Prosecutors, Chief Prosecutors and Ministers of Justice, to be held in Doha in November 2005;

2. *Requests* the United Nations Office on Drugs and Crime, subject to the availability of extrabudgetary resources for that purpose, to assist the Government of Qatar in the preparation and substantive servicing of the Summit;

3. *Invites* the Summit to ensure that its programme is targeted to further strengthening international cooperation in criminal matters, taking into account the crucial role of prosecutors in enhancing law enforcement cooperation under the rule of law;

4. *Calls upon* the Summit to ensure that its conclusions and recommendations make a substantive contribution to the work of the Conference of the Parties to the United Nations Convention against Transnational Organized Crime, as well as to advance the ratification process of the United Nations Convention against Corruption and the universal instruments against terrorism;

5. *Requests* the Secretary-General to bring the conclusions and recommendations of the Summit to the attention of the Commission on Crime Prevention and Criminal Justice.

Human resources development

UN Institute for Training and Research

In response to General Assembly resolution 58/223 [YUN 2003, p. 1161], the Secretary-General submitted an August report [A/59/230] on the United Nations Institute for Training and Research (UNITAR). The report reviewed UNITAR's ongoing programmes, highlighting the main features of each and placed special emphasis on the strengthening of partnerships between the Institute and other UN system organizations and bodies achieved in the framework of each of the programmes. Some 130 seminars, workshops and conferences were organized by UNITAR, benefiting 7,800 persons. In 2004, programmes offered included: multilateral diplomacy and international affairs management; peacemaking and preventive diplomacy; correspondence instruction in peacekeeping operations; women and children in and after conflict; environmental law; climate change; chemicals and waste management; decentralized cooperation; and the legal aspects of debt and financial management.

In an August note [A/59/271] on the financial viability of UNITAR, submitted in response to Gen-

eral Assembly resolution 58/272 [YUN 2003, p. 1417], the Secretary-General transmitted the decision of the UNITAR Board of Trustees, at its forty-second session (Geneva, 27-29 April), on the issue of rental and maintenance costs charged to the Institute. To rationalize the financial structure of the Institute, the Board directed the Executive Director to continue to insist that donors of special purpose grants obtain full recovery of the programme support costs (overhead), and bring such recovery in line with the standard UN rate of 13 per cent; make sure that any further expansion of training programmes, especially those offered free of charge, would be commensurate with the level of resources available for both direct and administrative and common-service costs involved; and consider the possible downsizing of staff remunerated by the General Fund.

GENERAL ASSEMBLY ACTION

On 22 December [meeting 75], the General Assembly, on the recommendation of the Second Committee [A/59/490/Add. 1], adopted **resolution 59/252** without vote [agenda item 92 *(a)*].

United Nations Institute for Training and Research

The General Assembly,

Recalling its resolutions 51/188 of 16 December 1996, 52/206 of 18 December 1997, 53/195 of 15 December 1998, 54/229 of 22 December 1999, 55/208 of 20 December 2000, 56/208 of 21 December 2001, 57/268 of 20 December 2002 and 58/223 of 23 December 2003,

Having considered the reports of the Secretary-General and the Executive Director of the United Nations Institute for Training and Research,

Acknowledging the work of the Board of Trustees of the United Nations Institute for Training and Research on the functioning of the Institute,

Noting the continued progress made by the Institute in its various programmes and activities, including the strengthened cooperation with other organizations of the United Nations system and with regional and national institutions,

Expressing its appreciation to the Governments and private institutions that have made or pledged financial and other contributions to the Institute,

Noting that the bulk of the resources contributed to the Institute are directed to the Special Purpose Grants Fund rather than to the General Fund, stressing the need to address that unbalanced situation, and also noting that the participation of the developed countries in training programmes in New York and Geneva is increasing,

Noting also that the Institute is self-funded, not receiving any kind of subsidies from the United Nations regular budget, and delivers, free of charge, training courses to diplomats and delegates accredited to United Nations Headquarters in New York and to the United Nations offices at Geneva, Vienna and Nairobi,

Noting further the various ongoing training programmes of the Institute, including those in the field of sustainable development,

Reiterating that training activities should be accorded a more visible and larger role in support of the management of international affairs and in the execution of the economic and social development programmes of the United Nations system,

1. *Reaffirms* the importance of a coordinated United Nations system-wide approach to research and training, based on an effective coherent strategy and an effective division of work among the relevant institutions and bodies;

2. *Also reaffirms* the relevance of the United Nations Institute for Training and Research, in view of the growing importance of training within the United Nations and the training requirements of States, and the relevance of the training-related research activities undertaken by the Institute within its mandate;

3. *Welcomes* the progress made in building partnerships between the Institute and other organizations and bodies of the United Nations system with respect to their training programmes, and in this context underlines the need to develop further and to expand the scope of those partnerships, in particular at the country level;

4. *Notes with appreciation* the activities of the Institute's Regional Office for Asia and the Pacific in Hiroshima, Japan, during its first year of existence;

5. *Welcomes* the establishment of the Institute's Project Field Office in Dushanbe;

6. *Requests* the Board of Trustees of the Institute to continue to ensure fair and equitable geographical distribution and transparency in the preparation of the programmes and in the employment of experts, and in this regard stresses that the courses of the Institute should focus primarily on development issues and the management of international affairs;

7. *Renews its appeal* to all Governments, in particular those of developed countries, and to private institutions that have not yet contributed financially or otherwise to the Institute, to give it their generous financial and other support, and urges the States that have interrupted their voluntary contributions to consider resuming them in view of the successful restructuring and revitalization of the Institute;

8. *Encourages* the Board of Trustees to consider diversifying further the venues of the events organized by the Institute and to include the cities hosting regional commissions, in order to promote greater participation and reduce costs;

9. *Notes with appreciation* the one-time provision to cancel the Institute's past debts decided upon in section XIV of General Assembly resolution 58/272 of 23 December 2003;

10. *Stresses* the need for continued consideration of the issues related to the Institute's rent, rental rates and maintenance costs, taking into account its financial situation, with a view to its expeditious resolution;

11. *Encourages* the Board of Trustees of the Institute to continue its efforts to resolve the critical financial situation of the Institute, in particular with a view to broadening its donor base and to further increasing the contributions to the General Fund;

12. *Requests* the Secretary-General to submit to the General Assembly at its sixtieth session a report on the implementation of the present resolution, including details on the status of contributions to and the financial situation of the Institute, and decides to consider the issue of the periodicity of the agenda item entitled "Training and research" at its sixtieth session.

On the same date, the Assembly took note of the report [A/59/490] of the Second Committee, containing its decision to include in the agenda of its fifty-ninth (2004) session the item on UNITAR (**decision 59/541**).

On 23 December, the Assembly, in **resolution 59/276**, section X (see p. 1386), noted the conclusions of the UNITAR Board of Trustees and requested the Secretary-General to submit a report on the Institute's finances, including proposals for addressing the funding of rent and maintenance costs, at the beginning of its sixtieth (2005) session and prior to the introduction of the proposed 2006-2007 programme budget.

United Nations University

The Council of the United Nations University (UNU), at its fifty-first session (Helsinki, Finland, 6-10 December), reviewed the University's activities over the past year and assessed the financial situation and investment of the UNU Endowment Fund.

During the year, UNU continued to focus on peace and governance, and environment and development, and it worked on critical issues relating to key problem areas identified in the Millennium Development Goals (MDGs) [YUN 2000, p. 51]. It revised its strategic plan entitled "UNU Strategic Directions (2005-2008)", which would serve as a basis for the preparation of the 2006-2007 programme budget. In March, the Institute of Advanced Studies moved from Tokyo to Yokohama, which would help it to develop a clearer institutional profile for its work. In June, the Institute for Environment and Human Security was formally established in Bonn, Germany, and two operating units of the Institute for Natural Resources in Africa became operational in Yaoundé, Cameroon, and Cocody, Côte d'Ivoire.

In November [A/59/566], the Secretary-General provided a comprehensive report on UNU activities in 2003 and 2004.

GENERAL ASSEMBLY ACTION

On 22 December [meeting 75], the General Assembly, on the recommendation of the Second Committee [A/59/490/Add. 2], adopted **resolution 59/253** without vote [agenda item 92 *(b)*].

United Nations University

The General Assembly,

Reaffirming its previous resolutions on the United Nations University, including resolution 57/267 of 20 December 2002,

Having considered the report of the Council of the United Nations University, as presented by the Rector of the University on 16 November 2004, and the report of the Secretary-General,

Bearing in mind the importance of the intellectual contributions made by the University for the United Nations system,

Expressing its deep appreciation for the voluntary contributions made by Governments and other public and private entities in support of the University,

1. *Notes with satisfaction* the implementation of the "Strategic Plan, 2000", which lays out broad programmatic orientations with special focus on the priority concerns of the United Nations and the need to bring together theory and practice in a global perspective, and requests the United Nations University to continue to attach importance to the priority agendas of the United Nations system;

2. *Highly appreciates* the successful steps taken by the University to promote the work and visibility of the University, including its research and training centres and programmes, to strengthen interaction with and contributions to the work of the United Nations system and to create new networks of activity with the academic communities in host countries, including Japan, and encourages the University to continue with such efforts;

3. *Expresses particular appreciation* of the University's support to scholars from developing countries and the countries with economies in transition, especially young scholars, through its capacity and network development activities;

4. *Notes with interest* the inauguration of the new research and training programme in Bonn, Germany, and encourages the University to continue with efforts towards creating a critical mass of viable research and training centres and programmes around the world, focused in particular on meeting the urgent needs and concerns of developing countries;

5. *Welcomes* the adoption and use by the University of computer-mediated dissemination and learning technologies through the United Nations University Online Learning initiative, and in particular the establishment of the Global Virtual University, which facilitates the intensification of activities in the areas of education and training, and encourages the further strengthening of these activities;

6. *Takes note with satisfaction* of the consolidation of the joint initiative by the University and the United Nations Office at Geneva to convene a yearly research and policy dialogue that is thematically focused and involves the United Nations system and other entities engaged in policy research and analysis;

7. *Encourages* the University to continue its efforts to implement the Secretary-General's suggestion on innovative measures to improve interaction and communication between the University and other United Nations entities, in particular by identifying and giving priority to common themes of interest;

8. *Requests* the Secretary-General to encourage other bodies of the United Nations system to utilize more fully the capacity of the University for mobilizing a worldwide network of applied policy researchers

to assist the United Nations, through research and capacity development, in resolving pressing global problems;

9. *Appreciates* the efficiency gains achieved by the University in order to make optimal use of modest and limited resources, and emphasizes the continuing need for cost-effectiveness in conducting the activities of the University;

10. *Welcomes* the University's increasing efforts to widen and diversify its financial base, and invites the international community to make voluntary contributions to the University, in particular to its Endowment Fund, as a means of consolidating the distinctive identity of the University in the United Nations system and the international academic community;

11. *Decides* to include in the provisional agenda of its sixty-first session the sub-item entitled "United Nations University".

International Year of Physics, 2005

On 10 June [meeting 90], the General Assembly adopted **resolution 58/293** [draft: A/58/L.62 & Add. 1] without vote [agenda item 169].

International Year of Physics, 2005

The General Assembly,

Recognizing that physics provides a significant basis for the development of the understanding of nature,

Noting that physics and its applications are the basis of many of today's technological advances,

Convinced that education in physics provides men and women with the tools to build the scientific infrastructure essential for development,

Being aware that the year 2005 is the centenary of seminal scientific discoveries by Albert Einstein which are the basis of modern physics,

1. *Welcomes* the proclamation of 2005 as the International Year of Physics by the United Nations Educational, Scientific and Cultural Organization;

2. *Invites* the United Nations Educational, Scientific and Cultural Organization to organize activities celebrating the International Year of Physics, in collaboration with physics societies and other groups throughout the world, including in the developing countries;

3. *Proclaims* 2005 the International Year of Physics.

Education for all

JIU report. In April [A/59/76], the Secretary-General transmitted the report of the Joint Inspection Unit (JIU) on achieving the universal primary education goal [YUN 2000, p. 52] of the Millennium Declaration: new challenges for development cooperation. The report examined whether necessary conditions were in place for attaining the goal of universal primary education—that by 2015 children everywhere could enjoy their human right to a quality education and complete a full course of primary schooling. It also examined whether the international community could ensure that girls and boys would have equal access to all levels of education by that date.

According to JIU, education statistics showed that 104 million children were currently deprived of access to primary education, and the majority of children out of school were girls. Other challenges to be addressed were the shortage of teachers and the HIV/AIDS epidemic, which threatened gains already made. While many countries had made progress towards meeting the two MDGs, many others, especially the least developed countries, were seriously off track. JIU concluded that there was a real danger the MDGs on education and gender equality would not be met unless the international community strongly resolved to live up to its pledges made at the 2000 World Education Forum [YUN 2000, p. 1081]. In that regard, the report discussed the contributions of bilateral donors and prominent actors in education, such as the European Commission's Development Assistance Committee, as well as UN agencies, including UNESCO, the United Nations Children's Fund, the United Nations Population Fund, the International Labour Organization, the World Food Programme, the World Bank Group and the International Monetary Fund. The report made a number of recommendations to the Assembly and the Economic and Social Council on ways to speed up progress towards universal primary education.

In July [A/59/76/Add.1 & Corr.1], the Secretary-General transmitted his comments and those of the United Nations Chief Executives Board for Coordination (CEB) on the JIU report.

UN Literacy Decade. In accordance with General Assembly resolution 57/166 [YUN 2002, p. 1135], the Secretary-General transmitted, in August [A/59/267], a report by the UNESCO Director-General on the implementation of the International Plan of Action for the United Nations Literacy Decade (2003-2012), proclaimed by the Assembly in resolution 56/116 [YUN 2001, p. 1052]. The report addressed international, regional and national activities to launch the Decade, provided information on the activities of UN organizations and other partners to advance literacy during 2003 and up to May 2004 and on current literacy projects to advance the objectives of the Decade at all levels, and made recommendations for strengthening the Literacy Decade effort. The meeting of the United Nations Inter-Agency Working Group, established by UNESCO to share information on the Decade (Geneva, 6-7 April), decided that the theme for the first biennium (2003-2004) of the Decade would be "Literacy and gender".

According to the report, the UN Literacy Decade faced many challenges, especially at the national level and particularly in those countries where the levels of illiteracy were highest. There was also a growing concern that the issue was not sufficiently high on the agendas of both developed and developing countries. During the first stage of the Decade, attention was focused on its launch, involving sizeable human and financial investments. However, it was too soon to tell how much the Decade's call to action had elicited increased resources and heightened levels of activity, although some literacy partners were preparing to make greater efforts. While positive actions reported provided a basis for some optimism, current trends indicated that the world was unlikely to meet the literacy challenges, either by the end of the Decade in 2012 or by the target date for the achievement of the education-for-all goals of 2015. Current estimates put the number of illiterate adults worldwide at roughly 800 million, the majority of which (63 per cent) were women.

The Secretary-General recommended, among other things, that countries mobilize the political will and financial resources required to meet the literacy challenges they faced, especially investments in basic education for children, youth and young adults. The international community should support those efforts and address the need for an effective and substantive integration of the UN Literacy Decade efforts with the education-for-all and MDG processes, and for an enhanced linkage between the Decade and other global initiatives.

GENERAL ASSEMBLY ACTION

On 20 December [meeting 74], the General Assembly, on the recommendation of the Third Committee [A/59/492], adopted **resolution 59/149** without vote [agenda item 94 (b)].

United Nations Literacy Decade: education for all

The General Assembly,

Recalling its resolution 56/116 of 19 December 2001, by which it proclaimed the ten-year period beginning on 1 January 2003 the United Nations Literacy Decade, and its resolution 57/166 of 18 December 2002, in which it welcomed the International Plan of Action for the United Nations Literacy Decade,

Recalling also the United Nations Millennium Declaration, in which Member States resolved to ensure that, by 2015, children everywhere, boys and girls alike, will be able to complete a full course of primary schooling and that girls and boys will have equal access to all levels of education, which requires a renewed commitment to promote literacy for all,

Reaffirming that a basic education is crucial to nation-building, that literacy for all is at the heart of basic education for all and that creating literate environments and societies is essential for achieving the goals of eradicating poverty, reducing child mortality, curbing population growth, achieving gender equality and ensuring sustainable development, peace and democracy,

Convinced that literacy is crucial to the acquisition by every child, youth and adult of the essential life skills that will enable them to address the challenges that they can face in life, and represents an essential step in basic education, which is an indispensable means for effective participation in the societies and economies of the twenty-first century,

Affirming that the realization of the right to education, especially for girls, contributes to the promotion of gender equality and the eradication of poverty,

Welcoming the considerable efforts that have been made to address the objectives of the Decade at various levels,

Noting with concern that over 100 million children are not in school and some 800 million adults are illiterate today, that the issue of illiteracy may not be sufficiently high on national agendas to generate the kind of political and economic support required to address global illiteracy challenges, and that the world is unlikely to meet those challenges if the present trends continue,

Deeply concerned about the persistence of the gender gap in education, which is reflected by the fact that nearly two thirds of the world's adult illiterates are women,

1. *Takes note* of the report of the Secretary-General, prepared in cooperation with the Director-General of the United Nations Educational, Scientific and Cultural Organization, on the implementation of the International Plan of Action for the United Nations Literacy Decade, as well as the report prepared by the Joint Inspection Unit on achieving the universal primary education goal of the United Nations Millennium Declaration;

2. *Welcomes* the efforts made so far by Member States and the international community in launching the Decade and implementing the International Plan of Action;

3. *Appeals* to all Governments to develop reliable literacy data and information and to further reinforce political will, mobilize adequate national resources, develop more inclusive policy-making environments and devise innovative strategies for reaching the poorest and most marginalized groups and for seeking alternative formal and non-formal approaches to learning with a view to achieving the goals of the Decade;

4. *Urges* all Governments to take the lead in coordinating the activities of the Decade at the national level, bringing all relevant national actors together in a sustained dialogue and collaborative action on policy formulation, implementation and evaluation of literacy efforts;

5. *Appeals* to all Governments and professional organizations to strengthen national and professional educational institutions in their countries with a view to expanding their capacity and promoting the quality of education, with particular focus on literacy;

6. *Appeals* to all Governments and to economic and financial organizations and institutions, both national and international, to lend greater financial and material support to the efforts to increase literacy and achieve the goals of Education for All and those of the Decade, through, inter alia, the 20/20 initiative, as appropriate;

7. *Invites* Member States, the specialized agencies and other organizations of the United Nations system, as well as relevant intergovernmental and non-governmental organizations, to intensify their efforts to implement effectively the International Plan of Action, and to integrate substantially those efforts in the Education for All process and other initiatives and activities of the United Nations Educational, Scientific and Cultural Organization and within the framework of the internationally agreed development goals, including those contained in the United Nations Millennium Declaration;

8. *Requests* the United Nations Educational, Scientific and Cultural Organization to reinforce its lead coordinating role in stimulating and catalysing the activities undertaken at the international level within the framework of the Decade in a manner that is complementary to and coordinated with the ongoing Education for All process, with the internationally agreed development goals, including those contained in the Millennium Declaration, and with other global initiatives;

9. *Requests* all relevant entities of the United Nations system, particularly the United Nations Educational, Scientific and Cultural Organization, in cooperation with national Governments, to take immediate, concrete steps to address the needs of countries with high illiteracy rates and/or with large populations of illiterate adults, with particular regard to women;

10. *Requests* the Secretary-General, in cooperation with the Director-General of the United Nations Educational, Scientific and Cultural Organization, to seek the views of Member States on the progress achieved in implementing their national programmes and plans of action for the Decade and to submit progress reports on the implementation of the International Plan of Action to the General Assembly on a biennial basis, beginning in 2006;

11. *Decides* to include in the provisional agenda of its sixty-first session, under the item entitled "Social development, including questions relating to the world social situation and to youth, ageing, disabled persons and the family", the sub-item entitled "United Nations Literacy Decade: education for all".

Chapter X

Women

In 2004, the United Nations continued to promote the advancement of the status of women and ensure their rights within the framework of the Beijing Declaration and Platform for Action, adopted at the Fourth (1995) World Conference on Women, and the outcome of the General Assembly's twenty-third (2000) special session, which reviewed progress in their implementation (Beijing+5). In July, the Economic and Social Council agreed that, on the occasion of the tenth anniversary of the Beijing Declaration and Platform for Action and the fifth anniversary of the Assembly's twenty-third special session, in 2005, the Commission on the Status of Women should convene a high-level plenary meeting at its forty-ninth session to review the implementation of both instruments and consider the current challenges and forward-looking strategies for the advancement of women. The Assembly, in welcoming that decision in December, called upon Governments, UN system entities and civil society, including non-governmental organizations (NGOs), to continue to take action to implement the Beijing Declaration and Platform for Action and the outcome of the twenty-third special session. The Assembly also adopted resolutions on violence against women, crimes against women and girls committed in the name of honour, and trafficking in women and girls.

The Commission on the Status of Women, at its forty-eighth session in March, recommended to the Economic and Social Council for action agreed conclusions on the thematic issues of the role of men and boys in gender equality, and women's equal participation in conflict prevention, management and resolution. The Council endorsed those agreed conclusions in July. It also adopted resolutions on women and girls in Afghanistan; Palestinian women; the release of women and children taken hostage; mainstreaming a gender perspective into UN policies and programmes; women, the girl child and AIDS; and the revitalization of the International Research and Training Institute for the Advancement of Women (INSTRAW).

The United Nations Development Fund for Women (UNIFEM) focused on the implementation of the first year of its 2004-2007 multi-year funding framework, targeting goals in the key areas of feminized poverty, violence against women, the spread of HIV/AIDS, and gender equality in democratic governance and in post-conflict countries. UNIFEM also chaired the newly launched task force on gender equality and convened the first conference on gender justice in post-conflict situations in September.

INSTRAW completed the first phase of its revitalization process. The Institute's new Executive Board held its first session in July and October, at which it approved the 2004-2007 strategic framework, and the programme of work and budget for 2005. However, INSTRAW's financial situation remained precarious at year's end.

In August the Secretary-General presented the fifth update of the *World Survey on the Role of Women in Development*, which focused on women and international migration, and announced the appointment of Rachel Mayanja as the new Special Adviser on Gender Issues and Advancement of Women.

Follow-up to the Fourth World Conference on Women and Beijing+5

During 2004, the Commission on the Status of Women, the Economic and Social Council and the General Assembly continued to consider follow-up to the 1995 Fourth World Conference on Women, in particular, the implementation of the Beijing Declaration and Platform for Action [YUN 1995, p. 1170], and the political declaration and further actions and initiatives to implement the Beijing Declaration and Platform for Action, adopted at the twenty-third (2000) special session of the General Assembly (Beijing+5) by resolution S/23-2 [YUN 2000, p. 1084]. The political declaration had reaffirmed the commitment of Governments to the goals and objectives of the Fourth World Conference and to implementation of the 12 critical areas of concern set forth in the Platform for Action: women and poverty; education and training of women; women and health; violence against women; women and armed conflict; women and the economy; women in power and decision-making; institutional mechanisms for the advancement of women; human rights and women; women and the media; women and the environment; and the girl child (see p. 777). The issue of mainstreaming a gender perspective into UN policies and programmes continued to be addressed (see p. 1166).

Commission action. In March, The Commission on the Status of Women, in resolution [E/2004/27 (res. 48/5)] adopted in March, decided that the review at its forty-ninth (2005) session of the implementation of the Beijing Declaration and Platform for Action and the outcome documents of the General Assembly's twenty-third session would focus on a more interactive dialogue among delegations, civil society and organizations within the United Nations, with an emphasis on the sharing of experiences and good practices in overcoming the remaining implementation challenges. The Commission recommended that the Economic and Social Council recommend to the Assembly the convening of a high-level plenary meeting of the Commission during its forty-ninth session on implementation of the Beijing Platform and the outcome of the Assembly's twenty-third session.

By **decision 2004/309** of 23 July, the Economic and Social Council took note of Commission resolution 48/5 (see above) and decided that the Commission would convene, at its forty-ninth session, a high-level plenary meeting open to all Member States, the outcome of which would be transmitted by the Chairperson, through the Council, to the Assembly's sixtieth (2005) session, including to its high-level event on the review of the Millennium Declaration.

Report of Secretary-General. In response to General Assembly resolution 58/148 [YUN 2003, p. 1165], the Secretary-General, in an August report [A/59/214], reviewed steps taken by the Assembly and its Main Committees, the Economic and Social Council and the Office of the Special Adviser on Gender Issues and Advancement of Women in support of gender mainstreaming in all UN programmes and policies. The report highlighted action taken relating to the World Summit on the Information Society [YUN 2003, p. 857]; follow-up to major international conferences and summits; and the São Paulo Consensus [TD/410], adopted by the eleventh session of the United Nations Conference on Trade and Development (UNCTAD XI) (see p. 954), which recognized that gender equality was essential for sustained economic growth, poverty eradication and employment creation.

The Secretary-General concluded that there was still limited qualitative attention to gender perspectives in reports submitted to the various committees, and few contained gender analysis and recommendations for further action. The

situation was no better with respect to gender perspectives in Assembly resolutions. He recommended that the Assembly continue to call for the inclusion of gender equality in reports submitted to it and its subsidiary bodies and gender perspectives in draft resolutions adopted by its subsidiary bodies, in particular concrete recommendations for action, and that it encourage reporting on progress made. The Assembly should ensure gender mainstreaming in the implementation of and follow-up to major international conferences and summits, in particular the review, in 2005, of the implementation of the 2000 United Nations Millennium Declaration [YUN 2000, p. 49].

On 20 December [meeting 74], the General Assembly, on the recommendation of the Third (Social, Humanitarian and Cultural) Committee [A/59/497], adopted **resolution 59/168**, without vote [agenda item 99].

Follow-up to the Fourth World Conference on Women and full implementation of the Beijing Declaration and Platform for Action and the outcome of the twenty-third special session of the General Assembly

The General Assembly,

Recalling its previous resolutions on the question, including resolution 58/148 of 22 December 2003,

Recalling also the contributions of the four World Conferences on Women, held in Mexico City, Copenhagen, Nairobi and Beijing, to the advancement of women and the promotion of gender equality,

Deeply convinced that the Beijing Declaration and Platform for Action and the outcome of the twenty-third special session of the General Assembly, entitled "Women 2000: gender equality, development and peace for the twenty-first century", are important contributions to the advancement of women worldwide in the achievement of gender equality and must be translated into effective action by all States, the United Nations system and other organizations concerned,

Reaffirming its commitment to the full and effective implementation of the Beijing Declaration and Platform for Action and the outcome document of the twenty-third special session, including the twelve critical areas of concern, namely women and poverty, education and training of women, women and health, violence against women, women and armed conflict, women and the economy, women in power and decision-making, institutional mechanisms for the advancement of women, human rights of women, women and the media, women and the environment and the girl child,

Also reaffirming its commitment to overcoming obstacles encountered in the implementation of the Beijing Declaration and Platform for Action and the outcome of the twenty-third special session and to strengthening a national and international enabling environment in this regard,

Recognizing that the responsibility for the implementation of the Beijing Declaration and Platform for Action and the outcome of the twenty-third special session rests primarily at the national level and that strengthened efforts are necessary in this respect, and reiterating that enhanced international cooperation is essential for the effective implementation of the Beijing Declaration and Platform for Action and the outcome of the twenty-third special session,

Welcoming the increased attention to the situation of women and girls and the integration of gender perspectives in the work of the United Nations, in particular in the outcomes of major conferences, special sessions and summit conferences and their follow-up processes, as well as the review and appraisal by the Economic and Social Council of the system-wide implementation of its agreed conclusions 1997/2 of 18 July 1997 on mainstreaming a gender perspective into all policies and programmes in the United Nations system, the inclusion of the question of gender mainstreaming in its agenda, the consideration of annual progress made in gender mainstreaming and the attention given to the gender perspective in the outcomes of its substantive session of 2004,

Reaffirming the primary and essential role of the General Assembly and the Economic and Social Council in promoting the advancement of women and gender equality, while noting the open debate on women and peace and security held in the Security Council on 28 October 2004, as well as previous debates,

Bearing in mind its relevant resolutions and Security Council resolution 1325(2000) of 31 October 2000,

1. *Takes note with appreciation* of the report of the Secretary-General on measures taken and progress achieved in follow-up to the implementation of the Beijing Declaration and Platform for Action and the outcome of the twenty-third special session of the General Assembly;

2. *Reaffirms* the goals, objectives and commitments contained in the Beijing Declaration and Platform for Action and in the political declaration and further actions and initiatives to implement the Beijing Declaration and Platform for Action adopted by the General Assembly at its twenty-third special session;

3. *Stresses* the need to undertake further action to ensure the full and accelerated implementation of the Beijing Declaration and Platform for Action and the outcome of the twenty-third special session, inter alia, through the promotion and protection of all human rights and fundamental freedoms, the mainstreaming of gender perspectives into all policies and programmes and the promotion of full and equal participation and empowerment of women and enhanced international cooperation for the full implementation of the Beijing Platform for Action;

4. *Underlines* the significance of the forty-ninth session of the Commission on the Status of Women, which will mark the tenth anniversary of the Beijing Declaration and Platform for Action and the fifth anniversary of the twenty-third special session, and at which the Commission will review the implementation of the Beijing Declaration and Platform for Action and the outcome of the twenty-third special session and consider the current challenges and forward-looking strategies for the advancement of women, as well as the comprehensive report of the Secretary-General;

5. *Stresses* the importance of strong, sustained political will and commitment at the national, regional and international levels for achieving full and accelerated implementation of the Beijing Declaration and Platform for Action and the outcome of the twenty-third special session;

6. *Welcomes* the opportunity provided by the forty-ninth session of the Commission on the Status of Women to demonstrate continued and full commitment to the full and effective implementation of the Beijing Declaration and Platform for Action and the outcome of the twenty-third special session;

7. *Encourages* participation in the forty-ninth session of the Commission on the Status of Women at a high political level;

8. *Invites* States and the United Nations system to publicize the forthcoming session of the Commission on the Status of Women, including through consultation with civil society;

9. *Calls upon* Governments, the relevant entities of the United Nations system, within their respective mandates, and all relevant actors of civil society, including non-governmental organizations, to continue to take effective action to achieve the full and effective implementation of the Beijing Declaration and Platform for Action and the outcome of the twenty-third special session;

10. *Emphasizes* that the creation of an enabling environment at the national and international levels, including by ensuring the participation of women on an equal basis with men at all levels of decision-making, is necessary to ensure the full participation of women in all aspects of social, political and economic activities, and in this regard calls upon States to remove obstacles to the full implementation of the Beijing Declaration and Platform for Action and the outcome of the twenty-third special session;

11. *Emphasizes also* the importance of men and boys taking joint responsibility with women and girls in the promotion of gender equality, taking into account the agreed conclusions adopted by the Commission on the Status of Women at its forty-eighth session on 12 March 2004;

12. *Welcomes* the contributions of the Commission on the Status of Women to the follow-up and review of the implementation of the commitments made in the Beijing Declaration and Platform for Action and the outcome of the twenty-third special session, reaffirms that the Commission will continue to play a central role in this regard, and encourages Governments, the relevant specialized agencies, funds and programmes of the United Nations system and civil society to continue to support its work;

13. *Stresses* the importance of implementing the agreed conclusions adopted by the Commission on the Status of Women since its fortieth session;

14. *Reaffirms* its decision that the General Assembly, the Economic and Social Council and the Commission on the Status of Women, in accordance with their respective mandates and with General Assembly resolutions 48/162 of 20 December 1993 and 57/270 B of 23 June 2003 and other relevant resolutions, constitute a three-tiered intergovernmental mechanism that plays the primary role in overall policy-making and follow-up and in coordinating the implementation and moni-

toring of the Beijing Platform for Action and the outcome of the twenty-third special session;

15. *Recalls* that, in accordance with resolution 57/270 B, the follow-up to the Fourth World Conference on Women and the twenty-third special session will continue to be undertaken within the framework of an integrated and coordinated follow-up to major international conferences and summits in the economic, social and related fields, and also recalls in this regard the request to each functional commission of the Economic and Social Council to examine its methods of work in order to better pursue the implementation of the outcomes of major United Nations conferences and summits and report to the Council no later than 2005 on the outcome of this examination;

16. *Recognizes* the importance attached to the regional and subregional monitoring of the global and regional platforms for action and of the implementation of the outcome of the twenty-third special session by regional commissions and other regional or subregional structures, within their mandates, in consultation with Governments, calls for the promotion of further cooperation in that respect among Governments and, where appropriate, national machineries of the same region, and welcomes in this regard the contributions of the United Nations regional commissions to the forty-ninth session of the Commission on the Status of Women;

17. *Encourages* the Economic and Social Council to reiterate its request to the regional commissions that have not yet done so, within their respective mandates and resources, to intensify efforts to build up a database, to be updated regularly, in which all programmes and projects carried out in their respective regions by organizations or bodies of the United Nations system are listed, and to facilitate the dissemination of information on such programmes and projects, as well as the evaluation of their impact on the empowerment of women through the implementation of the Beijing Platform for Action;

18. *Welcomes* Economic and Social Council decision 2004/309 of 23 July 2004, in which the Chairperson of the forty-ninth session of the Commission on the Status of Women is requested to submit the outcome of the session, through the Economic and Social Council, to the General Assembly at its sixtieth session, including to the high-level event of the Assembly on the review of the United Nations Millennium Declaration;

19. *Emphasizes* that the full and effective implementation of the Beijing Declaration and Platform for Action and the promotion of gender equality and of women's empowerment and participation, together with the mainstreaming of a gender perspective, are among the essential elements for advancing the implementation of the Millennium Declaration, with a view, in particular, to achieving the internationally agreed development goals, including those contained in the Millennium Declaration and the outcomes of United Nations summits, conferences and special sessions;

20. *Recognizes* that adequate mobilization of resources at the national and international levels, as well as new and additional resources for the developing countries, including the least developed countries and countries with economies in transition, from all available funding mechanisms, including multilateral, bilateral and private sources, will also be required;

21. *Requests* the Secretary-General to highlight the contribution of the Beijing Declaration and Platform for Action to the implementation of the Millennium Declaration and to integrate gender perspectives in his preparations, including reports, for the review of the Millennium Declaration;

22. *Calls upon* Member States to incorporate gender perspectives in their preparations for the review of the Millennium Declaration;

23. *Requests* the Secretary-General to include in his report on the follow-up to the Millennium Declaration an assessment of the progress made in promoting the goal of gender equality, in particular in relation to the development goals set forth in the Millennium Declaration, and recommendations to improve the measurement and coverage of indicators so that progress towards gender equality can be evaluated over time;

24. *Invites* States parties to the Convention on the Elimination of All Forms of Discrimination against Women to include information on measures taken to implement the outcome of the twenty-third special session, as well as the Beijing Platform for Action, in their reports to the Committee on the Elimination of Discrimination against Women under article 18 of the Convention;

25. *Urges* States parties to comply fully with their obligations under the Convention on the Elimination of All Forms of Discrimination against Women and those that have not yet done so to consider signing, ratifying or acceding to the Optional Protocol thereto;

26. *Recognizes* the important role of law, including legislation, in the promotion of gender equality and the implementation of the Beijing Platform for Action, commends the progress made by States in the area of legal reform, and calls upon States to continue their efforts to repeal laws and eradicate practices that discriminate against women and to adopt laws and promote practices that protect the rights of women and promote gender equality;

27. *Urges* Member States to consider signing, ratifying or acceding to the United Nations Convention against Transnational Organized Crime and the Protocols thereto, in particular the Protocol to Prevent, Suppress and Punish Trafficking in Persons, Especially Women and Children, supplementing the United Nations Convention against Transnational Organized Crime;

28. *Calls upon* Governments, the United Nations system and all other relevant actors to continue to integrate gender perspectives into the implementation of and follow-up to recent United Nations conferences, summits and special sessions;

29. *Affirms* that, in order to ensure the effective implementation of the strategic objectives of the Beijing Platform for Action and the outcome of the twenty-third special session, the United Nations system should continue to promote an active and visible policy of mainstreaming gender perspectives, including through the work of the Division for the Advancement of Women and the Office of the Special Adviser on Gender Issues and Advancement of Women and the maintenance of gender units, focal points and gender specialists, and with the active support of all United Nations bodies, including by ensuring that all United Nations personnel, especially in the field, receive training on gender perspectives in their work, including gender impact analysis, and that appropriate follow-up training is provided;

30. *Recognizes* the need to further include gender perspectives in the work of its Main Committees and other intergovernmental bodies;

31. *Requests* all bodies that deal with programme and budgetary matters, including the Committee for Programme and Coordination, to ensure that all programmes, plans and programme budgets visibly mainstream gender perspectives;

32. *Encourages* the Economic and Social Council to continue its efforts to ensure that gender mainstreaming is an integral part of all activities in its work and that of its subsidiary bodies, through, inter alia, the system-wide implementation of its agreed conclusions 1997/2 and its resolution 2004/4 of 7 July 2004;

33. *Welcomes* the convening of the World Summit on the Information Society in Tunis in 2005, and encourages Governments and all other stakeholders to integrate a gender perspective into the preparatory processes and outcome documents, taking into account the agreed conclusions adopted by the Commission on the Status of Women at its forty-seventh session on 14 March 2003;

34. *Recognizes* the important role of women in the prevention and resolution of conflicts and in peace-building, and urges Governments and the United Nations system to take further steps to ensure the integration of gender perspectives and the full and equal participation of women at all levels of decision-making and implementation in all aspects of conflict prevention and resolution and peacebuilding activities and to ensure that efforts to strengthen the rule of law and transitional justice in conflict and post-conflict situations incorporate gender perspectives, with a view to achieving gender equality in constitutional, legislative and judicial reform;

35. *Strongly encourages* Governments to continue to support the role and contribution of civil society, in particular non-governmental organizations and women's organizations, in the implementation of the Beijing Declaration and Platform for Action and the outcome of the twenty-third special session;

36. *Requests* the Secretary-General to continue to promote the Beijing Declaration and Platform for Action and the outcome of the twenty-third special session and to disseminate those documents as widely as possible in all the official languages of the United Nations;

37. *Also requests* the Secretary-General to report annually to the General Assembly, the Economic and Social Council and the Commission on the Status of Women on the follow-up to and progress made in the implementation of the Beijing Declaration and Platform for Action and the outcome of the twenty-third special session, with an assessment of progress made in mainstreaming a gender perspective within the United Nations system, including by providing information on key achievements, lessons learned and best practices, and to recommend further measures and strategies for future action within the United Nations system;

38. *Decides* to include in the provisional agenda of its sixtieth session the item entitled "Implementation of the outcome of the Fourth World Conference on Women and of the twenty-third special session of the General Assembly, entitled 'Women 2000: gender equality, development and peace for the twenty-first century' ".

Critical areas of concern

Violence against women

In response to General Assembly resolutions 57/181 [YUN 2002, p. 1139] and 58/185 [YUN 2003, p. 1172], the Secretary-General submitted an August report [A/59/281] providing information about legislative, policy and other measures undertaken by 26 Member States, and by UN bodies and entities to combat all forms of violence against women, including honour crimes (see p. 1150). Those included action taken to adhere to international and regional human rights instruments issues, including those specifically addressing the rights of women, the elaboration of new national action plans to combat violence against women, and campaigns to raise public awareness about domestic violence and discriminatory practices against women. The report discussed issues and considered measures taken by the Commission on the Status of Women at its forty-eighth session (2004), the Commission on Human Rights, human rights treaty bodies and UN system organizations. Among notable UN system activities were the World Health Organization (WHO) multi-country study on women's health and domestic violence against women, and its research on sexual violence. The report also provided an update on the preparation of the Secretary-General's in-depth study on all forms of violence against women, for which a funding proposal outlining the framework for the study, the areas to be studied, the scope and methodology and efforts to identify a project officer was prepared.

The Secretary-General recommended that Governments accelerate the preparation of comprehensive legislative frameworks to criminalize all forms of violence against women, including honour crimes; put in place adequate penalties for perpetrators; and ensure that violence against women was prosecuted and punished. Priority attention should be given to adequate funding for the implementation of legislation, in addition to efforts to monitor and assess the impact of actions taken; raise awareness about all forms of violence against women as a violation of human rights of women; and improve data collection in all areas of violence against women. Support should be provided for anti-violence networks, and partnerships should be encouraged between governmental and non-governmental actors working for attitudinal and legislative change.

UNIFEM activities. In compliance with General Assembly resolution 50/166 [YUN 1995,

p. 1188], the Secretary-General transmitted a December report [E/CN.6/2005/7-E/CN.4/2005/70] of the United Nations Development Fund for Women (UNIFEM) on the elimination of violence against women, which covered its 2004 activities undertaken in that regard (see p. 1171). Those activities concentrated on specific thematic interlinkages with gender-based violence, with grant-making during the year focusing on strategies to prevent and respond to gender-based violence in conflict and post-conflict settings. In October, the Trust Fund in Support of Actions to Eliminate Violence against Women provided $900,000 to 17 initiatives in 21 countries, bringing the total awarded since its inception in 1997 to $8.3 million in grants to 175 initiatives in more than 96 countries.

GENERAL ASSEMBLY ACTION

On 20 December [meeting 74], the General Assembly, on the recommendation of the Third Committee [A/59/497], adopted **resolution 59/167** without vote [agenda item 99].

Elimination of all forms of violence against women, including crimes identified in the outcome document of the twenty-third special session of the General Assembly, entitled "Women 2000: gender equality, development and peace for the twenty-first century"

The General Assembly,

Recalling the purposes and principles of the Charter of the United Nations, which, inter alia, calls for international cooperation in promoting and encouraging respect for human rights and fundamental freedoms for all without distinction as to race, sex, language or religion,

Recalling also the Universal Declaration of Human Rights, the Declaration on the Elimination of Discrimination against Women, the Declaration on the Elimination of Violence against Women, the United Nations Declaration on the Elimination of All Forms of Racial Discrimination, the Beijing Declaration and Platform for Action adopted by the Fourth World Conference on Women, the Vienna Declaration and Programme of Action, adopted on 25 June 1993 by the World Conference on Human Rights and the United Nations Millennium Declaration,

Recalling further its resolution 57/181 of 18 December 2002 and the agreed conclusions adopted by the Commission on the Status of Women at its forty-eighth session on 12 March 2004,

Reaffirming the obligations of all States to promote and protect human rights and fundamental freedoms, as enunciated in the Charter, and reaffirming also the obligations of States parties under international human rights instruments, in particular the International Covenant on Civil and Political Rights, the International Covenant on Economic, Social and Cultural Rights, the Convention on the Elimination of All Forms of Discrimination against Women, the International Convention on the Elimination of All Forms of Racial Discrimination, the Convention on the Rights of the Child, the Convention against Torture and Other

Cruel, Inhuman or Degrading Treatment or Punishment and the International Convention on the Protection of the Rights of All Migrant Workers and Members of Their Families,

Reaffirming also the outcome document of the twenty-third special session of the General Assembly, entitled "Women 2000: gender equality, development and peace for the twenty-first century",

Reaffirming further the call for the elimination of violence against women and girls, especially all forms of commercial sexual exploitation as well as economic exploitation, including trafficking in women and children, female infanticide, crimes committed in the name of honour, crimes committed in the name of passion, racially motivated crimes, the abduction and sale of children, dowry-related violence and deaths, acid attacks and harmful traditional or customary practices, such as female genital mutilation and early and forced marriage,

Stressing the importance of the empowerment of women as a tool to eliminate all forms of violence against women, including crimes identified in the outcome document of the twenty-third special session,

1. *Welcomes* the report of the Secretary-General;

2. *Expresses deep concern* at the persistence of various forms of violence and crimes against women in all parts of the world, especially all forms of commercial sexual exploitation as well as economic exploitation, including trafficking in women and children, female infanticide, crimes committed in the name of honour, crimes committed in the name of passion, racially motivated crimes, the abduction and sale of children, dowry-related violence and deaths, acid attacks and harmful traditional or customary practices, such as female genital mutilation and early and forced marriage;

3. *Stresses* that all forms of violence against women, including crimes identified in the outcome document of the twenty-third special session of the General Assembly, are obstacles to the advancement and empowerment of women, and reaffirms that violence against women both violates and impairs or nullifies the enjoyment by women of their human rights and fundamental freedoms;

4. *Also stresses* the need to treat all forms of violence against women and girls of all ages as a criminal offence punishable by law, including violence based on all forms of discrimination;

5. *Welcomes* specific legal and comprehensive legislative measures being enacted or contemplated, in particular with regard to various forms of violence against women and girls;

6. *Also welcomes* in this regard the launching of various initiatives, strategies and action plans aimed at, among other things, eradication, prevention, promotion, information, legislation, protection and welfare, education and research, enhancement of the economic capacity of women and the monitoring of the various forms of violence against women;

7. *Reaffirms* that there is increased awareness of and commitment to preventing and combating violence against women, including crimes identified in the outcome document of the twenty-third special session, welcomes in this context various legal, administrative and other measures taken by Governments for their prevention and elimination, and calls for high priority to be attached to the further strengthening of such measures;

8. *Urges* Member States to strengthen awareness and preventive measures for the elimination of all forms of violence against women, whether occurring in public or private life, by encouraging and supporting public campaigns to enhance awareness about the unacceptability and the social costs of violence against women, inter alia, through educational and media campaigns in cooperation with educators, community leaders and the electronic and print media;

9. *Calls upon* States to encourage and support the active participation of men and boys in the prevention and elimination of all forms of violence, especially gender-based violence, and to increase the awareness of men and boys of their responsibility in ending violence against women;

10. *Expresses its appreciation* of the work being done by non-governmental organizations, including women's organizations, community-based organizations and individuals, in raising awareness about the economic, social and psychological costs of all forms of violence against women, including crimes identified in the outcome document of the twenty-third special session, and in this regard encourages Governments to continue their support for the work of the non-governmental organizations in addressing this issue;

11. *Calls upon* States to fulfil their obligations under the relevant human rights instruments and to implement the Beijing Platform for Action as well as the outcome document of the twenty-third special session;

12. *Encourages* States parties to include in their reports to the Committee on the Elimination of Discrimination against Women and other relevant treaty bodies, wherever possible, sex-disaggregated data and information on measures taken or initiated to eliminate all forms of violence against women, including crimes identified in the outcome document of the twenty-third special session;

13. *Urges* relevant entities of the United Nations system, within their mandates, to assist countries, upon their request, in their efforts to prevent and eliminate all forms of violence against women, including crimes identified in the outcome document of the twenty-third special session, and in this regard expresses its appreciation of the work being done by the United Nations Population Fund, the United Nations Children's Fund and the United Nations Development Fund for Women and other relevant funds and programmes aimed at preventing and eliminating violence against women and girls;

14. *Invites* the Special Rapporteur of the Commission on Human Rights on violence against women, its causes and consequences to further devote equal attention to all forms of violence against women, including crimes identified in the outcome document of the twenty-third special session, in her work and her reports, within her mandate, to the Commission on Human Rights and the General Assembly;

15. *Requests* the Secretary-General to submit a comprehensive report on the matter to the General Assembly at its sixtieth session.

Honour crimes

The Secretary-General, in his August report [A/59/281] on violence against women (see p. 1148), provided information on measures taken by 23 Member States and the UN system to eliminate honour crimes against women, including resolutions adopted in April by the Commission on Human Rights relating to honour crimes and to violence against women migrant workers (see p. 777). Several Member States indicated that crimes committed in the name of honour did not exist, or were not known to exist, and were not covered by any specific legislation, while other States did not distinguish them from other crimes of violence against women and dealt with them under the relevant provisions of their criminal code. In some countries, policies and measures were being developed to provide greater insight into the nature and scale of honour and honour-related violence. Guidelines were also being developed to give more adequate protection to women in the asylum process. The Secretary-General recommended that crimes against women committed in the name of honour, where reported, should be criminalized and speedily prosecuted.

GENERAL ASSEMBLY ACTION

On 20 December [meeting 74], the General Assembly, on the recommendation of the Third Committee [A/59/496], adopted **resolution 59/165** without vote [agenda item 98].

Working towards the elimination of crimes against women and girls committed in the name of honour

The General Assembly,

Reaffirming the obligation of all States to promote and protect human rights and fundamental freedoms, including the right to life, liberty and security of person, as stated in the Universal Declaration of Human Rights, and reaffirming also the obligations of States parties under human rights instruments, in particular the International Covenant on Economic, Social and Cultural Rights, the International Covenant on Civil and Political Rights, the Convention on the Elimination of All Forms of Discrimination against Women and the Convention on the Rights of the Child,

Reaffirming also the Vienna Declaration and Programme of Action and the Declaration on the Elimination of Violence against Women, as well as the goals and commitments contained in the Beijing Declaration and Platform for Action adopted at the Fourth World Conference on Women, and the outcome document of the special session of the General Assembly entitled "Women 2000: gender equality, development and peace for the twenty-first century",

Recalling its resolutions 57/179 of 18 December 2002 and 58/147 of 22 December 2003, as well as Commission on Human Rights resolution 2004/46 of 20 April 2004,

Recalling also its resolution 58/185 of 22 December 2003, in which it called for an in-depth study on violence against women, including crimes committed in the name of honour, as well as its resolution 57/190 of 18 December 2002, in which it called for an in-depth study on violence against children,

Bearing in mind that States have an obligation to exercise due diligence to prevent, investigate and punish the perpetrators of crimes against women and girls committed in the name of honour and to provide protection to the victims, and that not doing so violates and impairs or nullifies the enjoyment of their human rights and fundamental freedoms,

Stressing the need to treat all forms of violence against women and girls, including crimes committed in the name of honour, as a criminal offence, punishable by law,

Stressing also the need to identify and effectively address the root causes of violence against women, in particular crimes committed in the name of honour, which take many different forms,

Aware that inadequate data on violence against women, including crimes committed in the name of honour, hinder informed policy analysis, at both the domestic and the international levels, and efforts to eliminate such violence,

Deeply concerned that women and girls continue to be victims of these crimes, as described in the relevant sections of the reports of the Human Rights Committee, the Committee on the Elimination of Discrimination against Women, the Committee on the Rights of the Child and the Committee on Economic, Social and Cultural Rights, and noting in this regard successive reports of the Special Rapporteur of the Commission on Human Rights on violence against women, its causes and consequences,

Emphasizing that such crimes are incompatible with all religious and cultural values,

Emphasizing also that the elimination of crimes against women and girls committed in the name of honour requires greater efforts and commitment on the part of Governments and the international community, inter alia, through international cooperation efforts, and civil society, including non-governmental organizations, and that fundamental changes in societal attitude are required,

Underlining the importance of the empowerment of women and their effective participation in decision-making and policy-making processes as one of the critical tools to prevent and eliminate crimes against women and girls committed in the name of honour,

1. *Welcomes:*

(a) The report of the Secretary-General on violence against women;

(b) The activities and initiatives of States aimed at the elimination of crimes against women committed in the name of honour, including the adoption of amendments to relevant national laws relating to such crimes, the effective implementation of such laws and educational, social and other measures, including national information and awareness-raising campaigns, as well as activities and initiatives of States aimed at the elimination of all other forms of violence against women;

(c) The efforts, such as projects, undertaken by United Nations bodies, funds and programmes, including the United Nations Population Fund, the United Nations Children's Fund and the United Nations Development Fund for Women, to address the issue of crimes against women committed in the name of honour, and encourages them to coordinate their efforts;

(d) The work carried out by civil society, including non-governmental organizations, such as women's or-

ganizations, grass-roots movements and individuals, in raising awareness of such crimes and their harmful effects;

2. *Expresses its concern* that women continue to be victims of crimes committed in the name of honour, and at the continuing occurrence in all regions of the world of such violence, which takes many different forms, and at failures to prosecute and punish perpetrators;

3. *Calls upon* all States:

(a) To fulfil their obligations under the relevant international human rights instruments and to implement the Beijing Declaration and Platform for Action and the outcome document of the special session of the General Assembly;

(b) To continue to intensify efforts to prevent and eliminate crimes against women and girls committed in the name of honour, which take many different forms, by using legislative, administrative and programmatic measures;

(c) To investigate promptly and thoroughly, prosecute effectively and document cases of crimes against women and girls committed in the name of honour and punish the perpetrators;

(d) To intensify efforts to raise awareness of the need to prevent and eliminate crimes against women and girls committed and condoned in the name of honour, with the aim of changing the attitudes and behaviour that allow such crimes to be committed by involving, inter alia, community leaders;

(e) To intensify efforts to raise awareness about the responsibility of men to promote gender equality and bring about change in attitudes to eliminate gender stereotypes, including, specifically, their role in preventing crimes against women and girls committed in the name of honour;

(f) To encourage the efforts of the media to engage in awareness-raising campaigns;

(g) To encourage, support and implement measures and programmes aimed at increasing the knowledge and understanding of the causes and consequences of crimes against women and girls committed in the name of honour, including the provision of training for those responsible for enforcing the law, such as police personnel and judicial and legal personnel, and to strengthen their capacity to respond to complaints of such crimes in an impartial and effective manner and take necessary measures to ensure the protection of actual and potential victims;

(h) To continue to support the work of civil society, including non-governmental organizations, in addressing this issue and to strengthen cooperation with intergovernmental and non-governmental organizations;

(i) To establish, strengthen or facilitate, where possible, support services to respond to the needs of actual and potential victims by, inter alia, providing for them the appropriate protection, safe shelter, counselling, legal aid, health-care services, including in the areas of sexual and reproductive health, psychological health and other relevant areas, rehabilitation and reintegration into society;

(j) To address effectively complaints of crimes against women and girls committed in the name of honour, inter alia, by creating, strengthening or facilitating institutional mechanisms so that victims and others can report such crimes in a safe and confidential environment;

(k) To gather and disseminate statistical information on the occurrence of such crimes, including information disaggregated by sex and age, and to make any such information available to the Secretariat for use in the in-depth study on violence against women, in accordance with resolution 58/185, and the in-depth study on violence against children, in accordance with resolution 57/190;

(l) To include, where appropriate, in their reports to the human rights treaty bodies information on legal and policy measures adopted and implemented in their efforts to prevent and eliminate crimes against women and girls committed in the name of honour;

4. *Invites:*

(a) The international community, including relevant United Nations bodies, funds and programmes, inter alia, through technical assistance and advisory services programmes, to support the efforts of all countries, at their request, aimed at strengthening institutional capacity for preventing crimes against women and girls committed in the name of honour and at addressing the root causes of such crimes;

(b) The relevant human rights treaty bodies, where appropriate, and the Special Rapporteur of the Commission on Human Rights on violence against women, its causes and consequences to continue to address this issue;

5. *Requests* the Secretary-General to report on the implementation of the present resolution in his report on the question of violence against women to the General Assembly at its sixtieth session.

Women, peace and security

In response to Security Council resolution 1325(2000) on women and peace and security [YUN 2000, p. 1113], the Secretary-General reported in October [S/2004/814] on progress achieved thus far and identified gaps and challenges in the implementation of that resolution within the intergovernmental processes, and in the areas of conflict prevention and early warning; peace processes and negotiations; peacekeeping operations; humanitarian response; post-conflict reconstruction; disarmament, demobilization and reintegration; prevention of and response to gender-based violence in armed conflict; gender balance in recruitment; coordination and partnership; monitoring and reporting; and information dissemination and exchange.

Initiatives were taken to develop policies, action plans, guidelines and indicators, increase access to gender expertise, provide training and promote consultation with and participation of women, increase attention to human rights and support women's groups. Gaps and challenges remained in relation to women's participation in conflict prevention and peace processes, and attention to the contribution and needs of women in decision-making positions.

The Secretary-General said that he intended to develop system-wide strategies and action plans for increasing attention to gender perspectives in conflict prevention and for mainstreaming them into peacekeeping activities, particularly in the planning of new operations, and to review recent peace processes and analyse the obstacles to and missed opportunities for women's full participation in negotiations and develop strategies accordingly. He also intended to routinely incorporate gender perspectives in all thematic and country reports to the Security Council and urged Member States, UN entities and civil society to develop guidelines and training initiatives based on the model provisions on promoting gender equality in peace agreements and guidelines for increasing attention to the needs and contribution of women and girls in disarmament, demobilization and reintegration programmes. He made other recommendations for action by Member States, the General Assembly, the Security Council, civil society and UN system organizations.

He concluded that, since the adoption of resolution 1325(2000), a positive shift had taken place in international understanding of the importance of women's participation as equal partners in all areas related to peace and security. However, the real test of the adequacy of efforts so far taken was in their impact on the ground. Gender perspectives were not systematically incorporated in planning, implementation, monitoring and reporting. Increasing the number of women in high-level, decision-making positions in peacekeeping operations was a challenge, as was the protection and promotion of the human rights of women and girls in armed conflicts. Inadequate resource allocation had also contributed to the slow progress in implementing the resolution. He recommended that budgetary resources be specifically allocated for gender mainstreaming and initiatives targeted at women and girls.

SECURITY COUNCIL ACTION

On 28 October [meeting 5066], following consultations among Security Council members, the President made statement **S/PRST/2004/40** on behalf of the Council:

> The Security Council reaffirms its commitment to the continuing and full implementation of its resolution 1325(2000), and welcomes the increasing focus on the situation of women and girls in armed conflict since the adoption of resolution 1325(2000) in October 2000. The Council recalls the statement by its President of 31 October 2002 and the meeting held on 29 October 2003 as valuable demonstrations of that commitment.

The Council also recalls the Beijing Declaration and Platform for Action and the outcome document of the twenty-third special session of the General Assembly, entitled "Women 2000: gender equality, development and peace for the twenty-first century", in particular the commitments concerning women and armed conflict.

The Council welcomes the report of the Secretary-General on women and peace and security, and expresses its intention to study its recommendations. The Council welcomes the efforts of the United Nations system, Member States, civil society and other relevant actors, to promote the equal participation of women in efforts to build sustainable peace and security.

The Council strongly condemns the continued acts of gender-based violence in situations of armed conflict. The Council also condemns all violations of the human rights of women and girls in situations of armed conflict and the use of sexual exploitation, violence and abuse. The Council urges the complete cessation by all parties of such acts with immediate effect. It stresses the need to end impunity for such acts as part of a comprehensive approach to seeking peace, justice, truth and national reconciliation. The Council welcomes the efforts of the United Nations system to establish and implement strategies and programmes to prevent and report on gender-based violence, and urges the Secretary-General to further his efforts in this regard. The Council requests the Secretary-General to ensure that human rights monitors and members of commissions of inquiry have the necessary expertise and training in gender-based crimes and in the conduct of investigations, including in a culturally sensitive manner favourable to the needs, dignity and rights of the victims. The Council urges all international and national courts specifically established to prosecute war-related crimes to provide gender expertise, gender training for all staff and gender-sensitive programmes for victims and witness protection. It emphasizes the urgent need for programmes that provide support to survivors of gender-based violence. The Council further requests that appropriate attention be given to the issue of gender-based violence in all future reports to it.

The Council reaffirms the important role of women in the prevention of conflict and supports the Secretary-General's intention to develop a comprehensive system-wide strategy and action plan for increasing attention to gender perspectives in conflict prevention. The Council urges all relevant actors to work collaboratively, including through strengthened interaction with women's organizations, to ensure the full participation of women and the incorporation of a gender perspective in all conflict prevention work.

The Council also welcomes the Secretary-General's intention to develop a comprehensive strategy and action plan for mainstreaming a gender perspective into all peacekeeping activities and operations and to incorporate gender perspectives in each thematic and country report to the Council. In support of this process, the Council reaffirms its commitment to integrate fully gender perspectives into the mandates of all peacekeeping missions. It recognizes the con-

tribution of the gender adviser within the Department of Peacekeeping Operations to advancing the implementation of resolution 1325 (2000), and requests the Secretary-General to consider an equivalent arrangement within the Department of Political Affairs to further support such implementation.

The Council considers that an increase in the representation of women in all aspects of conflict prevention, peacekeeping and peacebuilding operations and humanitarian response is urgently needed. To that end, the Council urges the Secretary-General to strengthen his efforts to identify suitable female candidates, including, as appropriate, from troop-contributing countries, in conformity with Article 101 of the Charter of the United Nations and taking into account the principle of equitable geographical balance. Such efforts should include the implementation of targeted recruitment strategies and also seek to identify candidates for senior level positions, including in the military and civilian police services.

The Council recognizes the vital contribution of women in promoting peace and their role in reconstruction processes. The Council welcomes the Secretary-General's intention to develop strategies to encourage the full participation of women in all stages of the peace process. The Council also requests the Secretary-General to encourage gender mainstreaming in disarmament, demobilization and reintegration programmes by developing guidelines to increase attention to the needs of women and girls in such programmes. It further requests the Secretary-General to mainstream a gender perspective in all aspects of post-conflict reconstruction programmes, including through the strengthening of gender theme groups in countries emerging from conflict, and to ensure that all policies and programmes in support of post-conflict constitutional, judicial and legislative reform, including truth and reconciliation and electoral processes, promote the full participation of women, gender equality and women's human rights.

The Council recognizes the important contribution of civil society to the implementation of resolution 1325(2000), and encourages Member States to continue to collaborate with civil society, in particular with local women's networks and organizations, in order to strengthen implementation. To that end, the Council welcomes the efforts of Member States in implementing resolution 1325(2000) at the national level, including the development of national action plans, and encourages Member States to continue to pursue such implementation.

The Council recognizes that significant progress has been made in the implementation of resolution 1325(2000) in certain areas of United Nations peace and security work. The Council expresses its readiness to further promote the implementation of this resolution, and in particular through active cooperation with the Economic and Social Council and the General Assembly. In order to further consolidate this progress, the Council requests the Secretary-General to submit to it in October 2005 an action plan, with time lines, for implementing resolution 1325(2000) across the United Nations system, with a view to strengthening commitment and accountability at the highest levels, as well as to allow for improved accountability, monitoring and reporting on progress on implementation within the United Nations system.

Conflict prevention, management and resolution

On 2 March [E/2004/27], the Commission on the Status of Women held a panel discussion on women's equal participation in conflict prevention, management and conflict resolution in post-conflict peace-building. It had before it a report of the Secretary-General on the subject [E/CN.6/2004/10]. The report was based on the recommendations of an expert group meeting (10-13 November 2003, Ottawa, Canada) on the theme "Peace agreements as a means for promoting gender equality and ensuring participation of women—a framework of model provisions" [EMG/PEACE/2003/REPORT]; case studies and contributions provided by regional experts, UN entities and civil society; and the Secretary-General's study and report on women, peace and security [YUN 2002, p. 1142]. It covered UN peace and security initiatives, and the role of peace agreements in promoting gender equality and the participation of women in peace processes.

According to the report, although there was increasing understanding of the important contribution of women to peace-building, they continued to be largely absent from formal peace negotiations. Support by donors and the international community of women's efforts for their effective engagement in formal peace processes was often lacking, provided late or not sustained long enough to have an impact. Customs, traditions and stereotypes also limited or narrowly defined women's roles in public life and decision-making. Women were often excluded from internationally sponsored peace processes because they were not political leaders or political decision-makers, nor had they participated in conflicts as combatants. Even when women did participate in formal peace agreements, they often lacked the capacity to contribute to shaping the agenda of such negotiations and a mandate to speak on behalf of the majority of women. Moreover, issues related to equality and the position of women within post-conflict society were typically excluded from peace agreements, as gender relations were rarely perceived as central to the causes of conflict and hence the solution.

The expert group meeting (above) identified the obligations of various actors in peace processes to enhance attention to gender equality and participation of women, and with regard to the gender-sensitive implementation of peace agreements. The Secretary-General recommended that the Commission take note of the recommendations of the expert group and call for their systematic use by all actors, or consider the actions he was recommending in his report to strengthen the use of peace agreements as tools for the promotion of gender equality and the participation of women. It might also wish to invite different actors, particularly UN entities, to use the Secretary-General's recommendations as a guide for action in all peace processes.

Also before the Commission was the report of an expert group meeting on enhancing women's participation in electoral processes in post-conflict countries (New York, 19-22 January) [E/CN.6/2004/CRP.7], which made recommendations on the incorporation of gender perspectives into the phases of elections and the roles of a diverse range of actors in support of women's full participation.

ECONOMIC AND SOCIAL COUNCIL ACTION

On 21 July [meeting 47], the Economic and Social Council, on the recommendation of the Commission on the Status of Women [E/2004/27], adopted **resolution 2004/12** without vote [agenda item 14 *(a)*].

Agreed conclusions of the Commission on the Status of Women on women's equal participation in conflict prevention, management and resolution and in post-conflict peace-building

The Economic and Social Council

Endorses the following agreed conclusions adopted by the Commission on the Status of Women at its forty-eighth session with respect to women's equal participation in conflict prevention, management and resolution and in post-conflict peace-building:

1. The Commission on the Status of Women recalls and reiterates the strategic objectives and actions of the Beijing Declaration and Platform for Action, the outcome document of the twenty-third special session of the General Assembly entitled "Women 2000: gender equality, development and peace for the twenty-first century", and its agreed conclusions on women and armed conflict adopted at its forty-second session in 1998. It also recalls the Convention on the Elimination of All Forms of Discrimination against Women, Security Council resolution 1325(2000) of 31 October 2000 on women and peace and security and all relevant resolutions of the General Assembly, including resolution 58/142 of 22 December 2003 on women and political participation.

2. The Commission calls for the full respect of international human rights law and international humanitarian law, including the four Geneva Conventions of 12 August 1949, in particular Geneva Convention relative to the Protection of Civilian Persons in Time of War.

3. The Commission calls for the promotion and protection of the full enjoyment of all human rights and fundamental freedoms by women and girls at all times, including during conflict prevention, conflict management and conflict resolution and in post-conflict peacebuilding. It further calls for protection and security for women and girls under threat of vio-

lence and their freedom of movement and participation in social, political and economic activities.

4. The Commission recognizes that the root causes of armed conflict are multidimensional in nature and thus require a comprehensive and integrated approach to the prevention of armed conflict.

5. International cooperation based on the principles of the Charter of the United Nations enhances women's full and equal participation in conflict prevention, conflict management and conflict resolution and in post-conflict peacebuilding and contributes to the promotion of sustainable and durable peace.

6. To achieve sustainable and durable peace, the full and equal participation of women and girls and the integration of gender perspectives in all aspects of conflict prevention, management and resolution and in post-conflict peacebuilding is essential. Yet women continue to be underrepresented in the processes, institutions and mechanisms dealing with these areas. Further effort is therefore needed to promote gender equality and ensure women's equal participation at all levels of decision-making in all relevant institutions. Further effort, including consideration of adequate resourcing, is also needed to build and consolidate the capacity of women and women's groups to participate fully in these processes, as well as to promote understanding of the essential role of women. In this regard, the international community should use lessons learned from actual experience to identify and overcome barriers to women's equal participation.

7. The Commission recognizes that while both men and women suffer from the consequences of armed conflict, there is a differential impact on women and girls, who are often subject to, and affected by, particular forms of violence and deprivation. The Commission calls for measures to prevent gender-based violence, including sexual violence against women and girls, as well as trafficking in human beings, especially trafficking in women and girls, arising from armed conflict and in post-conflict situations and to prosecute perpetrators of such crimes.

8. The Commission encourages the collection and dissemination of sex-disaggregated data and information for planning, evaluation and analysis in order to promote the mainstreaming of a gender perspective into conflict prevention, management and resolution and in post-conflict peace-building.

9. Peace agreements provide a vehicle for the promotion of gender equality and the participation of women in post-conflict situations. Significant opportunities for women's participation arise in the preparatory phase leading up to a peace agreement. The content of a peace agreement likewise offers significant scope for ensuring that the rights, concerns and priorities of women and girls are fully addressed. Finally, once a peace agreement has been concluded, its implementation should be pursued with explicit attention to women's full and equal participation and the goal of gender equality.

10. Women's full and equal participation and the integration of gender perspectives are crucial to democratic electoral processes in post-conflict situations. A gender-sensitive constitutional and legal framework, especially electoral laws and regulations, is necessary to ensure that women can fully participate in such processes. Political parties can play a crucial role in promoting women's equal participation. Steps are also necessary to ensure that women participate fully in, and that a gender perspective is incorporated throughout, the design and implementation of voter and civic education programmes and in election administration and observation.

11. Governments in particular, as well as the United Nations system, especially those United Nations entities having a mandate with regard to peace and security, and other relevant international, regional and national actors, including civil society, have a responsibility for advancing gender equality and ensuring women's full and equal participation in all aspects of peace processes and in post-conflict peacebuilding, reconstruction, rehabilitation and reconciliation, where they are participants in these processes.

12. In regard to conflict prevention, the Commission calls upon Governments, as well as all other relevant participants in these processes:

(*a*) To improve the collection, analysis and inclusion of information on women and gender issues as part of conflict prevention and early warning efforts;

(*b*) To ensure better collaboration and coordination between efforts to promote gender equality and efforts aimed at conflict prevention;

(*c*) To support capacity-building, especially for civil society, in particular for women's organizations, in order to increase community commitment to conflict prevention;

(*d*) To continue to make resources available nationally and internationally for the prevention of conflict and ensure women's participation in the elaboration and implementation of strategies for preventing conflict.

13. In regard to peace processes, the Commission calls upon Governments, as well as all other relevant participants in these processes:

(*a*) To promote women's full, equal and effective participation as actors in all peace processes, in particular negotiation, mediation and facilitation;

(*b*) To ensure that peace agreements address, from a gender perspective, the full range of security aspects, including legal, political, social, economic and physical, and also address the specific needs and priorities of women and girls;

(*c*) To ensure, in the implementation phase of a peace agreement, that all provisions concerning gender equality and the participation of women are fully complied with and that all provisions of the peace agreement, including those concerning demobilization, disarmament, reintegration and rehabilitation, are implemented in a manner that promotes gender equality and ensures women's full and equal participation;

(*d*) To promote women's full and equal access to public information relative to peace processes;

(*e*) To review, on a regular basis, their contributions to the promotion of gender equality and the full and equal participation of women, and to fulfil their monitoring, accountability and reporting obligations in the implementation of peace agreements;

(*f*) With regard to gender mainstreaming, to ensure and support the full participation of women at all levels of decision-making and implementation in development activities and peace processes, including conflict prevention and resolution, post-conflict reconstruction, peacemaking, peacekeeping and peace-building and, in this regard, support the involvement of women's organizations, community-based organizations and non-governmental organizations;

(g) To develop and strengthen the provision of gender advisory capacity and gender-sensitive training programmes for all staff in missions relating to armed conflicts. In this regard, the Commission takes note of the report of the Secretary-General.

14. In regard to post-conflict peacebuilding, the Commission calls upon Governments, as well as all other relevant participants in these processes,

Concerning elections:

(a) To ensure equal access of women in all stages of the electoral process and to consider the adoption of measures for increasing women's participation in elections through, inter alia, individual voter registration, temporary gender-specific positive actions and access to information, representation on bodies administering elections and as election monitors and observers, as well as encouraging political parties to involve women fully and equally in all aspects of their operations;

(b) To ensure equal access for women to voter and civic education, to provide women candidates with full support, training and financial resources and to eliminate discriminatory practices hampering women's participation either as voters or candidates.

Concerning reconstruction and rehabilitation:

(a) To ensure the full participation of women on an equal basis in the reconstruction and rehabilitation process;

(b) To ensure the equal access of women to social services, in particular in the areas of health and education, and, in this regard, to promote the provision of adequate health care and health services, assistance for women and girls in conflict and post-conflict situations and counselling for post-conflict trauma;

(c) To facilitate equal employment opportunities for women to achieve economic empowerment.

15. The realization and the achievement of the goals of gender equality, development and peace need to be supported by the allocation of the necessary human, financial and material resources for specific and targeted activities to ensure gender equality at the local, national, regional and international levels, as well as by enhanced and increased international cooperation.

16. The Commission requests the Secretary-General to disseminate the present agreed conclusions widely, including to the high-level panel on global security threats and reform of the international system.

The Conference on Gender Justice in Post-Conflict Situations (New York, 15-17 September) [S/2004/862], organized by UNIFEM and the International Legal Assistance Consortium (ILAC), brought together women legal and judicial officials from over twelve conflict-affected countries and regions, UN officials, Member States' representatives, regional organizations, academic institutions, foundations and private entities. The Conference considered: the reform of national laws (including customary/traditional systems) and constitutions in order to address discrimina-

tory practices and gaps and to advance the protection of women's rights; the establishment of more gender-sensitive justice and transitional justice mechanisms and the provision of reparations and rehabilitative services to victims; rehabilitation and reform of the judicial infrastructure, institutions and processes to enhance women's involvement in, and their access to, justice; increased employment and specialized training for women judges, prosecutors and lawyers; establishing/strengthening of institutions, mechanisms, policies and strategies to redress gender-based disparities; addressing the factors preventing equal access to public services and economic opportunities; increased participation of women in peace-making processes and negotiation of peace agreements and their implementation; participation of women and incorporation of gender dimensions in the planning and implementation of UN peace operations; enhancing responsibility and accountability of UN peacekeeping and humanitarian personnel in relation to the female population in deployed areas; and the prioritization of gender justice within the UN system and new structures to accelerate progress on gender justice.

The conference recommended the establishment of a high-level mechanism to determine the issues and recommendations requiring follow-up action, and to discuss the need for a separate UN office to coordinate assistance for justice systems and related institutions, including gender justice requirements.

Women and children taken hostage

In response to Commission resolution 46/1 [YUN 2002, p. 1144], the Secretary-General transmitted a report [E/CN.6/2004/6 & Corr.1] on the release of women and children taken hostage, including those subsequently imprisoned, in armed conflicts, which summarized information provided by 11 Member States and relevant UN system entities. He recommended that the Commission might wish to renew its commitment to resolution 46/1 and encourage Governments to report on its implementation and relevance in the context of the follow-up to Security Council resolution 1325(2000).

Communication. On 4 March [E/CN.6/2004/13], Armenia drew attention to a number of allegations contained in the Secretary-General's report (see p. 1154), which, it said, were against it. Armenia refuted those allegations.

Commission action. In a March resolution [E/2004/27 (res. 48/3)], the Commission emphasized the importance of objective, responsible and impartial information on hostages, verifiable by international organizations, in facilitating their release, and called for assistance to those organizations in that regard. It requested the Secretary-General and international organizations to facilitate the release of civilian women and children taken hostage. It further requested the Secretary-General to submit a report to the Commission at its fiftieth (2006) session on the implementation of the resolution.

Gender equality

Role of men and boys

In March [E/2004/27], the Commission on the Status of Women reviewed the role of men and boys in achieving gender equality. It had before it a summary of its 2 March panel discussion [E/CN.6/ 2004/14/CRP.10] and the Secretary-General's report [E/CN.6/2004/9] on the subject, which focused on the role of men and boys in achieving gender equality in socialization and education; as agents of change in the labour market and workplace; in the sharing of family responsibilities, including caring roles; and the prevention of HIV/AIDS. The report concluded that, since men had the potential to bring about change in attitudes, roles and relationships, they should be actively involved in developing and implementing legislation and policies to foster gender equality, and in providing positive role models for doing so in the family, workplace and society at large. The report provided specific recommendations for action by Governments, international organizations, including the United Nations, non-governmental organizations (NGOs), the private sector, the media and other stakeholders.

On 12 March, the Commission took note of the Secretary-General's report.

ECONOMIC AND SOCIAL COUNCIL ACTION

On 21 July [meeting 47], the Economic and Social Council, on the recommendation of the Commission on the Status of Women [E/2004/27], adopted **resolution 2004/11** without vote [agenda item 14(*a*)].

Agreed conclusions of the Commission on the Status of Women on the role of men and boys in achieving gender equality

The Economic and Social Council

Endorses the following agreed conclusions adopted by the Commission on the Status of Women at its forty-eighth session with respect to the role of men and boys in achieving gender equality:

1. The Commission on the Status of Women recalls and reiterates that the Beijing Declaration and Platform for Action encouraged men to participate fully in all actions towards gender equality and urged the establishment of the principle of shared power and responsibility between women and men at home, in the community, in the workplace and in the wider national and international communities. The Commission also recalls and reiterates the outcome document adopted at the twenty-third special session of the General Assembly entitled "Women 2000: gender equality, development and peace for the twenty-first century", which emphasized that men must take joint responsibility with women for the promotion of gender equality.

2. The Commission recognizes that, while men and boys sometimes face discriminatory barriers and practices, they can and do make contributions to gender equality in many capacities, including as individuals and as members of families, social groups and communities, in all spheres of society.

3. The Commission recognizes that gender inequalities still exist and are reflected in imbalances of power between women and men in all spheres of society. The Commission further recognizes that everyone benefits from gender equality and that the negative impacts of gender inequality are borne by society as a whole and emphasizes, therefore, that men and boys, by taking responsibility themselves and working jointly in partnership with women and girls, are essential to the achievement of the goals of gender equality, development and peace. The Commission recognizes the capacity of men and boys to bring about change in attitudes, relationships and access to resources and decision-making, which are critical for the promotion of gender equality and the full enjoyment of all human rights by women.

4. The Commission acknowledges and encourages men and boys to continue to take positive initiatives to eliminate gender stereotypes and promote gender equality, including combating violence against women, through networks, peer programmes, information campaigns and training programmes. The Commission acknowledges the critical role of gender-sensitive education and training in achieving gender equality.

5. The Commission also recognizes that the participation of men and boys in achieving gender equality must be consistent with the empowerment of women and girls, and acknowledges that efforts must be made to address the undervaluation of many types of work, abilities and roles associated with women. In this regard, it is important that resources for gender equality initiatives for men and boys do not compromise equal opportunities and resources for women and girls.

6. The Commission urges Governments and, as appropriate, the relevant funds, programmes and organizations and the specialized agencies of the United Nations system, the international financial institutions, civil society, including the private sector and non-governmental organizations, and other stakeholders to take the following actions:

(*a*) Encourage and support the capacity of men and boys to foster gender equality, including by acting in partnership with women and girls as agents for change and providing positive leadership, in particular where men are still key decision makers, responsible for policies, programmes and legislation, as well as holders of economic and organizational power and public resources;

(*b*) Promote understanding of the importance of fathers, mothers, legal guardians and other caregivers for the well-being of children and the promotion of gender equality, and the need to develop policies, programmes and school curricula that encourage and maximize their positive involvement in achieving gender equality and positive results for children, families and communities;

(c) Create and improve training and education programmes to enhance awareness and knowledge among men and women of their roles as parents, legal guardians and caregivers and the importance of sharing family responsibilities, and include fathers as well as mothers in programmes that teach infant childcare and development;

(d) Develop and include in education programmes for parents, legal guardians and other caregivers information on ways and means to increase the capacity of men to raise children in a manner oriented towards gender equality;

(e) Encourage men and boys to work with women and girls in the design of policies and programmes for men and boys aimed at gender equality, and foster the involvement of men and boys in gender mainstreaming efforts in order to ensure improved design of all policies and programmes;

(f) Encourage the design and implementation of programmes at all levels to accelerate a sociocultural change towards gender equality, especially through the upbringing and educational process and by changing harmful traditional perceptions of and attitudes regarding male and female roles in order to achieve the full and equal participation of women and men in society;

(g) Develop and implement programmes for preschools, schools, community centres, youth organizations, sport clubs and centres and other groups dealing with children and youth, including training for teachers, social workers and other professionals who deal with children, in order to foster positive attitudes and behaviour with regard to gender equality;

(h) Promote critical reviews of school curricula, textbooks and other information, education and communication materials at all levels in order to recommend ways to strengthen the promotion of gender equality that involves the engagement of boys as well as girls;

(i) Develop and implement strategies to educate boys and girls and men and women about tolerance, mutual respect for all individuals and the promotion of all human rights;

(j) Develop and utilize a variety of methods in public information campaigns on the role of men and boys in promoting gender equality, including through approaches specifically targeting boys and young men;

(k) Engage media, advertising and other related professionals, through the development of training and other programmes, on the importance of promoting gender equality, the non-stereotypical portrayal of women and girls and men and boys and on the harm caused by portraying women and girls in a demeaning or exploitative manner, as well as on the enhanced participation of women and girls in the media;

(l) Take effective measures, to the extent consistent with freedom of expression, to combat the growing sexualization of, and use of pornography in, media content and in the rapid development of information and communication technology, encourage men in the media to refrain from presenting women as inferior beings and exploiting them as sexual objects and commodities, combat information and communications technology- and media-based violence against women,

including criminal misuse of information and communication technology for sexual harassment, sexual exploitation and trafficking in women and girls, and support the development and use of such technology as a resource for the empowerment of women and girls, including those affected by violence, abuse and other forms of sexual exploitation;

(m) Adopt and implement legislation and/or policies to close the gap between women's and men's pay, and promote reconciliation of occupational and family responsibilities, including through the reduction of occupational segregation, the introduction or expansion of parental leave, and flexible working arrangements, such as voluntary part-time work, teleworking and other home-based work;

(n) Encourage men, through training and education, to participate fully in the care and support of others, including older persons, persons with disabilities and sick persons, in particular children and other dependants;

(o) Encourage the active involvement of men and boys, through education projects and peer-based programmes, in eliminating gender stereotypes as well as gender inequality, in particular in relation to sexually transmitted infections, including HIV/AIDS, as well as their full participation in prevention, advocacy, care, treatment, support and impact evaluation programmes;

(p) Ensure men's access to and utilization of reproductive and sexual health services and programmes, including HIV/AIDS-related programmes and services, and encourage men to participate with women in programmes designed to prevent the transmission and treat all forms of HIV/AIDS and other sexually transmitted infections;

(q) Design and implement programmes to encourage and enable men to adopt safe and responsible sexual and reproductive behaviour and to use effectively methods to prevent unwanted pregnancies and sexually transmitted infections, including HIV/AIDS;

(r) Encourage and support men and boys to take an active part in the prevention and elimination of all forms of violence, especially gender-based violence, including in the context of HIV/AIDS, and increase awareness of men's and boys' responsibility in ending the cycle of violence, inter alia, through the promotion of attitudinal and behavioural change, integrated education and training prioritizing the safety of women and children, the prosecution and rehabilitation of perpetrators of violence and support for survivors, recognizing that men and boys also experience violence;

(s) Encourage increased understanding among men of how violence, including trafficking for the purposes of commercialized sexual exploitation, forced marriage and forced labour, harms women, men and children and undermines gender equality, and consider measures aimed at eliminating the demand for trafficked women and children;

(t) Encourage and support both women and men in leadership positions, including political leaders, traditional leaders, business leaders, community and religious leaders, musicians, artists and athletes, to provide positive role models of gender equality;

(u) Encourage men in leadership positions to ensure equal access for women to education, property rights and inheritance rights and to promote equal access to information technology and business and economic opportunities, including in international trade, in order to provide women with the tools to enable them to take part fully and equally in economic and political decision-making processes at all levels;

(v) Identify and fully utilize all contexts in which a large number of men can be reached, particularly in male-dominated institutions, industries and associations, in order to sensitize men on their roles and responsibilities in the promotion of gender equality and the full enjoyment of all human rights by women, including in relation to HIV/AIDS and violence against women;

(w) Develop and use statistics to support and/or carry out research, inter alia, on the cultural, social and economic conditions that influence the attitudes and behaviour of men and boys towards women and girls, their awareness of gender inequalities and their involvement in promoting gender equality;

(x) Carry out research on the views of men and boys on gender equality and their perceptions of their roles, through which further programmes and policies can be developed, identify and widely disseminate good practices, and assess the impact of efforts undertaken to engage men and boys in achieving gender equality;

(y) Promote and encourage the representation of men in institutional mechanisms for the advancement of women;

(z) Encourage men and boys to support the equal participation of women in conflict prevention, management and resolution and in post-conflict peace-building;

7. The Commission urges all entities within the United Nations system to take into account the recommendations contained in the present agreed conclusions and to disseminate the agreed conclusions widely.

Women's health

Women, the girl child and HIV/AIDS

In a March resolution on women, the girl child and HIV/AIDS [E/2004/27 (res. 48/2)], the Commission on the Status of Women stressed that gender equality and the empowerment of women and girls were fundamental elements in the reduction of their vulnerability to HIV/AIDS and that their advancement was key to reversing the pandemic. It welcomed the launch in February by the Joint United Nations Programme on HIV/AIDS (UNAIDS) and its partners, of the Global Coalition on Women and AIDS to raise awareness of the effects of HIV/AIDS on women and girls and to stimulate the fight against the disease. It called for enhanced efforts by all relevant actors to include a gender perspective in the development of HIV/AIDS programmes and policies and in the training of personnel involved in their implementation, and requested the Secretary-General to do so when preparing his report on the implementation of the 2001 Declaration of Commitment on HIV/AIDS, adopted by the twenty-sixth

special session of the General Assembly in resolution S-26/2 [YUN 2001, p. 1126].

Traditional practices affecting the health of women and girls

By **decision 2004/276** of 22 July, the Economic and Social Council endorsed the decision of the Commission on Human Rights to renew for a further three years the mandate of the Special Rapporteur on traditional practices affecting the health of women and the girl child (see p. 777).

Women and human rights

Trafficking in women and girls

In July [A/59/185 & Corr.1], the Secretary-General, responding to General Assembly resolution 57/176 [YUN 2002, p. 1146], reported on trafficking in women and girls, focusing on information provided by 41 Member States on their legal and policy measures. He also reported on the activities of the UN system and other organizations to combat trafficking in women and girls, including the adoption by the Commission on Human Rights, at its sixtieth (2004) session, of a resolution on the trafficking in women and girls [E/2004/23 (res. 2004/45)], and a decision establishing the mandate of a new Special Rapporteur for three years to focus on the human rights aspects of trafficking in persons victims, especially women and children [dec. 2004/110] (see p. 778).

The Secretary-General concluded that to successfully combat trafficking, the prosecution of traffickers had to go hand in hand with the protection of the victims. He recommended that States continue to ratify international instruments and conclude agreements to ensure and facilitate the prosecution of offenders, and seek international cooperation for assistance and in the exchange of information on good practices against trafficking; place emphasis on adopting and enforcing anti-trafficking legislation; and address the root causes of trafficking in women. He emphasized that all actors, including judicial and law enforcement personnel, migration authorities, academic institutions, NGOs and civil society groups, should collaborate at the national level in the development and implementation of a comprehensive and interdisciplinary approach to trafficking, and that measures to combat trafficking should be continuously monitored to assess their impact.

GENERAL ASSEMBLY ACTION

On 20 December [meeting 74], the General Assembly, on the recommendation of the Third Committee [A/59/496], adopted **resolution 59/166** without vote [agenda item 98].

Trafficking in women and girls

The General Assembly,

Recalling all previous resolutions on the problem of trafficking in women and girls adopted by the General Assembly and the Commission on Human Rights, including their reaffirmation of the principles set forth in relevant human rights instruments and declarations, as well as the Optional Protocol to the Convention on the Rights of the Child on the sale of children, child prostitution and child pornography, the Optional Protocol to the Convention on the Elimination of All Forms of Discrimination against Women and the Convention for the Suppression of the Traffic in Persons and of the Exploitation of the Prostitution of Others,

Welcoming the entry into force of the United Nations Convention against Transnational Organized Crime on 29 September 2003 and of the Protocol to Prevent, Suppress and Punish Trafficking in Persons, Especially Women and Children, supplementing the United Nations Convention against Transnational Organized Crime on 25 December 2003 and the Protocol against the Smuggling of Migrants by Land, Sea and Air, supplementing the United Nations Convention against Transnational Organized Crime on 28 January 2004,

Recalling the United Nations Millennium Declaration, in particular the resolve expressed by Heads of State and Government to intensify efforts to fight transnational organized crime in all its dimensions, including trafficking in human beings,

Reaffirming the provisions pertaining to trafficking in women and girls contained in the outcome documents of relevant international conferences and summits, in particular the strategic objective on the issue of trafficking contained in the Beijing Declaration and Platform for Action adopted by the Fourth World Conference on Women,

Acknowledging the inclusion of gender-related crimes in the Rome Statute of the International Criminal Court, which entered into force on 1 July 2002,

Recognizing the need to address the impact of globalization on the particular problem of trafficking in women and children, in particular girls,

Bearing in mind that all States have an obligation to exercise due diligence to prevent, investigate and punish perpetrators of trafficking in persons and to provide protection to the victims and that not doing so violates and impairs or nullifies the enjoyment of their human rights and fundamental freedoms,

Seriously concerned that an increasing number of women and girls from developing countries and from some countries with economies in transition are being trafficked to developed countries, as well as within and between regions and States, and that men and boys are also victims of trafficking, including for sexual exploitation,

Recognizing that victims of trafficking are particularly exposed to racism, racial discrimination, xenophobia and related intolerance and that women and girl victims are often subject to multiple forms of discrimination on the grounds of their gender as well as their origins,

Acknowledging that women and girl victims of trafficking, on account of their gender, are further disadvantaged and marginalized by a general lack of information or awareness and recognition of their human rights, as well as by the obstacles they meet in gaining access to information and recourse mechanisms in cases of violation of their rights, and that special measures are required for their protection and to increase their awareness,

Recognizing the importance of bilateral, subregional and regional cooperation mechanisms and initiatives of Governments and intergovernmental and non-governmental organizations to address the problem of trafficking in persons, especially women and children,

Recognizing also that global efforts, including international cooperation and technical assistance programmes, to eradicate trafficking in persons, especially women and children, demand the strong political commitment, shared responsibility and active cooperation of all Governments of countries of origin, transit and destination,

Recognizing further that policies and programmes for prevention, rehabilitation and reintegration should be developed through a child- and gender-sensitive, comprehensive and multidisciplinary approach involving all actors in countries of origin, transit and destination,

Concerned about the use of new information technologies, including the Internet, for purposes of exploitation of the prostitution of others and for child pornography, paedophilia and any other forms of sexual exploitation of children, trafficking in women as brides and sex tourism,

Concerned also at the increasing activities of transnational criminal organizations and others that profit from international trafficking in persons, especially women and children, without regard to dangerous and inhumane conditions and in flagrant violation of domestic laws and international standards,

Convinced of the need to protect and assist all victims of trafficking, with full respect for their human rights,

1. *Takes note with appreciation* of the report of the Secretary-General;

2. *Welcomes* the efforts of Governments, United Nations bodies and agencies and intergovernmental and non-governmental organizations to address the particular problem of trafficking in women and girls, and encourages them to continue doing so and to share their knowledge and best practices as widely as possible;

3. *Also welcomes* the appointment of the Special Rapporteur of the Commission on Human Rights on trafficking in persons, especially women and children;

4. *Urges* Governments to take appropriate measures to address the root factors, including poverty and gender inequality, as well as external factors that encourage the particular problem of trafficking in women and girls for prostitution and other forms of commercialized sex, forced marriage and forced labour, in order to eliminate such trafficking, including by strengthening existing legislation with a view to providing better protection of the rights of women and girls and to punishing perpetrators, through both criminal and civil measures;

5. *Also urges* Governments to devise, enforce and strengthen effective measures to combat and eliminate all forms of trafficking in women and girls, including for sexual exploitation, as part of a comprehensive anti-trafficking strategy that integrates a gender and human rights perspective, and to draw up, as appropriate, national action plans in this regard;

6. *Further urges* Governments to consider signing and ratifying and States parties to implement relevant United Nations legal instruments such as the United Nations Convention against Transnational Organized Crime and the Protocols thereto, in particular the Protocol to Prevent, Suppress and Punish Trafficking in Persons, Especially Women and Children, supplementing the United Nations Convention against Transnational Organized Crime, the Convention on the Elimination of All Forms of Discrimination against Women, the Convention on the Rights of the Child, the Optional Protocol to the Convention on the Elimination of All Forms of Discrimination against Women and the Optional Protocol to the Convention on the Rights of the Child on the sale of children, child prostitution and child pornography, as well as the Convention concerning Discrimination in respect of Employment and Occupation, 1958 (Convention No. 111) and the Convention concerning the Prohibition and Immediate Action for the Elimination of the Worst Forms of Child Labour, 1999 (Convention No. 182), of the International Labour Organization;

7. *Encourages* Member States to conclude bilateral, subregional, regional and international agreements, as well as to undertake initiatives, including regional initiatives, to address the problem of trafficking in persons, and to ensure that such agreements and initiatives pay particular attention to the problem of trafficking in women and girls;

8. *Calls upon* all Governments to criminalize all forms of trafficking in persons, recognizing its increasing occurrence for purposes of sexual exploitation and sex tourism, and to condemn and penalize all those offenders involved, including intermediaries, whether local or foreign, through the competent national authorities, either in the country of origin of the offender or in the country in which the abuse occurs, in accordance with due process of law, while also ensuring that the victims of those practices are not penalized for being trafficked, and to penalize persons in authority found guilty of sexually assaulting victims of trafficking in their custody;

9. *Invites* Governments to strengthen international cooperation aimed at preventing and combating corruption and the laundering of proceeds derived from trafficking, including for purposes of commercialized sexual exploitation;

10. *Also invites* Governments to consider setting up or strengthening a national coordinating mechanism, for example, a national rapporteur or an inter-agency body, with the participation of civil society, including non-governmental organizations, to encourage the exchange of information and to report on data, root causes, factors and trends in violence against women, in particular trafficking;

11. *Encourages* Governments and relevant United Nations bodies, within existing resources, to take appropriate measures to raise public awareness of the issue of trafficking in persons, particularly in women and girls, including to address the demand side of the problem and to publicize the laws, regulations and penalties relating to this issue, and to emphasize that trafficking is a crime, in order to eliminate the demand, including by sex tourists, recognizing that the majority of trafficked victims are women and girls;

12. *Urges* concerned Governments, in cooperation with intergovernmental and non-governmental organizations, to support and allocate resources for programmes to strengthen preventive action, in particular education and campaigns to increase public awareness of the issue at the national and grass-roots levels;

13. *Calls upon* concerned Governments to allocate resources, as appropriate, to provide comprehensive programmes for the physical, psychological and social recovery of victims of trafficking, including through job training, legal assistance and health care, including for HIV/AIDS, and by taking measures to cooperate with intergovernmental and non-governmental organizations to provide for the social, medical and psychological care of the victims;

14. *Encourages* Governments, in cooperation with intergovernmental and non-governmental organizations, to undertake campaigns aimed at clarifying opportunities, limitations and rights in the event of migration so as to enable women to make informed decisions and to prevent them from becoming victims of trafficking;

15. *Also encourages* Governments to intensify collaboration with non-governmental organizations to develop and implement programmes for effective counselling, training and reintegration into society of victims of trafficking and programmes that provide shelter and helplines to victims or potential victims;

16. *Calls upon* Governments to take steps to ensure that the treatment of victims of trafficking, as well as all measures taken against trafficking in persons, in particular those that affect the victims of such trafficking, pay particular attention to the needs of women and girls and are applied with full respect for the human rights of those victims and are consistent with internationally recognized principles of non-discrimination, including the prohibition of racial discrimination and the availability of appropriate legal redress, which may include measures that offer victims the possibility of obtaining compensation for damage suffered;

17. *Invites* Governments to take steps to ensure that criminal justice procedures and witness protection programmes are sensitive to the particular situation of trafficked women and girls and that they are enabled to make complaints to the police or other authorities, as appropriate, and to be available when required by the criminal justice system, and to ensure that during this time they have access to protection and social, medical, financial and legal assistance, as appropriate;

18. *Also invites* Governments to consider preventing, within the legal framework and in accordance with national policies, victims of trafficking in persons, in particular women and girls, from being prosecuted for their illegal entry or residence, bearing in mind that they are victims of exploitation;

19. *Further invites* Governments to encourage Internet service providers to adopt or strengthen self-regulatory measures to promote the responsible use of the Internet with a view to eliminating trafficking in women and children, in particular girls;

20. *Invites* the business sector, in particular the tourism and telecommunications industries, including mass media organizations, to cooperate with Governments in eliminating trafficking in women and children, in particular girls, including through the dissemination by the media of information regarding the

rights of trafficked persons and services available to victims of trafficking;

21. *Stresses* the need for systematic data collection and comprehensive studies at both the national and the international levels and the development of common methodologies and internationally defined indicators to make it possible to develop relevant and comparable figures, and encourages Governments to enhance information-sharing and data-collection capacity as a way of promoting cooperation to combat the trafficking problem;

22. *Urges* Governments to strengthen national programmes to combat trafficking in persons, especially women and girls, through increased bilateral, regional and international cooperation, taking into account innovative approaches and best practices, and invites Governments, United Nations bodies and organizations, intergovernmental and non-governmental organizations and the private sector to undertake collaborative and joint research and studies on trafficking in women and girls that can serve as a basis for policy formulation or change;

23. *Invites* Governments, with the support of the United Nations as required, and other intergovernmental organizations, taking into account best practices, to formulate training manuals for law enforcement and medical personnel and judicial officers, with a view to sensitizing them to the special needs of women and girl victims;

24. *Urges* Governments to provide or strengthen training for law enforcement, immigration and other relevant officials in the prevention and combating of trafficking in persons, including the sexual exploitation of women and girls, which should focus on methods used in preventing such trafficking, prosecuting the traffickers and protecting the rights of victims, including protecting the victims from traffickers, to ensure that the training includes human rights and child- and gender-sensitive perspectives, and to encourage cooperation with non-governmental organizations, other relevant organizations and other elements of civil society;

25. *Invites* States parties to the Convention on the Elimination of All Forms of Discrimination against Women, the Convention on the Rights of the Child and the International Covenants on Human Rights to include information and statistics on trafficking in women and girls as part of their national reports to their respective committees and to work towards developing a common methodology and statistics to obtain comparable data;

26. *Requests* the Secretary-General to compile, as reference and guidance, successful interventions and strategies in addressing the various dimensions of the particular problem of trafficking in women and children, in particular girls, based on reports, research and other materials from within the United Nations, including the United Nations Office on Drugs and Crime, as well as from outside the United Nations, and to submit a report on the implementation of the present resolution to the General Assembly at its sixty-first session.

Women in Afghanistan

In response to Economic and Social Council resolution 2003/43 [YUN 2003, p. 1175], the Secretary-General submitted to the Commission a report [E/CN.6/2004/5] on the situation of women and girls in Afghanistan, which provided information on the political, social and economic developments affecting Afghan women in 2003. It detailed steps taken by the Afghan Transitional Administration (TA), the UN system and other actors to empower women and strengthen their status, particularly women's representation and participation in constitutional and electoral processes. The report revealed that women participated in significant numbers in the public consultations on the draft constitution for Afghanistan. To ensure that their voices were heard, a diverse group of women, meeting in Kahandar in September 2003, issued an Afghan Women's Bill of Rights, calling for the inclusion in the constitution of such rights as the right to education, protection and security, freedom of speech and the right to vote. Women were also represented in the Constitutional Loya Jirga (grand council) convened to draft the constitution. In that regard, a Committee for the Protection of Women's Rights in the Constitution was established to formulate a platform of action for women delegates to the Loya Jirga.

In preparation for the holding of general elections in October (see p. 318), tribal and religious community leaders and Afghan civil society organizations were being mobilized to encourage women to participate in the electoral process. The United Nations Assistance Mission in Afghanistan (UNAMA) electoral component reported that gender issues were fully taken into consideration in the planning of the voter registration exercise. It also developed a 2004 mission implementation plan to integrate gender perspectives throughout all aspects of its work in support of the Afghan Government's development policies and strategies. The Afghan Ministry of Education, with the United Nations Children's Fund (UNICEF), launched the Back-to-School campaign, which resulted in 4.2 million children being enrolled in schools, while the World Food Programme provided school feeding as an incentive to encourage girls' enrolment. Other areas addressed in the report included women's human rights and violence against women; disarmament and reintegration; return of refugees and displaced persons; narcotics trade; mine action; health; and employment. The Secretary-General made a number of recommendations to the TA and future Government, the UN system, donors and civil society to further strengthen the status of women and girls in Afghanistan and their full participation in the reconstruction and development of their country (see also p. 777).

ECONOMIC AND SOCIAL COUNCIL ACTION

On 21 July [meeting 47], the Economic and Social Council, on the recommendation of the Commission on the Status of Women [E/2004/27], adopted **resolution 2004/10** without vote [agenda item 14 (a)].

Situation of women and girls in Afghanistan

The Economic and Social Council,

Guided by the Charter of the United Nations, the Universal Declaration of Human Rights, the International Covenants on Human Rights, the Convention against Torture and Other Cruel, Inhuman or Degrading Treatment or Punishment, the Convention on the Elimination of All Forms of Discrimination against Women, the Declaration on the Elimination of Violence against Women, the Convention on the Rights of the Child and the Optional Protocols thereto on the involvement of children in armed conflict and on the sale of children, child prostitution and child pornography, the Beijing Declaration and Platform for Action, the further actions and initiatives to implement the Beijing Declaration and Platform for Action, adopted by the General Assembly at its twenty-third special session, accepted humanitarian rules as set out in the Geneva Conventions of 12 August 1949, and other instruments of human rights and international law,

Recalling that Afghanistan is a party to the Convention on the Prevention and Punishment of the Crime of Genocide, the International Covenant on Civil and Political Rights, the International Covenant on Economic, Social and Cultural Rights, the Convention against Torture and Other Cruel, Inhuman or Degrading Treatment or Punishment, the Convention on the Elimination of All Forms of Discrimination against Women, the Convention on the Rights of the Child and the Optional Protocols thereto, the Geneva Conventions of 12 August 1949 and the Rome Statute of the International Criminal Court,

Reaffirming that all States have an obligation to promote and protect human rights and fundamental freedoms,

Recalling the importance of the implementation of Security Council resolutions 1325(2000) of 31 October 2000, on women and peace and security and 1460(2003) of 30 January 2003, on children and armed conflict, and in this context recalling also the Security Council mission to Afghanistan from 31 October to 7 November 2003, which reviewed, inter alia, the humanitarian and human rights situation of women,

Welcoming the entry into force on 26 January 2004 of a new Constitution following the successful outcome of the Constitutional Loya Jirga, in which women played a prominent and crucial role, and also welcoming, in particular, the provisions of the new Constitution which state that the citizens of Afghanistan, whether men or women, are equal before the law, and guarantee the right of women to serve in the National Assembly,

Welcoming also the continuing commitment of the Transitional Administration of Afghanistan to the full enjoyment of all human rights and fundamental freedoms by women and girls, the restoration of the active participation of Afghan women in political, economic and social life, the education of girls as well as boys and the opportunity for women to work outside the home,

Welcoming further the fact that the Back-to-School campaign launched by the Ministry of Education and the United Nations Children's Fund has been a major success and that 4.2 million children are now enrolled in school, while recognizing the need for the enrolment rate of girls in school to improve considerably,

Welcoming the inclusion of women in the Transitional Administration, the Judicial Reform Commission, the Independent Human Rights Commission, the Constitutional Commission and the Secretariat of the Constitutional Loya Jirga, and stressing the importance of the full and effective participation of women in all decision-making processes regarding the future of Afghanistan,

Welcoming also the fact that the National Development Framework of the Transitional Administration reflects the needs of, and the importance of the role to be taken by, women and girls in the process of peace-building, reconstruction and development, and welcoming in this regard the assistance provided by the international community to achieve these goals,

Welcoming further the efforts of Afghanistan's neighbouring countries, which host millions of Afghan refugees, especially women and children, and have provided humanitarian assistance in many areas, such as education, health and other basic services,

Recognizing that, in spite of recent improvements, women in Afghanistan continue to face serious violations of their rights in many parts of the country, in particular in rural areas,

Recognizing also that Afghan women are primary stakeholders and agents of change, who must have the opportunity to identify their own needs, interests and priorities in all sectors of society as full partners in the rebuilding of their society,

Strongly emphasizing that a safe environment, free from violence, discrimination and abuse, for all Afghans, is essential for a viable and sustainable recovery and reconstruction process,

1. *Welcomes:*

(a) The ongoing commitments made by the Transitional Administration of Afghanistan to recognize, protect and promote all human rights and fundamental freedoms and to respect and promote respect for international humanitarian law;

(b) The provisions of the new Constitution which state that the citizens of Afghanistan, whether men or women, are equal before the law and that at least two women are to be elected to the Wolesi Jirga (Lower House of Parliament) from each province, as a national average, and which provide for half of the President's nominees to the Meshrano Jirga (Upper House of Parliament) to be women;

(c) The ongoing security sector reform processes being undertaken by the Transitional Administration with the support of the international community, including the demobilization, disarmament and reintegration of former combatants and the recruitment of a new cadre of women police;

2. *Also welcomes* the report of the Secretary-General to the Commission on the Status of Women;

3. *Urges* the Transitional Administration and future Government:

(a) To ensure that the provisions of the new Constitution are implemented fully and that any legislative, administrative and other measures support the full enjoyment by women and girls of human rights and fundamental freedoms, including by mainstreaming gender issues into the activities of all Transitional Administration ministries;

(b) To enable the full, equal and effective participation of women and girls in civil, cultural, economic, political and social life throughout the country at all levels;

(c) To protect the right to freedom of movement, expression and association for women and girls;

(d) To implement fully its obligations under the Convention on the Elimination of All Forms of Discrimination against Women and prepare the initial report due in March 2004 and to raise awareness and strengthen the knowledge of women and girls and their families about their rights, including the full enjoyment of all human rights by women and girls;

(e) To ensure that the electoral processes, including those in 2004, are carried out and monitored closely to make certain that women are able to register and participate fully, and to support special measures that would guarantee that they are represented in local, provincial and national government positions;

(f) To ensure that the Ministry of Women's Affairs, the Independent Human Rights Commission and the permanent Afghan judicial institutions have adequate human and financial resources to fulfil their mandates and address gender perspectives in line with international standards;

(g) To continue its efforts to re-establish the rule of law, in accordance with international standards, inter alia, by ensuring that law enforcement agencies respect and uphold human rights and fundamental freedoms, with a particular emphasis on access to justice for women;

(h) To continue its efforts to reflect a gender perspective in the training and activities of its police, army, prosecutors and judiciary and to promote the recruitment of Afghan women in all ranks;

(i) To review and improve the practices of law enforcement personnel when dealing with women victims of violence, including domestic and sexual violence, and trafficking, in particular those accused of offences based on tradition or imprisoned for social reasons;

(j) To strengthen efforts, including through legislative measures, to prevent and eliminate violence against women, including domestic and sexual violence and trafficking, inter alia, by raising awareness of the need to prevent and eliminate violence against women, with the aim of changing the attitudes and behaviour that allow such crimes to take place;

(k) To ensure that gender-sensitive approaches are applied in the development and application of procedures during data collection for the census and the registration of voters to deliver universal suffrage and the full participation of women in the national elections in 2004;

(l) To ensure the equal rights of women and girls to education, the effective functioning of schools throughout the country and the admission of women and girls to all levels of education, in a safe and secure environment, and to support the educational needs of those women and girls who were excluded from education in the past;

(m) To respect the equal right of women to work and promote their reintegration in employment in all sectors and at all levels of Afghan society;

(n) To protect the equal right of women and girls to security of person and to bring to justice those responsible for violence against women and girls;

(o) To continue demobilization and disarmament and facilitate the reintegration into society and work of women and girls who have been affected by war;

(p) To ensure the effective and equal access of women and girls, on the basis of equality among all Afghans, to the facilities necessary to protect the right to the enjoyment of the highest attainable standard of physical and mental health, in accordance with the obligations of Afghanistan under the International Covenant on Economic, Social and Cultural Rights;

(q) To ensure the equal right of women to own land and other property, inter alia, through the right to inheritance, and to undertake administrative reforms and other necessary measures to give women the same rights as men to credit, capital, appropriate technologies and access to and control over natural resources, as well as access to markets and information;

(r) To consider implementing gender budgeting in the national budget and in all budgets of ministries;

(s) To ensure that Afghan women are well represented at international conferences and that during the Berlin Conference adequate attention is given to issues relating to the rights of women and girls;

(t) To support measures to ensure the full enjoyment of human rights and fundamental freedoms by women and girls, to hold accountable those who were responsible for gross violations of human rights in the past and to ensure that full investigations are conducted and the perpetrators brought to justice, in accordance with international standards, in order to combat impunity;

4. *Encourages* the continuing efforts of the United Nations and its agencies, donors and civil society, guided by Security Council resolution 1325(2000):

(a) To provide financial and technical assistance, including support to the Ministry of Women's Affairs and the Independent Human Rights Commission, to ensure the full enjoyment of human rights and fundamental freedoms by women and girls so as to strengthen the capacity of Afghan women to participate fully and effectively in conflict resolution and peacebuilding efforts and in civil, political, economic, cultural and social life;

(b) To support fully the Transitional Administration regarding the participation of women in society, inter alia, by providing support to ministries to develop their capacity to mainstream gender issues into their programmes;

(c) To support capacity-building for Afghan women to enable them to participate fully in all sectors, with special emphasis on ensuring the participation and representation of women in all aspects of the 2004 electoral process;

(d) To provide technical and other relevant assistance so that the judicial system has the capacity to adhere to international human rights standards;

5. *Invites* the United Nations system, international and non-governmental organizations, and donors:

(a) To ensure a human rights-based approach and coherent policy and resources for gender mainstreaming in all programmes and operations, based on

the principles of non-discrimination and equality between women and men, and to ensure that women benefit equally with men from such programmes in all sectors;

(b) To ensure the full and effective participation of Afghan women in all stages of humanitarian assistance, recovery, reconstruction and development, including planning, programme development, implementation, monitoring and evaluation;

(c) To support the elements of civil society active in the field of human rights and encourage the involvement of women therein;

(d) To ensure that all their international and national personnel, prior to beginning their service, receive training in gender equality, as well as appropriate training in the history, culture and traditions of Afghanistan, and are fully familiar with and guided by international human rights standards;

(e) To integrate efforts to improve the health status of women into all reconstruction efforts, especially through access to skilled prenatal care, increased access to skilled birth attendance, education programmes on basic health issues, community information activities and emergency obstetric care;

(f) To continue to support measures for the employment of women and the integration of a gender perspective into all social, development and reconstruction programmes, taking into account the special needs of widows and returning refugee and displaced women and girls, as well as those living in rural areas;

6. *Strongly urges* the Secretary-General to ensure that the important post of Senior Gender Adviser in the United Nations Assistance Mission in Afghanistan is filled immediately and with due regard to the need for continuity in this task;

7. *Requests* the Secretary-General to continue to review the situation of women and girls in Afghanistan and to submit to the Commission on the Status of Women at its forty-ninth session a report on progress made in the implementation of the present resolution.

Palestinian women

In response to Economic and Social Council resolution 2003/42 [YUN 2003, p. 494], a report of the Secretary-General [E/CN.6/2004/4] summarized the situation of and assistance to Palestinian women during the period from September 2002 to September 2003 (see p. 483). It indicated that living conditions had drastically declined and recommended that UN entities continue to operate in the Occupied Palestinian Territory and refugee camps. Further opportunities should be sought to highlight the ways in which the crisis impacted on women as compared to men so that targeted actions could be taken to mitigate the gender-specific impacts.

On 23 July, the Economic and Social Council, in **resolution 2004/56**, took action on the situation of and assistance to Palestinian women (see p. 484).

Women and development

World survey and international migration

The Commission considered a note [E/CN.6/2004/CRP.4] by the Secretary-General, which responded to the General Assembly's request in resolution 54/210 [YUN 1999, p. 1097] for an update to the *World Survey on the Role of Women in Development* for consideration at its fifty-ninth (2004) session. The Secretary-General indicated that the *Survey* would address the increased movement of people, particularly women, within and across national borders, from a gender perspective.

Report of Secretary-General. Responding to General Assembly resolution 58/206 [YUN 2003, p. 1178], the Secretary-General submitted to the Assembly, in September, the *World Survey on the Role of Women in Development: Women and International Migration* [A/59/287/Add.1], together with an August summary of the key elements contained therein [A/59/287]. The *Survey* focused on women and international migration and presented key issues on labour migration; family formation and reunification; rights of migrant women, refugees and displaced persons; and trafficking in women and girls. The *Survey* revealed that, as at 2000, 49 per cent of all international migrants were women or girls and the proportion of females among international migrants had reached 51 per cent in more developed regions. Refugee women and girls faced particular problems regarding their legal and physical protection; an increasing area of concern was the trafficking of people, especially women, for prostitution and forced labour. International migration affected gender roles and opportunities for women in destination countries, and some countries had laws that particularly disadvantaged women migrants and native spouses of male migrants. The *Survey* concluded that the mobility of women affected the roles of both female and male migrants, the families left behind in the migration process and societies in the source and destination countries of migrants. Migration of women within and from developing countries affected the development process in those countries and also raised challenges to immigration and refugee policies. The *Survey* set out recommendations for improving the situation of migrant, refugee and trafficked women, including the ratification and implementation of all international legal instruments that protected the rights of migrant women and girls; review of national emigration and immigration laws and policies to identify discriminatory provisions that undermined the rights of migrant women; development of policies that enhanced employment opportunities, access to safe housing, education, language training in the host country, health care and other services; education and communication programmes to inform migrant women of their rights and responsibilities; and research and data collection that improved understanding of the causes of female migration and its impact on women, their countries of origin and their countries of destination to provide a basis for the formulation of appropriate policies and programmes.

GENERAL ASSEMBLY ACTION

On 22 December [meeting 75], the General Assembly, on the recommendation of the Second (Economic and Financial) Committee [A/59/487/Add.2], adopted **resolution 59/248**, without vote [agenda item 89 (*b*)].

World Survey on the role of women in development

The General Assembly,

Recalling its resolutions 54/210 of 22 December 1999 and 58/206 of 23 December 2003 and all its other resolutions on the integration of women in development,

1. *Takes note* of the report of the Secretary-General entitled "World Survey on the Role of Women in Development", which focuses on women and international migration, and decides to consider the report at its sixtieth session under the sub-item entitled "Women in development";

2. *Requests* the Secretary-General to update the *World Survey on the Role of Women in Development* for the consideration of the General Assembly at its sixty-fourth session, noting that the survey should continue to focus on selected emerging development themes that have an impact on the role of women in the economy at the national, regional and international levels, to be identified at its sixtieth session.

Eradication of poverty

Communication. A letter [E/CN.6/2004/12] from the President of the Economic and Social Council informed the Commission on the Status of Women of the themes for the Council's 2004 high-level segment (Resources mobilization and enabling environment for poverty eradication in the context of the implementation of the Programme of Action for the Least Developed Countries (LDCs) for the Decade 2001-2010 [YUN 2001, p. 771]) and coordination segment (Review and appraisal of the system-wide implementation of the Council's agreed conclusions 1997/2 on mainstreaming gender perspective into all programmes and policies of the United Nations (see p. 1427) and Coordinated and integrated UN system approach to promote rural development in developing countries, with due consideration for least developed countries, for poverty eradication and sustainable development (see p. 827)). The Council President requested the Commis-

sion's early consideration of the themes to ensure that the Commission's concerns were fully reflected in the Council's work. A Secretariat note [E/CN.6/2004/CRP.6], which discussed gender-equality and poverty eradication in least developed countries and gender-responsive poverty eradication, including poverty and rural women, creating an enabling environment for poverty eradication and mobilization of domestic and international resources, was submitted to assist the Commission should it consider providing input to the high-level segment.

Institutional mechanisms for the advancement of women

Inter-Agency Network. The United Nations Inter-Agency Network on Women and Gender Equality (IANWGE), at its third session (New York, 23-26 February) [IANWGE/2004/REPORT], endorsed decisions and recommendations made by task forces and working groups regarding gender and the Millennium Development Goals (MDGs); gender and information and communication technologies; women, peace and security; mainstreaming a gender perspective in development programming processes; gender mainstreaming in programme budgets; database activities, including WomenWatch, an Internet portal to UN gender sources; gender and trade; gender and water; the ten-year review of the Beijing Platform of Action; new task forces; and the review and appraisal of the system-wide implementation of Economic and Social Council Agreed Conclusions 1997/2 on mainstreaming a gender perspective into all UN system policies and programmes. The Network established new task forces on indigenous women and on gender mainstreaming in evaluation, monitoring and programme reporting. It also held a workshop on mainstreaming a gender perspective in evaluation, monitoring and programme reporting. Network members selected "Women and HIV/AIDS" as the theme for International Women's Day, celebrated on 8 March.

Report of Secretary-General. In January, pursuant to Commission resolution 47/2 [YUN 2003, p. 1188], the Secretary-General submitted a report [E/CN.6/2004/3] on measures taken and progress achieved in the follow-up to the Fourth World Conference on Women in mainstreaming a gender perspective in entities of the UN system, which was based on an analysis of inputs received from UN entities and the findings of the Office of the Special Adviser on Gender Issues and Advancement of Women and the Inter-Agency Network on Women and Gender Equality. The Secretary-General concluded that, although policies and strategies were in place in many entities and there had been increased focus on the development of training, methodologies and tools, a large gap remained between policy and practice. Constraints to full implementation of gender mainstreaming included inadequate support for and follow-up to gender equality policies and strategies; poor utilization of gender analysis; inadequate monitoring mechanisms, including indicators for assessing progress; and institutional constraints, such as the lack of competence and poor accountability. He added that considerable work remained to be done on developing awareness, commitment and capacity among UN staff, as the existence of policies and strategies had not always led to the desired change in attitudes or practices and methodologies. Resources were also not being utilized to the fullest extent. Increased explicit support from senior management levels in clarifying responsibilities demanding accountability and providing support would be critical for moving forward. The report also provided further measures the Commission might wish to recommend to enhance implementation and impact of the gender mainstreaming strategy.

Commission on Status of Women. In March [E/2004/27 (res. 48/4)], the Commission invited the UN system to link gender equality policies to organizational goals, develop and strengthen strategies and action plans and assess the impact of such policies and strategies to identify constraints to their full implementation. It recommended that the Economic and Social Council incorporate an assessment of the remaining gaps in the frameworks for gender equality policies and strategies in its review and appraisal of the implementation of its agreed conclusions 1997/2. The Secretary-General should include an assessment of the implementation of the Commission's resolution in his report on the follow-up to the Fourth World Conference on Women at the Commission's forty-ninth (2005) session.

Further report of Secretary-General. In response to Economic and Social Council resolution 2003/49 [YUN 2003, p. 1188], the Secretary-General, in a May report [E/2004/59] on the review and appraisal of the system-wide implementation of the Council's agreed conclusions 1997/2, provided an analysis and highlighted continuing gaps in and challenges to mainstreaming gender perspectives in UN system policies and programmes and at the intergovernmental level. The report concluded that the agreed conclusions remained a valid framework for gender mainstreaming in the United Nations and that progress made in mainstreaming gender perspectives at the intergovernmental level had had an important impact on efforts throughout the UN system. However, initiatives needed to be taken at all levels to increase the active and visible use of gender mainstreaming as a complement to women-focused strategies, in addition to increased inter-agency collaboration, particularly at operational levels. Recommendations to the Council included encouraging UN entities to establish gender equality policy frameworks linked to overall organizational policies and regularly assessing their impact; fully incorporating gender perspectives in all reports prepared for intergovernmental bodies, including the Security Council, its functional commissions, and the General Assembly; and increasing awareness of the responsibilities of all staff for gender mainstreaming, including senior management, and developing effective accountability mechanisms. In addition to Council suggestions to the Commission on the Status of Women, the Assembly, the Security Council, IANWGE and governing bodies of agencies, funds and programmes, the report recommended that the Economic and Social Council establish gender mainstreaming as a regular agenda item in meetings of its bureau with those of its functional commissions.

UNDP consideration. The United Nations Development Programme/United Nations Population Fund (UNDP/UNFPA) Executive Board requested UNDP to prepare a detailed plan of action on gender mainstreaming for review in 2005 [E/2004/35 (dec. 2004/21)] (see p. 883). It also requested that the UNDP organizational scorecard on gender balance be presented at that time [ibid., (dec. 2004/22)] (see p. 884), and that UNDP submit, in 2005, more detailed information on specific gender indicators, and an update on the progress achieved in the partnership between UNDP and UNIFEM [ibid., (dec. 2004/38)] (see p. 883).

ECONOMIC AND SOCIAL COUNCIL ACTION

On 7 July [meeting 27], the Economic and Social Council adopted **resolution 2004/4** [draft: E/2004/L.14] without vote [agenda item 4 (a)].

Review of Economic and Social Council agreed conclusions 1997/2 on mainstreaming the gender perspective into all policies and programmes in the United Nations system

The Economic and Social Council,

Recalling its agreed conclusions 1997/2 of 18 July 1997 on mainstreaming the gender perspective into all policies and programmes in the United Nations system, and its decision 2003/287 of 24 July 2003, in which it decided to undertake, during the coordination segment of its substantive session of 2004, a review and appraisal of the system-wide implementation of the agreed conclusions,

Recalling also its resolution 2001/41 of 26 July 2001, in which it decided to establish a regular sub-item entitled "Mainstreaming a gender perspective into all policies and programmes of the United Nations system", as well as its resolutions 2002/23 of 24 July 2002 and 2003/49 of 24 July 2003,

Reaffirming that gender mainstreaming constitutes a major strategy for the full implementation of the Beijing Platform for Action and the outcome of the twenty-third special session of the General Assembly, as a complement to strategies for the empowerment of women,

Underlining the catalytic role played by the Commission on the Status of Women, as well as the important role played by the Economic and Social Council and the General Assembly, in promoting and monitoring gender mainstreaming within the United Nations system,

1. *Reaffirms* its agreed conclusions 1997/2 as a valid framework for promoting and monitoring the implementation of gender mainstreaming within the United Nations system;

2. *Welcomes* the report of the Secretary-General on the review and appraisal of the system-wide implementation of Economic and Social Council agreed conclusions 1997/2 on mainstreaming the gender perspective into all policies and programmes of the United Nations system;

3. *Notes with appreciation* the progress made by the United Nations in mainstreaming gender perspectives into policies and programmes since 1997, including the ongoing activities of and efforts made by the entities of the United Nations system, both individually and through inter-agency cooperation;

4. *Recognizes* that mainstreaming the gender perspective into all aspects of the work of the United Nations is an ongoing process and that further concrete steps are required, as a matter of urgency, to ensure full implementation of agreed conclusions 1997/2;

5. *Recommends* that the General Assembly encourage its committees and other intergovernmental bodies to take further measures to integrate systematically gender perspectives into all areas of their work, including the integrated and coordinated implementation of and follow-up to the outcomes of major United Nations summits and conferences, and in particular the 2005 high-level event planned in pursuance of General Assembly resolution 58/291 of 6 May 2004;

6. *Reaffirms its commitment* to ensuring systematic attention to gender perspectives in all aspects of its work;

7. *Encourages* the governing bodies of United Nations agencies, funds and programmes to ensure that gender perspectives are integrated into all aspects of their monitoring functions in relation to policies and strategies, medium-term plans, multi-year funding frameworks and operational activities, including those relating to the implementation of the United Nations Millennium Declaration and the outcomes of major United Nations conferences and summits in the economic and social fields;

8. *Calls upon* its functional commissions to take further measures to incorporate recommendations on their areas of work provided by the Commission on the Status of Women and fully to integrate gender perspectives into their work, including through their annual or multi-year programmes of work and in the integrated and coordinated follow-up to major United Nations conferences and summits, and, to that end, requests its Bureau to strengthen further the regular dialogue with the bureaux of the functional commissions on the issue of gender mainstreaming;

9. *Requests* all entities of the United Nations system to enhance the effectiveness of gender specialist resources, gender focal points and gender theme groups by establishing clear mandates, by ensuring adequate training and access to information and to adequate and stable resources, and by increasing the support and participation of senior staff;

10. *Encourages* the Commission on the Status of Women to continue its catalytic role in relation to United Nations entities and intergovernmental bodies and to provide further practical guidance on gender mainstreaming;

11. *Requests* all entities of the United Nations system, including funds and programmes, fully to incorporate gender perspectives in their programmes and operational activities and to ensure, within their mandates, systematic integration of reporting on their efforts in mainstreaming gender into existing evaluation and monitoring processes within the United Nations system, including those relating to the development goals contained in the Millennium Declaration;

12. *Recommends* that all entities of the United Nations system continue to promote cooperation, coordination, sharing of methodologies and good practices, including through the development of tools and effective processes for monitoring and evaluation within the United Nations, in the implementation of agreed conclusions 1997/2, in particular through the Inter-agency Network on Women and Gender Equality, and recommends further that all inter-agency mechanisms pay attention to gender perspectives in their work;

13. *Takes note* of work already undertaken to implement General Assembly resolution 58/144 of 22 December 2003, and urges continued efforts towards its full implementation;

14. *Also takes note* of work already undertaken to implement Security Council resolution 1325(2000) of 31 October 2000 on women and peace and security, and urges continued efforts towards its full implementation;

15. *Requests* the Secretary-General to ensure that all entities of the United Nations system develop action plans with time lines for implementing agreed conclusions 1997/2 which address the gap between policy and practice identified in the report of the Secretary-General, with a view to strengthening commitment and accountability at the highest levels within the United Nations system as well as to establishing mechanisms to ensure accountability, systematic monitoring and reporting on progress in implementation;

16. *Also requests* the Secretary-General to continue to review the implementation of agreed conclusions 1997/2 within the framework of his annual reports to the Commission on the Status of Women, the Economic and Social Council and the General Assembly on the follow-up to and progress made in the implementation by United Nations entities and intergovernmental bodies of the Beijing Declaration and Platform for Action and the outcome of the twenty-third special session of the General Assembly, with a particular focus on bridging the gap between policies and practice on the basis of gender mainstreaming action plans;

17. *Decides* to undertake a further review and appraisal of the implementation of its agreed conclusions 1997/2 at a future session before 2010.

By **decision 2004/317** of 23 July, the Council also took note of the Secretary-General's report on the review and appraisal of the system-wide implementation of the Economic and Social Council's agreed conclusions 1997/2 on mainstreaming the gender perspective into all policies and programmes of the United Nations (see p. 1166).

Status of women in the United Nations

In response to General Assembly resolution 58/144 [YUN 2003, p. 1449], the Secretary-General presented a report [A/59/357] on progress made in the representation of women within the UN system as at 31 December 2003 and in the UN Secretariat from 1 July 2003 to 30 June 2004 (see p. 1428).

In **resolution 59/164** of 22 December (see p. 1429), the Assembly requested the Secretary-General to provide a verbal update to the Commission on the Status of Women at its forty-ninth (2005) and fiftieth (2006) sessions and to report to the Assembly at its sixty-first (2006) session.

UN machinery

Convention on the elimination of discrimination against women

As at 31 December 2004, 179 States were parties to the 1979 Convention on the Elimination of All Forms of Discrimination against Women, adopted by the General Assembly in resolution 34/180 [YUN 1979, p. 895]. During the year, Kiribati, the Federated States of Micronesia, Swaziland and the United Arab Emirates acceded to it. At year's end, 45 States parties had also accepted the amendment to article 20, paragraph 1, of the Convention in respect of the meeting time of the Committee on the Elimination of Discrimination against Women, which was adopted by the States parties in 1995 [YUN 1995, p. 1178]. The amendment would enter into force when accepted by a two-thirds majority of States parties.

The Optional Protocol to the Convention, adopted by the Assembly in resolution 54/4 [YUN 1999, p. 1100] and which entered into force in 2000 [YUN 2000, p. 1123], had 70 States parties by year's end.

Meeting of States parties. The thirteenth meeting of States parties to the Convention (New York, 5 August) [CEDAW/SP/2004/4] elected 11 CEDAW members to replace those members whose terms were to expire on 31 December 2004. The newly elected members would serve from 1 January 2005 to 31 December 2007. The meeting had before it a June document [CEDAW/SP/2004/2] containing declarations, reservations, objections and notifications of withdrawal of reservations relating to the Convention.

CEDAW

In 2004, the Committee on the Elimination of Discrimination against Women (CEDAW), established in 1982 [YUN 1982, p. 1149] to monitor compliance with the 1979 Convention, held two regular sessions in New York [A/59/38].

At its thirtieth session (12-30 January), CEDAW reviewed the initial/periodic reports of Belarus, Bhutan, Ethiopia, Germany, Kyrgyzstan, Kuwait, Nigeria and Nepal on measures they had taken to implement the Convention. CEDAW considered a Secretariat report on ways and means of expediting its work [CEDAW/C/2004/I/4] and notes by the Secretariat on an overview of the current working methods of the Committee [CEDAW/C/2004/I/4 & Add.1] and on enhancing the working methods of the Committee under article 18 of the Convention [CEDAW/C/2004/I/4 & Add.2]. By three decisions, CEDAW adopted general recommendation 25 on article 4, paragraph 1 of the Convention, on temporary special measures [A/59/38 (dec. 30/I)]; decided to mark the twenty-fifth (2004) anniversary of the adoption of the Convention with an event at the fifty-ninth (2004) session of the General Assembly [ibid., (dec. 30/II)]; and adopted a statement on the situation of women in Iraq [ibid., (dec. 30/III)], which was annexed to the report. In other action, the Committee took note of the report and decisions of the Working Group on Communications under the Optional Protocol, in respect of issues arising from article 2, and continued its work under article 8 of the Optional Protocol.

At its thirty-first session (6-23 July), CEDAW reviewed the initial or periodic reports of Angola, Argentina, Bangladesh, Dominican Republic, Equatorial Guinea, Latvia, Malta and Spain. It also considered the report on ways and means of expediting the work of the Committee [CEDAW/C/2004/II/4] and the reports of specialized agencies [CEDAW/C/2004/II/3 & Adds.1-4] on the implementation of the Convention in areas falling within the scope of their activity. The Committee requested the General Assembly to authorize the Committee to meet for an additional week at its thirty-third, thirty-fourth and thirty-fifth sessions (July 2005 and January and July 2006) and to hold three annual sessions of three weeks each, with a one-week pre-sessional working group for each session, effective January 2007 [A/59/38 (dec. 31/I)]. The Committee also adopted a statement on the situation of women in Iraq [ibid., (dec. 31/II)] and measures to further enhance and strengthen its working methods [ibid., (dec. 31/III)]. In a summary of Committee activities concerning the inquiry of allegations of abduction, rape and murder of women in the Ciudad Juarez area of Chihuahua, Mexico, the Committee noted that it would consider follow-up measures taken by the Government at its thirty-second (2005) session and issue a summary of its findings and recommendations and the Government's response at a future date.

By **decision 59/524** of 20 December, the General Assembly took note of the report of CEDAW on the work of its thirtieth and thirty-first sessions.

Commission on the Status of Women

The Commission on the Status of Women, at its forty-eighth session (New York, 1-12 March) [E/2004/27], recommended four draft resolutions to the Economic and Social Council for adoption on the situation of women and girls in Afghanistan (see p. 1162) and the situation of and assistance to Palestinian women (see p. 484), and its agreed conclusions on the role of men and boys in achieving gender equality (see p. 1157) and on women's equal participation in conflict prevention, management and resolution and in post-conflict peace-building (see p. 1154). It also recommended a draft decision for Council adoption on the report of the Commission's forty-eighth (2004) session and the provisional agenda for its forty-ninth (2005) session (see below). The Commission adopted and brought to the Council's attention resolutions on the revitalization and strengthening of INSTRAW (see p. 1173); the release of women and children taken hostage in armed conflict (see p. 1156); women, the girl child and HIV/AIDS (see p. 1159); mainstreaming a gender perspective in all UN system policies and programmes (see p. 1166); and preparations for its forty-ninth (2005) session (see p. 1171). The Commission adopted three decisions, which were brought to the Council's attention, regarding its working methods [dec. 48/101] (see below); the future work of the Working Group on Communications [dec. 48/103] (see below); and documents before the Commission under agenda item 3 on women's equal participation in conflict prevention, management and conflict resolution and in post-conflict peace-building [dec. 48/102].

By **decision 2004/239** of 21 July, the Economic and Social Council took note of the Commis-

sion's report on its forty-eighth session and approved the provisional agenda for its forty-ninth (2005) session.

Review of working methods

Report of Secretary-General. In response to General Assembly resolution 57/270 B [YUN 2003, p. 1468], the Secretary-General submitted a January report [E/CN.6/2004/2] on the review of the working methods of the Commission on the Status of Women in the context of integrated and coordinated implementation of, and follow-up to, the outcomes of major UN conferences and summits in the economic and social fields. The Secretary-General recommended that the Commission ensure that the outcomes of its examination of thematic issues contained policy developments and recommendations for action; developed ways to effectively incorporate emerging issues into future multi-year work programmes; strengthened linkages with other functional commissions; increased the contributions of the regional commissions in the work of the Commission; encouraged increased involvement by the entities of the UN system and further participation of all stakeholders in expert panel and round-table discussions; and found innovative means of supporting and monitoring gender mainstreaming.

Communications on the status of women

Report of Secretary-General. As requested by the Commission at its forty-seventh session [YUN 2003, p. 1193], the Secretary-General transmitted a report [E/CN.6/2004/11 & Add.1,2] on the future work of the Working Group on Communications on the Status of Women, established in 1993 [YUN 1993, p. 1050] to consider ways of making the communications procedure more transparent and efficient. The report was based on preliminary discussions held at that session and the written views of Member States. The issues raised related to the criteria for inclusion of communications, their volume and sources and continuity of the term of membership of the Working Group. Among the recommendations made were that the Commission elaborate criteria for screening out communications that fell outside the scope of the procedure and criteria for selecting communications; expand and specify the sources of communications; and extend the term of members of the Working Group to two or more years and stagger the nominations.

Working Group. At two meetings in March [E/2004/27], including one closed meeting, the Commission considered the report of the Working Group. The Working Group considered 15 confidential communications received directly by the Division for the Advancement of Women and seven confidential communications received by the Office of the High Commissioner for Human Rights (OHCHR). No non-confidential communications were received. The Group noted that one communication that had been selected from the 1503 procedure material had also been submitted directly to the Division. The Working Group noted that Governments had replied to five of the 15 communications received by the Division and to six of the seven transmitted by OHCHR. The Group ascertained that communications were most frequently submitted on discriminatory application of punishments in law based on sex, including corporal and capital punishment; sexual violence and threats of sexual violence against women; violations of the rights of female human rights defenders and women participating in political life; violations of the rights of women belonging to ethnic or religious minorities, particularly the widespread use of rape, involving extreme brutality, and discrimination against such women, for example, in relation to access to health care; violations of women's human rights during armed conflict, including multiple rapes, sexual mutilation, sexual slavery, and forced pregnancies and abortions; acid attacks against women stemming from rejected offers of marriage and dowry and property disputes; violence, degrading treatment and discrimination based on religious beliefs against women prisoners committed by guards; violations of human rights of migrant women and trafficked women; and denial of visitation rights (visas) and humiliating treatment of spouses of foreign male inmates. The Working Group was concerned about the application under law of certain forms of criminal punishment of women that constituted cruel, inhuman or degrading treatment; the application of criminal punishment based on sex, where only women were punished for certain crimes or sentenced to harsher punishments than men committing the same crime; lack of due diligence in investigating and prosecuting violence, including rape, against migrant women and women victims of trafficking; and the impunity and inadequate punishment of the perpetrators of such violence or those involved in trafficking.

In a March decision [E/2004/27 (dec. 48/103)], the Commission decided to postpone until its fiftieth (2006) session further consideration of the Secretary-General's report on the future work of the Working Group, and the views and proposals put forward by Member States.

Participation of NGOs in the Commission's forty-ninth session

Economic and Social Council consideration. On 23 July, the Economic and Social Council considered a draft resolution [E/2004/L.51] on participation of non-governmental organizations (NGOs) in the forty-ninth (2005) session of the Commission. The Netherlands, speaking on behalf of the European Union, emphasized the valuable contribution of civil society and NGOs to the outcomes of major UN conferences and summits and requested that the draft resolution address the possibility of accrediting additional NGOs to the Commission's 2005 session.

ECONOMIC AND SOCIAL COUNCIL ACTION

On 23 July [meeting 51], the Economic and Social Council adopted **resolution 2004/57** [draft: E/2004/L.51] without vote [agenda item 14 (a)].

Participation of non-governmental organizations in the forty-ninth session of the Commission on the Status of Women

The Economic and Social Council,

Underlining the significance of the forty-ninth session of the Commission on the Status of Women, to be held in 2005, which will mark the tenth anniversary of the adoption of the Beijing Declaration and Platform for Action, the twentieth anniversary of the adoption of the Nairobi Forward-looking Strategies for the Advancement of Women and the thirtieth anniversary of the World Conference of the International Women's Year, held in Mexico City from 19 June to 2 July 1975,

Noting that the Commission on the Status of Women will undertake, at its forty-ninth session, a review of the implementation of the Beijing Platform for Action and the outcome documents of the twenty-third special session of the General Assembly, entitled "Women 2000: gender equality, development and peace for the twenty-first century", and will consider current challenges and forward-looking strategies for the advancement and empowerment of women and girls,

1. *Decides,* on an exceptional basis, to invite those non-governmental organizations that were accredited to the Fourth World Conference on Women or to the twenty-third special session of the General Assembly to attend the forty-ninth session of the Commission on the Status of Women;

2. *Urges* that, in recognition of the importance of equitable geographical participation of non-governmental organizations in the forty-ninth session of the Commission on the Status of Women, relevant bodies of the United Nations system assist those non-governmental organizations that do not have resources, in particular non-governmental organizations from developing countries, including the least developed countries and countries with economies in transition, to participate in the forty-ninth session of the Commission.

UN Development Fund for Women (UNIFEM)

In January [E/2004/35 (dec. 2004/10)], the Executive Board of the United Nations Development Programme and of the United Nations Population Fund (UNDP/UNFPA) endorsed the strategic direction and priorities of the UNIFEM multi-year funding framework (MYFF), 2004-2007 [DP/2004/5 & Corr.1] and approved the 2004-2007 integrated resources framework contained therein. It requested UNIFEM, in collaboration with UNDP/UNFPA, and in consultation with Member States, to explore options for harmonized reporting of the results of its implementation and to report on the issue at the Board's annual session in 2004. In June [ibid., (dec. 2004/20)], the Board adopted the joint UNDP/UNFPA/UNIFEM proposal [DP/2004/4] for reporting on the multi-year funding framework.

UNIFEM activities. In 2004 [A/60/274], UNIFEM focused on the implementation of the first year of the 2004-2007 MYFF, which contained a strategic results framework highlighting four key UNIFEM goals: reducing feminized poverty and exclusion; ending violence against women; halting and reversing the spread of HIV/AIDS; and achieving gender equality in democratic governance and in post-conflict countries. Reports from the first year of implementation of the 2004-2007 MYFF reflected 41 instances in which UNIFEM contributed to strengthening policies and laws to enhance the empowerment and rights of women; 77 instances in which it contributed to strengthening the capacity of key institutions to deliver on commitments to gender equality; 64 instances in which it expanded the capacity of governmental and non-governmental organizations and networks to advocate for gender equality; and 16 instances in which it contributed to reversing harmful practices that discriminated against women and girls.

UNIFEM efforts to achieve its performance goals resulted in support of programmes in 43 countries and the provision of technical advice and/or catalytic funding in 40 others; coordination of gender theme groups in 11 countries; input into the MDG processes in 20 countries; participation in common country assessment/United Nations Development Assistance Framework processes and in the UN response to the Indian Ocean tsunami in December (see p. 952); establishment of UNIFEM as the chair of the United Nations Development Group task force on gender equality; enhanced cooperation with UNDP, UNAIDS, UNICEF and UNFPA; and revised guidelines on the operational relationship between UNDP and UNIFEM, signed by both parties

on 7 June (see p. 883). Other UNIFEM activities included the convening in September of the first conference on "Gender Justice in Post-Conflict Situations", in collaboration with the International Legal Assistance Consortium and an independent assessment of UNIFEM [A/60/62-E/2005/10] commissioned by the Consultative Committee, which highlighted opportunities lost due to the failure to strengthen its positioning and resources.

In 2004, UNIFEM resources totaled $50.3 million, an increase of $14 million over the 2003 figure, of which $23.2 million was in core resources and $25.5 million in non-core resources.

By **decision 59/540** of 22 December, the General Assembly took note of the report [A/59/135] on UNIFEM's 2003 activities [YUN 2003, p. 1193], transmitted by the Secretary-General in July.

International Research and Training Institute (INSTRAW)

A May report of the Director of INSTRAW [E/2004/66], submitted in accordance with Economic and Social Council resolution 2003/57 [YUN 2003, p. 1195], covered the Institute's activities for the period from December 2003 to May 2004. The report dealt with developments related to the Institute's institutional structure in line with Council resolution 2003/57, including the election of the members of the new Executive Board; development of a strategic plan for 2004-2007 to be presented to the Executive Board at its first session for approval; convening of a meeting (11 March) for donors and other interested parties; publication of a paper on "overcoming the gender digital divide"; and the reinstatement of the Institute's internship programme.

Commission on Status of Women. In a March resolution [E/2004/27 (res. 48/1)] on the revitalization and strengthening of INSTRAW, the Commission on the Status of Women welcomed the appointment by the Secretary-General of the Director of the Institute on 4 December 2003 and noted his plan to develop a targeted work programme and funding activities. It invited voluntary contributions by Member States to the United Nations Trust Fund for INSTRAW. The Commission encouraged efforts to revitalize INSTRAW and monitor its progress during its forty-ninth (2005) session.

Note of Secretary-General. In response to General Assembly resolution 57/311 [YUN 2003, p. 1200], the Secretary-General transmitted a November report [A/59/560] of the Director of INSTRAW on its work programme and on the implementation of the recommendations contained in the report of the Office of Internal Oversight

Services (OIOS) on the audit of INSTRAW [YUN 2002, p. 1165]. The report indicated that the INSTRAW Executive Board, at its first session on 27 July, approved the 2004-2007 strategic framework, which identified four strategic areas of work: research; information and communication; capacity-building/training; and institutional development. At the resumed session on 1 October, the Board approved the 2005 programme of work, which encompassed both core and project activities and contained the financial requirements for the Institute's operations. However, the Board pointed out that there were no resources in the INSTRAW Trust Fund to finance those requirements. INSTRAW developed 16 project profiles, totalling $7.7 million, which it had submitted to several financial partners for funding.

The report also detailed measures taken by the Institute to implement OIOS recommendations, including the revision of INSTRAW's statute; replacement of the Board of Trustees by an Executive Board; redesign of the Institute's website; and development of a draft strategic framework and portfolio of projects for consideration by donors.

Future of INSTRAW

Report of Secretary-General. In response to General Assembly resolution 58/244 [YUN 2003, p. 1199] and Economic and Social Council resolution 2003/57 [ibid., p. 1195], the Secretary-General submitted an August report [A/59/313] on the future operation of INSTRAW. As part of the revitalization process, INSTRAW had undertaken several important initiatives, including the launching of a redesigned website, strengthening cooperative arrangements with UN entities, expanding its research programme, intensifying its fund-raising campaign and enhancing communications with Governments, civil society, academia and the private sector. With the preparation of the programme of work, the related budget and portfolio of projects, the first phase of the revitalization of the Institute would be completed. However, full implementation of the revitalization process depended on the support of Governments, including making available the financial resources for the operation of the Institute.

GENERAL ASSEMBLY ACTION

On 23 December [meeting 76], the General Assembly, on the recommendation of the Third Committee [A/59/496], adopted **resolution 59/260**, by a recorded vote of 125 to 10, with 30 abstentions [agenda item 98].

Future operation of the International Research and Training Institute for the Advancement of Women

The General Assembly,

Recalling all of its previous resolutions on the situation of the International Research and Training Institute for the Advancement of Women, in particular resolutions 55/219 of 23 December 2000, 56/125 of 19 December 2001, 57/175 of 18 December 2002 and 58/244 of 23 December 2003,

Reaffirming its resolution 57/311 of 18 June 2003 on the financial situation of the Institute,

Recalling Economic and Social Council resolution 2003/57 of 24 July 2003, in which the Council decided to amend articles III and IV of the statute of the Institute,

Welcoming the constitution of the Executive Board of the Institute, in particular the important results of its first session, held on 27 July 2004, and its resumed first session, held on 1 October 2004,

Welcoming also the adoption by the Executive Board of the framework of the strategic plan for the Institute, 2004–2007,

Bearing in mind the recommendation made by the Executive Board at its resumed first session that the report of the Director of the Institute, the proposed operational budget for 2005 and other relevant documents be submitted to the General Assembly,

Taking note with appreciation of a number of important strategic initiatives, including the redesign of the web site of the Institute, the strengthening of cooperative arrangements with entities of the United Nations system, the expansion of the research programme of the Institute, the intensification of its fund-raising campaign, the enhancement of communications with governmental agencies, civil society, academia and the private sector, and the strengthening of the training, capacity-building and outreach activities undertaken by the Institute,

1. *Welcomes* the report of the Secretary-General;

2. *Welcomes also* the fact that the first phase of the revitalization process has been completed with the preparation of the programme of work, portfolio of projects and related budget of the International Research and Training Institute for the Advancement of Women, as noted by the Secretary-General in his report, and decides that all of its projects should be fully implemented in order to strengthen the Institute, thus enabling it to carry out effectively its mandate, in particular to address the challenges facing women in developing and least developed countries in all regions;

3. *Recognizes* that the implementation of the programme of work and strategic plan for the Institute will contribute to the review and appraisal of the implementation of the Beijing Declaration and Platform for Action and the outcome document of the twenty-third special session of the General Assembly;

4. *Requests* the Institute, in accordance with its mandate, to actively participate in and contribute to the review and appraisal of the implementation of the Beijing Declaration and Platform for Action and the outcome document of the twenty-third special session of the General Assembly in the context of the forty-ninth session of the Commission on the Status of Women;

5. *Also requests* that the Institute, in the formulation of future programmes and projects, take into account

the particular challenges facing women in developing and least developed countries in the different regions;

6. *Stresses* the critical importance of voluntary financial contributions by Member States to the United Nations Trust Fund for the International Research and Training Institute for the Advancement of Women to enable it to carry out its mandate;

7. *Urges* Member States to make voluntary contributions to the Trust Fund, particularly during this critical transitional period;

8. *Decides* to provide its full support to the current efforts to revitalize the Institute and, in this regard, to ensure that the Institute will be able to continue functioning for a period of at least one year;

9. *Requests* the Secretary-General to report to the General Assembly at its sixtieth session on the implementation of the present resolution.

In favour: Algeria, Andorra, Antigua and Barbuda, Argentina, Armenia, Azerbaijan, Bahamas, Bahrain, Bangladesh, Barbados, Belarus, Belize, Benin, Bhutan, Bolivia, Bosnia and Herzegovina, Brazil, Brunei Darussalam, Burkina Faso, Burundi, Cambodia, Cameroon, Cape Verde, Central African Republic, Chile, China, Colombia, Comoros, Congo, Costa Rica, Cuba, Cyprus, Democratic People's Republic of Korea, Democratic Republic of the Congo, Djibouti, Dominica, Dominican Republic, Ecuador, Egypt, El Salvador, Eritrea, Fiji, Ghana, Grenada, Guatemala, Guinea, Guyana, Haiti, Honduras, India, Indonesia, Iran, Iraq, Italy, Jordan, Kazakhstan, Kenya, Kuwait, Kyrgyzstan, Lao People's Democratic Republic, Lebanon, Lesotho, Liberia, Libyan Arab Jamahiriya, Madagascar, Malaysia, Maldives, Mali, Malta, Marshall Islands, Mauritius, Mexico, Micronesia, Monaco, Mongolia, Morocco, Mozambique, Myanmar, Namibia, Nepal, Nicaragua, Niger, Nigeria, Oman, Pakistan, Panama, Papua New Guinea, Paraguay, Peru, Philippines, Portugal, Qatar, Rwanda, Saint Lucia, Saint Vincent and the Grenadines, Saudi Arabia, Senegal, Serbia and Montenegro, Sierra Leone, Singapore, Slovakia, Solomon Islands, South Africa, Spain, Sri Lanka, Sudan, Suriname, Syrian Arab Republic, Thailand, The former Yugoslav Republic of Macedonia, Timor-Leste, Togo, Tonga, Trinidad and Tobago, Tunisia, Turkmenistan, Uganda, United Arab Emirates, United Republic of Tanzania, Uruguay, Venezuela, Viet Nam, Yemen, Zambia, Zimbabwe.

Against: Australia, Canada, Denmark, Finland, Japan, Latvia, New Zealand, Sweden, United Kingdom, United States.

Abstaining: Albania, Austria, Belgium, Bulgaria, Croatia, Czech Republic, Estonia, France, Georgia, Germany, Hungary, Iceland, Ireland, Israel, Liechtenstein, Lithuania, Luxembourg, Netherlands, Norway, Poland, Republic of Korea, Republic of Moldova, Romania, Russian Federation, San Marino, Slovenia, Switzerland, Turkey, Ukraine, Uzbekistan.

By **decision 2004/317** of 23 December, the Council also took note of the Secretary-General's note transmitting the report of the INSTRAW Director on the revitalization and strengthening of the Institute (see p. 1172).

Financial situation

Report of Secretary-General. In an October report [A/59/433] on the financial situation of INSTRAW, the Secretary-General indicated that, because of additional voluntary contributions received in December 2003 and lower than anticipated expenses in November-December 2003, the available balance of the INSTRAW Trust Fund as at 31 December 2003 amounted to $843,417. For the period 1 January to 30 September 2004, $109,100 in additional income was received in the

Trust Fund, comprising $101,706 in voluntary contributions and $7,394 in miscellaneous income. As the Fund balance as at 30 September was estimated at $314,420 and anticipated expenditures for October-December at $290,703, it was determined that the Institute would have adequate resources to function until the end of 2004, with a projected closing balance of $23,717. Core requirements for the 2005 budget were estimated at $1,183,760. However, funds had neither been pledged nor received to finance operations in 2005. The Secretary-General concluded that, under the circumstances, the General Assembly would need to consider the future viability of the Institute.

Communication. On 4 October [A/C.3/59/2], Spain, on behalf of the Executive Board of INSTRAW, informed the General Assembly that the Institute's Trust Fund did not contain sufficient resources to meet its financial requirements for the 2005 proposed work plan and budget approved by the Executive Board in October. The Executive Board had called on the Assembly to provide financial assistance to the Institute.

Statement of Secretary-General. In a November statement [A/C.5/59/16] on programme budget implications of draft resolution [A/C.3/59/L.26], the Secretary-General indicated that financial requirements for 2005 were estimated at $1,183,700. Taking into account $67,613 in additional contributions to the INSTRAW Trust Fund in October, resulting in a projected balance of $91,300 in the Fund as at 31 December 2004, an additional amount of $1,092,400 might be required from the UN regular budget to maintain the Institute in 2005.

ACABQ report. In November [A/59/579], the Advisory Committee on Administrative and Budgetary Questions, recommended that the Fifth (Administrative and Budgetary) Committee inform the General Assembly that should it adopt the draft resolution (above), an additional provision of up to $1,092,400 would arise under Section 9, Economic and social affairs, of the 2004-2005 programme budget.

Fifth Committee consideration. In December [A/59/641], the Fifth Committee informed the Assembly accordingly and recommended that the Secretary-General be requested to report to the Assembly, as a matter of priority, during the main part of its sixtieth (2005) session on the Institute's overall financial situation.

Chapter XI

Children, youth and ageing persons

In 2004, the United Nations Children's Fund (UNICEF) continued to work with diverse partners to ensure that children worldwide were given the best start in life—immunization against vaccine-preventable diseases; accurate information about HIV/AIDS prevention; a quality primary school education; and protection from harm, abuse, violence and discrimination, including during times of war and in emergencies.

Significant progress was made towards mainstreaming children's priorities into national policy. At least 170 of the 190 countries that had adopted "A world fit for children"—the outcome document of the General Assembly's twenty-seventh (2002) special session on children—had taken action on or planned to initiate policies to put the goals of the session into action, and some 105 countries had incorporated those commitments into poverty-reduction strategies, national development plans or sector plans. In February, the General Assembly decided to hold a commemorative plenary meeting in 2007 to chart further progress.

UNICEF continued work on its five organizational priorities for 2002-2005: girls' education; fighting HIV/AIDS; integrated early childhood development; immunization "plus"; and improved protection of children from violence, exploitation, abuse and discrimination.

United Nations policies and programmes on youth continued to focus on efforts to implement the 1995 World Programme of Action for Youth to the Year 2002 and Beyond. In December, the General Assembly decided to hold two follow-up plenary meetings at its sixtieth (2005) session to evaluate progress in implementation, which would be preceded by an interactive round table. The third meeting of the High-level Panel of the Youth Employment Network focused on promoting development and financing of youth employment in national action plans prior to the five-year review of the Millennium Development Goals in 2005.

In 2004, United Nations efforts to implement the 2002 Madrid International Plan of Action on Ageing continued through the road map drafted in 2003, and in his report on progress, the Secretary-General called for greater efforts to link ageing to development policy.

Children

Follow-up to the 2002 General Assembly special session on children

Pursuant to its decision 58/565 [YUN 2003, p. 1203], the General Assembly considered, at its resumed fifty-eighth (2004) session, follow-up to the Assembly's twenty-seventh (2002) special session on children [YUN 2002, p. 1168], including progress in realizing the commitments of the session's final document, "A world fit for children", consisting of a Declaration and Plan of Action, adopted in resolution S-27/2 [ibid., p. 1169]. The Assembly had before it the Secretary-General's 2003 report [YUN 2003, p. 1202] on the follow-up, which highlighted action taken under the four major goals of the Plan of Action.

GENERAL ASSEMBLY ACTION

On 9 February [meeting 80], the General Assembly adopted **resolution 58/282** [draft: A/58/L.58] without vote [agenda item 41].

Follow-up to the outcome of the special session on children

The General Assembly,

Reaffirming the Declaration and the Plan of Action contained in the final document of the special session of the General Assembly on children, entitled "A world fit for children", and recognizing that their implementation is a major contribution to protecting the rights and promoting the well-being of children,

Recalling the Convention on the Rights of the Child, the most universally embraced human rights treaty in history, and the Optional Protocols thereto,

Recalling also its resolutions on the special session on children, including resolution 57/190 of 18 December 2002, in which, inter alia, it decided to include in the agenda of its fifty-eighth session the item entitled "Follow-up to the outcome of the special session on children", and allocated its consideration to the plenary,

Recalling further its resolution 57/270 B of 23 June 2003 on the integrated and coordinated implementation of and follow-up to the outcomes of the major United Nations conferences and summits in the economic and social fields,

Bearing in mind that, by 2007, several of the time-bound and quantified commitments set out in the Declaration and the Plan of Action should have been met, and that other targets are to be met by 2010 and 2015,

1. *Welcomes* the report of the Secretary-General;

2. *Takes note* of the initial progress made in the implementation of the Declaration and the Plan of Action by Governments, as well as by intergovernmental organizations and non-governmental organizations, and the support provided to them by relevant United Nations agencies, funds and programmes;

3. *Calls upon* Member States that have not yet done so to prepare or strengthen national action plans and, where appropriate, regional action plans, with a set of specific time-bound and measurable goals and targets, and in this context encourages cooperation with civil society actors, including non-governmental organizations working for and with children, as well as children themselves, in order to implement the commitments made at the special session on children and at other relevant major United Nations conferences and summits, in particular the Millennium Summit;

4. *Urges* all relevant specialized agencies, funds and programmes of the United Nations system, and invites intergovernmental organizations, non-governmental organizations and civil society, to lend their full support to implementing the commitments made in the final document of the twenty-seventh special session, entitled "A world fit for children", and to keep the Secretary-General informed of their actions;

5. *Requests* the United Nations Children's Fund to continue to prepare and disseminate, in close collaboration with Governments, relevant specialized agencies, funds and programmes of the United Nation system and all other relevant actors, as appropriate, information on the progress made in the implementation of the Plan of Action;

6. *Requests* the governing bodies of the relevant specialized agencies to ensure that, within their mandates, the agencies give their fullest possible support for the achievement of the goals outlined in the Plan of Action and to keep the General Assembly fully informed, through the Economic and Social Council, of progress and additional action required using existing reporting frameworks and procedures;

7. *Requests* the Secretary-General to continue to report regularly to the General Assembly on the progress made in implementing the Declaration and the Plan of Action;

8. *Decides* to convene a commemorative plenary meeting in 2007, on a date to be decided at its sixtieth session, devoted to the follow-up to the outcome of its twenty-seventh special session and the progress made in implementing the Declaration and the Plan of Action, based on a report to be prepared by the Secretary-General, and invites the President of the General Assembly to finalize organizational matters in consultation with Member States;

9. *Decides also* to include in the provisional agenda of its fifty-ninth session the item entitled "Follow-up to the outcome of the special session on children".

Report of Secretary-General. In response to General Assembly resolutions 58/157 [YUN 2003, p. 701] and 58/282 (above), the Secretary-General issued his second report [A/59/274] on follow-up to the Assembly's special session on children.

The report updated progress achieved in realizing the commitments outlined in the session's final document, entitled "A world fit for children", which committed Governments to a time-bound set of goals for children, with a focus on health, education, protection from abuse, exploitation and violence, and combating HIV/AIDS. The report also identified problems and constraints, and recommended actions needed to achieve further progress.

In 2004, the overall rate of progress was more encouraging than the previous year. Some 105 countries had incorporated national policy instruments such as poverty-reduction strategies, national development plans or sector plans into the follow-up process, and at least 170 countries had taken or intended to take action to put the special session's goals into operation. UNICEF, as at the end of May, indicated that 25 countries had completed national action plans for children since the special session; 55 countries were in the process of doing so; and another 32 foresaw developing such plans. The report covered regional trends, noting outstanding progress in Central and Eastern Europe, the Commonwealth of Independent States (CIS) and the Baltic States; widespread efforts to develop or improve national action plans in Latin America and the Caribbean and Asia and the Pacific; and efforts to integrate the special session's goals into poverty reduction strategies among two-thirds of the countries in sub-Saharan Africa. However, it noted limited progress in the Middle East and North Africa.

The report highlighted strengths and weaknesses in the follow-up process to incorporate goals for children into local and national strategies and policies; involve civil society; reach the most disadvantaged groups; foster synergy between the Millennium Development Goals (MDGs) [YUN 2000, p. 49] and the goals of the special session; allocate funds to meet those goals; and link national action plans with the 1989 Convention on the Rights of the Child [YUN 1989, p. 560] (see p. 667).

In some countries, the special session appeared to have promoted stronger monitoring mechanisms of child-related goals. Widespread national reporting in the last few years on the MDGs indicated a positive response to monitoring child-related goals. Some 73 countries had issued monitoring reports on the MDGs as of July 2004. However, even though some countries had well-established monitoring systems for health and education indicators, few had disaggregated data on all the priority areas identified in the special session, particularly child protection.

UN agencies and other international actors were collaborating to achieve a consolidated statistical system to monitor and report on the relevant MDGs. UNICEF was developing multiple indicator cluster surveys (MICs) that would provide the largest single source of data for charting progress in reaching child-related MDGs and the goals of "A world fit for children." It also worked with demographic and health surveys sponsored by the United States Agency for International Development (USAID) to ensure that comparable child-related data were produced. More than 40 countries had adopted the *ChildInfo/DevInfo* database system for compiling child related data and that number was expected to double by the end of 2004. The system, a user-friendly technology platform which encouraged dialogue among stakeholders and facilitated reporting, was developed with UNICEF sponsorship.

The Secretary-General concluded that since the 2002 special session there had been numerous, but often isolated, examples of rapid progress in countries and regions, demonstrating that accelerated progress was possible, but it would require increased resource allocations and political action. Of the 190 countries that had adopted the "A world fit for children" Plan of Action, at least 169 had taken or were planning action to achieve related goals. However, many countries had yet to link such plans to national budgeting and monitoring mechanisms. The fact that the MDGs did not explicitly include child protection targets raised the challenge of ensuring that the relevant issues were appropriately considered in national planning processes, including strategies to end child trafficking, child labour and violence against children. Greater efforts were needed to ensure adequate and sustained national budget allocations for children, supplemented by donor funding when necessary. In many countries, weaknesses in institutional capacity, and in some cases conflict and instability, would challenge implementation of programmes for children.

As a way forward, the Secretary-General recommended the establishment of national councils for children, capacity-building of national child agencies and collaboration with parliamentarians and civil society organizations to promote child-focused budgets. He emphasized the importance of civil society involvement in mobilizing resources for children's rights and noted the participation of children and young people as a major constituency in many government-led decision-making processes, which had proliferated in the two years since the special session. He called on countries to report regularly to the public on progress in implementing the MDGs and the goals of "A world fit for children" as a means of social mobilization for those goals and to strengthen accountability. In addition, assistance should be provided to civil society and com-

munity groups to enable them to generate information on specific groups, such as children orphaned by AIDS.

The Secretary-General also proposed that regional mechanisms be utilized to encourage countries to share experiences and good practices in child-related programmes and that the Committee on the Rights of the Child promote closer linkages between follow-up to the special session, the MDGs and States parties' periodic reports on the Convention on the Rights of the Child. He indicated that further updates on progress in implementing the Declaration and Plan of Action would be provided to the General Assembly in 2005 and 2006, and a more detailed analysis in 2007.

On 23 December, the Assembly decided that its agenda item entitled "follow-up to the outcome of the special session on children" would be considered during its resumed fifty-ninth (2005) session (**decision 59/552**).

United Nations Children's Fund

UNICEF was committed to achieving the MDGs [YUN 2000, p. 51] and the goals set by the Assembly's twenty-seventh (2002) special session on children [YUN 2002, p. 1168] in its outcome document, "A world fit for children" [ibid., p. 1169]. Its mission was to defend children's rights, help meet their basic needs, ensure their survival and increase their opportunities to flourish; rally political will to invest in children's well-being; respond to emergencies and strengthen the ability of children and their families to handle crisis, including armed conflict, natural disasters and HIV/AIDS; assist countries in transition to protect young people's rights and provide vital services to children and their families; advance equal rights for boys and girls and encourage their full participation in developing their communities; and work towards the human development goals adopted by the world community and the peace, justice and social progress enshrined in the Charter of the United Nations.

UNICEF's annual flagship publication, *The State of the World's Children 2004,* emphasized the importance of girls' education to development and sought to draw attention to the plight of girls who, in most countries, were the most disadvantaged in regard to education. Millions of them never attended school; millions more never completed their education; and countless others never received quality education. Ill prepared as women to participate in the political, social and economic development of their communities, such uneducated or poorly educated girls—and their children—were at higher risk for poverty,

HIV/AIDS, sexual exploitation, violence and abuse. Girls' education raised economic productivity, reduced infant and maternal mortality, improved nutrition and promoted health, including helping to prevent the spread of HIV/AIDS. Noting that some 121 million children were out of school, and 65 million of them were girls, the report stressed the urgency of eliminating gender disparity in primary and secondary schools by 2005 as the first step towards meeting the MDGs relating to education.

In 2004, UNICEF cooperated with 157 countries, areas and territories: 45 in sub-Saharan Africa; 35 in Latin America and the Caribbean; 34 in Asia; 20 in the Middle East and North Africa; and 23 in Central and Eastern Europe, and the Baltic States.

Total expenditures, including write-offs, amounted to $1,606 million (compared to $1,480 million in 2003), of which 93.9 per cent ($1,508 million) was for programme assistance and support; 5.7 per cent ($92 million) for management and administration; and 0.4 per cent ($6 million) for write-offs. (For programme expenditures by priority, see p. 1181.) UNICEF operations in 2004 were described in the *UNICEF Annual Report* covering the period 1 January to 31 December 2004; the annual report of its Executive Director [E/ICEF/2005/3]; and a report of the Executive Director [E/ICEF/2005/6] on results achieved for children during the year in support of UNICEF's 2002-2005 medium-term strategic plan (MTSP), which was approved by the Executive Board in 2001 [YUN 2001, p. 1094].

The UNICEF Executive Board held its first regular session of 2004 (19-23 and 26 January), its annual session (7-11 June) and its second regular session (13-16 September), all in New York [E/2004/34/Rev.1]. The Board adopted 17 decisions during those sessions.

By **decision 2004/232** of 12 July, the Economic and Social Council took note of the Board's report on its first regular session; the Board's decisions at its annual session; and the annual report of the Executive Director covering the year 2003 [E/2004/3], which was transmitted to the Council in accordance with a January decision of the Board [E/2004/34/Rev.1 (dec. 2004/3)].

On 22 January [dec. 2004/4], the Board requested that the Bureau continue its lead role in exploring approaches to further improve working methods and to submit specific recommendations. In June the Board reviewed the Bureau's report on methods [E/ICEF/2004/CRP.10]; took note of the Bureau's recommendations; and indicated it would do its best to implement them.

On 16 September, the Executive Board adopted the programme of work and dates for its 2005 sessions [dec. 2004/17].

Programme policies

In December, the Executive Director transmitted to the Economic and Social Council her annual report [E/2005/6-ICEF/2005/3], which described UNICEF efforts to implement the Secretary-General's reform programme (see p. 1359) and the provisions of the triennial comprehensive policy review (TCPR) of operational activities for development of the UN system (see p. 1866). The report covered the areas of structures and mechanisms; funding for operational activities; capacity-building; the resident coordinator system; common country programming; common premises and common services; monitoring and evaluation; gender mainstreaming; and collaboration with the World Bank. It also discussed follow-up to international conferences, including the General Assembly's special session on children (see p. 1175).

Other issues highlighted the Greentree Report, produced at a private meeting (New York, 6 January) of the Executive Heads of the United Nations Development Group (UNDG); the progressive implementation of the new common country programming process and the 15 countries in 2004 that made up the first group of countries applying the full common country programming process; efforts to develop national plans of action (NPAs) for orphaned children; the participation of more than 400 national professionals and UN staff from 120 countries in introductory workshops on *DevInfo*, a tool adapted from the *ChildInfo* technology (see p. 1177).

Medium-term strategic plan (2002-2005)

In March, the Executive Director submitted a report [E/ICEF/2004/9] on the results achieved for children in 2003 in support of UNICEF's medium-term strategic plan (MTSP) (2002-2005), which provided information on progress, partnerships, constraints and key results achieved in 2002-2003 in the plan's five priority areas of girls' education, early childhood development (ECD), immunization "plus", fighting HIV/AIDS, and protection of children from violence, abuse, exploitation and discrimination. The report also presented UNICEF income and expenditures in 2003.

The report indicated that the second year (2003) of the MTSP period saw growing achievements from UNICEF's partnerships in the five priority areas. The linkages between priorities, such as the integration of actions against HIV/AIDS and for child protection in sectoral programmes, had become stronger. Within the MTSP framework, emergency assistance was provided to children and their families in 55 crisis-affected countries across the globe. Progress was made in operational areas, including an improvement in key performance indicators in the UNICEF global supply system. The introduction of matrices setting out strategic outcomes had assisted in the drive for results-oriented programmes. As the MTSP progressed, UNICEF would need to define more clearly its role and articulate its contributions to the Millennium Agenda [YUN 2000, p. 49] and the UN reform process—both overall and in specific areas such as early childhood and the struggle against HIV/AIDS. UNICEF would also need to focus on improving the quality of its publications, donor reporting and country programme management; ensuring a scaled-up response to the orphan crisis and HIV infection among young people through further cooperation with the World Health Organization (WHO) to expand access to treatment; and strengthening other areas, such as, expanded immunization services, supply of bednets and vitamin supplements, and enhanced efforts against child trafficking, child soldiery and gender-based violence.

Mid-term review. A July UNICEF report [E/ICEF/2004/13] on the MTSP mid-term review summarized the views of external partners and UNICEF field offices on their experience of MTSP so far; discussed key issues which had increased in prominence in the first two years of the plan; assessed organizational performance and lessons learned in the five priority areas and supporting strategies of the plan; and presented proposed adjustments to the current MTSP and implications for the next one.

The report recommended that UNICEF maintain strengths identified in the current MTSP, such as the emphasis on clear organization priorities coupled with a flexible approach that responded to national conditions, increased emphasis on results-based management, dynamic linkages among the priorities and between community-based and policy-oriented work, and a more coherent approach to external communication and fund-raising. Only limited adjustments to the MTSP were envisaged. The review confirmed that UNICEF should further specify its role in the development and implementation of poverty reduction strategy papers and sector-wide approach processes (SWAps).

In general, UNICEF staff and a number of external partners envisaged a high degree of continuity in the organizational priorities for the next plan. Suggested changes included more focus on young child survival and development, as well as quality education and issues of inequality in the discussion on girls' education. Other areas that needed more attention were water, sanitation and nutrition; emergency response; work in post-conflict transitions; humanitarian response; streamlining of programming and operational procedures; recruitment and retention of high-quality staff; and development of a fund-raising strategy, with a focus on a balance between regular and other resources.

On 16 September [dec. 2004/16], the Executive Board took note of the conclusions of the report on the mid-term review of the UNICEF MTSP and requested the Executive Director to report on progress in effecting the recommended adjustments at its annual session in 2005.

Medium-term financial plan (2004-2007)

At its September session, the Executive Board considered the MTSP: financial plan and related recommendation for 2004-2007 [E/ICEF/2004/AB/L.4], which provided a flexible framework of projections for that period, including the preparation of up to $492 million in programme expenditures from regular resources to be submitted to the Board in 2005. That amount was subject to the availability of resources and to the condition that income and expenditure estimates in the plan continued to be valid.

On 16 September [dec. 2004/14], the Executive Board approved the medium-term financial plan as a framework of projections.

Evaluation system

As requested by the Executive Board [YUN 2002, p. 1184], the UNICEF Secretariat issued an April progress report [E/ICEF/2004/11] on its evaluation function, which provided an overview of the evaluation system, of progress made in strengthening the evaluation function and of evaluations conducted by the Evaluation Office. The report noted that during the 2002-2003 period, some 2,435 evaluative exercises were registered in the database, of which 576 or 24 per cent were evaluation reports. The rest were surveys or research studies. Sixty-three per cent of the evaluation reports were related to organizational priorities of the MTSP, and of those, 42 per cent dealt with child protection, 20 per cent with early childhood development, 19 per cent with HIV/AIDS, 11 per cent with immunization, and 8 per cent with girls' education.

In 2003, the Evaluation Office conducted a meta-evaluation of one half of the evaluation reports received in 2001 and 2002 and found that the quality of evaluations supported by UNICEF country offices was inconsistent. Approximately 20 per cent were excellent, but one-third were poorly executed. UNICEF cited measures it would take to improve the quality of the bottom third of the evaluations and its overall evaluation function process. On 11 June [dec. 2004/9], the Executive Board, while commending UNICEF's progress in evaluation, noted that work remained to be done, including sharpening the strategic focus of evaluation work plans, improving efficiency and raising the standards of evaluation work. It emphasized that the evaluation function should be carried out in consultation with national authorities. Recommending areas for further strengthening the evaluation function, the Board requested the Executive Director to report on evaluation at its annual session in 2006 and to present key findings of evaluations of the MTSP thematic areas when they became available.

Health coordinating committee. At its January session, the Executive Board considered a note [E/ICEF/2004/6] on the evaluation of the WHO/UNICEF/United Nations Population Fund (UNFPA) Coordinating Committee on Health (CCH). On 21 January [dec. 2004/1], the Board endorsed the note's recommendation to discontinue CCH and recommended that those three organizations continue to strengthen coordination in health.

Emergency assistance

A July report [E/ICEF/2004/14] on the updated humanitarian priorities of UNICEF indicated that in 2003-2004, one third of the countries in which UNICEF operated were responding to crises and emergencies, and approximately 25-30 per cent of UNICEF funding was allocated for emergencies. As the organization's income had increased, so had the portion for emergencies, from $116 million in 1998 to $443 million in 2003. That illustrated the significant rise in the scale and nature of emergencies, especially large-scale displacement of populations, the breakdown of State institutions and community structures, political turbulence, human rights violations, disruption of social service systems, the lack of governance and presence of non-State entities. In recent years, the context for humanitarian action had changed, and both the number and complexity of emergencies had increased.

In 2003, UNICEF had updated its Core Commitments for Children in Emergencies (CCCs) in order to enhance the timeliness, effectiveness and predictability of its humanitarian response, and to reinforce its role in protecting women and children's rights. The revised CCCs covered four main areas: rapid assessment, including an objective analysis of the capacity to manage and re-spond to the situation; coordination and partnerships formed with other organizations to ensure achievement of the CCCs, particularly through initial emergency response commitments in the first six to eight weeks; programmatic response to attain the required minimum intervention in various sectors; and the operational capacities, procedures and resources to ensure that the funds, staff and supplies required were available on a timely basis. Focusing greater attention on HIV/AIDS prevention, strengthening child protection and increasing support for post-conflict transition periods, the new CCC format provided guiding principles for UNICEF to follow in an emergency. UNICEF applied the CCC format a number of times during 2004 in Caribbean countries ravaged by natural disasters and man-made crises—floods, hurricanes and political unrest—particularly in the Dominican Republic, Grenada, Haiti and Jamaica. The organization also responded to the terrorist attack on 1 September against a school in Beslan, Russian Federation (see p. 73), with emergency medical and school supplies, and to the devastating earthquake in Bam, Iran, on 26 December 2003, by supplying emergency water, medicines, tents and generators, as well as counseling to many of the 80,000 survivors. The wartorn Darfur region of the Sudan (see p. 235) remained a challenge throughout the year, due to insecurity and the remote locations of displaced people. UNICEF provided emergency health kits, primary health care and vaccinations, safe drinking water, latrines, food, shelter, blankets, mosquito nets and soap to many of those affected. It also assisted in providing education and psychosocial support, especially to child victims of violence.

In its resolution 59/173 (see p. 485), the General Assembly, concerned about the continued deterioration of the situation of children in the Occupied Palestinian Territory, called upon the international community to urgently provide needed assistance and services to alleviate the dire humanitarian crisis affecting Palestinian children and their families.

UNICEF programmes by region

A report of the Executive Director [E/ICEF/2005/6] indicated that in 2004, UNICEF regional programme expenditures totalled $1,344 million, of which $317 million (24 per cent) went to programmes in Eastern and Southern Africa; $266 million (20 per cent) to Western and Central Africa; $241 million (18 per cent) to South Asia; $215 million (16 per cent) to the Middle East and North Africa; $122 million (9 per cent) to East Asia and the Pacific; $84 million (6 per cent) to the Americas and the Caribbean; $58 million

(4 per cent) to the Commonwealth of Independent States (CIS) and the Baltic States; and $40 million (3 per cent) to interregional programmes. Programme support costs totalled an additional $164 million. The percentage of programme expenditure to sub-Saharan Africa as a whole was 48 per cent.

Programme expenditures were highest in countries with low income and high, or very high, under-five mortality rates. The 63 low-income countries—defined as those with a per capita gross national income of $735 or less—which had a total child population in 2002 of 1 billion, or 56 per cent of all children worldwide, received 66 per cent of total programme expenditures.

Field visits

Executive Board members who visited the Democratic Republic of the Congo (13-23 March) reported [E/ICEF/2004/CRP.7] that UNICEF played a lead role in responding to the needs of the community where many children and women faced some of the worst conditions in the world, including HIV/AIDS, rape and other violence, high infant and child mortality rates, recruitment of child soldiers and poor education. Members concluded that urgent attention was required and the Board called for the immediate cessation of all acts of violence against women and children; legal action against sexual violence perpetrators; disarmament, demobilization and reinsertion into communities of children associated with armed groups; an internationally supported post-conflict transition process; increased funding for community-focused activities; and reinforcement of UNICEF programme activities.

In a report [E/ICEF/2004/CRP.8] on the joint visit to Guatemala (21 March–2 April) by members of the Executive Boards of UNICEF, the United Nations Development Programme (UNDP), UNFPA and the World Food Programme (WFP), the participants concluded that there was a need to strengthen the functions of the resident coordinator and the UN funds, agencies and programmes in Guatemala, as the United Nations Verification Mission in Guatemala (MINUGUA) would end on 31 December 2004 (see p. 286). Members called for an assessment to determine which resources and infrastructure could be transferred from MINUGUA to the Resident Coordinator's office so that it could fulfil its new responsibilities. The report concluded that the United Nations should continue its advocacy and support for legislative and judicial frameworks that progress in such areas as, water and sanitation, food security and reform of the legal framework regulating adoption of children. Public policies, capacity-building at all levels and social

investments benefiting children also needed improvement. Responding to the rapid spread of HIV/AIDS in Guatemala, especially among women in recent years, Board members called for extending nationwide coverage of programmes to stop mother-to-child transmission of the disease.

Members of the Bureau of the UNICEF Executive Board travelled to Guyana (30 May–4 June) and reported [E/ICEF/2004/CRP.9] on UNICEF-supported projects and how the country programme implemented the MTSP priorities in that country. Key achievements included UNICEF's catalytic role in supporting pilot projects in national programmes and government programme integration, such as the incorporation of the "Prevention of Mother-to-Child Transmission of HIV" project into a national programme, and of the *Escuela Nueva* and Child-Friendly Schools approach into Guyana's education strategic plan and the Education for All (EFA) Fast Track Initiative. To strengthen weak areas, the members recommended that UNICEF introduce results-based management and an integrated monitoring and evaluation plan; develop a communication strategy focusing on behavioural change; and create opportunities for the development and participation of children. Particular attention was needed for the "forgotten group" of children ages 7 to 12 to prevent the spread of HIV/AIDS, teen pregnancies, school drop-outs and violence. The report also noted the establishment of a child protection monitoring database through UNICEF's technical support, which would help to improve social statistics, and the ability of non-governmental organizations (NGOs) to attract additional resources from funding agencies, thus developing broad-based partnerships in the country.

In a July report [E/ICEF/2004/19] on proposed guidelines for field visits by Board members, UNICEF provided a flexible frame of reference for preparing visits, which would specify the type and number of visits, the selection of the countries and the purpose and scope of visits. On 15 September [dec. 2004/13], the Board adopted the proposed guidelines.

UNICEF programmes by sector

In 2004, UNICEF programme expenditures, which were linked to the five organizational priorities established in 2001 under the 2002-2005 MTSP [YUN 2001, p. 1093], totalled $1,344 million, a 10 per cent increase over 2003 [E/ICEF/2005/6]. The largest share of total expenditures, $459 million (34 per cent), was spent early childhood development (ECD); followed by $293 million (22 per cent) for immunization "plus"; $282 million (21 per cent) for girls' education; $140 million (10 per cent) for child protection; $115 million (9 per cent) for HIV/AIDS prevention; and $55 million (4 per cent) for other matters. Programme support costs amounted to an additional $164 million.

The total share for girls' education and ECD had risen significantly since 2002. Decisions on contributions for other purposes by UNICEF funding partners and patterns of spending in emergencies had a growing effect on those shares. In 2004, it was notable that girls' education and HIV/AIDS prevention accounted for a significantly higher share of regular resources programme expenditures (25 and 13 per cent, respectively) than of total expenditures.

Early childhood development

An intensive review in 2004 of early childhood development (ECD) resulted in UNICEF modifications to its approach and possible changes to its next MTSP, including greater focus on young children's survival and development, and support for families and marginalized groups. Service delivery in basic health, and water and sanitation had improved, as had parenting programmes, birth registration and centre-based childcare, and efforts to strengthen breast-feeding practices had begun. UNICEF continued to cooperate with a number of national agencies, UN organizations, Governments and NGOs in supporting programmes in those areas.

In 2004, an estimated 34 countries had national ECD policies, up from 17 in 2002, which resulted in family issues and child development being more fully incorporated into national programmes. In partnership with the Netherlands, UNICEF supported innovative ECD programmes in 21 countries. It supported several countries in developing policies for: nutrition and infant and young child feeding, including in Kenya, Madagascar, Rwanda and Timor-Leste; water and sanitation, in Eritrea, Nepal, Nicaragua and Zimbabwe; early childhood education in Ghana, Mozambique and Uganda; and a stronger UN focus on young children through common country assessments (CCAs) and the United Ntions Development Assistance Framework (UNDAF). Many countries were using Sector-wide approaches (SWAps) to fill major gaps in national policy or to deal with new challenges, such as the HIV/AIDS impact on young children. Some 90 countries were implementing the Integrated Management of Childhood Illness (IMCI) and the Accelerated Child Survival and Development (ACSD) initiatives, reaching an estimated 124 million people in an expanded coverage of health and nutrition interventions to tackle major causes of child death.

UNICEF joined national aid agencies and others in supporting community programmes for pneumonia treatment in Senegal and Uganda, and training healthcare workers in new diarrhoea treatments in Cambodia, Ethiopia, Ghana and elsewhere. The organization distributed insecticide-treated nets (ITNs) to prevent malaria in 35 African countries and in parts of Asia and the Pacific, and also teamed with WHO to introduce artemisinin-based combination therapy (ACT) for malaria in many countries. As the world's largest supplier of ITNs, UNICEF procured $32 million worth of ITNs and insecticide in 2004, up from $17.2 million in 2003, and $6.7 million worth of ACTs (11.6 million treatments), up from $1 million in 2003. Declines in malaria-related deaths and illness were reported in Eritrea, Sierra Leone and Zambia.

Through partnerships with other agencies, NGOs and the African Development Bank, UNICEF helped upgrade 121 facilities for emergency treatment and care for pregnant women in Senegal, and teamed with others to upgrade 470 such facilities in South Asia. It helped 84 countries strengthen policies or services for infant and young child feeding, and promoted the "Baby-Friendly" Hospital Initiative in 50 countries. Due to the growing interest in food supplements and flour fortification to prevent anaemia and thus maintain women's health and the intellectual development of infants and young children, UNICEF collaborated with private-sector partners, the Fortification Initiative, the Micronutrient Initiative, the Global Alliance for Improved Nutrition and the Asian Development Bank, in a number of activities, including food fortification testing in China and Viet Nam.

UNICEF's 15-year leadership of the global campaign to eliminate iodine deficiency disorders, the most widespread cause of preventable mental retardation in children, resulted in a drop in the number of countries with iodine deficiency as a public health problem from 110 in 1993 to 54 in 2003. Deficiency levels in 40 of the 54 countries were mild.

In 2004, UNICEF supported water, sanitation and hygiene programmes in 93 countries, ranging from national policy development to service delivery in focus districts. Support to schools in 76 countries was provided in hygiene education and construction of water, sanitation and washing facilities. It also supported birth registration campaigns in 90 countries, particularly in West and Central Africa; a "catch-up" campaign in India, which issued some 25 million birth certificates; and campaigns in Afghanistan linked to immunization, which registered 2.7 million children since 2003.

By 2004, 94 countries, up from 67 in 2002, had developed a set of family and community practices for child survival, growth and development—fundamental to realizing the MDGs on child mortality reduction and education. UNICEF supported a community-oriented approach to IMCI in 85 countries and parenting programmes in 56 countries on early learning, psychosocial care, child health and nutrition. Sixty-five countries used baseline surveys and other data to evaluate existing family-care practices. Further deepening of the evidence base was needed, in particular for assessing the role of fathers in child care, which UNICEF promoted in 13 countries, and on how families were coping with conflict and HIV/AIDS.

UNICEF supported home-based care programmes in 70 countries and centre-based care in 84 countries. Efforts to include young children in conflict, with disabilities or affected by HIV/AIDS in childcare programmes grew significantly, and it appeared that, gradually, local childcare programmes were reaching more marginalized children. UNICEF continued to try to improve the quality of early learning programmes as a tool for improving school achievement and, in the longer run, for breaking the cycle of poverty. In some 53 countries, UNICEF-assisted early learning programmes specifically supported girls' preparation for school.

Immunization "plus"

Routine immunization in recent years reached about 75 per cent of the world's children. That strategy of immunizing as many children as possible, combined with routine services and accelerated disease control programmes, prevented an estimated 2.5 million child deaths annually. However, over 29 million children had no access to routine immunization and unless the gap was closed, 2 million children under five years of age would continue to die annually from vaccine-preventable diseases. UNICEF and WHO, with other partners, worked in 2004 to develop a Global Immunization Vision and Strategy (GIVS) for 2006-2015. At least 125 countries had adopted multi-year, comprehensive national immunization action plans.

Global coverage for three doses of the diphtheria/pertussis/tetanus vaccine (DPT3) was 78 per cent, reaching 98 million children in 2003, and the accelerated measles mortality reduction programme made exceptional progress. The Measles Partnership, involving a number of national organizations, including UNICEF and WHO, supported measles vaccination in priority countries in Africa. During 2001-2004, an additional 200 million children in sub-Saharan Africa were vaccinated, reducing measles deaths from an estimated 482,000 in 1999 to fewer than 240,000 in 2004 and achieving the target of halving measles mortality. The Global Polio Eradication Initiative achieved an almost 50 per cent decline in reported cases in Asia in 2004, but an outbreak of polio in Nigeria spread to 13 previously polio-free African countries. UNICEF played a role in the effort to stem the ensuing epidemic in 23 countries. As part of its advocacy programme, it encouraged African religious and traditional leaders to support immunization, notably during the "Pan-African Forum on Building Trust for Immunization and Child Survival" (Dakar, Senegal, October). By 2004, 89 countries had established national communication strategies for immunization. UNICEF continued to support vaccination drives in 41 countries to eliminate maternal and neonatal tetanus (MNT), which still existed in 58 countries, but uncertain funding for the future jeopardized that goal. Seventy-two UNICEF-assisted countries were currently using auto-disable syringes with injectable vaccines and other safer injection practices for routine immunizations, compared to 45 countries in 2002.

Vaccine availability rose significantly in 2004 due to the collective effort of donors, UNICEF, WHO and other partners. Only 35 per cent of countries covered by field reports had national vaccine stock-outs in their routine immunization programmes, down from 44 per cent in 2002. Routine vaccine costs were fully covered by national budgets in 75 per cent of the countries for which information was available, suggesting gradual, but clear, gains in national capacities for routine immunization across the developing world.

UNICEF supported the inclusion of vitamin A supplements in 89 countries with high child mortality, and more than two thirds of children in least developed countries received vitamin A supplements. Twenty-one countries achieved over 70 per cent coverage of children under five years, with two rounds of supplementation, thereby conferring full life-saving protection.

During 2002-2004, UNICEF provided measles vaccines and vitamin A supplements to an estimated 100 million children in 25 countries affected by emergencies. Within a week of the tsunami disaster in late December, UNICEF began providing measles vaccines to children in camps and high-risk areas in India and Indonesia. It also provided vitamin A to those in affected areas, as well as in Kenya and the Sudan's Darfur region. Large-scale UNICEF support sustained immunization services in post-conflict Iraq for over 5 million children, despite insecurity in some areas. In 2004, some 90 UNICEF-assisted countries had national strategies to reach marginalized groups with life-saving intervention. The "Reaching Every District" plan, promoted jointly by UNICEF and WHO, contributed to increased immunization coverage, including by 5 to 10 per cent in 20 countries from 2001 to 2003.

Girls' education

In 2004, efforts to show the urgency of achieving the millennium target for gender parity in basic education by 2015 [YUN 2000, p. 52] helped create a climate for action in most regions, and UNICEF focused on supporting capacities in national systems. Political commitment to girls' education was growing, both as a result of advocacy and in response to problems, such as HIV/AIDS. Some 79 countries had national plans relating to the EFA goal, which included explicit measures to reduce the numbers of girls out of school and to create opportunities to incorporate health, nutrition, water, sanitation and protection initiatives in schools.

UNICEF supported Governments in their applications for EFA Fast Track Initiative (FTI) funds and other funding for girls' education. In several African countries, girls' education clubs helped to enrol girls and encourage them to complete their education. Consultative meetings or launches of the United Nations Girls' Education Initiative (UNGEI) were held in Kenya, Lesotho, Malawi, Rwanda, South Africa, Uganda, United Republic of Tanzania and Zimbabwe.

In crisis and post-conflict situations in 2004, as in Burundi, Liberia and parts of the Middle East and North Africa, humanitarian response programmes included education as a force for normalization and healing. Further opportunities for boosting access were provided through engagement with SWAps, which helped address gender disparities in access to and quality of education, while gender reviews and advocacy helped remove financial barriers for poor families to send girls to school.

In 2004, 55 countries, up from 47 in 2002, took steps to boost girls' progression to post-primary education and reduce drop-out rates. However, sexual exploitation and violence continued to pose obstacles. In parts of the Middle East, the lack of post-school opportunities and life skills among adolescent girls tended to offset the high levels of girls' enrolment. UNICEF supported "second chance" initiatives for girls in several countries.

By 2004, some 41 countries, compared to 33 in 2002, had adopted national standards to promote child-friendly, gender-sensitive school environments, which were often based on lessons learned from UNICEF-supported pilot projects and were being developed in nearly 50 other countries. UNICEF also procured $71 million worth of education materials during the year, up from $56 million in 2003, due to special emphasis on accelerating girls' education in 25 countries.

As part of its contribution to the implementation of the International Plan of Action for the United Nations Literacy Decade (2003-2012) [A/59/267] (see p. 1142), UNICEF focused on the theme "literacy, girls and women". Among related activities, UNICEF supported programmes in Kosovo, which provided literacy to 2,300 women and girls, as well as projects in Bolivia, Burkina Faso, Kazakhstan, Pakistan, Uganda and Yemen, which linked literacy for women to other programmes, such as early childcare, life skills, income generating activities, and vocational and management training.

Protection from violence, abuse, exploitation and discrimination

The growth in information and promising initiatives, combined with continued advocacy for policy reform had helped raise awareness of violence, exploitation and abuse against children. Global initiatives such as the mid-term review of the Yokohama Commitments [YUN 2001, p. 1097], had also increased attention to child protection. The most prominent gaps in protecting children worldwide were in the areas of sexual abuse and exploitation, including in armed conflict, trafficking, the use of children as soldiers, harmful practices, and the situation of children not in the care of their families or in conflict with the law.

The "protective environment" approach continued to be an important vehicle for making responses more strategic and UNICEF's cooperation had shifted from programmes primarily for specific groups of children, to fostering institutional and attitudinal change, with emphasis on prevention strategies. In emergencies, immediate protection continued to focus on unaccompanied and separated children, and where necessary, on child soldiers, in line with the CCCs.

In April, the "Handbook for Parliamentarians on Child Protection", launched by UNICEF and the Inter-Parliamentary Union, created momentum for partnerships at regional and country levels, as illustrated by the first conference on child protection for Arab parliamentarians (Amman, Jordan, 22-23 November). An Arabic-language version of the handbook was presented at the conference.

A child protection analysis had either been completed or was under development in 113 countries in 2004, compared to 91 in 2002. Indicators on juvenile justice and formal care were developed by a wide range of partners and field tested during the year. Tools for measuring violence against children were also under development. In 2005-2006, MICs would collect data on child labour, birth registration, child marriage, female genital mutilation/cutting (FGM/C), prevalence of orphans, child discipline and childhood disability. A management information system to monitor progress in combating commercial sexual exploitation of children was being tested in the East Asia and Pacific region and a similar system was envisaged in Latin America and the Caribbean.

In 2004, UNICEF continued to cooperate with the International Labour Organization (ILO) to combat child labour in 62 countries, and by the end of the year, 151 countries had ratified ILO Convention 182 on the worst forms of child labour. An estimated 57 Governments in UNICEF programme countries monitored the most egregious forms of child labour through regular data gathering. The year also saw a number of initiatives against trafficking, especially through cross-border collaboration. Partnerships to address violence and trafficking had been pursued with UN agencies and regional governmental organizations, such as the League of Arab States and the Council of Europe. In 2004, UNICEF successfully promoted the inclusion of key child protection standards in the Council of Europe's draft convention against trafficking in human beings.

Advocacy related to children affected by armed conflict was carried out by 54 UNICEF offices, with 23 offices focusing specifically on the demobilization of child soldiers. UNICEF supported demobilization and reintegration of child soldiers in conflict and post-conflict transition countries, including some 15,000 demobilized in Burundi, Liberia and southern Sudan, and some 8,500 child soldiers in Afghanistan, as well as, war-affected children and young people enrolled in reintegration programmes in that country. By 2004, legal standards protecting children from violence had been reviewed in 87 countries and 102 UNICEF country offices had worked to change attitudes towards violence. With UNICEF support, 90 countries responded to a questionnaire of the Independent Expert for the Study on Violence against Children. UNICEF also increased its focus on violence in schools, resulting in improved data and school-based initiatives.

In April, the Security Council addressed the issue of children in armed conflict and in its resolution 1539(2004) (see p. 787), condemned the recruitment and use of child soldiers by parties to armed conflict and other violations of children's human rights. In a September report [A/59/331] on the assessment of the UN system response to children affected by armed conflict (see p. 789),

the Secretary-General stated that UNICEF, as well as NGOs, had contributed to the development of a robust framework for norms and standards related to such children.

UNICEF worked with partners in 23 African countries to end the practice of FGM/C, which remained widespread in many parts of the continent. Djibouti and Ethiopia passed laws against the practice. A UNICEF-assisted project in Senegal to promote change through a community-based approach was being replicated in Burkina Faso, Guinea, Mali and the Sudan.

UNICEF developed training materials for use by partners and staff to increase awareness of the Secretary-General's Bulletin on Special Measures for Protection from Sexual Exploitation and Abuse [ST/SGB/2003/13], which set standards of behaviour for UN personnel. A child protection training package for peacekeepers was finalized, together with the Office of the Special Representative of the Secretary-General for Children in Armed Conflict (see p. 786) and Save the Children (Sweden). Training for humanitarian personnel and peacekeepers was conducted in collaboration with UN country teams, mainly in sub-Saharan Africa.

UNICEF worked on combating threats posed to children by landmines in 34 countries. With its support, a national mine action strategy was developed in Angola and a centre for mine action was established in Burundi. Mine-risk education was integrated into primary school curricula in Afghanistan and Eritrea. UNICEF helped Sri Lanka educate 20,000 children, using child-to-child techniques, about the risks of landmines, and more than 200,000 people participated in community awareness programmes. A programme was developed in Chad to protect refugees and local communities, and in Liberia, UNICEF supported UN peacekeeping operations in undertaking mine awareness. UNICEF also developed standards for mine-risk education, which were endorsed by the United Nations, as part of the International Mine Action Standards.

HIV/AIDS

As a co-sponsor of the Joint United Nations Programme on HIV/AIDS (UNAIDS), UNICEF remained active in the response to the epidemic, working to stop its spread and to ensure care for children affected by it. In 2004, an estimated 510,000 children below 15 years of age died of AIDS and 640,000 were newly infected with HIV, mostly through a lack of prevention of mother-to-child transmission (PMTCT). In sub-Saharan Africa, about 1.9 million children under 15 years of age were living with HIV by the end of the year. In the 20 worst-affected countries, the epidemic was taking a toll most heavily on young people 15-24 years old, especially young women. While UNICEF had stepped up efforts to combat HIV/AIDS, total expenditures on HIV/AIDS remained at around 9 per cent of programme spending, compared to 13 per cent of regular resources expenditures, owing to the limited availability of other resources for that priority. The "three ones" principles, which called for support to one national plan, one coordinating mechanism and one monitoring evaluation system per country (see p. 1219), was adopted by developing countries and key partners in 2004.

A national situation analysis on HIV/AIDS and its impact on children and young people had been undertaken in 78 countries. UNICEF advocated for increased investment for children and young people in poverty reduction strategies. Major new comprehensive approaches to children and HIV/AIDS were adopted by countries in 2004, including 89 that had adopted national strategies for PMTCT; 89 for the prevention of HIV infection among young people; 79 for school-based life skills education; and 47 for the protection and care of orphans and vulnerable children (OVCs). While progress had been encouraging, greater efforts were needed, particularly in countries with low prevalence, to establish baselines and improve understanding of the impact of HIV/AIDS on children. An in-depth review of the effectiveness of the school-based life skills programme in reducing HIV transmission in the United Republic of Tanzania had disappointing results and pointed to the need for community awareness-raising. Following the mid-term review, UNICEF attempted to ensure that life-skills programmes were better focused on risks specific to the HIV context of each country.

Other highlights included peer education activities supported by 63 UNICEF country offices; collaboration by UNICEF and UNFPA in 15 countries to support national consultations with young people on HIV prevention; UNICEF's scaled up promotion of PMTCT programmes, particularly in developing countries, which provided support in 88 countries in 2004 compared with 58 in 2002; and the collaborative search by UNICEF, WHO and USAID for solutions to the challenges of paediatric HIV care and the cost of paediatric formulations of anti-retroviral drugs (ARVs). The three organizations also convened in Zambia to review accelerated actions to treat children with HIV/AIDS in the Southern African region. China's Ministry of Health and UNICEF, in partnership with the Clinton Foundation, launched the country's first paediatric AIDS care and treatment initiative.

UNICEF supported the development of infant feeding and PMTCT policies in 72 countries, as well as measures to provide help to HIV-positive women in using safe child feeding options in 60 countries. UNICEF and WHO organized 13 country orientations on the UN framework on infant feeding and HIV/AIDS. UNICEF, the Food and Agriculture Organization (FAO) and WFP supported nutritional security initiatives for children affected by HIV/AIDS. In 2004, UNICEF procurement services for ARV prophylaxis had grown extraordinarily, to an estimated $18.4 million worth of supplies, and an additional $2.9 million worth of HIV/AIDS-related test kits and diagnostic equipment were also supplied.

UNICEF continued to serve as a global convener and leader on issues concerning OVCs. More than half of UNICEF-assisted programmes for home-based and centre-based care for young children included children affected by HIV/AIDS. In parts of Africa, such centres were increasingly the first line of food, healthcare and other support for such children. UNICEF, UNAIDS, USAID and WFP joined national task forces in rapid assessment, analysis and action planning exercises in 16 African countries to increase interventions and funding for OVCs. UNICEF and partners also developed cost estimates for the protection, care and support services for OVCs in sub-Saharan Africa, which would be used for planning and leveraging resources. A UNICEF/World Bank partnership on ECD and HIV/AIDS was launched in five African countries to increase awareness of the needs of young children affected by HIV/AIDS.

UNAIDS programme coordination

A July report [E/ICEF/2004/15] on UNICEF's follow-up to the fourteenth meeting of the UNAIDS Programme Coordinating Board [YUN 2003, p. 1248] summarized UNICEF efforts to track costs and assess global resource needs; assist countries in accessing new resources; promote issues relating to women and girls in response to HIV/AIDS; integrate emergency, humanitarian and development response; and reduce the stigma and discrimination associated with the disease. The Executive Board considered the report at its second regular session in September.

Operational and administrative matters

UNICEF finances

In 2004, UNICEF's income totalled $1,978 million, an increase of $290 million (17 per cent) over 2003, resulting from substantial growth in contributions to other regular resources (non-emergency) from both governmental and private-sector sources. The increase in those contributions was partly offset by a $72 million reduction in government contributions to other resources (emergency). Total 2004 contributions were 17 per cent higher than forecast in the financial plan. UNICEF derived its income primarily from Governments, which contributed $1,339 million (68 per cent), and from private-sector or intergovernmental sources, which provided $578 million (29 per cent). The balance of $61 million (3 per cent) came from other sources.

During its September session, the Executive Board considered UNICEF's financial report and statements for the biennium ended 31 December 2003 [E/ICEF/2004/AB/L.6]. However, it deferred action until its first regular (2005) session in order to consider the discussion of the document by the General Assembly's Fifth (Administrative and Budgetary) Committee.

Budget appropriations

In June [dec. 2004/6], the Executive Board approved recommendations for the aggregate indicative budgets for 23 country programmes, amounting to the following totals for regular and other resources, respectively, by region: Africa, $63,663,000 and $151,450,000; the Americas and the Caribbean, $5,900,000 and $18,800,000; Asia, $13,070,000 and $33,500,000; Central and Eastern Europe, The Commonwealth of Independent States (CIS) and the Baltic States, $51,230,000 and $114,460,000; and the Middle East and North Africa, $11,752,000 and $202,200,000. It further approved a $140,000,000 increase in the other resources ceiling for the 2004 Iraq country programme.

On 15 September [dec. 2004/10], the Board approved a recommendation for the aggregate indicative budget for Guatemala's 2005-2008 country programme in the amount of $3,648,000 in regular resources and $18,478,000 in other resources. On the same date [dec. 2004/11], it approved allocations of additional regular resources for a number of countries, amounting to the following totals by region: Central and Eastern Europe, The Commonwealth of Independent States (CIS) and Baltic States, $38,234; East Asia and the Pacific, $116,000; and Eastern and Southern Africa, $531,000. The Board also confirmed [dec. 2004/12] a recommendation to increase other resources ceilings for approved country programmes to the following levels: Dominican Republic, $13,400; Cambodia, $64,000; Sri Lanka, $20,000; and Malawi, $52,120.

Budget approval process

In response to a 2003 Executive Board decision [YUN 2003, p. 1211], the Executive Director submitted a March report [E/ICEF/2004/AB/L.2] on the timing of the approval of the UNICEF biennial support budget. The report cited factors affecting the timing of the presentation of the biennial support budget, including those relating to the submission of draft country documents to the Executive Board prior to the commencement of a new programme cycle and the approval of future biennial support budgets before the end of the preceding biennium. The Executive Director recommended that the biennial support budget be reviewed at the Board's first regular (January) session of the first year of the biennium, and that during its second regular (September) session preceding the new biennium, the Board approve an advance allocation for spending for the month of January.

ACABQ action. In May [E/ICEF/2004/AB/L.3], the Advisory Committee on Administrative and Budgetary Questions (ACABQ) considered the Executive Director's report on the timing of the approval of the budget (above) and expressed its view that the review of the support budget should start before the beginning of UNICEF's financial period. It noted that the time line schedule annexed to the report for the integrated programme and budget planning and approval process had built-in flexibility for timing adjustments for some of the steps. If needed, the Committee would review the UNICEF budget in September rather than October of the year before the beginning of the biennium, and the informal briefing with Board members on budget proposals could be conducted in November, prior to the December Executive Board meeting.

On 10 June [dec. 2004/7], the Board decided that the biennial support budget for 2006-2007 would be reviewed at its first regular (January) session in 2006, and that at its second regular (September) session in 2005, an advance allocation would be approved for spending for January 2006, based on expenditures for January 2005.

Audits

In a June report [E/ICEF/2004/AB/L.7] to the UN Board of Auditors, UNICEF described measures taken or planned in response to the recommendations of the Board of Auditors on UNICEF accounts for the 2001-2002 biennium. The report focused on those recommendations that were either not implemented or only partially implemented at the time of the Board's previous report [YUN 2003, p. 1212].

OIA report. In a July report [E/ICEF/2004/AB/L.8] on internal audit activities in 2003, the seventh annual report of the secretariat, the Office of Internal Audit (OIA) indicated that it had completed 33 audits in 2003, including two audits of regional offices and one global summary report. Overall, UNICEF controls in country offices were generally satisfactory, although there was room for improving management of some aspects of finance and accounts and supply assistance, which were weak in almost half of all country offices audited. In 2003, UNICEF had strengthened its guidance to country offices to address common weaknesses in programme and operations management. However, scope remained for improving the programme and operations support provided by regional offices, as well as the regional and global monitoring of country office practices in areas of common weakness. The Executive Board took note of the report in September.

Recovery policy

In September, the Executive Board considered a July update [E/ICEF/2004/AB/L.5] on the UNICEF recovery policy for support costs for programmes funded from other resources, which was approved in 2003 [YUN 2003, p. 1212] as an interim measure. The report provided status updates on harmonization discussions among UN organizations and on UNICEF recovery policy, as well as information on thematic contributions and recovery rates.

Highlights of the report included the positive trend towards the goal of eliminating the subsidy of other resources from regular resources and increasing funding for regular resources programmes, as well as the positive response to the 4 per cent recovery rate reduction offered to donors making thematic contributions to reflect the lowered transaction costs attributable to the flexibility of strategic earmarking and donors' acceptance of consolidated reporting. The report indicated that as of mid-June, $34.8 million had been received in thematic contributions—surpassing the total amount of $26 million received in 2003—and during the previous 12 months, thematic funding had grown to $64.4 million.

In 2003, the Executive Board had established a 12 per cent recovery rate for non-thematic contributions and additional reductions of 1 per cent for 90 per cent upfront payment; 1 per cent for contributions over $500,000; 2 per cent for contributions over $2 million; 3 per cent for contributions over $10 million; and, as a transitional arrangement for 2004, a 4 per cent reduction for contributions over $40 million. The Executive Director recommended that the 4 per cent reduction for contributions over $40 million be continued beyond 2004 so that a comprehensive proposal could be prepared for the Board's review in 2005, taking into account the results of the harmonization discussions and UNICEF's experience

in implementing the Board's 2003 decision on recovery policy.

On 16 September [dec. 2004/15], the Executive Board noted the positive trend in recovering indirect costs attributed to the management of other resources contributions, expressed appreciation for the progress made with other UN organizations to harmonize the recovery methodology and encouraged UNICEF to continue active involvement in the working group of the High-Level Committee on Management on cost recovery. It also decided that the 4 per cent reduction in the recovery rate for contributions over $40 million would be maintained after 2004.

Resource mobilization and allocation

UNICEF continued to collaborate with Governments to mobilize regular and other resources. At the annual January pledging event, 55 countries pledged a total of $257.3 million and by year's end, 93 countries (35 high-income, 41 middle-income and 17 low-income countries) had contributed to regular resources. Some 18 Governments increased their contributions to regular resources in local currency and 14 Governments increased their amounts by 7 per cent or more. The United States remained the largest donor to regular resources with a contribution of $119.3 million, followed by Norway ($48.3 million), Sweden ($45.1 million), the Netherlands ($35.2 million), the United Kingdom ($34.5 million), Denmark ($29.7 million), Japan ($23.4 million), Finland ($16 million), Switzerland ($14.4 million) and Italy ($13.5 million).

Thematic funding for medium-term strategic plan (MTSP) priorities, particularly for girls' education and humanitarian response, increased rapidly in 2004. Some $157.7 million was mobilized, up from $29 million in 2003. Seven donor Governments and 34 national committees contributed $107 million and $47 million respectively, with Norway ($57 million) and Sweden ($44 million) providing the bulk of thematic contributions. Some 41 per cent of donors gave at the global level, 12 per cent at the regional level and 47 per cent at the country level. Those funds enabled UNICEF to programme more responsively, based on country and global priorities, without having to negotiate project agreements and conditions on individual contributions. A total of 23 Governments contributed other resources for emergencies, compared to 32 in the previous year, with the United Kingdom, Canada and the Netherlands as the top three donors. Funding of the UNICEF component of the 2004 consolidated appeals reached 63 per cent of the target, recovering to the level of 2002, but 11 out of 23 consolidated appeals were funded below 50 per cent of their targets, indicating that a number of emergency situations continued to receive inadequate attention.

Executive Director report. In response to a 2003 Executive Board request [YUN 2003, p. 1212], the Executive Director submitted a July report [E/ICEF/2004/16] on an analysis of the use of regular and other resources by country and by aggregate for each priority area of the UNICEF MTSP during 2002 and 2003. That included an analysis of the patterns of country programme allocations and expenditures in relation to the target allocation of 60 per cent of all regular resources to the least developed countries (LDCs) by 2005. Fifty-seven per cent of such resources were allocated to LDCs in 2004, and the target of 60 per cent was expected to be reached in 2005. The goal of allocating 50 per cent of regular resources to sub-Saharan Africa by 2005, was met in 2003; that allocation reached 51 per cent in 2004; and was projected to reach 52 per cent in 2005. The report also indicated that the increase in the amount of programme expenditures in 2003 as compared to 2002, in four out of the five priority areas, was due to a roll-over of unspent resources in country programmes and substantial increases in contributions. It concluded that the current systems for the allocation and expenditure of regular and other resources were consistent with the approved directives of the Executive Board. Stagnation in regular resources income, however, compromised the ability of UNICEF to be more responsive and effective in implementing Board directives. The allocation of other resources was uneven among country programmes, with some consistently and seriously underfunded, but the report indicated that those gaps between approved planning levels and allocations were beyond the control of UNICEF. The Executive Board took note of the report at its second regular session in September.

Private Sector Division

Net income from UNICEF Private Sector Division (PSD) activities for the year ended 31 December 2004 totalled $291.1 million for regular resources, which was $1.7 million (0.6 per cent) higher than the $289.4 million achieved in 2003 [E/ICEF/2005/AB/L.5]. That amount included $55.9 million from UNICEF cards and gift sales, $250.7 million from private sector fund-raising activities, a negative exchange rate adjustment of $1.3 million, and investment fund expenditures of $14.2 million. In addition, $218.8 million ($172.2 million in 2003) was raised from private sector fund-raising activities that were earmarked for other resources. The net consolidated income, including both regular and other resources,

amounted to $509.9 million, an increase of $48.3 million compared to the 2003 net consolidated income of $461.6 million.

On 21 January [dec. 2004/2], the Executive Board approved budgeted expenditures of $89 million for the PSD work plan for 2004 [E/ICEF/2004/AB/L.1] and authorized the Executive Director to redeploy resources between various budget lines up to a maximum of 10 per cent of the amounts approved, and to spend, when necessary, an additional amount between Executive Board sessions up to the amount resulting from currency fluctuations, to implement the 2004 approved work plan. The Board renewed investment funds with $16.4 million established for 2004; authorized the Executive Director to incur expenditures in 2004 relating to the cost of goods delivered (production/purchase of raw materials, cards and other products) for 2005, up to $31 million; and approved the PSD medium-term plan for 2005-2008.

In September, the Board took note of the PSD financial report and statements for the year ended 31 December 2003 [E/ICEF/2004/AB/L.9].

Joint programming

In response to a 2003 Executive Board request [YUN 2003, p. 1213], the Executive Director submitted a March report [E/ICEF/2004/10] on the assessment of UNICEF experience in joint programming and other innovative and collaborative approaches to improve programming effectiveness and reduce transaction costs for programme countries. The report discussed the rights-based approach to programming and goals for children, including advocacy and planning; support for programme implementation and management; and joint programme monitoring and evaluation. It also presented the experiences of the five pilot countries whose new programme cycles began in 2004—Benin, Ecuador, Kenya, Niger and Pakistan—and were the first to use some of the harmonized country programme tools, including the revised CCA/UNDAF guidelines.

On 11 June, the Executive Board [dec. 2004/8] took note of the report and deferred consideration of a decision on joint programming to 2005.

JIU report

In January, the Executive Board considered a secretariat note [E/ICEF/2004/5] on the activities of the Joint Inspection Unit (JIU) of specific relevance to UNICEF. The document provided information on reports prepared during 2002, action taken by UNICEF, and the views of the UNICEF Executive Director on the issues raised by the JIU inspectors. At its January session, the Board took note of the report.

Human resources

In September, the Executive Board took note of a July update on developments in human resources [E/ICEF/2004/17], which provided information on UNICEF staff composition and structure, and summarized human resources in the context of inter-agency collaboration and UN reform. The report also covered strategic initiatives aimed at ensuring adequate human resources capacity to achieve MTSP and MDG targets, such as the Brasilia resources change plan and the introduction of a new human resources management system.

As of May, UNICEF staff totalled 8,311 personnel. While the distribution of staff reflected the field-based nature of the organization and indicated that significant progress had been made in achieving gender diversity, challenges remained in achieving the same at senior managerial levels, and in achieving greater staff representation from programme countries. A projection of retirements within the next five years (2004-2008) highlighted the need to find timely replacements for retiring staff to ensure continuity in management and programme implementation. The report called for better change management, including improved accountability at all levels in overseeing the process.

Youth

Implementation of the World Programme of Action for Youth

In 2004, UN policies and programmes on youth continued to focus on efforts to implement the 1995 World Programme of Action for Youth to the Year 2000 and Beyond, adopted by the General Assembly in resolution 50/81 [YUN 1995, p. 1211]. The Programme of Action addressed problems faced by youth worldwide and identified ways to enhance youth participation in national and international policy- and decision-making.

The United Nations Programme on Youth, in partnership with interregional advisers of the Department of Economic and Social Affairs (DESA), organized several workshops to deepen understanding of youth issues and mobilize local, national and regional action, including the "Youth and Employment in Post-Conflict Situations in the Arab Region" workshop (Beirut, Lebanon, 28-30 January), where youth from Algeria,

Egypt, Jordan, Lebanon and Syria assessed policies and programmes for youth employment focusing on employability, equal opportunity, entrepreneurship and job creation; the "Global Media-Driven Youth Culture" workshop (New York, 28-29 April), which explored the impact of a powerful global media culture on young people and how it had affected their socialization and values; the "Strategies for Creating Urban Youth Employment in Africa" workshop (Nairobi, Kenya, 21-25 June),which brought together experts in youth employment from various regions of the world, as well as young people from African countries, who addressed the challenges of urban youth employment; and the "Youth in Poverty in Southeast Asia" workshop (Yogyakarta, Indonesia, 2-4 August), which focused on developing policies and programmes for poor youth in the region.

The Policy Workshop on HIV/AIDS and Family Well-being (Windhoek, Namibia, 28-30 January) brought together representatives of Governments, NGOs, and academic experts and practitioners from southern African countries to discuss the impact of HIV/AIDS on families in the region, to consider how families and communities were coping with the disease, and contribute to the development of strategic policy to help Governments strengthen the capacity of families and family networks to cope.

GENERAL ASSEMBLY ACTION

On 20 December [meeting 74], the General Assembly, on the recommendation of the Third (Social, Humanitarian and Cultural) Committee [A/59/492], adopted **resolution 59/148** without vote [agenda item 94 (*a*)].

Policies and programmes involving youth: tenth anniversary of the World Programme of Action for Youth to the Year 2000 and Beyond

The General Assembly,

Recalling its resolution 50/81 of 14 December 1995, by which it adopted the World Programme of Action for Youth to the Year 2000 and Beyond, annexed thereto,

Recalling also its resolution 58/133 of 22 December 2003, in which it, inter alia, recommended devoting two plenary meetings at its sixtieth session, in 2005, to review the situation of youth and achievements attained in the implementation of the World Programme of Action ten years after its adoption,

Recognizing the importance of the full and effective participation of young people and youth organizations at the local, national, regional and international levels in promoting and implementing the World Programme of Action and in evaluating the progress achieved and the obstacles encountered in its implementation,

1. *Decides* to convene, at its sixtieth session, two plenary meetings of the General Assembly devoted to the

evaluation of the progress made in the implementation of the World Programme of Action for Youth to the Year 2000 and Beyond, to be held during the general debate of the Third Committee under the agenda item entitled "Social development, including questions relating to the world social situation and to youth, ageing, disabled persons and the family";

2. *Decides also* to hold, prior to the plenary meetings, an informal, interactive round-table discussion on the theme "Young people: making commitments matter", which will be open to the participation of Member States, observers, organizations of the United Nations system and non-governmental youth organizations;

3. *Decides further* that one youth representative from a Member State shall orally present a summary of the informal round-table discussion to the General Assembly at the beginning of the plenary meeting;

4. *Urges* Member States to consider being represented by youth representatives to address the plenary on this occasion, as well as in the above-mentioned informal round-table discussion, bearing in mind the principle of gender balance;

5. *Decides* to facilitate access to United Nations Headquarters by the non-governmental organizations that were accredited to the World Conference of Ministers Responsible for Youth in 1998 and interested non-governmental organizations that are neither in consultative status with the Economic and Social Council nor were accredited to the World Conference to participate in the informal round-table discussions and side events to be held during the tenth anniversary of the World Programme of Action;

6. *Urges*, in recognition of the importance of ensuring the equitable geographical participation of non-governmental youth organizations in the tenth anniversary of the World Programme of Action, relevant United Nations entities to assist non-governmental organizations that do not have the resources, in particular non-governmental organizations from developing countries, including the least developed countries and countries with economies in transition, to participate in the tenth anniversary;

7. *Requests* the Secretary-General to disseminate widely to the community of non-governmental youth organizations all available information on the events associated with the tenth anniversary of the World Programme of Action;

8. *Decides* that the arrangements outlined in paragraph 5 above shall in no way create a precedent for other similar events;

9. *Notes with appreciation* the ongoing efforts of the United Nations system to solicit input from youth organizations and young people into the current review of the World Programme of Action, as requested by the General Assembly in paragraph 14 of its resolution 58/133, and invites the Secretary-General to provide an overview of the input gathered from youth organizations as a supplement to his report to the Assembly at its sixtieth session.

Youth employment

DESA and the World Bank hosted the third meeting of the High-level Panel of the Youth Employment Network (YEN) (Washington, D.C., 27-28 September). Participants sought to catalyse the development and financing of national action plans (NAPs) on youth employment and to mobilize Governments in the lead countries to prepare NAPs in time for the five-year review of the MDGs in 2005. During the meeting, YEN launched the "Youth Consultative Group", comprising representatives of international and regional youth organizations, who worked to represent the concerns of young people on the function, direction and priorities of the Network. Other issues discussed by the meeting included the development of a joint ILO-World Bank support programme within the framework of the Network; a letter from the High-level Panel to the Secretary-General requesting a meeting to discuss how youth employment could be strengthened in the five-year review of MDGs; and the Panellists' call on the Network's Core Partners to highlight the importance of youth employment in global development strategies based on the MDGs, including poverty reduction.

Ageing persons

Follow-up to the Second World Assembly on Ageing (2002)

Note by Secretariat. The Commission for Social Development, at its forty-second session (New York, 21 February 2003 and 4-13 and 20 February 2004) [E/2004/26] (see p. 1092), considered a Secretariat note [E/CN.5/2004/6] on modalities for the review and appraisal of the Madrid International Plan of Action on Ageing [YUN 2002, p. 1194], adopted by the Second World Assembly on Ageing in 2002 [ibid., p. 1193]. The Economic and Social Council, in resolution 2003/14 [YUN 2003, p. 1219] had invited Governments, the UN system and civil society to participate in a "bottom-up" approach to the review and appraisal of the Plan of Action through the sharing of ideas, data collection and best practices, which sought to link local and national activities to UN regional intergovernmental bodies and global processes of review and appraisal. The note reviewed recent progress in defining those modalities and proposed, for the Commission's consideration, an approach for the review and appraisal at national, regional and international levels.

The note recommended that the monitoring process include a feedback mechanism so that policy could be adjusted as necessary and that an advocacy campaign lead to the assessment of local needs, the setting of targets and the formulation of appropriate programmes of action. In conclusion, the Secretariat proposed that the Commission request Governments to: include ageing-specific policies and ageing-mainstreaming efforts in their national review and appraisal exercise; identify a lead agency to coordinate the national mainstreaming process; establish a national coordinating body to facilitate implementation of the Madrid Plan of Action, including its review and appraisal; and adopt the bottom-up approach to review and appraisal, with focus on the key elements of awareness-raising, assessing needs and setting targets, gathering information, distilling local findings into policy-relevant formats, and adjusting policies and programmes. The Commission was urged to request UN regional commissions to facilitate the review and appraisal by: promoting networking and the sharing of information; assisting Governments in the gathering, distillation and analysis of information; and developing a regional analysis and defining priorities for future policies.

The Secretariat also recommended that the Commission hold a series of informal discussions and consultations, such as round tables, symposiums and workshops, bringing together all major stakeholders. The outcome of the Commission's review and appraisal would be the identification of achievements and obstacles and the establishment of priorities for future international cooperation in implementing the Madrid Plan. It proposed that the Commission undertake its review and appraisal every five years and that it select a specific theme emanating from the Madrid Plan for each review cycle. That theme would then be adopted by Governments and regional commissions in initiating the bottom-up participatory process.

Commission action. In a February resolution [E/2004/26 (res. 42/1)] on modalities for the review and appraisal of the Madrid International Plan of Action on Ageing, the Commission, taking note of the Secretariat's note (see p. 1191), called on all actors to participate in implementing the Madrid Plan; decided to review and appraise it every five years; and requested the Secretary-General, through DESA, to facilitate and promote the Plan, including by proposing guidelines for policy development and implementation, advocating means to mainstream ageing issues into development agendas, engaging in dialogue with civil society and the private sector and promoting information exchange. The Secretary-General was also requested to propose guidelines for the review and appraisal process, taking into account the views of Member States, civil society and the private sector, and to report on the Plan's implementation to the Commission in 2005. Regional commissions were requested to promote and fa-

cilitate the implementation, review and appraisal of the Plan at the regional level by assisting national institutions, and UN bodies were requested to support national review and appraisal efforts by providing technical assistance, including for developing modalities for disaggregating statistics by age and sex.

Report of Secretary-General. In response to General Assembly resolution 58/134 [YUN 2003, p. 1220], the Secretary-General submitted a July report [A/59/164] on follow-up to the Second World Assembly on Ageing (2002), which summarized efforts and activities of the Secretariat and the funds, programmes and specialized agencies of the UN system, as well as major international NGOs, to implement the Madrid Plan of Action. Based on input from 14 UN-system focal points on ageing and NGOs, the report highlighted progress made and obstacles encountered in implementing the Plan of Action's road map [YUN 2003, p. 1219] and provided recommendations for consideration by the General Assembly.

The report noted that the Commission on Social Development (see p. 1191) had encouraged Member States to devise ageing-specific policies and ageing-mainstreaming efforts for review and appraisal of the Plan of Action. The Committee on the Elimination of All Forms of Discrimination against Women (CEDAW) (see p. 1169), which had consistently paid attention to the situation of older women, expressed concern over inadequate pension schemes, health, education and employment opportunities for women, particularly in rural areas, as well as the lack of statistics on older women in some countries. The Commission on the Status of Women (see p. 1167) urged Governments to train and educate men to participate fully in the care and support of others, including older persons, persons with disabilities and sick persons, in particular children and other dependants.

The Secretary-General indicated that capacity-building and mainstreaming ageing into national development agendas were essential to promote and implement the Plan of Action. He suggested that the Assembly encourage Governments to support the trust fund on ageing to enable DESA to expand assistance to countries, and recommended that ongoing efforts to achieve the MDGs include the plight of older persons; ensure the integration of ageing issues into policies and programmes; and provide opportunities for older persons to participate in decision-making and other activities.

Noting that the Economic Commission for Europe, the Economic Commission for Latin America and the Caribbean and the Economic and Social Commission for Asia and the Pacific had formed regional strategies to implement the Plan of Action, the report suggested that the Assembly encourage other regional commissions to do the same. Further, it recommended that the Assembly invite Governments, intergovernmental organizations and NGOs to support comprehensive, diversified and specialized research on ageing, particularly in developing countries, which should include international research with a view to promoting international research coordination, exchange knowledge and support policy responses to ageing.

The report concluded that although some progress had been achieved since 2002, notably on linking ageing and development within the programmes of the organizations and bodies of the UN system, much remained to be done, particularly to implement the development perspective of ageing policy at the national level. Other challenges that impeded progress in activities dedicated to ageing issues included limited UN human and financial resources and the perception in development policy discussions that older persons were among the most marginalized groups because they were vulnerable, dependent on resources, unproductive, and that they would continue to be cared for by their families. The lack of reliable age- and sex-aggregated data in most developing countries for determining poverty rates and whether older persons should be included in poverty reduction strategies contributed to the perception, as did inadequate data on their health-care needs, social integration, employment and roles as both providers and recipients of family and community support.

The report recommended that the Assembly invite the functional commissions of the Economic and Social Council to integrate population and individual ageing issues into their work programmes in order to implement the Plan of Action, and to reiterate its call for full-time, adequately funded focal points on ageing within the UN system.

GENERAL ASSEMBLY ACTION

On 20 December [meeting 74], the General Assembly, on the recommendation of the Third Committee [A/59/493], adopted **resolution 59/150** without vote [agenda item 95].

Follow-up to the Second World Assembly on Ageing

The General Assembly,

Recalling its resolution 57/167 of 18 December 2002, in which it endorsed the Political Declaration and the Madrid International Plan of Action on Ageing, 2002, as well as its resolution 58/134 of 22 December 2003, in which it took note, inter alia, of the road map for the implementation of the Madrid Plan of Action,

Recalling also Economic and Social Council resolution 2003/14 of 21 July 2003, in which the Council invited Governments, the United Nations system and civil society to participate in a "bottom-up" approach to the review and appraisal of the Madrid Plan of Action,

Recalling further Commission for Social Development resolution 42/1 of 13 February 2004, entitled "Modalities for the review and appraisal of the Madrid International Plan of Action on Ageing, 2002", in which the Commission decided to undertake a review and appraisal of the Madrid Plan of Action every five years, with each review and appraisal cycle to focus on one of the priority directions of the Madrid Plan of Action,

1. *Recommends* that ongoing efforts to achieve the internationally agreed development goals, including those contained in the United Nations Millennium Declaration, take into account the situation of older persons;

2. *Calls upon* Governments and the agencies and organizations of the United Nations system, within their mandates, and encourages the non-governmental community, to ensure that the challenges of population ageing and the concerns of older persons are adequately incorporated into their programmes and projects;

3. *Invites* Member States and the organizations and bodies of the United Nations system to take into account the needs and concerns of older persons in decision-making at all levels;

4. *Stresses* the need for additional capacity-building at the national level in order to promote and facilitate the implementation of the Madrid International Plan of Action on Ageing, 2002, and in this connection, encourages Governments to support the United Nations Trust Fund for Ageing to enable the Department of Economic and Social Affairs of the Secretariat to provide expanded assistance to countries, upon their request;

5. *Invites* Governments, intergovernmental organizations and non-governmental organizations to encourage and support comprehensive, diversified and specialized research on ageing in all countries;

6. *Invites* the functional commissions of the Economic and Social Council to integrate the issues of population and individual ageing into their work in order to promote the implementation of the Madrid Plan of Action;

7. *Recommends* that the Commission on the Status of Women continue to consider the situation of older women, in particular those who are most vulnerable, including those living in rural areas;

8. *Encourages* those regional commissions that have not yet done so to elaborate a regional strategy for the implementation of the Madrid Plan of Action;

9. *Takes note* of Commission for Social Development resolution 42/1, and in this context requests the Secretary-General to present his proposals for conducting the review and appraisal exercise at the regional and global levels to the Commission at its forty-fourth session;

10. *Requests* the organizations and bodies of the United Nations system to continue to strengthen the capacity of the focal points on ageing and to provide them with adequate resources for the further imple-

mentation of the Madrid Plan of Action, in particular through appropriate mainstreaming action;

11. *Stresses* the importance of the collection of data and population statistics disaggregated by age and sex on all aspects of policy formulation by all countries, and encourages the relevant entities of the United Nations system to support national efforts in capacity-building, especially those of developing countries and countries with economies in transition, takes note in this context of the establishment by the United Nations of an Internet-accessible database on ageing, and invites States to submit, whenever possible, information for inclusion in the database;

12. *Takes note* of the report of the Secretary-General, and requests that it be forwarded to the Commission for Social Development at its forty-third session in order to assist the Commission in its deliberations;

13. *Requests* the Secretary-General to report to the General Assembly at its sixtieth session on the implementation of the present resolution.

Chapter XII

Refugees and displaced persons

In 2004, the total number of persons of concern to the Office of the United Nations High Commissioner for Refugees (UNHCR) increased by some 13 per cent to 19.2 million, from 17 million in 2003. An estimated 1.5 million refugees returned to their places of origin during the year, while hundreds of thousands of others were driven out by conflicts and related instability in various parts of the world. UNHCR made progress in seeking durable solutions for those affected, but its efforts were undermined in some areas by such obstacles and challenges as new refugee outflows, attacks on humanitarian personnel, measures that eroded the international protection regime, the increasing volume and complexity of migratory flows and difficulties in sustaining voluntary repatriation.

During the year, repatriation was one of the key areas of UNHCR focus. Through its efforts, momentum in the repatriation of Afghan refugees was maintained, with some 1 million returning home—the highest number of returns during the year—despite persisting instability in parts of the country. Similar repatriation operations resulted in thousands returning to their places of origin in Angola, Bosnia and Herzegovina, Burundi, the Democratic Republic of the Congo (DRC), Iraq, Liberia, Rwanda, Sierra Leone, Somalia and Sri Lanka. The Office helped to resettle approximately 30,000, as compared to 26,000 in 2003, and worked to reduce statelessness and protect stateless persons, estimated at over 1 million worldwide. However, despite UNHCR's concerted efforts, millions of others—some two thirds of the global refugee population—remained out of reach of durable solutions and continued to suffer in protracted refugee situations, most notably Myanmar refugees in Bangladesh, Bhutanese nationals in Nepal and Saharawi refugees in Algeria. An estimated 2 million internally displaced persons (IDPs) in Colombia and hundreds of thousands of other IDPs and refugees were awaiting solutions in Africa, Asia, Europe and the Middle East. In many cases, already complex situations were exacerbated by fresh refugee outflows that sometimes created large-scale emergencies, as in the Darfur region of the Sudan; in the DRC, where 20,000 persons fled the outbreak of fighting in the town of Bukavu; and in Somalia, where tension caused 19,000 persons

to flee their homes. Other outflows included nationals of Côte d'Ivoire, Iraq and Yemen.

In continuing efforts to implement the "Convention Plus" initiative launched in 2003 to help strengthen the commitment of States and other partners to resolving refugee situations through multilateral action plans, UNHCR established in June a Framework of Understandings on the strategic use of resettlement and developed a methodology for assessing gaps in protection capacity. In October, the Joint Inspection Unit (JIU), following its review of UNHCR's management and administration, recommended measures for their improvement, including streamlining and rationalizing its organizational structure. In December, the General Assembly encouraged UNHCR to continue to improve its management systems. To enhance protection and durable solutions to refugee problems, UNHCR proposed the establishment of a post of Assistant High Commissioner (Protection) to oversee protection and the related advocacy role of the Office. As part of its ongoing headquarters review process, UNHCR re-examined its security procedures and made recommendations for improvement, which complemented the UN-wide changes in security management practices.

Office of the United Nations High Commissioner for Refugees

Programme policy

Executive Committee action. At its fifty-fifth session (Geneva, 4-8 October) [A/59/12/Add.1], the Executive Committee of the UNHCR Programme, in a conclusion on international protection, emphasized the continuing importance of the Agenda for Protection [YUN 2002, p. 1205], the multi-year programme of action for improving the protection of refugees and asylum-seekers. It acknowledged the increasing complexities of the international protection environment and the many challenges facing States and UNHCR in ensuring and providing protection for refugees and other persons of concern. The Committee expressed concern at the persecution, violence and human rights violations perpetuating the displacement of populations within and beyond national borders and increasing the challenges to durable solutions. It called on States to address those challenges, and on UNHCR to strengthen its protection presence in the field. The Committee also adopted conclusions on international cooperation and burden- and responsibility-sharing in mass influx situations and on legal safety issues in the context of the voluntary repatriation of refugees. Decisions were adopted on administrative, programme and financial, and institutional matters.

In his opening statement to the Committee, the High Commissioner drew attention to the crisis in the Sudan, particularly in the Darfur region, and to the challenges facing UNHCR in its response, as part of the wider UN effort. To oversee that response, a Director of Operations for the Sudan situation was appointed. Elsewhere in Africa, the number of repatriation programmes reached record levels. UNHCR continued to assist Burundian refugees, who were returning home at the rate of some 10,000 monthly, as well as hundreds of thousands of displaced persons to return to Angola, Eritrea, Liberia and Sierra Leone. It also helped some 14,000 refugees to return to Iraq from neighbouring countries, and about 775,000 to Afghanistan, despite the deteriorating security situation there, bringing the total repatriated since 2002 to over 3.5 million. In Western Sahara, UNHCR's oldest caseload, the year witnessed a breakthrough with the first exchange of visits between family members separated for decades by the conflict there. Unfortunately, no such progress was made in the Middle East, where UNHCR continued to address the potential for population displacement. In Europe, the number of displaced persons and refugees returning home to Bosnia and Herzegovina reached 1 million. UNHCR increased its field presence in the Russian Federation and the Commonwealth of Independent States (CIS), thus enabling it to find solutions to a range of problems and to make significant progress in capacity-building in the asylum field. However, in the North Caucasus, which continued to be plagued by insecurity and conflict, UNHCR was committed to working with the Russian Federation in responding to displacements from Chechnya. In Asia, while developments in Myanmar provided a rationale for planning the eventual return of 120,000 refugees from Thailand, less encouraging was the situation of Bhutanese people in camps in Nepal. Other situations of displacement requiring attention included those in Sri Lanka, the plight of North Korean asylum-seekers in China, and protection and resettlement issues in Latin America, which was commemorating the twentieth anniversary of the 1984 Cartagena Declaration—a regional initiative for refugee welfare.

One of UNHCR's global operational challenges was translating its priority commitments on refugee women into action in all its operations, especially their participation in food distribution. It reviewed its security procedures and made recommendations complementing anticipated UN system-wide changes, as part of the overall review of the Organization's global security management practices. Other notable operational developments during the year included proposals by the Joint Inspection Unit (JIU) relating to UNHCR's organizational structure, budget planning, and the work of its Inspector-General, (see p. 1199), and the High Commissioner's proposal for the establishment of a new position of Assistant High Commissioner for Protection (see p. 1200). UNHCR also made efforts to improve the use of partnerships, including with UN bodies and non-governmental organizations (NGOs). The High Commissioner reported that, for the first time in recent memory, UNCHR did not face a funding crisis, owing to increased donor support and better financial management.

GENERAL ASSEMBLY ACTION

On 20 December [meeting 74], the General Assembly, on the recommendation of the Third (Social, Humanitarian and Cultural) Committee [A/59/498], adopted **resolution 59/170** without vote [agenda item 100].

Office of the United Nations High Commissioner for Refugees

The General Assembly,

Having considered the report of the United Nations High Commissioner for Refugees on the activities of his Office and the report of the Executive Committee of the Programme of the United Nations High Commissioner for Refugees on the work of its fifty-fifth session and the conclusions and decisions contained therein,

Recalling its previous annual resolutions on the work of the Office of the High Commissioner since its establishment by the General Assembly,

Recalling also its resolution 58/153 of 22 December 2003 on implementing actions proposed by the High Commissioner to strengthen the capacity of his Office to carry out its mandate,

Expressing its appreciation for the leadership shown by the High Commissioner, commending the staff and implementing partners of the Office of the High Commissioner for the competent, courageous and dedicated manner in which they discharge their responsibilities, and underscoring its strong condemnation of all forms of violence to which humanitarian personnel and United Nations and associated personnel are increasingly exposed,

1. *Endorses* the report of the Executive Committee of the Programme of the United Nations High Commissioner for Refugees on the work of its fifty-fifth session;

2. *Welcomes* the important work undertaken by the Office of the United Nations High Commissioner for Refugees and the Executive Committee in the course of the year, and notes in this context the adoption of the general conclusion on international protection, the conclusion on international cooperation and burden- and responsibility-sharing in mass influx situations and the conclusion on legal safety issues in the context of voluntary repatriation of refugees, which are aimed at strengthening the international protection regime, consistent with the Agenda for Protection, and at assisting Governments in meeting their protection responsibilities in today's changing international environment;

3. *Reaffirms* the 1951 Convention relating to the Status of Refugees and its 1967 Protocol as the foundation of the international refugee protection regime, and recognizes the importance of their full and effective application by States parties and the values that they embody, notes with satisfaction that one hundred and forty-five States are now parties to one instrument or to both, encourages States not parties to consider acceding to those instruments, underlines in particular the importance of full respect for the principle of non-refoulement, and recognizes that a number of States not parties to the international refugee instruments have shown a generous approach to hosting refugees;

4. *Notes* that fifty-seven States are now parties to the 1954 Convention relating to the Status of Stateless Persons and that twenty-nine States are parties to the 1961 Convention on the Reduction of Statelessness, and encourages the High Commissioner to continue his activities on behalf of stateless persons;

5. *Notes also* that 2004 marks the twentieth anniversary of the Cartagena Declaration on Refugees and that States convened in Mexico City in November 2004 to commemorate this anniversary, recalls the contribution to refugee protection which regional approaches can make, and encourages States to strengthen further international protection of refugees in the region, in conjunction with relevant international organizations as well as representatives of civil society;

6. *Re-emphasizes* that the protection of refugees is primarily the responsibility of States, whose full and effective cooperation, action and political resolve are required to enable the Office of the High Commissioner to fulfil its mandated functions;

7. *Urges* all States and relevant non-governmental and other organizations, in conjunction with the Office of the High Commissioner and in a spirit of international solidarity and burden- and responsibility-sharing, to cooperate and to mobilize resources with a view to enhancing the capacity of, and reducing the heavy burden borne by, countries that have received large numbers of refugees and asylum-seekers, including by holding international consultations aimed at developing a comprehensive plan of action, as appropriate, to respond to a specific mass influx or protracted refugee situation, and calls upon the Office to continue to play its catalytic role in mobilizing assistance from the international community to address the root causes as well as the economic, environmental and so-cial impact of large-scale refugee populations in developing countries, in particular the least developed countries, and countries with economies in transition;

8. *Emphasizes* that international protection of refugees is a dynamic and action-oriented function that is at the core of the mandate of the Office of the High Commissioner and that includes, in cooperation with States and other partners, the promotion and facilitation of, inter alia, the admission, reception and treatment of refugees and the ensuring of durable, protection-oriented solutions, bearing in mind the particular needs of vulnerable groups, and notes in this context that the delivery of international protection is a staff-intensive service that requires adequate staff with the appropriate expertise, especially at the field level;

9. *Welcomes* the progress attained so far in regard to the High Commissioner's Convention Plus initiative, including the development of the Multilateral Framework of Understandings on the strategic use of resettlement, and encourages the High Commissioner and interested States to strengthen the international protection regime through the development of comprehensive approaches to resolving refugee situations, including improving international burden- and responsibility-sharing and realizing durable solutions that give due regard to the importance of both protection and, where possible, refugee self-reliance;

10. *Recalls* the important role of effective partnerships and coordination in meeting the needs of refugees and other displaced persons and in finding durable solutions to their situations, welcomes the efforts under way, in cooperation with refugee-hosting countries and countries of origin, including their respective local communities, United Nations agencies and other development actors, to promote a framework for durable solutions, particularly in protracted refugee situations, which includes the "4Rs" approach (repatriation, reintegration, rehabilitation and reconstruction) to sustainable return, and encourages States, in cooperation with United Nations agencies and other development actors, to support, inter alia, through the allocation of funds, the development and implementation of the 4Rs and of other programming tools to facilitate the transition from relief to development;

11. *Strongly reaffirms* the fundamental importance and the purely humanitarian and non-political character of the function of the Office of the High Commissioner of providing international protection to refugees and seeking permanent solutions to refugee problems, and recalls that these solutions include voluntary repatriation and, where appropriate and feasible, local integration and resettlement in a third country, while reaffirming that voluntary repatriation, supported by necessary rehabilitation and development assistance to facilitate sustainable reintegration, remains the preferred solution;

12. *Recognizes* the desirability of countries of origin, in cooperation with the Office of the High Commissioner, other States and other concerned actors, as necessary and appropriate, addressing, at an early stage, issues of a legal and administrative nature which are likely to hinder voluntary repatriation in safety and dignity, bearing in mind that some legal safety or administrative issues may be addressed only over time and that voluntary repatriation can and does take place

without all legal and administrative issues having first been resolved;

13. *Emphasizes* the obligation of all States to accept the return of their nationals, calls upon States to facilitate the return of their nationals who have been determined not to be in need of international protection, and affirms the need for the return of persons to be undertaken in a safe and humane manner and with full respect for their human rights and dignity, irrespective of the status of the persons concerned;

14. *Condemns* all acts that pose a threat to the personal security and well-being of refugees and asylum-seekers, such as refoulement, unlawful expulsion and physical attacks, deplores, in particular, the armed attacks that took place in the Gatumba transit centre in Burundi in August 2004, calls upon all States of refuge, in cooperation with international organizations, where appropriate, to take all necessary measures to ensure respect for the principles of refugee protection, including the humane treatment of asylum-seekers, notes with interest that the High Commissioner has continued to take steps to encourage the development of measures to better ensure the civilian and humanitarian character of asylum, and encourages the High Commissioner to continue those efforts in consultation with States and other relevant actors;

15. *Encourages* the Office of the High Commissioner to continue to improve its management systems and to ensure effective and transparent use of its resources, recognizes that adequate and timely resources are essential for the Office to continue to fulfil the mandate conferred upon it through its statute and by subsequent General Assembly resolutions on refugees and other persons of concern, recalls its resolutions 58/153 and 58/270 of 23 December 2003 concerning the implementation of paragraph 20 of the statute of the Office, and urges Governments and other donors to respond promptly to the annual and supplementary appeals issued by the Office for requirements under its programmes;

16. *Requests* the High Commissioner to report on his activities to the General Assembly at its sixtieth session.

Strengthening UNHCR

Oral report of High Commissioner. In response to General Assembly resolution 58/153 [YUN 2003, p. 1226] on strengthening UNHCR's capacity to carry out its mandate, the UNHCR representative, in an oral report to the Economic and Social Council on 22 July [E/2004/SR.48], said that the Office had worked with the Executive Committee on Humanitarian Affairs (ECHA) and the Inter-Agency Standing Committee (IASC) to strengthen refugee protection through cooperation, particularly by contributing to the work of the IASC Task Force on Protection from Sexual Exploitation and Abuse in Humanitarian Crises and to the inter-agency review of the collaborative approach on internally displaced persons (IDPs). UNHCR developed a Framework for Durable Solutions under the key strategies of repatriation, reintegration, rehabilitation and

reconstruction (the "4Rs"); development through local integration; and development assistance for refugees. Regarding security issues, UNHCR worked with the Office of the United Nations Security Coordinator, IASC and ECHA to develop a clearer vision and strategy for managing increased risks to humanitarian personnel. It also worked with other UN bodies to address refugee welfare, including the Joint United Nations Programme on HIV/AIDS (UNAIDS), the World Food Programme (WFP), the International Labour Organization (ILO), the United Nations Volunteers (UNVs) and the International Organization for Migration (IOM). In April, the High Commissioner and the Under-Secretary-General of the UN Department of Peacekeeping Operations (DPKO) signed a joint letter on enhanced cooperation, particularly regarding security for refugees, IDPs and returnees, among other areas.

Addressing Africa's refugee situation, the High Commissioner highlighted UNHCR's various repatriation operations on the continent, in particular those in Angola, Burundi, Eritrea, Rwanda, Sierra Leone and Somalia; its enhanced resettlement operations; and the development of a methodology for comprehensive plans of action for specific refugee situations. UNHCR recognized that it could not address the challenge of the reintegration of returnees alone, as rapidly evolving situations in Africa called for a strong emergency preparedness and response capacity. It had built innovative partnerships with regional and subregional organizations, with which it was advocating for the recognition of good governance, peace and security, and conflict resolution as preconditions for sustainable development and successful repatriation on the continent. The Office was chairing the sub-cluster on humanitarian response and post-conflict recovery under the New Partnership for Africa's Development (NEPAD) (see p. 920).

By **decision 2004/317** of 23 July, the Economic and Social Council took note of the High Commissioner's oral report on coordination aspects of UNHCR's work and on assistance to refugees, returnees and displaced persons in Africa.

Coordination of emergency humanitarian assistance

In 2004 [A/60/12], UNHCR continued to collaborate in the development of more effective UN system inter-agency coordination, particularly within the context of the humanitarian response review commissioned by the UN Emergency Relief Coordinator. The Office remained committed to the collaborative approach to internal displacement, adopting a more active and predictable disposition to address related protection challenges. As part of inter-agency efforts to develop guidelines and training support, UNHCR developed emergency team leadership training and helped to address such aspects as HIV/AIDS field training, an early warning/early action system, and gender-based violence interventions in humanitarian settings. Regarding collaboration on lessons learned, a key function of inter-agency forums, UNHCR participated in reviewing and adjusting the needs-assessment framework into a more analytical tool. The Office commented on a DPKO/Office for the Coordination of Humanitarian Affairs (OCHA) study of UN integrated missions, and was promoting and implementing the Secretary-General's bulletin on sexual exploitation and abuse [YUN 2003, p. 1238]. UNHCR and DPKO agreed to enhance cooperation in refugee/returnee security; the rule of law; disarmament, demobilization and reintegration; mine action; and technical cooperation. As part of efforts to develop a more systematic and timely system for reporting on key protection concerns in situations of armed conflict, UNHCR convened an expert meeting (Geneva, 9-11 June) on maintaining the civilian and humanitarian character of asylum, which was part of the process of developing operational guidelines. In related action, UNHCR was preparing operational guidelines on the separation of armed elements from refugee populations.

Bilateral partnerships to assist displaced persons improved in 2004. UNHCR and WFP were developing a joint donor communication strategy to address the challenges of securing acceptable levels of food and water for refugees, and agreed that WFP would participate in all future UNHCR appeals and reports. Cooperation with the Food and Agriculture Organization of the United Nations (FAO) and ILO increased in the area of refugee welfare. Partnerships with NGOs also grew, as those organizations were more actively involved in the assessment, planning, implementation and evaluation phases of UNHCR operations. In 2004, implementation agreements were signed with over 600 of them, and the Office was establishing guidelines to help build their capacity at the national level to respond to protection and assistance needs in field operations.

Evaluation activities

UNHCR, in a July report [A/AC.96/994] on its evaluation function, stated that interest had grown in inter-agency collaboration in joint evaluation activities, as the UNHCR Evaluation and Policy Analysis Unit (EPAU), together with the WFP evaluation service, began a joint evaluation of five pilot countries in which WFP was responsible for food distribution to refugees. The find-

ings would help determine whether or not to replicate the arrangement globally. EPAU and the Technical Support Section, in coordination with the Inter-Agency Working Group on Reproductive Health Services for Refugees, led an inter-agency global evaluation of reproductive health services for refugees and IDPs, the final report of which was expected in September. EPAU was also cooperating with the European Commission Humanitarian Office (ECHO) in developing an evaluation methodology for ECHO's 2004 evaluation of the effectiveness of its financial support to UNHCR. The findings of its 2002 evaluations, including those on refugee children and women and on community services [YUN 2002, p. 1201], informed changes to UNHCR's operational policies and implementation procedures. The Office intended to ensure that evaluation findings were more widely discussed and that lessons learned were fully absorbed. EPAU was developing an electronic follow-up mechanism for compiling and cataloguing evaluation recommendations, so that their impact could be better measured against policy changes in the respective functional areas.

Evaluation projects undertaken or initiated in 2004 related to the needs of IDPs, real-time evaluations of emergency operations, refugee livelihoods, reintegration, a Canadian Government-sponsored pilot project on Royal Canadian Mounted Police secondment to UNHCR field operations in Guinea, UNHCR's worldwide vehicle fleet, and building capacity through training. Evaluations were conducted on regional resettlement activities in West Africa to ascertain the validity of some of the assumptions underpinning the regional resettlement scheme, and on enhancing UNHCR's capacity to monitor the protection, rights and well-being of refugees, based on a review of the Office's multiple roles in both protection and programme monitoring.

Inspections

In 2004 [A/60/12], standard inspections of UNHCR activities by its Inspector General's Office (IGO) were conducted in Japan, Sierra Leone and Spain, while ad hoc inspections were undertaken in Kazakhstan, Uganda and Uzbekistan. Operational reviews were undertaken in Armenia, Azerbaijan, Georgia, Somalia, Sri Lanka and the Sudan to assess specific operational strategies, focusing on finding solutions to refugee problems and on the effectiveness of UNHCR's partnerships with other organizations. In 2004, IGO received 105 complaints of alleged misconduct. Some one third of them, where the investigation supported a finding of misconduct, were forwarded to the Division of Human Resources

Management for disciplinary action. The Investigation Unit produced a number of management implication reports to highlight vulnerabilities in UNHCR operations and to help managers adjust their actions accordingly. In September, UNHCR's Oversight Committee, whose terms of reference were revised and strengthened, was reconstituted as a decision-making body, chaired by the Deputy High Commissioner, with the mandate to decide on and oversee administrative measures to be taken in cases of continuing failure to comply with oversight recommendations. IGO no longer served as the secretariat of the Oversight Committee.

The UN Office of Internal Oversight Services (OIOS) audited UNHCR operations and activities involving expenditure of $362 million, or 34 per cent of UNHCR's total expenditure of $1,063 million in 2004. Those audits covered operations in 26 countries, as well as the payroll, mobility and hardship allowances and the headquarters management systems renewal project. OIOS also reviewed the functions of headquarters desk officers, and of two international NGOs to assess their systems and procedures and to advise on ways of complying with UN auditing requirements.

Enlargement of the Executive Committee

On 21 July, the Economic and Social Council, by **decision 2004/238**, took note of requests from Romania [E/2004/49] and Ghana [E/2004/76] for admission to membership in the UNHCR Executive Committee and recommended that the General Assembly take a decision at its fifty-ninth (2004) session on the question of enlarging the Committee's membership from 66 to 68 States.

GENERAL ASSEMBLY ACTION

On 20 December [meeting 74], the General Assembly, on the recommendation of the Third Committee [A/59/498], adopted **resolution 59/169** without vote [agenda item 100].

Enlargement of the Executive Committee of the Programme of the United Nations High Commissioner for Refugees

The General Assembly,

Taking note of Economic and Social Council decision 2004/238 of 21 July 2004 concerning the enlargement of the Executive Committee of the Programme of the United Nations High Commissioner for Refugees,

Taking note also of the requests regarding the enlargement of the Executive Committee contained in the letter dated 23 March 2004 from the Permanent Representative of Romania to the United Nations addressed to the Secretary-General and the letter dated 2 June 2004 from the Permanent Representative of Ghana to the United Nations addressed to the Secretary-General,

1. *Decides* to increase the number of members of the Executive Committee of the Programme of the United Nations High Commissioner for Refugees from sixty-six to sixty-eight States;

2. *Requests* the Economic and Social Council to elect the additional members at its resumed organizational session for 2005.

Financial and administrative questions

UNHCR's initial annual programme budget target for 2004 was set at $923 million by the Executive Committee in 2003 [YUN 2003, p. 1227]. Total income for 2004 amounted to $1,001.2 million, comprising $805.2 million in contributions and miscellaneous income (including currency exchange gains) for the annual programme budget, $10 million for the Junior Professional Officer (JPO) programme, $27.7 million provided by the UN regular budget, and $158.3 million in contributions for the 2004 supplementary programmes. Expenditures totalled $1,062.6 million, of which Africa accounted for some $468.3 million; Central Asia, South-West Asia, North Africa and the Middle East, $192.5 million; Europe, $114.3 million; Asia and the Pacific, $50.8 million; and the Americas, $28.5 million.

In October, the Executive Committee approved the revised 2004 annual programme budget, amounting to $955.8 million, including the UN regular budget contribution of $25.8 million, which, with the provision of $7 million for JPOs and $170.6 million for the supplementary programmes, brought total requirements for 2004 to $1,126 million.

The Committee approved $974.6 million for the 2005 annual programme budget, including an operational reserve of $62.5 million, or 7.5 per cent, of programme activities, and $50 million, continued on a further trial basis to provide appropriation authority for fully funded additional activities. Those provisions, together with $7 million for the JPO programme, brought total requirements in 2005 to $981.6 million. The Committee authorized the High Commissioner, within the total appropriation, to effect adjustments in regional and global programmes and in headquarters budgets, and to create supplementary programmes and issue corresponding special appeals to meet any additional new emergency needs that could not be filled from the operational reserve.

The Committee noted the proposal to create a post of Assistant High Commissioner (Protection) [A/AC.96/992/Add.1], at the Assistant Secretary-General level, for which an amount of $300,000 had been included in the annual programme budget. It stated that no expenditure should be charged against the item until the matter had been discussed by the Standing Committee in 2005 and a decision taken by the Executive Committee. In that regard, the Committee requested UNHCR to provide more detailed terms of reference for the proposed position. It requested UNHCR to commission an independent evaluation of the operational reserve, category II, including a review of the criteria for accepting contributions. The Committee welcomed the High Commissioner's initiative to consolidate UNHCR's information technology functions within the new Division of Information Systems and Technology.

Implementation of article 20 of the UNHCR statute

In response to General Assembly resolution 58/270 [YUN 2003, p. 1399], the Secretary-General, in August [A/59/294], described efforts made over the past two bienniums to progressively implement article 20 of the UNHCR statute, which required that no expenditure other than administrative expenditures relating to the functioning of the Office should be borne by the UN regular budget and that all other expenditures be borne by voluntary contributions. Towards meeting that goal, the Assembly had approved some $2 million in increases to UNHCR's proposed 2002-2003 and 2004-2005 programme budgets to meet management and administrative post and non-post costs, using a ratio of 50.8 per cent. For future bienniums, the Secretary-General proposed increased contributions similar to that applied for the 2002-2003 and 2004-2005 bienniums.

In November [A/C.5/59/SR.26], the ACABQ Chairman, in an oral statement to the Fifth Committee, recommended that the Assembly note the Secretary-General's report, with the understanding that proposals for subsequent increases in UN contributions to UNHCR's management and administrative costs would be submitted for its review in the context of the proposed programme budget for future bienniums.

The Assembly, in Part III of **resolution 59/276** of 23 December (see p. 1384), took note of the Secretary-General's report and ACABQ's related comments and recommendations. It requested the Secretary-General to include in the programme budget proposals for progressive increases of contributions from the UN regular budget to UNHCR, with a view to the full implementation of article 20 of the statute of the Office and to report in 2005 on progress made in the context of the 2006-2007 proposed programme budget, while recognizing that the 50.8 percentage referred to in his report did not represent a ceiling. The Assembly called on UNHCR to keep its support costs, including management and administration, under review, with the objective

of reducing them as a percentage of total budget expenditure.

Accounts (2003)

The audited financial statements of voluntary funds administered by UNHCR for the year ended 31 December 2003 [A/59/5/Add.5] showed total expenditures of some $957.4 million and total income of $981.2 million, with a reserve balance of $171 million.

The Board of Auditors found that: the unallocated available reserves at the end of 2003 ($78 million) were insufficient to cover the staff termination liabilities of some $290 million; the value of the non-expendable property as at 31 December 2003 remained inaccurate due to errors in data entry and non-recording of assets; the 2003 operational expenditure not unsupported by implementing partners' financial reports totalled $9.6 million as at 15 June 2004, an improvement over previous years; the accounting of unliquidated obligations still suffered from inaccurate disclosure; after spending some $13 million on the decentralization of its Africa Bureau (1999-2001), UNHCR recentralized its structure; UNHCR did not fully monitor the management of its many offices and buildings around the world and had no proactive policy to comply with UN common premises policy; and the Office had not developed a plan against the risk of corruption and fraud. The Board made recommendations for improving financial management and reporting, information technology and programme management, while noting that UNHCR had, in some respects, responded to the recommendations, although some had yet to be implemented.

In an October report [A/59/400], the Advisory Committee on Administrative and Budgetary Questions (ACABQ) expressed concern at the level of cash assistance from UNHCR implementing partners not yet justified, and over the extent of continued overstatement of unliquidated obligations. ACABQ was also concerned that UNHCR did not have a clear picture of its numerous buildings worldwide and had no proactive policy to comply with UN instructions on common premises at the country level.

The Executive Committee, in a decision on administrative, financial and programme matters [A/59/12/Add.1], requested that it be informed regularly on measures taken to address the recommendations and observations made by the Board of Auditors and ACABQ.

Management and administrative review

JIU report. On 1 October [A/59/394], the Secretary-General transmitted a report of the

Joint Inspection Unit (JIU) on its review of UNHCR's management and administration, as part of the ongoing reform to improve the functioning of the Office. JIU focused on UNHCR's organizational structure; planning, programming, budgeting, monitoring and evaluation activities; information management; human resources management; oversight activities; and field operations, using Tanzania as a case study. It took into consideration, for benchmarking purposes, the management practices of other UN system organizations.

The Inspectors found that UNHCR's management was characterized by multiple managerial policies and guidelines, formulated through various internal committees and boards. Its current organizational structure was fragmented and revealed shortcomings related to functional duplications between departmental units, the placement of some functional units, and non-uniformity in the organizational nomenclature. The structure was also anomalous in terms of the functional hierarchy, with the Deputy High Commissioner responsible for management and administration and the Assistant High Commissioner overseeing programmes and operations, both employed at the Assistant Secretary-General level. The structure suffered from a cumbersome, lengthy and expensive programme and budget process, a multitude of separate information systems with a proliferated information structure, a problematic flow of communication technology information, a failure to fully recognize results-based management in developing the Enterprise Resource Planning System, shortcomings in its internal oversight system, a lack of correlation between refugee caseloads and structural staffing levels of the different field offices, and high vacancy rates at some duty stations classified as family-duty stations.

JIU proposed that the Executive Committee recommend that the General Assembly authorize the creation of a second Deputy High Commissioner post by upgrading the existing Assistant High Commissioner position, resulting in two Deputies—one in charge of programme/operations and the other in charge of administration/management, with the understanding that such a measure would have no financial implications, and that the UNHCR Statute would be amended accordingly. The High Commissioner should present to the Executive Committee a streamlined and rationalized structure of the UNHCR secretariat, consolidating functions and relocating some organizational units, based on a uniform organizational nomenclature. The Executive Committee should modify the programme budget cycle from the current annual to a bien-

nial cycle, in alignment with the UN regular budget. To further enhance the results-based approach to planning, programming, budgeting, monitoring and evaluation, the High Commissioner should apply the UN logical framework to the UNHCR budget; integrate the Management Systems Renewal Project (MSRP) into the results-based management process; incorporate evaluation findings and recommendations into planning, programming, budgeting and monitoring; and enhance real-time evaluation. The High Commissioner should submit to the Executive Committee a long-term strategic framework containing UNHCR's guiding principles, organizational priorities and strategic goals, linked to activities, indicators of achievement, and target dates for completion. The High Commissioner should prepare a comprehensive information management strategy, consolidate information and communication technology (ICT) related functions into a centralized organizational entity and appoint a Chief Information Officer as the head of that entity. The Division of Human Resources should prepare a comprehensive strategic corporate policy on human resources management for submission to the Executive Committee in 2005, and an annual report on the composition of the secretariat. The High Commissioner should strengthen the role of the Oversight Committee, and the Executive Committee should approve a non-career five-year, non-renewable Inspector General position. JIU made a number of other recommendations to help strengthen UNHCR's human resources management and field operations.

In a September report [A/AC.96/992/Add.2], ACABQ concurred with JIU on the need for UNHCR to modify its programme cycle from annual to biennial but was not convinced of UNHCR's concern that biennialization would lead to loss of flexibility in responding to emergencies and possible resistance by donors who had annual budgets. UNHCR needed to move towards longer-term planning and strategic goals, particularly with its change from a five-year mandate to an open-ended one, pursuant to General Assembly resolution 58/153 [YUN 2003, p. 1226]. Regarding the creation of the additional post of Deputy High Commissioner, ACABQ, while favouring the proposal, believed that UNHCR should await the results of its headquarters review before establishing another top management post. ACABQ encouraged UNHCR to support the JIU recommendations on its oversight activities, especially that relating to the Office of the Inspector General.

A December report of the Secretary-General [A/59/394/Add.1], containing his comments on the

JIU report, indicated UNHCR's general agreement with most of the findings and recommendations of the Inspectors, and the High Commissioner's intention to take them into account during the review of the Office.

Standing Committee

The UNHCR Standing Committee held three meetings in 2004 (9-11 March [A/AC.96/988]; 29 June-1 July [A/AC.96/998]; and 23-24 September [A/AC.96/1001]). It considered issues relating to UNHCR's programmes, budgets and funding; international protection; protection/programme policy; coordination; management, finance, oversight and human resources; governance; and consultations.

In October [A/59/12/Add.1], the Executive Committee adopted the following items for the Standing Committee's 2005 programme of work: international protection; protection programme policy; programme budgets and funding; regional activities and Global Programmes; management, financial control, administrative oversight and human resources; coordination; and governance. The Standing Committee was authorized to add or delete items, as appropriate, to its intersessional work programme.

Staff safety

At the September meeting of the Standing Committee (23-24 September) [A/AC.96/1001], the Director of UNHCR's Emergency and Security Service (ESS), in an update on staff safety and security management, stated that UNHCR was taking innovative measures to meet its safety obligations to staff. The High Commissioner was considering some 80 recommendations made by the Steering Committee on Security Policy and Policy Implementation, which had conducted a comprehensive review of the issue. The policy changes envisaged would enable UNHCR to: integrate security considerations fully into its operations, including through a restructured ESS; train staff in effective security management concepts; emphasize levels of accountability; promote the conduct of operations from a risk management and risk mitigation perspective; and ensure its role within the wider scope of the United Nations' global security management. UNHCR's reforms, which would complement those of the United Nations, would require additional resources, with significant initial requirements particularly in the field of telecommunications. In addition to the estimated funding needs presented in the 2005 annual programme budget, further requirements were being quantified in

relation to the needs outlined in the Steering Committee's report.

ACABQ, in its September report [A/AC.96/992/Add.2], noted that $28.9 million had been included in the 2005 programme budget for security, which did not include an additional estimated $17.5 million to implement the Steering Committee's recommendations. ACABQ was of the opinion that the UNHCR security arrangements and related resource requirements should be kept under review to ensure that they were in harmony with the overall UN system security plan as might be adopted by the General Assembly, following consideration of the Steering Committee's report.

Refugee protection and assistance

Protection issues

In his annual report covering 2004 [A/60/12], the High Commissioner described the main challenges facing UNHCR and the international community to protect refugees, including concerns about terrorism and the confusion between migration and asylum issues, which affected the international protection regime and the right of refugees to seek asylum. UNHCR was working to preserve access to asylum for those seeking it on the basis of a well-founded fear of persecution. By mainstreaming the goals and objectives of the 2002 Agenda for Protection [YUN 2002, p. 1205], UNHCR had reinforced links between its Department of International Protection and its field operations, thereby helping to give focus to protection interventions. The physical security of refugees remained an issue of central concern for UNHCR during the year, particularly the rape of refugee women as a weapon of conflict and the abduction and humiliation of refugee children in displacement situations. There were also worrisome instances of refoulement, occasionally carried out under curious arrangements between asylum host States and countries of origin. The Office closely monitored developments in migration-related forums to ensure that the protection needs of the forcibly displaced were met. It developed a comprehensive framework for assessing protection capacity needs and facilitated a consultative process to develop activities to address the gaps identified. Particular efforts were made to enhance the protection of refugee women and children through a pilot project on age, gender and diversity mainstreaming, launched in February in 16 countries. UNHCR continued to promote accession to the 1951 Convention relating to the Status of Refugees [YUN 1951, p. 520] and its 1967 Protocol [YUN 1967, p. 477], and the 1954 Convention relating to the Status of Stateless Persons [YUN 1954, p. 416] and other related instruments.

In a July note on international protection [A/AC.96/989], the High Commissioner stated that, despite positive developments, particularly the repatriation of significant numbers of refugees, the movement of several countries towards peace and the impetus to implement the 1951 Convention in many regions, major challenges persisted due to non-existent or weak legal frameworks, measures taken that undermined the protection regime, the increasing volume and complexities of migratory flows and the difficulties associated with ensuring the sustainability of voluntary repatriation. The High Commissioner noted that protection responses were intrinsically linked, and the successful implementation of each element of the Agenda for Protection helped to reinforce the international protection regime as a whole. The strength and effectiveness of the regime would grow proportionately with the political and operational commitment of States and actors to resolving long-standing refugee situations, and the improvement of the conditions on which humanitarian action depended, among other factors.

The Executive Committee, in October [A/59/12/Add.1], acknowledged the increasing complexities of the environment in which international protection was provided and the many challenges faced by States and UNHCR in ensuring the protection of refugees and other persons of concern. Recognizing that the delivery of international protection was resource-intensive, the Committee reaffirmed the need for UNHCR to address protection in a holistic manner, and called on States to support it through the timely and predictable provision of resources. The Committee emphasized the continuing importance of the Agenda for Protection and encouraged all concerned actors to provide timely information on their follow-up initiatives to enable UNHCR to keep it informed on implementation initiatives.

International instruments

As at 31 December 2004, the number of States parties to both the 1951 Convention relating to the Status of Refugees [YUN 1951, p. 520] and to its 1967 Protocol [YUN 1967, p. 477] stood at 142. The accessions of the Czech Republic and Uruguay to the 1954 Convention relating to the Status of Stateless Persons [YUN 1954, p. 416], and of Liberia and the Libyan Arab Jamahiriya to the 1961 Convention on the Reduction of Statelessness [YUN 1961, p. 533], increased the number of States parties to those instruments to 57 and 29, respectively.

Convention Plus

In 2004, the "Convention Plus" initiative, launched in 2003 [YUN 2003, p. 1229] to help strengthen the commitment of States and UNHCR partners to resolving refugee situations, continued to provide the basis for action on behalf of refugees through enhanced burden sharing. Activities designed to make international cooperation more robust and effective in that regard included the establishment in June of a Framework of Understandings on Resettlement and discussions on irregular secondary movement of asylum-seekers and refugees and targeting development assistance to achieve durable solutions to refugee problems. Future efforts would focus on situation-specific approaches, notably for protracted refugee situations. Another innovative initiative under Convention Plus was the project on strengthening protection capacity, which helped develop a comprehensive methodology for assessing gaps in protection capacity and generated multilateral approaches to enhancing the protection capacity of host countries. In October, the High Commissioner's Forum, a mechanism for engaging States and humanitarian actors in dialogue on refugee issues, considered a methodology for making comprehensive approaches to resolving refugee problems more systematic.

Assistance measures

According to the High Commissioner's 2004 report [A/60/12], the global population of concern to UNHCR rose to 19.2 million in 2004, from 17 million in 2003. Despite the repatriation of significant numbers of refugees to their countries of origin in 2004, following the resolution of many conflict situations, new mass outflows resulted from other conflicts and human rights abuses around the world, with over 232,000 refugees fleeing their countries. The main refugee outflows comprised hundreds of thousands of Sudanese forced by militia attacks in that country's Darfur region to flee to Chad, Uganda and Kenya, resulting in one of the most complex and demanding UNHCR humanitarian operations in 2004. Others affected elsewhere included 37,900 who fled the DRC into Burundi, Rwanda, Zambia and Uganda; 19,000 from Somalia to Yemen and Kenya; and 5,500 from Côte d'Ivoire to Liberia. Another outflow was the movement of Iraqis fleeing to Syria, Lebanon and Jordan. The main IDP situations of concern were in Colombia, estimated to have over 2 million displaced persons, the Sudan's Darfur region and Liberia. During the year, an estimated 1.5 million refugees repatriated voluntarily to their countries of origin, of whom the largest number (approximately 1 million) returned to Afghanistan from Iran and Pakistan. Others returned to Angola (80,000), Burundi (90,000), the DRC (13,800), Iraq (194,000), Liberia (56,900), Rwanda (14,100), Sierra Leone (26,300), Somalia (18,100) and Sri Lanka (10,000). The number of those resettled during the year rose to approximately 30,000, from 26,000 in 2003, while the number of stateless persons was estimated at 1.5 million.

Refugees and the environment

In 2004, UNHCR continued to incorporate environmental concerns into all aspects of refugee operations. It updated sectoral guidelines on forestry and livestock management and publications on permaculture in refugee situations and sustainable land use. It enhanced technical support in operations in Africa and Asia, notably in Chad, where it collaborated with the Government on an environmental assessment in refugee-hosting areas. In cooperation with the United Nations Educational, Scientific and Cultural Organization (UNESCO) Programme for Education for Emergencies and Reconstruction, UNHCR continued environmental education for refugees to raise awareness and compliance with environmental strategies.

Refugees and HIV/AIDS

In 2004, as one of the co-sponsors of UNAIDS, UNHCR facilitated synergy and coordination of action in combating HIV/AIDS among persons of concern. Issues relating to conflicts, displacement and refugees featured more prominently in global and regional strategies on prevention, education, food and nutrition, and in interventions in emergency settings. UNHCR staff worked to improve measures to reduce stigmatization or discrimination against refugees affected by HIV/AIDS and to increase refugee access to public sector care and treatment programmes, including anti-retroviral therapy. Collaboration with partners and Governments on subregional initiatives was prioritized, and in that regard, UNHCR signed a memorandum of understanding with the participating States of the Great Lakes Initiative on AIDS and developed similar initiatives in West and Central Africa for improving continuity of services to mobile populations. The strategy involved building agreements on diagnostic and treatment protocols, bulk ordering of medi-

cation and supplies, and helping with repatriation planning and implementation.

Refugee women

During the year, UNHCR launched a pilot project on age, gender and diversity mainstreaming in 16 countries, through multifunctional teams and country-level work plans to promote gender equality and the rights of refugees of all ages. Initial results indicated that the project had helped boost awareness of gender issues in refugee situations and facilitated interaction between UNHCR staff and refugee men and women, better knowledge of refugee concerns and the identification of protection risks and gaps by age and gender. UNHCR supplemented its Guidelines for Prevention and Response to Sexual and Gender-based Violence in refugee and refugee-like settings with regular capacity-building sessions for its staff and those of its partners. In mid-2004, a joint UNHCR-WFP study on effective operational practices in relation to women's control of food and participation in food distribution identified ways to further secure women's interests in that regard. In collaboration with ILO, UNHCR secured technical support for refugee women entrepreneurship and economic empowerment in several countries.

Refugee children

In 2004, UNHCR promoted a rights-based approach to enhancing the protection and care of refugee children and adolescents. The strategy included the continuing prioritization of protection concerns, such as separation; sexual exploitation, abuse and violence; military recruitment; education; and the specific needs of adolescents. In collaboration with other humanitarian agencies and NGOs, the Office published a global registration form for unaccompanied and separated children, and through the inter-agency Action for the Rights of Children, undertook field-focused capacity-building initiatives in Africa, Latin America and Asia. UNHCR continued to support the education of persons of concern, with particular focus on access to primary education. It launched a number of capacity-building projects, and pursued the development of educational tools and the provision of scholarships for secondary and post-secondary education. Innovative strategies, undertaken in partnership with others, including through private sector funding and support, showed positive results in Kenya, demonstrating the value of affirmative action for girls' education.

Regional activities

Africa

In 2004, the total population of concern to UNHCR in Africa, excluding North Africa, totalled 4.5 million, of whom 2.8 million were refugees, 1 million IDPs and 199,603 asylum-seekers, compared to 3.3 million in 2003 [YUN 2003, p. 1232].

The Secretary-General, in an August report submitted in response to General Assembly resolution 58/149 [YUN 2003, p. 1234], updated information on assistance provided by UNHCR to refugees, returnees and displaced persons in Africa [A/59/317], covering 2003 and the first half of 2004. He noted that, despite the continuing decrease in the number of refugees in Africa in 2004, their situation and that of displaced persons in many parts of the continent remained precarious, especially in the Darfur province of the Sudan, from where some 200,000 refugees had fled into Chad and up to 1.5 million were displaced in the Sudan itself (see p. 235). UNHCR assisted hundreds of thousands of refugees on the continent to repatriate to their countries of origin, mainly nationals of Angola, Burundi, Eritrea, Liberia, Rwanda, Sierra Leone and Somalia. The main refugee groups continued to originate from some of those countries, and from the Sudan and the DRC, which recorded major new outflows during 2004.

In East Africa and the Horn of Africa, UNHCR assisted over 17,000 of the 770,517 refugees registered in the region to repatriate to Eritrea from the Sudan, and supported the Eritrean Government in protecting and assisting other camp-based refugees and asylum-seekers inside Eritrea. In Ethiopia, the deterioration of the security situation in the western region of Gambella hampered UNHCR's access to refugee camps and affected humanitarian assistance. However, the Office assisted refugees in other parts of the country and promoted the voluntary repatriation of thousands of Somali refugees there. In Kenya, where some 240,000 refugees were in camps, an expanded multisectoral approach to combating HIV/AIDS increased awareness of preventive patient care among the camp population. Over 10,000 Somali refugees repatriated voluntarily from neighbouring countries, but the return programme was undermined by continuing instability in most parts of southern Somalia, the lack of social services and economic prospects upon return, severe drought in the north and endemic human rights violations. The deteriorating security situation hampered humanitarian access to the 200,000 refugees from the Darfur region living in Chad and malnourished IDPs. In Uganda, an estimated 1.6 million

people were displaced as a result of the conflict between the Government and the rebel Lord's Resistance Army, whose continuing operation around settlements in the north of the country remained a major constraint for refugee programmes.

In the Central Africa and Great Lakes subregion, host to some 1.3 million refugees, some 55,000 Burundians and 23,300 Rwandans were assisted in returning to their places of origin. However, hopes for the further repatriation of hundreds of thousands more refugees as a result of the improved political climate in Burundi and the DRC were not realized owing to continuing instability in some areas, including northern Central African Republic, where tension prevented some 41,000 of its nationals from repatriating from Chad. Meanwhile, the situation in Chad was further aggravated by the new influx of Sudanese fleeing from the Darfur region. UNHCR relocated 122,000 refugees to safer locations away from the border in eastern Chad during the first half of 2004. At mid-year, the Office faced another challenging situation, following the outbreak of fighting in the DRC town of Bukavu, which resulted in a fresh outflow of an estimated 20,000 refugees to Rwanda and Burundi (see p. 124).

In West Africa, where 471,328 refugees resided, the continuing instability in Côte d'Ivoire limited access to refugee-hosting areas, a situation further aggravated by the involvement of Liberian fighters in the Ivorian conflict, which fuelled animosity towards Liberian refugees in the country. An emergency resettlement programme for some 8,000 of those refugees was initiated in the United States. In Liberia itself, marked improvement in the security situation, following the deployment of UN peacekeepers, facilitated the spontaneous return of 50,000 refugees and several thousand IDPs. The challenge facing the international community was the return and reintegration of another 300,000 Liberian refugees in neighbouring countries and 260,000 IDPs residing in camps in the country. Similar progress in the peace process in Sierra Leone (see p. 212) facilitated the repatriation of some 270,000 refugees, mainly from Guinea and Liberia. Reintegration programmes for the returnees would continue throughout 2004 and into 2005.

In Southern Africa, host to some 245,064 refugees, organized return programmes in Angola resumed in May, allowing some 8,000 refugees to be repatriated with UNHCR assistance. However, the lack of access to some parts of the country, owing to landmines and poor infrastructure, prevented repatriation to some 40 per cent of the key areas of refugee return. Another major constraint was the lack of adequate implementing partners. In South Africa, host to the largest number of urban refugees in the subregion, the phenomenon of mixed migration movements continued to pose a major challenge. Syndicates engaged in illegal activities abused the asylum system, thereby tarnishing the image of refugees and contributing to xenophobia, which prompted UNHCR to embark on a sensitization drive to raise government awareness and mobilize civil society support. In Zambia, the Office protected and assisted an estimated 200,000 refugees and promoted repatriation and resettlement programmes for many of them, particularly those returning mostly to Angola. Others opting to remain in Zambia benefited from economic and social empowerment programmes.

The Secretary-General also described interagency cooperation efforts to protect and assist refugees and displaced persons in Africa, and UNHCR's cooperation with regional bodies and initiatives. In that regard, UNHCR seconded one of its staff to the African Union (AU) to help build that organization's capacity to respond effectively to issues relating to refugees, IDPs and returnees in the continent. In collaboration with the African Parliamentary Union, UNHCR organized a regional conference on refugees in Africa: the challenges of protection and solutions (Cotonou, Benin, 1-3 June), which adopted a declaration and programme of action on ways to promote solutions to refugee problems on the continent, including through heightened awareness of international and regional refugee law.

UNHCR report. According to UNHCR's *Global Report 2004*, which provided information to the end of the year, UNHCR assisted almost 130,000 people to return to their countries in Central Africa and the Great Lakes subregion. However, the instability in eastern DRC and the insurrection by elements of the Congolese army in Bukavu in May/June led to an exodus of refugees into Rwanda and Burundi. Militia groups operating from the DRC attacked refugee sites in Gatumba in Burundi, killing some 160 refugees (see p. 149). In Gabon where repatriation was not successful, UNHCR made progress with local economic integration as the most durable solution. In the Sudan, UNHCR also maintained efforts in search of durable solutions for thousands of refugees from other countries, most notably Eritrea, and for an estimated 80,000 IDPs. One of the main constraints to its programmes in that country was its simultaneous involvement in three operations in the east, west and north, which overstretched its resources.

Repatriation programmes in East Africa and the Horn of Africa were facilitated by increased prospects for stability in Somalia, owing to the formation of the Transitional Federal Government of Somalia and significant international impetus to peace processes in the subregion. UNHCR assisted approximately 18,000 refugees to return to the Somaliland region from Ethiopia and Djibouti, and another 9,900 to repatriate to Eritrea from the Sudan. The Office continued to use resettlement as a tool to enhance the physical safety and security of refugees at risk, and succeeded in resettling, in the United States, thousands of refugees from Ethiopia. In West Africa, increasing stability in Sierra Leone and Liberia enabled UNHCR to assist the repatriation of 26,000 Sierra Leonean and some 72,000 Liberian refugees from neighbouring countries. Nonetheless, the subregion still hosted over 400,000 refugees from various conflicts on the continent. In some cases, particularly in protracted refugee situations, resettlement was considered a viable durable solution, with over 7,300 persons submitted for resettlement in Australia, Canada, Denmark, Finland, the Netherlands, Norway, Sweden and the United States. UNHCR's overriding concerns in the subregion were conflict prevention and the negative effects of socio-economic and political instability, as well as food insufficiency. The main challenges for the reintegration of returnees were the absence of employment opportunities and the implementation of the regional disarmament, demobilization, rehabilitation and reintegration process. In Southern Africa, UNHCR concentrated on durable solutions for the protracted refugee situations in various countries of asylum in the region. The integration of HIV/AIDS programmes into refugee operations remained a high priority, as did effective resource management. Progress was made with the repatriation of Angolan refugees, some 90,000 of whom returned from Botswana, the DRC, Namibia, the Republic of the Congo, South Africa and Zambia. For those who did not wish to repatriate, local integration schemes were initiated in Malawi, Mozambique and Zambia, for implementation in 2005. However, the backlog of asylum applications remained a serious challenge, as did the continuing reluctance of Rwandan refugees to repatriate; the outbreak of a meningitis epidemic in Namibia, which disrupted the return programme to Angola; and the general lack of facilities and hardship in areas of return in Angola, which discouraged voluntary returns.

UNHCR assisted 1.4 million persons in Central Africa and the Great Lakes region, which received $185.4 million in agency expenditures; East Africa and the Horn of Africa, $111 million for 1.5 million persons of concern; West Africa, some $118 million for 1.1 million persons in need;

and Southern Africa, $54.2 million for 463,202 persons of concern.

Other developments. The Executive Council of the African Union (AU), at its fifth ordinary session (Addis Ababa, 30 June–3 July), adopted decision EX.CL/Dec.127(V) on the situation of refugees, returnees and IDPs in Africa, reaffirming the importance of voluntary repatriation and urging AU member States to create conditions conducive to the repatriation and sustainable reintegration of refugees in their communities.

GENERAL ASSEMBLY ACTION

On 20 December [meeting 74], the General Assembly, on the recommendation of the Third Committee [A/59/498], adopted **resolution 59/172** without vote [agenda item 100].

Assistance to refugees, returnees and displaced persons in Africa

The General Assembly,

Recalling its resolution 58/149 of 22 December 2003,

Recalling also the Organization of African Unity Convention governing the specific aspects of refugee problems in Africa of 1969 and the African Charter on Human and Peoples' Rights,

Reaffirming that the 1951 Convention relating to the Status of Refugees, together with the 1967 Protocol thereto, as complemented by the Organization of African Unity Convention of 1969, remains the foundation of the international refugee protection regime in Africa,

1. *Takes note* of the reports of the Secretary-General and the United Nations High Commissioner for Refugees;

2. *Notes* the need for African States to address resolutely the root causes of all forms of forced displacement in Africa and to foster peace, stability and prosperity throughout the African continent so as to forestall refugee flows, and calls upon the international community, including States, the Office of the United Nations High Commissioner for Refugees, and other relevant United Nations organizations, within their respective mandates, to take concrete action to meet the protection and assistance needs of refugees, returnees and displaced persons and to contribute generously to projects and programmes aimed at alleviating their plight and facilitating durable solutions for refugees and displaced persons;

3. *Welcomes* decision EX.CL/Dec.127(V) on the situation of refugees, returnees and displaced persons in Africa adopted by the Executive Council of the African Union at its fifth ordinary session, held at Addis Ababa from 30 June to 3 July 2004;

4. *Takes note* of the holding of the conference organized by the African Parliamentary Union and the United Nations High Commissioner for Refugees on "Refugees in Africa: the challenges of protection and solutions" at Cotonou, Benin, from 1 to 3 June 2004;

5. *Expresses its appreciation* for the leadership shown by the High Commissioner since assuming office in January 2001, and commends the Office of the High Commissioner for its ongoing efforts, with the support of the international community, to assist African coun-

tries of asylum and to respond to the protection and assistance needs of refugees, returnees and displaced persons in Africa;

6. *Encourages* the Office of the United Nations High Commissioner for Refugees to continue to cooperate with the Office of the United Nations High Commissioner for Human Rights and the African Commission on Human and Peoples' Rights, in conjunction with relevant agencies of the United Nations system and intergovernmental organizations, within their respective mandates, in the promotion and protection of the human rights and fundamental freedoms of refugees, returnees and displaced persons in Africa, and welcomes in this regard the appointment by the African Commission on Human and Peoples' Rights of its Special Rapporteur on refugees and internally displaced persons in Africa;

7. *Recognizes* that, among refugees, returnees and internally displaced persons, women and children are the majority of the population affected by conflict and bear the brunt of atrocities and other consequences of conflict, and in this regard takes note of the report of the Secretary-General on women and peace and security submitted to and discussed by the Security Council;

8. *Reiterates* the importance of the full and effective implementation of standards and procedures to better address the specific protection needs of refugee children and adolescents and to safeguard rights and, in particular, to ensure adequate attention to unaccompanied and separated children and former child soldiers in refugee settings, as well as in the context of voluntary repatriation and reintegration measures;

9. *Notes with great concern* that, despite all of the efforts made so far by the United Nations, the African Union and others, the situation of refugees and displaced persons in Africa remains precarious, calls upon States and other parties to armed conflict to observe scrupulously the letter and the spirit of international humanitarian law, bearing in mind that armed conflict is one of the principal causes of forced displacement in Africa, and welcomes in this regard the appointment by the African Union of its Special Representative on the protection of civilians in armed conflict;

10. *Recognizes* the importance of early registration and effective registration systems and censuses as a tool of protection and as a means to enable the quantification and assessment of needs for the provision and distribution of humanitarian assistance and to implement appropriate durable solutions;

11. *Also recognizes* the need to strengthen the capacity of States to provide assistance to and protection for refugees, returnees and displaced persons, and calls upon the international community, in the context of burden- and responsibility-sharing, to increase its material, financial and technical assistance in countries affected by refugees, returnees and displaced persons, to address simultaneously the inadequacies of existing assistance arrangements and to support initiatives in this regard;

12. *Reaffirms* that host States have the primary responsibility to ensure the civilian and humanitarian character of asylum, and calls upon States, in cooperation with international organizations, within their mandates, to take all necessary measures to ensure re-

spect for the principles of refugee protection and, in particular, to ensure that the civilian and humanitarian nature of refugee camps is not compromised by the presence or the activities of armed elements or used for purposes that are incompatible with their civilian character;

13. *Condemns* all acts that pose a threat to the personal security and well-being of refugees and asylumseekers, such as refoulement, unlawful expulsion and physical attacks, deplores, in particular, the armed attacks that took place in the Gatumba transit centre in Burundi in August 2004, calls upon States of refuge, in cooperation with international organizations, where appropriate, to take all necessary measures to ensure respect for the principles of refugee protection, including the humane treatment of asylum-seekers, notes with interest that the United Nations High Commissioner for Refugees has continued to take steps to encourage the development of measures to better ensure the civilian and humanitarian character of asylum, and encourages the High Commissioner to continue these efforts in consultation with States and other relevant actors;

14. *Deplores* the deaths, injuries and other forms of violence sustained by staff members of the Office of the High Commissioner and other humanitarian organizations, urges States, parties to conflict and all other relevant actors to take all necessary measures to protect activities related to humanitarian assistance, prevent attacks on and kidnapping of national and international humanitarian workers and ensure their safety and security, calls upon States to investigate fully any crime committed against humanitarian personnel and bring to justice the persons responsible for such crimes, and calls upon organizations and aid workers to abide by the national laws and regulations of the countries in which they operate;

15. *Calls upon* the Office of the High Commissioner, the African Union, subregional organizations and all African States, in conjunction with agencies of the United Nations system, intergovernmental and non-governmental organizations and the international community, to strengthen and revitalize existing partnerships and forge new ones in support of the international refugee protection system, and welcomes in this regard the High Commissioner joining the Joint United Nations Programme on HIV/AIDS in 2004 as a co-sponsor;

16. *Calls upon* the Office of the High Commissioner, the international community and other concerned entities to intensify their support to African Governments through appropriate capacity-building activities, including training of relevant officers, disseminating information about refugee instruments and principles, providing financial, technical and advisory services to accelerate the enactment or amendment and implementation of legislation relating to refugees, strengthening emergency response and enhancing capacities for the coordination of humanitarian activities, and welcomes in this regard the conclusion on international cooperation and burden- and responsibility-sharing in mass influx situations adopted by the Executive Committee of the Programme of the United Nations High Commissioner for Refugees at its fifty-fifth session;

17. *Reaffirms* the right of return and the principle of voluntary repatriation, appeals to countries of origin and countries of asylum to create conditions that are conducive to voluntary repatriation, and recognizes that, while voluntary repatriation remains the pre- eminent solution, local integration and thirdcountry resettlement, where appropriate and feasible, are also viable options for dealing with the situation of African refugees who, owing to prevailing circumstances in their respective countries of origin, are unable to return home;

18. *Notes with satisfaction* the voluntary return of thousands of refugees to their countries of origin, and welcomes in this regard the conclusion on legal safety issues in the context of voluntary repatriation of refugees adopted by the Executive Committee of the Programme of the United Nations High Commissioner for Refugees at its fifty-fifth session;

19. *Reaffirms* that voluntary repatriation should not necessarily be conditioned on the accomplishment of political solutions in the country of origin in order not to impede the exercise of the refugees' right to return, and recognizes that the voluntary repatriation and reintegration process is normally guided by the conditions in the country of origin, in particular that voluntary repatriation can be accomplished in conditions of safety and dignity;

20. *Welcomes* the development by the High Commissioner, in cooperation with other United Nations agencies and development actors, of the framework for durable solutions, aimed at promoting lasting solutions, particularly in protracted refugee situations, including the "4Rs" approach (repatriation, reintegration, rehabilitation and reconstruction) to sustainable return;

21. *Appeals* to the international community to respond positively, in the spirit of solidarity and burdenand responsibility-sharing, to the third-country resettlement needs of African refugees, and in this regard notes with interest the development of the Multilateral Framework of Understandings on the strategic use of resettlement in the context of the High Commissioner's Convention Plus initiative;

22. *Calls upon* the international donor community to provide financial and material assistance that allows for the implementation of community-based development programmes that benefit both refugees and host communities, as appropriate, in agreement with host countries and consistent with humanitarian objectives;

23. *Also calls upon* the international donor community to provide material and financial assistance for the implementation of programmes intended for the rehabilitation of the environment and infrastructure affected by refugees in countries of asylum;

24. *Urges* the international community, in the spirit of international solidarity and burden-sharing, to continue to fund generously the refugee programmes of the Office of the High Commissioner and, taking into account the substantially increased needs of programmes in Africa, to ensure that Africa receives a fair and equitable share of the resources designated for refugees;

25. *Expresses grave concern* about the plight of internally displaced persons in Africa, calls upon States to take concrete action to pre-empt internal displacement and to meet the protection and assistance needs of in-

ternally displaced persons, recalls in that regard the Guiding Principles on Internal Displacement, and urges the international community, led by relevant United Nations organizations, to contribute generously to national projects and programmes aimed at alleviating the plight of internally displaced persons;

26. *Invites* the Representative of the Secretary-General on the human rights of internally displaced persons to continue his ongoing dialogue with Member States and the intergovernmental and nongovernmental organizations concerned, in accordance with his mandate, and to include information thereon in his reports to the Commission on Human Rights and the General Assembly;

27. *Requests* the Secretary-General to submit a comprehensive report on assistance to refugees, returnees and displaced persons in Africa to the General Assembly at its sixtieth session, taking fully into account the efforts expended by countries of asylum, under the item entitled "Report of the United Nations High Commissioner for Refugees, questions relating to refugees, returnees and displaced persons and humanitarian questions", and to present an oral report to the Economic and Social Council at its substantive session of 2005.

The Americas

Notable developments in North America and the Caribbean during the year included the entry into force of the 2002 "safe third country" agreement (STCA) between Canada and the United States [YUN 2002, p. 1212], the implementation of which UNHCR was formally invited to monitor. In both countries, UNHCR remained active on the issue of access and undertook missions to various ports of entry, particularly land borders, which would be the focus of its monitoring role within the STCA framework. In Canada, the Office worked to ensure that asylum-seekers were guaranteed legal aid, advocated for the protection of victims of human smuggling and/or trafficking and intercepted persons, and helped resettle some 7,400 persons of concern. A major development in the region was the exodus of an estimated 2,500 to 3,000 Haitian refugees who fled the political violence sparked by the departure of President Jean-Bertrand Aristide (see p. 292). Most were intercepted and returned home by the United States Coast Guard. UNHCR assisted those who sought refuge in neighbouring islands, particularly Cuba and Jamaica. In another development, the United States reinvigorated its resettlement programme, admitting over 53,000 refugees during the year. However, concern about international terrorism and national security in the country resulted in consideration by the United States House of Representatives of asylum and immigration measures that would be detrimental to refugees and asylum-seekers. Policy changes were also expected in Canada, where UNHCR worked closely with the authorities to en-

sure that persons of concern were not adversely affected. In Central America and Mexico, which recorded 2,010 new refugee arrivals during the year, UNHCR assisted Belize, Costa Rica, El Salvador, Guatemala, Honduras, Mexico and Nicaragua to strengthen their national institutions to protect and assist asylum-seekers and refugees, with special attention to women and children, to manage fair and efficient refugee status determination procedures, to interpret international refugee law and to improve related national legal frameworks. UNHCR's direct assistance to refugees in the subregion included the provision of food, lodging and other necessities. A notable challenge in the subregion was irregular migration northwards through Mexico, forcing regional States to apply restrictive measures, which made the identificaton of asylum-seekers difficult. In South America, the conflict in Colombia led over half a million of its citizens to seek protection in neighbouring Ecuador (250,000), Costa Rica (50,000), Panama (100,000) and Venezuela (270,000). In all refugee-receiving countries, the Office helped to strengthen and increase access to national protection regimes and to improve refugees' self-reliance through community-based projects. It facilitated resettlement programmes in Brazil, Canada, Chile and the United States, promoted refugee education in Ecuador and Venezuela, and implemented refugee welfare pilot programmes on gender and age in a number of subregional States. Elsewhere in South America, UNHCR focused on intra-regional debates on migration and human rights and helped register and assist new arrivals of asylum-seekers, mostly in Argentina, Brazil and Chile. At events organized in collaboration with UNHCR to commemorate the twentieth anniversary of the Cartagena Declaration (Mexico City, 16 November), the Mexico Declaration and Plan of Action for strengthening the international protection of refugees in Latin America were adopted. Under the Plan of Action, resettlement programmes in Brazil and Chile were accelerated during the year. In a related development, the regional States established a common agenda on the development of refugee legislation, local integration and resettlement.

Total UNHCR expenditure in the Americas in 2004 was $28.5 million, for a population of concern numbering 2.4 million.

Asia and the Pacific and the Arab States

In 2004, UNHCR spent approximately $51 million on activities in Asia and the Pacific, for a total population of concern of 1.3 million. For operations in Central Asia, South-West Asia, North Africa and the Middle East, a total of $192.5 million was spent for a population of concern of 4.2 million.

South Asia

In late 2004, UNHCR responded, as part of the overall UN effort, to the devastation caused by the Indian Ocean tsunami (see p. 952) in Sri Lanka, Indonesia's Aceh province and Bangladesh, where the protracted nature of the operation resulted in increased security problems in the refugee camps, disrupting programme delivery. At the end of the year, some 20,300 refugees remained in two camps in Bangladesh, and UNHCR worked closely with WFP to assist them, as well as over 11,000 other Afghan and Myanmar refugees in India. In Nepal, where UNHCR had accorded a high priority to ending the protracted plight of Bhutanese refugees, not much progress was made in securing durable solutions, partly owing to security. In Sri Lanka, 33,700 IDPs were repatriated to their places of origin, relatively fewer than in previous years, owing to human rights violations and other protection problems. Durable solutions were yet to be found for another 353,000 IDPs and 61,000 refugees living in camps.

East Asia and the Pacific

In East Asia and the Pacific, UNHCR, in cooperation with the Government of Myanmar, gained access to the main areas of origin of 140,000 Myanmar refugees in Thailand and assisted the return of IDPs to those areas. In Malaysia, progress was made in protecting persons of concern through greater government involvement and increased public awareness and visibility of refugee issues. In other regional States, including Cambodia, China, Fiji, Indonesia, Mongolia, Papua New Guinea, the Republic of Korea, Thailand and Timor-Leste, the Office undertook a variety of activities to assist and protect refugees. Notably, it initiated a five-point plan in Indonesia to ensure the effective local integration of East Timorese remaining in the country, and assisted with the family reunification of over 2,350 formerly separated children and the local integration of another 1,100 children. UNHCR also strengthened mechanisms for addressing issues related to sexual and gender-based violence for refugees and asylum-seekers in the subregion. Operational challenges concerned the status of North Koreans seeking refuge and asylum in China, the lack of a legal framework in the Hong Kong region of China for determining asylum and refugee status, the lack of durable solutions for mandate refugees in Japan and strained relations with Viet Nam and Cambodia over asylum issues.

Central Asia, South-West Asia, North Africa and the Middle East

In Central Asia, UNHCR assisted Turkmenistan to initiate the registration of all refugees in the country, to be completed in 2005, including the estimated 12,100 Tajik and 1,000 Afghan refugees in the country. UNHCR planned to discuss with the Turkmenistan Government durable solutions for them. In Uzbekistan, the Office successfully implemented a project funded by the European Union (EU) to rehabilitate two border crossing points in the country, which subsequently led to an agreement by the EU on technical assistance to the Commonwealth of Independent States for funding a regional project to strengthen protection capacity and support asylum systems in the subregion. In other action, UNHCR undertook an initiative in Central Asia to assess refugee protection gaps and identify solutions thereto, for discussion at a regional conference of Central Asian Governments. During the year, 605 refugees were repatriated, including nationals of Turkmenistan (249), Kyrgyzstan (174), Uzbekistan (89), Tajikistan (66) and Kazakhstan (27). Local integration in Turkmenistan and Kyrgyzstan through citizenship was pursued on behalf of some 2,863 refugees, while resettlement, mostly in Canada and the United States, was sought for other refugees. Despite the progress made, operational challenges remained in efforts to strengthen asylum institutions and in achieving durable solutions. In South-West Asia, the repatriation programme for Afghan refugees, mostly from Iran and Pakistan, continued, facilitated by presidential elections in the country, the formation of the national army and police, accelerated demobilization and disarmament programmes and the strengthening of regional trade relations. Overall, approximately 761,000 Afghan refugees returned to their places of origin during the year. However, despite its relative economic and social recovery, conditions inside Afghanistan remained difficult, making the provision of incentives for voluntary repatriation a daunting task.

UNHCR's primary focus in North Africa remained the protracted plight of the Saharawi refugees in the Tindouf camps in Algeria, and while a political solution remained elusive, the Office continued to implement its basic humanitarian assistance activities for refugees. Owing to a marked increase in the mixed flow of asylum-seekers and economic migrants transiting through North Africa in an attempt to enter Europe illegally, the five countries of the Union of the Arab

Maghreb took measures to stem migratory flow through their territories. As many as 120,000 people, of whom 35,000 were of sub-Saharan origin, were estimated to have attempted to cross the Mediterranean during the year through unseaworthy vessels, which resulted in the drowning of some migrants. A strategy for addressing the phenomenon and for strengthening the institution of asylum were among UNHCR's concerns in the subregion, as was the fragility of the refugee protection framework in most of the subregional States.

In the Middle East, events in Iraq remained prominent in subregional operations. Although a small number of Iraqi refugees and IDPs had repatriated during the year, unfavourable conditions in parts of the country resulted in fresh outflows of thousands of other Iraqis, who fled mostly to Syria, Jordan and Lebanon. The outbreak of fighting in Yemen in the summer of 2004 between Government forces and dissidents displaced several thousand Yemeni nationals, even as thousands of other asylum-seekers and refugees from Ethiopia and Somalia continued to embark on risky sea journeys to Yemen. In Egypt, the refugee status determination of Sudanese asylum-seekers was suspended in June, in view of progress towards peace in southern Sudan. Some 4,000 of those refugees who had already been recognized were resettled in Australia, Canada, Finland and the United States. During the year, UNHCR piloted a project in Egypt, Jordan, Lebanon and Syria, aimed at enhancing a community development approach to protection and assistance operations for refugees, and at mainstreaming age and gender concerns in related activities.

Europe

In 2004, UNHCR's expenditure for activities in Europe totalled $114.2 million, for a population of concern numbering over 5 million. Nearly half of that amount ($52 million) was spent for approximately 1 million persons of concern in South-Eastern Europe.

Western, Central and Eastern Europe

In Western Europe, asylum claims continued to drop markedly, with the 25 EU countries receiving 19 per cent fewer claims than the 288,100 recorded in 2003 [YUN 2003, p. 1239]. The drop, however, was uneven in individual States, and in a number of cases, claims actually increased. In leading asylum destinations, including Germany, the Netherlands, the United Kingdom and Switzerland, claims declined by 30 per cent or more, while in other popular destinations, particularly

France, which received the highest number of asylum applications (61,600), a 3 per cent rise in claims was recorded. Applications also increased by some 4 per cent on average for the 10 new EU member States. The largest group of asylum-seekers (30,100) were nationals of the Russian Federation, of whom the majority were reportedly Chechens. Others came from Serbia and Montenegro, particularly the province of Kosovo (22,300); China (19,700); Turkey (16,200); and India (11,900). In April, the first phase of the EU asylum harmonization process was completed with a political agreement on asylum procedures, comprising the establishment of databases and regulations that were designed to determine which EU member State would be responsible for examining asylum applications in another member State and a number of other directives relating to key aspects of asylum/refugee status. In November, EU member States adopted the Hague Programme, which, among other things, set out the parameters for the second phase in developing a common asylum system. While endorsing the initiative, UNHCR encouraged the EU to develop appropriate systems of responsibility/burden sharing in addressing asylum claims and hoped that the special needs of refugees and other persons of concern would be taken into consideration. The Office continued to concentrate on protection and advocacy, focusing on monitoring and commenting on legislative proposals at the national and regional levels. The operational challenges it confronted included more restrictive asylum laws and policies in some regional States, despite the declining number of asylum claims; poor reception and prolonged detention of asylum-seekers; abuse of the asylum procedure; variations in refugee recognition among the regional States; and aspects of the first phase of EU harmonization of the asylum system which might lead to breaches of international law.

In Central Europe and the Baltic States, where asylum claims increased slightly to 43,390 from 43,370 in 2003, the experience of individual countries also differed sharply. Contrary to the situation of Cyprus, which saw a dramatic 124 per cent increase in applications, and of Poland and Slovakia, where significant increases had also occurred, the Czech Republic experienced a 52 per cent decline, while in Bulgaria, Hungary, Lithuania and Romania, asylum applications dropped by over 20 per cent. The Central European countries that acceded to the EU in May 2004 began to enhance their structures and capacities as destination countries for asylum-seekers. UNHCR made considerable progress in strengthening asylum procedures and enhancing relevant skills, which enabled more asylum-seekers to gain access to refugee status determination procedures and helped improve the quality of judicial reviews. Also, as a result of UNHCR's advocacy, NGOs and border guard agencies in 12 regional States were able to collaborate effectively, thereby enhancing their protection role and involvement in border monitoring. Despite the progress made, challenges remained, such as obstacles to the implementation of legislation by some regional States to enhance integration; the tenuous capacity of the new EU member States in the region to manage secondary movements and monitor irregular migration on the Union's eastern border; the tendency in some regional States to detain asylum-seekers; lengthy and cumbersome procedures in processing asylum claims; and the failure of some States to follow the legal procedure in determining the best interests of the child when assigning them to foster care.

In Eastern Europe, despite widespread violence and insecurity linked to the conflict in the Chechnya republic of the Russian Federation, some 19,000 Chechen IDPs returned to their homes during the year, while those left in Ingushetia moved closer to full integration. Other refugees repatriated from Ukraine, Belarus and the Republic of Moldova. Some 400 refugees found solutions through integration in Belarus, as did 255 others in Ukraine. In Georgia, where the international community continued to promote peace in its two breakaway provinces, UNHCR began verifying IDP registration to prepare for voluntary return programmes, should they become viable. The Office also helped to ensure more effective and targeted assistance to Chechen refugees in Georgia's Pankisi Valley region and assisted the displaced and other persons of concern in the Russian Federation's northern Caucasus, Azerbaijan, Armenia and the Republic of Moldova. In May, it held discussions with CIS members, and began a detailed gaps analysis to define areas where further action was needed. The *Söderköping process*—the regional cross-border cooperation mechanism managed jointly by UNHCR, IOM and the Swedish Migration Board—expanded its activities in helping regional States strengthen asylum, migration, protection and border management. However, ongoing conflicts, particularly in Georgia, and the

restructuring of refugee and asylum services in Belarus and Ukraine hampered asylum system development in those countries. An additional source of concern was UNHCR's lack of sufficient funds, which limited its capacity to assist IDPs, particularly in Azerbaijan.

South-Eastern Europe

In South-Eastern Europe, where progress was maintained in securing durable solutions in the Balkans, over 20,000 persons of concern, including 2,400 refugees from abroad, returned to their places of origin in Bosnia and Herzegovina, bringing to over 1 million the total number of those who had returned since the signing of the General Framework Agreement for Peace in Bosnia and Herzegovina [YUN 1995, p. 544]. Others returned to Croatia (over 7,400), Serbia and Montenegro (129) and The former Yugoslav Republic of Macedonia (725). UNHCR facilitated the return process, assisted the returnees, and helped to secure alternative options for durable solutions and to strengthen the regional asylum system. In Serbia and Montenegro, UNHCR enhanced its protection activities with the publication of a study, "Analysis of the situation of internally displaced persons from Kosovo: law and practice", which identified areas where action was needed to improve protection for IDPs. Another UNHCR publication facilitated asylum registration in the country. In Serbia itself, the Office helped the authorities provide alternative durable solutions to over 400 refugees and IDPs, and assisted with refugee registration, designed to review refugee status so as to reduce substantially the 275,000 refugees currently in the country. In the Serbian province of Kosovo, where the outbreak of inter-ethnic violence in March displaced some 4,200 ethnic minorities, UNHCR led efforts to provide emergency assistance to those affected. However, the violence and its aftermath, coupled with continuing uncertainties over Kosovo's future status (see p. 404), posed the greatest challenge to UNHCR's activities in Serbia and Montenegro and neighbouring countries, as they hampered minority returns, which fell to some 2,400 in 2004, from 3,800 in 2003. The prospects for finding durable solutions for displaced Kosovars in general were also diminished.

Chapter XIII

Health, food and nutrition

In 2004, the United Nations continued to promote human health, coordinate food aid and food security, and support research in nutrition.

By the end of the year, close to 40 million people were living with the human immunodeficiency virus (HIV) and approximately 3 million died as a result of acquired immune deficiency syndrome (AIDS)-related illnesses. The incidence of malaria showed no evidence of diminishing and tuberculosis infection rates were only reduced by a small margin in most parts of the world. Although stopping the spread of HIV/AIDS, malaria, tuberculosis and other major diseases received political and financial support from donors, annual funding remained short. In an effort to meet the UN Millenium Development Goal of halting and beginning to reverse the spread of HIV/AIDS by 2015, the General Assembly decided to hold a high-level meeting in June 2005 to examine constraints in realizing the commitments set out in the Declaration of Commitment on HIV/AIDS, which was adopted during its twenty-sixth special session in 2001 and served as a blueprint for global action against AIDS. The results of that meeting would, in turn, contribute to the review of progress on the United Nations Millennium Declaration, scheduled for the Assembly's sixtieth session in 2005. The Joint United Nations Programme on HIV/AIDS (UNAIDS), which continued to coordinate UN activities for AIDS prevention and control, sought to address the duplication of effort and fragmentation of resources through the "Three Ones" principle, adopted at a high-level meeting in Washington, D.C. By that principle, the donors gathered at the meeting agreed to coordinate their work, to promote a unified AIDS policy at the country level, and to seek a national evaluation system. The Economic and Social Council requested the United Nations Office of Drugs and Crime (UNODC) to guide Governments in dealing with HIV/AIDS in pre-trial and correctional facilities.

In support of the Decade to Roll Back Malaria in Developing Countries, Particularly in Africa, 2001-2010, the General Assembly called on the international community to commit funds to develop new anti-malarial medicines that were effective against resistant strains of malaria. The Assembly also called for improved global road safety and invited the World Health Organization (WHO) to coordinate road safety issues within the UN system. With regard to tobacco control, the fortieth instrument of ratification for the WHO Framework Convention on Tobacco Control, negotiated among WHO member States more than four years earlier, was deposited in November, enabling the treaty to enter into force in 2005.

The World Food Programme (WFP) delivered 50 per cent of the year's global food aid, reaching 113 million people in 80 countries. The Food and Agriculture Organization of the United Nations (FAO) continued efforts to implement the Plan of Action adopted at the 1996 World Food Summit, which called on the international community to fulfil the Summit's pledge to halve the number of hungry people by 2015, and cooperated with WHO, among others, to tackle the current outbreak of avian influenza.

Health

Follow-up to Millennium Summit

The Secretary-General, in response to General Assembly resolution 56/95 [YUN 2001, p. 1279], submitted in August [A/59/282 & Corr.1] the third annual report on progress achieved by the UN system and Member States in implementing the Millennium Development Goals (MDGs) [YUN 2000, p. 51]. With regard to progress in achieving the goal on health, specifically to halve by 2015 the number of new cases of certain diseases, the Secretary-General noted that the number of new HIV/AIDS infections was higher than ever before, raising concerns about development prospects in the affected regions. The prevalence of infection declined in countries where prevention, testing and control programmes had been adopted, notably in Uganda; nevertheless, interventions continued to fall short, particularly in sub-Saharan Africa. The incidence of malaria showed no evidence of diminishing, and once again, sub-Saharan Africa was the most affected area. Tuberculosis infection rates were also on the increase in that region, and they had only been reduced by a small margin in most other regions.

Global health was threatened by outbreaks of new and re-emerging diseases. To respond to such threats, WHO and UN partners worked with Governments, particularly in least developed countries, to improve the preparedness of national health systems through capacity-building, exchange of information, and building up laboratory and epidemiological capacity.

At the global level, new initiatives, such as the Global Outbreak Alert and the Response Network, established in 2000 by WHO, were bringing more than 120 partners together to provide timely, high-quality technical support. It had become clear that WHO International Health Regulations, which served as a global regulatory framework for addressing global health security and epidemic alert and response, needed to adapt to the health challenges of the twenty-first century.

Although stopping the spread of HIV/AIDS, malaria, tuberculosis and other major diseases had received greater political and financial support from donors, annual funding remained short of the estimated $12 billion needed in 2005, and the $20 billion for 2006. Though spending on HIV/AIDS more than doubled in 2003, national commitment remained inadequate to effect any major global success. The report also noted that in almost no country had the spread of HIV/AIDS been definitely stopped, and there was no region where HIV/AIDS was not a potential serious threat to the population.

GENERAL ASSEMBLY ACTION

On 23 November [meeting 60], the General Assembly adopted **resolution 59/27** [draft: A/59/L.30 & Add.1, orally revised] without vote [agenda item 55].

Enhancing capacity-building in global public health
The General Assembly,

Recalling the United Nations Millennium Declaration, adopted by Heads of State and Government at the Millennium Summit of the United Nations, and the development goals contained therein, in particular the health-related development goals, and its resolutions 55/162 of 14 December 2000, 56/95 of 14 December 2001, 57/144 of 16 December 2002 and 58/3 of 27 October 2003,

Recalling also World Health Assembly resolutions 48.13 of 12 May 1995, 54.14 of 21 May 2001 and 56.28 and 56.29 of 28 May 2003,

Taking note of the report of the Secretary-General on the implementation of the Millennium Declaration,

Recognizing that Member States have to strengthen their efforts to halt and begin to reverse, by 2015, the spread of HIV/AIDS and the incidence of malaria and other major diseases,

Reaffirming its Declaration of Commitment on HIV/AIDS,

Recognizing that the globalization of trade and increased international travel have increased the risk of a rapid worldwide spread of infectious diseases, posing new challenges to public health,

Noting with concern the deleterious impact on humankind of HIV/AIDS, tuberculosis, malaria and other major infectious diseases and epidemics, and the heavy disease burden borne by poor people, especially in developing countries, including the least developed countries, as well as countries with economies in transition, and in this regard noting with appreciation the work of the Joint United Nations Programme on HIV/AIDS, its co-sponsoring agencies and the Global Fund to Fight AIDS, Tuberculosis and Malaria, and the holding of the XV International AIDS Conference in Bangkok, from 11 to 16 July 2004, with the theme of "Access for all" in respect of people living with HIV/AIDS,

Also noting with concern the recent outbreak of avian influenza, recognizing its impact on human health as well as on the economy, and welcoming the Joint Ministerial Statement on the Current Poultry Disease Situation,

Welcoming the current success of the affected countries in combating the severe acute respiratory syndrome, which illustrates the importance of political commitment and strong leadership by affected countries and the role of the World Health Organization in controlling such epidemics, while mindful of the fact that the fight against new and re-emerging diseases such as the severe acute respiratory syndrome and avian influenza is far from over,

Noting new initiatives at the global level responding to public health threats, such as the Global Outbreak Alert and the Response Network, which brings together more than one hundred and twenty partners to provide timely and high-quality technical support,

Convinced that strengthening public health systems is critical to the development of all Member States, and that economic and social development are enhanced through measures that strengthen capacity-building in public health, including systems of prevention and of immunization against infectious diseases,

Emphasizing that Member States have primary responsibility for strengthening their capacity-building in public health to detect and respond rapidly to outbreaks of major infectious diseases, through the establishment and improvement of effective public health mechanisms, while recognizing that the magnitude of the necessary response may be beyond the capabilities of many developing countries,

Convinced that the control of outbreaks of diseases, particularly new diseases whose origins remain unknown, requires international and regional cooperation, and noting in this regard, inter alia, the holding of the fifty-fifth session of the World Health Organization Regional Committee for the Western Pacific in Shanghai, China, from 13 to 17 September 2004,

Recognizing the need for greater international and regional cooperation to meet new and existing challenges to public health, in particular in promoting effective measures such as safe, affordable and accessible vaccines, as well as assisting developing countries in securing vaccines against preventable infectious diseases and supporting the development of new vaccines,

Recognizing also the expertise of the World Health Organization and its role in, inter alia, coordinating actions with Member States in the areas of information exchange, personnel training, technical support, resource utilization, the improvement of global public health preparedness and response mechanisms and stimulating and advancing work on the prevention, control and eradication of epidemic, endemic and other diseases, as well as the work of the World Health Organization office dedicated to communicable disease surveillance and response,

Underscoring the continued importance of the International Health Regulations as an instrument for ensuring the maximum possible protection against the international spread of diseases with minimum interference in international traffic, and urging Member States to give high priority to the work on the revision of the Regulations,

Welcoming the efforts of the World Health Organization, in cooperation with Member States, the United Nations system, the Bretton Woods institutions, the private sector and civil society, in enhancing capacity-building in global public health and in promoting public health at the country level,

Welcoming also the Doha Declaration on the Agreement on Trade-Related Aspects of Intellectual Property Rights and Public Health, adopted on 14 November 2001, and noting the decision of the World Trade Organization General Council of 30 August 2003 on the implementation of paragraph 6 of the Declaration,

Recognizing the need to strengthen national health and social infrastructures to reinforce measures to eliminate discrimination in access to public health, information and education for all people, and especially for the most underserved and vulnerable groups,

1. *Urges* Member States to further integrate public health into their national economic and social development strategies, including through the establishment and improvement of effective public health mechanisms, in particular networks of disease surveillance, response, control, prevention, treatment and information exchange and the recruitment and training of national public health personnel;

2. *Calls upon* Member States and the international community to raise awareness of good public health practices, including through education and the mass media;

3. *Emphasizes* the importance of active international cooperation in the control of infectious diseases, based on the principles of mutual respect and equality, with a view to strengthening capacity-building in public health, especially in developing countries, including through the exchange of information and the sharing of experience, as well as research and training programmes focusing on surveillance, prevention, control, response, and care and treatment in respect of infectious diseases, and vaccines against them;

4. *Calls for* the improvement of the global public health preparedness and response systems, including systems of prevention and monitoring of infectious diseases, to better cope with major diseases, including in cases of global outbreaks of new diseases;

5. *Encourages* Member States to participate actively in the verification and validation of surveillance data and information concerning public health emergencies of international concern and, in close collaboration with the World Health Organization, to exchange information and experience in a timely and open manner on epidemics and the prevention and control of emerging and re-emerging infectious diseases that pose a risk to global public health;

6. *Invites* the regional commissions of the Economic and Social Council, as appropriate, to cooperate closely with Member States, the private sector and civil society, when requested, in their capacity-building in public health, as well as in regional cooperation to diminish and eliminate the deleterious impact of major infectious diseases;

7. *Encourages* Member States, as well as United Nations agencies, bodies, funds and programmes, in accordance with their respective mandates, to continue to address public health concerns in their development activities and programmes, and to actively support capacity-building in global public health and health-care institutions, such as through the provision of technical and other relevant assistance to the developing countries, as well as countries with economies in transition;

8. *Requests* the Secretary-General to include observations on the issue of enhancing capacity-building in global public health in his report on the follow-up to the outcome of the Millennium Summit of the United Nations to be submitted to the General Assembly at its sixtieth session.

AIDS prevention and control

Follow-up to the twenty-sixth special session

The Declaration of Commitment on HIV/AIDS, adopted at the twenty-sixth special session of the General Assembly by resolution S-26/2 [YUN 2001, p. 1126], called for an expanded global response to the epidemic and established time-bound targets relating to HIV/AIDS prevention, care and treatment, and impact alleviation for those made vulnerable by the disease. The special session's participants pledged to devote at least one full day of the Assembly's annual session to review progress on the Declaration's implementation. Accordingly, the fifty-eighth session of the General Assembly held a day-long, high-level review on 22 September 2003 [YUN 2003, p. 1244], and in resolution 58/236 [ibid., p. 1245], it requested the Secretary-General to report on progress. On 1 July 2004, the Assembly, in resolution 58/313 (below), decided that the next high-level review would be held on 2 June 2005.

GENERAL ASSEMBLY ACTION

On 1 July [meeting 92], the General Assembly adopted **resolution 58/313** [draft: A/58/L.65] without vote [agenda item 47].

Organizational arrangements for the high-level meeting to review the progress achieved in realizing the commitments set out in the Declaration of Commitment on HIV/AIDS

The General Assembly,

Recalling its resolution S-26/2 of 27 June 2001, entitled "Declaration of Commitment on HIV/AIDS", in which it decided to devote sufficient time and at least one full day of the annual session of the General Assembly to review and debate a report of the Secretary-General,

Bearing in mind that the Declaration of Commitment contains time-bound commitments to be met by 2005, and noting that more complete data on fulfilment of the 2005 targets will be available for comprehensive review in 2006,

Recalling that in its resolution 58/236 of 23 December 2003, entitled "Follow-up to the outcome of the twenty-sixth special session: implementation of the Declaration of Commitment on HIV/AIDS", the General Assembly decided to hold a high-level meeting in 2005 to review the progress achieved in realizing the commitments set out in the Declaration of Commitment, and decided also that the scheduling, format, participation, including civil society participation, and other organizational details would be further considered during the fifty-eighth session of the General Assembly,

Recalling also its resolution 58/291 of 6 May 2004 entitled "Follow-up to the outcome of the Millennium Summit and integrated and coordinated implementation of and follow-up to the outcomes of the major United Nations conferences and summits in the economic and social fields",

1. *Decides* that the high-level meeting to review the progress achieved in realizing the commitments set out in the Declaration of Commitment on HIV/AIDS will be convened on 2 June 2005 and will have a technical focus with the aim of identifying the level of progress achieved, problems and constraints facing the full realization of those commitments and the prospects for achieving them and for sharing best practices;

2. *Decides also* that the review will, inter alia, contribute to the high-level plenary meeting, to be held in New York at the commencement of the sixtieth session of the General Assembly in 2005, to undertake a comprehensive review of the progress made in the fulfilment of all the commitments contained in the United Nations Millennium Declaration, including the internationally agreed development goals and the global partnership required for their achievement, and of the progress made in the integrated and coordinated implementation of the major United Nations conferences and summits in the economic, social and related fields;

3. *Decides further* that the organizational arrangements for the high-level meeting will be as follows:

(*a*) The high-level meeting will comprise opening and closing plenary meetings and interactive round tables covering areas related to the implementation of the Declaration of Commitment, particularly prevention, treatment, care and support, human rights including gender, orphans and resources;

(*b*) The opening plenary meeting will set the stage for the subsequent discussions and feature statements by the President of the General Assembly, the Secretary-General and the Executive Director of the Joint United Nations Programme on HIV/AIDS;

(*c*) A representative nominated by each of the five regional groups will chair each round table, with the support of the executive heads of the co-sponsoring agencies of the Joint Programme;

(*d*) In addition to Member States, observers, representatives of the entities of the United Nations system, non-governmental organizations in consultative status with the Economic and Social Council and non-governmental members of the Programme Coordinating Board of the Joint Programme, invitations to the round tables will be extended to the Global Fund to Fight AIDS, Tuberculosis and Malaria and not more than fifteen civil society representatives of international, national or community organizations, including those representing and working for people living with HIV/AIDS, and the private sector, including pharmaceutical companies. The President of the General Assembly, following appropriate consultations with Member States, will draw up a list of those civil society representatives, on the basis of the recommendations of the Joint Programme and taking into account the principle of geographical representation, and will submit the list to Member States for consideration on a no-objection basis for a final decision by the Assembly on participation;

(*e*) In order to ensure interactive and substantive discussions of high quality, participation in each round table will be limited to a maximum of forty to forty-five participants;

(*f*) Every effort will be made to ensure equitable geographical representation in each round table, while taking into account the importance of ensuring a mix of countries in terms of size, HIV prevalence rates and levels of development;

(*g*) Participation of Member States and observers will be limited to one round table, and each Member State representative may be accompanied by two advisers;

(*h*) Participation by accredited and invited civil society representatives will be limited to one round table, and participation will not exceed five representatives in each round table;

(*i*) The Chairmen of the round tables will submit summaries to the President of the General Assembly reflecting the views expressed during the discussions;

(*j*) The President of the General Assembly will present the summaries of the round-table discussions to the closing plenary meeting, and they will be submitted to the 2005 high-level event planned in pursuance of resolution 58/291;

4. *Decides* that the arrangements outlined in paragraph 3 (*d*) above shall in no way create a precedent for other similar events;

5. *Decides also* that the President of the General Assembly, with support from the Joint United Nations Programme on HIV/AIDS and in consultation with Member States, will finalize the details and scheduling of the round tables, several of which are expected to take place concurrently, and any outstanding organizational matters.

On 23 December, the Assembly, by **decision 59/552**, decided that the item on the follow-up to the outcome of the twenty-sixth special session and implementation of the Declaration of Commitment on HIV/AIDS would remain for consideration at its resumed fifty-ninth (2005) session.

Global Media AIDS Initiative. More than 20 of the world's leading media executives and producers joined the Global Media AIDS Initiative (GMAI), launched by the Secretary-General on 15 January, with the goal of mobilizing the media around the world in the HIV/AIDS response. The UN Headquarters meeting was held by the Joint

United Nations Programme on HIV/AIDS (UNAIDS), the UN Department of Public Information and the Kaiser Family Foundation, with additional support from the Bill and Melinda Gates Foundation. Members of the Initiative made commitments to integrate HIV messaging into television programming, give air time and page space to the issue, put in place HIV policies and training for staff, and establish a formal corporate position on the commitments.

Fifteenth International AIDS Conference. On 13 July, GMAI was showcased at the International AIDS Society's Fifteenth International AIDS Conference (Bangkok, Thailand, 11-16 July), a biennial meeting organized in part by UNAIDS. Also at the Conference, the International Labour Organization (ILO) launched a report, "HIV/AIDS and work: Global estimates, impact and response 2004", to be issued biennially as part of its programme on HIV/AIDS and the world of work.

IASC Task Force. During the year, the Inter-Agency Standing Committee (IASC) Task Force on HIV/AIDS in Emergency Settings, formally established by the IASC working group in 2002 as a reference group [YUN 2002, p. 1220], published its guidelines for HIV/AIDS interventions in emergency situations. Designed to help Governments and cooperating agencies give the minimum required multisectoral response to HIV/AIDS during the early phase of an emergency situation, the guidelines contained a planning and response matrix incorporating various sectors: coordination; assessment and monitoring; protection; water and sanitation; food security and nutrition; shelter and site planning; health; education; communication behaviour change; and HIV/AIDS in the workplace. As a Task Force member, the United Nations Population Fund (UNFPA) collaborated in the development and field-testing of the guidelines.

Economic and Social Council. On 21 July, the Economic and Social Council, in **resolution 2004/35** (see p. 1137) on combating the spread of HIV/AIDS in criminal justice pre-trial and correctional facilities, requested UNODC to analyse the situation of HIV/AIDS in pre-trial and correctional facilities with a view to providing programmatic and policy guidance to Governments. Appropriate training for managers and wardens of pre-trial and correctional facilities was also suggested as part of the effort to combat the spread of the disease in those facilities.

Joint UN Programme on HIV/AIDS

UNAIDS, which became fully operational in 1996 [YUN 1996, p. 1121] and served as the main advocate for global action on HIV/AIDS, had ten co-

sponsors: UNFPA, UNODC, the United Nations Children's Fund (UNICEF), the United Nations Development Programme (UNDP), the United Nations Office of the High Commissioner for Refugees (UNHCR), ILO, the United Nations Educational, Scientific and Cultural Organization (UNESCO), the World Food Programme (WFP), the World Health Organization (WHO) and the World Bank. UNAIDS was mandated to lead, strengthen and support an expanded response to the epidemic, with the aim of preventing the transmission of HIV, providing care and support, reducing the vulnerability of individuals and communities to HIV/AIDS, and alleviating the impact of the epidemic.

Trends

According to UNAIDS, at the end of 2004, close to 40 million people were living with HIV and approximately 3 million died during the year as a result of AIDS-related illnesses. Of those with HIV, 37 million were adults and just over 2 million were children under the age of 15. The number of new infections during the year was estimated at 5 million.

The epidemic continued to expand in sub-Saharan Africa, where an estimated 3 million people became infected in 2004 and roughly 2 million Africans died of the disease. The number of people living with HIV in that region was estimated to be over 25 million. However, some countries in East Africa showed signs of declines in HIV infection levels, in particular Uganda, where national adult HIV prevalence fell from 13 per cent in the early 1990s to 4 per cent by the end of 2003. In Asia, roughly 1 million people became infected during 2004, and just over 8 million people were living with HIV. East Asia experienced the fastest-growing epidemic, mainly due to the high rate of infection in China, where the estimated number of people living with HIV— 840,000 in 2004—could grow to 10 million by 2010 if no immediate action was taken. India's national adult HIV prevalence rate was estimated at less than 1 per cent, or 5 million people. In Cambodia and Thailand, where large-scale prevention programmes had addressed sexual transmission of HIV, there were declining levels of new HIV infections. Although Oceania had low levels of infection, Papua New Guinea's high prevalence rate elicited concern; an estimated 16,000 out of 2.6 million adults were living with HIV at the beginning of the year. In the Middle East and North Africa, an estimated 92,000 people acquired the virus in 2004, bringing the total number of people living with HIV to 540,000. In Eastern Europe and Central Asia, 1.4 million people were living with HIV, of whom more than 80 per cent were under 30 years of age. An estimated 210,000 people became infected and 60,000 died of AIDS. In Latin America, around 1.7 million people were living with HIV, with 240,000 new infections and 95,000 deaths during the year. The Caribbean had the second highest rate of HIV prevalence among the world's regions, at 2.3 per cent, with 440,000 people living with the virus and some 53,000 newly infected.

In high-income countries—where 65,000 people became infected and an estimated 1.6 million people lived with HIV—antiretroviral therapy had reduced AIDS-related mortality and led to a decline in the number of reported deaths. Demographic data showed heterosexual transmission increasing sharply in those countries, coupled with a progressive shift of the epidemic into poorer and marginalized sectors of the community.

The growing feminization of AIDS continued in 2004, largely as a consequence of the low social, economic and legal status of women in many countries. While women made up 41 per cent of adults living with the virus in 1998, that number increased to 50 per cent during 2004. The ratio tilted further towards women in the Caribbean (52 per cent) and in Africa (58 per cent). Male-to-female transmission during sex was about twice as likely to occur as female-to-male. Among people younger than 24, girls and young women made up nearly two thirds of those living with HIV. Inadequate knowledge about AIDS, insufficient access to HIV prevention services, inability to negotiate safer sex, and a lack of female-controlled prevention methods, such as microbicides, heightened women's vulnerability to the virus.

UNAIDS activities

As a vehicle for addressing the growing feminization of the AIDS epidemic, UNAIDS launched the Global Coalition on Women and AIDS (2 February, London), a network of civil society groups, Governments, UN agencies and concerned citizens, to focus on HIV prevention for women and girls, promoting access to treatment and prevention, protecting women's property and inheritance rights, and reducing violence against women. The Coalition was highlighted in the Secretary-General's message on International Women's Day (8 March), which carried the theme "Women and HIV/AIDS".

UNAIDS, joined by UNICEF and WHO, organized a ministerial conference on "Breaking the Barriers—Partnership to Fight HIV/AIDS in Europe and Central Asia" (Dublin, Ireland, 23-24 February), which was co-hosted by Development Cooperation Ireland and Ireland's Department of Health and Children. Concerned about the high number of HIV infections in Europe and Central Asia, participants, in the conference's Dublin Declaration, agreed on ways to accelerate the implementation of the UN Declaration of Commitment on HIV/AIDS.

Two months later, UNAIDS, the United Kingdom and the United States co-hosted a high-level meeting (Washington, D.C., 25 April), at which key donors endorsed the "Three Ones"—a single strategy for planning and promoting three principles: *one* agreed HIV/AIDS action framework to coordinate the work of all partners; *one* national AIDS coordinating authority with a broad-based multisectoral mandate; and *one* agreed country-level monitoring and evaluation system. The intent was to optimize coordination, reduce duplication of effort, achieve the most efficient use of resources and ensure rapid action and results-based management.

At its fifteenth meeting, the UNAIDS Programme Coordinating Board (PCB) (Geneva, 23-24 June) [DP/2004/CRP.9] endorsed the UNAIDS decision to include activities of the "Three Ones" in the Programme's 2006-2007 unified budget and work plan [UNAIDS/PCB(15)/04.4]. The Board also supported UNAIDS' development of a revitalized prevention strategy, incorporating prevention, treatment and impact alleviation, in particular stigma and discrimination, with a clear link to sexual and reproductive health and basic health services. It agreed with the bid to include the UNAIDS Country Coordinator in the UN country team to implement joint programming. The Board urged UNAIDS to promote discussions within countries to propose legislation against discrimination, and to provide assistance to countries that wished to declare HIV and AIDS a health emergency. In addition, the Board supported UNAIDS efforts to strengthen policy work and country analysis generating aggregate indicators and plans to address the problems of insufficient institutional and human resources of countries to respond to the epidemic.

At its sixteenth meeting and thematic session (Montego Bay, Jamaica, 14-15 December) [DP/2005/40], the Board focused on the growth of the AIDS epidemic in the Caribbean; discussed the theme of women, gender and AIDS; and reviewed the unified budget and work plan. It urged UNAIDS to play a leading role in making the "Three Ones" a reality, and it requested UNAIDS to ensure that the prevention strategy was based on evidence, integrated with global and national prevention, care and treatment initiatives, and grounded in a human-rights approach that addressed the needs of those at risk of HIV exposure.

UNDP/UNFPA consideration. In following up key decisions taken at the fourteenth PCB meeting in June 2003 [YUN 2003, p. 1248], both UNDP [DP/2004/13] and UNFPA [DP/FPA/2004/5] issued reports on their responses and implementation of the PCB recommendations. UNDP described its interventions in the areas of technical support at the country level, financial and technical resources, addressing the feminization of the epidemic, HIV/AIDS and food insecurity, combating stigma and discrimination, development of country-level leadership, and support to vulnerable groups, among others. For its part, UNFPA reported on activities in the areas of improving focus at the country level, scaling up national responses, addressing the feminization of the disease, increased access to affordable preventive commodities, responding to the crisis in southern Africa, intensified action in Asia and the Pacific, tracking resource flows, accessing resources, and improving management and performance monitoring. The UNDP/UNFPA Executive Board, on 30 January [E/2004/35 (dec. 2004/5)], welcomed the UNDP and UNFPA reports as a step towards a more consistent UN system response to the pandemic and requested them to provide more detailed information in their annual reports on how the two organizations would act on the PCB recommendations.

Consequently, UNDP [DP/2004/CRP.9] and UNFPA [DP/FPA/2004/CRP.6] submitted further reports in September on implementing the PCB recommendations, providing details of their activities in numerous countries. UNDP, for example, described its leadership development programmes for action on the epidemic in Botswana, Cambodia, the Dominican Republic, Ethiopia, Ghana, Haiti, India, Malaysia, Nepal, South Africa, Senegal, Swaziland and Ukraine, and a regional leadership development programme for six Caribbean countries. In addressing the needs of women and girls, UNFPA, while supporting the ABC approach for HIV prevention—abstinence, be faithful and condom use—had found that it was not always a viable option, and it continued to strengthen national capacities to provide reproductive health services.

Taking note of the reports, the Executive Board, on 24 September [dec. 2004/40], urged the two agencies to continue to strengthen the UNAIDS partnership, especially at the country level, thereby contributing to a comprehensive response to HIV/AIDS. The agencies were also urged to ensure the inclusion of the UNAIDS country coordinator as a member of the UN country team and to develop an outcome-oriented format for their annual reports on HIV/AIDS activities to PCB, in cooperation with the UNAIDS secretariat and other co-sponsors. The Board recognized the importance of the "Three Ones" framework as a framework for coordinating the work of all partners.

HIV/AIDS and food security

The High-level Committee on Programmes (HLCP) of the United Nations System Chief Executives Board for Coordination (CEB), at its seventh session (Beirut, Lebanon, 26-27 February) [CEB/2004/4], discussed the UN system's response to the linked threats of HIV/AIDS, food security and governance. An ad hoc inter-agency task group led by UNAIDS and WFP had prepared a framework, endorsed by CEB at its September 2003 session [YUN 2003, p. 1250], to guide the response. The process was led by the United Nations Development Group (UNDG) in coordination with IASC and in consultation with the Regional Inter-Agency Coordination and Support Office. CEB called on its members to provide the necessary support to carry out the measures recommended by the task group.

The UNDG Chairman (also the Administrator of UNDP) continued to lead the process for ensuring implementation of the measures at the country level, especially through UN representatives in countries of the Southern African Development Community, where special focal points were established to work closely with UNAIDS and WFP. At UNDG's request, the twenty-third meeting of the UNAIDS Committee of Co-sponsoring Organizations (CCO) (Zambia, 1-4 March), attended by a wide group of UNDG members, discussed implementation, monitoring and follow-up. The CCO meeting endorsed UNDG instructions to the UN country teams, and began assessing the country teams' capacities to implement the recommendations. Joint missions would review CEB recommendations and decisions with all country teams and make proposals on how best to support them, including the mobilization of resources to meet capacity gaps, the development of reform pilot initiatives, and the organization of a Regional Director's meeting to report on progress.

At its eighth session (Florence, Italy, 15-17 September) [CEB/2004/7], HLCP noted the summary prepared by UNAIDS entitled "Review of the United Nations progress on the 'triple threat' of food insecurity, weakened capacities for governance and AIDS in eastern and southern Africa" [CEB/2004/HLCP/VIII/CRP.6/Add.3], as well as its update on the fifteenth International Conference on AIDS (Bangkok, Thailand, 11-16 July).

Tobacco

The World Health Assembly unanimously adopted the WHO Framework Convention on Tobacco Control (FCTC) in 2003 [YUN 2003, p. 1251], with WHO as the interim secretariat. Negotiated among WHO members States for over four years, the Convention committed States parties to eliminating tobacco advertising, promotion and sponsorship within five years; requiring warning labels on cigarette packs; prohibiting misleading tobacco product descriptors such as "light" and "mild"; and protecting non-smokers from tobacco smoke in public places. The Convention urged strict regulation of tobacco product contents, higher tobacco taxes, global coordination to fight tobacco smuggling, and promotion of tobacco prevention, cessation and research programmes. On 29 November 2004, Peru deposited the fortieth instrument of ratification, enabling the treaty to enter into force in February 2005. As at 31 December 2004, there were 49 parties to the Convention. Pursuant to a World Health Assembly resolution [WHA56.1], the first session of the Open-ended Intergovernmental Working Group on the Framework Convention took place in Geneva (21-25 June) to prepare for the first session of the Conference of the Parties (Geneva, 6-17 February 2006).

Ad Hoc Inter-Agency Task Force

In accordance with Economic and Social Council decision 2002/242 [YUN 2002, p. 1222], the Secretary-General submitted an April report [E/2004/55] on progress made by the Ad Hoc Inter-Agency Task Force on Tobacco Control, established under the leadership of WHO in 1999 [YUN 1999, p. 1151]. The report linked tobacco with the adverse impact on health, economic development, poverty, malnutrition, education and environment. It stressed that tobacco control should be recognized as a factor in poverty reduction and the achievement of the MDGs. Tobacco-related diseases had a negative impact on labour productivity, while illicit trade and aggressive marketing only led to increased production and consumption of tobacco products. The report recommended that UNDG nurture collaboration between Government agencies to implement the Framework Convention at the country level, and that tobacco control be included on the agendas of regional commissions.

At the sixth session (Geneva, 30 November) of the Task Force, co-hosted by ILO and WHO, participants discussed smoke-free workplaces, the illicit trade of tobacco products, the link between tobacco control and economic development, and

preparations for FCTC implementation in member countries.

ECONOMIC AND SOCIAL COUNCIL ACTION

On 23 July [meeting 51], the Economic and Social Council adopted **resolution 2004/62** [draft: E/2004/L.49] without vote [agenda item 7 (h)].

Tobacco control

The Economic and Social Council,

Noting with profound concern the escalation in smoking and other forms of tobacco use worldwide,

Recognizing the adverse impact of tobacco consumption on public health, as well as its social, economic and environmental consequences, including for efforts towards poverty alleviation,

Acknowledging that tobacco control at all levels, particularly in developing countries and in countries with economies in transition, requires financial and technical resources commensurate with the current and projected need for tobacco control activities,

Recognizing the need for strong political commitment, at all levels, for effective tobacco control, consistent with the provisions of the World Health Organization Framework Convention on Tobacco Control,

Mindful of the social and economic difficulties that tobacco control programmes may engender in the medium and long term in some developing countries and countries with economies in transition, and recognizing their need for technical and financial assistance in the context of nationally developed strategies for sustainable development,

Noting with appreciation the report of the Secretary-General on the activities of the Ad Hoc Inter-Agency Task Force on Tobacco Control,

Welcoming the adoption, by consensus, of the Framework Convention by the fifty-sixth World Health Assembly,

Emphasizing the need for the expeditious entry into force of the Framework Convention and its effective implementation,

1. *Calls upon* Member States that have not yet done so to consider ratifying, accepting, approving or acceding to the World Health Organization Framework Convention on Tobacco Control at the earliest opportunity, with a view to bringing it into force as soon as possible;

2. *Urges* Member States to strengthen tobacco control measures;

3. *Calls upon* the relevant United Nations agencies, funds and programmes, and invites other relevant international organizations, to continue to provide support for strengthening national and international tobacco control programmes;

4. *Requests* the Secretary-General to submit a report on the work of the Ad Hoc Inter-Agency Task Force on Tobacco Control to the Economic and Social Council at its substantive session of 2006.

Roll Back Malaria initiative

In an August report [A/59/261], the Secretary-General provided an update prepared by WHO of the implementation of General Assembly resolution 57/294 [YUN 2002, p. 1223] on the Decade to Roll Back Malaria in Developing Countries, Particularly in Africa (2001-2010), which was proclaimed by the Assembly in resolution 55/284 [YUN 2001, p. 1139]. The report analysed the problem of increased resistance to conventional anti-malarial medicines, discussed alternative treatments and the continuing effectiveness of insecticide-treated nets, and highlighted efforts to reduce the impact of malaria on pregnant women and infants through intermittent preventive treatments during pregnancy. While noting that WHO had recommended a change in the treatment policy for malaria, the report remarked on significant problems, mainly relating to the lack of resources that prevented the widespread use of newer, more effective treatments. Describing malaria as preventable, treatable and curable, the report called on the international community to expand access to new treatments for populations at risk of falciparum malaria in Africa, to support development of new medicines and insecticides for malaria control and to improve the monitoring of interventions.

The Roll Back Malaria Partnership (RBM), founded by WHO in 1998 [YUN 1998, p. 1384] with the goal of halving the world's malaria burden by 2010, was restructured in 2002 to include a Partnership Board, a secretariat and thematic working groups. The Board oversaw the work of RBM, and brought together parties at the country-level involved with scaling up malaria control efforts. The secretariat took charge of partnership development and networking, country support development, communication and advocacy, and resource mobilization and financing. Thematic groups were used to establish consensus on best practices for increasing use of insecticide-treated nets, malaria treatment during pregnancy, and other areas, while the Monitoring and Evaluation Reference Group—established in 2003 [YUN 2003, p. 1251] and co-chaired by WHO and UNICEF—developed a malaria indicator survey for use at the country level.

The report concluded that major advances in malaria control could be rapidly achieved in many countries using existing tools; however, more resources were required from Governments to achieve that end. For Africa alone, only one quarter of the $2 billion per year needed to combat malaria had been made available. The report recommended that the General Assembly call upon the international community to commit new funds and establish innovative financial and procurement mechanisms for the cause.

GENERAL ASSEMBLY ACTION

On 23 December [meeting 76], the General Assembly adopted **resolution 59/256** [draft: A/59/L.56 & Add.1] without vote [agenda item 46].

2001-2010: Decade to Roll Back Malaria in Developing Countries, Particularly in Africa

The General Assembly,

Recalling its resolutions 49/135 of 19 December 1994, 50/128 of 20 December 1995, 55/284 of 7 September 2001, 57/294 of 20 December 2002 and 58/237 of 23 December 2003 concerning the struggle against malaria in developing countries, particularly in Africa,

Bearing in mind the relevant resolutions of the Economic and Social Council relating to the struggle against malaria and diarrhoeal diseases, in particular resolution 1998/36 of 30 July 1998,

Taking note of the declarations and decisions on health issues adopted by the Organization of African Unity, in particular the declaration and plan of action on the "Roll Back Malaria" initiative adopted at the Extraordinary Summit of Heads of State and Government of the Organization of African Unity, held in Abuja on 24 and 25 April 2000, as well as decision AHG/Dec.155(XXXVI) concerning the implementation of that declaration and plan of action, adopted by the Assembly of Heads of State and Government of the Organization of African Unity at its thirty-sixth ordinary session, held in Lomé from 10 to 12 July 2000,

Also taking note of the Maputo Declaration on Malaria, HIV/AIDS, Tuberculosis and Other Related Infectious Diseases, adopted by the Assembly of the African Union at its second ordinary session, held in Maputo from 10 to 12 July 2003,

Recognizing the linkages in efforts being made to reach the targets set at the Abuja Summit as necessary and important for the attainment of the "Roll Back Malaria" goal and the targets of the United Nations Millennium Declaration by 2010 and 2015, respectively,

Also recognizing the urgent need for scaling up national malaria control programmes if African countries are to meet the intermediate target set by the Abuja Summit for the five-year period 2000-2005,

Further recognizing that malaria-related ill health and deaths throughout the world can be eliminated with political commitment and commensurate resources if the public is educated and sensitized about malaria and appropriate health services are made available, particularly in countries where the disease is endemic,

Emphasizing the importance of implementing the Millennium Declaration, and welcoming in this connection the commitment of Member States to respond to the specific needs of Africa,

Commending the efforts of the World Health Organization, the United Nations Children's Fund and other partners to fight malaria over the years, including the launching of the Roll Back Malaria Partnership in 1998,

1. *Takes note* of the note by the Secretary-General transmitting the report of the World Health Organization, and calls for support for the recommendations contained therein;

2. *Calls upon* the international community to continue to support the "Roll Back Malaria" partner organizations, including the World Health Organization and the United Nations Children's Fund, as vital com-

plementary sources of support for the efforts of malaria-endemic countries to combat the disease;

3. *Appeals* to the international community to ensure increased support for bilateral and multilateral assistance to combat malaria, including support for the Global Fund to Fight AIDS, Tuberculosis and Malaria, in order to assist in the development of sound national plans to control malaria in malaria-endemic countries and their implementation in a sustained and equitable way that, inter alia, contributes to health system development;

4. *Urges* malaria-endemic countries to increase domestic resource allocation to malaria control;

5. *Encourages* all African countries that have not yet done so to implement the recommendations of the Abuja Summit to reduce or waive taxes and tariffs for nets and other products needed for malaria control, both to reduce the price of nets to consumers and to stimulate free trade in insecticide-treated nets;

6. *Calls upon* malaria-endemic countries, in particular those in sub-Saharan Africa, to establish and strengthen policies and programmes to ensure a rapid scale-up in the coverage of insecticide-treated nets to at least 60 per cent of those at risk, wherever the use of such nets is the vector-control method of choice, by applying expeditious approaches, including targeted free or highly subsidized distribution to vulnerable groups;

7. *Expresses its concern* about the increase in resistant strains of malaria in several regions of the world;

8. *Encourages* all Member States experiencing resistance to conventional monotherapies to replace them with combination therapies, as recommended by the World Health Organization, in a timely manner;

9. *Recognizes* the importance of the development of effective vaccines and new medicines to prevent and treat malaria and the need for further and accelerated research, including through effective global partnerships such as the various malaria vaccine initiatives and the Medicines for Malaria Venture, where necessary stimulated by new incentives to secure their development;

10. *Reiterates* the need for expanded public-private partnerships for malaria control and prevention, and in this context urges petroleum companies operating in Africa to consider providing polymer for the manufacture of mosquito nets at reduced prices as a contribution to rolling back malaria in Africa;

11. *Calls upon* the international community to support investment in the development of new anti-malarial medicines and insecticides for the effective control of malaria in view of the challenging resistance of the parasite to anti-malarial medicines and the resistance of mosquitoes to insecticides;

12. *Also calls upon* the international community to support ways to expand access to artemisinin-based combination therapy for populations at risk of exposure to resistant strains of falciparum malaria in Africa, including the commitment of new funds, innovative mechanisms for the financing and national procurement of artemisinin-based combination therapy and the scaling up of artemisinin production to meet the increased need;

13. *Further calls upon* the international community to support coordinated efforts to improve surveillance, monitoring and evaluation systems so as to better track and report changes in the coverage of recommended "Roll Back Malaria" interventions and subsequent reductions in the burden of malaria;

14. *Requests* the Secretary-General, in close collaboration with the World Health Organization, the United Nations Children's Fund, developing countries and regional organizations, including the African Union, to conduct in 2005 an evaluation of the measures taken and progress made towards the achievement of the mid-term targets, the means of implementation provided by the international community in this regard and the overall goals of the Decade, and to report thereon to the General Assembly at its sixtieth session;

15. *Also requests* the Secretary-General to report to the General Assembly at its sixtieth session on the implementation of the present resolution under the agenda item entitled "2001-2010: Decade to Roll Back Malaria in Developing Countries, Particularly in Africa".

Access to medication

On 16 April [E/2004/23 (res. 2004/26)], the Commission on Human Rights, in a resolution on access to medication in the context of pandemics such as HIV/AIDS, tuberculosis and malaria, called on Governments to pursue policies to make pharmaceutical products and medical technologies for treating HIV/AIDS, tuberculosis and malaria available in sufficient quantities for all (see also p. 770). The Commission called upon Governments to refrain from denying or limiting equal access to such products or technologies, and urged them to consider adapting national laws in the light of the World Trade Organization's 2003 decision to support related aspects dealt with in the 2001 Doha Declaration on the Agreement on Trade-Related Aspects of Intellectual Property Rights and Public Health [YUN 2001, p. 1432].

Road safety

Pursuant to General Assembly resolution 57/309 [YUN 2003, p. 1257] on the global road safety crisis, WHO designated road safety as the theme of World Health Day 2004 (7 April), with the slogan "Road safety is no accident". At a World Health Day event in Paris, WHO and the World Bank launched a joint report entitled "World Report on Road Traffic Injury Prevention", highlighting recommendations proven to reduce road-related deaths, including setting and enforcing laws on seat-belts, child restraints, helmets and drunk driving, and promoting daytime running lights and improving road visibility. In addition to enacting laws and raising awareness, countries were urged to formulate policies promoting safer vehicles, traffic management and road design. The report estimated that road traffic crashes had cost $518 billion globally, and predicted that road traffic injuries would become the third largest contributor to the global burden of disease by 2020, putting a strain on health-care budgets worldwide.

Building on the events of World Health Day, and in accordance with resolution 58/9 [YUN 2003, p. 1258], the General Assembly held a plenary meeting on 14 April to raise awareness of the road traffic injury problem and its magnitude. It called for global road safety to be improved and invited WHO to coordinate road safety issues within the UN system (see below).

GENERAL ASSEMBLY ACTION

On 14 April [meeting 84], the General Assembly adopted **resolution 58/289** [draft: A/58/L.60/Rev.1] without vote [agenda item 160].

Improving global road safety

The General Assembly,

Recalling its resolutions 57/309 of 22 May 2003 and 58/9 of 5 November 2003,

Having considered the report of the Secretary-General on the global road safety crisis,

Noting the recommendation contained in the report of the Secretary-General that a coordinating body be identified within the United Nations system to provide support in this field and the recommendation that the United Nations regional commissions undertake certain activities,

Convinced that responsibility for road safety rests at the local, municipal and national levels,

Recognizing that many developing countries and countries with economies in transition have limited capacities to address these issues, and underlining, in this context, the importance of international cooperation towards further supporting the efforts of developing countries, in particular, to build capacities in the field of road safety, and of providing financial and technical support for their efforts,

Commending the initiative of the Government of France, the World Health Organization and the World Bank in launching the *World Report on Road Traffic Injury Prevention* in Paris on 7 April 2004, in observance of World Health Day, with the theme "Road safety is no accident", which contains a number of recommendations,

Also commending the United Nations regional commissions and their subsidiary bodies for responding to the above-mentioned resolutions and to the report of the Secretary-General,

1. *Takes note* of the recommendations contained in the *World Report on Road Traffic Injury Prevention*;

2. *Invites* the World Health Organization, working in close cooperation with the United Nations regional commissions, to act as a coordinator on road safety issues within the United Nations system;

3. *Requests* the Secretary-General, in submitting his report to the General Assembly at its sixtieth session in accordance with resolution 58/9, to draw upon the expertise of the United Nations regional commis-

sions, as well as the World Health Organization and the World Bank;

4. *Underlines* the need for the further strengthening of international cooperation, taking into account the needs of developing countries, to deal with issues of road safety.

To complement the General Assembly plenary session of 14 April, in which only Member States could participate, a stakeholders' forum was held at UN Headquarters (15 April) where over 100 participants spoke on multisectoral strategies to address the crisis, on behalf of numerous organizations, including public health, transportation and finance organizations; non-governmental organizations, advocacy groups and researchers; international organizations; and the private sector. A report documenting stakeholders' efforts to stimulate action on road safety, entitled "The Global Road Safety Crisis: We Should Do Much More", was submitted to the WHO Executive Director on 1 October.

Inter-agency coordination in health policy

The WHO/UNICEF/UNFPA Coordinating Committee on Health (CCH), established in 1997 [YUN 1997, p. 1255] to coordinate the three agencies' health policies, reported in January 2004 [DP/FPA/2004/CRP.1] to the UNDP/UNFPA Executive Board on its review of its current terms of reference, roles, functions and methods of work, in order to assess its relevance and value. The report outlined the changing dynamics of cooperation in health among the three agencies, highlighting in particular the reforms initiated by the Secretary-General and a range of new collaborative mechanisms used by the organizations at global and country levels. It explored the implications of those developments for the future of CCH in relation to its effectiveness and resource costs, and recommended that CCH be discontinued and that the secretariats of the three organizations continue to strengthen coordination.

On 30 January [E/2004/35 (dec. 2004/11)], the UNDP/UNFPA Executive Board endorsed the recommendation.

Food and agriculture

Food aid

World Food Programme

In July, the Economic and Social Council had before it two reports relating to the World Food Programme (WFP): the annual report of the WFP

Executive Director for 2003 [E/2004/14] and a report of the WFP Executive Board containing the decisions and recommendations of its 2003 sessions [E/2004/36]. By **decision 2004/232** of 12 July, the Council took note of those reports.

The WFP Executive Board decided on organizational and programme matters and approved a number of projects at its 2004 sessions [E/2005/36] held in Rome; first regular session (23-26 February), annual session (24-26 May), second regular session (26-27 May) and third regular session (11-14 October). In October, the Board approved the 2005-2006 provisional biennial work programme.

WFP activities

The WFP strategic plan (2004-2007) and biennial management plan (2004-2005), approved by the Board in October 2003 [YUN 2003, p. 1259], established 2004 as the initial year for the Programme to report on achievements under the new governance framework, making WFP's 2004 Annual Performance Report (APR) [WFP/EB.A/2005/4] a major accountability tool and the first to contain results-based reporting under new strategic and management priorities.

According to the 2004 APR, global food aid deliveries amounted to 7.5 million tons in 2004, a decrease of about 27 per cent from the 10.3 million tons delivered in 2003. By year's end, WFP delivered $2.9 billion worth of food aid to 113 million people in 80 countries. The year opened with WFP providing relief to thousands of earthquake victims in Bam, Iran, and as 2005 approached, it was responding to the needs in tsunami-ravaged areas throughout the Indian Ocean region. During the year, it responded to numerous challenges, including those in the Darfur region of the Sudan and Chad, bringing food aid to millions of people displaced by conflict, hunger and extreme poverty. Of the people aided by WFP in 2004, 89 million were women and children, including 8.7 million boys and 7.9 million girls assisted through school feeding programmes. Some 2.8 million beneficiaries were refugees and 6.9 million were internally displaced persons. Nearly 51 per cent of food aid deliveries went to sub-Saharan Africa, 26 per cent to South and East Asia, 9 per cent to Latin America and the Caribbean, 8 per cent to North Africa and the Middle East and 6 per cent to Europe and the Commonwealth of Independent States. Almost 84 per cent of WFP's food deliveries in 2004, excluding food provided for the Iraq bilateral operation, was directed to emergency and protracted relief and recovery operations. The ten largest relief operations delivered emergency food aid to 41 million people in Afghanistan,

Bangladesh, Burundi, the Democratic People's Republic of Korea (DPRK), Ethiopia, Indonesia, southern Africa, the Sudan, Uganda and the United Republic of Tanzania. In 21 of the 29 such operations, the prevalence of acute malnutrition declined, as did crude mortality rates in four of nine African operations.

Through its wider development operations to support longer term food security, WFP assisted 24 million people in 52 countries, of whom 94 per cent were in low income food deficit countries.

WFP operations helped to improve the nutrition and health of women, children and other vulnerable people. For example, the proportion of chronically malnourished or stunted children in the DPRK declined from 42 per cent in 2002 to 37 per cent in 2004, with acute malnutrition or wasting declining from 9 to 7 per cent. In Afghanistan, WFP treated nearly 4.5 million children in a de-worming campaign at 8,000 schools. WFP special operations, designed to enhance logistical coordination, provided support to 11 protracted relief and recovery operations and 16 emergency operations in 2004.

Administrative and financial matters

The Executive Boards of UNDP/UNFPA, UNICEF and WFP, at a joint meeting in New York (23-26 January), reviewed the implementation of the declaration adopted by UN regional directors at a meeting in Maputo, Mozambique (July 2003), to accelerate country and regional action on HIV/AIDS in Southern and Eastern Africa and implications for the different UN organizations. The Boards assessed progress on the simplification and harmonization process undertaken by UNDG in June 2002, reviewed the Resident Coordinator Assessment Centre and the function of the Resident Coordinator, and received a briefing on staff security and developments in the UN security management system.

At the World Leaders Meeting on Action Against Hunger and Poverty (New York, 20 September), attended by 50 heads of State and Government, WFP reviewed new ways to finance the fight against hunger and poverty.

Resources and financing

WFP operational expenditures for 2004 amounted to $2.9 billion, a decrease from the previous year's $3.3 billion [WFP/EB.A/2005/4]. Confirmed contributions in 2004 totalled $2.2 billion, also a decrease from the $2.6 billion received the year before. The United States continued to be the largest contributor, providing $1 billion to the Programme. Of the total contributed, $1.1 billion went to the International Emergency Food Reserve, $616 million to protracted relief and recovery operations, $276 million to development activities, $95 million to special operations and $25 million to the Immediate Response Account.

Food security

Follow-up to the 1996 World Food Summit

At its 2004 session in (Rome, 22-27 November) , the Council of the Food and Agriculture Organization of the United Nations (FAO) considered a report of the FAO Committee on World Food Security [CFS:2004/3-Rev.1] on the implementation of the Plan of Action adopted at the 1996 World Food Summit [YUN 1996, p. 1129]. The Plan of Action called on countries to halve the number of undernourished people by 2015. According to the report, in 1999-2001, the number of undernourished people in developing countries stood at 798 million—only 19 million below the 1990-1992 estimate. To achieve the 2015 goal, annual reductions of 26 million were required worldwide. While the number of undernourished declined in Asia and the Pacific and Latin America, undernourishment increased in sub-Saharan Africa, the Near East and North Africa. At the national level, the number of undernourished declined in only 19 countries and increased in 26 countries.

The Council agreed with the Committee's decision to hold a multi-stakeholder dialogue during its thirty-first session (2005) to prepare for a Special Forum in 2006 that would review implementation of the Plan of Action [CL 127/10]. It also adopted voluntary guidelines [CFS: 2004/6] developed by the Intergovernmental Working Group for the Elaboration of a Set of Voluntary Guidelines to Support the Progressive Realization of the Right to Adequate Food in the Context of National Food Security, established by the Council in 2002 [YUN 2002, p. 1225].

World Food Day. During the observance of World Food Day 2004 at FAO Headquarters (Rome, Italy, 15 October), which carried the theme "Biodiversity for Food Security", farmers spoke of their experience in enhancing biodiversity and increasing food production in a sustainable way. Addressing the meeting, the FAO Director-General remarked that as agricultural biodiversity declined, the food supply became more vulnerable. Agriculture was less able to adapt to environmental changes, such as global warming or the appearance of new pests and diseases. Farmers' rights to use genetic resources for food and agriculture, to be involved in policy discussions and decision-making, and to use, save,

sell and exchange seeds in accordance with national laws were recognized in the Treaty on Plant Genetic Resources for Food and Agriculture, which entered into force on 29 June. The Treaty was approved by FAO Conference resolution 3/2001, adopted in November 2001.

International Year of Rice (2004)

As part of the International Year of Rice 2004, declared by the General Assembly in resolution 57/162 [YUN 2002, p. 1226], FAO convened a two-day international rice conference (Rome, 12-13 February), where experts discussed the challenges faced in the global market for rice and in sustainable rice-based production systems. The strategy of the Year of Rice was to use the Year as a catalyst for country-driven programmes throughout the world. FAO projections showed that, by 2030, total demand for rice would be 38 per cent higher than that of the years 1997 to 1999. More than 50 per cent of the 840 million people suffering from chronic hunger lived in areas dependent on rice production for food, income and employment, while more than 2 billion people in developing nations depended on the rice-based system for their economic livelihood. Because rice did not contain all the elements of a balanced diet, rice producers were encouraged to intensify their system of rice production and their capacity to raise fish and livestock.

Avian influenza

According to FAO, an outbreak of avian influenza occurred in Asia in 2003 and continued in 2004. As a result of the outbreak, FAO estimated that around 20-25 million birds had been culled in the region as at the end of January 2004. That figure accounted for less than one per cent of the region's total inventories. The impact was potentially devastating to local economies and to both commercial poultry operations and small farmers, particularly in Thailand, where the industry was heavily reliant on trade. In 2003, poultry exports from Thailand accounted for nearly 7 per cent of global poultry meat trade, with an export value of approximately $1 billion.

Particularly concerned over the outbreak of avian influenza in East Asia, FAO issued a joint statement with WHO and the World Organization for Animal Health (OIE) in January calling for international collaboration to fight the disease, including a targeted poultry vaccination campaign in affected countries. An agreement to strengthen cooperation in tackling transboundary animal diseases was signed by the FAO and OIE in May. In 2004, FAO provided $1.6 million in emergency assistance to Cambodia, Laos, Pakistan and Viet

Nam to combat avian influenza. Research showed that avian influenza viruses did not normally infect species other than birds and pigs, but there were some cases of infection of humans.

Nutrition

Standing Committee on Nutrition

The United Nations System Standing Committee on Nutrition (SCN), at its thirty-first session (New York, 22-26 March), held a symposium on "Nutrition and the Millennium Development Goals", at which participants discussed the links between nutrition and human rights, economics, the environment and health. A presentation on SCN's *Fifth Report on the World Nutrition Situation* summarized nutrition trends and described how health sector reform, poverty reduction, trade liberalization and governance could become more effective with attention to nutrition. The Committee reviewed reports of working groups on breastfeeding and complementary feeding; capacity development in food and nutrition; household food security; nutrition and HIV/AIDS; nutrition in emergencies; nutrition, ethics and human rights; micronutrients; nutrition of school-age children; and nutrition throughout the life-cycle.

UNU Activities

The United Nations University Food and Nutrition Programme for Human and Social Development (UNU-FNP) assisted developing regions to enhance individual, organizational and institutional capacity, carried out coordinated global research activities and served as the academic arm for the UN system in areas of food and nutrition that were best addressed in a non-regulatory, non-normative environment.

In 2004, UNU-FNP worked with WHO to develop new growth standards for infants and young children in a six-year project backed by a $6.5 million grant from the Bill and Melinda Gates Foundation. The project would use growth and development data gathered from a study of 8,500 children in Brazil, Ghana, India, Norway, Oman and the United States. The standards would enable researchers to recognize when children were becoming under-nourished or overweight, assess their motor development and track progress in reaching a range of health and social equity goals. The 99 countries that currently used the international references were expected to begin using the new standards by 2010, with help from the project.

Under the University's capacity development programme, plans to provide leadership training for mid-career professionals were discussed at a July meeting of the Middle East Capacity Development Task Force in Cairo, Egypt. Regional task forces in leadership training exercises for food and nutrition professionals were also held in Africa and Latin America. During the year, 50 former fellows of UNU-FNP met at the congress of the Latin American Nutrition Society in Acapulco, Mexico (November) and decided to provide capacity-building assistance to the Nutrition Institute of Central America and Panama in Guatemala, established in 1949.

Cooperation between UNU and FAO in nutrition data management continued with a three-week course on production and the use of food composition data in nutrition (Beijing, China, October-November). Five fellows began a year-long training programme in food science and technology organized by UNU at the National Food Research Institute in Tsukuba, Japan; five others completed their training and received grants to return to their home countries for follow-up research projects. UNU continued its quarterly publication of the *Food and Nutrition Bulletin* and the *Journal of Food Composition and Analysis*.

Chapter XIV

International drug control

During 2004, the United Nations, through the Commission on Narcotic Drugs, the International Narcotics Control Board (INCB) and the United Nations Office on Drugs and Crime (UNODC), reaffirmed its commitment to strengthen international cooperation and increase efforts to counter the world drug problem. UN system drug control activities focused mainly on carrying out the 1999 Action Plan for the Implementation of the Declaration on the Guiding Principles of Drug Demand Reduction, which served as a guide for Member States in adopting strategies and programmes for reducing illicit drug demand in order to achieve significant results by 2008.

UNODC continued to promote the mainstreaming of drug control matters into the work of UN organizations, strengthen the international drug control system and support the international community in achieving the objectives and measures adopted by the General Assembly at its twentieth special session on the world drug problem, held in 1998. In 2004, the Office assisted States in complying with international drug control treaties and supported INCB in monitoring their implementation. It also helped States in establishing new law enforcement mechanisms and national drug abuse information systems and in improving data collection and analysis. Its integrated portfolio of global programmes and regional and country projects included legislative and capacity-building assistance in addressing problems involving drugs, crime, corruption and terrorism. Focusing its work on the area of sustainable livelihoods, it promoted best practices in alternative development and supported projects in key illicit drug production areas.

The Commission on Narcotic Drugs—the main UN policy-making body dealing with drug control—recommended a number of draft resolutions to the Economic and Social Council and adopted resolutions on demand reduction and the prevention of drug abuse, illicit drug trafficking and supply, regional cooperation and strengthening UN international drug control machinery. In July, the Council urged Governments to continue contributing to the maintenance of a balance between the licit supply of and demand for opiate raw materials for medical and scientific needs. It requested Member States to develop programmes to reduce the illicit supply of and demand for amphetamine-type stimulants, and called on the international community to enhance support to Afghanistan in the implementation of its drug control strategy. The Council requested UNODC to support the strengthening of strategies for the eradication of cannabis crops, and to assist countries emerging from conflict in their drug control efforts.

INCB analysed the interaction between illicit drug supply and demand, emphasizing the need for a balanced and integrated approach. It continued to oversee the implementation of the three major international drug control conventions, analyse the drug situation worldwide and draw Governments' attention to weaknesses in national control and treaty compliance, making suggestions and recommendations for improvements at the national and international levels.

Follow-up to the twentieth special session

In response to General Assembly resolution 58/141 [YUN 2003, p. 1263], the Secretary-General, in a July report [A/59/188], gave an overview of the implementation of mandates relating to international drug control, in particular the outcome of the Assembly's twentieth special session on countering the world drug problem [YUN 1998, p. 1135], and the Action Plan for the Implementation of the Declaration on the Guiding Principles of Drug Demand Reduction, adopted by the Assembly in resolution 54/132 [YUN 1999, p. 1157]. The report reviewed the follow-up by the Commission on Narcotic Drugs; demand reduction; the Action Plan against Illicit Manufacture, Trafficking and Abuse of Amphetamine-type Stimulants and Their Precursors, adopted by Assembly resolution S-20/4 A [YUN 1998, p. 1139]; judicial and law enforcement cooperation; countering money-laundering; and illicit crop eradication and alternative development. The Secretary-General also reported on action taken by the UN system, including UNODC organizational arrangements, promulgated in March 2004.

The Secretary-General concluded that the results achieved so far in implementing the outcome of the Assembly's twentieth special session had been mixed and he appealed to Member States to strengthen their efforts in that regard. He called on relevant UN entities, other international organizations and financial institutions to mainstream drug control issues into their programmes.

On 18 and 19 March [E/2004/28 & Corr.1], the Commission on Narcotic Drugs considered the agenda item on follow-up to the twentieth special session: general overview and progress achieved by Governments in meeting the goals and targets for the years 2003 and 2008 set out in the Political Declaration adopted by the Assembly at that session.

GENERAL ASSEMBLY ACTION

On 20 December [meeting 74], the General Assembly, on the recommendation of the Third (Social, Humanitarian and Cultural) Committee [A/59/495], adopted **resolution 59/163** without vote [agenda item 97].

International cooperation against the world drug problem

The General Assembly,

Recalling the United Nations Millennium Declaration, its resolution 58/141 of 22 December 2003 and its other previous resolutions,

Reaffirming its commitment to the outcome of the twentieth special session of the General Assembly, devoted to countering the world drug problem together, held in New York from 8 to 10 June 1998, and welcoming the continuing determination of Governments to overcome the world drug problem by a full and balanced application of national, regional and international strategies to reduce the demand for, production of and trafficking in illicit drugs,

Reaffirming the importance of the commitments of Member States in meeting the objectives targeted for 2003 and 2008, as set out in the Political Declaration adopted by the General Assembly at the twentieth special session, and welcoming the guidelines and elements recommended by the Commission on Narcotic Drugs to the Executive Director of the United Nations International Drug Control Programme for the preparation of subsequent reports on the follow-up to the twentieth special session,

Emphasizing the importance of the Action Plan for the Implementation of the Declaration on the Guiding Principles of Drug Demand Reduction, which introduces a new global approach balanced between illicit supply and demand reduction, under the principle of shared responsibility, and of the Action Plan on International Cooperation on the Eradication of Illicit Drug Crops and on Alternative Development, which recognizes the importance of supply reduction as an integral part of a balanced drug control strategy,

Recognizing the efforts of all countries, in particular those that produce narcotic drugs for scientific and medical purposes, and of the International Narcotics Control Board in preventing the diversion of such substances to illicit markets and in maintaining production at a level consistent with licit demand, in line with the Single Convention on Narcotic Drugs of 1961 and the Convention on Psychotropic Substances of 1971,

Aware that progress has been uneven in meeting the goals set in the Political Declaration, as also reflected in the biennial reports of the Executive Director of the United Nations Office on Drugs and Crime, and recognizing that the drug problem is still a global challenge that constitutes a serious threat to public health and safety and the well-being of humankind, in particular children and young people, and that it undermines socio-economic and political stability and sustainable development, including efforts to reduce poverty, and causes violence and crime, including in urban areas,

Concerned by the increase in the abuse of illicit drugs among children, including adolescents, and young people,

Concerned also by the challenges posed by links between the spread of HIV/AIDS and injecting drug use,

Concerned further by the serious challenges and threats posed by the continuing links between illicit drug trafficking and terrorism and other national and transnational criminal activities, such as trafficking in human beings, especially women and children, money-laundering, corruption, trafficking in arms and trafficking in chemical precursors, and reaffirming that strong and effective international cooperation is needed to counter these threats,

Concerned about policies and activities in favour of the legalization of illicit narcotic drugs and psychotropic substances that are not in accordance with the international drug control treaties and that might jeopardize the international drug control regime,

Concerned also by the increase in the diversion of chemical precursors used in the illicit manufacture of drugs,

Acknowledging that international cooperation in countering drug abuse and illicit production and trafficking has shown that positive results can be achieved through sustained and collective efforts, and expressing its appreciation for the initiatives in this regard,

I

Respect for the principles enshrined in the Charter of the United Nations and international law in countering the world drug problem

1. *Reaffirms* that countering the world drug problem is a common and shared responsibility that must be addressed in a multilateral setting, requires an integrated and balanced approach, and must be carried out in full conformity with the purposes and principles of the Charter of the United Nations and international law, and in particular with full respect for the sovereignty and territorial integrity of States, the principle of non-intervention in the internal affairs of States and all human rights and fundamental freedoms, and on the basis of the principles of equal rights and mutual respect;

2. *Urges* all States to ratify or accede to, and States parties to implement all the provisions of, the Single Convention on Narcotic Drugs of 1961 as amended by the 1972 Protocol, the Convention on Psychotropic

Substances of 1971 and the United Nations Convention against Illicit Traffic in Narcotic Drugs and Psychotropic Substances of 1988;

3. *Invites* all States, as a matter of priority, to sign, ratify or accede to, and States parties to implement, the United Nations Convention against Transnational Organized Crime and the Protocols thereto and the United Nations Convention against Corruption, in order to counter comprehensively the transnational criminal activities that are related to illicit drug trafficking;

II

International cooperation to counter the world drug problem and follow-up to the twentieth special session

1. *Reaffirms* the Joint Ministerial Statement and further measures to implement the action plans emanating from the twentieth special session of the General Assembly, adopted during the ministerial segment of the forty-sixth session of the Commission on Narcotic Drugs, which emphasizes that the world drug problem must be addressed in multilateral, regional, bilateral and national settings and that, in order to succeed, action to counter it has to involve all Member States, that action must be supported by strong international and development cooperation and must be further included in national development priorities, and that it requires a balance between supply reduction and demand reduction, as well as a comprehensive strategy that combines alternative development, including, as appropriate, preventive alternative development, eradication, interdiction, law enforcement, prevention, treatment and rehabilitation as well as education;

2. *Calls upon* all States to strengthen their efforts in the fight against the world drug problem, in order to achieve the objectives targeted for 2008 in the Political Declaration adopted by the General Assembly at the twentieth special session;

3. *Calls upon* all relevant actors to continue their close cooperation with Governments in promoting and implementing the outcome of the twentieth special session and the ministerial segment of the forty-sixth session of the Commission on Narcotic Drugs;

4. *Stresses* that data collection, analysis and evaluation of the results of ongoing national and international policies are essential tools for further developing sound, evidence-based drug control strategies;

Demand reduction

5. *Urges* all Member States to implement the Action Plan for the Implementation of the Declaration on the Guiding Principles of Drug Demand Reduction and to strengthen their national efforts to counter the abuse of illicit drugs in their population, in particular among children and young people;

6. *Urges* States, in order to achieve a significant and measurable reduction of drug abuse by 2008:

(a) To further implement comprehensive demand reduction policies and programmes, including research, covering all the drugs under international control, in order to raise public awareness of the drug problem, paying special attention to prevention and education and providing, especially to young people and others at risk, information on developing life skills, making healthy choices and engaging in drug-free activities;

(b) To further develop and implement comprehensive demand reduction policies, including risk reduction activities, that are in line with sound medical practice and the international drug control treaties and that reduce the adverse health and social consequences of drug abuse, and to provide a wide range of comprehensive services for the treatment, rehabilitation and social reintegration of drug abusers, with appropriate resources being devoted to such services, since social exclusion constitutes an important risk factor for drug abuse;

(c) To enhance early intervention programmes that dissuade children and young people from using illicit drugs, including polydrug use and the recreational use of substances such as cannabis and synthetic drugs, especially amphetamine-type stimulants, and to encourage the active participation of the younger generation in campaigns against drug abuse;

(d) To provide a comprehensive range of services for preventing the transmission of HIV/AIDS and other infectious diseases associated with drug abuse, including education, counselling and drug abuse treatment, and in particular to assist developing countries in their efforts to deal with these issues;

Illicit synthetic drugs

7. *Urges* States to renew their efforts, at the national, regional and international levels, to implement the comprehensive measures covered in the Action Plan against Illicit Manufacture, Trafficking and Abuse of Amphetamine-type Stimulants and Their Precursors, to make special efforts to counter the abuse and recreational use of amphetamine-type stimulants, especially by young people, and to disseminate information on the adverse health, social and economic consequences of such abuse;

Control of substances

8. *Encourages* States to establish or strengthen mechanisms and procedures to ensure strict control of substances that are listed in the international drug treaties and are used to manufacture illicit drugs of natural and synthetic origin, and to support international operations aimed at preventing their diversion, including through coordination and cooperation between regulatory and enforcement services involved in their control;

Control of precursors

9. *Encourages* States to establish or strengthen mechanisms and procedures to ensure strict control of chemical precursors used to manufacture illicit drugs, to support international operations aimed at preventing the diversion of chemical precursors, including through coordination and cooperation between regulatory and enforcement services involved in precursor control, in cooperation with the International Narcotics Control Board, and to counter smuggling networks effectively, inter alia, by conducting backtracking law enforcement investigations;

Judicial cooperation

10. *Calls upon* all States to strengthen international cooperation among judicial and law enforcement authorities at all levels in order to prevent and combat illicit drug trafficking and to share and promote best

operational practices in order to interdict illicit drug trafficking, including by establishing and strengthening regional mechanisms, providing technical assistance and establishing effective methods for cooperation, in particular in the areas of air, maritime, port and border control and in the implementation of extradition treaties;

Countering money-laundering

11. *Urges* States to strengthen action, in particular international cooperation and technical assistance aimed at preventing and combating the laundering of proceeds derived from drug trafficking and related criminal activities, with the support of the United Nations system, international institutions such as the World Bank and regional development banks, to develop and strengthen comprehensive international regimes to combat money-laundering, and to improve information-sharing among financial institutions and agencies in charge of preventing and detecting the laundering of those proceeds;

12. *Calls upon* States to consider including provisions in their national drug control plans for the establishment of national networks to enhance their respective capabilities to prevent, monitor, control and suppress serious offences connected with money-laundering and the financing of terrorist acts, and in general to counter all acts of transnational organized crime, and to supplement existing regional and international networks dealing with money-laundering;

International cooperation in illicit crop eradication and alternative development

13. *Recognizes* the efforts made by States to implement innovative alternative programmes, inter alia, in reforestation, agriculture and small and medium enterprise, and stresses the importance of the United Nations system and the international community contributing to the economic and social development of the communities that benefit from such programmes;

14. *Calls upon* States, where appropriate:

(a) To enhance support, including, where appropriate, through the provision of new and additional financial resources, for alternative development, environmental protection and eradication programmes undertaken by countries affected by the illicit cultivation of cannabis, especially in Africa, of opium poppy and of coca bush, in particular national programmes that seek to reduce social marginalization and promote sustainable economic development;

(b) To enhance joint strategies, through international and regional cooperation, to strengthen, including by training, education and providing technical assistance, alternative development, eradication and interdiction capacity, with the aim of eliminating illicit crop cultivation and fostering economic and social development;

(c) To encourage international cooperation, including, as appropriate, preventive alternative development, to prevent illicit crop cultivation from emerging in or being relocated to other areas;

(d) To provide, in accordance with the principle of shared responsibility, greater access to their markets for products of alternative development programmes, which are necessary for the creation of employment and the eradication of poverty;

(e) To establish or reinforce, where appropriate, national mechanisms to monitor and verify illicit crops;

(f) To continue to contribute to the maintenance of a balance between the licit supply of and demand for opiate raw materials used for medical and scientific purposes and to cooperate in preventing the proliferation of sources of production of opiate raw materials;

(g) To share their experience, expertise and best practices in the eradication of illicit drug crops and the implementation of alternative development programmes with affected States;

15. *Calls upon* the international community to enhance financial and technical support for Afghanistan in order to enable the Government to implement successfully its national drug control strategy;

III

Action by the United Nations system

1. *Emphasizes* that the multidimensional nature of the world drug problem calls for the promotion of integration and coordination of drug control activities throughout the United Nations system, including in the follow-up to major United Nations conferences, as well as in other relevant multilateral institutions and organizations;

2. *Reaffirms its resolve* to continue to strengthen the United Nations machinery for international drug control, in particular the Commission on Narcotic Drugs, the United Nations International Drug Control Programme and the International Narcotics Control Board, in order to enable them to fulfil their mandates, bearing in mind the recommendations contained in Economic and Social Council resolution 1999/30 of 28 July 1999 and the measures taken and recommendations adopted by the Commission on Narcotic Drugs at its forty-fourth, forty-fifth, forty-sixth and forty-seventh sessions, aimed at the enhancement of its functioning;

3. *Encourages* the Commission on Narcotic Drugs, as the global coordinating body in international drug control and as the governing body of the United Nations International Drug Control Programme, and the International Narcotics Control Board to continue their useful work on the control of precursors and other chemicals used in the illicit manufacture of narcotic drugs and psychotropic substances;

4. *Notes* that the International Narcotics Control Board needs sufficient resources to carry out all its mandates, including those that will enable it to perform effectively its task within the framework of Operation Purple, Operation Topaz and Project Prism, and therefore urges Member States to commit themselves in a common effort to assigning adequate and sufficient budgetary resources to the Board, in accordance with Economic and Social Council resolution 1996/20 of 23 July 1996, emphasizes the need to maintain its capacity, inter alia, through the provision of appropriate means by the Secretary-General and adequate technical support by the United Nations International Drug Control Programme, and calls for enhanced cooperation and understanding between Member States and the Board in order to enable it to implement all its mandates under the international drug control conventions;

5. *Welcomes* the efforts of the United Nations Office on Drugs and Crime to implement its mandate, and requests the Office to continue:

(a) To strengthen dialogue with Member States and also to ensure continued improvement in management, so as to contribute to enhanced and sustainable programme delivery and further encourage the Executive Director to maximize the effectiveness of the drug programme of the United Nations Office on Drugs and Crime, inter alia, through the full implementation of Commission on Narcotic Drugs resolutions, in particular the recommendations contained therein;

(b) To strengthen cooperation with Member States and with United Nations programmes, funds and relevant agencies, as well as relevant regional organizations and agencies and non-governmental organizations, and to provide, on request, assistance in implementing the outcome of the twentieth special session;

(c) To increase its assistance, within the available voluntary resources, to countries that are deploying efforts to reduce illicit crop cultivation by, in particular, adopting alternative development programmes, and to explore new and innovative funding mechanisms;

(d) To allocate, while keeping the balance between supply and demand reduction programmes, adequate resources to allow it to fulfil its role in the implementation of the Action Plan for the Implementation of the Declaration on the Guiding Principles of Drug Demand Reduction, and support countries, upon their request, to further develop and implement drug demand reduction policies;

(e) To develop action-oriented strategies to assist Member States to implement the Action Plan for the Implementation of the Declaration, and to report to the Commission on Narcotic Drugs at its forty-eighth session on the follow-up to the Action Plan;

(f) To strengthen dialogue and cooperation with multilateral development banks and with international financial institutions so that they may undertake lending and programming activities related to drug control in interested and affected countries to implement the outcome of the twentieth special session, and to keep the Commission on Narcotic Drugs informed of further progress made in this area;

(g) To take into account the outcome of the twentieth special session, to include in its report on the illicit traffic in drugs an updated, objective and comprehensive assessment of worldwide trends in illicit traffic and transit in narcotic drugs and psychotropic substances, including methods and routes used, and to recommend ways and means of improving the capacity of States along those routes to address all aspects of the drug problem;

(h) To publish the *World Drug Report*, with comprehensive and balanced information about the world drug problem, and to seek additional extrabudgetary resources for its publication in all the official languages;

(i) To provide technical assistance, from available voluntary contributions for that purpose, to those States identified by relevant international bodies as the most affected by the transit of drugs, in particular developing countries in need of such assistance and support;

(j) To provide assistance, at the request of States and respecting fully their sovereignty and territorial integrity, and with the support of the United Nations

Office for Outer Space Affairs and the European Space Agency, among others, in detecting on time the emergence or relocation of illicit crop cultivation;

6. *Welcomes also* the follow-up, led by the United Nations Office on Drugs and Crime, to the 2003 Paris Conference on Drug Routes from Central Asia to Europe (the Paris Pact), and encourages the Office and other relevant international institutions to continue their efforts;

7. *Welcomes further* the decision of the Commission on Narcotic Drugs, at its forty-seventh session, to select the topic "Preventing HIV/AIDS and other blood-borne diseases in the context of drug abuse prevention" as part of the thematic debate of its forty-eighth session, in 2005;

8. *Requests* the United Nations Office on Drugs and Crime, subject to the availability of resources and the Commission on Narcotic Drugs guidelines for the use of general-purpose funds, together with international financial institutions and the organizations involved in preventing and suppressing money-laundering and drug trafficking, to facilitate the provision of training and advice through technical cooperation in States, when requested, taking into account, inter alia, the recommendations on money-laundering and the financing of terrorism formulated by the Financial Action Task Force on Money Laundering and its regional groups;

9. *Urges* all Governments to provide the fullest possible financial and political support to the United Nations International Drug Control Programme by widening its donor base and increasing voluntary contributions, in particular general-purpose contributions, to enable it to continue, expand and strengthen its operational and technical cooperation activities, and recommends that a sufficient share of the regular budget of the United Nations be allocated to the Programme to enable it to fulfil its mandates and to work towards securing assured and predictable funding;

10. *Encourages* the meetings of Heads of National Drug Law Enforcement Agencies and of the Subcommission on Illicit Drug Traffic and Related Matters in the Near and Middle East of the Commission on Narcotic Drugs to continue to contribute to the strengthening of regional and international cooperation, taking into account the outcome of the twentieth special session and the ministerial segment of the forty-sixth session of the Commission;

11. *Calls upon* the relevant United Nations agencies and entities, other international organizations and international financial institutions, including regional development banks, to mainstream drug control issues into their programmes, and calls upon the United Nations Office on Drugs and Crime to maintain its leading role by providing relevant information and technical assistance;

12. *Takes note* of the report of the Secretary-General, and, taking into account the promotion of integrated reporting, requests the Secretary-General to submit to the General Assembly at its sixtieth session a report on the implementation of the present resolution.

Conventions

International efforts to control narcotic drugs were governed by three global conventions: the 1961 Single Convention on Narcotic Drugs [YUN 1961, p. 382], which, with some exceptions of detail, replaced earlier narcotics treaties and was amended by the 1972 Protocol [YUN 1972, p. 397] to strengthen the role of the International Narcotics Control Board (INCB); the 1971 Convention on Psychotropic Substances [YUN 1971, p. 380]; and the 1988 United Nations Convention against Illicit Traffic in Narcotic Drugs and Psychotropic Substances [YUN 1988, p. 690].

As at 31 December 2004, 176 States were parties to the 1961 Convention, as amended by the 1972 Protocol. During the year, the Congo acceded to the Convention.

The number of parties to the 1971 Convention stood at 175 as at 31 December 2004, with the accession of the Congo during the year.

At year's end, 170 States and the European Community were parties to the 1988 Convention, with the Congo, the Lao People's Democratic Republic and Micronesia acceding in 2004.

Commission action. At its forty-seventh session in March [E/2004/28 & Corr.1], the Commission on Narcotic Drugs reviewed implementation of the international drug control treaties. It had before it the INCB report covering 2003 activities [YUN 2003, p. 1270] and the 2003 INCB technical report on the implementation of article 12 of the 1988 Convention entitled "Precursors and Chemicals Frequently Used in the Illicit Manufacture of Narcotic Drugs and Psychotropic Substances" [Sales No. E.04.XI.4].

The Commission welcomed INCB efforts to promote the global balance between the supply of and demand for opiates used for medical and scientific purposes, as required under the 1961 Convention as amended by the 1972 Protocol, and called on States to contribute to the maintenance of that balance and to cooperate in preventing the proliferation of sources of production of opiate raw materials. Concerned over the large number of Internet pharmacies trafficking in internationally controlled drugs, the Commission encouraged Governments to take action against them. It stressed the importance of adherence to and full implementation of the provisions of the international drug control treaties, and encouraged Member States to provide technical assistance to other Governments to strengthen the required regulatory controls. Regarding implementation of article 12 of the 1988 Convention, the Commission acknowledged the success

achieved under Operation Purple, Operation Topaz and Project Prism (see, p. 1237), but was concerned that, without additional resources, the Board would have to curtail its involvement in those operations. It agreed that the General Assembly should be requested to provide those resources. Noting that Governments continued to implement and update legislation relating to the control of precursor chemicals, the Commission emphasized the need for mechanisms to monitor both imports to and exports from national territories, and called on countries to establish networks among Governments and within countries to respond quickly to, and exchange information on, cross-border smuggling. The Commission noted that, in specific regions, pharmaceutical preparations were increasingly diverted from licit trade for use in the illicit manufacture of amphetamine-type stimulants, and called on Governments to introduce mechanisms to prevent the diversions of pharmaceutical preparations from international trade and from domestic distribution channels.

INCB action. In its report covering 2004 [Sales No. E.05.XI.3], INCB called on States that had not done so to become parties to the 1961 Convention and to accede to or ratify the 1972 Protocol amending it. The Board urged States concerned to implement the 1971 Convention and become parties without delay, as well as the 1988 Convention to implement the provisions of article 12. It noted that, with the exception of Switzerland, all States that were major manufacturers, exporters and importers of scheduled chemicals were parties to the 1988 Convention.

ECONOMIC AND SOCIAL COUNCIL ACTION

On 21 July [meeting 47], the Economic and Social Council, on the recommendation of the Commission on Narcotic Drugs [E/2004/28 & Corr.1], adopted **resolution 2004/43** without vote [agenda item 14 *(d)*].

Demand for and supply of opiates used to meet medical and scientific needs

The Economic and Social Council,

Recalling its resolution 2003/40 of 22 July 2003 and previous relevant resolutions,

Emphasizing that the need to balance the global licit supply of opiates against the legitimate demand for opiates used to meet medical and scientific needs is central to the international strategy and policy of drug control,

Noting the fundamental need for international cooperation with the traditional and established supplier countries in drug control to ensure the universal application of the provisions of the Single Convention on Narcotic Drugs of 1961 and that Convention as amended by the 1972 Protocol,

Reiterating that a balance between consumption and production of opiate raw materials was achieved in the past as a result of efforts made by the two traditional supplier countries, India and Turkey, together with other producer countries,

Expressing deep concern at the continued increase in the global production of opiate raw materials and the significant accumulation of stocks over the past few years as a consequence of the operation of market forces, which is causing a mismatch and is now upsetting the delicate balance between the licit supply of and demand for opiates used to meet medical and scientific needs,

Emphasizing the importance of adhering to the estimates furnished to and confirmed by the International Narcotics Control Board on the extent of cultivation and production of opiate raw materials, particularly in view of the current oversupply,

Recalling the Joint Ministerial Statement adopted during the ministerial segment of the forty-sixth session of the Commission on Narcotic Drugs, in which ministers and other government representatives called upon States to continue to contribute to the maintenance of a balance between the licit supply of and demand for opiate raw materials used for medical and scientific purposes and to cooperate in preventing the proliferation of sources of production of opiate raw materials,

Reiterating the importance of medically appropriate use of opiates in pain relief therapy as advocated by the World Health Organization,

Noting that countries differ significantly in their level of consumption of narcotic drugs and that in most developing countries the use of narcotic drugs for medical purposes has remained at an extremely low level,

1. *Urges* all Governments to continue to contribute to maintaining a balance between the licit supply of and demand for opiate raw materials used to meet medical and scientific needs, the achievement of which would be facilitated by maintaining, insofar as their constitutional and legal systems permit, support to the traditional and established supplier countries, and to cooperate in preventing the proliferation of sources of production of opiate raw materials;

2. *Urges* the Governments of all producer countries to adhere strictly to the provisions of the Single Convention on Narcotic Drugs of 1961 and that Convention as amended by the 1972 Protocol and to take effective measures to prevent the illicit production or diversion of opiate raw materials to illicit channels, especially when increasing licit production, invites the relevant Governments to contribute to the study being carried out by the International Narcotics Control Board on the relative merits of different methods of producing opiate raw materials, and encourages producer countries to adopt best practices in the cultivation and production of opiate raw materials;

3. *Urges* the Governments of consumer countries to assess their licit needs for opiate raw materials realistically and to communicate those needs to the International Narcotics Control Board in order to ensure easy supply, calls upon all Governments of countries producing opium poppy to limit the cultivation of opium poppy, taking into account the current level of global stocks, to the estimates furnished to and confirmed by the Board, in accordance with the requirements of the Single Convention on Narcotic Drugs of 1961, and calls

upon producer countries, in providing estimates of such cultivation, to consider the specific demand requirements of consumer countries;

4. *Urges* the Governments of all countries where, in the past, opium poppy has not been cultivated for the licit production of opiate raw materials, in the spirit of collective responsibility, to refrain from engaging in the commercial cultivation of opium poppy in order to avoid the proliferation of supply sites;

5. *Commends* the International Narcotics Control Board for its efforts in monitoring the implementation of the relevant Economic and Social Council resolutions and, in particular:

(a) In urging the Governments concerned to adjust global production of opiate raw materials to a level corresponding to actual licit needs and to avoid unforeseen imbalances between the licit supply of and demand for opiates caused by the exportation of products manufactured from seized and confiscated drugs;

(b) In inviting the Governments concerned to ensure that opiates imported into their countries for medical and scientific use do not originate in countries that transform seized and confiscated drugs into licit opiates;

(c) In arranging informal meetings, during sessions of the Commission on Narcotic Drugs, with the main States that import and produce opiate raw materials;

6. *Requests* the International Narcotics Control Board to continue its efforts in monitoring the implementation of the relevant Economic and Social Council resolutions in full compliance with the Single Convention on Narcotic Drugs of 1961 and that Convention as amended by the 1972 Protocol;

7. *Requests* the Secretary-General to transmit the text of the present resolution to all Governments for consideration and implementation and to report on the implementation of the resolution to the Commission on Narcotic Drugs at its forty-eighth session.

On the same date [meeting 47], the Council, on the recommendation of the Commission [E/2004/28 & Corr.1], adopted **resolution 2004/38** without vote [agenda item 14 (d)].

Follow-up on strengthening the systems of control over chemical precursors and preventing their diversion and trafficking

The Economic and Social Council,

Recommends to the General Assembly the adoption of the following draft resolution:

[For text, see General Assembly resolution 59/162 below.]

GENERAL ASSEMBLY ACTION

On 20 December [meeting 74], the General Assembly, on the recommendation of the Third Committee [A/59/495], adopted **resolution 59/162** without vote [agenda item 97].

Follow-up on strengthening the systems of control over chemical precursors and preventing their diversion and trafficking

The General Assembly,

Concerned about the continued diversion and misuse of precursors and the fact that, despite efforts undertaken by all States, including the producing, exporting, importing and transit States, chemical substances are increasingly feeding the manufacture of illicit drugs of natural or synthetic origin, a problem that deserves the utmost attention of all States,

Recalling the Political Declaration adopted by the General Assembly at its twentieth special session, devoted to countering the world drug problem together, in which Member States decided to establish 2008 as a target date for States to eliminate or considerably reduce the diversion of precursors,

Recalling also the Joint Ministerial Statement and further measures to implement the action plans emanating from the twentieth special session of the General Assembly, adopted during the ministerial segment of the forty-sixth session of the Commission on Narcotic Drugs,

Stressing the importance of Economic and Social Council resolutions 2003/32 and 2003/35 of 22 July 2003 on training in precursor control, countering money-laundering and drug abuse prevention, and on strengthening the prevention and suppression of illicit drug trafficking,

Recalling article 12, paragraphs 1, 9 *(c)* and 10, of the United Nations Convention against Illicit Traffic in Narcotic Drugs and Psychotropic Substances of 1988,

Reaffirming the importance of using all available legal means or measures to prevent the diversion of chemicals from legitimate trade to illicit drug manufacture as an essential component of comprehensive strategies against drug abuse and trafficking and of preventing access to chemical precursors by those engaged in or attempting to engage in the processing of illicit drugs,

Reiterating the importance of the effective and real-time exchange of information relating to the interdiction, diversion and suspected diversion of precursors, as an essential component of strategies to facilitate comprehensive investigations into cases relating to such diversion, including the identification of the modus operandi and entities involved and the initiation of appropriate legal action,

Encouraging Member States to conduct backtracking law enforcement investigations in order to counter organized smuggling networks effectively,

Also encouraging Member States to facilitate the exchange of information between the relevant agencies in order to identify the sources of seized precursor chemicals and those responsible for the shipping and diversion of those substances and to identify the sources of pharmaceutical preparations misused for illicit drug manufacture,

Noting that links are increasingly being uncovered between the smuggling of drugs and the smuggling of precursor chemicals, including the use of similar modi operandi to conceal consignments in order to avoid detection,

Welcoming with satisfaction the results achieved so far under Operation Purple and Operation Topaz and the new initiative called Project Prism, which were launched by the International Narcotics Control Board, in cooperation with Member States, to enhance controls over chemicals used in the illicit manufacture of cocaine, heroin and amphetamine-type stimulants respectively,

Concerned that, without additional resources, the International Narcotics Control Board will not be able to carry out its important functions under the above-mentioned operations,

1. *Urges* all Member States to put in place systems and procedures to ensure that the details of any interdiction, seizure, diversion or attempted diversion of precursors are communicated expeditiously to all Governments concerned and the International Narcotics Control Board and, insofar as possible, share relevant information so that methods frequently used for national and international trafficking in chemicals may be identified, pursuant to article 12 of the United Nations Convention against Illicit Traffic in Narcotic Drugs and Psychotropic Substances of 1988;

2. *Reiterates* the importance of applying the know-your-customer principle referred to in Economic and Social Council resolution 2003/39 of 22 July 2003, and stresses the necessity of strengthening the use of the mechanism of pre-export notifications, including by providing timely responses, especially through the efficient sharing of information;

3. *Invites* those States which do not have mechanisms to enable the real-time exchange of information under the current international operations to consider establishing a national focal point or central national authority in line with the standard operating procedures of the international operations, through which all information on licit and illicit consignments can be channelled, and invites all Member States to contribute to updating the directory of competent national authorities under the international drug control treaties, with a view to implementing article 12 of the 1988 Convention;

4. *Recommends* that Member States develop or further adapt, where necessary, their regulatory and operational control procedures to counter the diversion of chemical substances into illicit drug production or manufacture, and encourages authorities to initiate or further strengthen coordination and cooperation between all regulatory and enforcement services involved in precursor control;

5. *Invites* Member States and appropriate international and regional bodies to review intelligence on the smuggling of drugs and the smuggling of precursor chemicals, in order to identify common links and to plan appropriate operations to stop such activities;

6. *Encourages* Member States to ensure that stopped diversion attempts receive the same investigative attention that would be afforded to a seizure of the same substance, since such cases could provide valuable intelligence that could prevent diversions elsewhere;

7. *Emphasizes* the need to ensure that adequate mechanisms are in place, where necessary and to the extent possible, to prevent the diversion of preparations containing chemicals listed in tables I and II of the 1988 Convention, pertaining to illicit drug manufacture, in particular those containing ephedrine and pseudoephedrine;

8. *Encourages* Member States, in order to counter smuggling networks effectively, to conduct backtracking law enforcement investigations and, where appropriate, to identify the source of the seized chemical precursors and those responsible for the consignment and ultimately the diversion;

9. *Also encourages* Member States to investigate the possibility of establishing operational chemical profiling programmes, and invites all States to support, to the extent possible, such programmes;

10. *Requests* the International Narcotics Control Board, pursuant to Economic and Social Council reso-

lution 1995/20 of 24 July 1995, to monitor international trade so that diversion attempts can be identified, preventing chemical precursors from reaching the illicit market;

11. *Urges* the International Narcotics Control Board to continue to follow up all such cases of diversion by facilitating investigations by national authorities and to make its findings available to Governments through its annual report;

12. *Requests* the Secretary-General to provide the necessary resources to the International Narcotics Control Board to enable it to continue its work effectively under Operation Purple, Operation Topaz and Project Prism;

13. *Requests* the Executive Director of the United Nations Office on Drugs and Crime, within the framework of his biennial reports on the implementation of the outcome of the twentieth special session of the General Assembly and taking into account the relevant resolutions adopted on the subject since the special session, to include in his report on the control of precursors, starting with his report to be submitted to the Commission on Narcotic Drugs at its forty-eighth session, recommendations on how to strengthen the use of the pre-export notification mechanism and ensure timely responses.

Internet drug sales

On 21 July [meeting 47], the Economic and Social Council, on the recommendation of the Commission on Narcotic Drugs [E/2004/28 & Corr.1], adopted **resolution 2004/42** without vote [agenda item 14 (d)].

Sale of internationally controlled licit drugs to individuals via the Internet

The Economic and Social Council,

Recognizing that unauthorized trade in internationally controlled licit drugs ordered via the Internet has reached epidemic proportions,

Strongly suggesting that Member States prohibit the international sale of internationally controlled licit drugs via the Internet and that, when permitted, the sale of such drugs via the Internet within their national borders be strictly regulated, while acknowledging that some Member States already have laws that preclude the sale of internationally controlled substances via the Internet,

Aware that the non-prescribed or falsely prescribed use of internationally controlled licit drugs constitutes a serious risk to public health and that such use is facilitated by the Internet,

Noting that the Commission on Narcotic Drugs, in its resolution 43/8 of 15 March 2000, encouraged Member States to consider taking measures to prevent the diversion of internationally controlled licit drugs via the Internet,

Noting also that the Secretary-General submitted to the Commission on Crime Prevention and Criminal Justice at its eleventh session a report on effective measures to prevent and control computer-related crime, in which he recognized the use of online pharmacies to procure internationally controlled licit drugs without medical supervision as an emerging problem for law enforcement, regulatory and health authorities,

Further noting the frequent calls made by the International Narcotics Control Board in 2001, 2002 and 2003 for Governments to take measures to prevent the misuse of the Internet for the illegal offer, sale and distribution of internationally controlled licit drugs,

Recognizing that the procurement of internationally controlled licit drugs over the Internet is illegal in all cases when an international treaty or national legislation is contravened,

Recalling the successes that have been realized in the control of domestic and international diversion of licit pharmaceuticals, pursuant to the provisions of the relevant conventions,

1. *Encourages* Member States to consider new means and strategies to establish avenues of cooperation in order to prohibit the international offering and acquisition by individuals of internationally controlled licit drugs acquired illegally over the Internet;

2. *Calls upon* Member States to enforce, as appropriate, the provisions of article 30 of the Single Convention on Narcotic Drugs of 1961 and article 10 of the Convention on Psychotropic Substances of 1971 as they apply to pharmacies within their territory, specifically with regard to the need:

(a) To license those that distribute internationally controlled licit drugs via the Internet and to require them to disclose information regarding the identity of the parties responsible and their legal location;

(b) To actively pursue those that are in violation of the importing and exporting provisions of those conventions;

3. *Urges* Member States to develop, as appropriate, well-coordinated and focused policies to identify and take appropriate measures to terminate Internet sites used to offer internationally controlled licit drugs in an unauthorized way, through greater coordination between the judicial, police, postal, customs and other competent agencies;

4. *Encourages* Member States to enact or, where appropriate, to enhance sanctions or penalties for providing internationally controlled licit drugs over the Internet without a valid prescription within their national borders;

5. *Also encourages* Member States to identify those who operate web sites that illegally offer internationally controlled licit drugs by, for example, seeking the cooperation and support of Internet service providers;

6. *Encourages* Member States that do not have laws that preclude trade in internationally controlled licit drugs via the Internet to establish, as appropriate, laws or regulations governing the sale of such drugs via the Internet, with a view to minimizing the risks, including, as a minimum:

(a) The obligation for companies within their national borders offering internationally controlled licit drugs via the Internet to have preliminary operating licences;

(b) The necessity for those companies within their national borders to supply internationally controlled licit drugs via the Internet only to persons who have met all the medical and legal obligations required to obtain such substances;

(c) The prohibition of authorized companies within their national borders from making direct deliveries of internationally controlled licit drugs outside their national borders when such deliveries are made to individual persons or companies not authorized to import such drugs, as opposed to being made to authorized companies in accordance with the relevant international conventions;

(d) The necessity for suppliers to keep records of all acquisitions and deliveries of internationally controlled licit drugs for a period of at least two years, in accordance with the relevant international conventions;

7. *Encourages* the competent national authorities to increase public awareness of the risks associated with the unauthorized acquisition of internationally controlled licit drugs via the Internet, in particular with regard to the uncertain quality of the products and the disadvantage that there is no accompanying medical supervision;

8. *Requests* the Secretary-General to transmit the text of the present resolution to all Member States for consideration.

International Narcotics Control Board

The 13-member International Narcotics Control Board held its seventy-ninth (9-13 February), eightieth (17-28 May) and eighty-first (27 October–12 November) sessions, all in Vienna.

In performing the tasks assigned to it under the international conventions, the Board maintained a permanent dialogue with Governments, and used the information received from them to identify the enforcement of treaty provisions requiring them to limit to medical and scientific purposes the licit manufacture of, trade in and distribution and use of narcotic drugs and psychotropic substances. The Board, which was requested by the international drug control treaties to report annually on the drug control situation worldwide, noted weaknesses in national control and treaty compliance and made recommendations for improvements at the national and international levels.

The Board's 2004 report [Sales No. E.05.XI.3] reviewed the interaction between illicit drug supply and demand strategies, emphasizing the need for policy makers, national authorities and others to utilize balanced, combined and integrated approaches at all levels for maximum effectiveness. It also examined the operation of the drug control system. The Board recommended that supply reduction activities should be integrated into and coordinated with demand reduction activities; a central national authority with a balanced representation of supply and demand reduction agencies should be considered; strategies and training programmes on the interaction of both dimensions of the problem should be developed; and research and analysis of existing programmes should be conducted. Governments should compile effective experiences of supply and demand strategies and exchange them with local, national, regional and international authorities. The eradication of illicit crop cultivation and interdiction in source areas should be accompanied by parallel social and alternative development programmes.

In its analysis of the operation of the international drug control system, the Board expressed concern that several States, including some major manufacturers, importers, exporters or users of narcotic drugs, did not comply with their treaty obligation to submit timely annual statistical reports. It urged States and territories concerned to establish their own estimates of narcotic drug requirements for 2005 and furnish them to the Board as soon as possible.

INCB, noting that the diversion of pharmaceutical products containing narcotic drugs from licit domestic distribution channels and their abuse remained problems in both developing and some developed countries, urged the World Health Organization (WHO) and UNODC to assist Governments in preventing their diversion and abuse and in monitoring trends in that area. Reports in various countries on the abuse of psychotropic substances and their seizure indicated that the diversion of pharmaceuticals containing such substances from licit domestic distribution channels had become the most important source for illicit drug suppliers.

With regard to precursors, INCB continued to act as the international focal point for the exchange of information under Project Prism, Operation Purple and Operation Topaz. During 2004, the activities of Project Prism, the international initiative against diversion of precursors of amphetamine-type stimulants, focused on the monitoring of international trade in safrole, preventing diversions of pharmaceutical preparations containing pseudoephedrine, and locating laboratories involved in the illicit manufacture of 1-phenyl-2-propanone. Operation Purple continued to be useful to Governments in preventing the diversion of potassium permanganate for use in the illicit manufacture of cocaine. The Board noted the increase in shipments of potassium permanganate to non-participating countries in Africa. Concerned at the limited reporting on its trafficking in countries in Central and South America, it urged them to establish mechanisms for providing information on seizures of the drug. Shipments of acetic anhydride to West Asia remained a special focus of Operation Topaz. The Board urged Governments to make full use of the mechanisms established for addressing the issue of heroin manufacture in West Asia. It emphasized the usefulness of operational meetings such as the one hosted by Austria in Vienna in June, to exchange information on investigations and decide on action for dismantling trafficking activities.

As to ensuring the availability of drugs for medical purposes, INCB urged producing countries to maintain opiate raw materials production at actual worldwide requirement levels. The low consumption of opioid analgesics for the treatment of moderate to severe pain, especially in developing countries, continued to be a matter of concern. The Board called on Governments to maintain a balance between the licit supply of and demand for opiate raw materials and to cooperate in preventing the proliferation of sources of their production. It urged producing countries to review the adequacy of controls over the licit cultivation of opium poppy in their territories. INCB convened two meetings (Vienna, May and October) with permanent representatives to the United Nations to examine the system for balancing the supply of and demand for opiates and to raise awareness of the necessity of measuring actual medical needs. Governments that had not done so were encouraged to examine the extent to which their health-care systems and laws and regulations permitted the use of opioids for medical purposes, to identify impediments thereto and to develop plans for long-term pain management strategies so as to facilitate the supply and availability of narcotic drugs.

The illicit sale of pharmaceuticals containing internationally controlled narcotic drugs and psychotropic substances through the Internet and by mail had become a global problem. Some 90 per cent of such sales by Internet pharmacies were without prescriptions, with substances of high abuse potential, such as certain opioids, stimulants and benzodiazepines, and health risks, such as fentanyl and secobarbital, being among those frequently traded. In October, the Board convened an expert group in Vienna to consider the problem, which recommended several measures to combat it. The Board emphasized the need for a mechanism to ensure the sharing of experience and the exchange of information on specific cases and the standardization of data collected. Urgent action was required specifically for sharing information on national legislation regarding Internet pharmacies and individual mail order shipments, which should be supported by the universal application of international regulations. Weaknesses in national regulatory systems for domestic distribution should be identified, and countries should cooperate with the pharmaceutical industry and Internet service providers.

The INCB report was supplemented by three technical reports: *Narcotic Drugs: Estimated World Requirements for 2005; Statistics for 2003* [E/INCB/2004/2]; *Psychotropic Substances: Statistics for 2003; Assessments of Medical and Scientific Requirements for*

Substances in Schedules II, III and IV [E/INCB/2004/3]; and *Precursors and Chemicals Frequently Used in the Illicit Manufacture of Narcotic Drugs and Psychotropic Substances: Report of the International Narcotics Control Board for 2004 on the Implementation of Article 12 of the United Nations Convention against Illicit Traffic in Narcotic Drugs and Psychotropic Substances of 1988* [E/INCB/2004/4].

By **decision 2004/245** of 21 July, the Economic and Social Council took note of the INCB report for 2003 [YUN 2003, p. 1270].

World drug situation

In its 2004 report [Sales No.E.05.XI.3], INCB presented a regional analysis of world drug abuse trends and control efforts, so that Governments would be kept aware of situations that might endanger the objectives of international drug control treaties.

Africa

Africa's limited institutional and technical capacity to deal with the drug issue in an effective and comprehensive manner had impacted negatively on national drug control strategies. Mechanisms or skilled human resources to counter drug trafficking were insufficient, and counselling, treatment and rehabilitation facilities for drug abusers were inadequate, as was the investment by Governments to deal with the situation, making the continent a very weak link in international drug control. The uncontrolled sale in licensed pharmacies of prescription medication containing narcotic drugs and psychotropic substances, the proliferation of illegal retail pharmaceutical outlets and the diversion from licit distribution channels of such products into street markets continued. Most African countries had no adequate legislative framework, lacked administrative mechanisms for the control of precursor chemicals, and were increasingly targeted by traffickers attempting to obtain the chemicals needed for illicit drug manufacture.

Cannabis remained the major drug of concern throughout the continent, but trafficking in and abuse of cocaine, heroin and amphetamine-type stimulants were increasing, as was drug use by injection. The abuse of psychotropic substances was facilitated by the absence of licit control measures in most African countries.

The region continued to be a major source of the cannabis found in its illicit markets or smuggled out, mainly into Europe. Cannabis production and trafficking were reported in all countries, while the production of cannabis resin was concentrated in Morocco, which accounted for 40 per cent of its global production, and 60 per cent of that seized worldwide. Cannabis herb remained the most abused illicit drug in most countries. Its cultivation for commercial purposes increased in several countries, especially in Eastern Africa, as a result of declining prices for other agricultural products. There was evidence to suggest that some civil conflicts in Africa were funded by profits from cannabis trafficking.

Cocaine originating in South America continued to enter Southern and Western Africa on its way to Europe and North America. Several countries reported seizures of cocaine, the largest being recorded in 2004 in the Gulf of Guinea. Cocaine abuse was relatively small in Africa, mainly confined to Nigeria, Senegal and South Africa, and transit countries, notably Cape Verde. Heroin originating in South-East and South-West Asia was smuggled into Eastern and Western Africa on its way to Europe and, to a lesser extent, North America. While there was an upward trend in trafficking, the quantities involved remained small and Africa accounted for only 0.5 per cent of all the heroin seized worldwide. A number of countries reported growing heroin abuse, albeit at a low level, most of it being smoked, but its use by injection was increasingly reported in Eastern and Southern Africa.

The abuse of pharmaceutical products, particularly those containing psychotropic substances, remained a matter of concern, as they were increasingly sold without medical prescription or adequate control measures. Ephedrine and diazepam were often sold by street vendors or in neighbourhood shops in several Western and Central African countries. In South Africa, the abuse in the Cape Town area of methamphetamine hydrochloride (commonly called "ice") and the growing availability of methcathinone (commonly called "cat") increased. The abuse of methylenedioxymethamphetamine (MDMA) (Ecstasy) seemed to be confined to South Africa. Amphetamine and methamphetamine tablets were smuggled from West Africa, via the Sudan, to Saudi Arabia and other countries in the Persian Gulf. Khat, which was not under international control, continued to be cultivated in Ethiopia and Kenya, the Comoros, Madagascar and the United Republic of Tanzania but abused mainly in Djibouti, Ethiopia and Somalia.

As to regional cooperation, the Board noted the continuing commitment of the African Union (AU) to drug control, and the steps taken to create a sustainable drug control coordination and advisory capacity and a review and monitoring system throughout Africa. Regional collaboration in drug control was achieved through regular meetings of regional law enforcement authorities. INCB and UNODC organized a training seminar on licit drug control for Eastern African countries in Nairobi, Kenya, in January. Activities against money-laundering were also initiated in a number of subregions: the Groupe intergouvernemental d'action contre le blanchiment d'argent en Afrique de l'Ouest (GIABA) (Dakar, Senegal, 22-25 June) approved the formal establishment of the GIABA secretariat and its 2004-2006 work plan; the countries in Central Africa inaugurated the Action Group against Money-Laundering in Central Africa (Bangui, Central African Republic, March); and the Eastern and Southern Africa Anti–Money Laundering Group held a meeting in Cape Town in May to assist its member States in the drafting and finalization of national plans to counter money-laundering and the financing of terrorism. At the national level, several African countries, including Algeria, Cape Verde, Madagascar and Mauritius, took steps to establish and implement national drug control master plans. In June, INCB sent missions to Madagascar and South Africa and a technical mission to Mauritania.

Americas

Central America and the Caribbean

Cannabis cultivation occurred in most Central American and Caribbean countries, most of which was abused locally or smuggled into neighbouring countries. Despite some success in eliminating illicit cannabis cultivation, Jamaica remained a major source. The subregion was also affected by large-scale cocaine trafficking and its increased abuse. In response to rigorous efforts by law enforcement agencies, drug trafficking organizations in some countries were adapting their methods, such as increasing their use of air and sea routes in Honduras and small boats in Jamaica, to transport illicit consignments.

Heroin abuse was relatively low, but the situation was changing as drug trafficking throughout the region increased, especially in the Dominican Republic and El Salvador. The abuse of pharmaceutical medications containing psychotropic substances was at a high level in certain countries, in particular flunitrazepam and diazepam, which were the main drugs of abuse among street children in Port-au-Prince, Haiti. Those substances were mostly diverted from the licit market or international donations, or were smuggled from Costa Rica, the Dominican Republic, the Netherlands Antilles, Panama and Venezuela. During the year, several countries took steps to strengthen the control of precursors. Guatemala adopted new regulations and established an inter-ministerial committee to coordinate its action, while Honduras commenced implementation of its national action plan to strengthen precursor control. The Bahamas adopted a national drug control plan for 2003-2008, and Jamaica implemented stricter controls over the shipment of controlled chemical substances at authorized ports of entry, but the lack of resources created difficulties for it in pursuing such operations. Concrete information on drug abuse in many Central American and Caribbean countries remained scarce.

North America

North America was the largest market in the world for illicit drugs. Cannabis, the most abused drug, was produced in significant amounts in all three countries in the region. In Canada, debate continued regarding proposed legislation for reducing the sanctions for the possession of small amounts of cannabis from criminal prosecution to a fine. Cocaine was trafficked in large quantities throughout North America, with the United States being the largest market for the drug. It was also abused in Canada and, to a lesser extent, in Mexico. The amount of cocaine seized by Mexico increased significantly and there were indications that the country was being used as a transit point for cocaine destined for Europe. In the United States, cocaine (in powder or crack form) continued to be regarded as the drug that posed the greatest threat.

In the United States, the abuse or misuse, especially by youth, of prescription drugs under international control, including oxycodone and hydrocodone used for pain treatment, was an increasing problem. The majority of prescription drugs abused were diverted from the licit market and obtained through Internet pharmacies. The illicit manufacture of methamphetamine in North America had increased, and its abuse in the United States remained at a high level. In Canada, the abuse of amphetamine-type stimulants (ATS), including MDMA (Ecstasy) and methamphetamine, had also increased.

The three countries in North America continued their cooperation, in particular in the area of law enforcement, registering major successes against international drug trafficking organizations and dismantling money-laundering rings. At the national level, Canada commenced the first national survey on drug abuse since 1994, and Mexico continued its law enforcement efforts against drug trafficking organizations. The Board noted that the large amount of drugs trafficked through Mexico left it vulnerable to the spillover effect, and there were high rates of abuse for some drugs in the northern part of the country. The Board encouraged the Government to continue strengthening its efforts in demand reduction. The rate of drug abuse in the United States remained high, and the Board encouraged the Government to continue its efforts in drug abuse prevention and to take the differences in drug abuse among various ethnic groups into account in formulating and implementing demand reduction programmes. In July 2004, law enforcement authorities in the country closed down several websites used to sell controlled psychotropic substances.

South America

In South America, drug control continued to be an issue of considerable political importance, not only to the region but also to the rest of the world. Drug trafficking, and the money-laundering and corruption associated with it, continued to endanger stability in the region, and traffickers responded to interdiction efforts by using different trafficking routes, entering into new strategic alliances with trafficking organizations from other regions and merging organizations. Several Governments in the region achieved considerable success against drug trafficking networks as a result of strengthened regional and bilateral cooperation in interdiction efforts. In Colombia, the Government made progress in combating drug trafficking and the guerrilla and paramilitary groups involved.

Illicit cultivation of cannabis continued to be detected in most countries and increased in several of them. However, cannabis herb and resin were not the primary drugs of abuse. In Venezuela, they were second only to cocaine abuse, and in Brazil they ranked second after benzodiazepines.

In 2003, the total area under coca bush cultivation in Bolivia, Colombia and Peru decreased by 11 per cent compared with 2002. However, that reduction appeared to be offset by increasing agricultural yields. In Colombia, where the total area under cultivation decreased the most, mainly due to strict law enforcement and crop spraying, increases were recorded in certain parts of the country and was no longer confined to remote areas. There was also a shift towards smaller plots and high-yield varieties. In Peru, the reduction in the area under cultivation was partly offset by higher yields, resulting from improved farming techniques, as was the case in Bolivia, where the yield of coca leaf was greater than in previous years. In Ecuador and Venezuela, illicit coca bush cultivation continued to be reported in border areas close to Colombia. The

Board emphasized that the continued reduction of coca bush cultivation, either voluntarily or as a result of interdiction efforts, would depend on the ability to offer sustainable alternative livelihoods to farmers in the producing countries. The international community should therefore continue to support and expand alternative development initiatives. In Bolivia and Peru, numerous effective alternative development schemes were under way; however, too many coca bush farmers remained dependent on income from such illicit cultivation. In Bolivia, clashes between growers and the Government, which was trying to reduce such cultivation, continued. In Peru, the frequency and violence of such clashes increased, and some federations of coca bush growers were demanding the legalization of such cultivation.

Cocaine trafficking, mainly of transit trafficking of consignments destined for the United States or, increasingly, Europe, mostly affected Brazil, Ecuador and Venezuela, although it increased in other countries in the region, such as Argentina and Chile. Increasing amounts from Brazil and Colombia were smuggled through Portugal into Portuguese-speaking countries in Africa, primarily Angola and Mozambique, and also into South Africa. Cocaine from South America was also trans-shipped via several African countries to Europe.

Heroin manufacture continued, mainly in Colombia, most of which was destined for the United States. Heroin was smuggled out of the region through Venezuela. The illicit manufacture of psychotropic substances in the region was limited, but stimulants, mainly smuggled out of Europe, continued to be seized in some countries. The diversion and over-prescription of a variety of psychotropic substances also continued.

As to regional cooperation, countries in South America continued to participate in the multilateral cooperation mechanisms of the Inter-American Drug Abuse Control Commission of the Organization of American States, the main regional forum for coordinating drug control issues in the Americas. In addition, many States with common geographical characteristics or shared borders entered into bilateral or multilateral agreements, to which they continued to adhere. The United States and countries in Europe provided resources for drug control in South America through bilateral and multilateral agreements. At the national level, in Bolivia, the 2004-2008 integrated strategy to fight drug trafficking was approved in September and the 2004-2008 national plan for alternative development in May. Peru's 2002-2007 national drug control strategy was approved in January, while in Ecuador, the decree on the national policy to fight drugs strengthened the role of the competent authority and provided for a balanced approach between demand and supply reduction activities.

The Board encouraged Brazil, to which it had sent a mission in December 2003, to continue to attach high priority to drug control issues and, in particular, to ensure that all bodies involved in drug-related issues had adequate resources. It should also monitor and analyse prescription patterns more closely, especially those for medicines such as benzodiazepines or medications containing codeine, and to ensure cooperation between the regulatory and law enforcement authorities involved in the control of precursors.

Asia

East and South-East Asia

In East and South-East Asia, cannabis continued to be cultivated and abused, especially in Brunei Darussalam, Indonesia, Malaysia, Mongolia, the Philippines and the Republic of Korea. Meanwhile, illicit opium poppy production continued to decline, mainly in the Lao People's Democratic Republic and Myanmar, where, as a result of continued government efforts, the total area under cultivation was reduced by a further 45 per cent and 28 per cent, respectively; total production of raw opium also declined by some 64 per cent and 54 per cent, respectively, compared to the previous year. Thailand was no longer a major source of illicit opium and heroin, but small-scale opium poppy cultivation took place in remote areas in the northern part of the country. Seizures of opium were reported in several countries, including Japan, the Lao People's Democratic Republic, Malaysia, Myanmar, the Republic of Korea and Viet Nam.

Opiates were the most abused drugs in the region, the highest prevalence being reported in the Lao People's Democratic Republic, Myanmar and Thailand. Opium abuse increased in Hong Kong, China, as well as in Malaysia and the Republic of Korea. Some 70 per cent of China's registered drug addicts were heroin abusers, and Cambodia, Japan, Malaysia, Myanmar, Thailand and Viet Nam reported increased heroin abuse. Increased cocaine abuse was reported in a few countries; in the region as a whole, however, cocaine trafficking and abuse remained limited. Most of the countries in the region, including China, Japan, Malaysia, Myanmar, the Philippines and the Republic of Korea, reported a significant increase in the amount of ATS seized. The East and South-East Asia region accounted for nearly 90 per cent of all seizures worldwide, with large seizures of crystallized methamphetamine being reported in Japan, Myanmar, the Philippines and Thailand. The Lao People's Democratic Republic emerged as an important transit country for the trafficking of ATS illicitly manufactured in the border areas of Myanmar and destined for Thailand. Cambodia was also increasingly used as a transit country. A significant increase in the amount of MDMA (Ecstasy) seized was reported in the majority of countries in 2003. While its abuse remained relatively low compared with that of methamphetamine, it increased in Cambodia, China, Thailand and Viet Nam.

At the regional level, the Board welcomed continued cooperation under the Association of South-East Asian Nations and the China Cooperative Operations in Response to Dangerous Drugs Plan of Action, including the signing, in January, of a memorandum of understanding to develop strategies for combating transnational crime, including drug trafficking, terrorism and money-laundering. The annual meeting (Krabi, Thailand, 17-19 May) of senior officials of the signatories of the 1993 memorandum of understanding on drug control between the countries in the Mekong area (Cambodia, China, Lao People's Democratic Republic, Myanmar, Thailand, Viet Nam) agreed to strengthen regional cooperation and establish institutional links to share innovative approaches and best practices in the areas of community-based alternative development and the elimination of illicit opium poppy cultivation.

INCB sent missions to Indonesia in March and to Thailand in May. It also made a technical visit to Timor-Leste in March.

South Asia

South Asia continued to experience increased drug availability and abuse because of its proximity to the major opiate production areas, the Golden Crescent (Afghanistan, Iran, Pakistan) and the Golden Triangle (Laos, Myanmar, Thailand), widespread cultivation of cannabis and increasing diversion of pharmaceutical products.

Cannabis was produced and abused in large quantities, with Bangladesh and India being important sources for cannabis herb and Nepal a major source for cannabis resin. The flow of heroin from Afghanistan towards South Asia increased. In India, quantities of licitly produced opium continued to be diverted into illicit channels, for local abuse or for processing into heroin to be sold on illicit markets outside the area. A low-quality heroin, known as "brown sugar" was sold locally or smuggled into Maldives and Sri Lanka. The trafficking and abuse of pharmaceuticals containing narcotic drugs, such as co-

deine, remained widespread in the region. In India, because of its lower price and easy availability, propoxyphene abuse by injection was as prevalent as that of heroin. Pharmaceutical preparations containing psychotropic substances, notably benzodiazepines and analgesics, were diverted from licit distribution channels and smuggled through South Asia into countries outside the region, such as the Russian Federation and Scandinavian countries. The abuse of analgesics, anxiolytics and sedative hypnotics increased in the region, as well as buprenorphine.

India was the world's largest illicit manufacturer of methaqualone (Mandrax), destined for South Africa. Laboratories illicitly manufacturing methaqualone were also used for the illicit manufacture of other psychotropic substances, notably MDMA (Ecstasy) and amphetamines. The anaesthetic ketamine was abused in India's Goa tourist area, while inhalants were abused by the poorer segments of society and street children.

At the regional level, India and Pakistan identified focal points for sharing information and operational intelligence on drug trafficking, and customs officials from India and Sri Lanka adopted operational-level strategies to combat drug smuggling, while India and Maldives decided to establish contact point for law enforcement activities, including for drug smuggling. Noting that controls over the licit manufacture of, trade in and distribution of narcotic drugs and psychotropic substances in India needed to be strengthened, the Board called on the Government to step up its law enforcement activities, especially at the retail level, and to carry out education and information campaigns regarding the abuse liability of narcotic drugs and psychotropic substances.

West Asia

The central elements of the drug situation in West Asia were Afghanistan's opium production and its impact on peace and security, as illicit drug production and related activities reached an unprecedented level in 2004, threatening the country's stability. The widespread cultivation of opium poppy, the processing of and trafficking in opiates and the illicit drug trade dominated Afghanistan's economic, social and political life, and despite the efforts of the Government, assisted by the international community, the drug control situation continued to deteriorate. In other countries in the region, drug trafficking and abuse increased, undermining social and economic stability. In Central Asia, concerns were raised over trafficking in and abuse of Afghan opiates and the illicit movement of acetic anhydride, while injecting drug abuse became the main contributory factor to the spread of HIV/AIDS. Countries on the Arabian peninsula were more frequently used as transit points for heroin and cannabis destined for Europe, while precursors were smuggled in the opposite direction. The abuse of opiates, especially heroin, increased in the subregion, as did the already widespread abuse of synthetic drugs.

Cannabis, the most widely available and abused drug in West Asia, was illicitly cultivated in several countries and grown wild in others, including Afghanistan, Pakistan and Kazakhstan, where the Government was developing new strategies to prevent its illegal harvesting.

In Afghanistan, the illicit cultivation of opium poppy continued unabated, reaching an estimated 3,600 tons in 2003, more than three quarters of the world's illicit production, and 4,200 tons in 2004, despite efforts to counter the trend; the total area under cultivation increased from 80,000 hectares in 2003 to over 130,000 hectares in 2004. Eradication efforts were limited to only one province. In Pakistan, illicit opium poppy cultivation, which had re-emerged in 2003 after years of decline, continued in 2004, mostly in non-traditional growing areas. The processing of opium into heroin continued on a large scale in many countries, including in Afghanistan, the main producer. Trafficking in opiates from Afghanistan, and cannabis resin originating in various West Asian countries, to, or through, other countries in the region and to Europe, continued on a large scale, while synthetic drugs and precursors were frequently smuggled in the opposite direction. The main transit countries were Iran and Pakistan, the countries of Central Asia and increasingly those in the Persian Gulf, such as Kuwait and the United Arab Emirates, as well as Turkey.

Drug abuse was a serious concern in many countries in West Asia. Iran reported an increase in heroin consumption, including injecting drug use, and opium remained the most widely used drug in that country. Pakistan had one of the highest prevalence rates for heroin abuse in the world, where cannabis was also widely abused. Countries in the eastern Mediterranean and on the Arabian peninsula experienced an increase in the abuse of opiates, especially heroin, in addition to the widespread abuse of synthetic drugs. As a consequence of large quantities of illicit drugs being trafficked throughout Central Asia, there was a rising incidence of heroin, opium and cannabis abuse. The abuse of psychotropic substances, mainly benzodiazepines and barbiturates, which were often freely available and obtained without prescription, increased, particularly among women. Of increasing concern in many countries was the abuse of inhalants, mainly by youth, especially street children.

At the regional level, Afghan representatives, in July, participated in the Intergovernmental Technical Committee meeting, a forum for the exchange of drug law enforcement information in the region. In August, Pakistan hosted a seminar for member States of the South Asian Association for Regional Cooperation to review progress in achieving the goals related to precursor control set by the General Assembly's twentieth special session [YUN 1998, p. 1135]. A number of bilateral and multilateral agreements were adopted by countries in the region to intensify cooperation among national drug control agencies, promote joint law enforcement operations, harmonize national drug control legislation and build capacities. On 17 June, the member States of the Shanghai Cooperation Organization (China, Kazakhstan, Kyrgyzstan, Russian Federation, Tajikistan, Uzbekistan) adopted the Tashkent Declaration, expressing their common objective at joint efforts to counter new threats, including illicit drug trafficking, and to foster cooperation.

Noting the lack of long-term and sustainable solutions to the development of alternative livelihoods in opium-producing areas in Afghanistan, the Board emphasized the need to address that situation in a comprehensive manner, with support from the international community.

In July, an INCB mission visited Pakistan. The Board encouraged that Government to, among other things, monitor the domestic manufacture and distribution of narcotic drugs and psychotropic substances, while ensuring availability of and accessibility to controlled drugs for medical purposes. The Board, which visited Turkmenistan in December 2003, stressed that, in view of its proximity to Afghanistan, it was important that the country complied with its obligations under international treaties, took efforts against illicit drug trafficking and cooperated with the international community.

Afghanistan

The Secretary-General, in his March report on the situation in Afghanistan [A/58/742-S/2004/230], said that the international counter-narcotics conference on Afghanistan, organized by Afghanistan's Counter-Narcotics Directorate, the United Kingdom and UNODC (Kabul, 8-9 February), identified the priorities for: mainstreaming drug control into all development sectors; improving coordination among principal ministries and donors; extending Afghanistan's counter-narcotics police to priority regions; and providing effective drug-awareness programmes and skill-based training.

At the Berlin Conference on Afghanistan (31 March–1 April), the Transitional Authority of Afghanistan and its six neighbours (China, Iran, Pakistan, Tajikistan, Turkmenistan, Uzbekistan) adopted the Berlin Declaration on Counter-Narcotics within the Framework of the Kabul Declaration on Good-Neighbourly Relations, which provided, among other things, for increased collaboration in the fight against narcotics and the establishment of a security belt around Afghanistan.

The Board called on the Government of Afghanistan and the international community to continue to accord drug control the highest priority and to strengthen efforts to address the drug problem in a comprehensive manner, within the framework of overall development plans and programmes, to establish law and order throughout the country and make alternative development in areas under drug crop cultivation more effective.

ECONOMIC AND SOCIAL COUNCIL ACTION

On 21 July [meeting 47], the Economic and Social Council, on the recommendation of the Commission on Narcotic Drugs [E/2004/28 & Corr.1], adopted **resolution 2004/37** without vote [agenda item 14 (d)].

Providing support to the Government of Afghanistan in its efforts to eliminate illicit opium and foster stability and security in the region

The Economic and Social Council

Recommends to the General Assembly the adoption of the following draft resolution:

[For text, see General Assembly resolution 59/161 below.]

GENERAL ASSEMBLY ACTION

On 20 December [meeting 74], the General Assembly, on the recommendation of the Third Committee [A/59/495], adopted **resolution 59/161** without vote [agenda item 97].

Providing support to the Government of Afghanistan in its efforts to eliminate illicit opium and foster stability and security in the region

The General Assembly,

Recalling the United Nations Millennium Declaration outlining the interrelated commitments, goals and targets to be achieved on, inter alia, development, peace and security and setting the required framework for international cooperation for achieving those goals,

Recognizing that the threat emanating from illicit opium poppy cultivation and production of and trafficking in illicit opium, as addressed at the Conference on Drug Routes from Central Asia to Europe, held in Paris on 21 and 22 May 2003, is a serious challenge to the security and stability of Afghanistan, its neighbouring countries and the region and poses a problem for countries throughout the world,

Taking note of *Afghanistan: Opium Survey 2003*, published by the United Nations Office on Drugs and Crime,

Recognizing the strong and continuing commitment made by the Transitional Administration of Afghanistan at the institutional, legal and administrative levels to eliminate opium poppy cultivation by 2013,

Reaffirming the commitments undertaken by Member States in the Political Declaration adopted by the General Assembly at its twentieth special session, in which Member States recognized that action against the world drug problem was a common and shared responsibility and expressed their conviction that it must be addressed in a multilateral setting,

Recalling that the Security Council, on 17 June 2003, called upon the international community to provide assistance to the Transitional Administration of Afghanistan in collaboration with the United Nations Office on Drugs and Crime and in line with the national drug control strategy,

Recalling also that, in section II of its resolution 58/141 of 22 December 2003, the General Assembly reaffirmed the Joint Ministerial Statement and further measures to implement the action plans emanating from the twentieth special session of the General Assembly, adopted during the ministerial segment of the forty-sixth session of the Commission on Narcotic Drugs, and recommended that adequate help be provided to Afghanistan in support of the commitment of the Transitional Administration of Afghanistan to eliminate illicit opium,

Stressing the importance and urgency of the implementation of the five action plans adopted by the International Counter-Narcotics Conference on Afghanistan, held in Kabul on 8 and 9 February 2004, which were to form part of the discussion at the international conference entitled "Afghanistan and the International Community: a Partnership for the Future", held in Berlin on 31 March and 1 April 2004, and the conclusion of the Kabul conference that the illicit drug issue is a top priority of all those interested in securing the future of Afghanistan,

Recalling that, in the Joint Ministerial Statement and further measures to implement the action plans emanating from the twentieth special session of the General Assembly, the ministers and other government representatives participating in the ministerial segment of the forty-sixth session of the Commission on Narcotic Drugs recommended that adequate help be provided to Afghanistan within the framework of the comprehensive international strategy carried out, inter alia, under the auspices of the United Nations and through other multilateral forums, in support of the commitment of the Transitional Government of Afghanistan to eliminate the illicit cultivation of opium poppy and in response to the unique situation of that country, reaffirmed that that should help the provision of alternative livelihoods and the fight against illicit trafficking in drugs and precursors within Afghanistan and in neighbouring States and countries along trafficking routes, including the strengthening of "security belts" in the region, and that extensive efforts had to be made to reduce the demand for drugs globally in order to contribute to the sustainability of the elimination of illicit cultivation in Afghanistan and, in that context, affirmed that their response to that unique situation would not detract from their commitment and resources devoted to the fight against drugs in other parts of the world,

Recalling also that the International Narcotics Control Board, in its report for 2003, pointed out that trade in Afghan opiates generated funds that corrupted institutions, financed terrorism and insurgency and led to destabilization of the region,

Recalling further the appeal to the international community made by the International Narcotics Control Board on 12 February 2004 to support fully the Afghan authorities in addressing the drug control situation, in order to meet the requirements of the international drug treaties, including article 14 of the Single Convention on Narcotic Drugs of 1961 and that Convention as amended by the 1972 Protocol,

1. *Welcomes* the bilateral and multilateral support being provided by the international community, through the United Nations Office on Drugs and Crime and other organizations;

2. *Expresses its support* for the efforts of Member States aimed at strengthening regional cooperation in order to counter the threat to the international community posed by the illicit cultivation of opium poppy in Afghanistan and its illicit trade;

3. *Calls upon* the international community to enhance financial and technical support to Afghanistan in order to enable the Government to implement successfully its national drug control strategy and thereby reduce the demand for illicit drugs in Afghanistan and the threat that illicit opium poppy cultivation and illicit opium trade have created to the peace, stability and socio-economic recovery of Afghanistan and to the security of the region and the other parts of the world;

4. *Urges* all stakeholders to accelerate efforts to implement a combined strategy, comprising law enforcement, eradication, interdiction, demand reduction and awareness-building, including alternative livelihoods conceived in a broader development context than currently understood, with a view to creating sustainable livelihoods, independent of illicit opium;

5. *Encourages* the Transitional Administration of Afghanistan to accelerate the implementation of the commitment that it courageously made to the five action plans adopted by the International Counter-Narcotics Conference on Afghanistan, held in Kabul on 8 and 9 February 2004;

6. *Reaffirms* the need to strengthen measures to reduce the global demand for illicit drugs, in order to support and contribute to the sustainability of efforts to eliminate illicit opium in Afghanistan;

7. *Requests* the United Nations Office on Drugs and Crime, subject to the availability of voluntary funds, which might be either from general-purpose funds, in accordance with the Commission on Narcotic Drugs guidelines for the use of general-purpose funds, or from earmarked funds, and encourages concerned Member States, international organizations and financial institutions to routinely mainstream counter-narcotics measures as part of their development cooperation strategies, in coordination with the development objectives of the Government of Afghanistan, so that sustainable alternative livelihoods are created in Afghanistan.

Europe

Cannabis was the most widely abused illicit drug in Europe, accounting for an estimated 20 per cent of its abuse worldwide. It was cultivated and trafficked in Western Europe, mainly in the Netherlands and, to a lesser extent, in Switzerland. Cannabis herb was increasingly cultivated locally, particularly in the European Union (EU) countries, while Morocco and the Russian Federation were major sources of cannabis resin. Albania and other Balkan countries (Bulgaria, Croatia, Serbia and Montenegro and The former Yugoslav Republic of Macedonia) plus the Russian Federation and Slovenia remained the main suppliers to Eastern Europe.

Portugal and Spain, the main points of entry for cocaine from South America, accounted for 5 per cent of the cocaine seized worldwide. The amount of cocaine seized in some Western European countries (Belgium, France, Italy) increased, as well as in Eastern Europe, albeit at a lower level. Cocaine abuse also increased in Europe, although the level of abuse in Eastern Europe was well below that of Western Europe.

Whereas heroin abuse was stable or declining in Western Europe, it increased in Eastern Europe and in the Commonwealth of Independent States (CIS). Some 4 million people in Europe abused opiates, two thirds of whom were in Eastern Europe, primarily in the Russian Federation, which had become the largest heroin market in Europe. In Western Europe, in descending order, Luxembourg, Portugal, the United Kingdom, Italy and Switzerland had the highest level of abuse. Illicit opium poppy cultivation was at a low level in Central and Eastern Europe and in the CIS States, but the trafficking volume was high. Heroin seizures increased in Europe, 90 per cent of which came from Afghanistan. The northern and southern branches of the Balkan route continued to supply up to 80 per cent of the heroin distributed in Europe.

The illicit manufacture and abuse of ATS in Europe were significant. While the abuse level stabilized in Western Europe, Eastern Europe was becoming increasingly important in terms of the manufacture and abuse potential of amphetamines and MDMA (Ecstasy). The Netherlands remained their main source of supply, although increasing amounts originated from Central and Eastern Europe, especially Estonia and Poland. Preparations containing psychotropic substances were abused in several countries in Europe.

Regional cooperation remained strong with the eastward expansion of the EU, and Southern European and CIS countries were becoming increasingly open to regional partnerships. The Russian Federation joined Operation Purple, and Serbia and Montenegro joined Operation Topaz. Ukraine participated in Project Prism and Operation Purple and took part in Operation Topaz as an observer. Joint efforts were undertaken in implementing measures against illicit drug supply and money-laundering, while emphasizing the drug abuse prevention and treatment components of national strategies and integrating drug control activities of the national authorities of the new EU member States into the framework of the European Monitoring Centre for Drugs and Drug Addiction.

In 2004, INCB sent missions to Belgium, Denmark, Portugal and Sweden, examined the drug situations in Albania and Serbia and Montenegro, and reviewed Ukraine's progress in implementing its recommendations.

Oceania

In Australia, hydroponic cultivation, because of its higher yield and the perceived reduced risk of detection, continued to be the most common method for cultivating cannabis for the domestic market. In New Zealand, cannabis growers were also involved in the illicit manufacture of methamphetamine in clandestine laboratories. Heroin abuse declined in Australia, but the purity of seized heroin increased slightly. Most of the heroin abused in Australia originated in South-East Asia. Heroin detection increased, while there was a decrease in the amount of heroin seized, suggesting a shift in methods used by traffickers. However, the reduction in its availability resulted in heroin abusers turning to other drugs.

Demand for ATS, including MDMA (Ecstasy), remained high in Australia and New Zealand, where ATS illicit manufacture and abuse increased. The two countries accounted for the majority of the drug and precursor seizures made in Oceania. Trafficking organizations based outside New Zealand shipped large quantities of ATS into the country. ATS precursors, such as ephedrine and pseudoephedrine, were increasingly seized at the borders; medicines containing those substances were smuggled into New Zealand by mail and air passengers from China and South-East Asian countries for use in the illicit manufacture of methamphetamine. In Australia, the increasing abuse of *gamma*-hydroxybutyric acid, ketamine and various anti-depressants was cause for concern, as was the abuse of several benzodiazepines diverted from licit distribution channels. Most of the Pacific island countries remained vulnerable to drug transit trafficking and to ATS abuse.

At the regional level, the Board welcomed the launching in the Cook Islands of a Combined Law Agency Group, and the establishment in Suva, Fiji, in June, of the Pacific Transnational Crime Coordination Centre. Cooperation between law enforcement agencies in Australia and police authorities from several countries, including Cambodia, Peru and the Philippines, resulted in major drug seizures. The Board encouraged Australia to intensify its cooperation with countries in South America to fight cocaine trafficking and abuse. At the national level, Australia adopted a national drug strategy for 2004-2009.

UN action to combat drug abuse

UN Office on Drugs and Crime

The United Nations Office on Drugs and Crime (UNODC) implemented the Organization's drug programme and crime programme (see p. 1110) in an integrated manner, addressing the interrelated issues of drug control, crime prevention and international terrorism in the context of sustainable development and human security. The drug programme continued to be implemented in accordance with General Assembly resolution 45/179 [YUN 1990, p. 874]. The Office served as the central drug control entity responsible for coordinating all UN drug control activities, and as the repository of technical expertise in international drug control for the UN Secretariat. It acted on behalf of the Secretary-General in fulfilling his responsibilities under the terms of international treaties and resolutions relating to drug control; and provided services to the General Assembly, the Economic and Social Council, and committees and conferences dealing with drug control matters. On 15 March, the Secretary-General issued a bulletin setting out the organizational structure of the Office [ST/SGB/2004/6].

The UNODC Executive Director described the Office's 2004 activities in a report to the Commission on Narcotic Drugs and to the Commission on Crime Prevention and Criminal Justice [E/CN.7/2005/6-E/CN.15/2005/2]. UNODC supported the implementation of the three international drug control conventions and provided legal assistance, working with national and international partners to help jurisdictions establish and run drug treatment courts. Programme delivery was decentralized through its presence in the field and through regional and country initiatives. In Afghanistan, legal assistance activities supported authorities in implementing the new drug control law and strengthening the drug control machinery, including the training of judges, prosecutors and law enforcement personnel. In the Caucasus and Eastern Europe, the Office assisted task groups in developing workplans for drug law reform and in drafting amendments to their drug control laws. In law enforcement, UNODC focused on training officials in specialized investigative techniques and advanced intelligence software. It promoted best practices in policing and facilitated cross-border cooperation. Through its Laboratory and Scientific Support Programme, UNODC enhanced national capacity for drug-testing, and provided technical assistance to strengthen national laboratories and related institutions in Africa, Asia, the Caucasus, Latin America and the Russian Federation. To support law enforcement agencies in countering illicit drug production, manufacture and trafficking, the Office produced and distributed field test kits for the rapid detection of controlled drugs and precursors, and developed new tests for identifying non-scheduled chemicals used in clandestine heroin processing.

UNODC also focused on sustainable livelihoods, supporting the implementation of alternative development programmes and projects in all key illicit drug-producing regions. It assisted Afghanistan to establish institutional capacities on alternative development; supported Andean countries in generating agro-industries with proven markets; and helped the Lao People's Democratic Republic and Myanmar in further reducing opium poppy cultivation, with a focus on food security, health and improved market access. UNODC also assisted Morocco in revising its development plan for the northern region to address the problem of cannabis cultivation. It supported Afghanistan, Bolivia, Colombia, the Lao People's Democratic Republic, Morocco, Myanmar and Peru in carrying out monitoring surveys of illicit crops. The UNODC Illicit Crop Monitoring Programme assisted the international community and Governments concerned to monitor the extent and evolution of the illicit cultivation of narcotic crops, and to assess the progress of the measures implemented to eliminate or reduce illicit crop cultivation by 2008. It also assisted the Governments concerned to plan and deliver alternative development and poverty alleviation interventions. The Office strengthened inter-agency collaboration in alternative development, developing, with the United Nations Industrial Development Organization, a joint project in the Lao People's Democratic Republic, and implementing alternative development projects jointly with the Food and Agriculture Organization of the United Nations, the International Labour Organization and other aid agencies.

As to public health promotion and drug demand reduction, the Office, in collaboration with Governments in all regions, implemented projects to expand and improve drug dependence treatment and rehabilitation services. Under the Global Assessment Programme on Drug Abuse, it provided technical assistance in training, situation analysis and network establishment to 51 countries.

UNODC made the African region a priority and cooperated with partners in programme delivery. It provided technical and advisory services to the AU under the New Partnership for Africa's Development [YUN 2001, p. 899], and, in collaboration with the Economic Community of West African States and the Southern African Development Community, ran subregional drug demand reduction expert networks in Eastern, Northern and Western Africa. In August, UNODC launched a new Africa-wide project on the prevention of drug abuse and HIV/AIDS. It also strengthened the capacity of treatment and rehabilitation centres.

UNODC restructured its operations and streamlined its processes, emphasizing a new integrated approach on drugs and crime and the critical role of prevention in combating them. Reforms were initiated in the areas of human resources, finance and information technology. In July, UNODC established a partnership with the World Bank on money-laundering, terrorist financing, corruption, HIV/AIDS and alternative livelihoods.

In June, UNODC published the first annual *World Drug Report 2004* [Sales No. E.04.XI.16] which merged the former *Global Illicit Drug Trends* with the *World Drug Report*.

Administrative and budgetary matters

A February report by the Executive Director [E/CN.7/2004/11] provided an overview on the status of implementation of Commission resolution 46/9 [YUN 2003, p. 1281] on securing assured and predictable funding for the United Nations International Drug Control Programme (UNDCP). Among the important developments, the Executive Director noted, in respect of the adequacy of the resources provided to the programme, that the General Assembly, in resolution 58/270 [YUN 2003, p. 1399] on the 2004-2005 programme budget, had approved real resource growth of only 1.1 per cent, rejecting additional posts proposed by the Secretary-General. In the new 2006-2007 strategic framework (see below), the Executive Director intended to request additional resources; consultation in that regard would be held in early 2005 during preparation of the 2006-2007 regular budget. As to exploring ways of obtaining financial donations, significant success had been recorded in mobilizing resources under cost-sharing arrangements with a number of countries, and negotiations were ongoing with other States. Direct contributions were also made by some organizations. As a result of good governance during the 2002-2003 biennium, general-purpose income increased by 23 per cent, which, coupled with cost-saving measures, prevented a potential deficit and restored the general-purpose fund above the minimum of $8 million.

In a March note to the Commission on Narcotic Drugs and to the Commission on Crime Prevention and Criminal Justice [E/CN.7/2004/12-E/CN.15/2004/13], prepared pursuant to Assembly resolution 58/269 [YUN 2003, p. 1395], the Secretary-General submitted the programme on drugs and crime of the proposed UN strategic framework for the 2006-2007 biennium (see p. 1400). The framework consisted of a plan outline, reflecting longer-term objectives of the Organization, and a two-year biennial programme plan. The two Commissions were invited to review the proposed biennial programme plan for the programme on drugs and crime, annexed to the note, and to provide comments to the Secretary-General.

On 19 March [E/2004/28 & Corr.1], the Commission was unable to undertake detailed consideration of the proposed 2006-2007 framework, due to limited time; a detailed discussion was to take place later.

Commission on Narcotic Drugs

The Commission on Narcotic Drugs held its forty-seventh session in Vienna from 15 to 19 March, during which it recommended five resolutions and two decisions for adoption by the Economic and Social Council and three resolutions for recommendation by the Council to the General Assembly. It also adopted six resolutions to be brought to the attention of the Council.

Following the closure of the forty-seventh session on 19 March, the Commission opened its forty-eighth session to elect the new chairman and other bureau members.

By **decision 2004/244** of 21 July, the Council took note of the Commission's report on its forty-seventh session [E/2004/28 & Corr.1] and approved the provisional agenda and documentation for the forty-eighth (2005) session, on the understanding that they would be finalized at intersessional meetings, to be held in Vienna at no additional cost.

Drug demand reduction and drug abuse

In 2004, the Commission on Narcotic Drugs had before it a January report by the Secretariat [E/CN.7/2004/2], which provided an overview of

the world situation with regard to drug abuse and trends between 1998 and 2002 and the mechanisms used to measure trends and improve the global database. The analysis was based on information provided by 106 countries and territories (a response rate of 55 per cent) that had completed and returned part II of the annual reports questionnaire for 2002 by 16 December 2003, in compliance with their obligations under the international treaties. Analysis of the reported trends indicated that cannabis abuse increased in most countries; however, in those countries with high prevalence and long-term prevention efforts, prevalence stabilized or even declined. Abuse of opioids also increased in most regions, with significant differences within the various regions. Amphetamine-type stimulants (ATS) were a major drug of choice and abuse increased in all regions. Cocaine abuse was not very widespread, although it increased slightly in the Americas, the main region of consumption. The report also examined the role of the biennial reports for assessing progress in demand reduction and the annual reports questionnaire for assessing progress with regard to drug abuse. It was noted that not all countries were in a position to provide data on all the key indicators, but were doing their best to improve their data collection systems. However, to address the problem, a proactive approach was required. UNODC, through the Global Assessment Programme on Drug Abuse and other programmes, was providing advice in that regard.

The Commission, by a 19 March resolution [E/2004/28 & Corr.1 (res. 47/1)] on optimizing integrated drug information systems, requested UNODC to promote the development of integrated drug information systems by utilizing data on both the demand for and the supply of illicit drugs and by strengthening collaboration with INCB, WHO and other international bodies. It asked UNODC and regional organizations to continue providing expert advice to States on epidemiological methods of collecting information. The UNODC Executive Director was encouraged to strengthen the Global Assessment Programme on Drug Abuse to improve data collection and analysis on the extent and patterns of and trends in drug abuse and the related negative health consequences, taking into account regional initiatives and using epidemiologically sound and cost-effective methods, and to report in 2005.

HIV/AIDS and other blood-borne viruses

As requested by the Commission in its resolution 46/2 [YUN 2003, p. 1284], the Executive Director submitted a January report [E/CN.7/2004/3 & Corr.1], which reviewed the status of the HIV/AIDS epidemic and its linkages with drug use, highlighting some UNODC programme activities in support of Member States. It described collaborative efforts with the Joint United Nations Programme on HIV/AIDS (UNAIDS) and its co-sponsors and UNODC activities to strengthen its capacity to address HIV/AIDS issues as they related to drug use.

According to the report, there were some 12.6 million injecting drug users in the world; in some areas, up to 80 per cent of them were HIV-positive. In a number of countries (Indonesia, Myanmar, Russian Federation, Ukraine, Viet Nam), the majority of people living with HIV/AIDS were injecting drug users; and in others (India, Thailand, Ukraine, Viet Nam), the epidemic started in the drug injecting population and moved to the general public. It was estimated that at least 10 per cent of people living with HIV/AIDS worldwide were injecting drug users. UNODC, as co-sponsor of UNAIDS, was the convening agency for all matters pertaining to injecting drug use as it related to HIV/AIDS. Over the past two years, it had assumed a leadership role in terms of information development, advocacy and capacity-building. It had also informed its staff in the field about how to address HIV/AIDS issues among injecting drug users, emphasizing the need to address HIV/AIDS issues related to drug use in a comprehensive and holistic manner. UNODC was significantly strengthening its capacity to respond to HIV/AIDS issues related to drug use, by establishing an HIV/AIDS unit within the Division of Operations, which was to be operational by March 2004. At the regional level, it was placing HIV/AIDS advisers in its regional offices in Bangkok, Moscow and Tashkent, and planned organizing capacity-building events, including in-house information-sharing and training in addressing HIV/AIDS issues related to drug abuse, for staff in countries where drug use was a significant route of HIV transmission.

On 19 March [E/2004/28 & Corr.1 (res. 47/2)], the Commission urged that studies and research be conducted to identify vulnerable groups and the extent and patterns of risk-taking behaviour. It also urged the strengthening of health policies that promoted the diagnosis and treatment of drug dependence and infection by HIV and other blood-borne diseases and addressed risk-taking behaviour. The Commission encouraged the strengthening of civil society activities for promoting the health care and social support of drug users and their families. It reinforced the necessity of access for drug users to information on HIV prevention. UNODC, with UNAIDS, WHO and other relevant organizations, should study the effectiveness of drug-related HIV/AIDS prevention programmes, convene an intergovernmental expert group meeting in Vienna to assist in developing a programme on HIV/AIDS and drug abuse, and report to the Commission in 2005.

Drug control and related crime prevention assistance

On 21 July [meeting 47], the Economic and Social Council, on the recommendation of the Commission on Narcotic Drugs [E/2004/28 & Corr.1], adopted **resolution 2004/39** without vote [agenda item 14 (d)].

Drug control and related crime prevention assistance for countries emerging from conflicts

The Economic and Social Council,

Bearing in mind the provisions of the Single Convention on Narcotic Drugs of 1961 as amended by the 1972 Protocol, the Convention on Psychotropic Substances of 1971 and the United Nations Convention against Illicit Traffic in Narcotic Drugs and Psychotropic Substances of 1988,

Recalling the Declaration on the Guiding Principles of Drug Demand Reduction adopted by the General Assembly at its twentieth special session, and the Action Plan for the Implementation of the Declaration on the Guiding Principles of Drug Demand Reduction,

Bearing in mind that, in the Political Declaration adopted by the General Assembly at its twentieth special session, the Assembly set goals and targets to be met by Member States by 2003 and 2008,

Recalling Commission on Narcotic Drugs resolution 42/5 of 25 March 1999 on international action to mitigate the effects of the relationship between drug abuse, illicit trafficking and conflict situations and resolution 43/4 of 15 March 2000 on international cooperation for the prevention of drug abuse among children,

Fully aware that the international community is confronted with the problem of conflict and war in some parts of the world, especially in Africa, Asia, Latin America and the Caribbean and Oceania, and with the threat to civil society posed by illicit drugs,

Concerned that the demand for, production of and trafficking in illicit narcotic drugs and psychotropic substances by organized criminal groups continue to pose a serious threat to the socio-economic and political systems, stability, national security and sovereignty of an increasing number of States, especially those emerging from conflict and war,

Concerned also about the activities of national and international organized criminal groups engaged in drug trafficking and, in particular, about the destabilizing impact of those activities on peacekeeping and reconstruction efforts,

Concerned further about reports of widespread abuse of drugs in countries emerging from conflict and war, among the general population and soldiers, especially child soldiers,

Aware that, in treating victims of conflict or war, self-medication or the long-term prescription of drugs by medical personnel may lead to drug dependence,

Convinced of the priority that must be assigned to the prevention of drug use and abuse among children, within the framework of the Action Plan for the Implementation of the Declaration on the Guiding Principles of Drug Demand Reduction,

Recognizing the social, political, economic and other post-conflict challenges to reconstruction faced by countries emerging from conflict, in particular with regard to meeting the targets set out in the Political Declaration adopted by the General Assembly at its twentieth special session,

Recognizing also the importance of the rule of law for post-conflict reconstruction,

Noting with satisfaction the steady progress being made towards restoring peace in a number of conflict zones around the world, especially in Africa, Asia, Latin America and the Caribbean and Oceania,

Mindful of the need to ensure that effective measures for the protection, rehabilitation, physical and psychological recovery and reintegration of women and children are systematically incorporated into all stages of the peace process, including peacekeeping and peacebuilding programmes,

Convinced that extending support for drug control will facilitate the consolidation of peace in countries emerging from conflict,

1. *Requests* the United Nations Office on Drugs and Crime to consider specific strategies to assist countries emerging from conflict in their drug control and related crime prevention efforts, in collaboration with the Governments of the affected countries and other relevant United Nations entities involved in the peace process, and to give priority to those countries, subject to the availability of voluntary funds, which might be from general-purpose funds, in accordance with the Commission on Narcotic Drugs guidelines for the use of general-purpose funds, or from earmarked funds;

2. *Calls upon* the United Nations Office on Drugs and Crime to facilitate the mainstreaming of drug control programmes in the development efforts of countries emerging from conflict;

3. *Urges* Member States emerging from conflict to give adequate priority to addressing the drug problem and related crime in their post-conflict reconstruction efforts and to collaborate with the United Nations Office on Drugs and Crime and other development partners in order to address those problems in an integrated and comprehensive manner;

4. *Urges* Member States providing development assistance to countries emerging from conflict to increase, where relevant, their bilateral assistance in drug control and related crime prevention to those countries;

5. *Requests* the Executive Director of the United Nations Office on Drugs and Crime to report to the Commission on Narcotic Drugs at its forty-eighth session on the progress made in the implementation of the present resolution.

Guidelines for travellers

A January report by the Executive Director [E/CN.7/2004/8] reviewed provisions regarding travellers under medical treatment with drugs containing narcotic drugs and psychotropic substances under international control. The report, submitted to the Commission on Narcotic Drugs pursuant to its resolution 46/6 [YUN 2003, p. 1284], stated that the 2002 guidelines [YUN 2002, p. 1249]

had been published in the form of a multilingual booklet in the six UN official languages and distributed to the national authorities. They were also available in English, French and Spanish on the INCB website. INCB intended to publish regularly details of communications from States on restrictions currently applicable in their countries to such travellers in the list of narcotic drugs (the "Yellow List") and the list of psychotropic substances (the "Green List") under international control and on the INCB website.

Guidelines for pharmacological treatment of opioid dependency

On 21 July [meeting 47], the Economic and Social Council, on the recommendation of the Commission on Narcotic Drugs [E/2004/28 & Corr.1], adopted **resolution 2004/40** without vote [agenda item 14 *(d)*].

Guidelines for psychosocially assisted pharmacological treatment of persons dependent on opioids

The Economic and Social Council,

Recognizing the existence of a large number of persons dependent on opioids, who are either receiving or are in need of treatment for their opioid dependence,

Respecting the sovereign right of Member States to establish and implement effective treatment strategies,

Noting the evidence on the effectiveness of various treatments, inter alia, abstinence therapy,

Recognizing the existence of a wide range of evidence-based treatment options,

Emphasizing that psychosocially assisted pharmacological treatment is one of the treatment options available for improving the health, well-being and social functioning of persons dependent on opioids and for preventing the transmission of HIV and other blood-borne diseases,

Acknowledging that the present resolution may be applicable only to Member States that are providing or planning psychosocially assisted pharmacological treatment for opiate addiction,

Recalling the Single Convention on Narcotic Drugs of 1961 as amended by the 1972 Protocol, in particular article 38 thereof, on measures against the abuse of drugs,

Recalling also the Declaration on the Guiding Principles of Drug Demand Reduction adopted by the General Assembly at its twentieth special session,

Taking into account the conclusions and recommendations adopted by the World Health Organization in 1993 after the twenty-eighth meeting of the Expert Committee on Drug Dependence, on the need to increase access to effective treatment,

Taking note of the report of the International Narcotics Control Board for 2003, in particular paragraphs 222 and 328 thereof,

Taking note also of the position paper of the World Health Organization, the United Nations Office on Drugs and Crime and the Joint United Nations Programme on HIV/AIDS (UNAIDS) on substitution maintenance therapy in the management of opioid dependence and HIV/AIDS prevention,

Acknowledging that work has been undertaken on psychosocially assisted pharmacological treatment in different regions,

Invites the World Health Organization, in collaboration with the United Nations Office on Drugs and Crime, subject to the availability of voluntary funds, which might be either from general-purpose funds, in accordance with the Commission on Narcotic Drugs guidelines for the use of general-purpose funds, or from earmarked funds, to develop and publish minimum requirements and international guidelines on psychosocially assisted pharmacological treatment of persons dependent on opioids, taking into account regional initiatives in this field, in order to assist the Member States concerned.

Illicit cultivation, manufacture and trafficking

At its forty-seventh session, the Commission considered a January report by the Executive Director on international assistance to the States affected by the transit of illicit drugs [E/CN.7/2004/7], prepared in response to Economic and Social Council resolution 2003/34 [YUN 2003, p. 1285]. The report reviewed UNODC activities to assist States through programmes in Africa, Asia and the Pacific, Central and Eastern Europe, Central Asia, and Latin America and the Caribbean. Assistance was provided to upgrade legislation and judicial procedures; strengthen the technical skills of law enforcement agencies; improve data collection by national agencies to support informed responses to combat illicit drug trafficking and the problems associated with it; provide equipment to front-line operations; and strengthen cross-border and regional cooperation and assistance to develop self-sustaining training in the best operating practices for government law enforcement services.

Another January report by the Executive Director [E/CN.7/2004/6], submitted in response to Commission resolution 45/9 [YUN 2002, p. 1249], analysed connections between organized criminal groups trafficking in drugs and those involved in other types of illicit trafficking, and reviewed UNODC activities in counteracting such criminality. UNODC assisted Governments in upgrading their professional skills and introducing new approaches and procedures to break the link between drug trafficking and cross-border criminality. It provided training and assistance in special investigative techniques, and helped law enforcement agencies to upgrade their technical capacity so as to keep pace with the sophisticated technology used by organized criminal groups. The Office placed special emphasis on the use and promotion of controlled delivery in dismantling trafficking networks and in identifying and prosecuting criminal groups. In that regard, it assisted States in drafting and introducing legislation.

On 19 March [E/2004/28 & Corr.1 (res. 47/5)], the Commission affirmed the need to develop and harmonize the illicit drug profiling activities of the international drug law enforcement community, and requested UNODC, in cooperation with Member States, to prepare a report identifying drug profiling initiatives and best practices. It encouraged Member States to enhance their capacity to undertake profile analysis of seized illicit drugs; participate in the international exchange of drug profile analysis information and samples; and review their legislation to facilitate the exchange of drug profiling information and samples with other States. Member States were invited to promote the utilization of laboratory data to support the work of regulatory and health authorities and to establish programmes and law enforcement frameworks for that purpose.

Also on 19 March [res. 47/6], the Commission invited Member States to adopt or review national laws and procedures on controlled delivery operations; strengthen internal cooperation and coordination and establish joint training courses on controlled delivery. It requested UNODC to consider preparing a training manual on controlled delivery operations and compile, in conjunction with relevant international organizations and with the assistance of Member States, all relevant information. UNODC was requested to report on the progress made in 2005.

ECONOMIC AND SOCIAL COUNCIL ACTION

On 21 July [meeting 47], the Economic and Social Council, on the recommendation of the Commission on Narcotic Drugs [E/2004/28 & Corr.1], adopted **resolution 2004/41** without vote [agenda item 14 (d)].

Control of the manufacture of, trafficking in and abuse of synthetic drugs

The Economic and Social Council,

Concerned at the escalation of the problem of illicit supply of, trafficking in and diversion of synthetic drugs and the expansion of the illicit market for such drugs,

Noting that the supply of illicit drugs, including synthetic drugs, is harmful to public health and that the demand for such drugs is prevalent among young people,

Recognizing that education and training are prerequisites for the efficient performance of the various tasks that institutions and their officials must carry out in order to deal with the world drug problem,

Deeply concerned that an increasing number of people are placing their health at risk by abusing amphetamine-type stimulants because they do not recognize or are not aware of the health hazards associated with the abuse of such stimulants, in particular the abuse of methylenedioxymethamphetamine, commonly known as Ecstasy,

Noting that reducing both the illicit demand for and the illicit supply of amphetamine-type stimulants in a comprehensive and proactive manner requires strong political commitment,

Noting also that strategies to reduce the illicit demand for and supply of amphetamine-type stimulants require accurate information, including data on the manufacture of, trafficking in and abuse of such stimulants,

Considering that, in view of the extent of the abuse of amphetamine-type stimulants among young people and among persons in certain occupational groups, there is a need for more systematic research into the health hazards of the abuse of such stimulants that will contribute to improving the design of health education and prevention programmes, as well as treatment services, to meet the needs of all persons abusing amphetamine-type stimulants,

Considering also that systematic research into the health hazards of the abuse of amphetamine-type stimulants is crucial to assessments of the broader health and social implications of the specific patterns of abuse of such stimulants,

Acknowledging the importance of early warning mechanisms and rapid and global dissemination of information on new drugs, drug combinations and drug abuse patterns and more detailed information, such as the dyes, logos, machinery and other equipment used in the manufacture of amphetamine-type stimulants,

1. *Expresses its gratitude* to the United Nations Office on Drugs and Crime for the publication of *Ecstasy and Amphetamines: Global Survey 2003*, which provides a quantitative assessment of the extent of manufacture of, trafficking in and abuse of amphetamine-type stimulants throughout the world;

2. *Requests* Member States to continue to develop programmes to reduce both the illicit supply of and the illicit demand for amphetamine-type stimulants;

3. *Urges* Member States to take the steps necessary to ensure that their national drug control agencies are aware of and well trained in the recognition of amphetamine-type stimulants and the current modi operandi used to smuggle such stimulants and are also well trained in the interdiction of consignments of illicitly manufactured amphetamine-type stimulants;

4. *Also urges* Member States to monitor changing patterns in the abuse and availability of synthetic drugs, including methylenedioxymethamphetamine, commonly known as Ecstasy;

5. *Calls upon* Member States to include, in a multi-faceted strategy, action against the illicit manufacture of, trafficking in and abuse of amphetamine-type stimulants and to identify and dismantle clandestine laboratories manufacturing such stimulants;

6. *Encourages* Member States to provide their full and active support to Project Prism, an initiative of the International Narcotics Control Board, to address the illicit manufacture of amphetamine-type stimulants by following the twofold approach of the Project, namely, by establishing mechanisms to prevent precursor chemicals from being diverted from licit international trade or domestic distribution channels and by launching backtracking investigations of seizures and interceptions to identify the illicit sources and the persons involved;

7. *Urges* Member States to provide accurate evidence-based information on the harmful effects of amphetamine-type stimulants, through education and information campaigns to increase public knowledge and awareness of those harmful effects, with a view to decreasing the demand for such stimulants, particularly among young people;

8. *Urges* States engaged in the licit manufacture, import, export and transit of precursor chemicals used in the illicit manufacture of amphetamine-type stimulants to implement fully the United Nations Convention against Illicit Traffic in Narcotic Drugs and Psychotropic Substances of 1988 and, where appropriate, to strengthen controls over those substances, in conformity with that Convention;

9. *Urges* the relevant international organizations to consider providing support for training and other forms of technical assistance aimed at countering the threat of synthetic drugs, including by strengthening preventive measures;

10. *Encourages* the relevant international organizations and other entities, in particular the United Nations Office on Drugs and Crime, to continue to recognize the serious global threat posed by synthetic drugs and to pursue appropriate action to ameliorate the situation;

11. *Requests* the Executive Director of the United Nations Office on Drugs and Crime to report to the Commission on Narcotic Drugs at its forty-eighth session on the implementation of the present resolution.

On the same day [meeting 47], the Council, on the recommendation of the Commission [E/2004/28 & Corr.1], adopted **resolution 2004/36** without vote [agenda item 14 (*d*)].

Control of cultivation of and trafficking in cannabis

The Economic and Social Council

Recommends to the General Assembly the adoption of the following draft resolution:

[For text, see General Assembly resolution 59/160 below.]

GENERAL ASSEMBLY ACTION

On 20 December [meeting 74], the General Assembly, on the recommendation of the Third Committee [A/59/495], adopted **resolution 59/160** without vote [agenda item 97].

Control of cultivation of and trafficking in cannabis

The General Assembly,

Recalling the Single Convention on Narcotic Drugs of 1961, that Convention as amended by the 1972 Protocol, the Convention on Psychotropic Substances of 1971 and the United Nations Convention against Illicit Traffic in Narcotic Drugs and Psychotropic Substances of 1988,

Recalling also Commission on Narcotic Drugs resolution 45/8 of 15 March 2002 on the control of cannabis in Africa,

Concerned that, of all the substances listed in the international drug control treaties, cannabis is by far the most widely and most frequently abused, especially among young people,

Concerned also that the abuse of cannabis, especially among young people, often leads to risk-taking behaviour,

Concerned further that cultivation of and trafficking in cannabis are on the increase in Africa partly as a result of extreme poverty and the absence of any viable alternative crop and partly because of the profitability of such activity and the high demand for cannabis in other regions of the world,

Noting with concern that increased cultivation of cannabis in Africa is extremely dangerous for the ecosystem because it leads to extensive use of fertilizers, overexploitation of the soil and destruction of forests to make room for new cannabis fields, thus accelerating soil erosion,

Taking note of the report of the International Narcotics Control Board for 2003, in which the Board confirmed that the production of, trafficking in and abuse of cannabis continued to pose a serious problem in various regions of the world,

Aware of the importance of programmes promoting alternative development, including, where appropriate, preventive alternative development,

Emphasizing the primary importance of international cooperation in combating drug trafficking and drug abuse,

1. *Welcomes* the 2003 cannabis survey conducted by Morocco in cooperation with the United Nations Office on Drugs and Crime;

2. *Requests* the United Nations Office on Drugs and Crime, subject to the availability of voluntary funds, which might be either from general-purpose funds, in accordance with the Commission on Narcotic Drugs guidelines for the use of general-purpose funds, or from earmarked funds, to begin a global survey of cannabis, initially with a market survey, before the forty-eighth session of the Commission on Narcotic Drugs;

3. *Also requests* the United Nations Office on Drugs and Crime to support the creation or strengthening of national and subregional strategies and plans of action for the eradication of cannabis crops, subject to the availability of voluntary funds, which might be either from general-purpose funds, in accordance with the Commission on Narcotic Drugs guidelines for the use of general-purpose funds, or from earmarked funds;

4. *Urges* Member States, in accordance with the principle of shared responsibility and as a sign of their commitment to the fight against illicit drugs, to extend cooperation to affected States, particularly in Africa, in the area of alternative development, including funding for research into crops offering viable alternatives to cannabis, environmental protection and technical assistance;

5. *Encourages* Member States with experience and expertise in the eradication of illicit drug crops and alternative development programmes to share their experience and expertise with affected States, particularly in Africa;

6. *Urges* all Member States to encourage appropriate access to international markets for products of alternative development projects in order to support efforts aimed at eliminating the production of narcotic drugs and promoting sustainable development;

7. *Encourages* Member States to apply new strategies and tools to complement existing ones in efforts to combat trafficking in cannabis;

8. *Calls upon* all States to ensure strict compliance with all the provisions of the Single Convention on Narcotic Drugs of 1961, that Convention as amended by the 1972 Protocol, the Convention on Psychotropic Substances of 1971 and the United Nations Convention against Illicit Traffic in Narcotic Drugs and Psychotropic Substances of 1988;

9. *Requests* the Executive Director of the United Nations Office on Drugs and Crime to report to the Commission on Narcotic Drugs at its forty-eighth session on the implementation of the present resolution.

Secretariat report. A report by the Secretariat [E/CN.7/2005/4] described global trends and patterns in illicit drug crop cultivation and production of plant-based drugs during 2003-2004 and in illicit drug trafficking up to 2003, and summarized the information received from Governments and elsewhere. The primary sources of information were from the UNODC illicit crop monitoring surveys, the replies to the annual reports questionnaire and reports on significant drug seizures. The information received was as at 10 November 2004. The report also gave an overview on drug-related crime and other types of crime and provided information pursuant to Commission resolutions 47/5 and 47/6 (see p. 1251).

Cannabis continued to be the world's most trafficked drug, accounting for over two thirds of global drug seizures in 2003. It was the most seized drug in Africa and the Americas, while cannabis resin was the most seized drug in Asia and Europe. Trafficking in cannabis herb seriously affected countries in Africa and the Americas, where it accounted for 26 and 68 per cent, respectively, of global seizures. Trafficking routes for cannabis herb were more diffuse than for other illicit drugs because of the large number of source countries. Opiates, followed by cocaine, remained the principal problem drugs in the world. Global seizures of opiates (heroin, morphine and opium converted into heroin equivalents) increased 33 per cent, with Asia accounting for 76 per cent, Europe 17 per cent, the Americas 6 per cent and Africa and Oceania less than 1 per cent. Cocaine traffickers continued to target countries in the Americas and, increasingly, markets in Western Europe. Both continents accounted for the bulk of the cocaine seizures worldwide, with Colombia and the United States reporting 52 per cent of global seizures in 2003. Brazil and Venezuela were affected by trafficking in cocaine bound for the United States and Europe. ATS accounted for 3.5 per cent of global drug seizures, of which methamphetamine was responsible for 69 per cent, followed by amphetamine (14 per cent) and Ecstasy (13 per cent). East and South-East Asia were the most affected subregions.

In its conclusion, the report stated that future trends in trafficking in opiates would be determined by events in Afghanistan, where the development of that country's legitimate economy through private sector investment would provide the conditions for alternative sustainable livelihoods. Also of concern were opium poppy cultivation in Colombia and Mexico and the spread of coca bush to fragile ecosystems and Indian lands in the Andean subregion. The spread of illicit cannabis cultivation and the consequent increase in cannabis users worldwide would require further attention from the international community. The relatively low volume of seizures in certain subregions, in particular in Africa, was not indicative of the absence of trafficking, but of underreporting of seizures or inadequate resources available by Governments and the international community to law enforcement agencies. Interdiction figures for ATS in 2003 pointed to a regained momentum in its illicit manufacturing and trafficking and called for renewed efforts by Governments in the regions concerned.

Regional cooperation

A December report by the Secretariat [E/CN.7/2005/5] reviewed action taken by the Commission's subsidiary bodies in 2004. Following a review of drug trafficking trends and regional and subregional cooperation, each subsidiary body addressed drug law enforcement issues of priority in its region and made recommendations. The thirty-ninth session of the Subcommission on Illicit Drug Traffic and Related Matters in the Near and Middle East (Beirut, Lebanon, 26-29 October) [UNODC/SUBCOM/2004/5] considered trafficking in opiates and the heightened need for coordination between States and law enforcement agencies across the region; current regional trends in the illicit manufacture of and trafficking in ATS; and combating corruption through effective and uncompromising law enforcement. The fourteenth meeting of Heads of National Drug Law Enforcement Agencies (HONLEA), Africa (Cairo, Egypt, 30 May–3 June) [UNODC/HONLAF/2004/6] considered drug trafficking, conflict and violence: the challenge to law enforcement in conflict and post-conflict situations; emerging trafficking challenges; and cannabis: the African connection. The fourteenth meeting of HONLEA, Latin America and the Caribbean (Mexico City, 11-15 October) [UNODC/HONLAC/2004/5] examined effective measures against cocaine manufacture and trafficking; procedures to identify, seize and confiscate goods and assets derived from crime; and drug trafficking by sea: a review of controls over the sea container traffic in Latin America and the Caribbean. The twenty-eighth meeting of HONLEA, Asia and the Pacific (Bangkok, Thailand, 29 November–3 December) [UNODC/HONLAP/2004/5] considered detecting and dis-

mantling clandestine drug laboratories; effective measures to counter heroin trafficking; effective procedures to identify, seize and confiscate goods and assets derived from crime; and a regional approach to strategic planning to counter cross-border organized crime.

On 19 March [E/2004/28 & Corr.1 (res. 47/4)], the Commission affirmed the relevance of measures that facilitated effective cooperation in international investigations of cases involving illicit drugs, in conformity with treaties on mutual legal assistance, and encouraged Member States to utilize established liaison channels and to develop new channels to enhance their capacity to participate in joint and/or coordinated targeting initiatives and international cooperation in investigating cases involving illicit drug trafficking.

Strengthening UN mechanisms

The Commission on Narcotic Drugs had before it a January report by the Executive Director on strengthening UNDCP and the role of the Commission [E/CN.7/2004/10]. The report, prepared in response to Commission resolution 46/8 [YUN 2003, p. 1288], reviewed action taken to facilitate dialogue between Member States and UNDCP, and the Programme's operations, management and funding.

On 19 March [E/2004/28 & Corr.1 (res. 47/3)], the Commission welcomed the UNODC restructuring and ongoing process of reform, which should continue so as to maintain a culture of continuous improvement. It encouraged the Executive Director to facilitate dialogue with Member States on programmatic and management issues and on the reform process, and welcomed the measures taken to ensure good governance within UNODC and the establishment of the new independent evaluation unit. It called for continued transparency in the management of human resources. Reaffirming its governing role in the UNODC budget process, the Commission requested UNODC to facilitate that role by continuing to present timely briefings and reports to Member States. It encouraged the Executive Director to expand on the strategic framework called for in Assembly resolution 58/269 [YUN 2003, p. 1395] and to develop a plan for UNODC that would provide medium- and long-term strategic direction. The Commission welcomed the development of a transparent financial system and supported the efforts of the Executive Director to ensure that issues on the fight against drugs and related crime were included in sustainable development policies. The Executive Director was requested to report in 2005.

Chapter XV

Statistics

During 2004, the United Nations continued to broaden its work in the area of statistics, mainly through the activities of the Statistical Commission and the United Nations Statistics Division. In March, the Statistical Commission recommended the establishment of an expert group to focus on the next (2010) round of population and housing censuses; requested the expansion of the Statistics Division website; and endorsed two new United Nations Human Settlements Programme initiatives—the Monitoring Urban Inequities Programme and the Geographic Information System to 1,000 Cities Programme. It welcomed the findings of the Friends of the Chair on health statistics, calling for a review of international health statistics programmes and the establishment of an intersecretariat working group. The Commission approved changes to the 2004-2005 work programme of the Statistics Division and the strategic framework for the 2006-2007 biennium.

The Commission reviewed the work of groups of countries and international organizations in various areas of economic, social, demographic and environment statistics and made specific recommendations and suggestions.

Work of Statistical Commission

The Statistical Commission, in accordance with Economic and Social Council **decision 2004/215** of 13 February, held its thirty-fifth session in New York from 2 to 5 March [E/2004/24 & Corr.1]. Actions included: endorsement of the recommendations of the Expert Group on International Economic and Social Classifications; agreement with the proposed work plan for revision of the International Standard Industrial Classification of All Economic Activities (ISIC) and the Central Product Classification (CPC); a request to the Statistics Division to find a forum of coordination, to be decided on at the next Committee for the Coordination of Statistical Activities (CCSA) meeting; and acknowledgement of the work of the World Tourism Organization.

Having reviewed the statistical work of groups of countries and international organizations, the Commission took note of steps taken by the

World Health Organization (WHO) to address health statistics concerns; progress achieved towards the preparation of a poverty statistics handbook; and the issuance of the *Handbook of National Accounting on the System of Integrated Environmental and Economic Accounting, 2003* (SEEA-2003) on the Statistics Division web site. Welcoming the work of CCSA and progress made in the implementation of the Fundamental Principles of Official Statistics, the Commission emphasized the need for a coordinated effort to further develop indicators on information and communication technologies. It supported the work programme and timetable for updating the System of National Accounts, 1993 [YUN 1993, p. 1112] and the Organisation for Economic Co-operation and Development (OECD) proposal on coordination of services statistics. The Commission reaffirmed its support for the International Comparison Programme and emphasized the usefulness of purchasing power parities. It concluded that further investment in the development of sustainable statistical capacity would be required if availability of statistics, including those needed to monitor the Millennium Development Goals (MDGs) [YUN 2000, p. 51], was to be achieved. In support of coordinated follow-up to UN conferences and summits, the Commission asked its Bureau to examine the Commission's working methods and to present the outcome at its thirty-sixth (2005) session. The Commission approved changes to the 2004-2005 Statistics Division work programme and endorsed the proposed 2006-2007 programme plan.

On 13 February (**decision 2004/215**), the Council noted the Commission's report on its thirty-fourth session [YUN 2003, p. 1289]. On 20 July (**decision 2004/236**), it noted the Commission's report on its thirty-fifth session (above), decided that the thirty-sixth session should be held in New York from 1 to 4 March 2005 and approved the provisional agenda and documentation for that session.

Economic statistics

National accounts

In response to a 2003 Statistical Commission request [YUN 2003, p. 1290], the Secretary-General transmitted the report of the Intersecretariat Working Group on National Accounts (ISWGNA) [E/CN.3/2004/10]. The report examined the work programme for the 2008 update of the System of National Accounts, 1993 (1993 SNA) [YUN 1993, p. 1112], including issues relating to selection criteria, the governance and decision-making process, a timetable for consultations and comments from Commission members. It also discussed the assessment of the implementation of the 1993 SNA, particularly compliance with the 1993 SNA concepts, the scope of the accounts and quality issues.

The Commission expressed satisfaction with progress achieved during the first meeting (Washington, D.C., 16-20 February) of the Advisory Expert Group on National Accounts. Reconfirming the importance of updating the 1993 SNA, it supported the detailed work programme and noted the adequateness of the governance structure and decision-making mechanism. It reiterated that the revision process should build upon the conceptual basis of the 1993 SNA and reconfirmed the eligibility criteria for issues to be updated. The Commission also reiterated the need for maintaining consistency with ongoing revisions of the *Balance of Payments Manual* and related public sector accounting frameworks, and for coherence with business accounting standards. Emphasizing the need for transparency and involvement of the global statistical community in the updating process, the Commission suggested using electronically circulated questionnaires to record member States' opinions and strengthening the consultation process through additional regional workshops. In regard to funding the 1993 SNA updating programme, the Commission welcomed the financial and human resources commitments of member countries and encouraged additional funding to supplement resources committed by international agencies. The Commission, while noting progress in the implementation of the 1993 SNA and the increased compliance with its recommendations, called for further technical support to countries not yet in a position to adopt it. The Commission suggested further research into factors that impeded SNA implementation and requested the Statistics Division, in collaboration with regional offices, to draft an action plan for that purpose and seek the necessary funding.

Service statistics

In March, the Commission had before it the 2003 report of the Voorburg Group on Service Statistics [E/CN.3/2004/11], focusing on the core areas of: producer price indices, classifications of service activities and products, and information society statistics, and other issues such as turnover by product, strategy, and products, and activities for the Group's 2004 meeting.

It also had before an interim OECD report on service statistics [E/CN.3/2004/12], submitted in response to a 2003 Statistical Commission request [YUN 2003, p. 1291], which described the OECD project to improve the coordination of international development work in service statistics and outlined ideas for developing a strategic approach. OECD proposed that its coordination role should be light and feasible by identifying issues and contact persons to provide annual reports on progress and new outputs for the Commission and the Voorburg Group, coordinate with other non-OECD expert groups, maintain a web page with outputs and information and contribute ideas and proposals on service statistics. The OECD Statistics Directorate would integrate those reports in an annual report to the Commission and the Voorburg Group. A draft proposal for developing a matrix of issues/groups/coordinators and relevant information was set out in the report. The report also set out a timetable for preparing a proposal on service coordination and strategy development for presentation to the Commission and OECD in 2004 and other service activities.

The Commission also considered a report of the Inter-Agency Task Force on Statistics of International Trade in Services, which discussed implementation of the guidelines contained in the *Manual on Statistics of International Trade in Services.* The Task Force held its nineteenth meeting in Paris on 13 and 14 September.

The Commission welcomed the reports of OECD and the Voorburg Group. While expressing appreciation for the work of the Voorburg Group and supporting strategic discussions planned for its next meeting, the Commission cautioned against expanding the topics discussed by the Group. It supported the OECD proposal for a light approach to coordination and noted the desire of countries and regional bodies to participate in future OECD and Voorburg Group meetings. The OECD 2005 strategy paper, the Commission emphasized, should provide guidance to the service statistics agenda, including the Voorburg Group agenda.

International Comparison Programme

The Secretary-General submitted the World Bank report on the International Comparison Programme (ICP) [E/CN.3/2004/14], which detailed the establishment of the ICP international secretariat (Global Office) and its Executive Board—a consortium of national, regional and international institutions, including OECD and the Statistical Office of the European Communities (Eurostat). In addition to coverage of the first meeting of the ICP Technical Advisory Group (TAG) (Washington, D.C., 21-23 May 2003), the report summarized the TAG review of the ICP handbook, the creation of the ICP tool pack software system, efforts to compute poverty-specific purchasing power parities (PPPs), features of the new ICP website and a new approach to product description called structured product description. The Programme faced a $6.8 million funding shortfall.

In March, the Commission reaffirmed its support for ICP, emphasizing the usefulness of PPPs in poverty issues analysis and the Programme's potential for capacity-building in consumer price and national accounts statistics. It appreciated the progress achieved in the implementation of the 2004-2006 round of ICP, welcomed the wider dissemination of Programme information through the enhanced ICP web site and noted the progress in the preparation of the ICP handbook and development of ICP software. The Commission acknowledged the World Bank's role in the coordination of ICP, the guidance provided by the Executive Board and TAG, as well as the cooperation of OECD and Eurostat, efforts of regional coordinating agencies, the contribution of donor agencies and the work of participating countries. The Commission underlined the importance of the timely release of results to maximize the usefulness of data and noted that the effect of rapid price increases on the results of affected countries needed to be taken into account. Supporting the view that seeking funding, rather than reducing or limiting the Programme's goals, was the preferred approach, the Commission recommended that efforts to secure additional funding and in-kind support should be intensified to overcome the shortfall.

A December World Bank report [E/CN.3/2005/7] indicated that the Programme's financial status had improved due to a contribution from the World Bank's internal data budget, which reduced the deficit to about $1.1 million through fiscal year 2007.

Other economic statistics

Tourism statistics

The Statistical Commission had before it the report of the World Tourism Organization (WTO/OMT) on the development of tourism statistics [E/CN.3/2004/13]. The report discussed the implementation of the main functions of WTO/OMT and its 2004-2006 work programme, which

included proposed initiatives for updating the conceptual framework of tourism statistics, deepening the relationship between the tourism satellite account and the 1993 SNA, providing countries with guidelines for setting up a tourism satellite account and disseminating international guidelines for the presentation of statistical data and metadata.

The Commission acknowledged work done by WTO/OMT to develop and promote implementation of standards and disseminate tourism statistics, to provide training and capacity-building assistance in new areas, such as tourism satellite accounts, and to improve the international comparability and quality of tourism data. Noting the need for an international exchange of experiences in the compilation of tourism statistics, the Commission asked WTO/OMT to facilitate an exchange of best practices. To address the need for stronger coordination in tourism statistics and in the periodic revision of international recommendations, the Commission requested the Statistics Division to facilitate finding an appropriate coordination forum to be decided on by CCSA.

Statistics of science and technology

The Commission took note of the report of the United Nations Educational, Scientific and Cultural Organization and OECD on statistics of science and technology [E/CN.3/2004/15], which was transmitted by the Secretary-General, describing current work in that area, highlighting challenges faced and outlining expected future developments.

Information and communication technologies statistics

The Statistical Commission considered the report of the International Telecommunication Union (ITU) on information and communication technologies (ICT) statistics [E/CN.3/2004/16]. It discussed the OECD definition of ICT, ways of organizing ICT statistics for analytical purposes and the role of ICT in achieving the MDGs [YUN 2000, p. 51].

The Commission took note of the ITU report and emphasized the need for a coordinated effort to further develop indicators on ICT. It expressed the need for capacity-building, particularly in developing countries, and noted the suggestion that measures of ICT use should also include the government sector.

Business surveys and informal sector statistics

The Commission noted the report of the Round Table on Business Survey Frames [E/CN.3/2004/17] and recommended that it should review its priorities and focus on issues such as adequate business register frames for the service industries. It also noted underrepresentation of developing countries at Round Table meetings and encouraged their closer involvement in the future work of the group.

Taking note of the report of the Delhi Group on Informal Sector Statistics [E/CN.3/2004/18], the Commission acknowledged the progress achieved in the development and refinement of a harmonized definition of the informal sector and its measurement methods. It supported the Group's planned activities and expressed the need for building on existing household survey capability of national statistical offices. The Commission took note of the adoption by the International Labour Organization (ILO) of revised guidelines on informal employment and plans for the Statistics Division and the Delhi Group to prepare jointly a recommendation on the informal sector as part of the updating of the 1993 SNA.

Environmental statistics

The Commission had before it the report of the London Group on Environmental Accounting [E/CN.3/2004/19], which summarized its work programme and organizational structure, and the report of the Inter-Agency Working Group on Environment Statistics [E/CN.3/2004/20], established in 2003 [YUN 2003, p. 1293].

The Commission welcomed the report of the London Group, endorsed its organization and means of operation and supported its strategic directions. It also supported the preparation of an issue paper on the possible expansion of SEEA-2003 to include social aspects. It noted developing countries' success in the implementation of water and other natural resources accounting and stressed the usefulness of the accounts as tools for integrated resource management and dialogue with policy makers.

It also noted the report of the Inter-Agency Working Group.

Demographic and social statistics

Population and housing censuses

In March, the Statistical Commission [E/2004/24 & Corr.1] recommended the establishment of an international expert group to focus on planning issues related to the next (2010) round of population and housing censuses. It agreed to consider a resolution in 2005 requesting the Secretary-General to proceed with the development of a 2010 World Population and Housing Census Programme and recommended that Member States

carry out population and housing censuses during the period 2005-2014. Recognizing that the Statistics Division decennial census programme could not cover all emerging topics, the Commission asked the expert group to set priorities at its first meeting. It welcomed action 2 of the Marrakesh Action Plan for improving development statistics in support of preparation for the 2010 census round (see p. 1261).

At the global level, the Statistics Division conducted the United Nations Symposium on Population and Housing Censuses (New York, 13-14 September), which outlined a range of activities relevant to the 2010 Programme and the United Nations Expert Group Meeting to Review Critical Issues Relevant to the Planning of the 2010 Round of Population and Housing Censuses (New York, 15-17 September), which produced a set of recommendations on technical and scientific aspects of emerging issues [E/CN.3/2005/11 & Corr.1].

Human settlements statistics

The Statistical Commission had before it the report of the United Nations Human Settlements Programme (UN-Habitat) on human settlements statistics [E/CN.3/2004/5].

UN-Habitat pursued a two-pronged strategy. It continued to collect and report on official city statistics, including the preparation of the *Compendium of Human Settlements Statistics* [YUN 1999, p. 1196], and to reform its Urban Indicators Programme, and launched two new programmes: the Monitoring of Urban Inequities Programme (MUIP), under which Urban Inequities Household Surveys would be conducted in 35 cities in Asia, Latin America and Africa, and the Geographic Information System (GIS) to 1,000 cities, a capacity-building project, which supported the implementation of urban information systems at the local level using GIS technology.

The Commission endorsed the MUIP and GIS to 1,000 cities initiatives and noted points in the UN-Habitat report that needed reconsideration, including consideration of extra-legal aspects under country-specific conditions; the definition of slums and their determinants; and the proposed classification used for human settlements (urban, rural and slums). It also recognized the need for capacity-building of the national statistical offices to generate urban settlements statistics and indicators.

Health statistics

The Commission had before it the report of the Friends of the Chair on health statistics [E/CN.3/2004/4], established in response to a 2003

Commission request [YUN 2003, p. 1294] to examine coordination among and between international organizations and national statistical offices in health statistics and to recommend improvements.

The report discussed the official statistics framework, databases, technical resource requirements, the role of national statistical offices and areas of mutual interest, such as health surveys and the development of core health indicators.

The Commission welcomed the findings of the Friends of the Chair and noted the steps taken by WHO to address such concerns as the establishment of the Health Metrics Network; the proposed meeting of stakeholders on methods used to compile and generate mortality and health statistics; and the proposed joint Economic Commission for Europe (ECE)/WHO/Eurostat meeting to enhance consultation, coordination and collaboration in health statistics (see below). It underscored that the Fundamental Principles of Official Statistics should be applied in the development of official health statistics and requested that the declaration of principles under preparation by CCSA take into account relevant issues listed in the Friends of the Chair report. It also underscored the need to strengthen national capacities in health statistics.

The Commission called for a strategic review of international programmes on the production of health statistics and for an intersecretariat working group on health statistics to develop a coordinated agenda for the production of health statistics and to agree on standard definitions, classifications and methodologies. It also called on WHO to prepare an annual report on progress on specific initiatives in support of harmonization and improved coordination of health statistics. Reiterating its interest in being informed on alternative methods of estimating the prevalence of HIV/AIDS, the Commission requested closer cooperation at the regional level among WHO, its regional offices and other health statistics agencies.

A joint ECE/WHO/Eurostat meeting [E/CN.3/2005/12] on the measurement of health status (Geneva, 24-26 May) agreed on the WHO conceptual framework to measure health.

In June, WHO organized a one-day meeting of agency, donor and academic experts to address the requests made by participants at the high-level forum on health-related MDGs (Geneva, January).

Drug statistics

The Commission had before it the report of the United Nations Office on Drugs and Crime (UNODC) on statistics of drugs and drug use [E/CN.3/2004/6], which provided a summary of the 2003 edition of its annual statistical publication, *Global Illicit Drug Trends*. The Commission took note of UNODC's work on drug statistics, the need for national capacity-building to produce reliable statistics and the need for further development of methods for measuring various components of the world drug problem.

Labour statistics

Having considered the report of the Paris Group on Labour and Compensation [E/CN.3/2004/7], the Commission endorsed the activities proposed by the Group related to the outcome of the Seventeenth International Conference of Labour Statisticians (Geneva, 24 November-3 December 2003). It recommended work programme topics for the Group to explore, suggested that it continue to work with ILO in developing international standards in "working time", and requested it to encourage greater participation of developing countries in its deliberations.

Poverty statistics

The Commission had before it the report of the Secretary-General on poverty statistics [E/CN.3/2004/8] and the report of the Rio Group on Poverty Statistics [E/CN.3/2004/9].

The Commission noted the progress made in the preparation of a handbook on poverty statistics and expressed appreciation for the broad consultative process put in place by the Statistics Division for its further elaboration. The handbook should be a practical guide to poverty measurements based on country practices, address specific analytical aspects and broaden its focus to include best practices of poverty measurements in developed countries.

The Commission noted the continuing preparation by the Rio Group of a compendium on best practices of poverty statistics and welcomed the Statistics Division's intention to work with the Group on a joint publication.

Social statistics

The Commission had before it the Secretary-General's report on social statistics (programme review) [E/CN.3/2004/2], which described activities carried out by the Statistics Division in 2003 and its proposed 2004-2014 work programme, including plans to establish a social statistics forum to review the international work programme for social statistics; expand the web site on international statistics; conduct an integrated review of international principles and recommendations; and undertake a thorough review of the *Demo-*

graphic Yearbook work programme for 2004-2005. It also considered the report of the Siena Group for Social Statistics [E/CN.3/2004/3].

The Commission endorsed the proposal presented by the Statistics Division for replacing the proposed social statistics forum and related activities set out in the Secretary-General's report. It requested that the Division, as part of its alternative dissemination programme for the *Demographic Yearbook*, establish a well-structured web site to ensure the exchange of census and other data free of charge.

The Commission took note of the report of the Siena Group and requested that it focus on key issues, such as considering the possibility of developing model survey modules for social statistics and contributing to Commission activities by identifying a clear list of deliverable outputs and lead members. The Commission also noted the inadequate participation of developing countries in the Group's meetings.

Disability statistics

The Commission had before it the "Executive summary of the Third Meeting of the Washington Group on Disability Statistics" (Brussels, Belgium, 19-20 February). It took note of the presentation made and of progress being made by the Group.

Other statistical activities

International economic and social classifications

The Statistical Commission had before it a January report of the Secretary-General on international economic and social classifications [E/CN.3/2004/22], which outlined how Commission recommendations on international statistical classifications had been addressed since its 2003 session.

The Commission endorsed the recommendations of the Expert Group on International Economic and Social Classifications and its Technical Subgroup on the revision of ISIC and CPC, including the proposed ISIC high-level structure as a basis for detailed work on the classification. It agreed with the proposed work plan for the revisions and supported the development of a limited top-level structure for ISIC in conjunction with the ISWGNA. The Commission noted the efforts of the Food and Agriculture Organization of the United Nations to work on the classification of agricultural activities and products as part of the ISIC and CPC revisions and endorsed the work undertaken to ensure the consistency of ISIC and the Statistical Classification of Eco-

nomic Activities in the European Community. It noted ILO plans for revising the International Standard Classification of Occupations by 2007, and agreed with the International Merchandise Trade Statistics Task Force that the fourth revision of the Standard International Trade Classification should be prepared for 2007.

Official statistics

The Secretary-General submitted a report on the result of a survey on the implementation of the Fundamental Principles of Official Statistics [E/CN.3/2004/21], prepared by ECE and adopted by the Statistical Commission in 1994 [YUN 1994, p. 1265].

The Commission, while welcoming the progress made in the implementation of the Principles, expressed disappointment that only 58 per cent of all countries (50 per cent of developing countries and 31 per cent of least developed countries) had responded to the survey. It considered it important to obtain information from those that had not responded, study the implementation in greater depth for a sample of countries and analyse the variations in implementation to determine what action to take. It reaffirmed that the Principles should be broadly applied by all national statistical systems. The Commission considered that a compendium of best practices would be helpful to countries in their implementation efforts and that more advocacy efforts were needed. It identified areas in the Principles and related issues for additional thought and research, and considered it useful to survey the extent to which statistical services in the international organizations had implemented them.

Statistical capacity-building

The Commission considered a report of the Secretary-General on indicators for monitoring the implementation of the MDGs [E/CN.3/2004/23], submitted in response to a 2003 Commission request [YUN 2003, p. 1295], which described Statistics Division activities in leading inter-agency monitoring of the achievement of the MDGs, reviewed data availability and problems in compiling MDG indicators and described the activities of the Inter-Agency Expert Group on MDG Indicators for improving the situation. The Commission also had before it the report of the Advisory Committee on Indicators [E/CN.3/2004/24], the report of the Steering Committee of the Partnership in Statistics for Development in the Twenty-first Century (PARIS 21) [E/CN.3/2004/25], which presented the results of an independent evaluation of the PARIS 21 programme and its 2003 activities, and a World Bank document entitled "The Marrakesh Action Plan for Statistics: Better Data for Better Results: An Action Plan for Improving Development Statistics", adopted at the Second International Round Table on Managing for Development Results (Marrakesh, 4-5 February)".

The Commission concluded that the Advisory Committee recommendations on the harmonization of indicators should be accepted and that the Commission should carefully consider further international work to improve methods and technical specifications for development indicators to ensure a transparent process, with greater involvement of developed and developing countries and competent international agencies. Work on information technologies statistics and indicators should be coordinated and further investment in developing sustainable statistical capacity would be required to improve the availability of statistics at national and international levels, including those needed to monitor implementation of the MDGs.

The Commission encouraged further progress in the PARIS 21 programme and the proposed activities related to the Partnership Library of Statistical System Documentation. It concluded that statistical capacity-building should continue to feature in its agenda. Statistical capacity-building in developing countries should be stressed, as well as the support from developed countries and donors in that regard. The importance of the Marrakesh Action Plan should be noted also.

Standards for data dissemination and exchange

The Commission had before it an OECD report on the presentation of statistical data and metadata [E/CN.3/2004/26], which outlined proposals for the preparation of a manual containing guidelines and recommended best practice for presenting statistical data and metadata disseminated by national agencies and international organizations, and links to related international initiatives, including the statistical data and metadata exchange (SDMX) project—a consortium of international organizations working to develop a set of common business practices in statistical information sharing. The Commission also considered the report of the task force to establish standards on data and metadata exchange [E/CN.3/2004/27], detailing the first phase (2001-2003) and future plans (2004-2005) of the SDMX initiative.

The Commission took note of the OECD work and that of the task force in the presentation of and common open standards for the exchange and sharing of statistical data and metadata.

Coordination and integration of statistical programmes

The Commission considered the report of Committee for the Coordination of Statistical Activities (CCSA) on its first (New York, 3 March 2003) and second (Geneva, 8-10 September 2003) meetings [E/CN.3/2004/29], which covered aggregation of national data to regional and global estimates; harmonization of base years for index numbers; development of international guidelines for the presentation of statistical data and metadata; good practices in citation in the outputs of international statistical offices; strengthening governance of statistical systems; statistics at the subnational level; and new initiatives planned by organizations. The Commission welcomed the work of the Committee.

CCSA held its third (1 March) and fourth (1-3 September) meetings in New York, which addressed, respectively, plans for and follow-up to the Q2004 satellite conference on data quality (Wiesbaden, Germany, 27-28 May) [E/CN.3/2005/24].

Follow-up to Economic and Social Council policy decisions

The Commission had before it a note by the Secretary-General on the policy decisions of the Economic and Social Council that were relevant to the Commission's work [E/CN.3/2004/28].

The Commission agreed that the actions outlined in the Secretary-General's note were consistent with the Council's requests and reflected the work being undertaken and planned by the Commission and the Statistics Division. It asked the Bureau to examine the Commission's working methods in support of the coordinated follow-up to UN conferences and summits and to report thereon in 2005.

Programme and institutional questions

The Commission approved changes to the 2004-2005 Statistics Division work programme [YUN 2003, p. 1296] and the revised list of expert group meetings and workshops to be held in 2004/05 [E/CN.3/2004/30], and endorsed the proposed programme plan set out in the document "Proposed strategic framework for the biennium 2006-2007".

The Commission also approved its multi-year (2004-2007) work programme [E/CN.3/2004/31], as amended; took note of the activities of the Commission on Sustainable Development; recommended that its thirty-sixth session be held in New York from 1 to 4 March 2005; and approved the provisional agenda and documentation for that session.

PART FOUR

Legal questions

Chapter I

International Court of Justice

In 2004, the International Court of Justice (ICJ) delivered nine Judgments and one Advisory Opinion, made 6 Orders and had 21 contentious cases and one request for an advisory opinion pending before it. In a 4 November address to the General Assembly, the ICJ President underlined the role of the Court and its contribution to the promotion and development of a unified international legal system, both by the adjudication of contentious disputes between States and by the exercise of its advisory function. He noted the increased use of the Court by States in recent years and recalled that, in order to meet the growing demand and fulfil its judicial responsibilities, the Court had taken further steps to improve its judicial efficiency.

Judicial work of the Court

During 2004, the Court delivered a Judgment on the merits in the case concerning *Avena and other Mexican Nationals (Mexico v. United States of America)*, eight Judgments on the preliminary objections raised by the respondent Party in each of the cases concerning *Legality of Use of Force (Serbia and Montenegro v. Belgium)*, *(Serbia and Montenegro v. Canada)*, *(Serbia and Montenegro v. France)*, *(Serbia and Montenegro v. Germany)*, *(Serbia and Montenegro v. Italy)*, *(Serbia and Montenegro v. Netherlands)*, *(Serbia and Montenegro v. Portugal)* and *(Serbia and Montenegro v. United Kingdom)*, and one Advisory Opinion in the case concerning *Legal Consequences of the Construction of a Wall in the Occupied Palestinian Territory (Request for advisory opinion)*.

During the year, the Court was seized of one new case: *Maritime Delimitation in the Black Sea (Romania v. Ukraine)*.

The Court and its President made Orders on the conduct of the proceedings in the cases concerning *Certain Criminal Proceedings in France (Republic of the Congo v. France)*; *Maritime Delimitation in the Black Sea (Romania v. Ukraine)* and *Legal Consequences of the Construction of a Wall in the Occupied Palestinian Territory (Request for advisory opinion)* and one Order in the case concerning the *Frontier Dispute (Benin/Niger)*.

The Court held hearings in the cases concerning *Legality of Use of Force (Serbia and Montenegro v. Belgium)*, *(Serbia and Montenegro v. Canada)*, *(Ser-*

bia and Montenegro v. France), *(Serbia and Montenegro v. Germany)*, *(Serbia and Montenegro v. Italy)*, *(Serbia and Montenegro v. Netherlands)*, *(Serbia and Montenegro v. Portugal)* and *(Serbia and Montenegro v. United Kingdom)*; and *Certain Property (Liechtenstein v. Germany)* and on the request of the General Assembly for an advisory opinion in the case concerning *Legal Consequences of the Construction of a Wall in the Occupied Palestinian Territory*.

During the year, there were no new developments in the cases concerning *Application of the Convention on the Prevention and Punishment of the Crime of Genocide (Bosnia and Herzegovina v. Serbia and Montenegro)* [YUN 1993, p. 1138], *Ahmadou Sadio Diallo (Guinea v. Democratic Republic of the Congo)* [YUN 1998, p. 1190], *Armed Activities on the Territory of the Congo (Democratic Republic of the Congo v. Uganda)* [YUN 1999, p. 1209], *Application of the Convention on the Prevention and Punishment of the Crime of Genocide (Croatia v. Serbia and Montenegro)* [YUN 1999, p. 1210], *Maritime Delimitation between Nicaragua and Honduras in the Caribbean Sea (Nicaragua v. Honduras)* [YUN 1999, p. 1210] and *Armed Activities on the Territory of the Congo (New Application: 2002) (Democratic Republic of the Congo v. Rwanda)* [YUN 2002, p. 1271].

ICJ activities in 2004 were covered in two reports to the General Assembly, for the periods 1 August 2003 to 31 July 2004 [A/59/4] and 1 August 2004 to 31 July 2005 [A/60/4]. On 4 November 2004, the Assembly took note of the 2003/2004 report (**decision 59/508**).

Use of force (Serbia and Montenegro v. Belgium), (Serbia and Montenegro v. Canada), (Serbia and Montenegro v. France), (Serbia and Montenegro v. Germany), (Serbia and Montenegro v. Italy), (Serbia and Montenegro v. Netherlands), (Serbia and Montenegro v. Portugal), (Serbia and Montenegro v. Spain), (Serbia and Montenegro v. United States) and (Serbia and Montenegro v. United Kingdom)

Serbia and Montenegro, then known as the Federal Republic of Yugoslavia, instituted proceedings on 29 April 1999 [YUN 1999, p. 1207] against Belgium, Canada, France, Germany, Italy, the Netherlands, Portugal, Spain, the United Kingdom and the United States for alleged violation of the obligation not to use force. In the cases against Belgium, Canada, the Netherlands, Portugal, Spain and the United Kingdom, Serbia and Montenegro invoked the jurisdiction of the Court based on Article 36, paragraph 2, of the Statute of the Court and on article IX of the 1948 Convention on the Prevention and Punishment of the Crime of Genocide (the Genocide Convention), adopted by the General Assembly in resolution 260 A (III) [YUN 1948-49, p. 959], and, in the cases against France, Germany, Italy and the United States, on article IX of the Convention and Article 38, paragraph 5, of the Rules of Court.

In its Applications, Serbia and Montenegro stated that the disputes involved acts of the respondent States concerned, by which they had violated the international obligation banning the use of force against another State, the obligation not to intervene in the internal affairs of another State, the obligation not to violate the sovereignty of another State, the obligation to protect the civilian population and civilian objects in wartime, the obligation to protect the environment, the obligation relating to free navigation on international rivers, the obligation regarding fundamental human rights and freedoms, the obligation not to use prohibited weapons and the obligation not to deliberately inflict conditions of life calculated to cause the physical destruction of a national group.

Also on 29 April 1999 [YUN 1999, p. 1208], Serbia and Montenegro submitted, in each of the cases, a request for the indication of provisional measures, asking the Court to indicate that "the [respondent State concerned] shall cease immediately its acts of use of force and shall refrain from any act of threat or use of force" against Serbia and Montenegro. Hearings on the requests for the indication of provisional measures were held between 10 and 12 May 1999.

On 2 June 1999 [ibid.], the Court delivered eight Orders, by which, in the cases *(Serbia and Montenegro v. Belgium), (Serbia and Montenegro v. Canada), (Serbia and Montenegro v. France), (Serbia and Montenegro v. Germany), (Serbia and Montenegro v. Italy), (Serbia and Montenegro v. Netherlands), (Serbia and Montenegro v. Portugal)* and *(Serbia and Montenegro v. United Kingdom)*, the Court rejected the requests for the indication of provisional measures and reserved the subsequent procedure for further decision. In the cases of *(Serbia and Montenegro v. Spain)* and *(Serbia and Montenegro v. United States of America)*, the Court— having found that it manifestly lacked jurisdiction to entertain Serbia and Montenegro's Application, and that, within a system of consensual jurisdiction, to maintain on the General List a case upon which it appeared certain that the

Court would not be able to adjudicate on the merits and would most assuredly not contribute to the sound administration of justice—rejected Serbia and Montenegro's requests for the indication of provisional measures and ordered that those cases be removed from the List.

Following the filing of the Memorial of Serbia and Montenegro, in each of the eight cases maintained on the Court's List, within the prescribed time limit of 5 Janaury 2000, each of the respondent States raised preliminary objections of lack of jurisdiction and admissibility. By virtue of Article 79, paragraph 3, of the Rules of Court, the proceedings were accordingly suspended.

By an Order of 8 September 2000 [YUN 2000, p. 1217], the Court fixed 5 April 2001 as the time limit for the filing, in each of the cases, of a written statement by Serbia and Montenegro on the preliminary objections raised by the respondent State. By Orders of 21 February 2001 [YUN 2001, p. 1190] and 20 March 2002 [YUN 2002, p. 1267], the Court, in each of the cases, extended the time limit to 5 April 2002 and 7 April 2003, respectively. On 20 December 2002, within the extended time limit, Serbia and Montenegro filed a written statement on the preliminary objections raised by the respondent State concerned in each of the cases [ibid.].

Public hearings were held from 19 to 23 April 2004 on the preliminary objections raised by each of the respondent States. At the conclusion of the hearings, the parties presented their final submissions to the Court.

For the reasons set out in its preliminary objections and those set out during the oral submissions on 19 and 22 April 2004, Belgium requested the Court to remove from the List the case brought against it by Serbia and Montenegro, and, in the alternative, to rule that the Court lacked jurisdiction in the case and/or that the case was inadmissible.

Canada requested the Court to adjudge and declare that the Court lacked jurisdiction because the Applicant had abandoned all the grounds of jurisdiction originally specified in its Application pursuant to Article 38, paragraph 2, of the Rules of the Court and had identified no alternative grounds of jurisdiction. In the alternative, Canada requested the Court to adjudge and declare that: the Court lacked jurisdiction over the proceedings brought by the Applicant against Canada on 29 April 1999 on the basis of the purported declaration of 25 April 1999; the Court also lacked jurisdiction on the basis of article IX of the Genocide Convention; the new claims respecting the period beginning 10 June 1999 were inadmissible because they would transform the subject of the dispute originally brought before the Court; and the claims in their entirety were inadmissible because the subject matter of the case required the presence of essential third parties that were not before the Court.

France, for the reasons it had set out orally and in its written pleadings, requested the Court: principally, to remove the case from the List; in the alternative, to decide that it lacked jurisdiction to rule on the Application filed by Serbia and Montenegro against France; and in the further alternative, to decide that the Application was inadmissible.

Germany requested the Court to dismiss the Application for lack of jurisdiction and, additionally, as being inadmissible on the grounds it had stated in its preliminary objections and during its oral pleadings.

Italy, for the reasons set out in its preliminary objections and oral statements, requested the Court to adjudge and declare, principally, that no decision was called for on the Application filed in the Registry of the Court on 29 April 1999 [YUN 1999, p. 1207] by Serbia and Montenegro against Italy for "violation of the obligation not to use force", as supplemented by the Memorial filed on 5 January 2000 [YUN 2000, p. 1216], inasmuch as there was no longer any dispute between Serbia and Montenegro and Italy or as the subject matter of the dispute had disappeared. In the alternative, Italy requested the Court to adjudge and declare that: the Court lacked jurisdiction *ratione personarum* to decide the case, since Serbia and Montenegro was not a party to the Statute when the Application was filed and did not consider itself a party to a "treaty in force" such as would confer jurisdiction on the Court, in accordance with Article 35, paragraph 2, of the Statute; the Court lacked jurisdiction *ratione materiae* to decide the case, since Serbia and Montenegro did not regard itself as bound by article IX of the Genocide Convention, to which it made a reservation upon giving notice of accession in March 2001 [YUN 2001, p. 1184] and since, in any event, the dispute arising from the terms of the Application instituting proceedings, as supplemented by the Memorial, was not a dispute relating to "the interpretation, application or fulfilment" of the Genocide Convention, as provided in article IX; Serbia and Montenegro's Application, as supplemented by the Memorial in its entirety, was inadmissible, inasmuch as Serbia and Montenegro sought thereby to obtain from the Court a decision regarding the legality of action undertaken by subjects of international law not present in the proceedings or not all so present; and Serbia and Montenegro's Application was inadmissible with respect to the eleventh submission, mentioned for the first time in the Memorial, inasmuch as

Serbia and Montenegro sought thereby to introduce a dispute altogether different from the original dispute deriving from the Application.

The Netherlands requested the Court to adjudge and declare that the Court had no jurisdiction or should decline to exercise jurisdiction, as the parties in fact agreed that the Court had no jurisdiction or as there was no longer a dispute between the parties on the jurisdiction of the Court. Alternatively, the Netherlands asked the Court to adjudge and declare that: Serbia and Montenegro was not entitled to appear before the Court; the Court had no jurisdiction over the claims brought against the Netherlands by Serbia and Montenegro; and/or the claims brought against the Netherlands by Serbia and Montenegro were inadmissible.

Portugal requested the Court to adjudge and declare that the Court was not called upon to give a decision on the claims of Serbia and Montenegro; or, alternatively, that the Court lacked jurisdiction, either under Article 36, paragraph 2, of the Statute or under article IX of the Genocide Convention, and the claims were inadmissible.

The United Kingdom, for the reasons given in its written preliminary objections and at the oral hearing, requested the Court to remove the case from its List; or, in the alternative, to adjudge and declare that it lacked jurisdiction over the claims brought against the United Kingdom by Serbia and Montenegro and/or that those claims were inadmissible.

Serbia and Montenegro, for the reasons given in its pleadings, and, in particular, in its written observations, subsequent correspondence with the Court and at the oral hearing, requested the Court to: adjudge and declare on its jurisdiction *ratione personae* in the current cases; dismiss the remaining preliminary objections of the respondent States; and order proceedings on the merits if it found that it had jurisdiction *ratione personae*.

On 15 December 2004, the Court delivered its Judgment in each of the cases. The Court found that it had no jurisdiction to entertain the claims made in the Application filed by Serbia and Montenegro on 29 April 1999.

In each of the cases, Vice President Ranjeva and Judges Guillaume, Higgins, Kooijmans, Al-Khasawneh, Buergenthal and Elaraby appended a joint declaration to the Judgment, and Judge Koroma appended a declaration. Judges Higgins, Kooijmans and Elaraby and Judge ad hoc Kreca appended separate opinions.

Certain property (Liechtenstein v. Germany)

On 1 June 2001 [YUN 2001, p. 1194], Liechtenstein filed an Application instituting proceedings against Germany concerning Germany's decisions to treat certain property of Liechtenstein nationals as German assets, seized for the purposes of reparation or restitution as a consequence of the Second World War, without ensuring any compensation.

In the Application, Liechtenstein requested the Court to adjudge and declare that Germany had incurred international legal responsibility and was bound to make appropriate reparation to Liechtenstein for the damage and prejudice suffered. Liechtenstein further requested that the nature and amount of such reparation should, in the absence of agreement between the Parties, be assessed and determined by the Court, if necessary, in a separate phase of the proceedings. As a basis for the Court's jurisdiction, Liechtenstein invoked article 1 of the European Convention for the Peaceful Settlement of Disputes, signed at Strasbourg, France, on 29 April 1957.

By an Order of 28 June 2001 [ibid.], the Court fixed 28 March and 27 December 2002, respectively, as the time limits for the filing of a Memorial by Liechtenstein and of a Counter-Memorial by Germany. The Memorial was filed within the fixed time limit.

On 27 June 2002 [YUN 2002, p. 1271], Germany filed certain preliminary objections to the jurisdiction of the Court and the admissibility of the Application; the proceedings on the merits were suspended in accordance with Article 79 of the Rules of the Court. Within the 15 November 2002 time limit fixed by the President of the Court, Liechtenstein filed a written statement of its observations and submissions with regard to the preliminary objections raised by Germany.

Public hearings on the preliminary objections raised by Germany were held from 14 to 18 June 2004, at the conclusion of which the Parties presented their final submissions to the Court.

Germany requested the Court to adjudge and declare that it lacked jurisdiction over the claims brought against Germany by Liechtenstein, which were referred to it by Liechtenstein's 2001 Application [YUN 2001, p. 1194], and that those claims were inadmissible to the extent specified in its preliminary objections.

Liechtenstein requested the Court to adjudge and declare that the Court had jurisdiction over the claims presented in its Application and that they were admissible, and, accordingly, to reject Germany's preliminary objections in their entirety.

The Court deliberated its Judgment.

Territorial and maritime dispute (Nicaragua v. Colombia)

In 2001 [YUN 2001, p. 1195], Nicaragua instituted proceedings against Colombia in respect of a dispute concerning "a group of related legal issues subsisting" between the two States "concerning title to territory and maritime delimitation". In its Application, Nicaragua first requested the Court to adjudge and declare that Nicaragua had sovereignty over the islands of Providencia, San Andres and Santa Catalina and all the appurtenant islands and keys, and also over the Roncador, Serrana, Serranilla and Quitasueño keys (insofar as they were capable of appropriation); and, second, in the light of the determinations concerning the title requested above, asked the Court to determine the course of the single maritime boundary between the areas of the continental shelf and the exclusive economic zone appertaining respectively to Nicaragua and Colombia, in accordance with equitable principles and relevant circumstances recognized by general international law as applicable to such a delimitation of a single maritime boundary. Nicaragua reserved the right to claim compensation for elements of unjust enrichment consequent upon Colombian possession of the islands of San Andres and Providencia, as well as the keys and maritime spaces up to the 82 meridian, in the absence of lawful title. It also reserved the right to claim compensation for interference with fishing vessels of Nicaraguan nationality or vessels licensed by Nicaragua.

By an Order of 26 February 2002 [YUN 2002, p. 1271], the Court fixed 28 April 2003 and 28 June 2004, respectively, as the time limits for the filing of a Memorial by Nicaragua and of a Counter-Memorial by Colombia. The Memorial of Nicaragua was filed within the time limit [YUN 2003, p. 1305].

On 21 July 2003 [ibid.], Colombia filed preliminary objections to the jurisdiction of the Court; under Article 79 of the Rules of Court, proceedings on the merits were suspended accordingly. Nicaragua filed a written statement of its observations and submissions on the preliminary objections raised by Colombia within the time limit of 26 January 2004, fixed by the Court by an Order of 24 September 2003.

Frontier dispute (Benin/Niger)

In 2002 [YUN 2002, p. 1271], Benin and the Niger jointly notified the Court of a Special Agreement, which was signed between them on 15 June 2001 and entered into force on 11 April 2002. Under article 1 of the Agreement, the Parties agreed to submit their boundary dispute to a chamber to be formed by the Court, pursuant to Article 26, paragraph 2, of the Court's Statute, and that each of them would choose a judge ad hoc. Article 2 of the Agreement stated that the Court was requested to determine the course of the boundary between Benin and the Niger in the River Niger sector; specify which State owned each of the islands in the River Niger, in particular Lété Island; and determine the course of the boundary between the two States in the River Mekrou sector. Article 10 contained a "special undertaking" as follows: "Pending the judgment of the Chamber, the Parties undertake to preserve peace, security and quiet among the peoples of the two States".

By an Order of 27 November 2002 [ibid.], the Court decided to accede to the Parties' request and form a special chamber of five judges; the Court formed a Chamber of three members of the Court together with two judges ad hoc chosen by the Parties. The Court fixed 27 August 2003 as the time limit for the filing of a Memorial by each Party. The Memorials were filed within the time limit.

By an Order of 11 September 2003 [YUN 2003, p. 1305], the President of the Chamber fixed 28 May 2004 as the time limit for the filing of a Counter-Memorial by each of the Parties; the Counter-Memorials were filed within the time limit fixed. On 20 November 2003 [ibid.], the Chamber held its first public sitting to enable the two judges ad hoc to make the solemn declaration required by the Statute and the Rules of Court.

By an Order of 9 July 2004, the President of the Chamber, taking into account the wish of the Parties to be authorized to submit a third pleading as provided for by the Special Agreement, authorized the submission of a Reply by each of the Parties and fixed 17 December 2004 as the time limit for the filing of that pleading. The Replies were deposited within the time limit thus prescribed.

Certain criminal proceedings in France (Republic of the Congo v. France)

On 9 December 2002 [YUN 2002, p. 1263], the Republic of the Congo filed an Application by which it sought to institute proceedings against France seeking the annulment of the investigation and prosecution measures taken by the French judicial authorities further to a complaint for crimes against humanity and torture filed by various associations against the President of the Congo, Denis Sassou Nguesso, the Congolese Minister of the Interior, Pierre Oba, and other individuals, including General Norbert Dabira, Inspector General of the Congolese Armed Forces. The Application further stated that, in connection with the proceedings, an investigating judge of the Meaux (France) tribunal de grande instance had issued a warrant for the President of the Congo to be examined as witness.

The Congo contended that by "attributing to itself universal jurisdiction in criminal matters and by arrogating to itself the power to prosecute and try the Minister of the Interior of a foreign State for crimes allegedly committed by him in connection with the exercise of his powers for the maintenance of public order in his country", France violated "the principle that a State may not, in breach of the principle of sovereign equality among all Members of the United Nations . . . exercise its authority on the territory of another State". The Congo further submitted that, in issuing a warrant instructing police officers to examine the President of the Congo as witness in the case, France violated "the criminal immunity of a foreign head of State, an international customary rule recognized by the jurisprudence of the Court".

In its Application, the Congo indicated that it sought to found the jurisdiction of the Court, pursuant to Article 38, paragraph 5, of the Rules of Court, "on the consent of the French Republic, which will certainly be given". In accordance with that provision, the Application by the Congo was transmitted to France and no further action was taken in the proceedings at that stage.

By an 8 April 2003 letter [YUN 2003, p. 1308], France stated that it "consent [ed] to the jurisdiction of the Court to entertain the Application pursuant to Article 38, paragraph 5". That consent made it possible to enter the case in the Court's List and to open the proceedings. In its letter, France added that its consent to the Court's jurisdiction applied strictly within the limits "of the claims formulated by the Republic of the Congo" and that "Article 2 of the Treaty of Co-operation signed on 1 January 1974 by the French Republic and the People's Republic of the Congo, to which the latter refers in its Application, does not constitute a basis of jurisdiction for the Court in the present case".

The Application of the Congo was accompanied by a request for the indication of a provisional measure "seek [ing] an order for the immediate suspension of the proceedings being conducted by the investigating judge of the Meaux tribunal de grande instance".

Taking into account the consent given by France and in accordance with Article 74, paragraph 3, of the Rules of Court, the President of the Court fixed 28 April 2003 as the date for the opening of the public hearings on the request for the indication of a provisional measure submitted by the Congo. The hearings were held on 28 and 29 April 2003 [ibid.].

On 17 June 2003 [ibid.], the President of the Court read the Order, by which the Court found, by 14 votes to 1, that the circumstances, as they presented themselves to the Court, were not such as to require the exercise of its power under Article 41 of the Statute of the Court to indicate provisional measures. Judges Koroma and Vereshchetin appended a joint separate opinion to the Order, and Judge ad hoc de Cara a dissenting opinion.

By an Order of 11 July 2003 [ibid.], the President of the Court fixed 11 December 2003 as the time limit for the Memorial of the Congo and 11 May 2004 as the time limit for the Counter-Memorial of France. The Memorial was filed within the time limit.

By an Order of 17 June 2004, the Court, taking account of the agreement of the Parties and of the particular circumstances of the case, authorized the submission of a Reply by the Congo and a Rejoinder by France, and fixed 10 December 2004 and 10 June 2005 as the respective time limits for the filing of those pleadings. By Orders of 8 and 29 December 2004, the President of the Court, taking account of the reasons given by the Congo and of the agreement of the Parties, extended to 10 January and 10 August 2005 those respective time limits.

Avena and other Mexican nationals (Mexico v. United States)

On 9 January 2003 [YUN 2003, p. 1306], Mexico instituted proceedings before the Court against the United States in a dispute concerning alleged violations of articles 5 and 36 of the 1963 Vienna Convention on Consular Relations [YUN 1963, p. 510] with respect to 54 Mexican nationals who had been sentenced to death in the States of Arizona, Arkansas, California, Florida, Illinois, Nevada, Ohio, Oklahoma, Oregon and Texas. In its Application, Mexico maintained that the 54 cases (later adjusted by Mexico to 52) illustrated the systemic nature of the United States violation of its obligation under article 36 of the Vienna Convention to inform nationals of Mexico of their right to consular assistance and to provide relief adequate to redress such a violation. Mexico claimed that in at least 49 of the cases it had found no evidence that the competent United States authorities attempted to comply with article 36 before Mexico's nationals were tried, convicted and sentenced to death. It further noted that in four cases, some attempt was apparently made to comply with article 36 but the authorities still failed to provide the required notification "without delay"; and in one case, the detained national was informed of his rights to consular notification and access in connection with immigration proceedings, but not in connection with pending capital charges. Mexico invoked as a basis for the Court's jurisdiction arti-

cle I of the Vienna Convention's Optional Protocol concerning the Compulsory Settlement of Disputes [YUN 1963, p. 512], which provided that "disputes arising out of the interpretation or application of the Convention shall lie within the compulsory jurisdiction of the International Court of Justice".

Also on 9 January 2003 [YUN 2003, p. 1307], Mexico filed an urgent request for the indication of provisional measures. At hearings held on 21 January 2003, Mexico confirmed that request, while the United States asked the Court to reject it and not to indicate any such measures.

On 5 February 2003 [ibid.], the Court unanimously adopted an Order indicating provisional measures. In the Order, it decided that the United States should take "all measures necessary" to ensure that César Roberto Fierro Reyna, Roberto Moreno Ramos and Osvaldo Torres Aguilera, of Mexican nationality, were not executed pending a final judgment of the Court; the United States should inform the Court of all measures taken to implement the Order; and the Court would remain seized of the matters which formed the subject of the Order until it had rendered its final judgment.

In a further separate Order of 5 February 2003 [ibid.], the Court fixed 6 June 2003 as the time limit for the filing of a Memorial by Mexico and 6 October 2003 as the time limit for the filing of a Counter-Memorial by the United States. By an Order of 22 May 2003, the President of the Court, at the joint request of the Parties, extended the time limits to 20 June 2003 for the Memorial of Mexico and to 3 November 2003 for the Counter-Memorial of the United States. The Memorial and Counter-Memorial were filed within the extended time limits. At the conclusion of public hearings held from 15 to 19 December 2003, the Parties presented final submissions to the Court.

In its Judgment of 31 March 2004, the Court, by 13 votes to 2, rejected Mexico's objection to the admissibility of the objections presented by the United States to the jurisdiction of the Court and the admissibility of the Mexican claims. It rejected unanimously the four objections by the United States to the jurisdiction of the Court and the five objections by the United States to the admissibility of Mexico's claims. By six separate votes of 14 to 1, the Court found that: by not informing, without delay upon their detention, the 51 Mexican nationals referred to in paragraph 106 (1) of the Judgment of their rights under article 36, paragraph 1 (b), of the 1963 Vienna Convention, the United States breached the obligations incumbent upon it under that subparagraph; by not notifying the appropriate Mexican consular post without delay of the detention of the 49 Mexican nationals referred to in paragraph 106 (2) of the Judgment and thereby depriving Mexico of the right, in a timely fashion, to render the assistance provided for by the Vienna Convention to the individuals concerned, the United States breached the obligations incumbent upon it under article 36, paragraph 1 *(b)*; in relation to the 49 Mexican nationals referred to in paragraph 106 (3) of the Judgment, the United States deprived Mexico of the right, in a timely fashion, to communicate with and have access to those nationals and to visit them in detention, and thereby breached the obligations incumbent upon it under article 36, paragraph 1 *(a)* and *(c)*, of the Vienna Convention; in relation to the 34 Mexican nationals referred to in paragraph 106 (4) of the Judgment, the United States deprived Mexico of the right, in a timely fashion, to arrange for legal representation of those nationals, and thereby breached the obligations incumbent upon it under article 36, paragraph 1 *(c)*, of the Convention; by not permitting the review and reconsideration, in the light of the rights set forth in the Convention, of the conviction and sentences of César Roberto Fierro Reyna, Roberto Moreno Ramos and Osvaldo Torres Aguilera, after the violations referred to in subparagraph (4) of the Judgment had been established in respect of those individuals, the United States breached the obligations incumbent upon it under article 36, paragraph 2, of the Convention; and the appropriate reparation in that case consisted in the United States obligation to provide, by means of its own choosing, review and reconsideration of the convictions and sentences of the Mexican nationals referred to in subparagraphs (4), (5), (6) and (7) of the Judgment, by taking account both of the violation of the rights set forth in article 36 of the Convention and of paragraphs 138 to 141 of the Judgment. Unanimously, the Court took note of the commitment undertaken by the United States to ensure implementation of the specific measures adopted in performance of its obligations under article 36, paragraph 1 *(b)*, of the Convention; found that the commitment had to be regarded as meeting Mexico's request for guarantees and assurances of non-repetition; and found that, should Mexican nationals nonetheless be sentenced to severe penalties, without their rights under article 36, paragraph 1 *(b)*, of the Convention having been respected, the United States would provide, by means of its own choosing, review and reconsideration of the conviction and sentence, so as to allow full weight to be given to the violation of the rights set forth in the Convention, taking account of paragraphs 138 to 141 of the Judgment.

President Shi and Vice President Ranjeva appended declarations to the Judgment; Judges Vereshchetin, Parra-Aranguren and Tomka and Judge ad hoc Sepúlveda appended separate opinions.

Sovereignty over Pedra Branca/Pulau Batu Puteh, Middle Rocks and South Ledge (Malaysia/Singapore)

On 24 July 2003 [YUN 2003, p. 1308], Malaysia and Singapore jointly notified the Court of a Special Agreement, which was signed between them on 6 February 2003 at Putrajaya, Malaysia, and entered into force on 9 May 2003. In article 2 of the Special Agreement, the Parties requested the Court to determine whether sovereignty over Pedra Branca/Pulau Batu Puteh, Middle Rocks and South Ledge belonged to Malaysia or Singapore. In article 6, the Parties agreed to accept the judgment of the Court as final and binding upon them. The Parties further set out their views on the procedure to be followed.

By an Order of 1 September 2003 [ibid., p. 1309], the Court, taking into account the provisions of article 4 of the Special Agreement, fixed 25 March 2004 and 25 January 2005 as the respective time limits for the filing, by each of the Parties, of a Memorial and of a Counter-Memorial. The Memorials were filed within the time limit.

Maritime delimitation in the Black Sea (Romania v. Ukraine)

On 16 September, Romania filed an Application instituting proceedings against Ukraine in respect of a dispute concerning the establishment of a single maritime boundary between the two States in the Black Sea, thereby delimiting the continental shelf and the exclusive economic zones appertaining to them.

In its Application, Romania explained that Ukraine and itself signed, on 2 June 1997, a Treaty on Relations of Co-operation and Good Neighbourliness, and concluded an Additional Agreement by exchange of letters between their respective Ministers for Foreign Affairs. Both instruments entered into force on 22 October 1997. By those agreements, the two States assumed the obligation to conclude a treaty on the State Border Regime between them, as well as an agreement for the delimitation of the continental shelf and the exclusive economic zones in the Black Sea. At the same time, the Additional Agreement provided for the principles to be applied in the delimitation of the above-mentioned areas, and set out the commitment of the two countries that the dispute could be submitted to the Court, subject to the fulfilment of certain conditions. Between 1998 and 2004, 24 rounds of negotiations were held. However, according to Romania, no result was obtained and an agreed delimitation of the maritime areas in the Black Sea was not accomplished. Romania brought the matter before the Court "in order to avoid the indefinite prolongation of discussions that, in [its] opinion, obviously cannot lead to any outcome".

Romania requested the Court to draw, in accordance with international law, and specifically the criteria laid down in article 4 of the Additional Agreement, a single maritime boundary between the continental shelf and the exclusive economic zone of the two States in the Black Sea.

As a basis for the Court's jurisdiction, Romania invoked article 4 *(h)* of the Additional Agreement, which provided that, if the negotiations should not determine the conclusion of an agreement on the delimitation of the continental shelf and the exclusive economic zones in the Black Sea in a reasonable period of time, not later than two years after their initiation, Romania and Ukraine would agree that the delimitation problem would be solved by ICJ, at the request of any of the Parties, provided that the treaty on the regime of the State border between Romania and Ukraine had entered into force. However, should ICJ consider that the delay of the entry into force of the treaty on the border regime was the result of the other Party's fault, it might examine the request concerning the delimitation before the entry into force of the treaty.

Romania contended that the two conditions set out in article 4 *(h)* of the Additional Agreement had been fulfilled, since the negotiations had by far exceeded two years and the Treaty on the Romanian-Ukrainian State Border Régime had entered into force on 27 May 2004.

In its Application, Romania further provided an overview of the applicable law for solving the dispute, citing a number of provisions of the Additional Agreement of 1997, as well as the 1982 United Nations Convention on the Law of the Sea [YUN 1982, p. 181], to which both Ukraine and Romania were parties, together with other relevant instruments binding the two countries.

By an Order of 19 November 2004, the Court, taking into account the views of the Parties, fixed 19 August 2005 and 19 May 2006, respectively, as the time limits for the filing of a Memorial by Romania and a Counter-Memorial by Ukraine.

Legal consequences of the construction of a wall in the Occupied Palestinian Territory

In response to General Assembly resolution ES-10/14 [YUN 2003, p. 480], which requested the Court urgently to render an advisory opinion on the legal consequences arising from the construction of the wall being built by Israel in the Occupied Palestinian Territory, ICJ, by an Order of 19 December 2003 [ibid., p. 1309], decided that the United Nations and its Member States were likely, in accordance with Article 66, paragraph 2, of the ICJ Statute, to be able to furnish information on all aspects raised by the question submitted to the Court for an advisory opinion and fixed 30 January 2004 as the time limit within which written statements might be submitted, in accordance with Article 66, paragraph 4, of the Statute. By the same Order, the Court further decided that, in the light of resolution ES-10/14 and the report of the Secretary-General transmitted with the request [ibid, p. 478], and taking into account the fact that the Assembly had granted Palestine a special status of observer and that the latter was co-sponsor of the draft resolution requesting the advisory opinion, Palestine might also submit a written statement on the question within the time limit. Also by the Order, the Court decided, in accordance with Article 105, paragraph 4, of the Rules of Court, to hold public hearings, during which oral statements and comments might be presented to it by the United Nations and its Member States, regardless of whether or not they had submitted written statements, and fixed 23 February 2004 as the date for the opening of the hearings. In the Order, the Court also decided that, for the reasons set out above, Palestine might take part in the hearings. By letters of 19 December 2003 [ibid., p. 1309], the Registrar informed them of the Court's decisions and transmitted to them a copy of the Order.

Ruling on requests submitted subsequently by the League of Arab States (LAS) and the Organization of the Islamic Conference (OIC), the Court decided, in accordance with Article 66 of its Statute, that those two organizations were likely to be able to furnish information on the question submitted to the Court, and that, consequently, they might, for that purpose, submit written statements within the time limit fixed by the Court in its Order of 19 December 2003 and take part in the hearings. Pursuant to Article 65, paragraph 2, of the Statute, the Secretary-General communicated to the Court a dossier of documents likely to throw light upon the question.

By an Order of 30 January 2004 regarding its composition in the case, the Court decided that the matters brought to its attention by the Government of Israel in a letter of 31 December 2003, and in a confidential letter of 15 January 2004 addressed to the President pursuant to Article 34, paragraph 2, of the Rules of Court, were not such as to preclude Judge Elaraby from sitting in the case.

Within the time limit fixed by the Court for that purpose, written statements were filed by, in order of their receipt: Guinea, Saudi Arabia, LAS, Egypt, Cameroon, Russian Federation, Australia, Palestine, United Nations, Jordan, Kuwait, Lebanon, Canada, Syrian Arab Republic, Switzerland, Israel, Yemen, United States, Morocco, Indonesia, OIC, France, Italy, Sudan, South Africa, Germany, Japan, Norway, United Kingdom, Pakistan, Czech Republic, Greece, Ireland on its own behalf, Ireland on behalf of the European Union, Cyprus, Brazil, Namibia, Malta, Malaysia, Netherlands, Cuba, Sweden, Spain, Belgium, Palau, Federated States of Micronesia, Marshall Islands, Senegal and Democratic People's Republic of Korea.

In the course of hearings held from 23 to 25 February 2004, the Court heard oral statements, in the following order, by: the Palestinian Authority, South Africa, Algeria, Saudi Arabia, Bangladesh, Belize, Cuba, Indonesia, Jordan, Madagascar, Malaysia, Senegal, Sudan, LAS and OIC.

At a public sitting held on 9 July 2004, the Court delivered its Advisory Opinion. The Court found unanimously that it had jurisdiction to give the advisory opinion requested and, by a vote of 14 to 1, decided to comply with that request. In four separate votes of 14 to 1, the Court replied that: the construction of the wall being built by Israel, the occupying Power, in the Occupied Palestinian Territory, including in and around East Jerusalem, and its associated regime, were contrary to international law; Israel was under an obligation to terminate its breaches of international law, and was under an obligation to cease forthwith the works of construction of the wall being built in the Occupied Palestinian Territory, including in and around East Jerusalem, dismantle forthwith the structure therein situated, and repeal or render ineffective forthwith all legislative and regulatory acts relating thereto, in accordance with paragraph 151 of the Opinion; Israel was under an obligation to make reparation for all damage caused by the construction of the wall in the Occupied Palestinian Territory, including in and around East Jerusalem; and the United Nations, and especially the Assembly and the Security Council, should consider what further action was required to bring to an end the illegal situation resulting from the construction of the wall and the associated regime, taking due account of the Advisory Opinion. By a vote of 13 to 2, the Court replied that all States were under an obligation not to recognize the illegal situation resulting from the construction of the wall and not to render aid or assistance in maintaining the situation created by such construction; all States parties to the 1949 Geneva Convention relative to the Protection of Civilian Persons in Time of War (Fourth Geneva Convention) had in addition the obligation, while respecting the UN Charter and international law, to ensure compliance by Israel with international humanitarian law as embodied in that Convention.

Judges Koroma, Higgins, Kooijmans and Al-Khasawneh appended separate opinions to the Advisory Opinion; Judge Buergenthal appended a declaration; and Judges Elaraby and Owada appended separate opinions.

The Assembly, in **resolution ES-10/15** of 20 July (see p. 465), acknowledged the Court's Advisory Opinion.

Other questions

Composition of the Court

On 21 October [S/2004/830], the Secretary-General informed the Security Council that Judge Gilbert Guillaume, a former President of the Court whose term of office as a Court member was to expire on 5 February 2009, intended to resign effective 11 February 2005. He drew the Council's attention to Articles 14 and 5 of the Statute of the Court regarding the fixing of a date for the election to fill the vacancy. Noting that the date of the election was to be fixed by the Council, the Secretary-General suggested that it might wish to consider the question at an early meeting.

Also in October [A/59/237], the Secretary-General informed the General Assembly of the vacancy.

On 23 December, the Assembly decided that the agenda item on the election of a member of ICJ would remain for consideration during its resumed fifty-ninth (2005) session (**decision 59/552**).

SECURITY COUNCIL ACTION

On 4 November [meeting 5070], the Security Council adopted **resolution 1571(2004)** without vote. The draft [S/2004/879] was prepared during Council consultations.

The Security Council,

Noting with regret the resignation of Judge Gilbert Guillaume, to take effect on 11 February 2005,

Noting that a vacancy in the International Court of Justice for the remainder of the term of office of Judge Gilbert Guillaume will thus occur and must be filled in accordance with the terms of the Statute of the Court,

Noting also that, in accordance with Article 14 of the Statute, the date of the election to fill the vacancy shall be fixed by the Security Council,

Decides that the election to fill the vacancy shall take place on 15 February 2005 at a meeting of the Security Council and at a meeting of the General Assembly at its fifty-ninth session.

Rules of the Court

Practice Directions

In the ongoing review of its procedures and working methods, the Court took further measures to increase its productivity. The new measures mostly concerned the Court's internal functioning and provided practical methods for increasing the number of decisions rendered each year, including shortening the period between the closure of written proceedings and the opening of oral proceedings and stricter application of the Court's procedures. In addition, the Court amended Practice Direction V, which limited the period for the presentation by a party of its observations and submissions on preliminary objections to four months. It promulgated three new Practice Directions: Practice Direction X requesting the agents of parties to attend, without delay, any meeting called by the ICJ President whenever a decision on a procedural issue needed to be made in a case; Practice Direction XI limiting parties in oral proceedings on provisional measures to what was relevant to the criteria for the indication of such measures; and Practice Direction XII establishing the procedure to be followed with regard to written statements and/or documents submitted by international non-governmental organizations in connection with advisory proceedings.

Trust Fund to Assist States in the Settlement of Disputes

In September [A/59/372], the Secretary-General reported on the activities and status of the Trust Fund to Assist States in the Settlement of Disputes through ICJ since the submission of his 2003 report [YUN 2003, p. 1309]. The Fund, established in 1989 [YUN 1989, p. 818], provided financial assistance to States for expenses incurred in connection with a dispute submitted to ICJ by way of a special agreement or the execution of a judgment resulting from such an agreement.

During the period under review (1 July 2003–30 June 2004), the Fund received one joint application from Benin and the Niger to defray the expenses incurred in connection with the submission of their boundary dispute to the Court (see p. 1268). On the recommendation of the Panel of Experts set up in accordance with the Fund's terms of reference, the Secretary-General awarded financial assistance in the amount of $350,000 to each applicant.

Three States contributed to the Fund, which, as at 30 June, had a total balance of $1,936 million.

As a result of a review conducted by the UN Office of Legal Affairs, in consultation with the Court's Registry and the Controller, the Fund's Terms of Reference were revised. The revised terms of reference were annexed to the report.

Chapter II

International tribunals

In 2004, the International Tribunal for the Prosecution of Persons Responsible for Serious Violations of International Humanitarian Law Committed in the Territory of the Former Yugoslavia since 1991 (ICTY) completed remaining investigations and subsequently filed indictments for war crimes, thereby meeting the first of three deadlines set out in its 2002 completion strategy to accomplish its mandate by 2010. The other two deadlines were to complete first instance trials by 2008 and the rest of its work by 2010. The International Criminal Tribunal for the Prosecution of Persons Responsible for Genocide and Other Serious Violations of International Humanitarian Law Committed in the Territory of Rwanda and Rwandan Citizens Responsible for Genocide and Other Such Violations Committed in the Territory of Neighbouring States between 1 January and 31 December 1994 (ICTR) formalized and revised its completion strategy, based on the same objectives and targets as those of ICTY. It met its first deadline of completing investigations by year's end. Both Tribunals focused efforts during the year on the implementation of other deadlines under their respective completion strategies. In May and November progress reports, they detailed specific measures being taken in that regard and potential obstacles. In August, the Security Council encouraged them to remain on track for meeting the relevant target dates.

In related developments, the Office of the Prosecutor of ICTY developed measures to enhance its operations and streamline its procedures under the leadership of a new Deputy Prosecutor and a new Chief of Prosecutions, while the Registrar, mandated to support and facilitate the work of ICTY's other organs, began to implement an action plan to enforce sentences. ICTY also made efforts to increase the cooperation of relevant countries, which resulted in numerous arrests and a number of fugitive surrenders. In October, the review functions performed by the ICTY Prosecutor, which had enabled the Tribunal to oversee prosecutions by national authorities under the 1996 Rome Agreement (known as the "Rules of the Road"), were transferred to the State Prosecutor of Bosnia and Herzegovina. In November, the General Assembly elected 14 permanent judges to ICTY, to replace those whose terms would expire in November 2005.

During the year, ICTR achieved its full complement of nine ad litem judges, which enabled it to initiate four new trials and to maintain its 2003 record of five trial judgements within a single year. To further facilitate its work, ICTR established an Appeals Section in the Office of the Prosecutor and enhanced its tracking activities to ensure that as many fugitives as possible were arrested in good time to enable trials to be completed before the end of 2008.

International Tribunal for the Former Yugoslavia

In 2004, the International Tribunal for the Former Yugoslavia (ICTY) pushed forward with the implementation of its completion strategy [YUN 2002, p. 1275], adopting further reforms to ensure compliance with Security Council resolutions 1503(2003) [YUN 2003, p. 1330] and 1534(2004) (see p. 1292). In April, ICTY amended the following Rules of Procedure and Evidence: rule 28 (A), to ensure that all indictments confirmed by the Tribunal met the Council's directive that they concentrate, prima facie, on one or more of the most senior leaders suspected of being most responsible for crimes within the Tribunal's jurisdiction; and rule 11 bis, to facilitate the referral of cases involving intermediate- and lower-level accused by increasing the jurisdictions available to receive its cases. The latter amendment authorized the Trial Chambers to refer a case to any jurisdiction in which the accused could be tried fairly and where the death penalty would not be imposed. In December, rule 98 bis, which concerned a Trial Chamber's oral decision after hearing oral submissions of the parties at the close of the prosecutor's case, was also amended.

ICTY continued its work in preparing the States in the Balkan region for the prosecution of war crimes cases. To advance the establishment of a special chamber for that purpose in the State Court of Bosnia and Herzegovina, it formed working groups comprising representatives from the office of the President, the Registry, the Office of the Prosecutor and the Office of the High Representative for the Implementation of the Peace Agreement for Bosnia and Herzegovina, which made substantial progress with regard to legal reform, witness protection and detention facilities. ICTY also conducted a number of training seminars in Croatia to ensure the trial-readiness of its courts.

Investigations were streamlined to concentrate on the highest-level political and military leaders responsible for having committed the gravest crimes. Particular efforts were mounted to achieve the first major deadline foreseen by the completion strategy, namely, completion by year's end of pre-indictment investigations of all remaining suspects. However, the strategy posed a number of challenges relating to the transfer of cases to courts in the former Yugoslavia, and to human resources, scheduling and legacy issues. Attention was moreover drawn to the budget limitations for the Investigations Section of the Office of the Prosecutor, the shortfall in contributions and the associated recruitment freeze amidst an increasing vacancy rate throughout ICTY, all of which could result in serious obstacles to achieving the completion schedule set by the Council.

The activities of ICTY, established by Council resolution 827(1993) [YUN 1993, p. 440], were covered in two reports to the Council and the General Assembly, for the periods 1 August 2003 to 31 July 2004 [A/59/215-S/2004/627] and 1 August 2004 to 31 July 2005 [A/60/267-S/2005/532 & Corr.1]. On 15 November, the Assembly took note of the 2003/2004 report (**decision 59/511**).

The Chambers

The judicial activities of the Tribunal's three Trial Chambers, which ran six trials simultaneously during the year, and of its Appeals Chamber included first instance and appeals proceedings against judgements, interlocutory decisions and State requests for review; proceedings concerning the Tribunal's primacy; and contempt cases. ICTY had a total of 25 judges—14 permanent judges, 2 judges from ICTR serving in the Appeals Chamber and 9 ad litem judges.

New arrests, surrenders and indictments

On 3 March, the following officials of the former self-proclaimed "Croatian Union of Herceg-Bosna" [YUN 1993, p. 460] and of Croatia were indicted jointly for crimes committed against Serbs in the Croatian-held part of northern Bosnia in 1992 and 1993: Jadranko Prlic (Prime Minister), Bruno Stojic (Head, Ministry of Defence) and

Valentin Coric (Head, Military Police); and Slobodan Praljak (Croatia's Deputy Defence Minister and Military Commander, Croatian Defence Council (HVO)), Milivoj Petkovic (Chief, HVO military staff) and Berislav Pusic (Head, HVO Commission for Exchange of Prisoners). They surrendered to the Tribunal on 5 April and pleaded not guilty at their initial appearance the following day to 26 counts of war crimes (wilful killing, torture, inhumane treatment, extensive destruction of property, plunder, unlawful labour and attacks on civilians), violations of the laws and customs of war (wanton destruction of cities and villages) and crimes against humanity (persecution, murder, torture, inhumane treatment, imprisonment and deportation). On 30 July, the Trial Chamber granted the applications of all six co-accused for provisional release on the grounds that they posed no threat to victims, witnesses and other persons and that they would appear for trial. However, 16 preliminary motions filed on 15 December by defence counsel challenging the form of the indictment and the Tribunal's jurisdiction, and calling for severance of the cases, were denied by the Chamber. A request for certification to appeal that decision was filed.

Ivan Cermak and Mladen Markac, whose indictment was confirmed on 24 February, surrendered in Croatia on 11 March. At their initial appearance on 12 March, they pleaded not guilty to seven counts of crimes against humanity and violations of the laws or customs of war (persecutions; murder; plunder of property; wanton destruction of cities, towns or villages; deportation and forced displacement; and other inhumane acts) committed against the Serb population in the Krajina region of Croatia. On 1 April, the Trial Chamber granted protective measures to victims and witnesses, and on 29 April, it denied motions for provisional release filed by the accused, who again filed similar motions in July and alleged defects in the form of the indictment. On 2 December, the Appeals Chamber overturned the Trial Chamber's decision and ordered that the accused be provisionally released under various terms and conditions.

On 11 May, Colonel Mirko Norac, who was serving a national prison sentence imposed on him in Croatia for other war crimes, was indicted with two counts of crimes against humanity (persecutions and murder) and three counts of violations of the laws and customs of war (murder, plunder of property and wanton destruction of cities) committed against Serb civilians during the military operation in the Medak pocket in Croatia [YUN 1993, p. 490]; he pleaded not guilty. On 27 May, the Prosecutor filed a motion for joinder with the case against General Rahim Ademi

[YUN 2001, p. 1199; YUN 2003, p. 1313], with the intention of seeking referral of the joint case to a Court in Croatia. On 30 July, the Trial Chamber granted the joinder application and, on 2 September, the Prosecutor moved for referral of the joint case. The referral bench was currently deliberating.

Ljubisa Beara, Chief of Security in the Bosnian Serb Army, who was arrested in Serbia and transferred to the Tribunal on 10 October, made his initial appearance on 11 November and pleaded not guilty of crimes in Srebrenica, for which he was indicted.

Beqe Beqaj, indicted on 21 October for contempt or attempted contempt for allegedly interfering or attempting to interfere with potential witnesses in the trial against Fatmir Limaj, Haradin Bala and Isak Musliu [YUN 2003, p. 1311], was arrested by the international security force (KFOR) in Kosovo on 4 November and made his initial appearance on 5 November.

Miroslav Bralo, member of the HVO Special Forces Unit, whose indictment was made public in October, surrendered voluntarily on 12 November and was transferred to the Tribunal the following day. At his initial appearance on 13 December, he pleaded not guilty to eight counts of crimes in Lasva River Valley, Bosnia and Herzegovina.

Dragomir Milosevic, Chief Commander, Romanija Corps of the Bosnian Serb Army, who was indicted in 1999 for crimes in Sarajevo and who remained at large until 2004, arrived at the Tribunal on 3 December and made his initial appearance on 7 December.

In 2004, public indictments were made against Goran Hadzic and Stojan Zupljanin (Commander of the Serb-operated Regional Security Services Centre), both of whom remained at large.

Ongoing cases and trials

On 12 January, Milan Babic, indicted in 2003 for a crime against humanity and violations of the laws and customs of war [YUN 2003, p. 1312], filed a joint plea agreement with the Prosecutor, in exchange for cooperation with the prosecution in other cases. As part of the plea agreement, Mr. Babic pleaded guilty as an aider and abettor of a joint criminal enterprise, for which the prosecutor recommended a sentence not exceeding 11 years' imprisonment. He later changed his plea. On 29 June 2004, he was sentenced to 13 years in prison. The accused appealed the judgement.

In the case against Mitar Rasevic, who was indicted with other accused, and for whom the judge in 2003 entered pleas of not guilty [YUN 2003, p. 1312], a motion for leave to amend the in-

dictment was filed on 2 December 2003 by the prosecution. The defence did not oppose the motion but filed, on 12 January 2004, a fresh preliminary motion on the form of the indictment. On 28 April, the Trial Chamber granted the motion to amend the indictment. On 12 May, the prosecution filed an amended indictment, and on 10 June, the defence filed a further motion challenging parts of the amended indictment, which was denied on 27 July. In November, the prosecution moved for referral of the case to the authorities of Bosnia and Herzegovina.

Vojislav Seselj, charged in 2003 [YUN 2003, p. 1311] in a 14-count indictment alleging crimes against humanity and violations of the laws or customs of war, filed an interlocutory appeal on 12 January 2004, following the Trial Chamber's rejection of his request for permission to be visited in detention by a representative of his religion. On 29 January, the Appeals Chamber dismissed the appeal, having considered that the determination of visits an accused was allowed to receive while at the detention unit fell within the competence of the Registry and not of the Chambers. On 15 January, Mr. Seselj filed a motion challenging the Tribunal's jurisdiction and parts of the indictment. On 26 May, the Trial Chamber rejected the first part of the motion concerning the Tribunal's jurisdiction and most of the complaints of the accused about the indictment, and ordered the prosecution to amend the indictment, as the crimes for which Mr. Seselj was held responsible, committed in Vojvodina, were not properly charged. On 28 June, the prosecution filed an interlocutory appeal from the Trial Chamber's decision, submitting that the Chamber had applied an incorrect and narrow standard for the jurisdictional elements charged under article 5 of the ICTY statute; had interpreted too narrowly the words "committed in armed conflict"; and for those reasons, had erred when it held that article 5 could apply to crimes that allegedly occurred in Vojvodina only if an armed conflict existed there at the relevant time. The prosecution sought clarification from the Appeals Chamber of the phrase "committed in armed conflict", and a finding that the Trial Chamber had erred in requiring an armed conflict in Vojvodina to have occurred. On 29 July, the Appeals Chamber decided that the appeal was validly filed.

On 13 January, Blagoje Simic, found guilty of a crime against humanity and sentenced to 17 years in prison in 2003 [YUN 2003, p. 1315], was granted an extension to file his appeal brief, which he did on 17 June 2004. On 25 June, he filed a motion for disclosure of documents, and on 22 September, he filed an amended notice of appeal. On

21 October, Mr. Simic was granted provisional release from 4 to 7 November to attend a memorial service for his father.

In the case against Dragoljub Ojdanic, charged jointly with Milan Milutinovic, Slobodan Milosevic, Nikola Sainovic and Vlajko Stojiljkovic in 1999 [YUN 1999, p. 1214], a scheduled appeal briefing resumed on 16 January 2004 regarding the Trial Chamber's dismissal of Mr. Ojdanic's motion challenging ICTY's jurisdiction. Mr. Ojdanic submitted that the Trial Chamber had erred in finding that the Tribunal had jurisdiction to try him for crimes allegedly committed in the territory of Kosovo as the Security Council did not have the power to vest the Tribunal with jurisdiction over the territory of the Federal Republic of Yugoslavia (currently known as Serbia and Montenegro), which, at that time, was not a Member of the United Nations. On 12 May (with reasons issued on 8 June), the Appeals Chamber dismissed the appeal. Pre-trial briefs were filed by the prosecution on 14 June, and by the defence on 13 September. In December, Mr. Milutinovic filed his second, Mr. Ojdanic his fourth, and Mr. Sainovic his third application for provisional release.

On 16 January, Dragan Nikolic, convicted and sentenced to 23 years in prison [YUN 2003, p. 1314], filed a notice of appeal from the judgement on 16 January 2004 and an appeal brief on 30 June.

Enver Hadzihasanovic and Amir Kubura, who had pleaded not guilty in 2001 [YUN 2001, p. 1199] and, by a third amended indictment, were further charged in 2003 with violations of the laws or customs of war [YUN 2003, p. 1314], were granted provisional release from 18 to 20 January 2004 and from 13 to 15 March, respectively, to attend the funerals of relatives in Bosnia and Herzegovina. On a defence motion relating to the scope of prosecution examination of its witnesses, the Trial Chamber ruled on 16 March that, in the absence of an explicit mention in the third amended indictment, a charge of cruel treatment did not include allegations of inhuman treatment consisting of the use of detainees to carry out forced labour (trench digging). On 2 April, the Appeals Chamber reversed the Trial Chamber's 2003 decision [ibid.] barring the prosecution from showing one of its witnesses written extracts from his previous statement to refresh his memory. On 23 July 2004, the prosecution closed its case, having called 99 prosecution witnesses and one court witness. Mr. Hadzihasanovic's defence opened its case on 18 October.

In the case against Slobodan Milosevic [YUN 1999, p. 1214; YUN 2001, p. 1201; YUN 2002, p. 1277], the Trial Chamber had granted the accused an adjournment of three months to prepare his defence, and required him to present within six weeks a list of witnesses and evidentiary exhibits. In an appeal, the amici curiae argued that both periods were unreasonably short for the accused to prepare a meaningful defence, given that the case had come to trial in a relatively short period of time, that the prosecution had had a considerable amount of time available to it and that the accused was suffering from ill health. On 20 January, the Appeals Chamber dismissed the appeal and held that the Trial Chamber had acted with proper sensitivity to the concerns of a self-representing defendant and that there had been no violation of the right of the accused to a fair trial by the time limits imposed. On 25 February, the prosecution rested its case-in-chief, subject to several matters pertaining to the admission of documents and its case in rebuttal. The accused opened his case on 31 August. However, owing to frequent interruptions and delays caused by his chronic health condition, the Trial Chamber decided that, in order to safeguard his right to a fair trial, it was necessary to assign him counsel to assist him in his defence. Subsequently, two amici curiae were appointed as counsel for the defence. Following a challenge of that decision by the accused, the Appeals Chamber upheld the assignment of counsel in November, but reversed a subsequent order of the Trial Chamber regarding the modalities by which assigned counsel would fulfil their mandate.

An amended indictment, dated 23 January, brought further charges against Mile Mrksic, Miroslav Radic and Veselin Sljivancanin, who had been indicted jointly with other accused in 1997 [YUN 1997, p. 1322] for the alleged execution in Ovcara (near Vukovar, Croatia) of some 200 Croatian and other non-Serb persons removed from Vukovar Hospital in 1991. Mr. Radic and Mr. Sljivancanin had made initial appearances before the Tribunal in 2003 [YUN 2003, p. 1311]. In its decision authorizing additional charges, the Trial Chamber upheld challenges from the accused and ordered the prosecution to amend the indictment in a manner that complied with the Tribunal's pleading principles. A further decision on the form of the indictment, issued on 20 July 2004, which partly granted motions by the accused, directed the prosecution to amend and re-file the indictment no later than 17 August.

Sentencing hearings were held on 27 January and 5 March in the case of Miroslav Deronjic, who was arrested in 2002 [YUN 2002, p. 1276] and pleaded guilty in 2003 [YUN 2003, p. 1315] to charges brought against him. On 30 March 2004, the Trial Chamber entered a single conviction against the accused for persecutions, a crime against humanity, and sentenced him to 10 years in prison.

The presiding judge, in his dissent, held that the accused deserved a sentence of no less than 20 years' imprisonment. On 28 April, Mr. Deronjic filed a notice of appeal from the judgement.

Ivica Rajic, who pleaded not guilty in 2003 [YUN 2003, p. 1311], entered the same plea on 29 January 2004 to an amended indictment alleging five counts of war crimes (wilful killing, inhumane treatment and sexual assault, unlawful confinement, appropriation of property and wanton destruction) and five counts of violations of the laws and customs of war (murder, outrages upon personal dignity, cruel treatment, plunder, wanton destruction of towns and unjustified devastation). In response to a defence motion on the form of the second indictment, the Trial Chamber ordered the Prosecutor on 27 April to clarify a number of allegations in the indictment.

In January, Franko Simatovic and Jovica Stanisic, who pleaded not guilty in 2003 to four counts of crimes against humanity and one count of violating the laws or customs of war [YUN 2003, p. 1311], filed applications for provisional release, which were granted on 28 July 2004, based mainly on expert evidence as to the medical condition of Mr. Stanisic. On 29 July, the Trial Chamber, upon request from the prosecution, ordered the stay of the decisions to enable the prosecution to seek leave to appeal. On 3 December, the Appeals Chamber dismissed the prosecution's appeal and ordered the provisional release of both accused.

The trial of Momcilo Krajisnik, who pleaded not guilty to charges of genocide and other crimes in 2000 [YUN 2000, p. 1221], began on 3 February 2004 with the prosecution's opening arguments and presentation of evidence. By 27 February, seven witnesses had testified for the prosecution, including an expert witness on the Bosnian Serb leadership. The proceedings were adjourned several times to allow the defence team time to prepare its case and for the two sides to negotiate the number of crime-based and expert witnesses.

In the case against General Pavle Strugar, accused, in a third amended indictment, of crimes against persons and crimes against property [YUN 2003, p. 1314], the Trial Chamber, on 26 May, denied a 3 February motion by the defence, which again sought to terminate the trial based on a claim that the accused was unfit to stand trial. The prosecution case, comprising 29 viva voce witnesses and over 200 exhibits, concluded on 18 May. The defence case commenced on 28 June and concluded on 22 July.

Milomir Stakic, found guilty and sentenced in 2003 [YUN 2003, p. 1313] to life imprisonment, with a minimum term of 20 years, filed his appeal brief and a motion for the admission of additional evidence on 3 February 2004; he re-filed the appeal on 9 March. On 8 June, the prosecution filed a motion to strike an alleged new ground of appeal of the defendant raised in the reply brief, which the Appeals Chamber granted on 20 July.

In the case against Milka Maglov, who had pleaded not guilty in December 2003 to two counts of contempt of court for allegedly intimidating a witness in the Radoslav Brdanin case (see p. 1280), in which she had formerly served as defence co-counsel, the Trial Chamber, on 6 February 2004, upheld a motion by the amicus curiae Prosecutor to amend the indictment. The amendment added a third charge of attempted interference or intimidation. The prosecution case was heard from 16 to 19 February. On 19 March, a motion for acquittal brought by Ms. Maglov was dismissed, and her request for certification to appeal the decision was denied. The defence case was delayed by a confidential application, which was dismissed, seeking the disqualification and withdrawal of some judges, and the filing of an unopposed motion on 15 July for continuance on the basis that she was unfit to stand trial. On the same day, the Trial Chamber adjourned the case and directed the Registry to identify a psychiatrist who could establish the respondent's fitness to stand trial.

In the trial of Sefer Halilovic, who was charged with one count of violation of the laws of war and was granted provisional release in 2001 [YUN 2001, p. 1199], the Trial Chamber dismissed, on 16 February 2004, a defence motion for subpoenas to be issued so that certain prosecution witnesses could be interviewed by the defence. On appeal by the defence, the Appeals Chamber, with one of the judges dissenting, allowed the appeal in part, on 21 June, having found that the Trial Chamber had erred in rejecting the defence request for subpoenas solely on the basis that the defence would have the opportunity to cross-examine the witnesses, and should have examined whether the defence had presented reasons for the need to interview those witnesses, which went beyond the need to prepare a more effective cross examination. The Appeals Chamber directed the Trial Chamber to reconsider the matter and to issue subpoenas if its re-examination disclosed a need to interview the witnesses. Other issues that preoccupied the defence and prosecution related to counsel, assistance in obtaining access to material and information, and disclosures of materials and further investigations in the case.

On 16 February, the Appeals Chamber dismissed motions for additional evidence presented by Mlado Radic, Dragoljub Prcac and Zoran Zigic, who were sentenced with other accused to prison terms in 2001 [YUN 2001, p. 1201]. However, the Appeals Chamber found two pieces of evidence presented by Mr. Zigic admissible as additional evidence on appeal, and two witnesses were called to testify in that regard.

Dario Kordic and Mario Cerkez, sentenced in 2001 [YUN 2001, p. 1200] to 25 and 15 years' imprisonment, respectively, for crimes against humanity and violations of the laws and customs of war, appealed the judgement. In that regard, Mr. Kordic filed a supplemental appeal brief on 23 February 2004. On 26 March, the Appeals Chamber dismissed motions by Mr. Cerkez for the admission of additional evidence, and on 16 April, rejected his motion for admission of a witness transcript. On 17 December, the Appeals Chamber rendered its final judgement on the appeals of the accused; it rejected Mr. Kordic's first, second, fifth and sixth grounds of appeal, as well as his appeal concerning his responsibility for crimes committed in various locations. The Chamber did allow Mr. Kordic's appeal concerning his responsibility for crimes committed in other locations, and accordingly, pursuant to article 7 (1) of the ICTY statute, reversed his convictions under eight counts of the indictment relating to the respective locations in question, but affirmed his convictions with regard to 12 other counts. The Chamber also reversed his remaining convictions under count 1 and affirmed the sentence of 25 years' imprisonment. Regarding Mr. Cerkez, the Appeals Chamber allowed his appeal in part, rejecting a number of his grounds of appeal but allowing his appeal concerning his responsibility for certain crimes. It reversed his conviction, imposing a new sentence of 6 years' imprisonment.

On 25 February, the Appeals Chamber dismissed the appeal filed by Mitar Vasiljevic, who was sentenced to 20 years in prison in 2002 [YUN 2002, p. 1280]. However, the Chamber reduced his sentence to 15 years' imprisonment, having found, contrary to the Trial Chamber's findings, with one of the judges dissenting, that he was responsible as an aider and abettor, and not as a co-perpetrator, to murder as a violation of the laws or customs of war under article 3 of the ICTY statute, and to persecution under article 5.

In the trial, which began in 2003 [YUN 2003, p. 1312], of Vidoje Blagojevic and Dragan Jokic, charged jointly with other accused in 2001 [YUN 2001, p. 1199] for their alleged involvement in events in and around Srebrenica in 1995 [YUN 1995, p. 529], the prosecution's case concluded on 27 February 2004, and that of the defence for the two accused on 25 June and 23 July, respectively. The trial ended on 1 October, and judgement was expected in 2005.

The trial of Fatmir Limaj, Haradin Bala and Isak Musliu, arrested in 2003 with other accused for alleged crimes against Kosovo Serbs [YUN 2003, p. 1311], began on 15 November 2004; pre-trial briefs were filed by the prosecution on 28 February and the accused on 1 June.

Following a February defence motion seeking dismissal of the contempt of court charge against Dusko Jovanovic, a media practitioner, the prosecution filed a request in March to withdraw the indictment, on the understanding, as agreed between the parties, that the accused would publish a written statement acknowledging full personal and professional responsibility for publishing the details of a protected witness, in violation of protective measures orders issued by the Trial Chamber. Following the publication of the agreed statement on 19 April, the prosecution motion to withdraw the indictment was granted and the proceedings against Mr. Jovanovic were terminated.

The prosecution, in the case of Stanislav Galic, sentenced to 20 years in prison in 2003 [YUN 2003, p. 1315], with one of the judges filing a separate and partially dissenting opinion, with an alternative recommendation of 10 years in prison, filed its appeal brief on 2 March 2004. In response, Mr. Galic filed a notice of appeal on 4 May, and on 18 June, a motion for the admission of additional evidence.

In the case against Naser Oric, who was arrested in 2003 [YUN 2003, p. 1311] and pleaded not guilty to six counts of violations of the laws or customs of war, the defence filed its pre-trial brief on 4 March 2004. The trial commenced on 6 October.

On 11 March, Ranko Cesic, arrested in 2002 [YUN 2002, p. 1276], pleaded guilty under a plea agreement to all 12 counts charged in the indictment against him and was sentenced to 18 years in prison.

Miodrag Jokic, who entered into a plea agreement in 2003 [YUN 2003, p. 1314], according to which he pleaded guilty to six counts in an amended indictment, was sentenced to seven years in prison on 18 March 2004. Mr. Jokic filed a notice of appeal from the sentencing judgement on 16 April, two motions for the admission of additional evidence on 2 and 21 June, and his appeal brief on 30 June. The Appeals Chamber denied those motions on 31 August.

In the trial of Radoslav Brdanin, which began in 2002 [YUN 2002, p. 1277] on charges of genocide and crimes against humanity, the Appeals Chamber ruled on 19 March 2004 on a prosecution motion requesting the reversal of the Trial Chamber's 2003 decision [YUN 2003, p. 1313] to grant a defence motion for acquittal of genocide in the context of the third category of joint criminal enterprise liability. The Appeals Chamber allowed the prosecution's appeal, reversed the decision of the Trial Chamber and reinstated the charge of genocide, having found that the Trial Chamber had erred by conflating the mens rea requirement of the crime of genocide with the mental requirement of the mode of liability. Closing arguments in the case were heard in April 2004. On 1 September, the Trial Chamber acquitted Mr. Brdanin of genocide, complicity in genocide and extermination, but found him guilty of persecutions as a crime against humanity. He was sentenced to 32 years' imprisonment. Notices of appeal were filed by the Prosecutor on 30 September, and by Mr. Brdanin on 1 October.

On 31 March, Darko Mrda, who was charged in 2002 [YUN 2002, p. 1276] and pleaded guilty in 2003 [YUN 2003, p. 1313] to murder and inhuman acts under a plea agreement, was sentenced to 17 years' imprisonment.

Pre-trial briefs were filed by the prosecution on 1 April, and by the defence on 21 June in the case against Radovan Stankovic, charged in 2002 along with other accused [YUN 2002, p. 1277] of crimes against humanity and violations of the laws or customs of war for acts allegedly committed against Muslim women. On 21 September 2004, the Prosecutor moved for referral of the case to the State Court of Bosnia and Herzegovina in Sarajevo. That decision was appealed on its merits by the accused, while the Prosecutor appealed the part of the decision ordering it to monitor the process in Sarajevo and report regularly to the Referral Bench. On 29 November, the Prosecutor moved again for the referral of the case to Bosnia and Herzegovina.

On 19 April, the Appeals Chamber rendered its judgement in the case of Radislav Krstic, who had filed appeal briefs in 2002 [YUN 2002, p. 1278] against his conviction and sentencing in 2001 [YUN 2001, p. 1201]. The Appeals Chamber set aside Mr. Krstic's conviction as a participant in a joint criminal enterprise to commit genocide and his conviction as a participant in murder under article 3 of the ICTY statute, committed between 13 and 19 July 1995. He was found guilty, however, of aiding and abetting in genocide and murder as a violation of the laws or customs of war. The Appeals Chamber confirmed his conviction for participation in murder committed at other times (between 10 and 13 July 1995) as a violation of the laws or customs of war and as persecution. The Appeals Chamber further held that the Trial Chamber had incorrectly disallowed Mr. Krstic's convictions as a participant in extermination and persecution (on the grounds that they were cumulative with his conviction for genocide), but

that his level of responsibility was that of an aider and abettor in extermination and persecution as crimes against humanity. Appeals by both Mr. Krstic and the prosecution were otherwise dismissed, and Mr. Krstic was sentenced to 35 years' imprisonment. One of the judges appended a partial dissenting opinion.

In the case against Zeljko Mejakic, Momcilo Gruban, Dusen Fustar and Dusko Knezevic, charged jointly in 2002 [YUN 2002, p. 1279] with Pedrag Banovic, who was sentenced to eight years in prison in 2003 [YUN 2003, p. 1311], the Trial Chamber ruled in April 2004 on a prosecution motion to admit 252 facts that were the subject of prior adjudication by Trial Chambers in three other cases. It granted the prosecution's request in part, excluding those facts that were too broad, too tendentious, not sufficiently significant or not sufficiently relevant to the case; it also rejected facts that were derived from a judgement based on a plea agreement. On 17 June, the Chamber ruled, on the question of a potential conflict of interest arising from the appointment by the Registrar as counsel for Mr. Mejakic the same counsel already assigned as lead counsel to Dragoljub Prcac, that in the light of the hypothetical nature of the application, the matter was best left to the relevant Trial Chamber to decide when and if it arose. On 13 July, the prosecution filed an appeal brief submitting that the Trial Chamber erred in law in finding that the representation of two accused by one and the same counsel was not likely to affect the integrity of the proceedings or otherwise irreversibly prejudice the administration of justice. On 2 September, the Prosecutor filed a motion requesting referral of the case against the four accused to the authorities of Bosnia and Herzegovina.

On 7 May, the prosecution filed its pre-trial brief in the case against Milan Martic, who pleaded not guilty in 2003 [YUN 2003, p. 1315] to 10 counts of crimes against humanity and nine charges of violations of the laws or customs of war. The defence appealed the Trial Chamber's 1 July 2004 decision to uphold the Registrar's determination of the level of complexity of the case. The defence was given until 15 September to file its pre-trial brief.

On 24 May, Momir Nikolic, who was sentenced to 27 years in prison in 2003 [YUN 2003, p. 1313], filed an appeal against the sentence. On 8 June 2004, the prosecution filed a motion to strike out parts of the appeal, and, on 18 June, Mr. Nikolic filed a motion for the admission of additional evidence.

In the case against Vladimir Kovacevic and Milan Zec [YUN 2001, p. 1200], Mr. Kovacevic was released provisionally on 2 June and, on 7 June, he was transferred to a mental institution in Belgrade for psychiatric treatment for an initial period of six months to ascertain whether he would be fit to stand trial. On 28 October, the Prosecutor moved for referral of the case to Serbia and Montenegro, but the Referral Bench refrained from considering the motion until the question of Mr. Kovacevic's fitness to stand trial was determined.

On 18 June, Dragan Obrenovic, who was sentenced to 17 years in prison in 2003 [YUN 2003, p. 1313], was transferred to Norway to serve his sentence.

In the case of Pasko Ljubicic, the prosecution and defence filed pre-trial briefs in 2003 [YUN 2003, p. 1313], but Mr. Ljubicic was not deemed ready for trial until documents sought by the defence were produced by the Governments of Bosnia and Herzegovina and Croatia. The defence declared on 23 July 2004 that the accused was ready to go to trial even if not all the documents had been produced.

Regarding the notices of appeal filed by Tihomir Blaskic [YUN 2000, p. 1223; YUN 2002, p. 1280] following his 1999 trial [YUN 1999, p. 1216], the Appeals Chamber delivered its judgement on 29 July 2004; it allowed by majority, with one of the judges dissenting, Mr. Blaskic's grounds of appeal concerning his responsibility for the crimes committed in Ahmici, Santici, Pirici and Nadioi on 16 April 1993 and reversed his convictions pursuant to articles 7 (1) and 7 (3) of the ICTY statute. It also unanimously allowed his appeal against his convictions for a number of other counts in the indictment, but affirmed his conviction for the detention-related crimes committed in detention facilities, for ordering the use of protected persons for the construction of defensive military installations and for the inhuman treatment of detainees occasioned by their use as human shields, but dismissed his appeal in all other respects. It did, however, allow in part Mr. Blaskic's grounds of appeal against his sentence and imposed on him, by majority, with one of the judges dissenting, a new sentence of nine years' imprisonment. The dissenting judge appended a partial dissenting opinion and another judge appended a separate opinion limited to the sentence. On 29 July 2004, Mr. Blaskic was granted early release, effective 2 August.

On 20 October, the Appeals Chamber dismissed rule 115 motions on the admission of additional evidence filed by Vinko Martinovic and Mladen Naletilic in connection with their appeal of the Trial Chamber's sentence in 2003 [YUN 2003, p. 1312] of 18 years and 20 years in prison, respectively. In November 2004, the accused filed

further motions with the same request, which were being considered by the Appeals Chamber.

Election of judges

Permanent judges

On 5 April [S/2004/288], the Secretary-General informed the Security Council President that Judge Richard May (United Kingdom) had resigned as a permanent judge of ICTY, effective 31 May, and that the United Kingdom had presented Iain Bonomy to replace him. Annexed to the letter was Lord Bonomy's curriculum vitae.

Following consultations with Council members, the Council President, on 8 April [S/2004/289], informed the Secretary-General that he supported his intention to appoint Lord Bonomy as a permanent judge of ICTY.

In September [S/2004/754] and October [A/59/438], the Secretary-General forwarded to the Council and the General Assembly, respectively, the list of candidates nominated to replace the 14 permanent judges of ICTY whose terms would expire on 16 November 2005. The memorandum also contained the procedure for electing them. By a 21 October note [A/59/439], the Secretary-General submitted to the Assembly the curricula vitae of the 22 nominated candidates.

SECURITY COUNCIL ACTION

On 14 October [meeting 5057], the Security Council unanimously adopted **resolution 1567(2004)**. The draft [S/2004/813] was prepared in consultations among Council members.

The Security Council,

Recalling its resolutions 827(1993) of 25 May 1993, 1166(1998) of 13 May 1998, 1329(2000) of 30 November 2000, 1411(2002) of 17 May 2002, 1481(2003) of 19 May 2003, 1503(2003) of 28 August 2003 and 1534(2004) of 26 March 2004,

Having considered the nominations for Permanent Judges of the International Tribunal for the Former Yugoslavia received by the Secretary-General,

Forwards the following nominations to the General Assembly in accordance with Article 13 bis, paragraph 1 *(d)*, of the statute of the International Tribunal:

    Mr. Carmel A. Agius (Malta)
    Mr. Jean-Claude Antonetti (France)
    Mr. Iain Bonomy (United Kingdom of Great Britain and Northern Ireland)
    Mr. Liu Daqun (China)
    Mr. Mohamed Amin El-Abbassi El Mahdi (Egypt)
    Mr. Elhagi Abdulkader Emberesh (Libyan Arab Jamahiriya)
    Mr. Rigoberto Espinal Irias (Honduras)
    Mr. O-gon Kwon (Republic of Korea)
    Mr. Theodor Meron (United States of America)
    Mr. Bakone Melema Moloto (South Africa)
    Ms. Prisca Matimba Nyambe (Zambia)
    Mr. Alphonsus Martinus Maria Orie (Netherlands)

Mr. Kevin Horace Parker (Australia)
Mr. Fausto Pocar (Italy)
Mr. Yenyi Olungu (Democratic Republic of the Congo)
Mr. Sharada Prasad Pandit (Nepal)
Ms. Vonimbolana Rasoazanany (Madagascar)
Mr. Patrick Lipton Robinson (Jamaica)
Mr. Wolfgang Schomburg (Germany)
Mr. Mohamed Shahabuddeen (Guyana)
Ms. Christine Van den Wyngaert (Belgium)
Mr. Volodymyr A. Vassylenko (Ukraine)

On the same day [A/59/437], the Council President transmitted the text of the Council's resolution to the General Assembly.

GENERAL ASSEMBLY ACTION

On 19 November [meeting 57], the General Assembly adopted **decision 59/406** without vote [agenda item 18].

Election of judges of the International Tribunal for the Prosecution of Persons Responsible for Serious Violations of International Humanitarian Law Committed in the Territory of the Former Yugoslavia since 1991

At its 57th plenary meeting, on 19 November 2004, the General Assembly, pursuant to article 13 bis of the statute of the International Tribunal for the Prosecution of Persons Responsible for Serious Violations of International Humanitarian Law Committed in the Territory of the Former Yugoslavia since 1991, elected the following fourteen permanent judges for a four-year term of office beginning on 17 November 2005:

Mr. Carmel AGIUS (Malta)
Mr. Jean-Claude ANTONETTI (France)
Mr. Iain BONOMY (United Kingdom)
Mr. O-gon KWON (Republic of Korea)
Mr. LIU Daqun (China)
Mr. Theodor MERON (United States)
Mr. Bakone Melema MOLOTO (South Africa)
Mr. Alphonsus Martinus Maria ORIE (Netherlands)
Mr. Kevin Horace PARKER (Australia)
Mr. Fausto POCAR (Italy)
Mr. Patrick Lipton ROBINSON (Jamaica)
Mr. Wolfgang SCHOMBURG (Germany)
Mr. Mohamed SHAHABUDDEEN (Guyana)
Ms. Christine VAN DEN WYNGAERT (Belgium)

Office of the Prosecutor

During the year, the efficiency and work of the Office of the Prosecutor improved markedly, as it completed remaining investigations and the subsequent filing of the indictments for war crimes, thereby enabling it to meet the first deadline of the completion strategy initiated in 2002 [YUN 2002, p. 1275]. Also, as part of the strategy, the Prosecutor filed motions for the transfer of 10 cases concerning 18 accused to be tried by national jurisdictions in Bosnia and Herzegovina, Croatia, or Serbia and Montenegro. The transfer of four of those cases had been granted, one was denied and the outcome on the others was pending. The

Office continued its pre-trial, trial and appeals activities. It enhanced its operations and streamlined its procedures under the leadership of a new Deputy Prosecutor and a new Chief of Prosecutions, both of whom were appointed during the reporting period.

Efforts were made to increase the cooperation of relevant countries, resulting in numerous arrests and some fugitive surrenders. Cooperation with Croatia remained satisfactory in terms of requests for assistance, information, archives, witnesses and suspects, but no progress was made regarding that country's efforts to arrest Ante Gotovina, one of the high-profile fugitives accused of serious violations of international humanitarian law. Cooperation by Serbia and Montenegro improved late in the year, but was still not complete, consistent and speedy. Problems persisted with respect to the production of sensitive documents, and although the Government had secured surrenders of outstanding and new accused—a total of 14 accused were transferred from or through Belgrade—its reluctance to execute Tribunal arrest warrants continued.

In Bosnia and Herzegovina, cooperation by the entity government of the Federation of Bosnia and Herzegovina was satisfactory. However, cooperation by the other entity, the Republika Srpska, though improved, was still insufficient, particularly with regard to the transfer of fugitives and wartime documentation. To further cooperation, the Office of the High Representative promoted and implemented the Monitoring Group on Cooperation with the Tribunal, formed in 2003 [YUN 2003, p. 408], involving all relevant entities and State structures. In October 2004, the Prosecutor's review functions, which had enabled ICTY to oversee the prosecution of accused persons by relevant national authorities under the 1996 Rome Agreement [YUN 1996, p. 1187] (also known as the "Rules of the Road"), were transferred to the State Prosecutor of Bosnia and Herzegovina.

There were no problems regarding cooperation with the former Yugoslav Republic of Macedonia, enabling the Office of the Prosecutor to complete all investigations concerning that country.

Communication. On 6 May [S/2004/353], the President of the Tribunal transmitted to the Security Council President the report of the Prosecutor regarding the non-compliance by Serbia and Montenegro with its obligation to cooperate with ICTY. According to the Prosecutor, the level of that cooperation had declined since December 2003, particularly its failure to execute Tribunal arrest warrants, cooperate with the Prosecutor in securing the testimony of witnesses and documentary evidence, and respond to the Registrar's requests for an explanation of those failures, which could impinge on the Tribunal's ability to meet the expectations of its completion strategy.

The Registry

The Registry continued its managerial, administrative and judicial support functions to facilitate the work of the Chambers, the Office of the Prosecutor and the defence. It also managed the Detention Unit, the Victims and Witnesses Section, the legal aid office and the interpretation and translation service. The Registry also facilitated the implementation of the Tribunal's completion strategy, initiated in 2002 [YUN 2002, p. 1275], including an action plan to enforce sentences and relocate protected witnesses and their families. Consistent with Security Council resolution 1534(2004) (see p. 1292), the Registrar, in consultation with the President of the Tribunal and the Prosecutor, launched an initiative to convince more States to accept convicted persons to serve sentences in their respective territories. In that regard, on 11 March 2004, the Tribunal signed, on behalf of the United Nations, an agreement on the enforcement of sentences with the United Kingdom, the tenth UN Member State to conclude such an agreement; other States indicated their willingness to do the same.

As recommended in Council resolution 1503 (2003) [YUN 2003, p. 1330], the Tribunal continued to develop and improve its outreach programme as part of its completion strategy, with special attention paid to improving the capacity of national jurisdictions to prosecute war crimes cases. The programme significantly enhanced its activities in that regard. It assisted in the establishment of a responsible body of lawyers, prosecutors and other legal professionals in the former Yugoslavia, and organized in Croatia between May and October training seminars for judges and prosecutors likely to participate in the trial of war crimes cases. In efforts to engage victims across the region, particularly those whose communities were most affected by the crimes under the Tribunal's jurisdiction, the programme held the first in a series of community events in Bosnia and Herzegovina, intended to promote better local visibility of justice served, prevent historical revisionism and foster reconciliation.

Financing

2004-2005 biennium

Report of Secretary-General. The first performance report of ICTY for the 2004-2005

biennium [A/59/547], submitted by the Secretary-General in response to General Assembly resolution 58/255 [YUN 2003, p. 1318], reflected a requirement of additional appropriations of $26.8 million, net of staff assessment, over the initial appropriation for that biennium. The increased requirement included, among other things, changes with respect to exchange rates resulting from the weakening of the United States dollar vis-à-vis the euro and changes in inflation ($22,579,200), and provision for the Investigations Division for 2005 ($15,240,400), including staff and travel costs. The Assembly was requested to revise the appropriation for 2004-2005 in the amount of $329,501,900 gross ($298,437,000 net) to the ICTY Special Account.

ACABQ report. In November [A/59/561], the Advisory Committee on Administrative and Budgetary Questions (ACABQ) recommended approval of the Secretary-General's proposed staffing and travel requirements for ICTY's Investigations Division for 2005.

Board of Auditors

The Secretary-General submitted his financial report on the ICTY accounts for the 2002-2003 biennium, including the report of the Board of Auditors for the same period [A/59/5/Add.12].

The budget for the biennium totalled $288.3 million, with actual expenditures amounting to $284.3 million, leaving an unencumbered balance of $4.0 million. The total expenditure represented an increase of 35.8 per cent over total expenditures for 2000-2001.

Following a review of the operations of ICTY and an audit of its financial statements for the year ended 31 December 2003, the Board of Auditors was concerned about the level of unpaid assessed contributions, which stood at $53.3 million. It found that: the balance of reserves showed a shortfall of $12.6 million; procedures in place had led to an initial understatement of $79.0 million in deferred charges; liabilities for judges' pensions were neither assessed nor disclosed in financial statements; the usual UN staff medical standards were not applied to candidates for a judgeship; and the criteria for assigning counsel to indigent accused were still to be completed. In addition, while responsibility for the United Nations House in Sarajevo had been transferred to the Tribunal, no entity had been specified for handover in 2006, when the Tribunal was scheduled to downsize its Sarajevo site. The Board recommended that the Tribunal liaise with UN Headquarters to improve the rate of occupancy of the building and to transfer its management to another entity before the Tribunal left the premises. The Board remained concerned that the

2010 deadline set by the completion strategy might not be met. It recommended that the Tribunal develop efforts to collect outstanding contributions from Member States and review procedures for reporting on deferred charges. It further recommended that the Tribunal liaise with UN Headquarters to account for the liability relating to judges' pensions and plan for the transfer of pension commitments to a permanent entity at the termination of the Tribunal. In addition, the Tribunal should ensure that amendments were made to ICTY's Rules of Procedure and Evidence concerning the conditions for the designation of counsel by the accused, and consider applying the usual UN staff medical standards to candidates for judgeship.

GENERAL ASSEMBLY ACTION

On 23 December [meeting 76], the General Assembly, on the recommendation of the Fifth (Administrative and Budgetary) Committee [A/59/604], adopted **resolution 59/274** without vote [agenda item 122].

Financing of the International Tribunal for the Prosecution of Persons Responsible for Serious Violations of International Humanitarian Law Committed in the Territory of the Former Yugoslavia since 1991

The General Assembly,

Having considered the reports of the Secretary-General, namely the first performance report for the biennium 2004-2005 on the International Tribunal for the Prosecution of Persons Responsible for Serious Violations of International Humanitarian Law Committed in the Territory of the Former Yugoslavia since 1991 and the report on biennial budgeting at the Tribunals,

Having also considered the report of the Board of Auditors and the recommendations contained therein,

Having further considered the related report of the Advisory Committee on Administrative and Budgetary Questions,

Recalling its resolution 47/235 of 14 September 1993 on the financing of the Tribunal and its subsequent resolutions thereon, the most recent of which were resolutions 58/254 and 58/255 of 23 December 2003,

1. *Takes note* of the first performance report of the Secretary-General for the biennium 2004-2005 on the International Tribunal for the Prosecution of Persons Responsible for Serious Violations of International Humanitarian Law Committed in the Territory of the Former Yugoslavia since 1991 and his report on biennial budgeting at the Tribunals;

2. *Endorses* the conclusions and recommendations contained in the report of the Advisory Committee on Administrative and Budgetary Questions;

3. *Notes with concern* the precarious financial situation of the Tribunal;

4. *Also notes with concern* the levels of unpaid assessed contributions, and urges Member States to pay their assessed contributions on time, in full and without conditions;

5. *Further notes with concern* the resulting freeze imposed by the Secretariat on the Tribunal and the negative impact it is having on the completion strategy schedule, and requests the Secretary-General, in consultation with the Tribunal, to submit proposals on ways to ameliorate the staffing situation at the Tribunal in the context of the proposed budget for the biennium 2006–2007;

6. *Requests* the Secretary-General to ensure that areas critical to the successful completion of the mandate of the Tribunal, in accordance with the completion strategy, are exempt from any freezes;

7. *Also requests* the Secretary-General to make every effort to reduce the vacancy rate and improve staff retention at the Tribunal, including through extending contracts of staff performing functions that are central to the implementation of the completion strategy beyond the period of the current budget;

8. *Decides* to approve the proposed post and non-post resources for the Investigations Division for 2005;

9. *Also decides* on a revised appropriation to the Special Account for the International Tribunal for the Prosecution of Persons Responsible for Serious Violations of International Humanitarian Law Committed in the Territory of the Former Yugoslavia since 1991 of a total amount of 329,317,900 United States dollars gross (298,437,000 dollars net) for the biennium 2004-2005;

10. *Further decides,* for the year 2005, to apportion among Member States, in accordance with the scale of assessments applicable to the regular budget of the United Nations for the year, the amount of 90,148,375 dollars gross (81,300,850 dollars net), including 15,637,800 dollars gross (13,383,200 dollars net), being the increase in assessments;

11. *Decides,* for the year 2005, to apportion among Member States, in accordance with the rates of assessment applicable to peacekeeping operations for the year, the amount of 90,148,375 dollars gross (81,300,850 dollars net), including 15,637,800 dollars gross (13,383,200 dollars net), being the increase in assessments;

12. *Also decides* that, in accordance with the provisions of its resolution 973(X) of 15 December 1955, there shall be set off against the apportionment among Member States, as provided for in paragraphs 10 and 11 above, their respective share in the Tax Equalization Fund in the amount of 17,695,050 dollars, including 4,509,200 dollars, being the increase in the estimated staff assessment income approved for the Tribunal for the biennium 2004-2005.

Annex

Financing for the biennium 2004-2005 of the International Tribunal for the Prosecution of Persons Responsible for Serious Violations of International Humanitarian Law Committed in the Territory of the Former Yugoslavia since 1991

	Gross	*Net*
	(United States dollars)	
1. Initial appropriation for the biennium 2004-2005 (resolution 58/255)	298 226 300	271 854 600
Add:		
2. Proposed changes for the biennium 2004-2005 (A/59/547)	38 023 300	33 514 100

	Gross	Net
	(United States dollars)	

Less:

3. One-time adjustment reflecting projected savings for 2004 (A/59/547) — (6 747 700) — (6 747 700)

4. Estimated income for the biennium 2004-2005 — (184 000) — (184 000)

5. Proposed revised appropriation for the biennium 2004-2005 — 329 317 900 — 298 437 000

6. Assessment for 2004 — (149 021 150) — (135 835 300)

7. Balance to be assessed for 2005 — 180 296 750 — 162 601 700

Including:

8. Contributions assessed on Member States in accordance with the scale of assessments applicable to the regular budget of the United Nations for 2005 — 90 148 375 — 81 300 850

9. Contributions assessed on Member States in accordance with the rates of assessment applicable to peacekeeping operations of the United Nations for 2005 — 90 148 375 — 81 300 850

Also on 23 December, the Assembly decided that the item on the financing of ICTY would remain for consideration during its resumed fifty-ninth (2005) session (**decision 59/552**).

International Tribunal for Rwanda

In 2004, the International Criminal Tribunal for Rwanda (ICTR), in Arusha, the United Republic of Tanzania, rendered five trial judgements, the same as in the previous year [YUN 2003, p. 1320]. The number of ad litem judges serving ICTR rose to nine—the maximum number permitted under Security Council resolution 1512(2003) [ibid., p. 1324]. That enabled the Tribunal to increase the number of new trials initiated during the year to four, concerning seven accused, bringing the total number of persons on trial to 25. In April [S/2004/341], as requested in Security Council resolution 1503(2003) [ibid., p. 1330], the ICTR President submitted an updated and revised version of the ICTR completion strategy (see p. 1292), which was further revised in November [S/2004/921].

The 2004 activities of ICTR, established by Council resolution 955(1994) [YUN 1994, p. 299], were covered in two reports to the Council and the General Assembly, for the periods 1 July 2003 to 30 June 2004 [A/59/183-S/2004/601] and 1 July 2004 to 30 June 2005 [A/60/229-S/2005/534]. On 15 November, the Assembly took note of the 2003/04 report (**decision 59/510**).

The Chambers

New cases

On 25 February, Ephrem Setako, former senior official in the Rwanda Armed Forces, was arrested in the Netherlands, and he was transferred to ICTR on 17 November. He made his initial appearance on 22 November.

Yusuf Munyakazi, a businessman and leader of a militia group in Cyangugu Prefecture, who was arrested in the Democratic Republic of the Congo on 5 May, was transferred to ICTR on 7 May and made his initial appearance on 12 May.

On 16 July, Gaspard Kanyarukiga was arrested in South Africa and was transferred to the Tribunal on 19 July. At his initial appearance on 22 July, he pleaded not guilty to charges of genocide, complicity in genocide, conspiracy to commit genocide and extermination as a crime against humanity.

Ongoing trials

On 22 January, Jean de Dieu Kamuhanda, who pleaded not guilty in 2000 to charges of genocide and crimes against humanity [YUN 2000, p. 1225] and whose trial was held in 2001 [YUN 2001, p. 1208] and 2002 [YUN 2002, p. 1285], was convicted and sentenced to life in prison. The accused appealed the judgement.

In the case of Juvénal Kajelijeli, who was sentenced in 2003 [YUN 2003, p. 1321] to three concurrent sentences (a life sentence each for genocide and for a crime against humanity and 15 years in prison for direct and public incitement to commit genocide), and who had appealed the judgement at the time, the Appeals Chamber, on 23 January 2004, denied the prosecution's motion for acceptance of its notice of appeal out of time, stating that the prosecution's failure to file a timely notice was not excused by "good cause".

On 12 February, the Appeals Chamber dismissed the prosecution's appeal against the Trial Chamber's decision denying leave to amend the indictment in the case against Casimir Bizimungu, Justin Mugenzi, Jérôme Bicamumpaka and Prosper Mugiraneza, referred to as the "Government II" case [YUN 1999, pp. 1222 & 1223], and whose trial began in 2003 [YUN 2003, p. 1321]. On 15 July 2004, the Appeals Chamber rendered a decision on Mr. Mugiraneza's appeal against the decision of the Trial Chamber on exclusion of evidence and directed that the request of the accused be reconsidered. The Prosecutor's counter-appeal was dismissed.

In the trial against Edouard Karemera, Andre Rwamakuba, Matthieu Ngirumpatse and Joseph Nzirorera, which began in 2003 [YUN 2003, p. 1321] and was referred to as the "Government I" case [YUN 1999, pp. 1222 & 1223], the Appeals Chamber granted the prosecution's appeal against a decision to deny leave to amend the indictment. On 13 February 2004, the indictment was amended, and an initial appearance was held on 23 February to enable the accused to plead the new charges. On 29 March, the defence filed motions for the disqualification of the three judges on the case for alleged bias; those motions were dismissed. However, one of the judges elected to withdraw and the remaining two decided to continue the trial with a substitute judge. By a decision of 21 June, the Appeals Chamber allowed the appeals of Messrs. Rwamakuba, Karemera and Ngirumpatse challenging the decision of the remaining judges, who were found to have erred in law by deciding to continue the trial without giving the accused the opportunity to be heard. The matter was remanded to the remaining judges for reconsideration. Following an appeal filed by the defence, the Appeals Chamber, in its decision of 28 September and reasons of 22 October, disqualified the three judges engaged in the trial and ordered that the trial start de novo before a newly constituted Trial Chamber. Other appeals by Messrs. Karemera, Ngirumpatse and Nzirorera challenging the indictment, ICTR's jurisdiction and a number of other decisions relating to the case were dismissed.

On 25 February, the Chamber rendered a judgement in the joint trial of Samuel Imanishimwe, Emmanuel Bagambiki and André Ntagerura, referred to as the "Cyangugu" case [YUN 1999, p. 1222], which began in 2000 [YUN 2000, p. 1226] and terminated in 2003 [YUN 2003, p. 1321]. Mr. Imanishimwe, former officer in the Rwandan Armed Forces, was sentenced to 27 years in prison, while Messrs. Bagambiki, former Prefect of Cyangugu, and Ntagerura, former Minister of Transport, were both acquitted. Mr. Imanishimwe and the prosecution appealed the judgement.

In the case against Mikaeli Muhimana, who was arrested in 1999 [YUN 1999, p. 1223] and charged with genocide, crimes against humanity and violations of the Geneva Conventions, the trial began on 29 March 2004, and on 30 April, the prosecution closed its case. The defence case was scheduled to start later in the year.

On 26 March, the Trial Chamber granted the prosecution's motion for leave to amend the indictment in the case against Augustin Bizimungu, former Chief of Staff of the Rwandan Army, who was arrested in 2002 [YUN 2002, p. 1285], Augustin Ndindiliyimana, former Chief of Staff of the Gendarmerie, Francois-Xavier Nzuwonemeye, former Commander of the 42

Battalion, and Innocent Sagahutu, former Second-in-Command of the Reconnaissance Battalion, all of whom were arrested in 2000 [YUN 2000, p. 1225], in a case consolidated as the "Military II" case. On 31 March 2004, the prosecution filed the amended indictment, and further initial appearances were held on 30 April. The joint trial of the accused began on 20 September.

On 9 July, the Appeals Chamber upheld the conviction and affirmed the life sentence imposed on Eliezer Niyitegeka in 2003 [YUN 2003, p. 1321]. The appellant was currently seeking a review of the appeal judgement on the grounds that the prosecutor failed to disclose to him alleged exculpatory statements by witnesses, which were disclosed in another case. The briefing was ongoing.

On 4 June, the Appeals Chamber dismissed in part the appeal against the Trial Chamber's decision on the preliminary defence motion regarding defects in the form of the indictment in the case of Aloys Simba, who had pleaded not guilty in 2002 [YUN 2002, p. 1285] to charges of genocide or complicity in genocide. On 29 July 2004, a further appeal by the accused challenging the indictment was also dismissed, and on 30 August his trial began. On 30 September, the Appeals Chamber dismissed Mr. Simba's appeal challenging the decision of the Trial Chamber, which had found that the second indictment adequately pleaded the mens rea for joint criminal enterprise and that the allegations relating to murder as a crime against humanity were adequately connected to the widespread and systemic attack that had occurred. The prosecution closed its case on 10 November, and, on 13 December, the defence case began.

On 17 June, Sylvestre Gacumbitsi, who had pleaded not guilty in 2001 [YUN 2001, p. 1207] and whose trial began in 2003 [YUN 2003, p. 1321], was convicted of genocide and crimes against humanity (extermination and rape), but acquitted of a crime against humanity (murder). He was sentenced to 30 years' imprisonment.

In the joint trial against Pauline Nyiramasuhuko, Arsène Shalom Ntahobali, Sylvain Nsabimana, Alphonse Nteziryayo, Joseph Kanyabashi and Elie Ndayambaje, referred to as the "Butare" case, which began in 2001 [YUN 2001, p. 1208], the Appeals Chamber partially granted appeals by Ms. Nyiramasuhuko and Mr. Ntahobali against the Trial Chamber's decision to declare parts of the evidence of certain witnesses inadmissible. On 27 September, the Appeals Chamber dismissed Ms. Nyiramasuhuko's request for reconsideration of the appeal, and on 4 October, it also dismissed her appeal concerning a decision to admit as evidence a diary allegedly belonging to her. On 4 November, the prosecution closed its case.

Appeals were heard from 7 to 9 July in the case against Elizaphan Ntakirutimana and his son, Gérard Ntakirutimana, who were sentenced in 2003 to 10 and 25 years' imprisonment, respectively [YUN 2003, p. 1320]. On 13 December 2004, the Appeals Chamber rendered its judgement; it quashed a number of the convictions against both appellants, but affirmed the sentences imposed on them.

Emmanuel Ndindabahizi, a former Minister of Finance, who was arrested and pleaded not guilty in 2001 [YUN 2001, p. 1207], and whose trial began in 2003 [YUN 2003, p. 1321], was convicted on 15 July 2004 of genocide and crimes against humanity (extermination and murder) and sentenced to life in prison.

On 20 September, the trial began against Athanase Seromba, the Catholic priest of Nyange Parish in the Kivumu Commune, Kibuye Prefecture, who surrendered to ICTR in 2002 [YUN 2002, p. 1285].

On 14 October 2004, the prosecution closed its case in the joint trial, begun in 2002 [YUN 2002, p. 1285], of four senior Rwandan military officers (Théoneste Bagosora, Gratien Kabiligi, Anatole Nsengiyumva, Aloys Ntabakuze), consolidated in 1999 [YUN 1999, p. 1222] and currently referred to as the "Military I" case. Defence motions for acquittal were denied, and the defence case was scheduled for 2005.

On 8 December 2004, Vincent Rutaganira, who had pleaded not guilty in 2002 [YUN 2002, p. 1285], entered a guilty plea for crimes against humanity (extermination). As he had been indicted jointly with other accused, the Trial Chamber ordered the severance of the indictment against him. The parties presented their submissions on sentencing, and a joint recommendation was made for a term of imprisonment ranging from six to eight years.

In the case of Laurent Semanza, whose trial began in 2000 [YUN 2000, p. 1226] and was ongoing in 2001 [YUN 2001, p. 1208] and 2002 [YUN 2002, p. 1286], the Appeals Chamber granted a motion for admission of additional evidence. Hearings were heard on 13 and 14 December 2004.

Election of judges

By a 23 July letter [S/2004/619] to the President of the Security Council, the Secretary-General informed the Council of the resignation, effective 30 June, of Judge Asoka Gunawardana (Sri Lanka) as a permanent judge of ICTR. To replace him, the Government of Sri Lanka had presented the candidacy of Judge J. Asoka de Silva, whose curriculum vitae was annexed to the letter and who, in the view of the Secretary-General, met the qualifications prescribed in article 12 of the ICTR statute.

On 27 July [S/2004/620], the Council President, having consulted with Council members, expressed support for the Secretary-General's intention to appoint Judge de Silva.

On 3 August [S/2004/621], the Secretary-General appointed Judge de Silva as a permanent judge of ICTR, for the remainder of the term of office of Judge Gunawardana, which would expire on 24 May 2007.

Office of the Prosecutor

The Office of the Prosecutor, in a continuing effort to implement the ICTR completion strategy, established an Appeals Section in January. Investigations were completed to meet the new targets within the completion strategy deadline of 31 December 2004, and the Office stepped up its tracking activities to ensure that as many fugitives as possible were arrested sufficiently early to enable trials to be completed before the end of 2008. The Prosecutor continued to focus attention on accused persons who were allegedly in positions of leadership and who bore the gravest responsibility for the crimes committed. Other suspects alleged to have been mid- to low-level participants would be transferred to national jurisdictions, including Rwanda, for trial. The Prosecutor believed it was important to explore the idea of transferring cases to those African countries where certain suspects currently lived. In that regard, the possibility of transferring cases to Rwanda raised a number of issues, including the question of the death penalty, which had been imposed in genocide cases; the capacity of that country's judicial system to handle transferred cases at a time when it faced difficulties in coping with tens of thousands of local cases relating to genocide; and the issue of resources. It was decided that the transmission of the files of suspects and transfer of current detainees to Rwanda should await the resolution of those issues. Moreover, in preliminary discussions with national authorities, the Office of the Prosecutor found that the laws of the State in which a suspect was present might not confer jurisdiction over the suspect or the crime. Should it, therefore, not be possible to transfer cases to national jurisdictions, the Prosecutor would make alternative proposals to the Security Council and highlight related budgetary implications.

As part of global activities to mark the tenth anniversary of the Rwandan genocide (see p. 159), the Office of the Prosecutor hosted a colloquium of prosecutors of international criminal tribunals (Arusha, United Republic of Tanzania, 25-27 November), attended by representatives of ICTR, ICTY, the International Criminal Court and the Special Court for Sierra Leone, and legal practitioners from 12 countries. The aim was to discuss common problems, share ideas and solutions and adopt best practices. Participants discussed how to better prepare themselves for meeting the challenges of delivering international criminal justice. On 27 November, they issued a joint statement reaffirming commitment to ending impunity, deterring crimes against humanity, instituting a culture of accountability and bringing about peace and reconciliation in post-conflict societies. They also called on national and international authorities to assist the Tribunals by arresting and transferring indicted fugitives for trial.

The Registry

The Registry continued to support the judicial process by servicing the Tribunal's other organs and by participating in implementing the completion strategy. During the year, it signed a wide range of agreements with States and institutions concerning the reinforcement of sentences, the movement and relocation of witnesses and financial support for activities not covered by the regular budget. On 17 March and 27 April, Italy and Sweden became the fifth and sixth countries, respectively, to sign an agreement with the Tribunal on the enforcement of sentences imposed by ICTR. Between 20 and 22 September, top-level Rwandan Government officials and senior ICTR members discussed practical modalities for an agreement between the Rwandan Government and the United Nations regarding enforcement of ICTR sentences in Rwanda, pursuant to article 26 of the ICTR statute. The European Union also finalized details for an agreement to fund projects strengthening the managerial and operational capacity of the Tribunal.

Financing

2004-2005

Report of Secretary-General. In November [A/59/549], the Secretary-General submitted, in response to General Assembly resolution 58/253 [YUN 2003, p. 1327], the first performance report of ICTR for the 2004-2005 biennium. The report reflected a requirement of additional appropriations of $18.2 million, net of staff assessment. The increased requirements reflected changes arising from variations to budgetary assumptions ($10,705,600 net) and the provision of resources

for the Tribunal's Investigations Division for 2005 ($12,587,400 net), including provision for the staffing component approved for 2004, comprising 106 temporary posts (88 in the Professional and higher categories and 18 in the General Service category), and proposed resource requirements for investigative travel in the amount of $550,000. It also reflected projected savings of $5,062,000. The Secretary-General recommended that the Assembly approve the proposed staffing and resource requirements for the Division, and revise the appropriation for 2004-2005 in the amount of $255,909,500 gross ($231,506,500 net) to the Special Account for ICTR.

ACABQ report. In November [A/59/561], ACABQ recommended approval of the Secretary-General's proposed staffing and travel requirements for ICTR's Investigative Division for 2005.

Board of Auditors

The Secretary-General submitted his financial report on the ICTR accounts for the 2002-2003 biennium, including the report of the Board of Auditors for the same period [A/59/5/Add.11].

Against a budget of $208.5 million for the biennium, actual expenditures amounted to $208.4 million, leaving an unencumbered balance of $0.1 million. The total expenditure represented an increase of 15.9 per cent over total expenditures for 2000-2001.

The Board of Auditors, having reviewed ICTR's operations and audited its financial statements for the year ended 31 December 2003, found that its total reserves and fund balances decreased by approximately 52 per cent, from $5.5 million in 2000-2001 to $2.6 million in 2002-2003, and that its financial position had significantly worsened due to an increase in unpaid assessed contributions, which stood at $34.8 million. The Board also found that amounts owed to the Organization were reflected in accounts payable, while amounts owed by the Organization were reflected in accounts receivable, resulting in the netting-off of payables against receivables, which contravened UN system accounting standards, and the Tribunal's reserves were inadequate to cover its end-of-service and post-retirement benefit liabilities of $27.4 million. It did not seem possible that ICTR would be able to complete its work by 2010, and there was a risk that many of the indictees might never be brought to trial owing to the closure in April of the Investigations Unit at Kigali, Rwanda. The Board further found that the impact of initiatives to improve the Tribunal's legal aid system was yet to be evaluated; requests for the translation of documents that were apparently of no probative value to cases before the Tribunal added to the already heavy workload of the Language Services Section; and procurement contracts or extensions thereto were, in some instances, signed after the commencement date of the contract or not at all.

The Board recommended measures to improve the presentation and disclosure of the Tribunal's financial statements, review the funding mechanism for end-of-service and post-retirement benefit liabilities, monitor progress in implementing the completion strategy, intensify efforts to gain the cooperation of States, continue to monitor and limit defence counsel expenditures, prevent the translation of non-essential documents, shorten the procurement lead time and improve the process of approving contracts.

GENERAL ASSEMBLY ACTION

On 23 December [meeting 76], the General Assembly, on the recommendation of the Fifth Committee [A/59/603], adopted **resolution 59/273** without vote [agenda item 121].

Financing of the International Criminal Tribunal for the Prosecution of Persons Responsible for Genocide and Other Serious Violations of International Humanitarian Law Committed in the Territory of Rwanda and Rwandan Citizens Responsible for Genocide and Other Such Violations Committed in the Territory of Neighbouring States between 1 January and 31 December 1994

The General Assembly,

Having considered the reports of the Secretary-General, namely the first performance report for the biennium 2004-2005 on the International Criminal Tribunal for the Prosecution of Persons Responsible for Genocide and Other Serious Violations of International Humanitarian Law Committed in the Territory of Rwanda and Rwandan Citizens Responsible for Genocide and Other Such Violations Committed in the Territory of Neighbouring States between 1 January and 31 December 1994 and the report on biennial budgeting at the Tribunals,

Having also considered the report of the Board of Auditors and the recommendations contained therein,

Having further considered the related report of the Advisory Committee on Administrative and Budgetary Questions,

Recalling its resolution 49/251 of 20 July 1995 on the financing of the Tribunal and its subsequent resolutions thereon, the latest of which were resolutions 58/252 and 58/253 of 23 December 2003,

1. *Takes note* of the first performance report of the Secretary-General for the biennium 2004-2005 on the International Criminal Tribunal for the Prosecution of Persons Responsible for Genocide and Other Serious Violations of International Humanitarian Law Committed in the Territory of Rwanda and Rwandan Citizens Responsible for Genocide and Other Such Violations Committed in the Territory of Neighbouring

States between 1 January and 31 December 1994 and his report on biennial budgeting at the Tribunals;

2. *Endorses* the conclusions and recommendations contained in the report of the Advisory Committee on Administrative and Budgetary Questions;

3. *Notes with concern* the precarious financial situation of the Tribunal;

4. *Also notes with concern* the levels of unpaid assessed contributions, and urges Member States to pay their assessed contributions on time, in full and without conditions;

5. *Further notes with concern* the resulting freeze imposed by the Secretariat on the Tribunal and the negative impact it is having on the completion strategy schedule, and requests the Secretary-General, in consultation with the Tribunal, to submit proposals on ways to ameliorate the staffing situation at the Tribunal in the context of the proposed budget for the biennium 2006-2007;

6. *Requests* the Secretary-General to ensure that areas critical to the successful completion of the mandate of the Tribunal, in accordance with the completion strategy, are exempt from any freezes;

7. *Also requests* the Secretary-General to make every effort to reduce the vacancy rate and improve staff retention at the Tribunal, including by extending contracts of staff performing functions that are central to the implementation of the completion strategy beyond the period of the current budget;

8. *Further requests* the Secretary-General to submit the reports requested in paragraphs 17 and 23 of resolution 58/253 in the context of the proposed budget of the Tribunal for the biennium 2006-2007;

9. *Welcomes* the efforts of the Tribunal, in accordance with its statute, to assist the Government of Rwanda in strengthening its judiciary, and requests the Tribunal to increase its capacity-building efforts for the judiciary of Rwanda, including through recruitment of Rwandan legal professionals and training and attachment programmes, in view of the intention to transfer cases for prosecution to Rwanda as from 2005;

10. *Recognizes* the importance of carrying out an effective outreach programme within the overall mandate of the Tribunal and its completion strategy, and requests the Tribunal, in accordance with its mandate, to develop and implement outreach programmes that are proactive, utilizing available resources optimally, and that contribute to the reconciliation process by effectively developing an increased understanding of its work among Rwandans;

11. *Requests* the Secretary-General to report on the outreach programme of the Tribunal and on future measures to ensure the smooth transfer of cases to national jurisdiction in the context of the proposed budget of the Tribunal for the biennium 2006-2007;

12. *Decides* to approve the proposed post and non-post resources for the Investigations Division for 2005;

13. *Decides also* on a revised appropriation to the Special Account for the International Criminal Tribunal for the Prosecution of Persons Responsible for Genocide and Other Serious Violations of International Humanitarian Law Committed in the Territory of Rwanda and Rwandan Citizens Responsible for Genocide and Other Such Violations Committed in the Territory of Neighbouring States between 1 Janu-

ary and 31 December 1994 of a total amount of 255,909,500 United States dollars gross (231,506,500 dollars net) for the biennium 2004-2005;

14. *Decides further*, for the year 2005, to apportion among Member States, in accordance with the scale of assessments applicable to the regular budget of the United Nations for the year, the amount of 69,123,700 dollars gross (62,434,375 dollars net), including 10,292,650 dollars gross (9,115,500 dollars net), being the increase in assessments;

15. *Decides*, for the year 2005, to apportion among Member States, in accordance with the rates of assessment applicable to peacekeeping operations for the year, the amount of 69,123,700 dollars gross (62,434,375 dollars net), including 10,292,650 dollars gross (9,115,500 dollars net), being the increase in assessments;

16. *Decides also* that, in accordance with the provisions of its resolution 973(X) of 15 December 1955, there shall be set off against the apportionment among Member States, as provided for in paragraphs 14 and 15 above, their respective share in the Tax Equalization Fund in the amount of 13,378,650 dollars, including 2,354,300 dollars, being the increase in the estimated staff assessment income approved for the Tribunal for the biennium 2004-2005.

Annex

Financing for the biennium 2004-2005 of the International Criminal Tribunal for the Prosecution of Persons Responsible for Genocide and Other Serious Violations of International Humanitarian Law Committed in the Territory of Rwanda and Rwandan Citizens Responsible for Genocide and Other Such Violations Committed in the Territory of Neighbouring States between 1 January and 31 December 1994

	Gross	*Net*
	(United States dollars)	
1. Initial appropriation for the biennium 2004-2005 (resolution 58/253)	235 324 200	213 275 500
Add:		
2. Proposed changes for the biennium 2004-2005 (A/59/549)	25 647 300	23 293 000
Less:		
3. One-time adjustment reflecting projected savings for 2004 (A/59/549)	(5 062 000)	(5 062 000)
4. Proposed revised appropriation for the biennium 2004-2005	255 909 500	231 506 500
5. Assessment for 2004	(117 662 100)	(106 637 750)
6. Balance to be assessed for 2005	138 247 400	124 868 750
Of which:		
7. Contributions assessed on Member States in accordance with the scale of assessments applicable to the regular budget of the United Nations for 2005	69 123 700	62 434 375
8. Contributions assessed on Member States in accordance with the rates of assessment applicable to peacekeeping operations of the United Nations for 2005	69 123 700	62 434 375

Also on 23 December, the Assembly decided that the item on financing of ICTR would remain for consideration during its resumed fifty-ninth (2005) session (**decision 59/552**).

Functioning of the Tribunals

Office of the Prosecutor

GENERAL ASSEMBLY ACTION

On 8 April [meeting 83], the General Assembly, having considered the 2003 report of the Office of Internal Oversight Services (OIOS) on its review of the Office of the Prosecutor of ICTY and ICTR [YUN 2003, p. 1331], on the recommendation of the Fifth Committee [A/58/752], adopted **resolution 58/287** without vote [agenda items 131 & 132].

Review of the Office of the Prosecutor at the International Criminal Tribunal for Rwanda and the International Tribunal for the Former Yugoslavia

The General Assembly,

Recalling its resolutions 48/218 B of 29 July 1994 and 54/244 of 23 December 1999,

Recalling also its resolutions 57/289 of 20 December 2002 and 58/253 and 58/255 of 23 December 2003,

Having considered the report of the Office of Internal Oversight Services on the review of the Office of the Prosecutor at the International Criminal Tribunal for Rwanda and the International Tribunal for the Former Yugoslavia,

Takes note of the report of the Office of Internal Oversight Services on the review of the Office of the Prosecutor at the International Criminal Tribunal for Rwanda and the International Tribunal for the Former Yugoslavia.

Biennial budgeting

Report of Secretary-General. In response to General Assembly resolutions 58/253 [YUN 2003, p. 1327] and 58/255 [ibid., p. 1318], the Secretary-General submitted a July report [A/59/139] on the results of the biennialization of the budgets of ICTR and ICTY, introduced at the United Nations in 1974 but only used in the Tribunals for the 2002-2003 biennium. The Secretary-General noted that the implementation of the biennial budgeting cycle had saved the Tribunals time and effort, providing them a greater scope for planning, managing and coordinating their activities, and had enabled them to become more focused on the realization of their completion strategy. Biennialization was also helping to alleviate the heavy agenda of the legislative and expert bodies, thereby allowing more time for the review of budget performance and evaluation, among other things. Returning to annual budgets would imply the issuance of yearly staff contracts, thereby exacerbating the already difficult situation of staff retention, and have a negative impact on staff morale and the functioning of the Tribunals and their completion strategies. The Secretary-General therefore proposed that the Assembly maintain a biennial budget presentation for the Tribunals.

Annexed to the report were the views of the Board of Auditors, which concurred with the Secretary-General's proposal.

ACABQ report. In November [A/59/561], ACABQ also supported the Secretary-General's proposal that the Assembly maintain the biennial format for the presentation of the Tribunals' budgets.

Implementation of completion strategies

Following its consideration in March of the work of ICTY and ICTR, the Security Council emphasized the importance of fully implementing the completion strategies, as set out in Council resolution 1503(2003) [YUN 2003, p. 1330], which called for completing investigations by the end of 2004, first instance trials by 2008 and the work of both Tribunals by 2010. The Council requested each Tribunal to provide, by 31 May and every six months thereafter, assessments of progress made in that regard (see below).

SECURITY COUNCIL ACTION

On 26 March [meeting 4935], the Security Council unanimously adopted **resolution 1534(2004)**. The draft [S/2004/232] was prepared in consultations among Council members.

The Security Council,

Recalling its resolutions 827(1993) of 25 May 1993, 955(1994) of 8 November 1994, 978(1995) of 27 February 1995, 1165(1998) of 30 April 1998, 1166(1998) of 13 May 1998, 1329(2000) of 30 November 2000, 1411 (2002) of 17 May 2002, 1431(2002) of 14 August 2002 and 1481(2003) of 19 May 2003,

Recalling and reaffirming in the strongest terms the statement of 23 July 2002 made by the President of the Security Council endorsing the International Tribunal for the Former Yugoslavia Completion Strategy, and its resolution 1503(2003) of 28 August 2003,

Recalling that resolution 1503(2003) called upon the International Tribunal for the Former Yugoslavia and the International Tribunal for Rwanda to take all possible measures to complete investigations by the end of 2004, to complete all trial activities at first instance by the end of 2008, and to complete all of its work in 2010 (the completion strategies), and requested the Presidents and Prosecutors of the Tribunals, in their annual reports to the Council, to explain their plans to implement the completion strategies,

Welcoming the presentations made by the Presidents and Prosecutors of the Tribunals to the Security Council on 9 October 2003,

Commending the important work of both Tribunals in contributing to lasting peace and security and national reconciliation and the progress made since their inception, commending them on their efforts so far to give effect to the completion strategies, and calling upon them to ensure effective and efficient use of their budgets, with accountability,

Reiterating its support for the Prosecutors of the Tribunals in their continuing efforts to bring at-large indictees before the Tribunals,

Noting with concern the problems highlighted in the presentations to the Security Council on 9 October 2003 in securing adequate regional cooperation,

Also noting with concern indications in the presentations made on 9 October that it might not be possible to implement the completion strategies set out in resolution 1503(2003),

Acting under Chapter VII of the Charter of the United Nations,

1. *Reaffirms* the necessity of trial of persons indicted by the International Tribunal for the Former Yugoslavia, reiterates its call upon all States, especially Serbia and Montenegro, Croatia, and Bosnia and Herzegovina, and on the Republika Srpska within Bosnia and Herzegovina, to intensify cooperation with and render all necessary assistance to the Tribunal, particularly to bring Radovan Karadzic and Ratko Mladic, as well as Ante Gotovina and all other indictees, to the Tribunal, and calls upon all at-large indictees of the Tribunal to surrender to it;

2. *Reaffirms* the necessity of trial of persons indicted by the International Tribunal for Rwanda, reiterates its call upon all States, especially Rwanda, Kenya, the Democratic Republic of the Congo and the Republic of the Congo, to intensify cooperation with and render all necessary assistance to the Tribunal, including on investigations of the Rwandan Patriotic Army and efforts to bring Felicien Kabuga and all other such indictees to the Tribunal, and calls upon all at-large indictees of the Tribunal to surrender to it;

3. *Emphasizes* the importance of fully implementing the completion strategies as set out in paragraph 7 of resolution 1503(2003), which calls upon the Tribunals to take all possible measures to complete investigations by the end of 2004, to complete all trial activities at first instance by the end of 2008 and to complete all of its work in 2010, and urges each Tribunal to plan and act accordingly;

4. *Calls upon* the Prosecutors of the Tribunals to review the case load of the International Tribunal for the Former Yugoslavia and the International Tribunal for Rwanda, respectively, in particular with a view to determining which cases should be proceeded with and which should be transferred to competent national jurisdictions, as well as the measures which will need to be taken to meet the completion strategies referred to in resolution 1503(2003), and urges them to carry out this review as soon as possible and to include a progress report in the assessments to be provided to the Council under paragraph 6 of the present resolution;

5. *Calls upon* each Tribunal, in reviewing and confirming any new indictments, to ensure that any such indictments concentrate on the most senior leaders suspected of being most responsible for crimes within the jurisdiction of the relevant Tribunal, as set out in resolution 1503(2003);

6. *Requests* each Tribunal to provide to the Council, by 31 May 2004 and every six months thereafter, assessments by its President and Prosecutor, setting out in detail the progress made towards the implementation of the Completion Strategy of the Tribunal, explaining what measures have been taken to implement the Completion Strategy and what measures remain to be taken, including the transfer of cases involving intermediate- and lower-rank accused to competent national jurisdictions; and expresses the intention of the Council to meet with the President and the Prosecutor of each Tribunal to discuss these assessments;

7. *Declares* the determination of the Council to review the situation, and, in the light of the assessments received under the foregoing paragraph, to ensure that the time frames set out in the Completion Strategies and endorsed in resolution 1503(2003) can be met;

8. *Commends* those States which have concluded agreements for the enforcement of sentences of persons convicted by the International Tribunal for the Former Yugoslavia or the International Tribunal for Rwanda or have otherwise accepted such convicted persons to serve their sentences in their respective territories; encourages other States in a position to do so to act likewise; and invites the International Tribunal for the Former Yugoslavia and the International Tribunal for Rwanda to continue and intensify their efforts to conclude further agreements for the enforcement of sentences or to obtain the cooperation of other States in this regard;

9. *Recalls* that the strengthening of competent national judicial systems is crucially important to the rule of law in general and to the implementation of the International Tribunal for the Former Yugoslavia and the International Tribunal for Rwanda completion strategies in particular;

10. *Welcomes*, in particular, the efforts of the Office of the High Representative, the International Tribunal for the Former Yugoslavia and the donor community to create a war crimes chamber in Sarajevo; encourages all parties to continue efforts to establish the chamber expeditiously; and encourages the donor community to provide sufficient financial support to ensure the success of domestic prosecutions in Bosnia and Herzegovina and in the region;

11. *Decides* to remain actively seized of the matter.

Progress assessment

In response to Security Council resolution 1534(2004) (see p. 1292), the Presidents of ICTY and ICTR submitted May and November reports containing revised and updated versions of their completion strategies and detailing progress made towards implementing them.

The May report on ICTY [S/2004/420] reviewed the progress of proceedings regarding first instance trials and cases on appeal. It outlined measures taken to implement the completion strategy, including the referral of cases involving lower- and intermediate-rank accused to competent national jurisdictions, compliance with the requirement of seniority contained in Council resolution 1534(2004), operation of the Trial

Chambers at full capacity, efforts to make interlocutory appeals more effective and to shorten appeal judgements, and the establishment of a working group on scheduling cases, tasked with improving the efficiency of scheduling trials. The report also provided an updated prognosis of ICTY's ability to realize the completion strategy under current conditions, emphasizing that the Tribunal, in order to meet its mandate, needed to be able to try the most senior fugitives accused of serious violations of international humanitarian law, particularly Radovan Karadzic and Ratko Mladic, both of whom were indicted in 1995 [YUN 1995, p. 1314], as well as Ante Gotovina, indicted in 2001 [YUN 2001, p. 1199]. Although the unsealing of new indictments in March and April 2004 had created additional uncertainties for the completion strategy, the Tribunal was still in a position to try all accused currently in detention and on provisional release by the end of 2008, including Mr. Gotovina, provided he arrived in The Hague before 2006. However, because the new indictments would likely result in two new trials involving eight new defendants, it was unlikely that the Tribunal would be able to try within the completion strategy deadlines any other fugitives or new indictees, including Messrs. Karadzic and Mladic, unless some cases could be resolved through referral to a domestic jurisdiction or by a guilty plea. Other measures, including enhanced cooperation by Member States in transferring the high-profile fugitives and eliminating delays due to the election of new judges in 2005, would help the Tribunal meet the goals set out in the completion strategy. Such other measures as the general freeze on hiring personnel were bound to interfere with the Tribunal's work and with the completion strategy. It was, therefore, imperative that the Tribunal be in a position to replace departing essential staff, particularly in the Chambers. ICTY's November report [S/2004/897] updated information provided in May and demonstrated that the implementation of the completion strategy was on course. The first deadline would be met with the completion of all new investigations by year's end, when 11 motions requesting the transfer of cases to be tried by local jurisdictions would have been filed. However, the successful implementation of the completion strategy called for further increasing the Tribunal's efficiency. In that regard, the freeze on new recruitment needed to be lifted as soon as possible, and States of the former Yugoslavia needed to arrest and transfer all remaining 20 fugitives promptly.

The May report on ICTR [S/2004/341] outlined the Tribunal's completion strategy, based on the information available as at 26 April and taking into account the deadlines set in Council resolutions 1503(2003) [YUN 2003, p. 1330] and 1534(2004). The report reviewed recent judgements and trials in progress; the status of detainees awaiting trial; the Tribunal's workload relating to detainees currently in Arusha, United Republic of Tanzania, persons at large and other trial work; the transfer of cases to national jurisdictions; and past and current strategies. It was projected that by 2008 ICTR could complete trials and judgements relating to 65 to 70 persons, depending on the progress of current and future trials. Assessing ICTR's human resources needs, the report noted that the prosecution envisaged a substantial increase in the number of trial attorneys, an expansion of the Tribunal's Appeals Section and investigative and administrative support. The prosecution expected that at the anticipated conclusion of investigations at year's end, some posts currently held by investigators could be redeployed to increase the number of trial attorneys, legal advisers and other staff required for trial. The November report on ICTR [S/2004/921], which revised its completion strategy based on information available as at 19 November, noted, however, that in order to adhere to the time frames set out in relevant Council resolutions, ICTR needed to continue to receive the necessary resources. In that regard, the recruitment of new staff had been frozen because some Member States had failed to pay their assessed contributions.

SECURITY COUNCIL ACTION

On 4 August [meeting 5016], following consultations among Security Council members, the President made statement **S/PRST/2004/28** on behalf of the Council:

The Security Council takes note of the letter dated 21 May 2004 from the President of the International Tribunal for the Prosecution of Persons Responsible for Serious Violations of International Humanitarian Law Committed in the Territory of the Former Yugoslavia since 1991 addressed to the President of the Security Council.

The Council also takes note of the letter dated 30 April 2004 from the President of the International Criminal Tribunal for the Prosecution of Persons Responsible for Genocide and Other Serious Violations of International Humanitarian Law Committed in the Territory of Rwanda and Rwandan Citizens Responsible for Genocide and Other Such Violations Committed in the Territory of Neighbouring States between 1 January and 31 December 1994 addressed to the President of the Security Council.

The Council thanks the Presidents and Prosecutors of the two Tribunals for these assessments requested by resolution 1534(2004), as supplemented by their oral reports at the 4999th meeting of the Council on 29 June 2004.

The Council reaffirms its support for the two Tribunals and welcomes their efforts to carry out their completion strategies. The Council strongly encourages the Tribunals to make every effort to ensure that they remain on track to meet the target dates of the completion strategies.

The Council stresses that the full cooperation of all States with the Tribunals is not only a mandatory obligation of all States under its resolutions 827(1993) and 955(1994) and the statutes of the Tribunals, but is also an essential element in realizing the completion strategies. In this regard, the Council takes careful note of the assessments presented with respect to the level of cooperation by the authorities of Serbia and Montenegro and the Republika Srpska within Bosnia and Herzegovina with the International Tribunal for the Former Yugoslavia. We welcome as well the commitments made by the new Government in Serbia regarding cooperation with the International Tribunal for the Former Yugoslavia. The Council takes note of developments in Croatian and Rwandan cooperation with the International Tribunal for the Former Yugoslavia and the International Criminal Tribunal for the Rwanda, respectively.

The Council reiterates its call upon all States, especially Serbia and Montenegro, Croatia, Bosnia and Herzegovina, and the Republika Srpska within Bosnia and Herzegovina, to intensify cooperation with and render all necessary assistance to the International Tribunal for the Former Yugoslavia, particularly to bring Radovan Karadzic and Ratko Mladic, as well as Ante Gotovina and all other such indictees to the Tribunal.

The Council reiterates its call upon all States, especially Rwanda, Kenya, the Democratic Republic of the Congo and the Republic of the Congo, to intensify cooperation with and render all necessary assistance to the International Criminal Tribunal for Rwanda, including on investigations of the Rwandan Patriotic Army and efforts to bring Felicien Kabuga and all other such indictees to the Tribunal.

The Council notes with concern that the shortfall in financial contributions from Member States is having a disruptive effect on the work of the Tribunals and urges Member States to fulfil their commitments in a timely manner.

The Council emphasizes the importance of the referral of cases involving lower- and intermediate-rank accused to competent national jurisdictions in achieving the completion strategies and recalls the provisions of its resolutions 1503(2003) and 1534 (2004), including the call for assistance to ensure the success of this effort.

The Council also notes the concerns expressed by the President of the International Tribunal for the Former Yugoslavia on the effect the expiry of the terms of permanent judges may have on case management and takes note of the letter of 15 July 2004 from the Acting Legal Counsel bringing forward an invitation to Member States to submit nominations for permanent judges of the Tribunal before 13 September 2004.

The Council encourages further dialogue between the Tribunals and its Working Group on matters of mutual concern.

The Council will remain seized of the matter.

Chapter III

Legal aspects of international political relations

In 2004, the International Criminal Court (ICC), established by the 1998 Rome Statute of the International Criminal Court, focused on meeting its primary objective of becoming an independent and credible institution of international criminal justice. Significant developments included the adoption in May of the Regulations of the Court and the creation of an operational Office of the Prosecutor. In July, the Prosecutor opened the first ICC investigations, which concerned alleged crimes falling within the Court's jurisdiction committed in the territory of the Democratic Republic of the Congo. On 4 October, the Relationship Agreement between ICC and the United Nations, which set out a legal framework for their cooperation in the effective discharge of their respective responsibilities, entered into force. In December, the General Assembly called on States not yet parties to the Rome Statute to consider acceding to it. In other action, the Assembly adopted the United Nations Convention on Jurisdictional Immunities of States and Their Property, the draft of which had been prepared by the Ad Hoc Committee established in 2000 to elaborate the Convention.

The International Law Commission continued to examine topics suitable for the progressive development and codification of international law, provisionally adopting additional draft guidelines on reservations to treaties, as well as draft articles on diplomatic protection and draft principles on the allocation of loss in the case of transboundary harm arising out of hazardous activities.

The Ad Hoc Committee on the convention for suppression of nuclear terrorism and the Sixth (Legal) Committee of the General Assembly continued to elaborate a comprehensive convention on international terrorism and to resolve outstanding issues related to the preparation of a draft international convention for the suppression of acts of nuclear terrorism.

The Ad Hoc Committee on the Scope of Legal Protection under the 1994 Convention on the Safety of United Nations and Associated Personnel continued to consider measures to enhance the existing protective legal regime for UN and associated personnel.

Establishment of the International Criminal Court

The 1998 Rome Statute of the International Criminal Court [YUN 1998, p. 1209], which established ICC as a permanent institution with jurisdiction over persons accused of the most serious crimes of international concern—genocide, crimes against humanity, war crimes and the crime of aggression—entered into force on 1 July 2002 [YUN 2002, p. 1298]. As at 31 December 2004, the Statute had 139 signatories and 97 States parties.

During 2004, the Assembly of States Parties to the Rome Statute, the management oversight and legislative body of ICC, agreed on the future composition of ICC's Bureau and approved the negotiated draft Relationship Agreement between the United Nations and the Court (for more on the Assembly's deliberations, see p. 1296).

In 2004, the Security Council did not renew the request it had made in previous years that ICC delay, for a 12-month period, investigation or prosecution of any case involving officials or personnel from a State not party to the Rome Statute, in respect of acts or omissions relating to an operation authorized or established by the UN. That development represented a significant contribution to the Organization's efforts to promote justice and the rule of law in international affairs.

Relationship Agreement between the UN and ICC

Pursuant to General Assembly resolution 58/79 [YUN 2003, p. 1333], the Secretary-General, by an August note [A/58/874], submitted to the Assembly the draft Relationship Agreement between the United Nations and ICC, which would enter into force upon signature and approval by the General Assembly and the Assembly of States Parties to the Rome Statute. On 7 June, the text of the negotiated draft Agreement was initialed by the Secretary-General's Acting Legal Counsel and by the Chef de Cabinet of the ICC President in The Hague (Netherlands).

In an 8 September addendum to his note [A/58/874/Add.1], the Secretary-General said that he had been advised by the President of the Assembly of States Parties to the Rome Statute of ICC that the Assembly had approved the Agreement. On 13 September, the General Assembly, in **resolution 58/318** (below), also approved the Relationship Agreement, allowing ICC to attend and participate in its work as an observer.

On 4 October, the Relationship Agreement entered into force. It set out the legal framework for cooperation between the United Nations and the Court, in order to facilitate the effective discharge of their respective responsibilities. Under the Agreement, the United Nations might provide, at the request of ICC or the Prosecutor, information and documents that were relevant to the Court's work.

GENERAL ASSEMBLY ACTION

On 13 September [meeting 95], the General Assembly adopted **resolution 58/318** [draft: A/58/L.68] without vote [agenda item 154].

Cooperation between the United Nations and the International Criminal Court

The General Assembly,

Recalling its resolution 58/79 of 9 December 2003, in which it invited the Secretary-General to take steps to conclude a relationship agreement between the United Nations and the International Criminal Court and to submit the negotiated draft relationship agreement to the General Assembly for approval,

Noting the initialling of the negotiated draft Relationship Agreement between the United Nations and the International Criminal Court on 7 June 2004 in The Hague,

Taking note of the decision of 7 September 2004 taken by the Assembly of States Parties to the Rome Statute of the International Criminal Court at its third session to approve the negotiated draft Relationship Agreement, as noted by the Secretary-General,

Having considered the negotiated draft Relationship Agreement,

1. *Approves* the draft Relationship Agreement between the United Nations and the International Criminal Court;

2. *Decides* to apply the Relationship Agreement provisionally pending its formal entry into force;

3. *Also decides* that all expenses resulting from the provision of services, facilities, cooperation and any other support rendered to the International Criminal Court or the Assembly of States Parties to the Rome Statute of the International Criminal Court, including under any arrangements that may be otherwise agreed under article 10 of the Relationship Agreement, that may accrue to the United Nations as a result of the implementation of the Relationship Agreement shall be paid in full to the Organization.

Assembly of States Parties

The Assembly of States Parties to the Rome Statute of the International Criminal Court met in The Hague for its third annual session (6-10 September) [ICC-ASP/3/25].

The Assembly took note of its President's report on the activities of the Bureau, which, during the second year (September 2003-September 2004), held meetings aimed at assisting the Assembly in carrying out its activities under the Statute. The Assembly also heard statements by, among others, the Court's President, Judge Philippe Kirsch (Canada), and the Court's Prosecutor, Luis Moreno-Ocampo (Argentina). It elected as Deputy Prosecutor, Fatou Bensouda (the Gambia), for a nine-year term, with effect from 1 November 2004, and six members of the Committee on Budget and Finance, whose term of office would commence on 21 April 2005.

The Assembly approved by consensus the Court's programme budget for 2005, with total appropriations of 66,784,200 euros for the major programmes. It took note of the reports of external auditors on the audit of the Court's financial statements for the period 1 September 2002 to 31 December 2003 and of the Trust Fund for Victims financial statements for the same period. It requested ICC and the auditors to follow up on matters identified in the report of the Committee on Budget and Finance on its third session. In particular, ICC was encouraged to implement risk management procedures in its operations and to ensure better planning and implementation of procurement. Other areas warranting future attention from the auditors–results-based budgeting, information technology investment and human resources management–were also identified.

The Assembly considered, among other reports, the Registrar's reports on activities regarding defence counsel, including legal representation of victims and the process of consultation followed, and on the participation of and reparations to victims; the report of the Board of Directors of the Trust Fund for Victims; and the report of the Special Working Group on the Crime of Aggression.

The Assembly approved the negotiated draft Relationship Agreement between ICC and the United Nations (see above). It also agreed on the following future composition of the Bureau: five seats each for the Group of Western European and other States, and the Group of African States; four seats each for the Group of Latin American and Caribbean States, and the Group of Eastern European States; three seats for the Group of Asian States, on the understanding that the next Chair of the Credentials Committee would be elected from a State Party belonging to the Asian Group and who was not a Bureau member, and that the Bureau would extend to the next Chair a standing invitation to participate in its meetings, but without voting rights. That compromise, however, should not extend beyond the term of office of the next Bureau (2005-2008).

The Assembly considered and adopted by consensus the Bureau's proposal on the procedure for the nomination and election of ICC judges. It also adopted, among other things, the conditions of service and compensation of judges, as well as decisions on tax reimbursement of ICC staff and officials, the protection of the Court's name, the Staff Pension Committee and the Code of professional conduct for counsel. The Assembly agreed to intensify dialogue with the Court and welcomed the establishment of a Trust Fund for the participation of least developed countries in its activities.

At the same meeting, the Assembly amended rule 29 of its Rules of Procedure, elected by acclamation Bruno Stagno Ugarte (Costa Rica) as President for its fourth to sixth sessions and decided to hold its fourth session in The Hague in November 2005. It also decided that the Committee on Budget and Finance would meet in The Hague in April 2005.

ICC report. In July, ICC submitted a report [ICC-ASP/3/10] for consideration by the Assembly of States Parties (see p. 1296) at its September session, describing the Court's activities since September 2003. Significant developments included: the adoption by ICC judges of the Regulations of the Court; the creation of an operational Office of the Prosecutor, including staff recruitment, development of structures, priorities, policies and procedures and commencement of operations; the receipt by the Office of the Prosecutor of two referrals from States Parties (Uganda and the Democratic Republic of the Congo) on situations within their territories; the first meeting of members of the Board of Directors of the Trust Fund for Victims; the recruitment of an appropriate level of staff for the institution as a whole; the development of policies and procedures pertaining to issues essential for the future functioning of the Court, including matters relating to the defence, detention, victims, witnesses, counsel, court management and information technology; and the initialling of the Relationship Agreement between ICC and the United Nations. The Court's overall focus had been on meeting the primary objective of being an independent and credible institution of international criminal justice.

Report of Secretary-General (August). In an August report [S/2004/616] on the rule of law and transitional justice in conflict and post-conflict societies (see also p. 65), the Secretary-General noted that the most significant recent development in the international community's struggle to advance the cause of justice and rule of law was the establishment of ICC. The Court was making an impact by putting would-be violators on notice that impunity was not assured and by serving as a catalyst for enacting national laws against the gravest international crimes. It was crucial to ensure that ICC had the requisite resources, capacities, information and support to investigate, prosecute and bring to trial those responsible for war crimes, crimes against humanity and genocide, in situations where national authorities were unable or unwilling to do so. The Security Council had a particular role to play in that regard, given that it was empowered to refer situations to ICC, even in cases where the countries concerned were not States Parties to the Court's Statute.

Note of Secretary-General (September). In a September note [A/59/356], the Secretary-General summarized the activities undertaken by the Secretariat to facilitate an orderly and smooth transition of work from the UN Secretariat to the secretariat of the Assembly of States Parties to the Rome statute of ICC, as called for in General Assembly resolution 58/79 [YUN 2003, p. 1333]. The Secretariat ceased to serve as the provisional secretariat of the Assembly of States Parties on 31 December 2003. In addition to material transmitted previously to the Court's Registrar, the Secretariat facilitated the transfer of documents concerning the second session of the Assembly of States Parties, held in 2003 [ibid., p. 1332], and other material relevant to assisting the Assembly's secretariat in its future work, particularly regarding preparations for its third session (see p. 1296). The Secretariat also took steps to close trust funds administered by the Secretary-General relating to the establishment of ICC and its subsequent activities.

The Security Council, in presidential statement S/PRST/2004/34 of 6 October (see p. 66), thanked the Secretary-General for his August report (see above) and reaffirmed the importance it attached to promoting justice and the rule of law. It would consider, as appropriate, the recommendations contained in the report.

GENERAL ASSEMBLY ACTION

On 2 December [meeting 65], the General Assembly, on the recommendation of the Sixth (Legal) Committee [A/59/512], adopted **resolution 59/43** without vote [agenda item 146].

The General Assembly,

Recalling its resolutions 47/33 of 25 November 1992, 48/31 of 9 December 1993, 49/53 of 9 December 1994, 50/46 of 11 December 1995, 51/207 of 17 December 1996, 52/160 of 15 December 1997, 53/105 of 8 December 1998, 54/105 of 9 December 1999, 55/155 of 12 December 2000, 56/85 of 12 December 2001, 57/23 of 19 November 2002 and 58/79 of 9 December 2003,

Noting that the Rome Statute of the International Criminal Court was adopted on 17 July 1998 and entered into force on 1 July 2002,

Noting also the adoption of the Regulations of the International Criminal Court, the entry into force of the Agreement on the Privileges and Immunities of the Court, the opening of the first investigations by the Prosecutor and the constitution of the Pre-Trial Chambers of the Court,

Acknowledging the Relationship Agreement between the United Nations and the International Criminal Court ("Relationship Agreement") as approved by the Assembly of States Parties on 7 September 2004 and by the General Assembly in its resolution 58/318 of 13 September 2004, including paragraph 3 of the resolution with respect to the full reimbursement of expenses resulting from the implementation of the Relationship Agreement, and signed by the United Nations and the Court on 4 October 2004, thereby entering into force,

Reiterating the historic significance of the adoption of the Rome Statute of the International Criminal Court,

1. *Calls upon* all States that are not yet parties to the Rome Statute of the International Criminal Court to consider ratifying or acceding to it without delay, and encourages efforts aimed at promoting awareness of the results of the United Nations Diplomatic Conference of Plenipotentiaries on the Establishment of an International Criminal Court, held in Rome from 15 June to 17 July 1998, the provisions of the Statute and the process leading to the establishment of the International Criminal Court;

2. *Calls upon* all States to consider becoming parties to the Agreement on the Privileges and Immunities of the International Criminal Court without delay;

3. *Welcomes* the holding of the third session of the Assembly of States Parties in The Hague from 6 to 10 September 2004, and also welcomes the election of the new President of the Assembly of States Parties, new members to the Committee on Budget and Finance and the second Deputy-Prosecutor, and the important decisions taken on that occasion, including the establishment of the secretariat of the Board of Directors of the Trust Fund for Victims, as well as the adoption of a number of resolutions;

4. *Recalls* the establishment of the Special Working Group on the Crime of Aggression by the Assembly of States Parties to the Rome Statute of the International Criminal Court, open to all States on an equal footing;

5. *Expresses its appreciation* to the Secretary-General for providing effective and efficient assistance in the establishment of the International Criminal Court;

6. *Takes note* of the statement by the President of the Security Council of 6 October 2004, in which the Secretary-General is thanked for his report on the rule of law, in which reference was made to a number of efforts, in particular by the International Criminal Court to promote justice and the rule of law;

7. *Welcomes* the report of the Secretary-General on the work of the Organization, in which references were made to the International Criminal Court;

8. *Welcomes also* the steps taken as explained in the note by the Secretariat on the International Criminal Court, amongst which were those to close the various trust funds administered by the Secretary-General re-

lating to the establishment of the Court and subsequent activities;

9. *Recalls* that pursuant to article 4, paragraph 2, of the Relationship Agreement, the International Criminal Court may attend and participate in the work of the General Assembly in the capacity of observer and that pursuant to article 6 of the Relationship Agreement the Court may submit reports on its activities to the fifty-ninth and following sessions of the General Assembly;

10. *Decides* to include in the provisional agenda of its sixtieth session an item entitled "Report of the International Criminal Court", under which shall be considered, with the Court invited to attend and to participate, pursuant to article 4, paragraph 2, of the Relationship Agreement, any report of the International Criminal Court, pursuant to article 6 of the Relationship Agreement.

On 23 December, the Assembly, decided that the agenda item on ICC remained for consideration during its resumed fifty-ninth (2005) session (**decision 59/552**).

International Law Commission

The International Law Commission (ILC) held its fifty-sixth session in Geneva in two parts (3 May–4 June; 5 July–6 August) [A/59/10]. During the second part, the International Law Seminar held its fortieth session, which was attended by 24 participants, mostly from developing countries. They observed ILC meetings, attended specially arranged lectures and participated in working groups on specific topics.

ILC, assisted by working groups and a Drafting Committee, continued to advance its work on reservations to treaties by provisionally adopting further guidelines on widening the scope of a reservation, modification and withdrawal of interpretative declarations. It also adopted draft articles on diplomatic protection and on responsibility of international organizations, as well as draft principles on allocation of loss in the case of transboundary harm arising out of hazardous activities. In addition, ILC considered draft articles on the topics of shared natural resources and of unilateral acts of States. It considered the Special Rapporteur's report, which contained a survey of State practice in respect of unilateral acts. Subsequently, the Commission reconstituted a working group to consider specific examples of such acts. It also reconstituted the study group on the topic of fragmentation of international law: difficulties arising from the diversification and expansion of international law, to further study the *lex specialis* rule and the question of self-contained regime.

In furtherance of cooperation with other bodies concerned with international law, ILC continued its traditional information exchanges with the International Court of Justice, the Inter-American Judicial Committee, the Asian-African Legal Consultative Organization, the European Committee on Legal Cooperation and the Committee of Legal Advisers on Public International Law. ILC members also held informal meetings with other bodies and associations on matters of mutual interest.

Among its other decisions, ILC reconstituted the working group on its long-term programme of work, decided to include in its current work programme two new topics on "expulsion of aliens" and "effects of armed conflicts on treaties", and appointed as Special Rapporteurs Maurice Kamto (Cameroon) and Ian Brownlie (United Kingdom), to consider them, respectively. ILC noted with approval the Strategic Framework (2006-2007) for the programme on progressive development and codification of international law, prepared by the Secretary-General (see p. 1400) pursuant to General Assembly resolution 58/269 [YUN 2003, p., 1395]. Reflecting on Assembly resolution 58/250 [ibid., p. 1486], ILC emphasized the importance of summary records, which it considered a vital requirement for establishing the procedures and methods of its work and an indispensable part of the process of progressive development of international law. It also stressed that the reduction of the payment of honorariums to the nominal amount of $1 in Assembly resolution 56/272 [YUN 2002, p. 1402] mostly affected Special Rapporteurs, particularly those from developing countries, as it compromised support for their research. ILC decided to hold its fifty-seventh session in two parts: from 2 May to 3 June and from 4 July to 5 August.

GENERAL ASSEMBLY ACTION

On 2 December [meeting 65], the General Assembly, on the recommendation of the Sixth Committee [A/59/510], adopted **resolution 59/41** without vote [agenda item 144].

Report of the International Law Commission on the work of its fifty-sixth session

The General Assembly,

Having considered the report of the International Law Commission on the work of its fifty-sixth session,

Emphasizing the importance of furthering the codification and progressive development of international law as a means of implementing the purposes and principles set forth in the Charter of the United Nations and in the Declaration on Principles of International Law concerning Friendly Relations and Co-operation among States in accordance with the Charter of the United Nations,

Recognizing the desirability of referring legal and drafting questions to the Sixth Committee, including topics that might be submitted to the International Law Commission for closer examination, and of enabling the Sixth Committee and the Commission to enhance further their contribution to the progressive development of international law and its codification,

Recalling the need to keep under review those topics of international law which, given their new or renewed interest for the international community, may be suitable for the progressive development and codification of international law and therefore may be included in the future programme of work of the International Law Commission,

Welcoming the holding of the International Law Seminar, and noting with appreciation the voluntary contributions made to the United Nations Trust Fund for the International Law Seminar,

Stressing the usefulness of focusing and structuring the debate on the report of the International Law Commission in the Sixth Committee in such a manner that conditions are provided for concentrated attention to each of the main topics dealt with in the report and for discussions on specific topics,

Wishing to enhance further, in the context of the revitalization of the debate on the report of the International Law Commission, the interaction between the Sixth Committee as a body of governmental representatives and the Commission as a body of independent legal experts, with a view to improving the dialogue between the two bodies,

Welcoming initiatives to hold interactive debates, panel discussions and question time in the Sixth Committee, as envisaged in resolution 58/316 of 1 July 2004 on further measures for the revitalization of the work of the General Assembly,

1. *Takes note* of the report of the International Law Commission on the work of its fifty-sixth session, and recommends that the Commission continue its work on the topics in its current programme, taking into account the comments and observations of Governments, whether submitted in writing or expressed orally in debates in the General Assembly;

2. *Expresses its appreciation* to the International Law Commission for the work accomplished at its fifty-sixth session, in particular for the completion of the first reading of draft articles on Diplomatic protection and of the draft principles on the allocation of loss in the case of transboundary harm arising out of hazardous activities;

3. *Draws the attention* of Governments to the importance for the International Law Commission of having their views on the various aspects involved in the topics on the agenda of the Commission identified in chapter III of its report and in particular on:

(a) The draft articles and commentary on Diplomatic protection;

(b) The draft principles on Allocation of loss in the case of transboundary harm arising out of hazardous activities;

4. *Invites* Governments, within the context of paragraph 3 above, to provide information to the International Law Commission regarding:

(a) Their practice, bilateral or regional, relating to the allocation of groundwaters from transboundary aquifer systems and the management of non-renewable transboundary aquifer systems relating to the topic currently entitled "Shared natural resources";

(b) State practice on the topic "Unilateral acts of States";

5. *Endorses* the decision of the International Law Commission to include in its agenda the topics "Expulsion of aliens" and "Effects of armed conflicts on treaties";

6. *Takes note* of paragraphs 362 and 363 of the report of the International Law Commission with regard to its long-term programme of work and the syllabus on the new topic annexed to the report;

7. *Invites* the International Law Commission to continue taking measures to enhance its efficiency and productivity;

8. *Encourages* the International Law Commission to continue taking cost-saving measures at its future sessions;

9. *Takes note* of paragraph 370 of the report of the International Law Commission, and decides that the next session of the Commission shall be held at the United Nations Office at Geneva from 2 May to 3 June and from 4 July to 5 August 2005;

10. *Welcomes* the enhanced dialogue between the International Law Commission and the Sixth Committee at the fifty-ninth session of the General Assembly, stresses the desirability of further enhancing the dialogue between the two bodies, and in this context encourages, inter alia, the continued practice of informal consultations in the form of discussions between the members of the Sixth Committee and the members of the Commission attending the sixtieth session of the Assembly;

11. *Encourages* delegations, during the debate on the report of the International Law Commission to adhere as far as possible to the structured work programme agreed to by the Sixth Committee and to consider presenting concise and focused statements;

12. *Encourages* Member States to consider being represented at the level of legal adviser during the first week in which the report of the International Law Commission is discussed in the Sixth Committee (International Law Week) to enable high-level discussions on issues of international law;

13. *Requests* the International Law Commission to continue to pay special attention to indicating in its annual report, for each topic, any specific issues on which expressions of views by Governments, either in the Sixth Committee or in written form, would be of particular interest in providing effective guidance for the Commission in its further work;

14. *Takes note* of paragraphs 371 to 376 of the report of the International Law Commission with regard to cooperation with other bodies, and encourages the Commission to continue the implementation of article 16, paragraph (e), and article 26, paragraphs 1 and 2, of its statute in order to further strengthen cooperation between the Commission and other bodies concerned with international law, having in mind the usefulness of such cooperation;

15. *Notes* that consulting with national organizations and individual experts concerned with international law may assist Governments in considering whether to make comments and observations on drafts submitted by the International Law Commission and in formulating their comments and observations;

16. *Reaffirms* its previous decisions concerning the indispensable role of the Codification Division of the Office of Legal Affairs of the Secretariat in providing assistance to the International Law Commission;

17. *Approves* the conclusions reached by the International Law Commission in paragraph 367 of its report and reaffirms its previous decisions concerning the documentation and summary records of the International Law Commission;

18. *Expresses the hope* that the International Law Seminar will continue to be held in connection with the sessions of the International Law Commission and that an increasing number of participants, in particular from developing countries, will be given the opportunity to attend the Seminar, and appeals to States to continue to make urgently needed voluntary contributions to the United Nations Trust Fund for the International Law Seminar;

19. *Requests* the Secretary-General to provide the International Law Seminar with adequate services, including interpretation, as required, and encourages him to continue considering ways to improve the structure and content of the Seminar;

20. *Also requests* the Secretary-General to forward to the International Law Commission, for its attention, the records of the debate on the report of the Commission at the fifty-ninth session of the General Assembly, together with such written statements as delegations may circulate in conjunction with their oral statements, and to prepare and distribute a topical summary of the debate, following established practice;

21. *Requests* the Secretariat to circulate to States, as soon as possible after the conclusion of the session of the International Law Commission, chapter II of its report containing a summary of the work of that session, chapter III containing the specific issues on which the views of Governments would be of particular interest to the Commission and the draft articles adopted on either first or second reading by the Commission;

22. *Recommends* that the debate on the report of the International Law Commission at the sixtieth session of the General Assembly commence on 24 October 2005.

International liability

Under the topic of international liability for injurious consequences arising out of acts not prohibited by international law, ILC considered the second report by Special Rapporteur Pemmaraju Sreenivasa Rao (India) on the legal regime for the allocation of loss in case of transboundary harm arising out of hazardous activities [A/CN.4/540]. The report, which analysed comments submitted by States on the main issues concerning allocation of loss, also contained 12 draft principles proposed by the Special Rapporteur. ILC established a Working Group to examine those proposals and subsequently referred eight draft principles submitted by the Group to the Drafting Committee and also adopted a set of draft principles on allocation of loss in the case of transboundary harm arising out of hazardous activities.

Unilateral acts of States

ILC considered the seventh report on unilateral acts of States [A/CN.4/542 & Corr.1-3] by Special Rapporteur Victor Rodríguez Cedeño (Venezuela). The report, which was an initial study on the practice of States regarding unilateral acts, took account of the need to identify the relevant rules for codification and progressive development. In order to determine the criteria for the classification of acts and declarations that might represent the practice of States, the Special Rapporteur examined the following three categories: acts by which a State assumed obligations (promise and recognition); acts by which a State waived a right or a legal claim (waiver); and acts by which a State reaffirmed a right or a legal claim (protest). The report also examined conduct that could produce legal effects similar to unilateral acts, and in that context, analysed silence, consent and estoppel and their relationship with unilateral acts and described the practice of some international courts. The report concluded that unilateral acts and declarations of States were mostly addressed to other States and occasionally to other subjects, such as international organizations. They were usually formulated individually or otherwise issued by groups of States, and most were formulated by persons authorized to act at the international level on behalf of the State, such as the head of State or Government, the Minister for Foreign Affairs, ambassadors, heads of delegation and representatives of the State. It could be affirmed, however, that some existing rules were generally applicable to all unilateral acts and forms of conduct. Highlighting the difficulty involved in differentiating conducts from acts and in comparing both, the report advocated the elaboration of a draft definition based on the draft adopted in 2003 [YUN 2003, p. 1336] by the Working Group on Unilateral Acts. ILC reconstituted the Group to focus on a detailed consideration of specific examples of such acts. Other questions, such as that of the bodies which had the power to bind States by unilateral acts, could be settled by reference to the 1969 Vienna Convention on the Law of Treaties [YUN 1969, p. 734].

Communication. On 12 July [A/59/140], Cuba transmitted its observations to ILC on the topic of unilateral acts of States, in response to General Assembly resolution 58/77 [YUN 2003, p. 1334].

Responsibility of international organizations

ILC considered the second report on the topic of responsibility of international organizations [A/CN.4/541] by Special Rapporteur Giorgio Gaja (Italy). The report proposed articles 4 to 7, relating to attribution of conduct, conduct of organs or agents, excess of authority and conduct acknowledged and adopted, which ILC referred to the Drafting Committee. On the Committee's recommendation, ILC adopted the four articles and the commentaries thereto.

ILC also had before it a June report [A/CN.4/545] submitted pursuant to General Assembly resolution 58/77 [YUN 2003, p. 1334], which contained information received from the UN Secretariat and ten international organizations concerning their practice relevant to the topic of responsibility of international organizations, including cases in which States members of such an organization might be regarded as responsible for the organization's actions.

Fragmentation of international law

In 2004, ILC reconstituted the study group established in 2002 [YUN 2002, p. 1304] on the topic of fragmentation of international law: difficulties arising from the diversification and expansion of international law. The group considered the preliminary report on the study on the functions and scope of the *lex specialis* rule and the question of self-contained regimes, as well as outlines on the study on the application of successive treaties relating to the same subject matter (article 30 of the 1969 Vienna Convention on the Law of Treaties); on the study concerning the modification of multilateral treaties between certain parties only (article 41 of the Vienna Convention); on the study on the interpretation of treaties in the light of "any relevant rules of international law applicable in relations between parties" (article 31 (3) (c) of the same Convention); and on the study on hierarchy in international law: *jus cogens*, obligations *erga omnes*, Article 103 of the Charter of the United Nations, as conflict rules.

Based on the studies it had considered, the group agreed to draw conclusions regarding the nature and consequences of the phenomenon of "fragmentation" of international law, with the intention of developing a collective document that would be submitted to ILC in 2006. The document would comprise a substantive study on fragmentation and a concise summary containing the proposed conclusions and, if appropriate, guidelines on how to deal with such fragmentation.

Shared natural resources

In March and April, ILC considered the second report on shared natural resources [A/CN.4/539 & Add.1] by Special Rapporteur Chusei Yamada (Japan). In view of the opinions expressed both in ILC and the Sixth Committee on the use of the term "shared resources", which might refer to the common heritage of mankind or to the notion of shared ownership, the report focused on the sub-topic of transboundary groundwaters without using the term "shared". The report contained several draft articles formulated to generate comments and more concrete proposals, and to identify additional areas to be addressed. ILC established an open-ended Working Group on Transboundary Groundwaters and agreed that a questionnaire, prepared by the Special Rapporteur, be circulated to Governments and relevant intergovernmnetal organizations seeking their views and information regarding groundwaters. In particular, ILC would welcome information on Governments' practice that might be relevant to the principles to be incorporated in the draft articles, particularly on bilateral or regional practice relating to the allocation of groundwaters from transboundary aquifer systems, and to the management of non-renewable transboundary aquifer systems.

International State relations and international law

State succession

The Sixth Committee, on 28 October and 17 November, considered the item on nationality of natural persons in relation to the succession of States. For its consideration of the item, the Committee had before it a note by the Secretariat containing the comments and observations of nine Governments on the question of a convention on the nationality of natural persons in relation to the succession of States [A/59/180 & Add. 1, 2], submitted in response to General Assembly resolutions 54/112 [YUN 1999, p. 1230] and 55/153 [YUN 2000, p. 1242]. ILC, at its fifty-first session in 1999 [YUN 1999, p. 1230], had adopted draft articles on the item and recommended that they be adopted by the Assembly in the form of a declaration. Subsequently, the Assembly, in the resolutions mentioned above, invited Governments to submit comments and observations, with a view to considering the elaboration of such a convention at a future session.

On 2 December [meeting 65], the Assembly, on the recommendation of the Sixth Committee [A/59/504], adopted **resolution 59/34** without vote [agenda item 138].

Nationality of natural persons in relation to the succession of States

The General Assembly,

Having examined the item entitled "Nationality of natural persons in relation to the succession of States",

Recalling its resolution 54/112 of 9 December 1999, in which it decided to consider at its fifty-fifth session the draft articles on nationality of natural persons in relation to the succession of States prepared by the International Law Commission,

Recalling also its resolution 55/153 of 12 December 2000, the annex to which contains the articles on nationality of natural persons in relation to the succession of States,

Taking into consideration the comments and observations of Governments and the discussion held in the Sixth Committee at the fifty-ninth session of the General Assembly on the question of nationality of natural persons in relation to the succession of States, in particular, to preventing the occurrence of statelessness as a result of a succession of States,

Taking note, in this regard, of the efforts made at the regional level towards the elaboration of a legal instrument on the avoidance of statelessness in relation to State succession,

1. *Reiterates its invitation* to Governments to take into account, as appropriate, the provisions of the articles contained in the annex to resolution 55/153, in dealing with issues of nationality of natural persons in relation to the succession of States;

2. *Encourages* States to consider, as appropriate, at the regional or subregional levels, the elaboration of legal instruments regulating questions of nationality of natural persons in relation to the succession of States, with a view, in particular, to preventing the occurrence of statelessness as a result of a succession of States;

3. *Invites* Governments to submit comments concerning the advisability of elaborating a legal instrument on the question of nationality of natural persons in relation to the succession of States, including the avoidance of statelessness as a result of a succession of States;

4. *Decides* to include in the provisional agenda of its sixty-third session the item entitled "Nationality of natural persons in relation to the succession of States".

State responsibility

Pursuant to General Assembly resolution 56/83 [YUN 2001, p. 1218], the item on responsibility of States for internationally wrongful acts was included in the provisional agenda of the Assembly's fifty-ninth (2004) session. The item was considered and discussed by the Sixth Committee on 28 and 29 October and on 9 and 17 November.

On 2 December [meeting 65], the General Assembly, on the recommendation of the Sixth Committee [A/59/505], adopted **resolution 59/35** without vote [agenda item 139].

Responsibility of States for internationally wrongful acts

The General Assembly,

Recalling its resolution 56/83 of 12 December 2001, the annex to which contains the text of the articles on responsibility of States for internationally wrongful acts,

Emphasizing the continuing importance of the codification and progressive development of international law, as referred to in Article 13, paragraph 1 (*a*), of the Charter of the United Nations,

Noting that the subject of responsibility of States for internationally wrongful acts is of major importance in relations between States,

1. *Commends once again* the articles on responsibility of States for internationally wrongful acts to the attention of Governments, without prejudice to the question of their future adoption or other appropriate action;

2. *Requests* the Secretary-General to invite Governments to submit their written comments on any future action regarding the articles;

3. *Also requests* the Secretary-General to prepare an initial compilation of decisions of international courts, tribunals and other bodies referring to the articles and to invite Governments to submit information on their practice in this regard, and further requests the Secretary-General to submit this material well in advance of its sixty-second session;

4. *Decides* to include in the provisional agenda of its sixty-second session the item entitled "Responsibility of States for internationally wrongful acts".

Jurisdictional immunities of States and their property

In accordance with General Assembly resolution 58/74 [YUN 2003, p. 1337], the Ad Hoc Committee on Jurisdictional Immunities of States and Their Property, established by Assembly resolution 55/150 [YUN 2000, p. 1246], reconvened (New York, 1-5 March) to formulate a preamble and final clauses, with a view to completing a convention on jurisdictional immunities of States and their property.

The Working Group of the Whole proceeded with the formulation of a preamble and final clauses for a draft Convention, based on written and oral proposals submitted by delegations, as well as the suggestions of the Committee Chairman. The issues considered included the relationship between the draft articles and the understandings, as well as the provisions of the preamble and final clauses (relationship between the draft Convention and other international agreements; settlement of disputes; signature; ratification, acceptance, approval or accession;

entry into force; denunciation; depositary and notifications; authentic texts; and reservations). The Working Group agreed on a preamble and final clauses, as well as the chapeau for the understandings regarding certain provisions of the draft Convention (annex I). It was also agreed that the draft should be entitled United Nations Convention on Jurisdictional Immunities of States and Their Property. The Working Group, while emphasizing the general understanding that the draft Convention did not cover criminal proceedings, noted that a more appropriate placement for that issue was in a General Assembly resolution.

On 5 March, the Ad Hoc Committee adopted its report [A/59/22], which contained the text of the draft Convention.

The Sixth Committee considered the item on the Convention on 25 and 26 October and on 5 and 9 November. On 25 October, the Chairman of the Ad Hoc Committee introduced the Committee's report and proposed some corrections to the draft Convention. He said that the Committee had based its work on the draft articles on jurisdictional immunities of States adopted by ILC in 1991 at its forty-third session [YUN 1991, p. 829], and on the discussions of an open-ended working group of the Sixth Committee established by resolution 53/98 [YUN 1998, p. 1215]. The draft Convention was therefore the culmination of 27 years of sometimes difficult work by ILC, the Sixth Committee and the Ad Hoc Committee. The drafting of the text had been possible only because several States belonging to different legal systems and regions had made considerable concessions and demonstrated great flexibility, which was not easy when domestic legislation was already in force. The Chairman, further noting that one of the issues raised was whether military activities were covered by the Convention, clarified that the general understanding had always prevailed that they were not. However, reference should be made to ILC's 1991 commentary on article 12, stating that "neither did the article affect the question of diplomatic immunities, as provided in article 3, nor did it apply to situations involving armed conflicts". In addition, according to the preamble, the rules of customary international law continued to govern matters not regulated by the provisions of the Convention. In fact, that was the general approach of the Convention: it did not apply where there was a special immunity regime, including immunities *ratione personae* (*lex specialis*).

On 2 December [meeting 65], the General Assembly, on the recommendation of the Sixth

Committee [A/59/508], adopted **resolution 59/38** without vote [agenda item 142].

United Nations Convention on Jurisdictional Immunities of States and Their Property

The General Assembly,

Bearing in mind Article 13, paragraph 1 (*a*), of the Charter of the United Nations,

Recalling its resolution 32/151 of 19 December 1977, in which it recommended that the International Law Commission take up the study of the law of jurisdictional immunities of States and their property with a view to its progressive development and codification, and its subsequent resolutions 46/55 of 9 December 1991, 49/61 of 9 December 1994, 52/151 of 15 December 1997, 54/101 of 9 December 1999, 55/150 of 12 December 2000, 56/78 of 12 December 2001, 57/16 of 19 November 2002 and 58/74 of 9 December 2003,

Recalling also that the International Law Commission submitted a final set of draft articles, with commentaries, on the law of jurisdictional immunities of States and their property in chapter II of its report on the work of its forty-third session,

Recalling further the reports of the open-ended Working Group of the Sixth Committee, as well as the report of the Working Group on Jurisdictional Immunities of States and Their Property of the International Law Commission, submitted in accordance with General Assembly resolution 53/98 of 8 December 1998,

Recalling that in its resolution 55/150 it decided to establish the Ad Hoc Committee on Jurisdictional Immunities of States and Their Property, open also to participation by States members of the specialized agencies, to further the work done, consolidate areas of agreement and resolve outstanding issues with a view to elaborating a generally acceptable instrument based on the draft articles on jurisdictional immunities of States and their property adopted by the International Law Commission and also on the discussions of the open-ended Working Group of the Sixth Committee,

Having considered the report of the Ad Hoc Committee on Jurisdictional Immunities of States and Their Property,

Stressing the importance of uniformity and clarity in the law of jurisdictional immunities of States and their property, and emphasizing the role of a convention in this regard,

Noting the broad support for the conclusion of a convention on jurisdictional immunities of States and their property,

Taking into account the statement of the Chairman of the Ad Hoc Committee introducing the report of the Ad Hoc Committee,

1. *Expresses its deep appreciation* to the International Law Commission and the Ad Hoc Committee on Jurisdictional Immunities of States and Their Property for their valuable work on the law of jurisdictional immunities of States and their property;

2. *Agrees* with the general understanding reached in the Ad Hoc Committee that the United Nations Convention on Jurisdictional Immunities of States and Their Property does not cover criminal proceedings;

3. *Adopts* the United Nations Convention on Jurisdictional Immunities of States and Their Property, which is contained in the annex to the present resolu-

tion, and requests the Secretary-General as depositary to open it for signature;

4. *Invites* States to become parties to the Convention.

Annex

United Nations Convention on Jurisdictional Immunities of States and Their Property

The States Parties to the present Convention,

Considering that the jurisdictional immunities of States and their property are generally accepted as a principle of customary international law,

Having in mind the principles of international law embodied in the Charter of the United Nations,

Believing that an international convention on the jurisdictional immunities of States and their property would enhance the rule of law and legal certainty, particularly in dealings of States with natural or juridical persons, and would contribute to the codification and development of international law and the harmonization of practice in this area,

Taking into account developments in State practice with regard to the jurisdictional immunities of States and their property,

Affirming that the rules of customary international law continue to govern matters not regulated by the provisions of the present Convention,

Have agreed as follows:

Part I
Introduction

Article 1
Scope of the present Convention

The present Convention applies to the immunity of a State and its property from the jurisdiction of the courts of another State.

Article 2
Use of terms

1. For the purposes of the present Convention:

(*a*) "court" means any organ of a State, however named, entitled to exercise judicial functions;

(*b*) "State" means:

(i) the State and its various organs of government;

(ii) constituent units of a federal State or political subdivisions of the State, which are entitled to perform acts in the exercise of sovereign authority, and are acting in that capacity;

(iii) agencies or instrumentalities of the State or other entities, to the extent that they are entitled to perform and are actually performing acts in the exercise of sovereign authority of the State;

(iv) representatives of the State acting in that capacity;

(*c*) "commercial transaction" means:

(i) any commercial contract or transaction for the sale of goods or supply of services;

(ii) any contract for a loan or other transaction of a financial nature, including any obligation of guarantee or of indemnity in respect of any such loan or transaction;

(iii) any other contract or transaction of a commercial, industrial, trading or professional nature, but not including a contract of employment of persons.

2. In determining whether a contract or transaction is a "commercial transaction" under paragraph 1 (*c*), ref-

erence should be made primarily to the nature of the contract or transaction, but its purpose should also be taken into account if the parties to the contract or transaction have so agreed, or if, in the practice of the State of the forum, that purpose is relevant to determining the non-commercial character of the contract or transaction.

3. The provisions of paragraphs 1 and 2 regarding the use of terms in the present Convention are without prejudice to the use of those terms or to the meanings which may be given to them in other international instruments or in the internal law of any State.

Article 3
Privileges and immunities not affected by the present Convention

1. The present Convention is without prejudice to the privileges and immunities enjoyed by a State under international law in relation to the exercise of the functions of:

(a) its diplomatic missions, consular posts, special missions, missions to international organizations or delegations to organs of international organizations or to international conferences; and

(b) persons connected with them.

2. The present Convention is without prejudice to privileges and immunities accorded under international law to Heads of State *ratione personae.*

3. The present Convention is without prejudice to the immunities enjoyed by a State under international law with respect to aircraft or space objects owned or operated by a State.

Article 4
Non-retroactivity of the present Convention

Without prejudice to the application of any rules set forth in the present Convention to which jurisdictional immunities of States and their property are subject under international law independently of the present Convention, the present Convention shall not apply to any question of jurisdictional immunities of States or their property arising in a proceeding instituted against a State before a court of another State prior to the entry into force of the present Convention for the States concerned.

Part II
General principles

Article 5
State immunity

A State enjoys immunity, in respect of itself and its property, from the jurisdiction of the courts of another State subject to the provisions of the present Convention.

Article 6
Modalities for giving effect to State immunity

1. A State shall give effect to State immunity under article 5 by refraining from exercising jurisdiction in a proceeding before its courts against another State and to that end shall ensure that its courts determine on their own initiative that the immunity of that other State under article 5 is respected.

2. A proceeding before a court of a State shall be considered to have been instituted against another State if that other State:

(a) is named as a party to that proceeding; or

(b) is not named as a party to the proceeding but the proceeding in effect seeks to affect the property, rights, interests or activities of that other State.

Article 7
Express consent to exercise of jurisdiction

1. A State cannot invoke immunity from jurisdiction in a proceeding before a court of another State with regard to a matter or case if it has expressly consented to the exercise of jurisdiction by the court with regard to the matter or case:

(a) by international agreement;

(b) in a written contract; or

(c) by a declaration before the court or by a written communication in a specific proceeding.

2. Agreement by a State for the application of the law of another State shall not be interpreted as consent to the exercise of jurisdiction by the courts of that other State.

Article 8
Effect of participation in a proceeding before a court

1. A State cannot invoke immunity from jurisdiction in a proceeding before a court of another State if it has:

(a) itself instituted the proceeding; or

(b) intervened in the proceeding or taken any other step relating to the merits. However, if the State satisfies the court that it could not have acquired knowledge of facts on which a claim to immunity can be based until after it took such a step, it can claim immunity based on those facts, provided it does so at the earliest possible moment.

2. A State shall not be considered to have consented to the exercise of jurisdiction by a court of another State if it intervenes in a proceeding or takes any other step for the sole purpose of:

(a) invoking immunity; or

(b) asserting a right or interest in property at issue in the proceeding.

3. The appearance of a representative of a State before a court of another State as a witness shall not be interpreted as consent by the former State to the exercise of jurisdiction by the court.

4. Failure on the part of a State to enter an appearance in a proceeding before a court of another State shall not be interpreted as consent by the former State to the exercise of jurisdiction by the court.

Article 9
Counterclaims

1. A State instituting a proceeding before a court of another State cannot invoke immunity from the jurisdiction of the court in respect of any counterclaim arising out of the same legal relationship or facts as the principal claim.

2. A State intervening to present a claim in a proceeding before a court of another State cannot invoke immunity from the jurisdiction of the court in respect of any counterclaim arising out of the same legal relationship or facts as the claim presented by the State.

3. A State making a counterclaim in a proceeding instituted against it before a court of another State cannot invoke immunity from the jurisdiction of the court in respect of the principal claim.

Part III
Proceedings in which State immunity cannot be invoked

Article 10
Commercial transactions

1. If a State engages in a commercial transaction with a foreign natural or juridical person and, by virtue of the applicable rules of private international law, differences relating to the commercial transaction fall within the jurisdiction of a court of another State, the State cannot invoke immunity from that jurisdiction in a proceeding arising out of that commercial transaction.

2. Paragraph 1 does not apply:

(a) in the case of a commercial transaction between States; or

(b) if the parties to the commercial transaction have expressly agreed otherwise.

3. Where a State enterprise or other entity established by a State which has an independent legal personality and is capable of:

(a) suing or being sued; and

(b) acquiring, owning or possessing and disposing of property, including property which that State has authorized it to operate or manage, is involved in a proceeding which relates to a commercial transaction in which that entity is engaged, the immunity from jurisdiction enjoyed by that State shall not be affected.

Article 11
Contracts of employment

1. Unless otherwise agreed between the States concerned, a State cannot invoke immunity from jurisdiction before a court of another State which is otherwise competent in a proceeding which relates to a contract of employment between the State and an individual for work performed or to be performed, in whole or in part, in the territory of that other State.

2. Paragraph 1 does not apply if:

(a) the employee has been recruited to perform particular functions in the exercise of governmental authority;

(b) the employee is:

(i) a diplomatic agent, as defined in the Vienna Convention on Diplomatic Relations of 1961;

(ii) a consular officer, as defined in the Vienna Convention on Consular Relations of 1963;

(iii) a member of the diplomatic staff of a permanent mission to an international organization or of a special mission, or is recruited to represent a State at an international conference; or

(iv) any other person enjoying diplomatic immunity;

(c) the subject-matter of the proceeding is the recruitment, renewal of employment or reinstatement of an individual;

(d) the subject-matter of the proceeding is the dismissal or termination of employment of an individual and, as determined by the Head of State, the Head of Government or the Minister for Foreign Affairs of the employer State, such a proceeding would interfere with the security interests of that State;

(e) the employee is a national of the employer State at the time when the proceeding is instituted, unless this person has the permanent residence in the State of the forum; or

(f) the employer State and the employee have otherwise agreed in writing, subject to any considerations of public policy conferring on the courts of the State of the forum exclusive jurisdiction by reason of the subject-matter of the proceeding.

Article 12
Personal injuries and damage to property

Unless otherwise agreed between the States concerned, a State cannot invoke immunity from jurisdiction before a court of another State which is otherwise competent in a proceeding which relates to pecuniary compensation for death or injury to the person, or damage to or loss of tangible property, caused by an act or omission which is alleged to be attributable to the State, if the act or omission occurred in whole or in part in the territory of that other State and if the author of the act or omission was present in that territory at the time of the act or omission.

Article 13
Ownership, possession and use of property

Unless otherwise agreed between the States concerned, a State cannot invoke immunity from jurisdiction before a court of another State which is otherwise competent in a proceeding which relates to the determination of:

(a) any right or interest of the State in, or its possession or use of, or any obligation of the State arising out of its interest in, or its possession or use of, immovable property situated in the State of the forum;

(b) any right or interest of the State in movable or immovable property arising by way of succession, gift or *bona vacantia*; or

(c) any right or interest of the State in the administration of property, such as trust property, the estate of a bankrupt or the property of a company in the event of its winding up.

Article 14
Intellectual and industrial property

Unless otherwise agreed between the States concerned, a State cannot invoke immunity from jurisdiction before a court of another State which is otherwise competent in a proceeding which relates to:

(a) the determination of any right of the State in a patent, industrial design, trade name or business name, trademark, copyright or any other form of intellectual or industrial property which enjoys a measure of legal protection, even if provisional, in the State of the forum; or

(b) an alleged infringement by the State, in the territory of the State of the forum, of a right of the nature mentioned in subparagraph (a) which belongs to a third person and is protected in the State of the forum.

Article 15
Participation in companies or other collective bodies

1. A State cannot invoke immunity from jurisdiction before a court of another State which is otherwise competent in a proceeding which relates to its participation in a company or other collective body, whether incorporated or unincorporated, being a proceeding concerning the relationship between the State and the body or the other participants therein, provided that the body:

(a) has participants other than States or international organizations; and

(b) is incorporated or constituted under the law of the State of the forum or has its seat or principal place of business in that State.

2. A State can, however, invoke immunity from jurisdiction in such a proceeding if the States concerned have so agreed or if the parties to the dispute have so provided by an agreement in writing or if the instrument establishing or regulating the body in question contains provisions to that effect.

Article 16
Ships owned or operated by a State

1. Unless otherwise agreed between the States concerned, a State which owns or operates a ship cannot invoke immunity from jurisdiction before a court of another State which is otherwise competent in a proceeding which relates to the operation of that ship if, at the time the cause of action arose, the ship was used for other than government non-commercial purposes.
2. Paragraph 1 does not apply to warships, or naval auxiliaries, nor does it apply to other vessels owned or operated by a State and used, for the time being, only on government non-commercial service.
3. Unless otherwise agreed between the States concerned, a State cannot invoke immunity from jurisdiction before a court of another State which is otherwise competent in a proceeding which relates to the carriage of cargo on board a ship owned or operated by that State if, at the time the cause of action arose, the ship was used for other than government non-commercial purposes.
4. Paragraph 3 does not apply to any cargo carried on board the ships referred to in paragraph 2, nor does it apply to any cargo owned by a State and used or intended for use exclusively for government non-commercial purposes.
5. States may plead all measures of defence, prescription and limitation of liability which are available to private ships and cargoes and their owners.
6. If in a proceeding there arises a question relating to the government and non-commercial character of a ship owned or operated by a State or cargo owned by a State, a certificate signed by a diplomatic representative or other competent authority of that State and communicated to the court shall serve as evidence of the character of that ship or cargo.

Article 17
Effect of an arbitration agreement

If a State enters into an agreement in writing with a foreign natural or juridical person to submit to arbitration differences relating to a commercial transaction, that State cannot invoke immunity from jurisdiction before a court of another State which is otherwise competent in a proceeding which relates to:

(a) the validity, interpretation or application of the arbitration agreement;

(b) the arbitration procedure; or

(c) the confirmation or the setting aside of the award, unless the arbitration agreement otherwise provides.

Part IV
State immunity from measures of constraint in connection with proceedings before a court

Article 18
State immunity from pre-judgment measures of constraint

No pre-judgment measures of constraint, such as attachment or arrest, against property of a State may be taken in connection with a proceeding before a court of another State unless and except to the extent that:

(a) the State has expressly consented to the taking of such measures as indicated:

   (i) by international agreement;

   (ii) by an arbitration agreement or in a written contract; or

   (iii) by a declaration before the court or by a written communication after a dispute between the parties has arisen; or

(b) the State has allocated or earmarked property for the satisfaction of the claim which is the object of that proceeding.

Article 19
State immunity from post-judgment measures of constraint

No post-judgment measures of constraint, such as attachment, arrest or execution, against property of a State may be taken in connection with a proceeding before a court of another State unless and except to the extent that:

(a) the State has expressly consented to the taking of such measures as indicated:

   (i) by international agreement;

   (ii) by an arbitration agreement or in a written contract; or

   (iii) by a declaration before the court or by a written communication after a dispute between the parties has arisen; or

(b) the State has allocated or earmarked property for the satisfaction of the claim which is the object of that proceeding; or

(c) it has been established that the property is specifically in use or intended for use by the State for other than government non-commercial purposes and is in the territory of the State of the forum, provided that post-judgment measures of constraint may only be taken against property that has a connection with the entity against which the proceeding was directed.

Article 20
Effect of consent to jurisdiction to measures of constraint

Where consent to the measures of constraint is required under articles 18 and 19, consent to the exercise of jurisdiction under article 7 shall not imply consent to the taking of measures of constraint.

Article 21
Specific categories of property

1. The following categories, in particular, of property of a State shall not be considered as property specifically in use or intended for use by the State for other than government non-commercial purposes under article 19, subparagraph *(c)*:

(a) property, including any bank account, which is used or intended for use in the performance of the functions of the diplomatic mission of the State or its consular posts, special missions, missions to international organizations or delegations to organs of international organizations or to international conferences;

(b) property of a military character or used or intended for use in the performance of military functions;

(c) property of the central bank or other monetary authority of the State;

(d) property forming part of the cultural heritage of the State or part of its archives and not placed or intended to be placed on sale;

(e) property forming part of an exhibition of objects of scientific, cultural or historical interest and not placed or intended to be placed on sale.

2. Paragraph 1 is without prejudice to article 18 and article 19, subparagraphs *(a)* and *(b)*.

Part V
Miscellaneous provisions

Article 22
Service of process

1. Service of process by writ or other document instituting a proceeding against a State shall be effected:

(a) in accordance with any applicable international convention binding on the State of the forum and the State concerned; or

(b) in accordance with any special arrangement for service between the claimant and the State concerned, if not precluded by the law of the State of the forum; or

(c) in the absence of such a convention or special arrangement:

(i) by transmission through diplomatic channels to the Ministry of Foreign Affairs of the State concerned; or

(ii) by any other means accepted by the State concerned, if not precluded by the law of the State of the forum.

2. Service of process referred to in paragraph 1 *(c)* (i) is deemed to have been effected by receipt of the documents by the Ministry of Foreign Affairs.

3. These documents shall be accompanied, if necessary, by a translation into the official language, or one of the official languages, of the State concerned.

4. Any State that enters an appearance on the merits in a proceeding instituted against it may not thereafter assert that service of process did not comply with the provisions of paragraphs 1 and 3.

Article 23
Default judgment

1. A default judgment shall not be rendered against a State unless the court has found that:

(a) the requirements laid down in article 22, paragraphs 1 and 3, have been complied with;

(b) a period of not less than four months has expired from the date on which the service of the writ or other document instituting a proceeding has been effected or deemed to have been effected in accordance with article 22, paragraphs 1 and 2; and

(c) the present Convention does not preclude it from exercising jurisdiction.

2. A copy of any default judgment rendered against a State, accompanied if necessary by a translation into the official language or one of the official languages of the State concerned, shall be transmitted to it through one of the means specified in article 22, paragraph 1, and in accordance with the provisions of that paragraph.

3. The time-limit for applying to have a default judgment set aside shall not be less than four months and shall begin to run from the date on which the copy of the judgment is received or is deemed to have been received by the State concerned.

Article 24
Privileges and immunities during court proceedings

1. Any failure or refusal by a State to comply with an order of a court of another State enjoining it to perform or refrain from performing a specific act or to produce any document or disclose any other information for the purposes of a proceeding shall entail no consequences other than those which may result from such conduct in relation to the merits of the case. In particular, no fine or penalty shall be imposed on the State by reason of such failure or refusal.

2. A State shall not be required to provide any security, bond or deposit, however described, to guarantee the payment of judicial costs or expenses in any proceeding to which it is a respondent party before a court of another State.

Part VI
Final clauses

Article 25
Annex

The annex to the present Convention forms an integral part of the Convention.

Article 26
Other international agreements

Nothing in the present Convention shall affect the rights and obligations of States Parties under existing international agreements which relate to matters dealt with in the present Convention as between the parties to those agreements.

Article 27
Settlement of disputes

1. States Parties shall endeavour to settle disputes concerning the interpretation or application of the present Convention through negotiation.

2. Any dispute between two or more States Parties concerning the interpretation or application of the present Convention which cannot be settled through negotiation within six months shall, at the request of any of those States Parties, be submitted to arbitration. If, six months after the date of the request for arbitration, those States Parties are unable to agree on the organization of the arbitration, any of those States Parties may refer the dispute to the International Court of Justice by request in accordance with the Statute of the Court.

3. Each State Party may, at the time of signature, ratification, acceptance or approval of, or accession to, the present Convention, declare that it does not consider itself bound by paragraph 2. The other States Parties shall not be bound by paragraph 2 with respect to any State Party which has made such a declaration.

4. Any State Party that has made a declaration in accordance with paragraph 3 may at any time withdraw that declaration by notification to the Secretary-General of the United Nations.

Article 28
Signature

The present Convention shall be open for signature by all States until 17 January 2007, at United Nations Headquarters, New York.

Article 29
Ratification, acceptance, approval or accession
1. The present Convention shall be subject to ratification, acceptance or approval.
2. The present Convention shall remain open for accession by any State.
3. The instruments of ratification, acceptance, approval or accession shall be deposited with the Secretary-General of the United Nations.

Article 30
Entry into force
1. The present Convention shall enter into force on the thirtieth day following the date of deposit of the thirtieth instrument of ratification, acceptance, approval or accession with the Secretary-General of the United Nations.
2. For each State ratifying, accepting, approving or acceding to the present Convention after the deposit of the thirtieth instrument of ratification, acceptance, approval or accession, the Convention shall enter into force on the thirtieth day after the deposit by such State of its instrument of ratification, acceptance, approval or accession.

Article 31
Denunciation
1. Any State Party may denounce the present Convention by written notification to the Secretary-General of the United Nations.
2. Denunciation shall take effect one year following the date on which notification is received by the Secretary-General of the United Nations. The present Convention shall, however, continue to apply to any question of jurisdictional immunities of States or their property arising in a proceeding instituted against a State before a court of another State prior to the date on which the denunciation takes effect for any of the States concerned.
3. The denunciation shall not in any way affect the duty of any State Party to fulfil any obligation embodied in the present Convention to which it would be subject under international law independently of the present Convention.

Article 32
Depositary and notifications
1. The Secretary-General of the United Nations is designated the depositary of the present Convention.
2. As depositary of the present Convention, the Secretary-General of the United Nations shall inform all States of the following:
   (a) signatures of the present Convention and the deposit of instruments of ratification, acceptance, approval or accession or notifications of denunciation, in accordance with articles 29 and 31;
   (b) the date on which the present Convention will enter into force, in accordance with article 30;
   (c) any acts, notifications or communications relating to the present Convention.

Article 33
Authentic texts
The Arabic, Chinese, English, French, Russian and Spanish texts of the present Convention are equally authentic.

IN WITNESS WHEREOF, the undersigned, being duly authorized thereto by their respective Governments, have signed this Convention opened for signature at United Nations Headquarters in New York on 17 January 2005.

Annex to the Convention

Understandings with respect to certain provisions of the Convention

The present annex is for the purpose of setting out understandings relating to the provisions concerned.

With respect to article 10

The term "immunity" in article 10 is to be understood in the context of the present Convention as a whole.

Article 10, paragraph 3, does not prejudge the question of "piercing the corporate veil", questions relating to a situation where a State entity has deliberately misrepresented its financial position or subsequently reduced its assets to avoid satisfying a claim, or other related issues.

With respect to article 11

The reference in article 11, paragraph 2 (d), to the "security interests" of the employer State is intended primarily to address matters of national security and the security of diplomatic missions and consular posts.

Under article 41 of the 1961 Vienna Convention on Diplomatic Relations and article 55 of the 1963 Vienna Convention on Consular Relations, all persons referred to in those articles have the duty to respect the laws and regulations, including labour laws, of the host country. At the same time, under article 38 of the 1961 Vienna Convention on Diplomatic Relations and article 71 of the 1963 Vienna Convention on Consular Relations, the receiving State has a duty to exercise its jurisdiction in such a manner as not to interfere unduly with the performance of the functions of the mission or the consular post.

With respect to articles 13 and 14

The expression "determination" is used to refer not only to the ascertainment or verification of the existence of the rights protected, but also to the evaluation or assessment of the substance, including content, scope and extent, of such rights.

With respect to article 17

The expression "commercial transaction" includes investment matters.

With respect to article 19

The expression "entity" in subparagraph (c) means the State as an independent legal personality, a constituent unit of a federal State, a subdivision of a State, an agency or instrumentality of a State or other entity, which enjoys independent legal personality.

The words "property that has a connection with the entity" in subparagraph (c) are to be understood as broader than ownership or possession.

Article 19 does not prejudge the question of "piercing the corporate veil", questions relating to a situation where a State entity has deliberately misrepresented its financial position or subsequently reduced its assets to avoid satisfying a claim, or other related issues.

International terrorism

Conventions on international terrorism and for suppression of acts of nuclear terrorism

Ad Hoc Committee

In accordance with General Assembly resolution 58/81 [YUN 2003, p. 1339], the Ad Hoc Committee on the convention for suppression of nuclear terrorism, established by Assembly resolution 51/210 [YUN 1996, p. 1208], held its eighth session (New York, 28 June–2 July) to continue, within the framework of a working group of the Sixth Committee, to elaborate a draft comprehensive convention on international terrorism, with appropriate time allocated to the continued consideration of outstanding issues relating to the elaboration of a draft international convention for the suppression of acts of nuclear terrorism. It kept on its agenda the question of convening a high-level conference under UN auspices to formulate a joint organized response of the international community to terrorism in all its forms and manifestations.

The Ad Hoc Committee held a general exchange of views on issues within its mandate and proceeded with informal consultations regarding the draft comprehensive convention on international terrorism and on outstanding issues pertaining to articles 18 and 2 *bis* of the draft international convention for the suppression of acts of nuclear terrorism. The Chairman informed the Committee that, although some delegations had informal contacts on the question of convening a high-level conference under the auspices of the United Nations to formulate a joint organized response of the international community to terrorism in all its forms and manifestations, no specific proposals on the issue were set forth. The Chairman also informed the Committee that the Bureau had prepared a text of the draft international convention for the suppression of acts of nuclear terrorism, in order to facilitate discussion on the matter.

On 2 July, the Ad Hoc Committee adopted its report [A/59/37], to which were annexed the Chairman's informal summary of the general discussion, the coordinators' reports and amendments and proposals submitted to the Committee in connection with the draft international convention for the suppression of acts of nuclear terrorism. The Ad Hoc Committee recommended that the Sixth Committee, at the Assembly's fifty-ninth (2004) session, establish a working group to continue the elaboration of the two draft conventions and to keep on its agenda the question of convening a high-level conference.

Sixth Committee working group

As recommended by the Ad Hoc Committee (see above), the Sixth Committee established an open-ended working group on measures to eliminate international terrorism, which held two meetings (New York, 5 and 8 October). Before it were the reports of the Ad Hoc Committee on its sixth [YUN 2002, p. 1306], seventh [YUN 2003, p. 1338] and eighth sessions (see above); the 1998 report of the Sixth Committee working group [YUN 1998, p. 1216], as well as the 2000 [YUN 2000, p. 1248], 2001 [YUN 2001, p. 1225], 2002 [YUN 2002, p. 1307] and 2003 [YUN 2003, p. 1338] reports.

The working group held informal consultations on outstanding issues on the two draft conventions, and on 8 October, the coordinators orally reported on the results of those consultations. The working group was informed by its Chairman that several delegations had indicated that consultations on the question of convening a high-level conference were continuing at the political level in their capitals. Also on 8 October, the group adopted its report [A/C.6/59/L.10], which it referred to the Sixth Committee with a recommendation that work on finalizing the texts of the two draft conventions continue, building on what had already been accomplished.

Measures to eliminate terrorism

In accordance with General Assembly resolution 50/53 [YUN 1995, p. 1330], the Secretary-General, in August, issued his annual report [A/59/210 & Corr.1] containing information on measures taken at the national and international levels by 20 States and 8 UN system entities to implement the 1994 Declaration on Measures to Eliminate International Terrorism, approved by Assembly resolution 49/60 [YUN 1994, p. 1294] and Security Council resolution 1269(1999) [YUN 1999, p. 1240]. It listed 22 international instruments pertaining to terrorism, indicating the status of State participation in each, and also provided information on workshops and training courses on combating terrorism by three UN bodies. The report noted that the Secretariat had prepared the material to be published in the second volume of the *United Nations Legislative Series* entitled "National Law and regulations on the Prevention and Suppression of International Terrorism, Part II".

Further measures

In other action, the Commission on Crime Prevention and Criminal Justice, at its thirteenth session (11-20 May) [E/2004/30], recommended to the Economic and Social Council for approval a draft resolution for adoption by the General Assembly entitled "Strengthening international cooperation and technical assistance in promoting the implementation of the universal conventions and protocols related to terrorism within the framework of the activities of the United Nations Office on Drugs and Crime". The resolution was approved on 21 July by the Council as **resolution 2004/19** (see p. 1125) and adopted on 20 December by the Assembly as **resolution 59/153** (see p. 1125).

GENERAL ASSEMBLY ACTION

On 2 December [meeting 65], the General Assembly, on the recommendation of the Sixth Committee [A/59/514], adopted **resolution 59/46** without vote [agenda item 148].

Measures to eliminate international terrorism

The General Assembly,

Guided by the purposes and principles of the Charter of the United Nations,

Recalling the Declaration on the Occasion of the Fiftieth Anniversary of the United Nations,

Recalling also the United Nations Millennium Declaration,

Recalling further the Declaration on Measures to Eliminate International Terrorism, contained in the annex to General Assembly resolution 49/60 of 9 December 1994, and welcoming the celebration this year of the tenth anniversary of its adoption, and recalling the Declaration to Supplement the 1994 Declaration on Measures to Eliminate International Terrorism, contained in the annex to resolution 51/210 of 17 December 1996,

Recalling all General Assembly and Security Council resolutions on measures to eliminate international terrorism,

Convinced of the importance of the consideration of measures to eliminate international terrorism by the General Assembly as the universal organ having competence to do so,

Deeply disturbed by the persistence of terrorist acts, which have been carried out worldwide,

Reaffirming its strong condemnation of the heinous acts of terrorism that have caused enormous loss of human life, destruction and damage, including those which prompted the adoption of General Assembly resolution 56/1 of 12 September 2001, as well as Security Council resolutions 1368(2001) of 12 September 2001, 1373(2001) of 28 September 2001 and 1377(2001) of 12 November 2001, and those that have occurred since the adoption of General Assembly resolution 58/81 of 9 December 2003,

Recalling the strong condemnation of the atrocious and deliberate attack against the headquarters of the United Nations Assistance Mission for Iraq in Baghdad on 19 August 2003 in General Assembly resolution 57/338 of 15 September 2003 and Security Council resolution 1502(2003) of 26 August 2003,

Affirming that States must ensure that any measure taken to combat terrorism complies with all their obligations under international law and should adopt such measures in accordance with international law, in particular international human rights, refugee and humanitarian law,

Stressing the need to strengthen further international cooperation among States and among international organizations and agencies, regional organizations and arrangements and the United Nations in order to prevent, combat and eliminate terrorism in all its forms and manifestations, wherever and by whomsoever committed, in accordance with the principles of the Charter, international law and the relevant international conventions,

Noting the role of the Security Council Committee established pursuant to resolution 1373(2001) concerning counter-terrorism in monitoring the implementation of that resolution, including the taking of the necessary financial, legal and technical measures by States and the ratification or acceptance of the relevant international conventions and protocols,

Mindful of the need to enhance the role of the United Nations and the relevant specialized agencies in combating international terrorism, and of the proposals of the Secretary-General to enhance the role of the Organization in this respect,

Mindful also of the essential need to strengthen international, regional and subregional cooperation aimed at enhancing the national capacity of States to prevent and suppress effectively international terrorism in all its forms and manifestations,

Reiterating its call upon States to review urgently the scope of the existing international legal provisions on the prevention, repression and elimination of terrorism in all its forms and manifestations, with the aim of ensuring that there is a comprehensive legal framework covering all aspects of the matter,

Emphasizing that tolerance and the enhancement of dialogue among civilizations are among the most important elements in promoting cooperation and success in combating terrorism,

Reaffirming that no terrorist act can be justified in any circumstances,

Taking note of the Final Document of the Thirteenth Conference of Heads of State or Government of Non-Aligned Countries, adopted in Kuala Lumpur on 25 February 2003, which reiterated the collective position of the Movement of Non-Aligned Countries on terrorism and reaffirmed the previous initiative of the Twelfth Conference of Heads of State or Government of Non-Aligned Countries, held in Durban, South Africa, from 29 August to 3 September 1998, calling for an international summit conference under the auspices of the United Nations to formulate a joint organized response of the international community to terrorism in all its forms and manifestations, as well as other relevant initiatives,

Bearing in mind the recent developments and initiatives at the international, regional and subregional levels to prevent and suppress international terrorism, including those identified in the annex to the present resolution,

Recalling its decision in resolutions 54/110 of 9 December 1999, 55/158 of 12 December 2000, 56/88 of 12 December 2001, 57/27 of 19 November 2002 and 58/81 that the Ad Hoc Committee established by General Assembly resolution 51/210 of 17 December 1996 should address, and keep on its agenda, the question of convening a high-level conference under the auspices of the United Nations to formulate a joint organized response of the international community to terrorism in all its forms and manifestations,

Aware of its resolutions 57/219 of 18 December 2002 and 58/187 of 22 December 2003,

Noting regional efforts to prevent, combat and eliminate terrorism in all its forms and manifestations, wherever and by whomsoever committed, including through the elaboration of and adherence to regional conventions,

Having examined the report of the Secretary-General, the report of the Ad Hoc Committee established by resolution 51/210 and the report of the Working Group of the Sixth Committee established pursuant to resolution 58/81,

1. *Strongly condemns* all acts, methods and practices of terrorism in all its forms and manifestations as criminal and unjustifiable, wherever and by whomsoever committed;

2. *Reiterates* that criminal acts intended or calculated to provoke a state of terror in the general public, a group of persons or particular persons for political purposes are in any circumstances unjustifiable, whatever the considerations of a political, philosophical, ideological, racial, ethnic, religious or other nature that may be invoked to justify them;

3. *Reiterates its call upon* all States to adopt further measures in accordance with the Charter of the United Nations and the relevant provisions of international law, including international standards of human rights, to prevent terrorism and to strengthen international cooperation in combating terrorism and, to that end, to consider in particular the implementation of the measures set out in paragraphs 3 *(a)* to *(f)* of resolution 51/210;

4. *Also reiterates its call upon* all States, with the aim of enhancing the efficient implementation of relevant legal instruments, to intensify, as and where appropriate, the exchange of information on facts related to terrorism and, in so doing, to avoid the dissemination of inaccurate or unverified information;

5. *Reiterates its call upon* States to refrain from financing, encouraging, providing training for or otherwise supporting terrorist activities;

6. *Urges* States to ensure that their nationals or other persons and entities within their territory that wilfully provide or collect funds for the benefit of persons or entities who commit, or attempt to commit, facilitate or participate in the commission of terrorist acts are punished by penalties consistent with the grave nature of such acts;

7. *Reminds* States of their obligations under relevant international conventions and protocols and Security Council resolutions, including Security Council resolution 1373(2001), to ensure that perpetrators of terrorist acts are brought to justice;

8. *Reaffirms* that international cooperation as well as actions by States to combat terrorism should be conducted in conformity with the principles of the Charter, international law and relevant international conventions;

9. *Urges* all States that have not yet done so to consider, as a matter of priority, and in accordance with Security Council resolutions 1373(2001), and 1566 (2004) of 8 October 2004, becoming parties to the relevant conventions and protocols as referred to in paragraph 6 of General Assembly resolution 51/210, as well

as the International Convention for the Suppression of Terrorist Bombings and the International Convention for the Suppression of the Financing of Terrorism, and calls upon all States to enact, as appropriate, the domestic legislation necessary to implement the provisions of those conventions and protocols, to ensure that the jurisdiction of their courts enables them to bring to trial the perpetrators of terrorist acts, and to cooperate with and provide support and assistance to other States and relevant international and regional organizations to that end;

10. *Urges* States to cooperate with the Secretary-General and with one another, as well as with interested intergovernmental organizations, with a view to ensuring, where appropriate within existing mandates, that technical and other expert advice is provided to those States requiring and requesting assistance in becoming parties to and implementing the conventions and protocols referred to in paragraph 9 above;

11. *Notes with appreciation and satisfaction* that, consistent with the call contained in paragraph 7 of resolution 58/81, a number of States became parties to the relevant conventions and protocols referred to therein, thereby realizing the objective of wider acceptance and implementation of those conventions;

12. *Reaffirms* the Declaration on Measures to Eliminate International Terrorism and the Declaration to Supplement the 1994 Declaration on Measures to Eliminate International Terrorism, and calls upon all States to implement them;

13. *Calls upon* all States to cooperate to prevent and suppress terrorist acts;

14. *Urges* all States and the Secretary-General, in their efforts to prevent international terrorism, to make the best use of the existing institutions of the United Nations;

15. *Welcomes* the continuing efforts of the Terrorism Prevention Branch of the United Nations Office on Drugs and Crime in Vienna, after reviewing existing possibilities within the United Nations system, to enhance, through its mandate, the capabilities of the United Nations in the prevention of terrorism, and recognizes, in the context of Security Council resolution 1373(2001), its role in assisting States in becoming parties to and implementing the relevant international conventions and protocols relating to terrorism;

16. *Invites* regional intergovernmental organizations to submit to the Secretary-General information on the measures they have adopted at the regional level to eliminate international terrorism, as well as on intergovernmental meetings held by those organizations;

17. *Notes* the progress attained in the elaboration of the draft comprehensive convention on international terrorism and the draft international convention for the suppression of acts of nuclear terrorism during the meetings of the Ad Hoc Committee established by General Assembly resolution 51/210 of 17 December 1996 and the Working Group of the Sixth Committee established pursuant to General Assembly resolution 58/81;

18. *Decides* that the Ad Hoc Committee shall, on an expedited basis, continue to elaborate the draft comprehensive convention on international terrorism and to resolve the outstanding issues relating to the elaboration of the draft international convention for the

suppression of acts of nuclear terrorism as a means of further developing a comprehensive legal framework of conventions dealing with international terrorism, and shall keep on its agenda the question of convening a high-level conference under the auspices of the United Nations to formulate a joint organized response of the international community to terrorism in all its forms and manifestations;

19. *Decides also* that the Ad Hoc Committee shall meet from 28 March to 1 April 2005 in order to fulfil the mandate referred to in paragraph 18 above, and that the work shall continue, if necessary, during the sixtieth session of the General Assembly, within the framework of the Working Group of the Sixth Committee;

20. *Requests* the Secretary-General to continue to provide the Ad Hoc Committee with the necessary facilities for the performance of its work;

21. *Also requests* the Secretary-General to make a comprehensive inventory of the response of the Secretariat to terrorism as part of his report on measures to eliminate international terrorism;

22. *Requests* the Ad Hoc Committee to report to the General Assembly at its fifty-ninth session in the event of the completion of the draft comprehensive convention on international terrorism or the draft international convention for the suppression of acts of nuclear terrorism;

23. *Also requests* the Ad Hoc Committee to report to the General Assembly at its sixtieth session on progress made in the implementation of its mandate;

24. *Decides* to include in the provisional agenda of its sixtieth session the item entitled "Measures to eliminate international terrorism".

Annex

African Union

Second High-Level Intergovernmental Meeting on the Prevention and Combating of Terrorism in Africa, and inauguration of the African Centre for Studies and Research on Terrorism, Algiers, 13 and 14 October 2004

Andean Community

Subregional workshop on the regional fight against terrorism, Lima, 26 and 27 January 2004

Association of Southeast Asian Nations

Fourth ASEAN Ministerial Meeting on Transnational Crime, Bangkok, 8 January 2004

First ASEAN Plus Three Ministerial Meetings on Transnational Crime, Bangkok, 10 January 2004

European Union

European Council meetings with a focus on terrorism, Brussels, 25 and 26 March and 17 and 18 June 2004

Organization of American States

Fourth regular session of the Inter-American Committee against Terrorism, Montevideo, 28-30 January 2004

Shanghai Cooperation Organization

Summit Meeting of the Shanghai Cooperation Organization for the establishment of the Regional Anti-Terrorism Structure, Tashkent, 17 June 2004

South Asian Association for Regional Cooperation

Twelfth SAARC Summit, Islamabad, 4-6 January 2004

Other meetings

Bali Regional Ministerial Meeting on Counter-Terrorism, convened by Indonesia and Australia, Bali, Indonesia, 4 and 5 February 2004

On 23 December, the Assembly, by **decision 59/552**, decided that the item on measures to eliminate international terrorism would remain for consideration during its resumed fifty-ninth (2005) session.

Additional Protocols I and II to the 1949 Geneva Conventions

In response to General Assembly resolution 57/14 [YUN 2002, p. 1309], the Secretary-General submitted a September report with a later addendum [A/59/321 & Add.1] on the status of the two 1977 Protocols Additional to the Geneva Conventions of 12 August 1949 and relating to the protection of victims of armed conflicts [YUN 1977, p. 706], as well as on measures taken to strengthen the existing body of international humanitarian law with respect to, among other things, its dissemination and implementation at the national level, based on information received from a total of 19 States and the International Committee of the Red Cross. Annexed to the report was a list of 162 States parties to one or both of the Protocols as at 2 June 2004.

GENERAL ASSEMBLY ACTION

On 2 December [meeting 65], the General Assembly, on the recommendation of the Sixth Committee [A/59/506], adopted **resolution 59/36** without vote [agenda item 140].

Status of the Protocols Additional to the Geneva Conventions of 1949 and relating to the protection of victims of armed conflicts

The General Assembly,

Recalling its resolutions 32/44 of 8 December 1977, 34/51 of 23 November 1979, 37/116 of 16 December 1982, 39/77 of 13 December 1984, 41/72 of 3 December 1986, 43/161 of 9 December 1988, 45/38 of 28 November 1990, 47/30 of 25 November 1992, 49/48 of 9 December 1994, 51/155 of 16 December 1996, 53/96 of 8 December 1998, 55/148 of 12 December 2000 and 57/14 of 19 November 2002,

Having considered the report of the Secretary-General,

Thanking Member States and the International Committee of the Red Cross for their contribution to the report of the Secretary-General,

Convinced of the continuing value of established humanitarian rules relating to armed conflicts and the need to respect and ensure respect for those rules in all circumstances within the scope of the relevant international instruments, pending the earliest possible termination of such conflicts,

Stressing the possibility of making use of the International Fact-Finding Commission in relation to an armed conflict, pursuant to article 90 of Protocol I to the Geneva Conventions of 1949,

Stressing also the possibility for the International Fact-Finding Commission to facilitate, through its good offices, the restoration of an attitude of respect for the Geneva Conventions and Protocol I,

Stressing further the need to consolidate the existing body of international humanitarian law through its universal acceptance and the need for wide dissemination and full implementation of such law at the national level, and expressing concern about all violations of the Geneva Conventions and the two Additional Protocols,

Noting with satisfaction the increasing number of national commissions and other bodies involved in advising authorities at the national level on the implementation, dissemination and development of international humanitarian law,

Noting with appreciation the meetings of representatives of those bodies organized by the International Committee of the Red Cross to facilitate the sharing of concrete experience and the exchange of views on their roles and on the challenges they face,

Mindful of the role of the International Committee of the Red Cross in offering protection to the victims of armed conflicts,

Noting with appreciation the continuing efforts of the International Committee of the Red Cross to promote and disseminate knowledge of international humanitarian law, in particular the Geneva Conventions and the two Additional Protocols,

Recalling that the Twenty-eighth International Conference of the Red Cross and Red Crescent stressed the need to reinforce the implementation of and respect for international humanitarian law,

Noting the fiftieth anniversary of the Convention for the Protection of Cultural Property in the Event of Armed Conflict, adopted at The Hague in 1954, which was observed in May 2004, as well as the commemorative events organized in particular by or in cooperation with the United Nations Educational, Scientific and Cultural Organization and the International Committee of the Red Cross, and recalling the important achievement of enhancing the protection of cultural property in the event of armed conflicts,

Recalling the entry into force, on 9 March 2004, of the second Protocol to the 1954 Hague Convention, and appreciating the ratifications received so far,

Acknowledging the fact that the Rome Statute of the International Criminal Court, which entered into force on 1 July 2002, includes the most serious crimes of international concern under international humanitarian law, and that the Statute, while recalling that it is the duty of every State to exercise its criminal jurisdiction over those responsible for such crimes, shows the determination of the international community to put an end to impunity for the perpetrators of such crimes and thus to contribute to their prevention,

Acknowledging also the usefulness of discussing in the General Assembly the status of instruments of international humanitarian law relevant to the protection of victims of armed conflicts,

1. *Appreciates* the virtually universal acceptance of the Geneva Conventions of 1949, and notes the trend towards a similarly wide acceptance of the two Additional Protocols of 1977;

2. *Calls upon* all States parties to the Geneva Conventions that have not yet done so to consider becoming parties to the Additional Protocols at the earliest possible date;

3. *Calls upon* all States that are already parties to Protocol I, or those States not parties, on becoming parties to Protocol I, to make the declaration provided for under article 90 of that Protocol;

4. *Calls upon* all States that have not yet done so to consider becoming parties to the Convention for the Protection of Cultural Property in the Event of Armed Conflict and the two Protocols thereto, and to other relevant treaties on international humanitarian law relating to the protection of victims of armed conflict;

5. *Calls upon* all States parties to the Protocols Additional to the Geneva Conventions to ensure their wide dissemination and full implementation;

6. *Notes with appreciation* the Declaration and Agenda for Humanitarian Action adopted by the Twenty-eighth International Conference of the Red Cross and Red Crescent, which noted that all States must take national measures to implement international humanitarian law, including training of the armed forces and making this law known among the general public, as well as the adoption of legislation to punish war crimes in accordance with their international obligations;

7. *Affirms* the necessity of making the implementation of international humanitarian law more effective;

8. *Welcomes* the advisory service activities of the International Committee of the Red Cross in supporting efforts made by Member States to take legislative and administrative action to implement international humanitarian law and in promoting the exchange of information on those efforts between Governments;

9. *Also welcomes* the increasing number of national commissions or committees for the implementation of international humanitarian law and for promoting the incorporation of treaties on international humanitarian law into national law and disseminating the rules of international humanitarian law;

10. *Calls upon* States to consider becoming parties to the Optional Protocol to the Convention on the Rights of the Child on the involvement of children in armed conflict;

11. *Requests* the Secretary-General to submit to the General Assembly at its sixty-first session a report on the status of the Additional Protocols relating to the protection of victims of armed conflicts, as well as on measures taken to strengthen the existing body of international humanitarian law, inter alia, with respect to its dissemination and full implementation at the national level, based on information received from Member States and the International Committee of the Red Cross;

12. *Decides* to include in the provisional agenda of its sixty-first session the item entitled "Status of the Protocols Additional to the Geneva Conventions of 1949 and relating to the protection of victims of armed conflicts".

Safety and security of United Nations and associated personnel

Ad Hoc Committee consideration. The Ad Hoc Committee on the Scope of Legal Protection under the 1994 Convention on the Safety of United Nations and Associated Personnel [YUN 1994, p. 1289], established by General Assembly resolution 56/89 [YUN 2001, p. 1227], held its third session (New York, 12-16 April) on ways to expand the scope of the legal protection under the Convention, including by means of a legal instrument.

Accordingly, a working group of the whole Committee deliberated on the relation between a possible protocol and the Convention and the definition of UN operations, to ascertain which UN operations would fall within the expanded scope of the Convention. The group also deliberated on the respective responsibilities of host States and personnel engaged in UN operations and the scope of legal protection under the Convention in relation to international humanitarian law. It had before it two proposals: one by New Zealand, containing a draft optional additional protocol aimed at preserving the Convention's regime for States preferring to be bound exclusively by its provisions, while allowing those wishing to expand the Convention's scope to do so by becoming parties to the protocol as well as to the Convention; and a second by Costa Rica, which sought to delineate the scope of application of the mutually exclusive regimes of international humanitarian law and the Convention's protective regime.

On 16 April, the Ad Hoc Committee adopted its report [A/59/52], which annexed the proposals and recommended that the Assembly renew its mandate for 2005, to enable it to continue its work to expand the scope of legal protection under the Convention.

Report of Secretary-General. In response to General Assembly resolution 58/82 [YUN 2003, p. 1342], the Secretary-General submitted a report on the scope of legal protection under the Convention on the Safety of United Nations and Associated Personnel [A/59/226]. The report discussed developments concerning the incorporation of key provisions of the Convention into status-of-forces and status-of-mission agreements; circumstances supporting a declaration of exceptional risk pursuant to article 1 (c) (ii) of the Convention; the provision of information on matters of fact relevant to the Convention's application; the provision, to requesting Member States, of the list of non-governmental organizations (NGOs) contractually linked to the Organization; and practical measures taken to strengthen the protection of UN personnel, particularly locally recruited staff.

The Secretary-General observed that the Convention's core provisions had been introduced into a growing number of recently concluded status-of-forces and status-of-mission agreements, effectively extending its scope of application to UN operations in respect of which no declaration was made, or in countries which were not signatories to the Convention. However, the General Assembly should continue to pressure Member States to prosecute those responsible for crimes against UN and associated personnel, thus ensuring full application of the Convention in theory and practice. Noting that no declarations of a "risky operation" had been made, including in Afghanistan, where UN operations remained risky, the Secretary-General said efforts to expand the Convention's scope of application to all UN operations by means of a legal instrument dispensing with the need for a declaration should be encouraged.

No request for information in matters relevant to the Convention's application had been received by the UN Secretariat, and few States had requested to be provided with the list of NGOs contractually linked to the United Nations. Such requests had been met at both the field and Headquarters levels. In most cases, however, tripartite agreements concluded between a UN agency, the Government and the NGO implementing partner had obviated the need for such a request. Since locally recruited personnel remained vulnerable to attacks, additional measures, short of evacuation, had been taken to strengthen their security.

Sixth Committee working group. On 4 October, the Sixth Committee established a working group to continue the work of the Ad Hoc Committee. The report on the group's work [A/C.6/59/L.9] contained details of its discussions on expansion of the scope of legal protection under the Convention, on the basis of the Chairman's text, which was annexed to the report, and on the revised text of a proposal by Costa Rica (see above) concerning the relationship between the Convention and international humanitarian law. Delegations, voicing concern over continued attacks and acts of violence against UN and associated personnel, expressed support for the preparation of an additional protocol to the Convention, which would broaden the scope of its protective regime, cover certain UN operations other than peacekeeping operations and dispense with the requirement for a declaration of exceptional risk. The working group recommended that the Chairman's text be used as the basis for the Ad Hoc Committee's work and that the proposal by Costa Rica be considered by the Committee separately.

On 2 December [meeting 65], the General Assembly, on the recommendation of the Sixth Committee [A/59/515 & Corr.1], adopted **resolution 59/47** without vote [agenda item 149].

Scope of legal protection under the Convention on the Safety of United Nations and Associated Personnel

The General Assembly,

Recalling its resolution 58/82 of 9 December 2003 on the scope of legal protection under the Convention on the Safety of United Nations and Associated Personnel, as well as the adoption by the Security Council of resolution 1502(2003) on 26 August 2003,

Recalling also its resolution 57/338 of 15 September 2003, in which it strongly condemned the atrocious and deliberate attack against the headquarters of the United Nations Assistance Mission in Iraq in Baghdad on 19 August 2003,

Recalling further its resolution 49/59 of 9 December 1994, by which it adopted the Convention on the Safety of United Nations and Associated Personnel,

Recalling the letter dated 24 October 2000 addressed to the President of the Security Council on behalf of the global staff of the United Nations system, drawing attention to the safety and security problems faced by United Nations and associated personnel,

Recalling also the report of the Secretary-General on the scope of legal protection under the Convention on the Safety of United Nations and Associated Personnel and the recommendations contained therein, and also recalling the further report of the Secretary-General on this issue,

Reaffirming the need to promote and ensure respect for the principles and rules of international law, including international humanitarian law, as well as relevant provisions of human rights and refugee law,

Reaffirming also the obligation of all humanitarian personnel and United Nations and associated personnel to respect the national laws of the country in which they are operating, in accordance with international law and the Charter of the United Nations,

Deeply concerned by the increasing dangers and security risks faced by United Nations and associated personnel at the field level, and mindful of the need to provide the fullest possible protection for their security,

Expressing its concern that locally recruited personnel are particularly vulnerable to attacks directed at the United Nations,

Paying tribute to the courage of those who have served and who continue to serve in United Nations operations throughout the world, in particular those who have lost their lives in the course of their duties,

Deeply concerned that perpetrators of attacks against United Nations and associated personnel seemingly operate with impunity,

Welcoming the tenth anniversary of the adoption of the Convention, which entered into force on 15 January 1999, and noting that the Convention has been rati-

fied or acceded to by seventy-seven States as at the date of the present resolution,

Underlining the need to promote the universality of the Convention and thereby strengthen the safety and security of United Nations and associated personnel,

Having considered the report of the Ad Hoc Committee on the Scope of Legal Protection under the Convention on the Safety of United Nations and Associated Personnel, established pursuant to resolution 56/89 of 12 December 2001, and the report of the Working Group of the Sixth Committee, and bearing in mind the recommendations of the Working Group contained in paragraphs 7 and 8 of its report,

1. *Expresses its appreciation* for the work done by the Ad Hoc Committee on the Scope of Legal Protection under the Convention on the Safety of United Nations and Associated Personnel;

2. *Urges* States to take all necessary measures, in accordance with their international obligations, to prevent crimes against United Nations and associated personnel from occurring;

3. *Also urges* States to ensure that crimes against United Nations and associated personnel do not go unpunished and that the perpetrators of such crimes are brought to justice;

4. *Affirms* the obligation of all States to comply fully with their obligations under the relevant rules and principles of international law in relation to the safety and security of United Nations and associated personnel;

5. *Calls upon* all States to consider becoming parties to and to respect fully their obligations under the relevant international instruments, in particular the Convention on the Safety of United Nations and Associated Personnel;

6. *Recommends* that the Secretary-General continue to seek the inclusion of, and that host countries include, key provisions of the Convention, including those regarding the prevention of attacks against members of an operation, the establishment of such attacks as crimes punishable by law and the prosecution or extradition of offenders, in future as well as, if necessary, in existing status-of-forces, status-of-mission and host country agreements negotiated between the United Nations and those countries, mindful of the importance of the timely conclusion of such agreements;

7. *Recommends also* that, consistent with his existing authority, the Secretary-General advise the Security Council or the General Assembly, as appropriate, where in his assessment circumstances would support a declaration of exceptional risk for the purposes of article 1 *(c)* (ii) of the Convention;

8. *Confirms* that, consistent with his existing authority, the Secretary-General, who has knowledge of the facts and easy access to the information, may provide information, upon the request of a State, on matters of fact relevant to the application of the Convention, such as the fact and content of any declaration of exceptional risk by the Security Council or the General Assembly or any agreement concluded between the United Nations and a humanitarian non-governmental organization or agency;

9. *Notes* that the Secretary-General has prepared a standardized provision for incorporation into the agreements concluded between the United Nations

and humanitarian non-governmental organizations or agencies for the purposes of clarifying the application of the Convention to persons deployed by those organizations or agencies, and requests the Secretary-General to make available to Member States the names of organizations or agencies that have concluded such agreements;

10. *Urges* the Secretary-General and relevant bodies to continue to take such other practical measures as are within their authority and existing institutional mandates to strengthen protection for United Nations and associated personnel, including locally recruited personnel, who are particularly vulnerable and account for the majority of casualties among United Nations or associated personnel;

11. *Decides* that the Ad Hoc Committee established under resolution 56/89 shall reconvene for one week, from 11 to 15 April 2005, with a mandate to expand the scope of legal protection under the Convention on the Safety of United Nations and Associated Personnel, including, inter alia, by means of a legal instrument, and that the work shall continue during the sixtieth session of the General Assembly within the framework of a working group of the Sixth Committee;

12. *Requests* the Ad Hoc Committee to submit a report on its work to the General Assembly at the sixtieth session;

13. *Requests* the Secretary-General to report to the General Assembly at its sixtieth session on the measures taken to implement the present resolution;

14. *Decides* to include in the provisional agenda of its sixtieth session the item entitled "Scope of legal protection under the Convention on the Safety of United Nations and Associated Personnel".

Diplomatic relations

Protection of diplomatic and consular missions and representatives

As at 31 December 2004, the States parties to the following conventions relating to the protection of diplomats and diplomatic and consular relations were: 181 States parties to the 1961 Vienna Convention on Diplomatic Relations [YUN 1961, p. 512], 50 parties to the Optional Protocol concerning the acquisition of nationality [ibid., p. 516] and 62 parties to the Optional Protocol concerning compulsory settlement of disputes [ibid.].

The 1963 Vienna Convention on Consular Relations [YUN 1963, p. 510] had 166 parties, the Optional Protocol concerning the acquisition of nationality [ibid.,p. 512] had 39 and the Optional Protocol concerning the compulsory settlement of disputes [ibid.] had 46.

Parties to the 1973 Convention on the Prevention and Punishment of Crimes against Internationally Protected Persons, including Diplomatic Agents [YUN 1973, p. 775], numbered 147.

Report of Secretary-General. In a July report with a later addendum [A/59/125 & Add.1], the Secretary-General summarized information received from 13 States pursuant to paragraphs 10 and 12 of General Assembly resolution 57/15 [YUN 2002, p. 1313]. Five reported instances of serious violations of the protection, security and safety of diplomatic and consular missions and representatives.

The report also updated the status of State participation in the conventions named above.

ILC consideration. ILC, at its fifty-sixth session [A/59/10], had before it the fifth report of Special Rapporteur Christopher John R. Dugard (South Africa) on diplomatic protection [A.CN.4/538]. The report addressed issues relating to the protection of persons in a territory controlled or occupied by a State or administered by an international intergovernmental organization and the delegation or transfer of the right of diplomatic protection. It also proposed, for ILC's consideration, several draft articles dealing with the subject of competing claims to the protection of an individual by an international organization and a State, and the protection of a ship's crew by the flag State. ILC, following its deliberations, referred to the Drafting Committee draft articles 26 and 21 addressing human rights, diplomatic protection and a general saving clause, with a view to reformulating draft article 21 on the specific subject of *lex specialis*. The Commission requested that the Drafting Committee consider elaborating a provision on the connection between the protection of ships' crews and diplomatic protection, and to consider also the possible relationship between the clean hands doctrine and diplomatic protection, for discussion at the Commission's next session. ILC adopted on first reading 19 draft articles on diplomatic protection and decided to transmit them, through the Secretary-General, to Governments for comments.

GENERAL ASSEMBLY ACTION

On 2 December [meeting 65], the General Assembly, on the recommendation of the Sixth Committee [A/59/507], adopted **resolution 59/37** without vote [agenda item 141].

Consideration of effective measures to enhance the protection, security and safety of diplomatic and consular missions and representatives

The General Assembly,

Having considered the report of the Secretary-General,

Conscious of the need to develop and strengthen friendly relations and cooperation among States,

Convinced that respect for the principles and rules of international law governing diplomatic and consular relations is a basic prerequisite for the normal conduct of relations among States and for the fulfilment of the purposes and principles of the Charter of the United Nations,

Alarmed by the recent acts of violence against diplomatic and consular representatives, as well as against representatives of international intergovernmental organizations and officials of such organizations, which have endangered or taken innocent lives and seriously impeded the normal work of such representatives and officials,

Expressing sympathy for the victims of such illegal acts,

Concerned at the failure to respect the inviolability of diplomatic and consular missions and representatives,

Recalling that, without prejudice to their privileges and immunities, it is the duty of all persons enjoying such privileges and immunities to respect the laws and regulations of the receiving State,

Recalling also that diplomatic and consular premises must not be used in any manner incompatible with the functions of diplomatic and consular missions,

Emphasizing the duty of States to take all appropriate measures as required by international law, including measures of a preventive nature, and to bring offenders to justice,

Welcoming measures already taken by States to this end in conformity with their international obligations,

Convinced that the role of the United Nations, which includes the reporting procedures established pursuant to General Assembly resolution 35/168 of 15 December 1980 and further elaborated in subsequent Assembly resolutions, is important in promoting efforts to enhance the protection, security and safety of diplomatic and consular missions and representatives,

1. *Takes note* of the report of the Secretary-General;

2. *Strongly condemns* acts of violence against diplomatic and consular missions and representatives, as well as against missions and representatives of international intergovernmental organizations and officials of such organizations, and emphasizes that such acts can never be justified;

3. *Urges* States to strictly observe, implement and enforce the principles and rules of international law governing diplomatic and consular relations and, in particular, to ensure, in conformity with their international obligations, the protection, security and safety of the missions, representatives and officials mentioned in paragraph 2 above officially present in territories under their jurisdiction, including practical measures to prohibit in their territories illegal activities of persons, groups and organizations that encourage, instigate, organize or engage in the perpetration of acts against the security and safety of such missions, representatives and officials;

4. *Also urges* States to take all necessary measures at the national and international levels to prevent any acts of violence against the missions, representatives and officials mentioned in paragraph 2 above, and to ensure, with the participation of the United Nations where appropriate, that such acts are fully investigated with a view to bringing offenders to justice;

5. *Recommends* that States cooperate closely through, inter alia, contacts between the diplomatic and consular missions and the receiving State with regard to practical measures designed to enhance the protection, security and safety of diplomatic and consular missions and representatives and with regard to the exchange of information on the circumstances of all serious violations thereof;

6. *Urges* States to take all appropriate measures, in accordance with international law, at the national and international levels, to prevent any abuse of diplomatic or consular privileges and immunities, in particular serious abuses, including those involving acts of violence;

7. *Recommends* that States cooperate closely with the State in whose territory abuses of diplomatic and consular privileges and immunities may have occurred, including by exchanging information and providing assistance to its juridical authorities in order to bring offenders to justice;

8. *Calls upon* States that have not yet done so to consider becoming parties to the instruments relevant to the protection, security and safety of diplomatic and consular missions and representatives;

9. *Calls upon* States, in cases where a dispute arises in connection with a violation of their international obligations concerning the protection of the missions or the security of the representatives and officials mentioned in paragraph 2 above, to make use of the means available for peaceful settlement of disputes, including the good offices of the Secretary-General, and requests the Secretary-General, when he deems it appropriate, to offer his good offices to the States directly concerned;

10. *Requests*:

(a) All States to report to the Secretary-General as promptly as possible serious violations of the protection, security and safety of diplomatic and consular missions and representatives as well as missions and representatives with diplomatic status to international intergovernmental organizations;

(b) The State in which the violation took place—and, to the extent possible, the State where the alleged offender is present—to report to the Secretary-General as promptly as possible on measures taken to bring the offender to justice and eventually to communicate, in accordance with its laws, the final outcome of the proceedings against the offender, and to report on measures adopted with a view to preventing a repetition of such violations;

(c) The States so reporting to consider using or taking into account the guidelines prepared by the Secretary-General;

11. *Requests* the Secretary-General:

(a) To send, without delay, a circular note to all States reminding them of the request contained in paragraph 10 above;

(b) To circulate to all States, upon receipt, the reports received by him pursuant to paragraph 10 above, unless the reporting State requests otherwise;

(c) To draw the attention, when appropriate, of the States directly concerned to the reporting procedures provided for in paragraph 10 above, when a serious violation has been reported pursuant to paragraph 10 (a) above;

(d) To address reminders to States where such violations have occurred if reports pursuant to paragraph 10 (a) above or follow-up reports pursuant to paragraph 10 (b) above have not been made within a reasonable period of time;

12. *Also requests* the Secretary-General to invite States, in the circular note referred to in para-

graph 11 *(a)* above, to inform him of their views with respect to any measures needed or already taken to enhance the protection, security and safety of diplomatic and consular missions and representatives as well as missions and representatives with diplomatic status to international intergovernmental organizations;

13. *Further requests* the Secretary-General to submit to the General Assembly at its sixty-first session a report containing:

(a) Information on the state of ratification of, and accessions to, the instruments referred to in paragraph 8 above;

(b) A summary of the reports received and views expressed pursuant to paragraphs 10 and 12 above;

14. *Invites* the Secretary-General to include in his report to the General Assembly any views he may wish to express on the matters referred to in paragraph 13 above;

15. *Decides* to include in the provisional agenda of its sixty-first session the item entitled "Consideration of effective measures to enhance the protection, security and safety of diplomatic and consular missions and representatives".

Treaties and agreements

Reservations to treaties

ILC, at its fifty-sixth session [A/59/10], considered the ninth report of Special Rapporteur Alain Pellet (France) relating to the object and definition of objections [A/CN.4/544], which complemented his eighth report [YUN 2003, p. 1343] on the formulation of objections to reservations and interpretative declarations. Following its consideration of the report, ILC decided to refer to the Drafting Committee draft guidelines 2.6.1 (definition of objections to reservations) and 2.6.2 (objections to the late formulation of widening of the scope of a reservation). It considered and provisionally adopted the following draft guidelines that had been referred to the Drafting Committee in 2003 [ibid.]: 2.3.5 (widening of the scope of a reservation), 2.4.9 (modification of an interpretative declaration), 2.4.10 (limitation and widening of the scope of a conditional interpretative declaration), 2.5.12 (withdrawal of an interpretative declaration), and 2.5.13 (withdrawal of a conditional interpretative declaration). ILC also adopted the commentaries to those draft guidelines and reproduced in its report the text of the draft guidelines to treaties it had adopted, together with the commentaries thereto.

Treaties involving international organizations

The 1986 Vienna Convention on the Law of Treaties between States and International Organizations or between International Organizations [YUN 1986, p. 1006], which had not yet entered into force, had 39 States parties as at 31 December 2004.

Registration and publication of treaties by the United Nations

During 2004, 1,388 international agreements were received and 1,125 subsequent actions were registered or filed and recorded by the Secretariat. In addition, 890 formalities concerning agreements for which the Secretary-General performed depositary functions were registered. Twelve issues of the *Monthly Statement of Treaties and International Agreements* were published.

In addition, the texts of international agreements registered or filed and recorded were published in the UN *Treaty Series (UNTS)* in 84 volumes in the original languages, with translations into English and French where necessary. The United Nations Treaty Collection on the Internet (UNTC), which contained published UNTS volumes up to 2004, the *League of Nations Treaty Series*, the *Treaty Handbook*, the *Handbook of Final Clauses*, *Multilateral Treaties deposited with the Secretary-General*, the *Summary of Practice of the Secretary-General as Depositary of Multilateral Treaties*, the Focus Books, information on training and a range of materials on treaty law and practice, received an average of 1.7 million hits per month in 2004.

Multilateral treaties

The UN *Treaty Series* and the regularly updated status of multilateral treaties deposited with the Secretary-General were available on the Internet at the UN Treaty Collection website (http://untreaty.un.org).

New multilateral treaties concluded under UN auspices

The following treaties, concluded under UN auspices, were deposited with the Secretary-General during 2004:

United Nations Convention on Jurisdictional Immunities of States and Their Property, adopted in New York on 2 December 2004

Amendment to the Convention on Environmental Impact Assessment in a Transboundary Context, adopted in Cavtat, Croatia, on 4 June 2004

Amendments to Articles 25 and 26 of the Convention on the Protection and Use of Transboundary Watercourses and International Lakes, adopted in Geneva on 17 February 2004

Multilateral treaties
deposited with the Secretary-General

At the end of 2004, the Secretary-General performed depositary functions for 512 multilateral treaties. During the year, 184 signatures were affixed to treaties for which he performed depositary functions and 1,487 instruments of ratification, accession, acceptance and approval were deposited.

The following multilateral treaties, among others, in respect of which the Secretary-General acted as depositary, came into force in 2004:

International Convention on Maritime Liens and Mortgages, adopted in Geneva on 6 May 1993

Protocol against the Smuggling of Migrants by Land, Sea and Air, supplementing the United Nations Convention against Transnational Organized Crime, adopted by General Assembly resolution 55/25 of 15 November 2000

Agreement on the Privileges and Immunities of the International Criminal Court, adopted in New York on 9 September 2002

Amendment to the Convention on Prohibitions or Restrictions on the Use of Certain Conventional Weapons which may be Deemed to be Excessively Injurious or to have Indiscriminate Effects, adopted in Geneva on 21 December 2001

Rotterdam Convention on the Prior Informed Consent Procedure for Certain Hazardous Chemicals and Pesticides in International Trade, adopted in Rotterdam, the Netherlands, on 10 September 1998

Stockholm Convention on Persistent Organic Pollutants, adopted in Stockholm, Sweden, on 22 May 2001

Agreement on Succession Issues, adopted in Vienna on 29 June 2001

Special Protocol concerning Statelessness, adopted in The Hague, the Netherlands, on 12 April 1930

Information for 2004 regarding all multilateral treaties deposited with the Secretary-General was contained in *Multilateral Treaties Deposited with the Secretary-General: Status as at 31 December 2004,* Vols. I & II [ST/LEG/SER.E/23], Sales No. E.05.V.3.

Chapter IV

Law of the sea

The United Nations continued in 2004 to promote universal acceptance of the 1982 United Nations Convention on the Law of the Sea and its two implementing Agreements on the conservation and management of straddling fish stocks and highly migratory fish stocks and on the privileges and immunities of the International Tribunal for the Law of the Sea.

The three institutions created by the Convention—the International Seabed Authority, the International Tribunal for the Law of the Sea and the Commission on the Limits of the Continental Shelf—held sessions during the year.

The tenth anniversary of the Convention's entry into force was marked on 16 November 2004. The Secretary-General stated that the challenge during the anniversary year was for States and organizations to implement the Convention's provisions fully in their legislation, administrations and daily practice, and in cooperation with other States.

UN Convention on the Law of the Sea

Signatures and ratifications

In 2004, Denmark and Latvia ratified or acceded to the United Nations Convention on the Law of the Sea (UNCLOS), bringing the number of parties to 147. The Convention, which was adopted by the Third United Nations Conference on the Law of the Sea in 1982 [YUN 1982, p. 178], entered into force on 16 November 1994 [YUN 1994, p. 1301].

Meeting of States Parties

The fourteenth Meeting of States Parties to the Convention (New York, 14-18 June) [SPLOS/119 & Corr.1] discussed the 2003 activities of the International Tribunal for the Law of the Sea [YUN 2003, p. 1353] and took action on financial and administrative issues, including: approving the first biennial budget for 2005-2006 in the amount of 15.5 million euros; approving the establishment of a trust fund financed by the Korea International Cooperation Agency to support the participation of interns from developing countries in the Tribunal's internship programme; author-

izing the financing of overexpenditures in 2004 by transfers between appropriation sections as far as possible and, if necessary, by using savings up to $500,000; authorizing the appointment of an Auditor to examine the Tribunal's 2004 financial statement; and approving the Tribunal's financial rules and the inclusion of budget lines in the 2005-2006 budget for the reimbursement of national taxes levied on the remuneration of Tribunal members and officials. Also discussed were the 2004 activities of the International Seabed Authority (see p. 1329) and of the Commission on the Limits of the Continental Shelf (see p. 1331), and the possible inclusion in the agenda of future meetings of issues arising from the implementation of UNCLOS. A symposium on maritime delimitation, organized in commemoration of the tenth anniversary of the Convention's entry into force, took place on the premises of the Tribunal on 25 and 26 September. On 14 December, the headquarters agreement between the Tribunal and the host country, Germany, was signed.

Agreement relating to the Implementation of Part XI of the Convention

During 2004, the number of parties to the 1994 Agreement relating to the Implementation of Part XI of the Convention (governing exploitation of seabed resources beyond national jurisdiction), adopted by General Assembly resolution 48/263 [YUN 1994, p. 1301], reached 119. The Agreement, which entered into force on 28 July 1996 [YUN 1996, p. 1215], was to be interpreted and applied together with the Convention as a single instrument, and, in the event of any inconsistency between the Agreement and Part XI of the Convention, the provisions of the Agreement would prevail. Any ratification of or accession to the Convention after 28 July 1994 represented consent to be bound by the Agreement also. Parties to the Convention prior to the Agreement's adoption had to deposit a separate instrument of ratification of or accession to the Agreement.

Agreement relating to conservation and management of straddling fish stocks and highly migratory fish stocks

As at 31 December 2004, the number of parties to the 1995 Agreement for the Implementation of the Provisions of the United Nations Convention on the Law of the Sea of 10 December 1982 relating to the Conservation and Management of Straddling Fish Stocks and Highly Migratory Fish Stocks [YUN 1995, p. 1334] reached 52. Referred to as the Fish Stocks Agreement, it entered into force on 11 December 2001 [YUN 2001, p. 1232].

Report of Secretary-General. In response to General Assembly resolution 58/14 [YUN 2003, p. 1347], the Secretary-General submitted an August report [A/59/298] on the status and implementation of the Fish Stocks Agreement. The report contained information on steps and initiatives taken or recommended by the international community to improve the conservation and management of fishery and other marine living resources with a view to achieving sustainable fisheries and protecting marine ecosystems and biodiversity. It included a specific consideration of risks to the marine biodiversity of vulnerable marine ecosystems related to fishing activities and provided a review of existing conservation and management measures at the global, regional, subregional or national levels that addressed those issues.

The report concluded that one of the main tasks of fishery managers was to mitigate the impact of fishing activities on marine ecosystems, while maintaining fishing as a viable economic activity. The report emphasized the importance of the full implementation by States of all international fishery instruments, whether legally binding or voluntary, which provided for conservation and management measures and sustainable use of marine living resources. It also invited States to cooperate in all aspects of fishery conservation and management, including the establishment of new regional fisheries management organizations where none existed in a particular region or subregion; apply the precautionary and ecosystem approaches; and collect and exchange fishery data and statistics. The report further pointed out that regional and subregional fisheries-management organizations and arrangements were required to adopt effective conservation and management measures for fishery resources under their competence; improve fishery data to ensure the availability of the best scientific evidence; adopt effective monitoring, control and surveillance policies; and agree on effective decision-making procedures.

GENERAL ASSEMBLY ACTION

On 17 November [meeting 56], the General Assembly adopted **resolution 59/25** [draft: A/59/L.23 & Add.1] without vote [agenda item 49 (b)].

Sustainable fisheries, including through the 1995 Agreement for the Implementation of the Provisions of the United Nations Convention on the Law of the Sea of 10 December 1982 relating to the Conservation and Management of Straddling Fish Stocks and Highly Migratory Fish Stocks, and related instruments

The General Assembly,

Reaffirming its resolutions 46/215 of 20 December 1991, 49/116 and 49/118 of 19 December 1994, 50/25 of 5 December 1995 and 57/142 of 12 December 2002, as well as other resolutions on large-scale pelagic driftnet fishing, unauthorized fishing in zones of national jurisdiction and on the high seas, fisheries by-catch and discards, and other developments, its resolutions 56/13 of 28 November 2001 and 57/143 of 12 December 2002 on the Agreement for the Implementation of the Provisions of the United Nations Convention on the Law of the Sea of 10 December 1982 relating to the Conservation and Management of Straddling Fish Stocks and Highly Migratory Fish Stocks ("the Agreement"), and its resolution 58/14 of 24 November 2003,

Recalling the relevant provisions of the United Nations Convention on the Law of the Sea ("the Convention"), and bearing in mind the relationship between the Convention and the Agreement,

Recognizing that, in accordance with the Convention, the Agreement sets forth provisions concerning the conservation and management of straddling fish stocks and highly migratory fish stocks, including provisions on subregional and regional cooperation in enforcement, binding dispute settlement and the rights and obligations of States in authorizing the use of vessels flying their flags for fishing on the high seas, and specific provisions to address the requirements of developing States in relation to the conservation and management of straddling fish stocks and highly migratory fish stocks and the development of fisheries for such stocks,

Noting that the Code of Conduct for Responsible Fisheries of the Food and Agriculture Organization of the United Nations ("the Code") and its associated international plans of action set out principles and global standards of behaviour for responsible practices for the conservation of fisheries resources and the management and development of fisheries,

Noting with concern that effective management of marine capture fisheries has been made difficult in some areas by unreliable information and data caused by unreported and misreported fish catch and fishing effort and the contribution this lack of data makes to continued overfishing in some areas,

Noting with satisfaction the Strategy for Improving Information on Status and Trends of Capture Fisheries recently adopted by the Food and Agriculture Organization of the United Nations, and recognizing that the long-term improvement of the knowledge and understanding of fishery status and trends is a fundamental basis for fisheries policy and management for implementing the Code,

Recognizing the need to implement, as a matter of priority, the Plan of Implementation of the World Summit on Sustainable Development ("Johannesburg Plan of Implementation"), in relation to achieving sustainable fisheries,

Deploring the fact that fish stocks, including straddling fish stocks and highly migratory fish stocks, in many parts of the world are overfished or subject to sparsely regulated and heavy fishing efforts, mainly as a result of, inter alia, unauthorized fishing, inadequate regulatory measures, harmful fisheries subsidies and excess fishing capacity,

Concerned that illegal, unreported and unregulated fishing threatens seriously to deplete populations of certain fish species and to significantly damage marine ecosystems, to the detriment of sustainable fisheries as well as the food security and the economies of many States, particularly developing States,

Noting with satisfaction resolution 6/2003 of 9 December 2003, adopted by the Conference of the Food and Agriculture Organization of the United Nations, relating to preventing, deterring and eliminating illegal, unreported and unregulated fishing,

Recognizing that the problem of overfishing continues to be exacerbated by inadequate flag State control over fishing vessels, including those fishing for straddling fish stocks and highly migratory fish stocks, and insufficient monitoring, control and surveillance measures,

Recognizing also that the interrelationship between ocean activities, such as shipping and fishing, and environmental issues needs further consideration,

Noting that the contribution of aquaculture to global fish supplies continues to increase its potential in developing countries to enhance local food security and poverty alleviation and meet future demands in fish consumption, bearing in mind article 9.1.4 of the Code,

Calling attention to the circumstances affecting fisheries in many developing States, in particular African States and small island developing States, and recognizing the urgent need for capacity-building to assist such States in meeting their obligations under international instruments and realizing the benefits from fisheries resources,

Noting the obligation of all States, pursuant to the provisions of the Convention, to cooperate in the conservation and management of straddling fish stocks and highly migratory fish stocks, and recognizing the importance of coordination and cooperation at the global, regional, subregional as well as national levels in the areas, inter alia, of data collection, information-sharing, capacity-building and training for the conservation, management and sustainable development of marine living resources,

Recognizing the duty provided in the Convention, the Agreement to Promote Compliance with International Conservation and Management Measures by Fishing Vessels on the High Seas ("the Compliance Agreement"), the Agreement and the Code for flag States to exercise effective control over fishing vessels flying their flag and vessels flying their flag which provide support to such vessels, and to ensure that the activities of such vessels do not undermine the effectiveness of conservation and management measures taken in accordance with international law and adopted at the national, subregional, regional or global levels,

Recognizing also the urgent need for action at all levels to ensure the long-term sustainable use and management of fisheries resources through the wide application of a precautionary approach and appropriate measures to reduce pollution and waste, and other factors, such as discards and catch by lost or abandoned gear, which adversely affect fish stocks,

Recognizing further the economic and cultural importance of sharks in many countries, the biological importance of sharks in the marine ecosystem, the vulnerability of some shark species to over-exploitation, the need for measures to promote the long-term sustainability of shark populations and fisheries and the relevance of the International Plan of Action for the Conservation and Management of Sharks, adopted by the Food and Agriculture Organization of the United Nations in 1999, in providing development guidance of such measures,

Reaffirming its support for the initiative of the Food and Agriculture Organization of the United Nations and relevant regional and subregional fisheries management organizations and arrangements on the conservation and management of sharks, while noting with concern that only a small number of countries have implemented the International Plan of Action for the Conservation and Management of Sharks,

Noting with satisfaction the outcomes of the third round of informal consultations of States parties to the Agreement, held in New York on 8 July 2004,

Taking note with appreciation of the report of the Secretary-General, including the section outlining current risks to the marine biodiversity of vulnerable marine ecosystems related to fishing activities, and conservation and management measures in place at the global, regional, subregional or national levels addressing these issues, in particular the useful role of the report in gathering and disseminating information on or relating to the sustainable development of the world's marine living resources,

Expressing concern that the practice of large-scale pelagic drift-net fishing remains a threat to marine living resources, although the incidence of this practice has continued to be low in most regions of the world's oceans and seas,

Emphasizing that efforts should be made to ensure that the implementation of resolution 46/215 in some parts of the world does not result in the transfer to other parts of the world of drift nets that contravene the resolution,

Expressing concern, while recognizing considerable efforts to reduce by-catch in longline fishing through various regional fisheries management organizations, at the reports of continued loss of seabirds, particularly albatrosses, as a result of incidental mortality from longline fishing operations, and the loss of other marine species, including sharks, fin-fish species and marine turtles, as a result of incidental mortality,

Welcoming the fact that a growing number of States, and entities referred to in the Convention and in article 1, paragraph 2 *(b)*, of the Agreement, as well as regional and subregional fisheries management organizations and arrangements, have taken measures, as appropriate, towards the implementation of the provisions of the Agreement,

Recognizing the significant contribution of sustainable fisheries to food security, income and wealth for present and future generations,

I
Achieving sustainable fisheries

1. *Reaffirms* the importance it attaches to the long-term conservation, management and sustainable use of the marine living resources of the world's oceans and seas and the obligations of States to cooperate to this end, in accordance with international law, as reflected in the relevant provisions of the Convention, in particular the provisions on cooperation set out in Part V and Part VII, section 2, of the Convention, and where applicable, the Agreement;

2. *Calls upon* all States that have not done so, in order to achieve the goal of universal participation, to become parties to the Convention, which sets out the legal framework within which all activities in the oceans and seas must be carried out, taking into account the relationship between the Convention and the Agreement;

3. *Reaffirms* the importance of the Johannesburg Plan of Implementation in relation to fisheries, in particular the commitment made therein to restore depleted fish stocks on an urgent basis and, where possible, not later than 2015;

4. *Urges* all States to apply the precautionary approach and the ecosystem approach widely to the conservation, management and exploitation of fish stocks, including straddling fish stocks and highly migratory fish stocks, and also calls upon States parties to the Agreement to implement fully the provisions of article 6 of the Agreement as a matter of priority;

II
Implementation of the 1995 Agreement for the Implementation of the Provisions of the United Nations Convention on the Law of the Sea of 10 December 1982 relating to the Conservation and Management of Straddling Fish Stocks and Highly Migratory Fish Stocks

5. *Calls upon* all States, and entities referred to in the Convention and in article 1, paragraph 2 *(b)*, of the Agreement, that have not done so to ratify or accede to the Agreement and in the interim to consider applying it provisionally;

6. *Emphasizes* the importance of the effective implementation of the provisions of the Agreement, including those provisions relating to bilateral, regional and subregional cooperation in enforcement, and urges continued efforts in this regard;

7. *Welcomes* the entry into force of the Convention on the Conservation and Management of Highly Migratory Fish Stocks in the Western and Central Pacific Ocean on 19 June 2004, and encourages relevant States to become Parties to that Convention in accordance with its terms;

8. *Also welcomes* the inaugural meeting at Swakopmund, Namibia, from 9 to 13 March 2004 of the Commission of the South-East Atlantic Fisheries Organization as well as its continual operationalization and assumption of full competence for the conservation and management of resources that fall under its responsibility within the area of the Convention on the Conservation and Management of Fishery Resources in the South-East Atlantic Ocean, and encourages signatory States and other States with real interest whose vessels fish in that Convention area for fishery resources covered by that Convention to become parties

to the Convention and, in the interim, to consider applying it and the measures adopted thereunder provisionally, to ensure that vessels entitled to fly their flags apply such measures;

9. *Calls upon* all States to ensure that their vessels comply with the conservation and management measures that have been adopted by subregional and regional fisheries management organizations and arrangements in accordance with relevant provisions of the Convention and of the Agreement;

10. *Urges* States parties to the Agreement, in accordance with article 21, paragraph 4, thereof to inform, either directly or through the relevant regional or subregional fisheries management organization or arrangement, all States whose vessels fish on the high seas in the same region or subregion of the form of identification issued by those States parties to officials duly authorized to carry out boarding and inspection functions in accordance with articles 21 and 22 of the Agreement;

11. *Also urges* States parties to the Agreement, in accordance with article 21, paragraph 4, to designate an appropriate authority to receive notifications pursuant to article 21 and to give due publicity to such designation through the relevant subregional or regional fisheries management organization or arrangement;

12. *Invites* States and international financial institutions and organizations of the United Nations system to provide assistance according to Part VII of the Agreement, including, if appropriate, the development of special financial mechanisms or instruments to assist developing States, in particular the least developed among them and small island developing States, to enable them to develop their national capacity to exploit fishery resources, including developing their domestically flagged fishing fleet, value-added processing and the expansion of their economic base in the fishing industry, consistent with the duty to ensure the proper conservation and management of those fisheries resources;

13. *Recalls* paragraph 10 of its resolution 58/14, in which it decided to establish an Assistance Fund under Part VII of the Agreement to assist developing States parties in the implementation of the Agreement, and encourages States, intergovernmental organizations, international financial institutions, national institutions, non-governmental organizations, as well as natural and juridical persons to make voluntary financial contributions to the Fund;

14. *Notes with satisfaction* the conclusion of an arrangement between the United Nations and the Food and Agriculture Organization of the United Nations regarding the administration of the Assistance Fund;

15. *Emphasizes* the importance of outreach to potential donor organizations to contribute to the programme of assistance, including the Assistance Fund;

16. *Requests* the Secretary-General to convene, pursuant to article 36 of the Agreement, a one-week review conference in the first part of 2006, with a view to assessing the effectiveness of the Agreement in securing the conservation and management of straddling fish stocks and highly migratory fish stocks, and to render the necessary assistance and provide such services as may be required for the review conference;

17. *Also requests* the Secretary-General to present to the conference a comprehensive report, prepared in

cooperation with the Food and Agriculture Organization of the United Nations, in accordance with paragraph 2 of article 36 of the Agreement;

18. *Recalls* paragraph 6 of its resolution 56/13, and requests the Secretary-General to convene a fourth round of informal consultations of States parties to the Agreement, to consider, principally, but not exclusively, issues related to preparation for the review conference to be convened by the Secretary-General pursuant to article 36 of the Agreement, and to make any appropriate recommendation to the General Assembly;

19. *Requests* the Secretary-General to invite States, and entities referred to in the Convention and in article 1, paragraph 2 *(b)*, of the Agreement, not party to the Agreement, as well as the United Nations Development Programme, the Food and Agriculture Organization of the United Nations and other specialized agencies, the Commission on Sustainable Development, the World Bank, the Global Environment Facility and other relevant international financial institutions, subregional and regional fisheries management organizations and arrangements, other fisheries bodies, and relevant non-governmental organizations to attend the fourth round of informal consultations of States parties to the Agreement as observers;

III
Related fisheries instruments

20. *Emphasizes* the importance of the effective implementation of the provisions of the Compliance Agreement, and urges continued efforts in this regard;

21. *Calls upon* all States and other entities referred to in article X, paragraph 1, of the Compliance Agreement that have not yet become parties to that Agreement to do so as a matter of priority and, in the interim, to consider applying it provisionally;

22. *Urges* parties to the Compliance Agreement to exchange information in the implementation of that Agreement;

23. *Urges* States and subregional and regional fisheries management organizations and arrangements to implement and promote the application of the Code within their areas of competence;

24. *Urges* States, as a matter of priority, to support implementation of the Strategy for Improving Information on Status and Trends of Capture Fisheries at the national and regional levels, giving particular emphasis to capacity-building in developing countries;

25. *Also urges* States to develop and implement, as a matter of priority, national and, as appropriate, regional plans of action to put into effect the international plans of action of the Food and Agriculture Organization of the United Nations;

IV
Illegal, unreported and unregulated fishing

26. *Emphasizes once again its serious concern* that illegal, unreported and unregulated fishing remains one of the greatest threats to marine ecosystems and continues to have serious and major implications for the conservation and management of ocean resources, and renews its call upon States to comply fully with all existing obligations and to combat such fishing and urgently to take all necessary steps to implement the International Plan of Action to Prevent, Deter and Eliminate Illegal, Unreported and Unregulated Fishing of

the Food and Agriculture Organization of the United Nations;

27. *Calls upon* States not to permit vessels flying their flag to engage in fishing on the high seas or in areas under the national jurisdiction of other States, unless duly authorized by the authorities of the States concerned and in accordance with the conditions set out in the authorization, without having effective control over their activities, and to take specific measures, including deterring the reflagging of vessels by their nationals, in accordance with the relevant provisions of the Convention, the Agreement and the Compliance Agreement, to control fishing operations by vessels flying their flag;

28. *Affirms* the need to strengthen, where necessary, the international legal framework for intergovernmental cooperation, in particular at the regional and subregional levels, in the management of fish stocks and in combating illegal, unreported and unregulated fishing, in a manner consistent with international law, and for States and entities referred to in the Convention and in article 1, paragraph 2 *(b)*, of the Agreement to collaborate in efforts to address these types of fishing activities, including, inter alia, the development and implementation of vessel monitoring systems and the listing of vessels in order to prevent illegal, unreported, and unregulated fishing activities and, where appropriate and consistent with international law, trade monitoring schemes, including to collect global catch data, through subregional and regional fisheries management organizations and arrangements;

29. *Encourages* States to consider becoming members of the International Monitoring, Control and Surveillance Network for Fisheries-Related Activities, a voluntary network of monitoring, control and surveillance professionals designed to facilitate exchange of information and to support countries in discharging their obligations pursuant to international agreements, in particular the Compliance Agreement;

30. *Requests* the Secretary-General to report to the General Assembly at its sixty-first session on the study undertaken by the International Maritime Organization, in cooperation with other competent international organizations, following the invitation extended to it in resolution 58/14 and resolution 58/240 of 23 December 2003, to examine and clarify the role of the "genuine link" in relation to the duty of flag States to exercise effective control over ships flying their flag, including fishing vessels, and the potential consequences of non-compliance with the duties and obligations of flag States prescribed in the relevant international instruments;

31. *Calls upon* flag and port States to take all measures consistent with international law necessary to prevent the operation of sub-standard vessels and illegal, unreported and unregulated fishing activities;

32. *Encourages* the Food and Agriculture Organization of the United Nations and subregional and regional fisheries management organizations and arrangements to develop further ideas to devise means of discouraging owners and operators from non-compliance with the requirements imposed by flag States in carrying out their duties and obligations under relevant international instruments;

33. *Recognizes* the commitment made in the Johannesburg Plan of Implementation for States urgently to

develop and implement national and, where appropriate, regional plans of action, to put into effect by 2004 the International Plan of Action to Prevent, Deter and Eliminate Illegal, Unreported and Unregulated Fishing, and to establish effective monitoring, reporting, enforcement and control of fishing vessels, including by flag States, to further the International Plan of Action, and calls upon States to adhere to this commitment as a matter of priority;

34. *Also recognizes* that common means of conducting illegal, unreported and unregulated fishing involves the unreported or misreported transshipments of fish at sea, and urges States, either directly or through relevant subregional and regional fisheries management organizations and arrangements, to establish comprehensive systems, where appropriate, for monitoring and control of transshipments on the high seas;

35. *Urges* relevant regional and subregional fisheries management organizations and arrangements to implement effective measures against illegal, unreported and unregulated fishing, inter alia, by compiling a record of vessels authorized to fish in their area of competence, in accordance with the Code;

36. *Commends* the Food and Agriculture Organization of the United Nations for its activities in combating illegal, unreported and unregulated fishing, including its initiative to organize the intergovernmental technical consultation on the role of the port State in combating illegal, unreported and unregulated fishing, held from 31 August to 2 September 2004, and welcomes the outcome of the consultation;

37. *Urges* States to eliminate subsidies that contribute to illegal, unreported and unregulated fishing, while completing the efforts undertaken at the World Trade Organization to clarify and improve its disciplines on fisheries subsidies, taking into account the importance of this sector to developing countries;

38. *Recognizes* the need for enhanced port State controls to combat illegal, unreported and unregulated fishing, urges States to cooperate, in particular at the regional level, and through regional and subregional fisheries management organizations and arrangements, as well as through participation, where appropriate, in the efforts of the Food and Agriculture Organization of the United Nations in cooperation with the International Maritime Organization to address substantive issues relating to the role of the port State, noting that such efforts include the elaboration of a draft model scheme on port State measures to prevent, deter and eliminate illegal, unreported and unregulated fishing;

V
Fishing overcapacity

39. *Calls upon* States and relevant regional and subregional fisheries management organizations and arrangements, as a matter of priority, to take effective measures to improve the management of fishing capacity and to put into effect by 2005 the International Plan of Action for the Management of Fishing Capacity, taking into account the need, through these actions, to avoid the transfer of fishing capacity to other fisheries or areas including, but not limited to, those areas where fish stocks are overexploited or in a depleted condition;

40. *Urges* States to eliminate subsidies that contribute to fishing overcapacity, while completing the efforts undertaken at the World Trade Organization to clarify and improve its disciplines on fisheries subsidies, taking into account the importance of this sector to developing countries;

41. *Notes with satisfaction* that information about more than 5,500 fishing vessels authorized to fish on the high seas has been provided to the Food and Agriculture Organization of the United Nations by at least seventeen flag States and entered on the High Seas Vessels Authorization Record established by the Organization in accordance with article VI of the Compliance Agreement, and urges those States and other entities referred to in article X, paragraph 1, of the Compliance Agreement that have become parties to it to establish a record of fishing vessels authorized to fish on the high seas and, pursuant to articles IV and VI thereof, to make such a record available to the Organization as a matter of priority, and promptly to notify the Organization of any modifications to such a record;

42. *Calls upon* all States to assist this work of the Food and Agriculture Organization of the United Nations, and to take measures to halt the increase of large-scale fishing vessels in accordance with the International Plan of Action for the Management of Fishing Capacity;

43. *Welcomes* the significant outcomes of the Technical Consultation to Review Progress and Promote the Full Implementation of the International Plan of Action to Prevent, Deter and Eliminate Illegal, Unreported and Unregulated Fishing and the International Plan of Action for the Management of Fishing Capacity of the Food and Agriculture Organization of the United Nations, held from 24 to 29 June 2004, which recommended specific actions to the Committee on Fisheries of the Food and Agriculture Organization of the United Nations and other relevant regional and subregional fisheries management organizations and arrangements with regard to illegal, unreported and unregulated fishing and fishing overcapacity, and also suggested measures to be taken by States and fishing entities regarding expanding fishing capacity by certain fishing operations in the Central and Western Pacific Ocean;

VI
Large-scale pelagic drift-net fishing

44. *Reaffirms* the importance it attaches to continued compliance with its resolution 46/215 and other subsequent resolutions on large-scale pelagic drift-net fishing, and urges States and entities referred to in the Convention and in article 1, paragraph 2 *(b)*, of the Agreement to enforce fully the measures recommended in those resolutions;

VII
Fisheries by-catch and discards

45. *Urges* States, relevant international organizations and regional and subregional fisheries management organizations and arrangements that have not done so to take action to reduce or eliminate by-catch, catch by lost or abandoned gear, fish discards and post-harvest losses, including juvenile fish, consistent with international law and relevant international instruments, including the Code, and in particular to

consider measures including, as appropriate, technical measures related to fish size, mesh size or gear, discards, closed seasons and areas and zones reserved for selected fisheries, particularly artisanal fisheries, the establishment of mechanisms for communicating information on areas of high concentration of juvenile fish, taking into account the importance of ensuring confidentiality of such information, and support for studies and research that will reduce or eliminate by-catch of juvenile fish;

46. *Encourages* States and entities referred to in the Convention and in article 1, paragraph 2 *(b)*, of the Agreement to give due consideration to participation, as appropriate, in regional and subregional organizations with mandates to conserve non-target species taken incidentally in fishing operations, and notes in particular the Inter-American Convention for the Protection and Conservation of Sea Turtles and Their Habitats, regional sea turtle conservation instruments in the West African, the wider Caribbean, and the Indian Ocean/ South-East Asia regions, the work of the Southeast Asian Fisheries Development Centre on turtle conservation and management, the Agreement on the Conservation of Small Cetaceans of the Baltic and North Seas, and the Agreement on the Conservation of Cetaceans of the Black Sea, Mediterranean Sea and Contiguous Atlantic Area in this regard;

47. *Notes with satisfaction* the entry into force on 1 February 2004 of the Agreement on the Conservation of Albatrosses and Petrels under the Convention on the Conservation of Migratory Species of Wild Animals, and encourages relevant States which have not already done so to become parties to that Agreement in accordance with its terms;

48. *Also notes with satisfaction* the activities of the Food and Agriculture Organization of the United Nations, in cooperation with relevant United Nations agencies and programmes, in particular the United Nations Environment Programme and the Global Environment Facility, aimed at promoting the reduction of by-catch and discards in fisheries activities;

49. *Notes* the Technical Consultation on Sea Turtles Conservation and Fisheries to be organized by the Food and Agriculture Organization of the United Nations from 29 November to 2 December 2004, and encourages States to participate actively in this work;

VIII
Subregional and regional cooperation

50. *Urges* coastal States and States fishing on the high seas, in accordance with the Convention and the Agreement, to pursue cooperation in relation to straddling fish stocks and highly migratory fish stocks, either directly or through appropriate subregional or regional fisheries management organizations or arrangements, to ensure the effective conservation and management of such stocks;

51. *Encourages* States fishing for straddling fish stocks and highly migratory fish stocks on the high seas, and relevant coastal States, where a subregional or regional fisheries management organization or arrangement has the competence to establish conservation and management measures for such stocks, to give effect to their duty to cooperate by becoming members of such an organization or participants in such an arrangement, or by agreeing to apply the conservation

and management measures established by such an organization or arrangement;

52. *Invites*, in this regard, subregional and regional fisheries management organizations and arrangements to ensure that all States having a real interest in the fisheries concerned may become members of such organizations or participants in such arrangements, in accordance with the Convention and the Agreement;

53. *Encourages* relevant coastal States and States fishing on the high seas for a straddling fish stock or a highly migratory fish stock, where there is no subregional or regional fisheries management organization or arrangement to establish conservation and management measures for such stock, to cooperate to establish such an organization or enter into another appropriate arrangement to ensure the conservation and management of such stocks, and to participate in the work of the organization or arrangement;

54. *Welcomes* the initiation of negotiations and ongoing preparatory work to establish regional and subregional fisheries management organizations or arrangements in several fisheries, and urges participants in those negotiations to apply provisions of the Convention and the Agreement to their work;

55. *Notes with satisfaction*, in this regard, the recent recommendation of the Western Central Atlantic Fisheries Commission that established an intersessional working group tasked to study the feasibility of strengthening regional fisheries management in that region, encourages relevant States and organizations to work actively to fulfil the recommendation, and notes the important contribution of the Caribbean Regional Fisheries Mechanism to this process;

56. *Encourages* States to develop ocean policies and mechanisms on integrated management, including at the subregional and regional levels, and also including assistance to developing States in accomplishing these objectives, as well as by promoting improved cooperation between regional fisheries management organizations and other regional entities, such as the United Nations Environment Programme regional seas programmes and conventions;

57. *Encourages* subregional or regional fisheries management organizations or arrangements and States and entities referred to in the Convention and in article 1, paragraph 2 *(b)*, of the Agreement that are members of or participate in such organizations or arrangements, to consider adopting, where appropriate and in accordance with international law, conservation and management measures for fish stocks that fall within the competence of such organizations and/or arrangements but are not yet managed by them, in particular for those stocks that have vulnerable life histories, that scientific data indicate are in decline and/or are subject to an international plan of action of the Food and Agriculture Organization of the United Nations;

IX
Responsible fisheries in the marine ecosystem

58. *Encourages* States to apply by 2010 the ecosystem approach, notes the Reykjavik Declaration on Responsible Fisheries in the Marine Ecosystem and decision VII/ 11 and other relevant decisions of the Conference of the Parties to the Convention on Biological Diversity, notes the work of the Food and Agriculture

Organization of the United Nations related to guidelines for the implementation of the ecosystem approach to fisheries management, and also notes the importance to this approach of relevant provisions of the Agreement and the Code;

59. *Also encourages* States to increase scientific research in accordance with international law on the marine ecosystem;

60. *Calls upon* States, the Food and Agriculture Organization of the United Nations, the International Maritime Organization, the United Nations Environment Programme, in particular its Regional Seas programme, regional and subregional fisheries management organizations and arrangements and other appropriate intergovernmental organizations that have not yet done so to take action to address the issue of lost or abandoned fishing gear and related marine debris, including through the collection of data on gear loss, economic costs to fisheries and other sectors, and the impact on marine ecosystems;

61. *Requests* the Secretary-General, in his next report concerning fisheries, to include information on the actions taken by the Food and Agriculture Organization of the United Nations, the United Nations Environment Programme, in particular its Regional Seas programme, the International Maritime Organization, regional and subregional fisheries management organizations and arrangements, and other appropriate intergovernmental organizations, to give effect to paragraph 60 above;

62. *Urges* States to ratify and implement relevant international agreements, including annex V to the International Convention for the Prevention of Pollution from Ships, 1973, as modified by the Protocol of 1978 relating thereto;

63. *Calls upon* States, where relevant, to establish systems for retrieving lost gear and nets;

64. *Notes* that 2005 will mark the ten-year anniversary of the adoption of the Global Programme of Action for the Protection of the Marine Environment from Land-based Activities, and urges all States to implement the Global Programme of Action and to accelerate activity to safeguard the marine ecosystem, including fish stocks, against pollution and physical degradation;

65. *Calls upon* States, the Food and Agriculture Organization of the United Nations and other specialized agencies of the United Nations, subregional and regional fisheries management organizations and arrangements, where appropriate, and other appropriate intergovernmental bodies, to cooperate in achieving sustainable aquaculture, including through information exchange, developing equivalent standards on such issues as aquatic animal health and human health and safety concerns, assessing the potential positive and negative impacts of aquaculture, including socio-economics, on the marine and coastal environment, including biodiversity, and adopting relevant methods and techniques to minimize and mitigate adverse effects;

66. *Calls upon* States, either by themselves or through regional fisheries management organizations or arrangements, where these are competent to do so, to take action urgently, and consider on a case-by-case basis and on a scientific basis, including the application of the precautionary approach, the interim prohi-

bition of destructive fishing practices, including bottom trawling that has adverse impacts on vulnerable marine ecosystems, including seamounts, hydrothermal vents and cold water corals located beyond national jurisdiction, until such time as appropriate conservation and management measures have been adopted in accordance with international law;

67. *Calls upon* regional fisheries management organizations or arrangements with the competence to regulate bottom fisheries urgently to adopt, in their regulatory areas, appropriate conservation and management measures, in accordance with international law, to address the impact of destructive fishing practices, including bottom trawling that has adverse impacts on vulnerable marine ecosystems, and to ensure compliance with such measures;

68. *Calls upon* members of regional fisheries management organizations or arrangements without the competence to regulate bottom fisheries and the impacts of fishing on vulnerable marine ecosystems to expand the competence, where appropriate, of their organizations or arrangements in this regard;

69. *Calls upon* States urgently to cooperate in the establishment of new regional fisheries management organizations or arrangements, where necessary and appropriate, with the competence to regulate bottom fisheries and the impacts of fishing on vulnerable marine ecosystems in areas where no such relevant organization or arrangement exists;

70. *Requests* the Secretary-General, in cooperation with the Food and Agriculture Organization of the United Nations, to include in his next report concerning fisheries a section on the actions taken by States and regional fisheries management organizations and arrangements to give effect to paragraphs 66 to 69 above, in order to facilitate discussion of the matters covered in those paragraphs;

71. *Agrees* to review within two years progress on action taken in response to the requests made in paragraphs 66 to 69 above, with a view to further recommendations, where necessary, in areas where arrangements are inadequate;

72. *Calls upon* States, the Food and Agriculture Organization of the United Nations and subregional or regional fisheries management organizations and arrangements to implement fully the International Plan of Action for the Conservation and Management of Sharks as a matter of priority, inter alia, by conducting assessments of shark stocks and developing and implementing national plans of action, recognizing the need of some States, in particular developing States, for assistance in this regard;

73. *Urges* States, including those working through subregional or regional fisheries management organizations and arrangements in implementing the International Plan of Action for the Conservation and Management of Sharks, to collect scientific data regarding shark catches and to consider adopting conservation and management measures, particularly where shark catches from directed and non-directed fisheries have a significant impact on vulnerable or threatened shark stocks, in order to ensure the conservation and management of sharks and their long-term sustainable use, including by banning directed shark fisheries conducted solely for the purpose of harvesting shark fins and by taking measures for other fisheries to minimize

waste and discards from shark catches, and to encourage the full use of dead sharks;

74. *Requests* the Food and Agriculture Organization of the United Nations to develop programmes to assist States, including developing States, in carrying out the tasks mentioned in paragraph 73 above, in particular the adoption of appropriate conservation and management measures, including the banning of directed shark fisheries conducted solely for the purpose of harvesting shark fins;

75. *Reaffirms* the requests contained in paragraph 50 of its resolution 58/14, and invites the Food and Agriculture Organization of the United Nations to report to the Secretary-General, for inclusion in his report on sustainable fisheries, on progress regarding the preparation of the study mentioned therein, as well as the programmes mentioned in paragraph 74 above, and to consider at the sixty-second session of the General Assembly whether additional action is required;

X
Capacity-building

76. *Reiterates* the crucial importance of cooperation by States directly or, as appropriate, through the relevant regional and subregional organizations, and by other international organizations, including the Food and Agriculture Organization of the United Nations through its FishCODE programme, including through financial and/or technical assistance, in accordance with the Agreement, the Compliance Agreement, the Code and the International Plan of Action to Prevent, Deter and Eliminate Illegal, Unreported and Unregulated Fishing and the International Plan of Action for the Conservation and Management of Sharks, to increase the capacity of developing States to achieve the goals and implement the actions called for in the present resolution;

77. *Invites* States and relevant intergovernmental organizations to develop projects, programmes and partnerships with relevant stakeholders and mobilize resources for the effective implementation of the outcome of the African Process for the Protection and Development of the Marine and Coastal Environment, and to consider the inclusion of fisheries components in this work;

78. *Also invites* States and relevant intergovernmental organizations to further implement sustainable fisheries management and improve financial returns from fisheries by supporting and strengthening relevant regional fisheries management organizations, as appropriate, such as the Caribbean Regional Fisheries Mechanism and such agreements as the Convention on the Conservation and Management of Highly Migratory Fish Stocks in the Western and Central Pacific;

XI
Cooperation within the United Nations system

79. *Requests* the relevant parts of the United Nations system, international financial institutions and donor agencies to support increased enforcement and compliance capabilities for regional fisheries management organizations and their member States;

80. *Invites* the Food and Agriculture Organization of the United Nations to continue its cooperative arrangements with United Nations agencies on the implementation of the international plans of action and to report to the Secretary-General, for inclusion in his annual report on sustainable fisheries, on priorities for cooperation and coordination in this work;

81. *Invites* the Division for Ocean Affairs and the Law of the Sea of the Office of Legal Affairs of the Secretariat, the Food and Agriculture Organization of the United Nations and other relevant bodies of the United Nations system to consult and cooperate in the preparation of questionnaires designed to collect information on sustainable fisheries, in order to avoid duplication;

XII
Sixtieth session of the General Assembly

82. *Requests* the Secretary-General to bring the present resolution to the attention of all members of the international community, relevant intergovernmental organizations, the organizations and bodies of the United Nations system, regional and subregional fisheries management organizations and relevant non-governmental organizations, and to invite them to provide the Secretary-General with information relevant to the implementation of the present resolution;

83. *Also requests* the Secretary-General to submit to the General Assembly at its sixtieth session a report on "Sustainable fisheries, including through the 1995 Agreement for the Implementation of the Provisions of the United Nations Convention on the Law of the Sea of 10 December 1982 relating to the Conservation and Management of Straddling Fish Stocks and Highly Migratory Fish Stocks, and related instruments", taking into account information provided by States, relevant specialized agencies, in particular the Food and Agriculture Organization of the United Nations, and other appropriate organs, organizations and programmes of the United Nations system, regional and subregional organizations and arrangements for the conservation and management of straddling fish stocks and highly migratory fish stocks, as well as other relevant intergovernmental bodies and non-governmental organizations, and consisting, inter alia, of elements provided in relevant paragraphs in the present resolution;

84. *Decides* to include in the provisional agenda of its sixtieth session, under the item entitled "Oceans and the law of the sea", the sub-item entitled "Sustainable fisheries, including through the 1995 Agreement for the Implementation of the Provisions of the United Nations Convention on the Law of the Sea of 10 December 1982 relating to the Conservation and Management of Straddling Fish Stocks and Highly Migratory Fish Stocks, and related instruments".

Institutions created by the Convention

International Seabed Authority

Through the International Seabed Authority, established by UNCLOS and the 1994 Implementation Agreement [YUN 1994, p. 1301], States organized and conducted exploration of the resources of the seabed and ocean floor and subsoil beyond the limits of national jurisdiction. In 2004, the Authority, which had 147 members as at 31 December, held its tenth session (Kingston, Jamaica, 24 May–4 June) [ISBA/10/A/12]. Its subsidiary bodies, namely, the Assembly, the Council, the Legal and Technical Commission and the Finance Committee, also met during the session. On 25 and 26 May, the Authority held a commemorative special session to celebrate the tenth anniversary of the Authority's establishment.

The Assembly considered the annual report of the Authority's Secretary-General [ISBA/10/A/3], which recapitulated the work of the Authority since its inception in November 1994. He noted that the organizational phase was complete and that the Authority had entered a new substantive phase. During the next three-year (2005-2007) period, the secretariat's work programme would focus mainly on the Authority's supervisory functions with respect to exploration contracts, the preparation of an appropriate regulatory regime for the future development of sea floor sulphides and deposits of cobalt-rich crusts of the Area (the seabed area beyond the limits of national jurisdiction), and the promotion and encouragement of marine scientific research. A key component of the work programme would be the establishment of a geological model of polymetallic nodule deposits in the Clarion-Clipperton Fracture Zone of the Pacific Ocean; all but one of the seven exploration contracts issued by the Authority were for mining operations there. During 2005-2007, the secretariat would explore the possibility of obtaining funds from the Global Environment Facility to further the international collaborative work required to manage environmental impacts from deep seabed mining, while the Secretary-General would explore the possible secondment of specialized scientific and technical staff from relevant national and international institutions to carry out specific projects within the scope of the work programme and to strengthen the Authority's technical capabilities.

The Assembly considered and approved the Finance Committee's report on the Authority's 2005-2006 budget in the amount of $10,816,700 [ISBA/10/A/6-ISBA/10/C/7]. It elected the Secretary-General of the Authority, Satya N. Nandan (Fiji), to serve a third four-year term, as well as 20 members of the 36-member Council for the period from 1 January 2005 to 31 December 2008. In addition, it approved the December 2003 Supplementary Agreement between the Authority and the Government of Jamaica regarding the headquarters of the Authority and the use of the Jamaica Conference Centre complex [YUN 2003, p. 1353].

The Legal and Technical Commission, reporting to the Council on its work during the current session [ISBA/10/C/4], stated that, as at 19 April 2004, the third set of annual reports had been received from all seven contractors engaged in the exploration of polymetallic nodules, namely: Deep Ocean Resources Development Ltd., the Government of the Republic of Korea, China Ocean Mineral Resources Research and Development Association, State Enterprise Yuzhmorgeologiya (Russian Federation), Interoceanmetal Joint Organization, and l'Institut français de recherche pour l'exploration de la mer/l'Association française pour l'étude et la recherche des nodules [YUN 2001, p. 1235]; and the Government of India [YUN 2002, p. 1321]. Most of the contractors followed the format and structure for annual reports recommended by the Commission in 2002 [ibid.]. The Commission's report and recommendations on the evaluation of the annual reports were contained in a May document [ISBA/10/LTC/3].

During its deliberations on the draft regulations for prospecting and exploration for polymetallic sulphides and cobalt-rich ferromanganese crusts in the Area, the Commission benefited from the advice of three internationally renowned experts who had reviewed the draft, specifically with regard to the size of the exploration area, the system of exploration to be recommended in the light of experience with the system for polymetallic nodules, and the related option. In the light of the advice provided, the Commission reviewed the draft regulations and proposed a size of exploration area for both resources of 10,000 square kilometres, which had the potential for localizing a mineable area with at least 40 million tons of core for each resource and a mining operation lasting 20 years.

International Tribunal for the Law of the Sea

The International Tribunal for the Law of the Sea held its seventeenth (22 March–2 April) and eighteenth (20 September–1 October) sessions at its seat in Hamburg, Germany [SPLOS/122].

The Tribunal met from 30 November to 18 December to deal with the *"Juno Trader" case (Saint Vincent and the Grenadines v. Guinea-Bissau), Prompt Release*. On 18 November, an application under article 292 of the Convention was filed on behalf of Saint Vincent and the Grenadines against Guinea-Bissau for the release of the vessel *Juno Trader*, flying the flag of Saint Vincent and the Grenadines, and its crew. By an Order dated 19 November, the Tribunal's President fixed 1 and 2 December as the dates for the hearing. On 26 November, the agent of Guinea-Bissau requested a postponement of the hearing and, on 29 November, the agent of Saint Vincent and the Grenadines transmitted his observations on that request. Oral proceedings were opened at a public sitting on 1 December, at which the President read the Order of the Tribunal of the same date concerning Guinea-Bissau's request for postponement. By that Order, the Tribunal postponed the continuation of the hearing to 6 December and extended the time limit for the filing of a statement by Guinea-Bissau to 2 December. Oral statements were made by representatives of the parties at four public sittings held on 6 and 7 December. On 18 December, the Tribunal delivered its judgement in the case.

In 2004, the Tribunal received communications from parties on matters relating to compliance with judgements and orders with respect to the *Case concerning Land Reclamation by Singapore in and around the Straits of Johor (Malaysia v. Singapore)* [YUN 2003, p. 1353]. By a joint communication dated 9 January, Malaysia and Singapore submitted to the Tribunal the initial report referred to in article 95, paragraph 1, of the Rules, pursuant to paragraph 106 (3) of the Order of the Tribunal of 8 October 2003. By a joint communication from the parties dated 24 September 2004, the Tribunal received the interim report regarding works in Area D at Pulau Tekong referred to in paragraph 106 (1) (a) (ii) of the Order of the Tribunal dated 8 October 2003. By a joint communication of 8 October 2004, the parties informed the Tribunal that the group of experts established to conduct the study referred to in paragraph 106 (1) (a) (i) of the Tribunal's Order had requested an extension of the deadline for the completion of the study. The Tribunal received the final study of the group of experts by a joint communication from the parties dated 8 November.

On 14 December, the Agreement between the International Tribunal for the Law of the Sea and the Federal Republic of Germany regarding the Headquarters of the Tribunal was signed. The Agreement defined the legal status of the Tribunal in Germany and regulated the relations between them.

Commission on the Limits of the Continental Shelf

In 2004, the Commission on the Limits of the Continental Shelf, established in 1997 [YUN 1997, p. 1362], held its thirteenth (26-30 April) [CLCS/39] and fourteenth (30 August–3 September) [CLCS/42] sessions in New York.

At its thirteenth session, the Commission finalized the review of its procedures by adopting a revised set of Rules of Procedures [CLCS/40], annex III of which contained the "Modus Operandi for the consideration of a submission made to the Commission on the Limits of the Continental Shelf", consolidating the Modus Operandi of the Commission. In addition, the Commission adopted several amendments to the Rules of Pro-

cedure. The revision process was carried out on the basis of the practical experience gained from examining the first (2003) submission, by the Russian Federation, regarding the establishment of the outer limits of the continental shelf beyond 200 nautical miles. The consolidation of all existing procedural rules into a single document would make them easier to understand and facilitate their application and interpretation by coastal States wishing to make submissions.

The Commission was informed that the development of a training manual to assist States in acquiring the knowledge and skills necessary to prepare a submission was at an advanced stage. It was under preparation by the Division for Ocean Affairs and the Law of the Sea of the Office of Legal Affairs, with the assistance of two Commission members as coordinators.

The Commission also signed a letter for transmittal to the Russian Federation in response to its questions regarding the recommendations made on its submission.

At its fourteenth session, the Commission considered, among other agenda items, a submission by Brazil, the training manual on submissions, the projected workload of the Commission and its need for appropriate facilities, the consolidation of the rules of procedure, the election of officers, and vacancies in the subcommission established to consider the Russian Federation's submission.

The nineteenth Hamilton Shirley Amerasinghe Fellowship, established in 1981 [YUN 1981, pp. 130 & 139], was awarded to Milinda Gunetilleke of Sri Lanka.

Other developments related to the Convention

In response to General Assembly resolution 58/240 [YUN 2003, p. 1355], the Secretary-General submitted a March report with a later addendum on oceans and the law of the sea [A/59/62 & Add.1], in which he described the status of UNCLOS and its two implementing Agreements, and discussed issues related to marine space; developments relating to the institutions established by UNCLOS since 1994; capacity-building; developments relating to international shipping activities; maritime security and crimes at sea; the marine environment, marine resources and sustainable development; new sustainable use of the oceans, including the conservation and management of the biological diversity of the seabed in areas beyond national jurisdiction; and international cooperation and coordination.

The Secretary-General noted that maritime security and assistance to persons in distress at sea dominated discussions in several forums in the area of navigation. He said it was paramount for States to take all necessary action to strengthen maritime security to ensure that ships were not used for terrorist or criminal purposes and emphasized that captains of merchant ships were duty-bound to assist persons in distress at sea regardless of their nationality or status.

The Secretary-General further emphasized that increasing awareness of the rich biological diversity of the areas beyond the limits of national jurisdiction, as well as concerns regarding the threats posed to it by human activities, had led to closer examination of the existing conservation and management regimes. UNCLOS had set out a legal framework within which all activities in the oceans were to be conducted, including in areas beyond national jurisdiction, which was supplemented by a number of international instruments adopted at the global and regional levels. He suggested that the General Assembly consider what further action was required, keeping in mind that the protection of vulnerable marine ecosystems and biodiversity depended on the specificities of particular marine areas and on the type of activities that would need to be regulated. As a first step, the location of ecosystems or species and their degree of sensitivity to threats, the specific threats to which such ecosystems or species were highly sensitive, and the activities posing such threats needed to be clearly identified on the basis of sound science and the precautionary approach. Second, priorities for action should include the identification of existing and/or required mechanisms to confront and alleviate threats in those areas and of the authorities responsible for dealing with those threats.

The Secretary-General recommended that States parties review their national legislation to ensure its conformity with the Convention; review any declarations made at the time of signature or ratification or accession to ensure that they were in accordance with the Convention; and submit the charts and/or coordinates required under the Convention. Other recommendations called on States to deposit their oceans-related legislation with the Division for Ocean Affairs and the Law of the Sea for publication in the Law of the Sea Bulletin and on its website; endeavour to establish the limits of their maritime zones and to settle any maritime boundaries with their neighbours; consider establishing national marine policies integrating all aspects of ocean affairs; endeavour to coordinate better the work of their various departments dealing with ocean affairs in order to manage the areas and activities under their national jurisdiction in an integrated manner; and be guided by those same consistent,

integrated oceans policies in their cooperation with other States. International organizations were to collect national legislation in their areas of competence for publication on their websites. Since some States might lack the technical, administrative or financial capacity to implement the Convention, capacity-building by the United Nations and other international organizations was essential to assist individual States and to ensure the development of an integrated global regime for the oceans.

Marine environment: Global Marine Assessment

Further responding to General Assembly resolution 58/240 [YUN 2003, p. 1355], the Secretary-General submitted a July report [A/59/126] providing an account of the discussions that took place at the Global Marine Assessment (GMA) International Workshop (New York, 8-11 June), convened in conjunction with the fifth meeting of the United Nations Open-ended Informal Consultative Process on Oceans and the Law of the Sea (7-11 June). The Workshop further considered and reviewed a draft document [A/AC.271/WP.1] prepared by a group of experts, as requested by resolution 58/240, on the scope, general framework and outline of the regular process of GMA reporting; peer review; secretariat; capacity-building; and funding. It also considered the comments sent by States, intergovernmental organizations and non-governmental organizations (NGOs) [A/AC.271/WP.2 & Add.1].

The GMA Workshop recommended that the Assembly invite the Secretary-General to establish an inter-agency task force to initiate and coordinate the next stage of preparatory work necessary to establish the formal GMA and inform Member States accordingly. For the start-up phase, the task force should first organize an "Assessment of Assessments" aimed at: assembling information about scientific assessments (including assessments covering social and economic issues) relevant to GMA that had already been carried out under the purview of UN agencies and global treaty organizations, regional organizations, national Governments and other organizations as appropriate; making a critical appraisal of those assessments; and assessing how well they had been communicated to policy makers at the national, regional and global levels. Second, in the light of that assessment, the task force should consult with Member States and relevant regional organizations to identify where the technical or scientific capacity to undertake marine assessments needed strengthening. Third, it should prepare summary information on relevant existing intergovernmental regional organizations and arrangements, and current scientific work. In carrying out its work, the task force should conform to the 2002 Johannesburg Plan of Implementation [YUN 2002, p. 822] and relevant Assembly resolutions. It should communicate its plans and progress to all Member States on a regular basis and provide them the opportunity to comment on and contribute to the development of the work at appropriate points.

United Nations Open-ended Informal Consultative Process

In accordance with General Assembly resolution 58/240 [YUN 2003, p. 1355], the fifth meeting of the United Nations Open-ended Informal Consultative Process on Oceans and the Law of the Sea (New York, 7-11 June) [A/59/122] focused its discussions on new sustainable uses of the oceans, including the conservation and management of the biological diversity of the seabed in the areas beyond national jurisdiction. It also discussed the report of the Consultative Group on Flag State Implementation [A/59/63 & Corr.1], which conducted a thorough investigation into all aspects—political, legal, economic and social—of the issues raised by the lack of control by flag States over their vessels, in contravention of international rules and standards. The Group's report contained a list of flag State obligations under UNCLOS, the United Nations Fish Stocks Agreement and a broad range of other international instruments. Based on its discussions and also with respect to Assembly resolution 54/14 [YUN 2003, p. 1347], the Consultative Process presented a series of agreed recommendations for the Assembly's consideration.

Established by Assembly resolution 54/33 [YUN 1999, p. 994] to facilitate the Assembly's annual review of developments in ocean affairs, the Consultative Process noted that the period since its fourth meeting [YUN 2003, p. 1355] had seen increasing concerns expressed by many States, scientists and several NGOs over the ineffective conservation and management of the biodiversity of the seabed beyond national jurisdiction. That was a part of the ocean environment that remained largely unexplored but contained areas rich in unique and diverse species and ecosystems, with high levels of endemism and, in some instances, with a relationship to the non-living resources of the Area.

GENERAL ASSEMBLY ACTION

On 17 November [meeting 56], the General Assembly adopted **resolution 59/24** [draft: A/59/L.22 & Add.1] by recorded vote (141-1-2) [agenda item 49 (a)].

Oceans and the law of the sea

The General Assembly,

Recalling its resolutions 49/28 of 6 December 1994, 52/26 of 26 November 1997, 54/33 of 24 November 1999, 57/141 of 12 December 2002, 58/240 of 23 December 2003 and other relevant resolutions adopted subsequent to the entry into force of the United Nations Convention on the Law of the Sea ("the Convention") on 16 November 1994,

Emphasizing the universal and unified character of the Convention and its fundamental importance for the maintenance and strengthening of international peace and security, as well as for the sustainable development of the oceans and seas,

Reaffirming that the Convention sets out the legal framework within which all activities in the oceans and seas must be carried out and is of strategic importance as the basis for national, regional and global action and cooperation in the marine sector, and that its integrity needs to be maintained, as recognized also by the United Nations Conference on Environment and Development in chapter 17 of Agenda 21,

Noting with satisfaction the tenth anniversary of the entry into force of the Convention on 16 November 2004, and recognizing the pre-eminent contribution provided by the Convention to the strengthening of peace, security, cooperation and friendly relations among all nations in conformity with the principles of justice and equal rights and to the promotion of the economic and social advancement of all peoples of the world, in accordance with the purposes and principles of the United Nations as set forth in the Charter of the United Nations,

Conscious that the problems of ocean space are closely interrelated and need to be considered as a whole through an integrated, interdisciplinary and intersectoral approach,

Reaffirming the need to improve cooperation and coordination at all levels, in accordance with the Convention, in order to address all aspects of oceans and seas in an integrated manner and to promote the integrated management and sustainable development of the oceans and seas,

Recalling the essential role of international cooperation and coordination at all levels to support and supplement the efforts of each State in promoting the implementation and observance of the Convention, including the integrated management and sustainable development of coastal and marine areas,

Reiterating the essential need for capacity-building to ensure that all States, especially developing countries, in particular the least developed countries and small island developing States, as well as coastal African States, are able both to implement the Convention and to benefit from the sustainable development of the oceans and seas, as well as to participate fully in global and regional forums and processes dealing with oceans and law of the sea issues,

Recognizing the important role that the competent international organizations have in relation to ocean affairs, in implementing the Convention and in promoting the sustainable development of the oceans and seas,

Emphasizing the need to strengthen the ability of competent international organizations to contribute, at the global, regional, subregional and bilateral levels, through cooperation programmes with Governments, to the development of national capacity in marine science and the sustainable management of the oceans and their resources,

Recalling that marine science, by improving knowledge, through sustained research efforts and the evaluation of monitoring results, and applying such knowledge to management and decision-making, is important for eradicating poverty, contributing to food security, conserving the world's marine environment and resources, helping to understand, predict and respond to natural events, and promoting the sustainable development of the oceans and seas,

Recalling also its decision to establish a regular process under the United Nations for global reporting and assessment of the state of the marine environment, including socio-economic aspects, both current and foreseeable, building on existing regional assessments, in its resolutions 57/141 and 58/240, as recommended by the World Summit on Sustainable Development, noting the work of the International Workshop, held in conjunction with the fifth meeting of the United Nations Open-ended Informal Consultative Process on Oceans and the Law of the Sea ("the Consultative Process") held from 8 to 11 June 2004, reaffirming its support for this objective, and noting the need for cooperation among all States to this end,

Reiterating its concern at the adverse impacts on the marine environment and biodiversity, in particular on vulnerable marine ecosystems, including corals, of human activities, such as overutilization of living marine resources, the use of destructive practices, physical impacts by ships, the introduction of alien invasive species and marine pollution from all sources, including from land-based sources and vessels, in particular through the illegal release of oil and other harmful substances and from dumping, including the dumping of hazardous waste such as radioactive materials, nuclear waste and dangerous chemicals,

Recognizing that hydrographic surveys and nautical charting are critical to the safety of navigation and life at sea, environmental protection, including vulnerable marine ecosystems and the economics of the global shipping industry, and recognizing in this regard that the move towards electronic charting not only provides significantly increased benefits for safe navigation and management of ship movement, but also provides data and information that can be used for sustainable fisheries activities and other sectoral uses of the marine environment, the delimitation of maritime boundaries and environmental protection,

Noting the important role of the Commission on the Limits of the Continental Shelf ("the Commission") in assisting States parties in the implementation of the Convention, through the examination of submissions by coastal States regarding the outer limits of the continental shelf beyond 200 nautical miles, and also noting the need to ensure the effective functioning of the Commission and its subcommissions, in particular the participation of the members of the Commission in its subcommissions,

Taking note of the report on the work of the fifth meeting of the Consultative Process, established by the General Assembly in its resolution 54/33 in order to facilitate the annual review by the Assembly of developments in ocean affairs and extended for three years by its resolution 57/141,

Taking note also of the report of the Secretary-General, and emphasizing in this regard the critical role of the annual comprehensive report of the Secretary-General, which integrates information on developments relating to the implementation of the Convention and the work of the Organization, its specialized agencies and other institutions in the field of ocean affairs and the law of the sea at the global and regional levels, and as a result constitutes the basis for the annual consideration and review of developments relating to ocean affairs and the law of the sea by the General Assembly as the global institution having the competence to undertake such a review,

Noting the responsibilities of the Secretary-General under the Convention and related resolutions of the General Assembly, in particular resolutions 49/28, 52/26 and 54/33, and in this context the increase in responsibilities of the Division for Ocean Affairs and the Law of the Sea of the Office of Legal Affairs of the Secretariat, in particular in view of the growing involvement of the Division with new developments such as the regular process for the global reporting and assessment of the state of the marine environment, including socio-economic aspects, with increasing capacity-building activities and assistance to the Commission, and the role of the Division in inter-agency coordination and cooperation,

Emphasizing that ships and watercraft of all descriptions and ages hold essential information on the history of humankind and that archaeological heritage is a non-renewable resource, deposited over thousands of years, but vulnerable to destruction through modern technologies,

I

Implementation of the Convention and related agreements and instruments

1. *Calls upon* all States that have not done so, in order to achieve the goal of universal participation, to become parties to the Convention, and the Agreement relating to the Implementation of Part XI of the United Nations Convention on the Law of the Sea of 10 December 1982 ("the Agreement");

2. *Reaffirms* the unified character of the Convention;

3. *Calls upon* all States that have not done so to become parties to the Agreement for the Implementation of the Provisions of the United Nations Convention on the Law of the Sea of 10 December 1982 relating to the Conservation and Management of Straddling Fish Stocks and Highly Migratory Fish Stocks ("the Fish Stocks Agreement");

4. *Once again calls upon* States to harmonize, as a matter of priority, their national legislation with the provisions of the Convention, to ensure the consistent application of those provisions and to ensure also that any declarations or statements that they have made or make when signing, ratifying or acceding to the Convention do not purport to exclude or to modify the legal effect of the provisions of the Convention in their application to the State concerned and to withdraw any such declarations or statements;

5. *Calls upon* States parties to the Convention to deposit with the Secretary-General charts or lists of geo-

graphical coordinates, as provided for in the Convention;

6. *Requests* the Secretary-General to improve the existing Geographic Information System for the deposit by States of charts and geographical coordinates concerning maritime zones, including lines of delimitation, submitted in compliance with the Convention, and to give due publicity thereto, in particular by implementing, in cooperation with relevant international organizations, such as the International Hydrographic Organization, the technical standards for the collection, storage and dissemination of the information deposited, in order to ensure compatibility among the Geographic Information System, electronic nautical charts and other systems developed by these organizations;

7. *Urges* all States to cooperate, directly or through competent international bodies, in taking measures to protect and preserve objects of an archaeological and historical nature found at sea, in conformity with article 303 of the Convention;

II
Capacity-building

8. *Calls upon* bilateral and multilateral donor agencies and international financial institutions to keep their programmes systematically under review to ensure the availability in all States, particularly in developing States, of the economic, legal, navigational, scientific and technical skills necessary for the full implementation of the Convention and the objectives of the present resolution as well as the sustainable development of the oceans and seas nationally, regionally and globally, and in so doing to bear in mind the rights of landlocked developing States;

9. *Encourages* intensified efforts to build capacity for developing countries, in particular for the least developed countries and small island developing States, as well as coastal African States, to improve hydrographic services and the production of nautical charts, including the mobilization of resources and building of capacity with support from international financial institutions and the donor community, recognizing that economies of scale can apply in some instances at the regional level through shared facilities, technical capabilities and information for the provision of hydrographic services and the preparation of and access to nautical charts;

10. *Calls upon* States and international financial institutions, including through bilateral, regional and global cooperation programmes and technical partnerships, to continue to strengthen capacity-building activities, in particular in developing countries, in the field of marine scientific research by, inter alia, training the necessary skilled personnel, providing the necessary equipment, facilities and vessels and transferring environmentally sound technologies;

11. *Encourages* the Intergovernmental Oceanographic Commission of the United Nations Educational, Scientific and Cultural Organization to continue to disseminate and implement the Criteria and Guidelines on the Transfer of Marine Technology, approved by the Assembly of the Oceanographic Commission at its twenty-second session, in 2003;

12. *Encourages* States to assist developing States, and especially the least developed States and small island developing States, as well as coastal African States, on a bilateral and, where appropriate, regional level, in the preparation of submissions to the Commission, including the assessment of the nature of the continental shelf of a coastal State made in the form of a desktop study, and the mapping of the outer limits of its continental shelf;

III
Trust funds and fellowships

13. *Welcomes* recent capacity-building initiatives, and in this context takes note with satisfaction of the conclusion of an arrangement between the United Nations and the Food and Agriculture Organization of the United Nations regarding the administration of the Assistance Fund established under Part VII of the Fish Stocks Agreement, and the conclusion of a capacity-building trust fund project agreement between the United Nations and the Nippon Foundation of Japan, focusing on human resources development for developing coastal States parties and non-parties to the Convention in the field of ocean affairs and the law of the sea or related disciplines;

14. *Recognizes* the importance of assisting developing States, in particular the least developed States and small island developing States, in implementing the Convention, and urges States, intergovernmental organizations and agencies, national institutions, nongovernmental organizations and international financial institutions, as well as natural and juridical persons, to make voluntary financial or other contributions to the trust funds, as referred to in resolution 57/141, established for this purpose;

15. *Also recognizes* the importance of the Hamilton Shirley Amerasinghe Memorial Fellowship Programme on the Law of the Sea established by the General Assembly in its resolution 35/116 of 10 December 1980, and urges Member States and others in a position to do so to contribute to the further development of the Fellowship Programme;

IV
Meeting of States Parties

16. *Takes note* of the report of the fourteenth Meeting of States Parties to the Convention;

17. *Requests* the Secretary-General to convene the fifteenth Meeting of States Parties to the Convention in New York from 16 to 24 June 2005 and to provide the services required;

V
Settlement of disputes

18. *Notes with satisfaction* the continued and significant contribution of the International Tribunal for the Law of the Sea ("the Tribunal") to the peaceful settlement of disputes in accordance with Part XV of the Convention, and underlines the important role and authority of the Tribunal concerning the interpretation or application of the Convention and the Agreement;

19. *Equally pays tribute* to the important and longstanding role of the International Court of Justice with regard to the peaceful settlement of disputes concerning the law of the sea;

20. *Encourages* States parties to the Convention that have not yet done so to consider making a written declaration choosing from the means set out in article 287 of the Convention for the settlement of disputes con-

cerning the interpretation or application of the Convention and the Agreement;

21. *Recalls* the obligation under article 296 of the Convention requiring all parties to a dispute before a court or a tribunal referred to in article 287 of the Convention to comply promptly with any decisions rendered by such court or tribunal;

22. *Encourages* States parties to the Convention that have not yet done so to nominate conciliators and arbitrators in accordance with annexes V and VII to the Convention, and requests the Secretary-General to continue to update and circulate lists of these conciliators and arbitrators on a regular basis;

VI
The Area

23. *Notes with satisfaction* the progress of the discussions on issues relating to the regulations for prospecting and exploration for polymetallic sulphides and cobalt-rich ferromanganese crusts in the Area, and reiterates the importance of the ongoing elaboration by the International Seabed Authority ("the Authority"), pursuant to article 145 of the Convention, of rules, regulations and procedures to ensure the effective protection of the marine environment, the protection and conservation of the natural resources of the Area and the prevention of damage to its flora and fauna from harmful effects that may arise from activities in the Area;

24. *Takes note* of the Workshop for the establishment of environmental baselines at deep seafloor cobalt-rich crusts and deep seabed polymetallic sulphide mine sites in the Area for the purpose of evaluating the likely effects of exploration and exploitation on the marine environment, held in Kingston from 6 to 10 September 2004;

VII
Effective functioning of the Authority and the Tribunal

25. *Appeals* to all States parties to the Convention to pay their assessed contributions to the Authority and to the Tribunal in full and on time;

26. *Calls upon* States that have not done so to consider ratifying or acceding to the Agreement on the Privileges and Immunities of the Tribunal and to the Protocol on the Privileges and Immunities of the Authority;

VIII
The continental shelf and the work of the Commission

27. *Encourages* States parties to the Convention that are in a position to do so to make every effort to make submissions to the Commission regarding the establishment of the outer limits of the continental shelf beyond 200 nautical miles within the time period established by the Convention, taking into account the decision of the eleventh Meeting of States Parties to the Convention;

28. *Notes with satisfaction* the progress in the work of the Commission, especially that the consideration of the first submissions regarding the establishment of the outer limits of the continental shelf beyond 200 nautical miles has begun, and that a number of States have advised of their intention to make submissions in the near future;

29. *Approves* the convening by the Secretary-General of the fifteenth session of the Commission in New York from 4 to 22 April 2005, and of the sixteenth session of the Commission from 29 August to 16 September 2005, on the understanding that the second and third weeks of each session will be used by the Commission for a technical examination of submissions at the Geographic Information System Laboratory and other technical facilities at the Division for Ocean Affairs and the Law of the Sea;

30. *Urges* the Secretary-General to take all necessary actions to ensure that the Commission can fulfil the functions entrusted to it under the Convention;

31. *Requests* the Secretary-General to submit to the General Assembly at its sixtieth session proposals on how the requirements of the Commission could be best accommodated, taking into account the concerns expressed in the statement by the Chairman of the Commission at its fourteenth session, regarding the expectation that new submissions will require concomitant meetings of several subcommissions for their examination;

32. *Also requests* the Secretary-General, in cooperation with States and relevant international organizations and institutions, to consider developing and making available training courses, based on the outline for a five-day training course prepared by the Commission in order to facilitate the preparation of submissions in accordance with its Scientific and Technical Guidelines, and welcomes the progress made by the Division for Ocean Affairs and the Law of the Sea in preparing a training manual to assist States in preparation of submissions to the Commission;

33. *Encourages* States to exchange views in order to increase understanding of issues arising from the application of article 76 of the Convention, thus facilitating preparation of submissions by States, in particular developing States, to the Commission, and welcomes initiatives in this regard, including the Conference on Legal and Scientific Aspects of Continental Shelf Limits, held in Reykjavik from 25 to 27 June 2003, the proceedings of which have been published and distributed worldwide;

IX
Maritime safety and security and flag State implementation

34. *Encourages* States to ratify or accede to international agreements addressing the safety and security of navigation and to adopt the necessary measures consistent with the Convention, aimed at implementing and enforcing the rules contained in those agreements;

35. *Welcomes* the adoption by the International Maritime Organization of Guidelines on Places of Refuge for Ships in Need of Assistance, encourages States to draw up plans and to establish procedures to implement those Guidelines, and invites States to participate in the consideration of those instruments by the International Maritime Organization;

36. *Invites* the International Hydrographic Organization and the International Maritime Organization to continue their coordinated efforts, to jointly adopt measures with a view to encouraging greater international cooperation and coordination for the transition to electronic nautical charts and to increase the coverage of hydrographic information on a global basis, es-

pecially in the areas of international navigation and ports and where there are vulnerable or protected marine areas;

37. *Welcomes* the adoption by the General Conference of the International Atomic Energy Agency at its forty-eighth session of resolution GC(48)/RES/10, concerning measures to strengthen international cooperation in nuclear, radiation and transport safety and waste management, including those aspects relating to maritime transport, and also welcomes the approval of the Action Plan for the Safety of Transport of Radioactive Materials by the Board of Governors of the Agency in March 2004;

38. *Once again urges* flag States without an effective maritime administration and appropriate legal frameworks to establish or enhance the necessary infrastructure, legislative and enforcement capabilities to ensure effective compliance with, and implementation and enforcement of, their responsibilities under international law and, until such action is undertaken, to consider declining the granting of the right to fly their flag to new vessels, suspending their registry or not opening a registry;

39. *Welcomes* the report of the Consultative Group on Flag State Implementation, and invites all concerned organizations to disseminate it widely;

40. *Also welcomes* the progress made by the International Maritime Organization on the establishment and further development of a voluntary International Maritime Organization member State audit scheme, in such a manner as not to exclude the possibility in the future of it becoming mandatory;

41. *Requests* that the Secretary-General report to the General Assembly at its sixty-first session on the study undertaken by the International Maritime Organization in cooperation with other competent international organizations following the invitation extended to it in resolution 58/240 and resolution 58/14 of 24 November 2003 to examine and clarify the role of the "genuine link" in relation to the duty of flag States to exercise effective control over ships flying their flag, including fishing vessels, and the potential consequences of non-compliance with duties and obligations of flag States described in relevant international instruments;

42. *Encourages* relevant international organizations to further develop ideas to devise means of discouraging owners and operators from non-compliance with the requirements imposed by flag States in carrying out their duties and obligations under relevant international instruments;

43. *Welcomes* the progress made by the International Labour Organization in the preparation of a consolidated maritime labour convention;

44. *Recognizes* the important role of port State control in promoting the effective enforcement by flag States of, and compliance by shipowners and charterers with, flag States' and internationally agreed safety, labour and pollution standards, as well as maritime security regulations and conservation and management measures, and encourages Member States to improve the exchange of appropriate information between port States control authorities;

45. *Invites* the International Maritime Organization to take steps within its mandate to harmonize, coordinate and evaluate port State control in relation to

safety and pollution standards, as well as maritime security regulations and, in collaboration with the International Labour Organization, labour standards so as to promote the implementation of globally agreed minimum standards by all States, and invites the Food and Agriculture Organization of the United Nations to continue its work in promoting port State measures in relation to fishing vessels in order to combat illegal, unreported and unregulated fishing;

46. *Calls upon* flag and port States to take all measures consistent with international law necessary to prevent the operation of sub-standard vessels and illegal, unreported and unregulated fishing activities;

47. *Urges* all States, in cooperation with the International Maritime Organization, to combat piracy and armed robbery at sea by adopting measures, including those relating to assistance with capacity-building through training of seafarers, port staff and enforcement personnel in the prevention, reporting and investigation of incidents, bringing the alleged perpetrators to justice, in accordance with international law, and by adopting national legislation, as well as providing enforcement vessels and equipment and guarding against fraudulent ship registration;

48. *Welcomes* the progress in regional cooperation in the prevention and suppression of piracy and armed robbery at sea in some geographical areas, and urges States to give urgent attention to promoting, adopting and implementing cooperation agreements, in particular at the regional level in high-risk areas;

49. *Notes* the concerns of the Council and the Secretary-General of the International Maritime Organization with regard to keeping shipping lanes of strategic importance and significance safe and open to international maritime traffic and thereby ensuring the uninterrupted flow of traffic, and welcomes the request of the Council in this regard that the Secretary-General of the International Maritime Organization continue work on the issue in collaboration with parties concerned and report developments to the Council at its next session;

50. *Urges* States to become parties to the Convention for the Suppression of Unlawful Acts against the Safety of Maritime Navigation and its Protocol, invites States to participate in the review of those instruments by the Legal Committee of the International Maritime Organization to strengthen the means of combating such unlawful acts, including terrorist acts, and also urges States to take appropriate measures to ensure the effective implementation of those instruments, in particular through the adoption of legislation, where appropriate, aimed at ensuring that there is a proper framework for responses to incidents of armed robbery and terrorist acts at sea;

51. *Welcomes* the entry into force of the International Ship and Port Facility Security Code and related amendments to the International Convention for the Safety of Life at Sea on 1 July 2004, as well as the adoption by the International Maritime Organization of the theme "International Maritime Organization 2004: Focus on Maritime Security" for the twenty-seventh World Maritime Day, and urges all States to work with that organization to promote safe and secure shipping while ensuring freedom of navigation;

52. *Also welcomes* the entry into force of the Protocol against the Smuggling of Migrants by Land, Sea and

Air, supplementing the United Nations Convention against Transnational Organized Crime and of the Protocol to Prevent, Suppress and Punish Trafficking in Persons, Especially Women and Children, supplementing the United Nations Convention against Transnational Organized Crime, and urges States that have not yet done so to become parties to the Protocols and to take appropriate measures to ensure their effective implementation;

53. *Further welcomes* the adoption by the International Maritime Organization of amendments to the International Convention on Maritime Search and Rescue and to the International Convention for the Safety of Life at Sea relating to the delivery of persons rescued at sea to a place of safety and of the associated Guidelines on the Treatment of Persons Rescued at Sea;

X

Marine environment, marine resources, marine biodiversity and the protection of vulnerable marine ecosystems

54. *Emphasizes once again* the importance of the implementation of Part XII of the Convention in order to protect and preserve the marine environment and its living marine resources against pollution and physical degradation, and calls upon all States to cooperate and take measures, directly or through competent international organizations, for the protection and preservation of the marine environment;

55. *Calls upon* all States that have not yet done so to become parties to and implement the 1996 Protocol to the Convention on the Prevention of Marine Pollution by Dumping of Wastes and Other Matter, 1972, and protect and preserve the marine environment from all sources of pollution and take effective measures, according to their scientific, technical and economic capabilities, to prevent, reduce and, where practicable, eliminate pollution caused by dumping or incineration at sea of wastes or other matter;

56. *Welcomes* the adoption by the International Maritime Organization of amendments to the International Convention for the Prevention of Pollution from Ships of 1973, as modified by the Protocol of 1978 relating thereto, providing for the accelerated phase-out of single-hull tankers and a phase-out scheme for the carriage of heavy grade fuel oil in single-hull tankers;

57. *Also welcomes* the adoption by the International Maritime Organization of the International Convention for the Control and Management of Ships' Ballast Water and Sediments, and calls upon States to become parties to that Convention;

58. *Calls upon* all States that have not yet done so to become parties to the International Convention on the Control of Harmful Anti-fouling Systems on Ships;

59. *Welcomes* the adoption of the Protocol establishing an International Oil Pollution Compensation Supplementary Fund, and calls upon States to become parties to that Protocol;

60. *Encourages* States, in accordance with the Convention and other relevant instruments, either bilaterally or regionally, to jointly develop and promote contingency plans for responding to pollution incidents, as well as other incidents that are likely to have significant adverse effects on the marine environment and biodiversity;

61. *Notes with interest* the decision taken at the fifty-second session of the Marine Environment Protection Committee of the International Maritime Organization to designate the Western European Waters as a particularly sensitive sea area;

62. *Welcomes* the entry into force of the Stockholm Convention on Persistent Organic Pollutants, and calls upon all States that have not yet done so to become parties to that Convention;

63. *Calls upon* States to continue to prioritize action on marine pollution from land-based sources as part of their national sustainable development strategies and programmes, in an integrated and inclusive manner, and to advance the implementation of the Global Programme of Action for the Protection of the Marine Environment from Land-based Activities and the Montreal Declaration on the Protection of the Marine Environment from Land-based Activities;

64. *Welcomes* the adoption of resolution A.962(23) by the International Maritime Organization on 5 December 2003, entitled "International Maritime Organization Guidelines on Ship Recycling", and calls upon States to follow these Guidelines in order to minimize marine pollution;

65. *Also welcomes* the continued work of States, the United Nations Environment Programme and regional organizations in the implementation of the Global Programme of Action for the Protection of the Marine Environment from Land-based Activities, and encourages increased emphasis on the link between freshwater, the coastal zone and marine resources in the implementation of international development goals, including those contained in the United Nations Millennium Declaration and of the time-bound targets in the Plan of Implementation of the World Summit on Sustainable Development ("Johannesburg Plan of Implementation"), in particular the target on sanitation, and the Monterrey Consensus of the International Conference on Financing for Development;

66. *Calls upon* States to implement strategies and programmes for an integrated ecosystem-based approach to management, developed by the Conference of the Parties to the Convention on Biological Diversity, the Food and Agriculture Organization of the United Nations and other relevant global and regional organizations, and urges those organizations to cooperate in the development of practical guidance to assist States in this regard;

67. *Takes note* of part two of the addendum to the report of the Secretary-General on oceans and the law of the sea describing the threats and risks to vulnerable and threatened marine ecosystems and biodiversity in areas beyond national jurisdiction, as well as details of conservation and management measures addressing these issues, prepared pursuant to the request contained in paragraph 52 of resolution 58/240;

68. *Reaffirms* the need for States and competent international organizations to urgently consider ways to integrate and improve, on a scientific basis and in accordance with the Convention and related agreements and instruments, the management of risks to the marine biodiversity of seamounts, cold water corals, hydrothermal vents and certain other underwater features;

69. *Welcomes* decision VII/5 on marine and coastal biological diversity adopted at the seventh meeting of

the Conference of the Parties to the Convention on Biological Diversity;

70. *Calls upon* States and international organizations to urgently take action to address, in accordance with international law, destructive practices that have adverse impacts on marine biodiversity and ecosystems, including seamounts, hydrothermal vents and cold water corals;

71. *Welcomes* decision VII/28 adopted at the seventh meeting of the Conference of the Parties to the Convention on Biological Diversity in which the Conference decided to establish an ad hoc open-ended working group on protected areas, and encourages the participation of oceans experts in the working group;

72. *Reaffirms* the need for States to continue their efforts to develop and facilitate the use of diverse approaches and tools for conserving and managing vulnerable marine ecosystems, including the possible establishment of marine protected areas, consistent with international law and based on the best scientific information available, and the development of representative networks of any such marine protected areas by 2012;

73. *Decides* to establish an Ad Hoc Open-ended Informal Working Group to study issues relating to the conservation and sustainable use of marine biological diversity beyond areas of national jurisdiction:

(a) To survey the past and present activities of the United Nations and other relevant international organizations with regard to the conservation and sustainable use of marine biological diversity beyond areas of national jurisdiction;

(b) To examine the scientific, technical, economic, legal, environmental, socio-economic and other aspects of these issues;

(c) To identify key issues and questions where more detailed background studies would facilitate consideration by States of these issues;

(d) To indicate, where appropriate, possible options and approaches to promote international cooperation and coordination for the conservation and sustainable use of marine biological diversity beyond areas of national jurisdiction;

74. *Requests* the Secretary-General to report on the issues referred to in paragraph 73 above in the context of his report on oceans and the law of the sea to the General Assembly at its sixtieth session, in order to assist the Ad Hoc Open-ended Informal Working Group in preparing its agenda, in consultation with all relevant international bodies; to convene the meeting of the Working Group in New York not later than six months after the release of the report; and to arrange support for the performance of its work to be provided by the Division for Ocean Affairs and the Law of the Sea;

75. *Encourages* States to include relevant experts in their delegations attending the meeting of the Working Group;

76. *Recognizes* the importance of making the outcomes of the Working Group widely available;

77. *Urges* States and relevant global and regional bodies to enhance their cooperation in the protection and preservation of mangroves, seagrass beds and coral reefs, including through the exchange of information;

78. *Reiterates its support* for the International Coral Reef Initiative, takes note of the tenth International Coral Reef Symposium, held in Okinawa, Japan, in 2004, supports the work under the Jakarta Mandate on Marine and Coastal Biological Diversity, and the elaborated Programme of Work on Marine and Coastal Biological Diversity, and notes the progress that the International Coral Reef Initiative and other relevant bodies have made to incorporate cold water coral ecosystems into their programmes;

79. *Encourages* States to cooperate, directly or through competent international bodies, in exchanging information in the event of accidents involving foreign vessels on coral reefs and in promoting the development of economic assessment techniques for both restoration and non-use values of coral reef systems;

80. *Emphasizes* the need to mainstream sustainable coral reef management and integrated watershed management into national development strategies, as well as into the activities of relevant United Nations agencies and programmes, international financial institutions and the donor community;

XI
Marine science

81. *Calls upon* States, individually, or in collaboration with each other or with relevant international organizations and bodies, to improve understanding and knowledge of the deep sea, including, in particular, the extent and vulnerability of deep sea biodiversity and ecosystems, by increasing their marine scientific research activities in accordance with the Convention;

82. *Notes* the potential for gas hydrates as one source for energy development, as well as the possible associated risks, including those in the context of climate change, and encourages States and, if appropriate, the Authority and the international scientific community to continue to cooperate in deepening the understanding of the issues and in investigating the feasibility, methodology, safety and environmental impacts of the extraction of gas hydrates from the seabed, their distribution and their use;

83. *Also notes* the potential for cobalt-rich ferromanganese crusts and polymetallic sulphides as important sources of minerals, and in this context encourages States, the Authority and the scientific community to cooperate to explore this potential and to minimize the environmental impacts of the exploration;

XII
Regular process for global reporting and assessment of the state of the marine environment, including socio-economic aspects

84. *Takes note* of the report on the International Workshop on the regular process for global reporting and assessment of the state of the marine environment, including socio-economic aspects ("the regular process"), including its draft conclusions, convened to consider and review the draft document prepared by the group of experts;

85. *Recognizes* the urgent need to initiate a start-up phase, the "Assessment of Assessments", as a preparatory stage towards the establishment of the regular process provided for in the Johannesburg Plan of Implementation and resolutions 57/141 and 58/240;

86. *Requests* the Secretary-General to convene the second International Workshop on the regular process for global reporting and assessment of the state of the marine environment, including socio-economic aspects, from 13 to 15 June 2005 with representatives from States, relevant organizations, agencies and programmes of the United Nations system, other competent intergovernmental organizations and relevant non-governmental organizations, to continue considering issues relating to the establishment of the process, including the scope of the process and a task force to initiate the start-up phase, the "Assessment of Assessments";

87. *Also requests* the Secretary-General to report on progress relating to establishment of the aforementioned regular process in his annual report to the General Assembly at its sixtieth session;

XIII
Regional cooperation

88. *Emphasizes once again* the importance of regional organizations and arrangements for cooperation and coordination in integrated oceans management, and, where there are separate regional structures for different aspects of oceans management, such as environmental protection and conservation of marine ecosystems, fisheries management, navigation, scientific research and maritime delimitation, calls for those different structures, where appropriate, to work together for optimal cooperation and coordination;

89. *Notes* that there have been a number of initiatives at the regional level, in various regions, to further the implementation of the Convention, takes note in this context of the Caribbean-focused Assistance Fund, which is intended to facilitate, mainly through technical assistance, the voluntary undertaking of maritime delimitation negotiations between Caribbean States, takes note once again of the Fund for Peace: Peaceful Settlement of Territorial Disputes, established by the General Assembly of the Organization of American States in 2000 as a primary mechanism, given its broader regional scope, for the prevention and resolution of pending territorial, land border and maritime boundary disputes, and calls upon States and others in a position to do so to contribute to these funds;

XIV
Open-ended informal consultative process on oceans and the law of the sea

90. *Requests* the Secretary-General to convene the sixth meeting of the Consultative Process in New York from 6 to 10 June 2005 and to provide it with the necessary facilities for the performance of its work and to arrange for support, as appropriate;

91. *Recalls* its decision to further review the effectiveness and utility of the Consultative Process at its sixtieth session;

92. *Recommends* that, in its deliberations on the report of the Secretary-General on oceans and the law of the sea at its meeting, the Consultative Process should organize its discussions around the following areas:

(*a*) Fisheries and their contribution to sustainable development;

(*b*) Marine debris;

as well as issues discussed at previous meetings;

XV
Inter-agency coordination and cooperation

93. *Notes* the establishment of the Oceans and Coastal Areas Network (UN-Oceans), a new inter-agency mechanism for coordination and cooperation on issues relating to oceans and coastal issues, called for in paragraph 69 of resolution 58/240;

94. *Urges* the close and continuous involvement in UN-Oceans of all relevant United Nations programmes, funds and the specialized agencies and other organizations of the United Nations system and the participation of international financial institutions, relevant intergovernmental and other organizations, as well as the Authority and the secretariats of multilateral environmental agreements;

95. *Requests* the Secretary-General to bring the present resolution to the attention of heads of intergovernmental organizations, the specialized agencies and funds and programmes of the United Nations engaged in activities relating to ocean affairs and the law of the sea, drawing their attention to paragraphs of particular relevance to them, and underlines the importance of their constructive and timely input for the report of the Secretary-General on oceans and the law of the sea and of their participation in relevant meetings and processes;

96. *Invites* the competent international organizations, as well as funding institutions, to take specific account of the present resolution in their programmes and activities and to contribute to the preparation of the comprehensive report of the Secretary-General on oceans and the law of the sea;

97. *Encourages* the sponsoring organizations of the Joint Group of Experts on the Scientific Aspects of Marine Environmental Protection to continue to support and provide the necessary assistance to the process of restructuring the Group of Experts;

XVI
Activities of the Division for Ocean Affairs and the Law of the Sea

98. *Expresses its appreciation* to the Secretary-General for the annual comprehensive report on oceans and the law of the sea and its addendum, prepared by the Division for Ocean Affairs and the Law of the Sea, as well as for the other activities of the Division, in accordance with the provisions of the Convention and the mandate set forth in resolutions 49/28, 52/26, 54/33, and 56/12 of 28 November 2001;

99. *Requests* the Secretary-General to continue to carry out the responsibilities entrusted to him in the Convention and related resolutions of the General Assembly, including resolutions 49/28 and 52/26, and to ensure that appropriate resources are made available to the Division for Ocean Affairs and the Law of the Sea for the performance of such responsibilities under the approved budget for the Organization;

100. *Invites* Member States and others in a position to do so to support the capacity-building activities of the Division for Ocean Affairs and the Law of the Sea, including, in particular, the training activities to assist developing States in the preparation of their submission to the Commission, and the TRAIN-SEA-COAST Programme of the Division;

XVII
Sixtieth session of the General Assembly

101. *Requests* the Secretary-General to report to the General Assembly at its sixtieth session on the implementation of the present resolution, including other developments and issues relating to ocean affairs and the law of the sea, in connection with his annual comprehensive report on oceans and the law of the sea, and to provide the report in accordance with the modalities set out in resolutions 49/28, 52/26 and 54/33, and also requests the Secretary-General to make the report available, in its current comprehensive format, at least six weeks in advance of the meeting of the Consultative Process;

102. *Notes* that the report referred to in paragraph 101 above will also be presented to States parties pursuant to article 319 of the Convention regarding issues of a general nature that have arisen with respect to the Convention;

103. *Decides* to include in the provisional agenda of its sixtieth session the item entitled "Oceans and the law of the sea".

RECORDED VOTE ON RESOLUTION 59/24:

In favour: Algeria, Andorra, Antigua and Barbuda, Argentina, Armenia, Australia, Austria, Bahamas, Bahrain, Bangladesh, Belgium, Belize, Bolivia, Bosnia and Herzegovina, Botswana, Brazil, Brunei Darussalam, Bulgaria, Cameroon, Canada, Chile, China, Congo, Costa Rica, Côte d'Ivoire, Croatia, Cuba, Cyprus, Czech Republic, Democratic Republic of the Congo, Denmark, Djibouti, Dominican Republic, Ecuador, Egypt, El Salvador, Ethiopia, Fiji, Finland, France, Gabon, Gambia, Georgia, Germany, Ghana, Greece, Guatemala, Guinea, Guinea-Bissau, Guyana, Honduras, Iceland, India, Indonesia, Iran, Iraq, Ireland, Israel, Italy, Jamaica, Japan, Jordan, Kazakhstan, Kenya, Kuwait, Lao People's Democratic Republic, Latvia, Libyan Arab Jamahiriya, Liechtenstein, Lithuania, Madagascar, Malaysia, Maldives, Mali, Malta, Marshall Islands, Mauritius, Mexico, Micronesia, Monaco, Mongolia, Morocco, Myanmar, Namibia, Nauru, Nepal, Netherlands, New Zealand, Nicaragua, Nigeria, Oman, Pakistan, Palau, Panama, Paraguay, Peru, Philippines, Poland, Portugal, Qatar, Republic of Korea, Republic of Moldova, Romania, Russian Federation, Samoa, San Marino, Saudi Arabia, Senegal, Serbia and Montenegro, Seychelles, Sierra Leone, Singapore, Slovakia, Slovenia, Solomon Islands, South Africa, Spain, Sri Lanka, Sudan, Suriname, Sweden, Switzerland, Thailand, The former Yugoslav Republic of Macedonia, Timor-Leste, Togo, Tonga, Trinidad and Tobago, Tunisia, Tuvalu, Uganda, Ukraine, United Arab Emirates, United Kingdom, United Republic of Tanzania, United States, Uruguay, Viet Nam, Yemen, Zambia, Zimbabwe.

Against: Turkey.

Abstaining: Colombia, Venezuela.

Division for Ocean Affairs and the Law of the Sea

During 2004, the Division for Ocean Affairs and the Law of the Sea of the Office of Legal Affairs continued to fulfil its role as the substantive unit of the UN Secretariat responsible for reviewing and monitoring all developments related to the law of the sea and ocean affairs, as well as for the implementation of UNCLOS and related General Assembly resolutions.

Under its TRAIN-SEA-COAST programme [YUN 1998, p. 1232], designed to build in-country capacity to improve skills in integrated coastal and ocean management, the Division conducted a training course for project managers in the South Pacific (Suva, Fiji, 9-27 February), entitled "Economics in community-based management projects". Another training course for project managers on improving waste-water management in coastal cities was also delivered (Rio Grande, Brazil, 21-25 June).

Chapter V

Other legal questions

The Special Committee on the Charter of the United Nations and on the Strengthening of the Role of the Organization continued in 2004 to consider, among other items, proposals relating to the maintenance of international peace and security in order to strengthen the Organization and the implementation of Charter provisions on assistance to third States affected by the application of sanctions under Chapter VII.

The Committee on Relations with the Host Country continued to address complaints by permanent missions to the United Nations. Matters discussed included transportation and parking issues, delays in issuing visas, travel regulations and acceleration of immigration and customs procedures.

The Sixth (Legal) Committee continued consideration of an international convention against reproductive cloning of human beings and recommended the establishment of a working group to finalize the text of a UN declaration on human cloning.

The United Nations Commission on International Trade Law adopted the Legislative Guide on Insolvency Law and requested the Secretary-General to transmit it to Governments and other interested bodies. The Commission decided to undertake a revision of its Model Law on Procurement of Goods, Construction and Services to reflect new practices, including those resulting from the use of electronic communications in public procurement.

The General Assembly noted the progress achieved towards enhancing cooperation between the United Nations and the Asian-African Legal Consultative Organization.

International organizations and international law

Strengthening the role of the United Nations

Special Committee on United Nations Charter

In accordance with General Assembly resolution 58/248 [YUN 2003, p. 1364], the Special Committee on the Charter of the United Nations and on the Strengthening of the Role of the Organization, at its fifty-ninth session (New York, 29 March–8 April) [A/59/33], continued to consider proposals relating to: the maintenance of international peace and security, according priority to the implementation of the provisions of the Charter of the United Nations on assistance to third States affected by the application of sanctions; the peaceful settlement of disputes between States; the future of the Trusteeship Council; the improvement of the Committee's working methods; and the status of the publications *Repertory of Practice of United Nations Organs* and *Repertoire of the Practice of the Security Council*.

With regard to the first item, the Russian Federation introduced a revision of its working paper entitled "Declaration on the basic conditions and standard criteria for the introduction of sanctions and other coercive measures and their implementation", reflecting amendments previously proposed, including those at the first reading [YUN 2003, p. 1363]. The Special Committee's working group of the whole completed a paragraph-by-paragraph reading of the paper, subject to additional amendments. Accordingly, the sponsor on 5 April submitted a new revised version for the Committee's consideration in 2005.

The Libyan Arab Jamahiriya observed that the Russian Federation's paper already included two of the three principles proposed in Libya's own revised working paper (2002) on the strengthening of certain principles concerning the impact and application of sanctions; namely, that sanctions constituted exceptional action of last resort and that their imposition should not place economic or humanitarian burdens on the targeted State. Nonetheless, the third principle, on the right of compensation for any unlawful damage done to a targeted State by sanctions imposed without good grounds, deserved further discussion, considering that it related to the topic "Responsibility of international organizations" currently on the work programme of the International Law Commission (see p. 1298).

Regarding the proposal submitted by the Russian Federation (1998) entitled "Fundamentals of the legal basis for United Nations peacekeeping operations in the context of Chapter VI of the Charter of the United Nations", the sponsor stressed that, while the practical issues of peacekeeping were discussed in other UN bodies, the Committee should not be precluded from dealing with its legal aspects. As for referring the working paper to the Special Committee on Peacekeeping Operations and exploring possible cooperation with it towards the preparation of a joint declaration on the subject as suggested by the sponsor, the Chairman pointed out that the Committee had no mandate for such a referral, nor was there a practical need for it.

In regard to the working papers submitted by Cuba (1997 and 1998) entitled "Strengthening the role of the Organization and enhancing its effectiveness", the sponsor pointed out that its proposal contained all of the basic criteria for the revision of the procedures and practices of the Assembly and other UN organs with respect to the maintenance of international peace and security and as such merited discussion by the Committee, notwithstanding the work of other bodies within the Organization on the subject.

Libya stated that its revised proposal (1998) on strengthening the role of the United Nations in the maintenance of international peace and security aimed at analysing the relationship between the Assembly and the Security Council and offering a precise definition of such a relationship. Libya reiterated the imperative of considering its proposal and suggested that it be taken into account, along with Cuba's proposal, in the reform process of those two principal organs, and that the Sixth Committee consider the legal aspects of both proposals and make appropriate recommendations to the Assembly.

Regarding the revised working paper jointly submitted by Belarus and the Russian Federation (2001) proposing that an advisory opinion be sought from the International Court of Justice (ICJ) on the legal consequences of a State's resort to the use of force without prior Council authorization, except in the exercise of the right to self-defence, Belarus pointed to the recent emergence of what it called new approaches to interpreting the Charter provisions on the use of armed force, such as the expansive interpretation of the right to self-defence for the purpose of combating international terrorism. An ICJ opinion would help answer the question of the legality of such approaches and contribute to a uniform interpretation and application of the relevant Charter provisions. It would moreover affirm the Council's key role in legitimizing any enforcement action or use of armed force by individual or groups of States, and regional and subregional bodies.

During the exchange of views on the peaceful settlement of disputes, the point was made that the Committee should identify proposals for discussion on the subject, since it was in that area that it had registered some impressive and valuable successes. The Committee was challenged to be innovative in devising ways of enhancing the various methods of resolving disputes elaborated in the *Handbook on the peaceful settlement of disputes between States* [Sales No. E.92.V.7], specifically with respect to facilitating resort to arbitration, by drawing attention to texts of compromissory clauses adopted after the publication of the *Handbook* and other instruments for arbitrating disputes that had since been adopted.

On the future of the Trusteeship Council, it was reiterated that it would be premature to abolish it or change its status since its existence entailed no financial implications for the United Nations, and the purpose for which it had been established remained relevant.

A revised working paper on measures to improve the Special Committee's working methods, currently sponsored by Australia, Japan, the Republic of Korea, Thailand and Uganda, was introduced in March. Shortly after its review by the working group, the sponsors, taking account of the various points of view expressed during informal consultations coordinated by Japan, submitted a further revised version of the working paper for consideration in 2005. The text of the agreed points was reproduced in the Committee's report.

As to the *Repertory of Practice of United Nations Organs* and *Repertoire of the Practice of the Security Council*, an oral report on the status of the *Repertoire* was made by the Deputy Director of the Security Council Affairs Division of the Department of Political Affairs, who said the Secretariat was developing a two-track approach for future volumes by simultaneously drafting a supplement covering the period 1996-1999 and a volume covering 2000-2003. This would help address the backlog in the publication by producing a streamlined version of the *Repertoire* and focus on the contemporary practice and procedure of the Council. The intention was to post individual chapters of the publication, once approved, on the UN website in an advance version. Supplement No. 11 should begin to be available in that format in the spring of 2004; chapters of Supplement No. 12 should follow shortly. Supplement No. 10, covering 1985-1988, had been published in all official languages. Member States were urged to make further contributions to the trust fund for the *Repertoire*, which was currently depleted.

The Assistant Secretary-General, Officer-in-Charge of the Office of Legal Affairs, reported on the status of the *Repertory of Practice of United*

Nations Organs. He provided information on progress achieved in 2003, including the finalization and submission for publication of four volumes and the preparation of numerous studies for several other volumes; the overall status of the *Repertory,* comprising 24 published volumes and five volumes submitted for publication; and the UN website for the *Repertory* providing access to studies from all 29 volumes and to studies on individual Charter Articles from volumes not yet completed. A pilot project was undertaken in cooperation with academia in early 2004 involving a group of externs.

Because the Assembly had not provided for the *Repertory* as an output of the Organization for 2004-2005, the Special Committee recommended that the Assembly, at its fifty-ninth (2004) session, review at the appropriate technical level the possibility of establishing a trust fund for the preparation, updating and publication of the *Repertory,* which should accept only voluntary contributions by States, private institutions and individuals.

Report of Secretary-General. In response to General Assembly resolution 58/248 [YUN 2003, p. 1364], the Secretary-General submitted a July report [A/59/189] outlining the efforts taken by the Secretariat to reduce the backlog in the publication of both the *Repertory* and the *Repertoire.* The Assembly was invited to consider the Special Committee's recommendation on establishing a trust fund for the *Repertory* and encouraging contributions to another trust fund for updating the *Repertoire.*

GENERAL ASSEMBLY ACTION

On 2 December [meeting 65], the General Assembly, on the recommendation of the Sixth Committee [A/59/513], adopted **resolution 59/44** without vote [agenda item 147].

Report of the Special Committee on the Charter of the United Nations and on the Strengthening of the Role of the Organization

The General Assembly,

Recalling its resolution 3499(XXX) of 15 December 1975, by which it established the Special Committee on the Charter of the United Nations and on the Strengthening of the Role of the Organization, and its relevant resolutions adopted at subsequent sessions,

Recalling also its resolution 47/233 of 17 August 1993 on the revitalization of the work of the General Assembly,

Recalling further its resolution 47/62 of 11 December 1992 on the question of equitable representation on and increase in the membership of the Security Council,

Taking note of the report of the Open-ended Working Group on the Question of Equitable Representation on and Increase in the Membership of the Security Council and Other Matters Related to the Security Council,

Recalling the elements relevant to the work of the Special Committee contained in its resolution 47/120 B of 20 September 1993,

Recalling also its resolution 51/241 of 31 July 1997 on the strengthening of the United Nations system and its resolution 51/242 of 15 September 1997, entitled "Supplement to an Agenda for Peace", by which it adopted the texts on coordination and the question of sanctions imposed by the United Nations, which are annexed to that resolution,

Recalling further that the International Court of Justice is the principal judicial organ of the United Nations, and reaffirming its authority and independence,

Considering the desirability of finding practical ways and means to strengthen the Court, taking into consideration, in particular, the needs resulting from its increased workload,

Taking note of the ongoing debate on the revised working papers on the working methods of the Special Committee,

Taking note also of the report of the Secretary-General on the *Repertory of Practice of United Nations Organs* and the *Repertoire of the Practice of the Security Council,*

Recalling its resolution 58/248 of 23 December 2003,

Having considered the report of the Special Committee on the work of its session held in 2004,

Noting with appreciation the work done by the Special Committee to encourage States to focus on the need to prevent and to settle peacefully their disputes which are likely to endanger the maintenance of international peace and security,

1. *Takes note* of the report of the Special Committee on the Charter of the United Nations and on the Strengthening of the Role of the Organization;

2. *Decides* that the Special Committee shall hold its next session from 14 to 24 March 2005;

3. *Requests* the Special Committee, at its session in 2005, in accordance with paragraph 5 of General Assembly resolution 50/52 of 11 December 1995:

(*a*) To continue its consideration of all proposals concerning the question of the maintenance of international peace and security in all its aspects in order to strengthen the role of the United Nations and, in this context, to consider other proposals relating to the maintenance of international peace and security already submitted or which may be submitted to the Special Committee at its session in 2005;

(*b*) To continue to consider, on a priority basis and in an appropriate substantive manner and framework, the question of the implementation of the provisions of the Charter of the United Nations related to assistance to third States affected by the application of sanctions under Chapter VII of the Charter based on all of the related reports of the Secretary-General and the proposals submitted on the question;

(*c*) To keep on its agenda the question of the peaceful settlement of disputes between States;

(*d*) To continue to consider proposals concerning the Trusteeship Council in the light of the report of the Secretary-General submitted in accordance with General Assembly resolution 50/55 of 11 December 1995, the report of the Secretary-General entitled "Renewing the United Nations: a programme for reform" and the views expressed by States on this subject at previous sessions of the Assembly;

(e) To continue to consider, on a priority basis, ways and means of improving its working methods and enhancing its efficiency with a view to identifying widely acceptable measures for future implementation;

4. *Invites* the Special Committee at its session in 2005 to continue to identify new subjects for consideration in its future work with a view to contributing to the revitalization of the work of the United Nations;

5. *Notes* the readiness of the Special Committee to provide, within its mandate, such assistance as may be sought at the request of other subsidiary bodies of the General Assembly in relation to any issues before them;

6. *Requests* the Special Committee to submit a report on its work to the General Assembly at its sixtieth session;

7. *Takes note* of paragraphs 10 and 17 of the report of the Secretary-General;

8. *Endorses* the efforts of the Secretary-General to eliminate the backlog in the publication of the *Repertoire of the Practice of the Security Council*;

9. *Requests* the Secretary-General to establish a trust fund to eliminate the backlog of the *Repertory of Practice of United Nations Organs*, which shall accept voluntary contributions by States, private institutions and individuals;

10. *Also requests* the Secretary-General to continue his efforts, within the level of the currently approved budget, towards making available electronically all versions of the *Repertory of Practice of United Nations Organs* as early as possible;

11. *Further requests* the Secretary-General to submit a report on both the *Repertory of Practice of United Nations Organs* and the *Repertoire of the Practice of the Security Council* to the General Assembly at its sixtieth session;

12. *Decides* to include in the provisional agenda of its sixtieth session the item entitled "Report of the Special Committee on the Charter of the United Nations and on the Strengthening of the Role of the Organization".

Charter provisions relating to sanctions

Special Committee consideration. During the Special Committee's consideration of the implementation of the Charter provisions related to assistance to third States affected by sanctions [A/59/33], support was expressed for the continuing consideration of the matter through a working group of the Sixth Committee. Reference was made to the need for pre-assessment and ongoing assessment reports on potential and actual unintended impact of sanctions on those States. To alleviate the hardships they encountered, a number of relief measures were reiterated or advanced, among them the provision of international assistance, the establishment of a fund or a permanent consultative mechanism, multichannel financial arrangements or economic assistance to minimize losses incurred, and facilitating applications for compensation. Delega-

tions welcomed the continuing recourse by the Council to targeted sanctions and encouraged it to continue making further refinements to sanctions regimes to avoid unintended consequences.

The Committee recommended that the Assembly continue to consider the results of the 1998 expert group's deliberations and findings on developing a methodology for assessing the consequences incurred by third States as a result of preventive or enforcement measures [YUN 1998, p. 1235], taking into account the Committee's current debate; views presented in the Secretary-General's 1999 [YUN 1999, p. 1252] and 2000 [YUN 2000, p. 1271] reports; his views on the main findings of the ad hoc expert group [YUN 2002, p. 1333]; information he was to submit on the follow-up to a 1999 Security Council note [YUN 1999, p. 1252]; and the implementation of the Charter provisions related to assistance to third States affected by the application of sanctions called for by Assembly resolutions yearly since 1995, the latest being resolution 58/80 [YUN 2003, p. 1367].

Security Council consideration. By a January note [S/2004/5], the President of the Security Council announced the Council's agreement that Joël W. Adechi (Benin) would serve as Chairman of the informal working group of the Security Council on general issues relating to sanctions, established in 2000 [YUN 2000, p. 1270], until 31 December 2004. He further announced, by a 23 December note [S/2004/1014], that the Council had extended the working group's mandate until 31 December 2005.

In addition to its original mandate of developing general recommendations on how to improve the effectiveness of UN sanctions, the group was also mandated to address the following sanctions-related issues: improving cooperation among sanctions committees, the duration and lifting of sanctions, assessments of the unintended impact of sanctions, improving national implementation of sanctions, enforcement of targeted sanctions, de-listing procedures in relation to the implementation of targeted sanctions, secondary sanctions against States violating sanctions, and improving Secretariat archives and databases, including the Roster of Experts.

Report of Secretary-General. In response to General Assembly resolution 58/80 [YUN 2003, p. 1367], the Secretary-General submitted a September report [A/59/334] highlighting measures for further improving the procedures and working methods of the Security Council and its sanctions committees related to assistance to third States affected by the application of sanctions. It reviewed recent developments on the roles of the Assembly, the Economic and Social Council and the Committee for Programme and Coordination in that regard, as well as the Secretariat's capacity and modalities for implementing intergovernmental mandates and the recommendations of the 1998 ad hoc expert group meeting [YUN 1998, p. 1235] on assistance to such States.

By **decision 2004/301** of 23 July, the Economic and Social Council took note of the Secretary-General's note on assistance to third States affected by the application of sanctions and of his 2003 report on the implementation of the Charter provisions related to such assistance.

GENERAL ASSEMBLY ACTION

On 2 December [meeting 65], the General Assembly, on the recommendation of the Sixth Committee [A/59/513], adopted **resolution 59/45** without vote [agenda item 147].

Implementation of the provisions of the Charter of the United Nations related to assistance to third States affected by the application of sanctions

The General Assembly,

Concerned about the special economic problems confronting certain States arising from the carrying out of preventive or enforcement measures taken by the Security Council against other States, and taking into account the obligation of Members of the United Nations under Article 49 of the Charter of the United Nations to join in affording mutual assistance in carrying out the measures decided upon by the Security Council,

Recalling the right of third States confronted with special economic problems of that nature to consult the Security Council with regard to a solution of those problems, in accordance with Article 50 of the Charter,

Recognizing the desirability of the consideration of further appropriate procedures for consultations to deal in a more effective manner with the problems referred to in Article 50 of the Charter,

Recalling:

(a) The report of the Secretary-General entitled "An Agenda for Peace", in particular paragraph 41 thereof,

(b) Its resolution 47/120 A of 18 December 1992, entitled "An Agenda for Peace: preventive diplomacy and related matters", its resolution 47/120 B of 20 September 1993, entitled "An Agenda for Peace", in particular section IV thereof, entitled "Special economic problems arising from the implementation of preventive or enforcement measures", and its resolution 51/242 of 15 September 1997, entitled "Supplement to an Agenda for Peace", in particular annex II thereto, entitled "Question of sanctions imposed by the United Nations",

(c) The position paper of the Secretary-General entitled "Supplement to an Agenda for Peace",

(d) The statement by the President of the Security Council of 22 February 1995,

(e) The report of the Secretary-General prepared pursuant to the statement by the President of the Security Council regarding the question of special economic problems of States as a result of sanctions imposed under Chapter VII of the Charter,

(f) The annual overview reports of the Administrative Committee on Coordination for the period from 1992 to 2000 and the annual overview reports of the United Nations System Chief Executives Board for Coordination for 2001 to 2003, in particular the sections on assistance to countries invoking Article 50 of the Charter,

(g) The reports of the Secretary-General on economic assistance to States affected by the implementation of the Security Council resolutions imposing sanctions against the Federal Republic of Yugoslavia and General Assembly resolutions 48/210 of 21 December 1993, 49/21 A of 2 December 1994, 50/58 E of 12 December 1995, 51/30 A of 5 December 1996, 52/169 H of 16 December 1997, 54/96 G of 15 December 1999, 55/170 of 14 December 2000 and 56/110 of 14 December 2001,

(h) The reports of the Special Committee on the Charter of the United Nations and on the Strengthening of the Role of the Organization on the work of its sessions held in the years 1994 to 2004,

(i) The reports of the Secretary-General on the implementation of the provisions of the Charter related to assistance to third States affected by the application of sanctions under Chapter VII of the Charter,

(j) The report of the Secretary-General to the Millennium Assembly of the United Nations, in particular section IV.E thereof, entitled "Targeting sanctions",

(k) The United Nations Millennium Declaration, in particular paragraph 9 thereof,

(l) The report of the Secretary-General entitled "Road map towards implementation of the United Nations Millennium Declaration", in particular paragraphs 56 to 61 thereof,

(m) The report of the Committee for Programme and Coordination on the work of its forty-third session, in particular the recommendation that the Chief Executives Board play a role in better coordinating the analysis of the problems of the countries invoking Article 50 of the Charter, and the development of new methodologies to identify the damage to affected States and new mechanisms to determine the appropriate compensation for them,

Taking note of the report of the Secretary-General on the work of the Organization, in particular paragraphs 78 to 81 thereof,

Recalling that the question of assistance to third States affected by the application of sanctions has been addressed recently in several forums, including the General Assembly, the Security Council, the Economic and Social Council and their subsidiary organs,

Recalling also the measures taken by the Security Council, in accordance with the statement by the President of the Security Council of 16 December 1994, that, as part of the effort of the Council to improve the flow of information and the exchange of ideas between members of the Council and other States Members of the United Nations, there should be increased recourse to open meetings, in particular at an early stage in its consideration of a subject,

Recalling further the measures taken by the Security Council in accordance with the note by the President of the Security Council of 29 January 1999 aimed at improving the work of the sanctions committees, including increasing the effectiveness and transparency of those committees,

Stressing that, in the formulation of sanctions regimes, due account should be taken of the potential effects of sanctions on third States,

Stressing also, in this context, the powers of the Security Council under Chapter VII of the Charter and the primary responsibility of the Council under Article 24 of the Charter for the maintenance of international peace and security in order to ensure prompt and effective action by the United Nations,

Recalling that, under Article 31 of the Charter, any Member of the United Nations that is not a member of the Security Council may participate, without vote, in the discussion of any question brought before the Council whenever the latter considers that the interests of that Member are specially affected,

Recognizing that the imposition of sanctions under Chapter VII of the Charter has been causing special economic problems in third States and that it is necessary to intensify efforts to address those problems effectively,

Taking into consideration the views of third States which could be affected by the imposition of sanctions,

Recognizing that assistance to third States affected by the application of sanctions would further contribute to an effective and comprehensive approach by the international community to sanctions imposed by the Security Council,

Recognizing also that the international community at large and, in particular, international institutions involved in providing economic and financial assistance should continue to take into account and address in a more effective manner the special economic problems of affected third States arising from the carrying out of preventive or enforcement measures taken by the Security Council under Chapter VII of the Charter, in view of their magnitude and of the adverse impact on the economies of those States,

Recalling the provisions of its resolutions 50/51 of 11 December 1995, 51/208 of 17 December 1996, 52/162 of 15 December 1997, 53/107 of 8 December 1998, 54/107 of 9 December 1999, 55/157 of 12 December 2000, 56/87 of 12 December 2001, 57/25 of 19 November 2002 and 58/80 of 9 December 2003,

1. *Renews its invitation* to the Security Council to consider the establishment of further mechanisms or procedures, as appropriate, for consultations as early as possible under Article 50 of the Charter of the United Nations with third States which are or may be confronted with special economic problems arising from the carrying out of preventive or enforcement measures imposed by the Council under Chapter VII of the Charter, with regard to a solution of those problems, including appropriate ways and means for increasing the effectiveness of its methods and procedures applied in the consideration of requests by the affected States for assistance;

2. *Welcomes* the measures taken by the Security Council since the adoption of General Assembly resolution 50/51, most recently the note by the President of the Security Council of 18 December 2003, whereby the members of the Security Council agreed to extend the mandate of the informal working group of the Council established in 2000 to develop general recommendations on how to improve the effectiveness of United Nations sanctions, looks forward to the adoption of the proposed outcome document of the working group, in particular those provisions thereof regarding the issues of the unintended impact of sanctions and assistance to States in implementing sanctions, and strongly recommends that the Council continue its efforts to enhance further the effectiveness and transparency of the sanctions committees, to streamline their working procedures and to facilitate access to them by representatives of States that find themselves confronted with special economic problems arising from the carrying out of sanctions;

3. *Invites* the Security Council, its sanctions committees and the Secretariat to continue to ensure, as appropriate, that:

(*a*) Both pre-assessment reports and ongoing assessment reports include as part of their analysis the likely and actual unintended impact of the sanctions on third States and recommend ways in which the negative impact of sanctions can be mitigated;

(*b*) Sanctions committees provide opportunities for third States affected by sanctions to brief them on the unintended impact of sanctions they are experiencing and on assistance needed by them to mitigate the negative impact of sanctions;

(*c*) The Secretariat continues to provide, upon request, advice and information to third States to help them to pursue means to mitigate the unintended impact of sanctions, for example, on invoking Article 50 of the Charter for consultation with the Security Council;

(*d*) Where economic sanctions have had severe effects on third States, the Security Council is able to request the Secretary-General to consider appointing a special representative or dispatching, as necessary, fact-finding missions on the ground to undertake necessary assessments and to identify, as appropriate, possible ways of assistance;

(*e*) The Security Council is able, in the context of situations referred to in subparagraph (*d*) above, to consider establishing working groups to consider such situations;

4. *Requests* the Secretary-General to pursue the implementation of General Assembly resolutions 50/51, 51/208, 52/162, 53/107, 54/107, 55/157, 56/87, 57/25 and 58/80 and to ensure that the competent units within the Secretariat develop the adequate capacity and appropriate modalities, technical procedures and guidelines to continue, on a regular basis, to collate and coordinate information about international assistance available to third States affected by the implementation of sanctions, to continue developing a possible methodology for assessing the adverse consequences actually incurred by third States and to explore innovative and practical measures of assistance to the affected third States;

5. *Welcomes* the report of the Secretary-General containing a summary of the deliberations and main findings of the ad hoc expert group meeting on developing a methodology for assessing the consequences incurred by third States as a result of preventive or enforcement measures and on exploring innovative and practical measures of international assistance to the affected third States, and renews its invitation to States and relevant international organizations within and outside the United Nations system that have not yet done so to provide their views regarding the report of the ad hoc expert group meeting;

6. *Takes note* of the most recent report of the Secretary-General on this question and, in particular, of his views on the deliberations and main findings, including the recommendations of the ad hoc expert group on the implementation of the provisions of the Charter related to assistance to third States affected by the application of sanctions, as well as the views of States, the organizations of the United Nations system, international financial institutions and other international organizations, as contained in the previous reports of the Secretary-General;

7. *Reaffirms* the important role of the General Assembly, the Economic and Social Council and the Committee for Programme and Coordination in mobilizing and monitoring, as appropriate, the economic assistance efforts of the international community and the United Nations system on behalf of States confronted with special economic problems arising from the carrying out of preventive or enforcement measures imposed by the Security Council and, as appropriate, in identifying solutions to the special economic problems of those States;

8. *Takes note* of the decision of the Economic and Social Council, in its resolution 2000/32 of 28 July 2000, to continue its consideration of the question of assistance to third States affected by the application of sanctions, invites the Council, at its organizational session for 2005, to make appropriate arrangements for this purpose within its programme of work for 2005, further invites the Council to continue its consideration of the question of assistance to third States affected by the application of sanctions, and decides to transmit the most recent report of the Secretary-General on the implementation of the provisions of the Charter related to assistance to third States affected by the application of sanctions, together with the relevant background materials, to the Council at its substantive session of 2005;

9. *Invites* the organizations of the United Nations system, international financial institutions, other international organizations, regional organizations and Member States to address more specifically and directly, where appropriate, the special economic problems of third States affected by sanctions imposed under Chapter VII of the Charter and, for this purpose, to consider improving procedures for consultations to maintain a constructive dialogue with such States, including through regular and frequent meetings, as well as, where appropriate, special meetings between the affected third States and the donor community, with the participation of United Nations agencies and other international organizations;

10. *Requests* the Special Committee on the Charter of the United Nations and on the Strengthening of the Role of the Organization, at its session in 2005, to continue to consider on a priority basis and in an appropriate substantive manner and framework the question of the implementation of the provisions of the Charter related to assistance to third States affected by the application of sanctions under Chapter VII of the Charter based on all of the related reports of the Secretary-General, in particular the 1998 report containing a summary of the deliberations and main findings of the ad hoc expert group meeting convened pursuant to paragraph 4 of General Assembly resolution 52/162, together with the most recent report of the Secretary-

General on this question, taking into consideration the forthcoming report of the informal working group of the Security Council on general issues relating to sanctions, the proposals submitted on the question, the debate on the question in the Sixth Committee during the fifty-ninth session of the Assembly and the text on the question of sanctions imposed by the United Nations contained in annex II to Assembly resolution 51/242, as well as the implementation of the provisions of Assembly resolutions 50/51, 51/208, 52/162, 53/107, 54/107, 55/157, 56/87, 57/25, 58/80 and the present resolution;

11. *Decides* to consider within the Sixth Committee or a working group of the Committee, at the sixtieth session of the General Assembly, further progress in the elaboration of effective measures aimed at the implementation of the provisions of the Charter related to assistance to third States affected by the application of sanctions under Chapter VII of the Charter;

12. *Requests* the Secretary-General to submit a report on the implementation of the present resolution to the General Assembly at its sixtieth session, under the item entitled "Report of the Special Committee on the Charter of the United Nations and on the Strengthening of the Role of the Organization".

Cooperation with Asian-African Legal Consultative Organization

Pursuant to General Assembly resolution 57/36 [YUN 2002, p. 1337], the Secretary-General submitted a report on cooperation between the United Nations and the Asian-African Legal Consultative Organization (AALCO), which was included in his September consolidated report [A/59/303] on cooperation between the United Nations and regional and other organizations. The report covered AALCO's activities during the biennium July 2002–July 2004. In line with the cooperative framework agreed upon by the two organizations, both routinely consulted and exchanged information and documentation on matters of common interest in the area of international law, including international trade law and the environment; aspects of refugee, human rights and humanitarian laws; and the peaceful settlement of disputes. AALCO continued to orient its work programme in order to accord priority to issues of concern to the United Nations and to initiate action aimed at strengthening its role.

The report provided details on AALCO representation at UN meetings and conferences and UN representation at AALCO sessions; measures taken by AALCO to further the work of the Assembly's Sixth Committee, to monitor the progress of the work of the United Nations Commission on International Trade Law and to promote the ratification and implementation of the 1982 United Nations Convention on the Law of the Sea [YUN 1982, p. 181]; and AALCO's ongoing study of refugee law and work, in close cooperation with the Office of the United Nations High Commissioner for Refugees. Also described were activities relating to issues on AALCO's agenda, including environment and sustainable development; extraterritorial application of national legislation: sanctions imposed against third parties; deportation of Palestinians and other Israeli practices; cooperation in combating trafficking in women and children; legal protection of migrant workers; international terrorism; recent developments related to the work of the International Criminal Court; elaboration of an international legal instrument against corruption; promotion of international arbitration, research and training projects at the AALCO Centre for Research and Training; and AALCO's annual publications.

In his statement before the Assembly on 22 October [meeting 40], the AALCO Secretary-General affirmed AALCO's dedication to enhancing and contributing to the work of the United Nations, underlining its efforts to act as a forum for the exchange of views among Asian and African countries on issues of international law.

GENERAL ASSEMBLY ACTION

On 22 October [meeting 40], the General Assembly adopted **resolution 59/3** [draft: A/59/L.1 & Add.1] without vote [agenda item 56 (*b*)].

Cooperation between the United Nations and the Asian-African Legal Consultative Organization

The General Assembly,

Recalling its resolutions 36/38 of 18 November 1981, 37/8 of 29 October 1982, 38/37 of 5 December 1983, 39/47 of 10 December 1984, 40/60 of 9 December 1985, 41/5 of 17 October 1986, 43/1 of 17 October 1988, 45/4 of 16 October 1990, 47/6 of 21 October 1992, 49/8 of 25 October 1994, 51/11 of 4 November 1996, 53/14 of 29 October 1998, 55/4 of 25 October 2000 and 57/36 of 21 November 2002,

Having considered the report of the Secretary-General on cooperation between the United Nations and the Asian-African Legal Consultative Organization,

Having heard the statement made by the Secretary-General of the Asian-African Legal Consultative Organization on the steps taken by the Consultative Organization to ensure continuing, close and effective cooperation between the two organizations,

Acknowledging in particular the close interaction between the Consultative Organization and the Sixth Committee,

1. *Takes note with appreciation* of the report of the Secretary-General;

2. *Notes with satisfaction* the continuing efforts of the Asian-African Legal Consultative Organization towards strengthening the role of the United Nations and its various organs in enhancing the rule of law and wider adherence to related international instruments;

3. *Also notes with satisfaction* the commendable progress achieved towards enhancing cooperation between the United Nations, its agencies, other international organizations and the Consultative Organization;

4. *Notes with appreciation* the work of the Consultative Organization aimed at strengthening the efforts of the United Nations in respect of issues such as combating corruption, international terrorism and trafficking, as well as human rights issues;

5. *Also notes with appreciation* the initiative and efforts the Consultative Organization has undertaken to promote the objectives and principles set out in the United Nations Millennium Declaration, including wider acceptance of treaties deposited with the Secretary-General;

6. *Recommends* that, with a view to promoting close interaction between the Consultative Organization and the Sixth Committee, the consideration of the sub-item entitled "Cooperation between the United Nations and the Asian-African Legal Consultative Organization" should be scheduled to coincide with the deliberations of the Committee on the work of the International Law Commission;

7. *Requests* the Secretary-General to submit to the General Assembly at its sixty-first session a report on cooperation between the United Nations and the Consultative Organization;

8. *Decides* to include in the provisional agenda of its sixty-first session the sub-item entitled "Cooperation between the United Nations and the Asian-African Legal Consultative Organization".

Host country relations

In three meetings held in New York (29 April, 26 July and 13 October), the Committee on Relations with the Host Country considered the following aspects of relations between the UN diplomatic community and the United States, the host country: transportation issues regarding the use of motor vehicles, parking and related matters; acceleration of immigration and customs procedures; entry visas to the host country; and host country travel regulations. The recommendations and conclusions on those items, approved by the Committee at its October meeting, were incorporated in its report [A/59/26].

Transportation

As recommended by the Legal Counsel in 2002 [YUN 2002, p. 1338], the Committee, at its April meeting, circulated a comprehensive database of submissions from permanent missions to the United Nations on their experience with the implementation of the Parking Programme for Diplomatic Vehicles in force since November 2002 [ibid.]. The Committee Secretary summarized the issues raised as follows: failure to uphold the availability of the designated spaces 24 hours a day, seven days a week, as stipulated in the Programme; failure to ticket or tow unauthorized vehicles parked in those spaces; insufficient education of law enforcement officials and the general public on the Programme's provisions and on the status of, and treatment to be accorded to, the diplomatic community; failure of review and appeals panels to uphold the deadlines provided for in the Programme; failure of such panels to provide the grounds and explanations for their conclusions; the invalidity/contestability of most summonses issued; and problems with the operation and effectiveness of the tow hotline and website.

The questions raised outside the scope of the Programme concerned the legality of subjecting the permanent missions to the jurisdiction of the host city; the non-transferability of decals; the inadequate number of parking spaces and decals; and the absence of designated spaces at diplomatic residences. Many delegations had protested the burdensome nature of the Programme, characterizing it as an impediment to their functions and security in contravention of the host country's obligation to facilitate the work of the missions.

To address the problems identified, the New York City Commissioner for the United Nations, Consular Corps and Protocol reported that the city had increased the number of tow trucks assigned to remove unauthorized vehicles from diplomatic spaces and patrols to issue summonses to unauthorized users; issued new city policies and procedures on the use of decals in other locations and on the unauthorized use of diplomatic spaces by construction companies; initiated a city training programme to promote due respect for diplomatic status; and improved response time and compliance with deadlines in the review and appeals process.

The Committee requested the host country to continue to bring to the attention of New York City officials reports on other problems experienced by the permanent missions or their staff regarding the Programme in order to improve its functioning and promote compliance with international norms concerning diplomatic privileges and immunities.

Acceleration of immigration and customs procedures

The Committee heard a complaint from Turkey regarding new customs procedures for the import of household effects. The complaint concerned two of its diplomats whose containers were put on hold for x-ray purposes beyond the four-day grace period for holding cargo, thereby incurring additional storage and demurrage charges. A request for reimbursement to the Office of Foreign Missions was denied. While expressing sympathy with the need of the host country to enhance security, Turkey urged it to ensure that such searches be conducted in the presence of a diplomatic agent of the countries concerned, that they

be exempted from any related charges and that the grace period be extended.

The United States responded that, as the matter had not been drawn to the attention of the United States Mission but rather to the competent authorities in Washington, D.C., it would have to await a reply from them.

Entry visas

The Committee heard a complaint from the Russian Federation regarding delays in issuing entry visas to Russian experts assigned to attend official UN meetings in New York, stating that the host country was not complying with its own time frames for issuing visas. The United States responded that applications for such persons were handled by the consulates in the countries concerned, and that, unless problems or delays were promptly brought to the attention of the United States Mission, it would not be able to intervene with the competent authorities.

The Committee anticipated that the host country would enhance its efforts to ensure the timely issuance of entry visas to representatives of Member States pursuant to article IV, section II, of the Agreement between the United Nations and the United States of America regarding the Headquarters of the United Nations [YUN 1947-48, p. 199].

Travel regulations

The Committee heard a complaint from Cuba regarding the host country's travel restrictions on its mission personnel, in particular the denial of a Cuban delegate's request to travel beyond the 25-mile radius to attend an informal meeting at Princeton University, in New Jersey. The United States reiterated that it regarded its obligations as host country very seriously but recalled that such obligations arose only in respect of formal UN meetings. Cuba responded that the host country's position violated customary diplomatic standards.

The Committee, noting that some travel restrictions had been removed, continued to urge the host country to remove the remaining travel restrictions as soon as possible.

GENERAL ASSEMBLY ACTION

On 2 December [meeting 65], the General Assembly, on the recommendation of the Sixth Committee [A/59/511], adopted **resolution 59/42** without vote [agenda item 145].

Report of the Committee on Relations with the Host Country

The General Assembly,

Having considered the report of the Committee on Relations with the Host Country,

Recalling Article 105 of the Charter of the United Nations, the Convention on the Privileges and Immunities of the United Nations, the Agreement between the United Nations and the United States of America regarding the Headquarters of the United Nations and the responsibilities of the host country,

Recalling also that, in accordance with paragraph 7 of General Assembly resolution 2819(XXVI) of 15 December 1971, the Committee should consider, and advise the host country on, issues arising in connection with the implementation of the Agreement between the United Nations and the United States of America regarding the Headquarters of the United Nations,

Recognizing that effective measures should continue to be taken by the competent authorities of the host country, in particular to prevent any acts violating the security of missions and the safety of their personnel,

1. *Endorses* the recommendations and conclusions of the Committee on Relations with the Host Country contained in paragraph 26 of its report;

2. *Considers* that the maintenance of appropriate conditions for the normal work of the delegations and the missions accredited to the United Nations and the observance of their privileges and immunities, which is an issue of great importance, are in the interest of the United Nations and all Member States, and requests the host country to continue to solve, through negotiations, problems that might arise and to take all measures necessary to prevent any interference with the functioning of missions;

3. *Notes* that the Committee conducted an initial detailed review of the implementation of the Parking Programme for Diplomatic Vehicles, as recommended by the Legal Counsel in his opinion on 24 September 2002, with a view to addressing the problems experienced by some permanent missions during the first year of the Programme and continuously ensuring its proper implementation in a manner that is fair, non-discriminatory, effective and therefore consistent with international law, and that it shall remain seized of the matter;

4. *Expresses its appreciation* for the efforts made by the host country, and hopes that the issues raised at the meetings of the Committee will continue to be resolved in a spirit of cooperation and in accordance with international law;

5. *Notes* that during the reporting period some travel restrictions previously imposed by the host country on staff of certain missions and staff members of the Secretariat of certain nationalities were removed, and requests the host country to consider removing the remaining travel restrictions, and in this regard notes the positions of affected States, of the Secretary-General and of the host country;

6. *Notes also* that the Committee anticipates that the host country will enhance its efforts to ensure the issuance, in a timely manner, of entry visas to representatives of Member States, pursuant to article IV, section 11, of the Agreement between the United Nations and the United States of America regarding the Headquarters of the United Nations, inter alia, for the purpose of their attending official United Nations meetings;

7. *Requests* the Secretary-General to remain actively engaged in all aspects of the relations of the United Nations with the host country;

8. *Requests* the Committee to continue its work in conformity with General Assembly resolution 2819 (XXVI);

9. *Decides* to include in the provisional agenda of its sixtieth session the item entitled "Report of the Committee on Relations with the Host Country".

International law

International bioethics law

Convention against cloning of human beings

Pursuant to General Assembly decision 58/523 [YUN 2003, p. 1374], the Sixth Committee met (21-22 October and 19 November) [A/59/516 & Corr.1] to continue its consideration, begun in 2002 [YUN 2002, p. 1339], of an international convention against the reproductive cloning of human beings. Among the documents before the Committee was a paper submitted by the Holy See [A/C.6/59/INF.1]. Following informal consultations, the Committee adopted a draft decision for consideration by the Assembly.

On 23 December, the Assembly, by **decision 59/547**, took note of the Sixth Committee's decision to establish a Working Group open to all States Members of the United Nations or members of specialized agencies or of the International Atomic Energy Agency to finalize the text of a UN declaration on human cloning, based on the draft resolution entitled "United Nations Declaration on Human Cloning" and report to the Committee during the current session. The Group would meet on 14, 15 and 18 February 2005, and the Committee in the afternoon of 18 February to take action on the Group's report. The Sixth Committee Chairman would be Chairman of the Working Group and members of the Committee's Bureau would serve as Friends of the Chairman.

Also on 23 December, the Assembly, by **decision 59/552**, decided that the agenda item entitled "International Convention against reproductive cloning of human beings" would remain for consideration during its fifty-ninth (2005) session.

International economic law

In 2004, legal aspects of international economic law continued to be considered by the United Nations Commission on International

Trade Law (UNCITRAL) and by the Sixth Committee of the General Assembly.

International trade law

At its thirty-seventh session (New York, 14-25 June), UNCITRAL finalized and adopted the UNCITRAL Legislative Guide on Insolvency Law. It continued its work on arbitration, transport law, electronic commerce and security interests. It reviewed the implementation of the 1958 New York Convention on the Recognition and Enforcement of Foreign Arbitral Awards (the New York Convention) [YUN 1958, p. 390], the work on the collection and dissemination of case law on UNCITRAL texts (CLOUT), and training and technical assistance activities. It also considered possible future work in public procurement.

The report on the session [A/59/17] described actions taken on those topics (for details, see below).

GENERAL ASSEMBLY ACTION

On 2 December [meeting 65], the General Assembly, on the recommendation of the Sixth Committee [A/59/509], adopted **resolution 59/39** without vote [agenda item 143].

**Report of the United Nations Commission on
International Trade Law on the work
of its thirty-seventh session**

The General Assembly,

Recalling its resolution 2205(XXI) of 17 December 1966, by which it established the United Nations Commission on International Trade Law with a mandate to further the progressive harmonization and unification of the law of international trade and in that respect to bear in mind the interests of all peoples, in particular those of developing countries, in the extensive development of international trade,

Reaffirming its belief that the progressive modernization and harmonization of international trade law, in reducing or removing legal obstacles to the flow of international trade, especially those affecting the developing countries, would contribute significantly to universal economic cooperation among all States on a basis of equality, equity and common interest and to the elimination of discrimination in international trade and, thereby, to the well-being of all peoples,

Having considered the report of the Commission on its thirty-seventh session,

Reiterating its concern that activities undertaken by other bodies in the field of international trade law without adequate coordination with the Commission might lead to undesirable duplication of efforts and would not be in keeping with the aim of promoting efficiency, consistency and coherence in the unification and harmonization of international trade law,

Reaffirming the mandate of the Commission, as the core legal body within the United Nations system in the field of international trade law, to coordinate legal activities in this field, in particular to avoid duplication of efforts, including among organizations formulating

rules of international trade, and to promote efficiency, consistency and coherence in the modernization and harmonization of international trade law, and to continue, through its secretariat, to maintain close cooperation with other international organs and organizations, including regional organizations, active in the field of international trade law,

1. *Takes note with appreciation* of the report of the United Nations Commission on International Trade Law on its thirty-seventh session;

2. *Commends* the Commission for the completion and adoption of its Legislative Guide on Insolvency Law;

3. *Also commends* the Commission for the progress made in the work on a draft convention on electronic contracting, on a draft instrument on transport law, on a draft legislative guide on secured transactions and on model legislative provisions on interim measures in international commercial arbitration, and for the Commission's decision to undertake a revision of its Model Law on Procurement of Goods, Construction and Services to reflect new practices, including those resulting from the increasing use of electronic communications in public procurement;

4. *Endorses* the efforts and initiatives of the Commission, as the core legal body within the United Nations system in the field of international trade law, aimed at increasing coordination of and cooperation on legal activities of international and regional organizations active in the field of international trade law, and in this regard appeals to relevant international and regional organizations to coordinate their legal activities with those of the Commission, to avoid duplication of efforts and to promote efficiency, consistency and coherence in the modernization and harmonization of international trade law;

5. *Reaffirms* the importance, in particular for developing countries, of the work of the Commission concerned with training and legislative technical assistance in the field of international trade law, and in this connection:

(*a*) Welcomes the Commission's initiatives towards expanding, through its secretariat, its training and legislative technical assistance programme;

(*b*) Expresses its appreciation to the Commission for organizing seminars and briefing missions in Azerbaijan, Colombia, Serbia and Montenegro, the Sudan, Thailand, Venezuela and Yemen;

(*c*) Expresses its appreciation to the Governments whose contributions enabled the seminars and briefing missions to take place, and appeals to Governments, the relevant bodies of the United Nations system, organizations, institutions and individuals to make voluntary contributions to the United Nations Commission on International Trade Law Trust Fund for Symposia and, where appropriate, to the financing of special projects, and otherwise to assist the secretariat of the Commission in carrying out training and legislative technical assistance activities, in particular in developing countries;

(*d*) Reiterates its appeal to the United Nations Development Programme and other bodies responsible for development assistance, such as the World Bank and regional development banks, as well as to Governments in their bilateral aid programmes, to support the training and legislative technical assistance programme of the Commission and to cooperate and co-ordinate their activities with those of the Commission;

6. *Takes note with regret* that, since the previous session of the Commission, no contributions have been made to the trust fund established to provide travel assistance to developing countries that are members of the Commission, at their request and in consultation with the Secretary-General, stresses the need for contributions to the trust fund in order to increase expert representation from developing countries at sessions of the Commission and its working groups, and reiterates its appeal to Governments, the relevant bodies of the United Nations system, organizations, institutions and individuals to make voluntary contributions to the trust fund;

7. *Decides*, in order to ensure full participation by all Member States in the sessions of the Commission and its working groups, to continue, in the competent Main Committee during the fifty-ninth session of the General Assembly, its consideration of granting travel assistance to the least developed countries that are members of the Commission, at their request and in consultation with the Secretary-General;

8. *Recalls* its resolutions on partnerships between the United Nations and non-State actors, in particular the private sector, and in this regard welcomes the Commission's consideration of the means of actively engaging non-State actors in its work, and encourages the Commission to further explore different approaches to the use of partnerships with non-State actors in the implementation of its mandate, in particular in the area of training and technical assistance, in accordance with the applicable principles and guidelines and in cooperation and coordination with other relevant offices of the Secretariat;

9. *Approves*, in conformity with its resolutions on documentation-related matters, which, in particular, emphasize that any reduction in the length of documents should not adversely affect either the quality of the presentation or the substance of the documents, the conclusions reached by the Commission in paragraphs 124 to 128 of its report regarding the imposition of page limits on its documentation, and requests the Secretary-General to bear in mind the particular characteristics of the mandate and work of the Commission in implementing page limits with respect to the documentation of the Commission;

10. *Also approves* the conclusions of the Commission in paragraph 130 of its report regarding the need for the continuing provision of summary records of its meetings relating to the formulation of normative texts;

11. *Stresses* the importance of bringing into effect the conventions emanating from the work of the Commission for the global unification and harmonization of international trade law, and, to this end, urges States that have not yet done so to consider signing, ratifying or acceding to those conventions;

12. *Notes* that 2005 will mark the twenty-fifth anniversary of the adoption of the United Nations Convention on Contracts for the International Sale of Goods and the twentieth anniversary of the adoption of the Model Law on International Commercial Arbitration of the United Nations Commission on International Trade Law, and in this regard welcomes initiatives being undertaken to organize conferences and similar

events to provide a forum for assessing the experience, in particular of courts and arbitral tribunals, with those texts;

13. *Expresses its appreciation* for the preparation of a digest of case law on the United Nations Convention on Contracts for the International Sale of Goods, intended to assist in the dissemination of information on the Convention and promote its adoption, use and uniform interpretation, and for the progress of work on a digest of case law relating to the Model Law on International Commercial Arbitration.

International commercial arbitration

UNCITRAL [A/59/17] took note of the reports of Working Group II (Arbitration and Conciliation) on its thirty-ninth (Vienna, 10-14 November 2003) [A/CN.9/545] and fortieth (New York, 23-27 February 2004) [A/CN.9/547] sessions. At those sessions, the Group continued deliberations on a draft text for a revision of article 17 of the UNCITRAL Model Law on International Commercial Arbitration on the power of an arbitral tribunal to grant interim measures of protection, and on a draft provision on the recognition and enforcement of such measures (for insertion as a new article of the Model Law, tentatively 17 bis). UNCITRAL commended the Group for the progress accomplished so far and hoped for an early consensus on the contentious issue of ex parte interim measures.

UNCITRAL observed that the Group had yet to complete its work on a draft article dealing with interim measures issued by State courts in support of arbitration (tentatively 17 ter) and in relation to the "writing requirement" contained in article 7, paragraph 2, of the Model Law, and article II, paragraph 2, of the Convention on the Recognition and Enforcement of Foreign Arbitral Awards (the New York Convention).

UNCITRAL was informed that the Working Group had been invited to consider the possible inclusion of the New York Convention in the list of international instruments to which the draft convention on the use of electronic communications in international contracts applied (see below). That question, in addition to the continued discussion on draft article 17, was considered by the Group at its forty-first session (Vienna, 13-17 September) [A/CN.9/569].

Implementation of the 1958 New York Convention

Under the ongoing project approved by UNCITRAL in 1995 [YUN 1995, p. 1364], aimed at monitoring the legislative implementation of the 1958 New York Convention [YUN 1958, p. 390], UNCITRAL [A/59/17] noted that, as at 8 April, replies from 75 States parties to the Convention (out of the current 134) had been received to the questionnaire relating to the legal regime in those States governing the recognition and enforcement of foreign arbitral awards. UNCITRAL called on the remaining States parties to submit their replies and invited the Secretariat to produce a preliminary analysis of those received for UNCITRAL's consideration in 2005.

Transport law

UNCITRAL [A/59/17] considered the reports of Working Group III (Transport Law) on its twelfth (Vienna, 6-17 October 2003) [YUN 2003, p. 1377] and thirteenth (New York, 3-14 May 2004) [A/CN.9/552] sessions, describing its continuing work on the provisions of a draft instrument on the carriage of goods [wholly or partly] [by sea]. It noted that, at the second reading of the draft, the Group had made progress on the scope of the instrument's application and on key liability provisions. An informal consultation group was created to meet between Working Group sessions so as to accelerate the exchange of views and arrive at a consensus in preparation for a third and final reading of the draft instrument. UNCITRAL agreed that 2006 was a desirable time frame for completing the project, but would revisit the matter of a deadline in 2005.

The Working Group, at its fourteenth session (Vienna, 29 November–10 December) [A/CN.9/572], continued to review the draft instrument based on a first revision of the draft prepared by the Secretariat and proposed interim redrafts of articles considered at the Group's previous two sessions. On the basis of its deliberations and conclusions, the Group requested the Secretariat to prepare a revised draft of a number of provisions.

Electronic commerce

UNCITRAL [A/59/17] took note of the reports of Working Group IV (Electronic Commerce) on its forty-second (Vienna, 17-21 November 2003) [YUN 2003, p. 1377] and forty-third (New York, 15-19 March 2004) [A/CN.9/548] sessions, during which it reviewed articles 1-15 and articles X and Y of the preliminary draft convention on electronic commerce dealing with selected issues related to electronic contracting. The Group's focus was to incorporate in the draft convention provisions aimed at removing possible legal obstacles to electronic commerce that might arise under existing international trade-related instruments and to formulate a broader legal framework for electronic contracting.

At its forty-fourth session (Vienna, 11-22 October) [A/CN.9/571], the Group resumed deliberations on a newly revised preliminary draft convention. It adopted articles 1-14, 18 and 19, and

exchanged views on the preamble and final clauses, including proposals for additional provisions in chapter IV. In the light of its deliberations on chapters I to III and articles 18 and 19, the Group asked the Secretariat to make the consequential changes in the draft final provisions of chapter IV and to insert within square brackets the draft provisions proposed for addition to the final revised version of the draft convention for submission to UNCITRAL. The Group further asked the Secretariat to circulate the final revised version of the draft convention to Governments and international organizations for their comments, and for submission to UNCITRAL.

UNCITRAL took note of various suggestions for future work, among them the preparation of guidelines to assist States in establishing a comprehensive legal framework to facilitate the use of electronic commerce.

Insolvency law

Legislative Guide on Insolvency Law

Working Group V (Insolvency Law), at its thirtieth session (New York, 29 March–2 April) [A/CN.9/551], completed its deliberations on the substantive parts of the draft legislative guide on insolvency law; for lack of time, however, it could not finalize its consideration of the glossary. The Group's deliberations were informed by those of its joint session with Working Group VI (Security Interests) (see p. 1355).

In addition, the Group noted a proposal to jointly publish the World Bank's *Principles and Guidelines for Effective Insolvency and Creditor Rights System*, currently under revision, and the finalized UNCITRAL Legislative Guide on Insolvency Law to form a unified standard on insolvency and creditor rights.

UNCITRAL in June [A/59/17] considered the draft legislative guide. It had before it a Secretariat note [A/CN.9/559 & Add.1,2] setting forth the terms of the glossary that were finalized by Working Group V and those that were not, as well as the Model Law on Cross-Border Insolvency and the Guide to Enactment of the Model Law [YUN 1997, p. 1379]. Having approved the substance of Parts One and Two, together with amendments and revisions, UNCITRAL concluded its review of the draft guide. It asked the Secretariat to edit and finalize the text in the light of its deliberations and to undertake any further revision required to align the commentary with the recommendations in the document.

On 25 June, UNCITRAL adopted the Legislative Guide on Insolvency Law, annexing the Model Law on Cross-Border Insolvency and the Guide to Enactment, and requested the Secretary-General to transmit it to Governments and other interested bodies. It recommended that all States utilize the Legislative Guide to assess the economic efficiency of their insolvency law regimes and give favourable consideration to the Legislative Guide when revising or adopting legislation relevant to insolvency. It further recommended that all States continue to consider implementing the UNCITRAL Model Law on Cross-Border Insolvency.

GENERAL ASSEMBLY ACTION

On 2 December [meeting 65], the General Assembly, on the recommendation of the Sixth Committee [A/59/509], adopted **resolution 59/40** without vote [agenda 143].

Legislative Guide on Insolvency Law of the United Nations Commission on International Trade Law

The General Assembly,

Recognizing the importance to all countries of strong, effective and efficient insolvency regimes as a means of encouraging economic development and investment,

Noting the growing realization that reorganization regimes are critical to corporate and economic recovery, the development of entrepreneurial activity, the preservation of employment and the availability of finance in the capital market,

Noting also the importance of social policy issues to the design of an insolvency regime,

Noting with satisfaction the completion and adoption of the Legislative Guide on Insolvency Law of the United Nations Commission on International Trade Law by the Commission at its thirty-seventh session, on 25 June 2004,

Believing that the Legislative Guide, which includes the text of the Model Law on Cross-Border Insolvency and the Guide to Enactment recommended by the General Assembly in its resolution 52/158 of 15 December 1997, contributes significantly to the establishment of a harmonized legal framework for insolvency and will be useful both to States that do not have an effective and efficient insolvency regime and to States that are undertaking a process of review and modernization of their insolvency regimes,

Recognizing the need for cooperation and coordination between international organizations active in the field of insolvency law reform to ensure consistency and alignment of that work and to facilitate the development of international standards,

Noting that the preparation of the Legislative Guide was the subject of due deliberations and extensive consultations with Governments and international intergovernmental and non-governmental organizations active in the field of insolvency law reform,

1. *Expresses its appreciation* to the United Nations Commission on International Trade Law for the completion and adoption of its Legislative Guide on Insolvency Law;

2. *Requests* the Secretary-General to publish the Legislative Guide and to make all efforts to ensure that it becomes generally known and available;

3. *Recommends* that all States give due consideration to the Legislative Guide when assessing the economic efficiency of their insolvency regimes and when revising or adopting legislation relevant to insolvency;

4. *Recommends also* that all States continue to consider implementation of the Model Law on Cross-Border Insolvency of the United Nations Commission on International Trade Law.

Security interests

UNCITRAL [A/59/17] took note of the reports of Working Group VI (Security Interests) on its fourth (Vienna, 8-12 September 2003) [YUN 2003, p. 1378] and fifth (New York, 22-25 March) sessions [A/CN.9/549], at which the Working Group continued its work on the development of an efficient legal regime for security rights in goods involved in a commercial activity, in the form of a legislative guide. Also noted was the report of the Group's second joint session (New York, 26-29 March) [A/CN.9/550] with Working Group V (Insolvency Law), at which the two Groups continued deliberations on the treatment of security interests in case of insolvency proceedings.

UNCITRAL commended Working Group VI for completing the second reading of the draft legislative guide on secured transactions, including the chapters on the introduction, key objectives and creation of security rights; and the third reading of the chapters on publicity, priority, insolvency and conflict of laws. In that connection, UNCITRAL noted the Group's agreement that publicity be a precondition of the effectiveness of security rights against third parties and of ensuring the protection of third parties.

UNCITRAL noted the progress made in the coordination of the Group's work on conflict of laws with the Hague Conference on Private International Law, the International Institute for the Unification of Private Law (Unidroit) and the World Bank, in particular for the agreement that the relevant sections of the Bank's *Principles* would form with the draft legislative guide on secured transactions, once finalized, a single international standard on the subject.

At its sixth session (Vienna, 27 September–1 October) [A/CN.9/570], the Working Group continued its work on the chapters of the draft legislative guide on secured transactions, including basic approaches to security, pre-default rights and obligations, transition (from the old to the new legislative regime), default and enforcement, and effectiveness of security rights against third parties.

Case law on UNCITRAL texts

UNCITRAL [A/59/17] noted the ongoing work under the established system for the collection and dissemination of case law on UNCITRAL texts (CLOUT), consisting of the preparation of case abstracts and of research aids and analytic tools, such as thesauri and indices, and the compilation of full texts of decisions. A total of 42 issues of CLOUT, dealing with 489 cases, had been published.

UNCITRAL expressed its appreciation to the national correspondents for their work in selecting decisions and preparing case abstracts. CLOUT was an important aspect of the overall training and technical assistance information activities undertaken by UNCITRAL. Its wide distribution in both print and electronic formats promoted the uniform interpretation and application of UNCITRAL texts by facilitating access to decisions and awards from other jurisdictions.

Training and technical assistance

UNCITRAL [A/59/17] considered a Secretariat note [A/CN.9/560] describing training and technical assistance activities undertaken since 2003 and the direction of future activities under its expanded functions. Reported, among other things, were 13 seminars and briefing missions organized to promote understanding of international commercial law conventions, model laws and other legal texts, and participation in 37 seminars, conferences and courses examining UNCITRAL texts for possible adoption or use. UNCITRAL also co-sponsored the eleventh Willem C. Vis International Commercial Arbitration Moot (Vienna, 2-8 April) to disseminate information about uniform law texts and teaching international trade law.

UNCITRAL reiterated its appeal to all States, international organizations and other interested entities to consider making contributions to its trust funds to enable it to meet increasing demands on its training and technical assistance programme. It requested the Secretariat to prepare a work programme and timetable for implementing its expanded technical assistance function, identifying national and regional needs, technical legal assistance requirements in international trade law reform and opportunities for developing joint programmes in that area.

Future work

Public procurement

UNCITRAL [A/59/17] discussed its future work in public procurement based on a Secretariat note [A/CN.9/539 & Add.1] submitted in response to its 2003 request [YUN 2003, p. 1379]. UNCITRAL agreed that the Model Law on Procurement of Goods, Construction and Services [YUN 1994, p. 1328] would benefit from being updated to reflect new practices, particularly those resulting from the use of electronic communications in public procurement, experiences gained from the use of the Model Law and possible additional issues. It entrusted the preparation of proposals for revising the Model Law to its Working Group I (Procurement), with a flexible mandate to identify the issues to be addressed. It requested the Secretariat to prepare detailed studies and proposals on the issues outlined in its note for the Group's consideration.

Working Group I began its work on the elaboration of proposals for the revision of the Model Law at its sixth session (Vienna, 30 August–3 September) [A/CN.9/568]. It gave preliminary consideration to the electronic publication of procurement-related information; the use of electronic communications in the procurement process and controls over such use; electronic reverse auctions; the use of suppliers' lists; framework agreements; procurement of services; evaluation and comparison of tenders and the use of procurement to promote industrial, social and environmental policies; remedies and enforcement; alternative methods of procurement; community participation in procurement; simplification and standardization of the Model Law; and legalization of documents. The Group would proceed with in-depth consideration of those topics at its future sessions.

PART FIVE

Institutional, administrative and budgetary questions

Chapter I

Strengthening and restructuring of the United Nations system

In 2004, the implementation of the Secretary-General's reform proposals to further improve the work of the Organization was largely completed. Notable achievements included the alignment of the Organization's activities with the priorities agreed upon at the Millennium Summit in 2000 and at the global conferences of the 1990s, a major reorganization of two large Departments—the Department for General Assembly and Conference Management and the Department of Public Information—as well as reforms at the Office of the United Nations High Commissioner for Refugees. Regarding planning and budgeting, a two-year strategic framework replaced the four-year medium-term plan, with good results. The processes for programme planning and resource allocation became better aligned, and the intergovernmental review process, streamlined.

In June, a 12-member panel of eminent persons established by the Secretary-General to review the relationship between the United Nations and civil society within the context of UN reform made recommendations for enhancing the Organization's capacity to engage relevant actors in tackling global problems. In December, the High-level Panel on Threats, Challenges and Change, appointed in 2003 to evaluate how the UN addressed current threats, also recommended measures to strengthen the Organization, including the establishment of an additional Deputy Secretary-General position to assist the Secretary-General.

The Assembly decided to convene in 2005 a high-level plenary meeting to undertake a comprehensive review of progress made in fulfilling the commitments contained in the Millennium Declaration. It also adopted a text regarding further measures to revitalize its own work. It urged the Open-ended Working Group on the Question of Equitable Representation and Increase in the Membership of the Security Council and Other Matters Related to the Security Council to make progress in considering all issues relevant to the question. While stressing the importance of the evaluation work of the Office of Internal Oversight Services, the Assembly decided to review at its sixty-fourth (2009) session the functions and reporting procedures of that Office.

Programme of reform

General aspects

In his annual report on the work of the Organization (see p. 3), the Secretary-General stated that the implementation of his reform proposals, initiated in 2002 [YUN 2002, p. 1352], to further improve the work of the Organization was largely complete. Notable achievements included the alignment of the Organization's activities with the priorities agreed upon at the 2000 Millennium Summit [YUN 2000, p. 45] and at the global conferences of the 1990s, the reorganization of the Department for General Assembly and Conference Management (DGACM) [YUN 2003, p. 1486] and the Department of Public Information (DPI) [YUN 2002, p. 585], and reforms in the Office of the United Nations High Commissioner for Refugees (UNHCR) (see p. 1195). Other positive developments included the discontinuation of a large number of reports, meetings and activities of marginal utility, the reallocation of over $100 million within or between programmes and the approval of significant increases in funds for improving information and communication technology services and related staff training. With regard to planning and budgeting, a two-year strategic framework replaced the four-year medium-term plan (see p. 1400), while the processes for programme planning and resource allocation had become better aligned and the intergovernmental review process streamlined. The implementation of the integrated human resources management reform programme (see p. 1416) continued with the further refinement of practices and procedures, and progress in implementing the Organization's human resources strategy. The administration of justice had also become more efficient. Improvements were made in client servicing, and efforts continued to implement the capital master plan (see p. 1473), improve financial management and enhance the Organization's accountability and oversight functions. In view of increasing threats to the Organization and its staff, measures were taken to enhance security at Headquarters and in field offices.

UN system funds and programmes continued to strengthen their presence at the country level and to address the issues of joint programming and management of resources.

Agenda for change

Strengthening of the UN system

Panel of eminent persons

By a June note [A/58/817 & Corr.1], the Secretary-General transmitted the report of the Panel of Eminent Persons on United Nations-Civil Society Relations entitled "We the peoples: civil society, the United Nations and global governance". First proposed in his 2002 report on strengthening of the United Nations : an agenda for further change [YUN 2002, p. 1352] and endorsed by the General Assembly in resolution 57/300 [ibid., p. 1353], the Secretary-General asked the Panel, among other things, to review guidelines, decisions and practices that affected civil society organizations' access to and participation in UN deliberations and processes, to identify new and better ways to interact with them, especially those from developing countries, and to review the Secretariat's organizational structure for facilitating, managing and evaluating UN relationships with civil society.

The Panel, chaired by Fernando Henrique Cardoso (Brazil), recognized that civil society organizations, through their global networks of activists, websites and other channels, were creating a new phenomenon, the global public opinion, which was shaping the political agenda and generating a set of norms and citizen demands that transcended national boundaries and had contributed to the opening of a global public space for debate. Over the years, the United Nations had consistently promoted the participation of civil society in its deliberative processes, leading to the emergence of values and norms, especially in the areas of human rights, gender relations, governance and the environment. However, the Panel questioned whether the United Nations had been clear enough in articulating its case for enhancing such engagement. The Panel found that civil societies and other constituencies were important to the United Nations because of their experience and social connections that could help the Organization work better, improve its legitimacy, identify priorities and connect it with public opinion. They could also raise new issues, focus attention on the moral and ethical dimensions of decisions in the public sphere, expand resources and skills, challenge basic assumptions and priorities and protest unfair decisions. En-

hanced engagement, carefully planned, would make the United Nations more effective in its actions and contributions to global governance, empower it, and increase its relevance to the issues of our times. The Panel established four paradigm shifts to guide the United Nations in strengthening its relations with civil society and other constituencies: becoming an outward-looking organization; embracing a plurality of constituencies; connecting the local with the global; and helping to reshape democracy for the twenty-first century.

The Panel made 30 proposals for reform in several areas. It proposed the creation of global policy networks of Government and others sharing specific concerns to promote global debate and/or pilot activities to combat problems directly, and that the United Nations be more proactive in bringing together all constituencies relevant to global issues and galvanize appropriate networks for effective results. In that regard, the Assembly should include civil society more regularly in its affairs, and public hearings involving a full range of relevant constituencies could be used for reviving progress on agreed global goals. Other proposed reforms concerned the need to invest more in partnerships, including the establishment by the Secretary-General of a Partnership Development Unit and the identification of partnership focal points throughout all UN organs and agencies. At the country level, the United Nations Development Group should ensure that all constituencies contributed to the goals of the United Nations by, among other actions, enhancing the capacity of UN resident coordinators' offices to identify, convene and broker partnerships to meet the main challenges and build consensus on country-specific goals. The Security Council should be enabled to draw from the experience of civil society organizations, and discuss with elected representatives issues of emerging importance, and convene independent commissions of inquiry after Council-mandated operations. The United Nations should encourage national parliaments to debate major matters on its agendas, and the Secretary-General should form an Elected Representatives Liaison Unit to provide information to parliaments and help create more effective opportunities for parliamentarians to take part in UN forums. The United Nations should streamline and depoliticize accreditation and access issues, including widening the access of civil society organizations beyond Economic and Social Council forums, and create a single UN accreditation process. The review of applications for accreditation should be shifted to the Secretariat and an accreditation unit established within DGACM to advise an Assembly Committee, which would decide on accreditation. The Secretary-General should initiate a review on UN accreditation, based on which proposals would be made to the Assembly for revising accreditation categories. The Secretary-General should appoint an Under-Secretary-General in charge of the new Office of Constituency Engagement and Partnerships, which would be responsible for formulating and implementing the UN strategy for engagement with constituencies. It would comprise a Civil Society Unit, which would absorb the Non-Governmental Liaison Service; a Partnership Development Unit to absorb the United Nations Fund for International Partnerships; the Elected Representative Liaison Unit; the Global Compact Office; and the secretariat of the Permanent Forum of Indigenous Issues. The Secretary-General should appoint 30 to 40 constituency engagement specialists in the offices of resident coordinators, and make redressing North-South imbalances a priority in enhancing UN-civil society relations. The United Nations should establish a fund to enhance the capacity of civil society in developing countries to engage in UN processes and partnerships.

Report of Secretary-General. In a September report [A/59/354], the Secretary-General commended the Panel's recommendations to the General Assembly for consideration. He welcomed the majority of those recommendations, which he supplemented with several of his own. In terms of increasing the participation of non-governmental organizations (NGOs) in intergovernmental bodies, the Secretary-General proposed the convening of a two-day, informal, interactive hearing with them prior to the opening of the Assembly each year, beginning on a trial basis at the Assembly's sixtieth (2005) session, to coincide with the 10-year review of the MDGs [YUN 2000, p. 51]. The Security Council could adopt the practice of conducting an assessment, with NGO participation, following completion of each peace mission, while reserving the Panel's proposal for an independent commission of inquiry after Council-mandated operations for special cases. The Assembly could recommend, organize or support meetings of parliamentarians at the national, regional or global levels in 2006 to provide input to the meeting to review the Declaration of Commitment on HIV/AIDS (see p. 1216). The Secretary-General said that he would create a single trust fund to support NGO participation in intergovernmental meetings, subsuming existing funds into it, and develop a detailed cost plan for administering it. He encouraged Member States to contribute to the fund. The Secretary-General said that there was not much

merit in consolidating the various UN accreditation processes or the structures for handling them. However, the Assembly could assume responsibility for a single accreditation system, with the General Committee being charged with that responsibility. The Secretary-General promised to review Secretariat experiences with NGOs in tandem with the Panel's proposals, with a view to determining how best to intensify dialogue with them. He would also establish a trust fund to enhance NGO capacity at the country level and to finance additional capacity in the office of the resident coordinator.

The Secretary-General did not agree with the Panel's proposal to incorporate the secretariat of the Permanent Forum of Indigenous Issues into the new Office of Constituency Engagement and Partnerships.

By **decision 59/552** of 23 December, the Assembly decided that the item on strengthening of the UN system would remain for consideration during its resumed fifty-ninth (2005) session.

High-level Panel on Threats, Challenges and Change

The High-level Panel on Threats, Challenges and Change, in its report transmitted by the Secretary-General in December [A/59/565 & Corr.1] (see p. 54), discussed, among other proposals for strengthening the Organization, institutional reform for a more effective United Nations in the twenty-first century. The Panel looked at the institutional weaknesses in current responses to threats in the functioning of the General Assembly, the Security Council, the arrangements for addressing countries under stress, as well as the economic and social threats to international security, and to a legitimacy deficit regarding the functioning of the United Nations Commission on Human Rights.

The Panel recommended reform initiatives for addressing those weaknesses. It proposed that Member States renew efforts to enable the Assembly to function as the main deliberative organ, including better conceptionalization and shortening of its agenda, smaller and more tightly focused committees to sharpen and improve resolutions, and the establishment of a better mechanism to enable systematic engagement with civil society. A decision on the enlargement of the Council was a necessity based on the membership models proposed: model A provided for six new permanent seats with no new veto and three new two-year term non-permanent seats, divided among regional areas; while model B provided for no new permanent seats, but created a new category of eight four-year renewable-term seats and one new two-year non-permanent (non-renewable seat), divided among major regional areas. The Panel also recommended that the composition of the Council should be reviewed in 2020, there should be no expansion of the veto, and introduction of a system of "indicative voting" (public indication of positions on a proposed action) should be introduced. Proposals were also made for strengthening the Council's relations with regional organizations. The Panel recommended that the Economic and Social Council establish a Committee on the Social and Economic Aspects of Security Threats and provide a regular venue for engaging the development community at the highest level by transforming itself into a "development cooperation forum". To that end, it should create an executive committee to provide orientation and direction.

Regarding reform of the Secretariat, the Panel recommended strengthening support for the Secretary-General, primarily through the establishment of an additional Deputy Secretary-General position responsible for peace and security. The Secretary-General should also be provided with the requisite resources to do his job effectively. In that regard, Member States should commit themselves to articles 100 and 101 of the Charter relating to the duties of the Secretary-General and increase his flexibility in managing the staff, subject to his accountability to the Assembly. The Secretary-General's 1997 [YUN 1997, p.1389] and 2002 [YUN 2002, p.1352] reform proposals should be fully implemented, and there should be a one-time review and replacement of personnel, including through early retirement, to ensure that the Secretariat was staffed with the right people to undertake the task at hand. In addition, the Secretary-General should be provided with 60 posts for the purpose of increasing the Secretariat's capacity as proposed in the report. In addition to any amendment of Article 23 of the UN Charter required by the proposed reform of the Security Council, the Panel suggested that articles 53 and 107 referring to "enemy States" should be revised; and Chapter XIII (the Trusteeship Council) should be deleted, as well as article 47 (the Military Staff Committee) and all references to it in Articles 26, 45 and 46.

Implementation of the Millennium Declaration

Report of Secretary-General. In his August report [A/59/282 & Corr.1] on the implementation of the United Nations Millennium Declaration [YUN 2000, p. 49], the Secretary-General reviewed progress made and the results achieved by the UN system and by Member States in peace and security, especially in the areas of peacekeeping

and curbing transnational crime, meeting the MDGs and protecting the vulnerable.

In the area of security, the Secretary-General reported that, since his last report, UN peace operations had achieved significant success in Afghanistan, Ethiopia and Eritrea, Georgia, the Kosovo province of Serbia and Montenegro and Sierra Leone. However, 2004 saw the establishment of new missions in Burundi, Côte d'Ivoire and Haiti in the space of six months and planning for new or expanded operations in Iraq and the Sudan. That surge in demand for peacekeeping went beyond the needs envisaged in the reforms and the capacities that had been built. The Department of Peacekeeping Operations (DPKO) was addressing the new challenges, but critical gaps remained and further reforms were required. Careful political management and coordination were called for since each new or planned mission was complex and multidimensional.

Across the globe, the growth of transnational criminal activity was having a significant impact on peace and development, prospects for economic growth, human rights, democracy and good governance. The nature of criminal organizations involved in such activities, with the associated problems of corruption and linkages to terrorism, constituted one of the key security challenges facing the global community. The increasingly global nature of organized crime required a global response, of which the key instrument was the United Nations Convention against Transnational Organized Crime and its supplementary Protocols, which came into force in 2003 [YUN 2003, p. 1125]. Similarly, the adoption of the United Nations Convention against Corruption, adopted by the General Assembly in resolution 58/4 [ibid., p. 1127], was a significant achievement. In April 2004, the United Nations System Chief Executives Board for Coordination endorsed immediate and medium-term measures to ensure more effective action against organized crime in sectors where UN agencies were active.

In the area of development, in the four years since the adoption of the Millennium Declaration, the eight MDGs derived from it had transformed global development cooperation, generating unprecedented, coordinated action within the UN system, including the Bretton Woods institutions (the World Bank Group and the International Monetary Fund), the wider donor community and developing countries themselves. The commitment of Governments to the MDGs and their integration into national and international development strategies, policies and actions were expected to produce improved development results. Data available as at 2002 suggested that developing countries fell into three broad groups in terms of their progress towards meeting the MDGs: those in Asia and Northern Africa, which were largely on track to meeting the targets of halving extreme poverty by 2015 and achieving many of the social targets; those, mainly in West Asia and Latin America and the Caribbean, which were making good progress towards some individual goals, such as universal primary education, but were less successful in reducing poverty; and those, largely comprising countries in sub-Saharan Africa and least developed countries in other regions, which were far from making adequate progress on most of the goals.

In protecting the vulnerable, the report noted that the consequences of disasters resulting from environmental hazards continued to fall disproportionally on the world's poor, and trends suggested that the frequency of and vulnerability to such hazards would only get worse, with significant implications for humanitarian and development actors. Vulnerability to conflict continued to be widespread also, as prolonged violence significantly altered political, social and economic relations, with immediate and long-term implications. Some progress was made in strengthening support and protecting the internally displaced and ensuring more focused planning and funding of post-crisis transition, especially in Liberia and Sierra Leone. However, much more needed to be done by the international community to harmonize transition planning and fundraising, bring coherence to needs assessment and build local institutions.

The Secretary-General observed that, in order to succeed, the United Nations required a range of key inputs, including vision and political support, adequate financing, staff of the highest calibre, adequate security and institutional agility to adapt to changing circumstances in the world. The institutional arrangements required to achieve the goals contained in the Millennium Declaration also had to be agile. As the primary actors and stakeholders in the international system, Member States would have to be flexible in their own approaches. While major headway had been made on reform and revitalization in recent years, adaptation was a constant process as new realities called for new solutions in terms of mechanisms and processes.

Review of the Millennium Declaration (2005)

High-level plenary meeting of the General Assembly

On 6 May [meeting 86], the General Assembly adopted **resolution 58/291** [draft: A/58/L.8/Rev.1] without vote [agenda items 50 & 60].

Follow-up to the outcome of the Millennium Summit and integrated and coordinated implementation of and follow-up to the outcomes of the major United Nations conferences and summits in the economic and social fields

The General Assembly,

Recalling its resolutions 57/144 of 16 December 2002 on follow-up to the outcome of the Millennium Summit and 57/270 A of 20 December 2002 and 57/270 B of 23 June 2003 on integrated and coordinated implementation of and follow-up to the outcomes of the major United Nations conferences and summits in the economic and social fields,

1. *Decides* to convene in New York in 2005, at the commencement of the sixtieth session of the General Assembly, a high-level plenary meeting of the Assembly with the participation of heads of State and Government, on dates to be decided by the Assembly at its fifty-ninth session;

2. *Also decides* that this major event will undertake a comprehensive review of the progress made in the fulfilment of all the commitments contained in the United Nations Millennium Declaration, including the internationally agreed development goals and the global partnership required for their achievement, and of the progress made in the integrated and coordinated implementation, at the national, regional and international levels, of the outcomes and commitments of the major United Nations conferences and summits in the economic, social and related fields, on the basis of a comprehensive report to be submitted by the Secretary-General;

3. *Requests* the Secretary-General to submit to the General Assembly at its fifty-ninth session a report on suggested modalities, format and organization of this major event for consideration and a final decision by the Assembly, taking into account the open-ended consultations to be carried out by the President of the Assembly.

CEB consideration. The United Nations System Chief Executives Board (CEB), at its second regular session (New York, 29-30 October) [CEB/2004/2], discussed the 2005 comprehensive review of follow-up to the Millennium Declaration, particularly the UN system response. CEB discussed the themes and messages that should be given prominence in the Secretary-General's report for the high-level meeting scheduled for 2005, focusing on the progress made in implementing the Millennium Declaration, the key conditions to be highlighted for future progress and how the report might best convey UN system contributions in implementing the Declaration.

CEB also considered the reports of its High-level Committee on Programmes (HLCP) on its seventh (Beirut, Lebanon, 26-27 February) [CEB/2004/4], inter-sessional (Frascati, Italy, 31 May–1 June) [CEB/2004/5] and eighth (Florence, Italy, 15-17 September) [CEB/2004/7] sessions regarding its preparatory work for the 2005 comprehensive review. HLCP focused on articulating UN system contributions in implementing the Declaration, to be presented as an "accountability report", a draft of which was annexed to the report of its eighth session. CEB invited the Committee to continue its work on the report and to pursue a related proposal by the Director-General of the United Nations Industrial Development Organization for renewing the role of the UN in the field of economic development as a means of advancing the achievement of the MDGs.

Report of Secretary-General. In response to General Assembly resolution 58/291 (see above), the Secretary-General submitted a November report [A/59/545] on the modalities, format and organization of the high-level plenary meeting of the Assembly—a summit—to be held at the commencement of its sixtieth (2005) session. The report made suggestions regarding the duration, participation and preparatory process for the meeting, which the Secretary-General observed would be an event of decisive importance, given that the decisions taken there might determine the Organization's future. He urged Member States to take an active and positive interest in the issues before the summit, and to prepare for it at the highest level.

In a 16 December statement on programme budget implications [A/C.5/59/25], the Secretary-General informed the Assembly that the planned high-level plenary meeting would give rise to additional requirements estimated at $1,060,700 under the 2004-2005 programme budget, to be charged against the contingency fund and, as such, would require a related increase in appropriations for that biennium. Efforts would be made to absorb the $317,100 for the change in venue of the 2005 substantive session of the Economic and Social Council from Geneva to New York.

Report of ACABQ. The Advisory Committee on Administrative and Budgetary Questions (ACABQ), in its report of the same date, [A/59/613], recommended that every effort be made to absorb the amount requested and that the Fifth (Administrative and Budgetary) Committee inform the Assembly that, should it adopt draft resolution [A/59/L.53], no additional appropriation would arise at that time, pending the submission of the second performance report on the 2004-2005 programme budget.

GENERAL ASSEMBLY ACTION

On 17 December [meeting 73], the General Assembly adopted **resolution 59/145** [draft: A/59/L.53] without vote [agenda items 44 & 55].

Modalities, format and organization of the High-level Plenary Meeting of the sixtieth session of the General Assembly

The General Assembly,

Recalling its resolution 58/291 of 6 May 2004 by which it decided to convene in New York in 2005, at the commencement of the sixtieth session of the General Assembly, a high-level plenary meeting of the Assembly with the participation of Heads of State and Government, on dates to be decided by the Assembly at its fifty-ninth session,

Recalling that in its resolution 58/291 it also decided that the High-level Plenary Meeting would undertake a comprehensive review of the progress made in the fulfilment of all the commitments contained in the United Nations Millennium Declaration, including the internationally agreed development goals and the global partnership required for their achievement, and of the progress made in the integrated and coordinated implementation, at the national, regional and international levels, of the outcomes and commitments of the major United Nations conferences and summits in the economic, social and related fields, on the basis of a comprehensive report to be submitted by the Secretary-General,

Welcoming the report of the Secretary-General entitled "Modalities, format and organization of the high-level plenary meeting of the sixtieth session of the General Assembly" requested in its resolution 58/291 and following informal consultations convened by the President of the General Assembly,

Convinced that the High-level Plenary Meeting will constitute a significant event,

1. *Decides* that the High-level Plenary Meeting of the sixtieth session of the General Assembly shall be held from 14 to 16 September 2005 in New York;

2. *Reiterates* that the High-level Plenary Meeting will be held with the participation of Heads of State and Government, and encourages all Member States to be represented at that level;

3. *Decides* that the High-level Plenary Meeting will be composed of six plenary meetings, on the basis of two meetings a day, and four interactive round-table sessions, and also that each round-table session will cover the entire agenda of the High-level Plenary Meeting and will be held in concurrence with a plenary meeting;

4. *Decides also* to hold the High-level Dialogue on Financing for Development on 27 and 28 June 2005 in New York immediately prior to the high-level segment of the 2005 substantive session of the Economic and Social Council in order for the recommendations of the High-level Dialogue to be considered in the preparatory process for the High-level Plenary Meeting and also decides to hold a separate meeting on Financing for Development within the framework of the High-level Plenary Meeting;

5. *Decides further* to change the venue of the 2005 substantive session of the Economic and Social Council from Geneva to New York on an exceptional basis and that the venue for the 2006 and 2007 substantive sessions of the Council shall be Geneva in order to resume the alternation in 2008, as established by the General Assembly;

6. *Decides* to hold the general debate at its sixtieth session from Saturday, 17 September, to Friday, 23 September, and from Monday, 26 September, to Wednesday, 28 September 2005, on the understanding that these arrangements shall in no way create a precedent for the general debate at future sessions;

7. *Notes* that, prior to the High-level Plenary Meeting, the second World Conference of Speakers of Par-

liament will be convened from 7 to 9 September 2005 at United Nations Headquarters;

8. *Requests* the President of the General Assembly, in consultation with representatives of non-governmental organizations, to organize informal interactive hearings in June 2005 in New York with representatives of non-governmental organizations, civil society organizations and the private sector, as an input to the preparatory process of the High-level Plenary Meeting;

9. *Looks forward* to the comprehensive report requested in its resolution 58/291, which the Secretary-General will submit in March 2005 and which will serve as the basis for the consultations leading to the High-level Plenary Meeting;

10. *Strongly urges* all Member States to take a positive interest in the process of formal and informal consultations leading to the High-level Plenary Meeting and to engage actively, at the highest level of government, with a view to reaching a successful outcome of the High-level Plenary Meeting;

11. *Requests* the President of the General Assembly to continue to hold consultations with all Member States in an open-ended manner, with a view to taking decisions on all process-related outstanding issues of the High-level Plenary Meeting.

On 23 December, the Assembly decided that the item on the follow-up to the outcome of the Millennium Summit would remain for consideration during its resumed fifty-ninth (2005) session (**decision 59/552**).

Managerial reform and oversight

Procurement

JIU report. During the year, the Joint Inspection Unit (JIU) reviewed procurement practices within the UN system [JIU/REP/2004/9 & Corr.1] to identify opportunities for increasing procurement efficiency in the common system, through productivity enhancement, improved cooperation and coordination and technological innovations. The review, which focused on the cost-effectiveness of common system organizations' procurement services, provided an overview of procurement operations in 2002, particularly the aggregate procurement value and trends, the distribution of procurement activities, procurement expenditures, geographic distribution, procurement from programme countries, common and specialized items, and major clients. Also examined were issues relating to the training of procurement staff; cooperation and coordination among common system organizations, including on the question of policy and related mechanisms; electronic procurement (e-procurement); and capacity-building in public procurement, particularly in recipient client countries.

JIU found that the procurement function had evolved over the previous ten years from a rela-

tively obscure administrative activity to a financially high-profile and high-risk function, accounting in 2002 for about $4.6 billion or 37 per cent of the organizations' combined regular and extrabudgetary resources. However, while procurement operations at Headquarters had been streamlined under a reform programme [YUN 1996, p. 1381] mandated and guided by the General Assembly in resolutions 49/216 C [YUN 1994, p. 1369] and 51/231 [YUN 1997, p. 1395], such reform measures were yet to filter down to other major duty stations, including field offices and the collective membership of the Inter-Agency Procurement Working Group (IAPWG)—the only inter-agency procurement forum involving virtually all common system organizations. JIU concluded that IAPWG had not done enough to research and develop procurement performance benchmarks or efficiency and quality paradigms to guide performance of the procurement function within the UN system, with special attention on related facilities and practices at field level. In addition, there was a need for rationalization, particularly the procurement of common user items, and increased outsourcing of procurement tasks among organizations as a means for reducing overlap and competition within the procurement community. Other shortcomings included the inadequacy of financial resources devoted to the training of procurement staff; the lack of central policy guidance in procurement; and major constraints that undermined the potential benefits of e-procurement.

JIU recommended that the Secretary-General continue to evaluate the results achieved by the Procurement Working Group of the Task Force on Common Services at Headquarters and other locations, including its findings on procurement performance benchmarks and other best practices resulting from procurement reforms, and that the evaluation report be discussed by the High-level Committee on Management of CEB and by IAPWG, which should, in turn, adopt recommendations for the procurement community. IAPWG should adopt and implement the concept of lead agency and promote a division of labour among common system organizations, aimed at the further rationalization of procurement practices by its members. Other recommendations advocated the establishment of a unified system of reporting and accountability for procurement services of the International Civil Aviation Organization, the International Telecommunications Union and the Universal Postal Union; staff training in the legal aspects of procurement; increasing procurement training budgets and related training initiatives; expanding training in e-procurement; the development of e-procurement solutions; the provision of procurement manuals in the working languages of common system organizations and the development of a generic system-wide policy and procedures manual; and formalizing the mandate of the inter-agency cooperation and coordination role of IAPWG and requiring it to report annually and to make action-oriented proposals on continuous improvements in the management, performance measurement and coordination of procurement services. In addition, JIU recommended further strengthening procurement reform at Headquarters through the establishment of a central procurement facility by 2010 to provide a frame of reference for similar streamlining of procurement services at other duty stations; avoiding overlap between the United Nations Office for Project Services procurement service and the Inter-Agency Procurement Services Office, including the option of merging the two entities; and capacity-building in public procurement agencies in recipient developing countries to strengthen their ability to participate in procurement.

Report of Secretary-General. In response to General Assembly resolution 57/279 [YUN 2002, p. 1358], the Secretary-General, in an August report [A/59/216], described the progress made since his 2002 report [YUN 2002, p. 1357] in procurement reform, in the areas of procurement opportunities for vendors from developing countries and countries with economies in transition, harmonization of the procurement process, the operation of air transportation service, audit observations, field procurement, efficiency in procurement, procurement training, vendor management, contract award and the work of the Committee on Rules of Origin. Annexed to the report were procurement statistics covering 1999 to 2003 and country procurement value by procurement division and local peacekeeping mission in 2002 and 2003, respectively.

The Secretary-General reported that the Secretariat had strengthened its cooperation with other UN system organizations through IAPWG and the Common Services Procurement Working Group. A newly designed web-based vendor registration system, designated the United Nations Global Marketplace, was launched in February to help harmonize the procurement process by simplifying the registration component. In terms of vendor management, IAPWG agreed that in future, different organizations would take the lead in evaluating and pre-qualifying vendors: the United Nations would take the lead in air charter services, information technology and communication goods and services; the United Nations Population Fund, in reproductive health items; the United Nations Children's Fund and the

World Health Organization, in medical items and pharmaceuticals; and the World Food Programme and the United Nations Relief and Works Agency for Palestine refugees in the Near East (UNRWA), in basic food commodities. That would eliminate administrative duplication and make the registration process more efficient and timely. The UN Secretariat and other system organizations created a standing working group to coordinate activities related to business seminars, including the development of guidelines, the prioritization of requests and the coordination of representation in an effort to further promote procurement opportunities for vendors from developing countries and countries with economies in transition. The Secretariat's Procurement Division revised the Procurement Manual. In terms of developing a code of conduct for procurement staff, the Secretariat had developed ethical guidelines, which the Inter-Agency Procurement Working Group agreed, in May, would be used by UN organizations to develop common guidelines for all. To improve the efficiency of the procurement decision-making process, the Secretariat further developed a system, known as the eHCC system, to process presentations to the Headquarters Committee on Contracts electronically. That would allow peacekeeping missions to submit local procurement cases to be reviewed by Headquarters directly to the Procurement Division for immediate review and processing. The Division also introduced electronic procurement data monitoring tools, a requisition tracking system and a workload monitoring system.

The Secretary-General concluded that the report demonstrated the Secretariat's commitments and collaborative efforts to increase transparency, fairness and responsiveness in the procurement process, as well as to enlist the collaboration and support of other common system organizations in developing a harmonized approach for improving efficiency in the procurement practices of the entire UN system.

ACABQ report. ACABQ, in an October report [A/59/540], acknowledged the Secretariat's efforts to promote procurement from developing countries, particularly through seminars. It encouraged the exploration of other avenues, including an analysis of the current approach to seminars, in order to make them more results-oriented, and recommended that follow-up mechanisms be considered. ACABQ welcomed initiatives developed to improve efficiency, including the review of vendor management and implementation of related recommendations. On the question of accountability, the Advisory Committee requested that related information be provided in the Secretary-General's next report and recommended that weaknesses in the procurement process identified by the Board of Auditors be addressed. Concerning the training of field procurement staff, ACABQ was of the opinion that training programmes should focus on a train-the-trainers approach, through which large numbers of junior personnel could be trained in a more cost-effective and efficient way. It recalled that it had drawn attention in its 2003 report [YUN 2003, p. 82] to the need to monitor and evaluate training needs in that regard.

Oversight activities

Internal oversight

At its resumed fifty-eighth session, the General Assembly had before it the OIOS report on its activities for the period from 1 July 2002 to 30 June 2003 [YUN 2003, p. 1386]. By **decision 58/564 B** of 8 April, the Assembly decided to defer consideration of the report until its fifty-ninth (2004) session.

The Assembly also had before it OIOS reports on the evaluation of the impact of the recent restructuring of DPKO (see p. 102); the follow-up review of the status of OIOS recommendations on mission liquidation activities at the United Nations [YUN 2003, p. 94]; the administration of Peacekeeping trust funds [ibid, p. 90]; and the investigation into the fraudulent diversion of $4.3 million by a senior staff member of the reconstruction pillar of the United Nations Interim Administration Mission in Kosovo [ibid., p. 427].

GENERAL ASSEMBLY ACTION

On 18 June [meeting 91], the General Assembly, on the recommendation of the Fifth (Administrative and Budgetary) Committee [A/58/582/Add.2], adopted **resolution 58/299** without vote [agenda item 134].

Reports of the Office of Internal Oversight Services

The General Assembly,

Recalling its resolutions 48/218 B of 29 July 1994, 54/244 of 23 December 1999, 56/241 and 56/246 of 24 December 2001 and 57/278 B of 18 June 2003,

Having considered the reports of the Office of Internal Oversight Services on the evaluation of the impact of the recent restructuring of the Department of Peacekeeping Operations, the follow-up review of the status of recommendations of the Office of Internal Oversight Services on mission liquidation activities at the United Nations, the administration of peacekeeping trust funds, and the investigation into the fraudulent diversion of 4.3 million United States dollars by a senior staff member of the reconstruction pillar of the United Nations Interim Administration Mission in Kosovo,

1. *Takes note* of the reports of the Office of Internal Oversight Services on the evaluation of the impact of the recent restructuring of the Department of Peacekeeping Operations, the follow-up review of the status of recommendations of the Office of Internal Oversight Services on mission liquidation activities at the United Nations, the administration of peacekeeping trust funds, and the investigation into the fraudulent diversion of 4.3 million dollars by a senior staff member of the reconstruction pillar of the United Nations Interim Administration Mission in Kosovo;

2. *Decides* to revert to the consideration of the report of the Office of Internal Oversight Services on the audit of the policies and procedures for recruiting staff for the Department of Peacekeeping Operations, during its fifty-ninth session, in the context of its consideration of the items entitled "Human resources management" and "Administrative and budgetary aspects of the financing of the United Nations peacekeeping operations";

3. *Notes* that the Board of Auditors will act upon General Assembly resolution 57/318 of 18 June 2003 once it has considered the report of the Office of Internal Oversight Services and assessed what additional evaluation it might provide, and also notes that the General Assembly may revert at that time to the report of the Office of Internal Oversight Services.

At its fifty-ninth session, the Assembly continued consideration of the reports of OIOS on its activities for the period from 1 July 2002 to 30 June 2003 [YUN 2003, p. 1386] and on the review of the structure and operations of the United Nations Information Centres [ibid., p. 636]. It also had before it the OIOS report on its audit of regional commissions (see p. 992).

OIOS activities. In October, the Secretary-General transmitted the tenth annual report of OIOS covering its activities from 1 July 2003 to 30 June 2004 [A/59/359]. During the reporting period, OIOS issued several reports, which the Secretary-General transmitted to the General Assembly. Those issued in 2004, in addition to its report on its own activities, were on: the review of the Office of the Prosecutor at the International Criminal Tribunals for Rwanda and for the former Yugoslavia [A/58/677]; audit of the policies and procedures for recruiting DPKO staff [A/58/704]; strengthening the investigation functions in the United Nations [A/58/708]; evaluation of the impact of the recent restructuring of DPKO [A/58/746]; the implementation of the recommendations of OIOS on the Investment Management Service of the United Nations Joint Staff Pension Fund [A/58/725]; audit of the regional commissions [A/58/785]; programme performance of the United Nations for the biennium 2002-2003 [A/59/69]; strengthening the role of evaluation findings in programme design, delivery and policy directives [A/59/79]; integration of global management of conference services [A/59/133 & Corr.1];

follow-up audit of DPKO policies and procedures for recruitment [A/59/152]; inspection of programme management and administrative practices of the International Trade Centre sponsored by the United Nations Conference on Trade and Development and the World Trade Organization (UNCTAD/WTO) [A/59/229]; audit of safeguarding air safety standards while procuring air services for UN peacekeeping missions [A/59/347]; review of the operation and management of United Nations Libraries [A/59/ 373]; impact of the human resources management reform [A/59/253]; report on the availability in local labour markets of the skills for which international recruitment for the General Service category took place [A/59/388]; report on the utilization and management of funds appropriated during the 2002-2003 biennium for strengthening the security and safety of United Nations premises [A/59/396]; management review of the appeals process at the United Nations [A/59/408]; the United Nations capital master plan for the period August 2003-July 2004 [A/59/420]; and first year of experience of regional investigations in two hubs, Vienna and Nairobi [A/59/546].

One OIOS report, transmitted to the Economic and Social Council, was on the evaluation of the United Nations Voluntary Fund for Victims of Torture [E/CN.4/2005/55].

Those for transmittal to the Committee for Programme and Coordination (CPC) were on: further development of topics for a pilot thematic evaluation [E/AC.51/2004/2]; in-depth evaluation of the programme on public administration, finance and development [E/AC.51/2004/3]; and triennial reviews of the implementation of the recommendations made by CPC in 2001 on the in-depth evaluation of sustainable development [E/AC.51/2004/4] and of the population programme [E/AC/51/2004/5].

During the period under review, OIOS issued 1,515 recommendations, of which 473 or 35.7 per cent were classified as critical. The overall implementation rate for all recommendations was 52.3 per cent. As at 30 June 2004, the implementation of 80 (including four critical) recommendations issued during 2001/02 and 114 recommendations (including 22 critical) issued during 2002/03 had not started owing to their complexity or to lengthy negotiations on the modalities for implementation. Of the 473 critical recommendations issued, 49 per cent were aimed at improving operational efficiency and effectiveness; 33 per cent, administration and management; 14 per cent, accuracy of management information; and 4 per cent, security and disclosure of mismanagement, misconduct or fraud. Savings and recoveries from OIOS audits and investigations

totalled $26.6 million, compared to $15.4 million in the previous reporting period [YUN 2003, p. 1387].

The report highlighted the oversight results for various high-risk areas, which were the outcome of audits, evaluation, inspection, investigation and management consulting activities undertaken to mitigate the risks identified. In that context, the report provided the definitions of *risk* and *risk management* and described the OIOS planning process. The caseload for investigation continued to rise during the reporting period, and the consequent backlog of cases in the Investigations Division presented a risk in terms of the ability of the Office to provide adequate professional investigative services to the Organization.

Between November 2003 and June 2004, OIOS conducted an Office-wide review of its activities to assist the General Assembly in its five-year evaluation and review of the Office, in accordance with resolution 54/244 [YUN 1999, p. 1274]. The review indicated that OIOS achievements and strengths derived from its operational independence, reporting procedures and functions (audit, monitoring/evaluation/consulting and investigations) and the risk mitigation component of its strategy for internal oversight. One of the most important findings of the review was the value that client departments placed on ongoing dialogue with OIOS on constructive teamwork in the common quest for good governance of the Organization. The review enabled OIOS to identify lessons learned and best practices aimed at improving its internal management, make proposals for enhancing its efficiency and effectiveness, and assist the Organization in addressing the opportunities and risks it faced.

Appointment of Under-Secretary-General. The Assembly, by **decision 59/552** of 23 December, decided that the item on the appointment of the Under-Secretary-General for Internal Oversight Services remained for consideration during its resumed fifty-ninth (2005) session.

GENERAL ASSEMBLY ACTION

On 23 December [meeting 76], the General Assembly, on the recommendation of the Fifth Committee [A/59/648], adopted two resolutions related to the activities of OIOS. The Assembly adopted **resolution 59/270** without vote [agenda item 118].

Reports of the Secretary-General on the activities of the Office of Internal Oversight Services

The General Assembly,

Recalling its resolutions 48/218 B of 29 July 1994 and 54/244 of 23 December 1999,

Recalling also its resolutions 56/246 of 24 December 2001 and 58/101 B of 9 December 2003,

Having considered the annual report of the Office of Internal Oversight Services for the period 1 July 2002 to 30 June 2003 and the report of the Office of Internal Oversight Services on the review of the structure and operations of United Nations information centres,

1. *Notes with appreciation* the work of the Office of Internal Oversight Services;

2. *Takes note* of the annual report of the Office of Internal Oversight Services;

3. *Requests* the Secretary-General to ensure that the Office of Internal Oversight Services continues to provide internal oversight of the entire claims process of the United Nations Compensation Commission and to report regularly thereon in the context of the annual reports of the Office;

4. *Recalls* regulation 1.2 of the Staff Regulations and Rules of the United Nations, and requests the Secretary-General to provide information to the General Assembly at its sixty-first session in the context of its consideration of matters related to procurement reform on actions taken to prevent recurrence of incidents of possible conflict of interest and inappropriate procurement practices;

5. *Notes* the description of the mission of the Office of Internal Oversight Services, as outlined in its annual report, and in this regard stresses that the mission of the Office should be in full conformity with its mandate, as approved by the General Assembly in its resolution 48/218 B;

6. *Requests* the Secretary-General to ensure that the Office of the United Nations High Commissioner for Refugees develops and utilizes comprehensive policy guidelines for the selection and management of consultants to ensure transparency and objectivity in their engagement, monitoring and evaluation as well as to make greater efforts to ensure a geographical balance in the use of qualified consultants, in accordance with the relevant resolutions of the General Assembly, and to report thereon to the Assembly at its sixty-first session;

7. *Endorses* the relevant recommendations of the Office of Internal Oversight Services regarding improvement of internal controls in management, accounting and reporting of assets of all United Nations field missions to establish reliable records, and requests the Secretary-General to ensure their full implementation and to report thereon to the General Assembly at the second part of its resumed sixtieth session;

8. *Requests* the Secretary-General to codify appropriate procedures for the purchase and utilization of vehicles and other equipment by United Nations field missions to ensure compliance by all missions with the procedures and to report thereon to the General Assembly at the second part of its resumed sixtieth session;

9. *Notes with concern* the contents of paragraph 97 of the annual report of the Office of Internal Oversight Services on the management and control of United Nations laissez-passer, and requests the Secretary-General to ensure the development of appropriate Organization-wide rules, policies and procedures for managing laissez-passer and to report thereon to the General Assembly, as appropriate;

10. *Recalls* paragraph 38 of General Assembly resolution 58/101 B, and takes note of the report of the Office of Internal Oversight Services on the review of the structure and operations of United Nations information centres.

The Assembly adopted **resolution 59/271** without vote [agenda item 118].

Report of the Secretary-General on the activities of the Office of Internal Oversight Services

The General Assembly,

Recalling its resolutions 48/218 B of 29 July 1994 and 54/244 of 23 December 1999,

Having considered the annual report of the Office of Internal Oversight Services for the period 1 July 2003 to 30 June 2004,

1. *Notes with appreciation* the work of the Office of Internal Oversight Services;

2. *Takes note* of the annual report of the Office of Internal Oversight Services;

3. *Notes* the description of the mission of the Office of Internal Oversight Services, as outlined in its annual report, and in this regard stresses that the mission of the Office should be in full conformity with its mandate, as approved by the General Assembly in its resolution 48/218 B;

4. *Notes also* the information provided by the Office of Internal Oversight Services on the economies and savings generated by its recommendations, and requests the Office to explain its guidelines for measuring the impact of such economies and/or savings and to report to the General Assembly thereon in its next annual report;

5. *Requests* the Secretary-General, with regard to paragraph 53 of the annual report of the Office of Internal Oversight Services, to ensure strict conformity with the highest standards of quality when recruiting staff to fill language posts, in accordance with legislative mandates;

6. *Notes with concern* the findings of the Office of Internal Oversight Services on investigations, as reflected in paragraphs 42 to 47 of its annual report, as well as the fact that some of them reflect serious managerial problems and lack of control;

7. *Stresses*, in this regard, the crucial importance of establishing an effective and efficient system of accountability throughout the Secretariat in order to prevent such problems and to make programme managers accountable;

8. *Takes note* of the report of the Office of Internal Oversight Services on its audit of the regional commissions, and requests the Secretary-General to report to the General Assembly at its sixtieth session on the actions taken by the legislative bodies of the regional commissions with regard to the recommendations of the report;

9. *Takes note also* of paragraph 63 of the annual report, relating to the audit of the non-governmental organization accreditation process;

10. *Reiterates*, in the context of paragraphs 8 and 9 above, paragraph 8 of its resolution 54/244, in which it emphasized that the approval, change and discontinuation of legislative mandates are the exclusive prerogatives of intergovernmental legislative bodies;

11. *Concurs* with the observation of the Office of Internal Oversight Services in paragraph 55 of its annual report, and requests the Secretary-General to ensure that the Office continues to provide internal oversight of the entire claims process of the United Nations Compensation Commission and to report regularly thereon in the context of the annual reports of the Office.

On the same date, the Assembly decided that the item on the report of the Secretary-General on the activities of the Office of Internal Oversight Services would remain for consideration during its resumed fifty-ninth (2005) session (**decision 59/552**).

OIOS reporting procedures

On 23 December [meeting 76], the General Assembly, on the recommendation of the Fifth Committee [A/59/649], adopted **resolution 59/272** without vote [agenda item 119].

Review of the implementation of General Assembly resolutions 48/218 B and 54/244

The General Assembly,

Recalling its resolutions 48/218 B of 29 July 1994 and 54/244 of 23 December 1999,

1. *Decides* to maintain the reporting procedures for the Office of Internal Oversight Services in full compliance with its resolutions 48/218 B and 54/244, and in this context requests the Secretary-General to ensure that:

(*a*) Annual reports submitted by the Office of Internal Oversight Services to the General Assembly contain the titles and brief summaries of all reports of the Office issued during the year;

(*b*) Semi-annual reports of the Office of Internal Oversight Services contain the titles and brief summaries of all other reports of the Office issued in the reporting period;

(*c*) Original versions of the reports of the Office of Internal Oversight Services not submitted to the General Assembly are, upon request, made available to any Member State;

2. *Also decides* that when access to a report would be inappropriate for reasons of confidentiality or the risk of violating the due process rights of individuals involved in Office of Internal Oversight Services investigations, the report may be modified, or withheld in extraordinary circumstances, at the discretion of the Under-Secretary-General for Internal Oversight Services, who will provide reasons for this to the requesting party;

3. *Further decides* that reports of the Office of Internal Oversight Services shall be submitted directly to the General Assembly as submitted by the Office and that the comments of the Secretary-General may be submitted in a separate report;

4. *Affirms* its primary role in the consideration of and action taken on the reports submitted to it;

5. *Notes* that no mechanism has been established for the follow-up to Office of Internal Oversight Services recommendations, including those considered by the General Assembly;

6. *Emphasizes* the importance of establishing real, effective and efficient mechanisms for responsibility and accountability;

7. *Regrets* that despite previous information provided by the Secretary-General on the establishment of accountability mechanisms, including the accountability panel, such mechanisms are not in place, thereby affecting the efficient and effective functioning of the Organization;

8. *Takes note* of paragraph 129 (*b*) of the annual report of the Office of Internal Oversight Services, and concurs with the view that a high-level follow-up mechanism under the authority of the Secretary-General should be established in the Organization to effectively feed findings and recommendations of the Office, as well as relevant findings of the Joint Inspection Unit and the Board of Auditors, into the executive management processes;

9. *Requests* the Secretary-General to submit annually to the General Assembly a report under the agenda item entitled "Review of the efficiency of the administrative and financial functioning of the United Nations" addressing the measures implemented with the aim of strengthening accountability in the Secretariat and the results achieved;

10. *Also requests* the Secretary-General to establish the aforementioned follow-up mechanism as soon as possible and to report to the General Assembly on the results achieved in the context of the report referred to in paragraph 9 above, with specific reference to:

(*a*) The composition of such a mechanism, including the seniority of the Chair and members;

(*b*) Terms of reference of the mechanism and frequency of its meetings;

(*c*) The inclusion in the mechanism of one or more participants with relevant expertise from United Nations-system oversight bodies;

(*d*) Reporting procedures;

11. *Reaffirms* the role of the Board of Auditors and the Joint Inspection Unit as external oversight bodies, and, in this regard, affirms that any external review, audit, inspection, monitoring, evaluation or investigation of the Office can be undertaken only by such bodies or those mandated to do so by the General Assembly;

12. *Also reaffirms* the importance of effective coordination, in the implementation of their respective mandates, between the Joint Inspection Unit, the Board of Auditors and the Office of Internal Oversight Services, in order to maximize the use of resources and share experiences, knowledge, best practices and lessons learned;

13. *Stresses* the vital importance of the evaluation function of the Office of Internal Oversight Services, and requests the Secretary-General to better reflect the objectives, expected accomplishments and performance indicators related to this function in future biennial programmes and budgetary submissions of the Office;

14. *Reaffirms* its oversight role as well as the role of the Fifth Committee in administrative and budgetary matters;

15. *Notes* paragraph 129 (*a*) of the annual report of the Office of Internal Oversight Services, and in this context requests the Secretary-General to report to the General Assembly at its sixtieth session, taking into account the views of external oversight bodies, on how to guarantee the full operational independence of the Office within the context of its resolution 48/218 B;

16. *Decides* to evaluate and review at its sixty-fourth session the functions and reporting procedures of the Office of Internal Oversight Services and any other matter which it deems appropriate, and to that end to include in the provisional agenda of that session an item entitled "Review of the implementation of Gen-

eral Assembly resolutions 48/218 B, 54/244 and 59/272".

Also on 23 December, the Assembly decided that the item on review of the implementation of General Assembly resolutions 48/218 B [YUN 1994, p. 1362] and 54/244 [YUN 1999, p. 1274] would remain for consideration during its resumed fifty-ninth (2005) session (**decision 59/552**).

Strengthening the investigations function

In response to General Assembly resolution 57/282 [YUN 2002, p. 1393], the Secretary-General, by a February note [A/58/708], transmitted a report of OIOS on strengthening the investigation function in the United Nations. OIOS reviewed 59 UN departments, offices, funds, programmes and missions to obtain information that would permit an assessment of the nature and extent of investigations conducted in 2002, the role played by management, whether guidelines existed and were followed, and the nature of any training. The review sought to determine whether programme managers involved in investigative processes retained the requisite independence in their administrative and managerial functions, had been given sufficient and proper investigative training and had used appropriate written procedures for investigations.

OIOS found, among other things, that: few investigations were done despite the yearly increase in serious matters reported by the offices reviewed; none of the offices reported having had any formal training programmes other than those provided by OIOS; and written procedures were not common, even though guidelines had been developed by OIOS and formally endorsed by UN system oversight offices. OIOS reaffirmed the importance of the 2001 JIU recommendations [YUN 2001, p. 1284] for training and procedures for those performing investigations. It intended, in coordination with other UN oversight bodies and relevant departments, to develop a policy on the role of programme managers in investigative activities; address how basic training could be provided for those responsible, including security officers and any other personnel assigned to conduct basic investigations; prepare procedures for handling less complex matters; further the development of the independent investigation function in the UN system; and conduct a follow-up review and report thereon to the Assembly.

Responses by the offices reviewed were included in the report, to which were also annexed the investigations conducted in 2002 by UN programme managers and the text for uniform guidelines for investigations proposed by OIOS.

By **decision 58/564 B** of 8 April, the Assembly deferred until its fifty-ninth session consideration of the item related to the OIOS report on strengthening the investigation functions in the United Nations.

External oversight

Joint Inspection Unit

At its resumed fifty-eighth session, the General Assembly had before it the 2002 report of JIU [YUN 2002, p. 1361] and notes by the Secretary-General transmitting: JIU's work programme for 2003 [YUN 2003, p. 1388], the preliminary list of reports for potential inclusion in its work programme for 2004 and beyond [ibid.], JIU reports on the preliminary and in-depth reviews of its statute and working methods [ibid. & A/58/343/Add/2] and the Secretary-General's 2003 report on the status of implementation of JIU recommendations [ibid.].

GENERAL ASSEMBLY ACTION

On 8 April [meeting 83], the General Assembly, on the recommendation of the Fifth Committee [A/58/751], adopted **resolution 58/286** without vote [agenda item 129].

Joint Inspection Unit

The General Assembly,

Reaffirming its previous resolutions on the Joint Inspection Unit, in particular resolutions 50/233 of 7 June 1996, 54/16 of 29 October 1999, 55/230 of 23 December 2000, 56/245 of 24 December 2001 and 57/284 A and B of 20 December 2002,

Having considered the report of the Joint Inspection Unit for 2002, the note by the Secretary-General transmitting the programme of work of the Unit for 2003, the note by the Secretary-General transmitting the preliminary listing of reports for potential inclusion in the programme of work of the Unit for 2004 and beyond, the report of the Secretary-General on the implementation of the recommendations of the Unit, the note by the Secretary-General transmitting the report of the Unit on the preliminary review of its statute and working methods and notes by the Secretary-General transmitting the reports of the Unit on the in-depth review of its statute and working methods,

1. *Takes note with appreciation* of the report of the Joint Inspection Unit for 2002;

2. *Takes note* of the note by the Secretary-General transmitting the programme of work of the Unit for 2003;

3. *Also takes note* of the note by the Secretary-General transmitting the preliminary listing of reports for potential inclusion in the programme of work of the Unit for 2004 and beyond;

4. *Further takes note* of the report of the Secretary-General on the implementation of the recommendations of the Unit;

5. *Takes note with appreciation* of the active contribution of the Unit to the review of its statute and working methods;

6. *Welcomes* the internal reform process undertaken by the Unit, including its strategic framework and its internal working procedures, and urges the Unit to continue these efforts;

7. *Requests* the secretariats of the United Nations and all participating organizations to facilitate the work of the Unit, including in particular by offering full access to all information, as required by the Unit;

8. *Reiterates once again its request* to the executive heads of the participating organizations that have not yet done so to take the steps necessary to facilitate the consideration of and action on the system of follow-up to the reports of the Unit, and invites the legislative organs concerned to consider the system and take action in that regard;

9. *Decides* to revert to the issue of the reform of the Unit at its fifty-ninth session.

JIU activities. In its annual report to the General Assembly [A/60/34], JIU gave an overview of its activities in 2004, during which it issued reports on: multilingualism and access to information: case study on the International Civil Aviation Organization [JIU/REP/2004/1]; a review of Headquarters agreements concluded by UN system organizations: human resources issues affecting staff [JIU/REP/2004/2]; administration of justice: harmonization of the statutes of the United Nations Administrative Tribunal and the International Labour Organization Administrative Tribunal [JIU/REP/2004/3]; a review of management and administration in the Office of the United Nations High Commissioner for Refugees [JIU/REP/2004/4]; an overview of the series of reports on managing for results in the UN system [JIU/REP/2004/5]: implementation of results-based management in UN organizations [JIU/REP/2004/6], delegation of authority and accountability [JIU/REP/2004/7], and managing performance and contracts [JIU/REP/2004/8]; procurement practices within the UN system [JIU/REP/2004/9]; harmonization of the conditions of travel throughout the UN system [JIU/REP/2004/10]; and knowledge management at the International Labour Organization [JIU/NOTE/2004/1].

During 2004, JIU continued to review its statute and working methods. The progress achieved in that regard was described in a February report [A/58/343/Add.2] to the Assembly. Pending an Assembly decision on some of the proposals outlined in its 2003 reports on the subject [YUN 2003, p. 1388], JIU continued to implement changes in other fields that did not require legislative approval or direction. Among those changes were the adoption of internal working procedures; the development of new mechanisms to implement the strategic framework adopted by JIU in 2003

[ibid.], particularly concerning risk assessment, selecting topics for reports and improving the quality of reports; pilot risk assessment exercises; and the initiation of the peer review process foreseen in the new internal working procedures, through which JIU would exercise collective responsibility for the preparation of reports, notes and confidential letters. The February report was complemented by a September conference room paper [A/C.5/59/CRP.1].

On 22 April [A/59/75], the Secretary-General transmitted to the Assembly the JIU work programme for 2004. On 10 September [A/59/349], he also transmitted information on the status of implementation of the recommendations contained in JIU reports on: administration of justice at the United Nations [YUN 2000, p 1359]; delegation of authority for management of human and financial resources in the UN Secretariat [ibid., 1350]; results-based budgeting: the experience of UN system organizations [YUN 1999, p. 1284]; and young professionals in selected organizations of the UN system: recruitment, management and retention [YUN 2001, p. 1352].

By a December note [A/59/617], the Secretary-General transmitted a JIU report entitled "Overview of the series of reports on managing for results in the United Nations system".

Appointment of JIU members. By an April note [A/59/108], the Secretary-General noted that four persons would be needed to fill the vacancies on JIU that would arise as at 31 December 2005.

On 23 December, the Assembly, by **decision 59/552**, decided that the item on the appointment of members of JIU would remain for consideration during its resumed fifty-ninth (2005) session.

GENERAL ASSEMBLY ACTION

On 23 December [meeting 76], the General Assembly, on the recommendation of the Fifth Committee [A/59/646], adopted **resolution 59/267** without vote [agenda item 115].

Reports of the Joint Inspection Unit

The General Assembly,

Reaffirming its previous resolutions on the Joint Inspection Unit, in particular resolutions 31/192 of 22 December 1976, 50/233 of 7 June 1996, 54/16 of 29 October 1999, 55/230 of 23 December 2000, 56/245 of 24 December 2001, 57/284 A and B of 20 December 2002 and 58/286 of 8 April 2004,

Having considered the report of the Joint Inspection Unit for 2003, the note by the Secretary-General transmitting the programme of work of the Joint Inspection Unit for 2004 and the report of the Secretary-General on the implementation of the recommendations of the Joint Inspection Unit,

Noting with appreciation the recent adoption by the Joint Inspection Unit of internal working procedures and mechanisms to complement its standards and guidelines, which are aimed at improving the quality and impact of the Unit's activities,

Recognizing that in order for the Unit to further improve its effectiveness, the provisions of the statute of the Unit should be fully implemented,

1. *Takes note with appreciation* of the report of the Joint Inspection Unit for 2003;

2. *Takes note* of the note by the Secretary-General transmitting the programme of work of the Unit for 2004;

3. *Also takes note* of the report of the Secretary-General on the implementation of the recommendations of the Unit;

4. *Decides* to discontinue the requirement for the report of the Secretary-General on the implementation of the recommendations of the Unit;

5. *Considers* that the implementation in full of the provisions of the statute of the Unit should contribute to the enhancement of its role and an increase in the effectiveness of its activities;

6. *Urges* Member States requested to propose candidates for membership in the Unit to strictly adhere to the qualifications and experience outlined in article 2, paragraph 1, of the statute;

7. *Stresses* the importance of ensuring that candidates have experience in at least one of the fields illustrated as follows: oversight, audit, inspection, investigation, evaluation, finance, project evaluation, programme evaluation, human resources management, management, public administration, monitoring and/ or programme performance, as well as knowledge of the United Nations system and its role in international relations;

8. *Invites* the President of the General Assembly to ensure the full implementation of the procedures and mechanisms for reviewing the qualifications of proposed candidates as outlined in article 3, paragraph 2, of the statute of the Unit, including through joint consultations with the President of the Economic and Social Council and the Chairman of the United Nations System Chief Executives Board for Coordination, as well as drawing, as appropriate, on relevant expertise from expert and intergovernmental bodies concerned with budgetary and human resources matters, and with consultations with the States concerned, after which the President of the Assembly submits the list of such candidates to the Assembly for appointment;

9. *Also invites* the President of the General Assembly to review the procedures followed by the Assembly for the appointment of inspectors, with a view to enhancing the efficiency of the application of article 3, paragraph 2, of the statute, bearing in mind the procedures followed for the selection of members of other expert bodies and to report to the Assembly at the first part of its resumed sixtieth session for its decision, as appropriate;

10. *Reaffirms* article 11, paragraph 2, of the statute of the Unit, and requests that the Unit, as a whole, also take responsibility in the exercise of its collective wisdom with regard to all its reports, notes and recommendations, in order to improve the effectiveness of the Unit;

11. *Re-emphasizes* paragraph 9 of its resolution 56/245;

12. *Decides* that the Unit shall perform its functions and responsibilities strictly in accordance with the provisions of its statute;

13. *Also decides* that the programme of work of the Unit shall be collectively approved, providing the rationale for choice as well as the relevance of the envisaged outcome to improving management and methods and promoting greater coordination between organizations;

14. *Affirms* that, in the implementation of article 18 of the statute of the Unit, the Chair shall be responsible for overseeing the Unit's programme of work, including, in the event of disagreement, the division of assignments, and for enforcing the internal working procedures of the Unit to ensure, through collective responsibility, the quality of its reports;

15. *Welcomes* the peer review system established by the Unit, and decides that if, in the opinion of the majority of the inspectors, the report in question does not meet the established quality standards, the Chair shall reflect such views and the reasons therefor in the introduction to the report;

16. *Emphasizes* the desirability of continuity in the term of office of the Chair and Vice-Chair, and calls upon the Unit to bear this in mind in implementing article 18 of the statute, so as to re-elect the Chairman and the Vice-Chairman for overlapping terms, thereby balancing the need for institutional memory and reasonable rotation;

17. *Also emphasizes* the need to assess resource management from a system-wide perspective, including the contribution of, and coordination between, organizations;

18. *Decides* that the Unit shall mainly focus on identifying means to improve management and to ensure that optimum use is made of available resources, as stipulated in article 5, paragraphs 1 to 3, of the statute, and to this end the Unit will set out management criteria and methods for assessment of management performance and effectiveness relevant to participating organizations;

19. *Also decides* that the Unit shall include, in its annual reports, information on implementation and the results achieved by organizations in respect of their follow-up to the recommendations of the Unit, as endorsed by their legislative bodies, and the arrangements put in place by participating organizations for reporting thereon;

20. *Further decides* that the Unit, as part of its focus on management issues, should assess the development and application in participating organizations of the principle of accountability in its relevant reports;

21. *Decides* that the Unit shall undertake inspections with a sharp focus on the areas stipulated in article 5, paragraphs 1 to 3, of the statute, bearing in mind paragraphs 18 and 20 above;

22. *Invites* the Committee for Programme and Coordination, in performing its programmatic, coordination, monitoring and evaluation functions, as contained in its mandate, to consider relevant reports of the Unit;

23. *Requests* the Secretary-General to ensure that the staff recruited according to article 19 of the statute fully meet the qualifications and have proven experience in specific areas required to assist the Unit in the

fulfilment of its functions, namely, inspection, investigation and evaluation;

24. *Reaffirms* that the working languages of the General Assembly are those of the Unit, in application of article 51 of the rules of procedure of the Assembly, and also reaffirms that the working languages of the Secretariat of the United Nations are those of the secretariat of the Unit, in application of Assembly resolution 2(I) of 1 February 1946;

25. *Decides* to continue providing translation in all official languages for the reports of the Unit and also to provide interpretation, as necessary, within existing resources;

26. *Reaffirms its request* to the Secretariat and all participating organizations to facilitate the work of the Unit, including, in particular, through offering full access to all relevant information, as required by the Unit;

27. *Also reaffirms its request* to the executive heads of the participating organizations that have not yet done so to take the steps necessary to facilitate the consideration of and action on the system of follow-up to the reports of the Unit, and invites the legislative organs concerned to consider the system and take action in that regard;

28. *Emphasizes* the need to ensure respect for the separate and distinct roles and functions of external and internal oversight mechanisms and also to strengthen the external oversight mechanisms;

29. *Decides* to consider the implementation of the provisions of the present resolution, which are aimed at increasing the effectiveness of the Unit, at its sixty-first session.

By **decision 59/552** of 23 December, the Assembly decided that the item on the Joint Inspections Unit would remain for consideration during its resumed fifty-ninth (2005) session.

The Assembly, in **section VIII of resolution 59/276** of the same date (see p. 1385), approved the gross budget for JIU for 2005 in the amount of $5,385,700 and to appropriate the amount of $1,712,700 under section 31, Jointly financed administrative activities, for the financing of JIU in 2005.

Intergovernmental machinery

Revitalization of the work of the General Assembly

At its resumed fifty-eighth session, the General Assembly adopted a text regarding further measures for the revitalization of its work. It also had before it Secretariat notes, submitted in response to resolution 58/216 [YUN 2003, p. 1389], on: options for the rescheduling of the Assembly's main Committees [A/58/CRP.3]; an illustrative agenda of the Assembly [A/58/CRP.4] and an analysis of its agenda [A/58/CRP.6]; a historical and ana-

lytical note on the practices and working methods of the Main Committees [A/58/CRP.5]; and control and limitation of documentation [A/58/CRP.7].

On 1 July [meeting 92], the General Assembly adopted **resolution 58/316** [draft A/58/L.66] without vote [agenda item 55].

Further measures for the revitalization of the work of the General Assembly

The General Assembly,

Recalling its resolution 58/126 of 19 December 2003 on the revitalization of the work of the General Assembly,

Recalling also its previous resolutions relating to the revitalization of its work,

1. *Decides* to adopt the text contained in the annex to the present resolution;

2. *Determines* to continue with efforts for the revitalization of its work;

3. *Requests* the Secretary-General to report on all aspects of the implementation of resolution 58/126 and the present resolution to the General Assembly at its sixtieth session.

Annex

A. Reordering the work of the General Assembly

1. Recalling section B, paragraph 2, of the annex to General Assembly resolution 58/126 of 19 December 2003, and having reviewed the note by the Secretariat entitled "Options for the rescheduling of the Main Committees of the General Assembly", it is decided that:

(*a*) The consideration of the implementation of paragraph 2 of section B of the annex to resolution 58/126 shall be deferred until its fifty-ninth session, taking into account the views expressed as well as the suggestions made by Member States in the context of the deliberations of the open-ended meetings of the General Committee during the fifty-eighth session;

(*b*) With effect from the fifty-ninth session of the General Assembly, the meetings of the plenary Assembly shall normally be held on Mondays and Thursdays.

B. Organization of the agenda of the General Assembly

2. Recalling section B, paragraph 4, of the annex to resolution 58/126, and having reviewed the note by the Secretariat entitled "Illustrative agenda of the General Assembly", and taking into account the views expressed by Member States on the matter, it is decided that:

(*a*) Pursuant to paragraph 4 of section B of the annex to resolution 58/126, the agenda of the General Assembly shall be organized under headings corresponding to the priorities of the Organization, as contained in the medium-term plan for the period 2002-2005 (or in the strategic framework, as appropriate), with an additional heading for "Organizational, administrative and other matters" for the purpose of giving a sense of structure to the work of the Assembly, achieving a better presentation of the issues and challenges with which the Assembly deals and making the work of the Assembly more accessible, with the understanding that the new arrangement will not prejudice the way in which the work of the Assembly is organized and carried out;

(b) The headings of the agenda shall consequently be:

(i) Maintenance of international peace and security;

(ii) Promotion of sustained economic growth and sustainable development in accordance with the resolutions of the General Assembly and recent United Nations conferences;

(iii) Development of Africa;

(iv) Promotion of human rights;

(v) Effective coordination of humanitarian assistance efforts;

(vi) Promotion of justice and international law;

(vii) Disarmament;

(viii) Drug control, crime prevention and combating international terrorism in all its forms and manifestations;

(ix) Organizational, administrative and other matters;

(c) The General Committee shall make recommendations, after consultation with Member States, to the General Assembly at its fifty-ninth session on the placement of the agenda items for the fifty-ninth session under the headings set out above, with a view to making the new arrangement effective;

(d) The provisions of the present section shall be reviewed by the General Assembly at its sixty-first session with a view to making further improvements, as appropriate.

C. Practices and working methods of the Main Committees

3. Recalling section B, paragraph 8, of the annex to resolution 58/126, and having reviewed the note by the Secretariat entitled "Historical and analytical note on the practices and working methods of the Main Committees", recalling that the Main Committees are bound by the rules of procedure of the General Assembly, and taking into account the views expressed by Member States on the matter, it is decided that:

(a) Main Committees shall give specific attention to the rationalization of their future agendas by the biennialization, triennialization, clustering and elimination of items, and make recommendations to the plenary Assembly for its decision by 1 April 2005;

(b) Main Committees shall adopt a provisional programme of work at the end of the session for the next session to help them better to plan, prepare and organize and, in this context, review the related documentation requirements;

(c) The practice of interactive debates and panel discussions shall be utilized or expanded, as appropriate, by all Main Committees so as to enhance informal, in-depth discussions and to bring together experts from various fields without prejudicing the progress of the substantive work of the Main Committees;

(d) The practice of "question time" shall be introduced, as appropriate, in all Main Committees to enable a dynamic and candid exchange with heads of departments and offices, representatives of the Secretary-General and special rapporteurs;

(e) The web sites of the Main Committees shall be enhanced and thereafter regularly updated and their content maintained by the secretariats of the Main Committees;

(f) The bureaux-elect of the Main Committees shall meet immediately after their election in order to discuss the organization and division of their work;

(g) With a view to ensuring the continuity and the effective organization of their work, the incoming bureaux of the Main Committees shall, no later than two weeks after their election, meet with the outgoing bureaux in order to consult on and review issues relating to the efficient functioning of the Main Committees;

(h) Prior to the opening of each session, informal briefings of each Main Committee shall be convened to discuss the organization of work.

D. Review of the agenda of the General Assembly

4. Recalling section B, paragraph 5, of the annex to resolution 58/126, having reviewed the note by the Secretariat entitled "Analysis of the agenda of the General Assembly", which provides factual information on the frequency of consideration, origin and history of action on the 333 items and sub-items on the agenda, taking into account the views expressed by Member States, and following consultations with concerned Member States, it is decided that:

(a) The items entitled "Launching of global negotiations on international economic cooperation for development" and "Restructuring and revitalization of the United Nations in the economic, social and related fields" shall be eliminated from the agenda;

(b) The items entitled "Question of Cyprus", "Armed aggression against the Democratic Republic of the Congo", "Question of the Falkland Islands (Malvinas)", "The situation of democracy and human rights in Haiti", "Armed Israeli aggression against the Iraqi nuclear installations and its grave consequences for the established international system concerning the peaceful uses of nuclear energy, the non-proliferation of nuclear weapons and international peace and security", "Consequences of the Iraqi occupation of and aggression against Kuwait", and "Declaration of the Assembly of Heads of State and Government of the Organization of African Unity on the aerial and naval military attack against the Socialist People's Libyan Arab Jamahiriya by the present United States Administration in April 1986" shall remain on the agenda for consideration upon notification by a Member State;

(c) The item entitled "Report of the Economic and Social Council" shall be considered in its entirety in plenary;

(d) While remaining on the agenda of the plenary, the sub-item entitled "Sport for peace and development: building a peaceful and better world through sport and the Olympic ideal" shall be considered every other year and the items entitled "Return or restitution of cultural property to the countries of origin" and "Elimination of unilateral extraterritorial coercive economic measures as a means of political and economic compulsion" shall be considered every three years;

(e) The item entitled "Information and communication technologies for development" and the sub-item entitled "Strengthening of the coordination of humanitarian and disaster relief assistance of the United Nations, including special economic assistance: special economic assistance to individual countries or regions" shall be allocated for annual consideration in the Second Committee;

(f) The item entitled "Towards global partnerships" shall be allocated for consideration every other year in the Second Committee;

(g) The sub-item entitled "Strengthening of the coordination of humanitarian and disaster relief assistance of the United Nations, including special economic assistance: participation of volunteers, 'White Helmets', in the activities of the United Nations in the field of humanitarian relief, rehabilitation and technical cooperation for development" shall be allocated for consideration every three years in the Second Committee;

(h) The item entitled "Global road safety crisis" shall be allocated for consideration every other year in the Third Committee;

(i) The item entitled "Implementation of the Declaration on the Granting of Independence to Colonial Countries and Peoples" shall be allocated for annual consideration in the Special Political and Decolonization Committee (Fourth Committee);

(j) The item entitled "Assistance in mine action" shall be allocated for consideration every other year in the Special Political and Decolonization Committee (Fourth Committee);

(k) The item entitled "University for Peace" shall be allocated for consideration every three years in the Special Political and Decolonization Committee (Fourth Committee);

(l) Bearing in mind that the General Assembly decided in resolution 55/285 of 7 September 2001 to cluster all cooperation items under one item, to make individual cooperation items sub-items and to hold a joint debate for all sub-items, the Secretary-General shall submit a single consolidated report under the item entitled "Cooperation between the United Nations and regional and other organizations";

(m) The adjustments outlined in the paragraphs above shall take effect beginning with the fifty-ninth session of the General Assembly;

(n) The General Assembly shall monitor the effects of the adjustments outlined in the paragraphs above and continue to make efforts, as appropriate, to further streamline the agenda of the plenary.

E. General Committee

5. Recalling section B, paragraph 1, of the annex to resolution 58/126, having conducted a review of the work of the General Committee, and taking into account the views expressed by Member States on the matter, it is decided that:

(a) The work of the General Committee shall be carried out in accordance with section VI of the rules of procedure of the General Assembly;

(b) The General Committee shall continue to meet throughout the session and to play the leading role in advising the General Assembly on the efficient organization, coordination and management of its work;

(c) To ensure the effective implementation of rule 42 of the rules of procedure of the General Assembly, the General Committee shall meet regularly throughout the session with the bureaux of the Main Committees to review the progress of the work of the Main Committees and to make recommendations for furthering such progress;

(d) In July of each year, the General Committee shall conduct a review of the proposed programme of work for the forthcoming session of the General Assembly, on the basis of a report to be submitted by the Secretary-General, and submit recommendations on the matter to the forthcoming Assembly. The report of the Secretary-General shall include information on the status of documentation to be issued during the forthcoming session;

(e) The General Committee, meeting in open-ended consultations, shall continue to consider the further biennialization, triennialization, clustering and elimination of items on the customary agenda of the General Assembly and make recommendations thereon to the Assembly during its fifty-ninth session;

(f) On the basis of proposals from the President of the General Assembly, and in the light of the positive experience during the fifty-eighth session, the General Committee shall be encouraged, as appropriate, to continue to schedule informal briefings on topical issues;

(g) At the beginning of each session, the General Committee, following recommendations from the President of the General Assembly, shall recommend to the Assembly a programme of, and format for, interactive debates on the items on its agenda;

(h) The General Committee shall continue to consider ways and means to further improve its working methods to increase its efficiency and effectiveness in all aspects, and make recommendations on the matter to the General Assembly for its decision by 1 April 2005.

F. Documentation

6. In the light of its decision in section B, paragraph 7, of the annex to resolution 58/126 that the heavy volume of documentation that is submitted to the General Assembly for its consideration should be reduced, the Secretary-General is requested:

(a) To update the note by the Secretariat entitled "Control and limitation of documentation", in the light of the provisions of the present resolution;

(b) To submit the updated version of the note by the Secretariat for the consideration of the General Committee, meeting in open-ended consultations, so that it may make recommendations to the General Assembly at its fifty-ninth session;

(c) To take the necessary action to initiate the implementation of the provisions of paragraph 20 of resolution 57/300 of 20 December 2002, in which the General Assembly requested the Secretary-General to start, on a trial basis, a consultative process with the President of the General Assembly and the Chairmen of the Main Committees of the Assembly at the end of the main part of each session of the Assembly, with a view to consolidating reports on related subjects, if decided by the Main Committees.

Report of Secretary-General. In response to General Assembly resolution 58/316 (see above), the Secretary-General submitted a 30 July report [A/58/864] containing the provisional agenda of the Assembly's fifty-ninth (2004) session [A/59/150]; the provisional agenda of the same session organized under headings corresponding to the priorities of the 2002-2005 medium-term plan; the draft programme of work of the Assembly plenary and of the six main Committees; and the status of documentation to be issued during the fifty-ninth session.

By **decision 59/552** of 23 December, the Assembly decided that the item on the revitalization of the work of the General Assembly would remain for consideration during its resumed fifty-ninth (2005) session.

Improving the methods of work of the First Committee

In response to General Assembly resolution 58/41 [YUN 2003, p. 1390], the Secretary-General, in a July report with later addenda [A/59/132 & Adds. 1, 2 & Corr.1, Adds. 3-6], presented the views of 17 Member States and the Non-aligned Movement on appropriate options for improving the effectiveness of the methods of work of the First (Disarmament and International Security) Committee.

GENERAL ASSEMBLY ACTION

On 3 December [meeting 66], the General Assembly, on the recommendation of the First Committee [A/59/459 and Corr.1], adopted **resolution 59/95** without vote [agenda item 65 *(k)*].

Improving the effectiveness of the methods of work of the First Committee

The General Assembly,

Recalling its resolutions 48/87 of 16 December 1993, 49/85 of 15 December 1994, 57/300 of 20 December 2002, 58/41 of 8 December 2003, 58/126 of 19 December 2003 and 58/316 of 1 July 2004,

Affirming that its rules of procedure permit the Main Committees to undertake organizational refinements to improve the effectiveness of their methods of work, and noting with satisfaction that the First Committee already has done so,

Emphasizing that improved functioning of the First Committee should be considered in an integrated and comprehensive manner through the existing three stages, namely general debate, thematic/structured debate, and consideration of and action on draft resolutions,

Determining to continue its efforts to improve the efficiency and effectiveness of the methods of work of the First Committee, as a means to enhance the role of the General Assembly in promoting international peace and security,

1. *Invites* Member States to consider the biennialization or triennialization of the agenda items discussed in the First Committee, on a voluntary basis, and particularly when no specific action is required for the implementation of relevant resolutions;

2. *Also invites* Member States to continue to hold interactive debates based on a programme and format elaborated through informal consultations between the Bureau and Member States in advance of each First Committee session;

3. *Further invites* Member States to submit draft resolutions in a more concise, focused and action-oriented manner and, where practical, to consider the possibility of submitting draft decisions;

4. *Recommends* that the respective sponsors of draft resolutions hold informal consultations, both before and during First Committee meetings, with the participation of all interested Member States for furthering discussions on draft resolutions already submitted or yet to be submitted to the Committee;

5. *Encourages* Member States to introduce draft resolutions on related or complementary issues to find commonalities in the language and purpose of those draft resolutions, and invites Member States to consider pursuing mergers of such texts through consultations with all sponsors;

6. *Also encourages* Member States, in particular those that present any draft resolution, to follow up on the agreed resolution in order to contribute to the achievement of the objective of such resolution;

7. *Encourages* the First Committee to introduce presentations of, and focus discussions on, reports on the work of expert groups, the United Nations regional centres for peace and disarmament, the United Nations Institute for Disarmament Research and the Advisory Board on Disarmament Matters initiated by the Committee;

8. *Reiterates* that the Secretary-General, in accordance with rule 154 of the rules of procedure of the General Assembly, shall keep all Committees, including the First Committee, informed of the detailed estimated cost of all resolutions and decisions that have been recommended by the Committees for approval by the Assembly;

9. *Requests* the First Committee, in the light of the growing interconnectedness of issues before the General Assembly, to explore the forms of mutual cooperation with other Main Committees;

10. *Decides* to develop further, within existing resources, the electronic support for the work of the First Committee, in particular through the existing web sites;

11. *Decides also* to review regularly the implementation of the present resolution.

Review of Security Council membership and related matters

The Open-ended Working Group on the Question of Equitable Representation on and Increase in the Membership of the Security Council and Other Matters related to the Security Council submitted a report on its work during three substantive sessions and nine rounds of informal consultations held between 19 February and 21 July [A/58/47 & Corr.1]. In the light of the Chairman's view that the Group should adopt an approach in its work that would create new opportunities for progress in the consideration of Council reform, the Group agreed to proceed with informal consultations, contrary to its approach in previous sessions when it considered proposals and/or position papers in two clusters on the questions of the increase in membership of the Council and related matters, its working methods and the transparency of its work. The Group also discussed separately in informal sessions held between 26 March and 8 April, the five topics proposed by the Bureau: an enlarged Security Council; the question of regional representation; criteria for membership; on the relationship between the General Assembly and the Security Council; and accountability. On the proposal of the Chairman, a sixth topic on the use of the veto was discussed on 19 April. The Chairman's summary of those discussions was annexed to the Group's report. In addition, delegates raised issues related to the reform of the Council, including its meetings with troop-contributing countries and the Secretariat, its annual report to the Assembly, further transparency of the Council vis-à-vis the wider membership of the United Nations, and the role of the Council in setting international legal norms. On 14 May, the Group held an formal exchange of views with the Council President and three other Council members on the topics discussed during the sessions. On 21 July, the Group considered and adopted its report to the Assembly.

By **decision 58/572** of 13 September, the Assembly took note of the Working Group's report and the six topics discussed by the Group; urged the Group to continue to work towards achieving progress in the consideration of all issues relevant to the question of equitable representation on and increase in the Council's membership and other related matters; and decided that the Group should continue its work, taking into account the progress achieved during the forty-eighth (1993) through the fifty-eighth (2003) Assembly sessions, and the views to be expressed on the question during the fifty-ninth (2004) session, and to report to the Assembly before the end of that session.

On 23 December, the Assembly decided that the item on the question of equitable representation on and increase in the membership of the Security Council and related matters would remain for consideration during its resumed fifty-ninth (2005) session (**decision 59/552**).

Revitalization of the United Nations in the economic, social and related fields

Work of the functional commissions

The Economic and Social Council, by **decision 2004/218** of 27 February, took note of the 2003 reports of the Secretary-General on the work of its functional commissions [YUN 2003, p. 1392] and on progress in implementing its agreed conclusions 2002/1 [YUN 2002, p. 1365] and related provisions of General Assembly resolution 50/227 [YUN 1996, p. 1249].

Report of Secretary-General. The Secretary-General, responding to the Council's agreed conclusions 2002/1, submitted a consolidated report [E/2004/81] in June on the work of the functional commissions of the Council in 2004. The report focused on the commissions' contributions to the achievement of various aspects of the MDGs [YUN 2000, p. 51] relevant to their areas of activity, aimed at assisting the Council in providing policy guidance regarding the commission's contributions to the high-level plenary meeting of the Assembly, scheduled for 2005. The report also examined the commissions' contributions to the Council's work and follow-up action by them to policy guidance provided by the Council in 2003, and reviewed key issues relating to coordination or procedural aspects of the Commission's work in 2004.

The Secretary-General recommended that the Council request its functional commissions and other relevant subsidiary bodies to contribute to the Council's High-level segment and other segments dealing with themes relating to the 2005 high-level plenary meeting of the Assembly; encourage the commissions to further promote synergies among themselves regarding their work towards the achievement of the MDGs; encourage the Commission on the Status of Women to continue its catalytic role and to contribute to the work of other functional commissions; request all international organizations to ensure coherence and collaboration with requests for data on conference indicators; and encourage further investment in sustainable statistical capacities. In other recommendations, the Council was encouraged to consider ways of promoting closer interaction between the functional commissions and governing bodies of UN funds and programmes; invite its commissions and their secretariats to clearly identify the operational implications of their work and bring them to the attention of the governing bodies of funds and programmes for their consideration and guidance on operational activities; continue to examine their methods of work in order to better implement the outcomes of major UN conferences and summits; and adhere to the guidelines regarding their reports to the Council. The Council should encourage its subsidiary bodies to present oral reports on issues that did not require extensive deliberations by the Council, consolidate reports that dealt with closely related topics and encourage the bureaux of the functional commissions to focus their joint meetings and meetings with the Bureau of the Council on cross-cutting issues in order to develop a common approach to work.

ECONOMIC AND SOCIAL COUNCIL ACTION

On 23 July [meeting 51], the Economic and Social Council adopted **resolution 2004/63** [draft E/2004/L.48] without vote [agenda items 13 and 14].

Promoting coordination and consolidation of the work of the functional commissions

The Economic and Social Council,

Recalling General Assembly resolutions 50/227 of 24 May 1996 and 52/12 B of 19 December 1997, and resolution 57/270 B of 23 June 2003, entitled "Integrated and coordinated implementation of and follow-up to the outcomes of the major United Nations conferences and summits in the economic and social fields",

Recalling also its agreed conclusions 2002/1 of 26 July 2002 on strengthening further the role of the Economic and Social Council,

1. *Takes note with appreciation* of the consolidated report of the Secretary-General on the work of the functional commissions of the Economic and Social Council in 2004;

2. *Welcomes* the contribution of the functional commissions to the substantive session of the Economic and Social Council of 2004, and requests the functional commissions and other relevant subsidiary bodies to contribute to the substantive session of the Council of 2005 and, in accordance with the modalities to be set out by the General Assembly at its fifty-ninth session, to contribute, through the Council, to the high-level plenary meeting of the Assembly;

3. *Requests* its functional commissions, in their review of conference implementation in 2005, to promote complementarity in their work and to follow the guidance of the Economic and Social Council and the General Assembly;

4. *Also requests* its commissions, in their reports, to identify clearly the operational implications of their work for consideration and appropriate action by the governing bodies of the United Nations funds and programmes;

5. *Encourages* greater cooperation between its functional commissions and the regional commissions;

6. *Invites* its Bureau to give due regard in its consultations with the bureaux of the functional commissions to their contributions to the various segments of the substantive session of the Economic and Social Council;

7. *Requests* the Chairpersons of the functional commissions to communicate to the President of the Economic and Social Council the issues requiring special attention or action by the Council, as determined by the commissions;

8. *Requests* the Secretary-General to submit to the Economic and Social Council a consolidated report on the work of the functional commissions in 2005, focusing on the substantive aspects of their activities so as to complement the report on the role of the Council in the implementation of General Assembly resolutions 50/227, 52/12 B and 57/270 B.

Review of structure and functions of liaison offices

Report of Secretary-General. In response to General Assembly resolution 58/270 [YUN 2003, p. 1399], the Secretary-General, in an October report [A/59/395], reviewed the structure and functions of all liaison or representation offices in New York of organizations headquartered elsewhere but funded by the regular budget. Those organizations included UNCTAD, the United Nations Environment Programme (UNEP), the United Nations Human Settlements Programme (UN-HABITAT), UNRWA, the Office of the United Nations High Commissioner for Human Rights (OHCHR), the United Nations Office at Vienna (UNOV), the United Nations Office on Drugs and Crime (UNODC) and the New York office of the regional commissions. The report also described the functions and level of staff resources of those offices.

The Secretary-General observed that it was evident from the review that representative offices in New York provided substantive contributions to the work programme of their parent offices, while maintaining a much smaller portion of traditional liaison functions. Activities focused on matters requiring the representatives' participation in meetings, both at the intergovernmental level and within the Secretariat. Those offices were operating with the benefit of current technology and were striving to be as effective as possible within the limited budgetary resources available to them.

ACABQ report. ACABQ, in a 3 November report [A/59/552], recommended that the Assembly take note of the Secretary-General's report (see above). It intended to revert to the issue and examine the functions and levels of staff resources of the liaison offices in New York in the context of its examination of the proposed programme budget for the 2006-2007 biennium.

Chapter II

United Nations financing and programming

The financial situation of the United Nations continued to improve in 2004 despite some areas of concern. By the end of the year, unpaid assessments almost doubled, compared to 2003, and the number of Member States paying their contributions to the regular budget in full and on time fell. While aggregate cash increased slightly, the Organization was still obliged to cross-borrow from other accounts and was still using reserves at the end of the year. Unpaid assessments reached $2.9 billion, compared to $1.6 billion in 2003, and debt to Member States for troops and contingent-owned equipment was $549 million, against $449 million in 2003.

In December, the General Assembly adopted revised budget appropriations for the 2004-2005 biennium of $3,608,173,900, an increase of $428,977,800 over the revised appropriation of $3,179,196,100 approved in June, to provide for the strengthening of UN security management. It invited the Secretary-General to prepare his proposed 2006-2007 programme budget on the basis of a preliminary estimate of $3,621,900,000.

The Committee on Contributions considered the methodology for calculating future scales of assessments, the criteria for ad hoc adjustments to assessments and measures to encourage the payment of arrears in contributions to the UN budget, including multi-year payment plans.

The Assembly also examined the proposed strategic framework for 2006-2007, which replaced the four-year medium-term plan, and endorsed the proposed biennial programme plan for that period.

Financial situation

Although the overall financial situation of the United Nations showed some improvement in 2004, serious problems remained. In October [A/59/524], the Secretary-General reported that aggregate assessments increased significantly to $5.9 billion as at 15 October (compared to $3.9 billion in 2003). Cash availability under the regular budget and related reserve accounts at the beginning of the year stood at $23 million, and only for two weeks in September was it neces-

sary to engage in cross-borrowing. Based on information provided by the major contributor, a positive cash balance of $96 million was projected for the end of the year.

As at 15 October, unpaid assessments for the regular budget, peacekeeping and the two international tribunals (see p. 1275) totalled $3.3 billlion, which included: $2.5 billion for peacekeeping (compared to $1.6 billion in 2003), $725 million for the regular budget ($32 million more than in 2003) and some $80 million for the tribunals ($37 million less than in 2003). Amounts that would be owed to Member States by 31 December were forecast to total $605 million, primarily due to the deployment of three new peacekeeping missions in Burundi, Côte d'Ivoire and Haiti. Member States that had paid their assessments in full as at 15 October numbered 111 (two less than at the same date in 2003).

In his end-of-year review of the financial situation [A/59/524/Add.1], the Secretary-General noted that the performance of the four indicators of the Organization's financial health was mixed: aggregate cash available amounted to $1.8 billion, with the tribunals showing a net balance of $5 million, the regular budget $192 million, and peacekeeping $1.6 billion. Nonetheless, the Organization was still obliged to cross-borrow from other accounts in November for the regular budget and was still using reserves at year's end. Total unpaid assessments decreased slightly to $2.9 billion and the actual debt to Member States amounted to $549 million. The number of Member States paying their regular budget assessments in full and on time fell to 124, down from 131 in 2003.

On 13 September, the General Assembly deferred consideration of the agenda item on improving the financial situation of the United Nations and included it in the draft agenda of its fifty-ninth (2004) session (**decision 58/575**). It further decided on 23 December that the item would remain for consideration at its resumed fifty-ninth (2005) session (**decision 59/552**).

Budget for 2004-2005

Revised appropriations

In April [A/58/756], the Secretary-General submitted revised estimates of $85,965,800 net

($92,433,500 gross) to finance the immediate and long-term measures he had proposed for strengthening the security and safety of the United Nations (see p. 1434) under sections 3, 4, 5, 7, 18, 19, 21, 22, 26, 28, 29A, 29C-G, 31, 33 and 34 and income sections 1 and 2 of the 2004-2005 programme budget, the budget for the International Criminal Tribunal for Rwanda (ICTR), and the relevant budgets of UN peacekeeping operations. The Advisory Committee on Administrative and Budgetary Questions (ACABQ) recommended [A/58/758] that the General Assembly appropriate $40 million (gross) under the 2004-2005 programme budget to implement those measures. ACABQ further recommended that the estimated expenses of $4.9 million in respect of peacekeeping operations and ICTR be accommodated within existing budgets, and that some $8.9 million of the provision for the Office of the United Nations Security Coordinator be borne by the participating organizations under existing cost-sharing arrangements. To strengthen security of UN operations, the General Assembly, in **resolution 58/295** of 18 June (see p. 1476), decided to appropriate $2,583,000, being the portion of costs normally attributable to the United Nations and to revert to the required residual funding of $8,162,100 at its fifty-ninth session when determining cost-sharing arrangements. It approved an additional appropriation of $18,287,100 under the budget sections identified by the Secretary-General and $48,700 under staff assessment.

In the first performance report on the 2004-2005 programme budget [A/59/578], the Secretary-General identified adjustments to the level of appropriations as a result of variations in the rates of inflation and exchange and in the standards assumed in the calculation of the initial appropriations.

The adjustments yielded revised expenditures of $3,351.1 million, an increase of $172 million, as compared with a revised appropriation level of $3,179.2 million approved by resolution 58/295, and an increase in income of $9.4 million, resulting in a revised income estimate of $424.7 million. The revised net estimate for the 2004-2005 biennium therefore amounted to $2,926.4 million, an increase of $162.5 million over the appropriation approved in Assembly resolutions 58/271 A and B [YUN 2003, p. 1414] and 58/295.

ACABQ recommended in December [A/59/601] that, with the exception of $815,000 related to staffing in the Office of the President of the General Assembly, the Assembly approve the revised estimates submitted by the Secretary-General, subject to adjustments resulting from its consideration of matters currently before it, including estimates related to special political missions and security, and to the consolidated statement of revised estimates and programme budget implications.

GENERAL ASSEMBLY ACTION

On 23 December, the General Assembly, on the recommendation of the Fifth (Administrative and Budgetary) Committee [A/59/448/Add.2], adopted **resolution 59/277 A-C** [agenda item 108].

Programme budget for the biennium 2004-2005

A

REVISED BUDGET APPROPRIATIONS FOR THE BIENNIUM 2004-2005

The General Assembly

Resolves that, for the biennium 2004-2005, the amount of 3,179,196,100 United States dollars appropriated by it in its resolutions 58/271 A of 23 December 2003 and 58/295 of 18 June 2004 shall be adjusted by 428,977,800 dollars, as follows:

Budget section	Amount approved in resolutions 58/271 A and 58/295[a]	Increase/ (decrease)	Revised appropriation
	(United States dollars)		
Part I. *Overall policy-making, direction and coordination*			
1. Overall policy-making, direction and coordination			
2. General Assembly affairs and conference services	58 504 400	3 038 800	61 543 200
	533 574 800	26 681 700	560 256 500
Total, part I	592 079 200	29 720 500	621 799 700
Part II. *Political affairs*			
3. Political affairs			
4. Disarmament	242 461 500	185 165 700	427 627 200
5. Peacekeeping operations	18 118 400	621 500	18 739 900
6. Peaceful uses of outer space	89 898 300	2 961 500	92 859 800
	5 484 400	419 500	5 903 900
Total, part II	355 962 600	189 168 200	545 130 800
Part III. *International justice and law*			
7. International Court of Justice			
8. Legal affairs	31 621 900	3 314 100	34 936 000
	39 303 000	1 331 000	40 634 000
Total, part III	70 924 900	4 645 100	75 570 000
Part IV. *International cooperation for development*			
9. Economic and social affairs			
	137 739 400	5 288 300	143 027 700

Budget section	Amount approved in resolutions 58/271 A and 58/295ª	Increase/ (decrease)	Revised appropriation
	(United States dollars)		
10. Least developed countries, landlocked developing countries and small island developing States	4 231 900	126 700	4 358 600
11. United Nations support for the New Partnership for Africa's Development	9 344 000	231 000	9 575 000
12. Trade and development	106 241 800	8 560 500	114 802 300
13. International Trade Centre UNCTAD/WTO	23 472 200	2 664 100	26 136 300
14. Environment	10 530 100	385 700	10 915 800
15. Human settlements	15 536 200	476 600	16 012 800
16. Crime prevention and criminal justice	9 392 800	647 400	10 040 200
17. International drug control	20 006 900	1 469 200	21 476 100
Total, part IV	**336 495 300**	**19 849 500**	**356 344 800**
Part V. *Regional cooperation for development*			
18. Economic and social development in Africa	95 672 700	569 300	96 242 000
19. Economic and social development in Asia and the Pacific	67 236 900	(2 169 800)	65 067 100
20. Economic development in Europe	50 196 800	4 565 000	54 761 800
21. Economic and social development in Latin America and the Caribbean	80 884 900	4 486 500	85 371 400
22. Economic and social development in Western Asia	52 713 800	(1 718 200)	50 995 600
23. Regular programme of technical cooperation	42 871 500	–	42 871 500
Total, part V	**389 576 600**	**5 732 800**	**395 309 400**
Part VI. *Human rights and humanitarian affairs*			
24. Human rights	56 794 500	7 776 800	64 571 300
25. Protection of and assistance to refugees	56 731 900	9 512 000	66 243 900
26. Palestine refugees	33 851 800	789 200	34 641 000
27. Humanitarian assistance	23 292 300	983 000	24 275 300
Total, part VI	**170 670 500**	**19 061 000**	**189 731 500**
Part VII. *Public information*			
28. Public information	156 056 100	6 266 500	162 322 600
Total, part VII	**156 056 100**	**6 266 500**	**162 322 600**
Part VIII. *Common support services*			
29. Management and central support services	525 139 700	(47 993 900)	477 145 800
Total, part VIII	**525 139 700**	**(47 993 900)**	**477 145 800**
Part IX. *Internal oversight*			
30. Internal oversight	23 227 200	959 800	24 187 000
Total, part IX	**23 227 200**	**959 800**	**24 187 000**
Part X. *Jointly financed administrative activities and special expenses*			
31. Jointly financed administrative activities	25 573 200	(15 128 000)	10 445 200
32. Special expenses	79 455 100	1 800 800	81 255 900
Total, part X	**105 028 300**	**(13 327 200)**	**91 701 100**
Part XI. *Capital expenditures*			
33. Construction, alteration, improvement and major maintenance	58 651 300	45 915 300	104 566 600
Total, part XI	**58 651 300**	**45 915 300**	**104 566 600**
Part XII. *Staff assessment*			
34. Staff assessment	382 319 400	28 874 800	411 194 200
Total, part XII	**382 319 400**	**28 874 800**	**411 194 200**
Part XIII. *Development Account*			
35. Development Account	13 065 000	–	13 065 000
Total, part XIII	**13 065 000**	**–**	**13 065 000**
Part XIV. *Safety and security*			
36. Safety and security	–	140 105 400	140 105 400
Total, part XIV	**–**	**140 105 400**	**140 105 400**
Grand total	**3 179 196 100**	**428 977 800**	**3 608 173 900**

B

REVISED INCOME ESTIMATES FOR THE BIENNIUM 2004-2006

The General Assembly

Resolves that, for the biennium 2004-2005, the estimates of income of 415,340,500 United States dollars approved by it in its resolutions 58/271 B of 23 December 2003 and 58/295 of 18 June 2004 shall be increased by 28,511,400 dollars, as follows:

[see table on next page]

C

FINANCING OF THE APPROPRIATIONS FOR THE YEAR 2005

The General Assembly

Resolves that, for the year 2005:

1. Budget appropriations totalling 2,027,743,750 United States dollars and consisting of 1,580,430,150 dollars, being half of the appropriation initially approved for the biennium 2004-2005 in its resolution 58/271 A of 23 December 2003, 18,335,800 dollars, be-

ing the additional appropriation approved for the bi-ennium 2004-2005 in its resolution 58/295 of 18 June 2004, and 428,977,800 dollars, being the increase ap-proved in resolution A above, shall be financed in ac-cordance with regulations 5.1 and 5.2 of the Financial Regulations and Rules of the United Nations, as fol-lows:

(a) 29,509,150 dollars, consisting of:

(i) 14,400,050 dollars, being half of the estimated income other than income from staff assess-ment approved for the biennium 2004-2005 in its resolution 58/271 B of 23 December 2003;

(ii) Less 561,900 dollars, being the decrease ap-proved in resolution B above;

(iii) 15,671,000 dollars, being the balance in the sur-plus account as at 31 December 2003;

(b) 1,998,234,600 dollars, being the assessment on Member States in accordance with its resolution 58/1 B of 23 December 2003;

2. There shall be set off against the assessment on Member States, in accordance with the provisions of General Assembly resolution 973(X) of 15 December 1955, their respective share in the Tax Equalization Fund in the total amount of 218,725,650 dollars, con-sisting of:

(a) 193,245,850 dollars, being half of the estimated staff assessment income approved by the Assembly in its resolution 58/271 B;

(b) 48,700 dollars, being the estimated staff assess-ment income approved by the Assembly in its resolu-tion 58/295;

(c) 29,073,300 dollars, being the estimated increase in income from staff assessment approved in resolu-tion B above;

(d) Less 3,642,200 dollars, being the decrease in in-come from staff assessment for the biennium 2002-2003 compared with the revised estimates approved by the Assembly in its resolution 58/267 B of 23 Decem-ber 2003.

Income section	Amount approved in resolutions 58/271 B and 58/295	Increase/ (decrease)	Revised income estimates
	(United States dollars)		
1. Income from staff assessment	386 540 400	29 073 300	415 613
Total, income section 1	**386 540 400**	**29 073 300**	**415 613**
2. General income	24 043 200	(33 700)	24 009 500
3. Services to the public	4 756 900	(528 200)	4 228 700
Total, income sections 2 and 3	**28 800 100**	**(561 900)**	**28 238 200**
Grand total	**415 340 500**	**28 511 400**	**443 851**

Questions relating to the 2004-2005 programme budget

The Fifth Committee considered a number of questions related to the 2004-2005 programme budget, among them revised estimates resulting from resolutions and decisions by the Economic and Social Council in 2004, unforeseen and ex-traordinary expenses, estimates in respect of spe-cial political missions, good offices and other political initiatives authorized by the General Assembly and/or the Security Council, the first

performance report of the programme budget for the 2004-2005 biennium, and the contingency fund: consolidated statement of programme budget implications and revised estimates.

Other subjects covered concerned the Interna-tional Trade Centre of the United Nations Con-ference on Trade and Development (UNCTAD) and the World Trade Organization (WTO) (see p. 965), the Office of the United Nations High Commissioner for Refugees (see p. 1195), the United Nations Institute for Disarmament Re-search (see p. 584), the construction of additional conference centre facilities at the Vienna Inter-national Centre (see p. 1384), the Department of Public Information websites (see p. 629), the United Nations Institute for Training and Re-search (see p. 1139), UN security management system (see p. 1387), and the International Civil Service Commission (see p. 1407).

GENERAL ASSEMBLY ACTION

On 23 December, the General Assembly, on the recommendation of the Fifth Committee [A/59/448/Add.2], adopted **resolution 59/276** [agenda item 108].

Questions relating to the programme budget for the biennium 2004-2005

The General Assembly,

I

Administrative arrangements for the International Trade Centre UNCTAD/WTO

Recalling its decision 57/572 of 20 December 2002 and its resolutions 57/312 of 18 June 2003, 48/218 B of 29 July 1994 and 54/244 of 23 December 1999,

1. *Takes note* of the report of the Secretary-General on administrative arrangements for the International Trade Centre UNCTAD/WTO and of the related report of the Advisory Committee on Administrative and Budgetary Questions, and endorses the recommenda-tions contained therein;

2. *Also takes note* of the report of the Office of Inter-nal Oversight Services on the inspection of pro-gramme management and administrative practices of the International Trade Centre UNCTAD/WTO, and re-quests the Secretary-General to ensure that the recom-mendations contained therein are implemented expe-ditiously;

II

Revised estimates resulting from resolutions and decisions adopted by the Economic and Social Council at its substantive session and resumed substantive sessions of 2004

Takes note of the report of the Secretary-General on the revised estimates resulting from resolutions and decisions adopted by the Economic and Social Council at its substantive and resumed substantive sessions of 2004 and the related reports of the Advisory Commit-tee on Administrative and Budgetary Questions, on the understanding that such appropriations as may be nec-essary and not exceeding 573,600 United States dollars will be requested by the Secretary-General in the context of a consolidated statement of programme budget implications and revised estimates to be submitted to the General Assembly;

III

Progressive implementation of article 20 of the statute of the Office of the United Nations High Commissioner for Refugees

Recalling paragraph 49 of its resolution 58/270 of 23 December 2003,

1. *Takes note* of the report of the Secretary-General on the progressive implementation of article 20 of the statute of the Office of the United Nations High Commissioner for Refugees and the related report of the Advisory Committee on Administrative and Budgetary Questions presented orally by its Chairman;

2. *Requests* the Secretary-General to include in the programme budget proposals for progressive increases for contributions from the regular budget to the Office of the High Commissioner with a view to the full implementation of article 20 of the statute of the Office and to report on the progress made to the General Assembly at its sixtieth session in the context of the proposed programme budget for the biennium 2006-2007, while recognizing that the percentage referred to in paragraph 6 of the report of the Secretary-General does not represent a ceiling;

3. *Calls upon* the Office of the High Commissioner to keep its support costs, including management and administration, under review with the objective of reducing these as a percentage of total budget expenditure, and welcomes the decision of the Office to initiate a headquarters process review with the aim of simplifying and streamlining administration;

4. *Requests* the Secretary-General to include in the proposed programme budget for the biennium 2006-2007 a transparent presentation of the purposes for which regular budget funds are proposed, including the composition of administrative costs and information on efficiency measures;

5. *Also requests* the Secretary-General to ensure that oversight and accountability mechanisms in the Office of the High Commissioner are operating effectively with the required independence, authority and transparency;

IV

Unforeseen and extraordinary expenses

Having considered the report of the Secretary-General on the comprehensive review of the resolution on unforeseen and extraordinary expenses relating to expenses certified by the President of the International Court of Justice and the related report of the Advisory Committee on Administrative and Budgetary Questions,

1. *Approves* the request to change the ceiling to 200,000 dollars under the resolution on unforeseen and extraordinary expenses for expenses that may be certified by the President of the Court without prior concurrence of the Advisory Committee on Administrative and Budgetary Questions in connection with the designation of ad hoc judges with effect from the biennium 2006-2007;

2. *Also approves* the proposal to maintain an amount of 400,000 dollars in the regular budget of the Court

to accommodate the recurring requirements for ad hoc judges, with effect from the biennium 2006-2007, to be included in the proposed programme budget for the biennium 2006-2007;

V

Request for a subvention to the United Nations Institute for Disarmament Research resulting from the recommendations of the Board of Trustees of the Institute on the programme of work of the Institute for 2005

Recalling its resolution 58/272 of 23 December 2003,

1. *Takes note* of the note by the Secretary-General on the request for a subvention to the United Nations Institute for Disarmament Research resulting from the recommendations of the Board of Trustees of the Institute on the programme of work of the Institute for 2005 and of the related report of the Advisory Committee on Administrative and Budgetary Questions;

2. *Approves* the request for a subvention to the Institute of 227,600 dollars, to be recosted, for 2005 from the regular budget of the United Nations, on the understanding that no additional appropriation would be required under section 4, Disarmament, of the programme budget for the biennium 2004-2005;

3. *Requests* the Secretary-General to make proposals in the context of the proposed programme budget for the biennium 2006-2007 for biennial review and approval by the General Assembly of subvention requirements of the Institute beginning with the biennium 2006-2007;

VI

Construction of additional conference facilities at the Vienna International Centre

Having considered the note by the Secretary-General on the construction of additional conference facilities at the Vienna International Centre and the related report of the Advisory Committee on Administrative and Budgetary Questions presented orally by its Chairman,

1. *Takes note with appreciation* of the proposal of the Government of Austria to construct a new conference facility within the boundaries of the Vienna International Centre;

2. *Approves* the participation of the United Nations, along with the other organizations located in the Vienna International Centre, in the arrangements for the proposed new conference facility on the terms proposed by the Secretary-General in his note;

3. *Entrusts* the Secretary-General to determine, in cooperation with the other three organizations located at the Vienna International Centre, the cost-sharing arrangements for potential future costs arising from the project within the amount indicated in his note, on the understanding that the related financial requirements will be dealt with in the context of the proposed programme budget for the respective bienniums, and to report thereon to the General Assembly for its review and decision;

4. *Requests* the Secretary-General to report on the progress in the project implementation to the General Assembly at its sixty-first session;

VII

Estimates in respect of special political missions, good offices and other political initiatives authorized by the General Assembly and/or the Security Council

Having considered the report of the Secretary-General on estimates in respect of special political missions, good offices and other political initiatives authorized by the General Assembly and/or the Security Council and on the request for a subvention to the Special Court for Sierra Leone, as well as the related report of the Advisory Committee on Administrative and Budgetary Questions,

Reaffirming section VI of its resolution 45/248 B of 21 December 1990,

1. *Takes note* of the report of the Secretary-General on estimates in respect of special political missions, good offices and other political initiatives authorized by the General Assembly and/or the Security Council;

2. *Endorses* the observations and recommendations of the Advisory Committee on Administrative and Budgetary Questions contained in its report, subject to the provisions of the present resolution;

3. *Notes* that the charging of expenditures against the appropriation for special political missions would be subject to the extension of the respective mandates;

4. *Reaffirms*, in the context of all Security Council decisions on special political missions, the prerogatives of the General Assembly in issues related to administrative and budgetary matters;

5. *Reiterates* that, in accordance with the Financial Regulations and Rules of the United Nations, the submission of the budget proposals is a prerogative of the Secretary-General;

6. *Invites* the Secretary-General to provide all intergovernmental bodies with the required information regarding procedures for administrative and budgetary matters;

7. *Regrets* the late issuance of the reports of the Secretary-General on estimates in respect of special political missions, and requests the Secretary-General, in the future, to present budget proposals for special political missions at an earlier date, in order to facilitate proper consideration by the General Assembly;

8. *Approves* the budgets of the 25 special political missions presented in table 1 of the report of the Secretary-General;

9. *Decides* to appropriate under the procedures provided for in paragraph 11 of annex I to its resolution 41/213 of 19 December 1986, under section 3, Political affairs, of the programme budget for the biennium 2004-2005 an amount of 678,600 dollars for the three special political missions presented in table 1, part A, of the report of the Secretary-General, emanating from the decisions taken or to be taken by the General Assembly;

10. *Also decides* to appropriate under the procedures provided for in paragraph 11 of annex I to resolution 41/213, under section 3 of the programme budget an amount of 161,936,100 dollars for the 22 special political missions presented in table 1, part B, of the report of the Secretary-General, emanating from the decisions taken or to be taken by the Security Council;

11. *Further decides* to appropriate an amount of 12,132,500 dollars under section 34, Staff assessment, to be offset by a corresponding amount under income section 1, Income from staff assessment, of the programme budget for the biennium 2004-2005;

12. *Requests* the Secretary-General, in preparing the next budget proposals for the Counter-Terrorism Committee Executive Directorate, to review and consider possible streamlining of the structure and level of positions, bearing in mind its temporary nature and its status as a subsidiary body of the Security Council, as well as to address its relationship with the Department of Political Affairs of the Secretariat;

13. *Decides* to approve the proposed waiver requested for the implementation of section III.B, paragraph 26, of resolution 51/226 of 3 April 1997, on an exceptional and extraordinary basis, and requests the Secretary-General to report in the next budget submission on how many consultants given such waiver were recruited, along with their nationalities and functions performed;

14. *Requests* the Secretary-General to recruit staff for the Counter-Terrorism Committee Executive Directorate in full compliance with relevant resolutions of the General Assembly;

15. *Decides* that the use of experts and consultants for the Counter-Terrorism Committee Executive Directorate and for the Security Council Committee established pursuant to Council resolution 1540(2004) of 28 April 2004 should also be in full compliance with the relevant resolutions of the General Assembly;

16. *Takes note* that the commitment authority authorized in resolution 58/284 of 8 April 2004 and valid through 31 December 2004 to support a subvention for the Special Court for Sierra Leone has been held unused in view of the continued dependence of the Court on voluntary contributions during the period and is being surrendered;

17. *Authorizes* the Secretary-General to enter into commitments in an amount not to exceed 20 million dollars to supplement the financial resources of the Special Court for Sierra Leone, with effect from 1 January to 30 June 2005, under special political missions of section 3, Political affairs, of the programme budget for the biennium 2004-2005;

18. *Requests* the Secretary-General, in concert with the Management Committee of the Special Court for Sierra Leone, to continue efforts to raise voluntary contributions to support the work of the Court and to report to the General Assembly at its resumed fifty-ninth session on progress made;

19. *Appeals* to Member States, as a matter of urgency, to contribute voluntary funds in support of the Court and to honour existing pledges;

20. *Requests* the Secretary-General to submit to the General Assembly at its resumed fifty-ninth session a progress report in respect of the Special Court for Sierra Leone;

21. *Requests* the President of the General Assembly to bring to the attention of the President of the Security Council the contents of the present resolution;

VIII

First performance report on the programme budget for the biennium 2004-2005

Having considered the first performance report of the Secretary-General on the programme budget for the biennium 2004-2005 and the related report of the Advisory Committee on Administrative and Budgetary Questions,

Recalling its resolutions 58/270 and 58/271 A to C of 23 December 2003 and 58/295 of 18 June 2004,

1. *Reaffirms* the budgetary process as approved in its resolution 41/213 and as reaffirmed in subsequent resolutions;

2. *Takes note* of the first performance report of the Secretary-General on the programme budget for the biennium 2004-2005 and the addendum on the implementation of the United Nations Official Document System, and endorses the observations and recommendations contained in the related report of the Advisory Committee on Administrative and Budgetary Questions, subject to the provisions of the present resolution;

3. *Reaffirms* the importance that Member States attach to the work of the Office of the President of the General Assembly in support of the activities carried out by the President of the General Assembly;

4. *Recalls* paragraph 10 of the annex to its resolution 58/126 of 19 December 2003, notes the assurances given by the Secretariat that the three remaining positions, namely, one D-2, one D-1 and one General Service, needed to strengthen the Office of the President of the General Assembly will be provided, and in this context requests the Secretary-General to ensure its full and expeditious implementation;

5. *Requests* the Secretary-General to report to the General Assembly on the implementation of paragraph 4 above in the context of the second performance report;

6. *Decides* to approve a gross budget for the Joint Inspection Unit for the year 2005 in the amount of 5,385,700 dollars and to appropriate the amount of 1,712,700 dollars under section 31, Jointly financed administrative activities, for the financing of the Joint Inspection Unit in 2005;

7. *Notes* the contents of paragraph 42 of the report of the Secretary-General and requests the Secretary-General to report to the General Assembly comprehensively on this issue at the beginning of its sixtieth session;

8. *Recalls* paragraph 9 of its resolution 58/270, and notes that its implementation resulted in a decrease of 4,007,000 dollars from the original proposed appropriation in section 23, Regular programme of technical cooperation;

9. *Requests* the Secretary-General to fill expeditiously vacant positions for web-site assistants in all official languages from external candidates, utilizing general temporary assistance;

10. *Recalls* paragraph 44 of its resolution 58/270 and takes note of the relevant paragraph of the Secretary-General's report regarding the *Repertory of Practice of the United Nations Organs*, and requests the Secretary-General to keep the matter under review and to report thereon to the General Assembly in the context of the proposed programme budget for the biennium 2006-2007;

11. *Approves* a net increase of 172,851,200 dollars in the appropriation approved for the biennium 2004-2005 and a net increase of 9,406,800 dollars in the estimates of income for the biennium, to be apportioned among expenditure and income sections as indicated in the report of the Secretary-General and amended to reflect the recommendation of the Advisory Committee;

IX

Strengthening the Department of Public Information, within the existing capacity, in order to support and enhance the United Nations web site in all official languages of the Organization: status of implementation

Having considered the report of the Secretary-General entitled "Strengthening the Department of Public Information, within the existing capacity, in order to support and enhance the United Nations web site in all official languages of the Organization: status of implementation" and the related report of the Advisory Committee on Administrative and Budgetary Questions,

Recalling paragraph 42 of its resolution 58/270 and paragraph 95 of its resolution 59/126 B of 10 December 2004, in which it requested the Secretary-General to strengthen the web site through further redeployment to the required language posts,

Reaffirming the need to achieve full parity among the six official languages on the United Nations web site,

Also reaffirming its request to the Secretary-General to ensure that the Department of Public Information has appropriate staffing capacity in all official languages of the United Nations to undertake all its activities,

1. *Takes note* of the report of the Secretary-General and paragraphs 19 to 23 of the report of the Advisory Committee on Administrative and Budgetary Questions;

2. *Requests* the Secretary-General to submit proposals to strengthen the United Nations web site within the context of the proposed programme budget for the biennium 2006-2007;

X

Financial viability of the United Nations Institute for Training and Research

Recalling section XIV of its resolution 58/272 of 23 December 2003,

Having considered the note by the Secretary-General on the financial viability of the United Nations Institute for Training and Research, transmitting the note by the Board of Trustees of the Institute on the rationalization of the financial structure of the Institute, and the related report of the Advisory Committee on Administrative and Budgetary Questions presented orally by its Chairman,

1. *Takes note with concern* of the observations and conclusions of the Board of Trustees of the United Nations Institute for Training and Research transmitted under the cover of the note by the Secretary-General;

2. *Stresses* the importance of maintaining the current level of the training programmes of the Institute, and requests the Board of Trustees to make every effort to ensure that in 2005 the level of training programmes will be maintained;

3. *Stresses also* the need for continued consideration of the issues related to the Institute's rent, rental rates and maintenance costs, taking into account its financial situation, with a view to its expeditious resolution;

4. *Requests* the Secretary-General to submit, as a priority, to the General Assembly at the beginning of its sixtieth session, and prior to the introduction of the proposed programme budget for the biennium 2006-2007, a comprehensive report on all aspects of the financial situation of the Institute, including proposals which would address the long-term, sound and predictable funding of rent and maintenance costs;

5. *Decides* to consider the outcome of its consideration of that report in the context of the proposed programme budget for the biennium 2006-2007;

XI

Strengthened and unified security management system for the United Nations

Recalling its resolutions 56/255 of 24 December 2001, 56/286 of 27 June 2002, 57/305 of 15 April 2003, 58/270 of 23 December 2003, 58/295 of 18 June 2004 and all relevant resolutions regarding the security and safety of United Nations operations, staff and premises,

Having considered the report of the Secretary-General on a strengthened and unified security management system for the United Nations and the report of the Office of Internal Oversight Services on the utilization and management of funds appropriated during the biennium 2002-2003 for strengthening the security and safety of United Nations premises,

Having also considered the report of the Advisory Committee on Administrative and Budgetary Questions,

Underlining the importance of achieving the highest levels of professionalism and expertise within United Nations security management,

Reaffirming Article 97 of the Charter of the United Nations,

Reaffirming also the role of the General Assembly in carrying out a thorough analysis and approval of posts and financial resources as well as human resources policies with a view to ensuring the full implementation of all mandated programmes and activities and the implementation of all policies in this regard,

Reaffirming further that the Fifth Committee is the appropriate Main Committee of the General Assembly responsible for administrative and budgetary matters,

1. *Takes note* of the report of the Secretary-General;

2. *Reaffirms* the importance of ensuring the safety and security of United Nations staff, operations and premises;

3. *Emphasizes* that the primary responsibility for ensuring the safety and security of United Nations staff and premises rests with the host country, and also emphasizes the role of the relevant host country agreements in defining this responsibility;

4. *Recognizes* the need for the urgent implementation of a unified and strengthened security management system in order to ensure the safety and security of United Nations staff, operations and premises at United Nations Headquarters and main duty stations, as well as in the field;

5. *Stresses* that the effective functioning at the country level of security operations on a decentralized basis as proposed by the Secretary-General requires a unified capacity for policy, standards, coordination, communication, compliance and threat and risk assessment;

6. *Endorses* the conclusions and recommendations of the Advisory Committee on Administrative and Budgetary Questions, subject to the provisions of the present resolution;

7. *Decides*, bearing in mind the observations of the Advisory Committee on Administrative and Budgetary Questions contained in paragraph 64 of its report and General Assembly resolution 32/204 of 21 December 1977 on organizational nomenclature in the Secretariat, to establish a Department of Safety and Security;

8. *Welcomes* the report of the Office of Internal Oversight Services on the utilization and management of funds appropriated by the General Assembly in its resolution 56/286 in response to concerns about delays and cost escalation, notes the progress made more recently in the implementation of these projects, and urges the Secretary-General to complete their implementation expeditiously;

9. *Notes with concern* the delays, cost escalation and deficiencies in planning and administering security-strengthening projects, particularly at Headquarters and at the United Nations Office at Geneva, in relation to funds appropriated by the General Assembly in its resolution 56/286, as set out by the Office of Internal Oversight Services in its report, and requests the Secretary-General to ensure that in the implementation of Assembly resolution 58/295, as well as the present resolution, funds appropriated for security-strengthening projects are managed and disbursed with great oversight, efficiency and effectiveness and in a timely manner;

10. *Requests* the Secretary-General to report on the implementation of recommendations contained in the report of the Office of Internal Oversight Services and also to entrust the Office of Internal Oversight Services to report on the utilization and management of funds approved by the General Assembly in its resolution 58/295 and in the present resolution for security-strengthening projects for submission to the Assembly at its sixtieth session;

11. *Emphasizes* the need for an enhanced culture of security awareness on the part of all staff and compliance with safety and security rules and procedures throughout the United Nations system, as well as clear lines of authority and accountability;

12. *Affirms* that United Nations security management requires clear lines of authority and accountability at all managerial levels at Headquarters and in the field for the implementation of safety and security rules and procedures;

13. *Requests* the Secretary-General to submit to the General Assembly at its sixtieth session an accountability framework for the United Nations security management system as a whole, which would, inter alia:

(a) Update the report on field security;

(b) Make clear the role of each responsible official;

(c) Provide information on how non-military lines of security-related authority lead to the head of the Department of Safety and Security;

14. *Also requests* the Secretary-General, in consultation with the executive heads of United Nations funds and programmes that maintain their own security personnel in the field, to elaborate in the updated accountability framework on how such security staff are integrated into the unified security management structure at the country level under the authority of

the designated official and to clarify the authority of the designated official over such staff;

15. *Further requests* the Secretary-General, in order to strengthen security compliance, to apply available measures for disciplinary action to be taken at all levels, especially at the managerial level, in all departments for non-compliance with security standards, norms and procedures, and to report thereon to the General Assembly at its sixtieth session;

16. *Requests* the Secretary-General, in order to strengthen security compliance, as Chairman of the United Nations System Chief Executives Board for Coordination, to propose to the executive heads of agencies, funds and programmes that participate in the United Nations security management system that they apply available measures for disciplinary action to be taken at all levels for non-compliance with security standards, norms and procedures;

17. *Reaffirms* Article 101 of the Charter of the United Nations;

18. *Urges* the Secretary-General to preserve the international character of the Organization in the recruitment of relevant categories of safety and security staff;

19. *Recognizes* that the Professional posts created by the present resolution under the regular budget would be added to the pool of posts subject to the system of geographical distribution in accordance with established procedures;

20. *Urges* the Secretary-General to ensure that recruitment to Professional and higher categories is made on a wide geographical basis;

21. *Requests* the Secretary-General to elaborate further on his proposals concerning career development, a new profile for security officers and the further professionalization of security personnel referred to in paragraphs 25 and 31 of his report, to submit detailed proposals on retirement policy given the special requirements for security staff and to report thereon to the General Assembly at its sixtieth session;

22. *Decides,* on an exceptional basis and without setting any precedent, that the Under-Secretary-General for Safety and Security shall serve for one non-renewable term not exceeding five years;

23. *Also decides* that the Under-Secretary-General for Safety and Security shall be appointed with full respect for the principle of equitable geographical representation and guided by its resolution 46/232 of 2 March 1992, whereby the General Assembly decided, inter alia, that as a general rule no national of a Member State should succeed a national of that State in that post and that there should be no monopoly on senior posts by nationals of any State or group of States;

24. *Further decides* to establish a D-2 post of deputy to the Under-Secretary-General and to review the post in the context of the implementation report to be submitted by the Secretary-General to the General Assembly at its sixtieth session;

25. *Decides* to establish the post of the head of the Division of Safety and Security Services at the D-2 level and to review the post in the context of the implementation report to be submitted by the Secretary-General to the General Assembly at its sixtieth session;

26. *Also decides* to establish 383 new security and safety officer posts within the General Service and re-

lated categories, of which 249 are established posts and 134 are on a temporary post basis;

27. *Further decides* to review the newly approved posts referred to in paragraph 26 above in the light of a comprehensive report to be submitted by the Secretary-General to the General Assembly at its sixtieth session addressing all elements contributing to the security planning of the Organization, including the updating and revision of host country agreements as well as the different capacities of host countries to provide security to the United Nations, as outlined in paragraphs 19 and 20 of the report of the Advisory Committee on Administrative and Budgetary Questions;

28. *Decides* to establish an Executive Office in the Department of Safety and Security consisting of 17 posts to handle its administrative support functions;

29. *Also decides* to appropriate 500,000 dollars under general temporary assistance to provide surge capacity for the Department of Safety and Security;

30. *Further decides* to approve the creation of the posts proposed by the Secretary-General in field locations;

31. *Recognizes* the need for the security and safety sections at the eight headquarters and main duty stations of the United Nations to convey threat and risk assessments through the appropriate regional desks;

32. *Notes* that threat and risk assessments will be conducted primarily by the field offices and reviewed by the regional desks;

33. *Decides* to enhance the capacity for threat and risk assessment by establishing one P-4, two P-3 and one General Service post in addition to the existing P-5 post, and further decides that this capacity will be located in the Office of the Director of Regional Operations;

34. *Reaffirms* paragraph 2 of its resolution 58/295;

35. *Notes* that in paragraph 54 of his report, the Secretary-General proposed getting input on threats and risks from sources other than international organizations and Governments, and emphasizes that it is incumbent on the Department of Safety and Security, in making its objective judgement, to weigh the reliability and responsibility of the source as well as the reliability and validity of the information being used in order to produce threat and risk assessments;

36. *Decides,* in this context, that threat and risk assessments to be provided to Headquarters should be prepared by country offices and other components of the United Nations system, on an objective basis and in full cooperation with the national authorities of host countries;

37. *Reaffirms,* in this context, Article 100 of the Charter of the United Nations;

38. *Requests* the Secretary-General to strengthen the process for the continuous review of threat and risk assessment so as to enable timely, systematic and periodic review of the phases, and requests the Secretary-General to keep the respective national Governments apprised in a timely manner of any changes resulting from such review;

39. *Also requests* the Secretary-General to provide information, upon request by Member States, about the methodology used for determining phases of threat and risk assessment;

40. *Further requests* the Secretary-General to provide, in the context of the implementation report, information on strengthening the cooperation between the Department of Safety and Security and the Department of Peacekeeping Operations with respect to security decisions that may affect the conduct of peacekeeping operations, in the framework of the unified security management system, which would be led by the Department of Safety and Security under the provisions of the present resolution;

41. *Notes* that the malicious acts insurance policy has a worldwide coverage except in headquarters countries, namely, Austria, Canada, France, Germany, Italy, Japan, the Netherlands, Switzerland, the United Kingdom and the United States of America;

42. *Notes with concern* that there are some staff in the United Nations system who are working in the field and are not covered by the malicious acts insurance policy or a comparable scheme;

43. *Requests* the Secretary-General, as Chairman of the United Nations System Chief Executives Board for Coordination, to address this matter in the context of the Board and to report to the General Assembly thereon at its sixtieth session with a view to ensuring that all staff are covered;

44. *Decides* to defer until the second part of the resumed fifty-ninth session of the General Assembly consideration of the proposal of the Secretary-General on the global access control system, pending the receipt of a detailed report by the Secretary-General, which will include the following:

(a) Integration with projects approved by the General Assembly in previous resolutions, including those in the context of the overall information technology strategy;

(b) The impact of implementing the global access control system on human resources requirements in the area of safety and security;

(c) The individual characteristics of each United Nations headquarters and main duty station;

(d) The implications of the global access control system for the capital master plan;

(e) Detailed information regarding the global identity management system, including the principles and guidelines for sharing the information obtained through the system, the level of centralization needed for managing this information and who would have access to the information;

(f) The time frame for implementation of the system;

45. *Decides also* to defer consideration of the expansion of the security service fitness facility and to revert to this issue in the context of its consideration of the scope of work of the capital master plan;

46. *Requests* the Secretary-General to ensure that infrastructure projects approved for Headquarters under the present resolution should not, pending a decision on the capital master plan, incur additional unnecessary costs at a later date under the capital master plan;

47. *Also requests* the Secretary-General to submit to the General Assembly at its sixtieth session the results of the technical study on information and communication technology security, business continuity and disaster recovery, with detailed costing and a timetable;

48. *Decides* to maintain existing arrangements with regard to cost-sharing for safety and security;

49. *Requests* the Secretary-General, in his capacity as the Chairman of the United Nations System Chief Executives Board for Coordination, while fully implementing the decision of the General Assembly to maintain the current cost-sharing arrangements, to submit a report to the General Assembly at its sixty-first session on measures taken to improve the operational administration of existing cost-sharing arrangements;

50. *Stresses* the importance that all entities participating in specific arrangements in place at headquarters duty stations for sharing the costs of the central security and safety services should provide prompt and secure funding for such arrangements;

51. *Decides* that the present cost-sharing arrangements relating to field security for those organizations which are not part of the United Nations system should be retained;

52. *Invites* those organizations of the United Nations system which are currently in arrears with their contributions to the United Nations under the present cost-sharing arrangements to take steps to ensure prompt payment of the outstanding sums;

53. *Decides* to approve an additional appropriation under the regular budget in the amount of 53,633,300 dollars, as detailed in the annex to the present section;

54. *Also decides* to approve an additional appropriation in the amount of 6,069,700 dollars under section 34, Staff assessment, of the programme budget for the biennium 2004-2005, to be offset by an equivalent amount of income under income section 1, Income from staff assessment;

55. *Recognizes* the need for a clearer presentation of security spending by each organization of the United Nations system, and requests the Secretary-General, as Chairman of the United Nations System Chief Executives Board for Coordination, to inform the General Assembly at its sixtieth session on this issue;

56. *Requests* the Secretary-General to examine the possibility for further integration and rationalization of the security management system and to report thereon to the General Assembly at its sixty-first session;

57. *Also requests* the Secretary-General to submit to the General Assembly at its sixtieth session a report on the implementation of the present resolution;

Annex

Additional appropriations for the strengthened and unified security management system for the United Nations, at revised 2004-2005 rates, by section of the programme budget for the biennium 2004-2005

(*Thousands of United States dollars*)

Budget section	Additional
3. Political affairs	147.2
4. Disarmament	50.5
5. Peacekeeping operations	1 612.6
13. International Trade Centre UNCTAD/WTO	669.4
18. Economic and social development in Africa	(2 383.0)
19. Economic and social development in Asia and the Pacific	(4 775.9)
21. Economic and social development in Latin America and the Caribbean	(2 960.3)
22. Economic and social development in Western Asia	(3 833.7)
24. Human rights	45.4

Budget section	Additional
25. Protection of and assistance to refugees	5 103.2
26. Palestine refugees	708.4
28. Public information	223.1
29D. Office of Central Support Services	(36 240.0)
29E. Administration, Geneva	(19 601.5)
29F. Administration, Vienna	(5 609.8)
29G. Administration, Nairobi	(5 835.0)
31. Jointly financed administrative activities	(17 796.1)
33. Construction, alteration, improvement and major maintenance	4 003.4
36. Safety and security	140 105.4
Total	**53 633.3**
34. Staff assessment	6 069.7
Income section 1. Income from staff assessment	(6 069.7)

XII

Administrative and financial implications of decisions and recommendations of the International Civil Service Commission for 2004

Recalling its resolution 59/268 of 23 December 2004 on the United Nations common system,

Takes note of the statement submitted by the Secretary-General on the administrative and financial implications of the decisions and recommendations contained in the report of the International Civil Service Commission for 2004 and the related report of the Advisory Committee on Administrative and Budgetary Questions;

XIII

Contingency fund: consolidated statement of programme budget implications and revised estimates

Decides to appropriate the required amounts, as contained in the report of the Secretary-General;

Notes that a balance of 7,854,800 dollars remains in the contingency fund.

On 23 December, the Assembly decided that the item on the programme budget for the 2004-2005 biennium would remain for consideration at its resumed fifty-ninth (2005) session (**decision 59/552**).

Revised estimates resulting from Economic and Social Council action

In a September report [A/59/393], the Secretary-General submitted expenditure requirements resulting from resolutions and decisions adopted by the Economic and Social Council at its 2004 substantive and first resumed substantive sessions relating to activities in the areas of indigenous issues, ad hoc advisory groups of the Council on African countries emerging from conflict, and human rights. Those requirements were estimated at $1,537,600, of which $964,000 could be absorbed within resources approved for the 2004-2005 biennium.

ACABQ, in its October report [A/59/542], recommended that the Fifth Committee take note of the estimate of $573,600, on the understanding that the Secretary-General would request any required appropriations in the context of the consolidated statement of programme budget implications and revised estimates to be submitted to the General Assembly.

In a later addendum [A/59/393/Add.1], the Secretary-General presented details of additional expenditure requirements arising from the Council's adoption of **resolution 2004/69**, relating to activities in the area of international cooperation in tax matters (see p. 985), estimated at $294,900 for 2005, which could be absorbed within approved 2004-2005 resources. The related requirements of $589,800 for the 2006-2007 biennium would be included in the proposed programme budget for that biennium and subsequent bienniums.

In December [A/59/597], ACABQ recommended approval of the Secretary-General's proposals.

Inflation and currency fluctuations

In December [A/C.5/59/24], the Secretary-General submitted adjustments to the revised estimates and programme budget implications that were subject to recosting, as indicated in the first performance report for the 2004-2005 biennium (see p. 1380). The adjustments, which were the result of the application of the new costing parameters approved by the General Assembly in the context of its consideration of the first performance report, showed an overall increase of $2,951,600, reflecting net increased requirements of $2,047,900 due to exchange rate fluctuation, with inflation and other standards adjustments amounting to $903,700, and an increase in staff assessment requirements of $159,300, to be offset by a corresponding increase under the income section.

The ACABQ Chairman, in an oral report to the Fifth Committee on 31 December [A/C.5/59/SR.31], recommended approval of the revised estimates submitted by the Secretary-General.

By **decision 59/550** of 23 December, the Assembly approved the adjustments, subject to the approval of related amounts for individual revised estimates and statements of programme budget implications.

Unforeseen and extraordinary expenses

Under the terms of resolution 58/273 [YUN 2003, p. 1422], the Secretary-General was authorized by the General Assembly to enter into commitments to meet unforeseen and extraordinary expenses arising either during or subsequent to the 2004-2005 biennium without prior ACABQ concurrence for certain specific commitments, including for expenses certified by the President of the International Court of Justice (ICJ). In a May report [A/59/90], the Secretary-General reviewed the adequacy of the provisions of the resolution as they related to ICJ and recommended that the Assembly approve his proposal to change the ceiling for expenses that might be certified by the ICJ President without prior ACABQ concurrence, with effect from the 2006-2007 biennium, and to maintain an amount of $400,000 in the regular ICJ budget to accommodate the recurring requirements for ad hoc judges, with effect from the same biennium, while adjusting the ceiling under that component of the resolution on unforeseen and extraordinary expenses from $330,000 to $200,000. No change was proposed for the 2004-2005 biennium.

ACABQ recommended in November [A/59/551] that the Assembly take note of the Secretary-General's report and approve his proposal.

Revised estimates in respect of matters of which the Security Council was seized

The Secretary-General, in November [A/59/534/Add.1], submitted proposed additional requirements for the period until 31 December 2005 for 25 political missions authorized by the Security Council and/or the General Assembly estimated at $162,614,700 net ($174,747,200 gross), after taking account of the balances expected to remain unencumbered for those missions at the end of their mandate periods, totalling an estimated $14,932,900.

In an interim progress report of 7 December [A/59/534/Add.2] on the implementation of Assembly resolution 58/284 (see p. 222), the Secretary-General recommended that the Assembly take note that the commitment authority valid through 31 December to support a subvention for the Special Court for Sierra Leone had been unused and was being surrendered in lieu of a request for an appropriation in 2005; it might also wish to decide to appropriate $20 million, with effect from 1 January through 30 June 2005, under special political missions of section 3, Political affairs, of the 2004-2005 programme budget, and revert to this matter at its resumed (2005) fifty-ninth session.

ACABQ pointed out that it could not make a detailed recommendation as to the level of financial assistance for the Special Court, since a fully justified presentation of its 2004-2005 budget would not be submitted to the Assembly until its resumed fifty-ninth (2005) session. In the meantime, and despite the perceived difficulty of fund-raising, ACABQ urged renewed and continued effort to mobilize voluntary resources. Should the Assembly agree to another subven-

tion, ACABQ recommended that a commitment authority be granted in an amount not to exceed $20 million to allow the Court to continue its operations to 30 June 2005 [A/59/569/Add.2].

In other related action, the Assembly authorized the Secretary-General to enter into commitments in the amount of $6 million to support the Cameroon-Nigeria Mixed Commission until 30 November (**resolution 58/294**) (see p. 231). Based on revised requirements of $5,419,300 for the period 1 June to 31 December submitted by the Secretary-General [A/58/886] and on the recommendation of ACABQ [A/59/411& Corr.1], the Assembly approved that amount, to be charged against the unallocated balance under section 3, Political affairs, of the 2004-2005 programme budget, for special political missions (**resolution 59/12**) (see p. 232).

Following the Council's establishment in June of an advance team to the Sudan, the Secretary-General, in October [A/59/534], proposed resource requirements for the 90-day extension of the team in the amount of $21,789,400 gross ($21,008,100 net), which the Assembly approved, to be charged against the balance for special political missions under section 3, Political affairs, of the 2004-2005 programme budget (**resolution 59/58**) (see p. 248).

Contingency fund

The contingency fund, established by General Assembly resolution 41/213 [YUN 1986, p. 1024], accommodated additional expenditures relating to each biennium that derived from legislative mandates not provided for in the proposed programme budget or from revised estimates. Guidelines for its use were annexed to Assembly resolution 42/211 [YUN 1987, p. 1098].

The Fifth Committee considered the Secretary-General's December report [A/C.5/59/27] containing a consolidated statement of all programme budget implications and revised estimates falling under the guidelines for the use of the fund. The consolidated amount of new and potential charges of $3,888,200 at revised 2004-2005 rates were within the available balance of the fund.

Programme budget implications of CPC recommendations

The Secretary-General submitted to the Fifth Committee in November [A/C.5/59/13] a statement of programme budget implications of the recommendations contained in the report of the Committee for Programme and Coordination (CPC) on its forty-fourth session (New York, 7 June–2 July) [A/59/16], concerning programme 24, as follows: Management and support services, of the proposed 2006-2007 strategic framework; Management and central support services, of the revised 2002-2005 medium-term plan; and section 29, Management and central support services, of the 2004-2005 programme budget.

The CPC recommendation for a biennial report on the improvement of management practices and for a time-bound plan for the reduction of duplication, complexity and bureaucracy in UN administrative processes and procedures could be prepared from existing resources of the 2004-2005 programme budget; the recommendation for a feasibility study to analyse available cost-accounting techniques and their applicability for identifying and analysing the costs of UN activities and outputs, drawing on best international practices, required an estimated $500,000 in additional appropriation under section 29B, Office of Programme Planning, of the 2004-2005 budget, representing a charge against the contingency fund. To reflect those recommendations, the programme of work under section 29 (see above) would have to be modified accordingly.

ACABQ in November [A/59/567] recommended that the Fifth Committee inform the General Assembly that its endorsement of the CPC recommendations would entail the additional appropriation and modification mentioned above.

The Assembly, by **decision 59/549** of 23 December, endorsed ACABQ's observations and recommendations. It noted that, should it adopt the draft resolution on programme planning [A/C.5/ 59/L.20], the progamme of work under section 29 would be modified as indicated in the Secretary-General's statement, and an additional amount of $500,000 at initial 2004-2005 rates would be required under section 29B, subject to the procedures for the use of the contingency fund. The Assembly also noted the possible substantial financial costs related to the implementation of a cost accounting system and requested of the Secretary-General a full presentation, at its sixtieth (2005) session, of the financial implications of options for the possible implementation of such a system.

Programme budget outline for 2006-2007

Report of Secretary-General. In October [A/59/415], the Secretary-General presented the proposed programme budget outline for 2006-2007, describing preliminary estimate of resources, priorities reflecting trends of a broad sectoral nature, real growth compared with the previous budget, and the size of the contingency fund as a percentage of the overall level of resources. The preliminary estimate for the 2006-2007 biennium, expressed in 2004-2005 prices, amounted to $3,359.2 million.

Recosted for inflation but not for exchange rates, the total requirements for 2006-2007 would amount to $3,556.9 million. The programme budget for 2006-2007 would reflect the priorities proposed in the strategic framework for that biennium (see p. 1400).

The preliminary estimate before the inclusion of special political missions maintained the level of 2004-2005 regular budget activities, which was equivalent to zero real growth. Once account was taken of the full inclusion of required provisions for those missions, the total preliminary estimate of $3,359.2 million would represent an increase of $180 million, or 5.7 per cent, compared with existing 2004-2005 provisions.

Noting that the size of the contingency fund was set at 0.75 per cent of the overall resource level, the Secretary-General recommended that the fund again be set at the same rate, or at $25.2 million, for the 2006-2007 biennium.

ACABQ report. ACABQ, in its December report [A/59/600], recommended that the General Assembly adopt a preliminary estimate of $3,760 million for the 2006-2007 biennium at revised 2004-2005 rates. That figure took into account adjustments consequential to the first performance report for the 2004-2005 biennium (see p. 1381), and requirement proposals for security, special political missions and other revised estimates and programme budget implications currently before the Fifth Committee, totalling $261.9 million as at 6 December. The total figure amounted to $3,745.6 million, rounded up to $3,760 million.

GENERAL ASSEMBLY ACTION

On 23 December [meeting 76], the General Assembly, on the recommendation of the Fifth Committee [A/59/652], adopted **resolution 59/278** without vote [agenda item 107].

Proposed programme budget outline for the biennium 2006-2007

The General Assembly,

Reaffirming its resolution 41/213 of 19 December 1986, in which it requested the Secretary-General to submit in off-budget years an outline of the proposed programme budget for the following biennium,

Reaffirming also section VI of its resolution 45/248 B of 21 December 1990,

Reaffirming further rule 153 of its rules of procedure,

Recalling its resolution 58/269 of 23 December 2003,

Having considered the report of the Secretary-General on the proposed programme budget outline for the biennium 2006-2007 and the related recommendations of the Advisory Committee on Administrative and Budgetary Questions,

1. *Endorses* the observations and recommendations of the Advisory Committee on Administrative and Budgetary Questions;

2. *Reaffirms* that the proposed programme budget outline shall contain an indication of the following:

(a) A preliminary estimate of resources needed to accommodate the proposed programme of activities during the biennium;

(b) Priorities, reflecting general trends of a broad sectoral nature;

(c) Real growth, positive or negative, compared with the previous budget;

(d) Size of the contingency fund expressed as a percentage of the overall level of resources;

3. *Also reaffirms* that the budget outline should provide a greater level of predictability of resources required for the following biennium and promote greater involvement of Member States in the budgetary process, thereby facilitating the broadest possible agreement on the programme budget;

4. *Further reaffirms* that the budget proposals of the Secretary-General should reflect resource levels commensurate with mandates for their full, efficient and effective implementation;

5. *Notes* that the budget outline is a preliminary estimate of resources;

6. *Invites* the Secretary-General to prepare his proposed programme budget for the biennium 2006-2007 on the basis of a preliminary estimate of 3,621,900,000 United States dollars at revised 2004-2005 rates;

7. *Decides* that the proposed programme budget for the biennium 2006-2007 shall contain provisions for recosting on the basis of the existing methodology;

8. *Decides also* that the priorities for the biennium 2006-2007 shall be the following:

(a) Maintenance of international peace and security;

(b) Promotion of sustained economic growth and sustainable development, in accordance with the relevant resolutions of the General Assembly and recent United Nations conferences;

(c) Development of Africa;

(d) Promotion of human rights;

(e) Effective coordination of humanitarian assistance efforts;

(f) Promotion of justice and international law;

(g) Disarmament;

(h) Drug control, crime prevention and combating international terrorism in all its forms and manifestations;

9. *Requests* the Secretary-General, in view of his preliminary indicative estimates contained in the proposed budget outline, to reflect the priorities outlined in paragraph 8 above when presenting the proposed programme budget for the biennium 2006-2007;

10. *Decides* that the contingency fund shall be set at the level of 0.75 per cent of the preliminary estimate, namely, at 27.2 million dollars, that this amount shall be in addition to the overall level of the preliminary estimate and that it shall be used in accordance with the procedures for the use and operation of the contingency fund.

Contributions

According to the Secretary-General's report on improving the financial situation of the United Nations [A/59/524/Add.1], unpaid assessed contributions to the UN budget at the end of 2004 totalled $2.887 million (compared to $1,603 million in 2003); outstanding peace-keeping arrears totalled $2,500 million (compared to $1,066 million in 2003); and total unpaid assessments to the international tribunals were reduced to $30 million (compared to $88 million in 2003).

The number of Member States paying their regular budget assessments in full decreased to 124 (compared to 131 at the end of 2003).

Assessments

Application of Article 19

Committee on Contributions. The Committee on Contributions, at its sixty-fourth session (New York, 7-25 June) [A/59/11], reviewed requests from 10 Member States for exemption under Article 19 of the United Nations Charter, whereby a Member would lose its vote in the General Assembly if the amount of its arrears should equal or exceed the amount of contributions due from it for the preceding two full years. The Committee duly noted the Members' written and oral representations and evaluated them against their payment records and economic and political circumstances.

The Committee noted that Burundi's request stemmed from its expectation that it would be unable to pay, before 2005, the necessary $14,100 to avoid application of the Article. It further noted that the Central African Republic had still not submitted its promised multi-year payment plan, nor had it made payments against its unpaid assessed contributions since 1994, apart from the $512,567 paid in 1998. In the light of the information that the newly elected parliament of the Comoros was considering the question of its arrears with the expectation that the current exemption request would be the last, the Committee understood that the Comoros would not be able to pay before 31 December the amount necessary to avoid application of the Article. It encouraged Guinea-Bissau, whose outstanding assessments had steadily increased since 1997, to resume reducing them and promptly to submit its intended multi-year payment plan. It encouraged Iraq, which faced exceptional problems, to do likewise.

Niger had submitted a payment plan under which it had already made the first payment. The Republic of Moldova, despite its continuing problems, had more than met its scheduled payments for 2001-2003 and had made an initial payment in 2004. Somalia's inability to meet its assessments was due principally to the devastating impact of civil war raging in the country since 1991 and of the current drought. Tajiskistan, which faced severe economic and social problems, had fulfilled its commitments under its payment plan, exceeding those scheduled for 2000-2004.

The Committee concluded that, since Burundi did not fall under the provisions of Article 19 in 2004, no Assembly action was required in its case. It recalled the Article's provision that a Member might be permitted to vote if the Assembly was satisfied that its failure to pay the full minimum amount of arrears to avoid application of the Article was due to conditions beyond its control. In that context, it determined that that was true in the cases of the Central African Republic, the Comoros, Guinea-Bissau, Iraq, Niger, the Republic of Moldova, Sao Tome and Principe, Somalia and Tajikistan; it therefore recommended that those nine Members be allowed to vote until 30 June 2005.

At the end of the Committee's session on 25 June 2004, seven Member States—Benin, Cape Verde, Chad, Iraq, Liberia, Malawi and Mauritania—were in arrears in the payment of their assessed contributions under the terms of Article 19 and had no vote in the Assembly. In addition, nine Members—the Central African Republic, the Comoros, Georgia, Guinea-Bissau, the Niger, the Republic of Moldova, Sao Tome and Principe, Somalia and Tajikistan—were similarly in arrears but had been permitted to vote until 30 June 2004 pursuant to Assembly resolution 58/1 A [YUN 2003, p. 1424].

The Committee noted that Cyprus, Morocco, Pakistan and Trinidad and Tobago, availing themselves of the opportunity afforded by Assembly resolution 55/5 B [YUN 2000, p. 1311], had paid the equivalent of $2,069,770.03 in non-United States dollar currencies.

Report of Secretary-General. During the year, the Secretary-General reported on payments made by certain Member States to reduce the level of their arrears below that specified in Article 19, so that they could vote in the Assembly. As at 19 January [A/58/688], 26 Member States were below the gross amount assessed for the preceding two full years (2002-2003). That number was reduced to 16 by 29 June [A/58/855] and to 13 by 10 September [A/59/350], remaining at that number by 11 October [A/59/430].

Communications. On 6 January [A/58/674], Azerbaijan requested, in the light of its continued good payment record, that it be included in the list posted on the website of the Office of the Spokesman for the Secretary-General of countries that had paid their contributions in full and on time to the UN budget for 2004.

On 1 July [A/C.5/58/40], the Assembly President transmitted to the Fifth Committee a 28 June letter from the Chairman of the Committee on Contributions regarding its report on the requests from Member States concerned for exception under Article 19.

Statements by Georgia and Liberia. During the Fifth Committee's consideration of the item on the scale of assessment for the apportionment of the expenses of the United Nations on 4 October [A/C.5/59/SR.2], Georgia expressed surprise that it should be deprived of its right to vote in the Assembly since, for the first time, it had discharged its obligation in full under its multi-year payment plan but, for reasons beyond its control resulting from the political upheaval in the country in 2003, it had been unable to meet the deadline for submitting the necessary information to the Committee on Contributions. Georgia thus hoped that the Fifth Committee would again authorize its full participation in the work of the United Nations.

At the Committee's 7 October meeting [A/C.5/59/SR.4], Liberia requested that it be exempted from the application of Article 19 and its right to vote restored for the current Assembly session. It had not been able to pay its assessed contributions owing to the protracted conflict in the country, but would draw up a repayment plan as soon as possible, of which it would inform the Committee on Contributions.

GENERAL ASSEMBLY ACTION

On 11 October [meeting 24], the General Assembly, on the recommendation of the Fifth Committee [A/59/421], adopted **resolution 59/1 A** without vote [agenda item 113].

Scale of assessments for the apportionment of the expenses of the United Nations: request under Article 19 of the Charter

The General Assembly,

Having considered the letter dated 1 July 2004 from the President of the General Assembly to the Chairman of the Fifth Committee transmitting a letter dated 28 June 2004 from the Chairman of the Committee on Contributions regarding the recommendations of the Committee on Contributions on requests for exemption under Article 19 of the Charter of the United Nations and the statements by the representatives of Georgia and Liberia,

Reaffirming the obligation of Member States under Article 17 of the Charter to bear the expenses of the Organization as apportioned by the General Assembly,

1. *Reaffirms* its role in accordance with the provisions of Article 19 of the Charter of the United Nations and the advisory role of the Committee on Contributions in accordance with rule 160 of the rules of procedure of the General Assembly;

2. *Also reaffirms* its resolution 54/237 C of 23 December 1999;

3. *Agrees* that the failure of the Central African Republic, the Comoros, Guinea-Bissau, Iraq, the Niger, the Republic of Moldova, Sao Tome and Principe, Somalia and Tajikistan to pay the full minimum amount necessary to avoid the application of Article 19 of the Charter was due to conditions beyond their control;

4. *Decides* that the Central African Republic, the Comoros, Guinea-Bissau, Iraq, the Niger, the Republic of Moldova, Sao Tome and Principe, Somalia and Tajikistan should be permitted to vote in the General Assembly until 30 June 2005;

5. *Takes note* of the information provided by Georgia and Liberia;

6. *Concludes* that the failure of Georgia and Liberia to pay the full minimum amount necessary to avoid the application of Article 19 of the Charter was due to conditions beyond their control, and invites Georgia and Liberia to submit appropriate information to the Committee on Contributions if similar circumstances prevail in the future;

7. *Decides* that Georgia and Liberia should be permitted to vote in the General Assembly until 30 June 2005.

Other matters related to payment of assessed contributions

The General Assembly also considered the recommendations of the Committee on Contributions on the methodology for future scale of assessments, the criteria for ad hoc adjustments of the rates of assessments and multi-year payment plans, and the treatment of the outstanding assessed contributions of the former Yugoslavia [YUN 2003, p. 1428] (see sections below).

GENERAL ASSEMBLY ACTION

On 23 December [meeting 76], the General Assembly, on the recommendation of the Fifth Committee [A/59/421/Add.1], adopted **resolution 59/1 B** without vote [agenda item 113].

Scale of assessments for the apportionment of the expenses of the United Nations

The General Assembly,

Recalling its resolutions 55/5 B and C of 23 December 2000, 56/243 A of 24 December 2001, 56/243 B of 27 March 2002, 57/4 B of 20 December 2002, and 58/1 B of 23 December 2003,

Recalling also rule 160 of the rules of procedure of the General Assembly,

Having considered the report of the Committee on Contributions on the work of its sixty-fourth session,

Having also considered the report of the Secretary-General on multi-year payment plans, the letter dated 27 December 2001 from the Secretary-General addressed to the President of the General Assembly and the related note by the Secretary-General,

1. *Takes note* of the report of the Committee on Contributions;

2. *Takes note also* of the report of the Secretary-General on multi-year payment plans;

3. *Urges* all Member States to pay their assessed contributions in full, on time and without imposing conditions;

4. *Reaffirms* paragraph 1 of its resolution 57/4 B;

5. *Decides* to defer until the first part of its resumed fifty-ninth session consideration of the question of the outstanding assessed contributions of the former Yugoslavia.

On 23 December, the Assembly decided that the item on the scale of assessments for the apportionment of the expenses of the United Nations would remain for consideration during its resumed fifty-ninth (2005) session (**decision 59/552**).

Scale Methodology

Committee on Contributions. Pursuant to General Assembly resolution 58/1 B [YUN 2003, p. 1424], the Committee on Contributions continued to review the methodology for future scales of assessments in respect of its different elements, as well as the pattern of major scale-to-scale changes in Member States' rates of assessments in recent scales. In concluding that changes in scale methodology were a significant factor in many cases, it recalled that, while the scale methodology should not be so rigid as to fail to accommodate changes in economic and technical circumstances, part of the Committee's mandate was to promote stability in the scale methodology, and any proposals for changes in it should be seen in that light.

The Committee undertook an initial review of the criteria for deciding when to replace market exchange rates (MERs) with price-adjusted rates of exchange (PAREs) or other appropriate conversion rates for purposes of preparing the scale of assessment; it would consider the matter further at its 2005 session on the basis of additional information from the UN Statistics Division. Based on its finding that the revised method of calculating PAREs had serious shortcomings as a tool for adjusting exchange rates, the Committee decided not to consider that method further; instead, it would consider, at its session in 2005, the concept of relative PARE, a comparatively simple method reflecting the movement of domestic prices relative to those of the United States, rather than their absolute movement. It decided to review, also in 2005, other elements of the scale methodology so as to reach agreement on the scale of assessments for the 2007-2009 period, to assist the Assembly in considering the question.

Criteria for ad hoc adjustments

The Committee on Contributions [A/59/11], in considering the question of criteria for ad hoc adjustments of the rates of assessment, focused on two recent, distinct requests for such adjustment: one called for a correction stemming from problems with data used in preparing the assessment scale; the other called for an adjustment to reflect substantive changes in relative capacity to pay since the adoption of the scale. The Committee concluded that, because of their exceptional and extraordinary nature, such cases should be considered on a case-by-case basis. It was therefore not feasible to elaborate more specific standard criteria for determining future ad hoc adjustments.

Measures to encourage payment of arrears

Committee on Contributions. The Committee on Contributions [A/59/11], in considering the question of measures to encourage the payment of arrears, had before it updated information on measures used by the UN system to encourage the payment of assessed contributions, which was annexed to its report, and a case study on the impact of incentive measures on the timely payment of assessed contributions in the World Health Organization. The Committee reaffirmed its earlier conclusion that it might be prudent to fix the deadline for timely payment from the date of issuance of the assessments, rather than from the date of their receipt, and to extend the deadline from 30 to 35 days. The Committee decided not to consider further the proposals for incentive payments based on the payment status of Member States, and for priority reimbursements of troop and equipment costs to Member States that were current in their payments to the United Nations, pending more specific guidance from the General Assembly. On the question of interest on or indexation of arrears, the Committee agreed that interest applied to arrears arising after the adoption of the related Assembly decision should also apply to any similar measures that the Assembly might adopt. It decided to consider further, based on information from the Secretariat, the suggestion of a composite approach, whereby payments received within a specified period after the issuance of the assessment would attract a rebate or share of interest income, while payment received after such period would attract a penalty. The Committee recommended that the Assembly encourage Member States with outstanding assessed contributions and credit balances to authorize the Secretariat to apply such credits towards reducing their outstanding assessed contributions.

The Committee also had before it the Secretary-General's March report [A/59/67] on multi-year payment plans prepared in response to Assembly resolutions 57/4 B [YUN 2002, p. 1385] and 58/1 B [YUN 2003, p. 1424]. Information was provided on the payment plans/schedules submitted by Georgia, the Niger, the Republic of Moldova, Sao Tome and Principe and Tajikistan and on the status of their implementation as at 31 December 2003. During the 2001-2003 period, Tajikistan, the Republic of Moldova, and Sao Tome and Principe had made payments exceeding that foreseen in their schedules. The schedule submitted by Niger and the most recent revision of Georgia's payment plan only began in 2004.

The Committee took note of the payment plan submitted by the Niger in March; of a long-term calendar of debt payments under preparation by the Central African Republic and soon to be announced; and that Guinea-Bissau, which had the issue of multi-year payment plans under continuous consideration, would, as the country's situation normalized, establish such a plan as a matter of priority. No further plans had been submitted.

The Committee also noted the considerable effort made by those Member States that had honoured their payment plan commitments and urged those that had not yet done so to do likewise so as to reduce their outstanding assessed contributions.

Accounts and auditing

The General Assembly, at its resumed fifty-eighth (2004) session, considered the report of the Board of Auditors on UN peacekeeping operations for the period 1 July 2002 to 30 June 2003 [A/58/5, vol. II], together with the Secretary-General's report on the implementation of the Board's recommendation thereon [A/58/737], and ACABQ's related comments and recommendations [A/58/759]. On 18 June, the Assembly, in **resolution 58/249 B**, endorsed the Board's report (see p. 97).

Board of Auditors report. The Chairman of the Board of Auditors transmitted to the Secretary-General the financial reports and audited financial statements for the biennium ended 31 December 2003 on the United Nations [A/59/5, vol. I], and on the following entities: the International Trade Centre UNCTAD/WTO [A/59/5, vol. III], the United Nations University [A/59/5, vol. IV], the United Nations Development Programme (UNDP) [A/59/5/Add.1], the United Nations Children's Fund (UNICEF) [A/59/5/Add.2], the United Nations Relief and Works Agency for Palestine Refugees in the Near East [A/59/5/Add.3], the United Nations Institute for Training and Research [A/59/5/Add.4], the voluntary funds administered by the Office of the United Nations High Commissioner for Refugees [A/59/5/Add.5], the Fund of the United Nations Environment Programme (UNEP) [A/59/5/Add.6], the United Nations Population Fund (UNFPA) [A/59/5/Add.7], the United Nations Human Settlements Programme (UN-Habitat) [A/59/5/Add.8], the United Nations International Drug Control Programme (UNDCP) [A/59/5/Add.9], the United Nations Office for Project Services (UNOPS) [A/59/5/Add.10], the International Criminal Tribunal for the Prosecution of Persons Responsible for Genocide and Other Serious Violations of International Humanitarian Law Committed in the Territory of Rwanda and Rwandan Citizens Responsible for Genocide and Other Such Violations Committed in the Territory of Neighbouring States between 1 January and 31 December 1994 (ICTR) [A/59/5/Add.11], and the International Tribunal for the Prosecution of Persons Responsible for Serious Violations of International Humanitarian Law Committed in the Territory of the Former Yugoslavia since 1991 (ICTY) [A/59/5/Add.12]. The Board also submitted, through the Secretary-General, its report on the financial statements of the United Nations Compensation Commission for the biennium ended 31 December 2003 [S/2004/789].

Introducing the reports in the Fifth Committee [A/C.5.59/SR.10], the Chairman of the Board drew attention to the progress made by the United Nations and its funds and programmes in the implementation of previous Board recommendations, of which 46 per cent had been fully implemented for the 2000-2001 biennium. At the same time, he underscored the principal shortcomings revealed by the audit. According to the Chairman, the Board had modified its audit report on the financial statements of UNDP, UNDCP, UNFPA and UNOPS. It did not express an opinion on the UNOPS statement as it was unable to obtain adequate assurances regarding a number of issues; it was concerned that failure by UNOPS to meet its 2004 targets could result in deficits that might not be absorbed by its operational reserve and that no proper system was in place to give reliable estimates of the cost of services provided. While the modified report had not affected the Board's audit opinion on the financial statements of the three other entities, concerns remained, notably the lack of adequate controls at UNDP and UNFPA even after the introduction of the new enterprise resource planning system known as Atlas and of procedures at

UNDCP to ensure the complete and timely recording of field obligations.

The Board had made various recommendations for improving the presentation and disclosure of financial statements and reports, but noted that none of the organizations had addressed the General Assembly's request in its resolution 57/278 A [YUN 2002, p. 1389] that they examine UN system governance structures, principles and accountability throughout the UN system and make proposals for a future report format. Unfunded end-of-service and post-retirement benefits were also a cause for concern, given that, as at 31 December 2003, an aggregate amount of over $3 billion remained unfunded, as did non-expendable equipment of some $1.1 billion. The Board had again noted weaknesses at the United Nations, UNDP, UNFPA, UN-Habitat and UNOPS relating to inadequate physical inventory counts and inaccurate and unreliable inventory records.

Monitoring and control of programme expenditure for several funds and programmes had improved, including efforts to simplify and harmonize resource transfer modalities. As to project management, it had been difficult to compare financial versus technical implementation, with the resultant risk that financial resources could be depleted before projects were completed or that excess resources might not be reprogrammed appropriately. Some projects that were operationally closed remained open in financial terms for long periods. The Board was concerned that 63 UN trust funds, with combined reserves and fund balances of $54 million as at 31 December 2003, did not show any expenditures for the 2002-2003 biennium, except for transactions pertaining to the investment and other related accounts.

The Board noted that the return on the significant funds in short- or medium-term financial assets or investments managed by the United Nations and by several of its funds and programmes had been generally close to benchmark, and, in the case of UNICEF, the Board's previous recommendations on funds management had been implemented. In other instances, however, it had found a number of problems relating to guidelines and management: the United Nations Office at Geneva managed an investment portfolio of $375 million (as at 31 December 2003) without an investment policy or committee, and, while over 75 per cent of that portfolio came from Geneva-based funds and programmes, formal guidelines or reporting procedures for their respective shares were non-existent; the former Director of the Investment Management Service of the United Nations Joint Staff Pension Fund had not provided a proper audit trail for the real estate investments he had personally managed, nor had the purchase of an office building in New York been conducted in a consistent manner; moreover, the UN system maintained a large number of bank accounts that had encountered problems of disclosure and reconciliation. Further steps had also to be taken to improve the efficiency of inter-agency transactions, since the Board had found a difference of some $22 million between the accounting records of Headquarters and of UNDP.

While recognizing the recent initiatives to improve coordination in information and communication technology, the Board was of the view that a comprehensive, system-wide initiative needed to be implemented. It recognized the need for the United Nations and its funds and programmes to establish a comprehensive fraud prevention policy. While some organizations had instituted measures in that regard, they seldom included formal corruption and fraud risk assessment mechanisms or a fraud prevention committee. Mechanisms for resolving incidents and allegations of corruption and fraud were not always designed or implemented efficiently.

The level of unpaid contributions to ICTR and ICTY, amounting to $34.8 million and $53 million, respectively, had significantly worsened their financial positions, leading to cross-borrowing from peacekeeping operations. The Board remained concerned that those tribunals might not be able to complete their work by the 2010 deadline.

By a July note [A/59/162], the Secretary-General transmitted to the Assembly a summary of the Board's principal findings, conclusions and recommendations, classified by audit area. He also submitted his first report [A/59/318 & Add.1] on measures taken to implement the Board's recommendations on the accounts for the biennium ended 31 December 2003. The related comments and observations of ACABQ were contained in its 1 October report [A/59/400].

GENERAL ASSEMBLY ACTION

On 23 December [meeting 76], the General Assembly, on the recommendation of the Fifth Committee [A/59/588], adopted **resolution 59/264** without vote [agenda item 106].

Financial reports and audited financial statements, and reports of the Board of Auditors

The General Assembly,

Reaffirming its resolutions 50/222 of 11 April 1996, 51/218 E of 17 June 1997, 52/212 B of 31 March 1998, 53/204 of 18 December 1998, 53/221, section VIII, of 7 April 1999, 54/13 B of 23 December 1999, 55/220 A of 23 December 2000, 55/220 B and C of 12 April and 14 June 2001 and 57/278 A of 20 December 2002,

Having considered, for the period ended 31 December 2003, the financial reports and audited financial statements and the reports and audit opinions of the Board of Auditors on the United Nations, the International Trade Centre UNCTAD/WTO, the United Nations University, the United Nations Development Programme, the United Nations Children's Fund, the United Nations Relief and Works Agency for Palestine Refugees in the Near East, the United Nations Institute for Training and Research, the voluntary funds administered by the United Nations High Commissioner for Refugees, the Fund of the United Nations Environment Programme, the United Nations Population Fund, the United Nations Human Settlements Programme, the Fund of the United Nations International Drug Control Programme, the United Nations Office for Project Services, the International Criminal Tribunal for the Prosecution of Persons Responsible for Genocide and Other Serious Violations of International Humanitarian Law Committed in the Territory of Rwanda and Rwandan Citizens Responsible for Genocide and Other Such Violations Committed in the Territory of Neighbouring States between 1 January and 31 December 1994, and the International Tribunal for the Prosecution of Persons Responsible for Serious Violations of International Humanitarian Law Committed in the Territory of the Former Yugoslavia since 1991, the concise summary of principal findings, conclusions and recommendations contained in the reports prepared by the Board of Auditors, the reports of the Secretary-General on the implementation of the recommendations of the Board of Auditors by the United Nations and its funds and programmes and the report of the Advisory Committee on Administrative and Budgetary Questions,

1. *Accepts* the financial reports and audited financial statements and the reports and audit opinions of the Board of Auditors for the above-mentioned organizations, with the exception of the financial statements of the United Nations Office for Project Services;

2. *Notes with concern* that the Board of Auditors was unable to express an opinion on the financial statements of the United Nations Office for Project Services, and acknowledges the comprehensive steps taken by the Office to address the issues raised by the Board;

3. *Notes* the view of the Board of Auditors that it would be premature to conduct an audit in 2005 of the financial statements of the United Nations Office for Project Services for 2004 owing to the time needed to address the critical issues raised in the Board's report, and decides to revert to the issue, at its sixtieth session, in the context of the report of the Board of Auditors on the implementation of its recommendations relating to the biennium 2002-2003;

4. *Approves* the recommendations and conclusions contained in the reports of the Board of Auditors and endorses the observations and recommendations contained in the report of the Advisory Committee on Administrative and Budgetary Questions, with the proviso that, should the need arise, the recommendations and conclusions of the Board of Auditors and the comments thereon by the Advisory Committee, including those on the International Criminal Tribunal for Rwanda, the International Tribunal for the Former Yugoslavia, the capital master plan and the United

Nations Joint Staff Pension Fund, will be considered under the respective agenda items;

5. *Commends* the Board of Auditors for the superior quality of its reports, in particular with respect to its comments on the management of resources and improving the presentation of financial statements;

6. *Notes with concern* the late issuance of the reports of the Board of Auditors despite the timely submission of these reports to the Secretariat, and requests the Secretary-General to ensure sufficient priority in completing their editing and translation in order that they may be submitted to the General Assembly in accordance with the six-week rule;

7. *Takes note* of the reports of the Secretary-General on the implementation of the recommendations of the Board of Auditors by the United Nations and its funds and programmes, and invites the Board of Auditors, in consultation with the Secretary-General and the executive heads of the funds and programmes, to categorize the recommendations according to their priority for implementation;

8. *Requests* the Secretary-General and the executive heads of the funds and programmes of the United Nations to indicate an expected time frame for the implementation of the recommendations of the Board of Auditors, including the office holders to be held accountable;

9. *Reiterates its request* to the Secretary-General and the executive heads of the funds and programmes of the United Nations to examine governance principles and to report thereon to the General Assembly at its sixty-first session, through the respective governing bodies of the funds and programmes of the United Nations;

10. *Requests* the Secretary-General and the executive heads of the funds and programmes of the United Nations also to consider strengthening the internal control framework, harmonizing the administrative mechanisms that would systematically act upon the findings and recommendations of oversight bodies and improving financial reporting, as well as the proper forums for the consideration of the reports of the Board of Auditors by the respective executive boards and the General Assembly, and to report thereon to the General Assembly at its sixty-first session;

11. *Notes* that the Secretariat has been collecting information on the experiences of audit committees within the United Nations system and other international organizations, and requests the Secretary-General to report on and provide an assessment of its findings to the General Assembly at its sixtieth session.

On 23 December, the Assembly decided that the item on the financial reports and audited financial statements, and the Board of Auditors would remain for consideration at its resumed fifty-ninth (2005) session (**decision 59/552**).

Administrative and budgetary coordination

The General Assembly, at its resumed fifty-eighth session had before it the Secretary-General's note transmitting the report of the Joint Inspection Unit (JIU) on support costs re-

lated to the extrabudgetary activities in UN system organizations [YUN 2002, p. 1391], the comments of ACABQ [A/57/434] and those of the Secretary-General and the United Nations System Chief Executives Board for Coordination (CEB) [YUN 2003, p. 1429] on the recommendations contained in the report, and a note by JIU [A/59/714] containing further clarifications on its recommendations 1, 4, 6, 8 and 9 as requested by the Assembly in decision 58/560 [YUN 2003, p. 1429].

GENERAL ASSEMBLY ACTION

On 8 April [meeting 83], the General Assembly, on the recommendation of the Fifth Committee [A/58/572/Add.2], adopted **resolution 58/283** without vote [agenda item 120].

Report of the Joint Inspection Unit on support costs related to extrabudgetary activities in organizations of the United Nations system

The General Assembly,

Recalling its decision 58/560 of 23 December 2003,

Having considered the report of the Joint Inspection Unit on support costs related to extrabudgetary activities in organizations of the United Nations system, the note by the Secretary-General transmitting his comments and those of the United Nations System Chief Executives Board for Coordination thereon and the related report of the Advisory Committee on Administrative and Budgetary Questions, as well as the note by the Joint Inspection Unit submitted in response to General Assembly decision 58/560, clarifying further some of the recommendations contained in its report,

1. *Concurs* with the observations and recommendations of the Advisory Committee on Administrative and Budgetary Questions contained in its report, subject to the provisions of the present resolution;

2. *Takes note* of the comments of the Secretary-General and those of the United Nations System Chief Executives Board for Coordination;

3. *Endorses* the recommendations contained in the report of the Joint Inspection Unit on support costs related to extrabudgetary activities in organizations of the United Nations system to the extent that they apply to the United Nations, subject to the provisions of the present resolution;

4. *Recognizes* that recommendations 2, 3, 5, 6, 8 and 10 are directed to executive heads, and invites executive heads to consider those recommendations;

5. *Takes note* of recommendation 1, and agrees with the Joint Inspection Unit that governing bodies should take the steps they consider necessary to ensure that extrabudgetary resources are accepted for purposes that are consistent with programme priorities and approved mandates;

6. *Also takes note* of recommendation 4, and draws the attention of legislative organs to the practice of the United Nations Children's Fund under which interest earned on some extrabudgetary contributions is retained by the organization, and invites legislative organs to consider the applicability or relevance of this practice to them;

7. *Further takes note* of recommendation 9, and agrees with the Joint Inspection Unit that legislative organs should enact support cost policies to ensure that extrabudgetary resources continue to be mobilized and deployed effectively so as to further the mandated activities in developmental, humanitarian and other substantive areas, and also agrees that those policies should be straightforward, transparent, easy to administer and must provide for a consistent and equitable approach to special arrangements.

CEB report. By a September note [A/59/315], the Secretary-General transmitted to the General Assembly the CEB statistical report on the budgetary and financial situation of the organizations of the UN system. The Assembly took note of the report on 23 December **(decision 59/548)**.

Also on 23 December, the Assembly decided that the items on the review of the efficiency of the administrative and financial functioning of the United Nations, and on the administrative and budgetary coordination of the United Nations with the specialized agencies and the International Atomic Energy Agency would remain for consideration at its resumed fifty-ninth (2005) session **(decision 59/552)**.

Programme planning

Strategic framework for 2006-2007

In May, the Secretary-General submitted the proposed strategic framework for 2006-2007 [A/59/6 (Part One) & Corr.1], which represented a translation of legislative mandates into programmes and subprogrammes. As affirmed by the General Assembly in its resolution 58/269 [YUN 2003, p. 1395], the strategic framework, to replace the four-year medium-term plan, constituted the principal policy directive of the United Nations and served as the basis for programme planning, budgeting, monitoring and evaluation.

The framework comprised two parts. Part one was a plan outline reflecting the longer-term objectives of the internationally agreed development goals, including those contained in the United Nations Millennium Declaration [YUN 2000, p. 49] and the outcomes of major UN conferences and international agreements since 1992. It also included the priorities for the 2006-2007 biennium, proposed for reaffirmation by the Assembly: maintenance of international peace and security; promotion of sustained economic growth and development; development of Africa; promotion of human rights; coordination of humanitarian assistance; promotion of justice and international

law; disarmament; and drug control, crime prevention and combating international terrorism.

Part two was the biennial programme plan, covering 26 programmes structured as in the current (2002-2005) medium-term plan, each corresponding to the work to be carried out by an organizational entity, usually at the departmental level, and subdivided into subprogrammes, each corresponding to an organizational entity, generally at the division level. The international drug control programme and the crime prevention and criminal justice programme were combined into the international drug control, crime prevention and criminal justice programme (new programme 11). The Management and support services programme (programme 24) was modified to include in greater depth the work of UN offices away from Headquarters: Geneva, Vienna and Nairobi. A new programme (programme 26) was included to reflect the work of the International Civil Service Commission, JIU and the Office of the United Nations Security Coordinator.

CPC [A/59/16], having examined the Secretary-General's proposed 2006-2007 strategic framework, recommended that the Assembly review part one at its fifty-ninth (2004) session and approve the programme narrative of 21 of the 26 programmes in part two, with certain modifications. It further recommended that the Assembly allocate, for consideration and action prior to submission to the Fifth Committee, programme 3, Disarmament, to the First (Disarmament and International Security) Committee; programme 10, Trade and development, to the Second (Economic and Financial) Committee, following its consideration in the light of the recommendations of the Working Party on the Medium-term Plan and the Programme Budget of UNCTAD made at its resumed forty-second session; programme 19, Human rights, to the Third (Social, Humanitarian and Cultural) Committee; programme 23, Public information, to the Fourth (Special Political and Decolonization) Committee; and review programme 25, Internal oversight, at its fifty-ninth session.

On 4 [A/C.5/59/14], 9 [A/C.5/59/15] and 16 November [A/C.5/59/17], and 20 December [A/C.5/59/26], the Assembly President submitted to the Chairman of the Fifth Committee the revised versions of programmes 23, 10, and 3 and 19 of the 2006-2007 strategic framework as approved by the respective Assembly Committee.

On 22 December, the Assembly took note of the report of the Second Committee [A/59/610] **(decision 59/542)**, and on 23 December, the reports of the First Committee [A/59/618] **(decision 59/544)**, the Fourth Committee [A/59/621] **(deci-**

sion 59/545) and the Third Committee [A/59/609] **(decision 59/546).**

GENERAL ASSEMBLY ACTION

On 23 December [meeting 76], the General Assembly, on the recommendation of the Fifth Committee [A/59/651], adopted **resolution 59/275** without vote [agenda item 109].

Programme planning

The General Assembly,

Recalling its resolutions 37/234 of 21 December 1982, 38/227 A of 20 December 1983, 41/213 of 19 December 1986, 55/234 of 23 December 2000, 56/253 of 24 December 2001, 57/282 of 20 December 2002 and 58/268 and 58/269 of 23 December 2003,

Having considered the report of the Committee for Programme and Coordination on the work of its forty-fourth session, the proposed strategic framework for the period 2006-2007: part one: plan outline and part two: biennial programme plan and the reports of the Secretary-General on the programme performance of the United Nations for the biennium 2002-2003 and on priority-setting, as well as the report of the Office of Internal Oversight Services on strengthening the role of evaluation findings in programme design, delivery and policy directives,

Appreciating the letters from the President of the General Assembly transmitting the recommendations of the First Committee concerning programme 3, Disarmament, the Second Committee concerning programme 10, Trade and development and the Special Political and Decolonization Committee (Fourth Committee) concerning programme 23, Public information, and concerning programme 19, Human rights,

Emphasizes the role of the plenary and the Main Committees in reviewing and taking action on the appropriate recommendations of the Committee for Programme and Coordination relevant to their work, in accordance with regulation 4.10 of the Regulations and Rules Governing Programme Planning, the Programme Aspects of the Budget, the Monitoring of Implementation and the Methods of Evaluation;

Strategic framework for the period 2006-2007

Recalling paragraph 5 of its resolution 58/269, in which it requested the Secretary-General to prepare, on a trial basis, a strategic framework, which would comprise in one document a plan outline, reflecting the longer-term objectives of the Organization, and a biennial programme plan, to cover two years,

1. *Notes* that the proposed strategic framework for the period 2006-2007 constitutes the first proposal submitted since the adoption of its resolution 58/269;

2. *Also notes* that the Committee for Programme and Coordination at its forty-fourth session recommended that the General Assembly review part one, plan outline, of the proposed strategic framework for the period 2006-2007;

3. *Recalls* its decision in resolution 58/269 to review, with a view to taking a final decision at its sixty-second session, the format, content and duration of the strategic framework, including the necessity of maintaining part one;

4. *Decides,* in view of the differences between Member States on the content of part one: plan outline of the proposed strategic framework for the period 2006-2007, to take no decision on part one;

5. *Requests* the Secretary-General to prepare and propose a plan outline, reflecting the longer-term objectives of the Organization, and a biennial programme plan in the context of the strategic framework for the biennium 2008-2009, based, inter alia, on the following principal criteria:

   (a) The longer-term objectives consistent with all the relevant legislative mandates in all areas of the activities of the United Nations;

   (b) Outcomes of the intergovernmental conferences and summits;

   (c) Inputs from relevant programme managers;

   (d) Use of intergovernmentally agreed terms and expressions;

6. *Invites* the Committee for Programme and Coordination to consider at its forty-fifth session additional guidelines, if any, for the preparation of the plan outline;

7. *Decides* that the priorities for the period 2006-2007 shall be the following:

   (a) Maintenance of international peace and security;

   (b) Promotion of sustained economic growth and sustainable development in accordance with the relevant resolutions of the General Assembly and recent United Nations conferences;

   (c) Development of Africa;

   (d) Promotion of human rights;

   (e) Effective coordination of humanitarian assistance efforts;

   (f) Promotion of justice and international law;

   (g) Disarmament;

   (h) Drug control, crime prevention and combating international terrorism in all its forms and manifestations;

8. *Requests* the Secretary-General to prepare the proposed programme budget for the biennium 2006-2007 based on the above priorities and the biennial programme plan as adopted in the present resolution;

9. *Also requests* the Secretary-General to issue in one document, before the forty-fifth session of the Committee for Programme and Coordination, only the priorities and the biennial programme plan, as adopted in the present resolution;

10. *Endorses* the conclusions and recommendations of the Committee for Programme and Coordination on the proposed biennial programme plan for the period 2006-2007 contained in the report of the Committee on the work of its forty-fourth session, those of the First Committee regarding programme 3, Disarmament, those of the Second Committee regarding programme 10, Trade and development, those regarding programme 19, Human rights and those of the Special Political and Decolonization Committee (Fourth Committee) regarding programme 23, Public information, subject to the provisions of the present resolution and the additional modifications contained in the annex hereto;

11. *Requests* the Secretary-General to propose a relevant indicator of achievement for programme 1, General Assembly and Economic and Social Council affairs and conference management, section A, Conference management, New York, subprogramme 4, Meetings

and publishing services, in the context of the proposed programme budget for the biennium 2006-2007;

12. *Notes* that the overall system of the administration of justice in the Secretariat will be considered by the General Assembly at its fifty-ninth session;

13. *Requests* the Secretary-General to make recommendations to the General Assembly by the end of its fifty-ninth session on how to ensure the ongoing discharge of key functions of the Office for the Coordination of Humanitarian Affairs of the Secretariat at Headquarters as defined by the Committee for Programme and Coordination;

Programme performance report

14. *Takes note* of the report of the Secretary-General on the programme performance of the United Nations for the biennium 2002-2003;

15. *Endorses* the conclusions and recommendations of the Committee for Programme and Coordination regarding the report of the Secretary-General;

16. *Stresses* that, while future reports on programme performance will be more aligned with the objectives, expected accomplishments and indicators of achievement, information on the outputs shall continue to be provided in the reports;

17. *Requests* the Secretary-General to ensure that future programme performance reports provide more detailed information on the reasons for less-than-full implementation of programmed outputs, or the postponement and termination thereof;

Evaluation

18. *Recalls* paragraph 19 of its resolution 58/269, in which it emphasized the need to strengthen the monitoring and evaluation system;

19. *Re-emphasizes* the importance of the contribution of the relevant intergovernmental bodies, in particular the Main Committees of the General Assembly, in reviewing the relevant recommendations on evaluation;

20. *Reiterates* section III of its resolution 57/282 on evaluation;

21. *Requests* the General Committee to take fully into account the above-mentioned resolutions in the allocation of agenda items to the Main Committees;

22. *Endorses* the conclusions and recommendations of the Committee for Programme and Coordination on strengthening the role of evaluation findings in programme design, delivery and policy directives, on in-depth evaluation of the programme on public administration, finance and development, on the triennial review of the implementation of the recommendations made by the Committee on the in-depth evaluation of sustainable development and on the triennial review of the implementation of the recommendations made by the Committee on the in-depth evaluation of the population programme, and on the further development of topics for a pilot thematic evaluation;

Improving the working methods and procedures of the Committee for Programme and Coordination within the framework of its mandate

23. *Requests* the Secretary-General to schedule the organizational session of the forty-fifth session of the Committee for Programme and Coordination as soon as possible at the resumed session of the Fifth Committee at the fifty-ninth session;

24. *Recalls* paragraph 18 of its resolution 58/269, in which it invited the Committee for Programme and Coordination to submit, at its forty-fourth session, recommendations on improving its working methods;

25. *Welcomes* the decision of the Committee for Programme and Coordination to revert to the agenda item entitled "Improving the working methods and procedures of the Committee for Programme and Coordination within the framework of its mandate", as a matter of priority, at the beginning of its forty-fifth session;

Other conclusions and recommendations of the Committee for Programme and Coordination

26. *Endorses* the conclusions and recommendations of the Committee for Programme and Coordination regarding the annual overview report of the United Nations System Chief Executives Board for Coordination for 2003, and its conclusions and recommendations regarding the report of the Secretary-General on United Nations system support for the New Partnership for Africa's Development;

27. *Also endorses* the recommendation of the Committee for Programme and Coordination on the report of the Secretary-General on priority-setting;

Other matters

28. *Invites* the Committee for Programme and Coordination to take appropriate measures to ensure that the discussion sections of the report of the Committee are drafted so as to reflect fully the opinions expressed by delegations.

Annex

Additional modifications to the proposed biennial programme plan for the period 2006-2007

Programme 1
General Assembly and Economic and Social Council affairs and conference management

Overall orientation

In the second sentence of paragraph 1.3, after "the control and limitation of documents," add "in accordance with legislative mandates,".

A. Conference management, New York

Subprogramme 4
Meetings and publishing services

Delete indicator of achievement *(b)* (ii) and delete "(i)" in indicator of achievement *(b)* (i).

A, B, C and D. Conference management, New York, Geneva, Vienna and Nairobi

Subprogramme 2
Planning, development and coordination of conference services

Under *Strategy*, replace the text of paragraphs 1.5 *(e)*, 1.7 *(c)*, 1.10 *(e)* and 1.13 *(c)* of sections A, B, C and D, respectively, with the following: "Upgrading, pursuant to the managerial responsibilities of the Secretary-General, the technological capacity in conference services in line with new developments in technology, in accordance with legislative mandates, while keeping the General Assembly aware of new technologies that can be issued in the Organization to achieve timeliness and better quality of services provided".

At the end of expected accomplishment *(b)*, add "where feasible and more cost-effective, without adversely affecting the quality of services provided".

Subprogramme 4
Meetings and publishing services

Under *Strategy*, in paragraphs 1.7 *(b)*, 1.9 *(b)*, 1.12 *(b)* and 1.15 *(b)* of sections A, B, C and D, respectively, after "documentation publishing", add "to achieve better quality, and timeliness".

Programme 21
Palestine refugees

Overall orientation

After the first sentence of paragraph 21.2, add the following sentence: "In its resolution 3331 B(XXIX) of 17 December 1974, the General Assembly decided that, with effect from 1 January 1975, the expenses relating to the emoluments of international staff in the service of the United Nations Relief and Works Agency for Palestine Refugees in the Near East, which would otherwise have been charged to voluntary contributions, should be financed by the regular budget of the United Nations for the duration of the Agency's mandate."

Programme 25
Internal oversight

Overall orientation

Replace the first sentence of paragraph 25.1 with the following: "The overall purpose of the programme is to enhance effectiveness in the implementation of all programmes through continually improved internal control mechanisms within the Organization. The mandate for the programme derives from the responsibility of the Secretary-General as the chief administrative officer of the United Nations, entrusted to him under Article 97 of the Charter of the United Nations."

Paragraph 25.3 should read as follows: "The Office assists Member States and the Organization in protecting its assets, and ensuring the compliance of programme activities with resolutions, regulations, rules and policies, and the more efficient and effective delivery of the Organization's activities; preventing and detecting fraud, waste, abuse, malfeasance or mismanagement; and improving the delivery of the Organization's programmes and activities to enable it to achieve better results by determining all factors affecting the efficient and effective implementation of programmes."

In the second sentence of paragraph 25.4, replace "ensure" with "assist".

The second sentence of paragraph 25.5 should read as follows: "In addition, the Office assists the Organization in achieving better results by determining the factors affecting the efficient and effective implementation of programmes in accordance with, inter alia, the internationally agreed development goals, including those contained in the United Nations Millennium Declaration and in the outcomes of the major United Nations conferences and international agreements since 1992."

Subprogramme 1
Internal audit

The objective of the Organization should read as follows: "To ensure efficient and effective implementation and management of programmes, activities and operations by programme managers, in accordance with the relevant legislative mandates, regulations and rules."

Expected accomplishment *(c)* should read as follows: "Improved levels of efficiency and effectiveness in the implementation of programmes, and enhanced accountability by programme managers."

Subprogramme 2
Monitoring, evaluation and consulting

The objective of the Organization should read as follows: "To strengthen programme implementation by monitoring the delivery of the programmes using results-based management methods as well as their outputs and to determine whether they are adequate, timely and in accordance with the mandates, whether they address effectively the objectives of the programmes and whether the resources are used efficiently."

Subprogramme 3
Investigations

The objective of the Organization should read as follows: "To ensure compliance with regulations and rules of the United Nations and to minimize the occurrence of fraud, violations of regulations and rules of the United Nations, mismanagement, misconduct, waste of resources and abuse of authority."

Expected accomplishment *(a)* should read as follows: "Better protection of the Organization's assets and resources and greater compliance with the Organization's rules and regulations."

Also on 23 December, the Assembly decided that the item on programme planning would remain for consideration at its resumed fifty-ninth (2005) session (**decision 59/552**).

Priority-setting

The Secretary-General submitted a May report [A/59/87], prepared in response to General Assembly resolution 58/268 [YUN 2003, p. 1430], which described the experience with priority-setting since the introduction of programme planning and budgeting in 1974, gave a brief historical background of matters related to its implementation and discussed a number of related issues. Annexed to the report were: a list of the designated priorities for the medium-term plan and related parts of the programme budget for 1998-2001 and 2002-2005; and a series of extracts on priority-setting from the Regulations and Rules Governing Programme Planning, the Programme Aspects of the Budget, the Monitoring of Implementation and the Methods of Evaluation [ST/SGB/2000/8].

According to the report, the system of priority-setting as a guide for focusing on issues considered by Member States as requiring specific attention and for allocating resources had encountered difficulties related to the structure of planning and budget documents as well as to questions of definition, criteria for designating priorities, political considerations, governance mechanisms, level of activity, unforeseen events and limited resources. While different criteria had been applied over the years, the problem was not how to implement the designated priorities but how to identify, agree upon and designate them, which was basically a political one. Moreover, the link between the designation of priorities and the level of resources was not always obvious, and technical budgetary issues unrelated to priority-setting for programmes could affect relative resource allocations. At the level of the programe budget, therefore, the determination of whether or not priorities established by Member States had been adequately reflected required careful scrutiny and analysis.

The Secretary-General recommended that the Assembly, taking into account the recommendations in resolution 58/269 [YUN 2003, p. 1395] and bearing in mind the most recent changes to the planning and budgeting process (see above), might wish to decide that priorities reflecting general trends of a broad sectoral nature would continue to be established for the strategic framework, on the recommendation of CPC; that the priorities in the budget outline would be in conformity with those contained in the strategic framework; and that both strategic framework and budget outline, once approved, would serve as the basis for the Secretary-General's proposed programme budget.

CPC [A/59/16] decided to continue consideration of the Secretary-General's report at its 2005 session and recommended that the Assembly defer its consideration of the report also to 2005.

Programme performance

In an April report [A/59/69] on the programme performance of the United Nations for the 2002-2003 biennium, the Secretary-General gave an overview of key results achieved, delivery of outputs, and resource utilization and proposals for strengthening results-based monitoring and reporting. Under the 2002-2003 programme budget, a total of 33,131 outputs had been committed for implementation, including 27,611 programmed outputs, 626 carried over from the previous biennium, 2,957 added by legislative bodies and 1,937 by the Secretariat. Of the total, 22,706 were implemented, 643 were postponed to the next biennium and 4,324 were terminated. The implementation rate for mandated outputs was 84 per cent, while

the total rate was 85 per cent. Of the 27 budget sections, 17 achieved implementation rates of 90 per cent or higher; only two sections registered markedly below-average rates. The most important factor affecting implementation rates was the number of outputs terminated, with the Department of General Assembly and Conference Management and the Department of Disarmament Affairs having the largest absolute and relative number of terminations, namely, 1,139 and 1,051, respectively, accounting for 50.6 per cent of all outputs terminated by the Secretariat. Implementation utilized 530,693 work-months.

The Secretary-General said that, during the 2002-2003 biennium, results of the Organization's activities were demonstrated in areas that ranged from facilitating new international agreements in all priority areas, setting up reliable mechanisms for monitoring their implementation and assisting in enhancing national and regional capacities to translate them into reality, to developing stronger peacemaking, peacekeeping and peace-building capacity, providing humanitarian assistance, assisting in the development of economic and social policies and building capacity, and advising on policy choices in support of sustainable development and environmental protection. Furthermore, the robust and extensive use of information technology during the biennium had greatly improved programme performance.

The distinguishing feature of the overview of achievements was that, for the first time, the programme performance report followed the results-based-budgeting approach. Efforts to create a results-based culture resulted in greater awareness of the importance of tracking the progress of results as they materialized and in more streamlined monitoring and reporting procedures. However, the degree of acceptance and ownership of the results-based concept and of its mastery varied significantly between departments and offices.

One of the main challenges in preparing the report was finding an effective means of tackling deficiencies and weaknesses in expected accomplishments and achievement indicators formulated more than two years ago. That was achieved by invoking relevant supplementary evidence and encouraging departments and offices to factor in the results of relevant evaluations into their performance reporting. The lessons from that experience led to the establishment of performance measures for the indicators of achievement in the proposed 2004-2005 programme budget and were taken into account in the development of the 2006-2007 strategic framework (see p. 1400).

The experience during the biennium highlighted the crucial importance of programme managers taking ownership of the objectives, expected accomplishments and indicators of achievement, and motivating their staff to focus on results. It had become clear that multifaceted efforts to strengthen results-based performance management, monitoring and reporting were not resource-neutral. Conceptual development, improvement of methods, strengthening of data collection and continuous and thorough training in all aspects of that enterprise required investment at the level of departments and offices and at the central monitoring and reporting point.

CPC consideration. CPC [A/59/16] took note of the performance report, particularly its improved format and sharper focus on results. It recommended that the Assembly request the Secretary-General to continue to explore ways to streamline and modernize future performance reports, including through greater use of electronic documentation and support materials; improve the implementation of results-based budgeting and management of programmes, with increased emphasis on results; and provide support and guidance to all departments in managing for results, including the issuance of guidelines, handbooks or manuals for the monitoring and evaluation of work undertaken so as to determine its continued relevance, usefulness, efficiency and effectiveness. CPC also recommended that future reporting on programme performance be more closely aligned with the objectives, expected accomplishments and indicators of achievement. Noting the inclusion in the report of a list of subprogrammes under each programme with highlights of programme results and subsections on subprogramme accomplishments, CPC requested that the 2004-2005 performance report include in each section a brief description of challenges, obstacles and unmet goals in order to facilitate the evaluation of issues affecting programme performance.

Evaluation

OIOS report. In May [A/59/79], the Secretary-General transmitted to the General Assembly, through CPC, the report of the Office of Internal Oversight Services (OIOS) presenting an overview for 2002-2003 of the Secretariat's evaluation capacity and the application of evaluation findings in programme design and delivery and policy directives. It examined the progress in implementing action called for in the Secretary-General's 2002 report [YUN 2002, p. 1368] that envisaged a strengthened results-oriented evaluation and monitoring system to better measure the impact of the Organization's work. It described five

specific actions under way in the Secretariat to define roles and responsibilities for monitoring and evaluation, and for developing a stronger evaluation capacity within its programmes. The review concluded that the Secretariat's evaluation capacity was sustained by reasonably sound institutional arrangements and evaluation practices which could nevertheless be improved in the short term.

In its conclusions and recommendations, OIOS stated that the strengthening of monitoring and evaluation envisaged by the Secretary-General should include addressing the following key issues by programme managers: ensuring that the organizational placement and arrangements for the evaluation function were revisited in each programme; establishing the practice of reviewing evaluation results by senior management; identifying resources for carrying out monitoring and evaluation functions in all sections of the proposed 2006-2007 programme budget; and ensuring the preparation of evaluation plans for each programme along with the 2006-2007 budget proposals. OIOS would issue guidelines on evaluation planning in conjunction with the 2006-2007 budget instructions and would lead the production of a glossary of evaluation terms to be used uniformly in the Secretariat.

To help managers and Member States assess results and use lessons learned when making decisions on future plans, a revised time line of activities had been developed to enhance the availability and use of programme and performance evaluation for planning and budgeting, which involved the preparation of preliminary performance assessments by programme managers in the last quarter of the biennium prior to formulating strategic frameworks at the end of the biennium. Programme managers should emphasize reliance on baselines, benchmarks, performance measures and other qualitative indicators in carrying out evaluation; formulate lessons learned based on evaluation findings; draw up action plans for follow-up on lessons learned, with concrete responsibilities and deadlines; incorporate lessons learned into training activities; and monitor the implementation of evaluation recommendations and assign accountability for it.

CPC consideration. CPC [A/59/16] requested OIOS to include in future in-depth and thematic evaluations and triennial reviews, a section on questions regarding which intergovernmental guidance and follow-up would be useful, focusing on practical and policy issues, the solution of which required cooperation between the Secretariat and intergovernmental bodies. It took note of actions identified in the report to define roles and responsibilities for monitoring and evaluation, and recommended that the action calling for the recruitment, selection and assessment of programme managers with monitoring and evaluation skills and for the development of a suitable training programme be considered at the Assembly's fifty-ninth (2004) session in the context of the agenda item on human resources management. It endorsed the suggestion on support from intergovernmental bodies.

CPC also recommended that the relevant programme of the proposed strategic framework be considered in conjunction with the corresponding section of the programme performance report; since that report covered a period of two bienniums prior to the biennium covered by the proposed strategic framework, the Secretariat should present updated information on the relevant parts of the performance report.

Other OIOS reports submitted to CPC by the Secretary-General included reports on: further

development of topics for a pilot thematic evaluation [E/AC.51/2004/2]; in-depth evaluation of the programme on public administration, finance and development [E/AC.51/2004/3] (see p. 852); triennial review of the implementation of the recommendations made by CPC at its forty-first (2001) session on the in-depth evaluation of sustainable development [E/AC.51/2004/4] (see p. 833); and the triennial review of the implementation of CPC recommendations made at the same session on the in-depth evaluation of the population programme [E/AC.51/2004/5 & Corr.1] (see p. 1087).

CPC selected the theme "Political affairs" for its in-depth evaluation in 2006, and agreed that OIOS should undertake a thematic evaluation on the theme "Linkages between headquarters and field activities: a review of best practices for poverty eradication in the framework of the United Nations Millennium Declaration" [YUN 2000, p. 49].

Chapter III

United Nations staff

In 2004, the work of the International Civil Service Commission (ICSC), the body which examined and made recommendations on the conditions of service of the staff of the UN common system, was reviewed by the Panel on the Strengthening of the International Civil Service, appointed by the Secretary-General. The Panel made recommendations for improving the functioning of the Commission, including proposals for enhancing the consultative process, facilitating the selection of high-level experts to bring to the Commission a mix of knowledge and expertise and limiting the terms of office of its members and the length of its sessions.

The General Assembly, through ICSC, continued to review the conditions of service of staff of the UN common system. The Assembly adopted ICSC recommendations relating to the level of the education grant, paternity leave, the base/floor salary scale and the level of children's and secondary dependants' allowances. It took note of the progress made in the review of the pay and benefits system, and requested ICSC to enhance transparency and administrative simplicity in that system. The Assembly took note of the progress made in establishing the Senior Management Service and requested the Secretary-General to redesignate that Service to enhance the managerial capacity of senior staff. The Assembly expressed concern that only limited progress had been made towards the advancement of women in the UN common system.

The Secretary-General reported on: the conditions of service and compensation of members of the International Court of Justice, judges of the International Tribunal for the Former Yugoslavia and the International Criminal Tribunal for Rwanda, and ad litem judges of both Tribunals; compensation of members of the United Nations Administrative Tribunal (UNAT); human resources management reform; improving gender distribution in the UN Secretariat; new contractual arrangements; staff composition; the use of consultants and individual contractors; recruitment of nationals of unrepresented and underrepresented Member States; the use of retired personnel; the improvement of the status of women in the UN system; special measures for protection from sexual exploitation and sexual abuse; updated information on threats against the safety and security of UN personnel; a strengthened and unified security management system for the United Nations; implementation of the 2003 recommendations of the Office of Internal Oversight Services (OIOS) on the Investment Management Services of the United Nations Joint Staff Pension Fund; standards of accommodation for air travel; the administration of justice in the Secretariat; the work and role of the Panels on Discrimination and Other Grievances; the work of the Joint Appeals Board; and the financial independence of UNAT. In cooperation with OIOS and the Joint Inspection Unit (JIU), the Secretary-General also reported on measures to prevent discrimination on the basis of nationality, race, gender, religion or language in the United Nations.

OIOS evaluated the implementation of Assembly provisions on human resources management, the availability in local labour markets of the skills for which international recruitment for the General Service category took place, and reported on the management review of the appeals process at the United Nations. JIU reported on the harmonization of the Statutes of UNAT and the International Labour Organization Administrative Tribunal.

To strengthen the safety and security of UN staff and associated humanitarian personnel, the Assembly called on all Governments and parties in complex humanitarian emergencies to cooperate fully with the United Nations to ensure the safe and unhindered access of humanitarian personnel in order to allow them to perform their task efficiently, and requested the Secretary-General to take the necessary measures to ensure full respect for the human rights, privileges and immunities of UN and other personnel carrying out activities in fulfilment of the mandate of a UN operation.

Conditions of service

International Civil Service Commission

The International Civil Service Commission (ICSC) continued to regulate and coordinate the conditions of service and the salaries and allowances of the UN common system. ICSC held its fifty-eighth (Paris, France, 29 March–16 April) and fifty-ninth (New York, 12-30 July) sessions, at which it considered, in addition to organizational matters, the conditions of service applicable to both Professional and General Service categories of staff, and those relating specifically to the Professional and higher categories and to the General Service and other locally recruited categories.

The deliberations, recommendations and decisions of ICSC on those matters were detailed in its thirtieth annual report to the General Assembly [A/59/30 (Vols. I & II)] (see sections below).

In a 12 October statement on the administrative and financial implications of ICSC decisions and recommendations for the 2004-2005 programme budget [A/59/429], the Secretary-General estimated the additional resulting requirements at $ 2,267,700, net of staff assessment.

On 21 October [A/59/522], the Advisory Committee on Administrative and Budgetary Questions (ACABQ) recommended approval of the Secretary-General's recommendation to accommodate the estimated supplementary requirements from within the common staff costs provision in the 2004-2005 programme budget.

GENERAL ASSEMBLY ACTION

The General Assembly, in section XII of **resolution 59/276** of 23 December (see p. 1383), took note of the Secretary-General's statement, the recommendations contained in ICSC's report and the related ACABQ report.

Also on 23 December [meeting 76], the General Assembly, on the recommendation of the Fifth (Administrative and Budgetary) Committee [A/59/647], adopted **resolution 59/268** without vote [agenda item 116].

United Nations common system: report of the International Civil Service Commission

The General Assembly,

Recalling its resolutions 51/216 of 18 December 1996, 52/216 of 22 December 1997, 53/209 of 18 December 1998, 55/223 of 23 December 2000, 56/244 of 24 December 2001, 57/285 of 20 December 2002 and 58/251 of 23 December 2003,

Having considered the report of the International Civil Service Commission for 2004, the note by the Secretariat submitting the report of the Panel on the Strengthening of the International Civil Service and the note by the Secretary-General on the findings and recommendations of the Panel,

Reaffirming its commitment to a single, unified United Nations common system as the cornerstone for the regulation and coordination of the conditions of service of the United Nations common system,

Convinced that the common system constitutes the best instrument through which to secure staff with the highest standards of efficiency, competence and integ-

rity for the international civil service, as stipulated in the Charter of the United Nations,

Reaffirming the statute of the Commission and the central role of the Commission and the General Assembly in the regulation and coordination of the conditions of service of the United Nations common system,

Takes note of the report of the International Civil Service Commission for 2004;

I

Conditions of service applicable to both categories of staff

A. Review of the pay and benefits system

1. *Notes* the information provided on the pilot study on broad banding and pay-for-performance;

2. *Also notes* that if all three models of the pay-for-performance system were not tested, this could diminish the value of the pilot project and requests the Commission to keep this in mind in its further consideration of the issue, and encourages volunteering organizations to test all three models;

3. *Recognizes* that an effective and credible performance appraisal system is the key for the possible introduction of a pay-for-performance system, and requests the Commission to ensure that the performance appraisal systems in volunteer organizations are developed, in full consultation with staff members, and are clear, effective and credible for all the parties concerned, including Member States;

4. *Looks forward* to receiving from the Commission annual updates on the pilot studies on broad banding and pay-for-performance;

5. *Decides* that no new strategy or pilot project in broad banding or pay-for-performance should be undertaken until the General Assembly has had an opportunity to review the results of the pilot study on broad banding and pay-for-performance being conducted by the Commission;

6. *Requests* the Commission to report on the contemporary rationale for separate salary scales for single staff and those with dependants in the context of its report on pay and benefits review;

B. Contractual arrangements

Recalling section I.A, paragraph 4, of its resolution 57/285 of 20 December 2002,

Notes the intention of the Commission to submit to the General Assembly at its sixtieth session a final report on contractual arrangements;

C. Mobility and hardship allowance

Recalling section VI of its resolution 51/216 of 18 December 1996, section I.C of its resolution 55/223 of 23 December 2000, and section II.A, paragraph 7, of its resolution 57/285 of 20 December 2002,

1. *Recognizes* the work undertaken by the Commission in reviewing the current mobility and hardship scheme in the context of the pay and benefits review;

2. *Takes note* of the decision taken by the Commission in paragraph 137 of its annual report;

D. Hazard pay

Recalling sections I.D of its resolutions 57/285 of 20 December 2002 and 58/251 of 23 December 2003,

Takes note of the decision of the Commission contained in paragraph 147 of its annual report;

E. Review of the level of the education grant

Recalling section IV of its resolution 51/216 of 18 December 1996, section III.A of its resolution 52/216 of 22 December 1997 and section I.E of its resolution 57/285 of 20 December 2002,

1. *Approves* the increases in the maximum reimbursement levels for fifteen countries, as well as other recommendations in respect of the reimbursement of expenses under the education grant, as recommended by the Commission in paragraphs 166 *(a)* to *(f)* of its annual report;

2. *Reiterates its request* to the organizations of the common system to bring the matter of the payment of the education grant to staff members living in their own countries to the attention of their governing bodies, with a view to harmonizing the staff rules and regulations along the lines of those of the United Nations, and invites governing bodies to take the relevant actions;

3. *Requests* the Commission to inform the General Assembly at its sixtieth session as to the practices of other relevant civil services and international organizations concerning the provision of education grants;

F. Review of pensionable remuneration

Recalling section II, paragraph 6, of its resolution 51/217 of 18 December 1996,

Takes note of the decision of the Commission contained in paragraph 181 of its annual report;

G. Review of allowances

1. *Requests* the Commission, in reviewing and modernizing the system of grants and allowances, to attach priority to enhancing transparency and administrative simplicity;

2. *Also requests* the Commission to inform the General Assembly at its sixtieth session on which entities it uses as comparators for the determination of entitlements such as leave and allowances, and to advise the Assembly on the merits and disadvantages of applying as a point of departure the practices of the civil service of the country used as comparator for salary purposes;

H. Common scale of staff assessment

Recalling its resolution 51/216 of 18 December 1996,

Takes note of the decision of the Commission contained in paragraph 188 of its annual report;

I. Paternity leave

Takes note of the decision contained in paragraph 211 of the annual report of the Commission, and confirms its recommendations to have paternity leave implemented throughout the common system within the parameters set forth in the report;

II
Conditions of service of staff in the Professional and higher categories

A. Examination of the Noblemaire principle and its application

Recalling its resolution 44/198 of 21 December 1989 and other relevant resolutions,

1. *Reaffirms* the continuing application of the Noblemaire principle;

2. *Also reaffirms* the need to continue to ensure the competitiveness of the conditions of service of the United Nations common system;

3. *Takes note* of the decision of the Commission contained in paragraph 273 of its annual report;

B. Grade equivalencies between the United States federal civil service and the United Nations common system

Recalling section I.A of its resolution 50/208 of 23 December 1995, section II.B of its resolution 55/223 of 23 December 2000, and section I.A, paragraph 7, of its resolution 57/285 of 20 December 2002,

1. *Takes note* of the decision of the Commission contained in paragraph 276 of its annual report;

2. *Requests* the Commission to include the review of grade equivalency in the study to determine the highest paid civil service on its work programme for 2005–2006;

C. Evolution of the margin

Recalling section I.B of its resolution 51/216 of 18 December 1996 and the standing mandate from the General Assembly, in which the Commission is requested to continue its review of the relationship between the net remuneration of the United Nations staff in the Professional and higher categories in New York and that of the comparator civil service (the United States federal civil service) employees in comparable positions in Washington, D.C. (referred to as "the margin"),

1. *Notes* that the margin between net remuneration of the United Nations staff in grades P-1 to D-2 in New York and that of officials in comparable positions in the United States federal civil service in Washington, D.C. for the period from 1 January to 31 December 2004 is 110.3, as shown in annex V to the annual report of the Commission;

2. *Reaffirms* that the range of 110 to 120 for the margin between the net remuneration of officials in the Professional and higher categories of the United Nations in New York and the officials in comparable positions in the comparator civil service should continue to apply, on the understanding that the margin would be maintained at a level around the desirable midpoint of 115 over a period of time;

D. Base/floor salary scale

Recalling its resolution 44/198 of 21 December 1989, by which it established a floor net salary level for staff in the Professional and higher categories by reference to the corresponding base net salary levels of officials in comparable positions serving at the base city of the comparator civil service (the United States federal civil service),

Approves, with effect from 1 January 2005, as recommended by the Commission, the revised base scale of gross and net salaries for staff in the Professional and higher categories, as contained in annex VI to the annual report of the Commission;

E. Review of the level of children's and secondary dependants' allowances

Recalling section II.F of its resolution 47/216 of 23 December 1992,

Approves the recommendations of the Commission contained in paragraph 244 of its annual report;

III

A. Senior Management Service

Recalling section I.A, paragraphs 5 and 6, of its resolution 57/285 of 20 December 2002,

1. *Recalls* that, in section I.A, paragraph 5, of its resolution 57/285 of 20 December 2002, it requested the Commission to review the proposal for the introduction of the Senior Management Service, as described in

paragraph 80 of the annual report of the Commission, in view of its intention to consider the question at its fifty-eighth session;

2. *Also recalls* that the Commission requested the United Nations System Chief Executives Board for Coordination to keep it informed and to report appropriately about the related developmental work proceeding under the auspices of the Board;

3. *Further recalls* its decision 55/488 of 7 September 2001;

4. *Reaffirms* articles 9 and 10 of the statute of the Commission;

5. *Recognizes* that measures to improve management capacity and performance among senior staff are highly desirable;

6. *Affirms* that the Commission is the only body responsible for recommending to the General Assembly the establishment of a separate category of staff for the common system;

7. *Requests* the Commission to continue to monitor the project regarding the improvement of management capacity and performance among senior staff by the United Nations System Chief Executives Board for Coordination, and to advise and make recommendations to the General Assembly as appropriate;

8. *Requests* the Secretary-General, in his capacity as Chairman of the United Nations System Chief Executives Board for Coordination, to redesignate the Senior Management Service to reflect its character as a set of collaborative efforts to enhance the managerial capacity and performance of senior staff by respective executive heads and to report to the General Assembly at its sixtieth session, clarifying the scope and content of such efforts, for consideration and action if it deems it necessary;

B. Gender balance in the United Nations system

1. *Notes with concern*, as pointed out by the Commission with regard to the organizations of the United Nations common system, that the rate of advancement of women had slowed over the years and that only limited progress had been made;

2. *Takes note* of the decision of the Commission in paragraph 297 of its annual report, and requests it to provide information on the outcome of its consideration of the report on further progress in this field;

IV
Strengthening of the international civil service
Decides to revert to the consideration of the report of the Panel on the Strengthening of the International Civil Service and the recommendations therein and the note by the Secretary-General on the findings and recommendations of the Panel during the first part of its resumed fifty-ninth session.

Also on 23 December, the Assembly decided that the agenda item on the UN common system would remain for consideration during its resumed fifty-ninth (2005) session (**decision 59/552**).

Functioning of ICSC

Strengthening of ICSC

In response to General Assembly resolution 57/285 [YUN 2002, p. 1397], the Secretary-General,

in June [A/59/153], submitted the report of the Panel on the Strengthening of the International Civil Service. The Panel, chaired by Mary Chinery-Hesse (Ghana), examined ways to further strengthen ICSC in the context of its statute, maximize its ability to support the Assembly in guiding the UN common system and enhance ICSC's contribution to modernizing and reinforcing the international civil service. The Panel found that the success of the reform efforts under way throughout the Organization to enhance its ability to deliver the programmes mandated by Member States depended largely on the performance of the international civil service. To improve the effectiveness of the service, the system had to be able to attract, develop, motivate and retain staff of the highest calibre from all regions of the world. The main challenges facing ICSC were: supporting the Assembly in leading the current change management process; and being a proactive partner with executive heads in the reform process. The Panel proposed, among its recommendations, strengthening ICSC's capacity as a source of technical expertise and policy advice, and reinforcing its collaboration with Member States, system organizations and the staff association. It recommended that the revised ICSC working methods be fully reflected in its rules of procedure annexed to the report, so as to formalize the consultative process in the establishment of its agenda, greater use be made of working groups to strengthen the relationship between consultative partners, the ICSC statute be strictly applied in respect of the qualifications and the process of consultations for membership in the Commission, as provided for in articles 3 and 4, and specific criteria be introduced, as set out in the annex to the report, to assist in focusing all phases of the selection process. Member States should take those requirements and criteria into full consideration when submitting and electing candidates, and the Secretary-General should draw on them to improve the consultative process and facilitate the selection of high-level experts in different management areas to bring the Commission an effective mix of expertise, knowledge and experience. The Panel also proposed that the Assembly limit ICSC appointments to two terms; each ICSC session be limited to a maximum of ten working days, while making greater use of informal working groups; a system of performance-based pay be introduced; the application of the Noblemaire principle be reviewed to determine the extent of the competitiveness of the common system; and action be taken by the Assembly to restore and preserve that competitiveness. Consultative partners should ensure greater cohesiveness in the organizations' contractual arrangements, and UN system organizations should use the various contractual arrangements for their intended purpose and avoid continual extension of short-term contracts for long periods. The Panel also recommend that the Commission's future work programme should place special emphasis on inter-agency mobility and ensure that effective incentives were in place; and that the Commission undertake a comprehensive reassessment of the compensation policy and incentives for service in difficult and hazardous conditions.

ICSC report. ICSC, in its comments on the report (see above), submitted in August [A/59/30 (Vol. II)], noted that, while many of the Panel's recommendations were in line with decisions adopted at its most recent sessions, others would weaken ICSC and the future of the international civil service. In particular, some recommendations seemed to be in direct contravention of ICSC's statute. ICSC considered that the Panel's report should have specifically addressed the ways in which ICSC should be strengthened to assist the Secretary-General and the Assembly in meeting their objective relative to the regulation and coordination of the conditions of service of the UN common system. In particular, ICSC objected to the Panel's recommendations on the criteria and process for the selection of ICSC members; the length of their term of office; the frequency and length of ICSC sessions; and the recommendations on enhancing ICSC's capacity to strengthen the international civil service.

Note of Secretary-General. The Secretary-General and the United Nations System Chief Executives Board for Coordination (CEB), in their comments on the Panel's report, submitted in October [A/59/399], stated that the broader recommendations of the Panel were in line with the reform process under way in most of the organizations of the system and related to policies and practices that were, for the most part, being addressed in varying degrees of priority in the Commission's work programme. In terms of thespecific recommendations, they shared the Panel's assessment that recent practices adopted by the Commission, including the establishment of working groups, had proved helpful in improving the consultative process, but they were disappointed that ICSC saw no need to formalize those improvements. Concerning the Panel's recommendations on the criteria for the selection of ICSC members and the length of their term of office, the Secretary-General and CEB considered them crucial in reinforcing the Commission and its capacity to support the Assembly. The recommendation for limiting membership on the Commission to two terms should be acceptable to the

Assembly, since it constituted an appropriate balance between continuity and the renewal and updating of expertise, experience and knowledge, as well as maximizing the independence of those who served. CEB welcomed the recommendation to limit the length of the annual sessions to 10 working days, and found the Panel's recommendations for strengthening the international civil service constructive, responsive to, and supportive of, the reforms under way in most organizations of the system. They agreed especially on the need for greater focus on performance in the determination of pay and, among other things, in strengthening managerial capacity, including through the development of a senior management service, and shared the Panel's concern about the erosion of some elements of conditions of employment. It welcomed the recommendation for a review of the Noblemaire principle. CEB made a number of recommendation for assisting the Assembly in its response to the recommendations of the Panel.

CEB consideration. The High-level Committee on Management (HLCM) of CEB, at its eighth session (Rome, 5-6 October) [CEB/2004/6], endorsed the Secretary-General's comments on the Panel's report (see above), and recommended to CEB members that they convey to ICSC its strong disappointment at ICSC's comments on the Panel's report and the expectation that the Assembly would respond positively to the Panel's key recommendations.

CEB, at its second regular session of 2004 (New York, 29-30 October) [CEB/2004/2], endorsed HLCM's conclusions.

Remuneration issues

Pursuant to the standing mandate in General Assembly resolutions 47/216 [YUN 1992, p. 1055] and 55/223 [YUN 2000, p. 1331], ICSC continued to review the relationship between the net remuneration of UN staff in the Professional and higher categories (grades P-1 to D-2) in New York, and that of the current comparator, the United States federal civil service employees in comparable positions in Washington, D.C. (referred to as the margin). In its 2004 report to the Assembly [A/59/30 (Vols. I & II)], ICSC noted that a net remuneration margin of 110.3 was forecast for 2004, based on existing grade equivalencies between United Nations and United States officials in comparable positions, as shown in annex V to its report. The actual year-to-year (2003-2004) gross increase for Washington D.C., taking into account the employment cost index and locality pay adjustment of the United States general schedule, was 4.42 per cent, effective 1 January 2004.

In view of the movement of the federal civil service salaries in the United States as from 1 January 2004, an adjustment of the UN common system's scale of 1.88 per cent would be necessary in 2005 in order to maintain the base/floor scale in line with the comparator. ICSC therefore recommended that the base/floor salary for the Professional and higher categories be increased to 1.88 per cent through standard consolidation procedures, on a no-loss/no-gain basis, with effect from 1 January 2005. ICSC decided to further study the possibility of lowering the level of the base/floor salary scale, with the remaining portion of salary provided through the post adjustment, to address the issue of duty stations that had no or very low post adjustment, as shown in annex VI to the report.

On the basis of the 1997 revised methodology for surveys of best prevailing conditions of employment at Headquarters and non-Headquarters duty stations [YUN 1997, p. 1453], ICSC conducted a survey of best prevailing conditions of service for General Service staff in Madrid, Spain, with a reference date of April 2004. The survey resulted in the recommendation of a new salary scale, as reproduced in annex VII to the ICSC report, and of revised rates for dependency allowances.

The Commission also reviewed the level of children's and secondary dependant's allowances (see p. 1414).

Noblemaire principle

In 2004, ICSC undertook an in-depth review of the Noblemaire principle and its application [A/59/30 (Vol. I)]. The last review was conducted in 1995 [YUN 1995, p. 1404]. The Commission acknowledged that the Noblemaire principle, intended to ensure the competitiveness of UN compensation and recruitment from all Member States, including the one with the highest-paid civil service, had served the organizations well and should not be set aside. ICSC should be considering how to make it continue to serve the common system, but needed more facts and analyses before it could determine whether the current application of the principle was effective. Repeating its view that salaries alone should not be used to measure whether the United Nations was a competitive employer, ICSC was of the opinion that the appropriate means of doing so was to evaluate recruitment and retention in organizations to identify difficulties in attracting and retaining highly qualified staff. In that regard, organizations had not responded to its repeated requests for such analyses over the past 10 years. ICSC decided to report to the General Assembly that, in applying the Noblemaire principle, its practice of using the highest-paid national civil service, combined

with a reference check with international organizations, was sound. ICSC had on its work programme for 2005-2006 a study to determine the highest-paid civil service, including a total comparison between the United Nations and the United States federal civil service.

Grade equivalencies

In 2004, ICSC was informed of a number of changes in the UN common system and the United States federal civil service, requiring a re-examination of the procedure for determining grade equivalencies. The Commission decided that a grade equivalency study should be conducted for the revised structure of the comparator's Senior Executive Service, using two comparison methods: one which assigned a midpoint or average salary to all members of the United States Senior Executive Service positions; and the other which would link the common system grades with the comparator's performance-based Senior Executive Service salaries. The results of the study should be reported to the Commission in 2005. A grade equivalency study should also be conducted for all other comparator pay systems in 2005.

Common staff assessment scale

In accordance with a 1997 recommendation of the United Nations Joint Staff Pension Board for a biennial update of the common staff assessment scale for all staff categories for determining pensionable remuneration levels, ICSC, at its fifty-ninth session, examined tax changes at the duty stations concerned between 2001 and 2003 [A/59/30 (Vol. I)]. Having found that average taxes had increased or decreased only minimally at the relevant income levels during that period, ICSC recommended continued application of the current common scale of staff assessment, which should be reviewed during the next comprehensive review of pensionable remuneration, scheduled for 2005-2006.

Other remuneration issues

Conditions of service and compensation for non-Secretariat officials

Judges of ICJ and the international tribunals

Report of Secretary-General. In September [A/C.5/59/2 & Corr.1], the Secretary-General submitted a report on the conditions of service and compensation of members of the International Court of Justice (ICJ), judges of the International Tribunal for the Former Yugoslavia (ICTY) and of the International Criminal Tribunal for Rwanda (ICTR), and ad litem judges for both Tribunals. The emoluments of the members of the Court and the judges of the Tribunals had remained at $160,000 since January 1999, while the consumer price index for the Netherlands had increased by 17.4 per cent for the period between then and May 2004 and during the past two years the United States dollar had lost, on average, 26.8 per cent against the euro. Accordingly, for 2004, the floor rate was frozen at the 2003 level. While the application of the floor/ceiling mechanism at the 2003 rates provided significant protection against the weakening United States dollar vis-à-vis the euro, it did not provide total protection and, in real terms, the salaries of the judges lost 4.35 per cent. In addition, the base salaries of staff at the Under-Secretary-General level were increased by 6.3 per cent. Accordingly, the Secretary-General proposed that Member States consider increasing the annual emoluments of the members of the Court, the judges of ICTY and ICTR and the ad litem judges from $160,000 to $177,000 (10.6 per cent), and that the same floor/ceiling mechanism should continue to be applied to the emoluments of the judges.

Based on the proposed increase in the base salary of ICJ members, it was recommended that pensions in payment be increased by 10.6 per cent, effective 1 January 2005. The Secretary-General was of the view that consideration be given to applying the floor/ceiling mechanism to pensions in payment to former judges and their survivors residing in euro zone countries to protect the level of pensions from further erosion as a result of the devaluation of the United States dollar vis-à-vis the euro.

The Secretary-General also proposed that the level of the education grant, including that for disabled children, approved by the General Assembly in resolution 57/285 [YUN 2002, p. 1397], and effective from the school year in progress on 1 January 2003, should be extended, under the same conditions, to members of the Court and judges of the Tribunals, as well any decision taken at the Assembly's fifty-ninth session to update the level of the grant and provisions regarding disabled children.

The Secretary-General proposed that no change be effected in the arrangements for ad hoc judges, and that any increase in the annual emoluments decided upon for ICJ members and the judges of the Tribunals be extended to the ad litem judges of the Tribunals, effective 1 January 2005.

The Secretary-General observed that, should the Assembly approve his proposals, the programme budget implications would amount to an

estimated $2,320,600 for the 2004-2005 biennium, which would be reported in the context of the performance report.

ACABQ report. In November [A/59/557], ACABQ recommended that the annual salary of ICJ members be set at $177,000 effective 1 January 2005. The Secretary-General should be requested to make proposals for the future, taking into account the uncertainties with regard to the current system, as the cost of living did not fluctuate evenly at all places where the members of ICJ and judges of the Tribunals sat. ACABQ had no objection to the Secretary-General's proposals regarding the education grant (including that for disabled children) and retirement benefits. ACABQ recommended further elaboration of the proposal to apply a floor/ceiling mechanism to pensions in payment to former judges and their survivors, including other options for protecting those pensions. The results of such a review should be presented to the Assembly at its resumed fifty-ninth (2005) session.

On 23 December, the Assembly deferred until its resumed fifty-ninth (2005) session, consideration of the Secretary-General's report on the conditions of service and compensation for ICJ members and judges and ad litem judges of ICTY and ICTR and the related ACABQ report (**decision 59/551**).

Members of the UN Administrative Tribunal

Communication. In a letter to the Chairman of the Fifth Committee [A/C.5/58/16], the President of the United Nations Administrative Tribunal (UNAT) requested the Secretary-General to take whatever steps were deemed appropriate to provide remuneration to the members of UNAT equivalent to that received by the judges of the Administrative Tribunal of the International Labour Organization (ILOAT).

Note of Secretary-General. In October [A/C.5/59/12], the Secretary-General noted that should the General Assembly decide that UNAT members were to be compensated in a manner comparable to ILOAT judges, it might wish to consider honorariums as follows: the UNAT member drafting a judgment would receive $1,000; and the two members signing the judgment would receive $250 for each case. On the assumption that implementation would take effect from 1 January 2005, additional requirements of $210,000 would arise under section 8, Legal Affairs, of the 2004-2005 programme budget. (For more information on UNAT, see p. 1443.)

On 23 December, the Assembly deferred consideration of the letter of the President of UNAT to the Chairman of the Fifth Committee and the

Secretary-General's note on compensation for officials other than Secretariat officials: members of UNAT, to its resumed fifty-ninth (2005) session (**decision 59/551**).

Dependency allowances

For its biennial review of dependency allowances for the Professional and higher categories, ICSC considered details of the percentage change required in the children's and secondary dependants' allowances based on changes in the tax abatement and social legislation for headquarters duty stations between 1 January 2002 and 1 January 2004 [A/59/30 (Vol. I)]. ICSC recommended to the General Assembly that, starting from the current review, those allowances should be determined on the basis of the value of tax abatements and social security payments in the countries of the eight headquarters duty stations, including Spain, and their current levels should remain unchanged. The current list of duty stations where the allowances were payable in local currencies should be maintained, pending a review of the methodology for determining them, and the dependency allowances payable to eligible common system staff be reduced by the amount of any direct payment received from Governments in respect of dependants.

Education grant

Based on the revised methodology for determining the education grant levels, endorsed by the General Assembly in resolution 52/216 [YUN 1997, p. 1454], ICSC reviewed the operation of the grant. It had before it a related study by the Human Resources Network, which analysed 12,799 claims for the academic year 2002/03 in the 17 individual countries/currency areas in which the grant was applied.

ICSC recommended to the Assembly that, in areas where education-related expenses were incurred in the euro (Austria, Belgium, Denmark, France, Germany, Ireland, Italy, the Netherlands, Spain and Sweden), Swiss francs, the Japanese yen, pounds sterling and United States dollars (inside and outside the United States), the levels of maximum admissible expenses and the maximum grant should be set as shown in table 1 of annex IV to its report [A/59/30 (Vol. I)]. Other recommendations were that the maximum amount of admissible expenses and the maximum grant should remain at the current level for the countries/currency areas of Finland and Norway; the flat rates for boarding to be taken into account within the maximum admissible educational expenses and the additional amounts for reimbursement of boarding costs over and above the

maximum grant payable to staff members at designated duty stations should be revised as shown in table 2 of annex IV to its report; and the amount of the special education grant for each disabled child should be equal to 100 per cent of the revised amounts of the maximum allowable expenses for the regular grant. For China, Indonesia, Romania and the Russian Federation, organizations would be allowed to reimburse 75 per cent of actual expenses up to and not exceeding the level of maximum admissible expenses in force for the United States dollar area inside the United States. All of the foregoing measures would apply as from the school year in progress on 1 January 2005.

Paternity leave

ICSC, in its review of policies designed to reconcile work and family life responsibilities, considered proposals for establishing the duration of paternity leave, separate conditions for that entitlement and measures for dealing with exceptional circumstances [A/59/30 (Vol. I)]. The Commission in 2002 had agreed that paternity leave of reasonable duration could be introduced in the common system under a uniform policy, superseding existing paternity leave entitlements in those organizations that had already introduced them. At its 2004 session, the Commission decided that up to four weeks paid leave for paternity purposes should be granted to staff at headquarters and family duty stations and up to eight weeks for staff at non-family duty stations or in exceptional circumstances, such as incapacity or death of a mother, inadequate medical facilities or complications encountered at the time of pregnancy. Those provisions should supersede existing paternity leave arrangements, and the administrative details covering the management of paternity leave should be determined at the level of the organizations. It also decided that the provisions for adoption leave should not be subsumed under the provisions for paternity leave.

Mobility and hardship allowance

ICSC, in its ongoing review of the mobility and hardship scheme, approved in 1989 [YUN 1989, p.885] to compensate staff for service at difficult duty stations and to encourage operational mobility, was presented with a number of options for delinking the scheme from the annual adjustment procedure applied to the base/floor scale, in response to its request [YUN 2003, p. 1439] to its secretariat to present alternative approaches to compensation for mobility and hardship in the context of the ongoing review of pay and benefits. ICSC noted that, while cognizant of the General Assembly's concern at the increasing costs generated by linking the allowance to the base/floor salary scale, it could not consider the linkage in isolation, but together with all aspects of the mobility and hardship scheme and organizations' mobility and rotation policies and their effects on career development before it could take a meaningful decision regarding linkage. The Commission therefore decided that the mobility and hardship scheme should be examined in the context of the pay and benefits reform. In that context, it was of the opinion that the primary incentive for staff mobility was career advancement and that the management of the mobility scheme should be approached differently from the scheme that compensated hardship. Although hardship had been equated with mobility in the past, they were not equal elements, nor were they linked, contrary to the organizations' belief.

The Commission decided to separate the mobility element from the hardship element; delink both the mobility and hardship allowances from the base/floor salary scale; defer the implementation of those two decisions until a new system had been put into place; and establish a working group to develop options for compensating staff for service in hardship duty stations and for encouraging mobility, and to estimate the cost of those options, and submit recommendations to the Commission at its sixtieth (2005) session.

Lump-sum payments for relocation grant

CEB action. The High-level Committee on Management (HLCM) of CEB, at its eighth session (Rome, 5-6 October) [CEB/2004/6], considered the findings of the review of the pilot phase of the relocation grant, which confirmed that, overall, the lump sum scheme had proved to be an effective new approach to entitlement design and administration for organizations and staff alike. It had contributed to organizational effectiveness in meeting the critical challenge of moving staff quickly and efficiently to new duty stations; enhanced staff satisfaction and morale; met with positive feedback from human resources administrators and practitioners; and yielded a favourable cost-benefit ratio, particularly if indirect cost savings and intangible benefits were added to the direct cost calculations. HLCM endorsed the lump sum approach as an option for staff in those organizations who felt ready for its formal introduction, and encouraged each agency to report in 2005 to the Human Resources Network on its decisions and experience within their specific organizational context.

Hazard pay

Pursuant to General Assembly resolution 58/251 [YUN 2003, p. 1432], ICSC reviewed the terms for granting hazard pay—payment for employment under conditions where war or active hostilities prevailed and the evacuation of families and non-essential staff had taken place—for local staff. The Commission decided that the level of hazard pay granted to locally recruited staff should be increased to 25 per cent of the midpoint of the local salary scale and that the decision be implemented with effect from 1 June 2004.

Pensionable remuneration

As requested by the General Assembly in resolution 51/217 [YUN 1996, p. 1334], ICSC, in cooperation with the United Nations Joint Staff Pension Fund (UNJSPF), undertook a comprehensive review, originally scheduled for 2002, of the methodologies for determining the pensionable remuneration of staff in the Professional and higher categories, and for the adjustment of pensionable remuneration between comprehensive reviews [A/59/30 (Vol. I)]. The Chief Executive Officer of the Pension Board presented specific modalities for the review and a detailed timetable. The items considered by the Pension Board included: a non-pensionable component; double taxation; reverse application of the special index for pensioners (at high-tax locations); and the impact of steep devaluation of local currency and/or high inflation. In addition, the Board considered that income replacement ratios, United States/ United Nations pension benefit comparisons and the impact of the pay and benefits review on pension benefits also needed close attention in the review. The Board proposed a collaborative work schedule extending from the autumn and winter of 2004-2005 to the completion of joint ICSC/Pension Board recommendations to the Assembly in 2006. In the context of the review, the Board recommended a formal joint ICSC-Pension Board Working Group and a Contact Group to facilitate communication prior to the establishment of the Working Group.

ICSC concurred with the Pension Board's proposals with regard to the terms of reference of the Working Group and modalities for cooperation.

Other staff matters

Senior Management Service

CEB action. The High-level Committee on Management (HLCM) of CEB, at its seventh session (London, 8-9 March) [CEB/2004/3], considered the report of the Human Resources Network on the establishment of a Senior Management Service. The Service was intended to build managerial capacity throughout the UN system in order to improve organizational performance, and contribute to the creation of a common managerial culture. It would complement existing management development programmes in organizations and would not diminish the prerogative of executive heads to create posts or appoint staff. The implementation of the Service was ongoing and could be extended to include, among other things, the development of an assessment approach for movement of staff into and out of the Service, and models/frameworks for performance accountability contracts and other tools for organizations. HLCM recommended that CEB approve the establishment of a Senior Management Service in the UN common system. It requested all organizations to establish and implement such a service; the Human Resources Network to continue to refine the competency map and to develop a learning framework for a leadership and management development programme together with the United Nations System Staff College; and the CEB's secretariat to follow up and provide support to the creation of the Senior Management Service.

CEB, at its first regular session of 2004 (Vienna, 2-3 April) [CEB/2004/1] approved HLCM's recommendation to establish a Senior Management Service.

At its eighth session (Rome, 5-6 October) [CEB/2004/6], HLCM received an update from CEB's secretariat on the establishment of the Senior Management Service. A working group of the Human Resources Network was collaborating with the UN Staff System College to prepare the bid proposals for the design and delivery of the leadership development programme. An evaluation committee comprising the Staff College and Human Resources Network representatives would review the proposals received and make the final selection. It was hoped that the programme would be ready for delivery in the first half of 2005.

Personnel policies

Human resources management

The General Assembly, by **decision 58/564** of 8 April, deferred to its fifty-ninth (2004) session consideration of the Secretary-General's reports on amendments to the 100 and 200 series of Staff Rules [YUN 2003, p. 1452] and on staff composition in 2003 [ibid., p. 1446]; the list of staff of the Secreta-

riat for 2003 [A/C.5/58/L.13]; and notes by the Secretary-General transmitting the report of the Office of Internal Oversight Services (OIOS) on possible discrimination due to nationality, race, sex, religion and language in recruitment, promotion and placement and the comments of the Joint Inspection Unit (JIU) thereon [YUN 2002, p. 1406].

At its fifty-ninth session, in addition to those reports, the Assembly had before it the Secretary-General's reports on measures to prevent discrimination on the basis of nationality, race, sex, religion and language in the United Nations [A/59/211]; amendments to the Staff Rules [A/59/213 & Add.1]; consultants and individual contractors [A/59/217]; the employment of retired former staff [A/59/222]; human resources management reform [A/59/263]; new contractual arrangements [A/59/263/Add.1]; proposals to improve gender distribution in the Secretariat [A/59/263/Add.2]; improving the equitable geographic representation in the Secretariat to include the development of a more robust capability in the Office of Human Resources Management (OHRM) to enable it to reduce the level of underrepresentation and the number of unrepresented Member States [A/59/264]; staffing of field missions, including the use of the 300 and 100 series of appointments (see p. 105); the composition of the Secretariat [A/59/299]; and the improvement of the status of women in the UN system [A/59/357] and the related ACABQ report [A/59/446]. It also had before it notes by the Secretary-General transmitting OIOS reports on the audit of the policies and procedures for recruiting Department of Peacekeeping Operations (DPKO) staff (see p. 103), the follow-up audit of DPKO policies and procedures for recruiting international civilian staff for field missions (see p. 104), the impact of human resources management reform [A/59/253], as well as a study on the availability in local labour markets of the skills for which international recruitment for posts in the General Service category took place [A/59/388], and the views of the staff representatives of the Secretariat [A/C.5/59/4] and a JIU report on the management review of the Office of the High Commissioner for Human Rights (see p. 650) and the comments of the Secretary-General thereon (see p. 651).

Reports of Secretary-General. In response to General Assembly resolutions 57/305 [YUN 2003, p. 1440] and 57/300 [YUN 2002, p.1353], the Secretary-General submitted an August report [A/59/263] on progress achieved in consolidating and expanding the human resources management reform programme, outlined in his 1997 [YUN 1997, p. 1390] and 2002 [YUN 2002, p. 1352] reports on UN reform, and some of the challenges faced in that process.

Significant progress was made in bringing about the changes envisioned in the integrated reform programme based on 10 key building blocks: human resources planning; streamlined rules and procedures; recruitment, placement and promotion; mobility; competencies and continuous learning; performance management; career development; conditions of service; contractual arrangements; and administration of justice. Follow-up activities were carried out on the actions set out in the Secretary-General's 2002 report that fell within the human resources management reform programme, including action on conditions of service in the field, expanding opportunities for General Service staff and HIV/AIDS.

According to the Secretary-General, major achievements included the introduction of a system of human resources planning providing workforce profiles and trends; streamlining of policies and rules and the launching of an electronic Human Resources Handbook; a new staff selection system, which, with its supporting electronic tool, Galaxy e-staffing, had speeded up the selection process, while improving efficiency and transparency; a policy on organizational mobility aimed at developing a more versatile, multiskilled and experienced international civil service; definition and strengthening of organizational core values and core and managerial competencies; promotion of continuous learning and strengthening of core organizational competencies, which included the development of a plan for enhancing opportunities for the General Service staff; an enhanced performance appraisal system; human resources monitoring; and greater attention to work and life issues.

Developing and implementing the reform initiatives had presented considerable challenges. A key area remaining to be addressed was that of contractual arrangements, for which the Secretary-General had made a number of proposals to the General Assembly (see below). Other areas needing attention were the continued disparity in conditions of service among Secretariat staff and those of other organizations serving in the field and the limited career prospects for General Service staff.

Human resources management reform necessitated a paradigm shift in underlying principles, attitudes and work methods, making some of the initiatives difficult to reconcile with the priorities of staff, managers and Member States. The reform was also affected by operational challenges, such as the lack of dedicated reform, and the difficulty of consulting staff representatives at a time when the consultative machinery was not fully operational.

The Organization's human resources management programme would continue to focus on ensuring that its policies and practices were fully in line with operational needs and worldwide standards of good practice. Special emphasis would be placed, in the coming years, on the implementation of the managed mobility policy; the strengthening of the staff selection system and performance management; further enhancement of management capacity; increased monitoring, particularly of delegated authority; improving OHRM's client orientation and communication with staff; and the improvement of its electronic tools and the introduction of new ones. There would be continuing close cooperation with other common system organizations and ICSC in developing and enhancing a competitive package of conditions of service.

On 1 October [A/C.5/59/4], the Secretary-General transmitted to the Fifth Committee the views of the staff representatives of the UN Secretariat.

OIOS report. As requested by the General Assembly in resolution 57/305 [YUN 2003, p. 1440], the Secretary-General submitted, in September [A/59/253], an OIOS report on the impact of human resources management reform. OIOS found that, although the reform had achieved significant success to date, including a decrease in the time to fill a vacancy and greater organizational focus on creating opportunities for staff mobility and career development, its potential impact was not yet fully realized. Though OHRM's initiatives had started a cultural change, staff and managers were not fully committed to the nature, scope and purpose of reform. As a result, there was inconsistent prioritization of responsibilities and accountability for people management. OIOS recommended that OHRM address that lack of confidence in the reform initiatives. An organizational focus on effective performance management and strategic planning, rather than compliance, would enhance the ultimate success of the OHRM's integrated policy framework. OHRM also needed to improve its ability to measure and monitor human resources indicators. Although the new staff selection system had significantly enhanced opportunities to apply and enlarge the pool of applicants, neither the quality of candidates nor career prospects for junior staff had improved. The effectiveness of central review bodies was diminished by a lack of information relevant to reviewing evaluations and proposals. The new mobility policy had yet to result in reduced vacancy rates at duty stations with chronic vacancy issues. The organizational culture needed to shift from a compliance perspective to promulgating mobility strategies that satisfied operational requirements and benefitted staff careers. OIOS recommendations included specific suggestions designed to build upon the policies, tools and infrastructure currently in place. In addition to proposals for shortening the recruitment process, developing proactive recruiting strategies, increasing capacity to assess operational needs and tracking indicators at the department/office and individual levels, OIOS suggested steps to increase staff and manager commitment to the most challenging aspects of reform: mobility and performance management.

ACABQ report. In an October report [A/59/446], ACABQ said that the Secretary-General's report on human resources management reform was rather general and lacking in analysis, particularly with regard to progress achieved in implementation, problems encountered and measures planned to redress them. That was particularly the case with the issue of compliance. Not enough attention was given to setting criteria to monitor the quality of decisions made by programme managers rather than merely quantifying mechanical adherence to procedures as measured by raw statistics. In that connection, ACABQ stressed the importance of monitoring and recalled that the Assembly, in resolution 57/305, had endorsed the development of a more robust monitoring capacity in OHRM. The Committee trusted that the sample monitoring template and a sample human resources action plan provided at its request would streamline the reporting process and make it more effective. The Committee was of the opinion that, to succeed, such broad human resources management reforms had to be accompanied by close staff/management cooperation and consultation. Noting that relations between the two over human resources management had broken down somewhat, ACABQ encouraged the Secretary-General and OHRM to take a fresh look at ways to involve staff meaningfully so as to take into account their concerns, and trusted that management and staff would make concerted efforts to work together constructively in the best interest of the Organization.

The Committee requested that statistics on the length of the placement process be quantified as a basis for analysing and correcting problems. ACABQ regretted that more progress had not been made in screening the increased number of applications for vacant positions since the introduction of the Galaxy system. It emphasized that, unless such problems were resolved, the effectiveness of Galaxy would be compromised and its cost-effectiveness called into question. It recommended approval of the Secretary-General's proposal to further shorten vacancy advertising

from 60 to 45 days, with the understanding that paper copies of vacancy announcements would also be provided, and expected the widest possible timely circulation of those announcements so as to attract qualified personnel from unrepresented or underrepresented countries. Effective implementation of the roster management module in Galaxy, including automatic electronic notification of programme managers concerning eligible roster candidates, could shorten the recruitment timeline. As to succession planning, not enough was being done to initiate the process for filling vacancies in a timely manner and thus reduce the long period that posts remained vacant. For internal candidates, improvement had to be made to ensure the timely release of the successful candidate to his or her new function.

With regard to the examination for recruitment from the General Service to the Professional category (G-P) and the national competitive recruitment examination, ACABQ noted that the limited number of posts available pointed to a larger problem, namely, the very small number of entry level (P-1/P-2) Professional posts in the Secretariat. To resolve the problem, the issue of redressing the imbalance in the grading pyramid would first need to be addressed, and the G-P roster used to help fill posts at duty stations with chronically high vacancy rates. ACABQ called upon the Secretariat to review the efficacy of the procedure of having staff members serve on the examinations boards on a voluntary basis outside of their regular functions.

ACABQ encouraged the Secretary-General to continue his efforts towards achieving gender parity, including at the Under-Secretary-General and Assistant Secretary-General levels. Care had to be taken, however, to ensure that such efforts did not unduly affect the timely filling of vacancies and were in conformity with Article 101, paragraph 3, of the UN Charter.

The Committee also considered the Secretary-General's comprehensive report on the staffing for field missions, including the use of 300 and 100 series appointments (see p. 105), and made a number of recommendations (see p. 106).

GENERAL ASSEMBLY ACTION

On 23 December [meeting 76], the General Assembly, on the recommendation of the Fifth Committee [A/59/650], adopted **resolution 59/266** without vote [agenda item 114].

Human resources management

The General Assembly,

Recalling Articles 8, 97, 100 and 101 of the Charter of the United Nations,

Recalling also its resolutions 49/222 A and B of 23 December 1994 and 20 July 1995, 51/226 of 3 April

1997, 52/219 of 22 December 1997, 52/252 of 8 September 1998, 53/221 of 7 April 1999, 55/258 of 14 June 2001, 57/305 of 15 April 2003 and 58/296 of 18 June 2004, as well as its other relevant resolutions and decisions,

Having considered the relevant reports on human resources management questions submitted to the General Assembly for its consideration and the related report of the Advisory Committee on Administrative and Budgetary Questions,

I
Human resources management reform

1. *Reaffirms* the principles set out in sections I and II of its resolution 53/221 and section I of its resolution 55/258 concerning human resources management and the role of the Office of Human Resources Management of the Secretariat;

2. *Affirms* that the Office of Human Resources Management shall remain the central authority within the Secretariat for the interpretation and enforcement of the Staff Regulations and Rules, without prejudice to regulation 12.3;

3. *Stresses* the crucial importance of a transparent and timely flow of information from the Secretariat to Member States in matters related to human resources management reform;

4. *Requests* the Secretary-General in future reports on mandated human resources management reform to include full information on achievements and the impact of its implementation;

5. *Stresses* that any proposals for changes in the building blocks of reform should be accompanied by transparent information for Member States on those changes;

6. *Recalls* section VII of its resolution 55/258, in which the General Assembly, inter alia, requested the Secretary-General to ensure that well-designed mechanisms of accountability are put in place before delegating authority to programme managers;

7. *Stresses* the need to ensure that adequate mechanisms are in place to ensure the accountability of programme managers for the implementation of human resources policies and the achievement of objectives contained in human resources action plans;

8. *Emphasizes* that effective accountability mechanisms are an integral and essential element of human resources management reform, and requests the Secretary-General to strengthen such mechanisms throughout the Organization;

9. *Requests* the Secretary-General to continue to improve the effectiveness of human resources action plans for achieving the human resources objectives of the Organization, including with respect to equitable geographical distribution and gender representation, as mandated by the General Assembly, and further requests him to report thereon to the Assembly at its sixty-first session;

10. *Also requests* the Secretary-General to reconstitute the Accountability Panel so as to strengthen the internal system of accountability, including with respect to human resources policies and objectives, and to ensure that the Panel has the authority necessary to hold programme managers accountable for their performance in achieving the objectives contained in human resources action plans;

11. *Stresses* that the staff selection system must provide transparency and fairness;

12. *Emphasizes* the importance of the participation of staff representatives in the work of the central review bodies, and requests the Secretary-General and invites staff representatives to engage in a consultative process with a view to resuming the participation of staff representatives in the work of the central review bodies;

13. *Requests* the Secretary-General to make every effort to ensure that the central review bodies discharge fully and effectively their roles in the staff selection system, as foreseen in annex II to the report of the Secretary-General entitled "Human resources management reform" and subsequently approved by the General Assembly in its resolution 55/258, including by addressing the deficiencies identified in the report of the Office of Internal Oversight Services, and to make proposals to amend the terms of reference of the central review bodies as necessary in the light of experience;

14. *Recalls its request* to the Secretary-General contained in section II, paragraph 2, of its resolution 51/226, as reiterated in section IV, paragraph 10, of its resolution 53/221, section VII of its resolution 55/258 and section III of its resolution 57/305, to enhance managerial accountability with respect to human resources management decisions, including imposing sanctions in cases of demonstrated mismanagement of staff and wilful neglect of, or disregard for, established rules and procedures, while safeguarding the right of due process of all staff members, including managers, and requests the Secretary-General to report comprehensively thereon to it at its sixty-first session;

15. *Requests* the Secretary-General to continue his efforts, as described in paragraphs 130 to 132 of his report, to report to the General Assembly on the experiences gained in the implementation of such measures and to make additional proposals for action by the Assembly as appropriate;

16. *Notes with concern* paragraph 91 of the report of the Secretary-General, and requests the Secretary-General to reassess the situation:

II
Recruitment and placement

1. *Requests* the Secretary-General to ensure that the highest standards of efficiency, competence and integrity serve as the paramount consideration in the employment of staff, with due regard for the principle of equitable geographical distribution, in accordance with Article 101, paragraph 3, of the Charter of the United Nations;

2. *Recognizes* the value of a transparent process of recruitment, placement and promotion in the Organization;

3. *Notes* the proposal of the Secretary-General, on the recommendation of the Office of Internal Oversight Services, to reduce the time required for advertising a vacancy from 60 to 45 days, and decides to revert to this issue in the context of a comprehensive study addressing all factors contributing to the process of selection, recruitment and placement at its sixty-first session;

4. *Requests* the Secretary-General to continue his efforts to reduce the period required to fill vacancies by addressing all factors contributing to delays in the process of selection, recruitment and placement and to re-

port thereon to the General Assembly at its sixty-first session;

5. *Also requests* the Secretary-General to continue to maintain a system of circulating printed copies of all vacancy announcements, in accordance with its resolution 57/305, for distribution to all delegations, except those which indicate otherwise;

6. *Reaffirms* the need to respect the equality of each of the two working languages of the Secretariat, reaffirms also the use of additional working languages in specific duty stations as mandated, and in this regard requests the Secretary-General to ensure that vacancy announcements specify the need for either of the working languages of the Secretariat unless the functions of the post require a specific working language;

7. *Requests* the Secretary-General to report on the definition of language posts to the General Assembly at its sixty-first session in the context of his report on the composition of the Secretariat;

8. *Expresses its concern* over the deficiencies in the recruitment of international civilian staff in peacekeeping missions as referred to by the Office of Internal Oversight Services in its report, and requests the Secretary-General to make efforts to rectify the situation and to report thereon to the General Assembly at its sixty-first session;

9. *Notes with concern* the range of weaknesses related to the Galaxy support tool identified by the Office of Internal Oversight Services in its report;

10. *Requests* the Secretary-General to fully develop the Galaxy support tool and make it more efficient and user-friendly for the purpose of efficient recruitment, as embodied in Article 101 of the Charter, and to ensure that all applicants are informed about the final result of their applications in a timely fashion;

11. *Also requests* the Secretary-General to ensure the conversion of all printed applications into electronic form upon their submission for inclusion in the Galaxy system and to ensure that those applications are considered in the filling of advertised vacancies, and to report thereon to the General Assembly at its sixty-first session;

12. *Further requests* the Secretary-General to continue to develop screening mechanisms that ensure that all applications submitted in the Galaxy system are treated fairly, that well-qualified candidates are given due consideration and that keywords outside of the vacancy announcements are not used to exclude well-qualified candidates;

13. *Requests* the Secretary-General to continue to take the steps necessary to ensure that Galaxy is available in both of the working languages of the Organization;

14. *Reiterates its requests* to the Secretary-General to inform Member States monthly, through the Internet, through the United Nations public web site and, upon request, in printed form of appointments made;

III

National competitive examination and General Service to Professional examination

1. *Reiterates its decision* that the recruitment of qualified staff from the General Service to the Professional category should be limited to the P-1 and P-2 levels and should be permitted for up to 10 per cent of the appointments at those levels;

2. *Authorizes* the Secretary-General to appoint to posts not subject to geographical distribution at the P-2 level up to seven successful candidates from the General Service to Professional examination each year;

3. *Also authorizes* the Secretary-General to appoint to P-2 posts in duty stations with chronically high vacancy rates up to three successful candidates from the General Service to Professional examination each year when no successful candidates from the national competitive examination are available;

4. *Requests* the Secretary-General to make special efforts to appoint to the relevant vacant posts in the Secretariat successful candidates from unrepresented and underrepresented Member States who have passed the national competitive examination;

5. *Also requests* the Secretary-General to ensure the expeditious placement in appropriate posts of as many candidates as feasible who have been placed on the roster following the successful completion of national competitive examinations;

6. *Reiterates* section II, paragraph 43, of its resolution 57/305, and requests the Secretary-General to apply strictly the relevant administrative instruction for recruitment at the P-3 level and to report thereon to the General Assembly at its sixty-first session;

IV

Measures to improve equitable geographical distribution

1. *Notes with appreciation* the progress made since 1994 in reducing the number of countries that are unrepresented and underrepresented;

2. *Requests* the Secretary-General to continue his ongoing efforts to attain equitable geographical distribution in the Secretariat and to ensure as wide a geographical distribution of staff as possible in all main departments and offices of the Secretariat;

3. *Welcomes* the continuing efforts of the Secretary-General to improve the situation of unrepresented and underrepresented Member States and of those in danger of becoming underrepresented under the system of desirable ranges;

4. *Notes* the low percentage of appointments of staff from unrepresented and underrepresented Member States to posts subject to geographical distribution in 2004;

5. *Notes with concern* the decline in the proportion of nationals of developing countries in posts at the senior and policy-making levels of the Secretariat;

6. *Reiterates its request* that the Secretary-General take all measures necessary to ensure, at the senior and policy-making levels of the Secretariat, equitable representation of Member States, especially those with inadequate representation at those levels, including unrepresented and underrepresented States, in particular developing countries, in accordance with the relevant resolutions of the General Assembly, and to continue to include relevant information thereon in all future reports on the composition of the Secretariat;

7. *Notes* that the system of geographic ranges was designed to apply to countries rather than regions or groups;

8. *Recalls* section II, paragraph 30, of its resolution 57/305, and reiterates its request that the Secretary-General include an analysis of the level of under-

representation in his next report on the composition of the Secretariat;

9. *Authorizes* the Secretary-General, for a trial period of two years during which the procedures would be fully developed, to establish a special roster of candidates from unrepresented and underrepresented Member States, as proposed in paragraphs 21 and 22 of his report, for a number of posts at the P-4 and P-5 levels only, until such Member States are within the desirable ranges, and requests the Secretary-General to report thereon to the General Assembly at its sixty-first session;

10. *Welcomes* the practice of conducting recruitment missions to unrepresented and underrepresented Member States, and requests the Secretary-General to intensify those efforts in order to increase the number of recruits from those Member States after going through the regular recruitment procedures for advertised vacancies;

11. *Reiterates its request* contained in section II, paragraph 29, of its resolution 57/305 that the Secretary-General set specific targets as well as develop a programme for achieving equitable geographical representation;

12. *Notes* the number of overrepresented countries under the system of desirable ranges, and requests the Secretary-General to provide the General Assembly with analytical information on this issue in the framework of his report on the composition of the Secretariat;

13. *Reaffirms* that, in accordance with its resolutions 41/206 B of 11 December 1986, 53/221, 55/258 and 57/305, no post should be considered the exclusive preserve of any Member State or group of States, including at the highest levels, and reiterates its request that the Secretary-General ensure that, as a general rule, no national of a Member State succeeds a national of that State in a senior post and that there is no monopoly on senior posts by nationals of any State or group of States, and to report thereon to the General Assembly at its sixty-first session;

V
System of equitable geographical distribution

1. *Reiterates its request* that the Secretary-General, as approved in its resolution 42/220 A of 21 December 1987, fully reach the level of posts subject to geographical distribution, which currently stands at 2,783;

2. *Also reiterates its request* that the Secretary-General submit the report requested in section IX, paragraph 2, of its resolution 57/305, which will include an assessment of the issues related to possible changes in the number of posts subject to the system of geographical distribution, and requests the Secretary-General to submit the report to the General Assembly by the second part of its resumed fifty-ninth session;

3. *Recalls* section IX, paragraph 1, of its resolution 57/305, and decides to revert to this subject at its sixty-first session;

4. *Requests* the Board of Auditors to conduct an audit of the implementation of the principle of equitable geographical representation in the Secretariat at all levels, as set out in relevant resolutions of the General Assembly, and to verify the application of established measures of transparency and accountability at all levels of the selection, recruitment and placement process in compliance with relevant resolutions of the Assembly;

5. *Also requests* the Board of Auditors to submit its findings and recommendations to the General Assembly at its sixty-first session for consideration and action;

VI
Gender representation

1. *Reaffirms* the goal of 50/50 gender distribution in all categories of posts within the United Nations system, especially at the senior and policy-making levels, with full respect for the principle of equitable geographical distribution, in conformity with Article 101 of the Charter, and regrets that progress towards attaining this goal has been slow;

2. *Expresses concern* at the continuing low proportion of women in the Secretariat, in particular the low proportion among them of women from developing countries, especially at the senior levels, and stresses that the continuing lack of representation or underrepresentation of women from certain countries, in particular from developing countries, should be taken into account and that those women should be accorded equal opportunities in the recruitment process, in full conformity with relevant resolutions;

3. *Notes with concern* that, in posts subject to the system of desirable ranges, 26 women from developing countries were recruited between 1 July 2003 and 30 June 2004 among the 86 women appointed during that period;

4. *Requests* the Secretary-General to increase his efforts to attain and monitor the goal of gender parity in the Secretariat, in particular at senior levels, and in this context to ensure that women, especially those from developing countries and countries with economies in transition, are appropriately represented within the Secretariat, and to report thereon to the General Assembly at its sixty-first session;

5. *Also requests* the Secretary-General, in the context of attaining this goal, to develop and implement recruitment targets, time frames for meeting those targets and accountability measures;

6. *Further requests* the Secretary-General to clarify the role of departmental focal points, including in the context of the staff selection system, and their participation in the development and monitoring of the departmental human resource action plans;

7. *Encourages* Member States to support the efforts of the Secretary-General by identifying more women candidates and encouraging them to apply for appointment to positions in the Secretariat and by creating awareness among their nationals, particularly women, of vacancies in the Secretariat;

VII
Post structure

Requests the Secretary-General to make proposals to the General Assembly, as appropriate, to reform the post structure with a view to considering a possible increase in the proportion of P-2 and P-3 posts, taking advantage of the opportunity provided by the retirement of many senior staff in the coming years;

VIII
Mobility

1. *Reaffirms* section V of its resolution 55/258, as well as the segment on mobility contained in section II

of its resolution 57/305, and notes its previous requests to the Secretary-General in this regard;

2. *Stresses*, in this regard, that when implementing mobility policies, the Secretary-General should ensure that:

(a) Mobility does not negatively affect the continuity and the quality of services and the institutional memory and capacity of the Organization;

(b) Mobility does not lead to the transfer or abolition of posts as a result of vacancies;

(c) Mobility has a positive impact in filling existing high vacancy rates at some United Nations duty stations and regional commissions;

(d) There is a clear differentiation between mobility within duty stations and mobility across duty stations and that the latter is a more important factor in career development;

(e) Mobility is encouraged for all posts in the Professional and higher categories;

3. *Notes* that the implementation of mobility policies, while recognizing their anticipated positive effects, may also give rise to problems and challenges that should be addressed;

4. *Requests* the Secretary-General to take the steps necessary to ensure that mobility is not used as an instrument of coercion against staff and to ensure that appropriate monitoring and accountability measures are in place;

5. *Notes* the measures to facilitate the implementation of mobility policies set out in paragraph 85 of the report of the Secretary-General, and requests the Secretary-General to develop a strategic plan with indicators, benchmarks, time lines and clear criteria for the implementation of mobility policies and to report thereon, including with information on the financial implications, to the General Assembly at its sixty-first session for its consideration and action in order to solve any problems;

6. *Requests* the Secretary-General to continue to consult with staff in the development of mobility policies;

7. *Requests* the International Civil Service Commission, within its mandate, to keep under review the question of mobility in the United Nations common system, including its implications for career development, and to make recommendations to the General Assembly, as appropriate, in the context of its annual reports;

8. *Requests* the Secretary-General to consider the use of incentives with a view to encouraging staff to move to duty stations with chronically high vacancy rates;

9. *Reiterates* section II, paragraph 51, of its resolution 57/305, in which the General Assembly encouraged the Secretary-General to expedite, as appropriate, agreements between the Secretariat and the United Nations funds and programmes and the specialized agencies for all staff levels in relation to mobility, and requests the Secretary-General to report thereon to the Assembly at its sixty-first session;

10. *Invites* host countries, as appropriate, to review their policies for granting work permits to spouses of United Nations staff;

11. *Invites* the Secretary-General to continue to explore ways of assisting spouses to find employment opportunities, in consultation with host Governments where necessary, including by taking measures to expedite the issuance of work permits;

12. *Acknowledges* that mobility needs to be supported through greater efforts to improve conditions of life and work at the various duty stations;

IX
Contractual arrangements

Takes note of the report of the Secretary-General on contractual arrangements, and decides to revert to the issue at its sixtieth session in the context of its consideration of the report of the International Civil Service Commission on contractual arrangements with a view to taking a decision;

X
Use of appointments under the 100 and 300 series of the Staff Rules in the staffing of field missions

1. *Decides* to continue to suspend the application of the four-year maximum limit for appointments of limited duration under the 300 series of the Staff Rules in peacekeeping operations until 30 June 2005;

2. *Authorizes* the Secretary-General, bearing in mind paragraph 1 above, to reappoint under the 100 series of the Staff Rules those mission staff whose service under 300-series contracts has reached the four-year limit by 31 December 2004 or later, pending a decision by the General Assembly, provided that their functions have been reviewed and found necessary and their performance has been confirmed as fully satisfactory, and requests him to report thereon to the General Assembly at the second part of its resumed fifty-ninth session;

3. *Requests* the Secretary-General to submit proposals for which functions are relevant for reappointment under the 100 series for consideration and action by the General Assembly at the second part of its resumed fifty-ninth session;

4. *Also requests* the Secretary-General to continue the practice of using 300 series contracts as the primary instrument for the appointment of new mission staff, pending a decision by the General Assembly on the report requested above;

5. *Requests* the International Civil Service Commission, as a matter of high priority, to review the contractual instruments available for the employment of common system staff in the field, including the practice of conversion to the 100 series from other contractual arrangements, and requests the Commission to present an analysis to the General Assembly at its sixty-first session of the desirability and feasibility of harmonizing conditions of service in the field, including at non-family duty stations, and to provide full details of the financial implications;

6. *Requests* the Secretary-General to submit to the General Assembly at its sixty-first session a comprehensive report with proposals for conditions of field service addressing, inter alia, the feasibility and desirability of conditions of service distinct to peacekeeping operations and the feasibility and desirability of harmonized conditions of field service in the United Nations;

7. *Recognizes* the authority of the Secretary-General to assign and deploy staff according to the operational needs of the Organization, and requests him to limit the assignment of staff, in particular General Service staff, from Headquarters and other established offices to field missions unless required by operational necessity or the unavailability of requisite skills in local labour markets;

XI
Consultants and individual contractors

1. *Endorses* the observations and recommendations of the Advisory Committee on Administrative and Budgetary Questions contained in paragraphs 59 to 61 of its report, and requests the Secretary-General to report to the General Assembly at its sixty-first session on the use of consultants and individual contractors, including actions taken to improve the monitoring capacity of the Office of Human Resources Management on this issue;

2. *Reaffirms* that consultants shall not perform functions of staff members of the Organization or have any representative or supervisory responsibility;

3. *Reiterates* that the Secretary-General should refrain from using consultants to carry out functions assigned to established posts and that consultants should be hired only in strict accordance with existing rules and relevant General Assembly resolutions and where expertise is not available within the Organization;

4. *Also reiterates* that in areas where consultants are frequently hired for a period of more than one year, the Secretary-General should submit proposals, where necessary, for the establishment of posts and should report thereon to the General Assembly at its sixty-first session;

XII
Employment of retired former staff

1. *Notes with concern* the increased use of retired former staff members in substantive areas and in decision-making positions;

2. *Also notes with concern* that the lack of proper succession planning has a negative impact on the rejuvenation of the Organization and on attaining core human resources targets;

3. *Endorses* the views expressed by the Advisory Committee on Administrative and Budgetary Questions in paragraphs 63 and 65 of its report;

4. *Reiterates its request* to the Secretary-General to ensure that the employment of retired former staff has no adverse effects on the career planning and mobility of other United Nations staff members;

5. *Requests* the Secretary-General to have recourse to the employment of retired former staff only if the operational requirements of the Organization cannot be met by existing staff;

6. *Stresses* that the hiring of retired former staff should be on an exceptional basis, and in this regard encourages the Secretary-General to fill vacant posts at senior and decision-making levels through the established staff selection process;

7. *Requests* the Secretary-General to report to the General Assembly at its sixty-first session on the use of retired former staff and to develop clear criteria for the selection of the retired former staff, in particular in the Professional category;

XIII
Study of availability of skills in local labour markets

Having considered the report of the Office of Internal Oversight Services on the availability in local labour markets of the skills for which international recruitment for General Service staff takes place,

1. *Requests* the Secretary-General to conduct a study on the availability of skills in local labour markets for which international recruitment for General Service

staff takes place and, drawing on the findings, to reassess the determination made in 1975 that recruitment from outside the area of the duty station is necessary to staff the text-processing units, bearing in mind the need for the highest standards of quality relevant to the language function, and to report to the General Assembly at its sixtieth session;

2. *Decides* to revert to its consideration of the issue and of the report of the Office of Internal Oversight Services at its sixtieth session in the context of its consideration of the report requested in paragraph 1 above;

XIV
Office of the United Nations High Commissioner for Human Rights

1. *Welcomes* the report of the Joint Inspection Unit on its management review of the Office of the United Nations High Commissioner for Human Rights, and notes the observations of the Secretary-General on the report and the actions of the Office to implement the recommendations of the Joint Inspection Unit;

2. *Emphasizes* that recruitment in the Office of the United Nations High Commissioner for Human Rights should be done in full consultation with and under the guidance of the Office of Human Resources Management, consistent with the provisions of the present resolution and other relevant legislative mandates;

3. *Notes* that the Joint Inspection Unit will submit a follow-up report on this issue to the General Assembly at its sixty-first session for consideration under relevant agenda items;

XV
Measures to prevent discrimination

1. *Takes note* of the report of the Secretary-General on measures to prevent discrimination on the basis of nationality, race, gender, religion or language in the United Nations, and requests him to develop further measures, as necessary, in cooperation with the Office of Internal Oversight Services and the Joint Inspection Unit, to prevent such discrimination, in accordance with the principles of the Charter and the provisions of the Staff Regulations and Rules of the United Nations, and to report thereon to the General Assembly at its sixty-first session;

2. *Decides* to revert to the consideration of the report of the Secretary-General in the context of the agenda item entitled "Administration of justice at the United Nations" during the first part of its resumed fifty-ninth session;

XVI
Staff-management consultations

1. *Takes note* of the views expressed by staff representatives in the Fifth Committee, stresses the importance of a meaningful dialogue on human resources management issues between staff and management, and calls upon both parties to intensify efforts to overcome differences and to resume the consultative process;

2. *Reiterates its requests* that the Secretary-General take into account the views of staff representatives, in accordance with article VIII of the Staff Regulations and Rules and resolution 35/213 of 17 December 1980;

XVII
Other matters

1. *Stresses* that all administrative issuances of the Secretary-General related to the implementation of resolutions and decisions of the General Assembly shall be in full compliance with such resolutions and decisions and shall be reported to the Assembly in conformity with the established regulations, rules and procedures;

2. *Reaffirms* that, in accordance with staff regulation 1.2, staff members shall not be actively associated with the management of, or hold a financial interest in, any profit-making, business or other concern if it were possible for the staff member or the profit-making, business or other concern to benefit from such association or financial interest by reason of his or her position with the United Nations;

XVIII
Reporting

Requests the Secretary-General to submit to the General Assembly for consideration at its sixty-first session consolidated reports, as appropriate, on the results of the implementation of the present resolution.

On 23 December, the Assembly decided that the agenda item on human resources management would remain for consideration during its resumed fifty-ninth (2005) session (**decision 59/552**).

Pay and benefits system

ICSC, in its ongoing review of the UN pay and benefits system, reviewed the status of the pilot study on broadbanding and pay-for-performance, decided on in 2003 [YUN 2003, p. 1445]. It agreed that the study should commence on 1 July 2004 for a three-year period, and include four volunteer bodies (the World Food Programme, the International Fund for Agricultural Development, the Joint United Nations Programme on HIV/AIDS, and the United Nations Development Programme). It later agreed to include the United Nations Educational, Scientific and Cultural Organization's International Centre for Theoretical Physics as of 1 July 2005.

ICSC commenced its comprehensive review of the allowances and benefits payable in the UN common system, with a review of the education grant, and the mobility and hardship scheme. The Commission noted that since several of the allowances and benefits were linked, it would prefer to look at those together, and decided on a schedule for considering the allowances and benefits in related groupings.

Regarding the implications of the enlargement of the European Union (EU) on the operation of the mobility and hardship scheme and on the post adjustment system, ICSC decided that, for post adjustment purposes, the 10 countries joining the EU on 1 May 2004 (Cyprus, Czech Re-public, Estonia, Hungary, Latvia, Lithuania, Malta, Poland, Slovakia and Slovenia) should be considered as Group I duty stations, starting with the implementation of new place-to-place surveys; those surveys should be conducted in 2004 for all 10 countries; organizations should start paying salaries for staff in the Professional and higher categories in local currencies, starting with the implementation of new place-to-place surveys for respective duty stations; a modification of the rental subsidy scheme corresponding to Group I duty stations should be introduced at the time of the implementation of new place-to-place surveys; the change from "A" to "H" in the classification of those duty stations under the mobility and hardship scheme should be applied with effect from 1 January 2005.

Contractual arrangements

ICSC consideration. As requested by ICSC [YUN 2003, p. 1445], its secretariat submitted a model for three contractual categories (continuing appointments, fixed-term appointments and temporary appointments) proposed in 2003 [ibid.], among the ever increasing types of contracts used in UN system organizations, including details on conditions of employment such as: duration of tenure; mobility requirements; probationary period; procedures for progression to other contract types; the compensation package; social security and health insurance provisions; and conditions for extension and/or termination.

ICSC, noting that significant progress had been made in categorizing contracts across organizations, decided to report to the General Assembly that there was a model within which to apply some definition to the varying contractual arrangements across the UN common system. It requested its secretariat to refine the model and to provide a revised version, as well as information on the distribution of all staff in the organizations by contractual category to ICSC, and a final report to the Assembly, all in 2005.

Report of Secretary-General. In accordance with Assembly resolution 57/305 [YUN 2003, p. 1440], the Secretary-General submitted, in September [A/59/263/Add.1], definitive proposals on new contractual arrangements for simplifying the existing system through the use of only three types of appointments for all Secretariat functions, departments, duty stations and field missions: a short-term appointment, up to a maximum of six months, for staff appointed to meet seasonal or peak workloads and specific short-term requirements; a fixed-term appointment, which could be renewed or extended to cover a maximum period of five years and during which time, staff members' performance and competencies would be thoroughly assessed; and a continuing appointment which, subject to the needs of service, would be granted to staff members who had served on fixed terms for five years, provided they had demonstrated adherence to the highest standards of efficiency, competence and integrity required by the UN Charter. Annex II to the report contained proposed amendments to the Staff Regulations and to the 100 series of the Staff Rules that would be necessary to implement the proposal.

The Secretary-General stated that the replacement of permanent appointments by continuing appointments would allow greater weight to be given to the needs of the Organization when an appointment was terminated, greatly assist the Secretary-General in his determination to enhance staff mobility, which was a major goal of his reform of human resources management, and remove the perception that there was a privileged group of staff in the Organization. Conversion to continuing appointment after five years of service on fixed-term appointments with the Organization, subject to performance and the continued needs of the service, would also be in the interest of the staff at large as it would ensure equal treatment.

To protect the acquired rights of staff in service at the time the amended regulations and rules came into force, there would be no change to the contractual status of staff with a permanent appointment, and those already serving on a probationary appointment would retain the right to a permanent appointment at the end of their probationary period. No new probationary appointment would be given after the effective date of the amended regulations and rules, and there would be a one-time review of staff members appointed under the 100 series of the Staff Rules for consideration of conversion of their contracts to permanent appointment. In order for the contracts to be converted, staff members would have to meet certain conditions, such as five years of continuous service on fixed-term appointments and outstanding performance.

The Secretary-General invited the Assembly to approve the proposal and the proposed amendments to the Staff Regulations contained in annex II to his report, and to take note of the proposed amendments to the 100 series of the Staff Rules also contained in annex II.

ACABQ report. ACABQ, in October [A/59/446], said that, should the Assembly approve those changes, care should be taken to handle the interim arrangements in an equitable and sensitive manner, with measures in place to ensure the application of objective criteria in considering con-

versions of probationary and fixed-term contracts into permanent appointments for eligible staff. The Committee welcomed the intention of the Secretariat to ensure that all options for placing staff would be considered carefully before termination was decided upon.

Measures to improve mobility

The Secretary-General, in his August report on progress in implementing human resources management reform in the United Nations [A/59/263], stated that the mobility policy, applied to all staff from G-5 to D-2, had been established as an integral part of the staff selection system. It set limits to post occupancy, as at 1 May 2002, of either five years up to the P-5 level or six above that level, and established minimum post occupancy of two years, or one year after a prior lateral move. The new policy linked mobility to career development, requiring two lateral moves before promotion to the P-5 level. All staff recruited at the P-2 level were required to serve in two different functions within their first five years of service. Over 100 staff at that level had moved successfully through the two mandatory managed reassignment exercises and five voluntary exercises held to date. An implementation plan leading up to the time of the first expiration of post occupancy limits in 2007 or 2008 was developed, which envisaged several pilot voluntary managed reassignment exercises prior to 2007. Starting in May 2007, mandatory managed reassignment exercises would be conducted to facilitate lateral moves of staff whose post occupancy deadlines had expired. There was clearly some resistance to the idea on the part of some staff and managers, but changing a culture and a mindset could only happen over time, and the experience with staff at the P-2 level was encouraging. Measures were being taken to inform and support staff and to ensure the maintenance of continuity, quality of service and institutional memory, through the implementation of knowledge management practices.

ACABQ, in its October report [A/59/446], requested the Secretary-General to pursue the development and implementation of the managed reassignment programmes for entry level and other staff and to budget the required posts accordingly. In his next report on human resources management, he should report on the concerns raised by the Assembly in resolutions 51/226, 53/221 [YUN 1999, p. 1324], 55/258 [YUN 2001, p. 1337] and 57/305 [YUN 2003, p. 1440], and address the financial implications of the reassignment programme. In particular, ACABQ pointed to the need to ensure that mobility would not be used as an instrument of coercion against staff, to recognize the difference between movement within a duty station and mobility across duty stations, and to ensure that lateral mobility would not negatively affect the continuity and quality of the services required for the implementation of mandated programmes and activities. The Committee also reiterated its view that staff members requested by the Organization to remain on mission assignment, whatever the period of time, should be guaranteed the ability to return to a job in their occupational network and duty station.

HLCM, at its seventh session (London, 8-9 March) [CEB/2004/3], considered measures to improve system-wide mobility, including the progress report on inter-agency mobility of the Working Group on Mobility. It requested the CEB secretariat, through a questionnaire-based exercise, to determine the baseline for organizations to increase or facilitate inter-agency mobility and to present its findings, in the form of a matrix, at its fall session.

At its eighth session (Rome, 5-6 October) [CEB/2004/6], HLCM approved the inter-agency mobility accord presented by the Food and Agriculture Organization of the United Nations (FAO) on behalf of the Working Group on Mobility and requested the CEB secretariat, in consultation with the Human Resources Network, to refine it and ensure its timely finalization. HLCM also considered the results of the questionnaire-based exercise it had requested in March. Noting that interorganizational mobility remained limited, HLCM encouraged organizations to promote it through suitable policies, practices and systems. It requested that thet CEB secretariat undertake a follow-up survey to the baseline in early 2007.

Family status

CEB consideration. HLCM, at its seventh session (London, 8-9 March) [CEB/2004/3], reached general agreement on principles with respect to the recognition of marriage and domestic partnerships, as part of the measures to improve mobility (see above). Those included: family status for the purpose of entitlements determined by reference to the law of nationality of the staff member concerned; a marriage recognized as valid under the law of the country of nationality of a staff member would qualify that staff member to receive the entitlements provided for eligible family members; and a legally recognized domestic partnership contracted by a staff member under the laws of the country of his or her nationality would qualify the staff member to receive the entitlements provided for eligible family members. Each organization would implement the principles, having regard to its own circumstances and requirements. Organizations

would also share information, through the High Level Committee on Management Human Resources Network, on the issue. HLCM requested CEB's secretariat to consult with the United Nations Joint Staff Pension Fund secretariat on the implementation of that policy by the Fund.

CEB, at its first regular session for 2004 (Vienna, 2-3 April) [CEB/2004/1], noted the general principles on domestic partnerships submitted by HLCM, and requested the Committee to inform it in 2005 on developments in that regard, including the decision to be adopted by the General Assembly (see below), relevant outcomes of agency governing bodies, the experience of organizations applying the policy, and other implications.

Secretary-General's bulletin. The Assembly, at its resumed fifty-eighth session in April, had before it a bulletin by the Secretary-General on family status for purposes of United Nations entitlements [ST/SGB/2004/4]. Some Member States expressed concern with paragraph 4 of the bulletin, which noted that a legally recognized domestic partnership contracted by a staff member under the law of the country of his or her nationality would also qualify that staff member to receive the entitlements provided for eligible family members.

GENERAL ASSEMBLY ACTION

On 8 April [meeting 83], the General Assembly, on the recommendation of the Fifth Committee [A/58/750], adopted **resolution 58/285** without vote [agenda item 127].

Human resources management

The General Assembly,

Reaffirming the Charter of the United Nations, in particular Articles 101 and 97,

Reaffirming also the Staff Regulations and Rules of the United Nations,

Reaffirming further the prerogative of Member States to supplement or amend the Staff Regulations, in accordance with regulation 12.1,

Reaffirming that the Secretary-General, as the Chief Administrative Officer of the Organization, shall provide and enforce staff rules consistent with the broad principles of personnel policy for the staffing and administration of the Secretariat,

Reaffirming also that all provisional rules and/or amendments to the Staff Rules should be consistent with the intent and purposes of the Staff Regulations and should be reported to the General Assembly in accordance with regulation 12.3,

1. *Notes* the practice in the Organization of determining personal status for the purpose of entitlements as are set out in the Staff Regulations and Rules of the United Nations by reference to the law of nationality of the staff member concerned;

2. *Invites* the Secretary-General to reissue Secretary-General's bulletin ST/SGB/2004/4 after re-

viewing its contents, taking into account the views and concerns expressed by Member States thereon;

3. *Notes* the absence of the terms referred to in paragraph 4 of the bulletin in the context of the existing Staff Regulations and Rules, and decides that the inclusion of those terms shall require the consideration of and necessary action by the General Assembly.

Staff composition

In an August annual report on the UN Secretariat's staff composition [A/59/299], the Secretary-General updated information on the demographic characteristics of the Secretariat's staff and on the system of desirable ranges for geographical distribution. As at 30 June 2004, Secretariat staff numbered 14,823, some 259 less than at 30 June 2003. Of that total, 5,325 were in the Professional and higher categories, 8,623 were in the General Service and related categories and 875 were project personnel; 7,602 were paid from the regular budget and 7,221 from extrabudgetary sources. Staff in posts subject to geographical distribution numbered 2,515, of whom 1,063 (42.3 per cent) were female. Fifteen Member States were unrepresented in all staff categories, while 10 were underrepresented, compared to 17 and 10, respectively, in 2003. Appointments to posts subject to geographical distribution between 1 July 2003 and 30 June 2004 totalled 208. Of those, 12 (5.8 per cent) were nationals of underrepresented Member States, 136 (65.4 per cent) of within-range Member States, and 60 (28.8 per cent) of overrepresented Member States. Changes in representation status resulted from appointments or separation from service, adjustments to desirable ranges, owing to an increase or decrease in the number of posts subject to geographical distribution, changes in the number of Member States, scale of assessments, population of Member States and status of individual staff members.

The report also gave information on the demographic profile of Secretariat staff, staff movement from 1 July 2003 to 30 June 2004, and forecasts of anticipated retirements between 2004 and 2008.

Equitable geographical representation

Report of Secretary-General. In response to General Assembly resolutions 57/305 [YUN 2003, p. 1440] and 58/270 [YUN 2003, p. 1399], the Secretary-General submitted an August report [A/59/264] on progress made in the recruitment of nationals of unrepresented and underrepresented Member States from June 1994 to June 2004. The number of unrepresented Member States declined from 28 in 1994, to 15 in 2004, while the number of underrepresented Member

States decreased from 25 in 1994 to 10 in 2004. However, of the 28 unrepresented Member States in June 1994, five continued to be unrepresented (Brunei Darussalam, Marshall Islands, Monaco, Sao Tome and Principe and Turkmenistan), and of the 25 underrepresented Member States in June 1994, three were currently still underrepresented (Japan, Norway and Saudi Arabia). For posts subject to geographical distribution, on average, 22 per cent, or more than one of every five recruitments, had been from an unrepresented or underrepresented Member State. Of the 534 successful national competitive examination candidates recruited over the past 10 years, 141 were from those States, reflecting a significant increase in both the number of Member States participating in the examination and in the number of candidates convoked to sit it. The OHRM human resources action plans, which included targets for the improvement of equitable geographical representation, had also contributed to the improved situation. To further improve representation, the Secretariat proposed the introduction of a fast-track recruitment procedure for candidates from unrepresented and underrepresented Member States to posts at the P-4 level and above in line with the overall principles and procedures of the staff selection system. The procedure would include targeted recruitment campaigns in partnership with departments and concerned Member States. OHRM proposed that relevant permanent missions should identify focal points with which the Secretariat would work on increasing their representation. A focal point was being established in OHRM for the systematic development and implementation of strategies to pursue the recruitment of candidates from unrepresented and underrepresented Member States at the P-5 level.

ACABQ report. In October [A/59/446], ACABQ expressed the hope that the measures that were being taken to improve equitable geographical representation would be pursued vigorously and would have concrete results.

Status of women

ICSC consideration. Under its standing mandate to review the status of women in the organizations of the common system, ICSC, at its fifty-ninth session [A/59/30 (Vol. I)], reviewed a statistical report submitted by its secretariat on gender balance at all levels in the common system organizations, including with regard to ungraded officials. ICSC expressed disappointment that the rate in the advancement of women had slowed over the years and that only limited progress had been made. It requested its secretariat to report on further progress in 2006, including information on the representation of women by region and on organizations' gender plans and their development, implementation and effectiveness.

Reports of Secretary-General. In response to General Assembly resolution 57/305 [YUN 2003, p. 1440], the Secretary-General submitted a September report [A/59/263/Add.2] on improving gender distribution in the UN Secretariat. The report complemented the Secretary-General's report on the improvement of the status of women in the UN system (see below). As at 30 June 2004, women comprised 37.4 per cent of staff in the Professional and higher categories with appointments of one year or more, a 1.7 per cent increase over the previous year, and the highest annual change since 1998. They also accounted for 42.5 per cent of recruitments into the Professional category between 1 July 2003 and 30 June 2004, with 37.7 per cent at the Director level; and 47.2 per cent of promotions, with 47.5 per cent at the Director level. The goal of gender parity had been achieved at the junior Professional level and in the General Service category. As at 30 June 2004, 50.8 per cent of staff at the P-2 level were women and 62.1 per cent in the General Service category. The Secretary-General was committed to ensuring that the progress achieved would not be eroded by the separation from the Organization of women staff members, particularly in the next five years (2004-2008), when, 1,689 staff members of the current work force (14.6 per cent), or one of every three retirements in the Professional and higher categories (697) and more than one of every two in the General Service and related categories (992) would be a female staff member. That would be an opportune time to increase recruitment of women candidates.

Efforts to improve gender distribution had focused on increasing the number of women recruited, promoted and placed; raising gender sensitivity among programme managers and the staff at large; providing appropriate work/life policies to attract and retain staff, particularly women; enhancing career development opportunities for all staff; and establishing mechanisms to monitor progress towards the achievement of the gender parity goal. Several key initiatives introduced under the current human resources management reform programme contained features or provisions that sought to contribute to the improvement of gender distribution, including the human resources action plans, the staff selection system, work/life policies, performance management, career development programmes and gender sensitivity training. Human resources action plans, established jointly by heads of departments and offices and the Assistant Secretary-General for Human Resources Management, contained specific targets, such as the selection of women for at least 50 per cent of vacancies resulting from retirements, new posts, and posts vacated for other reasons, in order to reach gender balance in all categories of staff. Twenty departments or offices had met that target in the 2001-2002 biennium, and in the 2003-2004 biennium, those departments and offices that had not achieved gender parity were to reach and maintain an average annual increase of at least 2 per cent for female staff in the Professional and higher categories.

However, several factors had affected progress towards the achievement of the 50/50 gender goal, such as the need for: strengthened accountability for achieving gender balance; better forecasting of future workforce needs, including completion of a skills inventory to identify women with leadership potential, and for succession planning; better coordination in policy implementation among stakeholders; specific support strategies for departments facing problems in meeting their gender targets, for more targeting of women, especially for senior-level posts and for occupational groups where women were chronically underrepresented; better online monitoring tools to provide heads of departments and offices with timely information; and the limited advancement opportunity for the internal pool of qualified women in the General Service and related categories.

Specific actions to improve gender distribution focused on accountability, human resources planning, policy implementation and review, specific support to departments and offices, an expanded pool of qualified women candidates and online monitoring tools.

In response to General Assembly resolution 58/144 [YUN 2003, p. 1449], the Secretary-General submitted a September report [A/59/357] on the improvement of the status of women in the UN system. He noted that at the senior policy-making levels (D-1 level and above), the representation of women increased by 3.1 per cent from 33.3 to 36.4 per cent, with the largest increases at the Assistant Secretary-General (from 23.5 to 29.4 per cent) and D-1 levels (from 36.3 to 39.4 per cent). At the Under-Secretary-General level, the proportion of women increased from 20.8 to 22.7 per cent and at the D-2 level, from 31.2 to 33.86 per cent. At the P-1 to P-5 levels, the proportion of women comprised 43.2 per cent, with the only increase, from 37.2 to 39.5 per cent, at the P-4 level. All other levels showed negative growth.

The Secretary-General concluded that the overall representation of women still fell short of a 50/50 gender balance, and projections were that the attainment of gender balance would remain a challenge. Despite the significant gains achieved to attain gender balance systemwide, UN entities, including the Secretariat, had a long way to go to effectively integrate gender balance considerations into institutional and attitudinal systems and human resources management policies of the Organization.

The report also presented the analysis carried out by the Office of the Special Adviser on Gender Issues and Advancement of Women on the causes of the slow progress in the improvement of the status of women in the Secretariat, which revealed that gender imbalance was a multidimensional and systemic problem which required a systemic and integrated response. As candidates for recruitment, women were discriminated against by unfavourable external factors and within the Organization, by recruitment strategies, promotion and retention policies, career development, justice and anti-harassment policies, human resources and succession planning, work/family policies, management culture and mechanisms for accountability needed to be reviewed to ensure that they did not directly or indirectly disadvantage women. Legislative bodies had not effectively addressed the problem of the disproportionately small number of women entering the UN system. At the entry level, the current staffing system was neither proactive nor targeted enough and relied too much on web-based vacancy announcements. Also, there was no accountability, particularly at the level of programme managers, for gender balance. Improved transparency and monitoring were also required. In that context, the new terms of reference of the departmental focal points were expected to include full access to data for purposes of regular monitoring of gender balance status, access to and regular consultations with programme managers and heads of departments or offices on human resources action plans and gender targets, and giving advice on the selection of women candidates.

The report identified several problems related to the retention of women, especially in the General Service category. Progression for that category of staff was severely restricted, owing to the need to pass the General to Professional (G-P) examination and the fact that only 10 per cent of vacant P-2 posts were allotted to them. The report revealed mismatches between formal and informal systems of selection and career development. Another key component of career progression was the impact of the working climate and culture. The report noted that the objective of introducing work/life policies to attract and retain

quality staff, especially women, had not yet impacted the current managerial culture within the Secretariat, which continued to view those policies as a barrier to efficiency and productivity and as incompatible with career advancement and the performance of managerial level posts.

The Secretariat's gender balance system needed to be enhanced by special measures adapted to the current staff selection system and by clearly defined organizational responsibilities for gender balance at all levels throughout the Secretariat. The Secretary-General remained firmly committed to reaching the goal of 50/50 gender balance at all levels and in all categories of posts and would ensure that heads of departments and offices and central monitoring offices intensified efforts and strengthened measures towards that end.

GENERAL ASSEMBLY ACTION

On 20 December [meeting 74], the General Assembly, on the recommendation of the Third (Social, Humanitarian and Cultural) Committee [A/59/496], adopted **resolution 59/164** without vote [agenda item 98].

Improvement of the status of women in the United Nations system

The General Assembly,

Recalling Articles 1 and 101 of the Charter of the United Nations, as well as Article 8, which provides that the United Nations shall place no restrictions on the eligibility of men and women to participate in any capacity and under conditions of equality in its principal and subsidiary organs,

Recalling also the goal, contained in the Platform for Action adopted by the Fourth World Conference on Women, of achieving overall gender equality, particularly at the Professional level and above, by 2000 and the further actions and initiatives set out in the outcome document adopted by the General Assembly at its twenty-third special session, entitled "Women 2000: gender equality, development and peace for the twenty-first century",

1. *Takes note with appreciation* of the report of the Secretary-General;

2. *Welcomes:*

(a) The commitment of the Secretary-General to meeting the goal of gender equality and his assurance that gender balance will be given the highest priority in his continuing efforts to bring about a new management culture in the Organization;

(b) The new initiatives and strategies undertaken system-wide and at the Secretariat level to achieve gender balance, including paying special attention to the identification of suitably qualified women candidates, strengthening of recruitment sources for women, development of recruitment strategies in substantive areas, enhancing women's career development, fostering attitudinal changes and introducing family-friendly policies;

(c) The increase in the proportion of women in the Professional and higher categories of staff with appointments of one year or more;

3. *Regrets* that the goal of 50/50 gender distribution has not been met and that overall progress in achieving this goal remains limited;

4. *Notes with concern* the continuing lack of representation of women at higher levels of decision-making, especially at the Under-Secretary-General level;

5. *Notes with particular concern* that gender balance considerations have yet to be effectively integrated throughout the human resources management policies of the United Nations;

6. *Reaffirms* the urgent goal of achieving 50/50 gender distribution in all categories of posts within the United Nations system, especially at senior and policy-making levels, with full respect for the principle of equitable geographical distribution, in conformity with Article 101, paragraph 3, of the Charter of the United Nations;

7. *Stresses* the need to address the continuing lack of representation or underrepresentation of women from certain countries, in particular from developing and least developed countries, from countries with economies in transition and from unrepresented or largely underrepresented Member States;

8. *Reaffirms* the need to continue to develop innovative recruitment strategies to identify and attract suitably qualified women candidates, in particular from, and in, developing and least developed countries and countries with economies in transition and other Member States that are unrepresented or underrepresented in the Secretariat;

9. *Reaffirms also* its resolution 58/144 of 22 December 2003, and requests increased and sustained efforts towards its full implementation;

10. *Requests* the Secretary-General and the executive heads of the organizations of the United Nations system to ensure that recruitment strategies, promotion and retention policies, career development, justice, anti-harassment and sexual harassment policies, human resources and succession planning, work/family policies, management culture and mechanisms for managerial accountability accelerate the goal of 50/50 gender distribution;

11. *Urges* the Secretary-General and the executive heads of the organizations of the United Nations system to redouble their efforts to realize significant progress towards the goal of 50/50 gender distribution in the very near future;

12. *Requests* the Secretary-General to enable the Office of the Special Adviser on Gender Issues and Advancement of Women to effectively contribute to, monitor and facilitate the setting and achievement of gender targets in human resource action plans, including by ensuring access to the information required to carry out that work;

13. *Strongly encourages* Member States to support the efforts of the United Nations and the specialized agencies, funds and programmes to achieve the goal of 50/50 gender distribution, especially at senior and policy-making levels, by identifying and regularly submitting more women candidates for appointment to positions in the United Nations system, by identifying and proposing national recruitment sources in cooperation with national women's machineries and pro-

fessional organization networks and by encouraging more women to apply for positions within the Secretariat, the specialized agencies, funds and programmes and the regional commissions, including in areas in which women are underrepresented, such as peacekeeping, peacebuilding and other non-traditional areas;

14. *Requests* the Secretary-General to provide an oral report to the Commission on the Status of Women at its forty-ninth and fiftieth sessions and to report to the General Assembly at its sixty-first session on the implementation of the present resolution, including by providing up-to-date statistics on all levels of the United Nations system.

Study of availability of skills in local labour markets

OIOS report. In response to General Assembly resolution 58/270 [YUN 2003, p. 1399], the Secretary-General transmitted a September OIOS report [A/59/388] on the availability in local labour markets, of the skills for which international recruitment for the General Service category took place. The Secretariat currently employed 6,761 staff in the General Service category, 304 of whom received international benefits. Of those receiving benefits, two-thirds were language staff working in the Department for General Assembly and Conference Management (DGACM), in New York and Geneva. OIOS assessed the granting of those benefits to staff in the General Service category throughout the Organization, which cost an estimated $9.25 million per biennium. The study also reviewed the rules governing local recruitment and its consequences, especially for DGACM's Text Processing Section in New York.

OIOS found that the determination regarding the absence of skills in the local labour market at Headquarters was not based on sufficient or up-to-date evidence about the characteristics of that market. Data indicated that the local labour market might have the skills required to fill posts expected to become vacant in the Arabic, Chinese, French, Spanish and Russian Text Processing Units. A definitive determination as to whether that was so should only be made on the basis of an examination for all four categories of skills required of editorial clerks/assistants, in addition to a systematic, aggressive outreach effort in the New York labour market. The United Nations Office at Geneva conducted such an outreach campaign and concluded that candidates with sufficient skills were available and, therefore, recruited staff in the General Service category for the Text Processing Units locally.

OIOS recommended that the Organization change the basis of recruitment for the General Service category to grant international status only to those recruited from outside the area of the duty station; require documentation to determine whether the local labour market contained the skills required in anticipation of vacancies; specify that staff members be regarded as locally recruited if recruited within the vicinity or country of the duty station; and amend Appendix B to the Staff Rules to clarify that payment of international benefits was subject to the determination that a particular post had been filled by international recruitment and/or could not be filled through local recruitment and discontinue such payment if the staff member moved to a post that could be filled locally. OHRM should pursue proactive recruitment strategies in New York, document the outcome of enhanced recruitment efforts for the Text Processing Units at Headquarters, ensure that adequate resources were provided for testing and create a trainee programme and short-term contract opportunities to develop a pool of eligible local candidates, especially in New York.

Consultants and individual contractors

Report of Secretary-General. In response to General Assembly 57/305 [YUN 2003, p. 1440] and 53/221 [YUN 1999, p. 1324], the Secretary-General, in August [A/59/217], submitted a biennial report on the use of consultants and individual contractors during 2002 and 2003. The report included statistics on the number of persons hired, the number and type of contracts awarded, the number of days worked, the total fees paid, the nationality of the persons hired, the purpose of engagement, occupational groups recruited, the duration of contracts, time actually worked, hiring departments, gender, level of education, performance evaluation, funding source and aggregate data for each duty station.

In 2002, a total of 3,307 consultants and 1,443 individual contractors were hired, accounting for 4,381 and 2,902 contracts, respectively, while in 2003, 3,543 consultants and 1,401 individual contractors were engaged under 4,693 and 2,652 contracts respectively. Overall, during the biennium, the number of consultants engaged increased by 243, or 7.1 per cent, compared to 2001, and individual contractors by 147, or 3.1 per cent. The average duration of all contracts was shorter, and the average individual cost of a consultant went down, whereas the cost of an individual contractor went up slightly. Fees for both categories amounted to $52 million in 2002 and $47.1 million in 2003, a total increase of 0.3 per cent, as compared to 2001. Of the 163 countries from which consultants were hired in 2002, 19 accounted for 57 per cent of all persons engaged, while individual contractors came from 108

countries, 11 of which accounted for 67 per cent of all engagements. In 2003, consultants were hired from 167 countries, with 19 of them accounting for 54 per cent of all consultations, and individual contractors from 114 countries, of which 11 accounted for 60 per cent of all engagements. Female representation increased, in the case of consultants to 29.7 per cent and of individual contractors to 54.8 per cent. Consultants and individual contractors were used mainly for advisory services, programme implementation, special analytical studies and the preparation of meetings, working as professionals, managers or technicians, and as economists and in technical cooperation related areas.

ACABQ report. In October [A/59/446], ACABQ found the information of limited value. It requested OHRM to broaden the scope of the report in the future to include more analysis and to assess the compliance of practice in the hiring of experts and consultants with existing rules and regulations. It also requested OHRM to complete the staff skills inventory expeditiously.

Employment of retirees

Report of Secretary-General. Pursuant to General Assembly resolution 57/305 and decision 51/408 [YUN 1996, p. 1329], the Secretary-General submitted an August report on the use of retired personnel, covering the 2002-2003 biennium [A/59/222]. The report provided statistical data on the use of persons who retired after ages 60 or 62, excluding those engaged by the United Nations Joint Staff Pension Fund, by the number of retirees engaged, the type and category of engagement, the departments and offices involved, and the retirees' nationality, gender, functions, age group, days worked and fees or salaries paid.

During 2002-2003, 620 retired staff were engaged by the Organization, a 65 per cent increase over the 2000-2001 biennium. The number of days worked increased by 99 per cent, as did the cost, from $10.5 million in 2000-2001 to $26.9 million in 2002-2003, an increase of 156 per cent. A total of 42 per cent of the engagements were in the Professional and higher categories and 25 per cent in the Field Service and General Service and related categories. Some 32 per cent of the engagements were by special service agreement, covering both consultants and individual contractors, and 54 per cent were on a short-term basis. The overall trend was an increase along all parameters (number engaged, days worked and fees) since 1998: 81 per cent more engagements, 86 per cent more days worked and a 162 per cent increase in cost.

The increases during the 2002-2003 biennium were due to an increase in the number of meetings and required documentation at major duty stations at a time when there was a simultaneous increase in the number of retirements, necessitating the hiring of retirees with specialized skills, such as translators, interpreters and editors, for limited periods, while the regular staff selection process was under way. There were also major increases in peacekeeping and humanitarian activities in the field, which required rapid reinforcement of backstopping capacity in the relevant departments. In both cases, the use of retirees was considered to be the most cost-effective way to meet short-term operational needs.

The three main groups of functions for which retired former staff were engaged in 2002-2003 were: language services (35 per cent), in particular revisers and interpreters; administrative functions (26 per cent); and political, economic, social, environmental, humanitarian, advisory and technical assistance functions (23 per cent).

ACABQ report. In October [A/59/446], ACABQ cautioned that the hiring of retirees to meet immediate organizational requirements did not obviate the need for proper succession planning. Progress in the streamlining of the staff selection process should also have an impact on the need for retirees. It recommended that greater efforts be made to hire qualified and skilled young persons to carry out functions for which the Secretariat was using retired staff. That might mean re-evaluating the levels of posts vacated by retirees prior to initiating recruitment procedures.

Discrimination

Pursuant to Assembly resolution 57/305 [YUN 2003, p. 1440], the Secretary-General submitted an August report, prepared in cooperation with OIOS and JIU, on measures to prevent discrimination on the basis of nationality, race, gender, religion or language in the United Nations [A/59/211]. The Secretary-General outlined the measures he had initiated to prevent or correct discrimination, or to create an environment free of discrimination. Those measures included: the definition of organizational core values and core and managerial competencies to build organizational capacity and promote shared values and common standards; issuance of a circular recalling that the core values of the Organization prohibited discrimination and harassment; the launching of an organizational integrity initiative; the establishment of monitoring and accountability mechanisms in the recruitment, promotion and placement processes; the enhancement of multilingualism, which minimized the likelihood of discrimination based on linguistic differences;

the issuance of clear guidance for conflict resolution and complaint mechanisms, which included the establishment of the Office of the Ombudsman, panels on discrimination and other grievances, and revision of procedures to address all forms of discrimination and harassment.

Protection from sexual exploitation and sexual abuse

Report of Secretary-General. In response to General Assembly resolution 57/306 [YUN 2003, p. 1237], the Secretary-General submitted an April report [A/58/777], containing information on the responses by 48 UN entities to the Secretariat's query regarding investigations into cases of sexual exploitation or sexual abuse. In 2003, forty-two entities reported that they had received no reports of sexual exploitation or abuse, and six reported the opening of investigations into newly reported cases. DPKO reported 24 new cases, and in two of the five cases where the alleged perpetrators were civilian personnel, serious misconduct was found to have occurred and appropriate disciplinary action taken. Of the 19 cases in which military personnel were allegedly involved, investigations revealed serious misconduct in eight. The Office for the Coordination of Humanitarian Affairs reported one case, which had been closed. The Office of the United Nations High Commissioner for Refugees reported 24 new cases, of which 22 had been closed and 2 remained under investigation. The United Nations Relief and Works Agency for Palestine Refugees in the Near East reported 2 cases; one was closed and the other was under investigation. The United Nations Children's Fund and the World Food Programme reported one case each, both of which were under investigation.

The Secretariat was aware that the data gathered might not reflect the true extent of those incidents, and complaint procedures and victim support mechanisms were not yet adequate. In many cases, victims were reportedly too frightened or ashamed to lodge a complaint, and once reported, some victims failed to provide evidence during the investigation phase due to confusion or intimidation. In addition, staff members might not yet be fully aware of the responsibilities placed on them by the Secretary-General's October 2003 bulletin [ST/SGB/2003/13] on special measures for protection from sexual exploitation and sexual abuse.

Additional efforts were required to establish a system within which misconduct of that kind was systematically reported and effectively followed up, while safeguarding the rights of the victims. Measures were put in place in 2004 to help improve the situation, including enhanced sensitization on the issue for managers and staff, particularly those in the field, and the development of tools and guidelines for the appropriate handling of complaints of sexual exploitation and abuse. The Inter-Agency Standing Committee Task Force on Protection from Sexual Exploitation and Abuse in Humanitarian Crises completed guidelines designed to assist with implementation of the measures outlined in the Secretary-General's bulletin. The Task Force also finalized model complaints procedures and investigative protocols.

On 18 June, the Assembly took note of the Secretary-General's report (**decision 58/568**).

Multilingualism

The Secretary-General transmitted to the Assembly his comments and those of CEB [A/58/93/Add.1] on the 2003 JIU report on the implementation of multilingualism in the UN system [YUN 2003, p. 1451]. CEB members generally concurred with the findings and conclusions of the report. Regarding the capabilities to provide language services, they said that system organizations were not quite as competitive as they could be in view of the prevailing salary conditions, and observed that considerable difficulty was still being encountered in the recruitment and retention of staff with the necessary language skills.

The General Assembly, on 5 August, at the request of France [A/58/862], on behalf of the States members of the Intergovernmental Agency of La Francophonie, decided to defer consideration of the item on multilingualism and to include it in the draft agenda of its fifty-ninth (2004) session, on the understanding that the biennial character of the item would not be called into question and the item would be considered next at the sixty-first (2006) session (**decision 58/571**).

On 23 December, the General Assembly decided that the agenda item on multilingualism would remain for consideration at its fifty-ninth (2005) session (**decision 59/552**).

Staff rules and regulations

In accordance with staff regulations 12.3 stipulating that the full text of provisional staff rules and amendments should be reported annually to the General Assembly, the Secretary-General, in August [A/59/213 & Add.1], outlined amendments to the 100, 200 and 300 series of Staff Rules, together with the rationale for the changes. Amendments to the 100 series related to sick leave, official travel, due process, and the Joint Disciplinary Committees. Amendments under the 200 and 300 series related to sick leave.

The Secretary-General recommended that the Assembly take note of the amendments in the annex to the report, which he proposed to implement as from 1 January 2005.

Headquarters agreements

JIU report. In October [A/59/526], the Secretary-General transmitted the JIU report entitled "Review of the Headquarters Agreements concluded by the organizations of the United Nations system: human resources issues affecting staff". The objective of the investigation was to identify where adjustments in headquarters agreements might be advisable, with an emphasis on areas essential for the reform of human resources management, and to contribute to the elaboration of model rules for future headquarters agreements and possible amendments to existing ones. JIU traced the evolution of headquarters agreements and its implications for current agreements, and addressed selected work/life issues requiring review in terms of their relevance to the agreements and their interpretation and implementation in host countries. Among the issues were: work permits for spouses and children, domestic helpers and non-dependent family members of staff; the acquisition, rental and sale of real estate by staff; staff integration into the social security system of host countries; staff retirement in host countries; and the payment of value added tax and similar taxes, and income taxation issues.

Recognizing that the employment of spouses of UN staff members was a concern that needed to be addressed if the UN system was to attract, employ and retain the best candidates for jobs in UN organizations worldwide, JIU recommended that legislative bodies of organizations bring to the attention of host countries the desirability of adopting more liberal policies regarding the granting of work permits or establishing similar arrangements for spouses of staff members and officials. It also recognized the need to reassess the procedures of host countries to facilitate the exercise of privileges, immunities and other facilities to ensure efficient and timely processing. In that regard, JIU recommended that legislative bodies of organizations remind host countries of the importance of fully implementing headquarters agreements and ensuring the use of simplified procedures to facilitate the exercise of those privileges, immunities and benefits, including those work/life issues mentioned above. To better acquaint staff, particularly new recruits and arrivals at a duty station, of the contents of host country agreements, executive heads were requested to issue comprehensive information and publicize the privileges, immunities and other benefits granted staff, and staff obligations. Host countries should likewise inform their local administrations, public services and business communities, especially those situated outside the capital or seat of the various organizations. Host countries should be reminded that any additional facilities granted to intergovernmental organizations should be extended to all UN system organizations, their staff and officials located in that territory. The Secretary-General should request CEB to coordinate the formulation of a model framework headquarters agreement, or standard articles ensuring uniformity, for approval by the Assembly, and which would be used to guide the conclusion of future and/or updating of existing headquarters agreements. Host countries should also be reminded of the significance of simplified procedures to ensure the speedy processing of visas for staff and officials travelling on mission for UN organizations, so as to prevent undue delays in the substantive work of the organization and possible financial losses.

Safety and security

Reports of Secretary-General. In response to General Assembly resolution 58/122 [YUN 2003, p. 1453], the Secretary-General, in September [A/59/332], updated information on threats against the safety and security of UN personnel between 1 July 2003 and 30 June 2004. He stated that, since 1992, 218 United Nations civilian staff members had been killed as a result of malicious acts. During the reporting period, 22 staff members were killed, the majority of whom were victims of the bomb attack on the UN headquarters in Baghdad in 2003 [YUN 2003, p. 346]. More than 120 incidents of assault, including 10 cases of rape or sexual assault on UN personnel were recorded, and at least 139 incidents of harassments at checkpoints or against convoys or other activities. There were also two serious incidents of kidnapping in Somalia, and four bomb threats against field offices in Ethiopia, Georgia, Guatemala and Pakistan. Attacks on UN premises and properties in the field were of increasing concern, with seven violent attacks against UN compounds and convoys, 52 reported forceful incursions into UN compounds, and more than 1,256 incidents of theft involving office equipment, official vehicles, staff residences and personal belongings.

The report described efforts to improve the security management system, including the results of the security evaluation conducted following the August 2003 attack against the UN premises in Baghdad. Immediate actions completed at Headquarters included the development and promulgation of an enhanced standardized pro-

cedure for conducting threat and risk assessment, upgrading of the Minimum Operating Security Standards (MOSS); dispatch of 19 support missions of the Office of the United Nations Security Coordinator (UNSECOORD) to countries of particular concern; elaboration by DPKO of specific security measures, including country-specific MOSS; a study on crisis management lessons; and a request to the Assembly (see p. 1380) for additional resources to fulfil immediate needs for security personnel and facilities protection at Headquarters and in field locations. To address in a comprehensive and integrated manner the issue of longer-term concepts and requirements for the entire United Nations, a separate report [A/59/356 & Corr.1 & Add.1] (see p. 1478) proposing a unified and strengthened UN security management system was submitted to the Assembly. Throughout the reporting period, UN organizations funds and programmes and UNSECOORD actively recruited, trained and deployed skilled field security coordination officers and agency field security officers. In terms of accountability, on 29 March, the Secretary-General announced disciplinary measures, following the release of the report by an investigative panel that had identified institutional and individual failures in assessing the security situation in Baghdad prior to the August 2003 attack.

The Secretary-General observed that the period under review was particularly difficult, forcing the UN system to reflect seriously on the future of its security management arrangements at all levels. There was a need for a proactive approach, which would allow the United Nations to monitor its environment more systematically. The Organization had to anticipate security incidents and plan for them in advance, as well as enhance its readiness and protection through training, equipment and physical security measures. That demanded a cultural change within the UN system. To ensure success, managers and staff had to be be equally committed to the process.

CEB consideration. HLCM, at its eighth session (Rome, 5-6 October) [CEB/2004/6], welcomed the Secretary-General's proposals for a strengthened and unified security management system for the United Nations to be funded under the UN regular budget (see above), including the new organizational structure and approach to financing, and agreed that all organizations should be proactive in seeking the support of Member States in their governing bodies or executive boards; took note of further work to be undertaken on such issues as governance, an implementation strategy for the new security management system and strengthened coordination at all headquarters locations, including how to maximize partnerships and collaboration with the specialized agencies; noted that the new United Nations Security Directorate would not be responsible for security at the headquarters locations of the specialized agencies, which would continue their relationships with host Governments, the latter being ultimately responsible for the security and safety of personnel; and requested that security networks, both in the field and at headquarters, submit proposals to HLCM on mechanisms that would ensure a robust, well-coordinated global security management system.

HLCM endorsed the report of the Inter-Agency Security Management Network on its May 2004 meeting and approved its key recommendations related to security threat and risk assessments, minimum operating security standards, aviation safety, medical emergencies involving mass casualties, security training and accountability. HLCM also endorsed the revised MOSS policy document as the new baseline standard for security at the field level. Those baseline standards, combined with the outcome of the threat and risk assessment for specific local conditions should be incorporated into a location-specific MOSS. It agreed that compliance evaluations of and assistance with the implementation of MOSS should be undertaken by UNSECOORD. HLCM reiterated that security training was mandatory for all staff members depending on their individual specific needs, whether in the field or at headquarters and called on each organization to ensure adherence; agreed that staff should refresh their CD-ROM security training every three years on a mandatory basis; and agreed that all designated officials had to undergo mandatory security briefing and training prior to assuming their assignment.

HLCM also considered an update of a document presented at its fifth session [YUN 2003, p. 1453] on actions taken by individual organizations to improve their security and emergency preparedness so as to provide guidance for those organizations that had yet to complete their emergency preparedness and business continuity planning in the hope that experience gained by organizations might serve as a useful reference for others.

CEB, at its second regular session for 2004 (New York, 29-30 October) [CEB/2004/2], welcomed the progress in HLCM's work, the outcome of the 2004 census of UN system staff members and the situation of contingency planning and emergency preparedness in the organizations and bodies of the system.

On 20 December [meeting 74], the General Assembly adopted **resolution 59/211** [draft: A/59/L.51 & Add.1] without vote [agenda item 39].

Safety and security of humanitarian personnel and protection of United Nations personnel

The General Assembly,

Reaffirming its resolution 46/182 of 19 December 1991 on strengthening of the coordination of humanitarian emergency assistance of the United Nations,

Recalling all relevant resolutions on safety and security of humanitarian personnel and protection of United Nations personnel, including its resolution 58/122 of 17 December 2003, Economic and Social Council resolution 2004/50 of 23 July 2004 and Security Council resolution 1502(2003) of 26 August 2003,

Taking note of all resolutions and presidential statements of the Security Council and reports of the Secretary-General to the Council on the protection of civilians in armed conflict,

Recalling all relevant provisions of international law, including international humanitarian law and human rights law, as well as all relevant treaties,

Reaffirming the need to promote and ensure respect for the principles and rules of international law, including international humanitarian law,

Recalling that primary responsibility under international law for the security and protection of humanitarian personnel and United Nations and its associated personnel lies with the Government hosting a United Nations operation conducted under the Charter of the United Nations or its agreements with relevant organizations,

Urging all parties involved in armed conflicts, in compliance with international humanitarian law, in particular their obligations under the Geneva Conventions of 12 August 1949 and the obligations applicable to them under the Additional Protocols thereto, of 8 June 1977, to ensure the security and protection of all humanitarian personnel and United Nations and its associated personnel,

Welcoming the fact that the number of States parties to the Convention on the Safety of United Nations and Associated Personnel, which entered into force on 15 January 1999, has continued to rise, the number now having reached seventy-seven, and mindful of the need to promote universality of the Convention,

Deeply concerned by the dangers and security risks faced by humanitarian personnel and United Nations and its associated personnel at the field level, as they operate in increasingly complex contexts, as well as the continuous erosion, in many cases, of respect for the principles and rules of international law, in particular international humanitarian law,

Expressing profound regret at the deaths of international and national humanitarian personnel and United Nations and its associated personnel involved in the provision of humanitarian assistance, and strongly deploring the rising toll of casualties among such personnel in complex humanitarian emergencies, in particular in armed conflicts and in post-conflict situations,

Strongly condemning acts of murder and other forms of violence, rape and sexual assault and all forms of violence committed in particular against women, and intimidation, armed robbery, abduction, hostage-taking, kidnapping, harassment and illegal arrest and detention to which those participating in humanitarian operations are increasingly exposed, as well as attacks on humanitarian convoys and acts of destruction and looting of property,

Commending the courage and commitment of those who take part in humanitarian operations, often at great personal risk, especially of locally recruited staff,

Expressing concern that the occurrence of attacks and threats against humanitarian personnel and United Nations and its associated personnel is a factor that increasingly restricts the ability of the Organization to provide assistance and protection to civilians in fulfilment of its mandate under the Charter,

Recalling the inclusion of attacks intentionally directed against personnel involved in a humanitarian assistance or peacekeeping mission in accordance with the Charter as a war crime in the Rome Statute of the International Criminal Court, and noting the role that the Court could play in appropriate cases in bringing to justice those responsible for serious violations of international humanitarian law,

Reaffirming the need to ensure adequate levels of safety and security for United Nations personnel and its associated humanitarian personnel, which constitutes an underlying duty of the Organization, and mindful of the need to promote and enhance the security consciousness within the organizational culture of the United Nations and a culture of accountability at all levels,

Emphasizing the urgent need to take concrete measures to strengthen the effectiveness of the security management system for the United Nations, and in this regard mindful of the report of the Secretary-General on a strengthened and unified security management system for the United Nations,

1. *Welcomes* the report of the Secretary-General on the safety and security of humanitarian personnel and protection of United Nations personnel;

2. *Urges* all States to take the necessary measures to ensure the full and effective implementation of the relevant principles and rules of international law, including international humanitarian law, human rights law and refugee law related to the safety and security of humanitarian personnel and United Nations personnel;

3. *Strongly urges* all States to take the necessary measures to ensure the safety and security of humanitarian personnel and United Nations and its associated personnel and to respect and ensure respect for the inviolability of United Nations premises, which are essential to the continuation and successful implementation of United Nations operations;

4. *Calls upon* all Governments and parties in complex humanitarian emergencies, in particular in armed conflicts and in post-conflict situations, in countries in which humanitarian personnel are operating, in conformity with the relevant provisions of international law and national laws, to cooperate fully with the United Nations and other humanitarian agencies and organizations and to ensure the safe and unhindered access of humanitarian personnel in order to allow them to perform efficiently their task of assisting the affected civilian population, including refugees and internally displaced persons;

5. *Calls upon* all States to consider becoming parties to and to respect fully their obligations under the relevant international instruments, in particular the Convention on the Safety of United Nations and Associated Personnel;

6. *Also calls upon* all States to consider becoming parties to and to respect fully their obligations under the Convention on the Privileges and Immunities of the United Nations and the Convention on the Privileges and Immunities of the Specialized Agencies, which have been ratified so far by one hundred and forty-eight States and one hundred and eight States, respectively;

7. *Further calls upon* all States to consider becoming parties to the Rome Statute of the International Criminal Court;

8. *Takes note with appreciation* of the important progress made by the working group and the Ad Hoc Committee on the Scope of Legal Protection under the Convention on the Safety of United Nations and Associated Personnel, and notes that the Ad Hoc Committee will reconvene from 11 to 15 April 2005 with a mandate to expand the scope of legal protection under the said Convention, including by means of a legal instrument;

9. *Expresses deep concern* that, over the past decade, threats against the safety and security of humanitarian personnel and United Nations and its associated personnel have escalated dramatically and that perpetrators of acts of violence seemingly operate with impunity;

10. *Strongly condemns* all threats and acts of violence against humanitarian personnel and United Nations and its associated personnel, affirms the need to hold accountable those responsible for such acts, strongly urges all States to take stronger actions to ensure that any such acts committed on their territory are investigated fully and to ensure that the perpetrators of such acts are brought to justice in accordance with international law and national law, and notes the need for States to end impunity for such acts;

11. *Calls upon* all States to provide adequate and prompt information in the event of the arrest or detention of humanitarian personnel or United Nations and its associated personnel, to afford them the necessary medical assistance and to allow independent medical teams to visit and examine the health of those detained, and urges them to take the necessary measures to ensure the speedy release of those who have been arrested or detained in violation of the relevant conventions referred to in the present resolution and applicable international humanitarian law;

12. *Calls upon* all other parties involved in armed conflicts to refrain from abducting humanitarian personnel or United Nations and its associated personnel or detaining them in violation of the relevant conventions referred to in the present resolution and applicable international humanitarian law, and speedily to release, without harm or requirement of concession, any abductee or detainee;

13. *Reaffirms* the obligation of all humanitarian personnel and United Nations and its associated personnel to observe and respect the national laws of the country in which they are operating, in accordance with international law and the Charter of the United Nations;

14. *Requests* the Secretary-General to take the necessary measures to ensure full respect for the human rights, privileges and immunities of United Nations and other personnel carrying out activities in fulfilment of the mandate of a United Nations operation, and also requests the Secretary-General to seek the inclusion, in negotiations of headquarters and other mission agreements concerning United Nations and its associated personnel, of the applicable conditions contained in the Convention on the Privileges and Immunities of the United Nations, the Convention on the Privileges and Immunities of the Specialized Agencies and the Convention on the Safety of United Nations and Associated Personnel;

15. *Recommends* that the Secretary-General continue to seek the inclusion of, and that host countries include, key provisions of the Convention on the Safety of United Nations and Associated Personnel, among others, those regarding the prevention of attacks against members of the operation, the establishment of such attacks as crimes punishable by law and the prosecution or extradition of offenders, in future as well as, if necessary, in existing status-of-forces, status-of-mission and host country agreements negotiated between the United Nations and those countries, mindful of the importance of the timely conclusion of such agreements;

16. *Requests* the Secretary-General to take the necessary measures, falling within his responsibilities, to promote and enhance the security consciousness and measures within the organizational culture of the United Nations system, agencies, funds and programmes, including by disseminating and ensuring the implementation of the security procedures and regulations and by ensuring accountability at all levels;

17. *Emphasizes* the importance of paying special attention to the safety and security of United Nations and its associated personnel engaged in United Nations peacekeeping and peacebuilding operations;

18. *Also emphasizes* the need to give further consideration to the safety and security of locally recruited humanitarian personnel, who account for the majority of casualties;

19. *Requests* the Secretary-General to take the necessary measures to ensure that United Nations and other personnel carrying out activities in fulfilment of the mandate of a United Nations operation are properly informed about and operate in conformity with the minimum operating security standards and relevant codes of conduct and are properly informed about the conditions under which they are called upon to operate and the standards that they are required to meet, including those contained in relevant national and international law, and that adequate training in security, human rights law and international humanitarian law is provided so as to enhance their security and effectiveness in accomplishing their functions, and reaffirms the necessity for all other humanitarian organizations to provide their personnel with similar support;

20. *Stresses* the importance of ensuring that humanitarian personnel and United Nations and associated personnel remain sensitive to national and local customs and traditions in their countries of assignment and communicate clearly their purpose and objectives to local populations;

21. *Also stresses* the need to ensure that all United Nations staff members receive adequate security training, including physical and psychological training, prior to their deployment to the field, the need to attach a high priority to the improvement of stress and trauma counselling services available to United Nations staff members, including through the implementation of a comprehensive security and stress and trauma management training, support and assistance programme for United Nations staff throughout the system, before, during and after missions, and the need to make available to the Secretary-General the means for that purpose;

22. *Recognizes* the need for a strengthened and unified security management system for the United Nations, both at the headquarters and the field levels, and requests the United Nations system, as well as Member States, to take all appropriate measures to that end;

23. *Takes note* of the report of the Secretary-General on a strengthened and unified security management system for the United Nations;

24. *Welcomes* the ongoing efforts of the Secretary-General to further enhance the security management system of the United Nations, and in this regard invites the United Nations and other humanitarian organizations to strengthen the analysis of threats to their safety and security in order to minimize security risks and to facilitate informed decisions on the maintenance of an effective presence in the field, inter alia, to fulfil their humanitarian mandate;

25. *Requests* the Secretary-General, inter alia, through the Inter-Agency Security Management Network, to promote increased cooperation and collaboration among United Nations agencies, funds and programmes, including between their headquarters and field offices, in the planning and implementation of measures aimed at improving staff security, training and awareness, and calls upon all relevant United Nations agencies, funds and programmes to support these efforts;

26. *Recognizes* the need for enhanced coordination and cooperation, both at the headquarters and the field levels, between the United Nations security management system and non-governmental organizations on matters relating to the safety and security of humanitarian personnel and United Nations and its associated personnel, with a view to addressing mutual security concerns in the field;

27. *Underlines* the need to allocate adequate and predictable resources to the safety and security of United Nations personnel, encourages all States to contribute to the Trust Fund for Security of Staff Members of the United Nations System and to meet requirements in the consolidated appeals, without prejudice to the outcome of the ongoing discussions in the General Assembly regarding the funding for safety and security;

28. *Recalls* the essential role of telecommunication resources in facilitating the safety of humanitarian personnel and United Nations and its associated personnel, calls upon States to consider acceding to or ratifying the Tampere Convention on the Provision of Telecommunication Resources for Disaster Mitigation and Relief Operations of 18 June 1998, and encourages them to facilitate and expedite, consistent with their national laws and regulations, the use of communications equipment in such operations, inter alia, through limiting and, whenever possible, lifting the restrictions

placed on the use of communications equipment by United Nations and its associated personnel;

29. *Requests* the Secretary-General to submit to the General Assembly at its sixtieth session a comprehensive and updated report on the safety and security of humanitarian personnel and protection of United Nations personnel and on the implementation of the present resolution.

UN Joint Staff Pension Fund

As at 31 December 2004, the United Nations Joint Staff Pension Fund (UNJSPF) had 88,356 active participants compared to 85,245 at the end of 2003; the number of periodic payments in award increased from 52,496 to 53,879 over the year. The breakdown of the periodic benefits in award was 17,338 retirement benefits; 12,092 early retirement benefits; 6,613 deferred retirement benefits; 8,676 widows' and widowers' benefits; 960 disability benefits; 8,156 children's benefits; and 44 secondary dependants' benefits.

The Fund was administered by the 33-member United Nations Joint Staff Pension Board (UNJSPB), which held its fifty-second session (Montreal, Canada, 13-23 July) [A/59/9 & Add.1] to consider actuarial matters, including the twenty-seventh actuarial valuation of the Fund as at 31 December 2003; management of the Fund's investments and reports on the investment strategies and performance for the biennium 2002-2003; administrative matters, including the revised budget estimates for the 2004-2005 biennium; the Fund's benefits provisions, including the methodology for the calculation of the final average remuneration and the comprehensive review of pensionable remuneration; and the size and composition of the Fund and its Standing Committee. The Board also examined and approved the financial statements and schedules for the biennium ended 31 December 2003 and considered the report of the Board of Auditors on the Fund's accounts and operations. In addition, the Board considered the proposed transfer agreement between the Fund and the Organization for Security and Cooperation in Europe and the World Trade Organization, the integration of the goals of sustainable development and the principles of the Global Compact into the Fund's operating processes and investment policies, and the possible applications of the Inter-Parliamentary Union, the International Organization for Migration and the International Commission for the Conservation of Atlantic Tunas for membership in the Fund.

ACABQ report. ACABQ, in October [A/59/447], concurred with the Pension Board's recommendation that the current contribution rate of 23.7 per cent of pensionable remuneration be re-tained. It also agreed with the Board's recommendations that the General Assembly approve a phased approach in the elimination of the 1.5 per cent reduction in the first consumer price index adjustments due after retirement; that the Pension Adjustment System be amended to provide for an adjustable minimum guarantee on the local-currency track of 80 per cent of the United States dollar-track amount, with effect from 1 April 2005, on a prospective basis only; and that the Assembly approve additional resources of $5,340,700 for the 2004-2005 biennium for the Fund's administrative costs. ACABQ expressed concern with the upward trend in the Fund's administrative expenditures and intended to revert to the matter in the context of its examination of the Fund's administrative budget proposal for the 2006-2007 biennium.

GENERAL ASSEMBLY ACTION

On 23 December [meeting 76], the General Assembly, on the recommendation of the Fifth Committee [A/59/606], adopted **resolution 59/269** without vote [agenda item 117].

United Nations pension system

The General Assembly,

Recalling its resolutions 51/217 of 18 December 1996, 53/210 of 18 December 1998, 55/224 of 23 December 2000 and 57/286 of 20 December 2002, section V of its resolution 54/251 of 23 December 1999 and of its resolution 56/255 of 24 December 2001, and section X of its resolution 58/272 of 23 December 2003,

Having considered the report of the United Nations Joint Staff Pension Board on its fifty-second session, the report of the Secretary-General on the investments of the United Nations Joint Staff Pension Fund and the related report of the Advisory Committee on Administrative and Budgetary Questions,

I

Actuarial matters

Recalling section I of its resolution 57/286,

Having considered the results of the actuarial valuation of the United Nations Joint Staff Pension Fund as at 31 December 2003 and the observations thereon by the Consulting Actuary of the Fund, the Committee of Actuaries and the United Nations Joint Staff Pension Board,

1. *Takes note* of the developments with respect to the actuarial surplus of the United Nations Joint Staff Pension Fund, which went from 0.36 per cent of pensionable remuneration as at 31 December 1997 to 4.25 per cent of pensionable remuneration as at 31 December 1999 to 2.92 per cent of pensionable remuneration as at 31 December 2001 and to 1.14 per cent of pensionable remuneration as at 31 December 2003, and, in particular, of the opinions on those developments provided by the Consulting Actuary and the Committee of Actuaries, as reproduced in annexes VII and VIII, respectively, to the report of the United Nations Joint Staff Pension Board on its fifty-second session;

2. *Also takes note* of the Board's agreement with the recommendation of the Committee of Actuaries that most of the surplus should be retained;

3. *Further takes note* of the view of the Committee of Actuaries and the recommendation of the Board that the current contribution rate of 23.7 per cent of pensionable remuneration should be maintained;

4. *Takes note* of the Board's approval of the terms of reference for the Committee of Actuaries, and notes that the Standing Committee of the Board will consider in 2005 provisions that would allow for the possible appointment of ad hoc members to the Committee of Actuaries;

5. *Concurs,* in accordance with article 13 of the Regulations of the Fund and with a view to securing continuity of pension rights:

   (a) With the revised transfer agreements of the Fund with the Organization for Security and Cooperation in Europe and the World Trade Organization, as approved by the Board and set out in annex IX to the report of the Board, which will supersede existing transfer agreements, effective 1 January 2005;

   (b) With the new transfer agreements of the Fund with the Universal Postal Union and the Preparatory Commission for the Comprehensive Nuclear-Test-Ban Treaty Organization, as approved by the Board and set out in annexes I and II, respectively, to the addendum to the report of the Board, which will become effective on 1 January 2005;

6. *Decides,* upon the affirmative recommendation of the Board, that the Inter-Parliamentary Union shall be admitted as a new member organization of the Fund, effective 1 January 2005;

II
Pension adjustment system

Recalling section II of its resolution 57/286,

Having considered the reviews carried out by the Consulting Actuary, the Committee of Actuaries and the United Nations Joint Staff Pension Board, as set out in the Board's report, of various aspects of the pension adjustment system,

1. *Takes note* of the recommendation of the United Nations Joint Staff Pension Board of a phased approach in the elimination of the 1.5 per cent reduction in the first consumer price index adjustments due after retirement, with effect from 1 April 2005, and also takes note of the Board's recommendation that the two-track pension adjustment system of the United Nations Joint Staff Pension Fund be amended to provide for an adjustable minimum guarantee at 80 per cent of the United States dollar-track amount, also with effect from 1 April 2005;

2. *Approves,* accordingly, with effect from 1 April 2005, the changes in the pension adjustment system set out in the annex to the present resolution, namely:

   (a) A phased approach in the elimination of the 1.5 per cent reduction in the first consumer price index adjustments;

   (b) The addition of a new provision under the two-track pension adjustment system for an adjustable minimum guarantee at 80 per cent of the United States dollar-track amount, with the understanding that, under the two-track pension adjustment system, benefits are subject to a maximum of 110 or 120 per cent of the local currency track, depending on the date of separation

from service, and that the Board will continue to review the costs/savings of all the modifications introduced since 1992 with respect to the two-track feature of the pension adjustment system and will report thereon to the General Assembly every two years on the occasion of the actuarial valuations of the Fund;

3. *Requests* the Board to review the benefit of the two-track system vis-à-vis the United States dollar track for both the beneficiaries and the Fund as a whole, taking into account the effect of the adjustable minimum guarantee at 80 per cent of the United States dollar-track amount on the utilization rate of the two-track system, and to report thereon to the General Assembly at its sixty-first session;

4. *Takes note* of the Board's intention to address in 2006, subject to a favourable actuarial valuation as at 31 December 2005, the possible total elimination of the balance of the 1.5 per cent reduction and, on an equal footing, the possible elimination of the limitation on the right to restoration based on length of prior service;

5. *Decides* not to consider any further proposals to enhance or improve pension benefits until action is taken on the issues contained in section I, paragraph 4, and section II, paragraphs 2 and 3, of its resolution 57/286;

6. *Invites* the Board to provide information on the special situation of pensioners living in countries having undergone dollarization and on possible proposals to attenuate the adverse consequences arising the refrom;

III
Financial statements of the United Nations Joint Staff Pension Fund and report of the Board of Auditors

Having considered the financial statements of the United Nations Joint Staff Pension Fund for the biennium ended 31 December 2003, the audit opinion and report of the Board of Auditors thereon, the information provided on the internal audits of the Fund and the observations of the United Nations Joint Staff Pension Board,

1. *Takes note* of the implementation of the recommendations of the Board of Auditors, as described in paragraphs 11 and 12 of its report on the accounts of the United Nations Joint Staff Pension Fund for the biennium ended 31 December 2003, and stresses the need for the Fund to comply fully and in a timely manner with all recommendations of the Board of Auditors;

2. *Takes note with satisfaction* of the approval of the United Nations Joint Staff Pension Board of an internal audit charter, which recognizes and incorporates policy changes for the Office of Internal Oversight Services of the Secretariat;

3. *Notes* that the Standing Committee of the United Nations Joint Staff Pension Board will consider, in 2005, the desirability of and possible terms of reference for an audit committee of the Board;

IV
Administrative arrangements of the United Nations Joint Staff Pension Fund

Recalling section VII of its resolution 51/217, section V of its resolutions 52/222, 53/210 and 54/251, section IV of its resolution 55/224, section V of its resolution 56/255, section IV of its resolution 57/286 and section X of its resolution 58/272 concerning the administrative arrangements and expenses of the United Nations Joint Staff Pension Fund,

1. *Takes note* of the information set out in paragraphs 134 to 136 of the report of the United Nations Joint Staff Pension Board on the revised budget estimates for the biennium 2004-2005;

2. *Also takes note* of the upward trend in the administrative expenses of the United Nations Joint Staff Pension Fund and of the intention of the Advisory Committee on Administrative and Budgetary Questions to further consider the matter in the context of the Fund's budget proposals for the biennium 2006-2007;

3. *Approves* additional resources in the amount of 5,340,700 United States dollars for the biennium 2004-2005 for administrative costs of the Fund, noting that the revised estimates for the biennium would amount to a total appropriation of 41,011,800 dollars for administrative costs;

4. *Takes note* of the arrangements for leasing office space to accommodate in New York, outside United Nations Headquarters, the Fund secretariat and the Investment Management Service;

V

Size and composition of the United Nations Joint Staff Pension Board and its Standing Committee

Stressing the importance of fair representation of participating organizations in the United Nations Joint Staff Pension Board and its Standing Committee,

1. *Takes note* of the information set out in paragraphs 200 to 210 of the report of the United Nations Joint Staff Pension Board concerning the review of the size and composition of the Board and its Standing Committee and the decision of the Board that the matter should be further studied by the Working Group established to carry out that review, for consideration by the Standing Committee in 2005 and the Board in 2006;

2. *Urges* the Board to explore the possibility of meeting annually for a shorter duration and to report its conclusions, including all financial and administrative implications associated with that possibility, to the General Assembly at its sixty-first session;

VI

Other matters

1. *Takes note* of the agreement of the United Nations Joint Staff Pension Board:

(a) To make no changes to the current methodology used in the determination of final average remuneration but to consider at the meeting of its Standing Committee in 2005 a study containing actuarial cost assessments of a proposed early retirement protection measure, together with both the positive features and the anomalies that might arise as a consequence;

(b) To consider at the meeting of its Standing Committee in 2005 a report on a possible provision to allow for the purchase by participants in the United Nations Joint Staff Pension Fund of additional years of contributory service;

(c) To consider at the meeting of its Standing Committee in 2005 possible applications for membership in the Fund from the International Organization for Migration and the International Commission for the Conservation of Atlantic Tunas;

(d) To consider at its session in 2006 a study on all benefit provisions relating to family benefits;

(e) To consider at its session in 2006 a study, to be carried out in consultation with the medical directors of the common system, on disability issues;

2. *Takes note with satisfaction* of the progress report on the Fund's management charter, which introduced specific goals and objectives, a detailed action plan for achieving such goals and the status report on the implementation of each goal;

3. *Takes note* of the arrangements with respect to the comprehensive review of pensionable remuneration that is to be carried out by the International Civil Service Commission in close cooperation with the Board, and also takes note of the timetable and framework for the required close collaboration between the two bodies;

VII

Investments of the United Nations Joint Staff Pension Fund

1. *Takes note* of the report of the Secretary-General on the investments of the United Nations Joint Staff Pension Fund, as well as the observations of the United Nations Joint Staff Pension Board set out in paragraphs 99 to 102 of its report;

2. *Also takes note* of the significant increase in the market value of the Fund's assets and the positive returns achieved during the biennium;

3. *Notes* that a comprehensive review will be carried out of the investment policies and practices of the Investment Management Service with a view to addressing the findings and recommendations contained in the audit reports of the Office of Internal Oversight Services of the Secretariat and the Board of Auditors;

4. *Takes note* of the Board's approval of the terms of reference for the Investments Committee, which will take effect on 1 January 2005;

VIII

Diversification of investments of the United Nations Joint Staff Pension Fund

Recalling its resolutions 36/119 A to C of 10 December 1981,

1. *Takes note* of the increase in investments of the United Nations Joint Staff Pension Fund in developing countries, and requests the Secretary-General to report to the General Assembly at its sixty-first session on the steps and efforts undertaken to increase, to the maximum extent possible, investments in developing countries;

2. *Reaffirms* the policy of diversification of the investments of the Fund across geographical areas, wherever this serves the interests of the participants and beneficiaries of the Fund, in accordance with the four criteria of safety, profitability, liquidity and convertibility;

IX

Implementation of the recommendations of the Office of Internal Oversight Services on the Investment Management Service of the United Nations Joint Staff Pension Fund

Recalling its resolution 58/279 of 23 December 2003,

Having considered the report of the Secretary-General,

Takes note of the report of the Secretary-General.

Annex

Changes to the pension adjustment system of the United Nations Joint Staff Pension Fund

Section H.   Subsequent adjustments of the benefit

Add the following new text at the end of paragraph 20:

"Effective 1 April 2005, the reduction in the initial adjustments due after separation shall be by 1.0 percentage point; with respect to benefits to which the 1.5 percentage point reduction was applied before 1 April 2005, there shall be a 0.5 percentage point increase in the first adjustments due on or after 1 April 2005."

Section I. Payment of the benefit

Add the following new text at the end of paragraph 23:

"The limitations described in (a) and (b) above shall not result in a benefit being smaller than either the United States dollar base amount determined in accordance with the Regulations of the Fund or 80 per cent of the adjusted United States dollar-track amount."

Also on 23 December, the Assembly, by **decision 59/552**, decided that the agenda item on the UN pension system would remain for consideration during its resumed fifty-ninth (2005) session.

Pension Fund investments

The market value of UNJSPF assets as at 31 December 2004 was $29.2 billion, an increase of about 13.6 per cent over the previous year. The Fund's investment assets were distributed in equities (62.5 per cent), bonds (25.7 per cent), real-estate related instruments (5.5 per cent) and short-term holdings (6.3 per cent). The total investment return, as at 31 March 2004, was 28.7 per cent, which after adjustment for the United States consumer price index, represented a real rate of 26.5 per cent.

In October [A/C.5/59/11], the Secretary-General described the economic and investment conditions prevailing in the reporting period ended 31 March 2004 and provided statistical information on the Fund's investment returns and diversification, including development-related investments.

Implementation of OIOS recommendations

In response to General Assembly resolution 58/279 [YUN 2003, p. 1458], the Secretary-General submitted a March report [A/58/725] on the implementation of the 2003 OIOS recommendations on the Investment Management Services of UNJSPF [YUN 2003, p. 1458]. The recommendations covered investment management and procurement and contract administration. Their implementation status was covered in an annex to the report.

On 8 April, the Assembly decided to defer until its fifty-ninth (2004) session consideration of the Secretary-General's report on the implementation of OIOS recommendations on the Investment Management Service of UNJSPF (**decision 58/564 B**).

Travel-related matters

In October, the Secretary-General submitted a biennial report on standards of accommodation for air travel [A/59/523], listing exceptions to those standards from 1 July 2002 to 30 June 2004 and comparative statistics for the two-year period ended 30 June 2002.

During the 2002-2004 period, the Secretary-General authorized 98 cases of first-class and 138 of business-class air travel, as exceptions to the standards of accommodations, and 87 and 74, respectively, during the 2000-2002 period. Included in the first-class group were the Deputy Secretary-General, the President of the General Assembly and the Secretary-General's personal aide/security officer.

ACABQ report. On 17 November [A/59/573], ACABQ reiterated its request for information on the date of booking, travel dates, itinerary and number of travel days and the nature of the event being attended. It was of the opinion that the time had come to reconsider the whole question of first-class travel. The Committee observed that, in recent years, many airlines had significantly cut back, if not entirely eliminated, first-class sections on aircraft. Instead, several varieties of enhanced business-class travel had been developed, and it appeared that differences in the level of accommodation between those classes and first class were minimal. Taking those developments into account, the General Assembly might wish to give further guidance on the future use of first-class travel with a view to its use in only the most exceptional circumstances.

Administration of justice

The General Assembly, at its resumed fifty-eighth session, had before it for consideration the 18 November 2003 letter from the President of the United Nations Administrative Tribunal addressed to the Chairman of the Fifth Committee [A/C.5/58/16] and the comprehensive report on the activities of the Tribunal [A/58/680] (see p. 1443). By **decision 58/576** of 13 September, the Assembly decided to defer consideration of the item entitled "Administration of justice at the United Nations" and to include it in the draft agenda of its fifty-ninth (2004) session.

Follow-up to resolution 57/307

The Secretary-General submitted an October report [A/59/449] on the administration of justice in the Secretariat, in which he outlined action taken to implement General Assembly resolution 57/307 [YUN 2003, p. 1459]. The report examined the findings of the management review of the appeals process conducted by OIOS (see below), alternatives for strengthening the administration of justice, and action taken in respect of the independence of the United Nations Administrative Tribunal (see p. 1443), proposals on the role and work of the Panels on Discrimination and other grievances (see below), activities of the United Nations Administrative Tribunal (see p. 1443), written notification of allegations to staff members, and personal financial responsibility of officials for financial losses to the Organization caused by gross negligence. The Secretary-General also reported on legal insurance schemes and provided statistics on the disposition of cases and work of the Panel of Counsel.

On 23 December, the Assembly deferred until its resumed fifty-ninth (2005) session consideration of the Secretary-General's report (**decision 59/551**). Also on the same date, the Assembly decided that the agenda item on the administration of justice at the United Nations would remain for consideration until its resumed fifty-ninth (2005) session (**decision 59/552**).

Panels on Discrimination and Other Grievances

Report of Secretary-General. In response to General Assembly resolution 57/307 [YUN 2003, p. 1459], the Secretary-General submitted an October report on the work and role of the Panels on Discrimination and Other Grievances [A/59/414]. He agreed with the assessment of the team, which had been requested by the Ombudsman to review the functions of the Panels, that they were not effective in their current form, though he recognized that many staff members valued their existence. After consulting with the Ombudsman and staff representatives, the Secretary-General proposed to the Assembly two options as to the future role of the Panels. Under option one, the Panels would be eliminated and their functions assumed by the Office of the Ombudsman. He believed that their elimination would not deprive staff of having their complaints considered by their peers, as that could be done informally, as part of the conciliation carried out by the Joint Appeals Board (JAB), and they could raise employment-related issues with the Ombudsman, which would be appealable to the formal recourse system. Option two would establish a successor mechanism to the Panels, by which the Panels would be abolished and some of their functions (notably, the functions of fact-finding and of writing recommendations) would be taken over by new joint bodies of peers, to be named joint grievance committees, which would be administratively attached to JAB. If the Assembly decided to endorse the second option, it would be

necessary that the members of the proposed joint grievance committees be provided with adequate resources in terms of training and administrative support, and would require system-wide consultation with the staff.

On 23 December, the Assembly deferred consideration of the Secretary-General's report until its resumed fifty-ninth (2005) session (**decision 59/551**).

Management review of the appeals process

OIOS report. Pursuant to General Assembly resolution 48/218 B [YUN 1994, p. 1362], 54/244 [YUN 1999, p. 1274] and 57/307, the Secretary-General transmitted an October report [A/59/408] on the management review of the appeals process at the United Nations carried out by OIOS from March to July 2004. In performing the review, OIOS focused on procedural and institutional matters. Accordingly, its findings could be grouped into four main categories: the time taken to complete the process; the institutional roles played by the various entities in the process; the resources available to the respective parties; and training and communication. With respect to the time taken to complete the process, OIOS found that the appeals process at most duty stations could be shortened, as during the past five years, the average time had ranged from 27 to 37 months for New York, 15 to 26 for Geneva, and 19 to 26 for Nairobi. Only in Vienna were appeals completed in 10 to 17 months. Such delays were attributed to gaps in the formal guidelines that governed the time lines for the process and bottlenecks in productivity caused by insufficient resources. OIOS recommended new time lines as set out in annex III to its report; the amendment of the staff rule 111.2 *(a)* to allow staff wishing to appeal an administrative decision to first address a letter to the Secretary-General, copied to the relevant department or office, requesting that the administrative decision be reviewed; and that the JAB secretariat be directed to amend the Rules of Procedure to allow for only one extension, of no more than one month, to the respondent for preparation of an initial reply.

Regarding the resources available to the respective parties, OIOS found that respondents had available to them the five staff members, including one P-5 and two P-4s, who comprised the Administrative Law Unit of the Office of Human Resources Management (OHRM). Appellants had only the two General Service staff members and the volunteers provided through the Panel of Counsel available to them. Appellants had to pay the costs of any outside legal assistance, while respondents' legal costs were borne by the Organization. OIOS recommended that OHRM assess after one year the extent to which extra staff had reduced the delays in preparation of the respondent's replies and consider the need to amend the Staff Rules, whereby the Secretary-General would approve by default the appellant's access to the Administrative Tribunal should the respondent fail to respond within the prescribed time frame. It also made specific recommendations for additional staff resources to strengthen the resources available to the appellants, such as the establishment of a full-time post of Secretary for the Vienna Appeals Board and recruitment of additional Professional staff for the Panel of Counsel in New York.

With respect to the institutional roles played by the several entities in the process, OIOS found that the Department of Management served as respondent, handling the appeals process through the Administrative Law Unit as representative of the Secretary-General, and took decisions on the recommendations of the JAB Panel on behalf of the Secretary-General. OIOS recommended clarification of accountability and measures to mitigate conflict of interest.

As to training and communication, OIOS found that there were shortcomings in the training provided to members of JAB and the Panel of Counsel. OIOS also found that there was scope for improving the access of staff to information about the status of their appeals through secure electronic means.

The Secretary-General concurred with the OIOS recommendations, subject to the observations provided by the Secretariat, which he further elaborated in his report on the administration of justice (see p. 1441).

On 23 December, the Assembly deferred consideration of the Secretary-General's report to its resumed fifty-ninth (2005) session (**decision 59/551**).

Joint Appeals Board

In response to section XI of General Assembly resolution 55/258 [YUN 2001, p. 1340], the Secretary-General submitted a March report [A/59/70] on the outcome of the work of JAB in 2003. He stated that 145 appeals and suspension-of-action cases were filed with JAB in New York, Geneva, Vienna and Nairobi in 2003, compared to 159 cases the previous year. JAB disposed of 131 cases compared to 119 in 2002. Regarding disciplinary cases, which were accorded priority, 18 such cases were considered in 2003, compared to 11 the previous year. The Secretary-General accepted fully or partially 84 per cent of unanimous JAB decisions favourable to appellants in 2003 and rejected 17 per cent, compared to 85 per

cent acceptances and 15 per cent rejections in 2002.

On 23 December, the Assembly deferred consideration of the Secretary-General's report to its resumed fifty-ninth (2005) session (**decision 59/551**).

UN Administrative Tribunal

In its annual note to the General Assembly [A/INF/59/5], the United Nations Administrative Tribunal (UNAT) reported in December, through the Secretary-General, that it delivered 59 judgements in 2004, relating to cases brought by staff against the Secretary-General or the executive heads of other UN bodies to resolve disputes involving terms of appointment and other issues. The Tribunal met in plenary in New York on 23 November and held two panel sessions (Geneva, 21 June–23 July; New York, 25 October–24 November).

UNAT report. Pursuant to Assembly resolution 57/307 [YUN 2003, p. 1459], UNAT submitted a January report [A/58/680] on its activities, which provided information on its organization, jurisdiction, functioning, judicial work and finances. The Tribunal supported the strengthening of the existing system and saw no great merit in radically modifying it or in creating a new one. UNAT stressed the importance of presenting an annual report to the Assembly, in order to keep it informed of emerging jurisprudence and of some of the possible conflictst between the Administration and staff members and to draw to its attention administrative practices that needed correction.

Report of Secretary-General. In response to General Assembly resolutions 57/307 and 58/270 [YUN 2003, p. 1399], the Secretary-General, in May [A/59/78], reported on the possibility of the financial independence of UNAT from the Office of Legal Affairs (OLA). The OLA Executive Office supported UNAT's secretariat in its day-to-day operations by providing administrative and logistical services as requested by the Executive Secretary. Without such service, UNAT's secretariat would need an entire administrative infrastructure of its own. UNAT was financially independent from OLA insofar as separate budgetary provisions were made for its operation under the heading "policy-making organs" of Section 8, Office of Legal Affairs, of the programme budget. However, to avoid any appearance of undue influence by the Respondent, the Secretary-General proposed that UNAT and its secretariat be included under Section 1, Overall policy-making, direction and coordination, of the programme budget. He recommended that the Assembly approve the transfer, effective with the beginning of the 2006-2007 biennium.

JIU report. In August [A/59/280 & Corr.1], the Secretary-General transmitted the Joint Inspection Unit (JIU) report on the harmonization of UNAT and the International Labour Organization Administrative Tribunal (ILOAT), prepared in response to General Assembly resolution 57/307. The objective of the report was to provide a definitive opinion of the feasibility of harmonizing the statutes of the two Tribunals. JIU concluded that there were only three major differences between the two Tribunals: selection and appointment of their members; authority of the Tribunals to order specific performance by the executive heads; and limitations on the amount of compensation that might be awarded by the Tribunals. Eliminating those discrepancies should close the gap between them, remove the perception of inequality within the UN internal justice system and strengthen the UN common system with regard to administration of justice. The Inspectors were of the view that all other differences in the statutes and practices of the two Tribunals were minor and did not materially affect the administration of justice, thus bringing the issue of any further harmonization of the statutes to a close.

JIU recommended that the Assembly should continue to keep under review the issue of selection and appointment of UNAT members with a view to bringing those practices into conformity with the statute and practices of ILOAT, and amend article 10 of UNAT's statute to bring it into conformity with ILOAT's statute and settle the issues of specific performance and compensation limitations. The Assembly should continue to treat, as a matter of priority, the improvement of other elements of the process of internal justice that preceded the Tribunal stage of a dispute, since those processes were slow and cumbersome, and expediting and improving them could lead to fewer cases being brought to the Tribunal and result in less costly decisions and procedures. The Secretary-General should invite CEB to develop a mechanism to enhance cooperation and facilitate professional exchange and regular dialogue between UNAT, ILOAT and other international administrative tribunals, particularly with respect to the uniform and consistent application of case law.

In an addendum [A/59/280/Add.1], the Secretary-General presented his comments on the JIU report, which he welcomed, and invited the Assembly to take into consideration the views expressed in his 2002 report on the administration of justice [YUN 2002, p. 1423].

On 23 December, the Assembly deferred consideration of the JIU report and the Secretary-General's comments thereon until its resumed fifty-ninth (2005) session (**decision 59/551**).

Chapter IV

Institutional and administrative matters

In 2004, the United Nations continued to address administrative and institutional matters in order to ensure the efficient functioning of the Organization. The General Assembly resumed its fifty-eighth session and its tenth emergency special session; it opened its fifty-ninth session on 14 September. The Assembly granted observer status to the Shanghai Cooperation Organization, the Southern African Development Community, the Collective Security Treaty Organization, the Economic Community of West African States, the Organisation of Eastern Caribbean States and the South Asian Association for Regional Cooperation. The Assembly also set out modalities for the participation of the Holy See in UN work.

The Security Council held 216 formal meetings to deal with regional conflicts, peacekeeping operations and other issues related to the maintenance of international peace and security. The Assembly again examined the question of expanding the Council's membership.

In addition to its organizational and substantive sessions, the Economic and Social Council held a special high-level meeting with the Bretton Woods institutions (the World Bank Group and the International Monetary Fund) and the World Trade Organization.

The Committee on Conferences examined requests for changes to the 2004 calendar of meetings and ways of improving the use of conference services and facilities. The Assembly noted the progress in the establishment of a task force to conduct a comprehensive study of workload standards and performance measurement with a view to making a recommendation to the Assembly on a comprehensive methodology. It requested the Secretary-General to elaborate all options for resolving the issue of the time frame for the provision of summary records, and to develop further the functions of the Electronic Meetings Planning and Resource Allocation System and the electronic documentation management concept.

The Secretary-General reported on progress in the implementation of the capital master plan for refurbishing the UN complex, including the offer by the host country of a loan for that purpose and other financing options, and on collaboration between the United Nations and the city and State of New York on arrangements for pro-

viding swing space during that period. He also reported on the implementation of the unified security management system for the United Nations and its financing.

On 23 December, the Assembly decided that the item entitled "Admission of new Members to the United Nations" would remain for consideration during its resumed fifty-ninth (2005) session (**decision 59/552**).

Institutional machinery

General Assembly

The General Assembly met throughout 2004; it resumed and concluded its fifty-eighth session and held the major part of its fifty-ninth session. The fifty-eighth session was resumed in plenary meetings on 9 and 25 February, 7-8 and 14 April, and 6 May. The fifty-ninth session opened on 14 September and continued until its suspension on 23 December.

The Assembly resumed the tenth emergency special session on 16 and 19-20 July to discuss "Illegal Israeli actions in Occupied East Jerusalem and the rest of the Occupied Palestinian Territory" (see p. 465).

Organization of Assembly sessions

2004 sessions

By **decision 59/501** of 14 September, the General Assembly authorized the Committee on Relations with the Host Country, the Committee on the Exercise of the Inalienable Rights of the Palestinian People, the Working Group on the Financing of the United Nations Relief and Works Agency for Palestine Refugees in the Near East, the Disarmament Commission, the Special Committee to Investigate Israeli Practices Affecting the Human Rights of the Palestinian People and Other Arabs of the Occupied Territories, the Executive Board of the United Nations Development Programme (UNDP) and of the United Nations Population Fund (UNFPA), and the Executive Boards of the United Nations Children's Fund (UNICEF) and the International Research and Training Institute for the Advancement of Women (INSTRAW) to meet during the main part of its fifty-ninth session; on 4 October, it authorized the United Nations Administrative Tribunal to do likewise.

By **decision 59/502** of 17 September, the Assembly adopted a number of provisions concerning the organization of the fifty-ninth session, as recommended by the General Committee [A/59/250 & Add.2-3]. On 14 October, the Assembly decided to hear a statement by UNFPA's Executive Director at the commemoration of the tenth anniversary (see p. 1078) of the 1994 International Conference on Population and Development [YUN 1994, p. 955], under the agenda item on integrated and coordinated implementation of and follow-up to the outcomes of the major UN conferences and summits in the economic, social and related fields. On 15 October, the Assembly decided to consider separately the agenda items on the role of diamonds in fuelling conflict and on the prevention of armed conflict. On 29 October, the Assembly decided to consider separately the agenda items on the situation in the Middle East and on the question of Palestine. On 10 and 20 December, the Assembly postponed the date of recess of the session to 20 and 23 December, respectively.

Credentials

The Credentials Committee, at its first meeting on 10 December [A/59/602], had before it a memorandum by the Secretary-General indicating that, to date, 133 Member States had submitted the formal credentials of their representatives. During the meeting, the Legal Counsel made a statement updating the information contained in the memorandum. Information concerning the representatives of 58 other Member States had been communicated also.

The Committee adopted a resolution accepting the credentials received and recommended a draft resolution to the General Assembly for adoption. On 20 December, the Assembly, by **resolution 59/208**, approved the Committee's report.

On 23 December, the Assembly decided that the agenda item on the report of the Credentials Committee would remain for consideration during the resumed fifty-ninth (2005) session (**decision 59/552**).

Agenda

During the resumed fifty-eighth (2004) session, the General Assembly, by **decision 58/503 B**, took a number of actions related to its agenda. It decided to reopen consideration of the agenda item on the implementation of the Declaration on the Granting of Independence to Colonial Countries and Peoples, in order to consider expeditiously a request by Saint Vincent and the Grenadines [A/58/692]; the item on support by the UN system of the efforts of Governments to promote and consolidate new or restored democracies, in order to consider expeditiously a draft resolution [A/58/L.57 & Add.1]; and the sub-item on the causes of conflict and the promotion of durable peace and sustainable development in Africa, in order to hold a plenary meeting to commemorate the International Day of Reflection on the 1994 Genocide in Rwanda. The Assembly also decided to reopen consideration of the sub-item on the further implementation of the Programme of Action for the Sustainable Development of Small Island Developing States and to examine it directly in plenary meeting, in order to consider expeditiously a draft resolution [A/58/L.63]; it agreed to proceed immediately to consideration of the sub-item. On the Secretary-General's proposal, the Assembly decided to include in its agenda the items on the financing of the United Nations Operation in Côte d'Ivoire [A/58/235], the United Nations Stabilization Mission in Haiti [A/58/236] and the United Nations Operation in Burundi [A/58/239], and to allocate those items to the Fifth (Administrative and Budgetary) Committee. On the recommendation of the General Committee [A/58/250/Add.3-4], the Assembly decided to include in the agenda the item on the International Year of Physics, 2005, and to consider it directly in plenary meeting, and to include the sub-item on the appointment of a member of the International Civil Service Commission and allocate it to the Fifth Committee. The Assembly also decided to submit to the Assembly section II of the Secretary-General's report [A/58/864] on the provisional agenda of the Assembly's fifty-ninth regular session organized under headings corresponding to the priorities of the Organization, as contained in the medium-term plan for the period 2002-2005; to submit to the Assembly annex I to the Secretary-General's report [ibid.] on the draft programme of work of the plenary of the Assembly at its fifty-ninth (2004) session, as orally revised; and that the item on the integrated and coordinated implementation of and follow-up to the outcomes of major UN conferences and summits in the economic, social and related fields should be considered jointly with the item on follow-up to the outcome of the Millennium Summit. It further decided to consider the agenda item on the International Criminal Court directly in plenary meeting in order to consider expeditiously a draft resolution [A/58/L.68].

On 8 April, the Assembly deferred until its fifty-ninth (2004) session consideration of the items on the review of the efficiency of the administrative and financial functioning of the United Nations, human resources management, and the Secretary-General's report on the activities of the Office of Internal Oversight Services (OIOS) (**decision 58/564 B**); the Secretary-General's report on the participation of United Nations Volunteers in peacekeeping operations and the report of the Advisory Committee on Administrative and Budgetary Questions (ACABQ) thereon (**decision 58/567**). On the same date, the Assembly postponed to the second part of the resumed fifty-eighth session consideration of the issue of financing the capital master plan (**decision 58/566**).

On 18 June, the Assembly deferred until its fifty-ninth session consideration of the items on the 2004-2005 programme budget and the administrative and budgetary aspects of the financing of UN peacekeeping operations (**decision 58/564 C**).

On 1 July, the Assembly, on the proposal of its President, decided to consider the report of the World Summit on the Information Society [YUN 2003, p. 857] directly in plenary meeting at its sixtieth (2005) session (**decision 58/569**).

On 5 August (**decision 58/571**), the Assembly deferred consideration of the item on multilingualism and included it in the draft agenda of its fifty-ninth session, on the understanding that the item's biennial character would be considered next at the sixty-first (2006) session.

On 13 September, the Assembly decided to consider the report of the Secretary-General on the implementation of resolution 56/212 on the Global Code of Ethics for Tourism [YUN 2001, p. 752] at its sixtieth (2005) session, instead of at its fifty-ninth (2004) session, pursuant to that resolution (**decision 58/573**). On the same date, the Assembly deferred consideration of, and included in the draft agenda of the fifty-ninth session, the items on: the confirmation of the appointment of the Secretary-General of the United Nations Conference on Trade and Development (UNCTAD) (**decision 58/574**), improving the financial situation of the United Nations (**decision 58/575**), administration of justice at the United Nations (**decision 58/576**), the financing of the United Nations Angola Verification Mission and the United Nations Observer Mission in Angola (**decision 58/577**), and the financing of the United Nations Mission in East Timor (**decision 58/578**).

The Assembly took a number of actions in respect of its fifty-ninth (2004) session agenda, as listed in **decision 59/503 A**. On 17 September, on the recommendation of the General Committee

[A/59/250], it adopted the agenda [A/59/251] and allocation of agenda items [A/59/252], and deferred consideration of, and included in the provisional agenda of its sixtieth (2005) session, the items "Question of the Comorian island of Mayotte" and "Question of the Malagasy islands of Glorieuses, Juan de Nova, Europa and Bassas da India". On 4 October, also on the recommendation of the General Committee [A/59/250/Add.1], the Assembly included in the agenda of its fifty-ninth (2004) session an additional item on observer status for the Economic Community of West African States in the Assembly and allocated it to the Sixth (Legal) Committee; included in the agenda an additional sub-item on cooperation between the United Nations and the community of Portuguese-speaking countries under the item "Cooperation between the United Nations and other organizations" and decided to consider it directly in plenary meeting; and allocated to the Third (Social, Humanitarian and Cultural) Committee the item on programme planning, with respect to programme 19 (Human rights) of the strategic framework for the period 2006-2007. On 15 October, the Assembly, on the recommendation of the General Committee [A/59/250/Add.2], included an additional item on observer status for the Organisation of Eastern Caribbean States in the Assembly and allocated it to the Sixth Committee. On 29 October, on the recommendation of the General Committee [A/59/250/Add.3], it included in the agenda of its fifty-ninth (2004) session and decided to consider in plenary meeting the additional items "Andean zone of peace" and "The situation in the occupied territories of Azerbaijan"; included in the agenda and allocated to the Sixth Committee the item "Observer status for the South Asian Association for Regional Cooperation in the General Assembly"; and included in the agenda an additional sub-item on the election of a member of the International Court of Justice under the item "Elections to fill vacancies in principal organs" and decided to consider it directly in plenary meeting. On 30 November, the Assembly, on the recommendation of the General Committee [A/59/250/Add.4], included in the agenda and allocated to the Second (Economic and Financial) Committee the additional sub-item on rendering assistance to the poor mountain countries to overcome obstacles in socio-economic and ecological areas under the item "Sustainable development".

The Assembly included in the provisional agenda of its sixtieth (2005) session the items "Establishment of a nuclear-weapon-free zone in Cental Asia" (**decision 59/513**), "United Nations conference to identify ways of eliminating nuclear dangers in the context of nuclear disarmament" (**decision 59/514**) (see p. 536), "Problems arising from the accumulation of conventional ammunition stockpiles in surplus" (**decision 59/515**), and "Assistance in mine action" (**decision 59/516**).

On 23 December, the Assembly deferred until its resumed fifty-ninth (2005) session consideration of the items on the 2004-2005 programme budget and the administration of justice at the United Nations (**decision 59/551 A**); retained 74 items for consideration during that session, including items on the election of its President and Vice-Presidents and the officers of its main committees (**decision 59/552**); and deferred consideration of, and included in the provisional agenda of its sixty-first (2006) session, the item on the role of the United Nations in promoting a new global human order (**decision 59/543**).

Resolutions and decisions
of the General Assembly

By **decision 59/509** of 8 November, the Assembly deferred consideration of the agenda item "Implementation of the resolutions of the United Nations" and included it in the provisional agenda of its sixtieth (2005) session.

Security Council

The Security Council held 216 formal meetings in 2004, adopted 59 resolutions and issued 48 presidential statements. It considered 51 agenda items (see APPENDIX IV). In a September note [A/59/335], the Secretary-General, in accordance with Article 12, paragraph 2 of the Charter of the United Nations and with the consent of the Council, notified the General Assembly of 61 matters relative to the maintenance of international peace and security that the Council had discussed since his previous annual notification [YUN 2003, p. 1465]. The Secretary-General also listed 85 matters that the Council had not discussed since then. The Assembly, on 11 October, took note of the Secretary-General's note (**decision 59/505**).

On 13 October, the Assembly took note of the Council's report for the period 1 August 2003 to 31 July 2004 [A/59/2] (**decision 59/506**). It decided on 23 December that the item on the Council's report would remain for consideration during its resumed fifty-ninth (2005) session (**decision 59/552**).

Membership

The General Assembly continued to examine the question of expanding the Security Council's membership. It considered the report of the Open-ended Working Group on the Question of Equitable Representation on and Increase in the Membership of the Security Council and Other Matters related to the Security Council [A/58/47]. (For details and related Assembly decisions, see p. 1378).

Economic and Social Council

The Economic and Social Council held its organizational session for 2004 on 21 January, 4 to 6, 13 and 27 February, 23 April, and 1 and 4 May; a resumed organizational session on 3, 15 and 23 June; and a special high-level meeting with the Bretton Woods institutions (the World Bank Group and the International Monetary Fund) and the World Trade Organization (WTO) on 26 April, all in New York. It held its substantive session from 28 June to 23 July and resumed substantive session on 16 September and on 5 and 11 November, all in New York.

On 21 January, the Council elected its Bureau (a President and four Vice-Presidents) for 2004 (see APPENDIX III) and adopted the agenda of its organizational session [E/2004/2 & Add.1].

On 4 February, the Council approved the change in the dates of its 2004 substantive session from 6 to 30 July to 28 June to 23 July (**decision 2004/202**), adopted the provisional agenda (**decision 2004/203**) and decided on the working arrangements for that session (**decision 2004/205**). On 28 June, it adopted the agenda [E/2004/100 & Corr. 2] and approved the proposed programme of work of that session [E/2004/L.7]. On 29 June, it approved the requests for hearings from nongovernmental organizations (NGOs) [E/2004/84] (**decision 2004/230**).

Sessions and segments

During 2004, the Economic and Social Council adopted 69 resolutions and 128 decisions. By **decision 2004/205** of 4 February, the Council decided that the high-level segment of its substantive session would be held from 28 to 30 June; the coordination segment from 1 to 7 July; the operational activities segment from 7 to 9 July; the humanitarian affairs segment from 10 to 14 July; and the general segment from 15 to 22 July. By **decision 2004/207** of the same date, the Council decided that its high-level meeting with the Bretton Woods institutions and WTO would be held in New York on 26 April.

The work of the Council in 2004 was covered in its report to the General Assembly [A/59/3 & Add.1-2]. On 23 December, the Assembly decided that the item on the Council's report would remain for consideration at its resumed fifty-ninth (2005) session (**decision 59/552**).

2004 and 2005 sessions

On 4 February (**decision 2004/206**), the Council decided that the work of its 2004 operational activities segment should be devoted to the triennial comprehensive policy review of operational activities for development of the UN system and the implementation of General Assembly resolution 56/201 [YUN 2001, p. 784] and Council resolution 2003/3 [YUN 2003, p. 883]. On 13 February, it decided that the theme for the regional cooperation item at its 2004 substantive session should be "Information technology for development: a regional perspective" (**decision 2004/213**). On 3 May, it decided that the theme for the 2004 humanitarian affairs segment would be "Strengthening of the coordination of humanitarian assistance of the United Nations: present and future challenges", and that it would convene two panels on the themes "Strengthening preparedness and response to natural disasters, with an emphasis on capacity-building" and "Field-level coordination for the purpose of continuing the presence and operation of United Nations humanitarian assistance missions in higher risk environments" (**decision 2004/219**).

On 23 July, the Council, by **decision 2004/294**, adopted the following theme for its high-level segment in 2005: "Achieving the internationally agreed development goals, including those contained in the Millennium Declaration, as well as implementing the outcomes of the major UN conferences and summits: progress made, challenges and opportunities". On the same date, it adopted the theme "Towards achieving internationally agreed development goals, including those contained in the Millennium Declaration" for the coordination segment in 2005, and decided to continue consultations on a multi-year work programme for that segment, with a view to finalizing the programme before the beginning of the next substantive session in 2005 (**decision 2004/292**).

Work programme

On 4 February, the Economic and Social Council, having considered its proposed basic programme of work for 2004 and 2005 [E/2004/1 & Corr.1], took note of the list of questions for inclusion in the programme of work for 2005 (**decision 2004/204**).

Coordination, monitoring and cooperation

Institutional mechanisms

CEB activities

According to its annual overview report [E/2005/63], the work of the United Nations System Chief Executives Board for Coordination (CEB) was dominated by preparations for the comprehensive review, to take place at the High-level Plenary Meeting of the General Assembly in 2005, of the implementation of the Millennium Declaration, adopted by the General Assembly in resolution 55/2 [YUN 2000, p. 49]. In that context, it took up the themes of curbing transnational crime, bridging the digital divide and fostering inter-agency collaboration in information and communication technology. It continued to consider the issues of conflict prevention; strengthening system-wide support for Africa's development and the New Partnership for Africa's Development (NEPAD); and increasing the effectiveness and coherence of UN system activities at the country level. In the area of management, CEB continued to focus on staff security and safety, human and financial resources management, and UN system oversight. In response to a request by the Committee for Programme and Coordination (see below), the overview report contained information on inter-agency collaboration to fight hunger.

CEB held two regular sessions in 2004: the first in Vienna, Austria, (2-3 April) [CEB/2004/1] and the second in New York (29-30 October) [CEB/2004/2]. Its principal subsidiary bodies met as follows: the High-level Committee on Management (HLCM), seventh (London, 8-9 March) [CEB/2004/3] and eighth (Rome, 5-6 October) [CEB/2004/6] sessions; the High-level Committee on Programmes (HLCP), seventh (Beirut, Lebanon, 26-27 February) [CEB/2004/4] and eighth (Florence, Italy, 15-17 September) [CEB/2004/7] sessions, with an intersessional meeting (Frascati, Italy, 31 May and 1 June) [CEB/2004/5].

Report for 2003

The Committee for Programme and Coordination (CPC) [A/59/16] considered CEB's annual overview report for 2003 [YUN 2003, p. 1466]. It underlined the importance of effective coordination of system-wide efforts against hunger and recommended that CEB include, in its annual overview report for 2004 (see above), information on existing mechanisms in that area and on any further initiatives envisaged. CPC called for a further strengthening of UN system support for Africa's development by, among other things, promoting synergies among the five inter-agency thematic clusters (infrastructure development; governance, peace and security; agriculture, trade and market access; environment, population and urbanization; human resources development/employment and HIV/AIDS); mainstreaming HIV/AIDS, gender and human rights into all cluster activities; enhancing support for the Commission of the African Union (AU) and NEPAD; and further clarifying the roles and responsibilities of the various agencies operating at the regional and subregional levels in Africa. It welcomed CEB's intention to undertake an in-depth review of UN system support for Africa's development and NEPAD, with a view to strengthening such support. CPC supported CEB's efforts to build a system-wide capacity for conflict prevention through comprehensive, multidimensional and country-based approaches, as well as through enhanced dialogue and improved information-sharing among the organizations concerned, and encouraged CEB to continue to pursue its efforts in that regard. It reiterated its concern over the increased threats to the safety and security of UN system staff and reaffirmed its full support for ongoing efforts to strengthen the security management system. CPC urged CEB to intensify inter-agency cooperation and exchange of information on practices in measuring programme performance and results, productivity in service functions, and on conference management. It recommended that the General Assembly revert to the issue of the establishment of the Senior Management Service at its fifty-ninth (2004) session, under the agenda item on the UN common system.

The Economic and Social Council, by **decision 2004/311** of 23 July, took note of CEB's 2003 report; welcomed progress in CEB's work, particularly as it related to harnessing UN system activities in support of the integrated follow-up to conferences and the Millennium Declaration [YUN 2000, p. 49]; and looked forward to further strengthening its dialogue with CEB members on all relevant aspects of UN system work and its effective coordination in the light of CEB's annual reports.

Programme coordination

The Committee for Programme and Coordination held an organizational meeting on 1 June and its forty-fourth session from 7 June to 2 July, all in New York [A/59/16].

CPC dealt with questions related to programme planning, UN programme perform-

ance for the 2002-2003 biennium, and the proposed strategic framework for 2006-2007. It considered OIOS reports on strengthening the role of evaluation findings in programme design, delivery and policy directives; further development of topics for a pilot thematic evaluation; the in-depth evaluation of the programme on public administration, finance and development; and two triennial reviews of the implementation of CPC recommendations on in-depth evaluations of sustainable development and the population programme. In addition to its review of CEB's 2003 annual report (see above), CPC also considered the Secretary-General's report on UN system support for NEPAD.

The Economic and Social Council, by **decision 2004/295** of 23 July, deferred consideration of the reports of coordination bodies and the proposed strategic framework for the 2006-2007 biennium. On 16 September (**decision 2004/318**), the Council took note of CPC's report.

Joint Inspection Unit

The Joint Inspection Unit (JIU), in its annual report to the General Assembly covering the period 1 January to 31 December 2003 [A/59/34], described its process of reform which began during that year [YUN 2003, p. 1388]. It discussed its reports issued in 2003, the establishment of the follow-up system for the systematic tracking of the status of JIU recommendations and the potential impact of the recommendations. JIU increased cooperation with other oversight bodies and systematically sought contacts with their representatives.

(For General Assembly action on the report, see **resolution 59/267** on p. 1373.)

Other coordination matters

Follow-up to international conferences

In response to General Assembly resolution 57/270 B [YUN 2003, p. 1468], the Secretary-General submitted a report outlining the overall approach and core elements for the integrated and coordinated follow-up to the outcomes of the major UN conferences and summits in the economic and social fields [A/58/359].

In a May report [E/2004/71], the Secretary-General identified steps that had been taken to implement the provisions of resolution 57/270 B that were relevant to the work of the Economic and Social Council and focused on areas that needed further action in order to promote coordinated implementation throughout the UN system. The report contained recommendations for: a Council review of conference implementation through a cross-sectoral approach and greater thematic unity and interlinkages between Council segments; guiding functional commissions to focus on implementation; promoting a coordinated UN system support to conference implementation; strengthening the relationship between the Council and financial and trade institutions; and complying with the specific mandates given to the Council in the outcomes of major UN conferences and summits, including the 2002 World Summit on Sustainable Development [YUN 2002, p. 821], the 2002 International Conference on Financing for Development [YUN 2002, p. 953], the Third (2001) United Nations Conference on the Least Developed Countries (LDCs) [YUN 2001, p. 770] and the 2003 International Ministerial Conference of Landlocked and Transit Developing Countries and Donor Countries and International Financial and Development Institutions on Transit Transport Cooperation [YUN 2003, p. 875]. The report also discussed the Council's contribution to the high-level plenary meeting of the Assembly scheduled to take place in 2005, which would undertake a comprehensive review of the progress achieved in implementing the commitments made in the Millennium Declaration. (For further information on preparations for the 2005 high-level plenary meeting, see p. 1363.)

By **decision 2004/310** of 23 July, the Council deferred until its resumed substantive session in September consideration of draft resolutions on the implementation of the Programme of Action for the Least Developed Countries for the Decade 2001-2010 [E/2004/L.39], adopted at the Third UN Conference on LDCs in 2001, and on the 2002 International Conference on Financing for Development [E/2004/L.47].

ECONOMIC AND SOCIAL COUNCIL ACTION

On 22 July [meeting 48], the Economic and Social Council adopted **resolution 2004/44** [draft: E/2004/L.24/Rev.1] without vote [agenda items 6 and 8].

Role of the Economic and Social Council in the integrated and coordinated implementation of the outcomes of and follow-up to major United Nations conferences and summits

The Economic and Social Council,

Recalling its agreed conclusions 1995/1 of 28 July 1995 and 2002/1 of 26 July 2002 and its relevant resolutions on the integrated and coordinated implementation of and follow-up to the outcomes of major United Nations conferences and summits,

Recalling also General Assembly resolutions 50/227 of 24 May 1996, 52/12 B of 19 December 1997 and 57/270 B of 23 June 2003,

Recalling further the internationally agreed development goals, including those contained in the United Nations Millennium Declaration, and the outcomes of the major United Nations conferences and summits and the reviews of their implementation in the economic, social and related fields,

Taking note of the report of the Secretary-General,

1. *Decides* to continue to take the steps necessary for the effective implementation of the provisions of resolutions 50/227, 52/12 B and 57/270 B, which are relevant to the work of the Economic and Social Council and its subsidiary machinery;

2. *Welcomes* General Assembly resolution 58/291 of 6 May 2004 on follow-up to the outcome of the Millennium Summit and integrated and coordinated implementation of and follow-up to the outcomes of the major United Nations conferences and summits in the economic and social fields, and decides to contribute to the overall preparation for the high-level plenary meeting of the Assembly in 2005, in accordance with the modalities to be set out by the Assembly at its fifty-ninth session;

3. *Requests,* in this regard, the functional commissions, the regional commissions and other relevant subsidiary bodies to contribute to the preparation of the input of the Economic and Social Council to the high-level plenary meeting of the General Assembly;

4. *Requests* the functional commissions and other relevant subsidiary bodies to continue to examine their methods of work, as mandated in resolution 57/270 B, in order better to pursue the implementation of the outcomes of major United Nations conferences and summits, and to submit their reports to the Council in 2005;

5. *Decides* to revise the title of agenda item 8 to read "Implementation of General Assembly resolutions 50/227, 52/12 B and 57/270 B" at the next substantive session of the Council in 2005;

6. *Requests* the Secretary-General to submit a report on the role of the Economic and Social Council in the implementation of General Assembly resolutions 50/227, 52/12 B and 57/270 B for consideration by the Council at its substantive session of 2005.

Report of Secretary-General. An August report of the Secretary-General [A/59/224] updated information on the implementation of General Assembly resolution 57/270 B [YUN 2003, p. 1468]. It described progress made by the intergovernmental bodies and the UN system in promoting an integrated and coordinated approach to the implementation of conference and summit outcomes, including the work of the Assembly and its Second and Third Committees, and made recommendations for further action in that regard. The report was to be read in conjunction with the Secretary-General's May report on the same subject (see p. 1450).

In February, the Economic and Social Council initiated consultations on the multi-year work programme for the coordination segment of its substantive session, based on a focused and balanced list of cross-sectoral thematic issues common to the outcomes of major UN conferences and summits. While the Council agreed on a cross-cutting theme focused on the Millennium Development Goals (MDGs) [YUN 2000, p. 51] and made some progress towards identifying themes for the multi-year programme, the consultations could not be finalized during the 2004 substantive session, thus the Council decided to continue consultations with a view to finalizing its programme before its 2005 substantive session. As requested in resolution 57/270 B, consultations were held between the presidents of the bureaux of the Assembly and Council to improve coordination between the two bodies in the consideration of the integrated coordinated implementation of and follow-up to conference outcomes. The functional commissions continued to examine their work methods in order to better implement conference outcomes, and were required to report to the Council no later than 2005 in that regard. The regional commissions were strengthening their role in linking global deliberations with regional implementation measures, while continuing to support subregional and regional integration and consensus-building. Further action was needed to strengthen the linkage between the Council's policy guidance and the operational activities of the UN system, in particular with regard to the coordinated implementation of conference outcomes. Under the aegis of the CEB High-Level Committee on Programmes (HLCP), work was under way on a system-wide contribution to the first comprehensive review of the implementation of the Millennium Declaration, to be undertaken during the high-level plenary meeting of the Assembly in 2005. The bureaux of the Second and Third Committees examined various aspects of their work during the fifty-eighth (2003) session and were expected to meet again during the fifty-ninth (2004) session, and the Assembly continued to explore ways and means of improving the work of its two Committees.

The Secretary-General concluded that ensuring a coherent and coordinated approach in the implementation of policies and actions to advance poverty eradication and sustainable development was more crucial than ever, and such an approach should facilitate the forming of coherent, cross-sectoral alliances around common themes and goals for joint action at the national and international levels. The guidance given to various entities by the Assembly was serving to reinforce the efforts of those institutions for more coordination and cooperation.

On 10 September, the Assembly decided that the agenda item on the integrated and coordinated implementation of and follow-up to the outcomes of the major UN conferences and summits in the economic, social and related fields should be considered jointly with the item on follow-up to the out-

come of the 2000 Millennium Summit [YUN 2000, p. 47] (**decision 58/503 B**).

On 23 December, the Assembly decided that the agenda item would remain for consideration during its resumed fifty-ninth (2005) session (**decision 59/552**).

The UN and other organizations

Requests for conversion to UN specialized agency

International Civil Defence Organization

The Economic and Social Council, by **decision 2004/209** of 4 February, deferred until further notice, at the request of the International Civil Defence Organization [E/2004/6], consideration of the request for conversion of the Organization, an intergovernmental body with observer status with the Council, to a specialized agency of the UN system [YUN 2002, p. 1437].

Cooperation with organizations

In response to General Assembly **resolution 58/316** (see p. 1374), the Secretary-General submitted a September consolidated report [A/59/303] on cooperation between the United Nations and regional and other organizations, including the African Union (see p. 283); the Association of Southeast Asian Nations (see p. 388); the Caribbean Community (see p. 306); the Council of Europe (see p. 450); the Economic Community of Central African States (see p. 999); the League of Arab States (see p. 1454); the Organization of the Islamic Conference (see p. 1453); the Organization of American States (see p. 307); the International Organization of la Francophonie (see p. 1456); the Organization for Security and Cooperation in Europe (see p. 451); the Pacific Islands Forum (see p. 387); the Southern African Development Community (see p. 999); the Asian-African Legal Consultative Organization (see p. 1348); the Black Sea Economic Cooperation Organization (see p. 1017); the Economic Cooperation Organization (see p. 1011); the Inter-Parliamentary Union (see p. 1455); the Latin American Economic System (see p. 1026); the Organization for the Prohibition of Chemical Weapons (see p. 558); and the Preparatory Commission for the Comprehensive Nuclear-Test-Ban Treaty Organization (see p. 539).

Organization of the Islamic Conference

In response to General Assembly resolution 57/42 [YUN 2002, p. 1438], the Secretary-General, in his September consolidated report [A/59/303], provided information on cooperation between the United Nations and the Organization of the Islamic Conference (OIC). Consultations at all levels continued to be held on a regular basis between the two organizations on political, economic, social and humanitarian issues, focusing on the situation in the Middle East, Iraq, Afghanistan and the Sudan, and on conflict prevention and the fight against terrorism. The general meeting to evaluate the existing mechanisms of cooperation between the United Nations and OIC (Vienna, 13-15 July) produced a number of proposals to enhance liaison and the exchange of expertise in the political field, and decided on a series of joint projects in areas including science, technology, trade, food security, agriculture, human resources development, environment, health, arts and promotion of heritage, and education. The United Nations and its institutions continued to undertake joint activities and programmes and to exchange information and documents with OIC's specialized and affiliated institutions and subsidiary organs in support of social, economic and cultural development.

GENERAL ASSEMBLY ACTION

On 22 October [meeting 40], the General Assembly adopted **resolution 59/8** [draft: A/59/L.12 & Add.1, orally revised] without vote [agenda item 56 (*p*)].

Cooperation between the United Nations and the Organization of the Islamic Conference

The General Assembly,

Recalling its resolutions 37/4 of 22 October 1982, 38/4 of 28 October 1983, 39/7 of 8 November 1984, 40/4 of 25 October 1985, 41/3 of 16 October 1986, 42/4 of 15 October 1987, 43/2 of 17 October 1988, 44/8 of 18 October 1989, 45/9 of 25 October 1990, 46/13 of 28 October 1991, 47/18 of 23 November 1992, 48/24 of 24 November 1993, 49/15 of 15 November 1994, 50/17 of 20 November 1995, 51/18 of 14 November 1996, 52/4 of 22 October 1997, 53/16 of 29 October 1998, 54/7 of 25 October 1999, 55/9 of 30 October 2000, 56/47 of 7 December 2001 and 57/42 of 21 November 2002,

Recalling also its resolution 3369(XXX) of 10 October 1975, by which it decided to invite the Organization of the Islamic Conference to participate in the sessions and the work of the General Assembly and of its subsidiary organs in the capacity of observer,

Having considered the report of the Secretary-General on cooperation between the United Nations and regional and other organizations,

Taking into account the desire of the two organizations to continue to cooperate closely in the political, economic, social, humanitarian, cultural and scientific fields and in their common search for solutions to global problems, such as questions relating to interna-

tional peace and security, disarmament, self-determination, decolonization, fundamental human rights and economic and social development,

Recalling the Articles of the Charter of the United Nations that encourage activities through regional cooperation for the promotion of the purposes and principles of the United Nations,

Noting the strengthening of cooperation between the United Nations, its funds and programmes and the specialized agencies and the Organization of the Islamic Conference, its subsidiary organs and its specialized and affiliated institutions,

Noting also the encouraging progress made in the ten priority areas of cooperation between the two organizations and their respective agencies and institutions, as well as in the identification of other areas of cooperation between them,

Convinced that the strengthening of cooperation between the United Nations and other organizations of the United Nations system and the Organization of the Islamic Conference and its organs and institutions contributes to the promotion of the purposes and principles of the United Nations,

Welcoming the results of the general meeting of the organizations and agencies of the United Nations system and the Organization of the Islamic Conference and its subsidiary organs and specialized and affiliated institutions, held in Vienna from 13 to 15 July 2004, and the fact that these meetings are now being held every two years, with the next one scheduled for 2006,

Noting with appreciation the determination of both organizations to strengthen further the existing cooperation by developing specific proposals in the designated priority areas of cooperation, as well as in the political field,

1. *Takes note with satisfaction* of the report of the Secretary-General;

2. *Notes with satisfaction* the active participation of the Organization of the Islamic Conference in the work of the United Nations towards the realization of the purposes and principles embodied in the Charter of the United Nations;

3. *Requests* the United Nations and the Organization of the Islamic Conference to continue to cooperate in their common search for solutions to global problems, such as questions relating to international peace and security, disarmament, self-determination, decolonization, fundamental human rights, emergency relief and rehabilitation, social and economic development and technical cooperation;

4. *Welcomes* the efforts of the United Nations and the Organization of the Islamic Conference to continue to strengthen cooperation between the two organizations in areas of common concern and to review and explore innovative ways and means of enhancing the mechanisms of such cooperation;

5. *Welcomes with appreciation* the continuing cooperation between the United Nations and the Organization of the Islamic Conference in the fields of peacemaking, preventive diplomacy, peacekeeping and peacebuilding, and notes the close cooperation between the two organizations in reconstruction and development in Afghanistan and Sierra Leone;

6. *Welcomes* the efforts of the secretariats of the two organizations to strengthen information exchange, co-

ordination and cooperation between them in areas of mutual interest in the political field and to develop practical modalities of such cooperation;

7. *Also welcomes* the periodic high-level meetings between the Secretary-General of the United Nations and the Secretary-General of the Organization of the Islamic Conference, as well as between senior secretariat officials of the two organizations, and encourages their participation in important meetings of the two organizations;

8. *Encourages* the specialized agencies and other organizations of the United Nations system to continue to expand their cooperation with the subsidiary organs and specialized and affiliated institutions of the Organization of the Islamic Conference, in particular by negotiating cooperation agreements, and through necessary contacts and meetings of the respective focal points for cooperation in priority areas of interest to the United Nations and the Organization of the Islamic Conference;

9. *Urges* the United Nations and other organizations of the United Nations system, especially the lead agencies, to provide increased technical and other forms of assistance to the Organization of the Islamic Conference and its subsidiary organs and specialized and affiliated institutions in order to enhance cooperation;

10. *Expresses its appreciation* to the Secretary-General for his continued efforts to strengthen cooperation and coordination between the United Nations and other organizations of the United Nations system and the Organization of the Islamic Conference and its subsidiary organs and specialized and affiliated institutions to serve the mutual interests of the two organizations in the political, economic, social, cultural, humanitarian and scientific fields;

11. *Requests* the Secretary-General to report to the General Assembly at its sixty-first session on the state of cooperation between the United Nations and the Organization of the Islamic Conference;

12. *Decides* to include in the provisional agenda of its sixty-first session the sub-item entitled "Cooperation between the United Nations and the Organization of the Islamic Conference".

League of Arab States

In response to General Assembly resolution 57/46 [YUN 2002, p. 1439], the Secretary-General, in his September consolidated report [A/59/303], provided information on the continuing and multifaceted cooperation between the United Nations and the League of Arab States (LAS). The two organizations agreed to enhance cooperation between the United Nations Industrial Development Organization and the Arab Industrial Development and Mining Organization in areas including the strengthening of technological capacity, development of a centre of training and excellence on industrial information and networks, and fostering a cleaner production concept in the Arab region in support of the implementation of multilateral environmental agreements.

On 22 October [meeting 40], the General Assembly adopted **resolution 59/9** [draft: A/59/L.13] without vote [agenda item 56 *(l)*].

Cooperation between the United Nations and the League of Arab States

The General Assembly,

Recalling its previous resolutions on cooperation between the United Nations and the League of Arab States,

Having considered the report of the Secretary-General on cooperation between the United Nations and regional and other organizations,

Recalling article 3 of the Pact of the League of Arab States, which entrusts the Council of the League with the function of determining the means whereby the League will collaborate with the international organizations which may be created in the future to guarantee peace and security and organize economic and social relations,

Noting the desire of both organizations to consolidate, develop and enhance further the ties existing between them in the political, economic, social, humanitarian, cultural, technical and administrative fields,

Taking into account the report of the Secretary-General entitled "An Agenda for Peace", in particular section VII, concerning cooperation with regional arrangements and organizations, and the "Supplement to an Agenda for Peace",

Convinced of the need for more efficient and coordinated utilization of available economic and financial resources in order to promote the common objectives of the two organizations,

Recognizing the need for the further strengthening of cooperation between the United Nations system and the League of Arab States and its specialized organizations for the realization of the common goals and objectives of the two organizations,

1. *Takes note with satisfaction* of the report of the Secretary-General;

2. *Commends* the continued efforts of the League of Arab States to promote multilateral cooperation among Arab States, and requests the United Nations system to continue to lend its support;

3. *Expresses its appreciation* to the Secretary-General for the follow-up action taken by him to implement the proposals adopted at the meetings between the representatives of the secretariats of the United Nations and other organizations of the United Nations system and the General Secretariat of the League of Arab States and its specialized organizations, including the sectoral meeting in 2004 on the theme "Achieving and financing the Millennium Development Goals and sustainable development for the members of the League of Arab States";

4. *Requests* the Secretariat of the United Nations and the General Secretariat of the League of Arab States, within their respective fields of competence, to intensify further their cooperation for the realization of the purposes and principles embodied in the Charter of the United Nations, the strengthening of international peace and security, economic and social development, disarmament, decolonization, self-determination and the eradication of all forms of racism and racial discrimination;

5. *Requests* the Secretary-General to continue his efforts to strengthen cooperation and coordination between the United Nations and other organizations and agencies of the United Nations system and the League of Arab States and its specialized organizations in order to enhance their capacity to serve the mutual interests and objectives of the two organizations in the political, economic, social, humanitarian, cultural and administrative fields;

6. *Calls upon* the specialized agencies and other organizations and programmes of the United Nations system:

(a) To continue to cooperate with the Secretary-General and among themselves, as well as with the League of Arab States and its specialized organizations, in the follow-up of multilateral proposals aimed at strengthening and expanding cooperation in all fields between the United Nations system and the League of Arab States and its specialized organizations;

(b) To strengthen the capacity of the League of Arab States and of its institutions and specialized organizations to benefit from globalization and information technology and to meet the development challenges of the new millennium;

(c) To step up cooperation and coordination with the specialized organizations of the League of Arab States in the organization of seminars and training courses and in the preparation of studies;

(d) To maintain and increase contacts and improve the mechanism of consultation with the counterpart programmes, organizations and agencies concerned regarding projects and programmes in order to facilitate their implementation;

(e) To participate whenever possible with organizations and institutions of the League of Arab States in the execution and implementation of development projects in the Arab region;

(f) To inform the Secretary-General of the progress made in their cooperation with the League of Arab States and its specialized organizations and, in particular, of the follow-up action taken on the multilateral and bilateral proposals adopted at the previous meetings between the two organizations;

7. *Also calls upon* the specialized agencies and other organizations and programmes of the United Nations system to increase their cooperation with the League of Arab States and its specialized organizations in the priority sectors of energy, rural development, desertification and green belts, training and vocational education, technology, environment, information and documentation, trade and finance, water resources, development of the agricultural sector, empowerment of women, transport, communications and information, promotion of the role of the private sector and capacity-building;

8. *Requests* the Secretary-General of the United Nations, in cooperation with the Secretary-General of the League of Arab States, to encourage periodic consultation between representatives of the Secretariat of the United Nations and of the General Secretariat of the League of Arab States in order to review and strengthen coordination mechanisms with a view to accelerating implementation of, and follow-up action on, the multilateral projects, proposals and recommen-

dations adopted at the meetings between the two organizations;

9. *Recommends* that the United Nations and all organizations of the United Nations system make the greatest possible use of Arab institutions and technical expertise in projects undertaken in the Arab region;

10. *Reaffirms* that, in order to enhance cooperation and for the purpose of the review and appraisal of progress, a general meeting between representatives of the United Nations system and the League of Arab States should be held once every two years and that joint inter-agency sectoral meetings should also be convened on a biennial basis to address priority areas of major importance to the development of Arab States, on the basis of agreement between the United Nations system and the League of Arab States and its specialized organizations;

11. *Also reaffirms* the importance of holding the next general meeting on cooperation between representatives of the secretariats of the organizations of the United Nations system and the General Secretariat of the League of Arab States and its specialized organizations during 2005;

12. *Requests* the Secretary-General to submit to the General Assembly at its sixty-first session a report on the implementation of the present resolution;

13. *Decides* to include in the provisional agenda of its sixty-first session the sub-item entitled "Cooperation between the United Nations and the League of Arab States".

Inter-Parliamentary Union

Pursuant to General Assembly resolution 57/47 [YUN 2002, p. 1441], the Secretary-General, in his September consolidated report [A/59/303], detailed the growing cooperation between the United Nations and the Inter-Parliamentary Union (IPU) in bringing a parliamentary dimension to UN work, including in the areas of peace and security, economic and social development, humanitarian affairs and crisis management, international law and human rights, democracy and gender issues. The report also addressed institutional efforts aimed at strengthening the relationship between the United Nations and IPU. The Secretary-General acknowledged IPU's contribution to meeting the major goals and objectives of the international community and welcomed the decision to hold, in August 2005, the Second Conference of Speakers of Parliaments, with a special focus on the contribution by parliaments in meeting the Millennium Development Goals (MDGs) [YUN 2000, p. 51], and on action and modalities to enhance the parliamentary dimension of international cooperation. He also looked forward to discussing the recommendations of the report of the Panel of Eminent Persons on United Nations-Civil Society Relations [A/58/817 & Corr.1] (see p. 1360) on engaging parliamentarians, parliaments and IPU more systematically in UN work.

On 8 November [meeting 50], the General Assembly adopted **resolution 59/19** [draft: A/59/L.5/ Rev.2 & Add.1] without vote [agenda item 56 (*j*)].

Cooperation between the United Nations and the Inter-Parliamentary Union

The General Assembly,

Having considered the report of the Secretary-General of 1 September 2004, which takes stock of the broad cooperation between the United Nations and the Inter-Parliamentary Union over the past two years,

Taking note of the resolutions adopted by the Inter-Parliamentary Union and circulated in the General Assembly and the activities undertaken by the organization over the past two years in support of the United Nations,

Welcoming the annual parliamentary hearings at the United Nations as a regular feature of the programme of events held at United Nations Headquarters on the occasion of the sessions of the General Assembly,

Taking into consideration the Cooperation Agreement between the United Nations and the Inter-Parliamentary Union of 1996, which laid the foundation for cooperation between the two organizations,

Recalling the United Nations Millennium Declaration, in which Heads of State and Government resolved to strengthen further cooperation between the United Nations and national parliaments through their world organization, the Inter-Parliamentary Union, in various fields, including peace and security, economic and social development, international law and human rights, and democracy and gender issues,

Also recalling its resolution 57/32 of 19 November 2002, in which the Inter-Parliamentary Union was invited to participate in the work of the General Assembly in the capacity of observer, as well as resolution 57/47 of 21 November 2002,

Taking note of the recommendations contained in the report of the Panel of Eminent Persons on United Nations-Civil Society Relations in regard to engaging parliamentarians more systematically in the work of the United Nations,

1. *Welcomes* the efforts made by the Inter-Parliamentary Union to provide for a greater parliamentary contribution and enhanced support to the United Nations;

2. *Welcomes with satisfaction* the decision to convene the second World Conference of Speakers of Parliament at United Nations Headquarters in September 2005, in follow-up to the first such conference held in New York in 2000 in conjunction with the Millennium Assembly of the United Nations;

3. *Calls upon* the host country to extend the usual courtesies to participants of all parliamentary delegations of States Members of the United Nations at the second World Conference of Speakers of Parliament;

4. *Takes note* of the efforts of the Inter-Parliamentary Union to consult parliaments on the recommendations contained in the report of the Panel of Eminent Persons in regard to engaging parliamentarians more systematically in the work of the United Nations, and looks forward to learning of the outcome of this process as a contribution to the deliberations of the General Assembly prior to a final decision on the recommendations of the Panel in regard to parliamentarians;

5. *Encourages* the United Nations and the Inter-Parliamentary Union to continue to cooperate closely in various fields, in particular peace and security, economic and social development, international law, human rights, and democracy and gender issues, bearing in mind the significant benefits of cooperation between the two organizations, to which the report of the Secretary-General attests;

6. *Decides* to include in the provisional agenda of its sixty-first session the sub-item entitled "Cooperation between the United Nations and the Inter-Parliamentary Union".

International Organization of la Francophonie

In response to resolution 57/43 [YUN 2002, p. 1442], the Secretary-General, in his September consolidated report on cooperation between the United Nations and regional and other organizations [A/59/303], provided information on cooperation between the United Nations and the International Organization of la Francophonie (OIF). A meeting held in New York in November 2003 between the UN Secretary-General and the Secretary-General of OIF led to strengthened collaboration between the two organizations in areas of common interest, including international peace and security. The report also covered cooperative activities in the areas of early warning and conflict prevention, elections, technical assistance, the rights of the child, human rights and education.

On 8 November [meeting 50], the General Assembly adopted **resolution 59/22** [draft: A/59/L.19 & Add.1] without vote [agenda item 56 (*i*)].

Cooperation between the United Nations and the International Organization of la Francophonie

The General Assembly,

Recalling its resolutions 33/18 of 10 November 1978, 50/3 of 16 October 1995, 52/2 of 17 October 1997, 54/25 of 15 November 1999, 56/45 of 7 December 2001 and 57/43 of 21 November 2002, as well as its decision 53/453 of 18 December 1998,

Considering that the International Organization of la Francophonie brings together a considerable number of States Members of the United Nations, among which it promotes multilateral cooperation in areas of interest to the United Nations,

Bearing in mind the Articles of the Charter of the United Nations which encourage the promotion of the purposes and principles of the United Nations through regional cooperation,

Bearing in mind also that, according to its charter, the objectives of the International Organization of la Francophonie are to assist in the establishment and development of democracy, the prevention of conflicts and support for the rule of law and for human rights, the intensification of dialogue between cultures and civilizations, the establishment of closer ties among peoples through mutual knowledge and strengthening of their solidarity through multilateral cooperation activities with a view to promoting the growth of their economies,

Welcoming the steps taken by the International Organization of la Francophonie to strengthen its ties with the organizations of the United Nations system and with international and regional organizations with a view to attaining its objectives,

Noting with satisfaction the commitment to multilateral cooperation in the search for solutions to the major international problems expressed by the Heads of State and Government of countries using French as a common language, at their ninth summit conference, held in Beirut from 18 to 20 October 2002, and their determination to extend the scope of francophone collaboration and cooperation in order to fight poverty and contribute to the emergence of a more equitable form of globalization that will bring progress, peace, democracy and human rights, in full respect for cultural and linguistic diversity, in the interests of the most vulnerable populations and the development of all countries,

Having considered the report of the Secretary-General on the implementation of resolution 57/43,

Noting with satisfaction the substantial progress achieved in cooperation between the United Nations, the specialized agencies and other United Nations bodies and programmes and the International Organization of la Francophonie,

Convinced that strengthening cooperation between the United Nations and the International Organization of la Francophonie serves the purposes and principles of the United Nations,

Noting the desire of the two organizations to consolidate, develop and strengthen the ties that exist between them in the political, economic, social and cultural fields,

1. *Takes note with satisfaction* of the report of the Secretary-General, and welcomes the increasingly close and productive cooperation between the United Nations and the International Organization of la Francophonie;

2. *Notes with satisfaction* that the International Organization of la Francophonie participates actively in the work of the United Nations, to which it makes a valuable contribution;

3. *Notes with great satisfaction* the initiatives taken by the International Organization of la Francophonie in the areas of conflict prevention, the promotion of peace and support for democracy, the rule of law and human rights, and commends it on the genuine contribution it makes, in cooperation with the United Nations, in Haiti, the Comoros, Côte d'Ivoire, Burundi, the Democratic Republic of the Congo and the Central African Republic;

4. *Welcomes* the initiation of cooperation between the United Nations and the International Organization of la Francophonie, with the participation of other regional and subregional organizations, as well as non-governmental organizations, in the fields of early warning and conflict prevention, and encourages the pursuit of this initiative with a view to formulating practical recommendations to facilitate the establishment of relevant operational mechanisms, where necessary;

5. *Expresses its gratitude* to the International Organization of la Francophonie for the steps it has taken in recent years to promote cultural and linguistic diversity and dialogue between cultures and civilizations;

6. *Expresses its appreciation* to the Secretary-General of the United Nations and the Secretary-General of the International Organization of la Francophonie for their sustained efforts to strengthen cooperation and coordination between the two organizations, thereby serving their mutual interests in the political, economic, social and cultural fields;

7. *Welcomes* the fact that the tenth summit conference of la Francophonie was devoted to solidarity for sustainable development, and calls upon the specialized agencies and the funds and programmes of the United Nations system to enhance their cooperation with the International Organization of la Francophonie in the area of sustainable development;

8. *Also welcomes* the involvement of the countries that use French as a common language, particularly through the International Organization of la Francophonie, in the preparation for, conduct of and follow-up to international conferences organized under United Nations auspices;

9. *Commends* the high-level meetings held periodically between the United Nations Secretariat and the Secretariat of the International Organization of la Francophonie, and advocates the participation of those Secretariats in major meetings of the two organizations;

10. *Expresses its appreciation* to the Secretary-General for including the International Organization of la Francophonie in the periodic meetings he holds with heads of regional organizations, and invites him to continue doing so, taking into account the role played by the International Organization of la Francophonie in conflict prevention and support for democracy and the rule of law;

11. *Notes with satisfaction* the continued collaboration between the United Nations and the International Organization of la Francophonie in the area of electoral monitoring and assistance, and advocates the strengthening of cooperation between the two organizations in that area;

12. *Requests* the Secretary-General of the United Nations, acting in cooperation with the Secretary-General of the International Organization of la Francophonie, to encourage the holding of periodic meetings between representatives of the United Nations Secretariat and representatives of the secretariat of the International Organization of la Francophonie in order to promote the exchange of information, coordination of activities and identification of new areas of cooperation;

13. *Invites* the Secretary-General of the United Nations to take the necessary steps, in consultation with the Secretary-General of the International Organization of la Francophonie, to continue to promote cooperation between the two organizations;

14. *Invites* the specialized agencies and funds and programmes of the United Nations system, as well as the regional commissions, including the Economic Commission for Africa, to collaborate to this end with the Secretary-General of the International Organization of la Francophonie by identifying new synergies in favour of development, in particular in the areas of

poverty elimination, energy, sustainable development, education, training and the development of new information technologies;

15.   *Requests* the Secretary-General to submit to the General Assembly at its sixty-first session a report on the implementation of the present resolution;

16.   *Decides* to include in the provisional agenda of its sixty-first session the sub-item entitled "Cooperation between the United Nations and the International Organization of la Francophonie".

Community of Portuguese-speaking Countries

In a 26 August letter to the General Assembly President [A/59/231], the eight member States of the Community of Portuguese-speaking Countries (CPLP)—Angola, Brazil, Cape Verde, Guinea-Bissau, Mozambique, Portugal, Timor-Leste, and Sao Tome and Principe—requested the inclusion of an item on cooperation between the United Nations and CPLP in the agenda of the Assembly's fifty-ninth session, and proposed a draft resolution on the issue. CPLP, which was founded in 1996, bringing together 240 million people of four continents, became a UN observer in 1999 [YUN 1999, p. 1360]. It devoted special attention to the political situation in Guinea-Bissau (see p. 223) through multilateralism and cooperation with the United Nations. CPLP sought to formalize that role and broaden cooperation by contributing to development and international security.

GENERAL ASSEMBLY ACTION

On 8 November [meeting 50], the General Assembly adopted **resolution 59/21** [draft: A/59/L.14] without vote [agenda item 56 *(t)*].

Cooperation between the United Nations and the Community of Portuguese-speaking Countries

The General Assembly,

Recalling its resolution 54/10 of 26 October 1999, by which it granted observer status to the Community of Portuguese-speaking Countries and considered it mutually advantageous to provide for cooperation between the United Nations and the Community of Portuguese-speaking Countries,

Recalling also the Articles of the Charter of the United Nations that encourage activities through regional cooperation for the promotion of the purposes and principles of the United Nations,

Considering that the activities of the Community of Portuguese-speaking Countries complement and support the work of the United Nations,

Welcoming the participation of the Community of Portuguese-speaking Countries in the fifth high-level meeting between the United Nations and regional organizations, held in New York on 29 and 30 July 2003,

1.   *Invites* the Secretary-General of the United Nations to undertake consultations with the Executive Secretary of the Community of Portuguese-speaking Countries, with a view to promoting cooperation between the secretariats of the two bodies, in particular by encouraging meetings that enable their representatives to consult one another on projects, measures and procedures that will facilitate and expand their mutual cooperation and coordination;

2.   *Requests* the specialized agencies and other bodies and programmes of the United Nations system to cooperate to this end with the Secretary-General and the Executive Secretary;

3.   *Requests* the Secretary-General to submit a report on the implementation of the present resolution to the General Assembly at its sixty-first session;

4.   *Decides* to include in the provisional agenda of its sixty-first session the sub-item entitled "Cooperation between the United Nations and the Community of Portuguese-speaking Countries".

Observer status

Shanghai Cooperation Organization

On 24 February [A/59/141], China requested the inclusion in the agenda of the General Assembly's fifty-ninth session of an item on observer status for the Shanghai Cooperation Organization (SCO) in the Assembly. An explanatory memorandum annexed to the request stated that SCO was founded in Shanghai, China, on 15 June 2001 by China, Kazakhstan, Kyrgyzstan, the Russian Federation, Tajikistan and Uzbekistan. SCO's main purposes were to strengthen mutual trust, good-neighbourliness and friendship among its members; develop effective cooperation in their political affairs, economic issues, trade, science and technology, culture, education, energy, transportation, environmental protection and other fields; work to maintain and guarantee regional peace, security and stability; and promote the creation of a new international political and economic order, with a focus on democracy and justice. SCO stated that, as an observer in the Assembly, it would take a more active part in international affairs, conduct wider cooperation with the United Nations and other organizations and countries in order to contribute to peace and security, as well as regional economic growth.

GENERAL ASSEMBLY ACTION

On 2 December [meeting 65], the General Assembly, on the recommendation of the Sixth (Legal) Committee [A/59/517], adopted **resolution 59/48** without vote [agenda item 151].

Observer status for the Shanghai Cooperation Organization in the General Assembly

The General Assembly,

Wishing to promote cooperation between the United Nations and the Shanghai Cooperation Organization,

1.   *Decides* to invite the Shanghai Cooperation Organization to participate in the sessions and the work of the General Assembly in the capacity of observer;

2.   *Requests* the Secretary-General to take the necessary action to implement the present resolution.

Southern African Development Community

On 15 April [A/59/142], the United Republic of Tanzania, on behalf of the Southern African Development Community (SADC), requested the inclusion in the agenda of the General Assembly's fifty-ninth session of an item on observer status for SADC in the Assembly. According to an explanatory memorandum annexed to the request, SADC was founded by a treaty signed in Windhoek, Namibia, on 17 August 1992. SADC's main objectives were to promote sustainable and equitable economic growth and socio-economic development in southern Africa, as well as common political values, systems and other shared values; consolidate, defend and maintain democracy, peace, security and stability; promote self-sustaining development on the basis of collective self-reliance and the interdependence of member States; achieve complementarity between national and regional strategies and programmes; promote and maximize productive employment and utilization of the region's resources; achieve sustainable utilization of natural resources and effective protection of the environment; strengthen and consolidate the long-standing historical, social and cultural affinities and links among the region's people; combat HIV/AIDS and other deadly and communicable diseases; ensure that poverty eradication was addressed in all SADC activities and programmes; and mainstream gender in the community-building process.

GENERAL ASSEMBLY ACTION

On 2 December [meeting 65], the General Assembly, on the recommendation of the Sixth Committee [A/59/518], adopted **resolution 59/49** without vote [agenda item 152].

Observer status for the Southern African Development Community in the General Assembly

The General Assembly,

Wishing to promote cooperation between the United Nations and the Southern African Development Community,

1. *Decides* to invite the Southern African Development Community to participate in the sessions and the work of the General Assembly in the capacity of observer;

2. *Requests* the Secretary-General to take the necessary action to implement the present resolution.

Collective Security Treaty Organization

On 10 August [A/59/195 & Corr.1], Armenia, Belarus, Kazakhstan, Kyrgyzstan, the Russian Federation and Tajikistan—the six member States of the Collective Security Treaty Organization (CSTO)—requested the inclusion in the agenda of the General Assembly's fifty-ninth session of an

item on observer status for CSTO in the Assembly. An explanatory memorandum annexed to the request contained information on the founding of CSTO as a regional organization on 18 September 2003. CSTO sought to strengthen peace and international and regional security and stability, and protect collectively the independence, territorial integrity and sovereignty of its member States. CSTO believed that the granting of observer status would make it possible to strengthen coordination between CSTO and the United Nations and expand their mutual capacities for ensuring peace, security and cooperation on a regional and global scale.

GENERAL ASSEMBLY ACTION

On 2 December [meeting 65], the General Assembly, on the recommendation of the Sixth Committee [A/59/519], adopted **resolution 59/50** without vote [agenda item 157].

Observer status for the Collective Security Treaty Organization in the General Assembly

The General Assembly,

Wishing to promote cooperation between the United Nations and the Collective Security Treaty Organization,

1. *Decides* to invite the Collective Security Treaty Organization to participate in the sessions and the work of the General Assembly in the capacity of observer;

2. *Requests* the Secretary-General to take the necessary action to implement the present resolution.

Economic Community of West African States

On 15 September [A/59/232], the States members of the Economic Community of West African States (ECOWAS) requested the inclusion in the agenda of the General Assembly's fifty-ninth session of an item on observer status for ECOWAS in the Assembly. An explanatory memorandum stated that a treaty signed in 1975 led to the establishment of ECOWAS, which arose from the determination to accelerate the economic and social development of the States of West Africa through effective cooperation. ECOWAS had as its principal aim the integration of the region's national economies into an economic and monetary union, for the purpose of raising the standard of living of its peoples, increasing and maintaining economic stability, fostering closer relationships among its members and contributing to the progress and development of the African continent. Over the years, ECOWAS had developed close working relations with the UN system. The ECOWAS Monitoring Group (ECOMOG) helped resolve civil conflicts in Liberia, Sierra Leone, Guinea-Bissau and Côte d'Ivoire. A regional early-warning system and a high-level mediation organ formed part of the ECOWAS conflict-prevention mechanism in West Africa. (For more information on ECOWAS conflict-prevention and conflict-resolution activities in Africa, see PART ONE, Chapter II.)

GENERAL ASSEMBLY ACTION

On 2 December [meeting 65], the General Assembly, on the recommendation of the Sixth Committee [A/59/520], adopted **resolution 59/51** without vote [agenda item 159].

Observer status for the Economic Community of West African States in the General Assembly

The General Assembly,

Wishing to promote cooperation between the United Nations and the Economic Community of West African States,

1. *Decides* to invite the Economic Community of West African States to participate in the sessions and the work of the General Assembly in the capacity of observer;

2. *Requests* the Secretary-General to take the necessary action to implement the present resolution.

Organisation of Eastern Caribbean States

On 4 October [A/59/233], Saint Lucia requested the inclusion in the agenda of the General Assembly's fifty-ninth session of an item on observer status for the Organisation of Eastern Caribbean States (OECS). An explanatory memorandum annexed to the request stated that OECS was established by the 1981 Treaty of Basseterre and comprised nine members, namely Antigua and Barbuda, Anguilla, the British Virgin Islands, Dominica, Grenada, Montserrat, Saint Kitts and Nevis, Saint Lucia, and Saint Vincent and the Grenadines. The main purposes of OECS were to promote cooperation, unity and solidarity among its members and defend their sovereignty, territorial integrity and independence; assist its members in the realization of their obligations and responsibilities to the international community; achieve the fullest possible harmonization of foreign policy; and promote economic integration among it members.

GENERAL ASSEMBLY ACTION

On 2 December [meeting 65], the General Assembly, on the recommendation of the Sixth Committee [A/59/521], adopted **resolution 59/52** without vote [agenda item 160].

Observer status for the Organisation of Eastern Caribbean States in the General Assembly

The General Assembly,

Wishing to promote cooperation between the United Nations and the Organisation of Eastern Caribbean States,

1. *Decides* to invite the Organisation of Eastern Caribbean States to participate in the sessions and the work of the General Assembly in the capacity of observer;

2. *Requests* the Secretary-General to take the necessary action to implement the present resolution.

South Asian Association for Regional Cooperation

On 12 October [A/59/234], Bangladesh, Bhutan, India, Maldives, Nepal, Pakistan and Sri Lanka—the seven member States of the South Asian Association for Regional Cooperation (SAARC)—requested the inclusion in the agenda of the General Assembly's fifty-ninth session of an item on observer status for SAARC in the Assembly. An explanatory memorandum annexed to the request provided information on SAARC's establishment in December 1985 and its objectives, which were to promote the welfare and improve the quality of life of the peoples of South Asia; accelerate economic growth, social progress and cultural development in the region and provide all individuals the opportunity to live in dignity and realize their full potential; promote and strengthen collective self-reliance among the countries of South Asia; contribute to mutual trust, understanding and appreciation of one another's problems; promote active collaboration and mutual assistance in the economic, social, cultural, technical and scientific fields; strengthen cooperation with other developing countries, and among States members in international forums on matters of common interests; and cooperate with international and regional organizations with similar aims and purposes. Poverty alleviation was the overarching goal of all SAARC activities. Granting SAARC observer status would enhance its profile in the international community and would act as an incentive to strengthen existing cooperation with UN agencies.

GENERAL ASSEMBLY ACTION

On 2 December [meeting 65], the General Assembly, on the recommendation of the Sixth Committee [A/59/544], adopted **resolution 59/53** without vote [agenda item 162].

Observer status for the South Asian Association for Regional Cooperation in the General Assembly

The General Assembly,

Wishing to promote cooperation between the United Nations and the South Asian Association for Regional Cooperation,

1. *Decides* to invite the South Asian Association for Regional Cooperation to participate in the sessions and the work of the General Assembly in the capacity of observer;

2. *Requests* the Secretary-General to take the necessary action to implement the present resolution.

Participation in UN work

Holy See

On 1 July [meeting 92], the General Assembly adopted **resolution 58/314** [draft: A/58/L.64] without vote [agenda item 59].

Participation of the Holy See in the work of the United Nations

The General Assembly,

Recalling that the Holy See became a Permanent Observer State at the United Nations on 6 April 1964, and since then has always been invited to participate in the meetings of all the sessions of the General Assembly,

Recalling also that the Holy See is a party to diverse international instruments, including the Vienna Convention on Diplomatic Relations, the Vienna Convention on the Law of Treaties, the Convention relating to the Status of Refugees and the Protocol thereto, the Convention on the Rights of the Child and the Optional Protocols thereto, the Convention against Torture and Other Cruel, Inhuman or Degrading Treatment or Punishment, the International Convention on the Elimination of All Forms of Racial Discrimination, the Convention for the Protection of Cultural Property in the Event of Armed Conflict, the Paris Convention for the Protection of Industrial Property, the Treaty on the Non-Proliferation of Nuclear Weapons, the main disarmament treaties and the Geneva Conventions and the Additional Protocols thereto,

Recalling further that the Holy See enjoys membership in various United Nations subsidiary bodies, specialized agencies and international intergovernmental organizations, including the Executive Committee of the Programme of the United Nations High Commissioner for Refugees, the United Nations Conference on Trade and Development, the World Intellectual Property Organization, the International Atomic Energy Agency, the Organization for the Prohibition of Chemical Weapons, the Preparatory Commission for the Comprehensive Nuclear-Test-Ban Treaty Organization and the International Committee of Military Medicine,

Aware that the Holy See actively participates as an observer in many of the specialized agencies, such as the Food and Agriculture Organization of the United Nations, the International Labour Organization, the World Health Organization, the United Nations Educational, Scientific and Cultural Organization, the United Nations Industrial Development Organization, the International Fund for Agricultural Development and the World Tourism Organization, as well as in the World Trade Organization, that it is a full member of the Organization for Security and Cooperation in Europe and a Guest of Honour in its Parliamentary Assembly, and that it participates as an observer in various other regional intergovernmental organizations, including the Council of Europe, the Organization of American States and the African Union, and is regularly invited to take part in the main meetings of the Asian-African Legal Consultative Organization,

Aware also that the Economic and Social Council, by its decision 244(LXIII) of 22 July 1977, recommended that the Holy See attend sessions of the regional commissions on a basis similar to that provided for in the relevant terms of reference applicable to States Members of the United Nations not members of the regional commissions,

Recalling that the Holy See contributes financially to the general administration of the United Nations in accordance with the rate of assessment for the Holy See as a non-member State, as adopted by the General Assembly in its resolution 58/1 B of 23 December 2003,

Considering that it is in the interest of the United Nations that all States be invited to participate in its work,

Desirous of contributing to the appropriate participation of the Holy See in the work of the General Assembly in the context of the revitalization of the work of the Assembly,

1. *Acknowledges* that the Holy See, in its capacity as an Observer State, shall be accorded the rights and privileges of participation in the sessions and work of the General Assembly and the international conferences convened under the auspices of the Assembly or other organs of the United Nations, as well as in United Nations conferences as set out in the annex to the present resolution;

2. *Requests* the Secretary-General to inform the General Assembly during the current session about the implementation of the modalities annexed to the present resolution.

Annex

The rights and privileges of participation of the Holy See shall be effected through the following modalities, without prejudice to the existing rights and privileges:

1. The right to participate in the general debate of the General Assembly;

2. Without prejudice to the priority of Member States, the Holy See shall have the right of inscription on the list of speakers under agenda items at any plenary meeting of the General Assembly, after the last Member State inscribed on the list;

3. The right to make interventions, with a precursory explanation or the recall of relevant General Assembly resolutions being made only once by the President of the General Assembly at the start of each session of the Assembly;

4. The right of reply;

5. The right to have its communications relating to the sessions and work of the General Assembly issued and circulated directly, and without intermediary, as official documents of the Assembly;

6. The right to have its communications relating to the sessions and work of all international conferences convened under the auspices of the General Assembly issued and circulated directly, and without intermediary, as official documents of those conferences;

7. The right to raise points of order relating to any proceedings involving the Holy See, provided that the right to raise such a point of order shall not include the right to challenge the decision of the presiding officer;

8. The right to co-sponsor draft resolutions and decisions that make reference to the Holy See; such draft resolutions and decisions shall be put to a vote only upon request from a Member State;

9. Seating for the Holy See shall be arranged immediately after Member States and before the other observers when it participates as a non-member State ob-

server, with the allocation of six seats in the General Assembly Hall;

10.　The Holy See shall not have the right to vote or to put forward candidates in the General Assembly.

In a 16 August note [A/58/871], the Secretary-General described the modalities, as set out in resolution 58/314 (above), through which the rights and privileges of participation of the Holy See, in its capacity as an Observer State, would be effected.

Intergovernmental organizations

On 4 February, the Economic and Social Council included in the agenda of its 2004 substantive session the application of the World Deserts Foundation [E/2004/7] for observer status with the Council (**decision 2004/208**). The Council granted observer status to the Foundation on 28 June (**decision 2004/231**).

Non-governmental organizations

Committee on NGOs

On the recommendations made by the Committee on Non-Governmental Organizations (NGOs) at its 2003 resumed session [YUN 2003, p. 1481], the Economic and Social Council, on 4 February, granted consultative status to 59 NGOs; placed ten others on the Roster; reclassified one from special to general consultative status and two from the Roster to special consultative status; and noted 51 quadrennial reports (**decision 2004/210**). It took note of the Committee's report on its resumed 2003 session [ibid, p. 1480]; decided on the dates for the Committee's 2004 session (see below); and approved the provisional agenda and documentation for the 2004 session (**decision 2004/211**).

The Committee, at its 2004 regular session (New York, 10-28 May and 23 June) [E/2004/32 & Corr.1], considered 171 applications for consultative status with the Council, including those deferred from its 1998-2003 sessions. It recommended 114 NGOs for consultative status, of which 19 were recommended ad referendum, and deferred 50 applications for further consideration at a later date. The Committee did not recommend four NGOs, closed consideration of three, and closed consideration of one complaint by a Member State. It recommended reclassification for four NGOs from roster to special status and three others from special to general consultative status. The Committee took note of 42 quadrennial reports and deferred consideration of six others.

The Committee recommended five draft decisions for action by the Council, including draft

decisions suspending the consultative status of two NGOs (see below), and adopted two decisions, which it brought to the Council's attention. By the first decision, the Committee acknowledged that the one-year suspension of the organization Reporters without Borders was due to come to an end on 24 July. By the second decision, the Committee requested that the International Council of the Associations for Peace in the Continents submit a special report, prior to the reinstatement of its consultative status, on its activities during the three years of suspension, the fulfilment in that period of the provisions of Council resolution 1996/31 [YUN 1996, p. 1360], the possible changes that had taken place in the organization and how it had overcome the reasons for its suspension.

The Committee reviewed its working methods relating to the implementation of Council resolutions 1996/31 [YUN 1996, p. 1360], including the process of NGO accreditation, and of decision 1995/304 [YUN 1995, p. 1445]. It also considered the implementation of Council decision 2001/295 [YUN 2001, p. 1377] relating to requests by those NGOs referred to in Council decision 1993/220 [YUN 1993, p. 668] to expand participation in other fields of the Council's work. During the Committee's consideration of the strengthening of the NGO section of the UN Department of Economic and Social Affairs (DESA), the chief of that section informed the Committee that the "Paperless Committee", a multifunctional, electronic meeting record management and archiving system introduced on a trial basis in 2003 [YUN 2003, p. 1481], was adopted as a normal mode of operation by the Committee on NGOs.

Following a request by the United States, the Committee, by a roll-call vote of 10 to 4, with 5 abstentions, recommended a draft decision for action by the Council to suspend for one year the consultative status of the Indian Movement "Tupaj Amaru". On 23 July, the Council, by a recorded vote of 28 to 4, with 22 abstentions, adopted the draft decision (**decision 2004/306**).

Following a request by Viet Nam, the Committee, by a roll-call vote of 9 to 8, with 2 abstentions, recommended a draft decision for action by the Council to suspend for three years the consultative status of the Transnational Radical Party. On 23 July, the Council, by a recorded vote of 22 to 20, with 11 abstentions, rejected the draft decision.

Also on 23 July, the Council granted special consultative status to 97 NGOs and placed 17 others on the Roster; reclassified three NGOs from special to general consultative status and four others from roster to special consultative status; and noted that the Committee had taken note of

42 quadrennial reports, closed consideration of requests by three NGOs for consultative status, decided not to grant consultative status to four, and closed the case of a complaint by a Member State against one NGO (**decision 2004/305**). On the same day, the Council took note of the report of the Committee on its 2004 session (**decision 2004/307**) and deferred until a resumed Council session action on the draft decision on the dates of the Committee's 2005 session and provisional agenda (**decision 2004/308**).

On 5 November, the Council decided that the Committee's 2005 regular session would be held from 5 to 18 January 2005 and its resumed session from 9 to 20 May 2005, and approved the provisional agenda for the Committee's 2005 session (**decision 2004/321**).

Requests for hearing

On 28 May, the Committee on NGOs approved 15 NGO requests to be heard during the Council's high-level segment and three during the coordination segment [E/2004/84].

Withdrawal of status

On 28 May, the Committee took note of the requests for withdrawal of status submitted by the International Committee for European Security and Cooperation, which informed the UN Secretariat of its dissolution, and the World Conservation Monitoring Centre, which informed the Secretariat that, as of 2000, it had become an office of the United Nations Environment Programme.

Conferences and meetings

Committee on Conferences

The Committee on Conferences held an organizational meeting on 25 March and its substantive session on 7, 8 and 10 September [A/59/32]. The Committee examined requests for changes to the approved calendar of conferences for 2004 [A/AC.172/2004/2] and the draft revised calendar for 2005 [A/59/159/Add.1]. On 8 September, the Committee, having considered the biennialization of the item entitled "Pattern of conferences" on the agenda of the General Assembly, recommended that the issue be referred to the Assembly in the light of the Committee's comments. The Committee also considered the utilization of conference-servicing resources and facilities, requests for exceptions to the Assembly's limitation on meetings during Assembly sessions [YUN 1985, p. 1256], documentation- and publication-

related matters, translation and interpretation-related matters and information technology. (The Committee's deliberations and recommendations on those matters are detailed in the sections below.)

The Committee approved requests from several bodies for changes to the approved calendar for 2004, and reviewed the draft revised calendar of conferences and meetings for 2005.

On 23 December [meeting 76], the General Assembly, on the recommendation of the Fifth Committee [A/59/644], adopted **resolution 59/265** without vote [agenda item 112].

Pattern of conferences

The General Assembly,

Recalling its relevant resolutions, including resolutions 40/243 of 18 December 1985, 41/213 of 19 December 1986, 43/222 A to E of 21 December 1988, 51/211 A to E of 18 December 1996, 52/214 of 22 December 1997, 53/208 A to E of 18 December 1998, 54/248 of 23 December 1999, 55/222 of 23 December 2000, 56/242 of 24 December 2001, 56/254 D of 27 March 2002, 56/262 of 15 February 2002, 56/287 of 27 June 2002, 57/283 A of 20 December 2002, 57/283 B of 15 April 2003 and 58/250 of 23 December 2003,

Reaffirming its resolution 42/207 C of 11 December 1987, in which it requested the Secretary-General to ensure the equal treatment of the official languages of the United Nations,

Having considered the report of the Committee on Conferences, the relevant reports of the Secretary-General, the report of the Joint Inspection Unit, the comments of the Secretary-General thereon, and the report of the Office of Internal Oversight Services,

Having also considered the reports of the Advisory Committee on Administrative and Budgetary Questions,

Reaffirming the provisions relevant to conference services of its resolutions on multilingualism,

I

Calendar of conferences and meetings

1. *Approves* the draft revised calendar of conferences and meetings of the United Nations for 2005, as submitted by the Committee on Conferences, taking into account the observations of the Committee, and subject to the provisions of the present resolution;

2. *Authorizes* the Committee on Conferences to make any adjustments to the calendar of conferences and meetings for 2005 that may become necessary as a result of actions and decisions taken by the General Assembly at its fifty-ninth session;

3. *Notes with satisfaction* that the Secretariat has taken into account the arrangements referred to in General Assembly resolutions 53/208 A, 54/248, 55/222, 56/242, 57/283 B and 58/250 concerning Orthodox Good Friday and the official holidays of Eid al-Fitr and Eid al-Adha, and requests all intergovernmental bodies to observe those decisions when planning their meetings;

4. *Notes* the outcome of the consultations between the Governing Council of the United Nations Human Settlements Programme and the Commission on Sustainable Development to avoid the overlap between the sessions of the Council and the Commission, and decides to reflect the results of those consultations in the revised calendar of conferences and meetings for 2005;

5. *Decides* that, in future, there should be an intervening period of at least two weeks after the closing of the sessions of relevant intergovernmental bodies and the beginning of the session of the Commission on Sustainable Development, in accordance with the multi-year programme of work of the Commission, and encourages such intergovernmental bodies and the Commission to closely coordinate meeting dates and programmes of work so as to avoid overlap between sessions;

II

A. Utilization of conference-servicing resources and facilities

1. *Notes* that the overall utilization factor at the four main duty stations in 2003 increased to 77 per cent, and encourages the bureaux and secretariats to meet the benchmark;

2. *Requests* the Committee on Conferences to continue to consult with those bodies that have consistently utilized less than the applicable benchmark figure of their allocated resources of the past three sessions with a view to making appropriate recommendations in order to achieve the optimum utilization of conference-servicing resources, and urges the secretariats and bureaux of bodies that underutilize their conference-servicing resources, with the assistance of the Department for General Assembly and Conference Management of the Secretariat, to consider changes to their programme of work, as appropriate, based on previous patterns for recurring agenda items, with a view to making improvements in their utilization factors;

3. *Requests* the Secretary-General to conduct systematic follow-up regarding the utilization of conference services by those bodies that consistently underutilize their conference-servicing resources over a longer period of time in order to identify the underlying causes for their being unable to reach the benchmark;

4. *Also requests* the Secretary-General to report in future statistics on reassignments of services to meetings both related and unrelated to the cancelling body;

5. *Welcomes* the efforts that are being made to improve the utilization of the conference facilities at the United Nations Office at Nairobi, as set out in the report of the Secretary-General;

6. *Reiterates its request* to the Secretary-General to continue to intensify the marketing efforts being made by the United Nations Office at Nairobi to attract more meetings to its facilities;

7. *Requests* the Secretary-General to ensure that conference management services at the United Nations Office at Nairobi are in line with other duty stations, taking into account the operational requirements of the Office, and to submit a report thereon to the General Assembly at its sixtieth session for its consideration;

8. *Recalls* its several resolutions, including resolution 57/283 B, section II.A, paragraph 9, and reaffirms that all meetings of Nairobi-based United Nations bodies shall take place in Nairobi, except as otherwise authorized by the General Assembly or the Committee on Conferences acting on its behalf, and requests the Secretary-General to report on the subject to the Assembly at its sixtieth session through the Committee on Conferences;

9. *Strongly discourages* any invitation to host meetings that would violate the headquarters rule, in particular for the United Nations Office at Nairobi and other United Nations centres with a low utilization level;

10. *Expresses deep concern* over the remaining vacancies in the interpretation and translation services, in particular at the United Nations Office at Nairobi, notes the efforts of the Secretary-General to fill the vacancies, and requests the Secretary-General to continue to report thereon to the General Assembly through the Committee on Conferences;

11. *Notes* the improvements in the utilization of the conference centre at the Economic Commission for Africa in response to section II.A, paragraph 1, of its resolution 58/250, and requests the Secretary-General to continue to explore all possible options to increase further the utilization of the conference centre;

12. *Welcomes* the efforts so far undertaken to increase utilization and to make more efficient use of the conference facilities at the Economic Commission for Africa, and urges the Secretary-General to sustain the marketing campaign efforts and to report on the outcome to the General Assembly at its sixtieth session;

13. *Requests* the Secretary-General to ensure that the conference centre at the Economic Commission for Africa establishes and develops linkages with other centres and bodies, introduces and utilizes an integrated conference management system and considers the implementation of other modern technology systems, as appropriate, for a more efficient delivery of services, and to report thereon to the General Assembly at its sixtieth session;

14. *Emphasizes* that all duty stations shall be given adequate resources for the effective and efficient discharge of their respective mandates, and in this respect welcomes the efforts of the Secretary-General to provide the available conference-servicing management tools and best practices to all duty stations;

15. *Recognizes* the importance of meetings of regional and other major groupings of Member States for the smooth functioning of the sessions of intergovernmental bodies, and requests the Secretary-General to ensure that, as far as possible, all requests for conference services for meetings of regional and other major groupings of Member States are met;

16. *Notes with concern* that the percentage of meetings held by regional and other major groupings of Members States that were provided with interpretation services during the reporting period from May 2003 to April 2004 decreased to 90 per cent from 92 per cent during the period from May 2002 to April 2003 for the four main duty stations;

17. *Notes* that, in absolute terms, the number of meetings provided with interpretation services was 10 per cent higher in the period 2003-2004 than in the period 2002-2003;

18. *Recalls* that meetings held by regional and other major groupings of Member States are provided with

interpretation services on an ad hoc basis, in accordance with established practice;

19. *Requests* the Secretary-General to review the current established practice concerning the provision of interpretation services for meetings of regional and other major groupings of Member States at Headquarters and other duty stations, with a view to improving the provision of interpretation services to those meetings;

B. Reform of the Department for General Assembly and Conference Management

1. *Reaffirms* that the Fifth Committee is the appropriate Main Committee of the General Assembly entrusted with responsibilities for administrative and budgetary matters;

2. *Notes* the steps taken by the Secretary-General in the implementation of the reform measures put forward in his report on the reform of the Department for General Assembly and Conference Management of the Secretariat in accordance with section II.B of its resolutions 57/283 B and 58/250, and encourages the continued implementation of the measures described in paragraph 65 of his report, subject to the provisions of the present resolution;

3. *Appreciates* the efforts of the Secretary-General in providing timely and detailed information during the consideration of the item entitled "Revitalization of the work of the General Assembly";

4. *Affirms* that the consideration of and decisions on the revitalization of the General Assembly remain its prerogative;

5. *Stresses* that the participation of the Department in the revitalization of the General Assembly should focus on the timely provision of the documentation needed in order to facilitate the intergovernmental negotiation process;

6. *Stresses also* that future reports on the reform of the Department should concentrate only on its effort to this end;

7. *Stresses further* that the reform of the Department is aimed at improving the quality of documents and their timely production and delivery as well as the quality of conference services provided to Member States, with a view to meeting their needs as efficiently and cost-effectively as possible and in accordance with the relevant resolutions of the General Assembly;

8. *Reiterates its request* contained in section II.B, paragraph 3, of its resolution 58/250;

9. *Notes* the ongoing efforts towards the establishment of the integrated global management system, and decides to consider at its sixtieth session the current outcomes in the light of the report of the Office of Internal Oversight Services on this issue;

10. *Also notes* the establishment by the Secretary-General of a Secretariat task force to conduct a comprehensive study of workload standards and performance measurement and the preliminary findings of the task force, and requests the Secretary-General to pursue the study of workload standards and performance measurement, in both qualitative and quantitative terms, with a view to submitting to the General Assembly a proposal for a comprehensive methodology for performance measurement and management from a full-system perspective, while also paying attention to the specificities of all the official languages and ensuring compliance with resolution 58/250;

11. *Reiterates its request* that the Secretary-General develop further effective measures to strengthen the responsibility and accountability system within the Secretariat, including the establishment of an interdepartmental mechanism to monitor the process in order to ensure the timely submission of documents for processing, and that he report comprehensively thereon to the General Assembly at its sixtieth session through the Committee on Conferences;

12. *Requests* the Secretary-General to pursue the delivery of summary records, a useful and vital tool for Member States, in particular in maintaining the institutional memory of the Organization, in a more efficient and cost-effective manner in full consultation with all the relevant intergovernmental bodies;

13. *Also requests* the Secretary-General to examine the option of setting a time frame for the publication of summary records, to study the related practical and financial implications and to present a pilot project to the General Assembly at its sixtieth session;

14. *Further requests* the Secretary-General to elaborate on all options, including those set out in paragraphs 59 to 63 of his report, in accordance with legislative mandates, and to report on their practical and financial implications to the General Assembly at its sixtieth session through the Committee on Conferences;

15. *Requests* the Secretary-General to develop further the functions of the Electronic Meetings Planning and Resource Allocation System (e-Meets) as the central tool for managing meetings to cover the entire spectrum of meeting-related activities and to continue consultations with other duty stations in order to expand its application across duty stations, or to integrate the system into other systems used in such offices;

16. *Also requests* the Secretary-General to continue his efforts to implement further the electronic documentation management concept (e-Doc), including the actual electronic transmission of documents through the documentation chain;

17. *Further requests* the Secretary-General to enhance the use of printing on demand for parliamentary documentation as a means of improving services provided to Member States, in full compliance with current legislative mandates, on the basis of experience gained and lessons learned, taking fully into account the special needs of developing countries and the views expressed by Member States, to consider the use of printing on demand for publications, and to report thereon to the General Assembly at its sixtieth session through the Committee on Conferences;

III
Documentation and publication-related matters

1. *Emphasizes* the paramount importance of the equality of the six official languages of the United Nations;

2. *Notes with concern* the delay in the issuance of verbatim and summary records, and in this regard requests the Secretary-General to take appropriate measures to ameliorate the situation, with a view to issuing them in a timely manner;

3. *Notes with deep concern* that the six-week rule for the issuance of documents is not fully complied with

owing to, inter alia, the continued late submission of documents by author departments, and requests the Secretary-General to take further urgent measures to ensure strict compliance with the six-week rule for the timely issuance of documentation in view of the impact of their late issuance on the functioning of intergovernmental and expert bodies, which was acutely felt during the main part of the fifty-ninth session;

4. *Notes* that the rate of compliance with the page limits remains only partial and that reports not originating in the Secretariat comprise the bulk of the documents issued, and requests the Secretary-General to encourage compliance with drafting guidelines as set out in paragraph 15 of its resolution 53/208 B, to the extent possible, for such documents and to report on the matter to the General Assembly through the Committee on Conferences;

5. *Recalls* section III, paragraphs 25 to 28, of its resolution 57/283 B and section III, paragraph 10, of its resolution 58/250, and urges the Secretary-General to continue the consultations referred to in this context with a view to considering the possible broadening of the electronic distribution of documentation while maintaining the distribution of printed copies, as required, and to report on the matter to the General Assembly through the Committee on Conferences;

6. *Notes with concern* the violations of the rule that parliamentary documents must be distributed simultaneously in all official languages;

7. *Requests* the Secretary-General to ensure that the rules concerning the simultaneous distribution of documents in all official languages are followed with respect to both the distribution of printed copies and the posting of parliamentary documentation on the Official Document System of the United Nations and the United Nations web site, in keeping with section III, paragraph 5, of resolution 55/222;

8. *Notes with concern* the non-compliance with rule 59 of the rules of procedure of the General Assembly, and requests the Secretary-General to ensure the communication of resolutions adopted by the Assembly to Member States within fifteen days after the closure of the session;

9. *Decides* that the issuance of documents on planning, budgetary and administrative matters requiring urgent consideration by the General Assembly shall be accorded priority;

IV
Translation and interpretation-related matters

1. *Requests* the Secretary-General to ensure the highest quality of interpretation and translation services in all official languages;

2. *Notes with appreciation* the continued practice of holding informational meetings with Member States to consult with them on the improvement of the language services and the intention to establish additional channels for communication on the terminology used and the quality of services rendered, and requests the Secretary-General to organize informational meetings twice a year and in a more appropriate setting, with interpretation provided on an as-available basis;

3. *Requests* the Secretary-General, when recruiting temporary assistance in language services, to ensure that all the language services are given equal treatment and are provided with equally favourable working conditions and resources with a view to achieving maximum quality of their services, with full respect for the specificities of the six official languages, taking into account their respective workloads;

4. *Reiterates its request* that the Secretary-General continue the efforts to explore the use of new technologies, such as computer-assisted translation, remote and off-site translation and speech recognition, in the six official languages so as to enhance further the quality and productivity of the conference services, and to keep the General Assembly informed of the introduction of any other new technology;

5. *Expresses deep concern* for the high level of self-revision, and requests the Secretary-General to submit a comprehensive report on the matter to the General Assembly at its sixtieth session through the Committee on Conferences;

6. *Reiterates its request* to the Secretary-General, in updating the workload standards, to address the question of the appropriate level of self-revision that is consistent with quality in all official languages and to report thereon to the General Assembly at its sixtieth session;

7. *Requests* the Secretary-General to make sure that terminology used in translation and interpretation services reflects the latest linguistic norms and terminology of the official languages in order to ensure the highest quality;

8. *Expresses deep concern* at the high vacancy rates in interpretation and translation services at the United Nations Office at Nairobi and especially the chronic difficulty in staffing the Arabic Interpretation Unit;

9. *Notes with concern* the sharp disparities in interpretation and translation vacancy rates between the United Nations Office at Nairobi and the other duty stations;

10. *Requests* the Secretary-General to pay greater attention to succession planning in order to fill emerging vacancies in language services in a timely manner through outreach to eligible applicants;

11. *Also requests* the Secretary-General to continue conducting competitive examinations in all official languages in order to fill emerging vacancies in language services in a timely manner;

V
Information technology

1. *Notes* the progress achieved thus far across duty stations in integrating information technology into management and documentation-processing systems and the global approach to sharing standards, good practices and technological achievements among the conference services at all duty stations;

2. *Welcomes* efforts undertaken by the Secretary-General at the United Nations Office at Nairobi to include the Office in sharing of standards, good practices and technological achievements with the other United Nations Offices, consistent with its operational requirements;

3. *Requests* the Secretary-General to intensify the efforts to strengthen the information technology capacity at the United Nations Office at Nairobi, to redeploy existing resources, as appropriate, to meet emerging priorities and to revert to this issue, as appropriate, in the context of the regular budget for the period 2006-2007;

4. *Also requests* the Secretary-General to ensure the compatibility of technologies used in all duty stations and to ensure that they are user-friendly for all official languages;

VI

1. *Notes* the comments in paragraphs 56 to 60 of the report of the Secretary-General, and paragraphs 12 to 14 of the report of the Committee on Conferences;

2. *Decides* to revert to the issue of biennialization of the agenda item entitled "Pattern of conferences" in the context of improving the working methods of the Fifth Committee.

Also on 23 December, the Assembly decided that the item "Pattern of conferences" would remain for consideration during its resumed fifty-ninth (2005) session (**decision 59/552**).

Reform of the Department for General Assembly and Conference Management

In response to General Assembly resolution 58/250 [YUN 2003, p. 1486], the Secretary-General reported in July [A/59/172] on the reform of the Department for General Assembly and Conference Management (DGACM), focusing on the technical secretariat support and conference services provided by the Department, and the three major studies undertaken during the past year—on integrated global management, workload standards and performance management, and summary records.

The Secretary-General observed that the momentum of the reform, which was in its second year, had been maintained and was fully integrated into the Department's daily operations. Its focus was on integrating and synchronizing the various projects envisioned at the beginning of the reform process and achieving synergy and full-system benefits by relying on management and technology. Highlighting the main achievements, the Secretary-General said that access to e-Meets, the electronic meetings management system, was provided to permanent missions in New York and UN programmes and organizations, and all servicing units outside DGACM were linked to the system. The Secretariat had also proceeded with the control and limitation of documentation by seeking reductions in the quantity, length and frequency of reports requested and by strictly enforcing page limits. The slotting mechanism for the submission of documents, part of e-Docs (the electronic documentation management system), was expanded in 2004 to cover all the pre-session documents of intergovernmental bodies. However, the mechanism was unable to cover all the documents processed by DGACM, including draft resolutions and decisions and force majeure documents, which would continue to impact on the timely issuance of documents submitted within the slotted time.

In the first of its three major studies, DGACM conducted a two-year project with the Office of Internal Oversight Services (OIOS) on integrated global management of conference services. Agreement was reached on a number of issues, laying the foundation for the full implementation of a global management approach to conference services (see below).

The second study, conducted by the Task Force on Workload Standards and Performance Management, reviewed existing workload standards for conference-servicing staff and the impact of the introduction of new technologies and working methods on staff performance. The Task Force feared that an exclusive emphasis on the productivity of individual staff members might obscure the more significant picture of full-system gains resulting from new technology. It noted, in particular, the case of editors, translators and interpreters, whose core functions were intellectual, and hence not amenable to automation. The Task Force believed that more work needed to be done to develop accurate performance measures to gauge the impact of changes as a result of new technology. It recommended that DGACM develop mechanisms for more systematically tracking user satisfaction of its products, and for analysing new developments and specific circumstances affecting the performance of conference-servicing staff and the regular exchange of information on workload standards and performance measurement.

In its study on summary records, DGACM confirmed the high costs of providing those records in all official languages. It presented several options, such as replacing summary records with digital recordings, reducing the number of bodies entitled to summary records, concentrating précis-writing in the English Translation Service to reduce delays in the translation of summary records, restricting the length of summary records, and eliminating publishing by keeping records only in electronic versions.

The Secretary-General said that the Department would follow-up on the study on integrated global management, begin implementation of the policies and measures agreed upon, and complete the project in 2005. It would pursue the study on workload standards and performance measurement with a view to presenting to the Assembly in 2005 a proposal for a comprehensive methodology from a full-system perspective.

The Committee on Conferences [A/59/32] said that there was need for a deliberate and balanced approach to reform that took into account the characteristics of the different Headquarters units and duty stations away from Headquarters. Innovations in technology and management should be considered from the perspective of full-system benefits, and pilot projects should be conducted over limited areas to ensure that mistakes did not negatively affect the entire system. It requested the Secretariat to pursue the delivery of summary records in a more efficient and cost-effective manner, including the options set out in the Secretary-General's report, to study their practical and financial implications and to make recommendations to the Assembly in 2005 for their implementation in the form of a pilot project.

Integration of global management of conference services

OIOS report. Pursuant to General Assembly resolution 58/250 [YUN 2003, p. 1485], the Secretary-General transmitted in July [A/59/133 & Corr.1] the OIOS report on the integration of global management of conference services. DGACM had requested OIOS to help identify ways of achieving better integration of the management of conference services at its four duty stations (New York, Geneva, Vienna, Nairobi) and to identify possible impediments.

OIOS found that authority within DGACM for policy-making and conference management was unclear, with some official documents providing for such authority to reside centrally in New York, while others provided for it to be decentralized. As a result of that inconsistency, the Under-Secretary-General of DGACM was responsible to the Secretary-General for budgets and expenditure of all four duty stations, with little authority over how those funds were spent. Moreover, inconsistent management practices had developed across all four duty stations in such areas as budgets and expenditures, staffing, workload standards, information technology, meeting planning, documentation management, outsourcing and examinations management.

To deal with those inconsistencies, OIOS proposed the establishment of a Cooperative Global Strategy, in which all duty stations would participate in setting policies and procedures that would be codified in a manual. The Strategy featured a consultative and cooperative culture; a focal point within the office of the Under-Secretary-General to promote the Strategy and act as a bridge between Headquarters and other duty stations; the establishment of cross-duty station task forces (on harmonization of statistical indicators, meeting and planning, human resources, contractual services, information technology, budget and finance, documentation and publishing, client orientation and examinations) to recommend

practical policies and procedures and the harmonization of the structures of all duty stations, including measures to standardize the budgetary sources of all duty stations. OIOS also recommended that DGACM promulgate mandatory reporting requirements for staff to ensure compliance with the manual of policies and procedures; that Directors General consult with the Under-Secretary-General on senior staff appointments in the four duty stations; and that DGACM consider a system of staff exchanges among duty stations. DGACM management endorsed the OIOS proposals and took action to implement many of them.

ACABQ report. The Advisory Committee on Administrative and Budgetary Questions (ACABQ), having considered the Secretary-General's report on DGACM reform (see p. 1467) and the OIOS report on the integration of global management of conference services (see above), noted in October [A/59/418] that an interdepartmental review group was being set up to address weaknesses in the document slotting system. ACABQ believed that more emphasis should be placed on the optimal use of allocated conference resources by measuring results achieved with available resources, and urged that the methodology for calculating the use of conference resources be revisited. It pointed out that the introduction of new technologies in DGACM had not automatically increased productivity in areas such as editing, translation and interpretation. It was concerned that measurable gains in productivity and quality had not been realized, despite the large investment in information technology (IT), and requested the Department to continue developing a practical, results-oriented IT strategy, while ensuring that the needs and experience of language staff were taken into account in the use of IT. It was of the view that DGACM should pay greater attention to succession planning by identifying suitable applicants in local markets and developing a roster of qualified candidates in all official languages. ACABQ intended to revert to the issues of succession planning and vacancies in its review of the Secretary-General's submission on human resources management to the Assembly's fifty-ninth (2004) session (see p. 1418). ACABQ was not convinced that DGACM had made sufficient efforts to raise the performance of individual staff members by linking staff training programmes to workload standards and performance management. It asked DGACM to report on the matter in the study on workload standards and performance management.

Use of conference services

The Committee on Conferences considered the Secretary-General's August report [A/59/159], in which he discussed improved utilization of conference-servicing resources and facilities, documentation and publication, translation and interpretation, and IT. The report also provided meeting statistics of a sample of UN bodies, statistics on conference services for meetings of regional and other groupings of Member States at the four duty stations from 1 May 2003 to 30 April 2004, and requests for meetings during the General Assembly's fifty-ninth (2004) session. The overall utilization factor for 2003 at the four duty stations was 77 per cent, lower than the benchmark of 80 per cent but higher than the rate for the previous two years. When information was included on the number of reassignments of services to related bodies, the overall utilization was 72 per cent. The Committee welcomed the improvement in utilization of conference-servicing resources and suggested that the Secretary-General consider alternative methods for calculating the utilization factor. The Committee Chairman reported on his consultations with bodies that had consistently utilized less than the benchmark figure of their allocated resources for the previous three sessions and made proposals for improving the utilization of those bodies.

Use of regional conference facilities

Nairobi

The Committee on Conferences was informed of the steady improvement in the utilization of conference-servicing facilities at Nairobi and that the modernization of the Nairobi conference facilities was well along in the planning stage [A/59/32]. Unlike the other headquarters, Nairobi received only half of its funding from regular budget allocations, resulting in the majority of language posts, except interpreter posts, being extrabudgetary, with no career prospects. The United Nations Office at Nairobi (UNON) intended to address the problem in the next budget cycle. The Committee expressed concern over the high proportion of extrabudgetary funding and about security. It noted the need for new methods for attracting more meetings to Nairobi, and the competition from other conference centres in Africa.

Economic Commission for Africa

The Secretary-General, in his August report on the pattern of conferences [A/59/159], indicated that, as requested by the General Assembly in resolution 58/250 [YUN 2003, p. 1486], improve-ments were made to increase utilization of the Conference Centre at the Economic Commission for Africa (ECA) (Addis Ababa, Ethiopia), including the finalization and implementation of an action plan and a marketing campaign, and teaming up with the Ethiopian Tourism Commission, Ethiopian Airlines and other players to attract internal and external clients. The Conference Centre looked to establish and develop linkages and networks with other UN conference centres and international convention centres, tourism boards, tour operators and exhibition organizers worldwide, and to introduce and utilize an integrated management system and other modern technology. However, the Centre continued to be hampered by competition from smaller conference venues in sub-Saharan Africa, lack of adequate infrastructure and logistical support in Addis Ababa, visa and immigration restrictions, and inadequate financial resources for implementing marketing programmes.

Interpretation for regional and other groupings

In August [A/59/159], the Secretary-General reported on the provision of interpretation services to meetings of regional and other major groupings of Member States for the period 1 May 2003 to 30 April 2004. The Committee on Conferences [A/59/32] noted that all requests by such groupings for meetings without interpretation services were met at the four duty stations (New York, Geneva, Vienna and Nairobi), and that of the requests for interpretation, 90 per cent were met, a decrease from 92 per cent for the previous 12 months, but an increase of 10 per cent in the total number of such meetings.

Construction of conference facilities

Additional conference rooms at Headquarters

The Capital Master Plan (CMP) for the UN Headquarters complex in New York, introduced in 2000 [YUN 2000, p. 1405], had identified the possibility of creating three new mid-sized conference rooms on the first basement level of the Headquarters building. The Secretary-General submitted a report [A/58/556] on plans and options for the three conference rooms and viable solutions for allowing natural light into them, as requested by the General Assembly in resolution 57/292 [YUN 2002, p. 1375]. The introduction of natural lighting would increase the cost of the rooms by between $0.7 million to $1.2 million.

ACABQ, in November [A/59/556], stated that, given the current uncertainties of the financing arrangements for CMP (see p. 1473), it was premature to make a recommendation on the layout of additional conference rooms.

By **decision 59/551** of 23 December, the General Assembly deferred consideration of the Secretary-General's report until its resumed fifty-ninth (2005) session.

Additional conference facilities at Vienna

The Secretary-General, reporting in December [A/C.5/59/23] on the construction of additional conference facilities at the Vienna International Centre, stated that the Centre's conference facilities were inadequate for the needs of the organizations headquartered there: the International Atomic Energy Agency, the United Nations Industrial Development Organization and the Preparatory Commission for the Comprehensive Nuclear-Test-Ban Treaty Organization, which had requested the host country to make additional conference facilities available. The Austrian Government offered to provide a new conference facility and signed a memorandum of understanding to that effect with the participating organizations in October. Under its terms, the new facility, of approximately 17,000 square metres, would have a ceiling cost of 52.5 million euros, of which 50 million euros would be provided by the Austrian Government and the remainder by the three organizations.

The Secretary-General recommended that the Assembly note the approval by the Vienna-based organizations of Austria's proposal for a new conference centre, approve the participation of the United Nations and those organizations in the proposed arrangements and entrust him with determining the cost-sharing arrangements for potential future costs.

The ACABQ Chairman, in an oral report to the Fifth Committee [meeting 31], recommended that the Assembly approve the Secretary-General's requests, which it did in **resolution 59/276** of 23 December (see p. 1383).

Documentation

In May [A/58/CRP.7], the Secretary-General submitted a note on the control and limitation of documentation, in response to General Assembly resolutions 58/126 [YUN 2003, p. 1389] and 58/250 [ibid. p. 1486], and Economic and Social Council agreed conclusions 2002/1 [YUN 2002, p. 1365] on the consolidation of reports on related subjects, compliance with the guidelines on page limits, and streamlining documentation, respectively. The note contained measures taken to comply with those requests, including guidelines issued by the Council and further steps that could be taken to limit the reports of functional commis-

sions and subsidiary bodies to the Council. After a review of all Secretariat departments and their mandates, it was believed that a consolidation of mandates could lead to a reduction of documentation of about 25 per cent.

The Assembly, in **resolution 58/316** of 1 July (see p. 1374), requested the Secretary-General to update his note on the control and limitation of documentation and to initiate implementation of resolution 57/300 [YUN 2002, p. 1353] with a view to consolidating reports on related subjects.

Official Document System

JIU report. The General Assembly considered the report [A/58/435] of the Joint Inspection Unit (JIU) entitled "From the Optical Disk System to the Official Documents System (ODS): status of implementation and evaluation", which assessed the status of implementation of ODS and identified remaining policy and management issues, which, if addressed, could help to widen its use as an archival and retrieval system of official documents for the United Nations and other interested organizations. JIU made a number recommendations for improving the system, to which the Secretary-General responded in a later report [A/58/435/Add.1]. ACABQ, in its comments [A/58/620] on the OIOS report, requested information on the financial implications of extending usage of the system.

Report of Secretary-General. Responding to Assembly resolution 58/270 [YUN 2003, p. 1399], the Secretary-General submitted a November report [A/59/578/Add.1] on progress made in implementation of ODS, reviewing the expansion of the system's use over the past two bienniums and the improvements under way to enhance its application. The Secretary-General reported that ODS, provided free of charge, was available worldwide. The Dag Hammarskjöld Library was gradually digitizing documentation issued prior to 1993 for loading onto ODS, which was expected to be completed in early 2005. Since June, all UN offices away from Headquarters had been loading their documents, and with the expected installation of a new document loading server, offices away from Headquarters would have access to a more reliable and faster loading process. Arrangements had yet to be worked out to reflect language parity in ODS since the majority of documents archived by offices away from Headquarters were available only in the working language of the duty station or of the intergovernmental body concerned.

ACABQ, in its comments on the first performance report on the 2004-2005 programme budget [A/59/601], recommended that DGACM consider the feasibility of ensuring full parity for language versions of all documents posted on ODS, which the Assembly endorsed in **resolution 59/276** (see p. 1383).

Translation and interpretation matters

Recruitment in language services

The Secretary-General reported in August [A/59/159] that several translation services at Headquarters continued to have relatively high vacancy rates as a result of retirements and other staff movements. While the situation at Geneva and Vienna was more stable, Nairobi's difficulties in filling translation and editorial vacancies mirrored those it faced in filling interpreters' posts. Recruitment to fill vacant posts would be speeded up, while special measures would be taken to mitigate the problems arising from the assimilation of large numbers of new staff over a relatively short period of time. In response to resolution 58/250, efforts had been made also to fill expeditiously the vacant posts in the interpretation and translation services at Nairobi.

The Committee on Conferences [A/59/32] expressed concern about the quality of translation and interpretation services, and the persistent vacancies in language service posts at Headquarters, and particularly at Nairobi.

Informational meetings

The Committee on Conferences [A/59/32] expressed support for holding informational meetings, organized in response to resolution 57/283 B [YUN 2003, p. 1481], to brief Member States on terminology and for consultations aimed at improving translation services. It proposed that they be held twice a year for each UN official language rather than once a year, and that interpretation services be provided on an as-available basis.

UN information systems

Information and communication technology

In September [A/59/265], the Secretary-General reported on progress in implementing the UN information and communication technology (ICT) strategy [YUN 2002, p. 1454] and on the impact of investments in ICT on the Organization's business processes. The report was made in line with General Assembly resolution 58/270 [YUN 2003, p. 1399].

The Secretariat had significantly upgraded its server and storage network infrastructures and the local area network at Headquarters. The in-

stallation of the Wi-Fi (wireless visitor network) public hotspots provided Internet access for portable devices in several areas in the Headquarter's building. To ensure security, the Organization had formally adopted the industry standard performance benchmark for security known as ISO-17799. Secretariat-wide planning activities were well under way to bring all offices into compliance with the standard and to obtain relevant certification. An ICT manual, constituting a compendium of policies, standards, procedures and plans for promoting best practices for ICT management and delivery, including security, was being prepared to comply with ISO-17799 requirements. The completed manual would become the operational guide by early 2005.

The governance of the ICT process was institutionalized by the Secretary-General [ST/SGB/2003/17] in setting up the Project Review Committee as a subsidiary body of the Information and Communications Technology Board. The Committee played a crucial role in applying the standards established by the Board, reviewing ICT initiatives and submitting recommendations on whether such initiatives should be implemented.

In terms of investments, during 2004, efforts and resources were devoted to further building the ICT infrastructure, as part of the ICT strategy. Although the aggregate figures on the positive return on those investments could not be produced, the methodology and mechanisms in place would allow the quantification of the return on investment at the individual project level.

ACABQ, in November [A/59/558], reviewed the implementation of the ICT strategy and recommended that the Assembly take note of the Secretary-General's report.

International cooperation in informatics

In response to Economic and Social Council resolution 2003/48 [YUN 2003, p. 1494], the Secretary-General submitted a May report [E/2004/78] on international cooperation in the field of informatics, which summarized the various activities in that field as reported by the Secretariat departments and the Ad Hoc Open-ended Working Group on Informatics. Activities of the Working Group included the circulation of the booklet entitled "Internet Services for Delegates", Andorra's initiative to allow delegates to download data onto their personal digital assistants, plans for improving ODS, and upgrading personal computer facilities for delegates. As of May, the Information Technology Services Division, in its efforts to provide connectivity and Internet access to all permanent and observer missions, had donated 1,157 personal computers and printers to missions.

On 23 July [meeting 50], the Economic and Social Council adopted **resolution 2004/51** [draft: E/2004/L.28] without vote [agenda item 7 (c)].

The need to harmonize and improve United Nations informatics systems for optimal utilization and accessibility by all States

The Economic and Social Council,

Welcoming the report of the Secretary-General on international cooperation in the field of informatics and the initiatives of the Ad Hoc Open-ended Working Group on Informatics,

Recognizing the interest of Member States in taking full advantage of information and communication technologies for the acceleration of economic and social development,

Recalling its previous resolutions on the need to harmonize and improve United Nations information systems for optimal utilization and access by all States, with due regard to all official languages,

Welcoming the intensification of efforts by the Information Technology Services Division of the Department of Management of the Secretariat to provide interconnectivity and unhindered Internet access to all Permanent and Observer Missions at the United Nations,

1. *Reiterates once again* the high priority that it attaches to easy, economical, uncomplicated and unhindered access for States Members and observers of the United Nations, as well as non-governmental organizations accredited to the United Nations, to the computerized databases and information systems and services of the United Nations, provided that the unhindered access of non-governmental organizations to such databases, systems and services will not prejudice the access of Member States nor impose an additional financial burden for their use;

2. *Requests* the President of the Economic and Social Council to convene the Ad Hoc Open-ended Working Group on Informatics for one more year to enable it to carry out, from within existing resources, the due fulfilment of the provisions of the Council resolutions on this item, to facilitate the successful implementation of the initiatives being taken by the Secretary-General with regard to the use of information technology and to continue the implementation of measures required to achieve its objectives, and, in this regard, requests the Working Group to continue its efforts in order to act as a bridge between the evolving needs of Member States and the actions of the Secretariat;

3. *Expresses its appreciation* to the Information Technology Services Division for the cooperation it extended to the Working Group in the production of the booklet entitled "Internet services for delegates" and to the Government of Andorra for its initiative on the personal digital assistant pilot project;

4. *Requests* the Secretary-General to extend full cooperation to the Working Group and to give priority to implementing its recommendations;

5. *Also requests* the Secretary-General to report to the Council at its substantive session of 2005 on action taken on the follow up to the present resolution, including the findings of the Working Group and an assessment of its work and mandate.

Other matters

Common services

Outsourcing practices

In response to General Assembly resolution 58/276 [YUN 2003, p. 1499], the Secretary-General submitted an August report on UN outsourcing practices [A/59/227]. Annexed to the report was a list of outsourced activities in 2002-2003, specifying the location and type of each activity and reasons for outsourcing, with the reported savings where outsourcing was initiated with that aim. The Secretary-General reiterated his commitment to ensuring that programme managers were guided by the four criteria set out in Assembly resolution 55/232 [YUN 2000, p. 1401]. He also informed the Assembly that supplier performance evaluation forms used by the Procurement Division had been shared with the members of the Inter-Agency Procurement Working Group.

ACABQ, in an October report [A/59/540], said that the information should be provided through a thematic approach by locality, instead of just a list of outputs, and should include an analysis of trends.

UN premises and property

Addis Ababa office facilities

In response to General Assembly resolution 56/270 [YUN 2002, p. 1459], the Secretary-General reported in October [A/59/444] that design activities for the construction of additional office facilities at the Economic Commission for Africa (ECA) in Addis Ababa were near completion. The final construction cost estimates were expected in December, and the construction contractor would be selected in May 2005. Construction was to be completed by mid-2007. However, the delay in project implementation and security-related enhancements to the building design might result in additional project costs. While every effort would be made to keep the total cost within the budget ($7.7 million) approved by the Assembly in resolution 56/270, any additional cost resulting from the design revisions would be reported to the Assembly in 2005.

ACABQ, in a November report [A/59/572], recommended that clear understandings be reached with the various UN entities involved to allow priority-oriented planning and to ensure the most efficient allocation of space, and that such information should be included in the next report of the Secretary-General.

Parking space at Headquarters

In response to General Assembly resolution 57/292 [YUN 2002, p. 1375], the Secretary-General submitted a February study [A/58/712] on viable options for ensuring sufficient parking space at UN Headquarters to meet current and future needs of diplomatic missions and Secretariat staff within the projected overall budget of the capital master plan (CMP) (see below). The study evaluated needs, described physical changes and gave estimated costs for a number of options. Taking into consideration costs and environmental and aesthetic impact, the study recommended the least expensive option, which would entail reorganization and rationalization of the existing garage and would add 66 parking spaces at a low initial cost and no additional operating costs.

ACABQ, in November [A/59/556], took note of the Secretary-General's report, but considered that given the current uncertainties of the financing for CMP, it was premature to make a recommendation on the options for increasing parking space at Headquarters.

By **decision 59/551** of 23 December, the Assembly deferred consideration of the Secretary-General's report until its resumed fifty-ninth (2005) session.

Capital master plan

Funding arrangements

As requested by the General Assembly in resolution 57/292 [YUN 2002, p. 1375], the Secretary-General reported in March [A/58/729] on the status of possible funding arrangements for the capital master plan (CMP). He stated that the host Government had informed the Secretariat on 20 February of its offer, subject to approval by the United States Congress, to lend the United Nations $1.2 billion to finance CMP at an interest rate of 5.54 per cent. During the construction phase, interest would be paid only on the advances received, and on the completion of construction, the loan would be based on the total amount, repayable over 25 years at the same interest rate, or $89,808,700 annually. The total sum to be repaid would amount to $2,511,137,500. The Secretary-General recommended that the Assembly note with appreciation the offer by the host country Government; note that the loan would increase the overall cost if interest rates were applied; and request him to consult further with the host country authorities on the exact terms of the loan, explore other funding opportunities, including contributions from public and private sources, and report to the Assembly at its fifty-ninth (2004) session.

By **decision 58/566** of 8 April, the Assembly postponed consideration of CMP financing to the second part of its resumed fifty-eighth (2004) session. It requested the Secretary-General to update section IV, entitled "Sources of funding, financing options and commercial borrowing" of his 2000 report on CMP [YUN 2000, p. 1405], and his report on the status of possible funding arrangements for CMP, and to submit all outstanding reports requested in resolution 57/292.

The Secretary-General, in his second annual report on the implementation of CMP, submitted in October [A/59/441] (see p. 1475) in response to resolution 57/292, stated that the Secretariat had sought more favourable financing options from the host country, which had since indicated that the maximum amount of the loan would be $1.2 billion and that the repayment period, including construction time, would be 35 years. Once approved by the Congress, a loan agreement between the United States and the United Nations should be entered into before 30 September 2005, or the offer would lapse. The loan could then be activated at any time over the next 35 years, with the United Nations drawing down all or part of it. The United Nations would incur no liability if it signed the loan agreement but did not activate the loan.

The Secretary-General sought advice on financing options from commercial financial institutions, which advised that the host country proposal was more favourable than a loan in capital markets. The Secretariat explored other options for reducing interest payments, such as taking advantage of short-term interest rates during the construction phase and using capital markets for longer-term borrowing. It determined, however, that the use of capital market alternatives would expose the United Nations to risk, especially with changes in interest rates on short-term borrowing.

The interest incurred on all financing proposals would be paid by Member States through the normal assessment process, with Member States having the option of paying the totality of their assessed share of the $1.2 billion prior to the start of construction, without any further obligation regarding future interest payments.

The Secretary-General said that the host country offer of an interest-bearing loan did not meet the Assembly's expectations. However, if accepted, it would allow the Organization to lock in the interest rate for the loan. The loan offer, when used as a guarantee, would enable the United Nations to have access to capital-market interest rates that could, particularly during construction, reduce the interest costs for the United Nations. A decision to use capital-market financing instead of the host country loan to finance either the CMP construction period or the permanent loan should be made prior to construction, when a more accurate comparison between the market interest rates and that offered by the host country could be made. Notwithstanding those options, the Secretary-General maintained the view that an interest-free loan would be the most advantageous option for the United Nations.

ACABQ, in November [A/59/556], said that since the proposed offer could not be formally made by the host country until the legislative process had been completed, it was not in a position to submit any views on it at that time, but would revert to the matter if and when a formal offer was made.

By **decision 59/551** of 23 December, the Assembly deferred until its resumed fifty-ninth (2005) session, the Secretary-General's report on possible funding arrangements for CMP and his second annual report on CMP.

Cooperation with the City of New York

In accordance with General Assembly resolution 57/292 [YUN 2002, p. 1375], the Secretary-General in April [A/58/799] provided an update on the status of the negotiations with the City and State of New York on implementation of the CMP project, which was initially reported on in 2003 [A/58/599]. Under the plan, a new building would be constructed by the United Nations Development Corporation (UNDC), to be known as the UNDC-5 building, to provide swing space during the implementation of CMP. The City had developed a plan to mitigate the effects of the construction on the community and was working with the New York State legislature, which was expected to enact a mitigation plan in 2005. UNDC was finalizing a contract for the construction with the architectural firm selected and design work was expected to begin immediately upon the signing of the contract. A study on security requirements for the building was nearing completion. Construction was scheduled to start in late 2005, pending the resolution of all related matters.

In his second annual report on the implementation of CMP, submitted in October [A/59/441], the Secretary-General stated that a formal contract was signed in April with the design architects, Maki and Associates (Japan), and consultations between the architect and the Secretariat began in May. The United Nations, UNDC, the architect and New York City representatives met in July to discuss security requirements, which resulted in significantly increased costs. Other options and designs would be studied. The cost of

the alternative building design by UNDC was estimated at $458.2 million, resulting in a fixed rent of $39.32 per square foot, compared to the preliminary estimate of $315.8 million prepared in 2002, with an estimated fixed rent of $27.59 per square foot. The Secretary-General recognized that the increase in the costs of the proposed building would impact on the overall cost of CMP and could call into question the viability of the building as swing space during the CMP construction phase. He would therefore evaluate other options for swing space during that period.

By **decision 59/551** of 23 December, the Assembly deferred until its resumed fifty-ninth (2005) session consideration of the Secretary-General's report on UN cooperation with the City and State of New York related to CMP.

Review of CMP

Report of Board of Auditors. In July [A/59/161], the Secretary-General transmitted to the General Assembly the report of the Board of Auditors on CMP for the biennium ended 31 December 2003, in response to Assembly resolution 57/292 [YUN 2002, p. 1375]. The review covered the design development and construction documentation phases. Expenditures of $4.3 million in 2002-2003 increased the total cumulative expenditure for CMP since its inception in December 2000 from $6.9 million to $11.2 million as at 31 December 2003. The Board found that delays in the initiation of the design and construction documentation phases might result in increases of some 3.5 per cent in design fees and of some $2.6 million per annum in administrative and operating expenses for the Office of the United Nations Capital Master Plan. The Board recommended that the Administration comply strictly with UN regulations and rules on procurement and contracting; address all causes of delay in the initiation of the design development and construction documentation phases; and adopt measures to minimize administrative and management costs.

OIOS report. In October [A/59/420], the Secretary-General, in response to Assembly resolution 57/292, forwarded the OIOS report on CMP for the period from August 2003 to July 2004. During that period, OIOS provided continuous audit coverage of CMP activities, including the construction phase of the security strengthening project. It reviewed contracts with an aggregate value of $59 million.

OIOS concluded that the resources appropriated by the Assembly for CMP activities were generally utilized in accordance with UN Financial Rules, however, UN operating procedures and documents related to construction contracts needed to be improved for the CMP project to be implemented efficiently and economically. OIOS expressed concern that the construction documents for the security-strengthening project might not be entirely adequate because the construction manager and contract administrator were not on board during the design stage. Also, inconsistencies in the construction documents and the potential for cost savings had not been addressed by the Office of the Capital Master Plan prior to the issuance of the request for proposals, and the contractor's guarantees for the performance of the security-strengthening construction were not adequate. OIOS stressed that the audit resources allocated to it for CMP were insufficient and that oversight resources should be increased to provide for adequate audit coverage.

By **decision 59/551** of 23 December, the Assembly deferred to its resumed fifty-ninth (2005) session consideration of the report of the Board of Auditors on CMP for the 2002-2003 biennium and the OIOS report on CMP for August 2003 to July 2004.

CMP implementation

In accordance with General Assembly resolution 57/292 [YUN 2002, p. 1375], the Secretary-General submitted his second annual report on the implementation of CMP [A/59/441]. The report discussed possible funding arrangements (see p. 1473), progress made by the United Nations Development Cooperation (see p. 1474), establishment of an advisory board, progress of the design work for the refurbishment of UN Headquarters, a procurement update and status of appropriations and expenditures.

As the Assembly requested, the Secretary-General established a CMP advisory board to advise on CMP, act as a sounding board on major project concepts and assist with decisions on financial issues. It would initially advise on commercial borrowing and other financing options, and on architectural issues.

Work on refurbishing Headquarters was in the design development phase. The first activity entailed confirmation of the details of the scope of the refurbishment. Each design firm would prepare a scope confirmation report of its work, which together would provide a coordinated framework for detailed design development. All design development was expected to be completed by September 2005. The functional programming process was well under way to determine the size and general location of space for functions at Headquarters. At the time of the report, 13 contracts, with a total value of $10.4 million, had been awarded, including five contracts for the design development phase and related ad-

visory services. Actual expenditure on CMP in 2003 amounted to $3.2 million. Expenditure for 2004 was projected at $19.4 million, of which $9.6 million had been spent by 31 July.

The Secretary-General recommended that the Assembly: decide, if a formal offer for the proposed loan from the host country was received, to take up the matter during its resumed fifty-ninth (2005) session; review at that session his proposals for the allocation of conference (see p. 1469) and parking space (see p. 1473) at Headquarters; encourage him to continue negotiations with the City and State of New York on the construction of a new building (UNDC-5) at a lease-purchase cost in line with the current lease costs of the UNDC-1 and UNDC-2 buildings, and in the light of those negotiations, to evaluate other options for swing space during the CMP construction phase; and convert into an appropriation for 2004-2005 an amount of $18,642,000 of the commitment authority of the $26 million approved in Assembly resolution 57/292, and to extend the validity of the residual balance of $7,358,000 into the 2006-2007 biennium so as to continue the design work and related project management and pre-construction services.

ACABQ, in its November report [A/59/556], stated that a number of the basic parameters had changed since the adoption of Assembly resolution 57/292, including the nature of the financing arrangements and the construction costs, which the Assembly might wish to take into account when considering the Secretary-General's recommendations. It recommended approval of his proposal concerning the commitment authority for the 2004-2005 and 2006-2007 bienniums.

By **decision 59/551** of 23 December, the Assembly deferred to its resumed fifty-ninth (2005) session the Secretary-General's second annual report on the implementation of CMP and the related ACABQ report.

Security

Strengthening security of UN operations, staff and premises

In April [A/58/756], the Secretary-General reported on strengthening the security and safety of UN operations, staff and premises. After the bombing of the UN facilities at Baghdad, Iraq, in August 2003 [YUN 2003, p. 346], he took a number of steps to strengthen the security and safety of the United Nations. In his April report, he proposed measures for the first phase of the long-term strengthening of security and safety, based on a review of arrangements at Headquarters and in the field. The total costs of the proposals were estimated at $92,433,500, including one-time requirements of $71,193,900 for upgrading the physical and security infrastructures, acquiring related equipment and other expenditures such as the interim strengthening of security staff using general temporary assistance. A net request for the appropriation of $85,965,800 was submitted for the Assembly's consideration, with the balance of $6,467,700 to be funded by Vienna-based organizations through cost-sharing.

ACABQ, having reviewed the Secretary-General's report in April [A/58/758], recommended that the Assembly appropriate $40 million (gross) under the 2004-2005 programme budget for the implementation of the measures proposed by the Secretary-General on an interim basis. It also recommended that for peacekeeping operations and the International Criminal Tribunal for Rwanda, expenses estimated at $4.9 million should be accommodated within existing budgets ($4.3 million for peacekeeping and $0.6 million for the Tribunal); such additional appropriations could be considered in the context of the relevant performance reports. Some $8.9 million of the provision for the Office of the United Nations Security Coordinator recommended by ACABQ would be borne by the participating organizations under cost-sharing arrangements. Compared with the Secretary-General's request for $85,965,800, ACABQ recommended a total of $63.0 million for the same functions.

GENERAL ASSEMBLY ACTION

On 18 June [meeting 91], the General Assembly, on the recommendation of the Fifth Committee [A/58/820], adopted **resolution 58/295** without vote [agenda items 121, 131, 134, 137, 138, 140, 141, 142, 145 *(a)* & *(b)*, 146, 147].

Strengthening the security and safety of United Nations operations, staff and premises

The General Assembly,

Recalling its resolutions 56/255 of 24 December 2001, 56/286 of 27 June 2002, 57/305 of 15 April 2003, 58/270 of 23 December 2003 and all relevant resolutions regarding the security and safety of United Nations operations, staff and premises,

Having considered the report of the Secretary-General on strengthening the security and safety of United Nations operations, staff and premises,

Having also considered the related report of the Advisory Committee on Administrative and Budgetary Questions,

1. *Endorses* the recommendations of the Advisory Committee on Administrative and Budgetary Questions contained in its report, subject to the provisions of the present resolution;

2. *Stresses* the need, for the purposes of objective analyses, for a dedicated functional staff at Headquarters to review the recommendations on country risk assessments made by security officers in the field with the assistance of and input from national authorities of the host country;

3. *Approves* the establishment of 58 new field security posts for the Office of the United Nations Security Coordinator, and decides, without prejudice to such decisions as may be arrived at regarding cost-sharing arrangements, to appropriate 2,583,000 United States dollars, being the portion of costs normally attributable to the United Nations using current formulas, and to revert to the required residual funding of 8,162,100 dollars at the fifty-ninth session when determining cost-sharing arrangements;

4. *Decides* to revert to the possible conversion of the 58 extrabudgetary field security posts for the Office of the United Nations Security Coordinator in the context of the comprehensive report at its fifty-ninth session;

5. *Authorizes* the Secretary-General to enter into commitments not to exceed 38,033,200 dollars for the financing of infrastructure projects;

6. *Requests* the Secretary-General to submit to it at its fifty-ninth session a comprehensive report on further strengthening the safety and security of United Nations operations, staff and premises, which should contain, inter alia, the following elements:

(a) Clearly established criteria for determining long-term needs;

(b) A rational framework for the enhancement of system-wide security arrangements, based on the completion of all ongoing reviews, including the change management study;

(c) Time frames for the completion of the various projects proposed in the report of the Secretary-General, as well as determinations as to which organizational units are responsible for their completion;

(d) Clearly established lines of accountability and responsibility and a clear chain of command for all participants in field security and at duty stations, including clarification of the relationship between all relevant United Nations entities and the Secretariat;

(e) Information on United Nations cooperation with and the role and responsibilities of host countries;

(f) Information on the need to ensure an enhanced professional capacity in the United Nations to conduct threat and risk assessment on a worldwide basis in order to address the issue raised in paragraph 18 of the report of the Secretary-General;

(g) Information on the utilization and cost of expertise sought on safety and security;

(h) Information on the need for adequate security-related training for all United Nations staff;

(i) Analysis of and recommendations on long-term funding arrangements for the Office of the United Nations Security Coordinator and related resource requirements;

7. *Decides* that the resource requirements in the requested report should be based on and justified in terms of the Secretary-General's comprehensive review of safety and security;

8. *Requests* the Secretary-General to entrust the Office of Internal Oversight Services with the conduct of an audit review of the utilization and management of the funds appropriated by the General Assembly in its resolution 56/286 for the implementation of measures to strengthen the security and safety of United Nations premises, including the causes for cost escalation and

compliance with procurement procedures, and to report to the Assembly at its fifty-ninth session in conjunction with the comprehensive report on strengthening the security and safety of United Nations operations, staff and premises;

9. *Decides* to approve an additional appropriation under the regular budget in the amount of 18,287,100 dollars, broken down by budget section as follows:

Section 3. Political affairs	2 866 100
Section 4. Disarmament	70 200
Section 5. Peacekeeping operations	3 774 100
Section 7. International Court of Justice	84 000
Section 18. Economic and social development in Africa	55 700
Section 19. Economic and social development in Asia and the Pacific	592 900
Section 21. Economic and social development in Latin America and the Caribbean	80 900
Section 22. Economic and social development in Western Asia	233 400
Section 28. Public information	186 200
Section 29A. Office of the Under-Secretary-General for Management	500 000
Section 29C. Office of Human Resources Management	326 800
Section 29D. Office of Central Support Services	1 672 100
Section 29E. Administration, Geneva	2 683 500
Section 29F. Administration, Vienna	1 931 900
Section 29G. Administration, Nairobi	646 300
Section 31. Jointly financed administrative activities	2 583 000
Total	18 287 100

On 23 December, the Assembly took related action on a strengthened and unified UN security management system in **resolution 59/276**, section XI (see p. 1383).

OIOS report. The Secretary-General transmitted in October [A/59/396] the OIOS report on the utilization and management of funds appropriated during the 2002-2003 biennium for strengthening the security and safety of UN premises, pursuant to General Assembly resolution 58/295 (see above). The OIOS audit of the $57.7 million appropriated during 2002-2003 for that purpose focused on determining whether the funds were utilized in accordance with the proposals contained in the Secretary-General's 2002 report on the subject [YUN 2002, p. 1460].

By 31 May 2004, $48.6 million of that amount had been spent. The delay in the signing of the main construction contract for projects at Headquarters, which was not finalized until 31 March, had led to further delays and increased costs. Proposed changes in specifications for the access control system would result in further cost escalation, and OIOS stated that the decision to modify the specifications should be supported by a cost benefit and risk analysis to justify the additional investment. OIOS considered that the unspent balance of $4.8 million for projects deferred to

CMP and pooled in a construction-in-progress account should be surrendered or used to reduce the additional funds requested in the current biennium. Noting that the guarantees provided by the contractor for the main construction contract were significantly lower than the Organization's requirements and industry standards, thereby exposing the United Nations to the risk of poor performance and payment defaults by the contractor, OIOS made recommendations for protecting more effectively the Organization's interests in future construction contracts.

The underutilization of about $9.6 million (or 62 per cent of the revised appropriation) for security-strengthening projects at the UN Office at Geneva (UNOG) resulted from the redesign and rescheduling of the projects owing to the increased level of threat to the United Nations following the incidents of 11 September 2001 [YUN 2001, p. 60] and 19 August 2003 [YUN 2003, p. 346]. UNOG expected most projects to be completed by December 2005. As projects were modified and the scope of work increased, the cost estimates more than doubled and further adjustments were likely. OIOS was of the opinion that, once all the security requirements were finalized, an up-to-date security strategy, a final plan and costing should be developed for each project. Senior management should ensure that the plan was respected and project objectives were achieved within the established costs and timelines. The steering committee established to oversee the projects should be revitalized to ensure a coordinated management decision-making process and to provide direction and oversight, and a dedicated project manager should be assigned to enhance UNOG project management capacity.

The value of the contract awarded for architectural/engineering work and overall supervision of the security projects increased from $670,000 to $4 million owing to a significant change in the scope of the work. It was expected that the fees would rise to $6.4 million because of a further increase in the scope of the construction work. In the opinion of OIOS, a market survey should be conducted to make certain that the total fees payable were still competitive.

Unified security management system

As requested in resolution 58/295 (see p. 1476), the Secretary-General reported in October [A/59/365] on the strengthened and unified security management system for the United Nations. The report examined the current state of the UN security system, reviewed changes made since his 2001 report on inter-organizational security measures [YUN 2001, p. 1348] and made recommendations for organizational reform aimed at better meeting the evolving security threat. Those recommendations called for the amalgamation of existing security components into a new Directorate of Security, to be headed by an Under-Secretary-General reporting directly to the Secretary-General; providing the Directorate with new capabilities in security threat and risk assessment, operational support in the field, policies and standards, compliance and evaluation, human resources management and training; increasing significantly the number of security personnel, particularly in the field; and phasing out the current cost-sharing arrangements for field security in favour of centrally funding security costs from assessed resources. In an addendum [A/59/365/Add.1 & Corr. 1] to the report, the Secretary-General proposed revised estimates under various sections of the 2004-2005 programme budget for the second phase of measures on the long-term strengthening of UN security and safety. The total gross costs of the proposed measures were estimated at $97.1 million, including one-time requirements of $29.6 million. Those resources would provide for the establishment of the Directorate of Security in New York, as well as activities to bring infrastructure and procedures up to a satisfactory standard of compliance with Headquarters minimum operating security standards.

ACABQ reviewed the recommendations in October [A/59/539] and stated that the new unified security management system should be focused primarily on the field, with a streamlined central capacity at Headquarters. It was of the view that the United Nations should enhance cooperation with national and/or local law enforcement agencies where host countries had well developed security structures, and make use of their capacity in security threat and risk assessment. In countries where that was absent, the United Nations should strengthen its ability to ensure its own security. Concerning accountability and responsibility, ACABQ said that it was still not clear how the lines of reporting and decision-making would work in complex operations involving regional commissions, peacekeeping activities, special political missions, and activities of UN agencies, funds and programmes. The role of each responsible official should be clarified, as well as their place in the security framework.

ACABQ recommended against the proposal to phase out the cost-sharing arrangements for field-related costs among organizations using the services of the field security management system, in favour of the United Nations appropriating the entire financial requirement, subject to proportional reimbursement from the agencies. According to ACABQ, it was not necessary for the proposed Directorate of Security to have an autonomous administrative and support capacity at Headquarters. The Headquarters operation should focus on policy guidance, general direction and monitoring functions. ACABQ expressed its firm view that the UN security system should be primarily focused on the field, with a streamlined central capacity at Headquarters. In that regard, ACABQ suggested a regional field presence, using national experience where relevant, in a structure to be accommodated within the total number of the proposed field desk posts. An additional 394 posts were proposed for the reinforcement of Security and Safety Services at Headquarters and at the other seven main UN locations.

In regard to the Secretary-General's proposal for a system to control access to UN premises, ACABQ requested him to submit for Assembly consideration a detailed blueprint of the system, with justification for the costs involved. He should be authorized to enter into commitments not exceeding $11.2 million for the planning and initial work pending consideration of the requested report.

ACABQ looked forward to the further refinement of the Secretary-General's security plan and to his implementation report which it had requested. It would revert to the matter of achieving economies in resources. The current request for appropriation would be adjusted to take into account the financial consequences of those ACABQ recommendations that the Assembly might adopt.

The Assembly took action on the reports of the Secretary-General on UN security and those of OIOS and ACABQ in **resolution 59/276**, section XI, of 23 December (see p. 1383).

Intergovernmental organizations related to the United Nations

Chapter I

International Atomic Energy Agency (IAEA)

In 2004, the International Atomic Energy Agency (IAEA) continued to act as a catalyst for the development and transfer of peaceful nuclear technologies; to build and maintain a global nuclear safety regime; and to assist in efforts to prevent the proliferation of nuclear weapons.

The forty-eighth session of the IAEA General Conference (Vienna, Austria, 20-24 September) adopted resolutions and decisions on strengthening IAEA's activities in nuclear science, technology and applications; strengthening international cooperation in nuclear, radiation, transport and waste safety; improving the effectiveness and efficiency of the safeguards system; strengthening IAEA technical cooperation activities; applying safeguards in the Middle East; implementing the safeguards agreement between IAEA and the Democratic People's Republic of Korea (DPRK); and measures to protect against nuclear and radiological terrorism.

In 2004, IAEA had 138 member States.

Activities

Nuclear safety and security

IAEA continued to support a global nuclear safety regime based on strong national safety infrastructures and widespread subscription to international legal instruments. During 2004, it published five standards dealing with the safety of nuclear installations. In December, IAEA and the European Commission signed a "Contribution Agreement", which established the modalities for the European Union's support, through the Nuclear Security Fund, to IAEA efforts to secure nuclear and other radioactive material and to enhance detection and response capabilities in a number of States across southeastern Europe and Central Asia. In 2004, 11 additional States became parties to the 1979 Convention on the Physical Protection of Nuclear Material [YUN 1979, p. 1239], making a total of 109 States Parties.

Radiation safety

IAEA's radiation safety programme continued to focus on the development of a unified set of safety standards and their application; the imple-

mentation of the Agency's radiation protection rules; and the provision of advice and services to member States. In 2004, the IAEA Board of Governors approved an action plan for the safety of transport of radioactive material, which provided direction for the Agency's transport safety activities over the next five years. The Board also approved an Agency policy for promoting effective and sustainable national regulatory infrastructures for the control of radiation sources. International consensus was reached with the publication of a *Safety Guide on the Application of the Concepts of Exclusion, Exemption and Clearance*, which established levels of radioactivity in materials such as wood and foodstuff below which regulatory controls needed not be applied. Also in 2004, the IAEA Commission on Safety Standards approved the Safety Guide on the categorization of radioactive sources.

Nuclear power

In 2004, IAEA continued to assist member States in planning and implementing programmes for the utilization of nuclear power, supported them in improving safety, and provided them with information and training. To mark the 50th anniversary of when electricity was first produced by nuclear energy—in Obninsk, Russian Federation—IAEA organized a conference entitled "Fifty Years of Nuclear Power—The Next Fifty Years" (Moscow/Obninsk, June–July). The Conference highlighted the vital role played by nuclear power in a number of countries and supported continued innovation in technology and infrastructure to advance spent fuel recycling and fast reactor and waste management technologies. In addition, the Agency undertook technical cooperation projects on integrated nuclear power and desalination system design and the simulation of a nuclear desalination plant.

Nuclear fuel cycle

In 2004, IAEA continued to publish reports on the uranium production cycle and the environment. Within the framework of its technical cooperation programme, expert teams visited Romania to review the status of a project on restructuring the uranium mining industry. Another team visited Argentina for a project on prospecting for uranium and other elements using gamma ray spectrometry surveys. In connection with its work on nuclear fuel performance and technology, IAEA assisted member States in enhancing the performance and reliability of zirconium alloy-clad fuel, and continued its work on spent fuel management and on nuclear fuel cycle issues and information systems.

Radioactive waste management

In 2004, IAEA's Board of Governors approved an action plan on the decommissioning of nuclear facilities. One of the first activities undertaken under the plan was the publication of a report on the *Status of the Decommissioning of Nuclear Facilities around the World*. During the year, the intercomparison of safety assessment methodologies was extended with the establishment of a new project known as Safety Assessment Driving Radioactive Waste Management Solutions. The project's goal was to examine different approaches to the safety assessment of activities involving the predisposal of radioactive waste, including waste conditioning and storage. In December, IAEA held an international symposium on the disposal of low activity radioactive waste (Cordoba, Spain, 13-17 December), which discussed policies and strategies for low level waste management.

Marine environment and water resources

In 2004, IAEA continued to promote the linkage between water and human development, and in that regard, it assisted Egypt, Chad, the Libyan Arab Jamahiriya and the Sudan to improve the management of the shared Nubian Aquifer System. During the year, IAEA convened a conference in Monaco on isotopes in environmental studies, which reviewed the latest applications of isotopes to marine geochemistry and biology, including pollution budgeting in coastal zones, marine food chain dynamics, and predictions of regional and global climate change using high resolution isotopic records in dated sediments and corals. In October, the Agency co-sponsored a roundtable meeting on the 'World Groundwater Vision', held in Zacatecas, Mexico, which was an important step in the development by international organizations of a global strategic vision for groundwater use and protection, to be launched at the fourth World Water Forum in 2006.

Food and agriculture

In 2004, IAEA's support regarding the use of nuclear techniques enabled member States to ad-dress some of the challenges associated with sustainable intensification of crop production systems, particularly concerning, among other things, the achievement of better soil, nutrient and water management practices to improve low crop yields. The Agency's efforts in the sustainable intensification of livestock production systems were directed at intensifying and disseminating nuclear technologies and related guidelines and standards that led to improvements in productivity and income generation from domestic and international trade in livestock and livestock products. IAEA's activities also focused on the use of nuclear and related analytical methods for ensuring compliance with maximum residue limits for pesticides and veterinary drugs, and integrated approaches to the application of agricultural countermeasures following a nuclear or radiological emergency.

Human health

In 2004, IAEA continued to promote professional training, innovative teaching technologies and the application of information and communication tools through technical cooperation projects on tele-nuclear medicine and distance assisted teaching. The Agency also addressed issues pertaining to applied radiation biology and radiotherapy, dosimetry and medical radiation physics, and nutrition and the effects of contaminants on human health.

Technical cooperation

In 2004, IAEA's secretariat delivered $75.6 million worth of training, expert services, equipment and other assistance to member States under its technical cooperation programme. New extra-budgetary resources remained at a level comparable with that of the previous year. Funds received in 2004 totalled $10.9 million, compared with $11.8 million in 2003. A total of $3.7 million was contributed as government cost-sharing by member States to support project activities in their own countries. During the year, IAEA began a phased restructuring of its Department of Technical Cooperation. The initial phase, reorganizing the Department's five regional sections into four (Africa, Asia and the Pacific, Europe and Latin America) had been completed.

Safeguard responsibilities

The year 2004 was marked by increased international attention on IAEA's verification programme, particularly its inspection activities relating to the compliance by a number of States with their safeguards agreements. The discovery of covert nuclear trade networks and continuing uncertainty regarding DPRK's nuclear capabilities also contributed to heighten awareness of the risk of nuclear weapons proliferation. Based on the information available to it, IAEA concluded that, except for the nuclear material in the DPRK, all nuclear material and other items placed under safeguards remained in peaceful nuclear activities or were otherwise adequately accounted for. The Agency was unable to verify the DPRK's nuclear material under safeguards and, therefore, could not draw any conclusions about the country's nuclear material or activities. During the year, safeguards were applied for 152 States with safeguards agreements in force with IAEA. In 21 of those States, IAEA was able to complete sufficient work to provide credible assurance regarding the absence of undeclared nuclear material and activities. Four States (Iran, the Libyan Arab Jamahiriya, the Republic of Korea and Egypt) had been found to have been previously engaged in nuclear activities of varying significance which they had failed to report; corrective actions were being taken by those States, while IAEA's efforts to verify the correctness and completeness of their respective declarations remained ongoing.

Nuclear information

The International Nuclear Information System (INIS), IAEA's largest database, continued to collect and distribute scientific information in all areas of nuclear science and technology published in member States. IAEA also maintained two other databases and one simulation system which were available online (http://www-nfcis.iaea.org): World Distribution of Uranium Deposits; Post-Irradiation Examination Facilities; and the Nuclear Fuel Cycle Simulation System.

Secretariat

At the end of 2004, IAEA secretariat staff totalled 2,244 for both the Professional and higher categories and the General Service category.

Budget

The 2004 regular budget amounted to $304 million. Actual budget expenditure amounted to $284 million. A total of $54.5 million in extrabudgetary funds was provided by member States, the United Nations, international organizations and other sources.

NOTE: For further information, see *Annual Report 2004*, published by IAEA.

HEADQUARTERS AND OTHER OFFICE

HEADQUARTERS
International Atomic Energy Agency
P.O. Box 100
Wagramerstrasse 5
A-1400 Vienna, Austria
Telephone: (43) (1) 2600-0
Fax: (43) (1) 2600-7
Internet: www.iaea.org
E-mail: Official.Mail@iaea.org

NEW YORK LIAISON OFFICE
IAEA Office at the United Nations
1 United Nations Plaza, Room 1155
New York, NY 10017, United States
Telephone: (1) (212) 963-6012/6011
Fax: (1) (917) 367-4046
Email: iaeany@un.org

Chapter II

International Labour Organization (ILO)

In 2004, the International Labour Organization (ILO) continued to promote social justice and economic stability and improve labour conditions. ILO's strategic objectives were to promote and realize fundamental principles and rights at work; create greater opportunities for women and men to secure decent employment and income; enhance the coverage and effectiveness of social protection; and strengthen tripartism and social dialogue.

In 2004, ILO membership increased to 178.

Meetings

The ninety-second session of the International Labour Conference (ILC) (Geneva, 1-17 June) adopted a new plan of action to ensure that migrant workers were covered by international labour standards, while benefiting from national labour and social laws. The plan called for the development of a non-binding multilateral framework for a rights-based approach to labour migration and the establishment of an ILO dialogue on migration, in partnership with international and multilateral organizations. ILC also adopted a new Recommendation on human resources development (see below) and a resolution on gender equality, pay equity, and maternity protection. The Conference made progress in forging new labour standards to improve the working conditions and safety of the world's 35 million fishing sector workers, and considered the situation of workers in the Occupied Palestinian Territory, forced labour in Myanmar, and rights at work in other countries.

As follow-up to the 1998 ILO Declaration of Fundamental Principles and Rights at Work [YUN 1998, p. 1375], the Director-General submitted to the Conference a global report entitled "Organizing for social justice", which indicated that, despite continued threats to workers and employers seeking to organize, global respect for fundamental rights at work was improving.

Sectoral and other meetings convened in Geneva during 2004 included: China Employment Forum (28-30 April); Preparatory Technical Maritime Conference (13-24 September); Tripartite Meeting on the Future of Work and Quality in the Information Society: The Media, Culture, Graphical Sector (18-22 October); and

Tripartite Meeting of Experts on the Fishing Sector (13-17 December).

International standards

During the year, ILO activities with regard to Conventions and Recommendations included standard-setting and the supervision and promotion of the application of standards. Supervisory bodies reviewed existing procedures and standard-setting policy, withdrawing outdated Recommendations.

In June, ILC adopted a new Recommendation on human resources development, focusing on education, training and lifelong learning.

Employment and development

ILO continued in 2004 to help constituents combat unemployment and poverty through the creation of employment opportunities and improvement of existing jobs. It provided advice and guidance on employment and labour market policies and on labour market information and statistical systems. Activities to promote employment included support to constituents to develop entrepreneurship through the creation of cooperatives and small and micro-enterprises.

Regarding human resources development, ILO emphasized the need for the adaptation of training policy and delivery to the rapidly changing skill requirements and special needs of vulnerable groups. It also responded to the needs of countries affected by conflict.

Field activities

In 2004, expenditure on technical cooperation programmes totalled $138.4 million, slightly more than the amount spent in 2003 [YUN 2003, p. 1508]. The leading fields of activity were: the standards and fundamental principles and rights at work sector, with 43.1 per cent ($59.6 million); followed by the employment sector, with 27.8 per cent ($38.5 million); the social protection sector, with 12.1 per cent ($16.7 million); and social dialogue, with 11 per cent ($15.3 million).

In terms of regional distribution, Africa accounted for 22.9 per cent of total expenditure ($31.7 million); Asia and the Pacific, 24.2 per cent ($33.5 million); Latin America and the Caribbean, 19.3 per cent ($26.7 million); Europe,

5.2 per cent ($7.2 million); and the Arab States, 1.5 per cent ($2.1 million). Interregional and global activities accounted for the greatest share, at 26.9 per cent ($37.2 million).

Educational activities

The Turin Centre and the International Institute for Labour Studies, both autonomous institutions within ILO, reported to the ILO Governing Body. The Centre continued to carry out training and related activities in a wide range of technical areas as an integral part of ILO technical cooperation activities. The Institute continued to conduct research, encouraged networking related to emerging labour policy issues, and acted as a catalyst for future ILO programme development. The Institute analysed the relationships between social exclusion, labour institutions and poverty, and explored the changing global organization of production and its social implications at the local level.

Secretariat

As at 31 December, ILO employed a total of 2,500 full-time staff, of whom 1,040 were in the Professional and higher categories and 1,460 were in the General Service category.

Budget

The ILO budget for 2004-2005, adopted by ILC in 2003 [YUN 2003, p. 1509], stood at $529.6 million.

NOTE: For further information on ILO, see *Report of the Director-General–ILO programme implementation, 2003-2004.*

HEADQUARTERS AND OTHER OFFICES

HEADQUARTERS

International Labour Organization
4, route des Morillons
CH-1211 Geneva 22, Switzerland
  Telephone: (41) (22) 799-6111
  Fax: (41) (22) 798-8685
  Internet: www.ilo.org
  E-mail: ilo@ilo.org

LIAISON OFFICE

International Labour Organization
Liaison Office with the United Nations
220 East 42nd Street, Suite 3101
New York, NY 10017, United States
  Telephone: (1) (212) 697-0150
  Fax: (1) (212) 697-5218
  Email: newyork@ilo.org

ILO maintained regional offices in Abidjan, Côte d'Ivoire; Bangkok, Thailand; Beirut, Lebanon; Geneva, Switzerland; and Lima, Peru.

Chapter III

Food and Agriculture Organization of the United Nations (FAO)

The Food and Agriculture Organization of the United Nations (FAO) continued to work towards achieving sustainable global food security by raising nutrition levels and living standards, improving agricultural productivity and advancing the condition of rural populations.

At its one hundred and twenty-seventh session (Rome, 22-27 November), the FAO Council adopted a set of voluntary guidelines aimed at providing practical guidance to States in implementing their obligations relating to the right to adequate food in the context of national food security and improving the chances of reaching the hunger reduction goals set by the 1996 World Food Summit [YUN 1996, p. 1129] and the United Nations Millennium Summit [YUN 2000, p. 49].

As part of the follow-up to the World Food Summits held in 1996 [YUN 1996, p. 1397] and 2002 [YUN 2002, p. 1225], FAO helped its members to prepare strategies in meeting the goal of halving the number of hungry by 2015 and in the preparation of medium-term food security and agricultural development programmes. With the collaboration of financial institutions, FAO also helped to formulate projects that would hasten a reversal of the declining resources to agriculture.

As lead agency for the International Year of Rice (2004), declared by the General Assembly in resolution 57/162 [YUN 2002, p. 1226], FAO worked with UN agencies, Governments and non-governmental organizations (NGOs) to increase global awareness and promote the importance of rice development and its positive consequences for poverty alleviation and global food security.

In 2004, FAO membership remained at 187 countries and the European Union.

World food situation

FAO estimated world cereal production at a record 2.042 million tonnes in 2004, 8.2 per cent higher than in 2003. Cereal output was forecast to exceed utilization in 2004/05, which could lead to an increase in stock for the first time in five years. World livestock production in 2004 was estimated at 258 million tonnes of meat, an increase of 2 per cent from the previous year. World fish output in 2003, the latest year for which data were available, stood at 132.5 million

tonnes, of which about 32 per cent was from aquaculture, a sub-sector under continuous expansion.

Activities

FAO continued to provide emergency assistance in the agriculture, livestock and fisheries sectors to developing countries affected by exceptional natural or man-made calamities. In 2004, FAO received $232 million to fund 250 emergency relief and rehabilitation projects in over 70 countries and regions. FAO missions toured countries hit by the Indian Ocean tsunami of 26 December (see p. 952) to assess damage to the agriculture and fisheries sectors and provide detailed information on the assistance needed.

Through its field programmes, FAO provided technical assistance in food and agriculture, fisheries, forestry and rural development totalling $368.3 million, of which $129.5 million was expended for its emergency agricultural rehabilitation programme and $238.8 million for development and technical support. FAO's Investment Centre assisted developing and transition countries to identify and assess investment opportunities, and formulated 163 investment projects worth $5.6 billion, of which $4.1 billion was provided through external loans from funding partners. The Special Programme for Food Security assisted developing countries, particularly low-income food-deficit countries, to improve national and household food security on an economically and environmentally sustainable basis. By the end of 2004, 101 countries were participating in the programme.

In 2004, FAO continued to participate in activities related to plant biological diversity, crop management and diversification, seed production and improvement, crop protection, agricultural engineering, the prevention of food losses, and food and agricultural industries. It also contributed to the development of animal production and health programmes through better resource utilization, improved processing and commercialization, and better control of animal diseases. The Global Rinderpest Eradication Programme continued to work to eliminate the fatal livestock virus by 2010. Asia was considered free of the disease and the only remaining suspect area was in the Horn of Africa.

The FAO Forestry Department continued its work in forest resource management, policy and planning, and forest products. FAO hosted the secretariat of the International Partnership for Sustainable Development in Mountain Regions and continued to work with NGOs, Governments and the private sector in promoting support for mountain livelihoods, especially for the 270 million mountain people who lived in developing and transition countries and suffered from hunger.

The FAO Fisheries Department promoted sustainable development of responsible fisheries and contributed to food security through activities in fishery resources, policy, industries and information. FAO's main priority was to enlist the international community in promoting more widespread adherence to the FAO Code of Conduct for Responsible Fisheries. In 2004, FAO established an advisory commission on fisheries management and development, known as the South-West Indian Ocean Fisheries Commission.

During the year, FAO provided technical assistance in plant breeding and the safe movement of germoplasm, as well as associated legislation.

The International Treaty on Plant Genetic Resources for Food and Agriculture, approved by the FAO Conference in 2001 [YUN 2001, p.1406], entered into force in 2004. The Treaty aimed at the conservation of plant genetic resources, their sustainable use, and the fair and equitable sharing of benefits resulting from commercialization.

In 2004, the Codex Alimentarius Commission, responsible for implementing the joint FAO/World Health Organization Food Standards Programme, adopted over 20 new and amended food standards. Among the new standards and other texts to protect consumers' health and facilitate fair practices in the food trade worldwide were those related to animal feeding, milk products and a newly adopted definition of traceability/product tracing.

Secretariat

As at 31 December 2004, FAO staff numbered 3,821, of whom 1,620 were in the Professional or higher categories, and 2,201 were in the General Service category.

Budget

The regular programme budget for the 2004-2005 biennium totalled $749.1 million.

HEADQUARTERS AND OTHER OFFICES

HEADQUARTERS

Food and Agriculture Organization of the United Nations
Viale delle Terme di Caracalla
00100 Rome, Italy
  Telephone: (39) (06) 57051
  Fax: (39) (06) 5705 3152
  Internet: www.fao.org
  E-mail: FAO-HQ@fao.org

NEW YORK LIAISON OFFICE

Food and Agriculture Organization
Liaison Office with the United Nations
1 United Nations Plaza, Room 1125
New York, NY 10017, United States
  Telephone: (1) (212) 963-6036
  Fax: (1) (212) 963-5425
  E-mail: FAO-LONY@fao.org

FAO also maintained liaison offices in Brussels, Geneva, Washington, D.C., and Yokohama, Japan; regional offices in Accra, Ghana; Bangkok, Thailand; Cairo, Egypt; and Santiago, Chile; and subregional offices in Apia, Samoa; Bridgetown, Barbados; Budapest, Hungary; Harare, Zimbabwe; and Tunis, Tunisia.

Chapter IV

United Nations Educational, Scientific and Cultural Organization (UNESCO)

The United Nations Educational, Scientific and Cultural Organization (UNESCO) continued in 2004 to promote cooperation in education, science, culture and communication among its member States. The General Conference, which met biennially to decide on policy, programme and budgetary matters, was scheduled to hold its thirty-third session in October 2005. The 58-member Executive Board held its one hundred and sixty-ninth (19-29 April) and one hundred and seventieth (4-14 October) sessions in Paris.

UNESCO membership remained at 190, with six associate members.

Activities

Education

As the lead agency for the United Nations Literacy Decade (2003-2012), launched on 13 February 2003 under the theme "Literacy as freedom", UNESCO continued to promote literacy as a human right and a prerequisite for participating in social, cultural and economic activities. In collaboration with the Organisation for Economic Co-operation and Development (OECD), UNESCO launched a global review on early childhood care and education. It promoted the increased enrolment of girls in primary and secondary education in sub-Saharan Africa and gave special attention to girls affected by HIV/AIDS to enable them to attend school.

UNESCO convened the fourth annual meeting of the High-level Group on Education for All (EFA) (Brasilia, Brazil, 8-10 November) [YUN 2001, p. 1408] and issued two publications: the third edition of the *Global Monitoring Report on EFA* and the *Minimum Standards for Education in Emergencies, Chronic Crises and Early Reconstruction*. To reinforce EFA progress, UNESCO launched three initiatives—the Literacy Initiative for Empowerment, the Teacher Training Initiative in Sub-Saharan Africa and the Global Initiative on HIV/AIDS and Education.

Meetings were held to develop joint UNESCO/ OECD guidelines on higher education and globalization, in addition to the First Colloquium on Research and Higher Education Policy (Paris, 1-3 December). UNESCO also organized meetings of the Interagency Task Team on Education and HIV/AIDS (Ottawa, Canada, 12-13 May). Progress was made in drafting the convention against doping in sport at the Fourth International Conference of Ministers and Senior Officials Responsible for Physical Education and Sport (Athens, Greece, 6-8 December).

Natural sciences

UNESCO's Intergovernmental Oceanographic Commission (IOC) and Natural Disaster Reduction team responded immediately to the Indian Ocean tsunami disaster in December (see p. 952). IOC coordinated United Nations activities in ocean and coastal issues and participated in drafting a ten-year plan for the implementation of the Global Earth Observing System of Systems, which was designed to help countries identify and address challenges such as climate change and natural disasters. Other natural sciences activities focused on the advancement and sharing of scientific and technical knowledge and on the capacity-building of scientists and engineers and of national Governments for science and technology policy-making and planning. The International Geoscience Programme continued to provide a multidisciplinary platform for scientists to exchange knowledge on global geological problems.

Social and human sciences

UNESCO, in its leading role as an ethical forum, drafted a declaration on universal norms on bioethics for submission to its General Conference in 2005. It also collaborated with the World Commission on the Ethics of Scientific Knowledge and Technology to establish a programme to develop national capacities in science and technology ethics and helped it raise public awareness on the ethical implications of scientific knowledge and technology and on the responsibility of science and technology professionals.

UNESCO collaborated with the City of Nantes (France) in organizing the World Forum on Human Rights (16-18 May), and under its International Coalition of Cities against Racism project, it successfully launched (Nuremburg, Germany,

10 December) the first regional coalition in Europe.

Culture

UNESCO continued its activities for safeguarding tangible cultural heritage in post-conflict situations. Within the framework of the 2003 UNESCO Convention for the Safeguarding of Intangible Cultural Heritage [YUN 2003, p. 1513], the Director General proclaimed 47 Masterpieces of the Oral and Intangible Heritage of Humanity to further raise awareness regarding the importance of safeguarding vulnerable expressions of cultural heritage. On 9 March, the Second Protocol to the 1954 Hague Convention for the Protection of Cultural Property in the Event of Armed Conflict entered into force; the Convention had taken effect in 1956 [YUN 1956, p 436]. In order to establish a new standard-setting instrument in the field of cultural diversity, UNESCO convened the first intergovernmental meeting (Paris, 20-24 September) to exchange views on the preliminary draft text of the Convention on the Protection of Diversity of Cultural Contents and Artistic Expressions. It also organized activities in recognition of the International Year to Commemorate the Struggle against Slavery and its Abolition, including an itinerant international exhibition, "Lest We Forget", organized by the Schomburg Center for Research on Black Culture.

UNESCO broadened the scope of its activities on the global agenda for Dialogue among Civilizations and Cultures, conducting conferences in Albania, France, Kyrgyzstan, Spain, Viet Nam and Yemen. It also continued its partnership with Daimler Chrysler, known as "Mondialogo", which promoted intercultural dialogue through an international school contest and an engineering award.

Communication

UNESCO continued to support and promote activities related to media development in developing countries, the celebration of World Press Freedom Day (3 May) and the empowerment of people to enable them to access and contribute to information and knowledge flows. UNESCO's Information for All Programme (IFAP) provided the policy framework for setting standards, raising awareness and monitoring progress in an effort to achieve universal access to information and knowledge. IFAP promoted the formulation of strategies and policies that conformed with the Principles and Action Plan adopted at the World Summit on the Information Society [YUN 2003, p. 857].

Supporting youth and a culture of peace

UNESCO continued its cooperation with youth and intergovernmental organizations and produced several publications on empowering youth, young people and the Universal Declaration on Cultural Diversity, and UNESCO's commitment to youth. On 10 May, a tool for measuring youth development—the Youth Development Index—was launched by the UNESCO office in Brasilia.

UNESCO promoted culture of peace activities within the context of the International Decade (2001-2010) for a Culture of Peace and Non-Violence for the Children of the World. It also organized the International Colloquium on Women in Service of Peace (Paris, 8 June).

Secretariat

As at 31 December 2004, UNESCO employed 2,181 full-time staff, of whom 1,066 were in the Professional or higher categories and 1,115 in the General Service category.

Budget

In October 2003, the UNESCO General Conference approved a budget of $610 million for the 2004-2005 biennium.

HEADQUARTERS AND OTHER OFFICES

HEADQUARTERS

UNESCO House
7, Place de Fontenoy
75352 Paris 07-SP, France
Telephone: (33) (1) 45-68-10-00
Fax: (33) (1) 45-67-16-90
Internet: www.unesco.org

UNESCO also maintained a liaison office in Geneva.

NEW YORK LIAISON OFFICE

United Nations Educational, Scientific and Cultural Organization
2 United Nations Plaza, Room 900
New York, NY 10017, United States
Telephone: (1) (212) 963-5995
Fax: (1) (212) 963-8014
E-mail: newyork@unesco.org

Chapter V

World Health Organization (WHO)

In 2004, the World Health Organization (WHO) continued to implement its corporate strategy by focusing on its core functions, which included efforts to stimulate and advance the eradication of epidemic, endemic and other diseases; promote and conduct research; propose conventions, agreements and regulations; promote cooperation and partnerships; provide information, counsel and assistance in the field of health; and develop, establish and promote relevant international standards on health issues.

The World Health Assembly, WHO's governing body, at its fifty-seventh session (Geneva, 17-22 May), adopted global strategies on diet, physical activity and health, aimed at combating cardiovascular disease, diabetes, cancers and obesity-related conditions, and on reproductive health, which targeted the priority aspects of reproductive and sexual health, including improving antenatal, delivery, postpartum and newborn care and providing high-quality services for family planning.

Both strategies were endorsed by the one hundred and thirteenth session of the WHO Executive Board (Geneva, 19-24 January), which also adopted resolutions relating to the control of *Mycobacterium ulcerans* disease (Buruli ulcer) and of human African trypanosomiasis (sleeping disease); the promotion of health and healthy lifestyles; road safety; genomics (the study of genes, their functions and related techniques); and human organ and tissue transplantation. At its one hundred and fourteenth session (Geneva, 19-24 May), the Board adopted resolutions on sustainable financing for tuberculosis control; cancer prevention and control; and disability, including prevention, management and rehabilitation.

In another development, the WHO *World Health Report 2004: Changing History* called for a comprehensive HIV/AIDS strategy linking prevention, treatment, care and support for people living with the disease, especially in developing countries. WHO designated road safety as the theme for World Health Day, 2004, marked globally on 7 April. The joint WHO/World Bank *World Report on Road Traffic Injury Prevention* highlighted evidence-based recommendations to reduce the death toll on roads.

As at 29 November, 40 countries had ratified the WHO Framework Convention on Tobacco Control, adopted in 2003 [YUN 2003, p. 1514] as the first global health treaty aimed at reducing global tobacco consumption and cutting the number of tobacco-related deaths. Consequently, the Convention would enter into force in February 2005, in accordance with the terms of article 36 (see also p. 1221).

In 2004, WHO membership remained at 192, with two associate members.

2004 activities

In 2004, the World Health Assembly established the Commission on Intellectual Property Rights, Innovation and Public Health. The Commission would summarize evidence on the prevalence of significant diseases, review the volume and distribution of existing research, analyse proposals for improvements to current incentive and funding regimes and formulate a final report with proposals for consideration in 2006.

WHO prepared and distributed new surveillance guidelines and a risk assessment and preparedness framework for severe acute respiratory syndrome (SARS), which had reappeared four times since July 2003, resulting in 17 cases. It continued to assess the risk of an avian influenza pandemic and supported national and international action in pandemic preparedness.

As part of its work in monitoring medicine quality, WHO pre-qualified 12 new products in 2004, nine of which were for the treatment of HIV/AIDS, one for malaria and two for tuberculosis. It also initiated systematic inspections of contract research organizations which had carried out bioequivalence studies for pre-qualified medicines, starting with priority medicines for treating HIV/AIDS.

The Indian Ocean tsunami of 26 December devastated coastal areas, killing hundreds of thousands of people and displacing millions more (see p. 952). Within hours of the tragedy, WHO staff were deployed to the affected regions, where they assessed the damage and identified needs. Early work to ensure adequate clean water and sanitation, including the delivery of millions of water purification tablets and health emergency kits, averted potential outbreaks of diarrhoeal diseases. WHO also facilitated information gathering and the coordination of health-related relief and recovery efforts.

Secretariat

As at 31 December 2004, WHO employed a staff of 4,017, of whom 1,565 were in the Professional and higher categories and 2,207 in the General Service category. The remaining 245 were employed under other contracts. In addition, 3,973 staff held temporary appointments, including consultancies.

Budget

The World Health Assembly appropriated a working budget of $880.1 million for the 2004-2005 biennium. Extrabudgetary resources were expected to be about $1,824.5 million, leading to a total effective budget of $2,704.6 million for that period.

NOTE: For further details on WHO activities, see the *World Health Report 2004*, published by the organization.

HEADQUARTERS AND OTHER OFFICES

HEADQUARTERS

World Health Organization
20, Avenue Appia
CH-1211 Geneva 27, Switzerland
 Telephone: (41) (22) 791-21-11
 Fax: (41) (22) 791-31-11
 Internet: www.who.int
 E-mail: info@who.int

WHO OFFICE AT THE UNITED NATIONS

2 United Nations Plaza, Room 970
New York, NY 10017, United States
 Telephone: (1) (212) 963-4388
 Fax: (1) (212) 963-8565

WHO also maintained regional offices in Brazzaville, Republic of the Congo; Cairo, Egypt; Copenhagen, Denmark; Manila, Philippines; New Delhi, India; and Washington, D.C.

Chapter VI

World Bank (IBRD and IDA)

The World Bank consisted of the International Bank for Reconstruction and Development (IBRD) and the International Development Association (IDA). Collectively, the following five institutions were known as the World Bank Group: IBRD, IDA, the International Finance Corporation (IFC) (see p. 1494), the Multilateral Investment Guarantee Agency (MIGA) and the International Centre for Settlement of Investment Disputes (ICSID).

In fiscal 2004 (1 July 2003–30 June 2004), the World Bank continued to promote sustainable economic development by providing loans, guarantees and related technical assistance for projects and programmes in developing countries. It also maintained a leading role in the debt relief process under the Heavily Indebted Poor Countries Initiative, in order to increase resources for poverty reduction. In June, the first Global Monitoring Report published by the Bank and IMF assessed progress on policies and actions for achieving the Millennium Development Goals (MDGs) [YUN 2000, p. 51].

In 2004, the Bank joined with several partner organizations to make generic HIV/AIDS drugs available in more than 100 poor countries. In cooperation with the United Nations, the Bank also produced a Joint Iraq Needs Assessment, which identified Iraq's reconstruction and development requirements and estimated its financing needs.

At the end of fiscal 2004, IBRD membership remained at 184.

Lending operations

IBRD continued to promote sustainable development through loans, guarantees and non-lending, including analytical and advisory services. As at 30 June 2004, its cumulative lending totalled $394 billion.

IBRD's loan commitment for fiscal 2004 totalled $11 billion for 87 new operations in 33 countries, compared to $11.2 billion in 2003 for 99 operations. In fiscal 2004, IBRD lending commitments were highest in Latin America and the Caribbean ($5 billion), followed by Europe and Central Asia ($3 billion), East Asia and the Pacific ($1.7 billion), the Middle East and North Africa ($1 billion) and South Asia ($.44 million). Public administration was the leading sector for

IBRD lending, with $2.7 billion, or about 24 per cent of the total, followed by transportation, with $2.5 billion, and health and social services, with $1.8 billion.

In fiscal 2004, the four largest borrowers were Argentina, Turkey, Brazil and China, which collectively accounted for 51 per cent of total IBRD lending.

International Development Association

Established in 1960 as the Bank's concessional lending arm, IDA provided interest-free loans and other services to low-income countries to reduce poverty and improve the quality of life. In fiscal 2004, IDA commitments totalled $9 billion for 158 operations in 62 countries, compared with $7.3 billion for 141 operations in 55 countries in fiscal 2003 [YUN 2003, p. 1516]. In addition, IDA provided $1.7 billion in grants and a guarantee for $70 million.

Lending to Africa constituted 45 per cent or $4.1 billion of total IDA commitments. South Asia and East Asia and the Pacific followed with $3 billion and $0.9 billion, respectively. Bangladesh, the Democratic Republic of the Congo, India, Pakistan and Vietnam represented the largest recipients of IDA financing.

In fiscal 2004, about 19 per cent of total IDA financing was provided in the form of grants to the following clients and projects: the poorest countries ($264 million); debt-vulnerable countries ($529 million); post-conflict countries ($536 million); HIV/AIDS projects and related components ($381 million); and natural disaster reconstruction projects ($2 million).

Public administration, including law and justice, was the leading sector for IDA support, receiving $2.3 billion, or 24 per cent, of the total.

At the end of fiscal 2004, IDA membership increased to 165 countries.

International Centre for Settlement of Investment Disputes

ICSID, established in 1966, continued to encourage foreign investments by providing international facilities for coordination and arbitration of investment disputes. In 2004, 30 new cases were registered with the Centre. ICSID also undertook research and publishing activities in arbitration and foreign investment law.

In 2004, ICSID membership increased to 140.

Multilateral Investment Guarantee Agency

The Multilateral Investment Guarantee Agency (MIGA), established in 1988, continued to encourage foreign direct investment in developing countries by providing guarantees to foreign investors against losses caused by non-commercial risks. It also provided technical assistance and advisory services to help developing countries strengthen the capacity of investment promotion intermediaries and disseminate information on investment opportunities.

In fiscal 2004, MIGA had 164 members and issued $1.1 billion in guarantee coverage, for a cumulative total of $13.5 billion.

World Bank Institute

In 2004, the World Bank Institute continued to organize global training activities in an effort to empower people through knowledge- and capacity-building. It also developed diagnostic and analytical tools that helped countries assess their governance practices and preparedness to compete in the global knowledge economy. As part of its efforts to decentralize its programmes, the Institute and the Middle East and North African region launched the Marseilles Knowledge Hub. In partnership with local training centres and through the Global Development Learning Network's distance learning facilities, the Institute delivered 1,016 training activities to 78,500 participants in some 124 countries.

Co-financing

Major co-financing partners included the Inter-American Development Bank, the European Commission and the British Department for International Development. By region, most of the co-financing went to Latin America and the Caribbean ($4 billion), followed by Africa ($3 billion) and South Asia ($1.3 billion).

Financial activities

During fiscal 2004, IBRD raised $13 billion in medium- and long-term debt, compared to $19 billion in fiscal 2003. The decrease in funding was primarily attributed to lower borrowing requirements as a result of the reduction in the loan portfolio. IBRD followed a strategy of selective bond issuance, composed of cost-effective private placements and public issues placed with large institutional investors, and those targeted to retail investors. During fiscal 2004, IBRD repurchased or called $4 billion of its outstanding borrowings (net of unamortized discounts, premiums, and issuance costs).

Capitalization

As at 30 June 2004, the total authorized capital of IBRD was $190,811 million, of which $189,718 million had been subscribed. Of the subscribed capital, $11,483 million had been paid in and $178,235 million was callable.

Income, expenditures and reserves

IBRD's net income was $2.4 billion in fiscal 2004, down from $5.34 billion in fiscal 2003. As at 30 June 2004, the Bank's liquid asset portfolio was $31 billion, up from $27 billion in fiscal 2003.

Secreteriat

At the end of fiscal 2004, IBRD's regular, fixed-term and long-term consultants and long-term temporary staff in Washington, D.C., and local offices numbered 9,758.

NOTE: For further details regarding the Bank's activities, see *The World Bank Annual Report 2004*.

HEADQUARTERS AND OTHER OFFICES

HEADQUARTERS

The World Bank
1818 H Street, NW
Washington, DC 20433, United States
Telephone: (1) (202) 473-1000
Fax: (1) (202) 477-6391
Internet: www.worldbank.org
E-mail: feedback@worldbank.org

LIAISON OFFICE

The World Bank Mission to the United Nations
1 Dag Hammarskjöld Plaza
885 Second Avenue, 26th floor
New York, NY 10017, United States
Telephone: (1) (212) 355-5112
Fax: (1) (212) 355-4523

The World Bank also maintained offices in Brussels, Belgium; Frankfurt, Germany; Geneva; London; Paris; Sydney, Australia; and Tokyo, Japan.

Chapter VII

International Finance Corporation (IFC)

The International Finance Corporation (IFC), part of the World Bank Group, continued in fiscal 2004 (1 July 2003–30 June 2004) to promote sustainable growth in developing countries by financing private sector investments, helping to mobilize capital in the international financial markets and providing technical assistance and advice to Governments and businesses. To address the environmental and social consequences of development, IFC continued to focus on sustainability as a top priority in its investment and advisory activities.

During fiscal 2004, IFC membership increased to 176.

Financial and advisory services

In fiscal 2004, IFC's total committed portfolio amounted to $17.4 million, of which $5.64 million was dedicated to 217 new projects in six regions. IFC aligned its network of small and medium enterprise facilities with its regional departments, reflecting the growing importance of providing technical assistance and advice in all regions. IFC also worked to standardize the procedures, data recording, partner relations and monitoring across all its donor-funded operations.

The Foreign Investment Advisory Service (FIAS) assisted Governments to develop policies and institutions to attract more foreign investment. FIAS completed 60 advisory projects in fiscal year 2004, with the largest number of programmes in Europe and Central Asia (17 projects), followed by Asia and the Pacific (16).

Throughout fiscal 2004, the donor community provided cumulative contributions of $188 million to support the technical assistance trust funds (TATF) programme, which included a budgetary allocation from IFC's own resources of $14.4 million. Since the inception of the programme in 1988, donors had approved more than 1,380 technical assistance projects. The TATF programme financed feasibility studies, sector studies, and advisory activities on privatization and on policies to strengthen the business environment in developing countries. It also assessed the environmental and social impacts of investment projects. Other funds provided by donors assisted small and medium enterprise project development facilities, such as IFC's new tech-

nical assistance initiatives in the Balkans and the Middle East. Cumulative contributions to all IFC managed technical assistance programmes reached $931 million in fiscal 2004.

Regional projects

In fiscal 2004, the new projects for which IFC committed $5.63 billion were grouped under six regions.

In order to address sub-Saharan Africa's development needs, IFC expanded its programmes for the smaller businesses that constituted much of Africa's private sector. For larger projects, the strategy targeted more support at the formative stages of project development, thus expanding IFC's role beyond the provision of finance. IFC's commitments in the region totalled $1.83 million for 25 projects in 12 countries.

In East Asia and the Pacific, IFC focused on improving the investment climate, developing local financial markets, and expanding private provision of physical and social infrastructure development. It also allocated more specialized resources for financial sector activities. IFC's commitments in the region totalled $3.8 million for 40 projects in seven countries.

In South Asia, IFC provided investments and technical assistance to help companies improve competitiveness, access longer-term funding, and reach new markets. It also helped build internationally competitive enterprises throughout South Asia. IFC's commitments in the region totalled $1.8 million for 19 projects in five countries.

In Europe and Central Asia, the largest share of funding went to the Russian Federation, reflecting the country's growth and stability and IFC's increasing work with local companies and firms based outside of Moscow. IFC also supported the private sector throughout Eastern Europe through advisory work and investment, with a focus on strengthening small businesses. IFC's commitments in the region totalled $5.5 million for 65 projects in 17 countries.

In Latin America and the Caribbean, IFC's strategy centered on added-value services tailored to specific market segments and on addressing social inequality through investments and technical assistance. IFC continued to emphasize increasing competitiveness and supported intraregional investments. IFC's commitments in the region totalled $8.6 million for 45 projects in 16 countries.

In the Middle East and North Africa, IFC focused on its technical assistance and advisory programme for the region, with an emphasis on creating greater synergies with its more traditional investment activities. The North Africa Enterprise Development facility, which operated in Algeria, Egypt and Morocco, completed its second year of work with small and medium enterprises. During fiscal year 2004, IFC launched the Private Enterprise Partnership for the Middle East, a facility to support private sector development in four frontier markets: Afghanistan, Iraq, the West Bank and Gaza, and Yemen. IFC's commitments in the region totalled $1.87 million for 18 projects in eight countries.

Financial performance

In fiscal 2004, IFC's operating income was $982 million, compared with $528 million in fiscal 2003. IFC's committed portfolio at the end of fiscal 2004 was $17.9 billion, up from $16.8 billion in fiscal 2003. The portfolio consisted of loans, equity investments, risk management products, and guarantees in 1,337 companies in 119 countries.

Capital and retained earnings

As at 30 June 2004, IFC's net worth reached $7.8 billion, compared with $6.8 billion at the end of fiscal 2003.

Secretariat

As at 31 December 2004, IFC employed 2,200 staff, of whom 1,276 were in the Professional or higher categories and 924 were in the General Service category.

NOTE: For further details of IFC activities, see *International Finance Corporation 2004 Annual Report*, published by the Corporation.

HEADQUARTERS AND OTHER OFFICE

HEADQUARTERS

International Finance Corporation
2121 Pennsylvania Avenue, NW
Washington, DC 20433, United States
  Telephone: (1) (202) 473-3800
  Fax: (1) (202) 974-4384
  Internet: http://www.ifc.org
  E-mail: webmaster@ifc.org

NEW YORK OFFICE

International Finance Corporation
c/o The World Bank, Office of the Special Representative to the UN
1 Dag Hammarskjöld Plaza
885 Second Avenue, 26th floor
New York, NY 10017, United States
  Telephone: (1) (212) 355-5112
  Fax: (1) (212) 355-5523

Chapter VIII

International Monetary Fund (IMF)

In 2004, the activities of the International Monetary Fund (IMF) related mainly to its responsibility for overseeing the international monetary system and the economic, financial and exchange rate policies of its member countries. The Fund continued to foster sustainable growth and financial stability, promote sound policies and assist in the global fight against poverty, particularly in low-income countries. Following the expiration of its contingent credit lines instrument, IMF began exploring the scope for adapting precautionary arrangements for crisis prevention and introduced ex post assessment of the programmes it supported. It also continued to emphasize financial sector surveillance and to combat money laundering.

In fiscal year 2004 (1 May 2003–30 April 2004), IMF membership remained at 184.

IMF facilities and policies

In fiscal 2004, IMF changed its lending policies and facilities and reviewed the design of several programmes and the policy conditions that borrowing countries were expected to meet. It completed an expanded review of its access policy in the credit tranches, the extended fund facility (EFF), the poverty reduction and growth facility (PRGF), and the exceptional access policy, which established a global limit on access to IMF's general resources account. The PRGF process continued to emphasize the need to build on progress in several areas, including designing policies to foster pro-poor economic growth, improving the quality and efficiency of government spending, coordinating programme design with the World Bank, and enhancing communication with the authorities, donors and civil society in PRGF countries.

The Independent Evaluation Office (IEO) issued reports on the role of IMF in the capital account crises of Brazil, Indonesia and the Republic of Korea, and on fiscal adjustment in IMF-supported programmes. IMF's Executive Directors noted that, while the Fund's efforts to deal with crises were appropriate, the crises highlighted the need for improvements in its policies and procedures. The Directors welcomed the conclusion of the latter report that there was no evidence that IMF-supported programmes were uniformly contradictory or caused a decline in social spending. The Directors supported IEO's recommendation that programme documentation provide a more coherent justification for the magnitude and pace of fiscal adjustment.

During the year, IMF's Executive Board discussed the Fund's support for trade-related balance of payments adjustments, particularly ways to give its member countries more confidence to pursue ambitious trade liberalization under the World Trade Organization's Doha (Qatar) round of trade negotiations (see p. 958). In April, the Board established the Trade Integration Mechanism, designed to mitigate the fear of some developing countries that their balance of payments position could suffer temporarily as multilateral liberalization changed their competitive position in world markets.

Financial assistance

New IMF lending commitments in fiscal 2004 declined to 14.5 billion special drawing rights (SDR) from SDR 29.4 billion in fiscal 2003. Commitments were largely dominated by Argentina and Brazil, which together accounted for over 90 per cent of the total new commitments. Burundi purchased SDR 9.6 million under the IMF policy of emergency assistance. No extended arrangements were approved and no commitments were made under the IMF's Compensatory Financing Facility (CFF).

IMF approved five new standby arrangements and an augmentation of existing arrangements totalling SDR 14.5 billion. Drawings under PRGF amounted to SDR 865 million compared with SDR 1.2 billion in fiscal 2003. IMF also committed SDR 1.8 billion in Highly Indebted Poor Countries Initiative grants to 28 countries, of which SDR 1.2 billion was disbursed.

As at April 2004, 13 standby arrangements and extended arrangements, and 36 PRGF arrangements were in effect, while outstanding IMF credit amounted to SDR 62.2 billion, compared with SDR 72.9 billion a year earlier.

Liquidity

As at 30 April, IMF's usable resources totalled SDR 103.8 billion, a slight increase from SDR 98 billion in fiscal 2003. Net uncommitted usable resources totalled SDR 70 billion at the end of fiscal 2004, compared with SDR 60.6 billion in fiscal 2003.

The Fund's liquid liability totalled SDR 63 billion, compared with SDR 68 billion in 2003, while the ratio of its net uncommited usable resources to its liquid liabilities increased to 119.4 per cent at the end of April 2004, from 89.1 per cent a year earlier.

SDR activity

In fiscal 2004, total transfers of SDRs declined to SDR 13.8 billion from SDR 15.6 billion in fiscal 2003.

Transfers of SDRs among participants and pre-scribed holders fell to SDR 2.4 billion in 2004 from SDR 6 billion the previous year. In contrast, transfers from participants to the general resources account (GRA) increased to SDR 5.5 billion from SDR 4.5 billion in fiscal 2003, due to increased payments for members' quotas. Drawings from IMF in SDRs increased to SDR 3.5 billion from SDR 2.2 billion in fiscal 2003.

IMF holdings of SDRs in the GRA declined to SDR 0.5 billion in fiscal 2004 from SDR 1 billion a year earlier, while SDRs held by prescribed hold-ers amounted to SDR 0.4 billion. SDR holdings by participants increased to SDR 20.6 billion from SDR 19.9 billion in fiscal 2003.

Policy on arrears

As at 30 April 2004, total overdue financial ob-ligations to IMF increased slightly to SDR 2.05 bil-lion, from SDR 2.01 billion. Almost all arrears were protracted (outstanding for more than six months) and over four-fifths of the debt was to GRA, and the remainder to the SDR and the PRGF Trust. The Sudan and Liberia maintained the largest arrears, accounting for 77 per cent of the overdue financial obligations to the Fund, with Somalia and Zimbabwe accounting for most of the remainder. The application of remedial measures against Iraq and Somalia continued to be delayed or suspended owing to ongoing civil conflicts, the absence of a functioning govern-ment, and/or international sanctions.

Despite approval by IMF's Board of Directors of the resumption of technical assistance to Libe-ria, that country, together with Somalia, the Su-dan and Zimbabwe, remained ineligible to use the Fund's general resources. In addition, Zim-babwe continued to be excluded from the PRGF list and the Board began consideration of its compulsory withdrawal from the Fund. Declara-tions of non-cooperation against Liberia and Zimbabwe remained in effect, and both countries had their voting and related rights suspended.

Technical assistance

During fiscal 2004, technical assistance in-creased for policy reform and capacity building, and for countries trying to meet international standards and codes and to promote financial sec-tor improvements. Sub-Saharan Africa continued to receive the largest share, although technical as-sistance to the Asia-Pacific region also increased, owing partly to the assistance provided to such post-conflict countries as Cambodia and Timor-Leste, and support for reforms in China, Indone-sia and Mongolia. Technical assistance was also provided to a number of countries in Central and Eastern Europe, in support of their preparations for European Union membership. In March, IMF's Executive Board reviewed the Fund's techni-cal assistance programme, particularly as it af-fected low-income countries, and emphasized that the Fund's main challenges in that regard were to ensure that such assistance was focused and that appropriate priorities were set.

The IMF Institute continued to expand its training, mainly through the Fund's six regional institutes and programmes, located in Austria, Brazil, China, Singapore, Tunisia and the United Arab Emirates.

Secretariat

As at 31 December 2004, IMF employed 2,712 staff members, of whom 1,994 were Professional staff and 718 assistant staff.

Budget

The fund's administrative budget for fiscal 2004 was approved at $837.5 million ($785.5 mil-lion net of estimated reimbursements). In April, the Board approved $905.1 million ($849.6 mil-lion net of estimated reimbursement) for 2005.

NOTE: For further details of IMF activities, see its *International Monetary Fund Annual Report 2004.*

HEADQUARTERS AND OTHER OFFICES

HEADQUARTERS

International Monetary Fund
700 19th Street, NW
Washington, DC 20431, United States
Telephone: (1) (202) 623-7000
Fax: (1) (202) 623-4661
Internet: www.imf.org
E-mail: publicaffairs@imf.org

IMF also maintained offices in Geneva, Paris and Tokyo.

IMF OFFICE, UNITED NATIONS, NEW YORK

International Monetary Fund
885 Second Avenue, 26th floor
New York, NY 10017, United States
Telephone: (1) (212) 893-1700
Fax: (1) (212) 893-1715

Chapter IX

International Civil Aviation Organization (ICAO)

The International Civil Aviation Organization (ICAO) continued in 2004 to promote the safety, security and efficiency of civil air transport by prescribing standards and recommending practices and procedures for facilitating international civil aviation operations. Its objectives were set forth in annexes to the Convention on International Civil Aviation, adopted in Chicago, United States, in 1944 (the Chicago Convention).

In 2004, domestic and international scheduled traffic of the world's airlines increased to some 457 billion tonne-kilometres. Overall, passenger traffic increased by about 9 per cent to some 1.8 billion, and freight carriage by about 9 per cent to some 38 million tonne-kilometres. The passenger load factor on scheduled services in 2004 increased to about 73 per cent. Air freight increased by almost 13 per cent to 140.9 billion tonne-kilometres, while there was little change in airmail traffic, which remained at about 4.6 billion tonne-kilometres. Overall passenger/freight/mail tonne-kilometres increased by some 13 per cent and international tonne-kilometres increased by about 14 per cent.

The thirty-fifth session of the ICAO Assembly (Montreal, Canada, 28 September–8 October) elected a new Council and adopted resolutions to strengthen and promote greater transparency in its global safety and security programmes, while endorsing long-term plans of action in other major areas of global air transport.

ICAO observed International Civil Aviation Day (7 December) under the theme "International Cooperation: Solutions to Global Aviation Challenges".

In 2004, ICAO membership remained at 188 countries.

Activities

Air navigation

ICAO continued to update and implement international specifications and regional plans, with particular emphasis on aviation safety, communications, and navigation and surveillance/air traffic management (CNS/ATM) systems. The specifications consisted of International Standards and Recommended Practices contained in 18 technical annexes to the Chicago Convention, and Procedures for Air Navigation Services (PANS). In that regard, the ICAO Council adopted amendments to nine annexes and approved amendments to three PANS documents.

Other projects that were given special attention in 2004 included: harmonization of ICAO safety management provisions; reduction of runway incursions; development of ATM system requirements, transition strategies and a performance framework in support of seamless, global ATM systems; development of material to facilitate the integration of new larger aircraft; passenger health issues, including the development of a harmonized contingency plan for airports to help prevent the spread of communicable diseases by air travel; and agreement on the implementation of a unified strategy for resolving safety deficiencies.

Air transport

ICAO's air transport programmes were directed towards economic analysis, policy, forecasting and planning; collection and publication of air transport statistics; financial management of airports and air navigation services, including user charges; economic aspects of CNS/ATM systems; environmental protection; facilitation of formalities for international air transport operations; and aviation security.

The sixth meeting of the Committee on Aviation Environmental Protection (Montreal, 2-12 February) developed recommendations concerning aircraft noise and the impact of aircraft engine emissions, market-based options, environmental goals and future work.

The twelfth session of the Facilitation Division (Cairo, Egypt, 22 March–1 April) recommended some 75 changes to standards in annex 9 on facilitation, to provide for the smoother passage of travellers through border controls, heightened aviation security and controls on travel document fraud and illegal migration.

Progress was made in the implementation of the ICAO Aviation Security Plan of Action. Through the Universal Security Audit Programme, 44 States were audited by ICAO aviation security audit teams, bringing the total number of States audited to 64 by year's end.

Further work was undertaken by the Aviation Security Panel on amendment 11 to annex 17 on security, on the development of guidance material, on the use of in-flight security officers, also called sky marshals, and on the development of national quality control tools and guidance material for States.

Legal matters

The Secretariat Study Group on Legal Aspects of CNS/ATM Systems, in its final report to the ICAO Council, covered consideration of a contractual framework and of an international convention relating to CNS/ATM systems. The Council submitted its report to the thirty-fifth session of the ICAO Assembly, and on that basis, the Assembly adopted resolution A35-3: A practical way forward on legal and institutional aspects of communications, navigation, surveillance/air traffic management systems.

The Legal Committee considered during its thirty-second session (Montreal, 15-21 March) the text of a draft Convention on Damage Caused by Foreign Aircraft to Third Parties. The ICAO Council considered the Legal Committee's report on the subject, which included the text of the draft Convention. The Council agreed that the text was not mature enough for submission to a diplomatic conference and required additional study. A Special Group on the Modernization of the Rome Convention of 1952 was established to advance the work.

In relation to the subject "International interests in mobile equipment (aircraft equipment)", the ICAO Secretary-General received the necessary start-up funding for the work of the Preparatory Commission for the International Registry, provided on a voluntary basis by Contracting States and interested private parties. The Preparatory Commission, in May, selected Aviareto (Ireland) as the entity to establish the International Registry and to act as the Registrar, in accordance with the 2001 Convention on International Interests in Mobile Equipment and the Protocol thereto on matters specific to aircraft equipment. The working group set up by the Preparatory Commission agreed on a set of draft regulations for the International Registry.

The Legal Committee also considered a draft amendment to the technical annex to the 1991 Convention on the Marking of Plastic Explosives for the Purpose of Detection and recommended that certain provisions of the Convention be applied, mutatis mutandis, without amending either the Convention or its technical annex. Based on that recommendation, as endorsed by the Council on 31 May, the thirty-fifth session of the Assembly adopted resolution A35-2: Application of article IV of the Convention on the Marking of Plastic Explosives for the Purpose of Detection.

Technical cooperation

In 2004, ICAO undertook 253 technical cooperation projects in 113 countries. The technical cooperation programmes financed by the United Nations Development Programme (UNDP) trust funds, management service agreements and the Civil Aviation Purchasing Service had total expenditures of $120.3 million. Over 95 per cent of that amount was provided by Governments to fund their own projects.

A total of 539 fellowships were awarded in 2004, of which 515 were implemented. ICAO employed 515 experts from 32 countries, of whom 51 were on assignment under UNDP and 464 worked on trust fund projects. There were 116 Governments and organizations registered with ICAO in 2004 under its Civil Aviation Purchasing Service. Equipment purchases in 2004 totalled $102.45 million, compared with $82.8 million in 2003.

Secretariat

As at 31 December 2004, ICAO employed 796 staff members, including 323 in the Professional and higher categories and 473 in the General Service and related categories.

Budget

Appropriations for the ICAO budget in 2004 were $61,001,778.

NOTE: For further details on the activities of ICAO in 2004, see *Annual Report of the Council, 2004.*

HEADQUARTERS AND REGIONAL OFFICES

International Civil Aviation Organization
999 University Street
Montreal, Quebec, Canada H3C 5H7
Telephone: (1) (514) 954-8219
Fax: (1) (514) 954-6077
Internet: www.icao.int
E-mail: icaohq@icao.int

ICAO maintained regional offices in Bangkok, Thailand; Cairo, Egypt; Dakar, Senegal; Lima, Peru; Mexico, D.F.; Nairobi, Kenya; and Paris.

Chapter X

Universal Postal Union (UPU)

In 2004, the Universal Postal Union (UPU) continued to promote an efficient and accessible universal postal service at affordable prices through international collaboration among its member countries. It assisted postal administrations to improve the quality of their service and to stimulate growth in mail traffic.

UPU's 190 member countries remained the largest physical distribution network in the world, with more than 5 million postal employees in some 660,000 post offices.

Activities of UPU organs

Universal Postal Congress

The Universal Postal Congress, UPU's supreme legislative authority, held its twenty-third session (Bucharest, Romania, 15 September–5 October). It adopted the Bucharest World Postal Strategy, a road map for action by Governments, postal administrations and UPU bodies. Related activities would focus on universal postal service and programmes to help member countries improve mail security, quality of service and the development of markets, including letter-mail, parcels, postal financial services and philately. The Congress established a new UPU body—the Consultative Committee—to give postal stakeholders other than public postal operators and regulators a voice in the organization's deliberations and to provide a framework for effective dialogue among those stakeholders.

The Congress decided that it would convene every four years instead of five.

Council of Administration

The Council of Administration, which ensured the continuity of the Union's work between Congresses and studied regulatory, administrative, legislative and legal issues of concern to the Union, held its annual session (Berne, Switzer-land, 10-13 February). It undertook, among other tasks, a study on extraterritorial offices of exchange and submitted several scenarios on that topic to the 2004 Bucharest Congress (see above).

Postal Operations Council

The Postal Operations Council, at its annual session (Berne, 29 January–9 February), endorsed the principles of the future terminal dues system (payments postal services made to each other for the delivery of inbound foreign mail) and finalized the quality link for industrialized countries, aimed at implementation of the country-specific terminal dues system adopted at the 2004 Bucharest Congress.

International Bureau

The UPU Bureau continued to provide support, liaison, information and consultation to the postal administrations of member countries. It studied developments in the postal environment, monitored the quality of global postal service and published information and statistics on international postal services. UPU's Postal Technology Centre introduced new technology applications and information technology solutions aimed at improving the quality, reliability and speed of national and international postal services.

As at 31 December 2004, the Bureau's permanent staff numbered 151, of whom 60 were in the Professional or higher categories and 91 were in the General Service category.

Budget

The Council of Administration approved a budget of 71.4 million Swiss francs for the 2005-2006 budget.

NOTE: For further details on UPU's 2004 activies, see *Universal Postal Union Biennial Report 2004-2005*, published by UPU.

HEADQUARTERS

Universal Postal Union
Weltpoststrasse 4
3015 Berne, Switzerland
Telephone: (41) (31) 350 31 11
Fax: (41) (31) 350 31 10
Internet: www.upu.int
E-mail: info@upu.int

Chapter XI

International Telecommunication Union (ITU)

The International Telecommunication Union (ITU) continued in 2004 to promote the worldwide development and efficient operation of telecommunication systems.

At its annual session (Geneva, 9-18 June), the ITU Council discussed preparations for the second phase of the World Summit on the Information Society (see p. 844), the biennial budget for 2004-2005, international telecommunication regulations, Internet issues, issues involving management of the Union, and forthcoming conferences and events.

During the year, the Union staged numerous events, including the World Telecommunication Standardization Assembly (Florianópilis, Brazil, 5-14 October), ITU TELECOM Africa 2004 (Cairo, Egypt, 4-8 May) and ITU TELECOM Asia 2004 (Busan, Republic of Korea, 7-11 September).

ITU membership remained at 189 in 2004.

Radiocommunication Sector

ITU's Radiocommunication Sector (ITU-R) reduced its backlog of satellite network filings as the processing time for most procedures was reduced to less than one year, down from two years at the end of 2003. Preparatory work for the 2007 World Radiocommunication Conference and Radiocommunication Assembly began, and dialogue was initiated with a number of organizations to finalize formal arrangements for facilitating access to their technical standards and for referencing them in ITU-R recommendations. Some 88 new and revised recommendations were published, including on compatibility between passive and active services based on band-by-band studies, digital sound broadcasting below 30 MHz, protection of passive services, spectrum and sharing issues concerning wireless access systems, use of earth stations onboard vessels, and future development of International Mobile Telecommunications 2000 (IMT-2000) and systems beyond IMT-2000. The Radiocommunication Bureau implemented a new component of TerRaSys to streamline workflows by making it possible to examine numerous pending notices related to shared bands more quickly and effectively, thus reducing the backlog in that area.

Telecommunication Standardization Sector

The Telecommunication Standardization Sector (ITU-T) continued to ensure the efficient and on-time production of high-quality standards covering all areas of telecommunications. In 2004, the World Telecommunication Standardization Assembly (Florianópolis, Brazil, 5-14 October) adopted 17 revised resolutions and 14 new ones in areas ranging from budgeting and operational planning to Internet top level domains, cyber security, spam, standardization issues for developing countries and gender issues in ITU-T work.

ITU-T also adopted 257 recommendations and supplements on a wide range of issues, including standards for security architecture for systems providing end-to-end communications, quadrupling fiber optic transmission capacity, lowering costs, and setting a standard that encouraged innovation in interactive television.

Telecommunication Development Sector

The Telecommunication Development Sector (ITU-D) continued in 2004 to promote investment and foster the expansion of telecommunication infrastructure in developing countries.

ITU-D's Telecommunication Development Bureau continued to assist countries to reform and restructure their telecommunication sectors through the introduction of new technologies, capacity development to ensure sustainability in management and operations, and by promoting financing and partnerships as a strategy to attract investment. The Bureau's Sector Reform Unit carried out an annual telecommunication regulation survey and published the sixth annual *Trends in Telecommunication Reform* report, which focused on licensing issues for regulators.

The fifth annual Global Symposium for Regulators (Geneva, 8-10 December) established a set of Best Practice Guidelines for the Promotion of Low-Cost Broadband and Internet Connectivity.

ITU-D published the Yearbook of Statistics, the leading source of information and communication technology (ICT) statistics, and the World Telecommunication Development Report 2004, which tracked trends in national, regional and international ICT development.

Secretariat

As at 31 December 2004, ITU had 742 staff members, comprising 5 elected officials, 299 in the Professional and higher categories and 438 in the General Service category.

Budget

The ITU Council in 2003 set the budget for 2004-2005 at 328,872,000 Swiss francs.

NOTE: For further details regarding ITU activities, see the *ITU 2004 Annual Report*, published by the Union.

HEADQUARTERS

International Telecommunication Union
Place des Nations
CH-1211, Geneva 20, Switzerland
Telephone: (41) (22) 730-6039
Fax: (41) (22) 733-7256
Internet: http://www.itu.int
E-mail: pressinfo@itu.int

Chapter XII

World Meteorological Organization (WMO)

In 2004, the World Meteorological Organization (WMO) facilitated worldwide cooperation in the generation and exchange of meteorological and hydrological information and the application of meteorology to aviation, shipping, water problems, agriculture and other activities. It also promoted operational hydrology and encouraged research and training in meteorology. Major new cross-cutting programmes—the WMO Space Programme and the Disaster Prevention and Mitigation Programme—became fully operational.

The WMO Executive Council, at its fifty-sixth session (Geneva, 8-18 July), reviewed the activities of WMO and National Meteorological and Hydrological Services (NMHSs). It addressed several issues, including redesigning the Global Observing System (GOS); improving the capabilities of WMO members in climate activities; establishing a WMO information system on hydrometeorological phenomena leading to natural disasters; and technical assistance to members.

WMO's membership remained at 181 States and six Territories at the end of 2004.

Observation systems

In 2004, GOS provided standardized observations of the atmosphere and ocean surfaces through surface- and space-based subsystems. The redesign and establishment of a future composite GOS as part of the modernization of WMO's World Weather Watch Programme were underway. The third WMO Workshop on the Impact of Various Observing Systems on Numerical Weather Prediction (Alpbach, Austria, 9-12 March) advanced the redesign process.

The Integrated Global Observing Strategy panel approved the Atmospheric Chemistry Theme Report, which critically evaluated requirements for accuracy/precision and spatial/temporal resolution and the state of modelling chemical cycles in forecast and climate models.

The Global Climate Observing System completed its 10-year implementation plan in support of the United Nations Framework Convention on Climate Change (see p. 1051). The plan contained a number of recommendations aimed at the parties to the Convention.

World Climate Programme

The World Climate Programme, which marked its twenty-fifth anniversary in 2004, continued to contribute to the infrastructure and human resources capacities of NMHSs in climate monitoring, prediction and data management for improved climate services, especially in developing countries. In the context of the Programme, WMO worked with the International Strategy for Disaster Reduction, other UN agencies, and international institutions to address climate issues. Emphasis was placed on understanding climate-related extreme events and their associated impacts.

Natural disaster prevention and mitigation

Following the Indian Ocean tsunami of 26 December (see p. 952), WMO, through its Natural Disaster Prevention and Mitigation Programme, mobilized efforts with key partners to establish a multi-hazard early warning system for areas at risk, building on the telecommunication and human resources infrastructure already in place for tropical cyclone and storm surge warnings. It also facilitated the reinforcement of preparedness measures.

WMO collaborated with UN system organizations on the proposed Global Disaster Alert System and on preparations for the World Conference on Disaster Reduction, scheduled to take place in Kobe, Japan, in January 2005.

In 2004, WMO worked on further developing the WMO Global Telecommunication System, especially on the Improved Main Telecommunication Network and the enhanced use of data-communication technologies.

Research

In 2004, WMO's Atmospheric Research and Environment Programme focused on research on the multi-hazard mitigation strategy and the establishment of an interdisciplinary, interactive global prediction system. The World Weather Research Programme (WWRP) launched the Beijing Olympics 2008 Project and the Sand and Dust Storm Project.

The Observing System Research and Predictability Experiment (THORPEX), a WWRP global atmospheric research programme, entered its implementation stage in December with approval of its International Research Implementation Plan. The first THORPEX International Science Symposium (Montreal, Canada, 6-10 December) discussed issues related to predictability, observing systems, data assimilation strategies and economic and societal applications.

WMO and the International Council for Science established the Joint Committee for the International Polar Year 2007-2008 (IPY), and WMO formed an inter-commission task group to coordinate IPY preparation and implementation activities in the two polar regions.

The World Climate Research Programme (WCRP) organized the First International Climate Variability and Predictability Science Conference (Baltimore, United States, 21-25 June), the largest climate research conference to date. The Third Stratospheric Processes and their Role in Climate General Assembly (Victoria, Canada, August) discussed climate and chemistry interaction. The WCRP Climate and Cryosphere project, initiated in 2003 [YUN 2003, p. 1528], began its implementation phase.

Applications of meteorology

The Applications of Meteorology Programme focused on enhancing the capability of WMO members to provide comprehensive weather and related services, stressing public safety and welfare, and helping the public better understand NMHS capabilities and how to benefit from them. The final phase of the World Area Forecast System, with a completion date of 1 July 2005, began on 25 November 2004. The Agricultural Meteorology Programme continued to promote weather and climate information applications in agriculture, forestry and fisheries. In the light of the locust infestation in West Africa in 2004, WMO and the Food and Agriculture Organization of the United Nations developed the Database of Meteorological Information for Locust Control to facilitate effective control operations.

Hydrology and water resources

The twelfth session of the WMO Commission for Hydrology (Geneva, 20-29 October) discussed water-resources development as a means of achieving socio-economic benefits. Hydrological networks in 11 countries in Africa were strengthened through the Volta and Niger Hydrological Cycle Observing Systems, and WMO introduced the Historical Hydrological Data Rescue project in Egypt and Nigeria. The report of the Integrated Global Water Cycle Observations theme of the Integrated Global Observing Strategy Partnership was published and the implementation phase began. A theme component, the Coordinated Enhanced Observing Period, collected global data on the hydrological cycle for two years, completing its main observation period in December. The *Water Resources Assessment—Handbook for Water Review of National Capabilities* was published jointly by WMO and the United Nations Educational, Scientific and Cultural Organization. Three regional workshops on flood forecasting and warning were held in Africa.

Technical cooperation

In 2004, WMO technical assistance, valued at $20.51 million, was financed by the WMO Voluntary Cooperation Programme ($8.57 million), the United Nations Development Programme ($3.32 million), trust funds ($7.89 million), and the WMO regular budget ($0.73 million).

The WMO Trust Fund for the Least Developed Countries was established during the year.

Secretariat

As at 31 December 2004, WMO staff totalled 244, including 112 in the Professional and higher categories and 132 in the General Service category.

Budget

A regular budget of 127,169,800 Swiss francs (SwF) for the 2004-2005 biennium was approved by the WMO Executive Council in 2003. The Fourteenth World Meteorological Congress, in 2003, approved a maximum expenditure of SwF 253,800,000 for the fourteenth financial period (2004-2007).

NOTE: For further details regarding WMO activities, see *World Meteorological Organization Annual Report 2004*, published by WMO.

HEADQUARTERS AND LIAISON OFFICE

World Meteorological Organization
7 bis, avenue de la Paix
(Case postale No. 2300)
CH-1211 Geneva 2, Switzerland
Telephone: (41) 22-730-8111
Fax: (41) (22)-730-8181
Internet: www.wmo.ch
E-mail: wmo@wmo.int

World Meteorological Organization Liaison Office at the United Nations
866 United Nations Plaza, Room A-302
New York, NY 10017, United States
Telephone: (1) (212) 963-9444
Fax: (1) (917) 367-9868
E-mail: zbatjargal@wmo.int

Chapter XIII

International Maritime Organization (IMO)

In 2004, the International Maritime Organization (IMO) continued to facilitate cooperation to improve the safety and security of international shipping and to protect the maritime environment. It adopted a convention on ballast water management, a key new instrument in the organization's work on the prevention of marine pollution by ships.

New measures to enhance maritime security and other amendments to the International Convention for the Safety of Life at Sea entered into force during 2004, as did the 1996 Protocol to the 1976 Convention on Limitation of Liability for Maritime Claims.

In 2004, IMO membership increased to 164 with three associate members.

Activities in 2004

Prevention of pollution

In February, IMO adopted the International Convention for the Control and Management of Ships' Ballast Water and Sediments, which aimed to prevent the potentially devastating effects of the spread of harmful aquatic organisms carried by ships' ballast water. The Convention would enter into force 12 months after ratification by 30 States, representing 35 per cent of world merchant shipping tonnage.

IMO also adopted revised Annexes I and II of the International Convention for the Prevention of Pollution from Ships, 1973, as modified by the Protocol of 1978 relating thereto (MARPOL 73/78). The Annexes, which contained regulations to prevent pollution by oil and noxious liquid substances, were expected to enter into force in 2007. IMO's Marine Environment Protection Committee (MEPC) designated the Oman Area of the Arabian Sea as a special area in Annex I of the MARPOL convention and the Western European Waters as a new Particularly Sensitive Sea Area.

Ship security and safety at sea

International maritime security measures for enhancing maritime security, the International Ship and Port Facility Security Code, entered into force on 1 August.

The Legal Committee continued the revision of the suppression of unlawful acts treaties and preparation for a conference in 2005 to adopt protocols to revise the Convention for the Suppression of Unlawful Acts against the Safety of Maritime Navigation, 1988, and its Protocol of 1988 relating to Fixed Platforms Located on the Continental Shelf. Uniform global rules for the safe transport by sea of dangerous goods and marine pollutants in packaged form became compulsory on 1 January. The IMO Maritime Safety Committee approved the Code of Security for Fisherman and Fishing Vessels, 2005, and the Voluntary Guidelines for the Design, Construction and Equipment of Fishing Vessels, 2005. Amendments to the International Conventions for the Safety of Life at Sea and on Maritime Search and Rescue concerning the treatment of persons rescued at sea, refugees and stowaways were adopted. IMO continued its work on passenger ship safety and on the development of new ship construction standards.

Secretariat

As at 31 December, IMO had 282 staff members, of whom 127 were in the Professional and higher categories and 155 were in the General Service category.

Budget

The IMO Assembly, in 2003, approved budget appropriations of 46,194,900 pounds sterling for the 2004-2005 biennium.

NOTE: For further information, see the organization's quarterly magazine, *IMO News*.

HEADQUARTERS

International Marine Organization
4 Albert Embankment
London SE1 7SR, United Kingdom
Telephone: (44) (207) 735-7611
Fax: (44) (207) 587-3210
Internet: www.imo.org
E-mail: info@imo.org

Chapter XIV

World Intellectual Property Organization (WIPO)

The World Intellectual Property Organization (WIPO) continued to help ensure that the rights of creators and owners of intellectual property (IP) were protected worldwide, thus ensuring that inventors and authors were recognized and rewarded for their ingenuity.

The governing bodies of WIPO and the Unions administered by the organization held their thirty-ninth (Geneva, 22 September–1 October 2003) and fortieth (Geneva, 27 September–5 October 2004) series of meetings.

During 2004, WIPO membership increased to 181. The number of States adhering to the treaties administered by WIPO increased: as at 31 December, 168 States were parties to the Paris Convention for the Protection of Industrial Property, 157 to the Berne Convention for the Protection of Literary and Artistic Works, and 124 to the Patent Cooperation Treaty (PCT).

World Intellectual Property Day was celebrated on 26 April, under the theme "Encouraging Creativity".

Activities in 2004

Development cooperation

During 2004, WIPO continued to assist developing countries in optimizing their intellecutal property systems for economic, social and cultural benefit. Some 12,000 representatives from 124 developing countries participated in WIPO activities in the areas of human capacity-building, institutional strengthening, public policy issues and business opportunities. The WIPO Worldwide Academy, through its distance learning programmes, reached out to 10,000 people, mostly from developing and transition countries, and provided professional training in intellectual property to officials from 83 developing and transition countries and a policy development programme for some 800 government officials, university professors and judges from over 40 countries. WIPO developed an audit tool to help Governments determine those components of their national intellectual property infrastructure that needed strengthening. It provided legal advice to 44 countries and worked on optimizing intellectual property use among enterprises to create employment and generate revenue. WIPO

evaluated the intellectual property situation in 10 African countries with a view to assisting them in formulating appropriate national strategies, and worked in partnership with regional institutions to ensure consistency with broader economic development goals. It assisted Egypt, Jordan, Lebanon, Morocco and Tunisia in realizing the economic potential of cultural industries, and helped Jordan formulate an intellectual property rights policy and set up a management office. WIPO worked in partnership with the Association of Southeast Asian Nations to launch a series of economic studies, and implemented specific projects throughout the Asia and Pacific region to improve productive links between research institutions and national intellectual property administrations, and to develop synergies between science, business and government support agencies. Industrial property offices of five Andean countries in Latin America adopted a common manual on the processing of patent applications, the result of four years of regional cooperation with WIPO's support.

Intellectual property law

The Standing Committee on the Law of Patents continued to discuss the provisions of the draft substantive patent law treaty. Work was directed towards agreeing on provisions which would enable patent applicants to rely on common requirements in different countries, improve the quality of granted patents and facilitate the sharing of results between interested member countries.

The Standing Committee on the Law of Trademarks, Industrial Design and Geographical Indication made substantive progress towards revising the 1994 Trademark Law Treaty (TLT) in order to introduce: modern and flexible rules concerning communications, including electronic communications; relief measures in case of failure to comply with time limits; rules on the recording of trademark licenses; and provisions concerning the establishment of a TLT Assembly with powers to amend the TLT regulations.

The Standing Committee on Copyright and Related Rights continued to develop a treaty on the protection of broadcasting organizations, taking into account the emergence of digital and other new technology and the spread of the Internet.

The Intergovernmental Committee on Intellectual Property and Genetic Resources, Traditional Knowledge and Folklore began work on international legal provisions, setting out objectives and principles for the protection of traditional knowledge and traditional cultural expressions.

Arbitration and Mediation Centre

In 2004, the Arbitration and Mediation Centre, the leading provider of services for domain name and other intellectual property disputes, received 1,178 new cases from 50 countries. It continued to assist administrators of country code Top Level Domains in establishing efficient procedures for the protection of intellectual property rights against abusive domain name registrations. Also, the center published practical guides and ran workshops based on material developed by its staff for IP specialists from 35 countries.

International registration activities

PCT. The year 2004 was a landmark for PCT, with the receipt of the one-millionth international patent application since the system began operation in 1978. The number of international patent applications filed in 2004 using PCT set an all time record of 120,000.

Madrid System. In the trademark system under the Madrid Agreement concerning the International Registration of Trademarks and its 1989 protocol, the number of international trademark applications filed totalled 29,482, signalling a major increase in use of the Madrid System in 2004.

Hague System. Under the Hague Agreement concerning industrial designs, nearly 35,000 international registrations were in force by the end of 2004. Two thirds of the total 2004 registrations were filed by Switzerland and Germany.

Lisbon System. In 2004, the International Bureau received five international applications, bringing the total number of internationally registered appellations of origin in force to 781.

Secretariat

As at 31 December 2004, WIPO employed 855 staff members, 380 of whom were in the Professional and higher categories and 475 in the General Service category.

Budget

The approved programme and budget for 2006-2007 amounted to 531 million Swiss francs. Contributions by member States represented 7 per cent of the overall budget. WIPO remained largely a self-funding agency, financing its activities from revenues acquired through the provision of services to the private sector.

NOTE: For further information, see *WIPO Annual Report 2004*, published by WIPO.

HEADQUARTERS AND OTHER OFFICE

HEADQUARTERS

World Intellectual Property Organization
34, Chemin des Colombettes (P.O. Box 18)
CH-1211 Geneva 20, Switzerland
 Telephone: (41) (22) 338-9111
 Fax: (41) (22) 733-5428
 Internet: www.wipo.int
 E-mail: wipo-mail@wipo.int

WIPO OFFICE AT THE UNITED NATIONS

2 United Nations Plaza, Suite 2525
New York, NY 10017, United States
 Telephone: (1) (212) 963-6813
 Fax: (1) (212) 963-4801
 Email: wipo@un.org

Chapter XV

International Fund for Agricultural Development (IFAD)

The International Fund for Agricultural Development (IFAD) continued in 2004 to promote the economic advancement of the rural poor by providing low-interest loans and grants.

The twenty-seventh session of the Governing Council (Rome, Italy, 18-19 February) focused on rural finance, rural enterprises, remittances, sector-wide approaches and access to markets. The Executive Board held three regular sessions (April, September, December) and approved loans for 25 programmes and projects, and 87 grants.

In 2004, IFAD membership remained at 163, of which 23 were in List A (developed countries), 12 in List B (oil-exporting developing countries) and 128 in List C (other developing countries). Of the latter, 49 were in Sub-List C1 (Africa), 48 in Sub-List C2 (Europe, Asia and the Pacific) and 31 in Sub-List C3 (Latin America and the Caribbean).

Resources

On 1 January 2004, IFAD entered the three-year period of its sixth replenishment. By year's end, pledges equivalent to $505.7 million had been received, representing over 90 per cent of the sixth replenishment target of $560 million. The 2004 programme of work was approved for $462.5 million.

Activities

In 2004, loans approved and finalized through IFAD totalled $433.4 million, and grants worth $33.3 million were also approved. The total cost of the 25 new projects and programmes that were approved was estimated at over $928 million, of which $176.2 million would be provided by other external financiers, and $316.1 million by financiers in the recipient countries—primarily Governments.

Regular Programme lending was distributed as follows: Asia and the Pacific, $127.9 million for six projects (29.3 per cent); Eastern and Southern Africa, $92.5 million for five projects (21.2 per cent); the Near East and North Africa, $91.2 million for six projects (20.9 per cent); Latin America and the Caribbean, $75 million for four projects (17.2 per cent); and Western and Central Africa, $49.8 million for four projects (11.4 per cent).

During 2004, 27 programmes and projects were completed; 192 were ongoing at the end of the year.

Secretariat

As at 31 December 2004, the IFAD secretariat had 316 staff members, comprising 143 in the Professional and higher categories and 172 in the General Service category.

Income and expenditure

At the end of 2004, IFAD's income from loans was $48 million and that from cash and investments was $115.2 million. Operating expenses for the year totalled $57 million.

NOTE: For further details on IFAD activities in 2004, see *Annual Report 2004*, published by the Fund.

HEADQUARTERS AND OTHER OFFICES

HEADQUARTERS

International Fund for Agricultural Development
Via del Serafico, 107
00142 Rome, Italy
  Telephone: (39) (06) 54591
  Fax: (39) (06) 5043463
  Internet: www.ifad.org
  E-mail: ifad@ifad.org

IFAD LIAISON OFFICE

2 United Nations Plaza, Room 1128-29
New York, NY 10017, United States
  Telephone: (1) (212) 963-0546
  Fax: (1) (212) 963-2787

  IFAD also maintained offices in Eschbom, Germany, and in Washington, D.C.

Chapter XVI

United Nations Industrial Development Organization (UNIDO)

The United Nations Industrial Development Organization (UNIDO) continued in 2004 to promote the sustainable industrial development of developing countries and countries in transition.

The Industrial Development Board, at its twenty-eighth session (Vienna, 25-27 May), considered UNIDO's medium-term programme framework (2004-2007), which focused on decentralization and field representation; UNIDO's financial situation; and the adoption of the draft statue of the International Centre for Science and High Technology. At its twenty-ninth session (Vienna, 9-11 November), member States considered recommendations of the Programme and Budget Committee on a number of issues and reviewed, among other things, decentralization, South-South cooperation and UNIDO activities in countries emerging from crisis situations. The eleventh session of the General Conference would take place in 2005.

UNIDO membership remained at 171 in 2004.

Global forum activities

Through its global forum activities, UNIDO continued to promote industrial development and cooperation between countries, partnerships, knowledge-sharing, technology and investment. It also assisted developing countries and countries with economies in transition in the implementation of multilateral environmental agreements.

Global forum activities included the compilation and dissemination worldwide of the 2004 edition of UNIDO's databases on industrial statistics through several media, including CD-ROM, hard copy publication and the Internet; the publication of the Industrial Development Report 2004; the continued implementation of a re-search programme on combating marginalization and poverty through industrial development; and the Global Biotechnology Forum (Concepción, Chile, 2-5 March). Cooperation arrangements continued between UNIDO and leading research institutions with a view to strengthening the Organization's global forum activities.

Technical cooperation

UNIDO continued to provide technical cooperation through its integrated programmes and country service frameworks, most of which dealt with capacity-building; many were geared towards increasing productivity and competitiveness with a particular emphasis on small and medium-sized enterprises and on environmental protection. During 2004, UNIDO's technical cooperation programmes and projects totalled some $117.2 million. Africa remained the focus of UNIDO's cooperation, with its share of the Organization's total services amounting to 47 per cent.

Secretariat

As at 31 December 2004, UNIDO employed a total of 646 staff members: 252 were in the Professional or higher categories, 386 were in the General Service category and 8 were national officers.

Budget

The tenth (2003) session of the UNIDO General Conference approved the 2004-2005 regular budget in the amount of 142,000,000 euros.

NOTE: For further information on UNIDO, see *Annual Report of UNIDO 2004*.

HEADQUARTERS AND OTHER OFFICES

HEADQUARTERS
United Nations Industrial Development Organization
Vienna International Centre
P.O. Box 300
A-1400 Vienna, Austria
 Telephone: (43) (1) 26026-0
 Fax: (43) (1) 269-26-69
 E-mail: unido@unido.org
 Internet: http://www.unido.org

LIAISON OFFICES

UNIDO Office at Geneva
Palais des Nations
Le Bocage, Pavillion 1
8, rue de Pregny
CH-1211 Geneva 10, Switzerland
  Telephone: (41) (22) 917-3364
  Fax: (41) (22) 917-0059
  E-mail: office.geneva@unido.org

UNIDO Office in New York
1 United Nations Plaza, Room DC1-1110
New York, NY 10017, United States
  Telephone: (1) (212) 963-6890
  Fax: (1) (212) 963-7904
  E-mail: office.newyork@unido.org

Chapter XVII

World Trade Organization (WTO)

During 2004, the World Trade Organization (WTO), the legal and institutional foundation of the multilateral trading system, continued to oversee the rules of international trade, settle trade disputes and organize trade negotiations.

Significant progress was made in advancing the Doha Development Agenda, adopted by WTO's Fourth (2001) Ministerial Conference [YUN 2001, p. 1432], following resolution, in July, of the deadlock in negotiations, which arose among WTO members during the Fifth (2003) Ministerial Conference [YUN 2003, p. 1535]. That enabled the adoption by WTO's General Council of framework agreements to advance negotiations in some of the most difficult areas, particularly agriculture and non-agricultural market access. Members also agreed on a package of measures on development issues, to begin negotiations on trade facilitation (see p. 958), to continue those negotiations beyond the timeframe of 1 January 2005 set in the Doha Ministerial Declaration [YUN 2001, p. 1432] and to schedule the next Ministerial Conference for December 2005 in Hong Kong, China.

WTO's General Council, the body overseeing the organization's work between meetings of the Ministerial Conference—its highest body—continued throughout the year to monitor the implementation and operation of the multilateral trading system embodied in the WTO Agreement [YUN 1994, p. 1474]. The Council played a key role in the negotiations and decisions that put the Doha Development Agenda work programme back on track in July. It also took decisions to improve transparency in WTO operations and to achieve better cooperation and coordination between the organization, the International Monetary Fund, the World Bank and other international organizations.

As at 31 December 2004, WTO membership (members and observers) totalled 148.

General activities

The three working groups established by the 1996 Ministerial Conference [YUN 1996, p. 1441], which met within the framework of the Doha Development Agenda, did not meet in 2004. In August, the General Council decided that the three issues they were set up to consider—the relationship between trade and investment, interaction between trade and competition policy, and transparency in government procurement—no longer formed part of the work programme set out in the Doha Ministerial Declaration. As such, no negotiation on those issues would take place within WTO during the Doha Round.

WTO continued to settle trade disputes between members covered by the Understanding on Rules and Procedures Governing the Settlement of Disputes and provided technical assistance and capacity-building to developing countries in that regard.

During the year, the Trade Policy Review Body carried out reviews of Belize, Benin, Brazil, Burkina Faso, the European Union, the Gambia, the Republic of Korea, Liechtenstein, Mali, Norway, Rwanda, Singapore, Sri Lanka, Suriname, Switzerland and the United States.

Trade in goods

During 2004, the Council for Trade in Goods (CTG) continued to monitor the implementation of multilateral trade agreements and examined and approved requests for waivers and waiver extensions from members in connection with the transposition of their schedules into the Harmonized System. It carried out a transitional review under the Protocol of accession of China, discussed the review of the operation of the Trade-Related Investment Measures Agreement and considered a request for extension of the transition period under the Agreement. CTG also conducted the third and final major review of the implementation of the Agreement on Textiles and Clothing, as 2004 was the last year of implementation. The Committee on Agriculture continued to review the implementation of WTO commitments resulting from the Uruguay Round agricultural reform programme, or from accession to WTO.

The Committee on Sanitary and Phytosanitary Measures monitored the implementation of the Agreement on the Application of Sanitary and Phytosanitary Measures, which set out the rights and obligations of members to ensure food safety, protect humans from plant- or animal-spread diseases, or protect plants and animals from pests and diseases.

The Committee on Safeguards continued to review national safeguard legislation and/or regulations.

Trade in services

In 2004, the Council for Trade in Services held seven formal meetings, which considered proposals for a technical review of the General Agreement on Trade in Services (GATS) provisions; Albania's request for a waiver from specific commitments under GATS; the deadline for negotiations on emergency safeguard measures under the Agreement; the European Community's request for continued restriction of the report of the Council's meeting in June; and issues submitted by India relating to the implementation of GATS. It also conducted the third transitional review under the Protocol of accession of China and the second review of most favoured nation (MFN) exemptions.

Intellectual property

The Trade-related Aspects of Intellectual Property Rights Agreement (TRIPS) provided for minimum international standards of protection in copyright, trademarks, geographic indications, industrial designs, patents, layout designs of integrated circuits and undisclosed information. In 2004, the Council for TRIPS continued to review national implementing legislation of developing countries and economies in transition.

Regional trade agreements

As at December 2004, WTO received notifications of 33 additional regional trade agreements, bringing the total number of notified agreements in force to 226.

Trade and development

In 2004, the Committee on Trade and Development continued to consider special and differential treatment of developing countries to facilitate their participation in world trade, technical cooperation and training, and market access for least developed countries. It also considered the declining terms of trade for primary commodities and its implication for the trade and development of primary commodity exporting countries.

Plurilateral agreements

The Committee on Government Procurement continued negotiations on expanding the coverage of the Agreement on Government Procurement, its simplification and improvement, including adaptation to advances in information technology, expansion of the coverage of the Agreement and the elimination of discriminatory measures and practices that distorted open procurement.

The Agreement on Trade in Civil Aircraft eliminated customs duties and other charges on imports of civil aircraft products and repairs, bound them at zero level and required the adoption or adaptation of end-use customs administration. Although it was part of the 1994 WTO Agreement, it remained outside the organization's framework. The Committee on Trade in Civil Aircraft discussed end-use customs administration, including a revised proposal concerning the definition of "civil" vs. "military" aircraft based on initial certification.

International Trade Centre

The International Trade Centre (ITC), operated jointly by WTO and the United Nations Conference on Trade and Development (see p. 954), continued to play a crucial role in trade-related technical cooperation and trade-related capacity-building. In 2004, it focused its technical assistance on helping businesses understand WTO rules, strengthening enterprises, competitiveness and developing new trade promotion strategies.

Budget

The WTO budget for 2004 was 161.7 million Swiss francs.

Secretariat

As at 31 December 2004, WTO staff numbered 630.

NOTE: For further information on WTO activities, see the organization's *Annual Report 2004*.

HEADQUARTERS

World Trade Organization
Centre William Rappard
154, rue de Lausanne
CH-1211 Geneva, 21, Switzerland
Telephone: (41) (22) 739-5111
Fax: (41) (22) 731-4206
Internet: www.wto.org
E-mail: enquiries@wto.org

Chapter XVIII

World Tourism Organization (UNWTO)

In 2004, the World Tourism Organization (UNWTO), recognized by the UN General Assembly in resolution 58/232 [YUN 2003, p. 1475] as a specialized agency of the United Nations, continued to play a central role in promoting responsible, sustainable and universally accessible tourism, with particular attention to the interests of developing countries. In its first year as a UN agency, UNWTO established links with similar organizations and sought to better align its work programme with UN strategies and campaigns.

The UNWTO General Assembly, its governing body, did not meet in 2004; its sixteenth session was scheduled to be held in Dakar, Senegal, in 2005. The UNWTO Executive Council, which met between Assembly sessions, held its seventy-third (Hyderabad, India, 8-9 July) and seventy-fourth (Salvador de Bahia, Brazil, 2-3 December) sessions. Other meetings of UNWTO organs convened in 2004 included a supplementary meeting of the Commission of the Americas (Costa Rica, October), a meeting of the Strategic Group (Monaco, October) and the second meeting of the Quality Support and Trade Committee (Madrid, Spain, November). During the year, UNWTO also organized a Tourism Policy Forum, in cooperation with the George Washington University, Washington, D.C., and a meeting among the tourism-related agencies and programmes of the UN system, designed to improve coordination among them.

World Tourism Day was commemorated on 27 September under the theme "Sport and tourism; two living forces for mutual understanding, culture and social development".

As at 31 December 2004, UNWTO comprised 144 member States, seven associate members and over 300 affiliate members, representing the private sector, educational institutions and destination management organizations.

Activities

One of UNWTO's main areas of focus in 2004 was a programme designed to develop sustainable tourism as a force for eliminating poverty, as part of its commitment to contribute to the implementation of the United Nations Millennium Development Goals [YUN 2000, p. 51]. The programme, known as the Sustainable Tourism—Eliminating Poverty (ST-EP) initiative, which was first launched at the World Summit for Sustainable Development [YUN 2002, p. 821] in cooperation with the United Nations Conference on Trade and Development (UNCTAD), was unanimously supported by the fifteenth UNWTO General Assembly in 2003.

In 2004, the UNWTO ST-EP Foundation was established in Seoul, Republic of Korea, as an institution aimed at encouraging international cooperation on sustainable tourism development for poverty elimination. Some $500,000 remaining from the execution of past technical cooperation activities was allocated to new projects within the Foundation's framework.

The World Committee on Tourism Ethics, established by the UNWTO Assembly in 2003 as an independent body to assist in implementing and monitoring the Global Code of Ethics for Tourism, at its second meeting (Madrid, Spain, 4-5 October), adopted its rules of procedure and guidelines relative to the dispute settlement procedure. A report on the Committee's work regarding the implementation of the Code was considered by the Executive Council, which met twice during the year (see above). Italy offered to host the Committee headquarters in Rome.

Other UNWTO activities addressed issues relating to cooperation for development, in terms of transferring tourism know-how to developing countries; quality in tourism development, with regard to measures to improve the design and supply of tourism products and services; sustainable tourism development, designed to ensure that the benefits of tourism could be enjoyed for generations; statistics, involving the provision of facts and figures that demonstrated the economic impact of tourism; market intelligence, in terms of identifying market trends, forecasting, research and analysis of key market issues and evaluation tools for promotional campaigns; human resource development, particularly regarding the preparation of professionals for leadership roles in the tourism sector of UNWTO member countries; and communications and documentation, in terms of increasing awareness of the importance of the tourism industry and related media activities.

Regional activities to strengthen and support national tourism were undertaken by UNWTO in Africa, the Americas, Asia and the Pacific, the Middle East and Europe.

During the year, UNWTO revised its "vision 2020" report, a long-term forecast and assessment of the development of tourism, covering the first 20 years of the new millennium. Based on the revision, a "provisional outlook for 2010" would be prepared.

Secretariat

As at 31 December 2004, UNWTO staff numbered 103, of whom 45 were in the Professional or higher categories and 58 were in the General Service category.

Budget

The UNWTO Executive Council approved a budget of 10,645,000 euros for 2005.

HEADQUARTERS

World Tourism Organization
Capitán Haya, 42
28020 Madrid, Spain
Telephone: (34) (91) 567-8100
Fax: (34) (91) 571-3733
Internet: www.world-tourism.org
E-mail: omt@world-tourism.org

The UNWTO secretariat maintained a regional support office for Asia-Pacific, in Osaka, Japan.

Appendices

Appendix I

Roster of the United Nations
There were 191 Member States as at 31 December 2004.

MEMBER	DATE OF ADMISSION	MEMBER	DATE OF ADMISSION	MEMBER	DATE OF ADMISSION
Afghanistan	19 Nov. 1946	El Salvador	24 Oct. 1945	Mauritania	27 Oct. 1961
Albania	14 Dec. 1955	Equatorial Guinea	12 Nov. 1968	Mauritius	24 Apr. 1968
Algeria	8 Oct. 1962	Eritrea	28 May 1993	Mexico	7 Nov. 1945
Andorra	28 July 1993	Estonia	17 Sep. 1991	Micronesia (Federated	
Angola	1 Dec. 1976	Ethiopia	13 Nov. 1945	States of)	17 Sep. 1991
Antigua and Barbuda	11 Nov. 1981	Fiji	13 Oct. 1970	Monaco	28 May 1993
Argentina	24 Oct. 1945	Finland	14 Dec. 1955	Mongolia	27 Oct. 1961
Armenia	2 Mar. 1992	France	24 Oct. 1945	Morocco	12 Nov. 1956
Australia	1 Nov. 1945	Gabon	20 Sep. 1960	Mozambique	16 Sep. 1975
Austria	14 Dec. 1955	Gambia	21 Sep. 1965	Myanmar	19 Apr. 1948
Azerbaijan	2 Mar. 1992	Georgia	31 July 1992	Namibia	23 Apr. 1990
Bahamas	18 Sep. 1973	Germany[3]	18 Sep. 1973	Nauru	14 Sep. 1999
Bahrain	21 Sep. 1971	Ghana	8 Mar. 1957	Nepal	14 Dec. 1955
Bangladesh	17 Sep. 1974	Greece	25 Oct. 1945	Netherlands	10 Dec. 1945
Barbados	9 Dec. 1966	Grenada	17 Sep. 1974	New Zealand	24 Oct. 1945
Belarus	24 Oct. 1945	Guatemala	21 Nov. 1945	Nicaragua	24 Oct. 1945
Belgium	27 Dec. 1945	Guinea	12 Dec. 1958	Niger	20 Sep. 1960
Belize	25 Sep. 1981	Guinea-Bissau	17 Sep. 1974	Nigeria	7 Oct. 1960
Benin	20 Sep. 1960	Guyana	20 Sep. 1966	Norway	27 Nov. 1945
Bhutan	21 Sep. 1971	Haiti	24 Oct. 1945	Oman	7 Oct. 1971
Bolivia	14 Nov. 1945	Honduras	17 Dec. 1945	Pakistan	30 Sep. 1947
Bosnia and Herzegovina	22 May 1992	Hungary	14 Dec. 1955	Palau	15 Dec. 1994
Botswana	17 Oct. 1966	Iceland	19 Nov. 1946	Panama	13 Nov. 1945
Brazil	24 Oct. 1945	India	30 Oct. 1945	Papua New Guinea	10 Oct. 1975
Brunei Darussalam	21 Sep. 1984	Indonesia[4]	28 Sep. 1950	Paraguay	24 Oct. 1945
Bulgaria	14 Dec. 1955	Iran (Islamic Republic of)	24 Oct. 1945	Peru	31 Oct. 1945
Burkina Faso	20 Sep. 1960	Iraq	21 Dec. 1945	Philippines	24 Oct. 1945
Burundi	18 Sep. 1962	Ireland	14 Dec. 1955	Poland	24 Oct. 1945
Cambodia	14 Dec. 1955	Israel	11 May 1949	Portugal	14 Dec. 1955
Cameroon	20 Sep. 1960	Italy	14 Dec. 1955	Qatar	21 Sep. 1971
Canada	9 Nov. 1945	Jamaica	18 Sep. 1962	Republic of Korea	17 Sep. 1991
Cape Verde	16 Sep. 1975	Japan	18 Dec. 1956	Republic of Moldova	2 Mar. 1992
Central African Republic	20 Sep. 1960	Jordan	14 Dec. 1955	Romania	14 Dec. 1955
Chad	20 Sep. 1960	Kazakhstan	2 Mar. 1992	Russian Federation[6]	24 Oct. 1945
Chile	24 Oct. 1945	Kenya	16 Dec. 1963	Rwanda	18 Sep. 1962
China	24 Oct. 1945	Kiribati	14 Sep. 1999	Saint Kitts and Nevis	23 Sep. 1983
Colombia	5 Nov. 1945	Kuwait	14 May 1963	Saint Lucia	18 Sep. 1979
Comoros	12 Nov. 1975	Kyrgyzstan	2 Mar. 1992	Saint Vincent and the	
Congo	20 Sep. 1960	Lao People's Democratic		Grenadines	16 Sep. 1980
Costa Rica	2 Nov. 1945	Republic	14 Dec. 1955	Samoa	15 Dec. 1976
Côte d'Ivoire	20 Sep. 1960	Latvia	17 Sep. 1991	San Marino	2 Mar. 1992
Croatia	22 May 1992	Lebanon	24 Oct. 1945	Sao Tome and Principe	16 Sep. 1975
Cuba	24 Oct. 1945	Lesotho	17 Oct. 1966	Saudi Arabia	24 Oct. 1945
Cyprus	20 Sep. 1960	Liberia	2 Nov. 1945	Senegal	28 Sep. 1960
Czech Republic[1]	19 Jan. 1993	Libyan Arab Jamahiriya	14 Dec. 1955	Serbia and Montenegro	1 Nov. 2000
Democratic People's		Liechtenstein	18 Sep. 1990	Seychelles	21 Sep. 1976
Republic of Korea	17 Sep. 1991	Lithuania	17 Sep. 1991	Sierra Leone	27 Sep. 1961
Democratic Republic of		Luxembourg	24 Oct. 1945	Singapore[5]	21 Sep. 1965
the Congo	20 Sep. 1960	Madagascar	20 Sep. 1960	Slovakia[1]	19 Jan. 1993
Denmark	24 Oct. 1945	Malawi	1 Dec. 1964	Slovenia	22 May 1992
Djibouti	20 Sep. 1977	Malaysia[5]	17 Sep. 1957	Solomon Islands	19 Sep. 1978
Dominica	18 Dec. 1978	Maldives	21 Sep. 1965	Somalia	20 Sep. 1960
Dominican Republic	24 Oct. 1945	Mali	28 Sep. 1960	South Africa	7 Nov. 1945
Ecuador	21 Dec. 1945	Malta	1 Dec. 1964	Spain	14 Dec. 1955
Egypt[2]	24 Oct. 1945	Marshall Islands	17 Sep. 1991	Sri Lanka	14 Dec. 1955

MEMBER	DATE OF ADMISSION	MEMBER	DATE OF ADMISSION	MEMBER	DATE OF ADMISSION
Sudan	12 Nov. 1956	Tonga	14 Sep. 1999	United Republic of	
Suriname	4 Dec. 1975	Trinidad and Tobago	18 Sep. 1962	Tanzania[7]	14 Dec. 1961
Swaziland	24 Sep. 1968	Tunisia	12 Nov. 1956	United States of America	24 Oct. 1945
Sweden	19 Nov. 1946	Turkey	24 Oct. 1945	Uruguay	18 Dec. 1945
Switzerland	10 Sep. 2002	Turkmenistan	2 Mar. 1992	Uzbekistan	2 Mar. 1992
Syrian Arab Republic[2]	24 Oct. 1945	Tuvalu	5 Sep. 2000	Vanuatu	15 Sep. 1981
Tajikistan	2 Mar. 1992	Uganda	25 Oct. 1962	Venezuela (Bolivarian	
Thailand	16 Dec. 1946	Ukraine	24 Oct. 1945	Republic of)	15 Nov. 1945
The former Yugoslav		United Arab Emirates	9 Dec. 1971	Viet Nam	20 Sep. 1977
Republic of Macedonia	8 Apr. 1993	United Kingdom of Great		Yemen[8]	30 Sep. 1947
Timor-Leste	27 Sep. 2002	Britain and Northern		Zambia	1 Dec. 1964
Togo	20 Sep. 1960	Ireland	24 Oct. 1945	Zimbabwe	25 Aug. 1980

[1]Czechoslovakia, which was an original Member of the United Nations from 24 October 1945, split up on 1 January 1993 and was succeeded by the Czech Republic and Slovakia.

[2]Egypt and Syria, both of which became Members of the United Nations on 24 October 1945, joined together—following a plebiscite held in those countries on 21 February 1958—to form the United Arab Republic. On 13 October 1961, Syria, having resumed its status as an independent State, also resumed its separate membership in the United Nations; it changed its name to the Syrian Arab Republic on 14 September 1971. The United Arab Republic continued as a Member of the United Nations and reverted to the name of Egypt on 2 September 1971.

[3]Through accession of the German Democratic Republic to the Federal Republic of Germany on 3 October 1990, the two German States (both of which became United Nations Members on 18 September 1973) united to form one sovereign State. As from that date, the Federal Republic of Germany has acted in the United Nations under the designation Germany.

[4]On 20 January 1965, Indonesia informed the Secretary-General that it had decided to withdraw from the United Nations. By a telegram of 19 September 1966, it notified the Secretary-General of its decision to resume participation in the activities of the United Nations. On 28 September 1966, the General Assembly took note of that decision and the President invited the representatives of Indonesia to take their seats in the Assembly.

[5]On 16 September 1963, Sabah (North Borneo), Sarawak and Singapore joined with the Federation of Malaya (which became a United Nations Member on 17 September 1957) to form Malaysia. On 9 August 1965, Singapore became an independent State and on 21 September 1965 it became a Member of the United Nations.

[6]The Union of Soviet Socialist Republics was an original Member of the United Nations from 24 October 1945. On 24 December 1991, the President of the Russian Federation informed the Secretary-General that the membership of the USSR in all United Nations organs was being continued by the Russian Federation.

[7]Tanganyika was admitted to the United Nations on 14 December 1961, and Zanzibar, on 16 December 1963. Following ratification, on 26 April 1964, of the Articles of Union between Tanganyika and Zanzibar, the two States became represented as a single Member: the United Republic of Tanganyika and Zanzibar; it changed its name to the United Republic of Tanzania on 1 November 1964.

[8]Yemen was admitted to the United Nations on 30 September 1947 and Democratic Yemen on 14 December 1967. On 22 May 1990, the two countries merged and have since been represented as one Member.

Appendix II

Charter of the United Nations and Statute of the International Court of Justice

Charter of the United Nations

NOTE: The Charter of the United Nations was signed on 26 June 1945, in San Francisco, at the conclusion of the United Nations Conference on International Organization, and came into force on 24 October 1945. The Statute of the International Court of Justice is an integral part of the Charter.

Amendments to Articles 23, 27 and 61 of the Charter were adopted by the General Assembly on 17 December 1963 and came into force on 31 August 1965. A further amendment to Article 61 was adopted by the General Assembly on 20 December 1971 and came into force on 24 September 1973. An amendment to Article 109, adopted by the General Assembly on 20 December 1965, came into force on 12 June 1968.

The amendment to Article 23 enlarges the membership of the Security Council from 11 to 15. The amended Article 27 provides that decisions of the Security Council on procedural matters shall be made by an affirmative vote of nine members (formerly seven) and on all other matters by an affirmative vote of nine members (formerly seven), including the concurring votes of the five permanent members of the Security Council.

The amendment to Article 61, which entered into force on 31 August 1965, enlarged the membership of the Economic and Social Council from 18 to 27. The subsequent amendment to that Article, which entered into force on 24 September 1973, further increased the membership of the Council from 27 to 54.

The amendment to Article 109, which relates to the first paragraph of that Article, provides that a General Conference of Member States for the purpose of reviewing the Charter may be held at a date and place to be fixed by a two-thirds vote of the members of the General Assembly and by a vote of any nine members (formerly seven) of the Security Council. Paragraph 3 of Article 109, which deals with the consideration of a possible review conference during the tenth regular session of the General Assembly, has been retained in its original form in its reference to a "vote of any seven members of the Security Council", the paragraph having been acted upon in 1955 by the General Assembly, at its tenth regular session, and by the Security Council.

WE THE PEOPLES
OF THE UNITED NATIONS
DETERMINED

to save succeeding generations from the scourge of war, which
  twice in our lifetime has brought untold sorrow to mankind, and
to reaffirm faith in fundamental human rights, in the dignity
  and worth of the human person, in the equal rights of men
  and women and of nations large and small, and
to establish conditions under which justice and respect for the
  obligations arising from treaties and other sources of international law can be maintained, and
to promote social progress and better standards of life in larger
  freedom,

AND FOR THESE ENDS

to practice tolerance and live together in peace with one
  another as good neighbours, and
to unite our strength to maintain international peace and security, and
to ensure, by the acceptance of principles and the institution of
  methods, that armed force shall not be used, save in the common interest, and
to employ international machinery for the promotion of the
  economic and social advancement of all peoples,

HAVE RESOLVED TO
COMBINE OUR EFFORTS TO
ACCOMPLISH THESE AIMS

Accordingly, our respective Governments, through representatives assembled in the city of San Francisco, who have exhib-
ited their full powers found to be in good and due form, have
agreed to the present Charter of the United Nations and do
hereby establish an international organization to be known
as the United Nations.

Chapter I
PURPOSES AND PRINCIPLES

Article 1

The Purposes of the United Nations are:

1. To maintain international peace and security, and to that end: to take effective collective measures for the prevention and removal of threats to the peace, and for the suppression of acts of aggression or other breaches of the peace, and to bring about by peaceful means, and in conformity with the principles of justice and international law, adjustment or settlement of international disputes or situations which might lead to a breach of the peace;

2. To develop friendly relations among nations based on respect for the principle of equal rights and self-determination of peoples, and to take other appropriate measures to strengthen universal peace;

3. To achieve international co-operation in solving international problems of an economic, social, cultural or humanitarian character, and in promoting and encouraging respect for human rights and for fundamental freedoms for all without distinction as to race, sex, language or religion; and

4. To be a centre for harmonizing the actions of nations in the attainment of these common ends.

Article 2

The Organization and its Members, in pursuit of the Purposes stated in Article 1, shall act in accordance with the following Principles:

1. The Organization is based on the principle of the sovereign equality of all its Members.

2. All Members, in order to ensure to all of them the rights and benefits resulting from membership, shall fulfil in good faith the obligations assumed by them in accordance with the present Charter.

3.   All Members shall settle their international disputes by peaceful means in such a manner that international peace and security, and justice, are not endangered.

4.   All Members shall refrain in their international relations from the threat or use of force against the territorial integrity or political independence of any state, or in any other manner inconsistent with the Purposes of the United Nations.

5.   All Members shall give the United Nations every assistance in any action it takes in accordance with the present Charter, and shall refrain from giving assistance to any state against which the United Nations is taking preventive or enforcement action.

6.   The Organization shall ensure that states which are not Members of the United Nations act in accordance with these Principles so far as may be necessary for the maintenance of international peace and security.

7.   Nothing contained in the present Charter shall authorize the United Nations to intervene in matters which are essentially within the domestic jurisdiction of any state or shall require the Members to submit such matters to settlement under the present Charter; but this principle shall not prejudice the application of enforcement measures under Chapter VII.

Chapter II
MEMBERSHIP

Article 3

The original Members of the United Nations shall be the states which, having participated in the United Nations Conference on International Organization at San Francisco or having previously signed the Declaration by United Nations of 1 January 1942, sign the present Charter and ratify it in accordance with Article 110.

Article 4

1.   Membership in the United Nations is open to all other peace-loving states which accept the obligations contained in the present Charter and, in the judgment of the Organization, are able and willing to carry out these obligations.

2.   The admission of any such state to membership in the United Nations will be effected by a decision of the General Assembly upon the recommendation of the Security Council.

Article 5

A Member of the United Nations against which preventive or enforcement action has been taken by the Security Council may be suspended from the exercise of the rights and privileges of membership by the General Assembly upon the recommendation of the Security Council. The exercise of these rights and privileges may be restored by the Security Council.

Article 6

A Member of the United Nations which has persistently violated the Principles contained in the present Charter may be expelled from the Organization by the General Assembly upon the recommendation of the Security Council.

Chapter III
ORGANS

Article 7

1.   There are established as the principal organs of the United Nations: a General Assembly, a Security Council, an Economic and Social Council, a Trusteeship Council, an International Court of Justice, and a Secretariat.

2.   Such subsidiary organs as may be found necessary may be established in accordance with the present Charter.

Article 8

The United Nations shall place no restrictions on the eligibility of men and women to participate in any capacity and under conditions of equality in its principal and subsidiary organs.

Chapter IV
THE GENERAL ASSEMBLY

Composition

Article 9

1.   The General Assembly shall consist of all the Members of the United Nations.

2.   Each Member shall have not more than five representatives in the General Assembly.

Functions and Powers

Article 10

The General Assembly may discuss any questions or any matters within the scope of the present Charter or relating to the powers and functions of any organs provided for in the present Charter, and, except as provided in Article 12, may make recommendations to the Members of the United Nations or to the Security Council or both on any such questions or matters.

Article 11

1.   The General Assembly may consider the general principles of co-operation in the maintenance of international peace and security, including the principles governing disarmament and the regulation of armaments, and may make recommendations with regard to such principles to the Members or to the Security Council or to both.

2.   The General Assembly may discuss any questions relating to the maintenance of international peace and security brought before it by any Member of the United Nations, or by the Security Council, or by a state which is not a Member of the United Nations in accordance with Article 35, paragraph 2, and, except as provided in Article 12, may make recommendations with regard to any such questions to the state or states concerned or to the Security Council or to both. Any such question on which action is necessary shall be referred to the Security Council by the General Assembly either before or after discussion.

3.   The General Assembly may call the attention of the Security Council to situations which are likely to endanger international peace and security.

4.   The powers of the General Assembly set forth in this Article shall not limit the general scope of Article 10.

Article 12

1.   While the Security Council is exercising in respect of any dispute or situation the functions assigned to it in the present Charter, the General Assembly shall not make any recommendation with regard to that dispute or situation unless the Security Council so requests.

2.   The Secretary-General, with the consent of the Security Council, shall notify the General Assembly at each session of any matters relative to the maintenance of international peace and security which are being dealt with by the Security Council and shall similarly notify the General Assembly, or the Members of the United Nations if the General Assembly is not in session, immediately the Security Council ceases to deal with such matters.

Article 13

1.   The General Assembly shall initiate studies and make recommendations for the purpose of:

   a.   promoting international co-operation in the political field and encouraging the progressive development of international law and its codification;

   b.   promoting international co-operation in the economic, social, cultural, educational and health fields, and assisting in the realization of human rights and fundamental freedoms for all without distinction as to race, sex, language or religion.

2. The further responsibilities, functions and powers of the General Assembly with respect to matters mentioned in paragraph 1 (b) above are set forth in Chapters IX and X.

Article 14

Subject to the provisions of Article 12, the General Assembly may recommend measures for the peaceful adjustment of any situation, regardless of origin, which it deems likely to impair the general welfare or friendly relations among nations, including situations resulting from a violation of the provisions of the present Charter setting forth the Purposes and Principles of the United Nations.

Article 15

1. The General Assembly shall receive and consider annual and special reports from the Security Council; these reports shall include an account of the measures that the Security Council has decided upon or taken to maintain international peace and security.

2. The General Assembly shall receive and consider reports from the other organs of the United Nations.

Article 16

The General Assembly shall perform such functions with respect to the international trusteeship system as are assigned to it under Chapters XII and XIII, including the approval of the trusteeship agreements for areas not designated as strategic.

Article 17

1. The General Assembly shall consider and approve the budget of the Organization.

2. The expenses of the Organization shall be borne by the Members as apportioned by the General Assembly.

3. The General Assembly shall consider and approve any financial and budgetary arrangements with specialized agencies referred to in Article 57 and shall examine the administrative budgets of such specialized agencies with a view to making recommendations to the agencies concerned.

Voting

Article 18

1. Each member of the General Assembly shall have one vote.

2. Decisions of the General Assembly on important questions shall be made by a two-thirds majority of the members present and voting. These questions shall include: recommendations with respect to the maintenance of international peace and security, the election of the non-permanent members of the Security Council, the election of the members of the Economic and Social Council, the election of members of the Trusteeship Council in accordance with paragraph 1 (c) of Article 86, the admission of new Members to the United Nations, the suspension of the rights and privileges of membership, the expulsion of Members, questions relating to the operation of the trusteeship system, and budgetary questions.

3. Decisions on other questions, including the determination of additional categories of questions to be decided by a two-thirds majority, shall be made by a majority of the members present and voting.

Article 19

A Member of the United Nations which is in arrears in the payment of its financial contributions to the Organization shall have no vote in the General Assembly if the amount of its arrears equals or exceeds the amount of the contributions due from it for the preceding two full years. The General Assembly may, nevertheless, permit such a Member to vote if it is satisfied that the failure to pay is due to conditions beyond the control of the Member.

Procedure

Article 20

The General Assembly shall meet in regular annual sessions and in such special sessions as occasion may require. Special sessions shall be convoked by the Secretary-General at the request of the Security Council or of a majority of the Members of the United Nations.

Article 21

The General Assembly shall adopt its own rules of procedure. It shall elect its President for each session.

Article 22

The General Assembly may establish such subsidiary organs as it deems necessary for the performance of its functions.

Chapter V

THE SECURITY COUNCIL

Composition

Article 23¹

1. The Security Council shall consist of fifteen Members of the United Nations. The Republic of China, France, the Union of Soviet Socialist Republics, the United Kingdom of Great Britain and Northern Ireland and the United States of America shall be permanent members of the Security Council. The General Assembly shall elect ten other Members of the United Nations to be non-permanent members of the Security Council, due regard being specially paid, in the first instance to the contribution of Members of the United Nations to the maintenance of international peace and security and to the other purposes of the Organization, and also to equitable geographical distribution.

2. The non-permanent members of the Security Council shall be elected for a term of two years. In the first election of the non-permanent members after the increase of the membership of the Security Council from eleven to fifteen, two of the four additional members shall be chosen for a term of one year. A retiring member shall not be eligible for immediate re-election.

3. Each member of the Security Council shall have one representative.

Functions and Powers

Article 24

1. In order to ensure prompt and effective action by the United Nations, its Members confer on the Security Council primary responsibility for the maintenance of international peace and security, and agree that in carrying out its duties under this responsibility the Security Council acts on their behalf.

2. In discharging these duties the Security Council shall act in accordance with the Purposes and Principles of the United Nations. The specific powers granted to the Security Council for the discharge of these duties are laid down in Chapters VI, VII, VIII and XII.

3. The Security Council shall submit annual and, when necessary, special reports to the General Assembly for its consideration.

Article 25

The Members of the United Nations agree to accept and carry out the decisions of the Security Council in accordance with the present Charter.

Article 26

In order to promote the establishment and maintenance of international peace and security with the least diversion for armaments of the world's human and economic resources, the Security Council shall be responsible for formulating, with the assistance of the Military Staff Committee referred to in Article

47, plans to be submitted to the Members of the United Nations for the establishment of a system for the regulation of armaments.

Voting

Article 27[2]

1. Each member of the Security Council shall have one vote.

2. Decisions of the Security Council on procedural matters shall be made by an affirmative vote of nine members.

3. Decisions of the Security Council on all other matters shall be made by an affirmative vote of nine members including the concurring votes of the permanent members; provided that, in decisions under Chapter VI, and under paragraph 3 of Article 52, a party to a dispute shall abstain from voting.

Procedure

Article 28

1. The Security Council shall be so organized as to be able to function continuously. Each member of the Security Council shall for this purpose be represented at all times at the seat of the Organization.

2. The Security Council shall hold periodic meetings at which each of its members may, if it so desires, be represented by a member of the government or by some other specially designated representative.

3. The Security Council may hold meetings at such places other than the seat of the Organization as in its judgment will best facilitate its work.

Article 29

The Security Council may establish such subsidiary organs as it deems necessary for the performance of its functions.

Article 30

The Security Council shall adopt its own rules of procedure, including the method of selecting its President.

Article 31

Any Member of the United Nations which is not a member of the Security Council may participate, without vote, in the discussion of any question brought before the Security Council whenever the latter considers that the interests of that Member are specially affected.

Article 32

Any Member of the United Nations which is not a member of the Security Council or any state which is not a Member of the United Nations, if it is a party to a dispute under consideration by the Security Council, shall be invited to participate, without vote, in the discussion relating to the dispute. The Security Council shall lay down such conditions as it deems just for the participation of a state which is not a Member of the United Nations.

Chapter VI
PACIFIC SETTLEMENT OF DISPUTES

Article 33

1. The parties to any dispute, the continuance of which is likely to endanger the maintenance of international peace and security, shall, first of all, seek a solution by negotiation, enquiry, mediation, conciliation, arbitration, judicial settlement, resort to regional agencies or arrangements, or other peaceful means of their own choice.

2. The Security Council shall, when it deems necessary, call upon the parties to settle their dispute by such means.

Article 34

The Security Council may investigate any dispute, or any situation which might lead to international friction or give rise to a dispute, in order to determine whether the continuance of the dispute or situation is likely to endanger the maintenance of international peace and security.

Article 35

1. Any Member of the United Nations may bring any dispute, or any situation of the nature referred to in Article 34, to the attention of the Security Council or of the General Assembly.

2. A state which is not a Member of the United Nations may bring to the attention of the Security Council or of the General Assembly any dispute to which it is a party if it accepts in advance, for the purposes of the dispute, the obligations of pacific settlement provided in the present Charter.

3. The proceedings of the General Assembly in respect of matters brought to its attention under this Article will be subject to the provisions of Articles 11 and 12.

Article 36

1. The Security Council may, at any stage of a dispute of the nature referred to in Article 33 or of a situation of like nature, recommend appropriate procedures or methods of adjustment.

2. The Security Council should take into consideration any procedures for the settlement of the dispute which have already been adopted by the parties.

3. In making recommendations under this Article the Security Council should also take into consideration that legal disputes should as a general rule be referred by the parties to the International Court of Justice in accordance with the provisions of the Statute of the Court.

Article 37

1. Should the parties to a dispute of the nature referred to in Article 33 fail to settle it by the means indicated in that Article, they shall refer it to the Security Council.

2. If the Security Council deems that the continuance of the dispute is in fact likely to endanger the maintenance of international peace and security, it shall decide whether to take action under Article 36 or to recommend such terms of settlement as it may consider appropriate.

Article 38

Without prejudice to the provisions of Articles 33 to 37, the Security Council may, if all the parties to any dispute so request, make recommendations to the parties with a view to a pacific settlement of the dispute.

Chapter VII
ACTION WITH RESPECT TO THREATS TO THE PEACE, BREACHES OF THE PEACE, AND ACTS OF AGGRESSION

Article 39

The Security Council shall determine the existence of any threat to the peace, breach of the peace, or act of aggression and shall make recommendations, or decide what measures shall be taken in accordance with Articles 41 and 42, to maintain or restore international peace and security.

Article 40

In order to prevent an aggravation of the situation, the Security Council may, before making the recommendations or deciding upon the measures provided for in Article 39, call upon the parties concerned to comply with such provisional measures as it deems necessary or desirable. Such provisional measures shall be without prejudice to the rights, claims or position of the parties concerned. The Security Council shall duly take account of failure to comply with such provisional measures.

Article 41

The Security Council may decide what measures not involving the use of armed force are to be employed to give effect to its decisions, and it may call upon the Members of the United Nations to apply such measures. These may include complete or partial interruption of economic relations and of rail, sea, air, postal, telegraphic, radio and other means of communication, and the severance of diplomatic relations.

Article 42

Should the Security Council consider that measures provided for in Article 41 would be inadequate or have proved to be inadequate, it may take such action by air, sea or land forces as may be necessary to maintain or restore international peace and security. Such action may include demonstrations, blockade, and other operations by air, sea, or land forces of Members of the United Nations.

Article 43

1. All Members of the United Nations, in order to contribute to the maintenance of international peace and security, undertake to make available to the Security Council, on its call and in accordance with a special agreement or agreements, armed forces, assistance and facilities, including rights of passage, necessary for the purpose of maintaining international peace and security.

2. Such agreement or agreements shall govern the numbers and types of forces, their degree of readiness and general location, and the nature of the facilities and assistance to be provided.

3. The agreement or agreements shall be negotiated as soon as possible on the initiative of the Security Council. They shall be concluded between the Security Council and Members or between the Security Council and groups of Members and shall be subject to ratification by the signatory states in accordance with their respective constitutional processes.

Article 44

When the Security Council has decided to use force it shall, before calling upon a Member not represented on it to provide armed forces in fulfilment of the obligations assumed under Article 43, invite that Member, if the Member so desires, to participate in the decisions of the Security Council concerning the employment of contingents of that Member's armed forces.

Article 45

In order to enable the United Nations to take urgent military measures, Members shall hold immediately available national air-force contingents for combined international enforcement action. The strength and degree of readiness of these contingents and plans for their combined action shall be determined, within the limits laid down in the special agreement or agreements referred to in Article 43, by the Security Council with the assistance of the Military Staff Committee.

Article 46

Plans for the application of armed force shall be made by the Security Council with the assistance of the Military Staff Committee.

Article 47

1. There shall be established a Military Staff Committee to advise and assist the Security Council on all questions relating to the Security Council's military requirements for the maintenance of international peace and security, the employment and command of forces placed at its disposal, the regulation of armaments, and possible disarmament.

2. The Military Staff Committee shall consist of the Chiefs of Staff of the permanent members of the Security Council or their representatives. Any Member of the United Nations not permanently represented on the Committee shall be invited by the Committee to be associated with it when the efficient discharge of the Committee's responsibilities requires the participation of that Member in its work.

3. The Military Staff Committee shall be responsible under the Security Council for the strategic direction of any armed forces placed at the disposal of the Security Council. Questions relating to the command of such forces shall be worked out subsequently.

4. The Military Staff Committee, with the authorization of the Security Council and after consultation with appropriate regional agencies, may establish regional sub-committees.

Article 48

1. The action required to carry out the decisions of the Security Council for the maintenance of international peace and security shall be taken by all the Members of the United Nations or by some of them, as the Security Council may determine.

2. Such decisions shall be carried out by the Members of the United Nations directly and through their action in the appropriate international agencies of which they are members.

Article 49

The Members of the United Nations shall join in affording mutual assistance in carrying out the measures decided upon by the Security Council.

Article 50

If preventive or enforcement measures against any state are taken by the Security Council, any other state, whether a Member of the United Nations or not, which finds itself confronted with special economic problems arising from the carrying out of those measures shall have the right to consult the Security Council with regard to a solution of those problems.

Article 51

Nothing in the present Charter shall impair the inherent right of individual or collective self-defence if an armed attack occurs against a Member of the United Nations, until the Security Council has taken measures necessary to maintain international peace and security. Measures taken by Members in the exercise of this right of self-defence shall be immediately reported to the Security Council and shall not in any way affect the authority and responsibility of the Security Council under the present Charter to take at any time such action as it deems necessary in order to maintain or restore international peace and security.

Chapter VIII
REGIONAL ARRANGEMENTS

Article 52

1. Nothing in the present Charter precludes the existence of regional arrangements or agencies for dealing with such matters relating to the maintenance of international peace and security as are appropriate for regional action, provided that such arrangements or agencies and their activities are consistent with the Purposes and Principles of the United Nations.

2. The Members of the United Nations entering into such arrangements or constituting such agencies shall make every effort to achieve pacific settlement of local disputes through such regional arrangements or by such regional agencies before referring them to the Security Council.

3. The Security Council shall encourage the development of pacific settlement of local disputes through such regional arrangements or by such regional agencies either on the initiative of the states concerned or by reference from the Security Council.

4. This Article in no way impairs the application of Articles 34 and 35.

Article 53

1. The Security Council shall, where appropriate, utilize such regional arrangements or agencies for enforcement action under its authority. But no enforcement action shall be taken under regional arrangements or by regional agencies

without the authorization of the Security Council, with the exception of measures against any enemy state, as defined in paragraph 2 of this Article, provided for pursuant to Article 107 or in regional arrangements directed against renewal of aggressive policy on the part of any such state, until such time as the Organization may, on request of the Governments concerned, be charged with the responsibility for preventing further aggression by such a state.

2. The term enemy state as used in paragraph 1 of this Article applies to any state which during the Second World War has been an enemy of any signatory of the present Charter.

Article 54

The Security Council shall at all times be kept fully informed of activities undertaken or in contemplation under regional arrangements or by regional agencies for the maintenance of international peace and security.

Chapter IX
INTERNATIONAL ECONOMIC AND SOCIAL CO-OPERATION

Article 55

With a view to the creation of conditions of stability and well-being which are necessary for peaceful and friendly relations among nations based on respect for the principle of equal rights and self-determination of peoples, the United Nations shall promote:

a. higher standards of living, full employment, and conditions of economic and social progress and development;

b. solutions of international economic, social, health, and related problems; and international cultural and educational co-operation; and

c. universal respect for, and observance of, human rights and fundamental freedoms for all without distinction as to race, sex, language, or religion.

Article 56

All Members pledge themselves to take joint and separate action in co-operation with the Organization for the achievement of the purposes set forth in Article 55.

Article 57

1. The various specialized agencies, established by inter-governmental agreement and having wide international responsibilities, as defined in their basic instruments, in economic, social, cultural, educational, health, and related fields, shall be brought into relationship with the United Nations in accordance with the provisions of Article 63.

2. Such agencies thus brought into relationship with the United Nations are hereinafter referred to as specialized agencies.

Article 58

The Organization shall make recommendations for the co-ordination of the policies and activities of the specialized agencies.

Article 59

The Organization shall, where appropriate, initiate negotiations among the states concerned for the creation of any new specialized agencies required for the accomplishment of the purposes set forth in Article 55.

Article 60

Responsibility for the discharge of the functions of the Organization set forth in this Chapter shall be vested in the General Assembly and, under the authority of the General Assembly, in the Economic and Social Council, which shall have for this purpose the powers set forth in Chapter X.

Chapter X
THE ECONOMIC AND SOCIAL COUNCIL

Composition

Article 61[3]

1. The Economic and Social Council shall consist of fifty-four Members of the United Nations elected by the General Assembly.

2. Subject to the provisions of paragraph 3, eighteen members of the Economic and Social Council shall be elected each year for a term of three years. A retiring member shall be eligible for immediate re-election.

3. At the first election after the increase in the membership of the Economic and Social Council from twenty-seven to fifty-four members, in addition to the members elected in place of the nine members whose term of office expires at the end of that year, twenty-seven additional members shall be elected. Of these twenty-seven additional members, the term of office of nine members so elected shall expire at the end of one year, and of nine other members at the end of two years, in accordance with arrangements made by the General Assembly.

4. Each member of the Economic and Social Council shall have one representative.

Functions and Powers

Article 62

1. The Economic and Social Council may make or initiate studies and reports with respect to international economic, social, cultural, educational, health, and related matters and may make recommendations with respect to any such matters to the General Assembly, to the Members of the United Nations, and to the specialized agencies concerned.

2. It may make recommendations for the purpose of promoting respect for, and observance of, human rights and fundamental freedoms for all.

3. It may prepare draft conventions for submission to the General Assembly, with respect to matters falling within its competence.

4. It may call, in accordance with the rules prescribed by the United Nations, international conferences on matters falling within its competence.

Article 63

1. The Economic and Social Council may enter into agreements with any of the agencies referred to in Article 57, defining the terms on which the agency concerned shall be brought into relationship with the United Nations. Such agreements shall be subject to approval by the General Assembly.

2. It may co-ordinate the activities of the specialized agencies through consultation with and recommendations to such agencies and through recommendations to the General Assembly and to the Members of the United Nations.

Article 64

1. The Economic and Social Council may take appropriate steps to obtain regular reports from the specialized agencies. It may make arrangements with the Members of the United Nations and with the specialized agencies to obtain reports on the steps taken to give effect to its own recommendations and to recommendations on matters falling within its competence made by the General Assembly.

2. It may communicate its observations on these reports to the General Assembly.

Article 65

The Economic and Social Council may furnish information to the Security Council and shall assist the Security Council upon its request.

Article 66

1. The Economic and Social Council shall perform such functions as fall within its competence in connexion with the carrying out of the recommendations of the General Assembly.

2. It may, with the approval of the General Assembly, perform services at the request of Members of the United Nations and at the request of specialized agencies.

3. It shall perform such other functions as are specified elsewhere in the present Charter or as may be assigned to it by the General Assembly.

Voting

Article 67

1. Each member of the Economic and Social Council shall have one vote.

2. Decisions of the Economic and Social Council shall be made by a majority of the members present and voting.

Procedure

Article 68

The Economic and Social Council shall set up commissions in economic and social fields and for the promotion of human rights, and such other commissions as may be required for the performance of its functions.

Article 69

The Economic and Social Council shall invite any Member of the United Nations to participate, without vote, in its deliberations on any matter of particular concern to that Member.

Article 70

The Economic and Social Council may make arrangements for representatives of the specialized agencies to participate, without vote, in its deliberations and in those of the commissions established by it, and for its representatives to participate in the deliberations of the specialized agencies.

Article 71

The Economic and Social Council may make suitable arrangements for consultation with non-governmental organizations which are concerned with matters within its competence. Such arrangements may be made with international organizations and, where appropriate, with national organizations after consultation with the Member of the United Nations concerned.

Article 72

1. The Economic and Social Council shall adopt its own rules of procedure, including the method of selecting its President.

2. The Economic and Social Council shall meet as required in accordance with its rules, which shall include provision for the convening of meetings on the request of a majority of its members.

Chapter XI

DECLARATION REGARDING
NON-SELF-GOVERNING TERRITORIES

Article 73

Members of the United Nations which have or assume responsibilities for the administration of territories whose peoples have not yet attained a full measure of self-government recognize the principle that the interests of the inhabitants of these territories are paramount, and accept as a sacred trust the obligation to promote to the utmost, within the system of international peace and security established by the present Charter, the well-being of the inhabitants of these territories and, to this end:

a. to ensure, with due respect for the culture of the peoples concerned, their political, economic, social, and educational advancement, their just treatment, and their protection against abuses;

b. to develop self-government, to take due account of the political aspirations of the peoples, and to assist them in the progressive development of their free political institutions, according to the particular circumstances of each territory and its peoples and their varying stages of advancement;

c. to further international peace and security;

d. to promote constructive measures of development, to encourage research, and to co-operate with one another and, when and where appropriate, with specialized international bodies with a view to the practical achievement of the social, economic, and scientific purposes set forth in this Article; and

e. to transmit regularly to the Secretary-General for information purposes, subject to such limitation as security and constitutional considerations may require, statistical and other information of a technical nature relating to economic, social, and educational conditions in the territories for which they are respectively responsible other than those territories to which Chapters XII and XIII apply.

Article 74

Members of the United Nations also agree that their policy in respect of the territories to which this Chapter applies, no less than in respect of their metropolitan areas, must be based on the general principle of good-neighbourliness, due account being taken of the interests and well-being of the rest of the world, in social, economic, and commercial matters.

Chapter XII

INTERNATIONAL TRUSTEESHIP SYSTEM

Article 75

The United Nations shall establish under its authority an international trusteeship system for the administration and supervision of such territories as may be placed thereunder by subsequent individual agreements. These territories are hereinafter referred to as trust territories.

Article 76

The basic objectives of the trusteeship system, in accordance with the Purposes of the United Nations laid down in Article 1 of the present Charter, shall be:

a. to further international peace and security;

b. to promote the political, economic, social, and educational advancement of the inhabitants of the trust territories, and their progressive development towards self-government or independence as may be appropriate to the particular circumstances of each territory and its peoples and the freely expressed wishes of the peoples concerned, and as may be provided by the terms of each trusteeship agreement;

c. to encourage respect for human rights and for fundamental freedoms for all without distinction as to race, sex, language, or religion, and to encourage recognition of the interdependence of the peoples of the world; and

d. to ensure equal treatment in social, economic, and commercial matters for all Members of the United Nations and their nationals, and also equal treatment for the latter in the administration of justice, without prejudice to the attainment of the foregoing objectives and subject to the provisions of Article 80.

Article 77

1. The trusteeship system shall apply to such territories in the following categories as may be placed thereunder by means of trusteeship agreements:

a. territories now held under mandate;

b. territories which may be detached from enemy states as a result of the Second World War; and

c. territories voluntarily placed under the system by states responsible for their administration.

2. It will be a matter for subsequent agreement as to which territories in the foregoing categories will be brought under the trusteeship system and upon what terms.

Article 78

The trusteeship system shall not apply to territories which have become Members of the United Nations, relationship among which shall be based on respect for the principle of sovereign equality.

Article 79

The terms of trusteeship for each territory to be placed under the trusteeship system, including any alteration or amendment, shall be agreed upon by the states directly concerned, including the mandatory power in the case of territories held under mandate by a Member of the United Nations, and shall be approved as provided for in Articles 83 and 85.

Article 80

1. Except as may be agreed upon in individual trusteeship agreements, made under Articles 77, 79 and 81, placing each territory under the trusteeship system, and until such agreements have been concluded, nothing in this Chapter shall be construed in or of itself to alter in any manner the rights whatsoever of any states or any peoples or the terms of existing international instruments to which Members of the United Nations may respectively be parties.

2. Paragraph 1 of this Article shall not be interpreted as giving grounds for delay or postponement of the negotiation and conclusion of agreements for placing mandated and other territories under the trusteeship system as provided for in Article 77.

Article 81

The trusteeship agreement shall in each case include the terms under which the trust territory will be administered and designate the authority which will exercise the administration of the trust territory. Such authority, hereinafter called the administering authority, may be one or more states or the Organization itself.

Article 82

There may be designated, in any trusteeship agreement, a strategic area or areas which may include part or all of the trust territory to which the agreement applies, without prejudice to any special agreement or agreements made under Article 43.

Article 83

1. All functions of the United Nations relating to strategic areas, including the approval of the terms of the trusteeship agreements and of their alteration or amendment, shall be exercised by the Security Council.

2. The basic objectives set forth in Article 76 shall be applicable to the people of each strategic area.

3. The Security Council shall, subject to the provisions of the trusteeship agreements and without prejudice to security considerations, avail itself of the assistance of the Trusteeship Council to perform those functions of the United Nations under the trusteeship system relating to political, economic, social, and educational matters in the strategic areas.

Article 84

It shall be the duty of the administering authority to ensure that the trust territory shall play its part in the maintenance of international peace and security. To this end the administering authority may make use of volunteer forces, facilities, and assistance from the trust territory in carrying out the obligations towards the Security Council undertaken in this regard by the administering authority, as well as for local defence and the maintenance of law and order within the trust territory.

Article 85

1. The functions of the United Nations with regard to trusteeship agreements for all areas not designated as strategic, including the approval of the terms of the trusteeship agreements and of their alteration or amendment, shall be exercised by the General Assembly.

2. The Trusteeship Council, operating under the authority of the General Assembly, shall assist the General Assembly in carrying out these functions.

Chapter XIII

THE TRUSTEESHIP COUNCIL

Composition

Article 86

1. The Trusteeship Council shall consist of the following Members of the United Nations:

a. those Members administering trust territories;

b. such of those Members mentioned by name in Article 23 as are not administering trust territories; and

c. as many other Members elected for three-year terms by the General Assembly as may be necessary to ensure that the total number of members of the Trusteeship Council is equally divided between those Members of the United Nations which administer trust territories and those which do not.

2. Each member of the Trusteeship Council shall designate one specially qualified person to represent it therein.

Functions and Powers

Article 87

The General Assembly and, under its authority, the Trusteeship Council, in carrying out their functions, may:

a. consider reports submitted by the administering authority;

b. accept petitions and examine them in consultation with the administering authority;

c. provide for periodic visits to the respective trust territories at times agreed upon with the administering authority; and

d. take these and other actions in conformity with the terms of the trusteeship agreements.

Article 88

The Trusteeship Council shall formulate a questionnaire on the political, economic, social, and educational advancement of the inhabitants of each trust territory, and the administering authority for each trust territory within the competence of the General Assembly shall make an annual report to the General Assembly upon the basis of such questionnaire.

Voting

Article 89

1. Each member of the Trusteeship Council shall have one vote.

2. Decisions of the Trusteeship Council shall be made by a majority of the members present and voting.

Procedure

Article 90

1. The Trusteeship Council shall adopt its own rules of procedure, including the method of selecting its President.

2. The Trusteeship Council shall meet as required in accordance with its rules, which shall include provision for the convening of meetings on the request of a majority of its members.

Article 91

The Trusteeship Council shall, when appropriate, avail itself of the assistance of the Economic and Social Council and of the specialized agencies in regard to matters with which they are respectively concerned.

Chapter XIV

THE INTERNATIONAL COURT OF JUSTICE

Article 92

The International Court of Justice shall be the principal judicial organ of the United Nations. It shall function in accordance with the annexed Statute, which is based upon the Statute of the Permanent Court of International Justice and forms an integral part of the present Charter.

Article 93

1. All Members of the United Nations are *ipso facto* parties to the Statute of the International Court of Justice.

2. A state which is not a Member of the United Nations may become a party to the Statute of the International Court of Justice on conditions to be determined in each case by the General Assembly upon the recommendation of the Security Council.

Article 94

1. Each Member of the United Nations undertakes to comply with the decision of the International Court of Justice in any case to which it is a party.

2. If any party to a case fails to perform the obligations incumbent upon it under a judgment rendered by the Court, the other party may have recourse to the Security Council, which may, if it deems necessary, make recommendations or decide upon measures to be taken to give effect to the judgment.

Article 95

Nothing in the present Charter shall prevent Members of the United Nations from entrusting the solution of their differences to other tribunals by virtue of agreements already in existence or which may be concluded in the future.

Article 96

1. The General Assembly or the Security Council may request the International Court of Justice to give an advisory opinion on any legal question.

2. Other organs of the United Nations and specialized agencies, which may at any time be so authorized by the General Assembly, may also request advisory opinions of the Court on legal questions arising within the scope of their activities.

Chapter XV

THE SECRETARIAT

Article 97

The Secretariat shall comprise a Secretary-General and such staff as the Organization may require. The Secretary-General shall be appointed by the General Assembly upon the recommendation of the Security Council. He shall be the chief administrative officer of the Organization.

Article 98

The Secretary-General shall act in that capacity in all meetings of the General Assembly, of the Security Council, of the Economic and Social Council, and of the Trusteeship Council, and shall perform such other functions as are entrusted to him by these organs. The Secretary-General shall make an annual report to the General Assembly on the work of the Organization.

Article 99

The Secretary-General may bring to the attention of the Security Council any matter which in his opinion may threaten the maintenance of international peace and security.

Article 100

1. In the performance of their duties the Secretary-General and the staff shall not seek or receive instructions from any government or from any other authority external to the Organization. They shall refrain from any action which might reflect on their position as international officials responsible only to the Organization.

2. Each Member of the United Nations undertakes to respect the exclusively international character of the responsibilities of the Secretary-General and the staff and not to seek to influence them in the discharge of their responsibilities.

Article 101

1. The staff shall be appointed by the Secretary-General under regulations established by the General Assembly.

2. Appropriate staffs shall be permanently assigned to the Economic and Social Council, the Trusteeship Council, and, as required, to other organs of the United Nations. These staffs shall form a part of the Secretariat.

3. The paramount consideration in the employment of the staff and in the determination of the conditions of service shall be the necessity of securing the highest standards of efficiency, competence, and integrity. Due regard shall be paid to the importance of recruiting the staff on as wide a geographical basis as possible.

Chapter XVI

MISCELLANEOUS PROVISIONS

Article 102

1. Every treaty and every international agreement entered into by any Member of the United Nations after the present Charter comes into force shall as soon as possible be registered with the Secretariat and published by it.

2. No party to any such treaty or international agreement which has not been registered in accordance with the provisions of paragraph 1 of this Article may invoke that treaty or agreement before any organ of the United Nations.

Article 103

In the event of a conflict between the obligations of the Members of the United Nations under the present Charter and their obligations under any other international agreement, their obligations under the present Charter shall prevail.

Article 104

The Organization shall enjoy in the territory of each of its Members such legal capacity as may be necessary for the exercise of its functions and the fulfilment of its purposes.

Article 105

1. The Organization shall enjoy in the territory of each of its Members such privileges and immunities as are necessary for the fulfilment of its purposes.

2. Representatives of the Members of the United Nations and officials of the Organization shall similarly enjoy such privileges and immunities as are necessary for the independent exercise of their functions in connexion with the Organization.

3. The General Assembly may make recommendations with a view to determining the details of the application of paragraphs 1 and 2 of this Article or may propose conventions to the Members of the United Nations for this purpose.

Chapter XVII

TRANSITIONAL SECURITY ARRANGEMENTS

Article 106

Pending the coming into force of such special agreements referred to in Article 43 as in the opinion of the Security Council enable it to begin the exercise of its responsibilities under Article 42, the parties to the Four-Nation Declaration, signed at Moscow, 30 October 1943, and France, shall, in accordance with the provisions of paragraph 5 of that Declaration, consult with one another and as occasion requires with other Members of the United Nations with a view to such joint action on behalf of the Organization as may be necessary for the purpose of maintaining international peace and security.

Article 107

Nothing in the present Charter shall invalidate or preclude action, in relation to any state which during the Second World War has been an enemy of any signatory to the present Charter, taken or authorized as a result of that war by the Governments having responsibility for such action.

Chapter XVIII

AMENDMENTS

Article 108

Amendments to the present Charter shall come into force for all Members of the United Nations when they have been adopted by a vote of two thirds of the members of the General Assembly and ratified in accordance with their respective constitutional processes by two thirds of the Members of the United Nations, including all the permanent members of the Security Council.

Article 109[1]

1. A General Conference of the Members of the United Nations for the purpose of reviewing the present Charter may be held at a date and place to be fixed by a two-thirds vote of the members of the General Assembly and by a vote of any nine members of the Security Council. Each Member of the United Nations shall have one vote in the conference.

2. Any alteration of the present Charter recommended by a two-thirds vote of the conference shall take effect when ratified in accordance with their respective constitutional processes by two thirds of the Members of the United Na-tions including all the permanent members of the Security Council.

3. If such a conference has not been held before the tenth annual session of the General Assembly following the coming into force of the present Charter, the proposal to call such a conference shall be placed on the agenda of that session of the General Assembly, and the conference shall be held if so decided by a majority vote of the members of the General Assembly and by a vote of any seven members of the Security Council.

Chapter XIX

RATIFICATION AND SIGNATURE

Article 110

1. The present Charter shall be ratified by the signatory states in accordance with their respective constitutional processes.

2. The ratifications shall be deposited with the Government of the United States of America, which shall notify all the signatory states of each deposit as well as the Secretary-General of the Organization when he has been appointed.

3. The present Charter shall come into force upon the deposit of ratifications by the Republic of China, France, the Union of Soviet Socialist Republics, the United Kingdom of Great Britain and Northern Ireland and the United States of America, and by a majority of the other signatory states. A protocol of the ratifications deposited shall thereupon be drawn up by the Government of the United States of America which shall communicate copies thereof to all the signatory states.

4. The states signatory to the present Charter which ratify it after it has come into force will become original Members of the United Nations on the date of the deposit of their respective ratifications.

Article 111

The present Charter, of which the Chinese, French, Russian, English, and Spanish texts are equally authentic, shall remain deposited in the archives of the Government of the United States of America. Duly certified copies thereof shall be transmitted by that Government to the Governments of the other signatory states.

IN FAITH WHEREOF the representatives of the Governments of the United Nations have signed the present Charter.

DONE at the city of San Francisco the twenty-sixth day of June, one thousand nine hundred and forty-five.

---

[1] Amended text of Article 23, which came into force on 31 August 1965.
(The text of Article 23 before it was amended read as follows:
   1. The Security Council shall consist of eleven Members of the United Nations. The Republic of China, France, the Union of Soviet Socialist Republics, the United Kingdom of Great Britain and Northern Ireland and the United States of America shall be permanent members of the Security Council. The General Assembly shall elect six other Members of the United Nations to be non-permanent members of the Security Council, due regard being specially paid in the first instance to the contributions of Members of the United Nations to the maintenance of international peace and security and to the other purposes of the Organization, and also to equitable geographical distribution.
   2. The non-permanent members of the Security Council shall be elected for a term of two years. In the first election of the non-permanent members, however, three shall be chosen for a term of one year. A retiring member shall not be eligible for immediate re-election.
   3. Each member of the Security Council shall have one representative.)

[2] Amended text of Article 27, which came into force on 31 August 1965.
(The text of Article 27 before it was amended read as follows:
   1. Each member of the Security Council shall have one vote.
   2. Decisions of the Security Council on procedural matters shall be made by an affirmative vote of seven members.
   3. Decisions of the Security Council on all other matters shall be made by an affirmative vote of seven members including the concurring votes of the permanent members; provided that, in decisions under Chapter VI, and under paragraph 3 of Article 52, a party to a dispute shall abstain from voting.)

[3] Amended text of Article 61, which came into force on 24 September 1973.
(The text of Article 61 as previously amended on 31 August 1965 read as follows:
   1. The Economic and Social Council shall consist of twenty-seven Members of the United Nations elected by the General Assembly.
   2. Subject to the provisions of paragraph 3, nine members of the Economic and Social Council shall be elected each year for a term of three years. A retiring member shall be eligible for immediate re-election.

3. At the first election after the increase in the membership of the Economic and Social Council from eighteen to twenty-seven members, in addition to the members elected in place of the six members whose term of office expires at the end of that year, nine additional members shall be elected. Of these nine additional members, the term of office of three members so elected shall expire at the end of one year, and of three other members at the end of two years, in accordance with arrangements made by the General Assembly.

4. Each member of the Economic and Social Council shall have one representative.)

[4] Amended text of Article 109, which came into force on 12 June 1968.
(The text of Article 109 before it was amended read as follows:

1. A General Conference of the Members of the United Nations for the purpose of reviewing the present Charter may be held at a date and place to be fixed by a two-thirds vote of the members of the General Assembly and by a vote of any seven members of the Security Council. Each Member of the United Nations shall have one vote in the conference.

2. Any alteration of the present Charter recommended by a two-thirds vote of the conference shall take effect when ratified in accordance with their respective constitutional processes by two thirds of the Members of the United Nations including all the permanent members of the Security Council.

3. If such a conference has not been held before the tenth annual session of the General Assembly following the coming into force of the present Charter, the proposal to call such a conference shall be placed on the agenda of that session of the General Assembly, and the conference shall be held if so decided by a majority vote of the members of the General Assembly and by a vote of any seven members of the Security Council.)

Statute of the International Court of Justice

Article 1

The International Court of Justice established by the Charter of the United Nations as the principal judicial organ of the United Nations shall be constituted and shall function in accordance with the provisions of the present Statute.

Chapter I
ORGANIZATION OF THE COURT

Article 2

The Court shall be composed of a body of independent judges, elected regardless of their nationality from among persons of high moral character, who possess the qualifications required in their respective countries for appointment to the highest judicial offices, or are jurisconsults of recognized competence in international law.

Article 3

1. The Court shall consist of fifteen members, no two of whom may be nationals of the same state.

2. A person who for the purposes of membership in the Court could be regarded as a national of more than one state shall be deemed to be a national of the one in which he ordinarily exercises civil and political rights.

Article 4

1. The members of the Court shall be elected by the General Assembly and by the Security Council from a list of persons nominated by the national groups in the Permanent Court of Arbitration, in accordance with the following provisions.

2. In the case of Members of the United Nations not represented in the Permanent Court of Arbitration, candidates shall be nominated by national groups appointed for this purpose by their governments under the same conditions as those prescribed for members of the Permanent Court of Arbitration by Article 44 of the Convention of The Hague of 1907 for the pacific settlement of international disputes.

3. The conditions under which a state which is a party to the present Statute but is not a Member of the United Nations may participate in electing the members of the Court shall, in the absence of a special agreement, be laid down by the General Assembly upon recommendation of the Security Council.

Article 5

1. At least three months before the date of the election, the Secretary-General of the United Nations shall address a written request to the members of the Permanent Court of Arbitration belonging to the states which are parties to the present Statute, and to the members of the national groups appointed under Article 4, paragraph 2, inviting them to undertake, within a given time, by national groups, the nomination of persons in a position to accept the duties of a member of the Court.

2. No group may nominate more than four persons, not more than two of whom shall be of their own nationality. In no case may the number of candidates nominated by a group be more than double the number of seats to be filled.

Article 6

Before making these nominations, each national group is recommended to consult its highest court of justice, its legal faculties and schools of law, and its national academies and national sections of international academies devoted to the study of law.

Article 7

1. The Secretary-General shall prepare a list in alphabetical order of all the persons thus nominated. Save as provided in Article 12, paragraph 2, these shall be the only persons eligible.

2. The Secretary-General shall submit this list to the General Assembly and to the Security Council.

Article 8

The General Assembly and the Security Council shall proceed independently of one another to elect the members of the Court.

Article 9

At every election, the electors shall bear in mind not only that the persons to be elected should individually possess the qualifications required, but also that in the body as a whole the representation of the main forms of civilization and of the principal legal systems of the world should be assured.

Article 10

1. Those candidates who obtain an absolute majority of votes in the General Assembly and in the Security Council shall be considered as elected.

2. Any vote of the Security Council, whether for the election of judges or for the appointment of members of the conference envisaged in Article 12, shall be taken without any distinction between permanent and non-permanent members of the Security Council.

3. In the event of more than one national of the same state obtaining an absolute majority of the votes both of the General Assembly and of the Security Council, the eldest of these only shall be considered as elected.

Article 11

If, after the first meeting held for the purpose of the election, one or more seats remain to be filled, a second and, if necessary, a third meeting shall take place.

Article 12

1. If, after the third meeting, one or more seats still remain unfilled, a joint conference consisting of six members, three appointed by the General Assembly and three by the Security Council, may be formed at any time at the request of either the General Assembly or the Security Council, for the purpose of choosing by the vote of an absolute majority one name for each seat still vacant, to submit to the General Assembly and the Security Council for their respective acceptance.

2. If the joint conference is unanimously agreed upon any person who fulfils the required conditions, he may be included in its list, even though he was not included in the list of nominations referred to in Article 7.

3. If the joint conference is satisfied that it will not be successful in procuring an election, those members of the Court who have already been elected shall, within a period to be fixed by the Security Council, proceed to fill the vacant seats by selection from among those candidates who have obtained votes either in the General Assembly or in the Security Council.

4. In the event of an equality of votes among the judges, the eldest judge shall have a casting vote.

Article 13

1. The members of the Court shall be elected for nine years and may be re-elected; provided, however, that of the judges elected at the first election, the terms of five judges shall expire at the end of three years and the terms of five more judges shall expire at the end of six years.

2. The judges whose terms are to expire at the end of the above-mentioned initial periods of three and six years shall be chosen by lot to be drawn by the Secretary-General immediately after the first election has been completed.

3. The members of the Court shall continue to discharge their duties until their places have been filled. Though replaced, they shall finish any cases which they may have begun.

4. In the case of the resignation of a member of the Court, the resignation shall be addressed to the President of the Court for transmission to the Secretary-General. This last notification makes the place vacant.

Article 14

Vacancies shall be filled by the same method as that laid down for the first election, subject to the following provision: the Secretary-General shall, within one month of the occurrence of the vacancy, proceed to issue the invitations provided for in Article 5, and the date of the election shall be fixed by the Security Council.

Article 15

A member of the Court elected to replace a member whose term of office has not expired shall hold office for the remainder of his predecessor's term.

Article 16

1. No member of the Court may exercise any political or administrative function, or engage in any other occupation of a professional nature.

2. Any doubt on this point shall be settled by the decision of the Court.

Article 17

1. No member of the Court may act as agent, counsel, or advocate in any case.

2. No member may participate in the decision of any case in which he has previously taken part as agent, counsel, or advocate for one of the parties, or as a member of a national or international court, or of a commission of enquiry, or in any other capacity.

3. Any doubt on this point shall be settled by the decision of the Court.

Article 18

1. No member of the Court can be dismissed unless, in the unanimous opinion of the other members, he has ceased to fulfil the required conditions.

2. Formal notification thereof shall be made to the Secretary-General by the Registrar.

3. This notification makes the place vacant.

Article 19

The members of the Court, when engaged on the business of the Court, shall enjoy diplomatic privileges and immunities.

Article 20

Every member of the Court shall, before taking up his duties, make a solemn declaration in open court that he will exercise his powers impartially and conscientiously.

Article 21

1. The Court shall elect its President and Vice-President for three years; they may be re-elected.

2. The Court shall appoint its Registrar and may provide for the appointment of such other officers as may be necessary.

Article 22

1. The seat of the Court shall be established at The Hague. This, however, shall not prevent the Court from sitting and exercising its functions elsewhere whenever the Court considers it desirable.

2. The President and the Registrar shall reside at the seat of the Court.

Article 23

1. The Court shall remain permanently in session, except during the judicial vacations, the dates and duration of which shall be fixed by the Court.

2. Members of the Court are entitled to periodic leave, the dates and duration of which shall be fixed by the Court, having in mind the distance between The Hague and the home of each judge.

3. Members of the Court shall be bound, unless they are on leave or prevented from attending by illness or other serious reasons duly explained to the President, to hold themselves permanently at the disposal of the Court.

Article 24

1. If, for some special reason, a member of the Court considers that he should not take part in the decision of a particular case, he shall so inform the President.

2. If the President considers that for some special reason one of the members of the Court should not sit in a particular case, he shall give him notice accordingly.

3. If in any such case the member of the Court and the President disagree, the matter shall be settled by the decision of the Court.

Article 25

1. The full Court shall sit except when it is expressly provided otherwise in the present Statute.

2. Subject to the condition that the number of judges available to constitute the Court is not thereby reduced below eleven, the Rules of the Court may provide for allowing one or more judges, according to circumstances and in rotation, to be dispensed from sitting.

3. A quorum of nine judges shall suffice to constitute the Court.

Article 26

1. The Court may from time to time form one or more chambers, composed of three or more judges as the Court may determine, for dealing with particular categories of cases; for example, labour cases and cases relating to transit and communications.

2. The Court may at any time form a chamber for dealing with a particular case. The number of judges to constitute such a chamber shall be determined by the Court with the approval of the parties.

3. Cases shall be heard and determined by the chambers provided for in this Article if the parties so request.

Article 27

A judgment given by any of the chambers provided for in Articles 26 and 29 shall be considered as rendered by the Court.

Article 28

The chambers provided for in Articles 26 and 29 may, with the consent of the parties, sit and exercise their functions elsewhere than at The Hague.

Article 29

With a view to the speedy dispatch of business, the Court shall form annually a chamber composed of five judges which, at the request of the parties, may hear and determine cases by summary procedure. In addition, two judges shall be selected for the purpose of replacing judges who find it impossible to sit.

Article 30

1. The Court shall frame rules for carrying out its functions. In particular, it shall lay down rules of procedure.

2. The Rules of the Court may provide for assessors to sit with the Court or with any of its chambers, without the right to vote.

Article 31

1. Judges of the nationality of each of the parties shall retain their right to sit in the case before the Court.

2. If the Court includes upon the Bench a judge of the nationality of one of the parties, any other party may choose a person to sit as judge. Such person shall be chosen preferably from among those persons who have been nominated as candidates as provided in Articles 4 and 5.

3. If the Court includes upon the Bench no judge of the nationality of the parties, each of these parties may proceed to choose a judge as provided in paragraph 2 of this Article.

4. The provisions of this Article shall apply to the case of Articles 26 and 29. In such cases, the President shall request one or, if necessary, two of the members of the Court forming the chamber to give place to the members of the Court of the nationality of the parties concerned, and, failing such, or if they are unable to be present, to the judges specially chosen by the parties.

5. Should there be several parties in the same interest, they shall, for the purpose of the preceding provisions, be reckoned as one party only. Any doubt upon this point shall be settled by the decision of the Court.

6. Judges chosen as laid down in paragraphs 2, 3 and 4 of this Article shall fulfil the conditions required by Articles 2, 17 (paragraph 2), 20, and 24 of the present Statute. They shall take part in the decision on terms of complete equality with their colleagues.

Article 32

1. Each member of the Court shall receive an annual salary.

2. The President shall receive a special annual allowance.

3. The Vice-President shall receive a special allowance for every day on which he acts as President.

4. The judges chosen under Article 31, other than members of the Court, shall receive compensation for each day on which they exercise their functions.

5. These salaries, allowances, and compensation shall be fixed by the General Assembly. They may not be decreased during the term of office.

6. The salary of the Registrar shall be fixed by the General Assembly on the proposal of the Court.

7. Regulations made by the General Assembly shall fix the conditions under which retirement pensions may be given to members of the Court and to the Registrar, and the conditions under which members of the Court and the Registrar shall have their travelling expenses refunded.

8. The above salaries, allowances, and compensation shall be free of all taxation.

Article 33

The expenses of the Court shall be borne by the United Nations in such a manner as shall be decided by the General Assembly.

Chapter II

COMPETENCE OF THE COURT

Article 34

1. Only states may be parties in cases before the Court.

2. The Court, subject to and in conformity with its Rules, may request of public international organizations information relevant to cases before it, and shall receive such information presented by such organizations on their own initiative.

3. Whenever the construction of the constituent instrument of a public international organization or of an international convention adopted thereunder is in question in a case before the Court, the Registrar shall so notify the public international organization concerned and shall communicate to it copies of all the written proceedings.

Article 35

1. The Court shall be open to the states parties to the present Statute.

2. The conditions under which the Court shall be open to other states shall, subject to the special provisions contained in treaties in force, be laid down by the Security Council, but in no case shall such conditions place the parties in a position of inequality before the Court.

3. When a state which is not a Member of the United Nations is a party to a case, the Court shall fix the amount which that party is to contribute towards the expenses of the Court. This provision shall not apply if such state is bearing a share of the expenses of the Court.

Article 36

1. The jurisdiction of the Court comprises all cases which the parties refer to it and all matters specially provided for in the Charter of the United Nations or in treaties and conventions in force.

2. The states parties to the present Statute may at any time declare that they recognize as compulsory *ipso facto* and without special agreement, in relation to any other state accepting the same obligation, the jurisdiction of the Court in all legal disputes concerning:

a. the interpretation of a treaty;

b. any question of international law;

c. the existence of any fact which, if established, would constitute a breach of an international obligation;

d. the nature or extent of the reparation to be made for the breach of an international obligation.

3. The declarations referred to above may be made unconditionally or on condition of reciprocity on the part of several or certain states, or for a certain time.

4. Such declarations shall be deposited with the Secretary-General of the United Nations, who shall transmit copies thereof to the parties to the Statute and to the Registrar of the Court.

5. Declarations made under Article 36 of the Statute of the Permanent Court of International Justice and which are still in force shall be deemed, as between the parties to the present Statute, to be acceptances of the compulsory jurisdiction of the International Court of Justice for the period which they still have to run and in accordance with their terms.

6. In the event of a dispute as to whether the Court has jurisdiction, the matter shall be settled by the decision of the Court.

Article 37

Whenever a treaty or convention in force provides for reference of a matter to a tribunal to have been instituted by the League of Nations, or to the Permanent Court of International Justice, the matter shall, as between the parties to the present Statute, be referred to the International Court of Justice.

Article 38

1. The Court, whose function is to decide in accordance with international law such disputes as are submitted to it, shall apply:
   a. international conventions, whether general or particular, establishing rules expressly recognized by the contesting states;
   b. international custom, as evidence of a general practice accepted as law;
   c. the general principles of law recognized by civilized nations;
   d. subject to the provisions of Article 59, judicial decisions and the teachings of the most highly qualified publicists of the various nations, as subsidiary means for the determination of rules of law.
2. This provision shall not prejudice the power of the Court to decide a case *ex aequo et bono*, if the parties agree thereto.

Chapter III
PROCEDURE

Article 39

1. The official languages of the Court shall be French and English. If the parties agree that the case shall be conducted in French, the judgment shall be delivered in French. If the parties agree that the case shall be conducted in English, the judgment shall be delivered in English.
2. In the absence of an agreement as to which language shall be employed, each party may, in the pleadings, use the language which it prefers; the decision of the Court shall be given in French and English. In this case the Court shall at the same time determine which of the two texts shall be considered as authoritative.
3. The Court shall, at the request of any party, authorize a language other than French or English to be used by that party.

Article 40

1. Cases are brought before the Court, as the case may be, either by the notification of the special agreement or by a written application addressed to the Registrar. In either case the subject of the dispute and the parties shall be indicated.
2. The Registrar shall forthwith communicate the application to all concerned.
3. He shall also notify the Members of the United Nations through the Secretary-General, and also any other states entitled to appear before the Court.

Article 41

1. The Court shall have the power to indicate, if it considers that circumstances so require, any provisional measures which ought to be taken to preserve the respective rights of either party.
2. Pending the final decision, notice of the measures suggested shall forthwith be given to the parties and to the Security Council.

Article 42

1. The parties shall be represented by agents.
2. They may have the assistance of counsel or advocates before the Court.
3. The agents, counsel, and advocates of parties before the Court shall enjoy the privileges and immunities necessary to the independent exercise of their duties.

Article 43

1. The procedure shall consist of two parts: written and oral.

2. The written proceedings shall consist of the communication to the Court and to the parties of memorials, counter-memorials and, if necessary, replies; also all papers and documents in support.
3. These communications shall be made through the Registrar, in the order and within the time fixed by the Court.
4. A certified copy of every document produced by one party shall be communicated to the other party.
5. The oral proceedings shall consist of the hearing by the Court of witnesses, experts, agents, counsel, and advocates.

Article 44

1. For the service of all notices upon persons other than the agents, counsel, and advocates, the Court shall apply direct to the government of the state upon whose territory the notice has to be served.
2. The same provision shall apply whenever steps are to be taken to procure evidence on the spot.

Article 45

The hearing shall be under the control of the President or, if he is unable to preside, of the Vice-President; if neither is able to preside, the senior judge present shall preside.

Article 46

The hearing in Court shall be public, unless the Court shall decide otherwise, or unless the parties demand that the public be not admitted.

Article 47

1. Minutes shall be made at each hearing and signed by the Registrar and the President.
2. These minutes alone shall be authentic.

Article 48

The Court shall make orders for the conduct of the case, shall decide the form and time in which each party must conclude its arguments, and make all arrangements connected with the taking of evidence.

Article 49

The Court may, even before the hearing begins, call upon the agents to produce any document or to supply any explanations. Formal note shall be taken of any refusal.

Article 50

The Court may, at any time, entrust any individual, body, bureau, commission, or other organization that it may select, with the task of carrying out an enquiry or giving an expert opinion.

Article 51

During the hearing any relevant questions are to be put to the witnesses and experts under the conditions laid down by the Court in the rules of procedure referred to in Article 30.

Article 52

After the Court has received the proofs and evidence within the time specified for the purpose, it may refuse to accept any further oral or written evidence that one party may desire to present unless the other side consents.

Article 53

1. Whenever one of the parties does not appear before the Court, or fails to defend its case, the other party may call upon the Court to decide in favour of its claim.
2. The Court must, before doing so, satisfy itself, not only that it has jurisdiction in accordance with Articles 36 and 37, but also that the claim is well founded in fact and law.

Article 54

1. When, subject to the control of the Court, the agents, counsel, and advocates have completed their presentation of the case, the President shall declare the hearing closed.

2. The Court shall withdraw to consider the judgment.

3. The deliberations of the Court shall take place in private and remain secret.

Article 55

1. All questions shall be decided by a majority of the judges present.

2. In the event of an equality of votes, the President or the judge who acts in his place shall have a casting vote.

Article 56

1. The judgment shall state the reasons on which it is based.

2. It shall contain the names of the judges who have taken part in the decision.

Article 57

If the judgment does not represent in whole or in part the unanimous opinion of the judges, any judge shall be entitled to deliver a separate opinion.

Article 58

The judgment shall be signed by the President and by the Registrar. It shall be read in open court, due notice having been given to the agents.

Article 59

The decision of the Court has no binding force except between the parties and in respect of that particular case.

Article 60

The judgment is final and without appeal. In the event of dispute as to the meaning or scope of the judgment, the Court shall construe it upon the request of any party.

Article 61

1. An application for revision of a judgment may be made only when it is based upon the discovery of some fact of such a nature as to be a decisive factor, which fact was, when the judgment was given, unknown to the Court and also the party claiming revision, always provided that such ignorance was not due to negligence.

2. The proceedings for revision shall be opened by a judgment of the Court expressly recording the existence of the new fact, recognizing that it has such a character as to lay the case open to revision, and declaring the application admissible on this ground.

3. The Court may require previous compliance with the terms of the judgment before it admits proceedings in revision.

4. The application for revision must be made at latest within six months of the discovery of the new fact.

5. No application for revision may be made after the lapse of ten years from the date of the judgment.

Article 62

1. Should a state consider that it has an interest of a legal nature which may be affected by the decision in the case, it may submit a request to the Court to be permitted to intervene.

2. It shall be for the Court to decide upon this request.

Article 63

1. Whenever the construction of a convention to which states other than those concerned in the case are parties is in question, the Registrar shall notify all such states forthwith.

2. Every state so notified has the right to intervene in the proceedings; but if it uses this right, the construction given by the judgment will be equally binding upon it.

Article 64

Unless otherwise decided by the Court, each party shall bear its own costs.

Chapter IV
ADVISORY OPINIONS

Article 65

1. The Court may give an advisory opinion on any legal question at the request of whatever body may be authorized by or in accordance with the Charter of the United Nations to make such a request.

2. Questions upon which the advisory opinion of the Court is asked shall be laid before the Court by means of a written request containing an exact statement of the question upon which an opinion is required, and accompanied by all documents likely to throw light upon the question.

Article 66

1. The Registrar shall forthwith give notice of the request for an advisory opinion to all states entitled to appear before the Court.

2. The Registrar shall also, by means of a special and direct communication, notify any state entitled to appear before the Court or international organization considered by the Court, or, should it not be sitting, by the President, as likely to be able to furnish information on the question, that the Court will be prepared to receive, within a time limit to be fixed by the President, written statements, or to hear, at a public sitting to be held for the purpose, oral statements relating to the question.

3. Should any such state entitled to appear before the Court have failed to receive the special communication referred to in paragraph 2 of this Article, such state may express a desire to submit a written statement or to be heard; and the Court will decide.

4. States and organizations having presented written or oral statements or both shall be permitted to comment on the statements made by other states or organizations in the form, to the extent, and within the time limits which the Court, or, should it not be sitting, the President, shall decide in each particular case. Accordingly, the Registrar shall in due time communicate any such written statements to states and organizations having submitted similar statements.

Article 67

The Court shall deliver its advisory opinions in open court, notice having been given to the Secretary-General and to the representatives of Members of the United Nations, of other states and of international organizations immediately concerned.

Article 68

In the exercise of its advisory functions the Court shall further be guided by the provisions of the present Statute which apply in contentious cases to the extent to which it recognizes them to be applicable.

Chapter V
AMENDMENT

Article 69

Amendments to the present Statute shall be effected by the same procedure as is provided by the Charter of the United Nations for amendments to that Charter, subject however to any provisions which the General Assembly upon recommendation of the Security Council may adopt concerning the participation of states which are parties to the present Statute but are not Members of the United Nations.

Article 70

The Court shall have power to propose such amendments to the present Statute as it may deem necessary, through written communications to the Secretary-General, for consideration in conformity with the provisions of Article 69.

Appendix III

Structure of the United Nations

General Assembly

The General Assembly is composed of all the Members of the United Nations.

SESSIONS
Resumed fifty-eighth session: 9 February–13 September 2004.
Resumed tenth emergency special session: 16, 19 and 20 July 2004 (suspended).
Fifty-ninth session: 14 September–23 December 2004 (suspended).

OFFICERS
Resumed fifty-eighth and tenth emergency special sessions
President: Julian R. Hunte (Saint Lucia).
Vice-Presidents: Cape Verde, China, Equatorial Guinea, France, Haiti, Honduras, Iran, Luxembourg, Madagascar, Malawi, Morocco, Myanmar, Netherlands, Russian Federation, Senegal, Slovenia, Tajikistan, Turkmenistan, United Kingdom, United States, Yemen.

Fifty-ninth session
President: Jean Ping (Gabon).[1]
Vice-Presidents:[2] Algeria, Antigua and Barbuda, Australia, Azerbaijan, Bangladesh, Belgium, Burkina Faso, China, Djibouti, El Salvador, France, Ghana, Iran, Kazakhstan, Nicaragua, Russian Federation, Syrian Arab Republic, United Kingdom, United States, Uzbekistan, Zambia.

The Assembly has four types of committees: (1) Main Committees; (2) procedural committees; (3) standing committees; (4) subsidiary and ad hoc bodies. In addition, it convenes conferences to deal with specific subjects.

Main Committees

Six Main Committees have been established as follows:

Disarmament and International Security Committee (First Committee)
Special Political and Decolonization Committee (Fourth Committee)
Economic and Financial Committee (Second Committee)
Social, Humanitarian and Cultural Committee (Third Committee)
Administrative and Budgetary Committee (Fifth Committee)
Legal Committee (Sixth Committee)

The General Assembly may constitute other committees, on which all Members of the United Nations have the right to be represented.

OFFICERS OF THE MAIN COMMITTEES

Resumed fifty-eighth session

Fifth Committee[3]
Chairman: Hynek Kmonícek (Czech Republic).
Vice-Chairpersons: Abdelmalek Bouheddou (Algeria), Ronald Elkhuizen (Netherlands), Asdrúbal Pulido León (Venezuela).

Rapporteur: Fouad A. Rajeh (Saudi Arabia).
Fifty-ninth session[1]

First Committee
Chairman: Luis Alfonso De Alba (Mexico).
Vice-Chairmen: Dziunik Aghajanian (Armenia), Alon Bar (Israel), Sylvester Ekundayo Rowe (Sierra Leone).
Rapporteur: Mohamed Ali Saleh Alnajar (Yemen).

Fourth Committee
Chairman: Kyaw Tint Swe (Myanmar).
Vice-Chairmen: Eduardo Calderón (Ecuador), Helfried Carl (Austria), Andrej Droba (Slovakia).
Rapporteur: Kais Kabtani (Tunisia).

Second Committee
Chairman: Marco Balarezo (Peru).
Vice-Chairpersons: Ewa Anzorge (Poland), Antonio Bernardini (Italy), Majdi Ramadan (Lebanon).
Rapporteur: Azanaw T. Abreha (Ethiopia).

Third Committee
Chairman: Valery P. Kuchinsky (Ukraine).
Vice-Chairmen: Astanah Banu Shri Abdul Aziz (Malaysia), Rachel Groux (Switzerland), Mavis Esi Kusorgbor (Ghana).
Rapporteur: Carlos Enrique García González (El Salvador).

Fifth Committee
Chairman: Don MacKay (New Zealand).
Vice-Chairmen: Mhd. Najib Elji (Syrian Arab Republic), Karen Lock (South Africa), Karla G. Samayoa-Recari (Guatemala).
Rapporteur: Denisa Hutanová (Slovakia).

Sixth Committee
Chairman: Mohamed Bennouna (Morocco).
Vice-Chairmen: Ram Babu Dhakal (Nepal), Carlos Fernando Díaz Paniagua (Costa Rica), Csaba Simon (Hungary).
Rapporteur: Anna Sotaniemi (Finland).

Procedural committees

General Committee
The General Committee consists of the President of the General Assembly, as Chairman, the 21 Vice-Presidents and the Chairmen of the six Main Committees.

Credentials Committee
The Credentials Committee consists of nine members appointed by the General Assembly on the proposal of the President.

Resumed fifty-eighth session
Antigua and Barbuda, Cape Verde, China, Costa Rica, Ethiopia, Fiji, New Zealand, Russian Federation, United States.

Fifty-ninth session[5]
Benin, Bhutan, China, Ghana, Liechtenstein, Russian Federation, Trinidad and Tobago, United States, Uruguay.

Standing committees

The two standing committees consist of experts appointed in their individual capacity for three-year terms.

Advisory Committee on Administrative and Budgetary Questions (ACABQ)

To serve until 31 December 2004: Michiel W. H. Crom (Netherlands); Nazareth A. Incera (Costa Rica); Richard Moon (United Kingdom); Rajat Saha (India); Sun Minqin (China); Jun Yamazaki (Japan).

To serve until 31 December 2005: Homero Luis Hernandez (Dominican Republic); Vladimir V. Kuznetsov (Russian Federation); Thomas Mazet (Germany); Susan M. McLurg (United States); Mounir Zahran (Egypt).

To serve until 31 December 2006: Andrzej T. Abraszewski (Poland); Manlan Narcisse Ahounou (Côte d'Ivoire); Collen V. Kelapile (Botswana); E. Besley Maycock (Barbados); Murari Raj Sharma (Nepal).

On 8 December 2004 (dec. 59/407), the General Assembly appointed the following for a three-year term beginning on 1 January 2005 to fill the vacancies occurring on 31 December 2004: Ronald Elkhuizen (Netherlands), Jorge Flores Callejas (Honduras), Jerry Kramer (Canada), Rajat Saha (India), Sun Minqin (China), Jun Yamazaki (Japan).

Committee on Contributions

To serve until 31 December 2004: David Dutton (Australia); Bernardo Greiver, *Vice-Chairman* (Uruguay); Hassan Mohammed Hassan (Nigeria); Eduardo Iglesias (Argentina); Omar Kadiri (Morocco); Eduardo Manuel da Fonseca Fernandes Ramos (Portugal).

To serve until 31 December 2005: Alvaro Gurgel de Alencar Netto (Brazil); Sergei I. Mareyev (Russian Federation); Bernard Meijerman (Netherlands); Hae-yun Park (Republic of Korea); Ugo Sessi, *Chairman* (Italy); Wu Gang (China).

To serve until 31 December 2006: Kenshiro Akimoto (Japan); Meshal Al-Mansour (Kuwait); Petru Dumitriu (Romania); Haile Selassie Getachew (Ethiopia); Ihor V. Humenny (Ukraine); David A. Leis (United States).

On 8 December 2004 (dec. 59/408), the General Assembly appointed the following for a three-year term beginning on 1 January 2005 to fill the vacancies occurring on 31 December 2004: David Dutton (Australia), Paul Ekorong B Dong (Cameroon), Bernardo Greiver (Uruguay), Hassan Mohammed Hassan (Nigeria), Eduardo Iglesias (Argentina), Eduardo Manuel da Fonseca Fernandes Ramos (Portugal).

By the same decision, the Assembly appointed Vyacheslav A. Logutov (Russian Federation) for a one-year term beginning on 1 January 2005, as a result of the resignation of Sergei I. Mareyev effective 31 December 2004.

Subsidiary and ad hoc bodies

The following is a list of subsidiary and ad hoc bodies functioning in 2004, including the number of members, dates of meetings/sessions in 2004, document numbers of reports (which generally provide specific information on membership), and relevant decision numbers pertaining to elections.

Ad Hoc Committee on a Comprehensive and Integral International Convention on Protection and Promotion of the Rights and Dignity of Persons with Disabilities

Sessions: Third and fourth, New York, 24 May–4 June and 23 August–3 September
Chairman: Luis Gallegos Chiriboga (Ecuador)
Membership: Open to all Member States and observers of the United Nations
Reports: A/AC.265/2004/5, A/59/360

Ad Hoc Committee established by General Assembly resolution 51/210 of 17 December 1996

Session: Eighth, New York, 28 June–2 July
Chairman: Rohan Perera (Sri Lanka)
Membership: Open to all States Members of the United Nations or members of the specialized agencies or of IAEA
Report: A/59/37

Ad Hoc Committee on the Indian Ocean

Meeting: Did not meet in 2004
Membership: 43

Ad Hoc Committee on Jurisdictional Immunities of States and Their Property

Session: Third, New York, 1-5 March
Chairman: Gerhard Hafner (Austria)
Membership: Open to all States Members of the United Nations and members of the specialized agencies
Report: A/59/22

Ad Hoc Committee on the Scope of Legal Protection under the Convention on the Safety of United Nations and Associated Personnel

Session: Third, New York, 12-16 April
Chairman: Christian Wenaweser (Liechtenstein)
Membership: Open to all States Members of the United Nations or members of the specialized agencies or of IAEA
Report: A/59/52

Advisory Committee on the United Nations Programme of Assistance in the Teaching, Study, Dissemination and Wider Appreciation of International Law

Session: Thirty-ninth, New York, 11 November
Chairman: Robert Tachie-Menson (Ghana)
Membership: 25
Report: A/60/441

Board of Auditors

Sessions: Special session, Paris, 15 December
Chairman: François Logerot (France)
Membership: 3

Committee on Conferences

Sessions: New York, 25 March (organizational), 7, 8 and 10 September (substantive)
Chairman: Enno Drofenik (Austria)
Membership: 21
Report: A/59/32
Decision: GA 59/405

Committee on the Exercise of the Inalienable Rights of the Palestinian People

Meetings: Throughout the year
Chairman: Paul Badji (Senegal)
Membership: 24 (23 from 1 May)
Report: A/59/35

Committee on Information

Session: Twenty-sixth, New York, 26 April–7 May
Chairman: Iftekhar Ahmed Chowdhury (Bangladesh)
Membership: 102 (107 from 10 December)
Report: A/59/21
Decision: GA 59/413

Committee on the Peaceful Uses of Outer Space

Session: Forty-seventh, Vienna, 2-11 June
Chairman: Adigun Ade Abiodun (Nigeria)
Membership: 65
Report: A/59/20 & Corr.1,2

Committee for Programme and Coordination (CPC)

Session: Forty-fourth, New York, 1 June (organizational), 7 June–2 July (substantive)
Chairman: Nonye Udo (Nigeria)

Membership: 34
Report: A/59/16
Decisions: ESC 2004/201 C & D, GA 59/404

Committee on Relations with the Host Country

Meetings: New York, 29 April, 26 July, 13 October
Chairman: Andreas D. Mavroyiannis (Cyprus)
Membership: 19 (including the United States as host country)
Report: A/59/26

Committee for the United Nations Population Award

Meetings: New York, 7 and 21 April
Chairman: Iftekhar Ahmed Chowdhury (Bangladesh)
Membership: 10 (plus 5 honorary members, the Secretary-General and the UNFPA Executive Director)
Report: A/59/160

Disarmament Commission

Sessions: New York, 5-23 April (substantive), 22 December (organizational)
Chairman: Revaz Adamia (Georgia) (substantive), Sylvester Ekundayo Rowe (Sierra Leone) (organizational)
Membership: All UN Members
Reports: A/59/42, A/60/42

High-level Committee on the Review of Technical Cooperation among Developing Countries

Session: Did not meet in 2004
Membership: All States participating in UNDP

International Civil Service Commission (ICSC)

Sessions: Fifty-eighth, Paris, 29 March–16 April; fifty-ninth, New York, 12-30 July
Chairman: Mohsen Bel Hadj Amor (Tunisia)
Membership: 15
Report: A/59/30, vol. I
Decisions: GA 58/421, 59/412

ADVISORY COMMITTEE ON POST ADJUSTMENT QUESTIONS
Session: Twenty-sixth, Geneva, 9-16 February
Chairman: Eugeniusz Wyzner (Poland)
Membership: 6

International Law Commission

Session: Fifty-sixth, Geneva, 3 May–4 June and 5 July–6 August
Chairman: Theodor Viorel Melescanu (Romania)
Membership: 34
Report: A/59/10

Investments Committee

Meetings: New York, 9-10 February, 10 May, 13 September, 22 November; Montreal, Canada, 12-13 July (UNJSPB)
Chairman: Emmanuel Noi Omaboe (Ghana)
Membership: 9
Decision: GA 59/409

Joint Advisory Group on the International Trade Centre UNCTAD/WTO

Session: Thirty-seventh, Geneva, 26-30 April
Chairman: Henrik Rée Iversen (Denmark)
Membership: Open to all States members of UNCTAD and all members of WTO
Report: ITC/AG(XXXVII)/200

Joint Inspection Unit (JIU)

Chairman: Ion Gorita (Romania)
Membership: 11
Report: A/60/34
Decision: GA 58/422

Office of the United Nations High Commissioner for Refugees (UNHCR)

EXECUTIVE COMMITTEE OF THE HIGH COMMISSIONER'S PROGRAMME

Session: Fifty-fifth, Geneva, 4-8 October
Chairman: Hernán Escudero Martínez (Ecuador)
Membership: 61
Report: A/59/12/Add.1
Decision: ESC 2004/201 C

High Commissioner: Ruud Lubbers

Panel of External Auditors

Membership: Members of the UN Board of Auditors and the appointed external auditors of the specialized agencies and IAEA

Special Committee on the Charter of the United Nations and on the Strengthening of the Role of the Organization

Meetings: New York, 29 March–8 April
Chairman: Carl J. M. Peersman (Netherlands)
Membership: Open to all States Members of the United Nations
Report: A/59/33

Special Committee to Investigate Israeli Practices Affecting the Human Rights of the Palestinian People and Other Arabs of the Occupied Territories

Meetings: Geneva, 19-25 March and 24 May; Beirut, Lebanon, 25-28 May; Cairo, Egypt, 28 May–4 June; Damascus, Syrian Arab Republic, 4-8 June
Chairperson: C. Mahendran (Sri Lanka) (March), Bernard A. B. Goonetilleke (Sri Lanka) (May/June)
Membership: 3
Report: A/59/381

Special Committee on Peacekeeping Operations

Meetings: New York, 29 March–16 April
Chairperson: Permanent Representative of the Permanent Mission of Nigeria to the United Nations
Membership: 113
Report: A/58/19

Special Committee to Select the Winners of the United Nations Human Rights Prize

Meeting: Did not meet in 2004
Membership: 5

Special Committee on the Situation with regard to the Implementation of the Declaration on the Granting of Independence to Colonial Countries and Peoples

Session: New York, 11 February and 6 April (first part), 7, 8, 14, 16, 17, 18, 21 and 22 June (second part)
Chairman: Robert Guba Aisi (Papua New Guinea)
Membership: 25 (27 from 10 December)
Report: A/59/23
Decisions: GA 58/411 B, 59/414

United Nations Administrative Tribunal

Sessions: Geneva, 21 June–23 July; New York, 25 October–24 November
President: Julio Barboza (Argentina)
Membership: 7
Report: A/INF/59/5
Decision: GA 59/410

United Nations Capital Development Fund (UNCDF)

EXECUTIVE BOARD

The UNDP/UNFPA Executive Board acts as the Executive Board of the Fund.

Managing Director: Mark Malloch Brown (UNDP Administrator)

United Nations Commission on International Trade Law (UNCITRAL)
Session: Thirty-seventh, New York, 14-25 June
Chairman: Wisit Wisitsora-At (Thailand)
Membership: 60
Report: A/59/17

United Nations Conciliation Commission for Palestine
Membership: 3
Report: A/59/260

United Nations Conference on Trade and Development (UNCTAD)
Session: Eleventh, São Paulo, Brazil, 13-18 June
President: Celso Amorim (Brazil)
Membership: Open to all States Members of the United Nations or members of the specialized agencies or of IAEA
Report: TD/412

Secretary-General of UNCTAD: Rubens Ricupero (until 15 September), Carlos Fortin Cabezas (from 15 September) (Officer-in-Charge)

TRADE AND DEVELOPMENT BOARD
Sessions: Thirty-fourth executive, 10 March; twenty-first special, 14 May; thirty-fifth executive, 21 September; thirty-third executive (second part), 30 September; fifty-first, 4-15 October; all in Geneva
President: Sha Zukang (China) (thirty-third to thirty-fifth executive and twenty-first special sessions), Mary Whelan (Ireland) (fifty-first session)
Membership: Open to all States members of UNCTAD
Report: A/59/15

SUBSIDIARY ORGANS OF THE
TRADE AND DEVELOPMENT BOARD

COMMISSION ON ENTERPRISE,
BUSINESS FACILITATION AND DEVELOPMENT
Session: Eighth, Geneva, 12-15 January
Chairperson: Luciano Barillaro (Italy)
Membership: Open to all States members of UNCTAD
Report: TD/B/COM.3/64

COMMISSION ON INVESTMENT,
TECHNOLOGY AND RELATED FINANCIAL ISSUES
Session: Eighth, Geneva, 26-30 January
President: Trevor Clarke (Barbados)
Membership: Open to all States members of UNCTAD
Report: TD/B/COM.2/60 & Corr.1

Intergovernmental Group of Experts
on Competition Law and Policy
Session: Sixth, Geneva, 8-10 November
Chairperson: Amina Mohamed (Kenya)
Membership: Open to all States members of UNCTAD
Report: TD/B/COM.2/CLP/48

Intergovernmental Working Group of Experts on
International Standards of Accounting and Reporting
Session: Twenty-first, Geneva, 27-29 October
Chairperson: Abbas Ali Mirza (Saudi Arabia)
Membership: 34
Report: TD/B/COM.2/ISAR/26
Decisions: ESC 2004/201 A, C & F

COMMISSION ON TRADE IN
GOODS AND SERVICES, AND COMMODITIES
Session: Eighth, Geneva, 9-13 February
Chairperson: Dimiter Tzantchev (Bulgaria)
Membership: Open to all States members of UNCTAD
Report: TD/B/COM.1/67 & Corr.1

WORKING PARTY ON THE MEDIUM-TERM PLAN AND THE PROGRAMME BUDGET
Sessions: Forty-second, Geneva, 4 June and 6 July; forty-third, Geneva, 13-17 September
Chairperson: Naïm Akibou (Benin) (forty-second session), Mariano Payá (Spain) (forty-third session)
Membership: Open to all States members of UNCTAD
Reports: TD/B/WP/173, TD/B/WP/176 & Corr.1

United Nations Development Fund for Women (UNIFEM)

CONSULTATIVE COMMITTEE
Session: Forty-fourth, New York, 15-16 March
Chairperson: Prince Zeid Ra'ad Zeid Al-Hussein (Jordan)
Membership: 5

Executive Director of UNIFEM: Noeleen Heyzer

United Nations Environment Programme (UNEP)

GOVERNING COUNCIL
Session: Eighth special/Global Ministerial Environment Forum, Jeju, Republic of Korea, 29-31 March
President: Arcado Ntagazwa (United Republic of Tanzania)
Membership: 58
Report: A/59/25

Executive Director of UNEP: Klaus Töpfer

United Nations Human Settlements Programme (UN-Habitat)

GOVERNING COUNCIL
Session: Did not meet in 2004
Membership: 58
Decisions: ESC 2004/201 C & D
Executive Director of UN-Habitat: Anna Kajumulo Tibaijuka

United Nations Institute for Disarmament Research (UNIDIR)

BOARD OF TRUSTEES
Sessions: Forty-second, New York, 4-6 February; forty-third, Geneva, 30 June–2 July
Chairman: Harald Müller (Germany)
Membership: 22, plus 1 ex-officio member (Director of UNIDIR)
Report: A/59/361

Director of UNIDIR: Patricia Lewis
Deputy Director: Christophe Carle

United Nations Institute for Training and Research (UNITAR)

BOARD OF TRUSTEES
Session: Forty-second, Geneva, 27-29 April
Chairman: Arthur C. I. Mbanefo (Nigeria)
Membership: Not less than 11 and not more than 30, plus 4 ex-officio members

Executive Director of UNITAR: Marcel A. Boisard

United Nations Joint Staff Pension Board
Session: Fifty-second, Montreal, Canada, 13-23 July
Chairman: A. Busca (Italy)
Membership: 33
Report: A/59/9

United Nations Relief and Works Agency for Palestine Refugees in the Near East (UNRWA)

ADVISORY COMMISSION OF UNRWA
Meeting: Amman, Jordan, 30 September
Chairperson: Abdul Karaim Abu Al-Haija (Jordan)
Membership: 10
Report: A/59/13

WORKING GROUP ON THE FINANCING OF UNRWA
Meetings: New York, 7 and 15 October
Chairman: Ümit Pamir (Turkey)
Membership: 9
Report: A/59/442

Commissioner-General of UNRWA: Peter Hansen
Deputy Commissioner-General: Karen Koning AbuZayd

United Nations Scientific Committee on the Effects of Atomic Radiation

Session: Fifty-second, Vienna, 26-30 April
Chairman: Yasuhito Sasaki (Japan)
Membership: 21
Report: A/59/46

United Nations Staff Pension Committee

Meetings: New York, Geneva and Santiago, Chile, 30 January; New York and Geneva, 19 May; New York, Geneva and Santiago, 17 November (all via videoconference)
Chairperson: Jean-Michel Jakobowicz (France)
Membership: 12 members and 8 alternates
Decision: GA 59/411

United Nations University (UNU)

COUNCIL OF THE UNITED NATIONS UNIVERSITY
Session: Fifty-first, Helsinki, Finland, 6-10 December
Chairperson: Vappu Taipale (Finland)

Membership: 24 (plus 3 ex-officio members and the UNU Rector)
Report: A/56/566

Rector of the University: Johannes A. van Ginkel

United Nations Voluntary Fund for Indigenous Populations

BOARD OF TRUSTEES
Session: Seventeenth, Geneva, 11-19 March
Chairperson: Victoria Tauli-Corpuz (Philippines)
Membership: 5
Report: E/CN.4/Sub.2/AC.4/2004/8

United Nations Voluntary Fund for Victims of Torture

BOARD OF TRUSTEES
Session: Twenty-third, Geneva 4-8 October
Chairman: Jaap Walkate (Netherlands)
Membership: 5
Report: A/60/215

United Nations Voluntary Trust Fund on Contemporary Forms of Slavery

BOARD OF TRUSTEES
Session: Ninth, Geneva, 26-30 January
Chairman: Swami Agnivesh (India)
Membership: 5
Report: A/59/309

Security Council

The Security Council consists of 15 Member States of the United Nations, in accordance with the provisions of Article 23 of the United Nations Charter as amended in 1965.

MEMBERS
Permanent members: China, France, Russian Federation, United Kingdom, United States.
Non-permanent members: Algeria, Angola, Benin, Brazil, Chile, Germany, Pakistan, Philippines, Romania, Spain.

On 15 October 2004 (dec. 59/402), the General Assembly elected Argentina, Denmark, Greece, Japan and the United Republic of Tanzania for a two-year term beginning on 1 January 2005, to replace Angola, Chile, Germany, Pakistan and Spain whose terms of office were to expire on 31 December 2004.

PRESIDENT
The presidency of the Council rotates monthly, according to the English alphabetical listing of its member States. The following served as President during 2004:

Month	Member	Representative
January	Chile	Heraldo Muñoz
		Soledad Alvear Valenzuela
February	China	Wang Guangya
March	France	Jean-Marc de La Sablière
		Pierre-André Wiltzer
April	Germany	Gunter Pleuger
		Kerstin Müller
May	Pakistan	Munir Akram
		Khurshid M. Kasuri

Month	Member	Representative
June	Philippines	Lauro L. Baja, Jr.
		Delia Domingo Albert
July	Romania	Mihnea I. Motoc
		Adrian Nastase, Mircea Geoana
August	Russian Federation	Andrey Denisov
September	Spain	Juan Antonio Yáñez-Barnuevo
		Miguel Angel Moratinos Cuyaubé
October	United Kingdom	Sir Emyr Jones Parry, KCMG
		Bill Rammell
November	United States	John C. Danforth
December	Algeria	Abdallah Baali
		Abdelaziz Belkhadem

Military Staff Committee
The Military Staff Committee consists of the chiefs of staff of the permanent members of the Security Council or their representatives. It meets fortnightly.

Standing committees
Each of the three standing committees of the Security Council is composed of representatives of all Council members:

Committee of Experts (to examine the provisional rules of procedure of the Council and any other matters entrusted to it by the Council)
Committee on the Admission of New Members
Committee on Council Meetings Away from Headquarters

Subsidiary bodies

Counter-Terrorism Committee (CTC)

Chairman: Inocencio F. Arias (Spain) (until 27 May), Alexander V. Konuzin (Russian Federation) (from 28 May to 2 August), Andrey I. Denisov (Russian Federation) (from 3 August).

United Nations Compensation Commission

Executive Secretary: Rolf Goran Knutsson.

United Nations Monitoring, Verification and Inspection Commission (UNMOVIC)

Acting Executive Chairman: Demetrius Perricos.

1540 Committee[6]

Chairman: Mihnea Ioan Motoc (Romania).

Peacekeeping operations

United Nations Truce Supervision Organization (UNTSO)

Chief of Staff: Major General Carl Dodd (until 30 September), Brigadier General Clive William Lilley (from October).

United Nations Military Observer Group in India and Pakistan (UNMOGIP)

Chief Military Observer: Major General Pertti Juhani Puonti (until August), Major General Guido Palmieri (from September).

United Nations Peacekeeping Force in Cyprus (UNFICYP)

Special Adviser to the Secretary-General on Cyprus: Alvaro de Soto.
Special Representative of the Secretary-General and Chief of Mission: Zbigniew Wlosowicz.
Force Commander: Major General Herbert Joaquin Figoli Almandos.

United Nations Disengagement Observer Force (UNDOF)

Force Commander: Major General Franciszek Gagor (until 16 January), Major General Bala Nanda Sharma (from 17 January).

United Nations Interim Force in Lebanon (UNIFIL)

Personal Representative of the Secretary-General for Southern Lebanon: Staffan de Mistura.
Force Commander: Major General Lalit Mohan Tewari (until 17 February), Major General Alain Pellegrini (from 18 February).

United Nations Mission for the Referendum in Western Sahara (MINURSO)

Personal Envoy of the Secretary-General: James A. Baker III (until June).
Special Representative of the Secretary-General and Chief of Mission: Alvaro de Soto.
Force Commander: Major General Gyorgy Száraz.

United Nations Observer Mission in Georgia (UNOMIG)

Special Representative of the Secretary-General and Head of Mission: Heidi Tagliavini.
Chief Military Observer: Major General Kazi Ashfaq Ahmed (until 24 May), Major General Hussein Ahmed Eissa Ghobashi (from 25 May).

United Nations Interim Administration Mission in Kosovo (UNMIK)

Special Representative of the Secretary-General and Head of Mission: Harri Holkeri (until June), Srren Jessen-Petersen (from 16 June).
Principal Deputy Special Representative: Charles Brayshaw (until September), Lawrence Rossin (from 1 October).
Deputy Special Representative for Police and Justice: Jean-Christian Cady (until 15 December).

Deputy Special Representative for Civil Administration: Francesco Bastagli.

United Nations Mission in Sierra Leone (UNAMSIL)

Special Representative of the Secretary-General and Head of Mission: Daudi Ngelautwa Mwakawago.
Deputy Special Representative: Alan Claude Doss (until June), José Vitor da Silva Angelo (from 1 July).
Force Commander: Major General Sajjad Akram.

United Nations Organization Mission in the Democratic Republic of the Congo (MONUC)

Special Envoy of the Secretary-General: Mustapha Niasse.
Special Representative of the Secretary-General and Chief of Mission: William Lacy Swing.
Deputy Special Representatives: Behrooz Sadry, Lena Sundh (until 12 July), Ross Mountain (from 15 November).
Force Commander: Major General Samaila Iliya.

United Nations Mission in Ethiopia and Eritrea (UNMEE)

Special Envoy for Ethiopia and Eritrea: Lloyd Axworthy (from 30 January)
Special Representative of the Secretary-General: Legwaila Joseph Legwaila.
Deputy Special Representatives: Cheikh Tidiane Gaye, Angela Kane (until March), Sissel Ekaas (from 17 November).
Force Commander: Major General Robert Gordon (until July), Major General Rajender Singh (from 27 July).

United Nations Mission of Support in East Timor (UNMISET)

Special Representative of the Secretary-General and Head of Mission: Kamalesh Sharma (until May), Sukehiro Hasegawa (from May).
Force Commander: Lieutenant General Khairuddin Mat Yusof.
Chief Military Observer: Brigadier General Pedro Rocha Pena Madeira.

United Nations Mission in Côte d'Ivoire (MINUCI)[7]

Special Representative of the Secretary-General and Chief of Mission: Albert Tévoédjré.
Chief Military Liaison Officer: Brigadier General Abdul Hafiz.

United Nations Mission in Liberia (UNMIL)

Special Representative of the Secretary-General and Head of Mission: Jacques Paul Klein.
Deputy Special Representatives: Abou Moussa, Souren Seraydarian.
Force Commander: Lieutenant General Daniel Ishmael Opande.

United Nations Operation in Côte d'Ivoire (UNOCI)[8]

Special Representative of the Secretary-General and Chief of Mission: Albert Tévoédjré.
Principal Deputy Special Representative: Alan Claude Doss.
Force Commander: Major General Abdoulaye Fall.

United Nations Operation in Burundi (ONUB)[9]

Special Representative of the Secretary-General and Chief of Mission: Carolyn McAskie.
Deputy Special Representatives: Ibrahima Fall, Nureldin Satti.
Force Commander: Major General Derrick Mbuyiselo Mgwebi.

United Nations Stabilization Mission in Haiti (MINUSTAH)[10]

Special Representative of the Secretary-General: Juan Gabriel Valdés.
Principal Deputy Special Representative: Hocine Medili.
Deputy Special Representative: Adama Guindo.
Force Commander: Lieutenant General Augusto Heleno Ribeiro Pereira.

Political, peace-building and other missions

United Nations Office in Burundi (UNOB) [1]
Special Representative of the Secretary-General and Head of UNOB: Berhanu Dinka.

United Nations Political Office for Somalia (UNPOS)
Representative of the Secretary-General and Head of UNPOS: Winston A. Tubman.

Office of the Special Representative of the Secretary-General for the Great Lakes Region
Special Representative: Ibrahima Fall.

United Nations Observer Mission in Bougainville (UNOMB)
Head of Mission: Tor Stenbock (from 1 March).

United Nations Peace-building Support Office in Guinea-Bissau (UNOGBIS)
Representative of the Secretary-General and Head of UNOGBIS: David Stephen (until September), Jono Bernardo Honwana (from 15 September).

Office of the United Nations Special Coordinator for the Middle East (UNSCO)
Special Coordinator for the Middle East Peace Process and Personal Representative of the Secretary-General to the Palestine Liberation Organization and the Palestinian Authority: Terje Roed-Larsen.

United Nations Peace-building Office in the Central African Republic (BONUCA)
Representative of the Secretary-General and Head of BONUCA: General Lamine Cissé.

United Nations Tajikistan Office of Peace-building (UNTOP)
Representative of the Secretary-General: Vladimir Sotirov.

Office of the Special Representative of the Secretary-General for West Africa
Special Representative of the Secretary-General: Ahmedou Ould-Abdallah.

United Nations Assistance Mission in Afghanistan (UNAMA)
Special Representative of the Secretary-General and Head of UNAMA: Lakhdar Brahimi (until 6 January), Jean Arnault (from 11 February).
Principal Deputy Special Representative: Ameerah Haq (from 8 June).
Deputy Special Representative: Filippo Grandi (from 1 June).

United Nations Assistance Mission for Iraq (UNAMI)
Special Representative of the Secretary-General for Iraq: Ross Mountain (Acting) (until July), Ashraf Qazi (from 12 July).

Economic and Social Council

The Economic and Social Council consists of 54 Member States of the United Nations, elected by the General Assembly, each for a three-year term, in accordance with the provisions of Article 61 of the United Nations Charter as amended in 1965 and 1973.

MEMBERS
To serve until 31 December 2004: Australia, Bhutan, Burundi, Chile, China, El Salvador, Finland, Ghana, Guatemala, Hungary, India, Libyan Arab Jamahiriya, Qatar, Russian Federation, Sweden, Ukraine, United Kingdom, Zimbabwe.
To serve until 31 December 2005: Azerbaijan, Benin, Congo, Cuba, Ecuador, France, Germany, Greece, Ireland, Jamaica, Japan, Kenya, Malaysia, Mozambique, Nicaragua, Saudi Arabia, Senegal, Turkey.
To serve until 31 December 2006: Armenia, Bangladesh, Belgium, Belize, Canada, Colombia, Indonesia, Italy, Mauritius, Namibia, Nigeria, Panama, Poland, Republic of Korea, Tunisia, United Arab Emirates, United Republic of Tanzania, United States.

On 28 and 29 October 2004 (dec. 59/403), the General Assembly elected the following for a three-year term beginning on 1 January 2005 to fill the vacancies occurring on 31 December 2004: Albania, Australia, Brazil, Chad, China, Costa Rica, Democratic Republic of the Congo, Denmark, Guinea, Iceland, India, Lithuania, Mexico, Pakistan, Russian Federation, South Africa, Thailand, United Kingdom.

By the same decision, on 28 October, the Assembly elected Spain for the remainder of the term of Greece, beginning on 1 January 2005.

SESSIONS
Organizational session for 2004: New York, 21 January, 4-6, 13 and 27 February, 23 April and 1 and 4 May.
Resumed organizational session for 2004: New York, 3, 15 and 23 June.
Special high-level meeting with the Bretton Woods institutions and the World Trade Organization: New York, 26 April.
Substantive session of 2004: New York, 28 June–23 July.

Resumed substantive session of 2004: New York, 16 September and 5 and 11 November.

OFFICERS
President: Marjatta Rasi (Finland).
Vice-Presidents: Yashar Aliyev (Azerbaijan), Jagdish Koonjul (Mauritius), Stafford O. Neil (Jamaica), Daw Penjo (Bhutan).

Subsidiary and other related organs

SUBSIDIARY ORGANS

The Economic and Social Council may, at each session, set up committees or working groups, of the whole or of limited membership, and refer to them any items on the agenda for study and report.

Other subsidiary organs reporting to the Council consist of functional commissions, regional commissions, standing committees, expert bodies and ad hoc bodies.

The inter-agency United Nations System Chief Executives Board for Coordination also reports to the Council.

Functional commissions

Commission on Crime Prevention and Criminal Justice
Session: Thirteenth, Vienna, 11-20 May
Chairman: Pavel Vacek (Czech Republic)
Membership: 40
Report: E/2004/30
Decision: 2004/243

Commission on Human Rights
Sessions: Sixtieth, Geneva, 19 January and 15 March–23 April
Chairperson: Mike Smith (Australia)
Membership: 53
Report: E/2004/23
Decision: ESC 2004/201 C

SUBCOMMISSION ON THE PROMOTION
AND PROTECTION OF HUMAN RIGHTS
Session: Fifty-sixth, Geneva, 26 July–13 August

Chairperson: Soli Jehangir Sorabjee (India)
Membership: 26
Report: E/CN.4/2005/2

Commission on Narcotic Drugs

Session: Forty-seventh, Vienna, 15-19 March
Chairperson: Alfred T. Moleah (South Africa)
Membership: 53
Report: E/2004/28

Commission on Population and Development

Session: Thirty-seventh, New York, 22-26 March and 6 May
Chairman: Alfredo Chuquihuara (Peru)
Membership: 47
Report: E/2004/25
Decisions: ESC 2004/201 C, D & F

Commission on Science and Technology for Development

Session: Seventh, Geneva, 24-28 May
Chairman: Arnoldo Ventura (Jamaica)
Membership: 33
Report: E/2004/31
Decisions: ESC 2004/201 C & D

Commission for Social Development

Session: Forty-second, New York, 4-13 and 20 February
Chairperson: Jean-Jacques Elmiger (Switzerland)
Membership: 46
Report: E/2004/26
Decisions: ESC 2004/201 C-E

Commission on the Status of Women

Session: Forty-eighth, New York, 1-12 March
Chairperson: Kyung-wha Kang (Republic of Korea)
Membership: 45
Report: E/2004/27
Decision: ESC 2004/201 C

Commission on Sustainable Development

Session: Twelfth, New York, 14-30 April
Chairperson: Brrge Brende (Norway)
Membership: 53
Report: E/2004/29
Decision: ESC 2004/201 C

Statistical Commission

Session: Thirty-fifth, New York, 2-5 March
Chairman: Katherine Wallman (United States)
Membership: 24
Report: E/2004/24 & Corr.1
Decision: ESC 2004/201 C

United Nations Forum on Forests

Session: Fourth, Geneva, 3-14 May
Chairman: Yuriy N. Isakov (Russian Federation)
Membership: Open to all States Members of the United Nations and members of the specialized agencies
Report: E/2004/42 & Corr.1

Regional commissions

Economic Commission for Africa (ECA)

Session: Thirty-seventh session of the Commission/Conference of African Ministers of Finance, Planning and Economic Development, Kampala, Uganda, 18-22 May
Membership: 53

Economic Commission for Europe (ECE)

Session: Fifty-ninth, Geneva, 24-26 February
Chairman: Clyde Kull (Estonia)
Membership: 55
Report: E/2004/37

Economic Commission for Latin America and the Caribbean (ECLAC)

Session: Thirtieth, San Juan, Puerto Rico, 28 June–2 July
Chairperson: Puerto Rico
Membership: 41 members, 7 associate members
Report: LC/G.2267

Economic and Social Commission for Asia and the Pacific (ESCAP)

Session: Sixtieth, Shanghai, China, 22-28 April
Chairperson: Li Zhaoxing (China)
Membership: 53 members, 9 associate members
Report: E/2004/39

Economic and Social Commission for Western Asia (ESCWA)

Session: Did not meet in 2004
Membership: 13

Standing committees

Committee on Non-Governmental Organizations

Session: New York, 10-28 May and 23 June
Chairperson: Paimaneh Hasteh (Iran)
Membership: 19
Report: E/2004/32 & Corr.1

Committee for Programme and Coordination (CPC)

Sessions: Forty-fourth, New York, 1 June (organizational), 7 June–2 July (substantive)
Chairman: Nonye Udo (Nigeria)
Membership: 34
Report: A/59/16
Decisions: ESC 2004/201 C & D, GA 59/404

Expert bodies

Ad Hoc Group of Experts on International Cooperation in Tax Matters

Meeting: Did not meet in 2004
Membership: 25

Committee for Development Policy

Session: Sixth, New York, 29 March–2 April
Chairperson: Suchitra Punyaratabandhu (Thailand)
Membership: 24
Report: E/2004/33
Decision: ESC 2004/201 A

Committee on Economic, Social and Cultural Rights

Sessions: Thirty-second and thirty-third, Geneva, 26 April–14 May and 8-26 November
Chairperson: Virginia Bonoan-Dandan (Philippines)
Membership: 18
Report: E/2005/22
Decision: ESC 2004/201 C

Committee of Experts on Public Administration

Session: Third, New York, 29 March–2 April
Chairperson: Apolo Nsibambi (Uganda)
Membership: 24
Report: E/2004/44
Decision: ESC 2004/201 A

Committee of Experts on the Transport of Dangerous Goods and on the Globally Harmonized System of Classification and Labelling of Chemicals

Session: Second, Geneva, 10 December
President: K. Headrick (Canada)
Membership: 35
Report: ST/SG/AC.10/32 & Add.1-3 & Add.3/Corr.1
Decision: ESC 2004/201 A

Permanent Forum on Indigenous Issues

Session: Third, New York, 10-21 May
Chairperson: Ole Henrik Magga (Norway)
Membership: 16
Report: E/2004/43
Decisions: ESC 2004/201 C, E & F

United Nations Group of Experts on Geographical Names

Session: Twenty-second, New York, 20-29 April
Chairperson: Helen Kerfoot (Canada)
Membership: Representatives of the 22 geographical/linguistic divisions of the Group of Experts
Report: GEGN/22

Ad hoc body

Commission on Sustainable Development acting as the preparatory meeting for the International Meeting to Review the Implementation of the Programme of Action for the Sustainable Development of Small Island Developing States
Session: New York, 14-16 April
Chairperson: Brrge Brende (Norway)
Report: A/CONF.207/3

United Nations System Chief Executives Board for Coordination

Sessions: Vienna, 2-3 April; New York, 29-30 October
Chairman: The Secretary-General
Membership: Organizations of the UN system
Reports: CEB/2004/1, CEB/2004/2

Other related bodies

International Research and Training Institute for the Advancement of Women (INSTRAW)

EXECUTIVE BOARD
Session: First session, New York, 27 July; resumed session, New York 1 October
Membership: 10 plus 8 ex-officio members
Report: E/2004/66
Decisions: ESC 2004/201 A, B & D

Director of INSTRAW: Carmen Moreno

Joint United Nations Programme on Human Immunodeficiency Virus/Acquired Immunodeficiency Syndrome (UNAIDS)

PROGRAMME COORDINATING BOARD
Meetings: Fifteenth, Geneva, 23-24 June; sixteenth, Montego Bay, Jamaica, 14-15 December
Chairperson: Aileen Carroll (Canada)

Membership: 22
Reports: UNAIDS/PCB(15)/04.15, UNAIDS/PCB(15)/04.16
Decisions: ESC 2004/201 C-E

Executive Director of UNAIDS: Dr. Peter Piot

United Nations Children's Fund (UNICEF)

EXECUTIVE BOARD
Sessions: First and second regular, New York, 19-23 and 26 January, 13-16 September; annual, New York, 7-11 June
President: Lebohang K. Moleko (Lesotho)
Membership: 36
Report: E/2004/34/Rev.1
Decision: ESC 2004/201 C

Executive Director of UNICEF: Carol Bellamy

United Nations Development Programme (UNDP)/ United Nations Population Fund (UNFPA)

EXECUTIVE BOARD
Sessions: First and second regular, New York, 23-30 January, 20-24 September; annual, Geneva, 14-23 June
President: Abdullah M. Alsaidi (Yemen)
Membership: 36
Report: E/2004/35
Decision: ESC 2004/201 C

Administrator of UNDP: Mark Malloch Brown
Associate Administrator: Zéphirin Diabré
Executive Director of UNFPA: Thoraya Obaid

United Nations Research Institute for Social Development (UNRISD)

BOARD OF DIRECTORS
Session: Forty-second, Geneva, 23 April
Chairperson: Emma Rothschild (United Kingdom)
Membership: 11 (plus 7 ex-officio members)

Director of UNRISD: Thandika Mkandawire

World Food Programme (WFP)

EXECUTIVE BOARD
Sessions: First, second and third regular, Rome, Italy, 23-26 February, 26-27 May, 11-14 October; annual, Rome, 24-26 May
President: Miguel Barreto (Peru)
Membership: 36
Report: E/2005/36
Decisions: ESC 2004/201 B & C

Executive Director of WFP: James T. Morris

Trusteeship Council

Article 86 of the United Nations Charter lays down that the Trusteeship Council shall consist of the following:

Members of the United Nations administering Trust Territories;
Permanent members of the Security Council that do not administer Trust Territories;

As many other members elected for a three-year term by the General Assembly as will ensure that the membership of the Council is equally divided between United Nations Members that administer Trust Territories and those that do not.[12]

Members: China, France, Russian Federation, United Kingdom, United States.

International Court of Justice

Judges of the Court

The International Court of Justice consists of 15 Judges elected for nine-year terms by the General Assembly and the Security Council.

The following were the Judges of the Court serving in 2004, listed in the order of precedence:

Judge	Country of nationality	End of term [13]
Shi Jiuyong, *President*	China	2012
Raymond Ranjeva, *Vice-President*	Madagascar	2009
Gilbert Guillaume	France	2009
Abdul G. Koroma	Sierra Leone	2012
Vladlen S. Vereshchetin	Russian Federation	2006
Rosalyn Higgins	United Kingdom	2009
Gonzalo Parra-Aranguren	Venezuela	2009
Pieter H. Kooijmans	Netherlands	2006
Francisco Rezek	Brazil	2006
Awn Shawkat Al-Khasawneh	Jordan	2009
Thomas Buergenthal	United States	2006
Nabil Elaraby	Egypt	2006
Hisashi Owada	Japan	2012
Bruno Simma	Germany	2012
Peter Tomka	Slovakia	2012

Registrar: Philippe Couvreur.
Deputy Registrar: Jean-Jacques Arnaldez.

Chamber of Summary Procedure

Members: Shi Jiuyong (ex officio), Raymond Ranjeva (ex officio), Gonzalo Parra-Aranguren, Awn Shawkat Al-Khasawneh, Thomas Buergenthal.
Substitute members: Nabil Elaraby, Hisashi Owada.

Chamber for Environmental Matters

Members: Shi Jiuyong (ex officio), Raymond Ranjeva (ex officio), Gilbert Guillaume, Pieter H. Kooijmans, Francisco Rezek, Bruno Simma, Peter Tomka.

Parties to the Court's Statute

All Members of the United Nations are ipso facto parties to the Statute of the International Court of Justice.

States accepting the compulsory jurisdiction of the Court

Declarations made by the following States, a number with reservations, accepting the Court's compulsory jurisdiction (or made under the Statute of the Permanent Court of International Justice and deemed to be an acceptance of the jurisdiction of the International Court) were in force at the end of 2004:

Australia, Austria, Barbados, Belgium, Botswana, Bulgaria, Cambodia, Cameroon, Canada, Costa Rica, Côte d'Ivoire, Cyprus, Democratic Republic of the Congo, Denmark, Dominican Republic, Egypt, Estonia, Finland, Gambia, Georgia, Greece, Guinea, Guinea-Bissau, Haiti, Honduras, Hungary, India, Japan, Kenya, Lesotho, Liberia, Liechtenstein, Luxembourg, Madagascar, Malawi, Malta, Mauritius, Mexico, Nauru, Netherlands, New Zealand, Nicaragua, Nigeria, Norway, Pakistan, Panama, Paraguay, Peru, Philippines, Poland, Portugal, Senegal, Serbia and Montenegro, Slovakia,[14] Somalia, Spain, Sudan, Suriname, Swaziland, Sweden, Switzerland, Togo, Uganda, United Kingdom, Uruguay.

United Nations organs and specialized and related agencies authorized to request advisory opinions from the Court

Authorized by the United Nations Charter to request opinions on any legal question: General Assembly, Security Council.

Authorized by the General Assembly in accordance with the Charter to request opinions on legal questions arising within the scope of their activities: Economic and Social Council, Trusteeship Council, Interim Committee of the General Assembly, ILO, FAO, UNESCO, ICAO, WHO, World Bank, IFC, IDA, IMF, ITU, WMO, IMO, WIPO, IFAD, UNIDO, IAEA.

Committees of the Court

BUDGETARY AND ADMINISTRATIVE COMMITTEE

Members: Shi Jiuyong (ex officio) (Chair), Raymond Ranjeva (ex officio), Gilbert Guillaume, Abdul G. Koroma, Vladlen S. Vereshchetin, Pieter H. Kooijmans, Awn Shawkat Al-Khasawneh.

COMMITTEE ON RELATIONS

Members: Gonzalo Parra-Aranguren (Chair), Francisco Rezek, Awn Shawkat Al-Khasawneh, Hisashi Owada.

COMPUTERIZATION COMMITTEE

Members: Raymond Ranjeva (Chair); open to all interested members of the Court.

LIBRARY COMMITTEE

Members: Abdul G. Koroma (Chair), Pieter H. Kooijmans, Francisco Rezek, Thomas Buergenthal, Peter Tomka.

RULES COMMITTEE

Members: Rosalyn Higgins (Chair), Thomas Buergenthal, Nabil Elaraby, Hisashi Owada, Bruno Simma, Peter Tomka.

Other United Nations–related bodies

The following bodies are not subsidiary to any principal organ of the United Nations but were established by an international treaty instrument or arrangement sponsored by the United Nations and are thus related to the Organization and its work. These bodies, often referred to as "treaty organs", are serviced by the United Nations Secretariat and may be financed in part or wholly from the Organization's regular budget, as authorized by the General Assembly, to which most of them report annually.

Committee on the Elimination of Discrimination against Women (CEDAW)

Sessions: Thirtieth and thirty-first, New York, 12-30 January and 6-23 July
Chairperson: Feride Acar (Turkey)

Membership: 23
Report: A/59/38

Committee on the Elimination of Racial Discrimination (CERD)

Sessions: Sixty-fourth and sixty-fifth, Geneva, 23 February–12 March and 2-20 August
Chairperson: Mario Jorge Yutzis (Argentina)
Membership: 18
Report: A/59/18

Committee on the Protection of the Rights of All Migrant Workers and Members of Their Families

Session: First, Geneva, 1-5 March
Chairperson: Prasad Kariyawasam (Sri Lanka)

Membership: 10
Report: A/59/48

Committee on the Rights of the Child

Sessions: Thirty-fifth, thirty-sixth and thirty-seventh, Geneva,
12-30 January, 17 May–4 June and 13 September–1 October
Chairperson: Jakob Egbert Doek (Netherlands)
Membership: 10
Reports: CRC/C/137, CRC/C/140, CRC/C/143

Committee against Torture

Sessions: Thirty-second and thirty-third, Geneva, 3-21 May and
16-26 November
Chairperson: Fernando Mariño (Spain)
Membership: 10
Reports: A/59/44, A/60/44

Conference on Disarmament

Meetings: Geneva, 19 January–26 March, 10 May–25 June, 26
July–8 September

President: Kenya, Malaysia, Mexico, Mongolia, Morocco,
Myanmar (successively)
Membership: 61
Report: A/59/27

Human Rights Committee

Sessions: Eightieth, eighty-first and eighty-second, Geneva, 15
March–2 April, 5-30 July and 18 October–5 November
Chairperson: Abdelfattah Amor (Tunisia)
Membership: 18
Reports: A/59/40, vol. I

International Narcotics Control Board (INCB)

Sessions: Eighty-first, Vienna, 2-11 November
President: Hamid Ghodse
Membership: 13
Report: E/INCB/2004
Decision: Economic and Social Council 2004/201 C

Principal members of the United Nations Secretariat

(as at 31 December 2004)

Secretariat

The Secretary-General: Kofi A. Annan
Under-Secretary-General, Deputy Secretary-General: Louise
Fréchette

Executive Office of the Secretary-General

Under-Secretary-General, Chef de Cabinet: S. Iqbal Riza
*Under-Secretary-General, Special Adviser to the Secretary-
General:* Lakhdar Brahimi
Assistant Secretary-General, Deputy Chef de Cabinet: Elisa-
beth Lindenmayer
Assistant Secretary-General for Policy Planning: Robert Orr

Office of Internal Oversight Services

Under-Secretary-General: Dileep Nair

Office of Legal Affairs

Under-Secretary-General, Legal Counsel: Nicolas Michel
Assistant Secretary-General: Ralph Zacklin

Department of Political Affairs

Under-Secretary-General: Kieran Prendergast
*Assistant Secretary-General, Executive Director, Counter-
Terrorism Committee:* Javier Rupérez
Assistant Secretaries-General: Tuliameni Kalomoh, Danilo
Türk

Department for Disarmament Affairs

Under-Secretary-General: Nobuyasu Abe

Department of Peacekeeping Operations

Under-Secretary-General: Jean-Marie Guéhenno
Assistant Secretaries-General: Hédi Annabi, Jane Holl Lute

Office for the Coordination of Humanitarian Affairs

*Under-Secretary-General for Humanitarian Affairs, Emergency
Relief Coordinator:* Jan Egeland
*Assistant Secretary-General, Deputy Emergency Relief Coor-
dinator:* Margareta Wahlstrom

Department of Economic and Social Affairs

Under-Secretary-General: José Antonio Ocampo
*Assistant Secretary-General, Special Adviser on Gender
Issues and Advancement of Women:* Rachel Mayanja
Assistant Secretary-General: Patrizio M. Civili

Department for General Assembly and Conference Management

Under-Secretary-General: Jian Chen
Assistant Secretary-General: Angela Kane

Department of Public Information *Under-Secretary-General for
Communications and Public Information:* Shashi Tharoor

Department of Management

Under-Secretary-General: Catherine Bertini

OFFICE OF PROGRAMME PLANNING, BUDGET AND ACCOUNTS
Assistant Secretary-General, Controller: Jean-Pierre Halbwachs

OFFICE OF HUMAN RESOURCES MANAGEMENT
Assistant Secretary-General: Rosemary McCreery

OFFICE OF CENTRAL SUPPORT SERVICES
Assistant Secretary-General: Andrew Toh

CAPITAL MASTER PLAN PROJECT
Assistant Secretary-General, Executive Director: Vacant

Office of the United Nations Ombudsman

Assistant Secretary-General, Ombudsman: Patricia M. Durrant

Office of the Iraq Programme

Under-Secretary-General, Executive Director: Benon V. Sevan
*Assistant Secretary-General, Humanitarian Coordinator in
Iraq:* Ramiro Lopes da Silva

Economic Commission for Africa

Under-Secretary-General, Executive Secretary: K. Y. Amoako

Economic Commission for Europe

Under-Secretary-General, Executive Secretary: Brigita
Schmögnerová

Economic Commission for Latin America and the Caribbean

Under-Secretary-General, Executive Secretary: José Luis
Machinea

Economic and Social Commission for Asia and the Pacific

Under-Secretary-General, Executive Secretary: Kim Hak-Su

Economic and Social Commission for Western Asia

Under-Secretary-General, Executive Secretary: Mervat Tallawy

United Nations Office at Geneva

Under-Secretary-General, Director-General of the United Nations Office at Geneva: Sergei Ordzhonikidze

Office of the United Nations High Commissioner for Human Rights

Under-Secretary-General, High Commissioner: Louise Arbour

Assistant Secretary-General, Deputy High Commissioner: Mehr Khan Williams

United Nations Office at Vienna

Under-Secretary-General, Director-General of the United Nations Office at Vienna and Executive Director of the United Nations Office on Drugs and Crime: Antonio Maria Costa

International Court of Justice Registry

Assistant Secretary-General, Registrar: Philippe Couvreur

Secretariats of subsidiary organs, special representatives and other related bodies

International Trade Centre UNCTAD/WTO

Executive Director: J. Denis Bélisle

Office of the High Representative for the Least Developed Countries, Landlocked Developing Countries and Small Island Developing States

Under-Secretary-General, High Representative: Anwarul Karim Chowdhury

Office of the Special Adviser to the Secretary-General on Africa

Under-Secretary-General, Special Adviser: Mohamed Sahnoun

Office of the Special Adviser to the Secretary-General on Colombia

Under-Secretary-General, Special Adviser: James LeMoyne

Office of the Special Adviser to the Secretary-General for Special Assignments in Africa

Under-Secretary-General, Special Adviser: Ibrahim Gambari

Office of the Special Envoy of the Secretary-General for Myanmar

Under-Secretary-General, Special Envoy: Razali Ismail

Office of the Special Representative of the Secretary-General for Children and Armed Conflict

Under-Secretary-General, Special Representative: Olara A. Otunnu

Office of the Special Representative of the Secretary-General for the Great Lakes Region

Assistant Secretary-General, Special Representative: Ibrahima Fall

Office of the Special Representative of the Secretary-General for West Africa

Under-Secretary-General, Special Representative: Ahmedou Ould-Abdallah

Office of the United Nations High Commissioner for Refugees

Under-Secretary-General, High Commissioner: Ruud Lubbers

Office of the United Nations Special Coordinator for the Middle East

Under-Secretary-General, Special Coordinator for the Middle East Peace Process and Personal Representative of the Secretary-General to the Palestine Liberation Organization and the Palestinian Authority: Terje Roed-Larson

Special Adviser to the Secretary-General on European Issues

Under-Secretary-General, Special Adviser: Jean-Bernard Merimée

Special Adviser to the Secretary-General on Latin American Issues

Under-Secretary-General, Special Adviser: Diego Cordovez

Special Envoy of the Secretary-General for the Commonwealth of Independent States

Under-Secretary-General, Special Envoy: Yuli Vorontsov

Special Envoy of the Secretary-General for Humanitarian Affairs in the Sudan

Under-Secretary-General, Special Envoy: Tom Eric Vraalsen

Special Representative of the Secretary-General for the Sudan

Under-Secretary-General, Special Representative: Johannes Pronk

Assistant Secretary-General, Principal Deputy Special Representative: Taye Zerihoun

United Nations Assistance Mission in Afghanistan

Under-Secretary-General, Special Representative of the Secretary-General: Jean Arnault

United Nations Assistance Mission for Iraq

Under-Secretary-General, Special Representative of the Secretary-General for Iraq: Ashraf Qazi

United Nations Children's Fund

Under-Secretary-General, Executive Director: Carol Bellamy

Assistant Secretaries-General, Deputy Executive Directors: Kul Gautam, Toshiyuki Niwa, Karin Sham Poo

United Nations Compensation Commission

Assistant Secretary-General, Executive Secretary: Rolf Goran Knutsson

United Nations Conference on Trade and Development

Assistant Secretary-General, Officer-in-Charge: Carlos Fortin Cabezas

United Nations Development Programme

Administrator: Mark Malloch Brown

Under-Secretary-General, Associate Administrator: Zéphirin Diabré

Assistant Administrator and Director, Bureau for Crisis Prevention and Recovery: Julia V. Taft

Assistant Administrator and Director, Bureau of Management: Jan Mattsson

Assistant Administrator and Director, Bureau for Development Policy: Shoji Nishimoto

Assistant Administrator and Regional Director, UNDP Africa: Abdoulie Janneh

Assistant Administrator and Regional Director, UNDP Arab States: Khalaf Rima Hunaidi

Assistant Administrator and Regional Director, UNDP Asia and the Pacific: Hafiz Pasha

Assistant Administrator and Regional Director, UNDP Europe and the Commonwealth of Independent States: Kalman Mizsei

Assistant Administrator and Regional Director, UNDP Latin America and the Caribbean: Elena Martinez

United Nations Disengagement Observer Force

Assistant Secretary-General, Force Commander: Major General Bala Nanda Sharma

United Nations Environment Programme

Under-Secretary-General, Executive Director: Klaus Töpfer

Assistant Secretary-General, Deputy Executive Director: Shafqat S. Kakakhel

Assistant Secretary-General, Executive Secretary: Hamdallah Zedan

United Nations Human Settlements Programme (UN-Habitat)

Under-Secretary-General, Executive Director: Anna Kajumulo Tibaijuka

United Nations Institute for Training and Research

Assistant Secretary-General, Executive Director: Marcel A. Boisard

United Nations Interim Administration Mission in Kosovo

Under-Secretary-General, Special Representative of the Secretary-General and Head of Mission: Srren Jessen-Petersen

Assistant Secretary-General, Principal Deputy Special Representative: Lawrence Rossin

Assistant Secretaries-General, Deputy Special Representatives: Jean-Christian Cady, Francesco Bastagli

United Nations Interim Force in Lebanon

Assistant Secretary-General, Personal Representative of the Secretary-General for Southern Lebanon: Staffan de Mistura

Assistant Secretary-General, Force Commander: Major General Alain Pellegrini

United Nations Joint Staff Pension Fund

Assistant Secretary-General, Chief Executive Officer: Bernard G. Cochemé

United Nations Military Observer Group in India and Pakistan

Chief Military Observer: Major General Guido Palmieri

United Nations Mission in Ethiopia and Eritrea

Under-Secretary-General, Special Representative of the Secretary-General: Legwaila Joseph Legwaila

Assistant Secretaries-General, Deputy Special Representatives: Sissel Ekaas, Cheikh Tidiane Gaye

Force Commander: Major General Rajender Singh

United Nations Mission in Liberia

Under-Secretary-General, Special Representative of the Secretary-General and Head of Mission: Jacques Paul Klein

Assistant Secretary-General, Deputy Special Representative: Abou Moussa

Assistant Secretary-General, Force Commander: Lieutenant General Daniel Ishmael Opande

United Nations Mission for the Referendum in Western Sahara

Under-Secretary-General, Special Representative of the Secretary-General and Chief of Mission: Alvaro de Soto

Force Commander: Major General Gyorgy Száraz

United Nations Mission in Sierra Leone

Under-Secretary-General, Special Representative of the Secretary-General and Chief of Mission: Daudi Ngelautwa Mwakawago

Assistant Secretary-General, Deputy Special Representative: José Vitor da Silva Angelo

Assistant Secretary-General, Force Commander: Major General Sajjad Akram

United Nations Mission of Support in East Timor

Assistant Secretary-General, Special Representative of the Secretary-General and Head of Mission: Sukehiro Hasegawa

Force Commander: Lieutenant General Khairuddin Mat Yusof

Chief Military Observer: Brigadier General Pedro Rocha Pena Madeira

United Nations Monitoring, Verification and Inspection Commission

Assistant Secretary-General, Acting Executive Chairman: Demetrius Perricos

United Nations Observer Mission in Bougainville

Head of Mission: Tor Stenbock

United Nations Observer Mission in Georgia

Assistant Secretary-General, Special Representative of the Secretary-General and Head of Mission: Heidi Tagliavini

Chief Military Observer: Major General Hussein Ahmed Eissa Ghobashi

United Nations Office for Project Services

Assistant Secretary-General, Executive Director: Nigel Fisher

United Nations Operation in Burundi

Under-Secretary-General, Special Representative of the Secretary-General and Head of Mission: Carolyn McAskie

Assistant Secretary-General, Principal Deputy Special Representative: Nureldin Satti

United Nations Operation in Côte d'Ivoire

Under-Secretary-General, Special Representative of the Secretary-General and Chief of Mission: Albert Tévoédjré

Assistant Secretary-General, Principal Deputy Special Representative: Alan Claude Doss

Force Commander: Major General Abdoulaye Fall

United Nations Organization Mission in the Democratic Republic of the Congo

Under-Secretary-General, Special Envoy of the Secretary-General: Mustapha Niasse

Under-Secretary-General, Special Representative of the Secretary-General and Chief of Mission: William Lacy Swing

Assistant Secretary-General, Deputy Special Representative: Ross Mountain

Force Commander: Major General Samaila Iliya

United Nations Peace-building Office in the Central African Republic

Representative of the Secretary-General and Head of Office: General Lamine Cissé

United Nations Peace-building Support Office in Guinea-Bissau

Representative of the Secretary-General and Head of Office: Jono Bernardo Honwana

United Nations Peacekeeping Force in Cyprus

Under-Secretary-General, Special Adviser to the Secretary-General on Cyprus: Alvaro de Soto

Assistant Secretary-General, Special Representative of the Secretary-General and Chief of Mission: Zbigniew Wlosowicz

Force Commander: Major General Herbert Joaquin Figoli Almandos

United Nations Political Office for Somalia

Representative of the Secretary-General and Head of Office: Winston A. Tubman

United Nations Population Fund

Under-Secretary-General, Executive Director: Thoraya Obaid

Deputy Executive Director, Management: Imelda Henkin

Deputy Executive Director, Programme: Kunio Waki

United Nations Relief and Works Agency for Palestine Refugees in the Near East

Under-Secretary-General, Commissioner-General: Peter Hansen

Assistant Secretary-General, Deputy Commissioner-General: Karen Koning AbuZayd

United Nations Stabilization Mission in Haiti

Under-Secretary-General, Special Representative of the Secretary-General: Juan Gabriel Valdés

Assistant Secretary-General, Principal Deputy Special Representative: Hocine Medili

Assistant Secretary-General, Deputy Special Representative: Adama Guindo

Force Commander: Lieutenant General Augusto Heleno Ribeiro Pereira

United Nations Tajikistan Office of Peace-building

Assistant Secretary-General, Representative of the Secretary-General: Vladimir Sotirov

United Nations Truce Supervision Organization

Assistant Secretary-General, Chief of Staff: Brigadier General Clive William Lilley

United Nations University

Under-Secretary-General, Rector: Johannes A. van Ginkel

Director, World Institute for Development Economics Research: Anthony F. Shorrocks

United Nations Verification Mission in Guatemala

Representative of the Secretary-General and Chief of Mission: Tom Koenigs

On 31 December 2004, the total number of staff of the United Nations Secretariat with continuous service or expected service of a year or more was 15,191. Of these, 5,385 were in the Professional and higher categories, 910 were experts (200-series Project Personnel staff) and 8,896 were in the General Service and related categories.

[1]Elected on 10 June 2004 (dec. 58/418).
[2]Elected on 10 June 2004 (dec. 58/420).
[3]The only Main Committee to meet at the resumed session.
[4]Chairmen elected by the Committees; announced by the Assembly President on 10 June 2004 (dec. 58/419).
[5]Appointed on 14 September 2004 (dec. 59/401).
[6]Established by resolution 1540(2004) of 28 April 2004.
[7]Replaced by UNOCI on 4 April 2004.
[8]Established on 4 April 2004.
[9]Established on 1 June 2004.
[10]Established on 1 June 2004.
[11]Absorbed into ONUB on 1 June 2004.
[12]During 2004, no Member of the United Nations was an administering member of the Trusteeship Council, while five permanent members of the Security Council continued as non-administering members.
[13]Term expires on 5 February of the year indicated.
[14]Declaration deposited on 28 May 2004.

Agendas of United Nations principal organs in 2004

This appendix lists the items on the agendas of the General Assembly, the Security Council and the Economic and Social Council during 2004. For the Assembly, the column headed "Allocation" indicates the assignment of each item to plenary meetings or committees.

Agenda item titles have been shortened by omitting mention of reports, if any, following the subject of the item. Where the subject matter of an item is not apparent from its title, the subject is identified in square brackets; this is not part of the title.

General Assembly

Agenda items remaining for consideration at the resumed fifty-eighth session
(9 February–13 September 2004)

Item No.	Title	Allocation
2.	Minute of silent prayer or meditation.	Plenary
4.	Election of the President of the General Assembly.	Plenary
6.	Election of the Vice-Presidents of the General Assembly.	Plenary
8.	Organization of work, adoption of the agenda and allocation of items.	Plenary
10.	Report of the Secretary-General on the work of the Organization.	Plenary
11.	Report of the Security Council.	Plenary, 4th,
12.	Report of the Economic and Social Council.	2nd, 3rd, 5th
17.	Appointments to fill vacancies in subsidiary organs and other appointments:	Plenary
	(h) Appointment of a member of the Joint Inspection Unit;	
	(i) Confirmation of the appointment of the Secretary-General of the United Nations Conference on Trade and Development;	Plenary 5th
	(j) Appointment of a member of the International Civil Service Commission.[1]	Plenary
18.	Admission of new Members to the United Nations.	Plenary, 4th
19.	Implementation of the Declaration on the Granting of Independence to Colonial Countries and Peoples.	
20.	Support by the United Nations system of the efforts of Governments to promote and consolidate new or restored democracies.	Plenary Plenary
21.	The role of diamonds in fuelling conflict.	
23.	Sport for peace and development:	Plenary
	(a) Building a peaceful and better world through sport and the Olympic ideal.	Plenary
25.	University for Peace.	Plenary
28.	The situation in Afghanistan and its implications for international peace and security.	2
30.	Question of Cyprus.	Plenary
31.	Armed aggression against the Democratic Republic of the Congo.	Plenary
33.	The situation of democracy and human rights in Haiti.	Plenary
37.	The situation in the Middle East.	Plenary
38.	Question of Palestine.	
39.	New Partnership for Africa's Development: progress in implementation and international support:	Plenary
	(b) Causes of conflict and the promotion of durable peace and sustainable development in Africa.	
40.	Strengthening of the coordination of humanitarian and disaster relief assistance of the United Nations, including special economic assistance.	Plenary Plenary
41.	Follow-up to the outcome of the special session on children.	Plenary
44.	Culture of peace.	
47.	Follow-up to the outcome of the twenty-sixth special session: implementation of the Declaration of Commitment on HIV/AIDS.	Plenary Plenary
49.	Information and communication technologies for development.	
50.	Integrated and coordinated implementation of and follow-up to the outcomes of the major United Nations conferences and summits in the economic, social and related fields.	Plenary

Item No.	Title	Allocation
55.	Revitalization of the work of the General Assembly.	Plenary
56.	Question of equitable representation on and increase in the membership of the Security Council and related matters.	Plenary
57.	United Nations reform: measures and proposals.	Plenary
58.	Restructuring and revitalization of the United Nations in the economic, social and related fields.	Plenary
59.	Strengthening of the United Nations system.	Plenary
60.	Follow-up to the outcome of the Millennium Summit.	Plenary
61.	Multilingualism.	Plenary
83.	United Nations Relief and Works Agency for Palestine Refugees in the Near East.	4th
85.	Comprehensive review of the whole question of peacekeeping operations in all their aspects.	4th
94.	Environment and sustainable development:	
	(d) Further implementation of the Programme of Action for the Sustainable Development of Small Island Developing States.	2nd
117.	Human rights questions.	3rd
118.	Financial reports and audited financial statements, and reports of the Board of Auditors.	5th
119.	Review of the efficiency of the administrative and financial functioning of the United Nations.	5th
120.	Programme budget for the biennium 2002-2003.	5th
121.	Programme budget for the biennium 2004-2005.	5th
122.	Programme planning.	5th
123.	Improving the financial situation of the United Nations.	5th
124.	Scale of assessments for the apportionment of the expenses of the United Nations.	5th
125.	Pattern of conferences.	5th
127.	Human resources management.	5th
128.	Administration of justice at the United Nations.	5th
129.	Joint Inspection Unit.	5th
131.	Financing of the International Criminal Tribunal for the Prosecution of Persons Responsible for Genocide and Other Serious Violations of International Humanitarian Law Committed in the Territory of Rwanda and Rwandan Citizens Responsible for Genocide and Other Such Violations Committed in the Territory of Neighbouring States between 1 January and 31 December 1994	5th
132.	Financing of the International Tribunal for the Prosecution of Persons Responsible for Serious Violations of International Humanitarian Law Committed in the Territory of the Former Yugoslavia since 1991.	5th
133.	Scale of assessments for the apportionment of the expenses of United Nations peacekeeping operations.	5th
134.	Administrative and budgetary aspects of the financing of the United Nations peacekeeping operations.	5th
135.	Financing of the United Nations Angola Verification Mission and the United Nations Observer Mission in Angola.	5th
136.	Financing of the United Nations Mission in Bosnia and Herzegovina.	5th
137.	Financing of the United Nations Peacekeeping Force in Cyprus.	5th
138.	Financing of the United Nations Organization Mission in the Democratic Republic of the Congo.	5th
139.	Financing of the United Nations Mission in East Timor.	5th
140.	Financing of the United Nations Mission of Support in East Timor.	5th
141.	Financing of the United Nations Mission in Ethiopia and Eritrea.	5th
142.	Financing of the United Nations Observer Mission in Georgia.	5th
143.	Financing of the activities arising from Security Council resolution 687(1991):	
	(a) United Nations Iraq-Kuwait Observation Mission.	5th
144.	Financing of the United Nations Interim Administration Mission in Kosovo.	5th
145.	Financing of the United Nations peacekeeping forces in the Middle East:	
	(a) United Nations Disengagement Observer Force;	5th
	(b) United Nations Interim Force in Lebanon.	5th
146.	Financing of the United Nations Mission in Sierra Leone.	5th
147.	Financing of the United Nations Mission for the Referendum in Western Sahara.	5th
154.	International Criminal Court.	6th
156.	Measures to eliminate international terrorism.	6th
160.	Global road safety crisis.	Plenary
161.	Financing of the United Nations Mission in Côte d'Ivoire.	5th
165.	Financing of the United Nations Mission in Liberia.	5th
167.	Financing of the United Nations Operation in Côte d'Ivoire.[3]	5th

Item No.	Title	Allocation
168.	Financing of the United Nations Stabilization Mission in Haiti.[3]	5th
169.	International Year of Physics, 2005.[3]	Plenary
170.	Financing of the United Nations Operation in Burundi.[3]	5th

Agenda item considered at the resumed tenth emergency special session
(16, 19 and 20 July 2004)

Item No.	Title	Allocation
5.	Illegal Israeli actions in Occupied East Jerusalem and the rest of the Occupied Palestinian Territory.	Plenary

Agenda of the fifty-ninth session[4]
(first part, 14 September–23 December 2004)

A. Maintenance of international peace and security

Item No.	Title	Allocation
11.	Report of the Security Council.	Plenary
20.	Implementation of the Declaration on the Granting of Independence to Colonial Countries and Peoples.	4th
21.	The role of diamonds in fuelling conflict.	Plenary
22.	Assistance in mine action.	4th
23.	Review of the implementation of the recommendations of the Third United Nations Conference on the Exploration and Peaceful Uses of Outer Space.	Plenary
24.	Prevention of armed conflict.	Plenary
26.	The situation in Central America: progress in fashioning a region of peace, freedom, democracy and development.	Plenary
27.	The situation in Afghanistan and its implications for international peace and security.	Plenary
28.	Necessity of ending the economic, commercial and financial embargo imposed by the United States of America against Cuba.	Plenary
29.	Question of Cyprus.	Plenary
30.	Armed aggression against the Democratic Republic of the Congo.	Plenary
31.	Question of the Falkland Islands (Malvinas).	Plenary
32.	Armed Israeli aggression against the Iraqi nuclear installations and its grave consequences for the established international system concerning the peaceful uses of nuclear energy, the non-proliferation of nuclear weapons and international peace and security.	Plenary
33.	Consequences of the Iraqi occupation of and aggression against Kuwait.	Plenary
34.	Declaration of the Assembly of Heads of State and Government of the Organization of African Unity on the aerial and naval military attack against the Socialist People's Libyan Arab Jamahiriya by the present United States Administration in April 1986.	Plenary
36.	The situation in the Middle East.	Plenary
37.	Question of Palestine.	Plenary
42.	The situation of democracy and human rights in Haiti.	Plenary
48.	Elimination of unilateral extraterritorial coercive economic measures as a means of political and economic compulsion.	Plenary
73.	Effects of atomic radiation.	4th
74.	International cooperation in the peaceful uses of outer space.	4th
75.	United Nations Relief and Works Agency for Palestine Refugees in the Near East.	4th
76.	Report of the Special Committee to Investigate Israeli Practices Affecting the Human Rights of the Palestinian People and Other Arabs of the Occupied Territories.	4th
77.	Comprehensive review of the whole question of peacekeeping operations in all their aspects.	4th
78.	Questions relating to information.	4th
79.	Information from Non-Self-Governing Territories transmitted under Article 73 *e* of the Charter of the United Nations.	4th
80.	Economic and other activities which affect the interests of the peoples of the Non-Self-Governing Territories.	4th

Item No.	Title	Allocation
81.	Implementation of the Declaration on the Granting of Independence to Colonial Countries and Peoples by the specialized agencies and the international institutions associated with the United Nations.	4th
82.	Offers by Member States of study and training facilities for inhabitants of Non-Self-Governing Territories.	4th
91.	Permanent sovereignty of the Palestinian people in the Occupied Palestinian Territory, including East Jerusalem, and of the Arab population in the occupied Syrian Golan over their natural resources.	2nd
100.	Report of the United Nations High Commissioner for Refugees, questions relating to refugees, returnees and displaced persons and humanitarian questions.	3rd
161.	Andean Zone of Peace.	Plenary
163.	The situation in the occupied territories of Azerbaijan.	Plenary

B. Promotion of sustained economic growth and sustainable development in accordance with the resolutions of the General Assembly and recent United Nations conferences

Item No.	Title	Allocation
12.	Report of the Economic and Social Council.	Plenary
35.	Culture of peace.	Plenary
40.	Follow-up to the outcome of the special session on children.	Plenary
41.	The role of the United Nations in promoting a new global human order.	Plenary
43.	Follow-up to the outcome of the twenty-sixth special session: implementation of the Declaration of Commitment on HIV/AIDS.	Plenary
44.	Information and communication technologies for development.	2nd
45.	Integrated and coordinated implementation of and follow-up to the outcomes of the major United Nations conferences and summits in the economic, social and related fields.	Plenary
46.	2001-2010: Decade to Roll Back Malaria in Developing Countries, Particularly in Africa.	Plenary
47.	Sport for peace and development: International Year of Sport and Physical Education.	Plenary
83.	Macroeconomic policy questions:	
(a)	International trade and development;	2nd
(b)	International financial system and development;	2nd
(c)	External debt crisis and development;	2nd
(d)	Commodities.	2nd
84.	Follow-up to and implementation of the outcome of the International Conference on Financing for Development.	2nd
85.	Sustainable development:	
(a)	Implementation of Agenda 21, the Programme for the Further Implementation of Agenda 21 and the outcomes of the World Summit on Sustainable Development;	2nd
(b)	Further implementation of the Programme of Action for the Sustainable Development of Small Island Developing States;	2nd
(c)	International Strategy for Disaster Reduction;	2nd
(d)	Protection of global climate for present and future generations of mankind;	2nd
(e)	Implementation of the United Nations Convention to Combat Desertification in Those Countries Experiencing Serious Drought and/or Desertification, Particularly in Africa;	2nd
(f)	Convention on Biological Diversity;	2nd
(g)	United Nations Decade of Education for Sustainable Development;	2nd
(h)	Rendering assistance to the poor mountain countries to overcome obstacles in socio-economic and ecological areas.	2nd
86.	Implementation of the outcome of the United Nations Conference on Human Settlements (Habitat II) and of the twenty-fifth special session of the General Assembly.	2nd
87.	Globalization and interdependence:	
(a)	Globalization and interdependence;	2nd
(b)	International migration and development;	2nd
(c)	Preventing and combating corrupt practices and transfer of funds of illicit origin and returning such assets to the countries of origin;	2nd
(d)	Culture and development;	2nd
(e)	Integration of the economies in transition into the world economy.	2nd
88.	Groups of countries in special situations:	
(a)	Third United Nations Conference on the Least Developed Countries;	2nd

Item No.	Title	Allocation

(b) Specific actions related to the particular needs and problems of landlocked developing countries: outcome of the International Ministerial Conference of Landlocked and Transit Developing Countries and Donor Countries and International Financial and Development Institutions on Transit Transport Cooperation.   2nd

89. Eradication of poverty and other development issues:

(a) Implementation of the first United Nations Decade for the Eradication of Poverty (1997-2006);   2nd

(b) Women in development;   2nd

(c) Industrial development cooperation.   2nd

90. Operational activities for development:

(a) Operational activities for development of the United Nations system;   2nd

(b) Triennial comprehensive policy review of operational activities for development of the United Nations system.   2nd

92. Training and research:

(a) United Nations Institute for Training and Research;   2nd

(b) United Nations University.   2nd

93. Implementation of the outcome of the World Summit for Social Development and of the twenty-fourth special session of the General Assembly.   3rd

94. Social development, including questions relating to the world social situation and to youth, ageing, disabled persons and the family:

(a) Social development, including questions relating to the world social situation and to youth, ageing, disabled persons and the family;   Plenary, 3rd

(b) United Nations Literacy Decade: education for all.   3rd

95. Follow-up to the International Year of Older Persons: Second World Assembly on Ageing.   3rd

98. Advancement of women.   3rd

99. Implementation of the outcome of the Fourth World Conference on Women and of the twenty-third special session of the General Assembly, entitled "Women 2000: gender equality, development and peace for the twenty-first century".   3rd

C. Development of Africa

38. New Partnership for Africa's Development: progress in implementation and international support:

(a) New Partnership for Africa's Development: progress in implementation and international support;   Plenary

(b) Causes of conflict and the promotion of durable peace and sustainable development in Africa.   Plenary

D. Promotion of human rights

101. Promotion and protection of the rights of children.   3rd

102. Programme of activities for the International Decade of the World's Indigenous People, 1995-2004.   3rd

103. Elimination of racism and racial discrimination:

(a) Elimination of racism and racial discrimination;   3rd

(b) Comprehensive implementation of and follow-up to the Durban Declaration and Programme of Action.   3rd

104. Right of peoples to self-determination.   3rd

105. Human rights questions:

(a) Implementation of human rights instruments;   3rd

(b) Human rights questions, including alternative approaches for improving the effective enjoyment of human rights and fundamental freedoms;   Plenary, 3rd

(c) Human rights situations and reports of special rapporteurs and representatives;   3rd

(d) Comprehensive implementation of and follow-up to the Vienna Declaration and Programme of Action;   3rd

(e) Report of the United Nations High Commissioner for Human Rights.   3rd

E. Effective coordination of humanitarian assistance efforts

39. Strengthening of the coordination of humanitarian and disaster relief assistance of the United Nations, including special economic assistance:

(a) Strengthening of the coordination of emergency humanitarian assistance of the United Nations;   Plenary

(b) Special economic assistance to individual countries or regions.   2nd

(c) Assistance to the Palestinian people;   Plenary

Item No.	Title	Allocation

(d) Emergency international assistance for peace, normalcy and reconstruction of war-stricken Afghanistan. — Plenary

F. Promotion of justice and international law

13. Report of the International Court of Justice. — Plenary

49. Oceans and the law of the sea:

  (a) Oceans and the law of the sea; — Plenary

  (b) Sustainable fisheries, including through the Agreement for the Implementation of the Provisions of the United Nations Convention on the Law of the Sea of 10 December 1982 relating to the Conservation and Management of Straddling Fish Stocks and Highly Migratory Fish Stocks, and related instruments. — Plenary

50. Report of the International Criminal Tribunal for the Prosecution of Persons Responsible for Genocide and Other Serious Violations of International Humanitarian Law Committed in the Territory of Rwanda and Rwandan Citizens Responsible for Genocide and Other Such Violations Committed in the Territory of Neighbouring States between 1 January and 31 December 1994. — Plenary

51. Report of the International Tribunal for the Prosecution of Persons Responsible for Serious Violations of International Humanitarian Law Committed in the Territory of the Former Yugoslavia since 1991. — Plenary

138. Nationality of natural persons in relation to the succession of States. — 6th

139. Responsibility of States for internationally wrongful acts. — 6th

140. Status of the Protocols Additional to the Geneva Conventions of 1949 and relating to the protection of victims of armed conflicts. — 6th

141. Consideration of effective measures to enhance the protection, security and safety of diplomatic and consular missions and representatives. — 6th

142. Convention on jurisdictional immunities of States and their property. — 6th

143. Report of the United Nations Commission on International Trade Law on the work of its thirty-seventh session. — 6th

144. Report of the International Law Commission on the work of its fifty-sixth session. — 6th

146. International Criminal Court. — 6th

147. Report of the Special Committee on the Charter of the United Nations and on the Strengthening of the Role of the Organization. — 6th

149. Scope of legal protection under the Convention on the Safety of United Nations and Associated Personnel. — 6th

150. International convention against the reproductive cloning of human beings. — 6th

G. Disarmament

14. Report of the International Atomic Energy Agency. — Plenary

57. Reduction of military budgets. — 1st

58. Maintenance of international security—good-neighbourliness, stability and development in South-Eastern Europe. — 1st

59. Verification in all its aspects, including the role of the United Nations in the field of verification. — 1st

60. Developments in the field of information and telecommunications in the context of international security. — 1st

61. Role of science and technology in the context of international security and disarmament. — 1st

62. Establishment of a nuclear-weapon-free zone in the region of the Middle East. — 1st

63. Conclusion of effective international arrangements to assure non-nuclear-weapon States against the use or threat of use of nuclear weapons. — 1st

64. Prevention of an arms race in outer space. — 1st

65. General and complete disarmament:

  (a) Notification of nuclear tests; — 1st

  (b) Further measures in the field of disarmament for the prevention of an arms race on the seabed and the ocean floor and in the subsoil thereof; — 1st

  (c) Disarmament and non-proliferation education; — 1st

  (d) Measures to uphold the authority of the 1925 Geneva Protocol; — 1st

  (e) Relationship between disarmament and development; — 1st

  (f) Mongolia's international security and nuclear-weapon-free status; — 1st

  (g) Missiles; — 1st

  (h) Compliance with arms limitation and disarmament and non-proliferation agreements; — 1st

  (i) Regional disarmament; — 1st

Item No.		Title	Allocation
	(j)	Conventional arms control at the regional and subregional levels;	1st
	(k)	Improving the effectiveness of the methods of work of the First Committee;	1st
	(l)	National legislation on transfer of arms, military equipment and dual-use goods and technology;	1st
	(m)	Confidence-building measures in the regional and subregional context;	1st
	(n)	Promotion of multilateralism in the area of disarmament and non-proliferation;	1st
	(o)	Observance of environmental norms in the drafting and implementation of agreements on disarmament and arms control;	1st
	(p)	Follow-up to the advisory opinion of the International Court of Justice on the *Legality of the Threat or Use of Nuclear Weapons;*	1st
	(q)	Reducing nuclear danger;	1st
	(r)	Measures to prevent terrorists from acquiring weapons of mass destruction;	1st
	(s)	Nuclear-weapon-free southern hemisphere and adjacent areas;	1st
	(t)	Towards a nuclear-weapon-free world: a new agenda;	1st
	(u)	Implementation of the Convention on the Prohibition of the Development, Production, Stockpiling and Use of Chemical Weapons and on Their Destruction;	1st
	(v)	Implementation of the Convention on the Prohibition of the Use, Stockpiling, Production and Transfer of Anti-personnel Mines and on Their Destruction;	1st
	(w)	Transparency in armaments;	1st
	(x)	Nuclear disarmament;	1st
	(y)	Assistance to States for curbing the illicit traffic in small arms and collecting them;	1st
	(z)	The illicit trade in small arms and light weapons in all its aspects;	1st
	(aa)	United Nations conference to identify ways of eliminating nuclear dangers in the context of nuclear disarmament;	1st
	(bb)	Establishment of a nuclear-weapon-free zone in Central Asia;	1st
	(cc)	Consolidation of peace through practical disarmament measures;	1st
	(dd)	Convening of the fourth special session of the General Assembly devoted to disarmament.	1st
66.		Review and implementation of the Concluding Document of the Twelfth Special Session of the General Assembly:	
	(a)	United Nations Disarmament Information Programme;	1st
	(b)	United Nations disarmament fellowship, training and advisory services;	1st
	(c)	United Nations Regional Centre for Peace, Disarmament and Development in Latin America and the Caribbean;	1st
	(d)	United Nations Regional Centre for Peace and Disarmament in Africa;	1st
	(e)	United Nations Regional Centre for Peace and Disarmament in Asia and the Pacific;	1st
	(f)	United Nations regional centres for peace and disarmament;	1st
	(g)	Convention on the Prohibition of the Use of Nuclear Weapons;	1st
	(h)	Regional confidence-building measures: activities of the United Nations Standing Advisory Committee on Security Questions in Central Africa.	1st
67.		Review of the implementation of the recommendations and decisions adopted by the General Assembly at its tenth special session:	
	(a)	Advisory Board on Disarmament Matters;	1st
	(b)	United Nations Institute for Disarmament Research;	1st
	(c)	Report of the Conference on Disarmament;	1st
	(d)	Report of the Disarmament Commission.	1st
68.		The risk of nuclear proliferation in the Middle East.	1st
69.		Convention on Prohibitions or Restrictions on the Use of Certain Conventional Weapons Which May Be Deemed to Be Excessively Injurious or to Have Indiscriminate Effects.	1st
70.		Strengthening of security and cooperation in the Mediterranean region.	1st
71.		Comprehensive Nuclear-Test-Ban Treaty.	1st
72.		Convention on the Prohibition of the Development, Production and Stockpiling of Bacteriological (Biological) and Toxin Weapons and on Their Destruction;	1st

H. Drug control, crime prevention and combating international terrorism in all its forms and manifestations

96.		Crime prevention and criminal justice.	3rd
97.		International drug control.	3rd
148.		Measures to eliminate international terrorism.	6th

Item No.	Title	Allocation
(g)	Cooperation between the United Nations and the Economic Community of Central African States;	Plenary
(h)	Cooperation between the United Nations and the Economic Cooperation Organization;	Plenary
(i)	Cooperation between the United Nations and the International Organization of la Francophonie;	Plenary
(j)	Cooperation between the United Nations and the Inter-Parliamentary Union;	Plenary
(k)	Cooperation between the United Nations and the Latin American Economic System;	Plenary
(l)	Cooperation between the United Nations and the League of Arab States;	Plenary
(m)	Cooperation between the United Nations and the Organization for the Prohibition of Chemical Weapons;	Plenary
(n)	Cooperation between the United Nations and the Organization for Security and Cooperation in Europe;	Plenary
(o)	Cooperation between the United Nations and the Organization of American States;	Plenary
(p)	Cooperation between the United Nations and the Organization of the Islamic Conference;	Plenary
(q)	Cooperation between the United Nations and the Pacific Islands Forum;	Plenary
(r)	Cooperation between the United Nations and the Preparatory Commission for the Comprehensive Nuclear-Test-Ban Treaty Organization;	Plenary
(s)	Cooperation between the United Nations and the Southern African Development Community;	Plenary
(t)	Cooperation between the United Nations and the Community of Portuguese-speaking Countries.	Plenary
106.	Financial reports and audited financial statements, and reports of the Board of Auditors:	
(a)	United Nations;	5th
(b)	United Nations Development Programme;	5th
(c)	United Nations Children's Fund;	5th
(d)	United Nations Relief and Works Agency for Palestine Refugees in the Near East;	5th
(e)	United Nations Institute for Training and Research;	5th
(f)	Voluntary funds administered by the United Nations High Commissioner for Refugees;	5th
(g)	Fund of the United Nations Environment Programme;	5th
(h)	United Nations Population Fund;	5th
(i)	United Nations Human Settlements Programme;	5th
(j)	Fund of the United Nations International Drug Control Programme;	5th
(k)	United Nations Office for Project Services;	5th
(l)	International Tribunal for the Prosecution of Persons Responsible for Serious Violations of International Humanitarian Law Committed in the Territory of the Former Yugoslavia since 1991;	5th
(m)	International Criminal Tribunal for the Prosecution of Persons Responsible for Genocide and Other Serious Violations of International Humanitarian Law Committed in the Territory of Rwanda and Rwandan Citizens Responsible for Genocide and Other Such Violations Committed in the Territory of Neighbouring States between 1 January and 31 December 1994;	5th
(n)	Capital master plan.	5th
107.	Review of the efficiency of the administrative and financial functioning of the United Nations.	5th
108.	Programme budget for the biennium 2004-2005.	5th
109.	Programme planning.	1st, 4th, 2nd, 3rd, 5th
110.	Improving the financial situation of the United Nations.	5th
111.	Administrative and budgetary coordination of the United Nations with the specialized agencies and the International Atomic Energy Agency.	5th
112.	Pattern of conferences.	5th
113.	Scale of assessments for the apportionment of the expenses of the United Nations.	5th
114.	Human resources management.	5th
115.	Joint Inspection Unit.	5th
116.	United Nations common system.	5th
117.	United Nations pension system.	5th
118.	Report of the Secretary-General on the activities of the Office of Internal Oversight Services.	5th
119.	Review of the implementation of General Assembly resolutions 48/218 B and 54/244.	5th
120.	Administration of justice at the United Nations.	5th
121.	Financing of the International Criminal Tribunal for the Prosecution of Persons Responsible for Genocide and Other Serious Violations of International Humanitarian Law Committed in the Territory of Rwanda and Rwandan Citizens Responsible for Genocide and Other Such Violations Committed in the Territory of Neighbouring States between 1 January and 31 December 1994.	5th
122.	Financing of the International Tribunal for the Prosecution of Persons Responsible for Serious Violations of International Humanitarian Law Committed in the Territory of the Former Yugoslavia since 1991.	5th

Item No.	Title	Allocation
123.	Administrative and budgetary aspects of the financing of the United Nations peacekeeping operations.	5th
124.	Financing of the United Nations Angola Verification Mission and the United Nations Observer Mission in Angola.	5th
125.	Financing of the United Nations Mission in Bosnia and Herzegovina.	5th
126.	Financing of the United Nations Peacekeeping Force in Cyprus.	5th
127.	Financing of the United Nations Organization Mission in the Democratic Republic of the Congo.	5th
128.	Financing of the United Nations Mission in East Timor.	5th
129.	Financing of the United Nations Mission of Support in East Timor.	5th
130.	Financing of the United Nations Mission in Ethiopia and Eritrea.	5th
131.	Financing of the United Nations Observer Mission in Georgia.	5th
132.	Financing of the activities arising from Security Council resolution 687(1991):	
	(a) United Nations Iraq-Kuwait Observation Mission;	5th
	(b) Other activities.	5th
133.	Financing of the United Nations Interim Administration Mission in Kosovo.	5th
134.	Financing of the United Nations Mission in Liberia.	5th
135.	Financing of the United Nations peacekeeping forces in the Middle East:	
	(a) United Nations Disengagement Observer Force;	5th
	(b) United Nations Interim Force in Lebanon.	5th
136.	Financing of the United Nations Mission in Sierra Leone.	5th
137.	Financing of the United Nations Mission for the Referendum in Western Sahara.	5th
145.	Report of the Committee on Relations with the Host Country.	6th
151.	Observer status for the Shanghai Cooperation Organization in the General Assembly.	6th
152.	Observer status for the Southern African Development Community in the General Assembly.	6th
153.	Financing of the United Nations Operation in Burundi.	5th
154.	Financing of the United Nations Operations in Côte d'Ivoire.	5th
155.	Financing of the United Nations Stabilization Mission in Haiti.	5th
156.	Multilingualism.	Plenary
157.	Observer status for the Collective Security Treaty Organization in the General Assembly.	6th
158.	Declaration by the United Nations of 8 and 9 May as days of remembrance and reconciliation.	Plenary
159.	Observer status for the Economic Community of West African States in the General Assembly.	6th
160.	Observer status for the Organisation of Eastern Caribbean States in the General Assembly.	6th
162.	Observer status for the South Asian Association for Regional Cooperation in the General Assembly.	6th
164.	Financing of the United Nations Mission in the Sudan.	6th

Security Council

Agenda items considered during 2004

Item No. [5]	Title

1. Threats to international peace and security caused by terrorist acts.
2. The situation in Afghanistan.
3. The situation concerning the Democratic Republic of the Congo.
4. The situation in the Middle East, including the Palestinian question.
5. Small arms.
6. The situation between Iraq and Kuwait.
7. Children and armed conflict.
8. Security Council mission [to West Africa, 26 June–5 July 2003; to Central Africa, 7-16 June 2003; to West Africa, 20-29 June 2004; to Central Africa, 21-25 November 2004].
9. Meeting of the Security Council with the troop-contributing countries [to UNOMIG, UNIFIL, MINURSO, UNMEE, UNAMSIL, UNMISET, UNFICYP, UNDOF, MONUC, UNMIL, MINUSTAH, ONUB].
10. Post-conflict national reconciliation: role of the United Nations.
11. The situation in Georgia.
12. The situation concerning Western Sahara.
13. The situation in the Middle East.

Item
No.^5   *Title*

14. The situation in Côte d'Ivoire.
15. Security Council resolutions 1160(1998), 1199(1998), 1203(1998), 1239(1999) and 1244(1999) [Kosovo].
16. The situation in Timor-Leste.
17. The situation in Somalia.
18. The question concerning Haiti.
19. The situation in Bosnia and Herzegovina.
20. The situation between Eritrea and Ethiopia.
21. The situation in Liberia.
22. Cross-border issues in West Africa.
23. International Tribunal for the Prosecution of Persons Responsible for Serious Violations of International Humanitarian Law Committed in the Territory of the Former Yugoslavia since 1991; International Criminal Tribunal for the Prosecution of Persons Responsible for Genocide and Other Serious Violations of International Humanitarian Law Committed in the Territory of Rwanda and Rwandan Citizens Responsible for Genocide and Other Such Violations Committed in the Territory of Neighbouring States between 1 January and 31 December 1994.
24. The situation in Sierra Leone.
25. The situation in Cyprus.
26. The role of business in conflict prevention, peacekeeping and post-conflict peace-building.
27. Decision of the Libyan Arab Jamahiriya to abandon its weapons of mass destruction programmes.
28. Non-proliferation of weapons of mass destruction.
29. Letter dated 31 March 1998 from the Chargé d'affaires a.i. of the Permanent Mission of Papua New Guinea to the United Nations addressed to the President of the Security Council [implementation of the Agreement on Peace, Security and Development on Bougainville (the Lincoln Agreement)].
30. Briefing by the Chairman-in-Office of the Organization for Security and Cooperation in Europe.
31. United Nations peacekeeping operations.
32. Briefing by the United Nations High Commissioner for Refugees.
33. The situation in Burundi.
34. Letter dated 25 May 2004 from the Permanent Representative of the Sudan to the United Nations addressed to the President of the Security Council [humanitarian situation in Darfur].
35. Complex crises and United Nations response.
36. Report(s) of the Secretary-General on the Sudan.
37. Protection of civilians in armed conflict.
38. The situation in Guinea-Bissau.
39. Role of civil society in post-conflict peace-building.
40. Cooperation between the United Nations and regional organizations in stabilization processes.
41. Civilian aspects of conflict management and peace-building.
42. The situation in Africa.
43. Consideration of the draft report of the Security Council to the General Assembly.
44. Justice and the rule of law: the United Nations role.
45. Security Council meetings in Nairobi (18-19 November 2004).
46. The situation in the Great Lakes region.
47. Women and peace and security.
48. The situation in the Central African Republic.
49. Date of election to fill a vacancy in the International Court of Justice.
50. Institutional relationship with the African Union.
51. Briefings by Chairmen of Security Council committees and working groups.

Economic and Social Council

Agenda of the organizational and resumed organizational sessions for 2004
(21 January, 4-6, 13 and 27 February, 23 April and 1 and 4 May; 3, 15 and 23 June)

Item
No.   *Title*

1. Election of the Bureau.
2. Adoption of the agenda and other organizational matters.
3. Basic programme of work of the Council.
4. Elections, nominations, confirmations and appointments.

Agenda of the substantive and resumed substantive sessions of 2004
(28 June–23 July; 16 September and 5 and 11 November)

Item
No.

Title

1. Adoption of the agenda and other organizational matters.

   High-level segment

2. Resources mobilization and enabling environment for poverty eradication in the context of the implementation of the Programme of Action for the Least Developed Countries for the Decade 2001-2010.

   Operational activities of the United Nations for international development cooperation segment

3. Operational activities of the United Nations for international development cooperation:

   (a) Follow-up to policy recommendations of the General Assembly and the Council;

   (b) Reports of the Executive Boards of the United Nations Development Programme and of the United Nations Population Fund, the United Nations Children's Fund and the World Food Programme;

   Coordination segment

4. Coordination of the policies and activities of the specialized agencies and other bodies of the United Nations system related to the following themes:

   (a) Review and appraisal of the system-wide implementation of the Council's agreed conclusions 1997/2 on mainstreaming a gender perspective into all policies and programmes in the United Nations system;

   (b) Coordinated and integrated United Nations system approach to promote rural development in developing countries, with due consideration to least developed countries, for poverty eradication and sustainable development.

   Humanitarian affairs segment

5. Special economic, humanitarian and disaster relief assistance.

   General segment

6. Implementation of and follow-up to major United Nations conferences and summits:

   (a) Follow-up to the International Conference on Financing for Development;

   (b) Review and coordination of the implementation of the Programme of Action for the Least Developed Countries for the Decade 2001-2010.

7. Coordination, programme and other questions:

   (a) Reports of coordination bodies;

   (b) Proposed strategic framework for the biennium 2006-2007;

   (c) International cooperation in the field of informatics;

   (d) Long-term programme of support for Haiti;

   (e) Mainstreaming a gender perspective into all policies and programmes in the United Nations system;

   (f) Ad hoc advisory groups on African countries emerging from conflict;

   (g) Information and Communication Technologies (ICT) Task Force;

   (h) Tobacco or health.

8. Implementation of General Assembly resolutions 50/227 and 52/12 B.

9. Implementation of the Declaration on the Granting of Independence to Colonial Countries and Peoples by the specialized agencies and the international institutions associated with the United Nations.

10. Regional cooperation.

11. Economic and social repercussions of the Israeli occupation on the living conditions of the Palestinian people in the Occupied Palestinian Territory, including Jerusalem, and the Arab population in the occupied Syrian Golan.

12. Non-governmental organizations.

13. Economic and environmental questions:

    (a) Sustainable development;

    (b) Science and technology for development;

    (c) Statistics;

    (d) Human settlements;

    (e) Environment;

    (f) Population and development;

    (g) Public administration and development;

    (h) International cooperation in tax matters;

    (i) United Nations Forum on Forests;

    (j) Assistance to third States affected by the application of sanctions;

    (k) Cartography;

    (l) Women and development.

14. Social and human rights questions:

    (a) Advancement of women;

Item
No.
Title

(b) Social development;

(c) Crime prevention and criminal justice;

(d) Narcotic drugs;

(e) United Nations High Commissioner for Refugees;

(f) Implementation of the Programme of Action for the Third Decade to Combat Racism and Racial Discrimination;

(g) Human rights;

(h) Permanent Forum on Indigenous Issues;

(i) Genetic privacy and non-discrimination.

[1] Sub-item added at the resumed session.

[2] Not allocated; consideration deferred to the fifty-ninth session.

[3] Item added at the resumed session.

[4] Further to resolution 58/316 of 1 July 2004, agenda items are organized under headings corresponding to the priorities of the Organization, as contained in the medium-term plan for the period 2002-2005.

[5] Numbers indicate the order in which items were taken up in 2004.

Appendix V

United Nations information centres and services

(as at 3 May 2006)

ACCRA. United Nations Information Centre
Gamel Abdul Nassar/Liberia Roads
(P.O. Box GP 2339)
Accra, Ghana

Serving: Ghana, Sierra Leone

ADDIS ABABA. United Nations Information Service, Economic Commission for Africa
P.O. Box 3001
Addis Ababa, Ethiopia

Serving: Ethiopia, ECA

ALGIERS. United Nations Information Centre
9a rue Emile Payen, Hydra
(Boîte postale 444, Hydra-Alger)
Algiers, Algeria

Serving: Algeria

ANKARA. United Nations Information Centre
Birlik Mahallesi, 2 Cadde No. 11
06610 Cankaya
(P.K. 407)
Ankara, Turkey

Serving: Turkey

ANTANANARIVO. United Nations Information Centre
22 rue Rainitovo, Antasahavola
(Boîte postale 1348)
Antananarivo, Madagascar

Serving: Madagascar

ASUNCION. United Nations Information Centre
Avda. Mariscal López esq. Saraví
Edificio Naciones Unidas
(Casilla de Correo 1107)
Asunción, Paraguay

Serving: Paraguay

BANGKOK. United Nations Information Service, Economic and Social Commission for Asia and the Pacific
United Nations Building
Rajdamnern Nok Avenue
Bangkok 10200, Thailand

Serving: Cambodia, Lao People's Democratic Republic, Malaysia, Singapore, Thailand, Viet Nam, ESCAP

BEIRUT. United Nations Information Centre/ United Nations Information Service, Economic and Social Commission for Western Asia
UN House
Riad El-Solh Square
(P.O. Box 11-8575-4656)
Beirut, Lebanon

Serving: Jordan, Kuwait, Lebanon, Syrian Arab Republic, ESCWA

BOGOTA. United Nations Information Centre
Calle 100 No. 8A-55, Piso 10
Edificio World Trade Center - Torre "C"
(Apartado Aéro 058964)
Bogotá 2, Colombia

Serving: Colombia, Ecuador, Venezuela

BRAZZAVILLE. United Nations Information Centre
Avenue Foch, Case ortf 15
(P.O. Box 13210 or 1018)
Brazzaville, Congo

Serving: Congo

BRUSSELS. Regional United Nations Information Centre
Résidence Palace
155 rue de la Loi
1040 Brussels, Belgium

Serving: Belgium, Cyprus, Denmark, Finland, France, Germany, Greece, Holy See, Iceland, Ireland, Italy, Luxembourg, Malta, Netherlands, Norway, Portugal, San Marino, Spain, Sweden, United Kingdom, European Union

BUCHAREST. United Nations Information Centre
c/o UN House
48 A Primaverii Blvd.
Bucharest 011975 1, Romania

Serving: Romania

BUENOS AIRES. United Nations Information Centre
Junín 1940, 1er piso
1113 Buenos Aires, Argentina

Serving: Argentina, Uruguay

BUJUMBURA. United Nations Information Centre
117 Avenue de la Révolution
(Boîte postale 2160)
Bujumbura, Burundi

Serving: Burundi

CAIRO. United Nations Information Centre
1 Osiris Street, Garden City
(Boîte postale 262)
Cairo, Egypt

Serving: Egypt, Saudi Arabia

COLOMBO. United Nations Information Centre
202/204 Bauddhaloka Mawatha
(P.O. Box 1505, Colombo)
Colombo 7, Sri Lanka

Serving: Sri Lanka

DAKAR. United Nations Information Centre
Rues de Thann x Dagorne
(Boîte postale 154)
Dakar, Senegal

Serving: Cape Verde, Côte d'Ivoire, Gambia, Guinea, Guinea-Bissau, Mauritania, Senegal

DAR ES SALAAM. United Nations Information Centre
Morogoro Road/Sokoine Drive
Old Boma Building (ground floor)
(P.O. Box 9224)
Dar es Salaam, United Republic of Tanzania

Serving: United Republic of Tanzania

DHAKA. United Nations Information Centre
IDB Bhaban (14th floor)
Begum Rokeya Sharani
Sher-e-Bangla Nagar
(G.P.O. Box 3658, Dhaka-1000)
Dhaka-1207, Bangladesh

Serving: Bangladesh

GENEVA. United Nations Information Service, United Nations Office at Geneva
Palais des Nations
1211 Geneva 10, Switzerland

Serving: Switzerland

HARARE. United Nations Information Centre
Sanders House (2nd floor)
Cnr. First Street/Jason Moyo Avenue
(P.O. Box 4408)
Harare, Zimbabwe
   Serving: Zimbabwe

ISLAMABAD. United Nations Information Centre
House No. 26, Street 88 G-6/3
(P.O. Box 1107)
Islamabad, Pakistan
   Serving: Pakistan

JAKARTA. United Nations Information Centre
Gedung Surya (14th floor)
Jl. M. H. Thamrin Kavling 9
Jakarta 10350, Indonesia
   Serving: Indonesia

KATHMANDU. United Nations Information Centre
Pulchowk, Patan
(P.O. Box 107, UN House)
Kathmandu, Nepal
   Serving: Nepal

KHARTOUM. United Nations Information Centre
United Nations Compound
Gamma'a Avenue
(P.O. Box 1992)
Khartoum, Sudan
   Serving: Somalia, Sudan

KINSHASA. United Nations Information Centre (temporarily inoperational)
Immeuble Losonia
Boulevard du 30 juin
B.P. 7248
Kinshasa 1, Democratic Republic of the Congo
   Serving: Democratic Republic of the Congo

LAGOS. United Nations Information Centre
17 Kingsway Road, Ikoyi
(P.O. Box 1068)
Lagos, Nigeria
   Serving: Nigeria

LA PAZ. United Nations Information Centre
Calle 14 esq. S. Bustamante
Edificio Metrobol II, Calacoto
(Apartado Postal 9072)
La Paz, Bolivia
   Serving: Bolivia

LIMA. United Nations Information Centre
Lord Cochrane 130
San Isidro (L-27)
(P.O. Box 14-0199)
Lima, Peru
   Serving: Peru

LOME. United Nations Information Centre
107 boulevard du 13 janvier
(Boîte postale 911)
Lomé, Togo
   Serving: Benin, Togo

LUSAKA. United Nations Information Centre
Revenue House (ground floor)
Cairo Road (Northend)
(P.O. Box 32905, Lusaka 10101)
Lusaka, Zambia
   Serving: Botswana, Malawi, Swaziland, Zambia

MANAGUA. United Nations Information Centre
Palacio de la Cultura
(Apartado Postal 3260)
Managua, Nicaragua
   Serving: Nicaragua

MANAMA. United Nations Information Centre
United Nations House
Bldg. 69, Road 1901
(P.O. Box 26004, Manama)
Manama 319, Bahrain
   Serving: Bahrain, Qatar, United Arab Emirates

MANILA. United Nations Information Centre
RCBC Plaza, Yuchengco Tower 30th floor (rooms 30-17 and 30-18)
Sen Gil Puyat Avenue, corner Ayala Avenue
Makati City, 1229
Metro Manila, Philippines
   Serving: Papua New Guinea, Philippines, Solomon Islands

MASERU. United Nations Information Centre
United Nations Road
UN House
(P.O. Box 301, Maseru 100)
Maseru, Lesotho
   Serving: Lesotho

MEXICO CITY. United Nations Information Centre
Presidente Masaryk 29-2do piso
Col. Chapultepec Morales
11570 México D.F., Mexico
   Serving: Cuba, Dominican Republic, Mexico

MONROVIA. United Nations Information Centre (temporarily inoperational)
UNDP—Simpson Building
P.O. Box 0274
Mamba Point
Monrovia, Liberia
(UNDP Liberia, Grand Central Station, P.O. Box 1608, New York, NY 10163)
   Serving: Liberia

MOSCOW. United Nations Information Centre
4/16 Glazovsky Pereulok
Moscow 121002, Russian Federation
   Serving: Russian Federation

NAIROBI. United Nations Information Centre
United Nations Office
Gigiri
(P.O. Box 30552)
Nairobi, Kenya
   Serving: Kenya, Seychelles, Uganda

NEW DELHI. United Nations Information Centre
55 Lodi Estate
New Delhi 110 003, India
   Serving: Bhutan, India

OUAGADOUGOU. United Nations Information Centre
14 Avenue de la Grande Chancellerie
Secteur no. 4
(Boîte postale 135)
Ouagadougou 01, Burkina Faso
   Serving: Burkina Faso, Chad, Mali, Niger

PANAMA CITY. United Nations Information Centre
Calle Gerardo Ortega y Ave. Samuel Lewis
Banco Central Hispano Building (1st floor)
(P.O. Box 6-9083 El Dorado)
Panama City, Panama
   Serving: Panama

PORT OF SPAIN. United Nations Information Centre
2nd floor, Bretton Hall
16 Victoria Avenue
(P.O. Box 130)
Port of Spain, Trinidad, W.I.
   Serving: Antigua and Barbuda, Bahamas, Barbados, Belize, Dominica, Grenada, Guyana, Jamaica, Saint Kitts and Nevis, Saint Lucia, Saint Vincent and the Grenadines, Suriname, Trinidad and Tobago

PRAGUE. United Nations Information Centre
nam. Kinskych 6
15000 Prague 5, Czech Republic
   Serving: Czech Republic

PRETORIA. United Nations Information Centre
Metro Park Building
351 Schoeman Street
(P.O. Box 12677)
Pretoria, South Africa
   Serving: South Africa

RABAT. United Nations Information Centre
6 Angle avenue Tarik Ibnou Ziyad et Ruet
   Roudana
(Boîte postale 601, Casier ONU, Rabat-
   Chellah)
Rabat, Morocco
   Serving: Morocco

RIO DE JANEIRO. United Nations Infor-
   mation Centre
Palácio Itamaraty
Av. Marechal Floriano 196
20080-002 Rio de Janeiro RJ, Brazil
   Serving: Brazil

SANA'A. United Nations Information
   Centre
Street 5, off Al-Bonyia Street
Handlal Zone, beside Handhal Mosque
(P.O. Box 237)
Sana'a, Yemen
   Serving: Yemen

SANTIAGO. United Nations Information
   Service, Economic Commission for
   Latin America and the Caribbean
Edificio Naciones Unidas
Avenida Dag Hammarskjöld, Vitacura
(Avenida Dag Hammarskjöld s/n,
   Vitacura Casilla 179-D)
Santiago, Chile
   Serving: Chile, ECLAC

SYDNEY. United Nations Information
   Centre
46-48 York Street (5th floor)
(G.P.O. Box 4045, Sydney, N.S.W. 2001)
Sydney, N.S.W. 2000, Australia
   Serving: Australia, Fiji, Kiribati, Nauru,
New Zealand, Samoa, Tonga, Tuvalu,
Vanuatu

TEHRAN. United Nations Information
   Centre
No. 39, Shahrzad Blv.
(P.O. Box 15874-4557, Tehran)
Darous, Iran
   Serving: Iran

TOKYO. United Nations Information
   Centre
UNU Building (8th floor)
53-70 Jingumae 5-chome, Shibuya-Ku
Tokyo 150-0001, Japan
   Serving: Japan

TRIPOLI. United Nations Information
   Centre
Khair Aldeen Baybers Street
Hay El-Andalous
(P.O. Box 286)
Tripoli, Libyan Arab Jamahiriya
   Serving: Libyan Arab Jamahiriya

TUNIS. United Nations Information Cen-
   tre
61 boulevard Bab-Benath
(Boîte postale 863)
Tunis, Tunisia
   Serving: Tunisia

VIENNA. United Nations Information
   Service, United Nations Office at Vienna
Vienna International Centre
Wagramer Strasse 5
(P.O. Box 500, A-1400 Vienna)
A-1220 Vienna, Austria
   Serving: Austria, Hungary, Slovakia,
Slovenia

WARSAW. United Nations Information
   Centre
A. Niepodleglosci 186
(UN Centre P.O. Box 1, 02-514 Warsaw
   12)
00-608 Warszawa, Poland
   Serving: Poland

WASHINGTON, D.C. United Nations
   Information Centre
1775 K Street, N.W., Suite 400
Washington, D.C. 20006, United States
   Serving: United States

WINDHOEK. United Nations Information
   Centre
372 Paratus Building
Independence Avenue
(Private Bag 13351)
Windhoek, Namibia
   Serving: Namibia

YANGON. United Nations Information
   Centre
6 Natmauk Road
Yangon, Myanmar
   Serving: Myanmar

YAOUNDE. United Nations Information
   Centre
Immeuble Tchinda, Rue 2044, derrière
   camp SIC TSINGA
(Boîte postale 836)
Yaoundé, Cameroon
   Serving: Cameroon, Central African
Republic, Gabon

For more information on UNICs, access the Internet: http://www.un.org/aroundworld/unics

Indexes

USING THE SUBJECT INDEX

To assist the researcher in reading and searching the *Yearbook* index, three typefaces have been employed.

ALL BOLD CAPITAL LETTERS are used for major subject entries, including chapter topics (e.g., **DEVELOPMENT**, **DISARMAMENT**), as well as country names (e.g., **TAJIKISTAN**), region names (e.g., **AFRICA**) and principal UN organs (e.g., **GENERAL ASSEMBLY**).

CAPITAL LETTERS are used to highlight major sub-topics (e.g., POVERTY), territories (e.g., MONTSERRAT), subregions (e.g., CENTRAL AMERICA) and official names of specialized agencies (e.g., UNIVERSAL POSTAL UNION) and regional commissions (e.g., ECONOMIC COMMISSION FOR EUROPE).

Regular body text is used for single entries and cross-reference entries, e.g., armed conflict, mercenaries, terrorism.

1—An asterisk (*) next to a page number indicates the presence of a text (reproduced in full) of General Assembly, Security Council or Economic and Social Council resolutions and decisions, or Security Council presidential statements.

2—Entries, which are heavily cross-referenced, appear under key substantive words, as well as under the first word of official titles.

3—United Nations bodies are listed under major subject entries and alphabetically.

Subject index

human rights, 673
refugees, 234, 239
and Sudan, 239
Charter of Economic Rights and Duties of States
(1974), 827
CHEMICALS
Committee of Experts on the Transport of Danger-
ous Goods and on the Globally Harmonized
System of Classification and Labelling of
Chemicals, 986-87
Consolidated List of Products Whose Consumption and/or Sale Have Been Banned, Withdrawn, Severely Restricted or Not Approved by
Governments, 1065
Convention on the Control of Transboundary
Movements of Hazardous Wastes and their Disposal (Basel, 1989), 767, 1066-67
Trust Fund to Assist Developing Countries and
Other Countries in Need of Technical Assistance in Implementation of, 1067
harmful products and waste, protection against,
*1063-68
cleaner production and sustainable consumption, 1067-68
international chemicals management, 1064
lead, 1064-65
mercury programme, 1065
persistent organic pollutants (POPs), 1066
Stockholm Convention on, 1046, 1066
Partnership for Clean Fuels and Vehicles, 1032,
1064
Rotterdam Convention on the Prior Informed
Consent (PIC) Procedure for Certain Hazardous
Chemicals and Pesticides in International Trade
(1998), 767, 1063
see also pollution
chemical weapons, 56, *556-58
Convention (1993), *556-58
Organization for the Prohibition of, 546, *557-58
CHILDREN, *729-90, *1175-90
abducted in Africa, 790
and armed conflict, *786-89, 811, 1177-78
child labour, 1185
GA special session (2002), *1175-77
the girl child, 777, 1156, *1159-62, 1184
guidelines on justice for child victims and witnesses, *1132-37
HIV/AIDS, 779, 1159, 1178-81, 1185-86
human rights, *779-90
International Decade for a Culture of Peace and
Non-Violence for the Children of the World
(2001-2010), *679-80
Pan-African Forum on Building Trust for Immunization and Child Survival, 1083
prostitution and child pornography, 785-86
refugees, 1165, 1205
rights of, 1022, *779-85
Committee on the Rights of the Child, 659, 667-
68, 811
Convention on the Rights of the Child (1989)
and Optional Protocols (2000), 659, 667-68,
*779-85

The State of the World's Children, 1177
trafficking, kidnapping and smuggling of, 330,
1156-57, *1159-62
Tunza children and youth strategy (UNEP), 1046-
47
International Children's Conference, 1047
violence against, 785
see also United Nations Children's Fund; youth
CHILE
development, right to, 745
torture and cruel treatment, 733
CHINA
human rights, 722, 806-807
CICIACS, see Commission for the Investigation of Illegal Groups and Clandestine Security Organizations
CIVIL AND POLITICAL RIGHTS, *709-44
democracy, right to, *724-26
disappearance of persons, *730-33
expression, freedom of, 736-38
Colombia, 737
conscientious objection, 738
Côte d'Ivoire, 737
Italy, 738
Serbia and Montenegro, 737-38
extralegal executions, *726-30
Sudan, 727
genocide, prevention of, 730
International Covenant on Civil and Political
Rights (1966) and Optional Protocols (1966,
1989), 659-60, 662-63, 702-704, 728, 806
justice, administration of, *714-24
arbitrary detention, 721-22
capital punishment, 724
civilians in armed conflict, *717-20
compensation for victims, *716
impunity, 722-23
judicial system independence, 723-24
missing persons, *719-20
rule of law, 716-17
self-determination, right to, *709-14
mercenaries impeding, *711-14
Palestinians, *710-11
Western Sahara, 711
and terrorism, *738-44
torture and cruel treatment, *733-36
see also human rights
civilians in armed conflict, *717-20
climate change
Assessment of Impacts and Adaptation to Climate
Change (UNEP), 1043
Intergovernmental Panel on, 946, 1043, 1057
UN Framework Convention on (1992), 946, 1046,
1051-52
Conference of the Parties to, *1051-52
Kyoto Protocol (1997), 55-56, 1051, 1056
see also environment; pollution; weather; World
Meteorological Organization
Collective Security Treaty Organization, *1459
COLOMBIA, 737, 792, 805-806
ICJ case (Nicaragua), 1268
commissions, see main part of name

Index of resolutions and decisions

Resolution/decision numbers in italics indicate that the text is summarized rather than reprinted in full. (For dates of sessions, refer to Appendix III.)

Index of 2004 Security Council presidential statements

Number	Subject	Date	Page
S/PRST/2004/34	Justice and the rule of law: the United Nations role	6 October	66
S/PRST/2004/35	The situation in Afghanistan	12 October	322
S/PRST/2004/36	The situation in the Middle East	19 October	508
S/PRST/2004/37	Threats to international peace and security caused by terrorist acts	19 October	78
S/PRST/2004/38	The situation in Somalia	26 October	262
S/PRST/2004/39	The situation in the Central African Republic	28 October	162
S/PRST/2004/40	Women and peace and security	28 October	1152
S/PRST/2004/41	The situation in Guinea-Bissau	2 November	227
S/PRST/2004/42	The situation in Côte d'Ivoire	6 November	186
S/PRST/2004/43	The situation in Somalia	19 November	263
S/PRST/2004/44	Institutional relationship with the African Union	19 November	282
S/PRST/2004/45	The situation concerning the Democratic Republic of the Congo	7 November	133
S/PRST/2004/46	Protection of civilians in armed conflict	14 November	717
S/PRST/2004/47	The situation in the Middle East	15 December	518
S/PRST/2004/48	The situation in Côte d'Ivoire	16 December	190

How to obtain volumes of the *Yearbook*

Recent volumes of the *Yearbook* may be obtained in many bookstores throughout the world, as well as from United Nations Publications, Room DC2-853, United Nations, New York, N.Y. 10017, e-mail (publications@un.org); or from United Nations Publications, Palais des Nations, CH-1211 Geneva 10, Switzerland, e-mail (unpubli@unog.ch).

Older editions are available in microfiche.

Yearbook of the United Nations, 2003
Vol. 57. Sales No. E.05.I.1 $150.

Yearbook of the United Nations, 2002
Vol. 56. Sales No. E.04.I.1 $150.

Yearbook of the United Nations, 2001
Vol. 55. Sales No. E.03.I.1 $150.

Yearbook of the United Nations, 2000
Vol. 54. Sales No. E.02.I.1 $150.

Yearbook of the United Nations, 1999
Vol. 53. Sales No. E.01.I.4 $150.

Yearbook of the United Nations, 1998
Vol. 52. Sales No. E.01.I.1 $150.

Yearbook of the United Nations, 1997
Vol. 51. Sales No. E.00.I.1 $150.

Yearbook of the United Nations, 1996
Vol. 50. Sales No. E.97.I.1 $150.

Yearbook of the United Nations, 1995
Vol. 49. Sales No. E.96.I.1 $150.

Yearbook of the United Nations, 1994
Vol. 48. Sales No. E.95.I.1 $150.

Yearbook of the United Nations, 1993
Vol. 47. Sales No. E.94.I.1 $150.

Yearbook of the United Nations, 1992
Vol. 46. Sales No. E.93.I.1 $150.

Yearbook of the United Nations, 1991
Vol. 45. Sales No. E.92.I.1 $115.

Yearbook of the United Nations, 1990
Vol. 44. Sales No. E.98.I.16 $150.

Yearbook of the United Nations, 1989
Vol. 43. Sales No. E.97.I.11 $150.

Yearbook of the United Nations, 1988
Vol. 42. Sales No. E.93.I.100 $150.

Yearbook of the United Nations, 1987
Vol. 41. Sales No. E.91.I.1 $105.

Yearbook of the United Nations
Special Edition
UN Fiftieth Anniversary
1945-1995
Sales No. E.95.I.50 $95

NOTES

NOTES